The Libraries Directory

A Guide to the Libraries and Archives of the United Kingdom and Ireland

49th Edition

Editor

IAIN WALKER

JAMES CLARKE & CO. LTD

CAMBRIDGE

James Clarke & Co. Ltd
P.O. Box 60
Cambridge
CB1 2NT
England

email: **publishing@jamesclarke.co.uk**
website: **http://www.jamesclarke.co.uk**

British Library Cataloguing in Publication Data
A catalogue record for this book is available from the British Library

ISBN 0 227 67972 5   Reference Version, Single user
ISBN 0 227 67973 3   Reference Version, Network
ISBN 0 227 67975 X   Marketing Version, Single user
ISBN 0 227 67974 1   Marketing Version, Network

ISSN 0961 4575
formerly The Libraries Yearbook (ISSN 0955 4645)

© James Clarke & Co. Ltd., 2004

Advertising Sales by Jilly Hanna

Printed by CLE Print Ltd

CONTENTS

PREFACE

The information contained in the new edition of *The Libraries Directory* is based upon feedback received from questionnaires sent out in 2002 and early 2003, and as always, we would like to express our gratitude and appreciation to the librarians, archivists and other officers contacted for their time and co-operation in completing and returning the questionnaires.

The new edition expands further upon the previous one, with over 500 new entries, an increase of some 15%. Most notably, our coverage of Archives has been increased by over 30%, including a number of business archives and local studies libraries not previously represented, and similar increases are to be found in the sections devoted to Library and Information Organisations. As well as expanding the range of the *Directory*, we have also improved the depth of its coverage, in particular through providing additional contact details for public library branches, and a wider selection of contact names, especially those officers responsible for stock acquisitions and equipment purchases. However, the biggest change to *The Libraries Directory* is that it is now available as a dual-format package, comprising a printed volume and a CD-ROM. We hope that the CD-ROM, with its hyperlink navigation and its search facilities based on the more detailed and wide-ranging indexing allowed by the electronic format, will provide a useful complement to the printed work. As ever, we welcome any comments and suggestions for further improvements.

The profusion of electronic publications in recent years has led to calls for the legal deposit status of such materials to be clarified. These calls have been answered by the introduction of the new Legal Deposit Libraries Act 2003, which makes the United Kingdom one of the first countries to widen the scope of legal deposit to include electronic and related non-print media. The Act permits copyright libraries to acquire and store materials such as CD-ROMs and e-journals, and to carry out the selective acquisition of information published on web sites with a .uk suffix. This is a welcome and timely development, as the number of e-journals published in the United Kingdom is rising rapidly, expected to reach nearly 200,000 by the end of 2005. Another welcome aspect of the new legislation is its forward looking, enabling nature. As new media are developed, legal deposit can be extended to include them as well. The introduction of the Act also raises questions of whether further revision of the more archaic aspects of existing legal deposit legislation may now be possible, for example regarding the requirement for UK publishers to provide six separate copies of each book rather than one.

The possibility of new legislation concerning archives is also under consideration. Since the Public Records Acts of 1958 and 1967, the rôle of public archives as a community resource has expanded considerably, and the growth of digital formats has created new challenges. Questions have therefore arisen regarding the adequacy of the existing legislative framework. The National Archives, formed in 2003 by the merger of the Public Record Office and the Historical Manuscripts Commission, has accordingly issued a public consultation document on the proposed revision of national records and archives legislation. The document highlights issues such as the scope of what is to count as a public record, accountability in the selection of records to be preserved, and the development of a national framework for public records management, particularly as regards records in digital format, including standards of practice and their enforcement. The question is also raised of whether local authority archives should be placed on a statutory footing, as is already the case for public libraries. The consultation period has only just ended, and definite proposals have yet to be put forward, but the National Archives' initiation of this discussion is very welcome, and it is to hoped that beneficial changes will follow.

In the public libraries sector, the perennial problems of declining issues and under-funding continue. The report *Building Better Library Services*, published by the Audit Commission in 2002, has highlighted the ongoing trend in recent years of falling loans and fewer people using libraries to borrow books, while a more recent report by Audit Scotland draws a similar picture for Scottish libraries. A feature of both reports is that this trend has been accompanied a decline in spending on book acquisitions, and that those library authorities that resist cuts in the Book Fund are those most likely to maintain steady borrowing levels. This link between falling loans and reduced spending has been recognised for some time, and it is discouraging to note that the problem remains acute. The Audit Commission in particular warns of libraries becoming an increasingly marginal service unless these trends can be reversed.

One area in which public library spending has held up is in multi-media provision, and it would be easy to blame the decline in traditional book-based services on the greater emphasis now placed on public libraries as user-friendly providers of internet and related facilities. There is indeed a risk that in expanding the scope of their services, a trade-off between different areas of provision may seem inevitable. However, the policy of trying to attract users with a wide range of services can pay dividends in terms of books issued. Tower Hamlets Libraries, in remodelling their libraries as community-friendly 'Idea Stores', might on the face of it seem to epitomise the caricature of a modern British public library as an internet café that just happens to stock books. Yet their success in attracting new users has also led to an increase in borrowing.

It seems quite plausible then that where borrowing has declined, it is due less to strategic choices forced by limited resources, than in a strategy that emphasises economies rather than the development of the library service as a whole. This is not to say that the pressure on library authorities to prioritise services is more apparent than real, but that the policies needed to reverse the decline must take a broad view of what libraries can offer and how they offer it. Quite

apart from maintaining investment in the Book Fund, measures that have been identified as beneficial include the more effective management of stock expenditure, the promotion of reader development activities, and an acquisitions policy that focuses more clearly on the books that people actually want to read. This third factor, of course, raises questions concerning the actual purpose of the public library as a provider of books – is it to educate or to entertain? The risk is that too populist an approach to acquisitions may lead to a downgrading of the book stock's educational potential, for while people may be able to find more of the books they want, there will be correspondingly fewer of the books that it might actually be more beneficial for them to read. However, the distinction between recreational and educational reading is not hard and fast, and if people are to take advantage of libraries as an educational resource, then they need to be encouraged to visit in the first place. And one important means of ensuring this is through an acquisitions policy that is responsive to their wishes. So as long as a balanced approach to book selection is maintained, this is another area in which attention paid to one aspect of the service may well pay dividends in another.

Stock development is just one of many issues addressed in the Department for Culture, Media and Sport's paper *Framework for the Future: Libraries, Learning and Information in the Next Decade*, which identifies the challenges facing the public library sector and the areas most in need of improvement. The report has been greeted with general approval by the library and information community for reaffirming the government's commitment to public libraries and for its strategic guidance for the future. However, the Chartered Institute of Librarians and Information Professionals has raised concerns about the document's failure to tackle the problem of sustaining progress through long-term funding, for although ready and willing to provide backing to libraries in their quest for funding from local authorities and through partnerships with business, the DCMS envisages no additional assistance from central government. This has potential ramifications not just for the long-term improvement of traditional core services, but also for the new electronic services that the government has been so keen to implement. For example, although the introduction of the People's Network has been backed by the New Opportunities Fund, it less clear where the money is to come from in order to maintain it. A related difficulty with the framework document is that it is also unclear how the performance of library authorities is to be assessed in future, which has led to concerns that libraries may find it difficult support their bids for additional local authority funding without reference to clear performance measures.

That strategic guidance and encouragement may be of limited benefit without the resources to back the vision can perhaps be seen in Northern Ireland, where the public library service is centrally funded through the Department of Culture, Arts and Leisure. The Department's recent report *Tomorrow's Libraries* has been praised for its wide range of concrete recommendations and initiatives. At the time of writing, however, public libraries are also facing a freeze in funding, and as a consequence, Northern Ireland's Education and Library Boards are warning of higher charges, substantial cuts in acquisitions, and possible branch closures. The outlook for public libraries in the Republic of Ireland is rather more encouraging, in part because the responsible governmental body, the Department of the Environment and Local Government, is able to complement local authority spending through direct grants for capital investment, computerisation of services, and the purchase of library vehicles. Grants have also been made available to assist library authorities in meeting book stock targets set by the Department, a clear case of strategy being followed up with the wherewithal to implement it.

Part of the difficulty faced by British libraries in securing government support lies in the fragmented nature of government responsibility for them. Unlike the case in Ireland, where the DELG has both political and financial responsibility for public libraries, in the UK political responsibility lies with the Department for Culture, Media and Sport, while central funding comes from the Office of the Deputy Prime Minister. This has obvious implications for the government's ability to adopt a co-ordinated approach to the disbursement of resources, and while *Framework for the Future* acknowledges this situation as a weakness in the system, it offers no indication as to how it might be overcome. In their response to the report, CILIP argue that because the public library service is a statutory one, it is surely entitled to adequate core funding from public expenditure in order to meet targets and maintain a consistent level of standards. The argument for improved central assistance for public libraries in the United Kingdom is a strong one, on the understanding that this assistance is complementary to the statutory duty of local authorities to provide a comprehensive and accessible library service, and not in any way a substitute source of funding. Even the step of uniting political and financial responsibility for public libraries in a single government department would be welcome. At a time when the government is asking libraries to manage themselves more effectively in order to make the most of their resources, it is surely not unreasonable for libraries to ask the same in return.

Questions of attracting investment are not restricted to Britain's public libraries alone. A survey carried out for CILIP by the Information Management Research Institute has revealed a worrying variation in standards of library provision in colleges of further education, with one of the key problems being a failure to invest in staffing and staff development. Proposed cuts in staffing also led to last year's furore over the threatened closure of York Minster's historic library, although for the meantime, that threat has fortunately turned out to be more apparent than real. There is a worry that even as libraries in all sectors seek to meet new challenges and to adapt their services to modern needs, they will struggle to do so if they are overlooked when prioritising resources. Whether their rôle is to act as a service to the community, as centres for learning and skill development, or as repositories of knowledge, libraries need to be valued and supported as the essential asset to our national life that they are.

Iain Walker

ABBREVIATIONS & COMMON ACRONYMS

A2A Access to Archives
ABTAPL Association of British Theological & Philosophical Libraries
ACLAIIR Advisory Council on Latin American & Iberian Information Resources
acq(s) acquisition(s)
activ(s) activity(ies)
ad adult
admin administration
adv advance(d)
AGLINET Agricultural Libraries Network
agric agriculture/agricultural
AHIS Animal Health Information Specialists
AIG Agency Information Group
AIL Association of Independent Libraries
ALA Associate member of the Library Association (now MCLIP)
ALAI Associate member of the Library Association of Ireland
ALCID Academic Libraries Co-operation in Dublin
ALCL Association of London Chief Librarians
ALLCU Association of Land-based Librarians in Colleges & Universities
ALF Ayrshire Libraries Forum
ALLIN Access to Libraries for Learning in Northamptonshire
ALLIS Accessing Lancashire Libraries & Information Services
ANGLES Anglian Libraries Information Exchange Scheme
anthro anthropology/anthropological
appl application
approx approximate
appt appointment
arch architecture
archaeo archaeology/archaeological
archv(s) archive(s)
ARIEL an internet document delivery service
ARLIS Art Libraries Society UK & Ireland
ARTEL Automated Request Transmission by Telephone
ASCEL Association of Senior Children's & Education Librarians
ASFIS Aquatic Sciences & Fisheries Information System
assoc(s) association(s)
asst assistant
ASTM American Society of Testing & Materials
ATLA American Theological Library Association
ATLIS Access to Libraries in Swansea
AUKML Association of UK Media Librarians
AULIC Avon University Libraries in Co-operation
auto automated
AV(s) audiovisual(s)
AWHILES All-Wales Health Library Extension Services
AWHL Association of Welsh Health Libraries
AYHJLS Associated Yorkshire & Humberside Joint Library Service

backgrnd background
BALBS Birmingham Academic Libraries Special Borrowing Scheme
BAPLA British Association of Picture Libraries & Agencies
BBBCLC Blackburn, Bolton & Bury Community Languages Consortium
BBI Beds & Bucks Information
BBOB Berkshire, Buckinghamshire & Oxfordshire Branch (Library Association)
BBSLG British Business Schools Librarians' Group
BBSRC Biotechnology & Biological Sciences Research Council
BCLIP Black Country Library & Information Providers
BEWHICH consortium of Library Authorities in North East London
BIALL British & Irish Association of Law Libraries
BIASLIC Britain & Ireland Association of Aquatic Sciences Libraries and Information Centres

biblio bibliographic(al)
BIDS Bath Information & Data Services
BIN Business & Information Network
bk(s) book(s)
bklet(s) booklet(s)
BL British Library
BLCMP Birmingham Libraries Co-operative Mechanisation Project
bldg building
BLDSC British Library Document Supply Centre
BLG Berkshire Libraries Group
BLIP Berkshire Library & Information Partnership
BLLD British Library Lending Division
BMA British Medical Association
BNB British National Bibliography
bnd bound
BRIL BBSRC Research Institute Libraries
BRISC BBSRC Research Institutes Serials Consortium
BSI British Standards Institution
BSRIA Building Services Research & Information Association
BT British Telecom
BUBL Bulletin Board for Libraries

c circa
C (e.g., 19C, 13C) century
CABBEG Co-operation & Access Bedfordshire & Buckinghamshire Education Group
CADIG Coventry & District Information Group
CAIRNS Co-operative Academic Information Retrieval Network for Scotland
CALIM Consortium of Academic Libraries in Manchester
CAMP Co-operative Africana Microform Project
CARN County Archives Research Network
cat catalogue
CBC Central Buying Consortium
CBI Confederation of British Industry
CC-IW Cydfenthyca Cymru – Interlending Wales (also IW-CC)
CCTV closed-circuit television
CEMARE Centre for Economics & Management of Aquatic Resources
CENTRAL Children's Education Needs Teaching Resources & Libraries
CERL Consortium of European Research Libraries
cert certificate
ch children
CHELPS Cumbria Higher Education Institution Library Partnership Scheme
chem chemistry
CHILL Consortium of Health Independent Information Libraries in London
CILIP Chartered Institute of Library & Information Professionals (formerly the Library Association & Institute of Information Scientists)
CILLA Co-operative of Indic Language LASER Authorities
classn classification
Co Company
C of E Church of England
C of I Church of Ireland
co-op co-operative
COFHE Colleges of Further & Higher Education (special interest group of CILIP)
coll(s) college(s)
colln(s) collection(s)
COLRIC Council for Learning Resources in Colleges
comm community
CONARLS Circle of Officers of National & Regional Library Systems
conc concessions
COPAC CURL Online Public Access Catalogue
copier photocopier
COPOL Council of Polytechnic Librarians
corp corporate/corporation
COSEELIS Council for Slavonic & East European Library & Information Services

CROESO a Welsh Library access scheme
cttee committee
CUC Cambridge Union Catalogue
CULS Cambridge Union List of Serials
CULT Clydeside University Libraries Together
CURL Consortium of University Research Libraries
CUSP Consortium of United Stock Purchasers
CWLIS Consortium of Welsh Library & Information Services

DDC Dewey Decimal Classification
dep deputy
dept department
DIG Derbyshire Information Group
Dip diploma
dir director
dist district
div(s) division(s)
DoH Department of Health
DTI Department of Trade & Industry
DUGS Dynix Users Group Scotland

E east/eastern
EAD Encoded Archival Description
EAHIL European Association of Health Information Libraries
EALCC former East Anglian Librarians Consultative Committee (now ELIPP)
EBHL European Botanical & Horticultural Libraries
EBSLG European Business Schools Librarians' Group
econ economics
ed edition/editor/edited
EDC European Documentation Centre
edu education
ELAN Essex Libraries Automated Network
elec electronic
ELIPP Eastern Library & Information Professionals Partnership (formerly EALCC)
ELISA East of England Library & Information Services
ELRS Education Libraries Resource Services
EMRLS East Midlands Regional Library System
EMUA East Midlands Universities' Association
eng engineering
enq(s) enquiry(ies)
EPIC European Public Information Centre
equip equipment
esp especially
ESRC Economic & Social Research Council
est estimated
ESTC Eighteenth Century Short-Title Catalogue
EU European Union
EULOS Essex Union List of Serials
EURASLIC European Association of Aquatic Sciences Libraries & Information Centres
excl excludes/excluding
exec executive
exhib(s) exhibition(s)
exp expenditure

FCLIP Fellow of the Chartered Institute of Library & Information Professionals (formerly FLA or FIInfSc)
FE further education
FEFC Further Education Funding Council
fig(s) figure(s)
FIInfSc Fellow of the Institute of Information Scientists (now FCLIP)
FIL Forum for Interlending
FIRST Forum for Information Resources in Staffordshire
FLA Fellow of the Library Association
FLAI Fellow of the Library Association of Ireland
FT full-time; *also* Financial Times
FTE full-time equivalent

GALW Gateways to Libraries in Wrexham
gen generated
genl general

geog geography
geol geology
GLAN Greater London Archives Network
GLASS Greater London Audio Specialisation Scheme
GMPLTC Greater Manchester Public Libraries Training Co-operative
govt government
grad(s) graduate(s)
GRIP Grimsby Regional Information Providers
gt great/greater

HA health authority
HATRICS Hampshire Technical, Research, Industrial & Commercial Services
hb hardback
HB health board
HE higher education
HeLIN Health Library Information Network
HERTIS Hertfordshire County Technical Interloan Scheme
HLN Health Libraries North; *also* Health Libraries Network
hol(s) holiday(s)
Hon honourable/honorary
hortic horticulture/horticultural
hosp(s) hospital(s)
housebnd housebound
hr hour
HULTIS Hull Libraries Technical Information Service

IAALD International Association of Agricultural Information Specialists
IAML (UK) International Association of Music Libraries, Archives & Documentation Centres (UK)
IAMSLIC International Association of Marine Sciences Libraries & Information Centres
IBSS International Bibliography of the Social Sciences
ICA International Council on Archives
IFLA International Federation of Library Associations & Institutions
IJFR(S) Irish Joint Fiction Reserve (Scheme)
ILIOS Insurance Libraries & Information Officers
ILL inter-library loan(s)
illust(s) illustration(s)/illustrated
inc income
incl includes/including
info information
inst(s) institute(s)
instn(s) institution(s)
internatl international
IRIS an Irish Joint OPAC
ISAD(G) International Standard for Archival Description (General)
ISTC Incunabula Short Title Catalogue
IT info technology
IW-CC Interlending Wales –Cydfenthyca Cymru (also CC-IW)

JANET Joint Academic Network
JFR Joint Fiction Reserve
JHLS Joint Healthcare Library Services
JISC Joint Information Systems Committee
jnr junior

keybd(s) keyboard(s)
KILN Kent Information & Library Network
KSS Kent Surrey Sussex Health Librarians

lab laboratory
LADSIRLAC Liverpool & District Scientific Industrial & Research Library Advisory Council
LAI Library Association of Ireland
LAILLAR Libraries Agreement in Leicestershire, Leicester & Rutland
LALIC Leeds Art Libraries in Co-operation
LALNET Lancashire Academic Libraries Network
LAMDA London & Manchester Document Access
LAN local area network
lang(s) languages

LASER former London & South Eastern (Library) Region
LASH Libraries Access Sunderland Scheme
LC Library of Congress
LCBS London Classification for Business Studies
lend lending
LENDIT Local Economic Development through Information Technology
lib(s) library(ies)
libn(s) librarian(s)
LIHNN Library & Information Health Network Northwest
LINC Library Information Network Cumbria
LINE Libraries & Information North East
LINNET Leicestershire Information Network
LISE Libraries of Institutes & Schools of Education
LISN Lincolnshire Information Services Network
LISTED Library Integrated System for Telegramatics-based Education
lit literature
LLiL Libraries & Learners in London
LOPS Librarians in Occupational & Physiotherapy Schools
LRC learning resource(s) centre
Ltd Limited

m metres
m- (e.g., m-fiche) micro or (e.g., m-reader) microform
maths mathematics
MBC Metropolitan Borough Council
MCHLG Mersey & Cheshire Health Libraries Group
MCLIP Member of the Chartered Institute of Library & Information Professionals (formerly ALA)
MDA Museum Documentation Association
MDEC Multi-Disciplinary Education Centre
MEC Medical Education Centre
mech mechanical
med medium
MELCOM Middle East Libraries Committee
memb(s) member(s)
membship membership
mgmt management
mgr manager
MIDAIG Midlands Agricultural Information Group
MIDIRS Midwives Information & Resource Service
MIInfSc Member of the Institute of Information Scientists (now MCLIP)
misc miscellaneous
MLA-WM Museums, Libraries & Archives Council West Midlands
mln million
mod modified
MoD Ministry of Defence
MRC Medical Research Council
MRLA Mersey Region Libraries Association
MS(S) manuscript(s)
MSC Metropolitan Special Collection
MUMLIB Multimedia Technology in Libraries
MWRLS Mid-Western Regional Libraries Scheme

N north/northern
N&YRLAS Northern and Yorkshire Regional Library Advisory Service
NAG National Acquisitions Group
NAPLIB National Association of Aerial Photographic Libraries
nat natural
natl national
NCL Northern Chief Librarians
NELLIE North East London Libraries Information Exchange
NEMLAC North East Museums, Libraries & Archives Council
NEPO North East Purchasing Organisation
NERC Natural Environment Research Council
NERLG North Eastern Regional Library Group
NERS North Eastern Regional Section
NETWORK a sub-group of NCL

NEWLIS Newport Libraries Information Service
NEYAL North East & Yorkshire Academic Libraries
NGO non-governmental organisation
NHS National Health Service
NI Northern Ireland
NILTA National Information & Learning Technologies Association
NISS National Information Services & Systems
NJFR Northern Joint Fiction Reserve
NLJWP Newcastle Libraries Joint Working Party
NLM National Library of Medicine
NLS National Library of Scotland
NLSLS National Library of Scotland Lending Scheme
NLW National Library of Wales
NOF New Opportunities Fund
NoWAL North West Academic Libraries
NRLB Northern Regional Library Board
NTRLIU North Thames Regional Library & Information Unit
NTRHLN North Thames Regional Health Libraries Network
NTRLIS North Thames Regional Library & Information Service
NTRLS North Thames Regional Library Service
NULJ Nursing Union List of Journals
NWHSLA North West Health Services Librarians Association
NWMHSL North West Midlands Health Service Libraries
NWRHS North West Regional Health Service
NWRLA North West Regional Library Association
NWRLB North West Regional Library Board
NWRLS North West Regional Library System

o/p out of print
oap(s) old age pensioner(s)
offcr officer
OLIS Oxford Libraries Information System
OPAC online public access catalogue
ORLIN Oxford Region Library & Information Network
OS Ordnance Survey

pa per annum
pamph(s) pamphlet(s)
pb paperback
PC personal computer
pd per day
periodcl(s) periodical(s)
pg page
PGMC Postgraduate Medical Centre
PGMEC Postgraduate Medical Education Centre
phil philosophy
PIR Public Information Relay
PLCS Psychiatric Libraries Co-operative Scheme
pop population
postgrad(s) postgraduate(s)
Pres President
PRISM Partnership for Regional Information & Systems Management
prof(s) professional(s)
Prof Professor
proj(s) project(s)
PSIB Public Services Information Bulletin
psy psychology
pt(s) point(s)
PT part-time
publ published/publisher
pubn(s) publication(s)
pw per week

RC Roman Catholic
RCGP Royal College of General Practitioners
RCN Royal College of Nursing
RCS(E) Royal College of Surgeons (of England)
rec(s) recreation(s)
rec mgmt records management
ref(s) reference(s)
req requests
res reservations

RESCOLINC Research Council Libraries & Information Consortium
RIDING academic library consortium in North East England
RLB Regional Library Board
RLG Research Libraries Group
RSC Royal Society of Chemistry
RSLP Research Support Libraries Programme
RSM Royal Society of Medicine
rsrch research
rsrcher(s) researcher(s)

S south/southern
SAIL Shropshire Access to Information for Learning
SALALM Seminar on the Acquisition of Latin American Library Materials
SALCGT Scottish Academic Libraries Co-operative Training Group
SALG Scottish Agricultural Librarians Group; *also* South Asia Library Group
SALSER Scottish Academic Libraries Serials database
SASLIC Surrey & Sussex Libraries in Co-operation
SBHILS Swansea Bay Health Information & Library Service
SCAN Scottish Archives Network
SCANDALS Suffolk, Cambridgeshire & Norfolk Direct Application Loan System
sci(s) science(s)
SCIP Strathclyde Community Information Points
SCL Society of Chief Librarians
SCOLMA Standing Conference on Library Materials on Africa
SCONUL Standing Conference of National & University Libraries
SCRAN Scottish Cultural Resources Access Network
SCURL Scottish Confederation of University & Research Libraries
SEAL South East Area Libraries
SEALS Selection, Acquisition & Loans Systems (part of WMRLS)
sec secretary
SELPIG South East Libraries Performance Improvement Group
SESLIN South East Scotland Library & Information Network
SET South East (Wales) Training Co-operative
SETG South East Training Group
SETRHA South East Thames Regional Health Authority
SETRLIS South East Thames Regional Library & Information Service
SFR Scottish Fiction Reserve
SHAIR Shropshire Access to Information Resources
SHIC Social History & Industrial Classification
SHINE Scottish Health Information Network
SHIRL Serial Holdings in Irish Libraries
SIBMAS Section Internationale des Bibliothèques et Musées des Arts du Spectacle
SILLR Scottish Inter-Library Loan Rates
SINTO Sheffield Information Organisation
SKILLS Sharing Knowledge & Information in London Libraries

SLIC Scottish Library & Information Council; *also* Southampton Libraries in Co-operation
snr senior
soc(s) society(ies)
SoPSE Sense of Place across South East England
SPICE Specialist Provision in Community Languages & English Group
spkn spoken
src source
STC Short Title Catalogue
STLIS South Thames Library & Information Service
STRLIS South Thames Regional Library and Information Service
sub subscription
subj(s) subject(s)
SUC Scottish Union Catalogue
SUfI Scottish University for Industry
SUPC Southern Universities Purchasing Consortium
suppl suppliers
SUSCAG Scottish Universities Special Collections & Archives Group
SVAG Scottish Visual Arts Group
svc(s) service(s)
SWALCAP South West Academic Libraries Co-operative Automation Project
SWEHSLinC South West England Health Service Libraries in Co-operation
SWELTEC South West London Teacher Education Consortium
SWHCLU South & West Health Care Libraries Unit
SWHELS South West Higher Education Libraries
SWRLS South West Regional Library System
SYALL South Yorkshire Access to Libraries for Learning
SWIFT South West London Information Providers
SWRLIN South West Regional Library & Information Network
SWRLS South West Regional Library System
SWTRLS South West Thames Regional Library Service
sys system

TALNET North West Wales Bibliographic Services
TAPS Training Access Points
tech technology
tel telephone
temp temporary
TLP-WM The Libraries Partnership - West Midlands
TRAHCLIS Trent Regional Allied Health Care Librarians & Information Specialists
TSO The Stationery Office
TWIRL Tyne & Wear Information Resources for Learning

UCABLIS Union Catalogue of Art Books in Scotland
UDC Universal Document Classification
UHI University of the Highlands & Islands
UK United Kingdom
UKOLUG UK Online User Group
UL University Library
ULNJ Union List of Nursing Journals

undergrad(s) undergraduate(s)
univ university

V3 inter-Library loan system, formerly VISCOUNT
vac vacation
VALNOW Virtual Academic Library of the North West
vol(s) volume(s)

W west/western
WALIA Welsh Academic Libraries Inter-Access
wd word
wd-proc word processor
WELLSTOC West London Libraries Stock Consortium
WILCO Wiltshire Libraries in Co-operation
WING Donald Wing short title catalogue
wk(s) week(s)
WMHEALG West Midlands Higher Education Association Libraries Group
WMHLN West Midlands Health Libraries Network
WMLCS West Midlands Libraries Co-operative Scheme
WMRHLN West Midlands Regional Health Libraries Network
WMRLS West Midlands Regional Library System
WRLS Wales Regional Library Service
WW1 World War One
WW2 World War Two
WWW World Wide Web

YADLOGIS Yorkshire & District Local Govt Information Service
YHBICN Yorkshire & Humberside Business Information Co-operative Network
YHFMP Yorkshire & Humberside Forum on Multicultural Provision
YHJLS Yorkshire & Humberside Joint Libraries Service
YHRLS Yorkshire & Humberside Regional Library Service
YHUA Yorkshire & Humberside Universities Association
YLI Yorkshire Libraries & Information
yr year
YRLS Yorkshire Regional Library Service

Addresses

Ave Avenue
Bldg Building
Blvd Boulevard
Cl Close
Ct Court
Dr Drive
Est Estate
Gdn(s) Garden(s)
Ln Lane
Pl Place
Rd Road
St Street
Ter Terrace

SECTION 1 – UK LEGAL DEPOSIT LIBRARIES

This section consists of the legal deposit or copyright libraries entitled to receive copies of all materials published in the United Kingdom:

National Libraries
L1   The British Library
L2   The National Library of Scotland
L3   The National Library of Wales

University Libraries
L4   The Bodleian Library
L5   Cambridge University Library

Each entry has the following general format:

An introductory paragraph, including a brief history of the Library.

General Information – including address and contact details; opening hours (if applicable to the Library as a whole); names of chief officers; staff numbers; general financial figures; stock and holdings; admissions policy; any other general points of relevance.

Structure of the Library – lists the main departments or divisions of the Library, including (where appropriate): address and contact details; opening hours; names of chief officers; a description of the functions of the department; details of stock and special collections; details of any other organisations or services for which the department is responsible.

Special Collections – if not covered by entries for individual departments. Please note that only major collections are included.

Electronic Information Resources – if not covered by entries for individual departments. Includes details of major resources available, such as online databases and CD-ROMs.

Dependent or Branch Libraries – including address and contact details; opening hours; names of chief officers; subjects covered; details of stock and special collections; details of services provided and online resources available.

Other Services – such as exhibitions and publications, if not covered by entries for individual departments.

Telephone and fax numbers are given in the form of area dialling codes within the United Kingdom. To telephone the UK from outside the country, dial 00-44 followed by the number, minus the initial 0.

L1 – THE BRITISH LIBRARY

THE BRITISH LIBRARY is the United Kingdom's national library. The foundation collections were established in the 18th century as British Museum's Departments of Manuscripts and of Printed Books. The collections expanded during the 19th century, and a new Department of Oriental Printed Books and Manuscripts was created in 1892. These Departments, along with the National Reference Library of Science and Invention, formed the core of the national library when it was established on 1 July 1973 by the British Library Act (1972), and a Lending Division was established in Boston Spa, Yorkshire. The Office of Scientific and Technical Information, the Library Association Library and the British National Bibliography were incorporated in 1974. The India Office Library and Records were acquired in 1982, and the British Institute of Recorded Sound was incorporated as the National Sound Archive in 1983. The Library is managed by the British Library Board.

GENERAL INFORMATION

The British Library, 96 Euston Rd, London, NW1 2DB (020-7412-7000)
Internet: http://www.bl.uk/

Chairman: Lord Eatwell
Chief Executive: Ms Lynne Brindley
Head of Corporate Secretariat: Mr Andrew Stephens
Total staff: 2,309
Grant in aid: £85,187,000 (2002-03)
Receipts: £37,200,000 (2002-03)
Expenditure: £111,500,000 (2002-03)
Holdings: 150 million items, including c18 million vols, with 2.6 million items added in 2001-02
Admission: admission to reading rooms and collections is by Reader's Pass. Passes are issued to those requiring access to material not readily available elsewhere, or whose work or studies require the facilities of a large research library. Passes can be applied for at:

Reader Admissions Office
(020-7412-7677; *fax:* 020-7412-7794)
Email: reader-admissions@bl.uk
Open: Mon 1000-1800, Tue-Thu 0930-1800, Fri-Sat 0930-1630

STRUCTURE OF THE LIBRARY

The British Library is divided into five directorates:

1. SCHOLARSHIP AND COLLECTIONS

Director: Dr Clive Field
Responsible for strategic and operational management of the Library's collections, and for the provision of a wide range of value added services to facilitate access to, interpretation and use of the collections by both scholarly and general audiences.

The British Library's collections are all of international renown and provide a wide range of expert advice and research services, as well as supplying content for exhibitions, publications and Web-based services.

ASIA, PACIFIC AND AFRICA COLLECTIONS
(020-7412-7873; *fax:* 020-7412-7641)
Email: oioc-enquiries@bl.uk
Internet: http://www.bl.uk/collections/orientalandindian.html
OIOC Reading Room: Mon 1000-1700, Tue-Sat 0930-1700

Holdings include 65,000 oriental MSS, 900,000 printed vols and 120,000 vols of oriental periodicals and newspapers in over 350 languages, as well as the India Office Records and Library. The main areas of the oriental collections are:

Judaeo-Christian - Comprise 7,000 MSS and 106,000 printed vols of Hebrew, Coptic, Syriac, Georgian, Armenian and Ethiopian materials, including ancient Christian MSS and illuminated Bibles and Gospels.
Islamic - Comprise 19,000 MSS and 108,000 printed vols in Arabic, Persian, Turkish and Central Asian Iranian and Turkic languages, including illuminated Korans.
South Asian - Comprise 20,000 MSS and 435,000 printed vols in Hindi, Urdu, Sanskrit, Bengali, Tamil, Sinhalese, Tibetan and other languages, including illustrated MSS and very early Central Asian documents.
South-East Asian - Comprise 1,500 MSS and 47,000 printed vols of Burmese, Thai, Vietnamese, Malay, Indonesian and Javanese materials, including fine illustrated Burmese and Thai MSS.

Far Eastern - Comprise 16,000 MSS and 195,000 printed vols of Chinese, Japanese, Korean, Mongol and Manchu materials, including the world's oldest printed documents from Japan and China.

The current emphasis is on acquiring modern literature and official documents and materials for the study of all aspects of contemporary as well as traditional Asia and North Africa. The section also houses the secretariat of the International Dunhuang Project (IDP), which promotes the study and preservation of MSS and printed materials from Dunhuang and other Central Asian sites.

India Office Records and Library
The India Office Records include 14km of shelving, 70,000 bound vols and 105,000 MS and printed maps, and comprise the archives of the East India Company (1600-1858), the Board of Control or Board of Commissioners for the Affairs of India (1784-1858), the India Office (1858-1947), the Burma Office (1937-1948) and other British agencies overseas linked to the four main bodies. The India Office Library also includes over 16,000 vols of private and family papers of individuals who served in India, 12,000 Indian paintings, 16,000 British drawings and 250,000 photographs.

BRITISH AND EARLY PRINTED COLLECTIONS
Reader Services (general enquiries): 020-7412-7676; *fax:* 020-7412-7609
Email: reader-services-enquiries@bl.uk

Early Printed Collections: 020-7412-7676; *fax:* 020-7412-7577
Email: rare-books@bl.uk
Internet: http://www.bl.uk/collections/early.html

Modern British Collections: 020-7412-7623; *fax:* 020-7412-7557
Email: modern-british@bl.uk
Internet: http://www.bl.uk/collections/british/britishandirish.html

Humanities Reading Rooms, Rare Books and Music Reading Room: Mon 1000-2000, Tue-Thu 0930-2000, Fri-Sat 0930-1700

These collections comprise the Library's printed materials produced in the British Isles and/or in English from all periods as well as its collections of historic printed materials from Western Europe until 1850. The British collection is the single largest collection of books and periodicals of its kind in the world and this is true of many of the west European collections too.

Books, periodicals and ephemera on all subjects are held in the Early Printed Collections areas. The holdings of incunabula, some 12,500 items, include more editions than any other collection in the world. For publications produced in the British Isles since 1914, the Modern British Collections cover all subjects in the humanities and social sciences. Dispersed throughout these collections there are outstanding examples of fine bindings.

Foundation collections include the Old Royal Library and the library of Sir Hans Sloane. Subsequent acquisitions include: the Ashley Library of English Literature; Sir Joseph Banks' Library (natural history); the Revd C.M. Cracherode Library; the Garrick Collection (early English drama); the Grenville Library (politics and literature); the King's Library of George III (history and topography); the Lawrence Durrell Collection; the George Orwell Collection; the John Osborne Collection; and the George Bernard Shaw Collection. These and many others are described on the Library's web pages.

MANUSCRIPTS COLLECTIONS
(020-7412-7513; *fax:* 020-7412-7745)
Email: mss@bl.uk
Internet: http://www.bl.uk/collections/manuscripts.html
MSS Reading Room: Mon 1000-1700, Tue-Sat 0930-1700

These collections form the chief national repository of MSS and private papers and archives, mainly in Western languages. Collections date from the third century BC, and include papyri in Latin and Greek, biblical MSS, MSS in Old English, medieval illuminated MSS and chronicles, seals, charters and manorial records, state papers (16C-17C), family papers (15C-20C), heraldic, antiquarian and genealogical collections, scientific and medical MSS, literary MSS and theatrical records, MS maps and topographical drawings, documents and papers of all periods relating to literary, cultural, social, economic and political history. The collections also include large numbers of facsimiles and photocopies of MSS, and is the place of deposit for scripts of plays performed in the UK.

Particularly important documents in the collections include: Lindisfarne Gospels (8C); Bede's History of the English Church and People (8C); Beowulf (11C); the Anglo-Saxon Chronicle (11C); The Articles of the Barons and two of the four surviving contemporary Exemplifications of Magna Carta (1215); Malory's Le Morte D'Arthur (15C).

Foundation collections include: Cotton MSS; Harley MSS; Sloane MSS. Other collections include: Arundel MSS; Ashley MSS (mainly 19C literary MSS); Blenheim Papers; Burney MSS; Cecil of Chelwood Papers; Egerton MSS; Gladstone Papers; Hargrave MSS (legal MSS); Lansdowne MSS (including the papers of William Cecil, Lord Burghley); the King's MSS (collected by George III); the Royal MSS; Stowe MSS; Yates Thompson MSS (illuminated MSS); Yelverton MSS; Zweig MSS.

The Manuscripts Reading Room also contains a variety of reference materials relating to the main collections on open access.

THE BRITISH LIBRARY SOUND ARCHIVE
(020-7412-7676; Listening and Viewing Service: 020-7214-7418; *fax:* 020-412-7441)
Email: sound-archive@bl.uk
Internet: http://www.bl.uk/nsa/
Humanities Reading Rooms (for Recorded Sound Information Service), Rare Books and Music Reading Room (for Listening and Viewing Service, available by appointment only): Mon 1000-2000, Tue-Thu 0930-2000, Fri-Sat 0930-1700

Houses over 1.2 million sound discs, 205,000 sound tapes and over 22,000 videos, as well as a growing number of recordings in digital format. Around 2.5 million recordings are catalogued on the archive's online catalogue database CADENSA. Main areas of the collections are:

Classical Music - covers music in the Western classical tradition including opera, liturgical music and Western European pre-Baroque repertoires.
Drama and Literature - audio and video recordings of performances and readings, including rare and historical recordings.
International Music Collection - covers traditional, folk and world music from all cultures, including music of most of the world's major religions, work songs, wedding and funeral music, instrumental music, and popular styles such as bhangra, rumba, soukouss, highlife, son, cumbia, tango and rembetika.
Oral History - holds audio and videotaped interviews covering such diverse subjects as British colonialism, religion, history of medicine, industry, politics, the arts, women's history and Jewish history. The archive also carries out its own fieldwork recording projects, and was a leading participant in the Millennium Memory Bank, the largest oral history project even mounted in Britain.
Popular Music - from early music hall recordings to the latest chart and dancefloor music, and including 7,000+ promotional videos.
Wildlife Sounds - over 130,000 recordings of all kinds of animals and their environments world-wide.

The Recorded Sound Information Service operates from the Humanities Reading Room, providing access to the archive's extensive printed collections, which include books and periodicals, discographies and commercial record catalogues dating back to the early 1900s. The Listening and Viewing Service, based in the Rare Books and Music Reading Room, gives access to the recorded collections, as well as providing public access to recordings in the BBC Sound Archives. The archive also maintains a charged Transcription Service providing copies of recordings in the

collections to users who are able to obtain the appropriate copyright clearance.
Northern Listening Service
Boston Spa, Wetherby, West Yorkshire, LS23 7BQ (01937-546070)
Provides access to the archive's recorded collections at the Boston Spa Reading Room. Access is by appointment only.

BRITISH LIBRARY NEWSPAPERS
Colindale Ave, London, NW9 5HE (020-7412-7353; *fax:* 020-7412-7379)
Email: newspaper@bl.uk
Internet: http://www.bl.uk/collections/newspapers.html
Reading Room: Mon-Sat 1000-1645; advance booking recommended

Comprises collections of UK, Irish and overseas newspapers and popular UK periodicals. Early collections date from the early 17C, while systematic collections date from 1822. Over 52,000 newspaper and journal titles are held, comprising 664,000 volumes and 370,000 reels of microfilm. An estimated 155,000 issues were collected by legal deposit in the 2001-02 period. Around 2,600 UK and Irish titles are received, along with 250 overseas titles in western, east European and Slavonic languages, which are received mainly on microfilm.

Foundation collections are the Thomason Tracts (Civil War and other 17C newsbooks and newspapers) and the Burney Collection (700 bound vols of newspapers, 1603-1817). Both of these are housed in the main library, although the Newspaper Library has the Burney Collection on microfilm. Other major collections on microform include: Northern Ireland Political Literature (1966-89); Francis Place Collection (press cuttings and ephemera relating to politics and economics, 1770-1853); Early American Newspapers (17C-19C); Underground and Alternative Press in Britain (1966-83); Tuskegee Institute News Clippings File (history of African-Americans, 1899-1966); Belgian Underground Press (1940-45); Dutch Underground Press (1940-45). Other collection strengths include mainly popular culture and entertainment subjects, particularly fashion, cinema, theatre and music hall, sports, hobbies, trade journals, children's magazines, women's magazines (from suffragette papers to today's glossies), radical and political papers (especially anarchist, Chartist and fascist), and exile and ethnic minority newspapers.

Facilities include 54 microfilm readers, 2 microfiche readers, 8 microfilm reader-printers, and 6 computer workstations with networked access to newspapers on CD-ROM or online, and the Internet.

Access is available to CD-ROMs of the British Humanities Index (1985-date), British Newspaper Index (1990-2000), Newspaper Abstracts (1988-date), the *Economist* (1987-date), the *Financial Times* (1990-date), the *Guardian* (1990-date), the *Independent* (1994-date), the *International Herald Tribune* (1994-date), the *Observer* (1994-date), the Official Index to the Times, the *Telegraph* (1991-date), the *Times* (1990-date) and many others. A range of reproduction services are also provided.

The British Library is a leading partner in NEWSPLAN, a co-operative project for the microfilming and preservation of newspapers in the UK and Ireland, and much of the microfilming carried out under the scheme has been done at the Newspaper Library. The current NEWSPLAN 2000 project, funded by the Heritage Lottery Fund and the UK Newspaper Industry, aims to preserve 1,600 rare or fragile local titles (covering some 33,000 volumes) throughout the UK's ten NEWSPLAN regions, and to provide microfilm copies for libraries throughout the UK.

EUROPEAN AND AMERICAN COLLECTIONS
Include:

American Collections
Email: americas@bl.uk
Covers research-level material in the humanities and social sciences published in Canada, the United States, Central and South America and the Caribbean. Also includes publications of international and inter-governmental organisations.

Slavonic and East European Collections
Email: slavonic@bl.uk
The Library's collections in Slavonic, East European and Soviet Studies are the largest in the UK. Policy is to acquire, as widely as possible, material of research value published in all Slavonic and East European languages covering subjects in the humanities and social sciences.

West European Collections
Internet: http://www.bl.uk/collections/westeuropean/westeuropean.html
Comprises research-level publications in the humanities and social sciences from continental Western Europe, including France, Germany, Italy, Spain and Portugal, the Benelux countries, Austria, Switzerland, Greece and Scandinavia. Material in English published in those countries is also collected. The collections are of international research importance, covering a wide range of disciplines.

THE MAP COLLECTIONS
(020-7412-7702; *fax:* 020-7412-7780)
Email: maps@bl.uk
Internet: http://www.bl.uk/collections/maps.html
Map Library Reading Room: Mon 1000-1700, Tue-Sat 0930-1700

This, the major cartographical collection in the British Isles, comprises about 4.5 million maps, atlases, globes, gazetteers, books on cartography dating from the 9C. It incorporates numerous medieval maps and early modern maps, almost all of the classic early modern European atlases, extensive holdings of cartographic ephemera (postcards, medals etc.), topographical prints and drawings, and the most comprehensive collection of OS maps in existence, from 18C Ordnance Surveyors Drawings and the mid-19C County Series to the modern National Grid Series and the latest editions in digital form. Other modern collections include: topographical maps from throughout the world; geological maps; fire insurance and shopping centre plans; and archival mapping from the Ministry of Defence. Digital mapping and cartographic web sites are being increasingly collected.

Antiquarian collections include: an outstanding collection of medieval mapping (notably the Anglo-Saxon world map of c1025 and the Psalter world map of c1260); the mapping of Matthew Paris (c1250); a large number of portolan charts and atlases 14C-17C; the Augustus series of the Cotton Collection, (c250 predominantly governmental British 16C and early 17C manuscript maps); the Beudeker Collection (Netherlands' cartographical material, predominantly 17C); the Bauza Collection (18C and early 19C maps of South America); Crace Collection (London plans and views, 16C-19C); King George III Topographical Collection (16C-early 19C atlases, maps, plans and views, 50,000 items); King George III Maritime Collection (c3000 charts and atlases, 16C-early 19C); RUSI Collections (18C-20C manuscript and printed military maps worldwide) and the map collections of the East India Company and the India Office. Most of the Library's MS maps are held in the Manuscripts and Asia, Pacific and Africa Collections.

THE MUSIC COLLECTIONS
(020-7412-7772; *fax:* 020-7412-7751)
Email: music-collections@bl.uk
Internet: http://www.bl.uk/collections/music.html
Rare Books and Music Reading Room: Mon 1000-2000, Tue-Thu 0930-2000, Fri-Sat 0930-1700

Comprises MS and printed music from all periods, with 12,000 volumes of MSS (100,000 single items), including many primary sources for the history of music in England, and c1.5 million items of printed music, with 4,000-5,000 added each year. MSS date from the early Middle Ages, printed music from the early 16C onwards.

Special collections include: Paul Hirsch Collection (20,000 items from all periods, especially music theory, opera full scores, 1st editions of Viennese classics); Royal Music Library (early printed music, Handel autographs, 5,000 items); The Royal Philharmonic Society Archive; Zweig Collection (musical autographs of major European composers). Important MSS include the Mulliner Book (16C keyboard music) and the Old Hall MS (medieval and early Renaissance English music).

THE PHILATELIC COLLECTIONS
(020-7412-7635/6; *fax:* 020-7412-7780)
Email: philatelic@bl.uk
Internet: http://www.bl.uk/collections/philatelic/
Philatelic Collections Researchers' Room: Mon-Fri 1000-1600; by appointment

Holdings include fiscal stamps and information on design, postage stamps and associated material from all over the world. 8,191,000 philatelic items, including over 30,000 volumes of philatelic literature, are kept at the London collection.

General collections include: Campbell-Johnston Collection (poster stamps, 1850s-1920s); Crawford Library (philatelic literature, 1861-1913, 4,500 vols); Crown Agents Collection (British Commonwealth); Crown Agents, Philatelic and Security Printing Archive (essays, artwork, proofs and associated records, British Commonwealth, 1900-recent); Foreign and Commonwealth Office Collection (c1890-1992); General Collection (small acquisitions worldwide from 1923); Harrison Collection (British Commonwealth die proofs, 1922-1937); Kay Collection (British colonial revenue stamps to c1940); Mosely Collection (British Africa); Supplementary Collection (British colonial material); Tapling Collection (worldwide, 1840-90); Turner Collection (forgeries, worldwide); Universal Postal Union Collection (specimen and unused stamps and postal stationery from UPU member states, from c1920 onwards); Wilson-Todd Collection (World War 1). There is also a photographic collection of materials not held by the Library.

The Directorate of Scholarship and Collections is also responsible for the selection, acquisition, cataloguing, processing, storage and preservation the Library's collections. Particular activities of note are:

LEGAL DEPOSIT
The British Library is charged with the responsibility for collecting and retaining a copy of everything published in the UK and, under reciprocal legislation, the Republic of Ireland.

NATIONAL PRESERVATION OFFICE
The Library houses and jointly funds the NPO which acts as the focal point in the UK for promoting good practices in preservation and security in libraries and archives. It administers the National Manuscripts Conservation Trust and provides an information and advice service.

2. FINANCE AND CORPORATE RESOURCES
Director: Mr Ian Millar
Responsible for the financial management and budgetary control of the Library. Embraces internal audit, risk management and corporate governance, as well as responsibility for developing corporate strategy and business planning, the maintenance and development of the Library's estate, and the maintenance and development of information systems to support the Library's services. Also acts as the focus of contact with the Department for Culture, Media and Sport, and heads the corporate secretariat.

3. OPERATIONS AND SERVICES
Director: Ms Natalie Ceeney
Provides reading room and document supply services to all user sectors across humanities, research, business use and innovation. Responsible for securing partnerships with publishers to enable distribution of material, plus promoting the sale of Library services. The directorate's responsibilities include:

SCIENCE, TECHNOLOGY AND INNOVATION (STI)
(020-7412-7288/7494; *fax:* 020-7412-7217/7495)
Email: scitech@bl.uk
Internet: http://www.bl.uk/collections/science.html
Science, Technology and Business Reading Rooms: Mon 1000-2000, Tue-Thu 0930-2000, Fri-Sat 0930-1700

Provides comprehensive reference sources of information in science, technology, business, patents and social policy. Simple enquiries can generally be answered free of charge, but more advanced enquiries involving online searches are charged. The following services are spread over five reading rooms:

Sciences and Technology
(020-7412-7288/7494; *fax:* 020-7412-7217)
Email: scitech@bl.uk
Covers all aspects of science, technology and medicine. Provides access to around 20,000 journals, books at professional/research level, reference works, technical standards and abstracting/indexing series; much available in electronic format. Accessed from the Science 2 South and Science 3 Reading Rooms.

Business Information Service (BIS)
(020-7412-7454; *fax:* 020-7412-7453)
Email: business-information@bl.uk
Holds the most comprehensive collection of business information literature in the UK, including journals, directories, market research reports, company reports, trade literature and CD-ROM services. Accessed from the Science 3 South Reading Room.

Social Policy Information Service (SPIS)
(020-7412-7536; *fax:* 020-7412-7761)
Email: social-policy@bl.uk
Provides information in the applied social sciences, including government and administration, education, welfare, employment, crime, housing, family and social life and health care policy. The Official Publications and Social Sciences Reading Area in the Science 2 North Reading Room also provides access to the Library's extensive collections of governmental, inter-governmental and other official publications.

Patents Information Services
(020-7412-7919/20; *fax:* 020-7412-7480)
Email: patents-information@bl.uk
The UK's national patents library, accessed from the Science 1 North and South Reading Rooms, with over 49 million British and foreign patents specifications, as well as abstracts, abridgements, official journals and gazettes, trade marks and designs.

Research Service
(020-7412-7903; *fax:* 020-7412-7840)
Email: research@bl.uk
Provides customised, priced online and desk research and updating services by experts in the fields of patents, scientific, technical and medical information.

DOCUMENT SUPPLY CENTRE
Boston Spa, Wetherby, West Yorkshire, LS23 7BQ (01937-546060; *fax:* 01937-546333)
Email: dsc-customer-services@bl.uk
Internet: http://www.bl.uk/services/document/dsc.html
Reading Room: Mon-Fri 0900-1630; last admittance 1600; pass not required

Provides a rapid national and international loan and photocopying service to 17,000 customers world-wide. The loan service varies in its coverage from a photocopy to supplying a whole archive, tailoring the service to the individual user.

The Document Supply Centre has over 250,000 journal titles in its collection, of which almost 40,000 are currently received, alongside its extensive collections of 3 million books, 400,000 conference proceedings, 4.9 million reports (some unique in the West) and 600,000 theses. It also houses the National Reports Collection and Focus on British Research. 95% of the 4 million requests received each year are satisfied from stock via either the standard service (where over 80% are satisfied from stock) or premium service (a fast response service via the user's preferred delivery medium).

The service has an extensive publishing programme providing information about the collection, available in a variety of formats.

NATIONAL BIBLIOGRAPHIC SERVICE
Boston Spa, Wetherby, West Yorkshire, LS23 7BQ (01937-546585; *fax:* 01937-546586)
Email: nbs-info@bl.uk
Internet: http://www.bl.uk/services/bibliographic/service.html

Develops and markets bibliographic products and services based upon the British National Bibliography (BNB), which the British Library makes available world wide, and upon the catalogues of the Library's collection.

BNB is a collection of bibliographic records of books and first issues of serial titles published in the UK and Ireland. It also holds details of forthcoming books and serial titles under the Cataloguing In Publication programme. Records are fully standardised in UKMARC format (with plans to move to the MARC 21 format in 2004), catalogued to AACR2 standard with full subject indexing. BNB is available on CD-ROM in a number of different packages. The records are also available online on the BLPC (British Library Public Catalogue).

The service distributes records, supports cataloguing activities, allows selection, record supply and online information retrieval via access to 21 databases with over 16 million bibliographical records, although some services can be provided via printed publications or CD-ROM.

4. STRATEGIC MARKETING AND COMMUNICATIONS
Director: Ms Jill Finney
Responsibilities include developing the marketing strategy for the Library's chosen markets and implementing the Library's brand strategy through design, marketing and publishing. Also responsible for internal communications and fund-raising, as well as co-operative programmes with partners to extend the Library's reach.

MARKETING
(020-7412-7468; *fax:* 020-7412-7807)
Head of Corporate and Public Marketing: Ms Heather Norman
Head of Marketing for Business: Ms Isabel Oswell
Head of Marketing Services: Ms Carol Meades

PUBLISHING
(020-7412-7704; *fax:* 020-7412-7768)
The Library has over 600 titles in print, both under its own imprint and is association with other publishers. Publications include bibliographies and reference works in both print and electronic media, as well as numerous general and illustrated books based mainly on the Library's historic collections.

EXHIBITIONS
(020-7412-7595; *fax:* 020-7412-7508)
Email: exhibitions@bl.uk
Gallery Opening Hours: Mon, Wed-Fri 0930-1800, Tue 0930-2000, Sat 0930-1700, Sun 1100-1700
The St Pancras building contains three exhibition galleries. The Library's treasures, including the Gutenberg Bible and Shakespeare's First Folio, are on display in the John Ritblat Gallery, as is the computer-based interactive "Turning the Pages" exhibition. Special exhibitions are held in the Pearson Gallery, and the Workshop of Words, Sounds and Images is an interactive gallery tracing the history of book production and recorded sound.

EVENTS
There are programmes of events (lectures, readings, performances, films etc) and activities for adults and children, including schools, and there is a web site devotes to resources for schools at: http://www.bl.uk/learning/.

PRESS AND PUBLIC RELATIONS
(020-7412-7111; *fax:* 020-7412-7168)
Email: press-and-pr@bl.uk
Head of Public Affairs: Mr Greg Hayman

DEVELOPMENT OFFICE
(020-7412-7030; *fax:* 020-7412 -7168)
Head: Ms Lara Jukes

5. e-STRATEGY AND PROGRAMMES
Director: Mr Richard Boulderstone
Responsibilities include the effective development, integration, and delivery of all electronic, online and IT functions, the development and implementation of e- and IT strategies for digital media, services, projects and programmes, managing the delivery of the e-strategy and the IT change programme, and leading the development of e-business methods and tools.

L2 - THE NATIONAL LIBRARY OF SCOTLAND

THE NATIONAL LIBRARY OF SCOTLAND was founded as the Advocate's Library in 1682, which was first given copyright status in 1710. It was established as the National Library of Scotland by an Act of Parliament in 1925. The Library is entitled under Copyright legislation to claim works published in the UK and Ireland. It is governed by The Board of Trustees and is funded by The Scottish Office.

GENERAL INFORMATION

National Library of Scotland, George IV Bridge, Edinburgh, EH1 1EW (0131-226-4531; *fax:* 0131-622-4803)
Email: enquiries@nls.uk
Internet: http://www.nls.uk/

Open: see times for individual reading rooms and departments; the Library is closed on public holidays and for one week in Sep/Oct.

Chair of the Board of Trustees: Prof Michael Anderson
National Librarian: Mr Martyn Wade
Secretary of the Library: Mr Martin C. Graham
Director of Special Collections: Dr Murray Simpson
Director of General Collections: Mrs Cate Newton
Director of Public Services: Dr Alan M. Marchbank
Director of Information and Communications Technology: Mr Fred Guy
Expenditure: £10,086,000 (running costs); £1,055,000 (purchases)
Holdings: 7 million printed items; 20,000 current periodical and newspaper titles; 120,000 vols of MSS; 1.6 million maps; plus microforms and other non-print materials. An average of 6,000 printed items are added every week, from books and pamphlets to maps and music. Popular and local material as well as scholarly works are preserved with a particular focus on Scotland and the Scots at home and abroad.
Admission: admission to reading rooms is by reader's ticket (certain restrictions apply to undergraduates and school students). Applicants must apply in person at one of the Library's service points, and proof of identity will be required. Note that the NLS is a library of last resort, and access is generally restricted to those carrying out research requiring material not readily available elsewhere.

STRUCTURE OF THE LIBRARY

The Library has 4 operational departments:

1. GEORGE IV BRIDGE

The reading rooms are for reference and research which cannot be conveniently pursued elsewhere.
Services: copying service; powerpoints for laptop PCs

GENERAL READING ROOM

Open: Mon-Tue, Thu-Fri 0930-2030, Wed 1000-2030, Sat 0930-1300
Used for the consultation of journals, newspapers and most post-1800 printed material from the Library's general collections, which are not dealt with by any of the other specialist, reading rooms. Scientific materials are also consulted here. A small collection of CD-ROMs is also available.

NORTH READING ROOM

Open: Mon-Tue, Thu-Fri 0930-2030, Wed 1000-2030, Sat 0930-1300
Used for the consultation of MSS, printed books from special collections including pre-1801 printed material, and photographs (including the Library's collections of early Scottish photographs).

MICROFORM READING ROOM

Open: Mon-Tue, Thu-Fri 0930-2000, Wed 1000-2000, Sat 0930-1230
Used for the consultation of the Library's microform collections.

Special collections include:

RARE BOOK COLLECTIONS

(0131-446-2806; *fax:* 0131-466-2807)
Email: rarebooks@nls.uk
Head of Rare Books: Dr Brian Hillyard

Collections include: Astorga Collection (Spanish books, 15C-19C, 3,617 vols); Walter Blaikie Collection (Jacobitism, 17C-18C, 1,076 items); Blairs College Collection (Libraries of Scottish Roman Catholic communities at home and abroad, on deposit, 27,000 vols); Graham Brown Collection (alpine and mountaineering, 16C-20C, c20,000 items); Bute Collection (1,266 English plays, 17C-18C); Cassidy Collection (religious works, 16C-19C, c5,000 vols); Castle Fraser Collection (18C-19C, 1,372 vols); Cowan Collection (Scottish liturgy, 16C-20C, 1,117 vols); Crawford Collections (15C-19C, c45,000 items); Dieterichs Collection (German Reformation, 16C-18C, c100,000 items); Drygrange Collection (Scottish Catholicism, 18C-19C, 2,300+ vols); John and Ljubica Erickson Collection (Soviet Union, c7,000 vols); Gray Collection (theology and classics, 15C-16C, c1,500 vols); Institute of Chartered Accountants Antiquarian Collection (accountancy, 15C-20C, 1,000+ items on deposit); Jolly Collection (theology, 16C-19C, 2,976 vols); Lauriston Castle Collection (Scottish books, chap-books, 17C-19C, 3,700 vols); Loyd Collection (alpine and mountaineering, 18C-20C, c2,000 items); Macadam Collection (baking and confectionary, 19C-20C, 1,619 vols); Eudo Mason Collection (children's books, mainly 19C, 3,600 items); Newbattle Collection (European literature and humanities, 15C-18C, 5,158 vols); Newhailes Library (18C library, c7,000 vols); Preshome Chapel Library (theology, 4,700+ items); Rosebery Collection (early and rare Scottish books and pamphlets, c3,120 items); Saltoun Manse Collection (17C-18C, c2,000 vols); Hugh Sharp Collection (English and American first editions, 17C-20C, 1,200 vols); Thorkelin Collection (Scandinavia, 16C-19C, c1,500 items); Warden Collection (shorthand, 16C-20C, c4,600 items); Wordie Collection (polar exploration, 17C-20C, 4,600+ items).

MANUSCRIPT AND ARCHIVAL COLLECTIONS

(0131-466-2812; *fax:* 0131-466-2811)
Email: manuscripts@nls.uk
Head of Manuscripts: Mr Iain Maciver

Collections include: medieval MSS; Gaelic MSS; Scottish literary MSS (15C-date): Robert Burns; James Hogg; Sir Walter Scott; J.G. Lockhart; Thomas Carlyle; R.L. Stevenson; Hugh MacDairmid & others; music MSS (early 16C onwards); Scottish historical documents: letters of Mary Queen of Scots and the Marquess of Montrose; copies of the National Covenant; Denmylne State Papers; archives of Scottish publishers: William Blackwood & Sons; Oliver & Boyd; W. & R. Chambers; political, military and diplomatic papers: Lord Milton; Henry Dundas; Sir Robert Liston; Sir George Murray; Lord Rosebery; Lord Haldane; Earl Haig; labour history collections (Scottish trade unions and political organisations); philosophical, scientific and engineering papers: David Hume; Alexander Campbell Fraser; John Rennie; Stevenson family archives; J.S. Haldane; J.B.S. Haldane; church history and missions: Robert Wodrow MSS; John Lee papers; David Livingstone papers; records of Church of Scotland and other missions; family and estate papers: Sunderland estate papers; Minto papers; Yester and Saltoun papers; Cadell of Grange papers; Dundas papers; Maxwell of Monreith papers; Lynedock papers; Asburton papers; sporting archives: Honourable Company of Edinburgh Golfers Archive; Camanachd Association Archive; Scottish Mountaineering Club Archive; cultural and theatre archives: Scottish Arts Council Archive; Edinburgh International Festival Society Archive; Edinburgh International Film Festival Archive.

PRINTED MUSIC COLLECTIONS

(0131-226-4531 x2328)
Email: music@nls.uk
Head of Music: Ms Almut M. Boehme

Collections comprise some 250,000 printed scores and 3,000 published recordings, and are particularly strong in Scottish music, especially traditional and folk music. Special collections include: Balfour Handel Collection (early editions of Handel, c500 scores, 100+ libretti); Glen Collection (Scottish music); Hopkinson Collections (contemporary and later editions of Berlioz and Verdi); Inglis Collection (Scottish music, 740 items); Murdoch Henderson Collection (Scottish music, 200+ vols, 556 printed music items). There are also about 5,000 published sound recordings. MS music is held by the Manuscripts Division.

OFFICIAL PUBLICATIONS
Email: p.wellburn@nls.uk
Head of Official Publications: Mr Peter Wellburn

Extensive collections covering both the UK and overseas include: publications of the Scottish Parliament; House of Commons Papers (1715 onwards); House of Lords Papers (1801 onwards); governmental publications from the Republic of Ireland; publications of the UN and its agencies; OECD publications (official repository); some EU materials; significant coverage of US official publications prior to 1993.

PHOTOGRAPHIC COLLECTIONS
General collections are mainly in the form of photographically-illustrated books and albums, relating to Scotland and Scottish photography from 1847 to the present day. Special collections held by the Manuscripts Division include early photography, documentary material relating to Scottish photographers (Hill and Adamson, David Brewster and others), and photographic archives, such as the Paul Schillabeer Archive.

2. MAP LIBRARY
Causewayside Bldg, 33 Salisbury Place, Edinburgh, EH9 1SL (0131-466-3813; *fax:* 0131-466-3812)
Email: maps@nls.uk
Open: Mon-Tue, Thu-Fri 0930-1700, Wed 1000-1700, Sat 0930-1300 (restricted service); reader's ticket not required, but users must have tried other sources first.
Head of Map Library: Mr D. Webster

Subjects: the largest and most comprehensive map collection in Northern Britain, with emphasis on Europe, North America, mountain areas of the world and also areas with Scottish association. Topographic but with a growing thematic collection to mirror world environmental issues.
Stock: 1,600,000 printed maps (30,000 are added each year); over 4,000 MSS; over 15,000 atlases; 100,000 Ordnance Survey microfilms; 4,000 reference books; gazetteers; CD-ROMs.
Collections: Bartholomew Archive (maps used and published by Edinburgh mapmaking firm); John Bartholomew Collection (36 atlases in 53 volumes, 1525-1865); Board of Ordnance Collection (375 18C military maps, mainly MS); Graham Brown Collection (370 mountain and polar maps); Marischal Collection (137 maps of Scotland, 1673-1873); Murray Collection (early 18C military maps); Newman Collection (British road books, itineraries and road maps, 17C-19C, c1,500 items); Wade Collection (18C maps and plans relating to military construction in the Highlands)
Services: microfilm and microfiche readers; reprographic and photocopying (b&w up to A0, colour up to A3); enquiry service; hire of transparencies and negatives; talks, visits and displays.

3. THE SCOTTISH BUSINESS INFORMATION SERVICE
(0131-225-8488; *fax:* 0131-466-2818)
Email: enquiries@scotbis.com
Internet: http://www.scotbis.com/
Head of Business Information: Mr John Coll

Acts as a national resource in the provision of company and market information. It holds over 1,200 trade directories and over 700 company directories (both UK and international), over 8,000 company annual reports and over 3,500 market research reports. Access is provided to a wide range of official and unofficial statistics, and to all major business online databases and CD-ROMs. Over 1,000 business and trade journals are available including the *Financial Times* and the *Wall Street Journal*.
Services: enquiry service; online searches; photocopying; fax; inter-library loans.

4. INTER-LIBRARY SERVICES
Causewayside Bldg, 33 Salisbury Place, Edinburgh, EH9 1SL (0131-466-3815; *fax:* 0131-466-3814)
Email: ils@nls.uk
Head of Inter-Library Services: Miss Patricia McKenzie

Founded in 1921 as the Scottish Central Library, merged with the National Library of Scotland in 1974. Co-ordinates interlibrary lending in Scotland and co-operation between collaborating libraries of all categories. Maintains the Scottish Union Catalogue (SUC) which contains about 200,000 entries, and Pool Lending Stock (c140,000 volumes and 1,500 microforms). Coordinates the Scottish Fiction Reserve Scheme. Accepts interlibrary loan requests on official pre-paid requisitions from all UK libraries and from overseas libraries.

OTHER SERVICES

ELECTRONIC INFORMATION RESOURCES
As well as online catalogues and indexes relating to its collections, the Library maintains a number of bibliographical databases:

Bibliography of Scotland (BOS)
Bibliography of Scottish Gaelic (BOSG)
Bibliography of Scottish Literature in Translation (BOSLIT)
Bibliography of the Scots Language (BOSLAN)
Union Catalogue of Art Books in Libraries in Scotland (UCABLIS)
Millgate Union Catalogue of Walter Scott Correspondence
US and Canadian Newspaper Holding in Scottish Libraries
Scottish Book Trade Index (SBTI)
Scottish Books 1505-1600
Scottish Academic Libraries Serials Database (SALSER)

EXHIBITIONS AND PUBLICATIONS
Regular exhibitions of Scottish interest are held in the exhibition hall in the George IV Building where there is also a bookshop. The Library also stages frequent touring exhibitions.

Publications include: Quarto: Newsletter of the National Library of Scotland; ILS Notes (Inter-Library Service newsletter); Annual Report; Bibliography of Scotland (updated annually); Scottish Gaelic Union Catalogue; Directory of Scottish Newspapers; Scottish Family Histories; numerous other bibliographical and reference works, as well as works of more general interest, exhibition catalogues, and facsimile maps and MSS.

L3 - NATIONAL LIBRARY OF WALES
(Llyfrgell Genedlaethol Cymru)

THE NATIONAL LIBRARY OF WALES was established by Royal Charter in 1907 and granted legal deposit privilege under the Copyright Act of 1911. Its function is to collect and preserve material relating to Wales, reflecting its history, culture, economy, geography and people, and to act as the major scholarly and reference library for Wales. It operates through the two official languages of Wales, Welsh and English, and is managed by a Court of Governors and a Council. The Library is funded by the National Assembly for Wales.

GENERAL INFORMATION
The National Library of Wales, Aberystwyth, Ceredigion, SY23 3BU (01970-632800; fax: 01970-615709)
Email: holi@llgc.org.uk
Internet: http://www.llgc.org.uk/

Open: Mon-Fri 0930-1800, Sat 0930-1700 (restricted service), closed Sun, public holidays and first full week of Oct.

President: Dr R. Brinley Jones MA, DPhil, FSA
Librarian and Chief Executive: Mr Andrew M.W. Green MA, DipLib, MCLIP
Director of Corporate Services: Mr Mark Mainwaring MA, Solicitor, MIMgt
Director of Finance: Mr D.H. Michael CPFA
Total staff: 270
Grant in aid: £9,671,000

Holdings: c5 million books, serials and newspapers; 4 million archive items; 40,000 vols of MSS; 1 million maps; 750,000 photographs; 200,000 hours of video recordings; c4 million ft of film; 150,000 hours of sound recordings; some 200,000 items are added annually.

Admission: by Reader's Ticket, valid for 5 years (application form available on request from the Director of Public Services). A temporary (1 month, non-renewable) Reader's Ticket is also available.

STRUCTURE OF THE LIBRARY

The library is divided into two main departments:

1. DEPARTMENT OF COLLECTION SERVICES

(01970-632803; *fax:* 01970-632882)
Director of Collection Services: Mr Gwyn Jenkins MA

The Department is responsible for all aspects of the Library's collections, their acquisition, description and preservation. Of the Library's 4.5 million printed works, there are many rare and important items including:

The first three books printed in Welsh (1546-1547)
The first book printed in Wales (1587)
The earliest Welsh Bibles

PRINTED BOOK COLLECTIONS

Special collections include: Anderson Collection (c140 works by or relating to John Donne); Arthurian Collection (Arthurian legends, c3,200 vols including the 1488 Lancelot du Lac); Baring-Gould Ballad Collection (19C ballads and street literature in English, c950 items); Idris Bell Collection (papyrological texts, classical history and literature, c1,500 items); Blondeau Collection (2,024 French dramatic texts, 1815-1914); Borg Collection (the Viking world, 400+ items); Bourdillon Collection (French medieval literature, early illustrated books, Arthuriana, classical and English authors, reference works, 150 MSS, 6,178 printed vols); Castell Gorford Collection (Welsh history, genealogy and topography, 1,500 items); Casell Gwyn Collection (English literature, mainly 18C, c1,500 vols); Children's Books, pre-1870 (c450 items); Chirk Castle Collection (18C parliamentary and other pamphlets, c500 pamphlets and c350 vols); Civil War Tracts (c600 items); Frances Power Cobbe Collection (theology, science, zoology, history, bibliography, mainly pre-1900, c2,500 vols); Lewis Weston Dillwyn Collection (botany, 16C-19C, c1,000 vols); Dunraven Collection (Oxford Movement and other religious movements of mid 19C, 78 vols, c350 monographs and pamphlets); Gladstone Collection (politics, education, religion, history, c4,000 items); Greenwell Collection (mining and coal industry, c1,000 items); Gregynog Collection (printing and book production, 282 vols); Gregynog Press Collection (c135 vols and some ephemera); Hawkes Collection (works in Chinese, Japanese and English, c4,500 vols); Incunabula Collection (c250 vols); David Jones Collection (art, literature, Wales and the Celts, religion, Roman history, c1,760 items); Llandaff Cathedral Library (mainly theology, c800 items); Robert Owen Collection (mainly 19C, c1,150 items); Plas Power Collection (mainly literature and history, 18C-19C, c220 vols); Private Press Collection (c1,800 vols); Bruce Rogers Collection (works of American typographer, 211 items); St Asaph Cathedral Library (c2,500 vols); 16C Continental Books (c2,500 items); Thomas-Stanford Euclid Collection (Euclid's works, including pre-1600 editions, 303 vols); Trefeca Collection (mainly theology, 1,500 vols); UCW Library (foundation collection, 16C-20C, c13,400 vols); Welsh Almanacs Collection (1681-1800, c250 items); Welsh Ballads Collection (18C-19C, c7,000 items); D.J. Williams Collection (Welsh children's books, c500 items); Griffith John Williams Collection (Welsh and Celtic studies, c5,000 monographs); Sir John Williams Collection (foundation collection, 16C-early 20C, c26,360 vols); World War 1 Collection (c8,000 vols).

PRINTED MUSIC

The Library's collection of printed music includes 300,000 pieces of sheet music, with 1,500 additions made annually. The collection is particularly strong in Welsh and Celtic music.

MAP COLLECTION

The collection of maps is unrivalled in Wales and is a rich source for atlases and antiquarian maps of Wales and the British Isles. It includes historical maps dating back to the 16C, Ordnance Survey maps at all scales (early 19C onwards), Ministry of Defence maps, maps of the Tithe survey, foreign maps and national atlases, sea charts, town plans, estate and farm plans, assuring it to be one of Britain's largest cartographical resources. Also held are enclosure awards and auctioneers' sales particulars. Special map collections include: Mervyn Prichard Collection (early geographies and atlases); modern Admiralty Charts.

PHOTOGRAPHIC COLLECTION

The collection concentrates on people and places in Wales and Welsh life in general, and contain 750,000 images from the earliest days of photography to the present. Major collections include: John Thomas Collection (1860s-90s, 3,500 negatives); Francis Frith & Co Collection (1860-1970, 35,000+ photos); Geoffrey Charles Collection (1939-1979, 150,000 negatives).

PICTURE COLLECTION

An extensive national collection of pictures, water colours and prints, including topographical prints and drawings, portraits, and various printed ephemera, such as posters, cards, scrap books and book marks. The Department is responsible for developing the Welsh Portrait Archive.

MANUSCRIPT COLLECTIONS

The MS collections held by the Department are described in the *Handlist of Manuscripts in the National Library of Wales (1940-)*. The collections as a whole are also surveyed in the *Guide to the Department of Manuscripts and Records* (1997).

Special MS collections include: The Hengwrt-Peniarth MSS (500+ vols); The Mostyn MSS; Llanstephan MSS; Panton MSS; Cwrtmawr MSS (only partially covered in the Handlist); Sir Lewis Morris MSS; Sir Henry Owen MSS; Sir Edward Anwyl MSS; Sir Daniel Lleufer Thomas MSS; Celynog MSS; Francis Bourdillon MSS; The Llanover MSS; The Gwysaney MSS, and others.

Archival collections include: a wide range of public records and documents, including the Great Sessions in Wales (1530-1830); ecclesiastical records: Anglican; Wesleyan Methodist; Calvinistic Methodist (Presbyterian Church of Wales); Baptist; Congregationalist and others; also the records of the Welsh Church Commission; estate and family archives: Badminton; Brogyntyn; Bronwydd; Bute; Chirk Castle; Dolaucothi; Penrice and Margam; Powis Castle; Tredegar; Wynnstay; industrial records: Beaumont Archive; Cyfarthfa Archive; Evans & Bevin Archive; Llandinam Archive; Nevill Archive; early industrial records can also be found in a number of estate archives; archives of institutions: Council for the Principality; Welsh Arts Council; National Eisteddfod; Honourable Society of Cymmrodorion; Royal Welsh Agricultural Society; personal papers of writers: David Jones; Vernon Watkins; Emlyn Williams; John Cowper Powys; personal papers of artists, musicians and scholars: Gwen John; Joseph Parry; David Vaughan-Thomas; Sir John Rhys; Sir Henry Lewis; O.T. Jones; and many others.

The Welsh Political Archive

Established by the Library in 1983 to co-ordinate the collection of all materials relating to politics in Wales. Party records include: Labour Party (Wales) Archive (1937-date); Welsh Liberal Party records (1960s-date); records of the SDP in Wales (1981-date); records of several Welsh Conservative and Unionist Associations (early 20C-date); Plaid Cymru Archives (1925-date). As well as those of David Lloyd George, papers of politicians include: Clement Davies Papers; T.E. Ellis Papers; Lord Elwyn-Jones Papers; Gwynfor Evans Papers; Thomas Jones CH Papers; Sir John Herbert Lewis Papers; Beata Brookes Papers; Leo Abse Papers; Dafydd Wigley Papers. The Archive also holds records of various organisations and pressure groups, including: the Welsh National Council of the United Nations Association (1923-56); Association of Welsh Local Authorities (1928-70); Parliament for Wales Campaign (1953-56). General election leaflets and other ephemera are also held.

2. DEPARTMENT OF PUBLIC SERVICES
(01970-632801; *fax:* 01970-632882)
Director of Public Services: Dr Rhidian Griffiths MA, MLitt, PhD, DipLib, MCLIP

The Department is responsible for the whole range of services to the public, including services to readers, public programmes (exhibitions and education), access and marketing, and publications.

GENEALOGICAL RESEARCH
The Department provides a genealogical search service for a fee, although some simple searches are free of charge. All three main departments hold some materials of use to genealogical researchers, although the most extensive are in the Department of Manuscripts and Records. Holdings of genealogical interest include: Anglican and Nonconformist records; wills; court records; poor law and parochial records; education records; manorial records; and pedigree books. Tithe maps and apportionment schedules are held in the Department of Pictures and Maps, while the Department of Printed Books holds electoral lists, newspapers and directories.

ELECTRONIC INFORMATION RESOURCES
There are many databases available for use by readers, either on CD-ROM, or online, including:

British Humanities Index
COPAC
Early English Books Online
ESTC (Eighteenth Century Short Title Catalogue)
Global Books in Print
Periodicals Contents Index
RLG Cultural Materials
UKOP (Catalogue of UK Official Publications)
Ulrichs

THE NATIONAL SCREEN AND SOUND ARCHIVE OF WALES
(01970-632828; *fax:* 01970-615709)
Email: agssc@llgc.org.uk
Internet: http://screenandsound.llgc.org.uk/
Open: Mon-Fri 0930-1730
Head of Archive: Mr Iestyn Hughes BLib, MCLIP

The Archive covers every aspect of Wales and Welsh life and culture, as chronicled by audiovisual media. The range of recording media varies from early wax cylinders to CDs and from turn-of-the-century ciné film to recent television broadcasts and digital recordings. Moving image materials held include feature films, documentaries, educational and amateur films, home movies, animation, television off-air recordings, including a number of unique unpublished recordings. Audio materials include radio broadcasts, classical and popular music and oral history. Unpublished sound and radio recordings include lectures, field recordings and off-air recordings. Some documentation (scripts, cuttings, etc.) also accompanies certain of the moving image collections. A Viewing and Listening Service is provided for visiting researchers. Other services include community screenings for groups and societies, assistance to production companies, licensing of images and sound, and limited loan services.

The collection comprises over 200,000 hours of video recordings, c4 million ft of film, over 150,000 hours of audio recordings, thousands of records and hundreds of CDs. The 78rpm Records Database and the Film Catalogue are also available online.

The Archive also operates on two other sites:

National Screen and Sound Archive of Wales, Unit 1, Science Park, Cefn Llan, Llanbadarn Fawr, Ceredigion, SY23 3AH
(01970-626007; *fax:* 01970-626008)

National Screen and Sound Archive of Wales, Sgrîn: Media Agency for Wales, The Bank, 10 Mount Stuart Square, Cardiff, CF10 5EE
(029-2033-3309; *fax:* 029-2033-3320)

The main site at The National Library of Wales should always be contacted first by those wishing to use the viewing and listening facilities. It is intended that the collection will be united at the main site in 2004.

OTHER SERVICES
The Library provides a range of reprographic services, and stages frequent exhibitions, some of which can be viewed on the Internet. It also maintains a programme of regular publications, including a Library Journal (2 pa).

L4 - THE BODLEIAN LIBRARY

THE BODLEIAN LIBRARY is the principal library of the University of Oxford. It was refounded in 1598 on the site of an earlier 15th century library by Sir Thomas Bodley, opened to readers in 1602 and has been a legal deposit library since 1610.

GENERAL INFORMATION
The Bodleian Library, Broad St, Oxford, OX1 3BG
(01865-277000; *fax:* 01865-277182)
Email: enquiries@bodley.ox.ac.uk
Internet: http://www.bodley.ox.ac.uk/

Director of University Library Services and Bodley's Librarian: Mr R.P. Carr MA, BA(Leeds), MA(Manc), MA(Camb), Hon DLitt (Leic), FRSA
Deputy: Mr R.R. Milne MA, MA(Edin), MA(Lond), FRSA, FCLIP
Keeper of Special Collections and Western Manuscripts: Mrs M. Clapinson MA, FSA, FRHistS
Keeper of Oriental Collections: Ms L.E. Forbes BA, DipLib, MCLIP
Total staff: 382
Holdings: 7,004,000 vols, including 187,000 vols of MSS, with 133,000 added in 2001-02; 59,250 current periodicals; 950,000 microforms
Expenditure: £15 million
Admission: on production of current Reader's card; outside applicants should bring written recommendations; visitors may be charged an admission fee - academic visitors from HEFCE institutions are exempt. For full details contact:

The Admissions Office (01865-277180; *fax:* 01865-277105)
Email: admissions@bodley.ox.ac.uk
Internet: http://www.bodley.ox.ac.uk/guides/admisfrm.htm
Open: Mon-Fri 0930-1630, Sat 0930-1230

THE STRUCTURE OF THE LIBRARY
The central library buildings include the Old Library, the New Library and the Radcliffe Camera. Also part of the Bodleian is the Nuneham Courtenay Book Repository, opened in 1975 to house less used materials.

THE OLD LIBRARY
Open: term: Mon-Fri 0900-2200, Sat 0900-1300; vac: Mon-Fri 0900-1900, Sat 0900-1300

LOWER READING ROOM
General catalogue of printed books, general reference and bibliography, patristics, classics, classical philosophy.

UPPER READING ROOM
Research collections for history and English language and literature.

DUKE HUMFREY'S LIBRARY
Restored in 1963 and again in 1999, this is the main reading room for bound manuscripts, papyri, Oxford Theses, material from the University Archives, printed books up to 1640 and other rare printed material. It also houses the four main catalogues for MSS:

The Quarto Catalogues - cover the major MS collections acquired in the 17C and 18C.
The Summary Catalogue - published between 1895 and 1953 and describes MSS acquired from the refoundation of the library from 1602-1915 except those entered in the quarto catalogues.

The Summary Catalogue of Post medieval Western Manuscripts ...Acquisitions 1916-1975 - The major post 1916 acquisitions excluding the large collections of modern political papers and all acquisitions of medieval MSS.

The Continuation of the Summary Catalogue - unpublished current catalogue of MSS acquired from 1975 (and including those MSS omitted from the Summary Catalogue 1916-1975).

Current cataloguing for MSS is undertaken and available online. See: http://www.bodley.ox.ac.uk/dept/scwmss/wmss/online/online.htm

THE NEW LIBRARY

Open: term: Mon-Fri 0900-2200, Sat 0900-1300; vac: Mon-Fri 0900-1900 (some reading rooms -1700 in Aug), Sat 0900-1300; Map Room, Music Room, Oriental Reading Room and Room 132 close at 1900 in term and vacations.

PPE READING ROOM
Politics, modern philosophy, economics, management studies.

MAP ROOM
(01865-277013; *fax:* 01865-277139)
Email: maps@bodley.ox.ac.uk
Map Librarian: Mr N. Millea BA, DipLib, FRGS
Houses 1,215,000 maps and 21,500 atlases. Collections include early cartographical works, portolan charts and estate maps, and one of the most comprehensive collections of OS maps in existence. Also held are a wide range of reference works on geography and cartography.

MUSIC ROOM
(01865-277063; *fax:* 01865-277182)
Email: music@bodley.ox.ac.uk
Music Librarian: Mr P.A. Ward Jones MA, FRCO
Music collections comprise c500,000 items of printed music; 3,500 music MSS; 800 microfilms; and 59,000 books and periodicals. Special collections include the musical sections of the Harding Collection, as well as opera and concert programmes, and press cuttings.

MODERN PAPERS AND JOHN JOHNSON READING ROOM (ROOM 132)
Modern MSS and unbound papers, mainly political and literary; small collection of reference material relating to modern MSS. Also the reading room for the John Johnson Collection of Printed Ephemera.

ORIENTAL READING ROOM
Catalogues of MSS in all Oriental languages except the languages of India; Oriental studies.

RADCLIFFE CAMERA

Open: term: Mon-Fri 0900-2200, Sat 0900-1300; vac: Mon-Fri 0900-1900, Sat 0900-1300

UPPER READING ROOM
Undergraduate material on history, art history, education, archaeology and anthropology.

S.T. LEE (LOWER) READING ROOM
Undergraduate material on theology and English; books and periodicals on Latin America; Official Papers; British government publications; publications of international organisations.

SPECIAL COLLECTIONS
Housed in the Department of Special Collections and Western Manuscripts, and the Department of Oriental Collections.

PRINTED BOOKS
Major collections include: Barlow Collection (17C tracts and pamphlets, early theology, 6,000 items); Bartholomew Pamphlets (17C- early 18C pamphlets, 50,000 items); Broxbourne Collection (incunabula and early printed books, historical bindings from the 12C-date, 4,000 items); Bywater Collection (history of classical scholarship, especially 16C Paris printing, 4,000 items); Clarendon Press Collection (3,200 classical texts and other books published by the Clarendon Press from 1720-1892); Douce Collection (romances, histories, and liturgical books from all periods, 17,000 vols); Dunston Collection (literature, botany, history and travel, 8,000 items); Godwyn Collection (18C English and general history, civil and ecclesiastical, 3,000 books and 38,000 pamphlets); Gough Collection (maps, prints and drawings, 3,700 items including 2500 books); Harding Collection (songbooks, English and French poetry, poetical miscellanies and English drama, 250,000 items); Jessel Collection (history and use of playing cards, 3,500 items); John Johnson Collection (16C-20C printed ephemera, 100,000 items); Malone Collection (mainly Elizabethan, Jacobean and Caroline Literature, 3,000 vols); Mason Collection (rare books and fine printing, mainly 16C-19C, in all languages, 8,000 vols); Opie Collection (17C-20C children's books and periodicals, mainly English, 20,000 items); Oppenheimer Collection (Hebrew literature, mainly pre-18C, c4,350 vols); Rawlinson Collection (almanacs, 1606-1747, 5,000 items); Selden Collection (books owned by famous scholars, covering 16C-17C, including medicine, science, theology, history, law and Hebrew studies, 8,000 vols); Toynbee Collection (rare editions of Italian authors, 16C Italian imprints, 3,700 vols).

MANUSCRIPT COLLECTIONS
Range from papyri from the 3C BC to modern correspondence and papers. Strengths include medieval MSS, 17C literary and historical collections, antiquarian and topographical MSS and modern scholarly, scientific, literary and political papers, as well as personal and research papers of individual members of the University. The medieval MSS of twelve Oxford colleges are also held on deposit. Access to the collections is largely restricted to graduate readers.

Modern political papers include the archives of the Conservative Party, as well as the papers of Prime Ministers Disraeli, Asquith, Attlee, Macmillan, Wilson and Callaghan. Over 400 other collections are held from 1840 onwards, which are listed in the Modern Politics Database (MODPOL). Other modern collections include papers of 19C-20C politicians, public servants, journalists, writers, philosophers, scientists and scholars, and the UN Career Records Project.

The Library's own administrative records (1602-date) are also held (access to some records less than 80 years old is restricted).

ELECTRONIC INFORMATION RESOURCES
The Library's Systems and Electronic Resources Section (01865-278170; *fax:* 01865-204937; *email:* helpline@sers.ox.ac.uk) is responsible for the Library's database network and web pages. Electronic media available include:

OxLIP (Oxford Libraries Information Platform)
Over 400 subscription databases and information services in electronic format including bibliographic information, abstracts and indices to periodicals, full texts of literary works, electronic versions of reference works, both on CD-ROM and available on the Internet, together with a variety of links to freely available Internet resources.

OLIS
- a computerised catalogue of libraries within Oxford University, containing 8 million copy records attached to over 5 million titles (including 5 million records for 4.2 million titles for the Bodleian Library alone).

REPROGRAPHIC SERVICES
The Imaging Services Section (01865-277061; *fax:* 01865-287127; *email:* repro@bodley.ox.ac.uk) is responsible for all photocopying, photographic, microfilming and digital imaging services.

DEPENDENT LIBRARIES
The Bodleian Library has seven dependent libraries:

BODLEIAN JAPANESE LIBRARY
Nissan Institute, 27 Winchester Rd, Oxford, OX2 6NA (01865-284506; *fax:* 01865-284500)
Email: japanese@bodley.ox.ac.uk
Open: term: Mon-Fri 0915-1900, Sat 0915-1300; vac: Mon-Fri 0915-1700

Librarian: Mrs I.K. Tytler MA status, BA, MA
Subjects: Japanese studies; humanities and social sciences relating to the history and culture of Japan; Japanese MSS, antiquarian printed books and modern publications; Western language materials relating to Japan.
Stock: 90,000 vols.

Collections: Wylie Collection (40 Japanese editions of Buddhist works); Satow Collection (328 vols of Buddhist literature); Japanese local history publications; IKEDA collection presented by the President of Soka Gakkai International covering serials and collected editions in the field of religion, philosophy, history and literature.
Services: self-service photocopying; reprographic services.
Electronic Resources: NACSIS-IR, Japanese Periodicals Index, UK union catalogue of Japanese books.

BODLEIAN LAW LIBRARY
St Cross Bldg, Manor Rd, Oxford, OX1 3UR (01865-271462; *fax:* 01865-271475)
Email: law.library@bodley.ox.ac.uk
Open: term: Mon-Fri 0900-2200, Sat 0900-1700, Sun 1100-1700; vac: Mon-Fri 0900-1900, Sat 0900-1300

Librarian: Miss B.M. Tearle LLB, MSt, MCLIP
Subjects: law; criminology; mainly post-1800. Houses the Bodleian Library's European Documentation Centre (edc@bodley.ox.ac.uk)
Stock: 250,000 vols.
Collections: Viner Collection (17C-18C); Kahn-Freund Collection (labour law); Bandar Collection of Islamic Law; Public, Local, Personal and Private Acts (17C onwards).
Services: self-service photocopying; microform reader/printer.
Electronic Resources: Lexis/Nexis, Lawtel, Legal Journals Index, Eurolaw

INDIAN INSTITUTE LIBRARY
New Library Bldg, Bodleian Library, Broad St, Oxford, OX1 3BG (01865-277081; *fax:* 01865-277182)
Email: indian.institute@bodley.ox.ac.uk
Open: term: Mon-Fri 0900-1900, Sat 0900-1300; vac: Mon-Fri 0900-1700, Sat 0900-1300

Librarian: Dr G.A. Evison MA, MPhil, DPhil
Subjects: history, social studies, religion, culture, language and literature of the countries of the Indian sub-continent and South East Asia. Newspapers and current affairs weeklies are collected from the Indian subcontinent along with back runs. The Institute is known as one of the most important centres for South Asian studies in Britain.
Stock: 116,000 vols.
Collections: Government publications (19C); The Lucknow Sparks Library of Hindi, Urdu and Persian Books.
Services: self-service photocopying; microfilm and microfiche facilities.

ORIENTAL INSTITUTE LIBRARY
Pusey Lane, Oxford, OX1 2LE (01865-278202; *fax:* 01865-278204)
Email: library@orinst.ox.ac.uk
Open: term: Mon-Fri 0915-1900, Sat 0915-1300; vac: Mon-Fri 0915-1700

Librarian: Mr M.J. Minty MA, MCLIP
Subjects: Oriental studies (except Chinese).
Stock: c47,000 vols.
Collections: private libraries of past professors, notably Margoliouth (Arabic) and Thomas (Sanskrit studies).
Services: self-service photocopying.

INSTITUTE FOR CHINESE STUDIES LIBRARY
Walton St, Oxford, OX1 2HG (01865-280430; *fax:* 01865-280431)
Email: chinese.studies.library@bodley.ox.ac.uk
Open: term: Mon-Fri 0915-1900, Sat 0915-1300; vac: Mon-Fri 0915-1700

Chinese Studies Librarian: Mr M. Chung MA status, BA(Durham), MA
Subjects: Chinese studies, excluding art and archaeology.
Stock: c35,000 vols.
Services: self-service photocopying; microform reader.

PHILOSOPHY LIBRARY
10 Merton St, Oxford, OX1 4JJ (01865-276927; *fax:* 01865-276932)
Email: phillib@bodley.ox.ac.uk
Open: term: Mon-Fri 0930-1730, Sat 0930-1200; vac: Mon-Fri 0930-1630

Librarian: Dr H.A. Wait MA, DPhil
Subjects: Western Philosophy from the classical period to the present day; philosophy of physics and science; logic and language; ethics; aesthetics; history; politics; religion; history of philosophy; medieval thought.
Stock: 27,000+ monographs; 100+ current periodicals.
Collections: small reference and archive collections; Fowler Collection (antiquarian logic books).
Services: self-service photocopying.
Electronic Resources: CD-ROM and networked databases, including the Philosopher's Index.

RADCLIFFE SCIENCE LIBRARY
Parks Rd, Oxford, OX1 3QP (01865-272800; *fax:* 01865-272821)
Email: rsl.enquiries@bodley.ox.ac.uk
Open: term: Mon-Fri 0900-2200, Sat 0900-1300; vac: Mon-Fri 0900-1900, Sat 0900-1300
Keeper of Scientific Books: Dr J. Palmer MA status, PhD, FCLIP, MIIS

Subjects: physical and biological sciences; medicine; experimental psychology; mathematics; computing science; history of science.
Stock: c900,000 vols.
Collections: CR (botany, natural history, natural sciences and medicine in European languages); Acland Collection (pamphlets on medicine, mainly printed 1830-1900); RR (rare books in all languages from all periods mainly on natural science and medicine, including bequests of James Gibbs and Richard Frewin).
Services: self-service photocopying; microform readers and reader/printer.
Electronic Resources: numerous scientific databases, including: Web of Science, EDINA, MIMAS and Ingenta Journals.

Also, in the same building:

Hooke Lending Library
South Parks Rd, Oxford, OX1 3UB (01865-272812; *fax:* 01865-272821)
Email: hooke@bodley.ox.ac.uk
Open: term: Mon-Fri 0900-1730, Sat 0900-1230; vac: closed

Librarian: Ms J.K.L. Ralph BA, MSc, MCLIP
Subjects: undergraduate lending library for the sciences, covering: anatomy; astronomy; astrophysics; biochemistry; biology; chemistry; earth sciences; engineering; human sciences; materials science; mathematics; pharmacology; physics; physiology; plant sciences; psychology; social studies; zoology.

BODLEIAN LIBRARY OF COMMONWEALTH AND AFRICAN STUDIES AT RHODES HOUSE (formerly Rhodes House Library)
South Parks Rd, Oxford, OX1 3RG (01865-270909; *fax:* 01865-270912)
Email: rhodes.house.library@bodley.ox.ac.uk
Open: term: Mon-Fri 0900-1900, Sat 0900-1300; vac: Mon-Thu 0900-1900 (-1700 Xmas vac), Fri 0900-1700, Sat 0900-1300

Librarian: Mr J.R. Pinfold MA
Subjects: the history and current affairs - political, economic and social - of the Commonwealth and sub-Saharan Africa (including the offshore islands). Some coverage of Sri Lanka shared with the Indian Institute Library.
Stock: c200,000 vols.
Collections: Scicluna Collection (history of Malta, 16C-20C); over 4,000 MSS collections, including papers of individuals and organisations: Cecil Rhodes; the Anti-Slavery Society; the Fabian Colonial Bureau; United Society for the Propagation of the Gospel; Sir Roy Welensky; the Anti-Apartheid Movement.
Services: self-service photocopying; microform reader/printer
Electronic Resources: statistical databases; electronic texts; periodical indexes; reference works; online catalogues from other libraries.

Also responsible for:

Vere Harmsworth Library
Rothermere American Institute, 1a South Parks Rd, Oxford, OX1 3TG (01865-282700; *fax:* 01865-282709)
Email: vhl@bodley.ox.ac.uk
Open: term: Mon-Fri 0900-1900, Sat 0900-1300; vac: Mon-Thu 0900-1900 , Fri 0900-1700, Sat 0900-1300

Librarian: Mr J.R. Pinfold MA
Subjects: the history and current affairs of the United States of America (formerly housed at Rhodes House)
Stock: c180,000 vols.
Collections: Aydelotte-Kieffer-Smith Collection (modern US publications)

OXFORD UNIVERSITY ARCHIVES

Old Library, Broad St, Oxford, OX1 3BG (*tel & fax:* 01865-277145)
Email: enquiries@oua.ox.ac.uk
Internet: http://www.oua.ox.ac.uk/
Open: term: Mon-Fri 0900-2200, Sat 0900-1300; vac: Mon-Fri 0900-1900, Sat 0900-1300

Keeper of the Archives: Mr S. Bailey BA
The University Archives are overseen by the University's Committee for the Archives, and so are not strictly part of the Bodleian Library. However, facilities for consulting the archives are provided through the Duke Humfrey's Library in the Old Library Building. Access is by advance appointment with the Archivist. Some restricted materials may require special permission in order to view them.

Stock: 2000 linear m of archives
Collections: records of Oxford University (1214-date), including: charters, statutes and title deeds; records of the Chancellor's Court; records of University legislative and executive bodies; financial and administrative records; student records; records of University committees; departmental and faculty records.
Services: photocopying; limited telephone enquiry service; photography and microfilming can also be undertaken by the Bodleian Library.

EXHIBITIONS AND PUBLICATIONS

The Bodleian Library houses regular exhibitions in its Exhibition Room (open to the public Mon-Fri 0930-1645, Sat 0930-1230).

Publications include: The Bodleian Library Record (2 pa, £18 pa); various guides and catalogues to the collections; Bodleian picture books; exhibition catalogues; facsimiles and colour transparencies.

The Bodleian Library Gift Shop is located in the main entrance to the Old Library, and is open Mon-Fri 0900-1800 (-1700 Jan-Mar), Sat 0900-1230.

L5 - CAMBRIDGE UNIVERSITY LIBRARY

CAMBRIDGE UNIVERSITY LIBRARY was formally established during the second decade of the 15C, although there is evidence for the ownership by the University of a small collection of books from the mid-14C. Major benefactions in the 17C were followed in 1715 by a gift from King George I of the library formed by John Moore, Bishop of Ely. In the 19C the effective working of the Copyright Act ensured continuing growth of the collection. In 1934 Cambridge University Library moved to its current site at West Road.

GENERAL INFORMATION

Cambridge University Library, West Road, Cambridge, CB3 9DR (01223-333030; *fax:* 01223-333160)
Email: library@lib.cam.ac.uk
Internet: http://www.lib.cam.ac.uk/

Librarian: P.K. Fox
Deputy Librarians: D.J. Hall and Ms A. Murray
Total staff: 358
Holdings: 5,568,000 books and pamphlets, and 1,270,000 periodical and serial vols (in 2002)
Expenditure: £9,061,442 (2001-02)
Open: Mon-Fri 0900-1900 (-2200 during Full Easter Term), Sat 0900-1700; *Main Reading Room and West Room:* Mon-Fri 0930-1900 (-2145 in Full Easter Term), Sat 0930-1645; *Map Room:* Mon-Thu 0930-1710, Fri 0930-1650, Sat 0930-1245; *Official Publications Reading Room, Digital Resources Area, Manuscripts Reading Room and Inter-Library Loans Reading Room:* Mon-Fri 0930-1850, Sat 0930-1245; *Other Reading Rooms:* Mon-Fri 0930-1850, Sat 0930-1630. The library is closed on Sundays, Christmas Eve and during the New Year public holiday, Good Friday and the following three days, August Bank Holiday and for one week in September for inventory purposes.
Admission: on production of a valid Reader's Ticket. Readers requiring a ticket should contact the library for advice on eligibility, and apply to:

The Admissions Office
(01223-333084)
email: admissions@lib.cam.ac.uk
Open: Mon-Fri 0930-1230, 1415-1615, Sat 0930-1230

STRUCTURE OF THE LIBRARY

The Library has eleven reading rooms: the Main Reading Room, which houses the main reference collections and general enquiry facilities, and specialist reading rooms. The Library is divided into seven divisions and has four dependent libraries:

1. ADMINISTRATION AND SERVICES DIVISION

Head of Administration and Services: D.J. Hall
Responsible for the following departments: Library Offices and Printing, Bindery and Conservation, Photography, Preservation Microfilming, Technical Maintenance, Cleaning and General Maintenance.

The Photography Department provides a variety of photographic reproduction services, including photocopying, through the Photocopying Room. There are also self-service photocopying machines available.

2. AUTOMATION DIVISION

Head of Automation: C.J. Sendall
Provides access to Newton, the online catalogue system for the University of Cambridge, as well as to hundreds of library catalogues throughout the world. The online catalogue can also be accessed via JANET (Joint Academic Network), and is also accessible over the Internet.

IT SERVICES DEPARTMENT

Email: it_services@lib.cam.ac.uk
Head of IT Services: Ms P. Killiard
Responsible for the provision of IT services and electronic information resources, including e-journals, online databases, electronic books, networked CD-ROMs, and digital images. Bibliographic and full-text database resources include services via BIDS (Bath Information and Data Services), OCLC FirstSearch, EDINA and MIMAS, as well as numerous CD-ROM titles.

Digital Resources Area

A dedicated area providing access to the Library's collection of digital resources. Facilities include 48 workstations with Microsoft Office software and networked printing. Users must apply for an account and password in order to access these facilities.

3. ACCESSIONS DIVISION

Email: accessions@lib.cam.ac.uk
Head of Division: Ms A. Murray
Head of Accessions Department: V.H. King
Responsible for accessions, copyright accessions and periodicals. The Division includes the Official Publications Department and the Periodicals Department:

THE OFFICIAL PUBLICATIONS DEPARTMENT

Email: offpub@lib.cam.ac.uk
Reading Room: Official Publications Room
Head of Department: W.A. Noblett

Includes publications of the governments of the United Kingdom, the Republic of Ireland, members of the Commonwealth and some

foreign countries, as well as publications of over fifty intergovernmental organisations including the UN and its specialised agencies and the EU. Also responsible for:

The Microform Reading Room
Microform and audiovisual materials are available here for consultation. The reading room houses a number of microfilm and microfiche readers and reader-printers.

THE PERIODICALS DEPORTMENT
Email: period@lib.cam.ac.uk
Reading Room: West Room
Head of Department: C.A. Simmonds

Houses the Library's collections of periodicals, newspapers, directories, travel guides and reports.

4. CATALOGUING DIVISION
Email: lib-cat-query@lists.cam.ac.uk
Head of Cataloguing: J.R.H. Taylor
The primary catalogues of the Library's holdings are:

The Main Catalogue - post-1977 books, some earlier books, music from 1990 (online and microfiche)
The Interim Catalogue - some pre-1978 materials (online)
The Pre-1978 General Catalogue - pre-1978 scholarly books (bound volumes)
The Supplementary Catalogues - pre-1978 non-scholarly books, sheaf catalogue for 1800-1905, card index for 1906-1977
Cambridge Union List of Serials (CULOS) - periodicals and journals (online and microfiche)

Special collections are covered by separate catalogues.

5. SPECIAL COLLECTIONS DIVISION
Head of Special Collections: B. Jenkins
Contains four main departments:

DEPARTMENT OF MANUSCRIPTS AND UNIVERSITY ARCHIVES
Reading Room: Manuscripts Reading Room
Email: mss@lib.cam.ac.uk
Keeper of Manuscripts & University Archives: Dr P.N.R. Zutshi

The Department's medieval manuscripts include survivors of the University's oldest collections, acquired in the 16C after the break-up of monastic libraries, including benefactions by Archbishop Matthew Parker (1574), Theodorus Beza (1581), and George I (known as the Royal Library). Other MSS include the medieval MSS of Pembroke and Peterhouse Colleges, held on deposit.

Other major collections include: the Hengrave Hall MSS; the Cholmondeley (Houghton) Papers (including the Sir Robert Walpole Papers); Cambridge verses for Queen Elizabeth I (1564); the collections of Lord Kelvin. Among the many collections of private papers held are those of Stanley Baldwin, Lord Randolph Churchill, Charles Darwin, Stefan Heym, James Clerk Maxwell, Sir Francis Meynell, G.E. Moore, Stanley Morison, Sir Isaac Newton, Spencer Perceval, Lord Rutherford, Siegfried Sassoon, Arthur Schnitzler, Adam Sedgwick, Sir George Stokes and Sir J.J. Thomson. Family and estate papers include: Buxton of Channons and Shadwell, Coke of Weasenham Hall and Vanneck of Heveningham Hall.

The Department is also responsible for the Library's archival collections, including the archives of the University itself. Other archives include: Queens' College Archives (on deposit); the Ely Dean and Chapter Archives; Ely Diocesan Records; Royal Greenwich Observatory Archives; 7:84 Theatre Company Archives; and several business archives, such as: Cambridge Scientific Instrument Co Archives; Curwen Press Archives; Jardine Matheson Archives; Jardine Skinner Archives; Phoenix Assurance Archives; Vickers Archives. The Department also holds copies of all Cambridge doctoral and some masters dissertations.

Cambridge University Archives
Email: archives@lib.cam.ac.uk
Deputy Keeper: Ms J. Cox

Contain records dating from the 13C, and which were transferred to the Library in 1972. Holdings include: Royal Charters and grants of

privileges; financial records; records of degrees; records of the Vice-Chancellor's and Commissary's Courts; Council of the Senate minutes; minutes and papers of Faculty Boards, Degree and Appointments Committees; records of the Cambridge University Press; records of the Botanic Garden; records of some University Departments.

DEPARTMENT OF MAPS
Email: maps@lib.cam.ac.uk
Reading Room: Map Room
Map Librarian: Miss A.E.M. Taylor

The Map Collections contain 1,100,000 British and foreign maps and several thousand atlases, as well as manuscript plans, development plans, gazetteers and books on cartography. The Department holds original maps and atlases by most of the principal map-makers from the 16C onwards; Ordnance Survey and other British official map series; sea charts and Admiralty charts; topographic views; estate plans; and others.

DEPARTMENT OF MUSIC
Reading Room: Anderson Room
Email: music@lib.cam.ac.uk
Music Librarian: R.M. Andrewes

Houses one of the country's largest collections of printed music, as well as MS music, books and periodicals on music and a small collection of sound recordings. Important collections include: F. T. Arnold Bequest (18C instrumental music, history of the thorough-bass); Marion Scott Bequest (early Haydn scores); Picken Collection (ethnomusicological literature); autograph music by James Hook, Alan Gray, C.B. Rootham, Peter Warlock and Peter Tranchell; scholarly transcriptions by E.J. Dent and J.B. Trend; MSS and papers of Sir Arthur Bliss, Roberto Gerhard and Alexander Goehr.

DEPARTMENT OF RARE BOOKS
Reading Room: Munby Rare Books Reading Room
Email: rarebooks@lib.cam.ac.uk
Head of Rare Books Department: Ms N. Thwaite

The foundations of this collection lie in the Royal Library and those printed books amassed before 1715. The collections include early English printing, Irish material, and illustrated books.

Major collections include: the Acton Library (mainly European and Church history, 15C-19C, 60,000 vols); Adams Collection (mainly science and astronomy, 15C-19C, 1,500 vols); Bensley Collection (Hebrew, Arabic, 19C, 1,500 vols); Bradshaw (Irish) Collection (Irish imprints, books of Irish interest, 14,000 items); Brett-Smith Collection (English plays, dramatic literature, poetical miscellanies, 1640-1750, 2,000 items); Cambridge Collection (Cambridge imprints, books about Cambridge, 16C-20C, 10,000 items); Chapbooks Collection (mostly English, 18C-19C, 5,000 items); Darwin Collection (annotated books from Charles Darwin's working library, 18C-19C, 2,500 vols); De Laszlo Collection (phytotherapy, 18C-20C, 2,000 items); Ely Collection (part of library of Ely Cathedral, 15C-19C, 1,500 volumes); Forster Collection (18C English verse, 1,300 volumes); Hisp Collection (16C-19C Spanish books, 4,000 vols); Hunter Collection (history of psychiatry, witchcraft and demonology, 16C-20C, 7,000 items); Incunabula (4,600 items); Keynes Collection (English authors, early medicine and surgery, 15C-20C, 8,000 vols); Leigh Collection (French history, literature and philosophy, mainly 18C, 8,000 items); Madden Collection (18C-19C broadside ballads, also on microfilm, 16,000 items); Morison Collection (typography, palaeography, some church history, mostly 19C-20C, 6,000 items); Munby Collection (library and auction catalogues, 1,800 items); Novels Collection (mainly 19C English novels, 2,000 vols); Pamphlet Collection (English and Foreign pamphlets, 1800-1960, 50,000 items); Peterborough Collection (pre-1800 books from Peterborough Cathedral Library, 7,200 vols); Pryme Collection (economics, political science, 18C-19C, 2,500 items); Romances Collection (romances and novels, mainly English from c1825, 2,500 vols); Rosenthal Collection (18C-19C Africana, 6,000 items); Sandars Collection (liturgies, fine bindings, 15C-19C, 1,460 vols); Society for Psychical Research Library and Archives (occultism, psychic phenomena, hypnotism, 16C-20C, 3,000 items); Venn Collection (logic, 16C-19C, 1,100 vols); Verney Collection (17C English pamphlets and broadsides, 1,400 items);

Waddleton Collection (illustrated books, 5,200 vols); White Collection (mathematics, physics, optics, 16C-18C, 1,350 vols); World War I Collection (printed works and ephemera, 10,000 items).

British and Foreign Bible Society Library and Archives
Reading Room: Anderson Room
Email: bslib@lib.cam.ac.uk
A sub-department of Rare Books. Deposited in 1984-5, the collections comprise c30,000 printed texts in over 2000 languages, and 500 MSS in the scripture library. The Society's archives consist of committee minutes, correspondence, financial records and deposited papers, dating back to the Society's foundation in 1804. A prior appointment is necessary to consult materials from these collections.

The Royal Commonwealth Society Library
Reading Rooms: Rare Books or Manuscripts Reading Rooms
Librarian: Miss R. Rowe
Acquired in 1993, the collections comprise c305,000 printed items, over 70,000 photographs, plus MSS and archives, covering the British Commonwealth and the former colonies of other European powers. Strengths include history, biography and politics, although its scope covers many subject areas. Special collections include: African Exploration; the Cobham Collection on the history of Cyprus.

6. ORIENTAL AND OTHER LANGUAGES DIVISION
Reading Rooms: East Asian Reading Room and Manuscripts Reading Room (for manuscripts)
Head of Division: Prof S.C. Reif
The main areas covered are:

THE CHINESE COLLECTION
Comprises over 100,000 printed vols (12C onwards) and over 1,000 current Chinese serials, covering all aspects of Chinese culture. Special collections include: the bequest of Sir Thomas Wade (mainly 19C Chinese history, 4,304 vols); Chinese inscribed oracle bones (13C BC, over 800 items); rare titles from the National Library of China (on microfilm, 3,000 titles).

THE JAPANESE COLLECTION
Holds c80,000 vols and 300 current Japanese periodicals. Special collections include: the W.G. Aston, Ernest Satow, and Heinrich Siebold Collections (pre-1868 Japanese books, c2,500 volumes); Japanese books of the Meiji Period (1868-1912), from the National Diet Library in Tokyo (on microfilm, 160,000 titles). This is one of the most important resources of its kind outside Japan.

THE KOREAN COLLECTION
Holds c3,000 books and 50 current Korean periodicals.

THE NEAR EASTERN COLLECTIONS
The collections include over 50,000 printed volumes and MSS, including over 1,500 Arabic codices, over 1,000 Hebrew codices, over 1,200 Persian codices, c300 Syriac codices and c450 Turkish codices. Major collections include: the E.G. Brown Collection (Arabic, Persian and Turkish codices, c4,300 items); the Michaelides papyri (c2,000 Arabic and Coptic fragments).

Taylor-Schechter Genizah Research Unit
Email: genizah@lib.cam.ac.uk
Director: Prof S.C. Reif
Project to conserve and catalogue the Taylor-Schechter Genizah collection of 140,000 fragments of Hebrew and Jewish literature and documents. The fragments cover all aspects of life in the Mediterranean area in the 9C-10C, including Jewish religious, communal and person life, Hebrew culture, settlement in Palestine and relations with Muslims and Christians.

THE INDIAN, TIBETAN AND SOUTHEAST ASIAN COLLECTIONS
Incorporate over 1,000 Sanskrit and Prakrit volumes, 111 Sinhalese, 109 Tibetan, 93 Malay, 64 Pali, 52 Malayalam, 50 Burmese, and smaller collections in other languages of the Indian sub-continent and Southeast Asia. Much of the focus of the collections is on Buddhist MSS. Significant collections include: Cecil Bendall and Daniel Wright Collections (Buddhist Sanskrit MSS, 200 items); Sir James George Scott Collection (significant material in Southeast Asian languages).

7. READER SERVICES DIVISION
Head of Reader Services: A.C. Harper
Responsible for the smooth running of reader services in the Library. It comprises the following departments: the Entrance Hall (includes the borrowing desk and Admissions Office), the Reference Department (Reading Room and West Room) and the Inter-Library Loans Department.

DEPENDENT LIBRARIES

BETTY AND GORDON MOORE LIBRARY
Wilberforce Rd, Cambridge, CB3 0WD (01223-765670; *fax:* 01223-765678)
Email: moore-library@lib.cam.ac.uk
Internet: http://www.lib.cam.ac.uk/BGML/
Open: term: Mon-Fri 0900-2100, Sat 0900-1300; vac: Mon-Fri 0900-1700, Sat 0900-1300
Head of Science Libraries: M.L. Wilson
Library Officers: Ms S.V. Lambert and Ms J.I. Booth

Stock: 24,000 vols; 2,000 periodicals; 40,100 journal vols.
Subjects: physics; astronomy; computer science; materials science; technology; engineering; pure and applied mathematics
Collections: former libraries of the Department of Applied Mathematics and the Department of Pure Mathematics and Mathematical Statistics.
Services: self-service photocopying; microform reader; computer and internet facilities.
Electronic Resources: full range of databases and e-journals via the University Library network.

UNIVERSITY MEDICAL LIBRARY
Box 111, New Addenbrooke's Hospital, Hills Road, Cambridge, CB2 2SP (01223-336750; *fax:* 01223-331918)
Email: library@medschl.cam.ac.uk
Internet: http://www.medschl.cam.ac.uk/library/library.html
Open: Mon-Fri 0800-2200, Sat 0900-2100, Sun 1400-1800
Librarian: P.B. Morgan
Deputy Librarian: Mrs F.W. Roberts

Subjects: clinical medicine; nursing; midwifery; psychiatry.
Stock: 41,000 books; c2,500 periodicals (current and non-current); 70,000 bound periodicals; some audiovisual materials
Collections: Cambridge MD and MChir theses.
Services: self-service photocopying; computer and internet facilities; online searching; report binding.
Electronic Resources: Medline; CINAHL; BIDS; BNI; Best Evidence; HMIC; Cochrane; in-house CD-ROMs; and others.

SQUIRE LAW LIBRARY
10 West Rd, Cambridge, CB3 9DZ (01223-330077; *fax:* 01223-330048)
Email: sql1@lib.cam.ac.uk
Open: term: Mon-Fri 0900-2100 (2200 in Easter term), Sat 0900-1800; vac: Mon-Fri 0900-1900 (2200 in Easter vac), Sat 0900-1300
Librarian: D.F. Wills
Deputy Librarian & Reader Services: P.J. Zawada

Stock: 142,000 vols; 1,300 periodicals in 91,000 vols.
Subjects: law
Collections: Roman law; legal history; comparative law; international law; environmental law; political biographies; law reports of most Commonwealth countries.
Services: self-service photocopying; microform reader; computer and internet facilities.
Electronic Resources: Lexis, Westlaw UK and others

SCIENTIFIC PERIODICALS LIBRARY
Bene't Street, Cambridge, CB2 3PY (01223-334742; *fax:* 01223-334748)
Email: lib-spl-enquiries@lists.cam.ac.uk
Internet: http://www.lib.cam.ac.uk/SPL/
Open: term: Mon-Fri 0900-2000, Sat 0900-1300; vac: Mon-Fri 0900-1800, Sat 0900-1300
Librarian: M.L. Wilson
Assistant Librarian: S.M. Dale

Stock: 6,000 periodical titles (2,000 current) in 118,000 vols; some scientific reference books; British Standards.
Subjects: biological, chemical, earth and environmental sciences.
Collections: Buttress Collection of Applied Biology (agricultural periodicals and monographs); collection of 3000 scientific books from 17C-19C.
Services: self-service photocopying; microfilm reader/printer.
Electronic Resources: full range of databases and e-journals via the University Library network.

EXHIBITIONS AND PUBLICATIONS
Regular exhibitions are held in the Library's Exhibition Centre.

Publications include: library guides; guides and catalogues to the collections; exhibition catalogues; the Historical Bibliography series; the Genizah Series; the Sandars Lectures in Bibliography; and others.

SECTION 2 – UK PUBLIC LIBRARIES

Entries are arranged alphabetically under local authority names.

Public libraries are not generally open on bank holidays.

Telephone and fax numbers are given in the form of area dialling codes within the United Kingdom. To telephone the UK from outside the country, dial 00-44 followed by the number, minus the initial 0.

Entries are based on the library authorities' responses to the following questions:

1. **Name of Library Service**

2. **Full address of administrative headquarters or central library** *(incl. postcode)*
   Tel & Fax *(incl. STD code)*
   Email: Electronic Mail
   Internet: Internet address

Local Auth: 3. **Name of governing Local Authority**

Pop: 4. **Population served**

Cttee: 5. **Committee responsible for libraries**

6. **Is library part of a larger department?** *(e.g., Amenities, Leisure Services)*
   If so please provide:
   Larger Dept: a) Name of department
   Dept Chief: b) Chief Officer *(give designation, name, qualifications)*

Chief: 7. **Chief Librarian/Officer** *(please state if responsible for a wider service than libraries alone)* Give designation, name, qualifications, email

Dep: 8. **Deputy** Give designation, name, qualifications, email

9. **Other Senior Staff** Give designations, names, qualifications, email

Main Libs: 10. **District/Area/Regional/Divisional Libraries** Give addresses, postcodes, tel & fax, email

Branch Libs: 11. **Branch (or Community) Libraries** *(open for 20 or more hrs per week)* Give addresses, postcodes, tel & fax, email

Svc Pts: 12. **Number of service points**
   PT: a) Part-time libraries *(open less than 20 hrs per week)*
   Mobile: b) Mobile libraries
   AV: c) Service points with audiovisual stock
   Computers: d) Service points with computer facilities
   Internet: e) Service points with internet facilities
   Other: f) Other *(please specify)*

Collns: 13. **Special Collections** *(incl. BSI, EDC, & collns held as part of a national co-operative scheme, e.g., SCOLMA: Kenya, or STD: M-Mi)* Give collection name, subject(s), location, brief details

Co-op Schemes: 14. **Co-operative schemes in which library participates** *(incl. any listed in Q13, using acronyms where possible)*

ILLs: 15. **Inter-library loans**

Loans: 16. **Loan period** For books, audios, videos, CD-ROMs, other

Charges: 17. **Loan charges or subscription** *(if any)* For audios, videos, CD-ROMs, other

Income Gen: 18. **Other charges and income generation** *(not fees for equipment & facilities, for which see Q20)* For requests, reservations, lost tickets, other

Fines: 19. **Fines** *(if fine is distinguished from loan charge)* For books (adults, children, OAPs), audios, videos, CD-ROMs, other
   Groups exempt from fines *(e.g., registered blind)*

Equip: 20. **Equipment & facilities available to library users** *(give numbers, and fees per item if any)*
   Disabled: **Equipment for disabled** *(please specify, e.g., Kurzweil)*
   Online: **Online information service available** *(e.g., Dialog, give fees)*
   Other *(please specify)*
   Offcr-in-Charge: **Officer in charge of equipment purchases** Give designation, name, email

21. **Stock & Issues**
   Stock: **Stock** *(for 2000 & 2001)*
   Issues: **Issues** *(during 1999-2000 & 2000-01)*
   ad lend: a) Adult lending
   ad ref: b) Adult reference
   ch: c) Children *(excl. d below)*
   schools: d) Schools
   instns: e) Institutions *(e.g., prisons)*
   audios: f) Audios *(incl. cassettes & CDs)*
   videos: g) Videos
   CD-ROMs: h) CD-ROMs
   periodcls: i) Periodicals *(titles currently taken)*
   archvs: j) Archives *(specify unit e.g., linear, cubic metre)*

Acqs: 22. **Acquisitions** *(during 1999-2000 & 2000-01)*
   bks: a) Books
   AVs: b) Audiovisuals
   Source: **Usual sources of acquisitions**
   Co-op: **Co-operative acquisitions programs**
   Offcr-in-Charge: **Officer in charge of acquisitions** Give designation, name, email

Classn: 23. **Classification method(s) used**

Cat: 24. **Catalogue**
   Type: **Type(s) of catalgue(s) used**
   Medium: **Medium on which the catalogue is kept**

Auto Sys: 25. **Automated Library system used** *(if any)*

Svcs: **Services**

Extramural: 26. **Extramural services**

Info: 27. **Information services** *(please specify, e.g., business, community, careers, etc.)*

Other: 28. **Other services provided** *(please specify, e.g., open learning, etc.)*

Activs: 29. **Activities & Entertainments** *(on a regular basis)*
   Offcr-in-Charge: **Officer in charge** Give designation, name, email

Enqs: 30. **Enquiries handled** 1999-2000 & 2000-01

Staff: 31. **Staff establishment** *(give full-time equivalent for part-time staff incl. vacancies)*
   Total number of:
   Libns: a) Professional librarians
   Other Prof: b) Professional staff other than a
   Non-Prof: c) Non-professional staff

32. **Finance** For 1999-2000 & 2000-01
   Inc from: **Income from:**
   local govt: a) Local Government
   fines/fees/sales: b) Fines, Fees & Sales
   total: c) Total Income *(incl. a, b & any other income)*
   Exp on: **Expenditure on:**
   bks: a) Books & Printed Stock *(incl. binding)*
   AV: b) Audiovisual Stock *(incl. CD-ROMs)*
   elec media: c) Electronic media & Services *(incl. internet)*
   activs: d) Cultural activities
   salaries: e) Salaries & wages *(incl. superannuation & insurance & training)*
   total: f) Total Expenditure *(incl. a to e & any other exp)*

Proj: 33. **Capital projects** *(name any capital project approved for start in 2001 or 2002 and costing more than £100,000)*

Further Info: 34. **Additional Information**

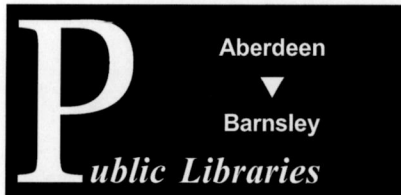

Public Libraries

Aberdeen ▼ Barnsley

Aberdeen

P1 Aberdeen City Council, Library and Information Services

Central Lib, Rosemount Viaduct, Aberdeen, AB25 1GW (01224-652500; *fax:* 01224-641985)
Email: centlib@arts-rec.aberdeen.net.uk
Internet: http://www.aberdeencity.gov.uk/

Local Auth: Aberdeen City Council *Pop:* 211300
Cttee: Edu & Leisure Cttee *Larger Dept:* Learning & Leisure *Dept Chief:* Corporate Dir: Mr John Stodter *Chief:* Principal Offcr, Lib & Info Svcs: Mr Neil Bruce MA, DipLib, LLM, MCLIP
Main Libs: CENTRAL LIB, addr as above
Branch Libs: AIRYHALL LIB, Springfield Rd, Aberdeen, AB15 7RF (01224-310536; *email:* airyhall@arts-rec.aberdeen.net.uk); BRIDGE OF DON LIB, Scotstown Rd, Aberdeen, AB22 8HH (01224-702800; *email:* bridge1@arts-rec.aberdeen. net.uk); BUCKSBURN LIB, Kepplehills Rd, Bucksburn, Aberdeen, AB21 9DG (01224-712016; *email:* bucks1@arts-rec.aberdeen.net.uk); CORN-HILL LIB, Cornhill Shopping Arcade, Cornhill Dr, Aberdeen, AB16 5UT (01224-696209; *email:* cornhill1@arts-rec.aberdeen.net.uk); COVE LIB, Cove Rd, Aberdeen, AB12 4NX (01224-897451; *email:* cove@arts-rec.aberdeen.net.uk); CULTER LIB, 189 North Deeside Rd, Culter, Aberdeen, AB14 0UJ (01224-732587; *email:* culter1@arts-rec.aberdeen.net.uk); CULTS LIB & LEARNING CENTRE, 429 North Deeside Rd, Cults, Aberdeen, AB15 9SX (01224-868346; *email:* cults1@arts-rec.aberdeen.net.uk); DYCE LIB, Riverview Dr, Aberdeen, AB21 7NF (01224-723015; *email:* dyce1@arts-rec.aberdeen.net.uk); FERRYHILL LIB, Fonthill Rd, Aberdeen, AB11 6UP (01224-581576; *email:* ferryhill1@arts-rec.aberdeen.net.uk); KAIMHILL LIB, Pitmedden Ter, Aberdeen, AB10 7HR (01224-325940); KINCORTH LIB, Provost Watt Dr, Aberdeen, AB12 5NA (01224-872572; *email:* kincorth1@arts-rec.aberdeen.net.uk); LINKSFIELD LIB, 520 King St, Aberdeen, AB24 5SS (01224-494092); MASTRICK LIB, Greenfern Rd, Aberdeen, AB16 6TR (01224-693623; *email:* mastrick1@arts-rec. aberdeen.net.uk); NORTHFIELD LIB, Byron Sq, Aberdeen, AB16 7LL (01224-695104; *email:* north1@arts-rec.aberdeen.net.uk); TILLYDRONE LIB, Pennan Rd, Aberdeen, AB24 2UD (01224-276975; *email:* tilly1@arts-rec.aberdeen.net.uk); TORRY LIB, Victoria Rd, Aberdeen, AB11 9NJ (01224-879037; *email:* torry1@arts-rec.aberdeen. net.uk); WOODSIDE LIB, 356 Clifton Rd, Aberdeen, AB24 4DX (01224-484534; *email:* woodside1@arts-rec.aberdeen.net.uk)
Svc Pts: PT: 2 Mobile: 1 AV: 18 Computers: 13 Internet: 13 Other: HOUSEBND LIB SVC, at Airyhall Lib; ABERDEEN ART GALLERY, JAMES MCBEY REF LIB, Schoolhill, Aberdeen, AB10 1FQ (see **S2**)
Collns: Scottish family hist; Oil/Business; BSI; British patents; Aberdeen newspapers; Walker Music Colln; Cosmo Mitchell Dance Colln; Murdoch Henderson Scottish Music Colln; George Washington Wilson photos; local studies: historical photos (c14000); European Public Info Centre; Scottish Parliament Info Centres (at Central Lib, Bridge of Don Lib & Kincorth Lib)
Co-op Schemes: Grampian Info *ILLs:* county, natl & internatl *Loans:* bks & audios/4 wks; videos & DVDs/1 wk *Charges:* cassettes/25p;

CDs & videos/50p; DVDs/£2; AV svcs/£25 pa sub; orchestral sets/£10 *Income Gen:* res/free-50p; ILLs/£6; lost ticket/£2; arts equip booking fee/£3 per item *Fines:* bks, audios & videos/ad & oap 30p per wk; DVDs/loan charge; under-12s exempt *Equip:* 4 m-readers, 3 m-printers (A4/10p), 2 fax (inland £1 per pg, overseas £2), 20 copiers (A4/10p, A3/20p), clr copier (A4/£1.50, A3/£2.50), 55 computers (all with wd-proc, internet & CD-ROM, print-outs 10p per A4), 18 scanners (3 A3, 15 A4), 18 webcams

Stock:	1 Apr 2000	1 Apr 2001
ad lend:	107014	108125
ch:	291766	279640
schools:	114522	112811
audios:	46241	63370
videos:	5863	11914
CD-ROMs:	-	403
periodcls:	376	303
archvs:	126 linear m	126 linear m

Issues:	1999-2000	2000-01
ad lend:	1111882	1007197
ch:	376556	330635
audios:	132920	208292
videos:	50252	78607

Acqs:	1999-2000	2000-01
bks:	30746	30610
AVs:	7686	81412

Acqs: Source: lib suppl & bksellers
Classn: DDC *Cat: Type:* author, classified, subj & title *Medium:* auto *Auto Sys:* Talis *Svcs: Extramural:* schools, old people's homes, housebnd, play groups *Info:* genl ref & local studies, business & technical, community *Other:* Arts Equip Lending Svc (video, photographic & digital); Learning Centre *Activs:* ch's activs, bk sales, temp exhibs, poetry readings, reading groups, writers' groups, talks, author visits
Enqs: 145924 (1999-2000); 129364 (2000-01)
Staff: Libns: 29 Non-Prof: 79.7

Inc from:	1999-2000
fines etc:	£157907

Exp on:	1999-2000
total:	£3160912

Aberdeenshire

P2 Aberdeenshire Library and Information Service

Meldrum Meg Way, The Meadows Industrial Est, Oldmeldrum, Aberdeenshire, AB51 0GN (01651-872707; *fax:* 01651-872142)
Email: ALIS@aberdeenshire.gov.uk
Internet: http://www.aberdeenshire.gov.uk/

Local Auth: Aberdeenshire Council *Pop:* 227200
Larger Dept: Edu & Rec *Dept Chief:* Dir of Edu & Rec: Mr Hamish Vernal *Chief:* Libs & Heritage Mgr: Mr Gerald Moore BA, MCLIP *Other Snr Staff:* Central Support Svcs Mgr: Ms Anne Harrison; Client Svc Libns: Mr Rufus de Silva & Ms Helen Dewar
Branch Libs: AABOYNE LIB, Community Centre, Bridgeview Rd, Aboyne, Aberdeenshire, AB34 5JN (013398-86004; *email:* aboyne.lib@ aberdeenshire.gov.uk); ALFORD LIB, Alford Academy, Murray Ter, Alford, Aberdeenshire, AB33 8PY (019755-63333; *email:* alford.lib@ aberdeenshire.gov.uk); BANCHORY LIB, Bridge St, Banchory, Aberdeenshire, AB31 3SU (01330-823784; *email:* banchory.lib@aberdeenshire. gov.uk); ELLON LIB, Station Rd, Ellon, Aberdeen-shire, AB41 9AE (01358-720865; *email:* ellon.lib@ aberdeenshire.gov.uk); FRASERBURGH LIB, King Edward St, Fraserburgh, Aberdeenshire, AB43 5PN (01346-518197; *email:* fraserburgh.lib@ aberdeenshire.gov.uk); HUNTLY LIB, The Square, Huntly, Aberdeenshire, AB54 5BR (01466-792179; *email:* huntly.lib@aberdeenshire.gov.uk);

INVERURIE LIB, Town Hall, Inverurie, Aberdeen-shire, AB51 3SN (01467-621619; *email:* inverurie. lib@aberdeenshire.gov.uk); MACDUFF LIB, High St, Macduff, Aberdeenshire, AB44 1LR (01261-833289; *email:* macduff.lib@aberdeenshire. gov.uk); MELDRUM LIB, Colpy Rd, Oldmeldrum, Aberdeenshire, AB51 0NT (01651-871307; *email:* meldrum.lib@aberdeenshire. gov.uk); PETER-HEAD LIB, St Peter St, Peterhead, Aberdeen-shire, AB42 6QD (01779-472554; *email:* peterhead. lib@aberdeenshire.gov.uk); STONEHAVEN LIB, Evan St, Stonehaven, Aberdeenshire, AB3 2ET (01569-762136; *email:* stonehaven.lib@ aberdeenshire.gov.uk); TURRIFF LIB, Grange Villa, The Sq, Turriff, Aberdeenshire, AB53 7AE (01888-562539; *email:* turriff.lib@aberdeenshire. gov.uk); WESTHILL LIB, Hay's Way, Westhill, Skene, Aberdeenshire, AB32 6XZ (01224-741312; *email:* westhill.lib@aberdeenshire. gov.uk)
Svc Pts: PT: 22 Mobile: 6 AV: 36 Computers: 36 Internet: 36 Other: MOBILE LIB SVCS, at Lib HQ (01651-871209); INFO SVCS, at Lib HQ (01651-871206); LOCAL STUDIES DEPT, at Lib HQ (01651-871219/20; *fax:* 01651-872142; *email:* local.studies@aberdeenshire.gov.uk)
Collns: George MacDonald Colln (Huntley); Strichen Estate papers; Scottish Parliament collns
Co-op Schemes: Grampian Info *ILLs:* county, natl & internatl *Loans:* bks, audios & videos/4 wks; DVDs & CD-ROMs/1 wk *Charges:* cassettes/30p; CDs & videos/60p; DVDs/£2; CD-ROMs/£1 *Income Gen:* req/most items free; lost ticket/50p *Fines:* bks/ad 30p pw (max 6 wks), ch & oap exempt for 1st 4 wks; audios/ad 30p pw (max 6 wks); videos/50p pw *Equip:* m-readers, m-printers (10p), fax (to send 50p per pg, higher overseas, to receive 20p 1st pg, 10p addl), copiers (10p), clr copier (50p), computers (incl wd-proc & internet)

Stock:	1 Apr 2000	1 Apr 2001
ad lend:	323556	398530
ad ref:	31915	32033
ch:	128335	153874
audios:	33532	36172
videos:	6081	8724
periodcls:	93	100

Issues:	1999-2000	2000-01
ad lend:	1096309	1069185
ch:	364703	303057
audios:	81815	85330
videos:	19087	21866

Acqs:	1999-2000	2000-01
bks:	38283	35260
AVs:	8615	3746

Acqs: Source: lib suppl, publ & bksellers
Classn: DDC *Cat: Type:* author, classified, subj & title *Medium:* auto *Auto Sys:* Talis *Svcs: Extramural:* schools, prisons, hosps, old people's homes, housebnd *Info:* business, community, council, careers, Scottish Parliament, European *Other:* Lifelong Learning *Activs:* bk sales, temp exhibs, poetry readings, talks, author visits
Enqs: 166816 (1999-2000); 174980 (2000-01)
Staff: 94 FTE in total

Inc from:	1999-2000	2000-01
local govt:	£2647736	£2651792
fines etc:	£101666	£127686
total:	£2749402	£2779478

Exp on:	1999-2000	2000-01
bks:	£273610	£297405
AVs:	£85745	£47485
salaries:	£1707847	£1626979
total:	£2749402	£2779478

Anglesey

P3 Anglesey Library, Information and Archive Service

Llangefni Central Lib, Lon-y-Felin, Llangefni, Ynys Môn, LL77 7RT (01248-752095; *fax:* 01248-750197)
Email: dhelh@anglesey.gov.uk
Internet: http://www.ynysmon.gov.uk/

Local Auth: Isle of Anglesey County Council *Pop:* 64847 *Cttee:* Leisure & Heritage Cttee *Larger Dept:* Edu & Leisure *Dept Chief:* Dir: Mr Richard Parry Jones *Chief:* Head of Lifelong Learning & Info: Mr John Rees Thomas BSc, DipLib, MCLIP (jrtlh@ynysmon.gov.uk) *Dep:* Principal Libn: Mr Rhys Bebb Jones (rbj@cybi.demon.co.uk) *Other Snr Staff:* Info & Local Studies Libn: Mr D. Handel Evans
Main Libs: LLANGEFNI LIB, contact details as above *Branch Libs:* AMLWCH LIB, Ffordd Parys, Amlwch, Ynys Môn, LL68 9EA (*tel & fax:* 01407-830145); HOLYHEAD LIB, Newry Fields, Caergybi, Holyhead, Ynys Môn, LL65 1LA (01407-762917; *fax:* 01407-769616; *email:* mon@cybi.demon.co.uk); MENAI BRIDGE LIB, Ffordd Y Ffair, Porthaethwy, Ynys Môn, LL59 5AS (*tel & fax:* 01248-712706)
Svc Pts: PT: 6 *Mobile:* 3 *AV:* 9 *Computers:* 2 *Internet:* 2 *Other:* HOUSEBND SVCS, at Llangefni Lib (01248-752098)
Collns: Local Studies Colln (Anglesey hist, at Llangefni Lib) *Co-op Schemes:* TALNET *ILLs:* natl *Loans:* bks & audios/3 wks; videos/1wk *Charges:* audios/60p; videos/£1-£2 *Income Gen:* req & res/50p within TALNET, £2 outside; lost tickets/£1 1st replacement, £2 subsequent *Fines:* bks/ad 10p-30p 1st wk, then 30p pw (max £3), ch exempt; videos/loan charge *Equip:* m-readers, copiers (A4/10p, A3/20p), fax (£1 per pg to send in UK, higher overseas, 50p per pg to receive), computers (incl wd-proc, internet & CD-ROM, printouts 10p), rooms for hire

Stock:	1 Apr 2000
bks:	350044

Issues:	1999-2000
bks:	520786
AVs:	13488

Acqs:	1999-2000
bks:	13423

Acqs: Source: lib suppl *Offcr-in-Charge:* Principal Libn, as above
Classn: DDC *Cat: Medium:* auto *Auto Sys:* Talis *Svcs: Extramural:* schools, old people's homes, housebnd *Info:* genl ref svc, business, educational, careers, community, current affairs, Welsh, European, local studies *Other:* Open Learning *Activs:* ch's activs, bk sales, temp exhibs, poetry readings, author visits
Enqs: 65106 (1999-2000)
Staff: Libns: 8 *Non-Prof:* 20

Exp on:	1999-2000	2000-01
stock & svcs:	£229870	£222630
salaries:	£341146	£352740

Angus

P4 Angus Libraries

Admin Unit, County Bldgs, Market St, Forfar, Angus, DD8 3WF (01307-461460; *fax:* 01307-462590)
Internet: http://www.angus.gov.uk/history/libraries/

Local Auth: Angus Council *Pop:* 112000 *Cttee:* Rec & Cultural Svcs Cttee *Larger Dept:* Leisure Svcs *Dept Chief:* Dir: Mr Norman K. Atkinson DipEd *Chief:* Libs Mgr: Mr John Doherty BSc, MCLIP (dohertyj@angus.gov.uk)

Other Snr Staff: Cultural Resources Mgr: Mr Colin Dakers BA, MCLIP (dakersc@angus.gov.uk) *Branch Libs:* ARBROATH LIB, Hill Ter, Arbroath, Angus, DD11 1AH (01241-872248; *email:* arbroath.library@angus.gov.uk); BRECHIN LIB, 10 St Ninian's Sq, Brechin, Angus, DD9 7AA (*email:* brechin.library@angus.gov.uk); CARNOUSTIE LIB, 21 High St, Carnoustie, Angus, DD7 6AN (01241-859620; *email:* carnoustie.library@angus.gov.uk); FORFAR LIB, 50-56 West High St, Forfar, Angus, DD8 1BA (01307-466071; *email:* forfar.library@angus.gov.uk); KIRRIEMUIR LIB, Town Hall, 28-30 Reform St, Kirriemuir, Angus, DD8 4BS (01575-572357; *email:* kirriemuir.library@angus.gov.uk); MONIFIETH LIB, High St, Monifieth, Angus, DD5 4AE (*email:* monifieth.library@angus.gov.uk); MONTROSE LIB, 214 High St, Montrose, Angus, DD10 8PH (01674-673256; *email:* montrose.library@angus.gov.uk)
Svc Pts: PT: 4 *Mobile:* 2 *AV:* 11 *Computers:* 11 *Internet:* 11 *Other:* SCHOOLS LIB SVC, Edu Resource Svcs, Bruce House, Wellgate, Arbroath, Angus, DD11 1TL (01242-435045) *Collns:* Montrose Subscription Lib (travel & lit, at Forfar Lib); John C. Ewing Colln (Scottish interest, at Forfar Lib); R.W. Inglis Free Lib (at Edzell Lib); local hist collns at all libs *Loans:* bks, audios & info videos/4 wks; entertainment videos & DVDs/1 wk *Charges:* audios/50p (talking bks free); videos/50p-£1.50; DVDs/£2 *Income Gen:* res/25p (under-16s & oaps exempt) *Fines:* bks & audios/ad 5p pd, under-16s 1p pd; videos & DVDs/ad 15p pd, under-16s 3p pd *Equip:* 4 m-printers (25p per sheet), 7 copiers (10p), 4 fax, rooms for hire (varies)

Stock:	1 Apr 2000	1 Apr 2001
ad lend:	193255	190910
ad ref:	5901	5042
ch:	67568	67830
audios:	18977	16876
videos:	7089	6817
periodcls:	110	110

Issues:	1999-2000	2000-01
ad lend:	745934	760754
ch:	157750	198743
audios:	56599	57859
videos:	43814	44102

Acqs:	1999-2000	2000-01
bks:	27894	27182
AVs:	3992	3365

Acqs: Source: lib suppl & bksellers *Offcr-in-Charge:* Libs & Info Svcs Mgr, as above
Classn: DDC *Cat: Type:* author, classified, subj & title *Medium:* auto *Auto Sys:* Dynix *Svcs: Extramural:* hosps, old people's homes, housebnd *Info:* community *Other:* Learning Centres at all libs *Activs:* ch's activs, bk sales, temp exhibs
Enqs: 130159 (1999-2000); 125188 (2000-01)
Staff: Libns: 14 *Non-Prof:* 28

Inc from:	1999-2000
fines etc:	£228000

Exp on:	1999-2000
bks:	£350600
salaries:	£1361000
total:	£1761600

Argyll and Bute

P5 Argyll and Bute Library and Information Service

Lib HQ, Highland Ave, Sandbank, Dunoon, Argyll, PA23 8PB (01369-703214; *fax:* 01369-705797)
Email: andy.ewan@argyll-bute.gov.uk
Internet: http://www.argyll-bute.gov.uk/content/leisure/libraries/

Local Auth: Argyll & Bute Council *Pop:* 91310 *Larger Dept:* Community Svcs *Dept Chief:* Dir of Community Svcs: Mr Douglas Hendry

Chief: Principal Lib & Info Svcs Offcr: Mr Andrew Ewan MCLIP *Dep:* Area Libn & IT Systems Development Mgr: Mr Patrick McCann BA, MCLIP *Main Libs:* CAMPBELTOWN LIB, Hall St, Campbeltown, Argyll, PA28 6BS (01586-552366 x2237; *fax:* 01586-552938; *email:* library@campbeltown.fsbusiness.co.uk); DUNOON LIB, 248 Argyll St, Dunoon, Argyll, PA23 7LT (01369-703735 x7522; *fax:* 01369-701323; *email:* pauline.flynn@argyll-bute.gov.uk); HELENSBURGH LIB, West King St, Helensburgh, Dunbartonshire, G84 8EB (01436-674626; *fax:* 01436-679567; *email:* pat.mccann@argyll-bute.gov.uk); OBAN LIB, Corran Halls, Oban, Argyll, PA34 5AB (01631-571444; *fax:* 01631-571372; *email:* kevinbaker@oban-library.fsbusiness.co.uk) *Branch Libs:* ROTHESAY LIB, The Moat Centre, Stuart St, Rothesay, Isle of Bute, PA20 0BX (01700-503266; *fax:* 01700-500511; *email:* rothesaylibrary@hotmail.com)
Svc Pts: PT: 8 *Mobile:* 5
Collns: Local Studies Colln (at Lib HQ, with smaller collns at branches) *Co-op Schemes:* SUC, SCIP *ILLs:* natl & internatl *Loans:* bks & audios/4 wks *Income Gen:* req & res/50p, conc 25p *Fines:* bks & audios/ad 6p pd, oap & conc 3p pd; ch exempt *Equip:* m-reader, 5 copiers, 5 fax (£1 per pg), 2 rooms for hire (various)

Stock:	1 Apr 2001
ad lend:	186435
ad ref:	4454
ch:	49112
audios:	10427
videos:	196
CD-ROMs:	207
periodcls:	40

Issues:	2000-01
ad lend:	494079
ch:	85018
audios:	35084
videos:	914
CD-ROMs:	475

Acqs:	2000-01
bks:	10306
AVs:	553

Acqs: Source: lib suppl & bksellers *Offcr-in-Charge:* Bibliographical Svcs Libn: Ms Karen Strutt (karen.strutt@argyll-bute.gov.uk)
Classn: DDC *Cat: Type:* author & classified *Medium:* cards & auto *Svcs: Extramural:* hosps, old people's homes, housebnd *Info:* community, European, Scottish Parliament *Other:* Learning Centres at all main libs & Rothesay & Lochgilphead Branch Libs; Learning Access Pts in all PT libs *Activs:* ch's activs, bk sales, temp exhibs
Enqs: 30048 (2000-01)
Staff: Libns: 10 *Non-Prof:* 24

Inc from:	2000-01
local govt:	£1201412
fines etc:	£36248
total:	£1237660

Exp on:	2000-01
bks:	£110930
AVs:	£15385
salaries:	£639578
total:	£1237660

Barnsley

P6 Barnsley Libraries

Central Lib, Shambles St, Barnsley, S Yorkshire, S70 2JF (01226-773930; *fax:* 01226-773955)
Email: BarnsleyLibraryEnquiries@barnsley.gov.uk
Internet: http://www.barnsley.gov.uk/service/libraries/

Public Libraries

Barnsley
▼
Birmingham

(Barnsley Libs cont)

Local Auth: Barnsley Metropolitan Borough Council **Pop:** 227200 **Cttee:** Cabinet Spokesperson for Edu **Larger Dept:** Edu **Dept Chief:** Exec Dir: Ms Jean Potter **Chief:** Chief Libs Offcr: Mr Steven Bashforth BA, MCLIP (stevebashforth@barnsley.gov.uk) **Dep:** Lending Svcs Offcr: Mrs Kathryn Green BA, MCLIP (KathrynGreen@barnsley.gov.uk)

Main Libs: BARNSLEY CENTRAL LIB, addr as above; GOLDTHORPE LIB, Barnsley Rd, Goldthorpe, Rotherham, S Yorkshire, S63 9NE (*tel & fax:* 01709-893278); PENISTONE LIB, High St, Penistone, Sheffield, S Yorkshire, S36 6BR (01226-762313); PRIORY INFO & RESOURCE CENTRE, Pontefract Rd, Lundwood, Barnsley, S Yorkshire, S71 4QP (01226-770616; *fax:* 01226-771425); ROYSTON LIB, Midland Rd, Royston, Barnsley, S Yorkshire, S71 4QP (01226-722870)

Branch Libs: CUDWORTH LIB, Barnsley Rd, Cudworth, Barnsley, S Yorkshire, S72 8SY (01226-710535); DARFIELD LIB, Church St, Darfield, Barnsley, S Yorkshire, S73 9LG (01226-752548); HOYLAND NETHER LIB, High Croft, Hoyland Nether, Barnsley, S Yorkshire, S74 9AF (01226-743434); MAPPLEWELL LIB, 22 Blacker Rd, Mapplewell, Barnsley, S Yorkshire, S75 6BP (01226-382309); ROUNDHOUSE LIB & LEARNING CENTRE, Laithes Cres, Athersley, Barnsley, S Yorkshire, S71 4AE (01226-281584); THURNSCOE LIFELONG LEARNING CENTRE, 2 Shepherd Ln, Thurnscoe, Rotherham, S Yorkshire, S63 0JS (01709-890001); WOMBWELL LIB, Station Rd, Wombwell, Barnsley, S Yorkshire, S70 3BA (01226-753846); WORSBROUGH LIB, Elm House Est, Queensway, Worsbrough, Barnsley, S Yorkshire, S70 5EN (01226-203372)

Svc Pts: PT: 4 Mobile: 2 **AV:** 12 **Computers:** 14 **Internet:** 14 **Other:** ARCHVS & LOCAL STUDIES, at Central Lib (see **A26**)

Collns: BSI; local author colln (at Local Studies Dept, Central Lib) **Co-op Schemes:** SINTO, SYALL, YLI **ILLs:** county, natl & internatl

Loans: bks & audios/3 wks; videos/3 days or 1 wk; Playstation games/1 wk; pictures/12 wks; Open Learning materials/3 wks **Charges:** cassettes/single 50p, double £1, set of 3+ £1.25; CDs/single 75p, double £1.50, set of 3+ £1.75; videos/premium £1.50 per 3 days, other £1 for 1 wk, double £2; Playstation games/£4 **Income Gen:** req/in stock 50p (conc 30p), not in stock 75p; lost ticket/£1.50 **Fines:** bks/ad & oap 10p pd, ch 5p pd (max for both £5); cassettes/10p pd (max £5); CDs/20p pd (max £8); videos/premium £1 pd, others 30p pd (max for both £12); Playstation games/£1 pd **Equip:** 14 m-readers, m-printer (30p), 4 fax (50p per pg + £1 admin fee to send), 11 copiers (A4/10p, A3/15p), clr copier (A4/£1, A3/£1.50), computers (incl 70 with wd-proc, 50 with CD-ROM & 70 with internet), rooms for hire (various) **Disabled:** Duo CCTV (enlarger for partially sighted), hearing loop **Online:** Artel

Stock:	1 Apr 2000	1 Apr 2001
ad lend:	208830	206500
ad ref:	56334	52151
ch:	78334	77493
audios:	11329	11823
videos:	4124	3999
CD-ROMs:	170	467
periodcls:	98	95
archvs:	2507 linear m	2535 linear m

Issues:	1999-2000	2000-01
ad lend:	967742	891981
ch:	214042	186402
audios:	29210	24416
videos:	16198	15267
CD-ROMs:	1706	3602

Acqs:	1999-2000	2000-01
bks:	25299	30135
AVs:	1239	1588

Acqs: Source: lib suppl **Offcr-in-Charge:** Support Svcs Offcr: Mr I. Stringer MCLIP **Classn:** DDC **Cat: Type:** author, classified, subj & title **Medium:** auto **Auto Sys:** Dynix **Svcs: Extramural:** hosps, old people's homes, housebnd **Info:** European, community, learning, business **Other:** Open Learning, study support centres **Activs:** ch's activs, bk sales, temp exhibs, reading groups, theatrical events & music concerts **Offcr-in-Charge:** Learning & Info Svcs Offcr: Mrs Jane Lee BA, MCLIP **Enqs:** 96772 (1999-2000); 84773 (2000-01) **Staff:** Libns: 20.6 Other Prof: 2 Non-Prof: 59.4

Inc from:	1999-2000	2000-01
local govt:	£1635016	£1763259
fines etc:	£132920	£109219
total:	£1946834	£2302757

Exp on:	1999-2000	2000-01
bks:	£47379	£161001
AVs:	£19804	£13610
salaries:	£1231460	£1337687
total:	£1946834	£2302757

Bath and NE Somerset

P7 Bath and North East Somerset Libraries

Bath Central Lib, 19 The Podium, Northsafe St, Bath, Somerset, BA1 5AN (01225-787400; *fax:* 01225-787426)
Email: bathlibraries@bathnes.gov.uk
Internet: http://www.bathnes.gov.uk/libraries/

Local Auth: Bath & NE Somerset Council **Pop:** 170238 **Larger Dept:** Corporate Support **Dept Chief:** Corporate Dir: Mrs Sarah Berry **Chief:** Head of Customer Svcs (Libs & Info): Mrs Julia Fieldhouse **Other Snr Staff:** Lib Planning & Development Mgr: Mrs Judith Dixon MCLIP (Judith_Dixon@bathnes.gov.uk); Lib Operations Mgr: Mrs June Brassington MCLIP (June_Brassington@bathnes.gov.uk); Lib Resources Mgr: Mr David Moger BA, DipLib, MCLIP (David_Moger@bathnes.gov.uk)

Main Libs: CENTRAL LIB, addr as above; KEYNSHAM LIB, The Centre, Keynsham, Somerset, BS31 1ED (01225-394191; *fax:* 01225-394195; *email:* keynsham_library@bathnes. gov.uk); MIDSOMER NORTON LIB, High St, Midsomer Norton, Somerset, BA3 2DF (01761-412024; *fax:* 01761-417841; *email:* midsomernorton_library@ bathnes.gov.uk)

Branch Libs: MOORLAND RD LIB, Moorland Rd, Bath, Somerset, BA1 3PI (01225-424357; *email:* moorlandroad_library@ bathnes.gov.uk); RADSTOCK LIB, The Street, Radstock, Somerset, BS3 3PR (01761-432315; *email:* radstock_library@bathnes.gov.uk); WESTON LIB, Church St, Weston, Bath, Somerset, BA1 4BU (01225-425452; *email:* weston_library@bathnes. gov.uk)

Svc Pts: PT: 2 Mobile: 2 **AV:** 10 **Computers:** 10 **Internet:** 10

Collns: local hist of Bath; colln on Napoleonic period **Co-op Schemes:** SWRLS-FOURSITE **ILLs:** county, natl & internatl **Loans:** bks, audios & CD-ROMs/3 wks; videos & Playstation games/1 wk; lang courses/3 or 6 wks **Charges:** spkn wd/£1.20; CDs/£1.60; videos/£1.30 or £2.60; DVDs/£2.80; CD-ROMs/£1.60; Playstation games/£3; lang courses/£1.20-£5 **Income Gen:** res/85p; lost tickets/£1, £2 after 1st replacement,

under-18s 50p **Fines:** bks & audios/ad & oap 15p pd (£5 max), ch 3p pd (£2.50 max); videos, DVDs & Playstation games/loan charge (£10.50 max); music & play sets/£1.50 pd **Equip:** 10 m-readers, 4 m-printers (50p), 4 copiers (A4/10p, A3/20p), 48 computers (incl 28 with CD-ROM & 20 with internet, access free, printouts 10p b&w, 50p clr), rooms for hire at all libs (various) **Disabled:** Kurzweil, text enlarger

Stock:	1 Apr 2000	1 Apr 2001
ad lend:	113681	115906
ad ref:	99715	102081
ch:	40872	41868
audios:	11997	10420
videos:	3154	3895
CD-ROMs:	124	288
periodcls:	182	260
archvs:	811 linear m	646 linear m

Issues:	1999-2000	2000-01
ad lend:	820217	763420
ch:	246538	249732
audios:	63463	63849
videos:	35602	33695
CD-ROMs:	2	1012

Acqs:	1999-2000	2000-01
bks:	28602	18180
AVs:	3622	3298

Acqs: Source: lib suppl **Offcr-in-Charge:** Stock Mgr: Mrs K. Alvey & Mrs E. Bevan **Classn:** DDC **Cat: Type:** author, classified, subj & title **Medium:** auto **Auto Sys:** DS **Svcs: Extramural:** old people's homes, housebnd **Info:** local, business, careers, family hist **Activs:** ch's activs, bk sales, temp exhibs, reading groups **Enqs:** 127954 (1999-2000); 114051 (2000-01) **Staff:** Libns: 14.5 Non-Prof: 47.5

Inc from:	1999-2000	2000-01
local govt:	£1836950	£1872000
fines etc:	£189446	£197317
total:	£2051099	£2119941

Exp on:	1999-2000	2000-01
bks:	£176930	£157085
AVs:	£27190	£26259
salaries:	£1229675	£1301955
total:	£2051099	£2119941

Bedfordshire

P8 Bedfordshire Libraries

County Hall, Cauldwell St, Bedford, MK42 9AP (01234-228752; *fax:* 01234-213006)
Email: BedfordshireLibraries@bedfordshire. gov.uk
Internet: http://www.bedfordshire.gov.uk/

Local Auth: Bedfordshire County Council **Pop:** 389200 **Cttee:** Exec Cttee **Chief:** Head of Libs: Mr Barry S. George MCLIP (georgeb@deal. bedfordshire.gov.uk)

Main Libs: BEDFORD CENTRAL LIB, Harpur St, Bedford, MK40 1PG (01234-350931; *fax:* 01234-342163); DUNSTABLE LIB, Vernon Pl, Dunstable, Bedfordshire, LU5 4HA (01582-608441; *fax:* 01582-471290); LEIGHTON BUZZARD LIB, Lake St, Leighton Buzzard, Bedfordshire, LU7 8RX (01525-371788; *fax:* 01525-851368); **Area Libs:** BIGGLESWADE LIB, Chestnut Ave, Biggleswade, Bedfordshire, SG18 0LL (01767-312324; *fax:* 01767-601802); FLITWICK LIB, Coniston Rd, Flitwick, Bedford, MK45 1QJ (01525-715268; *fax:* 01525-713897); HOUGHTON REGIS LIB, Bedford Sq, Houghton Regis, Dunstable, Bedfordshire, LU5 5ES (01582-865473; *fax:* 01582-868466); KEMPSTON LIB, Halsey Rd, Kempston, Bedford, MK42 8AU (01234-853092; *fax:* 01234-841476); PUTNOE LIB, Putnoe St, Bedford, MK41 8HF (01234-353422; *fax:* 01234-272833); SHEFFORD LIB, High St, Shefford, Bedfordshire, SG17 5DD (01462-639070; *fax:* 01462-639071)

Branch (Community) Libs: AMPTHILL LIB, Saunders Piece, Ampthill, Bedford, MK45 2NL (01525-402278; *fax:* 01525-840766); BARTON LIB, Bedford Rd, Barton, Bedford, MK45 4PP (*tel & fax:* 01582-881101); BROMHAM LIB, Springfield Dr, Bromham, Bedford, MK43 8LE (01234-824391); SANDY LIB, Market Sq, Sandy, Bedfordshire, SG19 1EH (01767-680384; *fax:* 01767-692438); STOTFOLD LIB, Hitchin Rd, Stotfold, Hitchin, Hertfordshire, SG5 4HP (01462-730695); TODDINGTON LIB, Market Sq, Toddington, Dunstable, Bedfordshire, LU5 6BP (*tel & fax:* 01525-873626); WOOTTON LIB, Lorraine Rd, Wootton, Bedfordshire, MK43 9LH (01234-766061)
Svc Pts: *PT:* 1 *Mobile:* 4 *Computers:* 17 *Internet:* 17 *Other:* 1 prison lib, 1 special client groups unit
Collns: Fowler Lib (medieval & modern hist); John Bunyan Collns (both at Bedford Central)
Co-op Schemes: Co-East *ILLs:* county & natl
Loans: bks & spkn wd/3 wks; music audios, videos & DVDs/1 wk *Charges:* spkn wd/cassettes 90p; CDs £1; music audios/cassettes 60p, CDs £1; videos/£2.20; DVDs/£2.30; half price for conc; registered blind, partially sighted & hearing impaired, housebnd & people with dyslexia exempt from some or all AV charges *Income Gen:* req & res/ad 90p, conc 45p, ch 10p (+90p out of county); lost ticket/£1 *Fines:* bks & spkn wd/ad 18p pd (max £5.40), ch 5p pd (max £1.50), conc 9p pd (£2.70 max); music & videos/loan charge; conc: people over 60, unemployed, those receiving income support or allowances *Equip:* m roaders, 4 m-printers, 12 fax (UK £1.15 1st pg, 55p addl, higher overseas), copiers (A4/10p, A3/15p), computers (incl wd-proc, internet & CD-ROM), room hire (various) *Disabled:* wheel-chairs at some libs, print enlargers, hearing loops

Stock:	1 Apr 2000	1 Apr 2001
ad lend:	332500	323926
ad ref:	44371	43554
ch:	144700	137683
audios:	37489	34731
videos:	9221	9041

Issues:	1999-2000	2000-01
ad lend:	2237823	2126707
ch:	947301	904101
audios:	211321	204030
videos:	74217	69309

Acqs:	1999-2000	2000-01
bks:	53812	58808
AVs:	5492	4726

Acqs: *Source:* lib suppl *Co-op:* LASER subj specialisation *Offcr-in-Charge:* Lib Resources Mgr: Mr Andy Baker
Classn: DDC *Cat: Type:* author, classified, subj & title *Medium:* auto *Auto Sys:* DS *Svcs: Extramural:* schools, prisons, hosps, old people's homes, housebnd *Info:* business, community, environmental *Other:* Open Learning, multicultural svcs *Activs:* ch's activs, bk sales, temp exhibs
Enqs: 568532 (1999-2000); 546616 (2000-01)
Staff: *Libns:* 29.5 *Non-Prof:* 137

Inc from:	1999-2000	2000-01
local govt:	£3912842	£4004789
fines etc:	£1011700	£1032095
total:	£4924542	£5036884

Exp on:	1999-2000	2000-01
bks:	£707836	£721122
salaries:	£2852778	£2966462
total:	£4924542	£5036884

Birmingham

P9 Birmingham Libraries

Central Lib, Chamberlain Sq, Birmingham, B3 3HQ (0121-303-4511; *fax:* 0121-233-9702)
Email: libraries@birmingham.gov.uk
Internet: http://www.birmingham.gov.uk/

Local Auth: Birmingham City Council *Pop:* 1013400 *Cttee:* Cabinet Memb for Leisure, Sport & Culture *Larger Dept:* Leisure & Culture *Dept Chief:* Dir: Mr Andrew Kerr *Chief:* Asst Dir, Lib & Info Svcs: Mr John Dolan BA, MCLIP (john. dolan@birmingham.gov.uk) *Other Snr Staff:* Head of Community Libs: Mr Geoff Mills (geoff. mills@birmingham.gov.uk); Head of Svcs for Ch, Youth & Edu: Mrs Patsy Heap (patsy.heap@ birmingham.gov.uk); Head of Performance Mgmt: Mrs Linda Butler BA, MBA, MCLIP (linda.butler@ birmingham.gov.uk)
Main Libs: CENTRAL LIB, addr as above
Branch (Community) Libs: ACOCKS GREEN LIB, Shirley Rd, Birmingham, B27 7XH (0121-464-1738; *fax:* 0121-464-0787; *email:* acocks.green. library@birmingham.gov.uk); ASTON LIB, Albert Rd, Birmingham, B6 5NQ (0121-464-1184; *fax:* 0121-464-0656; *email:* aston.library@birmingham. gov.uk); BALSALL HEATH LIB, Moseley Rd, Birmingham, B12 9BX (0121-464-1962; *fax:* 0121-464-0113; *email:* balsall.heath.library@birmingham. gov.uk); BARTLEY GREEN LIB, Adams Hill, Birmingham, B32 3QG (0121-464-4473; *fax:* 0121-464-0663; *email:* bartley.green.library@ birmingham.gov.uk); BIRCHFIELD LIB, Birchfield Rd, Birmingham, B20 3BX (0121-464-4202; *fax:* 0121-464-0802; *email:* birchfield.library@ birmingham.gov.uk); BLOOMSBURY LIB, Nechells Parkway, Birmingham, B7 4PT (0121-464-3466; *fax:* 0121-464-0640; *email:* bloomsbury. library@birmingham.gov.uk); BOLDMERE LIB, 119 Boldmere Rd, Sutton Coldfield, W Midlands, B73 5TU (0121-464-1048; *fax:* 0121-464-0666; *email:* boldmere.library@birmingham.gov.uk); CASTLE VALE LIB, Turnhouse Rd, Birmingham, B35 6PR (0121-464-7335; *fax:* 0121-464-0672; *email:* castle.vale.library@birmingham.gov.uk); DRUIDS HEATH LIB, Idmiston Croft, Birmingham, B14 7NJ (0121-303-7171; *fax:* 0121-464-0527; *email:* druids.heath.library@birmingham. gov.uk); ERDINGTON LIB, Orphanage Rd, Birmingham, B24 9HP (0121-464-0798; *fax:* 0121-464-0118; *email:* erdington.library@birmingham. gov.uk); FRANKLEY LIB, Frankley Community High School, New St, Birmingham, B45 0EU (0121-464-7676; *fax:* 0121-464-0679; *email:* frankley.library@birmingham.gov.uk); GLEBE FARM LIB, Glebe Farm Rd, Birmingham, B33 9NA (0121-464-4210; *fax:* 0121-464-0682; *email:* glebe.farm.library@birmingham.gov.uk); HALL GREEN LIB, 1221 Stratford Rd, Birmingham, B28 9AD (0121-464-6633; *fax:* 0121-464-0764; *email:* hall.green.library@birmingham.gov.uk); HANDSWORTH LIB, Soho Rd, Birmingham, B21 9DP (0121-464-1185; *fax:* 0121-464-0123; *email:* handsworth.library@birmingham.gov.uk); HARBORNE LIB, High St, Birmingham, B17 9QG (0121-464-1596; *fax:* 0121-464-0804; *email:* harborne.library@birmingham.gov.uk); HAWTHORN HOUSE LIB, Hamstead Hall Rd, Birmingham, B20 1HX (0121-464-6120; *fax:* 0121-464-0125; *email:* hawthorn.house.library@ birmingham.gov.uk); KENTS MOAT LIB, 55-57 The Poolway, Birmingham, B33 8NF (0121-464-5755; *fax:* 0121-464-0696; *email:* kents.moat.library@ birmingham.gov.uk); KINGS HEATH LIB, High St, Birmingham, B14 7SW (0121-464-1515; *fax:* 0121-464-0129; *email:* kings.heath.library@birmingham. gov.uk); KINGS NORTON LIB, Pershore Rd South, Birmingham, B30 3EU (0121-464-1532; *fax:* 0121-464-0249; *email:* kings.norton.library@ birmingham.gov.uk); KINGSTANDING LIB, Kingstanding Rd, Birmingham, B44 9ST (0121-464-5193; *fax:* 0121-464-0647; *email:* kingstanding.library@birmingham.gov.uk); MERE GREEN LIB, Mere Green Rd, Sutton Coldfield, W Midlands, B75 5BP (0121-464-4592; *fax:* 0121-464-0707; *email:* mere.green.library@ birmingham.gov.uk); NORTHFIELD LIB, 77 Church Rd, Birmingham, B31 2LB (0121-464-1007; *fax:* 0121-464-0803; *email:* northfield. library@birmingham.gov.uk); PERRY COMMON LIB, Coll Rd, Birmingham, B44 0HH (0121-464-

0481; *fax:* 0121-464-0139; *email:* perry.common. library@birmingham.gov.uk); QUINTON LIB, Ridgacre Rd, Birmingham, B32 2TW (0121-464-7400; *fax:* 0121-464-0772; *email:* quinton.library@ birmingham.gov.uk); SELLY OAK LIB, 669 Bristol Rd, Birmingham, B29 6AE (0121-464-0403; *fax:* 0121-464-0719; *email:* selly.oak.library@ birmingham.gov.uk); SHARD END LIB, Shustoke Rd, Birmingham, B34 7BA (0121-464-6779; *fax:* 0121-464-0725; *email:* shard.end.library@ birmingham.gov.uk); SHELDON LIB, Brays Rd, Birmingham, B26 2RJ (0121-464-3512; *fax:* 0121-464-0730; *email:* sheldon.library@birmingham. gov.uk); SMALL HEATH LIB, Muntz St, Birmingham, B10 9RX (0121-464-6155; *fax:* 0121-464-0153; *email:* small.heath.library@birmingham. gov.uk); SOUTH YARDLEY LIB, Yardley Rd, Birmingham, B25 8LT (0121-464-1944; *fax:* 0121-464-0160; *email:* south.yardley.library@ birmingham.gov.uk); SPARKHILL LIB, 641 Stratford Rd, Birmingham, B11 4EA (0121-303-0732; *fax:* 0121-303-0733; *email:* sparkhill.library@ birmingham.gov.uk); SPRINGHILL LIB, Spring Hill, Birmingham, B18 7BH (0121-464-7422; *fax:* 0121-464-0655; *email:* spring.hill.library@ birmingham.gov.uk); STIRCHLEY LIB, Bournville Ln, Birmingham, B30 2JT (0121-464-1534; *fax:* 0121-464-0733; *email:* stirchley.library@ birmingham.gov.uk); SUTTON COLDFIELD LIB, Lower Parade, Sutton Coldfield, W Midlands, B72 1XX (0121-464-2274; *fax:* 0121-464-0173; *email (lend):* sutton.coldfield.lending.library@ birmingham.gov.uk; *email (ref):* sutton.coldfield. reference.lib@birmingham.gov.uk); TOWER HILL LIB, Tower Hill, Birmingham, B42 1LG (0121-464-1948; *fax:* 0121-464-0740; *email:* tower.hill. library@birmingham.gov.uk); WALMLEY LIB, Walmley Rd, Sutton Coldfield, W Midlands, B76 8NP (0121-464-1842; *fax:* 0121-464-0741; *email:* walmley.library@birmingham.gov.uk); WARD END LIB, Washwood Heath Rd, Birmingham, B8 2HF (0121-464-0366; *fax:* 0121-464-0917; *email:* ward.end.library@birmingham.gov.uk); WEOLEY CASTLE LIB, 76 Beckbury Rd, Birmingham, B29 5HR (0121-464-1664; *fax:* 0121-464-0186; *email:* weoley.castle.library@ birmingham.gov.uk); WEST HEATH LIB, The Fordrough, Birmingham, B31 3LX (0121-464-7548; *fax:* 0121-464-0750; *email:* west.heath.library@ birmingham.gov.uk); YARDLEY WOOD LIB, Highfield Rd, Birmingham, B14 4DU (0121-464-2110; *fax:* 0121-464-0755; *email:* yardley.wood.library@birmingham.gov.uk)
Svc Pts: *PT:* 1 *Mobile:* 3 *AV:* 40 *Computers:* 40 *Internet:* 40 *Other:* ARTS, LANGS & LIT LIB, at Central Lib (0121-303-4227; *fax:* 0121-464-1005; *email:* arts.library@birmingham.gov.uk); LOCAL STUDIES & HIST LIB, at Central Lib (0121-303-4549; *fax:* 0121-464-0993; *email:* local.studies. library@birmingham.gov.uk); MUSIC LIB, at Central Lib (0121-303-2482; *fax:* 0121-464-1177; *email:* music.library@birmingham.gov.uk); BUSINESS INSIGHT, at Central Lib (0121-303-4531; *fax:* 0121-303-7828; *email:* business. library@birmingham.gov.uk); SCI, TECH & MGMT LIB, at Central Lib (0121-303-4537; *fax:* 0121-233-4458; *email:* science.library@birmingham.gov.uk); SOCIAL SCIS LIB, at Central Lib (0121-303-4545; *fax:* 0121-464-1178; *email:* social.sciences. library@birmingham.gov.uk); BIRMINGHAM CITY ARCHVS (see **A51**); CENTRE FOR THE CHILD, at Central Lib (0121-303-2421; *fax:* 0121-464-1006; *email:* centre.for.the.child@birmingham. gov.uk)
Collns: Boulton Watt Archv of the Industrial Revolution; Shakespeare Lib; Barry Jackson Colln (Archv of Birmingham Repertory Theatre); Early & Fine Printing Colln; Milton Colln; Johnson Colln; Cervantes Colln; War Poetry Colln; Parker Colln of Ch's Bks (all at Central Lib); Railways & Steam Engines Colln (at Acocks Green Lib); local hist collns *Co-op Schemes:* TLP-WM *Loans:* bks/4 wks; audios/2 wks; videos/2-7 days; CD-ROMs/1 wk ☛

Public Libraries

Birmingham
▼
Bournemouth

(Birmingham Libs cont)

Charges: audios/sub £25 pa or 75p per loan; videos/£1-£2.25; CD-ROMs/£1-£2 *Income Gen:* req & res/60p, conc 30p; lost ticket/£1-£2; lost bks/cost of replacement *Fines:* bks & audios/ad 10p pd 1st wk, then 50p pw (max £5), oap 2p pd 1st wk, then 10p pw (max £1); videos/loan charge; ch & under-18s exempt *Equip:* m-reader (50p/30 min), m-printer (A4/25p, A3/50p), fax (UK £2 1st pg, 50p addl), copier (A4/10p, A3/20p), clr copier (£1.50), 400 computers (incl 57 with wd-proc, 214 with CD-ROM & 234 with internet), rooms for hire *Disabled:* Kurzweil, videophone, textphone, induction loops, adjustable tables, access software *Online:* various (cost + 10% + VAT)

Stock:	1 Apr 2000	1 Apr 2001
ad lend:	876962	834017
ad ref:	1375688	1406316
ch:	337023	350538
audios:	72097	86786
videos:	5073	5093
CD-ROMs:	484	687
periodcls:	2471	2890

Issues:	1999-2000	2000-01
ad lend:	3581458	3275519
ch:	1358127	1234276
audios:	407329	435152
videos:	61886	67576
CD-ROMs:	11	3375

Acqs:	1999-2000	2000-01
bks:	192240	179589
AVs:	14487	17188

Acqs: Source: lib suppl, publ & bksellers *Co-op:* CBC *Offcr-in-Charge:* Head of Resources Mgmt: Ms C. Perry (cathy.perry@birmingham.gov.uk) *Classn:* DDC *Cat: Type:* author, subj & title *Medium:* auto *Auto Sys:* DS *Svcs: Extramural:* schools, prisons, housebnd, old people's homes, day centres, play groups *Info:* business, community, health, advice on edu, employment & training opportunities, Learning Shop, tourist, European Relay Pt, patent, Childcare Info Bureau, Youth Info Shop, Genealogist *Other:* Open Learning, Learning Centres, Arthritis Resource Centre *Activs:* ch's activs, bk sales, temp exhibs, poetry readings, reading groups, talks, author visits, Book Wks, homework clubs *Offcr-in-Charge:* Reader Development Offcr: Ms Anuradha Singh (anu.singh@birmingham.gov.uk) *Enqs:* 1529736 (1999-2000); 1465848 (2000-01) *Staff: Libns:* 123 *Other Prof:* 8 *Non-Prof:* 435

Inc from:	1999-2000	2000-01
local govt:	£15265397	£15703369
fines etc:	£1253328	£1237117
total:	£17854610	£18739134

Exp on:	1999-2000	2000-01
bks:	£1556275	£1755875
AVs:	£259379	£275590
elec media:	£25330	£29382
salaries:	£11054012	£11996288
total:	£17854610	£18739134

Blackburn with Darwen

P10 Blackburn with Darwen Library and Information Service

Blackburn Central Lib, Town Hall Street, Blackburn, Lancashire, BB2 1AG (01254-661221; *fax:* 01254-690539)
Email: library@blackburn.gov.uk
Internet: http://library.blackburnworld.com/

Local Auth: Blackburn with Darwen Borough Council *Pop:* 138399 *Cttee:* Community & Personnel Cttee *Larger Dept:* Community, Leisure & Sport *Dept Chief:* Dir: Mr Steve Rigby BEd(Hons), DMS, DipISRM *Chief:* Asst Dir (Community, Leisure & Sport): Mrs Norma Monks MCLIP (norma.monks@blackburn.gov.uk) *Dep:* Head of Lib & Info Svcs: Mrs Susan Law MCLIP (susan.law@blackburn.gov.uk) *Other Snr Staff:* Lending Svcs Mgr: Mrs Kath Sutton; Info & Development Mgr: Mr Ian Sutton; Ch's/Schools Libn: Miss Jean Gabbatt
Main Libs: CENTRAL LIB, addr as above *Branch Libs:* DARWEN LIB, Knott St, Darwen, Lancashire, BB3 3BU (01254-706021; *fax:* 01254-707177; *email:* darwen.library@blackburn.gov.uk); LIVESEY LIB, Cherry Tree Ln, Blackburn, Lancashire, BB2 5NX (01254-209442; *fax:* 01254-209596; *email:* Livesey.Library@blackburn.gov.uk); MILL HILL LIB, Mill Hill Community Centre, New Chapel St, Blackburn, Lancashire, BB2 4DT (01254-57584; *email:* Mill-Hill.Library@blackburn.gov.uk); ROMAN RD LIB, Fishmoor Dr, Blackburn, Lancashire, BB2 3UY (01254-682347; *fax:* 01254-51832; *email:* Roman-Road.Library@blackburn.gov.uk)
Svc Pts: Mobile: 1 *AV:* 5 *Computers:* 5 *Internet:* 5 *Other:* Schools' Lib Svc; ch's lib
Collns: Community Hist Colln (local studies)
Co-op Schemes: BBBCLC *ILLs:* county & natl
Loans: bks, spkn wd & music scores/3 wks; CDs, videos, DVDs & CD-ROMs/1 wk; lang courses/6 wks *Charges:* audios/50p; videos/£1, genl interest 50p; CD-ROMs/£1.50; DVDs/£2; music scores/£5 *Income Gen:* res/60p per item; lost tickets/£1 *Fines:* bks & spkn wd/10p pd; CDs, videos, DVDs & CD-ROMs/loan charge; over-65s, under-17s, long-term sick, disabled, housebnd, registered blind, learning disabled & mobile lib users all exempt *Equip:* 17 m-readers, 2 m-printers (20p), 3 copiers (10p), fax (UK 50p per sheet, overseas £1); 94 computers (incl 56 with wd-proc, 74 with CD-ROM & 70 with internet), 2 rooms for hire (£17 or £33 per session) *Disabled:* Kurzweil, video caption readers, braille & large print transcription svc *Online:* Dialog, Medline *Offcr-in-Charge:* Head of Lib & Info Svcs, as above

Stock:	1 Apr 2000	1 Apr 2001
ad lend:	160343	145173
ad ref:	83542	78684
ch:	48697	48976
schools:	36856	35060
audios:	8247	9346
videos:	2681	3227
CD-ROMs:	371	427
periodcls:	209	204

Issues:		2000-01
ad lend:		768725
ch:		236224
audios:		53163
videos:		27916
CD-ROMs:		1849

Acqs:	1999-2000	2000-01
bks:	21890	29577
AVs:	2298	3717

Acqs: Source: lib suppl & publ *Offcr-in-Charge:* Head of Lib & Info Svcs, as above
Classn: DDC *Cat: Type:* author, classified, subj & title *Medium:* auto *Auto Sys:* DS *Svcs: Extramural:* schools, old people's homes, housebnd, play groups *Info:* business, community

Other: Lifelong Learning, ethnic svcs, svcs to visually impaired *Activs:* ch's activs, bk sales, exhibs, reading groups, talks, author visits *Offcr-in-Charge:* Head of Lib & Info Svcs, as above
Enqs: 358384 (1999-2000); 415688 (2000-01)
Staff: Libns: 19.7 *Non-Prof:* 61.2

Inc from:	1999-2000	2000-01
local govt:	£2147048	£2151447
fines etc:	£108733	£182327
total:	£2255781	£2333774

Exp on:	1999-2000	2000-01
bks:	£309222	£292976
AVs:	£44302	£53968
elec media:	£1509	£853
salaries:	£1249900	£1281478
total:	£2255781	£2333774

Proj: refurbishing of Central Lib

Blaenau Gwent

P11 Blaenau Gwent Libraries

Community Svcs Admin HQ Central Depot, Barleyfield Industrial Est, Brynmawr, Blaenau Gwent, NP23 4YF (01495-355319; *fax:* 01495-312357)
Internet: http://www.blaenau-gwent.gov.uk/

Local Auth: Blaenau Gwent County Borough Council *Pop:* 73000 *Cttee:* Leisure, Amenities & Facilities Cttee *Larger Dept:* Community Svcs *Dept Chief:* Dir: Mr Robin Morrison BSc(Hons), CEng, MICE, DMS *Chief:* County Borough Libn: Mrs Mary Jones MLib, MCLIP
Main Libs: ABERTILLERY LIB, Station Hill, Abertillery, Blaenau Gwent, NP13 1TE (01495-212332; *fax:* 01495-320995); BRYNMAWR LIB, Market St, Brynmawr, Blaenau Gwent, NP23 4AJ (*tel & fax:* 01495-310045); EBBW VALE LIB, 21 Bethcar St, Ebbw Vale, Blaenau Gwent, NP23 6HS (01495-303069; *fax:* 01495-350547); TREDEGAR LIB, The Circle, Tredegar, Blaenau Gwent, NP22 3PS (01495-722687; *fax:* 01495-717018) *Branch Libs:* BLAINA LIB, Reading Inst, Blaina, Blaenau Gwent, NP13 3BN (*tel & fax:* 01495-290312); CWM LIB, Canning St, Cwm, Ebbw Vale, Blaenau Gwent, NP23 7RW (*tel & fax:* 01495-370454)
Svc Pts: PT: 1 *Mobile:* 2 *AV:* 7 *Computers:* 4 *Internet:* 4
ILLs: county & natl *Loans:* bks & spkn wd/3 wks; audios, videos & CD-ROMs/1 wk *Charges:* audios & foreign lang sets/75p; videos/£1.50; CD-ROMs/£2 *Income Gen:* req, res & lost tickets/£1, oap, unemployed & disabled 50p *Fines:* bks/ad 60p pw, oap 30p pw, ch exempt; audios, videos & CD-ROMs/loan charge; registered blind & 16-19 yr-olds in FT edu exempt *Equip:* m-reader, m-printer, 6 copiers (5p-10p), clr copier (A4/£1.50, A3 £2), 7 fax (£1), computers (incl wd-proc & internet, both free), 2 rooms for hire (£6 per hr) *Disabled:* Kurzweil, Voyager

Stock:	1 Apr 2000	1 Apr 2001
ad lend:	63187	61949
ad ref:	7382	7406
ch:	31901	29953
audios:	4756	5175
videos:	2161	1960
periodcls:	29	30

Issues:	1999-2000	2000-01
ad lend:	324554	302405
ch:	85893	87730
audios:	16026	16852
videos:	3978	3456

Acqs:	1999-2000	2000-01
bks:	10296	13855
AVs:	1277	996

Acqs: Source: lib suppl & local bksellers *Offcr-in-Charge:* Lib Mgrs: Mrs Anne Maund & Mrs Sue White
Classn: DDC *Cat: Type:* author, classified, subj & title *Medium:* auto *Auto Sys:* Dynix

Svcs: Extramural: schools served via joint svc led by Caerphilly Borough Council (see **P21**), cottage hosps, old people's homes, housebnd, day centres, play groups *Info:* community, European Relay Info Colln *Other:* 4 Open Learning centres (at Abertillery, Blaina, Brynmawr & Tredegar Libs) *Activs:* ch's activs, bk sales, temp exhibs, poetry readings, author visits, musical evenings *Offcr-in-Charge:* County Borough Libn, as above *Enqs:* 191973 (1999-2000); 233304 (2000-01) *Staff: Libns:* 8 *Other Prof:* 1 *Non-Prof:* 23

Inc from:	2000-01
local govt:	£935958
fines etc:	£54895
total:	£990853

Exp on:	2000-01
stock:	£109363
salaries:	£620437
total:	£990853

Bolton

P12 Bolton Libraries

Bolton Central Lib, Le Mans Cres, Bolton, Lancashire, BL1 1SE (01204-333173; *fax:* 01204-332225)
email: central.library@bolton.gov.uk
Internet: http://bold.bolton.gov.uk/library/

Local Auth: Bolton Metropolitan Borough Council *Pop:* 267600 *Cttee:* Edu & Arts Cttee *Larger Dept:* Edu & Arts *Dept Chief:* Dir of Edu & Arts: Mrs Margaret Blenkinsop MSc *Chief:* Asst Dir (Heritage, Info & Arts): post vacant *Dep:* Head of Libs & Archvs: Mrs Yvonne Gill-Martin BA(Hons), MCLIP, DMS (yvonne.gill-martin@bolton.gov.uk)
Main Libs: CENTRAL LIB, as above; FARNWORTH LIB, Market St, Farnworth, Bolton, Lancashire, BL4 7PG (01204-332344; *fax:* 01204-332346; *email:* farnworth.library@bolton.gov.uk); HARWOOD LIB, Gate Fold, Harwood, Bolton, Lancashire, BL2 3HN (01204-332340; *email:* harwood.library@bolton.gov.uk); HORWICH LIB, Jones St, Horwich, Bolton, Lancashire, BL6 7AJ (01204-332347; *fax:* 01204-332349; *email:* horwich.library@bolton.gov.uk); LITTLE LEVER LIB, Coronation Sq, Little Lever, Bolton, Lancashire, BL3 1LP (01204-332360; *fax:* 01204-332362; *email:* littlelever.library@bolton.gov.uk); WEST-HOUGHTON LIB, Library St, Westhoughton, Bolton, Lancashire, BL5 3AU (01942-634640; *fax:* 01942-634643; *email:* westhoughton.library@bolton.gov.uk) *Branch Libs:* ASTLEY BRIDGE LIB, Moss Bank Way, Bolton, Lancashire, BL1 8NP (01204-332350; *email:* astleybridge.library@bolton.gov.uk); BLACKROD LIB, Church St, Bolton, Lancashire, BL6 5EQ (01204-332380; *email:* blackrod.library@bolton.gov.uk); BREIGHT-MET LIB, Breightmet Dr, Bolton, Lancashire, BL2 6EE (01204-332352; *email:* breightmet.library@bolton.gov.uk); BROMLEY CROSS LIB, The Cres, Toppings Est, Bolton, Lancashire, BL7 9JU (01204-332354; *email:* bromley.cross.library@bolton.gov.uk); HALLIWELL LIB, Shepherd Cross St, Bolton, Lancashire, BL1 3EJ (01204-332367; *fax:* 01204-332383; *email:* halliwell.library@bolton.gov.uk); HEATON LIB, New Hall Ln, Bolton, Lancashire, BL1 5LF (01204-332356; *email:* heaton.library@bolton.gov.uk); HIGH ST LIB, High St, Bolton, Lancashire, BL3 6SZ (01204-332358; *email:* high.street.library@bolton.gov.uk); MARSH LN LIB, Marsh Ln, Farnworth, Bolton, Lancashire, BL4 0PA (01204-332363; *email:* marsh.lane.library@bolton.gov.uk); TONGE MOOR LIB, Tonge Moor Rd, Bolton, Lancashire, BL2 2LE (01204-332365; *email:* tonge.moor.library@bolton.gov.uk) *Svc Pts: Mobile:* 1 (at Westhoughton Lib) *AV:* 11 *Collns:* Whitman Colln (relating to the American poet); Catherall Colln (relating to local ch's author); JFR; Bolton Colln (local studies);

Crompton Papers (Samuel Crompton, inventor of the spinning mule); Bill Naughton Archv (playwright); Bolton Archvs (local archival colln); 42 deposit collns *Co-op Schemes:* BLCMP, GMPLTC, Libs North West *ILLs:* county, natl & internatl *Loans:* bks & audios/3 wks; videos/2 days or 1 wk *Charges:* audios/50-80p; videos/free, £1 or £1.50 *Income Gen:* req & res/60p; lost ticket/£1 *Fines:* bks & audio/ad 8p pd, ch 1p pd, oap 4p pd; video/loan charge; visually impaired, housebnd, mobile lib users & playgroups exempt *Equip:* 15 m-readers, m-printer (£1), video viewer, 5 fax (£1.50-£3 per pg), 16 copiers (10p-20p), clr copier (£1-£1.50), 33 computers (incl wd-procs, internet & CD-ROM), 4 rooms for hire (varies), hi-fi equip, slide projector, overhead projectors, photo booth (£2) *Disabled:* Kurzweil *Online:* available via Business Liaison Libn

Stock:	1 Apr 2000	1 Apr 2001
ad lend:	267029	264962
ad ref:	122578	113099
ch:	87863	90961
audios:	21996	23252
videos:	2872	3553
CD-ROMs:	287	435
periodcls:	296	293

Issues:	1999-2000	2000-01
ad lend:	1494529	1401714
ch:	465895	442436
audios:	104686	109632
videos:	55374	57199
CD-ROMs:	433	1925

Acqs:	1999-2000	2000-01
bks:	40819	42862
AVs:	3286	4522

Acqs: Source: lib suppl, publ & bksellers *Co-op:* JFR *Offcr-in-Charge:* Bibliographical & Support Svcs Libn: Mrs Marguerite Gracey (marguerite.gracey@bolton.gov.uk)
Classn: DDC *Cat: Medium:* cards & auto *Auto Sys:* Talis *Svcs: Extramural:* schools, old people's homes, housebnd *Info:* business, child-care, community, svc to minority communities, svc to sight & hearing impaired, Bolton Libs Database (BOLD) *Other:* Open Learning *Activs:* ch's activs, bk sales, temp exhibs, poetry readings, reading groups, talks author visits *Offcr-in-Charge:* Principal Arts Offcr: Mr A.C. Hughes BA *Enqs:* 308809 (1999-2000); 321985 (2000-01) *Staff: Libns:* 40 *Non-Prof:* 107

Inc from:	1999-2000	2000-01
local govt:	£3440189	£3590000
fines etc:	£428428	£435653
total:	£3871102	£4017746

Exp on:	1999-2000	2000-01
bks:	£476328	£444484
AVs:	£68773	£58604
salaries:	£2245699	£2161138
total:	£3871102	£4017746

Bournemouth

P13 Bournemouth Libraries

Leisure & Tourism Directorate, Town Hall, Bourne Ave, Bournemouth, Dorset, BH2 6DY (01202-451451; *fax:* 01202-454820)
Email: Bournemouth@bournemouthlibraries.org.uk
Internet: http://www.bournemouth.gov.uk/leisure/Libraries/

Local Auth: Bournemouth Borough Council *Pop:* 163600 *Cttee:* Cabinet Structure; Portfolio for Developing Communities & Tackling Crime *Larger Dept:* Leisure & Tourism Directorate *Dept Chief:* Dir: Mr Stephen Godsall *Chief:* Head of Arts, Libs & Museum Svcs: Ms Shelagh Levett BA, CertEd, MCLIP (Shelagh.Levett@bournemouthlibraries.org.uk)

Other Snr Staff: Principal Development & Support Svcs Mgr: Ms Elaine Arthur (Elaine.Arthur@bournemouthlibraries.org.uk); Principal Area Svcs Mgr: Ms Carolyn Date (Carolyn.Date@bournemouthlibraries.org.uk); Finance & Admin Offcr: Mr Tim Jones (tim.jones@bournemouthlibraries.org.uk)
Main Libs: BOURNEMOUTH LIB, 22 The Triangle, Bournemouth, Dorset, BH2 5RQ (01202-454848; *fax:* 01202-454830) *Branch Libs:* BOSCOMBE LIB, Heathcote Rd, Bournemouth, Dorset, BH5 1EZ (01202-396078; *fax:* 01202-396583); CHARMINSTER LIB, Strouden Ave, Bournemouth, Dorset, BH8 9HF (01202-510379; *fax:* 01202-530001); KINSON LIB, Wimborne Rd, Bournemouth, Dorset, BH11 9AW (01202-573180; *fax:* 01202-581081); SOUTHBOURNE LIB, Seabourne Rd, Bournemouth, Dorset, BH5 2HY (01202-428784; *fax:* 01202-432389); SPRING-BOURNE LIB, Holdenhurst Rd, Bournemouth, Dorset, BH8 8BX (01202-397115; *fax:* 01202-397358); STROUDEN LIB, Castlepoint, Castle Ln West, Bournemouth, Dorset, BH8 9UP (01202-451900; *fax:* 01202-451904); TUCKTON LIB, Wick Ln, Bournemouth, Dorset, BH6 4LF (01202-429521; *fax:* 01202-434950); WESTBOURNE LIB, Alum Chine Rd, Bournemouth, Dorset, BH4 8DX (01202-761845; *fax:* 01202-763287); WEST HOWE LIB, West Howe, Bournemouth, Dorset, BH11 8DU (01202-573665; *fax:* 01202-593638); WINTON LIB, Wimborne Rd, Winton, Bournemouth, Dorset, BH9 2EN (01202-528139; *fax:* 01202-534083)
Svc Pts: PT: 1 *AV:* 12 *Computers:* 12 *Internet:* 12
ILLs: county, natl & internatl *Loans:* bks/3 wks; audios, videos & DVDs/1 wk *Charges:* audios/up to 90p; videos/info £1, others up to £3; DVDs/up to £3; music sets/£11.50 per hire period; playsets/£5.75 per hire period *Income Gen:* req & res/up to 90p; lost ticket/£1.60 *Fines:* bks/ad & oap 12p pd (max £7.50), ch free; audios, videos & DVDs/loan charge; music & play sets/loan charge; housebnd exempt *Equip:* m-reader/printer (35p per pg), fax (UK £1.60 1st pg, 50p addl, higher overseas), copiers (A4/10p), 150 computers (all with wd-proc, internet & CD-ROM), rooms for hire (£9.50-£300 depending on room & duration of booking), scanner (10p-£5.75 depending on format & quality), map viewer (printouts 25p per sheet) *Disabled:* Easiplay cassette player, standard cassette players, minicom, closed caption decoders for subtitled videos, adaptive hardware & software *Offcr-in-Charge:* Finance & Admin Offcr, as above

Stock:	1 Apr 2000	1 Apr 2001
lend:	241778	240080
ref:	21509	36164
AVs:	37742	35960
periodcls:	127	124

Issues:	1999-2000	2000-01
bks:	1534648	1321783
AVs:	116019	114144

Acqs:	1999-2000	2000-01
bks:	23986	24659
AVs:	5315	4243

Acqs: Source: lib suppl *Co-op:* CUSP *Offcr-in-Charge:* Finance & Admin Offcr, as above
Classn: DDC *Cat: Type:* author, classified, subj & title *Medium:* m-form & auto *Auto Sys:* Talis *Svcs: Extramural:* old people's homes, housebnd *Info:* business, community, local studies *Other:* all libs registered as CALL UK online centres *Activs:* ch's activs, bk & video sales, temp exhibs, poetry readings, reading groups, writers' groups, talks, author visits, homework clubs, computer courses *Offcr-in-Charge:* Libs Offcr (Ch & Learning): Mrs Heather Young (Heather.young@bournemouthlibraries.org.uk); Area Libn South: Ms Tanya Butchers (Tanya.butchers@bournemouthlibraries.org.uk) ☛

Bournemouth ▼ Bristol

Public Libraries

(Bournemouth Libs cont)

Enqs: 158964 (1999-2000); 143429 (2000-01)
Staff: Libns: 19.5 *Other Prof:* 1 *Non-Prof:* 64.6

Inc from:	1999-2000	2000-01
local govt:	£2345782	£2892310
fines etc:	£167375	£289708
total:	£2513157	£3182018

Exp on:	1999-2000	2000-01
bks:	£260325	£234479
AVs:	£62400	£57353
salaries:	£1286350	£1343638
total:	£2513157	£3182018

Bracknell Forest

P14 Bracknell Forest Library and Information Service

Bracknell Lib, Town Sq, Bracknell, Berkshire, RG12 1BH (01344-423149; *fax:* 01344-411392)
Email: bracknell.library@bracknell-forest.gov.uk
Internet: http://www.bracknell-forest.gov.uk/libraries/

Local Auth: Bracknell Forest Borough Council *Pop:* 110636 *Cttee:* Select Cttee for Lifelong Learning *Larger Dept:* Leisure Svcs *Dept Chief:* Dir: Mr Vincent Paliczka *Chief:* Lib & Info Mgr: Ms Kay Chambers
Main Libs: BRACKNELL CENTRAL LIB, contact details as above *Branch Libs:* ASCOT HEATH LIB, Fernbank Rd, Ascot, Berkshire, SL5 8LA (*tel & fax:* 01344-884030); BINFIELD LIB, Benetfield Rd, Binfield, Berkshire, RG42 4JZ (01344-306663; *fax:* 01344-486467); BIRCH HILL LIB, Leppington, Birch Hill, Bracknell, Berkshire, RG12 7WW (*tel & fax:* 01344-456526); CROWTHORNE LIB, Lower Broadmoor Rd, Crowthorne, Berkshire, RG11 7LA (*tel & fax:* 01344-776431); SANDHURST LIB, The Broadway, Sandhurst, Camberley, Surrey, GU47 9BL (01252-870161; *fax:* 01252-878285); WHITEGROVE LIB, 5 County Ln, Warfield, Bracknell, Berkshire, RG42 3JP (01344-424211; *fax:* 01344-861233)
Svc Pts: PT: 2 *Mobile:* 2
ILLs: natl *Loans:* bks & audios/3 wks; videos & CD-ROMs/1 wk *Charges:* audios/£1-£2; videos/£1.50-£2; CD-ROMs/£1.50-£2.50 *Income Gen:* res/70p; lost ticket/£1.50 *Fines:* bks/ad 10p pd (£4 max), ch 5p pd (50p max); audios/as ad bks; videos & CD-ROMs/50p pd (£10 max); registered blind or partially sighted exempt from spkn wd charges *Equip:* m-reader, m-printer, 9 copiers (A4/10p), 11 fax, 50 computers (all with internet & CD-ROM, access free)

Stock:	1 Apr 2000	1 Apr 2001
ad lend:	94689	96444
ad ref:	7062	8440
ch:	46143	38722
audios:	7497	7363
videos:	3469	4177
CD-ROMs:	837	1077
periodcls:	84	84

Issues:	1999-2000	2000-01
ad lend:	483538	473218
ch:	218834	231655
audios:	28533	26953
videos:	47275	46978
CD-ROMs:	273	3265

Acqs:	1999-2000	2000-01
bks:	19276	28450
AVs:	3554	4105

Acqs: Source: lib suppl & bksellers *Offcr-in-Charge:* Stock Mgr: Mrs G. Norman
Classn: DDC *Cat: Type:* author, classified & title *Medium:* auto *Auto Sys:* Dynix *Svcs: Extramural:* schools, old people's homes, housebnd; extramural svcs provided under co-op joint arrangements *Info:* community, local govt *Other:* Webwise *Activs:* ch's activs, bk sales
Enqs: 97604 (1999-2000); 100620 (2000-01)
Staff: Libns: 15.5 *Non-Prof:* 26.9

Inc from:	2000-01
local govt:	£20726
fines etc:	£140528
total:	£164322

Exp on:	2000-01
bks:	£241180
AVs:	£46266
salaries:	£786021
total:	£1655213

Bradford

P15 Bradford Public Libraries

Central Lib, Prince's Way, Bradford, W Yorkshire, BD1 1NN (01274-753600; *fax:* 01274-395108)
Internet: http://www.bradford.gov.uk/

Local Auth: City of Bradford Metropolitan Dist Council *Pop:* 486000 *Cttee:* Exec Cttee; Portfolio Memb: Regeneration *Larger Dept:* Arts, Heritage & Leisure *Dept Chief:* Ms Jane Glaister *Chief:* Head of Libs, Archvs & Info Svc: Mr Ian Watson
Main Libs: CENTRAL LIB, addr as above; *Bradford East Area:* ECCLESHILL LIB, Bolton Rd, Eccleshill, Bradford, W Yorkshire, BD2 4SR (01274-431541; *fax:* 01274-431544); *Bradford West/Shipley Area:* SHIPLEY LIB, 2 Well Croft, Shipley, W Yorkshire, BD18 3QH (01274-437150; *fax:* 01274-530247); *Keighley/Ilkley Area:* KEIGHLEY LIB, North St, Keighley, W Yorkshire, BD21 3SX (01535-618212; *fax:* 01535-618214) *Branch Libs:* BAILDON LIB, Hallcliffe, Baildon, Shipley, W Yorkshire, BD17 6ND (01274-581425); BINGLEY LIB, Myrtle Walk, Bingley, W Yorkshire, BD16 1AW (01274-438780); CLAYTON LIB, Old School House, Clayton Ln, Bradford, W Yorkshire, BD14 6AY (01274-880689); GT HORTON LIB, Cross Ln, Bradford, W Yorkshire, BD7 3JT (01274-573175); HOLMEWOOD LIB, Broadstone Way, Holmewood, Bradford, W Yorkshire, BD4 9DY (01274-684012); ILKLEY LIB, Station Rd, Ilkley, W Yorkshire, LS29 8HA (01943-436225; *fax:* 01943-603795); LAISTERDYKE LIB, Manse St, Bradford, W Yorkshire, BD3 8RP (01274-434724); MANNINGHAM LIB, Carlisle Rd, Bradford, W Yorkshire, BD8 8BB (01274-543516; *fax:* 01274-484016); WIBSEY LIB, North Rd, Wibsey, Bradford, W Yorkshire, BD6 1TR (01274-679043); WYKE LIB, Huddersfield Rd, Wyke, Bradford, W Yorkshire, BD12 8HS (01274-676830)
Svc Pts: PT: 17 *Mobile:* 3 *AV:* 21 *Computers:* 14 *Internet:* 14
Collns: Photography; Film & Television; Oral Hist; Fine Art & Local Hist (all at Central Lib); Brontë Colln; Snowden Colln; Gordon Bottomley Bks; Local Archvs Colln (all at Keighley Lib)
Co-op Schemes: Bradford Accord, YHRLS, YHFMP, YHBICN, YLI, BIN *ILLs:* county, natl & internatl *Loans:* bks/3 wks; audios, videos & DVDs/1 wk *Charges:* cassettes/40p, sets 80p-£1.20; CDs/60p, sets £1.20-£1.80; videos/£1-£1.50 *Income Gen:* req/60p or £1; res/60p; lost ticket/50p or £1 *Fines:* bks/ad 7p pd 1st wk, then 20p pw + admin costs, ch & oap admin costs only; audios & videos/loan charge *Equip:* 24 m-readers, 2 m-printers (A4/40p, A3/80p), 10 fax (£1 1st pg, 75p addtl), 20 copiers (A4/10p, A3/20p), clr copier (A4/£1, A3/£2), computers (incl 120

internet & 120 CD-ROM readers), 10 rooms for hire (various) *Disabled:* Kurzweil, CCTV, braille embosser, Speech Synthesiser software, 2 minicom *Online:* Juniper, Waterlow, Companies House, Dun & Bradstreet, MINTEL

Stock:	1 Apr 2000	1 Apr 2001
ad lend:	409453	377256
ad ref:	190903	203791
ch:	132071	128753
audios:	45596	36492
videos:	20601	16596
CD-ROMs:	450	534
periodcls:	541	511
archvs:	306 linear m	310 linear m

Issues:	1999-2000	2000-01
ad lend:	1960620	1791360
ch:	580508	516615
audios:	153379	153199
videos:	80651	76530
CD-ROMs:	1363	2425

Acqs:	1999-2000	2000-01
bks:	32300	26492
AVs:	4343	4369

Acqs: Source: lib suppl, publ & bksellers *Co-op:* Yorkshire Bk Consortium *Offcr-in-Charge:* Principal Libn (Support Svcs): Mr R. Walters *Classn:* DDC *Cat: Type:* author, classified, subj & title *Medium:* cards & auto *Auto Sys:* BiblioMondo *Svcs: Extramural:* old people's homes, housebnd, day centres *Info:* business, community *Other:* LearnDirect *Activs:* ch's activs, bk sales, temp exhibs, poetry readings, reading groups, talks, author visits
Enqs: 545233 (1999-2000); 615836 (2000-01)
Staff: Libns: 32 *Non-Prof:* 161

Inc from:	1999-2000	2000-01
local govt:	£4241600	£3949579
fines etc:	£622240	£513325
total:	£4863840	£4462904

Exp on:	1999-2000	2000-01
bks:	£238217	£255368
AVs:	£33359	£40338
salaries:	£3105064	£3188154
total:	£4863840	£4462904

Bridgend

P16 Bridgend Library and Information Service

Coed Parc, Pk Street, Bridgend, Mid Glamorgan, CF31 4BA (01656-661813; *fax:* 01656-645719)
Email: blis@bridgend.gov.uk
Internet: http://www.bridgend.gov.uk/english/library/

Local Auth: Bridgend County Borough Council *Pop:* 131000 *Larger Dept:* Edu, Leisure & Community Svcs *Dept Chief:* Dir: Mr David Matthews *Chief:* County Borough Libn: Mr John Woods
Main Libs: BRIDGEND REF & INFO CENTRE (incl Local Studies Lib), addr as above *Branch Libs:* ABERKENFIG LIB, Heol-y-Llyfrau, Aberkenfig, Mid Glamorgan, CF32 9PT (01656-721622; *fax:* 01656-729121; *email:* abkenlib@bridgend.gov.uk); BETWS LIB, Betws Centre, Betws, Mid Glamorgan, CF32 8TB (01656-725696; *email:* bettwslib@bridgend.gov.uk); BRIDGEND LIB, Wyndham St, Bridgend, Mid Glamorgan, CF31 1EF (01656-653444; *fax:* 01656-667886; *email:* bridgendlib@bridgend.gov.uk); MAESTEG LIB, North's Ln, Maesteg, Mid Glamorgan, CF34 9AA (01656-733201; *fax:* 01656-731098; *email:* maestlib@bridgend.gov.uk); NANTYMOEL LIB, Berwyn Centre, Nantymoel, Mid Glamorgan, CF32 7SD (01656-840719; *email:* nantymoellib@bridgend.gov.uk); OGMORE VALE LIB, Ogmore Valley Life Centre, Cwrt Gwalia, Ogmore Vale, Mid Glamorgan, CF32 7AJ (01656-842153; *fax:* 01656-840367; *email:* ovalelib@bridgend.gov.uk);

PENCOED LIB, Penybont Rd, Pencoed, Mid Glamorgan, CF35 5RA (01656-860358; *fax:* 01656-863042; *email:* penclib@bridgend.gov.uk); PORTHCAWL LIB, Church Pl, Porthcawl, Mid Glamorgan, CF36 3AG (01656-782059; *fax:* 01656-772745; *email:* porthcawllib@bridgend.gov.uk); PYLE LIB, Pyle Life Centre, Helig Fan, Pyle, Mid Glamorgan, CF33 6BS (01656-740631; *fax:* 01656-744865; *email:* pylelib@bridgend.gov.uk)
Svc Pts: PT: 4 *Mobile:* 1 *AV:* 8 *Computers:* 13 *Internet:* 13 *Other:* 1 Booklink Svc to housebnd *Collns:* local & family hist *ILLs:* county & natl *Loans:* bks & audios/3 wks; videos & DVDs/1 wk *Equip:* m-readers, m-printers, fax, copiers, computers (with wd-proc, internet & CD-ROM), room hire at all libs *Disabled:* loop sys

Stock:	1 Apr 2001
ad:	179820
ch:	58291

Acqs: Source: lib suppl *Offcr-in-Charge:* Resources Development Offcr
Classn: DDC *Cat: Type:* author, classified & title *Medium:* auto *Auto Sys:* Geac *Svcs: Extramural:* old people's homes, housebnd *Info:* community, council *Other:* LearnDirect *Activs:* ch's activs, literary lecture series
Staff: Libns: 19 *Non-Prof:* 19.8

Exp on:	2000-01
bks:	£167811
AVs:	£24104

Brighton and Hove

P17 Brighton and Hove Libraries
Brighton Lib, Vantage Pt, New England Street, Brighton, E Sussex, BN1 1UE (01273-290800; *fax:* 01273-296951)
Email: libraries@brighton-hove.gov.uk
Internet: http://www.citylibraries.info/

Local Auth: Brighton & Hove Council *Pop:* 259900 *Cttee:* Libs & Museums Sub-Cttee *Larger Dept:* Culture & Regeneration *Dept Chief:* Strategic Dir: Ms Sarah Tamber *Chief:* Head of Libs & ITC: Ms Sally McMahon *Other Snr Staff:* Operational Resources Mgr: Ms Julia Hugall; Community & Development Mgr: Mr Alan Issler; Prof & Collns Mgr: Mr Nigel Imi
Main Libs: BRIGHTON LIB, addr as above
Branch Libs: HANGLETON LIB, West Way, Hangleton, Hove, E Sussex, BN3 8LD (01273-296904; *fax:* 01273-296903); HOVE LIB, 182-186 Church Rd, Hove, E Sussex, BN3 2EG (*lend:* 01273-296937; *ref:* 01273-296942; *fax:* 01273-296931); PORTSLADE LIB, 223 Old Shoreham Rd, Portslade, Brighton, E Sussex, BN4 1XR (01273-296914; *fax:* 01273-296913); PORTSLADE COMMUNITY COLL LIB, Chalky Rd, Portslade, E Sussex, BN41 2WS (01273-296916); WHITE-HAWK LIB, Whitehawk Community Centre, Whitehawk Rd, Brighton, E Sussex, BN2 5GZ (01273-296924; *fax:* 01273-296925)
Svc Pts: PT: 9 *Mobile:* 1 *Other:* LOCAL STUDIES LIB (see **A67**)
Collns: Arts & Antiques Colln; BBC Radio Brighton Tapes; Bloomfield Colln (MSS & early printed materials); Clericetti Colln (15C Italian writers); Cobden Colln; Elliott Theological Colln (from 15C); Erredge Colln (local author of local hist bks); Hack Colln; Halliwell-Phillips Colln (Shakespeare); Illusts Colln; Kipling Colln; Lewis Colln (foreign fine arts bks); Long Classics Colln; Matthews Colln (Hebrew & Oriental lit); Nat Hist Colln; Paine Colln; Politics Colln; Railway Photo Colln; Trade Union Collns; Victorian Fiction (all at Brighton Lib); Autograph Colln; BBC Radio Scripts; Ben Harland Slide Colln; Bk Plate Colln; Early Ch's Bk Colln; Early English Newspapers; Plays & Poetry; Underground & Alternative Press; Wolseley Colln (all at Hove Lib)
Co-op Schemes: WebsLink *ILLs:* county, natl

& internatl *Loans:* bks & talking bks/3 wks; music audios & videos/1 wk; toys/3 wks; jigsaws/6 wks *Charges:* audios/80p single issue, £20 annual sub; videos/films £2, non-fiction £1.50, ch 75p *Income Gen:* res/70p, £1.40 outside region; lost ticket/ad £1; rsrch/£20 per hr *Fines:* bks & audios/ad & oap 15p per item, ch 3p per item; videos/ad 40p, ch 15p; housebnd, instns & registered blind exempt *Equip:* 4 m-readers, 2 m-printers (25p per printout), 15 fax (UK 1st pg £2, £1 addl, higher charges overseas), 16 copiers (A4/10p, A3/15p), 2 clr copiers (A4/£1, A3/£1.50), 91 computers (incl wd-proc & internet) *Disabled:* Eazee reader, video caption decoder

Stock:	1 Apr 2000	1 Apr 2001
ad lend:	201797	208126
ad ref:	223559	225659
ch:	82643	-
audios:	20623	21923
videos:	10645	11708
periodcls:	122	225

Issues:	1999-2000	2000-01
ad lend:	971941	944915
ch:	357566	350205
audios:	107493	115170
videos:	73610	85990

Acqs:	1999-2000	2000-01
bks:	40191	36824
AVs:	4622	3949

Acqs: Source: lib suppl *Offcr-in-Charge:* Professional Svcs Mgr: Mr Nigel Imi
Classn: DDC *Cat: Type:* author, classified, dictionary, subj & title keyword *Medium:* printed & auto *Auto Sys:* DS Galaxy 2000 *Svcs: Extramural:* old people's homes, housebnd *Info:* European, Public Info Relay (PIR) Pt, business, community, local studies *Other:* Open Learning, rsrch svcs, email facilities, fax bureaux, local illustrations reproduction svc *Activs:* ch's activs, bk sales *Offcr-in-Charge:* Libn: Ms Jo Harvey
Enqs: 199732 (1999-2000); 201448 (2000-01)
Staff: Libns: 12.68 *Non-Prof:* 66.26

Inc from:	1999-2000	2000-01
local govt:	£3029657	£3037597
fines etc:	£226870	£265618
total:	£3256327	£3303215

Exp on:	1999-2000	2000-01
stock:	£496068	£462622
salaries:	£1572087	£1642048
total:	£3256327	£3303215

Proj: new Brighton Lib (opening 2004)

Bristol

P18 Bristol City Libraries
Central Lib, Coll Green, Bristol, BS1 5TL (0117-903-7200; *fax:* 0117-922-1081)
Email: bristol_library_service@bristol-city.gov.uk
Internet: http://www.bristol-city.gov.uk/

Local Auth: Bristol City Council *Pop:* 402300 *Larger Dept:* Environment, Transport & Leisure *Dept Chief:* Dir: Mr Stephen Wray *Chief:* Head of Libs: Ms Kate Davenport
Main Libs: CENTRAL LIB, addr as above
Branch Libs: BEDMINSTER LIB, East St, Bedminster, Bristol, BS3 4HY (0117-903-8529; *email:* bedminster_library@bristol-city.gov.uk); BISHOPSWORTH LIB, Bishopsworth Rd, Bishopsworth, Bristol, BS13 7LN (0117-903-8566; *email:* bishopsworth_library@bristol-city.gov.uk); CHELTENHAM RD LIB, Cheltenham Rd, Bristol, BS6 5QX (0117-903-8562; *email:* cheltenhamrd_library@bristol-city.gov.uk); CLIFTON LIB, Princess Victoria St, Clifton, Bristol, BS8 4BX (0117-903-8572; *email:* clifton_library@bristol-city.gov.uk); EASTVILLE LIB, Muller Rd, Eastville, Bristol, BS5 6XP (0117-903-8578; *email:* eastville_library@bristol-city.gov.uk); FILWOOD LIB, Filwood Broadway,

Filwood, Bristol, BS4 1JN (0117-903-8581; *email:* filwood_library@bristol-city.gov.uk); FISHPONDS LIB, Fishponds Rd, Fishponds, Bristol, BS16 3UH (0117-903-8560; *email:* fishponds_library@bristol-city.gov.uk); HARTCLIFFE LIB, Peterson Sq, Hartcliffe, Bristol, BS13 0EE (0117-903-8568; *email:* hartcliffe_library@bristol-city.gov.uk); HENBURY LIB, Crow Ln, Henbury, Bristol, BS10 7DR (0117-903-8522; *email:* henbury_library@bristol-city.gov.uk); HENLEAZE LIB, Northumbria Dr, Henleaze, Bristol, BS9 4HP (0117-903-8541; *email:* henleaze_library@bristol-city.gov.uk); HILLFIELDS LIB, Summerleaze, Hillfields, Bristol, BS16 4HL (0117-903-8576; *email:* hillfields_library@bristol-city.gov.uk); HORFIELD LIB, Filton Ave, Horfield, Bristol, BS7 0BD (0117-903-8538; *email:* horfield_library@bristol-city.gov.uk); KNOWLE LIB, Redcatch Rd, Knowle, Bristol, BS4 2EP (0117-903-8585; *email:* knowle_library@bristol-city.gov.uk); LAWRENCE WESTON LIB, Stile Acres, Lawrence Weston, Bristol, BS11 0QA (0117-982-2432; *email:* lawrencew_library@bristol-city.gov.uk); MARKS-BURY RD LIB, Marksbury Rd, Bedminster, Bristol, BS3 5LG (0117-903-8574; *email:* marksburyrd_library@bristol-city.gov.uk); REDLAND LIB, Whiteladies Rd, Redland, Bristol, BS8 2PY (0117-903-8549; *email:* redland_library@bristol-city.gov.uk); SEA MILLS LIB, Sylvan Way, Westbury on Trym, Bristol, BS9 2NA (0117-903-8555; *email:* seamills_library@bristol-city.gov.uk); SHIREHAMPTON LIB, Station Rd, Shirehampton, Bristol, BS11 9TU (0117-903-8570; *email:* shirehampton_library@bristol-city.gov.uk); SOUTHMEAD LIB, Greystoke Ave, Southmead, Bristol, BS10 6AS (0117-903-8583; *email:* southmead_library@bristol-city.gov.uk); ST GEORGE LIB, Church Rd, St George, Bristol, BS5 8AL (0117-903-8523; *email:* st_george_library@bristol-city.gov.uk); STOCK-WOOD LIB, Stockwood Rd, Stockwood, Bristol, BS14 8PL (0117-903-8546; *email:* stockwood_library@bristol-city.gov.uk); TRINITY RD LIB, Trinity Rd, Bristol, BS2 0NW (0117-903-8543; *email:* trinityrd_library@bristol-city.gov.uk); WESTBURY LIB, Falcondale Rd, Westbury on Trym, Bristol, BS9 3JZ (0117-903-8552; *email:* westbury_library@bristol-city.gov.uk); WICK RD LIB, Wick Rd, Brislington, Bristol, BS4 4HE (0117-903-8557; *email:* wickrd_library@bristol-city.gov.uk)
Svc Pts: PT: 1 *Mobile:* 1 *AV:* 25 *Computers:* 25 *Internet:* 25
Collns: Drama Colln (at Central Lib); BSI; Feminist Archv (at Trinity Rd Lib – see **A75**)
ILLs: county, natl & internatl *Loans:* bks/3 wks; audios/2 wks; videos/1 wk *Charges:* audios/70p; videos/£1-£2 *Income Gen:* req & res/75p-£1.50; lost ticket/£1 *Fines:* bks/ad & oap 10p pd; audios & videos/loan charge; housebnd & hard of hearing exempt *Equip:* m-readers, m-printers (A4/30p, A3/40p), fax (to send £1 UK, higher overseas, to receive 50p), teletext, copiers (A4/10p, A3/20p), clr copier (A4/£1.20, A3/£2.20), 200+ computers (incl wd-procs, internet & CD-ROM, access free, printouts 10p)

Stock:	1 Apr 2000	1 Apr 2001
ad lend:	302578	301532
ad ref:	268165	268877
ch:	95799	65134

Stock:	1 Apr 2000	1 Apr 2001
audios:	28763	28487
videos:	10901	9209
CD-ROMs:	426	515
periodcls:	230	243

Issues:	1999-2000	2000-01
ad lend:	1638606	1497704
ch:	371261	366937
audios:	145109	150768
videos:	83461	84554
CD-ROMs:	2189	5873

(Bristol City Libs cont)

Acqs:	1999-2000	2000-01
bks:	53714	42822
AVs:	5743	7021

Acqs: Source: lib suppl, publ & bksellers *Co-op:* CUSP *Offcr-in-Charge:* Acqs Offcr: Ms Kate Shaw (Kate_Shaw@bristol-city.gov.uk) *Classn:* DDC *Cat: Type:* author, classified, subj & title *Medium:* auto *Auto Sys:* Talis *Svcs: Extramural:* schools, prisons, old people's homes, housebnd, day centres, play groups *Info:* business, IT in the Community *Other:* Open Learning, Training Access Pt (TAP), local studies & family hist, svcs for ethnic minority groups *Activs:* ch's activs, temp exhibs, bk sales, reading groups, writers' groups, talks *Enqs:* 268167 (1999-2000); 324629 (2000-01) *Staff: Libns:* 37.7 *Non-Prof:* 139.5

Inc from:	1999-2000	2000-01
local govt:	£306832	£85456
fines etc:	£363648	£489829
total:	£670480	£572285

Exp on:	1999-2000	2000-01
bks:	£432700	£449601
AVs:	£70250	£73908
salaries:	£3296000	£3399123
total:	£5669533	£5963089

Proj: NOF-funded Peoples' Network installation of 240 computer terminals

Buckinghamshire

P19 Buckinghamshire County Library Service

Libs & Heritage, County Hall, Walton Street, Aylesbury, Buckinghamshire, HP20 1UU (01296-383206; *fax:* 01296-382259)
Email: library@buckscc.gov.uk
Internet: http://www.buckscc.gov.uk/libraries/

Local Auth: Buckinghamshire County Council *Pop:* 483129 *Larger Dept:* Community Svcs *Dept Chief:* Strategic Mgr: Mr Dean Taylor *Chief:* Head of Libs & Heritage: Mr Robert Strong BA, DipLib, MCLIP *Dep:* Libs Mgr: Mrs Jenny Varney MCLIP *Other Snr Staff:* Resources Development Libn: Mr Mark Bryant; Community Development Libn: Mr Peter Mussett; Learning Development Libn: Mr Mike Ryan
Main Libs: AMERSHAM LIB, Chiltern Ave, Amersham, Buckinghamshire, HP6 5AH (01494-586878; *fax:* 01494-586870; *email:* lib-ame@ buckscc.gov.uk); AYLESBURY LIB, Walton St, Aylesbury, Buckinghamshire, HP20 1UU (01296-382248; *fax:* 01296-382641; *email:* lib-ayl@ buckscc.gov.uk); BEACONSFIELD LIB, Reynolds Rd, Beaconsfield, Buckinghamshire, HP9 2NJ (01494-672295; *fax:* 01494-678772; *email:* lib-bea@buckscc.gov.uk); BUCKINGHAM LIB, Verney Cl, Buckingham, MK18 1JP (01280-813229 *fax:* 01280-823597; *email:* lib-buc@ buckscc.gov.uk); CHESHAM LIB, Elgiva Ln, Chesham, Buckinghamshire, HP5 2JD (01494-772322; *fax:* 01494-773074; *email:* lib-che@ buckscc.gov.uk); HAZLEMERE LIB, 312 Amersham Rd, Hazlemere, High Wycombe, Buckinghamshire, HP15 7PY (01494-815266; *fax:* 01494-816621; *email:* lib-haz@buckscc.gov.uk); HIGH WYCOMBE LIB, Queen Victoria Rd, High Wycombe, Buckinghamshire, HP11 1BD (01494-464004; *fax:* 01494-533086; *email:* lib-hiw@ buckscc.gov.uk); MARLOW LIB, Inst Rd, Marlow, Buckinghamshire, SL7 1BL (01628-486163; *fax:* 01628-476313; *email:* lib-mar@buckscc.gov.uk); COUNTY REF LIB, Walton St, Aylesbury, Buckinghamshire, HP20 1UU (01296-383252; *fax:* 01296-382405; *email:* countyreflib@buckscc. gov.uk) *Branch Libs:* BOURNE END LIB, Wakeman Rd, Bourne End, Buckinghamshire, SL8 5SX (01628-524814; *email:* lib-boe@buckscc. gov.uk); BURNHAM LIB, Windsor Ln, Burnham, Buckinghamshire, SL1 7HR (01628-662522; *fax:* 01628-603611; *email:* lib-bur@buckscc.gov.uk); CASTLEFIELD LIB, Combined School, Middle Way, Castlefield, High Wycombe, Buckinghamshire, HP12 3LE (01494-527288; *email:* lib-cas@ buckscc.gov.uk); Chalfont St Giles, High St, Chalfont St Giles, Buckinghamshire, HP8 4QA (01494-874732; *email:* lib-csg@buckscc.gov.uk); CHALFONT ST PETER LIB, High St, Chalfont St Peter, Buckinghamshire, SL9 9QA (01753-885991; *email:* lib-csp@buckscc.gov.uk); FARNHAM COMMON LIB, Victoria Rd, Farnham Common, Buckinghamshire, SL2 3NL (*tel & fax:* 01753-644088; *email:* lib-fac@buckscc.gov.uk); FLACK-WELL HEATH LIB, Carrington Jnr School, Chapel Rd, Flackwell Heath, Buckinghamshire, HP10 9AA (01628-521050; *email:* lib-flh@buckscc.gov.uk); GERRARDS CROSS LIB, 38 Station Rd, Gerrards Cross, Buckinghamshire, SL9 8EL (01753-885766; *fax:* 01753-890036; *email:* lib-gex@buckscc.gov.uk); GT MISSENDEN LIB, High St, Gt Missenden, Buckinghamshire, HP16 0AL (01494-864659; *email:* lib-mis@buckscc. gov.uk); HADDENHAM LIB, Churchway, Haddenham, Aylesbury, Buckinghamshire, HP17 8EE (01844-291527; *email:* lib-had@buckscc. gov.uk); IVER HEATH LIB, St Margaret's Cl, Iver Heath, Iver, Buckinghamshire, SL0 0DA (01753-650293; *email:* lib-ivh@buckscc.gov.uk); LITTLE CHALFONT LIB, Cokes Ln, Little Chalfont, Amersham, Buckinghamshire, HP7 9QA (01494-764602; *email:* lib-lit@buckscc.gov.uk); LONG CRENDON LIB, High St, Long Crendon, Aylesbury, Buckinghamshire, HP18 9AF (01844-208032; *email:* lib-lon@buckscc.gov.uk); PRINCES RISBOROUGH LIB, Bell St, Princes Risborough, Buckinghamshire, HP27 0AA (01844-343559; *fax:* 01844-347083; *email:* lib-prr@ buckscc.gov.uk); STOKE POGES LIB, Bell St, Stoke Poges, Buckinghamshire, SL2 4BY (01753-645485; *email:* lib-stp@buckscc.gov.uk); STOKENCHURCH LIB, Wycombe Rd, Stoken-church, High Wycombe, Buckinghamshire, HP14 3RG (01494-482560; *email:* lib-sto@buckscc. gov.uk); WENDOVER LIB, High St, Wendover, Aylesbury, Buckinghamshire, HP22 6DU (01296-623649; *email:* lib-wen@buckscc.gov.uk); WINSLOW LIB, Park Rd, Winslow, Buckingham, MK18 3DN (01296-383590; *email:* lib-wis@ buckscc.gov.uk)
Svc Pts: PT: 8 *Mobile:* 6 *Computers:* 35 *Internet:* 35 *Other:* CENTRE FOR BUCKINGHAMSHIRE STUDIES, at Libs & Heritage HQ (see **A19**); COUNTY RESERVE STOCK, at Libs & Heritage HQ (01296-382271; *fax:* 01296-382274)
Collns: Buckinghamshire Colln (local hist, at Centre for Buckinghamshire Studies); Early Ch's Bk Colln (c1500 items, at Chesham Lib); many rare, older & specialised items are held in the County Reserve Stock *Co-op Schemes:* BBI, Six Counties Ref Group *ILLs:* county, natl & internatl *Loans:* bks & prints/4 wks; audios & CD-ROMs/2 wks; videos, DVDs & Playstation games/1 wk *Charges:* cassettes/50p; CDs/90p; sets £1.60; spkn wd/90p-£2.50; videos, DVDs & CD-ROMs/90p-£2.50; Playstation games/£2.50-£4 *Income Gen:* req & res/80p, +£1.50 outside county, music scores £11 per set, ch's bks free; lost ticket/£2 *Fines:* bks/ad & oap 10p pd (max £5), ch 3p pd (max £1.50); audios & CD-ROMs/as ad bks; videos & DVDs/40p pd (max £8); Playstation games/£1 pd (max £20); registered blind & partially sighted exempt *Equip:* m-readers, m-printer, video viewer, fax (£1 per pg, higher overseas), copiers (A4/10p, A3/15p), clr copier (A4/£1, A3/£1.50), computers (incl wd-procs, internet & CD-ROM), rooms for hire (varies) *Disabled:* Visually Impaired Persons (VIP) Suite (software & computer facilities, at County Ref Lib)

Stock:	1 Apr 2000	1 Apr 2001
lend:	563641	536987
ref:	75996	77208
AVs:	114474	112400
periodcls:	530	522

Issues:	1999-2000	2000-01
bks:	4564424	4331441
AVs:	916443	892611

Acqs:	1999-2000	2000-01
bks:	133459	136997
AVs:	54421	49524

Acqs: Source: lib suppl & bksellers *Co-op:* CBC *Offcr-in-Charge:* Libs Mgr, as above *Classn:* DDC *Cat: Type:* author, classified, subj & title *Medium:* auto *Auto Sys:* ALS *Svcs: Extramural:* schools, prisons, old people's homes *Info:* business, community, careers, council, European *Other:* LearnDirect, Learning Link, People's Network *Activs:* ch's activs, bk sales, temp exhibs, evening promotional events *Enqs:* 362440 (1999-2000); 325884 (2000-01) *Staff: Libns:* 42.5 *Non-Prof:* 178.4

Inc from:	1999-2000	2000-01
local govt:	£5386653	£6258846
fines etc:	£1962805	£1704469
total:	£7349458	£7963315

Exp on:	1999-2000	2000-01
bks:	£974728	£979277
AVs:	£613863	-
elec media:	incl in AVs	-
salaries:	£3948773	-
total:	£7349458	£7963315

Bury

P20 Bury Public Library Service

Bury Central Lib, Manchester Rd, Market Street, Bury, Lancashire, BL9 0DR (0161-253-6077; *fax:* 0161-253-6003)
Email: information@bury.gov.uk
Internet: http://www.bury.gov.uk/

Local Auth: Bury Metropolitan Borough Council *Pop:* 183800 *Larger Dept:* Cultural Svcs *Chief:* Principal Libn: Mrs Diana Sorrigan (d.sorrigan@bury.gov.uk) *Dep:* Asst Principal Libns: Ms Lesley Kelly (s.l.kelly@bury.gov.uk) & Mr Tony Jowett (t.jowett@bury.gov.uk) *Other Snr Staff:* Housebnd & Special Svcs Libn: Ms Elizabeth Binns (e.binns@bury.gov.uk); Learning Support Libn: Ms Christine Almond (c.almond@ bury.gov.uk)
Main Libs: BURY CENTRAL LIB, addr as above (0161-253-5872/3; *fax:* 0161-253-5857; *email:* bury.lib@bury.gov.uk) *Branch Libs:* PRESTWICH LIB, Longfield Centre, Prestwich, Manchester, M25 1AY (0161-253-7214/6; *fax:* 0161-253-5372; *email:* prestwich.lib@bury.gov.uk); RADCLIFFE LIB, Stand Ln, Radcliffe, Manchester, M26 9WR (0161-253-7160; *fax:* 0161-253-7165; *email:* radcliffe.lib@bury.gov.uk); RAMSBOTTOM LIB, Carr St, Ramsbottom, Bury, Lancashire, BL0 9AE (01706-822484; *fax:* 01706-824638; *email:* ramsbottom.lib@bury.gov.uk); TOTTINGTON LIB, Town Hall, Market St, Tottington, Bury, Lancashire, BL8 3LN (01204-882839; *fax:* 01204-886517; *email:* tottington.lib@ bury.gov.uk); UNSWORTH LIB, Sunnybank Rd, Bury, Lancashire, BL9 8ED (0161-253-7560; *fax:* 0161-253-7566; *email:* unsworth.lib@bury.gov.uk);

WHITEFIELD LIB, Pinfold Ln, Whitefield, Manchester, M45 7NY (0161-253-7510; *fax:* 0161-253-7514; *email:* whitefield.lib@bury.gov.uk) *Svc Pts:* PT: 4 *AV:* 2 *Other:* VISUAL IMPAIRMENT UNITS, at Bury & Whitefield Libs; HEARING IMPAIRMENT UNIT, at Bury Lib; BURY ARCHV SVC (see **A82**); HOUSEBND & SPECIAL SVCS, at Bury Lib; LEARNING SUPPORT SVCS, at Unsworth Lib *Co-op Schemes:* Libs North West, JFR *ILLs:* natl *Loans:* bks & audios/3 wks; videos, DVDs & CD-ROMs/1 wk *Charges:* audios/£1.40; videos & DVDs/£1.70 *Income Gen:* res/60p-£1, leisure card half price; lost ticket/£1, under-16s, oaps, registered blind/partially sighted 50p; transcription svc/£10 per hr, charities £5 per hr, registered blind/partially sighted free *Fines:* bks/ ad 12p pd (max £5), leisure card holders 6p pd, ch & over 60s exempt; talking bks/15p pd (max £5); audios/30p pd (max £5); videos & DVDs/32p pd (max £5); registered blind exempt for AV items *Equip:* m-readers, m-printer, fax (UK £1.50 1st pg, £1 addl, higher charges overseas), video viewer, copiers (A4/10p. A3/20p), clr copier (A4/ £1, A3/£1.50), computers (incl wd-proc, internet & CD-ROM), rooms for hire (varies) *Disabled:* 2 visual impairment units, hearing impairment unit

Stock:	1 Apr 2000	1 Apr 2001
lend:	259155	265207
ad ref:	13173	13823
AVs:	24836	27271
periodcls:	141	132

Issues:	1999-2000	2000-01
bks:	1165509	1081250
AVs:	120097	105549

Acqs:	1999-2000	2000-01
bks:	22396	26283
AVs:	3274	3176

Acqs: Source: lib suppl *Co-op:* JFR *Classn:* DDC *Cat: Type:* classified & dictionary *Medium:* auto *Auto Sys:* Dorset *Svcs: Extramural:* schools, old people's homes, housebnd *Info:* community, environment, business, health, leisure, employment, European *Other:* Open Learning, Homework Centre *Activs:* ch's activs, bk sales, temp exhibs *Enqs:* 164164 (1999-2000); 207636 (2000-01) *Staff: Libns:* 20.5 *Non-Prof:* 61.92

Inc from:	1999-2000	2000-01
local govt:	£2126015	£2144214
fines etc:	£190684	£191604
total:	£2316699	£2335818

Exp on:	1999-2000	2000-01
bks:	£262036	£266797
AVs:	£37902	£28965
elec media:	£2522	£3308
salaries:	£1200302	£1318062
total:	£2316699	£2335818

Caerphilly

P21 Caerphilly County Borough Council Libraries

Lib HQ, Unit 7, Woodfieldside Business Pk, Penmaen Rd, Pontllanfraith, Blackwood, Mid Glamorgan, NP12 2DG (01495-235586; *fax:* 01495-235567) *Email:* libraries@caerphilly.gov.uk *Internet:* http://www.caerphilly.gov.uk/learning/ libraries/

Local Auth: Caerphilly County Borough Council *Pop:* 167300 *Cttee:* Edu & Leisure Cttee *Larger Dept:* Edu & Leisure *Dept Chief:* Head of Lifelong Learning & Leisure: Mr Peter Gomer *Chief:* Principal Offcr, Libs: Ms Mary Palmer MLib, MCLIP (palmem@caerphilly.gov.uk) *Main Libs:* BLACKWOOD LIB, 192 High St, Blackwood, Newport, NP12 1AJ (01495-233000;

fax: 01495-233002); CAERPHILLY LIB, Morgan Jones Pk, Caerphilly, Mid Glamorgan, CF83 1AP (029-2085-2543; *fax:* 029-2086-5585); RISCA LIB, Pk Pl, Risca, Newport, NP11 6AS (01633-600920; *fax:* 01633-600922) *Branch Libs:* ABER-BARGOED LIB, Pant St, Aberbargoed, Mid Glamorgan, CF81 9BB (*tel & fax:* 01443-875538); ABERTRIDWR LIB, Aberfawr Rd, Abertridwr, Caerphilly, Mid Glamorgan, CF83 2EJ (*tel & fax:* 029-2083-0790); BARGOED LIB, The Square, Bargoed, Mid Glamorgan, CF81 8QQ (01443-875548; *fax:* 01443-836057); BEDWAS LIB, Newport Rd, Bedwas, Mid Glamorgan, CF83 8BJ (*tel & fax:* 029-2085-2542); NELSON LIB, Commercial St, Nelson, Treharris, Mid Glamorgan, CF46 6NF (*tel & fax:* 01443-451632); NEW-BRIDGE LIB, Church Rd, Newbridge, Newport, NP11 4QP (*tel & fax:* 01495-243574); NEW TREDEGAR LIB, Duffryn Ter, New Tredegar, Newport, NP24 6DG (*tel & fax:* 01443-875550); OAKDALE LIB, Llwynon Rd, Oakdale, Blackwood, Newport, NP12 0LX (*tel & fax:* 01495-223545); PENGAM LIB, Ivor St, Pengam, Blackwood, Newport, NP12 3RF (*tel & fax:* 01443-831739); RHYMNEY LIB, Victoria Rd, Rhymney, Newport, NP22 5NU (01685-840606; *fax:* 01685-843237); YSTRAD MYNACH LIB, Bedwlwyn St, Ystrad Mynach, Hengoed, Mid Glamorgan, CF82 7BB (01443-812988; *fax:* 01443-862711) *Svc Pts:* PT: 5 *Mobile:* 4 *AV:* 23 *Computers:* 19 *Internet:* 19 *Collns:* Idris Davies Colln; Thomas Jones Colln (both at Rhymney Lib) *Co-op Schemes:* V3 Online *ILLs:* natl *Loans:* bks & lang courses/3 wks; audios, videos, CD-ROMs & software/1 wk *Charges:* audios/75p; videos/£1.50; CD-ROMs & software/£2; Playstation games/£2.50 *Income Gen:* req/80p, not in stock £2; lost ticket/£1 *Fines:* bks/ad 13p pd, oaps 6p pd; under 16s, unemployed & registered blind exempt *Equip:* 8 m-readers, m-printer (10p), 19 copiers (10p), clr copier (A4/£1, A3/£1.50), 19 fax, 201 computers (all with wd-proc, internet & CD-ROM *Disabled:* Loop Sys (in 1 lib only) *Offcr-in-Charge:* various

Stock:	1 Apr 2000	1 Apr 2001
ad lend:	163344	158749
ad ref:	9883	10491
ch:	79029	82540
audios:	10412	10981
videos:	4409	4993
periodcls:	100	106

Acqs:	1999-2000	2000-01
bks:	29083	29276
AVs:	2223	3151

Acqs: Source: lib suppl & bksellers *Offcr-in-Charge:* Support Svcs Libn: Mrs Elizabeth Roberts (robere@caerphilly.gov.uk) *Classn:* DDC *Cat: Type:* author, classified, subj & title *Medium:* auto *Auto Sys:* Geac *Svcs: Extramural:* schools, old people's homes, day centres, play groups *Info:* 3 Info Centres, 1 Business Centre, 1 European Info Centre, Natl Assembly linked lib *Other:* Open Learning (4 libs), family hist (1 lib) *Activs:* ch's activs, bk sales, temp exhibs, reading groups, talks, author visits *Offcr-in-Charge:* various offcrs *Enqs:* 144177 (1999-2000); 174109 (2000-01) *Staff: Libns:* 18 *Non-Prof:* 52

Inc from:	1999-2000	2000-01
local govt:	£1887808	£2135211
fines etc:	£132675	£203844
total:	£2020483	£2339065

Exp on:	1999-2000	2000-01
bks:	£243205	£234379
AVs:	£44875	£43877
elec media:	£4092	£7589
salaries:	-	£1375914
total:	£2020483	£2339065

Calderdale

P22 Calderdale Libraries Service

Calderdale Central Lib, Northgate House, Northgate, Halifax, W Yorkshire, HX1 1UN (01422-392630; *fax:* 01422-392615) *Email:* libraries@calderdale.gov.uk *Internet:* http://www.calderdale.gov.uk/libraries/

Local Auth: Calderdale Metropolitan Borough Council *Pop:* 193700 *Cttee:* Cabinet Memb (Community Svcs) *Larger Dept:* Leisure Svcs *Dept Chief:* Chief Leisure Svcs Offcr: Mr Paul Lucas *Chief:* Asst Chief Leisure Svcs Offcr (Libs): Mr Martin Stone BA, MCLIP (martin.stone@calderdale.gov.uk) *Dep:* Head of Central & Support Svcs: Mr David Duffy *Main Libs:* East Area HQ: CENTRAL LIB, addr as above; West Area HQ: HEBDEN BRIDGE LIB, Cheetham St, Hebden Bridge, Halifax, W Yorkshire, HX7 8EP (01422-842151/3993; *fax:* 01422-845224) *Branch Libs:* East Area: BRIGHOUSE LIB, Halifax Rd, Brighouse, W Yorkshire, HD6 2AF (01484-718639; *fax:* 01484-719222); ELLAND LIB, Coronation St, Elland, W Yorkshire, HX5 0DF (01422-374472; *fax:* 01422-370509); HIPPER-HOLME LIB, Council Offices, Leeds Rd, Hipperholme, Halifax, W Yorkshire, HX3 8ND (01422-202257); NORTHOWRAM LIB, Lydgate, Northowram, Halifax, W Yorkshire, HX3 7EJ (01422-202997); RASTRICK LIB, Crowtrees Ln, Rastrick, Brighouse, W Yorkshire, HD6 3NE (01484-714858); SKIRCOAT LIB, Skircoat Green Rd, Halifax, W Yorkshire, HX3 0LQ (01422-354828); West Area: AKROYD LIB, Bankfield, Boothtown Rd, Halifax, W Yorkshire, HX3 6HG (01422-352277); BEECHWOOD RD LIB, Beechwood Rd, Holmfield, Halifax, W Yorkshire, HX2 9BU (01422-244161); KING CROSS LIB, 237-9 King Cross Rd, Halifax, W Yorkshire, HX1 3JL (01422-361595); MIXENDEN LIB, Mixenden Rd, Mixenden, Halifax, W Yorkshire, HX2 8PU (01422-244694); SOWERBY BRIDGE LIB, Hollins Mill Ln, Sowerby Bridge, W Yorkshire, HX6 2QG (01422-831627; *fax:* 01422-832681); TODMORDEN LIB, Strand, Rochdale Rd, Todmorden, W Yorkshire, OL14 7LB (01706-815600; *fax:* 01706-819025) *Svc Pts:* PT: 11 *Mobile:* 2 *AV:* 24 *Computers:* 14 *Internet:* 14 *Other:* LOCAL STUDIES SECTION, at Central Lib *ILLs:* county, natl & internatl *Loans:* bks/3 wks; audios/cassettes & spkn wd 3 wks, CDs 1 wk; videos/2 days, special interest 3 wks; DVDs/2 days; CD-ROMs/1 wk; lang tapes/3 wks *Charges:* spkn wd/50p (sets £1); music audios/ cassettes 60p, CDs 80p (set £1.40); videos/ £1.50-£2.50, special interest 70p; DVDs/£2.50; CD-ROMs/80p-£1.95; lang tapes/60p *Income Gen:* res/60p, conc 35p, +50p for ILLs; lost ticket/£1.50 *Fines:* bks/ad 10p pd, oap 6p pd (with Passport to Leisure), under-16s exempt; spkn wd & music cassettes/10p pd; videos/£1.50-£2.50 pd, special interest 10p pd; DVDs/£2.50 pd; CDs & CD-ROMs/15p pd; blind & partially sighted exempt, conc on AV fines & charges for under-16s & Passport to Leisure holders *Equip:* m-readers, m-printers, fax (UK £1 per pg, £2 overseas), copiers (A4/10p, A3/20p), clr copier (A4/£1, A3/£1.50), computers (incl wd-procs, internet & CD-ROM), rooms for hire (various) *Disabled:* video caption reader, induction loop sys in all meeting rooms, sign lang interpreting svc

Stock:	1 Apr 2001
bks:	378500

Issues:	2000-01
bks:	1433380
AVs:	136560

Acqs:	2000-01
bks:	31960
AVs:	4450

Public Libraries

Calderdale
▼
Cheshire

(Calderdale Libs Svc cont)

Acqs: Source: lib suppl & bksellers *Offcr-in-Charge:* Bibliographical Svcs Libn: Mr Chris Kearns
Classn: DDC *Cat: Type:* author, classified & title *Medium:* m-form & auto *Auto Sys:* Dynix, Ameritech *Svcs: Extramural:* schools, hosps, old people's homes, housebnd *Info:* business, community, careers *Other:* Open Learning, LearnDirect *Activs:* ch's activs, bk sales, temp exhibs, poetry readings, readers groups *Offcr-in-Charge:* various
Enqs: 156700 (2000-01)
Staff: Libns: 21.8 *Non-Prof:* 67.8

Inc from:	1999-2000	2000-01
local govt:	£3231611	£3345513
fines etc:	£219504	£258115
total:	£3586304	£3746785

Exp on:	1999-2000	2000-01
stock:	£321476	£415446
salaries:	£1508186	£1551352
total:	£3586304	£3746785

Cambridgeshire

P23 Cambridgeshire Libraries and Information Service

Cambridgeshire County Council, Shire Hall, Castle Hill, Cambridge, CB3 0AP (01223-712000; *fax:* 01223-717079)
Email: libraries@cambridgeshire.gov.uk
Internet: http://www.camcnty.gov.uk/library/

Local Auth: Cambridgeshire County Council
Pop: 573700 *Cttee:* Edu, Libs & Heritage Cttee
Larger Dept: Edu, Libs & Heritage *Dept Chief:* Dir: Mr Andrew Baxter *Chief:* Head of Libs & Info: Mr Michael G. Hosking MCLIP, MIMgt
Main Libs: CAMBRIDGE CENTRAL LIB, 7 Lion Yard, Cambridge, CB2 3QD (01223-712000; *fax:* 01223-712018; *email:* cambridge.central.library@camcnty.gov.uk); *Dist Libs:* ELY LIB, 6 The Cloisters, Ely, Cambridgeshire, CB7 4ZH (01353-616158; *fax:* 01353-616164); HUNTINGDON LIB, Princes St, Huntingdon, Cambridgeshire, PE29 3PH (01480-375800; *fax:* 01480-459563); MARCH LIB, City Rd, March, Cambridgeshire, PE15 9LT (01354-754754; *fax:* 01354-754760); ST IVES LIB, Station Rd, St Ives, Huntingdon, Cambridgeshire, PE27 5BW (01480-398004; *fax:* 01480-386604); ST NEOTS LIB, Priory Ln, St Neots, Huntingdon, Cambridgeshire, PE19 2BH (01480-398006; *fax:* 01480-396006); WISBECH LIB, 1 Ely Pl, Wisbech, Cambridgeshire, PE13 1EU (01945-464009; *fax:* 01945-582784) *Branch Libs:* ARBURY CT LIB, Arbury Ct, Cambridge, CB4 2JQ (*tel & fax:* 01223-712080); BAR HILL LIB, Gladeside, Bar Hill, Cambridge, CB3 8DY (*tel & fax:* 01954-273318); BARNWELL RD LIB, Barnwell Rd, Cambridge, CB5 8RQ (*tel & fax:* 01223-712083); BURWELL LIB, Village College, Burwell, Cambridgeshire, CB5 0DU (*tel & fax:* 01638-613125); CHATTERIS LIB, 2 Furrowfields Rd, Chatteris, Cambridgeshire, PE16 6DY (01354-692485; *fax:* 01354-694549); CHERRY HINTON LIB, High St, Cherry Hinton, Cambridge, CB1 9HZ (*tel & fax:* 01223-712081); COTTENHAM LIB, Margett St, Cottenham, Cambridgeshire, CB4 8QY (*tel & fax:* 01954-273322); GT SHELFORD LIB, 10-12 Woollards Ln, Gt Shelford, Cambridge,

CB2 5LZ (*tel & fax:* 01223-508746); HISTON LIB, School Hill, Histon, Cambridge, CB4 9JE (*tel & fax:* 01223-712059); LINTON LIB, Cathodeon Centre, Linton, Cambridge, CB1 6JT (*tel & fax:* 01223-892227); LITTLEPORT LIB, Town Hall, Littleport, Cambridgeshire, CB6 1LU (*tel & fax:* 01353-860699); MILTON RD LIB, Asham Rd, Cambridge, CB4 2BD (*tel & fax:* 01223-712082); PAPWORTH LIB, Pendrill Ct, Papworth Everard, Cambridge, CB3 8UY (*tel & fax:* 01480-830940); RAMSEY LIB, School Ln, Ramsey, Huntingdon, Cambridgeshire, PE26 1AF (*tel & fax:* 01487-812575); ROCK RD LIB, Rock Rd, Cambridge, CB1 7UG (*tel & fax:* 01223-712084); SAWSTON LIB, Village Coll, New Rd, Sawston, Cambridge, CB2 4BP (*tel & fax:* 01223-712058); SOHAM LIB, Clay St, Soham, Cambridgeshire, CB7 5HJ (01353-720773; *fax:* 01353-642517); SOMER-SHAM LIB, Church St, Somersham, Huntingdon, Cambridgeshire, PE28 3EG (*tel & fax:* 01487-840266); WHITTLESEY LIB, Market St, Whittlesey, Peterborough, Cambridgeshire, PE7 1BA (*tel & fax:* 01733-202536); YAXLEY LIB, Lansdowne Rd, Yaxley, Peterborough, Cambridgeshire, PE7 3JL (*tel & fax:* 01733-241648)
Svc Pts: PT: 14 *Mobile:* 7 *AV:* 40 *Computers:* 41 *Internet:* 41
Collns: Cambridgeshire Colln (local studies); Sports Resources Colln (both at Cambridge Central Lib) *Co-op Schemes:* EMRLS, Co-East *ILLs:* county, natl & internatl *Loans:* bks, spkn wd & CD-ROMs/3 wks; audios, videos & DVDs/1 wk *Charges:* spkn wd/cassettes 60p, CDs/80p; music audios/cassettes 40p, CDs 90p; videos/full length £2.20, short £1.20; DVDs/£2.50; CD-ROMs/£3 *Income Gen:* req & res/ad £1, ch free; lost ticket/£1, 1st replacement free *Fines:* bks/ad & oap 15p pd (max £5 for bks), ch 5p pd (max £1.50); spkn wd/cassettes 15p pd (max £7.20), ch 5p pd (max £1.50), CDs 30p pd (max £12.60); music audios/cassettes 10p pd (max £4.80), CDs 15p pd (max £9); videos/full length 40p pd (max £12), short 20p pd (max £6.60); DVDs/40p pd (max £12); CD-ROMs/50p pd (max £12) *Equip:* m-readers, m-printers, 40 fax (£2 1st pg, £1 addl), copiers (A4/10p, A3/20p), clr copiers (A4/50p), 402 computers (incl wd-proc, internet & CD-ROM), rooms for hire (various) *Disabled:* Kurzweil, CCTV, text enlargers, video decoders, hearing loops, large screen, braille translator & printer, other specialised computer hardware & software *Online:* Infotrac, various resources on CD-ROM

Stock:	1 Apr 2000	1 Apr 2001
ad lend:	466824	451645
ad ref:	121544	119240
ch:	222442	213809
audios:	42546	41051
videos:	19006	18304
CD-ROMs:	354	332

Issues:	1999-2000	2000-01
ad lend:	3008948	2851483
ch:	1270599	1211893
audios:	286544	267079
videos:	154189	164301
CD-ROMs:	998	1892

Acqs:	1999-2000	2000-01
bks:	70988	84787
AVs:	13313	13521

Acqs: Source: lib suppl *Offcr-in-Charge:* County Stock Mgr: Miss N. Fairweather
Classn: DDC *Cat: Type:* author, classified & title *Medium:* auto *Auto Sys:* Dynix *Svcs: Extramural:* prisons, old people's homes, housebnd *Info:* business, community, careers, edu, legal, govt, council *Other:* LearnDirect Centres at 8 libs, Postal Tape Svcs (POTS) for people with visual handicaps *Activs:* ch's activs, bk sales, films, temp exhibs, poetry readings, reading groups
Enqs: 389463 (1999-2000); 349292 (2000-01)
Staff: 222 FTE in total

Inc from:	1999-2000	2000-01
local govt:	£5083714	£5246901
fines etc:	£1123090	£1134526
total:	£6678141	£6869114

Exp on:	1999-2000	2000-01
stock:	£1065750	£1071098
salaries:	£3576941	£3772651
total:	£6678141	£6869114

Cardiff

P24 Cardiff County Library Services

Cardiff Central Lib, St David's Link, Frederick Street, Cardiff, CF10 2DU (029-2038-2116; *fax:* 029-2087-1599)
Email: rboddy@cardiff.gov.uk
Internet: http://www.cardiff.gov.uk/libraries/

Local Auth: City & County of Cardiff Council
Pop: 320900 *Larger Dept:* Leisure & Lifelong Learning *Dept Chief:* Head of Svc: Mr Trevor Gough CertEd, DipMS *Chief:* Operational Mgr, Learning, Info & Community Arts: Ms Jenny Rickard *Dep:* Ms Elspeth Morris
Main Libs: CENTRAL LIB, addr as above
Branch Libs: CANTON LIB, Lib St, Canton, Cardiff, CF5 1QD (029-2022-9935); CATHAYS LIB, Fairoak Rd, Cardiff, CF24 4PW (029-2038-2172); ELY LIB, Grand Ave, Cardiff, CF5 4BL (029-2056-2064); FAIRWATER LIB, Doyle Ave, Cardiff, CF5 3HU (029-2056-4019); GRANGE-TOWN LIB, Redlaver St, Cardiff, CF11 7LY (029-2023-0526); LLANDAFF NORTH LIB, Gabalfa Ave, Cardiff, CF14 2HU (029-2061-3182); LLANEDEYRN LIB, 74 The Maelfa, Cardiff, CF23 9PL (029-2073-1428); LLANRUMNEY LIB, Countisbury Ave, Cardiff, CF3 5NQ (029-2077-7351); PENYLAN LIB, Penylan Rd, Cardiff, CF23 5HW (029-2048-4897); RADYR LIB, Park Rd, Cardiff, CF15 8DF (029-2084-2234); RHIWBINA LIB, Pen-y-Dre, Cardiff, CF14 6EH (029-2069-3276); RHYDYPENNAU LIB, Llandennis Rd, Cardiff, CR23 6EG (029-2075-4657); ROATH LIB, Newport Rd, Roath, Cardiff, CF24 0DF (029-2049-4538); RUMNEY LIB, Brachdy Rd, Cardiff, CF3 3BG (029-2079-5834); SPLOTT LIB, Star Centre, Splott Rd, Cardiff, CF2 2BZ (029-2046-2522); TROWBRIDGE & ST MELLONS LIB, 30 Crickhowell Rd, Cardiff, CF3 0EF (029-2077-9194); WHITCHURCH LIB, Park Rd, Cardiff, CF14 7XA (029-2062-8951)
Svc Pts: PT: 2 *Mobile:* 2 *Other:* SCHOOL LIB SVC, at Central Lib
Collns: Welsh lit; Welsh Bibles; Welsh early printed bks (all in Central Lib); Welsh hist & historical MSS *ILLs:* county, natl & internatl *Loans:* bks & audios/3 wks; videos & DVDs/1-2 wks, blockbusters overnight only; CD-ROMs & Playstation games/1 wk *Charges:* audios/90p; videos & DVDs/£1-£2, blockbusters £1.75; CD-ROMs/£2; Playstation games/£3.50; sub £18 pa non-resident membership *Income Gen:* req & res/80p; lost ticket/ad £1.75, ch 50p *Fines:* bks/ad & oap 10p pd, ch exempt; audios/20p pd; videos, DVDs & CD-ROMs/40p pd; Playstation games/60p pd; various groups exempt from fines *Equip:* 8 m-readers, 2 m-printers (printout 50p), fax (UK £1 per pg), 8 copiers (10p), clr copier (A4/£1, A3/£1.50), 112 computers (all with wd-proc & internet, 18 with CD-ROM), 4 rooms for hire (various) *Disabled:* CCTV

Stock:	1 Apr 2000	1 Apr 2001
lend:	549777	497085
ref:	24496	26043
AVs:	49044	41089
periodcls:	485	485

Issues:	1999-2000	2000-01
bks:	2067669	1971403
AVs:	149767	185015

Acqs:	1999-2000	2000-01
bks:	35494	57553
AVs:	6997	8551

Acqs: Source: lib suppl *Offcr-in-Charge:* Bibliographical Svcs Offcr: Ms Sian Best *Classn:* DDC, UDC *Cat: Type:* author, classified, subj & title *Medium:* auto *Auto Sys:* Sirsi Unicorn *Svcs: Extramural:* prisons, housebnd, old people's homes *Info:* business, community *Activs:* ch's activs, bk sales *Enqs:* 221936 (1999-2000); 190112 (2000-01) *Staff:* Libns: 32 *Non-Prof:* 101.3

Inc from:	1999-2000
local govt:	£3544356
fines etc:	£250911
total:	£3816596

Exp on:	1999-2000
bks:	£362195
AVs:	£43260
salaries:	£2298552
total:	£3816596

Carmarthenshire

P25 Carmarthenshire Library Service

Cultural Svcs, Parc Myrddin, Richmond Ter, Carmarthen, Carmarthenshire, SA31 1DS (01267-228205; *fax:* 01267-238584)
Email: DGriffiths@sirgar.gov.uk
Internet: http://www.carmarthenshire.gov.uk/

Local Auth: Carmarthenshire County Council *Pop:* 169100 *Cttee:* Cabinet *Larger Dept:* Edu & Community Svcs *Chief:* Cultural Svcs Mgr: Mr D.F. Griffiths FCLIP
Main Libs: AMMANFORD LIB, 3 Wind St, Ammanford, Carmarthenshire, SA18 3DN (01269-598150; *fax:* 01269-598151; *email:* WTPhillips@sirgar.gov.uk); CARMARTHEN LIB, St Peter's St, Carmarthen, SA31 1LN (01267-224830; *fax:* 01267-221839; *email:* DPThomas@sirgar.gov.uk); LLANELLI LIB, Vaughan St, Llanelli, Carmarthenshire, SA15 3AS (01554-773538; *fax:* 01554-750125; *email:* RichDavies@sirgar.gov.uk)
Branch Libs: BURRY PORT LIB, Brynmor House, Carway St, Burry Port, Carmarthenshire, SA16 0AE (01554-834478); LLANDEILO LIB, Crescent Rd, Llandeilo, Carmarthenshire, SA19 6HN (*tel & fax:* 01558-823659); LLWYNHENDY LIB, Heol Elfed, Llwynhendy, Llanelli, Carmarthenshire, SA14 9EA (01554-778402); PENDINE LIB, Museum of Speed, Old Caravan Pk, Pendine, Carmarthenshire, SA33 4NY (01994-453488)
Svc Pts: PT: 27 *Mobile:* 5
ILLs: natl *Loans:* bks & audios/4 wks; videos/1 wk; pictures/3 months *Charges:* audios/65p; videos/£1.50; CD-ROMs/£1
Income Gen: res/85p, ch exempt; lost ticket/£2.50 *Fines:* bks/ad 50p pw, ch 20p, oap exempt
Equip: 6 m-readers, m-printer (10p), fax (UK £1 per pg, higher overseas), copiers (A4/15p, A3/20p), computers (incl wd-procs & internet)
Disabled: VISTEL, Robotron, CCTV, sound enhancers, print magnifying sheets, pg turners

Stock:	1 Apr 2000	1 Apr 2001
ad lend:	482700	487204
ad ref:	85835	70316
ch:	133683	113358
audios:	32212	32953
videos:	4976	4975
CD-ROMs:	237	663
periodcls:	115	100

Issues:	1999-2000	2000-01
ad lend:	1412580	1460893
ch:	184172	133610
audios:	37476	37274
videos:	2625	4068
CD-ROMs:	145	472

Acqs:	1999-2000	2000-01
bks:	49366	33987
AVs:	2287	2328

Acqs: Source: lib suppl
Classn: UDC *Cat: Type:* author, classified, subj *Medium:* auto *Auto Sys:* Genesis *Svcs: Extramural:* schools, hosps, old people's homes, housebnd *Info:* business, community *Activs:* ch's activs, bk sales, temp exhibs, poetry readings
Enqs: 147521 (1999-2000); 150658 (2000-01)
Staff: Libns: 33.5 *Non-Prof:* 68.5

Inc from:	1999-2000
local govt:	£1848034
fines etc:	£85632
total:	£1933666

Exp on:	1999-2000
stock:	£494877
salaries:	£841629
total:	£1933666

Ceredigion

P26 Ceredigion Libraries

Ceredigion County Lib, Corp Street, Aberystwyth, Ceredigion, SY23 2BU (01970-633703/16; *fax:* 01970-625059)
Email: llyfrgell.library@ceredigion.gov.uk
Internet: http://www.ceredigion.gov.uk/libraries/

Local Auth: Ceredigion County Council *Pop:* 75384 *Cttee:* Lang & Culture *Larger Dept:* Edu *Dept Chief:* Dir of Edu: Mr Roger J. Williams MA *Chief:* Asst Dir, Edu & Community Svcs: Mr D. Geraint Lewis MA, MCLIP *Dep:* County Libs Offcr: Mr William H. Howells BA, MLib, MCLIP (williamh@ceredigion.gov.uk)
Main Libs: CEREDIGION COUNTY LIB, addr as above *Branch Libs:* ABERAERON LIB, County Hall, Stryd y Farchnad, Aberaeron, Ceredigion, SA46 0AT (01545-570382; *email:* aeronllb@ceredigion.gov.uk); CARDIGAN LIB, Canolfan Teifi, Pendre, Cardigan, Ceredigion, SA43 1JL (01239-612578; *fax:* 01239-612285; *email:* teifillb@ceredigion.gov.uk); LAMPETER LIB, Market St, Lampeter, Ceredigion, SA48 7DR (01570-423606; *email:* pedrllb@ceredigion.gov.uk); LLANDYSUL LIB, Canolfan Ceredigion, Llandysul, Ceredigion (01559-362899; *email:* tysulllb@ceredigion.gov.uk); TREGARON LIB, Secondary School, Tregaron, Ceredigion, SY25 6HG (*tel & fax:* 01974-298673; *email:* caronllb@ceredigion.gov.uk)
Svc Pts: PT: 1 *Mobile:* 6 *AV:* 6 *Computers:* 6 *Internet:* 6
Co-op Schemes: Interlending Wales *ILLs:* county, natl & internatl *Loans:* bks/3 wks; audios/2 wks; videos/1 wk *Charges:* audios/50p; videos/£1.50 pw *Income Gen:* req & res/50p; lost tickets/£1 *Fines:* bks/ad & oap 5p pd (max £3), ch 1p pd (max £1); audios/ad 5p pd, ch 1p pd; videos/5p pd; registered blind exempt
Equip: copiers (A4/10p, A3/20p), fax (£1-£5), 78 computers (incl wd-proc, internet & CD-ROM), 2 rooms for hire (£10 per half day)

Stock:	1 Apr 2000	1 Apr 2001
ad lend:	127929	128014
ad ref:	12830	12592
ch:	47592	50136
audios:	3633	3253
videos:	2689	2726
periodcls:	75	75

Issues:	1999-2000	2000-01
ad lend:	540336	531702
ch:	105837	95396
audios:	10140	10850
videos:	14772	14084

Acqs:	1999-2000	2000-01
bks:	17528	18500
AVs:	1083	1246

Acqs: Source: lib suppl, publ & bksellers *Offcr-in-Charge:* County Libs Offcr, as above
Classn: DDC *Cat: Type:* author, classified, subj & title *Medium:* auto *Auto Sys:* Geac

Svcs: Extramural: schools, hosps, old people's homes, housebnd *Info:* community *Other:* Open Learning *Activs:* bk sales, temp exhibs *Offcr-in-Charge:* Asst Libn (Reader Promotion & Ch's Svcs): N.P. Davies (nestpd@cerdigion.gov.uk)
Enqs: 81428 (1999-2000); 84224 (2000-01)
Staff: Libns: 11 *Non-Prof:* 19

Inc from:	1999-2000	2000-01
local govt:	£901353	£832179
fines etc:	£34401	£35983

Exp on:	1999-2000	2000-01
bks:	£114794	£127520
AVs:	£11601	£10399
culture:	£2500	£3000
salaries:	£468893	£478837
total:	£597787	£619756

Cheshire

P27 Cheshire Libraries, Information and Culture

Room 286, County Hall, Chester, Cheshire, CH1 1SF (01244-606034; *fax:* 01244-602767)
Internet: http://www.cheshire.gov.uk/library/

Local Auth: Cheshire County Council *Pop:* 674200 *Cttee:* Edu & Community Advisory Cttee *Larger Dept:* Edu & Community *Dept Chief:* Dir: Mr David Cracknell *Chief:* County Libn: Mr Ian Dunn (dunni@cheshire.gov.uk) *Dep:* Mgr Public Libs Operations: Mr Allan Bell (bellaw@cheshire.gov.uk) *Other Snr Staff:* Resources & Development Mgr: Mr Hedley Skinner (skinnerh@cheshire.gov.uk)
Main Libs: CHESTER LIB, Northgate St, Chester, CH1 2EF (01244-312935; *fax:* 01244-315534; *email:* chester.infopoint@cheshire.gov.uk); CONGLETON LIB, Market Sq, Congleton, Cheshire, CW12 1BU (01260-271141; *fax:* 01260-298774; *email:* congleton.infopoint@cheshire.gov.uk); CREWE LIB, Prince Albert St, Crewe, Cheshire, CW1 2DH (01270-211123; *fax:* 01270-256952; *email:* crewe.infopoint@cheshire.gov.uk); ELLESMERE PORT LIB, Civic Way, Ellesmere Port, Cheshire, CH65 0BG (0151-357-4684/85; *fax:* 0151-357-4683; *email:* eport.infopoint@cheshire.gov.uk); MACCLESFIELD LIB, 2 Jordangate, Macclesfield, Cheshire, SK10 1EE (01625-422512; *fax:* 01625-612818; *email:* macclesfield.infopoint@cheshire.gov.uk); NANTWICH LIB, Beam St, Nantwich, Cheshire, CW5 5LY (01270-624867; *fax:* 01270-610271; *email:* nantwich.infopoint@cheshire.gov.uk); NORTHWICH LIB, Wilton St, Northwich, Cheshire, CW9 5DR (01606-44221; *fax:* 01606-48396; *email:* northwich.infopoint@cheshire.gov.uk); WILMSLOW LIB, South Dr, Wilmslow, Cheshire, SK9 1NW (01625-528977; *fax:* 01625-548401; *email:* wilmslow.infopoint@cheshire.gov.uk) *Branch Libs:* ALDERLEY EDGE LIB, Heyes Ln, Alderley Edge, Cheshire, SK9 7JT (*tel & fax:* 01625-584487; *email:* alderleyedge.library@cheshire.gov.uk); ALSAGER LIB, Sandbach Rd North, Sandbach, Cheshire, ST7 2QH (01270-873552; *fax:* 01270-883093; *email:* alsager.infopoint@cheshire.gov.uk); BARNTON LIB, Townfield Ln, Barnton, Northwich, Cheshire, CW8 4LJ (*tel & fax:* 01606-77343; *email:* barnton.library@cheshire.gov.uk); BLACON LIB, Western Ave, Blacon, Chester, CH1 5QY (*tel & fax:* 01244-390628; *email:* blacon.library@cheshire.gov.uk); BOLLINGTON LIB, Palmerston St, Bollington, Macclesfield, Cheshire, SK10 5JX (*tel & fax:* 01625-573058; *email:* bollington.library@cheshire.gov.uk); DISLEY LIB, off Buxton Old Rd, Disley, Macclesfield, Cheshire, SK12 2BB (*tel & fax:* 01663-765635; *email:* disley.library@cheshire.gov.uk); FRODSHAM LIB, Rock Chapel, High St, Frodsham, Cheshire, WA6 7AN (01928-732775; *fax:* 01928-734214; *email:* frodsham.library@cheshire.gov.uk); ☛

Cheshire
▼
Coventry

Public Libraries

(Cheshire Libs, Info & Culture cont)
GT BOUGHTON LIB, Green Ln, Vicars Cross, Chester, CH3 5LB (*tel & fax:* 01244-320709; *email:* greatboughton.library@ cheshire.gov.uk); HANDFORTH LIB, The Green, Wilmslow Rd, Handforth, Cheshire, SK9 3ES (01625-528062; *fax:* 01625-524390; *email:* handforth.library@ cheshire.gov.uk); HELSBY LIB, Lower Robin Hood Ln, Helsby, Cheshire, WA5 0BW (01928-724659; *fax:* 01928-726947; *email:* helsby.library@ cheshire.gov.uk); HOLMES CHAPEL LIB, London Rd, Holmes Chapel, Crewe, Cheshire, CW4 7AP (01477-535126; *fax:* 01477-544193; *email:* holmeschapel.library@cheshire.gov.uk); HOOLE LIB, 91 Hoole Rd, Hoole, Chester, CH2 3NG (*tel & fax:* 01244-347401; *email:* hoole.library@ cheshire.gov.uk); HOPE FARM LIB, Bridge Meadow, Gt Sutton, Ellesmere Port, Cheshire, CH66 2LE (*tel & fax:* 0151-355-8923; *email:* hopefarm.library@cheshire.gov.uk); KNUTS-FORD LIB, Toft Rd, Knutsford, Cheshire, WA16 0PG (01565-632909; *fax:* 01565-653076; *email:* knutsford.infopoint@cheshire.gov.uk); LACHE LIB, Lache Pk Ave, Chester, CH4 8HR (*tel & fax:* 01244-683385; *email:* lache.library@cheshire. gov.uk); LITTLE SUTTON LIB, Chester Rd, Little Sutton, Cheshire, CH66 1QQ (*tel & fax:* 0151-339-3373; *email:* littlesutton.library@cheshire.gov.uk); MIDDLEWICH LIB, Lewin St, Middlewich, Cheshire, CW10 9AS (01606-832801; *fax:* 01606-833336; *email:* middlewich.library@cheshire. gov.uk); NESTON LIB, Parkgate Rd, Neston, Cheshire, CH64 6QE (0151-336-5486; *fax:* 0151-353-0973; *email:* neston.infopoint@cheshire. gov.uk); POYNTON LIB, Park Ln, Poynton, Stockport, Cheshire, SK12 1RB (01625-876257; *fax:* 01625-858027; *email:* pointon.infopoint@ cheshire.gov.uk); SANDBACH LIB, The Common, Sandbach, Cheshire, CW11 1FJ (01270-762309; *fax:* 01270-759656; *email:* sandbach.library@ cheshire.gov.uk); SANDIWAY LIB, Mere Ln, Cuddington, Northwich, Cheshire, CW8 2NS (01606-732558; *fax:* 01606-883743; *email:* sandiway.library@cheshire.gov.uk); UPTON LIB, Wealstone Ln, Upton by Chester, Cheshire, CH2 1HB (01244-380053; *fax:* 01244-377197; *email:* upton.library@cheshire.gov.uk); WEAVERHAM LIB, Russett Rd, Weaverham, Northwich, Cheshire, CW8 3HY (*tel & fax:* 01606-853359; *email:* weaverham.library@cheshire.gov.uk); WINSFORD LIB, High St, Winsford, Cheshire, CW7 2AS (01625-415037; *fax:* 01625-548401; *email:* winsford.infopoint@cheshire.gov.uk)
Svc Pts: PT: 12 *Mobile:* 6 *AV:* 38 *Computers:* 39 *Internet:* 39
Collns: Militaria Colln (at Chester Lib); Business Info & Rsrch Svc (at Ellesmere Port Lib); Special Needs Colln (at Libs HQ) *Co-op Schemes:* Libs North West, LADSIRLAC *ILLs:* county, natl & internatl *Loans:* bks/3 wks; audios, videos, DVDs & CD-ROMs/1 wk *Charges:* talking bks/ £1.10; videos & DVDs/£1.10-£2.20; CD-ROMs/ £2.20 *Income Gen:* req/75p; British Lib £1.60; lost ticket/£1.50 *Fines:* bks/ad & oap 11p pd (max £4.40), ch 5p pd (max £2.20); audios, videos, DVDs & CD-ROMs/ad & oap 22p pd (max £4.40), ch 11p pd (max £2.20); visually impaired exempt *Equip:* 37 fax (£1 per pg), 38 copiers (A4/10p, A3/20p), clr copier (A4/£1, A3/£1.50), 225 computers (all with wd-proc, internet & CD-ROM), 12 rooms for hire (various) *Disabled:* video magnifiers, ZoomText, JAWS, Smartreader/ Kurzweil, video caption readers, induction loops

Stock:	1 Apr 2000	1 Apr 2001
lend:	916626	872776
ad ref:	80195	73891
AVs:	49699	53548
Issues:	**1999-2000**	**2000-01**
bks:	6625900	6262311
AVs:	326511	392592
Acqs:	**1999-2000**	**2000-01**
bks:	161280	167195

Acqs: Source: lib suppl *Offcr-in-Charge:* Acqs Mgr: Mr Roy Walker (walkerrm@cheshire.gov.uk)
Classn: DDC *Cat: Type:* author, classified, subj & title *Medium:* auto *Auto Sys:* DS Galaxy
Svcs: Extramural: schools, prisons, hosps, old people's homes, housebnd *Info:* local govt, business, community *Other:* Open Learning
Activs: ch's activs, exhibs, reading groups, bk sales
Staff: Libns: 80.4 *Non-Prof:* 165

Inc from:	1999-2000
local govt:	£187618
fines etc:	£881392
total:	£1176586

Exp on:	1999-2000
bks:	£1394674
AVs:	£169346
elec media:	£65048
salaries:	£4476689
total:	£8979121

Clackmannanshire

P28 Clackmannanshire Libraries
Alloa Lib, 26-28 Drysdale Street, Alloa, Clackmannanshire, FK10 1JL (01259-722262; *fax:* 01259-219469)
Email: libraries@clacks.gov.uk
Internet: http://www.clacksweb.org.uk/

Local Auth: Clackmannanshire Council *Pop:* 48500 *Cttee:* Learning & Leisure *Larger Dept:* Svcs for People *Dept Chief:* Mr David Jones *Chief:* Snr Libn: vacant *Dep:* Team Leader, Community Svcs: Mr John Blake MA, DipLib, MCLIP *Other Snr Staff:* Team Leader: Mrs Anne Fulton
Main Libs: ALLOA LIB, addr as above *Branch Libs:* ALVA COMMUNITY ACCESS PT, 153 West Stirling St, Alva, Clackmannanshire, FK12 2EL (01259-760652; *fax:* 01259-760364); CLACKMANNAN COMMUNITY ACCESS PT, Main St, Clackmannan, Clackmannanshire, FK10 4JA (01259-721579; *fax:* 01259-212493); DOLLAR COMMUNITY ACCESS PT, Dollar Civic Centre, Pk Pl, Dollar, Clackmannanshire, FK14 7AA (01259-743253; *fax:* 01259-743328); MENSTRIE COMMUNITY ACCESS PT, Dumyat Leisure Centre, Main St East, Menstrie, Clackmannan-shire, FK11 7BJ (01259-769439; *fax:* 01259-762941); SAUCHIE COMMUNITY ACCESS PT, 42-48 Main St, Sauchie, Alloa, Clackmannanshire, FK10 3JY (01259-721679; *fax:* 01259-218750); TILLICOULTRY BRANCH LIB, 99 High St, Tillicoultry, Clackmannanshire, FK13 6DL (01259-751685); TULLIBODY BRANCH LIB, Leisure Centre, Abercromby Pl, Tullibody, Alloa, Clackmannanshire, FK10 2RS (01259-218725)
Svc Pts: Mobile: 1 *Computers:* 8 *Internet:* 8
Collns: Walter Murray Local Studies Colln (at Alloa Lib) *ILLs:* county, natl & internatl *Loans:* bks & audios/4 wks; Open Learning/8 wks
Income Gen: req & res/40p; lost ticket/£2
Fines: bks/10p 1st wk overdue (rising to max of 70p for 8th wk), ch 10p 4th wk overdue (rising to max of 50p for 8th wk); software/as bks *Equip:* 4 m-readers, m-printer (A4/20p), fax, copier (10p), clr copier, video viewer, computers (incl wd-proc, internet & CD-ROM) *Offcr-in-Charge:* Team Leader, Community Svc, as above

Stock:	1 Apr 2000	1 Apr 2001
ad lend:	156610	155947
ad ref:	5219	5571
ch:	85964	90857
audios:	13775	9786
periodcls:	73	66
Issues:	**1999-2000**	**2000-01**
ad lend:	303032	278993
ch:	87470	66857
audios:	15190	-
Acqs:	**1999-2000**	**2000-01**
bks:	15219	22468

Acqs: Source: lib suppl *Offcr-in-Charge:* Team Leader, Community Svcs, as above
Classn: DDC *Cat: Type:* author, classified, subj & title *Medium:* cards & auto *Auto Sys:* Citrix
Svcs: Extramural: schools, prisons, housebnd *Info:* ref, local studies, archvs *Other:* Open Learning *Activs:* ch's activs, bk sales, author visits
Staff: Libns: 6 *Non-Prof:* 21

Inc from:	2000-01
local govt:	£927711
fines etc:	£95351
total:	£1023062

Exp on:	2000-01
stock:	£169217
salaries:	£413802
total:	£1023062

Conwy

P29 Conwy Library, Information and Archive Service
Administrative HQ, Conwy County Borough Council, Bodlondeb, Conwy, LL32 8DU (01492-576140; *fax:* 01492-592061)
Email: llyfr.lib.pencadlys.hq@conwy.gov.uk
Internet: http://www.conwy.gov.uk/

Local Auth: Conwy County Borough Council *Pop:* 112700 *Cttee:* Cabinet, via Memb with portfolio for Leisure & Cultural Development (plus advisory Policy Panel on the same portfolio) *Larger Dept: Dept Chief:* County Sec: Mr Ronald Evans LLB *Chief:* County Libn & Archivist: Ms Rona Aldrich MLib, MCLIP (rona.aldrich@conwy. gov.uk)
Dep: Principal Libn: Ms Rhian Williams BA, DipLib, MCLIP (rhian.williams@conwy. gov.uk)
Other Snr Staff: Corporate Info Libn: Mr David Smith (david.smith@conwy.gov.uk); Snr Community Libn: Mr Malcolm Thomas (malcolm. thomas@conwy.gov.uk); Community Libn (Svcs to Ch & Yng People): Ms Tanis Jones (tanis. jones@conwy.gov.uk)
Branch Libs: ABERGELE LIB, Market St, Abergele, Conwy, LL22 7BP (01745-832638; *fax:* 01745-823376; *email:* llyfr.lib.abergele@conwy. gov.uk); COLWYN BAY LIB, Woodland Rd West, Colwyn Bay, Conwy, LL29 7DH (01492-532358; *fax:* 01492-534474; *email:* llyfr.lib.baecolwynbay@ conwy.gov.uk); CONWY LIB, Civic Hall, Castle St, Conwy, LL32 6AY (01492-596242; *fax:* 01492-582359; *email:* llyfr.lib.conwy@conwy.gov.uk); LLANDUDNO LIB, Mostyn St, Llandudno, Conwy, LL30 2RP (01492-574010/20; *fax:* 01492-876826; *email:* llyfr.lib.llandudno@conwy.gov.uk); LLANRWST LIB, Plas-yn-Dre, Station Rd, Llanrwst, Conwy, LL26 0DF (01492-640043; *fax:* 01492-642316; *email:* llyfr.lib.llanrwst@conwy. gov.uk); PENRHYN BAY LIB, Llandudno Rd, Penrhyn Bay, Conwy, LL30 3HN (01492-548873; *email:* llyfr.lib.baepenrhynbay@conwy.gov.uk)
Svc Pts: PT: 7 *Mobile:* 1 *AV:* 12 *Computers:* 6 *Internet:* 6
Co-op Schemes: TALNET, Interlending Wales *ILLs:* county & natl *Loans:* bks, audios & videos/3 wks; study extended loan available

Charges: audios/50p, set 75p, registered blind & partially sighted exempt; videos/£1; Open Learning packs/free *Income Gen:* req/80p + 50p outside TALNET, under 16s exempt; lost tickets/ad £2, ch 50p *Fines:* bks, audios & videos/ad 10p 1st day, 20p 2nd day, 30p 3rd day, 50p 4th-7th days, 60p pw thereafter (max £6), ch exempt *Equip:* m-readers, m-printers (30p per copy), fax (UK £1.50 1st pg, 50p addl, overseas £2), copiers (A4/10p, A3/15p), computers (incl internet & CD-ROM), rooms for hire (various) *Disabled:* minicom at Colwyn Bay Lib

Stock:	1 Apr 2000	1 Apr 2001
lend:	170529	175155
ref:	38251	24344
AVs:	10527	11206
periodcls:	28	28
Issues:	1999-2000	2000-01
bks:	738521	707012
AVs:	46367	49824
Acqs:	1999-2000	2000-01
bks:	9571	11408
AVs:	961	1136

Acqs: Source: lib suppl *Co-op:* TALNET *Offcr-in-Charge:* Principal Libn, as above
Classn: DDC *Cat: Type:* author, classified & keyword *Medium:* auto *Auto Sys:* Talis *Svcs: Extramural:* schools, hosps, old people's homes, housebnd, playgroups & nurseries *Info:* community, council, European Public Info Centre (at Colwyn Bay Lib), careers, travel, health, business, current affairs *Other:* Open Learning, archv access pts *Activs:* ch's activs, bk sales, temp exhibs, art & craft workshops
Enqs: 157924 (1999-2000); 124340 (2000-01)
Staff: Libns: 10 *Other Prof:* 1.8 *Non-Prof:* 28.2

Inc from:	1999-2000	2000-01
local govt:	£1147552	£1160897
fines etc:	£76340	£80581
total:	£1223892	£1241478
Exp on:	1999-2000	2000-01
stock:	£104141	£107178
salaries:	£704773	£700431
total:	£1223892	£1241478

Cornwall

P30 Cornwall Library Service
Unit 17, Threemilestone Industrial Est, Truro, Cornwall, TR4 9LD (01872-324316; *fax:* 01872-223509)
Email: library@cornwall.gov.uk
Internet: http://www.cornwall.gov.uk/library/

Local Auth: Cornwall County Council *Pop:* 500000 *Cttee:* Lifelong Learning Portfolio *Larger Dept:* Edu, Arts & Libs *Dept Chief: Dir:* Mr Geoff Aver *Chief: Asst Dir (Arts & Libs):* Mr Chris Ramsey *Other Snr Staff:* Area Mgr (East): Mr Philip Kerridge (based at Bodmin Lib); Area Mgr (West): Miss Pam Martindale (based at Redruth Lib); Head of New Initiatives: Mr John Stephens (based at HQ)
Branch Libs: BODMIN LIB, Lower Bore St, Bodmin, Cornwall, PL31 2JX (01208-72286; *email:* bodmin.library@cornwall.gov.uk); BUDE LIB, The Wharf, Bude, Cornwall, EX23 8LG (01288-352527; *email:* bude.library@cornwall.gov.uk); CALLINGTON LIB, Launceston Rd, Callington, Cornwall, PL17 7DR (01579-383236; *email:* callington.library@cornwall.gov.uk); CAMBORNE LIB, The Cross, Camborne, Cornwall, TR14 8HA (01209-713544; *email:* camborne.library@cornwall.gov.uk); CAMELFORD LIB, Town Hall, Market Pl, Camelford, Cornwall, PL32 9PD (01840-212409; *email:* camelford.library@cornwall.gov.uk); FALMOUTH LIB, Municipal Offices, The Moor, Falmouth, Cornwall, TR11 3QA (01326-314901; *email:* falmouth.library@cornwall.gov.uk); FOWEY LIB, Caffa Mill House, 2 Passage Ln, Fowey,

Cornwall, PL23 1JS (01726-832332; *email:* fowey.library@cornwall.gov.uk); HAYLE LIB, Commercial Rd, Hayle, Cornwall, TR27 4DH (01736-753196; *email:* hayle.library@cornwall.gov.uk); HELSTON LIB, Trengrouse Way, Helston, Cornwall, TR13 8AG (01326-572321; *email:* helston.library@cornwall.gov.uk); LAUNCESTON LIB, Bounsalls Ln, Launceston, Cornwall, PL15 9AB (01566-773306; *email:* launceston.library@cornwall.gov.uk); LISKEARD LIB, Barras St, Liskeard, Cornwall, PL14 6AB (01579-343285; *email:* liskeard.library@cornwall.gov.uk); LOOE LIB, Sea Front Ct, East Looe, Cornwall, PL13 1AL (01503-262365; *email:* looe.library@cornwall.gov.uk); LOSTWITHIEL LIB, Taprell House, North St, Lostwithiel, Cornwall, PL22 0BL (01208-872747; *email:* lostwithiel.library@cornwall.gov.uk); NEWQUAY LIB, Marcus Hill, Newquay, Cornwall, TR7 1BD (01637-873538; *email:* newquay.library@cornwall.gov.uk); PADSTOW LIB, The Institute, Padstow, Cornwall, PL28 8AL (01841-532387; *email:* padstow.library@cornwall.gov.uk); PAR LIB, Hamley's Corner, Eastcliff Rd, Par, Cornwall, PL24 2AH (01726-814853; *email:* par.library@cornwall.gov.uk); PENRYN LIB, St Thomas St, Penryn, Cornwall, TR10 8JN (01326-372203; *email:* penryn.library@cornwall.gov.uk); PENZANCE LIB, Morrab Rd, Penzance, Cornwall, TR18 4EY (01736-363954; *email:* penzance.library@cornwall.gov.uk); PERRANPORTH LIB, Oddfellows Hall, Ponsmere Rd, Perranporth, Cornwall, TR6 0BW (01872-572590; *email:* perranporth.library@cornwall.gov.uk); REDRUTH LIB, 2-4 Clinton Rd, Redruth, Cornwall, TR15 2QE (01209-219111; *email:* redruth.library@cornwall.gov.uk); SALTASH LIB, Callington Rd, Saltash, Cornwall, PL12 6DX (01752-842478; *email:* saltash.library@cornwall.gov.uk); ST AGNES LIB, The Car Pk, St Agnes, Cornwall, TR5 0TP (01872-553245; *email:* stagnes.library@cornwall.gov.uk); ST AUSTELL LIB, 2 Carlyon Rd, St Austell, Cornwall, PL25 4LD (01726-73348; *email:* staustell.library@cornwall.gov.uk); ST COLUMB LIB, The Town Hall, Market Pl, St Columb, Cornwall, TR9 6AN (01637-881480; *email:* stcolumb.library@cornwall.gov.uk); ST IVES LIB, Gabriel St, St Ives, Cornwall, TR26 2LX (01736-795377; *email:* stives.library@cornwall.gov.uk); ST JUST LIB, Market St, St Just, Cornwall, TR19 7HX (01736-788669; *email:* stjust.library@cornwall.gov.uk); TORPOINT LIB, Fore St, Torpoint, Cornwall, PL11 2AG (01752-812207; *email:* torpoint.library@cornwall.gov.uk); TRURO LIB, Union Pl, Pydar St, Truro, Cornwall, TR1 1EP (01872-279205; *email:* truro.library@cornwall.gov.uk); WADEBRIDGE LIB, Southern Way, Wadebridge, Cornwall, PL27 7BX (01208-812202; *email:* wadebridge.library@cornwall.gov.uk)
Svc Pts: PT: 1 *Mobile:* 6 *AV:* 29 *Other:* CORNISH STUDIES LIB, The Cornwall Centre, Alma Pl, Redruth, Cornwall, TR15 2AT (see **A430**); PERFORMING ARTS LIB, at St Austell Lib (01726-61702; *email:* performingarts.library@cornwall.gov.uk); REF & INFO LIB, at Truro Lib (01872-272702; *email:* reference.library@cornwall.gov.uk); EDU LIB SVC, at Lib HQ (01872-323456; *email:* els@cornwall.gov.uk)
Collns: Maritime Colln (at Falmouth Lib): boat-building, seamanship, shipwrecks, Lloyd's List (1914-date), voyages, naval hist, charts & almanacs, outboard manuals, fishing; Art Bks Colln (at St Ives & Penzance Libs): Cornish arts, 20C European art, art hist, world art, sculpture, pottery arch (at Penzance Lib), photography, fashion, design (at St Ives Lib); Cornish Newspapers (various titles, 1801-date, mostly on m-film, some paper copies in store for some titles, held at Cornish Studies Lib & various branches); music scores, playscripts, playsets & ref materials on music & drama (at Performing Arts Lib) *Co-op Schemes:* SWRLS, EARL *ILLs:* county, natl & internatl *Loans:* bks & audios/3 wks; videos, DVDs & CD-ROMs/1 wk; music sets/1 month; Linguaphone/2 months

Charges: audios/ad £1.10, ch 50p; videos/50p-£3; DVDs/£3; CD-ROMs/£2; music sets/£2.50-£5 *Income Gen:* res/ad 70p (50p if placed online), free to ch, housebnd & for large print, addl £2 for out of County (students £1), £10+ for internatl; lost tickets/ad £1.50, ch 50p *Fines:* bks/ad & oap 12p pd (max £6), ch 5p pd (max £2.50); audios, videos, DVDs & CD-ROMs/loan charge; under-5s, housebnd & mobile lib users exempt *Equip:* 79 m-readers, 4 m-printers (65p per pg), 4 video viewers, 32 fax (£1-£3 per pg), 31 copiers (A4/10p, A3/20p), clr copier (A4/£1, A3/£1.50), 199 computers (all with wd-proc, internet & CD-ROM, 1st half hr free, then £2 per hr, £3 for non-membs), 2 rooms for hire (£20-£25 pd) *Disabled:* software, RNID videos phones *Online:* Eurolaw

Stock:	1 Apr 2000	1 Apr 2001
ad lend:	548186	495812
ad ref:	95154	74643
ch:	145428	174813
audios:	32256	32782
videos:	11925	11433
CD-ROMs:	290	386
periodcls:	122	399
Issues:	1999-2000	2000-01
bks:	4832036	4479585
audios:	173721	180871
videos:	71016	62826
CD-ROMs:	209	1650
Acqs:	1999-2000	2000-01
bks:	75934	53140
AVs:	9155	8215

Acqs: Source: lib suppl, publ & bksellers *Co-op:* CUSP
Classn: DDC, McColvin (for music) *Cat: Type:* author & classified *Medium:* auto *Auto Sys:* Talis, Heritage (Edu Lib Svc) *Svcs: Extramural:* schools, hosps, old people's homes, housebnd, day centres, play groups *Info:* Business Info Unit (at Ref & Info Lib), CWIC (Countywide Info Cornwall – community info svc) *Other:* Link Into Learning, Surestart, BookStart *Activs:* ch's activs, bk sales, temp exhibs, poetry readings, reading groups, writers' groups, talks, author visits *Offcr-in-Charge:* Outreach Svcs Team
Enqs: 398181 (1999-2000); 409964 (2000-01)
Staff: Libns: 25.5 *Non-Prof:* 153.8

Coventry

P31 Coventry Libraries and Information Services
Central Lib, Smithford Way, Coventry, W Midlands, CV1 1FY (024-7683-2321; *fax:* 024-7683-2315)
Email: library.office@coventry.gov.uk
Internet: http://www.coventry.gov.uk/

Local Auth: Coventry Metropolitan Dist Council *Pop:* 303900 *Cttee:* Cabinet Memb (Edu & Lib Svcs) *Larger Dept:* Edu & Lib Svcs *Dept Chief:* Strategic Dir (Lifelong Learning): Ms Cathryn Goodwin MA *Chief: City Libn:* Mr Andrew Green BA, MA, MCLIP (andrew.green@coventry.gov.uk) *Other Snr Staff:* Strategic Mgr (Policy, Planning & Marketing): Mr Bob Parsons BA, DipLib, MA, MCLIP (bob.parsons@coventry.gov.uk); Strategic Mgr (Svc Delivery): Mr Simon Rice MBA, MCLIP (simon.rice@coventry.gov.uk); Strategic Mgr (Learning Partnerships): Mr Colin Scott BA, DipLib, MCLIP (colin.scott@coventry.gov.uk); Mgr (Admin & Support Svcs): Mr Bob Sidney BA, MA (bob.sidney@coventry.gov.uk)
Main Libs: CENTRAL LIB, addr as above (024-7683-2314; *fax:* 024-7683-2440; *email:* central.library@coventry.gov.uk) *Branch Libs:* BELL GREEN LIB, Roseberry Ave, Bell Green, Coventry, W Midlands, CV2 1NB (024-7668-8986; *fax:* 024-7666-3468); CANLEY LIB, Prior Deram Walk, Canley, Coventry, W Midlands, CV4 8FT (024-7667-3041; *fax:* 024-7671-7361); ☞

(Coventry Libs & Info Svcs cont)
COUNDON LIB, Moseley Ave, Radford, Coventry, W Midlands, CV6 1HT (024-7659-3496; *fax:* 024-7659-8768); EARLSDON LIB, Earlsdon Ave North, Earlsdon, Coventry, W Midlands, CV5 6FZ (024-7667-5359; *fax:* 024-7671-7958); FINHAM LIB, Droylsdon Pk Rd, Finham, Coventry, W Midlands, CV3 6EQ (024-7641-4050; *fax:* 024-7641-9524); FOLESHILL LIB, Broad St, Foleshill, Coventry, W Midlands, CV6 5BG (024-7668-7562; *fax:* 024-7666-4281; *email:* info.follib@ covnet.co.uk); HOLBROOK LIB, Briscoe Rd, Holbrook, Coventry, W Midlands, CV6 4JP (024-7668-7561; *fax:* 024-7666-3082); JUBILEE CRES LIB, Jubilee Cres, Radford, Coventry, W Midlands, CV6 3EX (024-7659-6762; *fax:* 024-7659-5728); STOKE LIB, Kingsway, Stoke, Coventry, W Midlands, CV2 4EA (024-7645-2059; *fax:* 024-7645-2567); TILE HILL LIB, Jardine Cres, Tile Hill, Coventry, W Midlands, CV4 9PL (024-7646-4994; *fax:* 024-7669-5774); WILLENHALL LIB, 192 Remem-brance Rd, Willenhall, Coventry, W Midlands, CV3 3DN (024-7630-2383; *fax:* 024-7630-2151)
Svc Pts: PT: 1 *Mobile:* 1 *AV:* 14 *Computers:* 13 *Internet:* 13
Colls: George Eliot Colln; Angela Brazil Colln; local studies (Coventry & Warwickshire); JFR: Mea-Mer; Tom Mann Colln; automobiles/bicycles colln; SEALS Foreign Fiction; Chinese/Vietnamese colln; Indic langs colln *Co-op Schemes:* TLP-WM, JFR, CILLA
ILLs: county, natl & internatl *Loans:* bks & talking bks/4 wks; audios, videos, DVDs & CD-ROMs/1 wk *Charges:* audios/55p, talking bks £1; videos & DVDs/£2.50; CD-ROMs/£2 *Income Gen:* req & res/60p; lost ticket/£1.50 *Fines:* bks/ad 14p pd, oap 7p pd, ch exempt; audios/14p pd, talking bks 26p pd; videos & DVDs/50p pd; CD-ROMs/40p pd; fines halved & no charge for talking bks for ch, oaps & Passport to Leisure holders *Equip:* 16 m-readers (free except 65p per half hr for St Catherine's Index), 2 m-printers (A4/20p, A3/40p), 13 fax (UK £1 1st pg, 50p per addl, overseas £1.50 1st pg, 75p per addl), 15 copiers (A4/10p, A3/20p), clr copier (A4/£1, A3/£1.50), 102 computers (all with wd-proc, internet & CD-ROM, access free), room for hire (£8 per hr)
Disabled: Kurzweil, talking teletext, minicom, Zoom software *Online:* Dialog, Dialtech, PFDS (biblio searches free, company searches at cost, in-house company database £20) *Offcr-in-Charge:* Mgr (Admin & Support Svcs), as above

Stock:	1 Apr 2000	1 Apr 2001
ad lend:	281077	260573
ad ref:	18423	16329
ch:	115065	96389
schools:	106875	53526
instns:	6007	5839
audios:	40277	33962
videos:	523	525
CD-ROMs:	523	495
periodcls:	260	260

Issues:	1999-2000	2000-01
ad lend:	1392186	1309266
ch:	417124	374369
audios:	133207	142908
videos:	2013	1344
CD-ROMs:	1836	5243

Acqs:	1999-2000	2000-01
bks:	39538	50469
AVs:	5509	5850

Acqs: Source: llb suppl, publ & bksellers *Co-op:* CBC *Offcr-in-Charge:* Bibliographical Svcs Libn: Ms Mandy Hayward (mandy.hayward@coventry. gov.uk)
Classn: DDC *Cat: Type:* author, classified, subj & title *Medium:* auto *Auto Sys:* Talis *Svcs: Extramural:* schools, hosps, old people's homes, housebnd, day centres, play groups *Info:* community (PeopleLink), business, careers *Other:* LearnDirect, Open Learning, RNIB talking bk svc *Activs:* ch's activs, bk sales, temp exhibs, poetry readings, reading groups, writers' groups, talks, author visits, Multicultural Festival *Offcr-in-Charge:* Strategic Mgr (Policy, Planning & Marketing), as above
Enqs: 301392 (1999-2000); 284483 (2000-01)
Staff: Libns: 31.9 *Non-Prof:* 112.6

Inc from:	1999-2000	2000-01
local govt:	£3281305	£3264304
fines etc:	£220631	£232254
total:	£3584197	£3607931

Exp on:	1999-2000	2000-01
bks:	£371366	£381356
AVs:	£69897	£79365
elec media:	£18842	£12390
culture:	£19278	£13920
salaries:	£2420867	£2536801
total:	£3584197	£3607931

Proj: Stoke Lib refurbishment (2001-02); People's Network implementation (2002-03)

Cumbria

P32 Cumbria Library Service

Lib Svc HQ, Arroyo Block, The Castle, Carlisle, Cumbria, CA3 8UR (01228-607295; *fax:* 01228-607299)
Internet: http://www.cumbria.gov.uk/libraries/

Local Auth: Cumbria County Council *Pop:* 487607 *Larger Dept:* Community, Economy & Environment *Dept Chief:* Dir: Mr R.P. Howard
Chief: Lib Svcs Mgr: Mr Alan Welton (alan.welton@cumbriacc.gov.uk) *Other Snr Staff:* Principal Administrative Offcr: Mr Paul Graham (paul.graham@cumbriacc.gov.uk); Libs Info & Monitoring Offcr: Ms Hazel Waiting (hazel.waiting@cumbriacc.gov.uk)
Main Libs: Barrow Group HQ: BARROW-IN-FURNESS LIB, Ramsden Sq, Barrow-in-Furness, Cumbria, LA13 1LL (01229-894370; *fax:* 01229-894371; *email:* barrow.library@cumbriacc.gov.uk); *Carlisle Group HQ:* CARLISLE LIB, 11 Globe Ln, Carlisle, Cumbria, CA3 8NX (01228-607310; *fax:* 01228-607333; *email:* carlisle.library@cumbriacc. gov.uk); *Kendal Group HQ:* KENDAL LIB, Stricklandgate, Kendal, Cumbria, LA9 4PY (01539-773520; *fax:* 01539-773544; *email:* kendal.library@cumbriacc.gov.uk); *Penrith Group HQ:* PENRITH LIB, St Andrews Churchyard, Penrith, Cumbria, CA11 7YA (01768-242100; *fax:* 01768-242101; *email:* penrith.library@cumbriacc. gov.uk); *Whitehaven Group HQ:* THE DANIEL HAY LIB, Lowther St, Whitehaven, Cumbria, CA28 7QZ (01946-852900; *fax:* 01946-852911; *email:* whitehaven.library@cumbriacc.gov.uk); *Workington Group HQ:* WORKINGTON LIB, Vulcans Ln, Workington, Cumbria, CA14 2ND (01900-325170; *fax:* 01900-325181; *email:* workington.library@cumbriacc.gov.uk) *Branch Libs:* Barrow Group: DALTON-IN-FURNESS LIB, Nelson St, Dalton-in-Furness, Cumbria, LA15 8AF (*tel & fax:* 01229-897921; *email:* daltoninfurness. library@cumbriacc.gov.uk); ROOSE LIB, Roose Rd, Barrow-in-Furness, Cumbria, LA13 9RJ (01229-894384; *fax:* 01229-894385; *email:* roose.library@cumbriacc.gov.uk); WALNEY LIB, Central Dr, Walney Island, Barrow-in-Furness, Cumbria, LA14 3HY (*tel & fax:* 01229-471742; *email:* walney.library@cumbriacc.gov.uk); *Carlisle Group:* HARRABY LIB, Edgehill Rd, Carlisle,

Cumbria, CA1 3SL (01228-607341; *email:* harraby.library@cumbriacc.gov.uk); *Kendal Group:* AMBLESIDE LIB, Kelsick Rd, Ambleside, Cumbria, LA22 0BZ (015394-32507; *fax:* 015394-31484; *email:* ambleside.library@cumbriacc. gov.uk); GRANGE OVER SANDS LIB, Grange Fell Rd, Grange over Sands, Cumbria, LA11 6BQ (015395-32749; *fax:* 015395-32409; *email:* grangeoversands.library@cumbriacc.gov.uk); ULVERSTON LIB, Kings Rd, Ulverston, Cumbria, LA12 0BT (01229-894151; *fax:* 01229-894152; *email:* ulverston.library@cumbriacc.gov.uk); WINDERMERE LIB, Ellerthwaite, Windermere, Cumbria, LA23 2AJ (01539-462400; *fax:* 01539-462401; *email:* windermere.library@cumbriacc. gov.uk); *Penrith Group:* APPLEBY LIB, Low Wiend, Appleby-in-Westmorland, Cumbria, CA16 6QP (*tel & fax:* 017683-51170; *email:* appleby. library@cumbriacc.gov.uk); KIRKBY STEPHEN LIB, 15 Market St, Kirkby Stephen, Cumbria, CA17 4QS (*tel & fax:* 017683-71775; *email:* kirkbystephen.library@cumbriacc.gov.uk); *Whitehaven Group:* CHARLES EDMONDS LIB, Wyndham School, Egremont, Cumbria, CA22 2DH (*tel & fax:* 01946-820464; *email:* egremont. library@cumbriacc.gov.uk); CLEATOR MOOR LIB, Market Sq, Cleator Moor, Cumbria, CA25 5AP (*tel & fax:* 01946-855030; *email:* cleatormoor. library@cumbriacc.gov.uk); FRIZINGTON LIB, Community Centre, Main St, Frizington, Cumbria, CA26 2DH (01946-810775; *fax:* 01946-814288; *email:* frizington.library@cumbriacc.gov.uk); MILLOM LIB, St George's Rd, Millom, Cumbria, LA18 4DD (*tel & fax:* 01229-772445; *email:* millom.library@cumbriacc.gov.uk); SEASCALE LIB, Gosforth Rd, Seascale, Cumbria, CA20 1PN (*tel & fax:* 019467-28487; *email:* seascale.library@ cumbriacc.gov.uk); *Workington Group:* ASPATRIA LIB, The Brandraw, Aspatria, Carlisle, Cumbria, CA5 3EZ (*tel & fax:* 016973-20515; *email:* aspatria.library@cumbriacc.gov.uk); COCKERMOUTH LIB, Main St, Cockermouth, Cumbria, CA13 9LU (01900-325990; *fax:* 01900-325991; *email:* cockermouth.library@cumbriacc. gov.uk); KESWICK LIB, Heads Ln, Keswick, Cumbria, CA12 5HD (017687-72656; *fax:* 017687-75323; *email:* keswick.library@cumbriacc.gov.uk); MARYPORT LIB, Lawson St, Maryport, Cumbria, CA15 6ND (01900-812384; *fax:* 01900-816803; *email:* maryport.library@cumbriacc.gov.uk); MOORCLOSE LIB, Needham Dr, Moorclose, Workington, Cumbria, CA14 3SE (01900-325190; *fax:* 01900-325191; *email:* moorclose.library@ cumbriacc.gov.uk); SILLOTH LIB, Silloth Community School, Liddell St, Silloth, Carlisle, Cumbria, CA5 4DD (016973-32195; *fax:* 016973-32613; *email:* silloth.library@cumbriacc.gov.uk); WIGTON LIB, High St, Wigton, Cumbria, CA7 9NJ (016973-66150; *fax:* 016973-66151; *email:* wigton.library@ cumbriacc.gov.uk)
Svc Pts: PT: 25 *Mobile:* 7 *Other:* LIB SVC FOR SCHOOLS, Botchergate, Carlisle, Cumbria, CA1 1RZ (01228-607276; *fax:* 01228-607275; *email:* lss@cumbriacc.gov.uk); HM PRISON LIB, Haverigg, Millom, Cumbria, LA18 4NE (01229-772131 x323; *fax:* 01229-770011)
Colls: JFR: E-F *Co-op Schemes:* NEMLAC
ILLs: county, natl & internatl *Loans:* bks & talking bks/3 wks; audios, videos, DVDs, CD-ROMs & Playstation games/1 wk *Charges:* audios/cassettes 50p, CDs 75p; videos & CD-ROMs/£1; DVDs & Playstation games/£1.50 *Income Gen:* req & res/60p, non-Cumbria stock £2.50; lost ticket/£1.50 *Fines:* bks/ad 8p pd, oap & ch exempt; talking bks/4p pd; audios/cassettes 9p pd, CDs 13p pd; videos & CD-ROMs/17p pd; DVDs/25p pd; Playstation games/35p pd *Equip:* 9 m-readers/printers (50p per pg), 42 fax (UK 50p per pg, higher overseas), 45 copiers (A4/10p, A3/20p), 5 clr copiers (A4/£1, A3/£1.50), computers (incl internet & CD-ROM, 50p per 15 min, £1 per half hr), rooms for hire *Disabled:* Kurzweil, Eazee reader

Stock:	1 Apr 2002
ad lend:	694575
ad ref:	31141
ch:	191015
audios:	46330
videos:	43059
CD-ROMs:	1970

Issues:	2001-02
ad lend:	2411660
ch:	607355
audios:	202259
videos:	364627
CD-ROMs:	7921

Acqs:	2001-02
bks:	85467
AVs:	21330

Acqs: Source: lib suppl & bksellers *Offcr-in-Charge:* Lib Svcs Mgr: Mr Alan Welton
Classn: DDC *Cat: Type:* author, classified, subj & title *Medium:* auto *Auto Sys:* Geac *Svcs: Extramural:* schools, prisons, hosps, old people's homes, housebnd *Info:* Cumbria local info pts (CLIPS), local govt, local socs database *Other:* Open Learning *Activs:* ch's activs, bk sales, temp exhibs *Offcr-in-Charge:* Lib Mgr: Mr Alan Welton
Staff: Libns: 44 *Other Prof:* 5 *Non-Prof:* 145

Inc from:	1999-2000	2000-01
local govt:	£4788000	£4910000
fines etc:	£701000	£728000
total:	£5925000	£6399000

Exp on:	1999-2000	2000-01
bks:	£799000	£826000
AVs:	£149000	£156000
salaries:	£3032000	£3147000
total:	£5925000	£6399000

Darlington

P33 Darlington Library Service

Crown Street Lib, Crown Street, Darlington, Co Durham, DL1 1ND (01325-462034; *fax:* 01325-381556)
Email: crown.street.library@darlington.gov.uk
Internet: http://www.darlington.gov.uk/Education/Library/Library.htm

Local Auth: Darlington Borough Council *Pop:* 100600 *Cttee:* Leisure Svcs Cttee *Larger Dept:* Edu *Dept Chief:* Mr Geoff Pennington *Chief:* Acting Libs Mgr: Mrs Lynne Litchfield *Main Libs:* CROWN ST LIB, addr as above (lend: 01325-349600; ref: 01325-349620) *Branch Libs:* COCKERTON LIB, Cockerton Green, Darlington, Co Durham, DL3 9AA (01325-461320; *email:* cockerton.library@darlington.gov.uk)
Svc Pts: Mobile: 1 *Other:* DARLINGTON CENTRE FOR LOCAL STUDIES, at Crown St Lib (see **A119**)
Co-op Schemes: JFR *ILLs:* county, natl & internatl *Loans:* bks/3 wks; audios/1 wk *Charges:* audios/65p *Income Gen:* res/60p (£2 for some ILL); lost tickets/£1 *Fines:* bks/10p pd, ch & oaps 5p pd; audios/10p pd; videos/varies *Equip:* m-reader; m-printer; fax, copiers (A4/10p, A3/20p), computers (incl internet & CD-ROM) *Disabled:* Visualtek reader for partially sighted

Stock:	1 Apr 2000	1 Apr 2001
lend:	77443	73943
ref:	112545	115804
AVs:	9997	8151
periodcls:	66	37

Issues:	1999-2000	2000-01
bks:	697737	685039
AVs:	41992	42579

Acqs:	1999-2000	2000-01
bks:	19044	17636
AVs:	1145	1441

Acqs: Source: lib suppl & bksellers
Classn: DDC *Cat: Type:* author, classified, subj & title *Medium:* auto *Auto Sys:* DS *Svcs: Extramural:* old people's homes, housebnd *Info:* business, community *Activs:* ch's activs, bk sales, temp exhibs, poetry readings
Enqs: 119253 (1999-2000); 145132 (2000-01)
Staff: Libns: 10 *Non-Prof:* 28.3

Inc from:	1999-2000	2000-01
local govt:	£989453	£967117
fines etc:	£86531	£89635
total:	£1075984	£1056752

Exp on:	1999-2000	2000-01
stock:	£193463	£157037
salaries:	£646215	£655208
total:	£1075984	£1056752

Denbighshire

P34 Denbighshire Library and Information Services

Yr Hen Garchar, Clwyd Street, Ruthin, Denbighshire, LL15 1HP (01824-708204; *fax:* 01824-708202)
Email: dcclib&infoservice@denbighshire.gov.uk
Internet: http://www.denbighshire.gov.uk/

Local Auth: Denbighshire County Council *Pop:* 91800 *Larger Dept:* Culture & Leisure *Chief:* Principal Libn: Mr R. Arwyn Jones DipLib, MCLIP *Branch Libs:* DENBIGH LIB, Hall Sq, Denbigh, LL16 3NU (01745-816313; *fax:* 01745-816427); LLANGOLLEN LIB, The Chapel, 19-21 Castle St, Llangollen, Denbighshire, LL20 8NY (01978-869600); PRESTATYN LIB, Nant Hall Rd, Prestatyn, Denbighshire, LL19 9LH (01745-854841; *fax:* 01745-855208); RHUDDLAN LIB, Vicarage Ln, Rhuddlan, Rhyl, Denbighshire, LL18 2UE (01745-590719); RHYL LIB, Church St, Rhyl, Denbighshire, LL18 3AA (01745-353814; *fax:* 01745-331438); RUTHIN LIB, Record St, Ruthin, Denbighshire, LL15 1DS (01824-705274; *fax:* 01824-702580); ST ASAPH LIB, The Roe, St Asaph, Denbighshire, LL17 0LU (01745-582253; *fax:* 01824-708402)
Svc Pts: PT: 1 *Mobile:* 2, incl 1 for housebnd *AV:* 7 *Computers:* 8 *Internet:* 8
Collns: Music Scores (vocal sets & orchestral parts, at Ruthin Lib) *ILLs:* county & natl *Loans:* bks, audios & videos/2 wks *Charges:* CDs/75p; videos/£1 *Income Gen:* req/free within Denbighshire & Flintshire, £2 outside; lost ticket/ad £1.50, 2ndary school ch 75p, primary school ch free *Fines:* all items/10p pd for 1st wk, then £1 for 1st wk + 50p per addl wk (max £3); ch exempt *Equip:* m-readers, copiers (A4/10p, A3/15p), clr copier (A4/£1, A3/£1.50), fax (50p per pg to send in UK, £1 overseas, 5p per pg to receive), computers (incl wd-proc, internet & CD-ROM), rooms for hire (various)

Stock:	1 Apr 2000	1 Apr 2001
ad lend:	89166	89183
ad ref:	14170	15144
ch:	41812	44838
audios:	4032	4009
videos:	790	1019
periodcls:	46	46

Issues:	1999-2000	2000-01
ad lend:	570364	508882
ch:	128038	133630
audios:	* 6512	19166
videos:	2954	3062

* music only; talking bks incl in ad lend

Acqs:	1999-2000	2000-01
bks:	10524	10342
AVs:	963	203

Acqs: Source: lib suppl & bksellers *Offcr-in-Charge:* Stock Mgmt Team

---

Classn: DDC *Cat: Type:* author, classified, subj & title *Medium:* auto *Auto Sys:* DS Galaxy *Svcs: Extramural:* old people's homes, housebnd *Info:* business, ch's, community, council *Other:* Open Learning, music scores, Welsh Lit *Activs:* ch's activs, bk sales, temp exhibs, reading groups, writers' groups, author visits, visual arts programme *Offcr-in-Charge:* various
Enqs: 104447 (1999-2000); 94757 (2000-01)
Staff: Libns: 15 *Non-Prof:* 30

Inc from:	1999-2000	
local govt:	£1340311	
fines etc:	£62062	
total:	£1402373	

Exp on:	1999-2000	
bks:	£118391	
salaries:	£813722	
total:	£1402373	

Derby

P35 Derby City Libraries

Lib HQ, 5th Floor, Celtic House, Heritage Gate, Friary Street, Derby, DE1 1QX (01332-716607; *fax:* 01322-715549)
Email: libraries@derby.gov.uk
Internet: http://www.visitderby.com/libraries/

Local Auth: Derby City Council *Pop:* 236300 *Larger Dept:* Development & Cultural Svcs *Dept Chief:* Dir: Mr Jonathan Guest BA, DipTP, MRTPI *Chief:* City Libn: Mr David Potton MA, DipLib, MCLIP (david.potton@derby.gov.uk) *Other Snr Staff:* Asst City Libn (Central Libs): Mr Bernard Haigh
Main Libs: DERBY CENTRAL LIB, The Wardwick, Derby, DE1 1HS (01332-255398/9; *fax:* 01322-369570; *email:* central.library@derby.gov.uk) *Branch Libs:* ALLESTREE LIB, Park Farm Centre, Birchover Way, Allestree, Derby, DE22 2QN (01332-559761; *email:* allestree.library@derby.gov.uk); ALVASTON LIB, Boulton Ln, Alvaston, Derby, DE24 0FD (01332-571971; *email:* alvaston.library@derby.gov.uk); BLAGREAVES LIB, Blagreaves Ln, Littleover, Derby, DE23 7PT (01332-255403; *fax:* 01332-255404; *email:* blagreaves.library@derby.gov.uk); CHADDESDEN LIB, Chaddesden Pk, Derby, DE21 6LN (01332-672352; *email:* chaddesden.library@derby.gov.uk); MICKLEOVER LIB, Station Rd, Mickleover, Derby, DE3 5GJ (01332-513076: *email:* mickleover.library@derby.gov.uk); PEARTREE LIB, Peartree Rd, Derby, DE23 8NQ (01332-344059; *email:* peartree.library@derby.gov.uk); SINFIN LIB, Dist Centre, Arleston Ln, Sinfin, Derby, DE24 3DS (01332-773773; *email:* sinfin.library@derby.gov.uk); SPONDON LIB, Sitwell St, Spondon, Derby, DE2 7FG (01332-662708; *email:* spondon.library@derby.gov.uk)
Svc Pts: Mobile: 1 (based at Blagreaves Lib) *AV:* 9 *Computers:* 9 *Internet:* 9 *Other:* HOME LIB SVC, at Blagreaves Lib (01332-255409; *email:* special.services@derby.gov.uk); LOCAL STUDIES LIB (see **A122**)
Collns: Joint Provincial Fiction Reserve (at Blagreaves Lib); Derby Local Studies Colln (at Local Studies Lib) *Co-op Schemes:* EMRLS *ILLs:* internatl *Loans:* bks & spkn wd/4 wks; audios/1 wk; DVDs/3 days *Charges:* spkn wd/70p, conc 35p, free to visually impaired; audios/£1, conc 50p; DVDs/£2, conc £1.50 *Income Gen:* req/80p; lost ticket/£1.20 *Fines:* bks & audios/ad & oap 15p pd, 12-18 years 2p pd, ch under 12 exempt *Equip:* m-readers, m-printers (printout 45p), fax (£1 per pg), copiers (A4/10p), computers (incl wd-proc, internet & CD-ROM), 3 rooms for hire (various) *Disabled:* induction loops, minicom, reading machine, large screen PC

☛

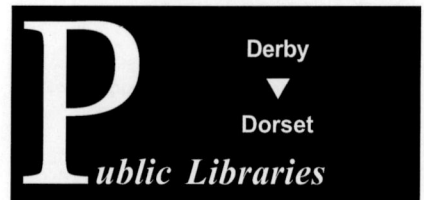

Public Libraries

Derby
▼
Dorset

(Derby City Libs cont)

Stock:	1 Apr 2000	1 Apr 2001
lend:	220556	213114
ref:	58863	71627
AVs:	-	15178

Issues:	1999-2000	2000-01
bks:	1372872	1264938
AVs:	74203	67015

Acqs:	1999-2000	2000-01
bks:	23491	39502
AVs:	-	2974

Acqs: Source: lib suppl *Co-op:* joint arrangement with Derbyshire County Council (see **P36**) *Classn:* DDC *Cat: Type:* classified *Medium:* m-form & auto *Auto Sys:* ALS *Svcs: Extramural:* schools, hosps, old people's homes, housebnd *Info:* business, community, tourist, careers *Other:* Lifelong Learning, Homework Centre, BookStart *Activs:* ch's activs, bk sales, temp exhibs, author visits, reading groups *Offcr-in-Charge:* Snr Libn (Access & Promotions): Miss Maureen King *Enqs:* 138531 (1999-2000); 130633 (2000-01) *Staff:* 95.6 FTE total

Inc from:	1999-2000	2000-01
fines etc:	£406608	£410217

Exp on:	1999-2000	2000-01
bks:	£274224	£528603
AVs:	£48698	£64037
salaries:	£1553148	£1614376

Derbyshire

P36 Derbyshire Libraries and Heritage

County Hall, Matlock, Derbyshire, DE4 3AG (01629-580000; *fax:* 01629-585363) *Email:* derbyshire.libraries@derbyshire.gov.uk *Internet:* http://www.derbyshire.gov.uk/

Local Auth: Derbyshire County Council *Pop:* 741500 *Cttee:* Cabinet memb for Community Svcs *Chief:* Dir of Libs & Heritage: Mr Martin Molloy BA, DipLib, MCLIP *Dep:* Dep Dir of Libs & Heritage: Ms Jaci Brumwell *Other Snr Staff:* Asst Dirs of Libs & Heritage: Mr Robert Gent & Mr George Jennings *Main Libs:* ALFRETON LIB, Severn Sq, Alfreton, Derby, DE55 7BQ (01773-833199; *fax:* 01773-521020); BOLSOVER LIB, Church St, Bolsover, Chesterfield, Derbyshire, S44 6HB (01246-823179; *fax:* 01246-827237); BUXTON LIB, Kents Bank School, Kents Bank Rd, Buxton, Derbyshire, SK17 9HW, (01298-25331; *fax:* 01298-73744); CHESTERFIELD LIB, New Beetwell St, Chesterfield, Derbyshire, S40 1QN (01246-209292; *fax:* 01246-209304); DRONFIELD LIB, Manor House, Dronfield, Sheffield, S Yorkshire, S18 6PY (01246-414001; *fax:* 01246-291489); ILKESTON LIB, Market Pl, Ilkeston, Derbyshire, DE7 5RN (0115-930-1104; *fax:* 0115-944-1226); MATLOCK LIB, Steep Turnpike, Matlock, Derbyshire, DE4 3DP (01629-582480; *fax:* 01629-760749); SWADLIN-COTE LIB, Civic Way, Swadlincote, Burton-on-Trent, Staffordshire, DE11 0AD (01283-217701; *fax:* 01283-216352)

Branch Libs: ASHBOURNE LIB, Cockayne Ave, Ashbourne, Derbyshire, DE6 1EJ (*tel & fax:* 01335-342702); BAKEWELL LIB, Orme Ct, Granby Rd, Bakewell, Derbyshire, DE45 1ES (01629-812267; *fax:* 01629-815337); BELPER LIB, Bridge St, Belper, Derby, DE56 1BA (01773-824333; *fax:* 01773-822172); BORROWASH LIB, Victoria Ave, Borrowash, Derby, DE72 3HE (*tel & fax:* 01332-663440); BRIMINGTON LIB, Church St, Brimington, Chesterfield, Derbyshire, S43 1JG (*tel & fax:* 01246-271547); CHAPEL-EN-LE-FRITH LIB, Town Hall, Chapel-en-le-Frith, High Peak, Derbyshire, SK23 0HP (*tel & fax:* 01298-812212); CLAY CROSS LIB, Kenning Pk, Holmgate Rd, Clay Cross, Chesterfield, Derbyshire, S45 9PH (*tel & fax:* 01246-862592); CLOWNE LIB, Rec Cl, Clowne, Chesterfield, Derbyshire, S43 4PL (01246-810675; *fax:* 01246-811131); CRESWELL LIB, Elmton Rd, Creswell, Worksop, Nottinghamshire, S80 4EY (*tel & fax:* 01909-721606); DUFFIELD LIB, Wirksworth Rd, Duffield, Belper, Derbyshire, DE56 4GH (01332-840324); ECKINGTON LIB, Market St, Eckington, Sheffield, S Yorkshire, S21 4JG (01246-433943; *fax:* 01246-431579); GAMESLEY LIB, Gamesley Primary School, Grindleford Grove, Gamesley, Glossop, Derbyshire, SK13 6HW (01457-860041); GLOSSOP LIB, Victoria Hall, Talbot St, Glossop, Derbyshire, SK13 7DQ (01457-852616; *fax:* 01457-856329); HEANOR LIB, Ilkeston Rd, Heanor, Derbyshire, DE75 7DX (01773-712482; *fax:* 01773-535465); KILLAMARSH LIB, Village Centre, Sheffield Rd, Killamarsh, Derbyshire, S21 1DY (*tel & fax:* 0114-248-5616); LONG EATON LIB, Tamworth Rd, Long Eaton, Nottingham, NG10 1JG (0115-973-5426; *fax:* 0115-946-5133); NEW MILLS LIB, Hall St, New Mills, High Peak, Derbyshire, SK22 4AR (*tel & fax:* 01663-743603); NEWBOLD LIB, Windermere Rd, Newbold, Chesterfield, Derbyshire, S41 8DU (*tel & fax:* 01246-277328); RIPLEY LIB, Grosvenor Rd, Ripley, Derbyshire, DE5 3JE (01773-743321; *fax:* 01773-741057); SANDIACRE LIB, Doncaster Ave, Sandiacre, Nottingham, NG10 5FJ (0115-939-6805; *fax:* 0115-949-1132); SHIREBROOK LIB, Main St, Shirebrook, Mansfield, Nottinghamshire, NG20 8AL (01623-742425; *fax:* 01623-744244); STAVELEY LIB, Hall Ln, Staveley, Chesterfield, Derbyshire, S43 3TP (01246-472448; *fax:* 01246-470132); WHALEY BRIDGE LIB, Mechanics Inst, Whaley Bridge, High Peak, Cheshire, SK23 7AA (*tel & fax:* 01663-732480); WIRKSWORTH LIB, Town Hall, Wirksworth, Matlock, Derbyshire, DE4 4EU (*tel & fax:* 01629-823173)

Svc Pts: PT: 13 *Mobile:* 13 *Other:* SCHOOL LIB SVCS (01332-371921); LOCAL STUDIES LIB, at Lib HQ (see **A374**); LOCAL STUDIES LIB, at Chesterfield Central Lib *Collns:* Natl Speleological Lib (incl British Cave Rsrch Assoc Lib); Peak Dist Mines Hist Soc Lib (both at Matlock Lib); George Stephenson Colln; Ashe Colln (both at Chesterfield Lib); Howitt Colln (at Heanor Lib); D.H. Lawrence Collns (at Ilkeston & Heanor Libs) *Co-op Schemes:* SINTO, YADLOGIS, EMRLS, CILLA *ILLs:* county, natl & internatl *Loans:* bks/3 wks; audios/1 wk; videos & DVDs/2 nights or 1 wk *Charges:* CDs/75p (conc 45p), sets £1.50 (conc 90p); cassettes/60p (conc 35p), sets £1.20 (conc 70p); spkn wd/60p (conc 35p, housebnd, under 18s, blind & sight impaired free); videos & DVDs/new films £2.50, older films £1-£2, other free-£1 *Income Gen:* req/80p + £1 for ILLs, over-60s 50p, housebnd, under-18s, blind & sight impaired exempt from bk res charges; lost ticket/£1 *Fines:* bks/ad, oap & 10p pd, 12-18 years olds 5p pd, postage & stationary charged for reminders, under-12s exempt; audios & videos/loan charge *Equip:* m-readers, m-printers, fax, copiers, clr copier, computers (incl wd-proc & internet), rooms for hire (varies) *Disabled:* Kurzweil, CCTV, microwriter, Viewscan, APH, Optacon, TLoop, brailler

Stock:	1 Apr 2000	1 Apr 2001
lend:	759762	757709
ref:	84732	84068
AVs:	-	46366

Issues:	1999-2000	2000-01
bks:	4709779	4712760
AVs:	403489	454237

Acqs:	1999-2000	2000-01
bks:	90339	117022
AVs:	14281	16761

Acqs: Source: lib suppl *Offcr-in-Charge:* Resources Mgr: Mrs Sue Weatherley *Classn:* DDC *Cat: Type:* author, classified, subj & title *Medium:* auto *Auto Sys:* BiblioMondo *Svcs: Extramural:* schools, prisons, hosps, old people's homes, housebnd *Info:* business, community, Marketing Info Centre (at Chesterfield Lib) *Other:* Open Learning, Bks for Babies *Activs:* ch's activs, bk sales, temp exhibs, poetry readings, reading groups, author visits *Staff: Libns:* 74 *Non-Prof:* 212

Inc from:	1999-2000	2000-01
local govt:	£8297000	£8305000
fines etc:	£552000	£590000
total:	£9257000	£9285000

Exp on:	1999-2000	2000-01
stock:	£1247000	£1253000
salaries:	£5079000	£5309000
total:	£9257000	£9285000

Devon

P37 Devon Library and Information Services

Barley House, Isleworth Rd, Exeter, Devon, EX4 1RQ (01392-384300; *fax:* 01392-384316) *Email:* devlibs@devon.gov.uk *Internet:* http://www.devon.gov.uk/library/

Local Auth: Devon County Council *Pop:* 700000 *Cttee:* Community Svcs Scrutiny Cttee & Exec Cttee *Larger Dept:* Edu, Arts, & Libs Directorate *Dept Chief:* Dir of Edu, Arts & Libs: Mr Tony Smith *Chief:* Head of Lib & Info Svcs: Mrs Lynn Osborne BA, MCLIP *Dep:* Quality, Performance & Development Libn: Mr Geraint Hughes BA, MA, DipLib, MCLIP (ghughes@devon.gov.uk) *Main (Group) Libs: N&W Devon Area:* BARNSTAPLE LIB, Tuly St, Barnstaple, Devon, EX31 1EL (*tel & fax:* 01271-388619); *S&E Devon Area:* EXETER CENTRAL LIB, Castle St, Exeter, Devon, EX4 3PQ (01392-384223; *fax:* 01392-384228) *Branch Libs:* ASHBURTON LIB, The Old Town Hall, North St, Ashburton, Newton Abbot, Devon, TQ13 7QG (01364-652896); AXMINSTER LIB, South St, Axminster, Devon, EX13 5AD (01297-32693); BIDEFORD LIB, New Rd, Bideford, Devon, EX39 2HR (*tel & fax:* 01237-476075); BOVEY TRACEY LIB, Abbey Rd, Bovey Tracey, Newton Abbot, Devon, TQ13 9HZ (01626-832026); BRAUNTON LIB, Challoners Rd, Braunton, Devon, EX33 2ES (01271-812808); BUDLEIGH SALTERTON LIB, Station Rd, Budleigh Salterton, Devon, EX9 6RH (01395-443245); CHUDLEIGH LIB, Fore St, Chudleigh, Newton Abbot, Devon, TQ13 0HL (01626-852469); CREDITON LIB, Belle Parade, Crediton, Devon, EX17 2AA (01363-772578); CULLOMPTON LIB, 2 Exeter Hill, Cullompton, Devon, EX15 1DH (01884-33628); DARTMOUTH LIB, 48 Newcomen Rd, Dartmouth, Devon, TQ6 9BJ (01803-832502); DAWLISH LIB, 1 Lawn Ter, Dawlish, Devon, EX7 9PY (01626-862529); EXMOUTH LIB, 40 Exeter Rd, Exmouth, Devon, EX8 1PS (01395-272677; *fax:* 01395-271426); HOLSWORTHY LIB, North Rd, Holsworthy, Devon, EX22 6HA (01409-253514); HONITON LIB, 48 New St, Honiton, Devon, EX14 1BS (01404-42818; *fax:* 01404-45326); ILFRACOMBE LIB, The Candar,

Ilfracombe, Devon, EX34 9DS (01271-862388; *fax:* 01271-866150); IVYBRIDGE LIB, 7a Keaton Rd, Plymouth, Devon, PL21 9DH (01752-893140); KINGSBRIDGE LIB, Ilbert Rd, Kingsbridge, Devon, TQ7 1EB (01548-852315); KINGSKERWELL LIB, 1 Newton Rd, Kingskerwell, Newton Abbot, Devon, TS12 5EH (01803-873723); KINGSTEIGNTON LIB, Newton Rd, Newton Abbot, Devon, TQ12 3AL (01626-367980); NEWTON ABBOT LIB, Market St, Newton Abbot, Devon, TQ12 2RJ (01626-206420; *fax:* 01626-206428); NORTHAM LIB, Fore St, Northam, Bideford, Devon, EX39 1AW (01237-475111); OKEHAMPTON LIB, 4 North St, Okehampton, Devon, EX20 1AR (01837-52805); OTTERY ST MARY LIB, Old Town Hall, Ottery St Mary, Devon, EX11 1DJ (01404-813838); SEATON LIB, 21-23 Queen St, Seaton, Devon, EX12 2NY (01297-21832); SIDMOUTH LIB, Blackmore Dr, Sidmouth, Devon, EX10 8LA (01395-512192); SOUTH MOLTON LIB, 1 East St, South Molton, Devon, EX36 3BU (01769-572128; *fax:* 01769-574233); ST THOMAS LIB, Cowick St, Exeter, Devon, EX4 1AF (01392-252783); TAVISTOCK LIB, The Quay, Plymouth Rd, Tavistock, Devon, PL19 8AB (01822-612218; *fax:* 01822-610690); TEIGNMOUTH LIB, Fore St, Teignmouth, Devon, TQ14 8DY (01626-774646); TIVERTON LIB, Angel Hill, Tiverton, Devon, EX16 6PE (01884-252937); TOPSHAM LIB, Nelson Cl, Topsham, Exeter, Devon, EX3 0DX (01392-874955); TORRINGTON LIB, The Sq, Torrington, Devon, EX38 8HD (01805-622107); TOTNES LIB, 27a High St, Totnes, Devon, TQ9 5NP (01803-862210)
Svc Pts: PT: 21 *Mobile:* 11 *AV:* 24 *Computers:* 56 *Internet:* 56
Collns: JFR; Ta-Ta & W; Westcountry Studies Lib (at Exeter Central Lib – see **A164**); Railway Studies (at Newton Abbot Lib) *Co-op Schemes:* SWRLS Subj Specialisation, JFR *ILLs:* county, natl & internatl *Loans:* bks/3 wks; audios, videos, DVDs & CD-ROMs/1 wk *Charges:* audios/85p, sets of 3+ £1.30, talking bks free for chronically sick or disabled; videos & DVDs/top titles £2.70, genl interest £2.20, special interest £1; CD-ROMs/£2; all charges incl VAT *Income Gen:* res/ad 75p (+£1 from outside Devon), ch's bks free, music & drama 75p; lost ticket/computer ad £1.50, ch 50p, other tickets 25p *Fines:* bks/ad 10p 1st day, 25p 2nd day, then 70p pw (incl initial fines), over 65s, chronically sick & disabled 10p 1st day, 15p 2nd day, then 30p pw (incl initial fine), under-16s 5p 1st day, 10p 2nd day, then 15p pw (incl initial fine); audios, videos & CD-ROMs/loan charge; lang sets/£1 pw (max £6) *Equip:* m-readers, m-printers (A4/30p, A3/40p), fax (UK 75p per pg, higher overseas, 75p to receive), video viewers, copiers (A4/12p, A3/24p), clr copier (A4/£1, A3/£1.50), computers (incl wd-procs, internet & CD-ROM, 1st half hr free, then £1.50 per half hr), rooms for hire (various) *Disabled:* local newspapers on cassette, high intensity reading lamps, induction loops, supercom tel terminal, reminiscence material, reading machines, large print bks, provision for housebnd *Online:* Dialog, Datastar, BLAISE, Dun & Bradstreet, Infocheck, FT Profile, Kompass, Waterlow Signature (all fees cost+10%+VAT)

Stock:	*1 Apr 2000*	*1 Apr 2001*
ad lend:	1024912	984397
ad ref:	109334	115407
ch:	278404	274283
audios:	73058	67728
videos:	12602	14172
periodcls:	340	343
Issues:	*1999-2000*	*2000-01*
ad lend:	4441445	4195289
ch:	1061306	992196
audios:	182167	202842
videos:	69416	75839
Acqs:	*1999-2000*	*2000-01*
bks:	101294	117320
AVs:	11002	10443

Acqs: Source: lib suppl, publ & bksellers *Co-op:* JFR, SWRLS Subj Specialisation *Offcr-in-Charge:* Stock Mgr: Mr John M. Stevens (jxstephe@devon.gov.uk)
Classn: DDC *Cat: Type:* author, classified, subj & title *Medium:* auto *Auto Sys:* DS *Svcs: Extramural:* schools, prisons, hosps, old people's homes, housebnd, day centres *Info:* business & commercial, community, travel, careers *Other:* Open Learning, public access PCs *Activs:* ch's activs, bk sales, temp exhibs, poetry readings, reading groups, talks, author visits
Enqs: 623918 (1999-2000); 608120 (2000-01)
Staff: Libns: 36 *Non-Prof:* 188.5

Doncaster

P38 Doncaster Library and Information Services

Central Lib, Waterdale, Doncaster, S Yorkshire, DN1 3JE (01302-734305; *fax:* 01302-369749)
Email: reference.library@doncaster.gov.uk
Internet: http://www.doncaster.gov.uk/education/libraries.htm

Local Auth: Doncaster Metropolitan Borough Council *Pop:* 290100 *Larger Dept:* Edu & Culture *Dept Chief:* Exec Dir: Mr Mark Eales *Chief:* Head of Lib & Info Svcs: Mrs G. Johnson MA, MCLIP
Main Libs: CENTRAL LIB, addr as above; *Area Lib HQs:* BENTLEY LIB, Cooke St, Bentley, Doncaster, S Yorkshire, DN5 0DP (tel & fax: 01302-873456; *email:* bentley.library@doncaster.gov.uk); MEXBOROUGH Lib, John St, Mexborough, Doncaster, S Yorkshire, S64 9HS (tel & fax: 01709-582037; *email:* mexborough.library@doncaster.gov.uk) *Branch Libs:* ARMTHORPE LIB, Church St, Armthorpe, Doncaster, S Yorkshire, DN3 3AL (tel & fax: 01302-833538; *email:* armthorpe.library@doncaster.gov.uk); ASKERN LIB, Station Rd, Askern, Doncaster, S Yorkshire, DN6 0JA (tel & fax: 01302-700324; *email:* askern.library@doncaster.gov.uk); BALBY LIB, High Rd, Balby, Doncaster, S Yorkshire, DN4 0PL (01302-853656; *email:* balby.library@doncaster.gov.uk); BAWTRY LIB, Doncaster Rd, Bawtry, Doncaster, S Yorkshire, DN10 6NE (01302-710858; *email:* bawtry.library@doncaster.gov.uk); CANTLEY LIB, Goodison Blvd, Cantley, Doncaster, S Yorkshire, DN4 6BT (tel & fax: 01302-535614; *email:* cantley.library@doncaster.gov.uk); CARCROFT LIB, Skellow Rd, Carcroft, Doncaster, S Yorkshire, DN6 8HF (01302-722327; *fax:* 01302-727293; *email:* carcroft.library@doncaster.gov.uk); CONISBROUGH LIB, Old Rd, Conisbrough, Doncaster, S Yorkshire, DN12 3NN (01709-869509; *fax:* 01709-869508); EDLINGTON LIB, 7 The Crescent, Edlington, Doncaster, S Yorkshire, DN12 1AJ (01709-863259; *email:* edlington.library@doncaster.gov.uk); HATFIELD LIB, High St, Hatfield, Doncaster, S Yorkshire, DN7 6RY (01302-842064; *fax:* 01302-350663); INTAKE LIB, Montrose Ave, Intake, Doncaster, S Yorkshire, DN2 6PL (01302-367225; *email:* intake.library@doncaster.gov.uk); ROSSINGTON LIB, McConnell Cres, Rossington, Doncaster, S Yorkshire, DN11 0PL (01302-868295; *email:* rossington.library@doncaster.gov.uk); SCAWTHORPE LIB, Amersall Rd, Scawthorpe, Doncaster, S Yorkshire, DN5 9PQ (01302-781786; *email:* scawthorpe.library@doncaster.gov.uk); SPROTBROUGH LIB, Sprotbrough Rd, Sprotbrough, Doncaster, S Yorkshire, DN5 8BA (01302-782436; *fax:* 01302-783460; *email:* sprotbrough.library@doncaster.gov.uk); STAINFORTH LIB, Church Rd, Stainforth, Doncaster, S Yorkshire, DN7 5PW (01302-841239; *email:* stainforth.library@doncaster.gov.uk); THORNE LIB, Fieldside, Thorne, Doncaster, S Yorkshire, DN8 4BQ (01405-812862; *email:* thorne.library@doncaster.gov.uk);

TICKHILL LIB, Castlegate, Tickhill, Doncaster, S Yorkshire, DN11 9QU (*tel & fax:* 01302-742871; *email:* tickhill.library@doncaster.gov.uk); WHEATLEY LIB, Parkway South, Wheatley, Doncaster, S Yorkshire, DN2 4JS (01302-361288; *email:* wheatley.lib1@doncaster.gov.uk); WOODLANDS LIB, Windmill Balk Ln, Woodlands, Doncaster, S Yorkshire, DN6 7SB (*tel & fax:* 01302-724293; *email:* woodlands.library@doncaster.gov.uk)
Svc Pts: PT: 4 *Mobile:* 2 *AV:* 25 *Computers:* 23 *Internet:* 23 *Other:* BIBLIOGRAPHICAL SVCS, Skellow Rd, Carcroft, Doncaster, S Yorkshire, DN6 8HF (01302-722327; *fax:* 01302-727293); SCHOOL LIB SVC HQ, Top Rd, Barnby Dun, Doncaster, S Yorkshire, DN3 1DB (*tel & fax:* 01302-881787; *email:* Education.YoungPeople@doncaster.gov.uk); ARCHVS SVC (see **A124**); DONCASTER ROYAL INFIRMARY PATIENTS' LIB, Thorne Rd, Doncaster, S Yorkshire, DN2 5LT (01302-366666 x3650; *email:* dri.library@doncaster.gov.uk); LINDHOLME HM PRISON LIB, Bawtry Rd, Hatfield Woodhouse, Doncaster, S Yorkshire, DN7 6EE (01302-846600 x283/272); MOOR-LANDS HM PRISON LIB, Bawtry Rd, Hatfield Woodhouse, Doncaster, S Yorkshire, DN7 6BW (01302-523129/30)
Collns: Horse Racing Colln; Railway Colln (both at Local Studies Lib, Central Lib) *Co-op Schemes:* YLI, SINTO *ILLs:* county, natl & internatl *Loans:* bks & audios/3 wks; videos & DVDs/1 wk *Charges:* cassettes/50p; CDs/90p; videos/£1.30 *Income Gen:* res/45p; lost ticket/1st time 50p, 2nd & subsequent £1 *Fines:* bks/ad & oap 6p pd; audios, videos & DVDs/loan charge; under-16s & print disabled exempt *Equip:* 2 m-readers, m-printer (20p), 12 fax, 18 copiers (A4/10p), clr copier (A4/£1, A3/£1.50), computers (incl wd-procs, internet & CD-ROM) *Disabled:* Kurzweil, CCTV magnifiers

Stock:	*1 Apr 2000*	*1 Apr 2001*
lend:	430681	428405
ref:	76195	75826
AVs:	46690	41790
periodcls:	368	381
Issues:	*1999-2000*	*2000-01*
bks:	1907349	1788807
AVs:	98941	104967
Acqs:	*1999-2000*	*2000-01*
bks:	48320	48371
AVs:	3508	5057

Acqs: Source: lib suppl & publ
Classn: DDC *Cat: Type:* author, classified, subj & title *Medium:* auto *Auto Sys:* Dynix *Svcs: Extramural:* schools, prisons, hosps, housebnd *Info:* business, community (Donfacts), tourist *Other:* 3 LearnDirect Centres *Activs:* ch's activs, bk sales, temp exhibs, poetry readings, readers groups
Enqs: 201136 (1999-2000); 208780 (2000-01)
Staff: Libns: 31.8 *Non-Prof:* 135.02

Inc from:	*1999-2000*	*2000-01*
fines etc:	£215246	£250381

Exp on:	*1999-2000*	*2000-01*
stock:	£713379	£743960
salaries:	£2474992	£2620830
total:	£4515597	£4634245

Dorset

P39 Dorset Libraries and Arts Service

County Lib HQ, Colliton Pk, Dorchester, Dorset, DT1 1XJ (01305-251000; *fax:* 01305-224344)
Email: dorsetlibraries@dorsetcc.gov.uk
Internet: http://www.dorset-cc.gov.uk/

(Dorset Libs & Arts Svc cont)
Local Auth: Dorset County Council *Pop:* 381930 *Cttee:* Corporate Svcs Overview & Policy Development Cttee *Larger Dept:* Corporate Svcs *Dept Chief:* Dir: Mrs Elaine M. Taylor LLB *Chief:* Head of Libs & Arts Svc: Mr Ian Lewis BA, MCLIP
Main Libs: DORCHESTER LIB, Colliton Pk, Dorchester, Dorset, DT1 1XJ (01305-224440/652; *fax:* 01305-225160; *email:* DorchesterLibrary@ dorsetcc.gov.uk); DORCHESTER REF LIB, at Dorchester Lib (01305-224448/501; *fax:* 01305-266120; *email:* DorchesterReferenceLibrary@ dorsetcc.gov.uk); FERNDOWN LIB, Penny's Walk, Ferndown, Dorset, BH22 9TH (01202-874542; *fax:* 01202-896097; *email:* FerndownLibrary@dorsetcc.gov.uk or FerndownReferenceLibrary@dorsetcc.gov.uk); WEYMOUTH LIB, Gt George St, Weymouth, Dorset, DT4 8NN (01305-762410; *fax:* 01305-762412; *email:* WeymouthLibrary@dorsetcc. gov.uk); WEYMOUTH REF LIB, at Weymouth Lib (01305-762418; *fax:* 01305-780316; *email:* WeymouthReferenceLibrary@dorsetcc.gov.uk)
Branch Libs: BLANDFORD LIB, The Tabernacle, Blandford, Dorset, DT11 7DW (01258-452075; *fax:* 01258-459795; *email:* BlandfordLibrary@ dorsetcc.gov.uk); BRIDPORT LIB, South St, Bridport, Dorset, DT6 3NY (01308-422778; *fax:* 01308-421039; *email:* BridportLibrary@dorsetcc. gov.uk); CHRISTCHURCH LIB, Druitt Bldgs, High St, Christchurch, Dorset, BH23 1AW (01202-485938; *fax:* 01202-490204; *email:* ChristchurchLibrary@dorsetcc.gov.uk); COLEHILL LIB, Middlehall Rd, Colehill, Wimborne, Dorset, BH21 2HL (01202-886676; *fax:* 01202-886593; *email:* ColehillLibrary@dorsetcc.gov.uk); CORFE MULLEN LIB, 54 Wareham Rd, Corfe Mullen, Wimborne, Dorset, BH21 3LE (01202-659755; *fax:* 01202-658395; *email:* CorfeMullenLibrary@dorsetcc.gov.uk); GILLINGHAM LIB, Chantry Fields, Gillingham, Dorset, SP8 4UA (01747-822180; *fax:* 01747-826237; *email:* GillinghamLibrary@dorsetcc. gov.uk); HIGHCLIFFE LIB, Gordon Rd, Highcliffe, Christchurch, Dorset, BH23 5HN (01425-272202; *fax:* 01425-279093; *email:* HighcliffeLibrary@dorsetcc.gov.uk); LITTLE-MOOR LIB, Louviers Rd, Weymouth, Dorset, DT3 6SF (01305-812350; *fax:* 01305-815926; *email:* LittlemoorLibrary@dorsetcc.gov.uk); LYME REGIS LIB, Silver St, Lyme Regis, Dorset, DT7 3HR (01297-443151; *fax:* 01297-444268; *email:* LymeRegisLibrary@dorsetcc.gov.uk); LYTCHETT MATRAVERS LIB, High St, Lytchett Matravers, Poole, Dorset, BH16 6BG (01202-621281; *fax:* 01202-620134; *email:* LytchettMatraversLibrary@ dorsetcc.gov.uk); PORTLAND TOPHILL LIB, The Straits, Portland, Dorset, DT5 1HG (01305-820171; *fax:* 01305-824916; *email:* PortlandTophillLibrary@dorsetcc.gov.uk); PORT-LAND UNDERHILL LIB, 28 Fortuneswell, Portland, Dorset, DT5 1LP (01305-820149; *fax:* 01305-824914; *email:* PortlandUnderhillLibrary@ dorsetcc.gov.uk); SHAFTESBURY LIB, Bell St, Shaftesbury, Dorset, SP7 8AE (01747-852256; *fax:* 01747-850154; *email:* ShaftesburyLibrary@ dorsetcc.gov.uk); SHERBORNE LIB, Digby Hall, Hound St, Sherborne, Dorset, DT9 3AA (01935-812683; *fax:* 01935-817623; *email:* SherborneLibrary@dorsetcc.gov.uk); STUR-MINSTER NEWTON LIB, Bath Rd, Sturminster

Newton, Dorset, DT10 1EH (01258-472669; *fax:* 01258-472596; *email:* SturminsterNewtonLibrary@ dorsetcc.gov.uk); SWANAGE LIB, High St, Swanage, Dorset, BH19 2NU (01929-423485; *fax:* 01929-475876; *email:* SwanageLibrary@dorsetcc. gov.uk); UPTON LIB, Corner House, Upton Cross, Poole, Dorset, BH16 5PW (01202-623744; *fax:* 01202-621925; *email:* UptonLibrary@ dorsetcc.gov.uk); VERWOOD LIB, 1 Manor Rd, Verwood, Wimborne, Dorset, BH31 6DS (01202-822972; *fax:* 01202-829939; *email:* VerwoodLibrary@dorsetcc.gov.uk); WAREHAM LIB, South St, Wareham, Dorset, BH20 4LR (01929-556146; *fax:* 01929-550672; *email:* WarehamLibrary@dorsetcc.gov.uk); WEST MOORS LIB, Station Rd, West Moors, Wimborne, Dorset, BH22 0JD (01202-873272; *fax:* 01202-871477; *email:* WestMoorsLibrary@dorsetcc. gov.uk); WIMBORNE LIB, Crown Mead, rear of 55-57 High St, Wimborne, Dorset, BH21 1HH (01202-882770; *fax:* 01202-880392; *email:* WimborneLibrary@dorsetcc.gov.uk); WYKE REGIS LIB, Portland Rd, Wyke Regis, Weymouth, Dorset, DT4 9BE (01305-760191; *fax:* 01305-768465; *email:* WykeRegisLibrary@ dorsetcc.gov.uk)
Svc Pts: PT: 9 *Mobile:* 6 (4 public svc, 1 domiciliary svcs, 1 schools) *Computers:* 34
Collns: Thomas Hardy Colln; Powys Colln; Dorset Colln of local hist (all at Dorchester Lib)
Co-op Schemes: SWRLS *ILLs:* county & natl
Loans: bks/3 wks; audios & videos/1 wk; lang courses/12 wks; music sets/13 wks *Charges:* CDs & talking bks/£1; cassettes/single 50p, sets £1; videos/info £1, entertainment £2.50; DVDs/ £2.50; CD-ROMs/£1.50; lang courses/£6; music sets/£10 *Income Gen:* res/ad fiction 80p, play sets 80p, music sets £2, other categories free; lost ticket/£1.50 *Fines:* bks/30p 1st wk, 50p pw thereafter, no charge for ch's bks; audios & videos/loan charge; admin charge of 25p for final reminders on all items; housebnd exempt from fines *Equip:* m-readers, 4 m-printers (20p), 34 fax (varies), 30 copiers (A4/10p, A3/20p), computers (incl 209 with internet & CD-ROM, access free, printouts 10p), rooms for hire (varies) *Disabled:* Eazee-readers, minicoms at 3 libs *Online:* LID (Local Info in Dorset)

Stock:	1 Apr 2000	1 Apr 2001
ad lend:	413822	405269
ad ref:	39483	41291
ch:	135784	131888
audios:	33104	34373
videos:	12561	13492
periodcls:	183	183

Issues:	1999-2000	2000-01
ad lend:	2979731	2881349
ch:	793012	732077
audios:	164784	167109
videos:	84186	74570

Acqs:	1999-2000	2000-01
bks:	73271	69150
AVs:	12217	12829

Acqs: Source: lib suppl *Offcr-in-Charge:* Svc Development Offcr: Mrs A. Evans
Classn: DDC *Cat: Medium:* auto & online *Auto Sys:* own *Svcs: Extramural:* schools, prisons, old people's homes, housebnd *Activs:* ch's activs, bk sales, temp exhibs, poetry readings, reading groups, author visits, Lit Promotions Offcr on staff *Offcr-in-Charge:* Snr Mgr: Ms Tracey Long, at Weymouth Lib; for arts events & promotions only, contact Cultural Svcs Offcr: Mr M. Hoskin BA(Hons)
Enqs: 278616 (1999-2000); 337064 (2000-01)
Staff: Libns: 44 *Other Prof:* 9 *Non-Prof:* 128; these figs incl School Lib & Div Svcs staff

Inc from:	1999-2000	2000-01
local govt:	£4651064	£5269069
fines etc:	£496232	£548774
total:	£5165156	£5880988

Exp on:	1999-2000	2000-01
bks:	£692281	£652026
AVs:	£131301	£168046
salaries:	£2636220	£3003088
total:	£5165156	£5880988

Dudley

P40 Dudley Library Services

Dudley Lib, St James's Rd, Dudley, W Midlands, DY1 1HR (01384-815568; *fax:* 01384-815543) *Internet:* http://www.dudley.gov.uk/libraries/

Local Auth: Dudley Metropolitan Borough Council *Pop:* 311500 *Larger Dept:* Directorate of Edu & Lifelong Learning *Dept Chief:* Dir: Mr John Freeman *Chief:* Head of Lib Svcs, Mr C.A. Wrigley BA, MCLIP (chris.wrigley@dudley.gov.uk)
Other Snr Staff: Asst Head of Libs (North): Mrs E.J. Woodcock BA (elizabeth.woodcock@ dudley.gov.uk); Asst Head of Libs (South): Mrs K.J. Millin BLib, MCLIP (kate.millin@dudley. gov.uk); Mgmt Support Offcr: Miss S.V. Helm BA, DipMS, MCLIP (s.helm@dudley.gov.uk)
Main Libs: Town Libs: BRIERLEY HILL LIB, High St, Brierley Hill, W Midlands, DY5 3ET (01384-812865; *fax:* 01384-812866; *email:* brierlib. pls@mbc.dudley.gov.uk); DUDLEY LIB, addr as above (*lend:* 01384-815560; *ref:* 01384-815557; *fax:* 01384-815543; *email:* dudlib.pls@mbc.dudley. gov.uk); HALESOWEN LIB, Queensway Mall, The Cornbow, Halesowen, W Midlands, B63 4AJ (01384-812980; *fax:* 01384-812981; *email:* hallib. pls@mbc.dudley.gov.uk); STOURBRIDGE LIB, Stourbridge Town Hall & Lib, Crown Centre, Stourbridge, W Midlands, DY8 1YE (01384-812945; *fax:* 01384-812946; *email:* stourlib.pls@ mbc.dudley.gov.uk); *Group Libs HQ (North):* SEDGLEY LIB, Ladies Walk, Sedgley, W Midlands, DY3 3UA (01384-812790; *email:* sedglib.pls@mbc.dudley.gov.uk); *Group Libs HQ (South):* KINGSWINFORD LIB, Market St, Kingswinford, W Midlands, DY6 9LG (01384-812740; *email:* kfordlib.pls@mbc.dudley.gov.uk)
Branch Libs: AMBLECOTE LIB, School Dr, Amblecote, Stourbridge, W Midlands, DY8 4JJ (01384-812760); COSELEY LIB, Old Meeting Rd, Coseley, Bilston, W Midlands, WV14 8HB (01384-812775); CRADLEY LIB, Colley Ln, Cradley, Halesowen, W Midlands, B63 2TL (01384-812885); DUDLEY WOOD LIB, Bush Rd, Dudley Wood, Dudley, W Midlands, DY2 0BH (01384-812890); GORNAL LIB, Abbey Rd, Lower Gornal, Dudley, W Midlands, DY3 2PG (01384-812755); LONG LN LIB, Long Ln, Halesowen, W Midlands, B62 9JY (01384-812880); LYE LIB, Chapel St, Lye, Stour-bridge, W Midlands, DY9 8BT (01384-812835); NETHERTON LIB, Halesowen Rd, Netherton, Dudley, W Midlands, DY2 9EP (01384-812845); QUARRY BANK LIB, High St, Quarry Bank, Brierley Hill, W Midlands, DY5 2JP (01384-812895); WALL HEATH LIB, Albion Parade, Wall Heath, Kingswinford, W Midlands, DY6 0NB (01384-812735); WOODSIDE LIB, Stourbridge Rd, Holly Hall, Dudley, W Midlands, DY1 2EG (01384-812840); WORDSLEY LIB, Wordsley Green, Wordsley, Stourbridge, W Midlands, DY8 5PD (01384-812765)
Svc Pts: Other: ARCHVS & LOCAL HIST SVC, Mount Pleasant St, Coseley, Dudley, W Midlands, WV14 9JR (see **A130**); SCHOOLS LIB & INFO SVC, Unit 29, Wallowes Industrial Est, Fens Pool Ave, Brierley Hill, W Midlands, DY5 1QA (01384-812850; *fax:* 01384-812851; *email:* edlib.pls@mbc. dudley.gov.uk)
Collns: Dudley Local Hist Colln; Francis Brett Young Colln; JFR; Earl of Dudley's Est archv
Co-op Schemes: BCLIP, WMRLS *Loans:* bks/4 wks; audios/2 wks; videos/1 wk *Charges:* cassettes/single 50p, double 75p, set of 3+ 90p; CDs/single 70p, double £1, set of 3+ £1.30; videos/75p-£2; linguaphone/£1.50; Key to Leisure holders charged at approx 50%

Income Gen: res/60p, Key to Leisure holders 30p; lost tickets/£1 *Fines:* bks & audios/ad 10p pd (max £3.60), over-60s 5p pd (max £1.80), ch exempt; videos/loan charge *Equip:* m-reader/printers (50p per sheet), fax, copiers (A4/10p, A3/15p), computers, rooms for hire (various) *Disabled:* access ramps, lifts, magnifier

Stock:	1 Apr 2000	1 Apr 2001
lend:	620520	609351
ref:	29449	29409
AVs:	38640	36997
periodcls:	-	138

Issues:	1999-2000	2000-01
bks:	2272548	2136616
AVs:	163283	173229

Acqs:	1999-2000	2000-01
bks:	43750	34981
AVs:	3971	7996

Acqs: Offcr-in-Charge: Central Svcs Libn: Ms Jane Callear (jcallear.pls@mbc.dudley.gov.uk) *Classn:* DDC *Cat: Type:* author & classified *Medium:* m-form & auto *Auto Sys:* DS Galaxy 2000 *Svcs: Extramural:* schools, old people's homes, housebnd *Info:* community, business *Other:* Open Learning *Activs:* ch's activs, bk sales, temp exhibs
Enqs: 547191 (1999-2000); 522187 (2000-01)
Staff: Libns: 34.4 *Other Prof:* 2 *Non-Prof:* 106.6

Inc from:	1999-2000	2000-01
local govt:	£3459185	£3599469
fines etc:	£299664	£298898
total:	£3963599	£3898367

Exp on:	1999-2000	2000-01
stock & materials:	£587832	£445656
salaries:	£2516374	£2513285
total:	£3963599	£3898367

Dumfries and Galloway

P41 Dumfries and Galloway Libraries, Information and Archives

Central Support Unit, Ewart Lib, Catherine Street, Dumfries, DG1 1JB (01387-253820; fax: 01387-260294)
Email: libs&i@dumgal.gov.uk
Internet: http://www.dumgal.gov.uk/

Local Auth: Dumfries & Galloway Council *Pop:* 147300 *Cttee:* Community Resources Cttee *Larger Dept:* Community Resources *Chief:* Libs & Info Mgr: Mr Alastair R. Johnston BA, MCLIP, FSAScot *Other Snr Staff:* Svc Support Libns: Mr Bill Millar & Ms Helen McArthur; Bibliographic Svcs Libn: Ms Kathleen Beattie; Schools Libn: Ms Janice Goldie; Resources Development Libn: Mr Graham Roberts *Branch Libs:* ANNAN LIB, Charles St, Annan, Dumfriesshire, DG12 5AG (tel & fax: 01461-202809; email: libannan@dumgal.gov.uk); CASTLE DOUGLAS LIB, Market Hill, King St, Castle Douglas, Kirkcudbrightshire, DG7 1AE (tel & fax: 01556-502643; email: libcastledouglas@dumgal.gov.uk); DALBEATTIE LIB, 23 High St, Dalbeattie, Kirkcudbrightshire, DG5 4AD (tel & fax: 01556-610898; email: libdalbeattie@dumgal.gov.uk); EWART LIB, addr as above; GEORGETOWN LIB, Gillbrae Rd, Georgetown, Dumfries, DG1 4EJ (01387-256059; fax: 01387-256059; email: libgeorgetown@dumgal.gov.uk); KIRKCUD-BRIGHT LIB, Sheriff Ct House, High St, Kirkcudbright, DG6 4JW (tel & fax: 01557-331240; email: libkirkcudbright@dumgal.gov.uk); LOCH-SIDE LIB, Lochside Rd, Dumfries, DG2 0LW (tel & fax: 01387-268751; email: liblochside@dumgal.gov.uk); LOCHTHORN LIB, Lochthorn, Dumfries, DG1 1UF (01387-265780; fax: 01387-266424; email: liblochthorn@dumgal.gov.uk); LOCKERBIE LIB, 31-33 High St, Lockerbie, Dumfriesshire, DG11 2JU (tel & fax: 01576-203380; email:

liblockerbie@dumgal.gov.uk); NEWTON STEWART LIB, Church St, Newton Stewart, Wigtownshire, DG8 6ER (01671-403450; fax: 01671-403450; email: libnewtonstewart@dumgal.gov.uk); STRANRAER LIB, North Strand St, Stranraer, Wigtownshire, DG9 7LD (01776-707400; fax: 01776-703565; email: libstranraer@dumgal.gov.uk)
Svc Pts: PT: 13 *Mobile:* 4 *Computers:* 21 *Internet:* 13 *Other:* ARCHV CENTRE (see **A133**) *Collns:* local colln; local photo colln; local map colln; R.C. Reid Genealogical Colln; Frank Miller Colln; Lockerbie Air Disaster Archv (all at Ewart Lib) *Loans:* bks & audios/3 wks (CDs 1wk); videos/2 days; CD-ROMs/1 wk *Charges:* req/50p *Fines:* bks/35p pw *Equip:* m-readers, m-printers, video viewers, fax, copiers, clr copier, 62 computers (all with CD-ROM, 27 with internet & 34 OPACs), rooms for hire

Stock:	1 Apr 2000
ad lend:	197123
ad ref:	48415
ch:	83223
audios:	14838
videos:	8012
CD-ROMs:	1470
periodcls:	53
archvs:	770 linear m

Issues:	1999-2000
ad lend:	1005251
ch:	226477
audios:	58232
videos:	59323
CD-ROMs:	4330

Acqs:	1999-2000
bks:	35060
AVs:	5425

Acqs: Offcr-in-Charge: Libs & Info Mgr, as above *Classn:* DDC *Svcs: Extramural:* schools, old people's homes *Info:* community, Council Info Svc, Membs Info Bulletin *Other:* Open Learning, CyberCentre *Activs:* ch's activs, temp exhibs
Enqs: 95355 (1999-2000)
Staff: Prof: 21.3 *Non-Prof:* 56.8

Inc from:	1999-2000
fines etc:	£255872

Exp on:	1999-2000
stock:	£91456
salaries:	£1252057
total:	£2384619

Dundee

P42 Dundee City Libraries

Communities Dept, Podium Block, Tayside House, Crichton Street, Dundee, DD1 3RA (01382-433250; fax: 01382-433871)
Email: nrdd.reception@dundeecity.gov.uk
Internet: http://www.dundeecity.gov.uk/

Local Auth: Dundee Council *Pop:* 142700 *Larger Dept:* Communities Dept *Dept Chief:* Head of Dept: Mr Stewart Murdoch *Chief:* Head of Lib & Info Svcs: Mrs Moira Methven MCLIP *Other Snr Staff:* Section Leader, Central Lib: Mrs Judy Dobbie
Main Libs: CENTRAL LIB & BIBLIO-GRAPHICAL SVCS, The Wellgate, Dundee, DD1 1DB (01382-434318; fax: 01382-434642; email: central.library@dundeecity.gov.uk) *Branch Libs:* ARDLER LIB, Turnberry Ave, Dundee, DD2 3TP (01382-432863; fax: 01382-432862; email: ardler.library@dundeecity.gov.uk); ARTHURSTONE LIB, Arthurstone Ter, Dundee, DD4 6RT (01382-438881; fax: 01382-438886; email: arthurstone.library@dundeecity.gov.uk); BLACKNESS LIB, 225 Perth Rd, Dundee, DD2 1EJ (01382-435843; fax: 01382-435942; email: blackness.library@dundeecity.gov.uk);

BROUGHTY FERRY LIB, Queen St, Broughty Ferry, Dundee, DD5 2HN (01382-436919; fax: 01382-436913; email: broughty.library@dundeecity.gov.uk); CHARLESTON LIB, 60 Craigowan Rd, Dundee, DD2 4NL (01382-432798; fax: 01382-432671; email: charleston.library@dundeecity.gov.uk); COLDSIDE LIB, 150 Strathmartine Rd, Dundee, DD3 7SE (01382-432849; fax: 01382-432850; email: coldside.library@dundeecity.gov.uk); DOUGLAS LIB, Balmoral Ave, Dundee, DD4 8SD (01382-436915; fax: 01382-436922; email: douglas.library@dundeecity.gov.uk); FINTRY LIB, Findcastle St, Dundee, DD4 9EW (01382-432560; fax: 01382-432559; email: fintry.library@dundeecity.gov.uk); HUB LIB, Pitkerro Rd, Dundee, DD4 8ES (01382-438648; fax: 01382-438627; email: hub.library@dundeecity.gov.uk); KIRKTON LIB, Derwent Ave, Dundee, DD3 0BW (01382-432851; fax: 01382-432852; email: kirkton.library@dundeecity.gov.uk); LOCHEE LIB, High St, Lochee, Dundee, DD2 3AU (01382-432675; fax: 01382-432677; email: lochee.library@dundeecity.gov.uk); MENZIES-HILL LIB, Orleans Pl, Dundee, DD2 4BN (01382-435965; fax: 01382-435992; email: menzieshill.library@dundeecity.gov.uk); WHITFIELD LIB, Whitfield Dr, Dundee, DD4 0DX (01382-432561; fax: 01382-432562; email: whitfield.library@dundeecity.gov.uk)
Svc Pts: Mobile: 1 *AV:* 14 *Computers:* 14 *Internet:* 14 *Other:* LOCAL STUDIES DEPT, at Central Lib (see **A136**); HOUSEBND LIB SVC (01382-434356; fax: 01382-434642)
Collns: Wighton Colln of Natl Scottish Music; Ivory Colln of mathematical & scientific printed works (both in Rare Bks Dept at the Central Lib); Lamb Colln of bks, pamphs & ephemera relating to Dundee (in Local Studies Dept, Central Lib) *ILLs:* county, natl & internatl *Loans:* bks & audios/3 wks (mobile lib 4 wks); videos/1 or 5 nights; CD-ROMs/1 wk *Charges:* audios & videos/50p per item or £10 pa sub (conc £2 pa) *Income Gen:* req/20p-45p; lost ticket/50p *Fines:* bks & audios/ad 20p pd (£2 max), ch & oap exempt, registered blind exempt from audio charges; videos/loan charge *Equip:* m-readers, m-printer (£1), fax (40p per A4 + £1 handling, higher charges overseas), copiers (A4/10p), clr copiers (A4/£1.50, A3/£2), 30 computers (incl wd-proc, internet & CD-ROM), 3 rooms for hire *Disabled:* Kurzweil, CCTV enlarger, reading edge machine

Stock:	1 Apr 2000	1 Apr 2001
lend:	315837	306959
ref:	130788	131720
AVs:	31407	33106
periodcls:	407	378

Issues:	1999-2000	2000-01
bks:	1005913	975611
AVs:	117366	109564

Acqs:	1999-2000	2000-01
bks:	33837	33699
AVs:	4236	4551

Acqs: Source: lib suppl & bksellers *Offcr-in-Charge:* Snr Lib & Info Worker: Ms Janis Milne *Classn:* DDC *Cat: Type:* author, classified & title *Medium:* auto *Auto Sys:* DS *Svcs: Extramural:* schools, hosps, old people's homes, housebnd *Info:* business, community, Scottish Parliament *Other:* Open for Learning, BookStart, Partnership with Dundee Coll *Activs:* ch's activs, bk sales, temp exhibs, reading groups, storytelling sessions, homework & study support
Enqs: 158308 (1999-2000); 145369 (2000-01)
Staff: Libns: 23 *Non-Prof:* 92.1

Inc from:	1999-2000	2000-01
local govt:	£3169416	£3171971
fines etc:	£114389	£111734
total:	£3283805	£3283705

☛

Dundee
▼
East Lothian

Public Libraries

(Dundee City Libs cont)

Exp on:	1999-2000	2000-01
stock:	£452788	£434236
salaries:	£1744281	£1764914
total:	£3283805	£3283705

Durham

P43 Durham County Libraries

Cultural Svcs, County Hall, Durham, DH1 5TY (0191-383-3595; *fax:* 0191-384-1336)
Internet: http://www.durham.gov.uk/

Local Auth: Durham County Council *Pop:* 493700 *Cttee:* Cabinet *Larger Dept:* Cultural Svcs *Chief:* Dir of Cultural Svcs: Mr Patrick Conway BA, FRSA
Main Libs: Northern Div: DURHAM CLAYPORT LIB, Millennium Sq, Durham, DH1 1WA (0191-386-4003; *fax:* 0191-386-0379; *email:* DurhamClayportLibrary@durham.gov.uk); *Eastern Div:* PETERLEE LIB, Burnhope Way, Peterlee, Co Durham, SR8 1NT (0191-586-2279; *fax:* 0191-586-6664; *email:* peterlee.lib@durham.gov.uk); *Western Div:* CROOK LIB, Market Pl, Crook, Co Durham, DL15 8QH (01388-762269; *fax:* 01388-766170; *email:* crook.lib@durham.gov.uk)
Branch Libs: Northern Div: ANNFIELD PLAIN LIB, North Rd, Annfield Plain, Stanley, Co Durham, DH9 8EZ (01207-234241; *email:* annfieldplain.lib@durham.gov.uk); BELMONT LIB, Cheveley Pk, Shopping Centre, Belmont, Co Durham, DH1 2AA (0191-384-3223; *email:* belmont.lib@durham.gov.uk); BOWBURN LIB, Durham Rd, Bowburn, Durham, DH6 5AB (0191-377-0693; *email:* bowburn.lib@durham.gov.uk); BRANDON LIB, Lowland Rd, Brandon, Durham, DH7 8NN (0191-378-0527; *email:* brandon.lib@durham.gov.uk); CHESTER-LE-STREET LIB, Station Rd, Chester-le-Street, Co Durham, DH3 3PB (0191-388-2015; *email:* chesterlest.lib@durham.gov.uk); ESH WINNING LIB, College View, Cemetery Rd, Esh Winning, Durham, DH7 9AD (0191-373-4412; *email:* eshwinning.lib@durham.gov.uk); NEWTON HALL LIB, Alnwick Rd, Newton Hall, Durham, DH1 5NL (0191-386-7695; *email:* newtonhall.lib@durham.gov.uk); PELTON LIB, Ouston Ln, Pelton, Chester-le-Street, Co Durham, DH2 1EZ (0191-370-0485; *email:* pelton.lib@durham.gov.uk); SACRISTON LIB, Plawsworth Rd, Sacriston, Durham, DH7 6HJ (0191-371-0550; *email:* sacriston.lib@durham.gov.uk); SOUTH MOOR LIB, Severn Cres, South Moor, Stanley, Co Durham, DH9 7PX (01207-235596; *email:* southmoor.lib@durham.gov.uk); STANLEY LIB, High St, Stanley, Co Durham, DH9 0DQ (01207-232128; *email:* stanley.lib@durham.gov.uk); *Eastern Div:* BLACKHALL LIB, Back Middle St, Blackhall Colliery, Hartlepool, Cleve-land, TS27 4HD (0191-586-3545; *email:* blackhall.lib@durham.gov.uk); CORNFORTH LIB, High St, West Cornforth, Ferryhill, Co Durham, DL17 9HP (01740-54320; *email:* cornforth.lib@durham.gov.uk); EASINGTON LIB, Seaside Ln, Easington Colliery, Peterlee, Co Durham, SR8 3PN (0191-527-0239; *email:* easingtoncoll.lib@durham.gov.uk); FERRYHILL LIB, North St, Ferryhill, Co Durham, DL17 8HX (01740-651236; *email:* ferryhill.lib@durham.gov.uk); HORDEN LIB, Sunderland Rd, Horden, Peterlee, Co Durham, SR8 4PF (0191-586-3887; *email:* horden.lib@durham.gov.uk); MURTON LIB,

Barnes Rd, Murton, Seaham, Co Durham, SR7 9QR (0191-526-2025; *email:* murton.lib@durham.gov.uk); SEAHAM LIB, St John's Sq, Seaham, Co Durham, SR7 7JE (0191-381-2034; *email:* seaham.lib@durham.gov.uk); SEDGEFIELD LIB, Front St, Sedgefield, Stockton-on-Tees, Cleveland, TS21 3AT (01740-620103; *email:* sedgefield.lib@durham.gov.uk); SHOTTON LIB, Coop Ter, Shotton Colliery, Durham, DH6 2LW (0191-526-1379; *email:* shotton.lib@durham.gov.uk); SPENNYMOOR LIB, 24 Cheapside, Spennymoor, Co Durham, DL16 6DJ (01388-814694; *email:* spennymoor.lib@durham.gov.uk); THORNLEY LIB, High St, Thornley, Durham, DH6 3EL (01429-821431; *email:* thornley.lib@durham.gov.uk); TRIMDON LIB, Church Rd, Trimdon, Co Durham, TS29 6PY (01429-880433; *email:* trimdon.lib@durham.gov.uk); WINGATE LIB, Front St, Wingate, Co Durham, TS28 5AA (01429-838339; *email:* wingate.lib@durham.gov.uk); *Western Div:* BARNARD CASTLE LIB, 2 Hall St, Barnard Castle, Co Durham, DL12 8JB (01833-638001; *email:* bdcaslibrary@durham.gov.uk); BISHOP AUCKLAND LIB, Town Hall, Market Pl, Bishop Auckland, Co Durham, DL14 7NP (01388-602610; *email:* BATH@durham.gov.uk); CHILTON LIB, Durham Rd, Chilton, Ferryhill, Co Durham, DL17 0EX (01388-720251; *email:* chilton.lib@durham.gov.uk); CONSETT LIB, Victoria Rd, Consett, Co Durham, DH8 5AT (01207-503606; *email:* consett.lib@durham.gov.uk); NEWTON AYCLIFFE LIB, Dalton Way, Newton Aycliffe, Co Durham, DL5 4PD (01325-312856; *email:* newtonayc.lib@durham.gov.uk); SHILDON LIB, Church St, Shildon, Co Durham, DL4 1DU (01388-772203; *email:* shildon.lib@durham.gov.uk); WILLINGTON LIB, 46a High St, Willington, Crook, Co Durham, DL15 0PG (01388-746341; *email:* willington.lib@durham.gov.uk); WOLSINGHAM LIB, Town Hall, Wolsingham, Bishop Auckland, Co Durham, DL13 3AB (01388-527625; *email:* wolsingham.lib@durham.gov.uk); WOODHOUSE CL LIB, Woodhouse Ln, Woodhouse Cl, Bishop Auckland, Co Durham, DL14 6JX (01388-604612; *email:* woodhousecl.lib@durham.gov.uk)
Svc Pts: PT: 2 *Mobile:* 10 mobile & trailer libs *AV:* 15 *Computers:* 38 *Internet:* 38
Collns: Co Durham local hist (at Durham Clayport Lib); BSI complete set (also on-line)
ILLs: county & natl *Loans:* bks & spkn wd/3 wks; audios & videos/1 wk *Charges:* audios/80p; spkn wd/£1; videos/75p-£2; visually impaired exempt *Income Gen:* res/50p, conc/25p; lost tickets/£1.50, ch & oap free *Fines:* bks, audios & spkn wd/12p pd, ch & oap 5p pd; videos/loan charge *Equip:* 6 m-readers, 3 m-printers (30p per copy), 6 fax (£1 per pg in UK), 38 copiers (A4/10p, A3/20p), clr copier (A4/10p, A3/20p), 237 computers (all with wd-proc, internet & CD-ROM), 3 rooms for hire (cost+50% for commercial use) *Disabled:* Supernova software, tracker ball & big key keyboards, PCs with touch screens

Stock:	1 Apr 2001	1 Apr 2002
ad lend:	358773	354626
ad ref:	30333	31134
ch:	140225	138555
schools:	114727	-
instns:	17178	16945
audios:	22756	25313
videos:	2580	3190
CD-ROMs:	-	318
periodcls:	305	311

Issues:	2000-01	2001-02
ad lend:	2956578	2755877
ch:	661538	610942
instns:	95741	75037
audios:	127324	123171
videos:	18263	17321

Acqs:	2000-01	2001-02
bks:	97904	86375
AVs:	5127	7401

Acqs: Source: lib suppl *Offcr-in-Charge:* Stock & Systems Mgr: Mr A.G. Raine (andy.raine@durham.gov.uk)
Classn: DDC *Cat: Type:* author & classified *Medium:* auto *Auto Sys:* in-house *Svcs: Extramural:* schools, prisons, hosps, old people's homes, housebnd *Info:* community, council *Other:* Open Learning, public info & training access pts *Activs:* ch's activs, bk sales, temp exhibs, poetry readings, author events, info events
Enqs: 609897 (2000-01); 688845 (2001-02)
Staff: Libns: 33 *Non-Prof:* 149.5

Inc from:	2000-01	2001-02
local govt:	£314413	£412926
fines etc:	£352134	£456083
total:	£666547	£869009

Exp on:	2000-01	2001-02
bks:	£858706	£790906
AVs:	£75971	£93448
elec media:	£60326	£61637
salaries:	£3177087	£3389654
total:	£6445776	£6920288

Proj: new libs in Trimdon & Wingate

East Ayrshire

P44 East Ayrshire Library, Registration and Information Services

The Dick Inst, Elmbank Ave, Kilmarnock, Ayrshire, KA1 3BU (01563-554300; *fax:* 01563-554311)
Email: libraries@east-ayrshire.gov.uk
Internet: http://www.east-ayrshire.gov.uk/

Local Auth: East Ayrshire Council *Pop:* 120630 *Cttee:* Community Svcs Cttee *Larger Dept:* Community Svcs *Dept Chief:* Dir of Community Svcs: Mr William Stafford MIWM, MREHIS *Chief:* Lib, Registration & Info Svcs Mgr: Mr Gerard Cairns BA, DipLib, MCLIP, DMS (gerard.cairns@east-ayrshire.gov.uk) *Dep:* Snr Libns: Mrs Elaine Gray MA, DipLib, MCLIP (elaine.gray@east-ayrshire.gov.uk) & Mr John Laurenson BSc, DipLib, MCLIP (john.laurenson@east-ayrshire.gov.uk) *Other Snr Staff:* Community Libn (Marketing): Mrs Geraldine Downie BA, MCLIP (geraldine.downe@east-ayrshire.gov.uk); Community Libn (Heritage Svcs): Ms Anne Geddes MCLIP (anne.geddes@east-ayrshire.gov.uk); Support Svcs Libn: Mrs Julia Harvey MA(Hons), DipLib, MCLIP (julia.harvey@east-ayrshire.gov.uk); Community Libn (Operations): Mr Hugh Maclean MA, DipLib, MCLIP (hugh.maclean@east-ayrshire.gov.uk); Community Libn (Staff Development): Ms Lynn Mee BA(Hons), MCLIP (lynn.mee@east-ayrshire.gov.uk); Edu Liaison Offcr: Ms Pat Standen BA, MCLIP (pat.standen@east-ayrshire.gov.uk); Info Offcr: Ms Dawn Vallance BA(Hons), DipLIS, MCLIP (dawn.vallance@east-ayrshire.gov.uk)
Main Libs: DICK INST LIB, addr as above; LIB HQ (SOUTH), Council Offices, Lugar, Cumnock, Ayrshire, KA18 3JQ (01563-555452; *fax:* 01563-555400) – admin centre only, lends Educational Resource Svc material; DIST HIST CENTRE & BAIRD INST MUSEUM, 3 Lugar St, Cumnock, Ayrshire, KA18 1AD (*tel & fax:* 01290-421701)
Branch Libs: AUCHINLECK LIB, Well Rd, Auchinleck, Cumnock, Ayrshire, KA18 2LA (01290-422829); BELLFIELD LIB, 79 Whatriggs Rd, Kilmarnock, Ayrshire, KA1 3RB (01563-534266); CROSSHOUSE LIB, 11-13 Gatehead Rd, Crosshouse, Kilmarnock, Ayrshire, KA2 0HN (01563-573640); CUMNOCK LIB, 25-27 Ayr Rd, Cumnock, Ayrshire, KA18 1EB (01290-422804); DALMELLINGTON LIB, Townhead, Dalmellington, Ayr, KA6 7QZ (01292-550159); DARVEL LIB, Town Hall, West Main St, Darvel, Ayrshire, KA17 0AQ (01560-322754); GALSTON LIB, Henrietta St,

Galston, Ayrshire, KA4 8HQ (01563-821994); HURLFORD LIB, Blair Rd, Hurlford, Kilmarnock, Ayrshire, KA1 5BN (01563-539899); KILMAURS LIB, Irvine Rd, Kilmaurs, Kilmarnock, Ayrshire, KA3 2RJ (01563-539895); NEW CUMNOCK LIB, Community Centre, The Castle, New Cumnock, Cumnock, Ayrshire, KA18 4AH (01290-338710); NEWMILNS LIB, Craigview Rd, Newmilns, Ayrshire, KA16 9DQ (01560-322890); STEWARTON LIB, Cunningham Inst, Stewarton, Kilmarnock, Ayrshire, KA3 5AB (01560-484385) *Svc Pts:* PT: 9 *Mobile:* 2 *AV:* 15 *Computers:* 23 *Internet:* 23
Collns: Burns Colln (life & works of Robert Burns, at Baird Inst & Dick Inst); Galt Colln (life & works of John Galt, at Dick Inst); James Boswell Colln (life & works of James Boswell of Auchinleck, at Baird Inst); James Keir Hardie Colln (life & works of James Keir Hardie, at Baird Inst); Ayrshire Colln; Braidwood Colln; Buchanan Bequest *Co-op Schemes:* SUC, ALF, CAIRNS, Ayrshire Archvs *ILLs:* county, natl & internatl *Loans:* bks, magazines & spkn wd/3 wks; audios, videos, DVDs, Playstation games & software/1 wk; open learning material/4 wks *Charges:* audios, videos, DVDs, Playstation games & software/ad 90p, conc 55p *Income Gen:* ILL req/£2.10, conc £1; res/ad 32p, conc 15p; lost tickets/£1; rsrch/local hist & genealogy £12.50, business, commercial & prof £49.50; sale of old stock/varies *Fines:* bks/ad 5p pd, oaps & other conc 3p pd, ch exempt; audios, videos, DVDs, Playstation games & software/ad 11p pd, conc 5p pd; registered blind exempt from all fines *Equip:* 8 m-readers, m-printer (10p per pg), 4 fax (to send UK £1 per pg, elsewhere £2, 10p per pg to receive), 8 copiers (A4/10p, A3/15p), 94 computers (all with wd-proc, internet & CD-ROM, printouts 10p b&w, 30p clr) *Disabled:* Echo-Loop 2000 induction loop in main lending lib *Online:* Emerald *Offcr-in-Charge:* Snr Libn, as above

Stock:	1 Apr 2000	1 Apr 2001
ad lend:	270628	263044
ad ref:	21690	18019
ch:	110097	105522
schools:	16893	17373
audios:	13309	13029
videos:	5106	5902
CD-ROMs:	-	85
periodcls:	76	98
archvs:	1953 linear m	1953 linear m

Issues:	1999-2000	2000-01
ad lend:	611355	545624
ch:	142083	129354
schools:	5882	10537
audios:	37208	36306
videos:	46189	45974
CD-ROMs:	-	5

Acqs:	1999-2000	2000-01
bks:	36743	36007
AVs:	4741	2938

Acqs: Source: lib suppl, publ & bksellers *Offcr-in-Charge:* Support Svcs Libn, as above
Classn: DDC *Cat: Type:* author, classified, subj & title *Medium:* auto *Auto Sys:* Unicorn *Svcs: Extramural:* schools (via Educational Resource Svc as an agency Svc), old people's homes, housebnd (in partnership with WRVS) *Info:* local hist & genealogy rsrch, business, commercial & professional rsrch *Other:* Open Learning, NOF Learning Centres *Activs:* ch's activs, bk sales, temp exhibs, reading groups, talks, author visits *Offcr-in-Charge:* Community Libn (Marketing), as above
Enqs: 58006 (1999-2000); 56278 (2000-01)
Staff: Libns: 10 *Other Prof:* 1 *Non-Prof:* 51.4

Inc from:	1999-2000	2000-01
local govt:	£1943633	£1928560
fines etc:	£64141	£93681
total:	£2007774	£2022241

Exp on:	1999-2000	2000-01
bks:	£246482	£252178
AVs:	£43636	£39174
elec media:	-	£4519
salaries:	£1097895	£1105721
total:	£2007774	£2022241

Proj: setting up People's Network Learning Centres in each lib

East Dunbartonshire

P45 East Dunbartonshire Information and Lifelong Learning

William Patrick Lib, 2-4 West High Street, Kirkintilloch, E Dunbartonshire, G66 1AD (0141-776-5666; *fax:* 0141-776-0408)
Email: libraries@eastdunbarton.gov.uk
Internet: http://www.eastdunbarton.gov.uk/

Local Auth: East Dunbartonshire Council *Pop:* 110800 *Cttee:* Edu & Cultural Svcs Cttee *Larger Dept:* Community Svcs *Dept Chief:* Strategic Dir: Ms Sue Bruce *Chief:* Info & Lifelong Learning Mgr: Ms Elizabeth Brown MA, MCLIP *Other Snr Staff:* Asst Mgr (Info & Archvs): Mr Don Martin; Asst Mgr (Learning & Outreach): Mr Gerry Kiernan
Main Libs: WILLIAM PATRICK LIB, addr as above (lend: 0141-776-7484; info: 0141-776-8090)
Branch Libs: BISHOPBRIGGS LIB, 170 Kirkintilloch Rd, Bishopbriggs, E Dunbartonshire, G64 2LX (0141-772-4513; fax: 0141-762-5363); BROOKWOOD LIB, 166 Drymen Rd, Bearsden, E Dunbartonshire, G61 3RJ (0141-942-6811; fax: 0141-943-1119); CRAIGHEAD LIB, Craighead Rd, Milton of Campsie, E Dunbartonshire, G66 8DL (01360-311925); LENNOXTOWN LIB, Main St, Lennoxtown, E Dunbartonshire, G66 7HA (tel & fax: 01360-311436); LENZIE LIB, 13-15 Alexandra Ave, Lenzie, E Dunbartonshire, G66 5BG (0141-776-3021); MILNGAVIE LIB, Allander Rd, Milngavie, E Dunbartonshire, G62 8PN (tel & fax: 0141-956-2776); WESTERTON LIB, 82 Maxwell Ave, Bearsden, E Dunbartonshire, G61 1NZ (0141-943-0780)
Svc Pts: Mobile: 2 *AV:* 8
Collns: McEwan Colln (Scottish transport photos, at William Patrick Lib) *Co-op Schemes:* SCIP, Proj Earl, CAIRNS, DUGS, SCRAN *ILLs:* natl & internatl *Loans:* bks & audios/3 wks; videos & software/1 wk *Charges:* audios & videos/50p; software/£1 *Income Gen:* req/30p; lost ticket/£1 *Fines:* bks/ad 5p pd, oap (except conc) 5p pd; ch, disabled & those on income support exempt *Equip:* m-readers, fax, copiers, computers (incl wd-proc, internet & CD-ROM)

Stock:	1 Apr 2000	1 Apr 2001
lend:	130420	189970
ref:	14397	20169
AVs:	19373	18477
periodcls:	120	120

Issues:	1999-2000	2000-01
bks:	865002	839887
AVs:	86946	89254

Acqs:	1999-2000	2000-01
bks:	32972	27801
AVs:	2902	2592

Acqs: Source: lib suppl *Offcr-in-Charge:* Bibliographical Svcs Libn: Ms Sandra Busby
Classn: DDC *Cat: Type:* author, classified, subj & title *Medium:* auto *Auto Sys:* Dynix *Svcs: Extramural:* schools, prisons, hosps, old people's homes, housebnd *Info:* business, community, edu, youth, European, Scottish Parliament *Other:* Open Learning, local pubns for sale *Activs:* ch's activs, bk sales, temp exhibs, talks, author visits, music evenings, reading groups *Offcr-in-Charge:* various offcrs
Enqs: 148252 (1999-2000); 109060 (2000-01)
Staff: Libns: 16 *Non-Prof:* 43.5

Exp on:	1999-2000	2000-01
total:	£2045219	£2089910

East Lothian

P46 East Lothian Libraries

Lib & Museum HQ, Dunbar Rd, Haddington, E Lothian, EH41 3PJ (01620-828200; fax: 01620-828201)
Email: jstevenson@eastlothian.gov.uk
Internet: http://www.eastlothian.gov.uk/libraries/

Local Auth: East Lothian Council *Pop:* 91300 *Cttee:* Edu & Community Svcs Cttee *Larger Dept:* Edu & Community Svcs *Dept Chief:* Cultural Svcs Mgr: Ms Margaret O'Connor *Chief:* Principal Libs Offcr: Mr David Moody MCLIP (dmoody@eastlothian.gov.uk) *Other Snr Staff:* Snr Libn (Adult Svcs): Ms Morag Tocher (mtocher@eastlothian.gov.uk); Snr Libn (Yng Peoples Svcs): Ms Ruth Collin (rcollin@eastlothian.gov.uk); Snr Libn (Local Hist & Promotions): Ms Veronica Wallace (vwallace@eastlothian.gov.uk); Snr Libn (Computer Svcs): Mr Andy Holmes (aholmes@eastlothian.gov.uk)
Branch Libs: DUNBAR LIB, Castellau, Belhaven Rd, Dunbar, E Lothian, EH42 1DA (01368-863521; email: dunbar.library@eastlothian.gov.uk); EAST LINTON LIB, 60a High St, East Linton, E Lothian, EH40 3BX (01620-860015; email: eastlinton.library@eastlothian.gov.uk); HADDINGTON LIB, Newton Port, Haddington, E Lothian, EH41 3NA (01620-822531; email: haddington.library@eastlothian.gov.uk); LONGNIDDRY LIB, Church Way, Longniddry, E Lothian, EH32 0LW (01875-852735; email: longniddry.library@eastlothian.gov.uk); MUSSELBURGH LIB, 10 Bridge St, Musselburgh, E Lothian, EH21 6AG (0131-665-2183; email: musselburgh.library@eastlothian.gov.uk); NORTH BERWICK LIB, The Old School, School Rd, North Berwick, E Lothian, EH39 4JU (01620-893470; email: northberwick.library@eastlothian.gov.uk); ORMISTON LIB, 5a Meadowbank, Ormiston, Tranent, E Lothian, EH35 5LQ (01875-616675; email: ormiston.library@eastlothian.gov.uk); PORT SETON LIB, Community Centre, South Seton Pk, Cockenzie, E Lothian, EH32 0BG (01875-811709; email: portseton.library@eastlothian.gov.uk); PRESTONPANS LIB, West Loan, Prestonpans, E Lothian, EH32 9NX (01875-810788; email: prestonpans.library@eastlothian.gov.uk); TRANENT LIB, 3 Civic Sq, Tranent, E Lothian, EH33 1LH (01875-610254; email: tranent.library@eastlothian.gov.uk)
Svc Pts: PT: 2 *Mobile:* 2 *Other:* LOCAL HIST CENTRE, at Haddington Lib (see A193)
Collns: local studies; local authors *ILLs:* internatl *Loans:* all items/3 wks *Income Gen:* req & res/25p *Fines:* all items/ad & oap 5p pd open, ch exempt *Equip:* 14 m-readers, m-printer (A4/10p), 3 fax, 13 copiers (A4/10p, A3/15p), computers (incl wd-proc, internet & CD-ROM), room for hire (£3 per hr)

Stock:	1 Apr 2000	1 Apr 2001
ad lend:	84652	100361
ad ref:	9927	9327
ch:	33802	38268
audios:	12273	15527
videos:	1402	2146
periodcls:	228	174

Issues:	1999-2000	2000-01
ad lend:	543129	505038
ch:	146540	135607
audios:	60708	60401
videos:	6589	9687

Acqs:	1999-2000	2000-01
bks:	29734	33216
AVs:	2759	incl in bks

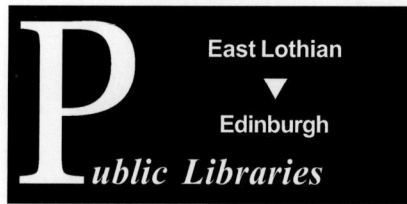

East Lothian
▼
Edinburgh

Public Libraries

(East Lothian Libs cont)
Acqs: Source: lib suppl *Offcr-in-Charge:* Snr Libn (Adult Svcs): Ms Morag Tocher & Snr Libn (Yng Peoples Svcs): Ms Ruth Collin; both as above *Classn:* DDC *Cat: Medium:* auto *Svcs: Extramural:* schools, hosps, old people's homes, housebnd, day centres *Info:* Scottish Parliament, business, community, European *Activs:* ch's activs, bk sales, temp exhibs, poetry readings, reading groups, writers' groups, talks, homework clubs *Enqs:* 57512 (2000-01)
Staff: Libns: 12 *Non-Prof:* 31

Inc from:	1999-2000	2000-01
local govt:	£1231709	£1235600
fines etc:	£55162	£68384
total:	£1286861	£1303984

Exp on:	1999-2000	2000-01
stock:	£237198	£234185
salaries:	£745595	£741173
total:	£1286861	£1303984

East Renfrewshire

P47 East Renfrewshire Libraries

Cultural Svcs HQ, Glen Street, Barrhead, E Renfrewshire, G78 1QA (0141-577-3500; *fax:* 0141-577-3501)
Email: informationservices@eastrenfrewshire. gov.uk
Internet: http://www.eastrenfrewshire.gov.uk/

Local Auth: East Renfrewshire Council *Pop:* 89410 *Cttee:* Community & Leisure Cttee *Larger Dept:* Community & Leisure *Dept Chief: Dir:* Mrs Ann Saunders BA, MIMgt, MILAM, MCLIP *Chief:* Head of Cultural Svcs: Mr Ken McKinlay MA(Hons), DipLib, MCLIP (mckinlayk@eastrenfreshire.gov.uk)
Branch Libs: BARRHEAD COMMUNITY LIB, Glen St, Barrhead, E Renfrewshire, G78 1QA (0141-577-3518; *email:* Barrhead.Library@eastrenfrewshire.gov.uk); BUSBY COMMUNITY LIB, Duff Memorial Hall, Main St, Busby, E Renfrewshire, G76 8DX (0141-577-4971; *fax:* 0141-577-4971; *email:* Busby.Library@eastrenfrewshire.gov.uk); CLARKSTON COMMUNITY LIB, Clarkston Rd, Clarkston, E Renfrewshire, G76 8NE (0141-577-4972; *fax:* 0141-577-4973; *email:* Clarkston.Library@eastrenfrewshire.gov.uk); EAGLESHAM COMMUNITY LIB, Montgomerie Hall, Gilmour St, Eaglesham, E Renfrewshire, G76 0LH (01355-302649; *fax:* 01355-302649; *email:* Eaglesham.Library@eastrenfrewshire.gov.uk); GIFFNOCK COMMUNITY LIB, Station Rd, Giffnock, E Renfrewshire, G46 6JF (0141-577-4976; *fax:* 0141-577-4978; *email:* Giffnock.Library@eastrenfrewshire.gov.uk); MEARNS COMMUNITY LIB, McKinley Pl, Newton Mearns, E Renfrewshire, G77 6EZ (0141-577-4974; *fax:* 0141-577-4980; *email:* Mearns.Library@eastrenfrewshire.gov.uk); NEILSTON COMMUNITY LIB, Main St, Neilston, E Renfrewshire, G38 3NN (0141-577-4981; *fax:* 0141-577-4982; *email:* Neilston.Library@eastrenfrewshire.gov.uk); THORNLIEBANK COMMUNITY LIB, 1 Spiersbridge Rd, Thornliebank, E Renfrewshire, G46 7SJ (0141-577-4983; *fax:* 0141-577-4816; *email:* Thornliebank.Library@eastrenfrewshire.gov.uk)
Svc Pts: PT: 2 *AV:* 10 *Computers:* 10 *Internet:* 10

Collns: local hist (at Giffnock Lib) *Co-op Schemes:* Proj Earl *ILLs:* county, natl & internatl *Loans:* bks/4 wks; audios, videos & DVDs/1 wk *Charges:* audios/50p; videos & DVDs/£1.25 *Income Gen:* req & res/50p; lost ticket/£1 *Fines:* bks & audios/ad 35p pw, oap & conc 20p pw; audios/10p pd; videos & DVDs/30p pd; under-18s exempt *Equip:* 2 m-readers, 8 fax (UK 1st pg £1, 25p per addl, overseas 1st pg £1.50, 50p per addl), 8 copiers (A4/10p, A3/20p), 78 computers (all with internet, 71 with wd-proc & 71 with CD-ROM) *Disabled:* ZoomText, large keyboards *Online:* Kompass, Xrefer, Know UK, Newsbank

Stock:	1 Apr 2000	1 Apr 2001
ad lend:	98676	100767
ad ref:	4305	4400
ch:	43417	46275
audios:	12763	11648
videos:	2389	2381
periodcls:	32	26

Issues:	1999-2000	2000-01
ad lend:	597300	546437
ch:	193357	177160
audios:	44117	44776
videos:	10739	9231

Acqs:	1999-2000	2000-01
bks:	21840	22016
AVs:	1695	1328

Acqs: Source: lib suppl
Classn: DDC *Cat: Type:* author, classified, subj & title *Medium:* auto *Auto Sys:* Talis *Svcs: Extramural:* old people's homes, housebnd, play groups *Info:* community, council *Other:* Open Learning *Activs:* ch's activs, bk sales, temp exhibs, reading groups, talks, author visits *Enqs:* 105040 (1999-2000); 119548 (2000-01)
Staff: Libns: 11.6 *Non-Prof:* 54.1

Exp on:	1999-2000	2000-01
bks:	£174224	£169335
AVs:	£21618	£19473
salaries:	£1025151	£1044705
total:	£1754897	£1733070

East Riding of Yorkshire

P48 East Riding Library and Information Service

Council Offices, Main Rd, Skirlaugh, E Riding of Yorkshire, HU11 5HN (01482-392740; *fax:* 01482-392710)
Email: alan.moir@eastriding.gov.uk
Internet: http://www.eastriding.gov.uk/learning/libraries.html

Local Auth: East Riding of Yorkshire Council *Pop:* 314817 *Cttee:* Lifelong Learning Cttee *Larger Dept:* Lifelong Learning *Dept Chief: Dir* of Lifelong Learning: Mr Jon Mager *Chief:* Libs, Museums & Archvs Mgr: Mr Alan Moir
Main Libs: BEVERLEY LIB, Champney Rd, Beverley, E Riding of Yorkshire, HU17 8HE (01482-392750; *email:* beverley.library@eastriding.gov.uk); BRIDLINGTON LIB, King St, Bridlington, E Riding of Yorkshire, YO15 2DF (01262-672917; *fax:* 01262-670208); GOOLE LIB, Carlisle St, Goole, E Riding of Yorkshire, DN14 5AA (01405-762187; *fax:* 01405-768329; *email:* goole.library@eastriding.gov.uk) *Branch Libs:* ANLABY LIB, North St, Anlaby, Hull, Humberside, HU2 8NJ (01482-657108); COTTINGHAM LIB, The Green, Cottingham, E Riding of Yorkshire, HU16 5QG (01482-392762); DRIFFIELD LIB, Cross Hill, Driffield, E Riding of Yorkshire, YO25 6RQ (01377-253393); HEDON LIB, St Augustine's Gate, Hedon, Hull, Humberside, HU12 8EX (01482-897651); HESSLE LIB, Southgate, Hessle, E Riding of Yorkshire, HU13 0RB (01482-640114; *email:* hessle.library@eastriding.gov.uk); HORNSEA LIB, Newbegin, Hornsea, E Riding of

Yorkshire, HU18 1PB (01964-532561; *email:* hornsea.library@eastriding.gov.uk); NORTH BRIDLINGTON LIB, Martongate, Bridlington, E Riding of Yorkshire, YO19 6YD (01262-671468); POCKLINGTON LIB, Station Sq, Pocklington, E Riding of Yorkshire, YO42 2SQ (01759-303373); WILLERBY LIB, The Inst, Main St, Willerby, E Riding of Yorkshire, HU10 6BZ (01482-658077); WITHERSEA LIB, Queen St, Withersea, E Riding of Yorkshire, HU19 2HH (01964-612537)
Svc Pts: PT: 14 *Mobile:* 6
Co-op Schemes: YLI *ILLs:* county, natl & internatl *Loans:* bks, audios & CD-ROMs/3 wks; videos/1 wk *Charges:* audios/25p-£1; videos/£1-£2.50; CD-ROMs/£1-£2 *Income Gen:* res/from 25p; lost tickets/£1.50 (computer tickets only) *Fines:* bks/ad 50p pw; audios, videos & CD-ROMs/loan charge; ch, yng adults, snr citizens & mobile lib users exempt *Equip:* 3 m-readers, 3 m-printers (50p per pg), 14 fax (from 50p per pg), 14 copiers (10p), 3 clr copiers (from £1), 110 computers (all with wd-proc, internet & CD-ROM), 5 rooms for hire (from £15) *Disabled:* hearing loop, disability access hardware & software *Online:* KnowUK, Xrefer (free)

Stock:	1 Apr 2000	1 Apr 2001
ad lend:	269650	253718
ad ref:	62361	63577
ch:	95080	95797
schools:	109556	109450
instns:	14139	13405
audios:	22269	19168
videos:	3311	3566
CD-ROMs:	-	281
periodcls:	157	161
archvs:	8 linear m	8 linear m

Issues:	1999-2000	2000-01
ad lend:	1483845	1433029
ch:	386133	347792
audios:	69671	70257
videos:	19252	19582
CD-ROMs:	-	1318

Acqs:	1999-2000	2000-01
bks:	38118	36137
AVs:	3468	2710

Acqs: Source: lib suppl & publ *Offcr-in-Charge:* Bibliographical Svcs Offcr: Mrs Margaret Sumner *Classn:* DDC *Cat: Type:* author, classified, subj & title *Medium:* auto *Auto Sys:* DS *Svcs: Extramural:* schools, prisons, old people's homes, housebnd, play groups *Info:* business, community, careers *Other:* homework centres, IT centres, Peoples Network *Activs:* ch's activs, bk sales, temp exhibs, reading groups, talks *Offcr-in-Charge:* Lib Mgr: Miss Margaret Slattery *Enqs:* 255788 (1999-2000); 268632 (2000-01)
Staff: Libns: 24.9 *Other Prof:* 2 *Non-Prof:* 94.1

Inc from:	1999-2000	2000-01
local govt:	£3450733	£3650152
fines etc:	£132757	£136259
total:	£3590117	£3853771

Exp on:	1999-2000	2000-01
bks:	£355491	£358690
AVs:	£49184	£39189
salaries:	£1776080	£1898118
total:	£3590117	£3853771

Proj: new PFI lib at North Bridlington (Oct 2002)

East Sussex

P49 East Sussex Libraries, Information and Arts

County Lib HQ, Southdown House, 44 St Anne's Cres, Lewes, E Sussex, BN7 1SQ (01273-481870; *fax:* 01273-480092)
Email: kate.nassir-pour@eastsussexcc.gov.uk
Internet: http://www.eastsussexcc.gov.uk/lia/

Local Auth: East Sussex County Council *Pop:* 498800 *Cttee:* Cabinet Memb for Community Svcs *Larger Dept:* Community Svcs *Chief:* Acting Head of Libs & Info: Mr Paul Leivers (paul.leivers@eastsussexcc.gov.uk) *Other Snr Staff:* Customer Svcs Mgr: Ms Helena Sykes (helena.sykes@eastsussexcc.gov.uk)

Main Libs: EASTBOURNE CENTRAL LIB, Grove Rd, Eastbourne, E Sussex, BN21 4TL (01323-434206; *fax:* 01323-649174; *email:* library. eastbourne@eastsussexcc.gov.uk); HASTINGS CENTRAL LIB, Brassey Inst, 13 Claremont, Hastings, E Sussex, TN34 1HE (01424-420501; *fax:* 01424-443289; *email:* library.hastings@ eastsussexcc.gov.uk) *Branch Libs:* BATTLE LIB, 7 Market Sq, Battle, E Sussex, TN33 0XA (*tel & fax:* 01424-772250; *email:* library.battle@ eastsussexcc.gov.uk); BEXHILL LIB, Western Rd, Bexhill-on-Sea, E Sussex, TN40 1DY (01424-212546; *fax:* 01424-733390; *email:* library.bexhill@ eastsussexcc.gov.uk); CROWBOROUGH LIB, Pine Grove, Crowborough, E Sussex, TN6 1DH (01892-664426; *fax:* 01892-667064; *email:* library. crowborough@eastsussexcc.gov.uk); HAILSHAM LIB, Western Rd, Hailsham, E Sussex, BN27 3DN (01323-840604; *fax:* 01323-844426; *email:* library.hailsham@eastsussexcc.gov.uk); HAMPDEN PK LIB, Brodrick Cl, Hampden Pk, Eastbourne, E Sussex, BN22 9NR (*tel & fax:* 01323-502485; *email:* library.hampdenpark@ eastsussexcc.gov.uk); HEATHFIELD LIB, 21 High St, Heathfield, E Sussex, TN21 8LU (01435-863975; *fax:* 01435-867798; *email:* library. heathfield@eastsussexcc.gov.uk); HOLLINGTON LIB, 96 Battle Rd, St Leonards-on-Sea, E Sussex, TN37 7AG (01424-421718; *email:* library. hollington@eastsussexcc.gov.uk); LANGNEY LIB, Unit 4 – The Shopping Centre, 110 Kingfisher Dr, Langney, E Sussex, BN23 7DR (01323-761214; *fax:* 01323-740783; *email:* library. langney@eastsussexcc.gov.uk); LEWES LIB, Albion St, Lewes, E Sussex, BN7 2ND (01273-474232; *fax:* 01273-477881; *email:* library.lewes@ eastsussexcc.gov.uk); NEWHAVEN LIB, 16 High St, Newhaven, E Sussex, BN9 9PD (01273-514468; *fax:* 01273-512343; *email:* Library. Newhaven@eastsussexcc.gov.uk); ORE LIB, Old London Rd, Ore, Hastings, E Sussex, TN35 5BP (01424-428316; *email:* library.ore@eastsussexcc. gov.uk); PEACEHAVEN LIB, Meridian Centre, Peacehaven, E Sussex, BN9 8BB (01273-583945; *fax:* 01273-589988; *email:* library.peacehaven@ eastsussexcc.gov.uk); PEVENSEY BAY LIB, Wallsend House, Richmond Rd, Pevensey Bay, E Sussex, BN24 6AU (01323-761708; *email:* library.pevensey@eastsussexcc.gov.uk); POLEGATE LIB, Windsor Way, Polegate, E Sussex, BN26 6QF (*tel & fax:* 01323-482155; *email:* library. polegate@eastsussexcc.gov.uk); RYE LIB, Lion St, Rye, E Sussex, TN31 7LB (01797-223355; *fax:* 01797-222913; *email:* library. rye@eastsussexcc.gov.uk); SEAFORD LIB, 17 Sutton Pk Rd, Seaford, E Sussex, BN25 1QX (01323-893420; *fax:* 01323-896952; *email:* library. seaford@eastsussexcc.gov.uk); UCKFIELD LIB, 75 High St, Uckfield, E Sussex, TN22 1AR (01825-763254; *fax:* 01825-769762; *email:* library. uckfield@ eastsussexcc.gov.uk); WILLINGDON LIB, Coppice Ave, Lower Willingdon, Eastbourne, E Sussex, BN20 9PN (*tel & fax:* 01323-482534; *email:* Library.Willingdon@eastsussexcc.gov.uk)

Svc Pts: PT: 10 *Mobile:* 2 *Computers:* 23 *Internet:* 23 *Other:* 3 music libs (at Eastbourne, Hastings & Lewes)

Collns: Budgen Bequest (slides of Eastbourne); Equal Access Svcs Colln; Health Info Pt; Loeb Classical Lib; Rice Bequest Colln (Sussex local studies); Statistics & Standardisation; Walking Guides (all in Eastbourne Area); Baines Colln (local authors); W.H. Borrow Colln (postcards of Sussex & Kent); Brett Local Studies Colln; Carpenter Shipping Colln; Channel Tunnel Colln; Harry Furniss Colln (local illustrator); Matilda Betham-Edwards Colln (France in 19C);

Military Hist Colln; Nuclear Energy Colln; Protheroe Colln (local & WW2 hist, all in Hastings area); Wolseley Crimean War Colln; Baxter Colln (early clr prints, both at Lewes) *Co-op Schemes:* SASLIC, Standing Cttee of Sussex Libns *ILLs:* county & natl *Loans:* bks & spkn wd/3 wks; music audios, videos & CD-ROMs/1 wk *Charges:* spkn wd/£1-£1.50; music audios/50p; videos/ad £2.50, ch £1.50; CD-ROMs/£2 *Income Gen:* res/75p, self-svc 60p, special £2; lost ticket/£1.25 *Fines:* bks, audios & videos/ad & oap 16p pd, ch 25p admin charge only; CD-ROMs/40p pd; housebnd exempt *Equip:* m-readers, m-printers (20p per pg), fax (various), copiers (A4/10p, A3/15p), clr copiers (up to £1.50), 222 computers (incl wd-proc, internet & CD-ROM, access free, printouts 10p), rooms for hire (various) *Disabled:* minicom, hand magnifiers, CCTV, large print bks, sub-titled videos *Online:* not available direct to public

Stock:	1 Apr 2000	1 Apr 2001
lend:	656589	722357
ref:	65845	69823
AVs:	68911	63704
periodcls:	251	238

Issues:	1999-2000	2000-01
bks:	3588367	3344668
AVs:	274505	279902

Acqs:	1999-2000	2000-01
bks:	71386	77430
AVs:	7045	8494

Acqs: Source: lib suppl *Co-op:* CBC *Classn:* DDC *Cat: Type:* author, classified, subj & title *Medium:* auto *Auto Sys:* DS Galaxy *Svcs: Extramural:* schools, prisons, hosps, old people's homes, housebnd *Info:* business, community, health *Other:* LearnDirect (at Uckfield Lib), homework support *Activs:* ch's activs, bk sales, temp exhibs, reading groups, writers' groups, yearly summer promotion *Enqs:* 361088 (1999-2000); 371592 (2000-01) *Staff:* 176.39 FTE in total

Inc from:	2000-01
local govt:	£5189972
fines etc:	£775634
total:	£5965606

Exp on:	2000-01
stock:	£734234
salaries:	£3273126
total:	£5965606

Edinburgh

P50 Edinburgh City Libraries and Information Services

Edinburgh Central Lib, 7-9 George IV Bridge, Edinburgh, EH1 1EG (0131-242-8000; *fax:* 0131-242-8009)
Email: eclis@edinburgh.gov.uk
Internet: http://www.edinburgh.gov.uk/libraries/

Local Auth: City of Edinburgh Council *Pop:* 450000 *Cttee:* Culture & Leisure Scrutiny Board *Larger Dept:* Culture & Leisure *Dept Chief:* Dir: Mr Herbert Coutts AMA, FMA, FSA *Chief:* Head of Libs & Info Svcs: Mr Bill Wallace MA, DipLib, MCLIP *Dep:* shared between Heads of Svcs *Main Libs:* CENTRAL LIB, addr as above, incl Ref Lib (0131-242-8060; *fax:* 0131-242-8009; *email:* central.reference.library@edinburgh.gov.uk) & Lending Lib (0131-242-8025; *fax:* 0131-242-8009; *email:* central.lending.library@edinburgh. gov.uk); *North Div:* LEITH LIB, 28-30 Ferry Rd, Edinburgh, EH6 4AE (0131-529-5517; *fax:* 0131-554-2720; *email:* leith.library@edinburgh.gov.uk); *South Div:* OXGANGS LIB, 343 Oxgangs Rd North, Edinburgh, EH13 9LY (0131-529-5549; *fax:* 0131-529-5554; *email:* oxgangs.library@edinburgh. gov.uk); *East Div:* PORTOBELLO LIB, 14 Rose-field Ave, Portobello, Edinburgh, EH15 1AU

(0131-529-5558; *fax:* 0131-669-2344; *email:* portobello.library@edinburgh.gov.uk); *West Div:* SIGHTHILL LIB, 6 Sighthill Wynd, Edinburgh, EH11 4BL (0131-529-5569; *fax:* 0131-529-5572; *email:* sighthill.library@edinburgh.gov.uk) *Branch Libs:* BALERNO LIB, 1 Main St, Balerno, Edinburgh, EH14 7EQ (0131-529-5500; *fax:* 0131-529-5502; *email:* balerno.library@edinburgh. gov.uk); BALGREEN LIB, 173 Balgreen Rd, Edinburgh, EH11 3AT (0131-529-5585; *email:* balgreen.library@edinburgh.gov.uk); BLACKHALL LIB, 56 Hillhouse Rd, Edinburgh, EH4 5EG (0131-529-5595; *fax:* 0131-336-5419; *email:* blackhall. library@edinburgh.gov.uk); COLINTON LIB, 14 Thorburn Rd, Edinburgh, EH13 0BQ (0131-529-5603; *fax:* 0131-529-5607; *email:* colinton.library@ edinburgh.gov.uk); CORSTORPHINE LIB, 12 Kirk Loan, Edinburgh, EH12 7HD (0131-529-5506; *fax:* 0131-529-5508; *email:* corstorphine.library@ edinburgh.gov.uk); CRAIGMILLAR LIB, 7 Niddrie Marischal Gdns, Edinburgh, EH16 4LX (0131-529-5597; *email:* craigmillar.library@edinburgh.gov.uk); CURRIE LIB, 210 Lanark Rd West, Currie, Edinburgh, EH14 5NN (0131-529-5609; *email:* currie.library@edinburgh.gov.uk); FOUNTAIN-BRIDGE LIB, 137 Dundee St, Edinburgh, EH11 1BG (0131-529-5616; *fax:* 0131-529-5621; *email:* fountainbridge.library@edinburgh.gov.uk); GILMERTON LIB, 13 Newtoft St, Edinburgh, EH17 8RG (0131-529-5628; *fax:* 0131-529-5627; *email:* gilmerton.library@edinburgh.gov.uk); GRANTON LIB, Wardieburn Ter, Edinburgh, EH5 1DD (0131-529-5630; *fax:* 0131-529-5634; *email:* granton.library@edinburgh.gov.uk); KIRKLISTON LIB, Station Rd, Kirkliston, Edinburgh, EH29 9BE (0131-529-5510; *fax:* 0131-529-5514; *email:* kirkliston.library@edinburgh.gov.uk); MCDONALD RD LIB, 2 McDonald Rd, Edinburgh, EH7 4LU (0131-529-5640; *fax:* 0131-529-5646; *email:* mcdonaldrd.library@edinburgh.gov.uk); MORE-DUN LIB, 92 Moredun Pk Rd, Edinburgh, EH17 7HL (0131-529-5652; *fax:* 0131-529-5651; *email:* moredun.library@edinburgh.gov.uk); MORNING-SIDE LIB, 184 Morningside Rd, Edinburgh, EH10 4PU (0131-529-5654; *fax:* 0131-447-4685; *email:* morningside.library@edinburgh.gov.uk); MUIR-HOUSE LIB, 15 Pennywell Ct, Edinburgh, EH4 4TZ (0131-529-5528; *fax:* 0131-529-5532; *email:* muirhouse.library@edinburgh.gov.uk); NEWING-TON LIB, 17-21 Fountain Hall Rd, Edinburgh, EH9 2LN (0131-529-5536; *fax:* 0131-667-5491; *email:* newington.library@edinburgh.gov.uk); PIERSHILL LIB, 30 Piersfield Ter, Edinburgh, EH8 7BQ (0131-529-5685; *fax:* 0131-529-5691; *email:* piershill. library@ edinburgh.gov.uk); RATHO LIB, 6 School Wynd, Edinburgh, EH28 8TT (*tel & fax:* 0131-333-5297; *email:* ratho.library@edinburgh.gov.uk); SOUTH QUEENSFERRY LIB, 9 Shore Rd, South Queensferry, Edinburgh, EH30 9RD (0131-529-5576; *fax:* 0131-529-5578; *email:* southqueensferry.library@edinburgh. gov.uk); STOCKBRIDGE LIB, Hamilton Pl, Edinburgh, EH3 5BA (0131-529-5665; *fax:* 0131-529-5681; *email:* stockbridge.library@edinburgh.gov.uk); WESTER HAILES LIB, 1 Westside Plaza, Edinburgh, EH14 2FT (0131-529-5667; *fax:* 0131-529-5671; *email:* westerhailes.library@edinburgh.gov.uk)

Svc Pts: Mobile: 3 *AV:* 1 *Computers:* 26 *Internet:* 26 *Other:* ACCESS SVCS HQ, 343 Oxgangs Rd, Edinburgh, EH13 9LT (0131-529-5683/4; *email:* access.services@edinburgh. gov.uk); RESOURCE CENTRE FOR DISABLED, at Central Lib (0131-242-8135; minicom: 0131-242-8126; *fax:* 0131-242-8009; *email:* resource. centre@edinburgh.gov.uk); 10 Learning Centres for group & indiv use

Collns: BSI; Krishnamurti Colln; Sir Arthur Conan Doyle Colln; Hill & Adamson Cellotype Colln; Robert Louis Stevenson Colln; Scottish family hist; prints, drawings & photos of Edinburgh *Co-op Schemes:* NLSLS, BLDSC, SCURL, UCABLIS, Scottish Visual Arts, ARLIS, IAML, Talis *ILLs:* county, natl & internatl

(Edinburgh City Libs & Info Svcs cont)
Loans: bks, audios, videos & CD-ROMs/3 wks
Charges: audios & DVDs/50p single, £1 double
Income Gen: res/50p; ILLs/£2; lost ticket/£1
Fines: all items/15p pd; ch, housebnd & disabled users exempt **Equip:** 6 m-readers, 6 m-printers (20p per pg), 25 fax (UK £1 per sheet; higher overseas), 30 copiers (A4/15p, A3/20p), video viewer, 400 computers (all with wd-proc, internet & CD-ROM), 9 rooms for hire (£20 non-commercial use, £60 commercial) *Disabled:* extensive range of resources throughout, plus dedicated Resource Centre *Online:* Kompass UK, KnowUK, Newsbank, Hydra, Lit Resource Centre & others

Stock:	1 Apr 2000	1 Apr 2001
ad lend:	675513	615888
ad ref:	383531	387780
ch:	201432	180890

Issues:	1999-2000	2000-01
ad lend:	2938884	2441874
ch:	676770	607415

Acqs:	1999-2000	2000-01
bks:	62351	86641

Acqs: Source: lib suppl, publ & bksellers *Offcr-in-Charge:* Bibliographic Svcs Offcr: Mrs M. Curry **Classn:** DDC, LC **Cat:** Type: author, classified, subj & title *Medium:* auto *Auto Sys:* Talis **Svcs:** Extramural: prisons, hosps, old people's homes, housebnd *Info:* community, business, careers & courses, European, on-line searching *Other:* Open Learning, educational liaison, translation svc, ethnic svc **Activs:** ch's activs, bk sales, temp exhibs
Enqs: 296164 (1999-2000); 376104 (2000-01)
Staff: Libns: 90 Non-Prof: 233

Inc from:	1999-2000
fines etc:	£561393

Exp on:	1999-2000
bks:	£887251
AVs:	£42609
elec media:	£63380
salaries:	£6417327
total:	£7410567

Essex

P51 Essex Libraries

Lib HQ, Goldlay Gdns, Chelmsford, Essex, CM2 0EW (01245-284981; *fax:* 01245-490199)
Email: essexlib@essexcc.gov.uk
Internet: http://www.essexcc.gov.uk/libraries/

Local Auth: Essex County Council *Pop:* 1316300 *Cttee:* Lifelong Learning & Libs Cttee **Larger Dept:** Learning Svcs *Dept Chief:* Dir: Mr Paul Lincoln MA **Chief:** Head of Libs, Heritage & Culture: Dr Margaret Keeling BA(Hons), MA, PhD, MCLIP (margaret.keeling@essexcc.gov.uk) **Dep:** Strategic Mgr (Svc Delivery): Ms Jenny Glazer MCLIP (jenny.glayzer@essexcc.gov.uk); Strategic Mgr (Policy & Development): Mr Geoff Elgar BA(Hons), DipLib, MCLIP (geoff.elgar@essexcc.gov.uk)
Main (Principal) Libs: BASILDON LIB, The Basildon Centre, St Martin's Sq, Basildon, Essex, SS14 1EE (01268-288533; *fax:* 01268-286326; *email:* Basildon.Library@essexcc.gov.uk); BRAIN-TREE LIB, Fairfield Rd, Braintree, Essex, CM7 3LY (01376-320752; *fax:* 01376-553316; *email:*

Braintree.Library@essexcc.gov.uk); CHELMS-FORD CENTRAL LIB, County Hall, Market Rd, Chelmsford, Essex, CM1 1LH (01245-492758; *fax:* 01245-492536; *email:* chelmsford.library@ essexcc.gov.uk); COLCHESTER LIB, Trinity Sq, Colchester, Essex, CO1 1JB (01206-245900; *fax:* 01245-245901; *email:* Colchester.Library@ essexcc.gov.uk); HARLOW LIB, The High, Harlow, Essex, CM20 1HA (01279-413772; *fax:* 01279-424612; *email:* Harlow.Library@essexcc. gov.uk) **Branch Libs:** BILLERICAY LIB, High St, Billericay, Essex, CM12 9AB (01277-624624; *fax:* 01277-654905); BRENTWOOD LIB, New Rd, Brentwood, Essex, CM14 4BP (01277-264290; *fax:* 01277-261638); BRIGHTLINGSEA LIB, New St, Bright-lingsea, Colchester, Essex, CO7 0BZ (01206-302399; *fax:* 01206-304775); BUCK-HURST HILL LIB, 165 Queens Rd, Buckhurst Hill, Essex, IG9 5AZ (020-8504-0810; *fax:* 020-8504-5886); BURNHAM LIB, 103 Station Rd, Burnham-on-Crouch, Essex, CM0 8HQ (01621-782006; *fax:* 01621-786179); CANVEY LIB, High St, Canvey Island, Essex, SS8 7RB (01268-683741; *fax:* 01268-681890); CHIGWELL LIB, Hainault Rd, Chigwell, Essex, IG7 6QX (020-8500-7809; *fax:* 020-8501-2082); CHIPPING ONGAR LIB, 'The Pleasance', High St, Chipping Ongar, Essex, CM5 9AB (01277-362616; *fax:* 01277-366231); CLACTON LIB, Station Rd, Clacton-on-Sea, Essex, CO15 1SF (01255-421207; *fax:* 01255-222531); DEBDEN LIB, Rectory Ln, Loughton, Essex, IG10 3RU (020-8508-5869; *fax:* 020-8508-1388); DUNMOW LIB, North St, Dunmow, Essex, CM6 1AZ (01371-873447; *fax:* 01371-878196); EPPING LIB, St Johns Rd, Epping, Essex, CM16 5DN (01992-573504; *fax:* 01992-570034); FRINTON LIB, 59 Old Rd, Frinton-on-Sea, Essex, CO13 9DA (01255-672581; *fax:* 01255-851825); FRYERNS LIB, Whitmore Way, Basildon, Essex, SS14 2NN (01268-521642; *fax:* 01268-522196); GALLEYWOOD LIB, Watchouse Rd, Galleywood, Chelmsford, Essex, CM2 8PU (01245-259042; *fax:* 01245-493520); GT BADDOW LIB, 27 High St, Gt Baddow, Chelmsford, Essex, CM2 7HH (01245-478032; *fax:* 01245-474583); GT PARN-DON LIB, Staple Tye, Harlow, Essex, CM18 7LZ (01279-435101); GT TARPOTS LIB, 127 London Rd, Benfleet, Essex, SS7 5UH (01268-757361; *fax:* 01268-759420); GREENSTEAD LIB, Hawthorn Ave, Colchester, Essex, CO4 3QE (01206-862758); HADLEIGH LIB, 180 London Rd, Hadleigh, Benfleet, Essex, SS7 2PD (01702-559676; *fax:* 01702-558824); HALSTEAD LIB, Bridge St, Halstead, Essex, CO9 1HU (01787-473431; *fax:* 01787-476148); HARWICH LIB, Upper Kingsway, Harwich, Essex, CO12 3JT (01255-503499; *fax:* 01255-551449); HOCKLEY LIB, Southend Rd, Hockley, Essex, SS5 4PZ (01702-203558; *fax:* 01702-207254); HOLLAND LIB, Public Hall, Frinton Rd, Holland-on-Sea, Essex, CO15 5UR (01255-812409); HULL-BRIDGE LIB, Ferry Rd, Hullbridge, Hockley, Essex, SS5 6ET (01702-230868; *fax:* 01702-233020); INGATESTONE LIB, High St, Ingate-stone, Essex, CM4 9EU (01277-354284; *fax:* 01277-354705); LAINDON LIB, 48 New Century Rd, Basildon, Essex, SS15 6AG (01268-542065; *fax:* 01268-548826); LOUGHTON LIB, Traps Hill, Loughton, Essex, IG10 1HD (020-8502-0181; *fax:* 020-8508-5041); MALDON LIB, Carmelite House, White Horse Ln, Maldon, Essex, CM9 5FW (01621-853556; *fax:* 01621-841086); MANNING-TREE LIB, High St, Manningtree, Essex, CO11 1AD (01206-392747; *fax:* 01206-391725); MARK HALL LIB, The Stow, Harlow, Essex, CM20 3AP (01279-425533; *fax:* 01279-421371); NORTH MELBOURNE LIB, Dickens Pl, Copperfield Rd, Chelmsford, Essex, CM1 4UU (01245-442292; *fax:* 01245-440701); NORTH WEALD LIB, 138 High Rd, North Weald, Epping, Essex, CM16 6BZ (01992-522896; *fax:* 01992-524865); OLD HARLOW LIB, 30 High St, Old Harlow, Harlow, Essex, CM17 0DW (01279-433170; *fax:* 01279-

635766); PITSEA LIB, Community Centre, off Maydells, Pitsea, Basildon, Essex, SS13 3DU (01268-552884; *fax:* 01268-581013); PRETTY-GATE LIB, Prettygate Rd, Colchester, Essex, CO3 4EQ (01206-563700; *fax:* 01206-571283); RAYLEIGH LIB, 132-4 High St, Rayleigh, Essex, SS6 7BX (01268-775830; *fax:* 01268-745067); ROCHFORD LIB, 26-28 West St, Rochford, Essex, SS4 1AJ (01702-546688; *fax:* 01702-545670); SAFFRON WALDEN LIB, 2 King St, Saffron Walden, Essex, CB10 1ES (01799-523178; *fax:* 01799-513642); SHENFIELD LIB, Hutton Rd, Shenfield, Brentwood, Essex, CM15 8NJ (01277-225540; *fax:* 01277-201275); SOUTH BENFLEET LIB, 264 High St, Benfleet, Essex, SS7 5HD (01268-758558; *fax:* 01268-750607); SOUTH WOODHAM FERRERS LIB, Trinity Sq, South Woodham Ferrers, Chelmsford, Essex, CM3 5JU (01245-329531; *fax:* 01245-328288); TIPTREE LIB, Rectory Rd, Tiptree, Colchester, Essex, CO5 0SX (01621-816458; *fax:* 01621-810321); TYE GREEN LIB, Bush Fair, Harlow, Essex, CM18 6LU (01279-425002; *fax:* 01279-421376); VANGE LIB, Southview Rd, Basildon, Essex, SS16 4ET (01268-281575; *fax:* 01268-287175); WALTHAM ABBEY LIB, 37 Sun St, Waltham Abbey, Essex, EN9 1EL (01992-713717; *fax:* 01992-718044); WALTON LIB, 52 High St, Walton on the Naze, Essex, CO14 8AE (01255-674619); WEST MERSEA LIB, 13 High St, West Mersea, Colchester, Essex, CO5 8QA (01206-383321; *fax:* 01206-386130); WICKFORD LIB, Market Rd, Wickford, Essex, SS12 0AG (01268-732354; *fax:* 01268-561963); WITHAM LIB, 18 Newland St, Witham, Essex, CM8 2AQ (01376-519625; *fax:* 01376-501913)
Svc Pts: PT: 19 *Mobile:* 16 *Computers:* 74 *Internet:* 74 *Other:* 9 village centres
Collns: Harsnett Colln (16C & 17C); Castle Colln (18C example lib, both at Colchester Lib); jazz archv colln of bks, magazines & some instruments; Victorian Studies (bks, photos & catalogues, at Saffron Walden Lib); music colln of 52000 music scores **Co-op Schemes:** BLDSC **ILLs:** county, natl & internatl **Loans:** bks, audios & CD-ROMs/3 wks; videos & DVDs/1 wk **Charges:** music cassettes/60p; spkn wd cassettes/sets of 1-2 65p, 3-7 £1.30, 8+ £1.50; CDs/90p; videos/entertainment £2.50, other £1; CD-ROMs & DVDs/£2.60 (software free to blind or partially sighted ch & yng adults); Playstation games/£3 **Income Gen:** res/60p using ELAN, 90p via staff; lost ticket/1st £1, 2nd £1.50; subj enq/£1 **Fines:** bks, audios & CD-ROMs/ad & oap 12p pd (max £5.04); videos & DVDs/loan charge; ch exempt for bks & audios, registered blind & partially sighted exempt for audios, deaf/hard of hearing exempt for sub-titled videos **Equip:** 67 fax, 87 copiers (10p), 3 clr copiers, 247 computers (incl wd-proc, internet & CD-ROM) *Disabled:* 4 reading machines, 14 CCTV, 4 text phones, braille embosser *Online:* variety of online hosts & databases, incl Dialog & Datastar

Stock:	1 Apr 2001
ad lend:	1341462
ad ref:	227225
ch:	589104
audios:	91638
videos:	64906
CD-ROMs:	4801
periodcls:	928

Issues:	2000-01
ad lend:	8884419
ch:	3154749
audios:	602538
videos:	475680
CD-ROMs:	32689

Acqs:	2000-01
bks:	417195
AVs:	46519

Acqs: Source: lib suppl, publ & bksellers *Co-op:* Co-East *Offcr-in-Charge:* Resources & Reader Development Mgr: Mr Martin Palmer (martin.palmer@essexcc.gov.uk)
Classn: DDC *Cat: Type:* author, classified, dictionary, subj & title *Medium:* auto *Auto Sys:* Geac *Svcs: Extramural:* prisons, hosps, old people's homes, housebnd *Info:* Business Info Unit, community, info for parents, carers & teachers, Answers Direct (staff only at present) *Other:* Peoples Network, homework centres
Activs: ch's activs, bk sales, temp exhibs, poetry readings, reading groups, writers' groups, author visits *Offcr-in-Charge:* various offcrs
Enqs: 1004406 (2000-01)
Staff: Libns: 125.1 *Non-Prof:* 458.3

Falkirk

P52 Falkirk Council Library Services

Victoria Bldgs, Queen Street, Falkirk, Stirlingshire, FK2 7AF (01324-506800; *fax:* 01324-506801)
Email: library.support@falkirk.gov.uk
Internet: http://www.falkirk.gov.uk/

Local Auth: Falkirk Council *Pop:* 144320
Cttee: Community & Citizen Development Cttee
Larger Dept: Community Svcs *Dept Chief:* Dir: post vacant *Chief:* Libs Mgr: post vacant *Dep:* Principal Libn: Mrs Irene McIntyre
Branch Libs: BO'NESS LIB, Scotland's Cl, Bo'ness, Falkirk, Stirlingshire, EH51 0AH (01506-778520; *email:* bo'ness.library@falkirk.gov.uk); BONNYBRIDGE LIB, Bridge St, Bonnybridge, Falkirk, Stirlingshire, FK4 1AD (01324-503295; *email:* bonnybridge.library@falkirk.gov.uk); DENNY LIB, 49 Church Walk, Denny, Falkirk, Stirlingshire, FK6 6DF (01324-504242; *email:* denny.library@falkirk.gov.uk); FALKIRK LIB, Hope St, Falkirk, Stirlingshire, FK1 5AU (01324-503605; *email:* falkirk.library@falkirk.gov.uk); GRANGEMOUTH LIB, Bo'ness Rd, Grangemouth, Falkirk, Stirlingshire, FK3 8AG (01324-504690; *email:* grangemouth.library@falkirk.gov.uk); LARBERT LIB, Main St, Stenhousemuir, Larbert, Falkirk, Stirlingshire, FK5 3JX (01324-503590; *email:* larbert.library@falkirk.gov.uk)
Svc Pts: PT: 1 *Mobile:* 2 *AV:* 6 *Computers:* 7 *Internet:* 7 *Other:* HOMEBND SVC, at Lib HQ; LIB SUPPORT FOR SCHOOLS, at Lib HQ
Collns: Aeneas Mackay Colln; Stirling Publishers' Colln *Co-op Schemes:* NLSLS, BLDSC *ILLs:* natl & internatl *Loans:* bks, audios & CD-ROMs/ 4 wks; videos/commercial 2 days, special interest 4 wks *Charges:* audios/50p or £15.75 sub pa; videos/commercial £2 + 80p for 2 days, special interest free *Income Gen:* req/ad 35p if not in stock; res/free; lost ticket/50p; sale of withdrawn stock/bks 30p or 60p, audios 75p, videos £3
Fines: bks, audios & CD-ROMs/ad & OAP 30p pw, ch 5p pw, videos/commercial £2 pd, older & ch's videos 80p pd, special interest 30p pw
Equip: 11 m-readers, 5 m-printers (A4/10p), 3 copiers (A4/10p), 43 computers (all with wd-proc & CD-ROM, 42 with internet), 2 rooms for hire (varies) *Disabled:* text enlarger, 18 text enlarged OPACs, induction loops in all facilities, adaptive PC tech in 5 facilities

Stock:	*1 Apr 2000*	*1 Apr 2001*
ad lend:	212822	210561
ad ref:	43872	44338
ch:	70744	68254
schools:	74825	72804
instns:	1000	1000
audios:	26119	25246
videos:	2702	3145
CD-ROMs:	136	577
periodcls:	785	785

Issues:	*1999-2000*	*2000-01*
ad lend:	1287740	1235396
ch:	279048	256092
schools:	43667	49735
audios:	163862	165123
videos:	49412	43896
CD-ROMs:	-	3041

Acqs:	*1999-2000*	*2000-01*
bks:	49194	45628
AVs:	5692	5595

Acqs: Source: lib suppl *Co-op:* joint contract with two other authorities for bk supply *Offcr-in-Charge:* Libns in charge of each lib
Classn: DDC *Cat: Type:* author, classified, dictionary & title *Medium:* auto *Auto Sys:* DS *Svcs: Extramural:* schools, prisons, old people's homes, housebnd *Info:* online community database *Activs:* ch's activs, bk sales, films, temp exhibs, poetry readings, reading groups, talks, author visits, internet & beginner computer training sessions
Enqs: 163702 (1999-2000); 160147 (2000-01)
Staff: Libns: 28 *Non-Prof:* 55

Inc from:	*1999-2000*
fines etc:	£169110

Exp on:	*1999-2000*
bks:	£574360
AVs:	£71250
elec media:	£4620
salaries:	£1443530
total:	£2093760

Fife

P53 Fife Libraries

Lib HQ (West), Dunfermline Carnegie Lib, 1 Abbot Street, Dunfermline, Fife, KY12 7NL (01383-312605; *fax:* 01383-314314)
Email: DCLib.Admin@fife.gov.uk
Internet: http://www.fifedirect.org.uk/

Local Auth: Fife Council *Pop:* 350400 *Cttee:* Social & Community Development Cttee & Area Community Svcs Cttee *Larger Dept:* Community Svcs *Dept Chief:* Head of Community Svcs: Mr David Somerville *Chief:* Svc Mgr, Arts, Libs & Museums: Mr Iain Whitelaw *Dep:* Libs Policy & Learning Svcs Co-ordinator: Mrs Dorothy Miller MBA, MA, MCLIP (Dorothy.Miller@smtp5.fife.gov.uk) *Other Snr Staff:* Libs Info Svcs Co-ordinator: Ms Aileen McLachlan (aileen.mcLachlan@smtp5.fife.gov.uk); Libs Cultural Svcs Co-ordinator: Mr David Spalding (David.Spalding@smtp5.fife.gov.uk)
Main Libs: Central Area: LIB HQ, 16 East Fergus Pl, Kirkcaldy, Fife, KY1 1XT (01592-412930; *fax:* 01592-412941); KIRKCALDY CENTRAL LIB, War Memorial Gdns, Kirkcaldy, Fife, KY1 1YG (01592-412878; *fax:* 01592-412750; *email:* Kirkcaldy.Library@fife.gov.uk); *East Area:* LIB HQ, County Bldgs, St Catherine St, Cupar, Fife, KY15 4TA (01334-412737; *fax:* 01334-412941); *West Area:* DUNFERMLINE CARNEGIE LIB & LIB HQ, addr as above (01383-312600; *fax:* 01383-312608; *email:* carnegie.library@fife.gov.uk) *Branch Libs: Central Area:* BURNTISLAND LIB, 102 High St, Burntisland, Fife, KY3 9AS (01592-872781; *fax:* 01592-872672; *email:* Burntisland.Library@fife.gov.uk); CADHAM LIB, 12 Cadham Centre, Glenrothes, Fife, KY7 6RU (01592-741784; *email:* Cadham.Library@fife.gov.uk); GLENWOOD LIB, Glenwood Centre, Glenrothes, Fife, KY6 1PA (01592-416840; *fax:* 01592-416843; *email:* Glenwood.Library@fife.gov.uk); LEVEN LIB, 16 Durie St, Leven, Fife, KY8 4HE (01333-592650; *fax:* 01333-592655; *email:* Leven.Library@fife.gov.uk); METHIL LIB, Wellesley Rd, Methil, Leven, Fife, KY8 3PA (01333-592470; *fax:* 01333-592415; *email:* Methil.Library@fife.gov.uk); PITTEUCHAR LIB, Glamis Centre, Glamis Rd,

Glenrothes, Fife, KY7 4RH (01592-771655; *email:* Pitteuchar.Library@fife.gov.uk); ROTHES HALLS LIB, Rothes Halls, Rothes Sq, Glenrothes, Fife, KY7 5NX (01592-415100; *fax:* 01592-415101; *email:* RothesHalls.Library@fife.gov.uk); SINCLAIRTOWN LIB, Lough-borough Rd, Kirkcaldy, Fife, KY1 3DB (01592-417900; *fax:* 01592-417905; *email:* Sinclairtown.Library@fife.gov.uk); TEMPLEHALL LIB, Beauly Pl, Kirkcaldy, Fife, KY2 6EX (01592-412696; *fax:* 01592-412697; *email:* Templehall.Library@fife.gov.uk); *East Area:* ANSTRUTHER LIB, Murray Lib Bldg, Shore St, Anstruther, Fife, KY10 3EA (01333-310111; *email:* anstrutherlibrary@talk21.com); CUPAR LIB, 33 Crossgate, Cupar, Fife, KY15 5AS (01334-412285; *fax:* 01334-412467; *email:* cupar.library@fife.gov.uk); ST ANDREWS LIB, Church Sq, St Andrews, Fife, KY16 9NN (01334-412688); *West Area:* ABBEYVIEW LIB, 38 Abbeyview, Dunfermline, Fife, KY11 4HA (01383-724697; *email:* abbeyview.library@fife.gov.uk); COWDEN-BEATH LIB, 95 High St, Cowdenbeath, Fife, KY4 9QA (01383-510457; *email:* cowdenbeath.library@fife.gov.uk); DALGETY BAY LIB, Regent's Way, Dalgety Bay, Fife, KY11 9UY (01383-318981; *fax:* 01383-318988; *email:* dalgetybay.library@fife.gov.uk); INVERKEITHING LIB, Church St, Inverkeithing, Fife, KY11 1LG (01383-414831; *email:* inverkeithing.library@fife.gov.uk); KELTY LIB, Cocklaw St, Kelty, Fife, KY4 0DD (01383-831809; *email:* kelty.library@fife.gov.uk); KINCARDINE LIB, 2 Keith St, Kincardine, Fife, FK10 4ND (01259-730796; *email:* kincardine.library@fife.gov.uk); LOCHGELLY LIB, 2-4 High St, Lochgelly, Fife, KY5 9JP (01592-780260; *email:* lochgelly.library@fife.gov.uk); LOCHORE LIB, 2 Ballingry Rd, Lochore, Lochgelly, Fife, KY5 8ET (01592-860273; *email:* lochore.library@fife.gov.uk); ROSYTH LIB, Parkgate, Rosyth, Dunfermline, Fife, KY11 2JW (01383-313560; *fax:* 01383-313562; *email:* rosyth.library@fife.gov.uk); TOWNHILL LIB, Main St, Townhill, Dunfermline, Fife, KY12 0EN (01383-724210)
Svc Pts: PT: 26 *Mobile:* 3 *Computers:* 41 *Internet:* 38 *Other:* SCHOOLS LIB SVC, Auchterderran Centre, 14 Woodend Rd, Carden-den, Lochgelly, Fife, KY5 0NE (01592-414612)
Collns: George Reid Colln (illuminated MSS); Murison Burns Colln; Robert Burns (all at Dunfermline Carnegie Lib); Scottish Community Drama Colln (at Sinclairtown Lib); Hay-Fleming Colln (at St Andrews Lib) *ILLs:* internatl *Loans:* bks & audios/3 wks; videos & CD-ROMs/1 wk *Charges:* audios/sub £12 (conc £6), charges 80p (conc 40p) *Income Gen:* req/£1 (conc 50p); lost tickets/£1 *Fines:* bks, audios & videos/ad & oap 32p pw, ch exempt *Equip:* 40 m-readers, 3 m-printers (50p), video viewer, 8 fax (£1), 15 copiers (A4/10p), 210 computers (with internet), 3 rooms for hire

Stock:	*1 Apr 2000*	*1 Apr 2001*
lend:	761982	681325
ref:	46408	47747
AVs:	65310	52572
periodcls:	88	90

Issues:	*1999-2000*	*2000-01*
bks:	2985884	2603957
AVs:	230154	210015

Acqs:	*1999-2000*	*2000-01*
bks:	82356	84426
AVs:	8470	9855

Acqs: Source: lib suppl *Offcr-in-Charge:* Systems Co-ordinator: Mr David Burns
Classn: DDC *Cat: Medium:* auto *Auto Sys:* Talis
Svcs: Extramural: schools, old people's homes, housebnd *Info:* council, community, local hist, family hist *Other:* 15 Open Learning Centres
Activs: ch's activs, bk sales, temp exhibs, poetry readings, author visits, Family Hist Fairs
Enqs: 384393 (1999-2000); 324276 (2000-01)
Staff: Libns: 33 *Non-Prof:* 153.6 ☛

(Fife Libs cont)

Inc from:	1999-2000	2000-01
local govt:	£4795923	£4935429
fines etc:	£300661	£269107
total:	£5096584	£5204536

Exp on:	1999-2000	2000-01
bks:	£835985	£824842
salaries:	£2972390	£3106296
total:	£5096584	£5204536

Proj: refurbishment of St Andrews Lib

Flintshire

P54 Flintshire Library and Information Service

Lib HQ, County Hall, Mold, Flintshire, CH7 6NW (01352-704403; *fax:* 01352-753662)
Email: libraries@flintshire.gov.uk
Internet: http://www.flintshire.gov.uk/

Local Auth: Flintshire County Council *Pop:* 148300 *Larger Dept:* Edu, Ch's Svcs & Rec *Dept Chief:* Dir: Mr John Clutton MScEd *Chief:* Head of Libs, Culture & Heritage: Mr Lawrence Rawsthorne MLib, MCLIP (lawrence_rawsthrone@ flintshire.gov.uk) *Dep:* Principal Libn (Community Libs & Arts): Mrs Sheila Kirby MCLIP (sheila_kirby@flintshire.gov.uk)
Main Libs: REF & INFO CENTRE, at above addr (01352-704411; *fax:* 01352-753662); *Group Libs:* BROUGHTON LIB, Broughton Hall Rd, Broughton, Chester, Cheshire, CH4 0QQ (*tel & fax:* 01244-533727); BUCKLEY LIB, The Precinct, Buckley, Flintshire, CH7 2EF (01244-549210; *fax:* 01244-548850); CONNAH'S QUAY LIB, Wepre Dr, Connah's Quay, Deeside, Flintshire, CH5 4HA (01244-830485; *fax:* 01244-836672); FLINT LIB, Church St, Flint, Flintshire, CH6 5AP (01352-703737; *fax:* 01352-703750); HOLYWELL LIB, North St, Holywell, Flintshire, CH8 7TQ (01352-713157; *fax:* 01352-710144); MOLD LIB, Museum & Gallery, Daniel Owen Centre, Earl Rd, Mold, Flintshire, CH7 1AP (01352-754791; *fax:* 01352-754655) *Branch Libs:* HAWARDEN LIB, The Old Rectory, Rectory Ln, Hawarden, Deeside, Flintshire, CH5 3NN (01244-532926); MANCOT LIB, Mancot Ln, Mancot, Deeside, Flintshire, CH5 2AH (01244-532430); MYNYDD ISA LIB, Community Centre, Mynydd Isa, Mold, Flintshire, CH7 6UH (01352-757903); QUEENSFERRY LIB, Queensferry Campus, Queensferry, Deeside, Flintshire, CH5 1SE (01244-812544; *fax:* 01244-831559)
Svc Pts: PT: 10 *Mobile:* 2 *AV:* 6 *Computers:* 21 *Internet:* 21
Collns: Arthurian Colln (Arthurian legends, at Ref & Info Centre) *Co-op Schemes:* UnityWeb, CONARLS *ILLs:* county, natl & internatl *Loans:* bks, audios & videos/3 wks *Charges:* audios & videos/60p *Income Gen:* req & res/ 60p; lost ticket/£1.50 or 45p *Fines:* all items/ad & oap 10p pd for 1st wk, then rising weekly to maximum of £4.10; under-17s, blind & partially sighted, housebnd exempt *Equip:* 25 m-readers, m-printer (30p per sheet), 7 copiers (10p+), 7 fax (£1.50+), 104 computers (all with wd-proc, internet & CD-ROM), rooms for hire (various) *Disabled:* Aladdin Video Magnifier at Flint Lib *Online:* Dialog, BLAISE *Offcr-in-Charge:* Principal Libn (Community Libs & Arts), as above

Stock:	1 Apr 2000	1 Apr 2001
ad lend:	127256	126724
ad ref:	31101	30994
ch:	71852	69139
audios:	7600	8734
videos:	1241	1621
CD-ROMs:	256	398
periodcls:	95	95

Issues:	1999-2000	2000-01
ad lend:	626472	617649
ch:	184292	173291
audios:	34529	43172
videos:	5575	7492

Acqs:	1999-2000
bks:	16793
AVs:	1505

Acqs: Source: lib suppl, publ & bksellers *Offcr-in-Charge:* Principal Libn (Community Libs & Arts), as above
Classn: DDC *Cat: Type:* author, classified, subj & title *Medium:* auto *Auto Sys:* DS Galaxy 2000 *Svcs: Extramural:* schools, hosps, old people's homes, housebnd *Info:* business, community, Wales European Info Centre *Other:* Open Learning *Activs:* ch's activs, bk sales, temp exhibs, poetry readings
Enqs: 107419 (1999-2000)
Staff: Libns: 13.6 *Non-Prof:* 40

Inc from:	1999-2000	2000-01
fines etc:	£154879	£127296

Exp on:	1999-2000	2000-01
bks:	£177019	£190409
AVs:	£23000	£24132
elec media:	£4096	£4499
salaries:	£940254	£1083311
total:	£1592300	£1670600

Gateshead

P55 Gateshead Arts and Libraries

Gateshead Central Lib, Prince Consort Rd, Gateshead, Tyne & Wear, NE8 4LN (0191-477-3478; *fax:* 0191-477-7454)
Email: enquiries@gateshead.gov.uk
Internet: http://www.gateshead.gov.uk/libraries/

Local Auth: Gateshead Metropolitan Borough Council *Pop:* 198900 *Cttee:* Portfolio memb of Cabinet *Chief:* Head of Cultural Development: Mr W.J. Macnaught MA, MCLIP *Dep:* Cultural Svcs Mgr (Libs, Arts & Tourism): Ms A. Borthwick BA, MCLIP *Other Snr Staff:* Lib Systems Mgr: Mr. Ian Carlton (IanCarlton@ gateshead.gov.uk)
Main Libs: GATESHEAD CENTRAL LIB, addr as above; BIRTLEY LIB, 16 Durham Rd North, Birtley, Chester le Street, Co Durham, DH3 1LE (0191-433-6101; *fax:* 0191-433-6106); BLAYDON LIB, Wesley Ct, Blaydon-on-Tyne, Tyne & Wear, NE21 5BT (0191-433-6201; *fax:* 0191-433-6206); FELLING LIB, Tarlton Cres, Felling, Gateshead, Tyne & Wear, NE10 9HU (0191-469-2906; *fax:* 0191-438-5538); WHICKHAM LIB, St Mary's Green, Whickham, Newcastle upon Tyne, NE16 4DN (0191-488-1262; *fax:* 0191-488-3926) *Branch Libs:* CHOPWELL LIB, Derwent St, Chopwell, Newcastle upon Tyne, NE17 7HZ (01207-561379; *fax:* 01207-560572); CRAWCROOK LIB, Main St, Crawcrook, Ryton, Tyne & Wear, NE40 4BN (0191-413-8164; *fax:* 0191-413-1433); DUNSTON LIB, Ellison Rd, Dunston, Gateshead, Tyne & Wear, NE11 9SS (0191-433-5690; *fax:* 0191-433-5691); LEAM LN LIB, Colegate, Leam Ln, Gateshead, Tyne & Wear, NE10 8PP (0191-469-3049; *fax:* 0191-495-2618); LOBLEY HILL LIB, Lobley Hill Rd, Gateshead, Tyne & Wear, NE11 0AL (*tel & fax:* 0191-460-4149); LOW FELL LIB, 710 Durham Rd, Low Fell, Gateshead, Tyne & Wear, NE9 6HT (*tel & fax:* 0191-487-9360); PELAW LIB, Joicey St, Pelaw, Gateshead, Tyne & Wear, NE10 0QS (0191-438-

0739; *fax:* 0191-469-6325); ROWLANDS GILL LIB, Norman Rd, Rowlands Gill, Tyne & Wear, NE39 1JT (01207-542372; *fax:* 01207-549191); RYTON LIB, Grange Rd, Ryton, Tyne & Wear, NE40 3LT (0191-413-2187); SUNDERLAND RD LIB, Herbert St, Gateshead, Tyne & Wear, NE8 3PA (0191-477-1841; *fax:* 0191-477-8836); WINLATON LIB, Church St, Winlaton, Blaydon-on-Tyne, Tyne & Wear, NE21 6AR (0191-414-3223; *fax:* 0191-414-0052); WREKENTON LIB, Ebchester Ave, Wrekenton, Gateshead, Tyne & Wear, NE9 7LP (*tel & fax:* 0191-487-6272)
Svc Pts: Mobile: 1 *AV:* 6 *Computers:* 18 *Internet:* 18
Collns: 41000 photos of local interest; hist of Gateshead & surrounding areas *Co-op Schemes:* NEMLAC, NCL, NETWORK *Loans:* bks/3 wks; audios & computer software/2 wks; videos/features 1 day, others 2 wks *Charges:* cassettes/40p; CDs/70p; videos/£1-£2.50 *Income Gen:* res/ad £1, conc 50p, ch 10p; lost ticket/£1 *Fines:* bks & audios/ad 12p pd, conc 6p, ch exempt; videos/loan charge *Equip:* 4 m-readers, m-printer (A4/10p), 18 fax (UK £1 pg to send), 18 copiers (A4/10p, A3/20p), clr copier (£1), computers (incl 152 with internet & 4 with CD-ROM), 8 rooms for hire *Disabled:* AIRS svc (talking newspaper), tape recorders, pg turners, magnifying glasses & sheets, bookstands *Online:* FT Profile, ESAIRS (staff use only) *Offcr-in-Charge:* Lib Systems Mgr, as above

Stock:	1 Apr 2000	1 Apr 2001
ad lend:	209521	209168
ad ref:	37052	19717
ch:	116560	109229
audios:	24845	26771
videos:	5748	3574
CD-ROMs:	176	577
periodcls:	214	339

Issues:	1999-2000	2000-01
ad lend:	1564260	1470548
ch:	314126	297090
audios:	148414	159010
videos:	45636	38996

Acqs:	1999-2000	2000-01
bks:	41645	65003
AVs:	4617	3982

Acqs: Source: lib suppl, publ *Offcr-in-Charge:* Lib Systems Mgr, as above
Classn: DDC *Cat: Type:* author, classified, subj & title *Medium:* auto *Auto Sys:* Talis *Svcs: Extramural:* schools, old people's homes, housebnd *Info:* public info sys, cable TV public info sys *Other:* Open Learning, Portcullis (local info sys), arts equip bank *Activs:* ch's activs, bk sales, temp exhibs, poetry readings, reading groups, writers' groups, talks, author visits *Offcr-in-Charge:* Arts Development Mgr: Ms Ednie Wilson BA & Reader Development Mgr: Ms Dorothy Cameron MCLIP
Enqs: 272872 (1999-2000); 343466 (2000-01)
Staff: Libns: 32.5 *Other Prof:* 8 *Non-Prof:* 118

Glasgow

P56 Glasgow City Libraries, Information and Learning

The Mitchell Lib, 201 North Street, Glasgow, G3 7DN (0141-287-2807; *fax:* 0141-287-2936)
Email: lil@cls.glasgow.gov.uk
Internet: http://www.glasgow.gov.uk/

Local Auth: Glasgow City Council *Pop:* 611000 *Cttee:* Cultural & Leisure Svcs Cttee *Larger Dept:* Cultural & Leisure Svcs *Dept Chief:* Dir: Mrs Bridget McConnell *Chief:* Head of Libs, Info & Archvs: Ms Karen Cunningham (karen. cunningham@cls.glasgow.gov.uk) *Other Snr Staff:* Info Svcs Mgr: Mr Gordon Anderson (gordon.anderson@cls.glasgow.gov.uk);

Community Libs Network Mgr: Ms Pamela Tulloch (pamela.tulloch@cls.glasgow.gov.uk); Community Learning Mgr: Ms Jane Edgar (jane.elgar@cls.glasgow.gov.uk) *Main Libs:* MITCHELL LIB, addr as above (0141-287-2999) *Branch Libs:* ANDERSTON LIB, Berkeley St, Glasgow, G3 7DN (*tel & fax:* 0141-287-2872); ANNIESLAND LIB, 833 Crow Rd, Glasgow, G13 (0141-954-5687; *fax:* 0141-954-5548); BAILLIESTON LIB, 141 Main St, Glasgow, G69 6AA (*tel & fax:* 0141-771-2433); BARMULLOCH LIB, 99 Rockfield Rd, Glasgow, G21 3DY (*tel & fax:* 0141-558-6185); BRIDGETON LIB, 23 Landressy St, Glasgow, G40 1BP (*tel & fax:* 0141-554-0217); CARDONALD LIB, 1113 Mosspark Dr, Glasgow, G52 3BU (0141-882-1318; *fax:* 0141-810-5490); CASTLEMILK LIB, 100 Castlemilk Dr, Glasgow, G45 9TN (*tel & fax:* 0141-634-2066); CASTLEMILK TOWER LIB, 55 Machrie Rd, Glasgow, G45 0AR (0141-634-7110; *fax:* 0141-634-7091); COUPER INST LIB, 84 Clarkston Rd, Glasgow, G44 3DA (*tel & fax:* 0141-637-1544); CRANHILL BEACON LIB, 200 Bellrock St, Glasgow, G33 3LZ (0141-774-3736; *fax:* 0141-774-5859); DENNISTOUN LIB, 2a Craigpark, Glasgow, G31 2NA (0141-554-0055; *fax:* 0141-551-9971); DRUMCHAPEL LIB, 65 Hecla Ave, Glasgow, G15 8LX (*tel & fax:* 0141-944-5698); EASTERHOUSE LIB, 65 Shandwick St, Glasgow, G34 9DP (0141-771-5986; *fax:* 0141-771-5643); ELDER PK LIB, 228a Langlands Rd, Glasgow, G51 3TZ (*tel & fax:* 0141-445-1047); GOMA: THE LEARNING GALLERY, Queen St, Glasgow, G1 3HA (0141-248-0143; *fax:* 0141-249-9943); GOVANHILL LIB, 170 Langside Rd, Glasgow, G42 7JU (*tel & fax:* 0141-423-0335); HILLHEAD LIB, 348 Byres Rd, Glasgow, G12 8AP (0141-339-7223; *fax:* 0141-337-2783); IBROX LIB, 31 Midlock St, Glasgow, G51 1SL (0141-427-5831; *fax:* 0141-427-1139); KNIGHTSWOOD LIB, 27 Dunterlie Ave, Glasgow, G13 3BB (*tel & fax:* 0141-959-2041); LANGSIDE LIB, 2 Sinclair Dr, Glasgow, G42 9QE (0141-632-0810; *fax:* 0141-632-8982); MARYHILL LIB, 1508 Maryhill Rd, Glasgow, G20 9AD (*tel & fax:* 0141-946-2348); MILTON LIB, 163 Ronaldsay St, Glasgow, G22 7AP (*tel & fax:* 0141-772-1410); PARKHEAD LIB, 64 Tollcross Rd, Glasgow, G31 4XA (*tel & fax:* 0141-554-0198); PARTICK LIB, 305 Dumbarton Rd, Glasgow, G11 6AB (*tel & fax:* 0141-339-1303); POLLOK LIB & LEISURE CENTRE, Cowglen Rd, Glasgow, G53 6DH (*tel & fax:* 0141-881-3540); POLLOKSHAWS LIB, 50-60 Shawbridge St, Glasgow, G43 1RW (*tel & fax:* 0141-632-3544); POLLOKSHIELDS LIB, 30 Leslie St, Glasgow, G41 2LF (*tel & fax:* 0141-423-1460); POSSILPARK LIB, 127 Allander St, Glasgow, G22 5JJ (*tel & fax:* 0141-336-8110); RIDDRIE LIB, 1020 Cumbernauld Rd, Glasgow, G33 2QS (*tel & fax:* 0141-770-4043); ROYSTON LIB, Royston Rd, Glasgow, G21 2QW (*tel & fax:* 0141-552-1657); SHETTLESTON LIB, 154 Wellshot Rd, Glasgow, G32 7AX (0141-778-1221; *fax:* 0141-778-9004); SIGHTHILL LIB, Fountainwell Sq, Glasgow, G21 1RF (0141-558-6910; *fax:* 0141-558-9087); SPRINGBURN LIB, 179 Ayr St, Glasgow, G21 4BW (*tel & fax:* 0141-558-5559); WHITEINCH LIB, 14 Victoria Park Dr South, Glasgow, G14 9RL (*tel & fax:* 0141-959-1376); WOODSIDE LIB, 343 St George's Rd, Glasgow, G3 3JQ (*tel & fax:* 0141-332-180) *Svc Pts:* Mobile: 3 *AV:* 34 *Computers:* 34 *Internet:* 34 *Other:* SPECIAL COLLNS SECTION, at Mitchell Lib (0141-287-2937/88; email: hist_and_glasgow@cls.glasgow.gov.uk) *Collns:* Scottish Poetry Colln (10600 items); Robert Burns Colln (bks, audio & cuttings, 4600 items); Glasgow Colln (material relating to Glasgow, 22000 items); Early Glasgow Printing Colln (bks printed in Glasgow, 4300 vols); Scottish Regimental Histories Colln (Scottish military hist, 1000 vols); Northern British Locomotive Colln (locomotive illusts, 13000 items); Jeffrey Ref Lib (fine bindings & illustrated works);

Slains Castle Colln (16C-18C); Henry Dyer Bequest (Scottish & Japanese hist & topography); Kidson Colln (folk music & song); Reid Memorial Angling Colln; large colln of medieval MSS & early printed bks; 19C illustrated works; all at the Mitchell Lib *Co-op Schemes:* NLS Co-op Acquisitions, BLDSC, Conspectus in Scotland, SCURL, Glasgow Digital Libs, Glasgow's Story, Access Glasgow, Newsplan Scotland *ILLs:* county, natl & internatl *Loans:* bks/4 wks; audios & videos/1 wk (4 wks for videos if no charge on item); reserved items/2 wks *Charges:* CDs/80p, conc 40p; cassettes/50p, conc 25p; videos/£1.60, conc 80p, ch 60p; DVDs/£3, conc £1.60, ch £1.20 *Income Gen:* req/£2; res/60p, conc 25p, ch exempt; lost ticket/£1.35, ch exempt *Fines:* bks/ad & oap 30p pw; audios/loan charge; videos & DVDs/loan charge (max £9); ch exempt *Equip:* 6 m-readers, m-printers (A4/£1), video viewer, 33 fax (varies), 37 copiers (A4/10p, A3/20p), clr copier (A4/£1, A3/£2), 282 computers (all with wd-proc, 238 with CD-ROM & 221 with internet), 2 piano practice rooms for hire *Disabled:* Visualtek, Kurzweil, Arkenstone, Optacon, Talking Teletext, 4 CCTV/video magnifiers, reading machine, 4 reading lamps, manual brailler, elec braille embosser *Online:* Dialog, Datastar, Questel, FT Profile, Context, Profound, Reuters *Offcr-in-Charge:* Purchasing Mgr: Mr James Meenan (james.meenan@cls.glasgow.gov.uk)

Stock:	1 Apr 2000	1 Apr 2001
ad lend:	679572	673236
ad ref:	1265923	1274751
ch:	215332	213078
audios:	79982	73789
videos:	17844	18900
CD-ROMs:	2725	1732
periodcls:	1927	1810

Issues:	1999-2000	2000-01
ad lend:	2664166	2509431
ch:	609494	553910
audios:	317596	308471
videos:	83756	77629
CD-ROMs:	3650	12336

Acqs:	1999-2000	2000-01
bks:	132180	146985
AVs:	8470	15224

Acqs: Source: lib suppl, publ & bksellers *Co-op:* NLS Co-op Purchase *Offcr-in-Charge:* Stock Development Co-ordinator: Ms Alyson Niven (alyson.niven@cls.glasgow.gov.uk) *Classn:* DDC *Cat: Type:* author, classified, subj & title *Medium:* cards, printed, m-form & auto *Auto Sys:* DS *Svcs: Extramural:* schools, old people's homes, play groups *Info:* business & marketing, patents & bespoke client svcs, careers advice *Other:* Open Univ Study Centre, all libs are becoming lib & lifelong learning centres, incorporating a range of ICT equip & software applications *Activs:* ch's activs, bk sales, temp exhibs, poetry readings, reading groups, talks, author visits *Offcr-in-Charge:* Adult Svcs Co-ordinator: Mr Ronnie Campbell (ronnie.campbell@cls.glasgow.gov.uk) & Yng People's Co-ordinator: Mrs Pamela McClean (pamela.mcclean@cls.glasgow.gov.uk) *Enqs:* 374162 (1999-2000); 330603 (2000-01) *Staff: Libns:* 67 *Non-Prof:* 320

Inc from:	1999-2000	2000-01
fines etc:	£234749	£282977
total:	£311888	£342879

Exp on:	1999-2000	2000-01
bks:	£1296304	£1278783
AVs:	£211055	£235458
elec media:	£14171	-
salaries:	£7243590	£6812759
total:	£13059836	£12513769

Proj: Gorbals Community Lib & Cyber Café; relocation of Springburn Lib to Leisure Centre;

Anniesland Community Lib; Barmulloch Learning & Community Centre; Easterhouse Cultural Campus, incl new lib; Mitchell Lib redevelopment; ongoing lib upgrade proj; development of Lifelong Learning Centres (roll out programme)

Gloucestershire

P57 Gloucestershire County Library Service

County Lib, Arts & Museum Svc HQ, Quayside House, Shire Hall, Gloucester, GL1 2HY (01452-425020; *fax:* 01452-425042)
Email: clams@gloscc.gov.uk
Internet: http://www.gloscc.gov.uk/aboutglo/moreinfo/library.htm

Local Auth: Gloucestershire County Council *Pop:* 565000 *Larger Dept:* Community Svcs *Dept Chief:* Exec Dir: Mr Peter Jones *Chief:* Head of Lib Svcs: Mr Colin Campbell BA, MBA, MCLIP (ccampel@gloscc.gov.uk) *Dep:* Asst County Libn: Mr John Holland BA, MBA, MCLIP (jholland@gloscc.gov.uk) *Other Snr Staff:* Asst County Libn (Development & Client): Ms Elizabeth Dubber
Main (Group) Libs: North: CHELTENHAM LIB, Clarence St, Cheltenham, Gloucestershire, GL50 3JT (*lend:* 01242-522476; *ref:* 01242-582269/515636; *fax:* 01242-510373); *West:* GLOUCESTER LIB, Brunswick Rd, Gloucester, GL1 1HT (*lend:* 01452-426973; *ref:* 01452-426977; *fax:* 01452-521468); *South:* STROUD LIB, Lansdown, Stroud, Gloucestershire, GL5 1BB (01453-751651; *fax:* 01453-762060) *Branch Libs:* BISHOPS CLEEVE LIB, Tobyfield Rd, Bishops Cleeve, Cheltenham, Gloucestershire, GL52 4NN (01242-672217; *fax:* 01242-679684); BROCKWORTH LIB, Moorfield Rd, Brockworth, Gloucester, GL3 4ET (01452-862730; *fax:* 01452-863751); CHARLTON KINGS LIB, Church St, Charlton Kings, Cheltenham, Gloucestershire, GL53 8AR (01242-243413; *fax:* 01242-527074); CHURCHDOWN LIB, Parton Rd, Churchdown, Gloucester, GL3 2AF (01452-712504); CINDERFORD LIB, Belle Vue Rd, Cinderford, Gloucestershire, GL14 2BZ (01594-822581; *fax:* 01594-824907); CIRENCESTER BINGHAM LIB, The Waterloo, Cirencester, Gloucestershire, GL7 2PZ (01285-659813; *fax:* 01285-640449); COLEFORD LIB, Bank St, Coleford, Gloucestershire, GL16 8BA (01594-833351; *fax:* 01594-836175); DURSLEY LIB, May Ln, Dursley, Gloucestershire, GL11 4JH (01453-543059; *fax:* 01453-548230); HESTERS WAY LIB, Goldsmith Rd, Hesters Way, Cheltenham, Gloucestershire, GL51 7RT (01242-514969); HUCCLECOTE LIB, Hucclecote Rd, Hucclecote, Gloucester, GL3 3RT (01452-619577; *fax:* 01452-615124); LONGLEVENS LIB, Church Rd, Longlevens, Gloucester, GL2 0AJ (01452-525952); LYDNEY LIB, Hill St, Lydney, Gloucestershire, GL15 5HW (01594-842769; *fax:* 01594-842377); MATSON LIB, Winsley Rd, Matson, Gloucester, GL4 6NG (01452-524370); MINCHINHAMPTON LIB, School Rd, Minchinhampton, Gloucestershire, GL6 9BP (01453-885497; *fax:* 01453-887793); NAILSWORTH LIB, Old Market, Nailsworth, Gloucestershire, GL6 0DU (01453-832747; *fax:* 01453-835360); NEWENT LIB, High St, Newent, Gloucestershire, GL18 1AS (01531-820447; *fax:* 01531-822240); PRESTBURY LIB, The Burgage, Prestbury, Cheltenham, Gloucestershire, GL52 3DN (01242-234540; *fax:* 01242-222063); QUEDGELEY LIB, Bristol Rd, Quedgeley, Gloucester, GL2 4PE (01452-721233; *fax:* 01452-722726); STONEHOUSE LIB, Elms Rd, Stonehouse, Gloucestershire, GL10 2NP (01453-823176; *fax:* 01453-823597); TEWKESBURY LIB, Sun St, Tewkesbury, Gloucestershire, GL20 5NX (01684-293086; *fax:* 01684-290125); TUFFLEY LIB, Windsor Dr, Tuffley, Gloucester, GL4 0RT (01452-522160); ☞

(Gloucestershire County Lib Svc cont)
UP HATHERLEY LIB, Safeway Centre, Caernarvon Rd, Up Hatherley, Gloucestershire, GL51 5BW (01242-863010; *fax:* 01242-862995); WINCHCOMBE LIB, Back Ln, Winchcombe, Gloucestershire, GL54 5PZ (01242-602772; *fax:* 01242-603043); WOTTON-UNDER-EDGE LIB, Ludgate Hill, Wotton-under-Edge, Gloucestershire, GL12 7JJ (01453-842115; *fax:* 01453-521428)
Svc Pts: PT: 12 *Mobile:* 6 *AV:* 39 *Computers:* 39 *Internet:* 39
Collns: Gloucestershire Colln; Hitchings Colln of Bibles; Hannam Clark Palestine Colln (all at Gloucester Lib); Birchall English Civil War Colln (at Stow Lib); Art Colln (at Cheltenham Lib) *Co-op Schemes:* BLCMP, SWRLS, JFR, CILLA (South West) *ILLs:* county, natl & internatl *Loans:* bks/3 wks; audios & videos/1 wk *Charges:* cassettes/50p; CDs & spkn wd/80p; videos/£1.50-£2; DVDs/£2.50; foreign standards/ £12; drama & music sets/£3 *Income Gen:* res/ ad 70p, mobile libs 50p; lost ticket/ad 70p; business card display/£10 or £6 pa *Fines:* bks/ ad & oap 40p pw, ch 5p pw; audios & videos/loan charge; wide range of exemptions incl disabilities & low income/unemployed *Equip:* 15 m-readers (60p), 9 m-printers (60p), 16 m-cameras (60p per sheet), 5 video viewers, 20 fax (UK £1, higher overseas), 33 copiers (A4/10p), clr copier (A4/ £1.20), 208 computers (all with wd-proc, internet & CD-ROM, printouts 10p per sheet), 39 rooms for hire (various) *Disabled:* minicom, CCTV *Online:* Dialog, BLAISE-LINE, HOLLIE, Blackwell's UnCover, Unity, TelMe, Compuserve, GlosNet *Offcr-in-Charge:* Snr Libn (Stock & Reader Development): Mrs Christine Nicholson (cnichols@gloscc.gov.uk)

Stock:	1 Apr 2000	1 Apr 2001
ad lend:	584917	563532
ad ref:	82464	84312
ch:	179838	185692
schools:	211559	179716
instns:	6340	7082
audios:	45692	47565
videos:	12295	12955
CD-ROMs:	720	740
periodcls:	187	187
archvs:	152779 items	154825 items

Issues:	1999-2000	2000-01
ad lend:	3187634	2973260
ch:	992863	953590
schools:	3087808	2986800
instns:	10992	14278
audios:	216309	212708
videos:	70870	82171
CD-ROMs:	2606	1843

Acqs:	1999-2000	2000-01
bks:	103035	80091
AVs:	11739	10857

Acqs: Source: lib suppl *Offcr-in-Charge:* Snr Libn (Stock & Reader Development): Mrs Christine Nicholson (cnichols@gloscc.gov.uk)
Classn: DDC *Cat: Type:* author, classified, subj & title *Medium:* auto *Auto Sys:* Talis *Svcs: Extramural:* schools, prisons, old people's homes, housebnd, playgroups *Info:* business, GlosNet (auto community svc), Daily Press svc for offcrs & membs, IAG *Other:* Open Learning, Clearvision for ch, special svcs for ethnic community groups, Share (mobile svc for under-8s)

Activs: ch's activs, bk sales, temp exhibs, performances, author visits, special events
Enqs: 554619 (1999-2000); 537228 (2000-01)
Staff: Libns: 47.2 *Other:* 151

Inc from:	1999-2000	2000-01
fines etc:	£529161	£758969

Exp on:	1999-2000	2000-01
bks:	£934620	£808849
AVs:	£115181	£134134
elec media:	£4879	£1257
culture:	£6910	£9562
salaries:	£3853512	£3973121
total:	£6631345	£6953893

Proj: Dursley replacement lib (£881000); Bishops Cleve Lib extension & refurbishment

Gwynedd

P58 Gwynedd Library and Information Service

Gwynedd Council, Council Offices, Shirehall Street, Caernarfon, Gwynedd, LL55 1SH (01286-679504)
Email: library@gwynedd.gov.uk
Internet: http://www.gwynedd.gov.uk/library/

Local Auth: Gwynedd Council *Pop:* 117000 *Cttee:* Edu, Culture & Svcs to Yng People *Larger Dept:* Edu, Culture & Leisure *Dept Chief:* Dir of Edu & Culture: Mr Dafydd Whittall BA *Chief:* Principal Libn: Mr Hywel James BA, MCLIP (HywelJames@gwynedd.gov.uk) *Dep:* Snr Libn: Mr Alun Williams (AlunHWilliams@ gwynedd.gov.uk)
Main Libs: CAENARFON LIB, Lon Pafiliwn, Caernarfon, Gwynedd, LL55 1AS (01286-675944; *email:* LlCaernarfon@gwynedd.gov.uk) *Branch Libs:* BANGOR LIB, Ffordd Gwynedd, Bangor, Gwynedd, LL57 1DT (01248-353479; *email:* LlBangor@gwynedd.gov.uk); BARMOUTH LIB, Station Rd, Abermaw, Gwynedd, LL42 1LU (01341-280258; *email:* LlAbermaw@gwynedd. gov.uk); BLAENAU FFESTEINIOG LIB, Canolfon Maenofferen, Blaenau, Gwynedd, LL41 3DL (01766-830415; *email:* LlBlaenau@gwynedd. gov.uk); DOLGELLAU LIB, Ffordd y Bala, Dolgellau, Gwynedd, LL40 2YF (01341-422771; *email:* LlDolgellau@gwynedd.gov.uk); PORTH-MADOG LIB, Stryd Wesla, Porthmadog, Gwynedd, LL49 9BT (01766-514091; *email:* LlPorthmadog@gwynedd.gov.uk); PWLLHELI LIB, Neuadd Dwyfor, Stryd Penlan, Pwllheli, Gwynedd, LL53 5DN (01758-612089; *email:* LlPwllheli@ gwynedd.gov.uk); TYWYN LIB, Ffordd Neifion, Tywyn, Gwynedd, LL36 9HA (01654-710104; *email:* LlTywyn@gwynedd.gov.uk)
Svc Pts: PT: 10 *Mobile:* 4 *AV:* 17 *Computers:* 17 *Internet:* 17
ILLs: county, natl & internatl *Loans:* bks & audios/3 wks; videos, CD-ROMs & DVDs/1 wk; lang tapes & Open Learning packs/12 wks *Charges:* audios/60p; videos/£1.50-£2; CD-ROMs/£1.50; DVDs/£2; lang tapes/£1 *Income Gen:* req & res/£1; lost ticket/£1 *Fines:* bks/ad & oap 15p pd, ch & registered blind exempt; audios/60p pw; videos/£1.50 pw *Equip:* 6 fax (£1.50), 8 copiers (A4/10p), 83 computers (all with wd-proc, internet & CD-ROM), 4 rooms for hire (£5) *Online:* TALNET Catalogue

Stock:	1 Apr 2000	1 Apr 2001
lend:	273734	274102
ref:	15889	17910
AVs:	15826	16886
periodcls:	-	106

Issues:	1999-2000	2000-01
bks:	771589	723510
AVs:	35251	35439

Acqs:	1999-2000	2000-01
bks:	25942	29143
AVs:	1655	1677

Acqs: Source: lib suppl & bksellers *Co-op:* TALNET (with Anglesey & Conwy) *Offcr-in-Charge:* Mgr (Acqs): Mr Rhion Pritchard *Classn:* DDC *Cat: Type:* author, classified, subj & title *Medium:* auto *Auto Sys:* Talis *Svcs: Extramural:* schools, old people's homes, housebnd, day centres, play groups *Info:* community *Other:* Lifelong Learning Centres
Activs: ch's activs, temp exhibs, poetry readings, reading groups, author visits
Enqs: 225870 (1999-2000)
Staff: Libns: 10 *Non-Prof:* 40

Inc from:	1999-2000
local govt:	£1231996
fines etc:	£76009
total:	£1308005

Exp on:	1999-2000
bks:	£202885
salaries:	£539398
total:	£1308005

Halton

P59 Halton Borough Council Library Service

Culture & Leisure Svcs, Town Hall, Heath Rd, Runcorn, Cheshire, WA7 5TD (0151-424-2061; *fax:* 0151-471-7303)
Internet: http://www.halton.gov.uk/libraries/

Local Auth: Halton Borough Council *Pop:* 118200 *Larger Dept:* Edu & Social Inclusion Directorate *Chief:* Lib Svcs Mgr: Ms Paula Reilly-Cooper (Paula.Reilly-Cooper@halton-borough.gov.uk) *Other Snr Staff:* Snr Libn (Runcorn): Ms Siobhan Kirk (Siobhan.Kirk@halton-borough.gov.uk); Snr Libn (Widnes): Ms Kay Marshall (Kay.Marshall@halton-borough.gov.uk); Specialist Svcs Mgr: Ms Julie Potter (Julie. Potter@halton-borough.gov.uk) & Mr Philip Cooke (Philip.Cooke@halton-borough.gov.uk)
Main Libs: HALTON LEA LIB, Halton Lea, Runcorn, Cheshire, WA7 2PF (01928-715351; *fax:* 01928-790221; *email:* haltonlea.library@halton-borough.gov.uk); WIDNES LIB, Victoria Sq, Widnes, Cheshire, WA8 7QY (0151-423-4818; *fax:* 0151-420-5108; *email:* widnes.library@halton-borough.gov.uk) *Branch Libs:* RUNCORN LIB, Egerton St, Runcorn, Cheshire, WA7 1JL (01928-574495; *fax:* 01928-569461; *email:* runcorn. library@halton-borough.gov.uk); DITTON LIB, Queens Ave, Ditton, Widnes, Cheshire, WA8 8HR (*tel & fax:* 0151-424-2459; *email:* ditton. library@halton-borough.gov.uk)
Svc Pts: Mobile: 1 (with Warrington Borough Council – see **P193**; own svc starting 2003-04) *AV:* 4 *Computers:* 4 *Internet:* 4
Collns: local studies collns at all libs; Railway Colln; Chemical Industry Colln *Co-op Schemes:* BLDSC, Libs North West, ASCEL, NAG, Time To Read, Merseyside Public Libs Partnership, North West SCL, Plus User Group, bk purchasing consortium with Cheshire & Warrington *Loans:* bks & talking bks/3 wks; CDs, videos & CD-ROMs/1 wk; DVDs/2 nights; Learning for Life/3 wks; bookstock videos/3 wks *Charges:* talking bks/£1, conc 50p, ch & reading impaired free; CDs/80p, conc 40p; videos, DVDs & CD-ROMs/ £2, conc £1; Learning for Life/£1 for non-bk items, conc free; bookstock videos/£1, conc free *Income Gen:* res/70p, conc 35p, ch free; BL req/£2.20-£3.20, conc £1.10-£1.60 *Fines:* bks, CDs, Learning for Life materials & bkstock videos/10p pd, conc 5p; videos & CD-ROMs/40p pd, conc 20p; DVDs/£1 per night, conc 50p per night; overdue reminders/30p admin charge; under-16s exempt from fines *Equip:* m-reader/ printer, copiers (10p per sheet), fax (varies), 54 computers (with wd-proc, internet & CD-ROM, access free, printouts 10p-20p), 2 scanners, 3 rooms for hire (£5.50-£5 per hr) *Disabled:* Eazeeread machine, video caption readers,

JAWS, ZoomText, Galileo reading machine, minicom, wheelchair access to all libs *Online:* Companies House, Local info database, Oxford English Dictionary Online & Oxford Ref Online, LearnDirect, Newsbank, London Gazette, Which Online

Stock:	1 Apr 2001
bks:	141579
AVs:	9090

Issues:	1999-2000	2000-01
bks:	-	699294
AVs:	34767	41574

Acqs: Co-op: consortium with Cheshire & Warrington for bk & AV contracts *Offcr-in-Charge:* Specialist Svcs Mgr, as above *Cat: Auto Sys:* Dynix *Svcs: Extramural:* old peoples homes, housebnd, community centres *Info:* community, business, European, careers, advice & guidance *Other:* Lifelong Learning, LearnDirect centres *Activs:* ch's activs, temp exhibs, readers' groups, Chatterbox clubs, SureStart Family Reader Development Workers, Halton Daemons Club *Enqs:* 171720 (2000-01) *Staff:* 38.9 FTE in total

Inc from:	1999-2000	2000-01
fines etc:	£130272	£108978

Exp on:	1999-2000	2000-01
stock & supplies:	-	£429140
salaries:	£711964	£750480

Hampshire

P60 Hampshire Library and Information Service

County Lib HQ, 81 North Walls, Winchester, Hampshire, SO23 8BY (01962-826600; *fax:* 01962-856615)
Email: library@hants.gov.uk
Internet: http://www.hants.gov.uk/library/

Local Auth: Hampshire County Council *Pop:* 1269502 *Cttee:* Rec & Heritage Cttee *Chief:* County Libn: Mr P.H. Turner BA, MCLIP *Dep:* Dep County Libn: Miss A.M. Watkins MCLIP *Main Libs:* BASINGSTOKE LIB, 19-20 Westminster House, Potters Walk, Basingstoke, Hampshire, RG21 7LS (01256-473901; *fax:* 01256-470666; *email:* clnobas@hants.gov.uk); FAREHAM LIB, Osborn Rd, Fareham, Hampshire, PO16 7EN (01329-282715; *fax:* 01329-221551; *email:* clsofhm@hants.gov.uk); LYMINGTON LIB, North Cl, Lymington, Hampshire, SO41 9BW (01590-673050; *fax:* 01590-676172; *email:* clwelym@hants.gov.uk); WINCHESTER LENDING LIB, Jewry St, Winchester, Hampshire, SO23 8RX (01962-862748; *fax:* 01962-841489; *email:* clcewin@hants.gov.uk); WINCHESTER REF LIB, Jewry St, Winchester, Hampshire, SO23 8BY (01962-826666; *fax:* 01962-856615; *email:* clceref@hants.gov.uk) *Branch Libs:* ALDERSHOT LIB, 109 High St, Aldershot, Hampshire, GU11 1DQ (01252-322456; *fax:* 01252-321008; *email:* clnoald@hants.gov.uk); ALRESFORD LIB, 20 Broad St, New Alresford, Hampshire, SO24 9AQ (01962-732706; *email:* clcealr@hants.gov.uk); ALTON LIB, Vicarage Hall, Alton, Hampshire, GU34 1HT (01420-83147; *fax:* 01420-544109; *email:* clcealt@hants.gov.uk); ANDOVER LIB, Chantry Centre, Andover, Hampshire, SP10 1LT (01264-352807; *fax:* 01264-365939; *email:* clceand@hants.gov.uk); BISHOPS WALTHAM LIB, Bank St, Bishops Waltham, Hampshire, SO32 1AN (01489-892871; *email:* clcebwm@hants.gov.uk); BORDON LIB, Forest Centre, Bordon, Hampshire, GU35 0TN (01420-489288; *email:* clcebor@hants.gov.uk); BRIDGMARY LIB, 74 Brewers Ln, Bridgemary, Gosport, Hampshire, PO13 0LA (01329-232940; *email:* clsobri@hants.gov.uk); CHANDLERS FORD LIB, Oakmount Rd,

Chandlers Ford, Eastleigh, Hampshire, SO53 2LH (023-8026-7393; *fax:* 023-8025-1327; *email:* clwechf@hants.gov.uk); CHINEHAM LIB, Chineham Dist Centre, Basingstoke, Hampshire, RG24 8BQ (01256-465643; *email:* clnochi@hants.gov.uk); EASTLEIGH LIB, Swan Centre, Eastleigh, Hampshire, SO50 5SF (023-8061-2513; *fax:* 023-8065-2931; *email:* clweeas@hants.gov.uk); ELSON LIB, 136 Chantry Rd, Gosport, Hampshire, PO12 4NG (023-9258-2162; *email:* clsoels@hants.gov.uk); EMSWORTH LIB, 23 High St, Emsworth, Hampshire, PO10 7AW (01243-372364; *email:* clsoems@hants.gov.uk); FARNBOROUGH LIB, Pinehurst, Farnborough, Hampshire, GU14 7JZ (01252-513838; *fax:* 01252-511149; *email:* clnofnb@hants.gov.uk); FLEET LIB, 236 Fleet Rd, Fleet, Hampshire, GU51 4BX (01252-614213; *fax:* 01252-627242; *email:* fleet.lib@hants.gov.uk); FORDINGBRIDGE LIB, Roundhill, Fordingbridge, Hampshire, SP6 1AQ (01425-652639; *email:* clwefor@hants.gov.uk); GOSPORT LIB, High St, Gosport, Hampshire, PO12 1BT (023-9252-3431; *fax:* 023-9250-1911; *email:* clsogos@hants.gov.uk); HAVANT LIB, Meridian Centre, Havant, Hampshire, PO9 1UN (023-9248-2032; *fax:* 023-9247-2853; *email:* clsohav@hants.gov.uk); HAYLING ISLAND LIB, Elm Grove, Hayling Island, Hampshire, PO11 9EE (023-9246-3921; *email:* clsohay@hants.gov.uk); HEDGE END LIB, 11 Upper Northam Rd, Hedge End, Hampshire, SO30 4DY (01489-783135; *email:* clcehed@hants.gov.uk); HYTHE LIB, Pylewell Rd, Hythe, Hampshire, SO45 6AP (023-8084-3574; *fax:* 023-8020-7859; *email:* clwehth@hants.gov.uk); LEE-ON-THE-SOLENT LIB, High St, Lee-on-the-Solent, Hampshire, PO13 9BZ (023-9255-0311; *email:* clsolee@hants.gov.uk); LEIGH PK LIB, 50 Pk Parade, Leigh Pk, Havant, Hampshire, PO9 5AB (023-9248-4519; *fax:* 023-9249-8918; *email:* clsolei@hants.gov.uk); LOCKSWOOD LIB, Lockswood Centre, Locks Heath Dist Centre, Hampshire, SO31 6DX (01489-583729; *email:* clsolcw@hants.gov.uk); NEW MILTON LIB, Gore Rd, New Milton, Hampshire, BH25 6RW (01425-613668; *fax:* 01425-620761; *email:* clwenwm@hants.gov.uk); PETERSFIELD LIB, 27 The Sq, Petersfield, Hampshire, GU32 3HH (01730-263451; *fax:* 01730-268121; *email:* clcepet@hants.gov.uk); PORTCHESTER LIB, West St, Portchester, Fareham, Hampshire, PO16 9TX (023-9237-9210; *email:* clsopch@hants.gov.uk); RINGWOOD LIB, Christchurch Rd, Ringwood, Hampshire, BH24 1DW (01425-474198; *fax:* 01425-475913; *email:* clwerin@hants.gov.uk); ROMSEY LIB, Station Rd, Romsey, Hampshire, SO51 8DN (01794-513299; *fax:* 01794-517838; *email:* clwerom@hants.gov.uk); SOUTH HAM LIB, Paddock Rd, South Ham, Basingstoke, Hampshire, RG22 6QB (01256-465102; *email:* clnosoh@hants.gov.uk); STUBBINGTON LIB, Stubbington Ln, Fareham, Hampshire, PO14 2PP (01329-663775; *fax:* 01329-663458; *email:* clsostu@hants.gov.uk); TADLEY LIB, Mulfords Hill, Tadley, Basingstoke, Hampshire, RG26 3JE (01189-814595; *fax:* 01189-811465; *email:* clnotad@hants.gov.uk); TOTTON LIB, Lib Rd, Totton, Southampton, Hampshire, SO40 3RS (023-8086-2203; *fax:* 023-8066-0203; *email:* clwetot@hants.gov.uk); WATERLOOVILLE LIB, The Precinct, Waterlooville, Hampshire, PO7 7DT (023-9225-4626; *fax:* 023-9226-3720; *email:* clsowvl@hants.gov.uk); YATELEY LIB, School Ln, Yateley, Hampshire, GU46 6NL (01252-873880; *fax:* 01252-890731; *email:* clnoyat@hants.gov.uk) *Svc Pts: PT:* 15 *Mobile:* 14 + 6 school lib svc vehicles *AV:* 41 *Computers:* 54 *Internet:* 54 *Collns:* BSI complete set (at 2 libs); NJRF (at HQ); Naval Colln (at Gosport Lib); Bible Colln (at HQ); HMSO Colln (at HQ); Hampshire Colln (at Winchester Lib); Military Colln (at Aldershot Lib); Aeronautical Colln (at Farnborough Lib) *Co-op Schemes:* HATRICS, Well-Worth Reading, NJFR, SWRLS, CBC *ILLs:* county, natl & internatl

Loans: bks & audios/3 wks; videos/popular 1 wk, info 3 wks *Charges:* cassettes/50p; CDs/£1; videos, DVDs & CD-ROMs/£1-£3.50 *Income Gen:* req & res/85p, not in stock £1.85; lost computer ticket/ad £1.50, ch 50p *Fines:* bks, audios & info videos/ad & oap 10p pd (max £4), ch 1p pd (max 40p); popular videos, DVDs & CD-ROMs/loan charge *Equip:* 150 m-readers, 15 m-printers (A4/30p, A3/60p), 21 fax (various), 42 copiers (A4/10p, A3/20p), computers (incl wd-proc, internet & CD-ROM), rooms for hire (various) *Disabled:* CCTV

Stock:	1 Apr 2000	1 Apr 2001
lend:	1580040	1552176
ref:	201737	201898
AVs:	148367	162899
periodcls:	728	712

Issues:	1999-2000	2000-01
bks:	11482526	11626742
AVs:	1086993	614272

Acqs:	1999-2000	2000-01
bks:	176989	195936
AVs:	28444	40322

Acqs: Source: lib suppl *Classn:* DDC *Cat: Type:* author, classified, subj & title *Medium:* m-form *Auto Sys:* DS Galaxy *Svcs: Extramural:* schools, prisons, hosps, old people's homes, housebnd *Info:* business, local pts, community, careers, edu *Activs:* ch's activs, bk sales, temp exhibs, bk fairs, author visits, talks *Enqs:* 1061933 (1999-2000); 1046248 (2000-01) *Staff: Libns:* 145.7 *Non-Prof:* 388.3

Inc from:	1999-2000	2000-01
local govt:	£13162000	£13599000
fines etc:	£1401000	£1427000
total:	£14563000	£15026000

Exp on:	1999-2000	2000-01
stock:	£2572000	£2642000
salaries:	£9199000	£9633000
total:	£14563000	£15026000

Hartlepool

P61 Hartlepool Borough Libraries

Hartlepool Central Lib, 124 York Rd, Hartlepool, Cleveland, TS26 9DE (01429-272905; *fax:* 01429-275685)
Email: reflib@hartlepool.gov.uk
Internet: http://www.hartlepool.gov.uk/services/libs/

Local Auth: Hartlepool Borough Council *Pop:* 92100 *Cttee:* Cabinet, under Lifelong Learning & Skills Portfolio *Larger Dept:* Community Svcs *Dept Chief:* Dir: Mrs Janet Barker MCLIP *Chief:* Borough Libn: Mrs Susan Atkinson BA, MCLIP, DipRSA (susan.atkinson@hartlepool.gov.uk) *Main Libs:* CENTRAL LIB, addr as above *Branch Libs:* OGGY FURZE LIB, Stockton Rd, Hartlepool, Cleveland, TS25 5BQ (01429-274095; *fax:* 01429-283401); OWTON MANOR LIB, Wynyard Rd, Hartlepool, Cleveland, TS25 3LQ (01429-272835; *fax:* 01429-283403); SEATON CAREW LIB, Station Ln, Seaton Carew, Hartlepool, Cleveland, TS25 1BN (01429-269808; *fax:* 01429-283405); THROSTON GRANGE LIB, Glamorgan Grove, Throston, Hartlepool, Cleveland, TS26 0XR (01429-263199; *fax:* 01429-283408); WEST VIEW LIB, Miers Ave, Hartlepool, Cleveland, TS24 9JQ (01429-268288; *fax:* 01429-283406; *email:* west.view.library@hartlepool.gov.uk) *Svc Pts: PT:* 1 *Mobile:* 2 *AV:* 8 *Computers:* 7 *Internet:* 7 *Collns:* Health Info Svc (at Cromwell St, Hartlepool, funded by former Cleveland Boroughs); Subtitled Videos Colln (300+ titles, administered on behalf of former Cleveland Boroughs); Reminiscence Therapy Colln ☛

(Hartlepool Borough Libs cont)
Co-op Schemes: joint arrangements for archvs & schools lib svc **ILLs:** county, natl & internatl **Loans:** bks/4 wks; audios/2 wks **Charges:** CDs/80p; spkn wd/35p-£1.40; lang courses/£1-40; Open Learning materials/£2.75 **Income Gen:** res/50p, conc 32p; lost tickets/£1.10, conc 60p; sale of old stock; sale of local hist bks **Fines:** bks/ad & oap 6p pd, ch exempt; audios/loan charge; visually impaired exempt from spkn wd charges **Equip:** 7 m-readers, 4 m-printers (45p per sheet), 3 copiers (10p), 8 fax (£1.50 per sheet), 34 computers (incl 10 with wd-proc, 26 with CD-ROM & 28 with internet), 2 rooms for hire (various) **Disabled:** CCTV, Tieman mini-reader

Stock:	1 Apr 2000	1 Apr 2001
ad lend:	158129	152208
ad ref:	20072	20099
ch:	47060	47281
audios:	15316	14609
videos:	439	567
CD-ROMs:	216	98

Issues:	1999-2000	2000-01
ad lend:	601630	565451
ch:	158881	143902
audios:	33029	32790
videos:	1023	1163

Acqs:	1999-2000	2000-01
bks:	35069	40479
AVs:	1891	2697

Acqs: Source: lib suppl & publ **Co-op:** subtitled videos for deaf people **Offcr-in-Charge:** Accessions & Req Offcr: Miss Pat Stearman (pat.stearman@hartlepool.gov.uk) **Classn:** DDC **Cat:** Type: author, classified, subj & title **Medium:** auto **Auto Sys:** Talis **Svcs: Extramural:** old people's homes, housebnd, day centres, playgroups **Info:** business, community, local studies, genealogical, statistics, European, health **Other:** Open Learning **Activs:** ch's activs, bk sales, temp exhibs, reading groups **Enqs:** 129350 (1999-2000); 108288 (2000-01) **Staff:** Libns: 12 Non-Prof: 36.6

Inc from:	2000-01
local govt:	£1715984
fines etc:	£81839
total:	£1797823

Exp on:	2000-01
bks:	£295359
AVs:	£28248
elec media:	£8150
salaries:	£857202
total:	£1797823

Herefordshire

P62 Herefordshire Libraries and Information Service

Admin HQ, Shirehall, Hereford, HR1 2HY (01432-359830; *fax:* 01432-260744)
Internet: http://www.libraries.herefordshire.gov.uk/

Local Auth: Herefordshire Council *Pop:* 169300 *Chief:* Libs & Info Mgr: Mr Mark Warren *Main (Group) Libs:* HEREFORD LIB, Broad St, Hereford, HR4 9AU (01432-272456; *fax:* 01432-359668; *email:* herefordlibrary@herefordshire.gov.uk); LEOMINSTER LIB, 8

Buttercross, Leominster, Herefordshire, HR6 8BN (01432-383290; *fax:* 01568-616025; *email:* leominsterlibrary@herefordshire.gov.uk) *Branch (Local) Libs:* KINGTON LIB, 64 Bridge St, Kington, Herefordshire, HR5 3DJ (01544-230427; *email:* kingtonlibrary@herefordshire.gov.uk); LEDBURY LIB, The Homend, Ledbury, Herefordshire, HR9 1BT (01531-632133; *email:* ledburylibrary@herefordshire.gov.uk); ROSS-ON-WYE LIB, Cantilupe Rd, Ross-on-Wye, Hereford-shire, HR9 7AN (01432-383280; *fax:* 01432-383282; *email:* rosslibrary@herefordshire.gov.uk) *Svc Pts:* PT: 5 *Mobile:* 3 *AV:* 10 *Computers:* 10 *Internet:* 10 *Other:* SCHOOLS LIB SVC, Shire-hall, Hereford, HR1 2HY (01432-260661; *fax:* 01432-260744; *email:* sls@herefordshire.gov.uk) *Collns:* A. Watkins & F.C. Morgan photo negative colln (at Hereford Lib); John Masefield Colln (at Ledbury Lib); local hist collns (each group & local lib); beekeeping **Co-op Schemes:** WMRLS **Loans:** bks/4 wks; audios/2 wks; videos/1 wk **Charges:** audios/£1-1.50; videos/£1-£2 **Income Gen:** res/ad 50p, ch 25p, £2 for out of county; lost ticket/ad £1, ch 1st replacement free, then 50p **Fines:** bks/ad 12p pd, ch 6p pd; audios & videos/loan charge; registered blind & handicapped exempt **Equip:** m-readers, m-printers (50p per pg), faxes, copiers (A4/10p), 60 computers (incl wd-proc & internet), rooms for hire (varies) **Disabled:** Alphavision reader

Stock:	1 Apr 2000	1 Apr 2001
lend:	206156	188369
ref:	11672	44574
AVs:	11943	13242
periodcls:	110	114

Issues:	1999-2000	2000-01
bks:	1257595	1146117
AVs:	47903	48120

Acqs:	1999-2000	2000-01
bks:	23039	21729
AVs:	1274	1331

Classn: DDC **Cat:** Auto Sys: Talis **Svcs: Extramural:** schools, prisons, old people's homes, housebnd **Other:** Open Learning (at Ross-on-Wye Lib) **Activs:** ch's activs, bk sales, temp exhibs, poetry readings, readers' groups **Enqs:** 90869 (1999-2000); 92711 (2000-01) **Staff:** Libns: 14.8 Non-Prof: 35.2

Inc from:	1999-2000	2000-01
fines etc:	£123389	£137662

Exp on:	1999-2000	2000-01
stock & supplies:	£408085	£453943
salaries:	£821622	£836796
total:	£1671037	£1795030

Hertfordshire

P63 Hertfordshire Libraries

Central Support Svcs, New Barnfield, Travellers Ln, Hatfield, Hertfordshire, AL10 8XG (01438-737333; *fax:* 01707-281514)
Internet: http://www.hertsdirect.org/infoadvice/libraries/

Local Auth: Hertfordshire County Council *Pop:* 1060200 *Cttee:* Community Svcs Cttee *Larger Dept:* Community Info (Libs) *Dept Chief:* Dir: Mr A. Robertson *Chief:* Libs Operations Mgr: Mrs Glenda Wood *Other Snr Staff:* Asst Dir: Mrs H. Ebrahim DipLib, BIBL; Info Svcs Mgr: Mr R.V. Breakey MCLIP; Yng People's & Community Svcs Mgr: Ms C. Hall BA, MCLIP; Head of Property & Operations: Mrs M. Hilton BA, DipLib, MCLIP; Stock Mgr: Mrs S. Valentine BA(Hons), MCLIP
Main Libs: CENTRAL RESOURCES LIB, at above addr (01438-737333; *fax:* 01707-281514; *email:* CentralResources.Library@hertscc.gov.uk); HEMEL HEMPSTEAD CENTRAL LIB, Combe St, Hemel Hempstead, Hertfordshire, HP1 1HJ;

ST ALBANS CENTRAL LIB, The Maltings, St Albans, Hertfordshire, AL1 3JQ; STEVENAGE CENTRAL LIB, Southgate, Stevenage, Hertfordshire, SG1 1HD; WATFORD CENTRAL LIB, Hempstead Rd, Watford, Hertfordshire, WD17 3EU *Branch Libs:* ABBOTS LANGLEY LIB, High St, Abbots Langley, Hertfordshire, WD5 0AP; BALDOCK LIB, Simpson Dr, Baldock, Hertfordshire, SG7 6DH; BERKHAMSTED LIB, Kings Rd, Berkhamsted, Hertfordshire, HP4 3BD; BISHOP'S STORTFORD LIB, The Causeway, Bishop's Stortford, Hertfordshire, CM23 2EJ; BOREHAMWOOD LIB, Elstree Way, Borehamwood, Hertfordshire, WD6 1JX; BOVINGDON LIB, Bovingdon High St, Boving-don, Hemel Hempstead, Hertfordshire, HP3 0HJ; BUNTINGFORD LIB, 77 High St, Buntingford, Hertfordshire, SG9 9AE; BUSHEY LIB, Sparrows Herne, Bushey, Watford, Hertfordshire, WD23 1FA; CHESHUNT LIB, Turners Hill, Cheshunt, Waltham Cross, Hertfordshire, EN8 8LB; CHORLEYWOOD LIB, Lower Rd, Chorleywood, Rickmansworth, Hertfordshire, WD3 5LB; CRANBORNE LIB, Mutton Ln, Potters Bar, Hertfordshire, EN6 3AA; CROXLEY GREEN LIB, Barton Way, Croxley Green, Rickmansworth, Hertfordshire, WD3 3HB; CUFFLEY LIB, Maynards Pl, Station Rd, Cuffley, Potters Bar, Hertfordshire, EN6 4HU; CUNNINGHAM LIB, 207 Cell Barnes Ln, St Albans, Hertfordshire, AL1 5PX; FLEETVILLE LIB, 237 Hatfield Rd, St Albans, Hertfordshire, AL1 4TB; GOFFS OAK LIB, Goffs Ln, Goffs Oak, Waltham Cross, Hertford-shire, EN7 5ET; HARPENDEN LIB, Vaughan Rd, Harpenden, Hertfordshire, AL5 4EN; HATFIELD LIB, Queensway, Hatfield, Hertfordshire, AL10 0LT; HERTFORD LIB, Old Cross, Hertford, SG14 1RF; HITCHIN LIB, Paynes Pk, Hitchin, Hertfordshire, SG5 1EW; HODDESDON LIB, 98a High St, Hoddesdon, Hertfordshire, EN11 8HD; KINGS LANGLEY LIB, The Nap, Kings Langley, Hertfordshire, WD4 8ET; KNEBWORTH LIB, 7 St Martins Rd, Knebworth, Hertfordshire, SG3 6ER; LETCHWORTH LIB, Broadway, Letchworth, Hertfordshire, SG6 3PF; LONDON COLNEY LIB, Community Centre, Caledon Rd, London Colney, St Albans, Hertfordshire, AL2 1PU; MARSHALS-WICK LIB, The Ridgeway, St Albans, Hertford-shire, AL4 9TU; NORTH WATFORD LIB, St Albans Rd, Watford, Hertfordshire, WD2 5RE; OAKMERE LIB, High St, Potters Bar, Hertford-shire, EN6 5BZ; OXHEY LIB, Bridlington Rd, South Oxhey, Watford, WD1 6AG; RADLETT LIB, 1 Aldenham Ave, Radlett, Hertfordshire, WD7 8HL; REDBOURN LIB, Lamb Ln, Redbourn, St Albans, Hertfordshire, AL3 7BP; RICKMANS-WORTH LIB, High St, Rickmansworth, Hertford-shire, WD3 1EH; ROYSTON LIB, Market Hill, Royston, Hertfordshire, SG8 9JN; SAWBRIDGE-WORTH LIB, The Forebury, Sawbridgeworth, Hertfordshire, CM21 9BD; TRING LIB, High St, Tring, Hertfordshire, HP23 4AF; WALTHAM CROSS LIB, 123 High St, Waltham Cross, Hertfordshire, EN8 7AN; WARE LIB, 87 High St, Ware, Hertfordshire, SG12 9AD; WELWYN GDN CITY LIB, Campus West, Welwyn Gdn City, Hertfordshire, AL8 6AE; WHEATHAMPSTEAD LIB, Memorial Hall, Marford Rd, Wheatham-stead, St Albans, Hertfordshire, AL4 8AY; WOOD-HALL LIB, Cole Green Ln, Welwyn Gdn City, Hertfordshire, AL7 3JA
Svc Pts: PT: 4 *Mobile:* 10 *Computers:* 52 *Internet:* 52 *Other:* HERTFORDSHIRE ARCHVS & LOCAL STUDIES, County Hall, Pegs Ln, Hertford, SG13 8EJ (see **A204**); LOCAL GOVT INFO SVC, County Hall, Hertford, SG13 8EJ *ILLs:* county, natl & internatl *Loans:* bks & spkn wd/3 wks; videos, music & CD-ROMs/1 wk; music sets/1-6 months; play sets/up to 6 months; linguaphone/13 wks *Charges:* music/75p or £1.50; spkn wd/60p or £1.20 (ch free); DVDs/feature films £2; videos/£1; CD-ROM/£2; orchestral & vocal scores & play sets/£1.50 per month (incl res fee); linguaphone/£7.50;

exemptions & conc on some charges for oap, ch, disabled & low income; specialist svcs to blind, deaf & housebnd free *Income Gen:* res/£1, +£3 for items outside Hertfordshire; lost ticket/£1.50; rsrch/1st 15 min free, addl £15+VAT for 15 min, or £60+VAT per hr *Fines:* bks/ad 15p pd 1st wk (max 75p), wks 2-10 75p pw (max £7.50), ch & oap 5p pd 1st wk (max 25p), 25p pw thereafter (max £2.50); audios, videos, CD-ROMs & DVDs/ loan charge; music & play sets returned incomplete/£10 + replacement costs; registered disabled exempt, conc for some users *Equip:* 40 m-readers, 11 m-printers, 52 fax (£1 to send, 50p to receive), 52 copiers (A4/10p), computers (incl wd-procs, internet & CD-ROM), rooms for hire (varies with user) *Disabled:* minicoms, hearing loops, CCTV print readers *Online:* Kompass, Dun & Bradstreet, Tradesmarkscan, ABI Inform; Biosis, CAB Abstracts, Enviroline; TextLine, PTS Prompt, Infomat; Inspec, Ei Compendex; Tenders Elec Daily, Spicers Centre for Europe, Spearhead, Delphes Business & Industry News (cost of time & printouts + 10%)

Stock:	1 Apr 2000	1 Apr 2001
bks:	1718864	1638197

Issues:	1999-2000	2000-01
bks:	8462669	-
others:	1051344	1066562

Acqs:	1999-2000	2000-01
bks:	185654	235379

Acqs: Source: lib suppl *Offcr-in-Charge:* Stock Mgr, as above
Classn: DDC *Cat: Type:* author, classified & title *Medium:* auto *Auto Sys:* ALS *Svcs: Extramural:* schools, prisons, old people's homes, housebnd *Info:* Business Info Pt, European Info Relay, InfoCentre (local & community database), all at Central Resources Lib *Other:* Open Learning, cassette svc for the blind, video svc for the deaf, OFL, LLIPs *Activs:* ch's activs, bk sales, temp exhibs, reading groups *Offcr-in-Charge:* Head of Communications: Mr B. Mayes *Enqs:* 2089984 (1999-2000); 1973362 (2000-01) *Staff: Libns:* 109 *Non-Prof:* 326

Inc from:	1999-2000
fines etc:	£1261293

Exp on:	1999-2000
bks:	£1567061
AVs:	£238623
salaries:	£8049136
total:	£14543607

Highland

P64 Highland Library and Information Services

Lib Support Unit, 31a Harbour Rd, Inverness, IV1 1UA (01463-235713; *fax:* 01463-236986)
Email: libraries@highland.gov.uk
Internet: http://www.highland.gov.uk/

Local Auth: The Highland Council *Pop:* 208600 *Larger Dept:* Edu, Culture & Sport *Dept Chief:* Dir: Mr Bruce Robertson *Chief:* Lib, Info & Archvs Mgr: Mr Christopher Philips BA, DipLib, MCLIP
Branch Libs: ALNESS LIB, Averon Centre, High St, Alness, Ross & Cromarty, IV17 0QB (01349-882674; *fax:* 01349-883587; *email:* alness.library@highland.gov.uk); BROADFORD LIB, Old Industrial Est, Broadford, Isle of Skye, IV49 9AB (01471-820075; *fax:* 01471-820076; *email:* broadford.library@highland.gov.uk); BRORA LIB, Gower St, Brora, Sutherland, KW9 6PD (01408-621128; *fax:* 01408-622064; *email:* brora.library@highland.gov.uk); CULLODEN LIB, Keppoch Rd, Culloden, Inverness, IV1 7LL (01463-792531; *fax:* 01463-793162; *email:* culloden.library@highland.gov.uk); DINGWALL LIB, Old Academy Bldgs, Tulloch St, Dingwall, Ross & Cromarty, IV15 9JZ

(01349-863163; *fax:* 01349-865239; *email:* dingwall.library@highland.gov.uk); DORNOCH LIB, Carnegie Bldgs, High St, Dornoch, Sutherland, IV25 3SH (*tel & fax:* 01862-811079; *email:* dornoch.library@highland.gov.uk); FORTROSE LIB, Fortrose Academy, Fortrose, Ross & Cromarty, IV10 8TW (*tel & fax:* 01381-622235; *email:* fortrose.library@highland.gov.uk); FORT WILLIAM LIB, Airds Crossing, Fort William, Inverness-shire, PH33 6EU (01397-703552; *fax:* 01397-703538; *email:* fortwilliam.library@highland.gov.uk); GAIRLOCH LIB, Gairloch High School, Gairloch, Ross & Cromarty, IV21 2BP (01445-712469; *fax:* 01445-712438; *email:* gairloch.library@highland.gov.uk); GLEN URQUHART LIB, Drumnadrochit, Inverness-shire, IV63 6XA (01456-459223; *email:* glenurquhart.library@highland.gov.uk); GRANTOWN ON SPAY LIB, 20 High St, Grantown on Spey, Morayshire, PH26 3HB (*tel & fax:* 01479-873175; *email:* grantownonspey.library@highland.gov.uk); INVERGORDON LIB, High St, Invergordon, Ross & Cromarty, IV18 0DG (*tel & fax:* 01349-852698; *email:* invergordon.library@highland.gov.uk); INVERNESS LIB, Farraline Pk, Inverness, IV1 1NH (01463-236463; *fax:* 01463-237001; *email:* inverness.library@highland.gov.uk); KINLOCHLEVEN LIB, The Visitor's Centre, Linnhe Rd, Kinlochleven, Argyll, PA40 4RP (*tel & fax:* 01855-831663; *email:* kinlochleven.library@highland.gov.uk); NAIRN LIB, 68 High St, Nairn, Inverness, IV12 4UA (01667-458506; *fax:* 01667-458548; *email:* nairn.library@highland.gov.uk); PORTREE LIB, Bayfield Rd, Portree, Isle of Skye, IV51 9EL (01478-612697; *fax:* 01478-613314; *email:* portree.library@highland.gov.uk); TAIN LIB, Stafford St, Tain, Ross & Cromarty, IV19 1AZ (*tel & fax:* 01862-892391; *email:* tain.library@highland.gov.uk); THURSO LIB, Davidsons Ln, Thurso, Caithness, KW14 7AF (01847-893237; *fax:* 01847-896114; *email:* thurso.library@highland.gov.uk); ULLAPOOL LIB, Ullapool High School, Mill St, Ullapool, Ross & Cromarty, IV26 2UN (*tel & fax:* 01854-612543; *email:* ullapool.library@highland.gov.uk); WICK LIB, Sinclair Ter, Wick, Caithness, KW1 5AB (01955-602864; *fax:* 01955-603000; *email:* wick.library@highland.gov.uk)
Svc Pts: PT: 22 *Mobile:* 8 *AV:* 30 *Computers:* 41 *Internet:* 41
Collns: Kirk Session Lib (hist & theology); Fraser-Mackintosh Colln (local hist); Gaelic Soc Lib; Scottish Community Drama Assoc (all at Inverness Lib); Mowat Colln (local hist, at Wick Lib); Miller Inst Lib (at Thurso Lib) *ILLs:* county, natl & internatl *Loans:* bks, audios & videos/4 wks *Charges:* cassettes/75p; CDs/£1.30; videos/ad £1.50, ch £1 *Income Gen:* req/ad 50p; lost ticket/£2 *Fines:* bks, audios & software/ad 15p pd open; videos/30p pd open; ch's materials & oaps exempt *Equip:* m-readers, m-printers, fax, copiers, clr copier, computers (incl wd-proc, internet & CD-ROM), rooms for hire

Stock:	1 Apr 2000	1 Apr 2001
ad lend:	202731	195542
ad ref:	37553	39628
ch:	95377	94482
audios:	8628	9083
videos:	5538	6452
periodcls:	106	186

Issues:	1999-2000	2000-01
ad lend:	1118286	1090333
ch:	392225	387471
audios:	29387	30954
videos:	26680	28189

Acqs:	1999-2000	2000-01
bks:	42702	51783
AVs:	3008	3494

Acqs: Source: lib suppl & publ
Classn: DDC *Cat: Type:* author, classified & title *Medium:* auto *Auto Sys:* Talis *Svcs: Extramural:* schools, old people's homes, housebnd *Info:* community, careers, Scottish

Parliament *Other:* archvs, genealogy, Open Learning *Activs:* ch's activs, bk sales, temp exhibs, poetry readings
Enqs: 91092 (1999-2000); 129818 (2000-01) *Staff: Libns:* 21 *Non-Prof:* 71.6

Inc from:	1999-2000	2000-01
local govt:	£2606205	£3184273
fines etc:	£146020	£177310
total:	£2752225	£3361583

Exp on:	1999-2000	2000-01
bks:	£421998	£458711
AVs:	£56948	£30664
salaries:	£1545517	£1604134
total:	£2752225	£3361583

Inverclyde

P65 Inverclyde Libraries

Central Lib, Clyde Sq, Greenock, Renfrewshire, PA15 1NA (01475-712323; *fax:* 01475-712334/9)
Email: library.central@inverclyde.gov.uk
Internet: http://www.inverclyde.gov.uk/

Local Auth: Inverclyde Council *Pop:* 89000
Chief: Acting Libs Mgr: Miss Sandra MacDougall MA, MCLIP (Sandra.MacDougall@inverclyde.gov.uk)
Main Libs: CENTRAL LIB, addr as above
Branch Libs: BOGLESTONE LIB, Dubbs Rd, Port Glasgow, Renfrewshire, PA14 5UD (01475-715620; *email:* Library.Boglestone@inverclyde.gov.uk); EAST BRANCH LIB, 30 Bawhirley Rd, Greenock, Renfrewshire, PA15 2BH (01475-715622; *email:* Library.EastBranch@inverclyde.gov.uk); GOUROCK LIB, Kempock Pl, Gourock, Renfrewshire, PA19 1QU (01475-632861; *fax:* 01475-637803; *email:* Library.Gourock@inverclyde.gov.uk); INVERKIP LIB, Inverkip School, Inverkip, Renfrewshire, PA16 0AY (01475-521557; *email:* Library.Inverkip@inverclyde.gov.uk); KILMACOLM LIB, Kilmacolm Inst, Kilmacolm, Renfrewshire, PA13 4HA (01505-873489; *fax:* 01505-873935; *email:* Library.Kilmacolm@inverclyde.gov.uk); PORT GLASGOW LIB, Fore St, Port Glasgow, Renfrewshire, PA14 5EX (01475-715629; *fax:* 01475-715632; *email:* Library.PortGlasgow@inverclyde.gov.uk); SOUTH WEST BRANCH LIB, Barr's Cottage, Greenock, Renfrewshire, PA16 9HG (01475-715667; *email:* Library.SWBranch@inverclyde.gov.uk); WATT LIB, 9 Union St, Greenock, Renfrewshire, PA16 8JH (01475-715628; *email:* Library.Watt@inverclyde.gov.uk)
Svc Pts: AV: 5 *Computers:* 5 *Internet:* 5
ILLs: county, natl & internatl *Loans:* bks & audios/3 wks; videos/1 wk *Charges:* CDs/ad 50p, oap 30p; videos/ad 90p, oap 60p *Income Gen:* req & res/ad 40p, oap 30p, ch 20p; lost ticket/ad £1, oap & ch 50p; ILLs/ad £3, oap £1.50 *Fines:* bks & audios/ad 5p pd (max £1 per item), ch 20p (teenage £1) for final overdue notice; videos/ad 50p pd (max £3 per item), teenage £1 for final overdue notice; oap & registered blind exempt *Equip:* 6 m-readers, m-printer (40p per pg), copiers (A4/10p, A3/20p), 4 fax (UK 50p per pg, internatl £1, receiving 50p), 27 computers (incl 14 with wd-proc & CD-ROM, 10 with internet)

Stock:	1 Apr 2000	1 Apr 2001
ad lend:	88326	86988
ad ref:	23175	22415
ch:	40144	34722
audios:	8411	8454
videos:	1445	1389
periodcls:	53	53

Issues:	1999-2000	2000-01
ad lend:	312548	301521
ch:	61002	58091
audios:	132818	30061
videos:	incl in audios	12638

(Inverclyde Libs cont)

Acqs:	1999-2000	2000-01
bks:	10647	10615
AVs:	1926	1492

Acqs: *Source:* lib suppl, publ & bksellers
Classn: DDC *Cat: Type:* author, classified, subj & title *Medium:* auto *Svcs:* Dynix *Extramural:* schools, prisons, hosps, old people's homes, housebnd, day centres, play groups *Info:* community *Activs:* ch's activs, bk sales, temp exhibs, author visits
Enqs: 42380 (2000-01)
Staff: *Libns:* 6 *Non-Prof:* 45

Inc from:	1999-2000	2000-01
local govt:	£1168759	£1288016
fines etc:	£60300	£38419
total:	£1432300	£1326435

Exp on:	1999-2000	2000-01
bks:	£141600	£104455
AVs:	£27900	£23876
salaries:	£904900	£805555
total:	£1432300	£1326435

Isle of Wight

P66 Isle of Wight Library Service

Lib HQ, Parkhurst Rd, Newport, Isle of Wight, PO30 5TX (01983-825717; *fax:* 01983-528047)
Email: tblackmore@iwight.gov.uk
Internet: http://www.iwight.gov.uk/

Local Auth: Isle of Wight Council **Pop:** 125000
Cttee: Edu & Community Development Cttee
Larger Dept: Edu & Community Development
Dept Chief: Dir: Mr Alan Kaye **Chief:** Head of Libs: Mr Tim Blackmore MCLIP (email as above)
Branch Libs: BEMBRIDGE LIB, Church Rd, Bembridge, Isle of Wight, PO35 5NA (*tel & fax:* 01983-873102); COWES LIB, Beckford Rd, Cowes, Isle of Wight, PO31 7SG (*tel & fax:* 01983-293341); EAST COWES LIB, The York Centre, 11 York Ave, East Cowes, Isle of Wight, PO32 6QY (*tel & fax:* 01983-293019); FRESH-WATER LIB, 41 School Green Rd, Freshwater, Isle of Wight, PO40 9AP (*tel & fax:* 01983-752377); LORD LOUIS LIB, Orchard St, Newport, Isle of Wight, PO30 1LL (01983-527655); RYDE LIB, 101 George St, Ryde, Isle of Wight, PO33 2JE (*tel & fax:* 01983-562170); SANDOWN LIB, High St, Sandown, Isle of Wight PO36 8AF (*tel & fax:* 01983-402748); SHANKLIN LIB, Victoria Ave, Shanklin, Isle of Wight, PO37 6PG (*tel & fax:* 01983-863126); VENTNOR LIB, High St, Ventnor, Isle of Wight, PO38 1LZ (01983-852039)
Svc Pts: *PT:* 2 *Mobile:* 3 *AV:* 5 *Other:* COUNTY RECORDS OFFICE (see **A392**); SCHOOLS & CH'S SVC; 3 Prison Libs
Co-op Schemes: HATRICS **ILLs:** county, natl & internatl **Loans:** bks/3 wks; audios & videos/1 wk **Charges:** audios/70p; videos/£1-£2 **Income Gen:** req & res/80p; lost ticket/£2, £1 conc **Fines:** bks/ad & oap 15p pd, ch 5p pd; audios/15p pd; videos/20p-40p pd; exempt from spkn wd & lang course loan charges: registered blind, partly sighted, registered disabled, housebnd, mobile svc **Equip:** 12 m-readers, m-printer, 11 fax (£1 per sheet), 11 copiers (A4/10p, A3/20p), 2 clr copiers (A4/£1, A3/£1.50), 3 wd-procs, 2 internet terminals **Disabled:** Kurzweil, Robotron Reader, Eazee Reader

Stock:	1 Apr 2000	1 Apr 2001
ad lend:	171152	201649
ad ref:	18545	14829
ch:	64278	67411
schools:	26354	25650
instns:	23347	20058
audios:	11735	13273
videos:	5314	6743
CD-ROMs:	481	785
periodcls:	449	355

Issues:	1999-2000	2000-01
ad lend:	1004384	919273
ch:	239047	229756
audios:	46034	46383
videos:	57893	62499
CD-ROMs:	1608	3022

Acqs:	1999-2000	2000-01
bks:	29287	23826
AVs:	3041	3250

Acqs: *Source:* lib suppl *Offcr-in-Charge:* Stock Mgr: Mr John English
Classn: DDC *Cat: Type:* author, classified, subj & title *Medium:* auto *Auto Sys:* DS *Svcs:* *Extramural:* schools, prisons, hosps, old people's homes, housebnd *Info:* local govt, European, ad literacy *Other:* Open Learning *Activs:* ch's activs, bk sales, temp exhibs
Enqs: 113239 (1999-2000); 120095 (2000-01)
Staff: *Libns:* 9 *Non-Prof:* 40

Inc from:	1999-2000	2000-01
fines etc:	£153981	£162649

Exp on:	1999-2000	2000-01
bks:	£227089	£235826
AVs:	£37737	£44325
elec media:	£550	£5056
salaries:	£852295	£886730
total:	£1606465	£1525564

Kent

P67 Kent Arts and Libraries

Arts & Libs HQ, Springfield, Maidstone, Kent, ME14 2LH (01622-696505; *fax:* 01622-696450)
Internet: http://www.kent.gov.uk/

Local Auth: Kent County Council **Pop:** 1335200
Larger Dept: Community Svcs Div **Chief:** Head of Arts & Libs: Ms Cath Anley MCLIP
Main (Group) Libs: COUNTY CENTRAL LIB, Springfield, Maidstone, Kent, ME14 2LH (01622-696511; *fax:* 01622-696494; *email:* countycentrallibrary@kent.gov.uk); ASHFORD LIB, Church Rd, Ashford, Kent, TN23 1QX (01233-620649; *fax:* 01233-620295; *email:* ashfordlibrary@kent.gov.uk); CANTERBURY LIB, High St, Canterbury, Kent, CT1 2JF (01227-463608; *fax:* 01227-768338; *email:* canterburylibrary@kent.gov.uk); DARTFORD LIB, Central Pk, Dartford, Kent, DA1 1EU (01322-221133; *fax:* 01322-278271; *email:* dartfordlibrary@kent.gov.uk); DEAL LIB, Broad St, Deal, Kent, CT14 6ER (01304-374726; *fax:* 01304-380821; *email:* deallibrary@kent.gov.uk); FOLKESTONE LIB, 2 Grace Hill, Folkestone, Kent, CT20 1HD (01303-850123; *fax:* 01303-242907; *email:* folkestonelibrary@kent.gov.uk); GRAVESEND LIB, Windmill St, Gravesend, Kent, DA12 1BE (01474-352758; *fax:* 01474-320284; *email:* gravesendlibrary@kent.gov.uk); MAID-STONE LIB, St Faith's St, Maidstone, Kent, ME14 1LH (01622-752344; *fax:* 01622-761699; *email:* maidstonelibrary@kent.gov.uk); MARGATE LIB, Cecil Sq, Margate, Kent, CT9 1RE (01843-223626; *fax:* 01843-293015; *email:* margatelibrary@kent.gov.uk); SEVENOAKS LIB, Buckhurst Ln, Sevenoaks, Kent, TN13 1LQ (01732-453118; *fax:* 01732-742682; *email:* sevenoakslibrary@kent.gov.uk); SITTINGBOURNE LIB, Central Ave, Sittingbourne, Kent, ME10 4AH (01795-476545; *fax:* 01795-428376; *email:* sittingbournelibrary@kent.gov.uk); TONBRIDGE LIB, Avebury Ave,

Tonbridge, Kent, TN9 1TG (01732-352754; *fax:* 01732-358300; *email:* tonbridgelibrary@kent.gov.uk); TUNBRIDGE WELLS LIB, Mount Pleasant Rd, Tunbridge Wells, Kent, TN1 1NS (01892-522352; *fax:* 01892-514657; *email:* tunbridgewellslibrary@kent.gov.uk) **Branch Libs:** ALLINGTON LIB, Castle Rd, Allington, Kent, ME16 0PR (*tel & fax:* 01622-683435); AYLESHAM LIB, Aylesham Community Centre, Ackholt Rd, Aylesham, Kent, CT3 3AJ (01304-841050; *fax:* 01304-840388); BEARSTED LIB, The Green, Bearsted, Maidstone, Kent, ME14 4DN (*tel & fax:* 01622-739774); BIRCHINGTON LIB, Alpha Rd, Birchington, Kent, CT7 9EG (01843-841883; *fax:* 01843-842206); BOROUGH GREEN LIB, High St, Borough Green, Sevenoaks, Kent, TN15 8BJ (*tel & fax:* 01732-884404); BROADSTAIRS LIB, The Broadway, Broadstairs, Kent, CT10 2BS (01843-862994; *fax:* 01843-861938); CHERITON LIB, Cheriton High St, Folkestone, Kent, CT19 4HB (01303-275163; *fax:* 01303-275049); CLIFTONVILLE LIB, Queen Elizabeth Ave, Cliftonville, Margate, Kent, CT9 3JX (01843-226979; *fax:* 01843-229031); COLDHARBOUR LIB, Coldharbour Rd, Northfleet, Kent, DA11 8AE (01474-534787; *fax:* 01474-361139); COXHEATH LIB, Heath Rd, Coxheath, Maidstone, Kent, ME17 4EH (*tel & fax:* 01622-744130); CRANBROOK LIB, Carriers Rd, Cranbrook, Kent, TN17 3JT (01580-712463; *fax:* 01580-715101); DOVER LIB, Dover Discovery Centre, Market Sq, Dover, Kent, CT16 1PH (01304-204241; *fax:* 01304-225914); EDENBRIDGE LIB, Church St, Edenbridge, Kent, TN8 5BD (*tel & fax:* 01732-862600); FAVERSHAM LIB, Newton Rd, Faversham, Kent, ME13 8DY (01795-532448; *fax:* 01795-591229); FLEETDOWN LIB, Swaledale Rd, Dartford, Kent, DA2 6JZ (*tel & fax:* 01322-225546); GREENHILL LIB, Greenhill Rd, Herne Bay, Kent, CT6 7PN (01227-374288); HARTLEY LIB, Ash Rd, Hartley, Longfield, Kent, DA3 8EL (*tel & fax:* 01474-704403); HAWKHURST LIB, Rye Rd, Highgate, Hawkhurst, Cranbrook, Kent, TN18 4EY (*tel & fax:* 01580-752064); HERNE BAY LIB, 124 High St, Herne Bay, Kent, CT6 5JY (01227-374896; *fax:* 01227-741582); HIGHAM LIB, Villa Rd, Higham, Kent, ME3 7BS (*tel & fax:* 01474-823822); HILDENBOROUGH LIB, Riding Ln, Hildenborough, Tonbridge, Kent, TN11 9HX (*tel & fax:* 01732-838729); HIVE HOUSE LIB, 10-11 The Hive, Hive Ln, Northfleet, Gravesend, Kent, DA11 9DE (*tel & fax:* 01474-534681); HYTHE LIB, 1 Stade St, Hythe, Kent, CT21 6BD (01303-267111; *fax:* 01303-230232); KEMSING LIB, Dippers Cl, Kemsing, Sevenoaks, Kent, TN15 6QD (*tel & fax:* 01732-762199); KINGS FARM LIB, Sun Ln, Gravesend, Kent, DA12 5HR (01474-365491); LARKFIELD LIB, Martin Sq, Larkfield, Maidstone, Kent, ME20 6QW (01732-842339; *fax:* 01732-521455); LENHAM LIB, 11 The Limes, The Sq, Lenham, Maidstone, Kent, ME17 2PQ (*tel & fax:* 01622-859140); LONGFIELD LIB, 49 Main Rd, Longfield, Kent, DA3 7QT (*tel & fax:* 01474-706507); LYMINGE LIB, 7-9 Station Rd, Lyminge, Folkestone, Kent, CT18 8HS (*tel & fax:* 01303-862180); MADGINFORD LIB, Egremont Rd, Madginford, Bearsted, Kent, ME15 8LH (*tel & fax:* 01622-730631); MEOPHAM LIB, Wrotham Rd, Meopham, Gravesend, Kent, DA13 0AH (01474-814636; *fax:* 01474-815371); MINSTER-IN-SHEPPEY LIB, Worcester Cl, Minster-in-Sheppey, Sheerness, Kent, ME12 3NP (01795-872363; *fax:* 01795-877355); MINSTER-IN-THANET LIB, 4a Monkton Rd, Minster-in-Thanet, Kent, CT12 4EA (01843-821442; *fax:* 01843-825869); NEW ASH GREEN LIB, New Ash Green, Longfield, Kent, DA3 8QT (*tel & fax:* 01474-872506); NEW ROMNEY LIB, 82 High St, New Romney, Kent, TN28 8AU (01797-363245; *fax:* 01797-361760); NEWINGTON LIB, Newington Rd, Ramsgate, Kent, CT12 6PX (*tel & fax:* 01843-594533); OTFORD LIB, High St, Otford, Sevenoaks, Kent, TN14 5PH (*tel & fax:* 01959-522488); PADDOCK WOOD LIB, 9 Commercial Rd, Paddock Wood,

Tonbridge, Kent, TN12 6EN (01892-832006; *fax:* 01892-832065); PEMBURY LIB, The Hop House, Henwood Green Rd, Pembury, Tunbridge Wells, Kent, TN2 4HS (*tel & fax:* 01892-822278); QUEENBOROUGH LIB, Railway Ter, Queenborough, Kent, ME11 5AY (*tel & fax:* 01795-663695); RAMSGATE LIB, Guildford Lawn, Ramsgate, Kent, CT11 9AY (01843-593532; *fax:* 01843-852692); RIVERHEAD LIB, 31 London Rd, Riverhead, Sevenoaks, Kent, TN13 2BU (01732-459218); RIVERVIEW PK LIB, The Alma, Leander Dr, Riverview Pk, Gravesend, Kent, DA12 4NG (01474-564181); RUSTHALL LIB, High St, Rusthall, Tunbridge Wells, Kent, TN4 8RZ (*tel & fax:* 01892-521667); SANDGATE LIB, James Morris Ct, High St, Sandgate, Folkestone, Kent, CT20 3RR (*tel & fax:* 01303-248563); SANDWICH LIB, 13 Market St, Sandwich, Kent, CT13 9DA (01304-613819; *fax:* 01304-614580); SHEERNESS LIB, Russell St, Sheerness, Kent, ME12 1PL (01795-662618; *fax:* 01795-583035); SHEPWAY LIB, 17 Northumberland Ct, Northumberland Rd, Shepway, Maidstone, Kent, ME15 7LW (*tel & fax:* 01622-751488); SHOWFIELDS LIB, Showfields Rd, Tunbridge Wells, Kent, TN2 5PR (*tel & fax:* 01892-532620); SNODLAND LIB, 15-17 High St, Snodland, Kent, ME6 5DA (*tel & fax:* 01634-243776); SOUTHBOROUGH LIB, Yew Tree Rd, Southborough, Tunbridge Wells, Kent, TN4 0AB (01892-529808; *fax:* 01892-540442); STANHOPE LIB, Stanhope Sq, Ashford, Kent, TN23 5SH (*tel & fax:* 01233-627591); STAPLEHURST LIB, The Parade, High St, Staplehurst, Kent, TN12 0LA (01580-891929; *fax:* 01580-890148); STURRY LIB, Chafy Cres, Sturry, Canterbury, Kent, CT2 0BA (01227-711479; *fax:* 01227-710768); SUMMERHOUSE DR LIB, Summerhouse Dr, Bexley, Kent, DA5 2EE (*tel & fax:* 01322-527604); SUTTON-AT-HONE LIB, Main Rd, Sutton-at-Hone, Dartford, Kent, DA4 9HS (*tel & fax:* 01322-863683); SWALECLIFFE LIB, 78 Herne Bay Rd, Swalecliffe, Kent, CT5 2LX (*tel & fax:* 01227-792645); SWANLEY LIB, London Rd, Swanley, Kent, BR8 7AE (01322-662570; *fax:* 01322-614519); TEMPLE HILL LIB, Temple Hill Sq, Dartford, Kent, DA1 5HY (*tel & fax:* 01322-226013); TENTERDEN LIB, 55 High St, Tenterden, Kent, TN30 6BD (01580-762558; *fax:* 01580-766990); TONBRIDGE NORTH LIB, 5 York Parade, Tonbridge, Kent, TN10 3NP (*tel & fax:* 01732-351918); WEST MALLING LIB, 22-24 High St, West Malling, Kent, ME19 6QR (*tel & fax:* 01732-842504); WESTERHAM LIB, London Rd, Westerham, Kent, TN16 1BD (*tel & fax:* 01959-562326); WESTGATE LIB, Minster Rd, Westgate-on-Sea, Kent, CT8 8BP (*tel & fax:* 01843-831017); WHITSTABLE LIB, 31-33 Oxford St, Whitstable, Kent, CT5 1DB (01227-273309; *fax:* 01227-771812); WOOD AVE LIB, Wood Ave, Folkestone, Kent, CT19 6HS (01303-254226; *fax:* 01303-227051)
Svc Pts: PT: 27 *Mobile:* 12 *AV:* 55 *Computers:* 106 *Internet:* 106 *Other:* CENTRE FOR KENTISH STUDIES (see **A362**); SCHOOL LIB SVC, Gibson Dr, West Malling, Kent, ME19 4AL (01622-605216; *fax:* 01622-605221)
Collns: English lit; music; performing arts; ancient lit (all at County Central Lib); Ashrail Railways Colln (at Ashford Lib) *Co-op Schemes:* SCL (South East Region), KILN *ILLs:* county, natl & internatl *Loans:* bks/4 wks; audios/2 wks; videos/2 days or 1 wk *Charges:* CDs/70p; cassettes/50p; videos/£1-£2.50 *Income Gen:* req & res/75p; lost ticket/50p *Fines:* bks & spkn wd/ad 15p pd, ch & OAP 2p pd; videos & audio/loan charge; housebnd, mobile lib users, users of branches open less than 10 hrs pw, registered blind & partially sighted exempt *Equip:* m-readers (free), m-printers, video viewers, fax, copiers (A4/10p, A3/15p-20p), clr copiers, computers (with wd-proc, internet & CD-ROM) *Disabled:* Kurzweil, Dolphin software, textphones, Eazee Readers, TV readers, hearing loops, CCTV

Stock:	1 Apr 2000	1 Apr 2001
lend:	1675853	1819191
ref:	161089	204912
AVs:	175463	170017

Issues:	1999-2000	2000-01
bks:	7974448	7716937
AVs:	985825	1046670

Acqs:	1999-2000	2000-01
bks:	141004	170581
AVs:	36791	34454

Acqs: Source: lib suppl & bksellers *Co-op:* CBC *Offcr-in-Charge:* Bibliographical Svcs Mgr: Mr Ken Jarvis
Classn: DDC *Cat: Type:* author, subj & title *Medium:* auto *Auto Sys:* DS *Svcs: Extramural:* schools, prisons, hosps, old people's homes, housebnd, sheltered housing *Info:* business, European, local govt, edu, careers *Other:* Open Learning *Activs:* ch's activs, bk sales, temp exhibs, poetry readings, reading groups, writers' groups, talks, author visits *Offcr-in-Charge:* organised at local level
Enqs: 894881 (1999-2000); 925181 (2000-01)
Staff: Libns: 135 *Non-Prof:* 457.3

Inc from:	1999-2000	2000-01
local govt:	£16577766	£15418824
fines etc:	£1728384	£1886361
total:	£18306150	£17305185

Exp on:	1999-2000	2000-01
stock:	£1153152	£1447924
salaries:	£9868992	£10374984
total:	£18306150	£17305185

Kingston upon Hull

P68 Kingston upon Hull City Libraries and Archives

Central Lib, Albion Street, Kingston upon Hull, Humberside, HU1 3TF (01482-210000; *fax:* 01482-616827)
Email: lending.library@hullcc.gov.uk
Internet: http://www.hullcc.gov.uk/libraries/

Local Auth: Kingston upon Hull City Council *Pop:* 254300 *Larger Dept:* Learning Svcs *Dept Chief:* Group Dir: Mr Peter Fletcher *Chief:* Head of Community Learning: Mr Brian Chapman MCLIP *Dep:* Principal Libs Offcr: Mrs Jo Edge (jo.edge@hullcc.gov.uk) *Other Snr Staff:* Central Svcs Mgr: Mrs Michelle Alford (michelle.alford@hullcc.gov.uk)
Main Libs: HULL CENTRAL LIB, addr as above *Branch Libs:* ANLABY PK LIB, The Greenway, Anlaby High Rd, Hull, Humberside, HU4 6TX (01482-505506); AVENUES LIB, 76 Chanterlands Ave, Hull, Humberside, HU5 3TS (01482-331280); BRANSHOLME LIB, Dist Centre, Goodhart Rd, Bransholme, Hull, Humberside, HU7 4EF (01482-331234); FRED MOORE LIB, Wold Rd, Derringham Bank, Hull, Humberside, HU5 5UN (01482-331239); GARDEN VILLAGE LIB, Shopping Centre, Gdn Village, Hull, Humberside, HU8 9QE (01482-781723); GIPSYVILLE LIB, Gipsyville Multi Purpose Centre, Hessle Rd, Hull, Humberside, HU4 6JA (01482-616973); GREENWOOD AVE LIB, Greenwood Ave, Hull, Humberside, HU6 9RU (01482-331257); HARRY LEWIS LIB, Annandale Rd, Hull, Humberside, HU9 5HD (01482-331264); INGS LIB, Savoy Rd, Hull, Humberside, HU8 0TX (01482-331250); JAMES RECKITT LIB, Holderness Rd, Hull, Humberside, HU9 1EA (01482-320015); KINGSWOOD HIGH LIB, Wawne Rd, Hull, Humberside, HU7 4WR (01482-331275); LONGHILL LIB, Shannon Rd, Longhill Est, Hull, Humberside, HU8 9RW (01482-331361); NORTHERN LIB, Beverley Rd, Hull, Humberside, HU3 1UP (01482-328397); PRESTON RD LIB, Preston Rd, Hull, Humberside, HU9 5UZ (01482-376266); WESTERN LIB, The Boulevard, Hessle Rd, Hull, Humberside, HU3 3ED (01482-320399)
Svc Pts: PT: 1 *AV:* 5 *Computers:* at all branches

Other: BUSINESS INFO CENTRE, at Central Lib; community centre
Collns: BSI; EPIC; Anthony Hedges Colln; Napoleonic Colln (Napoleon); Backgrnd Colln (bks publ 1740-59); Quakers deposit; mountaineering deposit (all at Arts & Humanities Lib); Winifred Holtby Colln; Slavery Colln; Whaling Colln; Andrew Marvell Colln; Fish Street Methodist Church deposit; Trades Council Papers (all at Local Studies Lib) *Co-op Schemes:* PRISM *ILLs:* county, natl & internatl *Loans:* bks, audios & CD-ROMs/3 wks; videos & DVDs/1 wk *Charges:* talking bks/45p; CDs/75p; videos/ £1.75; DVDs/£2; CD-ROMs/£2.50 *Income Gen:* res/25p; lost tickets/£1.50 *Fines:* bks/10p pd up to 40p, then 40p pw; audios/25p pd up to 75p, then 75p pw; videos/loan charge; CD-ROMs/50p pd up to £2.50, then £2.50 pw; ch, asylum seekers, blind & partially sighted exempt *Equip:* 32 m-readers, 3 m-printers (30p per pg), 17 copiers (10p), clr copier (A4/£1, A3/£1.50), 6 fax, 2 video viewers, computers (incl wd-procs, internet & CD-ROM), room for hire (varies) *Disabled:* Kurzweil, CCTV, computer with OCR scanner *Online:* Dialog, Dialtech, Companies House

Stock:	1 Apr 2000	1 Apr 2001
ad lend:	382415	300910
ad ref:	345179	339066
ch:	124448	101293
audios:	26417	24119
videos:	3489	3388
CD-ROMs:	478	409

Issues:	1999-2000	2000-01
ad lend:	1260970	1033508
ch:	274374	266002
schools:	101751	-
audios:	68027	43927
videos:	9295	10861
CD-ROMs:	748	1097

Acqs:	1999-2000	2000-01
bks:	24579	27896
AVs:	2639	3903

Acqs: Source: lib suppl, publ & bksellers *Co-op:* PRISM
Classn: DDC *Cat: Type:* author, classified, subj & title *Medium:* cards & auto *Auto Sys:* ALS *Svcs: Extramural:* schools, prisons, hosps, old people's homes, housebnd, play groups *Info:* business, community, genealogical, ch's *Other:* transcription svc, Open Learning, study support *Activs:* ch's activs, bk sales, films, temp exhibs, poetry readings, reading groups, writers' groups, talks, author visits, music events
Enqs: 499720 (1999-2000); 502060 (2000-01)
Staff: Libns: 29.5 *Non-Prof:* 125.1
Proj: refurbishment of Central Lib

Kirklees

P69 Kirklees Libraries

Cultural Svcs HQ, Red Doles Ln, Huddersfield, W Yorkshire, HD2 1YF (01484-226300; *fax:* 01484-226342)
Email: cultural.services@kirklees.gov.uk
Internet: http://www.kirkleesmc.gov.uk/

Local Auth: Kirklees Metropolitan Council *Pop:* 395100 *Larger Dept:* Cultural Svcs *Dept Chief:* Head of Cultural Svcs: Mr Jonathan Drake MA, AMA, MILAM, MIFA *Chief:* Asst Head of Cultural Svcs (Libs): Mr Rob Warburton BA(Hons), MCLIP (rob.warburton@kirklees.gov.uk)
Main Libs: BATLEY LIB, Market Pl, Batley, W Yorkshire, WF17 5DA (01924-326021; *tel:* 01924-326308; *email:* batley.library@kirklees.gov.uk); DEWSBURY LIB, Dewsbury Retail Pk, Railway St, Dewsbury, W Yorkshire, WF12 8EA (01924-325080; *fax:* 01924-325086; *email:* dewsbury.library@kirklees.gov.uk);

(Kirklees Libs cont)

HOLMFIRTH LIB, 47 Huddersfield Rd, Holmfirth, Huddersfield, W Yorkshire, HD9 3JH (01484-222430; fax: 01484-222435; email: holmfirth. library@kirklees.gov.uk); HUDDERSFIELD LIB, Princess Alexandra Walk, Huddersfield, W Yorkshire, HD1 2SU (lend: 01484-221959/60; ref: 01484-221967/8; fax: 01484-221952; email: hudlib.office@kirklees.gov.uk) **Branch Libs:** ALMONDBURY LIB, Stock Walk, Almondbury, Huddersfield, W Yorkshire, HD5 8XB (01484-223183; email: almondbury.library@kirklees. gov.uk); BIRSTALL LIB, Market St, Birstall, Batley, W Yorkshire, WF17 9EN (01924-326227; fax: 01924-326236; email: birstall.library@kirklees. gov.uk); CLECKHEATON LIB, Whitcliffe Rd, Cleckheaton, W Yorkshire, BD19 3DX (01274-335170; fax: 01274-335171; email: cleckheaton. library@kirklees.gov.uk); DENBY DALE LIB, Wakefield Rd, Denby Dale, Huddersfield, W Yorkshire, HD8 8RX (01484-222904; email: denbydale.library@kirklees.gov.uk); GOLCAR LIB, 12 Town End, Golcar, Huddersfield, W Yorkshire, HD7 4QD (01484-222138; email: golcar. library@kirklees.gov.uk); HECKMONDWIKE LIB, Walkley Ln, Heckmondwike, W Yorkshire, WF16 0LY (01924-325637; fax: 01924-325634; email: heckmondwike.library@kirklees.gov.uk); HONLEY LIB, West Ave, Honley, Huddersfield, W Yorkshire, HD9 6HF (01484-222340; email: honley. library@kirklees.gov.uk); KIRKBURTON LIB, 17 Turnshaws Rd, Kirkburton, Huddersfield, W Yorkshire, HD8 0RT (01484-222710; email: kirkburton. library@kirklees.gov.uk); LEPTON LIB, 56 Highgate Ln, Lepton, Huddersfield, W Yorkshire, HD8 0HB (01484-222711; email: lepton.library@ kirklees.gov.uk); LINDLEY LIB, Lidget St, Lindley, Huddersfield, W Yorkshire, HD3 3JP (01484-222172; fax: 01484-222139; email: lindley.library@ kirklees.gov.uk); MARSDEN LIB, Mechanics Hall, Peel St, Marsden, Huddersfield, W Yorkshire, HD7 6BW (01484-222555; email: marsden. library@kirklees.gov.uk); MELTHAM LIB, Carlisle St, Meltham, Huddersfield, W Yorkshire, HD9 4AG (01484-222606; email: meltham.library@ kirklees.gov.uk); MIRFIELD LIB, Eastthorpe Lodge, Huddersfield Rd, Mirfield, W Yorkshire, WF14 8AN (01924-326470; fax: 01924-326472; email: mirfield.library@kirklees.gov.uk); RAVENS-THORPE LIB, The Park, Huddersfield Rd, Ravensthorpe, Dewsbury, W Yorkshire, WF13 3JR (01924-325040; fax: 01924-324948; email: ravensthorpe.library@kirklees.gov.uk); SKELMANTHORPE LIB, 24 Commercial Rd, Skelmanthorpe, Huddersfield, W Yorkshire, HD8 9DA (01484-222905; fax: 01484-222957; email: skelmanthorpe.library@kirklees.gov.uk); SLAITH-WAITE LIB, 8 Britannia Rd, Slaithwaite, Huddersfield, W Yorkshire, HD7 5HG (01484-222500; email: slaithwaite.library@kirklees.gov.uk) **Svc Pts:** PT: 3 Mobile: 7 AV: 21 Computers: 23 Internet: 16 Other: COMMUNITY INFO & COMMUNICATION TECH CENTRE, Princess Rd, Chickenley, Dewsbury, W Yorkshire, WF12 8QT (01924-324961) **Co-op Schemes:** YADLOGIS, YLI **ILLs:** county, natl & internatl **Loans:** bks & talking bks/3 wks; music/1 wk; videos/blockbusters 1 day, others 1 wk; CD-ROMs/1 wk **Charges:** CDs/60p-£1.20; talking bks/£1; videos/blockbusters £2.50, features & non-fiction £2, ch £1; CD-ROM/£2 **Income Gen:** req & res/60p Kirklees stock, £2.50 elsewhere; lost ticket/£2.50; vocal scores & playsets/70p per copy; song parts, chamber music & orchestral parts/40p per copy **Fines:** bks/ad 30p per bk 1st 3 days, 10p pd thereafter, 30p charge for reminders; audios & videos/loan charge; oap, registered blind & ch exempt, but ch & oaps still liable for 30p reminder change **Equip:** m-readers, m-printers, fax, copiers (A4/10p, A3/20p), clr copiers (A4/80p, A3/£1.20), computers (incl wd-procs, internet & CD-ROM), rooms for hire **Disabled:** Kurzweil, induction loop, minicom, braille transcription svc

Stock:	1 Apr 2000	1 Apr 2001
bks:	488709	452746
AVs:	40105	38892
periodcls:	201	197

Issues:	1999-2000	2000-01
bks:	2578402	2387923
AVs:	177634	186063

Acqs:	1999-2000	2000-01
bks:	37048	60924
AVs:	4259	8483

Acqs: Source: lib suppl Offcr-in-Charge: Bibliographical Svcs Mgr
Classn: DDC **Cat:** Type: author, classified, subj & title Medium: auto **Auto Sys:** Dynix **Svcs:** Extramural: schools, housebnd **Info:** business, community Other: Open Learning **Activs:** ch's activs, bk sales, temp exhibs, poetry readings, reading groups Offcr-in-Charge: Unit Mgrs
Enqs: 313300 (1999-2000); 340184 (2000-01)
Staff: Libns: 41.9 Non-Prof: 116.2

Inc from:		2000-01
local govt:		£4636139
fines etc:		£468194
total:		£5104333

Exp on:		2000-01
bks:		£489134
AVs:		£67167
salaries:		£2715917
total:		£5104333

Knowsley

P70 Knowsley Library Service
Leisure & Community Svcs, PO Box 22, Municipal Bldgs, Archway Rd, Huyton, Merseyside, L36 9YX (0151-443-3459; fax: 0151-443-3492)
Internet: http://www.knowsley.gov.uk/leisure/libraries/

Local Auth: Knowsley Metropolitan Borough Council **Pop:** 154562 **Cttee:** Leisure Cttee
Larger Dept: Leisure & Community Svcs **Dept Chief:** Dir: Mr John Bell BSc, MSocSc, MILAM
Chief: Head of Libs: Mr Peter Marchant BA(Hons), DipLib, DM, MCLIP
Main Libs: HUYTON LIB (incl Ref Lib & Local Studies), Civic Way, Huyton, Liverpool, L36 9DG (0151-443-3734; ref: 0151-443-3738; fax: 0151-443-3739) **Branch Libs:** HALEWOOD LIB, Leathers Ln, Halewood, Liverpool, L26 0TS (0151-486-4442; fax: 0151-486-8101); KIRKBY LIB, Newtown Gdns, Kirkby, Liverpool, L32 8RR (0151-443-4290; fax: 0151-443-1453); PAGE MOSS LIB, Stockbridge Ln, Liverpool, L36 3SA (0151-489-9814; fax: 0151-480-9284); PRESCOT LIB, High St, Prescot, Merseyside, L34 3LD (0151-426-6449; fax: 0151-430-7548); STOCKBRIDGE VILLAGE LIB, The Withens, Stockbridge, Liverpool, L28 1SU (tel & fax: 0151-480-3925); WHISTON LIB, Dragon Ln, Whiston, Prescot, Merseyside, L35 3QW (0151-426-4757; fax: 0151-493-0191) **Svc Pts:** Mobile: 1 Computers: 7 Other: HOUSE-BND LIB SVC, at Kirkby Lib (0151-443-4223); LOCAL STUDIES & ARCHVS, at Huyton Lib (see **A222**) **Co-op Schemes:** Libs North West, LADSIRLAC, North West Training Consortium **Loans:** bks & talking bks/4 wks

Income Gen: req/ad 65p, conc 30p; ILLs/£5, conc £2.50; lost ticket/ad 65p, jnr 35p **Fines:** bks & talking bks/ad 12p pd 1st wk, 16p pd thereafter; under 18s, oap, housebnd, mobile lib users exempt **Equip:** m-readers, m-printers, 8 fax (£1.20 1st pg, 60p addl to send in UK), copiers (10p), computers (incl wd-proc, internet & CD-ROM) **Disabled:** text phones, induction loops, Robotron text reader, magnifier, tracker balls, touch screens, adapted keyboards **Online:** KnowUK, Infotrac etc

Stock:	1 Apr 2000	1 Apr 2001
bks:	322262	262292

Issues:	1999-2000	2000-01
bks:	865550	881000
AVs:	48996	64645

Acqs:	1999-2000	2000-01
bks:	53015	31222
AVs:	4482	3400

Acqs: Source: lib suppl, publ & bksellers
Classn: DDC **Cat:** Type: author, classified, dictionary, subj & title Medium: auto **Auto Sys:** Dynix **Svcs:** Extramural: schools, old people's homes, housebnd **Info:** community, edu, business, European, careers, tourist Other: Open Learning, homework clubs **Activs:** ch's activs, bk sales, temp exhibs, poetry readings, toy libs
Staff: Libns: 24 Non-Prof: 73

Inc from:	1999-2000	2000-01
local govt:	£2657811	£2932000
fines etc:	£192575	£225481
total:	£2850386	£3157481

Exp on:	1999-2000	2000-01
stock:	£719530	£780109
salaries:	£1407294	£1504079
total:	£2850386	£3157481

Lancashire

P71 Lancashire County Libraries
Room D21, Admin Section, PO Box 61, County Hall, Preston, Lancashire, PR1 8RJ (01772-264008; fax: 01772-264880)
Email: library@lcl.lancscc.gov.uk
Internet: http://www.lancashire.gov.uk/libraries/

Local Auth: Lancashire County Council **Pop:** 1140700 **Larger Dept:** Edu & Cultural Svcs Directorate **Chief:** County Lib Mgr: Mr David Lightfoot MA, DMS, MCLIP
Main Libs: North Lancashire Div: LANCASTER LIB, Market Sq, Lancaster, Lancashire, LA1 1HY (01524-580700; fax: 01524-580706; email: lancaster.library@lcl.lancscc.gov.uk); Central Lancashire Div: HARRIS PRESTON LIB, Market Sq, Preston, Lancashire, PR1 2PP (01772-532676; email: harris.reference@lcl.lancscc. gov.uk); South Lancashire Div: CHORLEY LIB, Union St, Chorley, Lancashire, PR7 1EB (01257-277222; fax: 01257-231730; email: chorley.enq@ lcl.lancscc.gov.uk); South East Lancashire Div: ACCRINGTON LIB, St James St, Accrington, Lancashire, BB5 1NQ (01254-872385; fax: 01254-301066; email: accrington.enq@lcl.lancscc. gov.uk); East Lancashire Div: BURNLEY LIB, Grimshaw St, Burnley, Lancashire, BB11 2BD (01282-437115; fax: 01282-452869; email: burnley.enq@lcl.lancscc.gov.uk) **Branch Libs:** North Lancashire Div: ANSDELL LIB, 59 Commonside, Ansdell, Lytham St Annes, Lancashire, FY8 1XX (01253-738554; fax: 01253-732160; email: ansdell.library@lcl.lancscc.gov.uk); BOLTON-LE-SANDS LIB, Main Rd, Bolton-le-Sands, Carnforth, Lancashire, LA5 8DN (tel & fax: 01524-823906; email: boltonlesands.library@ lcl.lancscc.gov.uk); CARNFORTH LIB, Lancaster Rd, Carnforth, Lancashire, LA5 9DZ (tel & fax: 01524-732815; email: carnforth.library@lcl. lancscc.gov.uk); CHATSWORTH AVE LIB, Chatsworth Ave, Fleetwood, Lancashire, FY7

8EG (01253-771601; *fax:* 01253-776787; *email:* chatsworth.library@lcl.lancscc.gov.uk); CLEVELEYS LIB, Rossall Rd, Thornton Cleveleys, Blackpool, Lancashire, FY5 1EE (01253-852114; *fax:* 01253-858834; *email:* cleveleys.library@lcl.lancscc.gov.uk); FLEET-WOOD LIB, North Albert St, Fleetwood, Lancashire, FY7 6AJ (01253-775800; *fax:* 01253-775804; *email:* fleetwood.library@lcl.lancscc. gov.uk); FRECKLETON LIB, Preston Old Rd, Freckleton, Preston, Lancashire, PR4 1PB (01772-635321; *fax:* 01772-632682; *email:* freckleton.library@lcl.lancscc.gov.uk); GARSTANG LIB, Windsor Rd, Garstang, Preston, Lancashire, PR3 1ED (01995-604052; *fax:* 01995-605247; *email:* garstang.library@lcl.lancscc. gov.uk); HEYSHAM LIB, Council Offices, Heysham Rd, Heysham, Lancashire, LA3 2BJ (*tel & fax:* 01524-851530; *email:* heysham. library@lcl.lancscc.gov.uk); KIRKHAM LIB, Station Rd, Kirkham, Preston, Lancashire, PR4 2HD (*tel & fax:* 01772-684479; *email:* kirkham. library@lcl.lancscc.gov.uk); KNOTT END LIB, Lancaster Rd, Knott End-on-Sea, Poulton-le-Fylde, Lancashire, FY6 0AU (*tel & fax:* 01253-810632; *email:* knott-end.library@lcl.lancscc. gov.uk); LYTHAM LIB, Clifton St, Lytham St Annes, Lytham, Lancashire, FY8 5EP (01253-736745; *fax:* 01253-796784; *email:* lytham. library@lcl.lancscc.gov.uk); MORECAMBE LIB, Central Dr, Morecambe, Lancashire, LA4 5DL (01524-415215; *fax:* 01524-415008; *email:* morecambe.library@lcl.lancscc.gov.uk); POULTON LIB, Blackpool Old Rd, Poulton-le-Fylde, Blackpool, Lancashire, FY6 7DH (01253-888900; *fax:* 01253-884132; *email:* poulton. library@lcl.lancscc.gov.uk); ST ANNES LIB, 254 Clifton Dr South, St Annes-on-Sea, Lancashire, FY8 1NR (01253-643900; *fax:* 01253-643909; *email:* st-annes.library@lcl.lancscc.gov.uk); THORNTON LIB, Victoria Rd, Thornton Cleveleys, Blackpool, Lancashire, FY5 3SZ (01253-869138; *fax:* 01253-827842; *email:* thornton.library@lcl.lancscc.gov.uk); *Central Lancashire Div:* BAMBER BRIDGE LIB, Station Rd, Bamber Bridge, Preston, Lancashire, PR5 6LA (01772-335402; *email:* bamber-bridge.library@lcl.lancscc.gov.uk); FULWOOD LIB, 294 Garstang Rd, Fulwood, Preston, Lancashire, PR2 9RX (01772-719082; *email:* fulwood.library@lcl.lancscc. gov.uk); INGOL LIB, Ventnor Pl, off Tag Ln, Ingol, Preston, Lancashire, PR2 3YX (01772-720483; *email:* ingol.library@lcl.lancscc.gov.uk); KINGS-FOLD LIB, Hawksbury Dr, Penwortham, Preston, Lancashire, PR1 9EJ (01772-744457; *email:* kingsfold.library@lcl.lancscc.gov.uk); LEYLAND LIB, Lancaster Gate, Leyland, Lancashire, PR25 1EX (01772-432804; *fax:* 01772-456549; *email:* leyland.library@lcl.lancscc.gov.uk); LONGRIDGE LIB, Berry Ln, Longridge, Preston, Lancashire, PR3 3JA (01772-782386; *fax:* 01772-782696; *email:* longridge.library@lcl.lancscc.gov.uk); LONGTON LIB, Liverpool Rd, Longton, Preston, Lancashire, PR4 5HA (01772-617401; *email:* longton.library@lcl.lancscc.gov.uk); LOSTOCK HALL LIB, Watkin Ln, Lostock Hall, Preston, Lancashire, PR5 5TU (01772-339775; *email:* lostock-hall.library@lcl.lancscc.gov.uk); PENWORTHAM LIB, Liverpool Rd, Penwortham, Preston, Lancashire, PR1 9XE (01772-744331; *email:* penwortham.library@lcl.lancscc.gov.uk); RIBBLETON LIB, Ribbleton Hall Dr, Ribbleton, Preston, Lancashire, PR2 6EE (01772-792632; *email:* ribbleton.library@lcl.lancscc.gov.uk); SAVICK LIB, West Pk Ave, Savick, Preston, Lancashire, PR2 1UH (01772-729119; *email:* savick.library@lcl.lancscc.gov.uk); SHAROE GREEN LIB, 8 Sharoe Green Ln, Fulwood, Preston, Lancashire, PR2 8ED (01772-719071; *email:* sharoe-green.library@lcl.lancscc.gov.uk); *South Lancashire Div:* ADLINGTON LIB, Railway Rd, Adlington, Chorley, Lancashire, PR6 9RG (01257-480525; *email:* adlington.library@lcl. lancscc.gov.uk); BURSCOUGH LIB, Mill Ln,

Burscough, Ormskirk, Lancashire, L40 5TJ (01704-892334; *email:* burscough.library@lcl. lancscc.gov.uk); CLAYTON GREEN LIB, Lib Rd, Clayton-le-Woods, Chorley, Lancashire, PR6 7EN (01772-321820; *email:* clayton-green.library@lcl. lancscc.gov.uk); COPPULL LIB, Spendmore Ln, Coppull, Chorley, Lancashire, PR7 5DF (01257-791426; *email:* coppull.library@lcl.lancscc.gov.uk); ECCLESTON LIB, The Green, Eccleston, Chorley, Lancashire, PR7 5TE (01257-451825; *email:* eccleston.library@lcl.lancscc.gov.uk); EUXTON LIB, St Mary's Gate, Euxton, Chorley, Lancashire, PR7 6AH (01257-265430; *email:* euxton.library@ lcl.lancscc.gov.uk); ORMSKIRK LIB, Burscough St, Ormskirk, Lancashire, L39 2EN (01695-573448; *fax:* 01695-580033; *email:* ormskirk. library@lcl.lancscc.gov.uk); PARBOLD LIB, The Common, Parbold, Wigan, Lancashire, WN8 7EA (01257-463769; *email:* parbold.library@lcl.lancscc. gov.uk); SKELMERSDALE LIB, Southway, Skelmersdale, Lancashire, WN8 6NL (01695-720312; *fax:* 01695-558627; *email:* skelmersdale. library@lcl.lancscc.gov.uk); TARLETON LIB, Mark Sq, Tarleton, Preston, Lancashire, PR4 6TU (01772-815179; *email:* tarleton.library@lcl. lancscc.gov.uk); UPHOLLAND LIB, Hall Green, Upholland, Skelmersdale, Lancashire, WN8 0PB (01695-622368; *email:* upholland.library@lcl. lancscc.gov.uk); *South East Lancashire Div:* BACUP LIB, St James Sq, Bacup, Lancashire, OL13 9AH (*tel & fax:* 01706-873324; *email:* bacup.library@lcl.lancscc.gov.uk); CLAYTON-LE-MOORS LIB, Pickup St, Clayton-le-Moors, Accrington, Lancashire, BB5 5NS (01254-236463; *email:* clayton-le-moors.library@lcl.lancscc. gov.uk); GT HARWOOD LIB, Queen St, Gt Harwood, Blackburn, Lancashire, BB6 7AL (01254-884733; *email:* great-harwood.library@lcl.lancscc. gov.uk); HASLINGDEN LIB, Deardengate, Haslingden, Rossendale, Lancashire, BB4 5QL (*tel & fax:* 01706-215690; *email:* haslingden. library@lcl.lancscc.gov.uk); OSWALDTWISTLE LIB, Union Rd, Oswaldtwistle, Accrington, Lancashire, BB5 3HS (01254-233823; *email:* oswaldtwistle.library@lcl.lancscc.gov.uk); RAWTENSTALL LIB, Queen's Sq, Haslingden Rd, Rawtenstall, Lancashire, BB4 6QU (01706-227911; *fax:* 01706-217014; *email:* rawtenstall.library@lcl. lancscc.gov.uk); RISHTON LIB, High St, Rishton, Blackburn, Lancashire, BB1 4LA (01254-885314; *email:* rishton.library@lcl.lancscc.gov.uk); WHIT-WORTH LIB, Lloyd St, Whitworth, Rochdale, Lancashire, OL12 8AA (01706-853261; *email:* whitworth.library@lcl.lancscc.gov.uk); *East Lancashire Div:* BARBON ST LIB, Barbon St, Burnley, Lancashire, BB10 1TS (01282-437051; *email:* barbon-street.library@lcl.lancscc.gov.uk); BARNOLDSWICK LIB, Fern Lea Ave, Barnolds-wick, Colne, Lancashire, BB8 5DW (01282-812147; *fax:* 01282-850791; *email:* barnoldswick. enq@lcl.lancscc.gov.uk); BARROWFORD LIB, Ann St, Barrowford, Nelson, Lancashire, BB9 8HQ (01282-613038; *email:* barrowford.library@lcl. lancscc.gov.uk); BRIERFIELD LIB, Colne Rd, Brierfield, Nelson, Lancashire, BB9 5HW (01282-615816; *email:* brierfield.library@lcl.lancscc. gov.uk); CLITHEROE LIB, Church St, Clitheroe, Lancashire, BB7 2DG (01200-428788; *fax:* 01200-443203; *email:* clitheroe.library@lcl.lancscc. gov.uk); COAL CLOUGH LIB, Coal Clough Ln, Burnley, Lancashire, BB11 4NW (01282-435573; *fax:* 01282-441236; *email:* coal-clough.library@ lcl.lancscc.gov.uk); COLNE LIB, Market Sq, Colne, Lancashire, BB8 0AP (01282-871155; *fax:* 01282-865227; *email:* colne.enq@lcl.lancscc. gov.uk); COLNE RD LIB, Colne Rd, Burnley, Lancashire, BB10 1LL (01282-422783; *email:* colne-road.library@lcl.lancscc.gov.uk); EARBY LIB, Coronation Hall, Cemetery Rd, Earby, Barnoldswick, Lancashire, BB18 6QX (01282-843470; *email:* earby.library@lcl.lancscc.gov.uk); IGHTENHILL LIB, Romford St, Burnley, Lanca-shire, BB12 8AS (01282-437979; *email:* ightenhill. library@lcl.lancscc.gov.uk); NELSON LIB, Market

Sq, Nelson, Lancashire, BB9 7PU (01282-692511; *fax:* 01282-449584; *email:* nelson.library@lcl. lancscc.gov.uk); PADIHAM LIB, Town Hall, Burnley Rd, Padiham, Burnley, Lancashire, BB12 8BS (01282-771640; *fax:* 01282-777956; *email:* padiham.library@lcl.lancscc.gov.uk); ROSE-GROVE LIB, Lowerhouse Ln, Rosegrove, Burnley, Lancashire, BB12 6HU (01282-423620; *email:* rosegrove.library@lcl.lancscc.gov.uk); WHALLEY LIB, Abbey Rd, Whalley, Blackburn, Lancashire, BB6 9RS (01254-822446; *fax:* 01254-825149; *email:* whalley.library@lcl.lancscc.gov.uk)
Svc Pts: PT: 22 *Mobile:* 11 *AV:* 71 *Computers:* 72 *Internet:* 72 *Other:* SCHOOL LIB SVC; BIBLIOGRAPHICAL SVCS
Collns: Dr Shepherd's Lib; Spencer Colln of early ch's bks (both at Harris Preston Lib); Stocks Massey Music Lib (at Burnley Lib); Fuller-Maitland Music Colln (at Lancaster Lib); Lancashire Authors' Assoc Colln; local studies (at Lancashire Record Office – see **A425**) *Co-op Schemes:* Libs North West, Lib Co-operation in Lancashire *ILLs:* county, natl & internatl *Loans:* bks & spkn wd/3 wks; audios, videos, DVDs & CD-ROMs/1 wk *Charges:* audios/50p; videos/entertainment £1-£1.50, genl interest 50p, public info free; DVDs/£2; CD-ROMs/£1.50 *Income Gen:* req & res/60p *Fines:* bks/ad 10p pd (£6 max); audios, videos & CD-ROMs/loan charge; various exemptions available to ch, oaps, long term sick or disabled, visually impaired, mobile lib users, housebnd *Equip:* m-readers, m-printers, fax, copiers (10p), clr copiers (£1), 751 computers (incl internet & CD-ROM), rooms for hire (various) *Disabled:* Kurzweil, CCTV, video caption readers, minicom, induction loops

Stock:	*1 Apr 2000*	*1 Apr 2001*
lend:	1614661	1560992
ref:	352546	324562
AVs:	112030	114106
periodcls:	574	781
Issues:	*1999-2000*	*2000-01*
bks:	9850979	9488076
AVs:	661793	687971
Acqs:	*1999-2000*	*2000-01*
bks:	191313	205563
AVs:	19357	22732

Acqs: Source: lib suppl, publ & bksellers *Classn:* DDC *Cat: Type:* author, classified, subj & title *Medium:* auto *Auto Sys:* Talis *Svcs: Extramural:* schools, prisons, old people's homes, housebnd *Info:* community, business, edu, info for visually impaired *Other:* Open Learning *Activs:* ch's activs, bk sales, temp exhibs, poetry readings, reading groups, annual lit festival, annual programme of arts *Enqs:* 852948 (1999-2000); 761280 (2000-01) *Staff: Libns:* 165 *Non-Prof:* 548

Inc from:	*1999-2000*	*2000-01*
local govt:	£15802701	£16622178
fines etc:	£830269	£844622
total:	£16968148	£17783568
Exp on:	*1999-2000*	*2000-01*
stock:	£2349107	£2396956
salaries:	£8556708	£8817348
total:	£16968148	£17783568

Leeds

P72 Leeds Library and Information Service

Lib HQ, 32 York Rd, Leeds, W Yorkshire, LS9 8TD (0113-214-3300; *fax:* 0113-214-3312)
Email: catherine.blanshard@leeds.gov.uk
Internet: http://www.leeds.gov.uk/library/library.html

Local Auth: Leeds City Council *Pop:* 727800 *Larger Dept:* Leisure Svcs *Dept Chief: Dir:* Mr John Davies ☛

(Leeds Lib & Info Svc cont)
Chief: Asst Dir & Head of Lib Svcs: Miss Catherine Blanshard BA, MCLIP
Main Libs: CENTRAL LIB, Municipal Bldgs, Calverley St, Leeds, W Yorkshire, LS1 3AB (0113-247-8274; *fax:* 0113-247-8271) **Branch Libs:** ARMLEY LIB, 2 Stocks Hill, Leeds, W Yorkshire, LS12 1UQ (0113-214-3545; *fax:* 0113-214-3546); ARMLEY HEIGHTS LIB, 36 Heights Dr, Leeds, W Yorkshire, LS12 3SU (*tel & fax:* 0113-214-3549); BEESTON LIB, Hugh Gaitskell School, St Anthony's Dr, Leeds, W Yorkshire, LS11 8AB (0113-214-1766; *fax:* 0113-214-1767); BELLE ISLE LIB, Aberfield Gate, Belle Isle Rd, Leeds, W Yorkshire, LS10 3QH (*tel & fax:* 0113-214-1768); BRAMLEY LIB, Hough Ln, Leeds, W Yorkshire, LS13 3ND (0113-214-6040; *fax:* 0113-214-6041); BURLEY LIB, Cardigan Rd, Leeds, W Yorkshire, LS6 1QL (*tel & fax:* 0113-214-4528); CALVERLEY LIB, Thornhill St, Calverley, Pudsey, Leeds, W Yorkshire, LS28 5PD (*tel & fax:* 0113-214-6043); CHAPEL ALLER-TON LIB, 106 Harrogate Rd, Leeds, W Yorkshire, LS7 4LZ (0113-214-5812; *fax:* 0113-214-5813); COMPTON RD LIB, Harehills Ln, Leeds, W York-shire, LS9 7BG (0113-214-3156; *fax:* 0113-214-3157); CROSSGATES LIB, Farm Rd, Leeds, W Yorkshire, LS15 7LB (0113-224-3328; *fax:* 0113-224-3316); DEWSBURY RD LIB, 118 Dewsbury Rd, Leeds, W Yorkshire, LS11 6XD (0113-224-3328; *fax:* 0113-224-3316); FARSLEY LIB, Old Rd, Farsley, Pudsey, Leeds, W Yorkshire, LS28 5DH (0113-214-6038; *fax:* 0113-214-6039); GARFORTH LIB, 1 Lidgett Ln, Garforth, Leeds, W Yorkshire, LS25 1EH (0113-224-3291; *fax:* 0113-224-3293); GUISELEY LIB, Otley Rd, Guiseley, Leeds, W Yorkshire, LS20 8AH (*tel & fax:* 01943-872675); HALTON LIB, 273 Selby Rd, Leeds, W Yorkshire, LS15 7JR (0113-214-1320; *fax:* 0113-214-1321); HEADINGLEY LIB, North Ln, Leeds, W Yorkshire, LS6 3HG (0113-214-4525; *fax:* 0113-214-4526); HOLT PK LIB, Ralph Thoresby High School, Village Sq, Farrar Ln, Leeds, W Yorkshire, LS16 7NQ (0113-214-1025; *fax:* 0113-214-1026); HORSFORTH LIB, Town St, Horsforth, Leeds, W Yorkshire, LS18 5BL (0113-214-4801; *fax:* 0113-214-4802); HUNSLET LIB, Waterloo Rd, Leeds, W Yorkshire, LS10 2NS (*tel & fax:* 0113-214-1764); KIPPAX LIB, Westfield Ln, Kippax, Leeds, W Yorkshire, LS25 7JP (*tel & fax:* 0113-214-6802); MIDDLETON LIB, St Georges Centre, St Georges Rd, Leeds, W Yorkshire, LS10 4UZ (0113-224-3119; *fax:* 0113-224-3121); MOOR ALLERTON LIB, Moor Allerton Centre, King Ln, Leeds, W Yorkshire, LS17 5NY (0113-214-5624/5/6; *fax:* 0113-214-5627); MORLEY LIB, Commercial St, Morley, Leeds, W Yorkshire, LS27 8HZ (0113-214-5418; *fax:* 0113-214-5419); OAKWOOD LIB, 1 Oakwood Ln, Leeds, W York-shire, LS8 2PZ (0113-214-4192; *fax:* 0113-214-4193); OTLEY LIB, 4 Boroughgate, Otley, Leeds, W Yorkshire, LS21 1AL (0113-224-3285; *fax:* 0113-224-3286); PUDSEY LIB, Church Ln, Pudsey, Leeds, W Yorkshire, LS28 7TY (0113-214-6035; *fax:* 0113-214-6036); RAWDON LIB, Micklesfield Pk, Rawdon, Leeds, W Yorkshire, LS19 6DF (0113-247-7621; *fax:* 0113-224-3290); ROTHWELL LIB, Marsh St, Rothwell, Leeds, W Yorkshire, LS26 0AE (*tel & fax:* 0113-224-3288); SEACROFT LIB, Seacroft Cres, Leeds, W Yorkshire, LS14 6PA (0113-214-4171; *fax:* 0113-214-4172);

WETHERBY LIB, 17 Westgate, Wetherby, Leeds, W Yorkshire, LS22 4LL (01937-583144; *fax:* 01937-586964); YEADON LIB, Town Hall Sq, Yeadon, Leeds, W Yorkshire, LS19 7PP (0113-214-6501; *fax:* 0113-214-6502)
Svc Pts: PT: 23 *Mobile:* 8 *AV:* 12 *Computers:* 55 *Internet:* 55 *Other:* ART LIB; MUSIC LIB; BUSINESS LIB (all at Central Lib)
Collns: Porton Colln (Judaism, 3500 items); Gascoigne Colln (military & naval hist, 3000 items); Gott Bequest (16C-18C gardening bks); Arthington Trust Colln (missionary work, early 20C, c1000 items); Sanderson Colln (19C-20C fashion); Taphouse Colln (17C-18C music); Yorkshire & local hist *Co-op Schemes:* BLDSC, CONARLS, LALIC *ILLs:* county & natl *Loans:* bks & talking bks/3 wks; audios & videos/1 wk; DVDs/2 nights or 1 wk *Charges:* talking bks/£1.50, free to visually impaired; CDs/80p, sets £1.50; videos/50p-£2; DVDs/£1.50-£3 *Income Gen:* req & res/70p, conc 50p, under-16s free, ILLs £3; lost ticket/£2, conc £1 *Fines:* bks/ad 15p pd, oap 10p pd; audios, videos & DVDs/loan charge; ch & registered blind exempt *Equip:* m-readers (50p per hr), m-printers (A4/50p), fax, copiers (A4/10p, A3/20p), clr copier (A4/£1, A3/£1.50), c500 computers (incl wd-proc, internet & CD-ROM), rooms for hire (varies) *Disabled:* Kurzweil, Dolphin Supernova

Stock:	1 Apr 2000	1 Apr 2001
ad lend:	516191	646133
ad ref:	302190	229622
ch:	215437	223725
audios:	21427	23149
videos:	11129	11677
periodcls:	714	815

Issues:	1999-2000	2000-01
ad lend:	3565713	3152411
ch:	1377023	956402
audios:	98612	107770
videos:	57718	57007

Acqs:	1999-2000	2000-01
bks:	126928	131114
AVs:	-	5053

Acqs: Source: lib suppl & bksellers *Offcr-in-Charge:* Stock & Finance Mgr: Mr Richard Fuller *Classn:* DDC *Cat: Type:* author, classified, subj & title *Medium:* auto *Auto Sys:* Talis *Svcs: Extramural:* schools, prisons, old people's homes, housebnd *Info:* business, council, careers, health, patents *Other:* Open Learning (at Central & Seacroft Libs), braille & Large Print Unit *Activs:* ch's activs, bk sales, temp exhibs, poetry readings, reading groups
Enqs: 516219 (1999-2000); 575315 (2000-01)
Staff: Libns: 74 *Non-Prof:* 270

Inc from:	1999-2000
local govt:	£7967384
fines etc:	£952108
total:	£8919492

Exp on:	1999-2000
stock:	£1207215
salaries:	£4811416
total:	£8919492

Leicester

P73 Leicester City Libraries
Edu & Lifelong Learning, Marlborough House, 38 Welford Rd, Leicester, LE2 7AA (0116-252-6762)
Email: libraries@leicester.gov.uk
Internet: http://www.leicester.gov.uk/

Local Auth: Leicester City Council *Pop:* 295700
Larger Dept: Edu & Lifelong Learning *Dept Chief: Dir:* Mr Stephen Andrews *Chief:* Head of Libs & Info Svcs: Ms Patricia Flynn
Main Libs: BEAUMONT LEYS LIB, Beaumont Way, Leicester, LE4 1DS, (0116-299-5460; *fax:*

0116-234-0078; *email:* beaumontleys.lib@leicester. gov.uk); CENTRAL LENDING LIB, 54 Belvoir St, Leicester, LE1 6QL (0116-255-5402; *fax:* 0116-255-5434; *email:* central.lending@leicester. gov.uk); REF & INFO LIB, Bishop St, Leicester, LE1 6AA (0116-299-5401; *fax:* 0116-299-5444; *email:* central.reference@leicester.gov.uk)
Branch Libs: AYLESTONE LIB, Richmond Rd, Leicester, LE2 8BB (*tel & fax:* 0116-283-2540); BELGRAVE LIB, Cossington St, Leicester, LE4 6JD (0116-299-5500; *fax:* 0116-266-0846); BRAUNSTONE LIB, Braunstone Ave, Leicester, LE3 1LE (*tel & fax:* 0116-299-5476); EVINGTON LIB, 200 Evington Ln, Leicester, LE5 6DH (*tel & fax:* 0116-273-9518; *email:* evington.lib@leicester. gov.uk); FOSSE LIB, Mantle Rd, Leicester, LE5 5HG (0116-225-4995); HIGHFIELDS LIB, 98 Melbourne Rd, Leicester, LE2 0DS (0116-299-5494; *fax:* 0116-253-7358; *email:* highfields.lib@ leicester. gov.uk); HUMBERSTONE LIB, Keyham Cl, Leicester, LE5 1FW (*tel & fax:* 0116-276-3106); KNIGHTON LIB, Clarendon Pk Rd, Leicester, LE2 3AJ (0116-299-5477; *fax:* 0116-299-5478; *email:* knighton.lib@leicester.gov.uk); NEW PARKS LIB, Dillon Rd, Leicester, LE3 9PF (*tel & fax:* 0116-287-2620); RUSHEY MEAD LIB, Lockerbie Walk, Leicester, LE4 7ZX (*tel & fax:* 0116-266-5112); ST BARNABAS LIB, French Rd, Leicester, LE5 4AH (0116-299-5450; *fax:* 0116-246-1163; *email:* barnabas.lib@leicester.gov.uk); ST MATTHEWS LIB & RESOURCE CENTRE, 50 Malabar Rd, Leicester, LE1 2PD (0116-223-2085); SOUTH-FIELDS LIB, Saffron Ln, Leicester, LE2 6QS (0116-299-5480; *fax:* 0116-299-5491; *email:* southfields.lib@leicester.gov.uk); WESTCOTES LIB, Narborough Rd, Leicester, LE3 0BQ (0116-299-5510; *fax:* 0116-255-8172; *email:* westcotes. lib@leicester.gov.uk)
Svc Pts: PT: 3 *Mobile:* 3 *Other:* GOLDSMITH MUSIC SVCS, at Central Lending Lib (0116-299-5435); AGE CONCERN LIB, Clarence House, 46 Humberstone Gate, Leicester, LE1 3PJ (0116-222-0580; *fax:* 0116-253-1995)
Collns: Burchell Colln (British films); Stretton Colln (British railways); Times Newspaper Colln *Co-op Schemes:* EMRLS *ILLs:* county & natl *Loans:* bks & talking bks/3 wks; audios, videos & DVDs/1 wk; lang courses/3-9 wks *Charges:* talking bks/50p-£1 (conc 35p-70p), free to registered visually impaired; LPs & cassettes/50p (conc 35p); CDs/70p-£1 (conc 50p-70p); videos/£1.25-£3 (conc 80p-£2), sets £2.50-£6 (conc £1.60-£4); lang courses/£1.10-£5 (conc 75p-£3.50) *Income Gen:* req & res/city residents 25p, county residents 80p (conc 50p); lost ticket/ad £1, ch 50p; various charges for lost or damaged stock *Fines:* bks/ad 14p pd open (max £4.20), ch aged 12-15 5p pd open (max £1.50), ch under 11 exempt; audios & videos/loan charge *Equip:* m-reader, m-printer (20p per sheet), 11 copiers (A4/10p, A3/20p), 2 clr copiers (A4/£1, A3/£1.50), 3 fax (UK 75p per pg, higher overseas, 50p per pg to receive), computers (incl wd-proc, internet & CD-ROM, access free, printouts same rate as photocopies) *Disabled:* minicom, CCTV *Online:* online enq svc available; charge made to recover costs

Stock:	1 Apr 2000	1 Apr 2001
lend:	447989	436064
ref:	137969	135670
AVs:	58057	50168
periodcls:	696	696

Issues:	1999-2000	2000-01
bks:	1707908	1571324
AVs:	-	149946

Acqs:	1999-2000	2000-01
bks:	49669	48053
AVs:	10078	5241

Acqs: Source: lib suppl *Co-op:* JFR (Jja-Jjo)
Offcr-in-Charge: Area Mgrs: Chris Ashton (ad bks) & Paul Gobey (jnr bks)

Classn: DDC **Cat: Type:** author, classified, title, Keyword & phrase **Medium:** auto **Auto Sys:** DS **Svcs: Extramural:** prisons, old people's homes, housebnd **Info:** business, community, European **Activs:** ch's activs, bk sales, temp exhibs, poetry readings, author visits **Offcr-in-Charge:** Head of Libs & Info Svcs, as above **Enqs:** 281904 (1999-2000); 289106 (2000-01) **Staff: Libns:** 40 **Non-Prof:** 81

Inc from:	2000-01
fines etc:	£346977

Exp on:	2000-01
stock:	£697308
salaries:	£2288630
total:	£4898537

Leicestershire

P74 Leicestershire Libraries and Information Service

4th Floor, County Hall, Glenfield, Leicester, LE3 8SS (0116-265-6988; fax: 0116-265-7370)
Email: libraries@leics.gov.uk
Internet: http://www.leics.gov.uk/

Local Auth: Leicestershire County Council **Pop:** 613400 **Cttee:** Arts, Libs & Museums Cttee **Chief:** Head of Svc: Ms M. Bellamy MBA, DMS, MCLIP (mbellamy@leics.gov.uk)
Main Libs: COUNTY HALL LIB, addr as above (email: countyhalllibrary@lelcs.gov.uk); HINCKLEY LIB, Lancaster Rd, Hinckley, Leicestershire, LE10 0AT (01455-635106; fax: 01455-251385; email: hinckleylibrary@leics. gov.uk); LOUGHBOROUGH LIB, Granby St, Loughborough, Leicestershire, LE11 3DZ (01509-212985/266436; fax: 01509-610594; email: loughboroughlibrary@leics.gov.uk); WIGSTON MAGNA LIB, Bull Head St, Wigston, Leicester-shire, LE18 1PA (0116-288-7381; fax: 0116-281-2985; email: wigstonlibrary@leics.gov.uk)
Branch Libs: ANSTEY LIB, Paper Mill Cl, Anstey, Leicester, LE7 7AU (0116-236-3796; fax: 0116-234-0147; email: ansteylibrary@leics. gov.uk); ASHBY-DE-LA-ZOUCH LIB, North St, Ashby-de-la-Zouch, Leicestershire, LE65 1HU (01530-413346; fax: 01530-560282; email: ashbydelazouchlibrary@leics.gov.uk); BARROW UPON SOAR LIB, North St, Barrow upon Soar, Loughborough, Leicestershire, LE12 8PZ (01509-413160; fax: 01509-621094; email: barrowuponsoarlibrary@leics.gov.uk); BARWELL LIB, Malt Mill Bank, Barwell, Leicestershire, LE9 8GS (tel & fax: 01455-842466; email: barwelllibrary@leics.gov.uk); BIRSTALL LIB, Wanlip Ln, Birstall, Leicester, LE4 4JU (0116-267-3494; fax: 0116-267-7212; email: birstalllibrary@ leics.gov.uk); BLABY LIB, Lutterworth Rd, Blaby, Leicester, LE8 4DW (0116-277-2868; fax: 0116-278-0245; email: blabylibrary@leics.gov.uk); BOTTESFORD LIB, Old Primary School, Grantham Rd, Bottesford, Nottinghamshire, NG13 0DF (tel & fax: 01949-842696; email: bottesfordlibrary@leics.gov.uk); BROUGHTON ASTLEY LIB, Green Rd, Broughton Astley, Leicester, LE9 6RA (tel & fax: 01455-283983; email: broughtonastleylibrary@leics.gov.uk); BURBAGE LIB, Church St, Burbage, Hinckley, Leicestershire, LE10 2DA (tel & fax: 01455-239245; email: burbagelibrary@leics.gov.uk); CASTLE DONINGTON LIB, Delven Ln, Castle Donington, Derbyshire, DE74 2LJ (tel & fax: 01332-810183; email: castledoningtonlibrary@ leics.gov.uk); COALVILLE LIB, High St, Coalville, Leicestershire, LE67 3EA (01530-835951; fax: 01530-832019; email: coalvillelibrary@leics. gov.uk); COSBY LIB, Pk Rd, Cosby, Leicester-shire, LE59 1RN (tel & fax: 0116-286-2967; email: cosbylibrary@leics.gov.uk); COUNTESTHORPE LIB, Station Rd, Countesthorpe, Leicestershire, LE8 5TB (0116-277-6010; fax: 0116-278-2187; email: countesthorpelibrary@leics.gov.uk);

DESFORD LIB, Main St, Desford, Leicestershire, LE9 9JP (tel & fax: 01455-822101; email: desfordlibrary@leics.gov.uk); EARL SHILTON LIB, Wood St, Earl Shilton, Leicester, LE9 7NE (01455-842467; fax: 01455-850931; email: earlshiltonlibrary@leics.gov.uk); ENDERBY LIB, Townsend Rd, Enderby, Leicester, LE19 4PG (tel & fax: 0116-286-2091; email: enderbylibrary@ leics.gov.uk); GLENFIELD LIB, Station Rd, Glenfield, Leicester, LE3 8BQ (0116-287-2934; fax: 0116-232-1917; email: glenfieldlibrary@leics. gov.uk); GROBY LIB, Leicester Rd, Groby, Leicestershire, LE6 0DQ (0116-287-6949; fax: 0116-287-8764; email: grobylibrary@leics.gov.uk); KIBWORTH LIB, Paget St, Kibworth, Leicester-shire, LE8 0HW (tel & fax: 0116-279-2141; email: kibworthlibrary@leics.gov.uk); KIRBY MUXLOE LIB, Station Rd, Kirby Muxloe, Leicestershire, LE9, 9EN (tel & fax: 0116-238-7343; email: kirbymuxloelibrary@leics.gov.uk); LEICESTER FOREST EAST LIB, Holmfield Ave West, Leicester, LE3 3FF (tel & fax: 0116-239-3765; email: leicesterforesteastlibrary@leics.gov.uk); LUTTERWORTH LIB, Coventry Rd, Lutterworth, Leicestershire, LE17 5SH (01455-552868; fax: 01455-559663; email: lutterworthlibrary@leics. gov.uk); MARKET BOSWORTH LIB, Station Rd, Market Bosworth, Nuneaton, Warwickshire, CV13 0NP (tel & fax: 01455-290149; email: marketbosworthlibrary@leics.gov.uk); MARKET HARBOROUGH LIB, Adam & Eve St, Market Harborough, Leicestershire, LE16 7LT (01858-821272; fax: 01858-821265; email: marketharboroughlibrary@leics.gov.uk); MARKFIELD LIB, Oakfield Ave, Markfield, Leicestershire, LE67 9WG (01530-244364; fax: 01530-249130; email: markfieldlibrary@leics. gov.uk); MELTON MOWBRAY LIB, Wilton Rd, Melton Mowbray, Leicestershire, LE13 0UJ (01664-560161; fax: 01664-410199; email: meltonmowbraylibrary@leics.gov.uk); MOUNT-SORREL LIB, Market Pl, Mountsorrel, Leicester-shire, LE12 7BA (0116-230-2834; fax: 0116-237-6619; email: mountsorrellibrary@leics.gov.uk); NARBOROUGH LIB, Station Rd, Narborough, Leicestershire, LE19 2HR (tel & fax: 0116-286-3051; email: narboroughlibrary@leics.gov.uk); NEWBOLD VERDON LIB, Sparkenhoe, Main St, Newbold Verdon, Leicestershire, LE9 9NP (tel & fax: 01455-823553; email: newboldverdonlibrary@ leics.gov.uk); OADBY LIB, Sandhurst St, Oadby, Leicester, LE2 5AR (0116-271-5066; fax: 0116-271-8163; email: oadbylibrary@leics.gov.uk); QUORN LIB, Rawlins Community Coll, Lough-borough Rd, Quorn, Leicestershire, LE12 8DY (tel & fax: 01509-414296; email: quornlibrary@leics. gov.uk); RATBY LIB, Main St, Ratby, Leicester-shire, LE6 0LL (tel & fax: 0116-239-4530; email: ratbylibrary@leics.gov.uk); ROTHLEY LIB, Mountsorrel Ln, Rothley, Leicestershire, LE7 7PS (0116-237-4407; fax: 0116-230-1728; email: rothleylibrary@leics.gov.uk); SAPCOTE LIB, Church St, Sapcote, Leicestershire, LE9 4FG (tel & fax: 01455-273666; email: sapcotelibrary@leics. gov.uk); SHEPSHED LIB, Hall Croft, Shepshed, Loughborough, Leicestershire, LE12 9AN (01509-502291; fax: 01509-507284; email: shepshedlibrary@leics.gov.uk); SILEBY LIB, Cossington Rd, Sileby, Loughborough, Leicester-shire, LE12 7RS (01509-812684; fax: 01509-816430; email: silebylibrary@leics.gov.uk); SOUTH WIGSTON LIB, Bassett St, South Wigston, Leicestershire, LE18 4PE (tel & fax: 0116-278-7108; email: southwigstonlibrary@ leics.gov.uk); SYSTON LIB, Upper Church St, Syston, Leicester, LE7 1HR (0116-260-7877; fax: 0116-269-8283; email: systonlibrary@leics. gov.uk); THURMASTON LIB, Church Hill Rd, Thurmaston, Leicester, LE4 8DE (0116-264-0270; fax: 0116-260-7961; email: thurmastonlibrary@ leics.gov.uk); WELCOMBE AVE LIB, Welcombe Ave, Leicester, LE3 2TA (tel & fax: 0116-289-0545; email: welcombeavenuelibrary@leics. gov.uk)

Svc Pts: PT: 11 **Mobile:** 8 **AV:** 16 **Computers:** 34 **Internet:** 23
Collns: hunting (at Melton Lib); Provincial JFR: Hard-Harz, Him-Hir (at County Reserve) **Co-op Schemes:** joint catalogue with Rutland County Council (see **P156**), LAILLAR, EMRLS, Provincial JFR **ILLs:** regional, natl & internatl **Loans:** bks & spkn wd/21 days; audio & videos/charged pw; music & plays/up to 3 months **Charges:** talking bks, vinyl disks & cassettes/ad 50p (sets £1), oaps, ch, unemployed & full-time students 25p (sets 50p), free for disabled, blind, partially sighted & learning difficulties; CDs/£1 (set £1.50); videos/£1-£3; DVDs/£1.50-£3; music & plays/12p pd **Income Gen:** req/£2.20 for ILL, £10 for overseas loan, £3.90 if requiring search; res/ad 90p, ch, full-time students, oap & unemployed 50p, free for disabled, blind, partially sighted & learning difficulties; lost ticket/ad £1-£2, ch 50p-£1 **Fines:** bks/ad & oap 15p pd open (max £4.50), under-16s 2p pd open (max 60p); talking bks/loan charge (max £2.50 for 1-2 cassettes, max £5 for 3+ cassettes, half for conc); records & cassettes/loan charge (max £4, £8 for set); CDs/loan charge (max £8, £12 for set); special interest videos & DVDs/loan charge (max £8, £16 for set); feature film videos & DVDs/loan charge (max £12-£24, £24-£40 for set); disabled, blind, partially sighted & learning difficulties exempt from fines on talking bks & special interest videos & DVDs **Equip:** 17 m-readers, 6 m-printers (20p per sheet), 48 fax (varies), 44 copiers (A4/10p, A3/20p), 127 computers (incl 65 wd-proc, 15 CD-ROM & 104 internet, access free, printouts 20p per sheet), 4 rooms for hire (varies) **Disabled:** minicom, induction loops, CCTV, subtitled videos, magnifier **Online:** BLAISE, Datastar, Dialog, Dialtech, FT Profile, TextLine, Volnet (at cost)

Stock:	1 Apr 2000	1 Apr 2001
ad lend:	481429	476531
ad ref:	32814	29199
ch:	211669	220776
instns:	12228	13793
audios:	42117	39813
videos:	10624	12083

Issues:	1999-2000	2000-01
ad lend:	2965685	2780910
ch:	1148582	1100164
instns:	70837	64174
audios:	163571	168731
videos:	112302	111839

Acqs:	1999-2000	2000-01
bks:	104413	114677
AVs:	14231	11507

Acqs: Source: lib suppl, publ & bksellers **Co-op:** SPICE **Offcr-in-Charge:** Bibliographical Svc Mgr: Mr Andrew Jackson (ajackson@leics.gov.uk)
Classn: DDC **Cat: Type:** author, classified, subj & title **Medium:** auto **Auto Sys:** Talis **Svcs: Extramural:** schools, prisons, old people's homes, housebnd, day centres **Info:** INFOLINX (local organisations & database); community legal svcs, svcs for local govt, local studies svcs (in partnership with Leicestershire Record Office – see **A227**), County Council Info Pts **Activs:** ch's activs, bk sales, temp exhibs, poetry readings, reading groups, writers' groups, talks, author visits **Offcr-in-Charge:** Asst Chief Libn, as above **Enqs:** 306651 (1999-2000); 358663 (2000-01) **Staff: Libns:** 57.4 **Other Prof:** 3 **Non-Prof:** 166.5

Inc from:	1999-2000	2000-01
local govt:	£6111808	£6656918
fines etc:	£617863	£593422
total:	£7260254	£7751081

Exp on:	1999-2000	2000-01
bks:	£792820	£891050
AVs:	£177044	£220437
salaries:	£3921018	£4160088
total:	£7260254	£7751081

Lincolnshire

P75 Lincolnshire Libraries

Edu & Cultural Svcs Directorate, County Offices, Newland, Lincoln, LN1 1YL (01522-552804; *fax:* 01522-552811)
Internet: http://www.lincolnshire.info/

Local Auth: Lincolnshire County Council *Pop:* 634000 *Cttee:* Edu Cttee *Larger Dept:* Edu & Cultural Svcs Directorate *Dept Chief:* Dir: Dr Cheryle Berry *Chief:* Asst Dir of Edu & Cultural Svcs: Ms Lorraine Jubb (lorraine.jubb@lincolnshire.gov.uk) *Other Snr Staff:* Operations Mgr: Ms Alison Peden (alison.peden@lincolnshire.gov.uk); Training & Development Mgr: Ms Jan Adams (adamsj@lincolnshire.gov.uk); Community Svcs Mgr: Ms Gill Fraser (fraserg@lincolnshire.gov.uk); Info Svcs Mgr: Ms Dianne Slapp (slappd@lincolnshire.gov.uk); Resources Mgr: Mr Gary Porter (gary.porter@lincolnshire.gov.uk) *Main (Area) Libs:* BOSTON LIB (South Area), County Hall, Boston, Lincolnshire, PE21 6DY (01205-310010; *fax:* 01205-357760; *email:* boston.library@lincolnshire.gov.uk); LINCOLN CENTRAL LIB (Lincoln Area), Free School Ln, Lincoln, LN2 1EZ (01522-510800; *fax:* 01522-575011; *email:* lincoln.library@lincolnshire.gov.uk); LOUTH LIB (North Area), Northgate, Louth, Lincolnshire, LN11 0LY (01507-602105/5907; *fax:* 01507-605907; *email:* louth.library@lincolnshire.gov.uk); SLEAFORD LIB (Mid-Lincolnshire Area), 13-16 Market Pl, Sleaford, Lincolnshire, NG34 7SR (01529-303394; *fax:* 01529-307973; *email:* sleaford.library@lincolnshire.gov.uk) *Branch Libs:* ALFORD LIB, 6 South Market Pl, Alford, Lincolnshire, LN13 9AF (*tel & fax:* 01507-463440; *email:* alford.library@lincolnshire.gov.uk); BIRCH-WOOD LIB, Jasmin Rd, Birchwood, Lincoln, LN6 0QB (01522-500065/685262; *fax:* 01522-688511; *email:* birchwood.library@lincolnshire.gov.uk); BOULTHAM LIB, Boultham Pk Rd, Lincoln, LN6 7ST (*tel & fax:* 01522-684802; *email:* boultham.library@lincolnshire.gov.uk); BOURNE LIB, South St, Bourne, Lincolnshire, PE10 9LY (01778-422264; *fax:* 01778-426002; *email:* bourne.library@lincolnshire.gov.uk); BRACEBRIDGE LIB, Newark Rd, Lincoln, LN5 8PE (*tel & fax:* 01522-520649; *email:* bracebridge.library@lincolnshire.gov.uk); BRANSTON COMMUNITY LIB, Branston Community Coll, Station Rd, Branston, Lincoln, LN4 1LH (*tel & fax:* 01522-791323; *email:* branston.library@lincolnshire.gov.uk); CAISTOR LIB, South Dale, Caistor, Market Rasen, Lincolnshire, LN7 6LS (*tel & fax:* 01472-851109; *email:* caistor.library@lincolnshire.gov.uk); CHERRY WILLINGHAM LIB, The Parade, Cherry Willingham, Lincoln, LN3 4JL (*tel & fax:* 01522-750124; *email:* Cherry_Willingham.Library@lincolnshire.gov.uk); CONINGSBY/TATTERSHALL LIB, Butt Ln, Tattershall, Lincoln, LN4 4NL (*tel & fax:* 01526-342910; *email:* coningsby.library@lincolnshire.gov.uk); DEEPINGS LIB, The Park, High St, Market Deeping, Peterborough, Cambridgeshire, PE6 8ED (01778-342772; *fax:* 01778-380221; *email:* deepings.library@lincolnshire.gov.uk); ERMINE LIB, Ravendale Dr, Lincoln, LN2 2BT (01522-523155; *fax:* 01522-514882; *email:* ermine.library@lincolnshire.gov.uk); GAINSBOROUGH LIB, Cobden St, Gainsborough, Lincolnshire, DN21 2NG (01427-614780; *fax:* 01427-810318; *email:* gainsborough.library@lincolnshire.gov.uk); GRANTHAM LIB, Isaac Newton Centre, Grantham, Lincolnshire, NG31 9LD (01476-591411; *fax:* 01476-592458; *email:* grantham.library@lincolnshire.gov.uk); HOLBEACH LIB, Church St, Holbeach, Spalding, Lincolnshire, PE12 7LL (01406-422785; *fax:* 01406-425082; *email:* holbeach.library@lincolnshire.gov.uk); HORNCASTLE LIB, Wharf Rd, Horncastle, Lincolnshire, LN9 5HL (01507-523480; *fax:* 01507-523750; *email:* horncastle.library@lincolnshire.gov.uk); KIRTON LIB, Station Rd, Kirton, Boston, Lincolnshire, PE20 1EF (01205-722438; *fax:* 01205-723806; *email:* Kirton.Library@lincolnshire.gov.uk); MABLETHORPE LIB, 32 Victoria Rd, Mablethorpe, Lincolnshire, LN12 2AQ (01507-472263; *fax:* 01507-472688; *email:* mablethorpe.library@lincolnshire.gov.uk); MARKET RASEN LIB, Mill Rd, Market Rasen, Lincolnshire, LN8 3BP (*tel & fax:* 01673-842586; *email:* Market_Rasen.Library@lincolnshire.gov.uk); METHERINGHAM LIB, High St, Metheringham, Lincoln, LN4 3DZ (*tel & fax:* 01526-320550; *email:* metheringham.library@lincolnshire.gov.uk); NETTLEHAM LIB, 1 East St, Nettleham, Lincoln, LN2 2SL (01522-751391; *fax:* 01522-751070; *email:* nettleham.library@lincolnshire.gov.uk); NORTH HYKEHAM LIB, Middle St, North Hykeham, Lincoln, LN6 9QX (*tel & fax:* 01522-681169; *email:* North_Hykeham.Library@lincolnshire.gov.uk); RUSKINGTON LIB, Station Rd, Ruskington, Sleaford, Lincolnshire, NG34 9DD (*tel & fax:* 01526-832536; *email:* ruskington.library@lincolnshire.gov.uk); SKEGNESS LIB, 23 Roman Bank, Skegness, Lincolnshire, PE25 2SA (01754-762475; *fax:* 01754-761013; *email:* skegness.library@lincolnshire.gov.uk); SPALDING LIB, Victoria St, Spalding, Lincolnshire, PE21 1EA (01775-769916; *fax:* 01775-768931; *email:* spalding.library@lincolnshire.gov.uk); SPILSBY LIB, 2 West End Villas, Spilsby, Lincolnshire, PE23 5ED (*tel & fax:* 01790-752386; *email:* spilsby.library@lincolnshire.gov.uk); STAMFORD LIB, High St, Stamford, Lincolnshire, PE9 2BB (01780-763442; *fax:* 01780-482518; *email:* stamford.library@lincolnshire.gov.uk); SUTTON-ON-SEA LIB, Broadway, Sutton-on-Sea, Mablethorpe, Lincolnshire, LN12 2JN (*tel & fax:* 01507-441392; *email:* Sutton_on_Sea.Library@lincolnshire.gov.uk); WADDINGTON LIB, Lower High St, Waddington, Lincoln, LN5 9QA (*tel & fax:* 01522-720346; *email:* waddington.library@lincolnshire.gov.uk); WASHINGBOROUGH LIB, School Ln, Washingborough, Lincoln, LN4 1BW (*tel & fax:* 01522-790119; *email:* washingborough.library@lincolnshire.gov.uk); WELTON LIB, Cliff Rd, Welton, Lincoln, LN2 3JJ (*tel & fax:* 01673-860046; *email:* welton.library@lincolnshire.gov.uk); WOODHALL SPA LIB, 2 Station Rd, Woodhall Spa, Lincolnshire, LN10 6QL (*tel & fax:* 01526-352808; *email:* Woodhall_Spa.Library@lincolnshire.gov.uk)
Svc Pts: PT: 10 *Mobile:* 11 *AV:* 44 *Computers:* 46 *Internet:* 46 *Other:* LIB SUPPORT SVCS, Brayford House, Lucy Tower St, Lincoln, LN1 1XN (01522-800921; *fax:* 01522-823022); SPECIAL NEEDS LIB SVC, Westholme House, Westgate, Sleaford, Lincolnshire, NG34 7PT (01529-302691; *fax:* 01529-413876; *email:* Library.Westholme@lincolnshire.gov.uk); SCHOOLS LIB SVC, Brayford House, Lucy Tower St, Lincoln, LN1 1XN (01522-800921; *fax:* 01522-823022; *email:* Schools.LibraryService@lincolnshire.gov.uk); YNG PEOPLE'S LIB SVC & MOBILE LIBS HQ, at Nettleham Lib (*tel & fax:* 01522-595766; *email:* lib.YPS@lincolnshire.gov.uk); TENNYSON RSRCH CENTRE, at Lincoln Central Lib (see **A235**)
Collns: Pye Colln; Armitage Colln; local studies colln (all at Lincoln Central Lib); Sir Joseph Banks Colln; Tennyson Colln (both at Tennyson Rsrch Centre); Wheeler Colln (at Boston Lib); Sir Isaac Newton Colln; Newcome Collns (both at Grantham Lib); Brace Colln (at Gainsborough Lib); R.W. Goulding & Binnell Collns (at Louth Lib) *Co-op Schemes:* EMRLS, BLLD *ILLs:* county & natl

Loans: bks & spkn wd/3 wks; audios, videos & CD-ROMs/1 wk *Charges:* CDs/50p; spkn wd/£1; videos/ad £1.50, ch 75p; CD-ROMs/£1.50 *Income Gen:* req & res/75p; lost ticket/£1 *Fines:* bks & spkn wd/ad 50p pw (max £4), ch £1 per 4 wks after 1st overdue notice; audios/50p pw; videos/ad £1.50 pw (max £12), ch 75p pw (max £6); CD-ROMs/£1.50 (max £6) *Equip:* m-readers, m-printers, fax, copiers (A4/10p), clr copiers (variable), computers (incl wd-proc, internet & CD-ROM), rooms for hire (variable) *Disabled:* CCTV, induction loops, mobile lib with lift, Teletext

Stock:	1 Apr 2000	1 Apr 2001
lend:	814669	818280
ref:	221667	222228
AVs:	56797	57627

Issues:	1999-2000	2000-01
ad lend:	4057957	3981559
ch:	1016874	956810
AVs:	353439	406199

Acqs:	1999-2000	2000-01
bks:	95413	91752
AVs:	13095	10421

Acqs: Source: lib suppl & bksellers *Co-op:* JFR *Offcr-in-Charge:* Resources Mgr, as above *Classn:* DDC *Cat: Type:* author, classified, subj & title *Medium:* auto *Auto Sys:* DS Galaxy *Svcs: Extramural:* schools, prisons, hosps, old people's homes, housebnd, day centres, sheltered housing *Info:* LINNET (Lincolnshire INformation NETwork), business, community, council, European, career, health *Other:* Open Learning *Activs:* ch's activs, bk sales, temp exhibs, poetry readings, lit festival, author visits, writers workshops, readers groups *Enqs:* 585000 (1999-2000); 406192 (2000-01) *Staff: Libns:* 64 *Non-Prof:* 251

Inc from:	1999-2000	2000-01
local govt:	£5511804	£5539924
fines etc:	£1437416	£1357588
total:	£6949220	£6897512

Exp on:	1999-2000	2000-01
stock:	£1160210	£1025280
salaries:	£4072516	£4186082
total:	£6949220	£6897512

Liverpool

P76 Liverpool Libraries and Information Services

Central Lib, William Brown Street, Liverpool, L3 8EW (0151-233-5829; *fax:* 0151-233-5824)
Email: refbt.central.library@liverpool.gov.uk
Internet: http://www.liverpool.gov.uk/

Local Auth: Liverpool City Council *Pop:* 457300 *Cttee:* Culture & Tourism *Larger Dept:* Edu & Lifelong Learning Svc *Chief:* Head of Lib Svcs: Ms Joyce Little BA, MBA, MCLIP *Main Libs:* CENTRAL LIB, addr as above *Branch Libs:* ALLERTON LIB, Allerton Rd, Liverpool, L18 9HJ (0151-724-2987; *email:* allerton.library@liverpool.gov.uk); BRECK RD LIB, Breck Rd, Liverpool, L5 6PX (0151-233-1795; *email:* breckroad.library@liverpool.gov.uk); CHILDWALL LIB, Childwall Fiveways, Liverpool, L16 6YG (0151-722-3214; *email:* childwall.library@liverpool.gov.uk); CROXTETH LIB, Croxteth Sports Centre, Altcross Rd, Liverpool, L11 0BS (0151-546-3964; *email:* croxteth.library@liverpool.gov.uk); DOVECOTT LIB, rear of Dovecott Parade, Liverpool, L14 9BA (0151-233-6455; *email:* dovecott.library@liverpool.gov.uk); EDGE HILL LIB, Lodge Ln, Liverpool, L8 0QH (0151-709-5213; *email:* edgehill.library@liverpool.gov.uk); FAZAKERLEY LIB, Longmoor Ln, Liverpool, L10 7LU (0151-525-1124; *email:* fazakerley.library@liverpool.gov.uk); GARSTON LIB, Bowden Rd, Liverpool, L19 1QN (0151-427-7422; *email:*

garston.library@liverpool.gov.uk); GT HOMER ST LIB, Gt Homer St, Liverpool, L5 3LF (0151-207-1432; *email:* ghomer.library@liverpool.gov.uk); HUNTS CROSS LIB, Hunts Cross School, Kingsthorne Rd, Liverpool, L25 0PJ (0151-486-9376; *email:* huntscross.library@liverpool.gov.uk); KENSINGTON LIB, Kensington, Liverpool, L7 2RJ (0151-233-4495; *email:* kensington.library@liverpool.gov.uk); LARKHILL LIB, Queens Dr, Liverpool, L13 0DB (0151-226-2057; *email:* larkhill.library@liverpool.gov.uk); LEE VALLEY LIB, Lee Valley Millennium Centre, Childwall Valley Rd, Liverpool, L25 2RF (0151-233-1950; *email:* leevalley.library@liverpool.gov.uk); LISTER DR LIB, Green Ln, Liverpool, L13 7EB (0151-228-3004; *email:* listerdrive.library@liverpool.gov.uk); NORRIS GREEN LIB, Townsend Ave, Liverpool, L11 5AF (0151-233-1090; *email:* norrisgreen. library@liverpool.gov.uk); OLD SWAN LIB, Prescot Rd, Liverpool, L13 5XG (0151-228-3187; *email:* oldswan.library@liverpool.gov.uk); SEFTON PK LIB, Aigburth Rd, Liverpool, L17 4JS (0151-727-1559; *email:* seftonpark.library@liverpool. gov.uk); SPEKE LIB, Central Ave, Liverpool, L24 0TW (0151-486-2227; *email:* speke.library@ liverpool.gov.uk); SPELLOW LIB, County Rd, Liverpool, L4 3QF (0151-525-5477; *email:* spellow.library@liverpool.gov.uk); TOXTETH LIB, Windsor St, Liverpool, L8 1XF (0151-709-7489; *email:* toxteth.library@liverpool.gov.uk); WALTON LIB, Evered Ave, Liverpool, L9 2AF (0151-525-6098; *email:* walton.library@liverpool.gov.uk); WAVER-TREE LIB, Picton Rd, Liverpool, L15 4LP (0151-225-8938; *email:* wavertree.library@ liverpool.gov.uk); WOOLTON LIB, Allerton Rd, Liverpool, L25 7RQ (0151-428-2235; *email:* woolton.library@liverpool.gov.uk)
Svc Pts: Mobile: 2
Collns: EC colln; patents; BSI; UN deposit colln; bookplates; Hornby Lib (rare bks & bindings); historical colln of ch's bks *Co-op Schemes:* Patents Network, LADSIRLAC, BLCMP, Libs North West, Libs Together *ILLs:* county, natl & internatl *Loans:* bks & audios/3 wks; videos, DVDs & CD-ROMs/1 wk *Charges:* CDs/£1-£1.50; videos & DVDs/£2-£2.50; music parts/£25-£55 pa *Income Gen:* req & res/ad 80p, conc 40p, ch 10p; inter-lib loans/£2.50 *Fines:* bks/ad 8p pd, oap 3p pd (£4 max), disabled exempt; audios, videos & DVDs/3p-50p pd *Equip:* m-readers, m-printers, video viewers, fax, copiers (A4/10p, A3/20p), clr copier (A4/£1.50, A3/£2.50), computers (incl wd-procs, CD-ROM & internet), rooms for hire *Disabled:* Kurzweil, CCTV, talking teletext, braille embosser, hearing loops, minicom, video conferencing facilities for deaf people

Stock:	1 Apr 2000	1 Apr 2001
ad lend:	622597	597193
ad ref:	339827	328894
ch:	158253	146012
audios:	31326	31586
videos:	3767	3874
CD-ROMs:	929	936
periodcls:	690	998
archvs:	8050 linear m	8050 linear m

Issues:	1999-2000	2000-01
ad lend:	1879403	2106045
ch:	408966	430176
instns:	17237	15979
audios:	98196	115305
videos:	13895	19623
CD-ROMs:	1930	3321

Acqs:	1999-2000	2000-01
bks:	77444	107371
AVs:	6425	6153

Acqs: Source: lib suppl *Offcr-in-Charge:* Team Leader (Stock Supply): Mrs Sue Finnesey (Sue.Finnesey@liverpool.gov.uk)
Classn: DDC *Cat: Type:* author, classified, dictionary, subj & title *Medium:* auto & sheaf catalogue *Auto Sys:* Talis *Svcs: Extramural:* schools, prisons, old people's homes, housebnd

Info: small business unit, MRLS (local govt svc), LADSIRLAC (info svc to industry) *Other:* 4 Open Learning Centres, patent clinics, UK Online computing centres, LearnDirect *Activs:* ch's activs, bk sales, temp exhibs, poetry readings *Enqs:* 919317 (1999-2000); 1051417 (2000-01)
Staff: Libns: 64.3 *Non-Prof:* 199.5

Inc from:	1999-2000	2000-01
local govt:	£7955892	£8382641
fines etc:	£425141	£327298
total:	£8520393	£8962401

Exp on:	1999-2000	2000-01
bks:	£751832	£931465
AVs:	£119089	£128650
elec media:	£6548	£6248
salaries:	£4329746	£4471791
total:	£8520393	£8962401

London: Barking and Dagenham

P77 Barking and Dagenham Library Services

Central Lib, Barking, Essex, IG11 7NB (020-8227-3604; *fax:* 020-8227-3699)
Email: libraries@barking-dagenham.gov.uk
Internet: http://www.barking-dagenham.gov.uk/

Local Auth: London Borough of Barking & Dagenham *Pop:* 164000 *Larger Dept:* Edu, Arts & Libs *Dept Chief:* Dir: Mr R. Luxton OBE *Chief:* Head of Lib Svcs: Mr Trevor Brown MCLIP (trevor.brown@lbbd.gov.uk) *Dep:* Principal Libn (Learning & Development): Mrs Susan Leighton MCLIP (sleighton@barking-dagenham.gov.uk) *Other Snr Staff:* Principal Libn (Info & Resources Mgmt): Mr Tony Clifford (tony. clifford@lbbd.gov.uk); Principal Libn (Customer & Professional Svcs): Ms Sylvia Currie (scurrie@ barking-dagenham.gov.uk); Principal Libn (Quality & Standards): Mr David Bailey (dbailey@barking-dagenham.gov.uk)
Main Libs: CENTRAL LIB, addr as above (020-8227-3604; *fax:* 020-8227-3625; *email:* barking. library@lbbd.gov.uk); RECTORY LIB, Rectory Rd, Dagenham, Essex, RM10 9SA (tel & fax: 020-8270-6233; *email:* rectory.library@lbbd.gov.uk); VALENCE LIB, Becontree Ave, Dagenham, Essex, RM8 3HT (020-8270-6864; *fax:* 020-8270-6869; *email:* valence.library@lbbd.gov.uk); WHALEBONE LIB, High Rd, Chadwell Heath, Romford, Essex, RM6 6AS (tel & fax: 020-8270-4305; *email:* whalebone.library@lbbd.gov.uk); WOODWARD LIB, Woodward Rd, Dagenham, Essex, RM9 4SP (tel & fax: 020-8270-4166; *email:* woodward.library@lbbd.gov.uk) *Branch Libs:* MARKYATE LIB, Markyate Rd, Dagenham, Essex, RM8 2LD (tel & fax: 020-8270-4137; *email:* markyate.library@lbbd.gov.uk); RUSH GREEN LIB, Dagenham Rd, Rush Green, Romford, Essex, RM7 0TL (tel & fax: 020-8270-4304; *email:* rushgreen.library@lbbd.gov.uk); THAMES VIEW LIB, 2a Farr Ave, Barking, Essex, IG11 0NZ (tel & fax: 020-8270-4164; *email:* thamesview. library@lbbd.gov.uk); WANTZ LIB, Rainham Rd North, Dagenham, Essex, RM10 7DX (tel & fax: 020-8270-4169; *email:* wantz.library@lbbd.gov.uk)
Svc Pts: PT: 2 *AV:* 11 *Computers:* 11 *Internet:* 11
Collns: JFR; special colln on printing, publishing, lithography & journalism (formerly part of LASER scheme); local hist (at Central & Valence Libs) *Co-op Schemes:* ELIT, GLASS *ILLs:* county, natl & internatl *Loans:* bks & audios/3 wks; videos/features 3 days, ch & special interest 7 days; lang courses/3-6 wks *Charges:* LPs/35p; cassettes/45p; CDs/70p, set £1.20; audio sub/£6 for 3 months, £10 for 6 months; lang courses/80p for 3 wks, £1.50 for 6 wks; videos/£1.10-£2.10 *Income Gen:* req/40p; lost ticket/50p; study carrels/50p *Fines:* bks & audios/ad & oap 10p pd

(£10 max); videos/loan charge; no charge for under 14s, blind exempt *Equip:* m-readers, m-printers (30p), fax, copiers (A4/10p, A3/20p), clr copier (£1), computers (incl internet & CD-ROM), rooms for hire (varies) *Disabled:* CCTV, personal communicators, minicom

Stock:	1 Apr 2000
lend:	380484
ref:	68120
AVs:	38517

Issues:	1999-2000
bks:	1187101
AVs:	412317

Acqs: Source: lib suppl *Co-op:* LASER, GLASS *Offcr-in-Charge:* Principal Libn (Info & Resources Mgmt), as above
Classn: DDC *Cat: Type:* author, classified, dictionary, subj & title *Medium:* auto *Auto Sys:* Dynix *Svcs: Extramural:* schools, old people's homes, housebnd *Info:* community, European, business, local & family hist (Essex) *Other:* Open Learning *Activs:* ch's activs, temp exhibs, lectures
Enqs: 164528 (1999-2000)
Staff: Libns: 31 *Non-Prof:* 53.5

London: Barnet

P78 Barnet Libraries

Barnet Cultural Svcs, The Old Town Hall, Friern Barnet Ln, London, N11 3DL (020-8359-3164; *fax:* 020-8359-3171)
Internet: http://www.libraries.barnet.gov.uk/

Local Auth: London Borough of Barnet *Pop:* 331500 *Cttee:* Rec, Leisure & Arts, Overview & Scrutiny Cttee *Larger Dept:* Cultural Svcs *Chief:* Head of Cultural Svcs: Mrs Pam Usher BA(Hons), DMS, MCLIP *Dep:* Svc Mgr (Operations & Development): Ms Tricia Little BA, MCLIP (tricia.little@barnet.gov.uk)
Main (Group) Libs: CHIPPING BARNET LIB, 3 Stapylton Rd, Barnet, Hertfordshire, EN5 4QT (020-8359-4040); CHURCH END LIB, 24 Hendon Ln, Finchley, London, N3 1TR (020-8346-5711); EDGWARE LIB, Hale Ln, Edgware, Middlesex, HA8 8NN (020-8359-2626; *fax:* 020-8359-2139); HENDON LIB, The Burroughs, London, NW4 4BQ (020-8359-2629) *Branch Libs:* BURNT OAK LIB, Watling Ave, Edgware, Middlesex, HA8 0UB (020-8959-3112); CHILDS HILL LIB, 320 Cricklewood Ln, London, NW2 2QE (020-8455-5390); EAST BARNET LIB, 85 Brookhill Rd, East Barnet, Hertfordshire, EN4 8SG (020-8440-4376; *fax:* 020-8449-1883); EAST FINCHLEY LIB, 225 High Rd, London, N2 9BB (020-8883-2664); FRIERN BARNET LIB, Friern Barnet Rd, London, N11 3DS (020-8368-2680); GOLDERS GREEN LIB, 156 Golders Green Rd, London, NW11 8HE (020-8359-2060; *fax:* 020-8359-2066); GRAHAME PK LIB, The Concourse, London, NW9 5XL (020-8200-0470); HAMPSTEAD GDN SUBURB LIB, 15 Market Pl, London, NW11 6LB (020-8455-1235); MILL HILL LIB, Hartley Ave, London, NW7 2HX (020-8959-5066); NORTH FINCHLEY LIB, Ravensdale Ave, London, N12 9HP (020-8445-4081); OSIDGE LIB, Brunswick Pk Rd, London, N11 1EY (020-8368-0532); SOUTH FRIERN LIB, Colney Hatch Ln, London, N10 1HD (020-8883-6513); TOTTERIDGE LIB, 109 Totteridge Ln, London, N20 8DZ (020-8445-5288)
Svc Pts: Mobile: 2 + mobile action pt vehicle *AV:* 17 *Other:* LOCAL STUDIES & ARCHVS (see **A255**); town hall info centre
Collns: GLASS: Chopin, Liszt, Jazz Me-Mo, stage musicals, Japanese folk music (both at Hendon Lib) *Co-op Schemes:* GLASS *ILLs:* county, natl & internatl *Loans:* bks & audios/3 wks; videos & DVDs/3 days or 1 wk; CD-ROMs/1 wk *Charges:* records/60p, set £1; cassettes/70p (ch's 30p), set £1.40 (ch's 60p); CD/80p, set £1.60; videos/£1-£3.50; CD-ROMs/£2.50 ☞

(Barnet Libs cont)
Income Gen: res/posted £1, collected 73p; lost ticket/£1.75, conc 45p; vouchers for audios/CDs £18, cassettes £16, records £10 (price for 25 vouchers) **Fines:** all items/15p pd (27p for overdue notice), registered blind exempt **Equip:** 5 m-readers, 3 m-printers (20p-40p), 6 fax (various); 3 video viewers; 19 copiers (A4/10p, A3/15p), 3 clr copiers (£1), computers (incl wd-proc, internet & CD-ROM), passport photo booth, 8 rooms for hire (various) **Disabled:** CCTV magnifiers, minicoms

Stock:	1 Apr 2000	1 Apr 2001
ad lend:	582865	557837
ad ref:	47591	47155
ch:	234479	236434
audios:	64580	62996
videos:	16219	17733
CD-ROMs:	802	1977

Issues:	1999-2000	2000-01
ad lend:	1889446	1686357
ch:	833558	742564
audios:	140429	127674
videos:	118515	155852
CD-ROMs:	1815	6302

Acqs:	1999-2000	2000-01
bks:	53176	73001
AVs:	7837	9985

Acqs: Source: lib suppl **Offcr-in-Charge:** Head of Bibliographical Svcs: Ms Mary Ross
Classn: DDC **Cat:** Type: author, classified & title **Medium:** auto **Auto Sys:** Geac **Svcs:** Extramural: old people's homes, housebnd **Info:** community, European, council **Other:** Open Learning
Activs: ch's activs, bk sales, temp exhibs
Staff: Libns: 65 Non-Prof: 117
Proj: refurbishment of Hendon Lib

London: Bexley

P79 Bexley Library Service
Thamesmead Centre, Yarnton Way, Erith, Kent, DA18 4DR (020-8320-4132; *fax:* 020-8320-4050)
Email: libraries@bexley.gov.uk
Internet: http://www.bexley.gov.uk/

Local Auth: London Borough of Bexley **Pop:** 220489 **Cttee:** Cabinet memb for Leisure, Arts & Libs **Larger Dept:** Corporate Svcs **Dept Chief:** Chief Exec & Dir of Corporate Svcs: Mr Chris Duffield **Chief:** Head of Lib & Info Svcs: Mr F.V. Johnston LLB, DMS, MILAM, MCLIP (fred.johnson@bexley.gov.uk) **Other Snr Staff:** Lib Development Mgr: Mr Hugh Paton BA, DipLib, MCLIP (hugh.paton@bexley.gov.uk); Principal Libn (Town & Community Svcs): Mrs Lynn Sawbridge BA, MCLIP (lynn.sawbridge@bexley. gov.uk); Principal Libn (Central & Neighbourhood Svcs): Mr Geoff Boulton BA, MCLIP (geoff. boulton@bexley.gov.uk)
Main Libs: CENTRAL LIB, Townley Rd, Bexleyheath, Kent, DA6 7HJ (*lend:* 020-8301-1066; *ref:* 020-8301-5151; *fax:* 020-8303-7872; *email:* BexleyCentralLibrary@bexley.gov.uk); SIDCUP LIB, Hadlow Rd, Sidcup, Kent, DA14 4AQ (020-8300-2958; *fax:* 020-8309-1351; *email:* SidcupLibrary@bexley.gov.uk); THAMESMEAD LIB, Binsey Walk, Thamesmead, London, SE2 9TS (020-8310-9944; *email:* ThamesmeadLibrary@ bexley.gov.uk); WELLING LIB, Bellegrove Rd,

Welling, Kent, DA16 3PA (020-8303-2788; *fax:* 020-8303-3926; *email:* WellingLibrary@bexley. gov.uk) **Branch Libs:** BEXLEY VILLAGE LIB, Bourne Rd, Bexley, Kent, DA5 1LU (01322-522168; *email:* BexleyVillageLibrary@bexley. gov.uk); BLACKFEN LIB, Cedar Ave, Sidcup, Kent, DA15 8NJ (020-8300-3010; *email:* BlackfenLibrary@bexley.gov.uk); BOSTALL LIB, King Harold's Way, Bexleyheath, Kent, DA7 5RE (020-8310-1779; *email:* BostallLibrary@bexley. gov.uk); CRAYFORD LIB, Crayford Rd, Crayford, Kent, DA1 4ER (01322-526050; *email:* CrayfordLibrary@bexley.gov.uk); ERITH LIB, Walnut Tree Rd, Erith, Kent, DA8 3HF (01322-336582; *email:* ErithLibrary@bexley.gov.uk); NORTH HEATH LIB, Mill Rd, Erith, Kent, DA8 1HW (01322-333663; *email:* NorthHeathLibrary@ bexley.gov.uk); SLADE GREEN LIB, Howbury Centre, Slade Green Rd, Erith, Kent, DA8 2HX (020-8319-9640; *email:* SladeGreenLibrary@ bexley.gov.uk); UPPER BELVEDERE LIB, Woolwich Rd, Upper Belvedere, Kent, DA17 5EQ (01322-439760; *email:* UpperBelvedereLibrary@ bexley.gov.uk)
Svc Pts: PT: 1 Mobile: 2 AV: 13 Computers: 13 Internet: 13 Other: LOCAL STUDIES CENTRE, at Central Lib (see **A47**)
Collns: JFR: Che-Cn; playsets & music sets (at Crayford Lib) **Co-op Schemes:** JFR, GLASS, SEAL, V3, SELPIG **ILLs:** county, natl & internatl
Loans: bks & audios/3 wks; videos, DVDs, CD-ROMs & Playstation games/1 wk; linguaphone courses/12 wks **Charges:** audios/80p-£2; videos/ recent £3, others £1.50; DVDs/recent £3, others £2; CD-ROMs/£1; Playstation games/£3; linguaphone courses/£10 **Income Gen:** req/65p; lost ticket/ad £2, ch £1 **Fines:** bks/ad & oap 18p pd, ch reminder letter only; audios/18p pd; videos, DVDs, CD-ROMs & Playstation games/loan charge; reminder letter/60p per notice sent; visually impaired exempt from talking bk charges **Equip:** 4 m-readers, 2 m-printers (10p per pg), 3 fax (UK £1 per pg, overseas £2), 13 copiers (A4/ 10p, A3/20p), clr copier (A4/£1, A3/£2), 137 computers (all with wd-proc & internet, 15 with CD-ROM), 3 rooms for hire (£6-£36) **Disabled:** Kurzweil, accessibility hardware & software for PCs

Stock:	1 Apr 2000	1 Apr 2001
ad lend:	198791	196164
ad ref:	171326	172954
ch:	91530	88005
audios:	12851	13099
videos:	10136	10305
CD-ROMs:	346	800
periodcls:	143	320
archvs:	422 linear m	842 linear m

Issues:	1999-2000	2000-01
ad lend:	1276248	1136922
ch:	487393	427297
audios:	56586	55735
videos:	69779	66427
CD-ROMs:	1588	2555

Acqs:	1999-2000	2000-01
bks:	39555	40953
AVs:	6966	6415

Acqs: Source: lib suppl & bksellers **Co-op:** SELPIG consortium stock purchasing **Offcr-in-Charge:** Bibliographical Svcs Mgr: Mrs Julia Peacock (julie.peacock@bexley.gov.uk)
Classn: DDC **Cat:** Type: author, classified, subj & title **Medium:** auto **Auto Sys:** Dynix **Svcs:** Extramural: hosps, old people's homes, housebnd, day centres, play groups **Info:** EU Info Relay, tourist, council, community **Other:** UKOnline, LearnDirect access pts **Activs:** ch's activs, bk sales, temp exhibs, reading groups, talks
Enqs: 308832 (1999-2000); 285611 (2000-01)
Staff: Libns: 35 Non-Prof: 95

Inc from:	1999-2000	2000-01
local govt:	£3562642	£3869000
fines etc:	£310026	£343098
total:	£3872668	£4212098

Exp on:	1999-2000	2000-01
bks:	£391751	£490392
AVs:	£81724	£90924
salaries:	£1992057	£2070936
total:	£3907649	£4211991

London: Brent

P80 Brent Library Service
Brent Lib HQ, 4th Floor, Chesterfield House, 9 Park Ln, Wembley, Middlesex, HA9 7RW (020-8937-3144; *fax:* 020-8937-3008)
Email: raj.phull@brent.gov.uk
Internet: http://www.brent.gov.uk/libraryservice/

Local Auth: London Borough of Brent **Pop:** 254900 **Larger Dept:** Dept of Edu, Arts & Libs **Dept Chief:** Dir: Mr John Christie **Chief:** Head of Lib Svcs: Ms Marianne Locke
Branch Libs: BARHAM PK LIB, Harrow Rd, Sudbury, Middlesex, HA0 2HB (020-8937-3550; *fax:* 020-8937-3553; *email:* barhamparklibrary@ brent.gov.uk); CRICKLEWOOD LIB, 152 Olive Rd, Cricklewood, London, NW2 8UY (020-8937-3540; *fax:* 020-8450-5211; *email:* cricklewoodlibrary@brent.gov.uk); EALING RD LIB, Coronet Parade, Ealing Rd, Wembley, Middlesex, HA0 4BR (020-8937-3560; *fax:* 020-8795-3425; *email:* ealingroadlibrary@brent.gov.uk); HARLESDEN LIB, Craven Park Rd, Harlesden, London, NW10 8SE (020-8965-7132; *fax:* 020-8838-2199; *email:* harlesdenlibrary@brent.gov.uk); KENSAL RISE LIB, Bathurst Gdns, Harlesden, London, NW10 5JA (020-8969-0942; *fax:* 020-8960-8399; *email:* kensalriselibrary@brent.gov.uk); KILBURN LIB, Salusbury Rd, Kilburn, London, NW6 6NN (020-8937-3530; *fax:* 020-7625-6387; *email:* kilburnlibrary@brent.gov.uk); KINGSBURY LIB, Stag Ln, Kingsbury, London, NW9 9AE (020-8937-3520; *fax:* 020-8905-0264; *email:* kingsburylibrary@brent.gov.uk); NEASDEN LIB, 277 Neasden Ln, Neasden, London, NW10 1QJ (020-8937-3580; *fax:* 020-8208-3909; *email:* neasdenlibrary@brent.gov.uk); PRESTON LIB, Carlton Ave East, Wembley, Middlesex, HA9 8PL (020-8937-3510; *fax:* 020-8908-6220; *email:* prestonlibrary@brent.gov.uk); TOKYNGTON LIB, Monks Pk, Wembley, Middlesex, HA9 6JE (020-8937-3590; *fax:* 020-89795-3440; *email:* tokyngtonlibrary@brent.gov.uk); TOWN HALL LIB, Brent Town Hall, Forty Ln, Wembley, Middlesex, HA9 9HV (020-8937-3500; *fax:* 020-8937-3504; *email:* townhalllibrary@brent.gov.uk); WILLESDEN GREEN LIB, 95 High Rd, Willesden Green, London, NW10 2ST (020-8937-3400; *fax:* 020-8937-3401; *email:* willesdengreenlibrary@ brent.gov.uk)
Svc Pts: Mobile: 2 Other: BRENT COMMUNITY HIST ARCHV, at Cricklewood Lib (see **A258**); HOMEBND & MOBILE LIB SVCS, 2-12 Grange Rd, Willesden, London, NW10 2QY (020-8937-3460)
Collns: local hist (at Cricklewood Lib & Archv); minority langs & lit (at Ealing Rd Lib); Fiction: authors Co-Col; GLASS: classical composers P-Sai; folk music of Ireland; Jazz T-Vau; music hall; theatre **Co-op Schemes:** GLASS, CILLA
Loans: bks & audios/3 wks; videos & DVDs/1 wk **Charges:** cassettes/30p; CDs/80p; videos/50p-£2 depending on category; DVDs/£2-£2.50 **Income Gen:** res/70p, oaps & 12-14 year olds 40p, under-12s exempt; lost ticket/ad £1, conc 50p; lost stock/full replacement cost (min £4) **Fines:** bks/15p pd, oaps & 12-14 year olds 8p pd, under-12s exempt; audios/15p pd; videos/ad 10p-40p pd; DVDs/40p-50p pd **Equip:** m-reader/ printer (50p), 10 fax (various), 8 copiers (A4/10p, A3/20p), 2 clr copiers (A4/£1, A3/£1.50), computers (incl wd-proc, CD-ROM & internet, access free, printouts 10p b&w, 50p clr), rooms for hire (various) **Disabled:** Kurzweil **Online:** lib catalogue

Stock:	1 Apr 2000	1 Apr 2001
lend:	518689	420176
ref:	13405	13559
AVs:	44192	37867
periodcls:	52	87

Issues:	1999-2000	2000-01
bks:	1094504	1055862
AVs:	159547	191757

Acqs:	1999-2000	2000-01
bks:	65333	35531
AVs:	7343	5900

Classn: DDC *Cat: Auto Sys:* Urica *Svcs:*
Extramural: old people's homes, housebnd *Info:*
business, community, European, Age Concern
Other: 4 IT Learning Centres, creche *Activs:* ch's
activs, bk sales, temp exhibs, poetry readings,
writers groups, Brent Festival, pensioners' events
Enqs: 105911 (1999-2000); 103909 (2000-01)
Staff: Libns: 25.4 *Non-Prof:* 84.6

Inc from:	1999-2000	2000-01
fines etc:	£525212	£576329

Exp on:	1999-2000	2000-01
stock:	£318654	£327292
salaries:	£1897059	£2126121
total:	£3752051	£4055204

London: Bromley

P81 Bromley Libraries

Central Lib, 100 High Street, Bromley, Kent, BR1
1EX (020-8460-9955; *fax:* 020-8313-9975)
Internet: http://bk.bromley.gov.uk/

Local Auth: London Borough of Bromley *Pop:*
297120 *Cttee:* Leisure & Community Svcs Cttee
Larger Dept: Leisure & Community Svcs *Dept
Chief:* Dir: Mr R. Stoakes MSc, MILAM *Chief:*
Chief Libn: Mr B. Walkinshaw BA(Hons), MCIM,
MCLIP, FRSA *Dep:* Lib Operations Mgr: Mr L. F.
Favret BA, DipMgt, MIMgt, MCLIP
Main Libs: CENTRAL LIB, addr as above (020-
8460-9955; *fax:* 020-8313-9975; *email:* reference.
library@bromley.gov.uk); BECKENHAM LIB,
Beckenham Rd, Beckenham, Kent, BR3 4PE
(020-8650-7292; *email:* beckenham.library@
bromley.gov.uk); ORPINGTON LIB, The Priory,
Church Hill, Orpington, Kent, BR6 0HH (01689-
831551; *email:* orpington.library@bromley.gov.uk);
PETTS WOOD LIB, Frankswood Ave, Petts
Wood, Orpington, Kent, BR5 1BP (01689-821607;
email: pettswood.library@bromley.gov.uk)
Branch Libs: ANERLEY LIB, Anerley Town Hall,
Anerley Rd, Anerley, London, SE20 8BD (020-
8778-7457; *email:* anerley.library@bromley.
gov.uk); BIGGIN HILL LIB, Church Rd, Biggin
Hill, Westerham, Kent, TN16 3LB (01959-574468;
email: biggin.hill@bromley.gov.uk); BURNT ASH
LIB, Burnt Ash Ln, Bromley, Kent, BR1 5AF (020-
8460-3405; *email:* burntash.library@bromley.
gov.uk); CHISLEHURST LIB, Red Hill, Chislehurst, Kent, BR7 6DA (020-8467-1318; *email:*
chislehurst.library@bromley.gov.uk); HAYES LIB,
Hayes St, Hayes, Bromley, Kent, BR2 7LH (020-
8462-2445; *email:* hayes.library@bromley.gov.uk);
MOTTINGHAM LIB, 31 Mottingham Rd, Mottingham, London, SE9 4QZ (020-8857-5406; *email:*
mottingham.library@bromley.gov.uk); PENGE
LIB, 186 Maple Rd, Penge, London, SE20 8HT
(020-8778-8772; *email:* penge.library@bromley.
gov.uk); ST PAUL'S CRAY LIB, Mickleham Rd, St
Paul's Cray, Bromley, Kent, BR5 2RW (020-8300-
5454; *email:* stpaulscray.library@bromley.gov.uk);
SHORTLANDS LIB, 110 Shortlands Rd, Bromley,
Kent, BR2 0JP (020-8460-9692; *email:* shortlands.
library@bromley.gov.uk); SOUTHBOROUGH LIB,
Southborough Ln, Bromley, Kent, BR2 8HP (020-
8467-0355; *email:* southborough.library@bromley.
gov.uk); WEST WICKHAM LIB, Glebe Way, West
Wickham, Kent, BR4 0SH (020-8777-4139; *email:*
westwickham.library@bromley.gov.uk)

Svc Pts: Mobile: 1 *AV:* 15 *Other:* LOCAL
STUDIES LIB (see **A79**)
Collns: BSI; H.G. Wells Colln; Walter de la Mare
Colln (all at Central Lib); Harlow Bequest Colln (at
Orpington Museum); GLASS: Composers E-Gl
minus Elgar; Jazz Composers R-S; Instructional
Recordings; Crystal Palace Colln (at Anerley Lib)
Co-op Schemes: GLASS, SEAL *ILLs:* county,
natl & internatl *Loans:* bks & audios/3 wks; ch's
cassettes/1 wk; videos/3 days or 3 wks; DVDs/3
days; CD-ROMs & Playstation games/1 wk
Charges: cassettes/40p, sets 90p-£1.40; ch's
cassettes/16p, sets 27p; CDs/£1, sets £1.70-
£3.15; videos/90p-£3.10 depending on type;
DVDs/£1.80, new titles £3.10; CD-ROMs/£1.40 or
£2.90; linguaphone & Open Learning/£3.70 per 3
wks *Income Gen:* res/80p-£1.20, oap 40p-60p,
ch free; lost ticket/ad £2.85, ch 80p, conc £1.45
Fines: bks, audios & special interest videos/16p
pd; ch's cassettes, linguaphone & Open Learning/
loan charge; videos/55p pd; new title videos,
DVDs, CD-ROMs & Playstation games/£1.15 pd;
postage charged on overdue notices *Equip:* 9
m-readers, 6 m-printers (20p per pg), fax (£1 per
pg), copier at each lib (A4/10p, A3/20p), clr
copiers (A4/£1, A3/£2), computers (incl wd-proc,
internet & CD-ROM, printouts 20p per pg)
Disabled: Kurzweil, CCTV, closed caption video
readers *Online:* Datastar, ESA-IRS, Dialog

Stock:	1 Apr 2000	1 Apr 2001
ad lend:	446577	477057
ad ref:	92005	62209
ch:	179140	198700
audios:	65048	54940
videos:	10634	16049
CD-ROMs:	1331	496

Acqs:	1999-2000	2000-01
all items:	72031	72647

Acqs: Source: lib suppl *Offcr-in-Charge:* Supply
Mgr
Classn: DDC, own *Cat: Medium:* auto *Auto
Sys:* Geac *Svcs: Extramural:* schools advice, old
people's homes, housebnd *Info:* business,
careers *Other:* Open Learning, Internet
Exchange, People's Network *Activs:* ch's activs,
bk sales, temp exhibs, coffee mornings, concerts
Offcr-in-Charge: Group Mgrs
Enqs: 314340 (1999-2000); 323690 (2000-01)
Staff: Libns: 54 *Non-Prof:* 131

London: Camden

P82 Camden Library Service

Crowndale Centre, 218 Eversholt Street, London,
NW1 1BD (020-7974-4058)
Email: david.jones@camden.gov.uk
Internet: http://www.camden.gov.uk/

Local Auth: London Borough of Camden *Pop:*
202826 *Larger Dept:* Leisure & Community
Svcs *Chief:* Head of Libs, Info & Community
Learning: Mr David Jones
Main Libs: HOLBORN LIB, 32-38 Theobalds Rd,
London, WC1X 8PA (020-7974-6345/6; *fax:* 020-
7974-6356; *email:* holbornlibrary@camden.gov.uk);
KENTISH TOWN LIB, 262-266 Kentish Town Rd,
London, NW5 2AA (020-7485-1121; *fax:* 020-7482-
5650; *email:* kentishtownlibrary@camden.gov.uk);
QUEEN'S CRES LIB, 165 Queen's Cres, London,
NW5 4HH (020-7974-6252; *fax:* 020-7974-6243;
email: queenscrescentlibrary@camden.gov.uk);
ST PANCRAS LIB, Camden Town Hall, Argyle St,
London, WC1H 8NN (020-7974-5833; *fax:* 020-
7974-5963; *email:* stpancraslibrary@camden.
gov.uk); SWISS COTTAGE CENTRAL LIB, 88
Ave Rd, London, NW3 3HA (020-7974-6522; *fax:*
020-7974-6532; *email:* swisscottagelibrary@
camden.gov.uk); WEST HAMPSTEAD LIB,
Dennington Pk Rd, London, NW6 1AU (020-7974-
6610; *fax:* 020-7974-6539; *email:*
westhampsteadlibrary@camden.gov.uk)

Branch Libs: BELSIZE LIB, Antrim Rd, London,
NW3 4XN (020-7974-6518; *fax:* 020-7974-6508;
email: belsizelibrary@camden.gov.uk); CAMDEN
TOWN LIB, Crowndale Centre, 218 Eversholt St,
London, NW1 1DB (020-7974-1563; *fax:* 020-
7974-1582; *email:*
camdentownlibrary@camden.gov.uk); CHALK
FARM LIB, Sharpleshall St, London, NW1 8YN
(020-7974-6526; *fax:* 020-7974-6502; *email:*
chalkfarmlibrary@camden.gov.uk); HEATH LIB,
Keats Grove, London, NW3 2RR (020-7974-6520;
fax: 020-7974-6618; *email:* heathlibrary@camden.
gov.uk); HIGHGATE LIB, Chester Rd, London,
N19 5DH (020-7974-5752; *fax:* 020-7974-5555;
email: highgatelibrary@camden.gov.uk); KILBURN
LIB, Cotleigh Rd, London, NW6 2NP (020-7974-
1965; *fax:* 020-7974-6524; *email:* kilburnlibrary@
camden.gov.uk); REGENTS PK LIB, Compton Cl,
Robert St, London, NW1 3QT (020-7974-1530;
fax: 020-7974-1531; *email:* regentsparklibrary@
camden.gov.uk)
Svc Pts: Mobile: 1 *AV:* 13 *Computers:* 11
Internet: 9 *Other:* HOME LIB SVC; SCHOOLS'
LIB SVC; LOCAL STUDIES & ARCHVS CENTRE
(see **A262**)
Collns: Phil & Psy Colln; Map Colln (both at
Swiss Cottage Lib); JFR: Go-Gre, Pid-Pz to 1988,
R-Rnz; GLASS: Beethoven (both at Holborn Lib);
local hist collns; Kate Greenaway Colln (at Keats
House – see **S1225**) *Co-op Schemes:* JFR,
GLASS, SKILLS, Central London Libs Learning
Partnership *ILLs:* county & natl *Loans:* bks,
audios & CD-ROMs/3 wks; videos & DVDs/3
days *Charges:* talking bks/50p; cassettes/40p;
CDs/80p-£1; videos/50p-£2.50; CD-ROMs/£2.50
Income Gen: res/80p, conc 40p; lost ticket/
£1.20, conc 60p *Fines:* bks, audios & videos/ad
12p pd, conc 6p pd; CD-ROMs/20p pd; ch exempt
Equip: m-readers, m-printers, video viewer, fax
(staff use), copiers (5p-15p), computers (incl wd-
proc, internet & CD-ROM) *Disabled:* videophone,
magnification software on PCs, ORC software
Online: KnowUK, Know Europe, UKOP, UK
Newstand

Stock:	1 Apr 2000	1 Apr 2001
lend:	349954	368756
ref:	52344	54373
AVs:	78225	84953
periodcls:	393	367

Issues:	1999-2000	2000-01
bks:	997243	949637
AVs:	189145	200429

Acqs:	1999-2000	2000-01
bks:	65337	42803
AVs:	14777	12166

Acqs: Source: lib suppl, publ & bksellers
Classn: DDC *Cat: Type:* author & classified
Medium: auto *Auto Sys:* Talis *Svcs: Extramural:*
schools, old people's homes, housebnd, day
centres, sheltered housing units *Info:* community,
tourist, council, business, European *Other:* Open
Learning, drop-in session for over 60s, Input-
Output Centre (at Swiss Cottage Central Lib)
Activs: ch's activs, bk sales, temp exhibs *Offcr-
in-Charge:* organised on a group basis
Enqs: 544982 (1999-2000); 549698 (2000-01)
Staff: Libns: 35.4 *Non-Prof:* 106.7

Inc from:	1999-2000	2000-01
local govt:	£6161000	£5974000
fines etc:	£225000	£288000
total:	£6589000	£6364000

Exp on:	1999-2000	2000-01
stock & svcs:	£1110000	£893000
salaries:	£3418000	£3513000
total:	£6589000	£6364000

Public Libraries

London: Croydon

P83 Croydon Library Service

Central Lib, Croydon Clocktower, Katharine Street, Croydon, Surrey, CR9 1ET (020-8760-5400; *fax:* 020-8253-1004)
Internet: http://www.croydon.gov.uk/

Local Auth: London Borough of Croydon *Pop:* 336000 *Cttee:* Cabinet memb for Culture *Larger Dept:* Cultural Svcs *Dept Chief:* Dir of Cultural Svcs: Mr Steve Halsey *Chief:* Asst Dir, Libs: Mrs Adie Scott BA, MCLIP (adie_scott@croydon.gov.uk) *Other Snr Staff:* Libs Operations Mgr: Mrs Brenda Constable (brenda_constable@croydon.gov.uk); Ref & Info Sources Mgr: Ms Heather Kirby (heather_kirby@croydon.gov.uk)
Main Libs: CROYDON CENTRAL LIB, addr as above (*email:* controldesk@croydononline.org)
Branch Libs: ASHBURTON LIB, Lower Addiscombe Rd, Croydon, Surrey, CR0 6RX (020-8656-4148; *email:* ashburton@croydononline.org); BRADMORE GREEN LIB, Bradmore Way, Coulsdon, Surrey, CR5 1PE (01737-553267; *email:* bradmoregreen@croydononline.org); BROAD GREEN LIB, 89 Canterbury Rd, Croydon, Surrey, CR0 3HH (020-8684-4829; *email:* broadgreen@croydononline.org); COULSDON LIB, Brighton Rd, Coulsdon, Surrey, CR5 2NH (020-8660-1548; *email:* coulsdon@croydononline.org); NEW ADDINGTON LIB, Central Parade, New Addington, Croydon, Surrey, CR0 0JB (01689-841248; *email:* newaddington@croydononline.org); NORBURY LIB, Beatrice Ave, Norbury, London, SW16 4UW (020-8679-1597; *email:* norbury@croydononline.org); PURLEY LIB, Banstead Rd, Purley, Surrey, CR8 3YH (020-8660-1171; *email:* purley@croydononline.org); SANDERSTEAD LIB, Farm Fields, Sanderstead, South Croydon, Surrey, CR2 0HL (020-8657-2882; *email:* sanderstead@croydononline.org); SELSDON LIB, Addington Rd, Selsdon, South Croydon, Surrey, CR2 8LA (020-8657-7210; *email:* selsdon@croydononline.org); SHIRLEY LIB, Wickham Rd/Hartland Way, Shirley, Croydon, Surrey, CR0 8BH (020-8777-7650; *email:* shirley@croydononline.org); SOUTH NORWOOD LIB, Lawrence Rd, South Norwood, London, SE25 5AA (020-8653-4545; *email:* southnorwood@croydononline.org); THORNTON HEATH LIB, Brigstock Rd, Thornton Heath, Surrey, CR7 7JB (020-8684-4432; *email:* thorntonheath@croydononline.org)
Svc Pts: Mobile: 1 *AV:* 13 *Computers:* 13 *Internet:* 13
Co-op Schemes: CILLA, SELPIG *ILLs:* county & natl *Loans:* bks & audios/4 wks; videos & CD-ROMs/1 wk *Charges:* cassettes/50p; CDs/70p; videos/varies; CD-ROMs/£1.50 *Income Gen:* res/60p, videos & DVDs £2; lost ticket/ad £1, ch 50p *Fines:* bks/ad & oap 11p pd; audios/11p pd; videos & CD-ROMs/loan charge; registered blind & ch exempt *Equip:* 6 m-readers, 6 m-printers (A4/10p), fax (£1 per pg), 16 copiers (A4/10p, A3/15p), clr copier (A4/£1, A3/£1.50), 203 computers (incl 69 with wd-procs, 46 with CD-ROM & 69 with internet, access free except £5 per hr for wd-procs) *Disabled:* Kurzweil, CCTV scanner, induction loops (all at Central Lib) *Online:* Companies House (cost + small fee), Lexis-Nexis (costs + £30 per hr) *Offcr-in-Charge:* Libs Operations Mgr, as above

Stock:	1 Apr 2000	1 Apr 2001
ad lend:	395883	367967
ad ref:	69262	65315
ch:	200823	173991
audios:	30141	30474
videos:	11371	11238
CD-ROMs:	425	842
periodcls:	509	491
archvs:	662.1 linear m	687.1 linear m

Issues:	1999-2000	2000-01
ad lend:	2043966	1799555
ch:	708704	658102
audios:	169216	167077
videos:	112928	105646
CD-ROMs:	3294	4122

Acqs:	1999-2000	2000-01
bks:	118114	93386
AVs:	10641	9670

Acqs: Source: lib suppl, publ & bksellers *Co-op:* working with SELPIG Consortium *Offcr-in-Charge:* Stock Svcs Mgr: Miss Gill Hyder (gill_hyder@croydon.gov.uk)
Classn: DDC *Cat: Type:* author, classified, subj & title *Medium:* auto *Auto Sys:* Geac *Svcs: Extramural:* old people's homes, housebnd *Info:* business, community, tourist, local studies & archvs *Other:* Open Learning, IT courses *Activs:* ch's activs, bk sales, temp exhibs, poetry readings, reading groups, author visits *Offcr-in-Charge:* Asst Dir, Libs, as above
Enqs: 677417 (1999-2000); 657046 (2000-01)
Staff: Libns: 54 *Other Prof:* 4 *Non-Prof:* 105

Inc from:	1999-2000	2000-01
lfines etc:	£489216	£400019

Exp on:	1999-2000	2000-01
bks:	-	£871702
AVs:	-	£219050
elec media:	-	£145247
salaries:	-	£3620054
total:	£5617357	£6643955

London: Ealing

P84 Ealing Library and Information Service

3SE Perceval House, 14 Uxbridge Rd, Ealing, London, W5 2HL (020-8825-5162)
Email: libuser@ealing.gov.uk
Internet: http://www.ealing.gov.uk/services/libraries/

Local Auth: London Borough of Ealing *Pop:* 311500 *Cttee:* Edu *Larger Dept:* Edu & Leisure *Dept Chief:* Dir of Edu: Mr Alan Parker *Chief:* Head of Lib & Info Svc: Ms Jane Battye
Main Libs: ACTON LIB, High St, Acton, London, W3 6NA (020-8752-0999; *fax:* 020-8992-6086); CENTRAL LIB, 103 Ealing Broadway Centre, Ealing, London, W5 5JY (020-8567-3670; ref: 020-8567-3656; *fax:* 020-8840-2351); GREENFORD LIB, Oldfield Ln South, Greenford, Middlesex, UB6 9LG (020-8578-1466; *fax:* 020-8575-7800); SOUTHALL LIB, Osterley Park Rd, Southall, Middlesex, UB2 4BL (020-8574-3412; *fax:* 020-8571-7629); WEST EALING LIB, Melbourne Ave, London, W13 9BA (020-8567-2812; *fax:* 020-8567-1736) *Branch Libs:* HANWELL LIB, Cherington Rd, Hanwell, London, W7 3HL (020-8567-5041); JUBILEE GDNS LIB, Southall, Middlesex, UB1 2TJ (020-8578-1067); NORTHFIELDS LIB, Northfield Ave, London, W5 4UA (020-8567-5700; *fax:* 020-8567-5572); NORTHOLT LIB, Church Rd, Northolt, Middlesex, UB5 5AS (020-8845-3380); PERIVALE LIB, Horsenden Ln South, Greenford, Middlesex, UB6 7NT (020-8997-2830); PITS-HANGER LIB, 143-145 Pitshanger Ln, Ealing, London, W5 1RH (020-8997-0230); WOOD END LIB, Whitten Ave West, Greenford, Middlesex, UB6 0EE (020-8422-3965)

Svc Pts: Mobile: 1 *AV:* 9 *Computers:* 12 *Internet:* 12 *Other:* HOME LIB SVC, at West Ealing Lib; SCHOOL LIB SVC, at West Ealing Lib; ST BERNARD'S HOSP PATIENTS' LIB
ILLs: natl *Loans:* bks/4 wks; audios/2 wks; videos/2 days or 2 wks *Charges:* cassettes/50p; CDs/£1; videos/£1.10-£1.60 *Income Gen:* res/74p, conc 27p, under-16s free; lost ticket/£1.80 *Fines:* bks & audios/ad & oap 14p pd (max £7), under-16s exempt; videos/ch & edu 14p pd, other £1 pd *Equip:* m-reader, m-printers, copiers, (A4/10p), clr copier, computers (incl wd-proc, internet & CD-ROM), rooms for hire

Stock:	1 Apr 2000	1 Apr 2001
ad lend:	325756	335260
ad ref:	70655	60822
ch:	166687	82328
audios:	24219	23032
videos:	7127	8061
periodcls:	765	782

Issues:	1999-2000	2000-01
ad lend:	970391	835264
ch:	505595	472242
audios:	45010	42482
videos:	44028	49799

Acqs:	1999-2000	2000-01
bks:	40347	51453
AVs:	3604	4197

Acqs: Source: lib suppl *Co-op:* CILLA
Classn: DDC *Cat: Type:* author, classified, subj & title *Medium:* printed, auto *Auto Sys:* DS *Svcs: Extramural:* schools, hosps, old people's homes, housebnd *Info:* community *Activs:* ch's activs, temp exhibs, reading groups
Enqs: 402740 (1999-2000); 414147 (2000-01)
Staff: Libns: 54 *Non-Prof:* 106.3

Inc from:	1999-2000	2000-01
fines etc:	£260010	£278481

Exp on:	1999-2000	2000-01
stock:	£546576	£553224
Asalaries:	£2886045	£3350183
total:	£5056291	£5669612

London: Enfield

P85 Enfield Libraries

Libs & Culture, 9th Floor, Civic Centre, PO Box 58, Silver Street, Enfield, Middlesex, EN1 3XJ (020-8379-3752; *fax:* 020-8379-3753)
Internet: http://www.enfield.gov.uk/

Local Auth: London Borough of Enfield *Pop:* 269500 *Larger Dept:* Leisure Svcs *Dept Chief:* Dir, Leisure Svcs: Ms Christine Neyndorff *Chief:* Asst Dir, Libs & Culture: Mrs Claire Lewis BA, MSc, MCLIP
Main Libs: ENFIELD CENTRAL LIB, Cecil Rd, Enfield, Middlesex, EN2 6TW (020-8379-8366; *fax:* 020-8379-8401; *email:* enfield.library@dial.pipex.com); EDMONTON GREEN LIB, 36-44 South Mall, Edmonton Green, London, N9 0TN (020-8379-2600; *fax:* 020-8379-2615; *email:* edmonton.green.library@enfield.gov.uk); ORDNANCE RD LIB, 645 Hertford Rd, Enfield, Middlesex, EN3 6ND (020-8379-1725/6; *fax:* 01992-788763); PALMERS GREEN LIB, Broomfield Ln, London, N13 4EY (020-8379-2711; *fax:* 020-8379-2712; *email:* palme@dial.pipex.com)
Branch Libs: BUSH HILL PK LIB, Agricola Pl, Enfield, Middlesex, EN1 1DW (020-8379-1709; *fax:* 020-8367-2213); ENFIELD HIGHWAY LIB, 258 Hertford Rd, Enfield, Middlesex, EN3 5BN (020-8379-1710; *fax:* 020-8443-5034); MERRY-HILLS LIB, Enfield Rd, Enfield, Middlesex, EN2 7HL (020-8379-1711; *fax:* 020-8367-4715); PONDERS END LIB, College Ct, High St, Ponders End, Middlesex, EN3 4EY (020-8379-1712; *fax:* 020-8443-5035); RIDGE AVE LIB, Ridge Ave, Winchmore Hill, London, N21 2RH (020-8379-1714; *fax:* 020-8364-1352);

SOUTHGATE CIRCUS LIB, High St, Southgate, London, N14 6BP (020-8350-1124; fax: 020-8886-3669); WEIR HALL LIB, Millfield Arts Complex, Silver St, Edmonton, London, N18 1PJ (020-8379-1717; fax: 020-8807-3193); WINCHMORE HILL LIB, Green Lanes, Winchmore Hill, London, N21 3AE (020-8379-1718; fax: 020-8364-1060)
Svc Pts: PT: 2 Mobile: 2 AV: 11
Collns: BSI; JFR: Ho-Hz (at Ordnance Rd Lib); GLASS: J.S. Bach; Jazz Baj-Bh; Folk (at lib resources unit) *Co-op Schemes:* GLASS *ILLs:* natl & internatl *Loans:* bks, cassettes & records/ 4 wks; CDs/2 wks; videos/1 wk; lang courses/3 wks *Charges:* records & cassettes/40p; CDs/ 80p; videos/£1.30 or £1.90; lang courses/£1 *Income Gen:* res & req/90p; lost ticket/£1.50; Open Learning/sub £20 *Fines:* bks & audios/ad 14p pd, oap 6p pd, ch & registered disabled pay reminder fee only; videos/40p pd; DVDs/45p pd *Equip:* 19 m-readers, 4 m-printers (printouts 10p), 14 fax (£1.50 1st pg, £1 addl, higher overseas), 14 copiers (A4/10p, A3/20p), 7 clr copiers (A4/£1, A3/£1.50), 36 wd-procs (£1.20 per half hr), 6 internet terminals (varies), 36 CD-ROM readers, 4 rooms for hire (varies) *Disabled:* CCTV, magnifier, open bk machine, Sir Jules Tuan IT/Multimedia Centre for people with sensory impairment *Online:* Companies House Direct, CCN Business Info, Dun & Bradstreet, Equifax, ICC, Kompass, small business register *Offcr-in-Charge:* Lib Resources Unit Mgr: Mrs Ruth Hellen

Stock:	*1 Apr 2000*	*1 Apr 2001*
ad lend:	342788	307572
ad ref:	60844	57204
ch:	140977	132837
schools:	37087	40577
audios:	45606	34458
videos:	13505	12667
CD-ROMs:	-	832
periodcls:	162	247
archvs:	133 linear m	133 linear m

Issues:	*1999-2000*	*2000-01*
ad lend:	1461999	1370384
ch:	599931	567887
audios:	179487	180900
videos:	84564	99817

Acqs:	*1999-2000*	*2000-01*
bks:	59029	51005
AVs:	10586	10073

Acqs: Source: lib suppl, publ & bksellers *Co-op:* LASER, GLASS *Offcr-in-Charge:* Lib Resources Unit Mgr: Mrs Ruth Hellen
Classn: DDC *Cat: Type:* author, classified, subj & title *Medium:* auto *Auto Sys:* DS *Svcs: Extramural:* schools, old people's homes, housebnd *Info:* business, First Stop (community) *Other:* Open Learning *Activs:* ch's activs, bk sales, temp exhibs, poetry readings *Offcr-in-Charge:* Area Lib Mgrs
Enqs: 415415 (1999-2000); 406792 (2000-01)
Staff: Libns: 56.5 *Other Prof:* 8 *Non-Prof:* 92.5

Inc from:	*1999-2000*	*2000-01*
fines etc:	£552941	£438053

Exp on:	*1999-2000*	*2000-01*
bks:	£556199	£491253
AVs:	£135849	£122985
elec media:	£1380	£6220
salaries:	£3182826	£3102255
total:	£5520245	£5277606

London: Greenwich

P86 Greenwich Libraries
Libs Support Svc, Plumstead Lib, 232 Plumstead High Street, London, SE18 1JL (020-8317-4466; fax: 020-8317-4868)
Email: libraries@greenwich.gov.uk
Internet: http://www.greenwich.gov.uk/

Local Auth: London Borough of Greenwich *Pop:* 218100 *Cttee:* Public Svcs Cttee *Larger Dept:* Community Svcs *Dept Chief:* Head of Commuity Svcs: Mrs Margaret Snook BLib, MCLIP *Chief:* Head of Community Svcs (as above) *Other Snr Staff:* Group Lib Mgrs: Mr Martin Stone MCLIP; Mr Steve Woods MCLIP; Mr Paul Clarke MCLIP
Main Libs: BLACKHEATH LIB, Old Dover Rd, Blackheath, London, SE3 7BT (020-8858-1131; fax: 020-8853-3615; email: blackheath.library@ greenwich.gov.uk); ELTHAM LIB, Eltham High St, London, SE9 1TS (020-8850-2268; fax: 020-8850-1368; email: eltham.library@greenwich.gov.uk); WOOLWICH LIB & REF LIB, Calderwood St, Woolwich, London, SE18 6QZ (020-8312-5750; ref: 020-8921-5748; fax: 020-8316-1645; email: woolwich.library@greenwich.gov.uk) *Branch Libs:* ABBEY WOOD LIB, Eynsham Dr, Abbey Wood, London, SE2 9PT (020-8310-4185; email: abbeywood.library@greenwich.gov.uk); CHARLTON LIB, Charlton Rd, London, SE7 8RE (020-8319-2525; email: charlton.library@ greenwich.gov.uk); CLAUDE RAMSEY LIB, Thamesmere Dr, Thamesmead, London, SE28 8DT (020-8310-4246; email: clauderamsey. library@greenwich.gov.uk); EAST GREENWICH LIB, Woolwich Rd, London, SE10 0RL (020-8858-6656; email: eastgreenwich.library@greenwich. gov.uk); FERRIER LIB, Telemann Sq, Kidbrooke, London, SE3 9YR (020-8856-5149; email: ferrier. library@greenwich.gov.uk); NEW ELTHAM LIB, Southwood Rd, London, SE9 3QT (020-8850-2322; email: neweltham.library@greenwich.gov.uk); PLUMSTEAD LIB, Plumstead High St, London, SE18 1JL (020-8854-1728; fax: 020-8317-4868; email: plumstead.library@greenwich.gov.uk); SLADE LIB, Erindale, London, SE18 2QQ (020-8854-7900; email: slade.library@greenwich. gov.uk); WEST GREENWICH LIB, Greenwich High Rd, London, SE10 8NN (020-8858-4289; email: westgreenwich.library@greenwich.gov.uk)
Svc Pts: PT: 1 Mobile: 2 AV: 8 *Other:* SCHOOLS LIB SVC, at West Greenwich Lib (020-8853-1691; fax: 020-8858-3512; email: projectloans.library@greenwich.gov.uk); MOBILE & HOME SVC HQ, at Plumstead Lib (020-8317-4466; email: mobile.library@greenwich.gov.uk); GREENWICH ETHNIC LIB SVC, at Plumstead Lib (020-8317-1544; email: gels.library@greenwich. gov.uk); LOCAL HIST LIB (see **A278**)
Collns: sports & games (former LASER colln); GLASS (Ravel; Schumann; English Folk; Jazz Composers M-Md; spkn wd: transport & communications) *Co-op Schemes:* GLASS *Loans:* bks & spkn wd/4 wks; audios, videos, DVDs & Playstation games/1 wk *Charges:* spkn wd/free; music cassettes/25p, conc 15p; CDs/ 40p, conc 25p; videos, DVDs & Playstation games/£1.80, conc £1.40 *Income Gen:* res/70p, conc 40p; lost ticket/£1.20 *Fines:* bks & audios/ ad & oap 15p pd (max £10), ch exempt; videos, DVDs & Playstation games/40p pd (max £10) *Equip:* 3 m-readers, 2 m-printers (A4/10p), 13 copiers (A4/5p), 3 clr copiers (A4/£1), computers (incl internet & CD-ROM)

Stock:	*1 Apr 2000*	*1 Apr 2001*
lend:	407739	384431
ref:	35175	36078
AVs:	66614	64778
periodcls:	327	317

Issues:	*1999-2000*	*2000-01*
bks:	1085857	983500
AVs:	185579	206947

Acqs:	*1999-2000*	*2000-01*
bks:	74978	24602
AVs:	17186	7453

Acqs: Source: lib suppl
Classn: DDC *Cat: Type:* author, classified, subj & title *Medium:* auto *Auto Sys:* Dynix *Svcs: Extramural:* schools, prisons, hosps, old people's

homes, housebnd, sheltered housing *Info:* community, council, European, careers *Other:* Open Learning *Activs:* ch's activs, bk sales, exhibs, reading groups, storytelling, talks, concerts
Enqs: 149681 (1999-2000); 169898 (2000-01)
Staff: Libns: 26 *Non-Prof:* 73.8

Inc from:	*2000-01*
local govt:	£3751972
fines etc:	£425077
total:	£4177049

Exp on:	*2000-01*
bks:	£324097
AVs:	£99454
salaries:	£2446646
total:	£4177049

London: Hackney

P87 Hackney Libraries Service
Central Lib, Tech & Learning Centre, 1 Reading Ln, London, E8 1GQ (020-8356-2560; fax: 020-8356-2531)
Internet: http://www.hackney.gov.uk/libraries.htm

Local Auth: London Borough of Hackney *Pop:* 198800 *Cttee:* Edu & Leisure Svcs *Larger Dept:* Cultural Svcs Div *Dept Chief:* Asst Dir: Ms Carol Stewart *Chief:* Head of Lib Svcs: Ms Joan Middleton (Joan.Middleton@hackney.gov.uk)
Main Libs: HACKNEY CENTRAL LIB, addr as above (020-8356-2542; fax: 020-8356-2446); HACKNEY REF LIB, at Central Lib (020-8356-4358/9; fax: 020-8356-2531; email: reference. library@hackney.gov.uk); SHOREDITCH LIB, 80 Huxton St, London, N1 6LP (020-8356-4350; fax: 020-8356-4353); STOKE NEWINGTON LIB, Stoke Newington Church St, London, N16 0JS (020-8356-5230/1; fax: 020-8356-5233) *Branch Libs:* C.L.R. JAMES LIB, 24-30 Dalston Ln, London, E8 3AZ (020-8356-1665; fax: 020-8254-4655); CLAPTON LIB, Northwold Rd, London, E5 8RA (020-8356-2570; fax: 020-8806-7849); HOMERTON LIB, Homerton High St, London, E9 6AS (020-8356-1690); STAMFORD HILL LIB, Portland Ave, London, N16 6SB (020-8356-2573; fax: 020-8809-5986)
Svc Pts: Mobile: 1 AV: 7 *Computers:* 7 *Internet:* 7 *Other:* MOBILE LIB SVC, at Stoke Newington Lib (020-8356-5238; fax: 020-8356-5237)
Collns: European Info Colln; London Hist Colln; Local Hist Colln (all at Ref Lib); Three Continents Liberation Colln (Africa, Asia & Latin America, at Central Lib); Torah Colln (Jewish studies, at Stamford Hill Lib); Islam Colln (at Clapton Lib); HIV/AIDS Colln (at Stoke Newington Lib) *Co-op Schemes:* NELLIE *ILLs:* county, natl & internatl *Loans:* bks & audios/3 wks; videos & DVDs/1 wk *Charges:* audios/50p-£1; videos/£1.50 *Income Gen:* res/60p; lost ticket/50p-£1 *Fines:* bks/ad 10p pd; audios/35p-£1.50; videos/£1-2; ch, oap & disabled exempt *Equip:* m-readers, m-printers, fax (UK £1 for 1st pg, addl 50p), copiers (A4/5p, A3/10p), clr copier (A4/£1, A3/£1.50), computers (incl wd-proc, internet & CD-ROM), rooms for hire *Disabled:* Kurzweil, exemption from most charges

Stock:	*1 Apr 2000*	*1 Apr 2001*
ad lend:	147415	101421
ad ref:	35230	19003
ch:	81370	83493
audios:	43048	40155
videos:	4693	4959
periodcls:	200	196

Issues:	*1999-2000*	*2000-01*
ad lend:	598861	554523
ch:	309358	289656
audios:	143777	141148
videos:	20590	20475

Acqs:	*1999-2000*	*2000-01*
bks:	43368	29781
AVs:	12299	5292

☛

(Hackney Libs Svcs cont)

Acqs: Source: lib suppl
Classn: DDC *Cat: Type:* author, classified, subj
& title *Medium:* auto *Auto Sys:* Dynix *Svcs:*
Extramural: hosps, old people's homes, housebnd
Info: business, community, European *Other:*
Open Learning *Activs:* ch's activs, bk sales,
temp exhibs, poetry readings, reading groups,
writers' groups
Enqs: 371750 (1999-2000); 364100 (2000-01)
Staff: Libns: 28 *Non-Prof:* 84.5

Inc from:	1999-2000	2000-01
fines etc:	£130000	£164420

Exp on:	1999-2000	2000-01
total:	£3826400	£3837010

London: Hammersmith and Fulham

P88 Hammersmith and Fulham Libraries

Hammersmith Lib, Shepherds Bush Rd, London,
W6 7AT (020-8753-3813; *fax:* 020-8753-3815)
Email: info@haflibs.org.uk
Internet: http://www.lbhf.gov.uk/

Local Auth: London Borough of Hammersmith &
Fulham *Pop:* 166200 *Cttee:* Edu *Larger Dept:*
Mgmt Support & Lib Svcs *Dept Chief:* Asst Dir of
Edu: Mr David Cross *Chief:* Head of Libs: Mr
David Herbert (d.herbert@libs.lbhf.gov.uk) *Other*
Snr Staff: Lib Development Mgr: Ms Amanda
Stirrup; Lib Operations Mgr: Mr Steven Liddle;
Support Svcs Mgr: Mr John Aquilina
Main Libs: HAMMERSMITH LIB, addr as above
(020-8753-3823; *fax:* 020-8753-3815); FULHAM
LIB, 598 Fulham Rd, London, SW6 5NX (020-
8753-3879; *fax:* 020-8736-3741) *Branch Libs:*
ASKEW RD LIB, 87-91 Askew Rd, London, W12
9AS (020-8753-3863); BARONS CT LIB, North
End Cres, London, W14 8TG (020-8753-3888);
SANDS END LIB, The Community Centre, 59-61
Broughton Rd, London, SW6 2LA (020-753-3885);
SHEPHERDS BUSH LIB, 7 Uxbridge Rd, London,
W12 8LJ (020-8753-3842; *fax:* 020-8740-1712)
Svc Pts: Mobile: 1 *AV:* 7 *Computers:* 6 *Internet:*
6 *Other:* OUTREACH SVCS, based at Barons Ct
Lib (020-7610-4251)
Collns: JFR: Cri-Del (at Hammersmith Lib);
MSC: Religion 200-299; (at Fulham Lib); GLASS:
Mendelssohn, Vaughan Williams; British poetry;
World Music: Iran, Iraq, Syria, Jordan, Lebanon;
Jazz Artistes Hp-Jef *Co-op Schemes:* GLASS
ILLs: county, natl & internatl *Loans:* bks &
audios/3 wks; videos/1 day or 1 wk; DVDs/3
days or 1 wk *Charges:* audios/50p-£1; videos/
£1-£2.50; DVDs/£1.50-£2.50 *Income Gen:* req
& res/70p; lost ticket/£3.50 *Fines:* bks & audios/
ad 10p pd (max £6 per item); videos/20p-£1 pd
(50p rewind charge); ch, oap & registered disabled
exempt *Equip:* 3 m-readers, m-printer (20p), 3
fax (£1-£6), 11 copiers (A4/10p, A3/20p), 1clr
copier (A4/£1, A3/£1.50), rooms for hire (various)
Disabled: Kurzweil *Online:* Lawtel

Stock:	1 Apr 2000	1 Apr 2001
ad lend:	145573	145390
ad ref:	78033	93041
ch:	65607	59552
schools:	31456	32968
instns:	17316	15924
audios:	18316	22963
videos:	5753	6992
periodcls:	493	453

Issues:	1999-2000	2000-01
ad lend:	493856	523606
ch:	160203	176326
schools:	17614	16712
instns:	11017	13718
audios:	66891	76973
videos:	37948	48990

Acqs:	1999-2000	2000-01
bks:	27056	31671
AVs:	4512	4088

Acqs: Source: lib suppl, publ & bksellers *Co-op:*
CBC *Offcr-in-Charge:* Lib Operations Mgr, Mr
Steven Liddle
Classn: DDC *Cat: Type:* author & classified
Medium: auto *Auto Sys:* Geac *Svcs: Extramural:*
prisons, housebnd, old people's homes, day
centres *Info:* Local Pages (community) *Other:*
Open Learning *Activs:* ch's activs, bk sales,
temp exhibs, reading groups, talks, author visits
Enqs: 132325 (1999-2000); 131969 (2000-01)
Staff: Libns: 28 *Non-Prof:* 69

Inc from:	1999-2000	2000-01
local govt:	£2971970	£3212919
fines etc:	£137723	£146356
total:	£3109693	£3359275

Exp on:	1999-2000	2000-01
bks:	£322631	£282888
AVs:	£42205	£45429
elec media:	£10259	£8627
culture:	£6697	£12114
salaries:	£2106792	£2232636
total:	£3109693	£3359275

Proj: installation of public toilets in 4 libs;
improved access for disabled in 2 libs

London: Haringey

P89 Haringey Libraries, Archives and Museum Service

Wood Green Central Lib, High Rd, Wood Green,
London, N22 6XD (020-8489-2700; *fax:* 020-8489-
2722)
Email: diana.edmonds@haringey.gov.uk
Internet: http://www.haringey.gov.uk/

Local Auth: London Borough of Haringey *Pop:*
225100 *Larger Dept:* Edu Svcs *Chief:* Interim
Mgr: Ms Diana Edmonds
Main Libs: WOOD GREEN CENTRAL LIB, addr
as above (020-8489-2780); HORNSEY LIB,
Haringey Pk, London, N8 9JA (020-8489-1425);
MARCUS GARVEY LIB, Tottenham Green Centre,
1 Phillip Ln, Tottenham, London, N15 4JA (020-
8489-5350) *Branch Libs:* ALEXANDRA PK LIB,
Alexandra Pk Rd, Wood Green, London, N22 7UJ
(020-8489-8770); COOMBES CROFT LIB, Totten-
ham High Rd, London, N17 8AG (020-8489-8771);
HIGHGATE LIB, Shepherds Hill, Highgate,
London, N6 5QJ (020-8489-8772); MUSWELL
HILL LIB, Queens Ave, Muswell Hill, London, N10
3PE (020-8489-8773); ST ANN'S LIB, Cissbury
Rd, Tottenham, London, N15 5PU (020-8489-
8775); STROUD GREEN LIB, Quernmore Rd,
London, N4 4QR (020-8489-8776)
Svc Pts: Mobile: 1 *AV:* 9 *Computers:* 9 *Internet:*
9 *Other:* HOUSEBND LIB SVC (020-8489-1425);
MOBILE LIB SVC (020-8489-1425); SCHOOLS
LIB SVC (020-8489-5043); HARINGEY MUSEUM
& ARCHV SVC (see **A283**)

Co-op Schemes: BEWHICH *ILLs:* county, natl
& internatl *Loans:* bks & audios/3 wks; videos/2
days or 1 wk *Charges:* cassettes/50p; CDs/80p;
videos/£1-£2.50 *Income Gen:* res/70p; lost
ticket/£1.50 *Fines:* bks & audios/ad 10p pd;
videos/loan charge; ch & oap exempt *Equip:*
m-reader/printers, fax, video viewers, copiers, clr
copiers, 165 computers (incl wd-proc, internet &
CD-ROM), room hire *Disabled:* Dolphin machine

Stock:	1 Apr 2000	1 Apr 2001
lend:	505294	426842
ref:	25120	25588
AVs:	67163	60399
periodcls:	290	278

Issues:	1999-2000	2000-01
bks:	773670	739542
AVs:	119057	137178

Acqs:	1999-2000	2000-01
bks:	14930	24947
AVs:	4678	5235

Acqs: Source: lib suppl & bksellers
Classn: DDC *Cat: Type:* author, classified, subj
& title *Medium:* auto *Auto Sys:* Talis *Svcs:*
Extramural: schools, old people's homes,
housebnd, sheltered housing *Info:* community
Activs: ch's activs, bk sales, temp exhibs,
poetry readings, reading groups, writers' groups
Enqs: 352716 (1999-2000); 291668 (2000-01)
Staff: Libns: 42 *Non-Prof:* 62

Inc from:		2000-01
fines etc:		£170401

Exp on:		2000-01
stock:		£456053
salaries:		£2070020
total:		£3677234

London: Harrow

P90 Harrow Libraries

Libs Admin, PO Box 4, Civic Centre, Station Rd,
Harrow, Middlesex, HA1 2UU (020-8424-1059/
1970; *fax:* 020-8424-1971)
Email: library@harrow.gov.uk
Internet: http://www.harrow.gov.uk/

Local Auth: London Borough of Harrow *Pop:*
214900 *Cttee:* Edu, Arts & Leisure Cttee *Larger*
Dept: Edu *Dept Chief:* Dir of Edu: Mr Paul
Osburn *Chief:* Lib Svcs Mgr: Mr Robert Mills
BSc, DMS, MCLIP *Other Snr Staff:* Principal
Libn (Ref & Info Svcs): Mr Paul Lane; Principal
Libn (Lending Svcs): Mr John Pennells
Main Libs: CIVIC CENTRE LIB (Central Ref
Lib), addr as above (020-8424-1055/6; *email:*
civiccentre.library@harrow.gov.uk); GAYTON LIB
(Central Lending Lib), Gayton Rd, Harrow, Middle-
sex, HA1 2HL (020-8427-8986/6012; *email:*
gayton.library@harrow.gov.uk) *Branch Libs:*
BOB LAWRENCE LIB, 6-8 North Parade, Mollison
Way, Edgware, Middlesex, HA8 5QH (020-8952-
4140; *email:* boblawrence.library@harrow.gov.uk);
HATCH END LIB, Uxbridge Rd, Hatch End,
Pinner, Middlesex, HA5 4EA (020-8428-2636;
email: hatchend.library@harrow.gov.uk); KENTON
LIB, Kenton Ln, Kenton, Harrow, Middlesex, HA3
8UJ (020-8907-2463; *email:* kenton.library@
harrow.gov.uk); NORTH HARROW LIB, 429-433
Pinner Rd, Harrow, Middlesex, HA1 4HN (020-
8427-0611; *email:* northharrow.library@harrow.
gov.uk); PINNER LIB, Marsh Rd, Pinner,
Middlesex, HA5 5NQ (020-8866-7827; *email:*
pinner.library@harrow.gov.uk); RAYNERS LN LIB,
226 Imperial Dr, Rayners Ln, Harrow, Middlesex,
HA2 7HJ (020-8866-9185; *email:* raynerslane.
library@harrow.gov.uk); ROXETH LIB, Northolt
Rd, Harrow, Middlesex, HA2 8EQ (020-8422-0809;
email: roxeth.library@harrow.gov.uk); STANMORE
LIB, 8 Stanmore Hill, Stanmore, Middlesex, HA7
3BQ (020-8954-9955; *email:* stanmore.library@
harrow.gov.uk); WEALDSTONE LIB, Grant Rd,

Wealdstone, Middlesex, HA3 7SD (020-8427-8670; *email:* wealdstone.library@harrow.gov.uk)
Svc Pts: AV: 11 *Computers:* 11 *Internet:* 11
Other: HOUSEBND LIB SVCS, at Libs Admin (020-8424-1058; *email:* housebnd.library@harrow.gov.uk); LOCAL HIST COLLN, at Civic Centre Lib (see **A196**); MUSIC LIB, at Gayron Lib (020-8427-8986/6012; *email:* music.library@harrow.gov.uk); SCHOOL LIB SVC, at Libs Admin (020-8424-1052/3; *email:* school.library.service@harrow.gov.uk); YNG PEOPLE'S SVCS, at Libs Admin (020-8424-1052/1267)
Collns: Town planning, arch, civil eng & bldg; JFR: Maz-Mn excluding Mc; local hist; GLASS: Strav-Z excluding Stravinsky, Tchaikovsky, Teleman, Vaughn Williams, Verdi, Vivaldi, Wagner (all at Gayton Lib); local hist (at Civic Centre Lib)
Co-op Schemes: GLASS, CILLA *ILLs:* county, natl & internatl *Loans:* bks & audios/3 wks
Charges: cassettes & vinyl/45p (90p for sets of 3+); CDs/80p (£1.10 for sets of 3+) *Income Gen:* req & res/65p; lost ticket/ad £1.25, ch 60p *Fines:* bks & audios/ad 13p pd; ch & disabled residents on social svcs register exempt *Equip:* m-readers, m-printers, copiers (A4/10p, A3/20p), clr copiers (A4/£1, A3/£1.50), computers (incl wd-proc, internet & CD-ROM), rooms for hire *Disabled:* magnifiers

Stock:	1 Apr 2000	1 Apr 2001
ad lend:	266202	258135
ad ref:	29306	32570
ch:	108344	105580
audios:	25892	26313
periodcls:	191	287

Issues:	1999-2000	2000-01
ad lend:	1413564	1333113
ch:	581221	543309
audios:	115147	107020

Acqs:	1999-2000	2000-01
bks:	46531	50678
AVs:	4685	5357

Acqs: Source: lib suppl & bksellers *Co-op:* GLASS, CILLA *Offcr-in-Charge:* Principal Libn (Stock Svcs): Mrs Nikki Copleston
Classn: DDC *Cat: Type:* author, classified, subj & title *Medium:* auto *Auto Sys:* Dynix *Svcs: Extramural:* schools, old people's homes, housebnd *Info:* business, community *Activs:* ch's activs, bk sales, temp exhibs, poetry readings, reading groups
Staff: Libns: 43.5 *Non-Prof:* 64.2

Inc from:	1999-2000	2000-01
local govt:	£3001752	£3149140
fines etc:	£226312	£232307
total:	£3228064	£3381447

Exp on:	1999-2000	2000-01
stock:	£507178	£477293
salaries:	£1794941	£1804945
total:	£3228064	£3381447

London: Havering

P91 Havering Library Services
Central Lib, St Edward's Way, Romford, Essex, RM1 3AR (01708-432394; *fax:* 01708-432391)
Email: info@havering.gov.uk
Internet: http://www.havering.gov.uk/

Local Auth: London Borough of Havering *Pop:* 230900 *Chief:* Borough Libn: Mr R. Worcester
Main Libs: CENTRAL LIB (incl Ref Lib), contact details as above *Branch Libs:* COLLIER ROW LIB, 45 Collier Row Rd, Collier Row, Romford, Essex, RM5 3NR (01708-760063); ELM PK LIB, St Nicholas Ave, Elm Pk, Hornchurch, Essex, RM12 4PT (01708-451270); GIDEA PK LIB, Balgores Ln, Gidea Pk, Romford, Essex, RM2 6BS (01708-441856); HAROLD HILL LIB, Hilldene Ave, Harold Hill, Romford, Essex, RM3 8DJ (01708-342749); HAROLD WOOD LIB, Arundel

Rd, Harold Wood, Romford, Essex, RM3 0RX (01708-342071); HORNCHURCH LIB, 44 North St, Hornchurch, Essex, RM11 1LW (01708-452248); RAINHAM LIB, 7-11 The Broadway, Rainham, Essex, RM13 9YW (01708-551905); SOUTH HORNCHURCH LIB, Rainham Rd, Rainham, Essex, RM13 7RD (01708-554126); UPMINSTER LIB, 26 Corbets Tey Rd, Upminster, Essex, RM14 2BB (01708-222864)
Svc Pts: AV: 10 *Computers:* 10 *Internet:* 10
Other: HOUSEBND LIB SVC, at Central Lib (01708-772388); SCHOOL LIB SVC, at Central Lib (01708-432397); FAMILY HIST CENTRE, at Central Lib
Collns: botany; palaeontology; JFR: Mam-May; GLASS: Bartok; Dvorak; Verdi; Shakespeare plays; music of Bali & Indonesia; Queen's Theatre Archv; Local Hist Colln; large print bks *Co-op Schemes:* GLASS, CILLA *ILLs:* county, natl & internatl *Loans:* bks & spkn wd/3 wks; audios & videos/1 wk *Charges:* audios/60p (spkn wd & lang recordings free); videos/£1-£2.50 *Income Gen:* res/75p-£2; lost ticket/£2.30, under-16s free *Fines:* bks & audios/ad & oap 10p pd, ch 1p pd; videos/loan charge; registered blind/partially sighted & housebnd exempt *Equip:* m-readers, m-printers, copiers (10p), clr copier (A4/£1, A3/£1.50), 116 computers (incl wd-proc, internet & CD-ROM), rooms for hire (varies) *Disabled:* Kurzweil, brailler, Jaws software, minicom *Online:* newspapers on CD-ROM

Stock:	1 Apr 2000	1 Apr 2001
lend:	326508	330252
ref:	45945	46419
AVs:	33921	32558
periodcls:	181	167

Issues:	1999-2000	2000-01
bks:	1548347	1437548
AVs:	160227	153917

Acqs:	1999-2000	2000-01
bks:	34175	44697
AVs:	7068	5514

Acqs: Source: lib suppl
Classn: DDC *Cat: Type:* author, classified, subj & title *Medium:* auto *Auto Sys:* Genesis *Svcs: Extramural:* schools, housebnd *Info:* business, community, European, tourist, family hist, medical, edu *Other:* Open Learning (at Central Lib) *Activs:* ch's activs, bk sales, temp exhibs, reading groups, Music Circle
Enqs: 235560 (1999-2000); 225732 (2000-01)
Staff: 95.5 FTE

Inc from:	1999-2000	2000-01
local govt:	£3078000	£3198000
fines etc:	£223000	£214000
total:	£3301000	£3412000

Exp on:	1999-2000	2000-01
stock & svcs:	£703000	£674000
salaries:	£1841000	£1819000
total:	£3301000	£3412000

London: Hillingdon

P92 Hillingdon Libraries, Arts and Information Service
Central Lib, 14-15 High St, Uxbridge, Middlesex, UB8 1HD (01895-250600; *fax:* 01895-239794)
Email: clibrary@hillingdongrid.org
Internet: http://www.hillingdon.gov.uk/libraries/

Local Auth: London Borough of Hillingdon *Pop:* 251200 *Larger Dept:* Edu, Youth & Leisure Svcs *Chief:* Asst Dir of Cultural Svcs: Mrs Trisha Grimshaw
Main Libs: CENTRAL LIB, addr as above; *Area Libs:* HAYES LIB, Golden Cres, Hayes, Middlesex, UB3 1AQ (020-8573-2855; *fax:* 020-8848-0269); MANOR FARM LIB (Ruislip), Bury St, Ruislip, Middlesex, HA4 7SU (01895-633651; *fax:* 01895-677555)

Branch Libs: EASTCOTE LIB, 88 Field End Rd, Eastcote, Pinner, Middlesex, HA5 1RL (020-8866-3668); HAREFIELD LIB, Park Ln, Harefield, Middlesex, UB9 6BJ (01895-822171); HARLINGTON LIB, Pinkwell Ln, Hayes, Middlesex, UB3 1PD (020-8569-1612; *fax:* 020-8569-1625); HAYES END LIB, 1346 Uxbridge Rd, Hayes, Middlesex, UB4 8JQ (020-8573-4209); ICKENHAM LIB, Long Ln, Ickenham, Middlesex, UB10 8RE (01895-635945); KINGSHILL LIB, Bury Ave, Hayes, Middlesex, UB4 8LF (020-8845-3773); NORTHWOOD HILLS LIB, Potter St, Northwood, Middlesex, HA6 1QQ (01923-824595); OAK FARM LIB, Sutton Court Rd, Hillingdon, Middlesex, UB10 9PB (01895-23469); OAKLANDS GATE LIB, Green Ln, Northwood, Middlesex, HA6 3AB (01923-826690); RUISLIP MANOR LIB, Victoria Rd, Ruislip Manor, Ruislip, Middlesex, HA4 9BW (01895-633668); SOUTH RUISLIP LIB, Victoria Rd, South Ruislip, Ruislip, Middlesex, HA4 0JE (020-8845-0188); WEST DRAYTON LIB, Station Rd, West Drayton, Middlesex, UB7 7JS (01895-443238); YEADING LIB, Yeading Ln, Hayes, Middlesex, UB4 4EW (020-8573-0261); YIEWSLEY LIB, High St, Yiewsley, West Drayton, Middlesex, UB7 0BE (01895-442539)
Svc Pts: Mobile: 1 *AV:* 17 *Computers:* 17 *Internet:* 17 *Other:* SCHOOLS' LIB SVC, at Central Lib (01895-250715; *fax:* 01895-811164); LOCAL STUDIES & ARCHVS, at Central Lib (see **A495**)
Collns: local hist colln *Co-op Schemes:* GLASS, CILLA, Proj Earl *ILLs:* county, natl & internatl *Loans:* bks & audios/3 wks; videos/1 wk; Open Learning & lang courses/3 wks *Charges:* cassettes/50p; CDs/£1.20; videos/ad £2, new releases £2.50, ch's £1.20; DVDs/£3; Open Learning & lang courses/£2; conc half price for all loan charges *Income Gen:* res/80p, self-svc 40p; lost ticket/ad £1.50, conc 75p *Fines:* bks, audios & lang courses/ad 13p pd, young ad & school students 3p pd; videos & DVDs/ad 85p pd, ch's videos 40p pd *Equip:* m-readers, m-printers, video viewer, fax (UK £1 1st pg to send, 50p addl, higher overseas), copiers (A4/10p, A3/20p), clr copier (A4/£1, A3/£1.50), 170+ computers (incl wd-proc, internet & CD-ROM), rooms for hire (£8-£15 per hr) *Disabled:* magnifiers, CCTV, minicom *Online:* Infotrac, KnowUK, XreferPlus

Stock:	1 Apr 2000	1 Apr 2001
ad lend:	265038	253925
ad ref:	27220	27354
ch:	107223	109596
audios:	17431	16804
videos:	6410	6933
periodcls:	140	140

Issues:	1999-2000	2000-01
ad lend:	1135769	1033042
ch:	458113	426553
audios:	58372	51995
videos:	40448	41240

Acqs:	1999-2000	2000-01
bks:	35611	34066
AVs:	2818	2671

Acqs: Source: lib suppl & bksellers *Co-op:* WELLSTOC *Offcr-in-Charge:* Stock & Community Svcs Mgr: Mrs C.M. Beaumond
Classn: DDC *Cat: Type:* author, classified, subj & title *Medium:* auto *Auto Sys:* Geac *Svcs: Extramural:* schools, old people's homes, housebnd *Info:* community, European, tourist, council, business, careers *Other:* Open Learning *Activs:* ch's activs, bk sales, temp exhibs, reading groups, homework club
Enqs: 297294 (1999-2000); 254077 (2000-01)
Staff: Libns: 34.8 *Non-Prof:* 74.47

Inc from:	1999-2000	2000-01
local govt:	£3610395	£3858670
fines etc:	£402333	£408854
total:	£4012728	£4267524

(Hillingdon Libs, Arts & Info Svcs cont)

Exp on:	1999-2000	2000-01
bks:	£361333	£316185
salaries:	£2240797	£2310589
total:	£4012728	£4267524

Proj: refurbishment of Yeading Lib

London: Hounslow

P93 Hounslow Libraries

CIP, Centrespace, Treaty Centre, High Street, Hounslow, Middlesex, TW3 1ES (020-8583-4545; *fax:* 020-8583-4595)
Internet: http://www.cip.org.uk/library/

Local Auth: London Borough of Hounslow *Pop:* 206100 *Larger Dept:* Community Initiative Partnerships (CIP) *Chief:* Dir of Culture & Heritage & Borough Libn: Ms Linda Simpson BA, MCLIP (linda-simpson@cip.org.uk) *Dep:* Principal Libn: Mrs Frances Stanbury MCLIP (frances-stanbury@cip.org.uk)
Main Libs: CHISWICK LIB, Duke's Ave, Chiswick, London, W4 2AB (020-8994-1008; *fax:* 020-8995-0016); FELTHAM LIB, 210 The Centre, High St, Feltham, Middlesex, TW13 4BX (020-8890-3506/5273; *fax:* 020-8893-2748); HOUNSLOW LIB, contact details as above *Branch Libs:* BEDFONT LIB, Staines Rd, Bedfont, Feltham, Middlesex, TW14 8DB (020-8890-6173); BRENTFORD LIB, Boston Manor Rd, Brentford, Middlesex, TW8 8DW (020-8560-8801); CRANFORD LIB, Bath Rd, Cranford, Hounslow, Middlesex, TW5 9TL (020-8759-0641); HANWORTH LIB, 2-12 Hampton Rd West, Hanworth, Feltham, Middlesex, TW13 6AW (020-8898-0256); HESTON LIB, New Heston Rd, Heston, Hounslow, Middlesex, TW5 0LW (020-8570-1028); ISLEWORTH LIB, Twickenham Rd, Isleworth, Middlesex, TW7 7EU (020-8560-2934); OSTERLEY LIB, St Mary's Cres, Hounslow, Middlesex, TW7 4NB (020-8560-4295)
Svc Pts: Mobile: 1 *Internet:* 1 *Other:* Feltham Cyberskills Centre
Collns: JFR authors: T-Th; geol colln (both at Hounslow Lib); Layton Colln of Local Studies; English topographical colln (8000 bks, 5000 maps & prints, c1570-1900); GLASS: Wagner, Debussy, Jazz (Cham-Col), Folk Music: Turkey (all at Hounslow) *Co-op Schemes:* JFR, GLASS
ILLs: internatl *Loans:* bks/4 wks; audios/2 wks; videos/entertainment 1 wk, non-fiction 4 wks
Charges: audios/50p (conc 40p); videos & DVDs/ad £1.80 (conc £1.20), ch £1.20 (conc 80p)
Income Gen: res/£1.50 conc 75p; lost ticket/£2.50 conc £1.50 *Fines:* bks & audios/ad & over-12s 12p pd open, ch of 12 or under 4p pd open, oap 8p pd (conc); videos/40p pd open, conc 30p *Equip:* 3 m-readers, 3 m-printers, 11 fax (£1.20-£3 to send; £1 to receive), 11 copiers (A4/10p), clr copier (A4/£1), computers (incl internet), 6 rooms for hire (various) *Disabled:* Kurzweil

Stock:	1 Apr 2000
ad lend:	275974
ad ref:	20971
ch:	108098
audios:	35035
videos:	12925
periodcls:	231
archvs:	118 linear m

Issues:	1999-2000
ad lend:	1230644
ch:	501987
audios:	138378
videos:	74470

Acqs:	1999-2000
bks:	47216
AVs:	6508

Acqs: Source: lib suppl *Offcr-in-Charge:* Strategic Lib Mgr (Stock & Reader Development): Ms Elizabeth Lee (elizabeth-lee@cip.org.uk)
Classn: DDC *Cat: Type:* author, classified & title *Medium:* auto *Auto Sys:* SBS Genesis
Svcs: Extramural: schools, prisons, old people's homes, housebnd *Other:* Input Output Centre, Feltham Cyberskills Centre *Activs:* ch's activs, temp exhibs
Enqs: 528517 (1999-2000)
Staff: 130 total

Inc from:	1999-2000
local govt:	£3432881
fines etc:	£341226
total:	£4093089

Exp on:	1999-2000
bks:	£539316
AVs:	£44517
salaries:	£2343853
total:	£4093089

Proj: new lib to replace Beavers Lib, to open Spring 2004

London: Islington

P94 Islington Library and Cultural Services

Central Lib, 2 Fieldway Cres, London, N5 1PF (020-7527-6900; *fax:* 020-7527-6902)
Email: library.information@islington.gov.uk
Internet: http://www.islington.gov.uk/

Local Auth: London Borough of Islington *Pop:* 178000 *Cttee:* Info & Customer Svcs Cttee *Larger Dept:* Info & Customer Svcs *Chief:* Head of Lib & Cultural Svcs: Ms Rosemary Doyle (hlcs@islington.gov.uk) *Other Snr Staff:* Principal Libn (Learning): Mr Brendan Redmond; Mgr, Svcs to Ch & Yng People: Mr Geoff James *Main Libs:* CENTRAL LIB, addr as above (*email:* centralref.library@islington.gov.uk) *Branch Libs:* ARCHWAY LIB, Hamlyn House, Highgate Hill, London, N19 5PH (020-7527-7820; *fax:* 020-7527-7833; *email:* archway.library@islington.gov.uk); ARTHUR SIMPSON LIB, Hanley Rd, London, N4 3DL (020-7527-7800; *fax:* 020-7527-7808; *email:* arthursimpson.library@islington.gov.uk); FINSBURY LIB, 245 St John St, London, EC1V 4NB (020-7527-7960; *fax:* 020-7527-7998; *email:* finsbury.library@islington.gov.uk); JOHN BARNES LIB, 275 Camden Rd, London, N7 0JN (020-7527-7900; *fax:* 020-7527-7907; *email:* johnbarnes.library@islington.gov.uk); LEWIS CARROLL CH'S LIB, Copenhagen St, London, N1 0ST (020-7527-7936; *fax:* 020-7527-7935; *email:* lewiscarroll.library@islington.gov.uk); MILDMAY LIB, 21-23 Mildmay Pk, London, N1 4NA (020-7527-7880; *fax:* 020-7527-7898; *email:* mildmay.library@islington.gov.uk); NORTH LIB, Manor Gdns, London, N7 6JX (020-7527-7840; *fax:* 020-7527-7854; *email:* north.library@islington.gov.uk); SOUTH LIB, 115-117 Essex Rd, London, N1 2SL (020-7527-7860; *fax:* 020-7527-7869; *email:* south.library@islington.gov.uk); WEST LIB, Bridgeman Rd, London, N1 1BD (020-7527-7920; *fax:* 020-7527-7929; *email:* west.library@islington.gov.uk)
Svc Pts: AV: 10 *Other:* HOME LIB SVC, at Finsbury Lib (020-7527-7980; *fax:* 020-7527-7999; *email:* home.libraryservice@islington.gov.uk)
Collns: JFR: Ha-Hwn (at Finsbury Lib); GLASS: Classical Gm-Kh (at Central Lib); Jazz Shb-Sm (at Finsbury Lib); Folk SE Europe; Illusts Colln (at

Finsbury Lib); Forgetfulness Colln (dementia & related topics, at Central & Finsbury Libs); hearing impairment (at North Lib); disability (at West Lib); local hist (at Central & Finsbury Libs)
Co-op Schemes: BEWHICH *Loans:* bks/3 wks; audios/2 wks; videos/features 1 day, non-features 1 wk; DVDs/1 day; CD-ROMs & Playstation games/1 wk *Charges:* CDs/50p, conc 30p; cassettes/20p, conc 10p; videos/new feature films £2, others £1; DVDs/£1-£2; CD-ROMs/£1; Playstation games/£2; conc available to registered disabled, unemployed & recipients of social, health or housing benefit *Income Gen:* res & req/85p, conc 45p; lost ticket/80p *Fines:* bks & audios/ad 10p pd (max £6), ch & oap exempt; videos, DVDs & CD-ROMs/loan charge *Equip:* m-readers, m-printers, fax, 10 copiers, 60+ computers (incl internet), 7 rooms for hire (various) *Disabled:* CCTV, OCR, typetalk phones, magnifiers, induction loop, captioned video facilities *Online:* local info database

Stock:	1 Apr 2000	1 Apr 2001
lend:	339307	330416
ref:	38369	43147
AVs:	84685	84179
periodcls:	348	352

Issues:	1999-2000	2000-01
bks:	857792	806970
AVs:	266335	322157

Acqs:	1999-2000	2000-01
bks:	43205	37866
AVs:	12664	12071

Acqs: Source: lib suppl
Classn: DDC *Cat: Type:* author & classified *Medium:* auto *Auto Sys:* Talis *Svcs: Extramural:* prisons, hosps, old people's homes, housebnd *Info:* community, European, tourist, careers, edu, local info database *Other:* Lifelong Learning, local hist, ethnic & women's svcs, computer clubs, Cyberskills Workshop (at Finsbury Lib) *Activs:* ch's activs, bk sales, temp exhibs, poetry readings, live music, author talks
Enqs: 400400 (1999-2000); 434122 (2000-01)
Staff: Libns: 35.3 *Non-Prof:* 89.2

Inc from:	1999-2000	2000-01
local govt:	£6146557	£5940421
fines etc:	£401222	£374737
total:	£6547779	£6315158

Exp on:	1999-2000	2000-01
stock:	£612614	£569305
salaries:	£3399745	£3264143
total:	£6547779	£6315158

London: Kensington and Chelsea

P95 Kensington and Chelsea Libraries and Information Services

Kensington Central Lib, Phillimore Walk, London, W8 7RX (020-7937-2542; *fax:* 020-7361-2976)
Email: information.services@rbkc.gov.uk
Internet: http://www.rbkc.gov.uk/libraries/general/

Local Auth: Royal Borough of Kensington & Chelsea *Pop:* 190300 *Cttee:* Cabinet Memb for Edu, Libs & Arts *Larger Dept:* Edu, Libs & Arts *Dept Chief:* Exec Dir: Ms Jacky Griffin MA *Chief:* Head of Libs & Arts: Mr John McEachen BSc, MCLIP
Main Libs: CENTRAL LIB, addr as above *Branch Libs:* BROMPTON LIB, 210 Old Brompton Rd, London, SW5 0BS (020-7373-3111); CHELSEA LIB, Kings Rd, London, SW3 5EE (020-7352-6056); NORTH KENSINGTON LIB, 108 Ladbroke Grove, London, W11 1PZ (020-7727-6583); NOTTING HILL GATE LIB, 1 Pembridge Sq, London, W2 4EW (020-7229-8574); KENSAL LIB, 20 Golborne Rd, London, W10 5PF (020-8969-7736)
Svc Pts: AV: 6

Collns: Biography Colln (80000 biographies, at Central Lib); JFR (Caq-Chd, Huz-Kel to Jan 1988); MSC (920-929) *Co-op Schemes:* BLLD, GLASS, Proj EARL *ILLs:* county, natl & internatl *Loans:* bks & audios/3 wks; videos/1 day or 1 wk *Charges:* cassettes/1-2 items 40p, set of 3+ 50p; CDs/1-2 discs 65p, set of 3+ 85p; videos/ new releases £3, older films & special interest £2, ch 50p; alternative sub/£17 pa *Income Gen:* res/62p, conc 36p; lost ticket/50p *Fines:* bks & audios/ad & oap 12p pd, 12-15s 6p pd, under 12s exempt; videos/loan charge *Equip:* 2 m-readers, 2 m-printers (10p), 8 copiers (10p), 2 clr copiers (£1), 4 rooms for hire (various), computers (incl wd-proc & CD-ROM)

Stock:	*1 Apr 2000*	*1 Apr 2001*
lend:	235774	406929
ref:	139461	113584
audios:	34494	52406
videos:	3389	3896
CD-ROMs:	306	346
periodcls:	503	544

Issues:	*1999-2000*	*2000-01*
bks:	996592	1270637
audios:	370890	514799
videos:	36881	56750
CD-ROMs:	1696	5090

Acqs:	*1999-2000*	*2000-01*
bks:	40376	55780
AVs:	5698	10957

Acqs: Source: lib suppl *Offcr-in-Charge:* Bibliographical Libn: M. Jackson
Classn: DDC *Cat: Medium:* auto *Auto Sys:* Dynix *Svcs: Extramural:* schools, old people's homes, housebnd *Info:* First Stop Council Info Pts, business, community *Other:* Employment Resource & Open Learning Centre, Input/Output Computer Centre, SPACE Centre (Supporting Parents As Co-Educators) *Activs:* ch's activs, bk sales, temp exhibs, poetry readings, reading groups, author talks
Enqs: 300508 (1999-2000); 240604 (2000-01)
Staff: Libns: 48 *Non-Prof:* 83.5

Inc from:	*1999-2000*
local govt:	£4985173
fines etc:	£394061
total:	£5379234

Exp on:	*1999-2000*
bks:	£382413
AVs:	£104115
salaries:	£2895872
total:	£5379234

London: Kingston upon Thames

P96 Kingston Libraries

Kingston Lib, Fairfield Rd, Kingston upon Thames, Surrey, KT1 2PS (020-8547-6400; *fax:* 020-8547-6401)
Email: kingston.library@rbk.kingston.gov.uk
Internet: http://www.kingston.gov.uk/Learning/ Libraries/

Local Auth: Royal Borough of Kingston upon Thames *Pop:* 151000 *Cttee:* Edu & Leisure Svc Cttee *Larger Dept:* Edu & Leisure Svc *Chief:* Head of Lib Svc: Miss Barbara Lee BA, MA, MCLIP
Main Libs: KINGSTON LIB, addr as above; SURBITON LIB, Ewell Rd, Surbiton, Surrey, KT6 6AG (020-8399-2331 *fax:* 020-8339-9805; *email:* surbiton.library@rbk.kingston.gov.uk); NEW MALDEN LIB, Kingston Rd, New Malden, Surrey, KT3 3LY (020-8547-6540 *fax:* 020-8547-6545; *email:* newmalden.library@rbk.kingston.gov.uk) *Branch Libs:* HOOK & CHESSINGTON LIB, Hook Rd, Hook, Chessington, Surrey, KT9 1EJ (020-8397-4931; *fax:* 020-8391-4416; *email:* hookandchess.library@rbk.kingston.gov.uk); OLD MALDEN LIB, Church Rd, Worcester Pk, Surrey, KT4 7RD (020-8337-6344; *fax:* 020-8330-3118; *email:* oldmalden.library@rbk.kingston.gov.uk); TOLWORTH COMMUNITY LIB, 37-39 The Broadway, Tolworth, Surrey, KT6 7DJ (020-8339-6950; *fax:* 020-8339-6955; *email:* tolworth.library@ rbk.kingston.gov.uk); TUDOR DR LIB, Tudor Dr, Kingston upon Thames, Surrey, KT2 5QH (020-8546-1198; *fax:* 020-8547-2295; *email:* tudordrive.library@rbk.kingston.gov.uk)
Svc Pts: Mobile: 1 *AV:* 7 *Computers:* 7 *Internet:* 7 *Other:* HOME LIB SVC, based at Surbiton Lib (020-8399-7900; *email:* homeandmobile@rbk.kingston.gov.uk)
Loans: bks & spkn wd/3 wks; audios, videos, DVDs & CD-ROMs/1wk; linguaphone/6 wks; music scores & play sets/3 months *Charges:* CDs/75p single, £1.25 double; lang cassettes/50p single, £1 double; spkn wd/55p, free to oaps & other categories; videos/£1.50 single, £2.25 double, ch's £1 single, £1.60 double; DVDs/£2 single, double £2.50; CD-ROMs/£1.50; linguaphone sets/£5; music scores & sets of plays/£5 *Income Gen:* res/in stock ad 70p, oaps 35p, ch free for ch's bks, no charge for registered disabled & unemployed, £1.20 if not in stock, £3 if reserved through natl interlending scheme; lost ticket/£1 *Fines:* bks/ad 15p pd open (max £5), oap/10p pd open (max £5), under 16s exempt; audios & videos/loan charge (max £6); linguaphone, music scores & play sets/loan charge (max £20) *Equip:* m-reader (15p), m-printer (15p), 5 fax (to send varies, to receive £1 for 1-6 sheets), copier (A4/5p, A3/10p), computers (incl internet, access free, printout 15p b&w, 25p-50p clr), room for hire (varies)

Stock:	*1 Apr 2000*	*1 Apr 2001*
ad lend:	143048	149070
ad ref:	9175	10064
ch:	71553	73772
audios:	11210	11669
videos:	7385	8502
CD-ROMs:	194	296
periodcls:	32	56

Issues:	*1999-2000*	*2000-01*
ad lend:	614774	529624
ch:	306365	273882
audios:	46469	46609
videos:	58905	55319
CD-ROMs:	384	907

Acqs:	*1999-2000*	*2000-01*
bks:	23984	24884
AVs:	4017	3953

Acqs: Source: lib suppl
Classn: DDC *Cat: Type:* author, classified, subj & title *Medium:* auto *Auto Sys:* Talis *Svcs: Extramural:* schools, old people's homes, housebnd, visually impaired *Info:* community *Other:* Open Learning Centre *Activs:* ch's activs, bk sales, reading groups
Enqs: 68050 (1999-2000); 88140 (2000-01)
Staff: Libns: 13 *Non-Prof:* 63.5

Inc from:	*1999-2000*	*2000-01*
fines etc:	-	£233080
total:	£253000	£250420

Exp on:	*1999-2000*	*2000-01*
bks:	-	£204524
AVs:	-	£32328
salaries:	£1311000	£1406417
total:	£2031000	£2170090

London: Lambeth

P97 Lambeth Libraries, Archives and Arts

3rd Floor, Internatl House, Canterbury Cres, Brixton, London, SW9 7QE (020-7926-0750; *fax:* 020-7926-0751)
Email: vmadden@lambeth.gov.uk
Internet: http://www.lambeth.gov.uk/

Local Auth: London Borough of Lambeth *Pop:* 275800 *Cttee:* Environment Cttee *Larger Dept:* Lambeth Environment Directorate *Dept Chief:* Dir: Mr Frank Quigg *Chief:* Head of Libs & Leisure: Mrs Lesli Good (Chief Commissioning Offcr); Head of Libs & Archvs: Mr David Jones (Chief Libs Offcr)
Main Libs: BRIXTON CENTRAL LIB, Brixton Oval, London, SW2 1JQ (*lend:* 020-7926-1056; *ref:* 020-7926-1067; *fax:* 020-7926-1070) *Branch Libs:* CLAPHAM LIB, 1 Northside, Clapham Common, London, SW4 0QW (020-7926-0717; *fax:* 020-7926-5804); DURNING LIB, 167 Kennington Ln, London, SE11 4HF (020-7926-8682; *fax:* 020-7926-8684); MINET LIB, 52 Knatchbull Rd, London, SE5 9QY (020-7926-6076; *fax:* 020-7926-6080); SOUTH LAMBETH LIB, 180 South Lambeth Rd, London, SW8 1QP (020-7926-0705; *fax:* 020-7926-8684); STREATHAM LIB, 63 Streatham High Rd, London, SW16 1PL (020-7926-6768; *fax:* 020-7926-5804); WATERLOO LIB, 114-118 Lower Marsh, London, SE1 7AQ (020-7926-8750; *fax:* 020-7926-8749); WEST NORWOOD LIB, Norwood High St, London, SE27 9JX (020-7926-8092; *fax:* 020-7926-8032)
Svc Pts: PT: 1 *Mobile:* 1 *AV:* 10 *Computers:* 10 *Internet:* 9 *Other:* LAMBETH ARCHVS DEPT, at Minet Lib (see A296); 270 community groups with 'outreach' collns
Collns: MSC 302-307 (at Tate Lib, Brixton); JFR: Kem-Kzz; Surrey Colln of Archvs; GLASS (Orchestral Recitals, 4+ composers; Jazz Bi-Bru; Mechanical Musical Instruments; Folk Music of West Africa & east to the Sahara); Royal Doulton Colln *Co-op Schemes:* CILLA, MSC, JFR, GLASS, SELPIG *ILLs:* natl & internatl *Loans:* bks & cassettes/4 wks; CDs/2 wks; videos/3 days; CD-ROMs & Playstation games/1 wk *Charges:* CDs & CD-ROMs/80p; videos/ individually priced *Income Gen:* res/50p; lost ticket/£1 (conc 50p) *Fines:* bks & audios/ad 10p pd (max £4.50), ch & oap exempt; videos & CD-ROMs/50p pd (max £5); under-16s & over-60s also exempt from charges *Equip:* 2 m-readers, 2 m-printers (10p), 8 fax (various), 8 copiers (A4/ 10p, A3/20p), computers (incl internet), 9 rooms for hire (various), cassette players for public use in all libs *Disabled:* Kurzweil, CCTV, reading aids, magnifiers & bk rests in all libs

Stock:	*1 Apr 2000*	*1 Apr 2001*
ad lend:	195743	202990
ad ref:	72999	81548
ch:	75300	92508
audios:	10277	17003
videos:	5822	4995
CD-ROMs:	-	389
periodcls:	295	239

Issues:	*1999-2000*	*2000-01*
ad lend:	431528	482690
ch:	254365	263830
audios:	41763	50013
videos:	22915	28951
CD-ROMs:		552

Acqs:	*1999-2000*	*2000-01*
bks:	49109	54097
AVs:	7199	6484

Acqs: Source: lib suppl, publ & bksellers *Offcr-in-Charge:* Head of Bibliographical Svcs: Mrs C. Stockbridge-Bland
Classn: DDC *Cat: Type:* author, classified, dictionary, subj & title *Medium:* auto *Auto Sys:* Talis *Svcs: Extramural:* schools, prisons, hosps, old people's homes, housebnd, nurseries & play groups, day centres *Info:* community database on OPACs *Other:* 'Outreach' svc to community groups, 2 computer centres *Activs:* ch's activs, bk sales, temp exhibs, poetry readings, reading groups, writers' groups, talks, author visits, promotional events
Enqs: 191256 (1999-2000); 155337 (2000-01)
Staff: 114.5 total

London: Lambeth

▼

London: Redbridge

Public Libraries

(Lambeth Libs, Archvs & Arts cont)

Inc from:	1999-2000	2000-01
fines etc:	£103307	£152058
total:	£4794781	£5763273

Exp on:	1999-2000	2000-01
bks:	£398620	£281914
AVs:	£76190	£72378
salaries:	£2681777	£3004338
total:	£4794781	£5763273

London: Lewisham

P98 Lewisham Library Service
Directorate of Edu & Culture, Laurence House, 1 Catford Rd, London, SE6 4SW (020-8314-6399; *fax:* 020-8314-1110)
Email: julia.newton@lewisham.gov.uk
Internet: http://www.lewisham.gov.uk/

Local Auth: London Borough of Lewisham *Pop:* 246000 *Cttee:* Exec Cttee *Larger Dept:* Edu & Culture *Dept Chief:* Exec Dir: Ms Frankie Sulke *Chief:* Head of Libs & Info: Ms Julia Newton MCLIP
Main Libs: CATFORD LIB, addr as above; FOREST HILL LIB, Dartmouth Rd, London, SE23 3HZ (020-8699-2065; *fax:* 020-8699-8296); LEWISHAM LIB (incl Ref Lib & Local Studies Centre), 199-201 Lewisham High St, London, SE13 6LG (020-8297-9677; ref: 020-8297-9430; *fax:* 020-8297-1169; *email:* reference.library@ lewisham.gov.uk); WAVELENGTHS LIB, Griffin St, Deptford, London, SE8 4RJ (020-8694-2535; *fax:* 020-8694-9652) *Branch Libs:* BLACK-HEATH VILLAGE LIB, 3-4 Blackheath Grove, London, SE3 0DD (020-8852-5309); CROFTON PK LIB, Brockley Rd, London, SE4 2AF (020-8692-1683); DOWNHAM LIB, 7 Moorside Rd, Downham, London, BR1 5EP (020-8698-1475; *fax:* 020-8695-5826); GROVE PK LIB, Somertrees Ave, London, SE12 0BX (020-8857-5794); MANOR HOUSE LIB, 34 Old Rd, Lee, London, SE12 5SY (020-8852-0357); NEW CROSS LIB, 283-285 New Cross Rd, London, SE14 6AS (020-8694-2534); SYDENHAM LIB, 210 Sydenham Rd, London, SE26 5SE (020-8778-7563); TORRIDON RD LIB, 103 Torridon Rd, Catford, London, SE6 1RQ (020-8698-1590)
Svc Pts: AV: 12 *Computers:* 12 *Internet:* 12 *Other:* HOUSEBND SVC, at Catford Lib
Collns: JFR: Che-Col & Mac-Mat; Edgar Wallace Colln; Henry Williamson Colln *Co-op Schemes:* BLDSC, JFR, GLASS, SELPIG *ILLs:* county & natl *Loans:* bks & audios/4 wks; videos, DVDs, CD-ROMs & Playstation games/varies *Income Gen:* req & res/50p; lost ticket/£1 *Fines:* bks & audios/ad 7p pd, oap 2p pd, ch & housebnd exempt; videos/7p pd *Equip:* m-readers, m-printers, video viewers, fax, copiers (A4/10p, A3/15p), clr copiers, computers (incl wd-procs, internet & CD-ROM), lang labs, CD players, darkrooms, dictaphones, 4 rooms for hire (varies) *Disabled:* Kurzweil, CCTV, minicom

Stock:	1 Apr 2000	1 Apr 2001
lend:	482140	401226
ref:	22449	35167
AVs:	56654	68019
periodcls:	544	398

Issues:	1999-2000	2000-01
bks:	1256178	1095739
AVs:	146551	206165

Acqs:	1999-2000	2000-01
bks:	50893	49260
AVs:	3610	5038

Acqs: Source: lib suppl & bksellers *Co-op:* GLASS, SELPIG Stock Consortium *Offcr-in-Charge:* Acqs Mgr
Classn: DDC *Cat: Type:* author, classified, dictionary, subj & title *Medium:* auto *Auto Sys:* Dynix *Svcs: Extramural:* old people's homes, housebnd *Info:* business, community, council, tourist *Other:* Open Learning *Activs:* ch's activs, bk sales, exhibs, reading groups, arts events
Enqs: 372684 (1999-2000); 345540 (2000-01)
Staff: 120.19 in total

Inc from:	2000-01
local govt:	£4065514
fines etc:	£227304
total:	£4292818

Exp on:	2000-01
stock:	£505284
salaries:	£2733798
total:	£4292818

London: London

P99 Corporation of London Libraries
Guildhall Lib, Aldermanbury, London, EC2P 2EJ (020-7606-3030; *fax:* 020-7600-3384)
Internet: http://www.cityoflondon.gov.uk/

Local Auth: Corp of London *Pop:* 6400 *Cttee:* Libs, Guildhall Art Gallery & Archvs Cttee *Larger Dept:* Libs & Guildhall Art Gallery *Chief:* Dir of Libs & Guildhall Art Gallery: Mr David Bradbury BA, MA, DipLib, MCLIP, FRSA (david.bradbury@corpoflondon.gov.uk) *Other Snr Staff:* Asst Dir (Libs & Archvs): Ms Lesley Blundell BA, MCLIP (lesley.blundell@ corpoflondon.gov.uk); Asst Dir (Art Gallery & Support Svcs): Mr Barry Cropper MA, MCLIP, MCIMgT (barry.cropper@corpoflondon.gov.uk)
Main Libs: GUILDHALL LIB, addr as above (020-7332-1868/70; email: printedbooks.guildhall@ corpoflondon.gov.uk) – see **A280** for MSS Section; BARBICAN CENTRE LIB, Barbican Centre, London, EC2Y 7EX (020-7638-0569; *fax:* 020-7638-2249; email: barbicanlib@corpoflondon. gov.uk); CITY BUSINESS LIB, 1 Brewers' Hall Gdn, London, EC2V 5BX (020-7638-8215; *fax:* 020-7332-1847; *email:* cbl@corpoflondon.gov.uk) *Branch Libs:* CAMOMILE ST LIB, 12-20 Camomile St, London, EC3A 7EX (020-7247-8895; *fax:* 020-7377-2972; email: Camomile@corpoflondon. gov.uk); SHOE LN LIB, Hill House, Little New St, London, EC4A 3JR (020-7583-7178; *fax:* 020-7353-0884; email: shoelane@cityoflondon.gov.uk); ST BRIDE PRINTING LIB (see **S1408**)
Svc Pts: AV: 3 *Computers:* 6 *Internet:* 6
Collns: Lloyd's Marine Colln; Clockmaker's Company Lib & Museum; Charles Lamb Soc Lib (see **S1064**); Stock Exchange historical colln; historical records relating to City of London; Gresham Coll Colln; Antiquarian Horological Soc Lib; Fletcher's Company Lib; Internatl Wine & Food Soc Lib; Inst of Masters of Wine Lib; Jane Grigson Colln; maps, prints & drawings (all at Guildhall Lib); Soc of Technical Analysts Lib; Gilbert & Sullivan Soc Lib; Music Performance Rsrch Centre archv (all at Barbican Lib); collns added in 2002 incl: Pepys Colln; Cock Colln (Thomas More); Wilkes Colln; Computer Auditers Colln *Co-op Schemes:* LibPAC V3 (inter-lib loans) *ILLs:* natl *Loans:* bks & CD-ROMs/3 wks; audios, videos & DVDs/1 wk *Charges:* audios & CD-ROMs/25p pw; videos/£1.80, educational free; DVDs/£2.50 *Income Gen:* res/80p; lost ticket/£1 1st time, £1.50 subsequent; lost items/replacement cost

Fines: bks & audios/ad & oap 14p pd open, ch exempt; audios & CD-ROMs/14p pd open; videos/70p pd; DVDs/90p pd *Equip:* 20 m-readers, 4 m-printers (20p), 7 copiers (10p), clr copier (20p), 65 computers (incl 41 with wd-proc, 8 with CD-ROM & 60 with internet) *Disabled:* Online Jaws (talking pages), Online Zoom (enlarges info for the partially sighted) *Online:* range of svcs available through the Business Info Svc at City Business Lib *Offcr-in-Charge:* Asst Dir (Art Gallery & Support Svcs), as above

Stock:	1 Apr 2000	1 Apr 2001
ad lend:	217239	212686
ad ref:	563857	290490
ch:	34919	36105
audios:	32273	41980
videos:	10018	10937
CD-ROMs:	478	748
periodcls:	2650	2650

Issues:	1999-2000	2000-01
ad lend:	680915	625849
ch:	67043	65836
audios:	209025	218768
videos:	56273	59881
CD-ROMs:	980	1812

Acqs:	1999-2000	2000-01
bks:	17865	18467
AVs:	4061	4124

Acqs: Source: lib suppl, publ & bksellers *Offcr-in-Charge:* selection decisions are at indiv lib level, procedures are dealt with by Bibliographical Svcs Libn: Mr C. A. Hall (chris.hall@corpoflondon. gov.uk)
Classn: DDC *Cat: Type:* author, classified, subj & title *Medium:* auto *Auto Sys:* Talis *Svcs: Extramural:* housebnd *Info:* Business Info Svc (FOCUS) *Activs:* ch's activs, bk sales, temp exhibs, reading groups *Offcr-in-Charge:* Barbican Libn: Mr John Lake BA, MCLIP (john.lake@ corpoflondon.gov.uk)
Enqs: 299416 (1999-2000); 280664 (2000-01)
Staff: Libns: 40 *Other Prof:* 20 *Non-Prof:* 95

Inc from:	1999-2000	2000-01
fines etc:	£392600	£519500

Exp on:	1999-2000	2000-01
bks:	£647000	£685800
AVs:	£38600	£49600
salaries:	£4147600	£4332100
total:	£8396600	£8315100

London: Merton

P100 Merton Library and Heritage Services
Apollo House, 66a London Rd, Morden, Surrey, SM4 5BE (020-8545-3783; *fax:* 020-8545-3237)
Internet: http://www.merton.gov.uk/libraries/

Local Auth: London Borough of Merton *Pop:* 189000 *Cttee:* Cabinet Portfolio for Regeneration *Larger Dept:* Edu, Leisure & Libs *Dept Chief:* Dir: Mrs Sue Evans *Chief:* Head of Lib & Heritage Svcs: Mr John Pateman (john.pateman@ merton.gov.uk)
Branch Libs: DONALD HOPE LIB, Cavendish House, High St, Colliers Wood, London, SW19 2HR (020-8542-1975; *fax:* 020-8543-9767; email: donaldhope.library@merton.gov.uk); MITCHAM LIB, London Rd, Mitcham, Surrey, CR4 2YR (020-8648-4070; *fax:* 020-8646-6360; *email:* mitcham. library@merton.gov.uk); MORDEN LIB, Merton Civic Centre, London Rd, Morden, Surrey, SM4 5DX (020-8545-4040; *fax:* 020-8545-4037; email: morden.library@merton.gov.uk); Pollards Hill, South Lodge Ave, Mitcham, Surrey, CR4 1LT (020-8764-5877; *fax:* 020-8765-0925; *email:* pollardshill.library@merton.gov.uk); RAYNES PK LIB, Approach Rd, London, SW20 8BA (020-8542-1893; *fax:* 020-8543-6132; *email:* raynespark. library@merton.gov.uk); WEST BARNES LIB, Station Rd, New Malden, Surrey, KT3 6JF (020-

8942-2635; *fax:* 020-8336-0554; *email:* westbarnes.library@merton.gov.uk); WIMBLE-DON LIB, 35 Wimbledon Hill Rd, London, SW19 7NB (020-8946-7432; *fax:* 020-8944-6804; *email:* wimbledon.library@merton.gov.uk)

Svc Pts: Mobile: 1 *AV:* 6 *Computers:* 7 *Internet:* 6 *Other:* OPEN LEARNING CENTRE, at Pollards Hill Lib; LOCAL STUDIES CENTRE, at Morden Lib (see **A385**)

Collns: MSC (900-909) & JFR (Ti-Trd): world hist, available for loan, held borough-wide; Gustav Mahler (music); Gioacchino Rossini (music); Jazz Colln, incl Alan Strugnell Colln (pre-1945); Nelson Colln (biographical materials on Horatio Nelson); William Morris Colln (all at Morden Lib) *Co-op Schemes:* MSC, JFR, GLASS, Proj EARL, WELLSTOC *ILLs:* county & natl *Loans:* bks & audios/3 wks; videos/2 nights-3 wks; Open Learning stock/4 wks *Charges:* cassettes & spkn wd/65p; CDs/95p, set £1.90; videos/50p-£2.50; lang courses/60p 1 item, set £5 *Income Gen:* req & res/70p, £4.35 via BLDSC; lost ticket/£1.05; video rewind charge/50p; annual sub to Open Learning Centre/£22, £5 for those on income support *Fines:* bks/14p pd for ad bks, no fine on ch's bks; audios/18p pd; videos/loan charge; registered disabled exempt *Equip:* 4 m-readers, 2 m-printers (printouts 25p), 7 fax (£2.50 + phone costs to send; £2 to receive), 9 copiers (A4/10p, A3/15p), 2 clr copiers (A4/£1, A3/£2), 102 computers (incl 47 with wd-proc & CD-ROM, 55 with internet) *Disabled:* magnifying aids, CCTV, 4 PCs adapted for disabled users

Stock:	1 Apr 2001
ad lend:	202275
ad ref:	76752
ch:	71096
audios:	25761
videos:	11527
CD-ROMs:	38
periodcls:	250

Issues:	2000-01
ad lend:	933274
ch:	309314
audios:	46507
videos:	55319

Acqs:	2000-01
bks:	25902
AVs:	3400

Acqs: Source: lib suppl, publ & bksellers *Co-op:* WELLSTOC *Offcr-in-Charge:* Strategy & Commissioning Offcr: Mr Gordon Brewin (gordon.brewin@merton.gov.uk)

Classn: DDC *Cat: Type:* author, classified, subj & title *Medium:* auto *Auto Sys:* DS Galaxy 2000 *Svcs: Extramural:* schools, old people's homes, housebnd, day centres, play groups *Other:* Open Learning Centre (at Pollards Hill Lib), LearnDirect Access Pts (at Mitcham & West Barnes Libs) *Activs:* ch's activs, bk sales, temp exhibs, poetry readings, reading groups, writers' groups, talks, author visits, story times *Enqs:* 152100 (2000-01) *Staff: Libns:* 26 *Other Prof:* 1 *Non-Prof:* 62

Inc from:	2000-01
fines etc:	£289926

Exp on:	2000-01
bks:	£338200
AVs:	£53010
salaries:	£1645780
total:	£3313600

London: Newham

P101 Newham Libraries

Libs Mgmt, Culture & Community Dept, 292 Barking Rd, London, E6 3BA (020-8430-2476; *fax:* 020-8557-8845)
Internet: http://www.newham.gov.uk/

Local Auth: London Borough of Newham *Pop:* 239527 *Cttee:* Cabinet *Larger Dept:* Culture & Community *Chief:* Head of Libs: Mr Adrian Whittle (adrian.whittle@newham.gov.uk) *Dep:* Svc Delivery Mgr: Ms Katherine Pedley (katherine.pedley@newham.gov.uk)

Main Libs: BECKTON GLOBE LIB, 1 Kingsford Way, London, E6 5JQ (020-8430-4063); EAST HAM LIB, High St South, London, E6 4EL (020-8430-3648; *fax:* 020-8503-5383); STRATFORD LIB, 3 The Grove, Stratford, London, E15 1EL (020-8430-6890) *Branch Libs:* CANNING TOWN LIB, Barking Rd, Canning Town, London, E16 4HQ (020-7476-2696; *fax:* 020-7511-8693); CUSTOM HOUSE LIB, Prince Regent Ln, London, E16 3JJ (020-7476-1565); FOREST GATE LIB, 38 Woodgrange Rd, Forest Gate, London, E7 0QH (020-8534-6952); GREEN ST LIB, 337-341 Green St, London, E13 9AR (020-8472-4101; *fax:* 020-8472-0927); MANOR PK LIB, Romford Rd, Manor Pk, London, E12 5JY (020-8478-1177; *fax:* 020-8514-8221); NORTH WOOLWICH LIB, St John's Centre, Albert Rd, North Woolwich, London, E16 2JD (020-7511-2387); PLAISTOW LIB, North St, London, E13 9HL (020-8472-0420; *fax:* 020-8471-3148)

Svc Pts: Mobile: 1 *AV:* 10 *Computers:* 9 *Internet:* 9 *Other:* ref libs at East Ham & Stratford

Collns: Historic Commercial Vehicle Colln (East Ham Lib, by appt); Archvs & Local Studies (at Stratford Lib – see **A315**) *Co-op Schemes:* GLASS, CILLA, EARL *ILLs:* internatl *Loans:* bks & audios/3 wks; videos & CD-ROMs/1 wk *Charges:* videos/£1.75 *Income Gen:* req/free in stock, £1 out of stock; lost ticket/£1.25 *Fines:* bks/ad 10p pd, ch exempt, oap 2 wks grace then 10p pd; audios/10p pd *Equip:* m-reader/printers, video viewer, 6 fax, 9 copiers (A4/10p, A3/15p), clr copier (A4/£1, A3/£1.50), computers (incl wd-procs, internet & CD-ROM, printouts 20p), room for hire *Disabled:* Kurzweil, magnifiers, profile pictures, bks in braille

Stock:	1 Apr 2000	1 Apr 2001
lend:	320762	434807

Issues:	1999-2000	2000-01
bks:	1328474	1328153
AVs:	173559	301774

Acqs:	1999-2000	2000-01
bks:	62567	117574
AVs:	10285	18507

Acqs: Source: lib suppl *Co-op:* BEWHICH Consortium *Offcr-in-Charge:* Finance & Bibliographical Svcs Libn: Ms Nicky Parker

Classn: DDC *Cat: Type:* author, classified, subj & title *Medium:* auto *Auto Sys:* Dynix *Svcs: Extramural:* schools, hosps, old people's homes, housebnd *Info:* community, business, legal, EU, govt, welfare *Other:* Open Learning (at Beckton Globe Lib) *Activs:* ch's activs, bk sales, temp exhibs, poetry readings, live music, author visits, theatre visits, reading groups *Offcr-in-Charge:* Principal Advisory Svcs Libn: Ms Jill Davies BSc, DipLib

Enqs: 98778 (1999-2000); 102769 (2000-01) *Staff:* 112.5 FTE in total

Exp on:	1999-2000
bks:	£626520
AVs:	£36570
elec media:	£50370
salaries:	£2296090
total:	£4256610

London: Redbridge

P102 Redbridge Libraries Service

Ilford Central Lib, Clements Rd, Ilford, Essex, IG1 1EA (020-8708-2436; *fax:* 020-8553-3299)
Internet: http://www.redbridge.gov.uk/

Local Auth: London Borough of Redbridge *Pop:* 231918 *Cttee:* Cabinet Memb for Culture & Leisure *Chief:* Chief Libn: Mr Martin Timms BA, MCLIP (martin.timms@redbridge.gov.uk) *Dep:* Central Lib Mgr: Mr Peter Ledger MCLIP

Main Libs: ILFORD CENTRAL LIB, addr as above; CENTRAL REF LIB, at Ilford Central Lib (020-8478-7145; *ref:* 020-8708-2420; *fax:* 020-8553-4185) *Branch Libs:* ALDERSBROOK LIB, 2a Park Rd, London, E12 5HQ (020-8496-0006; *fax:* 020-8596-0001); FULLWELL CROSS LIB, 140 High St, Barkingside, Ilford, Essex, IG6 2EA (020-8708-9281); GANTS HILL LIB, 490 Cranbrook Rd, Gants Hill, Ilford, Essex, IG2 6LA (020-8708-9274); GOODMAYES LIB, 76 Goodmayes Ln, Goodmayes, Ilford, Essex, IG3 9QB (020-8708-7750); HAINAULT LIB, 100 Manford Way, Chigwell, Essex, IG7 4DD (020-8708-9206); SOUTH WOODFORD LIB, 116 High Rd, London, E18 2QS (020-8708-9067); WANSTEAD LIB, Spratt Hall Rd, London, E11 2RQ (020-8708-7400); WOODFORD GREEN LIB, Snakes Ln, Woodford Green, Essex, IG8 0DX (020-8708-9055)

Svc Pts: Mobile: 3
Collns: GLASS: Haydn, Schoenberg, Miles Davis, Jazz E-F, folk music of Australia & Tasmania *Co-op Schemes:* ELIT, GLASS, CILLA *ILLs:* county, natl & internatl *Loans:* bks & audios/3 wks; videos, DVDs & CD-ROMs/1 wk *Charges:* audios/40p-£1.80; videos/70p-£2; CD-ROM/£2 *Income Gen:* res/£1 per item, oaps & income support 50p per item; lost ticket/ad £1.50, ch £1 *Fines:* bks & audios/ad 10p pd (max £4), ch 2p pw, oap 10p pd (max 80p); videos, DVDs & CD-ROMs/loan charge; registered disabled exempt *Equip:* m-readers, m-printers, fax, copiers (10p per copy), 2 clr copiers (£1 per copy), computers (incl wd-proc, internet & CD-ROM), room hire *Disabled:* CCTV

Stock:	1 Apr 2000	1 Apr 2001
lend:	453356	459631
ref:	38192	38989
AVs:	42316	44921
periodcls:	363	270

Issues:	1999-2000	2000-01
bks:	2005746	1898334
AVs:	111803	100180

Acqs:	1999-2000	2000-01
bks:	56832	47305
AVs:	4750	3437

Acqs: Source: lib suppl, publ & bksellers *Offcr-in-Charge:* Acq Asst: Mrs Helen Lyons
Classn: DDC *Cat: Type:* author, classified, subj & title *Medium:* auto *Auto Sys:* Geac *Svcs: Extramural:* housebnd *Info:* local studies, community, business *Other:* Open Learning (at Central Lib) *Activs:* ch's activs, bk sales, temp exhibs, reading groups
Enqs: 263813 (1999-2000); 264268 (2000-01) *Staff:* 117.5 FTE in total

Inc from:	1999-2000
fines etc:	£316000

Exp on:	1999-2000	2000-01
bks:	£590955	-
salaries:	£2242000	-
total:	£4587166	£4633017

London: Richmond upon Thames

P103 London Borough of Richmond upon Thames Library and Information Services

Edu, Arts & Leisure, Regal House, London Rd, Twickenham, Surrey, TW1 3QB (020-8940-0031; *fax:* 020-8891-7787)
Email: libraries@richmond.gov.uk
Internet: http://www.richmond.gov.uk/libraries/

London: Richmond

▼

London: Waltham Forest

Public Libraries

(Richmond Lib & Info Svcs cont)
Local Auth: London Borough of Richmond upon Thames *Pop:* 195126 **Larger Dept:** Edu, Arts & Leisure *Dept Chief:* Chief Edu Offcr: Ms Anji Phillips **Chief:** Head of Lib & Info Svcs: Ms Caroline Taylor (c.taylor@richmond.gov.uk) **Dep:** Asst Chief Libn: Ms Sheila Harden (s.harden@ richmond.gov.uk) **Other Snr Staff:** Asst Chief Libn (Yng People's Lib Svcs): Ms Sharon Kirkpatrick (s.kirkpatrick@richmond.gov.uk) **Main Libs:** CENTRAL LENDING LIB, Little Green, Richmond, Surrey, TW9 1QL (020-8940-0981/6857; *email:* richmond.library@richmond. gov.uk); CENTRAL REF LIB & INFO SVCS, Old Town Hall, Whittaker Ave, Richmond, Surrey, TW9 1TP (020-8940-5529; *fax:* 020-8940-6899; *email:* reference.services@richmond.gov.uk); EAST SHEEN DIST LIB, Sheen Ln, London, SW14 8LP (020-8876-8801; *email:* eastsheen. library@richmond.gov.uk); HAMPTON LIB, Rosehill, Hampton, Middlesex, TW12 2AB (020-8979-5110; *email:* hampton.library@richmond. gov.uk); TEDDINGTON DIST LIB, Waldegrave Rd, Teddington, Middlesex, TW11 8LG (020-8977-1284/8264; *email:* teddington.library@richmond. gov.uk); TWICKENHAM DIST LIB, Garfield Rd, Twicken-ham, Middlesex, TW1 3JT (020-8892-8091; *email:* twickenham.library@richmond. gov.uk); WHITTON LIB, 141 Nelson Rd, Whitton, Twickenham, Middlesex, TW2 7BB (020-8894-9828; *email:* whitton.library@richmond.gov.uk) **Branch Libs:** HAM LIB, Ham St, Richmond, Surrey, TW10 7HR (020-8940-8703; *email:* ham.library@richmond.gov.uk)
Svc Pts: PT: 5 *AV:* 13 *Computers:* 13 *Internet:* 13 *Other:* SCHOOLS' LIB & RESOURCE SVC
Collns: Sir Richard Burton Colln (artefacts & bks of the explorer of Africa & Middle East, at Richmond Local Studies Lib); Alexander Pope Colln (artefacts & bks of the poet & former resident of Twickenham, at Twickenham Local Studies Lib); Sladen Colln (letters etc, at Central Ref Lib); dyslexia collns (at 4 libs) **Co-op Schemes:** BLDSC, JFR, SOPSE, NOF **ILLs:** county & natl **Loans:** bks/3 wks; audios/2 wks; videos & DVDs/1 wk; lang courses/6 wks **Charges:** CDs & talking bks/90p; videos/80p-£3.50; DVDs/£3.50 **Income Gen:** res/90p, conc 50p, free to ch & at part-time libs; lost ticket/£1, under-18s 50p **Fines:** bks/ad & oap 10p for 1st wk, then 15p (£6 max), ch exempt; audio & videos/loan charge; registered blind & other registered disabled exempt **Equip:** 2 m-readers, 2 m-printers (20p), 13 copiers (A4/10p, A3/20p), clr copier (A4/£1, A3/£1.50), 150 computers (all with internet, 85 with wd-proc, 20 with CD-ROM), room for hire (various) **Disabled:** Dolphin Supernova **Online:** KnowUK, Xrefer, UKOP, Guardian/Observer Archv *Offcr-in-Charge:* Asst Chief Libn, as above

Stock:	1 Apr 2001
ad lend:	211175
ad ref:	24054
ch:	105123
audios:	20198
videos:	13898
CD-ROMs:	475
periodcls:	285

Issues:	2000-01
ad lend:	908094
ch:	400201
audios:	79492
videos:	108371
CD-ROMs:	1389

Acqs:	2000-01
bks:	31848
AVs:	7292

Acqs: *Source:* lib suppl *Offcr-in-Charge:* Info Svcs Mgr: Ms Kate Davenport
Classn: DDC *Cat: Type:* author, classified, Subj & title *Medium:* auto *Auto Sys:* DS *Svcs: Extra-mural:* schools, old people's homes, housebnd, play groups *Info:* tourist, council, community *Other:* lib svc for teachers, LearnDirect **Activs:** ch's activs, bk sales, temp exhibs, reading groups, talks, author visits, Book Now! lit festival *Offcr-in-Charge:* Asst Chief Libn, as above
Enqs: 405885 (2000-01)
Staff: Libns: 23.5 *Non-Prof:* 79.1

London: Southwark

P104 Southwark Libraries

Bibliographic Svcs, 15 Spa Rd, Bermondsey, London, SE16 3QW (020-7525-1574; *fax:* 020-7525-1505)
Email: adrian.olsen@southwark.gov.uk
Internet: http://www.southwark.gov.uk/

Local Auth: London Borough of Southwark *Pop:* 242311 **Larger Dept:** Edu & Culture *Dept Chief:* Dir: Mr Gordon Mott **Chief:** Lib Svcs Mgr: Mr Adrian Olsen BA, MCLIP **Dep:** Support Svcs Libn: Mr Stuart Woollard MCLIP
Main Libs: DULWICH LIB (incl Ref Lib), 368 Lordship Ln, London, SE22 8NB (020-8693-5171; ref: 020-8693-8312); NEWINGTON LIB (incl Ref Lib), 155-157 Walworth Rd, London, SE17 1RS (020-7703-3324; ref: 020-7708-0516); PECKHAM LIB, 122 Peckham Hill St, London, SE15 5JR (020-7525-0200) **Branch Libs:** BLUE ANCHOR LIB, Market Pl, Southwark Pk Rd, London, SE16 3UQ (020-7231-0475); BRANDON LIB, Maddock Way, Cooks Rd, London, SE17 3NH (020-7735-3430; *fax:* 020-7735-1664; *email:* brandon.library@ southwark.gov.uk); CAMBERWELL LIB, 17-21 Camberwell Church St, London, SE5 8TR (020-7703-3763); EAST ST LIB, 168-170 Old Kent Rd, London, SE1 5TY (020-7703-0395); GROVE VALE LIB, 25-27 Grove Vale, London, SE22 8EQ (020-8693-5734; *fax:* 020-8693-0755); JOHN HARVARD LIB (incl Local Studies Lib), 211 Borough High St, London, SE1 1JA (020-7407-0807); KINGSWOOD LIB, Seeley Dr, London, SE21 8QR (020-8670-4803); NUNHEAD LIB, Gordon Rd, London, SE15 3RW (020-7639-0264); ROTHERHITHE LIB, Albion St, London, SE16 1JA (020-7237-2010)
Svc Pts: Mobile: 1 *AV:* 12 *Computers:* 12 *Other:* SPECIAL LIB SVC (Housebnd & Bk Bus), at Rotherhithe Lib (020-7237-1487); EDU LIB SVC, Edu Resource Centre, Cator St, London, SE15 6AA (020-7525-2830; *fax:* 020-7525-2837)
Collns: GLASS: Berlioz & Messiaen, Jazz Joo-Led, Folk: South East Asia (at Dulwich Lib) **Co-op Schemes:** GLASS, BLCMP, ALCL, SEAL, SELPIG **ILLs:** natl **Loans:** bks/3 wks; audios & videos/1 wk **Charges:** audios/30p (sets 60p); videos/£1.50-£2 **Income Gen:** req/70p; res/85p, ch 42p; lost ticket/50p **Fines:** bks & audios/ad 10p pd; videos/30p-40p pd; ch, oap & registered disabled exempt **Equip:** m-readers, m-printers, fax, copiers (A4/10p), clr copiers (A4/£1), computers (with wd-proc, internet & CD-ROM), rooms for hire (various) **Disabled:** Kurzweil, Horizon & Dolphin CCTV magnifiers, induction loops, ZoomText, JAWS, Supernova

Stock:	1 Apr 2000	1 Apr 2001
lend:	424397	405016
ref:	27366	29608
AVs:	58334	61510
periodcls:	270	298

Issues:	1999-2000	2000-01
bks:	1059131	1256900
AVs:	208661	277049

Acqs:	1999-2000	2000-01
bks:	41957	45880
AVs:	7879	10625

Acqs: *Source:* lib suppl *Co-op:* SELPIG Stock Purchase Consortium *Offcr-in-Charge:* Snr Libn (Stock Development)
Classn: DDC *Cat: Type:* author, classified, subj & title *Medium:* auto *Auto Sys:* Talis *Svcs: Extramural:* schools, housebnd, day centres, sheltered housing *Info:* business, community *Other:* Learning Centres **Activs:** ch's activs, under-5s, pensioners' group, homework groups, reading groups, writer's groups
Enqs: 377312 (1999-2000); 423371 (2000-01)
Staff: Libns: 36.75 *Non-Prof:* 112.55

Inc from:	1999-2000	2000-01
local govt:	£4842674	£5204660
fines etc:	£253723	£413598
total:	£5096397	£5618258

Exp on:	1999-2000	2000-01
stock:	£662402	£501156
salaries:	£3194164	£3542435
total:	£5096397	£5618258

London: Sutton

P105 London Borough of Sutton Library Services

Central Lib, St Nicholas Way, Sutton, Surrey, SM1 1EA (020-8770-4700; *fax:* 020-8770-4777)
Email: sutton.library@sutton.gov.uk
Internet: http://www.sutton.gov.uk/lfl/librarie/

Local Auth: London Borough of Sutton *Pop:* 178737 **Cttee:** Learning for Life Performance Cttee **Larger Dept:** Learning for Life *Dept Chief:* Strategic Dir: Dr Ian Burnbaum **Chief:** Exec Head of Lib, Heritage & Registration Svcs: Mr T.J. Knight MLib, FCLIP (trevor.knight@sutton. gov.uk) **Dep:** Principal Libns: Mrs C. McDonough BSc, MCLIP & Mrs A. Fletcher BA, PGCE **Other Snr Staff:** Quality Svcs Mgr: Mr David Bundy BA, MCLIP (david.bundy@sutton.gov.uk)
Main Libs: CENTRAL LIB, addr as above **Branch Libs:** CARSHALTON LIB, The Sq, Carshalton, Surrey, SM5 3BN (020-8647-1151; *fax:* 020-8770-4849; *email:* carshalton.library@ sutton.gov.uk); CHEAM LIB, Church Rd, Cheam, Sutton, Surrey, SM3 8QH (020-8644-9377; *fax:* 020-8644-1311; *email:* cheam.library@sutton. gov.uk); MIDDLE-TON CIRCLE LIB, Green Wrythe Ln, Carshalton, Surrey, SM5 1JJ (*tel & fax:* 020-8648-6608; *email:* middleton.library@ sutton.gov.uk); RIDGE RD LIB, Ridge Rd, Sutton, Surrey, SM3 9LY (*tel & fax:* 020-8644-9696; *email:* ridge.library@sutton.gov.uk); ROUNDSHAW LIB, Mollison Dr, Roundshaw, Wallington, Surrey, SM6 9HG (020-8770-4901; *fax:* 020-8770-4896; *email:* roundshaw.library@ sutton.gov.uk); WALLINGTON LIB, Shotfield, Wallington, Surrey, SM6 0HY (020-8770-4900; *fax:* 020-8770-4884; *email:* wallington.library@ sutton.gov.uk); WORCESTER PK LIB, Windsor Rd, Worcester Pk, Surrey, KT4 8ES (020-8337-1609; *fax:* 020-8401-0835; *email:* worcester. library@sutton.gov.uk)
Svc Pts: PT: 1 *Mobile:* 2 *AV:* 9 *Computers:* 9 *Internet:* 9
Collns: JFR (X, Y, Z); GLASS (Bruckner; Choral Recitals; Jazz Gim-Hard; Folk: USA; plays in English except Shakespeare); astronomy colln; genealogy colln **Co-op Schemes:** JFR, GLASS

Loans: bks & audios/3 wks; videos/1 day or 1 wk; pictures/1 or 6 months *Charges:* cassettes/ ad 60p, ch 40p; CDs/90p; videos/50p-£2; pictures/£1.15 per month or £5.40 for 6 months *Income Gen:* req & res/85p in stock, £1.50 not in stock; lost ticket/ad £1.50, ch 50p *Fines:* bks & audios/ad & oap 12p pd; videos/loan charge *Equip:* 3 m-readers, 2 m-printers (£1.30 1st copy, 40p addl), fax (varies), copier in each lib (A4/10p, A3/20p), clr copier (A4/£1, A3/£1.50), room hire (varies), 75 computers (incl 4 wd-procs, charged at £2 per hr, 42 CD-ROM & 36 internet), 5 study carrels (£3.20 pd) *Disabled:* Kurzweil, CCTV *Offcr-in-Charge:* various offcrs

Stock:	1 Apr 2000	1 Apr 2001
ad lend:	320690	303117
ad ref:	51483	51274
ch:	96631	87279
schools:	120995	115000
audios:	35054	31507
videos:	10979	10956
CD-ROMs:	1364	2196
periodcls:	290	375

Issues:	1999-2000	2000-01
ad lend:	1252439	1178603
ch:	450006	454580
schools:	73360	70000
audios:	331232	364044
videos:	72265	72470
CD-ROMs:	6893	13253

Acqs:	1999-2000	2000-01
bks:	48611	45023
AVs:	7137	6235

Acqs: Source: lib suppl *Offcr-in-Charge:* Quality Svcs Mgr, as above
Classn: DDC *Cat: Type:* author, classified & title *Medium:* auto *Auto Sys:* Geac *Svcs: Extramural:* schools, old people's homes, housebnd *Info:* business, community *Other:* public computer centres for training, LearnDirect centre *Activs:* ch's activs, bk sales, temp exhibs, poetry readings, reading groups, talks, author visits *Offcr-in-Charge:* various offcrs
Enqs: 394680 (1999-2000); 343486 (2000-01)
Staff: Libns: 26 *Non-Prof:* 63.5

Inc from:	1999-2000	2000-01
local govt:	£3449253	£3564029
fines etc:	£402992	£405789
total:	£3852245	£3969818

Exp on:	1999-2000	2000-01
bks:	£412750	£401172
AVs:	£107200	£103700
elec media:	-	£15000
salaries:	£1874373	£1944036
total:	£3852245	£3969818

London: Tower Hamlets

P106 Tower Hamlets Libraries
Lib Administrative HQ, Bancroft Lib, 277 Bancroft Rd, London, E1 4DQ (020-8980-4366; *fax:* 020-8983-4510)
Internet: http://www.towerhamlets.gov.uk/

Local Auth: London Borough of Tower Hamlets *Pop:* 186700 *Larger Dept:* Customer Svcs Directorate *Dept Chief:* Corporate Dir: Mr Eric Bohl *Chief:* Head of Libs: Ms Anne Cunningham MCLIP (gdr43@dial.pipex.com) *Other Snr Staff:* Lib Mgr (Customer Svcs): Mr Steve Clarke (stevej.clarke@towerhamlets.gov.uk); Lib Mgr (Development): Mr Kate Pitman (kate.pitman@ towerhamlets.gov.uk) & Ms Sue Bridgwater (sue.bridgwater@towerhamlets.gov.uk); Lib Mgr (Operations): Mr John Hagerty (john.hagerty@ towerhamlets.gov.uk)
Branch Libs: BANCROFT LIB, addr as above (020-7364-1291/6; *fax:* 020-7364-1292; *email:* bancroftlibrary@towerhamlets.gov.uk); BETHNAL

GREEN LIB (incl Ref Lib), Cambridge Heath Rd, London, E12 0HL (020-8980-3902/6274; *fax:* 020-8980-1610; *email:* bethnalgreenlibrary@ towerhamlets.gov.uk); BOW IDEA STORE, Gladstone Pl, London, E3 5ES (020-7364-4332; *fax:* 020-7364-5773; *email:* bowideastore@ towerhamlets.gov.uk); CUBITT TOWN LIB, Strattondale St, London, E14 3HG (020-7987-3152; *fax:* 020-7538-2795; *email:* cubitttownlibrary@towerhamlets.gov.uk); LANSBURY LIB, 23-27 Market Way, London, E14 6AH (020-7987-3573; *fax:* 020-7538-5520; *email:* lansburylibrary@towerhamlets.gov.uk); LIME-HOUSE LIB, 638 Commercial Rd, London, E14 7HS (020-7364-2527; *fax:* 020-7364-2502); WATNEY MARKET LIB, 30-32 Watney Market, London, E1 2PR (020-7790-4039; *fax:* 020-7265-9401; *email:* watneymarketlibrary@towerhamlets. gov.uk); WHITECHAPEL LIB, 77 Whitechapel High St, London, E1 7QX (020-7247-5272/0265; *fax:* 020-7247-5731; *email:* whitechapellibrary@ towerhamlets.gov.uk)
Svc Pts: PT: 3 *Mobile:* 2 *AV:* 11 *Computers:* 11 *Internet:* 11 *Other:* OUTREACH LIB SVCS, at Bancroft Lib (020-8980-4366; *fax:* 020-8983-4510; *email:* outreachlibrary@towerhamlets.gov.uk); CH'S LIB SVCS, at Whitechapel Lib (020-7247-9510; *email:* childrenslibrary@towerhamlets. gov.uk)
Collns: MSC: French, German & Portuguese non-fiction; *JFR:* St-Sz, some Ben-Bor & P-Pic; GLASS: Schubert, Jazz artists Bru-Chal, humour, sporting events, Israeli folk music, Italian lit; art bks colln; Islamic collns *Co-op Schemes:* BLDSC, GLASS, CILLA, GLAN, BEWHICH, ALCL *ILLs:* county, natl & internatl *Loans:* bks, audios & videos/3 wks; DVDs & CD-ROMs/1 wk *Charges:* audios/£20 pa sub, or: cassettes/40p; CDs/70p; videos/£1; CD-ROMs/70p *Income Gen:* req & res/70p; lost tickets/ad £1, ch 50p *Fines:* bks/ad 10p pd; audios & videos/10p pd; CD-ROMs/loan charge; ch, over 60s, registered blind, deaf & housebnd exempt *Equip:* m-readers, m-printers (A4/20p), fax, copiers (A4/ 10p, A3/20p), clr copier (A4/£1), computers (incl wd-procs, internet & CD-ROM, printouts 10p), room for hire *Disabled:* minicom, Kurzweil, braille printer, Aladdin CCTV, tape recorders for housebnd

Stock:	1 Apr 2000	1 Apr 2001
lend:	355994	381122
ref:	45426	45037
AVs:	38027	43705
periodcls:	582	588

Issues:	1999-2000	2000-01
bks:	835991	846387
AVs:	63401	68055

Acqs:	1999-2000	2000-01
bks:	38757	59942
AVs:	2482	7079

Acqs: Source: lib suppl *Co-op:* CILLA
Classn: DDC *Cat: Type:* author, classified, subj & title *Medium:* auto *Auto Sys:* DS Galaxy *Svcs: Extramural:* hosps, old people's homes, housebnd, day centres, sheltered accommodation *Info:* council, community, business *Activs:* ch's activs, bk sales, temp exhibs, poetry readings, local hist walks & lectures, talks
Enqs: 198257 (1999-2000); 164008 (2000-01)
Staff: Libns: 38.5 *Other Prof:* 1 *Non-Prof:* 61

Inc from:	1999-2000	2000-01
local govt:	£3677000	£4052000
fines etc:	£64000	£74000
total:	£3741000	£4126000

Exp on:	1999-2000	2000-01
stock & svcs:	£621000	£699000
salaries:	£2365000	£2496000
total:	£3741000	£4126000

London: Upper Norwood

P107 Upper Norwood Joint Library
39 Westow Hill, Upper Norwood, London, SE19 1TJ (020-8670-2551; *fax:* 020-8670-5468)
Internet: http://www.virtualnorwood.com/ localinfo/unlibrary.shtml

Local Auth: jointly funded by London Boroughs of Croydon (see **P83**) & Lambeth (see **P97**) *Pop:* 40000 *Cttee:* Upper Norwood Joint Lib Cttee *Chief:* Chief Libn: Mr Bradley Millington *Open: Ad & Ref Libs:* Mon 1000-1900, Tue, Thu-Fri 0900-1900, Sat 0900-1700; *Ch's Lib:* Mon-Tue, Thu-Fri 1000-1800, Sat 0930-1700; closed Wed *Collns:* local hist colln covering all aspects of hist of Upper Norwood & neighbouring dists to a lesser extent; some material on the Crystal Palace & the Gt Exhib of 1851; J.B. Wilson Colln (personal colln of local historian J.B. Wilson, d 1949); Gerald Massey Colln (Victorian Chartist, poet, spiritualist & Egyptologist) *Co-op Schemes:* LASER, CLLUBS, BLLD *ILLs:* county & natl *Loans:* bks & cassettes/3 wks; CDs & DVDs/1 wk; videos/overnight or 1 wk *Charges:* lang cassettes/£1, ch, oap & visually impaired free; CDs/75p; videos/£1.80, ch & oap 90p; overnight loans £2; DVDs/£2.25 *Income Gen:* req & res/ad 80p, oap 40p, ch 20p; lost ticket/£1.50, oap & ch 75p *Fines:* bks & cassettes/ad 12p pd (£6 max), oap & young ad 5p pd (£2 max), ch free; CDs/ad 20p pd (max £8), oap & young adults 10p pd (max £4); videos/ 50p pd (max £10), oap & young ad 25p pd (max £5); DVDs/60p pd (max £12), oap & young ad 30p pd (max £6) *Equip:* fax (varies), copier (A4/ 5p, A3/10p), 6 computers (with wd-proc, internet & CD-ROM), laminator (a5/60p, A4/90p)
Acqs: Source: lib suppl, publ & bksellers *Offcr-in-Charge:* Chief Libn, as above
Classn: DDC *Cat: Type:* author, subj, title, series & keyword *Medium:* auto *Svcs: Extramural:* schools, old people's homes *Info:* business, community, local hist, tourist, careers *Other:* Learning Centre *Activs:* ch's activs, bk sales, temp exhibs *Offcr-in-Charge:* Chief Libn, as above
Staff: Libns: 4 *Non-Prof:* 7
Proj: refurbishment of lib in 2003 (closure of 4-6 months anticipated)

London: Waltham Forest

P108 Waltham Forest Libraries
Central Lib, High Street, Walthamstow, London, E17 7JN (020-8520-3031; *fax:* 020-8520-9693)
Email: libs.c@al.lbwf.gov.uk
Internet: http://www.lbwf.gov.uk/

Local Auth: London Borough of Waltham Forest *Pop:* 218800 *Cttee:* Leisure Cttee *Larger Dept:* Arts & Leisure *Chief:* Asst Dir, Arts & Leisure: Mr Colin Richardson MCLIP
Main Libs: CENTRAL LIB, High St, Waltham-stow, London, E17 7JN (020-8520-3031/4733; *fax:* 020-8520-9693); LEYTONSTONE LIB, Church Ln, Leytonstone, London, E11 1HG (020-8539-2730; *fax:* 020-8556-1026); NORTH CHINGFORD LIB, The Green, Chingford, London, E4 7EN (020-8529-2993) *Branch Libs:* HALE END LIB, Castle Ave, Highams Pk, London, E4 9QD (020-8531-6423); HARROW GREEN LIB, Cathall Rd, Leytonstone, London, E11 4LF (020-8539-5997); HIGHAM HILL LIB, North Countess Rd, Waltham-stow, London, E17 5HF (*tel & fax:* 020-8531-6424); LEA BRIDGE LIB, Lea Bridge Rd, Leyton, London, E10 7HU (020-8539-5652); LEYTON LIB, High Rd, Leyton, London, E10 5QH (020-8539-1223); ST JAMES ST LIB, Coppermill Ln, Walthamstow, London, E17 7HA (020-8520-1292); SOUTH CHINGFORD LIB, Hall Ln, Chingford, London, E4 8EU (020-8529-2332); WOOD ST LIB, Forest Rd, Walthamstow, London, E17 4AA (020-8521-1070) ☞

(Waltham Forest Libs cont)

Svc Pts: PT: 1 *Mobile:* 1 *AV:* 7 *Computers:* 5 *Internet:* 5 *Other:* YNG PEOPLE'S LIB SVC, at Central Lib (020-8520-8325); DOMICILIARY LIB SVC, at Wood Street Lib (020-8520-9875)
Collns: GLASS (Jazz K-O) *Co-op Schemes:* GLASS, CILLA, BEWHICH *ILLs:* county, natl & internatl *Loans:* bks & audios/3 wks; videos/1 wk *Charges:* cassettes/55p; CDs/80p; videos/ £1.80, ch's £1.25 *Income Gen:* res/ad 60p, conc 20p; lost ticket/£1.60 *Fines:* bks/10p pd, ch & oap exempt; audios & videos/loan charge *Equip:* m-readers, m-printers, copiers, fax, computers (incl wd-proc, internet & CD-ROM), rooms for hire *Disabled:* minicoms, CCTV, magnifiers

Stock:	1 Apr 2000	1 Apr 2001
ad lend:	253899	251476
ad ref:	16282	14838
ch:	107388	83661
AVs:	31725	24617
periodcls:	262	259

Issues:	1999-2000	2000-01
ad lend:	1012257	890085
ch:	374575	333407
AVs:	85044	82838

Acqs:	1999-2000	2000-01
bks:	49494	39328
AVs:	4103	6548

Acqs: Source: lib suppl & bksellers *Offcr-in-Charge:* Bibliographical Svcs Offcr
Classn: DDC *Cat: Type:* author, classified, subj & title *Medium:* auto *Auto Sys:* Dynix *Svcs: Extramural:* schools, hosps, old people's homes, housebnd *Info:* community, European, business, travel, council, edu, careers *Activs:* ch's activs, bk sales, temp exhibs
Enqs: 266032 (1999-2000); 237276 (2000-01)
Staff: 121.4 in total

Inc from:	2000-01
local govt:	£3661428
fines etc:	£250745
total:	£3912173

Exp on:	2000-01
stock:	£535404
salaries:	£2526484
total:	£3912173

London: Wandsworth

P109 Wandsworth Libraries

Leisure & Amenity Svcs, Room 223, The Town Hall, Wandsworth High Street, London, SW18 2PU (020-8871-6364; *fax:* 020-8871-7630)
Email: libraries@wandsworth.gov.uk
Internet: http://www.wandsworth.gov.uk/libraries/

Local Auth: London Borough of Wandsworth *Pop:* 260000 *Cttee:* Environment & Public Svcs Cttee *Larger Dept:* Leisure & Amenity Svcs *Dept Chief:* Dir: Mr Peter Brennan *Chief:* Head of Libs, Museum & Arts: Ms Jane Allen BA(Hons), DMS, MCLIP *Dep:* Asst Head of Libs: Ms Meryl Jones MCLIP
Main (Area) Libs: BALHAM LIB, Ramsden Rd, London, SW12 8QY (020-8871-7195; *fax:* 020-8675-4015); BATTERSEA LENDING LIB, Lavender Hill, London, SW11 1JB (020-8871-7466; *fax:* 020-7978-4376); PUTNEY LIB, Disraeli Rd,

London, SW15 2DR (020-8871-7090; *fax:* 020-8789-6175); REF LIB, Altenburg Gdns, London, SW11 1JQ (020-8871-7467; *fax:* 020-7978-4376) *Branch Libs:* ALVERING LIB, Allfarthing Ln, London, SW18 2PQ (020-8871-6398; *fax:* 020-8870-4599); BATTERSEA PK LIB, Battersea Pk Rd, London, SW11 4NF (020-8871-7468; *fax:* 020-7622-5459); EARLSFIELD LIB, Magdalen Rd, London, SW18 3NY (020-8871-6389; *fax:* 020-8944-6912); NORTHCOTE LIB, Northcote Rd, London, SW11 6QB (020-8871-7469; *fax:* 020-7228-6842); ROEHAMPTON LIB, Danebury Ave, London, SW15 4HD (020-8871-7091; *fax:* 020-8780-2719); SOUTHFIELDS LIB, Wimbledon Pk Rd, London, SW19 6NL (020-8871-6388; *fax:* 020-8780-9045); TOOTING LIB, Mitcham Rd, London, SW17 9PD (020-8871-7175; *fax:* 020-8672-3099); WEST HILL LIB, West Hill, London, SW18 1RZ (020-8871-6386; *fax:* 020-8877-3476); YORK GDNS LIB, Lavender Rd, London, SW11 2UG (020-8871-7471; *fax:* 020-7223-0864)
Svc Pts: AV: 13 *Computers:* 13 *Internet:* 13 *Other:* LOCAL HIST SVC, at Battersea Lib (see **A355**); ASIAN COMMUNITY LIB, at Tooting Lib; AFRICAN CARIBBEAN COMMUNITY LIB, at Battersea Lib
Collns: GLASS: Prokofiev, Rachmaninov, Jazz artists Lee-Lz, film soundtracks, Scottish folk music; Early Ch's Bks (7000 items); G.A. Henty Colln (all at Putney Lib); William Blake Colln; Edward Thomas Colln; Swinburne Colln; Occult Colln; Arch & Bldg Colln (all at Battersea Ref Lib); Regional Fiction Reserve: A-AL; European hist (at West Hill Lib) *ILLs:* natl & internatl *Loans:* bks/3 wks; audios/3 wks; videos/3 days-3 wks
Equip: m-readers, m-printers, 13 fax (scale of charges), 14 copiers (A4/10p, A3/20p), computers (incl wd-proc, internet & CD-ROM), electric typewriters, rooms for hire *Disabled:* hearing loop, minicom, video caption readers, Reading Edge print scanners, special hardware & software

Stock:	1 Apr 2000	1 Apr 2001
lend:	569970	570281
ref:	49892	37976
AVs:	51030	48198
periodcls:	318	322

Issues:	1999-2000	2000-01
ad lend:	1531337	1484665
ch:	747648	754891
AVs:	171319	189970

Acqs:	1999-2000	2000-01
bks:	76980	85633
AVs:	6840	8035

Acqs: Source: lib suppl
Classn: DDC *Cat: Medium:* auto *Auto Sys:* Epixtech *Svcs: Extramural:* prisons, hosps, old people's homes, housebnd *Info:* community, business *Other:* Computer Training Centres (at Putney & Battersea Libs) *Activs:* ch's activs, bk sales, temp exhibs, poetry readings, author talks, homework clubs, reading groups *Offcr-in-Charge:* Asst Head of Libs, as above
Enqs: 260468 (1999-2000); 263588 (2000-01)
Staff: Libns: 49.2 *Non-Prof:* 81.73

Inc from:	1999-2000	2000-01
local govt:	£5764000	£5691000
fines etc:	£653644	£796000
total:	£6418000	£6487000

Exp on:	1999-2000	2000-01
stock:	£686000	£727000
salaries:	£2925000	£2979000
total:	£6418000	£6487000

London: Westminster

P110 Westminster Libraries

Lib HQ, Charing Cross Lib, 4 Charing Cross Rd, London, WC2H 0HF (020-7641-6573; *fax:* 020-7641-6551)
Internet: http://www.westminster.gov.uk/el/
libraries/

Local Auth: City of Westminster *Pop:* 244597 *Cttee:* Cabinet Memb for Lifelong Learning *Larger Dept:* Edu *Dept Chief:* Dir of Edu: Mr John Harris BA(Hons), DipEd *Chief:* Westminster Libs Mgr: Mr Andrew Stevens BA, DipLib, MCLIP (a.stevens@dial.pipex.com)
Other Snr Staff: Customer Svcs Mgr: Ms Iona Cairns (ionacairns@dial.pipex.com); Lifelong Learning Mgr: Ms Sarah Wilkie (swilkie@dial.pipex.com); ICT Development Mgr: Mr Chris Lally (c.lally@dial.pipex.com)
Main Libs: CHARING CROSS LIB, addr as above (020-7641-4628; *fax:* 020-7641-4629); MARYLEBONE LIB, 109-117 Marylebone Rd, London, NW1 5PS (020-7641-1037; *fax:* 020-7641-1044); PADDINGTON LIB, Porchester Rd, London, W2 5DU (020-7641-4475; *fax:* 020-7641-4471); VICTORIA LIB, 160 Buckingham Palace Rd, London, SW1W 9UD (020-7641-4287; *fax:* 020-7641-4281); WESTMINSTER REF LIB, 35 St Martin's St, London, WC2H 7HP (020-7641-4636; *fax:* 020-7641-4606) *Branch Libs:* CHURCH ST LIB, Church St, London, NW8 8EU (020-7641-5479; *fax:* 020-7641-5482); MAIDA VALE LIB, Sutherland Ave, London, W9 2QT (020-7641-3659; *fax:* 020-7641-3660); MAYFAIR LIB, 25 South Audley St, London, W1Y 5DJ (020-7641-4903; *fax:* 020-7641-4901); PIMLICO LIB, Rampayne St, London, SW1V 2PU (020-7641-2983; *fax:* 020-7641-2980); QUEENS PK LIB, 666 Harrow Rd, London, W10 4NE (020-7641-4575; *fax:* 020-7641-4576); ST JAMES'S LIB, 62 Victoria St, London, SW1V 6QP (020-7641-2989; *fax:* 020-7641-2986); ST JOHN'S WOOD LIB, 20 Circus Rd, London, NW8 6PD (020-7641-5087; *fax:* 020-7641-5089)
Svc Pts: Mobile: 1 *AV:* at all libs *Computers:* at all libs *Internet:* at all libs *Other:* CHINESE LIB, at Charing Cross Lib (020-7641-4623); WESTMINSTER MUSIC LIB, at Victoria Lib (020-7641-4292); MARYLEBONE INFO SVC, at Marylebone Lib (020-7641-1039); HOME LIB SVC, at Church Street Lib (020-7641-4806); MOBILE LIB SVC (020-7641-5405); WESTMINSTER SCHOOLS LIB SVC, 62 Shirland Rd, London, W9 2EH (020-7641-4320/1; *fax:* 020-7641-4322; *email:* sls@dial.pipex.com); CITY OF WESTMINSTER ARCHVS CENTRE (see **A268**)
Collns: Sherlock Holmes Colln; Amnesty Internatl Archvs (both at Marylebone Info Svc); printed music & music bks (at Westminster Music Lib); GLASS (Mozart) *ILLs:* county, natl & internatl *Loans:* bks & audios/3 wks; videos/1 day or 1 wk; lang courses/3 months; orchestral sets/1 month *Charges:* audios/£8-£20 pa or 10p-60p; videos/80p-£3; lang course sets/£4-£10; orchestral sets/£12-£20 *Income Gen:* req/25p-80p, lost ticket/ad £3, ch 70p *Fines:* bks & audios/ad 15p pd (£5 max), ch 15-17 5p pd (£2 max), ch under 14 exempt; videos/loan charge; blind & partially sighted, home lib svc users exempt *Equip:* m-readers, m-printers (50p), fax (50p-£2), copiers (A4/10p), clr copier (A4/£1), computers (incl wd-procs, internet & CD-ROM) *Disabled:* Kurzweil, magnifiers at all sites, cassette loan for housebnd *Online:* BLAISE, Datastar, Profile, Justis-Celex

Stock:	1 Apr 2000	1 Apr 2001
ad lend:	297282	287797
ad ref:	490156	469977
ch:	81687	85211
audios:	40339	36589
videos:	15774	16385
CD-ROMs:	100	588
periodcls:	525	764
archvs:	3062 linear m	-

Issues:	1999-2000	2000-01
ad lend:	1623267	1563763
ch:	315428	292171
audios:	243252	203801
videos:	166821	157328
CD-ROMs:	830	415

Acqs:	1999-2000	2000-01
bks:	62010	61601
AVs:	10265	8651

Acqs: Source: lib suppl, publ & bksellers *Co-op:* GLASS *Offcr-in-Charge:* Stock Mgr: Ms Pat Chamberlain (pat.chamberlain@dial.pipex.com) *Classn:* DDC, local classifications for music & art *Cat: Type:* author, classified, dictionary, subj & title *Medium:* cards & auto *Auto Sys:* Geac *Svcs: Extramural:* schools, old people's homes, housebnd *Info:* Info for Business (IfB), European Deposit Colln, Performing Arts (all at Westminster Ref Lib), Info for the Community (all libs), health, careers *Other:* Open Learning (at Queens Pk Lib), Homework Clubs (at 4 libs) *Activs:* ch's activs, bk sales, temp exhibs, lunchtime concerts & recitals, reading groups, writers' groups *Offcr-in-Charge:* various front line staff *Enqs:* 392313 (1999-2000); 334586 (2000-01) *Staff: Libns:* 39.5 *Non-Prof:* 141

Inc from:	1999-2000	2000-01
local govt:	£7347083	£7548617
fines etc:	£696653	£835788
total:	£8090714	£8422942

Exp on:	1999-2000	2000-01
bks:	£736720	£767301
AVs:	£172079	£199591
elec media:	£3706	-
salaries:	£4266072	£4209514
total:	£8090714	£8422942

Proj: Lib Self Issue Terminals (in 2002-03)

Luton

P111 Luton Libraries

Central Lib, St George's Sq, Luton, Bedfordshire, LU1 2NG (01582-547440; *fax:* 01582-547461)
Email: lendinglibrary@luton.gov.uk
Internet: http://www.luton.gov.uk/libraries/

Local Auth: Luton Borough Council *Pop:* 183300 *Cttee:* Lifelong Learning Cttee *Larger Dept:* Lifelong Learning *Dept Chief:* Corporate Dir: Mr T. Dessant *Chief: Libs* Mgr: Ms Jean George BA, DMS, MCLIP
Main Libs: LUTON CENTRAL LIB, addr as above, incl Adult Lending Lib (01582-547418/9; *email:* as above), Ref Lib (01582-547420/1; *fax:* 01582-547450; *email:* referencelibrary@luton. gov.uk) & Ch's Lib (01582-547411; *email:* childrenslibrary@luton.gov.uk) *Branch Libs:* BURY PK LIB, 161 Dunstable Rd, Luton, Bedfordshire, LU1 1BW (01582-450194; *email:* BuryParkLibrary@luton.gov.uk); LEAGRAVE LIB, Marsh Rd, Leagrave, Luton, Bedfordshire, LU3 2NL (01582-597851; *fax:* 01582-560012; *email:* leagravelibrary@luton.gov.uk); LEWSEY LIB, Landrace Rd, Lewsey, Luton, Bedfordshire, LU4 0SW (*tel & fax:* 01582-696094; *email:* lewseylibrary@luton.gov.uk); MARSH FARM LIB, Purley Centre, Luton, Bedfordshire, LU3 3SR (*tel & fax:* 01582-574803; *email:* Marshfarmlibrary@ luton.gov.uk); STOPSLEY LIB, Hitchin Rd, Luton, Bedfordshire, LU2 7UG (*tel & fax:* 01582-722791; *email:* Stopsleylibrary@luton.gov.uk); SUNDON PK LIB, Hill Rise, Sundon Pk, Luton, Bedford-shire, LU3 3EE (*tel & fax:* 01582-574573; *email:* Sundonparklibrary@luton.gov.uk); WIGMORE LIB, Wigmore Centre, Wigmore Ln, Luton, Bedford-shire, LU3 8DJ (*tel & fax:* 01582-455228; *email:* Wigmorelibrary@luton.gov.uk)
Svc Pts: Mobile: 1 *AV:* 4 *Other:* HOUSEBND UNIT; SCHOOLS LIB SVC
Collns: local studies; car manuals (both at Central Lib) *Co-op Schemes:* Co-East *ILLs:* county, natl & internatl *Loans:* bks/3 wks; audios, videos & DVDs/1 wk *Charges:* cassettes/50p; CDs/75p; videos/£1 or £2; DVDs/ £2.50 *Income Gen:* req & res/50p (+50p for ILL); lost ticket/£1 *Fines:* bks/ad 12p pd, oap 6p pd; audios, videos & CD-ROMs/loan charge; ch, registered blind & housebnd exempt

Equip: m-readers, m-printers (10p), fax (varies), copiers (A4/10p, A3/15p), clr copier (A4/£1, A3/ £1.50), computers (incl internet), room for hire (varies) *Disabled:* Magnilink, video decoders, spkn wd cassettes, large print bks, Abilitynet PCs

Stock:	1 Apr 2000	1 Apr 2001
ad lend:	237941	221181
ch:	71638	66451
AVs:	19500	18867

Issues:	1999-2000	2000-01
ad lend:	979982	948546
ch:	407083	357861

Acqs: Source: lib suppl *Co-op:* joint arrangement with Bedfordshire County Council (see **P8**) *Offcr-in-Charge:* Principal Libns
Classn: DDC *Cat: Type:* author, classified, subj & title *Medium:* auto *Auto Sys:* DS, Viewpoint *Svcs: Extramural:* schools, old people's homes, housebnd *Info:* business, EU Public Info Relay, careers *Other:* IT suite *Activs:* ch's activs, bk sales, exhibs, poetry readings, reading groups *Staff: Libns:* 15 *Non-Prof:* 66.2

Inc from:	1999-2000	2000-01
local govt:	£2874624	£2931439
fines etc:	£292773	£295146
total:	£3167397	£3226585

Exp on:	1999-2000	2000-01
stock:	£412300	£370743
salaries:	£1391575	£1425731
total:	£3167397	£3226585

Manchester

P112 Manchester Library and Information Service

Manchester Central Lib, St Peter's Sq, Manchester, M2 5PD (0161-234-1900; *fax:* 0161-234-1963)
Email: mclib@libraries.manchester.gov.uk
Internet: http://www.manchester.gov.uk/libraries/

Local Auth: Manchester City Council *Pop:* 432641 *Cttee:* Exec Cttee *Larger Dept:* Libs & Theatres Dept *Dept Chief:* Acting Dir of Libs & Theatres: Mr Michael Curtis *Chief:* Acting Dir of Libs & Theatres, as above
Main Libs: MANCHESTER CENTRAL LIB, addr as above; *North Dist HQ:* CRUMPSALL LIB, Abraham Moss Centre, Cres Rd, Manchester, M8 5UF (0161-908-1900; *fax:* 0161-908-1912; *email:* crumpsal@libraries.manchester.gov.uk); *Central Dist HQ:* LONGSIGHT LIB, 519 Stockport Rd, Manchester, M12 4NE (0161-224-1411; *fax:* 0161-225-2119; *email:* longsite@libraries.manchester. gov.uk); *South Dist HQ:* WYTHENSHAWE LIB, The Forum, Manchester, M22 5RX (0161-935-4000; *fax:* 0161-935-4039; *email:* wythens@ libraries.manchester.gov.uk) *Branch Libs: North Dist:* BESWICK LIB, Grey Mare Ln, Manchester, M11 3AZ (0161-223-9614; *fax:* 0161-223-9614; *email:* beswick@libraries.manchester.gov.uk); CLAYTON LIB, 2 Clayton St, Manchester, M11 4BH (0161-223-2065; *email:* clayton@libraries. manchester.gov.uk); HARPURHEY LIB, Pk View, Manchester, M9 5TF (0161-205-2637; *fax:* 0161-205-2637; *email:* harpur@libraries.manchester. gov.uk); HIGHER BLACKLEY LIB, Victoria Ave, Manchester, M9 3RH (0161-740-1534; *fax:* 0161-740-1534; *email:* higherb@libraries.manchester. gov.uk); MILES PLATTING LIB, Varley St, Manchester, M40 8EE (0161-205-8956; *fax:* 0161-205-8956; *email:* miles_pl@libraries.manchester. gov.uk); MOSTON LIB, Moston Ln, Manchester, M40 9NB (0161-205-1064; *fax:* 0161-205-1064; *email:* moston@libraries.manchester.gov.uk); NEW MOSTON LIB, Nuthurst Rd, Manchester, M40 3PY (0161-688-6291; *fax:* 0161-688-6291; *email:* newmost@libraries.manchester.gov.uk); NEWTON HEATH LIB, Old Church St, Manchester, M40 2GB (0161-688-8513; *fax:* 0161-688-8513; *email:* newtonhe@libraries.manchester.

gov.uk); *Central Dist:* CHORLTON LIB, Manchester Rd, Manchester, M21 9PN (0161-881-3179; *fax:* 0161-860-0169; *email:* chorlton@ libraries.manchester.gov.uk); FALLOWFIELD LIB, Platt Ln, Manchester, M14 7FB (0161-224-4153; *email:* fallowf@libraries.manchester.gov.uk); GORTON LIB, Garrat Way, Manchester, M18 8HE (0161-223-0775; *fax:* 0161-230-8375; *email:* gorton@libraries.manchester.gov.uk); HULME LIB, Hulme Walk, Manchester, M15 5FQ (0161-226-1005; *fax:* 0161-232-7426; *email:* hulme@ libraries.manchester.gov.uk); LEVENSHULME LIB, Cromwell Grove, Manchester, M19 2QE (0161-224-2775; *email:* levenshu@libraries. manchester.gov.uk); MOSS SIDE POWER-HOUSE LIB, 140 Raby St, Manchester, M14 4SQ (0161-232-8327; *fax:* 0161-226-4969; *email:* mspl@libraries.manchester.gov.uk); *South Dist:* BARLOW MOOR LIB, 21 Merseybank Ave, Manchester, M21 7NN (0161-446-2061; *email:* b_moor@libraries.manchester.gov.uk); BURNAGE LIB, Burnage Ln, Manchester, M19 1EW (0161-442-9036; *email:* burnage@libraries.manchester. gov.uk); DIDSBURY LIB, 692 Wilmslow Rd, Manchester, M20 2DN (0161-445-3220; *email:* didsbury@libraries.manchester.gov.uk); NORTH-ENDEN LIB, Church Rd, Manchester, M22 4WL (0161-998-3023; *email:* northend@libraries. manchester.gov.uk); RACKHOUSE LIB, Yarmouth Rd, Manchester, M23 0BT (0161-998-2043; *email:* rackhous@libraries.manchester. gov.uk); WITHINGTON LIB, 410 Wilmslow Rd, Manchester, M20 3BN (0161-445-1991; *email:* withing@libraries.manchester.gov.uk)
Svc Pts: Mobile: 4 *AV:* 23 *Other:* Manchester prison
Collns: Gaskell Colln; De Quincey Colln; Coleridge Colln; Alexander Ireland Colln (at Lang & Lit Lib); Parliamentary papers & UN documents; 18C & 19C pamphs; natl newspapers on m-film (at Social Scis Lib); parish registers; local genealogical material; theatre colln (at Arts Lib); extensive map colln (at Local Studies Lib); Newman Flower Colln of Handel MSS (at Watson Music Lib); broadside & print colln (at Local Studies Lib); US, British & European patents (at Technical Lib) *Co-op Schemes:* Libs North West, Lancashire Bibliography *ILLs:* county, natl & internatl *Loans:* bks/4 wks; spkn wd/1 wk or 4 wks; audios & CD-ROMs/1 wk; videos & DVDs/1 day or 1 wk *Charges:* spkn wd/50p for 1 wk, £2 for 4 wks; music LPs & cassettes/30p; CDs/60p; videos/feature films £1.20-£1.70 pd, others £1 pw; DVDs/feature films £1.50-£2.50 pd, others £1 pw; CD-ROMs/£1.50 *Income Gen:* res/80p, conc 30p; lost ticket/£1.50 *Fines:* bks & audios/ad 10p pd; videos/30p pd for weekly charge items, loan charge for overnight loans; exemptions for under-13s, oaps & visually impaired (Manchester residents only) *Equip:* 75 m-readers, 7 m-cameras, 4 m-printers (A4/30p, A3/40p), 20 copiers (A4/10p self-svc,15p staff assisted), clr copier (A4/£1, A3/£2); computers (incl wd-proc, internet & CD-ROM) *Disabled:* Kurzweil, computers with packages to aid visually impaired, braille printer

Stock:	1 Apr 2000	1 Apr 2001
ad lend:	501697	483618
ad ref:	1028084	1031446
ch:	167144	169608
audios:	71717	67979
videos:	13771	15475
CD-ROMs:	1509	1609
periodcls:	1600	1418

Issues:	1999-2000	2000-01
ad lend:	1827456	1745559
ch:	521560	485499
audios:	251406	235722
videos:	130793	130668
CD-ROMs:	3117	3695

Acqs:	1999-2000	2000-01
bks:	74309	76870
AVs:	11868	11958

(Manchester Lib & Info Svc cont)
Acqs: *Source:* lib suppl, publ & bksellers
Classn: DDC **Cat:** *Type:* author, classified, subj
& title *Medium:* cards & auto *Auto Sys:* DS
Svcs: *Extramural:* prisons, old people's homes,
housebnd *Other:* Open Learning, homework
centres *Activs:* ch's activs, bk sales, temp
exhibs, poetry readings
Enqs: 550836 (2000-01)
Staff: *Libns:* 86 *Non-Prof:* 260.4

Inc from:	1999-2000	2000-01
local govt:	£9560828	£10086895
fines etc:	£584870	£568663
total:	£10203007	£10709106

Exp on:	1999-2000	2000-01
bks:	£878498	£1029988
AVs:	£197497	£193897
elec media:	£2021	-
salaries:	£5764262	£5968833
total:	£10203007	£10709106

Medway

P113 Medway Library, Information and Museum Service
Civic Centre, Strood, Rochester, Kent, ME2 4AU
(01634-306000)
Internet: http://www.medway.gov.uk/lims/

Local Auth: Medway Council **Pop:** 249502
Larger Dept: Edu & Leisure **Dept Chief:** Dir: Ms
Rose Collinson **Chief:** Lib, Info & Museum Svc
Mgr: Ms Gill Woodhams (gill.woodhams@medway.
gov.uk)
Main Libs: CHATHAM LIB, Riverside, Chatham,
Kent, ME4 4SN (01634-843589; *fax:* 01634-
827976; *email:* chatham.library@medway.gov.uk);
GILLING-HAM LIB, High St, Gillingham, Kent,
ME7 1BG (01634-281066; *fax:* 01634-855814;
email: gillingham.library@medway.gov.uk);
STROOD LIB, 32 Bryant Rd, Strood, Rochester,
Kent, ME2 3EP (01634-718161; *fax:* 01634-
297919; *email:* strood.library@medway.gov.uk)
Branch Libs: HOO LIB, Church St, Hoo,
Rochester, Kent, ME3 9AL (*tel & fax:* 01634-
250640); LORDSWOOD LIB, Kestrel Rd,
Lordswood, Chatham, Kent, ME5 8TH (01634-
862096; *fax:* 01634-681595); LUTON LIB, 2
Nelson Ter, Luton, Chatham, Kent, ME5 7LA
(01634-406923); RAINHAM LIB, Birling Ave,
Rainham, Gillingham, Kent, ME8 7LR (01634-
231745; *fax:* 01634-263415); ROCHESTER LIB,
Northgate, Rochester, Kent, ME1 1LU (01634-
842415; *fax:* 01634-843837); TWYDALL LIB, 14-
15 Twydall Green, Gillingham, Kent, ME8 6JY (*tel
& fax:* 01634-232488); WALDERSLADE HOOK
MEADOW LIB, King George Rd, Walderslade,
Chatham, Kent, ME5 0TZ (*tel & fax:* 01634-
861531); WALDERSLADE VILLAGE LIB,
Walderslade Centre, Walderslade Rd,
Walderslade, Chatham, Kent, ME5 9LR (01634-
686467; *fax:* 01634-681505); WIGMORE LIB, 208
Fairview Ave, Wigmore, Gillingham, Kent, ME8
0PX (01634-235576; *fax:* 01634-375064)
Svc Pts: *PT:* 4 *Mobile:* 1 *Computers:* 15 *Other:*
MEDWAY ARCHVS & LOCAL STUDIES CENTRE
(see **A435**)
Co-op Schemes: local arrangements with Kent
County Council (see **P67**) **Loans:** bks/4 wks;
audios/2 wks; videos/2 days-1 wk; DVDs/2 days;
CD-ROMs/1 wk

Equip: m-reader/printers, fax, copiers, clr copier,
computers (with internet) *Disabled:* Horizon TV
reader, easy reader sys, text phone, induction
loop, public access PCs with accessibility
adaptations

Stock:	1 Apr 2000	1 Apr 2001
lend:	325602	290921
ref:	41568	36253
AVs:	24861	25559
periodcls:	84	84

Issues:	1999-2000	2000-01
bks:	1336633	1286665
AVs:	151945	168629

Acqs:	1999-2000	2000-01
bks:	52303	42801
AVs:	6304	5779

Svcs: *Extramural:* prisons, old people's homes,
housebnd *Info:* community, business, careers,
EU, local govt *Other:* ethnic minority svcs,
postal cassette svc for the blind, local studies
Activs: ch's activs, temp exhibs, readers' groups,
lectures, BookStart, Surestart
Enqs: 116687 (1999-2000); 114103 (2000-01)
Staff: *Libns:* 22 *Non-Prof:* 55.1

Inc from:	1999-2000	2000-01
local govt:	£2795640	£2796097
fines etc:	£208179	£250675
total:	£3003819	£3046772

Exp on:	1999-2000	2000-01
bks:	£336832	£314078
AVs:	£33805	£41616
salaries:	£1537997	£1646525
total:	£3003819	£3046772

Merthyr Tydfil

P114 Merthyr Tydfil Libraries
Central Lib, High Street, Merthyr Tydfil, Mid
Glamorgan, CF47 8AF (01685-723057; *fax:*
01685-370690)
Email: central.library@merthyr.gov.uk

Local Auth: Merthyr Tydfil Council **Pop:** 58000
Larger Dept: Edu & Leisure **Dept Chief:** Dir of
Edu & Leisure: Mr Dewi Jones BA, MSc, DipEd,
MIMgt **Chief:** Head of Libs: Mr Geraint James
BA, MCLIP
Main Libs: CENTRAL LIB, addr as above; *Area
Libs:* DOWLAIS LIB, Church St, Dowlais, Merthyr
Tydfil, Mid Glamorgan, CF48 3HS (*tel & fax:*
01685-723051; *email:* dowlais.library@merthyr.
gov.uk); TREHARRIS LIB, Perrott St, Treharris,
Mid Glamorgan, CF46 5ET (*tel & fax:* 01443-
410517; *email:* treharris.library@merthyr.gov.uk)
Svc Pts: *Mobile:* 2
Collns: local hist colln of monographs, pamphs,
papers, theses, census records & newspapers;
Aberfan Disaster Archv **Co-op Schemes:**
WRLS, BLDSC **ILLs:** natl **Loans:** bks, audios
& videos/3 wks **Charges:** CDs/£5 pa + 30p per
loan; videos/£1 **Income Gen:** req & res/60p;
lost ticket/30p **Fines:** bks, audios & videos/ad &
oap 5p pd, ch exempt **Equip:** m-readers,
m-printers, video viewers, fax, copiers, clr copier,
computers (incl wd-proc, internet & CD-ROM),
rooms for hire *Disabled:* magnifiers, stair lift,
Dowlais

Stock:	1 Apr 2000
lend:	120862
ref:	11194
audios:	7536
videos:	74

Issues:	1999-2000
ad lend:	277960
ch:	89084
audios:	14959
videos:	121

Acqs:	1999-2000
bks:	11821
AVs:	845

Acqs: *Source:* lib suppl *Offcr-in-Charge:* Head of
Libs, as above
Classn: DDC **Cat:** *Type:* author, classified &
title *Medium:* cards **Svcs:** *Extramural:* schools,
old people's homes, housebnd *Info:* business,
community *Other:* Open Learning **Activs:** ch's
activs, bk sales, temp exhibs, poetry readings
Enqs: 34882 (1999-2000); 34950 (2000-01)
Staff: *Libns:* 5 *Non-Prof:* 16.5

Inc from:	1999-2000
local govt:	£584461
fines etc:	£19614
total:	£604075

Exp on:	1999-2000
bks:	£106443
AVs:	£14331
salaries:	£376203
total:	£604075

Middlesbrough

P115 Middlesbrough Libraries and Information
Central Lib, Victoria Sq, Middlesbrough, TS1 2AY
(01642-729416)
Internet: http://www.middlesbrough.gov.uk/

Local Auth: Middlesbrough Council **Pop:** 143900
Larger Dept: Housing, Regeneration & Culture
Directorate **Chief:** Head of Libs & Info: Ms
Chrys Mellor **Other Snr Staff:** Principal Libns:
Mr Jeremy Adler & Ms Jennifer Brittain
Main Libs: MIDDLESBROUGH CENTRAL LIB,
addr as above (lend: 01642-729002; ref: 01642-
729001; email: central_lending@middlesbrough.
gov.uk or reference_library@middlesbrough.
gov.uk) **Branch Libs:** ACKLAM LIB, Acklam Rd,
Middlesbrough, TS5 7AB (01642-817810; *fax:*
01642-270444); BERWICK HILLS LIB, Crossfell
Rd, Berwick Hills, Middlesbrough, TS3 7RL
(01642-246947; *fax:* 01642-218112); EASTERSIDE
LIB, Broughton Ave, Middlesbrough, TS4 3PZ
(01642-317535); GROVE HILL LIB, Eastbourne
Rd, Middlesbrough, TS4 6QS (01642-822555);
HEMLINGTON LIB, Crosscliff, Viewley Centre,
Hemlington, Middlesbrough, TS8 9JJ (01642-
591918); MARTON LIB, The Willows, Marton,
Middlesbrough, TS7 8BL (01642-300255); NORTH
ORMESBY LIB, Derwent St, North Ormesby,
Middlesbrough, TS3 6JB (01642-247980); RAIN-
BOW LIB, Parkway Centre, Coulby Newham,
Middlesbrough, TS8 0TJ (01642-593696; *email:*
rainbow_library@middlesbrough.gov.uk); THORN-
TREE LIB, Beresford Cres, Middlesbrough, TS3
9JN (*tel & fax:* 01642-242332)
Svc Pts: *PT:* 2 *Mobile:* 1 *AV:* 6 *Other:*
SCHOOLS RESOURCE SVC, Cooper Centre,
Beech Green, South Bank, Middlesbrough, TS6
6SU (01642-289199)
Collns: BSI (at Central Lib); Keith Teasdale Colln
(socialism); Kelly Colln (religion); Capt Cook
Colln; local & family hist **Co-op Schemes:**
NEMLAC, NCL, LINE **ILLs:** county, natl &
internatl **Loans:** bks/4 wks; audios/2 wks;
videos & CD-ROMs/1 wk; Playstation games/2
days **Charges:** cassettes/40p; CDs/65p; videos/
75p-£1.50; CD-ROMs/75p-£2.50 **Income Gen:**
res/in stock free, otherwise £1; lost ticket/£1
Fines: bks/ad 25p pw or part or wk, teenage 10p
pw or part of wk; under 13s & visually impaired
exempt **Equip:** m-reader, m-printers, copiers
(A4/10p), computers (incl wd-proc, internet & CD-
ROM), 5 rooms for hire

Stock:	1 Apr 2000	1 Apr 2001
bks:	231327	221648
AVs:	16002	15040
periodcls:	251	251

Issues:	1999-2000	2000-01
bks:	910647	839285
AVs:	35442	40747

Acqs:	1999-2000	2000-01
bks:	21946	29163
AVs:	2061	2554

Acqs: Source: lib suppl
Classn: DDC *Cat: Type:* author, classified, subj & title *Medium:* auto *Auto Sys:* DS Galaxy
Svcs: Extramural: hosps, old people's homes, housebnd, day centres *Info:* community, business, European *Activs:* ch's activs, bk sales, homework clubs
Enqs: 98462 (1999-2000); 109668 (2000-01)
Staff: 60.3 in total

Inc from:	1999-2000	2000-01
fines etc:	£46700	£46100

Exp on:	1999-2000	2000-01
stock:	£196000	£250000
salaries:	£1063000	£1115000
total:	£1894000	£2038000

Midlothian

P116 Midlothian Council Library Service

Lib HQ, 2 Clerk Street, Loanhead, Midlothian, EH20 9DR (0131-271-3980; *fax:* 0131-440-4635)
Email: library.hq@midlothian.gov.uk
Internet: http://www.midlothian.gov.uk/library/

Local Auth: Midlothian Council *Pop:* 82200
Cttee: Cabinet sys *Larger Dept:* Community Svcs *Dept Chief:* Dir: Mr Graeme Marwick
Chief: Lib Svcs Mgr: Mr Alan Reid MA(Hons), MCLIP (alan.reid@midlothian.gov.uk) *Dep:* Principal Libn: Mr Philip Wark MCLIP (philip.wark@midlothian.gov.uk)
Main Libs: BONNYRIGG LIB, Polton St, Bonnyrigg, Midlothian, EH19 3HB (0131-663-6762; *fax:* 0131-654-9019; *email:* bonnyrigg.library@midlothian.gov.uk); DALKEITH LIB, White Hart St, Dalkeith, Midlothian, EH22 1AE (0131-663-2083; *fax:* 0131-654-9029; *email:* dalkeith.library@midlothian.gov.uk) *Branch Libs:* DANDERHALL LIB, 1a Campview, Danderhall, Dalkeith, Midlothian, EH22 1QD (0131-663-9293; *email:* danderhall.library@midlothian.gov.uk); GOREBRIDGE LIB, Hunterfield Rd, Gorebridge, Midlothian, EH23 4TT (01875-820630; *fax:* 01875-823657; *email:* gorebridge.library@midlothian.gov.uk); LOANHEAD LIB, George Ave, Loanhead, Midlothian, EH20 9HD (0131-440-0824; *email:* loanhead.library@midlothian.gov.uk); MAYFIELD LIB, Stone Ave, Mayfield, Dalkeith, Midlothian, EH22 5PB (0131-663-2126; *email:* mayfield.library@midlothian.gov.uk); NEWTONGRANGE LIB, St Davids, Newtongrange, Dalkeith, Midlothian, EH22 4LQ (0131-663-1816; *fax:* 0131-654-1990; *email:* newtongrange.library@midlothian.gov.uk); PENICUIK LIB, Bellman's Rd, Penicuik, Midlothian, EH26 0AB (01968-672340; *fax:* 01968-679968; *email:* penicuik.library@midlothian.gov.uk)
Svc Pts: PT: 2 *Mobile:* 2 *AV:* 12 *Computers:* 9 *Internet:* 9 *Other:* MIDLOTHIAN RECORDS CENTRE & LOCAL STUDIES DEPT (see **A247**)
Collns: Marwick Colln (Scottish economic & labour hist); Midlothian Dist Archv Colln (records of Midlothian Council & predecessors); records of local socs; collns of personal papers etc; all at Records Centre & Local Studies *Co-op Schemes:* NLS, SESLIN *ILLs:* natl & internatl
Loans: all items/4 wks *Charges:* audios/25p per item *Income Gen:* req & res/20p, under-14s exempt; inter-lib loans/£2, under-14s, oaps & unemployed exempt; lost tickets/£1 *Fines:* all items/ad, ch & oap 5p pd (max £1) *Equip:* 12 m-readers, 2 m-printers (A4/10p), 6 fax (UK £1 per pg, Europe £1.50, internatl £2, £1 to receive), 10 copiers (A4/10p, A3/20p, 10+ copies A4/8p,

A3/16p), 4 rooms for hire (£2.30 per hr), 14 computers (all with wd-proc & CD-ROM, 12 with internet, printouts 5p-10p) *Disabled:* magnifiers *Offcr-in-Charge:* Principal Libn, as above

Stock:	1 Apr 2000	1 Apr 2001
ad lend:	89599	90295
ad ref:	10008	8305
ch:	59964	53423
schools:	24641	25875
audios:	10949	10805
videos:	2159	2125
CD-ROMs:	-	37
periodcls:	53	63
archvs:	1029 linear m	1241 linear m

Issues:	1999-2000	2000-01
ad lend:	405331	395150
ch:	131569	124208
schools:	33283	29441
audios:	27269	31845
videos:	9659	9987
CD-ROMs:	-	68

Acqs:	1999-2000	2000-01
bks:	22236	13574
AVs:	1451	1748

Acqs: Source: lib suppl, publ & bksellers *Offcr-in-Charge:* Principal Libn, as above
Classn: DDC *Cat: Type:* author, title & keyword *Medium:* auto *Auto Sys:* DS *Svcs: Extramural:* schools, hosps, old people's homes, housebnd, play groups, nurseries, childminders *Info:* European, careers, community *Other:* Open Learning, BookStart *Activs:* ch's activs, bk sales, films, temp exhibs, poetry readings, writers' workshops, reading groups, author visits, talks *Offcr-in-Charge:* Principal Libn, as above
Enqs: 72358 (1999-2000); 74204 (2000-01)
Staff: Libns: 8 *Other Prof:* 1 *Non-Prof:* 29.7

Inc from:	1999-2000	2000-01
fines etc:	£30235	£34416
total:	£32196	£37791

Exp on:	1999-2000	2000-01
bks:	£141207	£115762
AVs:	£7858	£6004
salaries:	£717125	£742789
total:	£1408269	£1518132

Milton Keynes

P117 Milton Keynes Council Library Service

Milton Keynes Central Lib, 555 Silbury Blvd, Saxon Gate East, Milton Keynes, Buckinghamshire, MK9 3HL (01908-254050; *fax:* 01908-254088)
Email: Central.Library@milton-keynes.gov.uk
Internet: http://www.mkweb.co.uk/library_services/

Local Auth: Milton Keynes Council *Pop:* 213186
Cttee: Learning, Community & Economic Development Overview Cttee *Larger Dept:* Learning & Skills *Dept Chief:* Learning & Skills Mgr: Ms Deborah Cooper BA, MEd, CertEd, DMS (deborah.cooper@milton-keynes.gov.uk) *Chief:* as above *Other Snr Staff:* Learning & Skills Libn (Central Lib Svcs): Ms Teresa Carroll MCLIP (teresa.carroll@milton-keynes.gov.uk); Learning & Skills Libn (Community Lib Svcs): Ms Barbara Merrifield BA, DipLib, MCLIP (barbara.merrifield@milton-keynes.gov.uk)
Main Libs: CENTRAL LIB, addr as above; BLETCHLEY LIB, Westfield Rd, Bletchley, Milton Keynes, Buckinghamshire, MK2 2RA (01908-372797; *fax:* 01908-645562; *email:* Bletchley.Library@milton-keynes.gov.uk) *Branch Libs:* NEWPORT PAGNELL LIB, St John St, Newport Pagnell, Milton Keynes, Buckinghamshire, MK16 8HQ (*tel & fax:* 01908-610933; *email:* NewportPagnell.Library@milton-keynes.gov.uk); OLNEY LIB, High St, Olney, Milton Keynes,

Buckinghamshire, MK46 4EF (*tel & fax:* 01234-711474; *email:* Olney.Library@milton-keynes.gov.uk); STONY STRATFORD LIB, 5-7 Church St, Stony Stratford, Milton Keynes, Buckinghamshire, MK11 1BD (*tel & fax:* 01908-562562; *email:* StonyStratford.Library@milton-keynes.gov.uk); WESTCROFT LIB, 17-18 Barnsdale Dr, Westcroft Dist Centre, Westcroft, Milton Keynes, Buckinghamshire, MK4 4DD (01908-507874; *fax:* 01908-507875; *email:* Westcroft.Library@milton-keynes.gov.uk); WOBURN SANDS LIB, Friends Meeting House, Hardwick Rd, Woburn Sands, Milton Keynes, Buckinghamshire, MK17 8QH (*tel & fax:* 01908-582033; *email:* WoburnSands.Library@milton-keynes.gov.uk); WOLVERTON LIB, 122 Church St, Wolverton, Milton Keynes, Buckinghamshire, MK12 5JR (*tel & fax:* 01908-312812; *email:* Wolverton.Library@milton-keynes.gov.uk)
Svc Pts: Mobile: 1 *AV:* 9 *Computers:* 8 *Internet:* 8 *Other:* BUSINESS LIB, at Milton Keynes Lib
Co-op Schemes: BIN, PIR, V3, CBC *ILLs:* county, natl & internatl *Loans:* bks/4 wks; magazines/1 wk; audios & CD-ROMs/2 wks; videos & DVDs/1 wk; prints/4 wks *Charges:* audios/60p-£1.20; videos/£1-£2.20; CD-ROMs/£1.70-£2.20 *Income Gen:* req/80p, ch's bks free; lost tickets/£1.50 *Fines:* bks/ad 14p pd (max £5.74); ch 4p pd (max £1.64); magazines/as ad bks; audios/as ad bks; videos, CD-ROMs, DVDs & prints/45p pd (max £9) *Equip:* 13 m-readers, 3 m-printers (40p), 9 fax (£1.25-£2 per pg to send, 50p per pg to receive), 10 copiers (A4/5p, A3/10p), 2 clr copiers (A4/£1, A3/£1.50), 47 computers (incl 20 with wd-proc, 9 with CD-ROM & 28 with internet, all charged at £1 per 20 min), room for hire (£2-£13 per hr) *Disabled:* ZoomText, enlarged keyboard *Online:* Companies Direct, BSI Online, BookFind *Offcr-in-Charge:* Snr Libn: Ms Sally Elson (sally.elson@milton-keynes.gov.uk)

Stock:	1 Apr 2000	1 Apr 2001
ad lend:	157185	155532
ad ref:	38886	38975
ch:	86702	84559
instns:	9523	10088
audios:	19317	20337
videos:	12620	11815
CD-ROMs:	1112	3944
periodcls:	380	340

Issues:	1999-2000	2000-01
ad lend:	1223290	1147896
ch:	593563	548606
audios:	141847	132695
videos:	177099	152838
CD-ROMs:	6893	25437

Acqs:	1999-2000	2000-01
bks:	38999	35845
AVs:	13129	7759

Acqs: Source: lib suppl *Co-op:* CBC *Offcr-in-Charge:* Snr Libn (Acqs): Mr Dave Quayle (dave.quayle@milton-keynes.gov.uk)
Classn: DDC *Cat: Type:* author, classified, subj & title *Medium:* auto *Auto Sys:* ALS *Svcs: Extramural:* schools, prisons, hosps, old people's homes, housebnd, day centres, play groups *Info:* local studies/family hist & Business Lib at Central Lib *Activs:* ch's activs, bk sales, temp exhibs, author visits, music concerts
Enqs: 317564 (1999-2000); 278824 (2000-01)
Staff: Libns: 16 *Non-Prof:* 58.5

Inc from:	1999-2000	2000-01
local govt:	£2392457	£2451692
fines etc:	£510422	£464916
total:	£2902807	£2960907

Exp on:	1999-2000	2000-01
bks:	£348833	£307357
AVs:	£113381	£112243
salaries:	£1415403	£1469229
total:	£2902807	£2960907

Monmouthshire

P118 Monmouthshire Libraries and Information Service

Chepstow Lib, Manor Way, Chepstow, Monmouthshire, NP16 5HZ (01291-635730; *fax:* 01291-635736)
Email: infocentre@monmouthshire.gov.uk
Internet: http://www.monmouthshire.gov.uk/leisure/libraries/

Local Auth: Monmouthshire County Council *Pop:* 87400 *Cttee:* Lifelong Learning & Leisure Cttee *Larger Dept:* Lifelong Learning & Leisure *Dept Chief:* Dir: Mr Phil Cooke *Chief:* Head of Libs & Culture: Mr Kevin Smith *Dep:* Principal Libn: Mrs Ann Jones *Other Snr Staff:* Info & Learning Mgr: Ms Sally Bradford & Ms Cathy Milby; Lib Resources Mgr: Ms Mary Rooney; Reading & Youth Mgr: Ms Fiona Ashley *Main Libs:* CHEPSTOW LIB, addr as above (chepstowlibrary@monmouthshire.gov.uk); ABERGAVENNY LIB, Baker St, Aber-gavenny, Monmouthshire, NP7 5BD (01873-735980; *fax:* 01873-735985; *email:* abergavennylibrary@monmouthshire.gov.uk); CALDICOT LIB, Woodstock Way, Caldicot, Newport, Monmouthshire, NP6 5DB (01291-426425; *fax:* 01291-426426; *email:* caldicotlibrary@monmouthshire.gov.uk); MONMOUTH LIB, Rolls Hall, Whitecross St, Monmouth, Monmouthshire, NP25 3BY (01600-775215; *fax:* 01600-775218; *email:* monmouthlibrary@monmouthshire.gov.uk) *Branch Libs:* USK LIB, 18a Maryport St, Usk, Monmouthshire, NP15 1AE (01291-674925; *fax:* 01291-674924; *email:* usklibrary@monmouthshire.gov.uk)
Svc Pts: PT: 1 *Mobile:* 3 *Other:* SCHOOL LIB SVCS, serving Monmouthshire, Torfaen (see **P188**) & Newport (see **P122**); 2 prison libs *Collns:* Chepstow Colln (colln of the Chepstow Soc, materials relating to Chepstow & dist, at Chepstow Lib) *Co-op Schemes:* SET, CWLIS, Proj Earl *ILLs:* natl *Loans:* bks/3 wks; audios, videos & CD-ROMs/1 wk *Charges:* audios/£1; spkn wd/50p; videos/£1.50 *Income Gen:* req & res/£3; lost tickets/£1.50; disks/£1.50 *Fines:* bks/ad 12p pd, oap 6p pd; audios & videos/loan charge; visually impaired & ch exempt *Equip:* 4 copiers (A4/10p), 2 clr copiers (A4/£1), 5 fax (75p), 82 computers (all with wd-proc & internet, 16 with CD-ROM), 3 rooms for hire (various)

Stock:	1 Apr 2000	1 Apr 2001
ad lend:	82665	97264
ad ref:	5414	3142
ch:	56608	54407
audios:	6896	6822
videos:	2821	2789
CD-ROMs:	514	537
periodcls:	75	75

Issues:	1999-2000	2000-01
ad lend:	582907	532560
ch:	207053	191335
audios:	33904	25828
videos:	12358	9738
CD-ROMs:	1841	1998

Acqs:	1999-2000	2000-01
bks:	12999	18381
AVs:	1211	1404

Acqs: Source: lib suppl *Offcr-in-Charge:* Resources Mgr: Mrs Mary Rooney

Classn: DDC *Cat: Type:* author, classified, subj & title *Medium:* auto *Auto Sys:* Dynix *Svcs: Extramural:* schools, prisons, old people's homes, housebnd *Info:* community info databases, Welsh Assembly & European Info collns (at Chepstow Lib), online databases, 1891 & 1901 census for Monmouthshire on m-fiche at Aber-gavenny & Chepstow Libs *Other:* Monmouthshire Online (82 People's Network computers with internet, MS Office & CD-ROM) *Activs:* ch's activs, bk sales, temp exhibs, poetry readings, music events, events for specific customers e.g., teenage *Offcr-in-Charge:* Community Lib Mgrs at Abergavenny, Caldicot, Chepstow & Monmouth Libs
Enqs: 91350 (1999-2000); 94239 (2000-01)
Staff: Libns: 14 *Non-Prof:* 40

Inc from:	1999-2000	2000-01
local govt:	£924331	£1062660
fines etc:	£127735	£108726
total:	£1052066	£1171386

Exp on:	1999-2000	2000-01
stock:	£156659	£218238
salaries:	£614600	£637758
total:	£1052066	£1171386

Moray

P119 Moray Libraries and Information Services

Libs Support, Elgin Lib, Cooper Pk, Elgin, Moray, IV30 1HS (01343-562600; *fax:* 01343-562640)
Internet: http://www.moray.org/

Local Auth: The Moray Council *Pop:* 86000 *Cttee:* Educational Svcs Cttee *Larger Dept:* Educational Svcs *Dept Chief:* Dir: Mr Donald Duncan *Chief:* Libs & Museums Mgr: Mr G. Alistair Campbell MA, BCom, MCLIP (campbea@moray.gov.uk) *Dep:* Principal Libn (Central Svcs): Mrs Sheila A. Campbell MCLIP (sheila.campbell@moray.gov.uk)
Main Libs: BUCKIE LIB, Cluny Pl, Buckie, Moray, AB56 1HB (01542-832121; *fax:* 01542-835237; *email:* buckie.library@moray.gov.uk); ELGIN LIB, addr as above (*email:* elgin.library@moray.gov.uk); FORRES LIB, Forres House, High St, Forres, Moray, IV36 1BU (01309-672834; *fax:* 01309-675084; *email:* forres.library@moray.gov.uk); KEITH LIB, Union St, Keith, Moray, AB55 5DP (01542-882223; *fax:* 01542-882177; *email:* keith.library@moray.gov.uk) *Branch Libs:* LOSSIEMOUTH LIB, Town Hall Ln, Lossiemouth, Moray, IV31 6DF (01343-813334; email: lossiemouth.library@moray.gov.uk)
Svc Pts: PT: 11 *Mobile:* 3 *AV:* 20 *Computers:* 17 *Internet:* 17 *Other:* GRANT LODGE LOCAL HERITAGE CENTRE (incl Archvs – see **A158**) *Collns:* local studies; Doig Colln & Whittet Colln (architect's plans, both at Local Heritage Centre) *ILLs:* internatl *Loans:* bks, audios & CD-ROMs/4 wks; videos & DVDs/2 wks; art prints/2 month *Charges:* audios/50p; videos/£1.50; DVDs/£2.50; no charge for CD-ROMs & art prints *Income Gen:* req/50p; lost ticket/£1 *Fines:* bks & audios/ad 25p pw, ch, oap, registered blind exempt; videos/£1 pw; DVDs/£1.50 pw *Equip:* 8 m-readers, m-printer (A4/40p), 7 video viewers, 10 fax (£1 per pg UK, £1.50 overseas, 50p per pg to receive), 14 copiers (A4/10p, A3/20p), clr copier (A4/£1, A3/£1.50), 75 computers (all with wd-procs, 67 with internet & 67 with CD-ROM, access free), 5 rooms for hire (charges vary), video conferencing facilities *Disabled:* Kurzweil & induction loop at main lib, access to all PCs *Online:* Proquest, Statistical Accounts, Kompass, Libindx (all free)

Stock:	1 Apr 2000	1 Apr 2001
ad lend:	136197	133967
ad ref:	18990	8008
ch:	52890	53127
audios:	14396	14529
videos:	2394	2360
periodcls:	123	123
archvs:	264 linear m	267 linear m

Issues:	1999-2000	2000-01
ad lend:	716953	668822
ch:	202183	182271
audios:	34643	34063
videos:	10112	9940

Acqs:	1999-2000	2000-01
bks:	28215	22175
AVs:	1660	1843

Acqs: Source: lib suppl & bksellers *Offcr-in-Charge:* Principal Libn (Central Svcs), as above *Classn:* DDC *Cat: Type:* author, classified, subj & title *Medium:* auto *Auto Sys:* Talis *Svcs: Extramural:* schools, hosps, old people's homes, housebnd, play groups *Info:* genealogical, business, community, European, careers, edu, govt, Scottish Parliament *Other:* LearnDirect Scotland Centres at 7 libs; SQA & ECDL Centre, at Elgin Lib *Activs:* ch's activs, bk sales, temp exhibs, poetry readings, art exhibs, reading groups, writers' groups, talks, author visits
Enqs: 68276 (1999-2000); 72228 (2000-01)
Staff: Libns: 8 *Non-Prof:* 39

Inc from:	1999-2000	2000-01
local govt:	£1303851	£1463629
fines etc:	£101867	£107713
total:	£1405718	£1571342

Exp on:	1999-2000	2000-01
bks:	£230018	£204724
AVs:	£22412	£25250
elec media:	-	£3767
salaries:	£758173	£787783
total:	£1405718	£1571342

Neath Port Talbot

P120 Neath Port Talbot Library and Information Services

County Borough Lib HQ, Reginald Street, Velindre, Port Talbot, W Glamorgan, SA13 1YY (01639-899829; *fax:* 01639-899152)
Email: npt.libhq@neath-porttalbot.gov.uk
Internet: http://www.neath-porttalbot.gov.uk/libraries/

Local Auth: Neath Port Talbot Council *Pop:* 138000 *Larger Dept:* Edu, Leisure & Lifelong Learning *Dept Chief:* Dir: Mr Karl Napieralla *Chief:* Co-ordinator of Cultural Svcs: Mr Lloyd Ellis BLib, MCLIP (j.l.ellis@neath-porttalbot.gov.uk) *Dep:* Snr Principal Lib Offcr: Mrs Virginia Jones BA, MCLIP (v.jones@neath-porttalbot.gov.uk)
Main Libs: NEATH LIB, Victoria Gdns, Neath, W Glamorgan, SA11 3BA (01639-644604/635017; *fax:* 01639-641912; *email:* neath.library@neath-porttalbot.gov.uk); PONTARDAWE LIB, Holly St, Pontardawe, W Glamorgan, SA8 4ET (01792-862261; *fax:* 01792-869688; *email:* pontardawe.library@neath-porttalbot.gov.uk); PORT TALBOT LIB, 1st Floor, Aberafan Shopping Centre, Port Talbot, W Glamorgan, SA13 1PB (01639-763490/1; *fax:* 01639-763489; *email:* porttalbot.library@neath-porttalbot.gov.uk) *Branch Libs:* BAGLAN LIB, Laurel Ave, Baglan, Port Talbot, W Glamorgan, SA12 8PA (*tel & fax:* 01639-813477); BRITON FERRY LIB, Neath Rd, Briton Ferry, Neath, W Glamorgan, SA11 2AQ (01639-813244; *fax:* 01639-765109); CWMAFAN LIB, Depot Rd, Cwmafan, Port Talbot, W Glamorgan, SA12 9DF (*tel & fax:* 01639-896532); GLYNNEATH LIB, Park Ave, Glynneath, Neath, W Glamorgan, SA11 5DW (*tel & fax:* 01639-720776); RESOLVEN LIB, Neath Rd, Resolven, Neath, W Glamorgan, SA11

4AA (*tel & fax*: 01639-710412); SANDFIELDS LIB, Morriston Rd, Sandfields, Port Talbot, W Glamorgan, SA12 6TG (*tel & fax*: 01639-883616); SKEWEN LIB, New Rd, Skewen, Neath, W Glamorgan, SA10 6UU (01792-813488; *fax*: 01792-815662); TAIBACH LIB, Commercial Rd, Taibach, Port Talbot, W Glamorgan, SA13 1LN (01639-883831; *fax*: 01639-895367)
Svc Pts: PT: 7 *Mobile*: 2 *AV*: 4 (at Port Talbot, Neath, Sandfields & Pontardawe Libs)
Collns: BSI (at Neath Lib); local studies colln (at Neath & Port Talbot Libs) *Co-op Schemes*: ELRS, mobile lib svc provided to part of neighbouring Powys County Council (see **P149**) *Loans*: bks & audios/3 wks; videos/1 wk *Charges*: audios/50p, visually impaired exempt; videos/£1 *Income Gen*: req & res/50p; ILLs/£2; lost ticket/50p *Fines*: bks/ad 8p pd, oap 4p pd, ch exempt; audios/50p pw; videos/£1 pw; visually impaired exempt from spkn wd charges, ch exempt from bk fines only *Equip*: m-reader (£1 per hr), 2 m-printers (30p per sheet), 5 fax (UK £1 per pg, overseas £3), 15 copiers (A4/5p, A3/10p), 2 clr copiers (A4/60p, A3/£1), computers (incl internet & CD-ROM), 4 rooms for hire *Disabled*: Robotron (in 3 libs), Eazee Readers (in 3 libs)

Stock:	1 Apr 2000	1 Apr 2001
lend:	293452	255766
ref:	24840	30587
AVs:	13084	12002
periodcls:	62	64

Issues:	1999-2000	2000-01
bks:	997810	934182
AVs:	36024	38966

Acqs:	1999-2000
bks:	27064
AVs:	1426

Acqs: Source: lib suppl, publ & bksellers *Offcr-in-Charge*: Snr Principal Lib Offcr, as above *Classn*: DDC *Cat: Type*: author, classified, dictionary, subj & title *Medium*: auto *Auto Sys*: Dynix *Svcs: Extramural*: old people's homes, housebnd, playgroups *Info*: community, business, youth, TEC *Other*: Open Learning, Storybag Schemes *Activs*: ch's activs, bk sales, temp exhibs, poetry readings, reading groups *Offcr-in-Charge*: Snr Principal Lib Offcr, as above *Enqs*: 185276 (1999-2000); 205140 (2000-01) *Staff: Libns*: 14 *Non-Prof*: 36.43

Inc from:	2000-01
local govt:	£1685374
fines etc:	£106950
total:	£1792324

Exp on:	2000-01
bks:	£243984
AVs:	£16836
salaries:	£938262
total:	£1792324

Newcastle upon Tyne

P121 Newcastle Libraries and Information Service

City Lib, Princess Sq, Newcastle upon Tyne, NE99 1DX (0191-277-4100; *fax*: 0191-277-4137)
Email: city.information@newcastle.gov.uk
Internet: http://www.newcastle.gov.uk/

Local Auth: Newcastle City Council *Pop*: 270500 *Cttee*: Leisure Svcs Cttee *Larger Dept*: Edu & Libs *Dept Chief*: Dir of Edu & Libs: Mr Phil Turner BPhil, MEd *Chief*: Head of Libs & Info: Mr Tony Durcan BA, MCLIP (tony.durcan@newcastle.gov.uk) *Dep*: Snr Lib & Info Mgr: Mr Allan Wraight BA, MCLIP, DMS (allan.wraight@newcastle.gov.uk) *Other Snr Staff*: Customer & Quality Svcs Mgr: Ms June Biggins BA, MCLIP (june.biggins@newcastle.gov.uk); Central Svcs Mgr: Ms Eileen Burt MCLIP (eileen.burt@newcastle.gov.uk); Info & e-Libs Mgr: Mr Andrew Fletcher BA (andrew.fletcher@newcastle.gov.uk)

Main Libs: CITY LIB, addr as above; *Central Group HQ*: GOSFORTH LIB, Regent Farm Rd, Gosforth, Newcastle upon Tyne, NE3 1JN (0191-285-4244; *fax*: 0191-213-0086); *East Group HQ*: WALKER LIB, Welbeck Rd, Walker, Newcastle upon Tyne, NE6 2PA (0191-265-7420; *fax*: 0191-276-4461); *Inner West Group HQ*: FENHAM LIB, Fenham Hall Dr, Fenham, Newcastle upon Tyne, NE4 9XD (0191-274-5837; *fax*: 0191-274-8225); *Outer West Group HQ*: DENTON PK LIB, West Denton Way, Newcastle upon Tyne, NE5 2QZ (0191-267-7922; *fax*: 0191-267-8612) *Branch Libs*: BENWELL LIB, Atkinson Rd, Benwell, Newcastle upon Tyne, NE4 8XS (0191-273-3220); BLAKELAW LIB, Binswood Ave, Newcastle upon Tyne, NE5 3PN (0191-286-9674); BRINKBURN CENTRE LIB, Brinkburn St, Byker, Newcastle upon Tyne, NE6 2AR (0191-278-4200); CRUDDAS PK LIB, Cruddas Pk Shopping Centre, Pk Rd, Newcastle upon Tyne, NE4 7QL (0191-273-5331); DENTON BURN LIB, West Rd, Denton Burn, Newcastle upon Tyne, NE15 7QQ (0191-274-2906); EAST END LIB, Corbridge Rd, Byker, Newcastle upon Tyne, NE6 3DY (0191-278-8444); FAWDON LIB, Fawdon Park Rd, Fawdon, Newcastle upon Tyne, NE3 2PE (0191-285-4415); HIGH HEATON LIB, Newton Pl, High Heaton, Newcastle upon Tyne, NE7 7HD (0191-281-1150); JESMOND LIB, St Georges Ter, Jesmond, Newcastle upon Tyne, NE2 2DL (0191-281-3774); KENTON LIB, Halewood Ave, Kenton, Newcastle upon Tyne, NE3 3RX (0191-286-9597); MOORSIDE LIB, Moorside Community High School, Beaconsfield St, Newcastle upon Tyne, NE4 5AW (0191-272 4312); NEWBIGGIN HALL LIB, Trevelyan Dr, Newbiggin Hall Est, Newcastle upon Tyne, NE5 4BR (0191-286-1889); NEWBURN LIB, High St, Newburn, Newcastle upon Tyne, NE15 8LN (0191-267-4833)
Svc Pts: PT: 4 *Mobile*: 1 *AV*: 21 *Computers*: 21 *Internet*: 21 *Other*: HOUSEBND READERS SVC, at Byker Branch Lib
Collns: Thomas Bewick Colln; Dr Thomlinson's Lib (18C bks); Joseph Cowan Colln (19C radicalism); UK/EU patents deposit colln; HMSO pubns (complete from 1957); illusts; films; glass plate negatives; local studies *Co-op Schemes*: NCL, NLJWP, JFR, Newcastle & Gateshead Libs Partnership *ILLs*: county, natl & internatl *Loans*: bks/4 wks; audios/2 wks; videos & DVDs/varies *Charges*: cassettes/60p; CDs/80p; videos/50p-£2.50 *Income Gen*: res/10p or 50p; lost ticket/£1.50; local hist rsrch/varies *Fines*: bks/ad & oap 6p pd, ch exempt; audios/12p pd; videos & DVDs/loan charge pd *Equip*: 20 m-readers, 7 m-printers (20p), 6 fax (50p-£2.50 per pg), 26 copiers (A4/10p, A3/20p), 3 clr copiers (£1), 248 computers (incl wd-proc, CD-ROM/DVD & internet), room hire *Disabled*: Voyager, minicom *Offcr-in-Charge*: Central Svcs Mgr, as above

Stock:	1 Apr 2000	1 Apr 2001
ad lend:	245870	245291
ad ref:	249211	250487
ch:	74326	72286
audios:	30868	32038
videos:	2677	5952
periodcls:	736	-

Issues:	1999-2000	2000-01
ad lend:	1498283	1372485
ch:	310816	327999
audios:	204675	205826
videos:	52305	50637

Acqs:	1999-2000	2000-01
bks:	46614	24434
AVs:	6428	6346

Acqs: Source: lib suppl, publ, & bksellers *Offcr-in-Charge*: Central Svcs Mgr, as above *Classn*: DDC *Cat: Type*: author & classified *Medium*: cards & auto *Auto Sys*: DS *Svcs: Extramural*: housebnd, old people's homes, day centres, play groups *Info*: Business Info (incl

patents advice, at City Lib) *Other*: virtual careers svcs, Open Learning, edu guidance unit *Activs*: ch's activs, bk sales, reading groups *Offcr-in-Charge*: professional staff at all svc pts *Staff: Libns*: 42 *Other Prof*: 10 *Non-Prof*: 126

Inc from:	1999-2000	2000-01
fines etc:	£619670	£958700

Exp on:	1999-2000	2000-01
stock:	£661700	£448100
salaries:	£3250500	£3452100
total:	£5097800	£4757100

Proj: Denton Pk Customer Svc Centre, to incl a new lib

Newport

P122 Newport Library and Information Service

Central Lib, John Frost Sq, Newport, South Wales, NP20 1PA (01633-265539; *fax*: 01633-222615)
Email: central.library@newport.gov.uk
Internet: http://www.newport.gov.uk/

Local Auth: Newport City Council *Pop*: 138500 *Cttee*: Culture & Rec *Larger Dept*: Continuing Learning & Leisure *Dept Chief*: Head of Continuing Learning & Leisure: Mr Iain Varah *Chief*: Borough Libn: Mrs Gillian John MBA, MCLIP (gill.john@newport.gov.uk) *Dep*: Operations Mgr: Mr John Abraham BLib, MCLIP (john.abraham@newport.gov.uk)
Main Libs: CENTRAL LIB, contact details as above (ref lib: 01633-211376) *Branch Libs*: BETTWS LIB, Shopping Centre, Bettws, Newport, NP20 6TN (01633-855245); CAERLEON LIB, Coldbath Rd, Caerleon, Newport, NP18 1NF (01633-420305); CARNEGIE LIB, Corp Rd, Newport, NP19 0GP (01633-244766); MAINDEE LIB, Chepstow Rd, Newport, NP19 8BY (01633-259108; *fax*: 01633-257439); MALPAS LIB, Malpas Community Centre, Pillmawr Rd, Newport, NP20 6WF (01633-821376); PILLGWENLLY LIB, Temple St, Newport, NP20 2GJ (01633-840324); RINGLAND LIB, Ringland Centre, Ringland, Newport, NP19 9PS (01633-273151); ROGERSTONE LIB, Tregwillym Rd, Rogerstone, Newport, NP10 9EL (01633-893613); STOW HILL LIB, 226 Stow Hill, Newport, NP20 4HA (01633-263870)
Svc Pts: Mobile: 3 *AV*: 13 *Computers*: 10 *Internet*: 10
Collns: Chartist Colln; Machen Colln (works by & about Arthur Machen, 600 items); Haines Colln (hist & topography of Monmouthshire, 2000 items); Monmouthshire Colln (local studies, 23000 items); Mary Delaney MSS (correspondence, 1720-88); all at Central Lib *Co-op Schemes*: Interlending Wales *ILLs*: county, natl & internatl *Loans*: bks, talking bks & lang tapes/3 wks; audios, videos, DVDs & CD-ROMs/1 wk *Charges*: audios/70p; videos/£1.40; CD-ROMs/£1.25; DVDs/£2 *Income Gen*: res/£1 for items in catalogue, £2 for others; lost ticket/£1.50 *Fines*: bks/ad & oap 15p pd; audios, videos, CD-ROMs & DVDs/loan charge; ch exempt *Equip*: 9 m-readers (5 fiche, 4 film, printout 60p), 2 fax (varies), 4 copiers (A4/10p, A3/20p), clr copier (A4/£1, A£/£1.50), computers (incl wd-proc, internet & CD-ROM), rooms for hire (varies) *Disabled*: portable hearing induction loop *Offcr-in-Charge*: Borough Libn, as above

Stock:	1 Apr 2000	1 Apr 2001
ad lend:	269526	235949
ad ref:	35869	36513
ch:	61933	71237
audios:	11467	10933
videos:	1810	2035
CD-ROMs:	192	518

☞

(Newport Lib & Info Svc cont)

Issues:	1999-2000	2000-01
ad lend:	846437	782267
ch:	243770	258479
audios:	58050	58846
videos:	14264	12905
CD-ROMs:	829	1866

Acqs:	1999-2000	2000-01
bks:	39422	37906
AVs:	1944	1892

Acqs: Source: lib suppl *Offcr-in-Charge:* Borough Libn, as above
Classn: DDC *Cat: Medium:* auto *Auto Sys:* Genesis *Svcs: Extramural:* old people's homes, housebnd, day centres, play groups *Info:* community, legal, EU, Natl Assembly for Wales *Other:* BookStart *Activs:* ch's activs, bk sales, temp exhibs, poetry readings, writers' groups, talks, author visits *Offcr-in-Charge:* Borough Libn, as above
Enqs: 168987 (1999-2000); 168376 (2000-01)
Staff: Prof: 14 *Non-Prof:* 36.8

Inc from:	1999-2000	2000-01
fines etc:	£116803	£169885

Exp on:		2000-01
total:		£2056970

Norfolk

P123 Norfolk County Council Library and Information Service

County Hall, Martineau Ln, Norwich, NR1 2UA (01603-222049; *fax:* 01603-222422)
Email: libraries@norfolk.gov.uk
Internet: http://www.library.norfolk.gov.uk/

Local Auth: Norfolk County Council *Pop:* 797900 *Cttee:* Edu & Cultural Svcs Review Panel *Larger Dept:* Cultural Svcs *Dept Chief:* Dir of Cultural Svcs: Mr Terry Turner BA, MCLIP *Chief:* Head of Libs & Info: Ms Jennifer Holland *Main (Tier A) Libs:* GT YARMOUTH CENTRAL LIB, Tolhouse St, Gt Yarmouth, Norfolk, NR30 2SH (01493-844551; *fax:* 01493-857628; *email:* yarmouth.lib@norfolk.gov.uk); KING'S LYNN CENTRAL LIB, London Rd, King's Lynn, Norfolk, PE30 5EZ (01553-772568; *fax:* 01553-769832; *email:* kings.lynn.lib@norfolk.gov.uk); NORFOLK & NORWICH MILLENNIUM LIB, The Forum, Millennium Plain, Norwich, NR2 1AW (01603-774774; *fax:* 01603-774775; *email:* millennium.lib@norfolk.gov.uk); THETFORD LIB, Raymond St, Thetford, Norfolk, IP24 2EA (01842-752048; *fax:* 01842-750125; *email:* thetford.lib@norfolk.gov.uk)
Branch Libs: ATTLEBOROUGH LIB, 33 Connaught Rd, Attleborough, Norfolk, NR17 2BW (01953-452319; *email:* attleborough.lib@norfolk.gov.uk); AYLSHAM LIB, 7 Hungate St, Aylsham, Norwich, NR11 6AA (01263-732320; *email:* aylsham.lib@norfolk.gov.uk); CAISTER LIB, Beach Rd, Caister-on-Sea, Gt Yarmouth, Norfolk, NR30 5EX (01493-720594; *email:* caister.lib@norfolk.gov.uk); COSTESSEY LIB, Breckland Rd, Norwich, NR5 0RW (01603-742669; *email:* costessey.lib@norfolk.gov.uk); CROMER LIB, Prince of Wales Rd, Cromer, Norfolk, NR27 9HS (01263-512850; *email:* cromer.lib@norfolk.gov.uk); DEREHAM LIB, Church St, Dereham, Norfolk, NR19 1DN (01362-693184; *fax:* 01362-691891;

email: dereham.lib@norfolk.gov.uk); DERSING-HAM LIB, Chapel Rd, Dersingham, King's Lynn, Norfolk, PE31 6PN (01485-540181; *email:* dersingham.lib@norfolk.gov.uk); DISS LIB, Church St, Diss, Norfolk, IP22 3DD (01379-642609; *email:* diss.lib@norfolk.gov.uk); DOWN-HAM MARKET LIB, 78 Priory Rd, Downham Market, Norfolk, PE38 9JS (01366-383073; *email:* downham.lib@norfolk.gov.uk); EARLHAM LIB, Colman Rd, Norwich, NR4 7GH (01603-454338; *email:* earlham.lib@norfolk.gov.uk); FAKENHAM LIB, Oak St, Fakenham, Norfolk, NR21 9DY (01328-862715; *email:* fakenham.lib@norfolk. gov.uk); GAYWOOD LIB, River Ln, King's Lynn, Norfolk, PE30 4HD (01553-768498; *email:* gaywood.lib@norfolk.gov.uk); GORLESTON LIB, 1 Lowestoft Rd, Gorleston, Gt Yarmouth, Norfolk, NR31 6SG (01493-662156; *fax:* 01493-446010; *email:* gorleston.lib@norfolk.gov.uk); HARLESTON LIB, Swan Ln, Harleston, Norfolk, IP20 9AW (01379-852549; *email:* harleston.lib@norfolk. gov.uk); HELLESDON LIB, Middletons Ln, Norwich, NR6 5SR (01603-427790; *email:* hellesdon.lib@norfolk.gov.uk); HETHERSETT LIB, Queen's Rd, Hethersett, Norwich, NR9 3DB (01603-810188; *email:* hethersett.lib@norfolk. gov.uk); HOLT LIB, 9 Church St, Holt, Norfolk, NR25 6BB (01263-712202; *email:* holt.lib@norfolk. gov.uk); HUNSTANTON LIB, Westgate, Hunstanton, Norfolk, PE36 5AL (01485-532280; *email:* hunstanton.lib@norfolk.gov.uk); LODDON LIB, 31 Church Plain, Loddon, Norwich, NR14 6EX (01508-520678; *email:* loddon.lib@norfolk.gov.uk); LONG STRATTON LIB, The St, Long Stratton, Norwich, NR15 2XJ (01508-530797; *email:* long. stratton.lib@norfolk.gov.uk); MILE CROSS LIB, Aylsham Rd, Norwich, NR3 2RJ (01603-425906; *email:* mile.cross.lib@norfolk.gov.uk); NORTH WALSHAM LIB, New Rd, North Walsham, Norfolk, NR28 9DE (01692-402482; *fax:* 01692-500597; *email:* north.walsham.lib@norfolk.gov.uk); PLUMSTEAD RD LIB, Plumstead Rd, Norwich, NR1 4JS (01603-433455; *email:* plumstead.road. lib@norfolk.gov.uk); ST WILLIAMS WAY LIB, St Williams Loke, Norwich, NR7 0AJ (01603-434123; *email:* st.williams.way.lib@norfolk.gov.uk); SHERINGHAM LIB, New Rd, Sheringham, Norfolk, NR26 8EB (01263-822874; *email:* sheringham.lib@norfolk.gov.uk); SPROWSTON LIB, Recreaction Ground Rd, Sprowston, Norwich, NR7 8EW (01603-408426; *email:* sprowston.lib@ norfolk.gov.uk); STALHAM LIB, High St, Stalham, Norwich, NR12 9AN (01692-580794; *email:* stalham.lib@norfolk.gov.uk); SWAFFHAM LIB, The Pightle, Swaffham, Norfolk, PE37 7DF (01760-721513; *email:* swaffham.lib@norfolk. gov.uk); TAVERHAM LIB, Sandy Ln, Taverham, Norwich, NR8 6JR (01603-260545; *email:* taverham.lib@norfolk.gov.uk); WATTON LIB, George Trollope Rd, Watton, Thetford, Norfolk, IP25 6AS (01953-881671; *email:* watton.lib@ norfolk.gov.uk); WELLS LIB, Station Rd, Wells-next-the-Sea, Norfolk, NR23 1EA (01328-710467; *fax:* 01328-710624; *email:* wells.lib@norfolk. gov.uk); WROXHAM LIB, Norwich Rd, Wroxham, Norwich, NR12 8RX (01603-782560; *email:* wroxham.lib@norfolk.gov.uk); WYMONDHAM LIB, Becket's Chapel, 2 Church St, Wymondham, Norfolk, NR18 0PH (01953-603319; *email:* wymondham.lib@norfolk.gov.uk)
Svc Pts: PT: 12 *Mobile:* 17 *AV:* 48 *Computers:* 48 *Internet:* 48
Collns: Colman & Rye Colln (at Norwich Lib); Thomas Paine Colln (at Thetford Lib); St Margaret's Colln (at Kings Lynn Lib) *Co-op Schemes:* EMRLS, Co-East *ILLs:* county & natl
Loans: bks/3 wks; audios & videos/1 wk
Charges: audios/40p-£1.25; videos/75p-£2; DVDs/£1-£2.50; Playstation games/£2-£2.50
Income Gen: res/60p self-svc, 85p staff assisted; lost ticket/ad £1, ch 35p *Fines:* bks/ad & ch various; housebnd, blind, oap, disabled, mobile lib users exempt *Equip:* 36 m-readers, 5 m-printers (50p), 6 fax, 18 copiers (A4/10p), 529

computers (incl 216 with wd-proc & 439 with internet), 5 rooms for hire *Disabled:* induction loops, CCTV

Stock:	1 Apr 2000	1 Apr 2001
ad lend:	859311	860790
ad ref:	156234	149860
ch:	213194	229796
schools:	-	163813
instns:	18892	19691
audios:	48968	53576
videos:	18361	22706
periodcls:	532	436

Issues:	1999-2000	2000-01
ad lend:	6248368	5779832
ch:	1371670	1235949
instns:	36577	26080
audios:	345394	350359
videos:	140221	199065

Acqs:	1999-2000	2000-01
bks:	149130	174766
AVs:	9870	22973

Acqs: Source: lib suppl *Offcr-in-Charge:* Bibliographical Svcs Team Leader: Mrs Pauline Montgomery (pauline.montgomery@norfolk. gov.uk)
Classn: DDC *Cat: Type:* author, classified, subj & title *Medium:* auto *Auto Sys:* DS *Svcs: Extramural:* schools, prisons, hosps, old people's homes, housebnd, day centres, play groups *Info:* Business Link, European Info Centre *Other:* Learning Centre (at Wells Lib) *Activs:* ch's activs, bk sales, temp exhibs, poetry readings, reading groups, writers' groups, talks, author visits
Enqs: 736528 (1999-2000); 669449 (2000-01)
Staff: Libns: 62 FTE *Non-Prof:* 231 FTE

Inc from:	1999-2000	2000-01
local govt:	£7958271	£9220135
fines etc:	£767299	£863703
total:	£8725570	£10083838

Exp on:	1999-2000	2000-01
bks:	£1418290	£1680631
AVs:	£175124	£286202
salaries:	£4902356	£5408364
total:	£8725570	£10083838

North Ayrshire

P124 North Ayrshire Library and Information Service

Lib HQ, 39-41 Princes Street, Ardrossan, Ayrshire, KA22 8BT (01294-469137; *fax:* 01294-604236)
Email: Libraryhq@north-ayrshire.gov.uk
Internet: http://www.north-ayrshire.gov.uk/

Local Auth: North Ayrshire Council *Pop:* 138850 *Cttee:* Educational Svcs Cttee *Larger Dept:* Educational Svcs *Dept Chief:* Corporate Dir: Mr John Travers *Chief:* Info & Resource Mgr: Mrs Marion McLarty MA, MCLIP (mmclarty@ north-ayrshire.gov.uk) *Dep:* Principal Offcr (Lib Operations): Miss Janice Martin MA, DipLib, MCLIP (jmartin@north-ayrshire.gov.uk) *Other Snr Staff:* Area Offcrs (Lib Operations): Mrs Marilyn Vint, MCLIP (mvint@north-ayrshire. gov.uk); Mr Paul Cowan BEd, DipLib, MCLIP (pcowan@north-ayrshire.gov.uk); Miss Sandra Kerr, MCLIP (skerr@north-ayrshire.gov.uk)
Main (Area) Libs: IRVINE LIB, Cunninghame House, Irvine, Ayrshire, KA12 8EE (01294-324251; *fax:* 01294-324252; *email:* IrvineLibrary@ north-ayrshire.gov.uk); KILWINNING LIB, St Winning's Ln, Kilwinning, Ayrshire, KA13 6EP (01294-554699; *fax:* 01294-557628; *email:* KilwinningLibrary@north-ayrshire.gov.uk); LARGS LIB, Allenpark St, Largs, Ayrshire, KA30 9AG (*tel & fax:* 01475-673309; *email:* LargsLibrary@north-ayrshire.gov.uk); SALTCOATS LIB, Springvale Pl, Saltcoats, Ayrshire, KA21 5LS (*tel & fax:*

01294-469546; *email:* SaltcoatsLibrary@north-ayrshire.gov.uk) **Branch Libs:** ARDROSSAN LIB, Princes St, Ardrossan, Ayrshire, KA22 8BT (*tel & fax:* 01294-469682; *email:* ArdrossanLibrary@north-ayrshire.gov.uk); ARRAN LIB, Brodick Hall, Brodick, Isle of Arran, Ayrshire, KA27 8DL (*tel & fax:* 01770-302835; *email:* ArranLibrary@north-ayrshire.gov.uk); BEATTIE LIB, 1 Main St, Stevenston, Ayrshire, KA20 3AA (*tel & fax:* 01294-469535; *email:* StevenstonLibrary@north-ayrshire.gov.uk); BEITH LIB, Main St, Beith, Ayrshire, KA15 2AD (01505-503613; *fax:* 01505-503417; *email:* BeithLibrary@north-ayrshire.gov.uk); BOUR-TREEHILL LIB, Cheviot Way, Bourtreehill, Irvine, Ayrshire, KA11 1HU (01294-216958; *email:* BourtreehillLibrary@north-ayrshire.gov.uk); DALRY LIB, 14 The Cross, Dalry, Ayrshire, KA24 5AW (*tel & fax:* 01294-833196; *email:* DalryLibrary@north-ayrshire.gov.uk); DREGHORN LIB, 159 Main St, Dreghorn, Ayrshire, KA11 4AQ (01294-211072; *email:* DreghornLibrary@north-ayrshire.gov.uk); KILBIRNIE LIB, Avils Pl, Kilbirnie, Ayrshire, KA25 6BL (*tel & fax:* 01505-684218; *email:* KilbirnieLibrary@north-ayrshire.gov.uk); WEST KILBRIDE LIB, Halfway St, W Kilbride, Ayrshire, KA23 9EG (01294-822987; *email:* WestKilbrideLibrary@north-ayrshire.gov.uk)
Svc Pts: PT: 4 *Mobile:* 2 *AV:* 14 *Computers:* 15 *Internet:* 15
Collns: Alexander Wood Colln (local hist) **Co-op Schemes:** ILL **Loans:** bks & spkn wd/4 wks; audios/2 wks; videos & CD-ROMs/1 wk
Charges: CDs/25p; videos/£1.20; CD-ROMs & Playstation games/£3; registered blind exempt from audio charges *Income Gen:* res/25p; lost tickets/£1 *Fines:* bks/ad 6p pd (max £3), ch 1p pd (max 50p), oap exempt; audios/6p pd (max £3); videos/loan charge (max £6); CD-ROMs & Playstation games/loan charge (max £15); 60+ exempt for bks & audios *Equip:* m-reader, 3 m-reader/printers (A4/30p), 11 fax (UK £1 to send, 50p to receive), 17 copiers (A4 & A3/10p), clr copier (A4/£1.20, A3/£2.40), 51 computers (all with wd-proc & CD-ROM, 48 with internet), 3 rooms for hire (various) *Offcr-in-Charge:* Principal Offcr (Lib Operations), as above

Stock:	1 Apr 2000	1 Apr 2001
ad lend:	152001	155137
ad ref:	16774	16465
ch:	67937	66160
audios:	15252	12937
videos:	5860	5717
CD-ROMs:	433	387
periodcls:	144	144
archvs:	52 linear m	52 linear m

Issues:	1999-2000	2000-01
ad lend:	815213	767199
ch:	155030	128662
audios:	70995	69727
videos:	36002	34142
CD-ROMs:	3321	2410

Acqs:	1999-2000	2000-01
bks:	31655	37009
AVs:	4453	4168

Acqs: Source: lib suppl *Offcr-in-Charge:* Area Offcrs (Lib Operations), as above
Classn: DDC *Cat: Type:* author, classified, keyword, title & ISBN *Medium:* auto *Auto Sys:* Talis *Svcs: Extramural:* old people's homes, housebnd, play groups *Other:* Open Learning, Computer Buddies scheme *Activs:* ch's activs, bk sales, temp exhibs, talks, author visits *Offcr-in-Charge:* Area Offcr (Lib Operations), as above & Ch's Resource Offcr: Mrs Irene Gilmour (igilmour@north-ayrshire.gov.uk)
Enqs: 93756 (1999-2000); 90948 (2000-01)
Staff: Libns: 10 *Non-Prof:* 52.5

Inc from:	1999-2000	2000-01
local govt:	£1840856	£1999833
fines etc:	£148662	£215663
total:	£1989518	£2216017

Exp on:	1999-2000	2000-01
bks:	£270176	£285722
AVs:	£48291	£64976
salaries:	£1089322	£1171278
total:	£1989518	£2216017

Proj: lib computerisation

North East Lincolnshire

P125 North East Lincolnshire Libraries and Museums Service
Grimsby Central Lib, Town Hall Sq, Grimsby, NE Lincolnshire, DN31 1HG (01472-323600; *fax:* 01472-323634)
Email: librariesandmuseums@nelincs.gov.uk
Internet: http://www.nelincs.gov.uk/

Local Auth: North East Lincolnshire Council *Pop:* 155189 *Chief:* Head of Libs & Museums: Mr Steve Hipkins MA, DipLib, MCLIP *Other Snr Staff:* Principal Libn (Customer Svcs): Ms Joan Sargent; Strategy & Support Mgr: Mr David Bell *Main Libs:* GRIMSBY CENTRAL LIB, addr as above *Branch Libs:* CLEETHORPES LIB, Alexandra Rd, Cleethorpes, NE Lincolnshire, DN35 8LG (01472-323648/50; *fax:* 01472-323652); GRANT THOROLD LIB, Durban Rd, Grimsby, NE Lincolnshire, DN32 8BX (01472-323631); HUMBERSTON LIB, Church Ln, Humberston, Grimsby, NE Lincolnshire, DN36 4WZ (01472-323682); IMMINGHAM LIB, Civic Centre, Pelham Rd, Immingham, NE Lincolnshire, DN40 1QF (01469-516050); NUNSTHORPE LIB, Sutcliffe Ave, Grimsby, NE Lincolnshire, DN33 1HA (01472-323636); SCARTHO LIB, St Giles Ave, Grimsby, NE Lincolnshire, DN33 2HB (01472-323638); WALTHAM LIB, High St, Waltham, NE Lincolnshire, DN37 0LL (01472-323656); WILLOWS LIB, Binbrook Way, Grimsby, NE Lincolnshire, DN37 9AS (01472-323679); YARBOROUGH LIB, Cromwell Rd, Grimsby, NE Lincolnshire, DN31 2BX (01472-323658)
Svc Pts: PT: 1 *Mobile:* 1, bought in from North Lincolnshire Libs (see **P127**) *AV:* 11 *Computers:* 11 *Other:* SCHOOLS LIB SVC, Broadway, Grimsby, NE Lincolnshire, DN34 5RS (01472-323654; *fax:* 01472-323653); HOME LIB SVC, at Cleethorpes Lib (01472-323651); LOCAL STUDIES LIB, at Central Lib
Collns: BSI on CD-ROM; European Info Relay; local photograph colln (all at Central Lib) *Co-op Schemes:* YLI, PRISM, Newsplan *ILLs:* county, natl & internatl *Loans:* bks & spkn wd/3 wks; audios, videos, DVDs & CD-ROMs/1 wk
Charges: spkn wd/50p, over-60s 25p, free to under-16s & visually impaired; music audios/75p; videos/ad £2, ch's £1; CD-ROM/£1 *Income Gen:* res/30p, £2.40 for external ILLs; lost ticket/£1.50 *Fines:* bks/ad 10p pd up to 50p, then 50p pw (max £5); audios, videos, DVDs & CD-ROMs/loan charge; over-60s, under-16s, registered blind & partially sighted exempt *Equip:* m-readers, m-printers, fax (50p per pg in UK, higher overseas), copiers (A4/10p), computers (incl wd-proc, internet & CD-ROM), rooms for hire *Disabled:* variety of aids for disabled to access PCs, induction loops

Stock:	1 Apr 2000	1 Apr 2001
lend:	200204	192435
ref:	62506	66888
AVs:	20135	23721
periodcls:	213	146

Issues:	1999-2000	2000-01
bks:	877755	847910
AVs:	77547	73209

Acqs:	1999-2000	2000-01
bks:	26145	24254
AVs:	2766	4166

Acqs: Source: lib suppl & bksellers *Co-op:* PRISM
Classn: DDC, Humberside Music Classn *Cat: Type:* author, subj & title *Medium:* auto *Auto Sys:* ALS *Svcs: Extramural:* schools, old people's homes, housebnd *Info:* business, community, council, European *Other:* Lifelong Learning, Training Access Pts *Activs:* ch's activs, temp exhibs, bk sales, reading groups
Enqs: 91650 (1999-2000); 108576 (2000-01)
Staff: 63.35 in total

Inc from:	1999-2000	2000-01
local govt:	£1924762	£2035166
fines etc:	£144025	£144175
total:	£2068787	£2179341

Exp on:	1999-2000	2000-01
bks:	£334073	£355804
elec media:	£19954	£3911
salaries:	£986506	£1038180
total:	£2068787	£2179341

North Lanarkshire

P126 North Lanarkshire Libraries and Information
Buchanan Tower, Cumbernauld Rd, Stepps, Glasgow, G33 6HR (0141-304-1800; *fax:* 0141-304-1859)
Email: libraries@northlan.gov.uk
Internet: http://www.northlan.gov.uk/

Local Auth: North Lanarkshire Council *Pop:* 327600 *Larger Dept:* Dept of Community Svcs, Community Resources Div *Chief:* Head of Community Resources: Mr Jim McGuinness *Dep:* Libs & Info Mgr: Mr John Fox DMS, MCLIP *Main Libs:* MOTHERWELL LIB, 35 Hamilton Rd, Motherwell, Lanarkshire, ML1 3BZ (01698-332626; *fax:* 01698-332624) *Branch Libs:* North Area: ABRONHILL LIB, 17 Pine Rd, Abronhill, Cumbernauld, Glasgow, G67 3BE (*tel & fax:* 01236-731503); CHRYSTON LIB, Chryston Valley Business Pk, Cloverhill Pl, Chryston, Glasgow, G69 9DH (*tel & fax:* 0141-779-4720); CONDORRAT LIB, North Rd, Condorrat, Cumbernauld, Glasgow, G68 9AE (*tel & fax:* 01236-736615); CUMBERNAULD LIB, 8 Allander Walk, Cumbernauld, Glasgow, G67 1EE (01236-725664; *fax:* 01236-458350); EASTFIELD LIB, 8 Ben Lawers Dr, Eastfield, Cumbernauld, Glasgow, G68 9HJ (*tel & fax:* 01236-720032); KILSYTH LIB, Burngreen, Kilsyth, Glasgow, G65 0HT (*tel & fax:* 01236-823147); MOODIESBURN LIB, Glenmanor Ave, Moodiesburn, Glasgow, G69 0LS (01236-874927; *fax:* 01236-875024); STEPPS LIB, School Rd, Stepps, Glasgow, G33 6HF (*tel & fax:* 0141-779-1050); *Central Area:* AIRDRIE LIB, Wellwynd, Airdrie, Lanarkshire, ML6 0AG (01236-758070; *fax:* 01236-758076); BELLSHILL CULTURAL CENTRE, John St, Bellshill, Lanarkshire, ML4 1RJ (01698-346770; *fax:* 01698-843509); CHAPELHALL LIB, 2 Honeywell Cres, Airdrie, Lanarkshire, ML6 8XW (01236-750099; *fax:* 01236-770055); COATBRIDGE LIB, Academy St, Coatbridge, Lanarkshire, ML5 3AW (01236-424150; *fax:* 01236-437997); NEW STEVENSON LIB, 228 Clydesdale St, New Stevenson, Lanarkshire, ML1 4JG (*tel & fax:* 01698-732745); OLD MONKLAND LIB, Marshall St, Coatbridge, Lanarkshire, ML5 5LU (01236-428018); PETERSBURN LIB, Four Isles Community Centre, Varmsdorf Way, Petersburn, Airdrie, Lanarkshire, ML6 8EQ (01236-755008); VIEWPARK LIB, Burnhead St, Viewpark, Tannochside, Glasgow, G71 5AT (01698-812801; *fax:* 01698-810311); WHIFFLET LIB, Easton Pl, Whifflet, Coatbridge, Lanarkshire, ML5 4EW (*tel & fax:* 01236-429118); *South Area:* CLELAND LIB, Main St, Cleland, Motherwell, Lanarkshire, ML1 5QW (*tel & fax:* 01698-860487); CRAIGNEUK LIB, 35 Shieldsmuir Rd, Craigneuk, Wishaw, Lanarkshire, ML2 7TJ (01698-376689);

☞

North Lanarkshire ▼ **North Yorkshire**

Public Libraries

(N Lanarkshire Libs & Info cont)
NEWARTHILL LIB, 1 Kirkhall Rd, Newarthill, Lanarkshire, ML1 5BB (*tel & fax:* 01698-732033); NEWMAINS LIB, 15 Manse Rd, Newmains, Wishaw, Lanarkshire, ML2 9AX (01698-385325; *fax:* 01698-385324); SHOTTS LIB, Benhar Rd, Shotts, Lanarkshire, ML7 5EN (*tel & fax:* 01501-821556); WISHAW LIB, Kenilworth Ave, Wishaw, Lanarkshire, ML2 7LP (01698-372325; *fax:* 01698-360534)
Svc Pts: Mobile: 6 + 1 housebound van *AV:* 24 *Computers:* 24 *Internet:* 24
Collns: Hamilton of Dalziel Papers; Duke of Hamilton Colln; Hurst Nelson Photo Colln (all at Motherwell Heritage Centre); Drumpellier Papers (MSS & maps); Alston Papers (MSS); Airdrie Weavers Colln (regalia, banners, MSS) *Co-op Schemes:* NLSLS, BLDSC *ILLs:* county, natl & internatl *Loans:* bks & audios/4 wks; videos & DVDs/2 days; software/1 wk *Charges:* audios/50p, conc 25p; videos/£1-£2; DVDs/£1.50-£2.50; software/70p-£1.50 *Income Gen:* req & res/50p, conc 25p, ch exempt; lost ticket/ad £1.80, ch £1.20 *Fines:* bks & free loan items/ad & oap 25p pw; audios, videos, DVDs & software/loan charge; ch, prisons, mobile users & housebnd exempt *Equip:* m-reader, m-printers, fax, copiers (A4/10p, A3/20p), computers (incl wd-proc, internet & CD-ROM), 9 rooms for hire (various)

Stock:	1 Apr 2000	1 Apr 2001
lend:	492318	516677
ref:	17010	17210
audios:	43065	40471
videos:	9027	9607
CD-ROMs:	4188	5227
periodcls:	132	354

Issues:	1999-2000	2000-01
bks:	2082527	1777823
audios: *	72724	63282
videos:	103048	111925
CD-ROMs:	48609	37923

* music only; spkn wd included in bks

Acqs:	1999-2000	2000-01
bks:	71890	46967
AVs:	11076	8709

Acqs: Source: lib suppl
Classn: DDC *Cat: Type:* author, classified, subj & title *Medium:* auto *Auto Sys:* Dynix *Svcs: Extramural:* prisons, old people's homes, housebnd, playgroups/nurseries *Info:* community, business, council *Other:* Open Learning *Activs:* ch's activs, bk sales, temp exhibs, poetry readings
Enqs: 215953 (1999-2000); 242141 (2000-01)
Staff: Libns: 35 *Non-Prof:* 133.8

Inc from:	1999-2000	2000-01
local govt:	£4982860	£5696260
fines etc:	£318102	£305651
total:	£5300962	£6001911

Exp on:	1999-2000	2000-01
stock:	£651289	£594922
salaries:	£2865212	£2900898
total:	£5300962	£6001911

North Lincolnshire

P127 North Lincolnshire Libraries and Information Services
Scunthorpe Central Lib, Carlton Street, Scunthorpe, N Lincolnshire, DN15 6TX (01482-860161; *fax:* 01482-859737)
Email: ref.library@northlincs.gov.uk
Internet: http://www.northlincs.gov.uk/ NorthLincs/Leisure/libraries/

Local Auth: North Lincolnshire Council *Pop:* 152500 *Larger Dept:* Edu & Personal Development *Chief:* Principal Libn: Mrs Margaret Carr BA, MCLIP (margaret.carr@northlincs. gov.uk) *Other Snr Staff:* Snr Libn (Svc Delivery): Ms Sandra Barker (sandra.barker@ northlincs.gov.uk); Snr Libn (Yng People's Svcs): Mr Colin Brabazon (colin.brabazon@northlincs. gov.uk); Snr Libn (Info Svcs): Ms Helen Rowe (helen.rowe@northlincs.gov.uk); Snr Libn (Stock & Svc Development): Ms Janet Stopper (janet. stopper@northlincs.gov.uk)
Main Libs: SCUNTHORPE CENTRAL LIB, addr as above *Branch Libs:* ASHBY LIB, Ashby High St, Scunthorpe, N Lincolnshire, DN16 2JX (01724-865490); BARTON LIB, Providence House, Holydyke, Barton upon Humber, N Lincolnshire, DN18 5PR (01652-632245; *fax:* 01652-632837); BRIGG LIB, 23 Old Courts Rd, Brigg, N Lincolnshire, DN20 8JW (01652-657006); RIDDINGS LIB, Willoughby Rd, Scunthorpe, N Lincolnshire, DN17 2NW (01724-865412)
Svc Pts: PT: 10 *Mobile:* 2 *AV:* 3 *Computers:* 15 *Internet:* 15 *Other:* EDU LIB SVC, Edu Development Centre, South Leys Campus, Enderby Rd, Scunthorpe, N Lincolnshire, DN17 2JL (01724-297165; *email:* els@northlincs.gov.uk)
Collns: Steel Industry Colln; Wesley Family Colln *Co-op Schemes:* BLDSC, PRISM, YLI *ILLs:* county & natl *Loans:* bks & audios/3 wks; videos/1 wk *Charges:* spkn wd/75p, conc 25p, free to housebnd & visually impaired; music audios/85p; videos/£1.65 *Income Gen:* req/75p, conc 35p, BL loans £2.10; lost ticket/£1.60 *Fines:* bks & audios/10p pd for 1st wk, then 40p pw; videos/loan charge; oaps, ch, under-18s, recipients of state benefit, mobile lib users & housebnd svc users exempt *Equip:* m-reader, m-printer, fax, copiers (10p), computers (incl wd-proc, internet & CD-ROM), room for hire *Disabled:* Kurzweil, braille printer

Stock:	1 Apr 2000	1 Apr 2001
ad lend:	157590	148034
ad ref:	16601	17076
ch:	66024	65282
audios:	12965	13270
videos:	1006	1040
periodcls:	228	207

Issues:	1999-2000	2000-01
ad lend:	649295	630678
ch:	163570	160555
audios:	35705	37615
videos:	3834	3336

Acqs:	1999-2000	2000-01
bks:	29040	21080
AVs:	1576	1530

Acqs: Source: lib suppl *Offcr-in-Charge:* Snr Libn (Stock & Svc Development), as above
Classn: DDC *Cat: Type:* author, classified, subj & title *Medium:* auto *Auto Sys:* BiblioMondo
Svcs: Extramural: schools, old people's homes, housebnd, day centres, sheltered housing *Info:* business, community, European, tourist *Other:* Lifelong Learning, theatre bookings *Activs:* ch's activs, temp exhibs *Offcr-in-Charge:* Snr Libn (Svc Delivery), as above
Enqs: 107984 (1999-2000); 237276 (2000-01)
Staff: Libns: 16 *Non-Prof:* 51.47

Inc from:	1999-2000	2000-01
local govt:	£1772390	£1866180
fines etc:	£83040	£115530
total:	£1958730	£2061250

Exp on:	1999-2000	2000-01
stock & equip:	£405270	£390570
salaries:	£1040420	£1092190
total:	£1958730	£2061250

North Somerset

P128 North Somerset Library Service
Town Hall, Walliscote Grove Rd, Weston-super-Mare, Somerset, BS23 1AE (01934-888888; *fax:* 01934-418194)
Internet: http://www.n-somerset.gov.uk/

Local Auth: North Somerset Council *Pop:* 192000 *Cttee:* Youth & Learning Portfolio *Larger Dept:* Development & Environment *Chief:* Libs & Museums Mgr: Mrs Jackie Petherbridge DMS, MIMgt, MCLIP (jackie. petherbridge@n-somerset.gov.uk)
Main Libs: North Area: CLEVEDON LIB, 37 Old Church Rd, Clevedon, Somerset, BS21 6NN (01275-874858; *fax:* 01275-343630; *email:* clevedon.library@n-somerset.gov.uk); *South Area:* WESTON-SUPER-MARE LIB, The Boulevard, Weston-super-Mare, Somerset, BS23 1PL (01934-636638; *fax:* 01934-413046; *email:* weston. library@n-somerset.gov.uk) *Branch Libs:* NAILSEA LIB, Somerset Sq, Nailsea, Somerset, BS48 1RQ (01275-854583; *fax:* 01275-858373; *email:* nailsea.library@n-somerset. gov.uk); PORTISHEAD LIB, High St, Portishead, Somerset, BS20 9EW (01275-843433; *fax:* 01275-847085; *email:* portishead.library@n-somerset. gov.uk); WINSCOMBE LIB, Woodborough Rd, Winscombe, Somerset, BS25 1AB (*tel & fax:* 01934-843069; *email:* winscombe.library@ n-somerset.gov.uk); WORLE LIB, The Maltings, High St, Worle, Somerset, BS22 6JB (01934-513732; *fax:* 01934-517531; *email:* worle.library@ n-somerset.gov.uk)
Svc Pts: PT: 6 *Mobile:* 2
Collns: North Somerset Local Studies Colln (all aspects of North Somerset, at Weston Lib)
ILLs: county, natl & internatl *Loans:* bks/3 wks; audios & videos/1 wk *Charges:* audios/75p-£2; videos/£1-£3 *Income Gen:* res/75p-90p; lost ticket/£1.50 *Fines:* bks & audios/ad & oap 10p pd; ch exempt *Equip:* 24 m-readers, m-printer (A4/30p), 12 copiers (A4/10p, A3/20p), 10 fax (£1-£2), 86 computers (incl wd-procs, internet terminals & CD-ROM), 2 rooms for hire (£5 per session) *Disabled:* 40x CCTV magnifier at Nailsea & Weston Libs

Stock:	1 Apr 2000	1 Apr 2001
bks:	275144	254366

Issues:	1999-2000	2000-01
bks:	1442210	1339763
AVs:	64431	74914

Acqs:	1999-2000	2000-01
bks:	35774	34721
AVs:	2810	3208

Acqs: Source: lib suppl *Co-op:* FOURSITE Consortium *Offcr-in-Charge:* Libs, Info & Support Offcr: Mrs Susan Rossiter
Classn: DDC *Cat: Type:* author, classified, subj & title *Medium:* m-form & auto *Auto Sys:* DS *Svcs: Extramural:* old people's homes, housebnd *Activs:* ch's activs, bk sales, temp exhibs
Enqs: 87656 (1999-2000); 96213 (2000-01)
Staff: Libns: 12.5 *Non-Prof:* 84

Exp on:	1999-2000
bks:	£223160
salaries:	£1083720
total:	£1395680

North Tyneside

P129 North Tyneside Libraries

Central Lib, Northumberland Sq, North Shields, Tyne & Wear, NE30 1QU (0191-200-5424; *fax:* 0191-200-6118)
Email: central.library@northtyneside.gov.uk
Internet: http://www.northtyneside.gov.uk/libraries/

Local Auth: North Tyneside Metropolitan Borough Council *Pop:* 194100 *Larger Dept:* Edu & Cultural Svcs *Dept Chief:* Dir: Ms Anne Marie Carrie *Chief:* Libs & Info Mgr: Mrs Julia Stafford BA, MCLIP
Main Libs: CENTRAL LIB, addr as above; WALLSEND LIB, Ferndale Ave, Wallsend, Tyne & Wear, NE28 7NB (0191-200-6968; *fax:* 0191-200-6967; *email:* wallsend.library@northtyneside. gov.uk) *Branch Libs:* FOREST HALL LIB, Whitfield Rd, Forest Hall, Newcastle upon Tyne, NE12 0LJ (0191-200-7839; *email:* foresthall. library@northtyneside.gov.uk); HOWDON LIB, Churchill St, Howdon, Wallsend, Tyne & Wear, NE28 7TG (0191-200-6979; *email:* howdon. library@northtyneside.gov.uk); KILLINGWORTH LIB, White Swan Centre, Citadel East, Killingworth, Newcastle upon Tyne, NE12 6SS (0191-200-8266; *email:* killingworth.library@ northtyneside.gov.uk); LONGBENTON LIB, Black Friars Way, Long-benton, Newcastle upon Tyne, NE12 8SY (0191-200-7865; *email:* longbenton. library@northtyneside. gov.uk); MONKSEATON LIB, Woodleigh Rd, Monkseaton, Whitley Bay, Tyne & Wear, NE25 8ET (0191-200-8538; *email:* Monkseaton.Library@northtyneside.gov.uk); WHITLEY BAY LIB, Pk Rd, Whitley Bay, Tyne & Wear, NE26 1EJ (0191-200-8500; *fax:* 0191-200-8536; *email:* whitleybay.library@northtyneside. gov.uk)
Svc Pts: PT: 8 *Mobile:* 1 *AV:* 1 *Other:* CH'S & YNG PEOPLE'S SVC, at Wallsend Lib
Collns: local studies; BSI *Co-op Schemes:* NEMLAC, JFR *ILLs:* county, natl & internatl *Loans:* bks/4 wks; audios/2 wks; videos, DVDs & CD-ROMs/1 wk *Charges:* cassettes/60p; CDs/80p; videos/85p; DVDs & CD-ROMs/£2 *Income Gen:* req & res/ad 50p, ch 25p; lost ticket/£1.50; registered blind & disabled exempt *Fines:* bks & audios/ad & oap 8p pd (max £4), ch, registered blind & disabled exempt; videos & DVDs/25p pd; CD-ROMs/40p pd *Equip:* 14 m-readers, 2 m-printers, 3 fax (£1-£2.50 per pg), 11 copiers (A4/10p, A3/20p), clr copier (£1), 124 computers (all with wd-proc, internet & CD-ROM) *Disabled:* CCTV, subtitled videos *Online:* Dialog

Stock:	1 Apr 2000	1 Apr 2001
ad lend:	325232	313500
ad ref:	20840	21748
ch:	94812	103545
audios:	60003	31514
videos:	11562	12036
CD-ROMs:	299	486

Issues:	1999-2000	2000-01
ad lend:	1227352	1116843
ch:	322396	246540
audios:	79167	69124
videos:	89769	82720
CD-ROMs:	2022	2380

Acqs:	1999-2000	2000-01
bks:	25086	23727
AVs:	3914	4466

Acqs: Source: lib suppl & bksellers *Offcr-in-Charge:* Snr Libn (Support Svcs): Mrs Anne Newbury
Classn: DDC *Cat: Type:* author, classified, subj & title *Medium:* auto *Auto Sys:* Talis *Svcs: Extramural:* schools, old people's homes, housebnd *Info:* community *Activs:* ch's activs, bk sales, temp exhibs, poetry readings, reading groups, author visits
Enqs: 97000 (1999-2000); 117000 (2000-01)
Staff: Libns: 20.5 *Other Prof:* 1 *Non-Prof:* 75.5

Inc from:	1999-2000	2000-01
fines etc:	£202705	£190152

Exp on:	1999-2000	2000-01
bks:	£290414	£201090
AVs:	£39548	£23861
elec media:	£1039	£1021
salaries:	£1669720	£1667219
total:	£2000072	£1893191

North Yorkshire

P130 North Yorkshire County Libraries

Libs & Arts HQ, 21 Grammar School Ln, Northallerton, N Yorkshire, DL6 1DF (01609-767800; *fax:* 01609-780793)
Email: libraries@northyorks.gov.uk
Internet: http://www.northyorks.gov.uk/

Local Auth: North Yorkshire County Council *Pop:* 575000 *Cttee:* Business & Community Svcs Cttee *Larger Dept:* Business & Community Svcs *Dept Chief:* Dir: Mr Gordon Cresty *Chief:* Head of Libs, Archvs & Arts: Ms Julie Blaisdale (julie.blaisdale@northyorks.gov.uk) *Dep:* Public Svcs Libn: Mr Mike Gibson BA, MCLIP (mike.gibson@northyorks.gov.uk) *Other Snr Staff:* Info Svcs Advisor: Ms Elizabeth Melrose (elizabeth.melrose@northyorks.gov.uk); Special Svcs Advisor: Ms June Scratchard (june.scratchard@northyorks.gov.uk); Arts Offcr (Strategy & Policy): Ms Gayle Sutherland (gayle.sutherland@northyorks.gov.uk); ICT Development Offcr: Mr Nigel Prince (nigel. prince@northyorks.gov.uk); ICT Training Offcr: Ms Donna Tonks (donna.tonks@northyorks. gov.uk); Support Svcs Mgr: Mr Chris Riley (chris.riley@northyorks.gov.uk)
Main (Group) Libs: HARROGATE GROUP HQ LIB, Victoria Ave, Harrogate, N Yorkshire, HG1 1EG (01423-720300; *fax:* 01423-523158; *email:* harrogate.library@northyorks.gov.uk); MALTON GROUP HQ LIB, St Michael St, Malton, N Yorkshire, YO17 7LJ (01653-692714; *fax:* 01653-691200; *email:* malton.library@northyorks.gov.uk); NORTHALLERTON GROUP HQ LIB, 1 Thirsk Rd, Northallerton, N Yorkshire, DL6 1PT (01609-767832; *fax:* 01609-780793; *email:* northallerton. library@northyorks.gov.uk); SCARBOROUGH GROUP HQ LIB, Vernon Rd, Scarborough, N Yorkshire, YO11 2NN (01723-383400; *fax:* 01723-353893; *email:* scarborough.library@ northyorks.gov.uk); SHERBURN GROUP HQ LIB, Finkle Hill, Sherburn-in-Elmet, Leeds, W Yorkshire, LS25 6EA (01977-682306; *fax:* 01977-685308; *email:* sherburn.library@ northyorks.gov.uk); SKIPTON GROUP HQ LIB, Water St, Skipton, N Yorkshire, BD23 1JX (01756-792926; *fax:* 01756-798056; *email:* skipton. library@northyorks.gov.uk) *Branch Libs:* AYTON LIB, 3 Pickering Rd, West Ayton, Scarborough, N Yorkshire, YO13 9JE (01723-863052; *email:* ayton.library@northyorks.gov.uk); BEDALE LIB, Bedale Hall, Bedale, N Yorkshire, DL8 1AA (01677-422053; *email:* bedale.library@ northyorks.gov.uk); BILTON LIB, The Old Vicarage, Bilton Ln, Harrogate, N Yorkshire, HG1 3DT (01423-563609; *email:* bilton.library@ northyorks.gov.uk); CROSSHILLS LIB, Main St, Crosshills, Keighley, N Yorkshire, BD20 8TQ (01535-632441; *email:* crosshills.library@ northyorks.gov.uk); EASINGWOLD LIB, Market Pl, Easingwold, N Yorkshire, YO61 3AN (01347-821706; *email:* easingwold.library@northyorks. gov.uk); EASTFIELD LIB, High St, Eastfield, Scarborough, N Yorkshire, YO11 3LL (01723-582401; *email:* eastfield.library@northyorks. gov.uk); FILEY LIB, Station Ave, Filey, N Yorkshire, YO14 9AE (01723-512328; *fax:* 01723-515786; *email:* filey.library@northyorks.gov.uk); GT AYTON LIB, 105b High St, Gt Ayton, Middlesbrough, TS9 6NB (01642-723268; *email:* greatayton.library@ northyorks.gov.uk);

INGLETON LIB, Ingleborough Community Centre, Main St, Ingleton, Lancashire, LA6 3HG (*tel & fax:* 01524-241758; *email:* ingleton.library@northyorks. gov.uk); KNARESBOROUGH LIB, Market Pl, Knaresborough, N Yorkshire, HG5 8AG (01423-863054; *fax:* 01423-861539; *email:* knaresborough. library@northyorks.gov.uk); NORTON LIB, Commercial St, Norton, Malton, N Yorkshire, YO17 9ES (01653-692960; *email:* norton.library@ northyorks.gov.uk); PICKERING LIB, The Ropery, Pickering, N Yorkshire, YO18 8DY (01751-472185; *fax:* 01751-476775; *email:* pickering.library@northyorks.gov.uk); RICHMOND LIB, Queen's Rd, Richmond, N Yorkshire, DL10 4AE (01748-823120; *fax:* 01748-826977; *email:* richmond.library@northyorks.gov.uk); RIPON LIB, The Arcade, Ripon, N Yorkshire, HG4 1AG (01765-604799; *fax:* 01765-608511; *email:* ripon.library@northyorks.gov.uk); SCALBY LIB, 450 Scalby Rd, Newby, Scarborough, N Yorkshire, YO12 6EE (01723-365671; *fax:* 01723-501295; *email:* scalby.library@northyorks.gov.uk); SELBY LIB, 52 Micklegate, Selby, N Yorkshire, YO8 4EQ (01757-702020; *fax:* 01757-705396; *email:* selby.library@northyorks.gov.uk); STARBECK LIB, The Avenue, Starbeck, Harrogate, N Yorkshire, HG1 4QB (01423-885450; *email:* starbeck.library@northyorks.gov.uk); STOKESLEY LIB, Manor House, Manor Cl, Stokesley, Middlesbrough, TS9 5AG (01642-711592; *email:* stokesley.library@northyorks.gov.uk); TADCASTER LIB, Station Rd, Tadcaster, N Yorkshire, LS24 9JG (01937-832518; *email:* tadcaster. library@northyorks.gov.uk); THIRSK LIB, Finkle St, Thirsk, N Yorkshire, YO7 1DA (01845-522268; *email:* thirsk.library@northyorks.gov.uk); WHITBY LIB, Windsor Ter, Whitby, N Yorkshire, YO21 1ET (01947-602554; *fax:* 01947-820288; *email:* whitby. library@northyorks.gov.uk)
Svc Pts: PT: 18 *Mobile:* 12 *AV:* all libs *Computers:* all libs *Internet:* all libs *Other:* SCHOOL LIB SVC, at Lib HQ
Collns: Early Church Bks; Petty Colln (English Civil War, both at Skipton Lib); Mineral Waters Colln (from 1572, at Harrogate Lib); Early Printing Colln (at Stokesley Lib); Alex MacLean Colln (salon music); Unné Colln (Yorkshire Photo Colln, both at Northallerton HQ) *Co-op Schemes:* YLI *ILLs:* county, natl & internatl *Loans:* bks & spkn wd/3 wks; music audios, videos, DVDs & Playstation games/1 wk *Charges:* audio sub/ spkn wd £10 pa, music £12.50 pa, both £15 pa, audios charged at 50% for subscribers; cassettes/70p (sets max £2.80); CDs/£1.10 (sets max £4.40); spkn wd/60p (sets max £2.40), ch story tapes 60p per title; videos/£2; DVDs/£2.60 *Income Gen:* req & res/60p, conc 50p; lost ticket/£2 *Fines:* bks/ad 12p pd to max 70p for 1st wk, then 70p pw to max £4.20, ch 5p per 3 days to max 10p for 1st wk, then 10p pw to max 50p; audios, videos & DVDs/loan charge (up to 6 loan periods) *Equip:* 50 m-readers, 12 m-printers (30p), 6 fax (£1 per pg, higher overseas), 35 copiers (A4/10p, A3/20p), clr copier (A4/£1.20, A3/ £2), 106 computers (incl 62 with wd-proc, 62 with CD-ROM & 62 with internet, access free, printouts 10p b&w, 20p clr), rooms for hire (various) *Offcr-in-Charge:* Support Svcs Mgr, as above

Stock:	1 Apr 2000	1 Apr 2001
ad lend:	496955	474719
ad ref:	135894	125405
ch:	149737	153057
audios:	40382	44126
videos:	12378	13525
CD-ROMs:	-	761

Issues:	1999-2000	2000-01
ad lend:	3200214	2989038
ch:	619864	612281
audios:	115558	126014
videos:	49196	61181
CD-ROMs:	680	3043

☞

(N Yorkshire County Libs cont)

Acqs:	1999-2000	2000-01
bks:	52590	61098
AVs:	10065	7724

Acqs: Source: lib suppl, publ & bksellers *Offcr-in-Charge:* Snr Libn (Bibliographical Svcs): Mr Mike Elder (mike.elder@northyorks.gov.uk)
Classn: DDC *Cat: Type:* author, classified, subj & title *Medium:* cards & auto *Auto Sys:* Genesis *Svcs: Extramural:* schools, prisons, hosps, old people's homes, housebnd *Info:* local *Activs:* ch's activs, bk sales, temp exhibs, poetry readings, picture loan, reading groups, talks, author visits *Offcr-in-Charge:* various offcrs
Staff: Libns: 49 *Non-Prof:* 141.8

Inc from:	1999-2000	2000-01
local govt:	£5233740	£5499774
fines etc:	£401149	£438337
total:	£5639447	£5991297

Exp on:	1999-2000	2000-01
bks:	£605142	£592340
AVs:	£108834	£110841
culture: *	£150781	£151088
salaries:	£3345947	£3568996
total:	£5639447	£5991297
* not included in total		

Proj: new lib at Ripon

Northamptonshire

P131 Northamptonshire Libraries and Information Service
Lib Svc HQ, PO Box 216, John Dryden House, 8-10 The Lakes, Northampton, NN4 7DD (01604-236236; *fax:* 01604-237937)
Email: nlis@northamptonshire.gov.uk
Internet: http://www2.northamptonshire.gov.uk/council/library/

Local Auth: Northamptonshire County Council *Pop:* 609400 *Larger Dept:* Svcs Northamptonshire *Dept Chief:* Acting Strategic Dir: Mr Michael Bordiss *Chief:* County Libs & Info Offcr: Mr Eric Wright MA, BPhil, BSocSc, MCLIP (ewright@northamptonshire.gov.uk) *Other Snr Staff:* Principal Libs & Info Offcr (Svc Delivery): Mr Nick Matthews (nmatthews@northamptonshire.gov.uk); Principal Libs & Info Offcr (Svc Development): Ms Evelyn Jarvis (ejarvis@northamptonshire.gov.uk)
Main (Area) Libs: DAVENTRY LIB, North St, Daventry, Northamptonshire, NN11 5PN (01327-703130; *fax:* 01327-300501; *email:* davlib@northamptonshire.gov.uk); KETTERING LIB, Sheep St, Kettering, Northamptonshire, NN16 0AY (01536-512315; *fax:* 01536-411349; *email:* KetLib@northamptonshire.gov.uk); CENTRAL LIB, Abington St, Northampton, NN1 2BA (01604-462040; *fax:* 01604-462055; *email:* CentLib@northamptonshire.gov.uk); WELLINGBOROUGH LIB, Pebble Ln, Wellingborough, Northamptonshire, NN8 1AS (01933-225365; *fax:* 01933-442060; *email:* WellLib@northamptonshire.gov.uk); WESTON FAVELL LIB, Weston Favell Centre, Northampton, NN3 8JZ (01604-403100; *fax:* 01604-403112; *email:* WestLib@northamptonshire.gov.uk) *Branch (Community) Libs:* ABINGTON LIB, Lindsay Ave, Northampton, NN3 2SJ (01604-401402; *fax:* 01604-416385); BRACKLEY LIB, Manor Rd, Brackley, Northamptonshire,

NN13 6AJ (01280-703455; *fax:* 01280-701627); BURTON LATIMER LIB, High St, Burton Latimer, Northamptonshire, NN15 5RH (01536-723357); CORBY LIB, 9 The Links, Queens Sq, Corby, Northamptonshire, NN17 1PZ (01536-203304; *fax:* 01536-400954; *email:* CorLib@northamptonshire.gov.uk); DESBOROUGH LIB, High St, Desborough, Northamptonshire, NN14 0QS (01536-761085); DUSTON LIB, Pendle Rd, Duston, Northampton, NN5 6DT (01604-585882; *fax:* 01604-758531); EARLS BARTON LIB, Broad St, Earls Barton, Northampton, NN6 0ND (01604-810726); FAR COTTON LIB, Towcester Rd, Far Cotton, Northampton, NN4 9LG (01604-762192); HIGHAM FERRERS LIB, Midland Rd, Higham Ferrers, Northamptonshire, NN10 8DN (01933-314842; *fax:* 01933-412246); HUNSBURY LIB, Overslade Cl, East Hunsbury, Northampton, NN4 0RZ (01604-702830; *fax:* 01604-702935; *email:* HunsLib@northamptonshire.gov.uk); IRTHLINGBOROUGH LIB, High St, Irthlingborough, Northamptonshire, NN9 5PU (01933-650641); KINGSTHORPE LIB, Welford Rd, Kingsthorpe, Northampton, NN2 8AG (01604-714021; *fax:* 01604-791692); OUNDLE LIB, Glapthorn Rd, Oundle, Northamptonshire, PE8 4JA (01832-272584; *fax:* 01832-274805); RAUNDS LIB, High St, Rotten Row, Raunds, Northamptonshire, NN9 6HT (01933-623671); ROTHWELL LIB, Market Hill, Rothwell, Northamptonshire, NN14 2EP (01536-711880); RUSHDEN LIB, Newton Rd, Rushden, Northamptonshire, NN10 0PT (01933-312754; *fax:* 01933-312944); ST JAMES LIB, 138 St James Rd, Northampton, NN5 5LQ (01604-751037); THRAPSTON LIB, High St, Thrapston, Northamptonshire, NN14 4JJ (01832-733251); TOWCESTER LIB, Richmond Rd, Towcester, Northamptonshire, NN12 7EX (01327-350794; *fax:* 01327-358263)
Svc Pts: PT: 11 *Mobile:* 6 *AV:* 29 *Other:* 2 prison libs
Collns: Northamptonshire Studies Colln; Northampton Footwear & Leather Colln; John Clare Colln; Tebbut Printed Music Colln (all at Central Lib); Frederick William Bull Colln (publicity material, 1840-1880); Gotch Family Colln (both at Kettering Lib); H.E. Bates Colln (at Rushden Lib); Lawson Pratt Colln (photos of Wellingborough); Mary Pendered Colln (local novelist & playwright, both at Wellingborough Lib) *Co-op Schemes:* EMRLS *ILLs:* county, natl & internatl *Loans:* bks/3 wks; audios, videos & CD-ROMs/1 wk; lang courses/single 1 wk, multi-part 3 wks *Charges:* cassettes/34p; CDs/90p; spkn wd/ad 92p, ch's 46p; videos/£1.90 *Income Gen:* req & res/75p; lost ticket/£1.43 *Fines:* bks/ad 50p pw, ch 25p pw; audios & videos/loan charge; reading impaired, learning difficulties, housebnd, old people's homes, hospices & prisons exempt
Equip: m-readers, m-printers (A4/62p),fax (UK £1.58 1st pg, addl 79p), copiers (A4/10p, A3/15p), clr copiers (A4/£1, A3/£1.50), computers (incl wd-proc, internet & CD-ROM) *Disabled:* CCTV, magnifiers, Aladdin, minicoms, Eazee Reader, reading edge machines, portable hearing loop

Stock:	1 Apr 2000	1 Apr 2001
ad lend:	688708	679760
ad ref:	52999	57004
ch:	289529	286772
schools:	417399	-
instns:	20097	23762
audios:	69843	67366
videos:	14272	18074
CD-ROMs:	1067	2177
periodcls:	403	575
archvs:	6 linear m	6 linear m

Issues:	1999-2000	2000-01
ad lend:	3311531	3112245
ch:	1461915	1330912
instns:	122858	102014
audios:	253133	247272
videos:	116571	130951
CD-ROMs:	3572	10481

Acqs:	1999-2000	2000-01
bks:	113742	104441
AVs:	14826	16846

Acqs: Source: lib suppl *Offcr-in-Charge:* Resources Mgr: Mr Hugh Marks
Classn: DDC *Cat: Type:* author, classified & title *Medium:* auto *Auto Sys:* Talis *Svcs: Extramural:* schools, prisons, hosps, old people's homes, housebnd *Info:* council, careers & employment, business, environmental *Activs:* ch's activs, bk sales, temp exhibs, poetry readings, talks, author visits
Enqs: 347464 (1999-2000); 326300 (2000-01)
Staff: Prof: 63.5 *Non-Prof:* 162

Exp on:	1999-2000	2000-01
total:	£7129169	£6848137

Northern Ireland: Belfast

P132 Belfast Education and Library Board
Belfast Central Lib, Royal Ave, Belfast, Northern Ireland, BT1 1EA (028-9050-9150; *fax:* 028-9033-2819)
Email: info.belb@ni-libraries.net
Internet: http://www.belb.org.uk/

Local Auth: Belfast Edu & Lib Board *Pop:* 287500 *Cttee:* Lib Cttee *Larger Dept:* Belfast Edu & Lib Board *Dept Chief:* Chief Exec: Mr David Cargo *Chief:* Chief Libn: Mrs Linda Houston BLS, MBA, MCLIP (linda.houston@ni-libraries.net) *Dep:* Asst Chief Libns: Mrs Katherine McCloskey (katherine.mccloskey@ni-libraries.net) & Mr David Jess (david.jess@ni-libraries.net)
Main Libs: BELFAST CENTRAL LIB, contact details as above *Branch Libs:* ANDERSONSTOWN LIB, Slievegallion Dr, Belfast, BT11 8JP (028-9050-9200); ARDOYNE LIB, 446-450 Crumlin Rd, Belfast, BT14 7GH (028-9050-9202); BALLYGOMARTIN LIB, Mount Gilbert Community School, Belfast, BT13 3NL (028-9050-9241); BALLYHACKAMORE LIB, 1-3 Eastleigh Dr, Belfast, BT4 3DX (028-9050-9204); BALLY-MACARRETT LIB, 19-35 Templemore Ave, Belfast, BT5 4FP (028-9050-9207); CAIRN-MARTIN LIB, Cairnmartin School, 13 Lyndhurst Gdn, Belfast, BT12 3NL (028-9050-9241); CHICHESTER LIB, Salisbury Ave, Belfast, BT15 5EB (028-9050-9210); FALLS RD LIB, 49 Falls Rd, Belfast, BT12 4PD (028-9050-9212); FINAGHY LIB, 13 Finaghy Rd South, Belfast, BT10 0BW (028-9050-9214); HOLYWOOD ARCHES LIB, 4-12 Holywood Rd, Belfast, BT4 1NT (028-9050-9216); LIGONIEL LIB, 53-55 Ligoniel Rd, Belfast, BT14 8BW (028-9050-9221); LISBURN RD LIB, 440 Lisburn Rd, Belfast, BT9 6GR (028-9050-9223); ORMEAU RD LIB, Ormeau Rd Embankment, Belfast, BT7 3GG (028-9050-9228); SANDY ROW LIB, 127 Sandy Row, Belfast, BT12 5ET (028-9050-9230); SHANKILL LIB, 298-300 Shankill Rd, Belfast, BT13 2BN (028-9050-9232); SKEGONEILL LIB, Skegoneill Ave, Belfast, BT15 3JN (028-9050-9244); SUFFOLK LIB, Stewartstown Rd, Belfast, BT11 9JP (028-9050-9234); WHITEROCK LIB, Whiterock Rd, Belfast, BT12 7FW (028-9050-9236); WOODSTOCK RD LIB, 358 Woodstock Rd, Belfast, BT6 9DQ (028-9050-9239)
Svc Pts: PT: 1 *Mobile:* 2 *AV:* 22 *Computers:* 21 *Internet:* 21 *Other:* MUSIC LIB, at Central Lib; BELFAST ULSTER & IRISH STUDIES LIB (see **A37**); SCHOOL LIB SVC, incl: Teachers' Ref Lib & NI Educational Film Lib
Collns: F.J. Biggar Lib & Archv; Fine Bk Room Colln (8500 vols); Nat Hist Colln; UK Govt pubns; patents *Co-op Schemes:* IJFR *Loans:* bks & audios/3 wks; videos/1 wk *Charges:* audios/£10 pa; videos/£1 per loan *Fines:* bks & audios/10p pw, videos/20p pd; ch, oap, blind & disabled exempt *Equip:* m-readers, m-printers, fax,

copiers, room hire, computers (incl wd-proc, internet & CD-ROM) *Online:* access to 400+ databases

Stock:	***1 Apr 2000***
lend:	340820
ref:	905482
AVs:	65723
periodcls:	830

Issues:	***1999-2000***
bks:	1533261
AVs:	95688

Acqs: Source: lib suppl
Classn: DDC *Cat: Type:* author & classified
Medium: cards, printed & auto *Auto Sys:* DS
Svcs: Extramural: schools, prisons, hosps, old people's homes, housebnd *Info:* business, community *Other:* Learning Gateway at Central Lib *Activs:* ch's activs, bk sales, temp exhibs, talks
Enqs: 626930 (1999-2000)
Staff: Libns: 34 *Non-Prof:* 121

Northern Ireland: North Eastern

P133 North Eastern Education and Library Board Library Service

Lib HQ, Demesne Ave, Ballymena, Co Antrim, Northern Ireland, BT43 7BG (028-2566-4100; *fax:* 028-2563-2038)
Email: Library.Enquiries@neelb.org.uk
Internet: http://www.neelb.org.uk/

Local Auth: North Eastern Edu & Lib Board
Pop: 375500 *Cttee:* Lib Cttee *Larger Dept:* North Eastern Edu & Lib Board *Dept Chief:* Chief Exec: Mr Gordon Topping BA, MSc, MBA, DipEd
Chief: Chief Libn: Mrs P. Valentine BA(Hons), FCLIP *Other Snr Staff:* Asst Chief Libn (Public Svcs): Mrs M. Bryson BA, MCLIP; Asst Chief Libn (Info & Support Svcs): Miss A. Peoples BA(Hons), MCLIP, DMS; Asst Chief Libn (Youth & Training): Mr M. McFaul DipLS, AMA, MBA
Main (Group) Libs: BALLYMENA LIB & GROUP HQ, 25-31 Demesne Ave, Ballymena, Co Antrim, BT43 7BG (028-2566-4110/1; *fax:* 028-2564-6680; *email:* Ballymena.Library@ni-libraries. net); ANTRIM GROUPHQ, Ballycraigy Primary School, Bracken Avenue, Antrim, BT41 1TU; CARRICKFERGUS LIB & GROUP HQ, 2 Joymount Ct, Carrickfergus, Co Antrim, BT38 7DQ (028-9336-2261; *fax:* 028-9336-0589; *email:* Carrickfergus.Library@ni-libraries.net); COLERAINE LIB, Queen St, Coleraine, Co Londonderry, BT52 1BE (028-7034-2561; *fax:* 028-7034-2561; *email:* Coleraine.Library@ ni-libraries.net); MAGHERAFELT LIB, 6 Church St, Magherafelt, Co Londonderry, BT45 6AN (028-7963-2278; *fax:* 028-7963-4887; *email:* Magherafelt.Library@ni-libraries.net) *Branch Libs:* AHOGHILL LIB, Brooke St, Ahoghill, Ballymena, Co Antrim, BT42 1LD (028-2587-1768; *email:* Ahoghill.Library@ni-libraries.net); ANTRIM LIB, 41 Church St, Antrim, BT41 4BE; BALLEE LIB, 2 Neighbourhood Ct, Ballee, Ballymena, Co Antrim, BT42 2SX (tel & fax: 028-2564-5761; *email:* Ballee.Library@ni-libraries.net); BALLYCASTLE LIB, 5 Leyland Rd, Ballycastle, Co Antrim, BT54 6DT (tel & fax: 028-2076-2566; *email:* Ballycastle.Library@ni-libraries.net); BALLYCLARE LIB, The Market House, School St, Ballyclare, Co Antrim, BT39 9BE (tel & fax: 028-9335-2269; *email:* Ballyclare.Library@ni-libraries. net); BALLYMONEY LIB, Rodden Foot, Queen St, Ballymoney, Co Antrim, BT53 6JB (tel & fax: 028-2766-3589; *email:* Ballymoney.Library@ni-libraries. net); BELLAGHY LIB, 22 Castle St, Bellaghy, Magherafelt, Co Londonderry, BT45 8LA (028-7938-6627; *email:* Bellaghy.Library@ ni-libraries.net); BROUGHSHANE LIB, Main St,

Broughshane, Ballymena, Co Antrim, BT42 4JW (tel & fax: 028-2586-1613; *email:* Broughshane. Library@ni-libraries.net); BUSHMILLS LIB, 44 Main St, Bushmills, Co Antrim, BT57 8QA (tel & fax: 028-2073-1424; *email:* Bushmills.Library@ ni-libraries.net); CARNLOUGH LIB, Town Hall, Carnlough, Ballymena, Co Antrim, BT44 0EU (tel & fax: 028-2888-5552; *email:* Carnlough.Library@ ni-libraries.net); CLOUGHFERN LIB, 2a Kings Cres, Newtownabbey, Co Antrim, BT37 0DH (tel & fax: 028-9085-4789; *email:* Cloughfern.Library@ ni-libraries.net); CRUMLIN LIB, Orchard Rd, Crumlin, Co Antrim, BT29 4SD (tel & fax: 028-9442-3066; *email:* Crumlin.Library@ni-libraries. net); CULLYBACKEY LIB, 153 Tobar Pk, Cullybackey, Co Antrim, BT42 1NW (tel & fax: 028-2588-1878; *email:* Cullybackey.Library@ ni-libraries.net); CUSHENDALL LIB, Mill St, Cushendall, Ballymena, Co Antrim, BT44 0RR (tel & fax: 028-2177-1297; *email:* Cushendall.Library@ ni-libraries.net); DRAPERSTOWN LIB, High St, Draperstown, Magherafelt, Co Londonderry, BT45 7AD (028-7962-8249; *email:* Draperstown.Library@ ni-libraries.net); GARVAGH LIB, Bridge St, Garvagh, Coleraine, Co Londonderry, BT51 5AF (028-2955-8500; *email:* Garvagh.Library@ ni-libraries.net); GLENGORMLEY LIB, 40 Carnmoney Rd, Newtownabbey, Co Antrim, BT36 6HP (tel & fax: 028-9083-3797; *email:* Glengormley. Library@ni-libraries.net); GREENISLAND LIB, 17 Glassillan Grove, Greenisland, Carrickfergus, Co Antrim, BT38 8PE (tel & fax: 028-9086-5419; *email:* Greenisland.Library@ni-libraries.net); GREYSTONE LIB, Greystone Rd, Antrim, BT41 1JW (tel & fax: 028-9446-3891; *email:* Greystone. Library@ni-libraries.net); KILREA LIB, Town Hall, 27 The Diamond, Kilrea, Coleraine, Co Londonderry, BT51 5QN (028-2954-0630; *email:* Kilrea. Library@ni-libraries.net); LARNE LIB, 36 Pound St, Larne, Co Antrim, BT40 1SQ (tel & fax: 028-2827-7047; *email:* Larne.Library@ni-libraries.net); MAGHERA LIB, 1 Main St, Maghera, Co Londonderry, BT46 5EA (tel & fax: 028-7964-2578; *email:* Maghera.Library@ni-libraries.net); MONKSTOWN LIB, Monkstown Secondary School, Bridge Rd, Monkstown, Newtownabbey, Co Antrim, BT37 0EG (tel & fax: 028-9085-3138; *email:* Monkstown. Library@ni-libraries.net); PORTGLENONE LIB, 19 Townhill Rd, Portglenone, Ballymena, Co Antrim, BT44 8AD (028-2582-2228; *email:* Portglenone. Library@ni-libraries.net); PORTRUSH LIB, Technical College, Dunluce St, Portrush, Co Antrim, BT56 8DN (tel & fax: 028-7082-3752; *email:* Portrush.Library@ni-libraries.net); PORT-STEWART LIB, Town Hall, The Crescent, Portstewart, Co Londonderry, BT55 7AB (tel & fax: 028-7083-2712; *email:* Portstewart.Library@ ni-libraries.net); RANDALSTOWN LIB, 34 New St, Randalstown, Co Antrim, BT41 3AF (tel & fax: 028-9447-2725; *email:* Randalstown.Library@ ni-libraries.net); RATHCOOLE LIB, 2 Rosslea Way, Rathcoole, Newtownabbey, Co Antrim, BT37 9BJ (tel & fax: 028-9085-1157; *email:* Rathcoole. Library@ni-libraries.net); WHITEHEAD LIB, 17b Edward Rd, Whitehead, Carrickfergus, Co Antrim, BT38 9QB (tel & fax: 028-9335-3249; *email:* Whitehead.Library@ni-libraries.net)
Svc Pts: PT: 4 *Mobile:* 8 + 2 housebnd *AV:* 24
Internet: at all branches from end of 2002
Collns: IJFR: D & G, Local; George Shiels Colln (at Ballymoney Lib); Ballymoney Special Colln (at Ballymoney Lib); Local Studies Colln (at Ballymena Lib) *Co-op Schemes:* IJFR *ILLs:* county, natl & internatl *Loans:* bks/3 wks; audios & videos/1 wk; Open Learning packs/12 wks *Charges:* CDs/60p; videos/£1.75 *Income Gen:* req/40p; res/free; ILL/£3 *Fines:* bks & audios/ad 20p pw; videos/loan charge; ch, oaps, registered blind exempt *Equip:* 4 m-printers, 29 fax (UK £1.50 to send, overseas £3) 2 video viewers, 16 copiers (A4/10p, A3/20p), 37 computers (all with internet, 20 with CD-ROM; internet free, £2.50 per half hr for non lib membs,

printouts A4/10p, A3/20p), 2 rooms for hire
Disabled: bk rests, magnifying glasses, earphones *Online:* Ulster-American Folk Park Database (emigration)

Stock:	***1 Apr 2001***
ad lend:	405779
ad ref:	45106
ch:	195230
audios:	13298
videos:	11662
CD-ROMs:	237
periodcls:	101

Issues:	***2000-01***
ad lend:	1643750
ch:	929681
audios:	24801
videos:	42737

Acqs:	***2000-01***
bks:	46132
AVs:	4466

Acqs: Source: lib suppl, publ & bksellers *Offcr-in-Charge:* Group Libns, Team Libns & Stock Libn
Classn: DDC *Cat: Type:* author, classified, subj & title *Medium:* auto *Auto Sys:* Galaxy DS
Svcs: Extramural: schools, hosps, old people's homes, housebnd *Info:* business, local studies *Other:* 5 Open Learning centres (at Ballee, Ballymoney, Ballymena, Carrickfergus & Greenisland Libs) *Activs:* ch's activs, bk sales, temp exhibs, reading groups, talks, author visits *Offcr-in-Charge:* various
Enqs: 243464 (2000-01)
Staff: Libns: 26 *Other Prof:* 1 *Non-Prof:* 131

Inc from:	***2000-01***
fines etc:	£180605

Exp on:	***2000-01***
bks:	£355812
AVs:	£50554
salaries:	£2601286
total:	£4093892

Proj: new Antrim Lib opened Dec 2002; Peoples Network to be extended to all libs by end of 2002; Galaxy DS to be installed in all libs by end of 2002

Northern Ireland: South

P134 Southern Education and Library Board

Lib HQ, 1 Markethill Rd, Armagh, Northern Ireland, BT60 1NR (028-3752-5353; *fax:* 028-3752-6879)
Email: info.selb@ni-libraries.net
Internet: http://www.selb.org/library/index.htm

Local Auth: Southern Edu & Lib Board *Pop:* 343500 *Cttee:* Lib Cttee *Larger Dept:* Southern Edu & Lib Board *Dept Chief:* Chief Exec: Mrs Helen McClenaghan *Chief:* Chief Libn: Mrs Kathleen Ryan BA, MBA, FCLIP *Dep:* Asst Chief Libn: Mr Philip Reid
Main (Group/Team) Libs: BANBRIDGE LIB, Scarva St, Banbridge, Co Down, BT32 3AD (028-4062-3973; *email:* BanbridgeLibrary@ni-libraries. net); COOKSTOWN LIB, Burn Rd, Cookstown, Co Tyrone, BT80 8BT (028-8663-3702; *email:* CookstownLibrary@ni-libraries.net); DUNGANNON LIB, Market Sq, Dungannon, Co Tyrone, BT70 1JD (028-8772-2952; *email:* DungannonLibrary@ ni-libraries.net); LURGAN LIB, Carnegie St, Lurgan, Co Armagh, BT66 6AS (028-3932-3912; *email:* LurganLibrary@ni-libraries. net); NEWRY LIB, 79 Hill St, Newry, Co Down, BT34 1DG (028-3026-4683; *fax:* 028-3025-1739; *email:* NewryLibrary@ni-libraries.net); WARRENPOINT LIB, Summerhill, Warrenpoint, Newry, Co Down, BT34 3JB (028-4175-3375; *email:* WarrenpointLibrary@ni-libraries.net) ☞

Northern Ireland: SELB
▼
Nottingham

Public Libraries

(Southern Edu & Lib Board cont)
Branch Libs: ARMAGH LIB, Market St, Armagh, BT61 7BU (028-3752-4072; *email:* ArmaghLibrary@ni-libraries.net); BESSBROOK LIB, Church Rd, Bessbrook, Newry, Co Down, BT35 7AQ (028-3083-0424; *email:* BessbrookLibrary@ni-libraries. net); BROWNLOW LIB, Brownlow Rd, Craigavon, Co Armagh, BT65 5DP (028-3834-1946; *email:* BrownlowLibrary@ ni-libraries.net); COALISLAND LIB, The Cornmill, Coalisland, Co Tyrone, BT71 4LT (028-8774-0569; *email:* CoalislandLibrary@ni-libraries.net); CRAIGAVON LIB, 113 Church St, Portadown, Craigavon, Co Armagh, BT62 3DB; CROSSMAGLEN LIB, The Square, Crossmaglen, Co Down, BT35 9AA (028-3086-1951; *email:* CrossmaglenLibrary@ni-libraries.net); DROMORE LIB, Town Hall, Dromore, Co Down, BT25 1AW (028-9269-2280; *email:* DromoreLibrary@ ni-libraries.net); FIVEMILETOWN LIB, Main St, Fivemiletown, Co Tyrone, BT75 0PG (028-8952-1409; *email:* FivemiletownLibrary@ni-libraries.net); GILFORD LIB, Main St, Gilford, Craigavon, Co Armagh, BT63 6HY (028-3883-1770; *email:* GilfordLibrary@ni-libraries.net); KEADY LIB, Market St, Keady, Armagh, BT60 3RP (028-3753-1365; *email:* KeadyLibrary@ni-libraries.net); KILKEEL LIB, Greencastle St, Kilkeel, Newry, Co Down, BT34 4BH (028-4176-2278; *email:* KilkeelLibrary@ni-libraries.net); MONEYMORE LIB, 8 Main St, Moneymore, Co Londonderry, BT45 7PD (028-8674-8380; *email:* MoneymoreLibrary@ni-libraries.net); MOY LIB, The Square, Moy, Co Tyrone, BT71 7SG (028-8778-4661; *email:* MoyLibrary@ni-libraries.net); PORTADOWN LIB, 24-26 Church St, Portadown, Co Armagh, BT63 3LQ (028-3833-6122; *fax:* 028-3833-5296; *email:* PortadownLibrary@ni-libraries. net); RATHFRILAND LIB, John St, Rathfriland, Co Down, BT34 5QH (028-4063-0661; *email:* RathfrillandLibrary@ni-libraries.net); RICHHILL LIB, 1 Maynooth Rd, Richhill, Co Armagh, BT61 9PE (028-3887-0639; *email:* RichillLibrary@ ni-libraries.net); TANDRAGEE LIB, Market St, Tandragee, Co Armagh, BT62 2BW (028-3884-0694; *email:* TandrageeLibrary@ni-libraries.net); WARINGSTOWN LIB, Village Hall, Waringstown, Craigavon, Co Armagh, BT66 7QH (028-3888-1077; *email:* WarringstownLibrary@ni-libraries.net)
Svc Pts: Mobile: 5 + 2 housebnd **AV:** 23 **Computers:** 6 **Internet:** 6 **Other:** IRISH & LOCAL STUDIES LIB (see **A17**); INFO SVC, at Portadown Lib; AV RECORDING SVC, at Lib HQ
Collns: Crossle Colln MSS (Newry families hist); IJFR: Ha-Hh (both at Lib HQ) **Co-op Schemes:** IJFR **Loans:** bks & cassettes/3 wks; CDs & videos/1 wk **Charges:** CDs/50p pw; videos/£1 pw **Income Gen:** req & res/ad 30p, ch & oap 15p; lost ticket/ £1; ILL/ £1, students 50p; printing of labels/1.5p-2p label. **Fines:** bks & audios/ad 20p pw, ch & oap exempt; videos/25p pd **Equip:** m-readers, m-printers, copiers (10p), computers (incl internet), scanners, rooms for hire (various)

Stock:	1 Apr 2000	1 Apr 2001
ad lend:	228318	233457
ad ref:	65893	72929
ch:	120358	128618
audios:	34899	34960
videos:	12832	13883
periodcls:	329	446

Issues:	1999-2000	2000-01
ad lend:	1145306	1381349
ch:	679082	691890
audios:	151922	133347
videos:	92426	75974

Acqs:	1999-2000	2000-01
bks:	45206	58757
AVs:	6527	6225

Acqs: *Source:* lib suppl **Offcr-in-Charge:** Stock Svcs Co-ordinator: Mr Paddy Pender
Classn: DDC **Cat:** *Type:* author & classified **Medium:** auto **Svcs:** *Extramural:* schools, hosps, old people's homes, housebnd, day centres, sheltered housing *Info:* business, community, European *Activs:* ch's activs, bk sales, temp exhibs
Enqs: 254956 (1999-2000); 276380 (2000-01)
Staff: Libns: 28 Non-Prof: 92.7

Inc from:	2000-01
local govt:	£3662162
fines etc:	£212970
total:	£3875132

Exp on:	2000-01
bks:	£393651
AVs:	£59426
salaries:	£2594143
total:	£3875132

Northern Ireland: South Eastern

P135 South Eastern Education and Library Board Library Service
Lib HQ, Windmill Hill, Ballynahinch, Co Down, Northern Ireland, BT24 8DH (028-9756-6400; *fax:* 028-9756-5072)
Email: libraries@seelb.org.uk
Internet: http://www.seelb.org.uk/

Local Auth: South Eastern Edu & Lib Board **Pop:** 387200 **Cttee:** Lib & Info Cttee **Larger Dept:** South Eastern Edu & Lib Board **Dept Chief:** Chief Exec: Mr J.B. Fitzsimons BSc, MBA, MIPD **Chief:** Chief Libn: Mrs Beth Porter BA(Hons), DipLS, MCLIP (beth.porter@seelb.org.uk) **Other Snr Staff:** Asst Chief Libn (East Svc Unit): Ms Adrienne Adair (adrienne.adair@seelb.org.uk); Asst Chief Libn (West Svc Unit): Mrs Laura Plummer (laura.plummer@seelb.org.uk); Snr Info Libn: Mr Malcolm Buchanan (malcolm.buchanan@ seelb.org.uk); Snr Stock Libn: Ms Geraldine Duffin (geraldine.duffin@seelb.org.uk); Marketing Mgr: Mr Derek Flack (derek.flack@seelb.org.uk); Special Svcs Libn: Mrs Hilary Glenn (hilary. glenn@seelb.org.uk); Snr Youth Libn: Mrs Marie Sloan (marie.sloan@seelb.org.uk); Lib ICT Adviser: Mr Noel Sloan (noel.sloan@seelb.org.uk); Snr Edu Libn: Ms Sandra Stokes (sandra.stokes@ seelb.org.uk); Group Lib Mgr (Down Group): Ms Pamela Cooper (pamela.cooper@seelb.org.uk); Group Lib Mgr (Lisburn Group): Mrs Margaret Bell (margaret.bell@seelb.org.uk); Group Lib Mgr (North Down & Ards Group): Mrs Norma Millar (norma.millar@seelb.org.uk); Group Lib Mgr (Castlereagh Group): Mrs Aileen McVey (aileen. mcvey@seelb.org.uk)
Main (Dist) Libs: BALLYNAHINCH LIB, Main St, Ballynahinch, Co Down, BT24 8DN (028-9756-6442; *fax:* 028-9756-4282); BANGOR LIB, Hamilton Rd, Bangor, Co Down, BT20 4LH (028-9127-0591; *fax:* 028-9146-2744; *email:* bangorlib@ hotmail.com); CREGAGH LIB, 409-413 Cregagh Rd, Belfast, BT6 0LF (028-9040-1365; *fax:* (028-9079-8911; *email:* cregaghlibrary@hotmail.com); DAIRY FARM LIB, Dairy Farm Centre, Unit 17, Stewartstown Rd, Dunmurry, Belfast, BT17 0AW (028-9043-1266; *fax:* 028-9043-1278; *email:* dfarmlib@hotmail.com); DOWNPATRICK LIB, Market St, Downpatrick, Co Down, BT30 6LZ (028-4461-2895; *fax:* 028-4461-9039; *email:*

dptklib@hotmail.com); LISBURN LIB, 29 Railway St, Lisburn, Co Antrim, BT28 1XP (028-9260-1749; *fax:* 028-9260-1239; *email:* lburnlib@hotmail.com); NEWTOWNARDS LIB, Queen's Hall, Regent St, Newtownards, Co Down, BT23 4AB (028-9181-4732; *fax:* 028-9181-0265; *email:* nardslib@ hotmail.com); TULLYCARNET LIB, Kinross Ave, Belfast, BT5 7GF (028-9048-5079; *fax:* 028-9048-2342; *email:* tullycarnetlib@hotmail.com) **Branch Libs:** BELVOIR PK LIB, Drumart Sq, Belfast, BT8 7EY (tel & fax: 028-9064-4331); BRANIEL LIB, Glenn Rd, Belfast, BT5 7JH (tel & fax: 028-9079-7420); CARRYDUFF LIB, Church Rd, Carryduff, Belfast, BT8 3DT (tel & fax: 028-9081-3568); CASTLEWELLAN LIB, Main St, Castlewellan, Co Down, BT31 9DA (tel & fax: 028-4377-8433); COMBER LIB, Newtownards Rd, Comber, Newtownards, Co Down, BT23 5AU (028-9187-2610; *fax:* 028-9187-1759); DONAGHADEE LIB, 5 Killaughey Rd, Donaghadee, Co Down, BT23 0BL (028-9188-2507; *fax:* 028-9188-4625); DUNDONALD LIB, 16 Church Rd, Dundonald, Belfast, BT16 2LN (028-9048-3994; *fax:* 028-9041-9509); DUNMURRY LIB, Upper Dunmurry Ln, Dunmurry, Belfast, BT17 0AA (tel & fax: 028-9062-3007); HOLYWOOD LIB, Sullivan Bldg, 86-88 High St, Holywood, Co Down, BT18 9AE (028-9042-4232; *fax:* 028-9042-4194; *email:* hwoodlib@ hotmail.com); KILLYLEAGH LIB, High St, Killyleagh, Downpatrick, Co Down, BT30 9QF (tel & fax: 028-4482-8407; *email:* kleaghlib@hotmail. com); LAURELHILL COMMUNITY LIB, 22 Laurelhill Rd, Lisburn, Co Antrim, BT28 2UH (tel & fax: 028-9266-4596); MOIRA LIB, Blackwood Rd, Moira, Co Antrim, BT67 0LJ (tel & fax: 028-9261-9330); NEWCASTLE LIB, 141-143 Main St, Newcastle, Co Down, BT33 0AE (028-4372-2710; *fax:* 028-4372-6518; *email:* ncastlib@hotmail.com); NEWTOWNBREDA LIB, Saintfield Rd, Belfast, BT8 7HL (028-9070-1620; *fax:* 028-9070-1780); POLEGLASS LIB, Youth & Lib Centre, Good Shepherd Rd, Poleglass, Belfast, BT17 0PP (tel & fax: 028-9062-9740); PORTAFERRY LIB, 74 High St, Portaferry, Newtownards, Co Down, BT22 1QU (tel & fax: 028-4272-8194); SAINTFIELD LIB, Ballynahinch Rd, Saintfield, Ballynahinch, Co Down, BT24 7AD (tel & fax: 028-9751-0550)
Svc Pts: PT: 1 **Mobile:** 5 **AV:** 31 **Computers:** 31 **Internet:** 31
Collns: IJFR: Hi-Hz; Irish & Local Studies; Health Care Colln **Co-op Schemes:** IJFR **ILLs:** county, natl & internatl **Loans:** bks & audios/3 wks; videos/1 wk; lang courses/3 wks; linguaphone/3 months **Charges:** videos/£1 **Income Gen:** req/30p (under-16s & over-60s exempt), ILLs £4; lost ticket/£2 **Fines:** bks & audios/20p pw (£2 max), ch charged only for ad stock, over 60s exempt; videos/£1 pw (£10 max) **Equip:** m-readers, 27 fax (50p svc charge + 50p per pg, internatl 50p + £1.50 per pg, to receive 50p per message), 29 copiers (A4/10p, A3/20p), 27 clr copiers (A4/75p, A3/£1.50), computers (with internet & CD-ROM, b&w printouts A4/10p, A3/20p, clr A4/40p, A3/80p), rooms for hire (varies) **Disabled:** adaptive tech in all libs by Dec 2002 **Online:** Reuters (staff use only) **Offcr-in-Charge:** Purchasing Offcr SEELB: Mr David Gilmore (david.gilmore@seelb.org.uk)

Stock:	1 Apr 2001
ad lend:	258247
ad ref:	15856
ch:	141576
audios:	26745
videos:	8479
CD-ROMs:	350
periodcls:	490

Issues:	2000-01
ad lend:	1129038
ch:	552583
schools:	421695
instns:	7893
audios:	108310
videos:	33326

Acqs: *2000-01*
bks: 26664
AVs: 2838

Acqs: Source: lib suppl *Offcr-in-Charge:* Snr Stock Libn: Ms Geraldine Duffin (geraldine.duffin@ seelb.org.uk) *Classn:* DDC *Cat: Type:* author, classified, title & keyword access *Medium:* auto *Auto Sys:* Galaxy DS *Svcs: Extramural:* schools, prisons, hosps, old people's homes, housebnd, day centres, play groups *Info:* health *Other:* homework centres, iCON at Bangor Lib (ICT suite) *Activs:* ch's activs, bk sales, temp exhibs, poetry readings, reading groups, writers' groups, talks, author visits *Offcr-in-Charge:* relevant Group Lib Mgr & Mr Derek Flack (Marketing Mgr) *Enqs:* 363373 (2000-01) *Staff: Libns:* 32 *Non-Prof:* 122

Northern Ireland: Western

P136 Western Education and Library Board

Lib HQ, Omagh Lib, 1 Spillars Pl, Omagh, Co Tyrone, Northern Ireland, BT78 1HL (028-8224-4821; *fax:* 028-8224-6716)
Email: omagh_library@welbni.org
Internet: http://www.welbni.org/libraries/homepage.htm

Local Auth: Western Edu & Lib Board *Pop:* 282100 *Cttee:* Lib Cttee *Larger Dept:* Edu & Lib Board *Dept Chief:* Chief Exec: Mr Joseph Martin BA, BD *Chief:* Chief Libn: Ms Helen Osbourn *Other Snr Staff:* Asst Chief Libn (Operational Svcs): Mr Leo Crossey; Asst Chief Libn (Support Svcs): Mrs Rosemary Adams *Main (Divisional) Libs: Fermanagh:* ENNIS-KILLEN LIB, Halls Ln, Enniskillen, Co Fermanagh, BT74 7DR (028-6632-2886; *fax:* 028-6632-4685; *email:* EnniskillenLibrary@ni-libraries.net); *Londonderry:* CENTRAL LIB, 35 Foyle St, Derry, BT48 6AL (028-7127-2300; *fax:* 028-7126-9084; *email:* DerryCentralLibrary@ni-libraries.net); *Tyrone:* OMAGH LIB, addr as above (028-8224-4821; *fax:* 028-8224-6772; *email:* OmaghLibrary@ni-libraries.net) *Branch Libs:* CASTLEDERG LIB, Main St, Castlederg, Co Tyrone, BT81 7AY (*tel & fax:* 028-8167-1419; *email:* CastledergLibrary@ni-libraries.net); CREGGAN LIB, 59 Central Dr, Creggan, Londonderry, BT48 9QH (028-7126-6168; *fax:* 028-7130-8939; *email:* CregganLibrary@ni-libraries.net); DUNGIVEN LIB, 74 Main St, Dungiven, Co Londonderry, BT47 4LD (*tel & fax:* 028-7774-1475; *email:* DungivenLibrary@ni-libraries.net); FINTONA LIB, 112-114 Main St, Fintona, Co Tyrone, BT78 2AE (*tel & fax:* 028-8284-1774; *email:* FintonaLibrary@ni-libraries.net); IRVINES-TOWN LIB, Main St, Irvinestown, Co Fermanagh, BT94 1GT (*tel & fax:* 028-6862-1383; *email:* IrvinestownLibrary@ni-libraries.net); LIMAVADY LIB, 5 Connell St, Limavady, Co Londonderry, BT49 0EA (028-7776-2540; *fax:* 028-7772-2006; *email:* LimavadyLibrary@ni-libraries.net); LISNASKEA LIB, Drumhaw, Lisnaskea, Co Fermanagh, BT92 0GT (*tel & fax:* 028-6772-1222; *email:* LisnaskeaLibrary@ni-libraries.net); NEWTOWNSTEWART LIB, Main St, Newtownstewart, Omagh, Co Tyrone, BT78 9AA (*tel & fax:* 028-8166-1245; *email:* NewtonstewartLibrary@ni-libraries.net); SHANTALLOW LIB, 92 Racecourse Rd, Shantallow, Londonderry, BT48 8DA (028-7135-4148; *fax:* 028-7135-4122; *email:* ShantallowLibrary@ni-libraries.net); SION MILLS LIB, Church Sq, Sion Mills, Strabane, Co Tyrone, BT82 9HD (*tel & fax:* 028-8165-8513; *email:* SionMillsLibrary@ni-libraries.net); STRABANE LIB, Butcher St, Strabane, Co Tyrone, BT82 8BJ (028-7188-3686; *fax:* 028-7138-2745; *email:* StrabaneLibrary@ni-libraries.net); STRATHFOYLE LIB, 22 Temple Rd, Strathfoyle, Londonderry, BT47 6TJ (*tel & fax:* 028-7186-0385; *email:*

StrathfoyleLibrary@ni-libraries.net); WATERSIDE LIB, 23 Glendermott Rd, Waterside, Londonderry, BT47 6BG (028-7134-2963; *fax:* 028-7131-8283; *email:* WatersideLibrary@ni-libraries.net)
Svc Pts: Mobile: 10 *AV:* 16 *Computers:* 16 *Internet:* 16
Collns: William Carleton Colln (works & commentaries, at Omagh Lib); Nawn Colln (Irish & local hist, at Enniskillen Lib); Irish Colln (at Londonderry Lib) *Co-op Schemes:* IJFR (A, F & T) *ILLs:* county, natl & internatl *Loans:* bks/4 wks; audios/2 wks; videos/1 day *Income Gen:* req/40p, ch 10p, addl charge of £2.50 for ILLs *Fines:* bks & audios/ad 20p pw, ch & oap exempt; videos/50p pd; homes, playgroups & registered blind exempt *Equip:* m-reader/printers, fax, copiers (A4/10p, A3/20p), computers (incl internet), scanners, rooms for hire

Stock:	1 Apr 2000	1 Apr 2001
lend:	384053	384761
ref:	61510	57399
AVs:	18144	16375
periodcls:	184	181

Issues:	1999-2000	2000-01
bks:	1236790	1140730
AVs:	37976	37712

Acqs:	1999-2000	2000-01
bks:	25945	12090
AVs:	953	1901

Acqs: Source: lib suppl, publ & bksellers *Classn:* DDC *Cat: Type:* author, classified, subj & title *Medium:* auto *Svcs: Extramural:* schools, prisons, hosps, old people's homes, housebnd, playgroups *Info:* business, community, local hist *Activs:* ch's activs, bk sales, films, temp exhibs, poetry readings, talks, yarnspinning, concerts *Enqs:* 234988 (1999-2000); 198380 (2000-01) *Staff: Libns:* 33 *Non-Prof:* 124

Inc from:	1999-2000	2000-01
fines etc:	£87797	£107762

Exp on:	1999-2000	2000-01
stock:	£344174	£161643
salaries:	£2081591	£2180351
total:	£3113831	£3121154

Northumberland

P137 Northumberland County Libraries

County Lib HQ, Central Lib, The Willows, Morpeth, Northumberland, NE61 1TA (01670-533000; *fax:* 01670-534521)
Email: pmcnabola@northumberland.gov.uk
Internet: http://www.northumberland.gov.uk/

Local Auth: Northumberland County Council *Pop:* 312000 *Larger Dept:* Edu *Dept Chief:* Dir of Edu: Dr K.L. Davies *Chief:* Divisional Dir, Libs, Arts & Heritage: Mr D.E. Bonser BA, MCLIP *Main Libs:* CENTRAL LIB, addr as above; ALNWICK LIB, Green Batt, Alnwick, Northumberland, NE66 1TU (01665-602689; *fax:* 01665-604740); ASHINGTON LIB, Kenilworth Rd, Ashington, Northumberland, NE63 8AA (01670-813245; *fax:* 01670-850500); CRAMLINGTON LIB, Forum Way, Cramlington, Northumberland, NE23 6QD (01670-714371; *fax:* 01670-737624); HEXHAM LIB, Queen's Hall, Beaumont St, Hexham, Northumberland, NE46 3LS (01434-652488; *fax:* 01434-652474) *Branch Libs:* AMBLE LIB, Middleton St, Amble, Morpeth, Northumberland, NE65 0ET (01665-710419); BEDLINGTON LIB, Glebe Rd, Bedlington, Northumberland, NE22 6JX (01670-822056; *fax:* 01670-829620); BEDLINGTON STATION LIB, Station Rd, Bedlington, Northumberland, NE22 5HB (01670-822211); BERWICK LIB, Walkergate, Berwick-upon-Tweed, Northumberland, TD15 1DB (01289-334051; *fax:* 01289-334057); BLYTH LIB, Bridge St, Blyth, Northumberland, NE24 2DJ

(01670-361352; *fax:* 01670-351269); CLEASWELL HILL LIB, The Square, Guide Post, Choppington, Northumberland, NE62 5BZ (01670-822745); HALTWHISTLE LIB, Mechanics' Inst, West Gate, Haltwhistle, Northumberland, NE49 0AX (01434-320462); NEWBIGGIN LIB, Gibson St, Newbiggin-by-the-Sea, Northumberland, NE64 6UZ (01670-818277; *fax:* 01670-857478); PONTELAND LIB, Thornhill Rd, Ponteland, Newcastle upon Tyne, NE20 9PZ (*tel & fax:* 01661-823594); PRUDHOE LIB, Front St, Prudhoe, Northumberland, NE42 5LN (01661-832540; *fax:* 01661-830126); SEATON VALLEY COMMUNITY LIB, Elsdon Ave, Seaton Delaval, Whitley Bay, Tyne & Wear, NE25 0BW (0191-237-1660)
Svc Pts: PT: 19 *Mobile:* 5 *AV:* 38 *Computers:* 35 *Internet:* 35
Collns: JFR (Ell-Ez); Northern Poetry Lib (modern poetry & English poetry database); film & cinema; postcards of Northumberland *Co-op Schemes:* NEMLAC, NCL *ILLs:* county, natl & internatl *Loans:* bks/3 wks; audios/2 wks; videos/varies *Charges:* audios/75p; videos/£1-£2 *Income Gen:* res/80p; lost ticket/£1; postal enq/£8 + VAT *Fines:* bks/ad & oap 8p pd; audios & videos/loan charge *Equip:* 11 m-readers, 3 m-printers (20p per sheet), 13 copiers (20p), 180 computers (all with wd-proc, internet & CD-ROM) *Disabled:* closed caption video players *Online:* COBRA

Stock:	1 Apr 2000	1 Apr 2001
ad lend:	350138	345691
ad ref:	37619	37530
ch:	136129	135646
schools:	233547	214082
audios:	19632	20123
videos:	16831	17008
CD-ROMs:	-	223
periodcls:	169	172

Issues:	1999-2000	2000-01
ad lend:	1923816	1737919
ch:	450396	463296
schools:	132577	-
audios:	253133	78110
videos:	72507	88312

Acqs:	1999-2000	2000-01
bks:	49833	50860
AVs:	8133	7901

Acqs: Source: lib suppl *Offcr-in-Charge:* Principal Lib Offcr: Mr M. Dimelow *Classn:* DDC *Cat: Type:* author & classified *Medium:* auto *Auto Sys:* Geac *Svcs: Extramural:* schools, prisons, play groups *Info:* business, local govt, European, IAC *Activs:* ch's activs, bk sales, temp exhibs, poetry readings, reading groups, author visits *Enqs:* 150821 (1999-2000); 151763 (2000-01) *Staff: Libns:* 20.5 *Other Prof:* 2 *Non-Prof:* 73

Nottingham

P138 Nottingham City Libraries

Central Lib, Angel Row, Nottingham, NG1 6HP (0115-915-2828; *fax:* 0115-950-2850)
Email: cenlib@notlib.demon.co.uk
Internet: http://www.nottinghamcity.gov.uk/

Local Auth: Nottingham City Council *Pop:* 282900 *Cttee:* Cultural & Community Svcs Strategic Board *Larger Dept:* Leisure & Community Svcs *Dept Chief:* Dir: Mr Michael Williams DMS, DMA, MILAM, MIMgt *Chief:* Asst Dir (Museums, Libs & Info Svcs): Mr Brian Ashley *Dep:* Svc Mgr (Community Libs): Ms Christina Dyer; Svc Mgr (Central Lib): Mr John Turner *Main Libs:* CENTRAL LIB, addr as above *Branch Libs:* ASPLEY LIB, 469 Nuthall Rd, Nottingham, NG8 5DD (0115-915-5700; *fax:* 0115-915-5701; *email:* aspley.library@nottinghamcity.gov.uk); BAKERSFIELD LIB, Watson Ave, Nottingham, NG3 7BN (0115-915-0199; *email:* bakersfield.library@nottinghamcity.gov.uk); ☜

(Nottingham City Libs cont)

BASFORD LIB, Vernon Rd, Nottingham, NG6 0AR (0115-915-5797; *email:* basford.library@nottinghamcity.gov.uk); BESTWOOD LIB, 516 Arnold Rd, Nottingham, NG5 5HL (0115-915-5799; *email:* bestwood.library@nottinghamcity.gov.uk); BILBOROUGH LIB, Bracebridge Dr, Nottingham, NG8 4PN (0115-915-5795; *email:* bilborough. library@nottinghamcity.gov.uk); BULWELL LIB, Highbury Vale, Nottingham, NG6 9AE (0115-915-5708; *fax:* 0115-915-5708; *email:* bulwell.library@nottinghamcity.gov.uk); CARLTON RD LIB, Carlton Rd, Nottingham, NG3 2EN (0115-915-1399; *email:* carlton_road.library@nottinghamcity.gov.uk); CLIFTON LIB, Southchurch Dr, Clifton, Nottingham, NG11 8AB (0115-915-2945; *fax:* 0115-915-2948; *email:* clifton.library@nottinghamcity.gov.uk); HYSON GREEN LIB, Gregory Blvd, Nottingham, NG7 6BE (0115-915-2483; *email:* hyson_green.library@nottinghamcity.gov.uk); MEADOWS LIB, Wilford Grove, Nottingham, NG2 2DR (0115-915-9279; *email:* meadows.library@nottinghamcity.gov.uk); RADFORD/LENTON LIB, Lenton Blvd, Nottingham, NG7 2BY (0115-915-1790; *email:* radford_lenton.library@nottinghamcity.gov.uk); ST ANN'S LIB, Robin Hood Chase, Nottingham, NG3 4EZ (0115-915-6941; *email:* st_anns.library@nottinghamcity.gov.uk); SHERWOOD LIB, Spondon St, Nottingham, NG5 4AB (0115-915-1155; *fax:* 0115-915-1166; *email:* sherwood.library@nottinghamcity.gov.uk); SNEINTON LIB, Sneinton Blvd, Nottingham, NG2 4FD (0115-915-1192; *email:* sneinton.library@nottinghamcity.gov.uk); STRELLEY RD LIB, Strelley Rd, Nottingham, NG8 3AP (0115-915-5788; *email:* strelley_road.library@nottinghamcity.gov.uk); TOP VALLEY LIB, Top Valley Dr, Top Valley, Nottingham, NG7 9AZ (0115-915-7504; *email:* top_valley.library@nottinghamcity.gov.uk); WESTERN BLVD LIB, Beechdale Rd, Nottingham, NG8 3LH (0115-915-5749; *email:* western_boulevard.library@nottinghamcity.gov.uk); WOLLATON LIB, Bramcote Ln, Nottingham, NG8 2NA (0115-915-5715; *email:* wollaton.library@nottinghamcity.gov.uk)

Svc Pts: PT: 1 *Mobile:* 1 (based at Aspley Lib) + 1 van for housebnd svc *Other:* LOCAL STUDIES CENTRE, at Central Lib

Collns: D.H. Lawrence Colln; Lord Byron Colln; Alan Sillitoe Colln; Stanley Middleton Colln; Robin Hood Colln; Theatre Colln (all at Local Studies Centre); Parents Colln (at Central Lib) *Co-op Schemes:* EMRLS, Earl, EPIC *ILLs:* natl *Loans:* bks/3 wks; audios, videos, DVDs & CD-ROMs/1 wk; spkn wd & lang courses/6 wks *Charges:* cassettes/40p; CDs/50p-£1.50; spkn wd/70p; lang course/£1; videos/40p-£2.70, public info videos free; DVDs/£1.75-£2.50; CD-ROMs/£1 *Income Gen:* req/80p, BL £1.80; lost ticket/£1.30 *Fines:* all items/ad 10p pd (max £2.80), over-60s & under-16s exempt; disabled, housebnd & asylum seekers exempt from all charges *Equip:* 20 m-readers, 3 m-printers (40p per sheet), 22 copiers (10p), clr copier (A4/£1, A3/£2), fax (£1 to send + 50p per addl sheet), 60 computers (all with wd-proc, internet & CD-ROM, access free, printouts 10p), 10 rooms for hire (varies, free to community groups) *Disabled:* Spectrum reading machine, minicom, induction loops, PCs with adapted keyboards

Stock:	1 Apr 2000	1 Apr 2001
ad lend:	674269	655913
ad ref:	24121	23475
ch:	124643	125836
audios:	40016	50545
videos & DVDs:	8603	10540
CD-ROMs:	764	708
periodcls:	2477	2477

Issues:		2000-01
all items:		2250130

Acqs:		2000-01
bks:		78057
AVs:		10523

Acqs: Co-op: joint purchasing with Nottinghamshire County Council (see **P139**) *Classn:* DDC *Cat: Type:* author & classified *Medium:* auto *Auto Sys:* Sirsi Unicorn *Svcs: Extramural:* schools, prisons, hosps, old people's homes, housebnd *Info:* business, community, internet-based *Other:* Open Learning Centre *Activs:* ch's activs, bk sales, temp exhibs, talks, poetry readings, reading groups, writers' groups *Enqs:* 260416 (1999-2000); 243591 (2000-01) *Staff: Libns:* 42 *Non-Prof:* 105

Nottinghamshire

P139 Nottinghamshire Libraries, Archives and Information

Community Svcs, 4th Floor, County Hall, West Bridgford, Nottingham, NG2 7QP (0115-977-4401; *fax:* 0115-977-2428)
Email: cslibraries@nottscc.gov.uk
Internet: http://www.nottscc.gov.uk/libraries/

Local Auth: Nottinghamshire County Council *Pop:* 750000 *Cttee:* Leisure Cttee *Larger Dept:* Community Svcs *Chief:* Asst Dir (Libs, Archvs & Info) Mr David Lathrope BSc, MCLIP, DMS (david.latrope@nottscc.gov.uk) *Other Snr Staff:* Principal Libs Offcr (Public Svcs, Operations & Quality): Mr Tony Cook; Principal Libs Offcr (Resources & Commissioning): Mr Philip Marshall *Main (Group HQ) Libs:* North Group: RETFORD LIB, Churchgate, Retford, Nottinghamshire, DN22 6PE (01777-708724; *fax:* 01777-710020; *email:* retford.library@nottscc.gov.uk); South Group: BEESTON LIB, Foster Ave, Beeston, Nottingham, NG9 1AE (0115-925-5168; *fax:* 0115-922-0841; *email:* beeston.library@nottscc.gov.uk); East Group: NEWARK LIB, Beaumond Gdns, Baldertongate, Newark-on-Trent, Nottingham-shire, NG24 1UW (01636-703966; *fax:* 01636-610045; *email:* newark.library@nottscc.gov.uk); West Group: MANSFIELD LIB, Four Seasons Centre, Westgate, Mansfield, Nottinghamshire, NG18 1NH (01623-627591; *fax:* 01623-629276; *email:* mansfield.library@nottscc.gov.uk); Central Group: ARNOLD LIB, Front St, Arnold, Nottingham, NG5 7EE (0115-920-2247; *fax:* 0115-967-3378; *email:* arnold.library@nottscc.gov.uk) *Branch Libs:* North Group: BIRCOTES LIB, Scrooby Rd, Bircotes, Doncaster, S Yorkshire, DN11 8AD (01302-742384; *email:* bircotes.library@nottscc.gov.uk); CARLTON-IN-LINDRICK LIB, Long Ln, Carlton-in-Lindrick, Worksop, Nottinghamshire, S81 9AR (01909-732275; *email:* carltoninlindrick.library@nottscc.gov.uk); WORKSOP LIB, Memorial Ave, Worksop, Nottinghamshire, S80 2BP (01909-472408; *fax:* 01909-501611; *email:* worksop.library@nottscc.gov.uk); South Group: BINGHAM LIB, Eaton Pl, Bingham, Nottingham, NG13 8BE (01949-837905; *fax:* 01949-837574; *email:* bingham.library@nottscc.gov.uk); COTGRAVE LIB, Cotgrave Shopping Centre, Cotgrave, Nottingham, NG12 3JQ (0115-989-2578; *email:* cotgrave.library@nottscc.gov.uk); EAST LEAKE LIB, Gotham Rd, East Leake, Loughborough, Leicestershire, LE12 6JG (01509-852349; *email:* eastleake.library@nottscc.gov.uk); KEYWORTH LIB, Church Dr, Keyworth,

Nottingham, NG12 5FF (0115-937-3509; *email:* keyworth.library@nottscc.gov.uk); RADCLIFFE-ON-TRENT LIB, New Rd, Radcliffe-on-Trent, Nottingham, NG12 2AJ (0115-933-2312; *email:* radcliffeontrent.library@nottscc.gov.uk); RUDDINGTON LIB, Church St, Ruddington, Nottingham, NG11 6HD (0115-921-2309; *email:* ruddington.library@nottscc.gov.uk); STAPLE-FORD LIB, Church St, Stapleford, Nottingham, NG9 8GA (0115-939-9178; *fax:* 0115-939-8405; *email:* stapleford.library@nottscc.gov.uk); TOTON LIB, Stapleford Ln, Toton, Nottingham, NG9 6GA (0115-972-6403; *email:* toton.library@nottscc.gov.uk); WEST BRIDGFORD LIB, Bridgford Rd, West Bridgford, Nottingham, NG2 6AT (0115-981-6506/6780; *fax:* 0115-981-3199; *email:* westbridgford.library@nottscc.gov.uk); *East Group:* BALDERTON LIB, Main St, Old Balderton, Newark, Nottinghamshire, NG24 3NP (01636-703930; *email:* balderton.library@nottscc.gov.uk); DUKERIES LIB, Whinney Ln, New Ollerton, Nottinghamshire, NG22 9TD (01623-862363; *fax:* 01623-836082; *email:* dukeries.library@nottscc.gov.uk); EDWINSTONE LIB, High St, Edwinstone, Mansfield, Nottinghamshire, NG21 9QS (01623-822280; *email:* edwinstowe.library@nottscc.gov.uk); OLLERTON LIB, Forest Rd, New Ollerton, Newark, Nottinghamshire, NG22 9PL (01623-860274; *fax:* 01623-861743; *email:* ollerton.library@nottscc.gov.uk); SOUTHWELL LIB, King St, Southwell, Nottinghamshire, NG25 0EN (01636-812148; *email:* southwell.library@nottscc.gov.uk); *West Group:* FOREST TOWN LIB, Clipstone Rd West, Forest Town, Mansfield, Nottinghamshire, NG19 0AA (01623-623395; *email:* foresttown.library@nottscc.gov.uk); KIRKBY-IN-ASHFIELD LIB, Ashfield Precinct, Kirkby-in-Ashfield, Nottinghamshire, NG17 7BQ (01623-753236; *fax:* 01623-759147; *email:* kirkbyinashfield.library@nottscc.gov.uk); LADY-BROOK LIB, Ladybrook Ln, Mansfield, Nottinghamshire, NG18 5JH (01623-622835; *email:* ladybrook.library@nottscc.gov.uk); MANSFIELD WOODHOUSE LIB, Church St, Mansfield Woodhouse, Nottinghamshire, NG19 8AH (01623-621781; *fax:* 01623-621120; *email:* mansfieldwoodhouse.library@nottscc.gov.uk); SELSTON LIB, Chapel Rd, Selston, Nottinghamshire, NG16 6BW (01773-810093; *email:* selston.library@nottscc.gov.uk); SKEGBY LIB, Mansfield Rd, Skegby, Sutton-in-Ashfield, Nottinghamshire, NG17 3EE (01623-554890; *email:* skegby.library@nottscc.gov.uk); SUTTON-IN-ASHFIELD LIB, Idlewells Precinct, Sutton-in-Ashfield, Nottinghamshire, NG17 1BP (01623-556296; *fax:* 01623-551962; *email:* sutton.library@nottscc.gov.uk); WARSOP LIB, High St, Warsop, Mansfield, Nottinghamshire, NG20 0AG (01623-842322; *email:* warsop.library@nottscc.gov.uk); *Central Group:* BLIDWORTH LIB, New Ln, Blidworth, Nottingham, NG21 0PW (01623-793775; *email:* blidworth.library@nottscc.gov.uk); BURTON JOYCE LIB, Meadow Ln, Burton Joyce, Nottingham, NG14 5EX (0115-931-3360; *email:* burtonjoyce.library@nottscc.gov.uk); CALVERTON LIB, St Wilfrid's Sq, Calverton, Nottinghamshire, NG14 6FP (0115-965-2580; *email:* calverton.library@nottscc.gov.uk); CARLTON LIB, Manor Rd, Carlton, Nottingham, NG4 3AY (0115-987-0276; *email:* carlton.library@nottscc.gov.uk); CARLTON HILL LIB, 341 Carlton Hill, Carlton, Nottingham, NG4 1JE (0115-987-3050; *email:* carltonhill.library@nottscc.gov.uk); EASTWOOD LIB, Wellington Pl, Eastwood, Nottingham, NG16 3GB (01773-712209; *fax:* 01773-761355; *email:* eastwood.library@nottscc.gov.uk); HUCKNALL LIB, South St, Hucknall, Nottinghamshire, NG15 7BS (0115-963-2035; *fax:* 0115-964-1476; *email:* hucknall.library@nottscc.gov.uk); KIMBERLEY LIB, Main St, Kimberley, Nottingham, NG16 2LY (0115-938-2322; *email:* kimberley.library@nottscc.gov.uk); MAPPERLEY LIB, 454 Westdale Ln, Mapperley, Nottingham, NG3 6DG (0115-962-1224; *email:* mapperley.library@nottscc.gov.uk);

RAVENSHEAD LIB, Milton Ct, Ravenshead, Nottingham, NG15 9BD (01623-794634; *email:* ravenshead.library@nottscc.gov.uk)
Svc Pts: PT: 20 *Mobile:* 7 *AV:* 59 *Computers:* 60 *Internet:* 60
Collns: D.H. Lawrence Colln (at Eastwood Lib); Eric Coates Colln (at Hucknall Lib); Pilgrim Fathers Colln (at Retford Lib); Arthur Mee Colln (at Stapleford Lib) *ILLs:* county, natl & internatl *Loans:* bks & audios other than CDs/3 wks; CDs, videos & DVDs/1 wk; lang courses/6 wks *Charges:* CDs/premium 85p (sets £1.50), standard 50p (sets £1); cassettes/60p; spkn wd/ 80p, over-60s 30p; records/40p (sets 80p); videos/50p-£2.30, public info free; DVDs/ premium £2.50 (£1.65 conc), standard £1.25 (95p conc); lang courses/£1, over-60s 50p *Income Gen:* res/80p; BL ILLs/£2.20; lost ticket/£1.30 *Fines:* all items/10p pd for 1st wk, then weekly charge rising to £2.80 for 7th wk; ch, oap, registered disabled exempt *Equip:* 14 m-reader/ printers (40p per pg), 18 fax (various charges), 31 copiers (A4/10p, A3/20p), clr copier (A4/£1, A3/ £2), 342 computers (all with wd-proc, internet & CD-ROM, access free, printouts 10p), 17 rooms for hire (various) *Disabled:* minicoms, induction loops, Easy Play cassette players, subtitled videos, signed videos, spkn wd audio bks, audio-described videos, closed caption videos *Offcr-in-Charge:* Operations Offcr: Ms Barbara Johnson (barbara.johnson@nottscc. gov.uk)

Stock:	1 Apr 2001
ad lend:	699084
ad ref:	55930
ch:	300466
audios:	57500
videos:	18047
periodcls:	600

Issues:	2000-01
ad lend:	4469068
ch:	1225887
audios:	330443
videos:	128928

Acqs:	2000-01
bks:	149198
AVs:	16770

Acqs: Offcr-in-Charge: Principal Bibliographical Offcr: Mrs Anne Corin (anne.corin@nottscc. gov.uk)
Cat: Medium: Auto *Auto Sys:* Geac *Svcs: Extramural:* prisons, hosps, old people's homes, housebnd, day centres, play groups *Info:* business *Other:* Open for Learning, Opportunities Database, County Contract *Activs:* ch's activs, bk sales, temp exhibs, poetry readings, reading groups, writers' groups, talks, author visits
Enqs: 530868 (2000-01)
Staff: 305.9 in total
Proj: replacement libs at Southwell & Bingham, starting 2002-04

Oldham

P140 Oldham Library and Information Service

Oldham Lib, Union Street, Oldham, Lancashire, OL1 1DN (0161-911-4643; *fax:* 0161-911-4630)
Email: ecs.reference.lib@oldham.gov.uk
Internet: http://www.oldham.gov.uk/

Local Auth: Oldham Metropolitan Borough Council *Pop:* 218100 *Larger Dept:* Edu & Culture *Chief:* Head of Libs, Info & Archvs: Mr Richard Lambert (ecs.richard.lambert@oldham. gov.uk) *Dep:* Lending Svcs Mgr: Mrs Judith Lamb (ecs.judy.lamb@oldham.gov.uk) *Other Snr Staff:* Info & Support Svcs Mgr: Ms Jane Barkess (ecs.jane.barkess@oldham.gov.uk); Outreach & Inclusion Mgr: Ms Linda Dawson (ecs.linda.dawson@oldham.gov.uk)

Main Libs: OLDHAM LIB, addr as above
Branch Libs: BROADWAY LIB, Whitegate Ln, Chadderton, Oldham, Lancashire, OL9 8LS (0161-624-7866; *email:* ecs.broadway.library@oldham. gov.uk); CHADDERTON LIB, Middleton Rd, Oldham, Lancashire, OL6 9JN (0161-665-2225; *email:* ecs.chadderton.library@oldham.gov.uk); CROMPTON LIB, Farrow St East, Oldham, Lancashire, OL2 8QY (01706-842184; *fax:* 01706-842505; *email:* ecs.crompton.library@oldham. gov.uk); DELPH LIB, Millgate, Delph, Oldham, Lancashire, OL3 5JG (*email:* ecs.delph.library@oldham.gov.uk); FAILSWORTH LIB, Main St, Failsworth, Manchester, M35 9DP (0161-681-2405; *fax:* 0161-688-7828; *email:* ecs.failsworth.library@oldham.gov.uk); FITTON HILL LIB, Fir Tree Ave, Fitton Hill, Oldham, Lancashire, OL8 2QP (0161-633-2011; *email:* ecs.fittonhill.library@oldham.gov.uk); GREEN-FIELD LIB, Chew Vale, Greenfield, Oldham, Lancashire, OL3 7EQ (01457-872472; *email:* ecs.greenfield.library@oldham.gov.uk); LEES LIB, Thomas St, Lees, Oldham, Lancashire, OL4 5DA (0161-633-5764; *email:* ecs.lees.library@oldham. gov.uk); LIMESIDE LIB, Whitebank Rd, Limeside, Oldham, Lancashire, OL8 3JY (0161-624-0351; *email:* ecs.limeside.library@oldham.gov.uk); NORTH-MOOR LIB, Chadderton Way, Oldham, Lancashire, OL9 6DH (0161-633-1168; *email:* ecs.northmoor.library@ oldham.gov.uk); ROYTON LIB, Rochdale Rd, Oldham, Lancashire, OL1 1DN (0161-911-3087; *fax:* 0161-911-3087; *email:* ecs.royton.library@oldham.gov.uk); STONELEIGH LIB, Vulcan St, Derker, Oldham, Lancashire, OL1 4LJ (0161-626-8455; *email:* ecs.stoneleigh.library@oldham.gov.uk); UPPER-MILL LIB, St Chad's, High St, Uppermill, Oldham, Lancashire, OL3 6AP (01457-872777; *email:* ecs.uppermill.library@ oldham.gov.uk)
Svc Pts: Mobile: 1 *AV:* 14 *Computers:* 14 *Internet:* 14 *Other:* SCHOOL LIB SVC, at Fitton Hill Lib; LOCAL STUDIES & ARCHVS (see **A408**)
Co-op Schemes: Libs North West, JFR *ILLs:* county, natl & internatl *Loans:* bks/3 wks; audios/1 wk, jnr cassettes 2 wks; videos & CD-ROMs/1 wk; DVDs/3 days; Open Learning/3 wks *Charges:* spkn wd/50p; music audios/cassettes 50p, CDs 80p; videos/£1.50; DVDs/2.50; CD-ROMs/£2 *Income Gen:* req & res/50p; lost ticket/£1.50 *Fines:* bks/ad 12p pd (£5 max), oap 2p pd (max £1); videos/loan charge; ch exempt *Equip:* m-readers, fax, copiers (A4/10p, A3/20p), clr copier, 100+ computers (all with wd-proc, internet & CD-ROM) *Disabled:* Supernova *Online:* FAME

Stock:	1 Apr 2001
ad lend:	260292
ad ref:	4536
ch:	99917
audios:	21292
videos:	3770
CD-ROMs:	140
periodcls:	197

Issues:	2000-01
ad lend:	1078935
ch:	285349
audios:	55380
videos:	15367
CD-ROMs:	267

Acqs:	2000-01
bks:	49853
AVs:	3480

Acqs: Offcr-in-Charge: Acqs Offcr: Mr John Lenton
Classn: DDC *Cat: Medium:* auto *Auto Sys:* ALS *Svcs: Extramural:* schools, hosps, old people's homes, housebnd *Info:* business, community, careers, edu, health, EU, 2 tourist info centres *Other:* Open Learning, local studies, computer training in Oldham Lib & 6 community libs

Activs: ch's activs, bk sales, temp exhibs, poetry readings, reading groups, writers' groups, talks, author visits
Enqs: 129740 (2000-01)
Staff: Libns: 25 *Non-Prof:* 68.39

Inc from:	1999-2000	2000-01
local govt:	£2355892	£2619248
fines etc:	£177393	£228646
total:	£2533285	£2847894

Exp on:	1999-2000	2000-01
supplies & svcs:	£683028	£707148
salaries:	£1282004	£1351816
total:	£2533285	£2847894

Orkney Islands

P141 Orkney Libraries

The Orkney Lib & Archv, 44 Junction Rd, Kirkwall, Orkney, KW15 1AG (01856-873166; *fax:* 01856-875260)
Email: general.enquiries@orkneylibrary.org.uk
Internet: http://www.orkneylibrary.org.uk

Local Auth: Orkney Islands Council *Pop:* 19500
Larger Dept: Edu & Rec Svcs Directorate
Chief: Chief Libn: Mr Robert Leslie MCLIP (robert.leslie@orkneylibrary.org.uk) *Dep:* Depute Libn: Mrs Karen Walker BA (karen.walker@ orkneylibrary.org.uk) *Other Snr Staff:* Asst Libn: Ms Karen Miller BSc(Econ), PGAG, MCLIP (karen.miller@orkneylibrary.org.uk)
Main Libs: THE ORKNEY LIB, addr as above
Branch Libs: STROMNESS BRANCH LIB, Hellihole Rd, Stromness, Orkney, KW16 3DE (01856-850907)
Svc Pts: Mobile: 2 *AV:* 2 *Computers:* 2 *Internet:* 2
Collns: Orkney Room Colln (local hist, at Orkney Lib) *Co-op Schemes:* SFR *ILLs:* county, natl & internatl *Loans:* bks/4 wks; audio/2 wks *Charges:* audios/60p *Income Gen:* req & res/ free; lost ticket/50p *Equip:* m-readers, m-printer, fax, copier, computers (incl internet), room for hire *Online:* KnowUK, Kompass UK, Newsbank

Stock:	1 Apr 2000	1 Apr 2001
lend:	114444	117897
ref:	3236	3166
audios:	2206	2307
periodcls:	104	107

Issues:	1999-2000	2000-01
bks:	231282	216767
audios:	5800	5967

Acqs:	1999-2000	2000-01
bks:	6634	7041
AVs:	257	327

Acqs: Source: lib suppl, publ & bksellers *Offcr-in-Charge:* Depute Libn, as above
Classn: DDC *Cat: Type:* dictionary *Medium:* auto *Auto Sys:* Talis *Svcs: Extramural:* schools, hosps, old people's homes, housebnd *Other:* Lifelong Learning *Activs:* ch's activs, bk sales, temp exhibs, reading groups, author visits *Offcr-in-Charge:* Asst Libn, as above
Staff: Libns: 6 *Non-Prof:* 9.4

Inc from:	1999-2000	2000-01
local govt:	£514819	£514515
fines etc:	£11701	£10940
total:	£526520	£525455

Exp on:	1999-2000	2000-01
bks:	£81516	£84240
AVs:	£2450	£1326
salaries:	£312032	£316259
total:	£526520	£525455

Oxfordshire

P142 Oxfordshire Library Service

Cultural Svcs, Central Lib, Westgate, Oxford, OX1 1DJ (01865-810191; *fax:* 01865-810187)
Email: andrew.coggins@oxfordshire.gov.uk
Internet: http://www.oxfordshire.gov.uk/

Local Auth: Oxfordshire County Council *Pop:* 632000 *Cttee:* Cultural Svcs Cttee *Larger Dept:* Cultural Svcs *Dept Chief:* Dir: Mr Richard Munro BA, DipLib, MCLIP *Chief:* County Libn: Mr Andrew Coggins MA, MCLIP *Dep:* Asst County Libn: Mr Charles Pettit
Main Libs: CENTRAL LIB, addr as above (01865-815509; *fax:* 01865-721694); ABINGDON LIB, The Charter, Abingdon, Oxfordshire, OX14 3LY (01235-520374; *fax:* 01235-532643); BANBURY LIB, Marlborough Rd, Banbury, Oxfordshire, OX16 5DB (01295-262282; *fax:* 01295-264331); COWLEY LIB, Temple Rd, Cowley, Oxford, OX4 2EZ (01865-777494; *fax:*01865-715102); DIDCOT LIB, Mereland Rd, Didcot, Oxfordshire, OX11 8BU (01235-813103; *fax:* 01235-811935); WITNEY LIB, Welch Way, Witney, Oxfordshire, OX28 6JH (01993-703659; *fax:* 01993-775993) *Branch Libs:* BENSON LIB, Castle Sq, Benson, Oxfordshire, OX10 6SD (01491-838474); BERINSFIELD LIB, Green Furlong, Berinsfield, Oxfordshire, OX10 7NR (01865-340771); BICESTER LIB, Old Place Yard, Bicester, Oxfordshire, OX26 6AU (01869-252181; *fax:* 01869-249658); BLACKBIRD LEYS LIB, Blackbird Leys Rd, Oxford, OX4 6HT (01865-770403); BOTLEY LIB, Elms Ct, Botley, Oxford, OX2 9LP (01865-248142); BURFORD LIB, 82 High St, Burford, Oxfordshire, OX18 4QF (01993-823377); CARTERTON LIB, 6 Alvescot Rd, Carterton, Oxfordshire, OX18 3JH (01993-841492; *fax:* 01993-845254); CHARLBURY LIB, Corner House, Market St, Charlbury, Chipping Norton, Oxfordshire, OX7 3PN (01608-811104); CHINNOR LIB, Station Rd, Chinnor, Oxfordshire, OX39 4PU (01844-351721); CHIPPING NORTON LIB, Goddards Ln, Chipping Norton, Oxfordshire, OX7 5NP (01608-643559); EYNSHAM LIB, 30 Mill St, Eynsham, Oxfordshire, OX29 4JS (01865-880525); FARINGDON LIB, Gloucester St, Faringdon, Oxfordshire, SN7 7HY (*tel & fax:* 01367-240311); GORING LIB, Station Rd, Goring-on-Thames, Oxfordshire, RG8 9ES (*tel & fax:* 01491-873028); GROVE LIB, Millbrook, Grove, Oxfordshire, OX12 7LB (*tel & fax:* 01235-763841); HEADINGTON LIB, Bury Knowle Pk, North Pl, Headington, Oxford, OX3 9HY (01865-762867; *fax:* 01865-308783); HENLEY LIB, Ravenscroft Rd, Henley-on-Thames, Oxfordshire, RG9 2DH (01491-575278; *fax:* 01491-576187); KIDLINGTON LIB, Ron Groves House, 23 Oxford Rd, Kidlington, Oxfordshire, OX5 2BP (01865-373067; *fax:* 01865-379898); NEITHROP LIB, Community Centre, Woodgreen Ave, Banbury, Oxfordshire, OX16 0AT (01295-264815); SONNING COMMON LIB, Grove Rd, Sonning Common, Oxfordshire, RG4 9RH (01189-722448); SUMMERTOWN LIB, South Parade, Oxford, OX2 7JN (01865-558290); THAME LIB, Southern Rd, Thame, Oxfordshire, OX9 2DY (01844-212288); WALLINGFORD LIB, High St, Wallingford, Oxfordshire, OX10 0DB (*tel & fax:* 01491-837395); WANTAGE LIB, Stirlings Rd, Wantage, Oxfordshire, OX12 7BB (01235-762291; *fax:* 01235-770951); WATLINGTON LIB, 35 High St, Watlington, Oxfordshire, OX49 5PZ

(01491-612241); WHEATLEY LIB, High St, Wheatley, Oxfordshire, OX33 1XP (01865-875267); WOODSTOCK LIB, Hensington Rd, Woodstock, Oxfordshire, OX20 1JQ (01993-812832)
Svc Pts: PT: 11 *Mobile:* 7 *AV:* 43 *Computers:* 43 *Internet:* 43
Collns: Centre for Oxfordshire Studies Colln (local & family hist); Business Info Pt (both at Central Lib) *Co-op Schemes:* SWRLS *ILLs:* county, natl & internatl *Loans:* bks & lang audios/3 wks; audios & videos/1 wk *Charges:* audios/50p-£2, spkn wd free to visually impaired; videos/£1-£3; CD-ROMs/£2.50 *Income Gen:* res/bks £1 (conc 50p), £2.50 outside South West region (conc £1.25), audios, videos & CD-ROMs £1.20 (conc 60p); lost tickets/£2; conc available for under 18s, chronically sick & disabled *Fines:* bks/ad 10p pd 1st wk, 2nd wk £1, then 40p pw (£4.60 max), under 18s 5p pd 1st wk, 2nd wk 50p, then 20p pw (£2.30 max), housebnd, chronically sick & disabled exempt; audios, videos & CD-ROMs/loan charge *Equip:* m-readers, m-printers, copiers (A4/10p, A3 20p), fax, computers (incl internet & CD-ROM) *Disabled:* minicom, screen magnifiers, magnifying sheets

Stock:	1 Apr 2000	1 Apr 2001
ad lend:	465914	449486
ad ref:	106748	109869
ch:	181618	180882
audios:	36879	35307
videos:	34392	35312
CD-ROMs:	444	932
periodcls:	695	710

Issues:	1999-2000	2000-01
ad lend:	2884270	2695759
ch:	1065073	1010315
audios:	190638	188452
videos:	299018	290709

Acqs:	1999-2000	2000-01
bks:	97192	97345
AVs:	18186	21497

Acqs: Source: lib suppl *Co-op:* CBC
Classn: DDC *Cat: Type:* author, classified & title *Medium:* auto *Auto Sys:* DS *Svcs: Extramural:* prisons, old people's homes, housebnd *Info:* business, community, council, European, legal, edu *Other:* Lifelong Learning *Activs:* ch's activs, bk sales, temp exhibs, poetry readings, talks, author visits
Enqs: 478616 (1999-2000); 442068 (2000-01)
Staff: 200.95 in total

Inc from:	1999-2000	2000-01
local govt:	£5850000	£6064000
fines etc:	£857000	£921000
total:	£6879000	£7138000

Exp on:	1999-2000	2000-01
stock & svcs:	£1524000	£1630000
salaries:	£3366000	£3619000
total:	£6879000	£7138000

Pembrokeshire

P143 Pembrokeshire Libraries

County Lib, Dew Street, Haverfordwest, Pembrokeshire, SA61 1SU (01437-762070; *fax:* 01437-769218)
Email: sandra.matthews@pembrokeshire.gov.uk
Internet: http://www.pembrokeshire.gov.uk/Libraries/

Local Auth: Pembrokeshire County Council *Pop:* 114500 *Cttee:* Cultural Svcs Sub-Cttee of Leisure & Development Cttee *Larger Dept:* Support & Cultural Svcs *Dept Chief:* Dir: Mr Huw James *Chief:* Head of Info & Cultural Svcs: Mr Neil Bennett BSc, MCLIP (neil.bennett@pembrokeshire.gov.uk) *Dep:* Group Libn (Central Svcs): Mrs Sandra Matthews MCLIP (sandra.matthews@pembrokeshire.gov.uk) *Other Snr Staff:* Group Libn (Northern): Mrs Anita Thomas MCLIP (anita.thomas@pembrokeshire.gov.uk);

Group Libn (Eastern): Mrs Eleri Evans; Group Libn (Haven): Mr Clive Richards MCLIP (clive.richards@pembrokeshire.gov.uk)
Main Libs: COUNTY LIB, addr as above
Branch Libs: FISHGUARD LIB, High St, Fishguard, Pembrokeshire, SA65 9AR (01348-872694); HAVERFORDWEST LIB, Dew St, Haverfordwest, Pembrokeshire, SA61 1SU (01437-762070); MILFORD HAVEN LIB, Hamilton Ter, Milford Haven, Pembrokeshire, SA73 3JP (01646-692892); PEMBROKE LIB, 38 Main St, Pembroke, SA71 4NP (01646-682973); PEMBROKE DOCK LIB, Water St, Pembroke, SA72 6DW (01646-686356); TENBY LIB, Greenhill House, Tenby, Pembrokeshire, SA70 7LB (01834-843934)
Svc Pts: PT: 9 *Mobile:* 3 *AV:* 14 *Computers:* 5 *Internet:* 5
Collns: Francis Green Colln (genealogy of Cardiganshire, Carmarthenshire & Pembrokeshire, 35 vols, some pedigree sheets), at Haverfordwest Lib *ILLs:* county, natl & internatl *Loans:* bks & audios/3 wks; videos/1 wk *Charges:* various charges for audios & videos; rsrch fees/£5 per hr *Income Gen:* lost tickets/£1; local hist postal rsrch fee/£12 *Fines:* bks/ad & oap 10p pd (max £5), ch 5p pd (max £1); audios/10p pd; videos/loan charge *Equip:* 4 m-readers, copiers (A4/10p, A3 20p), 2 fax (£1 UK, £2 elsewhere), 2 rooms for hire (various), 7 computers (all with wd-proc & CD-ROM, 6 with internet)

Stock:	1 Apr 2000	1 Apr 2001
lend:	171946	170922
ref:	28033	30925
audios:	6915	6951
videos:	3433	3234
periodcls:	52	49

Issues:	1999-2000	2000-01
bks:	901743	900336
audios:	13197	12399
videos:	10311	10074

Acqs:	1999-2000	2000-01
bks:	19540	20869
AVs:	680	676

Acqs: Source: lib suppl & publ *Offcr-in-Charge:* Group Libn (Central Svcs), as above
Classn: DDC *Cat: Type:* author *Medium:* cards & auto *Auto Sys:* Genesis *Svcs: Extramural:* schools, old people's homes *Info:* Genl Ref (incl business), Local Studies (incl community) *Activs:* ch's activs, bk sales, temp exhibs, talks *Offcr-in-Charge:* Group Libn (Central Svcs), as above
Enqs: 67496 (1999-2000)
Staff: Libns: 9 *Non-Prof:* 22.92

Inc from:	1999-2000
fines etc:	£67000

Exp on:	1999-2000
bks:	£202000
AVs:	£8000
salaries:	£591000
total:	£801000

Perth and Kinross

P144 Perth and Kinross Libraries

A.K. Bell Lib, 2-8 York Pl, Perth, PH2 8EP (01738-444949; *fax:* 01738-477010)
Email: library@pkc.gov.uk
Internet: http://www.pkc.gov.uk/library/

Local Auth: Perth & Kinross Council *Pop:* 134950 *Cttee:* Edu & Ch's Svcs Cttee *Larger Dept:* Edu & Ch's Svcs *Dept Chief:* Dir: Mr Bill Frew *Chief:* Head of Libs & Archvs: Mr Mark Moir BA, MCLIP (mmoir@pkc.gov.uk) *Dep:* Principal Libn: Mr Ian MacRae BA, MCLIP (imr@pkc.gov.uk)
Main Libs: A.K. BELL LIB, addr as above
Branch Libs: AUCHTERARDER LIB, Aytoun Hall, Chapel Wynd, Auchterarder, Perthshire, PH3

1BL (*tel & fax:* 01764-663850); BLAIRGOWRIE LIB, 46 Leslie St, Blairgowrie, Perthshire, PH10 6AW (*tel & fax:* 01250-872905); CRIEFF LIB, 6 Comrie St, Crieff, Perthshire, PH7 4AX (01764-653418; *fax:* 01764-653418); KINROSS LIB, County Bldgs, High St, Kinross, K13 7DA (01577-864202); SCONE LIB, Sandy Rd, Scone, Perth, PH2 6LJ (01738-553029; *fax:* 01738-553029); WEST MILL ST LIB, West Mill St, Perth, PH1 5QP (01738-638436)
Svc Pts: PT: 7 *Mobile:* 3 *AV:* 13 *Other:* 3 hosps, 24 old people's homes, 3 prisons
Collns: MacKintosh Colln (17C lib); Soutar Lib (William Soutar's personal lib, mostly lit); Atholl Colln (music) *Co-op Schemes:* V3 (inter-lib loans) *Loans:* bks/3 wks; audios, videos & CD-ROMs/1 wk *Charges:* cassettes/50p; CDs/80p; videos/£1.30, ch's 50p; DVDs/£2.50; CD-ROMs/£2; Playstation games/£3.50 *Income Gen:* req/50p; lost ticket/ad £2.50, ch exempt *Fines:* bks/ad & oap 10p pd, ch exempt; CDs/15p pd; cassettes/10p pd; videos/25p pd; DVDs/50p pd; CD-ROMs/40p pd; Playstation games/£1 pd *Equip:* m-reader (£1 per hr for non-residents), m-printer (A4/50p, A3/£1), fax (£1 per pg), 11 copiers (A4/10p, A3/30p), 2 clr copiers (A4/75p, A3/£1), computers (incl wd-procs, CD-ROM & 68 with internet, access free), CD-ROM reader, room for hire (charges on request)

Stock:	1 Apr 2000	1 Apr 2001
lend:	354385	-
ref:	52564	64000
AVs:	30528	-
periodcls:	108	-

Issues:	1999-2000	2000-01
bks:	1307000	1207512
AVs:	74949	-

Acqs: Source: lib suppl *Offcr-in-Charge:* Head of Libs & Archvs, as above
Classn: DDC *Cat: Medium:* auto *Auto Sys:* Talis *Svcs: Extramural:* schools, prisons, hosps, old people's homes, housebnd *Activs:* ch's activs, bk sales, temp exhibs, poetry readings, author visits, tape/slide presentations, annual festival *Enqs:* 85876 (1999-2000)
Staff: Libns: 16 *Non-Prof:* 43.5

Inc from:	1999-2000
fines etc:	£338000

Exp on:	1999-2000
bks:	£291000
AVs:	£21500

Peterborough

P145 Peterborough Libraries

Central Lib, Broadway, Peterborough, Cambridgeshire, PE1 1RX (01733-742700; *fax:* 01733-319140)
Email: libraryenquiries@peterborough.gov.uk
Internet: http://www.peterborough.gov.uk/subsites/libraries/

Local Auth: Peterborough City Council *Pop:* 156500 *Cttee:* Wellbeing Panel *Larger Dept:* Community Svcs Dept *Dept Chief:* Dir of Community Svcs: Ms Shelagh Grant *Chief:* Lib & Heritage Svcs Mgr: Ms Veronica Wellington (veronica.wellington@peterborough.gov.uk) *Other Snr Staff:* Reader Svcs Mgr: Ms Heather Walton (heather.walton@peterborough.gov.uk); Snr Lib Mgr: Ms Jane Brown (jane.brown@peterborough.gov.uk); Inclusion & Learning Mgr: Ms Barbara Lofthouse (barbara.lofthouse@peterborough.gov.uk); Enquiry Svcs Mgr: Ms Helen Sherley (helen.sherley@peterborough.gov.uk)
Main Libs: PETERBOROUGH CENTRAL LIB, addr as above; *Dist Libs:* BRETTON LIB, Bretton Centre, Bretton, Peter-borough, Cambridgeshire, PE3 8DS (01733-265519; *fax:* 01733-260417); ORTON LIB, Orton Centre, Orton, Peterborough, Cambridgeshire, PE2 5RQ (01733-234438; *fax:*

01733-361242); WERRINGTON LIB, Staniland Way, Werrington, Peterborough, Cambridgeshire, PE4 6JT (01733-576666; *fax:* 01733-324438)
Branch Libs: DOGSTHORPE LIB, Central Ave, Dogsthorpe, Peterborough, Cambridgeshire, PE1 4LH (*tel & fax:* 01733-565257); EYE LIB, Crowland Rd, Eye, Peterborough, Cambridgeshire, PE6 7IN (*tel & fax:* 01733-222531); STANGROUND LIB, Southfields Ave, Peterborough, Cambridge-shire, PE2 8RZ (*tel & fax:* 01733-568538); THORNEY LIB, Church St, Thorney, Peter-borough, Cambridgeshire, PE6 0QB (*tel & fax:* 01733-270395); WOODSTON LIB, Orchard St, Peterborough, Cambridgeshire, PE2 9AL (*tel & fax:* 01733-562258)
Svc Pts: Mobile: 2 *AV:* 9 *Computers:* 9 *Internet:* 9 *Other:* Librarylink to housebnd
Collns: local studies *Co-op Schemes:* Co-East, EMRLS, JFR, READEast, ELIPP, some joint arrangements with Cambridgeshire Libs (see **P23**) *ILLs:* county & natl *Loans:* bks, spkn wd & CD-ROMs/3 wks; music audios, videos & DVDs/1 wk *Charges:* spkn wd/cassettes 50p, CDs 90p, set of 5+ £2.50; music cassettes/40p, set of 3+ £1.20; music CDs/90p, set of 3+ £2.50; videos/£1.20-£2.20; DVDs/£2.50; CD-ROMs/£2.50, set of 2+ £6 *Income Gen:* req/£1; lost ticket/ad £1.50, jnr £1, 1st replacement free *Fines:* bks/ad 15p pd (max £5), ch 5p pd (max £1.50); spkn wd/cassettes 15p pd (max £7.20), CDs 30p pd (max £12.60); music audios/15p pd, sets 45p pd (max £5 cassettes, £9 CDs); videos/10p-40p pd depending on type (max £24); DVDs/40p pd (max £12); CD-ROMs/50p pd, sets £1 pd (max £12); housebnd, print disabled, over-60s exempt *Equip:* 5 m-readers, 4 m-printers (A4/20p, A3/40p), 9 fax (UK £1 per pg, higher overseas, 20p per pg to receive), 10 copiers (A4/10p, A3/20p), clr copier (A4/£1, A3/£1.50), 138 computers (all with wd-proc & internet) *Disabled:* hearing loop, Ability Net *Offcr-in-Charge:* Lib & Heritage Svcs Mgr, as above

Stock:	1 Apr 2000	1 Apr 2001
ad lend:	147806	126284
ad ref:	33540	47345
ch:	63069	60296
audios:	12444	19067
videos:	6491	5974
CD-ROMs:	545	455
periodcls:	497	351

Issues:	1999-2000	2000-01
ad lend:	905383	881437
ch:	315899	279193
audios:	82528	80952
videos:	35890	34999
CD-ROMs:	3444	1244

Acqs:	1999-2000	2000-01
bks:	21010	11878
AVs:	4413	2423

Acqs: Source: lib suppl & bksellers *Co-op:* consortium agreement with Cambridgeshire Libs *Offcr-in-Charge:* Reader Svcs Mgr, as above
Classn: DDC *Cat: Type:* author, classified, subj & title *Medium:* auto *Auto Sys:* Dynix *Svcs: Extramural:* housebnd, old people's homes, play groups *Info:* community, business, EU, careers, local studies, family hist *Other:* Open Learning *Activs:* ch's activs, bk sales, reading groups, Peterborough Film Soc weekly meetings at Central Lib *Offcr-in-Charge:* Reader Svcs Team *Enqs:* 1011081 (1999-2000); 1203109 (2000-01)
Staff: Libns: 11.5 *Non-Prof:* 50

Inc from:	1999-2000	2000-01
local govt:	£2208443	£1957793
fines etc:	£409686	£370873
total:	£2618129	£2328666

Exp on:	1999-2000	2000-01
bks:	£230947	£164365
AVs:	£38565	£30253
elec media:	£12828	£3652
salaries:	£1148789	£1234731
total:	£2618129	£2328666

Plymouth

P146 City of Plymouth Library and Information Services

Plymouth Central Lib, Drake Circus, Plymouth, Devon, PL4 8AL (01752-305923; *fax:* 01752-305976)
Email: library@plymouth.gov.uk
Internet: http://www.plymouthlibraries.info/

Local Auth: Plymouth City Council *Pop:* 256000 *Larger Dept:* Lifelong Learning *Chief:* City Libn: Mr Alasdair MacNaughtan *Other Snr Staff:* Public Svcs Libn: Mr Brian Holgate
Main Libs: PLYMOUTH CENTRAL LIB, addr as above; REF LIB, at Central Lib (01752-305907/8; *fax:* 01752-305905; *email:* ref@plymouth.gov.uk)
Branch Libs: CROWNHILL LIB, Cross Park Rd, Plymouth, Devon, PL6 5AN (01752-306248; *fax:* 01752-306252; *email:* Crownhill.Library@plymouth. gov.uk); EFFORD LIB, Efford Ln, Efford, Plymouth, Devon, PL3 6LT (*tel & fax:* 01752-773100; *email:* Efford.Library@plymouth.gov.uk); NORTH PROSPECT LIB, Wolseley Rd, Plymouth, Devon, PL2 3JQ (*tel & fax:* 01752-556778; *email:* NorthProspect.Library@plymouth. gov.uk); PEVERELL LIB, 242a Peverell Pk Rd, Peverell, Plymouth, Devon, PL3 4QF (*tel & fax:* 01752-706326; *email:* peverell.library@plymouth.gov.uk); PLYMPTON LIB, Harewood House, Plympton, Plymouth, Devon, PL7 2AS (01752-337867; *fax:* 01752-335247; *email:* plympton.library@plymouth. gov.uk); PLYMSTOCK LIB, Horn Cross Rd, Plymstock, Plymouth, Devon, PL9 9BU (01752-306606; *fax:* 01752-306608; *email:* plymstock. library@plymouth.gov.uk); ST BUDEAUX LIB, The Square, Victoria Rd, Plymouth, Devon, PL5 1RQ (01752-306237; *fax:* 01752-306238; *email:* stbudeaux.library@plymouth.gov.uk); SOUTH-WAY LIB, 351 Southway Dr, Plymouth, Devon, PL6 6QR (01752-776213; *fax:* 01752-795246; *email:* southway.library@plymouth.gov.uk); STOKE LIB, 21 Albert Rd, Plymouth, Devon, PL2 1AB (*tel & fax:* 01752-306239; *email:* Stoke. Library@plymouth.gov.uk); TOTHILL LIB, Tothill Community Centre, Knighton Rd, St Judes, Plymouth, Devon, PL4 9DA (*tel & fax:* 01752-667427; *email:* Tothill.Library@plymouth.gov.uk); WOODLAND FORT LIB, Crownhill Rd, Honick-nowle, Plymouth, Devon, PL5 3SQ (*tel & fax:* 01752-306241; *email:* WoodlandFort.Library@ plymouth.gov.uk)
Svc Pts: PT: 5 *Mobile:* 1 *AV:* 17 *Computers:* 16 *Internet:* 16 *Other:* CH'S LIB, at Central Lib (01752-305916; *fax:* 01752-305923; *email:* Childrens.Library@plymouth.gov.uk); MUSIC & DRAMA LIB, at Central Lib (*tel & fax:* 01752-305914; *email:* music@plymouth.gov.uk); LOCAL & NAVAL STUDIES LIB, at Central Lib (see **A420**); SCHOOLS LIB CENTRE, Chaucer Way, Manadon, Plymouth (01752-780713; *fax:* 01752-767623; *email:* sls@plymouth.gov.uk)
Collns: Naval Studies Colln; Devon & Cornwall Colln (local studies); Holcenburg Colln (Judaism, c1000 vols); Moxon Colln (rare travel & ornithology bks); Chinese Colln (bks in Cantonese); Foreign Lang Colln; Careers Colln; Illusts Colln *Co-op Schemes:* SWRLS, Learning Through Libs in Plymouth *ILLs:* county, natl & internatl *Loans:* bks/3 wks; audios, videos & DVDs/1 wk; lang courses/1 wk or 6 wks; music sets & play sets/2 months *Charges:* audios/75p, £1.20 for sets of 3+ items; lang courses/60p-£1.40 for 1 wk, special courses £8.40 for 6 wks; videos/£1.75, ch's 50p, info videos free; DVDs/£2; music sets/£1.50-£2 per 2 months; playsets/1st 2 months free, £1.50 per 2 months thereafter *Income Gen:* req/ad bks £1, conc 60p, ch's bks 25p; lost tickets/ad £1.50, conc 75p *Fines:* bks/ad 11p pd (max £4.50), oap 6p pd (max £2.50), conc 3p pd (max £1.20); audios, lang courses, videos & DVDs/loan charge; conc available to under-18s, over-65s & registered disabled ☛

(City of Plymouth Lib & Info Svcs cont)
Equip: m-readers, m-printers, copiers (A4/10p, A3/20p), clr copiers (A4/£1, A3/£1.50), scanners (£1 per image), fax (UK £1.25 per pg, higher overseas, 75p per pg to receive), computers (incl internet & CD-ROM), room for hire *Disabled:* CCTV *Online:* PLANet (Plymouth Libs Auto Network), database of local clubs & socs

Stock:	1 Apr 2000	1 Apr 2001
lend:	341397	357807
ref:	73969	74845
audios:	16318	16987
videos:	3924	4203
periodcls:	248	248

Issues:	1999-2000	2000-01
bks:	1827074	1612293
audios:	65733	76391
videos:	22321	21556

Acqs:	1999-2000	2000-01
bks:	35995	42815
AVs:	2851	4766

Acqs: Source: lib suppl, publ & bksellers *Co-op:* CUSP
Classn: DDC *Cat: Type:* author, classified, subj & title *Medium:* auto *Auto Sys:* DS Galaxy 2000 *Svcs: Extramural:* old people's homes, housebnd *Info:* community, business, legal, European, edu, employment, careers, tourist *Other:* Training Access Pts, local studies, Open Learning *Activs:* ch's activs, bk sales, temp exhibs, reading groups, art classes
Enqs: 203792 (1999-2000); 190192 (2000-01)
Staff: 100.28 in total

Inc from:	1999-2000	2000-01
local govt:	£2369353	£2294519
fines etc:	£157253	£173107
total:	£2633051	£2583992

Exp on:	1999-2000	2000-01
bks:	£394840	£458577
salaries:	£1709612	£1697290
total:	£2633051	£2583992

Poole

P147 Poole Libraries

Culture & Community Learning, Central Lib, Dolphin Centre, Poole, Dorset, BH15 1QE (01202-262440)
Email: centrallibrary@poole.gov.uk
Internet: http://www.poole.gov.uk/

Local Auth: Borough & County of the Town of Poole *Pop:* 140950 *Larger Dept:* Culture & Community Learning *Dept Chief:* Head of Culture & Community Learning: Ms Claire Chidley *Chief:* Lib Svc Mgr: Ms Fiona Williams (f.williams@poole.gov.uk) *Other Snr Staff:* Resources Offcr: Ms Gill Stockley (g.stockley@poole.gov.uk)
Main Libs: POOLE CENTRAL LIB, addr as above (01202-262421/4; *fax:* 01202-670253)
Branch Libs: BRANKSOME LIB, Ashley Rd, Branksome, Poole, Dorset, BH12 2BD (01202-748832; *fax:* 01202-744135; *email:* branksomelibrary@poole.gov.uk); BROADSTONE LIB, 10 Story Ln, Broadstone, Poole, Dorset, BH18 5EQ (01202-693504; *fax:* 01202-690537; *email:* broadstonelibrary@poole.gov.uk); CANFORD CLIFFS LIB, Western Rd, Canford Cliffs, Poole, Dorset, BH13 7BN (01202-707805; *fax:*

01202-709975; *email:* canfordcliffslibrary@poole.gov.uk); Canford Heath, Mitchell Rd, Canford Heath, Poole, Dorset, BH17 8UE (01202-678955; *fax:* 01202-669845; *email:* canfordheathlibrary@poole.gov.uk); CREEKMOOR LIB, 34 Northmead Dr, Creekmoor, Poole, Dorset, BH17 7XZ (01202-659289; *fax:* 01202-691256; *email:* creekmoorlibrary@poole.gov.uk); HAMWORTHY LIB, Blandford Rd, Hamworthy, Poole, Dorset, BH15 4BG (01202-672750; *fax:* 01202-669850; *email:* hamworthylibrary@poole.gov.uk); OAKDALE LIB, Wimborne Rd, Poole, Dorset, BH15 3EF (01202-674213; *fax:* 01202-669856; *email:* oakdalelibrary@poole.gov.uk); PARKSTONE LIB, Britannia Rd, Parkstone, Poole, Dorset, BH14 8AZ (01202-742218; *fax:* 01202-739862; *email:* parkstonelibrary@poole.gov.uk); ROSSMORE LIB, Herbert Ave, Parkstone, Poole, Dorset, BH12 4HU (01202-746023; *fax:* 01202-739956; *email:* rossmorelibrary@poole.gov.uk)
Svc Pts: Mobile: 1 *Computers:* 10 *Internet:* 10 *Other:* HOUSEBND SVC (01202-261660)
Collns: Healthpoint (health info, jointly funded with Dorset Health Authority); Local Studies Colln (both at Poole Lib) *Co-op Schemes:* SWRLS, CUSP *ILLs:* county & natl *Loans:* bks/3 wks; audios & videos/1 wk *Charges:* CDs/85p; videos & DVDs/£2.50; Playstation games/£3.50
Income Gen: res/fiction 75p, non-fiction free; lost ticket/£1.50; various charges for lost or damaged materials *Fines:* bks/ad 30p 1st wk, then 60p pw (max £6.90), ch 10p per item (max £1); audios & videos/loan charge; housebnd & disabled exempt (discretionary) *Equip:* m-readers, m-printer, fax (UK £1 1st pg, 50p addl, higher overseas, to receive £1 for any number of pages), copiers (A4/10p, A3/20p), computers (incl wd-proc, internet & CD-ROM), rooms for hire *Disabled:* closed-caption video readers

Stock:	1 Apr 2000	1 Apr 2001
lend:	163229	206096
ref:	59798	12738
AVs:	12986	14231
periodcls:	211	238

Issues:	1999-2000	2000-01
bks:	1173300	1102517
AVs:	81732	88575

Acqs:	1999-2000	2000-01
bks:	22639	19636
AVs:	4405	3130

Acqs: Source: lib suppl *Co-op:* joint purchase of music sets with Dorset (see **P39**) & Bournemouth (see **P13**) *Offcr-in-Charge:* Resources Offcr: Ms Gill Stockley (g.stockley@poole.gov.uk)
Classn: DDC *Cat: Type:* author, classified & subj *Medium:* m-form & auto *Auto Sys:* Talis *Svcs: Extramural:* old people's homes, housebnd *Info:* community, business, European, travel, edu, careers, legal, health *Activs:* ch's activs, poetry readings
Enqs: 101907 (1999-2000); 97032 (2000-01)
Staff: Libns: 17 *Non-Prof:* 39.7

Inc from:	1999-2000	2000-01
local govt:	£1986000	£1966000
fines etc:	£211000	£240000
total:	£2197000	£2206000

Exp on:	1999-2000	2000-01
stock & svcs:	£407000	£385000
salaries:	£986000	£1032000
total:	£2197000	£2206000

Portsmouth

P148 Portsmouth City Library Service

Central Lib, Guildhall Sq, Portsmouth, Hampshire, PO1 2DX (023-9281-9311; *fax:* 023-9283-9855)
Email: admin.library@portsmouthcc.gov.uk
Internet: http://www.portsmouthcc.gov.uk/library.htm

Local Auth: Portsmouth City Council *Pop:* 188700 *Cttee:* Cultural & Heritage Cttee *Larger Dept:* Leisure Svcs *Dept Chief:* Head of Leisure Svcs: Mr David Knight *Chief:* City Libn: vacant *Dep:* Principal Asst City Libn: Mr Colin Brown MCLIP *Other Snr Staff:* Asst City Libn (Bibliographic Svcs): Mr E. Ryan MA, MCLIP; Asst City Libn (Central Lib): Ms J. Painting MCLIP; Asst City Libn (Ch's Svcs): Mrs L. Elliott BA(Hons), MCLIP
Main Libs: CENTRAL LIB, as above (*email:* reference.library@portsmouthcc.gov.uk or lending.library@portsmouthcc.gov.uk) *Branch Libs:* ALBERMAN LACEY LIB, Tangier Rd, Copnor, Portsmouth, Hampshire, PO3 6HU (023-9282-3991; *email:* alderman.library@portsmouthcc.gov.uk); BEDDOW LIB, 180 Milton Rd, Milton, Portsmouth, Hampshire, PO4 8PR (023-9273-1848; *email:* beddow.library@portsmouthcc.gov.uk); CARNEGIE LIB, Fratton Rd, Fratton, Portsmouth, Hampshire, PO1 5EZ (023-9282-2581; *fax:* 023-9273-9244; *email:* carnegie.library@portsmouthcc.gov.uk); COSHAM LIB, Spur Rd, Cosham, Portsmouth, Hampshire, PO6 3ED (023-9237-6023; *fax:* 023-9237-1877; *email:* cosham.library@portsmouthcc.gov.uk); ELM GROVE LIB, Elm Grove, Southsea, Portsmouth, Hampshire, PO5 1LJ (023-9282-6058; *email:* elmgrove.library@portsmouthcc.gov.uk); NORTH END LIB, Gladys Ave, North End, Portsmouth, Hampshire, PO2 9AX (023-9266-2651; *fax:* 023-9266-8151; *email:* northend.library@portsmouthcc.gov.uk); PAULSGROVE LIB, Marsden Rd, Paulsgrove, Portsmouth, Hampshire, PO6 4JB (023-9237-7818; *email:* paulsgrove.library@portsmouthcc.gov.uk); PORTSEA LIB, St James St, Portsea, Portsmouth, Hampshire, PO1 3AP (023-9229-7072; *email:* johnpounds.library@portsmouthcc.gov.uk)
Svc Pts: Mobile: 2 *AV:* 9 *Internet:* 9
Collns: BSI; Patents (PIN); naval colln; genealogical colln; local studies colln; Reminiscence Colln; Dickens Colln (all at Central Lib) *Co-op Schemes:* HATRICS, PIN, DS User Group *ILLs:* county, natl & internatl *Loans:* bks, audios & info videos/4 wks; popular videos, DVDs, CD-ROMs & Playstation games/1 wk *Charges:* cassettes/40p; CDs/£1.20; videos/£1-£3; CD-ROMs/£1-£2.50; DVDs & Playstation games/£3 *Income Gen:* res/30p if in stock, 70p if not in stock; lost ticket/ad £1.50, under 18s 50p *Fines:* bks, audios & info videos/ad 10p pd 1st wk, then approx 40p pw from 2nd wk onwards (incl initial fine), 11-17s pay 50%; popular videos, DVDs, CD-ROMs & Playstation games/loan charge; under 11s exempt from fines *Equip:* 11 m-readers, m-reader/printer (A4/30p, A3/60p), 4 fax (UK £1 per pg, £1.50 overseas), 10 copiers (A4/10p, A3/20p), clr copier (A4/£1, A3/£1.50), 37 computers (all with internet, 6 with CD-ROM), 6 rooms for hire (varies) *Disabled:* Kurzweil, TV magnifier *Online:* Dialog, Dialtech, BLAISE, FT Profile (cost recovery) *Offcr-in-Charge:* Admin Offcr: Mrs Sue Main (smain@portsmouthcc.gov.uk)

Stock:	1 Apr 2000	1 Apr 2001
ad lend:	211873	216300
ad ref:	112227	113700
ch:	56893	61025
schools:	92304	94178
audios:	19123	20074
videos:	8206	8498
CD-ROMs:	384	971
periodcls:	238	242

Issues:	1999-2000	2000-01
ad lend:	1041580	951602
ch:	273878	272343
schools:	22818	22049
iaudios:	89047	92100
videos:	63786	64553
CD-ROMs:	1628	1624

Acqs:	1999-2000	2000-01
bks:	35670	33138
AVs:	7707	7320

Acqs: Source: lib suppl, publ & bksellers *Co-op:* CBC *Offcr-in-Charge:* Acqs Libn: Mrs T. Morgan (tmorgan@portsmouthcc.gov.uk)
Classn: DDC *Cat: Type:* author, classified & title *Medium:* auto *Auto Sys:* DS *Svcs: Extramural:* schools, prisons, old people's homes, housebnd *Info:* business, community, patent, careers *Other:* music lib, Open Learning Centre *Activs:* ch's activs, bk sales, temp exhibs, talks, author visits *Offcr-in-Charge:* Snr Libn of relevant dept
Enqs: 302990 (1999-2000); 292667 (2000-01)
Staff: Libns: 30.2 *Non-Prof:* 69.3

Inc from:	*1999-2000*	*2000-01*
local govt:	£2554374	£2488935
fines etc:	£245699	£264807
total:	£2821229	£2799396

Exp on:	*1999-2000*	*2000-01*
bks:	£355821	£339528
AVs:	£68344	£81552
elec media:	£11064	£774
salaries:	£1604260	£1654536
total:	£2821229	£2799396

Powys

P149 Powys Library and Archive Service

Svc HQ, Cefn Llys Ln, Llandrindod Wells, Powys, LD1 5LD (01597-826860; *fax:* 01597-826872)
Internet: http://www.powys.gov.uk/

Local Auth: Powys County Council *Pop:* 126800 *Cttee:* Lib & Cultural Svcs Cttee *Larger Dept:* Lifelong Learning & Community Svcs *Dept Chief:* Head of Lifelong Learning: Mr Mike Westhorpe *Chief:* County Libn (Libs & Archvs): Miss Tudfil L. Adams BA, MCLIP, MILAM
Main Libs: BRECON AREA LIB, Ship St, Brecon, Powys, LD3 9AE (01874-623346; *fax:* 01874-622818; *email:* breclib@powys.gov.uk); LLANDRINDOD WELLS AREA LIB, Cefn Llys Ln, Llandrindod Wells, Powys, LD1 5LD (01597-826870; *fax:* 01597-826872; *email:* llandod@ mail.powys.gov.uk); NEWTOWN AREA LIB, Park Ln, Newtown, Powys, SY16 1EJ (01686-626934; *fax:* 01686-624935; *email:* nlibrary@mail.powys. gov.uk) *Branch Libs:* BUILTH WELLS LIB, 20 High St, Builth Wells, Powys, LD2 3DN (01982-552722; *fax:* 01982-551084; *email:* builtlib@powys. gov.uk); CRICKHOWELL LIB, Silver St, Crick-howell, Powys, NP8 1BJ (*tel & fax:* 01873-810856; *email:* cricklib@powys.gov.uk); HAY-ON-WYE LIB, Chancery Ln, Hay-on-Wye, Hereford, HR3 5BL (*tel & fax:* 01497-820847; *email:* haylib@mail. powys.gov.uk); KNIGHTON LIB, West St, Knighton, Powys, LD7 1DN (*tel & fax:* 01547-528778; *email:* knighlib@mail.powys.gov.uk); RHAYADER LIB, West St, Rhayader, Powys, LD6 5AB (01597-810548; *email:* rhaylib@mail. powys.gov.uk); WELSHPOOL LIB, Brook St, Welshpool, Powys, SY21 7PH (01938-553001; *fax:* 01938-556625; *email:* welshlib@mail.powys. gov.uk); YSTRADGYNLAIS LIB, Temperance St, Ystradgynlais, Swansea, W Glamorgan, SA9 1JJ (01639-845353; *fax:* 01639-849312; *email:* ystradlib@mail.powys.gov.uk)
Svc Pts: PT: 6 *Mobile:* 5
Collns: local hist collns (at Brecon, Llandrindod Wells & Newtown Libs); Gregynog Press Colln of bks publ by the press, incl bks, pamphs, programmes & ephemera (at Newtown Lib) *Co-op Schemes:* WRLS *ILLs:* county, natl & internatl *Loans:* bks & audios/4 wks *Income Gen:* req/35p, exhib facilities/£2 pd *Fines:* bks, audios & videos/ad & oap 15p pw, ch exempt *Equip:* 5 m-readers, m-printer, 6 fax (£1 per sheet), 6 copiers (15p), room hire (£5/session), computers *Disabled:* CCTV, adapted tape players
Acqs: Source: lib suppl *Offcr-in-Charge:* Biblio-graphical Svcs Libn: Ms D. M. Hall

Classn: DDC *Cat: Type:* author & classified *Medium:* cards & auto *Svcs: Extramural:* schools, old people's homes, day centres, play groups *Info:* info for carers, local svcs *Other:* Open Learning, Basic Literacy skills, Welsh learners *Activs:* bk sales, temp exhibs, author visits & talks *Offcr-in-Charge:* Principal Libn (Field Svcs) Mrs Helen Edwards BLib, MCLIP
Staff: Libns: 18 *Non-Prof:* 37

Inc from:	*1999-2000*	*2000-01*
local govt:	£1593449	£1426049
fines etc:	£166211	£240793
total:	£1759650	£1666842

Exp on:	*1999-2000*	*2000-01*
stock:	£279881	£274015
salaries:	£940304	£881006
total:	£1759650	£1666842

Reading

P150 Reading Borough Libraries

Reading Central Lib, Abbey Sq, Reading, Berkshire, RG1 3BQ (0118-901-5950; *fax:* 0118-901-5954)
Email: info@readinglibraries.org.uk
Internet: http://www.readinglibraries.org.uk/

Local Auth: Reading Borough Council *Pop:* 147700 *Larger Dept:* Arts & Leisure *Dept Chief:* Dir: Ms Anita Cacchoili *Chief:* Head of Museums, Archvs & Libs: Mr Alec Kennedy BA(Hons), DMS, MCLIP (Alec.Kennedy@ reading.gov.uk) *Dep:* Lib Svcs Mgr: Mr Rhodri Thomas MCLIP (Rhodri.Thomas@reading.gov.uk)
Main Libs: READING CENTRAL LIB, as above *Branch Libs:* BATTLE LIB, 420 Oxford Rd, Reading, Berkshire, RG30 1EE (0118-901-5100; *fax:* 0118-901-5101); CAVERSHAM LIB, Church St, Caversham, Reading, Berkshire, RG4 8AU (0118-901-5103; *fax:* 0118-901-5104); PALMER PK LIB, St Bartholomew's Rd, Reading, Berkshire, RG1 3QB (0118-901-5106; *fax:* 0118-901-5107); SOUTHCOTE LIB, Southcote Ln, Reading, Berk-shire, RG30 3BA (0118-901-5109; *fax:* 0118-901-5110); TILEHURST LIB, School Rd, Tilehurst, Reading, Berkshire, RG31 5AS (0118-901-5112; *fax:* 0118-901-5113); WHITLEY LIB, Northumber-land Ave, Reading, Berkshire, RG2 7PX (0118-901-5115; *fax:* 0118-901-5116)
Svc Pts: Mobile: 2 *AV:* all libs *Internet:* all libs *Other:* BUSINESS LIB; LOCAL STUDIES LIB; MUSIC & DRAMA LIB (all at Reading Central Lib) *Collns:* Mary Mitford Colln; Frith Colln of photos of Berkshire (both at Local Studies Lib) *Co-op Schemes:* V3 (inter-lib loans) *ILLs:* county, natl & internatl *Loans:* bks & audios/3 wks; videos & DVDs/1 wk *Charges:* cassettes/from 55p, ch's 30p; CDs/from £1.55; videos/£1.60; DVDs/£2.60; conc available for Passport to Leisure holders *Income Gen:* req & res/in stock free, not in stock £1.50; lost ticket/£1.60 *Fines:* bks/ad 14p pd, ch 7p pd; audios/varies; videos & DVDs/75p pd; registered blind exempt *Equip:* 9 m-readers, m-printer, 9 copiers (A4/10p), 7 fax, computers (incl 3 wd-procs, 12 CD-ROM & 58 internet, access free), 2 rooms for hire

Stock:	*1 Apr 2000*	*1 Apr 2001*
ad lend:	182113	167011
ad ref:	48232	51171
ch:	42489	46689
audios:	18585	17532
videos:	4042	3973
periodcls:	409	400

Issues:		*2000-01*
ad lend:		763027
ch:		223061
audios:		66660
videos:		45607

Acqs:	*1999-2000*	*2000-01*
bks:	32583	24441
AVs:	3811	4068

Acqs: Source: lib suppl *Co-op:* Thames Valley Consortium for British Standards *Offcr-in-Charge:* Stock & Systems Mgr: Ms Alison England
Classn: DDC *Cat: Type:* author. classified, subj & title *Medium:* auto *Auto Sys:* Dynix *Svcs: Extramural:* prisons, housebnd, old people's homes *Info:* business, community, careers *Other:* Lifelong Learning *Activs:* ch's activs, temp exhibs, reading groups *Offcr-in-Charge:* Snr Yng Persons Libn: Ms Suzan Davis & Ms Nicci Shepherd
Enqs: 195728 (1999-2000); 193574 (2000-01)
Staff: Libns: 24 *Non-Prof:* 50

Redcar and Cleveland

P151 Redcar and Cleveland Libraries

Council Offices, Redcar & Cleveland House, Kirkleathen Street, Redcar, Cleveland, TS10 1YA (01642-444000; *fax:* 01642-444896)
Email: carol_barnes@redcar-cleveland.gov.uk
Internet: http://www.redcar-cleveland.gov.uk/

Local Auth: Redcar & Cleveland Borough Council *Pop:* 136382 *Larger Dept:* Neighbourhood Svcs *Chief:* Libs Offcr: Mrs Carol Barnes BA, DipLib, MCLIP
Main Libs: REDCAR CENTRAL LIB, Coatham Rd, Redcar, Cleveland, TS10 1RP (01642-472162; *ref:* 01642-489292; *fax:* 01642-492253; *email:* redcar_library@redcar-cleveland.gov.uk); GUIS-BOROUGH GROUP LIB, 90 Westgate, Guis-borough, Redcar, Cleveland, TS14 6AU (01287-632668; *email:* guisborough_library@ redcar-cleveland.gov.uk) *Branch Libs:* BROTTON LIB, High St, Brotton, Redcar, Cleveland, TS12 2PE (01287-676342; *email:* brotton_library@redcar-cleveland.gov.uk); DOR-MANSTOWN LIB, 3 Farndale Sq, Dormanstown, Redcar, Cleveland, TS10 5HE (01642-483626; *email:* dormanstown_library@redcar-cleveland. gov.uk); GRANGETOWN LIB, Birchington Ave, Grang-town, Middlesbrough, Cleveland, TS6 7LP (01642-454417; *email:* grangetown_library@redcar-cleveland.gov.uk); LABURNUM RD LIB, Laburnum Rd, Redcar, Cleveland, TS10 3QR (01642-484142; *email:* laburnum_library@redcar-cleveland.gov.uk); LOFTUS LIB, Hall Grounds, Loftus, Redcar, Cleveland, TS13 4HJ (01287-640582; *email:* loftus_library@redcar-cleveland. gov.uk); MARSKE LIB, Windy Hill Ln, Marske-by-Sea, Redcar, Cleveland, TS11 7BL (01642-485440; *email:* marske_library@redcar-cleveland. gov.uk); ORMESBY LIB, Sunnyfield, Ormesby, Middlesbrough, Cleveland, TS7 9BL (01642-314716; *email:* ormesby_library@redcar-cleveland.gov.uk); ROSEBERRY SQ LIB, Roseberry Sq, Redcar, Cleveland, TS10 4EL (01642-483326; *email:* roseberry_library@redcar-cleveland.gov.uk); SALTBURN LIB, Windsor Rd, Saltburn, Redcar, Cleveland, TS12 1AT (01287-623584; *email:* saltburn_library@ redcar-cleveland. gov.uk); SKELTON LIB, Coniston Rd, Skelton, Cleveland, TS12 2HN (01287-650487; *email:* skelton_library@redcar-cleveland.gov.uk); SOUTH BANK LIB, 248 Normanby Rd, Eston, Middlesbrough, Cleveland, TS6 6TD (01642-453461; *email:* south_bank_library@redcar-cleveland.gov.uk)
Svc Pts: Mobile: 2 *AV:* 13 *Computers:* 13 *Internet:* 13 *Other:* SPECIAL SVCS SECTION, at South Bank Lib (01642-464968; *email:* special_services@redcar-cleveland.gov.uk)
Collns: JFR: Fiction Fao-Fat, Fish-Flo (at South Bank Lib); playsets (at South Bank Lib, held in multiple copies) *Co-op Schemes:* ILL, JFR, NEMLAC, Newsplan, NCL, 3 co-operatives based on former Cleveland County Council: Health Info (led by Hartlepool Borough Council – see **P61**), School Resources Svc (led by Redcar & Cleveland Borough Council), Joint Archvs Svc (led by Middlesbrough Borough Council – see **P115** & **A379** for Archv Svc)

Public Libraries

Redcar & Cleveland
▼
Rotherham

(Redcar & Cleveland Libs cont)
ILLs: county, natl & internatl **Loans:** bks/4 wks; audios/2 wks; videos/1 wk or overnight; Open Learning & lang courses/4 wks **Charges:** cassettes & spkn wd/46p per item (max £1.84 for sets); CDs/92p per item (max £1.84 for sets); videos/£1.50-£2.50; Open Learning/free; lang courses/£1.64 **Income Gen:** req/80p, conc 40p, ch exempt; external ILLs/£1.18, conc 60p; lost ticket/£1, conc 50p **Fines:** bks/ad & oap 9p pd (max £8.10); audios/loan charge; videos/50p pd; ch exempt **Equip:** m-reader, m-printer (36p per sheet), copiers (A4/5p, A3/10pt), computers (incl internet & CD-ROM), rooms for hire (various)

Stock:	1 Apr 2000	1 Apr 2001
ad lend:	206049	196995
ad ref:	25683	26045
ch:	109077	103559
audios:	15816	15349
videos:	6060	5856
periodcls:	109	171

Issues:	1999-2000	2000-01
ad lend:	1015869	973558
ch:	272292	249443
audios:	40103	41146
videos:	10330	15019

Acqs:	1999-2000	2000-01
bks:	45039	34973
AVs:	2817	2888

Acqs: Source: lib suppl **Co-op:** JFR, local 4-borough co-op on collns (musical scores, playsets, subtitled videos etc)
Classn: DDC **Cat:** Type: author, classified & title Medium: auto **Auto Sys:** DS Galaxy **Svcs:** Extramural: schools, old people's homes, housebnd Info: community, council, business European **Activs:** ch's activs, bk sales **Offcr-in-Charge:** various offcrs
Enqs: 157053 (1999-2000); 154219 (2000-01)
Staff: Libns: 26 Non-Prof: 47.14

Inc from:	1999-2000	2000-01
local govt:	£2301111	£2240096
fines etc:	£190021	£210874
total:	£2491132	£2450970

Exp on:	1999-2000	2000-01
stock:	£329863	-
salaries:	£1227731	£1263200
total:	£2491132	£2450970

Renfrewshire

P152 Renfrewshire Libraries
Lib Svcs HQ, Abbey House, 8a Seedhill Rd, Paisley, Renfrewshire, PA1 1AJ (0141-840-3003; fax: 0141-840-3004)
Email: libraries.els@renfrewshire.gov.uk
Internet: http://www.renfrewshire.gov.uk/

Local Auth: Renfrewshire Council Pop: 177000
Cttee: Edu & Leisure Cttee **Larger Dept:** Edu & Leisure Svcs **Dept Chief:** Dir: Mrs Shelagh Rae **Chief:** Principal Libn: Ms Vivian Kerr BA, MCLIP, MIMgt
Main Libs: PAISLEY CENTRAL LIB, High St, Paisley, Renfrewshire, PA1 2BB (lend: 0141-887-3672; ref: 0141-889-2360; fax: 0141-887-6468; email: ce.els@renfrewshire.gov.uk or ref.els@renfrewshire.gov.uk) **Branch (Community) Libs:** BARGARRAN LIB, Barrhill Rd, Erskine, Renfrewshire, PA8 6BS (0141-812-2841; fax:

0141-812-5265); BISHOPTON LIB, 11 Greenock Rd, Bishopton, Renfrewshire, PA7 5JW (01505-862136; fax: 01505-862265); BRIDGE OF WEIR LIB, Main St, Bridge of Weir, Renfrewshire, PA11 3NR (01505-612220; fax: 01505-615052); ELDERSLIE LIB, Stoddard Sq, Elderslie, Renfrewshire, PA5 9AS (01505-322055; fax: 01505-327857); ERSKINE LIB, Bridgewater Pl, Erskine, Renfrewshire, PA8 7AA (0141-812-5331; fax: 0141-812-4977; email: er.els@renfrewshire.gov.uk); FERGUSLIE PK LIB, Tannahill Centre, Blackstoun Rd, Paisley, Renfrewshire, PA3 1NT (0141-887-6404; fax: 0141-849-0003); FOXBAR LIB, Ivanhoe Rd, Foxbar, Renfrewshire, PA2 0JX (01505-812353; fax: 01505-816989); GALLOW-HILL LIB, Netherhill Rd, Gallowhill, Renfrewshire, PA3 4SF (0141-889-1195; fax: 0141-889-0034); GLENBURN LIB, Fairway Ave, Paisley, Renfrewshire, PA2 8DX (0141-884-2874; fax: 0141-884-5758); JOHNSTONE LIB, Houston Ct, Johnstone, Renfrewshire, PA5 8DL (01505-329726; fax: 01505-336657; email: jo.els@renfrewshire.gov.uk); LINWOOD LIB, Ardlamont Sq, Linwood, Renfrewshire, PA3 3DE (01505-325283; fax: 01505-336150; email: lw.els@renfrewshire.gov.uk); LOCHWINNOCH LIB, Old School, High St, Lochwinnoch, Renfrewshire, PA12 4AB (01505-842305; fax: 01505-843780); RALSTON LIB, Community Centre, Allanton Ave, Paisley, Renfrewshire, PA1 3BL (0141-882-1879; fax: 0141-882-2325), RENFREW LIB, Paisley Rd, Moorpark, Renfrew, PA4 8LJ (0141-886-3433; fax: 0141-886-1660; email: rw.els@renfrewshire.gov.uk); SPATESTON LIB, Hallhill Rd, Johnstone, Renfrewshire, PA5 0SA (01505-704527; fax: 01505-706560); TODHOLM LIB, Lochfield Rd, Paisley, Renfrewshire, PA2 7JB (0141-887-3012; fax: 0141-889-6167)
Svc Pts: Mobile: 2 AV: 17 Other: small colln in HQ available on request; toy colln at Glenburn Community Centre, Fairway Ave, Paisley, Renfrewshire, PA2 8DX (0141-884-8000)
Collns: Paisley Pamphs Colln (80 vols of collected ephemera); Paisley Burns Club Colln (120 vols); Rowat Colln (300 vols); local govt archvs; Burgh Engineer Drawings; Cairn of Lochwinnoch (44 vols); Paisley Poor Law Records (50 vols); Dean of Guild Plans for Paisley (1888-1918) **Loans:** bks, audios & videos/4 wks **Charges:** audios/30p per item; videos/50p or £12 pa sub; CD-ROMs/£1; alternative AV sub charge of £12 pa **Income Gen:** req/20p; lost ticket/40p **Fines:** all items/ad 25p pw (£1.50 max), oaps & disabled 10p pw (60p max), ch exempt **Equip:** m-readers, m-printers, fax (UK £1 per pg, higher overseas), copiers (A4/10p, A3/20p), computers (incl wd-procs, internet & CD-ROM) **Disabled:** Aladdin personal readers, cassette players for home use by visually impaired

Stock:	1 Apr 2000	1 Apr 2001
lend:	368881	362972
ref:	39195	39623
AVs:	45924	38664
periodcls:	425	436

Issues:	1999-2000	2000-01
bks:	1257467	1188138
AVs:	129574	127192

Acqs:	1999-2000	2000-01
bks:	66812	61552
AVs:	8793	5710

Acqs: Source: lib suppl **Offcr-in-Charge:** Snr Libn (Bibliographical Svcs)
Classn: DDC **Cat:** Medium: auto **Auto Sys:** Geac **Svcs:** Extramural: hosps, old people's homes, housebnd Info: community, European, business, careers, travel, health, consumer Other: Lifelong Learning **Activs:** ch's activs, bk sales, temp exhibs, poetry readings, author visits
Enqs: 117073 (1999-2000); 92401 (2000-01)
Staff: Libns: 25 Non-Prof: 90

Inc from:	2000-01
local govt:	£3740176
fines etc:	£93810
total:	£3833986

Exp on:	2000-01
stock:	£390285
salaries:	£2174976
total:	£3833986

Rhondda Cynon Taff

P153 Rhondda Cynon Taff Libraries
The Edu Centre, Grawen St, Porth, Rhondda Cynon Taff, CF39 0BU (01443-687666; fax: 01443-680286)
Internet: http://www.rhondda-cynon-taff.gov.uk/libraries/

Local Auth: Rhondda Cynon Taff County Borough Council Pop: 240000 **Cttee:** Genl Policy Cttee (Cabinet), Edu/Leisure Scrutiny Cttee **Larger Dept:** Edu Dept **Dept Chief:** Dir: Ms Chris Berry **Chief:** County Borough Libn: Mrs Julie A. Jones BA, MCLIP (Julie.A.Jones@rhondda-cynon-taff.gov.uk) **Dep:** Principal Libn (Reader Svcs): Mrs Norma Jones MSc, MIMgt, MCLIP (Norma.D.Jones@rhondda-cynon-taff.gov.uk)
Main Libs: ABERDARE LIB, Green St, Aberdare, Rhondda Cynon Taff, CF44 7AC (01685 880050; fax: 01685-881181; email: Aberdare.Library@rhondda-cynon-taff.gov.uk); PONTYPRIDD LIB, Lib Rd, Pontypridd, Rhondda Cynon Taff, CF37 2DY (01443-486850; fax: 01443-493258; email: Pontypridd.Library@rhondda-cynon-taff.gov.uk); TREORCHY LIB, Station Rd, Treorchy, Rhondda, Rhondda Cynon Taff, CF42 6NN (01443-773204/592; fax: 01443-777047; email: Treorchy.Library@rhondda-cynon-taff.gov.uk) **Branch Libs:** ABERCYNON LIB, Ynysmeurig Rd, Abercynon, Mountain Ash, Rhondda Cynon Taff, CF45 4SU (01443-740486; email: Abercynon.Library@rhondda-cynon-taff.gov.uk); BEDDAU LIB, Parish Rd, Tynant, Beddau, Rhondda Cynon Taff, CF38 2DA (01443-202715; email: Beddau.Library@rhondda-cynon-taff.gov.uk); CHURCH VILLAGE LIB, Main Rd, Church Village, Pontypridd, Rhondda Cynon Taff, CF38 1PH (01443-202503; email: ChurchVillage.Library@rhondda-cynon-taff.gov.uk); CWMBACH LIB, Philip Row, Cwmbach, Aberdare, Rhondda Cynon Taff, CF44 0EF (01685-882441; email: Cwmbach.Library@rhondda-cynon-taff.gov.uk); FERNDALE LIB, High St, Ferndale, Rhondda Cynon Taff, CF43 4RH (01443-757557; email: Ferndale.Library@rhondda-cynon-taff.gov.uk); HIRWAUN LIB, High St, Hirwaun, Aberdare, Rhondda Cynon Taff, CF44 9SW (01685-811144; email: Hirwaun.Library@rhondda-cynon-taff.gov.uk); MOUNTAIN ASH LIB, Knight St, Mountain Ash, Rhondda Cynon Taff, CF45 4EY (01443-473200; email: MountainAsh.Library@rhondda-cynon-taff.gov.uk); PENRHIWCEIBER LIB, Rheola St, Penrhiwceiber, Mountain Ash, Rhondda Cynon Taff, CF45 3TA (01443-472424; email: Penrhiwceiber.Library@rhondda-cynon-taff.gov.uk); PENYGRAIG LIB, Tylacelyn Rd, Penygraig, Rhondda Cynon Taff, CF40 1LA (01443-430537; email: Penygraig.Library@rhondda-cynon-taff.gov.uk); PONTYCLUN LIB, Heol-Y-Felin, Pontyclun, Rhondda Cynon Taff, CF7 9BE (01443-237843; email: Pontyclun.Library@rhondda-cynon-taff.gov.uk); PORTH LIB, Pontypridd Rd, Porth, Rhondda Cynon Taff, CF39 9PG (01443-682785; email: Porth.Library@rhondda-cynon-taff.gov.uk); RHYDYFELIN LIB, Poplar Rd, Rhydyfelin, Pontypridd, Rhondda Cynon Taff, CF37 5LR (01443-486851; email: Rhydyfelin.Library@rhondda-cynon-taff.gov.uk); TAFFS WELL LIB, Cardiff Rd, Taffs Well, Rhondda Cynon Taff, CF15 7PL (029-2081-1079; email: TaffsWell.Library@rhondda-cynon-taff.gov.uk); TALBOT GREEN LIB, 3 Heol-Y-Gyfraith,

Talbot Green, Rhondda Cynon Taff, CF7 8AL (01443-237844; *email:* TalbotGreen.Library@rhondda-cynon-taff.gov.uk); TON PENTRE LIB, Church Rd, Ton Pentre, Rhondda Cynon Taff, CF41 7EF (01443-435428; *email:* TonPentre.Library@rhondda-cynon-taff.gov.uk); TONY-REFAIL LIB, High St, Tonyrefail, Rhondda Cynon Taff, CF39 8PG (01443-671249; *email:* Tonyrefail.Library@rhondda-cynon-taff.gov.uk); TONY-PANDY LIB, De Winton St, Tonypandy, Rhondda Cynon Taff, CF40 2QZ (01443-432251; *email:* Tonypandy.Library@rhondda-cynon-taff.gov.uk); TREHERBERT LIB, Bute St, Treherbert, Rhondda Cynon Taff, CF42 5NR (01443-771232; *email:* Treherbert.Library@rhondda-cynon-taff.gov.uk); TYLORSTOWN LIB, East Rd, Tylorstown, Rhondda Cynon Taff, CF43 3DA (01443-730298; *email:* Tylorstown.Library@rhondda-cynon-taff.gov.uk); YNYSYBWL LIB, 42 Robert St, Ynysybwl, Pontypridd, Rhondda Cynon Taff, CF37 3DY (01443-790394; *email:* Ynysybwl.Library@rhondda-cynon-taff.gov.uk)
Svc Pts: PT: 6 *Mobile:* 4 + 2 housebnd vehicles & 1 bookbus *AV:* at most libs
ILLs: county, natl & internatl *Loans:* all items/3 wks *Charges:* cassettes/25p; CDs/50p; videos/£1 *Income Gen:* res/40p; lost tickets/£1
Fines: bks/ad 30p pw, ch & oaps exempt; audios & videos/loan charge; registered blind & partially sighted exempt *Equip:* 6 m-readers, 4 m-printers (20p), 4 fax (£1 per pg to send, 50p per pg to receive), 14 copiers (A4/10p, A3/20p), 130 computers (incl wd-procs, internet & CD-ROM) *Disabled:* Aladdin magnifiers, stair lift at 2 branches

Stock:	1 Apr 2000	1 Apr 2001
ad lend:	406004	404282
ad ref: *	40665	45186
ch:	126677	133707
audios:	43727	45526
videos:	577	677
periodcls:	294	209
archvs:	15360 items	15955 items

* incl CD-ROMs

Issues:	1999-2000	2000-01
ad lend:	1382105	1264687
ch:	290953	247930
audios:	102134	96174
videos:	1847	2269

Acqs:	1999-2000	2000-01
bks:	59208	54511
AVs:	3814	3297

Acqs: Source: lib suppl *Offcr-in-Charge:* Principal Libn (Reader Svcs), as above
Classn: DDC *Cat: Type:* author, classified, dictionary, subj & title *Medium:* auto *Auto Sys:* Olib 6 *Svcs: Extramural:* schools, hosps, old people's homes, housebnd *Info:* community database *Other:* Open Learning *Activs:* ch's activs, temp exhibs
Enqs: 207428 (1999-2000)
Staff: Libns: 26 *Non-Prof:* 66.5

Inc from:	1999-2000	2000-01
local govt:	£2775693	£2563219
fines etc:	£8700	£81402
total:	£2862693	£2644621

Exp on:	1999-2000	2000-01
bks:	£577261	£416731
AVs:	£70359	£64968
elec media:	£102969	£89719
salaries:	£1681700	£1760753
total:	£2862693	£2644621

Rochdale

P154 Rochdale Library Service

Wheatsheaf Lib, Baillie Street, Rochdale, Lancashire, OL16 1JZ (01706-647474; *fax:* 01706-864992)
Email: library.service@rochdale.gov.uk
Internet: http://www.rochdale.gov.uk/

Local Auth: Rochdale Metropolitan Borough Council *Pop:* 210800 *Larger Dept:* Community Svcs *Dept Chief: Dir:* Mr Andy Wiggins BA *Chief: Principal Libn:* Mrs Sheila M. Sfrijan MCLIP *Other Snr Staff:* Bibliographical & Special Svcs Libn: Mrs Freda Fletcher MCLIP
Main (Area) Libs: HEYWOOD LIB, Church St, Heywood, Lancashire, OL10 1LL (01706-360947; *fax:* 01706-368683); LITTLEBOROUGH LIB, Hare Hall Pk, Littleborough, Lancashire, OL15 9HE (01706-378219); MIDDLETON LIB, Long St, Middleton, Manchester, M24 3DU (0161-643-5228; *fax:* 0161-654-0745); WHEATSHEAF LIB, addr as above (*lend:* 01706-864900; *ref:* 01706-864914; *fax:* 01706-864992) *Branch Libs:* ALKRINGTON LIB, Kirkway, Middleton, Manchester, M24 1LW (0161-643-7799); BALDERSTONE LIB, Balderstone Pk, Rochdale, Lancashire, OL11 2HD (01706-640438); CASTLETON LIB, 881 Manchester Rd, Rochdale, Lancashire, OL11 2ST (01706-633430); DARNHILL LIB, Argyle Parade, Heywood, Lancashire, OL10 3RY (01706-368142); LANGLEY LIB, Windermere Rd, Middleton, Manchester, M24 3PY (0161-654-8911); MILN-ROW LIB, Newhey Rd, Milnrow, Rochdale, Lancashire, OL16 3PS (01706-641563); SMALLBRIDGE LIB, Stevenson Sq, Halifax Rd, Rochdale, Lancashire, OL12 9SA (01706-659978); SPOTLAND LIB, Ings Ln, Rochdale, Lancashire, OL12 7AL (01706-648505)
Svc Pts: PT: 6 *Mobile:* 1 + 1 lib vehicle for housebnd
Collns: Co-operative Colln (co-op movement, c1600 items); various specialist archv collns at Local Studies Lib (see **A434**) *Co-op Schemes:* Libs North West, GMPLTC *ILLs:* county, natl & internatl *Loans:* bks/3 wks; audios/2 wks; videos/1 wk *Charges:* cassettes/65p; CDs/£1 *Income Gen:* res/60p, juniors & over-60s 30p; ILLs/£1; lost ticket/ad £1.50, juniors & conc 50p *Fines:* bks/ad 10p pd; audios/addl hire charge of 10p pd; registered blind & disabled, ch & oap exempt *Equip:* m-readers, m-printers (50p), fax, video viewers, copiers, computers (incl internet & CD-ROM), room for hire *Disabled:* Kurzweil, minicom, braille printer

Stock:	1 Apr 2000	1 Apr 2001
lend:	300205	308322
ref:	66807	57074
AVs:	11701	11961
periodcls:	218	208

Issues:	1999-2000	2000-01
bks:	1428004	1336933
AVs:	64986	66886

Acqs:	1999-2000	2000-01
bks:	36071	44775
AVs:	1100	740

Acqs: Source: lib suppl & bksellers *Offcr-in-Charge:* Bibliographical & Special Svcs Libn, as above
Classn: DDC *Cat: Type:* author, classified, subj & title *Medium:* auto *Auto Sys:* Dynix *Svcs: Extramural:* old people's homes, housebnd, playgroups, sheltered accommodation *Info:* business, community *Other:* Open Learning *Activs:* ch's activs, bk sales, temp exhibs, seasonal events/demos, author visits *Offcr-in-Charge:* Bibliographical & Special Svcs Libn, as above
Enqs: 146432 (1999-2000); 165932 (2000-01)
Staff: 86.2 in total

Inc from:	1999-2000	2000-01
local govt:	£2891292	£3078011
fines etc:	£94978	£88788
total:	£3259506	£3455382

Exp on:	1999-2000	2000-01
stock & svcs:	£854619	£887356
salaries:	£1276470	£1308205
total:	£3259506	£3455382

Rotherham

P155 Rotherham Library and Information Service

Central Lib & Arts Centre, Walker Pl, Rotherham, S Yorkshire, S65 1JH (01709-823611; *fax:* 01709-823650)
Email: central.library@rotherham.gov.uk
Internet: http://www.rotherham.gov.uk/

Local Auth: Rotherham Metropolitan Borough Council *Pop:* 253700 *Cttee: Edu*, Culture & Leisure Cttee *Larger Dept:* Edu, Culture & Leisure Svc *Dept Chief: Exec Dir:* Ms Di Billups *Chief: Mgr (Lib & Info Svcs):* Mr Keith Robinson (keith.robinson@rotherham.gov.uk) *Other Snr Staff:* Community & Community Lib Svcs Offcr: Ms Elenore Fisher; Inclusive & Development Svcs Offcr: Mr Kevin Smith; Stock Mgmt & Development Offcr: Ms Ruth Radford
Main Libs: CENTRAL LIB, addr as above; MALTBY LIB, High St, Maltby, Rotherham, S Yorkshire, S66 8LD (01709-812150); SWINTON LIB, Station St, Swinton, Mexborough, S Yorkshire, S64 8PZ (01709-583116); WATH LIB, Montgomery Rd, Wath-Upon-Dearne, Rotherham, S Yorkshire, S63 7RZ (01709-873542) *Branch (Community) Libs:* ASTON COMMUNITY LIB, Aughton Rd, Swallownest, Sheffield, S Yorkshire, S31 0TF (0114-2874225); DINNINGTON COMMUNITY LIB, Laughton Rd, Dinnington, Sheffield, S Yorkshire, S25 2PP (01909-562329); GREASBROUGH COMMUNITY LIB, Coach Rd, Greasbrough, Rotherham, S Yorkshire, S61 4PU (01709-551477); HERRINGTHORPE COMMUNITY LIB, Browning Rd, Herringthorpe, Rotherham, S Yorkshire, S65 2LG (01709-382952); KIMBERWORTH COMMUNITY LIB, Church St, Kimberworth, Rotherham, S Yorkshire, S61 1HA (01709-558581); KIMBERWORTH PK COMMUNITY LIB, Wheatley Rd, Rotherham, S Yorkshire, S61 3JU (01709-552799); KIVETON PK COMMUNITY LIB, Wales Rd, Kiveton Pk, Sheffield, S Yorkshire, S31 8RB (01909-771823); MOWBRAY GDNS COMMUNITY LIB, Herringthorpe Valley Rd, Rotherham, S Yorkshire, S65 8LD (01709-370038); RAWMARSH COMMUNITY LIB, Rawmarsh Hill, Parkgate, Rotherham, S Yorkshire, S62 6DS (01709-522588)
Svc Pts: PT: 2 *Mobile:* 4 + 1 special mobile to serve oap establishments *AV:* 5 *Computers:* 15 *Internet:* 15 *Other:* ARCHVS & LOCAL STUDIES (at Central Lib – see **A438**)
Co-op Schemes: YLI, SINTO *ILLs:* county, natl & internatl *Loans:* bks/3 wks; audios/1 wk; videos/2 days-1 wk; Playstation games/2 nights *Charges:* audios/55p; videos/£1.20-£2.30; CD-ROMs & Playstation games/£3 *Income Gen:* req & res/60p; lost ticket/£1 *Fines:* bks/ad 6p pd, ch, oap & registered disabled exempt; cassettes/10p pd; CDs/25p pd; videos/55p-$1.60 pd *Equip:* 5 m-readers, m-printer, 2 fax, 4 video viewers, 15 copiers, clr copier, 5 rooms for hire, computers (incl 24 with wd-proc & 24 with CD-ROM), digital mapping (at Archvs & Local Studies) *Disabled:* Kurzweil, CCTV, magnifiers *Online:* elec public info svc: Rotherview (at 27 sites), ICC (at Business Lib)

Stock:	1 Apr 2000
ad lend:	241287
ad ref:	14935
ch:	77967
audios:	9689
videos:	6466
periodcls:	70

Acqs:	1999-2000
bks:	23806

Acqs: Source: lib suppl & bksellers *Offcr-in-Charge:* Snr Libn, Bibliographical Svcs Unit: Ms Ruth M. Radford

(Rotherham Lib & Info Svc cont)
Classn: DDC **Cat:** *Type:* author & title *Medium:* auto *Auto Sys:* ALS **Svcs:** *Extramural:* schools, hosps, old people's homes, housebnd *Info:* business, community, tourist, local govt *Other:* Open Learning, homework clubs **Activs:** ch's activs, bk sales, temp exhibs, poetry readings, author visits, reading groups *Offcr-in-Charge:* Ms Marcia Newton (Ch & Yng Peoples Svcs); Ms Julie Hird (Reader Development)
Enqs: 201136 (1999-2000)
Staff: 115.46 in total

Rutland

P156 Rutland County Council Library Service

Rutland County Lib, Catmos Street, Oakham, Leicestershire, LE15 6HW (01572-722918; *fax:* 01572-724906)
Email: oakhamlibrary@rutnet.co.uk
Internet: http://www.rutnet.co.uk/

Local Auth: Rutland County Council *Pop:* 37800 **Cttee:** Cabinet **Larger Dept:** Edu, Youth & Culture *Dept Chief:* Dir: Ms C. Chambers **Chief:** Head of Cultural Svcs: Mr Roy Knight BA, MCLIP **Dep:** Lib Svcs Mgr: Mr Robert Clayton (rclayton@rutland.gov.uk)
Main Libs: RUTLAND COUNTY LIB, addr as above **Branch Libs:** UPPINGHAM LIB, Queen St, Uppingham, Rutland, LE15 9QR (01572-823218)
Svc Pts: *PT:* 2 *Mobile:* 1 *AV:* 2 *Computers:* 2 *Internet:* 2
Co-op Schemes: EMRLS **ILLs:** county, natl & internatl **Loans:** bks & talking bks/3 wks; audios, videos & CD-ROMs/1 wk **Charges:** cassettes/ 50p; talking bks/£1.20; CDs & videos/£1; CD-ROMs/£2 **Income Gen:** req & res/90p (conc 50p); lost ticket/plastic £1 (conc 50p), other 30p (conc 15p) **Fines:** bks/ad & oap 15p pd, ch 2p pd; audios, talking bks & videos/loan charge; special needs, special groups (nurseries etc), registered blind & playgroups exempt **Equip:** 4 m-readers, m-printer (20p per sheet), 4 copiers (A4/10p, A3/20p), fax (£1.70 + VAT), 7 computers (incl 4 wd-procs, 1 per half hr, 2 CD-ROM & 5 internet, internet free for 1st hr, then £1 per half hr) **Disabled:** disabled access *Online:* OPAC, Infolink, TAP *Offcr-in-Charge:* Lib Svcs Mgr, as above

Stock:	1 Apr 2000	1 Apr 2001
ad lend:	30108	29935
ad ref:	4540	5520
ch:	13750	14502
audios:	3173	2614
videos:	521	620
CD-ROMs:	132	139
periodcls:	34	33

Issues:		2000-01
ad lend:		199330
ch:		64112
audios:		9880
videos:		3414
CD-ROMs:		630

Acqs:	1999-2000	2000-01
bks:	6071	6747
AVs:	1112	503

Acqs: *Source:* lib suppl *Co-op:* JFR *Offcr-in-Charge:* all libns
Classn: DDC **Cat:** *Type:* author, classified, subj & title *Medium:* auto *Auto Sys:* Talis **Svcs:** *Extramural:* schools, prisons, old people's homes, housebnd *Info:* business, community *Other:* local studies, memb of govt's "IT for All" scheme **Activs:** ch's activs, bk sales, temp exhibs, reading groups, talks
Enqs: 25698 (1999-2000); 26704 (2000-01)
Staff: Libns: 3.7 *Non-Prof:* 7.5

Inc from:	1999-2000	2000-01
local govt:	£385058	£418831
fines etc:	£30643	£32648
total:	£445389	£481732

Exp on:	1999-2000	2000-01
bks:	£50901	£50344
AVs:	£14119	£13589
salaries:	£205703	£230140
total:	£445389	£481732

Further Info: biblio svcs, info systems, transport & prison lib svcs are provided through joint arrangements with Leicestershire County Council (see **P74**)

Salford

P157 Salford Libraries and Information Service

Swinton Lib, Chorley Rd, Swinton, M27 4AE (0161-793-3573)
Email: libraries@salford.gov.uk
Internet: http://www.salford.gov.uk/libraries/

Local Auth: City of Salford Metropolitan Council *Pop:* 225950 **Cttee:** Arts & Leisure Cttee **Larger Dept:** Edu & Leisure Dept *Dept Chief:* Dir of Edu & Leisure: Ms Jill Baker **Chief:** Libs & Info Svcs Mgr: Ms Sarah Spence BA, MCLIP (sarah. spence@salford.gov.uk)
Main (Divisional) Libs: BROADWALK LIB, Broadwalk, Salford, Lancashire, M6 5FX (0161-737-5802; *fax:* 0161-745-9157); ECCLES LIB, Church St, Eccles, Manchester, M30 0EP (0161-789-1430; *fax:* 0161-787-8430); SWINTON LIB, addr as above (0161-793-3560; *fax:* 0161-727-7071); WALKDEN LIB, Memorial Rd, Walkden, Worsley, Manchester, M28 3AQ (0161-790-4579; *fax:* 0161-703-8971) **Branch Libs:** BOOTHS-TOWN LIB, Community Centre, Standfield Dr, Boothstown, Worsley, Manchester, M28 4NB (*tel & fax:* 0161-799-6549); BROUGHTON LIB, 400-404 Bury New Rd, Salford, Lancashire, M7 4EY (0161-792-6640; *fax:* 0161-792-7193); CADISHEAD LIB, 126 Liverpool Rd, Cadishead, Manchester, M44 5AN (0161-775-3457); CHARLESTOWN LIB, Cromwell Rd, Salford, Lancashire, M6 6ES (0161-736-6834); HEIGHT LIB, King St, Salford, M6 7GY (0161-736-1907); HOPE LIB, Eccles Old Rd, Salford, Lancashire, M6 8FH (0161-789-2896); IRLAM LIB, Hurst Fold, Liverpool Rd, Irlam, Manchester, M44 6DF (0161-775-3566; *fax:* 0161-776-0279); LITTLE HULTON LIB, Longshaw Dr, Little Hulton, Manchester, M38 0AZ (0161-790-4201; *fax:* 0161-950-1776); ORDSALL LIB, 2 Robert Hall St, Salford, Lancashire, M5 3LT (0161-872-3884); WINTON LIB, Old Parrin Ln, Eccles, Manchester, M30 8BJ (0161-789-1431)
Svc Pts: *PT:* 2 *Mobile:* 2 *AV:* 9
Collns: Working Class Movement Lib (labour hist); Irish hist; Tom Paine Colln (held at: 51 Cres, Salford, M5 4PN) **Co-op Schemes:** Libs North West, GMPLTC **ILLs:** county & natl **Loans:** bks/3 wks; audios/2 wks; videos/1 wk **Charges:** audios/£1; videos/£1.50 **Income Gen:** res/70p **Fines:** bks/ad 10p pd; audios & videos/10p pd; ch, oap & registered disabled exempt **Equip:** 6 m-readers, m-printer (A4/10p), video viewer, 8 fax (50p-£2 pg), 14 copiers (A4/10p), clr copier (A4/ 50p-£2), 32 computers (incl wd-proc, internet & CD-ROM), 8 rooms for hire (£6.50/hr)

Stock:	1 Apr 2000	1 Apr 2001
lend:	271674	246188
ref:	6178	5216
AVs:	17732	15589
periodcls:	72	72

Issues:	1999-2000	2000-01
bks:	1088780	947058
AVs:	62432	65893

Acqs:	1999-2000	2000-01
bks:	26520	25028
AVs:	2422	2285

Acqs: *Source:* lib suppl *Offcr-in-Charge:* Principal Offcr (Acqs): Ms J. McFarland
Classn: DDC **Cat:** *Type:* author, classified, subj & title *Medium:* cards & auto *Auto Sys:* Talis **Svcs:** *Extramural:* schools, old people's homes, housebnd, sheltered accommodation units *Info:* Info Centre (at Broadwalk Lib) *Other:* Open Learning, homework clubs **Activs:** ch's activs, bk sales, temp exhibs
Enqs: 164840 (2000-01)
Staff: Libns: 25 *Non-Prof:* 70

Inc from:	1999-2000	2000-01
local govt:	£3017173	£3342986
fines etc:	£221109	£225440
total:	£3238282	£3568426

Exp on:	1999-2000	2000-01
bks:	£319584	£320000
AVs:	£58623	£56819
salaries:	£1542017	£1573675
total:	£3238282	£3568426

Sandwell

P158 Sandwell Library and Information Service

Central Lib, High Street, West Bromwich, W Midlands, B70 8DZ (0121-569-4911; *fax:* 0121-569-9465)
Email: information.service@sandwell.gov.uk
Internet: http://www.lea.sandwell.gov.uk/libraries/

Local Auth: Sandwell Metropolitan Borough Council *Pop:* 292800 **Cttee:** Youth & Community Svcs Cttee **Larger Dept:** Dept of Edu & Lifelong Learning **Chief:** Chief Libn: post vacant **Other Snr Staff:** Principal Libs Offcrs: Mr Tony Piorowski (tony.piorowski@sandwell.gov.uk), Mr Barry Clark (barry.clark@sandwell.gov.uk), Mrs Heather Vickerman (heather.vickerman@ sandwell.gov.uk) & Mrs Trish Fouracres (trish.fouracres@sandwell.gov.uk)
Main Libs: CENTRAL LIB (incl Info Svcs & Ref Lib), addr as above (0121-569-4904; *email:* central.library@sandwell.gov.uk) **Branch Libs:** BLACKHEATH LIB, Carnegie Rd, Rowley Regis, Warley, W Midlands, B65 8BY (*tel & fax:* 0121-559-1884; *email:* blackheath.library@sandwell. gov.uk); BLEAKHOUSE LIB, Bleakhouse Rd, Oldbury, W Midlands, B68 9DS (0121-422-2798; *email:* bleakhouse.library@sandwell.gov.uk); BRANDHALL LIB, Tame Rd, Oldbury, W Mid-lands, B68 0JT (*tel & fax:* 0121-422-5270; *email:* brandhall.library@sandwell.gov.uk); CRADLEY HEATH LIB, Upper High St, Cradley Heath, W Midlands, B64 5JU (*tel & fax:* 01384-569316; *email:* cradleyheath.library@sandwell.gov.uk); GLEBEFIELDS LIB, St Mark's Rd, Tipton, W Midlands, DY4 0SZ (*tel & fax:* 0121-557-8641; *email:* glebefields.library@sandwell.gov.uk); GT BARR LIB, Birmingham Rd, Gt Barr, Birmingham, B43 6NW (*tel & fax:* 0121-357-1340; *email:* greatbarr.library@sandwell.gov.uk); GT BRIDGE LIB, Sheepwash Ln, Tipton, W Midlands, DY4 7JF (*tel & fax:* 0121-557-3277; *email:* greatbridge. library@sandwell.gov.uk); HAMSTEAD LIB, Tanhouse Centre, Hamstead Rd, Gt Barr, Birming-ham, B43 5EL (0121-569-7866; *fax:* 0121-357-3578; *email:* hamstead.library@sandwell.gov.uk);

HILL TOP LIB, Park Bldgs, Hill Top, West Bromwich, W Midlands, B70 0RZ (tel & fax: 0121-556-0605; email: hilltop.library@sandwell.gov.uk); LANGLEY LIB, Barrs St, Oldbury, W Midlands, B68 8QT (tel & fax: 0121-552-1680; email: langley. library@sandwell.gov.uk); OAKHAM LIB, Poplar Rd, Tividale, W Midlands, B69 1RD (tel & fax: 01384-255563; email: oakham.library@sandwell. gov.uk); OLDBURY LIB, Church St, Oldbury, W Midlands, B69 3AF (tel & fax: 0121-552-5933; email: oldbury.library@sandwell. gov.uk); ROUNDS GREEN LIB, Martley Rd, Oldbury, W Midlands, B69 1DZ (tel & fax: 0121-552-2879; email: roundsgreen.library@sandwell. gov.uk); SMETHWICK LIB, High St, Smethwick, W Midlands, B66 1AB (0121-558-0497; fax: 0121-555-6064; email: smethwick.library@sandwell.gov.uk); STONE CROSS LIB, Beverley Rd, Stone Cross, W Bromwich, W Midlands, B71 2LH (tel & fax: 0121-588-2367; email: stonecross.library@ sandwell.gov.uk); THIMBLEMILL LIB, Thimblemill Rd, Smethwick, W Midlands, B67 5RJ (0121-429-2039; fax: 0121-429-2468; email: thimblemill. library@sandwell.gov.uk); TIPTON LIB, Victoria Rd, Tipton, W Midlands, DY4 8QL (0121-557-1796; fax: 0121-557-6459; email: tipton.library@ sandwell.gov.uk); WEDNESBURY LIB, Walsall St, Wednesbury, W Midlands, WS10 9EH (0121-556-0351; fax: 0121-505-2109; email: wednesbury. library@sandwell.gov.uk)
Svc Pts: Mobile: 2 *AV:* 22 *Computers:* 19 *Internet:* 19
Collns: JFR (at Wednesbury, Smethwick & West Bromwich Libs); BSI on m-fiche *Co-op Schemes:* WMRLS, ILL, Proj Earl *ILLs:* county, natl & internatl *Loans:* bks & spkn wd/4 wks; audios & CD-ROMs/2 wks; videos & DVDs/1 wk *Charges:* audios/50p, conc 25p; videos/75p-£2.25; DVDs/£1, conc 50p *Income Gen:* req & res/free if in stock, otherwise 50p, conc 25p, lost ticket/50p, conc 25p *Fines:* bks, audios & CD-ROMs/9p pd; videos/loan charge; under 18s, over-60s, students in HE & FE, recipients of various benefits all exempt *Equip:* 5 m-readers, m-printer (A4/40p), 24 fax (£1-£3 per pg), 21 copiers (A4/10p, A3 20p), 250 computers *Disabled:* CCTV, minicoms, cassette players, large print bks *Online:* Infocheck/Waterlow

Stock:	1 Apr 2000	1 Apr 2001
ad lend:	285087	245909
ad ref:	13416	24306
ch:	86262	80497
audios:	34456	18718
videos:	4636	4288
CD-ROMs:	234	200
periodcls:	216	153

Issues:	1999-2000	2000-01
ad lend:	1247406	1141880
ch:	406373	349142
audios:	86859	84692
videos:	21685	23926
CD-ROMs:	811	491

Acqs:	1999-2000	2000-01
bks:	59245	55088
AVs:	4894	3976

Acqs: Source: lib suppl *Offcr-in-Charge:* Principal Libs Offcr, as above
Classn: DDC *Cat: Type:* author, classified *Medium:* auto *Auto Sys:* Genesis *Svcs: Extramural:* schools, hosps, old people's homes, housebnd, day centres, playgroups *Info:* business, community, council *Other:* Open Learning *Activs:* ch's activs, bk sales, temp exhibs, poetry readings, talks, homework clubs, coffee mornings, Storytelling Cafe *Enqs:* 382655 (1999-2000); 393224 (2000-01) *Staff: Libns:* 28 *Non-Prof:* 101

Inc from:	1999-2000	2000-01
fines etc:	£185390	£252350

Exp on:	1999-2000	2000-01
bks:	£406586	£422033
AVs:	£88741	£86216

Scottish Borders

P159 Scottish Borders Council Library and Information Services
Lib Svc HQ, St Marys Mill, Selkirk, Scottish Borders, TD7 5EW (01750-20842; fax: 01750-22875)
Email: libraries@scotborders.gov.uk
Internet: http://www.scottishborders.gov.uk/libraries/

Local Auth: Scottish Borders Council *Pop:* 107000 *Cttee:* Edu & Lifelong Learning Cttee *Larger Dept:* Edu & Lifelong Learning *Dept Chief:* Acting Dir: Mr Colin Johnson *Chief:* Lib & Info Svcs Mgr: Miss Margaret Menzies BA, MLib, MCLIP (mmenzies@scotborders.gov.uk) *Dep:* Community & Operations Libn: Mrs Gillian McNay MA, MCLIP (gmcnay@scotborders.gov.uk) *Other Snr Staff:* Principal Libn, Yng People's Svcs: Miss Ruth Collin BA, MCLIP (rcollin@ scotborders.gov.uk); Info Svcs Libn: Mrs Sheena Milne MA, DipLib, MCLIP (smilne@scotborders. gov.uk); Area Libn (Galashiels): Miss Caroline Letton MA, FSA, MCLIP (cletton@scotborders. gov.uk); Area Libn (Hawick): Mr John Beedle BA, MCLIP (jbeedle@scotborders.gov.uk); Area Libn (Peebles): Mr Paul Taylor BSc, DipLib, MCLIP (ptaylor@scotborders.gov.uk) *Main Libs:* GALASHIELS LIB, Lawyers Brae, Galashiels, Scottish Borders, TD1 3JQ (01896-752512; fax: 01896-753575; email: Libgalashiels@ scotborders.gov.uk); HAWICK LIB, North Bridge St, Hawick, Scottish Borders, TD9 9QT (01450-372637; fax: 01450-370991; email: Libhawick@ scotborders.gov.uk); PEEBLES LIB, Chambers Inst, High St, Peebles, Scottish Borders, EH45 8AG (01721-720123; fax: 01721-724424; email: Libpeebles@scotborders.gov.uk) *Branch Libs:* DUNS LIB, 49 Newtown St, Duns, Scottish Borders, TD11 3AU (01361-882622; fax: 01361-884104; email: Libduns@scotborders.gov.uk); EYEMOUTH LIB, Manse Rd, Eyemouth, Scottish Borders, TD14 5JE (018907-50300; fax: 018907-51633; email: Libeyemouth@scotborders.gov.uk); JEDBURGH LIB, Castlegate, Jedburgh, Scottish Borders, TD8 6AS (tel & fax: 01835-863592; email: Libjedburgh@scotborders.gov.uk); KELSO LIB, Bowmont St, Kelso, Scottish Borders, TD5 7JH (01573-223171; fax: 01573-226618; email: Libkelso@scotborders.gov.uk); SELKIRK LIB, Ettrick Ter, Selkirk, Scottish Borders, TD7 4LE (tel & fax: 01750-20267; email: Libselkirk@ scotborders.gov.uk)
Svc Pts: PT: 4 *Mobile:* 6 *AV:* 13 *Computers:* 13 *Internet:* 13
Collns: SFR; Borders hist & archvs (at Lib HQ – see **A448**) *Co-op Schemes:* SILLR, CONARLS *ILLs:* county, natl & internatl *Loans:* bks & audios/4 wks; videos & CD-ROMs/1 wk *Charges:* CDs/70p; talking bks/free; videos/£1.80; CD-ROMs/£1.50 *Income Gen:* req/50p, conc 25p, juniors free; lost tickets/£1 *Fines:* bks/ad 15p pd, oaps 6p pd, ch exempt; talking bks/15p pd, conc 6p pd; CDs/70p pd; videos/£1.20 pd; CD-ROMs/£1 pd *Equip:* m-readers, m-printer (40p per sheet), copiers (A4/12p, A3/24p), 13 fax (varies to send, 10p per sheet to receive), computers (incl 29 with CD-ROM & 17 with internet) *Disabled:* Kurzweil *Offcr-in-Charge:* Lib & Info Svcs Mgr, as above

Stock:	1 Apr 2000	1 Apr 2001
ad lend:	136138	135541
ad ref:	38447	38092
ch:	41200	39327
audios:	6932	11104
videos:	1958	3441
CD-ROMs:	475	453
periodcls:	19	82
archvs:	3877 m	3877 m

Issues:	1999-2000	2000-01
ad lend:	596796	564528
ch:	112636	116637
audios:	33410	42517
videos:	3591	6428
CD-ROMs:	441	327

Acqs:	1999-2000	2000-01
bks:	15687	21067
AVs:	4250	4811

Acqs: Source: lib suppl *Offcr-in-Charge:* Lib & Info Svcs Mgr, as above
Classn: DDC *Cat: Type:* author, classified & title *Medium:* cards & auto *Auto Sys:* Dynix *Svcs: Extramural:* schools, hosps, old people's homes, housebnd, day centres, play groups *Info:* community, business, careers, tourist, genealogical *Activs:* ch's activs, bk sales, temp exhibs, reading groups, talks, author visits *Offcr-in-Charge:* Lib & Info Svcs Mgr, as above
Enqs: 35888 (1999-2000); 37985 (2000-01) *Staff: Libns:* 9.5 *Non-Prof:* 38

Inc from:	1999-2000	2000-01
local govt:	£1347112	£1440895
fines etc:	£67037	£90560
total:	£1414149	£1532332

Exp on:	1999-2000	2000-01
bks:	£136214	£176062
AVs:	£30100	£47628
elec media:	-	£4569
salaries:	£815578	£835124
total:	£1414149	£1532332

Sefton

P160 Sefton Library and Information Services
Lib Admin, Pavilion Bldgs, 99-105 Lord Street, Southport, Merseyside, PR8 1RH (0151-934-2380; fax: 0151-934-2370)
Email: library.service@leisure.sefton.gov.uk
Internet: http://www.sefton.gov.uk/leisure/libraries/

Local Auth: Sefton Metropolitan Borough Council *Pop:* 288856 *Cttee:* Leisure Ratification Cttee *Larger Dept:* Leisure Svcs *Dept Chief:* Leisure Dir: Mr G.L. Bayliss *Chief:* Head of Lib & Info Svcs: Mr John Hilton MCLIP (john.hilton@ leisure.sefton.gov.uk) *Branch Libs:* AINSDALE LIB, Liverpool Ave, Ainsdale, Southport, Merseyside, PR8 3NE (01704-577345; email: ainsdale.library@leisure. sefton.gov.uk); AINTREE LIB, Altway, Aintree, Liverpool, L10 6LF (0151-934-5790; email: aintree. library@leisure.sefton.gov.uk); BIRKDALE LIB, 240-244 Liverpool Rd, Birkdale, Southport, Merseyside, PR8 4PD (01704-567380; email: birkdale.library@leisure.sefton.gov.uk); BOOTLE LIB, 220 Stanley Rd, Bootle, Merseyside, L20 3EN (0151-934-5781; email: bootle.library@leisure. sefton.gov.uk); CHURCHTOWN LIB, Mill Ln, Churchtown, Southport, Merseyside, PR9 7PL (01704-228678; email: churchtown.library@leisure. sefton.gov.uk); COLLEGE RD LIB, College Rd, Crosby, Liverpool, L23 3DP (0151-934-5792; email: collegeroad.library@leisure.sefton.gov.uk); CROSBY LIB, Crosby Rd North, Waterloo, Liverpool, L22 0LQ (0151-934-5772; email: crosby. library@leisure.sefton.gov.uk); FORMBY LIB, Duke St, Formby, Liverpool, L37 4AN (01704-874177; email: formby.library@leisure.sefton. gov.uk); LITHERLAND LIB, Linacre Rd, Litherland, Liverpool, L21 6NR (0151-928-1357; email: litherland.library@leisure.sefton.gov.uk); MAGHULL LIB, Liverpool Rd North, Maghull, Liverpool, L31 2HJ (0151-934-5784; email: maghull.library@leisure.sefton.gov.uk); NETHERTON LIB, Glovers Ln, Netherton, Bootle, Merseyside, L30 3TL (0151-934-5786; email: netherton. library@leisure.sefton.gov.uk); ☞

(Sefton Lib & Info Svcs cont)
ORRELL LIB, Linacre Ln, Bootle, Merseyside, L20 6ES (0151-934-5796; *email:* orrell.library@leisure. sefton.gov.uk); SOUTHPORT LIB, Lord St, Southport, Merseyside, PR8 1DJ (0151-934-2118; *email:* Southport.library@leisure.sefton.gov.uk)
Svc Pts: Mobile: 1 *AV:* 13 *Computers:* 13 *Internet:* 13
Co-op Schemes: Libs North West, LADSIRLAC *ILLs:* county, natl & internatl *Loans:* bks/4 wks; audios & videos/1 wk; CD-ROMs/2 wks
Charges: audios/80p; videos/£1; CD-ROMs/£2 *Income Gen:* req & res/60p; lost ticket/£1; lost or damaged item/£1 admin charge; sale of old stock (60p-£2.25) *Fines:* bks/ad & oap 7p pd 1st 10 days, 70p pw thereafter (£60 max), ch 1p pd 1st 10 days, 10p wk thereafter (£1.20 max); audios, Videos & CD-ROMs/loan charge *Equip:* m-reader, m-printer (50p), copier (A4/10p, A3/ 25p), 120 computers (all with wd-proc, internet & CD-ROM), room hire (from £16.90 per hr)

Stock:	1 Apr 2000	1 Apr 2001
ad lend:	372529	367293
ad ref:	54210	64620
ch:	114606	127492
audios:	17981	21324
videos:	322	2252
CD-ROMs:	-	1656
periodcls:	185	185

Issues:	1999-2000	2000-01
ch:	395052	334264
audios:	144135	150644
videos:	-	20821

Acqs:	1999-2000	2000-01
bks:	57956	55021
AVs:	3662	7388

Acqs: Source: lib suppl, publ & bksellers *Offcr-in-Charge:* Head of Lib & Info Svcs, as above
Classn: DDC *Cat: Type:* author, classified, subj & title *Medium:* auto *Auto Sys:* DS *Svcs: Extramural:* schools, hosps, housebnd, play groups *Info:* community *Other:* LearnDirect Centre; UK Online Centres *Activs:* ch's activs, bk sales, temp exhibs, reading groups, talks, author visits, drama workshops
Staff: Libns: 23 *Other Prof:* 2 *Non-Prof:* 72

Inc from:	1999-2000	2000-01
local govt:	£3610918	£3966632
fines etc:	£159608	£187929
total:	£3839526	£4154561

Exp on:	1999-2000	2000-01
stock:	£615838	£617884
salaries:	£1595425	£1603772
total:	£3839526	£4154561

Sheffield

P161 Sheffield Libraries, Archives and Information

Central Lib, Surrey Street, Sheffield, S Yorkshire, S1 1XZ (0114-273-5052; *fax:* 0114-273-5009)
Internet: http://www.sheffield.gov.uk/

Local Auth: Sheffield Metropolitan Dist Council *Pop:* 529600 *Cttee:* Svc Standards Scrutiny Board *Larger Dept:* Leisure Svcs *Dept Chief:* Dir of Leisure Svcs: Mr Keith Crawshaw BA, MCLIP *Chief:* City Libn: Mrs Janice Maskort (janice.maskort@sheffield.gov.uk)

Other Snr Staff: Mgr (Policy & Development): Mr Martin Dutch; *Mgr* (Lifelong Learning): Mr David Isaac; *Mgr* (Operations): Ms Jo McCausland
Main Libs: Regional Libs: CENTRAL LIB, addr as above; *Dist Libs:* BROOMHILL LIB, Taptonville Rd, Sheffield, S Yorkshire, S10 5BR (0114-273-4276); CHAPELTOWN LIB, Nether Ley Ave, Sheffield, S Yorkshire, S35 1AE (0114-203-7000); CRYSTAL PEAKS LIB, 1-3 Peak Sq, Crystal Peaks, Sheffield, S Yorkshire, S20 7PH (0114-248-1127); DARNALL LIB, Britannia Rd, Sheffield, S Yorkshire, S9 5JG (0114-203-7429); FIRTH PK LIB, 443 Firth Park Rd, Sheffield, S Yorkshire, S5 6QG (0114-203-7433); HIGHFIELD LIB, London Rd, Sheffield, S Yorkshire, S2 4NF (0114-203-7204); HILLSBOROUGH LIB, Middlewood Rd, Sheffield, S Yorkshire, S6 4HD (0114-203-9529); MANOR LIB, Ridgeway Rd, Sheffield, S Yorkshire, S12 2SS (0114-203-7805); STOCKSBRIDGE LIB, Manchester Rd, Sheffield, S36 1DH (0114-273-4205); TOTLEY LIB, 205 Baslow Rd, Sheffield, S Yorkshire, S17 4DT (0114-236-3067); WOODSEATS LIB, Chesterfield Rd, Sheffield, S Yorkshire, S8 0SH (0114-274-9149) *Branch (Community) Libs:* BURNGREAVE LIB, 179 Spital Hill, Sheffield, S Yorkshire, S4 7LF (0114-203-9002); ECCLESFIELD LIB, High St, Sheffield, S Yorkshire, S35 9UA (0114-203-7013); FRECHEVILLE LIB, Smalldale Rd, Sheffield, S Yorkshire, S12 4YD (0114-203-7817); GLEAD-LESS LIB, White Ln, Sheffield, S12 3GH (0114-203-7804); GREENHILL LIB, Hemper Ln, Sheffield, S Yorkshire, S8 7FE (0114-203-7700); JORDANTHORPE LIB, 15 Jordanthorpe Centre, Sheffield, S Yorkshire, S8 8DX (0114-203-7701); LIMPSFIELD LIB, Limpsfield Middle School, Jenkin Ave, Sheffield, S Yorkshire, S9 1AN (0114-203-7430); NEWFIELD GREEN LIB, Gleadless Rd, Sheffield, S Yorkshire, S2 2BT (0114-203-7818); PARK LIB, Duke St, Sheffield, S Yorkshire, S2 5QP (0114-203-9000); PARSON CROSS LIB, Margetson Cres, Sheffield, S Yorkshire, S5 9ND (0114-203-9533); SOUTHEY LIB, Moonshine Ln, Sheffield, S Yorkshire, S5 8RB (0114-203-9531); STANNINGTON LIB, Uppergate Rd, Sheffield, S6 6BX (0114-232-6527); TINSLEY LIB, Tinsley Shopping Centre, Bawtrey Rd, Sheffield, S Yorkshire, S9 1UY (0114-203-7432); UPPERTHORPE LIB, Upperthorpe, Sheffield, S6 3NA (0114-203-9001); WALKLEY LIB, South Rd, Sheffield, S Yorkshire, S6 3TD (0114-203-9532); WOODHOUSE LIB, Tannery St, Sheffield, S Yorkshire, S13 7JU (0114-269-2607)
Svc Pts: Mobile: 5 *AV:* 31, incl 28 video *Computers:* 12 *Internet:* 11 *Other:* SHEFFIELD ARCHVS, 52 Shoreham St, Sheffield, S1 5BR (see **A452**); SCHOOLS LIB SVC, Bannerdale Centre, 125 Carter Knoele Rd, Sheffield, S7 2EX (0114-250-6840); 3 hosp libs
Collns: local hist photos (Sheffield & region); business & technical colln, incl patents, BSI & World Metal Index; Sports Lib & Info Svcs, incl Physical Edu Assoc Lib; European Public Info Centre (EPIC); botanical illusts; Alan Rouse Climbing Colln; Women's Health Colln; range of 19C journals *Co-op Schemes:* YLI, SINTO, Proj EARL, PIN *ILLs:* county, natl & internatl
Loans: bks/3 wks; audios/1 wk; videos & DVDs/ 1 day, 1 wk or 3 wks *Charges:* audios/free-80p; videos/free-£2.50 *Income Gen:* req & res/50p; lost ticket/50p *Fines:* bks/ad & oap 8p pd, audio, videos & DVDs/loan charge; ch & registered disabled exempt *Equip:* 12 m-reader/printers (20p), 28 fax (£1+) 30 copiers (5p-20p), 119 computers (incl 37 with wd-proc, 37 with CD-ROM & 37 with internet, access free, printouts 5p per pg), 6 rooms for hire (£3-£12)

Stock:	1 Apr 2000	1 Apr 2001
ad lend:	417061	424754
ad ref:	289547	286085
ch:	161717	163082
audios:	35527	34989
videos:	25674	28053
CD-ROMs:	97	97
periodcls:	750	750

Issues:	1999-2000	2000-01
ad lend:	1789996	1846827
ch:	680251	661576
audios:	204403	228640
videos:	270351	307985
CD-ROMs:	-	2312

Acqs:	1999-2000	2000-01
bks:	71554	51883
AVs:	12809	10310

Acqs: Source: lib suppl, publ & bksellers *Co-op:* Yorkshire Bk Consortium *Offcr-in-Charge: Mgr* (Stock & Collns): Miss Alison Jobey
Classn: DDC, Alpine Club's sys for climbing colln *Cat: Type:* author, classified, subj & title *Medium:* cards & auto *Auto Sys:* Epixtech *Svcs: Extramural:* schools, hosps, old people's homes, housebnd, play groups *Info:* business & technical svc, World Metal Index, community *Other:* learning centres, archvs *Activs:* ch's activs, bk sales, temp exhibs, reading groups, writers' groups, talks, author visits, Annual Bk Festival, Sheffield Ch's Bk Award, Local Hist Fair
Enqs: 390392 (1999-2000); 361812 (2000-01) *Staff: Libns:* 74.2 *Non-Prof:* 213.5

Inc from:	2000-01
local govt:	£7684486
fines etc:	£410987
total:	£8525981

Exp on:	2000-01
bks:	£1096448
AVs:	£93950
elec media:	£86765
salaries:	£4995740
total:	£8525981

Shetland Islands

P162 Shetland Islands Library Service

Lib HQ, Shetland Lib, Lower Hillhead, Lerwick, Shetland, ZE1 0EL (01595-693868; *fax:* 01595-694430)
Email: ShetlandLibrary@sic.shetland.gov.uk
Internet: http://www.shetland-library.gov.uk/

Local Auth: Shetland Islands Council *Pop:* 22400 *Larger Dept:* Community Svcs *Dept Chief:* Exec Dir: Ms Jacqui Watt *Chief:* Chief Libn: Ms Alison Hunter MCLIP *Dep:* Asst Chief Libns: Mr Douglas Gdn MA, MCLIP & Miss Elspeth Brown BA, DipLIS, MCLIP
Main Libs: SHETLAND LIB, addr as above
Svc Pts: PT: 2 *Mobile:* 2
Collns: E.S. Reid Tait Colln; Gilbert Goudie Colln (both collns of Shetlandiana, at Lib HQ) *ILLs:* county, natl & internatl *Loans:* bks, audios & videos/4 wks *Charges:* none *Fines:* none *Equip:* m-readers, copiers, computers (incl wd-proc & internet) *Disabled:* wheelchair access, external ramp

Stock:	1 Apr 2000
ad lend:	48288
ad ref:	9238
ch:	69677
AVs:	4248
periodcls:	108

Issues:	1999-2000
ad lend:	137616
ch:	91089
AVs:	8931

Acqs:	1999-2000
bks:	15555
AVs:	813

Acqs: Source: lib suppl
Classn: DDC *Cat: Type:* author, classified, subj & title *Medium:* auto *Auto Sys:* own (local company) *Svcs: Extramural:* schools (school svc integrated into public svc), hosps, old people's

homes, housebnd *Info:* business, community, council *Other:* Open Learning *Activs:* ch's activs, bk sales, temp exhibs, poetry readings *Enqs:* 12113 (1999-2000) *Staff:* Libns: 4 *Non-Prof:* 24

Inc from:	1999-2000	2000-01
local govt:	£753464	£806257
fines etc:	£47777	£3987
total:	£801241	£810244

Exp on:	1999-2000	2000-01
stock:	£175962	£168224
salaries:	£481883	£487245
total:	£801241	£810244

Shropshire

P163 Shropshire County Library Service

Shirehall, Abbey Foregate, Shrewsbury, Shropshire, SY2 6ND (01743-255000; *fax:* 01743-255050)
Email: libraries@shropshire-cc.gov.uk
Internet: http://www.shropshire-cc.gov.uk/

Local Auth: Shropshire County Council *Pop:* 284636 *Larger Dept:* Community & Environment Svcs *Dept Chief:* Corporate Dir: Ms Carolyn Downs *Chief:* Head of Libs & Info: Mr Jim Roads *Other Snr Staff:* Principal Libn (Development & Support): Mr Don Yuile; Principal Libn (Yng People & Access): Mr Gordon Dickins; Principal Libn (Shrewsbury): Ms Elaine Moss; Principal Libn (North): Ms Claire Cartlidge; Principal Libn (South): Mr Adrian Williams *Main Libs:* Shrewsbury Area HQ: SHREWSBURY LIB, Castle Gates, Shrewsbury, Shropshire, SY1 2AS (01743-255300; *fax:* 01743-255309); North Shropshire Area HQ: OSWESTRY LIB, Arthur St, Oswestry, Shropshire, SY11 1JN (01691-653211; *fax:* 01691-656994); South Shropshire Area HQ: BRIDGNORTH LIB, Listley St, Bridgnorth, Shropshire, WV16 4AW (01746-763358; *fax:* 01746-766625) *Branch Libs:* ALBRIGHTON LIB, Station Rd, Albrighton, near Wolverhampton, W Midlands, WV7 3QH (01902-372226; *fax:* 01902-373369); BAYSTON HILL LIB, Lythwood Rd, Bayston Hill, Shrewsbury, Shropshire, SY3 0NA (01743-872412); CHURCH STRETTON LIB, Church St, Church Stretton, Shropshire, SY6 5EL (01694-722535; *fax:* 01694-723045); ELLESMERE LIB, Fullwood House, Victoria St, Ellesmere, Shropshire, SY12 0EG (01691-622611); HARLESCOTT LIB, Meadow Dr Farm, Harlescott, Shrewsbury, Shropshire, SY1 4NG (01743-361822); LUDLOW LIB, 10 Old St, Ludlow, Shropshire, SY8 1NP (01584-813600; *fax:* 01584-813601); MARKET DRAYTON LIB, 51 Cheshire St, Market Drayton, Shropshire, TF9 1PH (01630-652105; *fax:* 01630-657688); SHIFNAL LIB, Broadway, Shifnal, Shropshire, TF11 8AZ (01952-461018; *fax:* 01952-463251); WEM LIB, Talbot House, High St, Wem, Shrewsbury, Shropshire, SY13 5AA (01939-236995; *fax:* 01939-236994); WHITCHURCH LIB, High St, Whitchurch, Shropshire, SY13 1AX (01948-662238; *fax:* 01948-665101) *Svc Pts:* PT: 9 *Mobile:* 7 *AV:* 23 *Computers:* 20 *Internet:* 20 *Other:* SCHOOLS LIB SVC; 2 prison libs
Collns: West Midlands Creative Lit Colln; Soc for Storytelling Lib (both at Shrewsbury Lib); Bridgnorth Historical Colln (at Bridgnorth Lib); Welsh Colln (at Oswestry Lib); Shropshire Parochial Libs; Records & Rsrch Colln (local studies & archvs) *Co-op Schemes:* JFR, WMRLS *ILLs:* natl & internatl *Loans:* bks & spkn wd/3 wks; audios, videos & CD-ROMs/1 wk *Charges:* audios & CD-ROMs/80p;spkn wd/£1 or £1.50; videos/£1.25 or £1.95; DVDs/£2.25 *Income Gen:* req/70p; lost ticket/£1 *Fines:* bks/ad 11p pd, ch 2p pd after 2nd wk; audios, videos & CD-ROMs/loan charge; blind & housebnd exempt *Equip:* 6

m-readers, 4 m-printers (10p), 14 fax (UK £1 per pg, higher overseas), 20 copiers (10p), clr copier (£1), 103 computers (all with wd-proc, 49 with CD-ROM & 43 with internet)

Stock:	1 Apr 2000	1 Apr 2001
ad lend:	279609	251350
ad ref:	95343	96429
ch:	75963	80601
audios:	23873	19086
videos:	5804	6815
CD-ROMs:	-	20
periodcls:	766	766

Issues:	1999-2000	2000-01
ad lend:	1493036	1419097
ch:	385005	373962
audios:	88474	87694
videos:	47433	38582

Acqs:	1999-2000	2000-01
bks:	29956	27598
AVs:	3644	5194

Acqs: Source: lib suppl & bksellers *Co-op:* consortium purchasing contracts awarded through West Mercia Supplies for supply to Herefordshire, Shropshire, Telford & Wrekin & Worcestershire *Offcr-in-Charge:* Snr Libn, Bibliographical Svcs: Mr Rob Woodward (rob.woodward@shropshire-cc.gov.uk)
Classn: DDC *Cat: Type:* author & classified *Medium:* auto *Auto Sys:* DS Galaxy *Svcs: Extramural:* schools, prisons, hosps, old people's homes, housebnd, sheltered accommodation, playgroups *Info:* business, community, careers *Other:* homework & study centres *Activs:* ch's activs, bk sales, temp exhibs, reading groups, writers' groups, talks, author visits *Enqs:* 251503 (1999-2000) 243503 (2000-01) *Staff:* Libns: 33.2 *Non-Prof:* 68.8

Inc from:	1999-2000	2000-01
local govt:	£2779937	£2911191
fines etc:	£249893	£271306
total:	£3156911	£3370501

Exp on:	1999-2000	2000-01
bks:	£323357	£322590
AVs:	£53711	£55216
salaries:	£1637280	£1701520
total:	£3156911	£3370501

Slough

P164 Slough Libraries and Information Service

Slough Central Lib, High Street, Slough, Berkshire, SL1 1EA (01753-535166; *fax:* 01753-825050)
Email: library@sloughlibrary.org.uk
Internet: http://www.sloughlibrary.org.uk/

Local Auth: Slough Borough Council *Pop:* 111100 *Cttee:* Community Svcs Cttee *Larger Dept:* Community Svcs *Dept Chief:* Chief Offcr: Mrs Janet Perez *Chief:* Head of Libs & Info: Mrs Yvonne M. Cope *Dep:* Lib Svcs Mgr (Strategy & Improvement): Ms Diane Flood BA(Hons), MCLIP, DMS (diane.flood@slough.gov.uk); Lib Svcs Mgr (Operations): Ms Jackie Menniss (jackie.menniss@slough.gov.uk)
Main Libs: SLOUGH CENTRAL LIB, addr as above *Branch Libs:* BRITWELL LIB, Wentworth Ave, Britwell, Slough, Berkshire, SL2 2AW (*tel & fax:* 01753-522869); CIPPENHAM LIB, Elmshott Ln, Cippenham, Slough, Berkshire, SL1 5RB (*tel & fax:* 01628-661745); LANGLEY LIB, Trelawney Ave, Langley, Slough, Berkshire, SL3 7UF (*tel & fax:* 01753-542153) *Svc Pts: Mobile:* 3, shared with Bracknell Forest (see **P14**) & Royal Borough of Windsor & Maidenhead (see **P202**) *Computers:* 4 *Internet:* 4
Collns: William Herschel Colln; Local Studies Colln (both at Central Lib) *Co-op Schemes:* HATRICS, CILLA, BLIP, BIN *ILLs:* county & natl

Loans: bks & audios/3 wks; videos, CD-ROMs & DVDs/1 wk; mixed-media packs/3 wks *Charges:* cassettes/50p, sets of 7+ £1; CDs & talking bks/ £1; videos/£1.50, ch's videos £1; CD-ROMs/ £1.50; DVDs/ad £2, ch £1.50; mixed-media packs/£1.50 *Income Gen:* res/ad 65p, large print & ch's bks 25p *Fines:* bks/ad 10p pd (£4 max), ch 4p pd (96p max); audios/as ad bks; videos & CD-ROMs/50p pd (£10 max) *Equip:* 3 m-readers, m-printer, 3 copiers (A4/10p, A3/20p), fax, 42 computers (all with wd-proc & internet, 12 with CD-ROM), room for hire (varies) *Disabled:* Aladdin Text Enlarger

Stock:	1 Apr 2000	1 Apr 2001
bks:	159317	184537

Issues:	1999-2000	2000-01
bks:	611050	588830

Acqs:	1999-2000	2000-01
all items:	30997	38330

Acqs: Source: lib suppl & bksellers *Offcr-in-Charge:* Stock Libn: Mrs Gail Stuckey *Classn:* DDC *Cat: Type:* author, classified & title *Medium:* auto *Auto Sys:* Dynix *Svcs: Extramural:* hosps, old people's homes, housebnd *Info:* business, careers, community, EU, tourist, local studies *Other:* Open Learning, UK Online Centre at Slough Lib *Activs:* ch's activs, bk sales, temp exhibs *Offcr-in-Charge:* Ms Zoe Dickens & Ms Gaynor Baveystock *Enqs:* 133764 (1999-2000); 130543 (2000-01) *Staff:* Libns: 15.8 *Non-Prof:* 41.8

Exp on:	1999-2000	2000-01
bks:	£333856	£295970

Solihull

P165 Solihull Libraries

Central Lib, Homer Rd, Solihull, W Midlands, B91 3RG (0121-704-6941; *fax:* 0121-704-6991)
Email: libraryarts@solihull.gov.uk
Internet: http://www.solihull.gov.uk/

Local Auth: Solihull Metropolitan Borough Council *Pop:* 205600 *Cttee:* Cabinet (Edu & Ch) *Larger Dept:* Edu, Libs & Arts *Dept Chief:* Dir: Mr Kevin Crompton *Chief:* Head of Libs & Arts: Mr Nigel Ward (nward@solihull.gov.uk)
Main Libs: CENTRAL LIB, addr as above *Branch Libs:* CASTLE BROMWICH LIB, Hurst Ln North, Castle Bromwich, Birmingham, B36 0EY (0121-747-3708; *fax:* 0121-748-5919); CHELMSLEY WOOD LIB, Stephenson Dr, Chelmsley Wood, Birmingham, B37 5TA (0121-788-4380; *fax:* 0121-788-4391; *email:* clamb@itpoint.org.uk); HOBS MOAT LIB, Ulleries Rd, Solihull, W Midlands, B92 8EB (0121-743-4592; *fax:* 0121-743-2473); KINGSHURST LIB, Marston Dr, Kingshurst, Birmingham, B37 6BD (0121-770-3451; *fax:* 0121-770-9388); KNOWLE LIB, Chester House, 1667-8 High St, Knowle, Solihull, W Midlands, B93 0LL (01564-775840; *fax:* 01564-770953); MERIDEN LIB, Arden Cottage, The Green, Meriden, Coventry, West Midlands, CV7 7LN (01676-522717; *fax:* 01676-521146); OLTON LIB, 169a Warwick Rd, Olton, Solihull, W Midlands, B92 7AR (0121-706-3038; *fax:* 0121-708-0549); SHIRLEY LIB, Church Rd, Shirley, Solihull, W Midlands, B90 2AY (0121-744-1076; *fax:* 0121-744-5047) *Svc Pts:* PT: 4 *Mobile:* 1 *AV:* 7 *Computers:* 7 *Internet:* 7
Collns: local studies colln; BSA archvs; local photo colln *Co-op Schemes:* BLCMP, ILL, JFR, Viscount, SEALS *Loans:* bks/4 wks; audios/2 wks *Charges:* cassettes/65p, conc 35p, set of 3+ £1.50, conc 75p; CDs/£1, conc 40p, set of 2+ £2, conc 75p; videos/£2, set of 2+ £3.50 *Income Gen:* res/75p, conc 50p, ch free; lost ticket/£1.50, conc £1, ch 50p *Fines:* bks/ad 15p pd (max £5), oap 5p pd (max £2.50), ch 2p pd (max £1); audios/10p pd (max £5); videos/£1 pd (max £10) 🖝

(Solihull Libs cont)
Equip: m-reader, m-printer (A4/30p), 8 fax (varies), 2 video viewers, 11 copiers (A4/10p, A3/20p), computers (incl wd-proc, internet & CD-ROM), rooms for hire (various)

Stock:	1 Apr 2000	1 Apr 2001
lend:	393077	374071
ref:	28284	28778
audios:	19366	18946
videos:	3762	3868
periodcls:	218	109

Issues:	1999-2000	2000-01
bks:	1221778	1072532
audios:	52719	52311
videos:	9512	8790

Acqs:	1999-2000	2000-01
bks:	19930	17961
AVs:	1933	1525

Acqs: Source: lib suppl
Classn: DDC **Cat:** Type: author, classified & title Medium: auto **Auto Sys:** Talis **Svcs:** Extramural: schools, old people's homes, housebnd, day centres **Info:** business, European, tourist, careers **Other:** Open Learning, special svcs database **Activs:** ch's activs, bk sales, films, temp exhibs, poetry readings, reading groups, concerts, plays, annual arts festival, coffee mornings
Enqs: 137020 (1999-2000); 155729 (2000-01)
Staff: Libns: 19 Non-Prof: 86

Inc from:	1999-2000	2000-01
local govt:	£3024463	£3107640
fines etc:	£333278	£268698
total:	£3357741	£3376338

Exp on:	1999-2000	2000-01
stock:	£281672	£278323
salaries:	£1957312	£2025882
total:	£3357741	£3376338

Proj: new Balsall Common Lib, opening summer 2002

Somerset

P166 Somerset Libraries, Arts and Information

Lib Admin Centre, Mount Street, Bridgwater, Somerset, TA6 3ES (01278-451201; fax: 01278-452787)
Email: librec@somerset.gov.uk
Internet: http://www.somerset.gov.uk/libraries/

Local Auth: Somerset County Council **Pop:** 496300 **Larger Dept:** Culture & Heritage Directorate **Dept Chief:** Dir: Ms Jane Murray **Chief:** County Libn: Mr Robert Froud BLib, DMS, MIMgt, MCLIP **Dep:** Principal Asst County Libn: Mr Ian Watson BA, MCLIP
Main (Area) Libs: BRIDGWATER LIB, Binford Pl, Bridgwater, Somerset, TA6 3LF (01278-458373; fax: 01278-451027; email: brwlib@somerset. gov.uk); CHARD LIB, Holyrood Lace Mill, Holyrood St, Chard, Somerset, TA20 2YA (01460-63321; fax: 01460-68125; email: chalib@ somerset.gov.uk); FROME LIB, Justice Ln, Frome, Somerset, BA11 1BE (01373-462215; fax: 01373-472003; email: frolib@somerset.gov.uk); MINEHEAD LIB, Bancks St, Minehead, Somerset,

TA24 5DJ (01643-702942; fax: 01643-707935; email: minlib@somerset.gov.uk); STREET LIB, 1 Leigh Rd, Street, Somerset, BA16 0HA (01458-442032; fax: 01458-440195; email: strlib@ somerset.gov.uk); TAUNTON LIB, Paul St, Taunton, Somerset, TA1 3XZ (01823-336334; fax: 01823-340302; email: taulib@somerset.gov.uk); YEOVIL LIB, King George St, Yeovil, Somerset, BA20 1PY (01935-423144; fax: 01935-431847; email: yeolib@somerset.gov.uk) **Branch Libs:** BURNHAM-ON-SEA LIB, Princess St, Burnham-on-Sea, Somerset, TA8 1EH (01278-780505; fax: 01278-794076; email: bhmlib@somerset.gov.uk); CASTLE CARY LIB, Bailey Hill, Castle Cary, Somerset, BA7 7AA (tel & fax: 01963-350483; email: ccylib@somerset.gov.uk); CHEDDAR LIB, Union St, Cheddar, Somerset, BS27 3NB (tel & fax: 01934-742769; email: chelib@somerset. gov.uk); CREWKERNE LIB, Falkland Sq, Crewkerne, Somerset, TA18 7JS (01460-74839; fax: 01460-76960; email: crwlib@somerset. gov.uk); DULVERTON LIB, 7-9 Fore St, Dulverton, Somerset, TA22 9EX (01398-323579; fax: 01398-324208; email: dullib@somerset. gov.uk); GLASTONBURY LIB, 1 Orchard Ct, The Archers Way, Glastonbury, Somerset, BA6 9JB (01458-832148; fax: 01458-837460; email: glalib@ somerset.gov.uk); ILMINSTER LIB, Ditton St, Ilminster, Somerset, TA19 0BW (tel & fax: 01460-52695; email: ilmlib@somerset.gov.uk); LANG-PORT LIB, Whatley, Langport, Somerset, TA10 9PR (01458-250152; fax: 01458-252869; email: lanlib@somerset.gov.uk); MARTOCK LIB, The Shopping Centre, Martock, Somerset, TA12 6DL (01935-822434; fax: 01935-826280; email: marlib@ somerset.gov.uk); NETHER STOWEY LIB, Castle St, Nether Stowey, Bridgwater, Somerset, TA5 1LN (tel & fax: 01278-732741; email: neslib@ somerset.gov.uk); PRIORSWOOD LIB, Eastwick Rd, Taunton, Somerset, TA2 7HD (tel & fax: 01823-272050; email: prwlib@somerset.gov.uk); SHEPTON MALLET LIB, 2 Market Pl, Shepton Mallet, Somerset, BA4 5AZ (01749-342354; fax: 01749-330042; email: shmlib@somerset.gov.uk); SOMERTON LIB, Cox's Yard, off West St, Somerton, Somerset, TA11 7PR (01458-272835; fax: 01458-274742; email: somlib@somerset. gov.uk); SOUTH PETHERTON LIB, St James's Corner, South Petherton, Somerset, TA13 5BS (tel & fax: 01460-240851; email: spnlib@somerset. gov.uk); WATCHET LIB, 11 The Esplanade, Watchet, Somerset, TA23 0AJ (tel & fax: 01984-631380; email: watlib@somerset.gov.uk); WELLINGTON LIB, 16 Fore St, Wellington, Somerset, TA21 8AQ (01823-662635; fax: 01823-665194; email: wlnlib@somerset.gov.uk); WELLS LIB, Union St, Wells, Somerset, BA5 2PU (01749-672292; fax: 01749-679218; email: wlslib@ somerset.gov.uk); WILLITON LIB, Killick Way, Williton, Somerset, TA4 4QA (01984-632651; fax: 01984-639185; email: willib@somerset.gov.uk); WINCANTON LIB, 7 Carrington Way, Wincanton, Somerset, BA9 9JS (01963-32173; fax: 01963-34555; email: winlib@somerset.gov.uk)
Svc Pts: PT: 8 **Mobile:** 7 + 1 travelling lib **AV:** 33 **Other:** ENQ CENTRE, at Taunton Lib (01823-336370; fax: 01823-272178; email: enquiry@ somerset.gov.uk); SOMERSET STUDIES LIB, at Taunton Lib (see **A488**); PERFORMING ARTS LIB, at Yeovil Lib (01935-472020; fax: 01935-429133; email: muslib@somerset.gov.uk)
Collns: local hist bks; historical ch's bks (both at Somerset Studies Lib); Tite Colln (local hist); Aviation Colln; Edu Special Colln (all at Yeovil Lib); Environmental Issues Colln (at Frome Lib); A.E. Houseman Colln (at Street Lib) **Co-op Schemes:** SWRLS, FOURSITE Consortium **ILLs:** county, natl & internatl **Loans:** bks & spkn wd/3 wks; audios/2 wks; videos, DVDs & computer games/1 wk **Charges:** cassettes/85p, sets of 3+ £1.60; CDs/£1, sets of 3+ £1.85; videos/non-fiction & short films £1, others £2; DVDs/£2; computer games/£2-£3

Income Gen: req/ad 85p (self-svc 50p), ch 35p (self-svc 25p); lost ticket/£1 **Fines:** bks & audios/ad 35p for 1st wk, 70p per addl wk (max £5.95), ch 15p for 1st wk, 30p per addl wk (max £2.55); videos & computer games/loan charge (max £10) **Equip:** m-readers, m-printers (50p per pg), fax (1st pg £1, addl 50p, higher overseas), copiers (10p), clr copier (A4/70p, A3/£1.20), computers (incl wd-proc, internet & CD-ROM), rooms for hire (varies) **Disabled:** reading edge scanner, magnifiers, disabled access to mobile libs

Stock:	1 Apr 2000	1 Apr 2001
ad lend:	490185	460232
ad ref:	129142	120875
ch:	152568	149688
audios:	37006	42284
videos:	13463	16454
periodcls:	225	183

Issues:	1999-2000	2000-01
ad lend:	3309659	3285164
ch:	883204	889484
audios:	177487	192754
videos:	129967	123702

Acqs:	1999-2000	2000-01
bks:	85684	109073
AVs:	10621	16038

Acqs: Source: lib suppl
Classn: DDC **Cat:** Type: author, classified & title Medium: m-form & auto **Auto Sys:** DS Galaxy 2000 **Svcs:** Extramural: schools, prisons, hosps, old people's homes, housebnd **Info:** business, community, tourist, European, careers, edu, council, environment **Other:** Open Learning (at Street Lib) **Activs:** ch's activs, bk sales, temp exhibs, poetry readings, plays
Enqs: 437789 (1999-2000); 478738 (2000-01)
Staff: Libns: 45.4 Non-Prof: 137.1

Inc from:	2000-01
local govt:	£4415764
fines etc:	£956437
total:	£5372201

Exp on:	2000-01
stock:	£832588
salaries:	£3205148
total:	£5372201

South Ayrshire

P167 South Ayrshire Library and Information Services

Lib HQ, 26 Green Street, Ayr, KA8 8AD (01292-288820; fax: 01292-619019)
Internet: http://www.south-ayrshire.gov.uk/libraries/

Local Auth: South Ayrshire Council **Pop:** 114200 **Cttee:** Lifelong Learning Cttee **Larger Dept:** Edu, Culture & Lifelong Learning **Dept Chief:** Dir: Mr Mike McCabe **Chief:** Libs & Galleries Mgr: Mr Charles Deas BA, MCLIP (charles.deas@south-ayrshire.gov.uk) **Dep:** Carnegie Libn: Mrs Jeanette Castle BA, MCLIP (jeanette.castle@south-ayrshire.gov.uk) **Other Snr Staff:** Enterprise Offcr: Ms Jean Inness MA, DipLib, MCLIP (jean.inness@south-ayrshire. gov.uk); ICT Systems Libn: Ms Michelle Jefford BA, MCLIP; Ch's Svcs Libn: Ms Geraldine Downie BA, MCLIP
Main Libs: CARNEGIE LIB, 12 Main St, Ayr, KA8 8AD (01292-286385; fax: 01292-611593; email: carnegie@south-ayrshire.gov.uk) **Branch Libs:** ALLOWAY LIB, Doonholm Rd, Alloway, Ayr, KA7 4QQ (01292-442395); COYLTON LIB, 28 Main St, Coylton, Ayr, KA6 6JW (01292-570867); FOREHILL LIB, 31 Mount Oliquant Cres, Ayr, KA7 3EN (01292-265591); GIRVAN LIB, Montgomerie St, Girvan, Ayrshire, KA26 9HE (01465-712813); JOHN POLLOCK LIB, Mainholm Campus, Mainholm Rd, Ayr (01292-294363);

MAYBOLE LIB, 70c High St, Maybole, Ayrshire, KA19 7AB (01655-883044; *email:* maybole@south-ayrshire.gov.uk); PRESTWICK LIB, 14 Kyle St, Prestwick, Ayrshire, KA9 1PQ (01292-476769); TROON LIB, 5 South Beach, Troon, Ayrshire, KA10 6ES (01292-315352)
Svc Pts: PT: 6 *Mobile:* 1 *AV:* 11 *Computers:* 13 *Internet:* 13 *Other:* CyberCentre, at Carnegie Lib *Collns:* Burns Colln; South Ayrshire local hist colln *Co-op Schemes:* ALF *ILLs:* natl & internatl *Loans:* bks & talking bks/4 wks; audios/ 2 wks; videos/1 wk *Charges:* audios/£1; videos/ £2 *Income Gen:* req/50p; lost ticket/£1 *Fines:* bks & audios/ad 30p pw, ch & oap 10p pw; audios & videos/50p pw *Equip:* 10 m-readers, 2 m-printers (50p per sheet), 14 fax (£1.50 per sheet), 9 copiers (A4/10p), 71 computers (all with wd-proc, internet & CD-ROM, access free), 4 rooms for hire (£10 per hr)

Stock:	1 Apr 2000	1 Apr 2001
ad lend:	180047	180476
ad ref:	21981	23061
ch:	66527	63492
audios:	11376	6972
videos:	3705	4301
CD-ROMs:	270	132
periodcls:	56	56

Issues:	1999-2000	2000-01
ad lend:	675300	630637
ch:	159241	142397
audios:	34104	33108
videos:	7220	7679
CD-ROMs:	413	178

Acqs:	1999-2000	2000-01
bks:	22153	29368
AVs:	2403	2228

Acqs: Source: lib suppl *Offcr-in-Charge:* Accessions Libn: Miss Lorraine Armstrong (lorraine.armstrong@south-ayrshire.gov.uk) *Classn:* DDC *Cat: Type:* author, classified, subj & title *Medium:* auto *Auto Sys:* ALS *Svcs: Extramural:* old people's homes, housebnd *Info:* community, web site *Other:* Open Learning *Activs:* ch's activs, bk sales, temp exhibs *Enqs:* 668980 (1999-2000); 632268 (2000-01) *Staff: Libns:* 8 *Non-Prof:* 51.5

Inc from:	1999-2000	2000-01
local govt:	£1646059	£1642997
fines etc:	£305800	£281200
total:	£1746600	£1723700

Exp on:	1999-2000	2000-01
bks:	£348900	£301700
AVs:	£13330	£4860
salaries:	£905800	£920000
total:	£1746600	£1723700

Proj: replacement of lib computer sys

South Gloucestershire

P168 South Gloucestershire Library Service

Civic Centre, High Street, Kingswood, S Gloucestershire, BS15 9TR (01454-865782; *fax:* 01454-868555)
Email: martin_burton@southglos.gov.uk
Internet: http://www.southglos.gov.uk/libs.htm

Local Auth: South Gloucestershire Council *Pop:* 243000 *Cttee:* Community Svcs Cttee *Larger Dept:* Community Svcs *Dept Chief:* Dir: Mr Steve Evans *Chief:* Head of Libs: Mr Martin Burton MCLIP (email as above) *Dep:* Team Leader (North): Mrs Anne Hartridge MCLIP (anne_hartridge@southglos.gov.uk); Team Leader (South): Mr M. Duffy MCLIP *Branch Libs:* BRADLEY STOKE LIB, Fiddlers Wood Ln, Bradley Stoke, S Gloucestershire, BS32 9BS (01454-865723; *fax:* 01454-865724; *email:* bradleystoke.library@southglos.gov.uk);

CADBURY HEATH LIB, School Rd, Cadbury Heath, S Gloucestershire, BS30 5EN (01454-865711; *email:* cadburyheath.library@southglos.gov.uk); DOWNEND LIB, Buckingham Gdns, Downend, S Gloucestershire, BS16 5TW (01454-865666; *email:* downend.library@southglos.gov.uk); EMERSONS GREEN LIB, Emersons Way, Emersons Green, S Gloucestershire, BS16 7AP (01454-865678; *email:* emersonsgreen.library@southglos.gov.uk); FILTON LIB, The Shield Retail Pk, Link Rd, Filton, S Gloucester-shire, BS34 7BR (01454-865670; *email:* filton.library@southglos.gov.uk); HANHAM LIB, High St, Hanham, S Gloucestershire, BS15 3EJ (01454-865678; *email:* hanham.library@southglos.gov.uk); KINGSWOOD LIB, High St, Kingswood, S Gloucestershire, BS15 4AR (01454-865650; *email:* kingswood.library@southglos.gov.uk); PATCHWAY LIB, Rodway Rd, Patchway, S Gloucestershire, BS34 5PE (01454-865674; *email:* patchway.library@southglos.gov.uk); STAPLE HILL LIB, The Square, Broad St, Staple Hill, S Gloucestershire, BS16 5LR (01454-865715; *email:* staplehill.library@southglos.gov.uk); THORNBURY LIB, St Mary St, Thornbury, S Gloucestershire, BS35 2AA (01454-865655; *email:* thornbury.library@southglos.gov.uk); WINTERBOURNE LIB, Flax Pits Ln, Winter-bourne, S Gloucestershire, BS36 1LA (01454-865654; *email:* winterbourne.library@southglos.gov.uk); YATE LIB, 44 West Walk, Yate, S Gloucestershire, BS37 4AX (01454-865661; *fax:* 01454-865665; *email:* yate.library@southglos.gov.uk)
Svc Pts: PT: 1 *Mobile:* 1
Co-op Schemes: SWRLS, FOURSITE *ILLs:* co *Loans:* bks & audios/3 wks; videos/1 wk *Charges:* audios/£1.20; videos & CD-ROMs/ £2.10 *Income Gen:* res/80p; lost ticket/50p *Fines:* bks/ad & oap 15p pd, ch exempt; audio/ 15p pd; housebnd exempt *Equip:* 12 copiers (A4/10p), 2 clr copiers (A4/£1), computers (incl 131 with internet, printouts 10p), 12 rooms for hire (£7.20 per hr) *Disabled:* Kurzweil at Thornbury Lib

Stock:	1 Apr 2000	1 Apr 2001
bks:	231503	239547
audios:	15807	17691
videos:	4116	5051

Issues:	1999-2000	2000-01
bks:	1519905	1522168
audios:	81983	85096
videos:	26903	34110

Acqs:	1999-2000	2000-01
bks:	46530	25334

Acqs: Source: lib suppl *Co-op:* to be established *Offcr-in-Charge:* Team Leaders, as above *Classn:* DDC *Cat: Type:* author, classified, subj & title *Medium:* auto *Auto Sys:* DS *Svcs: Extramural:* prisons, old people's homes, house-bnd *Info:* community *Other:* Open Learning *Activs:* ch's activs, bk sales, temp exhibs, poetry readings *Offcr-in-Charge:* local libns *Enqs:* 49585 (1999-2000); 48278 (2000-01) *Staff: Libns:* 14.3 *Non-Prof:* 40.85

Exp on:	1999-2000	2000-01
bks:	£389865	£247365

South Lanarkshire

P169 South Lanarkshire Libraries and Community Learning Service

Edu Resources, Floor 6, Council HQ, Almada Street, Hamilton, S Lanarkshire, ML3 0AE (01698-454412; *fax:* 01698-454398)
Internet: http://www.southlanarkshire.gov.uk/

Local Auth: South Lanarkshire Council *Pop:* 307400 *Larger Dept:* Edu Resources *Dept Chief:* Exec Dir: Ms Maggi Allen *Chief:* Libs & Community Learning Mgr: Ms Diana Barr BA, MIMgt, MCLIP

Main Libs: EAST KILBRIDE CENTRAL LIB, 40 The Olympia, E Kilbride, Glasgow, G74 1PG (01355-220046; *fax:* 01355-229365); HAMILTON CENTRAL LIB, 4 Auchingramont Rd, Hamilton, S Lanarkshire, ML3 6JT (01698-452411; *fax:* 01698-286334); LANARK CENTRAL LIB, 16 Hope St, Lanark, S Lanarkshire, ML11 7LZ (01555-661144; *fax:* 01555-665884); RUTHERGLEN LIB, 163 Main St, Rutherglen, Glasgow, G73 2HB (0141-613-5380; *fax:* 0141-647-5164) *Branch Libs:* BLANTYRE LIB, Calder St, Blantyre, Glasgow, G72 0AU (01698-823808); BOTHWELL LIB, The Donald Inst, Main St, Bothwell, Glasgow, G71 8RG (01698-853150); BURNBANK LIB, 76 Burnbank Centre, Burnbank, Hamilton, S Lanark-shire, ML3 0NA (01698-285730); CALDERWOOD LIB, Alison Lea, E Kilbride, Glasgow, G74 3HW (01355-224170); CAMBUSLANG LIB, 6 Glasgow Rd, Cambuslang, Glasgow, G72 7BW (0141-641-3909); CARLUKE LIB, Carnwath Rd, Carluke, S Lanarkshire, ML8 4DR (01555-772134); CATHKIN LIB, 21 Lovat Pl, Cathkin, Glasgow, G73 5HS (0141-634-1249); FAIRHILL LIB, Neilsland Rd, Hamilton, S Lanarkshire, ML3 8HF (01698-282054); FORTH LIB, Forth Primary School, Main St, Forth, S Lanarkshire, ML11 1AE (01555-811594); GREENHILLS LIB, Neighbour-hood Centre, E Kilbride, Glasgow, G75 8TT (01355-242951); HALFWAY LIB, 211 Hamilton Rd, Halfway, Glasgow, G72 7PJ (0141-641-2762); HILLHOUSE LIB, Hillhouse Rd, Hamilton, S Lanarkshire, ML3 9TX (01698-710400); KING'S PK LIB, 275 Castlemilk Rd, Glasgow, G44 4LE (01355-224837); LARKHALL LIB, Muir St, Larkhall, S Lanarkshire, ML9 2BG (01698-882867); LESMAHAGOW LIB, 48 Abbeygreen, Lesmahagow, S Lanarkshire, ML11 0EF (01555-892606); ST LEONARDS LIB, St Leonard's St, E Kilbride, Glasgow, G74 2AT (01355-241573); STONEHOUSE LIB, 4-5 The Cross, Stonehouse, S Lanarkshire, ML9 3LQ (01698-793984); STRATHAVEN LIB, Glasgow Rd, Strathaven, S Lanarkshire, ML10 6LZ (01357-521167); UDDINGTON LIB, 1 Main St, Uddington, Glasgow, G71 7ES (01698-813431); WESTWOOD LIB, 121 Westwood Sq, E Kilbride, Glasgow, G75 8JQ (01355-224837); WHITEHILL LIB, Margaret Rd, Hamilton, S Lanarkshire, ML3 0PT (01698-28328)
Svc Pts: Mobile: 5 + 3 housebnd vehicles & 1 delivery vehicle *Computers:* 25 *Internet:* 25 *ILLs:* county, natl & internatl *Loans:* bks & audios/4 wks; videos/1 wk *Charges:* audios/60p, spkn wd & lang tapes free; videos/£1 *Income Gen:* req & res/50p per item, + £2 for ILLs; lost tickets/£1; genealogical enqs/£5-£10 *Fines:* bks/ ad 10p pd (max £3), ch & oap 5p pd (max £1.50); audios/10p pd (max £3); videos/10p pd; conc based on 50% of standard ad rate *Equip:* m-readers, m-printers, fax, copiers (A4/10p, A3/ 20p), 123 computers (incl wd-proc, internet & CD-ROM), room hire (at discretion)

Stock:	1 Apr 2000	1 Apr 2001
lend:	629600	636914
ref:	22730	24304
audios:	44487	45450
videos:	14506	15558
periodcls:	-	130

Issues:	1999-2000	2000-01
bks:	2389492	2170015
audios:	131188	137635
videos:	110714	87720

Acqs:	1999-2000	2000-01
bks:	44931	50549
AVs:	3758	4547

Classn: DDC *Cat: Type:* author *Medium:* printed & auto *Auto Sys:* DS & Geac *Svcs: Extramural:* old people's homes, housebnd *Other:* 3 Open Learning centres *Activs:* ch's activs, bk sales, temp exhibs *Enqs:* 171042 (1999-2000); 178046 (2000-01) *Staff: Libns:* 37.5 *Non-Prof:* 149.5 ☛

Public Libraries

South Lanarkshire
▼
Staffordshire

(S Lanarkshire Libs cont)

Inc from:	1999-2000	2000-01
local govt:	£4467048	£4820005
fines etc:	£304752	£266823
total:	£4771800	£5086828

Exp on:	1999-2000	2000-01
bks:	£480346	£493992
salaries:	£3237878	£3383859
total:	£4771800	£5086828

South Tyneside

P170 South Tyneside Libraries

Central Lib, Prince George Sq, South Shields, Tyne & Wear, NE33 2PE (0191-427-1717/1818; fax: 0191-455-8085)
Email: reference.library@s-tyneside-mbc.gov.uk
Internet: http://www.southtyneside.info/

Local Auth: South Tyneside Metropolitan Borough Council *Pop:* 152785 *Larger Dept:* Lifelong Learning & Leisure *Dept Chief:* Exec Dir: Ms Barbara Hughes *Chief:* Libs Mgr: Mr Mark Freeman (mark.freeman@s-tyneside-mbc.gov.uk)
Main Libs: CENTRAL LIB, addr as above
Branch Libs: BOLDON LN LIB, Boldon Ln, South Shields, Tyne & Wear, NE34 0LZ (0191-456-2852; fax: 0191-496-7540); CLEADON PK LIB, Sunderland Rd, South Shields, Tyne & Wear, NE34 6AS (0191-455-2047; fax: 0191-496-7539); EAST BOLDON LIB, Boker Ln, East Boldon, Tyne & Wear, NE36 0RY (0191-536-2703; fax: 0191-519-3625); HEBBURN LIB, Station Rd, Hebburn, Tyne & Wear, NE31 1PN (0191-483-2088; fax: 0191-428-6219); JARROW LIB, Cambrian St, Jarrow, Tyne & Wear, NE32 3QN (0191-489-7786; fax: 0191-428-6227); WHITBURN LIB, Mill Ln, Whitburn, Sunderland, SR6 7EN (0191-529-3412; fax: 0191-529-2859)
Svc Pts: PT: 1 *AV:* 8 *Computers:* 8 *Internet:* 8
Collns: Fox & Wallace Colln (Westoe family archvs, 1790-1850); Flagg Colln (hist of South Shields & its industries); Kelly Colln (posters, 1790-1890); Photo Colln (South Tyneside, 1890-date) *Co-op Schemes:* NEMLAC *Loans:* bks & spkn wd/4 wks; music audios & CD-ROMs/2 wks; videos & DVDs/premier 1 day, others 1 wk
Charges: spkn wd/60p; music audios/cassettes 55p, CDs 80p; videos & DVDs/premier £1.50 pd, others £1 pw; CD-ROMs/£1.50 *Income Gen:* res/ad 55p, oap 25p, under-14s free *Fines:* bks & audios/10p pd, over-60s & under-14s exempt; videos, DVDs & CD-ROMs/loan charge *Equip:* m-readers, m-printers, fax, copiers, 75 computers (incl internet, access free), room for hire

Stock:	1 Apr 2000	1 Apr 2001
ad lend:	243591	237012
ad ref:	90120	82300
ch:	59867	60680
audios:	21892	21749
videos:	4104	4135
CD-ROMs:	935	1485
periodcls:	447	455

Issues:	1999-2000	2000-01
ad lend:	1013232	929335
ch:	183812	169434
audios:	63101	65808
videos:	42368	46093
CD-ROMs:	2378	6105

Acqs:	1999-2000	2000-01
bks:	29054	29141
AVs:	3261	4132

Classn: DDC *Cat:* Auto *Sys:* BiblioMondo *Svcs:* *Extramural:* old people's homes, housebnd *Info:* community *Other:* Open Learning, Community Edu, ESOL *Activs:* ch's activs, films, reading groups, writers' groups, talks, author visits, homework clubs
Enqs: 208270 (1999-2000); 210376 (2000-01)
Staff: Libns: 17 *Non-Prof:* 50.5

Inc from:	1999-2000	2000-01
local govt:	£2054170	£2155290
fines etc:	£155460	£158590
total:	£2278370	£2380450

Exp on:	1999-2000	2000-01
bks:	£319340	£309080
AVs:	£57230	£56900
salaries:	£1115630	£1139880
total:	£2278370	£2380450

Southampton

P171 Southampton City Libraries

Central Lib, Civic Centre, Southampton, Hampshire, SO14 7LW (023-8083-2664; fax: 023-8033-6305)
Email: t.richards@southampton.gov.uk
Internet: http://www.southampton.gov.uk/Libraries/

Local Auth: Southampton City Council *Pop:* 215500 *Chief:* Lib Svcs Mgr & City Libn: Mr Tony Richards *Dep:* Asst Lib Svcs Mgr & Asst City Libn: Mr David Baldwin
Main Libs: CENTRAL LIB, addr as above, incl Lending Lib (023-8083-2664; email: lending.library@southampton.gov.uk) & Ref & Info Svcs (023-8083-2462; email: reference.library@southampton.gov.uk) *Branch Libs:* BURGESS RD LIB, Burgess Rd, Southampton, Hampshire, SO16 3HF (023-8067-8873; email: burgess.road.library@southampton.gov.uk); COBBETT RD LIB, Cobbett Rd, Southampton, Hampshire, SO18 1HL (023-8022-5555; email: cobbett.road.library@southampton.gov.uk); EASTERN LIB, Bitterne Rd East, Southampton, Hampshire, SO18 5EG (023-8044-9909; email: eastern.library@southampton.gov.uk); LORDSHILL LIB, Lords Hill Dist Centre, Southampton, Hampshire, SO1 8HY (023-8073-2845; email: lordshill.library@southampton.gov.uk); PORTSWOOD LIB, Portswood Rd, Southampton, Hampshire, SO17 2NG (023-8055-4634; email: portswood.library@southampton.gov.uk); SHIRLEY LIB, Redcar St, Shirley, Southampton, Hampshire, SO15 5LL (023-8077-2136; email: shirley.library@southampton.gov.uk); THORNHILL LIB, 380 Hinkler Rd, Southampton, Hampshire, SO19 6DF (023-8044-7245; email: thornhill.library@southampton.gov.uk); WESTON LIB, 6 Wallace Rd, Southampton, Hampshire, SO16 9GX (023-8044-4363; email: weston.library@southampton.gov.uk); WOOLSTON LIB, Portsmouth Rd, Southampton, Hampshire, SO19 9AF (023-8044-8481; email: woolston.library@southampton.gov.uk)
Svc Pts: PT: 1 *Mobile:* 1 *AV:* 11 *Computers:* 11 *Internet:* 11 *Other:* CH'S SVCS, at Central Lib (023-8083-2598; email: children.library@southampton.gov.uk); SCHOOL LIB SVC
Collns: Local Studies Colln; Maritime Colln *Co-op Schemes:* HATRICS, Co-South, SLIC *ILLs:* county, natl & internatl *Loans:* bks & spkn wd/4 wks; audios/2 wks; videos, DVDs & CD-ROMs/1 wk *Charges:* spkn wd/cassettes 50p, CDs 90p, ch's & visually impaired free; music CDs/90p; cassettes/35p; videos/£1-£3; DVDs/£2-£3; CD-ROMs/£1-£2.50 *Income Gen:* res/70p, conc 50p, under-18s free; lost ticket/50p *Fines:* bks/ad 10p pd, oap 5p pd, ch 2p pd, after 1st 6 days weekly charges apply; audios, videos, DVDs & CD-ROMs/loan charge

Equip: m-readers, m-printers (A4/35p, A3/65p), copiers (A4/10p, A3/20p), computers (incl wd-proc, internet & CD-ROM), rooms for hire (free during lib hrs, otherwise negotiable) *Disabled:* CCTV text enlarger, text reader, induction loop, minicom, braille transcription svc *Online:* EBSCO, KnowUK, XreferPlus

Stock:	1 Apr 2000	1 Apr 2001
lend:	488249	415661
ref:	100452	100113
audios:	26572	19803
videos:	4139	4707
CD-ROMs:	352	749
periodcls:	346	346

Issues:	1999-2000	2000-01
bks:	1829918	1628327
audios:	106774	97531
videos:	33089	33725
CD-ROMs:	1127	1183

Acqs:	1999-2000	2000-01
bks:	34802	38358
AVs:	3755	3070

Acqs: Source: lib suppl
Classn: DDC *Cat: Type:* author, classified, subj & title *Medium:* auto *Auto Sys:* DS *Svcs:* *Extramural:* schools, hosps, old people's homes, housebnd *Info:* business, community, European Relay Centre *Other:* multicultural svcs, Open Learning *Activs:* ch's activs, bk sales, temp exhibs, author visits
Enqs: 290755 (1999-2000); 263520 (2000-01)
Staff: Libns: 29.2 *Non-Prof:* 78.9

Inc from:	1999-2000	2000-01
local govt:	£3462413	£3487847
fines etc:	£290578	£273812
total:	£3752991	£3761659

Exp on:	1999-2000	2000-01
stock:	£415256	£500369
salaries:	£1919786	£1739554
total:	£3752991	£3761659

Proj: refurbishment of Portswood Lib

Southend on Sea

P172 Southend on Sea Borough Libraries

Southend Lib, Victoria Ave, Southend on Sea, Essex, SS2 6EX (01702-612621; fax: 01702-469241)
Email: library@southend.gov.uk
Internet: http://www.southendlibrary.com/

Local Auth: Southend on Sea Borough Council *Pop:* 160000 *Larger Dept:* Leisure, Culture & Amenity Svcs *Dept Chief:* Dir: Mr John Dallaway *Chief:* Libs Svcs Mgr: Mr Simon May *Dep:* Head of Info & Resources: Mr Chris Hayes
Main Libs: SOUTHEND CENTRAL LIB, addr as above *Branch Libs:* FRIARS LIB, Constable Way, Shoeburyness, Essex, SS3 9TA (01702-294876; fax: 01702-298379); KENT ELMS LIB, 1 Rayleigh Rd, Leigh-on-Sea, Essex, SS9 5UU (01702-523803; fax: 01702-527196); LEIGH LIB, Broadway West, Leigh-on-Sea, Essex, SS9 2DA (01702-475929; fax: 01702-716151); SOUTH-CHURCH LIB, 221 Lifstan Way, Southend-on-Sea, Essex, SS1 2XG (01702-464959; fax: 01702-610796); THORPEDENE LIB, Delaware Rd, Thorpe Bay, Shoeburyness, Essex, SS3 9NW (01702-587761; fax: 01702-584503); WEST-CLIFFE LIB, 649 London Rd, Westcliffe-on-Sea, Essex, SS0 9PD (01702-341961; fax: 01702-213479)
Svc Pts: Mobile: 2 *Other:* Focal Pt Gallery; ESSEX RECORD OFFICE, SOUTHEND BRANCH, at Central Lib (see **A461**)

Collns: Arts Colln (art & art hist, at Central Lib); Rochford Hundred Colln (at Central Lib) *Co-op Schemes:* ELAN, with Essex County Council (see **P51**) & Thurrock Council (see **P186**); Co-East, ELISA *ILLs:* county, natl & internatl *Loans:* bks, audios & CD-ROMs/3 wks; videos & DVDs/1 wk *Charges:* audios/75p; videos & DVDs/£2.25; CD-ROMs/£2.50 *Income Gen:* req/60p; lost ticket/£1.50 *Fines:* bks/ad 55p pw; registered blind exempt *Equip:* m-reader, 2 m-printers (40p per copy), 7 fax, 2 video viewers, 9 copiers (10p), clr copier (£1.20), 42 computers (incl 25 with internet & 10 with CD-ROM), 2 rooms for hire (£8.50-£28) *Disabled:* Kurzweil, CCTV, wheelchair

Stock:	1 Apr 2000
lend:	343552
ref:	8930
AVs:	31341
periodcls:	378

Issues:	1999-2000
bks:	2212630
AVs:	165030

Acqs: Source: lib suppl, publ & bksellers *Co-op:* LASER *Offcr-in-Charge:* Head of Info & Resources, as above
Classn: DDC *Cat: Type:* author, classified, subj & title *Medium:* auto *Auto Sys:* Geac *Svcs: Extramural:* old people's homes, housebnd, BookStart *Info:* careers, business *Other:* Open Learning, Training Access Pt *Activs:* ch's activs, bk sales, temp exhibs, poetry readings *Offcr-in-Charge:* Marketing Offcr: Mr Matt Holmes
Enqs: 264056 (1999-2000)
Staff: Libns: 19 *Non-Prof:* 61.5

St Helens

P173 St Helens Library and Information Service

Central Lib, Victoria Sq, St Helens, Merseyside, WA10 1DY (01744-456954; *fax:* 01744-20836)
Email: criu@sthelens.gov.uk
Internet: http://www.sthelens.gov.uk/

Local Auth: St Helens Metropolitan Borough Council *Pop:* 179000 *Cttee:* Lifelong Learning Portfolio *Larger Dept:* Community, Edu & Leisure Svcs *Dept Chief:* Dir: Ms Susan Richardson *Chief:* Asst Dir (Community & Leisure): Mrs Dorothy Bradley BSc(Hons), DMS
Main Libs: CENTRAL LIB, addr as above
Branch Libs: BILLINGE LIB, Main St, Billinge, St Helens, Merseyside, WN5 7HA (01744-677535; *fax:* 01744-677536); CHESTER LN CENTRE LIB, Four Acre Ln, St Helens, Merseyside, WA9 4DA (01744-677081; *fax:* 01744-677874); ECCLESTON LIB, Broadway, Eccleston St, St Helens, Merseyside, WA10 5PJ (01744-677575; *fax:* 01744-677577); GARSWOOD LIB, School Ln, Garswood, St Helens, Merseyside, WA4 0TT (*tel & fax:* 01744-677797); HAYDOCK EAST LIB, Church Rd, Haydock, St Helens, Merseyside, WA11 0LY (01744-677801; *fax:* 01744-677802); MOSS BANK LIB, Eskdale Ave, Moss Bank, St Helens, Merseyside, WA11 7EJ (*tel & fax:* 01744-677988); NEWTON-LE-WILLOWS LIB, Crow Ln East, Newton-le-Willows, Merseyside, WA12 9TU (01744-677885; *fax:* 01744-677892); NEWTOWN LIB, Horace St, St Helens, Merseyside, WA10 4LZ (01744-677896; *fax:* 01744-677897); PARR LIB, Fleet Ln, St Helens, Merseyside, WA9 1SY (01744-677580; *fax:* 01744-677582); RAINFORD LIB, Church Rd, Rainford, St Helens, Merseyside, WA11 8HA (01744-677820; *fax:* 01744-677821); RAINHILL LIB, View Rd, Rainhill, Prescot, Merseyside, L35 0LE (01744-677822; *fax:* 01744-677823); THATTO HEATH LIB, Thatto Heath Rd, St Helens, Merseyside, WA10 3QX (01744-677842; *fax:* 01744-677841)
Svc Pts: AV: 12

Co-op Schemes: Libs North West *ILLs:* county, natl & internatl *Loans:* bks/3 wks; audios, videos, DVDs & CD-ROMs/2 wks *Charges:* cassettes/60p; CDs & CD-ROMs/£1; DVDs/£2 *Income Gen:* res/50p; lost ticket/£1 *Fines:* bks & audios/ad 7p pd, ch & oap exempt; visually impaired free audio svc *Equip:* 8 m-readers, m-printer, 13 fax (£1 per pg, higher overseas), 13 copiers (A4/5p, A3/10p), clr copier (A4/£1, A3/£1.50), computers (incl internet & CD-ROM) *Disabled:* Kurzweil

Stock:	1 Apr 2000	1 Apr 2001
lend:	353655	361140
ref:	41556	20108
AVs:	29911	29841
periodcls:	354	355

Issues:	1999-2000	2000-01
bks:	1619218	1567786
AVs:	130235	128819

Acqs:	1999-2000	2000-01
bks:	51932	53792
AVs:	4983	5966

Acqs: Source: lib suppl *Offcr-in-Charge:* Principal Offcr: Mrs S. Thomas
Classn: DDC *Cat: Medium:* auto *Auto Sys:* Dynix *Svcs: Extramural:* schools, old people's homes, housebnd, day centres *Info:* BSI *Other:* Open Learning *Activs:* ch's activs, bk sales, temp exhibs
Enqs: 317994 (1999-2000); 284058 (2000-01)
Staff: Libns: 23 *Non-Prof:* 79.37

Inc from:	2000-01
local govt:	£3257795
fines etc:	£303584
total:	£3561379

Exp on:	2000-01
stock:	£579244
salaries:	£1809332
total:	£3561379

Staffordshire

P174 Staffordshire Library and Information Services

16 Martin Street, Stafford, ST16 2LG (01785-278300; *fax:* 01785-276839)
Internet: http://www.staffordshire.gov.uk/

Local Auth: Staffordshire County Council *Pop:* 809700 *Cttee:* Cultural & Recreational Svcs Cttee *Larger Dept:* Cultural & Property Svcs *Dept Chief:* Dir: Mr Colin Savage *Chief:* County Libn: Ms Olivia Spencer (olivia.spencer@ staffordshire.gov.uk) *Dep:* Lead Offcr (Best Value Implementation): Ms Hilary Jackson (hilary.jackson@staffordshire.gov.uk) *Other Snr Staff:* Head of Operational Svcs (East): Ms Elizabeth Rees-Jones; Head of Operational Svcs (West): Ms Judy Goodson; Head of Lib Support Svcs: Ms Morna Williams
Main (Dist) Libs: BURTON LIB, Riverside, High St, Burton-on-Trent, Staffordshire, DE14 1AH (01283-239556; *fax:* 01283-239571; *email:* burton.library@staffordshire.gov.uk); CANNOCK LIB, Manor Ave, Cannock, Staffordshire, WS11 1AA (01543-510365; *fax:* 01543-510373; *email:* cannock.library@staffordshire.gov.uk); LEEK LIB, Nicholson Inst, Stockwell St, Leek, Staffordshire, ST13 6DW (01538-483209; *fax:* 01538-483216; *email:* leek.library@staffordshire.gov.uk); LICHFIELD LIB, The Friary, Lichfield, Staffordshire, WS13 6QG (01543-510700; *fax:* 01543-510716; *email:* lichfield.library@staffordshire.gov.uk); NEWCASTLE LIB, Ironmarket, Newcastle, Staffordshire, ST5 1AT (01782-297300; *fax:* 01782-297323; *email:* newcastle.library@ staffordshire.gov.uk); PERTON LIB, Severn Dr, Perton, Wolverhampton, W Midlands, WV6 7QU (01902-755794; *fax:* 01902-756123; *email:* perton.library@staffordshire.gov.uk); SHIRE HALL (STAFFORD) LIB, Market St, Stafford, ST16 2LQ

(01785-278585; *fax:* 01785-278599; *email:* stafford.library@staffordshire.gov.uk); TAMWORTH LIB, Corp St, Tamworth, Staffordshire, B79 7DW (01827-475645; *fax:* 01827-475658; *email:* tamworth.library@staffordshire.gov.uk)
Branch Libs: AUDLEY LIB, Hall St, Audley, Stoke-on-Trent, Staffordshire, ST7 8DB (01782-720527); BARLASTON LIB, The Green, Barlaston, Stoke-on-Trent, Staffordshire, ST12 9AB (01782-372703); BARTON LIB, Dunstall Rd, Barton-under-Needwood, DE13 8AX (01283-713753); BASWICH LIB, Lynton Ave, Baswich, Stafford, ST17 0EA (01785-663355); BIDDULPH LIB, Tunstall Rd, Biddulph, Stoke-on-Trent, Staffordshire, ST8 6HH (01782-512103); BLYTHE BRIDGE LIB, Uttoxeter Rd, Blythe Bridge, Stoke-on-Trent, Staffordshire, ST11 9JR (01782-392384); BRERETON LIB, Main Rd, Brereton, Rugeley, Staffordshire, WS15 1DY (01889-582574); BREWOOD LIB, Newport St, Brewood, Staffordshire, ST19 9DT (01902-850087); BURNTWOOD LIB, Sankey's Corner, Chase Ter, Walsall, W Midlands, WS7 8BX (01543-682447); CHEADLE LIB, 15-17 High St, Cheadle, Staffordshire, ST10 1AA (01538-483860; *fax:* 01538-483875); CHESLYN HAY LIB, High St, Cheslyn Hay, Walsall, W Midlands, WS56 7AE (01922-413956); CLAYTON LIB, Dartmouth Ave, Clayton, Newcastle, Staffordshire, ST5 3NR (01782-616074); CODSALL LIB, South Staffordshire Dist Council Offices, Wolverhampton Rd, Codsall, Wolverhampton, W Midlands, WV8 1PX (01902-842764); ECCLESHALL LIB, High St, Eccleshall, Staffordshire, ST21 6BZ (01785-850452); GLASCOTE LIB, Caledonian, Glascote, Tamworth, Staffordshire, B77 2ED (01827-284608); GT WYRLEY LIB, John's Ln, Gt Wyrley, Walsall, W Midlands, WS6 6BY (01922-414632); HEATH HAYES LIB, Hednesford Rd, Heath Hayes, Cannock, Staffordshire, WS12 5EA (01543-279675); HEDNESFORD LIB, Anglesey Cres, Hednesford, Cannock, Staffordshire, WD12 5AD (01543-422798); HOLMCROFT LIB, Holmcroft Rd, Stafford, ST16 1JG (01785-253908); KIDSGROVE LIB, Meadows Rd, Kidsgrove, Stoke-on-Trent, Staffordshire, ST7 1BS (01782-782445; *fax:* 01782-777508); KINVER LIB, Vicarage Dr, Kinver, Stourbridge, W Midlands, DY7 6HJ (01384-872348); NORTON CANES LIB, Burntwood Rd, Norton Canes, Cannock, Staffordshire, WS11 3RF (01543-279592); PENKRIDGE LIB, Bellbrook, Penkridge, Staffordshire, ST19 5DL (01785-712916); RISING BROOK LIB, Merrey Rd, Rising Brook, Stafford, ST17 9LX (01785-242155); RUGELEY LIB, Anson St, Rugeley, Staffordshire, WD15 2BB (01889-583237; *fax:* 01889-574515); SHENSTONE LIB, Main St, Shenstone, Lichfield, Staffordshire, WS14 0NF (01543-480915); SILVERDALE LIB, High St, Silverdale, Newcastle, Staffordshire, ST5 6LF (01782-624302); STONE LIB, High St, Stone, Staffordshire, ST15 8AT (01785-812745; *fax:* 01785-812626); TALKE LIB, Chester Rd, Talke, Stoke-on-Trent, Staffordshire, ST7 1SW (01782-782200); UTTOXETER LIB, Red Gables, High St, Uttoxeter, Staffordshire, ST14 7JQ (01889-256371; *fax:* 01889-256374); WERRINGTON LIB, Ash Bank Rd, Werrington, Stoke-on-Trent, Staffordshire, ST9 0JS (01782-302706); WILNECOTE LIB, Hockley Rd, Wilnecote, Tamworth, Staffordshire, B77 5RH (01827-475147); WOLSTANTON LIB, Bradwell Lodge, Bradwell Ln, Newcastle, Staffordshire, ST5 8PS (01782-636259); WOMBOURNE LIB, Windmill Bank, Wombourne, Wolverhampton, W Midlands, WV5 9JD (01902-892032)
Svc Pts: PT: 2 *Mobile:* 12 *AV:* 54 *Computers:* 43 *Internet:* 43
Collns: BSI; DTD Specifications; DEF Specifications; Victoria County Histories; large print bks; Citizens' Advice Bureaux files; Business Monitor Series; law reports; companies annual reports; statistics; statutes in force; govt pubns; librarianship (at staff lib); ☛

Staffordshire ▼ **Stoke-on-Trent**

ublic Libraries

(Staffordshire Lib & Info Svcs cont)
Collns (cont): local studies (at Dist Libs); County Fiction Reserve; Provincial JFR: Kb-Kel; Mam-Maq; May-Maz (all at Rugeley Lib); Kin-Kn (at Burton Lib); Lar-Led (at Newcastle Lib); Lia-Lis (at Lichfield Lib); Lit-Lod (at Leek Lib); Mar-Marn (at Tamworth Lib); David Garrick Colln; Elias Ashmole Colln; James Boswell Colln; Samuel Johnson Colln; Erasmus Darwin Colln; Annal Seward Colln; ecclesiastical hist; genea-logy; Shropshire (parts) (all at Lichfield Lib); Staffordshire hist (at Lichfield & Cannock Libs); playsets (at Stafford & Burton Libs); Polish; Hindi; Punjabi; Urdu; music scores; radio & tele-vision servicing data (all at Stafford Lib); Leicestershire (parts); brewing (both at Burton Lib); Vera Brittain Colln; pottery (both at New-castle Lib); illusts; coal mining (both at Cannock Lib); Wardle Colln (silk industry); Peak Dist of Derbyshire, Cheshire & Staffordshire (parts) (both at Leek Lib); Warwickshire (parts) (at Lichfield & Tamworth Libs); Sir Robert Peel Colln; workshop manuals (both at Tamworth Lib); Derbyshire (parts) (at Burton, Leek & Lichfield Libs); George Edalji Colln (at Gt Wyrley Lib) **Co-op Schemes:** ILL **ILLs:** county, natl & internatl **Loans:** bks & audios/3 wks; videos, CD-ROMs, DVDs & computer games/1 wk; lang courses/3-6 wks **Charges:** audios/80p, set £1.60; talking bks/1-2 tapes 50p, 2+ £1; lang courses/1-2 tapes for 3 wks £1, 2+ for 6 wks £3; videos/£1.60-£3, ch's 80p; DVDs/£1.60-£3; CD-ROMs & computer games/£2; half price conc available for audios & lang courses; visually impaired exempt from audio charges **Income Gen:** req/80p (conc 40p, ch's items free), out of county £2 (conc £1.20) **Fines:** bks & audios/ad 10p pd open (max £3.60), conc 5p pd open (max £1.80); videos & DVDs/loan charge (max £18); CD-ROMs & computer games/loan charge (max £12) **Equip:** 50 m-readers, 8 m-printers (75p), 34 copiers (A4/10p, A3/20p), 3 clr copiers (A4/£1.20, A3/£1.70), 120 computers (incl internet, access free, printouts 10p b&w, 50p clr), rooms for hire (various) **Disabled:** Kurzweil

Stock:	1 Apr 2000	1 Apr 2001
ad lend:	736176	706176
ad ref:	82320	81263
ch:	256151	256804
schools:	272147	253363
instns:	25210	26529
audios:	77329	63009
videos:	3837	12347
CD-ROMs:	458	2007
periodcls:	225	473

Issues:	1999-2000	2000-01
ad lend:	4257898	4246169
ch:	1282190	1236113
audios:	266706	287637
videos:	75927	92259
CD-ROMs:	5251	-

Acqs:	1999-2000	2000-01
bks:	120806	157074
AVs:	15944	16563

Acqs: Source: lib suppl **Offcr-in-Charge:** Svc Advisor (Stock Mgmt & Promotion): Mrs Jo Grocott (jo.grocott@staffordshire.gov.uk) **Classn:** DDC **Cat:** Type: author, classified, subj & title **Medium:** auto **Auto Sys:** Talis **Svcs:** Extramural: schools, prisons, old people's homes,

housebnd, day centres **Info:** business, comm-unity, European, environmental, legal, tourist **Other:** Open Learning **Activs:** ch's activs, bk sales, temp exhibs, poetry readings, reading groups, talks, author visits **Enqs:** 673712 (1999-2000); 626487 (2000-01) **Staff:** Libns: 78.6 Non-Prof: 277.2

Inc from:	1999-2000	2000-01
fines etc:	£202450	£209160
total:	£873774	£847613

Exp on:	1999-2000	2000-01
bks:	£1108616	£1366030
salaries:	£4760814	£4838258
total:	£8008194	£9379799

Proj: lib refurbishments

Stirling

P175 Stirling Council Libraries
Lib HQ, Borrowmeadow Rd, Springkerse Industrial Est, Stirling, FK7 7TN (01786-432383; *fax:* 01786-432395)
Email: libraryheadquarters@stirling.gov.uk
Internet: http://www.stirling.gov.uk/

Local Auth: Stirling Council **Pop:** 85200 **Cttee:** Community Svcs Cttee **Larger Dept:** Community Svcs **Dept Chief:** Dir: Ms Helen Munro **Chief:** Head of Libs, Heritage & Culture: Mr Allan Gillies MCLIP
Main Libs: CENTRAL LIB, Corn Exchange Rd, Stirling, FK8 2HX *(lend:* 01786-432107; *ref:* 01786-432106; *fax:* 01786-473094; *email:* centrallibrary@stirling.gov.uk) **Branch Libs:** BALFRON LIB, Buchanan St, Balfron, Glasgow, G63 0TW *(tel & fax:* 01360-440407; *email:* balfronlibrary@stirling.gov.uk); BANNOCKBURN LIB, Greenacre Pl, Bannockburn, Stirling, FK7 8HY *(tel & fax:* 01786-812286; *email:* bannockburnlibrary@stirling.gov.uk); BRIDGE OF ALLAN LIB, Fountain Rd, Bridge of Allan, Stirling, FK9 4AT *(tel & fax:* 01786-833680; *email:* bridgeofallanlibrary@stirling.gov.uk); CALLANDER LIB, South Church St, Callander, Perthshire, FK17 8BN *(tel & fax:* 01877-331544; *email:* callanderlibrary@stirling.gov.uk); CAMBUSBARRON LIB, Community Centre, Cambusbarron, Stirling, FK7 9NU *(tel & fax:* 01786-473873; *email:* cambusbarronlibrary@stirling.gov.uk); DRYMEN LIB, The Sq, Drymen, Glasgow, G63 0BL *(tel & fax:* 01360-660751; *email:* drymenlibrary@stirling.gov.uk); DUN-BLANE LIB, The Inst, High St, Dunblane, Perth-shire, FK15 0ER *(tel & fax:* 01786-823125; *email:* dunblanelibrary@stirling.gov.uk); FALLIN LIB, Stirling Rd, Fallin, Stirling, FK7 7JE *(tel & fax:* 01786-812492; *email:* fallinlibrary@stirling.gov.uk); KILLIN LIB, Primary School, Killin, Perthshire, FK21 8UW (tel & fax: 01567-820571; *email:* killinlibrary@stirling.gov.uk); ST NINIANS LIB, Mayfield Centre, Stirling, FK7 0DB *(tel & fax:* 01786-472069; *email:* stninianslibrary@stirling.gov.uk); STRATHBLANE LIB, Kirkburn Rd, Strathblane, Glasgow, G63 9ED *(tel & fax:* 01360-770737; *email:* strathblanelibrary@stirling.gov.uk) **Svc Pts:** PT: 3 Mobile: 2 **AV:** 15 **Computers:** 15 **Internet:** 15
Collns: local hist (at Central Lib) **Co-op Schemes:** SFR **ILLs:** natl & internatl **Loans:** bks/3 wks; audios, CD-ROMs & computer games/1 wk; videos/2 nights or 1 wk **Charges:** audios/40p single, 60p multiple; videos/75p-£2; CD-ROMs/£1; computer games/£2-£4 **Income Gen:** req & res/60p; lost ticket/£1 **Fines:** bks/ad & oap 11p pd (max £6), ch 3p pd (max £1.20); audios, videos, CD-ROMs & computer games/loan charge; mobile lib users exempt **Equip:** 4 m-readers, 3 m-printers (20p), 15 fax, 15 copiers (A4/10p, A3/20p, clr copier (A4/£1, A3/£2), 65 computers (incl 35 with wd-proc, 42 with CD-ROM, 34 with internet, access free)

Stock:	1 Apr 2000	1 Apr 2001
ad lend:	131789	151868
ad ref:	9795	10005
ch:	69649	72473
audios:	22260	20341
videos:	5021	5414
periodcls:	92	92

Issues:	1999-2000	2000-01
ad lend:	635001	600511
ch:	210424	210022
audios:	73996	66429
videos:	53217	46291

Acqs:	1999-2000	2000-01
bks:	25198	22659
AVs:	3809	2942

Acqs: Source: lib suppl & bksellers **Offcr-in-Charge:** Operations Libn: Mr Andrew Muirhead **Classn:** DDC **Cat:** Type: author, classified, subj & title **Medium:** auto **Auto Sys:** Dynix **Svcs:** Extramural: schools, prisons, old people's homes, housebnd **Info:** community (database of local clubs & orgs), business **Other:** Open Learning **Activs:** ch's activs, bk sales, temp exhibs **Enqs:** 41495 (1999-2000); 44862 (2000-01) **Staff:** Libns: 14.5 Non-Prof: 38.3

Inc from:	1999-2000	2000-01
fines etc:	£221999	£185566

Exp on:	1999-2000	2000-01
bks:	£307376	£285846
salaries:	£881304	£907039
total:	£1759050	£1737910

Stockport

P176 Stockport Library and Information Services
Community Svcs Div, 4th Floor, Stopford House, Piccadilly, Stockport, Cheshire, SK1 3XE (0161-474-4447)
Email: central.library@stockport.gov.uk
Internet: http://www.stockport.gov.uk/

Local Auth: Stockport Metropolitan Borough Council **Pop:** 291100 **Cttee:** Community Svcs **Larger Dept:** Community Svcs **Dept Chief:** Dir: Mr Ged Lucas FCIH, DipHS **Chief:** Head of Lib & Info Svcs: Mr John Condon (john.condon@stockport.gov.uk)
Main Libs: CENTRAL LIB, Wellington Rd South, Stockport, Cheshire, SK1 3RS (0161-474-4540/24/30 fax: 0161-474-7750) **Branch Libs:** East Area: BREDBURY LIB, George Ln, Bredbury, Stock-port, Cheshire, SK6 1DJ (0161-474-4545; *fax:* 0161-430-4384; *email:* bredbury.library@stockport.gov.uk); BRINNINGTON LIB, The Arcade, Taunton Ave, Stockport, Cheshire, SK5 8LR (0161-430-3909; *email:* brinnington.library@stockport.gov.uk); DIALSTONE LIB, Dialstone Centre, Lisburne Ln, Offerton, Stockport, Cheshire, SK2 7LL (0161-474-2255; *fax:* 0161-474-2210; *email:* dialstone.library@stockport.gov.uk); GT MOOR LIB, Gladstone St, Stockport, Cheshire, SK2 7QF (0161-483-3092; *email:* greatmoor.library@stockport.gov.uk); HAZEL GROVE LIB, Beech Ave, Hazel Grove, Stockport, Cheshire, SK6 6ER (0161-483-6437; *fax:* 0161-491-6516; *email:* hazelgrove.library@stockport.gov.uk); HIGH LN LIB, Buxton Rd, High Ln, Stockport, Cheshire, SK6 8DX (01663-765519; *email:* highlane.library@stockport.gov.uk); MARPLE LIB, Memorial Pk, Marple, Stockport, Cheshire, SK6 6BA (0161-427-3236; *fax:* 0161-426-0477; *email:* marple.library@stockport.gov.uk); West Area: BRAMHALL LIB, Bramhall Ln South, Bramhall, Stockport, Cheshire, SK7 2DU (0161-439-6067; *fax:* 0161-439-4437; *email:* bramhall.library@stockport.gov.uk); CHEADLE LIB, Ashfield Rd, Cheadle, Cheshire, SK8 1BB (0161-428-7169; *fax:* 0161-428-5843; *email:*

cheadle.library@stockport.gov.uk); CHEADLE HULME LIB, Mellor Rd, Cheadle Hulme, Cheadle, Cheshire, SK8 5AU (0161-485-2632; *email:* cheadlehulme.library@stockport.gov.uk); EDGELEY LIB, Alexandra Pk, Edgeley, Cheshire, SK3 9AB (0161-480-4319; *email:* edgeley.library@ stockport.gov.uk); HEALD GREEN LIB, Finney Ln, Heald Green, Cheadle, Stockport, Cheshire, SK8 3JB (0161-437-3201; *email:* healdgreen. library@stockport.gov.uk); THE HEATONS LIB, Thornfield Rd, Heaton Moor, Cheshire, SK4 3LD (0161-432-5109; *email:* heatons.library@stockport. gov.uk); REDDISH LIB, Gorton Rd, Stockport, Cheshire, SK5 6UG (0161-432-2568; *email:* reddish.library@stockport.gov.uk)
Svc Pts: Mobile: 2 *AV:* 16 *Other:* HOME LIB SVC; SCHOOL LIB SVC
Co-op Schemes: Libs North West, JFR *ILLs:* county, natl & internatl *Loans:* bks/3 wks; audios, videos & DVDs/1 wk *Charges:* cassettes/60p; CDs/£1; videos/£2.10; DVDs/£3
Income Gen: res & req/£1; lost ticket/£1 *Fines:* bks/ad 10p pd, oaps & under 18s 5p pd, under-13s exempt; cassettes/20p pd; CDs/30p pd; videos/65p pd; exempt: registered blind (audios only), ch with learning disabilities (audios, videos)
Equip: m-readers, m-printer, fax, copiers (A4/10p, A3/15p), 54 computers (incl internet & CD-ROM), rooms for hire *Disabled:* stairlift/ramp access, magnifiers, induction loop (at Edgeley Lib), minicom (at Central Lib) *Online:* business related svcs

Stock:	1 Apr 2000	1 Apr 2001
ad lend:	274527	318161
ad ref:	19464	16572
ch:	112734	110391
audios:	24170	21291
videos:	11277	12073
periodcls:	327	387
archvs:	520 linear m	543 linear m

Issues:	1999-2000	2000-01
ad lend:	2131340	2000093
ch:	673461	626122
audios:	84279	91395
videos:	68772	68120

Acqs:	1999-2000	2000-01
bks:	64988	50694
AVs:	9358	6651

Acqs: Source: lib suppl & publ *Offcr-in-Charge:* Snr Libn (Stock)
Classn: DDC *Cat: Type:* author, classified & subj *Medium:* auto *Auto Sys:* Talis *Svcs: Extramural:* schools, old people's homes, housebnd *Info:* community, business *Other:* Open Learning *Activs:* ch's activs, bk sales, temp exhibs, reading groups, talks
Enqs: 340444 (1999-2000); 302224 (2000-01)
Staff: Libns: 33 *Non-Prof:* 96.7

Inc from:	1999-2000	2000-01
local govt:	£3351000	£3587000
fines etc:	£278000	£340000
total:	£3629000	£3927000

Exp on:	1999-2000	2000-01
bks:	£654000	£657000
salaries:	£2044000	£2171000
total:	£3629000	£3927000

Stockton-on-Tees

P177 Stockton Borough Libraries

Municipal Bldgs, Church Rd, Stockton-on-Tees, TS18 1TU (01642-393939; *fax:* 01642-393924)
Internet: http://www.stockton-bc.gov.uk/

Local Auth: Stockton Borough Council *Pop:* 181000 *Cttee:* Edu & Lifelong Learning Select Cttee *Larger Dept:* Edu, Leisure & Cultural Svcs *Dept Chief:* Dir: Mr S. Bradford BSc(Hons), MA(Ed), MBA, CBiol, MBiol, MIMgt

Chief: Head of Cultural Svcs: Mrs Andrea Barker MCLIP (andrea.barker@stockton.gov.uk) *Dep:* Libs & Info Svcs Mgr: Ms Lesley King (lesley. king@stockton.gov.uk)
Main Libs: STOCKTON CENTRAL LIB, Church Rd, Stockton-on-Tees, TS18 1TV (01642-393998/9; *email:* stockton.library@stockton.gov.uk); CENTRAL REF LIB, at same addr (01642-393994; *fax:* 01642-393929; *email:* reference.library@ stockton.gov.uk) *Branch Libs:* BILLINGHAM LIB, Bedale Ave, Billingham, Stockton-on-Tees, TS23 1AJ (01642-397595; *email:* billingham. library@stockton.gov.uk); EGGLESCLIFFE LIB, Butterfield Dr, Orchard Est, Egglescliffe, Stockton-on-Tees, TS16 0EL (01642-391840; *email:* egglescliffe.library@stockton.gov.uk); FAIRFIELD LIB, Fairfield, Fairfield, Stockton-on-Tees, TS19 7AJ (01642-391750; *email:* fairfield.library@stockton.gov.uk); NORTON LIB, 87 High St, Norton, Stockton-on-Tees, TS20 1AE (01642-397592; *email:* norton.library@stockton. gov.uk); RAGWORTH LIB, St Johns Way, Stockton-on-Tees, TS19 0FB (01642-393990; *email:* ragworth.library@stockton.gov.uk); ROSEBERRY LIB, The Causeway, Billingham, Stockton-on-Tees, TS23 2LB (01642-397600; *email:* roseberry.library@stockton.gov.uk); ROSE-WORTH LIB, Redhill Rd, Stockton-on-Tees, TS19 9BX (01642-397604; *email:* roseworth.library@ stockton.gov.uk); THORNABY CENTRAL LIB, New Town Centre, Thornaby, Stockton-on-Tees, TS17 9EW (01642-391610; *email:* thornaby.central. library@stockton.gov.uk); THORNABY WEST-BURY ST LIB, Westbury St, Thornaby, Stockton-on-Tees, TS17 6PG (01642-393987; *email:* thornaby.library@stockton.gov.uk); YARM LIB, 41 High St, Yarm, Stockton-on-Tees, TS15 9BH (01642-391843; *email:* yarm.library@stockton. gov.uk)
Svc Pts: Mobile: 2 *AV:* 7 *Other:* 2 prisons, 1 housebnd svc
ILLs: county & natl *Loans:* bks/4 wks; audios/2 wks; videos/1wk *Charges:* CDs/91p; cassettes/41p; talking bks/£1.28, free to visually impaired; videos/£1.05, jnr 62p *Income Gen:* res/62p, conc & mobile lib users 32p; lost ticket/£1.59, conc 79p *Fines:* bks/ad 9p pd (max £5.40); audios, talking bks & videos/loan charge *Equip:* 16 m-readers, 3 m-printers (40p per sheet), 11 copiers (A4/10p, A3/20p), fax (various), computers (95 with wd-proc & internet, 11 with CD-ROM), room for hire (various) *Disabled:* Kurzweil, braille printer

Stock:	1 Apr 2000	1 Apr 2001
ad lend:	213010	205486
ad ref:	37232	37461
ch:	73275	69979
instns:	6863	8268
audios:	18005	18545
videos:	294	482
CD-ROMs:	233	539
periodcls:	220	220

Issues:	1999-2000	2000-01
ad lend:	1244054	1150110
ch:	301453	246960
instns:	64029	56338
audios:	38936	40195
videos:	1800	3213
CD-ROMs:	-	1751

Acqs:	1999-2000	2000-01
bks:	36065	37759
AVs:	1982	1744

Acqs: Source: lib suppl *Co-op:* NEPO *Offcr-in-Charge:* Bibliographical Svcs Mgr: Mrs Julia Greenwood (julia.greenwood@stockton.gov.uk)
Classn: DDC *Cat: Type:* author, classified, subj & title *Medium:* auto *Auto Sys:* Talis *Svcs: Extramural:* schools, prisons, hosps, old people's homes, housebnd *Info:* computerised community sys *Other:* lang courses, Open Learning, St Catherine's House Index, Open Tech Centre

Activs: ch's activs, bk sales, temp exhibs, poetry readings
Enqs: 147290 (1999-2000); 142064 (2000-01)
Staff: Libns: 25.5 *Non-Prof:* 57.5

Inc from:	1999-2000	2000-01
5fines etc:	£93006	£94889
total:	£155168	£165316

Exp on:	1999-2000	2000-01
bks:	£260770	£280219
AVs:	£27068	£34874
elec media:	£256896	£162354
salaries:	£1210279	£1288345
total:	£2432931	£2467274

Stoke-on-Trent

P178 Stoke-on-Trent Libraries, Information and Archives

Hanley Lib, Bethesda Street, Hanley, Stoke-on-Trent, Staffordshire, ST1 3RS (01782-238455; *fax:* 01782-238499)
Email: stoke.libraries@stoke.gov.uk
Internet: http://www.stoke.gov.uk/council/libraries/

Local Auth: Stoke-on-Trent City Council *Pop:* 249000 *Larger Dept:* Directorate of Edu & Lifelong Learning *Chief:* Head of Lib Svcs: Mrs Margaret Green BA, MLS, MCLIP *Other Snr Staff:* Strategy & Svc Development Mgr: Mr Ian Van Arkadie; Principal Operations Mgr: Ms Janet Simpson; Principal Libn (Central & Support Svcs): Ms Janet Thursfield; Principal Libn (Community Libs): Ms Heather Jones
Main Libs: HANLEY LIB, addr as above (01782-238455; *fax:* 01782-238434; *email:* hanley.library@ stoke.gov.uk) *Branch Libs:* BENTILEE LIB, Ubberley Rd, Bentilee, Stoke-on-Trent, Staffordshire, ST2 0EW (01782-238494; *email:* bentilee. library@stoke.gov.uk); BURSLEM LIB, Wedgewood Inst, Queen St, Burslem, Stoke-on-Trent, Staffordshire, ST6 3EF (*tel & fax:* 01782-238488; *email:* burslem.library@stoke.gov.uk); FENTON LIB, Baker St, Fenton, Stoke-on-Trent, Staffordshire, ST4 3AF (01782-238419; *email:* fenton. library@stoke.gov.uk); HAYWOOD LIB, City Learning Centre, Haywood Rd, Burslem, Stoke-on-Trent, Staffordshire, ST6 7AH (01782-233541; *email:* haywood.library@stoke.gov.uk); LONGTON LIB, Sutherland Inst, Lightwood Rd, Longton, Stoke-on-Trent, Staffordshire, ST3 4HY (01782-238424; *fax:* 01782-238429; *email:* longton. library@stoke.gov.uk); MEIR LIB, Sandon Rd, Meir, Stoke-on-Trent, Staffordshire, ST3 7DJ (01782-312706; *email:* meir.library@stoke.gov.uk); STOKE LIB, London Rd, Stoke-on-Trent, Staffordshire, ST4 7QE (01782-238446; *fax:* 01782-238449; *email:* stoke.library@stoke.gov.uk); TURNSTALL LIB, Victoria Inst, The Boulevard, Tunstall, Stoke-on-Trent, Staffordshire, ST6 6BD (01782-238471; *fax:* 01782-238475; *email:* tunstall. library@stoke.gov.uk)
Svc Pts: PT: 1 Mobile: 3 *AV:* 13 *Computers:* 10 *Internet:* 10 *Other:* ARCHVS SVC (see **A473**)
Collns: EPIC *Co-op Schemes:* WMRLS, V3, SEALS *ILLs:* county & natl *Loans:* bks & audios/3 wks; videos, DVDs & CD-ROMs/1 wk *Charges:* audios & CD-ROMs/80p; videos & DVDs/£1.60 *Income Gen:* req & res/80p; lost ticket/ad £1, ch & oap 50p *Fines:* bks & audios/ad 12p pd, oap 6p pd, ch exempt; videos, DVDs & CD-ROMs/loan charge; optional reduced rate for disabled, depending on nature of disability
Equip: 16 m-readers, 2 m-printers (A4/60p), 8 fax (£1 per pg), 11 copiers (A4/10p), clr copier (A4/£1.50), 100 computers (incl 86 with wd-proc, 96 with CD-ROM & 88 with internet), 4 rooms for hire *Disabled:* hearing loop, Kurzweil in some libs *Online:* BSI

Public Libraries

Stoke-on-Trent
▼
Surrey

(Stoke-on-Trent Libs, Info & Archvs cont)

Stock:	1 Apr 2000	1 Apr 2001
lend:	230911	228494
ref:	127769	126696
AVs:	33529	30391
periodcls:	234	222

Issues:	1999-2000	2000-01
bks:	1195655	1057400
AVs:	115363	107306

Acqs:	1999-2000	2000-01
bks:	35912	24246
AVs:	5136	4116

Acqs: Source: lib suppl *Co-op:* SEALS
Classn: DDC *Cat: Type:* author, classified, subj
& title *Medium:* auto *Auto Sys:* Geac *Svcs:*
Extramural: old people's homes, housebnd, day
centres, play groups *Info:* business, community,
European, legal, edu, careers *Other:* archv svc,
Open Learning *Activs:* ch's activs, bk sales,
temp exhibs, reading groups, talks, author visits
Enqs: 179920 (1999-2000); 136097 (2000-01)
Staff: Libns: 26 *Non-Prof:* 107

Inc from:	1999-2000	2000-01
local govt:	£2544251	£2507528
fines etc:	£180827	£200694
total:	£2725078	£2708222

Exp on:	1999-2000	2000-01
stock:	£435138	£282864
salaries:	£1582799	£1644894
total:	£2725078	£2708222

Suffolk

P179 Suffolk Libraries and Heritage

St Andrew House, County Hall, Ipswich, Suffolk,
IP4 2JS (01473-584564; *fax:* 01473-584549)
Email: asksuffolk@libher.suffolkcc.gov.uk
Internet: http://www.suffolkcc.gov.uk/
libraries_and_heritage/

Local Auth: Suffolk County Council *Pop:*
668548 *Cttee:* Libs & Heritage Cttee *Larger*
Dept: Libs & Heritage *Dept Chief: Asst Dir:* Ms
Guenever Pachent BA, DipLIS, MCLIP, MILAM
Chief: County Mgr, Libs & Heritage: Mr Roger
McMaster BA, MA, MCLIP (roger.mcmaster@
libher.suffolkcc.gov.uk) *Dep:* Head of Info &
Learning: Ms Margaret Davies MCLIP (margaret.
davies@libher.suffolkcc.gov.uk) *Other Snr*
Staff: Head of Localities: Ms Alison Wheeler
MCLIP (alison.wheeler@libher.suffolkcc.gov.uk);
Business Mgr: Mr Vincent McDonald BA, MCLIP
(vincent.mcdonald@ libher.suffolkcc.gov.uk);
School Lib Svc Mgr: Ms Helen Boothroyd BA,
MCLIP (helen.boothroyd@libher.suffolkcc.gov.uk)
Main Libs: IPSWICH COUNTY LIB, Northgate
St, Ipswich, Suffolk, IP1 3DE (*ref:* 01473-583705;
lend: 01473-583710; *fax:* 01473-583700; email:
Ipswich.Library@libher.suffolkcc.gov.uk); BURY
ST EDMUNDS LIB, Sergeant's Walk, off St
Andrews St North, Bury St Edmunds, Suffolk,
IP33 1TZ (01284-352545; *fax:* 01284-352566;
email: Bury.Library@libher.suffolkcc.gov.uk);
IXWORTH LIB, Village Hall, High St, Ixworth,
Suffolk, IP31 2HH (01359-231493; *email:*
Ixworth.Library@libher.suffolkcc.gov.uk);
LOWESTOFT LIB, Clapham Rd South, Lowestoft,
Suffolk, NR32 1DR (01502-405342; *fax:* 01502-

405350; *email:* Lowestoft.Library@libher.
suffolkcc.gov.uk); NEWMARKET LIB, 1a The
Rookery, Newmarket, Suffolk, CB8 8EQ (01638-
661216; *fax:* 01638-560818; *email:* Newmarket.
Library@libher.suffolkcc.gov.uk); STRAD-BROKE
LIB, Ct House, Queen St, Stradbroke, Suffolk,
IP21 5JG (01379-384768; *email:* Stradbroke.
Library@libher.suffolkcc.gov.uk) *Branch Libs:*
ALDEBURGH LIB, Victoria Rd, Aldeburgh,
Suffolk, IP15 5EG (01728-452502; *email:*
Aldeburgh.Library@libher.suffolkcc.gov.uk);
BECCLES LIB, Blyburgate, Beccles, Suffolk,
NR34 9TB (01502-714073/6471; *email:* Beccles.
Library@libher.suffolkcc.gov.uk); BRANDON LIB,
Community Centre, Bury Rd, Brandon, Suffolk,
IP27 0BU (01842-810184; *email:* Brandon.
Library@libher.suffolkcc.gov.uk); BUNGAY LIB,
Wharton St, Bungay, Suffolk, NR35 1EL (01986-
892748; *fax:* 01986-894008; *email:* Bungay.
Library@libher.suffolkcc.gov.uk); CAPEL ST
MARY LIB, Village Hall, The Street, Capel St
Mary, Suffolk, IP9 2EP (01473-311699; *email:*
Capel.Library@libher.suffolkcc.gov.uk);
CHANTRY LIB, Hawthorn Dr, Ipswich, Suffolk,
IP2 0QY (01473-685867; *email:* Chantry.Library@
libher.suffolkcc.gov.uk); ELMSWELL LIB,
Memorial Lib, Cooks Rd, Elmswell, Suffolk, IP33
9BX (01359-240974; *email:* Elmswell.Library@
libher.suffolkcc.gov.uk); EYE LIB, Buckshorn Ln,
Eye, Suffolk, IP23 7AZ (01379-870515; *email:*
Eye.Library@libher.suffolkcc.gov.uk); FELIX-
STOWE LIB, Crescent Rd, Felixstowe, Suffolk,
IP11 7BY (01394-625766; *fax:* 01394-625770;
email: Felixstowe.Library@libher.suffolkcc.
gov.uk); FRAMLINGHAM LIB, The Old Court
House, Bridge St, Framling-ham, Suffolk, IP13
9BA (01728-723735; *email:* Framlingham.Library@
libher.suffolkcc.gov.uk); GAINSBOROUGH LIB,
Clapgate Ln, Ipswich, Suffolk, IP3 0RL (01473-
588522; *email:* Gainsborough.Library@libher.
suffolkcc.gov.uk); GT CORNARD LIB, Upper
School, Head Ln, Gt Cornard, Suffolk, CO10 0JU
(01787-296085; *email:* Conard.Library@libher.
suffolkcc.gov.uk); HADLEIGH LIB, 29 High St,
Hadleigh, Suffolk, IP7 5AG (01473-823778; *fax:*
01473-822557; *email:* Hadleigh.Library@libher.
suffolkcc.gov.uk); HALESWORTH LIB, Bridge St,
Halesworth, Suffolk, IP19 8AD (01986-875095;
fax: 01986-875096; *email:* Halesworth.Library@
libher.suffolkcc.gov.uk); HAVERHILL LIB, Camps
Rd, Haverhill, Suffolk, CB9 8HB (01440-702638;
fax: 01440-703971; *email:* Haverhill.Library@
libher.suffolkcc.gov.uk); LEISTON LIB, Old Post
Office Sq, Main St, Leiston, Suffolk, IP16 4ER
(01728-831252; *fax:* 01728-832691; *email:* Leiston.
Library@libher.suffolkcc.gov.uk); MILDENHALL
LIB, Chestnut Cl, Mildenhall, Suffolk, IP28 7HL
(01638-713558; *fax:* 01638-510108; *email:*
Mildenhall.Library@libher.suffolkcc.gov.uk);
NEEDHAM MARKET LIB, School St, Needham
Market, Ipswich, Suffolk, IP6 8BB (01449-720780;
email: Needham.Library@libher.suffolkcc.gov.uk);
OULTON BROAD LIB, 92 Bridge St, Oulton Broad,
Lowestoft, Suffolk, NR32 3LR (01502-405522;
email: OultonBroad.Library@libher.suffolkcc.
gov.uk); ROSEHILL LIB, Tomline Rd, Ipswich,
Suffolk, IP3 8DB (01473-588518; *email:* Rosehill.
Library@libher.suffolkcc.gov.uk); SAXMUNDHAM
LIB, County Offices, St Farm Rd, Saxmundham,
Suffolk, IP17 1AL (01728-403094; *fax:* 01728-
403095; *email:* Saxmundham.Library@libher.
suffolkcc.gov.uk); SOUTHWOLD LIB, North
Green, Southwold, Suffolk, IP18 6AT (01502-
722519; *fax:* 01502-722519; *email:* Southwold.
Library@libher.suffolkcc.gov.uk); STOWMARKET
LIB, Milton Rd, Stowmarket, Suffolk, IP14 1EX
(01449-613143; *fax:* 01449-672629; *email:*
Stowmarket.Library@libher.suffolkcc.gov.uk);
SUDBURY LIB, Market Hill, Sudbury, Suffolk,
CO10 2EN (01787-296000; *fax:* 01787-296004;
email: Sudbury.Library@libher.suffolkcc.gov.uk);
WESTBOURNE LIB, Sherring-ton Rd, Ipswich,
Suffolk, IP1 4HT (01473-588000; *email:*
Westbourne.Library@libher.suffolkcc.gov.uk);

WOODBRIDGE LIB, New St, Woodbridge,
Suffolk, IP12 1DT (01394-625095; *fax:* 01394-
625091; *email:* Woodbridge.Library@libher.
suffolkcc.gov.uk)
Svc Pts: PT: 13 *Mobile:* 6 *AV:* 43 *Computers:* 43
Internet: 43 *Other:* MUSIC & DRAMA LIB, 5
Holywells Cl, Ipswich, Suffolk, IP3 0AW (01473-
583503)
Collns: racing colln (at Newmarket); Benjamin
Britten Colln (at Lowestoft); Cullum Colln (at Bury
St Edmunds); Edward Fitzgerald Colln; Seckford
Colln; Sutton Hoo Colln (all at Woodbridge);
Ipswich Old Town Lib (at Ipswich School, by appt
only); BSI on m-fiche (at Ipswich & Lowestoft);
HMSO Official Pubns; European Official Pubns
(both at Ipswich) *Co-op Schemes:* Co-East,
EMRLS, ANGLES, JFR *ILLs:* county, natl &
internatl *Loans:* bks/3 or 6 wks; audios/3 wks;
videos, DVDs & CD-ROMs/2 wks; lang courses/6
wks; Open Learning materials/12 wks *Charges:*
audios/£1-£2; videos/£1.90; DVDs/£2.50; CD-
ROMs/£1.50; lang courses/£2.60-£4; Playstation
games/£2.50 *Income Gen:* req & res/45p-75p,
priority svc £3; lost ticket/50p *Fines:* bks/ad &
oap 10p pd for 1st 2 days, then 55p pw), ch/1p pd
for 1st 2 days, then 6p pw); spkn wd/£1-£2.20 pw;
music audios/50p-£1.10 pw; videos, CD-ROMs &
Playstation games/loan charge; DVDs/£4 pw;
ABE tutors, playgroups, WEA, Home Lib Svc,
instns (prisons, hosps & residential homes)
exempt from fines *Equip:* 2 m-readers, 1 m-
printer, 17 fax (£1.50 1st pg, 75p addl, higher
charges overseas), 13 copiers, 3 clr copiers,
room hire, 322 computers (incl 23 with wd-proc,
173 with CD-ROM & 178 with internet) *Disabled:*
computers with large keyboards & specially
adapted mice at all libs *Online:* Companies
House, Dialog (cost of search + VAT) *Offcr-in-*
Charge: Head of Support Svcs: Mrs Sue Garbett
(sue.garbett@libher.suffolkcc.gov.uk)

Stock:	1 Apr 2000	1 Apr 2001
ad lend:	723705	734225
ad ref:	88779	91067
ch:	241326	245504
schools:	280434	289032
instns:	25107	29405
audios:	34200	35267
videos:	22966	22894
CD-ROMs:	1327	3665
periodcls:	374	382

Issues:	1999-2000	2000-01
ad lend:	4784177	4554388
ch:	1412313	1291261
audios:	197779	200532
videos:	160581	164379
CD-ROMs:	6770	16554

Acqs:	1999-2000	2000-01
bks:	172610	177631
AVs:	14304	13357

Acqs: Source: lib suppl, publ & bksellers *Offcr-in-*
Charge: Stock Mgr: Ms Elizabeth Brain (liz.brain@
libher.suffolkcc.gov.uk)
Classn: DDC *Cat: Type:* author, classified, subj
& title *Medium:* auto *Auto Sys:* DS *Svcs:*
Extramural: schools, prisons, hosps, old people's
homes, housebnd, day centres, play groups *Info:*
business, online local info database *Other:* Open
Learning, European Public Info Relay *Activs:*
ch's activs, bk sales, poetry readings, reading
groups, writers' groups, talks, author visits *Offcr-*
in-Charge: Arts Offcr (arts events): Ms Jayne
Knight BSc (jayne.knight@libher.suffolkcc.
gov.uk)
Enqs: 1032526 (1999-2000); 1069488 (2000-01)
Staff: Prof: 34 *Non-Prof:* 183

Inc from:	1999-2000	2000-01
local govt:	£6654640	£6546660
fines etc:	£1544000	£1733000
total:	£11558000	£11413000

Exp on:	1999-2000	2000-01
bks:	£2242000	£2104000
AVs:	£275000	£300000
elec media:	£36000	£31000
salaries:	£5681000	£5827000
total:	£11558000	£11413000

Proj: Lowestoft Learning Centre; Lowestoft Lib refurbishment

Sunderland

P180 City of Sunderland Public Libraries

City Lib & Arts Centre, Fawcett Street, Sunderland, Tyne & Wear, SR1 1RE (0191-514-1235; *fax:* 0191-514-8444)
Email: enquiry.desk@edcom.sunderland.gov.uk
Internet: http://www.sunderland.gov.uk/

Local Auth: City of Sunderland Council *Pop:* 289500 *Cttee:* Libs, Museums & Arts (Sub-Cttee of Leisure Cttee) *Larger Dept:* Community & Cultural Svcs *Dept Chief:* Acting Dir of Community & Cultural Svcs: Mr David Fleetwood *Chief:* Head of Libs, Arts & Info: Mrs Jane F. Hall MCLIP (jane.f.hall@edcom.sunderland.gov.uk) *Dep:* Asst Chief Libn: Mrs Valerie Craggs (valerie.craggs@edcom.sunderland.gov.uk)
Main Libs: CITY LIB, addr as above; WASHINGTON TOWN CENTRE LIB, Independence Sq, Washington, Tyne & Wear, NE38 7RZ (0191-219-3440; *fax:* 0191-219-3454; *email:* WashTown.Library@sunderland.gov.uk) *Branch Libs:* DOXFORD PK BRANCH LIB, Hillhead Rd, Doxford Pk, Sunderland, SR3 2ND (0191-553-5738); EASINGTON LN LIB, Easington Ln, Tyne & Wear, DH5 0JW (0191-553-6695); EAST HERRINGTON LIB, Atlantis Rd, East Herrington, Sunderland, SR3 3PF (0191-553-5885); FULWELL LIB, Dene Ln, Fulwell, Sunderland, SR6 8EH (0191-553-5260); GRINDON LIB, 31 Galashiels Rd, Sunderland, SR4 8JJ (0191-553-6894); HENDON LIB, Toward Rd, Sunderland, SR2 8JG (0191-553-2750); HETTON LIB, Houghton Rd, Hetton, Tyne & Wear, DH5 9PG (0191-553-6665); HOUGHTON LIB, 74 Newbottle St, Houghton, Tyne & Wear, DH4 4AF (0191-553-6475; *fax:* 0191-553-6478); HYLTON CASTLE LIB, Cranleigh Rd, Sunderland, SR5 3PQ (0191-553-5265); KAYLL RD LIB, Kayll Rd, Sunderland, SR4 7TW (0191-553-2760); MONKWEARMOUTH LIB, Church St, Sunderland, SR6 0DR (0191-553-2755); RYHOPE LIB, Ryhope St, Ryhope, Sunderland, SR2 0AB (0191-553-6245); SHINEY ROW LIB, Chester Rd, Shiney Row, Tyne & Wear, DH4 4RB (0191-382-3042); SILKSWORTH LIB, Vane St, Silksworth, Sunderland, SR3 1HW (0191-553-6170); SOUTHWICK LIB, Beaumont St, Southwick, Sunderland, SR5 2JR (0191-553-5270); WASHINGTON MILLENNIUM CENTRE COMMUNITY LIB, The Oval, Concord, Washington, Tyne & Wear, NE37 2QD (0191-219-3878); WASHINGTON GREEN LIB, The Green, Washington, Tyne & Wear, NE38 7AB (0191-219-3435)
Svc Pts: PT: 3 Mobile: 2 AV: 21 *Computers:* 21 *Internet:* 21 *Other:* SCHOOLS LIB SVC, Broadway Centre, Springwell Rd, Sunderland, SR4 8NW (0191-553-5646; *fax:* 0191-553-5645)
Collns: Lilburn Colln; Corder MSS *Co-op Schemes:* Info North, NETWORK *ILLs:* county, natl & internatl *Loans:* bks/3 wks; audios/2 wks; videos/1 day or 1 wk; CD-ROMs/1 wk *Charges:* audios/80p, conc 50p; talking bks/70p, conc 40p; videos/£1-£2.50; CD-ROMs/£2 *Income Gen:* res/70p, conc 40p; lost ticket/computer £1, Browne 50p *Fines:* bks/ad 10p pd, ch & oap 5p pd; audios/10p pd, conc 5p; videos & CD-ROMs/loan charge *Equip:* 2 m-readers, m-printer (50p), 2 fax (£2), 3 copiers (A4/10p, A3/25p), clr copier (A4/£1, A3/£1.50), video viewer, computers (incl

wd-proc, internet & CD-ROM, access free), room hire (£15-£30 per hr) *Disabled:* textphone, hearing loop sys *Offcr-in-Charge:* Admin Offcr: Mrs Anne Hall (anne.hall@edcom.sunderland.gov.uk)

Stock:	1 Apr 2000	1 Apr 2001
ad lend:	343114	318207
ad ref:	50082	48314
ch:	99328	97459
schools:	170968	166795
iaudios:	18717	16467
videos:	2359	1797
CD-ROMs:	1027	360
periodcls:	83	82
m-forms:	27517	27595
archvs:	52 linear m	52 linear m

Issues:	1999-2000	2000-01
ad lend:	1671549	1626034
ch:	282132	278645
schools:	71174	66176
audios:	86271	92221
videos:	18493	16697
CD-ROMs:	2643	2589

Acqs:	1999-2000	2000-01
bks:	53155	60538
AVs:	3340	3805

Acqs: Source: lib suppl *Offcr-in-Charge:* Acqs Offcr: Mrs Valerie Little (valerie.little@edcom.sunderland.gov.uk)
Classn: DDC *Cat: Type:* author, classified, subj & title *Medium:* auto *Auto Sys:* own *Svcs: Extramural:* schools, hosps, old people's homes, housebnd, day centres, play groups *Info:* business, community *Other:* Learning Centres, Elec Village Halls *Activs:* ch's activs, bk sales, temp exhibs, poetry readings, reading groups, writers' groups, talks, author visits, arts programme *Offcr-in-Charge:* Snr Libn (Reader Development): Mrs Joanne Parkinson (joanne.parkinson@edcom.sunderland.gov.uk)
Enqs: 145433 (1999-2000); 151151 (2000-01)
Staff: Libns: 23 *Non-Prof:* 115.2

Inc from:	1999-2000	2000-01
fines etc:	£387899	£426866

Exp on:	1999-2000	2000-01
bks:	£472581	£485759
AVs:	£126459	£61383
elec media:	£49210	£215720
salaries:	£2169174	£2294631
total:	£4027896	£4292822

Proj: Sandhill View PFI development (open Oct 2002); Metton Centre development (open Mar 2003) *Further Info:* Lib Svc recently achieved Beacon status for libs as a community resource

Surrey

P181 Surrey Libraries

Community Svcs, County Hall, Penrhyn Rd, Kingston-upon-Thames, Surrey, KT1 2DN (08456-009009; *fax:* 020-8541-9004)
Internet: http://www.surreycc.gov.uk/

Local Auth: Surrey County Council *Pop:* 1080600 *Larger Dept:* lib svcs are an integrated part of Community Svcs *Dept Chief:* Head of Community Svcs: Mr Nick Wilson *Chief:* Head of Libs: Mr Chris Norris *Dep:* for Area Offices, contact the Area Mgrs below
Area Offices: COMMUNITY SVCS, East Surrey Area Office, Omnibus Bldg, Lesbourne Rd, Reigate, Surrey, RH2 7JA (01737-737600/1; *fax:* 01737-737647), Area Mgr: Ms Hilary Ely; COMMUNITY SVCS, Mid Surrey Area Office, Bay Tree Ave, Kingston Rd, Leatherhead, Surrey, KT22 7SY (01372-371600), Area Mgr: Ms Sally Parker; COMMUNITY SVCS, NW Surrey Area Office, Runnymede Centre, Chertsey Rd, Addlestone, Surrey, KT15 2EP (01932-794179), Area Mgr: Ms Rose Wilson; COMMUNITY SVCS, SW Surrey Area Office, Grosvenor House, London Sq,

Guildford, Surrey, GU1 1FA (01483-517900/1; *fax:* 01483-517601), Area Mgr: Mr Chris Phillips
Branch Libs: ADDLESTONE LIB, Church Rd, Addlestone, Surrey, KT15 1RW (01932-843648; *fax:* 01932-857905); ASH LIB, Ash St, Ash, Aldershot, Hampshire, GU12 6LF (01252-321708; *fax:* 01252-314317); ASHFORD LIB, Church Rd, Ashford, Middlesex, TW15 2XB (01784-253651; *fax:* 01784-257603); ASHTEAD LIB, Woodfield Ln, Ashtead, Surrey, KT21 2BQ (01372-275875; *fax:* 01372-800335); BANSTEAD LIB, Bolters Ln, Banstead, Surrey, SM7 2AW (01737-351271; *fax:* 01737-373693); BOOKHAM LIB, Townshott Cl, Gt Bookham, Surrey, KT23 4DQ (01372-454440; *fax:* 01372-451433); BRAMLEY LIB, High St, Bramley, Guildford, Surrey, GU5 0HG (01483-892510; *fax:* 01483-892522); CAMBERLEY LIB, Knoll Rd, Camberley, Surrey, GU15 3SY (01276-63184; *fax:* 01276-65701); CATERHAM HILL LIB, Westway, Caterham, Surrey, CR3 5TP (01883-342008; *fax:* 01883-340885); CATERHAM VALLEY LIB, Stafford Rd, Caterham, Surrey, CR3 6JG (01883-343580; *fax:* 01883-330872); CHERTSEY LIB, Guildford St, Chertsey, Surrey, KT16 9BE (01932-564101; *fax:* 01932-565714); COBHAM LIB, Cedar Rd, Cobham, Surrey, KT11 2AE (01932-863292; *fax:* 01932-860443); CRANLEIGH LIB, High St, Cranleigh, Surrey, GU6 8AE (01483-272413; *fax:* 01483-271327); DITTONS LIB, Mercer Cl, Thames Ditton, Surrey, KT7 0BS (020-8398-2521; *fax:* 020-8339-0949); DORKING LIB, Pippbrook House, Dorking, Surrey, RH4 1SL (01306-882948; *fax:* 01306-875006); EGHAM LIB, High St, Egham, Surrey, TW20 9EA (01784-433904; *fax:* 01784-430156); EPSOM LIB, The Ebbisham Centre, 6 The Derby Sq, Epsom, Surrey, KT19 8AG (01372-721707; *fax:* 01372-744441); ESHER LIB, Old Church Path, Esher, Surrey, KT10 9NS (01372-465036; *fax:* 01372-467215); EWELL LIB, Bourne Hall, Spring St, Ewell, Epsom, Surrey, KT17 1UF (020-8394-0951; *fax:* 020-8873-1603); EWELL CT LIB, Ewell Court House, Lakehurst Rd, Ewell, Epsom, Surrey, KT19 0EB (020-8393-1069; *fax:* 020-8873-1602); FARNHAM LIB, Vernon House, 28 West St, Farnham, Surrey, GU9 7DR (01252-716021; *fax:* 01252-717377); FRIMLEY GREEN LIB, 2 Beech Rd, Frimley Green, Camberley, Surrey, GU16 6LQ (01252-835530; *fax:* 01252-834479); GODALMING LIB, Bridge St, Godalming, Surrey, GU7 1HT (01483-422743; *fax:* 01483-425480); GUILDFORD LIB, 77 North St, Guildford, Surrey, GU1 4AL (01483-568496; *fax:* 01483-579177); HASLEMERE LIB, 91 Wey Hill, Haslemere, Surrey, GU27 1HP (01428-642907; *fax:* 01428-641258); HERSHAM LIB, Molesey Rd, Hersham, Surrey, KT12 4RF (01932-226968; *fax:* 01932-230295); HORLEY LIB, Victoria Rd, Horley, Surrey, RH6 7AG (01293-784141; *fax:* 01293-820084); HORSLEY LIB, Parade Ct, Ockham Rd South, East Horsley, near Leatherhead, Surrey, KT24 6QR (01483-283870; *fax:* 01483-281358); LEATHERHEAD LIB, The Mansion, Church St, Leatherhead, Surrey, KT22 8DP (01372-373149; *fax:* 01372-376354); LINGFIELD LIB, The Guest House, Vicarage Ln, Lingfield, Surrey, RH7 6HA (01342-832058; *fax:* 01342-832517); MERSTHAM LIB, Weldon Way, Merstham, Surrey, RH1 3QB (01737-642471; *fax:* 01737-643912); MOLESEY LIB, The Forum, Walton Rd, W Molesey, Surrey, KT8 2HZ (020-8979-6348; *fax:* 020-8979-7398); NEW HAW LIB, The Broadway, New Haw, Addlestone, Surrey, KT15 3HA (01932-343091; *fax:* 01932-350946); OXTED LIB, 12 Gresham Rd, Oxted, Surrey, RH8 0BQ (01883-714225; *fax:* 01883-722742); REDHILL LIB, Warwick Quadrant, Redhill, Surrey, RH1 1NN (01737-763332; *fax:* 01737-772048); REIGATE LIB, Bancroft House, Bancroft Rd, Reigate, Surrey, RH2 7RP (01737-244272; *fax:* 01737-244405); SHEPPERTON LIB, High St, Shepperton, Middlesex, TW17 9AU (01932-225047; *fax:* 01932-245849); STAINES LIB, Friends Walk, Staines, Middlesex, TW18 4PG (01784-454430; *fax:* 01784-461780); ☞

(Surrey Libs cont)
STANWELL COMMUNITY LIB & INFO CENTRE, Hadrian Way, Stanwell, Middlesex, TW19 7HE (01784-244378; *fax:* 01784-253347); STONE-LEIGH LIB, 1 Stoneleigh Broadway, Stoneleigh, Epsom, Surrey, KT17 2JA (020-8394-0328; *fax:* 020-8873-1597); SUNBURY LIB, The Parade, Staines Rd West, Sunbury-on-Thames, Middlesex, TW16 7AB (01932-783131; *fax:* 01932-765963); TATTENHAMS LIB, Tattenham Cres, Epsom Downs, Epsom, Surrey, KT18 5NU (01737-354144; *fax:* 01737-219712); WALTON LIB, High St, Walton-on-Thames, Surrey, KT12 1HZ (01932-224818; *fax:* 01932-230296); WARLINGHAM LIB, Shelton Ave, Warlingham, Surrey, CR6 9NF (01883-622479; *fax:* 01883-622210); WEST BYFLEET LIB, The Corner, West Byfleet, Surrey, KT14 6NY (01932-343955; *fax:* 01932-343838); WEYBRIDGE LIB, Church St, Weybridge, Surrey, KT13 8DE (01932-843812; *fax:* 01932-850878); WOKING LIB, Gloucester Walk, Woking, Surrey, GU21 6EP (01483-770591; *fax:* 01483-756073)
Svc Pts: PT: 4 *Mobile:* 6 *AV:* 53 *Computers:* 52 *Internet:* 52 *Other:* PERFORMING ARTS LIB, Denbies Wine Est, London Rd, Dorking, Surrey (01306-875453; *fax:* 01306-875074); Local Hist Centres (at Caterham Valley, Cranleigh, Ewell, Horley, Lingfield & Redhill Libs)
Collns: BSI; TSO Colln (official pubns); Living with Disability Collns; Reminiscence Collns; environmental collns; homework collns for school ch *Loans:* bks/3 wks; audios, videos, CD-ROMs & DVDs/1 wk *Charges:* music CDs/60p single, 75p double; spkn wd/cassettes 40p-£1, CDs/75p-£1.50, ch's free; videos/info free, entertainment £1-£3; DVDs/£2; Playstation games/£3 *Income Gen:* req/ad bks 80p-£2, ch's 20p-£1.20, audios & videos £1; lost ticket/£1 *Fines:* bks/ad 12p pd (max £3.60), ch 2p pd (max 60p), over-70s exempt; audios & videos/loan charge *Equip:* m-readers, m-printers, fax, copiers, clr copiers, computers (incl internet & CD-ROM), rooms for hire, projection equip *Disabled:* CCTV, minicom, hearing loops *Online:* KnowUK, local info systems

Stock:	1 Apr 2000	1 Apr 2001
ad lend:	1491344	1343194
ad ref:	56555	54330
ch:	331781	425517
audios:	-	70739
videos:	-	42175
CD-ROMs:	-	2097
periodcls:	248	-

Issues:	1999-2000	2000-01
ad lend:	6193834	5921912
ch:	1959854	1922035
audios:	255441	253231
videos:	292977	308530
CD-ROMs:	4712	27422

Acqs:	1999-2000	2000-01
bks:	175193	124033

Acqs: Source: lib suppl (Surrey Lib Supply Agency) *Offcr-in-Charge:* Area Resources Mgrs for each of the 4 areas
Classn: DDC (modified) *Cat: Medium:* auto *Auto Sys:* DS Galaxy 2000 *Svcs: Extramural:* prisons, old people's homes, housebnd, informal contact with schools & hosps *Info:* community, business, environmental, European *Other:* Learning Centres at 11 libs

Activs: ch's activs, bk sales, temp exhibs, reader development, author visits
Enqs: 607620 (1999-2000); 584324 (2000-01)
Staff: Libns: 49.1 *Non-Prof:* 273.48

Inc from:	1999-2000
fines etc:	£1543366

Exp on:	1999-2000
bks:	£1927093
AVs:	£247361
salaries:	£5622675
total:	£13025000

Swansea

P182 Swansea Library and Information Service

County Lib HQ, County Hall, Swansea, W Glamorgan, SA1 3PN (01792-636430; *fax:* 01792-636235)
Email: Swansea.Libraries@swansea.gov.uk
Internet: http://www.swansea.gov.uk/libraries/

Local Auth: City & County of Swansea Council *Pop:* 230300 *Chief:* County Libn: Mr Michael J. Allen BA, MSc, MCLIP
Main Libs: SWANSEA CENTRAL LIB, Alexandra Rd, Swansea, W Glamorgan, SA1 5DX (*lend:* 01792-516750/1/2; *ref:* 01792-516753/7; *fax:* 01792-516759; *email:* Central.Library@ swansea.gov.uk); GORSEINON LIB, West St, Gorseinon, Swansea, W Glamorgan, SA4 4AA (01792-516780/1; *fax:* 01792-516782; *email:* gorseinon.library@swansea.gov.uk); MORRISTON LIB, Treharne Rd, Morriston, Swansea, W Glamorgan, SA6 7AA (01792-516770; *fax:* 01792-516771; *email:* morriston.library@swansea. gov.uk); OYSTERMOUTH LIB, Dunns Ln, Mumbles, Swansea, W Glamorgan, SA3 4AA (01792-368380; *fax:* 01792-369143; *email:* oystermouth.library@swansea.gov.uk) *Branch Libs:* BRYNHYFRYD LIB, Llangyfelach Rd, Brynhyfryd, Swansea, W Glamorgan, SA5 9LH (01792-650953; *fax:* 01792-641895; *email:* brynhyfryd.library@swansea.gov.uk); BRYNMILL LIB, Bernard St, Brynmill, Swansea, W Glamorgan, SA2 0DT (01792-466072; *email:* brynmill. library@swansea.gov.uk); CLYDACH LIB, High St, Clydach, Swansea, W Glamorgan, SA6 5LN (01792-843300; *fax:* 01792-844768; *email:* clydach.library@swansea.gov.uk); FFORESTFACH LIB, Kings Head Rd, Gendros, Swansea, W Glamorgan, SA5 8DA (01792-586978; *email:* fforestfach.library@swansea. gov.uk); GOWERTON LIB, Mansel St, Gowerton, Swansea, W Glamorgan, SA4 3BU (01792-873572; *fax:* 01792-874526; *email:* gowerton. library@swansea.gov.uk); KILLAY LIB (temp addr), St Hillary's Church, Gower Rd, Killay, Swansea, W Glamorgan, SA2 (*tel & fax:* 01792-203453; *email:* killay.library@swansea.gov.uk); LLANSAMLET LIB, 242 Peniel Green Rd, Llansamlet, Swansea, W Glamorgan, SA7 9BD (01792-771652); PENLAN LIB, Heol Frank, Penlan, Swansea, W Glamorgan, SA5 7AH (01792-584674; *email:* penlan.library@swansea. gov.uk); PENNARD LIB, Pennard Rd, Southgate, Pennard, Swansea, W Glamorgan, SA3 2AD (01792-233277; *email:* pennard.library@swansea. gov.uk); PONTARDDULAIS LIB, St Michaels Ave, Pontarddulais, Swansea, W Glamorgan, SA4 1TE (01792-882822; *email:* pontarddulais.library@ swansea.gov.uk); ST THOMAS LIB, Miers St, St Thomas, Swansea, W Glamorgan, SA1 8BZ (01792-655570; *email:* stthomas.library@swansea. gov.uk); SKETTY LIB, Vivian Rd, Sketty, Swansea, W Glamorgan, SA2 0UN (01792-202024; *fax:* 01792-206471; *email:* sketty.library@ swansea.gov.uk); TOWNHILL LIB, Paradise Pk, Powys Ave, Townhill, Swansea, W Glamorgan, SA1 6PH (01792-512370; *fax:* 01792-512371; *email:* townhill.library@swansea.gov.uk)

Svc Pts: PT: 1 *Mobile:* 2 *AV:* 1 *Other:* LOCAL STUDIES DEPT, at Swansea Central Lib (see **A479**)
Collns: Dylan Thomas Colln (c2000 items, at Swansea Central Lib) *ILLs:* county & natl *Loans:* bks & audios/3 wks *Charges:* audios/ £6+VAT *Income Gen:* res/40p *Fines:* bks/ad 20p pw, ch & oap 10p pw; audios/20p pw *Equip:* m-readers, m-printers, fax, copiers, clr copiers, computers (incl internet & CD-ROM)

Stock:	1 Apr 2000	1 Apr 2001
lend:	306700	331912
ref:	84313	86596
AVs:	17712	16227
periodcls:	320	221

Issues:	1999-2000	2000-01
bks:	1565277	1465021
audios:	91682	87350

Acqs:	1999-2000	2000-01
bks:	35734	31949
AVs:	1480	1998

Acqs: Source: lib suppl, publ & bksellers
Cat: Type: author, subj & title *Medium:* cards, m-form & auto *Svcs: Extramural:* hosps, housebnd, day centres *Info:* business, European *Activs:* ch's activs, bk sales, temp exhibs
Enqs: 255684 (1999-2000); 292552 (2000-01)
Staff: Libns: 17 *Non-Prof:* 66.3

Inc from:	1999-2000	2000-01
local govt:	£2350770	£2372195
fines etc:	£90311	£108471
total:	£2441081	£2480666

Exp on:	1999-2000	2000-01
bks:	£352513	£371013
salaries:	£1476235	£1434999
total:	£2441081	£2480666

Swindon

P183 Swindon Libraries

Central Lib, Regent Circus, Swindon, Wiltshire, SN1 1QG (01793-463230; *fax:* 01793-541319)
Email: libraries@swindon.gov.uk
Internet: http://www.swindon.gov.uk/libraries/

Local Auth: Swindon Borough Council *Pop:* 181700 *Larger Dept:* Cultural Svcs *Dept Chief:* Head of Cultural Svcs: Ms Julia Holberry *Chief:* Libs & Heritage Mgr: Mr David Allen MCLIP (dallen@swindon.gov.uk)
Main Libs: SWINDON CENTRAL LIB, addr as above (01793-463238; *ref:* 01793-463240; *email:* central.library@swindon.gov.uk) *Branch Libs:* COVINGHAM LIB, St Paul's Dr, Covingham, Swindon, Wiltshire, SN3 5BY (01793-520185; *email:* covingham.library@swindon.gov.uk); HIGH-WORTH LIB, Brewery St, Highworth, Wiltshire, SN6 7AJ (01793-463500; *email:* highworth.library@ swindon.gov.uk); LIDEN LIB, Barrington Cl, Liden, Swindon, Wiltshire, SN3 6HF (01793-463504; *email:* liden.library@swindon.gov.uk); MOREDON LIB, Church Walk North, Moredon Rd, Swindon, Wiltshire, SN25 3DJ (01793-464490; *email:* moredon.library@swindon.gov.uk); NORTH SWINDON LIB, Orbital Retail Pk, Thamesdown Dr, Swindon, Wiltshire, SN25 4AN (01793-707120; *email:* northswindon.library@swindon.gov.uk); PARK LIB, Cavendish Sq, Swindon, Wiltshire, SN3 2LP (01793-463501; *email:* park.library@ swindon.gov.uk); UPPER STRATON LIB, Beech-croft Rd, Swindon, Wiltshire, SN2 7QQ (01793-464495; *email:* stratton.library@swindon.gov.uk); WEST SWINDON LIB, Whitehill Way, Westlea, Swindon, Wiltshire, SN5 7DL (01793-465555; *email:* westswindon.library@swindon.gov.uk); WROUGHTON LIB, Ellendune Centre, Wrough-ton, Wiltshire, SN4 9LN (01793-464496; *email:* wroughton.library@swindon.gov.uk)
Svc Pts: PT: 7 *Mobile:* 2 *AV:* 16 *Computers:* 14 *Internet:* 14

Collns: Alfred Williams Colln; Richard Jefferies Colln **Co-op Schemes:** SWRLS, WILCO **ILLs:** natl & internatl **Loans:** bks & talking bks/3 wks; audios, videos, DVDs & Playstation games/1 wk **Charges:** talking bks/£1.30, ch's free; CDs/£1; videos/£1.50-£3; DVDs & Playstation games/ £2.50-£3.50 **Income Gen:** req/75p, 50p self-svc; ILLs/£2; lost ticket/ad £2, ch £1, 1st replacement free **Fines:** bks & talking bks/ad & oap 15p pd (max £5), ch 5p pd (max £1); audios, videos, DVDs & Playstation games/loan charge; registered blind & housebnd exempt **Equip:** m-readers, m-printers (80p per pg), copiers (A4/10p, A3/20p), clr copiers (A4/£1.50, A3/£2), computers (incl wd-proc & internet), rooms for hire (various)

Stock:	1 Apr 2000	1 Apr 2001
ad lend:	162436	149624
ad ref:	15513	27703
ch:	68210	66597
audios:	11608	11635
videos:	6477	6968
periodcls:	172	137

Issues:	1999-2000	2000-01
ad lend:	1064685	975065
ch:	354550	309910
audios:	65573	66849
videos:	55095	53887

Acqs:	1999-2000	2000-01
bks:	19320	23455
AVs:	3008	2889

Acqs: Source: lib suppl **Offcr-in-Charge:** Libs & Heritage Mgr, as above
Classn: DDC **Cat:** Type: author, classified, subj & title **Medium:** auto **Auto Sys:** Geac **Svcs:** Extramural: schools (joint arrangement), hosps, hospice, old people's homes, housebnd **Info:** business, community, European, edu **Activs:** ch's activs, bk sales, temp exhibs, poetry readings, reading groups, Lit Festival
Enqs: 286741 (1999-2000); 257985 (2000-01)
Staff: Libns: 17.9 Non-Prof: 62.1

Exp on:	1999-2000	2000-01
total:	£2325600	£2668220

Tameside

P184 Tameside Libraries and Leisure

Tameside Central Lib, Old Street, Ashton-under-Lyne, Lancashire, OL6 7SG (0161-342-2029/30; fax: 0161-330-4762)
Email: central.library@mail.tameside.gov.uk
Internet: http://www.tameside.gov.uk/

Local Auth: Tameside Metropolitan Borough Council **Pop:** 219312 **Larger Dept:** Edu & Cultural Svcs **Chief:** Head of Libs: Mrs Catherine Simensky MCLIP **Other Snr Staff:** Svc Unit Mgr (Libs & Heritage): Mr A. Collins DMS, MCLIP
Main Libs: TAMESIDE CENTRAL LIB, addr as above; DENTON LIB, Peel St, Denton, Manchester, M34 3JY (0161-336-8234/320-3202; fax: 0161-337-8931; email: denton.library@mail. tameside.gov.uk); DROYLSDEN LIB, Manchester Rd, Droylsden, Manchester, M43 6EP (0161-370-1282; fax: 0161-371-1886; email: droylsden. library@mail.tameside.gov.uk); HYDE LIB, Union St, Hyde, Cheshire, SK14 1NF (0161-368-2447/ 0909; fax: 0161-368-0205; email: hyde.library@ mail.tameside.gov.uk); STALYBRIDGE LIB, Trinity St, Stalybridge, Cheshire, SK15 2BN (0161-338-2708/3831; fax: 0161-303-8289; email: stalybridge. library@mail.tameside.gov.uk) **Branch Libs:** AUDENSHAW LIB, Manchester Rd, Audenshaw, Manchester, M34 5GJ (0161-370-4240; email: audenshaw.library@mail.tameside.gov.uk); DUKIN-FIELD LIB, Concord Way, Dukinfield, Cheshire, SK16 4DB (0161-330-3257; fax: 0161-330-3426; email: dukinfield.library@mail.tameside. gov.uk); HATTERSLEY LIB, Hattersley Rd East, Hattersley, Cheshire, SK14 3EQ (0161-368-8515;

email: hattersley.library@mail.tameside.gov.uk); HAUGHTON GREEN LIB, Mancunian Rd, Denton, Manchester, M34 1NP (0161-336-7193; fax: 0161-320-0902; email: haughtongreen.library@mail. tameside.gov.uk); HURST LIB, Hurst Cross, Ashton-under-Lyne, Lancashire, OL6 8EW (0161-330-3750; fax: 0161-343-6298; email: hurst. library@mail.tameside.gov.uk); MOSSLEY LIB, Wyre St, Mossley, Ashton-under-Lyne, Lancashire, OL5 0EU (01457-832467; fax: 01457-838671; email: mossley.library@mail.tameside. gov.uk); MOTTRAM LIB, Broadbottom Rd, Mottram, Hyde, Cheshire, SK14 6JA (01457-764144; email: mottram.library@mail.tameside. gov.uk); WEST END LIB, Windsor Rd, Denton, Manchester, M34 2HB (0161-336-2995; email: westend.library@mail.tameside.gov.uk)
Svc Pts: PT: 2 Mobile: 3 AV: 7 Computers: 15 Internet: 15 Other: CENTRE FOR VISUALLY IMPAIRED, at Dukinfield Lib; TAMESIDE LOCAL STUDIES LIB (see A469)
Co-op Schemes: Libs North West, JFR, CONARLS **ILLs:** county, natl & internatl **Loans:** bks/4 wks; audios & CD-ROMs/2 wks; videos/1 day or 1 wk; lang courses/4 wks **Charges:** audios & CD-ROMs/£1; videos/75p-£3; lang courses/£2 **Income Gen:** res/75p, outside Tameside £1.75; lost ticket/ad £1, ch 50p **Fines:** bks, audios & CD-ROMs/ad 10p pd, oap 5p pd; videos/varies according to loan charge; ch & registered blind exempt **Equip:** 3 m-readers, m-printer, fax, copiers (A4/10p), public access computers (incl wd-proc, internet & CD-ROM) **Disabled:** Kurzweil, braille printer, transcription equip, various low vision aids, Eazee reader **Online:** Infocheck, TelMe

Stock:	1 Apr 2000	1 Apr 2001
lend:	382106	319402
ref:	42293	38302
AVs:	28476	23500
periodcls:	215	215

Issues:	1999-2000	2000-01
bks:	1293843	1230284
AVs:	74606	78608

Acqs:	1999-2000	2000-01
bks:	41492	46183
AVs:	3093	3697

Acqs: Source: lib suppl **Offcr-in-Charge:** Work Group Mgr (Bibliographical Svcs): Mr G. Maddock **Classn:** DDC **Cat:** Type: author, classified, subj & title **Medium:** auto **Auto Sys:** Geac **Svcs:** Extramural: schools, hosps, old people's homes, housebnd **Info:** European, community, business, council, health, careers, travel, legal **Other:** Lifelong Learning **Activs:** ch's activs, bk sales, temp exhibs, BookStart, authors' visits, reading groups, lib clubs for over-60s
Enqs: 171108 (1999-2000); 162149 (2000-01)
Staff: 104.3 in total

Inc from:	1999-2000	2000-01
lfines etc:	£157749	£176317

Exp on:	1999-2000	2000-01
stock:	£368592	£420179
salaries:	£1766828	£1869971
total:	£3305700	£3148929

Telford and Wrekin

P185 Telford and Wrekin Libraries

Telford Lib, St Quentin Gate, Town Centre, Telford, Shropshire, TF3 4JG (01952-292151/38; fax: 01952-292078)
Email: telfordlibrary@hotmail.com
Internet: http://www.telford.gov.uk/

Local Auth: Telford & Wrekin Council **Pop:** 158200 **Cttee:** Leisure, Culture & Community Panel **Larger Dept:** Leisure, Culture & Community Svc **Dept Chief:** Head of Svc: Mr Graham Foster **Chief:** Libs & Heritage Mgr: Mrs Pat Davis MCLIP

Dep: Asst Mgr (Libs): Mrs Sharon Smith BA(Hons), MCLIP (sharon.smith@telford.gov.uk)
Main Libs: TELFORD LIB, addr as above **Branch Libs:** DAWLEY LIB, King St, Dawley, Telford, Shropshire, TF4 2AA (01952-505319; email: dawleylibrary@hotmail.com); MADELEY LIB, Russell Sq, Madeley, Telford, Shropshire, TF7 5BB (01952-586575; fax: 01952-587105; email: madeleylibrary@hotmail.com); NEWPORT LIB, High St, Newport, Shropshire, TF10 7AT (01952-811222; fax: 01952-814291; email: newportlibrary@hotmail.com); OAKENGATES LIB, 3-4 Limes Walk, Oakengates, Telford, Shropshire, TF2 6EP (01952-613534; email: oakengateslibrary@hotmail.com); STIRCHLEY LIB, The Upper School, Stirchley, Telford, Shropshire, TF3 1FA (01952-590352; fax: 01952-593913; email: stirchleylibrary@hotmail.com); WELLINGTON LIB, 23 Walker St, Wellington, Telford, Shropshire, TF1 1BD (01952-244013; fax: 01952-256960; email: wellingtonlibrary@hotmail. com)
Svc Pts: PT: 2 Mobile: 1 (based at Wellington Lib)
Collns: Music & Drama (at Wellington Lib) **Co-op Schemes:** SAIL, schools & some heritage svcs with Shropshire County Council (see P163) **Loans:** bks, audios, talking bks & lang courses/3 wks; videos & CD-ROMs/1 wk **Charges:** audios/ 75p; videos/£1.50; CD-ROMs/£2 **Income Gen:** req/65p; ILLs/£2.65, BL photocopy req £3.80 **Fines:** bks/ad & oap 14p pd, ch 1st wk free, then 4p pd; audios, videos & CD-ROMs/14p pd; under 5s & disabled exempt **Equip:** 7 m-readers, m-printer (50p), 5 fax (£1-£1.50), 9 copiers (A4/10p, A3/20p), 48 computers (all with wd-proc, internet & CD-ROM, access free, printouts 10p-20p per pg), 2 rooms for hire (various) **Disabled:** Supernova software on 5 PCs

Stock:		1 Apr 2001
ad lend:		128844
ad ref:		24066
ch:		32016
audios:		9305
videos:		2497
CD-ROMs:		339

Issues:	1999-2000	2000-01
bks:	720315	499448
instns:	38892	27614
audios:	28627	21610
videos:	14542	11115

Acqs:		2000-01
bks:		24196
AVs:		2248

Acqs: Source: lib suppl **Offcr-in-Charge:** Acq Mgr: Mrs M. Criddle
Classn: DDC **Cat:** Type: author, classified, subj & title **Medium:** auto **Auto Sys:** DS **Svcs:** Extramural: old people's homes, housebnd **Info:** community, local hist **Activs:** ch's activs, bk sales, temp exhibs
Enqs: 124529 (1999-2000); 102299 (2000-01)
Staff: Libns: 12 Non-Prof: 31

Inc from:	1999-2000	2000-01
fines etc:	£90899	£96337

Exp on:	1999-2000	2000-01
stock:	£164791	£189974
elec media:	£51132	£69717
salaries:	£653877	£695352
total:	£1287920	£1408356

Thurrock

P186 Thurrock Libraries

Grays Lib, Orsett Rd, Grays, Essex, RM17 5DX (01375-383611; fax: 01375-370806)
Email: grays.library@thurrock.gov.uk
Internet: http://www.thurrock.gov.uk/libraries/

(Thurrock Libs cont)

Local Auth: Thurrock Council *Pop:* 135000
Cttee: Cabinet *Larger Dept:* Libs & Cultural
Svcs *Dept Chief:* Libs & Cultural Svcs Mgr: Mr S.
Black *Chief:* Chief Libn: Mrs A. Halliday *Other
Snr Staff:* Info Svcs Mgr: Ms Alison Cairns; Ch's
Svcs Mgr: Ms Rosalyn Jones
Main Libs: GRAYS CENTRAL LIB, addr as
above *Branch Libs:* AVELEY LIB, Purfleet Rd,
Aveley, South Ockendon, Essex, RM15 4DJ
(01708-865667; *fax:* 01708-689891; *email:* aveley.
library@thurrock.gov.uk); BELHUS LIB, Derry
Ave, South Ockendon, Essex, RM15 5DX (01708-
852398; *fax:* 01708-851587; *email:* belhus.library@
thurrock.gov.uk); BLACKSHOTS LIB, Blackshots
Ln, Grays, Essex, RM16 2JU (01375-373244; *fax:*
01375-375325; *email:* blackshots.library@thurrock.
gov.uk); CHADWELL LIB, Brentwood Rd, Chadwell St Mary, Grays, Essex, RM16 4JP (01375-
842511; *fax:* 01375-856876; *email:* chadwell.
library@thurrock.gov.uk); CHAFFORD
HUNDRED CAMPUS LIB, Mayflower Rd,
Chafford Hundred, Grays, Essex, RM16 6SA
(01375-484594; *fax:* 01375-484596); CORRING-
HAM LIB, St John's Way, Corringham, Stanford-
le-Hope, Essex, SS17 7LJ (01375-678534; *fax:*
01375-641996; *email:* corringham.library@
thurrock.gov.uk); EAST TILBURY LIB, Princess
Ave, East Tilbury, Grays, Essex, RM18 8ST
(01375-844921; *fax:* 01375-857544; *email:*
easttilbury.library@thurrock.gov.uk); ORSETT
HOSP LIB, Main Concourse, Rowley Rd, Orsett,
Grays, Essex, RM16 3EU (01268-533911 x2380);
STANFORD-LE-HOPE LIB, High St, Stanford-le-
Hope, Essex, SS17 0HG (01375-672058; *fax:*
01375-644974; *email:* stanford.le.hope.library@
thurrock.gov.uk); TILBURY LIB, Civic Sq, Tilbury,
Essex, RM18 8AD (01375-842612; *fax:* 01375-
856477; *email:* tilbury.library@thurrock.gov.uk)
Svc Pts: Mobile: 1 *AV:* 10 *Computers:* 10
Internet: 10 *Other:* HOUSEBND SVC
Co-op Schemes: Co-East, ELAN, with Essex
County Council (see **P51**) & Southend on Sea
Borough Council (see **P172**) *ILLs:* county, natl &
internatl *Loans:* bks & talking bks/3 wks; audios,
videos, DVDs & Playstation games/1 wk; CD-
ROMs/3 wks (inter-lib loans); lang courses/3-12
wks *Charges:* audios/CDs 60p, spkn wd 50p-£2;
videos/£1.10-£2.25; CD-ROMs/£2.60; lang
courses/55p for 3 wks, £3 for 12 wks *Income
Gen:* req/85p staff assisted, 60p self-svc; lost
tickets/£1.50 *Fines:* bks/ad & oap 15p 1st day,
30p 2nd day, 40p 3rd day, then 50p pw; ch & print
disabled exempt *Equip:* 5 m-readers, m-printer
(30p per pg), 10 copiers (A4/5p-10p, A3/10p-20p),
clr copier, 10 fax, 29 computers (all with wd-proc,
CD-ROM & internet) *Offcr-in-Charge:* Ms Liz
Smith

Stock:	1 Apr 2000
ad lend:	113400
ad ref:	12072
ch:	64382
audios:	5447
videos:	5639
periodcls:	134

Issues:	1999-2000
ad lend:	637329
ch:	297254
audios:	32050
videos:	33781

Acqs:	2000-01
bks:	33354
AVs:	3686

Acqs: Source: lib suppl *Offcr-in-Charge:* Chief
Libn, as above
Classn: DDC *Cat: Type:* author, classified, subj
& title *Medium:* auto *Auto Sys:* Geac *Svcs:
Extramural:* schools, hosps, old people's homes,
housebnd, play groups *Info:* community *Activs:*
ch's activs, bk sales, talks
Enqs: 69420 (1999-2000)
Staff: Libns: 9 *Non-Prof:* 35.2

Torbay

P187 Torbay Libraries

Torquay Central Lib, Lymington Rd, Torquay,
Devon, TQ1 3DT (01803-208310; *fax:* 01803-
208311)
Email: tqreflib@torbay.gov.uk
Internet: http://www.torbay.gov.uk/

Local Auth: Torbay Borough Council *Pop:*
130000 *Cttee:* Edu/Learning for Life *Larger
Dept:* Edu Svcs Directorate *Dept Chief:* Dir of
Edu Svcs: Mr Frank Weeple *Chief:* Head of Lib
Svcs: Mr Peter Bottrill BA, MCLIP (peter.bottrill@
torbay.gov.uk) *Dep:* Professional Svcs Libn: Ms
K. Lusty MCLIP
Main Libs: TORQUAY CENTRAL LIB, addr as
above (*lend:* 01803-208300; *ref:* 01803-208305;
fax: 01803-208307) *Branch Libs:* BRIXHAM
LIB, Market St, Brixham, Devon, TQ5 8EU
(01803-853870; *fax:* 01803-853870); CHURSTON
LIB, Broadsands Rd, Paignton, Devon, TQ3 6LL
(01803-843757; *fax:* 01803-843482); PAIGNTON
LIB, Courtland Rd, Paignton, Devon, TQ3 2AB
(01803-208321; *fax:* 01803-664259)
Svc Pts: Mobile: 1 *AV:* 5
Collns: local studies colln (at Torquay Central
Lib) *Co-op Schemes:* SWRLS, some joint
arrangements with Devon County Council (see
P37) & Plymouth City Council (see **P146**) *ILLs:*
county, natl & internatl *Loans:* bks/3 wks;
audios, videos & CD-ROMs/1 wk; special lang
sets/6 wks or 12 wks; music sets & play sets/2
months *Charges:* CD music/80p, sets of 3+
£1.60; special lang sets/£7.20 or £14.40; videos/
50p-£3.00; vocal scores/£1.50 for 10 copies;
boxed music sets/£2 per box; play sets/free 1st 2
months, £1.50 per 2 months thereafter *Income
Gen:* res/ad 60p, ch free for Torbay items, scale
of charges apply for music & drama; lost tickets/
ad £2, ch 60p *Fines:* bks/ad 15p pd (max £3.60),
ch 5p pd (max £1.20), 16-17 year olds, over-65s
& disabled 8p pd (max £1.92), under-5s exempt;
audios, videos & CD-ROMs/loan charge; music
sets & play sets/£5 for incomplete return *Equip:*
m-readers, m-printers (A4/10p, A3/20p), fax (UK
£1.50 per pg, higher overseas, 75p per pg to
receive), copiers (A4/10p, A3/20p), computers
(incl internet & CD-ROM, access free, booking
systems apply for internet) *Disabled:* CCTV (at
Torquay & Paignton Libs), Kurzweil (at Brixham
Lib), ZoomText on public PCs with office software
Online: Britannica

Stock:	1 Apr 2001
ad lend:	83398
ad ref:	40085
ch:	27343
audios:	8649
videos:	2927
periodcls:	137

Issues:	1999-2000	2000-01
ad lend:	873561	816434
ch:	213616	194328
audios:	40431	42463
videos:	15570	16754

Acqs:	2000-01
bks:	21478
AVs:	1983

Acqs: Source: lib suppl & bksellers *Co-op:* CUSP
Offcr-in-Charge: Bibliographic Svcs Libn: Ms A.
Webb (alison.webb@torbay.gov.uk) & Ms R.
Bourne (rosalynd.bourne@torbay.gov.uk)
Classn: DDC *Cat: Type:* author, classified, subj
& title *Medium:* auto *Auto Sys:* DS *Svcs:
Extramural:* old people's homes, housebnd, day
centres, sheltered housing, nursing homes *Info:*
community, business, local clubs & socs
database *Activs:* ch's activs, bk sales, exhibs,
Reading scheme for ch, Blind Circle (at Torquay
Lib), Over 55s Club (at Paignton Lib), Music,
Rhythm & Rhyme for young ch
Enqs: 96524 (1999-2000); 93092 (2000-01)
Staff: Libns: 14.8 *Non-Prof:* 31.3

Inc from:	1999-2000	2000-01
fines etc:	£102382	£102269

Torfaen

P188 Torfaen Libraries

Lib HQ, Floor 6, Civic Centre, Pontypool,
Torfaen, NP4 6YB (01495-766311; *fax:* 01495-
766317)
Email: sue.johnson@torfaen.gov.uk
Internet: http://www.torfaen.gov.uk/

Local Auth: Torfaen County Borough Council
Pop: 90400 *Cttee:* Edu, Leisure & Yng People
Subj Cttee *Larger Dept:* Chief Exec's Dept
Dept Chief: Head of Leisure, Youth & Cultural: Mr
David Congreve MILAM, BA(Hons), MBA *Chief:*
Cultural Svcs Mgr: Ms Susan Johnson MCLIP
Dep: Principal Libn: Ms Christine George MCLIP
(christine.george@torfaen.gov.uk)
Main Libs: CWMBRAN LIB, Gwent House,
Cwmbran, Torfaen, NP44 1XQ (*info:* 01633-
867584; *lend:* 01633-483240; *fax:* 01633-838609;
email: cwmbran.library@torfaen.gov.uk); PONTY-
POOL LIB, Hanbury Rd, Pontypool, Torfaen, NP4
6JL (01495-762820; *fax:* 01495-752530; *email:*
pontypool.library@torfaen.gov.uk) *Branch Libs:*
ABERSYCHAN LIB, Brynteg, Abersychan,
Pontypool, Torfaen, NP4 7BG (01495-772261; *fax:*
01495-772269; *email:* abersychan.library@torfaen.
gov.uk); BLAENAVON LIB, Lion St, Blaenavon,
Torfaen, NP4 9QA (01495-791637; *fax:* 01495-
793240; *email:* blaenavon.library@torfaen.gov.uk)
Svc Pts: Mobile: 2 *AV:* 4
Collns: EPIC; Natl Assembly for Wales Documentation Colln *ILLs:* county & natl *Loans:*
bks & talking bks/3 wks; audios, videos & DVDs/
1 wk *Charges:* audios/75p; talking bks/75p, conc
40p; videos/£1-£2 *Income Gen:* req/85p, conc
55p; ILLs/£2.10, conc £1; lost ticket/£2, conc £1
Fines: bks/ad 11p pd, oap 6p pd; ch & mobile lib
users exempt; audios, talking bks & videos/loan
charge; registered blind exempt *Equip:* m-
reader, 4 fax (UK 75p per pg, £1 overseas), 5
copiers (A4 & A3/10p), clr copier (A4/£1, A3/
£1.50), 64 computers (all with wd-proc & CD-
ROM, 50 with internet), 2 rooms for hire *Disabled:*
lift, CCTV, hearing loop, sheet magnifiers, large
print bks & newspapers, Gwent Talking
Newspaper, subtitled videos *Online:* Viscount
Offcr-in-Charge: ICT Offcr: Mr Adrian Robinson
(adrian.robinson@torfaen.gov.uk)

Stock:	1 Apr 2000	1 Apr 2001
lend:	93217	101575
ref:	5743	5196
audios:	5392	5798
videos:	2194	2294
CD-ROMs:	138	115
periodcls:	67	37

Issues:	1999-2000	2000-01
bks:	561714	512199
audios:	25455	24756
videos:	8483	8677
CD-ROMs:	313	273

Acqs:	1999-2000	2000-01
bks:	16205	13819
AVs:	1364	1010

Acqs: Source: lib suppl & bksellers *Offcr-in-Charge:* Principal Libn, as above & Snr Libn: Mr Mark Tanner
Classn: DDC *Cat: Type:* author, classified, subj & title *Medium:* auto *Auto Sys:* Dynix *Svcs: Extramural:* schools, hosps, old people's homes, housebnd, play groups, sheltered housing *Info:* community, business, health *Other:* Open Learning, Key Skills, homework clubs *Activs:* ch's activs, temp exhibs, poetry readings, writers' groups, talks, author visits *Offcr-in-Charge:* Cultural Svcs Mgr, as above
Enqs: 69499 (1999-2000); 60804 (2000-01)
Staff: Libns: 10 *Non-Prof:* 30

Inc from:	1999-2000
fines etc:	£52913

Exp on:	1999-2000
stock:	£149149
salaries:	£601456
total:	£750605

Trafford

P189 Trafford Libraries

Edu, Arts & Leisure Dept, Trafford Town Hall, Talbot Rd, Stretford, Trafford, Manchester, M32 0TH (0161-912-1212; *fax:* 0161-912-4639)
Internet: http://www.trafford.gov.uk/

Local Auth: Trafford Metropolitan Borough Council *Pop:* 210161 *Cttee:* Arts, Leisure & Sports Development Cttee *Larger Dept:* Community Rights, Learning & Libs *Dept Chief:* Head of Svc: Mr Graham Luccock BA, MCLIP *Chief:* Principal Libn: Mrs Gill Fitzpatrick BA, MCLIP (gill.fitzpatrick@trafford.gov.uk) *Other Snr Staff:* Libs Resources Mgr: Mrs Judith Redhead (judith.redhead@trafford.gov.uk); Libs Operations Mgr: Ms Marie Tutton (marie.tutton@ trafford.gov.uk)
Main Libs: ALTRINCHAM LIB, 20 Stamford New Rd, Altrincham, Cheshire, WA14 1EJ (0161-912-5920; *fax:* 0161-912-5921); SALE LIB, Tatton Rd, Sale, Cheshire, M33 1YH (0161-912-3008; *fax:* 0161-912-3019); STRETFORD LIB, Kingsway, Stretford, Manchester, M32 8AP (0161-912-5150; *fax:* 0161-865-3835); URMSTON LIB, Crofts Bank Rd, Urmston, Manchester, M41 0TZ (0161-912-2727; *fax:* 0161-912-2947) *Branch Libs:* BOWFELL LIB, Urmston Leisure Centre, Bowfell Rd, Urmston, Manchester, M41 5RA (0161-912-2939; *fax:* 0161-912-2937); COPPICE LIB, Coppice Ave, Sale, Cheshire, M33 4ND (0161-912-3560; *fax:* 0161-912-3562); DAVYHULME LIB, Davyhulme Rd, Urmston, Manchester, M41 7BL (0161-912-2880; *fax:* 0161-912-2895); GREATSTONE LIB, Stretford Leisure Centre, Greatstone Rd, Stretford, Manchester, M32 0ZT (0161-912-4815; *fax:* 0161-912-4816); HALE LIB, Leigh Rd, Hale, Altrincham, Cheshire, WA15 9BG (0161-912-5966; *fax:* 0161-912-5967); LOSTOCK LIB, Selby Rd, Stretford, Manchester, M32 9PL (0161-912-5226; *fax:* 0161-912-5228); OLD TRAFFORD LIB, Community Centre, Shrewsbury St, Old Trafford, Manchester, M16 9AX (0161-912-4650; *fax:* 0161-912-4654); PARTINGTON LIB, Central Rd, Urmston, Manchester, M31 4EL (0161-912-5450; *fax:* 0161-912-5453); TIMPERLEY LIB, Stockport Rd, Timperley, Altrincham, Cheshire, WA14 7XR (0161-912-5600; *fax:* 0161-912-5604); WOODSEND LIB, Woodsend Rd, Fuxton, Manchester, M41 8GN (0161-912-2919; *fax:* 0161-912 2936)
Svc Pts: PT: 1 *Mobile:* 1 *AV:* 14 *Other:* SCHOOL LIB SVC, Hayeswater Rd, Davyhulme, Manchester, M41 7BL (0161-912-2891; *fax:* 0161-912-2895); LOCAL STUDIES CENTRE, at Altrincham Lib (see **A13**)
Co-op Schemes: Libs North West *ILLs:* county, natl & internatl *Loans:* bks & talking bks/3 wks; music audios, videos, DVDs & Playstation games/1 wk *Charges:* talking bks/ £1.50; CDs/£1; videos/£1.15 or £1.75; DVDs & Playstation games/£2.50 *Income Gen:* res/£1,

in stock free; lost ticket/50p, under 14s & disabled exempt *Fines:* bks/ad 10p pd (max £12), under-18s & over-60s exempt; audios, videos, DVDs & Playstation games/loan charge; disabled exempt from fines *Equip:* 4 m-readers, m-printer (A4/30p, A3/60p), 14 fax (£1 per pg), 14 copiers (A4/5p, A3/10p), clr copier (A4/£1.20, A3/ £1.75), 89 computers (all with wd-proc, internet & CD-ROM) *Disabled:* CCTV, magnifiers

Stock:	1 Apr 2000	1 Apr 2001
ad lend:	204480	219638
ad ref:	69513	27218
ch:	86975	89818
audios:	12850	12082
videos:	8441	8558
CD-ROMs:	52	86
periodcls:	302	182

Issues:	1999-2000	2000-01
ad lend:	1075159	979869
ch:	353855	322264
audios:	63100	48793
videos:	44123	45229

Acqs:	1999-2000	2000-01
bks:	27322	22735
AVs:	3235	3886

Acqs: Source: lib suppl & publ *Offcr-in-Charge:* Bibliographical & Schools Libn: Mr David Fitzpatrick (dave.fitzpatrick@trafford.gov.uk)
Classn: DDC *Cat: Type:* author, classified & title *Medium:* auto *Auto Sys:* Talis *Svcs: Extramural:* schools, old people's homes, housebnd, talking bks svcs for blind *Info:* business, council svc *Other:* Open Learning *Activs:* ch's activs, bk sales, temp exhibs
Enqs: 509184 (1999-2000); 450632 (2000-01)
Staff: Libns: 23 *Non-Prof:* 81

Inc from:	1999-2000	2000-01
local govt:	£2561198	£2756481
fines etc:	£273618	£286511
total:	£2857405	£3066651

Exp on:	1999-2000	2000-01
bks:	£275672	£248644
AVs:	£44388	£53429
elec media:	£13952	£12436
salaries:	£1582077	£1582331
total:	£2857405	£3066651

Vale of Glamorgan

P190 Vale of Glamorgan Libraries Service

Lib HQ, Barry Lib, Greenwood Street, Barry, Glamorgan, CF63 4RU (01446-735722; *fax:* 01446-709377)
Email: barrylibrary@valeofglamorgan.gov.uk
Internet: http://www.valeofglamorgan.gov.uk/

Local Auth: Vale of Glamorgan Council *Pop:* 122900 *Larger Dept:* Learning & Development *Dept Chief:* Dir: Mr Bryan Jeffreys *Chief:* Chief Libn: Mrs Sian E. Jones BSc(Econ), MSc(Econ), MCLIP *Dep:* Principal Libn: Mr Christopher Edwards BA(Hons), MCLIP
Main Libs: BARRY LIB, addr as above
Branch Libs: COWBRIDGE LIB, Old Hall, Cowbridge, Glamorgan, CF71 7AH (01446-773941; *fax:* 01446-771353); DINAS POWYS LIB, The Murch, Dinas Powys, Glamorgan, CF64 4QU (029-2051-2556; *fax:* 029-2051-5980); LLANTWIT MAJOR LIB, Boverton Rd, Llantwit Major, Glamorgan, CF61 1XZ (01446-792700; *fax:* 01446-790126); PENARTH LIB, Stanwell Rd, Penarth, Glamorgan, CF64 2YT (029-2070-8438; *fax:* 029-2070-6564)
Svc Pts: PT: 4 *Mobile:* 2
Co-op Schemes: Interlending Wales, SET *ILLs:* county & natl *Loans:* bks & audios/3 wks *Charges:* audios/50p *Income Gen:* req/50p; lost ticket/£1 *Fines:* bks/ad 20p pw, ch 10p pw; audios/30p pw *Equip:* m-readers, copiers, fax,

computers (incl wd-proc & CD-ROM), room for hire *Disabled:* hearing loops

Stock:	1 Apr 2000	1 Apr 2001
ad lend:	148940	154606
ad ref:	834	1061
ch:	46255	50916
audios:	9410	10782
videos:	47	46
periodcls:	79	79

Issues:	1999-2000	2000-01
ad lend:	711124	581658
ch:	205651	149993
AVs:	34887	36977

Acqs:	1999-2000	2000-01
bks:	10670	12390
AVs:	1143	1334

Acqs: Source: lib suppl
Classn: DDC *Cat: Type:* author, classified & title *Medium:* auto *Auto Sys:* Urica *Svcs: Extramural:* hosps, old people's homes *Info:* community, European, Natl Assembly of Wales, careers *Other:* Open Learning *Activs:* ch's activs, bk sales, temp exhibs, author visits
Enqs: 45180 (1999-2000); 60060 (2000-01)
Staff: Libns: 10 *Non-Prof:* 37

Inc from:	1999-2000	2000-01
local govt:	£1191683	£1138392
fines etc:	£65745	£79516
total:	£1257428	£1217908

Exp on:	1999-2000	2000-01
bks:	£113294	£87874
AVs:	£5701	£9586
salaries:	£763220	£758047
total:	£1257428	£1217908

Wakefield

P191 Wakefield Libraries and Information Services

Lib HQ, Balne Ln, Wakefield, W Yorkshire, WF2 0DQ (01924-302210; *fax:* 01924-302245)
Email: internet-libraries@wakefield.gov.uk
Internet: http://www.wakefield.gov.uk/

Local Auth: City of Wakefield Metropolitan Dist Council *Pop:* 320400 *Larger Dept:* Edu, Libs & Museums *Chief:* Libs & Info Svcs Mgr: Mr Colin MacDonald BA, MBA, DipLib, MCLIP
Main Libs: WAKEFIELD REF & INFO LIB, Balne Ln, Wakefield, W Yorkshire, WF2 0DQ (01924-302230/1; *fax:* 01924-298673; *email:* lib.reference@wakefield.gov.uk) *Branch Libs:* AIREDALE LIB, The Sq, Airedale, Castleford, W Yorkshire, WF10 3JJ (01977-724040); CASTLEFORD LIB, Carlton St, Castleford, W Yorkshire, WF10 1BB (01977-722085; *fax:* 01977-722080); CROFTON LIB, Crofton High School, Crofton, Wakefield, W Yorkshire, WF4 1NF (01924-303960; *email:* croftonlibrary@ hotmail.com); FEATHERSTONE LIB & COMMUNITY CENTRE, Victoria St, off Station Ln, Featherstone, Pontefract, W Yorkshire, WF7 5BB (01977-722745; *fax:* 01977-722749); FLANSHAW LIB, Flanshaw Ln, Dewsbury Rd, Wakefield, W Yorkshire, WF2 9JA (01924-302270; *fax:* 01924-302271; *email:* flanshawlibrary@hotmail. com); HAVERCROFT LIB, Cow Ln, Havercroft, Wakefield, W Yorkshire, WF4 2BE (01226-722152; *email:* havercroftlibrary@hotmail.com); HEMSWORTH LIB, Market St, Hemsworth, Pontefract, W Yorkshire, WF9 4JY (01977-722270; *email:* hemsworthlibrary@hotmail.com); HORBURY LIB, Westfield Rd, Horbury, W Yorkshire, WF4 6HP (01924-303060; *email:* horburylibrary@hotmail.com); KINSLEY LIB, Wakefield Rd, Kingsley, Pontefract, W Yorkshire, WF9 5BP (01977-722300; *email:* kinsleylibrary@ hotmail.com); KNOTTINGLEY LIB, Hill Top, Pontefract Rd, Knottingley, Pontefract, W Yorkshire, WF11 8EE (01977-722450); ☛

(Wakefield Libs & Info Svcs cont)
NORMANTON LIB, Market St, Normanton, W Yorkshire, WF6 2AR (01924-302525; *fax:* 01924-302532; *email:* normantonlibrary@ hotmail.com); OSSETT LIB, Station Rd, Ossett, W Yorkshire, WF5 8AB (01924-303040; *email:* ossettlibrary@hotmail.com); OUTWOOD LIB, Victorian St, Leeds Rd, Outwood, Wakefield, W Yorkshire, WF1 2NE (01924-303115); PONTE-FRACT LIB, Shoemarket, Pontefract, W York-shire, WF8 1BD (01977-727692; *fax:* 01977-727688); SANDAL LIB, Sparable Ln, Sandal, Wakefield, W Yorkshire, WF1 5LJ (01924-303355; *email:* sandallibrary@hotmail.com); SOUTH ELMSALL LIB, Barnsley Rd, South Elmsall, Pontefract, W Yorkshire, WF9 2AA (01977-723220; *email:* southelmsall@hotmail.com); SOUTH KIRKBY LIB, White Apron St, South Kirkby, Pontefract, W Yorkshire, WF9 3LD (01977-723370; *email:* librarysouthkirkby@ hotmail.com); STANLEY LIB & COMMUNITY CENTRE, Lake Lock Ln, Stanley, Wakefield, W Yorkshire, WF3 4HU (01924-303130; *fax:* 01924-870873); UPTON LIB, High St, Upton, Pontefract, W Yorkshire, WF9 1HG (01977-723285; *email:* uptonlibrary@hotmail.com); WAKEFIELD (DRURY LN) LIB, Drury Ln, Wake-field, W Yorkshire, WF1 2TE (01924-305376; *fax:* 01924-305378; *email:* drurylanelibrary@ hotmail.com)
Svc Pts: PT: 8 *Mobile:* 2 *AV:* 16 *Other:* MUSIC & DRAMA DEPT, at Lib HQ (01924-302229; *fax:* 01924-298673; *email:* lib.ylimusicanddrama@ wakefield.gov.uk); LOCAL HIST DEPT, at Lib HQ (01924-302224; *fax:* 01924-302245; *email:* wakehis@hotmail.com); SCHOOLS LIB SVC, at Lib HQ (01924-302238/9; *fax:* 01924-302245; *email:* lib.sls@wakefield.gov.uk)
Collns: George Gissing Colln (local hist); local hist colln (both at HQ, Local Hist Dept); JFR: N-S; HMSO (at HQ Ref & Info Lib); BSI (at HQ Ref & Info Lib) *Co-op Schemes:* YLI, YADLOGIS, JFR *ILLs:* county, natl & internatl *Loans:* bks & talking bks/3 wks; audios & CD-ROMs/2 wks; videos & DVDs/entertainment 2 days, leisure & learning 3 wks *Charges:* CDs/£1, sets £1.50; videos/entertainment £1-£2.50, leisure & learning free; DVDs/£2.50; CD-ROMs/£2 *Income Gen:* res/50p; ILLs/£2; lost ticket/computerised £1-£3, Browne 50p *Fines:* bks & talking bks/ad & oap 8p pd (max £4); audios & CD-ROMs/20p pd (max £10); videos/loan charge per night (max £20); ch borrowing jnr items exempt *Equip:* m-readers, m-printers (30p-40p per pg), fax, copiers (A4/10p, A3/20p), clr copier (A4/£1, A3/£1.50), computers (incl internet & CD-ROM), 8 rooms for hire *Disabled:* minicom, screen magnifiers, speech synthesisers

Stock:	1 Apr 2000	1 Apr 2001
lend:	407129	375405
ref:	16263	20539
AVs:	20671	23393
periodcls:	186	210

Issues:	1999-2000	2000-01
bks:	1550525	1484501
AVs:	99913	110559

Acqs:	1999-2000	2000-01
bks:	32421	62701
AVs:	4383	6414

Acqs: Source: lib suppl & bksellers
Classn: DDC *Cat: Type:* author, classified, subj & title *Medium:* m-form & auto *Auto Sys:* own

Svcs: Extramural: schools, prisons, hosps, old people's homes, housebnd *Info:* business, European, community *Other:* Open Learning, Reader in Residence, BookStart *Activs:* ch's activs, bk sales, temp exhibs, poetry readings, reading groups
Enqs: 284583 (1999-2000); 281853 (2000-01)
Staff: 121.13 in total

Inc from:	1999-2000	2000-01
local govt:	£3387458	£3572847
fines etc:	£283471	£308809
total:	£3670929	£3881656

Exp on:	1999-2000	2000-01
bks:	£350425	£486283
AVs:	£56739	£68807
salaries:	£2271412	£2323035
total:	£3670929	£3881656

Proj: refurbishment of Ackworth Lib

Walsall

P192 Walsall Libraries and Heritage
Leisure & Community Svcs, Civic Centre, Darwall Street, Walsall, W Midlands, WS1 1TZ (01922-653130; *fax:* 01922-721682)
Email: TheLibrarian@walsall.gov.uk
Internet: http://www.walsall.gov.uk/libraries/

Local Auth: Walsall Metropolitan Borough Council *Pop:* 260900 *Larger Dept:* Leisure Svcs *Chief:* Group Co-ordinator (Libs & Heritage): Ms Sue Grainger
Main (Divisional) Libs: CENTRAL LIB, Lich-field St, Walsall, W Midlands, WS1 1TR, incl Lending Lib (01922-653121; *fax:* 01922-722687; *email:* centrallendinglibrary@walsall.gov.uk) & Info Svcs (01922-653110; *fax:* 01922-654013; *email:* reference@walsall.gov.uk); ALDRIDGE LIB, Rookery Ln, Aldridge, Walsall, W Midlands, WS9 8LZ (01922-743601); BLOXWICH LIB, Elmore Row, Bloxwich, Walsall, W Midlands, WS3 2HR (01922-710059); BROWNHILLS LIB, Brickiln St, Brownhills, Walsall, W Midlands, WS8 6AU (01543-452017); DARLASTON LIB, 1 King St, Darlaston, Wednesbury, W Midlands, WS10 8DD (0121-526-4530; *fax:* 0121-526-2298); WILLEN-HALL LIB, Walsall St, Willenhall, W Midlands, WV13 2EX (01902-366513) *Branch Libs:* BEECHDALE LIB, Stephenson Sq, Beechdale Est, Walsall, W Midlands, WS2 7DX (01922-721431); BENTLEY LIB, Queen Elizabeth Ave, Bentley, Walsall, W Midlands, WS2 0HP (01922-721392); COAL-POOL LIB, Coalpool Ln, Walsall, W Midlands, WS3 1RF (01922-721325); FOREST GATE LIB, New Invention, Willenhall, W Midlands, WV12 5LF (01922-710208); PELSALL LIB, High St, Pelsall, Walsall, W Midlands, WS3 7LX (01922-682212); PHEASEY LIB, Collingwood Dr, Pheasey, Birmingham, B43 7NE (0121-366-6503); PLECK LIB, Darlaston Rd, Pleck, Walsall, W Mid-lands, WS2 9RE (01922-721307); RUSHALL LIB, Pelsall Ln, Walsall, W Midlands, WS4 1NL (01922-721310); SHELFIELD LIB, Birch Ln, Shelfield, Walsall, W Midlands, WS4 1AS (01922-682760); SOUTH WALSALL LIB, West Bromwich Rd, Walsall, W Midlands, WS5 4NW (01922-721347); STREETLY LIB, Blackwood Rd, Streetly, Sutton Coldfield, Birmingham, B74 3PL (0121-353-4230); WALSALL WOOD LIB, Lichfield Rd, Walsall Wood, Walsall, W Midlands, WS9 9NT (*tel & fax:* 01543-452517)
Collns: JFR (Mop-Mor) *Co-op Schemes:* JFR, SEALS, TLP-WM, CILLA *ILLs:* county, natl & internatl *Loans:* bks & audios/3 wks; videos/1 day, 1 wk or 3 wks *Charges:* talking bks/50p-60p, conc 25p-30p; cassettes/50p, conc 25p; CDs/70p, conc 35p; videos/90p-£2.50; registered blind exempt from audio charges, under-13s also exempt from talking bk charges *Income Gen:* res/80p, over-60s 40p, under-18s & mobile lib users exempt; lost ticket/£1, conc 50p

Fines: bks/ad 10p pd (max £5.50), under-18s & 60+ exempt; audios/10p pd (max £5.50); videos/loan charge *Equip:* m-readers, fax, copiers (A4/10p, A3/20p), clr copiers (A4/£1, A3/£1.50), computers (incl wd-proc, internet & CD-ROM) *Disabled:* CCTV, minicom, induction loops, text enlarger, speech synthesiser

Stock:	1 Apr 2001
bks:	552183
AVs:	50420

Issues:	2000-01
bks:	1825062
AVs:	123307

Acqs:	2000-01
bks:	57912
AVs:	5600

Acqs: Source: lib suppl *Co-op:* CILLA
Classn: DDC *Cat: Type:* author, classified & title *Medium:* auto *Auto Sys:* DS *Svcs: Extramural:* old people's homes, housebnd *Info:* business, community, European, council *Other:* Open Learning, homework centres *Activs:* ch's activs, bk sales, temp exhibs, poetry readings, author visits, ad storytelling, homework clubs, 50+ clubs, reading groups, local hist socs, clubs & socs fair
Enqs: 305864 (2000-01)
Staff: Libns: 31.5 *Other Prof:* 2 *Non-Prof:* 104.3

Inc from:	1999-2000	2000-01
local govt:	£3707000	£3561000
fines etc:	£114000	£108000
total:	£4153000	£3853000

Exp on:	1999-2000	2000-01
bks:	£399000	£423000
AVs:	£91000	£97000
salaries:	£2264000	£2168000
total:	£4153000	£3853000

Warrington

P193 Warrington Library and Information Services
Warrington Central Lib, Museum Street, Warrington, Cheshire, WA1 1JB (01925-442890; *fax:* 01925-411395)
Email: library@warrington.gov.uk
Internet: http://www.warrington.gov.uk/

Local Auth: Warrington Borough Council *Pop:* 191000 *Larger Dept:* Edu & Lifelong Learning *Dept Chief: Dir:* Mr Malcolm Roxburgh *Chief:* The Lib, Museum & Archvs Mgr: Mr Martin Gaw
Main Libs: WARRINGTON CENTRAL LIB, addr as above *Branch Libs:* BIRCHWOOD LIB, Brock Rd, Birchwood, Warrington, Cheshire, WA3 7PT (*tel & fax:* 01925-827491); CULCHETH LIB, Warrington Rd, Culcheth, Warrington, Cheshire, WA3 5SL (*tel & fax:* 01925-763293); LYMM LIB, Davies Way, off Brookfield Rd, Lymm, Cheshire, WA13 0QW (*tel & fax:* 01925-754367); ORFORD LIB, Poplars Ave, Orford, Warrington, Cheshire, WA2 9LW (*tel & fax:* 01925-812821); PADGATE LIB, Insall Rd, Padgate, Warrington, Cheshire, WA2 0HD (*tel & fax:* 01925-818096); PENKETH LIB, Honiton Way, Penketh, Warrington, Cheshire, WA5 2EY (01925-723730; *fax:* 01925-791264); STOCKTON HEATH LIB, Alexandra Pk, Stockton Heath, Warrington, Cheshire, WA4 2AN (*tel & fax:* 01925-261148); WESTBROOK LIB, Westbrook Centre, Westbrook Cres, Warrington, Cheshire, WA5 8UG (01925-416561; *fax:* 01925-230462); WOOLSTON LIB, Holes Ln, Woolston, Warrington, Cheshire, WA1 3UJ (*tel & fax:* 01925-816146)
Svc Pts: PT: 4 *Mobile:* 1 (at Stockton Heath Lib)
Collns: antiquarian bk colln; Warrington Academy Colln; MS colln; war-time posters colln; photo colln; Broadsides Colln of Ephemera *Co-op Schemes:* Libs North West, LADSIRLAC, ASCEL, North West SCL, PLUS User Group,

Time to Read, Proj Warmer *Loans:* bks & talking bks/3 wks; CDs, videos, DVDs & software/1 wk; Open Learning & lang courses/3 wks *Charges:* CDs & software/£1.08; videos & DVDs/£2.16 *Income Gen:* res/80p, conc 40p, under-17s exempt *Fines:* bks, talking bks & lang packs/ad 12p pd (max £4.32), conc 6p pd (max £1.14), CDs, videos, DVDs & software/loan charge; under-6s exempt *Equip:* copiers, 13 fax, 96 computers (all with wd-proc & internet) *Disabled:* Aladdin enlarger, video caption readers, minicom, large print newspapers, ch's bks in braille & Moon (all at Warrington Lib)

Stock:	1 Apr 2000	1 Apr 2001
ad lend:	159027	158386
ad ref:	50228	49880
ch:	86421	89899
audios:	5887	7748
videos:	3113	3442
CD-ROMs:	188	333
periodcls:	100	105

Issues:	1999-2000	2000-01
ad lend:	1052168	949426
ch:	453664	415009
audios:	33323	61234
videos:	16666	17296
CD-ROMs:	1378	5136

Acqs:	1999-2000	2000-01
bks:	48361	37609
AVs:	2060	4635

Acqs: Co-op: consortium with Cheshire County Libs (see **P27**) & Halton Borough Libs (see **P59**) *Classn:* DDC *Cat: Type:* author, classified, subj & title *Medium:* auto *Auto Sys:* Dynix *Svcs: Extramural:* schools, prisons, old people's homes, housebnd, sheltered housing *Info:* community, business, legal, careers, edu, EU, tourist, local hist *Other:* Open Learning, homework centres, bks available in Urdu, Gujarati, Bengali & Polish *Activs:* ch's activs, bk sales, temp exhibs, reading groups *Enqs:* 179348 (1999-2000); 156728 (2000-01) *Staff: Libns:* 18.6 *Non-Prof:* 41.4

Inc from:	1999-2000	2000-01
local govt:	£2483796	£2596917
fines etc:	£251820	£253726
total:	£2735616	£2850643

Exp on:	1999-2000	2000-01
bks:	£342408	£352512
salaries:	£1085700	£1204617
total:	£2735616	£2850643

Warwickshire

P194 Warwickshire Library and Information Service

Dept of Libs, Heritage & Trading Standards, Barrack Street, Warwick, CV34 4TH (01926-412550; *fax:* 01926-412471)
Email: librariesandheritage@warwickshire.gov.uk
Internet: http://www.warwickshire.gov.uk/

Local Auth: Warwickshire County Council *Pop:* 506200 *Cttee:* Learning & Overview Scrutiny Cttee *Larger Dept:* Directorate of Libs, Heritage & Trading Standards *Dept Chief:* Dir of Libs, Heritage & Trading Standards: Mr Noel Hunter *Chief:* Head of Libs & Info Svcs: Ms Kushal Birla
Main Libs: Central Area: LEAMINGTON LIB, Royal Pump Rooms, The Parade, Leamington Spa, Warwickshire, CV32 4AA (01926-742721/2; *fax:* 01926-742749; *email:* leamingtonlibrary@warwickshire.gov.uk); *East Area:* RUGBY LIB, Little Elborow St, Rugby, Warwickshire, CV21 3BZ (01788-533250; *fax:* 01788-533252; *email:* rugbylibrary@warwickshire.gov.uk); *North Area:* ATHERSTONE LIB, Long St, Atherstone, Warwickshire, CV9 1AX (01827-712395/034; *fax:*

01827-720285; *email:* atherstonelibrary@warwickshire.gov.uk); *Nuneaton & Bedworth Area:* NUNEATON LIB, Church St, Nuneaton, Warwickshire, CV11 4DR (024-7638-4027; *fax:* 024-7635-0125; *email:* nuneatonlibrary@warwickshire.gov.uk); *South Area:* STRATFORD LIB, 12 Henley St, Stratford on Avon, Warwickshire, CV37 6PZ (01789-292209/6904; *fax:* 01789-268554; *email:* stratfordlibrary@warwickshire.gov.uk) *Branch Libs:* ALCESTER LIB, Priory Rd, Alcester, Warwickshire, B49 5DZ (01789-762430; *fax:* 01789-766792); BEDWORTH LIB, 18 High St, Bedworth, Nuneaton, Warwickshire, CV12 8NF (024-7631-2267; *fax:* 024-7675-8006; *email:* bedworthlibrary@warwickshire.gov.uk); BIDFORD LIB & INFO CENTRE, Bramley Way, Bidford on Avon, Warwickshire, B50 4QG (*tel & fax:* 01789-773239); BULKINGTON LIB, School Rd, Bulkington, Nuneaton, Warwickshire, CV12 9JB (024-7631-4189; *fax:* 024-7631-1257); COLESHILL LIB, 141 High St, Coleshill, Birmingham, B46 3AY (01675-463307; *fax:* 01675-463986); DUNCHURCH LIB, The Green, Dunchurch, Rugby, Warwickshire, CV22 6PA (*tel & fax:* 01788-811355); KENILWORTH LIB, Smalley Pl, Kenilworth, Warwickshire, CV8 1QG (01926-748900/2; *fax:* 01926-748901); KINGSBURY LIB, Bromage Ave, Kingsbury, Tamworth, Staffordshire, B78 2HN (*tel & fax:* 01827-872333); LILLINGTON LIB, Valley Rd, Lillington, Leamington Spa, Warwickshire, CV32 7SJ (01926-422875; *fax:* 01926-338074); POLESWORTH LIB, Bridge St, Polesworth, Tamworth, Staffordshire, B78 1DT (01827-892587; *fax:* 01827-896301); SHIPSTON LIB, Church St, Shipston-on-Stour, Warwickshire, CV36 4AP (01608-661255; *fax:* 01608-664309); SOUTHAM LIB, High St, Southam, Leamington Spa, Warwickshire, CV47 0HB (01926-812523; *fax:* 01926-811668); WARWICK LIB, Barrack St, Warwick, CV34 4TH (01926-412189/488; *fax:* 01926-412784; *email:* warwicklibrary@warwickshire.gov.uk); WATER ORTON LIB, Mickle Meadow, Coleshill Rd, Water Orton, Birmingham, B46 1SN (0121-747-7460; *fax:* 0121-748-6735); WELLESBOURNE LIB, Kineton Rd, Wellesbourne, Warwick, CV35 9NF (*tel & fax:* 01789-840528); WHITNASH LIB, Franklin Rd, Whitnash, Leamington Spa, Warwickshire, CV31 2JH (*tel & fax:* 01926-421464)
Svc Pts: PT: 10 *Mobile:* 5 *AV:* 24 *Computers:* 32 *Internet:* 32 *Other:* 1 trailer lib
Collns: George Eliot Colln; Michael Drayton Colln (both at Nuneaton Lib); Warwickshire Colln (at Warwick Lib) *Co-op Schemes:* WMRLS, CADIG *ILLs:* county, natl & internatl *Loans:* bks & spkn wd/4 wks; CDs/1 wk; videos/4 nights-1 wk *Charges:* cassettes/60p-80p; CDs/90p-£1.35; videos/£1.50-£2.75 *Income Gen:* res/90p, ch 50p, mobile lib users 40p; lost ticket/£1 *Fines:* bks/ad 12p pd, oap & ch 6p pd; audios & videos/loan charge; housebnd, very young ch, foster ch & job seekers exempt *Equip:* 13 m-readers, 8 m-printers (30p), 33 fax (£1 1st pg, 75p addl, higher charges overseas), 33 copiers (A4/10p, A3/20p), computers (incl wd-procs, internet & CD-ROM, printouts 30p), 3 rooms for hire (various), *Disabled:* magnifiers, CCTV, minicom, tape players, induction loops, rising steps on mobiles *Online:* Dialog, Viscount (fees vary)

Stock:	1 Apr 2000	1 Apr 2001
bks:	1018340	971550

Issues:	1999-2000	2000-01
ad lend:	3189540	3173974
ch:	879384	880726
audios:	193338	206415
videos:	67864	100780

Acqs:	1999-2000	2000-01
bks:	99548	78030

Acqs: Source: lib suppl *Co-op:* SEALS (European Lang Fiction, part of WMRLS), JFR (Ked-Kim; Lah-Laq, Los-Mac B) *Offcr-in-Charge:* Principal Libn (Stock & Reader Development): Ms Alison MacKellar (alisonmackellar@warwickshire.gov.uk)

Classn: DDC *Cat: Type:* author, classified, dictionary, subj & title *Medium:* auto *Auto Sys:* Geac *Svcs: Extramural:* schools, old people's homes, housebnd *Info:* business, community, European, tourist, Parent Info Pts, Activ-Age Info Pts *Other:* Open Learning, Skills for Life, Council Help Pts, multicultural svcs *Activs:* ch's activs, bk sales, temp exhibs, arts events, coffee mornings
Enqs: 417864 (1999-2000); 462973 (2000-01) *Staff: Libns:* 54.75 *Non-Prof:* 134.55

Inc from:	1999-2000	2000-01
local govt:	£6391828	£6840571
fines etc:	£601550	£701769
total:	£6993378	£7542340

Exp on:	1999-2000	2000-01
bks:	£938765	£913539
AVs:	£109512	£105700
salaries:	£3654336	£3956934
total:	£6993378	£7542340

West Berkshire

P195 West Berkshire Libraries and Information

Council Offices, Market Street, Newbury, Berkshire, RG14 5LD (01635-519813)
Email: library@westberks.gov.uk
Internet: http://www.westberks.gov.uk/

Local Auth: West Berkshire Council *Pop:* 146600 *Chief:* Libs & Info Mgr: Mr Ken Richardson (krichardson@westberks.gov.uk) *Other Snr Staff:* Central Svcs Mgr: Ms Christine Owen (cowen@westberks.gov.uk); Info & Communication Mgr: Ms Jan Jones (jjones@westberks.gov.uk); Community Svcs Mgr: Mr Mike Brook (mbrook@westberks.gov.uk) *Main Libs:* NEWBURY CENTRAL LIB, The Wharf, Newbury, Berkshire, RG14 5AU (01635-519190; *fax:* 01635-519906; *email:* newburylibrary@westberks.gov.uk) *Branch Libs:* HUNGERFORD LIB, Church St, Hungerford, Berkshire, RG17 0JG (*tel & fax:* 01488-682660; *email:* hungerfordlibrary@westberks.gov.uk); MORTIMER LIB, 27 Victoria Rd, Mortimer, Reading, Berkshire, RG7 3SH (*tel & fax:* 0118-933-2882; *email:* mortimerlibrary@westberks.gov.uk); PANGBOURNE LIB, Reading Rd, Pangbourne, Reading, Berkshire, RG8 7LY (*tel & fax:* 0118-984-4117; *email:* pangbournelibrary@westberks.gov.uk); THATCHAM LIB, Bath Rd, Thatcham, Berkshire, RG18 3AG (01635-866049; *fax:* 01635-862583; *email:* thatchamlibrary@westberks.gov.uk); THEALE LIB, Church St, Theale, Reading, Berkshire, RG7 5BZ (*tel & fax:* 0118-930-3207; *email:* thealelibrary@westberks.gov.uk)
Svc Pts: PT: 2 *Mobile:* 2 *AV:* 8 *Computers:* 8 *Internet:* 8
Co-op Schemes: ILL *ILLs:* county & natl *Loans:* bks, talking bks & CD-ROMs/3 wks; audios, videos, DVDs & Playstation games/1 wk *Charges:* talking bks/75p-£1; CDs/£1.30; videos/£1.80-£2.80; DVDs/£2.30-£3.80; CD-ROMs/£1.70; Playstation games/£2.80-£3.90 *Income Gen:* res/in stock free, out of stock £1; lost ticket/£1.50 *Fines:* bks/ad 15p pd (£6 max), ch 7p pd (£2.80 max); audios/as ad bks; videos, DVDs, CD-ROMs & Playstation games/70p pd (£14 max) *Equip:* copiers, clr copier, fax, computers (incl internet)

Stock:	1 Apr 2000	1 Apr 2001
ad lend:	88055	106797
ad ref:	8970	8513
ch:	42101	50216
audios:	11212	14657
videos:	3609	5975
CD-ROMs:	280	877
periodcls:	163	163

Public Libraries

West Berkshire

▼

Wigan

(W Berkshire Libs & Info cont)

Issues:	1999-2000	2000-01
ad lend:	643923	640764
ch:	249546	291265
audios:	56714	63827
videos:	41522	57611
CD-ROMs:	-	1013

Acqs:	1999-2000	2000-01
bks:	22283	15985
AVs:	4515	2025

Acqs: Source: lib suppl
Classn: DDC *Cat: Type:* author, classified, subj
& title *Medium:* auto *Auto Sys:* Dynix *Svcs:*
Extramural: old people's homes, housebnd *Info:*
community, business, European *Other:*
Homework Club *Activs:* ch's activs, bk sales,
poetry readings, reading groups
Enqs: 67548 (1999-2000); 116636 (2000-01)
Staff: 74 in total

Inc from:	1999-2000	2000-01
local govt:	£1890844	£1769902
fines etc:	£115822	£165451
total:	£2006666	£1935353

Exp on:	1999-2000	2000-01
bks:	£245633	£222722
AVs:	£52095	£66863
salaries:	£942173	£1043010
total:	£2006666	£1935353

West Dunbartonshire

P196 West Dunbartonshire Libraries

Lib HQ, Levenford House, Helenslee Rd,
Dumbarton, Dunbartonshire, G82 4AH (01389-
608041/6; *fax:* 01389-608044)
Internet: http://www.west-dunbarton.gov.uk/
  library/

Local Auth: West Dunbartonshire Council *Pop:*
94600 *Cttee:* Cultural Svcs Cttee *Larger Dept:*
Edu & Cultural Svcs *Dept Chief: Dir:* Mr Ian
McMurdo *Chief:* Mgr, Lifelong Learning: Ms
Susan Carragher BA(Hons), MCLIP (susan.
carragher@west-dunbarton.gov.uk) *Other Snr*
Staff: Snr Offcr (Libs): Ms Fiona MacDonald
MA(Hons), DipLib, MCLIP (fiona.macdonald@
west-dunbarton.gov.uk); Snr Offcr (Libs): Mr Ian
Baillie (ian.baillie@west-dunbarton.gov.uk);
Network Co-ordinator: Mr Robert Ruthven
(robert.ruthven@west-dunbarton.gov.uk)
Main Libs: CLYDEBANK LIB, Dumbarton Rd,
Clydebank, Dunbartonshire, G81 1XH (0141-952-
1416/8765; *fax:* 0141-9551-8275); DUMBARTON
LIB, Strathleven Pl, Dumbarton, Dunbartonshire,
G82 1BD (01389-763129; *fax:* 01389-607302)
Branch Libs: ALEXANDRIA LIB, Gilmour St,
Alexandria, Dunbartonshire, G83 0DA (01389-
753425; *fax:* 01389-710550); BALLOCH LIB,
Carrochan Rd, Balloch, Dunbartonshire, G83 0BW
(01389-757026; *fax:* 01389-607911); DALMUIR
LIB, 3 Lennox Pl, Clydebank, Dunbartonshire,
G81 4HR (0141-952-3532; *fax:* 0141-952-6497);
DUNTOCHER LIB, Glenhead Leisure Centre,
Duntiglennan Rd, Duntocher, Clydebank,
Dunbartonshire, G81 6HF (01389-875728);
FAIFLEY LIB, Skypoint, Lennox Dr, Faifley,
Dunbartonshire, G81 5JY (tel & fax: 01389-
873490); LADYTON LIB, Ladyton Est, Bonhill,
Dunbartonshire, G83 9DZ (01389-753648);

PARKHALL LIB, Hawthorn St, Clydebank,
Dunbartonshire, G81 3EF (0141-952-3465)
Svc Pts: PT: 2 *Mobile:* 1 *AV:* 11 *Computers:* 6
Internet: 6
Collns: family hist & genealogy (at Dumbarton
Lib); local studies (at Clydebank & Dumbarton
Libs, with smaller collns at other branches) *ILLs:*
county, natl & internatl *Loans:* bks, audios &
CD-ROMs/4 wks; videos/2 days or 1 wk
Charges: audios, CD-ROMs & lang packs/free;
videos/feature films 50p or £1.25 per 2 day
period, ch's free *Income Gen:* req & res/40p;
lost ticket/adults £1, ch free *Fines:* videos/loan
charge; all other items/40p per reminder posted,
otherwise none *Equip:* 10 m-readers, 4 m-
printers, 7 fax (50p per pg), 11 copiers (A4/5p), 2
clr copiers (A4/60p), 24 computers (all with CD-
ROM, 20 with wd-proc, 19 with internet, access
free) *Disabled:* Qtronix reading aid *Offcr-in-*
Charge: Snr Offcr (Libs), as above

Stock:	1 Apr 2000	1 Apr 2001
ad lend:	215107	217387
ad ref:	14282	20045
ch:	83519	83314
audios:	18453	19630
videos:	2447	2651
CD-ROMs:	411	456
periodcls:	67	73
archvs:	55 linear m	55 linear m

Issues:	1999-2000	2000-01
ad lend:	483594	425567
ch:	111761	128086
audios:	43457	43695
videos:	33310	41821
CD-ROMs:	435	454

Acqs:	1999-2000	2000-01
bks:	17848	16309
AVs:	3646	4341

Acqs: Source: lib suppl *Offcr-in-Charge:* Biblio-
graphic Svcs Libn: Ms Linda Powers (linda.
powers@west-dunbarton.gov.uk)
Classn: DDC *Cat: Type:* author, classified &
title *Medium:* cards & auto *Auto Sys:* Dynix
Svcs: Extramural: old people's homes, housebnd,
play groups *Info:* community, Parliamentary Link
Libs for Scottish & European Parliaments (at
Clydebank & Dumbarton) *Other:* Adult Guidance
Unit (careers & courses), Genealogy Unit, Open
Learning *Activs:* ch's activs, bk sales, films,
temp exhibs, reading groups, talks, author visits
Offcr-in-Charge: Snr Offcr (Libs), as above
Enqs: 54444 (2000-01)
Staff: Libns: 13 *Other Prof:* 0.3 *Non-Prof:* 59

West Lothian

P197 West Lothian Library Services

Lib HQ, Connolly House, Hopefield Rd,
Blackburn, W Lothian, EH47 7HZ (01506-776336;
fax: 01506-776345)
Email: info@libhq.demon.co.uk
Internet: http://www.westlothian.gov.uk/libraries/

Local Auth: West Lothian Council *Pop:* 156700
Cttee: Ch & Lifelong Learning Cttee *Larger*
Dept: Edu *Dept Chief: Dir of Edu:* Mr Roger
Stewart MA *Chief:* Lib Svcs Mgr: Mr W.S.
Walker BA, MCLIP (bill.walker@westlothian.
gov.uk) *Other Snr Staff:* Area Mgrs: Ms Irene
Brough (irene.brough@westlothian.gov.uk), Ms
Anne Hunt (anne.hunt@westlothian.gov.uk) & Ms
Bernadette Main (bernadette.main@westlothian.
gov.uk)
Branch Libs: ALMONDBANK LIB, The Mall,
Craigshill, Livingston, W Lothian, EH54 5EJ
(01506-775000; *email:* almondbank.library@
westlothian.org.uk); ARMADALE LIB, West Main
St, Armadale, Bathgate, W Lothian, EH48 3JB
(01501-678400; *email:* armadale.library@
westlothian.org.uk); BATHGATE LIB, Hopetoun St,
Bathgate, W Lothian, EH48 4PD (01506-776400;
email: bathgate.library@westlothian.org.uk);

BLACKBURN LIB, Ash Grove, Blackburn, Bath-
gate, W Lothian, EH47 7LJ (01506-776500; *email:*
blackburn.library@westlothian.org.uk); BROX-
BURN LIB, West Main St, Broxburn, W Lothian,
EH52 5RH (01506-775600; *email:* broxburn.
library@westlothian.org.uk); CARMONDEAN LIB,
Carmondean Centre, Deans, Livingston,
W Lothian, EH54 8PT (01506-777602; *email:*
carmondean.library@westlothian.org.uk); EAST
CALDER LIB, 200 Main St, East Calder,
W Lothian, EH53 0EJ (01506-883633; *email:*
eastcalder.library@westlothian.org.uk); FAULD-
HOUSE LIB, Lanrigg Rd, Fauldhouse, Bathgate,
W Lothian, EH47 9JA (01051-770358; *email:*
fauldhouse.library@westlothian.org.uk);
LANTHORN LIB, Kenilworth Rise, Dedridge,
Livingstone, W Lothian, EH54 6JL (01506-777700;
email: lanthorn.library@westlothian.org.uk);
LINLITHGOW LIB, The Vennel, High St, Linlith-
gow, W Lothian, EH49 (01506-775490; *email:*
linlithgow.library@westlothian.org.uk); WEST
CALDER LIB, Main St, West Calder, W Lothian,
EH55 8BG (01506-871371; *email:* westcalder.
library@westlothian.org.uk); WHITBURN LIB,
Union St, Whitburn, Bathgate, W Lothian, EH47
0AR (01501-678050; *email:* whitburn.library@
westlothian.org.uk)
Svc Pts: PT: 2 *Mobile:* 2 *Other:* school lib svc
Collns: local studies colln *Loans:* bks & audios/
3 wks; videos/features 1 day, factual 3 wks
Charges: audios/£8 pa or 80p per loan; videos/
features £1 (50p on Wed) *Income Gen:* req/
35p, ch & oap free; lost ticket/£1 *Fines:* bks &
audios/ad 6p pd; videos/£1 pd; ch, oap & mobile
lib users exempt *Equip:* m-reader, m-printer
(15p), 2 copiers (A4/10p), computers (incl internet,
access free), room hire

Stock:	1 Apr 2000	1 Apr 2001
lend:	222332	190323
ref:	1693	1606
audios:	12198	8716
videos:	2308	1929
CD-ROMs:	1599	1188
periodcls:	142	-

Issues:	1999-2000	2000-01
bks:	1285724	1179904
audios: *	11556	10747
videos:	76088	60668
CD-ROMs:	2517	7398

* music only; spkn wd incl in bks

Acqs:	1999-2000	2000-01
bks:	38041	41860
AVs:	4636	2994

Classn: DDC *Cat: Auto Sys:* Dynix *Svcs:*
Extramural: schools, hosps, old people's homes,
housebnd, day centres, play groups *Info:*
community, EU *Activs:* ch's activs, bk sales,
temp exhibs
Enqs: 85000 (1999-2000); 72000 (2000-01)
Staff: Libns: 18 *Non-Prof:* 47

Inc from:	2000-01
local govt:	£2106201
fines etc:	£149805
total:	£2256006

Exp on:	2000-01
bks:	£374513
AVs:	£59546
salaries:	£1167885
total:	£2256006

West Sussex

P198 West Sussex Libraries and Information

Lib Admin Centre, Tower Street, Chichester, W
Sussex, PO19 1QJ (01243-756700; *fax:* 01243-
756014)
Email: county.libraries@westsussex.gov.uk
Internet: http://www.westsussex.gov.uk/
  librariesandarchives/libraries/

Local Auth: West Sussex County Council *Pop:* 751800 *Cttee:* Strategic, Environmental & Community Svcs Select Cttee *Chief:* County Libn: Mr Robert A. Kirk BA, MCLIP *Dep:* Dep County Libn: Mrs Susan Houghton
Main Libs: CHICHESTER LIB, Tower St, Chichester, W Sussex, PO19 1QJ (01243-777351; *fax:* 01243-531610; *email:* chichester.library@ westsussex.gov.uk); CRAWLEY LIB, County Bldgs, Northgate Ave, Crawley, W Sussex, RH10 1XG, (01293-895130; *fax:* 01293-895141; *email:* crawley.library@westsussex.gov.uk); EAST GRINSTEAD LIB, West St, East Grinstead, W Sussex, RH19 4SR (01342-410050; *fax:* 01342-410262; *email:* east.grinstead.library@ westsussex.gov.uk); HAYWARDS HEATH LIB, 34 Boltro Rd, Haywards Heath, W Sussex, RH16 1BN (01444-454607; *fax:* 01444-414294; *email:* haywards.heath.library@westsussex.gov.uk); HORSHAM LIB, Lower Tanbridge Way, Horsham, W Sussex, RH12 1PJ (01403-253939; *fax:* 01403-211972; *email:* horsham.library@westsussex. gov.uk); WORTHING LIB, Richmond Rd, Worthing, W Sussex, BN11 1HD (01903-206961; *fax:* 01903-821902; *email:* worthing.library@ westsussex.gov.uk) *Branch Libs:* ANGMERING LIB, Arundel Rd, Angmering, W Sussex, BN16 4JS (01903-772682; *fax:* 01903-859772); ARUNDEL LIB, Surrey St, Arundel, W Sussex, BN18 9DT (01903-883188; *fax:* 01903-884622); BILLINGSHURST LIB, Mill Ln, Billingshurst, W Sussex, RH14 9JZ (01403-783145; *fax:* 01403-786817); BOGNOR REGIS LIB, London Rd, Bognor Regis, W Sussex, PO21 1DE (01243-864638; *fax:* 01243-841698); BROADFIELD LIB, 46 Broadfield Barton, Broadfield, Crawley, W Sussex, RH11 9DA (01293-543298; *fax:* 01293-612411); BROADWATER LIB, Dominion Rd, Broadwater, W Sussex, BN14 8JL (*tel & fax:* 01903-233244); BURGESS HILL LIB, The Martlets, Burgess Hill, W Sussex, RH15 9NN (01444-235549; *fax:* 01444-230173); DURRING-TON LIB, Salvington Rd, Durrington, W Sussex, BN13 2JD (01903-260439; *fax:* 01903-693677); EAST PRESTON LIB, The Street, East Preston, W Sussex, BN16 1JJ (01903-786118; *fax:* 01903-850344); FERRING LIB, Ferring St, Ferring, W Sussex, BN12 5HL (01903-241811; *fax:* 01903-700953); FINDON VALLEY LIB, Lime Tree Ave, Findon Valley, W Sussex, BN14 0HD (01903-872213; *fax:* 01903-877804); GORING LIB, Mulberry Ln, Goring-by-Sea, W Sussex, BN12 4NR (01903-244300; *fax:* 01903-700430); HASSOCKS LIB, Stafford House, Keymer Rd, Hassocks, W Sussex, BN6 8QJ (01273-842779; *fax:* 01273-843112); HENFIELD LIB, off High St, Henfield, W Sussex, BN5 9HN (01273-493587; *fax:* 01273-494238); HURSTPIERPOINT LIB, Trinity Rd, Hurstpierpoint, W Sussex, BN6 9UY (01273-832609; *fax:* 01273-832194); LANCING LIB, Penstone Pk, Lancing, W Sussex, BN15 9DL (01903-753592; *fax:* 01903-763786); LITTLE-HAMPTON LIB, Maltravers Rd, Littlehampton, W Sussex, BN17 5NA (01903-716450; *fax:* 01903-733175); MIDHURST LIB, Knockhundred Row, Midhurst, W Sussex, GU29 9DQ (01730-813564; *fax:* 01730-815354); PETWORTH LIB, High St, Petworth, W Sussex, GU28 0AU (01798-342274; *fax:* 01798-342936); PULBOROUGH LIB, Brooks Way, off Lower St, Pulborough, W Sussex, RH20 2BP (01798-872891; *fax:* 01798-875419); RUSTINGTON LIB, Claigmar Rd, Rustington, W Sussex, BN16 2NL (01903-785857; *fax:* 01903-859877); SELSEY LIB, School Ln, Selsey, W Sussex, PO20 9EH (01243-602096; *fax:* 01243-607093); SHOREHAM LIB, St Mary's Rd, Shoreham, W Sussex, BN43 5ZA (01273-454438; *fax:* 01273-441231); SOUTHBOURNE LIB, First Ave, Southbourne, W Sussex, PO10 8HN (01243-375924; *fax:* 01243-378610); SOUTHWICK LIB, Southdown Rd, Southwick, W Sussex, BN42 4FT (01273-592150; *fax:* 01273-592983); STEYNING LIB, Church St, Steyning, W Sussex, BN44 3YB (01903-812751; *fax:* 01903-816827); STORRING-TON LIB, Ryecroft Ln, Storrington, W Sussex,

RH20 4NZ (01903-743075; *fax:* 01903-740175); WILLOWHALE LIB, Pryors Ln, Bognor Regis, W Sussex, PO21 4JF (01243-265712; *fax:* 01243-267022); WITTERINGS LIB, Oakfield Ave, Witterings, W Sussex, PO20 8BT (01243-673484; *fax:* 01243-671917)
Svc Pts: Mobile: 3 *Other:* HOME DELIVERY SVC (over 350 delivery pts)
Collns: BSI; local studies collns at all branches *Loans:* bks & audios/3 wks; videos/1 wk *Charges:* cassettes/30p-£1.20; CDs/80p; videos/ feature films £2.20, others £1.50; DVDs/£2.50; CD-ROMs/£1 *Income Gen:* res/60p; lost ticket/ £1.60; lost or damaged items/£1 + replacement cost *Fines:* bks/ad 13p pd, ch 1p pd; audios & CD-ROMs/13p pd; videos/feature films 50p pd, others 30p pd; spkn wd free for partially sighted *Equip:* m-readers, m-printers (25p) fax (£1.20 + 60p per pg in UK, + 80p per pg in EU), copiers (5p-£1.50), computers (incl CD-ROM & internet, access free) *Online:* Dialog, Datastar, FT Profile, ESA/IRS, Kompass Online (cost of search + £5 handling charge)

Stock:	1 Apr 2000	1 Apr 2001
ad lend:	734280	673789
ad ref:	143419	139331
ch:	239952	237095
audios:	76505	64049
videos:	11907	13402
CD-ROMs:	1105	980
periodcls:	1000	1025

Issues:	1999-2000	2000-01
ad lend:	5680722	5375791
ch:	1730149	1649064
audios:	460756	454709
videos:	132918	167157
CD-ROMs:	5815	6429

Acqs:	1999-2000	2000-01
bks:	140708	130303
AVs:	18256	17044

Cat: Auto Sys: DS *Svcs: Extramural:* housebnd *Info:* business (principally at Crawley, Chichester, Worthing & Horsham Libs), community, tourist, EU *Other:* Lifelong Learning *Activs:* ch's activs, temp exhibs, talks, demos, concerts
Enqs: 1050623 (1999-2000); 1000562 (2000-01)
Staff: Libns: 68 *Non-Prof:* 209

Inc from:		2000-01
fines etc:		£1023016

Exp on:		2000-01
stock & supplies:		£1854054
salaries:		£4262451
total:		£9042305

Western Isles

P199 Western Isles Libraries (Leabharlainn nan Eilean Siar)

Stornoway Lib, 19 Cromwell Street, Stornoway, Isle of Lewis, HS1 2DA (01851-708631; *fax:* 01851-708677)
Email: stornoway_library@cne-siar.gov.uk
Internet: http://www.cne-siar.gov.uk/

Local Auth: Comhairle nan Eilean Siar (Western Isles Council) *Pop:* 27180 *Cttee:* Arts & Leisure Cttee *Larger Dept:* Sustainable Communities *Dept Chief:* Dir: Mr Murdo Gold *Chief:* Chief Libn: Mr Robert M. Eaves BA, DipEd, MCLIP (bobeaves@cne-siar.gov.uk) *Dep:* Snr Libn (Adult Svcs): Mr David J. Fowler MCLIP (dfowler@cne-siar.gov.uk) *Other Snr Staff:* Snr Libn (Youth Svcs): Ms Mary Ferguson MA, MCLIP (mary-ferguson@cne-siar.gov.uk)
Main Libs: STORNOWAY LIB, addr as above *Branch Libs:* CASTLEBAY COMMUNITY LIB, Castlebay Community School, Castlebay, Isle of Barra, HS9 5XD (01871-810471; *fax:* 01871-810650; *email:* castlebaylibrary@eilanansiar. biblio.net); LIONACLEIT COMMUNITY LIB, Sgoil Lionacleit, Liniclate, Isle of Benbecula, HS7 5PJ

(01870-602211; *fax:* 01870-602817; *email:* fbramwell1a@eileanansiar.biblio.net); TARBERT COMMUNITY LIB, Sir E. Scott School, Tarbert, Isle of Harris, HS3 3BG (01859-502000; *email:* fmmorrison1b@eileanansiar.biblio.net)
Svc Pts: PT: 3 *Mobile:* 3 *AV:* 7
Collns: Western Isles Local Hist Colln (all locations; main ref colln at Stornoway Lib – see **A474**); An Comunn Gaidhealach Colln of Gaelic material & Highland hist in English (mainly at Stornoway & Lionacleit Libs); Gaelic Colln (all locations; main ref colln Stornoway Lib); T.B. Macaulay Photo Colln; Donald MacDonald Tolsta Papers; D.R. Morrison Scalpay Papers (Gaelic verse & English/Gaelic journalism, at Stornoway Lib) *ILLs:* natl & internatl *Loans:* bks & audios/ 3 wks; videos/1 wk; lang courses/8 wks *Income Gen:* req & res/50p; lost card/£5 *Fines:* bks & audios/ad 20p pw (£6 max); videos/50p pd; ch & blind or partially sighted exempt *Equip:* 4 m-readers, m-printer (10p), 2 fax (UK 75p pg, £1 internatl), 5 copiers (A4/10p, A3/15p), computers (incl internet & email) at all branches

Stock:	1 Apr 2000	1 Apr 2001
ad lend:	58436	61693
ad ref:	11575	11749
ch:	35353	34283
audios:	10346	10898
videos:	2198	2434
CD-ROMs:	12	12
periodcls:	35	35
archvs:	130 linear m	130 linear m

Issues:	1999-2000	2000-01
ad lend:	167645	155963
ch:	64260	49395
audios:	13215	11323
videos:	5571	3438

Acqs:	1999-2000	2000-01
bks:	11661	6848
AVs:	2748	1050

Acqs: Source: lib suppl *Offcr-in-Charge:* Snr Libns, as above
Classn: DDC *Cat: Type:* author & classified *Medium:* cards & auto *Auto Sys:* Dynix *Svcs: Extramural:* schools, hosps, old people's homes, housebnd *Info:* Gaelic Resources Database (both at Stornoway & Lionacleit Libs) *Activs:* ch's activs, bk sales, temp exhibs, author visits *Offcr-in-Charge:* Chief Libn, as above
Enqs: 50388 (1999-2000); 71542 (2000-01)
Staff: Libns: 5 *Non-Prof:* 14

Inc from:	1999-2000	2000-01
local govt:	£633938	£652390
fines etc:	£23740	£23482
total:	£748033	£788020

Exp on:	1999-2000	2000-01
bks:	£33657	£35941
AVs:	£1027	£2806
salaries:	£421718	£397505
total:	£748033	£788020

Wigan

P200 Wigan Libraries and Lifelong Learning

Wigan Leisure & Culture Trust, Indoor Sports Complex, Loire Dr, Robin Pk, Wigan, Lancashire, WN5 0UL (01942-244991; *fax:* 01942-828540)
Email: wiglib@wlct.org
Internet: http://www.wlct.org/Libraries/ libraries.htm

Local Auth: Wigan Metropolitan Borough Council *Pop:* 313000 *Larger Dept:* Wigan Leisure & Culture Trust *Chief:* Head of Libs & Lifelong Learning: Ms Kathryn Buddle (k.buddle@wlct.org)

Public Libraries

Wigan ▼ Wokingham

(Wigan Libs & Lifelong Learning cont)
Other Snr Staff: Head of Operational Svcs: Mrs Rosanne Patterson (r.patterson@wlct.org); Info Svcs & Learning Support Mgr: Mrs Susan Underwood (s.underwood@wlct.org); Svc Development Mgr: Mr Stephen Ruffley (s.ruffley@wlct.org)
Main Libs: *Central Libs:* WIGAN LIB, Coll Ave, Wigan, Lancashire, WN1 1NN (*info:* 01942-827619; *lend:* 01942-827621; *fax:* 01942-827640); LEIGH LIB, Civic Sq, Leigh, Lancashire, WN7 1EB (01942-404404; *fax:* 01942-404567); *Dist Libs:* ASHTON LIB, Wigan Rd, Ashton-in-Makerfield, Wigan, Lancashire, WN4 9BH (01942-727119; *fax:* 01942-276121); ATHERTON LIB, York St, Atherton, Manchester, M29 9JH (01942-404817); STANDISH LIB, Cross St, Standish, Wigan, Lancashire, WN6 0HQ (01257-400496; *fax:* 01257-400625) *Branch (Community) Libs:* ABRAM LIB, Vicarage Rd, Abram, Wigan, Lancashire, WN2 5QX (01942-866350; *fax:* 01942-515939); ASPULL LIB, Oakfield Cres, Aspull, Wigan, Lancashire, WN2 1XJ (01942-831303; *fax:* 01942-806262); BEECH HILL LIB, Buckley St West, Beech Hill, Wigan, Lancashire, WN6 7PQ (01942-747750; *fax:* 01942-209049); GOLBORNE LIB, Tanners Ln, Golborne, Warrington, Cheshire, WA3 3AW (01942-777800; *fax:* 01942-208630); HINDLEY LIB, Market St, Hindley, Wigan, Lancashire, WN2 3AN (01942-255287; *fax:* 01942-207520); INCE LIB, Smithy Green, Ince, Wigan, Lancashire, WN2 2AT (01942-324423; *fax:* 01942-730288); MARSH GREEN LIB, Harrow Rd, Marsh Green, Wigan, Lancashire, WN5 0QL (01942-760041; *fax:* 01942-511853); ORRELL LIB, Orrell Post, Orrell, Wigan, Lancashire, WN5 8LY (01942-705060; *fax:* 01942-510148); SHEVINGTON LIB, Gathurst Ln, Shevington, Wigan, Lancashire, WN6 8HA (01257-252618; *fax:* 01257-400013); TYLDESLEY LIB, Stanley St, Tyldesley, Manchester, M29 8AH (01942-882504; *fax:* 01942-638010)
Svc Pts: *Mobile:* 3 *AV:* 14 *Computers:* 16 *Internet:* 16 *Other:* WIGAN CH'S LIB, The Wiend Centre, The Wiend, Wigan, Lancashire, WN1 1PF (01942-828104); SCHOOLS LIB SVCS, based at Shevington Lib (01257-253269)
Collns: JFR *Co-op Schemes:* Libs North West, JFR *ILLs:* natl & internatl *Loans:* bks/3 wks; audios/2 wks; videos/2 days or 1 wk *Charges:* audios/£1; videos/£1.50 *Income Gen:* res/45p; ILLs/£1.20 *Fines:* bks/ad 10p pd, oaps 5p pd, ch exempt; audios/10p pd; videos/new releases £1.50 per 2 days, others 40p pd; registered blind, housebnd & mobile lib users exempt *Equip:* copiers, fax, computers (incl wd-procs, internet & CD-ROM), rooms for hire *Disabled:* Kurzweil, Eazee Readers, embossed button cassette players (& headphones), magnifiers, induction loops, minicom, sub-titled videos

Stock:	1 Apr 2000	1 Apr 2001
lend:	352342	344808
ref:	13944	14180
AVs:	23825	31005
periodcls:	152	153

Issues:	1999-2000	2000-01
bks:	1824206	1781954
AVs:	84255	89811

Acqs:	1999-2000	2000-01
bks:	63459	53148
AVs:	3803	4727

Acqs: *Source:* lib suppl
Classn: DDC *Cat: Type:* author, classified, subj & title *Medium:* auto *Svcs: Extramural:* schools, prisons, hosps, residential & nursing homes, housebnd *Info:* community, business, European, career, legal *Other:* Open Learning, picture loan, basic skills *Activs:* ch's activs, bk sales, films, temp exhibs, poetry readings, reading groups, homework clubs, BookStart Owl Club
Enqs: 153269 (1999-2000); 148562 (2000-01)
Staff: 105.1 in total

Exp on:	1999-2000	2000-01
total:	£3525163	£3792702

Wiltshire

P201 Wiltshire Libraries and Heritage

Libs & Heritage HQ, Bythesea Rd, Trowbridge, Wiltshire, BA14 8BS (01225-713701; *fax:* 01225-713993)
Email: librariesenquiries@wiltshire.gov.uk
Internet: http://www.wiltshire.gov.uk/

Local Auth: Wiltshire County Council *Pop:* 435900 *Cttee:* Community Svcs Advisory Panel *Larger Dept:* Edu & Libs *Dept Chief:* Chief Edu Offcr: Mr Robert Wolfson MA *Chief:* Head of Libs & Heritage: Mrs Pauline Palmer, MCLIP, DMS, MIMgt (paulinepalmer@wiltshire.gov.uk) *Dep:* Principal Libn: Mr Monte Little MPhil, MCLIP (montelittle@wiltshire.gov.uk) *Other Snr Staff:* Dist Libn (Kennet) & Branch Development Co-ordinator: Mr Maurice Chandler MCLIP (mauricechandler@wiltshire.gov.uk); Dist Libn (North Wiltshire): Ms Joan Davis BA, MCLIP (joandavis@wiltshire.gov.uk); Stock Mgr: Mr David Green BA, MCLIP (davidgreen@wiltshire.gov.uk); Dist Libn (Salisbury): Mr Chris Harling BA(Hons), MCLIP (chrisharling@wiltshire.gov.uk); County Ch's Libn: Miss Sarah Hillier BA, PGCE, MCLIP (sarahhillier@wiltshire.gov.uk); Dist Libn (West Wilts): Mrs Mary Liddle BA, MCLIP (maryliddle@wiltshire.gov.uk); Transport & Premises Mgr: Mr Keith Sheppard BIMgt, MITA, AMITM, MIPDM (keithsheppard@wiltshire.gov.uk); Info Svcs Mgr: Mr Chris Wildridge BA, MCLIP (christopherwildridge@wiltshire.gov.uk)
Main (Area) Libs: *North Wiltshire:* CHIPPENHAM LIB, Timber St, Chippenham, Wiltshire, SN15 3EJ (01249-650536; *fax:* 01249-443793); *Salisbury Dist:* SALISBURY LIB, Market Pl, Salisbury, Wiltshire, SP1 1BL (01380-324145; *fax:* 01722-413214); *West Wiltshire:* TROWBRIDGE LIB, Mortimer St, Cradle Bridge, Trowbridge, Wiltshire, BA14 8LD (01225-761171; *fax:* 01225-769447); *Kennet Dist:* DEVIZES LIB, Sheep St, Devizes, Wiltshire, SN10 1DL (01380-726878; *fax:* 01380-722161) *Branch Libs:* AMESBURY LIB, Smithfield St, Amesbury, Salisbury, Wiltshire, SP4 7AL (01980-623491; *fax:* 01980-626596); BRADFORD-ON-AVON LIB, Bridge St, Bradford-on-Avon, Wiltshire, BA15 1BY (01225-863280; *fax:* 01225-868647); CALNE LIB, The Strand, Calne, Wiltshire, SN11 0JU (01249-813128; *fax:* 01249-819468); CORSHAM LIB, Pickwick Rd, Corsham, Wiltshire, SN13 9BJ (01249-713159; *fax:* 01249-714076); CRICKLADE LIB, 113 High St, Cricklade, Swindon, Wiltshire, SN6 6AE (01793-750694; *fax:* 01793-750694); DOWNTON LIB, Barford Ln, Downton, Salisbury, Wiltshire, SP5 3QA (01725-511003); MALMESBURY LIB, Cross Hayes, Malmesbury, Wiltshire, SN16 9BG (01666-823611; *fax:* 01666-824953); MARLBOROUGH LIB, 91 High St, Marlborough, Wiltshire, SN8 1HD (01672-512663; *fax:* 01672-515896); MELKSHAM LIB, Lowbourne, Melksham, Wiltshire, SN12 7DZ (01225-702039; *fax:* 01225-707196); TIDWORTH LIB, Tidworth Leisure Centre, Nadder Rd, Tidworth, Hampshire, SP9 7QA (01980-843460); WARMINSTER LIB, Three Horseshoes Mall, Warminster, Wiltshire, BA12 9BT (01985-216022; *fax:* 01985-846332);

WESTBURY LIB, Westbury House, Edward St, Westbury, Wiltshire, BA13 3BD (01373-822294; *fax:* 01373-859208); WILTON LIB, South St, Wilton, Salisbury, Wiltshire, SP2 0JS (01722-743230; *fax:* 01722-743804); WOOTTON BASSETT LIB, Borough Fields, Wootton Bassett, Swindon, Wiltshire, SN4 7AX (01793-853249; *fax:* 01793-852807)
Svc Pts: *PT:* 12 *Mobile:* 4 *AV:* 30 *Computers:* 30 *Internet:* 11
Collns: Life of Christ (Christology, at Salisbury Lib); cricket (at Chippenham Lib); archvs & museums collns (at HQ in Trowbridge Lib); microbiology & anthro (at Amesbury Lib) *Co-op Schemes:* SWRLS Subj Specialisation, WILCO *ILLs:* county, natl & internatl *Loans:* bks, spkn wd & CD-ROMs/3 wks; music audios, videos, DVDs & Playstation games/1 wk *Charges:* spkn wd/£1.30 or annual sub £36; music audios/£1.40; videos, DVDs & Playstation games/£1.30-£2.60; CD-ROMs/£1.30 *Income Gen:* req & res/ad 50p + £2.20 for out of County, ch free; lost ticket/50p *Fines:* bks/ad & oap 11p pd open, ch 2p pd open; audios, videos, CD-ROMs, DVDs & Playstation games/loan charge; housebnd, blind & partially sighted exempt *Equip:* 28 m-readers (printouts A4/£1, A3/£1.50); 14 faxes (£1 per pg in UK); 19 copiers (10p, 50+ copies 8p each); 79 computers (incl 31 with wd-proc, 31 with CD-ROM, 30 with internet, access free), 14 rooms for hire (various) *Disabled:* CCTV Magnifiers, induction loops *Online:* Community Info *Offcr-in-Charge:* Principal Libn, as above

Stock:	1 Apr 2000	1 Apr 2001
ad lend:	330507	365283
ad ref:	130675	93699
ch:	121637	134747
instns:	4378	6544
audios:	25802	32997
videos:	16794	18310
CD-ROMs:	725	951
periodcls:	757	757

Issues:	1999-2000	2000-01
ad lend:	2529831	2341960
ch:	858285	773651
instns:	25490	22542
audios:	198131	195590
videos:	141824	139573
CD-ROMs:	2303	4612

Acqs:	1999-2000	2000-01
bks:	84802	84119
AVs:	13335	13093

Acqs: *Source:* lib suppl & publ *Co-op:* CUSP *Offcr-in-Charge:* Stock Mgr, as above
Classn: DDC *Cat: Type:* author, classified, subj & title *Medium:* auto *Auto Sys:* DS *Svcs: Extramural:* prisons, hosps, old people's homes, housebnd, day centres, play groups *Info:* community, business *Other:* Open Learning, art galleries *Activs:* ch's activs, bk sales, temp exhibs, poetry readings, reading groups, talks, author visits, class visits, workshops, demos, performance events *Offcr-in-Charge:* Principal Libn, as above
Enqs: 655088 (1999-2000); 378413 (2000-01)
Staff: Libns: 41 Non-Prof: 118.9

Inc from:	1999-2000	2000-01
local govt:	£4219898	£4619711
fines etc:	£548128	£530253
total:	£4781224	£5149964

Exp on:	1999-2000	2000-01
bks:	£546747	£655392
AVs:	£147009	£166302
elec media:	-	£11420
salaries:	£2771034	£2957438
total:	£4781224	£5149964

Proj: new libs at Cricklade & Downton; Disability Discrimination Access (DDA)

Windsor and Maidenhead

P202 Windsor and Maidenhead Library and Information Services

Maidenhead Lib, St Ives Rd, Maidenhead, Berkshire, SL6 1QU (01628-796969; *fax:* 01628-796971)
Email: maidenhead.library@rbwm.gov.uk
Internet: http://www.rbwm.gov.uk/libraries/

Local Auth: Royal Borough of Windsor & Maidenhead *Pop:* 133500 *Cttee:* Leisure & Cultural Svcs Board *Larger Dept:* Leisure, Cultural & Property Svcs Directorate *Dept Chief:* Dir: Mr David Oram *Chief:* Lib & Info Svcs Mgr: Mr Mark Taylor (mark.taylor@rbwm.gov.uk) *Dep:* Asst Lib & Info Svcs Mgr: Mr Brian Marpole (brian.marpole@rbwm.gov.uk) *Other Snr Staff:* Svc Development Mgr: Mrs Sara Hudson (sara. hudson@rbwm.gov.uk)
Main Libs: MAIDENHEAD CENTRAL LIB, addr as above *Branch Libs:* ASCOT DURNING LIB, Winkfield Rd, Ascot, Berkshire, SL5 7EX (*tel & fax:* 01344-620653; *email:* ascot.library@rbwm. gov.uk); COOKHAM LIB, High Rd, Cookham Rise, Maidenhead, Berkshire, SL6 9JF (*tel & fax:* 01628-526147; *email:* cookham.library@rbwm. gov.uk); DEDWORTH LIB, Dedworth County School, Smith's Ln, Windsor, Berkshire, SL4 5PE (*tel & fax:* 01753-868733; *email:* dedworth.library@ rbwm.gov.uk); SUNNINGHILL LIB, Reading Room, School Rd, Sunninghill, Ascot, Berkshire, SL5 7AA (*tel & fax:* 01344-621493; *email:* sunninghill.library@rbwm.gov.uk); WINDSOR LIB, Bachelors Acre, Windsor, Berkshire, SL4 1ER (01753-743940; *fax:* 01753-743942; *email:* windsor.library@rbwm.gov.uk)
Svc Pts: PT: 4 *Mobile:* 2, plus 1 Container visiting 4 lib sites weekly *AV:* 16 *Computers:* 14 *Internet:* 14
Colns: Royal Colln (at Windsor Lib); Thames Colln (at Maidenhead Lib) *ILLs:* natl & internatl *Loans:* bks, audios & mixed media/3 wks; videos, DVDs & CD-ROMs/1 wk *Charges:* audios/£1-£2.10; videos/£1.55-£2.10; DVDs/ £2.55-£3.20; CD-ROMs/£1.90-£2.10; mixed media/£1.50-£1.65 *Income Gen:* req & res/90p, ch 25p; lost ticket/£1.50 *Fines:* bks/ad & oaps 12p pd (£5.64 max), ch 4p pd (£1.88 max); audios/as ad bks; videos, DVDs & CD-ROMs/53p pd (£10.60 max) *Equip:* 4 m-readers, 4 m-printers (A4/50p), 3 copiers (A4/10p), 14 fax (from £1), 59 computers (incl 57 with wd-proc, 57 with internet & 37 with CD-ROM), 3 rooms for hire (varies) *Disabled:* Dolphin *Online:* Companies House(variable fees charged for downloading & printing), Gale/Infotrac, Oxford Online, XreferPlus, World Book On-line *Offcr-in-Charge:* Lib & Info Svcs Mgr, as above

Stock:	1 Apr 2000	1 Apr 2001
ad lend:	156682	141577
ad ref:	15136	14091
ch:	48580	49380
audios:	6999	8512
videos:	2466	4364
CD-ROMs:	560	1218
periodcls:	101	97

Issues:	1999-2000	2000-01
ad lend:	659174	583917
ch:	252774	246482
audios:	41316	37241
videos:	54515	53597
CD-ROMs:	4063	8081

Acqs:	1999-2000	2000-01
bks:	29079	28539
AVs:	3292	2865

Acqs: Source: lib suppl *Offcr-in-Charge:* Stock Svcs Offcr: Mr Paul Douch (paul.douch@rbwm. gov.uk)
Classn: DDC *Cat: Type:* author, classified & title *Medium:* auto *Auto Sys:* Dynix *Svcs: Extramural:* housebnd, old people's homes, day centres *Info:* council, community, careers (IAG), European (basic) *Activs:* ch's activs, bk sales, temp exhibs, reading groups, talks, author visits *Enqs:* 159952 (1999-2000); 180128 (2000-01)
Staff: Libns: 19 *Non-Prof:* 41

Inc from:	1999-2000	2000-01
fines etc:	£237960	£262324
total:	£1213077	£1319555

Exp on:	1999-2000	2000-01
bks:	£259162	£245626
AVs:	£65838	£78602
salaries:	£888077	£995327
total:	£1213077	£1319555

Proj: new bldg for Cookham Lib in 2001 (cost approx £500000)

Wirral

P203 Wirral Libraries

Edu & Cultural Svcs, Hamilton Bldg, Conway Street, Birkenhead, Merseyside, CH41 4FD (0151-666-2121; *fax:* 0151-666-4270)
Email: educ@wirral.gov.uk
Internet: http://www.wirral-libraries.net/

Local Auth: Wirral Metropolitan Borough Council *Pop:* 330700 *Larger Dept:* Edu & Cultural Svcs *Chief:* Snr Asst Dir (Lib, Info & Cultural Svcs): Mr Ian Coles DMS, MCLIP *Dep:* Principal Libn: Mr Owen Roberts DMS, MCLIP
Main (Central) Libs: BEBINGTON CENTRAL LIB, Civic Way, Bebington, Wirral, Merseyside, CH63 7SF (0151-643-7217; *fax:* 0151-645-2889; *email:* bebington@wirral-library.net); BIRKENHEAD CENTRAL LIB, Borough Rd, Birkenhead, Mersey-side, CH41 2XB (0151-652-6106; *fax:* 0151-653-7320; *email:* birkenhead@wirral-library.net); WALLASEY CENTRAL LIB, Earlston Rd, Wallasey, Merseyside, CH45 5DX (0151-639-2334; *fax:* 0151-691-2040; *email:* wallasey@wirral-library.net) *Branch Libs:* BEECHWOOD LIB, 8 Beechwood Dr, Greenfields, Beechwood, Wirral, Merseyside, CH43 4ZU (0151-677-3360; *email:* beechwood@wirral-library.net); BROMBOROUGH LIB, Allport Ln, Bromborough, Wirral, Merseyside, CH62 7HR (0151-334-1650; *email:* bromborough@ wirral-library.net); EASTHAM LIB, Mill Park Dr, Eastham, Wirral, Merseyside, CH62 9AL (0151-327-2289; *email:* eastham@wirral-library.net); GREASBY LIB, Greasby Rd, Greasby, Wirral, Merseyside, CH49 3AT (0151-677-5714; *email:* greasby@wirral-library.net); HESWALL LIB, Telegraph Rd, Heswall, Wirral, Merseyside, CH60 0AF (0151-342-4552; *email:* heswall@wirral-library. net); HIGHER BEBINGTON LIB, Higher Bebing-ton Rd, Higher Bebington, Wirral, Merseyside, CH63 2PT (0151-608-3430; *email:* higher. bebington@wirral-library.net); HOYLAKE LIB, Market St, Hoylake, Wirral, Merseyside, CH47 5AA (0151-632-2754; *email:* hoylake@wirral-library. net); IRBY LIB, Thurstaston Rd, Irby, Merseyside, CH61 0HE (0151-648-1348; *email:* irby@wirral-library.net); LEASOWE LIB, Twicken-ham Dr, Leasowe, Wirral, Merseyside, CH46 1PQ (0151-638-4013; *email:* leasowe@wirral-library.net); MORETON LIB, Pasture Rd, Moreton, Wirral, Merseyside, CH46 8SA (0151-677-5165; *email:* moreton@wirral-library.net); PENSBY LIB, Pensby Rd, Pensby, Wirral, Merseyside, CH61 9NE (0151-648-4537; *email:* pensby@wirral-library.net); PRENTON LIB, Dickens Ave, Prenton, Birken-head, Merseyside, CH43 0TQ (0151-608-2858; *email:* prenton@wirral-library.net); RIDGEWAY COMMUNITY LIB, Ridgeway High School, Noctorum Ave, Noctorum, Wirral, Merseyside, CH43 9EB (0151-641-8484; *email:* ridgeway@ wirral-library.net); ROCK FERRY LIB, 259 Old Chester Rd, Rock Ferry, Wirral, Merseyside, CH42 3TD (0151-641-2858; *fax:* 0151-641-2859; *email:* rock.ferry@ wirral-library.net); ST JAMES LIB, Laird St, Birkenhead, Merseyside, CH41 7AL (0151-652-2268; *email:* st.james@wirral-library. net); SEACOMBE LIB, Liscard Rd, Liscard, Wirral, Merseyside, CH44 6LT (0151-638-4475; *email:* seacombe@wirral-library.net); UPTON LIB, Ford Rd, Upton, Wirral, Merseyside, CH49 0TB (0151-677-5677; *email:* upton@wirral-library.net); WALLASEY VILLAGE LIB, St George's Rd, Wallasey Village, Wirral, Merseyside, CH45 3NE (0151-638-1024; *email:* wallasey. village@wirral-library.net); WEST KIRBY LIB, The Concourse, Grange Rd, West Kirby, Wirral, Merseyside, CH48 4HX (0151-929-7808; *email:* west.kirby@ wirral-library.net); WOODCHURCH LIB, Ganney's Meadow, New Hey Rd, Woodchurch, Birkenhead, Merseyside, CH49 8EB (0151-677-8068; *email:* woodchurch@wirral-library.net)
Svc Pts: PT: 1 *AV:* 4 *Other:* SCHOOLS LIB SVC (0151-346-6502; *fax:* 0151-346-6739; *email:* sls@ wirral.gov.uk)
Co-op Schemes: LADSIRLAC, Libs North West *ILLs:* natl *Loans:* bks/4 wks; audios/2 wks; videos/1-3 days; DVDs/3 days *Charges:* cassettes/65p, sets 80p-£1.55; CDs/90p, sets £1.25; videos/60p-£1, £1.60 for new feature films; DVDs/£1.60; blind & partially sighted exempt from charges on AV materials *Income Gen:* Video & DVD Lib membership/£7, conc £5; res/75p, conc 50p *Fines:* bks/ad 8p pd, oap 4p pd, ch 1p pd; audios/10p pd, videos & DVDs/loan charge; registered blind exempt *Equip:* m-readers, m-printers, fax, copiers (10p), 348 computers (incl wd-proc, internet & CD-ROM), room hire *Disabled:* Rainbow Reader, Supernova software

Stock:	1 Apr 2000	1 Apr 2001
lend:	560346	527594
ref:	112056	105921
AVs:	37052	35180
periodcls:	120	120

Issues:	1999-2000	2000-01
bks:	2409810	2273623
AVs:	93504	109272

Acqs:	1999-2000	2000-01
bks:	47266	48441
AVs:	1863	3697

Acqs: Source: lib suppl
Classn: DDC *Cat: Type:* classified *Medium:* auto *Auto Sys:* Talis *Svcs: Extramural:* schools, old people's homes, housebnd *Info:* community, business *Other:* Open Learning *Activs:* ch's activs, bk sales, films, temp exhibs, poetry readings, puppet shows, reading groups, writers' groups, computing courses
Enqs: 342056 (1999-2000); 341796 (2000-01)
Staff: Libns: 40 *Non-Prof:* 138.06

Inc from:	1999-2000	2000-01
local govt:	£4836248	£5240459
fines etc:	£231260	£261378
total:	£5067508	£5550864

Exp on:	1999-2000	2000-01
bks:	£526803	£513351
AVs:	£39053	£33661
salaries:	£2845521	£3062671
total:	£5067508	£5550864

Wokingham

P204 Wokingham Libraries and Information Service

Council Offices, Shute End, Wokingham, Berkshire, RG40 1BN (0118-978-6261; *fax:* 0118-978-6268)
Email: Libraries@wokingham.gov.uk
Internet: http://www.wokingham.gov.uk/libraries/

Local Auth: Wokingham Dist Council *Pop:* 146000 *Cttee:* Edu & Cultural Svcs Cttee *Larger Dept:* Edu & Cultural Svcs *Dept Chief:* Dir: Miss J.H. Ashmore MCLIP *Chief:* Head of Libs & Lifelong Learning: Mr C.J. Hamilton MCLIP

ublic Libraries

Wokingham ▼ York

(Wokingham Libs & Info Svc cont)
Main Libs: WOKINGHAM LIB, Denmark St, Wokingham, Berkshire, RG40 2BB (0118-978-1368; *fax:* 0118-989-1214) **Branch Libs:** LOWER EARLEY LIB, Chalfont Cl, Chalfont Way, Lower Earley, Berkshire, RG6 5HZ (0118-931-2150; *fax:* 0118-975-0162); MAIDEN ERLEGH LIB, Maiden Erlegh Dr, Earley, Berkshire, RG6 7HP (*tel & fax:* 0118-966-6630); SPENCERS WOOD LIB, Basingstoke Rd, Spencers Wood, Berkshire, RG7 1AJ (*tel & fax:* 0118-988-4771); TWYFORD LIB, Polehampton Cl, Twyford, Reading, Berkshire, RG10 9RP (0118-934-0800; *fax:* 0118-934-5399); WARGRAVE LIB, Church St, Wargrave, Berkshire, RG10 8EP (*tel & fax:* 0118-940-4656); WINNERSH LIB, Robin Hood Ln, Winnersh, Berkshire, RG41 5NE; WOODLEY LIB, Headley Rd, Woodley, Berkshire, RG5 4AJ (0118-969-0304; *fax:* 0118-969-9807)
Svc Pts: *PT:* 1 *Mobile:* 1 (based at Wokingham Lib) *Computers:* 9 *Internet:* 9
Collns: local hist colln (at Wokingham Lib) **Co-op Schemes:** BLIP **ILLs:** county & natl
Loans: bks, audios & mixed media items/3 wks; videos, CD-ROMs & DVDs/1 wk **Charges:** cassettes/sets of 1-2 75p, sets of 3-6 £1, sets of 7+ £1.50, ch's cassettes 50p; CDs/sets of 1-6 £1.50, sets of 7+ £2.50; videos/£1.60; CD-ROMs & DVDs/£2.50; mixed media items/£1.50; audio materials free for registered blind or partially sighted **Income Gen:** res/ad 30p (ILLs £2); lost ticket/£1.50 **Fines:** bks/ad 16p pd (£6.40 max), ch 4p pd (£2 max); audios/as ad bks; videos, CD-ROMs & DVDs/£1.10 pd (£13.20 max) **Equip:** m-readers, m-printers, copiers, computers (incl wd-proc & internet), fax

Stock:	1 Apr 2001
ad lend:	103078
ad ref:	7888
ch:	81337
audios:	14564
videos:	3954
CD-ROMs:	7327
periodcls:	106

Issues:	2000-01
ad lend:	665607
ch:	386682
audios:	49838
videos:	35106
CD-ROMs:	6695

Acqs:	1999-2000	2000-01
bks:	18482	23475
AVs:	-	2773

Classn: DDC **Cat:** *Type:* author, classified & title *Medium:* auto *Auto Sys:* Dynix **Svcs:** *Extramural:* housebnd, old people's homes, play groups *Info:* business, community, council **Activs:** ch's activs, bk sales, temp exhibs, reading groups, author visits
Enqs: 83460 (2000-01)
Staff: *Libns:* 9.5 *Non-Prof:* 36

Inc from:	2000-01
local govt:	£1818036
fines etc:	£164834
total:	£1982870

Exp on:	2000-01
bks:	£186588
AVs:	£41318
salaries:	£795554
total:	£1982870

Wolverhampton

P205 Wolverhampton Libraries and Information Services
Central Lib, Snow Hill, Wolverhampton, W Midlands, WV1 3AX (01902-552025; *fax:* 01902-552024)
Email: wolverhampton.libraries@dial.pipex.com
Internet: http://www.wolverhampton.gov.uk/

Local Auth: Wolverhampton Metropolitan Borough Council *Pop:* 240500 **Cttee:** Leisure Svcs Cttee **Larger Dept:** Leisure Svcs *Dept Chief:* Dir of Leisure Svcs: Miss S. Nixon BArch(Hons), MILAM **Chief:** City Libn: Mrs Karen Lees **Dep:** Asst City Libns: Mr Andrew Scragg & Mr Graeme Kent
Main Libs: CENTRAL LIB, addr as above
Branch Libs: ASHMORE PK LIB, Griffiths Dr, Wednesfield, Wolverhampton, W Midlands, WV11 2JW (01902-556296); BILSTON LIB, Mount Pleasant, Bilston, W Midlands, WV14 7LU (01902-556253); EASTFIELD LIB, Hurstbourne Cres, Wolverhampton, W Midlands, WV1 2EE (01902-556257); FINCHFIELD LIB, Whiteoak Dr, Finchfield, Wolverhampton, W Midlands, WV3 9AF (01902-556260); LONG KNOWLE LIB, Wood End Rd, Wednesfield, Wolverhampton, W Midlands, WV11 1YG (01902-556290); LOW HILL LIB, Showell Circus, Low Hill, Wolverhampton, W Midlands, WV10 9JJ (01902-556293); OXLEY LIB, Probert Rd, Oxley, Wolverhampton, W Midlands, WV10 6UF (01902-556287); PENDEFORD LIB, Whitburn Cl, Pendeford, Wolverhampton, W Midlands, WV9 5NJ (01902-556250); PENN LIB, Coalway Ave, Penn, Wolverhampton, W Midlands, WV3 7LT (01902-556281); SPRING VALE LIB, Bevan Ave, Wolverhampton, W Midlands, WV4 6SG (01902-556284); TETTENHALL LIB, Upper St, Tettenhall, Wolverhampton, W Midlands, WV6 8QF (01902-556308; *fax:* 01902-556318); WARSTONES LIB, Pinfold Grove, Penn, Wolverhampton, W Midlands, WV14 4PT (01902-556275); WEDNESFIELD LIB, Church St, Wednesfield, Wolverhampton, W Midlands, WV11 1SR (01902-556278); WHITMORE REANS LIB, Bargate Dr, Evans St, Wolverhampton, W Midlands, WV6 0QW (01902-556269)
Svc Pts: *PT:* 5 *Mobile:* 1 *AV:* 5
Collns: BSI; JFR (Lab-Lam, McE-McK); Asian Lang Colln; Public Info Relay (European info, at Central Lib) **Co-op Schemes:** WMRLS, JFR, SEALS, Proj EARL **ILLs:** county, natl & internatl
Loans: bks & audios/4 wks; videos/1 wk **Charges:** audios/£1, conc 50p; videos/£1.50, conc 75p **Income Gen:** res/75p, conc 30p; lost ticket/ad £1.50, ch 50p **Fines:** bks/ad & oap 12p pd, 13-17 year olds 6p pd; audios/12p pd; videos/£1.50 pw; ch under 13 exempt **Equip:** 2 m-readers, m-printer (A4/20p), 15 fax (£1 per pg), 14 copiers (A4/10p, A3/20p), clr copier (A4/£1, A3/£1.50), 125 computers (incl wd-proc, internet & CD-ROM, all free) **Disabled:** CCTV image enhancers, Kurzweil on 2 PCs, induction loops, minicom

Stock:	1 Apr 2000	1 Apr 2001
ad lend:	314983	316917
ad ref:	16994	23459
ch:	162329	159116
audios:	32011	31318
videos:	4554	4948
periodcls:	260	

Issues:	1999-2000	2000-01
ad lend:	1564824	1540973
ch:	582421	641293
audios:	129435	136480
videos:	14331	15667

Acqs:	1999-2000	2000-01
bks:	71709	75268
AVs:	5156	5482

Acqs: *Source:* lib suppl **Offcr-in-Charge:** Stock Mgr: Mrs Pat Holden
Classn: DDC **Cat:** *Type:* author, classified, subj & title *Medium:* auto *Auto Sys:* Talis **Svcs:** *Extramural:* schools, hosps, old people's homes, housebnd, day centres, play groups *Info:* business, community, European Public Relay Info *Other:* local studies, IT introduction packages available **Activs:** ch's activs, bk sales, temp exhibs, poetry readings, reading groups, writers' groups, author visits **Offcr-in-Charge:** Lit Development Worker: Mr Simon Fletcher (simon.fletcher@dial.pipex.com)
Enqs: 309296 (1999-2000); 288717 (2000-01)
Staff: *Libns:* 23 *Non-Prof:* 89.1

Worcestershire

P206 Worcestershire Libraries and Information Service
County Lib HQ, Cultural Svcs, County Hall, Spetchley Rd, Worcester, WR5 2NP (01905-766231; *fax:* 01905-766244)
Email: librarieshq@worcestershire.gov.uk
Internet: http://www.worcestershire.gov.uk/libraries/

Local Auth: Worcestershire County Council *Pop:* 542107 **Larger Dept:** Cultural Svcs Div **Chief:** Lib Svcs Mgr: Ms Cathy Evans (cevans@worcestershire.gov.uk) **Other Snr Staff:** Strategic Lib Mgr (North & Svcs to Yng People): Ms Carmel Reed; Strategic Lib Mgr (South, Stock & Social Inclusion): Mr Nigel Preedy; Strategic Lib Mgr (Info Svcs): Mr David Drewitt
Main Libs: BROMSGROVE LIB, Stratford Rd, Bromsgrove, Worcestershire, B60 1AP (*tel & fax:* 01527-575855; *email:* BromsgroveLib@worcestershire.gov.uk); EVESHAM LIB, Oat St, Evesham, Worcestershire, WR11 4PJ (01386-442291/41348; *fax:* 01386-765855; *email:* EveshamLib@worcestershire.gov.uk); KIDDERMINSTER LIB, Bromsgrove St, Kidderminster, Worcestershire, DY10 1PE (01562-824500; *fax:* 01562-512907; *email:* KidderminsterLib@worcestershire.gov.uk); MALVERN LIB, Graham Rd, Malvern, Worcestershire, WR14 2HU (01684-561223/573582; *fax:* 01684-892999; *email:* MalvernLib@worcestershire.gov.uk); REDDITCH LIB, 15 Market Pl, Redditch, Worcestershire, B98 8AR (01527-63291/2; *fax:* 01527-68571; *email:* RedditchLib@worcestershire.gov.uk); WORCESTER LIB, Foregate St, Worcester, WR1 1DT (01905-765312/765314; *fax:* 01905-726664; *email:* WorcesterLib@worcestershire.gov.uk)
Branch Libs: BEWDLEY LIB, Load St, Bewdley, Worcestershire, DY12 2EQ (01299-403303; *email:* BewdleyLib@worcestershire.gov.uk); BROADWAY LIB, Leamington Rd, Broadway, Worcestershire, WR12 7DZ (01386-858747; *email:* BroadwayLib@worcestershire.gov.uk); DROITWICH SPA LIB, Victoria Sq, Droitwich Spa, Worcestershire, WR9 8DQ (01905-773292/9970; *fax:* 01905-797401; *email:* DroitwichLib@worcestershire.gov.uk); HAGLEY LIB, Worcester Rd, Hagley, Stourbridge, W Midlands, DY9 0NW (01562-883441; *email:* HagleyLib@worcestershire.gov.uk); PERSHORE LIB, Church St, Pershore, Worcestershire, WR10 1DT (01386-553320; *email:* PershoreLib@worcestershire.gov.uk); RUBERY LIB, 7 Lib Way, Rubery, Rednal, Birmingham, B45 9JS (0121-453-2157; *email:* RuberyLib@worcestershire.gov.uk); ST JOHN'S LIB & INFO CENTRE, Glebe Cl, St John's, Worcester, WR2 5AX (01905-420400; *email:* StJohnsLib@worcestershire.gov.uk); STOURPORT-ON-SEVERN LIB, County Bldgs, Worcester St, Stourport-on-Severn, Worcestershire, DY13 9AA (01299-822866; *fax:* 01299-827464; *email:* StourportLib@worcestershire.gov.uk); TENBURY WELLS LIB, 24 Teme St, Tenbury Wells, Worcestershire, WR14 8BA

(01584-810285; email: TenburyLib@worcestershire.gov.uk); UPTON-ON-SEVERN LIB, School Ln, Upton-on-Severn, Worcestershire, WR8 0LE (01684-592176; email: UptonLib@worcestershire.gov.uk); WARNDON LIB, Cranham Dr, Warndon, Worcester, WR4 9PA (01905-453300; email: WarndonLib@worcestershire.gov.uk); WYTHALL LIB, May Ln, Hollywood, Birmingham, B47 5PD (01564-822980; email: WythallLib@worcestershire.gov.uk)
Svc Pts: PT: 4 *Mobile:* 5 (plus 1 spare) *AV:* 22 *Computers:* 22 *Internet:* 22 *Other:* COUNCIL INFO SHOP, at Kidderminster Lib; COUNCIL INFO SHOP, 44 High St, Droitwich, Worcestershire, WR9 8ES (01905-794272; *fax:* 01905-794245; *email:* droitwichshop@wychavon.gov.uk); EVESHAM COMMUNITY CONTACT CENTRE, 3 Abbey Rd, Evesham, WR11 5SS (01386-443322; *fax:* 01386-765915, *email:* service@theeveshamhub.org.uk); SCHOOLS LIB SVC, Sherwood Ln, Lower Wick, Worcester, WR2 4NU (01905-420273)
Collns: Housman Colln (at Bromsgrove Lib); Carpets & Textiles Colln (at Kidderminster Lib); Needle Industry Colln (at Redditch Lib); Willis Bund Colln; Soc of Friends Colln; Stuart Colln (all at Worcester Lib); local hist at most Group Libs, some smaller local studies collns at local libs; local newspapers on m-film *Co-op Schemes:* MLA-WM *Loans:* bks/4 wks; audios/2 wks; videos/1 wk *Charges:* audios/80p; videos/£1-£2; visually impaired & some disabled exempt from audio charges *Income Gen:* res/ad £1, ch 50p; lost ticket/ad £1, under-18s 50p; exhib booking fees/groups £25, indivs £10, 20% + VAT commission on sales; sales of withdrawn stock, pubns & other items *Fines:* bks/ad 16p pd, ch 8p pd; audios & videos/loan charge *Equip:* m-reader/printers (60p per pg), copiers (10p per pg), faxes (£1 for 1st pg, 50p per addl pg), computers (incl internet, access free, printouts 10p per pg), rooms for hire (varies)

Stock:	1 Apr 2000
bks:	652433
audios:	28902
videos:	10237

Issues:	1999-2000
bks:	4371072
audios:	116562
videos:	48602

Acqs: Offcr-in-Charge: selection panels
Classn: DDC *Cat: Medium:* auto *Auto Sys:* Talis
Svcs: Extramural: schools, housebnd *Info:* community *Other:* Open Learning (at Evesham Lib), Learning Centres, European Public Info Centre (at Kidderminster Lib) *Activs:* ch's activs, bk sales, temp exhibs
Enqs: 499876 (1999-2000)
Staff: Prof: 63.2 *Non-Prof:* 130

Inc from:	1999-2000
fines etc:	£992754

Exp on:	1999-2000
bks:	£689060
AVs:	£60020
salaries:	£2987141
total:	£4027053

Wrexham

P207 Wrexham Library and Information Service

Edu & Leisure Svcs, Ty Henblas, Queens Sq, Wrexham, LL13 8AZ (01978-297442)
Email: library@wrexham.gov.uk
Internet: http://www.wrexham.gov.uk/

Local Auth: Wrexham County Borough Council
Pop: 125700 *Larger Dept:* Edu & Leisure Svcs
Chief: Libs Offcr: Mr Dylan Hughes MCLIP

Main Libs: WREXHAM Lib, Llwyn Isaf, Rhosddu Rd, Wrexham, LL11 1AU (*lend:* 01978-292090; *ref:* 01978-292091; *fax:* 01978-292611) *Branch Libs:* BRYNTEG LIB, The Memorial Centre, Quarry Rd, Brynteg, Wrexham, LL11 6AB (01978-759523); CEFN MAWR LIB, Plas Kynaston, Cefn Mawr, Wrexham, LL14 3AT (01978-820938); COEDPOETH LIB, Park Rd, Coedpoeth, Wrexham, LL11 3TD (01978-753616); GRESFORD LIB, Vicarage Ln, Gresford, Wrexham, LL12 8UW (01978-852627); RHOS LIB, Princes Rd, Rhosllanerchrugog, Wrexham, LL14 1AB (01978-840328); RUABON LIB, High St, Ruabon, Wrexham, LL14 6NH (01978-822002)
Svc Pts: PT: 5 *Mobile:* 3 (incl housebnd vehicle) *AV:* 1 *Computers:* 12 *Internet:* 12
Collns: Japan Colln (at Wrexham Lib) *ILLs:* county & natl *Loans:* bks, audios & videos/3 wks; CD-ROMs/1 wk; extended loans possible for students *Charges:* audio & video/85p+VAT; CD-ROMs/£1 *Income Gen:* res/in stock free, out of stock 85p, free to under-16s; lost ticket/ad £2, ch £1 *Fines:* all items/10p pd for 1st 6 days, then 80p in total for 2nd wk, then 35p pw (max £3.60); ch, registered blind & housebnd exempt *Equip:* m-readers, m-printer, copiers (A4/10p, A3/15p), clr copier (A4/£1, A3/£1.50), fax, video viewers, computers (incl wd-proc, internet & CD-ROM), occasional room hire *Disabled:* Robotron scanner, induction loop, minicom

Stock:	1 Apr 2000	1 Apr 2001
lend:	170883	172745
ref:	21008	22966
AVs:	7800	8270
periodcls:	138	142

Issues:	1999-2000	2000-01
bks:	706570	655188
AVs:	32048	34247

Acqs:	1999-2000	2000-01
bks:	16959	15089
AVs:	608	554

Acqs: Source: lib suppl & bksellers
Classn: DDC *Cat: Type:* author, classified & title *Medium:* m-form & auto *Auto Sys:* DS
Svcs: Extramural: old people's homes, housebnd (part of mobile fleet) *Info:* business, community, ch's (aimed at parents/providers), health, travel, career, local hist, European *Other:* Lifelong Learning *Activs:* ch's activs, bk sales, temp exhibs, poetry readings, homework clubs
Enqs: 72712 (1999-2000); 71220 (2000-01)
Staff: Libns: 13 *Non-Prof:* 26

Inc from:	1999-2000	2000-01
fines etc:	£166539	£265227

Exp on:	1999-2000	2000-01
stock:	£163276	£152348
salaries:	£719743	£736949
total:	£1202792	£1464405

York

P208 York City Libraries

York Central Lib, Museum Street, York, YO1 7DS (01904-655631; *fax:* 01904-611025)
Internet: http://www.york.gov.uk/libraries/

Local Auth: City of York Council *Pop:* 179300
Cttee: Edu Svcs Cttee *Larger Dept:* Edu & Leisure Svcs *Dept Chief:* Dir: Mr Patrick Scott
Chief: Libs Mgr: Ms Janet Thompson BA, MCLIP
Main Libs: YORK CENTRAL LIB, addr as above, incl Lending Lib (01904-552813/5; *email:* lending@york.gov.uk) & Ref Lib (01904-552824/8; *email:* reference.library@york.gov.uk) *Branch Libs:* ACOMB LIB, Front St, Acomb, York, YO24 3BZ (01904-791135; *email:* acomb.library@york.gov.uk); BISHOPTHORPE LIB, Main St, Bishopthorpe, York, YO23 2RB (01904-705386; *email:* bishopthorpe.library@york.gov.uk); CLIFTON LIB, Rawcliffe Ln, Clifton, York, YO30 5SJ (01904-627464; *email:* clifton.library@york.gov.uk); COPMANTHORPE LIB, Village Centre, Main St, Copmanthorpe, York, YO23 3SU (01904-709457; *email:* copmanthorpe.library@york.gov.uk); DRING-HOUSES LIB, Tadcaster Rd, Dring-houses, York, YO24 1LR (01904-706046; *email:* dringhouses.library@york.gov.uk); HAXBY LIB, Station Rd, Haxby, York, YO32 3LT (01904-768811; *email:* haxby.library@york.gov.uk); HUNTINGTON LIB, Garth Rd, Huntington, York, YO32 9QJ (01904-768991; *email:* huntington.library@york.gov.uk); POPPLETON LIB, The Village, Upper Poppleton, York, YO26 6JT (01904-794877; *email:* poppleton.library@york.gov.uk); TANG HALL LIB, Fifth Ave, Tang Hall, York, YO31 0PR (01904-416429; *email:* tanghall.library@york.gov.uk)
Svc Pts: PT: 4 *Mobile:* 1 *AV:* 14 *Computers:* 14 *Internet:* 14
Collns: Marriot Colln (private lib, political & econ hist); Rowland Oboe Colln (oboe music); both held at York Lib *ILLs:* county, natl & internatl *Loans:* bks & spkn wd/3 wks; audios, videos & CD-ROMs/1 wk *Charges:* cassettes/60p, 30p with sub; CDs/90p, 45p with sub; spkn wd/£2, £1 with sub; ch's story tapes/50p; audio sub/£9 pa music or spkn wd only, £10.50 pa for both; videos/50p-£1.50; CD-ROMs/£2 *Income Gen:* res/ad 75p, conc 40p, surcharge outside York ad £2.20, conc £1.10, ch exempt; lost tickets/£1 *Fines:* bks/ad 10p pd for 1st 6 days to total of £1 for 2nd wk, then 50p pw (max £5), ch 5p 1st wk after 3rd day overdue, 10p 2nd wk, then 5p pw (max 50p); audios, videos & CD-ROMs/loan charge; registered blind exempt from audio charges *Equip:* m-readers, m-printers (A4/25p), copiers (A4/10p, A3/20p), fax (varies), 81 computers (incl wd-proc, internet & CD-ROM), scanners, room for hire *Disabled:* CCTV, Galileo Reading Machine, Aladdin Rainbow magnifiers, hearing loops, PCs with software for visually impaired

Stock:	1 Apr 2000	1 Apr 2001
lend:	209954	208604
ref:	59879	57729
AVs:	15833	17335
periodcls:	83	81

Issues:	1999-2000	2000-01
bks:	1351078	1250192
AVs:	75336	77568

Acqs:	1999-2000	2000-01
bks:	27667	23555
AVs:	2909	2405

Acqs: Source: lib suppl, publ & bksellers
Classn: DDC *Cat: Type:* author, classified & title *Medium:* auto *Auto Sys:* Sirsi Unicorn *Svcs: Extramural:* prison *Info:* business, community *Other:* Room 18 (ICT Learning Centre) *Activs:* ch's activs, bks sales, temp exhibs
Enqs: 171210 (1999-2000); 128531 (2000-01)
Staff: 68.1 in total

Inc from:	1999-2000	2000-01
local govt:	£2032000	£2066000
fines etc:	£160000	£166000
total:	£2406000	£2430000

Exp on:	1999-2000	2000-01
stock:	£338000	£326000
salaries:	£1004000	£1102000
total:	£2406000	£2430000

Isle of Man: Castletown
▼
Channel Islands: Jersey

Public Libraries

ISLE OF MAN

Castletown

P209 Castletown Library
Civic Centre, Farrants Way, Castletown, Isle of Man, IM9 1NR (01624-829355; *fax:* 01624-827134)
Email: library@castletown.org.im
Internet: http://www.castletown.org.im/

Local Auth: Castletown Commissioners *Pop:* 3000 *Chief:* Libn: Mrs Fenella Tasker *Dep:* Dep Libn: Mrs Pauline Cringle
Open: Mon 1500-1900, Tue 1000-1200, Wed 1300-1700, Thu 1700-1900, Fri-Sat 1000-1200
ILLs: natl *Loans:* bks/3 wks; audios & videos/2 wks *Charges:* videos/£1 *Income Gen:* membship sub/Castletown resident £6.50 (oap £4.00), out-of-town resident £7.50 (oap £5.50), jnr £1 *Fines:* bks/ad & oap 10p per wk, ch exempt; audios & videos/10p per wk *Equip:* computer terminal (with wd-proc, internet & CD-ROM, internet £1 for 15 min, £2 per half hr, £3 per hr), printer *Online:* internet *Offcr-in-Charge:* Libn, as above
Acqs: Source: lib suppl & publ *Offcr-in-Charge:* Libn, as above
Cat: Type: author, classified & subj *Medium:* cards *Activs:* bk sales, temp exhibs
Staff: Non-Prof: 2

Douglas

P210 Douglas Public Library
Ridgeway St, Douglas, Isle of Man, IM1 1EP (01624-623021; *fax:* 01624-662792)
Email: jbowring@douglas.org.im
Internet: http://www.douglas.org.im/

Local Auth: Douglas Corp *Pop:* 22000 *Cttee:* Leisure Svcs *Chief:* Borough Libn: Mr J.R. Bowring BA, MCLIP
Open: Mon-Sat 0915-1730
Collns: Manx Colln (local hist); cinema colln (bks on film & cinema to 1975); JFR (Caa-Cal) *Co-op Schemes:* BLDSC, ILL, JFR *Loans:* bks & audios/4 wks *Charges:* membship free to Douglas residents/ratepayers; £14 pa for other Isle of Man residents, £7 pa conc *Income Gen:* res/50p *Fines:* bks/ad 20p pd, ch & oap 10p pd *Equip:* Online: copier (A4/10p, A3/15p), 2 computers (incl internet)
Classn: DDC *Cat:* Type: author & classified *Medium:* auto *Auto Sys:* Heritage IV *Svcs:* Extramural: old people's homes
Staff: Libns: 1 Non-Prof: 4

Onchan

P211 Onchan Library
Willow House, 61-69 Main Rd, Onchan, Isle of Man, IM3 1AJ (01624-621228)
Email: onchan.library@onchan.org.im
Internet: http://www.onchan.org.im/

Local Auth: Onchan Dist Commissioners
Chief: Libn: Mrs Pamela Hand
Open: Mon-Wed, Fri 0930-1230, 1330-1700, Thu 0930-1230, 1400-1900, Sat 0930-1230, 1330-1630

Collns: Manx Colln (local studies); Manx Dyslexia Assoc Colln; minutes of Onchan Dist Commissioners public meetings; Tynwald Reports
Loans: bks/2 wks *Income Gen:* membship sub/Onchan residents £7.50 (oap £4.50), non-residents £12 (oap £7.50), students £2.50, ch £1 *Equip:* copier (A4/10p, A3/20p), fax, 2 computers (incl internet & wd-proc, internet £1 per 15 min), printer (10p b&w, 20p clr), scanner

Stock	1 Apr 2001
bks:	22752
audios:	662
videos:	400

Svcs: Info: careers info, tourist info *Activs:* ch's activs, temp exhibs, takes part in Natl Reading Challenge each summer
Staff: Libns: 1 Non-Prof: 3 part-time + 2 volunteers

Peel

P212 Ward Library
38 Castle St, Peel, Isle of Man, IM5 1AL (01624-843533)
Email: ward_library@hotmail.com

Local Auth: Peel Town Commissioners *Chief:* Libn: Mrs Carole Horton
Open: Mon, Wed 1400-1730, Fri 0930-1130, 1400-1800, Sat 1000-1200, 1400-1730 (closed Tue & Thu)
Collns: Manx Colln *Charges:* audios/free

Port Erin

P213 George Herdman Library
Bridson St, Port Erin, Isle of Man, IM9 6AL (01624-832365)
Email: gh_library@hotmail.com

Local Auth: Port Erin Town Commissioners
Chief: Libn: Miss A. Dryland
Open: Mon-Tue 1430-1700, Wed 1730-1930, Thu 1030-1230, Fri 1030-1230, 1430-1700, Sat 1000-1230

Ramsey

P214 Ramsey Town Library
Town Hall, Parliament Sq, Ramsey, Isle of Man, IM8 2LQ (01624-810146)
Email: rtc@mcb.net

Local Auth: Ramsey Town Commissioners
Pop: 7000 *Chief:* Libn: Mr Paul Boulton
Open: Mon-Sat 0900-1630
ILLs: natl *Loans:* all items/2 wks *Equip:* computer with internet (£1.50)
Classn: DDC *Cat:* Medium: auto *Auto Sys:* Heritage *Activs:* ch's activs

CHANNEL ISLANDS

Alderney

P215 Alderney Library
Island Hall, Royal Connaught Sq, Alderney, Channel Islands, GY9 3UE (01481-824178)

Local Auth: States of Alderney *Pop:* 2500
Cttee: Alderney Lib Cttee (voluntary org) *Chief:* contact the Chair of the Lib Cttee
Collns: Alderney hist; Island hist (bks & photos)
Co-op Schemes: liaison with Guernsey Guille-Alles Lib for bks, audios & videos *Loans:* bks, audios & videos/1 wk *Charges:* bks/20p; audios/40p; videos/£2 *Fines:* bks/ad 10p per wk, ch 5p per wk; audios/20p per wk; videos/£1 per wk
Acqs: Source: bksellers
Cat: Type: author, classified & title *Medium:* cards *Svcs:* Extramural: housebnd *Activs:* bk sales
Staff: Non-Prof: 42 volunteers
Proj: new purpose built lib with improved access, ref & ch's rooms & area for visually impaired

Guernsey

P216 Priaulx Library
Candie Rd, St Peter Port, Guernsey, Channel Islands, GY1 1UG (01481-721998; *fax:* 01481-713804)
Email: priaulx.library@gov.gg
Internet: http://www.gov.gg/priaulx/

Local Auth: States of Guernsey *Pop:* 80000
Cttee: Priaulx Lib Council *Chief:* Chief Libn: Mrs E.R. Harris MCLIP, CMS *Dep:* Snr Asst Rsrcher: Mrs J. Vidamour
Open: Mon-Sat 0930-1700
Collns: Channel Islands local hist; Guernsey shipowners & privateers; German occupation; local genealogical records (civil & ecclesiastical); local newspapers (1791-1994, some on m-film); local photos, prints, postcards & maps *ILLs:* county, natl & internatl *Loans:* bks/3 wks
Equip: 6 m-readers, 1 m-printer (50p), 2 copiers (A4/10p, A3/12p)

Stock	1 Apr 2000
all items:	c75000

Acqs: Source: bksellers *Offcr-in-Charge:* Chief Libn, as above
Classn: DDC *Cat:* Type: author, classified, subj & title *Medium:* auto *Auto Sys:* Talis *Svcs:* Info: some community info *Activs:* ch's activs, temp exhibs *Offcr-in-Charge:* Chief Libn, as above
Staff: Libns: 1 Non-Prof: 4
Proj: automation of lib catalogue & indexing sys using Talis

P217 Guille-Alles Library
Market St, St Peter Port, Guernsey, Channel Islands, GY1 1HB (01481-720392; *fax:* 01481-712425)
Email: ga@library.gg
Internet: http://www.library.gg/

Local Auth: States of Guernsey *Pop:* 80000
Cttee: Board of Mgmt, Guille-Alles Lib *Chief:* Principal Libn: Miss M.J. Falla BA, MA, MLib, MCLIP *Dep:* Dep Principal Libn: Miss L.B. Milligan BEd, MSc(Econ), DipLib, MCLIP
Open: Mon, Thu-Sat 0900-1700, Tue 1000-1700, Wed 0900-2000
Svc Pts: Other: SCHOOLS' LIB SVC, at same addr (01481-714098; fax: 01481-714436; email: sls@library.gg)
Collns: local studies colln *Co-op Schemes:* SWRLS, BLCMP *Loans:* bks & audios/3 wks; videos/1 wk *Charges:* audios/£10 sub for 2 years

Income Gen: req & res/40p; lost ticket/£1
Fines: bks & audios/ad 4p pd, ch 2p pd; videos/
4p pd *Equip:* 2 m-readers, m-printer (25p),
copier (A4 & A3/10p), computers (incl internet &
CD-ROM)
Acqs: Source: lib suppl & bksellers *Offcr-in-
Charge:* Principal Libn, as above
Classn: DDC *Cat: Type:* author, classified
Medium: auto *Auto Sys:* Talis *Svcs: Extramural:*
schools, prisons, hosps, old people's homes
Info: community *Activs:* ch's activs, bk sales,
temp exhibs
Staff: Libns: 7.5 *Non-Prof:* 23

Inc from:	2000
local govt:	£672728
fines etc:	£23610
total:	£700678

Exp on:	2000
bks:	£122750
AVs:	£11850
elec media:	£4500
salaries:	£470960
total:	£714605

Jersey

P218 Jersey Library
Halkett Pl, St Helier, Jersey, Channel Islands,
JE2 4WH (lending: 01534-759991; ref: 01534-
759992; *fax:* 01534-769444)
Email: jsylib@itl.net
Internet: http://www.jsylib.gov.je/

Local Auth: States of Jersey *Pop:* 87500
Cttee: Edu Cttee *Larger Dept:* Edu *Dept Chief:*
Dir of Edu: Mr Tom McKeon BEd, MBA, FRSA
Chief: Chief Libn: Mrs Maureen Corrigan MCLIP,
LLCM (m.corrigan03@jsylib.gov.je) *Dep:*
Principal Libn (Yng Peoples Svcs): Mrs Jaci
Graham MCLIP; Principal Libn (Info Svcs): Mrs
Sharon Jones BA, DipLib, MCLIP
Open: Mon, Wed-Fri 0930-1730, Tue 0930-1930,
Sat 0930-1600
Branch Libs: LES QUENNEVAIS BRANCH LIB,
Route Orange, St Brelade, Jersey, Channel
Islands (Mon-Fri 1400-1730, Sat 0930-1230) *Svc
Pts: Mobile:* 1
Collns: founder's colln; local studies colln *Co-
op Schemes:* SWRLS *ILLs:* county & natl
Loans: bks/4 wks; audios/2 wks; videos/1 wk
Income Gen: res/50p; lost ticket/ad £2, ch £1;
visitors ticket/£25 deposit; sale of withdrawn bks;
sale of phone cards *Fines:* bks/ad 5p pd, ch 2p
pd *Equip:* 4 m-readers, 4 m-printers (A4/20p), 3
copiers (A4/10p, A3/20p), 16 computers (incl wd-
proc, internet & CD-ROM) *Disabled:* Kurzweil,
Horizon CCTV
Acqs: Source: lib suppl, publ & bksellers *Offcr-
in-Charge:* Chief Libn, as above
Classn: DDC *Cat: Medium:* Auto *Auto Sys:*
Talis *Svcs: Extramural:* schools, prisons, old
people's homes, housebnd, day centres, play
groups *Info:* business info, careers info,
consumer info, legal info, travel info *Other:*
Online Learning, FCDC, LearnDirect *Activs:* ch's
activs, bk sales, temp exhibs, reading groups,
author visits *Offcr-in-Charge:* various offcrs
Enqs: 95590 (2000-01)
Staff: Libns: 7.5 *Non-Prof:* 21.86

Inc from:	2000-01
fines etc:	£33691

Exp on:	2000-01
bks:	£136000
elec media:	£55000
culture:	£5000
salaries:	£876992

Proj: Open Learning Centre in 2002

SECTION 3 – UK ARCHIVES AND LOCAL HISTORY

Entries are arranged alphabetically under town names. Institutions covered include governmental and local authority archives, local history and family history libraries and resources (both local authority and privately run), diocesan and other religious archives, museum archives, corporate archives and private archives.

Please note that many libraries also hold substantial archival and manuscript collections that are not listed in this section. See **Section 4 – UK Special Libraries**, or consult the **Index** for specific named collections.

Access to many archives and record offices is restricted, and entry may require an appointment in advance. Often identification will be required and a special need to use the collections will have to be demonstrated.

Telephone and fax numbers are given in the form of area dialling codes within the United Kingdom. To telephone the UK from outside the country, dial 00-44 followed by the number, minus the initial 0.

Entries are based on the institutions' responses to the following questions:

	1. **Official name of Institution**	*Svcs:*	15. **Services provided**
Type:	2. **Type of Institution** *(see also Key to Symbols below)*	*Stock:*	16. **Stock** *(give total quantities)*
	3. **Full postal address** *(incl. postcode)* Tel & fax numbers *(incl. STD code)*	archvs	**a)** Archives *(specify unit e.g., by linear, cubic metre)*
		rec mgmt	**b)** Records management holdings *(specify unit e.g., by linear, cubic metre)*
Email:	Electronic Mail	bks	**c)** Books *(incl bound periodicals)*
Internet:	Internet address	periodcls	**d)** Current periodical titles
Gov Body:	4. **Governing body** *(if any, e.g., local authority, university)*	photos	**e)** Photographs
		slides	**f)** Slides
		illusts	**g)** Illustrations
Chief:	5. **Officer in charge** *(give designation, name, qualifications & email address)*	pamphs	**h)** Pamphlets
		maps	**i)** Maps
Dep:	6. **Deputy** *(give designation, name, qualifications & email address)*	m-forms	**j)** Microforms
		audios	**k)** Audios
		videos	**l)** Videos
Other Snr Staff:	7. **Other Senior Staff** *(give designation, name, qualifications & email address)*	CD-ROMs	**m)** CD-ROMs
			n) Other *(please specify)*
Assoc Offices:	8. **Associate or Branch Offices** *(if any, give address, tel, fax & email address, plus designation, name & qualifications of officer in charge)*	*Acqs Offcr:*	**Officer in charge of stock acquisitions** *(give designation, name & email address)*
		Classn:	17. **Classification method(s) used** *(if applicable)*
Entry:	9. **Conditions for entry** *(e.g., reference only, advance appointment)*	*Auto Sys:*	18. **Automated Library system used** *(if any)*
Open:	10. **Opening hours** *(please use 24-hour clock, e.g., 0930-1730)*	*Pubns:*	19. **Publications** *(e.g., guides & handlists; give titles & prices)*
Subj:	11. **Main subjects covered** Geographical area, main types of archives covered	*Staff:*	20. **Staff establishment** *(give full-time equivalent for part-time staff incl. vacancies)* **Total number of:**
Collns:	12. **Special Collections** *(give subjects and brief details)*	*Archivists:*	**a)** Professional archivists
Bks & Pamphs:	**a)** Printed books & pamphlets	*Libns:*	**b)** Professional librarians
Archvs:	**b)** Archives	*Other Prof:*	**c)** Other professional staff
Other:	**c)** Other	*Non-Prof:*	**d)** Non-professional staff
Co-op Schemes:	13. **Co-operative schemes** *(in which institution participates, if any)*	*Exp:*	21. **Finance** *(expenditure on documents and/or books, incl. purchase & conservation)* **a)** 1999-2000 **b)** 2000-01
Equip:	14. **Equipment & facilities available to users** *(give numbers, and fees if appropriate)*	*Proj:*	22. **Capital projects** *(if any, starting in 2001 or 2002)*
Disabled:	**Equipment for disabled** *(e.g., Kurzweil)*	*Further Info:*	23. **Other Information**
Online:	**Online information services** *(e.g., Dialog; give fees)*		
Offcr-in-Charge:	**Officer in charge of equipment purchases** *(give designation, name & email address)*		

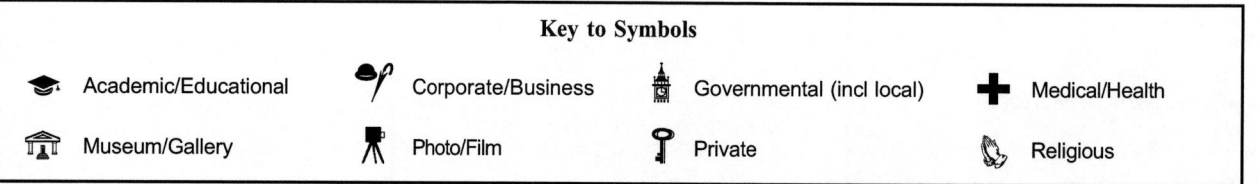

Key to Symbols

Academic/Educational   Corporate/Business   Governmental (incl local)   Medical/Health

Museum/Gallery   Photo/Film   Private   Religious

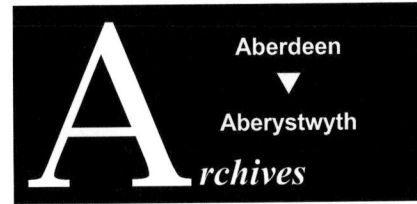

Aberdeen

A1 🗝

Aberdeen and North East Scotland Family History Society, Research Centre

158-164 King St, Aberdeen, AB24 5BD (01224-646323; *fax:* 01224-639096)
Email: enquiries@anesfhs.org.uk
Internet: http://www.anesfhs.org.uk/

Entry: rsrch centre open to membs; others on payment of a fee *Open:* Mon, Wed-Thu 1000-1600, Tue, Fri 1000-1600, 1900-2200, Sat 0900-1300; closed local & natl hols
Subj: NE Scotland: family hist; genealogy; church hist *Collns: Bks & Pamphs:* extensive collns on local & family hist *Archvs:* parish registers; census records (1881 census for whole of UK); poll bks for Aberdeenshire *Other:* OPR & IGI on m-film; monumental inscriptions & burial records (database of 60000+ entries); maps
Svcs: info, ref, rsrch (for membs, expenses charged)
Pubns: Soc Journal (quarterly, free to membs); Memorial Inscriptions series; Census Records series; Aberdeenshire Poll Bks series; Church Hist series; county & parish maps; many others
Staff: staffed by volunteers *Exp:* materials acquired as necessary

A2 🏛

Aberdeen City Archives

Town House, Aberdeen, AB10 1AQ (01224-522513; *fax:* 01224-522491)
Email: archives@legal.aberdeen.net.uk

Gov Body: Aberdeen City Council (see **P1**)
Chief: City Archivist: Miss Judith Cripps BA, DipAA
Assoc Offices: BRANCH OFFICE, Old Aberdeen House, Dunbar St, Aberdeen, AB24 3UJ (01224-481775; *fax:* 01224-495830)
Entry: adv appt *Open: Main Office:* Wed-Fri 0930-1630; *Branch Office:* Mon-Wed 0930-1300, 1400-1630
Subj: Aberdeen City & former Grampian Region (on behalf of new authorities): local authority archvs; parish records (city parishes only); estate archvs; business records *Collns: Archvs:* archvs of Aberdeen City Council & Aberdeenshire Council & predecessor authorities, incl the former Grampian Regional Archvs
Equip: m-reader, m-printer, 2 copiers, 2 computers (both with internet)
Classn: ISAD(G) *Pubns:* free info sheets
Staff: Archivists: 4 *Non-Prof:* 2

A3 🎓

Aberdeen University Historic Collections, Special Libraries and Archives

King's Coll, Aberdeen, AB24 3SW (01224-272598; *fax:* 01224-273891)
Email: speclib@abdn.ac.uk
Internet: http://www.abdn.ac.uk/diss/historic/speclib/

Gov Body: Univ of Aberdeen, Directorate of Info Systems & Svcs (see **S5**) *Chief:* Mgr: Dr Alan G. Knox BSc, PhD *Dep:* Reading Room Mgr: Mrs Jane Pirie MA
Entry: ref only, registration on arrival *Open:* Mon-Fri 0930-1630
Subj: NE Scotland: diocesan records; parish records; estate archvs; family papers; business records; personal papers; political papers; records of parent org; academic papers; historical papers; institutional records; genealogical papers; legal papers; local hist *Collns: Bks & Pamphs:* local colln; O'Dell Railway Colln; Cairngorm Club Lib; MacBean Jacobite Colln; Thomson Herald King Pamphs; Gregory Colln (early sci & medicine); Taylor Psalmody Colln; literary texts; sermons & liturgical texts *Archvs:* Univ of Aberdeen archvs (1860-date); archvs of predecessor colls: King's Coll (1495-1860); Marischal Coll (1593-1860); records of Episcopal Diocese of Aberdeen & Orkney; Duff House (Montcoffer) Papers; estate & family papers, incl: Arbuthnott; Keith of Kintore; Gordon of Cairness; Duff of Meldrum; Castle Fraser etc; papers of Thomas Reid (philosopher)
Other: George Washington Wilson Colln (glass plate negs); Aberdeen Harbour Board Colln (glass plate negs); musical compositions *Co-op Schemes:* Grampian Info
Equip: m-form reader/printers, copier (via staff), computers (incl internet & CD-ROM), UV lamp, light sheets *Svcs:* info, ref, photo reproduction
Stock: archvs/1410 linear m; rec mgmt/c360 linear m; bks/c150000 vols; periodcls/c50; photos/c48000; slides/c1000; illusts/c2000; pamphs/c25000; m-forms/c1700 film reels, c150 fiche; audios/c100; videos/10
Classn: DDC, fixed location & in-house classn
Auto Sys: Dynix, Clio
Pubns: Factsheet: Welcome to Special Collns & Archvs (free); Factsheet: 500 Years of Medicine (free); Univ of Aberdeen Historic Collns Newsletter (free); Rare & Fair: An Illustrated Hist of Aberdeen Univ Lib, by Colin McLaren (£2.99)
Staff: Libns: 3 *Other Prof:* 2 *Non-Prof:* 3

A4 ✚

Northern Health Services Archives

Aberdeen Royal Infirmary, Woolmanhill, Aberdeen, AB25 1LD (01224-663123)

Gov Body: Grampian Health Board *Chief:* Archivist: Miss Fiona Watson
Entry: by appt *Open:* Mon-Fri 0900-1700
Subj: Grampian & Highland area: local authority archvs (health function only); estate archvs; records of parent orgs & predecessor authorities
Collns: Bks & Pamphs: ref material: medical hist; NHS (incl Parliamentary acts, health svcs yearbks, medical registers, medical directories etc) *Archvs:* records of hosps & other health-related orgs in Grampian & Highland (1730s-date)
Co-op Schemes: Grampian Info, SCAN
Equip: m-reader, photocopies & photographic prints can be ordered
Stock: archvs/1500 ft; rec mgmt/500 ft; bks/50 ft
Pubns: The Hospitals of Peterhead (£1.50); Westburn Medical Group 1896-1996: A Practice Centenary (£3) *Staff: Other Prof:* 1

Aberystwyth

A5 🏛

Archifdy Ceredigion Archives

County Offices/Swyddfa'r Sir, Marine Terrace/Glan y Mor, Aberystwyth, Ceredigion, SY23 2DE (01970-633697; *fax:* 01970-633633)
Email: archives@ceredigion.gov.uk

Gov Body: Ceredigion County Council (see **P26**)
Chief: Archivist: Ms Helen Palmer BA, MA, DipAA
Entry: CARN ticket *Open:* Mon 1000-1300, 1400-1900, Tue-Fri 1000-1300, 1400-1600
Subj: Ceredigion (former Cardiganshire & part of Dyfed): local authority archvs; parish records (on m-film); estate archvs; family papers; business records *Collns: Archvs:* local govt records (County Councils, Rural Dist Councils, Urban Dist Councils, parishes, etc.); public records (Shipping Registers, Petty Sessions, Inland Revenue dist valuations, etc.); local newspapers; maps
Equip: 5 m-readers, m-printer, copier, computers (incl internet & CD-ROM) *Svcs:* info, rsrch
Stock: archvs/c130 cubic m; rec mgmt/c63 cubic m
Pubns: Genl Info leaflet (Welsh & English versions, free); Guide to Family Hist Sources at CRO (Welsh & English versions, free); An Introduction to Local Maps in Dyfed (25p); A Guide to Local Newspapers in Dyfed (25p); Parish Registers (25p)
Staff: Archivists: 2 *Non-Prof:* 2 *Exp:* £1000 (2000-01)

A6 🏛

National Monuments Record of Wales, Searchroom and Library

Royal Commission on the Ancient & Historical Monuments of Wales, Crown Bldg, Plas Crug, Aberystwyth, Ceredigion, SY23 1NJ (01970-621200; *fax:* 01970-627701)
Email: nmr.wales@rcahmw.org.uk
Internet: http://www.rcahmw.org.uk/

Gov Body: Royal Commission on the Ancient & Historical Monuments of Wales (RCAHMW)
Chief: Head of Info Mgmt: Mrs Hilary A. Malaws BLib, MIFA (hilary.malaws@rcahmw.org.uk)
Other Snr Staff: Head of Reader Svcs: Ms Tricia Moore (patricia.moore@rcahmw.org.uk); Archv Mgr: Mr Gareth Edwards (gareth.edwards@rcahmw.org.uk)
Entry: adv appt advised *Open:* Mon-Fri 0930-1600 (reduced svc 1300-1400) excl bank hols
Subj: Wales & adjacent territorial waters; records of RCAHMW; mainly modern records from many sources relating to archaeo, arch & hist *Collns: Bks & Pamphs:* 19C-early 20C eng bks; Welsh section of OS Archaeo Lib; A.H.A. Hogg Colln (bks, journals & offprints) *Archvs:* Welsh section of former Natl Bldgs Record; Welsh section of former OS Archaeo Div records; OS Colln (archaeo record cards covering 25000 sites, sketches, plans, photos etc); R.E. Kray Colln (archaeo notebks); excavation records (incl drawings, photos & slides); *Other:* Air Photo Collns (incl RAF & OS from 1940s onwards, Royal Commission from 1986, CUCAP pre-1980); Map Collns (mainly OS, incl original surveyors' copies); PSA Drawings Colln (5000 items); Arthur Chater Colln (photos of Cardiganshire sites & monuments, incl gravestone inscriptions); Rokeby Colln of Railway Photos
Equip: m-reader, photo svcs, computer (with wd-proc, internet & CD-ROM) *Online:* new web site being launched with email enq facility *Svcs:* assistance available in Welsh or English
Stock: archvs/270 linear m; rec mgmt/10 linear m; bks/12000 (incl guides & periodcls); photos/c250000; illusts/40000 drawings; maps/30000
Pubns: Cofnod (newsletter, for RCAHMW); Annual Report (for RCAHMW); NMRW Guide; various RCAHMW pubns
Staff: Other Prof: 3.5 *Non-Prof:* 1
See also NATL MONUMENTS RECORD (**A483**) & NATL MONUMENTS RECORD OF SCOTLAND (**A151**)

Welsh Political Archive

See NATL LIB OF WALES (**L3**)

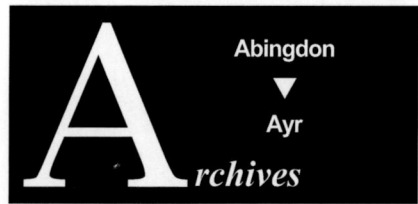

Abingdon
▼
Ayr

Abingdon

A7 🔑

St Peter's College, Radley, Archives
Radley Coll, Abingdon, Oxfordshire, OX14 2HR
(01235-543078; *fax:* 01235-543106)
Email: aem@radley.org.uk

Chief: Archivist: Mr A.E. Money MA
Entry: adv appt *Open:* Mon-Fri 0930-1730
during school terms
Subj: Radley Coll: estate archvs, some pre-1847
(founded); school records *Collns: Bks &
Pamphs:* school registers; hists; school magazine
(1864-date); bks written by founder Rev William
Sewell *Archvs:* diaries; letters home; files on
indiv boys/old boys; socs/games/punishment
bks; papers relating to wardens (Headmasters)
from foundation in 1847; files on chapel & other
bldgs; photo albums of various dates; lib of bks
by old Radleians *Other:* videos; BBC TV series
"Public School" 1980
Equip: fax, copier
Stock: archvs/40 linear m; rec mgmt/13 linear m
Pubns: Looking at Radley (£3); Football at
Radley (£3); Manly & Muscular Diversions: Public
Schools & the 19th Century Sporting Revival
(£14.99)

Alderley Edge

A8 🔑

Family History Society of Cheshire, Library and Research Centre
Festival Hall, Talbot Rd, Alderley Edge, Cheshire
(01625-599722)
Email: info@fhsc.org.uk
Internet: http://www.fhsc.org.uk/

Chief: Libn: Ms Lyn McCulloch *Dep:* Dep Libn:
Ms Sue Ritchie
Entry: membs of Soc only; non-membs can join
on arrival *Open:* Mon-Fri 1000-1600, Sat-Sun by
arrangement only; occasional late opening
Subj: Cheshire: local studies; family hist;
genealogy *Collns: Bks & Pamphs:* bks on local
hist; local directories; rsrch guides; monumental
inscriptions; journals of other Family Hist Socs
Archvs: 1881 census returns for England &
Wales; Indexes to Births, Marriages & Deaths for
England & Wales (1837-1900) *Other:* on m-form:
IGI; British Isles Genealogical Register; Bertram
Merrel Marriage Index (also on CD-ROM); 1891
census indexes (other census indexes also on
CD-ROM); trade directories; parish registers
Equip: 10 m-fiche readers, 6 m-film readers, m-
fiche printer, copier, 3 computers

Aldershot

A9 🏛🏛

Aldershot Military Museum, Library and Archives
Queens Ave, Aldershot, Hampshire, GU11 2LG
(01252-314598; *fax:* 01252-342942)
Email: museums@hants.gov.uk
Internet: http://www.hants.gov.uk/museum/
aldershot/

Type: local govt *Gov Body:* Hampshire County
Council (see **P60**) *Chief:* Curator: Mr Ian Maine
BA(Hons), MA
Assoc Offices: HAMPSHIRE COUNTY
COUNCIL MUSEUMS SVC LIB (see **A508**)
Entry: adv appt advisable *Open:* Mon-Fri 1000-
1700
Subj: Aldershot & Farnborough: local hist;
military hist *Collns: Bks & Pamphs:* pubns
relating to local & military hist of Aldershot &
Farnborough *Archvs:* listings of regiments &
corps (1856-1939, except WW1); some burial
records for Aldershot Military Cemetery; correspondence relating to Aldershot *Other:* oral hist
recordings; photographic colln (incl postcards,
albums & slides, 1850s-date); maps & plans
(1890s onwards); printed ephemera
Equip: copier
Stock: archvs/5000; various bks, maps & videos

Alloa

A10 🏛

Clackmannan Archives
26-28 Drysdale St, Alloa, Clackmannanshire,
FK10 1JL (01259-722262; *fax:* 01259-219469)
Email: libraries@clacks.gov.uk
Internet: http://www.clacksweb.org.uk/dyna/
archives/

Gov Body: Clackmannanshire Council (see **P28**)
Chief: Info Libn & Archivist: Mr Ian Murray
MA(Hons), DipLib, DipAA, MCLIP (imaurray@
clacks.gov.uk)
Entry: deliveries from archv store twice per
weekday; archv open on Sats but material must
be requested in adv *Open:* Mon, Wed-Fri 0930-
1900 (-1715 Thu-Fri in summer), Tue 0930-1630,
Sat 0900-1230
Subj: Clackmannanshire: local authority archvs;
family papers; business records; records of
parent org; records of local voluntary orgs
Collns: Bks & Pamphs: Walter Murray Local
Studies Colln; local business directories & journals
Archvs: records of Clackmannanshire Council &
predecessors (1660s onwards); private deposits
held incl: Alloa Grain Market records (1850-85);
Hunter & Donaldson records (textile firm, 1877-
1959); Glenochil Distillery records (1858-1949);
Clackmannan Agricultural Soc records (1886-
1964); Loyal Order of Ancient Shepherds records
(c1945-51); Alloa Allotments Assoc records (1909-
98); Tillicoultry Golf Club records (1899-1987);
Tullibody Poor Fund records (from 1704); Haig of
Dollarfield Papers (1768-1839); Bayne Family of
Kincardine Papers (1713-1972); Clackmannanshire
deeds & titles *Other:* parish registers (on m-film);
local newspapers (1840s-date, mainly on m-film);
map colln; arch plans (1849-c1904)
Equip: copier, clr copier, 15 computers (all with
wd-proc & internet, 2 with CD-ROM)
Stock: archvs/600 linear ft; rec mgmt/1200
linear ft
Staff: Archivists: 1 *Non-Prof:* 1

Alnwick

A11 🔑

Alnwick Castle Archives
Estates Office, Alnwick Castle, Alnwick,
Northumberland, NE66 1NQ (01665-602207/2068)

Chief: Collns Mgr: Ms Clare Baxter
Entry: adv appt only; please note that
uncatalogued papers & papers less than 100
years old are not available for rsrch
Subj: estate archvs; family papers *Collns:
Archvs:* estate, family & personal papers of the
Percy family (Dukes of Northumberland); papers
of other indivs associated with the family &
estate; some estate papers relating to the Russell

family (Dukes of Bedford) & Seymour family
(Dukes of Somerset); some deeds & papers
relating to Nevill family (Barons Latimer); for full
details refer to Principal Family & Estate Archvs
(Historical Manuscripts Commission, 1999)

Alton

A12 🏛🏛

Curtis Museum, Resource Room
High St, Alton, Hampshire, GU34 1BA (01420-
82802)
Internet: http://www.hants.gov.uk/museums/

Type: local authority *Gov Body:* Hampshire
County Council (see **P60**) *Chief:* Curator: Mr
Tony Cross
Assoc Offices: HAMPSHIRE COUNTY
COUNCIL MUSEUMS SVC LIB (see **A508**)
Entry: adv appt advised *Open:* Tue-Sat 1000-
1700
Subj: Alton & surrounding area: local hist
Pubns: Alton Papers (annual local hist pubn, £3)

Altrincham

A13 🏛

Trafford Local Studies Centre
Altrincham Lib, 20 Stamford New Rd, Altrincham,
Cheshire, WA14 1EJ (0161-912-1669)
Email: trafflocals@trafford.gov.uk

Gov Body: Trafford Metropolitan Borough
Council (see **P189**) *Chief:* Local Studies Libn: Ms
Pat Southern MPhil, MCLIP *Dep:* Supervisor:
Mrs Karen Cliff
Entry: Local Studies: no restrictions; *Archvs:* adv
appt, giving 24 hrs notice; booking sys for m-
readers *Open:* Mon, Wed, Fri 1000-1700, Tue,
Thu 1000-1930, Sat 1000-1600
Subj: Trafford Metropolitan Borough Council:
local authority archvs; diocesan & parish records
(on m-form); records of parent org; business
records (a few); records of local orgs; local hist
Collns: Bks & Pamphs: local hist bks & pamphs
Archvs: archvs of Trafford Metropolitan Borough
Council & predecessor authorities (19C onwards);
rate bks (from 1836) *Other:* maps & photos
Equip: m-readers, m-printer, fax, copier, public
access computers
Stock: archvs/6000; periodcls/40; m-forms/5000;
videos/100; CD-ROMs/35; AVs/35
Staff: Libns: 1 *Non-Prof:* 2.5 *Exp:* £7500 (2000-
01)
Further Info: Trafford Local Studies will be
based at Altrincham Lib while Sale Lib is being
rebuilt & refurbished

Andover

A14 🏛🏛

Andover Museum, Local Studies Room
6 Church Cl, Andover, Hampshire, SP10 1DP
(01264-366283; *fax:* 01264-339152)
Email: andover.museum@virgin.net
Internet: http://www.hants.gov.uk/museum/
andoverm/

Type: local govt *Gov Body:* Hampshire County
Council (see **P60**) *Chief:* Curator: Mr David Allen
Assoc Offices: HAMPSHIRE COUNTY
COUNCIL MUSEUMS SVC LIB (see **A508**)
Entry: adv appt *Open:* Tue-Sat 1000-1700
Subj: Andover: local hist; archaeo; nat hist
Collns: Bks & Pamphs: pubns relating to local
hist *Other:* maps, photos & videos
Staff: Other Prof: 1 *Non-Prof:* 3 *Exp:* £75
(2000-01)

 academic   corporate

 governmental   ➕ medical

Armagh

A15

Armagh County Museum, Archives

The Mall East, Armagh, BT61 9BE (028-3752-3070; *fax:* 028-3752-2631)
Email: acm.um@nics.gov.uk
Internet: http://www.magni.org.uk/

Gov Body: Museums & Galleries of Northern Ireland *Chief:* Curator: Ms Catherine McCullough MA, DipMan *Dep:* Dep Curator: Dr Greer Ramsey PhD, DipMan *Other Snr Staff:* Picture Lib Mgr: Ms Patricia McLean
Entry: adv appt; ref only *Open:* Mon-Fri 1000-1700, Sat 1000-1300, 1400-1700
Subj: Ulster, esp Co Armagh: local hist; personal papers *Collns: Bks & Pamphs:* Blacker Day Bks Colln (1798-1837) *Archvs:* Archv of Mr T.G.F. Paterson, 1st Curator of ACM, entitled 'Armachiana'; MSS Colln of George (AE) Russell (1867-1935, philosopher, artist, theosophist) *Other:* railway photos; maps; cuttings
Svcs: info, ref, rsrch
Pubns: Guide to ACM (free); Harvest Home: A Sample of the Collected Writings of T.G.F. Paterson
Staff: Sec & 3 warding staff

A16

Cardinal Tomás Ó Fiaich Memorial Library and Archive

(incorporating the Archvs of the RC Archdiocese of Armagh)
15 Moy Rd, Armagh, Co Armagh, BT61 7LY (028-3752-2981; *fax:* 028-3751-1944)
Email: ofiaichlibrary@btinternet.com

Gov Body: Trustees of The Cardinal Tomás Ó Fiaich Memorial Lib & Archv *Chief:* Libn: Mr Crónán Ó Doibhlin BA, MLib
Entry: letter of introduction required for some collns *Open:* Mon-Fri 0930-1300, 1400-1700
Subj: Ireland, particularly the North & the Diocese of Armagh: diocesan records; parish records; personal papers; Irish lang; Irish-European links; Irish Church hist; Irish hist; Irish games *Collns: Bks & Pamphs:* Lib of Cardinal Tomás Ó Fiaich *Archvs:* Armagh Catholic Diocese, diocesan & parish records; correspondence & other papers of Archbishops of Armagh (1787-1963); papers of Cardinal Tomás Ó Fiaich (1923-1990); Overseas Archv (papers relating to the Irish in Europe); papers of Micheline Kerney Walsh (former Dir of Overseas Archvs at Univ Coll Dublin) *Other:* photos relating to the careers of various Archbishops; O'Kane Colln of Audio-Tapes relating to Northern participants in the Irish War of Independence; newscuttings relating to careers of Archbishops *Co-op Schemes:* partnership with Univ Coll Dublin (see **IS148**)
Equip: copier, fax, computer (incl wd-proc), lecture hall for hire *Svcs:* info, ref, rsrch
Stock: archvs/455 linear m; bks/20000; periodcls/450; photos/4 linear m; maps/10 linear m; audios/15 linear m; videos/5 linear m
Classn: DDC *Staff: Libns:* 2 *Non-Prof:* 1

A17

Southern Education and Library Board, Irish and Local Studies Library

39c Abbey St, Armagh, BT61 7EB (028-3752-7851; *fax:* 028-3752-6879)
Email: mary.mcveigh@selb.org
Internet: http://www.selb.org/

Gov Body: Southern Edu & Lib Board (see **P134**)
Chief: Irish Studies Libn: Ms Mary McVeigh
Entry: ref only *Open:* Mon, Wed-Fri 0930-1300, 1400-1700, Tue 1400-1700

Subj: Ireland & SELB area (Co Armagh & parts of adjoining counties): local hist; Irish hist; geog; church hist; local arts & lit; Irish politics *Collns: Bks & Pamphs:* political pamphs (17C-20C); Parliamentary Papers (19C); local directories (early 19C-date) *Other:* Lawrence Colln (Irish photos, late 19C-early 20C); arch guides & plans; maps; local newspapers
Svcs: info, ref *Staff:* 3

Ashby-de-la-Zouch

A18

Ashby-de-la-Zouch Museum, Archives

North St, Ashby-de-la-Zouch, Leicestershire, LE65 5HU (01530-560090)

Gov Body: Trustees of Ashby-de-la-Zouch Museum (charitable status) *Chief:* Chairman: Mr Kenneth A. Hillier MA *Dep:* Hon Archivist: Mr D.J.H. Jackson
Open: Easter-Sep: Mon-Fri 1000-1300, 1400-1600, Sat 1000-1600, Sun 1400-1600; closed Oct-Easter but open by prior appt
Subj: Ashby-de-la-Zouch & dist: local hist; family papers *Collns: Bks & Pamphs:* local hist & topography colln *Archvs:* comprehensive archvs about Ashby-de-la-Zouch; part of Beaumont papers (Coleorton Hall); incomplete court records from 18C *Other:* extensive photographic archv of town
Equip: 2 m-readers, video viewer, computer (with wd-proc & CD-ROM) *Svcs:* info, ref
Pubns: Lord Loughborough, Ashby & the Civil War (75p); Ashby Girls Grammar School 1889-1989 (£2); Packington School: A History (£2); Napoleonic Prisoners of War in Ashby-de-la-Zouch (£5.95)
Staff: 40 PT volunteers

Aylesbury

A19

Centre for Buckinghamshire Studies

(incorporating the former Buckinghamshire Record Office & Buckinghamshire Local Studies Lib)
County Hall, Walton St, Aylesbury, Buckinghamshire, HP20 1UU (01296-382587; *fax:* 01296-382771)
Email: archives@buckscc.gov.uk
Internet: http://www.buckscc.gov.uk/archives/

Gov Body: Buckinghamshire County Council (see **P19**) *Chief:* County Archivist: Mr R.T. Bettridge BA, DipAS
Assoc Offices: LOCAL STUDIES DESK, at above addr (01296-382250; *email:* localstudies@buckscc.gov.uk); further local studies collns are held at: BUCKINGHAM LIB, Verney Cl, Buckingham, MK18 1JP (01280-813229; *fax:* 01280-823597; *email:* lib-buc@buckscc.gov.uk); CHESHAM LIB, Elgiva Ln, Chesham, Buckinghamshire, HP5 2JD (01494-772322; *fax:* 01494-773074; *email:* lib-che@buckscc.gov.uk); HIGH WYCOMBE LIB, Queen Victoria Rd, High Wycombe, Buckinghamshire, HP11 1BD (01494-464004; *fax:* 01494-533086; *email:* lib-hiw@buckscc.gov.uk)
Entry: CARN ticket for Archv Searchroom; adv booking also required for Archvs & for m-readers in Local Studies *Open:* Mon, Wed, Fri 0900-1730, Tue, Thu 0900-2000, Sat 0900-1600; Archv Searchroom closes 15 minutes earlier
Subj: historic County of Buckinghamshire: local authority archvs; diocesan records; parish records; estate archvs; family papers; business records; personal papers; political papers; records of parent org; nonconformist records; hosp records; solicitors records; school records;

police records; other public records; local studies; family hist *Collns: Bks & Pamphs:* comprehensive colln of printed bks on the hist of Buckinghamshire; trade directories *Archvs:* archvs of Buckinghamshire County Council (1889 onwards); Quarter Sessions records (1678-1889); records of Borough, Dist & Parish Councils; records of Poor Law Unions; records of Bucks Constabulary; Diocese of Oxford records (Archdeaconry of Buckingham) *Other:* materials on m-film or m-fiche (e.g., IGI, Natl Probate Index, census returns, parish registers); small misc collns of printed ephemera & auction sales particulars; local newspapers; map colln; photo colln *Co-op Schemes:* joint arrangement with Milton Keynes Council
Equip: 10 m-readers, 16 m-form reader/printers (40p per sheet), copier (A4/10p, A3/20p), 6 computers (all with CD-ROM, 3 with wd-proc & 3 with internet) *Disabled:* wheelchair access
Online: Family Search, 1881 Census, Vital Records, Natl Burial Index *Svcs:* info, rsrch
Stock: archvs/c275 cubic m
Classn: ISAD(G) *Auto Sys:* DS
Pubns: Buckinghamshire Sessions Records (various); The Buckinghamshire Sheriffs; Buckinghamshire Record Soc pubns; other items too numerous to mention incl maps; see web site for details
Staff: Archivists: 5.3 *Libns:* 1 *Other Prof:* 2 *Non-Prof:* 9.3

Ayr

A20

Ayrshire Archives

The Ayrshire Archvs Centre, Craigie Est, Ayr, KA8 0SS (01292-287584; *fax:* 01292-284918)
Email: archives@south-ayrshire.gov.uk
Internet: http://www.south-ayrshire.gov.uk/archives/ or http://www.ayrshirearchives.org.uk/

Gov Body: South Ayrshire Council (see **P167**), North Ayrshire Council (see **P124**) & East Ayrshire Council (see **P44**) *Chief:* Archivist: Mr Kevin Wilbraham MA, DipAA, FSA(Scot) *Dep:* Asst Archivist: Dr Christine Lodge BA(Hons), MA, PhD, DipAA
Entry: adv appt preferred *Open:* Tue-Thu 1000-1300, 1400-1630
Subj: Ayrshire: local authority archvs; parish records; estate archvs; family papers; business records; political papers; educational records; Church of Scotland records for Ayrshire; customs & excise records; health records; court records *Collns: Archvs:* archvs of South, East & North Ayrshire Councils & predecessors; records of Commissioners of Supply, incl minute bks (1713-1929); cttee minute bks (1854-1910); police cttee minute bks (1841-1890); abstracts of revenue & exp (1856-1890); lists of commissioners (1857-1898); valuation rolls (1705-1837); record of income & property appeals (1843-1895); Commissioners of the County Bldgs (1805-1900); Highway Authorities (1767-1883); Poorhouse records; records of School Boards & Edu Trusts; Parochial Board records; Customs & Excise records (1729-1975); Justice of the Peace records (1838-1975); Ayrshire & Arran Health Board records (1859-1972); Medical Offcr health reports; Kirk Session records (1615-1983); Earl of Glasgow correspondence & papers (1892-1918); Welbeck Estates (7th Duke of Portland) incl maps, mainly of NE Ayrshire (1798-1900); John MacIntosh, Architect (arch, 1863-1934); Dunlop of Doonside (1749-1874); Cunninghame of Auchen-harvie (1584-1954); Holms Estate (1860-1931); Fairlie Papers (1857-1930); Woodburn family papers (1795-1903); Kennedy of Kirkmichael (1432-1882); David Cathcart, Lord Alloway (correspondence, 1789-1828); Howieson-Crawford (family correspondence, 1830-1932);

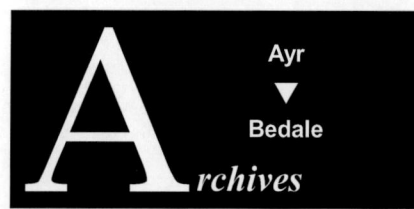

Archives

Ayr ▼ Bedale

(Ayrshire Archvs cont)
Collns: *Archvs (cont):* Brackenridge & Graham, Solicitors (various records); Independent Order of Rechabites, Galston (1885-1948); misc deeds *Other:* misc maps, incl turnpike & parish road systems (1852); maps & plans of coalworkings & railways (1841-1909) **Equip:** 2 m-readers, copier, 2 computers (both with wd-proc, internet & CD-ROM) **Classn:** MAD2, ISAD(G) & ISAAR(CPF) **Pubns:** Guide to Centre; Annual Report; info sheets **Staff:** *Archivists:* 2 *Non-Prof:* 3

A21
South Ayrshire Scottish and Local History Library
1st Floor, Carnegie Lib, 12 Main St, Ayr, KA8 8EB (01292-286385; *fax:* 01292-611593)
Email: localhistory@south-ayrshire.gov.uk
Internet: http://www.south-ayrshire.gov.uk/libraries/localhistory.htm

Gov Body: South Ayrshire Council (see **P167**)
Chief: Carnegie Libn: Mrs Jeanette Castle BA, MCLIP (jeanette.castle@south-ayrshire.gov.uk)
Assoc Offices: local authority & other archvs held at AYRSHIRE ARCHVS (see **A20**)
Entry: open to public, ref only **Open:** Mon-Tue, Thu-Fri 0900-1930, Wed, Sat 0900-1700
Subj: Scotland, Ayr & Ayrshire: local hist; family hist; genealogy; parish records; census records
Collns: *Bks & Pamphs:* bks & pamphs relating to Ayrshire; trade directories (1820s onwards); family hists; Robert Burns Colln; John Galt Colln *Other:* electoral rolls (1882-date); valuation rolls (Ayrshire, from 1899); Ayrshire parish registers (on m-film, 1624 onwards); census returns (1841-1901); Index of Wills for Scotland (1876-1936, 1948-1959); Indexes to Register of Sasines (1599-1609, 1617-60, 1781-1868); Retours & Svcs of Heirs (1544-1699); IGI (on m-fiche); photo colln; extensive map colln (Ayrshire, 1600 onwards); local newspapers (on m-film); monumental inscriptions
Equip: 3 m-readers, copier, 2 computers (with internet & CD-ROM) **Svcs:** info, ref, enq svc (fees vary)
Pubns: numerous pubns, prints & maps

Badminton

A22
Badminton Muniments
Badminton House, Badminton, S Gloucestershire, GL9 1DB (01454-218202/3; *fax:* 01454-218221)

Chief: Archivist: Mrs M.E. Richards MA
Assoc Offices: estate records prior to 1900 are deposited at GLOUCESTERSHIRE RECORD OFFICE (see **A185**)
Entry: by adv appt **Open:** Mon-Fri 0900-1700
Subj: Badminton: estate records; family papers
Collns: *Archvs:* records of Badminton estate (from 1900 onwards); papers & household records of Somerset family, Dukes of Beaufort
Equip: copier **Svcs:** info, rsrch
Stock: archvs/80 linear m; rec mgmt/40 linear m
Classn: own **Staff:** *Archivists:* 1

Ballymena

A23
North Eastern Education and Library Board, Local Studies Service
Ballymena Lib, 25-31 Demesne Ave, Ballymena, Co Antrim, N Ireland, BT43 7BG (028-2566-4125; *fax:* 028-2563-2038)
Email: local.studies@neelb.org.uk
Internet: http://www.neelb.org.uk/

Gov Body: NE Edu & Lib Board (see **P133**)
Chief: Local Studies Development Offcr: Ms Yvonne Hirst BEd, PGDipLIS (yvonne.hirst@neelb.org.uk)
Assoc Offices: smaller local studies collns are held at: CARRICKFERGUS LIB, 2 Joymount Ct, Carrickfergus, Co Antrim, BT38 7DQ (028-9336-2261; *fax:* 028-9336-0589; *email:* Carrickfergus.Library@neelb.org.uk); COLERAINE LIB, Queen St, Coleraine, Co Londonderry, BT52 1BE (028-7034-2561; *fax:* 028-7034-2561; *email:* Coleraine.Library@neelb.org.uk); & other local libs throughout the region
Entry: ref only **Open:** Mon, Thu-Fri 1000-2000, Tue-Wed 1000-1730, Sat 1000-1700
Subj: Co Antrim & Co Londonderry: local authority archvs; some school records; local studies; Irish hist & geog; family hist **Collns:** *Bks & Pamphs:* comprehensive range of local hist materials; journals of local historical socs; Irish historical & geographical journals *Archvs:* Borough Council minutes; Board of Guardian records (m-film); Grand Jury Presentments; Griffiths Valuation *Other:* census & statistical returns; local newspapers (m-film & bnd); photos & postcards; map colln (incl 1830 & 1857 OS & Griffiths Valuation maps)
Equip: 2 m-form reader/printers, copier, 4 computers (all with internet, access free to NEELB membs) **Disabled:** lift **Online:** access to the Ulster American Folk Park database **Svcs:** info, ref, rsrch, talks, workshops
Stock: archvs/c15000; photos/2000; maps/3000; m-forms/3200 **Acq Offcr:** Local Studies Development Offcr, as above
Classn: DDC (mod) **Auto Sys:** Talis, moving to Galaxy shortly

Bangor, *Gwynedd*

A24
Archive of Traditional Welsh Music
School of Music, Univ of Wales Bangor, College Rd, Bangor, Gwynedd, LL57 2DG (01248-382182)
Email: w.thomas@bangor.ac.uk
Internet: http://www.bangor.ac.uk/music/WMI/Archive.html

Gov Body: Univ of Wales Bangor & Welsh Arts Council **Chief:** Dir: Mr Wyn Thomas
Entry: ref only **Open:** Mon-Fri 0900-1700
Subj: Wales: ethnomusicology; music; folk music **Collns:** *Other:* commercial & field recordings of Welsh traditional music; oral recordings
Equip: copier (A4/7p, A3/14p), fax, video viewer, field tape recorders, turntables, minidisc recorders, DAT recorders **Svcs:** ref, rsrch
Acq Offcr: Dir, as above

A25
University of Wales Bangor, Department of Archives and Manuscripts
Main Lib, College Rd, Bangor, Gwynedd, LL57 2DG (01248-382966; *fax:* 01248-382979)
Email: issc04@bangor.ac.uk
Internet: http://www.bangor.ac.uk/is/library/archives.html

Gov Body: Univ of Wales Bangor (see **S76**)
Chief: Archivist: Mr Einion Wyn Thmoas BA, DipAA **Dep:** Asst Archivist: Miss Elen Wyn Hughes DipAA **Other Snr Staff:** Archivist's Assistant/Conservator: Miss Diana Clarke; Archvs Data Offcr: Ms Anne Lenaghan
Entry: upon entering name & addr in Register of Readers; access to Univ records only with permission of head of depositing dept **Open:** Mon-Fri 0900-1300, 1400-1700
Subj: North Wales: local hist & topography (13C-20C); records of parent org **Collns:** *Archvs:* archvs of UWB *Other:* MSS & printed maps
Stock: archvs/1850 linear m
Staff: *Archivists:* 2 *Non-Prof:* 1

Barnsley

A26
Barnsley Archives and Local Studies
Central Lib, Shambles St, Barnsley, S Yorkshire, S70 2JF (01226-773950; *fax:* 01226-773955)
Email: archives@barnsley.gov.uk
Internet: http://www.barnsley.gov.uk/

Gov Body: Barnsley Metropolitan Borough Council (see **P6**) **Chief:** Archvs & Local Studies Offcr: Ms Louise Whitworth MArAd **Dep:** Local Studies Libn: Mr M. Hepworth MCLIP; Snr Archvs Asst: Mrs G. Nixon
Entry: ref only **Open:** Mon, Wed 0930-1800, Tue, Fri 0930-1730, Sat 1000-1300
Subj: Barnsley area: local authority archvs; parish records; estate archvs; family papers; business records; nonconformist records; school records; records of local socs; local hist **Collns:** *Bks & Pamphs:* local hist bks (incl theses & dissertations); local pubns *Archvs:* archvs of Barnsley Metropolitan Borough Council & pre-decessors; papers of Lord Mason (former local Labour MP & Cabinet Minister); valuations of house contents (1829-1965); wills & deeds *Other:* local newspapers (mainly on m-film); census returns (m-forms); IGI for northern counties of England & Ireland; photos; OS & other maps **Co-op Schemes:** South Yorkshire Joint Archv Svc, with Doncaster (see **A124**), Rotherham (see **A438**) & Sheffield (see **A452**)
Equip: 10 m-readers, m-printer, copier, computer (with wd-proc, internet & CD-ROM) **Svcs:** info, ref
Stock: archvs/2556 linear m; bks/42499 (incl periodcls & pamphs); photos/11823 (incl illusts); slides/1696; maps/2537; m-forms/19537; audios/65; videos/19; CD-ROMs/6; posters/33
Classn: ISAD(G) **Auto Sys:** Dynix
Pubns: Family Hist Handbook (£3.50); Family Hist Starter Pack (£2.50)
Staff: *Archivists:* 1 *Libns:* 1 *Non-Prof:* 2.8 **Exp:** £2300 (2000-01)

Barnstaple

A27
North Devon Record Office
North Devon Local Studies Centre, Tuly St, Barnstaple, Devon, EX31 1EL (01271-388607; *fax:* 01271-388608)
Email: ndevrec@devon.gov.uk
Internet: http://www.devon.gov.uk/dro/

Gov Body: Devon County Council (see **P37**)
Chief: Snr Archivist: Mr T. Wormleighton
Assoc Offices: branch of DEVON RECORD OFFICE (see **A161**); office is one of 4 partners in the North Devon Local Studies Centre, along with: NORTH DEVON LOCAL STUDIES LIB (*email:* barnloc@devon.gov.uk); NORTH DEVON ATHENAEUM LIB (see **S88**); BEAFORD PHOTO-GRAPHIC ARCHV; all at above addr

Entry: CARN ticket or proof of ID; search room charge (with certain exemptions) **Open:** Mon-Tue, Thu-Fri 0930-1700, Wed 0930-1300, 2nd & 4th Sat of the month 0930-1600
Subj: Barnstaple & North Devon: local authority archvs; parish records; estate archvs; family papers; business records; personal papers **Collns:** Archvs: Barnstaple Borough Archvs; parish records (Archdeaconry of Barnstaple); estate collns; Dist Council records; school records etc for North Devon **Other:** Beaford Photographic Archv holds c10000 old photos of the North Devon & Torridge areas & more recent work by James Ravilious
Equip: 9 m-readers, copier, clr copier, video viewer, room for hire **Svcs:** info, ref, rsrch
Stock: archvs/800 linear m **Classn:** ISAD(G)
Staff: Archivists: 2 Non-Prof: 1

Barrow-in-Furness

A28
Cumbria Record Office and Local Studies Library, Barrow

140 Duke St, Barrow-in-Furness, Cumbria, LA14 1XW (01229-894363; fax: 01229-894364)
Email: barrow.record.office@cumbriacc.gov.uk
Internet: http://www.cumbria.gov.uk/archives/

Gov Body: Cumbria County Council (see **P32**)
Chief: Area Archivist: Mr A.C.J. Jones MA, DipAA, DMS **Other Snr Staff:** Asst Archivist: Miss E. Mullineaux BA, DipAA; Local Studies Libn: Mr G.A. Lang MA
Assoc Offices: branch office of CUMBRIA RECORD OFFICE, CARLISLE (see **A98**)
Entry: CARN ticket for Archvs, none for Local Studies collns **Open:** Archvs: Mon-Fri 0900-1700, also Wed 1700-1900 & Sat 0930-1600 by appt only; Local Studies: Mon-Wed, Fri 0930-1900, Thu 0930-1700, Sat 0930-1600
Subj: mainly SW Cumbria (Barrow-in-Furness, Dalton-in-Furness, Ulverston, Millom & surrounding villages): local authority archvs; diocesan records; parish records; estate archvs; family papers; business records; personal papers; political papers; records of parent org; local hist; topography **Collns:** Bks & Pamphs: Imperial War Graves Commission (printed registers relating to cemeteries of WW1); pubns of many local antiquarian socs; genl printed sources, chiefly for the hist & topography of the Furness area
Archvs: Diocese of Carlisle records (Barrow area); Vickers Shipbuilding & Eng Ltd, Barrow (plans & records, mainly from Armaments Drawings Office, 20C); Duke of Buccleuch's Furness Estate Colln (incl records of local iron industry, 19C-20C); J. Soulby, Jobbing Printer, Ulverston (handbills & trade cards, early 19C); Furness Railway minutes bks & records (mainly m-film, 1846-1923) **Other:** Genl Register Office Indexes (m-fiche, 1837-1996); local newspapers (m-film); census returns (m-film)
Equip: 8 m-readers, 2 m-printers, copier (via staff) **Svcs:** info, ref, rsrch
Stock: archvs/200 cubic m; bks/150 linear ft (in Search Room); periodcls/10 linear ft (in Search Room); photos/c5000, incl illusts; slides/c1000; maps/c400; m-forms/c900 reels; audios/c10-20
Classn: DDC for most lib stock, own sys for Local Studies (currently being transferred from card to computer) **Auto Sys:** CAIRS for Archvs, Geac for Local Studies
Pubns: Cumbrian Ancestors: Notes for Genealogical Searchers (£6.99 + p&p); The Ellen Rose Fieldhouse Colln (£4.95 + p&p); Local Src Guides for: Railways (£3); Ships & Shipbuilding (£2); Iron & Steel Industry (£2); free sheets on: Family Hist; House Hist; Town of Barrow; Local Industries; Maps & directories; Poor Relief; Local Manorial Records

Staff: Archivists: 2 Non-Prof: 2 (Archv Svc staff only; extra assistance from lib staff when required, incl Local Studies Libn on certain days)
Further Info: The record office & former local studies lib at the Central Lib in Barrow combined to share a joint search room in 1998. There is joint responsibility between the Archv Svc & the Lib Svc, with some sharing of staff. Stock collns are increasingly being unified, but details have not yet been finalised.

Basingstoke

A29
Milestones Living History Museum, Local Resource Collections

Leisure Pk, Churchill Way West, Basingstoke, Hampshire, RG21 6YR (01256-477766; fax: 01256-477784)
Email: musmlo@hants.gov.uk
Internet: http://www.milestones-museum.com/

Type: local authority **Gov Body:** Hampshire County Council (see **P60**) **Chief:** Curator: Mr Gary Wragg
Assoc Offices: HAMPSHIRE COUNTY COUNCIL MUSEUMS SVC LIB (see **A508**)
Entry: ref only **Open:** Tue-Fri 1000-1700, Sat-Sun 1100-1700
Subj: Hampshire: local studies; agricultural hist; hist of transport; hist of tech & industry; business records **Collns:** Bks & Pamphs: bks & other resources relating to museum's collns **Archvs:** Tasker Colln (eng drawings & photos from Taskers of Andover, agricultural implement manufacturers); Thornycroft Colln (drawings, photos, catalogues & archvs from Thornycrofts of Basingstoke, motor vehicle merchants)

A30
The Willis Museum, Archive Collections

Market Sq, Basingstoke, Hampshire, RG21 7QD (01256-465902; fax: 01256-471455)
Email: musmst@hants.gov.uk
Internet: http://www.hants.gov.uk/museum/willis/

Gov Body: Hampshire County Council (see **P60**)
Chief: Curator: Ms Sue Tapliss MSc
Assoc Offices: HAMPSHIRE COUNTY COUNCIL MUSEUMS SVC LIB (see **A508**)
Entry: free, no booking required **Open:** Mon-Fri 1000-1700, Sat 1000-1600
Subj: Basingstoke & Borough of Deane: diocesan records (some); parish records; family papers (m-fiche); personal papers (some); local hist **Collns:** Bks & Pamphs: trade directories **Archvs:** parish records for Basingstoke **Other:** maps, photos & ephemera
Equip: m-reader, copier, video viewer, computers (incl 2 wd-proc, internet & CD-ROM)
Svcs: info, ref
Stock: archvs/600; maps/100; audios/50; videos/12; CD-ROMs/12
Pubns: The Story of Basingstoke, by Anne Hawker (£6.95); Dear Mr Willis, by Derek Wren (£5.99); Motor Runs Round Basingstoke (reprint, £2) **Staff:** Other Prof: 1 Non-Prof: 7

Bath

A31
Bath Record Office

The Guildhall, High St, Bath, BA1 5AW (01225-477421; fax: 01225-477439)
Email: archives@bathnes.gov.uk
Internet: http://www.batharchives.co.uk/

Gov Body: Bath & NE Somerset Council (see **P7**) **Chief:** Principal Archivist: Mr C.A. Johnston BA(Hons), DipAA
Entry: no pre-conditions **Open:** Tue-Thu 0900-1300, 1400-1700, Fri 0900-1300, 1400-1630
Subj: Bath & NE Somerset: local authority archvs; parish records (registers only, m-fiche copies); family papers; business records **Collns:** Archvs: archvs of Bath & NE Somerset Council & predecessor authorities; Royal Bath & West of England Soc (records of agric soc, 1777-date)
Equip: 4 m-readers, m-printer, copier
Stock: archvs/1450 linear m **Staff:** Archivists: 2

A32
Sorabji Archive

Easton Dene, Bailbrook Ln, Bath, BA1 7AA (01225-852323; fax: 01225-852523)
Email: sorabi-archive@lineone.net
Internet: http://www.music.mcgill.ca/~schulman/sorabji.html

Chief: Curator/Dir: Mr Alistair Hinton ARCM, LRAM, AMusTCL, ATCL (alistair_hinton@compuserve.com)
Entry: adv appt
Subj: the music, writings & recordings of the composer Kaikhosru Sorabji (1892-1988) **Collns:** Archvs: music & literary MSS **Other:** recordings of Sorabji's works; info about Sorabji on computer
Equip: copier, 2 fax, 4 computers (all with wd-proc, internet & CD-ROM) **Offcr-in-Charge:** Curator/Dir, as above **Svcs:** info, ref, rsrch
Acq Offcr: Curator/Dir, as above
Pubns: Brochure; Performance/Broadcast Listing; etc **Staff:** Archivists: 1

Beckenham

A33
The Bethlem Royal Hospital Archives and Museum

Monks Orchard Rd, Beckenham, Kent, BR3 3BX (020-8776-4307; fax: 020-8776-4045)
Email: museum@bethlem.freeserve.co.uk

Gov Body: The Bethlem Art & Hist Collns Trust
Chief: Snr Archivist: Mr Colin Gale MPhil, DipAA
Entry: adv appt **Open:** Mon-Fri 0930-1700; closed bank hols
Subj: hist of Bethlem & Maudsley Hosps; hosp records **Collns:** Archvs: archvs of Bethlem Royal Hosp (the original 'Bedlam', founded 1247), Maudsley Hosp & Warlington Pk Hosp
Staff: Archivists: 2 Other Prof: 1 Non-Prof: 1

Bedale

A34
Bedale Museum, Local History Archive

Bedale Hall, Bedale, N Yorkshire, DL8 1AA (01677-423797; fax: 01677-425393)

Gov Body: Bedale Hall Trust **Chief:** Curator: Mr Alan Shinkfield
Entry: adv appt preferred **Open:** Easter-Oct: Mon-Wed, Fri 1400-1600, Sat 1000-1200; other times by appt
Subj: North Yorkshire: local hist; family hist
Collns: Archvs: extensive materials relating to local, family & area hist

Archives

Bedford
▼
Biggar

Bedford

A35 🏛

Bedfordshire and Luton Archives and Record Service

County Hall, Cauldwell St, Bedford, MK42 9AP (01234-228833/777; *fax:* 01234-228854)
Email: archive@csd.bedfordshire.gov.uk
Internet: http://www.bedfordshire.gov.uk/ (click on local svcs option for archv pgs)

Type: local authority *Gov Body:* Bedfordshire County Council (see **P8**) in partnership with Luton Borough Council (see **P111**) *Chief:* County Archivist: Mr K.T. Ward BA, DipAA (wardkt@csd.bedfordshire.gov.uk) *Other Snr Staff:* OPS Mgr (Customer Svcs & Outreach): Mr Nigel Lutt; OPS Mgr (Archvs Processing & Records Mgmt): Mr Martin Deacon
Entry: no restrictions *Open:* Mon-Fri 0900-1700 (1000-1700 on 1st Thu of month); no documents produced 1245-1400 or after 1630
Subj: historic Bedfordshire (incl Luton): local authority archvs; diocesan records; parish records; estate archvs; family papers; business records; personal papers; political papers; records of parent org; school records *Collns: Bks & Pamphs:* small ref lib of Bedfordshire & Luton material; local directories *Archvs:* Bedfordshire County Council archvs; Luton Borough Council archvs; Bedford Estate (Russells of Woburn) archvs; Lucas of Wrest Pk archvs; records of Bedford Archdeaconry (Diocese of St Albans), incl parish records; Bedfordshire & Hertfordshire Regiment archvs *Other:* local maps, photos & illusts; local newspapers
Equip: 12 m-readers, 3 m-printers (50p per copy), copier, clr copier, fax, computers (with internet) *Disabled:* induction loop, magnification sheets, VDU with magnifier *Svcs:* info, ref, rsrch svc (£24 per hr), copying
Stock: archvs/482 cubic m; rec mgmt/359 cubic m
Classn: ISAD(G) *Auto Sys:* Adlib
Pubns: Newsletter (4 pa, free); Tracing Ancestors in Bedfordshire, by C.R. Chapman (£4.50); Bedfordshire Sources for Women's Hist (£5); Bedfordshire Sources for Ethnic Minorities (£7); How to Trace the Hist of a House in Bedfordshire (£4.50)
Staff: Archivists: 5.5 *Other Prof:* 1 *Non-Prof:* 10
Further Info: 4 times winner of 'Charter Mark' for excellence in the provision of public svcs

Belfast

A36 🔑

Belfast Harbour Commissioners, Archives

Corporation Sq, Belfast, BT1 3AL (028-9055-4422; *fax:* 028-9055-4411)
Email: info@belfast-harbour.co.uk
Internet: http://www.belfast-harbour.co.uk/

Entry: adv appt
Subj: Irish hist; local hist; maritime hist; records of parent org *Collns: Bks & Pamphs:* colln of c800 vols donated over many years, incl old records of Belfast Harbour Commissioners

A37 🏛

Belfast Ulster and Irish Studies Library

2nd Floor, Belfast Central Lib, Royal Ave, Belfast, BT1 1EA (028-9050-9150; *fax:* 028-9031-2886)
Email: buis@libraries.belfast-elb.gov.uk
Internet: http://www.belb.org.uk/library/irishLocalStudies.htm

Gov Body: Belfast Edu & Lib Board (see **P132**)
Chief: Snr Lib Mgr (Ref Svcs): Ms Linda Greenwood *Dep:* Local Studies Libn: Ms Patricia Walker
Entry: ref only; no appt necessary *Open:* Mon, Thu 0930-2000, Tue-Wed, Fri 0930-1730, Sat 0900-1300
Subj: Belfast & Ulster: local studies; Irish studies; personal papers; literary papers; school records; records of some local orgs *Collns: Bks & Pamphs:* Horner Colln (19C textile manufacture); Irish Manuscripts Commission Colln (pubns of the Commission); Nat Hist Colln (c1000 vols, 17C-date); Tully Colln (WW1 pamphs); United Irishmen Colln (incl complete run of the Northern Star); British Official Pubns Colln; govt pubns from Northern Ireland & Irish Republic *Archvs:* Archaeo Colln (MSS etc relating to archaeo & antiquities in Ireland); Brown Street Natl School Archv (1826-1923); Royal Belfast Academical Instn Colln (1810-1910); records of Royal Belfast Botanic & Horticultural Company Ltd (19C); Andrade Colln (lit, hist of sci, 19C-20C); Bryson & MacAdam MSS (Irish lang MSS, 18C-19C); Barrington Baker Colln (mainly Irish lit & theatre, 19C-20C); F.J. Bigger Archv & Lib (Irish hist & culture, 40000 items, 18C-early 20C); J.S. Crone Archv (Irish literary journalist & writer, c10000 items); Lynn Doyle Colln (Ulster writer); A.S. Moore Colln (Belfast local hist); D.J. O'Donoghue Archv (Irish libn & writer); Bishop Reeves Archv (19C antiquarian & bishop); Forrest Reid Colln (Belfast writer); Alexander Riddel Colln (Ulster social & theatre hist, 19C-20C); Sam Thompson Colln (Belfast playwright); Ulster Writers Archv (MSS, typescripts, diaries & photographic memorabilia of Ulster authors); W.B. Yeats Archv (correspondence & cuttings) *Other:* Antiquarian Map Colln (16C-19C); Map Colln (OS & other modern surveys, 1830s onwards); photo colln; Cinema Colln (photos, cuttings & programmes relating to cinema in Ulster); Postcard Colln (early 20C-date); Newspaper Colln (largest historical colln of newspapers in Northern Ireland, 1790s onwards); Theatre Colln (c3000 Irish theatre bills, programmes & ephemera)
Classn: DDC *Auto Sys:* DS

A38 🖐

Down and Connor RC Diocesan Archives

73a Somerton Rd, Belfast, BT15 4DE (028-9077-6185; *fax:* 028-9077-9377)

Gov Body: RC Diocese of Down & Connor
Chief: Diocesan Archivist: Rev George O'Hanlon BA *Dep:* Asst Archivist: Rev Thomas McGlynn
Entry: adv appt *Open:* Mon-Fri 0900-1700
Subj: Diocese of Down & Connor: diocesan records; parish records

A39 🏛

General Register Office (Northern Ireland)

Oxford House, 49-55 Chichester St, Belfast, BT1 4HF (028-9025-2000; *fax:* 028-9025-2044)
Email: gronisra@dfpni.gov.uk
Internet: http://www.groni.gov.uk/

Gov Body: Northern Ireland Statistics & Rsrch Agency (NISRA) *Chief:* Registrar Genl: Dr Norman Caven *Dep:* Dep Registrar Genl: Mr George King
Assoc Offices: Registrar's Offices in each of the 26 Dist Councils in Northern Ireland
Entry: apply by post, phone or in person; genl searches by appt only *Open:* Mon-Fri 0930-1600
Subj: Northern Ireland: birth, death & marriage registrations *Collns: Bks & Pamphs:* annual report of Registrar Genl (1922-date); quarterly returns of the Registrar Genl (1922-date) *Archvs:* birth & death records & indexes (1864-date); marriage records & indexes (1922-date); original marriage registers (RC marriages from 1 Jan 1864, all others from 1 Apr 1845-date), not yet indexed & are held in local Registrar's Offices; Registers of Marine Deaths, of those born in Northern Ireland; Register of War Deaths (1939-1948); etc
Equip: m-reader, m-printer, fax, 2 copiers
Pubns: Registrar Genl's Annual Report for Northern Ireland (£25); Quarterly Returns of the Registrar Genl: period ending 30 June 1999 (free)
Proj: computerisation of indexes & current registrations

A40 🔑

North of Ireland Family History Society Library

c/o Graduate School of Edu, Queen's Univ of Belfast, 69 University St, Belfast, N Ireland, BT7 1HL
Internet: http://www.nifhs.org/

Assoc Offices: lib is held at: 45 Park Ave, off Holywood Rd, Belfast, BT4; please use above addr for correspondence
Entry: branch & associate membs of the Soc only; adv notice of visit preferred *Open:* Wed, Sat 1000-1300
Subj: Northern Ireland: family hist *Collns: Bks & Pamphs:* ref bks & journals from over 70 other socs throughout the UK, Canada, USA, Australia & New Zealand *Other:* large map colln
Equip: m-reader, copier
Staff: staffed by volunteers

A41 🏛

Public Record Office of Northern Ireland

66 Balmoral Ave, Belfast, BT9 6NY (028-9025-5905; *fax:* 028-9025-5999)
Email: proni@dcalni.gov.uk
Internet: http://www.proni.gov.uk/

Gov Body: Dept of Culture, Arts & Leisure (NI)
Chief: Chief Exec: Dr G.J. Slater
Assoc Offices: PUBLIC RECORD OFFICE OF NI LIB, at same addr
Entry: Archvs: photographic ID required; *Lib:* open to public *Open:* Mon-Wed, Fri 0915-1645, Thu 0915-2045
Subj: Northern Ireland: local authority archvs; diocesan records; parish records; estate archvs; family papers; political papers; business records; personal papers; political papers; records of parent org; records of Northern Irish govt depts; court records; records of other Northern Irish public bodies *Collns: Bks & Pamphs:* c4500 bks, some very rare, held separately in PRONI Lib *Archvs:* records of Northern Ireland Govt (from 1921); records of local councils & non-departmental public bodies; records of many landed families & estates; records of schools, hosps & courts (1700-1980s); others too numerous to mention *Other:* emigrant letters; photos; OS maps (1830-1960s); census returns
Equip: m-reader, m-camera, m-printer, video viewer, copier, computer

Stock: archvs/53 linear km; m-forms/c5000; plus photos, maps, audios, videos & AVs (exact quantities unknown)
Pubns: Edu Facsimile Packs (£3.50 each); Dep Keeper's Reports (prices vary); Annual & Statutory Reports (prices vary); PRONI Guide Series (prices vary); 18C Irish Official Papers in Great Britain, Vol 2 (£30); Road Versus Rail (a documentary hist of transport development in Northern Ireland, 1921-48) (£9); The Ulster Textile Industry: a Catalogue of Business Records in PRONI relating principally to the Linen Industry in Ulster (£2); Northern Ireland Town Plans (catalogue ofOS town plans) (£3); The Way We Were: Historic Armagh Photographs from the Allison Colln (£8.50); County Monaghan Sources in the Public Record Office of Northern Ireland; Tracing Your Ancestors in Northern Ireland; numerous others (full details from PRONI at above addr)
Staff: 80 in total

A42
Royal Ulster Rifles Museum, Library and Archives
5 Waring St, Belfast, BT1 2EW (028-9023-2086)
Email: rurmuseum@yahoo.co.uk
Internet: http://rurmuseum.tripod.com/

Type: regimental Gov Body: Royal Ulster Rifles Museum Trustees Chief: Curator: Capt J. Knox MBE (Rtd)
Entry: adv appt preferred Open: Mon-Thu 1000-1230, 1400-1600, Fri 1000-1230, 1400-1500
Subj: regimental records; business records; records of parent org (83rd Regiment, 86th Regiment, Royal Irish Rifles, Royal Ulster Rifles) Collns: Bks & Pamphs: army lists (c200 vols); regimental hists of Irish regiments; WW2 war diaries Archvs: muniments section of 5000 regimental interest items, incl: 83rd & 86th Regiment discharge records; record bks; medal rolls; casualty lists etc
Equip: m-reader, copier, computer (with internet & CD-ROM) Svcs: info, ref, rsrch
Stock: archvs/c180 box files; rec mgmt/several 1000 database records; bks/c1500; photos/c500; pamphs/c150; various maps, m-forms, audios & videos
Classn: Metric Auto Sys: MS Works 4.5a
Staff: Non-Prof: 1 full-time, 1 PT

A43
Ulster Historical Foundation
Balmoral Bldgs, 12 College Sq East, Belfast, BT1 6DD (028-9033-2288; fax: 028-9023-9885)
Email: enquiry@uhf.org.uk
Internet: http://www.ancestryireland.com/ or http://www.uhf.org.uk/

Type: educational charity Chief: Exec Dir: Mr Fintan Mullan BSSc(Hons), MSSc Other Snr Staff: Rsrch Dir: Dr Brian Trainor; Office Mgr: Ms Maura Cooke; Proj Offcr: Mr Andrew Vaughan
Entry: open to public Open: Mon-Fri 0930-1730
Subj: historic Ulster (Counties Antrim, Armagh, Cavan, Donegal, Down, Fermanagh, Londonderry, Monaghan & Tyrone): local hist; family hist; genealogy; local authority archvs; diocesan records; parish records; estate archvs; family papers Collns: Other: Irish Genealogical Proj database of historic genea-logical records for Co Antrim, Co Down & Belfast; gravestone inscriptions Co-op Schemes: Irish Genealogical Proj
Svcs: info, ancestral rsrch svc (fee based)
Pubns: numerous, incl: Irish Hist Series; Local & Family Hist Series; ref works; works on political hist; gravestone inscriptions; catalogue available on web site at http://www.ancestryireland.com/
Staff: Archivists: 1
See also ULSTER GENEALOGICAL & HISTORICAL GUILD (O406)

Berkhamsted
National Film and Television Archive
See BFI NATL LIB (S1013)

Berwick-upon-Tweed

A44
Berwick-upon-Tweed Record Office
Council Offices, Wallace Green, Berwick-upon-Tweed, Northumberland, TD15 1ED (01289-301865 or 01289-330044 x265; fax: 01289-330540)
Email: lb@berwick-upon-tweed.gov.uk
Internet: http://www.swinhope.demon.co.uk/NRO/

Gov Body: Northumberland County Council (see P137) & Berwick-upon-Tweed Borough Council
Chief: Borough Archivist: Mrs Linda A. Bankier MA, DipAA
Assoc Offices: branch office of NORTHUMBERLAND RECORD OFFICE (see A390)
Open: Wed & Thu 0930-1300, 1400-1700
Subj: Berwick-upon-Tweed area (i.e. North Northumberland): local authority archvs; parish records (m-films of registers only); estate archvs; family papers; business records Collns: Bks & Pamphs: North Northumberland local hist Archvs: Berwick Borough records, 16C-20C (incl guild, court, manor & financial records); estate records for Ford et al (18C-19C); estate records for Haggerston & Tillmouth (incl rentals & plans); port of Berwick shipping registers (1823-1910); Berwick Salmon Fisheries Co records (18C-20C) Other: census returns (1841-1901); St Catherine's House Indexes (1837-1993); transcripts of various North Northumberland Anglican & nonconformist registers
Equip: 6 m-readers, 2 computers (both with internet & CD-ROM) Svcs: info, ref, rsrch
Stock: archvs/1000 linear ft
Pubns: Family Hist Resources in Berwick-upon-Tweed Record Office (pamph, free); Berwick-on-Tweed Illustrated 1894-1994 (£5); various genealogical & family hist pubns available on m-fiche
Staff: Archivists: 1 Exp: £1000 (2000-01)

A45
King's Own Scottish Borders Archives
Regimental HQ, The Barracks, Berwick-upon-Tweed, Northumberland, TD15 1DG (01289-307426; fax: 01289-331928)

Type: military Gov Body: Regimental Trustees
Chief: Regimental Sec: Lt Col C.G.O. Hogg
Entry: adv appt Open: Mon-Sat 0900-1600; closed public hols & certain regimental days
Subj: regimental archvs; regimental hist Collns: Archvs: archvs of the King's Own Scottish Borderers (1689-date)
Svcs: info, ref Staff: Non-Prof: 2

Beverley

A46
East Riding of Yorkshire Archive Service
County Hall, Beverley, E Yorkshire, HU17 9BA (01482-885007; fax: 01482-885463)
Email: archives.service@east-riding-of-yorkshire.gov.uk

Gov Body: East Riding of Yorkshire Council (see P48) Chief: Area Archivist: Mr I. Mason BA, DipAA Dep: Snr Archivist: Mrs C.A. Boddington BA, DipAA

Entry: adv appt Open: Mon 1400-1645, Tue 0930-2000, Wed-Thu 0930-1645, Fri 0930-1600
Subj: East Riding of Yorkshire: local authority archvs; parish records; estate archvs; family papers; business records; records of parent org Collns: Archvs: archvs of East Riding of Yorkshire Council & predecessors; Archdiocese of East Riding parish records; records of East Riding Registry of Deeds (1708-1976)
Equip: 8 m-readers, 2 copiers
Pubns: various handlists etc (50p-£2.50)
Staff: Archivists: 3 Non-Prof: 5

Bexleyheath

A47
Bexley Local Studies and Archive Centre
Central Lib, Townley Rd, Bexleyheath, Kent, DA6 7HJ (020-8301-1545; fax: 020-8303-7872)
Email: archives@bexleycouncil.freeserve.co.uk
Internet: http://www.bexley.gov.uk/service/lib-localstudies.html

Gov Body: London Borough of Bexley (see P79)
Chief: Local Studies Mgr: Mr Simon McKeon
Dep: Archivist: Mr Oliver Wooller MA, DipAS
Entry: ref only Open: Mon-Wed, Fri 0930-1730, Thu 0930-2000, Sat 0930-1700, Sun 1000-1400
Subj: London Borough of Bexley: local authority archvs; parish records; estate archvs; family papers; personal papers; local hist; family hist Collns: Archvs: records of Bexley Borough & predecessors; parish records of Rochester & Southwark diocese; Hall Place Estate Archv; Danson Estate Archv; Foots Cray Place Estate Archv; Belvedere Estate Archv Other: local newspapers Co-op Schemes: LASER
Equip: 3 m-readers, 6 m-printers, copier, computer (with CD-ROM)
Stock: archvs/472.6 linear m; bks/9240; photos/21414; slides/5311; pamphs/4163; maps/1955; m-forms/902; CD-ROMs/7; postcards/3064; newspapers/38
Classn: DDC, ISAD(G) Auto Sys: Dynix, Adlib
Pubns: Bexley Pubs (£4.95); Bexley Village (£2.50); Bexley in Old Photographs (£9.99); Blendon (£6); Children of the Blitz (£3.60); Foots Cray (£1.50); From Country to Suburb (£4.95); Hist of Danson (£1.50); Hist of Erith Vol I-V (£5.50); Home Fires (£3.50); PLUTO (£3.95); Story of Barnehurst (£2.50); The Great Estates (£5.95); Bygone Bexley (video, £10); Erith (video, £10); numerous others; maps, postcards & prints
Staff: Archivists: 2 Non-Prof: 3 Exp: £29000 (2000-01)

Biggar

A48
The Albion Archive
9 Edinburgh Rd, Biggar, Lanarkshire, ML12 6AX (tel & fax: 01899-221497)
Email: sprocketlambie@aol.com
Internet: http://www.albion-trust.co.uk

Gov Body: The Biggar Albion Foundation Ltd
Chief: Volunteer Archivist: Mr Brian Lambie
Entry: adv appt preferred Open: Mon-Fri 0930-1700, weekends by appt only
Subj: commercial vehicles worldwide: business records Collns: Archvs: whole archv of Albion Motors (1899-1972, incl printed material & photos/drawings)
Equip: m-reader, copier, computer (incl CD-ROM) Svcs: info, ref, rsrch
Stock: archvs/c8000 negs; slides/c3000
Pubns: Quarterly Newsletter (£8 pa, £10 overseas) Staff: Non-Prof: 1
Proj: Albion Museum

Birkenhead
▼
Brecon

Archives

Birkenhead

A49 ✍ 🔑

Shrewsbury RC Diocesan Archives
c/o Curial Office, 2 Park Rd South, Prenton,
Birkenhead, Merseyside, CH43 4UX
Email: info@dioceseofshrewsbury.org

Gov Body: RC Diocese of Shrewsbury *Chief:*
Archivist: Canon John P. Marmion MA, MEd, PhD,
also contactable at: Our Lady of Pity RC Church,
The Presbytery, 24 Mill Lane, Greasby, Wirral,
Merseyside, CH49 3NN
Entry: by appt only *Open:* Thu only 0900-1400
Subj: RC Diocese of Shrewsbury: diocesan
records; parish records; local hist *Collns: Bks &
Pamphs:* small local hist colln *Archvs:* archvs of
RC Diocese of Shrewsbury (1850-20C); papers of
Bishops of Shrewsbury; for a full description see
Catholic Archvs No. 14 (1994)
Stock: archvs/500; photos/100; illusts/10;
pamphs/50; maps/10; audios/20; videos/2
Classn: CAS *Staff: Other Prof:* 4 *Non-Prof:* 2

A50 🏛

Wirral Archives Service
Town Hall, Hamilton Sq, Birkenhead, Merseyside,
CH41 5BR (0151-666-3903; *fax:* 0151-666-3065)
Email: archives@wirral-libraries.net
Internet: http://www.wirral-libraries.net/archives/

Gov Body: Wirral Metropolitan Borough Council
(see **P203**) *Chief:* Borough Archivist: Ms Janice
Taylor
Entry: appt advisable; ID with current addr
required *Open:* Thu-Fri 1000-1700, Sat 1000-
1300; tel queries: Mon-Fri 0900-1700
Subj: Metropolitan Borough of Wirral: local
authority archvs; estate archvs; family papers;
business records; political papers; records of
parent org; hosp records; court records *Collns:
Archvs:* archvs of Wirral Borough Council &
predecessors; Wirral Health Authority records
(incl local hosps); records of Birkenhead &
Wallasey magistrates; records of Birkenhead
Quarter sessions; records of Birkenhead County
Court; Cammall Laird Shipbuilders Ltd, Birkenhead
(large shipbldg archv); Unichema Chemicals Ltd,
Bromborough, Wirral (formerly Price's Patent
Candle Co Ltd); John Stafford Colln (Cheshire
documents)
Equip: 5 m-readers, m-printer (50p per sheet),
fax, copier (A4/10p, A3/20p), 4 computers (all with
wd-proc & CD-ROM, 3 with internet) *Offcr-in-
Charge:* Borough Archivist, as above *Svcs:* info,
ref, rsrch
Stock: archvs/588 cubic m *Acq Offcr:* Borough
Archivist, as above
Classn: ISAD(G) *Auto Sys:* DS
Pubns: Guide to Family Hist Sources (£2);
various lists & summary guides (free)
Staff: Archivists: 1 *Non-Prof:* 1

Birmingham

A51 🏛

Birmingham City Archives
Central Lib, Chamberlain Sq, Birmingham, B3
3HQ (0121-303-4217; *fax:* 0121-464-1176)
Email: archives@birmingham.gov.uk
Internet: http://www.birmingham.gov.uk/archives/

Gov Body: Birmingham City Council (see **P9**)
Chief: Central Lib Mgr: Mr Paul Hemmings *Dep:*
Snr Archivist: Ms Sian Roberts
Entry: CARN ticket *Open:* Mon-Tue, Fri-Sat
0900-1700, Thu 0900-2000; closed Wed
Subj: City of Birmingham (some collns also
relate to surrounding counties): local authority
archvs; diocesan records; parish records; estate
archvs; family papers; business records; records
of local charities & socs *Collns: Archvs:* archvs
of Birmingham City Council; Diocese of
Birmingham parish records; Boulton & Watt Archv
(steam engine manufacture, 1774-1890); Matthew
Boulton papers (personal & estate records, 18C-
19C); Metro-Cammell Archv (railway rolling stock
manufacture, c1860-1960); Cadbury family
papers (1809-c1970); Hagley Hall Estate records
(13C-17C); Charles Parker Archv (oral hist, folk
music revival, radical politics, c1950-80); IMI plc
(metalworking, c1860-1960); John Hardman & Co
(stained glass manufacture, 1839-1970), Albright
& Wilson (phosphorous manufacture, 1841-1940);
Brewery Hist Soc Archvs (hist of brewing)
Equip: 3 m-readers, copier, 2 computers (both
with internet, 1 with wd-proc), UV lamp, cassette
player
Stock: archvs/7630 linear m; rec mgmt/1750
linear m; bks/50 linear m
Pubns: Annual Report (free); Introductory Leaflet
(free); Guide to Collns (in preparation)
Staff: Archivists: 6.5 *Non-Prof:* 3.2

A52 🔑 ✍

Birmingham RC Archdiocesan Archives
Cathedral House, St Chad's Queensway,
Birmingham, B4 6EU (0121-230-6252; *fax:* 0121-
230-6279)
Email: archives@rc-birmingham.org

Gov Body: RC Archdiocese of Birmingham
Chief: Diocesan Archivist: Revd Dr John Sharp
Entry: adv appt *Open:* Wed-Fri 1100-1800
Subj: RC Diocese of Birmingham: diocesan
records; parish records & some registers; school
records; personal papers *Collns: Bks & Pamphs:*
bks of Roman Catholic hist pertaining to England
& Wales *Archvs:* records of Midland Dist (1688-
1840); records of Central Dist (1840-1850);
diocesan records of RC Diocese of Birmingham
(1850-date); archvs of Sedgley Park – Cotton
Coll (1763-1987); Besford Court School,
Worcestershire, archvs (1917-96); Oscott Coll
archvs (1794-date)
Equip: m-reader, copier, clr copier, fax, 3 computers
Stock: archvs/unquantified
Staff: Other Prof: 1 *Non-Prof:* 1

A53 🔑

British Association of Social Workers Archives
16 Kent St, Birmingham, B5 6RD (0121-622-3911)

Gov Body: BASW *Chief:* Hon Archivist: Prof
A.T. Collis BSc(Econ), DipSocSt
Collns: Archvs: records of predecessor orgs
(1890-1970), incl: Assoc of Child Care Workers;
Assoc of Family Case Workers (formerly Assoc
of Genl & Family Case Workers); Assoc of

Psychiatric Social Workers; Assoc of Social
Workers; Inst of Medical Social Workers
(formerly Inst of Almoners); Moral Welfare
Workers Assoc; Soc of Mental Welfare Offcrs;
Standing Conference of Orgs of Social Workers.
These records were transferred to the Modern
Records Centre at Univ of Warwick Lib (see
A114) in July 1997.
Pubns: Catalogue & Guide to the Archvs of the
Predecessor Orgs 1890-1970 (£35);
Supplementary Catalogue to the Archvs of the
Predecessor Orgs (£15); available from BASW
Pubns Dept at above addr

Blackburn, *Lancashire*

A54 🏛

Blackburn with Darwen Community History Department
Central Lib, Town Hall St, Blackburn, Lancashire,
BB1 2AG (01254-587920)
Email: diana.rushton@blackburn.gov.uk
Internet: http://library.blackburnworld.com/
our_services/genealogy/

Gov Body: Blackburn with Darwen Council (see
P10) *Chief:* Community Hist Mgr: Ms Diane
Rushton
Assoc Offices: archvs relating to Blackburn with
Darwen are held at LANCASHIRE RECORD
OFFICE (see **A425**)
Subj: Blackburn & Darwen: local studies; family
hist; genealogy *Collns: Bks & Pamphs:* trade
directories *Other:* Boyd's Marriage Index;
Internatl Genealogical Index; Blackburn Diocese
parish registers on m-film (CoE); 1901 Census on
m-form; register of electors (copies, 1841-date);
m-film copies of records of local cemeteries;
Blackburn & Darwen Rolls of Honour; Genl
Register Office indexes; newspapers, incl
Blackburn Mail (from 1793); Blackburn Times
(1855-1980); Lancashire Evening Telegraph/
Northern Daily Telegraph (1886-date); newspaper
cuttings colln
Equip: 12 m-readers (7 fiche, 5 film), m-reader/
printer (A4/20p), copier (A4/10p), 4 computers (all
with internet & CD-ROM)

A55 🔑 ✍

Cathedral Church of St Mary the Virgin, Archives
Cathedral Cl, Blackburn, Lancashire, BB1 5AA
(01254-57491)
Email: dean@blackburn.anglican.org

Gov Body: Blackburn Cathedral Chapter *Chief:*
Dean: Very Rev C. Armstrong *Dep:* Archivist:
Mr H.H. Thornber MSocArch
Assoc Offices: addl records, incl registers, are
held at LANCASHIRE RECORD OFFICE (see
A425)
Entry: by appt *Open:* normal church hrs: 0800-
1700
Subj: Parish Church of St Mary the Virgin &
Cathedral: parish records (1560 onwards)
Svcs: info
Pubns: various, from Cathedral Shop
Staff: Archivists: 1

Blackburn, *West Lothian*

A56 🏛

West Lothian Council Libraries, Local History Department
Lib HQ, Hopefield Rd, Blackburn, W Lothian,
EH47 7HZ (01506-776331; *fax:* 01506-776345)
Email: local.history@westlothian.gov.uk

Gov Body: West Lothian Council (see **P197**)
Chief: Head of Local Studies Svcs: Mrs M.S. Cavanagh MA, MCLIP *Dep:* Mrs E. Dunn
Assoc Offices: the main repository for local govt archvs in West Lothian is WEST LOTHIAN ARCHVS & RECORDS MGMT SVCS (see **A242**)
Open: Mon-Thu 0900-1700, Fri 0900-1600, 1st Sat of each month 0900-1300
Subj: West Lothian: local authority archvs (some); parish records; records of parent org; local hist; family hist *Collns: Bks & Pamphs:* various materials relating to W Lothian & its people *Archvs:* minute bks of old burgh & community councils; minute bks of West Lothian Dist & Lothian Regional Councils; valuation rolls (1855 onwards); electoral rolls; parish registers; census returns (1841-1901); confirmations & inventories (wills, 1876-1936) *Other:* photo colln; maps; videos; monumental inscriptions (pre-1855)
Equip: 3 m-readers, m-printer, copier
Stock: archvs/c57 linear m; other materials/c80 linear m
Pubns: West Lothian Local Hist Colln (free leaflet); various others
Staff: Libns: 1 *Non-Prof:* 0.5

Bolton

A57

Bolton Archive and Local Studies Service Library

Central Lib, Civic Centre, Le Mans Cres, Bolton, Lancashire, BL1 1SE (01204-332185; *fax:* 01204-332225)
Email: archives.library@bolton.gov.uk
Internet: http://bold.bolton.gov.uk/library/

Gov Body: Bolton Metropolitan Borough Council (see **P12**) *Chief:* Archivist: Ms Samantha Collenette BA, MARM (sam.collenette@bolton. gov.uk) *Dep:* Local Studies Libn: Mr B.D. Mills BA, MCLIP
Entry: ref only *Open:* Mon closed, Tue, Thu 0930-1930, Wed, Fri 0930-1730, Sat 0930-1700
Subj: Bolton Metropolitan Borough: local authority archvs; parish records (m-form only); estate archvs; family papers; personal papers; business records; records of parent org; records of local socs & charities; trade union records; public records; nonconformist records; records of employers' assocs *Collns: Bks & Pamphs:* Whitman Colln (material relating to American poet Walt Whitman); Lancashire dialect colln; local authors colln; local studies colln; local pubns colln *Archvs:* records of Samuel Crompton (inventor of the Mule, 1753-1827); Albinson Colln (maps & plans of John Albinson of Bolton, land surveyor, c1780-1850); Bill Naughton Archv (Bolton author & playwright) *Other:* Oral Hist Colln; photographic colln (1865-date); illusts; maps & plans, incl OS (1845 onwards) & MS maps (1620 onwards); census returns on m-form
Equip: 9 m-readers, m-printer, fax, copier, 2 computers
Stock: archvs/2000 linear m; rec mgmt/50 linear m; bks/300 linear m; photos/6 linear m; maps/3900; m-forms/5800; audios/328 oral hist tapes
Pubns: Handlist of Registers (£2 + 30p p&p); Guide to the Resources of Bolton Archv & Local Studies Unit (available on web site)
Staff: Archivists: 1 *Libns:* 1 *Non-Prof:* 3

Bootle

A58

Alliance & Leicester Group Archives

Girobank plc Paperstore, Dunnings Bridge Rd, Bootle, Merseyside, L30 6UT (0151-966-2822; *fax:* 0151-966-2831)

Chief: Archivist: Mr Nigel Hardman
Entry: adv appt; access currently available only for public records relating to Natl Giro (1965-69)
Open: Mon-Fri 1000-1600
Subj: business records; records of parent org

Bournemouth

A59

Bournemouth Local Studies Collection

2nd Floor, Bournemouth Lib, 22 The Triangle, Bournemouth, Dorset, BH2 5RQ (01202-454848; *fax:* 01202-454840)
Email: Bournemouth@bournemouthlibraries. org.uk
Internet: http://www.bournemouth.gov.uk/leisure/ Libraries/

Gov Body: Bournemouth Borough Council (see **P13**) *Chief:* Ref & Local Studies Libn: Mrs K. Spackman BLib, MCLIP
Entry: no restrictions, but adv appt appreciated
Open: Mon 1000-1900, Tue, Thu-Fri 0930-1900, Wed 0930-1700, Sat 1000-1400
Subj: Borough of Bournemouth: local hist & studies (published materials only); family hist; genealogy *Collns: Bks & Pamphs:* comprehensive colln of bks & pamphs about the past & continuing development of Bournemouth *Other:* census returns (1841-1901); electoral rolls (1890s-date); some parish registers; local newspapers on m-film (incl complete run of Bournemouth Echo, 1900 onwards); maps; photos, engravings & postcards (1860s onwards) *Co-op Schemes:* Newsplan
Equip: 5 m-readers, m-printer, copier *Svcs:* info, ref *Classn:* Brown (mod)

A60

Bournemouth University, Oral History Research Unit Archive

(incorporating the former Centre for the Hist of Defence Electronics)
Studland House, 12 Christchurch Rd, Bournemouth, Dorset, BH1 3NA (01202-503879; *fax:* 01202-503917)
Email: histru@bmth.ac.uk
Internet: http://chide.bournemouth.ac.uk/

Type: rsrch centre *Gov Body:* Bournemouth Univ (see **S1817**)
Entry: ref only, adv appt
Subj: hist of tech; hist of electronics; defence electronics *Collns: Archvs:* some text-based material *Other:* audio tapes of oral hist interviews, transcripts, videos & photographs
Auto Sys: Modes for Windows
Proj: ongoing cataloguing of archvs

Bracknell

A61

National Meteorological Archive

Scott Bldg, Sterling Centre, Eastern Rd, Bracknell, Berkshire, RG12 2PW (01344-855960; *fax:* 01344-855961)
Email: metarc@metoffice.com
Internet: http://www.metoffice.com/

Gov Body: The Met Office *Chief:* Archv Mgr: Mr Ian MacGregor *Dep:* Archv Supervisor: Mrs Marion James
Assoc Offices: MET OFFICE ARCHVS, Saughton House, Broomfield Dr, Edinburgh, EH11 3XQ (0131-244-8368; *fax:* 0131-244-8389); MET OFFICE ARCHVS, 32 College St, Belfast, BT1 6BQ (028-9032-8457; *fax:* 028-9031-3981); see also: NATL METEOROLOGICAL LIB (see **S210**)

Entry: Bracknell: adv appt preferred; *Edinburgh:* by prior appt only; *Belfast:* archvs held jointly with PRONI (see **A41**), contact Met Office or PRONI for advice before visiting *Open: Bracknell:* Mon-Fri 0830-1300, 1400-1630
Subj: England & Wales (some overseas): meteorological records *Collns: Archvs:* weather records from England & Wales (plus a few overseas) under the control of the Met Office (1850s-date); some private weather diaries (from later 18C); daily weather charts & weather summaries (from 1860s); meteorological ships logs (c150000, from 1850s); various papers, pictures & non-technical documents donated to Met Office; nearly all records are paper-based
Equip: m-reader, m-printer, copier *Svcs:* info
Stock: archvs/5000 linear m; maps/2.5 mln
Staff: Non-Prof: 3

Bradford

A62

West Yorkshire Archive Service: Bradford

15 Canal Rd, Bradford, W Yorkshire, BD1 4AT (01274-731931; *fax:* 01274-734013)
Email: bradford@wyjs.org.uk
Internet: http://www.archives.wyjs.org.uk/

Gov Body: West Yorkshire Joint Svcs Cttee
Chief: Principal Dist Archivist, Bradford: Mr Andrew George MA, DipAA
Assoc Offices: branch office of WEST YORKSHIRE ARCHV SVC HQ (see **A497**)
Entry: adv appt *Open:* Mon-Tue, Thu-Fri 0930-1300, 1400-1700; open until 2000 on alternate Thu
Subj: Metropolitan Dist of Bradford: local authority archvs; diocesan records; parish records; estate archvs; family papers; business records *Collns: Archvs:* archvs of Bradford Metropolitan Council & its predecessors; Anglican & nonconformist churches, incl many parishes in the Diocese of Bradford (Bradford Cathedral registers on m-fiche); family & estate records, incl: Spencer-Stanhope of Horsforth; Calverley & Eccleshill; Tempest of Tong; Ferrand of Bingley; Sharp Powell of Horton Hall; business records, incl: Salts of Saltaire; Drummond's of Lumb Lane; Bowling Iron Company; Hattersley & Sons (loom manufacturers); Bradford Canal Company; Leeds Liverpool Canal Company; Vint, Hill & Killick (Solicitors); records of many co-op socs; trade union & political records, incl papers on W.E. Forster & E.R. Hartley
Equip: 6 m-readers, m-printer, video viewer, fax, copier, computer
Stock: archvs/3000 linear m
Pubns: Guide for Family Historians (£9.99+p&p); Bradford Archvs 1974-1995: An Illustrated Guide to Bradford Dist Archvs (£11.95)
Staff: Archivists: 1.5 *Non-Prof:* 1.5

Brecon

A63

Brecknock Museum and Gallery, Archives

Captain's Walk, Brecon, Powys, LD3 7DW (01874-624121)
Email: brecknock.museum@powys.gov.uk

Gov Body: Powys County Council (see **P149**)
Chief: Curator: Mr David Moore
Entry: ref only; adv appt *Open:* Mon-Sat 1000-1700 (Sat closed 1300-1400), Sun 1200-1700 (Apr-Sep only)
Subj: Powys: local studies; personal papers; artists & sculptors *Collns: Archvs:* records of Brecknock Soc; Lt Col Sir John Conway Lloyd papers (1878-1954)

Brecon
▼
Bristol

Archives

A64

South Wales Borderers and Monmouthshire Regimental Museum, Archives

The Barracks, Brecon, Powys, LD3 7EB (01874-613310/1; *fax:* 01874-613275)
Email: swb@rrw.org.uk
Internet: http://www.rrw.org.uk/

Gov Body: Trustees *Chief:* Curator: Major Martin Everett MSA *Dep:* Customer Svcs Mgr: Mrs Celia Green
Entry: adv appt *Open: Archvs:* Mon-Fri 0900-1700; *Museum only:* Sat-Sun 0900-1700 during summer
Subj: campaigns of the South Wales Borderers (24th Regiment) & the Monmouthshire Regiment: regimental records; family papers; records of parent org *Collns: Archvs:* records of 24th Regiment (South Wales Borderers) & the Monmouthshire Regiment; of particular interest are papers relating to 1879 Anglo-Zulu War
Equip: m-reader, copier, fax, computers (incl wd-proc, internet & CD-ROM) *Svcs:* info, ref
Staff: Archivists: 1 *Other Prof:* 1 *Non-Prof:* 2
Exp: £1500 (2000-01); most stock acquired from donations from families & genl public

Brentwood

A65

Archive of the Diocese of Brentwood (RC)

Cathedral House, Ingrave Rd, Brentwood, Essex, CM15 8AT (01277-216116)

Gov Body: Diocesan Trustees *Chief:* Archivist of the Diocese: Miss Jane Neely BA(Hons) *Dep:* Rev Stewart Foster BA
Entry: adv appt *Open:* Mon-Fri 0930-1730
Subj: RC Diocese of Brentwood: diocesan records; parish records; personal papers *Collns: Other:* bldg plans; maps; photos
Equip: m-reader, copier *Svcs:* info, ref, rsrch
Stock: archvs/room size 14x10 ft
Staff: Non-Prof: 2 *Exp:* £200 (2000-01)

Bridgend

A66

Bridgend Local Studies Library

Bridgend Libs Ref & Info Centre, Coed Parc, Park St, Bridgend, Mid-Glamorgan, CF31 4BA (01656-767451; *fax:* 01656-645719)
Email: blis@bridgendlib.gov.uk
Internet: http://www.bridgend.gov.uk/english/library/

Gov Body: Bridgend County Borough Council (see **P16**)
Assoc Offices: local archvs are held at GLAMORGAN RECORD OFFICE (see **A97**)
Entry: open to public; adv appt advised for use of m-readers *Open:* Mon-Fri 0830-1900, Sat 0830-1700
Subj: Bridgend: local hist; family hist; personal papers *Collns: Bks & Pamphs:* bks by local

authors; directories for South Wales; local journals *Archvs:* MSS of local historians & politicians; census returns (on m-fiche & m-film)
Other: photo colln; maps, plans & surveys; oral hist recordings; local newspapers on m-film (1830s onwards); IGI (on CD-ROM & m-fiche); St Catherine's House Index (on m-fiche)
Equip: m-readers
Stock: archvs/7000+; photos/3000+

Brighton

A67

Brighton and Hove Local Studies Library

Brighton Lib, Church St, Brighton, BN1 1UE (01273-296971; *fax:* 01273-296965)
Internet: http://www.citylibraries.info/

Gov Body: Brighton & Hove Council (see **P17**)
Chief: Local Studies Mgr: Ms Sally Blann
Assoc Offices: HOVE LIB, 182-186 Church Rd, Hove, E Sussex, BN3 2EG (01273-296942; *fax:* 01273-296931)
Entry: ref only; access to rarer items requires membership of Rare Bks Membership Scheme
Open: Mon, Thu-Fri 0930-1700, Tue 0930-1900, Sat 0930-1600; closed Wed
Subj: Brighton & Sussex: local studies *Collns: Bks & Pamphs:* bks on the hist of the immediate area & of Sussex in genl, incl guides & descriptions of Brighton dating back to late 1700s; local hist periodcls & magazines, incl: Sussex Archaeological Collns (from 1848); Sussex County Magazine (1926-56); local school & church magazines *Archvs:* records of Brighton & Sussex trade unions *Other:* large colln of photographs, prints, drawings & postcards, incl: Brighton Herald Photo Colln (1934-70); Madgwick Colln of Railway Photographs; historic map colln (16C onwards); extensive colln of local newspapers (1749-date); several collns of cuttings, ephemera & extracts
Equip: copier
Proj: moving in 2003 to dedicated Local Studies Centre at Brighton Art Gallery & Museum (see **A68**)

A68

Brighton Art Gallery and Museum, Library and Archives

Church St, Brighton, E Sussex, BN1 1UE (01273-292765; *fax:* 01273-292841)
Email: richard.lesaux@brighton-hove.gov.uk
Internet: http://www.virtualmuseum.info/

Gov Body: Brighton & Hove Council (see **P17**)
Chief: Keeper of Local Hist & Archaeo: Mr Richard Lesaux
Entry: adv appt *Open:* Tue-Sat 1000-1700, Sun 1400-1700
Subj: local studies (Brighton); archaeo *Collns: Other:* oral hists; colln of local theatre ephemera
Proj: new Study Centre opening in 2003, incorporating Brighton & Hove Local Studies Collns (see **A67**)

A69

Design History Research Centre Archives

Univ of Brighton, 68 Grand Parade, Brighton, BN2 2LY (01273-643219/09; *fax:* 01273-643217)
Email: dhrc@brighton.ac.uk
Internet: http://www.dhrc.brighton.ac.uk/dca_web_site/

Gov Body: Design Council & Univ of Brighton, Faculty of Arts & Arch *Chief:* Curator: Dr Catherine Moriarty *Dep:* Asst Curator: Dr Lesley Whitworth

Assoc Offices: DESIGN COUNCIL SLIDE COLLN, Manchester Metropolitan Univ Slide Lib, Cavendish North Bldg, Manchester, contact: Mr John Davis (0161-247-1943/30; *email:* j.davis@mmu.ac.uk)
Entry: adv appt only; enqs may be made by post, tel or email
Subj: United Kingdom: all aspects of design; personal papers; records of parent org *Collns: Bks & Pamphs:* exhib catalogues *Archvs:* collns comprise a unique body of material that charts the hist of British design in the 20C, incl: Design Council Archv; James Gardner Archv (1908-1995); F.H.K. Henrion Archv & Rsrch Lib (1936-1990); Alison Settle Archv (1891-1980); Joseph Emberton Archv (1889-1956); Bernard Schottlander papers (1924-1999); Paul Clark Archv (b. 1940); W.H. Mayall papers (1923-1998); Vokins Archv *Other:* photos; posters; negs; prints

A70

Mass-Observation Archive

c/o Special Collns, Univ of Sussex Lib, Falmer, Brighton, BN1 9QL (01273-678157; *fax:* 01273-678441)
Email: library.specialcoll@sussex.ac.uk
Internet: http://www.sussex.ac.uk/library/massobs/

Gov Body: Trustees of the M-O Archv; part of Special Collns, Univ of Sussex Lib (see **S239**)
Chief: Archivist & Head of Special Collns: Ms Dorothy Sheridan MA, MBE *Dep:* Asst Archivist: to be appointed
Entry: adv appt *Open:* usually Mon-Fri 0915-1700
Subj: UK: family papers; personal papers; records of parent org; written materials by ordinary people on everyday life in Britain from 1937 *Collns: Bks & Pamphs:* complete colln of original Mass Observation pubns & small lib of related pubns covering Britain from 1937, with emphasis on documentary ordinary life, esp during WW2 *Archvs:* Mass Observation Papers (1937-date), incl: Worktown Colln (survey of Bolton & Blackpool, 1937-40); File Report Sequence (1937-60); diaries & 'directives' (1937-65); observational & survey materials on everyday life; Mass-Observation Proj (autobiographical writing on themes documenting life in contemporary Britain, 1981-date); variety of other collns, incl personal papers & diaries (see web site for full list of holdings)
Equip: m-reader, copier (via staff), 2 computers (all with wd-proc, internet & CD-ROM), seminar room *Disabled:* wheelchair access, Aladdin Rainbow reader & other assistive tech *Offcr-in-Charge:* Archivist, as above *Svcs:* info, seminars
Stock: archvs/c350 linear m of M-O material; some slides, m-forms, audios & videos *Acq Offcr:* Archivist, as above
Classn: in-house *Auto Sys:* Access & others
Pubns: regular newsletter; Mass-Observation File Report Handlist; Mass-Observation Archv Occasional Papers Nos 1-12; Mass-Observation Archv Teaching Bklets Nos 1-9; M-OA File Report Sequence (primary src media on m-fiche); various others; see web site for full lists & prices
Staff: Archivists: 1 *Libns:* 1 temp *Other Prof:* 1 temp *Non-Prof:* 4 FTE *Exp:* new materials come from donations of papers

A71

South East Film and Video Archive

Faculty of Arts & Arch, Univ of Brighton, Grand Parade, Brighton, E Sussex, BN2 2JY (01273-643213; *fax:* 01273-643214)
Email: sefva@brighton.ac.uk
Internet: http://www.bton.ac.uk/sefva/ or http://www.westsussex.gov.uk/RO/services/Film.htm

Gov Body: Univ of Brighton (see **S237**) & West Sussex Record Office (see **A106**) **Chief:** Dir: Mr Frank Gray **Dep:** Moving Image Archivist: Ms Ine van Dooren **Other Snr Staff:** Administrator: Ms Jane King; Conservation Offcr: Mr Rod Willerton
Assoc Offices: SEFVA REPOSITORY & CONSERVATION CENTRE, West Sussex Record Office, County Hall, Orchard St, Chichester, W Sussex, PO19 1RN (01243-753600; *fax:* 01243-533959; *email:* records.office@westsussex. gov.uk); contact the Moving Image Archivist: Ms Ine van Dooren
Entry: viewings by appt at the SEVFA Office at the Univ of Brighton & at West Sussex Record Office **Open:** *West Sussex Record Office:* Mon-Fri 0915-1645, Sat 0915-1630
Subj: SE England (Surrey, Kent, East & West Sussex, Brighton & Hove, Medway): soc & culture as recorded in moving images **Collns:** *Other:* over 1000 items of film, video & digital media made in or relating to SE England, incl: newsreels; corporate documentaries; promotional material; feature films from the Shoreham Film Studio; home movies; local footage from private collns; Bognor Regis Film Soc Colln
Pubns: Cinema West Sussex, by Allen Eyles, Frank Gray & Alan Readman (£15.95 + £3.65 p&p); West Sussex on the Silver Screen, by Martin OíNeill (£1.50 + 31p p&p); both available from West Sussex Record Office

Bristol

A72

Bristol Record Office
'B' Bond Warehouse, Smeaton Rd, Bristol, BS1 6XN (0117-922-4224; *fax:* 0117-922-4236)
Email: bro@bristol-city.gov.uk

Gov Body: Bristol City Council (see **P18**)
Chief: City Archivist: Mr John S. Williams BA, DipAA **Dep:** Snr Archivist: Mr Richard G. Burley BA, DipAA
Entry: prior appt advisable; ref only **Open:** Mon-Thu 0930-1645
Subj: City & County of Bristol: local authority archvs; diocesan records; parish records; estate archvs; family papers; business records; records of parent org; trade union records; school records; records of socs; public records (e.g., courts & hosps); shipping records & crew lists **Collns:** *Archvs:* archvs of Bristol City Council & predecessor authorities; Diocese of Bristol records (Archdeaconry of Bristol); W.D. & H.O. Wills Colln; J.S. Fry & Sons Colln; Smyth family of Ashton Court (correspondence from Tudor times); "Bishop's Transcripts" of parish registers; Quarter & Petty Sessions *Other:* films; photos
Equip: 27 m-readers, m-camera, m-printer, fax, video viewer, copier, clr copier, 4 computers (all with wd-proc, internet & CD-ROM)
Stock: archvs/800 cubic m; rec mgmt/330 cubic m; other materials/10 cubic m
Pubns: Bristol record Office Introductory Leaflet; 'B' Bond Bulletin: Bristol Record Office Newsletter (both free); Govt of Bristol 1373-1973 (£1); Civic Treasures of Bristol (£1.95 paperback, £4.95 hardback); Bristol Apprentice Bks 1566-1593 (4 vols, £4 each); Business in Avon & Somerset: a survey of archvs (£10); Antiquaries of Gloucestershire & Bristol (£7.50); The Inside Story of the Smyths of Ashton Court (£2.50); various info leaflets, handlists & rsrch aids (50p-£3); maps (35p-£1.55); postcards & posters; others too numerous to mention, list of pubns available
Staff: *Archivists:* 5 *Non-Prof:* 9.5

A73

Clerical Medical Investment Group Ltd, Archives
Customer Svc Support, Narrow Plain, Bristol, BS2 0JH (0117-955-5960; *fax:* 0117-955-5961)
Internet: http://www.clericalmedical.co.uk/

Chief: Archivist: Mr Nigel Wratten
Entry: adv appt **Open:** Mon-Fri 0900-1700
Subj: finance; investment; business records; records of parent org **Collns:** *Archvs:* Clerical Medical Investment Group Ltd Archvs (1824-1990); records of Genl Reversionary & Investment Co (1836-1989); records of Lands Improvement Co (1853-2000)

A74

Clifton RC Diocesan Archives
c/o St Bernadette's Presbytery, Wells Rd, Whitchurch, Bristol, BS14 9HU (0117-983-3699)

Gov Body: RC Diocese of Clifton **Chief:** Diocesan Archivist: Rev Dr J.A. Harding
Assoc Offices: Archvs are deposited at: Alexander House, 160 Pennywell Rd, Bristol, BS5 0TX; contact the Diocesan Archivist at the above addr in the first instance
Entry: adv appt
Subj: Diocese of Clifton: diocesan records; parish records; personal papers

A75

The Feminist Archive
Trinity Rd Lib, Trinity Rd, St Phillips, Bristol, BS2 0NW (0117-935-0025)
Email: femarch@femarch.freeserve.co.uk
Internet: http://www.femarch.freeserve.co.uk/

Type: registered charity 282681 **Chief:** Archv Mgr: Ms R. Jane Hargreaves BSc, MA **Dep:** Ms Ann Orchard BA
Entry: ref only **Open:** Wed 1400-1630
Subj: SW England, some natl & internatl material: feminism (mainly 1960s-date); women's issues; women's movement; personal papers; political papers **Collns:** *Bks & Pamphs:* Virago Fiction Colln; Spare Rib Colln *Archvs:* Dora Russell Colln (Women's Peace Caravan, 1958); Carole Harwood Greenham Common Archv; records of Bristol City Council Women's Unit; Spare Rib readers' letters; records of Bristol Women's Centre (incl Bristol Women's House refuge); Monica Sjöö Archv *Other:* oral hists of the second wave of feminism (1960s onwards); poster colln, incl Pen Dalton Archv; Bristol WLM newsletters; Greenham Common Colln (incl photos); some audios; ephemera
Equip: copier (10p per copy), computer (with wd-proc) **Svcs:** info, ref, rsrch
Stock: archvs/50 archv boxes; bks/32 linear m; periodcls/41 linear m; illusts/c800 posters; pamphs/15 linear m; grey lit/17 linear m
Classn: European Women's Thesaurus
Pubns: Dora Russell Peace Caravan (£1); Greenham Common Colln (£1); Oral Histories of the Second Wave of Feminism (£2-£3)
Staff: *Non-Prof:* 2 staffed by volunteers

A76

Scottish Courage Ltd Archives
PO Box 85, Bristol, BS99 7BT (0117-965-0723)
Email: moonbeam@easynet.co.uk

Chief: Company Archivist: Mr Ken Thomas BA(Hons), MA
Entry: by appt only
Subj: brewing; business records; records of parent org **Collns:** *Bks & Pamphs:* records of Courage Ltd (1870-1990); records of Courage

(Western) Ltd (18C-1983); minutes & records of numerous other brewing companies *Other:* photographs; news cuttings
Svcs: info, ref, rsrch
Stock: archvs/c300 linear m; rec mgmt/1200 boxes; photos/c1500
Classn: own **Staff:** *Archivists:* 1

A77

University of Bristol Information Services, Special Collections
Arts & Social Scis Lib, Tyndall Ave, Bristol, BS8 1TJ (0117-928-8014; *fax:* 0117-925-5334)
Email: special-collections@bris.ac.uk
Internet: http://www.bris.ac.uk/is/

Gov Body: Univ of Bristol **Chief:** Special Collns Libn: Mr Michael Richardson **Dep:** Archivist: Ms Hannah Lowery BLib(Hons), DipAA
Assoc Offices: Special Collns is a section of the Arts & Social Scis Lib, which is a branch of the UNIV OF BRISTOL INFO SVCS (see **S260**)
Entry: ref only; adv appt preferred; ID with permanent addr or from academic instn **Open:** Mon-Fri 0915-1645
Subj: personal papers; political papers; family papers; estate archvs; business records; records of parent org **Collns:** *Bks & Pamphs:* Special Collns also houses a very fine bk & pamph colln which is mainly catalogued on the Lib's auto catalogue *Archvs:* archvs of Bristol Univ Coll & Univ of Bristol (incomplete, 1876-date); papers relating to indivs associated with the Univ, incl: John Beddoe papers; Cecil Reginald Burch papers; A.R. Collar papers; Edward Conze papers; Basil Cottle papers; Sir Charles Frank papers; H.E. Hinton papers; Heinz London papers; Conwy Lloyd Morgan papers; Sir Philip Morris papers; Cecil Powell papers; C.H. Sisson papers; A.M. Tyndall papers; Roger Wilson papers; other collns incl: West Indies Papers (personal & estate records, 1663-1929); Brunel Colln (papers of Isambard Kingdom Brunel, Sir Marc Isambard Brunel & Brunel family, 1817-1903); Goldney Family Papers (1681-1891); Paget Family Papers (1270-1920); Pinney Family Papers (1650-1986); John Addington Symonds Papers & MSS (personal & family papers, 1884-1980); Worsley Family Papers; Clifton Suspension Bridge Trust Papers (1829-1939); Hamish Hamilton Ltd Editorial & Historical Archv (publishers, to 1970); Penguin Bks Ltd Editorial & Historical Archv (1935-70), incl papers of Allen Lane, Eunice Frost, Betty Radice & others associated with the company; records of Sir George H. Oatley & Partners (architects); Edward Conze Colln (oriental theology); Victor & Joan Eyles Papers (hist of geol); Dame Katherine Furse, correspondence (1887-1952); Matthew Blagden Hale Papers; Thomas Lloyd Humberstone Papers (1895-1955); David James Cathcart King Papers (relating to the medieval castle in England & Wales, 1939-89); Bryan Little Papers (1927-56); Philip Napier Miles Papers (1884-1951); Humphrey Repton Papers (1788-1814); Robin Tanner Papers (1920-88); Jane Cobden Unwin Papers (1880-1939); Bateman Colln (labour movement in 20C); Liberal Party Collns (numerous small collns, 19C-20C); Natl Liberal Club Papers; Women's Liberal Federation Papers (1888-1988); election addresses of all parties (1892-date); Moravian Church Colln (hist of Moravian Church on Maudlin St, Bristol, 1760-1893); Somerset Miners Assoc Colln (1868-1964); records of Sizewell 'B' Inquiry (1986); Kingswood Abbey Colln *Other:* Fry Portrait Colln (illustrated bks, prints & portraits, 16C-19C); Adey Horton Colln (reproductions of medieval art & arch); Teichman Bequest (prints of 18C Russia)
Equip: photocopying via staff; available elsewhere in lib: 4 m-readers, 2 m-printers, video viewer, computers (incl internet & CD-ROM)
Svcs: info, ref

Archives

Bristol ▼ Cambridge

(Univ of Bristol Info Svcs, Special Collns cont)
Stock: various printed bks & pamphs, periodcls, photos, slides, illusts, maps, m-forms & AVs
Classn: LC, ISAD(G) (being adopted), in-house
Auto Sys: Aleph
Pubns: Guide to Special Collns (free leaflet); Guide to Brunel Colln (free leaflet)
Staff: Archivists: 2 Libns: 1 Non-Prof: 1 PT asst

Brockenhurst

A78 🖤

Palace House (Beaulieu) Archive, Montagu Ventures Ltd

John Montagu Bldg, Beaulieu, Brockenhurst, Hampshire, SO42 7ZN (01590-612345; *fax:* 01590-612624)
Emall: Info@beaulleu.co.uk
Internet: http://www.beaulieu.co.uk/

Gov Body: Lord Montagu of Beaulieu **Chief:** Archivist & Heritage Edu Offcr: Miss Susan Tomkins BA(Hons), PGCE (susan.tomkins@ beaulieu.co.uk)
Entry: adv appt, ref only **Open:** Mon-Fri 1000-1500; tel enqs 0900-1700
Subj: The Beaulieu Estate: parish records; estate archvs; Montagu family papers; records of parent org (Montagu Ventures Ltd) **Collns:** Archvs: The Beaulieu Estate Archv (predominantly 18C onwards); Ditton Park, Slough (estate records); Montagu family papers; Beaulieu poor law records
Equip: fax, copier (via Archivist), room for hire (apply to Corporate Hospitality Dept at addr above) **Svcs:** photographic
Stock: archvs/110 m; bks/20 m
Pubns: The Beaulieu Record (£10.95); John Montagu of Beaulieu (£9.50); Buckler's Hard: A Rural Shipbuilding Centre (£6.95); Beaulieu: King John's Abbey (£4.75); An Album of Old Beaulieu & Buckler's Hard (£6.95); Beaulieu River Goes to War (£6.95); Beaulieu: The Finishing School for Secret Agents (£16.95); Wheels within Wheels: An Unconventional Life, by Lord Montague of Beaulieu (£20)
Staff: Other Prof: 1

Bromley

A79 🏛

Bromley Local Studies Library and Archives

Central Lib, High St, Bromley, Kent, BR1 1EX (020-8460-9955 x261; *fax:* 020-8313-9975)
Email: localstudies.library@bromley.gov.uk

Gov Body: London Borough of Bromley (see **P81**) **Chief:** Local Studies Libn: Mr Simon Finch BA, MCLIP, ACMI **Other Snr Staff:** Archivist: Miss E. Silverthorne MA, DipAS
Entry: appt advisable if consulting original documents **Open:** Mon, Wed & Fri 0930-1800, Tue & Thu 0930-2000, Sat 0930-1700
Subj: London Borough of Bromley: local authority archvs; parish records; estate archvs; family papers; records of parent org **Collns:** Bks & Pamphs: H.G. Wells Colln **Archvs:** archvs of London Borough of Bromley & predecessor authorities; census returns; electoral registers

Equip: 15 m-readers, 6 m-printers, copier, 4 computers (incl 3 with internet & 1 with CD-ROM)
Svcs: rsrch (limited svc)
Classn: Dewey 21 (mod) **Auto Sys:** Geac
Staff: Archivists: 1 Libns: 1 Non-Prof: 3 **Exp:** £12000 (1999-2000); £12000 (2000-01)

Burnley

A80 🔑 🐾

Salford RC Diocesan Archives

c/o St Mary's Presbytery, 3 Todmorden Rd, Burnley, Lancashire, BB10 4AU (01282-422007; *fax:* 01282-424622)
Email: davelannon@aol.com

Gov Body: Salford Roman Catholic Diocesan Trustees (Registered) **Chief:** Archivist: Rev Fr David Lannon MPhil
Entry: adv appt only
Subj: RC Diocese of Salford (Greater Manchester & East Lancashire): diocesan records; records of parent org **Collns:** Bks & Pamphs: The Harvest (diocesan magazine, 1887-1970); Catholic Directory (1818-date, some early gaps); Salford Diocesan Almanac (1877-date); Catholic record Soc pubns; early Catholic Social Guild pubns **Archvs:** archvs of the RC Diocese of Salford, incl much dealing with edu matters; Catholic Teachers' Federation records (1907 onwards); Catholic Federation records (incl copies of The Federationist, 1910-29)
Equip: 2 m-readers, computer
Stock: archvs/70 linear m; bks/80 linear m
Pubns: The Acta of Bishop Bilsborrow 1892-1903
Staff: Non-Prof: 3

Burton-upon-Trent

A81 🏛

Staffordshire and Stoke-on-Trent Archive Service, Burton-upon-Trent Archives

Burton Lib, Riverside, High St, Burton-upon-Trent, Staffordshire, DE14 1AH (01283-239556; *fax:* 01283-239571)
Email: burton.library@staffordshire.gov.uk
Internet: http://www.staffordshire.gov.uk/ archives/

Gov Body: part of Staffordshire & Stoke-on-Trent Archv Svc, run on behalf of Staffordshire County Council (see **P174**) & Stoke-on-Trent City Council (see **P178**) **Chief:** Archivist-in-Charge: Mr Martin Sanders BA, MPhil, DipAA
Assoc Offices: other Staffordshire & Stoke-on-Trent Archv Svc branches: STAFFORDSHIRE RECORD OFFICE (main office – see **A467**); LICHFIELD RECORD OFFICE (see **A232**); STOKE-ON-TRENT CITY ARCHVS (see **A473**); WILLIAM SALT LIB (see **A468**)
Entry: Archvs: Staffordshire & Stoke-on-Trent Archv Svc reader's ticket; adv appt essential; Local Studies Room: open to public for ref only **Open:** Mon, Wed-Fri 0900-1200, 1400-1800, Tue 1000-1200, 1400-1800
Subj: former County Borough of Burton: local authority archvs; business records; personal papers; school records; hosp records; nonconformist records; magistrates records; school records; poor law records; records of local orgs **Collns:** Archvs: records of County Borough of Burton-upon-Trent & predecessor authorities (16C onwards); records of Burton-upon-Trent Poor Law Union; records of Burton-upon-Trent Methodist Circuit **Other:** census returns, parish registers & local newspapers on m-film
Equip: m-readers **Disabled:** wheelchair access
Svcs: info, ref, postal enq svc, talks & exhibs

Bury

A82 🏛

Bury Archive Service

Edwin St, off Crompton St, Bury, Lancashire, BL9 0AS (0161-797-6697)
Email: archives@bury.gov.uk
Internet: http://www.bury.gov.uk/

Gov Body: Bury Metropolitan Borough Council (see **P20**) **Chief:** Archivist: Mr Kevin Mulley MA, DipAS
Entry: appt required except Tue **Open:** Mon-Fri 1000-1300, 1400-1700
Subj: Bury Metropolitan Borough: local authority archvs (1675-date); estate archvs (1654-date); family papers (late 18C-date); business records (1782-date); records of parent org; trade union records; records of sports clubs & social orgs; nonconformist records; school records **Co-op Schemes:** Greater Manchester Archivists' Group
Equip: m-reader, copier, computer **Disabled:** magnifying CCTV
Stock: archvs/55 cubic m
Classn: ISAD(G)
Pubns: Interim Guide (£2.50 + 50p p&p)
Staff: Archivists: 1 Non-Prof: 0.1 **Exp:** £200 (2000-01)

Bury St Edmunds

A83 🏛

Suffolk Record Office, Bury St Edmunds Branch

77 Raingate St, Bury St Edmunds, Suffolk, IP33 2AR (01284-352352; *fax:* 01284-352355)
Email: bury.ro@libher.suffolkcc.gov.uk
Internet: http://www.suffolkcc.gov.uk/ libraries_and_heritage/

Gov Body: Suffolk County Council, Libs & Heritage Dept (see **P179**) **Chief:** Public Svc Mgr: Mrs Sheila Reed (sheila.reed@libher.suffolkcc. gov.uk) **Other Snr Staff:** Local Studies Libn: Mr Ed Button BA, MCLIP (ed.button@libher. suffolkcc.gov.uk)
Assoc Offices: IPSWICH BRANCH (see **A215**); LOWESTOFT BRANCH (see **A361**)
Entry: CARN ticket required for access to archvs; booking sys for m-readers **Open:** Mon-Sat 0900-1700
Subj: West Suffolk: local authority archvs; diocesan records; parish records; estate records; family papers; business records; records of parent org; regimental records; records of local charities & socs **Collns:** Bks & Pamphs: Cullum Lib (18C-19C personal lib, c4000 vols); West Suffolk Local Studies Lib, incl Suffolk Inst of Archaeo Lib **Archvs:** Diocese of St Edmundsbury & Ipswich (Bury St Edmunds area) records; Suffolk Regiment Archvs; estate & family papers of the Dukes of Grafton; papers of Hervey family, Marquisses of Bristol (14C-20C); records of Robert Boby (engineers, 1866-1909) **Other:** local photo collns; 1901 Census for Suffolk (m-fiche)
Equip: 24 m-readers, 3 m-printers, copier (not self-svc), fax, computer (incl internet & CD-ROM)
Svcs: info, ref, rsrch, transcription, translation, m-fiche & m-film duplication
Stock: archvs/5875 ft; rec mgmt/900 ft; other materials/72 ft
Classn: DDC **Auto Sys:** DS CALM 2000
Pubns: Guide to Genealogical Sources (10 sections, priced individually or £22.50 for all 10, incl 2nd class p&p); Family Data Colln Pack (£2.75 incl p&p); Bowen's Map of Suffolk 1759 (£3 incl p&p); various leaflets on svcs (free)
Staff: Archivists: 1.4 Libns: 0.2 Non-Prof: 4.5

Caernarfon

A84
Gwynedd Archives and Museums Service

County Offices, Caernarfon, Gwynedd, LL55 1SH (01286-679093; *fax:* 01286-679637)
Email: archives@gwynedd.gov.uk
Internet: http://www.gwynedd.gov.uk/

Gov Body: Gwynedd Council (see **P58**) *Chief:* Principal Archivist & Heritage Offcr: Ms Ann Rhydderch MA, DipAA
Assoc Offices: MERIONETH AREA RECORD OFFICE (see **A123**)
Entry: CARN ticket *Open:* Tue-Fri 0930-1230, 1330-1700 (Wed -1900)
Subj: Gwynedd: local authority archvs; parish records; estate archvs; family papers; business records; maritime records; public records *Collns: Bks & Pamphs:* Lloyd's List of Registers; Welsh periodcls; Climbing Club pubns *Archvs:* strong in maritime matters; records of slate quarries *Other:* large collns of photos; oral hist tapes
Equip: 14 m-readers, 3 m-cameras, 2 m-printers, 2 video viewers, fax, 3 copiers *Online:* catalogue
Stock: archvs/451 cubic m; rec mgmt/173 cubic m; other materials/39 cubic m
Pubns: postcards, local hist bks etc
Staff: Other Prof: 4.9 *Non-Prof:* 12.1

A85
Royal Welch Fusiliers Museum Archives

The Castle, Caernarfon, Gwynedd, LL55 2AY (01286-673362; *fax:* 01286-677042)
Email: rwfusiliers@callnetuk.com
Internet: http://www.rwfmuseum.org.uk/

Chief: Curator: Mr P.A. Crocker
Entry: Museum: no restrictions; *Archvs:* adv appt
Open: Museum: Apr-May: Mon-Sun 0930-1700; Jun-Sep: Mon-Sun 0930-1800; Oct: Mon-Sun 0930-1700; Nov-Mar: Mon-Sat 0930-1600, Sun 1100-1600; *Archvs:* Mon-Fri 1000-1600
Subj: military hist; regimental hist; regimental records; personal papers; records of parent org
Collns: Archvs: records of Royal Welch Fusiliers/23rd Foot (1689-2000) & associated Militia, Volunteer, Yeomanry & Territorial regiments & battalions; papers relating to Genl Sir Hugh Stockwell (1903-1986), Robert Graves & David Jones
Equip: m-reader, copier (10p per sheet) *Svcs:* info, ref, rsrch *Staff: Non-Prof:* 1

Caithness

A86
North Highland Archive

Wick Lib, Sinclair Ter, Wick, Caithness, KW1 5AB (01955-606432; *fax:* 01955-603000)
Email: phil.astley@highland.gov.uk
Internet: http://www.northhighlandarchive.org/

Gov Body: Highland Council (see **P64**) *Chief:* North Highland Archivist: Mr Phil Astley *Dep:* Archv Asst: Mrs Gail Inglis
Assoc Offices: branch of HIGHLAND COUNCIL ARCHV (see **A213**)
Entry: free access; adv appt recommended
Open: Mon, Thu-Fri 1000-1300, 1400-1730, Tue 1000-1300, 1400-2000, Wed 1000-1300
Subj: former counties of Caithness & Sutherland: local authority archvs; parish records; estate archvs (one or two small collns); family papers (sparse); business records (one or two small collns); personal papers (sparse); political papers (ephemera only); records of parent org; harbour records; police records; parochial records;
customs & excise records; edu records (major holding); limited holdings in: archaeo; nursing; trade; agric *Collns: Bks & Pamphs:* Caithness Law Cases; Thomson's Acts of the Parliament of Scotland; Abridgements of Sasine (Caithness, 1648-1968); Calendar of Confirmations & Index to the Svcs of Heirs in Scotland (1876-1936 & 1847-1974); Valuation Rolls for Wick Burgh & Caithness County; John O'Groat's Journal (1836-date); Northern Ensign (1850-1922) *Archvs:* Burgh minutes of Wick (1660-date), Thurso (1866-date) & County of Caithness (1890-date); minutes of Commissioners of Supply, Road Trustees & JPs (Caithness); minutes of Trust Committees; private collns, incl Wick Harbour Trust; smaller collns from indivs, businesses & families *Other:* Old Parish Registers & census records for Caithness & Sutherland (m-form); OS Survey Name Bk (Caithness); OS maps of Caithness & Sutherland; 10ft maps of Wick; inland revenue maps; a few estate/crofting maps; arch plans; a few photos; small colln of audio tapes
Equip: 5 m-readers (3 film, 2 fiche), m-printer, copier, fax, computers (incl wd-proc, internet & CD-ROM) *Svcs:* info, ref, rsrch
Stock: archvs/120 linear m; bks/30 linear m; maps/20 linear m; m-forms/2 drawers
Pubns: Guide to the Collns of the North Highland Archv (free); numerous info sheets (free); Guide to Highland Council (in conjunction with Head Office at Inverness, £7); Guide to Printed Sources at the North Highland Archv (£2.50); Family Hist from Archvs & Ephemera (£1.50)
Staff: Archivists: 1 *Non-Prof:* 1 *Exp:* £7000 (2000-01)
Further Info: Caithness Hist Soc meets fortnightly in the Archv, hold regular exhibs & publishes quarterly newsletter

Cambridge

A87
Cambridgeshire County Record Office

Shire Hall, Castle Hill, Cambridge, CB3 0AP (01223-717281; *fax:* 01223-717823)
Email: county.records.cambridge@ cambridgeshire.gov.uk
Internet: http://edweb.camcnty.gov.uk/archives/

Gov Body: Cambridgeshire County Council (see **P23**) *Chief:* County Archivist: Mrs E. Stazicker MA, DipAA *Dep:* Dep County Archivist: Dr P.C. Saunders BA, DPhil
Assoc Offices: COUNTY RECORD OFFICE, Huntingdon (see **A211**)
Entry: CARN ticket, adv booking (esp for m-film & map users) advisable *Open:* Tue-Thu 0900-1245, 1345-1715, Fri 0900-1245, 1345-1615 (Tue 1715-2100 by appt only), closed Mon
Subj: former County of Cambridgeshire & Isle of Ely: local authority archvs; parish records; estate records; family papers; business records; records of parent org; local hist *Collns: Bks & Pamphs:* all aspects of local hist etc of former County of Cambridgeshire & Isle of Ely *Archvs:* archvs of Cambridgeshire County Council; probate records of the Diocese of Ely (1447-1857); parish records of Cambridgeshire & Isle of Ely; records of Bedford Level Corp (1663-1920); nearly complete series relating to land drainage in Fens
Equip: 7 m-readers, m-printer, copier, computer
Stock: archvs/597 cubic m; rec mgmt/238 cubic m; bks/1075 linear ft; periodcls/50 linear ft; photos/10000-15000; slides/500 (35mm); illusts/500; pamphs/4000; maps/50000; m-forms/10000; audios/30; videos/250; CD-ROMs/4; cine films/200
Classn: own *Auto Sys:* Access
Pubns: Guide to Edu Records in County Record Office, Cambridge (£1), Genealogical Sources in Cambridgeshire 1994 (£4 + 50p p&p inland, £1 p&p overseas)
Staff: Archivists: 5 *Other Prof:* 1 *Non-Prof:* 4

A88
Churchill Archives Centre

Churchill Coll, Storey's Way, Cambridge, CB3 0DS (01223-336087; *fax:* 01223-336135)
Email: archives@chu.cam.ac.uk
Internet: http://www.chu.cam.ac.uk/

Gov Body: Churchill Coll (see **S345**) *Chief:* Dir: Mr Allen Packwood *Other Snr Staff:* Archivist & Info Svcs Mgr: Ms Natalie Adams; Thatcher Archivist: Mr Andrew Riley (Thatcher.Archives@ chu.cam.ac.uk)
Entry: adv appt *Open:* Mon-Fri 0900-1700, closed bank hols
Subj: politics; diplomacy; foreign policy; internatl relations; defence policy; the military; sci; tech; WW1; WW2; journalism & lit; media & public relations; family papers; personal papers; political papers *Collns: Bks & Pamphs:* Roskill Lib (20C military & political hist) *Archvs:* papers & correspondence of Sir Winston Churchill (1874-1965); political papers of Lord Randolph Churchill (1849-1895); Wimborne Papers (Churchill family correspondence); other Churchill & Marlborough family papers; papers of private secretaries of Sir Winston Churchill; Thatcher Papers (incl correspondence, personal & official papers, photos, cuttings, audio & video recordings, c1 mln documents, 1920s-date); 300 other collns of private papers of scientists, public servants, diplomats, soldiers, sailors & airmen; see web site for full details *Other:* Broadwater Colln (Churchill famlily photograph albums & bks of press cuttings); press photos; press cuttings; audio & video recordings & transcripts for BBC series "Churchill"
Equip: 2 m-readers, 2 m-printers, copier, 2 computers (both with internet & CD-ROM) *Online:* online catalogue & educational resources; see web site for details
Stock: archvs/c300 linear m; bks/c5000
Classn: ISAD(G)
Pubns: Guide to Holdings (£3.50 + p&p); guides & online catalogue also available on web site
Staff: Archivists: 5 *Other Prof:* 1 conservator *Non-Prof:* 4

A89
Ely Diocesan Records

c/o Cambridge Univ Lib, West Rd, Cambridge, CB3 9DR (01223-333160)
Email: pmm1000@cam.ac.uk
Internet: http://www.lib.cam.ac.uk/

Gov Body: Diocese of Ely, administered by Cambridge Univ Lib (see **L5**) *Chief:* Keeper of Ely Diocesan Records: Mr Peter M. Meadows
Assoc Offices: also held at CAMBRIDGE UNIV LIB are the archvs & MSS of the Dean & Chapter of Ely (Keeper: Mr Peter M. Meadows); parish records are held at COUNTY RECORD OFFICES in Cambridge (see **A87**), Huntingdon (see **A211**), Wisbech (see **A512**) & Norwich (see **A400**)
Entry: adv appt (ring 01223-333030) *Open:* Mon-Fri 0930-1845, Sat 0930-1630
Subj: C of E Diocese of Ely: diocesan records; estate records *Collns: Archvs:* records of diocese & bishop's admin, incl: bishops' registers; visitation records; ecclesiastical & temporal court records; licenses & registers; estate & manorial records of Bishops of Ely
Pubns: A Catalogue of the Records of the Bishop & Archdeacon of Ely, by Dorothy M. Owen (1971)

Canterbury

A90 🍴 🖐

Canterbury Cathedral Archives

The Precincts, Canterbury, Kent, CT1 2EH
(01227-864330; *fax:* 01227-865222)
Email: archives@canterbury-cathedral.org
Internet: http://www.canterbury-cathedral.org/

Gov Body: Dean & Chapter of Canterbury & Kent County Council (see **P67**) *Chief:* Canon Libn: Canon Edward Condry; Cathedral Archivist: Ms Heather Forbes BA, MArAd *Dep:* Dep Cathedral Archivist: Dr M.T. Bateson BA, PhD, MArAd
Assoc Offices: CANTERBURY CATHEDRAL LIB (see **S404**)
Entry: CARN ticket required, adv appt advisable *Open:* Mon-Thu 0900-1700, 1ct, 3rd Sat of each month 0900-1300, closed 1st 2 wks of Jan
Subj: Canterbury & East Kent: local authority archvs; diocesan records; parish records; records of parent org *Collns: Archvs:* archvs of Canterbury City Council & predecessors; parish records of Archdeaconry of Canterbury (1538-date); MSS bks of monastic lib; medieval records of Priory of Christ Church; archvs of Dean & Chapter (1542-date); archvs of city (14C-date); archvs of Diocese of Canterbury & surrounding area (c1300-date)
Equip: 15 m-readers, m-camera, m-printer, copier, fax, computer (with internet & CD-ROM) *Svcs:* info, ref, rsrch
Stock: archvs/1300 linear m; maps/140 linear m; m-forms/750 reels
Classn: ISAD(G) *Auto Sys:* CALM 2000
Pubns: Canterbury Sources, incl: Vol 1: Bibliography of the Oxford Movement; Vol 2. In Foreign Parts; Vol 3. The Slave Trade
Staff: Archivists: 5, plus 3 archv assts, 2 conservators, 1 genealogical rsrcher, 1 reprographer

A91 🎓

Centre for the Study of Cartoons and Caricature, Archives

Templeman Lib, Univ of Kent at Canterbury, Canterbury, Kent, CT2 7NU (01227-823127; *fax:* 01227-823127)
Email: j.m.newton@ukc.ac.uk
Internet: http://library.ukc.ac.uk/cartoons/

Gov Body: Univ of Kent at Canterbury (see **S410**) *Chief:* Head of Centre: Dr N. Hiley PhD
Dep: Asst Head: Ms Jane Newton BA
Entry: adv appt advised; priority will be given to rsrchers with an appt *Open:* Mon-Fri 0900-1700
Subj: cartoons; cartoonists; caricature *Collns: Bks & Pamphs:* bks on cartoons & cartoonists; anthologies; ref works; Giles annuals (1954 onwards) *Archvs:* collns by over 60 cartoonists (1904-date), incorporating 85000+ pieces of original artwork; artists incl: W.K. Hasleden; Will Dyson; Sidney 'George' Strube; David Low; Vicky Emmwood; Michael Cummings; Ralph Steadman; Mel Calman; Nicholas Garland; Chris Riddell
Other: newspaper & journal cuttings; various AVs
Equip: copier, computer (incl internet) *Online:* online catalogue of 90000 British cartoons *Svcs:* rsrch, exhibs
Stock: archvs/2000; illusts/85000+
Pubns: exhib catalogues

A92 🍴 🖐

Franciscan Order of Friars Minor, Archives

Franciscan Internatl Study Centre, Giles Ln, Canterbury, Kent, CT2 7NA (01227-464939; *fax:* 01227-470496)
Email: narbuckle@yahoo.co.uk
Internet: http://www.friar.org/

Gov Body: Trustees of Order of Friars Minor
Chief: Archivist: Br Ninian Arbuckle OFM
Entry: by personal arrangement only
Subj: Gt Britain: Franciscan Order; personal papers; records of parent org *Collns: Bks & Pamphs:* works by Franciscan Friars (17C-20C)
Archvs: chapter & definitory minutes (1600-date); registers of acts of chapters, definitories & indiv minister provincials
Equip: 2 copiers (10p per copy), computer (with wd-proc, internet & CD-ROM) *Svcs:* info, ref, rsrch
Acq Offcr: Archivist, as above

Cardiff

A93 🏛

Cadw: The Welsh Historic Monuments Executive Agency

Crown Bldg, Cathays Pk, Cardiff, CF10 3NQ (029-2050-0200; *fax:* 029-2082-6375)
Email: cadw@wales.gsi.gov.uk
Internet: http://www.cadw.wales.gov.uk/

Gov Body: Natl Assembly for Wales
Assoc Offices: PHOTOGRAPHIC LIB, at same addr (029-2082-6395; *email:* photolib@wales.gsi.gov.uk)
Subj: Wales: ancient monuments; historical bldgs; conservation, presentation & promotion of the built heritage of Wales *Collns: Other:* photos of all the monuments in the care of Cadw
Svcs: loan of images

A94 🖐

Cardiff RC Archdiocesan Archive

Archbishop's House, Cathedral Rd, Cardiff, CF1 9HD (029-2022-0411; *fax:* 029-2034-5950)

Chief: contact the Diocesan Archivist
Entry: ref only; adv appt
Subj: RC Archdiocese of Cardiff: diocesan records; personal papers *Collns: Archvs:* records of the Roman Catholic Archdiocese of Cardiff; correspondence & papers of former Archbishops of Cardiff, incl: James Bilsborrow (1862-1931) & Francis Mostyn (1860-1939); correspondence & papers of former Bishops of Newport & Menevia, incl: Thomas Brown (1798-1880) & John Hedley (1837-1915)

A95 🎬 🎥

HTV Cymru Wales, Television Archive

TV Centre, Culverhouse Cross, Cardiff, CF5 6XJ (029-2059-0177/731; *fax:* 029-2059-0661)
Email: angela.jones@htv-wales.co.uk
Internet: http://www.htvwales.com/

Gov Body: HTV Cymru Wales *Chief:* Snr Lib Administrator: Ms Angela Jones
Entry: adv appt for rsrchers
Subj: television programmes in Welsh & English
Collns: Other: materials transmitted by predecessor TWW (1958-68); material transmitted by HTV (1968-date); news & current affairs programmes (1958-date); sports, light entertainment, dramas & documentaries (1970-date)

Stock: archvs/16mm film/10000 cans; 1" tapes/39000; betacam cassettes/50000+
See also HTV CYMRU WALES, CURRENT AFFAIRS LIB (**S418**)

A96 🍴 🏛

Welch Regiment Museum, Archives

Cardiff Castle, Cardiff, CF10 2RB (029-2022-9367)
Email: welch@rrw.org.uk
Internet: http://www.rrw.org.uk/museums/

Chief: Curator: Mr John Dart (john.dart@rrw.org.uk)
Entry: serious rsrchers by adv appt *Open:* Apr-Oct: Mon, Wed-Sun 1000-1800; Nov-Mar: Mon, Wed-Sun 1000-1630; closed Tue
Subj: regimental records; regimental hist; military hist *Collns: Archvs:* records relating to the Welch Regiment (41st/69th Foot, 1719-1969) & the Royal Regiment of Wales; genl order bk of the Royal Glamorgan Light Infantry Militia (1806-15)
Svcs: email enqs

A97 🏛

Glamorgan Record Office

The Glamorgan Bldg, King Edward VII Ave, Cathays Pk, Cardiff, CF10 3NE (029-2078-0282; *fax:* 029-2078-0284)
Email: glamro@cardiff.ac.uk
Internet: http://www.glamro.gov.uk

Gov Body: Glamorgan Archvs Joint Cttee, representing the following councils: City & County of Cardiff Council (see **P24**), Bridgend County Borough Council (see **P16**), Caerphilly County Borough Council (see **P21**), Merthyr Tydfil County Borough Council (see **P114**), Rhondda Cynon Taff County Borough Council (see **P153**) & Vale of Glamorgan County Borough Council (see **P190**)
Chief: Head Archivist: Ms Susan Edwards BA, DipAA *Dep:* Principal Archivist: Mrs Charlotte Hodgson BA, DipAA
Entry: ID required giving signature & current addr (essential for registering as a searcher); adv appt advised, esp for use of m-readers & for evening openings *Open:* Tue, Thu 0930-1700, Wed 0930-1900, Fri 0930-1630; closed Mon
Subj: former counties of Mid- & South Glamorgan, historic county of Glamorgan & successor authorities: local authority archvs; parish records (Diocese of Llandaff); estate archvs; family papers; business records; records of parent org; records of schools; hosp records; police records; Roman Catholic records; nonconformist records; synagogue records; Quaker records; records of socs & assocs
Collns: Bks & Pamphs: hist of Glamorgan & places within Glamorgan; directories; bks on genealogy & heraldry; bks on sources; pubns of local socs *Archvs:* Glamorgan County Council (1939-74); Mid- & South Glamorgan County Councils (1974-96); Glamorgan Quarter & Petty Sessions; Port of Cardiff Shipping Registers; records of RC Archdiocese of Cardiff, incl deaneries of Cardiff East, Cardiff West, Bridgend, Head of the Valleys & Pontypridd; Fonmon Castle (family & estate records); Nicholl of Merthyr Mawr (family & estate records); Dowlais Iron Co; Rhymney Iron Co; records of South Wales Coalfield *Other:* census returns for Glamorgan & Monmouthshire (m-film & m-fiche, 1841-1901); maps & plans; photos
Equip: 10 m-readers, m-printers (staff only), copier (staff only) *Disabled:* wheelchair access
Svcs: photographic, rsrch (£15 per hr)
Stock: archvs/10000 linear ft
Pubns: Guides to Rsrch; info sheets; leaflets; annual reports; Bridges of Merthyr Tydfil (£6); A Catalogue of Glamorgan Estate Maps (£6); Parish

---

Register of Wales (£14.95); Poor Relief in Merthyr Tydfil in Victorian Times (£6); Family Hist Rsrch in Glamorgan (£1.50); maps; prints & engravings; posters; postcards & greetings cards; numerous others
Staff: Archivists: 7 *Other Prof:* 1 *Non-Prof:* 8

Carlisle

A98

Cumbria Record Office, Carlisle

The Castle, Carlisle, Cumbria, CA3 8UR (01228-607285; *fax:* 01228-607270)
Email: carlisle.record.office@cumbriacc.gov.uk
Internet: http://www.cumbria.gov.uk/archives/

Gov Body: Cumbria County Council (see **P32**)
Chief: County Archivist: Ms A. Rowe BA, DipAA
Dep: Asst County Archivist: Mr D.M. Bowcock BA, DipAA
Assoc Offices: CUMBRIA RECORD OFFICE, KENDAL (see **A217**); CUMBRIA RECORD OFFICE, BARROW (see **A28**); CUMBRIA RECORD OFFICE, WHITEHAVEN (see **A507**)
Entry: CARN ticket *Open:* Mon-Fri 0900-1700
Subj: City of Carlisle, former County of Cumberland: local authority archvs; diocesan records; parish records; estate archvs; family papers; business records; records of parent org; records of schools, solicitors, socs etc *Collns: Archvs:* records of Sir Esme Howard (Lord Howard of Penrith) career diplomat (19C-20C); records of Catherine Marshall, suffragist & pacifist of Keswick (19C-20C); records of the Carlisle & Dist State Mgmt Scheme (1916-1973); records of the Dean & Chapter of Carlisle (13C-20C); Diocese of Carlisle (C of E) probate records (16C-mid 19C); Diocese of Bradford parish records (Carlisle area)
Equip: 12 m-readers, 2 m-printers, m-camera (staff operated), copier (staff operated), fax, room hire (max 15 persons) *Svcs:* historical rsrch svc (£19 per hr)
Stock: archvs/383.4 cubic m; other materials/33.9 cubic m
Auto Sys: CAIRS (being introduced)
Pubns: Cumbrian Ancestors: Notes for Genealogical Searchers (£6.99 + p&p); Vital Statistics: The Westmorland 'Census' of 1787, ed. Loraine Ashcroft (£9.50 + p&p); 'The Rake's Diary' – The Journal of George Hilton (£5.99. + p&p); Much Cry of Kendal Wool, compiled E.M. Wilson (£2.50 + p&p); The Ellen Rose Fieldhouse Colln (£4.95 + p&p); Fleming Senhouse Papers (£7.50 + p&p); Marriage License/Bonds Vol I 1668-1739 (£5.95 + p&p); Marriage License/Bonds Vol II 1740-1752 (£6 + p&p); West Cumbria – A Trip Back in Time (video, £11.99 + p&p); Source Guides (£2-£3 each + p&p); various maps & posters; full list available
Staff: Archivists: 5.6 *Non-Prof:* 4.8

Carmarthen

A99

Carmarthenshire Archive Service

(formerly part of Dyfed Archv Svc)
Parc Myrddin, Richmond Ter, Carmarthen, Carmarthenshire, SA31 1DS (01267-228232; *fax:* 01267-228237)
Email: archives@carmarthenshire.gov.uk
Internet: http://www.carmarthenshire.gov.uk/

Gov Body: Carmarthenshire County Council (see **P25**) *Chief:* County Archivist: Mr John Davies BA, DipAA *Dep:* Snr Archivist: Mr David Cooke MA
Entry: no restrictions; adv appt for m-readers
Open: Mon-Thu 0900-1645, Fri 0900-1615
Subj: Carmarthenshire: local authority archvs; diocesan records; parish records; estate archvs; family papers; business records; personal papers;

political papers; records of parent org; hosp records; solicitors' records; trade union records; records of local socs *Collns: Archvs:* records of Carmarthenshire County Council (1889-1974); records of Borough & Dist Councils; records of Carmarthenshire Quarter Sessions & Petty Sessions; Cawdor Estate Colln (Carmarthenshire & Pembrokeshire estates of the Vaughan & later the Campbell families, 13C-20C); Carmarthenshire Antiquarian Soc Colln; Felons Register (incl "mug shots", probably earliest in Britain, c1860s); shipping records for the ports of Llanelli & Carmarthen *Other:* census returns (1841-1901); OS map colln
Equip: m-reader, m-printer, copier, computer (with internet & CD-ROM)
Stock: archvs/300 cubic m; rec mgmt/150 cubic m
Pubns: Summaries of Main Collns (free); Tracing Your Family Hist at the Carmarthenshire Record Office (£1.60)
Staff: Archivists: 3 *Non-Prof:* 2

Chelmsford

A100

Essex Record Office

Wharf Rd, Chelmsford, Essex, CM2 6YT (01245-244644; *fax:* 01245-244655)
Email: ero.enquiry@essexcc.gov.uk
Internet: http://www.essexcc.gov.uk/

Gov Body: Essex County Council (see **P51**)
Chief: County & Hon Diocesan Archivist: Mr Ken Hall
Assoc Offices: COLCHESTER OFFICE (see **A111**); SOUTHEND OFFICE (see **A461**); SAFFRON WALDEN ARCHV ACCESS PT, Town Hall, Market St, Saffron Walden, Essex, CB10 1HR (01799-516821; *fax:* 01799-516822); HARLOW ARCHV ACCESS PT, Museum of Harlow, Muskham Rd, off First Ave, Harlow, Essex, CM20 2LF (01279-454959); also in same bldg as Main Record Office: ESSEX SOC FOR FAMILY HIST RSRCH CENTRE
Entry: Archvs: CARN ticket; *Lib Holdings:* ref only *Open:* Mon 0900-2030, Tue-Thu 0900-1700, Fri-Sat 0900-1600
Subj: County of Essex: local authority archvs; diocesan records; parish records; estate archvs; family papers; business records; records of parent org; school records; nonconformist records; records of local orgs *Collns: Bks & Pamphs:* extensive local hist lib; Essex biography; local directories *Archvs:* archvs of Essex County Council; records of dist, parish & borough councils; records of Poor Law Unions; records of Diocese of Chelmsford; title deeds & wills *Other:* Essex Sound Archv (1300+ oral hist & other sound recordings of local hist interest); maps & plans; photos & engravings; local newspapers; electoral registers
Equip: 50+ m-readers, 2 m-cameras, 2 m-printers, 4 copiers, 50 computer catalogue terminals, 6 listening booths for Sound Archv
Svcs: info, ref, rsrch (charged); svc for schools
Stock: archvs/999 cubic m; rec mgmt/602 cubic m; bks/15 cubic m
Classn: DDC, ISAD(G) *Auto Sys:* SEAX
Pubns: various, incl: local hist bks; photo bks; reproductions of county maps; greeting cards; catalogue available on request
Staff: Archivists: 12 *Other Prof:* 2 *Non-Prof:* 24.6

A101

Essex Regiment Museum, Regimental Archives

Oaklands Pk, Moulsham St, Chelmsford, Essex, CM2 9AG (01245-615101; *fax:* 01245-262428)
Email: pompadour@chelmsforddbc.gov.uk

Type: local govt *Gov Body:* Chelmsford Borough Council *Chief:* Keeper: Mr Ian Hook BA
Entry: by application to the Keeper; every effort is made to assist family historians & regimental rsrchers *Open: Museum:* Mon-Sat 1000-1700, Sun 1400-1700 (1300-1600 in winter); *Archvs:* by appt on weekdays only
Subj: Essex & area served by Essex regiment: regimental archvs; regimental hist; family hist *Collns: Archvs:* records of the Essex Regiment, incl both regular & auxiliary units
Equip: copier (fees vary) *Disabled:* wheelchair access *Svcs:* info, ref, rsrch, family hist searches
Staff: Other Prof: 1 curatorial *Non-Prof:* various volunteers

A102

Marconi and GEC Archives

(formerly GEC Archvs)
Marrable House, The Vineyards, Gt Baddow, Chelmsford, Essex, CM2 7QS (01245-707630; *fax:* 01245-707636)
Email: marconi.archives@marconi.com
Internet: http://www.marconicalling.com/

Gov Body: Marconi plc *Chief:* Company Archivist: Mrs Louise Jamison
Entry: adv appt; proof of ID & letter of introduction required *Open:* Mon-Fri 0900-1600
Subj: world-wide: business records (GEC & root companies); family papers; personal papers; records of parent org; company hist *Collns: Bks & Pamphs:* catalogues of GEC products from 1886; journals & pubns from GEC, English Electric, Marconi, BTH, Metropolitan Vickers & AEI *Archvs:* archvs documenting development of GEC from earliest known roots in 17C, through its foundation in 1886-date, incl personal colln of Hugo Hirst (Chairman of GEC, 1910-45); photo colln (GEC hist, personalities & branches); colln of company seal impressions *Other:* museum/display of GEC artifacts
Svcs: info, rsrch, reproductions by arrangement
Stock: archvs/90 linear m
Pubns: Archvs Handbook (complementary at discretion)
Staff: Other Prof: 2 *Non-Prof:* 1

Cheltenham

A103

Holst Birthplace Museum and Holst Archive

4 Clarence Rd, Cheltenham, Gloucestershire, GL52 2AY (01242-524846; *fax:* 01242-580182)
Email: holstmuseum@btconnect
Internet: http://www.holstmuseum.org.uk/

Gov Body: Holst Birthplace Museum & Cheltenham Borough Council *Chief:* Curator: Dr J. Archibald BA, MLitt, PhD
Assoc Offices: due to space restrictions the Holst Archv (except bks) is housed at: CHELTENHAM ART GALLERY & MUSEUM (see **S451**)
Entry: Museum: open to public; *Holst Archv:* by appt only *Open:* Tue-Sat 1000-1600, occasional Bank Hol opening; other times by appt
Subj: Gustav Holst; music *Collns: Bks & Pamphs:* pubns relating to Gustav Holst *Archvs:* archv relating to Gustav Holst, incl his scrapbk, MSS & publ material
Equip: m-reader, copier, fax
Stock: archvs/16 boxes (c1.26 cubic m in total); bks/110; illusts/100; m-forms/5; audios/50
Classn: by museum accession number
Staff: Archivists: 1 *Non-Prof:* 50

Archives

Chelmsford ▼ Cumbernauld

A104 🍳

The Planned Environment Therapy Trust, Archive and Study Centre

Church Ln, Toddington, Cheltenham, Gloucestershire, GL54 5DQ (01242-620125; *fax:* 01242-621200)
Email: archive@pettarchiv.org.uk
Internet: http://www.pettarchiv.org.uk/

Gov Body: Planned Environment Therapy Trust
Chief: Archivist: Dr Craig Fees
Entry: adv appt in writing, indicating nature of proposed rsrch *Open:* Mon-Fri 0900-1600
Subj: records & papers of indivs, instns & orgs involved in environment therapy, milieu therapy & therapeutic community work *Collns: Bks & Pamphs:* rsrch lib on environment/milieu therapy & therapeutic community work in schools, prisons & mental hosps; progressive, alternative & democratic edu; dissenting & alternative philosophies; journals; papers; theses etc *Archvs:* Marjorie Franklin Colln (incl 100+ paintings); W. David Wills Papers; Arthur T. Barron Colln; Charles Beedell Colln; papers relating to Assoc of Therapeutic Communities (esp those of Dr David Clark & Dr Robert Hinshelwood); archvs of: Red Hill School (1934-92); Sussex Youth Trust; Chalvington Trust; Chalvington School (1980-92); West Hope Manor/Shotton Hall School (1949-92); Arbours Assoc (1973-date); Q-Camps Cttee (1935-c1966); Homer Lane Soc; Homer Lane Trust; Inst of Phenomenological Studies; Wennington School; Birmingham Soc for the Care of Invalid & Nervous Children; significant colln relating to Assoc of Workers for Children with Emotional & Behavioural Difficulties (1951-date); various smaller collns *Other:* oral hist colln
Equip: copier, fax, video viewer, computers (incl wd-proc, internet & CD-ROM) *Svcs:* info, ref
Stock: archvs/several 1000 boxes; bks/5000+; periodcls/30; photos/1000s; slides/100s; illusts/100s; pamphs/100s; maps/10s; audios/c700; videos/c100; films/c20
Pubns: Newsletter
Staff: Archivists: 1 *Non-Prof:* 0,5

Chester

A105 🏛

Cheshire and Chester Archives and Local Studies

Cheshire Record Office, Duke St, Chester, Cheshire, CH1 1RL (01244-602574; *fax:* 01244-603812)
Email: recordoffice@cheshire.gov.uk
Internet: http://www.cheshire.gov.uk/recoff/home.htm

Gov Body: Cheshire County Council (see **P27**)
Chief: County Archivist: Mr Jonathan Pepler
Dep: Snr Archivist: Ms Katy Goodrum
Entry: adv appt *Open:* Mon 1330-1700, Tue-Wed, Fri 0900-1700, Thu 0900-1800, 3rd Sat of month 0900-1600
Subj: Cheshire & City of Chester: local authority archvs; diocesan records; parish records; estate archvs; family papers; business records; records of parent org; nonconformist records; poor law records; electoral records; hosp records; school records; court records; records of local socs

Collns: Bks & Pamphs: Cheshire Central Colln (3200 items) *Archvs:* archvs of Cheshire County Council; Diocese of Chester records; wills & probates (1492-1857); for full details see Cheshire Record Office Guide (1991) *Other:* maps & plans
Equip: 22 m-readers, m-printer, fax, copier, 3 computers (incl 1 with internet & 2 with CD-ROM), room for hire *Online:* own local studies database
Svcs: info, ref, enqs, rsrch
Stock: archvs/8000 linear m
Auto Sys: DS CALM 2000
Pubns: Cheshire Record Office Guide (£8.50p + £1.50p p&p); Ancient Parishes of Cheshire (£4.50 + 75p p&p); Cheshire Gazetteer (£4.50 + £1.05 p&p); full list available on application
Staff: Archivists: 7 *Libns:* 2 *Non-Prof:* 17

Chichester

A106 🏛

West Sussex Record Office

County Hall, Chichester, W Sussex, PO19 1RN (01243-753600; *fax:* 01243-533959)
Email: recordsoffice@westsussex.gov.uk
Internet: http://www.westsussex.gov.uk/librariesandarchives/recordoffice/

Gov Body: West Sussex County Council (see **P198**) *Chief:* County Archivist: Mr R. Childs BA, DipAA *Dep:* Dep County Archivist: Mr P.M. Wilkinson MA
Entry: CARN ticket *Open:* Mon-Fri 0915-1645, Sat 0915-1230, 1330-1630
Subj: Administrative County of West Sussex & C of E Diocese of Chichester: local authority archvs; diocesan records; parish records; estate archvs; family papers; business records *Collns: Bks & Pamphs:* Crookshank Lib (strong on Blake & Hayley & their circle & local printing); Fuller Lib; Hilda Johnstone Lib; W.D. Peckham Lib (Sussex antiquarian); Eric Gill Colln; Ronald Shephard Railway Colln (c1850-1980) *Archvs:* archvs of West Sussex County Council; Royal Sussex Regiment archvs; Diocese of Chichester records; Goodwood Estate records; Petworth House Estate records *Other:* Garland Photographic Colln (c70000 images reflecting rural life & crafts in West Sussex, 1920s-1978); SE Film & Video Archv (see **A71**) *Co-op Schemes:* SE Film & Video Archv
Equip: 24 m-readers, 2 m-printers (staff use), m-camera (staff use), 2 copiers (staff use), fax (staff use), video viewer, computer (incl CD-ROM), scanner & digital camera (staff use), 1 room for hire *Svcs:* rsrch
Stock: archvs/1557 cubic m; rec mgmt/340 cubic m; bks/54 cubic m; photos/c100000; slides/c5000; maps/c10000 printed, c3000 MS; m-forms/c10000; audios/c500; videos/c50
Pubns: Prints from the Past Series; Local Hist Mini-Guides to Sources (£1 each) (both publ jointly with County Lib Svc); Lists & Indexes (£2 + p&p each); The Greatham Archvs (£5); The Clough & Butler Archvs (£5); The Cobden Papers (currently o/p); A Catalogue of Sussex Estate & Tithe Award Maps, Vol 1 (£10); The Wilberforce Archvs (o/p); A Catalogue of the Records of the Bishop, Archdeacons & Former Exempt Juris-dictions (£15); A Catalogue of the Records of the Dean & Chapter, Vicars Choral, St Mary's Hosp, Colls & Schools (o/p); Petworth House Archvs, Vol 1 (£10); Goodwood Estate Archvs, Vol 1 (£15); The Royal Sussex Regiment: A Catalogue of Records (£25); numerous others, recent pubns incl: A Catalogue of Horsham Museum MSS (1995, £7.50); A Walk Around Chichester, City of Culture (1995, £1.50); With Treasures in Store: 50 Years of West Sussex Record Office (1996, £1); Recipes from the Archvs (1996, £3.95); Petworth House Archvs Vol 3 (£7.50); catalogue available
Staff: Archivists: 8 *Other Prof:* 2 *Non-Prof:* 20
Exp: £11400 (2000-01)

Christchurch

A107 🏛🏛

Red House Museum, Resource Room

Quay Rd, Christchurch, Dorset, BH23 1BU (01202-482860; *fax:* 01202-481924)
Email: museums@hants.gov.uk
Internet: http://www.hants.gov.uk/museum/redhouse/

Gov Body: Hampshire County Council (see **P60**) in partnership with Dorset County Council (see **P39**) & Christchurch Borough Council *Chief:* Curator: Mr Jim Hunter
Assoc Offices: HAMPSHIRE COUNTY COUNCIL MUSEUMS SVC LIB (see **A508**)
Entry: ref; adv appt advised for in-depth rsrch
Open: Tue-Sat 1000-1700, Sun 1400-1700
Subj: Christchurch Borough: local hist

Cirencester

A108 🏛🏛

Corinium Museum, Archives

Park St, Cirencester, Gloucestershire, GL7 2BX (01285-655611; *fax:* 01285-643286)
Email: judy.mills@cotswold.gov.uk
Internet: http://www.cotswold.gov.uk/

Gov Body: Cotswold Dist Council *Chief:* Collns Mgmt Offcr: Ms Judy Mills
Entry: ref only, adv appt; closed for redevelopment until Spring 2004 *Open:* Mon-Fri 1000-1700
Subj: Cotswolds: local studies; hist; archaeo
Svcs: ref
Stock: archvs/600+; photos/1000+; slides/1000+
Proj: major redevelopment of Museum; reopening Spring 2004

Clitheroe

A109 🎓

North West Sound Archive

Old Steward's Office, Clitheroe Castle, Clitheroe, Lancashire, BB7 1AZ (*tel & fax:* 01200-427897)
Email: nwsa@ed.lancscc.gov.uk
Internet: http://www.lancashire.gov.uk/education/d_lif/ro/content/sound/nwsound.asp

Gov Body: Council of NWSA *Chief:* Sound Archv Offcr: Mr Andrew Schofield BA *Dep:* Sound Archv Support Offcr: Mrs Lynda Yates
Assoc Offices: affiliated to LANCASHIRE RECORD OFFICE (see **A425**)
Entry: adv appt *Open:* Mon-Fri 0900-1700
Subj: NW England: oral hist records; sounds of the region, incl: local radio, music & dialect
Collns: Other: survey of English dialects; solidarity speeches; sounds of Jodrell Bank; Lancashire Theatre Organ Trust recordings
Equip: copier, fax, fully equipped sound studio
Svcs: info, ref, rsrch, loan svc
Stock: audios/110000 *Classn:* own
Pubns: compilations with transcripts; dialect dictionaries *Staff: Other Prof:* 2

Clydebank

A110 🏛

West Dunbartonshire Libraries, Clydebank Central Library - Local Collection and Archives

Dumbarton Rd, Clydebank, W Dunbartonshire, G81 1XH (0141-952-1416/8765; *fax:* 0141-951-8275)
Email: clydebank.local.history@west-dunbarton.gov.uk
Internet: http://www.west-dunbarton.gov.uk/

Gov Body: West Dunbartonshire Council (see **P196**) **Chief:** Info Svcs Libn: Ms Pat Malcolm MCLIP
Assoc Offices: INFO & LOCAL STUDIES, Dumbarton Lib (see **A131**)
Entry: for more complex enqs please tel first **Open:** Mon-Thu 0930-2000, Fri 0930-1700, Sat 1000-1700
Subj: Clydebank, Duntocher, Hardgate, Old Kilpatrick: local authority archvs; local hist
Collns: Bks & Pamphs: Clydebank Blitz 1941; shipbldg in Clydebank (John Brown, William Beardmore); Singer Manufacturing Co Ltd Archvs: minutes etc of West Dunbartonshire Council & predecessors; Clydebank Blitz 1941 archival colln Other: photos of local area
Equip: 3 m-readers, 2 m-printers, 2 copiers, clr copier, fax, 7 computers (all with wd-proc, internet & CD-ROM) **Svcs:** info, ref, rsrch
Classn: DDC (mod)
Pubns: various local hist pubns; list available
Staff: Libns: 1 Non-Prof: 1

Colchester

A111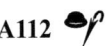

Essex Record Office, Colchester and North East Essex Branch
Stanwell House, Stanwell St, Colchester, Essex, CO2 7DL (01206-572099; fax: 01206-574541)
Email: ero.colchester@essexcc.gov.uk
Internet: http://www.essexcc.gov.uk/

Gov Body: Essex County Council (see **P51**)
Chief: Branch Archivist: Mr Paul Coverley MA
Assoc Offices: branch office of ESSEX RECORD OFFICE (see **A100**)
Entry: CARN ticket; adv appt strongly advised **Open:** Mon 1000-1715 (-2045 on 2nd Mon of each month), Tue-Thu 0915-1715, Fri 0915-1615
Subj: Essex (Colchester & Tendring Council areas): local authority archvs; parish records; estate archvs; family papers; business records; nonconformist church records; school records; records of socs & orgs **Collns:** Bks & Pamphs: small ref lib in search room Archvs: Colchester Borough records from early 14C; minutes & other records of Dist Councils up to 1974; records of Poor Law Unions; MSS of Philip Morant (Essex historian) Other: Internatl Genealogical Index (Essex only); Index to Essex wills (1400-1858); Index to 1851 & 1881 census returns for Essex; Calendar of rolls of Essex Quarter Sessions (to 1714); deeds & sale catalogues; maps & plans (incl historical OS maps)
Equip: 6 m-readers, staff-operated m-printer & copier
Stock: archvs/1150 linear m; bks/35 linear m
Pubns: various, incl: local hist bks; photo bks; reproductions of county maps; greeting cards
Staff: Archivists: 2 Non-Prof: 1

Coventry

A112 ✈℘

BP Archive
BP plc, Univ of Warwick, Coventry, CV4 7AL (024-7657-3929; fax: 024-7652-4523)
Email: BPArchive@bp.com
Internet: http://www.bp.com/company_overview/ history/bp/archive_unit.asp

Gov Body: BP plc **Chief:** Archvs & Records Mgr: Mr Peter Housego **Other Snr Staff:** Archivist: Ms Paula Brikci; Archivist: Miss Bethan Thomas
Entry: bona fide rsrchers, by appt **Open:** Mon-Thu 0900-1700, Fri 0900-1600
Subj: business records; records of parent org; oil industry; UK & internatl hist (esp of Middle East) relating to the oil industry

Collns: Bks & Pamphs: Company magazines; annual reports Archvs: relating to the hist & activs worldwide of BP & its predecessors & subsidiaries (1900-date, open to 1954); Kuwait Oil Co Archv (open to 1954); Iraq Petroleum Co Archv (30 yr rule); Shell-Mex & BP Ltd Archv (advertising records, 1931-1975); Burmah Oil Co (open to 1954, public access available after 2003) Other: photos; public relations material
Equip: Disabled: wheelchair access
Stock: archvs/4000 linear m
Staff: Archivists: 3 Non-Prof: 1

A113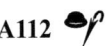

Coventry City Archives
Mandela House, Bayley Ln, Coventry, CV1 5RG (024-7683-2418; fax: 024-7683-2421)
Email: coventryarchives@discover.co.uk

Gov Body: Coventry Metropolitan Dist Council (see **P31**) **Chief:** City Archivist: Ms Susan Worrall MA(Hons), MArAd (susan.worrall@ coventry.gov.uk)
Assoc Offices: addl local & family hist materials are held at: COVENTRY LOCAL STUDIES LIB, Central Lib, Smithford Way, Coventry, CV1 1FY (024-7683-2336; fax: 024-7683-2440; email: central.library@coventry.gov.uk)
Entry: CARN ticket or other form of ID; access by appt only after 1645 on Mon **Open:** Mon 0930-2000, Tue-Fri 0930-1645
Subj: Coventry Metropolitan Dist: local authority archvs; parish records (on m-film only); estate archvs; family papers; business records; personal papers; political papers; records of parent org; nonconformist church records; court records; school records **Collns:** Bks & Pamphs: local directories Archvs: archvs of Coventry MDC & predecessors; Quarter Sessions & other court records for Coventry (15C-mid 20C); parish registers on m-film (Anglican & RC) Other: oral hist colln; vehicle registration cards; IGI on m-fiche; census returns for Coventry & Warwickshire (partial); index of apprentices' indentures (1781-1851); registers of burials (m-film); Registers of Electors & Burgess Rolls (partial); monumental inscriptions; computer database of Coventry inhabitants (30000 entries, medieval-present)
Equip: 5 m-readers, m-printer (20p per sheet), copier (A4/20p, A3/35p)
Stock: archvs/460 cubic m
Auto Sys: CALM 2000
Pubns: Brief Guides to Records (by subj & period, 60p each); Coventry Celebrates 650 Years of Civic Pride (20p); Coventry Martyrs (Protestant martyrs in the 16C, £1); Coventry at School (£1); People to Coventry (migration & settlement in Coventry from early times, £1); Criminals, Courts & Conflict, by Dr Arthur Gooder (£10.50); other City Council pubns relating to local hist; local hist leaflets by E. Castle & C. Kennedy; pubns by the Coventry Branch of the Historical Assoc; pubns of Coventry Family Hist Soc; numerous others; various maps, views, posters & postcards; a list of pubns produced & sold is available free
Staff: Archivists: 4 Other Prof: 1 Non-Prof: 3

A114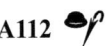

Modern Records Centre
Univ of Warwick Lib, Gibbet Hill Rd, Coventry, CV4 7AL (024-76524219; fax: 024-76524211)
Email: archives@warwick.ac.uk
Internet: http://www.warwick.ac.uk/services/ library/mrc/mrc.html

Gov Body: Univ of Warwick (see **S498**) **Chief:** Archivist: Christine Woodland
Entry: open to serious rsrchers, adv notice preferred; some collns can only be viewed with permission of depositor **Open:** Mon-Tue 0900-1700, Wed-Thu 0900-1900, Fri 0900-1600

Subj: Gt Britain: political hist; social hist; economic hist; labour hist; industrial relations; industrial politics; trade union records; employers' records; business records (esp motor industry); records of trade assocs; records of political orgs & interest groups **Collns:** Bks & Pamphs: trade union journals Archvs: numerous deposits incl: trade union minutes & correspondence files; TUC registry files (1920-90); British Assoc of Social Workers Archvs (see also **A53**); records of Confederation of British Industry & its predecessors (see **S1098** for CBI); Natl Cycle Archv; Gurharpal Singh Archv (communism in the Punjab, 1920s-1970s, held for Univ's Centre for Rsrch in Ethnic Relations) Other: political & trade union ephemera
Equip: m-reader, copier (staff only, limited facility), power pts for laptops
Stock: archvs/6800 linear m
Pubns: Guide to Holdings (£2.50); Supplement to Guide (£3); Summary Guide (£5); Info Bulletin (2 pa, back issues available on m-fiche); Notes for Rsrchers (free by post); Annual Reports; Trade Union & Related Records (6th ed, £3.50); The Confederation of British Industry & Predecessor Archvs (£5); The Internatl Transport Workers' Federation Archv (£2.25); The Trade Union Congress Archv 1920-60 (£4); Info Leaflet Series (10p-75p each); & others
Staff: Archivists: 2 full-time Non-Prof: 1

Croydon

A115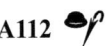

Croydon Local Studies Library and Archives Service
Croydon Clocktower, Katharine St, Croydon, CR9 1ET (020-8760-5400 x1112; fax: 020-8253-1012)
Email: localstudies@croydononline.org
Internet: http://www.croydon.gov.uk/localstudies/

Gov Body: London Borough of Croydon (see **P83**) **Chief:** Local Studies Libn: Mr Steve Roud
Dep: Borough Archivist: Mr Chris Bennett MA
Entry: ref only, open to public; adv appt required for most archival materials **Open:** Mon 0900-1900, Tue-Wed, Fri 0900-1800, Thu 0930-1800, Sat 0900-1700, Sun 1400-1700
Subj: London Borough of Croydon: local authority archvs; parish records; business records; school records; poor law records; local hist; family hist **Collns:** Bks & Pamphs: local hist colln; local directories Archvs: archvs of Croydon Borough Council & predecessors Other: IGI; census returns; electoral registers; parish registers; maps & plans; local newspapers
Equip: 7 m-form reader/printers (20p per pg), copier (A4/10p, A3/15p), video viewer, 6 computers (all with internet & CD-ROM) **Svcs:** info, ref, enqs
Stock: archvs/70 cubic m; photos/40000; videos/ 120
Classn: DDC **Auto Sys:** CALM 2000
Staff: Archivists: 1 Other Prof: 1.8 Non-Prof: 2.2

Cumbernauld

A116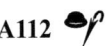

North Lanarkshire Archives
10 Kelvin Rd, Lenziemill Industrial Est, Cumbernauld, N Lanarkshire, G67 2BD (01236-737114; fax: 01236-781762)
Internet: http://www.northlan.gov.uk/

Gov Body: North Lanarkshire Council (see **P126**) **Chief:** Archivist: Mr John MacKenzie BA(Hons), HDipAS **Dep:** Archvs Asst: Mr Allan McKenzie
Entry: adv appt **Open:** Mon-Fri 0900-1700 ☞

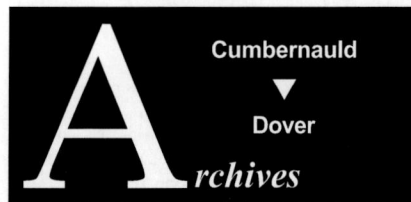

(N Lanarkshire Archvs cont)
Subj: North Lanarkshire: local authority archvs; estate archvs; family papers; business records; personal papers; records of parent org; local hist
Co-op Schemes: SCAN
Equip: copier, video viewer, fax, 3 computers (all with wd-proc, 1 with internet & 1 with CD-ROM)
Svcs: info, ref, rsrch
Stock: archvs/1500 linear m; rec mgmt/8000 linear m; photos/10 linear m; maps/50 linear m
Staff: Archivists: 1 Non-Prof: 3

Cwmbran

A117 🏛

Gwent Record Office

County Hall, Cwmbran, Gwent, NP44 2XH (01633-644886; *fax:* 01633-648382)
Email: gwent.records@torfaen.gov.uk

Gov Body: Gwent Joint Records Cttee, representing County Borough of Blaenau Gwent (see **P11**), Caerphilly County Borough Council (see **P21**), Monmouthshire County Council (see **P118**), Newport Council (see **P122**) & Torfaen County Borough Council (see **P188**) **Chief:** County Archivist: Mr David Rimmer BA, DipAA **Dep:** Dep County Archivist: Mr Anthony D.G. Hopkins BA, MA, DipAA **Other Snr Staff:** Records Mgmt Offcr: Ms Neta Whitehead
Entry: CARN ticket **Open:** Tue-Thu 0930-1700, Fri 0930-1600
Subj: County of Gwent: local authority archvs; diocesan records; parish records; estate archvs; family papers; business records; personal papers; political papers; records of parent org; hosp records; nonconformist records; Roman Catholic records; industrial records; manorial records; tithe records; local public records **Collns:** *Bks & Pamphs:* Gwent County Council Law Lib *Archvs:* archvs of former Gwent County Council & successor authorities (Blaenau Gwent, Caerphilly, Newport & Torfaen County Borough Councils & Monmouthshire County Council); archvs of former Monmouthshire County Council (1938-1974); diocesan & parish records of Diocese of Monmouth; parish records for Diocese of Swansea & Brecon (Llanelli & Brynmawr only); family & estate collns incl: Abergavenny; Hanbury of Pontypool; Rolls of the Hendre; Bosanquet; Jones of Llanarth; Herbert of Llanarth; Lewis of St Pierre; Addams-Williams; Piercefield Pk papers; business collns incl: records of Blaenavon Co Ltd (colliery proprietors, iron & steel manufacturers); records of Nantyglo & Blaina Ironworks Co Ltd; records of Webbs (Aberbeeg) Ltd (brewers); other collns incl: records of Monmouthshire Commissioners of the Sewers; Cwmbran New Town Development Corp archvs (restricted access); Pen-Y-Fal Hosp records; records of local Labour Party & trade unions; records of Quarter Sessions *Other:* local newspapers
Equip: 11 m-readers, m-printer (75p per copy), copier (40p-75p per copy), fax, computers (incl 2 with wd-proc, 1 with CD-ROM & 1 with internet)
Offcr-in-Charge: County Archivist, as above
Svcs: info, ref, rsrch, conservation
Stock: archvs/164.75 cubic m; rec mgmt/497.08 cubic m; bks/96 linear ft; m-forms/11 drawers; audios/c50; videos/12; CD-ROMs/1 *Acq Offcr:* County Archivist, as above

Pubns: Guides to Rsrch: 1) Poor Law (30p); 2) Hist of Edu (30p); 3) The Iron & Steel Industries (30p); 4) Hist of Houses (30p); 5) Shipping, Docks & Harbours (30p); 6) Crime & Punishment (50p); Guide to Sources for Family Hist (£2); Chartism: Guide to Documents & Printed Sources (£1); prices exclude p&p
Staff: Archivists: 5 Other Prof: 2 Non-Prof: 4.5
Exp: £18800 (1999-2000); £17400 (2000-01)

Dagenham

A118 🏛🏛

Barking and Dagenham Archives

Valence House Museum, Becontree Ave, Dagenham, Essex, RM8 3HT (020-8270-6865; *fax:* 020-8270-6868)
Email: localstudies@bardaglea.org.uk
Internet: http://www.barking-dagenham.gov.uk/

Gov Body: London Borough of Barking & Dagenham (see **P77**) **Chief:** Borough Archivist: Ms Judith Etherton MA, BA **Other Snr Staff:** Local Studies Libn: Ms Linda Rhodes BA, DipLib, MCLIP; Acting Museum Curator: Mr Mark Watson BA
Assoc Offices: LOCAL STUDIES CENTRE, addr as above (020-8270-6896; *fax:* 020-8270-6897)
Entry: adv appt requested, particularly for m-film readers **Open:** Mon-Tue, Fri 0930-1600, Thu 0930-1900; closed Wed
Subj: London Borough of Barking & Dagenham (incl historic parishes in Ilford): local authority archvs; parish records; family papers; business records; personal papers; records of parent org; local hist; family hist **Collns:** *Archvs:* archvs of London Borough of Barking & Dagenham; Fanshawe family papers, incl: 17C ambassadorial papers of Sir Richard Fanshawe (1608-66), ambassador to Portugal & Spain; business records, incl: Lawes Chemical Co; Samuel Williams & Sons Ltd
Equip: 5 m-readers, 2 m-printers, copier, 5 computers (incl 4 with internet & 4 with CD-ROM), room for hire **Disabled:** digitised colln of images (on ground floor), special-use m-reader **Svcs:** info, ref
Stock: archvs/300 linear m; rec mgmt/250 linear m; bks/500 linear m *Acq Offcr:* Borough Archivist or Local Studies Libn
Classn: DDC, ISAD(G), SHIC *Auto Sys:* Adlib
Pubns: numerous, incl: Barking & Dagenham Bldgs Past & Present (£4); A Brief Hist of Barking & Dagenham (£2.75); On the Home Front (£4.50); Residents & Visitors (£3.50); Views of Old Barking & Dagenham (£3.50); Fanshawe Family & Other Portraits: A Catalogue (£1); Barking & Ilford: An Extract from the Victoria of the County of Essex (£3.50); Dagenham: An Extract from the Victoria of the County of Essex (£2); Danger Over Dagenham (£2.50); On the Move: Views of Transport in Barking & Dagenham 1890-1959 (£3.50); The Papers of Sir Richard Fanshawe, Bart (£28); Recording the Past (£3); Footprints in Time, by Gillian Gillespie (£4.99)
Staff: Archivists: 1 Libns: 1 Other Prof: 1 Non-Prof: 5

Darlington

A119 🏛

Darlington Centre for Local Studies

Darlington Lib, Crown St, Darlington, Co Durham, DL1 1ND (01325-349630; *fax:* 01325-381556)
Email: local.studies@darlington.gov.uk
Internet: http://www.darlington.gov.uk/

Gov Body: Darlington Borough Council (see **P33**) **Chief:** Local Studies Libn: Miss K. Williamson BA
Entry: open to public, no restrictions; adv booking advised for m-readers & elec resources

Open: Mon-Tue, Thu 0930-1900, Wed, Fri 0930-1700, Sat 0930-1600
Subj: Darlington in particular, South Durham & NE England in genl: local hist; family hist; some local authority archvs; parish records; poor law records **Collns:** *Bks & Pamphs:* local hist colln; Quaker Colln; local trade & street directories (1828-1974) *Archvs:* Darlington Borough Council minutes & reports; records of Poor Law Unions for Darlington & Laughton-Le-Skerne *Other:* IGI; St Catherine's Index; Boyd's Marriage Index; parish registers (on m-film); electoral rolls; census returns; map colln (1826-date); photo colln; oral hist recordings; local newspapers (1847-date); monumental inscriptions; posters & ephemera
Co-op Schemes: Newsplan, Tomorrow's Hist (regional digitisation proj)
Equip: 15 m-readers, 3 m-printer, copier, fax, computers (incl 1 with internet & 2 with CD-ROM)
Online: Durham Record (database of 10000+ photos, maps & Sites & Monuments Record)
Svcs: info, ref
Stock: archvs/89000, incl pamphs; photos/18300, incl slides & illusts; maps/6790; m-forms/29600; audios/130; videos/35; CD-ROMs/60
Classn: Brown (mod) *Auto Sys:* DS
Pubns: Centre for Local Studies Guide (free); Newspapers Guide – Holdings in Darlington Local Studies Dept (30p); Stockton & Darlington Railway pubns; other handlists are for ref only
Staff: Libns: 2 Non Prof: 2

Dartmouth

A120 ✍

Plymouth RC Diocesan Archives

The Priest's House, 20 Newcomen Rd, Dartmouth, Devon, TQ6 9BN (01803-832860)
Internet: http://www.plymouth-diocese.org.uk/

Gov Body: RC Diocese of Plymouth **Chief:** Diocesan Archivist: Rev Christopher Smith
Entry: contact the Diocesan Archivist in adv
Subj: RC Diocese of Plymouth (counties of Cornwall, Devon & Dorset, & Isles of Scilly): diocesan records **Collns:** *Archvs:* correspondence & papers concerning the diocese since its foundation in 1851 (sorting & cataloguing still in progress)

Deeside

A121 ✍

Corus Colors Regional Records Centre

Shotton Works, Deeside, Flintshire, CH5 2NH (01244-892134/5/6; *fax:* 01244-892137)
Email: record.centre@corusgroup.com

Chief: Snr Records Advisor: Mr Rolf Holthöfer (rolf.holthofer@corusgroup.com) **Dep:** Supervisor: Miss Jean Needham
Assoc Offices: CORUS NORTHERN REGIONAL RECORDS CENTRE (see **A377**)
Entry: adv appt **Open:** Mon-Fri 0800-1545; closed bank hols
Subj: iron & steel industries; business records; records of parent org **Collns:** *Archvs:* minutes & other records of over 100 companies involved in iron & steel manufacture & related industries (19C-20C); British Iron & Steel Federation records (20C)
Equip: copier, fax
Stock: archvs/1000+; rec mgmt/148000 boxes
Staff: Other Prof: 1 Non-Prof: 6

 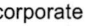

Derby

A122 🏛
Derby Local Studies Library
25b Irongate, Derby, DE1 3GL (01332-255393)
Email: localstudies.library@derby.gov.uk
Internet: http://www.derby.gov.uk/libraries/

Type: local authority *Gov Body:* Derby City Council (see **P35**) *Chief:* Snr Libn: Ms Tricia Kenny *Dep:* Libn: Mr Paul Hudson
Entry: ref only; adv advised for m-form facilities *Open:* Mon-Tue 0930-1900, Wed-Fri 0930-1700, Sat 0930-1300
Subj: Derbyshire: local authority archvs; family papers; business records; poor law records; local hist; family hist *Collns: Bks & Pamphs:* Duke of Devonshire Colln (Derby & Derbyshire, foundation colln); Sir Henry Howe Bemrose Colln (Derby & Derbyshire, foundation colln); local trade directories; local & family hist newsletters & journals; parish magazines; 19C broadsheets *Archvs:* records of Derby Borough; Derby China Factory records (1780s-1830s); Derby Canal Company records (1793-1974); Evans Cotton Mill records (1787-1923); notebks & correspondence of local figures (available on m-film); title deeds; chap bks *Other:* census returns (m-film, 1841-1901); electoral registers (1843-2001), plus some 18C poll bks; local newspapers (m-film, 1720s-date), incl the Derby Mercury (1732-1933); photo colln (19C-date), incl work by Richard Keene; map colln (1577 onwards)
Equip: m-readers, m-printers (50p per copy), copier (5p per copy), 2 computers (both with wd-proc, internet & CD-ROM) *Disabled:* wheelchair access, induction loop *Svcs:* info, ref, rsrch
Stock: archvs/c60000; photos/12000+; broadsheets/c3500
Classn: DDC

Dolgellau

A123 🏛
Merioneth Area Archives Office (Archifdy Meirion)
Swyddfeydd y Cyngor, Cae Penarlag, Dolgellau, Gwynedd, LL40 2YB (01341-424444; *fax:* 01341-424505)
Email: archives.dolgellau@gwynedd.gov.uk
Internet: http://www.gwynedd.gov.uk/archives/

Gov Body: Cyngor Gwynedd Council (see **P58**)
Chief: Area Archivist: Mr Merfyn Wyn Tomos BA, DipAA, MCLIP (merfynwyntomos@gwynedd.gov.uk)
Assoc Offices: part of GWYNEDD ARCHVS & MUSEUMS SVC (see **A84**)
Entry: CARN ticket; booking svc for m-readers
Open: Mon, Wed-Fri 0900-1300, 1400-1700, closed Tue & 1st full wk of Nov
Subj: former historic county of Merioneth: local authority archvs; parish records; estate archvs; family papers; business records; personal papers; political papers; records of parent org
Equip: m-reader, copier, computer (incl internet)
Svcs: rsrch (£12 per half hr)
Staff: Archivists: 1 *Non-Prof:* 2

Doncaster

A124 🏛
Doncaster Archives
King Edward Rd, Balby, Doncaster, S Yorkshire, DN4 0NA (01302-859811)
Email: doncaster.archives@doncaster.gov.uk
Internet: http://www.doncaster.gov.uk/doncasterarchives/

Gov Body: Doncaster Metropolitan Borough Council (see **P38**) *Chief:* Principal Archivist: Dr B.J. Barber BA, MA, PhD, DipAA
Entry: readers ticket (proof of ID required), appt advisable *Open:* Mon-Fri 0900-1245, 1400-1645
Subj: Doncaster: local authority archvs; parish records; estate archvs; family papers; business records; personal papers; political papers; records of parent org; public records, incl courts & hosps
Collns: Archvs: records of Doncaster Borough (1194-1974); records of Doncaster Metropolitan Dist Council (1974-1991); records of Rural Dist Councils; Diocesan Record Office for the Archdeaconry of Doncaster in the Diocese of Sheffield, incl records of 85 parishes (1538-date); manorial & tithe records; Bridon plc records (1751-1971); 10 estate collns (1265-1960); W. Aldam Papers (MP for Leeds 1841-46); W.B. Wrightson MP Papers *Co-op Schemes:* South Yorkshire Joint Archv Svc, with Barnsley (see **A26**), Rotherham (see **A438**) & Sheffield (see **A452**)
Equip: 6 m-readers, copier (A4/40p, A3/50p), computer (charge for printouts only) *Svcs:* ref, rsrch (£12.50 per half hr)
Stock: archvs/219.4 cubic m; rec mgmt/265 cubic m; CD-ROMs/6
Classn: ISAD(G)
Pubns: Guide to the Archvs Dept (2001 ed, £5 + £2 p&p)
Staff: Archivists: 2 *Non-Prof:* 2 *Exp:* £119320 (1999-2000); £135310 (2000-01)

Dorchester

A125 🏛
Dorset Archives Service
Dorset Record Office, Bridport Rd, Dorchester, Dorset, DT1 1RP (01305-250550; *fax:* 01305-257184)
Email: archives@dorset-c.gov.uk
Internet: http://www.dorsetcc.gov.uk/archives/

Type: local authority *Gov Body:* joint svc on behalf of Dorset County Council (see **P39**), Bournemouth Borough Council (see **P13**) & the Borough of Poole (see **P147**) *Chief:* County Archivist: Mr Hugh Jaques MA
Entry: adv appt advisable, ID required on first visit *Open:* Mon-Tue, Thu-Fri 0900-1700, Wed 1000-1700, Sat 0930-1230
Subj: mainly Dorset: local authority archvs; parish records; estate archvs; family papers; business records; personal papers; political papers; records of parent org *Collns: Archvs:* archvs of Dorset County Council; archvs of Bournemouth Borough Council; archvs of Borough of Poole; Diocese of Salisbury (Dorset area) records
Equip: 26 m-readers, m-printer, 2 m-cameras, copier, fax, video viewer, computer (incl CD-ROM), digital camera, lecture room *Svcs:* info, ref, rsrch, archvs & conservation advice & treatment, digital copying svc
Stock: archvs/698 cubic m; rec mgmt/426 cubic m
Classn: ISAD(G)
Pubns: Guide to the Location of the Parish Registers of Dorset (£2); Who's Afear'd of Family Hist (£6.95); Guide to the Location of Nonconformist & Roman Catholic Registers (£1.50); Guide to the Transcripts held in the Dorset Record Office (£1); List of Diaries & Memoirs held in the Dorset Record Office (50p); The Archvs of Dorset: Catalogue of an Exhib to mark the 30th Anniversary of Dorset Record Office 1986 (£2); other guides & catalogues; pubns of Dorset Record Soc; pubns of Somerset & Dorset Family Hist Soc; other pubns incl OS maps; postage charged at £1 for 1st item, 70p per addl
Staff: Archivists: 6 *Other Prof:* 2 *Non-Prof:* 16.1 3.5 proj staff, 1 museum staff *Exp:* £517300 (2000-01)

A126 🏛
The Keep Military Museum, Archives
Bridport Rd, Dorchester, Dorset, DT1 1RN (01305-264066; *fax:* 01305-250373)
Email: Keep.Museum@talk21.com
Internet: http://www.keepmilitarymuseum.org/

Gov Body: Ministry of Defence *Chief:* Curator: Lt Col R.A. Leonard (Rtd)
Entry: admission fee to Museum; access to archvs for rsrchers by appt *Open:* Apr-Sep: Mon-Sat 0930-1700, Sun (Jul-Aug only) 1000-1600; Oct-Mar: Tue-Sat 0930-1700; last admission 1 hr before closing
Subj: Devonshire & Dorset Regiments: military hist; regimental records *Collns: Archvs:* Dorset Regiment archvs; Devonshire Regiment archvs; Devon & Dorset Regiment archvs; Royal Devon Yeomanry archvs; Queen's Own Dorset Yeomanry archvs
Svcs: ref *Auto Sys:* Modes
Staff: staffed by up to 4 volunteers

Dorking

A127 🗝
Friends' Provident Life Insurance Archives
Secretariat Dept, Pixham End, Dorking, Surrey, RH4 1QA (01306-740123; *fax:* 01306-740150)

Chief: Archivist: Mr J.R. Murphy
Entry: adv appt
Subj: insurance; business records; records of parent org *Collns: Archvs:* records of Friends' Provident Life Insurance (1832-20C); records of Century Insurance Co Ltd (1885-1926)

Dover

A128 🏛
East Kent Archives Centre
Enterprise Zone, Honeywood Rd, Whitfield, Dover, Kent, CT16 3EH (01304-829306; *fax:* 01304-820783)
Email: EastKentArchives@kent.gov.uk

Gov Body: Kent County Council (see **P67**)
Chief: Mgr & Snr Archivist: Ms Alison Cable
Entry: CARN ticket; adv appt preferred, ref only
Open: Tue-Thu 0900-1700
Subj: Folkestone Borough & East Kent: local authority archvs; parish records (civil, not ecclesiastical); estate archvs; family papers; business records; personal papers; poor law records; nonconformist records; school records; hosp records; shipping records; port records
Collns: Archvs: Borough records (13C-20C), incl Deal, Dover, Folkestone, Hythe, Lydd, Margate, New Romney, Ramsgate & Sandwich; Rural Dist Council records (18C-20C), incl Dover, Eastry, Elham, Romney Marsh & Thanet; Urban Dist Council records, incl Broadstairs & St Peter's, Cheriton, Sandgate & Walmer; Liberty of Romney Marsh records; records of Land Drainage & Commissioners of Sewers (16C-20C); Eltham Poor Law Union records (1835-1966); Romney Marsh Poor Law Union records (1835-1931); records of Highway Boards (19C); records of Dover Harbour Board (c1520-1968); Cinque Ports Confederation records (1327-1959); Lord Warden of the Cinque Ports records (1498-1968); Natl Coal Board records (East Kent coalfields, to 1953); Royal Sea Bathing Hosp, Margate, records (1791-1939); East Kent Lunatic Asylum records (1854-1993); Kent & Canterbury Hosp records (1790-1990); Registers of British Shipping (East Kent area, 1786-1970); Kent shipping & fishing vessel records (1863-1914) ☛

Dover
▼
Durham

rchives

(East Kent Archvs Centre cont)
Equip: 2 m-readers, m-printer, copier, computer (with CD-ROM) *Disabled:* hearing loop, print magnification unit, disabled access, some leaflets in Braille *Svcs:* info, ref, rsrch, reprographic svcs
Stock: archvs/2000 linear m
Classn: ISAD(G) & in-house
Staff: Archivists: 2 Non-Prof: 2

Dudley

A129 🏛
Black Country Living Museum Archives
Tipton Rd, Dudley, W Midlands, DY1 4SQ (0121-557-9643; *fax:* 0121-557-4242)
Email: info@bclm.co.uk
Internet: http://www.bclm.co.uk/

Gov Body: Black Country Museum Trust *Chief:* Dir & Chief Exec: Mr Ian Walden OBE *Dep:* Curator: Mrs Kathleen Howe MA
Entry: by adv appt *Open:* Tue-Fri 1000-1600
Subj: Black Country (Midlands west of Birmingham): local studies; industry; social hist; industrial hist *Collns: Bks & Pamphs:* Keith Gale Lib (development of British iron & steel industry); Kenrick Colln (catalogues & design registrations & applications) *Other:* Braithwaite & Kirt Photographic Archv (bridge-bldg)
Equip: copier (A4/10p), room for hire *Disabled:* wheelchair access *Svcs:* ref
Stock: archvs/1500 items; bks/1500; photos/2000; maps/400
Staff: Other Prof: 3

A130 🏛
Dudley Archives and Local History Service
Mount Pleasant St, Coseley, Dudley, W Midlands, WV14 9JR (01384-812770; *fax:* 01384-812770)
Email: archives.pls@mbc.dudley.gov.uk
Internet: http://www.dudley.gov.uk/

Gov Body: Dudley Metropolitan Borough Council (see **P40**) *Chief:* Archivist: Mrs K.H. Atkins BA, DipAA
Entry: CARN ticket; appt advisable for m-form materials *Open:* Tue-Wed, Fri 0900-1700, Thu 0930-1900, 1st & 3rd Sat in month 0930-1230, by appt (limited svc 1300-1400)
Subj: area of present Dudley Metropolitan Borough: local authority archvs; parish records; estate archvs; family papers; business records; personal papers; records of parent org; nonconformist records; records of local orgs; local hist; family hist *Collns: Archvs:* Dudley Metro-politan Borough Council archvs; Diocese of Worcester (Dudley area) parish records; archv of the Earls of Dudley (12C-20C) *Other:* map colln
Equip: 16 m-readers, m-printer (via staff), video viewer, copier (via staff), photography by arrangement, room for hire *Svcs:* Family Hist rsrch svc (fee based)
Stock: archvs/c400 cubic m; photos/c1800; printed & local hist materials/c200 cubic m
Pubns: Handlist of Parish Registers; Handlist of Nonconformist Records; Brief Checklist of Sources for Genealogical Enquries; Census Enumerators Returns, Electoral Rolls & Rate Bks:

Lists of Holdings (all 30p, 55p by post); Directories: List of Holdings (50p, 75p by post); Reading List for Family Historians (£1.25, £1.75 by post); all of the above available as a pack for £2.50 (£3.75 by post); List of Principal Accessions of Records 30p, 55p by post)
Staff: Archivists: 2 Non-Prof: 4

Dumbarton

A131 🏛
West Dunbartonshire Libraries, Dumbarton Library - Information and Local Studies
Strathleven Pl, Dumbarton, W Dunbartonshire, G82 1BD (01389-733273; *fax:* 01389-607302)
Internet: dumbarton.local.history@west-dunbarton.gov.uk
Internet: http://www.west-dunbarton.gov.uk/

Gov Body: West Dunbartonshire Council (see **P196**) *Chief:* Info Svcs Libn: Mr Graham Hopner BA, MCLIP, AIL (graham. hopner@west-dunbarton.gov.uk) *Other Snr Staff:* Asst: Ms Rhoda MacLeod
Assoc Offices: LOCAL COLLN & ARCHVS, Clydebank Central Lib (see **A110**)
Entry: open access to all *Open:* Mon-Thu 0930-2000, Fri 0930-1700, Sat 1000-1700
Subj: West Dunbartonshire & the historical area of Lennox: local authority archvs; parish records; family papers; historical business records; personal papers; records of parent org *Collns: Bks & Pamphs:* comprehensive colln of local hist bks & pamphs; Watchmeal Colln (antiquarian deposit of local hist bks & MSS) *Archvs:* Dumbarton Town Council records (1579-1975); Dunbarton County Council minutes (1895-1975); Vale of Leven Dist Council minutes & relief applications (1930-75); Dumbarton Dist Council records (1975-1996); West Dunbartonshire Council records (1996-date) *Other:* Dunbarton-shire census (m-form, 1841-1901); West Stirling-shire census (m-form, 1841-1891); old parish registers for Dunbartonshire & beyond (m-form); local newspapers, incl: Dumbarton & Lennox Herald (1851-date); Reporter (1964-date); historical local map & photo collns
Equip: 8 m-readers, m-printer (25p per sheet), 2 copiers (5p per sheet), clr copier (60p per sheet), fax (50p per sheet), 2 computers (both with internet & CD-ROM, 1 with wd-proc, printouts 5p per sheet) *Disabled:* CCTV reader for visually impaired; wheelchair access *Offcr-in-Charge:* Info Svcs Libn, as above *Svcs:* info, ref rsrch
Stock: archvs/79 linear m; rec mgmt/5 linear m; bks/160 linear m; periodcls/2 linear m; photos/16 linear m; slides/1 linear m; illusts/1 linear m; pamphs/2 linear m; maps/6 cubic m; m-forms/10 linear m; audios/3 linear m; videos/2.5 linear m; CD-ROMs/3 linear m *Acq Offcr:* Info Svcs Libn, as above
Classn: DDC, Adlib cataloguing of local maerials starts 2004 *Auto Sys:* Dynix *Staff: Libns:* 1 Non-Prof: 1 (Info & Local Studies staff only)
Exp: £10000 (1999-2000); £10400 (2000-01)

Dumfries

A132 ✚ 🏛
Crichton Museum Archives
(incorporating the Dumfries & Galloway Health Board Archvs)
Easterbrook Hall, Bankend Rd, Dumfries, DG1 1SY (01387-244228; *fax:* 01387-26996)
Email: morag.williams@btinternet.com
Internet: http://www.chrichton.org.uk/

Gov Body: Crichton Development Company *Chief:* Archivist/Curator: Mrs Morag Williams MA, CertEd

Entry: adv appt
Subj: SW Scotland: health archvs; hosp records *Collns: Bks & Pamphs:* New Moon Lib (residual colln, 19C); pubns relating to hist of local hosps; reprints of hosp rsrch pamphs; Crichton Royal Hosp's in-house magazine (1844-1990s) *Archvs:* Dumfries & Galloway Health Board Archvs; archvs of local hosps (minute bks, registers, case bks, photos etc), incl: Crichton Royal Hosp; Dumfries & Galloway Royal Infirmary; Cresswell Maternity Hosp; Garrick Hosp, Stranraer; Thomas Hope Hosp, Langholm; Lochmaben Hosp; Newton Stewart Hosp; Kirkcudbright Hosp; Thornhill Hosp; Moffatt Hosp *Other:* patients' art therapy productions (mainly mid-19C); slides & photos; arch plans
Equip: copier (10p) *Svcs:* info, ref, rsrch
Stock: archvs/87.7 linear m; rec mgmt/3 linear m; bks/38 linear m; photos/2 linear m; slides/1 linear m; pamphs/1 linear m; maps/2 linear m; videos/0.5 linear m
Staff: Non-Prof: 1 *Exp:* £300 (1999-2000); £300 (2000-01)

A133 🏛
Dumfries and Galloway Archives
Archv Centre, 33 Burns St, Dumfries, DG1 2PS (01387-269254; *fax:* 01387-264126)
Email: libarchive@dgc.gov.uk
Internet: http://www.dumgal.gov.uk/

Type: local authority *Gov Body:* Dumfries & Galloway Council (see **P41**) *Chief:* Archivist: Miss Marion M. Stewart MA, MLitt, FSA(Scot)
Assoc Offices: extensive addl archvs held at EWART LIB (Dumfries & Galloway Lib HQ), Catherine St, Dumfries, DG1 1JB
Entry: adv appt advised *Open:* Tue-Wed, Fri 1100-1300, 1400-1700, Thu 1800-2100
Subj: mainly Dumfries Burgh & Nithsdale Dist but some material for rest of Dumfries & Galloway region: local authority archvs; parish records; estate archvs; family papers (various local families, 16C-20C); business records (18C-20C); personal papers; records of parent org; land ownership records (sasines); arch records; Customs & Shipping records; RC church records; nonconformist records *Collns: Bks & Pamphs:* lib of c900 bks as ref material; printed Poor Law Reports (1845-20C); misc pamphs (17C-20C) *Archvs:* local authority records for Burghs of Dumfries & Sanquhar (15C-20C); kirk session records of Dumfries (17C-20C); Court & Jail records (16C-20C); Sasine Indexes & Abridgements (17C-20C); Old Parish Registers on m-film for Dumfries-shire, Kirkcudbrightshire & Wigtown-shire; Methodist, RC & Free Church records as well as Church of Scotland parish records; Stewarts of Shambellie Estate Archv (18C-20C); Stair Estate Archv (19C); motor vehicle licensing records for Dumfries-shire & Kirkcudbrightshire (20C); records of Dumfries & Galloway Constab-ulary *Other:* 19C arch drawings; census returns for region; local newspapers (m-fiche, 18C-20C)
Equip: m-readers, copiers (not used by public but for public svc), computers (incl wd-procs, not for public use) *Svcs:* fee-based rsrch svc, available by post or personal consultation
Stock: archvs/c600 linear m; bks/898; photos/68; maps/2647 + c35000 arch plans
Classn: ISAD(G)
Pubns: Ancestor Hunting in Dumfries Archv Centre (60p); Census '57 Indexes for 6 parishes (5 at £2, 1 at £1); various bklets on types of records available or special subj src lists (10p-40p); all prices plus pubn list available
Staff: Archivists: 1 Non-Prof: 1 PT

---

 academic corporate

A134

Dumfries and Galloway Family History Society, Research Centre

9 Glasgow St, Dumfries, DG2 9AF (01387-248093)
Internet: http://www.dgfhs.org.uk/

Chief: Libn: Mr Gordon McKean
Entry: free to membs; £2 per hr for non-membs
Open: Apr-Oct: Tue-Fri 1000-1600, Sat 1000-1300; Nov-Mar: Tue-Fri 1100-1500, Sat 1000-1300
Subj: Dumfries & Galloway: family hist; genealogy; local hist; parish records *Collns: Bks & Pamphs:* ref colln; local directories; journals of other Scottish family hist socs *Other:* indexed records of memorial inscriptions; parish records (m-film); census indexes (m-form & CD-ROM); local newspapers (m-fiche)
Equip: m-fiche readers, m-film reader, computers (incl 2 with wd-proc, 2 with CD-ROM & 1 with internet) *Svcs:* info, ref, rsrch
Classn: DDC + regional code for local material
Staff: 25 volunteers

Dundee

A135

Dundee City Archives

Support Svcs, 21 City Sq, Dundee, DD1 3BY (01382-434494; *fax:* 01382-434666)
Email: archives@dundeecity.gov.uk
Internet: http://www.dundeecity.gov.uk/archives/ or http://www.fdca.org.uk/

Gov Body: Dundee City Council (see **P42**)
Chief: City Archivist: Mr Iain E.F. Flett MA, MPhil, DipAA, FSA(Scot) *Dep:* Archivist: Mr Richard Cullen MA, DipAA
Entry: adv appt; entry to Archvs is by 1 Shore Ter; no wheelchair access, but callers in wheelchairs can be interviewed at Helpline, City Sq, by appt Mon-Thu *Open:* Mon-Fri 0915-1300, 1400-1645
Subj: Dundee & Tayside: local authority archvs; parish records; estate archvs; family papers; business records *Collns: Bks & Pamphs:* Monthly Repository of Theology & Genl Lit (1806-27); The Christian Reformer or Unitarian Magazine (1835-63); Unitarian Review (1875-80); Dundee & Dist Jute & Flax Workers Guide (1916-27); Dundee Free Press (1926-33) *Archvs:* archvs of Dundee City Council & its predecessors (1327-date); records of Tayside Regional Council (1975-1996); Presbytery of Dundee parish records; Earls of Camperdown papers (19C); Dundee, Perth & London shipping papers (19C-20C); Dundee Port Authority papers (19C); Pearsie papers; Northesk papers (16C); Dundee Chamber of Commerce (formerly Forfarshire Chamber of Commerce, & Baltic Coffee House & Chamber of Commerce) records (1819-1960); Dundee Jute & Flax Union records (1906-1971), incl refs to jute industry in India; Geekie Family, Keillor, County Angus: correspondence, etc (1646-1850), incl letters from Alexander Geekie, surgeon in London (c1678-1724); papers of David Greig, FRCSEd (1850s, copies of his letters written while serving as asst surgeon in the Crimea)
Equip: m-reader
Stock: archvs/1475 linear m; rec mgmt/2159 linear m
Pubns: pamph guide (free)
Staff: Archivists: 2 Non-Prof: 2

A136

Dundee Local Studies Department

Central Lib, The Wellgate, Dundee, DD1 1DB (01382-434377; *fax:* 01382-434036)
Email: local.studies@dundeecity.gov.uk
Internet: http://www.dundeecity.gov.uk/nrd/

Gov Body: Dundee City Council (see **P42**)
Chief: Local Studies Libn
Entry: ref only *Open:* Mon-Tue, Fri 0930-1800, Wed 1000-1800, Thu 0930-2000, Sat 0930-1700
Subj: Dundee & Tayside: local hist; family hist
Collns: Bks & Pamphs: James Bowman Lindsay Colln; Ivory Colln (mathematical & scientific bks, 16C onwards, c300 vols); Mary Slessor Colln; Wighton Colln of Natl Music (620 vols) *Archvs:* Lamb Colln (450 boxes of bks, prints, maps, photos & ephemera relating to Dundee); William McGonagall Colln (works & MSS) *Other:* photographic collns, incl Alexander Wilson Bequest (several 1000 glass negs, 1870-1905); postcards; prints; maps & plans; local newspapers & periodcls (1803 onwards); Old Parish Registers; census returns
Stock: archvs/20000, incl pamphs

A137

Dundee University, Archive, Records Management and Museum Services

Univ of Dundee, Dundee, DD1 4HN (01382-344095; *fax:* 01382-345523)
Email: archives@dundee.ac.uk
Internet: http://www.dundee.ac.uk/armms/

Gov Body: Univ of Dundee (see **S561**) *Chief:* Univ Archivist & Head of Dept: Ms Patricia Whatley *Dep:* Dep Archivist: Ms Caroline Brown
Other Snr Staff: Museum Curator: Mr Matthew Jarron
Assoc Offices: RECORDS MGMT UNIT, at same addr (01382-345615)
Entry: adv appt advised; maps & plans should be ordered 24 hrs in adv *Open:* term: Mon-Wed 0900-1300, 1400-1800, Fri 0900-1300, 1400-1700, closed Thu; vac: Mon-Wed, Fri 0900-1300, 1400-1700
Subj: Dundee & Tayside: diocesan records (Brechin Diocese of the Scottish Episcopal Church); estate archvs; family papers; business records; personal papers; records of parent org; legal records; hosp records *Collns: Bks & Pamphs:* Kinnear Local Colln (local hist); Joan Auld Memorial Colln (labour & social hist) *Archvs:* records of Univ of Dundee & predecessors, Univ Coll Dundee & Queen's Coll Dundee; Dundee Town Council records; Brechin Diocesan Lib MSS; Tayside Health Board Archv; Thornton Colln (railways company records, family & estate papers & others); Dundee Inst of Architects records; Dundee Harbour Commissioners records; Sidlaw Industries Colln; A&S Henry & Co Ltd Colln; numerous other collns *Other:* Michael Peto Photographic Colln; maps & plans
Equip: 2 computers (all with wd-proc, internet & CD-ROM)
Proj: digitisation projs to provide access to collns via the internet

A138

Tay Valley Family History Society, Research Centre

179-181 Princes St, Dundee, DD4 6DQ (01382-461845)
Email: tayvalleyfhs@sol.co.uk
Internet: http://www.sol.co.uk/t/tayvalleyfhs/

Type: registered charity *Gov Body:* Tay Valley Family Hist Soc *Chief:* contact the Sec at above addr
Entry: free to membs; non-membs £2 per hr
Open: Mon, Thu 1000-1600, 1900-2100, Tue-Wed, Fri 1000-1600, Sat 1000-1300 (closed for 2 wks over Xmas & New Year)
Subj: counties of Angus (Forfarshire), Fife, Kinross & Perthshire: family hist; genealogy; some other Scottish, Irish & overseas material
Collns: Bks & Pamphs: ref lib of genealogical & local hist items; genealogical rsrch directories; local directories; journals of other family hist socs

Other: records of births, marriages & burials; Old Parish Registers; census indexes; Fife Shopkeepers & Traders (1820-70); Fife Deaths from Newspapers (1822-54); Fife Deaths Abroad (1855-1900)
Equip: m-reader, m-printer, copier *Svcs:* rsrch (membs only, £5 per hr)
Pubns: Tay Valley Family Historian (journal of soc, 3 pa, free to membs, some back issues available, £1 each); A Genealogist's Guide to Closes, Squares, Lanes & Entries in Dundee (£1); Census Index 1841 Angus (£10); Census Indexes 1851 for various parishes in Angus, Fife, Kinross, Perthshire (prices vary); Monumental Inscriptions Series (prices vary); full bkshop list available
Staff: staffed by volunteers

Dunfirmline

A139

Carnegie UK Trust

Comely Pk House, New Row, Dunfirmline, Fife, KY12 7EJ (01383-721445; *fax:* 01383-620682)
Internet: http://www.carnegieuktrust.org.uk/

Type: charitable trust *Gov Body:* Carnegie UK Trust *Chief:* Chief Exec: Mr C. John Naylor OBE
Dep: Exec Offcr: Miss Elizabeth East
Entry: adv appt by letter only
Subj: Carnegie UK Trust: minutes & grants; grant policy decisions *Collns: Bks & Pamphs:* Carnegie Colln of British Music (on permanent loan to KING'S COLL LONDON, SPECIAL COLLNS – see **S1227**); small office lib of reports, pubns etc relating to Trust policies *Archvs:* Trust Archvs are held at the NATL ARCHVS OF SCOTLAND (see **A150**)

Dunoon

A140

Argyll and Bute Library and Information Service, Local Studies Collection

Lib HQ, Highland Ave, Sandbank, Dunoon, Argyll, PA23 8PB (01369-703214; *fax:* 01369-705797)
Email: eleanor.harris@argyll-bute.gov.uk
Internet: http://www.argyll-bute.gov.uk/

Type: local authority *Gov Body:* Argyll & Bute Council (see **P5**) *Chief:* Local Studies Libn: Ms Eleanor Harris
Assoc Offices: small local studies colln at each branch lib; local archvs are held at ARGYLL & BUTE ARCHVS (see **A248**)
Entry: adv appt
Subj: Argyll & Bute: local studies; family hist
Collns: Other: map colln; postcards
Svcs: info, ref, local hist enq svc (excl genealogical rsrch)
Pubns: various local hist pubns, incl: Helensburgh Past & Present (£4.99); Images of Kintyre (video & bklet, £25); prices excl p&p

Durham

A141

Durham County Record Office

County Hall, Durham, DH1 5UL (0191-383-3253; *fax:* 0191-383-4500)
Email: record.office@durham.gov.uk
Internet: http://www.durham.gov.uk/

Gov Body: Durham County Council (see **P43**)
Chief: County Archivist: Miss J. Gill MA, DipAA
Dep: Snr Asst Archivist: Mr D.J. Butler BA, DipAA, DMS

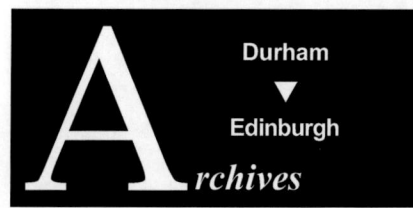

Archives
Durham ▼ Edinburgh

(Durham County Record Office cont)

Entry: adv appt, separate booking for Wed evenings **Open:** Mon-Tue, Thu 0845-1645, Wed 0845-2000, Fri 0845-1615, closed Sat
Subj: Co Durham: local authority archvs; diocesan records; parish records; family papers; hosp records; school records; nonconformist records **Collns:** Bks & Pamphs: small colln of local hist & genl ref bks in the fields of hist & record keeping *Archvs:* records relating to the county of Durham, incl: records of Durham County Council; records of dist councils; records of Diocese of Durham; parish registers; Londonderry & Strathmore family papers; other public records, incl: coroners records; Quarter Sessions records; Natl Coal Board records
Equip: 22 m-readers, m-printer, 3 computers (incl 2 with CD-ROM)
Stock: archvs/635 cubic m; rec mgmt/40 cubic m; bks/100 linear ft
Pubns: Parish Map, c1800 (50cm x 35 cm, £2); Streatlam & Gibside: the Bowes & Strathmore families in County Durham (£3.50); Catalogue of the Londonderry Papers (£4); Durham Places in the Mid-Nineteenth Century (£7.50); Durham Family Hist Gazetteer (£3.75); Cemeteries in County Durham (£2); Durham Collieries: A Listing (£6); numerous handlists, subj guides & user guides, available on receipt of 50p 10"x8" SAE
Staff: Other Prof: 4 Non-Prof: 7 **Exp:** £1220 pa

East Kilbride

A142

South Lanarkshire Council, Archives and Information Management Service
30 Hawbank Rd, College Milton, E Kilbride, S Lanarkshire, G74 5EX (01355-239193; *fax:* 01355-242365)
Email: frank.rankin@southlanarkshire.gov.uk

Gov Body: South Lanarkshire Council (see **P169**)
Chief: Archivist: Mr Frank Rankin MA, MArAd
Entry: adv appt **Open:** Mon-Thu 0930-1230, 1330-1630, Fri 0930-1230, 1330-1600
Subj: South Lanarkshire: local authority archvs; family papers; business records; records of parent org **Collns:** Archvs: records of South Lanarkshire Council & predecessors
Equip: m-reader, m-printer, copier (staff-operated), fax, computer (incl CD-ROM) **Svcs:** rsrch
Stock: archvs/150 linear m; rec mgmt/3000 linear m
Classn: ISAD(G) **Auto Sys:** MS Wd
Staff: Archivists: 1 Non-Prof: 2

Eastleigh

A143

Eastleigh Museum, Resource Room
25 High St, Eastleigh, Hampshire, SO50 5LF (023-8064-3026; *fax:* 023-8065-3582)
Email: museums@hants.gov.uk
Internet: http://www.hants.gov.uk/museum/eastlmus/

Type: local govt **Gov Body:** Hampshire County Council (see **P60**) **Chief:** Curator: Miss Susan Tapliss BA, MSc

Assoc Offices: HAMPSHIRE COUNTY COUNCIL MUSEUMS SVC LIB (see **A508**)
Entry: ref only; adv appt advised **Open:** Tue-Fri 1000-1700, Sat 1000-1600
Subj: Eastleigh Borough: local studies
Collns: Bks & Pamphs: local trade directories
Other: photographic colln; map colln; parish records & census data on m-fiche
Equip: m-reader, copier **Svcs:** info, ref
Stock: archvs/1000; slides/100; pamphs/200; maps/50
Classn: in-house **Staff:** Other Prof: 1

Edinburgh

A144

Edinburgh City Archives
Dept of Corporate Svcs, City Chambers, High St, Edinburgh, EH1 1YJ (0131-529-4616; *fax:* 0131-529-4957)

Gov Body: City of Edinburgh Council (see **P50**)
Chief: City Archivist: Mr Richard Hunter MA(Hons)
Entry: limited facilities; prior appt requested; 3 days notice required for some records **Open:** Mon-Thu 0900-1300, 1400-1630
Subj: past & present City of Edinburgh: local authority archvs; family papers; business records; personal papers; records of local orgs

A145

Edinburgh City Libraries, Edinburgh Room Collections
Edinburgh Central Lib, George IV Bridge, Edinburgh, EH1 1EG (0131-242-8030; *fax:* 0131-242-8035)
Email: edinburgh.room@edinburgh.gov.uk
Internet: http://www.edinburgh.gov.uk/libraries/

Gov Body: Edinburgh City Council (see **P50**)
Chief: Principal Lib Offcr: Ms Ann Nix
Entry: ref only; proof of ID requested for access to rare items; some items may require 2 days notice of visit **Open:** Mon-Thu 1000-2000, Fri 1000-1700, Sat 0900-1300
Subj: Edinburgh: local studies; family hist; some local authority archvs **Collns:** Bks & Pamphs: local studies materials; bks by Edinburgh-born novelists & poets; local directories *Archvs:* minutes of City of Edinburgh Council & predecessors **Other:** map colln (16C-date); local newspapers (mainly on m-film, 1719 onwards); Old Parish Registers (on m-film); census returns; monumental inscriptions; materials relating to Edinburgh Internatl Festival, Fringe & Sci Festival
Stock: archvs/100000+ bks, maps & other items; periodcls/c300

A146

General Register Office for Scotland
New Register House, Edinburgh, EH1 3YT (0131-334-0380; *fax:* 0131-314-4400)
Email: records@gro-scotland.gov.uk
Internet: http://www.gro-scotland.gov.uk/ or http://www.scotlandspeople.gov.uk/

Chief: Registrar Genl: Mr J.N. Randall **Dep:** Dep Registrar Genl: Mr P.M. Parr **Other Snr Staff:** Libn: Ms H. Borthwick
Entry: available to the public on payment of a fee (list of charges available); limited adv bookings taken **Open:** Mon-Fri 0900-1630
Subj: Scottish records **Collns:** Archvs: Statutory Registers of births, deaths & marriages (1855-date); Church of Scotland parish registers (1553-1854, incomplete); open Census records (1841-1901); minor records of births, deaths & marriages registered abroad (1855-date, Scottish nationals only)

Equip: m-readers, computer (incl CD-ROM)
Pubns: info leaflet, incl guidance for family historians (free), also available on web site
Staff: Archivists: 1 Libns: 1 Others: 245.74

A147

HBOS plc Group Archives
(formerly Bank of Scotland Archvs Dept)
12 Bankhead Crossway South, Sighthill, Edinburgh, EH11 4EN (0131-529-1288/1306; *fax:* 0131-529-1307)
Email: archives@HBOSplc.com

Gov Body: HBOS plc **Chief:** Archivist: Ms Helen Redmond-Cooper BA, DipAA **Dep:** Dep Archivist: Ms Seonaid McDonald
Entry: adv appt **Open:** Mon-Fri 0930-1630
Subj: Scotland & UK: banking & business records; records of parent org; banking & economic hist of Scotland; Scotland & Scottish investment in England & overseas; banking in Commonwealth **Collns:** Archvs: Bank of Scotland (1695-date) & banks which have been taken over, incl: Union Bank of Scotland; British Linen Bank
Equip: fax, copier, video viewer, computer
Stock: archvs/c8000 linear m
Staff: Other Prof: 3 Non-Prof: 1

A148

Heriot-Watt University Archive, Records Management and Museum Service
Cameron Smail Lib, Heriot-Watt Univ, Riccarton, Edinburgh, EH14 4AS (0131-451-3218/9; *fax:* 0131-451-3164)
Internet: http://www.hw.ac.uk/archive/

Gov Body: Heriot-Watt Univ (see **S604**) **Chief:** Univ Archivist: Ms Ann Jones (a.e.jones@hw.ac.uk) **Dep:** Archivist: Ms Pamela McIntyre (P.J.McIntyre@hw.ac.uk)
Assoc Offices: ARCHV OF HISTORICAL TEXTILE & BUSINESS RECORDS, Scottish Borders Campus, Netherdale, Galashiels, Selkirkshire, TD1 3HF; queries should be addressed to the Univ Archv at above addr
Entry: adv appt
Subj: Scotland: estate archvs; family papers; personal papers; business records; records of parent org; textiles; textile industry **Collns (Riccardon):** Archvs: archvs of Heriot-Watt Univ & predecessors (from 1821), incl: Edinburgh School of Arts (later the Watt Instn & School of Arts, 1821-1885); Heriot-Watt Coll (1885-1966); James Watt Archv (relating to the Scottish engineer); Gibson-Craig of Riccarton family & estate papers; John Tweedie Colln (local historian); Sir Robert Blair papers (educationalist); records of Leith Nautical Coll **Collns (Scottish Borders Campus):** Archvs: records of Scottish Borders Campus of Heriot-Watt Univ & predecessors (from 1889), incl: Galashiels Combined Technical School (1889-1900); South of Scotland Central Technical Coll (1906-22); Scottish Woollen Technical Coll (1922-65); Scottish Coll of Textiles (1965-98); business records of textile companies, incl: Robert Stocks & Co Ltd (1811-1956); R&A Sanderson (1852-1956); Blenkhorn Richardson (1883-1967) **Other:** 300+ pattern bks; fabric bks & samples; Lewis Anderson Tartan Colln

A149

Lothian Health Services Archive
Special Collns Div, Edinburgh Univ Lib, George Sq, Edinburgh, EH8 9LJ (0131-650-3392; *fax:* 0131-650-6863)
Email: lhsa@ed.ac.uk
Internet: http://www.lhsa.lib.ed.ac.uk/

Chief: Archivist: Dr. Michael Barfoot BA, MSc(Econ), PhD (m.barfoot@ed.ac.uk) **Other Snr Staff:** Asst Archivist: Ms Jenny McDermott MA, PGDip (jenny.mcdermott@ed.ac.uk) **Entry:** adv appt; access to some records restricted **Open:** term: Mon-Thu 0900-1900, Fri 0900-1700; vac: Mon-Fri 0900-1700 **Subj:** Edinburgh & Lothian: health svc records; hosp records; personal papers **Collns: Bks & Pamphs:** ref lib **Archvs:** chief repository for the archival records of hosps in the Edinburgh & Lothians (1690 onwards), incl administrative & legal records & records relating to patient care; personal papers of medical practitioners, nurses etc; papers of medical socs & instns; major collns incl: Royal Infirmary of Edinburgh records (1727-date); Royal Edinburgh Hosp for Sick Children records (1859-1992); Royal Edinburgh Hosp (1791-1985); Edinburgh Dental Hosp & School records (1862-1992); Lothian Health Board records (1912-date); City of Edinburgh Public Health Dept records (1865-1997); numerous others **Other:** large photo colln; paintings; medical artifacts **Svcs:** info **Staff:** 8 in total

A150

National Archives of Scotland

HM Genl Register House, Princes St, Edinburgh, EH1 3YY (0131-535-1314; *fax:* 0131-535-1360)
Email: research@nas.gov.uk
Internet: http://www.nas.gov.uk/

Gov Body: The Scottish Exec **Chief:** The Keeper of the Records of Scotland: Mr George P. MacKenzie BA, MLitt **Dep:** Dep Keepers: Dr Peter D. Anderson MA, PhD & Mr David Brownlee **Assoc Offices:** WEST REGISTER HOUSE, Charlotte Sq, Edinburgh, EH2 4DJ; THOMAS THOMSON HOUSE, 99 Bankhead, Crossway North, Sighthill, Edinburgh, EH11 4DX (please use main contact addr above for both offices) **Entry:** reader's permit on personal application & proof of ID **Open:** Mon-Fri 0900-1645 (closed part Nov for stocktaking) **Subj:** Scotland: public records (12C-21C); records of govt; Scottish central & local court records; church records; family papers; business records; personal papers; Scottish railway archvs; natl undertakings; maps & plans **Collns: Bks & Pamphs:** small ref lib for staff & readers using archival materials **Equip:** 8 m-film readers, 3 m-fiche readers, 2 m-film printers, 4 computers at Genl Register House, computer terminals at all desks at West Register House **Svcs:** ref **Stock:** archvs/60000 linear m **Pubns:** Guide to the Natl Archvs of Scotland (£50 + £5 p&p); Tracing Your Scottish Ancestors (£9.99 + £1.50 p&p); Tracing Scottish Local Hist (£9.99 + £1.50 p&p); List of Pubns & Other Items for Sale (free) **Staff:** Archivists: 40 Other Prof: 8 Non-Prof: 100 **Exp:** £5000 (2000-01, bk purchases only)

A151

National Monuments Record of Scotland Library

Royal Commission on the Ancient & Historical Monuments of Scotland, John Sinclair House, 16 Bernard Ter, Edinburgh, EH8 9NX (0131-662-1456; *fax:* 0131-662-1499)
Email: nmrs@rcahms.gpv.uk
Internet: http://www.rcahms.gov.uk/

Gov Body: Royal Commission on the Ancient & Historical Monuments of Scotland (RCAHMS) **Chief:** Sec & Curator: Mr R.J. Mercer MA, FSA, MIFA **Dep:** Dep Curator: Mrs Diana M. Murray MA, FSA, MIFA **Entry:** ref only; adv appt recommended for complex enqs **Open:** Mon-Fri 0930-1630; closed public hols

Subj: Scotland: archaeo; arch; arts; geog; hist **Collns: Bks & Pamphs:** archaeo & arch bks & periodcls **Archvs:** Arch Collns (early 18C-date), incl: survey records; arch drawings, photos, engravings, albums, bks & models; deposited arch collns incl: Royal Incorporation of Architects in Scotland Colln; Edinburgh City Architects Colln; Northern Lighthouse Board Colln; Archaeological Collns (relating to archaeo sites & monuments in Scotland, 19C-date), incl: RCAHMS survey drawings, photographs & notebks (1908-date); excavation & survey documentary archvs; Ordnance Survey (OS) Archaeo Branch records (1950-1983); personal rsrch archvs; important antiquarian material, incl the Soc of Antiquaries Colln **Other:** Air Photographs Colln (oblique & vertical photos, in b&w & clr, various scales, 1940s-date) **Equip:** m-reader, m-printer, copier, clr copier, computers **Online:** NMRS Database, available online via CANMORE (Computer Application for Natl MOnuments Record Enq) **Svcs:** info, ref **Stock:** archvs/165000; periodcls/259; photos/1500000; slides/70000; illusts/370000 prints & drawings; maps/80000; m-forms/1500 **Classn:** own **Staff:** Libns: 0.5 Other Prof: 15 Non-Prof: 2 See also NATL MONUMENTS RECORD (**A483**) & NATL MONUMENTS RECORD OF WALES (**A6**)

A152

National Trust For Scotland Archives

28 Charlotte Sq, Edinburgh, EH2 4ET (0131-243-9300; *fax:* 0131-243-9301)
Email: information@nts.org.uk
Internet: http://www.nts.org.uk/

Type: conservation charity **Chief:** Archivist: Miss Carolynn Bain MA(Hons), MArAd **Dep:** Archival Asst: Mr Iain Riches MA(Hons) **Entry:** adv appt **Open:** Mon-Fri 0930-1630 **Subj:** Scotland, esp land owned by NTS: records of parent org; personal papers; arts; hist; geog **Collns: Archvs:** organisational & administrative records of NTS; some private papers **Equip:** copier (free to students) **Svcs:** info, ref **Staff:** Archivists: 1 Non-Prof: 1

A153 ✚

Royal College of Nursing Archives

42 South Oswald Rd, Edinburgh, EH9 2HH (0131-662-6122/3; *fax:* 0131-662-1032)
Email: archives@rcn.org.uk
Internet: http://www.rcn.org.uk/

Chief: Archivist: Ms Susan McGann **Assoc Offices:** ROYAL COLL OF NURSING LIB & INFO SVCS (see **S1351**) **Entry:** adv appt **Open:** Mon-Fri 0930-1630 **Subj:** United Kingdom: nursing; hist of nursing; personal papers; records of parent org **Collns: Bks & Pamphs:** Historical Journals Colln **Archvs:** records of Royal Coll of Nursing (1916-date), incl minutes, reports, departmental papers, property records etc; records of other nursing orgs, incl: Natl Assoc of Chief & Principal Nursing Offcrs; Central Council for Dist Nursing in London; Commonwealth Nurses Federation; Florence Nightingale Colln; Florence Nightingale Internatl Foundation; Genl Nursing Council; Internatl Council for Nurses; Natl Council of Nurses; Natl Council of Women; Queen's Nursing Inst, Scotland; Royal British Nurses Assoc; Natl Assoc of State Enrolled Nurses; Standing Nursing Advisory Cttee; United Kingdom Central Council; personal records of nurses (19C onwards) **Other:** Oral Hist Colln (200 interviews, access at discretion of the Archivist) **Equip:** copier

A154

The Royal Scots Regimental Museum, Archives

RHQ The Royal Scots, The Castle, Edinburgh, EH1 2YT (0131-310-5016; *fax:* 0131-310-5019)
Email: rhqroyalscots@edinburghcastle.fsnet.co.uk
Internet: http://www.theroyalscots.co.uk/

Chief: Regimental Sec: Lt Col R.P. Mason **Dep:** Asst Regimental Sec: Capt W. Sutherland (Rtd) **Other Snr Staff:** Archivist: D. Murphy **Entry:** by appt; entry free if visiting Museum/Lib only, otherwise standard Castle entrance fees apply **Open:** Apr-Sep: Mon-Sun 0930-1730; Oct-Mar: Mon-Fri 0930-1600 **Subj:** regimental hist; regimental records **Collns: Bks & Pamphs:** war diaries of active svc battalions in 1st & 2nd World Wars; regimental hists; regimental magazine (1890s-date) **Archvs:** records relating to the Royal Scots **Other:** army lists; photographic colln; silver colln; medal colln **Equip:** copier (10p per copy) **Svcs:** info, ref

A155 ⚷ ✋

Scottish Catholic Archives

Columba House, 16 Drummond Pl, Edinburgh, EH3 6PL (0131-556-3661)

Gov Body: Scottish Catholic Bishops **Chief:** Keeper: Dr Christine Johnson MA, PhD **Entry:** not open to genl public; bona-fide academic rsrchers by adv appt only; please note that the Archv does not contain any genealogical info **Open:** Mon-Fri 0930-1300, 1400-1630 **Subj:** post-Reformation Scottish Roman Catholic Church; Scottish hist (for ref); family papers; personal papers; records of Scottish Roman Catholic orgs **Collns: Bks & Pamphs:** 19C Scottish Catholic pamphs **Archvs:** Archbishop James Beaton's personal papers (1540-1603) **Equip:** copier **Stock:** archvs/6000; letters/9000; some photos **Staff:** Other Prof: 1

A156 ⚷

Scottish Genealogy Society, Library and Family History Centre

15 Victoria Ter, Edinburgh, EH1 2JL (*tel & fax:* 0131-220-3677)
Email: info@scotsgenealogy.com
Internet: http://www.scotsgenealogy.com/

Chief: Hon Libn: Dr James Cranstoun **Entry:** membs of Soc free, non-membs charged £5 pd subj to space **Open:** Mon-Tue, Thu 1030-1730, Wed 1030-2030, Sat 1000-1700; closed Fri & on public hols, may close 1730 on Weds for Soc meetings **Subj:** Scotland: genealogy; family hist; local hist; Scottish hist; heraldry; church hist; biography; topography; parish records **Collns: Bks & Pamphs:** ref colln; Scottish family hist soc journals; rsrch aids; trade & county directories; emigration lists; topographies; gazetteers **Archvs:** MS materials relating to Scottish family hist; numerous secondary sources incl church records, burgess rolls, court records & records of births, marriages & deaths **Other:** Old Parish Registers of Scotland on m-film (70% coverage), incl Index to Births & Marriages; school & univ rolls; military records, incl rolls of honour, medal rolls, casualty lists & pensioners; extensive colln of Scottish monumental inscriptions; maps; pedigrees; rsrch notes; m-fiche & m-film colln; various resources on CD-ROM **Equip:** m-reader, m-printer, copier (A4/10p, A3/20p), computers (with CD-ROM) **Svcs:** enqs **Stock:** archvs/6000+ ☛

(Scottish Genealogy Soc Lib cont)

Pubns: Scottish Genealogist (4 pa, free to membs, £4.25 to non-membs); sales list of 300+ titles
Staff: 1 Hon Libn + volunteers

A157 🖋

Standard Life Assurance Company, Records Management and History Archives

1 Baileyfield Cres, Edinburgh, EH15 1ET (0131-245-1739)
Internet: http://www.standardlife.com/

Chief: Company Archivist: Mr David Steel MA(ARM)
Entry: by appt only
Subj: Standard Life: records of parent org; some historical actuarial material (pre-1950) **Collns:** Archvs: Standard Life Assurance Co Archvs; Colonial Life Assurance Co Archvs; Life Insurance Co of Scotland Archvs; archvs of some merger companies, incl: York & London Assurance Co; India Life Assurance Co; Minerva Life Assurance Co; small number of deposited collns relating to former staff membs
Svcs: info
Stock: archvs/350 linear m; photos/7000; audios/2 linear m; videos/5 linear m

Elgin

A158 🏛

Moray Local Heritage Centre

(incl collns of the former Moray Record Office)
Grant Lodge, Cooper Pk, Elgin, Moray, IV30 1HS (01343-562644; *fax:* 01343-569050)
Email: libstock@moray.gov.uk
Internet: http://www.moray.org/techleis/heritage_serv.html

Gov Body: Moray Council (see **P119**) **Chief:** Local Heritage Offcr: Mr Graeme Wilson MA (graeme.wilson@moray.gov.uk)
Open: Mon, Thu-Fri 1000-1700, Tue 1000-2000, Wed (May-Sep only) 1000-1700, Sat 1000-1200
Subj: Moray: local authority archvs; parish records; business records; records of parent org; genealogical records; local hist **Collns:** Bks & Pamphs: local hist bks & pamphs Archvs: records of Moray Dist Council & predecessors; presbytery & kirk sessions records; Fishery Office records; Customs & Excise records; Justice of the Peace Court records; motor vehicle licensing & drivers licenses (1904-1950) **Other:** extensive photo colln; maps & estate plans; arch plans (1840-1975), incl Doig Colln & Wittet Colln; back files of all local newspapers
Equip: 8 m-readers, m-printer, fax, 2 copiers, 5 computers (all with wd-proc, internet & CD-ROM) **Disabled:** available in adjacent public lib **Offcr-in-Charge:** Local Heritage Offcr, as above **Svcs:** info, ref, rsrch
Stock: archvs/700 linear m; rec mgmt/800 linear m; bks/8000; photos/20000+; slides/1000; maps/5000; m-forms/500; videos/60; CD-ROMs/20
Classn: DDC **Auto Sys:** in-house sys
Staff: Archivists: 1 Other Prof: 2

Ellesmere Port

A159 🔑 🏛

David Owen Waterways Archive

The Boat Museum, South Pier Rd, Ellesmere Port, Cheshire, CH65 4FW (0151-373-4378; *fax:* 0151-355-4079)
Email: doarchive@thewaterwaystrust.org
Internet: http://www.thewaterwaystrust.co.uk/archives/

Gov Body: The Waterways Trust **Chief:** Head of Archvs & Records: Mr Paul Sillitoe **Dep:** Archvs Offcr: Ms Diana Sumner
Assoc Offices: BRITISH WATERWAYS ARCHV (see **A183**); NATL WATERWAYS MUSEUM LIB (see **S749**)
Entry: ref only; prior appt advisable **Open:** Mon-Fri 1030-1630
Subj: England, Scotland & Wales: records relating to the mgmt, maintenance & operation of inland waterways (17C-20C) **Collns:** Bks & Pamphs: substantial lib of bks & periodcls on inland waterways Archvs: waterways archvs & MSS Other: maps, plans & drawings; photos; sound & video recordings; ephemera **Co-op Schemes:** partner in The Waterways Virtual Archv Catalogue Proj
Equip: 2 m-readers, m-printer, copier, fax, video viewor, 3 rooms for hire **Svcs:** info, ref, rsrch (limited svc)
Stock: archvs/c40 cubic m
Staff: Archivists: 0.5 Non-Prof: 1

Enniskillen

A160 🔑 🏛

Royal Inniskilling Fusiliers Museum, Regimental Archives

The Castle, Enniskillen, Co Fermanagh, BT74 7BB (028-6632-3142; *fax:* 028-6632-0359)

Chief: Curator: Major Jack Dunlop
Entry: by adv appt only
Subj: military hist; regimental hist; regimental records **Collns:** Archvs: records of the Royal Inniskilling Fusiliers/27th Foot (1775-1946), incl orders, letter bks, memoirs & diaries; records of Fermanagh Light Infantry (1855-1901); records of Royal Tyrone Militia (1793-1873)

Exeter

A161 🏛

Devon Record Office

Castle St, Exeter, Devon, EX4 3PU (01392-384253; *fax:* 01392-384256)
Email: devrec@devon.gov.uk
Internet: http://www.devon.gov.uk/dro/homepage.html

Gov Body: Devon County Council (see **P37**)
Chief: County Archivist: Mr J.M. Draisey MA, DipAA (jdraisey@devon.gov.uk) **Dep:** Snr Archivist: Mr J.D. Brunton BA, LLB (jbrunton@devon.gov.uk)
Assoc Offices: NORTH DEVON RECORD OFFICE (see **A27**); EXETER DEAN & CHAPTER ARCHVS (see **A163**); m-fiche records can also be consulted at svc pts at: NORTH DEVON MARITIME MUSEUM, Odun House, Odun Rd, Appledore, Devon (01237-474852); TORQUAY LOCAL HIST LIB (see **A491**); COLYTON LOCAL HIST CENTRE, St Andrews Churchyard, Colyton, Devon (01297-552828; *email:* jncochrane@roadgreen.fsnet.co.uk); TOTNES MUSEUM; MUSEUM OF DARTMOOR LIFE, West St, Okehampton, Devon (01837-52295); TAVISTOCK LIB, The Quay, Plymouth Rd, Tavistock, Devon,

PL19 8AB (01822-612218); TIVERTON MUSEUM, Beck's Sq, Tiverton, Devon (01884-520517); HOLSWORTHY MUSEUM, Manor Offices, Holsworthy, Devon (01409-259337; *email:* holsworthy@devonmuseums.net)
Entry: CARN ticket or proof of ID, fee charged (some exemptions, application forms available); some documents available only at 48 hrs notice
Open: Mon-Thu 1000-1700, Fri 1000-1630
Subj: Devon: local authority archvs; diocesan records; parish records; estate archvs; family papers; business records (mainly solicitors' firms, some manufacturing & retail); records of parent org **Collns:** Archvs: at main office in Exeter: Devon Quarter Sessions (1592-1971); Devon County Council (1889-1974); Dist Council records etc. for East, South & Mid Devon; Exeter City Archvs (incl exceptional coverage of medieval records from 12C onwards); Exeter Diocesan Archvs (13C-20C); records of Archdeaconry of Exeter; several large estate collns, incl: Bedford Estates; Courtenay of Powderham; Fortescue of Castle Hill; Acland of Killerton; Addington of Sidmouth; Rolle of St Giles; Petre of Axminster; Mallock of Cockington; Iddlesleigh of Upton Pyne; parish records (16C-date); nonconformist records (17C onwards); held separately: archvs of Exeter Dean & Chapter (see above)
Equip: 24 m-readers, m-camera, m-printer (30p per sheet), fax, copier **Offcr-in-Charge:** County Archivist, as above
Stock: archvs/10000 linear m; rec mgmt/1000 linear m **Acq Offcr:** County Archivist, as above
Classn: own sys
Pubns: Newsletter (biannual, free on receipt of SAE); Annual Reports (up to 1986-87, £1 each); List of Accessions (1987-88 to 1995-96, £2 each); Guides to Sources (free); Devon Record Office Handlists (prices vary); Stopping the Rot: Archv Preservation Good Practice (£3.50); Map of Devon Parishes (40p); numerous others
Exp: £4800 (1999-2000); £7600 (2000-01); exp on conservation only
Proj: construction of new record office in 2003 (£4994000)
See also WESTCOUNTRY STUDIES LIB (**A164**)

A162 🏛

Devonshire and Dorset Regiment Museum, Regimental Archives

Wyvern Barracks, Topsham Rd, Exeter, Devon, EX2 6AR (01392-492436)

Chief: Curator: Major C. Pape MBE **Dep:** Lt Col Squires **Other Snr Staff:** Museum Attendant & Archivist: Mr A. Cox BEM
Entry: adv appt **Open:** Mon-Fri 0830-1230
Subj: regimental hist; regimental records; records of parent org **Collns:** Bks & Pamphs: bks publ about the Devonshire Regiment Archvs: records of the battalions of the Devonshire Regiment
Svcs: info, rsrch
Acq Offcr: Lt Col Squires, as above
Classn: ISAD(G) **Auto Sys:** Dynix
Staff: Archivists: 1

A163 🙏

Exeter Cathedral Archives

Diocesan House, Palace Gate, Exeter, Devon, EX1 1HX (*mornings:* 01392-383063; *afternoons:* 01392-495954)
Email: catharchive@eurobell.co.uk

Gov Body: Exeter Dean & Chapter & Devon County Council (see **P37**) **Chief:** Cathedral Archivist: Mrs Angela Doughty BA(Hons), DipAA
Assoc Offices: EXETER CATHEDRAL LIB, at same addr (see **S665**); DEVON RECORD OFFICE (see **A161**)
Entry: adv appt only **Open:** Mon-Wed 1400-1700

Subj: Exeter Cathedral, Dean & Chapter properties in Exeter, Devon & Cornwall (plus a few in Dorset, Somerset & Oxford): records of parent org (cathedral archvs) **Collns:** *Archvs:* Dean & Chapter of Exeter Cathedral Archvs; records of Vicars Choral of Exeter Cathedral **Equip:** m-reader, copier, computer (incl internet) *Disabled:* no disabled access due to stairs **Stock:** archvs/831 linear ft (bks & boxes), 35 linear ft (maps & plans); rec mgmt/limited, variable quantity; photos/12 linear ft; slides/4 linear ft; maps/35 linear ft; videos/a few **Classn:** Archival Listing **Staff:** Archivists: 1 PT **Exp:** £500 on conservation (1999-2000); £500 on indexing (2000-01)

A164
Westcountry Studies Library
Exeter Central Lib, Castle St, Exeter, Devon, EX4 3PU (01392-384216; *fax:* 01392-384228)
Email: imaxted@devon.gov.uk
Internet: http://www.devon.gov.uk/library/locstudy/

Type: local authority **Gov Body:** Devon County Council (see **P37**) **Chief:** County Local Studies Libn: Mr Ian Maxted MA, MCLIP **Dep:** Westcountry Studies Libn: Mr Peter Waite MA & Mrs Kati Vámos MA, MCLIP (job share) **Assoc Offices:** NORTH DEVON LOCAL STUDIES CENTRE, Tuly St, Barnstable, Devon, EX31 1EL, Local Studies Libn: Ms Deborah Gahan (see also NORTH DEVON RECORD OFFICE – **A27** – also at same addr); smaller local collns in most branch libs, but no specialist staff **Entry:** ref only **Open:** Mon, Fri 0930-1800, Tue, Thu 0930-1900, Wed 1000-1700, Sat 0930-1600 **Subj:** the Westcountry, esp Devon: local hist; non-archival documentation on all aspects of the region, past & present; some personal & literary papers **Collns:** *Bks & Pamphs:* Pocknell Colln (shorthand); Brushfield Colln (Sir Walter Raleigh); local directories (1783-date); local hists (17C onwards); local guidebks (18C onwards) *Archvs:* historical MS papers, incl: James Davidson; Beatrix Cresswell; W.G. Hoskins; literary MS papers, incl: R.D. Blackmore; John Galsworthy; Eden Phillpotts; Devon & Cornwall Record Soc colln of transcripts of parish records etc (access for soc membs only); census returns; see DEVON RECORD OFFICE (**A161**) for local archvs *Other:* Heber Mardon Colln (Napoleonic prints); Brooking Rowe Colln (brass-rubbings & bkplates); Pike Ward Colln (Iceland); local newspapers (m-film, 1738-date, some earlier); map colln (1575 onwards); prints, drawings & photos of the county (18C-date); IGI **Co-op Schemes:** Newsplan **Equip:** 9 m-readers, 2 m-printers, copier, 6 computers (incl CD-ROM), room for hire **Svcs:** info, ref **Stock:** archvs/50000; periodcls/500; photos/50000; slides/10000; illusts/5000; pamphs/25000; maps/15000; m-forms/1500 reels, 5000 fiche; audios/100; videos/100; CD-ROMs/5; note that many of these figs are indicative only **Acq Offcr:** County Local Studies Libn, as above **Classn:** DDC **Auto Sys:** dBase **Pubns:** see web site for details **Staff:** Libns: 2 Non-Prof: 2.25

Falkirk

A165
Falkirk Council Archives
History Rsrch Centre, Callendar House, Callendar Pk, Falkirk, Stirlingshire, FK1 1YR (01324-503779; *fax:* 01324-503771)
Email: callendar.house@falkirk.gov.uk
Internet: http://www.falkirkmuseums.org/

Gov Body: Falkirk Council (see **P52**) **Chief:** Archivist: Ms Elspeth Reid MA(Hons), DipAA, RMSA **Dep:** Museums Asst: Miss Carol Sneddon **Entry:** ref only **Open:** Mon-Fri 1000-1230, 1330-1700; closed local & public hols **Subj:** Falkirk Dist: local authority archvs; parish records; estate archvs; family papers; business records; personal papers; records of parent org; trade union records; school records; local hist; industrial hist **Collns:** *Bks & Pamphs:* local studies ref colln *Archvs:* records of Falkirk Council & predecessors; Forbes Colln of Callendar Muniments *Other:* photo colln of c34000 items (local area); maps & plans; local newspapers on m-film **Equip:** m-printer, copier, slide viewer, light box **Svcs:** ref, rsrch **Stock:** archvs/730 linear m; bks/c3000; photos/34000; maps/c500 **Acq Offcr:** Archivist, as above **Classn:** ISAD(G) **Auto Sys:** Collns **Pubns:** unpublished finding aids & Guide to Archvs **Staff:** Archivists: 1 Non-Prof: 1 **Exp:** part of Falkirk Museums budget

Fareham

A166
Westbury Manor Museum, Local Studies Room
84 West St, Fareham, Hampshire, PO16 0JJ (01329-824895; *fax:* 01329-825917)
Email: musmjb@hants.gov.uk
Internet: http://www.hants.gov.uk/museum/westbury/

Gov Body: Hampshire County Council (see **P60**) & Fareham Borough Council **Chief:** Curator: Ms Julie Bibblecombe MA, AMA **Assoc Offices:** HAMPSHIRE COUNTY COUNCIL MUSEUMS SVC LIB (see **A508**) **Entry:** no restrictions; visitors researching a specific topic are advised to phone in adv **Open:** Mon-Fri 1000-1700, Sat 1000-1600 **Subj:** Borough of Fareham: local authority archvs; parish records; family papers; copies of material relating to area – originals in HAMPSHIRE RECORD OFFICE (see **A509**); local hist **Collns:** *Bks & Pamphs:* local material, mainly local hist; trade directories (from 1984) *Archvs:* parish records of area on m-fiche *Other:* maps (from 1610); photos **Equip:** m-reader, copier, computer **Svcs:** photographic copying svc **Stock:** archvs/2000+; slides/500+; maps/50 **Pubns:** free visitor guides; Fareham Past & Present (2 pa, £2, publ by Fareham Local Hist Group) **Exp:** £300 (2000-01)

Farnham

A167
Museum of Farnham, Local Studies Library
38 West St, Farnham, Surrey, GU9 7DX (01252-715094; *fax:* 01252-715094)
Email: fmuseum@waverley.gov.uk
Internet: http://www.waverley.gov.uk/museumoffarnham/

Gov Body: Waverley Borough Council **Chief:** Curator: Mrs Anne Jones BA, AMA **Dep:** Asst Curator: Mr Christopher Hellier BA, AMA **Entry:** ref only **Open:** Tue-Sat 1000-1700 **Subj:** Farnham, West Surrey & East Hampshire: local study; archaeo; hist **Collns:** *Bks & Pamphs:* colln of works by & about William Cobbett, incl The Political Register Vols 1-73, also State Trials by William Cobbett Vols 1-22

Archvs: local hist archv in museum colln accessed through lib ref *Other:* Farnham Parish Registers (on m-film); Farnham census returns (1841-1871, on m-film); Winchester pipe rolls (on m-film); map colln; large photographic colln, incl John Henry Knight Colln **Equip:** m-reader, copier **Svcs:** info, ref **Stock:** archvs/1000+; photos/150; maps/100 **Classn:** DDC **Staff:** Other Prof: 4 Non-Prof: 2

Frome

A168
Frome Museum Library
1 North Parade, Frome, Somerset, BA11 1AT (01373-463494)
Internet: http://www.fromemuseum.org.uk/

Gov Body: Trustees of Frome Museum **Chief:** Hon Libn: Mr Derek Gill **Entry:** adv appt **Open:** Tue-Sat 1100-1400; or by appt **Subj:** local studies (Frome & surrounding area); family hist; topography; local industry **Collns:** *Bks & Pamphs:* local hists, directories etc *Archvs:* materials relating of local businesses, esp Singer's Art Metalworks *Other:* photos; OS maps (1868 onwards) **Svcs:** ref **Stock:** archvs/various bks, photos, illusts & maps **Acq Offcr:** Hon Libn, as above **Staff:** Non Prof: 1 **Proj:** renovation of bldg & storage

Glasgow

A169
British Association of Academic Phoneticians Archive
Phonetics Laboratory, Dept of English Lang, Univ of Glasgow, Glasgow, G12 8QQ (0141-330-4596; *fax:* 0141-330-3531)
Email: m.macmahon@englang.arts.gla.ac.uk

Type: prof org **Chief:** Sec & Archivist: Prof M.K.C. MacMahon **Entry:** membs of BAAP, otherwise bona fide rsrchers **Open:** please contact Sec/Archivist **Subj:** business records: mainly papers relating to BAAP Colloquia (1950-date) **Staff:** Non-Prof: 1

A170
Centre for Political Song, Archives
Glasgow Caledonian Univ Lib, Cowcaddens Rd, Glasgow, G4 0BA (0141-331-3920)
Internet: http://www.gcal.ac.uk/

Type: sound archv **Gov Body:** Glasgow Caledonian Univ (see **S701**) **Chief:** Proj Mgr: Mr John Powles (J.Powles@gcal.ac.uk) **Dep:** Development Offcr: Ms Janis McNair (j.mcnair@gcal.ac.uk) **Subj:** hist of political song **Collns:** *Bks & Pamphs:* printed material relating to the hist of political song *Other:* recordings on vinyl, tape & video **Exp:** £7000 (2000-01); most material is acquired by donation

A171
East Dunbartonshire Information and Archives
William Patrick Lib, 2 West High St, Kirkintilloch, Glasgow, G66 1AD (0141-776-8090; *fax:* 0141-776-0408)
Email: libraries@eastdunbarton.gov.uk

(E Dunbartonshire Info & Archvs cont)
Gov Body: East Dunbartonshire Council (see **P45**) **Chief:** Archivist & Records Offcr: Ms Sarah Chubb
Assoc Offices: records relating to Bearsden & Milngavie are held at: BROOKWOOD LIB, 166 Drymen Rd, Bearsden, Glasgow (0141-942-6811; *fax:* 0141-943-1119)
Entry: no restrictions for local studies materials; form to fill in for archival materials & ID required
Open: Mon-Thu 1000-2000, Fri-Sat 1000-1700
Subj: East Dunbartonshire (former Strathkelvin & Bearsden & Milngavie districts): local authority archvs; parish records; estate archvs; family papers; business records; records of local socs; school records; local & family hist **Collns:** *Bks & Pamphs:* local hist bks; James F. McEwan Colln (Scottish transport hist, currently being catalogued); local directories (mainly at Brookwood Lib) *Archvs:* records of East Dunbartonshire Council & predecessor authorities (Strathkelvin Dist Council & Bearsden & Milngavie Dist Council); records of Kirkintilloch Dist Council; records of New Kilpatrick Dist Council; records of Burghs; records of School Boards & School Mgmt Committees; family & estate collns incl: Reid Family of Waterside papers; Goodwin Family of Kirkintilloch papers; Fraser of Westermains papers; Leitch Family of Kirkintilloch & Lenzie papers; Buchanan Family of Milton of Campsie papers; Cadder Estate archv; Lennox Estates archv *Other:* extensive photo colln (35000 + 25000 slides), incl aerial photos; census returns; electoral registers; valuation rolls; maps & plans; cemetery records
Svcs: postal enqs (no charge, but time limit on rsrch)
Staff: *Libns:* 3 *Non-Prof:* 1 + 2 assts shared with Lending Svc at Brookwood Lib

A172
East Renfrewshire District Archives
Giffnock Lib, Station Rd, Giffnock, Glasgow, G46 6JF (0141-577-4976; *fax:* 0141-577-4978)
Email: giffnock.library@eastrenfrewshire.gov.uk
Internet: http://www.eastrenfrewshire.gov.uk/

Gov Body: East Renfrewshire Council (see **P47**)
Chief: Info Svcs Libn: Mrs Maud Devine
Assoc Offices: small collns are also held at other East Renfrewshire Community Libs
Entry: adv appt **Open:** Mon, Wed 1000-2000, Tue, Thu-Fri 1000-1800, Sat 1000-1700
Subj: East Renfrewshire: local authority archvs; public records; personal papers; local hist; family hist **Collns:** *Bks & Pamphs:* local hist bks *Archvs:* records of East Renfrewshire Council & predecessors; census records (1841-91) *Other:* maps & photos; electoral registers; Old Parish Registers; valuation rolls
Equip: m-reader, fax, copier **Svcs:** info, ref, rsrch, school visits, talks, exhibs
Pubns: Dr Welsh, Eastwood Dist (£6.95); Fairest Parish: Hist of Mearns (£1.80); Crossroads Community: Hist of Clarkston (£1.80); Sandstone to Suburbia: Hist of Giffnock (£1.80); Planned Village: Hist of Eaglesham (£1.80); Hist of Busby (£1.50); Hist of Thornliebank (£1.50)
Staff: *Other Prof:* 2

A173
Glasgow and West of Scotland Family History Society, Research Centre
Unit 5, 22 Mansfield St, Glasgow, G11 5QP (0141-339-8303)
Internet: http://www.gwsfhs.org.uk/

Chief: Hon Libn: Dr H.E.C. Cargill Thompson MCLIP (Rtd)
Entry: open to membs; ref only **Open:** Tue 1400-1630, 1900-2130, Thu 1000-2130, Sat 1400-1630
Subj: Glasgow & West Scotland: family hist; genealogy; local hist **Collns:** *Bks & Pamphs:* ref works; publ records & indexes; exchange journals with other Family Hist Socs *Other:* IGI; Old Parish registers (Glasgow & West Scotland); census returns (all on m-form); map colln **Co-op Schemes:** indexing projs undertaken in co-operation with GLASGOW CITY ARCHVS (see **A174**) & the MITCHELL LIB (see **P56**)
Equip: 10 m-form readers, m-printer (50p per copy), copier (10p per copy), 5 computers (incl 2 with wd-proc, 2 with internet & 3 with CD-ROM, internet charged at £1.20 per hr) **Svcs:** info, ref, rsrch (available to membs only)
Stock: archvs/c1000, incl pamphs; maps/c150; m-forms/c300 film, c8000 fiche; CD-ROMs/35 titles **Acq Offcr:** Hon Libn, as above
Classn: own
Pubns: Newsletter (back issues also available); numerous family hist pubns, incl: 1841 Glasgow Police Return (£5); Burial Grounds in Glasgow (£2.40); Strathclyde Sources (£3.50); Argyll People (£3.50); Tracing Ancestors in Argyll (50p); Clock & Watch Makers of Glasgow & the West of Scotland (£4); Argyll 1841 Census Indexes (series of bklets, prices vary); m-fiche transcriptions of 1851 Census Index (prices vary)
Staff: *Libns:* 1 on very limited PT basis *Non-Prof:* 2 PT assts (staffed by volunteers) **Exp:** £2000 (1999-2000); £2500 (2000-01)

A174
Glasgow City Archives
The Mitchell Lib, North St, Glasgow, G3 7DN (0141-287-2913; *fax:* 0141-226-8452)
Email: archives@cls.glasgow.gov.uk
Internet: http://www.glasgowlibraries.org/

Gov Body: Glasgow City Council (see **P56**)
Chief: Principal Archivist: Mr A.M. Jackson MA, DipAA **Dep:** Asst Principal Archivist: Dr Irene O'Brien MA, PhD
Assoc Offices: SPECIAL COLLNS SECTION, at same addr (0141-287-2937/88; *email:* history_and_glasgow@cls.glasgow.gov.uk)
Open: Mon-Thu 0930-1645, Fri 0930-1600 & at other times by arrangement
Subj: Glasgow & parts of the former Strathclyde region: local authority archvs; diocesan records; parish records; estate archvs; family papers; business records; records of parent org; nonconformist records; shipping records; school records; poor law records; police records; records of clubs & socs **Collns:** *Bks & Pamphs:* local studies & family hist materials held by Special Collns Section *Archvs:* archvs of Glasgow Corp (1574 onwards) & successor authorities; records of burghs & other areas annexed to the city; Strathclyde Regional Council records; County Council records for Bute, Dunbartonshire, Lanarkshire, Renfrewshire & part of Stirlingshire, incl records for Commissioners of Supply (18C-early 20C); original registers of sasines for the Burgh of Glasgow (1694-1927); records of Diocese of Glasgow & Galloway (Episcopal Church of Scotland); records of Glasgow Presbytery (Church of Scotland, 16C-20C); family & estate records incl: Campbells of Succoth; Colquhouns of Luss; Maxwells of

Pollock; Stirlings of Keir; records of Glasgow & Strathclyde shipbldg industry (incl index of Clyde-built ships); records of Clyde Navigation Trust (1709-1988); Scottish Co-op Wholesale Soc records; papers held by Special Collns Section incl: Shawfield Papers (17C-18C business papers); Bogle Papers (tobacco merchants); Bedlay of Chryston papers; Brisbane of Largs papers; Scottish Women's Hosps Papers; modern Scottish literary MSS; papers of Scottish trade unions; various rare MSS *Other:* electoral & valuation rolls; arch plans; census returns (1841-1901)
Equip: 3 m-readers, fax, copier, computer (incl CD-ROM) **Svcs:** info, ref, rsrch
Stock: archvs/9000 linear m; rec mgmt/9000 linear m
Staff: *Archivists:* 5 *Non-Prof:* 9

Glasgow Caledonian University Archives
See GLASGOW CALEDONIAN UNIV, LIB & INFO CENTRE (**S701**)

A175
Glasgow RC Archdiocesan Archive
Archdiocesan Office, 196 Clyde St, Glasgow, G1 4JY (0141-226-5898 x154; *fax:* 0141-221-1962)
Internet: http://www.rcag.org.uk/Archives/

Gov Body: RC Archdiocese of Glasgow **Chief:** Archivist: Mary McHugh
Entry: adv appt
Subj: RC Archdiocese of Glasgow: diocesan records; personal papers

A176
Glasgow University Archive Services
13 Thurso St, Glasgow, G11 6PE (0141-330-5515; *fax:* 0141-330-2640)
Email: dutyarch@archives.gla.ac.uk
Internet: http://www.archives.gla.ac.uk/

Gov Body: Univ of Glasgow (see **S738**) **Chief:** Univ Archivist: Ms Lesley Richmond MA
Entry: adv appt, ID required for 1st visit **Open:** Mon 1300-1700, Tue-Wed, Fri 0930-1700, Thu 0930-2000
Subj: Univ of Glasgow: records of parent org; records of associated instns & related Scottish orgs; records of student clubs & socs; papers of staff & students; estate archvs; West of Scotland & elsewhere: business records; company records; personal papers **Collns:** *Bks & Pamphs:* technical & business hist lib (bks & periodcls) *Archvs:* Univ of Glasgow Archvs (from 1451); records of affiliated instns, incl: Anderson's Coll of Medicine; Trinity Coll; Glasgow Veterinary Coll; Queen Margaret Coll; Royal Scottish Academy of Music & Drama; Beith & other Ayrshire parish papers (1610-1924); Lumsden of Arden (stationers, 1661-1984); Garscube Estate Papers (1837-1960); over 400 business collns from 18C onwards, incl: House of Fraser Group Archvs; John Brown of Clydebank (shipbldg); William Denny of Dumbarton (shipbuilding); Lithgows of Port Glasgow (shipbldg); Scotts of Greenock (shipbldg); North British Locomotive Co; James Finlay & Sons (East India merchant); Gourock Ropeworks Co; J&P Coats (Paisley thread manufacturers); Highland Distillers Co; A&W Smith (machinery manufacturers); Anchor Line; Ivory & Sime (Edinburgh investment trust mgrs); Babcock & Wilcox (boiler makers); papers of indiv entrepreneurs, incl Viscount William Weir (1877-1959) & Sir James Lithgow (1883-1952) *Other:* photos; technical drawings; plans of Univ bldgs & lands
Equip: m-reader, computer **Online:** database of holdings **Svcs:** info, rsrch, photocopying, reprographic

Stock: archvs/4700 linear m; rec mgmt/1000 linear m; bks/6000; photos/100000; technical drawings/200000
Classn: ISAD(G) *Auto Sys:* EAD
Pubns: details on application
Staff: Archivists: 10 *Other Prof:* 3 *Non-Prof:* 10

A177
Greater Glasgow NHS Board Archive
Glasgow Univ Archvs Svcs, 77-81 Dumbarton Rd, Glasgow, G11 6PW (0141-330-4543; *fax:* 0141-330-4158)
Email: gghb@archives.gla.ac.uk
Internet: http://www.archives.gla.ac.uk/gghb/

Gov Body: Univ of Glasgow & Greater Glasgow NHS Board *Chief:* Archivist: Mr Alistair Tough
Assoc Offices: part of GLASGOW UNIV ARCHVS SVCS (see **A176**)
Entry: adv appt; access to some records may be restricted *Open:* Thu 0930-1645, Fri 0930-1600; at other times of the wk by appt with GGHB Archivist
Subj: Glasgow & Paisley area: health board records; medical records; hosp records; medical hist *Collns: Archvs:* prime records of former Western Regional HB; records of GGHB; records of Glasgow Royal Infirmary & other hosps (late 18C onwards), incl: minutes of governing bodies; patient records; accounts; reports & correspondence; historical archvs, incl: Lister Colln (antiseptic surgery); MacEwan Colln (aseptic surgery); Cameron Colln (caesarean delivery); McIntyre Colln (X-rays); T. McLurg Anderson Colln (physiotherapy); William Parry Jones Colln (psychiatry); materials on development of psychiatric care & nursing *Other:* arch drawings of hosps; photos
Pubns: Medical Archvs of Glasgow & Paisley – A Guide to the Greater Glasgow Heath Board Archv, by Alistair Tough (1993)

A178
John Dewar & Sons Ltd, Company Archives
1700 London Rd, Glasgow, G32 8XR (0141-551-4000; *fax:* 0141-551-4030)
Email: jseargeant@bacardi.com

Chief: Company Archivist: Ms Jacqui Seargeant
Entry: adv appt
Subj: whisky distilling; business records; records of parent org *Collns: Archvs:* records of John Dewar & Sons Ltd (whisky distillers, c1881-1977)

A179
Scottish Brewing Archive
Glasgow Univ Archv Svcs, 13 Thurso St, Glasgow, G11 6PE (0141-339-6079; *fax:* 0141-330-4158)
Email: w.redlich@archives.gla.ac.uk
Internet: http://www.archives.gla.ac.uk/

Gov Body: Univ of Glasgow *Chief:* Archivist: Ms Wiebke Redlich MA, MSc
Assoc Offices: part of GLASGOW UNIV ARCHV SVCS (see **A176**)
Entry: adv appt *Open:* Wed-Fri 0930-1700
Subj: Scottish brewing industry: all aspects (historical, scientific, economic, technological & political); family papers; business records (Scottish brewing companies) *Collns: Bks & Pamphs:* hist of brewing; company hists; technical & scientific texts; licensing; advertising antiques (all 1740s-date) *Archvs:* 120 collns incl records of: Aitken's of Falkirk; Fowlers of Prestonpans; Bernard's of Edinburgh; George Youngers of Alloa; Belhaven; Scottish Brewers; Alloa Brewery Co; Scottish & Newcastle; Tennant Caledonian *Other:* adverts; ephemera; label colln (Scottish beer labels, 1850s-date); brewing machinery

Equip: m-reader, 2 copiers, fax, video viewer, 2 computers (both with wd-proc, internet & CD-ROM) *Svcs:* info, ref, rsrch; clr copying, plan copying & photographic orders sent out
Stock: archvs/600 linear m; bks/1000; periodcls/1; photos/800; slides/100; pamphs/50; videos/250; various artifacts
Classn: ISAD(G)
Pubns: Annual Journal of the Scottish Brewing Archv (Vols 1-4 available, £4 each); Scottish Brewing Archv Newsletter (Vols 20-28 £4 each, Vols 29-41 £2 each); handlists in Search Room
Staff: Archivists: 1 PT

A180
Scottish Jewish Archives Centre
Garnethill Synagogue, 127 Hill St, Glasgow, G3 6UB (0141-332-4911)
Email: archives@sjac.fsbusiness.co.uk

Chief: Dir: Mr Harvey Kaplan
Entry: adv appt *Open:* Fri 0930-1330
Subj: Scotland: family papers; business records; personal papers; records of Jewish communities & orgs

A181 📷
Scottish Screen Archive
(formerly Scottish Film & Television Archv)
1 Bowmont Gdns, Glasgow, G2 4RB (0141-337-7400; *fax:* 0141-337-7413)
Email: archive@scottishscreen.com
Internet: http://www.scottishscreen.com/

Gov Body: Scottish Screen (see **S731**) *Chief:* Archivist: Ms Janet McBain BA *Dep:* Libn: Ms Ann Beaton MA, MCLIP
Entry: adv notice required, viewings by appt only
Open: Mon-Fri 0930-1230, 1400-1645
Subj: Scotland: records of parent org (Scottish Film Council, 1934-1997); actuality film of all aspects Scottish 20C life *Collns: Bks & Pamphs:* misc: related to hist of film production & cinema exhib *Archvs:* MSS, printed & photo ephemera
Equip: 2 video viewers, copier, 16mm & 35mm film viewing table
Stock: archvs/film/23000+ reels
Staff: Libns: 2 *Other Prof:* 4 *Non-Prof:* 3

A182 🎓
Scottish Theatre Archive
Dept of Special Collns, Glasgow Univ Lib, Hillhead St, Glasgow, G12 8QE (0141-330-6767; *fax:* 0141-330-3793)
Email: C.McKendrick@lib.gla.ac.uk
Internet: http://special.lib.gla.ac.uk/sta/

Chief: Snr Lib Asst: Ms Claire McKendrick
Entry: open to anyone with an interest in Scottish theatre; ref only *Open:* term: Mon-Thu 0900-2030, Fri 1000-1700, Sat 0900-1230; vac: Mon-Thu 0900-1700, Fri 1000-1700, Sat 0900-1230
Subj: Scottish theatre & drama; theatre records; personal papers *Collns: Bks & Pamphs:* BBC Scotland Radio & TV script colln; Eddie Boyd Script Colln; John Cairney Colln; Michael Elder Colln; Scottish Soc of Playwrights Colln; publ play texts *Archvs:* correspondence of Gordon Bottomley (poet & dramatist, 1874-1948); James Bridie Colln (dramatist & critic, 1888-1951); materials relating to various stage artists, incl Sir Harry Lauder (1870-1950); records of theatre companies, incl: Arts Theatre Group Archv; Citizens' Theatre Archv; Dundee Repertory Archv; Edinburgh Festival Fringe Archv; Gateway Theatre Archv; Glasgow Jewish Inst Players Archv; Glasgow Unity Theatre Archv; Royal Lyceum Theatre Archv; Scottish Actors Company Archv; Scottish Natl Players Archv; Scottish

Ballet Archv; Scottish Theatre Company Archv; 7:84 Theatre Group Archv; Western Theatre Ballet Archv; Wilson Barrett Company Archv; & others
Other: James Inglis Colln (photos & theatre programmes relating to performances of the Wilson Barrett Company); Menie Jamieson Colln (photos & prompt scripts of the Wilson Barrett Company); Jimmy Logan Colln (theatre memorabilia); stage designs & drawings colln
Svcs: reprographic

Gloucester

A183 🍷🔑
British Waterways Archive
7th Floor, Llanthony Warehouse, Gloucester Docks, Gloucester, GL1 2EJ (01452-318224; *fax:* 01452-318225)
Email: bwarchive@thewaterwaystrust.org
Internet: http://www.thewaterwaystrust.co.uk/archives/

Gov Body: The Waterways Trust/British Waterways *Chief:* Head of Archvs & Records: Mr Paul Sillitoe
Assoc Offices: DAVID OWEN WATERWAYS ARCHV (see **A159**); NATL WATERWAYS MUSEUM LIB (see **S749**); British Waterways Archv collns are dispersed around various centres across UK
Entry: ref only; prior appt essential *Open:* Mon-Fri 1000-1700
Subj: England, Scotland & Wales: records relating to the mgmt, maintenance & operation of inland waterways (17C-20C), for which British Waterways is the statutory undertaker; hist of canals & inland waterways in Gt Britain; canal company records; records of parent org *Collns: Archvs:* historical records of British Waterways & predecessor orgs (1750s-date) *Other:* arch drawings; photo colln (late 19C-date), incl: J.W. Millner Colln (1890s-1928); C. Arapoff Colln (1930s); A. Watts Colln (1952-72) *Co-op Schemes:* lead partner in The Waterways Virtual Archv Catalogue Proj
Equip: m-reader, m-printer, copier, fax *Svcs:* info, ref, rsrch (limited facility)
Stock: archvs/c80 cubic m
Staff: Archivists: 0.5 *Non-Prof:* 1

Ethnic Resources Archive
See THE TRADITIONS LIB & ETHNIC RESOURCES ARCHV (**S751**)

A184 🏛
Gloucestershire Libraries, Gloucestershire Collection
Gloucester Central Lib, Brunswick Rd, Gloucester, GL1 1HT (01452-426979; *fax:* 01452-521468)
Email: localstudies@gloscc.gov.uk
Internet: http://www.gloscc.gov.uk/

Gov Body: Gloucestershire County Council (see **P57**) *Chief:* Snr Libn (Local Studies): Mr Graham Baker MSc, MCLIP
Entry: visitors' bk, ref only; adv appt advised for use of machines *Open:* Mon-Tue, Thu 1000-1930, Wed, Fri 1000-1700, Sat 0900-1600
Subj: Gloucestershire: local studies *Collns: Bks & Pamphs:* comprehensive colln of printed material relating to Gloucestershire *Archvs:* Ivor Gurney Colln
Equip: 9 m-readers, 2 m-printers, copier, clr copier, computer (incl internet) *Svcs:* info, ref
Stock: archvs/134000 items in total
Classn: Austin Catalogue (in-house)
Pubns: leaflets: Your Local Lib; Routes to Roots
Staff: Libns: 2 *Non-Prof:* 3

 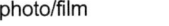

Archives

Gloucester
▼
Hastings

A185 🏛

Gloucestershire Record Office

Clarence Row, Alvin St, Gloucester, GL1 3DW (01452-425295; *fax:* 01452-426378)
Email: records@gloscc.gov.uk
Internet: http://archives.gloscc.gov.uk/

Gov Body: Gloucestershire County Council (see **P57**) *Chief:* County & Diocesan Archivist: Mr N.W. Kingsley MA, RMSA *Dep:* Dep County & Diocesan Archivist: Mr P.E. Bloomfield BA, CertEd, DipArch
Entry: customer registration & issue of Gloucestershire Record Office readers ticket (not CARN), entry charge is made *Open:* Mon 1000-1700, Tue-Wed, Fri 0900-1700, Thu 0900-2000
Subj: historic County of Gloucestershire (incl current county, South Gloucestershire & Diocese of Gloucester): local authority archve; diocesan records; parish records; estate archvs; family papers; business records; personal papers; political papers; records of parent org; health & hosp records; school records; coroners records; military records; public records; nonconformist records; RC ecclesiastical records; Jewish ecclesiastical records; records of socs, charities & voluntary orgs; solicitors' records *Collns: Bks & Pamphs:* Hyett Colln of Gloucestershire Bks; Sir Thomas Phillipps Antiquarian Colln *Archvs:* archvs of Gloucestershire County Council; Gloucester City Archvs (13C-20C); records of boroughs of Gloucester & Cheltenham; records of dist councils & predecessors; records of Guardians of the Poor; records of School Boards; records of Highway Boards; records of burial authorities; records of water authorities; Quarter Sessions Archvs; Diocese of Gloucester Archvs (from 1541); family & estate collns, incl: Bathurst of Cirencester; Beaufort of Badminton; Blathwayt of Dyrham; Codrington of Dodington, incl Wyatt arch drawings of Dodington House; Dent-Brocklehurst of Sudeley; Ducie of Tortworth; Dutton of Sherbourne; Hicks Beach of Coln St Aldwyn; Hyett & Dickinson of Painswick; Lloyd-Baker of Hardwicke Court, incl Granville-Sharp slavery papers; business records, incl: Fulljames & Waller; Gloucester Railway Carriage & Wagon Co; Dowty Group *Other:* m-films of Gloucestershire records (held offsite)
Equip: 44 m-readers, 2 m-cameras, 2 m-printers, digital camera, video viewer, fax, copier, computers (incl internet & CD-ROM) *Svcs:* info, ref, rsrch
Stock: archvs/1281 cubic m; rec mgmt/444 cubic m; bks/c5000
Classn: ISAD(G) *Auto Sys:* DS
Pubns: Handlist of the Contents of Gloucestershire Record Office (4th ed £15, supplement £3); Records of the Bishop & Archdeacons (£5); Records of the Dean & Chapter (£5); Gloucestershire Quarter Sessions 1660-1889 & Other Official records (£3); Handlist of Genealogical Sources (2nd ed, £8); Gloucestershire Family Hist (3rd ed, £4.50); Medieval Gloucester (£5.95); various maps (60p-£5); p&p extra
Staff: Archivists: 7.6 *Other Prof:* 2.7 *Non-Prof:* 13.1

A186 🔑

Gloucestershire Regimental Archives

Soldiers of Gloucestershire Museum, Custom House, Gloucester Docks, Gloucester, GL1 2HE (01452-522682; *fax:* 01452-311116)
Internet: http://www.glosters.org.uk/

Gov Body: Trustees of the Gloucestershire Regiment *Chief:* Hon Archivist: Major C.T.P. Rebbeck (Rtd) *Dep:* Curator: Mr George Streatfield
Entry: adv appt *Open: Archvs:* Tue only, by appt; *Museum:* Tue-Sun 1000-1700, also open Mon during Jun-Sep
Subj: Gloucestershire Regiment (28th Foot) since 1694: regimental hist; regimental records *Collns: Bks & Pamphs:* official manuals & records; privately & commercially produced pubns from late 18C onwards *Archvs:* official & personal records, diaries, accounts from 1750s onwards *Other:* photo colln (1850s-date)
Equip: copier *Staff: Other Prof:* 1

Gosport

A187 🏛 🏛

Gosport Museum, Local Resources Room

Walpole Rd, Gosport, Hampshire, PO12 1NS (023-9258-8035; *fax:* 023-9250-1951)
Internet: http://www.hants.gov.uk/museums/

Type: local authority *Gov Body:* Hampshire County Council (see **P60**) *Dep:* Curator: Ms Oonagh Palmer MA
Assoc Offices: HAMPSHIRE COUNTY COUNCIL MUSEUMS SVC LIB (see **A508**)
Entry: ref only; adv appt recommended *Open:* Tue-Fri 1015-1645
Subj: Hampshire & Gosport: local studies; geol *Collns: Bks & Pamphs:* trade directories (18C-20C); various historical printed materials *Archvs:* local parish records (m-fiche) *Other:* photograph colln; topographical prints & drawings; map colln (17C-date, incl OS)
Equip: m-reader, computer

Grays

A188 🏛

Thurrock Local Studies Department

Grays Lib, Orsett Rd, Grays, Essex, RM17 5DX (01375-383611; *fax:* 01375-380806)
Email: grays_library@hotmail.com
Internet: http://www.thurrock-community.org.uk/council/libraries/

Gov Body: Thurrock Council (see **P186**) *Chief:* Snr Mgr (Info): Ms Alison Cairns MCLIP (acairns@thurrock.gov.uk) *Other Snr Staff:* Local Studies Libn: Mr Victor Tucker MCLIP; Info Libn: Mr John Barrett MCLIP
Assoc Offices: small amount of local material at each branch lib
Entry: mainly ref; small lending colln (requires lib ticket) *Open:* Mon-Tue, Thu 0900-1900, Wed, Fri-Sat 0900-1700
Subj: Thurrock & local area: local authority archvs; parish records (m-form); estate archvs; family papers; business records; personal papers; harbour records; local hist; family hist *Collns: Bks & Pamphs:* pubns of Thurrock Local Hist Soc, incl Panorama (soc journal, 1956-date); local biographies *Archvs:* minutes of Thurrock Council; rate bks & electoral registers; local parish records on m-form (earliest times-1970s/80s); Barrett-Lennard (Belhus) family & estate papers; Rowley papers; notes of Revd W. Hayes; extensive records of Tilbury Docks & PLA generally;

annual reports of local firms *Other:* census returns (m-form, 1841-1901); Tithe Maps & Apportionments; colln of ancient & modern maps; illusts; local newspapers (incl Thurrock Gazette, 1884 onwards) *Co-op Schemes:* LASER
Equip: 5 m-readers, m-printer (30p), copier (A4/5p, A3/10p), clr copier (A4/£1, A3/£1.50), fax (£1.20 per pg to send), 20 computers (all with wd-proc & internet, 4 with CD-ROM) *Svcs:* info, ref
Classn: DDC *Auto Sys:* Geac

Greenford

A189 ☕🌾

Glaxo Wellcome Heritage Archives

Records Centre, Glaxo Wellcome plc, Greenford Rd, Greenford, Middlesex, UB6 0HE (020-8966-2581; *fax:* 020-8966-2240)
Email: UKRecordsCentreGreenford@glaxowellcome.co.uk

Chief: Site Mgr: Mr Phil Sawyer
Entry: adv appt
Subj: pharmaceuticals; business records; personal papers; records of parent org *Collns: Archvs:* records of Glaxo Wellcome & predecessor companies; records of Allen & Hanbury Ltd (manufacturing chemists, 1780-1880); correspondence & account bks of William Allen (Quaker scientist & philanthropist, 1770-1843); letter bks of Daniel Hanbury (pharmacist, 1825-1875)

Greenock

A190 🏛

Inverclyde Archives and Local History

Watt Lib, 9 Union St, Greenock, Renfrewshire, PA16 8JH (01475-715628; *fax:* 01475-731347 – at Museum)
Email: Library.Watt@inverclyde.gov.uk
Internet: http://www.inverclyde.gov.uk/Museum/

Gov Body: Inverclyde Council (see **P65**) *Chief:* Assistant-in-Charge: Mrs Betty Hendry
Entry: no restrictions *Open:* Mon, Thu 1400-1700, 1800-2000, Tue, Fri 1000-1300, 1400-1700, Wed, Sat 1000-1300
Subj: Inverclyde: local authority archvs; parish records; business records; hosp records; trade union records; records of local socs; local hist & genealogy *Collns: Bks & Pamphs:* local hist materials; local directories *Archvs:* archvs of Inverclyde Council & predecessors; council records for Greenock, Port Glasgow & Gourock (partial, 5th Dist) *Other:* local photo colln; local newspapers on m-film, incl: Greenock Telegraph; Greenock Advertiser; Gourock Times; Glasgow Express; local newspaper index; shipbldg index
Equip: 3 m-readers, m-printer, copier *Svcs:* ref, rsrch, genealogical enqs
Stock: archvs/1000; slides/200; pamphs/500; maps/100; m-forms/300; audios/12; videos/10
Staff: Other Prof: 1

Grimsby

A191 🏛

North East Lincolnshire Archives

Town Hall, Town Hall Sq, Grimsby, DN31 1HX (01472-323585; *fax:* 01472-323582)
Email: john.wilson@nelincs.gov.uk

Gov Body: NE Lincolnshire Council (see **P125**); also manages archvs on behalf of North Lincolnshire Council (see **P127**) *Chief:* Area Archivist: Mr John Wilson BA, DipAS
Entry: adv notice of visits is essential *Open:* Mon-Fri 1000-1230, 1330-1600

Subj: North & NE Lincolnshire, former South Humberside: local authority archvs; estate archvs; family papers; business records; records of parent org *Collns:* Archvs: archvs of NE Lincolnshire & North Lincolnshire Councils & predecessors in South Humberside area
Equip: 4 m-readers, copier
Stock: archvs/270 cubic m; rec mgmt/30 cubic m; photos/2000; maps/300; audios/150
Staff: Archivists: 1 *Other Prof:* 1 conservator
Non-Prof: 1 *Exp:* £600 (2000-01)

Guildford

A192

National Resource Centre for Dance, Archives

Univ of Surrey, Guildford, Surrey, GU2 5XH (01483-689316; *fax:* 01483-259500 – marked 'Attn NRCD')
Email: nrcd@surrey.ac.uk
Internet: http://www.surrey.ac.uk/NRCD/ nrcd.html

Gov Body: Univ of Surrey (see **S776**) *Chief:* Mgr: Ms Helen Roberts BA(Hons) (h.roberts@ surrey.ac.uk) *Dep:* Archv & Rsrch Offcr: Miss Chris Jones MA(Hons)
Entry: ref only; adv appt, rsrch fees apply
Open: Mon 1000-1630, Tue-Wed 0930-1630
Subj: performing arts; dance; movement; choreography; personal papers; records of dance companies *Collns: Bks & Pamphs:* South Asian Dance Colln; Valerie Booth Colln (ballet); British & foreign dance journals *Archvs:* Rudolf Laban Archv (4000+ files of papers, MSS, drawings, photos & bks); Lisa Ullmann Archv (papers, drawings, photos etc); Audrey Wethred & Chloë Gardner Colln (movement therapists); Betty Meredith-Jones Colln (dance therapist); Joan Russell Archv (choreographer); Maedée Duprès Archv (choreographer); Internatl Council for Kinetography Laban (ICKL) Archv; Laban Art of Movement Guild Archv; Nat Movement Archv; Bice Bellairs Colln of Revived Greek Dance; records of dance companies, incl: Dalcroze Soc Archv; Dance Adv Archv; Educational Dance-Drama Theatre Archv; EMMA/Midlands Dance Company Archv; Extempory Dance Theatre Archv; Green Candle Dance Company Archv; Janet Smith & Dancers Archv; Kickstart Dance Company Archv; Rosemary Butcher Dance Company Archv; Dance & the Child Internatl Archv; V-TOL Dance Company Archv *Other:* Audio Colln (dance music, interviews, off-air broadcasts & oral hist); Photographic Colln; Video & Film Colln; artwork relating to dance companies; posters; programmes; scores; newspaper cuttings; educational materials; examination papers; dissertations & theses; topic files; press releases & other publicity materials
Equip: copier, video viewer, computer (with internet) *Svcs:* info, ref
Classn: ISAD(G) *Auto Sys:* DS CALM 2000
Pubns: see web site
Staff: Other Prof: 2 *Non-Prof:* 3

Haddington

A193

East Lothian Libraries, Local History Centre

Haddington Lib, Newton Port, Haddington, E Lothian, EH41 3NA (01620-823307)
Email: localhistory@eastlothian.gov.uk
Internet: http://www.eastlothian.gov.uk/Libraries/ loch.html

Gov Body: East Lothian Council (see **P46**)
Chief: Snr Libn (Local Hist & Promotions): Ms Veronica Wallace (vwallace@eastlothian.gov.uk)

Entry: ref only *Open:* Mon 1400-1800, Tue 1000-1300, 1400-1900, Thu 1400-1900, Fri 1400-1700
Subj: East Lothian: local hist; family hist
Collns: Bks & Pamphs: local hist materials; bks by local authors; East Lothian Annual Registers & Year Bks (1820-1970, some gaps) *Other:* IGI on m-fiche; valuation rolls (1855-date, on m-film & m-fiche); census returns (1841-1901, on m-film); Old Parish Registers (c1650-1854, on m-film); photo colln (19C-20C); map colln (17C-20C); local newspapers (1850s-date); monumental inscriptions; ephemera
Equip: Offcr-in-Charge: Snr Libn (Local Hist & Promotions), as above *Svcs:* info, ref, brief searches if dates given, but no in-depth rsrch svc
Stock: various bks, photos, slides, pamphs & maps *Acq Offcr:* Snr Libn (Local Hist & Promotions), as above
Classn: in-house sys *Auto Sys:* Talis
Staff: Libns: 1 *Non-Prof:* 1 *Exp:* £4500 (1999-2000); £3500 (2000-01)

Halifax

A194

West Yorkshire Archive Service: Calderdale

Calderdale Central Lib, Northgate House, Northgate, Halifax, W Yorkshire, HX1 1UN (01422-392636; *fax:* 01422-341083)
Email: calderdale@wyjs.org.uk
Internet: http://www.archives.wyjs.org.uk/

Gov Body: West Yorkshire Joint Svcs Cttee
Chief: Principal Dist Archivist, Calderdale: Miss Pat Sewell BA, MArAd
Assoc Offices: branch office of WEST YORKSHIRE ARCHV SVC HQ (see **A497**); CALDERDALE LOCAL STUDIES SECTION, at same addr
Entry: adv appt *Open:* Mon-Tue, Thu-Fri by appt; documents on m-film may also be consulted Mon-Tue, Thu-Fri 1730-1900, Sat 1000-1700 in the Central Ref Lib
Subj: Metropolitan Dist of Calderdale: local authority archvs; parish records (m-film only); estate archvs; family papers; business records; nonconformist churches; trade union & political records *Collns: Bks & Pamphs:* local studies collns held at Local Studies Section *Archvs:* archvs of Calderdale Metropolitan Borough Council & predecessors; nonconformist churches; family & estate records, esp: Lister of Shibden Hall; Southowram; Stansfeld of Field House; Sowerby; Armitage of Kirklees Hall; Brighouse; Sunderland of Coley Hall; Hipperholme; business records (esp textile), incl: Samuel Hill of Soyland (clothier, 1736-1738); Cornelius Ashworth of Ovenden (farmer & handloom weaver, 1782-1816); Robert Parker (18C Halifax attorney); also banking, brewing, clock making, stone quarrying, wire manufacturing, local co-op socs etc; trade union & political records, incl some Anti-Corn Law League & Chartist; travel journals of Anne Lister (1806-1840); records of Halifax Antiquarian Soc; Halifax Loyal Georgian Soc (1799-1981); Nathaniel Waterhouse Charities (1635-1868); Diocese of Bradford parish records (Calderdale area, on m-film)
Equip: 13 m-readers, 2 m-printers, video viewer, fax, 3 copiers, computer (incl wd-proc)
Stock: archvs/3000 linear m
Pubns: Calderdale Archvs 1964-1989: An Illustrated Guide to Calderdale Dist Archvs (£6.95 + 75p p&p); Supplement 1990-1998 (£2.50 + 50p p&p)
Staff: Archivists: 1 *Non-Prof:* 2

Harlow

A195

Harlow Local History Library

Museum of Harlow, Muskham Rd, Harlow, Essex, CM20 2LF (01279-454959)
Internet: http://www.harlow.gov.uk/community/ histlib/historylib.htm

Type: local authority *Gov Body:* Harlow Council
Assoc Offices: HARLOW ARCHV ACCESS PT, at same addr (m-form copies of records only, joint svc with ESSEX RECORD OFFICE – see **A100**)
Entry: ref only, by adv appt *Open: Museum:* Tue-Sat 1000-1230, 1330-1700; *Harlow Archv Access Pt:* Tue-Fri 1000-1700, Sat 1000-1230, 1330-1700
Subj: Harlow: local studies *Collns: Archvs:* materials relating to local hist & archaeo; held on m-form only as part of Harlow Archv Access Pt: parish registers (Harlow Deanery & parish of Matching); records of the Barrington family (12C onwards); manorial records; Poor Law Guardians records; some school log bks; parish council records *Other:* maps & plans; programmes & scrapbks; c9000 photographs, slides, tapes & videos; local newspapers (complete, 1953-date); local census returns
Equip: copier (10p per copy)

Harrow

A196 [icon]

Harrow Local History Collection

PO Box 4, Civic Centre Lib, Civic Centre, Station Rd, Harrow, Middlesex, HA1 2UU (020-8424-1055/6; *fax:* 020-8424-1971)
Email: civiccentre.library@harrow.gov.uk
Internet: http://www.harrow.gov.uk/

Gov Body: London Borough of Harrow (see **P90**)
Chief: Local Hist Libn: Mr Bob Thomson *Dep:* Asst Local Hist Libn: Ms Amanda Wood
Open: Mon-Tue, Thu 0930-2000, Fri 0930-1300, Sat 0900-1700
Subj: London Borough of Harrow: local authority archvs; business records; records of local orgs; local hist *Collns: Bks & Pamphs:* local hist materials *Archvs:* records of the London Borough of Harrow *Other:* maps; photos; local newspapers; prints
Equip: 3 m-readers, 2 m-form reader/printers (40p per pg), copier (A4/10p, A3/20p), clr copier (A4/£1, A3/£1.50), 41 computers (all with wd-proc & internet, printouts A4/20p) *Svcs:* info, ref
Auto Sys: Dynix *Staff: Libns:* 2

Hastings

A197 [icon] [icon]

Hastings Museum and Art Gallery, Archives and Library

Johns Pl, Bohemia Rd, Hastings, E Sussex, TN34 1ET (01424-781155; *fax:* 01424-781165)
Email: museum@hastings.gov.uk
Internet: http://www.hastings.gov.uk/museum/

Type: local authority *Gov Body:* Hastings Borough Council *Chief:* Curator: Miss Victoria Williams BA, FRSA *Dep:* Asst Curator: Miss Catherine Walling MA *Other Snr Staff:* Archivist: Ms Sophie Houlton
Entry: ref only *Open: Museum:* Mon-Sat 1000-1700, Sun 1400-1700; *Local Studies Rsrch Room:* Wed 1000-1600, Fri 1000-1230, other times by appt

☞

(Hastings Museum & Art Gallery cont)
Subj: Hastings & Sussex: local authority archvs; family papers; business records; personal papers; records of parent org; records of local socs; local hist; nat hist; geog **Collns:** *Bks & Pamphs:* Marwick Nat Hist Soc Diaries & Lib (nat hist & travel, 18C-19C); local hists & biographies; local directories; journals of local hist socs *Archvs:* Hastings Borough Council Archvs; Hastings Corp records (copies & m-film); Burton Family Colln (arch drawings, documents & artifacts); John Manwaring Baines Colln; correspondence of John Logie Baird; archv of Volunteer Fire Brigade *Other:* Robert Tressal Colln (photos & socialist memorabilia); photographic colln; maps & plans of Hastings & St Leonards; theatre programmes; WW2 memorabilia
Equip: m-reader, copier, fax, room for hire
Svcs: info, ref, rsrch
Stock: archvs/200 linear ft; bks/4000; photos/3000; maps/600
Staff: Archivists: 0.5 Other Prof: 5 Non-Prof: 4

Havant

A198 🏛️🏛️

Havant Museum, Local Studies Room
East St, Havant, Hampshire, PO9 1BS (023-9245-1145; *fax:* 023-9249-8707)
Email: museums@hants.gov.uk
Internet: http://www.hants.gov.uk/museum/havant/

Gov Body: Hampshire County Council (see **P60**)
Chief: Curator: Ms Oonagh Palmer MA
Assoc Offices: HAMPSHIRE COUNTY COUNCIL MUSEUMS SVC LIB (see **A508**)
Entry: free entry; adv appt preferable **Open:** Tue-Sat 1000-1700
Subj: Borough of Havant: local hist; parish records (copies); family papers (copies); personal papers (copies) **Collns:** *Bks & Pamphs:* local hist bks & pamphs; magazine/journal articles; family hist src bks *Other:* local hist photos; various rsrch papers; videos
Equip: m-reader, copier (charged), video viewer
Svcs: info, ref
Staff: Other Prof: 1 Non-Prof: 2

Haverfordwest

A199 🏛️

The Pembrokeshire Record Office
The Castle, Haverfordwest, Pembrokeshire, SA61 2EF (01437-763707; *fax:* 01437-768539)
Email: record.office@pembrokeshire.gov.uk

Gov Body: Pembrokeshire Council (see **P143**)
Chief: County Archivist: Miss Claire Orr
Open: Mon-Thu 0900-1645, Fri 0900-1615, 1st Sat of month 0930-1230 (except bank hol weekends)
Subj: County of Pembrokeshire: local authority archvs; parish records; estate archvs; family papers; business records; hosp records; court records
Equip: 6 m-readers, m-printer, copier
Stock: archvs/1711 linear m; rec mgmt/329 linear m
Staff: Other Prof: 4 Non-Prof: 2

Hawarden

A200 🏛️

Flintshire Record Office
The Old Rectory, Hawarden, Flintshire, CH5 3NR (01244-532364; *fax:* 01244-538344)
Email: archives@flintshire.gov.uk
Internet: http://www.flintshire.gov.uk/

Gov Body: Flintshire County Council (see **P54**)
Chief: County Archivist: Mr Rowland Williams BA, DipAA
Assoc Offices: County Archivist acts as Hon Archivist to ST DEINIOL'S LIB (see **S523**)
Entry: CARN ticket; adv appt strongly recommended **Open:** Mon-Thu 0900-1645, Fri 0900-1615
Subj: Flintshire & NE Wales (but not exclusively): local authority archvs; parish records; estate archvs; family papers; business records; personal papers; political papers; records of parent org; antiquarian records; chapel & nonconformist records; court records; police records; shipping records; hosp records etc
Collns: *Archvs:* archvs of Flintshire County Council & predecessors (from 1888) *Other:* local newspapers; maps **Co-op Schemes:** archival & conservation support to St Deiniol's Lib
Equip: 7 m-readers (5 m-film, 2 m-fiche), m-printer (fees), copier (fees), clr copier (fees), video viewer, 3 computers (all with wd-proc, internet & CD-ROM) *Offcr-in-Charge:* County Archivist, as above **Svcs:** info, ref, limited rsrch svc
Stock: archvs/340 cubic m; rec mgmt/584 cubic m; various bks, periodcls, photos, slides, maps, pamphs, m-forms, audios, videos & CD-ROMs
Pubns: Guide to the Parish Records of Clwyd (£5.95); Industry in Clwyd: An Illustrated Hist (£4.50); Archvs Photographs Series: Flintshire, Buckley, Mold (£9.99); Bygone Flintshire (CD-ROM, £14.99); Mr Gladstone (CD-ROM, £35.25); numerous others
Staff: Archivists: 3 Other Prof: 1 Non-Prof: 4

Hayes

A201 ☕🎵

EMI Music Archives
EMI Group plc, Dawley Rd, Hayes, Middlesex, UB3 1HH (020-8848-2000; *fax:* 020-8848-2018/9)
Internet: http://www.emigroup.com

Gov Body: EMI Group Archv Trust **Chief:** Archv Mgr: Ms Ruth Edge BA(Hons) **Dep:** Snr Archv Asst: Mr Greg Burge
Entry: adv appt in writing; access for rsrchers is available only for printed materials **Open:** Tue-Thu 0930-1245, 1345-1630
Subj: hist of the recording industry, predominantly with ref to EMI Music; business records; records of parent org **Collns:** *Bks & Pamphs:* trade journals; house magazines; music biographies; trade catalogues; bks on hist of music industry *Archvs:* 102 years of corporate & business hist papers; records mgmt files on artists on EMI roster past & present; annual reports
Equip: m-reader, m-printer, copier **Svcs:** info, ref, biblio
Stock: archvs/12000 sq ft; photos/250000; slides/200000; m-forms/275 rolls; audios/500000; videos/35000; master tapes/400000; paper documents/6 mln
Classn: EMI own sys
Pubns: Since Records Began: EMI, The First 100 Years (£25); The Collector's Guide to His Master's Voice Nipper Souvenirs (£20+p&p); Abbey Road (£10.95)
Staff: Other Prof: 2 Non-Prof: 7

Hereford

A202 🏛️

Hereford Local Studies Library
Hereford Lib, Broad St, Hereford, HR4 9AU (01432-272456; *fax:* 01432-359668)
Email: herefordlibrary@herefordshire.gov.uk
Internet: http://www.libraries.herefordshire.gov.uk/

Type: local govt **Gov Body:** Herefordshire Council (see **P62**) **Chief:** Lib & Info Mgr: Ms Kate Murray
Assoc Offices: local archvs are held at: HEREFORDSHIRE RECORD OFFICE (see **A203**)
Entry: ref only **Open:** Tue-Thu 0930-1800, Fri 0930-2000, Sat 0930-1600
Subj: Herefordshire: local studies; family hist; some local authority archvs; personal papers; papers of orgs **Collns:** *Bks & Pamphs:* large printed colln relating to Herefordshire; Pilley Colln (c3000 items); Hopton Colln (local bks); Alfred Watkins Lib (early bks on beekeeping); Herd Bks for Hereford Cattle; county directories (19C-20C); property sale catalogues *Archvs:* local council minutes & papers; papers of the Old Straight Track Club; Bird MSS; Davies MSS *Other:* census returns (1841-1901); OS map colln (1880s-date); local newspapers (1770s-date); photo collns (10000+ negs), incl: F.C. Morgan Colln; Alfred Watkins Archv; some ephemera
Equip: copiers, computers

A203 🏛️

Herefordshire Record Office
The Old Barracks, Harold St, Hereford, HR1 2QX (01432-260750; *fax:* 01432-260006)
Internet: http://www.recordoffice.herefordshire.gov.uk/

Gov Body: Herefordshire Council (see **P62**)
Chief: Record Office Mgr: Miss Sue Hubbard MA, DipEd (shubbard@herefordshire.gov.uk)
Dep: Snr Conservator: Miss Lorna Lee (lolee@herefordshire.gov.uk) *Other Snr Staff:* Archivist: Mrs Elizabeth Semper O'Keefe BA, MARM (esemper@herefordshire.gov.uk)
Entry: CARN ticket **Open:** Mon-Fri 0915-1645
Subj: Herefordshire: local authority archvs; diocesan records; parish records; estate archvs; family papers; business records; personal papers; political papers; records of parent org **Collns:** *Archvs:* records of Herefordshire Council; Diocese of Hereford records
Equip: 18 m-readers, 2 m-printers, copier, computer (with internet & CD-ROM) *Offcr-in-Charge:* Record Office Mgr, as above **Svcs:** rsrch (fee payable)
Stock: archvs/310.9 cubic m, incl photos & maps
Acq Offcr: Archivist, as above
Pubns: Census Records Available at the Herefordshire Record Office (£1); School Records Available at the Herefordshire Record Office (£1); Parish Offcrs Records Available at the Herefordshire Record Office (£1); Parish Registers Available at the Herefordshire Record Office (£1)
Staff: Archivists: 2 Other Prof: 1 Non-Prof: 5.2
Exp: £2000 on purchases (2000-01)

Hertford

A204 🏛️

Hertfordshire Archives and Local Studies
Register Office Block, County Hall, Hertford, SG13 8EJ (01438-737333; *fax:* 01992-555113)
Email: hertsdirect@hertscc.gov.uk
Internet: http://www.hertsdirect.org/

Gov Body: Hertfordshire County Council (see **P63**) *Chief:* Heritage Svcs Mgr: Mrs Christine Shearman BA (christine.shearman@hertscc. gov.uk) *Dep:* Collns Mgr: Mrs Susan Flood BA, MSt, DipAA (susan.flood@hertscc.gov.uk) *Other Snr Staff:* Local Studies Libn: Dr Jill Barber BLib, PhD (jill.barber@hertscc.gov.uk); Svcs Mgr: Ms Sara Patterson (sarah.patterson@hertscc.gov.uk) *Entry:* CARN ticket for archvs; ref only for lib; adv appt advisable *Open:* Mon, Wed-Thu 0930-1730, Tue 1000-2000, Fri 0930-1630, Sat 0900-1300
Subj: Hertfordshire & pre-1965 Barnet & Totteridge: local authority archvs; diocesan records; parish records; estate archvs; family papers; business records; personal papers; records of parent org; family hist; local hist *Collns: Bks & Pamphs:* covering all aspects of Hertfordshire, incl many rare bks & pamphs from 1600 onwards; special collns incl: George Bernard Shaw Colln (lit & biographical works); William Blyth Gerish Colln (Hertfordshire); Reginald Hine Colln (Hitchin) *Archvs:* archvs of Hertfordshire County Council & predecessors; Diocese of St Albans (Hertford & St Albans Archdeaconries) records; principal family & estate archvs: Earl Cowper of Panshanger; Earl Lytton of Knebworth; Earl Verulam of Gorhambury; Ebenezer Howard papers *Other:* film archv; John Dickinson & Co photo archv (paper manufacturers); Family Hist Centre (m-form sources)
Equip: 26 m-readers, 5 m-printers, fax, video viewer, 2 copiers, 4 computers (incl 2 with wd-proc, 2 with internet & 1 with CD-ROM), room for hire (£10 per hr) *Svcs:* info, ref, postal rsrch *Stock:* archvs/992 cubic m; rec mgmt/343 cubic m; bks/30000+; illusts/29000; maps/10000; films & videos/600
Classn: ISAD(G) for archvs, DDC for bks *Auto Sys:* Concerto
Pubns: Brief Guide to the Hertfordshire Records Office (50p); Src Leaflets (£1 each): Sources for the Hist of Houses; C of E Parish Registers & Bishops Transcripts; Nonconformist Registers; Src Packs: Poverty & Welfare: The Old Poor Law 1601-1834 (£2.50); Markets & Fairs (£1.50); Public Health in Hertford 1830-1850 (£2.50); Hertfordshire in War & Peace 1938-1946 (£7.50); Child Labour (edu pack, £12); add 50p p&p to all above prices; various reproduction maps & prints (£3-£5); cards & postcards; list available
Staff: Archivists: 3 *Libns:* 3 *Other Prof:* 1 *Non-Prof:* 12.19 *Exp:* £4680 (2000-01), incl £1571 on documents & £3109 on conservation

Holywood

A205
BBC Northern Ireland Archives
c/o Ulster Folk & Transport Museum, Cultra, Holywood, Co Down, BT18 0EU (028-9042-8428; *fax:* 028-9042-8728)
Email: archives.ni@bbc.co.uk

Type: sound archv *Gov Body:* BBC Northern Ireland *Chief:* Broadcast Archivist: Ms Gráinne Loughran (grainne.loughran@bbc.co.uk)
Entry: ref only; adv appt; copying of materials is not permitted *Open:* Mon-Fri 0900-1700
Subj: Northern Ireland: local hist; life & culture; politics; customs & traditions; current affairs; social hist; lit; arts *Collns: Bks & Pamphs:* BBC pubns (c1930-90) *Other:* AV archvs of materials broadcast by or otherwise originating from BBC Northern Ireland (1924-date), incl: recordings of radio programmes (in analogue & digital formats, c1924-99); films (c1959-79); photos; early broadcast material; press releases & cuttings (c1930-2000)
Equip: listening facilities
Stock: archvs/c20000; audios/c8000 radio programmes; film/c500 cans
Auto Sys: Status IQ

Pubns: The Radio Catalogue: BBC Northern Ireland Archvs at the Ulster Folk & Transport Museum, edited by Gráinne Loughran & Marian McCavana (1993)

Hounslow

A206
Hounslow Local Studies Services
Hounslow Lib, Treaty Centre, Hounslow, Middlesex, TW3 1ES (0845-456-2800; *fax:* 0845-456-2880)
Internet: http://www.hounslow.gov.uk/

Gov Body: Community Initiative Partnership; provides local studies svc for London Borough of Hounslow (see **P93**) *Chief:* Snr Libn for Local Studies: Mr Jerome Farrell
Assoc Offices: LOCAL STUDIES SVCS, Chiswick Lib, Duke's Ave, London, W4 2AB, Local Studies Libn: Mrs C. Hammond (020-8994-1008; *fax:* 020-8995-0016); local studies colln also held at FELTNAM LIB (enqs via Hounslow Lib)
Entry: no restrictions, except adv appt required on Sat & on Mon & Fri before 1300; adv appt advised for non-local visitors at other times *Open:* Hounslow: Mon, Fri-Sat 1000-1300, 1400-1700, Tue 1000-1300, Thu 1400-2000, closed Wed; Chiswick: Mon, Thu 1000-1300, 1400-1700, Sat 1000-1300, closed Tue-Wed & Fri
Subj: London Borough of Hounslow & predecessor authorities: local authority archvs; local hist; misc material related to the Borough *Collns: Bks & Pamphs:* local hist bks; Layton Colln (printed bks, engravings, prints, & drawings, mainly 19C, some earlier); local directories *Archvs:* census returns (1841-1901) *Other:* Crickitt Colln (Hogarth engravings); photo colln (late 19C-date); maps (17C-date)
Equip: m-form reader/printer, copier *Svcs:* rsrch
Staff: Libns: 2.5

Hove

A207
Diocese of Arundel and Brighton (RC), Archives
Bishop's House, The Upper Drive, Hove, E Sussex, BN3 6NE (01273-506387; *fax:* 01273-501527)
Email: archives@dabnet.org

Gov Body: RC Diocese of Arundel & Brighton *Chief:* Archivist: Mrs Hazel State
Entry: by adv appt only
Subj: Diocese of Arundel & Brighton (West & East Sussex, Surrey outside Greater London boundary & Brighton & Hove Unitary Authority): diocesan records; some parish records
Svcs: info, rsrch
Classn: Catholic Archvs Soc Scheme

Huddersfield

A208
West Yorkshire Archive Service: Kirklees
Central Lib, Princess Alexandra Walk, Huddersfield, W Yorkshire, HD1 2SU (01484-221966)
Email: kirklees@wyjs.org.uk
Internet: http://www.archives.wyjs.org.uk/

Gov Body: West Yorkshire Joint Svcs Cttee *Chief:* Principal Dist Archivist, Kirklees: Miss Janet Burhouse BA
Assoc Offices: branch office of WEST YORKSHIRE ARCHV SVC HQ (see **A497**)
Entry: adv appt only *Open:* Mon-Tue, Thu-Fri

Subj: Kirklees Metropolitan Dist: local authority archvs; parish records (m-form only); estate archvs; family papers; business records; records of parent org; nonconformist records for over 120 chapels *Collns: Archvs:* Kirklees Metropolitan Council & predecessors; nonconformist churches; family & estate records, esp: Ramsden of Byram & Longley; Beaumont of Whitley; Thornhill of Fixby; Savile of Thornhill; business records, esp woollen, worsted & fancy cloth manufacturers in Huddersfield area & Shoddy, Mungo & rag merchants in Dewsbury & Batley area; co-op socs; trade unions; musical socs
Equip: 2 m-readers, m-printer, copier
Stock: archvs/3060 linear m
Pubns: Kirklees Archvs 1959-1989: An Illustrated Guide to Kirklees Dist Archvs (£5.95 + 75p p&p); Supplement 1989-1995 (£2.50 + 50p p&p)
Staff: Other Prof: 2 *Non-Prof:* 1

Hull

A209
Hull City Archives
79 Lowgate, Hull, HU1 1HN (01482-615102; *fax:* 01482-613051)
Email: City.Archives@hullcc.gov.uk
Internet: http://www.hullcc.gov.uk/libraries/hull_city_archives/

Gov Body: Kingston upon Hull City Council (see **P68**) *Chief:* City Archivist: Mr Martin Taylor MA, MArAd (Martin.Taylor@hullcc.gov.uk)
Assoc Offices: MEMORIAL OFFICES, Trippett St, Hull
Entry: adv appt *Open:* Tue, Thu 0900-1215, 1330-1645, Wed 0900-1215, Fri 0900-1215, 1330-1645; Memorial Offices: Wed 1345-1630 only
Subj: City of Hull & adjacent areas: local authority archvs; estate archvs; family papers; business records; personal papers; political papers; records of parent org; records of charities; school records; Methodist records
Collns: Bks & Pamphs: pamphs relating to Dock controversies (18C-19C) *Archvs:* records of Hull City Council & predecessors (from 1299); business colln incl: Hellyer Brothers (fishing industry); T. Harding & Co (fishing industry); BOEM Ltd (crushing industry); Hebblethwaites (land agents); records of dock undertakings & vessel registration *Other:* eng drawings of docks, bridges, trawler machinery etc (19C-20C); bldg control plans (19C-20C); OS maps for Hull & environs, most scales (1853-recent)
Equip: m-reader, m-printer (25p per sheet), copier, fax *Svcs:* info, ref
Stock: archvs/395 cubic m; various photos, maps & illusts
Classn: ISAD(G) *Auto Sys:* CALM 2000
Pubns: Guide to the Kingston upon Hull Record Office, Vol 1 (£1); Subj Guide – World War II (£1); Subj Guide – Transport by Sea, Rail & Inland Navigation (£1.60); Early Printers & Booksellers (£5); The Medical Profession in Hull (£4.40); Old Hull Borough Asylum (£2); posters; teaching & facsimile sets; various other pubns; list available
Staff: Archivists: 1 *Other Prof:* 1 *Non-Prof:* 3

A210
Reckitt's Heritage
Reckitt Benckiser plc, Dansom Ln, Hull, Humberside, HU8 7DS (01482-582910; *fax:* 01492-582532)
Email: Gordon.Stephenson@ReckittBenckiser.com
Internet: http://www.reckitt.com/

Gov Body: Reckitt Benckiser plc *Chief:* Mgr: Mr Gordon E. Stephenson DMS, MCLIP (Rtd) *Dep:* S.G. West

(Reckitt's Heritage cont)
Entry: adv appt **Open:** Wed-Thu 0930-1630
Subj: world-wide: business records; records of parent org **Collns:** Archvs: records of former Reckitt & Colman plc (manufacturers of household products, toiletries & pharmaceuticals, 19C-20C) **Other:** photos & ephemera
Equip: m-reader, copier, fax, video viewer, 2 computers (both with wd-proc) **Svcs:** info, ref, rsrch, business support
Stock: archvs/8 storage rooms; various photos, slides, illusts, pamphs, maps, audios & videos
Classn: own **Auto Sys:** MS Excel
Staff: Libns: 1 Other Prof: 1

Huntingdon

A211 ⚜
County Record Office, Huntingdon

4 Grammar School Walk, Huntingdon, Cambridgeshire, PE29 3LF (*tel & fax:* 01480-375842)
Email: County.Records.Hunts@cambridgeshire.gov.uk
Internet: http://www.cambridgeshire.gov.uk/

Gov Body: Cambridgeshire County Council (see **P23**) **Chief:** Snr Archivist: Mr Alan Akeroyd BA **Assoc Offices:** branch office of CAMBRIDGE-SHIRE COUNTY RECORD OFFICE (see **A87**)
Entry: CARN ticket **Open:** Tue-Thu 0900-1245, 1345-1715, Fri 0900-1245, 1345-1615, 2nd Sat in month 0900-1200 by appt only
Subj: Huntingdonshire & former Soke of Peterborough: local authority archvs; parish records; estate archvs; family papers; business records; records of predecessor authorities
Collns: Bks & Pamphs: published texts & guides, lists etc to records relating to Huntingdonshire Archvs: Huntingdon & Godmanchester Borough records; records of the Archdeaconry of Huntingdon (Diocese of Ely); family & estate collns: Montagu family, Earls & Dukes of Manchester, of Kimbolton; Fellowes family, Lords De Ramsey of Romsey; Montagu family, Earls of Sandwich; Cromwell-Bush family; business records: Peter-borough area brick companies; Brown Family (millers of Houghton) **Other:** Whitney Colln of photos; OS maps & plans of Huntingdonshire & Peterborough
Equip: 5 m-readers, m-printer, copier
Stock: archvs/1250 linear m; rec mgmt/260 linear m; bks/80 linear m; maps/2000 OS maps & plans
Pubns: Catalogue of Maps in the County Record Office Huntingdon (£1); Genealogical Sources (publ by Cambridge CRO, £4)
Staff: Archivists: 1 Non-Prof: 2

Ilford

A212 ⚜
Redbridge Local Studies and Archives

Local Hist Room, Ilford Central Lib, Clements Rd, Ilford, Essex, IG1 1EA (020-8708-2417; *fax:* 020-8553-3299)
Email: local.studies@redbridge.gov.uk
Internet: http://www.redbridge.gov.uk/learning/localstudies.cfm

Gov Body: London Borough of Redbridge (see **P102**) **Chief:** Archivist: Mr Tudor Allen **Other Snr Staff:** Local Studies Libn: Mr Ian Dowling
Entry: adv appt **Open:** Mon-Fri 0930-2000, Sat 0930-1600
Subj: London Borough of Redbridge: local authority archvs; family papers; business records; personal papers; local hist; family hist
Collns: Bks & Pamphs: local hist bks & periodcls; local directories Archvs: records of London Borough of Redbridge **Other:** maps; local newspapers; photos & illusts; census returns (m-film, 1841-1901); electoral registers
Classn: DDC
Pubns: Redbridge Aspects of Local Hist (50p); Conservation Areas & Listed Buildings (£1.50); Redbridge in WWII, A Perspective (20p); Return of the Mammoth: Fossil Mammal Remains from 19th Century Excavation in Redbridge (20p); Victory in 1945: How Local People Celebrated the End of World War II (£6.95); Ilford Past & Present (£9.95); Valentines Park Ilford: A Century of Hist (£4.95); It Happened Here: The Story of Civil Defence in Wanstead & Woodford (£4.99)
Staff: Archivists: 1 Libns: 1

Inverness

A213 ⚜
Highland Council Archive

Inverness Lib, Farraline Pk, Inverness, IV1 1NH (01463-220330; *fax:* 01463-711128)
Email: archives@highland.gov.uk
Internet: http://www.highland.gov.uk/

Gov Body: Highland Council (see **P64**) **Chief:** Archivist: Mr R.D. Steward BA, MCLIP, DipAA **Assoc Offices:** NORTH HIGHLAND ARCHV (see **A86**)
Entry: adv appt preferred **Open:** Mon-Thu 1000-1300, 1400-1700
Subj: Highland region: local authority archvs; parish records (m-film only); estate archvs; family papers; business records; records of parent org; school records **Collns:** Archvs: of Highland region, incl the records of the Counties of Caithness (held at North Highland Archv), Sutherland, Inverness-shire, Ross & Cromarty, Nairnshire from 1680, & Inverness burgh from 1556; family, business & estate collns, esp of Skye & Inverness; registers of sasines; shipping registers **Other:** maps & plans, incl full set of 2nd ed OS plans covering Highland region; D.C. Stewart's Tartan Archv; Highland Parish Registers on m-film (complete); census returns for the Highland Counties can also be made available
Equip: 8 m-readers, copier
Stock: archvs/1800 ft
Pubns: Family Hist Guide (free leaflet); Guide to the Highland Council Archv (£7.50 + £2.50 p&p)
Staff: Archivists: 2 Other Prof: 1 genealogist Non-Prof: 4

A214 🔑🏛
Regimental Museum of the Queen's Own Highlanders, Archives

c/o RHQ The Highlanders, Cameron Barracks, Inverness, IV2 3XD (01463-224380)

Gov Body: Regimental Trustees **Chief:** The Curator
Assoc Offices: museum addr is: Fort George, Ardersier, near Inverness, but contact the Curator at the above addr in the first instance
Entry: adv appt **Open:** Mon-Fri 0900-1700
Subj: regimental hist; regimental records
Collns: Archvs: records of the Queen's Own Highlanders, the Queen's Own Cameron Highlanders, the Seaforth Highlanders & the Lovat Scouts
Classn: own **Pubns:** price list on application

Ipswich

A215 ⚜
Suffolk Record Office, Ipswich Branch

Gatacre Rd, Ipswich, Suffolk, IP1 2LQ (01473-584541; *fax:* 01473-584533)
Email: ipswich.ro@libher.suffolkcc.gov.uk
Internet: http://www.suffolkcc.gov.uk/libraries_and_heritage/

Gov Body: Suffolk County Council, Libs & Heritage Dept (see **P179**) **Chief:** Public Svc Mgr: Ms Pauline Taylor (pauline.taylor@libher.suffolkcc.gov.uk) **Other Snr Staff:** Local Studies Libn: Mr Ed Button BA, MCLIP (ed.button@libher.suffolkcc.gov.uk)
Assoc Offices: BURY ST EDMUNDS BRANCH (see **A83**); LOWESTOFT BRANCH (see **A361**); LOCAL STUDIES LIB, at above addr
Entry: CARN ticket for access to original materials; booking sys for m-readers **Open:** Mon-Sat 0900-1700
Subj: Suffolk, esp former administrative county of East Suffolk: local authority archvs; diocesan records; parish records; estate archvs; family papers; personal papers; business records; records of parent org (East Suffolk County Council & Ipswich Borough); records of local charities & socs **Collns:** Bks & Pamphs: Local Studies Lib for Ipswich & eastern part of Suffolk, with good genl East Anglian coverage Archvs: archvs of former East Suffolk County Council; archvs of Ipswich Borough Council; Diocese of St Edmundsbury & Ipswich (Ipswich area) records; Sir Thomas Phillipps colln of Medieval MSS; Cornwallis Family Papers (incl letter-bk of 1st Marquis Cornwallis, Governor-Genl of Bengal); papers of Gathorne Hardy, 1st Earl of Cranbrook; papers of Earls of Albemarle; Admiral Viscount Keppel papers; Genl Sir William Keppel papers; Baron Egerton papers; Admiral Sir James Saumarez papers; Sir Philip Bowes Vere Broke papers; papers of George Pretyman, Bishop of Lincoln & Winchester; Mary Greenup papers (wife of Gen J.T. English); diaries of Canon J.H. Turner; papers of William Leathes, ambassador; estate collns incl: Long family; Gonning family; Boucherett family; Barne family; Hanbury-Bateman families; Kerrison family; Middleton family; Pretyman-Tomline families; Maynard family; Purcell-Fitzgerald family; Lord Rendlesham; business collns incl: Richard Garrett & Sons records (engineers); British Xylonite Company records; Hale End & Brantham records; Ransomes & Rapier records; Norsk Hydro Fertilisers Group records; Paul's Malt & Associated British Maltsters records **Other:** Oral Hist Tape Colln (600 items, with 300 transcripts); extensive photo colln; extensive holdings of local newspapers on m-film; Internatl Genealogical Index for the UK; 1881 Census Indexes for East Anglia & London; 1901 Census for Suffolk (m-fiche); Natl Probate Indexes (1858-1943)
Equip: 20 m-readers, 2 m-printers, copier, computers (incl internet & CD-ROM) **Svcs:** info, ref, rsrch, transcription, translation, m-fiche & m-film duplication
Stock: archvs/13457 linear ft; rec mgmt/9700 linear ft; other material/3397 linear ft (incl Local Studies Lib)
Classn: DDC **Auto Sys:** DS CALM 2000
Pubns: Guide to Genealogical Sources (10 sections, priced individually or £22.50 for all 10, incl 2nd class p&p); Family Data Colln Pack (£2.75 incl p&p); Bowen's Map of Suffolk 1759 (£3 incl p&p); various leaflets on svcs (free)
Staff: Archivists: 1.6 Libns: 0.2 Non-Prof: 5.5

Isleworth

A216
British and Foreign School Society Archive Centre
Brunel Univ, Osterley Campus, Borough Rd, Isleworth, Middlesex, TW7 5DU (020-8891-0121 x2615)
Email: bfss.archive@brunel.ac.uk
Internet: http://www.bfss.org.uk/archive/

Gov Body: British & Foreign School Soc & Brunel Univ (see **S2065**) *Chief:* Archivist: Mr B.A. York (Brian.York@brunel.ac.uk)
Entry: adv appt *Open:* Wed & Fri 1000-1600
Subj: hist of non-sectarian edu; personal papers; school records; records of parent org *Collns: Bks & Pamphs:* Annual Reports of the BFSS (1814-date); Educational Record (journal, 1848-1929); Joseph Lancaster Colln (19C); Salmon Colln (early 19C bks on elementary edu); George Bartle Colln; Susan Isaacs Colln (20C); Joan Cass Colln (20C) *Archvs:* records of the Soc (incl secs' papers, minutes, correspondence, reports etc); correspondence of Joseph Lancaster (19C educationalist & philanthropist); records of the Society's schools & colls, incl: Borough Road Coll, Southwark (19C-20C); Darlington Coll of Edu (1868-20C); Saffron Walden Coll (c1877-1979); Stockwell Coll (1858-1971); papers of Eric Hamilton (Principal of Borough Road Coll, 1893-1967); other misc records
Exp: £160 (1999-2000); £350 (2000-01)

Kendal

A217
Cumbria Record Office, Kendal
County Offices, Stricklandgate, Kendal, Cumbria, LA9 4RQ (01539-773540; *fax:* 01539-773538)
Email: kendal.record.office@cumbriacc.gov.uk
Internet: http://www.cumbria.gov.uk/archives/

Gov Body: Cumbria County Council (see **P32**)
Chief: Asst County Archivist: Ms Anne Rowe BA, DipAA
Assoc Offices: branch office of CUMBRIA RECORD OFFICE, CARLISLE (see **A98**)
Entry: CARN ticket *Open:* Mon-Fri 0900-1700
Subj: historic County of Westmorland, Lancashire North of the Sands (Furness & Cartmel), & Sedbergh-Dent area (formerly in West Riding of Yorkshire): local authority archvs; diocesan records; parish records; estate archvs; family papers; business records; records of parent org; nonconformist records; school records; records of local solicitors, socs & charities *Collns: Bks & Pamphs:* Lib of Capt J. Curwen; trade directories *Archvs:* Diocese of Bradford parish records (Kendal area); Diocese of Carlisle parish records (Kendal area); records of Westmorland Quarter Session; papers & plans of Thomas H. Mawson (landscape architect, 1861-1933); Fleming MSS of Rydal Hall (13C-20C), esp papers of Sir Daniel Fleming MP, JP (17C); Hothfield MSS of Appleby Castle (12C-20C), esp papers of Lady Anne Clifford (1590-1676) *Other:* maps; newspapers
Equip: 4 m-readers, copier
Stock: archvs/286 cubic m; rec mgmt/13.6 cubic m
Staff: Other Prof: 3 *Non-Prof:* 3

Kingsbridge

A218
William Cookworthy Museum, Local Heritage Resource Centre
The Old Grammar School, 108 Fore St, Kingsbridge, Devon, TQ7 1AW (01548-853235)
Email: wcookworthy@devonmuseums.net

Gov Body: William Cookworthy Museum Soc
Chief: Curator: Mr Kelvin Boot BSc, AMA
Entry: Museum: open to public; *Resource Centre:* ref only by appt *Open:* Mar-Oct: Mon-Fri 1030-1730 (-1630 during Oct) or by appt
Subj: South Hams of Devon: local hist; religion; geog; hist *Collns: Other:* m-film & paper originals of Kingsbridge Gazette
Equip: m-reader, computer
Stock: archvs/300
Classn: museum database, SHIC
Staff: Other Prof: 1

Kingston upon Thames

A219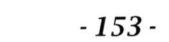
Kingston Museum and Heritage Service, Local History Room
North Kingston Centre, Richmond Rd, Kingston upon Thames, Surrey, KT2 5PE (020-8547-6738; *fax:* 020-8547-6747)
Email: local.history@rbk.kingston.gov.uk
Internet: http://www.kingston.gov.uk/museum/

Gov Body: Royal Borough of Kingston upon Thames (see **P96**) *Chief:* Archivist: Mrs Jill Lamb MA, DipAA *Dep:* Local Hist Offcr: Ms Emma Rummins MA, BA
Entry: no restrictions *Open:* Mon, Thu-Fri 1000-1300, 1400-1700, Tue 1000-1300, 1400-1900, closed Wed
Subj: Royal Borough of Kingston upon Thames: local authority archvs; personal papers; local hist *Collns: Bks & Pamphs:* local directories; local hist materials *Archvs:* archvs of Royal Borough of Kingston upon Thames (from 13C), incl: Borough Council minutes from 1680; records of former boroughs of Surbiton, Malden & Coombe; Eadweard Muybridge papers *Other:* photographic work & equip of Eadweard Muybridge; census returns; local newspapers; oral hist tapes; maps; photographs; ephemera
Equip: 2 m-fiche readers, m-film/fiche printer, copier, computers (incl internet via staff & CD-ROM) *Svcs:* info, ref, rsrch
Stock: archvs/c15000; periodcls/12; photos/6000; slides/1000; illusts/100; pamphs/1000; maps/500; m-forms/500; audios/10; videos/40; CD-ROMs/6
Classn: DDC *Auto Sys:* Adlib
Pubns: Guide to the Borough Archvs (£1); Eadweard Muybridge Catalogue (forthcoming)
Staff: Archivists: 1 *Libns:* 0.8 *Other Prof:* 3 in museum section *Non-Prof:* 2 in museum section
Exp: £3500 (2000-01)
Proj: possible digitisation of photos/illusts

Kirkcaldy

A220
Kirkcaldy Museum and Art Gallery, Archives
War Memorial Gdns, Kirkcaldy, Fife, KY1 1YG (01592-412860; *fax:* 01592-412870)
Email: dallas.mechan@fife.gov.uk

Type: local authority *Gov Body:* Fife Council (see **P53**) *Chief:* Museums Co-ordinator: Ms D.M. Mechan BSc, AMA
Entry: ref only; adv appt *Open:* Mon-Fri 1030-1700
Subj: Kirkcaldy: local hist; social hist; industrial hist; arts
Stock: archvs/35 linear m
Classn: own

Kirkwall

A221
Orkney Archives
Orkney Lib, 44 Junction Rd, Kirkwall, Orkney, KW15 1AG (01856-873166; *fax:* 01856-875260)
Email: orkney.archives@orkney.gov.uk
Internet: http://www.orkneylibrary.org.uk/

Gov Body: Orkney Islands Council (see **P141**)
Chief: Principal Archivist: Ms Alison Fraser MA
Dep: Archivist: Mr Phil Astley MA, DipAA (phil.astley@orkney.gov.uk)
Entry: adv appt essential (please incl return postage when writing) *Open:* Tue-Fri 0900-1300, 1400-1645
Subj: Orkney Island: local authority archvs; parish records; estate archvs; business records; personal papers; court records; census returns; electoral registers *Collns: Bks & Pamphs:* Peace's Almanacs (1869-1930) *Archvs:* records of Orkney Islands Council; records of Orkney Sheriff Court *Other:* local newspapers on m-film, incl: The Orcadian (1854-date); The Orkney Herald (1860-1960)
Equip: 2 m-readers, m-printer, computer (with wd-proc & CD-ROM)
Proj: move to new premises in summer 2003

Knowsley

A222
Knowsley Local Studies and Archives
Huyton Lib, Civic Way, Huyton, Knowsley, Merseyside, L36 9DG (0151-443-3738/4291; *fax:* 0151-443-3739)
Internet: http://www.knowsley.gov.uk/ or http://history.knowsley.gov.uk (local history)

Gov Body: Knowsley Metropolitan Borough Council (see **P70**) *Chief:* Local Studies & Archvs Libn: Mrs Eileen Hume CertEd, DipILM, MA, MCLIP
Assoc Offices: KNOWSLEY ARCHVS, Kirkby Lib, Newtown Gdns, Kirkby, Knowsley, Merseyside, L32 8RR (0151-443-4289; *fax:* 0151-546-1453); enqs should be directed via Huyton Lib (0151-443-4291)
Entry: ref only; adv appt required to consult archvs at Kirkby *Open:* Mon-Fri 1000-1900, Sat 1000-1600, Sun 1200-1600
Subj: Metropolitan Borough of Knowsley (Huyton, Kirkby, Halewood, Prescot, Cronton, Whiston, Knowsley village & Tarbock): local authority archvs (incl all predecessor authorities); parish records (on m-film); small local family papers; business records; personal papers; records of parent org; census returns; electoral registers; records of local clubs/socs; local hist; genealogy *Collns: Bks & Pamphs:* local hist colln; local directories *Archvs:* archvs of Knowsley Metropolitan Borough Council; Council minutes for Huyton-with-Robey, Kirkby & Prescot Urban Dist Councils; council minutes & Clerk's working papers for Whiston Rural Dist Council (c1890-1974); Prescot Grammar School archvs (15C-19C); NUM (Cronton Branch) minute bks (1952-1971); Huyton Cricket Club archvs (1860-c1970); Preston & Whiston Co-op Soc archvs (c19C-20C) *Other:* large photo colln; map colln; copies of tithe maps & awards; various parish registers (m-form); 1881 census (m-form); newspaper cuttings; local newspapers on m-film, incl Prescot Reporter; Huyton Reporter; Liverpool Echo
Equip: 6 m-fiche readers, 3 m-printers (laser), fax, copier, computer (with CD-ROM), also 40 computers in ref lib (incl wd-proc & internet)
Online: IGI on CD-ROM *Svcs:* info, ref, rsrch
Stock: archvs/250 linear m; bks/6500 vols; photos/7000; slides/500; maps/2500
Classn: DDC *Auto Sys:* Dynix

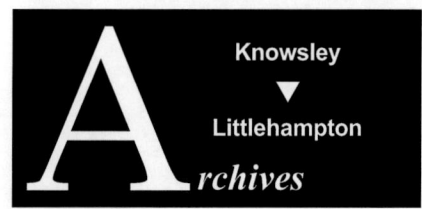

Knowsley
▼
Littlehampton

rchives

(Knowsley Local Studies & Archvs cont)
Pubns: Tracing Your Family Hist (free leaflet); Eye of the Eagle (local hist journal, 4 pa); Huyton with Roby; Kirkby Archv Photographs; Prescot of Yesteryear; Prescot Now & Then; Prescot Records – The Court Rolls; A Hist of Whiston; A Hist of Bowning Park; From Slacky Brow to Hope Street; Inns of Prescot & Whiston
Staff: Libns: 1 *Other Prof:* 1 PT (at ref lib) *Non-Prof:* 4 FTE, incl 2 PT

Lancaster

A223 🏛

King's Own Royal Regiment Museum, Regimental Archives

City Museum, Market Sq, Lancaster, LA1 1HT (01524-04037, *fax.* 01524-841692)
Email: kingsownmuseum@iname.com

Gov Body: Regimental Trustees **Chief:** Curator: Mr Peter Donnelly BA(Hons), AMA
Entry: adv appt **Open:** Mon-Fri 1000-1700; closed 24 Dec-2 Jan
Subj: military hist; regimental records **Collns:** *Archvs:* records of King's Own Royal Regiment **Equip:** copier, clr copier, fax **Svcs:** info, ref **Stock:** archvs/1000; photos/22000; slides/300; illusts/100; pamphs/2000; maps/100; videos/20
Staff: *Other Prof:* 1 *Exp:* £200 approx (2000-01)

Lancaster RC Diocesan Archives
See TALBOT LIB (**S1839**)

Leeds

The Henry Moore Institute Archives
See THE HENRY MOORE INST LIB (**S900**)

A224 🔑 ✍

Leeds Diocesan Archives (RC)

Hinsley Hall, 62 Headingley Ln, Leeds, W York-shire, LS6 2BX (0113-261-8031; *fax:* 0113-261-8035)
Email: refinnigan@hindsley-hall.co.uk
Internet: http://www.leeds-diocese.org.uk/

Gov Body: RC Diocese of Leeds **Chief:** Diocesan Archivist: Mgr George T. Bradley **Dep:** Asst Archivist: Mr Robert E. Finnigan, BSc MPhil
Entry: adv appt; bona fide students, by application to the Asst Archivist **Open:** Mon-Fri 1000-1600
Subj: Yorkshire (West Riding): diocesan records (Diocese of Beverley, 1850-1878; Diocese of Leeds, 1878-date) **Collns:** Bks & Pamphs: printed pastorals of bishops; small colln of theological pamphs for the period covered by the archvs **Archvs:** papers of the RC Church in Yorkshire (1688-date); some papers for other parts of Northern England before 1840; correspondence & papers of the Vicars Apostolic of the Northern Dist (1688-1840) & Yorkshire Dist (1840-50); papers of the Bishops of Beverley (1850-78) & Bishops of Leeds (1878-date); administrative records of the Dioceses of Beverley & Leeds (1850-date); 19C parish records (available on m-film, some exceptions); Hogarth

MSS (19C transcripts of papers of secular clergy in Yorkshire from 1660)
Equip: m-readers, copier **Svcs:** info, ref, rsrch **Pubns:** Leeds Cathedral Hist & Guide (£4.95); A Hist of the Soc of Yorkshire Brethren (£2.50); Four Essays in Yorkshire Catholic Hist (£3); Catholicism in Leeds: A Community of Faith 1794-1994 (£7.50)
Staff: *Other Prof:* 1

A225 🏛 ✍

Otley Museum Archives

Civic Centre, Cross Green, Otley, Leeds, W Yorkshire, LS21 1HD (01943-461052)

Type: registered charity **Chief:** contact the Sec: Mrs M. Hornsby
Entry: adv appt **Open:** Mon-Tue, Fri 1000-1230
Subj: Otley: local studies; social hist; industrial hist; printers' eng **Collns:** *Archvs:* colln relating to printers' eng industry founded in Otley; bldg records *Other:* photo colln relating to town; misc items relating to social hist of Otley
Equip: copier
Classn: own
Pubns: Otley & the Wharfdale Printing Machine (£2); Otley & Dist in Old Photographs (£5); Otley in Old Picture Postcards (£7); A Guide to the Landscape of Otley (£8.50); various other pubns relating to Otley's local hist
Staff: *Non-Prof:* c30 volunteers

A226 🏛

West Yorkshire Archive Service: Leeds

Chapeltown Rd, Sheepscar, Leeds, W Yorkshire, LS7 3AP (0113-214-5814; *fax:* 0113-214-5815)
Email: leeds@wyjs.org.uk
Internet: http://www.archives.wyjs.org.uk/

Gov Body: West Yorkshire Joint Svcs Cttee
Chief: Principal Dist Archivist (Leeds): Mr William J. Connor MA, DipAA
Assoc Offices: branch office of WEST YORKSHIRE ARCHV SVC HQ (see **A497**)
Entry: adv appt **Open:** Mon-Tue, Thu 0930-1700 (restricted svc 1200-1400), closed Wed
Subj: Leeds Metropolitan Dist & Yorkshire region: local authority archvs; diocesan records; parish records; estate archvs; family papers; business records; records of parent org; local voluntary orgs of all kinds; nonconformist churches
Collns: *Archvs:* archvs of Leeds City Council & predecessors, esp Leeds Corp (from 1662); records of boroughs of Morley & Pudsey; records of urban districts of Aireborough, Garforth, Horsforth, Otley & Rothwell; records of rural districts of Wetherby & Wharfdale; records of Leeds Board of Guardians & Public Assistance Cttee (1844-1948); records of Leeds School Board (1870-1903); Anglican & nonconformist churches, incl Diocese of Bradford, Diocese of Ripon & local parishes; probate records (Archdeaconry of Richmond, Eastern Deaneries & related particulars); manorial & tithe records; family & estate records, most notably: Fountains Abbey; Studley Royal; Ripley Castle; Nostell Priory; Temple Newsam; Newby Hall; Harewood; correspondence of Sir John Reresby (1639-1688); correspondence of George Canning (1780-1827); London port bks (1717-1720); additionally records concerning industry, commerce & local orgs of every kind, with archvs of courts, govt agencies & natl industries held under Public Records Acts
Equip: 6 m-readers, m-printer, fax, copier, computer **Svcs:** postal rsrch svc
Stock: archvs/5000 linear m
Pubns: Leeds Archvs 1938-1988: An Illustrated Guide (£5.95 + 75p p&p)
Staff: *Other Prof:* 3 *Non-Prof:* 2

Leicester

Cistercian Archives
See MOUNT ST BERNARD ABBEY LIB (**S930**)

A227 🏛

Leicestershire, Leicester and Rutland Record Office

Long St, Wigston Magna, Leicester, LE18 2AH (0116-257-1080; *fax:* 0116-257-1120)
Email: recordoffice@leics.gov.uk
Internet: http://www.leics.gov.uk

Gov Body: Leicestershire County Council (see **P74**) **Chief:** County Archivist: Mr Carl Harrison BA, DipAA **Dep:** Keeper of Archvs: Mr Robin P. Jenkins BA, MA, DipAS
Entry: CARN ticket **Open:** Mon-Tue, Thu 0915-1700, Wed 0915-1930, Fri 0915-1645, Sat 0915-1215; closed public hols & 1st full wk of Oct
Subj: Leicestershire (incl Rutland): local authority archvs; diocesan records; parish records; estate archvs; family papers; business records; personal papers; political papers; records of parent org **Collns:** Bks & Pamphs: Leicestershire Colln (County Local Studies Colln: bks, pamphs, illusts, sound recordings etc) **Archvs:** archvs of Leicestershire County Council & Leicester City Council; Diocese of Leicester records; Diocese of Peterborough parish records (parishes in Rutland) *Other:* maps, photos
Equip: 27 m-readers, m-camera, 2 m-printers, video viewer, fax, copier **Svcs:** info, ref, rsrch
Stock: archvs/930.6 cubic m; other materials/ 115.9 cubic m
Pubns: Handlist of Parish & Non-Conformist Church Records in the LRO (£3); The Way Back: A Guide to Tracing Your Family Tree (£3.75); Descent of Dissent: A Guide to Non-Conformist Records at the LRO (£3.50); Family & Estate Records in the LRO (£2.95)
Staff: *Archivists:* 6 *Libns:* 2 *Non-Prof:* 14
Proj: refurbishment of strongrooms (until Oct 2003)

Leigh

A228 🏛

Wigan Archives Service

Town Hall, Leigh, Lancashire, WN7 2DY (01942-404430; *fax:* 01942-404505)
Email: heritage@wiganmbc.gov.uk

Gov Body: Wigan Council (see **P200**) **Chief:** Archivist: Mr Alan Davies BA(Hons)
Entry: adv appt only **Open:** Tue, Thu 1000-1300, 1400-1630; other times by appt
Subj: Wigan Metropolitan Dist: local authority archvs; diocesan records; family papers; estate archvs; business records; trade union records; nonconformist records (Methodist, Presbyterian & Unitarian); school records **Collns:** *Archvs:* Wigan County Borough archvs; records of Leigh Municipal Borough Urban & Rural Districts; records of Boards of Guardians (Wigan, Leigh); Quarter & Petty Sessions records (Wigan, Leigh); records of Liverpool Diocese for parishes in Wigan dist; Edward Hall Colln (diaries etc); family & estate papers, incl: Holt Leigh; Standish; Crawford of Haigh *Other:* maps & plans
Equip: m-reader, m-printer (90p per copy), copier (A4/15p, A3/25p), fax, computer (with wd-proc, internet & CD-ROM) *Disabled:* wheelchair access
Svcs: info, ref
Stock: archvs/3860 linear m; bks/50 linear m; photos/c100000; pamphs/200; maps/1500; m-forms/500
Pubns: Guide to Genealogical Sources (£1.95); Guide to the Archvs (1996, £2.95); Those Dark Satanic Mills: An Illustrated Record of the

Industrial Revolution in South Lancashire (£2.50); Around Leigh (£9.95); The Wigan Coalfield (£9.95); Standish & Shevington (£9.95); Around Hindley & Abram (£9.95); Around Ashton-in-Makerfield (£9.95)
Staff: Archivists: 1

Lerwick

A229

Shetland Archives
44 King Harald St, Lerwick, Shetland Islands, ZE1 0EQ (01595-696247; *fax:* 01595-696533)
Email: shetland.archives@zetnet.co.uk
Internet: http://www.shetland.gov.uk/

Gov Body: Shetland Islands Council (see **P162**)
Chief: Archivist: Mr Brian Smith MA (brian.smith@sic.shetland.gov.uk)
Entry: appt preferred, not essential *Open:* Mon-Thu 0900-1300, 1400-1700, Fri 0900-1300, 1400-1600
Subj: Shetland: local authority archvs; parish records; estate archvs; family papers; business records; records of parent org; oral hist collns
Equip: m-reader, m-printer, copier, computer (incl wd-proc) *Disabled:* wheelchair access
Stock: archvs/2000 m
Staff: Archivists: 1 *Non-Prof:* 1

Lewes

A230

East Sussex Record Office
The Maltings, Castle Precincts, Lewes, E Sussex, BN7 1YT (01273-482349; *fax:* 01273-482341)
Email: archives@eastsussexcc.gov.uk
Internet: http://www.eastsussexcc.gov.uk/archives/

Gov Body: East Sussex County Council (see **P49**) *Chief:* County Archivist: Mrs E.M. Highes
Entry: CARN ticket *Open:* Mon-Tue, Thu 0845-1645, Wed 0930-1645, Fri 0845-1615, Sat please enquire
Subj: East Sussex: local authority archvs; parish records; estate archvs; family papers; business records; records of parent org *Collns: Archvs:* archvs of East Sussex County Council; Diocese of Chichester parish records (East Sussex area); Marquis of Abergavenny Archv; Earl of Ashburnham records; Battle Abbey Estate Archv; Earl of Chichester papers; Earl De La Warr records; Frewen Archv; Glynde Archv; Earl of Sheffield Archv; Shiffner Archv; records of William Figg (Lewes cartographer); Rye Borough Archv
Equip: m-reader, m-printer, copier
Stock: archvs/750 cubic m; rec mgmt/780 cubic m
Pubns: A Handlist of Registers of Births, Baptisms, Marriages, Deaths & Burials (£2 incl p&p); numerous others
Staff: Other Prof: 6 *Non-Prof:* 8.4

A231

Glyndebourne Archive
Glyndebourne, Lewes, E Sussex, BN8 5UU (01273-812321; *fax:* 01273-812783)
Email: julia.aries@glyndebourne.com
Internet: http://www.glyndebourne.co.uk/archive/

Gov Body: Glyndebourne Festival Opera *Chief:* Archivist: Miss J. Aries BA(Hons)
Entry: adv appt required *Open:* Mon-Fri 1000-1600
Subj: Glyndebourne: records of parent org; opera; music *Collns: Bks & Pamphs:* small colln of bks about Glyndebourne, opera & music

Archvs: programmes, printed lit, posters, press cuttings & correspondence relating to hist of Glyndebourne Festival Opera (1934-date) & Glyndebourne Touring Opera (1968-date) *Other:* coln of oral hist interviews on cassette
Equip: video viewer, copier
Stock: archvs/77 m; rec mgmt/10 m; other material/2 m
Pubns: Glyndebourne Archv Brochure (free with A4 SAE); Glyndebourne: Building a Vision (£16.95); Glyndebourne Recorded (£25); Glyndebourne Remembered (oral hist cassette) (£4.50)
Staff: Other Prof: 1 *Non-Prof:* 1 (temp only)

Lichfield

A232

Staffordshire and Stoke-on-Trent Archive Service, Lichfield Record Office
Lichfield Lib, The Friary, Lichfield, Staffordshire, WS13 6QG (01543-510720; *fax:* 01543-510715)
Email: lichfield.record.office@staffordshire.gov.uk
Internet: http://www.staffordshire.gov.uk/archives/

Gov Body: part of Staffordshire & Stoke-on-Trent Archv Svc, run on behalf of Staffordshire County Council (see **P174**) & Stoke-on-Trent City Council (see **P178**) *Chief:* Archivist-in-Charge: Mr Martin Sanders BA, MPhil, DipAA
Assoc Offices: other Staffordshire & Stoke-on-Trent Archv Svc branches: STAFFORDSHIRE RECORD OFFICE (see **A467**); BURTON-UPON-TRENT ARCHV (see **A81**); STOKE-ON-TRENT CITY ARCHVS (see **A473**); WILLIAM SALT LIB (see **A468**)
Entry: Staffordshire & Stoke-on-Trent Archv Svc Readers ticket & adv appt *Open:* Mon-Fri 0930-1700, 2nd Sat of each month 0930-1230
Subj: Diocese & City of Lichfield: local authority archvs; diocesan records; parish records; estate archvs; family papers; business records; personal papers; political papers *Collns: Archvs:* archvs of Lichfield City Council; Lichfield Rural Dist Council archvs; Lichfield Diocesan records, incl original wills (prior to 1858), bishops' transcripts of parish registers & marriage bonds; records of parishes in Lichfield city
Equip: 7 m-readers, copier
Stock: archvs/200 cubic m; bks/12 linear m
Classn: ISAD(G)
Staff: Archivists: 1 *Non-Prof:* 5

Lincoln

A233

Lincolnshire Archives
St Rumbold St, Lincoln, LN2 5AB (01522-526204; *fax:* 01522-530047)
Email: lincolnshire.archive@lincolnshire.gov.uk
Internet: http://www.lincolnshire.gov.uk/archives/

Gov Body: Lincolnshire County Council (see **P75**) *Chief:* Area Svc Mgr: Miss Stephanie Gilluly *Dep:* Principal Keeper (Archvs): Mrs S. Payne
Entry: adv appt advised, ref only; reader ticket requires 2 passport photos & proof of ID *Open:* Mon (Mar-Oct) 1300-1900 (Nov-Feb) 1100-1700, Tue-Fri 0900-1700, Sat 0900-1600
Subj: Lincolnshire & Diocese of Lincoln: local authority archvs; diocesan records; parish records; estate archvs; family papers; business records; personal papers; political papers; records of parent org *Collns: Bks & Pamphs:* Foster Lib (see **S951**); Soc for Lincolnshire Hist & Archaeo Lib *Archvs:* archvs of Lincolnshire County Council; records of Diocese of Lincoln; Dean & Chapter records of Lincoln Cathedral

Equip: 29 m-readers, m-printer, m-camera (via staff), copier (via staff), clr copier (via staff), video viewer, 2 computers, lecture room for hire
Svcs: info, ref, rsrch (charge for some svcs)
Stock: archvs/895 cubic m
Pubns: Deposited Parish Registers & BTS (£2 + 60p p&p); Poor Law Union Records: Lincolnshire (£2.50 + 60p p&p)
Staff: Archivists: 7 *Libns:* 0.5 *Other Prof:* 3 *Non-Prof:* 9 FT, 8 PT

A234

Royal Lincolnshire Regimental Museum, Regimental Archives
Museum of Lincolnshire Life, Burton Rd, Lincoln, LN1 3LY (01522-528448; *fax:* 01522-521264)
Email: lincolnshirelife_museum@lincolnshire.gov.uk

Gov Body: Lincolnshire County Council (see **P75**) *Chief:* Principal Keeper: Ms Janet Edmond (janet.edmond@lincolnshire.gov.uk)
Assoc Offices: some archival material held at ROYAL LINCOLNSHIRE REGIMENT, Sobraon Barracks, Burton Rd, Lincoln, Regimental Sec: Capt D.J. Lee (01522-525444); see also MUSEUM OF LINCOLNSHIRE LIFE (**S955**)
Entry: adv appt for use of ref material *Open:* Mon-Fri 1000-1700 (excl bank hols)
Subj: Royal Lincolnshire Regiment: military hist; regimental records *Collns: Archvs:* records of the Royal Lincolnshire Regiment
Equip: m-reader, copier
Stock: archvs/100; photos/1000; audios/3
Staff: Other Prof: 4

A235

Tennyson Research Centre
c/o Lib Support Svcs, Brayford House, Lucy Tower St, Lincoln, LN1 1XN (01522-552862; *fax:* 01522-552858)
Email: gatess@lincolnshire.gov.uk

Gov Body: Lincolnshire County Council (see **P75**) *Chief:* Curator: Miss S. Gates
Assoc Offices: the collns are held at LINCOLN CENTRAL LIB, Free School Ln, Lincoln, LN2 1EZ, but all enqs should be addressed as above
Entry: on written application to Miss S. Gates at above addr
Subj: Alfred Tennyson: life & works; personal papers; family papers *Collns: Bks & Pamphs:* George Clayton Tennyson Lib (Tennyson's father, 350 vols); Alfred Tennyson's own Lib (c2000 vols); 1st & other important eds of Tennyson's works; biography & criticism *Archvs:* MSS incl early drafts of poems & c200 proofs; Tennyson family diaries & notebks; journal of Emily Tennyson; letters to & from Tennyson (several 1000), incl correspondence with Browning, Gladstone, Lear & Fitzgerald *Other:* illusts & photos of Tennyson family

Littlehampton

A236

Littlehampton Museum Local Studies Room
Manor House, Church St, Littlehampton, W Sussex, BN17 5EW (01903-738100)
Email: littlehamptonmuseum@arun.gov.uk

Gov Body: Arun Dist Council *Chief:* Curator: Ms Rebecca Fardell
Subj: Littlehampton & dist: local studies (mainly 19C-20C); archaeo; social hist; geog *Collns: Archvs:* large amount of printed 2ndary materials with some MSS *Other:* local maps & 19C harbour plans; copies of historic newspapers; photo colln (8000+); local drawings, paintings & engravings

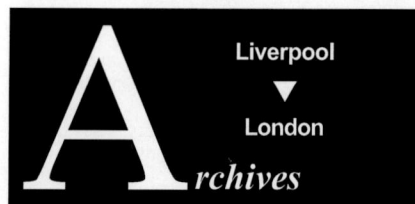

Liverpool

A237

Liverpool RC Archdiocesan Archive

Metropolitan Cathedral of Christ the King, Cathedral House, Mount Pleasant, Liverpool, L3 5TQ (0151-709-9222; *fax:* 0151-708-7274)
Email: met.cathedral@cwcom.net

Gov Body: Liverpool RC Diocesan Trustees
Chief: Archivist: Dr Meg Whittle PhD
Entry: adv appt *Open:* Mon-Wed 0930-1600
Subj: RC Archdiocese of Liverpool (between Mersey & Ribble, eastwards to Chorley, Wigan & Leigh, Isle of Man): diocesan records *Collns: Other:* Catholic Pictorial (weekly newspaper of the Archdiocese)
Equip: copier, computer *Svcs:* info, ref
Stock: archvs/c42 cubic m (1500 storage boxes)
Staff: staffed by volunteers

A238

Liverpool Record Office and Local Studies Department

Central Lib, William Brown St, Liverpool, L3 8EW (0151-233-5817; *fax:* 0151-233-5886)
Email: recoffice.central.library@liverpool.gov.uk
Internet: http://www.liverpool.gov.uk/ or http://www.pastliverpool.com/

Gov Body: Liverpool City Council (see **P76**)
Chief: Mgr Record Office: Mr D.A. Stoker BA, MArAd *Dep:* Team Leader Record Office: Ms R. Hobbins BA, MArAd
Assoc Offices: MERSEYSIDE RECORD OFFICE, at same addr (see **A240**)
Entry: authorised readers ticket; rare materials by personal application only with proof of ID (name & addr); adv appt essential for viewing m-forms (ring 0151-233-5811) *Open:* Mon-Thu 0900-2000, Fri 0900-1900, Sat 0900-1700, Sun 1200-1600; closed 3rd & 4th wks of Jun
Subj: Liverpool (also Cheshire & Lancaster): local authority archvs; diocesan records; parish records; estate archvs; family papers; business records; personal papers; trade union records; records of local charities, assocs & socs; local studies; family hist *Collns: Bks & Pamphs:* Historic Soc of Lancashire & Cheshire Lib; local street & trade directories (1766-1970) *Archvs:* local authority records from 1207 (minute bks from 1550); statutory bodies; ecclesiastical records: Anglican parishes (from 1586), RC parishes (from 1741), Nonconformist records (from 1787), Liverpool Diocesan Registry, Jewish records (from 1804); archvs of Edmund Kirby (architects & surveyors); family, estate (incl manorial) & personal papers, incl: Moore of Bank Hall; Plumbe-Tempest; Marquess of Salisbury; Norris of Speke Hall; William Roscoe; Earls of Derby etc; literary MSS *Other:* newspapers (1756-date); newscuttings; census returns; map colln; slides; photos; engravings; prints; water-colours; sound materials (incl the lib of BBC Radio Merseyside)
Equip: 14 m-readers, 6 m-printers, copier, clr copier (in Central Lib), 8 computers (incl internet & CD-ROM) *Svcs:* paid rsrch svc
Stock: archvs/885 cubic m; other materials/328 cubic m

Classn: ISAD(G) *Auto Sys:* DS
Pubns: Handlist of C of E Parish Records (£2.50 + p&p); Map of C of E Parishes in Liverpool & Dist c1900 (£3.99 + p&p); A Handlist of Roman Catholic Parish records (£3 + p&p); A Handlist of Cemetery & Burial Records (£2.50 + p&p); Info Leaflet Pack (50p + p&p); CD-ROM of Photographs of Old Liverpool (£15 + p&p); Catalogues & Indexes
Staff: Archivists: 4 *Libns:* 1.5 *Non-Prof:* 9.5

A239

Merseyside Maritime Museum, Maritime Archives and Library

Albert Dock, Liverpool, L3 4AQ (0131-478-4418; *fax:* 0131-478-4590)
Email: maritime.archives@nmgm.org.uk
Internet: http://www.nmgm.org.uk

Type: special rsrch lib & archv *Gov Body:* Natl Museums & Galleries on Merseyside *Chief:* Curator of Archvs: Ms Dawn Littler BA, DipAA
Dep: Libn: Mrs Helen Threlfall BA(Hons)
Assoc Offices: WALKER ART GALLERY ARCHVS (see **A241**); REGIONAL HIST DEPT, at above addr, contact Curator of Regional Hist (0151-207-0001)
Entry: Maritime Archvs & Lib: daily ticket 50p; annual reader's ticket £6; adv appt preferred; 2 wks notice to access reserve collns; *Regional Hist Dept:* adv appt required *Open: Maritime Archvs & Lib:* Tue-Thu 1030-1630; *Regional Hist Dept:* Mon-Fri 1000-1700
Subj: maritime hist; maritime records; business records *Collns (Maritime Archvs & Lib): Bks & Pamphs:* ref lib of printed bks, pamphs & periodcls, incl: Lloyd's Registers (from 1764); Lloyd's Lists (from 1741); Customs Bills of Entry (from 1820); museum catalogues; nat hist material (reserve colln) *Archvs:* Liverpool Registers of Merchant Ships; records of Mersey Docks & Harbour Company (from 1709); Mersey Docklands Hist Survey; seamen's charity & educational records; technical records; shipping company records, incl: Bibby; Booth; Brockle-bank; Ocean PSNC; Ellermans Lamport & Holt; some Cunard; shipping trading assoc records; Bills of Entry for British & Irish ports; Liverpool Nautical Rsrch Soc records; diaries of emigrants & seamen; accounts of slave traders; eng & other business archvs, incl: Meccano; BICC; Vulcan Locomotive Works; Fawcett Eng (all reserve collns); *Other:* Capt Beard Colln (compilation by name of sailing ship hists, compiled by Capt Jack Beard DSC); Cochrane Colln (compilation by name of steam ship hists, compiled by Douglas B. Cochrane); McRoberts Photo Colln; Stewart Bale Photo Colln (reserve colln); other photos, maps & charts *Collns (Regional Hist Dept): Archvs:* business archvs associated with museum's collns; records of Unity Theatre, Liverpool; King's Regiment Archv
Equip: 3 m-form reader/printers, m-fiche reader/printer, copier (staff use only) *Svcs:* info, ref, biblio, photographic, plan reproduction
Stock: archvs/5400; periodcls/25; photos/50000; slides/3000; pamphs/4000; maps/1000; m-forms/1400; audios/400; videos/400; AVs/11 linear m
Classn: own
Pubns: Guide to the Records of Merseyside Maritime Museum (£9.95)
Staff: Archivists: 2 *Libns:* 2 *Other Prof:* 1 *Non-Prof:* 3

A240

Merseyside Record Office

Central Lib, William Brown St, Liverpool, L3 8EW (0151-233-5817; *fax:* 0151-233-5886)
Email: recoffice.central.library@liverpool.gov.uk
Internet: http://www.liverpool.gov.uk/

Gov Body: Liverpool City Council (see **P76**)
Chief: Mgr, Liverpool Record Office: Mr D.A. Stoker BA, MArAd *Dep:* Archivist: Ms R. Hobbins BA, MArAd
Assoc Offices: LIVERPOOL RECORD OFFICE & LOCAL STUDIES DEPT, at same addr (see **A238**)
Entry: readers ticket (requires proof of name & addr); adv appt essential for viewing m-forms (ring 0151-233-5811) *Open:* Mon-Thu 0900-2000, Fri 0900-1900, Sat 0900-1700, Sun 1200-1600; closed 3rd & 4th wks of Jun
Subj: records relating to the county of Merseyside as a whole or to more than one metropolitan dist: local authority archvs; estate archvs; family papers; business records; records of parent org; hosp records; nonconformist records; records of social agencies *Collns: Archvs:* Merseyside Development Corp archvs; records of Merseyside Passenger Transport Exec; records of Merseyside Fire Svc (mid 19C-date); Methodist & United Reform church records; coroners records for Liverpool, Southport & Wirral
Equip: 14 m-readers, 6 m-printers, copier, clr copier (in Central Lib), computer (incl internet)
Svcs: paid rsrch svc
Stock: archvs/69 cubic m; rec mgmt/170 cubic m
Classn: ISAD(G) *Auto Sys:* DS
Pubns: Guide to Holdings; Guide to Genealogical Sources Available (both free)
Staff: Archivists: 2

A241

Walker Art Gallery Archives

William Brown St, Liverpool, L3 8EL (*Fine Art Dept:* 0151-478-4102; *fax:* 0151-478-4190)
Email: thewalker@nmgm.org
Internet: http://www.nmgm.org.uk/walker/

Gov Body: Natl Museums & Galleries on Merseyside
Assoc Offices: MERSEYSIDE MARITIME MUSEUM (see **A239**)
Entry: adv appt, with 1 wks notice; bona fide students only, with a serious need to consult the collns; contact the Fine Art Dept at the Walker Art Gallery as above *Open:* Mon-Fri 1000-1700
Subj: hist of Walker Art Gallery & its collns; the arts on Merseyside *Collns: Archvs:* Walker Gallery archvs; Liverpool Academy archvs; artists' papers & correspondence *Other:* photos of Merseyside sculpture
Exp: £9000 (2000-01)

Livingston

A242

West Lothian Archives and Records Management Service

7 Rutherford Sq, Brucefield Industrial Est, Livingston, W Lothian, EH54 9BU (01506-460020; *fax:* 01506-416167)

Gov Body: West Lothian Council (see **P197**)
Chief: Archivist & Records Mgr: to be appointed
Assoc Offices: other records relating to the area, incl genealogical materials, are held at WEST LOTHIAN LOCAL HIST DEPT (see **A56**)
Entry: adv appt only *Open:* Mon-Thu 0900-1600, Fri 0900-1500
Subj: West Lothian: local authority archvs; records of parent org *Collns: Archvs:* West Lothian Council Archvs (1890-1998, incl predecessor authorities); Livingston Development Corp Archvs (1732-1997)
Stock: archvs/c370 linear m

Llandrindod Wells

A243

Powys County Archives Office

County Hall, Llandrindod Wells, Powys, LD1 5LG
(01597-826088; *fax:* 01597-826087)
Email: archives@powys.gov.uk
Internet: http://archives.powys.gov.uk/

Gov Body: Powys County Council (see **P149**)
Chief: Archvs Mgr: Miss Catherine Richards BA,
MArAd
Entry: CARN ticket; ref only; adv appt **Open:**
Tue-Thu 1000-1230, 1330-1700, Fri 1000-1230,
1330-1600
Subj: Powys (incl old counties of Brecknock,
Radnor & Montgomery): local authority archvs;
parish records (on m-film); estate archvs; family
papers; business records; records of parent org;
census returns (on m-fiche)
Equip: 4 m-readers, m-printer, copier, computer
Stock: archvs/138 cubic m; rec mgmt/268
cubic m; bks/15 linear m; maps/3 cubic m
Pubns: office leaflets: genl, family hist sources,
house hist sources (free); A Guide to the Powys
County Archvs Office (1993, £4 by post)
Staff: Other Prof: 2 Non-Prof: 1

Llandudno

A244

Conwy Archive and Modern Record Service

The Old Board School, Lloyd St, Llandudno,
Conwy, LL30 2YG (*tel & fax:* 01492-860882)
Email: archifau.archives@conwy.gov.uk
Internet: http://www.conwy.gov.uk/archives/

Type: local govt *Gov Body:* Conwy County
Borough Council (see **P29**) *Chief:* County Libn &
Archivist: Ms Rona Aldrich MLib, MCLIP *Dep:*
Snr Archivist: Ms Susan Ellis BA, DipAA
Assoc Offices: Archv Svc Pts (archvs on m-
form & local hist materials): COLWYN BAY LIB,
Woodland Rd West, Colwyn Bay, Conwy, LL29
7DH (01492-532358; *fax:* 01492-534474; *email:*
llyfr.lib.baecolwynbay@conwy.gov.uk);
LLANDUDNO LIB, Mostyn St, Llandudno, Conwy,
LL30 2RP (01492-574010/20; *fax:* 01492-876826;
email: llyfr.lib.llandudno@conwy.gov.uk);
Entry: ref only **Open:** Mon-Wed 1000-1230,
1330-1630
Subj: Conwy (Aberconwy Dist of old Caernarfon-
shire & Colwyn Dist of old Denbighshire): local
authority archvs; parish records; estate archvs;
family papers; business records; personal papers;
school records; solicitors' records; nonconformist
records; local hist *Collns: Archvs:* records of
County Borough Council & predecessors, incl:
Aberconwy Council (1974-96); Colwyn Council
(1896-1995); Conwy Borough (17C-1835); records
of Urban & Rural Dist Councils; Conwy Poor Law
Union records; records of Abergele Town Council
(1985-94); parish council records; Gorddinog
Estate Archv; Porter Colln (solicitors' records);
records of Roberts & Rogers Jones (auctioneers
& valuers, Llanrwst); Colwyn Bay & Llandudno
Joint Water Supply records; records of MAFF
Rsrch Station, Conwy; records of Colwyn Bay &
Llandudno English Methodist Circuit *Other:* maps
& plans; electoral registers (1945-98); photos &
prints (at Llandudno Lib); local newspapers
Equip: available at both svc pts: 2 m-readers,
m-reader/printer, copier *Svcs:* info, ref, rsrch
Staff: Archivists: 1 Non-Prof: 1

Llangefni

A245

Anglesey County Record Office (Archifdy Ynys Môn)

Shirehall, Glanhwfa Rd, Llangefni, Ynys Môn,
LL77 7TW (01248-752080)
Email: avxed@anglesey.gov.uk
Internet: http://www.ynysmon.gov.uk/

Gov Body: Cyngor Sir Ynys Môn / Isle of
Anglesey County Council (see **P3**) *Chief:*
County Archivist: Ms Anne Venables BA, DipAA
Dep: Archvs Asst: Ms Gaynor Nice BA
Entry: CARN, booking recommended for m-
forms **Open:** Mon-Fri 0900-1300, 1400-1700;
closed 1st full wk of Nov
Subj: documentary heritage of Anglesey & its
people: local authority archvs; parish records;
estate archvs; family papers; business records;
personal papers; records of parent org; school
records; poor law records; nonconformist records;
police records *Collns: Archvs:* archvs of Isle of
Anglesey County Council & predecessors;
Quarter Sessions records *Other:* census returns
(m-form); local newspapers; maps; photos
Equip: 5 m-readers, copier *Svcs:* info, ref, rsrch
Stock: archvs/65 cubic m, incl photos, slides,
illusts, maps, m-forms, audios & videos; various
periodcls & pamphs
Pubns: Gwynedd Archvs & Museums Svc
pubns; Brief guides to particular topics (free);
Ynys Môn/Isle of Anglesey, compiled by Philip
Steele (Chalford)
Staff: Archivists: 1.25 Non-Prof: 1.5 *Exp:*
£5660 (2000-01)

A246

Oriel Ynys Môn, Archives and Local Studies Collection

Llangefni, Ynys Môn, LL77 7TQ (01248-724444;
fax: 01248-750282)
Email: OrielYnysMon@anglesey.gov.uk
Internet: http://www.ynysmon.gov.uk/english/
culture/oriel/oriel.htm

Chief: contact the Principal Heritage Offcr
Entry: ref only **Open:** Tue-Sat 1030-1700; also
open bank hols
Subj: Anglesey/Ynys Môn: local studies *Collns:*
Archvs: MSS, sketchbks, drawings, etc of
Charles Tunnicliffe (artist, 1901-1979)

Loanmead

A247

Midlothian Records Centre and Local Studies Department

2 Clerk St, Loanmead, Midlothian, EH20 9DR
(0131-271-3976; *fax:* 0131-440-4635)
Email: local.studies@midlothian.gov.uk
Internet: http://www.midlothian.gov.uk/Library/

Gov Body: Midlothian Council (see **P116**) *Chief:*
Archivist: Ms Ruth Calvert MA, DipMuseum/
GalleryStudies *Other Snr Staff:* Local Studies
Offcr: Ms Sheila Millar
Entry: ref only, proof of ID required **Open:** Mon
0900-1700 & 1800-2000, Tue-Thu 0900-1700, Fri
0900-1545
Subj: Midlothian area: local authority archvs;
estate archvs; family papers; personal papers;
records of local socs; local studies *Collns: Bks
& Pamphs:* Marwick Colln (Scottish economic &
labour hist); 19C directories; reports of the Royal
Commission on the Ancient & Historic Monuments
of Scotland *Archvs:* Midlothian Dist Archv Colln
(records of Midlothian Council & predecessors);

Black Colln (material on Penicuik) *Other:*
valuation rolls (1855-date); census returns; OS
maps; prints & photos; cuttings; local newspapers
Equip: 2 m-readers, m-printer, copier
Stock: archvs/206 linear m
Pubns: incl: The Dalkeith Tolbooth & Market
Cross (£5); Midlothian Gravestones (£6.95); The
Origins of Street Names in Dalkeith (£6.99); Early
Railways of the Lothians (£3.95); New Statistical
Account of Midlothian (Part 1 £2.75, Part 2 £2.95,
Part 3 £3.50); The Midlothian 2000 CD-ROM (£15)
Staff: Archivists: 1 Libns: 1

Lochgilphead

A248

Argyll and Bute Archives

Manse Brae, Lochgilphead, Argyll, PA31 8QU
(01546-604120; *fax:* 01546-606897)

Gov Body: Argyll & Bute Council (see **P5**)
Chief: Archivist: Mr Murdo McDonald
Entry: adv appt **Open:** Tue-Fri 1000-1300,
1400-1630
Subj: Argyll & Bute area: local authority archvs;
diocesan records; estate archvs; business
records; records of parent org; records of some
local clubs & socs *Collns: Bks & Pamphs:* small
ref lib *Archvs:* records of Argyll & Bute Council &
predecessors, incl Argyll & Bute County Council
records (1890-1975) & Argyll & Bute Dist Council
records (1975-1996); burgh records; records of
Episcopal Diocese of Argyll & the Isles (mid 19-
20C); major estate collns incl: Campbell of
Kilberry Papers (c1700-20C); Malcolm of
Poltalloch Papers (c1750-20C); business records
incl: records of Thomas Corson & Co (livestock
auctioneers); records of Campbeltown Coal Co;
records of Campbeltown Whisky Distilleries
Other: local newspapers; OS maps; valuation
rolls; electoral registers; monumental inscriptions
Equip: copier
Stock: archvs/360 linear m
Staff: Other Prof: 1 Non-Prof: 1 (PT)

London

A249

Alfred Dunhill Archive

27 Knightsbridge, London, SW1X 7YB (020-7838-
8233; *fax:* 020-7838-8556)
Email: peter.tilley@alfreddunhill.co.uk
Internet: http://www.dunhill.com/

Chief: Curator: Mr Peter Tilley
Entry: adv appt **Open:** Mon-Fri 0900-1700
Subj: business records; records of parent org
Collns: Archvs: records of Alfred Dunhill (retailer
of menswear & accessories, 1899-date)

A250

Archive of Art and Design

Blythe House, 23 Blythe Rd, London, W14 0QX
(020-7603-1514; *fax:* 020-7602-6907)
Email: archives@vam.ac.uk
Internet: http://www.nal.vam.ac.uk/

Gov Body: Victoria & Albert Museum *Chief:*
Head of Archvs: Ms Serena Kelly
Assoc Offices: the Archv is a section of the
NATL ART LIB (see **S1290**); V&A ARCHV, at
same addr (see **A353**)
Entry: by appt, proof of ID required **Open:**
Archv Reading Room: Thu-Thu 1000-1630; Paolozzi
Study Room: Thu 1000-1300 (appt only); closed
for 3 wks for stocktaking from the Sat before Aug
Bank Hol

(Archv of Art & Design cont)
Subj: exhibs & exhib design; fashion design; furniture design; graphic design; bk illust; interior design; metalwork design; stained glass design; textile design **Collns: Bks & Pamphs:** ref lib of bks & periodcls **Archvs:** over 200 archvs, incl: Ambassador (British Export magazine for textiles & fashion); Arts & Crafts Exhib Soc archvs; papers of Sir Cecil Beaton (photographer & stage designer); Crafts Council archvs; papers of John French (fashion photographer); papers of Eileen Gray (interior designer & architect); records of Heal & Son (bedding manufacturers & retailers); records of House of Worth, Paris (couture firm); records of Lilley & Skinner (shoe manufacturers & retailers); records of James Powell & Son (Whitefriars) Ltd (stained glass manufacturers); Sir Eduardo Paolozzi's Krazy Kat Arkive (20C popular culture); Royal Soc of British Artists Archv **Other:** printed ephemera
Equip: facilities for laptops **Svcs:** info, ref
Classn: ISAD(G), EAD
Pubns: Guide to the Archv of Art & Design, by Elizabeth Lomas (V&A Museum, 2000); various other pubns exist about the Archv or based on rsrch into its holdings

A251
Archive of the Society of Jesus in Britain
114 Mount St, London, W1Y 3AH (020-7493-7811)
Email: info@jesuit.org.uk

Gov Body: Trustees for Roman Catholic Purposes Registered **Chief:** Archivist: Thomas M. McCoog SJ
Entry: private archv; consultation only by appt
Subj: United Kingdom: official records of the British Province; personal papers of deceased membs of the Province **Collns: Bks & Pamphs:** extensive colln of post-Reformation religious works from the United Kingdom **Archvs:** historical papers of the British Jesuits
Equip: m-reader, copier **Staff:** Non-Prof: 1

A252
Archives of the Archdiocese of Southwark (RC)
Archbishop's House, 150 St Georges Rd, Southwark, London, SE1 6HX (020-7928-2495; *fax:* 020-7928-7833)
Email: michael_clifton@st-thomas-aquinas.co.uk

Gov Body: RC Archdiocese of Southwark
Chief: Archivist: Rev Michael Clifton
Entry: adv appt only
Subj: South London, Kent, Surrey, Sussex: diocesan records: of Southwark (RC); parish records of diocese **Collns: Bks & Pamphs:** bks on English & Scottish church hist **Archvs:** papers of Rev Percival Styche (d 1961): Elizabethan hist & Marian papers; Rev Godfrey Anstruther OP (d 1985): rsrch papers on RC English martyrs; papers of Canon Roy Fletcher (English church hist); papers of Geoffrey Parmenter (Elizabethan & Stuart Catholic hist); papers of Catholic Record Soc (English Catholic church hist)
Equip: m-fiche reader, fax, copier, clr copier
Svcs: info, ref, rsrch

Stock: archvs/30 m; bks/10 m
Pubns: Hist of the Archdiocese of Southwark, by Rev Michael Clifton (1999, £5)
Staff: Non-Prof: 2

A253
Bank of England Archive
Bank of England, Threadneedle St, London, EC2R 8AH (020-7601-5096; *fax:* 020-7601-4356)
Email: archive@bankofengland.co.uk
Internet: http://www.bankofengland.co.uk/

Gov Body: Bank of England **Chief:** Archivist: Ms Sarah Millard BA(Hons), DipAA
Assoc Offices: BANK OF ENGLAND INFO CENTRE (see **S1008**)
Entry: by prior arrangement only **Open:** Mon-Fri 1000-1630
Subj: internatl: records of parent org; banking; economic hist; finance & monetary **Collns: Archvs:** Bank of England records from 1694, incl: ledger series of customer accounts & govt stock holders; branch records; staff records; diaries & papers of staff membs; records of Bank's solicitors (incl case files on forgery & prisoners' correspondence) **Other:** arch plans & drawings
Stock: archvs/6000 linear m **Staff:** Archivists: 2

A254
Bankside Gallery Archives
48 Hopton St, Blackfriars, London, SE1 9JH (020-7928-7521; *fax:* 020-7928-2820)
Email: info@banksidegallery.com
Internet: http://www.banksidegallery.com/

Type: art gallery **Gov Body:** Bankside Gallery Trustees **Chief:** Archivist: Mr Simon Fenwick BA(Hons)
Entry: adv appt **Open:** on application
Subj: Gt Britain: business records; artistic socs **Collns: Bks & Pamphs:** catalogue colln of artists & artistic socs **Archvs:** Bankside Gallery archvs; archvs of Royal Watercolour Soc (founded 1804); archvs of Royal Soc of Painter-Printmakers (founded 1880) **Other:** Diploma collns of water-colour paintings & prints
Equip: copier, computer **Svcs:** info, ref, rsrch
Stock: archvs/60 ft; rec mgmt/150 ft; bks/50 ft
Pubns: The Business of Watercolour: A Guide to the Archvs of the RWS, by Simon Fenwick & Greg Smith (Ashgate, 1997)
Staff: Archivists: 1 Non-Prof: 1

A255
Barnet Archives and Local Studies Centre
c/o Hendon Lib, The Burroughs, London, NW4 4BQ (020-8359-2876; *fax:* 020-8359-2885)
Email: library.archives@barnet.gov.uk
Internet: http://www.barnet.gov.uk/

Gov Body: London Borough of Barnet (see **P78**)
Chief: Borough Archivist: Mr Andrew Mussell
Assoc Offices: Local Studies & Archvs Centre is located at: HENDON CATHOLIC SOCIAL CENTRE, Chapel Walk, Egerton Gdns, London, NW4 4EH; addr all enqs to Hendon Lib as above
Entry: adv appt required **Open:** Tue-Wed, Sat 0930-1230, 1330-1700, Thu 1230-1930; closed Mon & Fri
Subj: London Borough of Barnet: local authority archvs; parish records; estate archvs; family papers; business records; records of parent org; nonconformist church records; records of local insts & socs; hist & topography of area & material reflecting life in the borough **Collns: Bks & Pamphs:** Hendon Aerodrome Colln (bks, programmes of air shows & pageants, material on the aerodrome personnel etc); Golders Green

Hippodrome Colln (theatre programmes); local directories **Archvs:** official signed minutes & accounts of London Borough of Barnet Council & its predecessors **Other:** Mill Hill Historical Soc Colln (pamphs, photos, rsrch notes, cuttings); electoral registers; map colln; local newspapers (on m-film); illusts colln (paintings, photos & postcards)
Equip: m-form reader/printer, copier
Stock: archvs/1074 linear m
Pubns: Guide to London Local Hist Resources: London Borough of Barnet (free; currently o/p)
Staff: Archivists: 1 Non-Prof: 2

BBC Sound Archive
See BRITISH LIB SOUND ARCHV in British Lib entry (**L1**) for public access to the BBC's recorded sound archvs

A256
Black Cultural Archives
378 Coldharbour Ln, Brixton, London, SW9 8LF (020-7738-4591; *fax:* 020-7738-7168)
Email: info@aambh.org.uk

Gov Body: African Peoples Historical Monument Foundation **Chief:** Dir: Mr Sam Walker BA, PG DipLIS
Entry: adv appt **Open:** Mon-Fri 1000-1600
Subj: United Kingdom: records related to the hist & culture of Black people in Britain **Collns: Bks & Pamphs:** poems of Cain & Field, Paul Lawrence Dunbar 1899; Buxton on the slave trade 1839; Life & Times of Mary Seacole; Black People in Victorian Times for Primary Schools; Black People in London Transport **Archvs:** photos; documentation; original records of indentured slavery; Black newspapers; family papers; MSS **Other:** secondary src materials covering various aspects of Black life, hist & experiences; exhibs: Hist of the Black Presence in London; The Forgotten Blacks; Myth of the Motherland
Equip: video viewer, fax, copier, computer (with wd-proc) **Svcs:** info, ref, rsrch
Stock: archvs/c20000 documents & other items, incl printed materials, photos, audios & videos
Pubns: Life & Times of Mary Seacole (£11.99); Windrush Legacy (£3.50)
Staff: Non-Prof: 1 **Exp:** £3000 (2000-01)
Proj: Natl Museum & Archvs of Black Hist & Culture (a partnership proj with Middlesex Univ – see **S1282**); revenue grant of £344000 awarded to partnership proj to enhance access to & catalogue current holdings of Black Cultural Archvs

A257
The Board of Deputies of British Jews, Archives
6 Bloomsbury Sq, London, WC1A 2LP (020-7543-5400; *fax:* 020-7543-0010)
Email: info@bod.org.uk
Internet: http://www.bod.org.uk/

Chief: Dir Genl: Mr Neville Nagler **Dep:** Administrative Dir: Ms Sandra Clark
Assoc Offices: archvs are deposited at LONDON METROPOLITAN ARCHVS (see **A304**), but contact the Board of Deputies as above for access permission
Entry: permission is required in writing; application form available from Board of Deputies at above addr or on web site
Subj: records of parent org **Collns: Archvs:** archvs of The Board of Deputies of British Jews

A258

Brent Community History Archive

152 Olive Rd, Cricklewood, London, NW2 6UY
(020-8937-3541; *fax:* 020-8450-5211)
Email: archive@brent.gov.uk
Internet: http://www.brent.gov.uk/

Gov Body: London Borough of Brent (see **P80**)
Chief: Archivist: Mr Ian Johnston
Entry: no restrictions, but adv appt advised for complex enqs *Open:* Mon 1300-1700, Tue 1000-1700, Thu 1300-2000, Sat 0930-1700
Subj: London Borough of Brent: local authority archvs; parish records; family papers; business records; personal papers; political papers; records of parent org; local studies; borough hist *Collns: Archvs:* archvs of London Borough of Brent
Equip: m-printer, fax, copier, 2 computers (both with wd-proc, internet & CD-ROM) *Svcs:* info, ref, rsrch
Classn: ISAD(G) *Auto Sys:* Adlib
Staff: Archivists: 1 *Non-Prof:* 2

A259

British Museum Central Archives

Gt Russell St, Bloomsbury, London, WC1B 3DG
(020-7323-8224; *fax:* 020-7323-8118)
Email: archives@thebritishmuseum.ac.uk
Internet: http://www.thebritishmuseum.ac.uk/

Type: natl museum *Gov Body:* British Museum, Dept of Archvs & Libs (see **S1028**) *Chief:* Head of Archvs: Mr Christopher Date MA, RMSA (cdate@thebritishmuseum.ac.uk) *Dep:* Museum Records Mgr: Mr Stephen Plant MA (splant@thebritishmuseum.ac.uk)
Assoc Offices: records of the Museum's curatorial & admininstrative depts are held by those depts
Entry: adv appt only *Open:* Tue, Thu 1000-1300, 1400-1630
Subj: museology; personal papers; records of parent org *Collns: Archvs:* administrative records of the British Museum (1753-date), incl pre-1973 Reading Room records, covering meetings of Trustees, acquisitions, finance, bldgs, staff, exhibs, pubns & excavations; various other materials relating to the hist of the museum & its collns; personal archv of Charles Townley (antiquarian & collector of classical antiquities, 1737-1805), incl: autograph catalogues of his colln; annotated sales catalogues; travel diaries; correspondence with friends, collectors & dealers; papers of Baron d'Hancarville (Pierre Francois Hugues) *Other:* sketches, arch plans & drawings, scrapbks, press cuttings & photos
Equip: available to users: 2 m-readers, 2 m-printers; staff only: copier, fax, 5 computers (all with wd-proc, 3 with internet) *Online:* PROCAT (Public Record Office catalogue) *Svcs:* info, ref, rsrch
Stock: archvs/600 linear m; rec mgmt/3500 linear m; photos/c10000; illusts/c1000; audios/c50; arch plans & drawings/c3000
Classn: ISAD(G)
Pubns: Catalogue of the Townley Archv at the British Museum, by S.J. Hill (BM Press, 2002, £12); Building the British Museum, by M. Caygill & C. Date (BM Press, 1999, £8.50)
Staff: Archivists: 3 *Non-Prof:* 1 *Exp:* £1600 (2000-01)

A260

British Red Cross Museum and Archives

9 Grosvenor, London, SW1X 7EJ (020-7201-5153; *fax:* 020-7235-0876)
Email: enquiry@redcross.org.uk
Internet: http://www.redcross.org.uk/

Type: charity *Gov Body:* British Red Cross Soc *Chief:* Curator: Ms Elaine Fisher BA, MA
Dep: Archivist: Mrs Helen Pugh BA, DipAA
Entry: adv appt, ref only *Open:* Mon-Fri 1000-1300, 1400-1600
Subj: UK & Commonwealth: personal papers; records of parent org; first aid; nursing; medicine; biography; personal memoirs *Collns: Bks & Pamphs:* British Red Cross Soc Manuals (first aid, nursing etc.) from 1912; British Natl Soc for Aid to Sick & Injured in Work (BNAS) Reports (1870-1905); BRCS pubns, incl: Annual Reports, journals etc (1905-date); Review of the Internatl Cttee of the Red Cross (ICRC) (1919-date); Internatl Federation of Red Cross & Red Crescent Socs Weekly News (1982-date) *Archvs:* archvs & museum artifacts from British Red Cross Natl HQ, regions & branches (UK & overseas dependencies); papers of indivs who have served with the Soc, such as Lord Wantage, 1st Chairman BRCS (1870-1901)
Equip: video viewer, copier (via staff)
Classn: own
Pubns: Factsheets: No 1: Story of the Changi Quilts (£1.20); No 2: Indoor Uniform 1911-1980 (£1.20); No 3: Medals & Badges (£3)
Staff: Archivists: 1 *Other Prof:* 1 *Non-Prof:* 1

A261

BT Group Archives

3rd Floor, Holborn Tel Exchange, 268-270 High Holborn, London, WC1V 7EE (020-7492-8792; *fax:* 020-7242-1967)
Email: archives@bt.com
Internet: http://www.btplc.com/archives/

Gov Body: BT Group plc *Chief:* Head of Group Archvs: Mr David A. Hay BA, DipAA
Entry: adv appt *Open:* Tue, Thu 1000-1600
Subj: business records; records of parent org
Collns: Bks & Pamphs: historical telecommunications lib (18C-date), incl: tel directories (1879-date); printed journals & periodcls; historical & scientific works; local hists; BT & external pubns & reports *Archvs:* records relating to telecommunications function of Post Office & predecessor private companies (1830s-date); records of BT (1980-date) *Other:* visual materials lib (19C-date), incl photo, video & film collns
Equip: 4 m-readers, 4 m-printers, video viewer, 2 copiers, 2 computers (both with wd-proc & CD-ROM)
Stock: archvs/2000 linear m
Classn: ISAD(G) *Auto Sys:* DBTextworks
Pubns: User's Guide to the BT Archvs (leaflet, free); Guide to Events in Telecommunications Hist (leaflet, free); Historical Summary of BT (leaflet, free)
Staff: Archivists: 2 *Non-Prof:* 2

A262

Camden Local Studies and Archives Centre

Holborn Lib, 32-38 Theobalds Rd, London, WC1X 8PA (020-7974-6342; *fax:* 020-7974-6284)
Email: localstudies@camden.gov.uk
Internet: http://www.camden.gov.uk/localstudies/

Gov Body: London Borough of Camden (see **P82**) *Chief:* Principal Offcr, Local Studies & Archvs: Mr R.G. Knight BA, MCLIP
Entry: no restrictions *Open:* Mon, Thu 1000-1900, Tue, Fri 1000-1800, Sat 1000-1300, 1400-1700
Subj: London Borough of Camden: local authority archvs; parish records; estate archvs; family papers; business papers; personal papers; records of parent org; records of local socs; local studies *Collns: Bks & Pamphs:* Bellmoor Colln (hist of Hampstead, 21 vols); Eleanor Farjeon Colln (c150 vols); G.B. Shaw Colln (incl 1st eds, pamphs, photos & letters); Kate Greenaway Colln (printed items & illusts, c1400 items, by special application only); local studies vols; local directories *Archvs:* archvs of London Borough of Camden (1965-date) & predecessors; records of Metropolitan Boroughs of Hampstead, Holborn & St Pancras (1900-1965); parish records, excl parish registers (1617-1900); records of dist boards of works (1856-1900); records of local commissioners & boards (1850-1906); Hampstead Manor records; Highgate Cemetery records (1839-1894); title deeds; other documents *Other:* Dalziel Colln (c250 proof engravings); Heal Colln (ephemera, illusts maps etc about St Pancras to 1913); extensive colln of illusts, incl photos & slides; OS, parish & other maps; monumental inscriptions; local newspapers; cuttings; ephemera; oral hist tapes; census returns (1841-1901, on m-film)
Equip: 6 m-readers, m-printer, copier, fax, computers (incl internet) *Svcs:* info, ref
Stock: archvs/1584 linear m; bks/12000; periodcls/200; slides/5000; illusts/40000 incl photos; pamphs/13000; maps/3000; m-forms/12000; audios/200; videos/30
Classn: own
Pubns: Camden Past & Present: A Guide to the Camden Local Studies & Archvs Centre, edited by Mark Aston, Malcolm J. Holmes & Richard G. Knight (£2.95 + 75p p&p); info sheets on materials available (free)
Staff: Archivists: 2 *Libns:* 3 *Other Prof:* 0.5 (conservator) *Non-Prof:* 1

A263

Cameron Mackintosh Archive

1 Bedford Sq, London, WC1B 3RA (020-7637-8866; *fax:* 020-7436-2683)
Email: rosy@camack.co.uk

Chief: Archivist: Ms Rosy Runciman BA, MCLIP, FRSA
Entry: by prior appt *Open:* Mon-Thu 1000-1800
Subj: musicals; theatre; business records; records of parent org *Collns: Archvs:* archvs of Cameron Mackintosh Productions (1967-date), incl promptbks, correspondence, official documents & production materials etc *Other:* programmes; clippings; posters; technical plans & drawings; production photos; memorabilia; audio colln
Equip: copier *Svcs:* info, reprographic svc (fees)

CGU plc Archives

See AVIVA COMPANY ARCHV (**A396**)

A264

The Children's Society Archive

Record & Archv Centre, Floor 2, Block A, Tower Bridge Business Complex, 100 Clement's Rd, Bermondsey, London, SE16 4DG (020-7232-2966; *fax:* 020-7232-3902)
Email: archives@the-childrens-society.org.uk
Internet: http://www.the-childrens-society.org.uk/

Chief: Archivist: Mr Ian Wakeling BA(Hons), DipAA
Assoc Offices: CHILDREN'S SOC LIB (see **S1078**)
Entry: adv appt *Open:* Mon-Fri 1000-1630
Subj: social policy; social welfare; child care issues; fundraising; voluntary sector; religion *Collns: Bks & Pamphs:* pamphs: Supporter Magazines: Our Waifs & Strays (1882-1952); Gateway (1953-1993); Children in Focus (1993 to date); Brothers & Sisters (The Journal of the Children's Union, 1890-1970); Annual Reports (1882-1993); financial statements & accounts (1882-1993)

London
▼
London
Archives

(The Children's Soc Archv cont)

Collns: Archvs: selection comprises documents relating to the work of The Children's Soc since its founding in 1881; series incl material on the development & implementation of the Soc's social work policy & practice (incl case files & records of residential ch's homes & social work projs), & fundraising campaigns
Equip: 2 m-readers, fax, copier
Stock: archvs/1500 linear ft; rec mgmt/3500 linear ft; photos/10000; slides/500; videos/50
Auto Sys: MS Access cataloguing sys
Staff: Archivists: 2 *Non-Prof:* 2

A265
Christie's Archives
8 King St, St James's, London, SW1Y 6QT (020-7389-2617; *fax:* 020-7389-2998)
Email: lmcleod@christies.com
Internet: http://www.christies.com/

Chief: Libn: Miss Lynda McLeod *Dep: Archivist:* Mr Jeremy Rex-Parkes
Entry: ref only, adv appt, proof of ID *Open:* Mon-Fri 0900-1700
Subj: arts *Collns: Archvs:* Christie's sales catalogues (1766-date)
Equip: m-reader, m-printer, fax, copier (fee)
Svcs: info, ref *Staff: Libns:* 1 *Non-Prof:* 2

A266
Church of England Record Centre
15 Galleywall Rd, South Bermondsey, London, SE16 3PB (020-7898-1030; *fax:* 020-7394-7018)
Email: archivist@c-of-e.org.uk

Gov Body: Archbishops' Council of the C of E
Chief: Dir: Dr Wendy Sudbury MA, PhD *Other Snr Staff: Archivist & Records Mgr:* Mr Philip Gale BA, MArAd; *Systems Mgr:* Mr Tom Alves
Assoc Offices: held by the Record Centre: NATL SOC ARCHVS & LIB, *Archivist:* Miss Sarah Duffield BA, MArAd (see **A314**)
Entry: adv appt *Open:* Mon & Wed 1000-1630
Subj: England (England & Wales in the case of Natl Soc records): estate archvs; business records; political papers; records of parent org; religion *Collns: Archvs:* British Council of Churches Archv; archvs of the Church Commissioners (incl estates) & its predecessor orgs of the Ecclesiastical Commissioners (1835-1948) & the Queen Anne's Bounty (1704-1948); records of the Church Assembly (1919-1970); records of the Genl Synod (1970-date); business records of central Church bodies *Other:* back issues of Church Times
Equip: copier (30p per pg) *Svcs:* info, ref, rsrch
Stock: archvs/13700 linear m, incl records mgmt; bks/150 linear m; some photos
Classn: own *Auto Sys:* Idealist
Pubns: leaflets, mostly for internal use
Staff: Archivists: 3 *Non-Prof:* 8 *Exp:* archvs accrue from parent orgs & there is no separate conservation budget
Proj: renovation of existing premises, winter 2002-03
Further Info: The Public Search Room is expected to be relocated to Lambeth Palace Lib (see **S1234**) late in 2002 on an experimental basis; rsrchers should continue to contact the C of E Record Centre for bookings & enqs

A267
Cinema Museum, Ronald Grant Archive
The Master's House, 2 Dugard Way, London (020-7840-2200; *fax:* 020-7840-2299)
Email: martin@cinemamuseum.org.uk

Chief: Curator: Mr Martin Humphries
Entry: adv appt *Open:* Mon-Fri 0900-1700
Subj: film; cinema; drama; theatre; music hall; theatre arch; radio; television *Collns: Bks & Pamphs:* small lib of theatre bks, annuals, yearbks, magazines, biographies & ref works; Spotlight (casting directories) *Archvs:* minute bk of Una Plays Ltd; colln of Matheson Lang contracts; MSS & correspondence of actors & theatre personalities *Other:* theatre photos, prints & postcards (several 1000, 19C-date); theatre programmes (several 1000, 19C-date); theatre & variety posters (several 100); photos of theatre facades; clippings; designs & plans; sheet music from shows & musicals; audio & video colln, incl gramophone recordings of theatre personalities; costumes & memorabilia
Equip: copier

A268
City of Westminster Archives Centre
10 St Ann's St, London, SW1P 2DE (020-7641-5180; *fax:* 020-7641-5179)
Email: archives@westminster.gov.uk
Internet: http://www.westminster.gov.uk/archives/

Gov Body: Westminster City Council (see **P110**)
Chief: Acting City Archivist: Mr J. Sargent
Entry: ref only *Open:* Mon, Fri-Sat 0930-1700, Tue-Thu 0930-1900
Subj: City of Westminster (some items dating back to 13C): local authority archvs; diocesan records; parish records; estate archvs; family papers; business records; personal papers; political records; manorial records; military & militia records; nonconformist records; school records; hosp records; housing assoc records; records of local clubs & socs; local hist; family hist *Collns: Bks & Pamphs:* Westminster Hist Colln (local hist); Ashbridge Colln (private lib relating to Marylebone, 4630 items); Preston Blake Colln (on William Blake, c700 vols); ref colln relating to London generally; extensive pamph colln *Archvs:* archvs of Westminster City Council & predecessor bodies; records of the Diocese of Westminster; Grosvenor Estate Archvs (18000 deeds); records of Westminster Conservative Assoc (1863-1994); records of Union Soc of the City of Westminster (1836-1993); Royal Botanic Soc Archvs (1838-1931); Gillow Archvs (furniture makers, 1784-1905); Jaeger & Co Archvs (1883-date); Liberty & Co Archvs (1883-date); Watney Mann Archvs (brewers, 1784-1960); Royal Botanic Soc Archvs (Marylebone) *Other:* Theatre Colln (programmes & playbills); newspapers; prints & drawings; photos (incl aerial photos); maps & plans; electoral registers *Co-op Schemes:* London Discovery, Backstage, A2A
Equip: 14 m-readers (11 film, 3 fiche), 3 m-form reader/printers (2 film, 1 fiche), copier, 3 computers (all with CD-ROM, 2 with internet & 1 with wd-proc), room for hire *Disabled:* induction loop, wheelchair access *Svcs:* info, ref, photographic svc, talks, exhibs, ad edu courses, svcs to schools
Stock: archvs/737 cubic m; bks/23000; periodcls/116; slides/5548; illusts/c57000, incl prints & photos; maps/4500; m-forms/5722; theatre programmes/30000; cuttings/c32000
Classn: DDC (mod for local hist materials) *Auto Sys:* Geac, CALM

Pubns: numerous, incl: Blitz over Westminster (£4); Tracing the Hist of Your House (£3.50); Pineapples & Pantomime (£3.50); postcards; maps
Staff: Archivists: 4 *Libns:* 2 *Other Prof:* 1 conservator *Non-Prof:* 6 *Exp:* £20000 (2000-01)

A269
College of Arms, Archives
Queen Victoria St, London, EC4V 4BT (020-7248-2762; *fax:* 020-7248-6448)
Internet: http://www.college-of-arms.gov.uk/

Chief: Archivist: Mr R.C. Yorke
Entry: adv appt, proof of ID required; a fee may be payable *Open:* Mon-Fri 1000-1600
Subj: genealogy; heraldry; personal papers
Collns: Bks & Pamphs: genealogical & heraldic works *Archvs:* official records of the Coll (c750 MS vols), incl: registers of grants of arms; funeral certificates; records of heraldic visitations; changes of name & arms by Royal License; pedigree registers; unofficial & MS collns (from 14C onwards), incl working papers & other MSS of past heralds
Svcs: rsrch

A270
Corporation of London Records Office
PO Box 270, Guildhall, London, EC2P 2EJ (020-7332-1251; *fax:* 020-7710-8682)
Email: clro@corpoflondon.gov.uk
Internet: http://www.cityoflondon.gov.uk/archives/clro/

Gov Body: Corp of the City of London (see **P99**)
Chief: City Archivist: Mr J.R. Sewell MA, FSA, OBE *Dep: Dep City Archivist:* Mrs J.M. Bankes MA
Entry: ref only, adv notice appreciated *Open:* Mon-Fri 0930-1645
Subj: City of London (also some material for other areas of London, particularly Southwark): local authority archvs; estate archvs; records of parent org; hosp records; court records; school records; coroner's records *Collns: Archvs:* archvs of the Corp of the City of London, incl: charters (1067-1957); administrative records of the City (1275-date); financial records (1381-1942); judicial & court records (17C onwards); Freedom records (admissions to the Freedom of the City, 1681-1940); other collns incl: records of the Irish Soc (1613-20C, records of Plantation of Ulster & mgmt of estates there, with much material on Coleraine & Londonderry); records of the Guildhall School of Music & Drama (1876-1986); records of the City of London Lunatic Asylum/Mental Hosp (1866-1968); Bridge House Estates (medieval period-1942); City Lands (medieval period-1942); Finsbury Estate (16C-19C); Royal Contract Estates (mainly 17C); records relating to Southwark (incl coroner's, manorial & sessions records, 16C-20C); Thames Conservancy records (medieval-1857); Lieutenancy of London records (militia records, 17C-20C) *Other:* City Imperial Volunteers Colln (photos, publ material, insignia, medals etc, c1900 & later); arch plans & drawings (15C-date)
Equip: 3 m-readers, m-printer, photocopying through the Record Office staff *Disabled:* wheelchair access
Stock: archvs/6000 linear m; rec mgmt/340 linear m
Pubns: Calendar of Wills proved & rolled in the Court of Husting, London 1258-1688 (£40 per set); Calendar of Coroners Rolls of the City of London 1300-1378 (£15); Calendars of Pleas & Memoranda Rolls: Vol xxviii 1437-1457; Vol xxi 1458-1482 (£15 each – other vols o/p); The Fire Court: Calendar to the Decrees of the Court of Judicature on disputes as to rebuilding after the

Great Fire: Vols 1 & 2 1667-1668 (£10 each); Southwark & the City (£15); leaflets; numerous postcards & postcard sets
Staff: Archivists: 6 *Other Prof:* 2 *Non-Prof:* 3

A271

Coutts & Co, Archives Department
440 Strand, London, WC2R 0QS (020-7753-1000; *fax:* 020-7753-1051)
Internet: http://www.coutts.com/

Chief: Archivist: Miss Tracey Earl
Entry: by adv application in writing
Subj: banking; business records; records of parent org *Collns: Archvs:* records of Coutts & Co (bank, c1692-1980)

Docklands Archive
See DOCKLANDS LIB & ARCHV (**S1114**)

A272

The D'Oyly Carte Opera Company Archive
6 Sancroft St, London, SE11 5UD (020-7793-7100; *fax:* 020-7793-7300)
Email: mary@doylycarte.org.uk
Internet: http://www.doylycarte.org.uk/

Type: charitable trust *Gov Body:* D'Oyly Carte Opera Trust Ltd *Chief:* Archivist: Ms Mary Gilhooly MA
Entry: archvs are still being catalogued; not currently open to rsrchers
Subj: opera; business records; records of parent org *Collns: Archvs:* archvs of the D'Oyly Carte Opera Company (1880-date), incl: financial records (1890s onwards); company correspondence (1900s onwards) *Other:* press clippings (1900s onwards); company programmes (1930s onwards); production & publicity photographs; posters; promptbks
Svcs: limited enq svc (tel, email or written); a charge is made for rsrch undertaken

A273

The Drapers' Company Archive
Drapers' Hall, Throgmorton Ave, London, EC2N 2DQ (020-7588-5001; *fax:* 020-7628-1988)

Type: charity, livery company *Chief:* Archivist: Miss P.A. Fussell BA(Hons), MA, DipAS
Entry: by appt only after written application
Open: Mon-Fri 0930-1630
Subj: London: records of parent org; local studies; geog; hist *Collns: Bks & Pamphs:* bks by William Lambarde (1536-1601) incl his own copy of his 'Perambulation of Kent' 1576 *Archvs:* archvs of The Drapers' Company incl charters, minutes, accounts & title deeds (13C onwards)
Equip: m-film reader, copier (via staff)
Stock: archvs/900 linear ft; bks/1500; photos/600; slides/300; illusts/2000 plans & drawings; videos/3
Pubns: The Triple Crowns: A Narrative Hist of the Drapers' Company, 1364-1964 (£5); A Hist of the Drapers' Company (£35)
Staff: Archivists: 1

A274

Ealing Local History Centre
Central Lib, 103 Ealing Broadway Centre, Ealing, London, W5 5JY (020-8567-3656; *fax:* 020-8840-2351)
Email: joates@ealing.gov.uk
Internet: http://www.ealing.gov.uk/libraries/

Type: local govt *Gov Body:* London Borough of Ealing (see **P84**) *Chief:* Borough Archivist & Local Hist Libn: Dr Jonathan Oates BA, PhD, DipAA *Dep:* Asst Libn: Mr Terry Spencer
Entry: ref only, adv appt helpful but not essential
Open: Tue-Thu 0930-1945, Fri-Sat 0930-1700, closed Mon, occasional lunch time closure (1300-1400)
Subj: London Borough of Ealing: local authority archvs; parish records (no registers); estate archvs; family papers; personal papers (incl diaries); records of parent org *Collns: Bks & Pamphs:* various local hist materials *Archvs:* archvs of London Borough of Ealing & predecessors; Martinware Papers (ceramics); Genl Wetherall Papers (ADC to Queen Victoria's father)
Co-op Schemes: joint schemes with Ealing Libs (e.g., Natl Year of Reading), or with local museum
Equip: m-reader, m-printer, copier, computer (incl wd-proc), clr copier & fax available at Ref Lib
Svcs: info, ref, rsrch, talks/exhibs
Stock: archvs/60 linear m (main strong room), 228 linear m elsewhere; bks/92 linear m; periodcls/33 linear m; photos/10000; slides/c2800; illusts/1300 paintings; maps/c800; m-forms/810; audios/13; videos/2; scrapbks/16
Classn: own
Pubns: basic leaflet on holdings (free); Guide to Family Hist Resources (50p)
Staff: Archivists: 1 *Libns:* 2 *Exp:* most stock purchase via genl Lib funds

A275

English National Ballet Archive
Markova House, 39 Jay Mews, London, SW7 2ES (020-7581-1245; *fax:* 020-7225-0827)
Email: jane.prichard@ballet.org.uk

Gov Body: English Natl Ballet *Chief:* Archivist: Miss Jane Pritchard
Entry: bona fide rsrchers, by appt only
Subj: world-wide (wherever ENB has performed): records of parent org
Equip: video viewer, copier
Staff: Archivists: 0.8 (2 PT)

A276

English National Opera Archive
The ENO Works, 40 Pitfield St, London, N1 6EX (020-7729-9610; *fax:* 020-7729-9610)
Email: ccolvin@eno.org

Gov Body: English Natl Opera *Chief:* Archivist: Ms Clare Colvin MA, DipAA
Entry: by application to the Archivist
Subj: opera; records of parent org; theatre archvs *Collns: Archvs:* collns relating to Sadler's Wells Opera, English Natl Opera & the Coliseum Theatre, London; incl programmes, posters, photos, leaflets, press cuttings, administrative files & costume designs
Equip: copier *Staff: Archivists:* 1

A277

Granada Visual
16 Hatfields, London, SE1 8DJ (020-7633-2700; *fax:* 020-7633-2707)
Email: granada.visual@granadamedia.com
Internet: http://www.granadamedia.com/visual/

Gov Body: Granada Media *Chief:* Genl Mgr: Ms Amanda Deadman (amanda.deadman@granadamedia.com) *Other Snr Staff:* Head of Sales & Marketing: Mr Mark Leaver (mark.leaver@granadamedia.com)
Entry: operates commercially; appt necessary; business-to-business licensing only *Open:* Mon-Fri 0900-1800

Subj: visual archvs of parent org *Collns: Other:* film & video archvs of all companies owned by Granada Media, incl: Anglia Television; Border Television; HTV Network; Granada Television; Granada Wild; LWT; Meridian; Tyne Tees Television; Yorkshire Television

A278

Greenwich Local History Library
Woodlands, 90 Mycenae Rd, Blackheath, London, SE3 7SE (020-8858-4631; *fax:* 020-8293-4721)
Email: local.history@greenwich.gov.uk
Internet: http://www.greenwich.gov.uk/council/publicservices/lhistory.htm

Gov Body: London Borough of Greenwich (see **P86**) *Chief:* Snr Lib Mgr: Mr Julian Watson DMS, MCLIP *Dep:* Libn: post vacant
Entry: appt required for m-readers *Open:* Mon-Tue 0900-1730, Thu 0900-2000, Sat 0900-1700
Subj: London Borough of Greenwich: local authority archvs; parish records; family papers; business records; records of parent org; local hist; family hist *Collns: Bks & Pamphs:* A.R. Martin Colln (c10000 items relating to Blackheath, Greenwich, Charlton, Kidbrooke & Lewisham); local & London directories *Archvs:* records of London Borough of Greenwich & its predecessors (1635-date); records of the Blackheath Justices of the Peace (1743-1909); Charlton & Kidbrooke parish records (17C onwards); Martin Family Papers, records of Sykes Pumps; records of Combe Farm; records of Woolwich & Greenwich Labour Parties *Other:* IGI on m-fiche; Index to Births, Marriages & Deaths; census returns (1841-91); local newspapers (1834-date); prints & drawings; map colln (17C-date); photos; postcards
Equip: 4 m-readers, 4 m-printers, copier, clr copier, fax (staff only), computers (incl 2 with wd-proc & 2 with CD-ROM, staff only) *Svcs:* info, ref, copying svcs
Stock: archvs/350 linear m; bks/c8000; photos/14000; illusts/9000; pamphs/8000; maps/2500; audios/30; videos/30; CD-ROMs/6 *Acq Offcr:* Snr Lib Mgr, as above
Classn: DDC *Auto Sys:* Horizon/Sunrise
Pubns: Guide to Sources; Family Hist Guide; both available on the Greenwich Council web site
Staff: Libns: 2 *Non-Prof:* 3 *Exp:* £19000 (2000-01)

A279

The Guide Association Archive
17-19 Buckingham Palace Rd, London, SW1W 0PT (020-7834-6242 x255; *fax:* 020-7828-8317)
Email: chq@girlguiding.org.uk
Internet: http://www.girlguiding.org.uk/

Gov Body: Guide Assoc *Chief:* Archivist: Mrs Margaret Courtney
Entry: adv appt, personal refs necessary
Open: Mon-Fri 1000-1600
Subj: records of parent org (Guides Assoc)
Collns: Bks & Pamphs: Girl Guides Assoc (1910-date): biographies, hist, training; bnd journals, annual reports, subjs related to Girl Guide Movement, fiction (Girl Guide) *Archvs:* papers relating to all events & hist of movement *Other:* photographic colln
Equip: m-reader, m-printer, copier
Stock: archvs/45 linear m; bks/60 linear m; photos/8 linear m; slides/3 linear m; pamphs/5 linear m; m-forms/1 linear m; videos/5 linear m
Classn: own *Auto Sys:* Access
Pubns: Guiding (£1.40); Brownie (£1.30); pubns catalogue free on application
Staff: Archivists: 1 *Non-Prof:* 1
Proj: reorganisation of photo colln (2003)

Archives

A280

Guildhall Library, Manuscripts Section

Aldermanbury, London, EC2P 2EJ (020-7332-1863; *fax:* 020-7600-3384)
Email: manuscripts.guildhall@corpoflondon.gov.uk
Internet: http://ihr.sas.ac.uk/gh/

Gov Body: Corp of London (see **P99**) **Chief:** Dir of Libs & Guildhall Art Gallery: Mr David Bradbury BA, MA, DipLib, MCLIP, FRSA **Dep:** Keeper of MSS (for enqs): Mr S.G.H. Freeth BA, DipAA
Entry: appt not necessary, but 24 hr notice or proof of ID required for access to some items
Open: Mon-Sat 0930-1645 (last order for MSS 1630; no MSS on Sat 1200-1400)
Subj: City of London: local authority archvs; diocesan records; parish records; estate archvs; family papers; business records; personal papers; records of livery companies; schools records; records of local insts **Collns:** *Archvs:* administrative records of City of London wards & parishes (not Corp of London archvs); archvs of the Diocese of London; archvs of C of E Diocese in Europe; St Paul's Cathedral Archvs; City of London parish records, incl parish records of St Leonard, Shoreditch; records of 70+ of the City livery companies; some family & estate records; substantial commercial & business archvs, incl: London Stock Exchange records; Lloyds of London records; London Chamber of Commerce records; records of numerous banks, insurance companies, stockbrokers, merchants etc; records of several foundations originating in the City of London, incl: Christ's Hosp School records; Trinity House records; Bridewell Royal Hosp records
Equip: 13 m-readers, m-printer, copier
Stock: archvs/9265 linear m
Pubns: Guide to Archvs & Manuscripts at Guildhall Lib (o/p, but updated version from 1994 available on web site); numerous others
Staff: *Other Prof:* 7 *Non-Prof:* 13

A281

Hackney Archives Department

43 De Beauvoir Rd, London, N1 5SQ (020-7241-2886; *fax:* 020-7241-6688)
Email: archives@hackney.gov.uk
Internet: http://www.hackney.gov.uk/

Gov Body: London Borough of Hackney (see **P87**) **Chief:** Head of Archvs: Mr D.L. Mander MA, DipAA, DipLib **Dep:** Snr Archivist: Mr Edward Rogers BA, DipAA
Entry: adv appt **Open:** Mon-Tue, Thu 0930-1300, 1400-1700, Fri 0930-1300
Subj: area of London Borough of Hackney (as at 1965 boundaries): local authority archvs; parish records (mainly copies on m-film); estate archvs; family papers; business records; records of parent org; nonconformist records; school records
Collns: *Bks & Pamphs:* John Dawson Lib (18C lib bequeathed to parish of Shoreditch); street directories *Archvs:* archvs of the London Borough of Hackney & predecessors; deposited collns of local indivs, socs, religious bodies, insts & businesses; business collns strong, incl Bryant & May (match manufacturers); local theatre material (19C-20C); electoral registers; census

returns *Other:* local newspapers on m-film (1857-date), incl Hackney Gazette (1869-date)
Equip: 3 m-readers, m-printer, video viewer, copier, computers (all with internet)
Stock: archvs/183.58 cubic m, incl maps, audios & videos; rec mgmt/41.51 cubic m; bks/31 cubic m, incl periodcls & photos; m-forms/1403, excl newspapers
Pubns: Guide to London Local Hist Resources: Hackney (revised version, £7.50); Glimpses of Ancient Hackney & Stoke Newington (£5); Late Extra!: Hackney in the News (£10.99); A Hackney Century 1900-1999 (£14.99); Strength in the Tower: An Illustrated Hist of Hackney (£9.99); Hackney Hist (Journal of the Friends of Hackney Archvs, Vols 1-3 £3 each, Vols 4-7 £4 each); Black Londoners (£9.99); Under Hackney: The Archaeological Story (£4.95); How to Tackle Your Family Hist (guide, 65p); Registers & Burial Grounds (guide, 75p); OS maps – Godfrey Editions (reproductions with notes, £2.10 each); Hackney Soc pubns; East of London Family Hist Soc pubns; various maps & posters; various free info leaflets; numerous others
Staff: *Archivists:* 2.5 *Other Prof:* 1 + 2 PT **Exp:** £12950 (2000-01)

A282

Hammersmith and Fulham Archives and Local History Centre

The Lilla Huset, 191 Talgarth Rd, London, W6 8BJ (020-8741-5159; *fax:* 020-8741-4882)
Email: archives@lbhf.gov.uk
Internet: http://www.lbhf.gov.uk/

Gov Body: London Borough of Hammersmith & Fulham (see **P88**) **Chief:** Borough Archivist & Records Mgr: Miss Jane C. Kimber BA, MSc, DipAA **Dep:** Archivist, Public Svc: Mrs Anne Wheeldon BA, MA, DipAA
Entry: adv appt advisable **Open:** Mon 0930-2000, Tue & 1st Sat in month 0930-1300, Thu 0930-1630
Subj: London Borough of Hammersmith & Fulham: local authority archvs; parish records; estate archvs; business records; records of parent org; local hist **Collns:** *Bks & Pamphs:* Kelmscott Press (complete pubns of, 1891-98); extensive local hist collns *Archvs:* records of London Borough of Hammersmith & Fulham & predecessors; records of Fulham Pottery (1865-1968); records of Hammersmith Bridge Co (1824-1880); Sir William Bull Colln (antiquarian & other papers, 1882-1930); William Morris (1834-96) & Burne Jones (1833-98); misc papers; Fulham Bridge Company records (1729-1865); Fulham Manorial records (1810-1929); Bult family correspondence (1796-1846); estate papers: Dorville & Scott families (1607-1853); West London Hosp records (1866-1979) *Other:* colln of paintings & pottery, incl the Cecil French Bequest (works by Burne-Jones, Lord Leighton, Moore, Alma-Tadema, Waterhouse, Watts etc); pottery from Fulham Pottery & by De Morgan, Martin Brothers etc
Equip: m-reader, m-printer, copier
Stock: archvs/3000 linear m; rec mgmt/1000 linear m; bks/300 linear m
Classn: ISAD(G) **Auto Sys:** DS
Pubns: numerous local hist pubns; list available on request
Staff: *Archivists:* 2 *Libns:* 1 *Other Prof:* 1 *Non-Prof:* 1

A283

Haringey Museum and Archive Service

Bruce Castle Museum, Lordship Ln, London, N17 8NU (020-8808-8772; *fax:* 020-8808-4118)

Gov Body: London Borough of Haringey (see **P89**) **Chief:** Local Hist Offcr: Ms Rita Read
Entry: adv appt **Open:** Mon-Fri 0900-1900, Sat 0900-1700
Subj: London Borough of Haringey (incl old boroughs of Hornsey, Tottenham & Wood Green): local authority archvs; local hist **Collns:** *Bks & Pamphs:* monographs & serials *Archvs:* London Borough of Haringey Archvs *Other:* photos; slides; illusts; maps & plans; cuttings; ephemera
Equip: m-reader, copier **Staff:** *Other Prof:* 1 FT

A284

Harveian Society of London, Archives

Lettson House, 11 Chandos St, London, W1G 9EB (020-7580-1043; *fax:* 020-7580-5793)

Gov Body: Harveian Soc of London **Chief:** Hon Archivist: Dr Edith Gilchrist MB, BS, FFARCS
Dep: Exec Sec: Col Richard Kinsella-Bevan MA, FRGS
Assoc Offices: collns are housed with the LIB & ARCHVS OF THE MEDICAL SOC OF LONDON at same addr
Entry: private; offcrs & membs of Soc only
Subj: works of or about William Harvey; records of parent org **Collns:** *Archvs:* archvs of the Harveian Soc
Staff: *Other Prof:* 2

A285

Honourable Artillery Company Archives

Armoury House, City Rd, London, EC1Y 2BQ (020-7382-1541; *fax:* 020-7382-1538)

Type: unit of the Territorial Army **Gov Body:** Court of Assts **Chief:** Archivist: Mr James Armstrong MA(Hons), MArAd
Entry: by written appt only
Subj: hist of the Honourable Artillery Company & its membs; military hist; military records **Collns:** *Bks & Pamphs:* c150 early printed bks (1616-1800) *Archvs:* records of the Honourable Artillery Company (1656-date)
Equip: m-reader, copier, fax, computer (with wd-proc, internet & CD-ROM) **Svcs:** info
Staff: *Archivists:* 1 full-time

A286

House of Lords Record Office (The Parliamentary Archives)

House of Lords, Westminster, London, SW1A 0PW (020-7219-3074; *fax:* 020-7219-2570)
Email: hlro@parliament.uk
Internet: http://www.parliament.uk/

Gov Body: House of Lords **Chief:** Clerk of the Records: Mr S.K. Ellison BA, MSc
Entry: by prior appt, giving details of proposed rsrch **Open:** Mon-Fri 0930-1700
Subj: UK: records of both Houses of Parliament; political papers; personal papers **Collns:** *Bks & Pamphs:* Journals of both Houses of Parliament (1510-date); Hansard; Sessional Papers *Archvs:* Acts of Parliament (1497-date); papers laid before Parliament (1531-date); Peerage papers (1597-date); Judicial papers (1621-date); records of the Lord Gt Chamberlain & other records from within Palace of Westminster; private political papers, incl: Beaverbrook Papers; Bonar Law Papers; Lloyd George Papers *Other:* plans of canals, roads, railways & other public works deposited in connection with private membs' bills (1794-date); plans & illusts of Palace of Westminster
Equip: 2 m-form reader/printers, m-camera, copier, video viewer, computers (incl internet & CD-ROM), clr scanner **Svcs:** info, ref
Stock: archvs/300 linear m
Classn: ISAD(G)

Pubns: Guide to the Records of Parliament (£10 + p&p); Pubns List available free
Staff: Archivists: 10 Other Prof: 10 Non-Prof: 4
see also HOUSE OF LORDS LIB (**S1167**)

A287

HSBC Group Archives

HSBC Holdings plc, Level 36, 8 Canada Sq, London, E14 5HQ (020-7991-0645; fax: 020-7991-4883)
Email: edwingreen@hsbcgroup.com

Gov Body: HSBC Holdings plc **Chief:** Archivist: Mr Edwin Green **Dep:** Dep Archivists: Ms Sara Kinsey & Ms Tina Staples
Entry: by appt 1 wk in adv; new rsrchers should apply in writing describing nature of their rsrch; some records cannot be accessed for reasons of confidentiality **Open:** Mon-Fri 0900-1700
Subj: China, SE Asia, India & UK: banking; hist of banking; business hist; business records; records of parent org **Collns:** Bks & Pamphs: Midland Bank ref bks Archvs: historical records of: Hong Kong & Shanghai Banking Corp Ltd (ledgers, branch records, correspondence & photos, mainly 1920s-50s); HSBC Bank plc (minute bks, financial records, incl records of Midland Bank & its constituent banks, 1836 onwards, some older records); HSBC Bank Middle East (minute bks, progress reports, staff records & correspondence, incl records of Imperial Bank of Persia, 1889-1950s); former Mercantile Bank of India (staff registers, minute bks, correspond-ence, bldg records, 1850s-1960s); Edward Holden papers; papers of past chairmen of Midland Bank
Equip: copier, computer **Staff:** Archivists: 4

A288

Imperial War Museum, Department of Art, Archives

Lambeth Rd, London, SE1 6HZ (020-7416-5211/4/5; fax: 020-7416-5409)
Email: art@iwm.org.uk
Internet: http://www.iwm.org.uk/

Type: natl museum **Chief:** Keeper: Ms Angela Wright
Assoc Offices: DEPT OF DOCUMENTS (see **A289**); DEPT OF PRINTED BKS (see **S1182**); FILM & VIDEO ARCHV (see **A290**); PHOTO ARCHV (see **A291**); SOUND ARCHV (see **A292**)
Entry: adv appt **Open:** Mon-Fri 1000-1700
Subj: 20C warfare: art **Collns:** Archvs: corresp-ondence with artists commissioned under war artist schemes in both world wars Other: paintings; drawings; sculpture; posters; postcards; medallions; printed ephemera
Svcs: photographic svc, clr transparency loan svc to publishers

A289

Imperial War Museum, Department of Documents

Lambeth Rd, London, SE1 6HZ (020-7416-5221/2/3; fax: 020-7416-5374)
Email: docs@iwm.org.uk
Internet: http://www.iwm.org.uk/

Type: natl museum **Chief:** Keeper, Dept of Documents: Mr R.W.A. Suddaby MA
Assoc Offices: DEPT OF ART (see **A288**); DEPT OF PRINTED BKS (see **S1182**); FILM & VIDEO ARCHV (see **A290**); PHOTO ARCHV (see **A291**); SOUND ARCHV (see **A292**)
Entry: open to membs of public over age 15
Open: Mon-Sat 1000-1700; closed last 2 wks in Nov & bank hols
Subj: 20C warfare, all aspects: social; literary; political; econ; military; personal papers; literary papers **Collns:** Archvs: German documents of

WW2; records of major war crimes trials; private papers of membs of HM Forces & civilians in wartime (1914 onwards), incl: papers of Field Marshal Sir John French; papers of Field Marshal Sir Henry Wilson; papers of Field Marshal Viscount Montgomery of Alamein; MSS of Isaac Rosenberg; MSS of Siegfried Sassoon; various diaries & unpublished memoirs
Equip: 3 m-readers, m-printer (staff operated), 3 copiers (staff only)
Stock: archvs/4000 linear m
Pubns: Departmental Info leaflet (free)
Staff: Archivists: 5 Non-Prof: 3

A290

Imperial War Museum, Film and Video Archive

Lambeth Rd, London, SE1 6HZ (020-7416-5293/4; fax: 020-7416-5299)
Email: film@iwm.org.uk
Internet: http://www.iwm.org.uk/

Type: natl museum **Chief:** Keeper: Mr Roger Smither MA
Assoc Offices: DEPT OF ART (see **A288**); DEPT OF DOCUMENTS (see **A289**); DEPT OF PRINTED BKS (see **S1182**); PHOTO ARCHV (see **A291**); SOUND ARCHV (see **A292**)
Entry: adv appt, 5-7 days notice required for film viewing **Open:** Mon-Fri 1000-1700
Subj: 20C warfare **Collns:** Archvs: supporting documentation, incl cameramen's 'Dope-Sheets' for 2nd World War svc film units etc Other: moving images relating to conflict in which British or Commonwealth forces have served: actuality footage shot by svc cameramen; official films; amateur films & home movies; documentaries; television compilations; feature films; the Archv also holds the former film & video lib of NATO, documenting the diplomatic & military hist of European security to the end of the Cold War
Equip: m-readers, m-printer, video viewers, copier, room hire, computer (via staff except m-reader & video viewer, fees normally charged), small preview cinema **Svcs:** loans for HE instns
Stock: videos/6500 hrs; films/120+ mln ft
Pubns: A Working Guide to the Film Archv
Staff: Other Prof: 25

A291

Imperial War Museum, Photograph Archive

All Saints Annexe, Austral St, London, SE11 4SL (020-7416-5333; fax: 020-7416-5355)
Email: photos@iwm.org.uk
Internet: http://www.iwm.org.uk/

Type: natl museum **Chief:** Keeper: Mr Brad King **Dep:** Mr David Bell
Assoc Offices: DEPT OF ART (see **A288**); DEPT OF DOCUMENTS (see **A289**); DEPT OF PRINTED BKS (see **S1182**); FILM & VIDEO ARCHV (see **A290**); SOUND ARCHV (see **A292**)
Entry: adv appt **Open:** Mon-Fri 1000-1700
Subj: 20C British & Commonwealth military hist
Equip: copier, Pictrostat (instant photographic prints) Online: Museum database
Stock: archvs/5500000 images
Classn: War Office, MOD, IWM **Auto Sys:** DBTextworks
Staff: Other Prof: 12 + 9 photographers

A292

Imperial War Museum, Sound Archive

Lambeth Rd, London, SE1 6HZ (020-7416-5363; fax: 020-7416-5379)
Email: sound@iwm.org.uk
Internet: http://www.iwm.org.uk/

Type: natl museum **Chief:** Keeper of the Sound Archv: Dr Margaret Brooks PhD **Other Snr Staff:** Acquisitions Offcr: Ms Jo Lancaster BA (jlancaster@iwm.org.uk); Documentation Offcr: Mr Richard McDonough BA (rmcdonough@iwm.org.uk)
Assoc Offices: DEPT OF ART (see **A288**); DEPT OF DOCUMENTS (see **A289**); DEPT OF PRINTED BKS (see **S1182**); FILM & VIDEO ARCHV (see **A290**); PHOTO ARCHV (see **A291**)
Entry: free of charge, but by prior appt **Open:** Mon-Fri 1000-1700
Subj: all subjs: genl; GCSE & A level; undergrad; postgrad; local study (UK & sites of conflict); family hist; social hist (personal life stories); sci (as related to war); 20C warfare; oral hist (social & military); pacifism **Collns:** Archvs: recordings: oral hist; BBC World War II Sound Archv; Internatl Military Tribunal Nuremberg
Equip: copier (25p per pg), 3 computers (all with CD-ROM), audio playback equip Online: own database available to visitors free of charge
Svcs: info
Stock: archvs/36000+ hrs of audio recordings; bks & printed materials/1800 linear m **Acq Offcr:** Acquisitions Offcr, as above
Classn: own
Pubns: various catalogues & lists of recordings on various topics; latest catalogues incl: Spanish Civil War (£13); Special Operations Executive (£16); The Holocaust (£20); Korean War (£10)
Staff: Libns: 2 Other Prof: 2 Non-Prof: 1

A293

Independent Television Commission, Records Management Centre

33 Foley St, London, W1P 7LB (020-7306-7781; fax: 020-7306-7800)
Email: andrew.ledgard@itc.org.uk
Internet: http://www.itc.org.uk/

Type: public body **Gov Body:** ITC **Chief:** Records Mgr: Mr Andrew Ledgard
Entry: adv appt & proof of ID required **Open:** Mon-Fri 1200-1700
Subj: advertising; media; broadcasting; radio; television; records of parent org **Collns:** Archvs: administrative records of ITC & predecessors, incl: Independent Television Commission Archvs (1991-date); Independent Broadcasting Authority Archvs (1954-90); Cable Authority Archvs (1984-90) Other: large colln of press cuttings; audience rsrch reports
Svcs: rsrch

Institut Français Archives

See LA MÉDIATÈQUE DE L'INSTITUT FRANÇAIS (**S1231**)

A294

Institution of Electrical Engineers Archives

(incorporating the Natl Archv for Electrical Sci & Tech)
Savoy Pl, London, WC2R 0BL (020-7344-8436; fax: 020-7344-5395)
Email: archives@iee.org.uk
Internet: http://archives.iee.org/

Type: learned soc, prof body **Gov Body:** Instn of Elec Engineers **Chief:** Snr Archivist: L. Symons (lsymons@iee.org.uk) **Dep:** Asst Archivist: A. Locker (alocker@iee.org.uk)
Assoc Offices: INSTN OF ELECTRICAL ENGINEERS LIB (see **S1206**)
Entry: IEE membs; others by appt **Open:** Mon 1030-1700, Tue-Fri 0930-1700
Subj: IEE Archvs & Special MSS Collns: elec eng; hist of electrical eng & tech; records of parent org; personal papers;

London ▼ London Archives

(Instn of Elec Engineers Archvs cont)

Subj (cont): Natl Archv for Electrical Sci & Tech: electrical & elec eng; power generation; hist of electrical eng & tech; personal papers; company records *Collns (IEE Archvs & Special MSS): Archvs:* records of the Instn of Elec Engineers Archvs (official records incl minutes, correspondence files, working papers, membership application forms, 1871-date); records of Instn of Elec & Radio Engineers (IERE, formerly British Instn of Radio Engineers); records of Instn of Manufacturing Engineers (IMfgE, formerly Instn of Production Engineers); Special MSS Collns incl: Sir Francis Ronalds Papers (1788-1873); Sir William Fothergill Cooke Papers (development of telegraph in 19C, 7 vols); Jacob Brett Papers (6 vols); Blaikley Colln of Michael Faraday MSS (MS notebks & correspond-ence); Oliver Heaviside Papers (1850-1925); Silvanus P. Thompson Colln; 9 vols of other material on early telegraphy *Other:* historical photos of eminent engineers, IEE membs & electrical technologies; plans & photos of IEE bldgs; photos of 1881 Paris Electrical Exhib *Collns (Natl Archv for Electrical Sci & Tech): Archvs:* power station records; Eidsworth & Mudford records (consulting engineers, 1883-1929); Walters Electrical Manu-facturing Co Ltd records (1880-1960); private papers of Henry Boot, Douglas Chick & Sir Arthur Fleming; Women's Eng Soc records; Electrical Assoc for Women records; Dame Caroline Haslett Papers; numerous other records of elec eng & telecomm-unications companies & papers of elec engineers & scientists (19C-date) *Other:* Lucas & Pyke eng drawings (1890s-1930s); GEC Rugby Colln (13000 negs & 28 albums, covering electrical manu-facture & products, early GEC sites & British Thomson-Houston works)
Exp: £5800 (2000-01)

A295

Islington Local History Centre
Finsbury Ref Lib, 245 St John St, London, EC1V 4NB (020-7527-7988)
Email: local.history@islington.gov.uk
Internet: http://www.islington.gov.uk/

Gov Body: London Borough of Islington (see **P94**) *Chief:* Local Hist Libn: Mr Armand De Filippo *Other Snr Staff:* Asst Local Hist Libns: Mr Martin Banham & Ms Claire Frankland
Assoc Offices: parish records, school records & registers for the Borough are held at LONDON METROPOLITAN ARCHVS (see **A304**)
Entry: ref only, adv appt essential *Open:* Mon, Thu 0930-1300, 1400-2000, Tue 0930-1300, 1400-1700, Fri 0930-1300; also open on alternate Sats
Subj: London Borough of Islington: local authority archvs; parish records (limited); estates archvs; family papers; poor law records; local hist
Collns: Bks & Pamphs: local hist pubns; local directories; Joe Orton Colln; Sickert Colln (relating to Walter Sickert & Therese Lessore) *Archvs:* archvs of London Borough of Islington & predecessors, incl former Metropolitan Boroughs of Islington & Finsbury; rate bks (17C onwards); Sadler's Wells Theatre Archv (1740 onwards); Penton Family & Estate Papers *Other:* census returns; electoral registers; photos; cuttings; local newspapers & magazines (19C onwards); maps; paintings

A296

Lambeth Archives Department
Minet Lib, 52 Knatchbull Rd, London, SE5 9QY (020-7926-6076; *fax:* 020-7926-6080)
Email: archives@lambeth.gov.uk

Gov Body: London Borough of Lambeth (see **P97**) *Chief:* Archivists: Mr Jon Newman MA, DipAS & Ms Sue Mackenzie BA, DipAA (job share) *Dep:* Ms Gabrielle Bourne
Entry: adv appt preferred *Open:* Mon 1300-2000, Tue, Thu 1000-1800, Fri 1000-1300, Sat 0900-1700; closed Wed & bank & public hols
Subj: London Borough of Lambeth, Surrey: local authority archvs; parish records (civil parish only); estate archvs; family papers; business records; personal papers; records of parent org; records of local orgs; local hist *Collns: Bks & Pamphs:* William Minet Colln (bks, prints & MSS relating to hist of Lambeth, 19C); ref colln on Lambeth & London hist; local trade directories (19C onwards) *Archvs:* records of Lambeth Council & predecessors (16C-date); Clapham & Streatham parish records; Vauxhall Gdns records; Crystal Palace records *Other:* parish & cemetery registers (m-film); electoral registers (some on m-film); census returns (m-film, 1841-91); Lambeth Stoneware Pottery; oral hist materials; map colln; prints & photos; cuttings colln; ephemera colln
Equip: 4 m-readers, 2 m-printers, copier, comp-uters (with internet & CD-ROM) *Disabled:* wheel-chair access *Svcs:* info, ref, rsrch (fees), reprographic svcs, local hist talks
Stock: archvs/162 cubic m; bks/c10000; photos/c30000
Classn: Modes Plus (for archvs) *Auto Sys:* Talis (lib catalogue)
Pubns: Guide to Lambeth Archvs (£5); Born & Bred – Tracing Your Lambeth Family Hist (£3.50); House Hist at Lambeth Archvs (£1.50)
Staff: Archivists: 3 *Libns:* 1 *Non-Prof:* 3

A297

Lewisham Local Studies and Archives
Lewisham Lib, 199-201 Lewisham High St, London, SE13 6LG (020-8297-0682; *fax:* 020-8297-1169)
Email: local.studies@lewisham.gov.uk
Internet: http://www.lewisham.gov.uk/yourarea/

Gov Body: London Borough of Lewisham (see **P98**) *Chief:* Archivist: post vacant *Other Snr Staff:* Libn: Mr Keith Scott BA(Hons) (keith. scott@lewisham.gov.uk); Libn: Ms Melissa Wyatt BA(Hons), DipHE (melissa.wyatt@lewisham. gov.uk); Historian: Mr John Coulter (john.coulter@ lewisham.gov.uk)
Entry: ref only; adv appt for archvs, esp evenings, lunchtimes & Sat *Open:* Mon 1000-1700, Tue, Thu 0900-2000, Fri-Sat 0900-1700; Sun 1300-1600; closed Wed
Subj: London Borough of Lewisham: local authority archvs; diocesan records; parish records; estate archvs; family papers; business records; political papers; nonconformist records; school records; manorial records; military records; records of local charities, clubs & socs; local hist; family hist *Collns: Bks & Pamphs:* antiquarian collns; local & family hist pubns; bks by local authors; local & London directories; local hist periodcls *Archvs:* archvs of London Borough of Lewisham, incl predecessor authorities; records of Court of Law; records of Lewisham/Greenwich Board of Works; Lewisham Deanery records; parish records for: St Pauls (Deptford); St Margaret's (Lee); St Mary's (Lewisham); & others; L.A.J. Baxter Colln; estate & family collns, incl: Forster Estate Papers; Evelyn Estate Papers; Baring Estate Papers; Hadley Family Papers; Mavow Adams Family Papers; Walker Family Papers; Bowditch Papers; Margaret McMillan Papers; various business records incl agric firms,

---

biscuit manufacturers, dept stores, eng firms, estate agents & victualling firms; records of local political parties *Other:* census returns; electoral registers; OS & other maps; illusts; local photo collns, incl Millennium Portrait Photos of Borough of Lewisham; local newspapers (19C-date) *Co-op Schemes:* with Local Hist orgs
Equip: 2 m-readers, 2 m-printers (A4/20p), copier (A4/20p, A3/25p). 4 computers (incl 1 with CD-ROM & 2 with internet) *Disabled:* wheelchair access *Svcs:* info, rsrch, photocopying svc
Stock: archvs/stock currently being assessed
Classn: DDC *Auto Sys:* Dynix
Pubns: numerous, incl bks, maps, postcards & guides *Staff: Libns:* 2 *Other Prof:* 1

A298

Liddell Hart Centre for Military Archives
Room 302, Strand Bldg, King's Coll London, Strand, London, WC2R 2LS (020-7848-2015/2187; *fax:* 020-7848-2760)
Email: archives.web@kcl.ac.uk
Internet: http://www.kcl.ac.uk/lhcma/home.htm

Gov Body: King's Coll London (see **S1227**)
Chief: Dir of Archv Svcs: Miss Patricia Methven
Entry: by letter of introduction from a person of appropriate standing, & on completion of an admission form *Open:* term: Mon-Fri 0930-1730, vac: Mon-Fri 0930-1630; closed last 2 wks of Aug for stocktaking
Subj: military hist & related subjs (from second Boer War, 1899-1902, onwards); defence policy; weapons tech; nuclear hist; personal papers
Collns: Bks & Pamphs: personal lib of Capt Sir Basil Liddell Hart (military hist, late 19C-20C) *Archvs:* personal papers of over 600 snr British defence personnel, authors & commentators on internatl security & defence policy; archvs of television programmes relating to defence & conflict studies; m-forms of US official papers, incl records of Joint Chiefs of Staff & Natl Security Council *Other:* Location Register of 20C Defence Personnel (with Southampton Univ Lib – see **S1946**); Nuclear Hist database
Equip: m-form reader/printer, photocopying facilities available via staff, power pts for laptops
Online: access to Centre's own web site

A299

Lloyd's Register of Shipping
71 Fenchurch St, London, EC3M 4BS (020-7423-2475; *fax:* 020-7423-2039)
Email: info@lr.org
Internet: http://www.lr.org/

Chief: Snr Info Offcr & Archivist: Mrs B.E. Jones
Dep: Info Offcrs: Ms A. Cowne & Ms E. Taaffe
Entry: ref only *Open:* Mon-Fri 0930-1630
Subj: records of parent org; shipping records; shipping hist *Collns: Bks & Pamphs:* all Lloyd's Registers publ records (1760-date); colln of printed bks concerning shipping, shipbldg & shipping company hist *Archvs:* closed colln incl cttee minutes, other material concerning staff & genl business
Equip: copier (limited use)
Stock: archvs/120 linear m; bks/128 linear m
Classn: own
Pubns: Lloyd's Register of Ships (annual); List of Shipowners; Rules & Regulations for Classn of Ships; Statistical Tables; Casualty Return; Register of Internatl Shipowning Groups; prices on application *Staff: Other Prof:* 2 *Non-Prof:* 1

A300

Lloyds TSB Group Archives
Sec's Dept, 71 Lombard St, London, EC3P 3BS (020-7356-1032; *fax:* 020-7356-1038)

Gov Body: Lloyds TSB Group **Chief:** Group Archivist: Ms Karen Sampson MSc, BA, DipAA, RMSA (sampsok@lloydstsb.co.uk) **Dep:** Dep Group Archivist: Ms Natasha Cole-Jones BA, MA, RMSA (natasha.cole-jones@lloydstsb.co.uk) **Entry:** ref only by adv appt; closure period on some material **Open:** Mon-Fri 0930-1630, excl public hols
Subj: UK & internatl: business records; records of parent org; banking; local industry; social hist; economic hist; local hist **Collns:** *Bks & Pamphs:* banking periodcls; Bank of London & South America Dirs Lib (Latin American travel bks & hists, 19C-20C); hists of savings bank movement & indiv savings banks *Archvs:* archvs of Lloyds Bank & its constituent banks (1765-1995); archvs of TSB & its constituent savings banks (1816-1995); archvs of constituent building socs of Cheltenham & Gloucester Building Soc (1869-1985)
Equip: copier, clr copier **Svcs:** info, ref
Stock: archvs/c1200 linear m; bks/c1350; photos/c7000; artefacts/c800
Auto Sys: in-house Lotus Notes database
Staff: Archivists: 2 Non-Prof: 1

A301

London Archaeological Archive and Research Centre

Mortimer Wheeler House, 46 Eagle Wharf, London, N1 7FC (020-7490-8447; *fax:* 020-7490-5047)
Email: laarc@museumoflondon.org.uk
Internet: http://www.museumoflondon.org.uk/

Gov Body: Museum of London (see **S1288**)
Chief: Mgr (Snr Curator): Mr John Shepherd BA, FSA (jshepherd@museumoflondon.org.uk) **Entry:** adv appt **Open:** Mon-Fri 0900-1700; also open 1000-1600 on 1st & 3rd Sat of each month **Subj:** Greater London: archaeo; archaeo records; local hist **Collns:** *Bks & Pamphs:* London Soc Lib (see **S1267**); London & Middlesex Archaeological Soc Lib (available to membs only); periodcls & journals *Archvs:* repository for records relating to 5000 archaeo sites or projs in Greater London over the past 100 years; collns incl: Cottril Colln; Dunning Colln; Guildhall Museum Roman & Mediaeval records; London Excavation Council records; Grimes London Archv; Nonsuch Colln; Dept of Urban Archaeo records; Dept for Greater London Archaeo records; Inner London Archaeological Unit records **Co-op Schemes:** links with London Museums & Univ of London (see **S1440**)
Equip: m-reader, m-printer (10p per sheet), copier, 4 computers (all with wd-proc, internet & CD-ROM) *Disabled:* wheelchair access, induction loop in seminar room *Online:* access to site specific authorities *Offcr-in-Charge:* Mgr, as above **Svcs:** info, ref, rsrch
Stock: archvs/679 linear m; bks/103 linear m; periodcls/97 linear m; photos/96 linear m, incl slides; maps/3 linear m; m-forms/0.6 linear m; CD-ROMs/0.24 linear m
Auto Sys: bespoke
Pubns: Guides to the Records of Excavations by the Museum of London, incl: Archaeo in the City of London 1907-91 (Vol 1); Archaeo in Greater London 1965-90 (Vol 2); Post-War Archaeo in the City of London 1946-72 (Vol 3)
Staff: Archivists: 1

A302

London Borough of Enfield, Archives and Local History Unit

Southgate Town Hall, Green Lanes, London, N13 4XD (020-8379-2724; *fax:* 020-8379-2761)
Internet: http://www.enfield.gov.uk/library/lochist.htm

Gov Body: London Borough of Enfield (see **P85**)
Chief: Local Hist Offcr: Mr Graham Dalling MCLIP **Dep:** Local Hist Asst: Mrs Kate Godfrey **Entry:** by appt **Open:** Mon-Tue, Thu-Fri 1000-1700
Subj: London Borough of Enfield (Edmonton, Enfield & Southgate): local authority archvs; records of parent org; school records; manorial records; local hist **Collns:** *Bks & Pamphs:* local directories; auctioneers' catalogues *Archvs:* records of former boroughs of Edmonton, Enfield & Southgate *Other:* local newspapers; maps; extensive photo colln (1860s onwards); newspaper cuttings (c14000 items)
Equip: 2 m-readers, m-printer, copier, UV lamp
Stock: archvs/101 m; bks/106 m; photos/15000
Classn: UDC
Pubns: series of 12 Area Histories & 16 Fact Sheets designed for school proj work (free)
Staff: *Other Prof:* 1 *Non-Prof:* 2 *Exp:* £1500 (1999-2000); £1500 (2000-01)

A303

London Borough of Newham, Local History & Archaeology Resource Centre

(formerly Newham Museum Svc Lib)
31 Stock St, London, E13 0RY (020-7474-7244)
Email: susan.gosling@newham.gov.uk
Internet: http://www.newham.gov.uk/

Gov Body: London Borough of Newham (see **P101**), Heritage Svcs **Chief:** Heritage Svcs Mgr: Mr Séan Sherman MA (sean.sherman@newham.gov.uk) **Dep:** Sites & Exhibs Mgr: Ms Susan Kirby MA, AMA (sue.kirby@newham.gov.uk) *Other Snr Staff:* Collns Offcr: Ms Susan Gosling, email as above
Entry: by adv appt only; contact the Collns Offcr (020-8472-4795) **Open:** Wed 1000-1600; other days by arrangement
Subj: local study (London Borough of Newham, hist & archaeo) **Collns:** *Bks & Pamphs:* gas industry journals
Equip: copier (A4/10p) *Offcr-in-Charge:* Collns Offcr, as above **Svcs:** info
Classn: SHIC **Auto Sys:** CALM
Staff: *Other Prof:* 1 *Non-Prof:* 2
See also NEWHAM ARCHV & LOCAL STUDIES LIB (**A315**)

A304

London Metropolitan Archives

40 Northampton Rd, London, EC1R 0HB (020-7332-3820; *fax:* 020-7833-9136)
Email: lma@ms.corpoflondon.gov.uk
Internet: http://www.cityoflondon.gov.uk/lma/

Gov Body: Corp of London (see **P99**) **Chief:** Head Archivist: Dr Deborah G. Jenkins MA, PhD, DipAS **Dep:** Collns Development Mgr: Ms Emma Stewart MA
Entry: ref only **Open:** Mon, Wed, Fri 0930-1645, Tue, Thu 0930-1930; alternate Sats 0930-1645; closed part of Nov for stocktaking & over Xmas hol
Subj: Greater London: local authority archvs (London-wide); diocesan records; parish records; estate archvs; family papers; business records; records of parent org; records of charities **Collns:** *Bks & Pamphs:* pubns of Greater London Council & predecessors *Archvs:* records of former Greater London Council & predecessor authorities; records of Anglican Dioceses of London & Southwark; Royal Soc of Portrait Painters Archv *Other:* prints & printed map collns
Equip: 46 m-readers, video viewer, power pts for laptops
Stock: archvs/16256 cubic m; bks/203 cubic m
Classn: own

Pubns: various guides (free); info leaflets (free); We Think You Ought to Go: Evacuation of London in WWII (£5)
Staff: *Libns:* 2 *Other Prof:* 23, incl archivists *Non-Prof:* 27 *Exp:* £11000 (2000-01)

A305

Madame Tussaud's London, Archives

Marylebone Rd, London, NW1 5LR (020-7935-6861; *fax:* 020-7465-0862)

Chief: Archivist: Mrs Susanna Lamb
Entry: not open to public; in special circumstances limited access to rsrchers
Subj: business records; personal papers **Collns:** *Archvs:* records of Madame Tussaud's Ltd (1811-1964), incl accounts & ledgers; financial, business & personal papers of Anne Marie Tussaud (1760-1850); various letters & papers of Philippe Curtius (wax modeller, d 1794); some correspondence relating to famous criminals & other subjs of displays, incl Hawley Harvey Crippen (1862-1910)
Svcs: info, limited rsrch

A306

Marks and Spencer Company Archive

B169 Michael House, Baker St, London, W1U 8EP (020-7268-3115; *fax:* 020-7268-2643)
Email: rebecca.walker@marks-and-spencer.com
Internet: http://www.marks-and-spencer.com/

Chief: Company Archivist: Ms Rebecca Walker
Entry: adv appt
Subj: retailing; Zionism; family papers; business records; personal papers; records of parent org **Collns:** *Archvs:* records of Marks & Spencer plc (dept stores & retailers, 20C); records of Western Women's Internatl Zionist Org (1927-31); records of Zionist Commission to Palestine (1918); Simon Marks papers (businessman, 1888-1964); Harry Sacher papers (journalist & barrister, 1881-1971); Israel Sieff papers (businessman, 1889-1972); Rebecca Sieff papers (co-founder of WIZO, d1966); Chaim Weizmann correspondence (chemist, scholar & Zionist leader, 1874-1952) *Other:* photos; ephemera
Classn: ISAD(G)

A307

Mercers' Company Archive

Mercers' Company, Mercers' Hall, Ironmonger Ln, London, EC2V 8HE (020-7776-7244; *fax:* 020-7600-1158)

Type: archv & art colln **Gov Body:** Mercers' Company **Chief:** Archivist & Curator: Ms Ursula S. Carlyle BA, MA, DipAS
Entry: approved readers, by prior appt only
Open: Mon-Fri 0930-1700
Subj: London & England: estate archvs; family papers; business records; records of parent org **Collns:** *Archvs:* records of the Worshipful Company of Mercers, the premier City livery company & one of the ancient merchant guilds of London, & the Charitable Estates in its care, such as those of Richard Whittington, Dean Colet (founder of St Paul's School), Sir Thomas Gresham (founder of the Royal Exchange & Gresham Coll) & the Earl of Northampton
Equip: copier (via staff), computer
Stock: archvs/800 linear m; rec mgmt/100 linear m; small lib
Pubns: Some Account of St Thomas of Acon in the Cheap, London, & the Plate of the Mercers' Company, by J. Watney (1892); Acts of Court of the Mercers' Company 1453-1527, by L. Lyell & F.D. Watney (1936); Sir Thomas Gresham & His Trusts, by E. Featherstone (1952);

(Mercers' Company Archv cont)

Pubns (cont): The Charity of Richard Whittington 1424-1966 (1968), Thomas Becket, the Mercers' Company & the City of London (1970), The Mercers' Hall (1991), all by J.M. Imray; The Mercers' Company Plate, by R. Lane (1985); The Mercers' Company 1579-1959, by I. Doolittle (1994); Think & Thank God: The Mercers' Company & its Contribution to the Church & Religious Life since the Reformation, by G. Huelin (1994); The Mercers' Company's First Charter 1394, by A.F. Sutton (1994)
Staff: Archivists: 1 Non-Prof: 1

A308 ♀

Military Historical Society Archives

Natl Army Museum, Royal Hosp Rd, Chelsea, London, SW3 4HT (Soc: 01980-615689; *fax:* 01980-618746; *Museum:* 020-7730-0717; *fax:* 020-7823-6573)

Chief: Custodian: Mr Dennis Pillinger
Assoc Offices: MILITARY HISTORICAL SOC LIB is dispersed to military museums around the country; unique records held here at the Natl Army Museum
Entry: ref only
Subj: military records; British military hist
Collns: Archvs: Victoria Cross (VC) files; George Cross (GC) files
See also NATL ARMY MUSEUM, DEPT OF PRINTED BKS **(S1289)** & DEPT OF ARCHVS **(A311)**

A309 ♀ ✍

Moravian Church Archive and Library

Moravian Church House, 5-7 Muswell Hill, London, N10 3TJ (020-8883-3409; *fax:* 020-8365-3371)
Email: archive@moravianchurch.freeserve. co.uk
Internet: http://www.moravian.org.uk/

Gov Body: Moravian Church in Gt Britain & Ireland **Chief:** Archivist: Miss Lorraine Parsons MA(Archvs & Record Mgmt)
Entry: adv appt; if possible records should be ordered in adv **Open:** Mon-Tue 1000-1600; other days may be available upon request
Subj: Gt Britain: Moravian church records; church hist, esp hist of Moravian Church; Moravian theology **Collns:** Bks & Pamphs: Moravian Church hist bks; genl church hist, bibles & theological works; hymn & tune bks (both Moravian & other denominations); periodcls & pamphs incl both contemporary & past pubns; biographies; printed collns also serve as a rsrch tool for the archvs Archvs: archvs of the Moravian Church in Gt Britain & Ireland: records relating to certain congregations; synod minutes & resolutions; records of the administrative bodies of the British Province, the Moravian Union & Unitas Estates; mission records, incl material related to the Soc for the Furtherance of the Gospel (SFG)
Equip: m-reader, copier (15p per copy)
Stock: archvs/3800
Classn: ISAD(G) **Auto Sys:** DS
Staff: Archivists: 1

A310 🏛

The National Archives, Family Records Centre

1 Myddelton St, London, EC1R 1UW (020-8392-5300; *fax:* 020-8392-5307)
Email: frc@nationalarchives.gov.uk
Internet: http://www.familyrecords.gov.uk/frc/

Gov Body: Genl Register Office & the Natl Archvs (see **A432**) **Chief:** Centre Mgr for Natl Archvs: Ms Jill Albrooke **Other Snr Staff:** Centre Mgr for ONS: Ms Pauline Mason
Entry: no conditions **Open:** Mon, Wed, Fri 0900-1700, Tue 1000-1900, Thu 0900-1900, Sat 0930-1700
Subj: England & Wales: census records; records of births, marriages & deaths; family hist
Collns: Bks & Pamphs: family hist ref colln Archvs: census returns for England & Wales (1841-1901); wills & administrations from PPC (up to 1858); indexes of births, marriages & deaths in England & Wales (from 1837); indexes of legal adoptions in England & Wales (from 1927) Archvs: indexes of births, marriages & deaths of some British citizens abroad, incl deaths in two World Wars (from late 18C onwards); death duty registers (1796-1858) & indexes (1796-1903); records of nonconformist birth, baptisms & burials (mainly pre-1837) & marriages (mainly pre-1754)
Equip: 250 m-readers, 8 m-printers, copier, computers (incl 10 with CD-ROM) **Disabled:** various facilities available **Online:** indexes to Scottish registration & census records via Scot Link **Svcs:** info, advice on family hist rsrch
Pubns: various family hist pubns
Further Info: for Census enqs use contact numbers & email above; for enqs concerning Births, Marriages, Death, Adoptions & Overseas enqs (0870-243-7788; *fax:* 01704-550013; *email:* certificate.services@ons.gov.uk)

A311 🏛

National Army Museum, Department of Archives

Royal Hosp Rd, Chelsea, London, SW3 4HT (020-7730-0717; *fax:* 020-7823-6573)
Email: amassie@national-army-museum.ac.uk
Internet: http://www.national-army-museum. ac.uk/

Type: natl museum **Chief:** Head of Dept of Archvs: Dr Alastair Massie MA, DPhil
Assoc Offices: DEPT OF PRINTED BKS (see **S1289**)
Entry: by readers ticket; proof of ID & letter of recommendation required when applying **Open:** Tue-Sat 1000-1630; closed last 2 wks of Oct
Subj: British army; military hist; military records; regimental records; personal papers; records of svc orgs **Collns:** Archvs: relating to the British Army & earlier formations (15th-20C, with emphasis on 18C-19C); personal papers of army offcrs, incl: Genl Sir William Codrington papers; Field Marshal Sir George Nugent papers; Lord Fitzroy Somerset papers; Lt Genl Sir James Outram papers; Genl Henry Rawlinson papers; personal papers & memoirs of svc of indiv soldiers; Women's Royal Army Corps records; Royal Army Educational Corps records; United Svc Club records; regimental archvs incl: Surrey Yeomanry records; Middlesex Regiment records; Buffs Regiment records
Equip: Disabled: wheelchair access

A312 ☕🖋

National Farmers' Union, Archives

Agriculture House, 164 Shaftesbury Ave, London, WC2H 8HL (020-7331-7200; *fax:* 020-7331-7313)
Email: nfu@nfuonline.com
Internet: http://www.nfu.org.uk

Type: trade assoc **Gov Body:** NFU Council
Chief: Dir Genl: Mr Richard MacDonald **Dep:** Dep Dir Genl: Mr Ian Gardiner
Entry: archvs are primarily for internal use, but can be made available to genuine rsrchers (e.g., those preparing a PhD paper), strictly by appt only **Open:** Mon-Fri 0930-1700
Subj: records of parent org **Collns:** Archvs: NFU Archvs: most pre-1945 records held at RURAL HIST CENTRE (see **S1850**), catalogue available from Reading Univ; post-1945 & limited pre-1945 records under control of NFU but stored off-site, catalogue available from NFU
Equip: copier **Disabled:** wheelchair access
Stock: archvs/200+ archv boxes

A313 🏛🏛

National Portrait Gallery, Heinz Archive and Library

St Martins Pl, London, WC2H 0HE (020-7306-0055 x257; *fax:* 020-7306-0056)
Email: archive@npg.org.uk
Internet: http://www.npg.org.uk/archive.htm

Gov Body: Natl Portrait Gallery **Chief:** Head of Archv & Lib: Mr Robin Francis BSc, MA, MCLIP
Dep: Libn & Study Room Mgr: Miss Antonia Leak BA, MA
Entry: ref only, adv appt **Open:** Tue-Fri 1000-1700, closed 24 Dec-1 Jan, public hols & for 2 wk's stocktaking in Aug-Sep
Subj: arts; portraiture; records of parent org; personal papers (artists) **Collns:** Bks & Pamphs: various special collns, incl artists' sitter bks & sketchbks Archvs: muniments of the Natl Portrait Gallery; records of the Primary Colln of Portraits; artists' autograph letters; files of engravings, photos & reproductions held in collns world-wide Other: Photo Colln (160000+ original prints & negs of historic & contemporary portraits)
Equip: m-readers, copier, computer (with internet & CD-ROM)
Stock: archvs/35000; periodcls/70; illusts/800000, incl photos; some videos & m-forms; various archvs
Staff: Libns: 2 Other Prof: 4 Non-Prof: 2 **Exp:** £32017 (1999-2000); £32800 (2000-01)

A314 ♀ ✍

National Society Archives and Library

C of E Record Centre, 15 Galleywall Rd, Bermondsey, London, SE16 3PB (020-7898-1030; *fax:* 020-7394-7018)
Email: sarah.duffield@c-of-e.org.uk
Internet: http://www.natsoc.org.uk/wnsoffer/ archives.htm

Gov Body: Natl Soc for Promoting Religious Edu **Chief:** Archivist: Miss Sarah Duffield BA, MArAd
Assoc Offices: held as part of the C OF E RECORD CENTRE (see **A266**)
Entry: by appt **Open:** Mon & Wed 1000-1630
Subj: England & Wales: hist of C of E in edu; ch's lit; religious edu; Sunday schools; school records; records of parent org **Collns:** Bks & Pamphs: Natl Soc bks & pubns; St Katherine Cree Sunday School Lib (19C) Archvs: records of Natl Soc, incl cttee minute bks & complete set of annual reports (1811-date); records of the C of E Sunday School Inst; papers relating to indiv Anglican church schools (15000 files, from 1811), incl: correspondence, school annual reports, plans, letterheads & trust deeds Other: index of school teachers trained by the Soc (1812-1855)
Equip: copier (30p per pg) **Svcs:** info
Staff: 1 archivist
Further Info: The C of E Record Centre's Public Search Room is expected to be relocated to Lambeth Palace Lib (see **S1234**) late in 2002 on an experimental basis; rsrchers should continue to contact the Record Centre for bookings & enqs

A315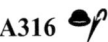

Newham Archive and Local Studies Library

Stratford Lib, 3 The Grove, Stratford, London, E15 1EL (020-8430-6881)
Email: richard.durack@newham.gov.uk
Internet: http://www.newham.gov.uk/leisure/libraries/local.htm

Gov Body: London Borough of Newham (see **P101**) *Chief:* Archivist: Mr Richard Durack
Entry: adv appt *Open:* Mon 1300-1730, Tue, Fri-Sat 0930-1730, Thu 0930-2000
Subj: London Borough of Newham: local authority archvs; parish records; family papers; business records; personal papers; census records; records of local orgs *Collns: Archvs:* records of London Borough of Newham & predecessors *Other:* local newspapers; historical map colln; electoral registers; parish registers; census returns

A316

News International Record Office

1 Virginia St, London, E1 9XY (020-7782-6890; *fax:* 020-7782-3967)
Email: eamon.dyas@newsint.co.uk

Chief: Group Records Mgr: Mr Eamon Dyas
Entry: adv appt
Subj: journalism; newspaper publishing; business records; family papers; personal papers *Collns: Archvs:* archvs of The Times newspaper (18C-20C); Walter family of Bear Wood papers (19C-20C); B.K. Long papers; Lord Rees-Mogg papers; papers of numerous Times correspondents & journalists

A317

Post Office Heritage

Freeling House, Mount Pleasant, Phoenix Pl, London, WC1X 0DL (020-7239-2570; *fax:* 020-7239-2576)
Email: heritage@royalmail.com
Internet: http://www.royalmailgroup.com/heritage/

Gov Body: Royal Mail *Chief:* Head of Archvs: Ms Vicky Parkinson (vicky.a.parkinson@royalmail.com)
Entry: proof of ID will be required & standard security procedures will apply *Open:* Mon-Fri 0900-1615 for public search room
Subj: UK, particularly London: archvs of the British Post Office from the 17C; business records; records of parent org; postal hist; local hist; family hist *Collns: Bks & Pamphs:* postal hist ref lib *Archvs:* Post Office Archvs (17C-date, comprehensive records from 1851); papers relating to Post Office Savings Bank; employee records; transport records; private papers of key indivs in development of postal svc; broadcasting & publicity records; records relating to hist of local postal svcs *Other:* large poster colln; photo lib; postal artifacts & artwork; philatelic colln
Equip: 5 m-readers, 3 m-printers (25p per copy), copier (40p per copy, no self-svc), 2 computers
Svcs: info, ref
Stock: archvs/2000 linear m; rec mgmt/6000 linear m; bks/200 linear m; photos/400000 prints & negs; illusts/6000, incl 5000 posters; maps/700
Acq Offcr: Head of Archvs, as above
Classn: ISAD(G) *Auto Sys:* DS CALM
Pubns: info sheets (free), also on web site
Staff: Archivists: 4 *Other Prof:* 7 *Non-Prof:* 6

A318

The Principal Probate Registry (The Principal Registry of the Family Division)

First Ave House, 42-49 High Holborn, London, WC1V 6NP (020-7947-7000; *fax:* 020-7947-6946)

Gov Body: The Court Svc Agency *Chief:* Dept Mgr: Mr Kevin Donnelly *Dep:* Probate Mgr: Ms Tina Constantinou
Open: Mon-Fri 1000-1630
Subj: wills; grants of probate; letters of admin
Equip: m-reader, computer

A319

Prospect Archives

(formerly the Instn of Profs, Mgrs & Specialists)
Prospect House, 75-79 York Rd, London, SE1 7AQ (020-7902-6600; *fax:* 020-7902-6667)
Email: enquiries@prospect.org.uk
Internet: http://www.prospect.org.uk/

Type: trade union *Chief:* Rsrch Offcr: Ms Mary Watkins BA(Hons), DipLib
Entry: ref only, adv appt *Open:* Mon-Fri 0900-1700
Subj: trade unions; industrial relations; collective bargaining; civil svc; records of parent org
Collns: Archvs: records of Instn of Profs, Mgrs & Specialists (1942-94), formerly the Instn of Prof Civil Servants
Equip: m-reader, m-printer, copier *Svcs:* info, ref, room hire
Classn: own *Auto Sys:* CardBox
Pubns: numerous, list of pubns available

A320

Prudential plc, Group Archives

Laurence Pountney Hill, London, EC4R 0EU (020-7548-3582; *fax:* 020-7548-3160)
Email: Group.Archives@prudential.co.uk
Internet: http://www.prudential.co.uk/prudentialplc/aboutpru/history/

Chief: Group Archivist: Mr David Carter (David.Carter@prudential.co.uk) *Dep:* Asst Archivist: Ms Clare Bunkham (Clare.Bunkham@prudential.co.uk)
Entry: adv appt
Subj: insurance; business records; records of parent org *Collns: Archvs:* records of Prudential plc (1848-date); minutes & other records of: British Industry Life Assurance Co; British Mutual Life Assurance Soc; British Widows Assurance Co Ltd; Consolidated Investment & Assurance Co; Hercules Insurance Co; Internatl Life Assurance Soc; Prince Fire Insurance Co; Scottish Amicable Life Assurance Soc; Mutual & Genl Securities Company Ltd; records of London Film Productions (1932-1960s)
Stock: archvs/600 linear m; bks/c1000; photos/c6000; videos/c1500
Classn: ISAD(G) *Auto Sys:* MS Access
Pubns: A Sense of Security: 150 Years of Prudential, by Laurie Dennett (1998)
Staff: Archivists: 2

A321

Rambert Dance Company Archive

94 Chiswick High Rd, London, W4 1SH (020-8630-0600; *fax:* 020-8747-8323)
Email: jdc@rambert.org.uk

Gov Body: Ballet Rambert Ltd *Chief:* Archivist: Miss Jane Pritchard
Entry: adv appt *Open:* Mon, Wed 1030-1700
Subj: world-wide, wherever Rambert Dance Company has performed: business records; records of parent org

Collns: Archvs: artistic & administrative records of the company; programmes (1926 onwards); press clippings (1937-49, 1958-date); other printed & MSS material, incl posters, advertising materials, ephemera *Other:* photo colln (c1910 onwards); sound, film & video recordings; costume designs
Equip: video viewer, copier
Stock: archvs/130 linear m; various printed bks, photos, designs, periodcls & MSS
Staff: Archivists: 1 PT

A322

Ramblers' Association Archives

1-5 Wandsworth Rd, London, SW8 2XX (020-7339-8500)
Internet: http://www.ramblers.org.uk/

Gov Body: Ramblers' Assoc *Chief:* post vacant
Entry: adv appt *Open:* Mon-Fri 0930-1730
Subj: records of parent org *Collns: Archvs:* archvs of the Ramblers' Assoc (1935-date)
Equip: copier

A323

Reuters Archive

85 Fleet St, London, EC4P 4AJ (020-7542-7132; *fax:* 020-7542-4066)
Email: john.ontwisle@reuters.com

Gov Body: Reuters Ltd *Chief:* Group Archivist: Mr John G. Entwisle LLB, DipAA
Assoc Offices: REUTERS NEWS AGENCY, EDITORIAL REF UNIT, at same addr (see **S1337**)
Entry: adv appt
Subj: business records; records of parent org (Reuters Ltd & associated activs, 1894-date) *Collns: Archvs:* Reuters Ltd archvs (news agency, c1862-1984); Eastern News Agency Ltd records (1910-60); Comtelburo Ltd records (telegraphic agents, 1890-1966) *Other:* training & corporate info videos; some film & m-forms
Equip: m-reader, m-printer, copier, clr copier, fax
Svcs: info, ref, rsrch
Stock: archvs/c550 linear m
Pubns: The Price of Truth, by J. Laurenson & L. Barber (1986); The Power of News, by D. Read (2nd edition, 1999); Reuters' Century 1851-1951, by G. Storey (1951)
Staff: Archivists: 1
Further Info: The Reuters Archv is one of the few major news agency archvs. It covers Reuters Internatl operations & the company's links with other news agencies throughout the world. It is of interest not only to those studying the hist & development of news agencies, but also to historians interested in major world events as reported by Reuters. Many well-known figures have worked for Reuters at some stage in their careers & biographers may find useful info.

A324

Rio Tinto plc, Archives

6 St James's Sq, London, SW1Y 4LD (020-7753-2123; *fax:* 020-7753-2211)
Email: fiona.maccoll@riotinto.com
Internet: http://www.riotinto.com/

Chief: Records Mgr: Ms Fiona Maccoll
Entry: adv appt; letter of introduction required
Subj: mining; business records; records of parent org *Collns: Archvs:* records of Rio Tinto plc (mine owners) & some of its subsidiaries & predecessors, incl: The Rio Tinto-Zinc Corporation/RTZ/Rio Tinto plc records (from 1962); The Rio Tinto Company records (from 1873); Pyrites Company records (from c1911); Zinc Corp records (from 1930s); ☛

(Rio Tinto plc, Archvs cont)

Collns: Archvs (cont): Consolidated Zinc Corp records (from 1949); Imperial Smelting Corp records (from 1929); Natl Smelting Company records (from 1917); Sulphide Corp records (from 1890s); Broken Hill Secretariat records (from 1948); Selection Trust records (from 1920s); Anglesey Aluminium records (from 1967); Kern River Oilfields of California records (from 1910); Tunnel Portland Cement Company records (from 1911); Capper Pass & Son (from 1894)

A325 ♀ ⌖♪

Rothschild Archive

New Ct, St Swithin's Ln, London, EC4P 4DU (020-7280-5874; *fax:* 020-7980-5657)
Email: info@rothschildarchive.org
Internet: http://www.rothschildarchive.org/

Gov Body: Rothschild Archv Trust (registered charity) *Chief:* Dir of Rothschild Archv: Mr Victor W. Gray
Entry: bona fide rsrchers by appt only *Open:* Mon-Fri 1000-1615
Subj: Rothschild Family & businesses in Britain, France, Austria & Germany: business records; family papers; estate archvs; personal papers
Collns: Archvs: records of N.M. Rothschild & Sons; records relating to the involvement of Rothschild family membs with cultural activs, philanthropic orgs, the development of Jewish colonies in Palestine, mgmt of estates & art collns

A326 ♀

Royal Albert Hall Archives

Kensington Gore, London, SW7 2AP (020-7589-3203; *fax:* 020-7823-7725)
Email: jackyc@royalalberthall.com
Internet: http://www.royalalberthall.com/

Gov Body: Corp of the Royal Albert Hall of Arts & Scis *Chief:* Archivist: Ms Jacky Cowdrey
Entry: adv appt only *Open:* Tue, Thu 1030-1730
Subj: music; performing arts; records of parent org *Collns: Archvs:* Corp of the Royal Albert Hal records (1868-date); assorted info relating to Royal Albert Hall *Other:* colln of c18000 programmes of events (1871-date); photos & clippings
Equip: copier *Disabled:* access facilities in Main Hall *Offcr-in-Charge:* Archivist, as above *Svcs:* info, ref, rsrch (charged on time basis, with 1st half hr free)
Acq Offcr: Archivist, as above
Classn: by date
Staff: Archivists: 1 *Non-Prof:* 1
Further Info: This is a small, specific archv run on a PT basis

A327 ⌖♪

Royal and Sun Alliance Insurance Group plc, Archives

Leadenhall Ct, 1 Leadenhall St, London, EC3V 1PP (020-7337-5196; *fax:* 020-7337-5188)
Email: martin.cruwys@rsa14.royalsun.com

Chief: Group Archivist: Mr Martin Cruwys
Entry: adv appt
Subj: insurance; business records; records of parent org & predecessors *Collns: Archvs:* records of Royal Insurance Co Ltd (1846-1896); records of London & Lancashire Insurance Co Ltd (1862-1962)

A328 ♀

Royal Anthropological Institute Archives

50 Fitzroy St, London, W1T 5BT (020-7323-8031/52; *fax:* 020-7388-8817)
Email: admin@therai.org.uk
Internet: http://www.therai.org.uk/

Gov Body: Royal Anthropological Inst *Chief:* Archivist: Mrs Sarah Walpole BA, DipLib *Other Snr Staff:* Lib Offcr: Mrs Janice Archer BSc (020-723-8052; *email:* jarcher@thebritishmuseum.ac.uk)
Assoc Offices: The Archvs are currently held at the BRITISH MUSEUM ANTHRO LIB (see **S1034**), but will be housed by the RAI elsewhere in late 2003
Entry: adv appt *Open:* Mon-Fri 1030-1645; closed public hols & last 2 wks of Sep
Subj: social sci; anthro; records of parent org
Collns: Archvs: Royal Anthropological Inst house archvs *Other:* MSS colln; field notes; theses; colonial reports; rsrch papers; maps & photos
Svcs: info, ref, biblio, rsrch
Stock: archvs/176 linear m
Classn: author & subj index
Pubns: handlists; Journal of the Royal Anthropological Inst; Anthro Today; occasional papers; annual report; Anthropological Index Online
Proj: rehousing of archvs in late 2003

A329 ⌖♪

The Royal Bank of Scotland plc, Group Archives

(incorporating the former NatWest Group Archvs)
Regent's House, 42 Islington High St, London, N1 8XL (020-7615-6127; *fax:* 020-7837-7560)
Email: archives@rbs.co.uk
Internet: http://www.rbs.co.uk/group_info/memorybank/

Gov Body: The Royal Bank of Scotland Group *Chief:* Group Archivist: Ms Alison Turton
Assoc Offices: LONDON READING ROOM, addr as above; EDINBURGH READING ROOM, 42 St Andrew Sq, Edinburgh, EH2 2AD (0131-556-7001)
Entry: bona fide rsrchers, by appt only; apply to Group Archvs for access application form in first instance; access to some records is restricted
Open: both Reading Rooms: Mon-Fri 0930-1630
Subj: banking: records of parent org & predecessors (mainly 18C-20C, but dating back to 1660s); hist of banking *Collns: Bks & Pamphs:* staff magazines; banking journals; bks on the hist of banking *Archvs:* historical archvs of The Royal Bank of Scotland Group & predecessors (over 200 businesses incl NatWest Group) in banking, incl foundation & corporate records; partners' papers; branch records (incomplete); staff records; records of premises (incl arch drawings & photos); advertising records *Other:* photos (1870s-date); banknotes (18C-early 20C); films & videos (1940-date, most from 1980s onwards)
Equip: m-film reader, copier *Svcs:* info
Stock: archvs/3500 linear m
Auto Sys: CALM
Pubns: A Guide to the Historical Records of The Royal Bank of Scotland (£6.00 incl p&p); The Ledgers of Edward Backwell – Banker of London (CD-ROM); online archv guide & historical info on web site

A330 🏛

Royal Borough of Kensington and Chelsea, Local Studies and Archives Service

Central Lib, Phillimore Walk, London, W8 7RX (020-7361-3038; *fax:* 020-7361-2976)
Email: information.services@rbkc.gov.uk
Internet: http://www.rbkc.gov.uk/libraries/localstudies/

Gov Body: Royal Borough of Kensington & Chelsea (see **P95**) *Chief:* Local Studies & Archvs Mgr: Ms Amber Baylis MA, MCLIP, MCMI
Assoc Offices: CHELSEA LOCAL STUDIES COLLN, Chelsea Ref Lib, Kings Rd, London, SW3 5EE (020-7352-6056), Ref Libn: Mr David Walker
Entry: Kensington: by adv appt only; *Chelsea:* adv appt advised *Open: Kensington:* Tue, Thu 1300-1830, Fri-Sat 1300-1700; *Chelsea:* Mon-Tue, Thu 1000-2000, Wed 1000-1300, Fri-Sat 1000-1700
Subj: Royal Borough of Kensington & Chelsea: local authority archvs; business records; estate archvs; family papers; local hist *Collns: Archvs:* council minutes & agendas; census returns; electoral registers *Other:* maps & illusts
Equip: m-form reader/printers, copier *Online:* Internatl Genealogical Index on CD-ROM
Stock: archvs/900 linear m
Staff: Libns: 2 *Non-Prof:* 1

Royal College of Obstetricians and Gynaecologists Archives

See ROYAL COLL OF OBSTETRICIANS & GYNAECOLOGISTS, MARKLAND LIB & INFO SVC (**S1352**)

A331 ♀

Royal Festival Hall Archive

Belvedere Rd, London, SE1 8XX (020-7921-0713; *fax:* 020-7928-0063)
Email: smiller@rfh.org.uk
Internet: http://www.rfh.org.uk

Chief: Archv Administrator: Mr Stephen Miller
Entry: adv appt in writing; proof of ID required
Open: Tue-Wed 1100-1700
Subj: opera; ballet; music; business records; records of parent org *Collns: Archvs:* records of Royal Festival Hall (1951-date); records relating to the Queen Elizabeth Hall, Purcell Room & the Jubilee Gdns; records relating to the Festival of Britain & to exhibs held at the South Bank Centre *Other:* photos; concert programmes & posters; ephemera
Equip: Disabled: wheelchair access

A332 ✚ 🎓

Royal Free Hospital Archives Centre

The Hoo, 17 Lyndhurst Gdns, London, NW3 5NU (*tel & fax:* 020-7794-0692)
Email: enquiries@royalfreearchives.org.uk
Internet: http://www.royalfreearchives.org.uk/

Gov Body: Royal Free Hampstead NHS Trust *Chief:* Archivist: Miss Victoria North MA
Entry: adv appt *Open:* Mon-Fri 1000-1700
Subj: London: hosp records; records of parent org *Collns: Bks & Pamphs:* small lib of health-related printed bks (17C-20C) *Archvs:* records of Royal Free Hosp & other hosps; records of London School of Medicine for Women (later Royal Free Hosp School of Medicine), incl some records relating to early women doctors (19C onwards); personal papers, mainly of former staff & students

Equip: m-reader, 2 copiers (A4/10p), fax *Svcs:* info, ref, rsrch
Classn: ISAD(G) *Auto Sys:* DS
Pubns: Illustrated Hist of the Royal Free Hosp, by Lynn A. Amidon (1996)
Staff: Archivists: 1

A333
Royal Fusiliers Museum and Archives
Tower of London, London, EC3N 4AB (020-7488-5612; *fax:* 020-7481-1093)

Chief: Hon Archivist: Miss F. Devereux
Entry: by appt only; letter of introduction required
Subj: regimental records; military hist *Collns: Archvs:* archvs of the Royal Regiment of Fusiliers

A334
Royal Geographical Society Archives
(incl the Inst of British Geographers Archvs)
Map Room, 1 Kensington Gore, London, SW7 2AR (020-7591-3050; *fax:* 020-7591-3001)
Email: archives@rgs.org
Internet: http://www.rgs.org/

Chief: Maps & Archvs Asst: Ms Sarah Strong
Assoc Offices: ROYAL GEOGRAPHICAL SOC LIB (see S1363)
Entry: open to fellows of the Soc & serious rsrchers by appt only; non-fellows are asked to pay £10 per visit; anyone wishing to make more than 3 visits should apply to join the Soc *Open:* Mon-Tue 1100-1700
Subj: worldwide: family papers; personal papers; records of parent org *Collns: Archvs:* large colln of autograph letters (1830-1950), mainly from Fellows of Soc to its Sec; various travel diaries & observation notebks; MSS submitted to the Geographical Journal; IGU (Internatl Geographical Union) papers (1956-92); Everest Expedition papers (1920-53); Mount Everest Foundation papers (1921-72); ; MSS of Soc's own Gold Medallists (not complete colln); misc MSS relating to geographical subjects/explorers; special collns: C.R. Markham MSS; D. Livingstone MSS; Dixon Denham MSS; Ney Elias MSS; F.W.H. Migeod MSS; E. Ommaney MSS; H.C. Rawlinson MSS; H.M. Stanley MSS
Equip: m-reader (in lib), video viewer (in lib), plug for laptop, photocopying svc available
Stock: archvs/500 linear m
Classn: own *Staff:* 1 PT

A335
Royal Institute of Painters in Watercolours Archives
c/o Federation of British Artists, 17 Carlton House Ter, London, SW1Y 5BD (020-7930-6844; *fax:* 020-7839-7830)

Chief: Archivist: Mr George Large RI, RBA
Entry: private; ref only, by appt
Subj: records of parent org *Collns: Bks & Pamphs:* catalogues, minutes etc *Archvs:* archvs of the RIPW from foundation in 1832

A336
Royal London Hospital Archives and Museum
Royal London Hosp, Whitechapel, London, E1 1BB (020-7377-7608; *fax:* 020-7377-7677)
Email: jonathan.evans@bartsandthelondon. nhs.uk
Internet: http://www.brlcf.org.uk/ archivesandmuseums/

Gov Body: Barts & The London NHS Trust
Chief: Trust Archivist: Mr Jonathan Evans BA, DipAA
Assoc Offices: located in the same bldg as THE LONDON HOSP MEDICAL COLL LIB
Entry: ref only & adv appt for archival users
Open: Mon-Fri 1000-1630
Subj: Tower Hamlets & Newham: estate archvs; business records; personal papers; records of parent org; hosp records; hist of nursing *Collns: Bks & Pamphs:* London Hosp "Old Londoner" Colln; H. Hamilton Bailey Colln (surgical author, 100 items); British Soc for the Study of Orthodontics Lib; small lib on hist of nursing *Archvs:* Royal London (previously The London) Hosp records (1740-date); Queen Elizabeth Hosp for Children, Hackney, records (1867-date); London Chest Hosp records (1848-date); records of several other hosps in Tower Hamlets & Newham; London Hosp Medical Coll records (1785-date); Edith Cavell (1865-1915), papers & artifacts; Eva Luckes (1854-1919), papers & artifacts, incl correspondence with Florence Nightingale; Sydney Holland, 2nd Viscount Knutsford (1855-1931), papers & artifacts
Equip: 2 m-readers, video viewer, 3 copiers
Stock: archvs/300 linear m; photos/20000; slides/2500; illusts/200; m-forms/8000; audios/20; videos/80; films/400
Pubns: London Pride: The Story of a Voluntary Hosp (£3.50p); LHMC 1785-1985: The Story of England's First Medical School (£7.95p); Edith Cavell: Her Life & Her Art (£2.95p); The Dental School of the London Hosp Medical Coll 1911-1991; A Hist of Radiotherapy at the London Hosp 1896-1996 (£12)
Staff: Archivists: 2 *Non-Prof:* 1
Further Info: A collection-level description of holdings can be found on the internet at: http://www.aim25.co.uk/

A337
Royal National Theatre Archive
Royal Natl Theatre, South Bank, London, SE1 9PX (020-7820-3512; *fax:* 020-7820-3512)
Email: archive@nationaltheatre.org.uk
Internet: http://www.nationaltheatre.org.uk/

Gov Body: Royal Natl Theatre *Chief:* Archivist: Ms Louise Ray
Assoc Offices: archvs are held at Salisbury House, Kennington Pk, 1-3 Brixton Rd, London, SW9 6DE; please use addr above for correspondence
Entry: adv appt; proof of ID required *Open:* Mon, Wed, Fri 1000-1700
Subj: UK: theatre; business records; records of parent org *Collns: Archvs:* administrative records of all depts of the Natl Theatre, incl annual reports & minutes; papers pertaining to establishment of a natl theatre from early 20C, incl: Shakespeare Memorial Natl Theatre papers; Sidney Bernstein Colln *Other:* production info (1963-date), incl: press cuttings; posters; programmes; press reviews; photos; prompt scripts; drawings; videos of NT productions from 1995 onwards
Svcs: photocopying svc
Classn: ISAD(G) *Auto Sys:* DS CALM
Staff: Archivists: 3

A338
Royal Opera House Archives
Covent Gdn, London, WC2E 7DD (020-7240-1200; *fax:* 020-7836-1762)
Internet: http://www.roh.org.uk/

Type: performing arts org *Chief:* Archivist: Ms Francesca Franchi *Dep:* Asst Archivist: Ms Jane Jackson
Entry: by appt only; a fee may be payable

Open: Mon-Tue, Thu-Fri 1030-1300, 1430-1730 (closed Wed)
Subj: records of parent org; opera; ballet; performing arts *Collns: Archvs:* archvs of the Royal Opera House & its performing companies, The Royal Ballet & The Royal Opera (incl playbills, programmes, photos, correspondence, designs & administrative files)
Equip: copier
Stock: archvs/900 linear m; bks/1000; periodcls/15; photos/500000; illusts/10000; press cuttings/56 linear m; costumes/200
Staff: Other Prof: 1 *Non-Prof:* 1.5

A339
Royal Statistical Society Archives
12 Errol St, London, EC1Y 8LX (020-7638-8998; *fax:* 020-7638-0946)
Email: j.foster@rss.org.uk
Internet: http://www.rss.org.uk/

Gov Body: Royal Statistical Soc *Chief:* Archvs Consultant: Ms Janet Foster
Entry: adv appt only
Subj: statistics; personal papers; records of parent org *Collns: Archvs:* archvs of Royal Statistical Soc (1834-date); William Newmarch papers (19C economist & statistician); Sir Arthur Lyon Bowley papers (20C economist & statistician); statistical papers of William Jevons (19C economist); Yule papers; Inst of Statisticians Archv
Staff: Archivists: 1 PT

A340
The Salters' Company Archive
Salters' Hall, 4 Fore St, London, EC2Y 5DE (020-7588-5216; *fax:* 020-7638-3679)
Email: company@salters.co.uk

Type: livery company *Chief:* Archivist: Mrs Katie George BA, DipAA
Entry: adv appt essential *Open:* varies
Subj: records of parent org *Collns: Archvs:* Archvs of the Salters' Company (13C-date), incl: minutes of Court of Assts (1627-date); minutes of various Company committees (19C-date); accounts (17C-date)
Staff: Archivists: 1

A341
Salvation Army, International Heritage Centre
William Booth Coll, Champion Pk, Denmark Hill, London, SE5 8BQ (020-7332-0101; *fax:* 020-7332-8064)
Email: heritage@salvationarmy.org

Gov Body: The Salvation Army UK Territorial HQ
Chief: Dir: Major James Bryden *Dep:* Archivist: Mr Gordon Taylor
Assoc Offices: SALVATION ARMY TERRITORIAL HQ LIB (see S1385); WILLIAM BOOTH COLL LIB, addr as above (see S1463)
Entry: rsrchers by appt in adv *Open:* Tue-Thu 0930-1530 excl public hols
Subj: internatl work of The Salvation Army; records of parent org
Equip: m-form reader/printer, copier
Classn: own

A342
Save the Children Fund, Archives
17 Grove Ln, Camberwell, London, SE5 8RD (020-7716-2269; *fax:* 020-7703-2278)
Email: s.sneddon@scfuk.org.uk
Internet: http://www.savethechildren.org.uk/

(Save the Children Fund, Archvs cont)
Type: charity **Gov Body:** Save the Children UK
Chief: Archivist & Records Mgr: Mrs Susan Sneedon BA, MArAd
Assoc Offices: SAVE THE CHILDREN FUND LIB, at same addr (020-7716-2263)
Entry: open to rsrchers, by adv appt only
Subj: Save the Children Fund: records of parent org; personal papers **Collns:** *Bks & Pamphs:* SCF pubns, incl The World's Children (1920-date) & annual reports (1920-date); bks & pamphs about or relating to SCF *Archvs:* minutes of Council (1922-1984, 1928 missing); minutes of various advisory & exec cttees (from 1920s); Eglantyne Jebb Papers (early SCF files, 1921-26); files of past Dir Genls (Sir Colin Thornley, Dir Genl 1965-74 & John Cumber, Dir Genl 1976-84); overseas papers; advertising & publicity materials *Other:* photo colln; film colln (1920s-1980s); video lib (incl more recent material)
Equip: photocopying svc **Svcs:** rsrch
Stock: archvs/150 linear m
Pubns: Archvs Guide; Archvs Papers (Nos 1-9); available on request
Staff: Archivists: 1

A343 🔑

The Scout Association, Archives Department

Gilwen Pk, Bury Rd, Chingford, London, E4 7QW (020-8433-7196; *fax:* 020-8433-7103)
Email: archives@scout.org.uk

Chief: Archivist: Mr P. Moynihan
Entry: ref only with adv appt **Open:** Mon-Fri 1000-1600
Subj: scouting; records of parent org; personal papers **Collns:** *Archvs:* correspondence & papers of Scout Assoc (1909-94); correspondence & papers of Robert Baden-Powell relating to Scouting, incl diaries, record bks & sketches
Equip: m-reader, copier
Stock: archvs/360 boxes; bks/4000; photos/10000; slides/4000; pamphs/1000; videos/200
Staff: Libns: 2

A344 🎓

The Serge Prokofiev Archive

Goldsmiths Coll, Univ of London, London, SE14 6NW (020-7919-7558; *fax:* 020-7919-7255)
Email: n.mann@gold.ac.uk
Internet: http://www.sprkfv.net/archive/archivehome.html

Chief: Curator: Mrs Noëlle Mann
Entry: ref only; adv appt
Subj: life & works of the composer Serge Prokofiev; family papers; personal papers
Collns: *Bks & Pamphs:* printed bks, mainly in English & Russian; Vladimir Blok Lib (Russian composer); publ scores; journals; doctoral theses on Prokofiev & 20C Russian music *Archvs:* music MSS, correspondence, business & private papers of Serge Prokofiev; addl collns & bequests of materials related to the composer incl: Lina Prokofiev Colln; Oleg Prokofiev Colln; Christopher Palmer Colln *Other:* photos; articles; press cuttings; concert programmes; audio colln, incl CDs, LPs & archival tape recordings; videos; memorabilia **Co-op Schemes:** collaborative projs with Russian counterparts

A345 🔑

Society for the Protection of Ancient Buildings, Archives

37 Spital Sq, London, E1 6DY (020-7377-1644; *fax:* 020-7247-5296)
Email: info@spab.org.uk
Internet: http://www.spab.org.uk/

Type: charity **Chief:** Archivist: Miss Cecily Greenhill
Entry: ref only, open to bona fide rsrchers by written appt only
Subj: historic bldgs; bldg conservation; hist of bldg conservation; records of parent org **Collns:** *Archvs:* about 15000 archv files relating to the work of the Soc (1877-date)
Equip: copier
Pubns: quarterly journal; Annual Report; pamphs on historic bldg repair methods
Staff: Archivists: 1 PT

A346 🔑 ✚

Society of Apothecaries Archives

Apothecaries' Hall, Black Friars Ln, London, EC4V 6EJ (020-7248-6648; *fax:* 020-7329-3177)
Email: archivist@apothecaries.org
Internet: http://www.apothecaries.org/

Type: city livery company **Gov Body:** The Worshipful Soc of Apothecaries of London
Chief: Archivist: Mrs Dee Cook BA, MA, DARM, RMSA
Entry: adv appt only **Open:** Mon-Fri 0930-1730
Subj: City of London: records of parent org
Collns: *Other:* The Soc maintains a small colln of printed bks, some rare, & some pamphs, relating to: medicine; pharmacy; hist of medicine & pharmacy; botany; other medical & associated orgs; the City of London; other livery companies; amongst its holdings are: short run of the Lancet (1823-43); almost complete set of the minutes of the Genl Medical Council (1858-date); almost complete set of medical directories (1846-date)
Svcs: info, rsrch
Stock: archvs/c200 linear ft, incl bnd vols, loose papers, legal documents, certificates, title deeds, cuttings & ephemera; also various photos, slides, illusts, pamphs, maps/plans, copperplates, collns of pharmaceutical, medical & surgical artifacts
Pubns: A Hist of the Soc of Apothecaries, by Penelope Hunting (Soc of Apothecaries, London, 1998); A Catalogue of Selected Portraits & Pictures at Apothecaries' Hall, by Dai Walters (Soc of Apothecaries, London, 1997)
Staff: Archivists: 1
Further Info: The Soc's Archvs are currently split between Apothecaries' Hall, where a new repository is in the process of being established, & Guildhall Lib (see **A280**)

A347 🏛

Southwark Local Studies Library

211 Borough High St, London, SE1 1JA (020-7403-3507; *fax:* 020-7403-8633)
Email: local.studies.library@southwark.gov.uk
Internet: http://www.southwark.gov.uk/

Gov Body: London Borough of Southwark (see **P104**) **Chief:** Local Studies Libn: post vacant
Dep: Archivist: Mr Stephen Humphrey MA
Entry: ref only, appt advised for m-readers
Open: Mon, Thu 0930-2000, Tue, Fri 0930-1700, Sat 0930-1300; closed Wed
Subj: London Borough of Southwark: local authority archvs; parish records (not registers); business records; political papers **Collns:** *Archvs:* London Borough of Southwark & preceding authorities; property deeds; other misc deposits
Equip: 4 m-readers, 3 m-printers (25p per copy), copier (A4/10p), clr copier (A4/£1), fax (£1 per pg

in UK), 3 computers (incl 2 with internet, printouts A4/10p), photograph copystand (£5 per hr) **Svcs:** info, ref, biblio, room hire
Stock: archvs/230 cubic m; bks/10000; periodcls/60; photos/20000; slides/4000; illusts/20000; pamphs/2000; maps/2000; m-forms/1300; videos/50; cuttings & ephemera/8 filing cases
Classn: DDC (mod) **Auto Sys:** SALIS
Pubns: Guide to the Archvs in the Southwark Local Studies Lib (£2.50); Southwark in Archvs (£4.95); London Borough of Southwark's Neighbourhood Series (£1.95-£4 each); Southwark – An Illustrated Hist (£6.95); Southwark at War (£2.50); Family Hist in Southwark (£1.95); Charles Dickens & Southwark (£2.50); The Mayflower & Pilgrim Story: Chapters from Rotherhithe & Southwark (£3); The Southwark Trail (£1.95); Southwark Park – A Brief Hist (£2.50); Postcard Sets (80p-£2 each); Reprint OS Maps (£1.95 each); other maps, greetings cards & other pubns available; contact Local Studies Lib for full list
Staff: Archivists: 1 **Libns:** 1 **Non-Prof:** 1.75
Exp: £4300 (2000-01)

A348 ✚

St George's Hospital Archive

Jenner Wing, Cranmer Ter, London, SW17 0RE (020-8725-3255; *fax:* 020-8767-4696)
Email: nthereka@sghms.ac.uk
Internet: http://www.sghms.ac.uk/depts/is/library/

Gov Body: free-standing, but memb of Federation of Univ of London (see **S1440**)
Chief: Bibliographic Svcs Libn: Mrs Nallini Thevakarrunai DipLib, MSc
Entry: ref only, adv appt; proof of ID required
Open: Mon-Fri 0900-1700; possible access during evenings & Sats
Subj: Wandsworth: personal papers; records of parent org; hosp records **Collns:** *Bks & Pamphs:* historical colln, incl bks by John Hunter, Edwards Jenner, Benjamin Brodie, Thomas Young & Everard Home; outsize bks of anatomical drawings *Archvs:* minute bks & student registers of St Georges Hosp (1733-1974); records of the St Georges Hosp Medical School & School of Nursing; Atkinson Morleys Hosp records & case hists (1846-1946); minute bks of Bolingbroke Hosp (1897-1948); records of Royal Victoria Hosp For Children; records of St Benedict's Hosp, Tooting; records of St James Hosp, Balham; Benjamin Brodie MSS; minutes of St George's Medical & Surgical Soc (later the Hunterian Soc); records of St George's Hosp Medical School Lib *Other:* photos, plans, misc papers etc
Equip: m-reader, m-printer, m-camera, copier, clr copier, fax, video viewer, computer (incl wd-proc, internet & CD-ROM), room for hire *Online:* Medline, CINAHL, IMIC, ASSIA, BNI, AHMED
Svcs: info, ref, rsrch (fee-based)
Stock: archvs/175 m; bks/1000; periodcls/800; slides/900; audios/70; videos/84
Classn: NLM **Auto Sys:** Unicorn (Sirsi)
Pubns: guides & handlists (Lib's Info Series)
Staff: Libns: 1 **Exp:** £1000 (2000-01)
Proj: movement of colln to purpose built accommodation & merging with Medical School Colln
See also ST GEORGE'S LIB (**S1410**)

A349 🔑 🏛

Tate Archive

Hyman Kreitman Rsrch Centre, Tate Britain, Millbank, London, SW1P 4RG (020-7887-8838; *fax:* 020-7887-8007)
Email: research.centre@tate.org.uk
Internet: http://www.tate.org.uk/collections/archive.htm

Gov Body: Trustees of the Tate Gallery **Chief:** Head of Archv & Registry: Mrs Jennifer Booth
Assoc Offices: TATE LIB, at same addr (see **S1418**)

Entry: ref only by adv appt; appointments may be made for morning or afternoon sessions, or for the whole day *Open:* Mon-Wed 1000 – 1700 *Subj:* British art & artists, collectors, critics, writers, galleries & instns (mainly 20C); personal papers; records of parent org *Collns: Bks & Pamphs:* artists' diaries *Archvs:* records of the Tate Gallery (1897-date), incl bldg deeds, acquisitions files, Board of Trustees minutes, exhib files & other materials relating to the hist of the Tate; Contemporary Art Soc Archv; Artists Internatl Assoc Archv; collns of papers of artists & other figs from the arts world incl: William Holman Hunt papers; Paul Nash papers; David Bomberg papers; Stanley Spencer papers; Alfred Turner papers; John Piper papers; Ben Nicholson papers; Kenneth Clark papers; Sir Jacob Epstein papers; Dame Barbara Hepworth papers; John Minton papers; Sir Eduardo Paolozzi papers; Walter Sickert papers; Charleston Papers (membs of the Bloomsbury Group); numerous others *Other:* Photo Colln (artists' photos & photos relating to the Tate); Audio Colln (incl oral hist recordings of artists & recordings of lectures & conferences held at the Tate); posters; press cuttings
Equip: m-reader, m-printer, copier (A4/20p, A3/40p), computers (incl 4 with internet), television, video viewer, DVD player, audio cassette players *Disabled:* no wheelchair access *Online:* Wilson Art Abstracts, Art Bibliographies Modern, Grove Dictionary of Art
Stock: archvs/c700 collns

A350
Tower Hamlets Local History Library and Archives

Bancroft Lib, 277 Bancroft Rd, London, E1 4DQ (020-8980-4366 x129; *fax:* 020-8983-4510)
Email: localhistory@towerhamlets.gov.uk

Gov Body: London Borough of Tower Hamlets (see **P106**) *Chief:* Local Hist Libn: Mr C.J. Lloyd BLib, MCLIP *Dep:* Asst Local Hist Libn: Mr D. Rich BA(Hons) *Other Snr Staff:* Archivist: Mr M. Barr-Hamilton BA, DipAS
Entry: ref only *Open:* Tue, Thu 0900-2000, Fri 0900-1800, Sat 0900-1700
Subj: Tower Hamlets: local authority archvs; estate archvs; local hist; shipping records
Collns: Archvs: local govt records relating to London Borough of Tower Hamlets & its predecessors; title deeds; lease bks for Cubitt Town Estate *Other:* shipping colln (mainly 19C merchant shipping): photos, press cuttings, files, various indexes
Equip: 4 m-readers, m-printer, video viewer, fax, copier, computer (incl wd-proc)
Stock: archvs/800 m; bks/11000; periodcls/250; photos/25000; slides/5000; pamphs/9000; maps/2300; m-forms/1800; audios/97; videos/65; cuttings/450 boxes
Classn: own
Pubns: All My Yesterdays: Autobiography of Patrick Hanshaw of Wapping (£5.99 + £1.09 p&p); Changing Places: A Short Hist of the Mile End Town Residents Assoc Area (£4.50 + 76p p&p); East End at Work (£9.99 + £1.58 p&p); East End Story: Autobiography of Alfred Gradner in Stepney, 1960s-1990s (£5.95 + £1.09 p&p); free leaflets: Brief Guide to Family Hist & Other Sources in Tower Hamlets Local Hist Lib & Archvs; Handlist 1: Personal Names Indexes; Handlist 2: Registers of Places of Worship; Handlist 3: Taxation, Rating & valuation Records
Staff: Archivists: 1 *Libns:* 2

Transport for London Archives and Records Management Service

See LONDON'S TRANSPORT MUSEUM, REF LIB (**S1268**)

A351 ✚
UCLH Archives

Info Mgmt Dept, Vezey Strong Wing, 112 Hampstead Rd, London, NW1 2LT (020-7387-9300 x3717)
Email: libby.adams@uclh.org
Internet: http://www.uclh.org/services/archives/

Gov Body: UCL Hosps NHS Trust *Chief:* Archivist: Ms Libby Adams
Assoc Offices: repositories holding archvs of other Trust hosps: UNIV COLL LONDON LIB SPECIAL COLLNS (see **S1433**); LONDON METROPOLITAN ARCHVS (see **A304**)
Entry: adv appt; proof of ID required; refs may be requested; patients' records less than 100 years old are closed, except to the indiv concerned or their next of kin; all records are only made available at the discretion of the Archivist
Open: Mon-Fri 0900-1700; closed Xmas & New Year, Easter & public hols
Subj: London: hosp records; health records
Collns: Archvs: records of existing & former hosps connected with the Trust, some dating from 1748, incl cttee minutes, photographs, staff records & patient records; collns incl: Middlesex Hosp archvs; Eastman Dental Hosp archvs; Middlesex Hosp Medical School archvs; St Peter's Hosp archvs; St Paul's Hosp archvs; St Philip's Hosp archvs; Hosp for Women, Soho Sq, archvs; Natl Temperance Hosp archvs
Equip: no copying facilities available; rsrchers may use lap-top computers *Svcs:* ref, enqs
Stock: archvs/c350 linear m
Staff: Archivists: 1

A352
Unilever Corporate Archives

Unilever House, Blackfriars, London, EC4P 4BQ (020-7822-5451/6642; *fax:* 020-7822-5616)

Chief: Corporate Archivist: Ms J. Strickland BA, MAA *Dep:* Snr Archivist: Mrs L.E. Owen-Edwards BA, DipAA
Assoc Offices: archvs are held at: The Lyceum, Bridge St, Port Sunlight, Merseyside, CH62 4UJ, but enqs & correspondence should be directed to the addr above
Entry: adv appt; proof of ID & a letter of intro-duction will be required *Open:* Mon-Fri 1000-1600 *Subj:* world-wide: business records; records of parent org *Collns: Bks & Pamphs:* company hists; biographies; subj-related textbks; in-house magazines; Unilever pubns *Archvs:* Unilever plc & UK concern companies
Equip: 2 m-readers
Classn: ISAD(G) *Auto Sys:* DS

A353
The V&A Archive

Blythe House, 23 Blythe Rd, London, W14 0QX (020-7602-8832/5886; *fax:* 020-7602-0980)
Email: archive@vam.ac.uk
Internet: http://www.nal.vam.ac.uk/

Gov Body: Victoria & Albert Museum *Chief:* Head of Archvs: Ms Serena Kelly *Dep:* Museum Archivist: Mr Christopher Marsden
Assoc Offices: the Archv is a section of the NATL ART LIB (see **S1290**); ARCHV OF ART & DESIGN, at same addr (see **A250**)
Entry: adv appt; all bona fide students & rsrchers; registration required, with proof of ID; records less than 30 years old can only be consulted with permission of head of relevant dept *Open:* Tue-Thu 1000-1630; closed for 3 wks for stocktaking from the Sat before August Bank Hol
Subj: Victoria & Albert Museum & its collns

Collns: Archvs: records documenting hist of Museum & its bldgs (1844-1956); records relaying to acq, disposal & loan of Museum's objects (1852 onwards), incl those acquired by Bethnal Green Museum of Childhood, Theatre Museum & Wellington Museum; departmental records, incl administrative papers, photos & bklets (1930s onwards); directorate records, incl papers of previous Dirs of the V&A, minutes of cttee meetings etc (1850s onwards); exhibition-related materials (1890 onwards); Natl Art Lib archvs, incl registers, inventories & catalogues (1853 onwards); papers of past Keepers of Museum collns (1950s onwards)
Equip: m-reader, video viewer, computer (incl internet) *Svcs:* info, ref
Classn: ISAD(G), EAD
Staff: Archivists: 2 *Non-Prof:* 3

A354
Waltham Forest Archives and Local Studies Library

Vestry House Museum, Vestry Rd, Walthamstow, London, E17 9NH (020-8509-1917)
Email: vestry.house@al.lbwf.gov.uk
Internet: http://www.lbwf.gov.uk/vestry/vestry.htm

Gov Body: London Borough of Waltham Forest (see **P108**) *Chief:* Archivist: Jo Parker BA, DipAS; Local Studies Libn: Mr David Pracy MA, MCLIP
Entry: adv appt *Open:* Tue-Wed, Fri 1000-1300, 1400-1715, Sat 1000-1300, 1400-1645
Subj: London Borough of Waltham Forest: local authority archvs; parish records; estate archvs; family papers; business records; political records; records of parent org; school records; charity records; records of nonconformist churches
Collns: Bks & Pamphs: hist of the area now comprised by London Borough of Waltham Forest *Archvs:* records of London Borough of Waltham Forest; records of former boroughs of Chingford, Leyton & Walthamstow; records of parishes of Waltham Forest Deanery; records of Chingford Mount Cemetery (1884-1970); MS works of John Drinkwater (1882-1937, from c1912-34) *Other:* historic maps of area; local newspapers; electoral registers; directories; ephemera
Equip: 3 m-readers, m-printer
Stock: archvs/43 cubic m; bks/119 linear m; pamphs/39 linear m
Staff: Archivists: 1 *Libns:* 0.5 *Non-Prof:* 0.5
Exp: £40780 (1999-2000); £40780 (2000-01); incl staff costs

A355
Wandsworth Local History Service

Battersea Lib, Lavender Hill, London, SW11 1JB (020-8871-7753; *fax:* 020-8978-4376)
Email: jgregson@wandsworth.gov.uk
Internet: http://www.wandsworth.gov.uk/libraries/

Gov Body: London Borough of Wandsworth (see **P109**) *Chief:* Local Hist Archivist: Miss Julie Gregson BA, MA *Dep:* Local Hist Libn: Ms Meredith Davies
Entry: adv appt preferred *Open:* Tue-Wed 1000-2000, Fri 1000-1700, Sat 0900-1300
Subj: London Borough of Wandsworth: local hist; local authority archvs; family papers; business records; personal papers; political papers; poor law records; charity records; records of local groups & orgs *Collns: Bks & Pamphs:* local hist materials; local directories (mainly mid 1880s-1930s); bnd electoral registers (late 19C-date, some gaps esp during world wars) *Archvs:* archvs of Wandsworth Borough Council & predecessor authorities; vestry minutes; cemetery registers; property deeds ☛

Archives

London ▼ Manchester

(Wandsworth Local Hist Svc cont)
Collns: *Other:* local newspapers, periodcls & newsletters; printed ephemera; scrapbks & cuttings collns; map colln; illusts colln (c20000, mainly photos c1870-date); IGI (on m-film); census returns (1941-1901, on m-film)
Equip: m-reader, 2 m-form reader/printers, copier (staff use only) **Svcs:** info, rsrch, photo reproduction, talks to local groups
Stock: archvs/c60 cubic m; bks/11 cubic m, incl pamphs; photos/2 cubic m, incl illusts; slides/1 cubic m; maps/1 cubic m; m-forms/0.5 cubic m
Classn: DDC **Auto Sys:** Dynix
Pubns: reproductions of postcards, prints & local hist pubns; details available on request
Staff: *Archivists:* 1 *Libns:* 0.5

Warburg Institute Archive
See WARBURG INST LIB (**S1456**)

A356 🔑 🖐
Westminster Diocesan Archives
16a Abingdon Rd, Kensington, London, W8 6AF (020-7938-3580)

Gov Body: Westminster RC Diocesan Trustees
Chief: Archivist: Fr Ian Dickie
Entry: adv appt **Open:** Mon-Fri 1030-1600
Subj: diocesan records **Collns:** *Bks & Pamphs:* Catholic pamphs (17C & 18C) *Archvs:* papers of the English Mission (c1568-1685); Vicars Apostolic (1687-1850); Archbishops of Westminster (1850-1963); St Edmunds Coll, Ware; The Old Chapter of England (The Old Brotherhood, 1623-1800)
Equip: copier

A357 🔑
The Worshipful Company of Leathersellers, Archive
15 St Helen's Pl, London, EC3A 6DQ (020-7330-1444; *fax:* 020-7330-1445)
Email: enquiries@leathersellers.co.uk
Internet: http://www.leathersellers.co.uk/

Type: livery company **Gov Body:** The Court of Assts **Chief:** Clerk to the Company: Capt Jonathan Cooke OBE, RN **Dep:** Archivist: Miss Wendy Hawke MArAd
Entry: private archv administered chiefly for the benefit of the Company; info can be provided to rsrchers, but personal callers are not encouraged; if necessary to call in person, admission is by adv appt with the Clerk **Open:** normal office hrs
Subj: records of parent org; estate records; charity records **Collns:** *Bks & Pamphs:* Lib of Abraham Colfe, Vicar of Lewisham (1604-1657) *Archvs:* private records of the Worshipful Company of Leathersellers, incl: govt of the Company; membership records; accounts; estate & charity records
Equip: lists & indexes available
Stock: archvs/225 linear ft
Classn: sys based on that used at Guildhall
Pubns: The Leathersellers' Company: A Hist, by Penelope Hunting (1994)
Staff: *Archivists:* 1

A358 🎩 🖊
Young & Co Breweries plc, Archives
Ram Brewery, Wandsworth High St, London, SW18 4JD (020-8875-7000; *fax:* 020-8875-7100)
Email: archives@youngs.co.uk
Internet: http://www.youngs.co.uk/

Chief: Archivist & Records Mgr: Ms H. Osborn
Entry: adv appt
Subj: brewing; business records; records of parent org **Collns:** *Archvs:* records of Young & Co Breweries (1692-1988), incl minutes, financial records, brewing bks, correspondence, property records etc; minutes of Foster-Probyn Ltd (beer bottlers, 1959-84)

Londonderry

A359 🙏
Diocese of Derry (RC) Archives
9 Steelstown Rd, Londonderry, Co Londonderry, BT48 9AP (028-7135-9809; *fax:* 028-7135-7098)
Email: Edward.Daly@btinternet.com

Gov Body: RC Diocese of Derry **Chief:** Diocesan Archivist: Bishop Edward Daly
Entry: adv appt **Open:** by arrangement
Subj: RC Diocese of Derry: diocesan records
Collns: *Bks & Pamphs:* small, limited colln *Archvs:* episcopal documents & diocesan records (primarily 20C)
Stock: archvs/limited; colln began in 1995

Loughton

A360 🔑
National Jazz Archive
Loughton Lib, Traps Hill, Loughton, Essex, IG10 1HD (020-8502-0181; *fax:* 020-8508-5041)
Email: david.nathan@essexcc.gov.uk
Internet: http://www.essexcc.gov.uk/libraries/

Gov Body: Cttee, incl representatives from Essex County Council Libs (see **P51**), Natl Sound Archv (see **L1**) & British Inst of Jazz Studies (see **S511**) **Chief:** Localities Mgr: Ms Elaine Adams
Dep: Archivist: Mr David Nathan
Open: Mon-Wed, Fri 1000-1300
Subj: music; jazz, mainly British but some foreign, esp American **Collns:** *Bks & Pamphs:* bks relating to jazz, incl many rare titles; disco-graphies; periodcls incl Melody Maker (complete run 1926-1981), Jazz Monthly, Jazz & Blues, Downbeat, Jazz Journal, Storyville, Crescendo, Cadence, Jazz News, Mississippi Rag & Wire, Record Changer *Other:* programmes; fanzines; photos; memorabilia; donations & bequests
Svcs: info, ref, enqs
Stock: archvs/1200; periodcls/4000

Lowestoft

A361 🕰
Suffolk Record Office, Lowestoft Branch
Clapham Rd, Lowestoft, Suffolk, NR32 1DR (01502-405357; *fax:* 01502-405350)
Email: lowestoftro@libher.suffolkcc.gov.uk
Internet: http://www.suffolkcc.gov.uk/libraries_and_heritage/

Gov Body: Suffolk County Council, Libs & Heritage Dept (see **P179**) **Chief:** Public Svc Mgr: Mrs Louise Clarke **Other Snr Staff:** Local Studies Libn: Mr Ed Button BA, MCLIP (ed.button@libher.suffolkcc.gov.uk)
Assoc Offices: BURY ST EDMUNDS BRANCH (see **A83**); IPSWICH BRANCH (see **A215**)

Entry: *Archvs:* CARN ticket, booking of m-reader advised; *Local Studies:* ref only, no ticket needed for open access materials **Open:** Mon, Wed-Fri 0915-1730, Tue 0915-1800, Sat 0915-1700
Subj: NE Suffolk, equivalent to Waveney Dist: local authority archvs; parish records; family papers; estate archvs; business records; shipping records; records of local charities & socs
Collns: *Bks & Pamphs:* Local Studies Lib incl: Benjamin Britten Colln (all publ scores up to 1973, bks on Britten etc); Suffolk Family Hist Soc Lib (on deposit) *Archvs:* Diocese of St Edmundsbury & Ipswich (Lowestoft area) records; Port of Lowestoft Rsrch Soc (photos & cards); Port of Lowestoft shipping records (c1750-1980s); Round Tower Churches Soc Colln (photos, notes, church guides etc); Adair of Flixton Hall family & estate records (13C-20C); records of the fishing industry (1862-1973); Mutford & Lothingland Half-Hundred Court records (13C-1936); Richard Clay Ltd of Bungay records (printers, 1816-1976) *Other:* photo colln; 1901 Census for Suffolk (m-fiche)
Equip: 11 m-readers, m-printer, fax, photocopying svc, computer (incl internet & CD-ROM) **Svcs:** info, ref, rsrch, transcription, translation, m-fiche & m-film duplication
Stock: archvs/2031 linear ft; bks/7500; pamphs/400; maps/1400
Classn: DDC **Auto Sys:** DS CALM 2000
Pubns: Guide to Genealogical Sources (10 sections, priced individually or £22.50 for all 10, incl 2nd class p&p); Family Data Colln Pack (£2.75 incl p&p); Bowen's Map of Suffolk 1759 (£3 incl p&p); various leaflets on svcs (free)
Staff: *Archivists:* 1.2 *Libns:* 0.2 *Non-Prof:* 3.5

Maidstone

A362 🏛
Centre for Kentish Studies
Sessions Hall, County Hall, Maidstone, Kent, ME14 1XQ (01622-694363; *fax:* 01622-694379)
Email: archives@kent.gov.uk
Internet: http://www.kent.gov.uk/arts/archives/

Gov Body: Kent County Council (see **P67**)
Chief: Asst Mgr: Ms Anne Atkinson
Assoc Offices: EAST KENT ARCHVS CENTRE (see **A128**)
Entry: CARN ticket; appt required for access to archival, local studies & m-form materials; no appt required for access to printed bk colln on open shelves **Open:** Tue-Wed, Fri 0900-1700, Thu 1000-1700, 2nd & 4th Sat 0900-1300; m-film facilities close 15 min before rest of Centre
Subj: Kent: local studies; genealogy; local authority archvs; parish records; estate records; family papers; records of charities & socs; hosp records; school records; business records; shipping records; taxation records; apprenticeship records; records of crime & punishment **Collns:** *Bks & Pamphs:* local hist colln *Archvs:* archvs of Kent County Council; Archdiocese of Canterbury (Archdeaconry of Maidstone) parish registers (16C-19C); Diocese of Rochester parish records; electoral registers for Kent (1832-1994); census returns for Kent (on m-film, 1841-1891); wills & inventories; manorial court rolls; school admission registers & logbks *Other:* Internatl Genealogical Index (for Kent, Surrey, Sussex & Essex, on m-fiche); extensive collns of maps & illusts
Stock: archvs/18000

Manchester

A363 🖊
Barclays Group Archives
Dallimore Rd, Wythenshawe, Manchester, M23 9JA (0161-946-3035; *fax:* 0161-946-0226)
Email: Jessie.Campbell@barclays.co.uk
Internet: http://www.personal.barclays.com/

Gov Body: Barclays plc *Chief:* Snr Archivist: Mrs J. Campbell
Entry: adv appt; proof of ID or letter of intro- duction required; closure periods apply to certain categories of record *Open:* Mon-Fri 1000-1600
Subj: business records; family papers; personal papers; records of parent org; banking records
Collns: Archvs: records of Barclays Bank (1896- date); records of founding banks (18C-1896); records of banks taken over since 1896 (incl Bank of Liverpool) & other banks amalgamated under the Barclays name; records of Barclays Bank Internatl (1925-date, incl much overseas material); family & estate records of Urry Family of Gatcombe; correspondence & papers of Sir Richard Biddulph Martin MP (late 19C-early 20C); family & other papers of George Stone (banker, 19C); correspondence & papers of John Thornhill (Dir of East India Company, early 19C)
Equip: m-reader, copier, fax, computer (with wd- proc)

A364

Greater Manchester County Record Office

56 Marshall St, New Cross, Manchester, M4 5FU (0161-832-5284; *fax:* 0161-839-3808)
Email: archives@gmcro.co.uk
Internet: http://www.gmcro.co.uk/

Gov Body: Manchester City Council (see **P112**)
Chief: County Archivist: Mr Vincent McKernan BA(Hons), MArAd *Dep:* Dep County Archivist: Ms Elizabeth Oxborrow-Cowan BA, MSc, RMSA
Entry: CARN ticket *Open:* Mon-Tue, Thu-Fri 0900-1700, Wed 0900-1300; 2nd & 4th Sat of the month 0900-1200, 1300-1600
Subj: County of Greater Manchester: local authority archvs; estate archvs; business records; records of parent org *Collns: Archvs:* Manchester Ship Canal Company records; Roch- dale Canal Company records; Assheton Family of Middleton papers; Wilton Family of Heaton Hall papers; Legh Family of Lyme Hall papers
Equip: 20 m-readers, copier, computer, room for hire
Stock: archvs/724 cubic m; rec mgmt/257 cubic m
Pubns: Guide to GMCRO (£3.95); Courier (bi- monthly newsletter, £2)
Staff: Prof: 5 *Non-Prof:* 3.5

A365

Labour History Archive and Study Centre

(formerly Natl Museum of Labour Hist)
103 Princess St, Manchester, M1 6DD (0161-228- 7212; *fax:* 0161-237-5965)
Email: LHASC@fs1.li.man.ac.uk
Internet: http://rylibweb.man.ac.uk/

Gov Body: Univ of Manchester (see **S1512**)
Chief: Asst Archivist: Mr Stephen Bird BA, MSc, MCLIP (sbird@fs1.li.man.ac.uk) *Dep:* Asst Archivist: Ms Janette Martin BA, MA, DipARC (jmartin@fs1.li.man.ac.uk) *Other Snr Staff:* Head of Archvs, John Rylands Lib: Mr John Hodgson
Entry: adv appt *Open:* Mon-Fri 1000-1700 (closed Xmas/New Year wk)
Subj: United Kingdom: political papers; personal papers; politics; labour hist; social hist; economic hist; women's hist & politics; European Community; foreign policy; race relations; immigration; fascism & anti-fascism; Labour Party; Communist Party; Chartism *Collns: Bks & Pamphs:* pamph colln; full set of Tribune
Archvs: Labour Party Archvs; politicians' private papers, incl: Ellen Wilkinson; Michael Foot; Judith Hart; Morgan Phillips; Eric Heffer; Bob Edwards;

Harry McShane; Hilary Wainwright; Communist Party of Gt Britain Archvs; minutes of some political parties, incl Parliamentary Labour Party & European Parliamentary Labour Party; some material on Labour & Socialist Internatl *Other:* newspapers; press clippings; photos
Equip: m-reader, m-printer, fax, copier, 2 computers (both with wd-proc, internet & CD- ROM) *Svcs:* info, ref, rsrch
Stock: archvs/800+ linear m; pamphs/15000+
Classn: IDAD(G)
Pubns: A Guide to the Labour Party Archv (1998)
Staff: Archivists: 2 *Non-Prof:* 0.5

A366

Manchester and Lancashire Family History Society, Library and Study Room

Clayton House, 59 Piccadilly, Manchester, M1 2AQ (0161-236-9750; *fax:* 0161-237-3812)
Email: office@mlfhs.org.uk
Internet: http://www.mlfhs.org.uk/

Entry: membs only; prospective membs can join at the lib *Open:* Mon, Fri 1015-1300, Tue, Thu 1015-1600; opening hrs on Wed & Sat vary depending on Soc meetings
Subj: Manchester & Lancashire: family hist; genealogy; local hist *Collns: Bks & Pamphs:* ref colln; journals of other Family Hist Socs *Other:* IGI on m-film; index to births, marriages & deaths for England & Wales (m-film, 1837-1920); census returns for Manchester & Salford (m-film); census indexes for Lancashire; parish register transcripts; monumental inscriptions
Equip: computers *Disabled:* no wheelchair access *Svcs:* ref, simple enq svc (membs only)
Pubns: Manchester Genealogist (4 pa, free to membs)

A367

Manchester Archives and Local Studies

Central Lib, St Peter's Sq, Manchester, M2 5PD *(local studies:* 0161-234-1979; *archvs:* 0161-234- 1980; *fax:* 0161-234-1927)
Email: lsu@libraries.manchester.gov.uk or archives@libraries.manchester.gov.uk
Internet: http://www.manchester.gov.uk/libraries/ arls/

Gov Body: Manchester City Council (see **P112**)
Chief: Local Studies Offcr: Mr R.J. Bond MA, DipAA
Assoc Offices: LIB OF LANCASHIRE & CHESHIRE ANTIQUARIAN SOC (see **S1513**), accessed through the Local Studies Lib
Entry: archv users may need to bk at least 24 hrs in adv *Open:* Mon-Thu 1000-2000, Fri-Sat 1000-1700; *Archvs:* Mon-Thu 1000-1630 only
Subj: Manchester & surrounding area, esp within a 25 mile radius: local authority archvs; diocesan records; parish records; estate archvs; family papers; business records; political papers; nonconformist records; Jewish records; hosp records; court records; trade union records; soc records; local hist *Collns: Bks & Pamphs:* ref colln; lending colln *Archvs:* archvs of Manchester City Council; Manchester Diocesan archvs; Women's Suffrage colln (1869-1919); Soc of Friends, Hardshaw & Hardshaw East records (17C-20C); records of Manchester & Stockport Methodist Dist; records of Manchester Chamber of Commerce; records of Strutt Mills in Derby- shire (1780-1936) & Gregg's Quarry, Bank Mill, Styal, Cheshire (1788-1937); letters to George Wilson, Chairman of the Anti-Corn Law League (1827-85); papers of Lord Simon *Other:* 6576 broadsides (18C-20C); maps; newspapers; press cuttings *Co-op Schemes:* various web projs, incl A2A & Spinning The Web

Equip: 32 m-readers, 3 m-printers, copier, 10 computers
Stock: archvs/3000 linear m; bks/19000 ref, 7000 lending; photos/145000 (77000 digitised); maps/13000; audios/100
Classn: DDC *Auto Sys:* DS
Pubns: Registers in the Local Studies Unit of Manchester Central Lib (£5 + 75p p&p in UK)
Staff: Libns: 4 *Other Prof:* 4 *Exp:* £5672 (2000- 01)

A368

Methodist Archives and Research Centre

John Rylands Univ Lib of Manchester, 150 Deansgate, Manchester, M3 3EH (0161-834- 5343/6765; *fax:* 0161-834-5574)
Email: pnockles@fs1.li.man.ac.uk
Internet: http://rylibweb.man.ac.uk/data1/dg/text/ method.html

Gov Body: Methodist Church of Gt Britain & John Rylands Univ Lib of Manchester (see **S1512**) *Chief:* Archivist: Dr Peter Knockles
Open: Mon-Fri 1000-1730, Sat 1000-1300
Subj: religion; Methodism; hist of Methodism & evangelical movements; local hist; personal papers; nonconformist records *Collns: Bks & Pamphs:* works of John Wesley (1300 items); libs of Charles Wesley & John Fletcher of Madeley (600 vols); 18C anti-Methodist printed material (1000s of items); tracts & pamphs colln (6000 items, 1568-1933); hymnals (5000+, 1737-date); bks on hist of Methodism & evangelical move- ments; modern pubns relating to Methodism; local hist colln (4500+ monographs & pamphs); British Methodist periodcls, incl Connexional magazines & news-papers (5000+ vols) *Archvs:* records of Methodist Conference & its committees; other institutional records deposited by administrative Divs of the Church; John & Charles Wesley & Wesley Family Papers & MSS (5000 items, 1700- 1865); John Fletcher of Madeley & Mary Bosanquet MSS (44 boxes); papers of other 18C Evangelicals, incl: George Whitefield (1714-70); Countess of Huntingdon (1707-91); Howell Harris (1714-73); Benjamin Ingham (1712-72); papers of c4000 ministers & lay-Methodists (18C-date), incl: Thomas Coke (1747-1814); Adam Clarke (1760- 1832); Hugh Bourne (1772-1852); Jabez Bunting (1779-1858); John Ernest Rattenbury (1870-1963); Dr Rupert Davies (1909-94) *Other:* 10000+ circuit plans
Stock: archvs/86000+ items
Pubns: guides & handlists for the collns

A369

National Archive for the History of Computing

John Rylands Univ Lib of Manchester, Oxford Rd, Manchester, M13 9PP (0161-275-8721; *fax:* 0161-273-7488)
Internet: http://www.chstum.man.ac.uk/nahc/

Gov Body: Univ of Manchester (see **S1512** for John Rylands Lib) *Chief:* Dir: Prof J.V. Pickstone (John.Pickstone@man.ac.uk) *Dep:* Librarian-in-Charge: Dr Barry White (Barry. White@man.ac.uk)
Entry: by adv appt with Librarian-in-Charge
Open: Mon-Fri 0930-1700
Subj: UK: hist of computing; personal papers; business records; institutional papers; scientific papers; technological papers; oral hist *Collns: Bks & Pamphs:* machine lit; trade catalogues
Archvs: numerous collns of records & papers of: UK computer manufacturers; UK computing pioneers (e.g., Alan Turing, F.C. Williams); UK computer depts *Other:* oral hist & video recordings; extensive photo colln
Stock: archvs/100 linear m; photos/3000
Staff: Other Prof: 1

A370 🎓 🔑

National Co-operative Archive

(formerly the Co-op Archv)
Co-op Coll, Holyoake House, Hanover St,
Manchester, M60 0AS (0161-246-2925; *fax:* 0161-
246-2946)
Email: archive@co-op.ac.uk
Internet: http://archive.co-op.ac.uk/

Gov Body: Co-op Union Ltd *Chief:* Archivist:
Mrs Gillian Lonergan BA(Hons), MCLIP (gillian@
co-op.ac.uk)
Entry: by appt, ref only *Open:* Mon-Fri 1000-
1700
Subj: hist of co-operation; hist of labour movement; socialism; politics; modern co-op movement; internatl co-op movement; personal papers;
political papers
Collns: Bks & Pamphs: hists of indiv co-op socs;
co-op edu; co-op plays & sketches; Co-op
Women's Guild; dividend & check systems; Co-
op Congresses; Co-op Party; periodcls & journals
of historical & co-op interest; Rochdale Equitable
Pioneers Soc; worker co-operatives *Archvs:*
correspondence & documents: Robert Owen
(1821-1858); G.J. Holyoake (1835-1906); E.O.
Greening (1850-1923) *Other:* commemorative
plateware
Equip: fax, copier (A4/15p, A3/30p) *Svcs:* info,
ref
Stock: archvs/c15000; periodcls/200; photos/
5000
Classn: UDC
Pubns: Holdings Lists for Special Collns (free)
Staff: Libns: 1

A371 🎓 🎥

North West Film Archive

The Manchester Metropolitan Univ, Minshull
House, 47-49 Chorlton St, Manchester, M1 3EU
(0161-247-3097; *fax:* 0161-247-3098)
Email: n.w.filmarchive@mmu.ac.uk
Internet: http://www.nwfa.mmu.ac.uk/

Type: public regional film archv *Gov Body:* The
Manchester Metropolitan Univ (see **S1519**)
Chief: Acting Dir: Ms Marion Hewitt BA, DipLib
Entry: viewings by adv appt *Open:* Mon-Fri
0900-1700
Subj: moving images relating to life in Greater
Manchester, Lancashire & Cheshire *Collns:*
Other: over 27000 moving image items (1897-
date), both prof & amateur; holdings incl: cinema
newsreels; documentaries; educational &
promotional films; regional TV programmes; home
movies; complementary collns of photos, taped
interviews & original documentation relating to film
& cinema industry in NW England & to the NW
Film Archv principal moving image colln
Equip: 2 video viewers, copier, computer, film
viewers, audiocassette player *Disabled:* minicom,
Magnilink magnification equip, Braille convertor &
printer, designated PC, screen reader, image
manipulation equip, large TV monitor, loop
systems *Online:* Online Film & Video catalogue
(4000 records) available on NWFA web site
Svcs: info, ref, rsrch, viewing/editing loans
Stock: archvs/27000 items of film & video
Classn: FIAF Standards
Pubns: The Picture House Bk (£6.95); Moving
Memories (series of compilation videos, £14.99);

specialist edu resources: 3 titles, details on
request; specialist transport merchandise: latest
title A North West Journey: Buses, Trams &
Trolleybuses 1927-35 (£19.50); Manchester Ship
Canal Centenary Video (£12.99); leaflets (free)
Staff: Libns: 2 *Other Prof:* 5 *Non-Prof:* 1 *Exp:*
£6000 (1999-2000); £23700 (2000-01)

Margate

A372 🏛

Margate Local Studies Library

Margate Central Lib, Cecil Sq, Margate, Kent, CT9
1RE (01843-223626; *fax:* 01843-293015)

Gov Body: Kent County Council Arts & Libs (see
P67) *Chief:* Team Libn, Local Studies: Ms Beth
Thomson BLib(Hons), MCLIP
Entry: ref only, appt advisable on Tue & Fri after
1400 *Open:* Mon-Thu 0930-1800, Fri 0930-1900,
Sat 0930-1700
Subj: Isle of Thanet: tourism; seaside; local hist;
illusts; family hist
Equip: 6 m-readers, m-printer, fax, 2 copiers, clr
copier, computers (incl wd-proc & CD-ROM)
Svcs: info, ref, rsrch (1st half hr free, then £24
per hr)
Classn: DDC, Brown's (mod) *Auto Sys:* DS
Pubns: Local Studies Collns in Thanet Libs;
Parish Registers in Thanet Libs (both free)
Staff: Libns: 1 *Non-Prof:* 0.5

Markinch

A373 🏛

Fife Council Archive Centre, Local Studies Services

Carleton House, Haig Business Pk, Balgonie Rd,
Markinch, Fife, KY7 6AQ (01592-413256/6504;
fax: 01592-417477)
Email: Andrew.Dowsey@fife.gov.uk

Type: local authority *Gov Body:* Fife Council
(see **P53**) *Chief:* Archivist: Mr Andrew Dowsey
Assoc Offices: local studies collns are also held
at: KIRKCALDY CENTRAL LIB, War Memorial
Gdns, Kirkcaldy, Fife, KY1 1YG (01592-412878;
fax: 01592-412750; *email:* Kirkcaldy.Library@fife.
gov.uk); DUNFERMLINE CARNEGIE LIB, 1
Abbot St, Dunfermline, Fife, KY12 7NL (01383-
312600; *fax:* 01383-312608; *email:* carnegie.
library@fife.gov.uk); CUPAR LIB, 33-35
Crossgate, Cupar, KY15 5AS (01334-412285; *fax:*
01334-412467; *email:* cupar.library@fife.gov.uk);
ST ANDREWS LIB, Church Sq, St Andrews, Fife,
KY16 9NN (01334-412688)
Entry: adv appt; proof of ID required *Open:*
Mon, Wed-Fri 0900-1700, Tue 0900-1915
Subj: Fife: local authority archvs; parish records;
estate archvs; business records; records of
parent org; school records; police records; local
hist *Collns: Bks & Pamphs:* local studies
materials for Central Fife (at Kirkcaldy Central
Lib), West Fife (at Dunfermline Central Lib) &
East Fife (at Cupar & St Andrews Libs) *Archvs:*
records of Fife Council & predecessor bodies
(1709 onwards), incl records of: Fife Regional
Council (1975-95); Fife County Council (1889-
1975); Kirkcaldy Dist Council (1975-95);
Dunfermline Dist Council (1975-95); NE Fife Dist
Council (1975-95); some Burgh & Town Council
records for Fife; records of Glenrothes Development Corp (1948-75); Quarter Sessions records
(18C-19C); burial records (18C-20C); Rothes
Estate papers (Leslie family, Earls of Rothes,
1640s-1960s); records of Largo Field Studies Soc
(1968-date) *Other:* maps; local newspapers;
photos; census returns; genealogical & other
indexes
Equip: m-readers, copiers

Matlock

A374 🏛

Derbyshire Local Studies Library

County Hall, Matlock, Derbyshire, DE4 3AG
(01629-585579; *fax:* 01629-585049)
Internet: http://www.derbyshire.gov.uk/librar/
locstu.htm

Gov Body: Derbyshire County Council (see **P36**)
Chief: County Local Studies Libn: Ms Ruth
Gordon
Assoc Offices: LOCAL STUDIES LIB, Chester-
field Lib, New Beetwell St, Chesterfield, Derby-
shire, S40 1QN (01246-209292; *fax:* 01246-
209304); local archvs are held at DERBYSHIRE
RECORD OFFICE (see **A375**)
Entry: ref only; adv appt (esp for use of m-form
& computer equip) *Open: Matlock:* Mon-Fri 0900-
1700, occasional opening on Sat mornings;
Chesterfield: Mon-Fri 0930-1900, Sat 0930-1600
Subj: Derbyshire: local studies; family hist
Collns: Bks & Pamphs: local hist materials; local
directories *Other:* census returns for Derbyshire
(m-film, 1841-1901); local newspapers; maps &
illusts
Equip: m-readers, m-printers (40p per copy),
copier (A4/10p), computers (with internet) *Svcs:*
info, ref, rsrch (fee based)

A375 🏛

Derbyshire Record Office

County Hall, Matlock, Derbyshire, DE4 3AG
(01629-585347; *fax:* 01629-57611)
Email: record.office@derbyshire.gov.uk

Gov Body: Derbyshire County Council (see **P36**)
Chief: County Archivist: Dr Margaret O'Sullivan
BA, PhD *Dep:* Snr Archivist: Mrs Judith Phillips
BA, MA
Entry: visitor registration (proof of ID required)
Open: Mon-Fri 0930-1645; restrictions 1300-1400
Subj: Derbyshire: local authority archvs;
diocesan records; parish records; estate archvs;
family papers; business records; records of
parent org; nonconformist records; court records;
school records; records of charities & voluntary
assocs, *Collns: Archvs:* archvs of Derbyshire
County Council; Diocese of Derby records; many
series of industrial records, incl: Stanton &
Staveley Iron & Coal Company (mid 19C-20C);
family archvs, incl: Harpur Crewe of Calke
Abbey; Gell of Hopton; Wilmot-Horton of Catton;
Fitzherbert of Tissington; Longsdon of Longstone
Equip: m-readers, m-form reader/printers, copier
(staff only) *Svcs:* rsrch
Pubns: Derbyshire Record Office Guide; Parish
& Nonconformist Registers; Tithe Maps;
Enclosure Maps; various guides to archvs
Staff: 6 archivists, 1 conservator + support staff

Menstrie

A376 🍸

Diageo Ltd, Archives

(formerly United Distillers & Vintners)
Glenochil House, Menstrie, Clackmannanshire,
FK11 7ES (01259-766886; *fax:* 01259-766888)
Email: Christine.Jones@diageo.com

Chief: Archivist: Ms Christine Jones
Entry: approved rsrchers on written application,
at the discretion of the company; email, tel &
postal enqs only for membs of genl public
Open: Mon-Fri 0900-1700
Subj: Scotland: business records; distilling &
distillers; blending; business; advertising;
packaging; etc *Collns: Bks & Pamphs:* relating to
all aspects of the drinks industry *Archvs:*
minutes & other records (19C-20C) of all

constituent distilling, blending, bottling & trading companies, incl: Associated Scottish Distilleries Ltd; Alexander Bonthrone & Sons Ltd (maltsters); Dailuaine-Talisker Distilleries Ltd; John Haig & Co Ltd (whisky distillers); WP Lowrie & Co Ltd (whisky distillers); Scottish Malt Distillers Ltd; Speyburn Glenlivet Distillery Co Ltd *Other:* photo colln
Equip: copier; clr copier, fax, 3 video viewers
Svcs: info, ref, rsrch, enq svc
Classn: ISAD(G) *Auto Sys:* DS
Staff: Archivists: 3
See also DIAGEO PLC, BRAND TECHNICAL CENTRE LIB (**S1541**)

Middlesbrough

A377
Corus Northern Regional Records Centre
Commerce Way, Skippers Ln Industrial Est, South Bank, Middlesbrough, TS6 6UT (01642-405814; *fax:* 01642-405854)
Email: Recordcentre.Teesside@corusgroup.com

Gov Body: Corus *Chief:* Co-ordinator & Administrator: Mrs Jenni Robinson (Jenni. Robinson@corusgroup.com) *Other Snr Staff:* Records Offcr: Mr Steve Dolphin
Assoc Offices: CORUS COLORS REGIONAL RECORDS CENTRE (see **A121**)
Entry: adv appt *Open:* Mon-Fri 0900-1700
Subj: Teesside & Cleveland: iron & steel industry; business records; some personal papers; very small quantity of local authority records (being handed over to local authority)
Collns: Archvs: minutes & other records of c40 companies & orgs involved in iron, steel & related industries in the North of England
Equip: copier, fax
Stock: archvs/52000 cubic ft *Staff: Non-Prof:* 3

A378
Middlesbrough RC Diocesan Archives
50a The Avenue, Linthorpe, Middlesbrough, TS5 6QT (01642-850505; *fax:* 01642-851404)
Email: archives@dioceseofmiddlesbrough.co.uk

Gov Body: Trustees of the Diocese of Middlesbrough *Chief:* Diocesan Archivist: Mr David Smallwood BSc
Entry: adv appt only
Subj: RC Diocese of Middlesbrough (East & most of North Riding of Yorkshire, incl Teesside, York & Hull): diocesan records; parish records
Collns: Archvs: records of the Roman Catholic Diocese of Middlesbrough (from 1878); parish records (from mid-18C)
Equip: copier (5p per pg), computer (with wd-proc, internet & CD-ROM) *Svcs:* info, ref, rsrch
Stock: archvs/70 linear m; rec mgmt/15 linear m; photos/3000 *Acq Offcr:* Diocesan Archivist, as above
Pubns: Middlesbrough Diocesan Archvs Catalogue (£5)
Staff: Non-Prof: 1

A379
Teesside Archives
Exchange House, 6 Marton Rd, Middlesbrough, TS1 1DB (01642-248321; *fax:* 01642-248931)
Email: teeside_archives@middlesbrough.gov.uk

Gov Body: lead authority for joint svc: Middlesbrough Borough Council (see **P115**); other authorities: Stockton Borough Council (see **P177**), Hartlepool Council (see **P61**) & Redcar & Cleveland Borough Council (see **P151**) *Chief:* Archivist: Mr D. Tyrell BA, DipAA *Dep:* Snr Asst Archivist: Mrs J. Baker MA, DipAA

Entry: CARN ticket *Open:* Mon, Wed & Thu 0900-1700, Tue 0900-2100, Fri 0900-1630
Subj: former Cleveland County, now covered by Middlesbrough, Stockton, Hartlepool & Redcar & Cleveland Boroughs: local authority archvs; parish records; estate records; family papers; business records; records of parent org *Collns: Archvs:* archvs of former Cleveland County Council; archvs of Middlesbrough, Stockton, Hartlepool & Redcar & Cleveland Borough Councils; Archdiocese of York (Cleveland area) parish records *Other:* Radio Cleveland Sound Archvs
Equip: 16 m-readers, m-printer (40p per sheet), copier (A4/15p, A3/25p)
Stock: archvs/450 cubic m
Pubns: various leaflets & guides, incl: C of E Parish Registers (£2.25); Methodist Registers (£1.20); Roman Catholic Registers (50p); Modern Transcripts for North Yorkshire & Co Durham (£1.20); Records of Burial/Cremation (£1.05); Monumental Inscriptions (£1.20); Tithe & Enclosure Maps (50p); Court Records (50p); Modern Transcripts & Indexes of Census Returns (£2.25); Registers of Electors & Burgess Rolls (£1); Miscellaneous Modern Transcripts & Indexes (50p); Starting Points for Family Hist (90p)
Staff: Archivists: 3 *Non-Prof:* 2 *Exp:* £4000 (1999-2000); £4000 (2000-01)

Milton Keynes

A380
Bedford Estate Archives
Woburn Abbey, Woburn, Milton Keynes, MK43 0TP (01525-290666; *fax:* 01525-290271)

Gov Body: Marquess of Tavistock & the Trustees of the Bedford Estate *Chief:* Archivist: Mrs Ann Mitchell BA(Hons), DipPAA
Entry: by appt with 2 refs *Open:* term: Mon-Fri 0930-1500; vac: limited svc during school hols
Subj: estate records; family papers; personal papers *Collns: Archvs:* personal & political papers of Earls & Dukes of Bedford; Bloomsbury Estate records (mid 16C-date)
Equip: copier
Stock: archvs/1100 linear ft
Classn: MAD *Staff: Archivists:* 1

Milton Keynes

A381
Milton Keynes Local Studies and Family History Library
c/o Central Lib, 555 Silbury Blvd, Saxon Gate East, Milton Keynes, Buckinghamshire, MK9 3HL (01908-254160; *fax:* 01908-254088)
Email: mklocal@milton-keynes.gov.uk
Internet: http://www.mkheritage.co.uk/mkl/

Type: local authority *Gov Body:* Milton Keynes Council (see **P117**) *Chief:* Snr Lib Asst (Local Studies): Mrs Ruth Meardon
Entry: ref only *Open:* Mon-Wed 0900-1800, Thu-Fri 0900-2000, Sat 0900-1700
Subj: Milton Keynes & North Buckinghamshire: local hist; parish records *Collns: Other:* no primary material, secondary sources only, incl: local newspapers on m-film; GRO indexes; IGI; 1881 census materials; map colln *Co-op Schemes:* Milton Keynes Heritage Assoc
Equip: 8 m-readers, 3 m-printers, copier, clr copier, fax, computers (incl 2 wd-procs, internet & CD-ROM) *Svcs:* ref
Classn: Bucks Bibliographical Classn Scheme *Auto Sys:* ALS *Staff: Non-Prof:* 1

Monmouth

A382
Monmouth Castle and Regimental Museum, Archives
The Castle, Monmouth, NP25 3BS (01600-772175)
Email: curator@monmouthcastlemuseum.org.uk
Internet: http://www.monmouthcastlemuseum. org.uk/

Chief: contact the Curator
Entry: ref only; adv appt *Open:* Apr-Oct: Mon-Sun 1400-1700; Nov-Mar: Sat-Sun 1400-1600
Subj: Monmouthshire: regimental records; military hist *Collns: Archvs:* records of the Royal Monmouthshire Royal Engineers (1799-20C)

A383
Nelson Museum and Local History Centre
Priory St, Monmouth, NP5 3XA (01600-713519)
Email: nelsonmuseum@monmouthshire.gov.uk
Internet: http://www.monmouth.org.uk/ nelson.htm

Chief: contact the Curator
Entry: ref only *Open:* Mon-Sat 1000-1300, 1400-1700, Sun 1400-1700
Subj: Monmouth. local studies; personal papers; naval records *Collns: Archvs:* logbks of HMS Victory & other vessels (18C-19C); correspondence & papers of Vice Admiral Horatio Nelson (1758-1805); correspondence of Emma Hamilton (c1761-1815); papers of Admiral Sir William Hoste (1780-1828); Charles Rolls Colln (aviator & engineer, 1877-1910)

Montrose

A384
Angus Archives and Local Studies Centre
Montrose Lib, 214 High St, Montrose, Angus, DD10 8PH (01674-671415; *fax:* 01674-671810)
Email: angus.archives@angus.gov.uk
Internet: http://www.angus.gov.uk/history/ archives/

Gov Body: Angus Council (see **P4**) *Chief:* Local Studies Librarian/Archivist: Mrs Fiona Scharlau MA(Hons), MCLIP *Dep:* Archv Asst: Heather Munro
Entry: adv appt, proof of ID required *Open:* Mon-Tue, Thu-Fri 0930-1700; Wed by appt only
Subj: Angus/Forfarshire: local authority archvs (all Angus burghs, Angus County Council, Angus Dist Council); family papers; business records; personal papers; records of parent org (Angus Council); nonconformist church records; records of local socs *Collns: Bks & Pamphs:* Rsrch Lib (ref works & historical rsrch files covering all aspects of life & work in Angus); Local Hist Colln (bks & ephemera); Genealogy Lib (genealogy bks & rsrch materials) *Archvs:* Arbroath Town Council (1563-1975); Kirriemuir Town Council (1834-1975); Brechin Town Council (1672-1975); Carnoustie Town Council (1895-1975); Forfar Town Council (1660-1975); Montrose Town Council (1617-1975); Monifieth Town Council (1895-1975); Angus County Council (1717-1975); Angus Dist Council (1975-1996); Trade Incorporation Records; 600+ MSS collns covering family papers, business records, music, socs, sermons, poems etc; various indexes, rolls, registers & transcripts *Other:* Slide Colln (historic bldgs, gravestones) *Equip:* m-reader, m-printer, copier, fax, computers (incl wd-proc)

Montrose
▼
Norwich

Archives

(Angus Archvs & Local Studies Centre cont)
Pubns: Angus Archvs: A Brief Outline (2nd class stamp + SAE); Angus Ancestors: How We Can Help You Find Them (2nd class stamp + SAE); List of Indexes, Transcripts & Databases (5 x 2nd class stamps + SAE)
Staff: Archivists: 2 Non-Prof: 2 + 4 volunteers

Morden

A385
Merton Library and Heritage Service, Local Studies Centre

Merton Civic Centre, London Rd, Morden, Surrey, SM4 5DX (020-8545-3239; fax: 020-8545-4037)
Email: Morden.Library@merton.gov.uk
Internet: http://www.merton.gov.uk/libraries/

Gov Body: London Borough of Merton (see **P100**) **Chief:** Libn: Ms Alison Williams
Entry: ref only **Open:** Mon-Fri 0930-2000, Sat 0930-1700
Subj: London Borough of Merton: local authority archvs; parish records; family papers; personal papers; records of parent org; local hist **Collns:** Bks & Pamphs: William Morris Colln; Lord Nelson Colln Archvs: records of London Borough of Merton Other: local maps & plans; local newspapers; ephemera; photos, incl Tom Francis Colln of Mitcham Photos **Co-op Schemes:** LASER, SHARE
Equip: 2 m-readers, m-printer (25p per copy), copier, 6 computers (all with internet, 2 with wd-proc, printouts 6p per sheet) **Svcs:** info, ref, rsrch
Classn: DDC (mod) **Auto Sys:** DS
Pubns: list of pubns for sale (free)

Morpeth

A386
Morpeth Records Centre

The Kylins, Loadsdean, Morpeth, Northumberland, NE61 2EQ (01670-504084; fax: 01670-514815)
Internet: http://www.swinhope.myby.co.uk/NRO/

Gov Body: Northumberland County Council (see **P137**) **Chief:** Snr Archivist: Mrs S. Wood BA, DipAA
Assoc Offices: branch of NORTHUMBERLAND RECORD OFFICE (see **A390**)
Entry: adv appt to view m-films **Open:** Mon, Wed 0930-1300, 1400-1700, Tue 0930-1300, 1400-2000 (closed Thu & Fri)
Subj: Northumberland: local authority archvs; diocesan records; parish records; records of parent org; hosp records **Collns:** Archvs: records of Northumberland County Council; records of Diocese of Newcastle; public records, incl records of pre-vesting coal companies (15C-20C); Quarter Sessions records; Petty Sessions records
Equip: 9 m-film readers (bookable), 3 m-fiche readers (not bookable), m-printer, fax, copier; self-svc printing & photocopying only at restricted times, facilities otherwise available via staff
Svcs: rsrch (£16 per hr)
Stock: archvs/237.27 cubic m; rec mgmt/241 cubic m
Staff: Archivists: 1.2 Non-Prof: 2.9

Much Hadham

The Henry Moore Archive
See The Henry Moore Foundation Lib (**S1562**)

Newcastle, Staffordshire

A387
Keele University, Air Photo Archive/Library

Brian Stokes Bldg, Newcastle, Staffordshire, ST5 5BG (01782-583395)
Email: m.c.beech@lib.keele.ac.uk

Gov Body: Keele Univ (see **S1572**) **Chief:** Archv Mgr: Mrs Marylyn C. Beech
Entry: strictly by appt with Archv Mgr; administrative search fee payable **Open:** Mon-Fri 0900-1300, 1400-1700
Subj: aerial photography **Collns:** Other: Allied Forces reconnaissance photos from World War II (covering Europe, but not the UK or any neutral country)
Svcs: copy print svc
Stock: archvs/5500000
Classn: catalogued by latitude & longitude
Staff: 1 archivist

Newcastle upon Tyne

A388
Hexham and Newcastle RC Diocesan Archives

Bishop's House, 800 West Rd, Newcastle upon Tyne, NE5 2BJ (0191-228-0003; fax: 0191-274-0432)
Email: archivist@rcdhn.org.uk
Internet: http://www.rcdhn.org.uk/looking_up_records.htm

Gov Body: RC Diocese of Hexham & Newcastle
Chief: Diocesan Archivist: Mr Robin M. Gard MA
Entry: adv appt only **Open:** Wed 1100-1700
Subj: Diocese of Hexham & Newcastle (Northumberland, Tyneside, Durham, part of Cleveland): diocesan records; Catholic hist **Collns:** Bks & Pamphs: Catholic Directories (1800-date); Local Div Yearbk (1869-date); small lib of standard Catholic hist ref bks Archvs: Hexham & Newcastle Diocesan Archvs, incl administrative records & records relating to the Bishops & diocesan clergy; Northern Brethren Fund records; St Mary's Cathedral Chapter records; records of the Apostleship of the Sea; Catholic Women's League records; records of some diocesan socs
Equip: copier
Stock: archvs/c150-200 linear m
Staff: Archivists: 1 voluntary PT

A389
Northumberland and Durham Family History Society, Library and Research Centre

2nd Floor, Bolbec Hall, Westgate Rd, Newcastle upon Tyne, NE1 1SE (0191-261-2159)
Email: 106251.1104@compuserve.com
Internet: http://www.ndfhs.org.uk/

Gov Body: Northumberland & Durham Family Hist Soc **Chief:** contact the Libn, NDFHS
Entry: membs of Soc; also open to non-membs (no fee, but donations welcome); adv booking for m-readers advised **Open:** Mon-Fri 1000-1600; addl hrs by appt only
Subj: Northumberland & Durham: family hist; genealogy; local hist; parish records

Collns: Archvs: large colln of transcripts of parish registers of churches & chapels in Northumber-land & Durham (bks & m-fiche) Other: census transcripts, incl 1881 Census for England & Wales (m-fiche) & 1851, 1891 & 1901 census returns for Northumberland & Durham (m-fiche); civil registration of birth, marriage & death indexes (m-fiche); monumental inscriptions
Equip: 15 m-readers, m-printer, 2 copiers **Svcs:** rsrch
Stock: archvs/c3000; m-forms/10000
Staff: Non-Prof: 20

A390
Northumberland Record Office

Melton Pk, North Gosforth, Newcastle upon Tyne, NE3 5QX (0191-236-2680; fax: 0191-217-0905)
Internet: http://www.swinhope.demon.co.uk/NRO/

Gov Body: Northumberland County Council (see **P137**) **Chief:** Snr Archivist: Mrs S. Wood BA, DipAA
Assoc Offices: BERWICK-UPON-TWEED RECORD OFFICE (see **A44**); MORPETH RECORDS CENTRE (see **A386**)
Entry: adv appt necessary for family historians, or to use m-readers **Open:** Wed 0930-1300, 1400-2000, Thu-Fri 0930-1300, 1400-1700 (closed Mon Tue)
Subj: Administrative County of Northumberland: estate archvs; family papers; business records; personal papers; political papers **Collns:** Archvs: records of the Soc of Antiquaries of Newcastle upon Tyne; records of the North of England Inst of Mining & Mechanical Engineers (15C-20C); substantial holdings of estate papers; other small private collns Other: main photo colln for the county: incl Gibson of Hexham & Blankenburg (mainly Kielder Forest & reservoir); main map colln for the county: incl enclosure awards, deposited plans, estate maps, tithe awards, OS maps; oral hist recordings
Equip: 3 m-readers, fax, copier (via staff)
Svcs: rsrch, photographic (not available for fragile documents)
Stock: archvs/286.83 cubic m
Pubns: free leaflet series, incl: Introduction to the Record Offices; Family Hist Resources for North Northumberland; Civil Cemetery Records; Northumberland Wills; Historic Census Returns for Northumberland 1841-1891; Historic Maps & Plans
Staff: Archivists: 1.8 Non-Prof: 3.1

A391
Tyne and Wear Archives Service

Blandford House, Blandford Sq, Newcastle upon Tyne, NE1 4JA (0191-232-6789 x407; fax: 0191-230-2614)
Email: twas@gateshead.gov.uk
Internet: http://www.thenortheast.com/archives/

Gov Body: Tyne & Wear Archvs Joint Cttee, Lead Dist: Gateshead Metropolitan Borough Council (see **P55**); also representing City of Newcastle upon Tyne (see **P121**), North Tyneside Metropolitan Borough Council (see **P129**), South Tyneside Metropolitan Borough Council (see **P170**) & City of Sunderland (see **P180**) **Chief:** Chief Archivist: Miss E.A. Rees BA, DipAA
Entry: adv booking for m-readers; observance of searchroom rules **Open:** Mon-Fri 0900-1715 (Tue -2030)
Subj: Tyne & Wear County Area: local authority archvs; family papers; business records; locally held public records; nonconformist records; records of Jewish community; school records; trade union records; business records; census records **Collns:** Archvs: archvs of Gateshead Metropolitan Borough Council, City of Newcastle upon Tyne, North Tyneside Metropolitan Borough

Council, South Tyneside Metropolitan Borough Council & City of Sunderland; Fenwick Colln (circuses & fairgrounds); also particularly strong on shipbldg & eng records *Other:* hosts part of Northern Region Film & Television Archv *Co-op Schemes:* Northern Region Film & Television Archv
Equip: 11 m-readers, m-camera, m-printer, video viewer, copier, 3 computers (all with CD-ROM), film viewing equip *Svcs:* rsrch
Stock: archvs/1432 cubic m; rec mgmt/358 cubic m
Classn: ISAD(G) *Auto Sys:* DS; CALM 2000 Plus
Pubns: User Guides on various types of records (free); Sources for Family Hist at Tyne & Wear Archvs Svc (£2.50); various others
Staff: Archivists: 5 *Other Prof:* 4 *Non-Prof:* 9

Newport, *Isle of Wight*

A392

Isle of Wight County Record Office
26 Hillside, Newport, Isle of Wight, PO30 2EB (01983-823820/1; *fax:* 01983-823820)
Email: record.office@iow.gov.uk

Gov Body: Isle of Wight Council (see **P66**) *Chief:* County Archivist: Mr R.H. Smout MA, DipAA *Dep:* Asst Archivist: Ms C. Dowland MA *Entry:* CARN ticket/day ticket; adv appt for m-readers *Open:* Mon 0930-1700, Tue-Fri 0900-1700; evening opening on 1st Wed of month 1700-1930, by appt only
Subj: Isle of Wight: local authority archvs; parish records; estate archvs; family papers; business records; records of parent org; nonconformist records (some); school records *Colln: Bks & Pamphs:* small ref & local hist colln *Archvs:* archvs of Isle of Wight Council & predecessors; Diocese of Portsmouth (Isle of Wight deaneries) parish records (1539 onwards); Oglander Colln (incl title deeds from 1200); diaries & notes of Sir John Oglander (17C antiquarian & first historian of the Isle of Wight); Barrington-Simeon Colln (estate records, from mid 16C); Seely estate archv; Ward estate archv; mid 18C-mid 20C family letters, of families related to Oglander of Nunwell, Glynn, Somerset etc *Other:* OS maps (1862-1971); tithe maps (1838-45); local prints & photos; electoral registers (1920s-70s); IGI (m-form); census returns (m-form); local newspapers on m-film, incl: County Press (1884-1996); Weekly Post (1976-86)
Equip: 5 m-readers, m-printer (A4/25p, A3/30p), copier (A4/20p, A3/25p), computer (with internet) *Svcs:* rsrch (£15 per hr to maximum of 3 hrs) *Stock:* archvs/220 cubic m, incl maps; rec mgmt/30 cubic m; bks/3 cubic m; photos/1 cubic m
Pubns: The Charters of Quarr Abbey (£18 + p&p); Cartulary of Carisbrooke Priory (£8 + p&p) *Staff: Archivists:* 2 *Non-Prof:* 2.5

Northallerton

A393

North Yorkshire County Record Office
County Hall, Northallerton, N Yorkshire, DL7 8AF (01609-777585; *fax:* 01609-777078)
Email: archives@northyorks.gov.uk
Internet: http://www.northyorks.gov.uk/archives/

Gov Body: North Yorkshire County Council (see **P130**) *Chief:* Acting County Archivist: Mrs Judith A. Smeaton BA, DipAA *Dep:* Acting Dep County Archivist: Miss M. Boustead BA, DipAA *Assoc Offices:* Record Office is located at: Malpas Rd, Northallerton; use above addr for correspondence

Entry: adv appt *Open:* Mon-Tue, Thu 0900-1645, Wed 0900-2045, Fri 0900-1615
Subj: North Yorkshire: local authority archvs; parish records; estate archvs; family papers; business records; personal papers; political papers; records of parent org *Collns: Archvs:* archvs of North Yorkshire County Council; Archdiocese of York parish records (North Yorkshire area); Diocese of Bradford parish records (North Yorkshire area); Diocese of Ripon parish records (North Yorkshire area)
Equip: 26 m-readers *Svcs:* info, ref, rsrch *Stock:* archvs/1261.35 cubic m; rec mgmt/86.66 cubic m
Pubns: leaflets covering opening hrs, copy charges, search fees & pubns (all free); Guides to Records (1-10, prices vary £1-£8); Review (vols 1994-2001 available, £2-£5); numerous others, incl offprints & guides to specific holdings; full list available
Staff: Archivists: 4 *Other Prof:* 1 conservator *Non-Prof:* 7.2

Northampton

A394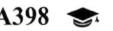

Northampton Diocesan Archives (RC)
Bishop's House, Marriot St, Northampton, NN2 6AW (01604-715635; *fax:* 01604-792186)

Gov Body: RC Diocese of Northampton *Chief:* Chancellor of Diocese: Rev D. Barrett *Dep:* Archivist: Mrs Margaret Osborne
Entry: adv appt *Open:* variable
Subj: RC Diocese of Northampton (North-amptonshire, Bedfordshire, Buckinghamshire, Huntingdonshire, Cambridgeshire, Norfolk & Suffolk): diocesan records *Collns: Bks & Pamphs:* Catholic Record Soc pubns *Archvs:* Fr Collin's collected papers on hist of Diocese & Midland dist from 16C *Other:* photo colln; parish magazines & other Diocesan pubns
Stock: archvs/c412 archv boxes; rec mgmt/12 catalogue bks & 13 card index boxes; videos/c12
Classn: Catholic Archv Soc scheme
Pubns: guide to archv publ in: Catholic Archvs No 21, p41-44 (2001)
Staff: Non-Prof: 1

A395

Northamptonshire Record Office
Wootton Hall Pk, Northampton, NN4 8BQ (01604-762129; *fax:* 01604-767562)
Email: archivist@northamptonshire.gov.uk
Internet: http://www2.northamptonshire.gov.uk/nro/

Gov Body: Northamptonshire County Council (see **P131**) *Chief:* County Archivist: Ms Sarah Bridges
Assoc Offices: NORTHAMPTONSHIRE RECORD SOC LIB, at same addr
Entry: no restrictions *Open:* Mon 1030-1645, Tue-Wed 0900-1645, Thu 0900-1945, Fri 0900-1615 (1st & 3rd Sat in month 0900-1215)
Subj: Northamptonshire & the Soke of Peter-borough: local authority archvs; diocesan records; parish records; estate archvs; family papers; business records; records of parent org; Northamptonshire orgs & socs; public records, incl court & hosp archvs *Collns: Bks & Pamphs:* Northamptonshire Antiquarian Soc Lib (mostly arch & archaeo bks & pamphs) *Archvs:* archvs of Northamptonshire County Council; Diocese of Peterborough parish records (parishes in Northamptonshire, former Soke of Peterborough & Rutland); records of Corby & Northampton Development Corps; estate archvs, incl: Spencer (Althorpe); Fitzwilliam (Milton); Finch Hatton *Other:* large photo & map collns
Equip: 31 m-readers, 3 m-printer, copier

Stock: archvs/7480 linear m; rec mgmt/5432 linear m; printed bks/150 linear m (not incl Northamptonshire Record Soc Lib)
Pubns: Tracing Your Northamptonshire Ancestors, by Colin Chapman (£3.25); A Short Guide to the Northamptonshire Record Office, by Philip Riden (£1)
Staff: Archivists: 6 *Other Prof:* 2 conservators *Non-Prof:* 11

Norwich

A396

Aviva Company Archive
(incorporating the former Norwich Union Archv & CGU plc Archv)
8 Surrey St, Norwich, Norfolk, NR1 3NG (01603-840498/687280; *fax:* 01603-840499)

Gov Body: Aviva plc *Chief:* Group Archivist: Mrs Anna Stone MAARM (anna_stone@aviva.com) *Dep:* Group Asst Archivist: Miss Sheree J. Leeds (sheree_leeds@aviva.com)
Entry: adv appt *Open:* Mon-Fri 0900-1630
Subj: insurance hist; family papers; business records; records of parent org & predecessors
Collns: Archvs: records of Group companies, incl: Norwich Union Archvs (1797 onwards); Commercial Union Archvs (1861-1988); Genl Accident Archvs (1885-1975); Scottish Union & Natl Insurance Co records (1813-1970); Yorkshire Insurance Co Archvs (1824-1968); Northern Assurance Archvs (1836-1968); North British & Mercantile Archvs (1809-1959); minutes, registers & accounts of 200+ smaller subsidiary companies (18C-20C); Bignold Family Papers
Equip: copier, fax, video viewer *Disabled:* wheelchair access *Svcs:* info, ref, rsrch
Auto Sys: CALM
Staff: Archivists: 1 *Non-Prof:* 1

A397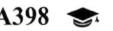

Diocese of East Anglia (RC), Diocesan Archives
Cathedral House, Unthank Rd, Norwich, Norfolk, NR2 2PA (01508-661082)
Email: office@east-angliadiocese.org.uk
Internet: http://www.eastangliadiocese.org.uk/

Gov Body: RC Diocese of East Anglia *Chief:* Diocesan Archivist: Rev Michael Edwards MA(Oxon), STL *Dep:* Asst Archivists: Mrs Dora Cowton & Mrs Sheila Monahan
Entry: adv appt *Open:* as arranged
Subj: RC Diocese of East Anglia: diocesan records; parish records; Catholic school records

A398

East Anglian Film Archive
Univ of East Anglia, Univ Plain, Norwich, Norfolk, NR4 7TJ (01603-592664; *fax:* 01603-458553)
Email: eafa@uea.ac.uk
Internet: http://www.uea.ac.uk/eafa/

Type: public regional film archv *Gov Body:* housed at Univ of East Anglia (see **S1631**), but raises its own money to pay staff & carry out preservation work *Chief:* Dir: Mr David Cleveland *Dep:* Dep Dir: Ms Jane Alvey *Entry:* by appt *Open:* Mon-Fri 0900-1700
Subj: Bedfordshire, Cambridgeshire, Essex, Hertfordshire, Norfolk & Suffolk: non-fiction film showing life in the region *Collns: Other:* all types of non-fiction film (1896-date), incl: prof films; home movies; television programmes; docu-mentaries; educational & instructional films; publicity films etc
Equip: 4 video viewers, film viewing facilities
Online: catalogue of part of colln on web site

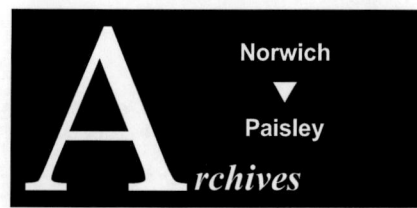

Norwich ▼ Paisley

Archives

(East Anglian Film Archv cont)
Svcs: info, ref, rsrch, film presentations, film conservation, film to video transfer, film printing
Stock: archvs/several 1000; film/25000 cans
Staff: Archivists: 6 Non-Prof: 1

A399 🔑

History of Advertising Trust Archive

12 HAT House, Raveningham Centre, Raveningham, Norwich, Norfolk, NR14 6NU (01508-548623; *fax:* 01508-548478)
Email: archive@hatads.demon.co.uk
Internet: http://www.hatads.org.uk/

Chief: Archv Mgr: Ms Margaret Rose **Dep:** Archv Curator: Ms Chloe Veale
Entry: adv appt; proof of ID required; a fee may be payable **Open:** Mon-Fri 0900-1700; closed public hols
Subj: hist of advertising, marketing, public relations & related subjs in UK; business records
Collns: Bks & Pamphs: various bks, industry data, consumer & trade journals (late 19C-date); store catalogues; Advertising Standards Colln (incl AA, ASA, IBA, ITC & other regulatory judgements from 1920s onwards) Archvs: archvs of advertising agencies (c1800-date), incl: R.F. White Archv (UK's first advertising agency); archvs of advertising industry bodies, incl: Advertising Assoc archvs (1926-89); Incorporated Soc of British Advertisers archvs; Direct Mail Assoc archvs; Periodical Publishers Assoc archvs; Inst of Public Relations archvs; Internatl Public Relations Assoc archvs; Publicity Club of London archvs; Women's Advertising Club of London archvs; Cinema Advertising Assoc Historic Archv; advertising archvs of leading UK companies, incl: Selfridges; Hovis Bread; Dairy Council; H.J. Heinz Company Ltd; HP Foods; SmithKline Beecham; Tefal; Compaq Computers; J Walter Thompson; HM Govt Advertising Colln (incl significant World War II colln); Political Advertising Colln; Image of Women Colln (women & advertising, 1870-date); Arthur Cain Colln (personal lib & papers, public relations); Other: AV collns of television, radio & cinema commercials, incl Saatchi & Saatchi Campaigns & Slides Colln; posters & press advertisements; illustrators' artwork; unpublished client rsrch & sales material
Equip: Disabled: wheelchair access **Svcs:** rsrch
Stock: archvs/2 mln+ items
Pubns: bks on the hist of British advertising; exhib teaching notes; postcards; newsletter

John Innes Centre Archives and Special Collections

See JOHN INNES CENTRE, THE LIB (**S1624**)

A400 🏛

Norfolk Record Office

The Archv Centre, Martineau Ln, Norwich, Norfolk, NR1 2DQ (01603-761349; *fax:* 01603-761885)
Email: norfrec.nro@norfolk.gov.uk
Internet: http://archives.norfolk.gov.uk/

Gov Body: Norfolk County Council (see **P123**)
Chief: County Archivist: Dr John Alban BA, DipAA, PhD

Entry: CARN ticket essential, adv appt advisable for users of original MSS only **Open:** Mon-Fri 0900-1700, Sat 0900-1200
Subj: County of Norfolk & Diocese of Norwich: local authority archvs; diocesan records; parish records; estate archvs; family papers (incl some literary & medical MSS); business records; hosp records; local police records; records of socs & voluntary orgs; antiquarian collns **Collns:** Archvs: archvs of Norfolk County Council; City of Norwich Archvs (12C onwards); Gt Yarmouth Borough Archvs (13C onwards); King's Lynn Borough Archvs (13C onwards); records of Dist Councils; Diocese of Norwich records (13C onwards); Diocese of Ely records (Deaneries of Feltwell & Fincham); Norwich Cathedral records (11C onwards)
Equip: 23 m-readers, m-camera, m-printer & copier available to staff only, but copies supplied to users
Stock: archvs/7619 linear m
Auto Sys: DS
Pubns: Parish Records & Transcripts in the Norfolk Record Office (£5); Free Church Registers & Related Records in the Norfolk Record Office (£1.50); Guide to Genealogical Sources (50p); Guide to the Records of Norwich Cathedral (£6.95); Norfolk Parish Map (50p); all prices exclusive of p&p
Staff: Archivists: 9 Other Prof: 3 Non-Prof: 9.5
Proj: move to new location at above addr in Spring-Summer 2003

A401 🎓

Norwich School (King Edward VI), Local History Library

69 The Close, Norwich, Norfolk, NR1 4DD (01603-623194; *fax:* 01603-627036)
Email: enquiries@norwich-school.org.uk
Internet: http://www.norwich-school.org.uk/

Chief: Keeper of Local Hist Colln: Dr Paul Cattermole PhD, BSc, DipEd
Entry: ref only, by appt **Open:** school term
Subj: Norfolk & Norwich: local hist **Collns:** Archvs: Norwich School Archvs
Stock: archvs/20 m; bks/2500

Nottingham

A402 🌽

The Boots Company plc, Company Archives

D122 Records Centre, Nottingham, NG90 4XY (0115-959-3413; *fax:* 0115-959-3704)

Gov Body: The Boots Company plc **Chief:** Company Archivist: Ms Judy Burg
Entry: limited access; strictly by prior arrangement & appt
Subj: business records; records of parent org
Collns: Archvs: records of The Boots Company Ltd & predecessors (1880-20C), incl corporate records, ledgers & production records **Other:** photo colln

A403 🎓 🎥

Media Archive for Central England

Inst of Film Studies, Univ of Nottingham, Univ Pk, Nottingham, NG7 2RD (0115-846-6448; *fax:* 0115-951-4270)
Internet: http://www.nottingham.ac.uk/film/mace/

Gov Body: Univ of Nottingham (see **S1647**)
Chief: Dir: Mr James Patterson (james.patterson@nottingham.ac.uk) **Dep:** Archivist: Mr James Taylor MA (james.taylor@nottingham.ac.uk)
Entry: adv appt **Open:** Mon-Fri 0900-1700
Subj: East & West Midlands: moving images

Collns: Other: film, video & other moving image material relating to the Midlands
Equip: video viewer **Svcs:** info, ref, rsrch
Staff: Archivists: 2

A404 🌽 🎥

Carlton Television, Image Rights Unit and Media Management Archive

Lenton Ln, Nottingham, NG7 2NA (*Image Rights:* 0115-964-5472; *Archv:* 0115-964-5476)

Chief: Libn: Mrs J. Pitts **Other Snr Staff:** Film Archivist: Mr James McDonald; Stills Archivist: Ms Emma Morley
Open: Mon-Fri 0930-1730
Subj: television; entertainment; programme production **Collns:** Archvs: Central & Carlton Television Productions Film & Stills Archvs (1982-date), programmes incl: Inspector Morse; Sharpe; Bramwell; Peak Practice; Crossroads; many others
Equip: m-reader, copier, fax, 3 video viewers
Svcs: info, ref, indexing
Stock: archvs/c1000; periodcls/12; photos/c15000; slides/c5000; m-forms/c10000
Classn: DDC **Auto Sys:** Status IQ
Staff: Libns: 1 Non-Prof: 12

A405 🙏

Nottingham RC Diocesan Archives

Willson House, Derby Rd, Nottingham, NG1 5AW (0115-953-9803)

Gov Body: RC Diocese of Nottingham **Chief:** Diocesan Archivist: Canon Anthony P. Dolan MA, STL **Dep:** Asst Archivist: Mr Graham Foster MA
Entry: by arrangement **Open:** variable
Subj: RC Diocese of Nottingham: diocesan records; parish records
Equip: m-reader, copier

A406 🏛

Nottinghamshire Archives

(incorporating Southwell Diocesan Record Office)
County House, Castle Meadow Rd, Nottingham, NG2 1AG (*archvs:* 0115-958-1634; *administrative enqs:* 0115-950-4524; *fax:* 0115-941-3997)
Email: archives@nottscc.gov.uk
Internet: http://www.nottscc.gov.uk/libraries/Archives/

Gov Body: Nottinghamshire County Council (see **P139**) **Chief:** Principal Archivist: Mr A. Henstock BA, DipAA, FRHistS **Dep:** Snr Archivists: Miss B. Sharp BA, DipAA & Mr C. Weir BA, DipAA
Assoc Offices: LORD BELPER LIB, at same addr (see **A407**)
Entry: CARN ticket for all users of original archvs only **Open:** Mon & Wed-Fri 0900-1645, Tue 0900-1915, Sat 0900-1245
Subj: Nottinghamshire (geographical county): local authority archvs; diocesan records; parish records; estate archvs; family papers; business records; personal papers; records of parent org; poor law records; probate records; court records
Collns: Archvs: Nottinghamshire County Council archvs; City of Nottingham archvs; local Borough & Dist Council archvs; Diocese of Southwell archvs; deposits of various bodies & indivs **Other:** maps & plans
Equip: 40 m-readers, m-printer, copier, 6 computers
Stock: archvs/890 cubic m
Pubns: Guide to the Nottinghamshire Record Office (o/p & out-of-date); various packs, bklets, posters, postcards etc for sale
Staff: Archivists: 10 archivists & conservators Non-Prof: 5.3

A407

Nottinghamshire Archives, Lord Belper Library

County House, Castle Meadow Rd, Nottingham, NG2 1AG (archvs: 0115-958-1634; administrative enqs: 0115-950-4524; *fax:* 0115-941-3997)
Email: archives@nottscc.gov.uk
Internet: http://www.nottscc.gov.uk/libraries/ Archives/

Gov Body: Nottinghamshire County Council (see **P139**) *Chief:* Principal Archivist: Mr A. Henstock BA, DipAA, FRHistS *Dep:* Snr Archivists: Ms B. Sharp BA, DipAA & Mr C. Weir BA, DipAA
Assoc Offices: NOTTINGHAMSHIRE ARCHVS (see **A406**)
Entry: none for lib users *Open:* Mon-Fri 0900-1645, Tue 0900-1915, Sat 0900-1245
Subj: Nottinghamshire local hist; genl local hist & genealogy; natl archv sources
Equip: 40 m-readers, m-printer, copier, 6 computers
Stock: archvs/6000; periodcls/6; illusts/500 engravings; pamphs/12000
Classn: Nottinghamshire Local Studies Scheme, DDC
Pubns: The Belper Lib of Nottinghamshire Bks & Prints (currently o/p & out-of-date)

Oldham

A408

Oldham Local Studies and Archives

84 Union St, Oldham, OL1 1DN (0161-911-4654; *fax:* 0161-911-4654)
Email: local.studies@oldham.gov.uk
Internet: http://www.oldham.gov.uk/local_studies/

Gov Body: Oldham Metropolitan Borough Council (see **P140**) *Chief:* Local Studies Offcr: Mrs Terry Berry MA, BLib, MCLIP (ecs.terry.berry@oldham. gov.uk) *Dep:* Archvs Offcr: Mr Roger Ivens BA, MSc(Econ), MARM (ecs.roger.ivens@oldham. gov.uk)
Entry: ref only, proof of ID to use archvs
Open: Mon, Thu 1000-1900, Tue 1000-1400, Wed, Fri 1000-1700, Sat 1000-1600
Subj: Oldham Metropolitan Borough: local authority archvs; parish records; family papers; business records; personal papers; nonconformist records; trade union records; hosp records; records of co-op socs & other local bodies; local hist *Collns: Bks & Pamphs:* Oldham local hist *Archvs:* Oldham Metropolitan Borough & pre-decessor authorities; records of Oldham Poor Law Union; records of Oldham Coroner; Oldham Walton Archv (printed & audio materials relating to Sir William Walton); parish registers (on m-film) *Other:* photo colln; map colln, incl latest eds of OS maps of the borough, along with earlier surveys dating back to 18C; indexed newspaper cuttings & obituaries; census returns (on m-film, 1841-1901); local newspapers on m-film, incl: Oldham Chronicle (1854-date); Oldham Standard (1859-1946)
Equip: 10 m-readers, m-printer, copier *Svcs:* info, ref
Stock: archvs/230 cubic m; bks/8350; periodcls/20; photos/16000; slides/1300; maps/2800; m-forms/3060; audios/135
Classn: own
Pubns: Taste of Oldham (£4.95); Going up Town: Shopping in Oldham (£3.50); Looking Back at Crompton (£3.50); Changing Face of Crompton (£5.95); Looking Back at Royton (£5.95); Failsworth Place & People (£7); Looking Back at Lees (£6.50); The Most Dismal Times: William Rowbottom's Diary 1787-1799 (£6); Oldham & Its People (£9.95); Cotton Mills of Oldham (£8.99); Oldham, Brave Oldham (£15); Going, Going, Gone: Disappearing Oldham (£5.50)
Staff: Archivists: 1 *Libns:* 1 *Non-Prof:* 2.5

A409

Saddleworth Museum Archive Department

High St, Uppermill, Saddleworth, Oldham, OL3 6HS (01457-874093)

Gov Body: The Trustees of the Saddleworth Museum *Chief:* Curator: Ms Kirsty Mairs MA(Hons), AGMS Dip *Dep:* Hon Archivist: Mr Maurice Dennett BA
Entry: adv appt *Open:* summer (Apr-Oct): 1000-1700, winter: 1300-1600
Subj: Saddleworth & adjacent districts: local authority archvs (yearbks); parish records (m-films: local churches); estate archvs (deeds); family papers (wills & deeds); business records (local mills); various local collns covering: geog; geol; nat hist; hist; topography; govt svcs; political elections; arch; health; edu; religion; festivals & customs; rec; arts; socs; industries, commerce & trade; transport & communications; war & military involvement *Collns: Bks & Pamphs:* large lib of bks on textile processes; Saddleworth Historical Soc Bulletins *Archvs:* Ammon Wrigley Colln (local poet, historian, archaeologist); photos & postcards; Tanner Colln (banking, military, churches, local industry, retailing, sports, arts) *Other:* bnd & misc newspapers from 1880
Equip: m-reader, copier, computer (incl wd-proc)
Stock: archvs/28 m; rec mgmt/2 m; bks/12 m
Staff: Other Prof: 1 *Non-Prof:* 1

Oxford

A410

Centre for Oxfordshire Studies

Central Lib, Westgate, Oxford, OX1 1DJ (01865-815749; *fax:* 01865-810187)
Email: cos@oxfordshire.gov.uk
Internet: http://www.oxfordshire.gov.uk/

Gov Body: Oxfordshire County Council (see **P142**) *Chief:* Head of Oxfordshire Studies: Mr Malcolm Graham
Entry: ref only, adv appt for use of equip advisable *Open:* Mon, Fri-Sat 0915-1700, Tue, Thu 0915-1900, closed Wed
Subj: Oxfordshire: local studies; family hist; local companies & business info; archaeo *Collns: Bks & Pamphs:* bks on local hist *Archvs:* oral hist archv; sites & monuments primary records *Other:* photo colln; maps
Equip: 23 m-readers, 2 m-printers, fax, copier, video viewer, 12 computers (incl 6 with internet & 6 with CD-ROM), 2 audio tape recorders
Stock: archvs/31000; periodcls/600; photos/414000; slides/4500; illusts/4000; pamphs/16000; maps/8500; m-forms/56000; audios/4000; videos/130; CD-ROMs/120; Sites & Monuments records/13000
Classn: DDC, Adept *Auto Sys:* Geac
Staff: Libns: 4 *Other Prof:* 4 *Non-Prof:* 6 *Exp:* £27000 (2000-01)
Further Info: houses the County Archaeo Svc, incl the Sites & Monuments Record

A411

Oxford University Press Archives

Gt Clarendon St, Oxford, OX2 6DP (01865-353527)
Internet: http://www.oup.com/

Gov Body: Oxford Univ (see **L4** for Bodleian Lib) *Chief:* Archivist: Dr Martin Maw PhD, MArAd (martin.maw@oup.com) *Dep:* Archvs Asst: Mr Tom McCulloch (tom.mcculloch@oup.com)
Entry: adv appt; letter of recommendation required; please note that a 30-yr closure rule applies to most archv items *Open:* Mon-Fri 0900-1700

Subj: publishing; business records; records of parent org *Collns: Bks & Pamphs:* Bible Lib (Oxford & non-Oxford titles, 16C-date) *Archvs:* records of Oxford Univ Press (publishers), incl: administrative records (17C-date); printing records (1668-1989); publishing records (19C-date); editorial files (c1900-date); editorial records of Oxford English Dictionary (19C-date); letter bks of OUP's work in Oxford & London (1868-1959); records of Wolvercote Paper Mill *Other:* Fell Type Colln (17C Dutch moulds & type-punches); Oxford Almanacks prints & plates (17C-date)
Equip: copier *Disabled:* wheelchair access
Offcr-in-Charge: Archivist, as above
Stock: archvs/c3000 linear m; rec mgmt/c200 linear m; bks/c1000 linear m; photos/c10 linear m; illusts/c20 linear m *Acq Offcr:* Archivist, as above
Classn: ISAD(G) *Auto Sys:* CALM
Pubns: OUP: An Informal Hist, by P. Sutcliffe (OUP, 1978); The Oxford Univ Press, by H. Carter (OUP, 1975)
Staff: Archivists: 1 *Libns:* 2 *Non-Prof:* 4

A412

Oxfordshire Record Office

St Lukes Church, Temple Rd, Cowley, Oxford, OX4 2EX (01865-398200; *fax:* 01865-398201)
Email: archives@oxfordshire.gov.uk
Internet: http://www.oxfordshire.gov.uk/

Gov Body: Oxfordshire County Council (see **P142**) *Chief:* County Archivist: Mr Carl A. Boardman MA, DipAS *Dep:* Snr Archivist: Mr Mark Priddey BA, DipAS
Entry: CARN ticket, adv appt advisable *Open:* Tue-Sat 0900-1700; closed bank hol weekends & Xmas-New Year
Subj: Oxfordshire: local authority archvs; diocesan records; parish records; estate archvs; family papers; business records; records of parent org; deposits by private indivs, groups & orgs *Collns: Bks & Pamphs:* Davenport Lib: secondary sources colln, incl Victoria County Hist of Oxfordshire vols, genl & local ref works *Archvs:* archvs of Oxfordshire County Council; Diocese of Oxford (Archdeaconry of Oxford) diocesan & parish records
Equip: 9 m-readers, m-printer, copier (staff operated), 5 computers, room for hire *Svcs:* info, ref, rsrch
Stock: archvs/306 cubic m; rec mgmt/92 cubic m; printed bks/13 cubic m
Classn: ISAD(G) *Auto Sys:* CALM
Pubns: Oxfordshire Parish Registers & Bishop's Transcripts (£4.50); Index to the Probate Records of Oxfordshire, 1733-1857, & the Oxfordshire Peculiars, 1547-1856; Gustavus Sneyd: A Scandal in the Parish (£1.95); Oxford Church Court Records Vols 1-6 (£3.95 each); A Handlist of Inclosure Acts & Awards relating to the County of Oxford (75p); The Oxfordshire Election of 1754 (75p); A Handlist of Plans, Sections & Bks of Ref for the Proposed Railways in Oxfordshire 1825-1936 (65p); Family Hist: A Guide to Resources (£1)
Staff: Archivists: 7 *Other Prof:* 1 *Non-Prof:* 6

Paisley

A413

Renfrewshire Local Studies Library

Central Lib & Museum Complex, High St, Paisley, Renfrewshire, PA1 2BB (0141-889-2360; *fax:* 0141-887-6468)
Email: locstuds.els@renfrewshire.gov.uk
Internet: http://www.renfrewshire.gov.uk/

Gov Body: Renfrewshire Council (see **P152**) *Chief:* Local Studies Libn: Ms Patricia Burke MCLIP *Dep:* Asst Libn: Mr David Weir

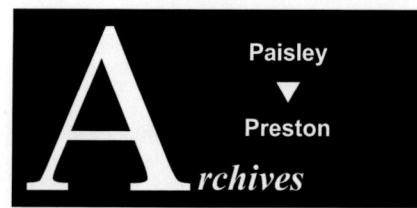

Archives

Paisley
▼
Preston

(Renfrewshire Local Studies Lib cont)

Open: Mon-Tue, Thu-Fri 1000-2000, Wed, Sat 1000-1700
Subj: Renfrewshire: local authority archvs; parish records; family papers; records of parent org; local hist *Collns: Bks & Pamphs:* The Paisley Pamphs (material, incl ephemera, 1739-1893); trade directories (1810-1937) *Archvs:* archvs of Renfrewshire Council & predecessors; Cairn of Lochwinnoch (45 vols of misc info about Lochwinnoch families); Poor Law records for Paisley & surrounding area; Paisley Weavers, Hammermen & Tailors records; sasines (1781-1947) *Other:* electoral & valuation rolls; local newspapers (1824-date); abstracts of earlier newspapers (1775 onwards); maps; photos; postcards; cuttings
Equip: 3 m-readers, 2 m-printers, copier, fax, computers (incl wd-proc & CD-ROM)
Staff: Libns: 1 *Other Prof:* 0.5 *Non-Prof:* 1.5

Penzance

A414
Cable and Wireless Archives

Eastern House, Porthcurno, Penzance, Cornwall, TR19 6JX (01736-810478; *fax:* 01736-810640)
Internet: http://www.porthcurno.org.uk/

Gov Body: Cable & Wireless Porthcurno & Collns Trust *Chief:* Curator: Ms Mary Godwin MA, AMA (mary.godwin@cw.com) *Dep:* Asst Curator: Mr Mark Steadman MSc
Entry: ref only, adv appt preferred *Open:* Mon-Fri 0900-1700
Subj: business records; records of parent org; marine records; telecommunications; telegraph; geog linked to growth of telecommunications network in British Empire & South America; hist of telecommunications; local studies (Porthcurno & Cornwall) *Collns: Bks & Pamphs:* ref colln, incl rare & early bks on hist of telecommunications; complete run of The Zodiac (staff magazine) & its successors; other professional journals relating to communications tech & eng *Archvs:* corporate archv of Eastern & Associated Telegraph Companies & Cable & Wireless plc (c1850-date), incl: records of Imperial Internatl Communications Ltd (1929-34); Marconi (mainly late 1920s); Cable & Wireless (from 1934); staff records (1860s onwards); financial records; brochures & sales records; maritime records & ephemera *Other:* press cuttings & releases (1850s onwards); photo colln (1870s onwards); film archv (1940s-date); map colln (1850s-date)
Equip: m-reader, m-printer (A4/10p), copier (A4/5p), room for hire *Offcr-in-Charge:* Curator, as above *Svcs:* info, ref, rsrch
Stock: archvs/565 linear m; bks/65 linear m; photos/40 linear m; videos/10 linear m *Acq Offcr:* Curator, as above
Classn: own *Auto Sys:* own
Pubns: Brief Guide to the Archv (free); Short Hist of C&W (free); various historical vols
Staff: Other Prof: 1

Perth

A415
The Black Watch Museum, Regimental Archives

Balhousie Castle, Hay St, Perth, PH1 5HR (0131-310-8530; *fax:* 0131-310-8525)

Gov Body: The Black Watch Trustees *Chief:* Curator: Major R.J.W. Proctor MBE
Open: May-Sep: Mon-Sat 1000-1630; Oct-Apr: Mon-Fri 1000-1530; closed 23rd Dec-4th Jan
Subj: regimental records; personal papers
Collns: Archvs: records of the Black Watch (Royal Highland Regiment)
Equip: m-reader, copier *Svcs:* info, ref, rsrch
Staff: Archivists: 1 *Non-Prof:* 2

A416
Perth and Kinross Council Archive

The AK Bell Lib, York Pl, Perth, PH2 8EP (01738-477012; *fax:* 01738-477010)
Email: archives@pkc.gov.uk
Internet: http://www.pkc.gov.uk/library/ archive.htm

Gov Body: Perth & Kinross Council (see **P144**)
Chief: Archivist: Mr Stephen Connelly (Registered Memb of the Soc of Archivists)
Dep: Asst Archivist: Dr Jan Merchant
Assoc Offices: LOCAL STUDIES SECTION, at same addr, Local Studies Libn: Mr Jeremy Duncan (01738-477062; *email:* jaduncan@pkc. gov.uk)
Entry: adv appt *Open:* Mon-Fri 0930-1700
Subj: Perth & Kinross Dist: local authority archvs; estate archvs; family papers; political papers; business records; records of parent org; legal records; school records; trade union records; records of local clubs & socs *Collns: Archvs:* records of Perth & Kinross Council & predecessors (1600 onwards); records of the burghs of Aberfeldy, Abernethy, Alyth, Auchterarder, Blairgowie & Rattray, Coupar Angus, Crieff, Kinross & Pitlochry; legal registers for Perth (1566 onwards); parish council registers of the poor (pre-1930); estate & family collns incl: Barons Kinnaird of Inchture; Drummond-Hays of Seggieden; Stewart-Meiklejohns of Edradynate; Fergussons of Baledmund; numerous business collns, incl: records of John Pullar & Sons Ltd *Other:* extensive colln of maps, plans & arch drawings
Co-op Schemes: SCAN
Equip: m-reader, fax, copier, Scottish Archv Network PC
Stock: archvs/c1500 linear m
Staff: Archivists: 1 *Non-Prof:* 2 *Exp:* £1000 (2000-01)

Peterborough

A417
Peterborough Local Studies Collection

Peterborough Central Lib, Broadway, Peterborough, Cambridgeshire, PE1 1RX (*switchboard:* 01733-742700; *fax:* 01733-555277)
Email: libraries@peterborough.gov.uk
Internet: http://www.peterborough.gov.uk/ subsites/libraries/

Gov Body: Peterborough City Council (see **P145**) *Chief:* Enquiry Svcs Libn (Local Studies): Mr Richard Hillier BA, MCLIP
Assoc Offices: for archival materials relating to Peterborough, see also NORTHAMPTONSHIRE RECORD OFFICE (**A395**), HUNTINGDON RECORD OFFICE (**A211**) & CAMBRIDGESHIRE RECORD OFFICE (**A87**)

Entry: ref only, adv appt for some non-bk items
Open: Mon, Fri-Sat 0930-1700, Tue-Thu 0930-1900
Subj: 10-15 mile radius of Peterborough: local hist; family hist; topography; biography *Collns: Bks & Pamphs:* local & family hist colln; local authors & their works; Peterborough Gentlemen's Soc Lib *Other:* IGI on m-fiche; census records (printed & m-form); church registers; wills & probate records; maps & plans; monumental inscriptions; engravings & lithographs; photos, incl Kitchin Colln (2000 negs of Peterborough, 1953-73); local newspapers & periodcls *Co-op Schemes:* Newsplan (m-filming of local newspapers)
Equip: 8 m-readers, 4 m-printers, copier, clr copier, fax, computers (incl 1 with CD-ROM), room for hire; some of these are genl Ref Lib svcs, not specific to Local Studies
Stock: archvs/10000; periodcls/10; photos/10000; illusts/1000; pamphs/3000; maps/3000; m-forms/15000 sheets/reels
Classn: own
Pubns: Guide to Peterborough Local Studies Colln (leaflet)
Staff: Libns: 1

A418
Thomas Cook Archives

The Thomas Cook Business Pk, 19-21 Coningsby Rd, Peterborough, Cambridgeshire, PE3 8SB (01733-402025; *fax:* 01733-402026)
Email: paul.smith@thomascook.com
Internet: http://www.thomascook.info/

Gov Body: Thomas Cook UK Ltd *Chief:* Company Archivist: Mr Paul Smith BA(Hons), MArAd
Entry: adv appt *Open:* Mon-Fri 1000-1600
Subj: worldwide: hist of travel & tourism; family papers; business records; personal papers; records of parent org *Collns: Bks & Pamphs:* guidebks; timetables; hol brochures; Cook's Excursions (newspaper); diaries of 19C travellers *Archvs:* operational records of Thomas Cook & Son Ltd (travel agents, 19C-20C); correspondence of Thomas Cook (tourist agent, 1808-1892); correspondence of John Cook (tourist agent, 1834-1899) *Other:* photo colln (of offices & travellers); travellers' ephemera; travel films
Equip: copier (A4/20p), video viewer *Offcr-in-Charge:* Company Archivist, as above *Svcs:* info, ref, rsrch
Stock: archvs/c200 linear m *Acq Offcr:* Company Archivist, as above
Classn: ISAD(G) *Staff: Archivists:* 1

Plymouth

A419
Plymouth and West Devon Record Office

Unit 3, Clare Pl, Coxside, Plymouth, Devon, PL4 0JW (01752-305940)
Email: pwdro@plymouth.gov.uk
Internet: http://www.plymouth.gov.uk/star/ archives.htm

Gov Body: City of Plymouth Council (see **P146**)
Chief: City Archivist: Ms M. Simms BA, DipAA
Dep: Archivist: Ms A. Morgan BA, PGCE, DipAA
Entry: proof of ID (incl CARN); adv appt; ref only; daily charge (£2) or annual (£25) or 6 month ticket (£13) *Open:* Tue-Thu 0930-1700, Fri 0930-1600
Subj: Plymouth & West Devon: local authority archvs; diocesan records; parish records; estate archvs; family papers; business records; personal papers; political papers; poor law records; school records; nonconformist records;

solicitors records; hosp records; coroners records; magistrates records; records of local clubs & socs; records of local charities & trusts; records of parent org *Collns: Archvs:* Plymouth City Council Archvs; West Devon Borough Council Archvs; records of rural & urban dist councils; Borough Quarter Sessions records; Plymouth Dock Labour Board records; Registers of Shipping; Archdeaconry of Plymouth records, incl parish records, poor law papers & churchwardens' records; estate collns, incl: Parker of Saltram; St Aubyn; Bastard of Kitley; Yonge of Puslinch; Lopes of Maristow; collns of private papers, incl: Clark Papers; Calmady Papers; Fox Papers; Seymour Papers; Hawkins Papers; Bayly Papers *Other:* Western Morning News photo colln (1942-1970); C of E & nonconformist registers (m-film); IGI for Devon & Cornwall (m-film); some census indexes; Plymouth Archvs Marriage Indexes (CD-ROM) *Equip:* 11 m-readers, m-printer *Svcs:* info, ref, postal photocopying svc *Stock:* archvs/2000 linear m (160 cubic m); rec mgmt/20 cubic m *Acq Offcr:* Snr Archvs Asst: Mrs D. Watson *Pubns:* Guide to Parochial & Non-Parochial Registers (£2 + p&p); Poor Law Records (£1) *Staff: Archivists:* 2 *Non-Prof:* 3

A420
Plymouth Local and Naval Studies Library
Central Lib, Drake Circus, Plymouth, Devon, PL4 8AL (01752-305909; *fax:* 01752-305905)
Email: localstudies@plymouth.gov.uk
Internet: http://www.pgfl.plymouth.gov.uk/ libraries/

Gov Body: Plymouth City Council (see **P146**) *Chief:* Local Studies Libn: Ms Joyce Brown *Assoc Offices:* local archvs are held at: PLYMOUTH & WEST DEVON RECORD OFFICE (see **A419**); addl local family records are held at: GENEALOGICAL BRANCH LIB, LDS Church, Mannamead Rd, Hartley, Plymouth (01752-668666) *Entry:* open to public, ref only; adv notice required to view rarer materials *Open:* Mon-Fri 0900-1900, Sat 0900-1600 *Subj:* Plymouth & West Devon: local hist; family hist; naval studies; transport; edu; geol; mining; genealogy; archaeo; biography *Collns: Bks & Pamphs:* Naval Studies Colln (naval hist, naval biography, ships' logs, naval periodcls etc); bks by Eden Phillpotts & Sabine Baring-Gould; Plymouth street directories (1812-1967); Devon trade directories (1823-1939); local journals *Archvs:* council minutes for Plymouth City Council, Devon County Council & Cornwall County Council *Other:* Naval Studies Colln (charts, illusts & photos, videos); Internatl Genealogical Index (m-fiche); electoral registers for Plymouth (1934-date); census returns for Plymouth (m-form, 1841-91); parish register transcripts (Devon & Cornwall); Naval Lists (1782 onwards); local newspapers on m-film, incl: Western Morning News (1860-date), Western Daily Mercury (1860-1920), Western Evening Herald (1895-date), Sherbourne Mercury (1737-1867); Map Colln (local maps, incl historical, geological & land use maps & navigation charts); Illusts Colln (photos, postcards & engravings of Plymouth, Devon & Cornwall); extensive cuttings colln; theatre programmes *Equip:* 5 m-readers, 6 m-printers, computer (with internet, staff only) *Stock:* archvs/35000 *Staff: Libns:* 1 *Non-Prof:* 2

A421
The South West Film and Television Archive
New Cooperage, Royal William Yard, Stonehouse, Plymouth, Devon, PL1 3RP (01752-202650; *fax:* 01725-205025)
Email: enquiries@tswfta.co.uk
Internet: http://www.tswfta.co.uk/

Type: independent charity *Gov Body:* TSW Archv Trust *Chief:* Curator: Ms Elayne Hoskin (elayne@tswfta.co.uk) *Entry:* viewing on premises by appt *Subj:* SW England: local life; people at work; urban life; rural life; special occasions & events; crafts & industries *Collns: Other:* TSW Film & Video Lib (incl Westward Television Film Lib); BBC South West Film Lib; over 500 other collns *Equip:* video & film viewing equip

Poole

A422
Poole Local History Centre
Waterfront Museum, 4 High St, Poole, Dorset, BH15 1BW (01202-262600)
Email: localhistory@poole.gov.uk
Internet: http://www.boroughofpoole.com/

Gov Body: Borough of Poole (see **P147**) *Chief:* Local Hist Resources Mgr: Mr David R. Watkins BA, AIFA *Dep:* Local Studies Offcr: Miss Pat Parker MCLIP *Assoc Offices:* Borough Archvs are held at DORSET ARCHVS SVC (see **A125**) *Entry:* ref only *Open:* Tue-Fri 1000-1500 *Subj:* Borough of Poole: local studies; family hist; parish records (m-film copies only); records of parent org (selective coverage) *Collns: Bks & Pamphs:* various, incl Mathews Colln *Archvs:* museum archvs *Other:* large photo archv; map colln; local newspapers (m-film); info files on local subjs & families *Equip:* 7 m-readers, 2 m-printers (30p per pg), copier (A4/10p, A3/20p), 4 computers (all with wd-proc, internet & CD-ROM) *Disabled:* disabled access *Svcs:* info, ref, rsrch *Stock:* archvs/c8000; photos/30000+; slides/2000; audios/100; videos/50 *Classn:* DDC with variations *Auto Sys:* Talis *Pubns:* Poole Census 1574; Poole Levee En Masse 1803: Vols 1-2 (£7.95 each); Book of the Staple 1589-1727 (£2.95) *Staff: Libns:* 1 *Other Prof:* 1

Portsmouth

A423
Portsmouth City Museums and Records Service
3 Museum Rd, Portsmouth, PO1 2LJ (023-9282-7261; *fax:* 023-9287-5276)
Email: info@portsmouthrecordsoffice.co.uk
Internet: http://www.portsmouthrecordsoffice. co.uk/

Gov Body: Portsmouth City Council (see **P148**) *Chief:* Museums & Records Offcr: Mrs S.E. Quail BA, DipAA *Entry:* CARN ticket *Open:* searchroom: Mon-Fri 1000-1700, excl public hols *Subj:* Portsmouth & SE Hampshire: local authority archvs; diocesan records; parish records; estate archvs; family papers; business records; personal papers; records of parent org; nonconformist records; records of local orgs *Collns: Archvs:* archvs of Portsmouth City Council & predecessor bodies (14C onwards);

records of Anglican Diocese of Portsmouth from 1927 onwards, incl parish records of Gosport, Fareham, Portsmouth, Havant & Alverstoke deaneries *Other:* map colln; census returns; photographs; postcards *Equip:* 9 m-readers, m-printer, video viewer, fax, copier, computer (Visual Images database) *Stock:* archvs/180 cubic m; rec mgmt/591 cubic m *Staff: Other Prof:* 6 *Non-Prof:* 4

A424
Portsmouth RC Diocesan Archives
St Edmund House, Edinburgh Rd, Portsmouth, PO1 3QA (023-9282-5430; *fax:* 023-9287-2424)
Email: finance@portsmouth-dio.org.uk

Gov Body: Portsmouth RC Diocesan Trustees Registered *Chief:* Diocesan Archivist: Rev Brian Croughan BA, MA, MTL *Dep:* Asst Archivist: Dr Val Fontana BSc, PhD *Entry:* adv appt by arrangement with the Archivists (call 023-9282-1560) *Open:* Mon-Fri 1000-1600 *Subj:* Diocese of Portsmouth (old counties of Berkshire, Hampshire, Isle of Wight & Channel Islands): diocesan records; parish records; some family papers; recusant hist *Collns: Bks & Pamphs:* Catholic & Diocesan directories *Equip:* copier (5p per pg) *Disabled:* wheelchair access *Svcs:* info, ref

Preston

A425
Lancashire Record Office
Bow Ln, Preston, Lancashire, PR1 2RE (01772-533039; *fax:* 01772-533050)
Email: record.office@ed.lancscc.gov.uk
Internet: http://www.lancashire.gov.uk/education/ d_lif/ro/

Gov Body: Lancashire County Council (see **P71**); also provides archv svc for Blackburn with Darwen Borough Council (see **P10**) & Blackpool Borough Council *Chief:* County Archivist: Mr B. Jackson MA, DipAA *Dep:* Asst County Archivist: Mrs J.M. Crosby MA, DipAS *Assoc Offices:* NORTH WEST SOUND ARCHV (see **A109**) *Entry:* CARN reader's ticket required *Open:* Mon, Wed, Fri 0900-1700, Tue 0900-2030, Thu 1000-1700 *Subj:* Lancashire (pre- & post-1974 boundary changes): local authority archvs; diocesan records; parish records; estate archvs; family papers; business records; records of parent org; RC & nonconformist records; hosp records; some trade union records *Collns: Bks & Pamphs:* Lancashire County Lib HQ Local Studies Colln is available for public use at the Record Office *Archvs:* archvs of Lancashire County Council; turnpike trusts; Quarter Sessions; Diocese of Blackburn parish records; Diocese of Bradford parish records (Lancashire area); estate archvs & family papers, incl: Earls of Derby; Earls of Sefton; Manor of Prescot; Blundell of Gt Crosby; Blundell of Ince Blundell; Scarisbrick of Scarisbrick *Equip:* 40 m-readers, 2 m-printers, 12 laptop sockets, computers (incl internet) *Stock:* archvs/1726 cubic m; rec mgmt/707 cubic m *Pubns:* Guide to the Lancashire Record Office (3rd edition, £12.75 + p&p); Guide to the Lancashire Record Office: A Supplement 1977-89 (£14.95 + p&p); Finding Folk: A Handlist of Genealogical Sources in Lancashire Record Office (£8.50 + £3 p&p) *Staff: Archivists:* 10 *Other Prof:* 2 *Non-Prof:* 15 *Exp:* £3700 (2000-01)

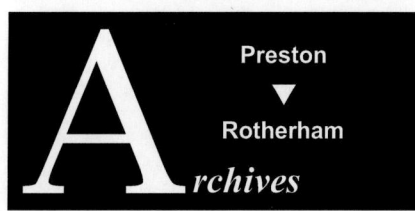

A426 🔑 🏛

Museum of the Queen's Lancashire Regiment

Fulwood Barracks, Preston, Lancashire, PR2 8AA
(01772-260362; fax: 01772-260583)
Email: rhq.qlr@talk21.com

Gov Body: Museum Trustees *Chief:* Curator: Lt Col M.J. Glover MA, AMA, PGCE *Dep:* Asst Curator: Mr G. Smith BA
Entry: ref only; adv appt *Open:* Tue-Thu 0930-1630; other times by appt
Subj: Lancashire & NW England: family papers; personal papers; records of parent org; regimental records *Collns: Bks & Pamphs:* 300 training/doctrine pamphs (1642-date) *Archvs:* papers covering the period 1689-date, relating to 30th, 40th, 47th, 59th, 81st & 82nd of Foot; East Lancashire Regiment; South Lancashire Regiment; Loyal Regiment (North Lancashire); Lancashire Regiment; Queen's Lancashire Regiment; associated militia, rifle volunteer, Territorial Army & Home Guard units *Other:* 200 battlefield maps
Equip: m-reader, copier, fax, video viewer, computers (incl wd-proc & CD-ROM), room for hire *Svcs:* info, ref, rsrch
Stock: archvs/131 cubic m
Staff: Other Prof: 2 *Exp:* £1500 (2000-01)

Ramsgate

A427 🏛

Ramsgate Library and Museum, Local Studies Collection

Guildford Lawn, Ramsgate, Kent, CT11 9AY
(01843-593532; fax: 01843-852692)
Internet: http://www.kent.gov.uk/e&l/artslib/reference/localstudies.html

Gov Body: Kent County Council (see **P67**)
Chief: Team Libn: Ms Beth Thomson BLib, MCLIP
Dep: Team Asst: Mrs Linda Kember
Entry: ref only *Open:* Thu 0930-1300, 1400-1800, 3rd Sat each month 0930-1300, 1400-1700
Subj: Ramsgate & Isle of Thanet: local studies
Collns: Archvs: archvs originally held here now transferred to EAST KENT ARCHVS CENTRE (see **A128**)
Equip: 6 m-readers, m-printer, copier, fax, computers (incl 3 wd-procs & 3 internet) *Svcs:* info, ref, rsrch
Stock: archvs/various bks, periodcls, photos, illusts, pamphs & maps
Staff: Libns: 2 *Non-Prof:* 1

Reading

A428 ✍ 🎓

BBC Written Archives Centre

Peppard Rd, Caversham Pk, Reading, Berkshire, RG4 8TZ (0118-948-6281; fax: 0118-946-1145)
Email: wac.enquiries@bbc.co.uk

Gov Body: British Broadcasting Corp *Chief:* Written Archivist: Mrs Jacqueline Kavanagh BA, DipAA *Dep:* Dep Written Archivist: Mr James Codd BA

Assoc Offices: BBC INFO & ARCHVS (see **S1009**); BBC PHOTO LIB (see **S1010**)
Entry: ref only; adv appt; charges made for certain svcs *Open:* Wed-Fri 0945-1700
Subj: postgrad; all subjs (excl sci & maths); broadcasting tech; broadcasting; 20C biography; business records; personal papers; records of parent org *Collns: Bks & Pamphs:* BBC pubns incl Radio Times, The Listener & BBC Schools pubns to date; press cuttings on broadcasting (1922-mid 1960s) *Archvs:* these are the written archvs of the BBC (1922-1979): correspondence, scripts, news bulletins etc relating to development & influence of BBC Radio & TV at home & abroad; major src for 20C social & political hist & the arts with particular importance for biographers
Equip: 5 m-readers, 2 m-printers, copier *Svcs:* info, ref, rsrch
Stock: archvs/20000 linear ft; bks/1000 linear ft; periodcls/500 linear ft; m-forms/21000 reels
Classn: archival
Staff: Other Prof: 7 *Non-Prof:* 4

A429 🏛

Berkshire Record Office

9 Coley Ave, Reading, Berkshire, RG1 6AF
(0118-901-5132; fax: 0118-901-5131)
Email: arch@reading.gov.uk
Internet: http://www.berkshirerecordoffice.org.uk/

Gov Body: Reading Borough Council (see **P150**), on behalf of the 6 unitary authorities of Berkshire *Chief:* County Archivist: Dr Peter Durrant BA, PhD *Dep:* Snr Archivist: Mr Mark Stevens LLB(Hons), DipARM
Entry: CARN ticket required; adv appt essential
Open: Tue, Wed 0900-1700, Thu 0900-2100, Fri 0900-1630
Subj: Berkshire (pre- & post-1974 boundary changes): local authority archvs; parish records; estate archvs; family papers; business records; records of parent org; school records; misc local public records; records of local socs *Collns: Bks & Pamphs:* local studies materials *Archvs:* archvs of former Berkshire County Council; Diocese of Oxford (Archdeaconry of Berkshire) parish records; Thames Conservancy records
Equip: 24 m-readers, m-printer, copier, 2 computers (both with internet & CD-ROM), room for hire *Disabled:* wheelchair access *Svcs:* info, ref, rsrch
Stock: archvs/425 cubic m; rec mgmt/630 cubic m; bks/13000; m-forms/17000
Classn: ISAD(G)
Pubns: Guide to Poor Law Records 1834-1948 (£1 + p&p); Finding Your Family: A Guide to Genealogical Sources (£1.95 + p&p)
Staff: Archivists: 7 *Other Prof:* 3 *Non-Prof:* 10.7

Redruth

A430 🏛

Cornish Studies Library

The Cornwall Centre, Alma Pl, Redruth, Cornwall, TR15 2AT (01209-216760; fax: 01209-210283)
Email: cornishstudies.library@cornwall.gov.uk
Internet: http://www.cornwall.gov.uk/

Type: special dept of public lib *Gov Body:* Cornwall County Council (see **P30**), Info Svcs Group *Chief:* Principal Lib Offcr, Cornish Studies: Mr Terry Knight MCLIP
Entry: adv appt advised for use of m-readers
Open: Mon-Fri 1000-1800, Sat 1000-1600
Subj: Cornwall & the Isles of Scilly: local studies; hist; industry; agric; mining; arts; lit; family hist; parish records *Collns: Bks & Pamphs:* Hambly & Rowe Colln; Ashley Rowe Colln; A.K. Hamilton Jenkin Colln; extensive colln of local journals; annual reports of Cornish orgs *Archvs:* parish

registers *Other:* photo colln, incl George Ellis Photo Archv (1939-c1980); local newspapers & newsletters; map colln; AV study collns on Cornish topics *Co-op Schemes:* SWRLS, ILL
Equip: 17 m-readers, 2 m-printers, copier, fax, 6 computers (all with wd-proc, internet & CD-ROM, £2 per hr), room for hire *Online:* Cornwall's community info database
Stock: archvs/19000; periodcls/200; photos/125000; pamphs/12000; maps/3000; m-forms/3500; videos/100; picture postcards/c50 albums
Classn: DDC *Auto Sys:* BLCMP Talis
Pubns: leaflets listing holdings (all free)
Staff: Libns: 3 *Non-Prof:* 2 *Exp:* £24300 (2000-01)
See also CORNWALL RECORD OFFICE (**A494**)

Richmond

A431 🏛

Historical Manuscripts Commission Searchroom

(formerly The Royal Commission on Historical MSS)
The Natl Archvs, Ruskin Ave, Kew, Richmond, Surrey, TW9 4DU (020-8876-3444; fax: 020-8392-5286)
Email: enquiry@nationalarchives.gov.uk
Internet: http://www.hmc.gov.uk/

Gov Body: Historical Manuscripts Commission (appointed by Royal Warrant in 1869); part of the Natl Archvs (see **A432**) *Chief:* Sec to the Commission: Dr C.J. Kitching BA, PhD, FSA
Open: Mon, Wed, Fri 0900-1700, Tue, Thu 1000-1900, Sat 0930-1700
Subj: info about British historical papers outside the public records *Collns: Bks & Pamphs:* own published guides & surveys of MSS *Other:* Natl Register of Archvs (43000+ unpublished catalogues indexed by person, family, company & org); Manorial Documents Register
Equip: 5 computers, all providing access to the Natl Register of Archvs database (also available on the Commission's web site)
Stock: archvs/a few available for public use; unpublished catalogues/43000
Staff: Other Prof: 18 *Non-Prof:* 7
Further Info: Merged with the Public Record Office on 1st Apr 2003 to form a new org, The Natl Archvs
See also **O226**

A432 🏛

The National Archives

Ruskin Ave, Kew, Richmond, Surrey, TW9 4DU (020-8876-3444; minicom: 020-8392-9198; fax: 020-8392-5286)
Email: enquiry@nationalarchives.gov.uk
Internet: http://www.nationalarchives.gov.uk/

Gov Body: Lord Chancellor's Dept *Chief:* Keeper of Public Records: Mrs Sarah Tyacke CB
Assoc Offices: HISTORICAL MSS COMMISSION SEARCHROOM, at same addr (see **A431**); FAMILY RECORDS CENTRE (see **A310**)
Entry: readers ticket issued subj to proof of ID
Open: Mon, Wed, Fri 0900-1700, Tue, Thu 1000-1900, Sat 0930-1700; closed 1st wk of Dec for stocktaking & on public hols
Collns: Archvs: natl archvs of England & UK dating from the Domesday Book (1086); modern, departmental & military records; medieval & early modern records; legal records; census records
Equip: m-readers, m-printers, copiers, clr copiers, computers (incl internet & CD-ROM)
Svcs: info, rsrch (fees vary), exhibs
Stock: archvs/92 miles
Pubns: Public Record Office Current Guide (personal orders £52, insts £75, m-fiche version available); Readers' Guides (Nos 1-3, 5-15, prices

vary); Special Pubns (guides to recently released documents, £3.25 each); Archvs in Edu (£9.95); Sussex Coroners' Inquests 1558-1603 (£20); Titanic: 14th-15th April 1912 – The Official Story (£14.99); Chancery Lane 1377-1977: "The Strongbox of the Empire" (£7.50); New to Kew? (first-time guide to PRO at Kew, £5.99); Battlefront: 1st July 1916 The First Day of the Somme (study pack, £9.99); Army Svc Records of the First World War (£5.99); PRO Texts & Calendars (prices vary); PROfiles 1964 (CD-ROM, £975 + VAT)
Staff: Archivists: 35 *Non-Prof:* 410
Proj: new Edu & Visitors Centre
Further Info: The Public Record Office merged with the Historical MSS Commission on 1st Apr 2003 to form a new org, The Natl Archvs

A433

Richmond upon Thames Archives and Local Studies Library

Old Town Hall, Whittaker Ave, Richmond, Surrey, TW9 1TP (020-8332-6820)
Email: localstudies@richmond.gov.uk
Internet: http://www.richmond.gov.uk/

Gov Body: London Borough of Richmond upon Thames (see **P103**) *Chief:* Local Studies Libn: Miss Jane Baxter BA, DipLib, MCLIP (j.baxter@ richmond.gov.uk) *Dep:* Snr Local Studies Asst: Mrs C. Turfitt (c.turfitt@richmond.gov.uk)
Open: Tue 1300-1700, Wed 1300-2000, Thu-Fri 1000-1200, 1300-1800, Sats 1000-1200, 1300-1700
Subj: London Borough of Richmond upon Thames: local authority archvs; family papers; business records; personal papers; local studies
Collns: Bks & Pamphs: Alexander Pope Colln; Horace Walpole Colln; Sir Richard Burton Colln (1821-90) *Archvs:* Douglas Sladen Colln (correspondence of editor of Who's Who 1897-99); Cole Family papers *Other:* Playbill Colln (Theatre Royal, Richmond)
Equip: 3 m-readers, m-printer, copier, 5 computers (incl 4 with wd-proc, 4 with internet & 4 with CD-ROM) *Svcs:* rsrch
Classn: DDC *Staff:* Libns: 1 *Non-Prof:* 1

Rochdale

A434

Rochdale Local Studies Library

Touchestone Rochdale, The Esplanade, Rochdale, Lancashire, OL16 1AQ (01706-864915)
Email: localstudies@rochdale.co.uk
Internet: http://www.rochdale.gov.uk/

Type: local govt *Gov Body:* Rochdale Metropolitan Borough Council (see **P154**) *Chief:* Local Studies Offcr: Mrs P. Godman BA(Librarianship) *Dep:* Asst Libn: Mrs S. Warburton MCLIP *Other Snr Staff:* Archivist: post vacant
Assoc Offices: HEYWOOD LOCAL STUDIES LIB, Heywood Central Lib, Church St, Heywood, Lancashire, OL10 1LL, Area Libn: Mr Alan Boughie (01706-360947; *fax:* 01706-368683; *email:* heywood.library@rochdale.gov.uk); MIDDLETON LOCAL STUDIES LIB, Middleton Central Lib, Long St, Middleton, Lancashire, M24 3DU, Area Libn: Mr Alan Boughie (0161-643-5228; *fax:* 0161-654-0745; *email:* middleton.library@rochdale.gov.uk)
Entry: no restrictions *Open:* Tue-Wed, Fri 1000-1730, Thu 1000-1930, Sat 1100-1630; closed Mon
Subj: Rochdale: local authority archvs; parish records; estate archvs; family papers; business records; personal papers; political papers; records of parent orgs; nonconformist records; trade union records

Collns: Bks & Pamphs: 'Tim Bobbin' (John Collier) Colln (dialect prints) *Archvs:* archvs of Rochdale Metropolitan Borough Council & predecessors; Co-operation Colln (minute bks of Rochdale Pioneers & various other local co-ops)
Equip: 6 m-readers, 3 m-printers (50p per sheet), copier (A4/10p, A3/20p), 12 computers (all with wd-proc & internet, printouts A4/10p) *Offcr-in-Charge:* Local Studies Offcr, as above *Svcs:* info, ref, rsrch on limited basis
Stock: archvs/106.76 cubic m; bks/13562 incl pamphs; periodcls/16; photos/10000+; slides/960; maps/1574; m-forms/7193; audios/163; videos/55; CD-ROMs/27 *Acq Offcr:* Asst Libn, as above
Classn: in-house scheme *Auto Sys:* Dynix (forthcoming)
Staff: Archivists: 1 *Libns:* 2 *Non-Prof:* 3 FTE
Exp: £7000 (1999-2000); £7000 (2000-01)
Proj: move back to refurbished Touchstones Rochdale (Arts & Heritage Centre)

Rochester

A435

Medway Archives and Local Studies Centre

(formerly Rochester-upon-Medway Studies Centre)
Civic Centre, Strood, Rochester, Kent, ME2 4AU (archvs: 01634-332714; local studies: 01634-332238; *fax:* 01634-297060)
Email: archives@medway.gov.uk or local.studies@medway.gov.uk
Internet: http://cityark.medway.gov.uk/

Gov Body: Medway Council (see **P113**) *Chief:* Local Head of Repository & City Archivist: Mr Stephen Dixon MA(Hons), DipAS *Other Snr Staff:* Local Studies Libn: Ms Norma Crowe
Entry: Archvs: CARN ticket & appt required; Local Studies: ref only, adv appt preferred but not essential *Open:* Mon, Thu-Fri 0900-1700, Tue 0900-1800, 0900-1600; closed Wed
Subj: Rochester-upon-Medway local authority area & Rochester Archdeaconry area: local authority archvs; parish records; estate archvs; family papers; business records; records of parent org; antiquarian records; records of charities; edu records; local hist; family hist; topography *Collns: Bks & Pamphs:* Medway Lib Group's Local Studies Collns, incl: Dickens Colln; Naval Colln; Chatham Dockyards Colln; Short Brothers Colln; Topographical Colln *Archvs:* Rochester City Council (1227-1974); Chatham Borough Council (1890-1974); Strood Rural Dist Council (1896-1974); Hoo Rural Dist Council (1897-1935); Kent County Council Edu records (schools in Medway); Diocese of Rochester (Rochester Archdeaconry) parish records (14C-20C); Medway Towns Methodists (1768-1986); Medway, Strood & Hoo Poor Law Unions (1835-1930); Watts Charity Rochester (1579 onwards); Hawkins' Hosp Chatham (16C-20C); St Bart's Hosp Rochester (1627-1948); Best family of Chatham/Boxley (1576-1905); Darnley of Cobham (1537-1974); Chatham Synagogue (1834-1972) *Other:* maps & plans; photos & engravings; local newspapers on m-film
Equip: 10 m-readers, m-printer, fax, copier, computers (incl wd-proc, internet & CD-ROM)
Disabled: adjustable table height for OPAC, lift, disabled toilet *Svcs:* info, ref, rsrch
Stock: archvs/950 linear m; bks/12000; periodcls/20; photos/8750; slides/350; illusts/1000; audios/100; videos/20; CD-ROMs/10
Pubns: Centre Leaflet (free); Archvs Subj Guide (£2.50); Local Military Family Hist (£2.50)
Staff: Archivists: 1 *Libns:* 2 PT *Non-Prof:* 3

A436

Rochester Bridge Trust Archives

The Bridge Chamber, 5 The Esplanade, Rochester, Kent, ME1 1QE (01634-846706; *fax:* 01634-840125)
Email: lewis@rochester-bridge-trust.freeserve. co.uk

Gov Body: Rochester Bridge Trust *Chief:* Bridge Clerk: M. Lewis *Dep:* Archivist: Dr James M. Gibson PhD
Entry: adv appt *Open:* Mon-Fri 0900-1300
Subj: Kent: estate archvs *Collns: Archvs:* minute bks, accounts, maps, plans, relating to the bldg & maintenance of Rochester Bridge & to the Bridge Estates (in Kent, Essex & London) from 14C onwards
Equip: video viewer, copier
Stock: archvs/100 linear m
Pubns: Traffic & Politics: The Construction & Mgmt of Rochester Bridge AD 43-1993 (£29.95); Crossing the Medway (£1)
Staff: Other Prof: 2 *Non-Prof:* 4

Romford

A437

Havering Local History Collection

Central Lib, St Edward's Way, Romford, Essex, RM1 3AR (01708-432393/4; *fax:* 01708-432391)
Email: romfordlib2@rmplc.co.uk

Gov Body: London Borough of Havering (see **P91**) *Chief:* Snr Libn: Mrs Julie Johns
Entry: ref only *Open:* Mon 1000-2000, Tue-Fri 0900-2000
Subj: London Borough of Havering, parts of Essex: local hist (primarily 19C-20C) *Collns: Bks & Pamphs:* genl local hist colln; Essex & Havering magazines; local directories *Other:* map colln (mainly 20C); local newspapers (from 1866); illusts; photos; postcards; slides
Equip: 5 m-readers, 2 m-printers, copier, clr copier, computer (with CD-ROM)

Rotherham

A438

Rotherham Archives and Local Studies Service

Central Lib, Walker Pl, Rotherham, S Yorkshire, S60 2AX (01709-823616; *fax:* 01709-823650)
Email: archives@rotherham.gov.uk
Internet: http://www.rotherham.gov.uk/

Gov Body: Rotherham Metropolitan Borough Council (see **P155**) *Chief:* Principal Offcr, Archvs & Local Studies: Mr Anthony P. Munford BA, RMSA *Dep:* Local Studies Libn: Miss C. Heron
Open: Tue-Wed, Fri 1000-1300, 1400-1700, Thu 1300-1900, Sat 0900-1300, 1400-1600 (closed Mon)
Subj: Metropolitan Borough of Rotherham: local authority archvs; parish records (transcripts & m-film only); estate archvs; family papers; business records; records of parent org *Collns: Bks & Pamphs:* bks, pamphs, newspapers etc relating to local hist of the area; bks by local authors *Archvs:* archvs of Rotherham Metropolitan Borough Council & predecessors; Effingham family papers; Bosville family papers; Verelst family papers; records of local iron & steel, coal, glass etc industries; other records relating to the area of the Metropolitan Borough of Rotherham *Other:* OS maps; m-film of census returns *Co-op Schemes:* South Yorkshire Joint Archv Svc, with Doncaster (see **A124**), Barnsley (see **A26**) & Sheffield (see **A452**) ☛

Archives

Rotherham
▼
Sheffield

(Rotherham Archvs & Local Studies Svc cont)
Equip: 5 m-readers, m-printer, copier, 5 computers (all with wd-proc, internet & CD-ROM) **Svcs:** info, ref, rsrch
Stock: archvs/220 cubic m; bks/c8000; photos/c20000; maps/3700; m-forms/4000 rolls & sheets
Classn: DDC **Auto Sys:** ALS
Pubns: Ivanhoe Review (1 pa); local hist titles
Staff: Archivists: 2 Libns: 1 Non-Prof: 2 **Exp:** £2000 (2000-01)

Runcorn

A439 🏛

Halton Local Studies and Family History Collections

Halton Lea Lib, Halton Lea, Runcorn, Cheshire, WA7 2PF (01928-715351; *fax:* 01928-790221)
Email: haltonlea.library@halton-borough.gov.uk
Internet: http://www.halton.gov.uk/libraries/local.asp

Type: local authority **Gov Body:** Halton Borough Council (see **P59**) **Chief:** Ref & Info Offcr: Ms Jean Bradburn (Jean.Bradburn@halton-borough.gov.uk)
Assoc Offices: HALTON LEA LIB, addr as above; WIDNES LIB, Victoria Sq, Widnes, Cheshire, WA8 7QY (0151-423-4818; *fax:* 0151-420-5108; *email:* widnes.library@halton-borough.gov.uk); local archvs are held at CHESHIRE & CHESTER ARCHVS & LOCAL STUDIES (see **A105**)
Entry: ref only **Open:** Halton Lea Lib: Mon-Wed 0930-1700, Thu-Fri 0930-1900, Sat 0930-1300; Widnes Lib: Mon, Wed 0930-1900, Tue, Fri 0930-1700, Thu, Sat 0930-1300
Subj: Runcorn & Widnes (North Cheshire): local studies; family hist **Collns:** Bks & Pamphs: local trade directories Other: parish registers; census returns (1841-1901, on m-form); local newspapers (from 1869, on m-film); map colln, incl Cheshire (17C onwards), Tithe Maps (1840s) & large scale maps of Runcorn & Widnes; large photo colln

Rushden

A440 ⚓

Random House Group Archive and Library

1 Cole St, Crown Pk, Rushden, Northamptonshire, NN10 6RZ (020-7840-8801; *fax:* 01933-419428)
Email: jrose@randomhouse.co.uk

Gov Body: Random House Group Ltd **Chief:** Lib Mgr: Mrs Jean E. Rose MCLIP
Entry: adv appt **Open:** Mon-Fri 0900-1700
Subj: UK: bk trade; publishing; publishing hist; business records; records of parent org **Collns:** Bks & Pamphs: pubns of Random House Group, Octopus Publishing, Methuen Publishing, Egmont Bks Ltd & Anderson Press Archvs: archvs of Random House Group, Methuen Publishing Children's Books & Anderson Press Other: Publishers Assoc; NDA files
Equip: 3 copiers (15p per pg), 2 fax, computers (incl wd-proc & CD-ROM) **Svcs:** info, ref, rsrch

Stock: archvs/100000 files; bks/650000 titles; periodcls/2
Classn: DDC **Auto Sys:** Soutron, InMagic
Staff: Libns: 2 Non-Prof: 9 **Exp:** £30000 (1999-2000); £50000 (2000-01)

Ruthin

A441 🏛

Denbighshire Record Office

46 Clwyd St, Ruthin, Denbighshire, LL15 1HP (01824-708250; *fax:* 01824-708258)
Email: archives@denbighshire.gov.uk
Internet: http://www.denbighshire.gov.uk/

Gov Body: Denbighshire County Council (see **P34**) **Chief:** County Archivist: Mr R. Kevin Matthias BA, DipAA
Entry: CARN ticket, adv appt for m-film use
Open: under review (contact Record Office)
Subj: present & historic county of Denbighshire & former county of Clwyd: local authority archvs; parish records; estate archvs; family papers; business records; records of parent org; hosp records **Collns:** Bks & Pamphs: local hist pubns; local hist soc transactions; annual reports Archvs: Denbighshire County Council motor taxation records; archvs of North Wales Hosp, Denbigh Other: OS maps; probate indexes (England & Wales, 1858-1928)
Equip: 7 m-readers, m-printer, video viewer, copier, computer (incl CD-ROM), UV reader
Stock: archvs/350 cubic m
Pubns: list of pubns available
Staff: Archivists: 4 Non-Prof: 4

Saffron Walden

A442 🏛🏛

Saffron Walden Museum, Archives

Museum St, Saffron Walden, Essex, CB10 1JL (01799-510333/4; *fax:* 01799-510333)
Email: museum@uttlesford.gov.uk

Type: local govt **Gov Body:** Uttlesford Dist Council **Chief:** Curator: Ms Carolyn Wingfield BA, FMA, DMS (cwingfield@uttlesford.gov.uk)
Other Snr Staff: Exhibs & Documentation Offcrs: Ms Julia Bazley MA (jbazley@uttlesford.gov.uk) & Ms Shirley Miller BA, PGDip (smiller@uttlesford.gov.uk)
Entry: small fee for entry to museum (ad £1, conc 50p); archvs available by adv appt only
Open: Mon-Sat 1000-1700, Sun & bank hols 1400-1700 (closes 1630 during Nov-Feb)
Subj: Saffron Walden & Uttlesford: estate archvs; family papers; business records; political papers; records of parent org; archaeo deposit records; local hist; archaeo; social hist; nat hist
Collns: Bks & Pamphs: wide colln of printed bks from 1485 onwards, esp Civil War pamphs & almanacs; Gabriel Harvey Colln (bks & marginalia); Thomas Bewick Colln (proof prints etc) Archvs: documents & records relating to Saffron Walden Museum (1835 onwards); Audley End Estate Colln; Gibson Papers; John Player Papers Other: Henry Winstanley Colln (prints); Robert Southey MSS Common Place Book; large colln of autographs
Equip: wheelchair access **Svcs:** info, rsrch
Stock: archvs/c11500 items; bks/500; photos/3000; pamphs/100; maps/100
Classn: Modes
Pubns: Brief Guide to Museum Collns
Staff: Other Prof: 8 Non-Prof: 3

A443 🏛

Saffron Walden Town Library and Victorian Studies Centre

(incorporating the Saffron Walden Literary & Scientific Inst Lib)
2 King St, Saffron Walden, Essex, CB10 1ES (01799-523178; *fax:* 01799-513642)
Email: SaffronWalden.Library@essexcc.gov.uk

Type: local authority **Gov Body:** Essex County Council (see **P51**) & Saffron Walden Town Lib Soc **Chief:** Local Studies Libn: Mr Martyn Everett (martyn.everett@essexcc.gov.uk)
Entry: ref only; appt advised **Open:** Mon-Tue, Thu 0900-1900, Fri 1000-1900, Sat 0900-1700
Subj: Saffron Walden: local studies; family hist; genealogy; hist; geog; Victorian studies **Collns:** Bks & Pamphs: antiquarian bks; bks on Essex & Cambridgeshire; Lib of the Saffron Walden Literary & Scientific Inst (c25000 vols, 1400-1920); wide range of academic journals Archvs: various local archival materials Other: census returns for Saffron Walden & dist; local newspapers on m-film; IGI; map colln; photo colln

Salford

A444 🏛

Salford City Archives Service

Salford Museum & Art Gallery, Peel Pk, The Crescent, Salford, Lancashire, M5 4WU (0161-736-2649; *fax:* 0161-745-9490)
Email: salford.museum@salford.gov.uk
Internet: http://www.salford.gov.uk/libraries/services/lhistory.shtm

Gov Body: City of Salford (see **P157**) **Chief:** Archivist: Mr A.N. Cross BA, DSRMA
Assoc Offices: SALFORD LOCAL HIST LIB, at same addr
Entry: adv appt **Open:** Mon-Fri 0900-1630
Subj: Archvs: present City of Salford: local authority archvs; estate archvs; family papers; business records; personal papers; records of parent org; civil parish records; nonconformist records; poor law records; trade union records; records of local socs & charities; Local Hist Lib: local hist; industrial hist; family hist **Collns:** Bks & Pamphs: local studies material, directories etc (at Local Hist Lib) Archvs: records of City of Salford Metropolitan Council & predecessors (urban districts of Salford, Eccles, Swinton, Irlam & Worsley) Other: maps, photos, newspapers & family hist resources (at Local Hist Lib)
Equip: photocopy orders taken
Stock: archvs/680 m; rec mgmt/200 m
Pubns: A Handlist of Salford City Archvs (free)
Staff: Archivists: 1

Salisbury

A445 🗝🏛

Royal Gloucestershire, Berkshire and Wiltshire Regiment (Salisbury) Museum, Regimental Archives

The Wardrobe Museum, 58 The Close, Salisbury, Wiltshire, SP1 2EX (01722-414536; *fax:* 01722-421626)
Internet: http://www.thewardrobe.org.uk/

Gov Body: RGBW Wardrobe Museum Trust
Entry: personal access only to serious rsrchers; adv appt in writing explaining reason for request; up to 4 wks notice required; access dependent on availability of staff **Open:** Feb-Mar & Nov: Tue-Sun 1000-1700; Apr-Oct: Mon-Sun 1000-1700; closed Dec-Jan
Subj: regimental hist; regimental records

Collns: *Archvs*: records of the Royal Berkshire Regiment (incl the 49th & 66th Regiments, militia & volunteers); records of the Wiltshire Regiment (incl the 62nd & 99th Regiments, militia & volunteers); historical records relating to Duke of Edinburgh's Royal Regiment
Svcs: postal enq svc

Sandwich

A446

Pfizer Ltd, Records Management
Central Rsrch, Ramsgate Rd, Sandwich, Kent, CT13 9NJ (01304-616161; *fax*: 01304-616221)
Internet: http://www.pfizer.co.uk/

Chief: Head of Records Mgmt: Mr Alan Murdock
Entry: adv appt
Subj: pharmaceuticals; business records
Collns: *Archvs*: records of British Alkaloids Ltd (manufacturing chemists, 1928-1966); records of Kemball, Bishop & Co Ltd (tartaric acid merchants, 1872-1968); records of John Bennet Lawes & Co Ltd (citric & tartaric acid manu-facturers, 1893-1958)

Scunthorpe

A447

North Lincolnshire Local Studies Library
Scunthorpe Ref Lib, Carlton St, Scunthorpe, N Lincolnshire, DN15 6TX (01724-860161; *fax*: 01724-859737)
Email: ref.library@northlincs.gov.uk
Internet: http://www.northlincs.gov.uk/library/local.htm

Gov Body: North Lincolnshire Council (see **P127**)
Chief: Snr Libn (Info Svcs): Ms Helen Rowe
Other Snr Staff: Local Studies Libn: Ms Carol Longbone
Assoc Offices: local archvs held at NE LINCOLNSHIRE ARCHVS (see **A191**)
Subj: North Lincolnshire, Lincolnshire & Humberside: local hist; family hist; parish records
Collns: *Bks & Pamphs*: local hist materials; trade directories; Steel Industry Colln; Wesley Family Colln *Other*: IGI on m-fiche; census returns (1841-1901); parish registers on m-fiche for Deaneries of Corringham, Haverstoe, Isle of Axholme, Lawres, Manlake & Yarborough; map colln (1891-date); local newspapers (from 1796, on m-film); photos; ephemera

Selkirk

A448

Scottish Borders Archive and Local History Centre
Lib HQ, St Mary's Mill, Selkirk, TD7 5EW (01750-20842; *fax*: 01750-22875)
Email: archives@scotborders.gov.uk
Internet: http://www.scottishborders.gov.uk/libraries/

Gov Body: Scottish Borders Council (see **P159**)
Entry: ref only, appt required for m-film materials
Open: Mon-Thu 0900-1300, 1400-1700, Fri 0900-1300, 1400-1530
Subj: Borders region (Roxburghshire, Peebles-shire, Berwickshire, Selkirkshire): local authority archvs; parish records; some business records; records of parent org; local hist; family hist
Collns: *Bks & Pamphs*: large colln of printed material covering the hist & way of life in the Borders Region; bks by & about local authors, incl Sir Walter Scott, James Hogg & Andrew Lang; colln of poetry by local poets *Archvs*: records of

Scottish Borders Council & predecessors, incl pre-1975 county councils & some records of Borders Regional Council; records of River Tweed Commissioners; Borders Police records (restricted access); Hawick Farmers Club records; Border Union Agricultural Soc records; Aimers McLean records (millwrights & engineers, incl eng plans & drawings); Selkirk Merchant Company records; papers of Earlston Women's War Work Party & WRVS *Other*: m-forms of Old Parish Registers; local newspapers, postcards & maps
Equip: 5 m-readers, 2 m-printers, copier, computer (with wd-proc, internet & CD-ROM)
Svcs: rsrch (postal rsrch svc £10 per half hr)
Stock: archvs/c45 cubic m; bks/c22000, incl pamphs
Staff: *Libns*: 1 *Non-Prof*: 0.94 *Exp*: £13753 (1999-2000); £12783 (2000-01)

Sevenoaks

A449

Sevenoaks Library and Museum
Buckhurst Ln, Sevenoaks, Kent, TN13 1LQ (01732-453118/452384; *fax*: 01732-742682)
Internet: http://www.kent.gov.uk/

Gov Body: Kent County Council (see **P67**)
Chief: Team Libn: Miss Ruth Marshall
Entry: ref only, adv appt *Open*: Mon-Wed, Fri 0930-1730, Thu 0930-1900, Sat 0900-1700, closed Sun
Subj: Sevenoaks Dist Council: local authority archvs; parish records (no originals); estate archvs; family papers; a few business records; Methodist circuit records *Collns*: *Other*: Gordon Ward Notebks (local hist)
Equip: m-reader, m-printer, fax, copier, computer (incl wd-proc)
Stock: archvs/1175 cubic m
Staff: *Libns*: 1 *Non-Prof*: 0.5

Sheffield

A450

Hallam RC Diocesan Archives
c/o Hallam Pastoral Centre, St Charles St, Sheffield, S Yorkshire (0114-256-6404; *fax*: 0114-256-2673)
Email: archives@hallam-diocese.com

Gov Body: RC Diocese of Hallam *Chief*: Diocesan Archivist: Fr Peter Kirkham PhL(Greg) Rome *Dep*: Asst Archivist: Mr Ian Battersby BA, CertEd
Entry: adv appt *Open*: Mon-Thu, Sat 0930-1930
Subj: Diocese of Hallam (South Yorkshire, North Derbyshire, North Nottinghamshire): diocesan records; parish records; personal papers; RC church hist; ecclesiastical biography; topography; liturgy *Collns*: *Bks & Pamphs*: liturgical bks; biographical & historical material *Archvs*: personal papers, bks & parish registers from RC Diocese of Hallam (c1690-1961) *Other*: varia: biography, photos, letters & newscuttings of Catholic interest
Svcs: info, ref, rsrch
Staff: *Archivists*: 2
Further Info: The majority of the Diocesan Archv is housed in the Sheffield Archvs (see **A452**). The Curia of the RC Diocese contains a variety of materials: bks, letters, liturgical texts, photos & newscuttings

A451

National Fairground Archive
Univ of Sheffield Lib, Western Bank, Sheffield, S Yorkshire, S10 2TN (0114-222-7231; *fax*: 0114-222-7290)
Email: fairground@shef.ac.uk
Internet: http://www.shef.ac.uk/nfa/

Gov Body: Univ of Sheffield (see **S1912**)
Chief: Rsrch Dir: Dr Vanessa Toulmin BA, PhD
Dep: Snr Asst & NFA Cataloguer: Ms Amanda Bernstein MA
Entry: by appt only; bookings should be made up to a wk in adv to avoid disappointment. *Open*: Mon-Fri 0930-1300, 1400-1630
Subj: UK: hist of fairs & fairgrounds; lifestyle, tradition & culture of travelling showpeople
Collns: *Bks & Pamphs*: c3000 monographs relating to fairs & the fairground community; journals & magazines *Archvs*: Billy Bellhouse Colln; R.A. Taylor Colln; Harry Lee Colln; Margaret Shufflebottom Colln; Waddington Colln *Other*: fairground ephemera, incl programmes, handbills, posters, charters, proclamations, plans & drawings; photographic collns, incl: Jack Leeson Colln (c5000 items); George Tucker Colln (c1400 items); audio & video colln; newspaper & cuttings colln, incl complete run of World's Fair
Equip: copier (A4/12p, A3/25p) *Svcs*: ref, reprographic svcs (fees)
Stock: archvs/80000+

A452

Sheffield Archives
52 Shoreham St, Sheffield, S Yorkshire, S1 4SP (0114-203-9395; *fax*: 0114-203-9398)
Email: sheffield.archives@dial.pipex.com

Gov Body: Sheffield City Council, Libs, Archvs & Info Svc (see **P161**) *Chief*: Archvs & Local Studies Mgr: Mr Len Reilly BA, MCLIP *Dep*: Snr Archivist: Ms R. Harman BA, DipAS
Assoc Offices: local studies colln at LOCAL STUDIES LIB, Central Lib, Surrey St, Sheffield, S1 1XZ (0114-273-4753)
Entry: readers ticket scheme (for archvs only); adv booking for m-form readers/printers strongly advised; all original documents required on Sat must be ordered by 1700 on Thu *Open*: Mon 1000-1730, Tue-Thu 0930-1730, closed Fri, Sat 0900-1300, 1400-1700; closed 2 wks Feb/Mar for annual stocktaking
Subj: Sheffield & South Yorkshire: local authority archvs; diocesan records; parish records; estate archvs; family papers; business records; personal papers; political papers; records of parent org; nonconformist records; school records; court records; hosp records; records of local firms; records of local instns & orgs
Collns: *Bks & Pamphs*: Transactions of the Hunter Archaeological Soc; small lib of publ works on local hist *Archvs*: archvs of Sheffield City Council & predecessors, incl former South Yorkshire County Council; Sheffield Quarter Sessions, Magistrates Courts & HM Coroners records; records of Natl Coal Board for South Yorkshire; records of Yorkshire Water Authority; Diocese of Sheffield (Archdeaconry of Sheffield) records; RC Diocese of Hallam records; Hunter Archaeological Soc (records of local hist rsrch, Hunter, Gatty, Ewing etc.); Guild of St George Archv; Fairbank family papers (map-makers & surveyors); Wentworth Woodhouse (Wentworth-Fitzwilliam) Muniments, incl personal papers of Earl of Strafford, 2nd Marquis of Rockingham & Edmund Burke; Arundel Castle MSS; Earls of Wharncliffe family papers; Venon-Wentworth family papers; Spencer Stanhope family papers; records of iron & steel, cutlers & coal industries; personal papers of Edward Carpenter, Mrs Gatty, David Blunkett MP & others *Collns*: *Other*: extensive colln of maps & surveys (mainly 18C & 19C); photo colln, incl aerial photos; audio recordings from Radio Sheffield *Co-op Schemes*: South Yorkshire Joint Archv Svc, with Doncaster (see **A124**), Barnsley (see **A26**) & Rotherham (see **A438**)
Equip: 17 m-readers, m-printer (30p per pg), copier (30p per pg), 6 computers (incl 4 with wd-proc, 4 with internet & 2 with CD-ROM), power pts for wd-processors/lap-tops *Svcs*: rsrch

Sheffield ▼ **Southport**

(Sheffield Archvs cont)

Stock: archvs/490 cubic m; rec mgmt/281 cubic m
Classn: ISAD(G)
Pubns: Guide to Manuscript Collns (1956, £2.50); Supplement to the Guide to Manuscript Collns (1976, £7); Catalogue of Arundel Castle Manuscripts (1965, £10); Guide to Fairbank Colln (1936, £2.50); Family Hist Guides (£1-£1.50 each); Local Hist Guide: Tracing the Hist of Your House (£1.50)
Staff: Archivists: 4 *Other Prof:* 4 conservators *Non-Prof:* 5

Shrewsbury

A453
Shropshire Records and Research Centre
Castle Gates, Shrewsbury, Shropshire, SY1 2AQ (01743-255350; *fax:* 01743-255355)
Email: research@shropshire-cc.gov.uk
Internet: http://www.shropshire-cc.gov.uk/research.nsf

Gov Body: Shropshire County Council (see **P163**) & Telford & Wrekin Council (see **P185**)
Chief: County Archivist: Miss M. McKenzie MA, MArAd *Dep:* Dep County Archivist: Mr A.M. Carr MA, MCLIP
Entry: ref only, own readers ticket (not CARN) to access original material (requires proof of ID & 2 photos) *Open:* Tue 1000-2100, Wed, Fri 1000-1700, Thu 1000-1300, Sat 1000-1600
Subj: Shropshire: local authority archvs; parish records; estate archvs; family papers; personal papers; records of parent org; nonconformist records; school records; records of local clubs & socs *Collns: Bks & Pamphs:* large colln of material on Shropshire; parochial libs colln; local directories *Archvs:* archvs of Shropshire County Council; Diocese of Lichfield (Archdeaconry of Salop) parish records; records of Shropshire regiments; Poor Law Union workhouse records *Other:* Shropshire census returns (1841-1901, on m-film); Genl Register Office indexes for England & Wales (1837-1980, on m-film); IGI for England & Wales; large photo colln; map colln, incl OS & tithe maps; Shrewsbury newspapers (from 1772) *Equip:* 29 m-readers, m-printer, m-camera, 2 copiers, 6 computers (incl 4 with CD-ROM & 2 with internet) *Disabled:* hearing loop, wheelchair access *Svcs:* rsrch, translation, transcription, conservation advice, edu, talks & courses
Stock: archvs/653 cubic m; rec mgmt/120 cubic m; bks/60000; periodcls/120; photos/25000; slides/4000; illusts/10000; pamphs/20000; maps/3000; m-forms/30000; audios/700; videos/50; CD-ROMs/50
Classn: Hobbs local classn *Auto Sys:* CALM 2000
Pubns: Shropshire Family Hist: A Guide to Sources in the Shropshire Records & Rsrch Centre (£3.50)
Staff: Archivists: 4 *Libns:* 2 *Other Prof:* 1 *Non-Prof:* 6.8 *Exp:* £291050 (2000-01)

Sidcup

A454 ✚
Gillies Archives
Charnley Lib, Queen Mary's Hosp, Sidcup, Kent, DA14 6LT (020-8308-3030; *fax:* 020-8308-3058)
Email: andrew.bamji@qms-tr.sthames.nhs.uk
Internet: http://website.lineone.net/~andrewbamji/

Gov Body: Queen Mary's Hosp, Charnley Lib (see **S1922**) *Chief:* Curator & Hon Consultant Archivist: Dr Andrew Bamji FRCP *Dep:* Hon Archivist: Ms Pat Howley
Entry: adv appt *Open:* Mon, Thu-Fri 1400-1700
Subj: medical records relating to WW1 & to plastic & facial surgery *Collns: Bks & Pamphs:* Gillies Lib (surgery & medicine of WW1, incl textbks, hosp journals, personal reminiscences, genl hist bks) *Archvs:* Gillies & Macalister Archvs (extensive WW1 casualties plastic surgery case records, incl models, paintings, pastels, case-notes, photos, illusts & x-rays); records from Rooksdown House, Basingstoke (1940-60)
Stock: archvs/5000+ case files
Exp: £3000 (1999-2000); £7000 (2000-01)

Solihull

A455
Solihull Heritage and Local Studies Department
Solihull Central Lib, Homer Rd, Solihull, W Midlands, B91 3RG (0121-704-6977; *fax:* 0121-704-6934)
Email: infols@solihull.gov.uk
Internet: http://www.solihull.gov.uk/

Gov Body: Solihull Metropolitan Borough Council (see **P165**) *Chief:* Head of Info & Local Studies: Mr David Gill
Assoc Offices: archival materials for Solihull can be found at: WARWICKSHIRE COUNTY RECORD OFFICE (see **A503**); LICHFIELD RECORD OFFICE (see **A232**); BIRMINGHAM CENTRAL LIB, LOCAL STUDIES DEPT, Chamberlain Sq, Birmingham, B3 3HQ (0121-303-4549); SHAKESPEARE BIRTHPLACE TRUST RECORD OFFICE (see **A476**)
Entry: ref only, adv appt for materials from strong room *Open:* Mon-Tue 0900-1730, Wed 1000-1730, Thu-Fri 0900-2000, Sat 0900-1700
Subj: Solihull Metropolitan Borough Council (some coverage of surrounding areas of Birmingham, Warwick & Stratford): local hist; geog; archaeo; arch; family hist *Collns: Bks & Pamphs:* good colln of bks & pamphs relating to present Solihull Metropolitan Borough Council at any period; some Warwickshire material; also: publ Council minutes for Solihull, Warwickshire & West Midlands; publ parish minutes from the Solihull area; annual reports of local companies & orgs; local directories *Archvs:* secondary sources only (see above for locations of original materials) *Other:* IGI on m-fiche; 19C census records for Solihull (m-form); local newspapers, incl: Warwick County News/Solihull News (1930-date) & Warwick & Warwickshire Advertiser (1806-1945); map colln (OS, Geol Survey, tithe, estate & antiquarian); photo & postcard colln (Solihull area, 1850s-date); paintings & drawings by local artists & of local subjs; ephemera *Co-op Schemes:* BL Newsplan (newspaper m-filming)
Equip: 5 m-fiche readers, 2 m-film readers, 3 m-fiche printers, m-film printer, 2 copiers, fax (via staff), computer (internal lib catalogue), 2 rooms for hire (study carrels, no charge, returnable deposit on key) *Svcs:* info, ref
Stock: archvs/9110; periodcls/50; photos/10000+, incl postcards; maps/3000; m-forms/650
Classn: DDC, internal classn for photo colln

Pubns: Guide to Solihull Local Studies Colln (free leaflet); Guide to Sources for Family Hist in Solihull Lib (free leaflet); Select List of Sources Relating to Solihull Metropolitan Borough Council in Solihull Local Studies Colln, compiled by Sue Bates (£1.50); Solihull in Wartime 1939-45, ed by Sue Bates (£6.95); Solihull: A Pictorial Hist, by Sue Bates (£11.99); Shirley: A Pictorial Hist, by Sue Bates (£11.99); Greater Solihull: Images of England, by Sue Bates (£8.99)
Staff: Libns: 3 *Non-Prof:* 6

South Croydon

A456
Girls' Day School Trust Archive
c/o Croydon High School GDST, Old Farleigh Rd, Selsdon, South Croydon, Surrey, CR2 8YB (020-8651-6647)

Gov Body: Council of the Girls' Day School Trust (founded 1872) *Chief:* Hon Trust Archivist: Miss M.C.M. Walker
Entry: adv appt; please note that material less than 50 yrs old is not normally made available *Open:* Tue-Thu 1030-1530, by arrangement only
Subj: England & South Wales: estate archvs; business records; records of parent org; girls' edu (1872-date); hist of schools currently & formerly membs of the Trust *Collns: Bks & Pamphs:* publ hists of the Trust & of indiv GDST schools (not a complete set) *Archvs:* records of the Girls' Public Day School Trust (1872-20C), incl: council minutes (handwritten 1872-77, printed 1877-date); minutes of council & other committees (1872 onwards); some personal details of early Headmistresses etc; records of negotiations with local & central govt with regard to grant aid
Equip: copier *Offcr-in-Charge:* Hon Trust Archivist, as above *Svcs:* info, rsrch
Classn: under reorganisation *Exp:* up to £5000
Proj: sorting & listing of material for both internal use & for the use of students & other rsrchers

South Shields

A457
South Tyneside Local History Library
Central Lib, Prince George Sq, South Shields, Tyne & Wear, NE33 2PE (0191-427-1717; *fax:* 0191-455-8085)
Email: localstudies.library@s-tyneside-mbc.gov.uk
Internet: http://www.southtyneside.info/

Gov Body: South Tyneside Metropolitan Borough Council (see **P170**) *Chief:* Local Hist Libn: Miss Doris Johnson
Assoc Offices: local archvs are held at TYNE & WEAR ARCHVS (see **A391**)
Open: Mon-Thu 0930-1900, Fri 0930-1700, Sat 0930-1300
Subj: South Tyneside: local hist; genealogy
Collns: Bks & Pamphs: local directories; Bldg Control Index for South Shields *Archvs:* papers of Amy Flagg (antiquary) *Other:* maps; historical photo colln, incl Jarrow March Colln; local newspapers (incl South Shields Gazette, 1849-date); census records for South Tyneside (1841-1901); St Catherine's Index (1837-1997); copies of older C of E church records for South Tyneside
Stock: various bks, pamphs, videos, posters, maps, photos & m-forms

---

Southampton

A458
Ancient Order of Foresters Heritage Trust

College Pl, Southampton, Hampshire, SO15 2FE
(023-8021-3811; *fax*: 023-8022-9657)
Email: mail@foresters.ws

Chief: Joint Trust Co-ordinators: Mrs Audrey Fisk BA (audrey@fisk72.fsnet.co.uk) & Mr R.I. Logan MA (roger.logan@virgin.net)
Entry: ref only through adv appt with the Joint Co-ordinators
Subj: UK: records of parent org; friendly soc records *Collns*: *Bks & Pamphs*: reports of governing council (1834 onwards); copies of Foresters Miscellany (house journal, 1838 onwards) *Archvs*: MS records of the Ancient Order of Foresters, mainly a selection of branch minutes & membership bks from the mid-19C
Svcs: info, rsrch
Acq Offcr: Joint Trust Co-ordinators, as above
Pubns: Hist of the Ancient Order of Foresters (1984, free); Grandfather was in the Foresters (1994, £2.50); AOF: Evolution 1834-2000 (2002, £2); By the Members for the Members (1996, £2); Friendly Societies Explained (1996, free)
Staff: *Non-Prof*: 2 voluntary co-ordinators
Proj: The primary aim of the Trust is the colln & preservation of surviving records

A459
Southampton Archives Services

Civic Centre, Southampton, Hampshire, SO14 7LY (023-8083-2251; *fax*: 023-8083-2156)
Email: city.archives@southampton.gov.uk
Internet: http://www.southampton.gov.uk/
education/libraries/arch.htm

Gov Body: Southampton City Council (see **P171**) *Chief*: Archvs Svcs Mgr: Mrs S.L. Woolgar BA, DipAA (s.woolgar@southampton. gov.uk) *Dep*: Asst Archivist: Miss J.E. Smith BA, DipAA (je.smith@southampton.gov.uk)
Entry: CARN ticket or Southampton City Council Lib Card *Open*: Tue-Fri 0930-1630 (1 late evening per month to 2100 by adv appt only)
Subj: City of Southampton: local authority archvs; parish records; estate archvs; family papers; business records; personal papers; political papers; records of parent org; nonconformist records; hosp records; solicitors' records; maritime records; wide range of deposited records of local orgs & socs; local hist *Collns*: *Bks & Pamphs*: Southampton street directories (1801-1975, some gaps); local & family hist pubns; Huguenot Soc pubns *Archvs*: archvs of Southampton City Council & predecessor authorities, incl Southampton Corp & other records of town admin dating back to 1199; Southampton Deanery (C of E) records, incl parish registers; Southampton Methodist circuit records & other non conformist records; Southampton Labour Party records; Southampton Conservative Party records; crew lists for Southampton registered merchant vessels (1863-1913); Central Index of Merchant Seamen (1918-1941) *Other*: Isherwood Colln (ships' drawings); OS maps (1846-1970); census indexes (1851, 1881 & 1881); Hampshire Wills Index; photo colln
Co-op Schemes: joint pubn with Univ of Southampton Records Series, producing eds of Southampton documents
Equip: 2 m-readers, m-printer (off-site, A4/60p, A3/£1.20), copier (A4/15p, A3/25p), clr copier (A4/£1, A3/£2), video viewer (by arrangement), computer (incl internet & access to CD-ROMs held in Archvs), room for hire (in Civic Centre, not Archvs) *Disabled*: magnifying lamps *Svcs*: info, ref, rsrch (£20 per hr)

Stock: archvs/176 cubic m; rec mgmt/135 cubic m; various bks & periodcls
Classn: ISAD(G) *Auto Sys*: DS Calm 2000
Pubns: Southampton Records 1: A Guide to the Records of Southampton Corp & Absorbed Authorities (£1); Sources for Family Hist in Southampton Archvs Office (£3, new ed in preparation); Southampton Crew Lists 1863-1913 (printed on request); Archvs Teaching Pack: Southampton in the Second World War (£15); Southampton Papers Series (£1-£2); numerous other pubns, incl maps & exhib catalogues
Staff: *Archivists*: 3.5 *Other Prof*: 1 conservator *Non-Prof*: 3

A460
West End Local History Society, Museum and Research Centre

c/o Mrs P. Berry, 16 Grosvenor Gdns, West End, Southampton, Hampshire, SO30 (023-8046-2490)
Email: westendlhs@aol.com
Internet: http://www.telbin.demon.co.uk/
westendlhs/

Chief: Soc Chairman: Mr Neville Dickinson
Dep: Museum Curator: Mr Nigel G. Wood
Assoc Offices: the museum is at: The Old Fire Station, High St, West End, Southampton, Hampshire, SO30 3FB; correspondence should be sent to the Sec at the above addr
Entry: no restrictions, donations accepted
Open: Sat 1000-1600, or by appt at other times
Subj: West End area, borough of Eastleigh, Hampshire: parish records; estate archvs; family papers; business records; personal papers (small holdings of each); records of local clubs & socs; local hist *Collns*: *Bks & Pamphs*: local hist bks; local directories; old business ledgers; diaries *Archvs*: files covering 30+ subj headings, incl materials on famous local residents: Capt Sir Arthur Rostron (Capt of the Carpathia); C.B. Fry (cricketer); & others *Other*: map colln; photos; local parish & community magazines *Co-op Schemes*: memb of Eastleigh & Dist Local Hist Forum
Equip: photocopying svc (A4/10p) *Disabled*: wheelchair access *Svcs*: info, ref, rsrch
Stock: archvs/c10 cubic m (artifacts only); bks/1 cubic m; maps & photos; small holdings of periodcls, pamphs, slides, audios & videos
Pubns: Tales of Old West End, by Charles Sillence (£3.50); I Remember, I Remember: Memories of Old West End, by Bob Moody (£4); Hatch Grange: A Stroll Back in Time, by Pauline Berry (£5.99); Townhill Park House, by R. Coney & J. Brown (£3); The Cholera Years, by John G. Avery (£6); The Mackay-Bennett, by John G. Avery (£1.50); Half a Loaf: South Stoneham Workhouse, by Eric Raffo (£9.50); Occasional Papers series, incl: Memories of Harefield Estate (£1.50); A New Church for Parish (£1); West End Natl School (£2.50); Sister Kate Oram (£4.99); soc newsletter; free pamphs
Staff: 1 voluntary archivist & 12+ volunteers
Exp: £1000 (2000-01); fig is approx; income depends on subscriptions, grants & donations

Southend-on-Sea

A461
Essex Record Office, Southend Branch

c/o Central Lib, Victoria Ave, Southend-on-Sea, Essex, SS2 6EX (01702-464278; *fax*: 01702-464253)
Email: ero.southend@essexcc.gov.uk
Internet: http://www.essexcc.gov.uk/

Gov Body: Essex County Council (see **P51**)
Chief: contact the Archivist-in-Charge

Assoc Offices: branch office of ESSEX RECORD OFFICE (see **A100**)
Entry: CARN ticket, adv appt; records should be ordered in adv *Open*: Mon 1000-1300, 1400-1715, Tue-Thu 0915-1300, 1400—1715, Fri 0915-1300, 1400-1615
Subj: Essex (Rochford Hundred): local authority archvs; estate archvs; family papers; business records *Collns*: *Other*: Essex parish records (on m-fiche); census indexes (1851 for Essex, 1881 for all English counties)
Equip: 9 m-readers, m-printer, copier
Stock: archvs/442 linear m; bks/65 linear m
Auto Sys: SEAX (Essex County Council)
Pubns: various, incl: local hist bks; photo bks; reproductions of county maps; greeting cards; catalogue available on request
Staff: *Other Prof*: 1 *Non-Prof*: 2

Southport

A462
Sefton Library and Information Services, Local History Administration

Pavilion Bldgs, 99-105 Lord St, Southport, Merseyside, PR8 1RH (0151-934-2380; *fax*: 0151-934-2370)
Email: library.service@leisure.sefton.gov.uk
Internet: http://www.sefton.gov.uk/leisure/
libraries/

Gov Body: Sefton Metropolitan Borough Council (see **P160**) *Chief*: Head of Lib & Info Svcs: Mr John Hilton MCLIP *Other Snr Staff*: Principal Lib Svcs Offcr (North): Mrs J. Stanistreet
Assoc Offices: CROSBY LIB (LOCAL HIST UNIT), Crosby Rd North, Waterloo, Liverpool, L22 0LQ (0151-257-6401; *fax*: 0151-934-5770; email: local-history.south@leisure.sefton.gov.uk); SOUTHPORT LIB (LOCAL HIST UNIT), Lord St, Southport, Merseyside, PR8 1DJ (0151-934-2119; *fax*: 0151-934-2115; *email*: local-history.north@leisure.sefton.gov.uk)
Entry: ref only, adv appt recommended for archival materials *Open*: *Crosby*: Mon, Wed, Fri 0930-2000, Tue 0930-1700, Thu, Sat 0930-1300; *Southport*: Mon-Tue, Fri 0930-1700, Wed-Thu: 0930-2000, Sat 0930-1300
Subj: Sefton: local authority archvs; local hist *Collns*: *Bks & Pamphs*: local hist bks *Archvs*: records of Sefton Metropolitan Borough Council & predecessor authorities (mid-19C onwards) *Other*: maps & photos
Equip: m-reader, m-printer (50p per sheet), copier (A4/10p, A3/20p), video viewer (at Crosby Lib only), People's Network PCs (incl wd-proc, internet & CD-ROM), room for hire
Svcs: info, ref, rsrch (written enqs from non-residents incurs a fee)
Classn: DDC *Auto Sys*: DS
Pubns: various brief guides to aspects of the local studies collns (free); local hist bks publ in-house, incl: The Great Lifeboat Disaster of 1886 (£5.85); Milestones in Maghull & Lydiate Hist (£3); Formby Reminiscences (£10.95); Churchtown in Camera (£3.90); Seaforth in Camera (£3.90); Crosby in Camera (£3.90); Descriptive Hist of Southport (£5); Birth of Waterloo (£5); Strange Story of the Bootle Corp Fraudulent Bonds (£1.50); bks are on sale in libs or by post (tel 0151-934-2385 for details)
Staff: *Libns*: 4

St Austell ▼ Stranraer

Archives

St Austell

A463 🗝 🏛

The China Clay Museum, Wheal Martyn, Archives

(formerly St Austell China Clay Museum)
Carthew, St Austell, Cornwall, PL26 8XG (01726-850362; *fax:* 01726-850362)
Email: info@wheal-martyn.com
Internet: http://www.wheal-martyn.com

Gov Body: St Austell China Clay Museum Ltd
Chief: Curator: Ms Elisabeth Chard BA (Lis@wheal-martyn.com) *Dep:* Dr Brian Strathen PhD (brian@wheal-martyn.com) *Other Snr Staff:* Chief Exec: Mr Peter J. Jennings
Entry: adv appt *Open:* Mon-Fri 0900-1600
Subj: local study (Mid-Cornwall, St Austell); china clay industry, esp in St Austell *Collns: Bks & Pamphs:* colln relating to china clay industry in Cornwall & Devon *Archvs:* document archv relating to china clay industry & hist of St Austell area *Other:* photo colln relating to china clay industry & hist of St Austell area
Equip: copier *Svcs:* info, ref
Stock: archvs/5 cubic m; bks/50; photos/1500; maps/100
Staff: Other Prof: 1

St Helens

A464 🏛

St Helens Local History and Archives Library

Central Lib, Gamble Inst, Victoria Sq, St Helens, Merseyside, WA10 1DY (01744-456952; *fax:* 01744-20836)
Internet: http://www.sthelens.gov.uk/

Gov Body: St Helens Metropolitan Borough Council (see **P173**) *Chief:* Local Hist Libn & Archivist: Ms Vivien Hainsworth MCLIP
Entry: ref only; adv appt for m-readers, computers & most archvs *Open:* Mon, Wed 0930-2000, Tue, Thu-Fri 0930-1700, Sat 0930-1600
Subj: modern Borough of St Helens: local authority archvs; parish records; estate archvs; family papers; business records; local hist
Collns: Archvs: mainly local authority archvs but several other collns: Beechams Pills Company Ltd; Sherdley Estate papers; Forster's Glass Company Ltd; Roby Iron Founders etc
Equip: 10 m-readers, m-printer, copier, clr copier (via lending lib), fax, computers (incl 3 CD-ROM)
Stock: archvs/over 700 linear m; bks/c8000; periodcls/16; photos/c10000; maps/c1200 OS maps; m-forms/c22000; audios/c150; CD-ROMs/c100
Classn: ISAD(G), HOBBS
Pubns: Tracing Your Family Tree (leaflet, free); Tracing Your Family Tree Overseas (leaflet, free); Mining Memories: An Illustrated Record of Coal Mining in St Helens (£6.95 + p&p); A Hist of St Helens Libs (£2.50 + p&p)
Staff: Other Prof: 3 Non-Prof: 2.5

St Ives

A465 🗝

St Ives Trust Archive Study Centre

The Lib, Gabriel St, St Ives, Cornwall, TR26 2LX (01736-796408)
Email: archive@stivestrust.co.uk
Internet: http://www.stivestrust.co.uk/

Gov Body: St Ives Trust (registered charity)
Open: Tue-Fri 1030-1700
Subj: St Ives: local hist; family hist; arts (strong coverage of artistic community in St Ives)
Collns: Archvs: 70 files on local galleries & socs; 350 files on artists & craftspeople who have lived or worked in St Ives (mid 19C-date) *Other:* photo colln (shipwrecks & other maritime subjs, 1920s-60s); audios & videos; press cuttings

Stafford

A466 🗝 🏛

The Harrowby Manuscripts at Sandon Hall

Sandon Hall, Sandon, Stafford, ST18 0BZ (01889-508004; *fax:* 01889-508004)
Email: info@sandonhall.co.uk

Gov Body: Harrowby MSS Trust *Chief:* Archivist & House Mgr: Mr Michael Bosson MA
Entry: by appt, subj to special conditions of access *Open:* normally Mon-Fri 1000-1600
Subj: estate archvs; family papers; political papers; arts; lit; hist *Collns: Archvs:* c1300 vols, most bnd, concerning the hist of the Harrowby family & their estates; much significant material on 19C British politics & some 90% of the original papers of Lady Mary Wortley Montagu
Svcs: genl support & advice on searching & subj matters, photocopying (by archivist, no self-svc)
Stock: archvs/c1300 vols; photos/200-300; slides/100; maps/100
Staff: Archivists: 1

Stafford

A467 🏛

Staffordshire and Stoke-on-Trent Archive Service, Staffordshire Record Office

Eastgate St, Stafford, ST16 2LZ (01785-278380; *fax:* 01785-278384)
Email: staffordshire.record.office@ staffordshire.gov.uk
Internet: http://www.staffordshire.gov.uk/ archives/

Gov Body: part of Staffordshire & Stoke-on-Trent Archv Svc, run on behalf of Staffordshire County Council (see **P174**) & Stoke-on-Trent City Council (see **P178**) *Chief:* Head of Archv Svcs: Mrs D.M.A. Randall BA, DipAS *Dep:* Principal Archivist: Mr M.S. Dorrington MA, DipAA
Assoc Offices: Staffordshire & Stoke-on-Trent Archv Svc branches: BURTON-UPON-TRENT ARCHV (see **A81**); LICHFIELD RECORD OFFICE (see **A232**); STOKE-ON-TRENT CITY ARCHVS (see **A473**); WILLIAM SALT LIB (see **A468**)
Entry: Staffordshire & Stoke-on-Trent Archv Svc reader's ticket; adv appt *Open:* Mon-Tue, Thu 0900-1700, Wed 0900-2000, Fri 0930-1630, Sat 0930-1230 (by appt)
Subj: Administrative County of Staffordshire: local authority archvs; parish records; estate archvs; family papers; business records; political papers; trade union records; school records; records of local clubs, socs, charities etc

Collns: Archvs: archvs of Staffordshire County Council & other local authorities; records of Quarter Sessions; parish records of Archdeaconries of Stoke, Lichfield & Walsall); many family papers of significance, incl: Bagot; Giffard; Dyott; Paget; Sutherland; Bradford; Talbot; Dartmouth; Hatherton; Shrewsbury; Sneyd-Kynnersley; Aqualate; Vernon; Wolseley; business collns incl: Birmingham City Rail Carriages & Wagons Company; Dormans Diesels; Joule's Brewery; Lotus Shoes; Baguley-Drewery Railcars *Other:* IGI on m-fiche; Staffordshire census returns on m-fiche
Equip: 17 m-readers, 2 m-printers
Stock: archvs/993 cubic m
Pubns: Kill or Cure, Medical Remedies of the 16th & 17th Centuries from the Staffordshire Record Office (£3.60); Family Hist Pack (£6); House Hist Pack (£5.50); A Staffordshire Christmas Stocking: A Celebration of Christmas from the Staffordshire Archv Svc (£2.50); Take 6 Eggs (£1.50); The Proof of the Pudding (£1.50); Guide to Sources No 1: Parish Registers & Bishops' Transcripts (£5); Guide to Sources No 2: Nonconformist Registers (£4.50); many other pubns, incl maps
Staff: Archivists: 5.25 *Libns:* 1 *Other Prof:* 2 *Non-Prof:* 6.5

A468 🗝

William Salt Library

19 Eastgate St, Stafford, ST16 2LZ (01785-278372; *fax:* 01785-278414)
Email: william.salt.library@staffordshire.gov.uk
Internet: http://www.staffordshire.gov.uk/ archives/salt.htm

Gov Body: William Salt Lib Trust *Chief:* Libn: Mrs D.M.A. Randall BA, DipAS
Assoc Offices: run in conjunction with STAFFORDSHIRE RECORD OFFICE, at adjacent addr (see **A467**)
Entry: reader's ticket *Open:* Tue-Thu 0900-1300, 1400-1700, Fri 0900-1300, 1400-1630, 1st Sat in month 0900-1300; closed public hols
Subj: Staffordshire: local studies; natl ref bks on hist; family papers *Collns: Bks & Pamphs:* William Salt's original Colln *Archvs:* William Salt's original Colln; Parker-Jervis Colln (family papers); Burne Colln (family papers) *Other:* Staffordshire Advertiser (from 1795)
Equip: copier (via staff)
Classn: own
Staff: Libns: 1 *Other Prof:* 1 *Non-Prof:* 1

Stalybridge

A469 🏛

Tameside Local Studies Library

Stalybridge Lib, Trinity St, Stalybridge, Cheshire, SK15 2BN (0161-338-2708/3831 or 0161-303-7937; *fax:* 0161-303-8289)
Email: localstudies.library@mail.tameside. gov.uk
Internet: http://www.tameside.gov.uk/history/

Gov Body: Tameside Metropolitan Borough Council (see **P184**) *Chief:* Local Studies Libn: Ms Alice Lock BA, MPhil, MCLIP *Dep:* Archivist: Mr Michael Keane BA, HDipAA
Entry: ref only, appt required for m-film use
Open: Mon-Wed, Fri 0900-1930, Sat 0900-1600
Subj: Tameside (incl Ashton-under-Lyne, Audenshaw, Denton, Droylsden, Dukinfield, Hyde, Longdendale, Mossley, Stalybridge): local authority archvs; parish records; family papers; business records; personal papers; church records; school records; hosp records; trade union records; records of co-op socs; records of local hist socs; economic & social hist of the area

---

Collns: Bks & Pamphs: good collns for the cotton industry & Lancashire dialect *Archvs:* records of local authorities that preceded Tameside; Manchester Regiment records; records of local Mechanics Insts; records of Turnpike Trusts; parish registers *Other:* m-films of local newspapers (1855-date), also Manchester Guardian (1821-1864) & Cotton Factory Times (1885-1937); m-films of census returns, incl indexes; maps (incl county maps from 1577 & OS maps & plans from 1843); photos & other illusts; oral hist recordings incl the Manchester Studies Unit colln (recorded 1974-1984) *Co-op Schemes:* small lending colln available through ILL, local A2A projs
Equip: 3 m-readers, m-printer, fax, copier, computers (incl internet & CD-ROM) *Svcs:* info, ref, biblio
Stock: archvs/1800 m; bks/1400; periodcls/120; photos/14000, plus 1750 negs; slides/2400; illusts/400; maps/1500; m-forms/1300; audios/2200; videos/20
Classn: DDC (mod)
Pubns: Guide to the Archv Svc (£12.95); Tameside Bibliography (o/p); 20+ local hist titles incl photo bks; postcards & prints; various advice leaflets (free); full pubn list available
Staff: Archivists: 1 *Libns:* 2 *Other Prof:* 1 *Non-Prof:* 2 *Exp:* £11000 (1999-2000); £13000 (2000-01)

Stevenage

A470
John Lewis Archive
Cavendish Rd, Stevenage, Hertfordshire, SG1 2EH (01438-312388; *fax:* 01438-794205)
Email: archives_stevenage@johnlewis.co.uk

Gov Body: John Lewis Partnership plc *Chief:* Company Archivist: Mrs Judith Faraday BA(Hons) (judy_faraday@johnlewis.co.uk)
Entry: adv appt *Open:* Mon-Thu 0930-1530
Subj: retailing; business records; estate archvs; records of parent org *Collns: Archvs:* records of John Lewis Partnership Ltd (19C-20C); records of associated stores & business, incl: Bannister Hall Print Works; John Barnes & Co Ltd (dept store); AH Bull Ltd (drapers & furnishers); Bainbridge (dept store, Newcastle); Bonds (dept store, Norwich); Caleus (dept store, Windsor); Cole Brothers (dept store, Sheffield); Findlater, Mackie Todd (wine merchants); Heelas Ltd (dept store); Jessops (dept store, Nottingham); Peter Jones (dept store, London); Jones Brothers (Holloway) Ltd (dept store); Knight & Lee (dept store, Southsea); Daniel Neal (childrenswear chain); Pratt's (Bon Marche Ltd) (dept store); Quin & Axtens (dept store); Robert Sayle (dept store, Cambridge); Stead, McAlpin & Co Ltd (calico printers); Charles Swainson & Co (calico printers); Trewins (dept store, Watford); Tyrrell & Green (dept store, Southampton); Waitrose (supermarket chain); Welwyn Dept Store; Leckford Estate Colln (papers, reports, surveys & photos, 1890-1990)
Equip: copier (3p per copy), clr copier, video viewer, 2 computers (both with wd-proc & CD-ROM, 1 with internet) *Svcs:* info, ref, rsrch
Auto Sys: Modes for Windows
Staff: Archivists: 1 PT *Non-Prof:* 1 PT
Proj: new racking in strongroom (Jan 2003)

Stirling

A471
Stirling Council Archives
Unit 6, Burghmuir Industrial Est, Stirling, FK7 7PY (01786-450745; *fax:* 01786-433005)
Email: archive@stirling.gov.uk

Gov Body: Stirling Council (see **P175**) *Chief:* Council Archivist: Dr John Brims MA, PhD *Dep:* Archivist: Mr Peter Clapham BA, MPhil
Open: Wed-Fri 1000-1230, 1330-1630
Subj: Stirling area: local authority archvs; parish records; family papers *Collns: Archvs:* archvs of Stirling Council & predecessors; Church of Scotland records (Stirling Presbytery); customs & excise records (Alloa, Grangemouth & Bo'ness); Justices of the Peace records (Stirlingshire & Clackmannanshire)
Equip: m-reader, m-printer, copier, computer (with wd-proc, internet & CD-ROM) *Svcs:* info, rsrch
Staff: Archivists: 2 *Non-Prof:* 1

Stockport

A472
Stockport Archive Service
Central Lib, Wellington Rd South, Stockport, Cheshire, SK1 3RS (0161-474-4530; *fax:* 0161-474-7750)
Email: localheritage.library@stockport.gov.uk

Gov Body: Stockport Metropolitan Borough Council (see **P176**) *Chief:* Archivist: Mrs M.J. Myerscough BA, DipAA
Entry: adv notice required for material kept in outstore *Open:* Mon 1000-2000, Tue, Fri 0900-2000, Wed-Thu 0900-1700, Sat 0900-1600
Subj: Stockport Metropolitan Borough: local authority archvs; family papers; business records; records of parent org; Methodist & some other Protestant nonconformist records; court records; hosp records *Collns: Archvs:* records of Stockport Metropolitan Borough; Stockport Magistrates Court records; Bradshaw-Isherwood family papers; Stockport Sunday School records; Christy & Co (hat manufacturers)
Equip: m-reader, m-printer, fax, copier
Stock: archvs/420 m
Pubns: Guide to Archv Calendars 1-14 (70p)
Staff: Archivists: 1

Stoke-on-Trent

A473
Staffordshire and Stoke-on-Trent Archive Service, Stoke-on-Trent City Archives
Hanley Lib, Bethesda St, Stoke-on-Trent, Staffordshire, ST1 3RS (01782-238420; *fax:* 01782-238499)
Email: stoke.archives@stoke.gov.uk
Internet: http://www.staffordshire.gov.uk/ archives/

Gov Body: part of Staffordshire & Stoke-on-Trent Archv Svc, run on behalf of Staffordshire County Council (see **P174**) & Stoke-on-Trent City Council (see **P178**) *Chief:* Snr Archivist: Mr C.S. Latimer MA, DipAA
Assoc Offices: other Archv Svc branches: STAFFORDSHIRE RECORD OFFICE (main office – see **A467**); BURTON-UPON-TRENT ARCHV (see **A81**); LICHFIELD RECORD OFFICE (see **A232**); WILLIAM SALT LIB (see **A468**)
Entry: Staffordshire & Stoke-on-Trent Archv Svc reader's ticket (requires current proofs of addr & signature); adv appt advisable *Open:* Tue, Thu-Fri 0930-1700, Wed 0930-1900, Sat 0930-1300
Subj: Stoke-on-Trent & North Staffordshire: local authority archvs; parish records; business records; nonconformist church records; trade union records; school records; police records; fire brigade records; records of local charities
Collns: Bks & Pamphs: extensive local studies colln; trade directories for the Potteries & Staffordshire (1798-date) *Archvs:* archvs of

County Borough & City of Stoke-on-Trent & predecessors, incl the Six Towns (Burslem, Fenton, Hanley, Longton, Stoke & Tunstall); local vehicle licensing records (1904-60); electoral registers; parish registers (North Staffordshire, also on m-form); Methodist Church archvs (North Staffordshire, later 18C onwards); Stoke-on-Trent Poor Law Union records; Burslem & Wolstanton Poor Law Union records; Solon Colln; Clarice Cliff Colln; Pottery Archvs (historical records of local potteries, incl pattern bks & designs); CATU records; NUM records; Hollow Ware Pressers Union records; North Staffordshire Chamber of Commerce archvs; Natl Council of the Pottery Industry archvs; Tile Fireplace Manufacturers Assoc archvs *Other:* photos; map colln (late 19C); local newspapers, incl: Staffordshire Advertiser (from 1795); Staffordshire Sentinel (1854-date)
Equip: m-readers, m-printer, copier *Svcs:* postal enqs; rsrch (fees charged); talks
Pubns: leaflets; guides to records; historical recipe bks; maps; greetings cards; list available

Stornoway

A474
Western Isles Libraries (Leabharlainn nan Eilean Siar), Local History Collection
Stornoway Public Lib, 19 Cromwell St, Stornoway, Isle of Lewis, HS1 2DA (01851-708631; *fax:* 01851-708677)
Internet: http://www.w-isles.gov.uk/w-isles/ library/locstud.htm

Gov Body: Western Isles Council/Comhairle nan Eilean Siar (see **P199**) *Chief:* Chief Libn: Mr Robert M. Eaves BA, DipEd, MCLIP (bobeaves@ cne-siar.gov.uk) *Dep:* Snr Libn, Adult Svcs: Mr David J. Fowler MCLIP (dfowler@cne-siar.gov.uk)
Assoc Offices: smaller collns & some school log bks at: COMMUNITY LIB, Castlebay Community School, Castlebay, Isle of Barra, HS9 5XD; COMMUNITY LIB, Sgoil Lionacleit, Liniclate, Isle of Benbecula, HS7 5PJ
Entry: ref only, prior appt advisable *Open:* Mon-Wed, Sat 1000-1700, Thu-Fri 1000-1800
Subj: Western Isles of Scotland: local hist; edu records *Collns: Bks & Pamphs:* Western Isles Local Hist Colln; Scottish Gaelic Colln; school log bks; School Board of Mgmt minute bks
Equip: m-reader, m-printer, copier, computers (incl wd-proc, internet & CD-ROM) *Svcs:* info, ref
Stock: archvs/21 linear m; photos/400; slides/100; maps/2140; m-forms/1750
Classn: DDC (archvs not classified) *Auto Sys:* Dynix

Stranraer

A475
Stranraer Museum, Archive Collections
55 George St, Stranraer, Wigtownshire, DG9 7JP (01776-705088; *fax:* 01776-705835)
Email: johnpic@dumgal.gov.uk

Gov Body: Dumfries & Galloway Council (see **P41**) *Chief:* Museums Curator: Mr John Pickin BA, AMA, MIFA
Entry: archv by adv appt *Open:* Mon-Fri 1000-1700
Subj: Wigtownshire: local authority archvs; local hist *Collns: Archvs:* records of Burghs of Wigtown, Whithorn, Stranraer & Newton Stewart, mostly post-1700, some earlier
Stock: archvs/1800 bundles & vols; photos/2000; maps/150
Classn: Natl Register of Archvs

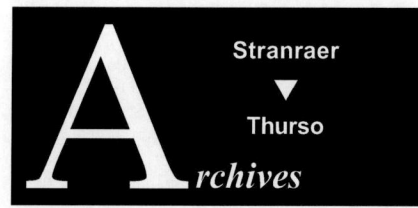

(*Stranraer Museum, Archv Collns cont*)
Pubns: Textile Industry in Wigtownshire (75p);
Castle of St John Guide (50p); Monuments &
Moorlands (£2); Ane Kirk: A Hist of the Stranraer
Churches (£1); John Livingstone's Diary (£3);
Through the Lens (£2.50); The Polar Rosses
(£2.50) **Staff:** Other Prof: 4

Stratford-upon-Avon

A476 ♀

Shakespeare Birthplace Trust Records Office

Shakespeare Centre, Henley St, Stratford-upon-
Avon, Warwickshire, CV37 6QW (01789-201816/
204016; *fax:* 01789-296083)
Email: records@shakespeare.org.uk
Internet: http://www.shakespeare.org.uk/
records.htm

Gov Body: Shakespeare Birthplace Trust **Chief:**
Head of Archvs & Local Studies: Dr Robert
Bearman PhD (robert.bearman@shakespeare.
org.uk)
Assoc Offices: SHAKESPEARE CENTRE LIB
(see **S1996**)
Entry: readers ticket issued on proof of ID
Open: Mon-Fri 0930-1700, Sat 0930-1230
Subj: Stratford-upon-Avon & surrounding area
(12C-20C): local hist; family hist; genealogy;
Shakespeare; local authority archvs; estate
archvs; family papers; parish records; poor law
records **Collns:** Bks & Pamphs: local hist &
genealogical sources; trade directories *Archvs:*
records of Stratford-upon-Avon Corp (1553-1835);
records of Stratford-upon-Avon Borough Council
(1836-1974); Gild of the Holy Cross records
(1328-1548); Stratford parish registers (1550s
onwards); estate & family papers of major
Warwickshire families, incl: Archer of Tanworth;
Ferrers of Baddesly Clinton; Gregory-Hood of
Stivichall; Lords Leigh of Stoneleigh Abbey;
Phillipps of Welcombe; Throckmorton of
Coughton Court; Lords Willoughby de Broke of
Compton Verney *Other:* monumental inscriptions;
photo colln (c10000 items); 1841 census returns;
maps colln (incl 1850s Ordnance Survey);
Stratford bldg plans (1851 onwards); local
newspapers (early 19C onwards)
Equip: m-reader, m-printer, copier, fax, video
viewer, computer (incl CD-ROM) *Disabled:* lift;
adv notification of visit helpful for wheelchair
users **Svcs:** info, ref, enq svc
Staff: Archivists: 2 Libns: 1 Other Prof: 1 Non-
Prof: 2
Proj: OPAC to be available on internet in 2003

Street

A477 ⚲⚱ 🏛

C&J Clark Ltd, Shoe Museum and Archives

Public Relations Dept, 40 High St, Street,
Somerset, BA6 8HS (01458-842169; *fax:* 01458-
842226)
Email: janet.targett@clarks.com
Internet: http://www.clarks.com/

Gov Body: C&J Clark Ltd **Chief:** Museum
Administrator: Ms Janet Targett

Entry: adv appt **Open:** Mon-Fri 1000-1645
Subj: hist of shoe manufacture; business
records; records of parent org **Collns:** Archvs:
historical & other records of C&J Clark Ltd (shoe
manufacturers, 19C-20C); records of Avalon
Leather Board Co Ltd (leather board manufacturers, c1882-1975); records of British Footwear Manufacturers Federation (20C); minutes of
Natl Inst of the Boot & Shoe Industry, Welsh &
Western branch (1948-65); records of Natl Union
of Boot & Shoe Operatives, Street Branch (1908-
77); minutes of Somerset West Liberal Assoc
(1882-1924); records of Shoe Museum (20C)

Sutton

A478 🏛

Sutton Archives and Local Studies

Level 5 West, Central Lib, St Nicholas Way,
Sutton, Surrey, SM1 1EA (020-8770-4747; *fax:*
020-8770-4777)
Email: local.studies@sutton.gov.uk
Internet: http://www.sutton.gov.uk/

Type: local govt **Gov Body:** London Borough of
Sutton (see **P105**) **Chief:** Borough Archivist &
Local Studies Mgr: Ms Kath Shawcross
Entry: proof of ID (e.g., lib ticket, driving
license, CARN ticket); 24 hrs notice required for
archvs **Open:** Tue 1400-1700, Thu 0930-1930,
Fri 0930-1230, 1st & 3rd Sat 0930-1300, 1400-
1645, 1st & 3rd Sun 1400-1700
Subj: London Borough of Sutton, Surrey &
Greater London (esp south of Thames): local
studies; local authority archvs; diocesan records;
parish records; estate archvs; family papers;
business records; personal papers; political
papers (few); poor law records; school records;
court records; manorial & tithe records **Collns:**
Bks & Pamphs: local hist materials; strong collns
of materials relating to Croydon Airport & to River
Wandle; local directories *Archvs:* archvs of
London Borough of Sutton & predecessors;
Carshalton Manorial Rolls (from 1346); Diocesan
Record Office for London Borough of Sutton;
large colln of copies of Surrey parish registers;
Wallington Magistrates Court records; Carews of
Beddington Manor estate papers (from 15C);
census returns (1841-1891); electoral registers
(1930s-date) *Other:* Dr Albert Peatling Colln
(materials relating to Carshalton); Bawtree Family
of Sutton Photo & Film Archv; photo colln
(c20000, 1860s onwards); maps (incl OS maps &
WW2 bomb maps of Sutton & Cheam); plans &
drawings of Sutton Gdn Suburb; local newspapers
(1860s onwards); cuttings (19C onwards)
Equip: 3 m-readers, m-printer, 2 computers (both
with internet); addl facilities in main lib incl: copier,
clr copier, fax, video viewer, addl m-readers &
computers, room for hire *Online:* Kurzweil (in
main lib) **Svcs:** info, ref, rsrch
Stock: archvs/c20000; various periodcls, slides,
illusts, pamphs, maps, m-forms, audios, videos,
other AVs & CD-ROMs (not counted) **Acq Offcr:**
Borough Archivist & Local Studies Mgr, as above
Classn: ISAD(G) **Auto Sys:** Geac
Staff: Archivists: 1 Libns: 0.5 Other Prof: 1
conservator Non-Prof: 0.75

Swansea

A479 🏛

City and County of Swansea Library Service, Local Studies Department

Central Lib, Alexandra Rd, Swansea, W Glam-
organ, SA1 5DX (01792-516753; *fax:* 01792-
516759)
Email: central.library@swansea.gov.uk
Internet: http://www.swansea.gov.uk/culture/
Libraries/LibraryIntro.htm

Type: local authority **Gov Body:** City & County
of Swansea Council (see **P182**) **Chief:** Local
Studies Libn: Mrs M.P. Jones **Other Snr Staff:**
Ref Libn: Mr P. Matthews
Assoc Offices: local archvs are held at WEST
GLAMORGAN ARCHV SVC (see **A481**)
Entry: ref only **Open:** Mon-Wed, Fri 0900-1900,
Thu, Sat 0900-1700
Subj: Wales (esp Swansea) & Celtic countries:
local studies; Welsh studies **Collns:** Bks &
Pamphs: Dylan Thomas Colln; Wales Colln;
Swansea Colln; wide range of local studies
material *Other:* Thomas Hornor Watercolours
Colln; maps & plans (1850-date); prints, photos &
postcards; local newspapers & periodcls; cuttings;
census returns for Swansea (1841-1901)
Stock: archvs/60000; pamphs/65000; newspaper
cuttings/c45000

A480 🏛🏛

Swansea Museum, Library and Archives

Victoria Rd, Maritime Quarter, Swansea, W Glamorgan, SA1 1SN (01792-653763; *fax:* 01792-
652585)
Email: swansea.museum@swansea.gov.uk
Internet: http://www.swansea.gov.uk/heritage/

Gov Body: City & County of Swansea (see
P182) **Chief:** Collns Access Offcr: Mr Andrew
Deathe BA(Hons), MA **Dep:** Asst Collns Access
Offcr: Ms Bernice Cardy BA
Assoc Offices: local archvs are held at WEST
GLAMORGAN ARCHV SVC (see **A481**)
Entry: ref only, adv appt for use of lib **Open:**
Tue-Fri 1030-1300, 1430-1630
Subj: Swansea & Dist (Gower, West Glamorgan):
family papers; personal papers; local hist;
topography; nat hist; geol; sci; industry; arts;
culture; biography; genealogy; archaeo **Collns:**
Bks & Pamphs: rare bks on Swansea & Dist local
hist; bks on various subjs written by local people
Archvs: archvs of Royal Instn of South Wales;
archvs of various local families & indivs *Other:*
prints & drawings; topographical paintings &
drawings; early photos; museum colln of artifacts
Equip: copier, room for hire
Stock: archvs/c5000; periodcls/c20; photos/
c3000; pamphs/c2000; maps/c200; audios/50
Acqs Offcr: Community Access Offcr: Mr
Michael Gibbs
Classn: DDC
Pubns: factsheets, bklets & info packs on local
hist & relating to the Museum & Art Gallery Collns
Staff: Other Prof: 2 Non-Prof: 1 **Exp:** £400
(2000-01)

A481 🏛

West Glamorgan Archive Service

County Hall, Oystermouth Rd, Swansea,
W Glamorgan, SA1 3SN (01792-636589; *fax:*
01792-637130)
Email: westglam.archives@swansea.gov.uk
Internet: http://www.swansea.gov.uk/archives/

Gov Body: archv svc for City & County of
Swansea (see **P182**) & County Borough of Neath
Port Talbot (see **P120**) **Chief:** County Archivist:
Miss Susan Beckby BA, DPAA, MCLIP
(susan.beckby@swansea.gov.uk) **Dep:** Principal
Archivist: Mr Kim Collis MA, DipAS (kim.collis@
swansea.gov.uk) **Other Snr Staff:** Principal
Archivist: Mr Robert Chell BA, MPhil, DPAA, FIAP
(robert.collis@swansea.gov.uk); Principal
Archivist: Mrs Rosemary Davies BA, DPAA
Assoc Offices: NEATH ARCHVS ACCESS PT,
Neath Mechanics Inst, Church Pl, Neath, West
Glamorgan, SA11 3LL, Principal Archivist: Mrs
Rosemary Davies, as above (*tel & fax:* 01639-
620139); PORT TALBOT ARCHVS ACCESS PT,
Port Talbot Lib, Aberafan Centre, Port Talbot,

W Glamorgan, SA13 1PB, Principal Archivist: Mrs Rosemary Davies (01639-763430)
Entry: ref only; adv booking required for m-readers; documents brought to Neath & Port Talbot Access Pts by adv arrangement *Open:* Swansea: Mon-Thu 0900-1700 (Mon 1730-1930 by appt); Neath: Tue-Fri 0930-1230, 1330-1700; Port Talbot: Mon-Tue, Thu-Fri 0930-1230, 1330-1730
Subj: former county of West Glamorgan & successor authorities: local authority archvs; parish records; estate archvs; family papers; business records; personal papers; political papers; records of parent org; records of law courts; hosp records; nonconformist (chapel) records; family hist *Collns: Archvs:* archvs of former West Glamorgan County Council; archvs of City & County of Swansea; archvs of County Borough of Neath Port Talbot; Swansea Borough Charters & other ancient muniments (1234-1902); Neath Abbey Foundation Charter (c1129); Neath Abbey Ironworks Colln (18C-19C eng drawings); correspondence & papers of Tennant Family of Neath, incl papers of the explorer Sir Henry Morton Stanley (1890-1904) *Other:* Genl Register Office Indexes of Births, Marriages & Deaths (1837-2000); photo colln; map colln
Equip: 18 m-readers (£1 per hr), 2 m-printers (30p per copy), 3 copiers (30p per copy), 5 computers (incl 4 with internet & 1 with CD-ROM)
Svcs: ref, rsrch
Stock: archvs/6000 linear m; rec mgmt/1500 linear m
Pubns: Guide to the Collns, by Kim Collis (£9.95); info leaflets; numerous others
Staff: Archivists: 7 *Non-Prof:* 9 *Exp:* £8000 (1999-2000); £10500 (2000-01)

Swindon

A482

Burmah Castrol Archives

Burmah Castrol House, Pipers Way, Swindon, Wiltshire, SN3 1RE (01793-452585/419; *fax:* 01793-453136/513506)
Email: vanna_skelley@burmahcastrol.com

Chief: Group Archivist: Miss Vanna Skelley
Entry: by adv appt only; apply to the Group Archivist in writing *Open:* Mon-Fri 1000-1600
Subj: petroleum industry; business records; records of parent org & predecessors *Collns: Archvs:* records of Burmah Oil Co Ltd (19C-20C); records of Castrol Ltd (1889-1997); records of Assam Oil Co Ltd (1893-1980); records of Anglo-Ecuadorian Oilfields Ltd (1919-1975); records of Atlas Preservative Co Ltd (1952-1979); records of Lobitos Oilfields Ltd (1908-1997); records of Manchester Oil Refinery (Holdings) Ltd (1930-1979); records of W.B. Dick & Co Ltd (lubricating oil manufacturers, 1859-1969)

A483

National Monuments Record

Kemble Dr, Swindon, Wiltshire, SN2 2GZ (01793-414600; *fax:* 01793-414606)
Email: nmrinfo@english-heritage.org.uk/
Internet: http://www.english-heritage.org.uk/

Gov Body: English Heritage *Chief:* Libn: Ms Felicity Gilmour (felicity.gilmour@rchme.co.uk)
Assoc Offices: LONDON SEARCH ROOM, 55 Blandford St, London, W1H 3AF (020-7208-8200; *fax:* 020-7224-5333)
Entry: free entry for public *Open:* Tue-Fri 0930-1700, occasional Sats
Subj: England: survey archv; archaeo & arch records; aerial photography throughout England *Collns: Bks & Pamphs:* substantial colln of bks & journals relating to archaeo & arch of England *Archvs:* archaeo & arch; air photos; maps, drawings & photos *Other:* listed bldgs records & archaeo records on database (600000 records)

Equip: m-reader, m-printer, copier, clr copier, computer (with Lib OPAC), stereoscopes
Stock: archvs/c10 mln items; bks/45000; periodcls/200
Pubns: various, catalogue available
Staff: Libns: 2 *Non-Prof:* 1
See also NATL MONUMENTS RECORD OF SCOTLAND (**A151**) & NATL MONUMENTS RECORD OF WALES (**A6**)

A484

W.H. Smith Archive Ltd

Greenbridge Rd, Swindon, Wiltshire, SN3 3LD (01793-616161)

Chief: Consultant Archivist: Mrs G. Collingburn
Entry: prior appt required
Subj: business records; family papers; personal papers; records of parent org *Collns: Archvs:* archvs of WH Smith & Son Ltd (19C-20C); personal & estate papers of the Smith family (Viscounts Hambleden); records of Bowes & Bowes (Cambridge) Ltd (bksellers, 1845-1951); records & correspondence of Pneumatic Despatch Co Ltd (1860-1868)

Tamworth

A485

Tamworth Castle and Museum Service, Archives

Tamworth Castle, The Holloway, Tamworth, Staffordshire, B79 7NA (01827-709626; *fax:* 01827-709630)
Email: heritage@tamworth.gov.uk

Gov Body: Tamworth Borough Council *Chief:* Heritage Svcs Mgr: Mr Frank Caldwell *Other Snr Staff: Collns Offcr:* Mrs Sarah Williams
Entry: ref only, adv appt *Open:* Tue-Sun 1200-1715 (last admissions 1630); extended hrs for schools & bank hols
Subj: Tamworth (Staffordshire) & 12 mile radius: local authority archvs; estate archvs; business records; local studies *Collns: Archvs:* Tamworth Borough Council records; Tamworth Castle Estate Archv; Gibbs & Canning Company minute bks *Other:* photo colln (Tamworth area) *Co-op Schemes:* Staffordshire Past Track
Equip: copier *Svcs:* ref, rsrch
Stock: archvs/45 linear m; bks/12 linear m; photos/17 linear m; slides/2 linear m; maps/2 linear m + 81 linear m of plans
Classn: MDA
Pubns: Tamworth Castle (official guidebk, £1.20)
Staff: Other Prof: 3 museum svc staff

Taunton

A486

Hydrographic Office, Hydrographic Data Centre

Admiralty Way, Taunton, Somerset, TA1 2DN (01823-337900 x4822; *fax:* 01823-323756)
Email: cmills@ukho.gov.uk

Gov Body: Ministry of Defence (see **S1284**)
Chief: Archvs & Acquisitions Mgr: Mr Chris Mills
Entry: not normally open to the public; visitors engaged on commercial or historical rsrch may consult documents in the Data Centre archvs, subj to certain restrictions; applications should be made in writing
Subj: hydrography; hydrographic charting & surveying; aerial photography *Collns: Bks & Pamphs:* atlases; publ chart catalogues *Archvs:* MS papers, letters, journal, logs etc (mainly 19C) *Other:* record copies of British Admiralty

navigational & other charts (c150000); foreign charts; Notices to Mariners (c1 mln); hydrographic surveys, reports & geodetic data (c100000); aerial photoplots (c2000); copper plates (c3500); ocean sounding sheets (c14000); hydrographic info files (several 100000)
Svcs: info, reprographic svc

A487

Somerset Archive and Record Office

Obridge Rd, Taunton, Somerset, TA2 7PU (01823-278805; *fax:* 01823-325402)
Email: archives@somerset.gov.uk
Internet: http://www.somerset.gov.uk/archives/

Gov Body: Somerset County Council (see **P166**)
Chief: County Archivist: Mr T.W. Mayberry MA
Entry: adv appt, ref only; CARN ticket accepted
Open: Mon 1030-1700, Tue-Fri 0900-1700, alternate Sats 0915-1215; closed Xmas, Easter & 2 wks in Nov-Dec for stock taking
Subj: Historic County of Somerset: local authority archvs; diocesan records; parish records; estate archvs; family papers; business records; records of parent org; poor law records; court records; hosp records; school records; solicitors' records; records of local socs & clubs; local studies *Collns: Bks & Pamphs:* lib of bks & pamphs relating to Somerset; trade directories *Archvs:* Somerset County Council archvs; Bath & Wells Diocesan records; records of Quarter & Petty Sessions; records of Poor Law Unions *Other:* maps & plans; electoral registers; census returns (1841-1901, on m-form)
Equip: 20 m-readers, 2 m-printers, fax, copier, computers (incl 2 internet) *Disabled:* wheelchair access *Svcs:* info, ref, rsrch, talks, exhibs, edu svc for schools & colls
Stock: archvs/850 cubic m; rec mgmt/200 cubic m
Pubns: Summary List of Parish Registers (£1.50); Your Somerset House (£3.50 incl p&p); Your Somerset Family (£3.50 incl p&p)
Staff: Archivists: 6 *Non-Prof:* 7

A488

Somerset Studies Library

Taunton Lib, Paul St, Taunton, Somerset, TA1 3XZ (01823-340300; *fax:* 01823-340301)
Email: somstud@somerset.gov.uk
Internet: http://www.somerset.gov.uk/libraries/

Gov Body: Somerset County Council (see **P166**)
Chief: Local Hist Libn: Mr David Bromwich MA, MCLIP
Assoc Offices: local archvs are held at SOMERSET RECORD OFFICE (see **A487**)
Open: Mon-Tue, Thu 0930-1730, Wed, Fri 0930-1900, Sat 0930-1600
Subj: Somerset: local hist & archaeo *Collns: Bks & Pamphs:* bks on all aspects of old Somerset; archaeo & other journals; access is also available to the private lib of the Somerset Archaeo & Nat Hist Soc *Other:* map colln (incl OS & tithe maps); photo collns (incl aerial photos); drawings; prints; postcards; local newspapers (m-film, 1737-date); birth, marriage & death registration indexes (1837-1998)

Thurso

A489

Caithness Family History Society Library

Thurso Lib, Davidsons Ln, Thurso, Caithness, KW14 7AF (01847-893237; *fax:* 01847-896114)
Email: Una.Vivers@ukgateway.net
Internet: http://www.caithnessfhs.org.uk/

Archives Thurso ▼ Warrington

(Caithness Family Hist Soc Lib cont)
Chief: Libn: Ms Una Vivers
Entry: membs only *Open:* Mon, Wed 1000-1800, Tue, Fri 1000-2000, Thu, Sat 1000-1300
Subj: Caithness & Scottish Highlands: family hist; genealogy; local hist *Collns: Other:* family trees; census records
Pubns: 1841 Census Returns for the County of Caithness (3 vols publ to date, £3.50 each to membs, £4.50 to non-membs)

Tonbridge

A490 🖋
Butterworth & Co (Publishers) Ltd, Archives
c/o 5 Higham Gdns, Tonbridge, Kent, TN10 4HZ (01732-354869)

Chief: Company Archivist: Mr R. Hedley-Jones
Entry: contact the Company Archivist at above addr
Subj: business records; publishing *Collns: Archvs:* records of Butterworth & Co (Publishers) Ltd (19C-20C), incl minutes, financial records, corporate plans, correspondence, registers & personnel records; misc papers relating to company hist; correspondence & papers relating to Coke Press (1893-1960)

Torquay, Devon

A491 🏛
Torbay Library Services, Local Studies Collections
Torquay Central Lib, Lymington Rd, Torquay, Devon, TQ1 3DT (01803-208305; *fax:* 01803-208307)
Email: tqreflib@torbay.gov.uk

Gov Body: Torbay Borough Council (see **P187**)
Chief: Ref & Info Svcs Libn: Mrs Anne Howard BA, MCLIP *Dep:* Central Ref Libn: Mrs Lesley Byers MCLIP (Lesley.Byers@torbay.gov.uk)
Assoc Offices: local archvs are held at DEVON RECORD OFFICE (see **A161**)
Entry: ref only *Open:* Mon, Wed, Fri 0930-1900, Tue 0930-1700, Thu 0930-1300, Sat 0930-1600
Subj: Torbay, South Hams & Teignbridge (major works on other parts of Devon, Cornwall & SW England): local studies; parish records (on loan from Devon Record Office); records of parent org *Co-op Schemes:* an archivist from Devon Record Office visits on a monthly basis
Equip: m-reader, 2-m-printers (film & fiche), copier, fax, computer (with internet), plus 19 other PCs with internet access elsewhere in the Ref Lib *Svcs:* info, ref
Stock: archvs/7050; periodcls/38; photos/8500 incl illusts, postcards & prints; pamphs/7392; m-forms/6268 fiche, 1685 film; CD-ROMs/2
Classn: DDC *Auto Sys:* DS
Staff: Libns: 2 *Non-Prof:* 6 (figs are for Ref Lib as a whole; Local Studies section is not staffed as a separate dept)

Torquay Museum Pictorial Records Archive
See TORQUAY NAT HIST SOC LIB & TORQUAY MUSEUM PICTORIAL RECORDS ARCHV (**S2049**)

Totnes

A492 🏛
Totnes Elizabethan House Museum, Study Centre
70 Fore St, Totnes, Devon, TQ9 5RU (01803-863821)
Email: totnesmuseum@btconnect.com
Internet: http://www.devonmuseums.net/totnes/

Gov Body: Totnes Town Council & Museum Trust
Chief: Museum Administrator: Mr Alan Langmaid
Other Snr Staff: Study Centre Mgr: Ms Sue King
Entry: informal; fee charged (£1.25 per hr for personal visits, £5 per hr for rsrch by staff)
Open: Wed, Fri 1000-1600, Thu 1400-2100; closed Mon-Tue
Subj: Totnes & surrounding area: local hist *Collns: Other:* census returns; parish registers; wills, leases, sales & ledgers; slide & photo colln; map colln; oral hist tapes; Totnes Times files (1860-1998)
Equip: 2 m-readers, copier, computer (with wd-proc & internet) *Offcr-in-Charge:* Museum Soc Chairman: Mrs Jill Drysdale (totnes.museum@virgin.net) *Svcs:* info, ref, biblio, indexing, abstracting, transcription, rsrch
Stock: archvs/c144 cubic m; various printed, AV, m-form & archival materials *Acq Offcr:* Museum Administrator, as above
Classn: SHIC *Auto Sys:* CardBox Plus
Pubns: Totnes Historian; various pubns by Museum Soc membs
Staff: Other Prof: 1 (museum); Study Centre staffed PT by volunteers

Trowbridge

A493 🏛
Wiltshire and Swindon Record Office
Libs HQ, Bythesea Rd, Trowbridge, Wiltshire, BA14 8BS (01225-713139; *fax:* 01225-713515)
Email: wrso@wiltshire.gov.uk

Gov Body: Wiltshire County Council (see **P201**)
Chief: Principal Archivist: Mr J.N. d'Arcy BA, DipAA
Entry: CARN readers ticket, no appt necessary
Open: Mon-Tue, Thu-Fri 0915-1700, Wed 0915-1945
Subj: County of Wiltshire: local authority archvs; diocesan records; parish records; estate archvs; family papers; business records; records of parent org *Collns: Archvs:* Wiltshire Quarter Sessions Archvs 16C-20C; Diocese of Salisbury Archvs 13C-20C, incl probate records 16C-19C; Diocese of Bristol records (Archdeaconry of Swindon); estate & family archvs, incl: Ailesbury family; Arundel family; Antrobus family; Hoare family; Long family; Methuen family; Radnor family; Somerset family; Talbot family; Troyte family; Bullock family
Equip: 18 m-readers, m-printer, copier, computers (incl 2 wd-proc)
Stock: archvs/851 cubic m; rec mgmt/55 cubic m
Pubns: Guide to the Records of the Quarter Sessions; Guide to the Records of the Diocese of Salisbury
Staff: Prof: 5 *Non-Prof:* 5

Truro

A494 🏛
Cornwall Record Office
County Hall, Truro, Cornwall, TR1 3AY (01872-323129; *fax:* 01872-270340)
Email: cro@cornwall.gov.uk
Internet: http://www.cornwall.gov.uk/cro/

Gov Body: Cornwall County Council (see **P30**)
Chief: County Archivist: Mr Paul Brough, BA, DipAA *Dep:* Archv Svcs Mgr: post vacant
Entry: CARN ticket; temp day tickets available; adv appt & ordering of documents advised
Open: Tue-Thu 0930-1700, Fri 0900-1600, Sat 0900-1200
Subj: Cornwall: local authority archvs; diocesan records; parish records; estate archvs; family papers; business records; records of parent org; metalliferrous mining records; maritime records
Collns: Archvs: quarter sessions order bks & deposited plans; County Council minutes; dist, borough parish council minutes, accounts & rate bks; school log bks, admissions registers & mgrs' minutes; records of hosps & turnpike trusts; census returns; Diocese of Truro records; parish registers, churchwardens' accounts & poor law records; wills & probate records; Methodist, Soc of Friends & other churches' registers, minutes & accounts; estate deeds, leases, rentals & plans; records of fishing, shipping, eng, shops & solicitors; programmes & minutes of clubs & socs; family correspondence & diaries *Other:* tithe maps; mine setts & cost bks; plans of abandoned mines
Equip: 16 m-readers, self-svc m-printer, m-printer, copier, fax, 2 computers (both with internet) *Svcs:* info, ref, rsrch
Stock: archvs/463 cubic m
Classn: ISAD(G)
Pubns: Sources for Cornish Family Hist (2002, £4.00); see web site for other pubns
Staff: Archivists: 6 *Other Prof:* 1 *Non-Prof:* 6.8
Exp: £380000 (1999-2000); £390000 (2000-01)

Royal Institution of Cornwall, Cornish History Research Centre
See ROYAL INSTN OF CORNWALL, COURTNEY LIB & CORNISH HIST RSRCH CENTRE (**S2056**)

Uxbridge

A495 🏛
Hillingdon Local Studies and Archives
Local Studies Lib, Central Lib, 14-15 High St, Uxbridge, Middlesex, UB8 1HD (01895-250702; *fax:* 01895-811164)
Email: archives@hillingdongrid.org
Internet: http://www.hillingdon.gov.uk/

Gov Body: London Borough of Hillingdon (see **P92**) *Chief:* Local Studies & Archvs Mgr: Mrs C. Cotton MA, BA, DipAA
Assoc Offices: MUSEUM COLLN (currently held in store, but temp exhibs regularly held in display area in Central Lib)
Entry: ref only, open to public, adv appt advised for archival material, 3 days notice required for official archvs held in store *Open:* Mon 0930-2000, Tue-Thu 1300-1730, Fri 1000-1230, 1330-1730, Sat 0930-1200, 1400-1600
Subj: London Borough of Hillingdon: local authority archvs; parish records; school records; local hist; family hist *Collns: Bks & Pamphs:* local studies colln; journals of local hist socs & other local groups; parish magazines of local parishes *Archvs:* archvs of London Borough of Hillingdon; census records; manorial records;

parish registers & transcripts *Other:* photo colln; IGI on m-fiche; local newspapers (mid 19C-date) *Equip:* 4 m-readers, 3 m-printers, 2 copiers, clr copier, fax, 18 computers (incl 2 wd-procs, 8 internet & 2 CD-ROM) *Disabled:* CCTV magnifier *Svcs:* info, ref *Stock:* archvs/75 cubic m; bks/7800; periodcls/70; photos/c10000; slides/c200; illusts/c200; pamphs/3000; maps/1000; m-forms/various; audios/70; videos/30; AVs/26 *Classn:* DDC, local topographical scheme *Auto Sys:* Adlib *Staff: Archivists:* 1 *Libns:* 1 *Other Prof:* 1 *Non-Prof:* 0.5 *Exp:* £1010 (1999-2000); £1010 (2000-01)

Wakefield

A496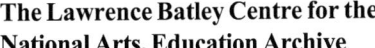

The Lawrence Batley Centre for the National Arts, Education Archive

Univ of Leeds, Bretton Hall Campus, W Bretton, Wakefield, W Yorkshire, WF4 4LG (01924-830261; *fax:* 01924-830521) *Internet:* http://naea.bretton.ac.uk/

Gov Body: Natl Arts Edu Archv (Trust) *Chief:* Asst Curator: Ms Sonja Kielty (S.Kielty@leeds.ac.uk) *Dep:* Centre Administrator: Mr Leonard Bartle (L.Bartle@leeds.ac.uk) *Entry:* ref only by adv appt *Open:* Mon-Thu 0845-1700, Fri 0845-1630 *Subj:* art edu; estate archvs *Collns: Archvs:* nearly 100 collns of complex & extensive material tracing the development of art edu in the UK, focus widened to incl other arts edu material, i.e., media edu, ballet, opera, theatre in edu etc; also holds the Bretton Estate Archv *Stock:* archvs/60000+ catalogued items

A497

West Yorkshire Archive Service Headquarters: Wakefield

Registry of Deeds, Newstead Rd, Wakefield, W Yorkshire, WF1 2DE (01924-305980; *fax:* 01924-305983) *Email:* archives@wyjs.org.uk or wakefield@wyjs.org.uk *Internet:* http://www.archives.wyjs.org.uk/

Gov Body: West Yorkshire Joint Svcs Cttee *Chief:* County Archivist: Mrs Sylvia Thomas MA DipAA *Dep:* Area Mgr: Mr Keith Sweetmore BA, DipAA *Other Snr Staff:* Principal Dist Archivist (Wakefield): Mrs Ruth Harris BA, MArAd *Assoc Offices:* WYAS BRADFORD (see **A62**); WYAS CALDERDALE (see **A194**); WYAS KIRKLEES (see **A208**); WYAS LEEDS (see **A226**); YORKSHIRE ARCHAEO SOC LIB (see **S919**) *Entry:* adv appt *Open:* Mon 0930-1300, 1400-2000, Tue, Thu 0930-1300, 1400-1700, 2nd Sat of each month 0930-1230 *Subj:* West Riding for some classes of records & Wakefield Metropolitan Dist for others: local authority archvs; diocesan records; parish records; estate archvs; family papers; business records; personal papers; records of parent org; hosp records; prison records; nonconformist records; court records; school records; trade union records; records of local socs & charities; central govt records deposited locally *Collns: Bks & Pamphs:* local Acts of Parliament (1815-1980); Public Genl Statutes (1215-1986) *Archvs:* West Riding Quarter Sessions records (1637-1970); West Riding County Council records (1889-1974); West Yorkshire Metropolitan County Council records (1974-1986); Wakefield Metro-politan Dist Council records (from 1974) & records of predecessor authorities (1894-1974); diocesan & parish records of Wakefield Diocese (from

1538); West Riding Registry of Deeds (1704-1970); records of motor taxation offices, probate registry, magistrates' courts, Ordnance Survey etc *Equip:* 13 m-readers, m-camera (via staff), m-printer (via staff), fax (via staff), copier (via staff), clr copier (via staff), computer (with internet & CD-ROM) *Svcs:* rsrch *Stock:* archvs/10000 linear m; other materials/50 linear m *Pubns:* Search Guide to the English Land Tax (£2.25 + 50p p&p); The West Riding County Council 1889-1974 (£2 + £1 p&p) *Staff: Archivists:* 3.5 *Other Prof:* 3 conservators *Non-Prof:* 5.5

Walsall

A498

Walsall Archives and Local History Centre

Essex St, Walsall, WS2 7AS (01922-721305/6; *fax:* 01922-634954) *Email:* localhistorycentre@walsall.gov.uk *Internet:* http://www.walsall.gov.uk/

Gov Body: Walsall Metropolitan Borough Council (see **P192**) *Chief:* Archivist/Local Studies Offcr: Miss Ruth F. Vyse BA(Hons), DipAS *Dep:* Archivist: Mr Matthew Blake Dip/MA Archvs & Records Mgmt *Other Snr Staff:* Local Studies Libn: Miss Cath Yates BLib(Hons); Conservator: Mrs Lisa Adye BA(Hons) *Entry:* ref only, booking for m-readers *Open:* Tue & Thu 0930-1730, Wed 0930-1900, Fri 0930-1700, Sat 0930-1300 *Subj:* Walsall Metropolitan Borough Council: local authority archvs; parish records; business records; hosp records; local hist *Collns: Archvs:* archvs of Walsall Metropolitan Borough Council & predecessors; local nonconformist church records (18C-20C); many important collns of records of local businesses, socs & orgs (mainly 19C-20C); Walsall Hosp records (19C-20C) *Other:* oral hist colln (400+ tapes); local photo colln *Equip:* 13 m-readers, m-printer, 2 video viewers, copier, room hire, tape recorder *Stock:* archvs/186.65 cubic m; rec mgmt/10 cubic m; bks/9625; periodcls/28; photos/12000+; maps/1411; m-forms/14674 *Classn:* DDC *Pubns:* numerous pubns concerning hist of Walsall area – list available on request *Staff: Archivists:* 2 *Libns:* 1 *Other Prof:* 1 *Non-Prof:* 6

Warley

A499

Sandwell Community History and Archives Service

Smethwick Lib, High St, Smethwick, Warley, W Midlands, B66 1AB (0121-558-2561; *fax:* 0121-555-6064) *Email:* archives.service@sandwell.gov.uk *Internet:* http://www.lea.sandwell.gov.uk/libraries/chas.htm

Gov Body: Sandwell Metropolitan Borough Council (see **P158**) *Chief:* Borough Archivist: Mr Huw Pierce Pritchard *Entry:* no restrictions, but booking recommended; proof of ID required *Open:* Mon, Wed, Fri 1000-1800, Tue 1030-1800, Sat 0930-1600; closed Thu *Subj:* Sandwell Metropolitan Borough: local authority archvs; parish records; business records; records of parent org *Collns: Bks & Pamphs:* local directories *Archvs:* archvs of Sandwell Metropolitan Borough Council; Diocese of Birmingham parish records for Sandwell area

Other: census returns; parish registers; electoral registers; map colln; photo colln (c15000 items); local newspapers & newspaper cuttings *Equip:* 8 m-readers, m-printer, copier, video viewer, fax

Warminster

Longleat House Archives

See LONGLEAT HOUSE, LIB & ARCHVS (**S2086**)

Warrington

A500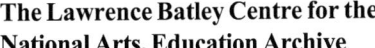

National Gas Archive

Unit 1, Europa Ct, Europa Blvd, Warrington, WA5 7TN (01925-425740; *fax:* 01925-425748) *Email:* enquiries@gasarchive.org

Gov Body: Transco plc *Chief:* Archv Mgr: Ms Helen Ford BLib, DipAA *Dep:* Archivist: Mrs Elaine Brison MA(Arch) *Entry:* by appt only *Open:* Mon-Fri 0900-1600 *Subj:* British gas industry (1812-date): business records; records of parent org & predecessors; hist of industry *Collns: Bks & Pamphs:* large colln of bks on gas, eng, chemical industry, coal/energy, social & domestic use of gas etc (19C-20C); technical papers; Acts of Parliament etc related to gas industry & regulation; commemor-ative bklets; bnd vols of technical periodcls, incl Gas Journal, Gas World & associated Yearbks & Directories; retail & domestic appliance cata-logues (early 20C onwards); lab bks from rsrch stations (1930s-70s) *Archvs:* administrative, financial, legal, technical, property & personnel records of the industry, incl: archvs of gas undertakings prior to nationalisation (1812-1949); archvs of Gas Council (1949-72); archvs of British Gas Corp (1972-86); archvs of British Gas (1986-97); archvs of BG plc (1997-2000); archvs of Lattice Group (2000-02); archvs of Natl Grid Transco (2002 onwards); regional gas records (1972-1995); papers & transactions of Instn of Gas Engineers *Other:* site plans of local gas works (19C onwards); technical drawings & specifications for bldg & plant; advertising & retail materials; extensive photo archv (covering technical, sites & works, personnel, transport, retail, appliances & machinery); large film & video colln, incl films produced by the Gas Council, the British Commercial Gas Assoc & British Gas Corp *Equip:* 3 m-form reader/printers, 2 copiers, fax, video viewer, computer *Svcs:* info, ref, rsrch, reprographic svc *Stock:* archvs/2500 linear m; photos/500000 *Classn:* ISAD(G) *Auto Sys:* CALM 2000 *Staff: Archivists:* 2 *Non-Prof:* 2 *Proj:* move to new bldg at above addr; starting records mgmt

A501

Warrington Libraries, Local and Family History Collection

Warrington Lib, Museum St, Warrington, Cheshire, WA1 1JB (01925-442890; *fax:* 01925-411395) *Email:* library@warrington.gov.uk *Internet:* http://www.warrington.gov.uk/

Gov Body: Warrington Borough Council (see **P193**) *Chief:* Libs & Info Svcs Offcr: Mr Martin Gaw *Dep:* Snr Libn: Mrs Joanne Unsworth *Assoc Offices:* small local hist collns at branch libs *Entry:* ref only, adv appt advisable *Open:* Mon-Tue, Fri 0900-1900, Wed 0900-1700, Thu, Sat 0900-1300

☛

Archives
Warrington ▼ Woking

(Warrington Libs, Local & family Hist Colln cont)
Subj: mainly Warrington & surrounding area: local authority archvs; parish records; estate archvs; family papers; business records; personal papers; political papers; records of parent org; local hist; family hist; genealogy **Collns:** Archvs: records of Borough Council, Rural Dist Council, surrounding townships & civil parishes; manorial & court records; militia records; estate & family deeds & papers; rental, maps & surveys; diaries & correspondence; electoral registers *Other:* photos; various materials on m-form, incl: census materials; local parish registers & Bishops' transcripts; local newspapers, incl Warrington Guardian Archv (from 1853); IGI for whole of UK **Co-op Schemes:** svc level agreement with Cheshire & Chester Archvs (see **A105**) **Equip:** 5 m-readers, m-printer, copier, fax, 10 computers (all with wd-proc, 9 with internet & 1 with CD-ROM) *Disabled:* Aladdin, Supernova

Warwick

A502 🗝🏛
The Queen's Own Hussars Regimental Museum, Archives
Lord Leycester Hosp, High St, Warwick, CV34 4BH *(tel & fax:* 01926-492035)
Email: trooper@qohm.tsnet.co.uk

Type: military **Chief:** Managing Trustee: Col H.M. Sandars **Dep:** Curator: Major P.J. Timmons (regsec@treenetname.co.uk)
Entry: archvs by appt **Open:** Summer: Tue-Sun 1030-1700; *Winter:* Tue-Sun 1030-1600
Subj: regimental hist; regimental records **Collns:** Archvs: records of 3rd Hussars, 7th Hussars & Queen's Own Hussars
Stock: archvs/252; bks/473 **Acq Offcr:** Curator, as above **Staff:** Non-Prof: 2

A503 🏛
Warwickshire County Record Office
Priory Pk, Cape Rd, Warwick, CV34 4JS (01926-412735; *fax:* 01926-412509)
Email: recordoffice@warwickshire.gov.uk
Internet: http://www.warwickshire.gov.uk/countyrecordoffice/

Gov Body: Warwickshire County Council (see **P194**) **Chief:** Head of Archv Svc: Miss Caroline Sampson BA(Hons), MArAd
Entry: CARN ticket **Open:** Tue-Thu 0900-1730, Fri 0900-1700, Sat 0900-1230
Subj: Warwickshire (pre-1974 boundaries): local authority archvs; diocesan records; parish records; estate archvs; family papers; business records; personal papers; political papers; records of parent org **Collns:** Bks & Pamphs: large local hist lib colln **Archvs:** archvs of Warwickshire County Council; Diocese of Coventry records; Diocese of Birmingham parish records (parishes in Warwickshire & Solihull area) *Other:* photo colln **Equip:** 22 m-readers, m-camera (not self-svc), m-printer, copier (not self-svc), fax (not self-svc), 20 computers (all with CD-ROM, 19 with internet) **Svcs:** rsrch (subj to payment of fee) **Stock:** archvs/520 cubic m; rec mgmt/82 cubic m; unquantified printed bks, photos, slides, illusts, pamphs, maps, audios & AVs

Pubns: Guide to Registers, Nonconformist Registers & Census Returns in the WCRO (£1.50 incl p&p)
Staff: Archivists: 6 Other Prof: 1 Non-Prof: 7
Proj: re-opening in Spring 2003 after extension & refurbishment

Welshpool

A504 🎓🗝
Clwyd-Powys Archaeological Trust, Archives
7a Church St, Welshpool, Powys, SY21 7DL (01938-553670; *fax:* 01938-552179)
Email: trust@cpat.org.uk
Internet: http://www.cpat.org.uk/

Type: archaeo svcs **Chief:** Dir: Mr William Britnell MA, MIFA (BillBritnell@cpat.org.uk) **Dep:** Dep Dir: Mr Robert Silvester BA, MIFA (BobSilvester@cpatfield.femon.co.uk) **Other Snr Staff:** Snr Proj Archaeologist: Mr Nigel Jones BA; Head of Curatorial Svcs: Mr Chris Martin BA; Development Control Offcr: Mr Mark Walters BA
Entry: adv appt **Open:** Mon-Fri 0900-1700
Subj: Clwyd, Powys & surrounding area: archaeo; excavation & survey records **Collns:** Bks & Pamphs: small archaeo lib; local & natl periodcls **Archvs:** Sites & Monuments Record for Powys, Flintshire, Denbighshire, Wrexham & part of Conwy & the River Conwy; records of excavations, surveys etc carried out by CPAT over the past 25 years, incl maps & photos **Equip:** copier (charged at cost) **Svcs:** info, rsrch **Stock:** archvs/held entirely on computer; rec mgmt/800 sets of records; bks/32 linear m; periodcls/7; photos/30000; slides/35000; maps/3000
Auto Sys: FoxPro
Staff: Other Prof: 12 Non-Prof: 1 **Exp:** £900 (1999-2000); £900 (2000-01)

Weybridge

A505 🏛
Brooklands Museum Trust Ltd, Archives
Brooklands Rd, Weybridge, Surrey, KT13 0QN (01932-857381; *fax:* 01932-855465)
Email: info@brooklandsmuseum.com
Internet: http://www.brooklandsmuseum.com/

Chief: Dir: Mr J. Michael Phillips **Other Snr Staff:** Curator of Motoring/Collns: Mr John Pulford (johnpulford@brooklandsmuseum.com); Curator of Aviation: Mr Julian C. Temple (juliantemple@brooklandsmuseum.com)
Entry: adv appt only **Open:** summer: Tue-Sun 1000-1700; winter: Tue-Sun 1000-1600
Subj: Brooklands Motor Circuit & Aerodrome & related sites: local hist; aviation; aircraft design, manufacture & test-flying; motor racing; estate archvs; family papers; business records; personal papers **Collns:** Bks & Pamphs: aircraft design manuals **Archvs:** records relating to British Aerospace & predecessor companies engaged in aircraft manufacture at Brooklands (1908-89); British Aircraft Corp records; Vickers-Armstrongs Ltd records; Hawker Aircraft & Hawker Siddeley Aviation Ltd records; records relating to motor racing at Brooklands (1907-39); papers of Sir George Edwards (aeronautical engineer); Sir Barnes Wallis Colln (aeronautical engineer, incl material on the Dambusters raid) *Other:* technical drawings
Equip: copier (fees) **Svcs:** info, ref, rsrch
Acq Offcr: Curator of Motoring/Collns & Curator of Aviation, as above
Staff: full-time curators supported by PT sec & small teams of PT volunteers

Whitby

A506 🎓🗝🏛
Whitby Archives and Heritage Centre
Flowergate, Whitby, N Yorkshire, YO21 3BA (01947-821364; *fax:* 01947-821436)
Email: info@whitbyarchives.freeserve.co.uk

Type: independent non-profit Trust **Gov Body:** Whitby Pictorial Archvs Trust **Chief:** Archvs Dir: Mrs S. Hutchinson **Other Snr Staff:** Trust President: C. Waters; Trust Chairman: D. Ingleton
Entry: entrance fee £1 (conc 50p); adv booking preferred for parties but not essential **Open:** Mon-Fri 1000-1600 (1100-1500 during winter); variable opening times at weekends
Subj: Whitby & surrounding area: local authority archvs; parish records; family papers; business records; genealogical records (in Family Hist Dept) **Collns:** Bks & Pamphs: Local Hist Series: a growing colln of factual hist bklets drawing on material from archvs **Archvs:** photo & pictorial archvs; various other collns incl family trees, newspapers, prints, posters & ephemera *Other:* growing colln of historical exhibits (special displays throughout the yr)
Equip: m-reader, copier, video viewer, computer (incl wd-proc), fax **Disabled:** facilities available
Svcs: info, ref, rsrch, exhibs
Pubns: Local Hist Series (see Collns above); Membs Newsletter; Heritage Shop stocks various selection of bks etc
Staff: c20 volunteers

Whitehaven

A507 🏛
Cumbria Record Office and Local Studies Library, Whitehaven
Scotch St, Whitehaven, Cumbria, CA28 7BJ (01946-852920; *fax:* 01946-852919)
Email: whitehaven.record.office@cumbriacc.gov.uk
Internet: http://www.cumbria.gov.uk/archives/

Gov Body: Cumbria County Council (see **P32**) **Chief:** Area Archivist: Mr Peter Eyre MA, DipAA **Dep:** Asst Archivist: Miss Catherine Clark BA, MArAd; Local Studies Libn: Miss Claire Caution MA, DipLib
Assoc Offices: branch office of CUMBRIA RECORD OFFICE, CARLISLE (see **A98**)
Entry: CARN ticket **Open:** Mon-Tue, Thu-Fri 0930-1700, Wed 0930-1900, Sat 0900-1300
Subj: Cumbria south & west of the River Derwent & north of the River Duddon: local authority archvs; parish records; estate archvs; family papers; business records; school records; shipping records; records of local socs & charities **Collns:** Bks & Pamphs: local studies colln concentrates on Whitehaven & area, but also provides less comprehensive coverage of the whole of Cumbria; particularly strong on mining, railways & shipping as well as biography, hist & topography. *Other:* 19C directories; OS maps, incl good coverage of County series Cumberland (Natl Grid Copeland BC only); 19C census for Cumberland; 1901 census for Cumbria
Equip: 14 m-readers, 2 m-printers, video viewer, copier **Svcs:** historical rsrch (£19 per hr + £1 p&p for UK, £2 overseas)
Stock: archvs/165 cubic m; bks/100 linear m; 50 file drawers of pamphs & ephemera
Pubns: as Cumbria Record Office, Carlisle
Staff: 3.5

🎓 academic   ✏ corporate   **- 194 -**   🏛 governmental   ✚ medical

Winchester

A508

Hampshire County Council Museums Service, Library

Chilcomb House, Chilcomb Ln, Winchester, Hampshire, SO23 8RD (01962-846700; *fax:* 01962-869836)
Email: gill.arnott@hants.gov.uk
Internet: http://www.hants.gov.uk/museums/

Type: local authority *Gov Body:* Hampshire County Council (see **P60**) *Chief:* Info Offcr & Libn: Mrs Gill Arnott
Assoc Offices: HAMPSHIRE RECORDS OFFICE (see **A509**); ALDERSHOT MILITARY MUSEUM LIB & ARCHVS (see **A9**); ANDOVER MUSEUM LOCAL STUDIES ROOM (see **A14**); CURTIS MUSEUM (see **A12**); EASTLEIGH MUSEUM RESOURCE ROOM (see **A143**); GOSPORT MUSEUM RESOURCES ROOM (see **A187**); HAVANT MUSEUM LOCAL STUDIES ROOM (see **A198**); MILESTONES LIVING HIST MUSEUM (see **A29**); RED HOUSE MUSEUM RESOURCE ROOM (see **A107**); WESTBURY MANOR MUSEUM LOCAL STUDIES ROOM (see **A166**); WILLIS MUSEUM LOCAL STUDIES ROOM (see **A30**); collns in nat sci & in arts & textiles are held at dept libs at Chilcomb House at the above addr
Entry: ref, by adv appt only *Open:* Mon-Fri 0830-1600
Subj: Hampshire: local studies; hist; topography
Collns: Bks & Pamphs: held in Nat Sci Dept Lib: Blair Colln (bks, journals, diaries & field notes associated with nat sci colln); archaeo field records & nat sci records *Archvs:* W.M. Curtis Archv (botanist & founder of Botanical magazine)
Equip: copier *Svcs:* info, ref
Stock: archvs/20000
Classn: DDC *Staff: Libns:* 1

A509

Hampshire Record Office

Sussex St, Winchester, Hampshire, SO23 8TH (01962-846154; *fax:* 01962-878681)
Email: enquiries.archives@hants.gov.uk
Internet: http://www.hants.gov.uk/record-office/

Gov Body: Hampshire County Council (see **P60**)
Chief: County Archivist: Miss Janet T. Smith
Entry: CARN ticket (proof of ID required for issue); adv booking necessary for m-form machines *Open:* Mon-Fri 0900-1900, Sat 0900-1600
Subj: Hampshire: local authority archvs; diocesan records; parish records; estate archvs; family records; business records; personal papers; political papers; records of parent org
Collns: Archvs: archvs of Hampshire County Council; Diocese of Portsmouth (deaneries of Bishop's Waltham & Petersfield) records; Diocese of Salisbury (Hampshire area) records; Diocese of Winchester records; Winchester Bishopric estate records, incl pipe rolls (1208-1711); political correspondence of George Tierney Snr (1761-1830); 3rd Baron Calthorpe (c1814-30); William Wickham (c1795-1830); 1st Baron Bolton (1764-1807); 1st Earl of Normanton (1767-1809); Harris/ Earl of Malmesbury papers (1732-1859); Bonham Carter family papers, incl correspondence with Florence Nightingale (18C-19C); Lempriére family papers relating to the Channel Islands (19C); Shelley-Rolls papers, incl papers relating to Percy Bysshe Shelley (1792-1822) *Other:* Wessex Film & Sound Archv (see **A510**)
Equip: 44 m-readers, m-camera (via staff), 2 m-printers, 3 video viewers, 2 copiers (via staff), 4 computers (for computerised document ordering), 3 cassette players *Disabled:* CCTV reader for magnifying documents, loop sys fitted in cinema & round enq desks *Online:* CALM 2000 archv catalogues from Hampshire available within office

Stock: archvs/1003.9 cubic m, incl photos, illusts, maps & AV materials; rec mgmt/178.5 cubic m; bks/77.6 cubic m
Auto Sys: CALM 2000 for Archvs
Pubns: Hampshire Record Series (Vols 1-15, £5-£15 each); Portsmouth Record Series (Vols 1-9, £15 each); Portsmouth Record Series Maps (1-14, £2 each); Hampshire Papers Series (23 issues, £1 each); Edu Svc resource packs & videos; various explanatory leaflets & guides to sources
Staff: Archivists: 14.2 *Other Prof:* 3 conservators *Non-Prof:* 15.5

A510

Wessex Film and Sound Archive

Hampshire Record Office, Sussex St, Winchester, Hampshire, SO23 8TH (01962-847742; *fax:* 01962-878681)
Email: david.lee@hants.gov.uk
Internet: http://www.hants.gov.uk/record-office/film/

Type: local govt *Gov Body:* Hampshire Record Office (see **A509**) *Chief:* Snr Archivist: Mr David Lee MLib
Entry: ref only *Open:* Mon-Fri 0900-1700
Subj: Wessex region (Hampshire, Dorset, Wiltshire, Berkshire & the Isle of Wight): local life as recorded on film, video & audio *Collns: Other:* prof & newsreel film of local events & personalities, incl military & maritime coverage, as shown in regional cinemas & halls; amateur film & video, showing many different aspects of life in the region; rsrch & advertising film produced by local businesses; videos reflecting life in the region; local radio tapes; music recordings of local interest; oral hist recordings
Co-op Schemes: arrangement with local TV companies (BBC South & Meridian Broadcasting) to make available copies of their documentaries
Equip: film & video viewing equip; audio players; 85-seat cinema for group viewing & listening
Disabled: wheelchair access
Stock: archvs/film & audio/c18000 items
Classn: ISAD(G) *Auto Sys:* DS CALM 2000
Pubns: A Guide to Wessex Film & Sound Archv Collns (£2.50 + 50p p&p); Oral Hist Guidelines (£2 + p&p)
Staff: Archivists: 1 *Non-Prof:* 1.5

A511

Winchester College Archives

College St, Winchester, Hampshire, SO23 9NA (school office: 01962-621100; *fax:* 01962-621106)
Email: sf@wincoll.ac.uk
Internet: http://www.winchestercollege.org/

Chief: Archivist: Ms Suzanne Foster
Assoc Offices: WARDEN & FELLOWS' LIB, at same addr (see **S2125**)
Entry: adv appt; access restricted *Open:* normal hrs during school term
Collns: Archvs: records of the Coll (to 20C); papers & correspondence of former staff & pupils, incl: Thomas Arnold (historian, 1795-1842); Francis Baigent (antiquary, 1830-1918); Sir Reginald Blomfield (architect, 1856-1942); Nathaniel Bond (politician, 1754-1823); William Butterfield (architect, 1814-1900); Thomas Cheyney (Dean of Winchester, d1760); Herbert Chitty (former archivist, 1863-1949); Samuel Taylor Coleridge (poet, 1772-1834); James Essex (architect, 1722-1784); Henry Gabell (former headmaster of Coll, 1764-1831); Henry Hill (architect, fl1884-1927); Benjamin Hoadly (Bishop of Winchester, 1676-1761); George Huntingford (Bishop of Hereford, 1748-1832); Henry Huntingford (classicist, 1787-1867); Thomas Huntingford (Precentor of Hereford Cathedral, c1783-1855); George Repton (architect, 1786-1858); George Ridding (Bishop of Southwell &

former headmaster of Coll, 1828-1904); John Scott, 1st Earl of Eldon (Lord Chancellor, 1751-1838); John Scott (architect, 1841-1913); Gavin Simonds (judge, 1881-1971); James Smith (politician, 1854-1929)

Wisbech

A512

Wisbech and Fenland Museum

Museum Sq, Wisbech, Cambridgeshire, PE13 1ES (01945-583817; *fax:* 01945-589050)
Email: wisbechmuseum@beeb.net

Gov Body: Museum Mgmt Cttee *Chief:* Curator & Libn: Dr Jane Hubbard
Entry: adv appt essential *Open: Museum:* Tue-Sat 1000-1700 (-1600 in winter); *Libs:* appt only
Subj: Fenland (Norfolk/Cambridgeshire): most subjs (mostly 18C-19C); some local authority records; diocesan records; parish records; estate archvs; family papers; records of parent org
Collns: Bks & Pamphs: Town Lib (founded c1654, formerly housed in church, mainly 16C-17C works in Latin, with some incunabula, MSS & other langs); Museum Lib, incl: Literary Soc Lib (founded 1781); Lib of The Revd Chauncey Townsend (12000+ vols) *Archvs:* Diocese of Ely (Deaneries of Wisbech & Lynn Marshland) parish registers, records & diaries; local deeds & indentures; Corp records & archv material; drainage records; medieval MSS (music & theology); Palmleaf MSS; archvs of Wisbech & Fenland Museum *Other:* tithe maps; maps; photo colln (1850-1950)
Equip: m-reader, m-printer, copier *Svcs:* rsrch
Stock: archvs/60 cubic m; bks/13100; photos/10000; illusts/500; pamphs/1000; maps/500; m-forms/50; Palmleaf MSS/10; some AV material

Woking

A513

Surrey History Centre

130 Goldsworth Rd, Woking, Surrey, GU12 6ND (01483-594594; *fax:* 01483-594595)
Email: shs@surreycc.gov.uk
Internet: http://www.surreycc.gov.uk/surreyhistoryservice/

Gov Body: Surrey County Council (see **P181**)
Chief: County Archivist: Mrs M. Vaughan-Lewis
Entry: Surrey County Lib ticket or CARN ticket; adv appt advised *Open:* Tue-Wed, Fri 0930-1700, Thu 0930-2130, Sat 0930-1600 (closed Mon)
Subj: County of Surrey: local authority archvs; estate archvs; parish records; nonconformist records; family papers; business records
Collns: Bks & Pamphs: Local Studies Colln for Surrey *Archvs:* records of Surrey County Council; Quarter Sessions; records of borough & districts; Anglican Diocese of Southwark records; Anglican Diocese of Guildford records; Charles L. Dodgson (Lewis Carroll) papers; family papers, incl: More Molyneaux of Losely Pk; Goulburn of Betchworth (& Jamaica); business records, incl: Broadwood of Lyne (piano manufacturers); records of Dennis Vehicles
Equip: 30 m-readers, 2 m-printers, 2 video viewers, 6 computers (incl 5 internet & 1 CD-ROM) *Svcs:* rsrch (fee based), room hire
Stock: archvs/full range of materials held
Auto Sys: DS (for lib materials)
Pubns: Guide to Parish Registers
Staff: Archivists: 10 *Libns:* 2 *Other Prof:* 4 *Non-Prof:* 15

Wolverhampton

A514

Tarmac plc Archives

Millfields Rd, Ettingshall, Wolverhampton, W Midlands, WV4 6JP
Internet: http://www.tarmac.co.uk/

Chief: Consultant Archivist & Historian: Revd Dr R.W.D. Fenn FSA, FRHistS, FLS
Entry: adv appt
Subj: construction materials; business records
Collns: Archvs: Cliffe Hill Granite Co Ltd records (1903-1965); Jee's Hartshill Granite & Brick Co Ltd records (quarry owners, 1728-1971); Lime Firms Ltd records (lime manufacturers, 1857-1987); Neuchatel Asphalte Co Ltd records (1873-1966); Northumberland Whinstone Co Ltd records (1876-1985); Ord & Maddison Ltd records (quarry owners, 1893-1971)
Pubns: The Tarmac Papers: The Hist Initiative & Archvs of Tarmac plc (occasional series, 4 vols publ to date)

A515

Wolverhampton Archives and Local Studies

42-50 Snow Hill, Wolverhampton, WV2 4AG
(01902-552480; *fax:* 01902-552481)
Email: wolverhamptonarchives@dial.pipex.com
Internet: http://www.wolverhampton.gov.uk/archives/

Gov Body: Wolverhampton City Council (see **P205**) *Chief:* City Archivist: Mr Peter Evans MA
Entry: CARN ticket; adv appt advised *Open:* Mon-Tue, Fri 1000-1700, Wed 1000-1900, 1st & 3rd Sat each month 1000-1700, closed Thu
Subj: Wolverhampton City, incl Bushbury, Penn, Heath Town, Wednesfield, Tettenhall, Bilston, Ettingshall & Bradley, also limited coverage of Willenhall & South Staffordshire: local authority archvs; parish records (m-form); family papers; business records; personal papers; records of parent org; school records; theatre records; court records; records of local clubs & socs *Collns: Bks & Pamphs:* various, relating to Wolverhampton & South Staffordshire; family hist guides; trade directories *Archvs:* archvs of Wolverhampton City Council & predecessors (1848-date); records of the Town Commissioners (1777 onwards); some records of other local authorities, incl Bilston, Heath Town, Tettenhall & Wednesfield; Wolverhampton Borough Quarter Sessions records (from 1864); records of John Thompson (local company); records of Goodyear (tire manufacturers); records of the Grand Theatre; records of Wolverhampton Naturalist & Archaeological Soc *Other:* Black & Ethnic Minority Experience (BEME) oral hist archv; Genl Register Office Indexes; Principal Probate Registry Indexes (m-fiche, 1858-1943); census returns for Wolverhampton area (1841-1901); electoral registers (1833-date, incomplete); photo colln (c10000); map colln (100s, 16C-date); local newspapers on m-film, incl: Wolverhampton Chronicle (from 1789); Express & Star (from 1882) *Co-op Schemes:* Black Country Archvs web portal (http://www.blackcountryarchives.co.uk), in assoc with Dudley (see **A130**), Sandwell (see **A499**) & Walsall (see **A498**)

Equip: 14 m-readers, 2 m-printers, video viewer, copier, 6 computers (incl 4 with wd-proc, 4 with internet & 4 with CD-ROM) *Svcs:* reprographic svcs, rsrch svc (fee based), educational advice
Stock: archvs/123.69 cubic m; rec mgmt/35.56 cubic m; printed bks & pamphs/16.9 cubic m
Classn: ISAD(G)
Pubns: free bklets: Summary of Collns; Registers of Baptisms, Marriages & Burials; 19 'Selections' bklets on different local topics; Bilston in the 19th Century (CD-ROM, £9.99); extensive local & family hist info on web site, incl 300000+ surname index
Staff: Archivists: 1 *Libns:* 1 *Other Prof:* 1 conservator *Non-Prof:* 2.7

Worcester

A516

Elgar Birthplace Museum Archives

Crown East Ln, Lower Broadheath, Worcester, WR2 6RH (01905-333224; *fax:* 01905-333426)
Email: birthplace@elgarmuseum.org
Internet: http://www.elgarmuseum.org/

Gov Body: Elgar Foundation & Birthplace Trust
Chief: Archivist: Ms Margaret Sanders
Entry: adv appt; a fee may be charged *Open:* Mon-Fri 1100-1300, 1400-1630
Subj: relating to Sir Edward Elgar; personal papers etc *Collns: Archvs:* papers, correspondence & musical MSS of Sir Edward Elgar (1857-1934); correspondence from various literary, musical & other figures, incl: G.B. Shaw; Arthur Benson; Fritz Volbach; Sir Henry Wood *Other:* scores & sheet music; concert programmes; press cuttings; photo colln; audio recordings

A517

Worcestershire Regiment Museum Archives

RHQ WFR, Norton Barracks, Worcester, WR5 2PA (01905-354359; *fax:* 01905-353871)
Email: rhq_wfr@lineone.net

Gov Body: Trustees of the Worcestershire Regiment Museum *Chief:* Curator & Regimental Sec: Major R.S. Prophet (Rtd)
Entry: by appt only *Open:* Mon-Fri 0900-1600
Subj: Worcestershire: regimental hist; military hist; regimental records *Collns: Archvs:* records of the Worcestershire Regiment
Equip: copier (5p per pg) *Svcs:* info, ref, rsrch
Acq Offcr: Curator & Regimental Sec, as above
Staff: Non-Prof: 1

A518

Worcestershire Record Office

County Hall, Spetchley Rd, Worcester, WR5 2NP (01905-766351; *fax:* 01905-766363)
Email: RecordOffice@worcestershire.gov.uk
Internet: http://www.worcestershire.gov.uk/records/

Gov Body: Worcestershire County Council (see **P206**) *Chief:* County Archivist: Mr A.M. Wherry BA, DipAA (twherry@worcestershire.gov.uk)
Dep: Snr Asst County Archivist: Mr R. Whittaker MA(Oxon), DipAA (rwhittaker@worcestershire.gov.uk) *Other Snr Staff:* Head of Repository (HQ Branch): Ms Margaret Tohill BA, DipAA (mtohill@worcestershire.gov.uk); Records Mgr (IT/IS): Ms Jo Terry BA, DipAA (jterry@worcestershire.gov.uk); Policy Offcr (Info): Ms Debbie Wilton BA, MA (dwilton@worcestershire.gov.uk)
Assoc Offices: MODERN RECORDS UNIT, County Hall, Worcester, WR5 2NP (not open to public), Head of Repository: Mr Adrian Gregson BA, DipAA (agregson@worcestershire.gov.uk);

WORCESTERSHIRE LIB & HIST CENTRE, Trinity St, Worcester, WR1 2PW, Head of Repository: Ms Teresa Nixon BA, DipAA (01905-765922; *email:* wlhc@worcestershire.gov.uk)
Entry: CARN ticket, adv booking for m-readers
Open: Record Office & Hist Centre: Mon, Fri 0930-1900, Tue-Thu 0930-1730, Sat 0930-1600
Subj: Worcestershire & Worcester Diocese: local authority archvs; diocesan records; parish records; estate archvs; family papers; business records; records of parent org *Collns: Archvs:* Borough records for Worcester, Droitwich & Bewdley; diocesan & parish records of Diocese of Worcester (excl Dudley parish); estate records for Bishop of Worcester; correspondence of Sir Edward Elgar; Worcestershire photo survey
Equip: 44 m-readers, 4 m-printers, 3 m-cameras, 2 copiers, 3 fax, video viewer, 18 computers (incl 2 with CD-ROM & 16 with internet) *Offcr-in-Charge:* County Archivist, as above *Svcs:* info, ref, rsrch
Stock: archvs/1300 cubic m; rec mgmt/850 cubic m; bks/164 cubic m *Acq Offcr:* County Archivist, as above
Classn: ISAD(G) (with new CALM sys) *Auto Sys:* Talis (current), CALM (forthcoming)
Pubns: Genealogical Resources in the Worcestershire Record Office No 1: Parish Registers & Transcripts (£4.25); No 2: Trade Directories & Almanacks (£3.99); info leaflets (all free on request): Using the Record Office for Family Hist Rsrch; House Hunting at the Worcestershire Record Office; A Guide to Adoption Records; Local Hist at Worcestershire Lib & Hist Centre; Searchroom Rules; Using the Worcestershire Lib & Hist Centre for Family Hist Rsrch; Tracing Missing Persons; The Photographic Survey; A Guide to Using FamilySearch
Staff: Archivists: 12 *Libns:* 1 *Non-Prof:* 25
Exp: £3170 (2000-01)

Wrexham

A519

Wrexham Archives Service, The A.W. Palmer Centre for Local Studies and Archives

Wrexham County Borough Museum, County Bldgs, Regent St, Wrexham, LL11 1RB (01978-317973; *fax:* 01978-317982)
Email: archives@wrexham.gov.uk or localstudies@wrexham.gov.uk
Internet: http://www.wrexham.gov.uk/

Gov Body: Wrexham County Borough Council
Chief: Archivist & Records Mgr: Ms Helen Gwerfyl BA, DipAA; Local Studies Libn: Miss Joy Thomas BA, MCLIP
Assoc Offices: collns are still being set up; most existing records relating to area are held in DENBIGHSHIRE RECORD OFFICE (see **A441**) & FLINTSHIRE RECORD OFFICE (see **A200**)
Entry: CARN ticket *Open:* Mon, Wed-Fri 1000-1700, Tue 1000-1900, Sat 1030-1500
Subj: Wrexham County Borough & area: local authority archvs; estate archvs; family papers; business records; personal papers *Collns: Bks & Pamphs:* Wrexham publishers & printers, esp Hughes & Son, Wrexham *Other:* various minor deposits/donations, acquired since 1996
Equip: 4 m-readers, copier, computer (with wd-proc, internet & CD-ROM) *Svcs:* info, ref
Stock: archvs/14 cubic m; rec mgmt/200 cubic m; bks/6800; periodcls/6; photos/470; maps/740; m-forms/617; audios/35; videos/56; CD-ROMs/4 *Acq Offcr:* Archivist & Records Mgr & Local Studies Libn, as above
Classn: DDC, ISAD(G) *Auto Sys:* DS
Staff: Archivists: 1 *Libns:* 1 *Non-Prof:* 2 PT
Exp: £1500 (1999-2000); £1500 (2000-01)

A520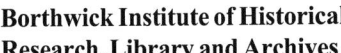

Wrexham RC Diocesan Archives

Bishop's House, Sontley Rd, Wrexham, Clwyd, LL13 7EW (01978-262726; *fax:* 01978-354257)
Email: diowxm@globalnet.co.uk

Gov Body: Trustees of the RC Diocese of Wrexham *Chief:* Diocesan Archivist: Mrs Kathryn Byrne BA
Entry: by adv appt
Subj: RC Diocese of Wrexham: diocesan records; parish records

Yate

A521

South Gloucestershire Local Studies Service

Yate Lib, 44 West Walk, Yate, S Gloucestershire, BS37 4AX (01454-865661; *fax:* 01454-865665)
Email: yate.library@southglos.gov.uk
Internet: http://www.southglos.gov.uk/

Gov Body: South Gloucestershire Council (see **P168**) *Chief:* Libn: Mr N. Weston BA, MA, MCLIP
Other Snr Staff: Local Studies Libn: Mrs Helen Egarr (at Downend Lib)
Assoc Offices: DOWNEND LIB, Buckingham Gdns, Downend, S Gloucestershire, BS16 5TW (01454-865666; *email:* downend.library@southglos.gov.uk); THORNBURY LIB, St Mary St, Thornbury, S Gloucestershire, BS32 2AA (01454-865655; *email:* thornbury.library@southglos.gov.uk)
Entry: no restrictions *Open: Yate:* Mon-Tue, Thu-Fri 0930-1900, Sat 0930-1700 (closed Wed); *Thornbury:* Mon-Tue 0930-1700, Wed, Fri 0930-1900, Sat 0930-1230, 1330-1700 (closed Thu)
Subj: South Gloucestershire: local studies
Collns: Other: local newspapers (back copies bnd, from 1975 onwards); oral hist tapes; photos; newspaper cuttings; ephemera
Equip: m-reader, copier *Disabled:* Kurzweil (at Thornbury Lib)
Stock: archvs/c1500
Classn: DDC *Auto Sys:* DS *Staff:* Libns: 20

York

A522

Borthwick Institute of Historical Research, Library and Archives

St Anthony's Hall, Peasholme Green, York, YO1 7PW (01904-642315)
Internet: http://www.york.ac.uk/inst/bihr/

Gov Body: York Univ (see **S2168**) *Chief:* Dir: Mr C.C. Webb MA, DipAA *Dep:* Archivist: post vacant
Assoc Offices: GURNEY LIB, at same addr (working lib for the larger archv collns)
Entry: adv appt for archv, lib open to all callers
Open: Mon-Fri 0930-1250, 1400-1650
Subj: GCSE & A level; undergrad; postgrad; religion; geog; hist; diocesan records; estate archvs; health records *Collns: Bks & Pamphs:* lib of the late Prof Sir Geoffrey Elton (new acq) *Archvs:* Archdiocese of York Archvs; Earls of Halifax Archvs; Carr-Brierly Architectural Archv; Centre for Southern African Studies; archvs of York NHS Trust & predecessor bodies; many smaller private & institutional archvs from medieval to modern
Equip: m-reader, copier *Svcs:* postal copying svc
Stock: archvs/650 cubic m; bks/20000
Classn: DDC (mod) *Auto Sys:* through Univ of York OPAC
Pubns: Guide to the Archv Collns
Staff: Prof: 6 *Non-Prof:* 7

A523

Castle Howard Archives

Estate Office, Castle Howard, York, YO60 7DA (01653-648444; *fax:* 01653-648529)
Internet: http://www.castlehoward.co.uk/

Gov Body: Castle Howard Estate Ltd *Chief:* Curator: Dr Christopher Ridgway
Entry: ref only for bona fide scholars & rsrchers, by appt 1 month in adv of planned visit; letter of recommendation required; daily reading charge of £25; Castle Howard is not normally able to accommodate applications to visit by genealogical rsrchers *Open:* Mon-Wed 1000-1600 during Mar-Oct on a limited basis
Subj: estate archvs; family papers
Svcs: rsrch, photocopying available at discretion of the Curator
Pubns: index to collns held at Natl Register of Archvs, London

A524

Prince of Wales's Own Regiment of Yorkshire Museum, Archives

3 Tower St, York, YO1 9SB (01904-662790; *fax:* 01904-658824)

Gov Body: MoD (see **S1284**) *Chief:* Curator: Lt Col T.C.E. Vines *Dep:* Asst: Mrs P. Boyd
Entry: adv appt for archvs *Open: Museum:* Mon-Sat 0930-1630
Subj: military hist; regimental records; personal papers *Collns: Bks & Pamphs:* WW1 war diaries of battalions of the West Yorkshire Regiment & the East Yorkshire Regiment *Archvs:* records of the Prince of Wales's Own Regiment of Yorkshire, the West Yorkshire Regiment & the East Yorkshire Regiment
Svcs: info, ref, rsrch, limited copying facilities (charged at cost)

A525

York City Archives Department

Art Gallery Bldg, Exhib Sq, York, YO1 2EW (01904-551878; *fax:* 01904-551877)
Email: archives@york.gov.uk
Internet: http://www.york.gov.uk/learning/libraries/archives/

Gov Body: York City Council (see **P208**) *Chief:* City Archivist: Mrs Rita J. Freedman BA, DipAA
Entry: adv appt advised *Open:* Mon-Wed, Fri 0900-1300, 1400-1700, Thu 0900-1300, 1400-1930
Subj: York: local authority archvs; some civil parish records; estate archvs; family papers; business records; personal papers; political papers; records of parent org (City depts); hosp records; trade union records; school records; solicitors records; manorial records; records of local socs & charities *Collns: Archvs:* York Civic Records; records of York City Courts; York Freeman Rolls (1272-1986); York Cemetery Company records (1837-1961); Robinson of Clifton & Rawcliffe family & estate records (16C-19C); Gray family papers (18C-19C); Munby family papers (18C-19C); John Goodricke papers (astronomy); meteorological records (18C-20C) *Other:* maps & plans; prints & photos
Equip: m-form reader/printers (25p), copier (A4/12p, A3/20p) *Svcs:* info, ref, rsrch (£10 per hr)
Pubns: Brief Guide (£2.40)
Staff: Archivists: 1 full-time *Non-Prof:* 2 PT archv assts, 1 admin asst

A526

Yorkshire Film Archive

York St John Coll, Lord Mayor's Walk, York, YO31 7EX (01904-716550)
Email: yfa@yorksj.ac.uk

Type: charitable trust *Chief:* Dir: Ms Sue Howard
Entry: adv appt
Subj: Yorkshire: crafts; traditions; local industry; leisure activs; family life etc *Collns: Other:* film relating to Yorkshire produced by prof & amateur filmmakers (late 19C-date)
Equip: copier, video & film viewing facilities, computers (incl wd-proc, internet & CD-ROM)
Svcs: ref, rsrch

York Minster Archives

See YORK MINSTER LIB (**S2174**)

ISLE OF MAN

Douglas

A527

Isle of Man General Registry

Civil Registry, Registries Bldg, Bucks Rd, Douglas, Isle of Man, IM1 3AR (*tel & fax:* 01624-687039)
Email: civil@registry.gov.im
Internet: http://www.gov.im/

Gov Body: Isle of Man Govt *Chief:* Registrar: Mrs Susan Cain *Dep:* Dep Registrar: Mrs Kathleen Chinn
Assoc Offices: RAMSEY REGISTRY OFFICE, Town Hall, Parliament Sq, Ramsey, Isle of Man, Registrar: Ms S. Willis & Ms L. Meechan; PEEL REGISTRY OFFICE, Town Hall, Derby Rd, Peel, Isle of Man, Registrar: Mr P. Leadley; CASTLE-TOWN REGISTRY OFFICE, Castle Rushen, Castletown, Isle of Man, Registrar: Mrs T. McKinlay
Entry: open to public *Open:* Douglas Registry: Mon-Fri 0900-1300, 1400-1700
Subj: Isle of Man: records of births, deaths & marriages; parish records (baptism, burials & marriages); family hist
Equip: 3 m-readers, 2 m-printers, copier (15p per copy) *Offcr-in-Charge:* Registrar:, as above
Svcs: info, ref, rsrch, provision of certified copies of entries
Acq Offcr: Registrar, as above
Staff: Non-Prof: 2 in Main Registry

A528

Isle of Man Public Record Office

Unit 3, Spring Valley Industrial Est, Braddan, Douglas, Isle of Man, IM2 2QR (01624-613383; *fax:* 01624-613384)
Email: public.records@registry.gov.im
Internet: http://www.gov.im/

Gov Body: Isle of Man Genl Registry (see **A527**) *Chief:* Public Records Offcr: Miss M.J. Critchlow *Dep:* Asst Public Records Offcr: Miss C. Mulcahy
Entry: adv appt essential *Open:* Mon-Thu 0900-1730, Fri 0900-1700
Subj: Isle of Man: govt records (mainly 20C); records of other public bodies
Further Info: Relatively new svc, with holdings still being collated & listed

A529

Manx National Heritage Library

Manx Museum & Natl Trust, Kingswood Grove, Douglas, Isle of Man, IM1 3LY (01624-648000; *fax:* 01624-648001)
Email: library@mnh.gov.im
Internet: http://www.gov.im/mnh/

Gov Body: trustees *Chief:* Dir & Inspector of Natl Monuments (Manx Natl Heritage): Mr S. Harrison BA, FSA, FMA, MBIM; Head of Library/Librarian-Archivist: Mr R. Sims BA, DipAA, DPESS *Dep:* Asst Libn: Mr Alan Franklin MA, MCLIP

Entry: ref only *Open:* Mon-Sat 1000-1700 & some bank hols
Subj: Isle of Man; local studies; family hist; diocesan records; personal papers; all types of record relating to Isle of Man incl legal, govt, private bodies & indivs (similar to a county record office) *Collns: Archvs:* Diocese of Sodor & Man records; ecclesiastical court records; manorial records; land & property records (16C-20C), incl Setting Bks (c1507-1911) & Wast Bks (1511-1916); wills (c1600-1910) & deeds (late 17C-1910) *Other:* Manx newspapers (late 18C onwards); census returns (m-form); parish registers (early 17C-1883); nonconformist registers; monumental inscriptions; maps & plans
Equip: 12 m-readers, m-form scanner/printer, video viewer, copier, 2 rooms for hire *Disabled:* wheelchair access *Svcs:* biblio
Stock: archvs/274 cubic m; bks/50000 incl pamphs; periodcls/121; photos/6000; maps/2000; m-forms/2000; videos/1000; films/100
Classn: DDC, Brown
Pubns: pubns too numerous to mention
Staff: Libns: 1 Other Prof: 3
Proj: fitting out of image store & revamp of film/archv store

Peel

A530

Isle of Man Family History Society Library

13 Michael St, Peel, Isle of Man, IM5 1HB (01624-843105/18)

Gov Body: Isle of Man Family Hist Soc *Chief:* Libn: Ms Veronica Vondy
Entry: by appt only *Open:* 3 afternoons per wk, 1400-1700
Subj: Isle of Man: family hist; genealogy
Collns: Other: IGI on m-fiche
Pubns: Fraueyn as Banglaneyn (journal, 4 pa)

CHANNEL ISLANDS

Guernsey

A531

The Greffe, Guernsey

Royal Court House, St Peter Port, Guernsey, Channel Islands, GY1 2PB (01481-725277; *fax:* 01481-715097)
Email: hm_greffier@court1.guernsey.gov.uk

Gov Body: Royal Court of Guernsey *Chief:* Her Majesty's Greffier: Mr K.H. Tough BA
Entry: written application to Her Majesty's Greffier; rsrchers from outside Guernsey should provide ID & letter of introduction *Open:* Mon-Fri 0900-1300, 1400-1600
Subj: Guernsey, Alderney & Sark: local authority archvs; parish records; family papers; records of parent org; all records prior to 1948 are in French *Collns: Archvs:* royal charters granted to the Bailiwick (from 1394); judicial records of the Royal Court of Guernsey (from 1526); legislative records (1553-date); Royal Court letter bks (from 1737); records of land conveyances etc (1576-date); records of the Assembly of the States of Guernsey (1605-date); registers of births, marriages & deaths (1840-date); Wills of Real Property (from 1841; Wills of Personalty are held by the Ecclesiastical Court 01481-721732); Company Registry (1883-date); documents issued by Royal Court (from c1350); feudal court registers (esp Cour St Michel, from 1537); Mont St Michel Colln (transcripts of originals destroyed in 1944); transcripts of minutes bks etc of Calvinist regime in Guernsey (c1558-1660); identity card files (1940-1945, c20000 personal forms & photos); private collns deposited by local families (esp de Sausmarez Papers)
Equip: m-form reader/printer, copiers (not available for delicate documents)
Stock: archvs/800 linear m; MSS/2700 vols; maps & plans/15000; company files/30000; documents/100000
Pubns: Lists of Records in the Greffe (ongoing Special Series, publ by List & Index Soc): i) Registers & Records in Vol Form (1969); ii) Single Documents under the Bailiwick Seal (1978); iii) Other Documents under Sign Manual, Signature or Seal (1983); Recueil d'Ordonnances de la Cour de l'Isle de Guernsey 1533- (25 vols to date); Actes des Etats de l'Île de Guernsey 1605-1843 (8 vols, thereafter publ as Billets d'État in annual vols to date); Recueil d'Ordres en Conseil d'un Intérêt Général enregistrés sur les Records de l'Île de Guernsey 1800- (31 vols to date)
Staff: Other Prof: 2 Non-Prof: 2

A532

Guernsey / Island Archives Service

29 Victoria Rd, St Peter Port, Guernsey, Channel Islands, GY1 1HU (01481-724512; *fax:* 01481-715814)

Gov Body: States of Guernsey *Chief:* Island Archivist: Dr D.M. Ogier BA, PhD(Warwick), FRHistS *Dep:* Asst Archivist: Mr Nathan Coyde
Assoc Offices: THE GREFFE, Guernsey (see **A531**)
Entry: adv appt preferred *Open:* Mon-Fri 0830-1630
Subj: Guernsey: local authority archvs (States of Guernsey); parish records (civil); estate archvs; family papers; business records; records of parent org *Collns: Archvs:* St Peter Port Hosp Archv (1741-1960); Royal Court records & collns (14C-20C); Stevens Guille Archv Colln (14C-19C); official records of States of Guernsey (generally open to 1948, closed post-1948)
Equip: m-reader, copier

Stock: archvs/2 km
Pubns: in house lists only
Staff: Archivists: 4.5

Jersey

A533

Jersey Archive

Clarence Rd, St Helier, Jersey, Channel Islands, JE2 4JY (01534-833300; *fax:* 01534-833301)
Email: archives@jerseyheritagetrust.org
Internet: http://www.jerseyheritagetrust.org/

Gov Body: States of Jersey **Chief:** Head of Archvs & Collns: Sue Groves **Other Snr Staff:** Snr Archivist: Ms Linda Myers BA, MSc, RMSA
Entry: Jersey Archvs reader card (obtainable from Archv on production of photographic ID)
Open: Tue-Sat 0900-1700; Reading Rooms closed 1300-1400
Subj: Jersey & Channel Islands: local authority archvs; parish & church records; estate archvs; family papers; business records; nonconformist records; personal papers; school records; records of local clubs & assocs **Collns:** *Archvs:* archvs of States of Jersey, State Committees, Depts & parishes; archvs of the Royal Court of Jersey; archvs of the Lt Governor of Jersey; collns relating to the Occupation 1940-45, incl: Bailiff of Jersey's Occupation Files (administrative records from during & after Occupation); Brigadier Snow Papers (plans for liberation of Channel Islands, maps, intelligence reports, RAF reconnaissance photos, war diaries, minutes of Rehabilitation Cttee) *Other:* Photographic, Film & Sound Archv; maps & plans
Equip: 6 m-readers, m-printer (A4/50p), video viewer, 5 computers (all with CD-ROM), 2 rooms for hire *Disabled:* wheelchair access, hearing loops, ZoomText programmes, large keyboard
Online: catalogue *Offcr-in-Charge:* Head of Archvs & Collns, as above **Svcs:** info, rsrch
Stock: archvs/310 cubic m; rec mgmt/5.67 cubic m; photos/61.7 cubic m; maps/c250; m-forms/0.3 cubic m; audios/50; videos/150 **Acq Offcr:** Snr Archivist, as above
Classn: ISAD(G) **Auto Sys:** Adlib
Pubns: genl info leaflets; Jersey Archv info leaflets, incl: Family Hist; House Hist; Royal Court Records; German Occupation; Preservation & Conservation
Staff: Archivists: 4 *Other Prof:* 1 *Non-Prof:* 7
Exp: £3327 (1999-2000); £5936 (2000-01)

A534

Jersey Public Registry Office

Judicial Greffe, Royal Court House, St Helier, Jersey, Channel Islands, JE1 1BA (01534-502318; *fax:* 01534-502399/0)
Internet: http://www.judicialgreffe.gov.je or http://www.jerseylegalinfo.je/

Gov Body: Judicial Greffe (Jersey), Judicial Greffier: Mr M. Wilkins **Chief:** Registrar of Deeds: Mrs J. Hume (J.Hume@gov.je) **Dep:** Asst Registrar: Mrs J. Le Breton (J.LeBreton@gov.je)
Entry: adv appt **Open:** Mon-Fri 0900-1300, 1400-1700
Subj: States of Jersey: land deeds & related documents **Collns:** *Archvs:* Deeds of Property (from 1602); Registrations of Partage; Wills of Immovable Estate; Records of the Royal Court (from 1506, discontinuous); Powers of Attorney, Tutelles & Curatelles
Svcs: limited searches

Sark

A535

The Greffe, Sark

Sark, Channel Islands
Internet: http://www.sark.gov.gg/

Chief: The Greffier
Subj: Sark: court records **Collns:** *Archvs:* Sark Court, registers of minutes of Chief Pleas & Acts of Court (1675-1991)

A536

Sark Seigneurie

Sark, Channel Islands
Email: seigneur@sark.gov.gg
Internet: http://www.sark.gov.gg/

Chief: contact the Seigneur
Subj: Sark: administrative records; estate archvs; court records; personal papers **Collns:** *Archvs:* Sark Court, minutes (copies & extracts, 1599-1657); Sark Seigneurie estate & administrative papers (1526-1927); Sark Seigneurie, Guernsey estate papers (1500-1927); Sark militia records (1859-1873); papers & correspondence of former Ministers of Sark & former Seigneurs (17C-19C)
Pubns: Calendar & Catalogue of Sark Seigneurie Archv 1526-1927, by Marie Axton & Richard Axton (List & Index Soc Special Series Vol 26, HMSO, 1991)

SECTION 4 – UK SPECIAL LIBRARIES

Entries are arranged alphabetically under town names. Within this framework, libraries within the same institution are grouped together. Libraries covered include governmental libraries, academic libraries (universities, schools and institutes of higher and further education), hospital and other medical libraries, corporate libraries, commercial libraries, libraries held by museums and art galleries, churches and other religious organisations, and numerous private libraries such as those held by learned or professional bodies, charities and stately homes.

Access to many special libraries (including academic libraries) is restricted, and entry may require an appointment in advance. Often identification will be required and a special need to use the collections will have to be demonstrated.

Telephone and fax numbers are given in the form of area dialling codes within the United Kingdom. To telephone the UK from outside the country, dial 00-44 followed by the number, minus the initial 0.

Entries are based on the libraries' responses to the following questions:

	1.	**Official name of Library/Institution**
Type:	2.	**Type of Institution** *(see also Key to Symbols below)*
	3.	**Full postal address** *(incl. postcode)* Tel & fax numbers *(incl. STD code)*
Email:		Electronic Mail
Internet:		Internet address
Gov Body:	4.	**Governing body** *(if any, e.g., local authority, university)*
Chief:	5.	**Chief Librarian/Officer** *(give designation, name, qualifications & email address)*
Dep:	6.	**Deputy** *(give designation, name, qualifications & email address)*
Other Snr Staff:	7.	**Other Senior Staff** *(give designation, name, qualifications & email address)*
Assoc Libs:	8.	**Associate/Dependent Libraries** *(if any, give address, tel, fax & email address, plus designation, name & qualifications of officer in charge)*
Entry:	9.	**Conditions for entry** *(e.g., reference only, advance appointment)*
Open:	10.	**Opening hours** *(please use 24-hour clock, e.g., 0930-1730)*
Subj:	11.	**Main subjects covered**
Collns:	12.	**Special Collections** *(give subjects and brief details)*
Bks & Pamphs:		**a)** Printed books & pamphlets
Archvs:		**b)** Archives
Other:		**c)** Other
Co-op Schemes:	13.	**Co-operative schemes** *(in which library participates, if any)*
Equip:	14.	**Equipment & facilities available to users** *(give numbers, and fees if appropriate)*
Disabled:		**Equipment for disabled** *(e.g., Kurzweil)*
Online:		**Online information services** *(e.g., Dialog; give fees)*
Offcr-in-Charge:		**Officer in charge of equipment purchases** *(give designation, name & email address)*

Svcs:	15.	**Services provided**
Stock:	16.	**Stock** *(give total quantities)*
bks		**a)** Books *(incl bound periodicals)*
periodcls		**b)** Current periodical titles
photos		**c)** Photographs
slides		**d)** Slides
illusts		**e)** Illustrations
pamphs		**f)** Pamphlets
maps		**g** Maps
m-forms		**h)** Microforms
audios		**i)** Audios
videos		**j)** Videos
CD-ROMs		**k)** CD-ROMs
archvs		**l)** Archives *(specify unit e.g., by linear, cubic metre)*
rec mgmt		**m)** Records management holdings *(specify unit e.g., by linear, cubic metre)*
		n) Other *(please specify)*
Acqs Offcr:		**Officer in charge of stock acquisitions** *(give designation, name & email address)*
Classn:	17.	**Classification method(s) used** *(if applicable)*
Auto Sys:	18.	**Automated Library system used** *(if any)*
Pubns:	19.	**Publications** *(e.g., guides & handlists; give titles & prices)*
Staff:	20.	**Staff establishment** *(give full-time equivalent for part-time staff incl. vacancies)*
		Total number of:
Libns:		**a)** Professional librarians
Other Prof:		**b)** Other professional staff
Non-Prof:		**c)** Non-professional staff
Exp:	21.	**Finance** *(expenditure on documents and/or books, incl. purchase & conservation)*
		a) 1999-2000 **b)** 2000-01
Proj:	22.	**Capital projects** *(if any, starting in 2001 or 2002)*
Further Info:	23.	**Other Information**

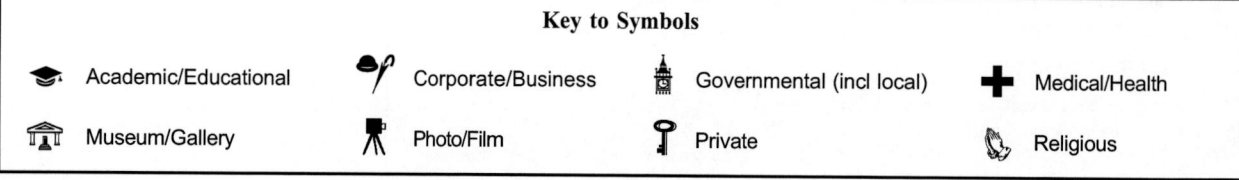

Academic/Educational	Corporate/Business	Governmental (incl local)	Medical/Health
Museum/Gallery	Photo/Film	Private	Religious

Key to Symbols

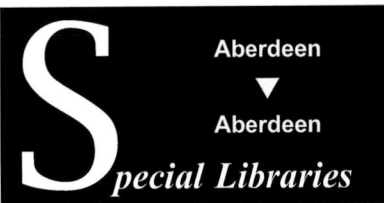

Special Libraries

Aberdeen

S1

Aberdeen and Grampian Chamber of Commerce, Information Centre
27 Albyn Pl, Aberdeen, AB10 1DB (01224-252727; *fax:* 01224-580055)
Email: sbg-grampian@scotent.co.uk
Internet: http://www.sbgateway.com/

Chief: Centre Mgr: Mrs Celia Hukins BA, MCLIP
Entry: adv appt *Open:* Mon-Fri 0900-1700
Subj: business info; mgmt; marketing; tech *Co-op Schemes:* Grampian Info
Equip: copier, computer (with wd-proc, internet & CD-ROM) *Online:* range of market rsrch databases, mostly free to users *Svcs:* info
Stock: bks/1000; periodcls/20; CD-ROMs/50
Classn: DDC
Staff: Libns: 3 *Other Prof:* 2 *Non-Prof:* 1

S2

Aberdeen Art Gallery, James McBey Art Reference Library
Schoolhill, Aberdeen, AB10 1FQ (01224-523700; *fax:* 01224-632133)
Email: info@aagm.co.uk
Internet: http://www.aagm.co.uk/

Gov Body: Aberdeen City Council (see **P1**)
Chief: Libn: Mr Jonathan Wilson BA(Hons), MA
Open: Mon-Fri 1000-1230, 1400-1630
Subj: arts; local study (Aberdeen, maritime)
Collns: Bks & Pamphs: James McBey Ex Libris Colln *Archvs:* William Dyce Papers
Equip: copier, 2 rooms for hire *Svcs:* info, ref
Stock: bks/10000; slides/2500
Classn: DDC *Auto Sys:* TMS
Staff: Other Prof: 0.2 *Non-Prof:* 1

S3

Aberdeen College Library
Gallowgate Centre, Gallowgate, Aberdeen, AB9 1DN (01224-612138; *fax:* 01224-612001)
Email: gallowlib@abcol.ac.uk
Internet: http://www.abcol.ac.uk/

Chief: Operations Mgr: Ms Kelly Friar BA (k.friar@abcol.ac.uk)
Assoc Libs: GALLOWGATE LIB, addr as above, Libn: Ms Kathryn Appleby MA, DipLib (k.appleby@abcol.ac.uk); CLINTERTY LIB, Clinterty, Kinellar, Aberdeenshire, Libn: Ms Sue Bowen BA, DipLib (s.bowen@abcol.ac.uk); ALTENS LIB, Hareness Rd, Aberdeen, Libn: Ms Sue Bowen (as above)
Entry: ref only to non-staff/students *Open:* term: Mon-Thu 0830-2130, Fri 0830-1700, Sat-Sun 0900-1700 (Gallowgate & Clinterty Libs only); vac: Mon-Fri 0830-1700, Sat-Sun 0900-1700
Subj: all subjs; genl; GCSE; A level; undergrad; vocational *Collns: Other:* BSI *Co-op Schemes:* Grampian Info, BLDSC
Equip: 4 video viewers, 4 copiers, 57 computers (all with wd-proc, internet & CD-ROM) *Disabled:* CCTV, text reader, trackballs, adapted keyboards *Online:* Dialog, KnowUK, GMID's Euromonitor, EBSCO UK/Eire, Reference Desk, mad.co.uk, Literature Online, Eurotext, City Mutual, Technical Indexes *Svcs:* info, ref

Stock: bks/50000; periodcls/200; audios/300; videos/800; CD-ROMs/50
Classn: DDC *Auto Sys:* Olib
Staff: Libns: 2 *Other Prof:* 2 *Non-Prof:* 10 *Exp:* £137450 (total exp, 2000-01)

S4

Aberdeen Maritime Museum Reference Library
Shiprow, Aberdeen, AB11 5BY (01224-337700; *fax:* 01224-213066)
Email: info@aagm.co.uk
Internet: http://www.aagm.co.uk/

Type: local authority *Gov Body:* Aberdeen City Council (see **P1**) *Chief:* Keeper of Sci & Maritime Hist: Mr John Edwards BA, AMA
Entry: free to museum, ref lib by appt *Open: Museum:* Mon-Sat 1000-1700, Sun 1200-1500
Subj: Aberdeen & North Sea: oil & gas; shipping; fishing; geog; hist
Equip: copier, computer (incl CD-ROM) *Svcs:* info, ref

S5

Aberdeen University, Directorate of Information Systems and Services
Queen Mother Lib, Meston Walk, Aberdeen, AB24 3UE (01224-272579; *fax:* 01224-487048)
Email: library@abdn.ac.uk
Internet: http://www.abdn.ac.uk/diss/

Gov Body: Univ of Aberdeen, Directorate of Info Systems & Svcs (DISS) *Chief:* Dir of DISS: Mr Graham Pryor *Dep:* Lib Svcs Mgr & Libn: Ms Carole Munro
Assoc Libs: TAYLOR LIB, Taylor Bldg, Old Aberdeen Campus, Aberdeen, AB24 3UB, Site Svcs Mgr: Ms Julie Oates (01224-272601; *fax:* 01224-273893; *email:* lawlib@abdn.ac.uk); MEDICAL LIB (see **S7**); EDU LIB (see **S6**); SPECIAL COLLNS & ARCHVS (see **A3**)
Entry: no charge for ref access; borrowing privileges through membership (incl external) only *Open:* term: Mon-Fri 0900-2200, Sat 0900-2200, Sun 1300-2200; vac: Mon-Thu 0900-2000, Fri 0900-1700, Sat 0900-1300
Subj: all subjs; undergrad; postgrad *Collns: Bks & Pamphs:* EDC; O'Dell Colln (railway); Sc Colln (hist of sci); MacBean Colln (Jacobite); Biesenthal Colln (Hebraica); Gregory Colln (hist of sci & medicine) *Archvs:* George Washington Wilson Photographic Archv (over 40000 glass plate negs); NAS-recognised repository for North East Scotland *Co-op Schemes:* BLDSC, NLSLS (SUC), Grampian Info
Equip: m-readers, m-cameras, m-printers, video viewers, fax, copiers, clr copiers, digital copiers, computers (incl internet & CD-ROM) *Online:* various (staff time + connect costs) *Svcs:* info, ref, binding svc, Business Info Svc
Stock: bks/1000000; periodcls/5800; photos/446000; slides/2000; pamphs/27500; maps/6000; m-forms/800; audios/1200; videos/300; archvs/c4000
Classn: DDC *Auto Sys:* Dynix
Pubns: George Washington Wilson photographic bklet series (12 titles, £4.95 each); Vanishing Edinburgh (£12.95); Vanishing Glasgow (£12.95); The Sparkling Cage (£6.95); Rare & Fair (£2.95)
Staff: 66.2 total (all sites)

S6

Aberdeen University, Education Library
(formerly Northern Coll of Edu)
Hilton Pl, Aberdeen, AB24 4FA (01224-283571; *fax:* 01224-283655)
Email: edulib@abdn.ac.uk

Chief: Site Svcs Mgr: Mrs Kit Corall MA, MCLIP (k.corall@abdn.ac.uk) *Other Snr Staff:* Faculty Info Adviser: Ms Claire Molloy (c.a.l.molloy@abdn.ac.uk)
Entry: staff & students of Univ; otherwise ref only *Open:* term: Mon-Fri 0845-2130, Sat 0930-1230; vac: Mon-Fri 0900-1700
Subj: edu *Co-op Schemes:* BLDSC
Classn: DDC *Auto Sys:* Dynix *Staff:* 10 in total

S7

Aberdeen University, Medical Library
Polwarth Bldg, Medical School, Foresterhill, Aberdeen, AB25 2ZD (01224-552488; *fax:* 01224-685157)
Email: medlib@abdn.ac.uk
Internet: http://www.abdn.ac.uk/diss/library/geninfo/sites/medical/

Gov Body: Univ of Aberdeen (see **S5**) *Chief:* Site Svcs Mgr: Mr Keith Nockels MA, DipLib, MCLIP *Other Snr Staff:* Faculty Info Consultant: Mrs Wendy Pirie MA, DipLib
Assoc Libs: ROYAL CORNHILL HOSP LIB, Clerkseat Bldg, Royal Cornhill Hosp, Aberdeen, AB25 225
Open: Mon-Thu 0845-2200, Fri 0845-2000, Sat 0900-1700, Sun 1300-2200
Subj: medicine; social sci; medical tech *Collns: Bks & Pamphs:* pre-1900 medical bks
Equip: m-reader, fax, video viewer, 7 copiers, clr copier, 94 computers (all with wd-proc & internet, 6 with CD-ROM), 2 rooms for hire *Disabled:* 2 PCs with large screen print *Svcs:* info, ref, biblio
Stock: bks/158100; periodcls/800; pamphs/2270; AVs/200
Classn: DDC *Auto Sys:* Dynix
Staff: Libns: 2 *Non-Prof:* 8.3 FTE

S8

Fisheries Research Services, Marine Laboratory Library
PO Box 101, 375 Victoria Rd, Aberdeen, AB9 8DB (01224-295391; *fax:* 01224-295511)
Email: heaths@marlab.ac.uk

Chief: Libn: Ms Sarah P. Heath BA(Hons) *Dep:* Asst Libn: Ms Elizabeth Richardson
Assoc Libs: FISHERIES RSRCH SVCS (see **S1803**)
Entry: adv appt, ref only *Open:* Mon-Fri 0830-1700
Subj: fisheries; fish cultivation; marine biology; oceanography; aquaculture; fishing methods & tech
Collns: Bks & Pamphs: Ogilvy Colln; extensive specialist pamph colln *Other:* maps & charts; ICES papers; cruise reports *Co-op Schemes:* ILL
Equip: m-printer, fax, copier, computer (incl CD-ROM) *Online:* Dialog, CORDIS, ASFA
Stock: bks/20000; periodcls/1200; pamphs/18000
Classn: UDC
Pubns: Marine Laboratory Annual Review; Freshwater Fisheries Laboratory Annual Review; Scottish Fisheries Rsrch Reports; Scottish Fisheries Info pamphs; Salmon Farming (price on appl)
Staff: Libns: 3 *Non-Prof:* 5

S9

Macaulay Land Use Research Institute Library
Craigiebuckler, Aberdeen, AB15 8QH (01224-318611; *fax:* 01224-311556)
Email: L.Robertson@macaulay.ac.uk
Internet: http://www.macaulay.ac.uk/

Aberdeen ▼ **Aldeburgh**

Special Libraries

(Macaulay Land Use Rsrch Inst Lib cont)
Chief: Libn: Mrs Lorraine Robertson BA, DipEd
Dep: Ms Jean MacGuinness BLib
Entry: adv appt **Open:** Mon-Fri 0845-1645
Subj: soil sci; geol; agric; ecology; forestry; environmental sci **Collns:** Bks & Pamphs: 10000 reprints **Co-op Schemes:** BLDSC, BRISC, SALG, Grampian Info
Equip: 3 m-readers, m-film reader, m-film copier, fax, copier, 4 computers (incl wd-proc, CD-ROM & internet), 2 rooms for hire **Online:** Web of Science, Biosis, CAB Abstracts, Agdex **Svcs:** info, ref, biblio
Stock: bks/15000; periodcls/200
Classn: UDC **Auto Sys:** Sydney Plus
Staff: Libns: 1.5

S10 🎓 🏛
Marischal Museum, Library and Archive
Marischal Coll, Univ of Aberdeen, Aberdeen, AB10 1YS (01224-274301; *fax:* 01224-274302)
Email: museum@abdn.ac.uk
Internet: http://www.abdn.ac.uk/marischal_museum/

Gov Body: Aberdeen Univ **Chief:** Snr Curator: Mr Neil Curtis MA, MLitt, AMA, AIFA, FSAScot
Entry: *Museum:* open access; *Archvs:* by appt only **Open:** Mon-Fri 1000-1700, Sun 1400-1700
Subj: local study (North East Scotland); geog; hist **Collns:** Archvs: records associated with Museum
Svcs: info, ref
Stock: bks/c2000; archvs/2 cubic m
Classn: by object number or donor
Staff: Other Prof: 3.5

S11 ✒
Mobil North Sea Ltd, Technical Library
Grampian House, Union Row, Aberdeen, AB10 1SA (01224-855325; *fax:* 01224-855300)

Gov Body: ExxonMobil **Chief:** Records Co-ordinator: Miss Jackie Adam **Dep:** Lib Asst: Mrs Rosemary Doherty
Entry: ref only, by adv appt **Open:** Mon-Fri 0800-1700
Subj: tech; oil industry **Collns:** Bks & Pamphs: BSI; API; ASME Standards **Co-op Schemes:** BLDSC, Grampian Info, ILL
Equip: m-reader, m-printer, copier, clr copier, fax, computers (incl wd-procs, internet & CD-ROM)
Svcs: ref
Stock: bks/1452; periodcls/50
Classn: UDC **Staff:** Non-Prof: 5

S12 🎓
The Robert Gordon University Library
Georgina Scott Sutherland Lib, Garthdee Rd, Aberdeen, AB10 7QE (01224-263450; *fax:* 01224-263455)
Email: library@rgu.ac.uk
Internet: http://www.rgu.ac.uk/library/

Gov Body: Governors of Robert Gordon Univ **Chief:** Chief Libn: Mrs Elaine Dunphy **Dep:** Dep Libn: Mrs Diane Devine **Other Snr Staff:** Snr Libns: Dr Susan Copeland & Ms Judith Brown

Assoc Libs: GEORGINA SCOTT SUTHERLAND LIB, addr as above; ST ANDREW ST LIB, 1 St Andrew St, Aberdeen, AB25 1HG, Site Libn: Mr Keith Fraser (01224-262888; *fax:* 01224-262889; *email:* saslibrary@rgu.ac.uk)
Entry: external & corporate membership available
Open: *Georgina Scott Sutherland Lib:* term: Mon-Thu 0900-2130, Fri 0900-1700, Sat-Sun 1000-1700; vac: Mon-Thu 0900-2100, Fri 0900-1700, Sat-Sun 1300-1700; *St Andrew St Lib:* term: Mon-Thu 0900-2130, Fri 0900-1715, Sat 1000-1645, Sun 1300-2030; vac: Mon-Tue, Thu-Fri 0900-1700, Wed 0900-2100, Sun 1300-1700
Subj: undergrad; postgrad; *Georgina Scott Sutherland Lib:* arch; art; surveying; design; business; media; mgmt; public admin; law; nursing; midwifery; psy; health mgmt; sociology; health edu; occupational therapy; physiotherapy; radiotherapy; hospitality mgmt; consumer studies; social sci; psy; food sci; textiles; tourism; travel; leisure; *St Andrew St Lib:* sci; eng; maths; tech; computing; pharmacy; food sci **Collns:** Bks & Pamphs: BSI; Soc of Petroleum Papers (from 1955); Company Reports; Arch & Construction Pamphs colln; antiquarian colln on arch & landscape arch **Other:** slide colln on art, arch & design **Co-op Schemes:** Grampian Info, BLDSC, ILL
Equip: m-readers, m-printer, video viewers, fax, copiers, clr copier, computers (incl internet & CD-ROM) **Disabled:** Kurzweil 3000, TextHelp Read & Write, Inspiration, ZoomText, Wordswork, CCTV Clearview Spectrum **Online:** various resources; see web site for full list
Stock: bks/202509; periodcls/4220; slides/c117000
Classn: DDC **Auto Sys:** Sirsi
Staff: Libns: 24 Non-Prof: 32 **Exp:** £712371 (1999-2000); £761177 (2000-01)

S13 🎓
Rowett Research Institute, Reid Library
Greenburn Rd, Bucksburn, Aberdeen, AB21 9SB (01224-712751; *fax:* 01224-715349)
Email: library@rri.sari.ac.uk
Internet: http://www.rri.sari.ac.uk/

Type: rsrch inst **Chief:** Snr Libn: Ms Mary W. Mowat BA, MLib, MCLIP
Entry: ref only, adv appt **Open:** Mon-Fri 0900-1730
Subj: at postgrad level: life sci; nutrition **Collns:** Archvs: relating to hist of the Inst; Boyd-Orr Archv **Co-op Schemes:** BLDSC, Grampian Info
Equip: m-reader, copier (5p), 5 computers (incl 2 wd-proc & 1 internet) **Online:** Dialog (not available to external users) **Svcs:** info, ref, biblio
Stock: bks/35000; periodcls/120; pamphs/10000; m-forms/50 **Acqs Offcr:** Snr Libn, as above
Classn: LC **Auto Sys:** SydneyPlus
Staff: Libns: 1 Non-Prof: 1

S14 ✒
Scottish Enterprise Grampian, Small Business Gateway Information Centre
(formerly Aberdeen Business Shop, Ref Lib)
27 Albyn Pl, Aberdeen, AB10 1DB (01224-575100; *fax:* 01224-580055)
Email: sbg-grampian@scotent.co.uk

Gov Body: Scottish Enterprise Grampian **Chief:** Ms Celia Hukins
Entry: provides info svcs to businesses in Grampian area, mainly via tel; visitor access to lib restricted due to space limitations
Subj: business; company info **Collns:** Bks & Pamphs: Grampian Enterprise & Scottish Enterprise Grampian pubns **Other:** Scottish companies database; various CD-ROMs
Equip: copier (free), computer (free) **Svcs:** info, ref

Classn: DDC **Auto Sys:** DBTextworks
Staff: Libns: 4 Other Prof: 2 Non-Prof: 1

Aberystwyth

S15 ✚
Bronglais Hospital Library Services
Bronglais Genl Hosp, Aberystwyth, Ceredigion, SY23 1ER (01970-635803; *fax:* 01970-635386)
Email: tricia.chapman@ceredigion-tr.wales.nhs.uk

Gov Body: Ceredigion & Mid Wales NHS Trust **Chief:** Lib Svcs Mgr: Ms Patricia Chapman MCLIP
Entry: lending to employees of Trust; others ref only **Open:** Mon-Fri 0900-1700
Subj: health svcs; medicine; nursing; allied health; genl practice **Co-op Schemes:** BLDSC, AWHL, AWHILES, BMA
Equip: fax, 2 copiers, video viewer, 8 computers (all with wd-proc, internet & CD-ROM) **Online:** HOWIS (Health of Wales Info Svc)
Stock: bks/4000; periodcls/100; pamphs/600; videos/100
Classn: NLM **Auto Sys:** Libero
Staff: Libns: 1 Non-Prof: 0.5 **Exp:** £16000 (1999-2000)

S16 🎓
Institute of Grassland and Environmental Research, Stapledon Library and Information Service
Plas Gogerddan, Aberystwyth, Ceredigion, SY23 3EB (01970-823000; *fax:* 01970-828357)
Email: igerlib.igerlib-wpbs@bbsrc.ac.uk
Internet: http://www.iger.bbsrc.ac.uk/igerweb/

Type: rsrch inst **Chief:** Inst Libn: Mr Steve Smith BSc, DipLib, MCLIP **Dep:** Collns Libn: Libn: Mr Paul Drew BLib, MPhil
Assoc Libs: IGER, NORTH WYKE RSRCH STATION LIB, Okehampton, Devon, EX20 2SB
Entry: by appt **Open:** *Stapledon:* Mon-Fri 0900-1700; *North Wyke:* Mon-Fri 1000-1300
Subj: sci; agric; botany; biology; environmental sci **Collns:** Bks & Pamphs: Stapledon Colln (works of Sir G. Stapledon, founder of WPBS) **Other:** herbarium (c300 grasses); Flora Colln (c300 monographs) **Co-op Schemes:** BLDSC, BBSRC ILL sys
Equip: copier (5p), 3 computers (all with wd-proc, internet & CD-ROM) **Online:** STN **Svcs:** info, ref, biblio
Stock: bks/c40000; periodcls/c300; slides/c1000; maps/c600
Classn: UDC
Pubns: Annual Report (free); IGER Innovations (£10); IGER Technical Review (irregular, price on appl)
Staff: Libns: 1 Non-Prof: 2

S17 🎓 🙏
United Theological College Library
King St, Aberystwyth, Ceredigion, SY23 2LT (01970-624574; *fax:* 01970-626350)
Email: esl998@aber.ac.uk

Gov Body: Presbyterian Church of Wales **Chief:** Libn: The Revd J.T. Williams MA, PhD **Dep:** Part-time Cataloguer: S.L. Hughes
Entry: by arrangement **Open:** term: Mon-Sat 0900-1600; vac: by arrangement
Subj: local study (Welsh hist & lit); religion **Collns:** Other: Ellis Lib (19C colln) **Co-op Schemes:** SWALCAP, ILL
Equip: m-reader, copier, computer (with internet), room for hire
Stock: bks/70000; periodcls/50
Classn: LC **Staff:** Libns: 1 Other Prof: 1

S18

University of Wales Aberystwyth, Hugh Owen Library

Penglais Campus, Aberystwyth, Ceredigion, SY23 3DZ (01970-622391; *fax:* 01970-622404)
Email: library@aber.ac.uk
Internet: http://www.aber.ac.uk/

Chief: Dir of Info Svcs: Dr Mike Hopkins BA, PhD, MCLIP *Dep:* Asst Dir: Mr Roger Matthews BSc
Assoc Libs: THOMAS PARRY LIB (see **S19**); OLD COLL LIB, King St, Aberystwyth, SY23 3AX (01970-622130); PHYSICAL SCIS LIB, Physical Scis Bldg, Penglais, Aberystwyth, SY23 3BZ (01970-622407)
Open: term: Mon-Thu 0900-2200, Fri 0900-1830, Sat-Sun 1200-1800; vac: Mon-Fri 0900-1730
Subj: all subjs; undergrad; postgrad *Collns: Bks & Pamphs:* Sir John Rhys Bequest (Celtic studies, 1916, c3000 vols, incorporated within the Lib's Celtic Colln); George Powell Colln (19C English & French Lit, fine art & music); James Camden Hotten Colln; Horton Colln (early ch's bks); Appleton Colln (Victorian printing & binding); Rudler Colln of Pamphs (geol); Duff Colln of Pamphs (classics); David de Lloyd Papers (Welsh folksongs); Lily Newton Papers (water pollution); Thomas Webster Letters (19C geol); British Soc of Rheology Lib; League of Nations & UN documents
Co-op Schemes: BLDSC, WALIA, UK Libs Plus & others
Equip: m-reader, m-printer, video viewer, copiers, clr copier, computers (incl wd-proc, internet & CD-ROM) *Disabled:* Kurzweil *Online:* numerous svcs
Svcs: info, ref, biblio
Stock: bks/700000; periodcls/4000
Classn: LC *Auto Sys:* Voyager

S19

University of Wales Aberystwyth, Thomas Parry Library

Llanbadarn Fawr, Aberystwyth, Ceredigion, SY23 3AS (01970-622417; *fax:* 01970-622190)
Email: parrylib@aber.ac.uk
Internet: http://www.inf.aber.ac.uk/tpl/

Gov Body: Univ of Wales Aberystwyth *Chief:* Librarian-in-Charge: Mr A.J. Clark BSocSc, DipLib, MCLIP
Assoc Libs: subsidiary of HUGH OWEN LIB (see **S18**)
Open: term: Mon-Thu 0900-2100, Fri 0900-1930, Sat 1200-1800; vac: Mon-Fri 0900-1730
Subj: all subjs; librarianship; info sci; mgmt; computing; media studies; agric; countryside mgmt; equine studies *Collns: Bks & Pamphs:* Appleton Colln (19C clr printing, c450 items); Oliver Simon Colln (fine printing); Whittinghams Colln (19C printing); Horton Colln (early ch's bks, c800 vols); Rare Bks Colln; Welsh Colln *Archvs:* Coll Farm records *Other:* map colln; press cuttings; theses *Co-op Schemes:* BLDSC, WRLS
Equip: m-readers, video viewers, copier, computers (incl CD-ROM)
Stock: bks/110000; periodcls/800; photos/2000; maps/300; m-forms/20000; audios/2500; videos/500
Classn: DDC *Auto Sys:* Libertas
Pubns: Lib Guide (Welsh & English); Resources & Svcs: A Brief Guide (Welsh & English); Aberystwyth & Dist Lib Resources
Staff: Libns: 3.5 *Non-Prof:* 6

S20

Welsh Books Council (Cyngor Llyfrau Cymru), Library

Castell Brychan, Aberystwyth, Ceredigion, SY23 2JB (01970-624151; *fax:* 01970-625385)
Email: wbc.children@cllc.org.uk
Internet: http://www.cllc.org.uk/

Chief: Dir: Miss Gwerfyl Pierce Jones
Assoc Libs: CHILDREN'S BKS DEPT, Head of Dept: Miss Menna Lloyd Williams
Entry: by appt *Open:* Mon-Fri 0900-1730
Subj: Welsh lang & Welsh interest children's bks (bks publ within the last 10 years)
Stock: bks/4000

Abingdon

S21

UKAEA Fusion Library

E6 Culham, Abingdon, Oxfordshire, OX14 3DB (01235-463347; *fax:* 01235-464385)
Email: helen.bloxham@ukaea.org.uk
Internet: http://www.ukaea.org.uk/

Gov Body: UK Atomic Energy Authority *Chief:* Lib Mgr: Miss Helen Bloxham MCLIP *Dep:* Asst: Ms Wendy Coombes
Entry: open to membership of contributing orgs
Open: Mon-Fri 0815-1630
Subj: tech
Equip: m-reader, m-printer, copier, fax, computers (incl wd-proc & CD-ROM) *Online:* EINS *Svcs:* info, ref, biblio, translation
Stock: bks/10000; periodcls/250; pamphs/3000; m-forms/10000
Classn: UDC *Staff: Libns:* 1 *Non-Prof:* 1 *Exp:* £90000 (1999-2000); £100000 (2000-01)

Accrington

S22

Accrington and Rossendale College Libraries

Sandy Ln, Accrington, Lancashire, BB5 2AW (01254-354041; *fax:* 01254-354151)
Internet: http://www.accross.ac.uk/LRC/

Chief: Head of Student Support Svcs: Mrs Ann M. Pilkington BA(Hons), PGCE *Dep:* Snr Libn: Ms Margery Airey MCLIP
Assoc Libs: RAWTENSTALL CENTRE LIB, Haslingden Rd, Rawtenstall, Lancashire, BB4 6RA (01254-354239)
Entry: staff & students *Open: Sandy Lane:* term: Mon-Thu 0845-2000, Fri 0845-1600; vac: Mon-Thu 0900-1630, Fri 0900-1600; *Rawtenstall:* term: Mon-Tue, Thu 0900-1630, Wed 0900-1900, Fri 0900-1600; vac: closed
Subj: most academic subjs; *Sandy Lane:* edu; business; sociology; cultural studies; statistics; tourism & leisure; construction; hotel & catering; motor vehicle studies; interior design; *Rawtenstall:* media; performing arts; hair & beauty *Co-op Schemes:* ILL
Equip: m-reader, copiers, clr copier, 45 computers (incl internet & CD-ROM), scanning facilities *Disabled:* 2 large screen PCs with Super Nova software, print enlarger *Online:* Infotrac Onefile, KnowUK, EBSCO
Stock: bks/c30000
Classn: DDC *Auto Sys:* Heritage
Pubns: various guides & leaflets

Addlestone

S23

Veterinary Laboratories Agency Library

New Haw, Addlestone, Surrey, KT15 3NB (01932-357314; *fax:* 01932-357608)
Email: enquiries@vla.defra.gsi.gov.uk

Gov Body: Dept for Environment, Food & Rural Affairs (see **S1110**) *Chief:* Chief Libn: Mrs Heather Hulse BA(Hons) *Dep:* Dep Libn: Miss Melanie French BA(Hons), PGDip

Entry: ref only, by appt *Open:* Mon-Fri 0930-1630
Subj: veterinary sci & medicine *Collns: Other:* full set of staff papers *Co-op Schemes:* BLDSC, LASER, SASLIC, AHIS
Equip: m-reader, m-printer, fax, 2 copiers, computers (incl wd-proc & 2 CD-ROM) *Online:* Dialog *Svcs:* info, ref, biblio, indexing, translation
Stock: bks/60000; periodcls/750; slides/3000; pamphs/2000; videos/30
Classn: Barnard *Auto Sys:* CAIRS LMS/IMS
Staff: Libns: 4 *Non-Prof:* 6

Airdrie

S24

Monklands Hospital Library

Monkscourt Ave, Airdrie, Lanarkshire, ML6 0JS (01236-748748; *fax:* 01236-713105)
Email: janet.jackson@laht.scot.nhs.uk

Gov Body: Monklands Hosp NHS Trust *Chief:* Libn: Ms Janet McLeod
Entry: ref & lending to hosp staff only *Open:* Mon-Thu 0900-1700, Fri 0900-1630; open 24 hrs for study
Subj: medicine; nursing; allied health sci; admin *Co-op Schemes:* SHINE, ILL
Equip: video viewer, copier, computers (incl wd-proc, internet & CD-ROM) *Online:* CINAHL, Medline, Embase, Cochrane
Stock: bks/4930; periodcls/102; slides/820; videos/52
Classn: NLM *Staff: Libns:* 1 *Non-Prof:* 1

Aldeburgh

S25

The Britten-Pears Library

The Red House, Golf Ln, Aldeburgh, Suffolk, IP15 5PZ (01728-451700; *fax:* 01728-453076)
Email: bpl@britten-pears.co.uk
Internet: http://www.britten-pears.co.uk/

Gov Body: The Britten-Pears Foundation *Chief:* Libn: Dr Christopher Grogan BMus, PhD, DipLIS (c.grogan@britten-pears.co.uk) *Other Snr Staff:* Ms Judith Tydeman MA, MArAd
Assoc Libs: THE HOLST LIB, Britten-Pears School for Advanced Music Studies, The Maltings, Snape, Suffolk, Curator: Mr Andrew Plant (lending lib for students attending the school)
Entry: prior appt *Open:* Mon-Fri 1000-1300, 1415-1715
Subj: music, esp works of Benjamin Britten & Peter Pears *Collns: Archvs:* Benjamin Britten's MSS (some on loan from British Lib – see **L1**); Britten's colln of printed music; Britten's personal papers (incl correspondence); printer's copies, proofs & early eds of Britten's works; Peter Pears' colln of printed music; Pears' personal papers (incl correspondence); English Opera Group/English Music Theatre Company Archvs; MSS of works of other composers, incl: Bax; Bedford; L. Berkeley; M. Berkeley; Bridge; Crosse; Maxwell Davies; C. Armstrong Gibbs; Greene; Harvey; Henze; G. Holst; I. Holst; Knussen; Lehmann; Lutoławski; Maconchy; C. Matthews; D. Matthews; Maw; Moeran; Nash; Oldham; Quilter; Rainier; Saxton; Seiber; Shostokovich; Stanford; Tippett; Turnage; Wier; Wellesz; Williamson; literary MSS, incl those of: W.H. Auden; Ronald Duncan; E.M. Forster; Thomas Hardy; Wilfred Owen; Myfanwy Piper; William Plomer; Edith Sitwell; materials on English song (16C-date); Julian Herbage material relating to Thomas Arne *Other:* extensive collns of audios & videos; archvs of press cuttings & programmes; photographic archvs (all chiefly relating to Britten & Pears) *Co-op Schemes:* BLDSC
Equip: 2 m-readers, video viewer, copier *Online:* online catalogue (see web site above) *Svcs:* info, ref, biblio

Special Libraries

Aldeburgh
▼
Armagh

(The Britten-Pears Lib cont)
Stock: various bks, periodcls, photos, m-forms, audios, videos & archvs
Classn: own **Auto Sys:** MikroMARC
Pubns: Benjamin Britten: A Catalogue of the Published Works; Britten & the Far East: Asian Influences in the Music of Benjamin Britten; Britten's Gloriana: Essays & Sources; A Britten Sourcebook; Music of Forty Festivals: A List of Works Performed at Aldeburgh Festivals from 1948-1987; The Making of 'Peter Grimes'; Travel Diaries of Peter Pears: 1936-1978; On Mahler & Britten: Essays in Honour of Donald Mitchell on his 70th Birthday; Prince of Hesse Memorial Lectures series
Staff: Libns: 1 Other Prof: 1 Non-Prof: 4

Aldershot

S26
Army Library Service, Prince Consort's Library
Knollys Rd, Aldershot, Hampshire, GU11 1PS (01252-349381; *fax:* 01252-349382)
Email: pcl@dera.gov.uk

Gov Body: Army Lib Svc (see **S995**)
Entry: ref only, adv appt **Open:** Mon-Thu 0900-1700, Fri 0900-1630
Subj: military sci; military theory; strategy; tactics; military eng; military hist; military tech; military life; recent conflicts; internatl relations; politics; geog; travel; hist **Collns:** Bks & Pamphs: military hist colln of Prince Albert; Army Lists; Navy Lists; Air Force Lists; Official Histories; London Gazettes; Regimental Histories **Co-op Schemes:** ILL
Equip: computers (incl CD-ROM) **Online:** MSLS (Military Studies Lib Svc)
Stock: bks/65000; periodcls/120; maps/100; CD-ROMs/20

Alloa

S27
Clackmannan College of Further Education, Learning Resource Services
Branshill Rd, Alloa, Clackmannanshire, FK10 3BT (01259-220512; *fax:* 01259-722879)
Email: learning@clacks.ac.uk
Internet: http://www.clacks.ac.uk/

Gov Body: Clackmannan Coll Board of Mgmt
Chief: Learning Resource Offcr: Mrs Margo Johnston BA, MCLIP (margo.johnston@clacks. ac.uk)
Open: term: Mom, Wed, Fri 0845-1630, Tue, Thu 0845-2030; vac: Mon-Fri 0845-1630
Subj: all subjs; genl; undergrad **Co-op Schemes:** BLDSC, NLSLS
Equip: 2 video viewers, fax, copier, 26 computers (all with wd-proc, internet & CD-ROM) **Online:** Proquest Learning News **Svcs:** info, ref, biblio, indexing, abstracting
Stock: bks/8000; periodcls/80; videos/100
Classn: DDC **Auto Sys:** Heritage
Staff: Libns: 2 Non-Prof: 2.5

S28
Scottish Police College Library
Tulliallan Castle, Kincardine, Alloa, Clackmannan-shire, FK10 4BE (01259-732073/29; *fax:* 01259-732285)
Internet: http://www.tulliallan.police.uk/

Gov Body: Scottish Exec **Chief:** Libn: Miss Polly St Aubyn MCLIP
Entry: req for permission to obtain access to lib must be made in writing to the Dir of the Coll
Open: Mon-Thu 0930-2000, Fri 0830-1530
Subj: criminal law; police studies; mgmt; politics; econ; criminology **Collns:** Archvs: materials relating to the hist of the Scottish Police Svc; Tulliallan Castle Estate Archv **Co-op Schemes:** BLDSC
Equip: m-reader, video viewer, copier, computers (incl wd-proc & internet)
Stock: bks & pamphlets/200 linear m; periodcls/ 134 linear m, 239 current titles; videos/150
Classn: UDC, Bramshill Scheme **Auto Sys:** Status **Staff:** Libns: 2

Alnwick

S29
Sanofi-Synthelabo Research Library
Willowburn Ave, Alnwick, Northumberland, NE66 2JH (01665-608300; *fax:* 01665-608315)

Entry: private company rsrch lib; not open to public
Subj: sci; maths; tech
Equip: copiers, computers (with wd-proc, internet & CD-ROM) **Online:** Datastar, Dialog, STN **Svcs:** info, ref, biblio
Stock: bks/2500; periodcls/150
Classn: UDC **Auto Sys:** own
Staff: Libns: 1 Other Prof: 1 Non-Prof: 2

Alton

S30
Oates Memorial Library and Museum and Gilbert White Museum
The Wakes, High St, Selborne, Alton, Hampshire, GU34 3JH (01420-511275; *fax:* 01420-511040)

Gov Body: Museum Trustees **Chief:** Museum Sec: Mrs Natalie E. Mees MA
Entry: adv appt **Open:** Mon-Fri 1100-1700
Subj: local study (Hampshire, relating to Gilbert White); sci; geog (East Africa, Antarctica) **Collns:** Bks & Pamphs: eds of "Nat Hist of Selborne" by Gilbert White; bks etc relating to Gilbert White & the Oates family **Archvs:** Oates family papers; White family papers
Equip: copier **Svcs:** info, ref
Stock: bks/2500; photos/some; pamphs/80
Classn: DDC **Staff:** Other Prof: 1

Ambleside

S31
Armitt Library and Museum Centre, Ambleside
Rydal Rd, Ambleside, Cumbria, LA22 9BL (01539-431212; *fax:* 01539-431313)
Email: mail@armitt.com
Internet: http://www.armitt.com/

Gov Body: The Armitt Trust **Chief:** Curator: Miss Michelle Kelly BA(Hons) **Other Snr Staff:** Custodian: Mr Ian Rollins
Entry: ref only; adv appt for material in archv store
Open: Mon-Fri 1000-1230, 1330-1600

Subj: Cumbria: local studies; nat hist; mycology; local art & artists; lit (local authors) **Collns:** Bks & Pamphs: guide bks to the Lakes (1750-1900); Fell & Rock Club Colln **Archvs:** Charlotte Mason Coll Archv; John Ruskin papers; papers relating to Ambleside
Equip: copier (20p per sheet) **Disabled:** chairlift to lib **Officer-in-Charge:** Custodian, as above
Stock: bks/10500; photos/c15000; maps/c150; archvs/c1000 MSS **Acqs Offcr:** Curator, as above
Classn: DDC, own **Auto Sys:** Modes for Windows
Staff: Other Prof: 1 Non-Prof: 25

S32
Freshwater Biological Association Library
(shared facility with CEH Windermere Laboratory)
The Ferry House, Far Sawrey, Ambleside, Cumbria, LA22 0LP (015394-42468; *fax:* 015394-46914)
Email: idm@ceh.ac.uk
Internet: http://www.fba.org.uk/Library/

Gov Body: joint facility shared by the Freshwater Biological Assoc & Centre for Ecology & Hydrology (see **S1786**) **Chief:** Libn: Mr Ian McCulloch
Other Snr Staff: Membership & Info Offcr: Dr Karen Rouen PhD (kjro@fba.org.uk)
Entry: any bona fide rsrcher with a specific non-profit rsrch need which cannot be easily met through their own org's resources may user the lib by adv appt **Open:** Mon-Thu 0830-1700, Fri 0830-1600
Subj: all aspects of freshwater ecology; freshwater biology; pollution; algology; invertebrate taxonomy; invertebrate ecology; microbiology; sediment & water chem; aquaculture; fisheries mgmt; hydro-logy; limnology; hydrobiology; phycology; aquatic microbiology; aquatic zoology; ichthyology; oceano-graphy; geog **Collns:** Bks & Pamphs: Fritsch Colln (illusts of freshwater algae); Leedale Colln (algal cytology)
Equip: fax, video viewer, copier, 2 computers (both with wd-proc, internet & CD-ROM) **Online:** Aquatic Sciences & Fisheries Abstracts, Science Citation Index, Water Resources Abstracts **Svcs:** info, ref, biblio, indexing, lit searches (fees, discounts for membs), document delivery
Stock: bks/c10000; periodcls/700+; maps/400; reprints & reports/c80000
Classn: in-house **Auto Sys:** Unicorn, CDS-ISIS
Staff: Libns: 2 Non-Prof: 1 FTE

S33
St Martin's College, Ambleside Library
Rydal Rd, Ambleside, Cumbria, LA22 9BB (015394-30274; *fax:* 015394-30371)
Email: amb.library@ucsm.ac.uk
Internet: http://www.ucsm.ac.uk/library/

Gov Body: St Martin's Coll **Chief:** Coll Libn: Mr David Brown **Dep:** Site Libn: Ms Lisa Bruce
Assoc Libs: HAROLD BRIDGES LIB (main lib, see **S886**); CARLISLE SITE LIB (see **S438**)
Entry: students of St Martin's Coll; external borrowers on payment of annual subscription
Open: term: Mon-Thu 0900-1945, Fri 0900-1715, Sat 1000-1545; vac: Mon-Fri 0900-1645
Subj: undergrad; local study (Cumbria local hist); edu; teaching; business; mgmt; accountancy; tourism; leisure mgmt; outdoor studies; environment **Collns:** Archvs: Charlotte Mason & P. Nell Archvs (held at Armitt Lib in Ambleside)
Equip: video viewer, copiers (A4/5p, A3/10p), 7 computers (incl 6 wd-proc, 6 internet & 1 CD-ROM) **Online:** Infotrac, SMART, CINAHL, BEI, Medline, ERIC, IBSS, Ingenta, SwetsNet Navigator, Zetoc, ASSIAnet, Newsbank, PSYCarticles, eBooks, LeisureTourism, European Business, PreMed, CommunityWise
Stock: bks/67000; periodcls/152; videos/60

Classn: Bliss *Auto Sys:* Talis
Staff: Libns: 2 *Other Prof:* 1 systems offcr *Non-Prof:* 6 *Exp:* £30000 (1999-2000); £30000 (2000-01)
Proj: new lib opening Jan 2003

S34 🏛️ 🎓
The Wordsworth Trust Library
Town End, Grasmere, Ambleside, Cumbria, LA22 9SH (01539-435544; *fax:* 01539-435748)
Email: enquiries@wordsworth.org.uk
Internet: http://www.wordsworth.org.uk/

Gov Body: The Wordsworth Trust *Chief:* Dir: Dr Robert Woof MA, DPhil *Dep:* Curator: Mr Jeffrey Cowton AMA
Entry: permission of trustees, adv appt *Open:* Mon-Fri 0930-1730, closed Xmas
Subj: arts (Romantic period), Lake Dist themes; lit; Romantic poets *Collns: Bks & Pamphs:* Lifetime Eds, critical works of 19C Romantic writers; bks owned & annotated by Wordsworth & other writers; Lake Dist guides, hists & works *Archvs:* major MS colln of Wordsworth, Coleridge & Wordsworth Circle; family papers of Wordsworth; significant autograph collns *Other:* paintings, drawings, prints from late 18C & 19C on Lake Dist themes; 19C photo archv
Equip: fax, video viewer, copier, computers (incl wd-proc, internet & CD-ROM)
Stock: bks/c8000; periodcls/5; photos/2000; illusts/60 paintings, 3000 prints & drawings; pamphs/1300; audios/500; archvs/32000 items
Classn: DDC (mod) *Auto Sys:* MODES for Windows
Pubns: exhib catalogues, incl: Walking to Paradise; Towards Tintern Abbey; John Keats; Romantic Icons; English Poetry 850-1850: The First Thousand Years; see pubns catalogue on web site
Staff: Other Prof: 7 *Non-Prof:* 20, incl PT & short-term; figs are for all staff, not just lib

Amersham

S35 ✚
South Buckinghamshire NHS Trust, Staff Library
Amersham Hosp, Whielden St, Amersham, Buckinghamshire, HP7 0JD
Email: aflo@amlib.demon.co.uk
Internet: http://www.wyclib.demon.co.uk/

Gov Body: South Buckinghamshire NHS Trust *Chief:* Staff Libn: Ms Ann Flood BA, MCLIP *Dep:* Lib Asst: Ms Diana Jones
Assoc Libs: CHILTERN MEDICAL LIB (see **S811**)
Entry: staff & students of South Buckinghamshire NHS Trust & Buckinghamshire Mental Health Trust; primary care staff in the area; nursing students at Univ of Luton *Open:* Mon-Fri 0900-1700; swipe card access for membs
Subj: medicine; nursing; psychiatry; psy; geriatrics
Equip: copier, computers (incl wd-proc, internet & CD-ROM) *Online:* Medline, Cochrane, Best Evidence, Embase Psychiatry, CINAHL, AMED, HMIC, BNI, RCN Bibliography, CareData, Bookfind
Svcs: info, ref, lit searches
Stock: bks/3600; periodcls/60
Classn: NLM *Staff: Libns:* 1 *Non-Prof:* 1

Andover

S36 🎓
Cricklade College, Learning Resources Centre
Charlton Rd, Andover, Hampshire, SP10 1EJ (01264-363311; *fax:* 01264-332088)
Internet: http://www.cricklade.ac.uk/

Gov Body: Cricklade Coll Corp *Chief:* Learning Resources Mgr: Ms R. Lynch BA, MA(Lib) *Dep:* Libns: Mrs C. Coleman BA, MA(Lib) & Mrs S. Smith BA, MCLIP
Entry: open to all students & staff of Coll; open to public with proof of ID & addr *Open:* term: Mon-Thu 0845-1900, Fri 0845-1630; vac: Mon-Fri 0930-1300
Subj: all subjs; GCSE; A level
Equip: video viewers, copier, computers (with internet & CD-ROM)
Stock: bks/23000; periodcls/80; maps/50; videos/60
Classn: DDC *Auto Sys:* CALM 2000 Plus
Staff: Libns: 3.5 *Non-Prof:* 1

Anstruther

S37 🗝️ 🏛️ 📷
The Scottish Fisheries Museum, Library and Photographic Archive
St Ayles, Harbourhead, Anstruther, Fife, KY10 3AB (01333-310628; *fax:* 01333-310628)
Email: andrew@scottish-fisheries.museum.org

Type: independent *Gov Body:* Scottish Fisheries Museum Trust Ltd *Chief:* Curator: Miss Linda McGowan MA, PGDip
Entry: ref only, adv appt *Open:* by appt Mon-Fri 1000-1700
Subj: Scotland: fisheries & associated industries
Collns: Bks & Pamphs: Scottish fishing industry; various fishing almanacs & other fishing related non-current periodcls *Archvs:* Miller Colln (plans & drawings, boat ledgers, cash bks, records, charts & office documents); other documents relating to all aspects of the Scottish fishing industry *Other:* photos & slides all relating to Scottish fishing industry; small audio & video colln
Equip: fax, copier, slide viewer *Svcs:* info, ref
Stock: bks/1500; periodcls/10; photos/10000+; slides/5000+; pamphs/50; audios/60; videos/60; maps & archvs still being catalogued
Staff: run by volunteers under direction of Museum Curator *Exp:* most bks acquired by donation

Antrim

S38 🎓 ✚
Antrim Healthcare Library
Fern House, Antrim Hosp, Antrim, BT41 2QB (028-9442-4232; *fax:* 028-9442-4496)
Email: AntrimHealthCare.Library@uh.n-i.nhs.uk

Gov Body: Queen's Univ of Belfast (see **S139**) *Chief:* Asst Libn: Mrs Mary Maguire BLS, MCLIP
Entry: open to all HPSS staff, particularly those in the Northern Health & Social Svcs Board; also open to those eligible to use the Queens Univ Lib *Open:* Mon, Wed 0900-1800, Tue, Thu 0900-1645, Fri 0900-1630
Subj: healthcare; nursing *Co-op Schemes:* ILL
Equip: copier (£1 per 20 copies), computers (incl 4 with wd-proc, 4 with internet & 4 with CD-ROM)
Svcs: info, ref
Stock: bks/5000; periodcls/40
Classn: LC *Auto Sys:* Talis
Staff: Libns: 1 *Non-Prof:* 3

Arbroath

S39 🎓
Angus College Library
Keptie Rd, Arbroath, Angus, DD11 3EA (01241-432600 x2200)
Email: library@angus.ac.uk
Internet: http://www.angus.ac.uk/

Chief: Learning Centre Mgr: Mr Charles Rosie MA
Dep: Learning Centre Administrator: Ms Cara Milne
Entry: staff & students of coll *Open:* term: Mon-Wed 0845-1900, Thu 0845-1700, Fri 0845-1630; vac: varies
Subj: genl; undergrad; further edu *Co-op Schemes:* ILL
Equip: video viewer, copier (5p per pg), computers (with internet & CD-ROM) *Disabled:* braille printer
Stock: bks/11674; periodcls/82; pamphs/1003; maps/123; videos/817
Classn: DDC *Auto Sys:* EASL
Staff: Libns: 1 *Non-Prof:* 1

Armagh

S40 🗝️ 🎓
Armagh Observatory Library
College Hill, Armagh, Northern Ireland, BT61 9DG (028-3752-2928; *fax:* 028-3752-7174)
Email: jmf@star.arm.ac.uk
Internet: http://www.arm.ac.uk/

Gov Body: Boards of Governors & Guardians *Chief:* Libn: Mr John McFarland BSc(Maths), BSc(Hons, Physics), MSc(Physics), MSc(Astronomy)
Entry: rsrch workers, adv appt *Open:* Mon-Fri 0900-1700 except Public/Bank Hols
Subj: astronomy; astrophysics; physics; maths
Collns: Bks & Pamphs: Thomas Romney Robinson Bk Colln (c200 vols); meteorological reports (1783 onwards) *Archvs:* MSS relating to founding, admin, governance, staffing of & rsrch at the Observatory (c1790-date) *Co-op Schemes:* BLDSC
Equip: m-reader, 2 copiers, fax, computers (incl wd-proc & CD-ROM) *Svcs:* info
Stock: bks/c18000; photos/c5000; slides/c1200
Classn: UDC
Pubns: Church, State & Astronomy in Ireland: 200 Years of Armagh Observatory (£7.50 + p&p); The Way to the Stars (£3 + p&p); Seeing Stars (£1 + p&p)
Staff: Other Prof: 1

S41 🎓 🏛️ 🙏
Armagh Public Library
43 Abbey St, Armagh, Northern Ireland, BT61 7DY (028-3752-3142; *fax:* 028-3752-4177)
Email: armroblib@aol.com
Internet: http://www.armaghrobinsonlibrary.org/

Gov Body: Governors & Guardians of the Lib *Chief:* Keeper: The Very Reverend Herbert Cassidy MA *Dep:* Asst Keeper: Ms Carol Conlin BA *Other Snr Staff:* Lib Adviser: Mr Harry Carson FCLIP, Hon FCLIP, FLAI; Curatorial Advisor: Ms Catherine McCullough, Curator of Armagh County Museum
Entry: ref only *Open:* Mon-Fri 0930-1300, 1400-1600
Subj: City, County & Diocese of Armagh: church hist; phil; religion; geog; hist *Collns: Bks & Pamphs:* c300 bks printed before 1640 *Archvs:* Armagh Corp records; Annals of Clonmacnoise; Church Lists; Clergy Lists *Other:* Rokeby Colln of prints; engravings (incl Piranesi)
Equip: copier, fax computers (incl wd-proc, internet & CD-ROM), room for hire *Officer-in-Charge:* Admin Offcr: Miss Lorraine Frazer *Svcs:* info, ref, biblio
Stock: bks/30000; periodcls/10; illusts/1000 prints & engravings; pamphs/2500; maps/20 *Acqs*
Offcr: Asst Keeper, as above
Auto Sys: local sys with public lib
Staff: Other Prof: 3

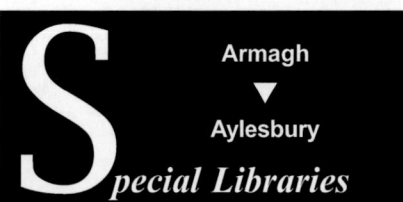

Special Libraries

Armagh
▼
Aylesbury

Cardinal Tomás Ó Fiaich Memorial Library

See CARDINAL TOMÁS Ó FIAICH MEMORIAL LIB & ARCHV (**A16**)

S42
Queen's University, Armagh Campus Library
39 Abbey St, Armagh, BT61 7EB (028-3751-0678; *fax:* 028-3751-0679)
Internet: http://www.armagh.qub.ac.uk/

Gov Body: Queen's Univ of Belfast (see **S139**)
Chief: User Svcs Libn: Ms Sue Mehrer (s.mehrer@qub.ac.uk) *Dep:* Lib Asst: Ms Colette Haughey (c.haughey@qub.ac.uk)
Entry: staff & students of Univ; adv appt for others *Open:* term: Mon-Tue 0900-2100, sat 0900-1300; vac: Mon-Fri 0900-1700
Subj: undergrad; postgrad; edu; social sci; econ; accounting; Irish studies; women's studies; gender studies; computing; mgmt; business studies; local studies *Collns: Bks & Pamphs:* Cardinal Daly Lib (theology, scripture, phil, Irish hist & culture, 9000 vols & 2000 periodcl issues)
Equip: copier (£1 per 20 copies), video viewer, 4 computers (with internet)

S43
Royal Irish Fusiliers Regimental Museum, Library and Archives
Sovereigns House, The Mall, Armagh, Northern Ireland, BT61 9DL (*tel & fax:* 028-3752-2911)
Email: amanda@rirfus-museum.freeserve.co.uk
Internet: http://www.rirfus-museum.freeserve.co.uk/

Chief: contact the Curator
Entry: adv appt *Open: Museum:* Mon-Fri 1000-1200, 13330-1600; also open Sat (Easter to end Aug) & on bank hols
Subj: military hist; regimental hist; regimental records *Collns: Archvs:* records of Royal Irish Fusiliers (former 87th & 89th Foot); records of Co Armagh militia (1793-1915); courts martial bk of Co Cavan militia (1855-65)

Arundel

S44
Duke of Norfolk's Library
Arundel Castle, Arundel, W Sussex, BN18 9AB (01903-882173; *fax:* 01903-884581)

Chief: Libn to His Grace The Duke of Norfolk: Dr J.M. Robinson, Maltravers Herald, MA, DPhil, DLitt, FSA
Entry: accredited scholars, adv written appt
Open: Tue-Wed 1000-1700
Subj: classics; arts; arch; religion; Catholicism; heraldry; topography; gardening; hortic; lit; biography; hist *Collns: Bks & Pamphs:* Catholic hist & Bibles; printed bks (15C-19C); clr plate folios; illuminated MSS *Archvs:* one of the most important private Family & Estate archvs: incl medieval deeds, Court Rolls, wills, later correspondence, arch drawings & maps & extensive estate papers

---

Equip: m-reader, fax, copier
Stock: bks/14000

Ascot

S45
Chartered Institute of Building, Library and Information Service
Englemere, King's Ride, Ascot, Berkshire, SL5 7TB (01344-630741; *fax:* 01344-630764)
Email: lis@ciob.org.uk
Internet: http://www.ciob.org.uk/

Chief: LIS Mgr: Ms Caroline Collier BA, MA
Entry: borrowing for membs only; non-membs by appt & subj to charge *Open:* Mon-Fri 0930-1630
Subj: construction; construction mgmt; site mgmt; contract law *Collns: Bks & Pamphs:* bldg law reports; construction law reports; Chartered Inst of Bldg pubns *Archvs:* bldg tech reps *Other:* Construction Mgmt Conference Proceedings (1970 onwards) *Co-op Schemes:* BLDSC
Equip: copier, computer (incl CD-ROM) *Svcs:* ref, lit searches
Stock: bks/12000; periodcls/42; audios/50; videos/160 *Acqs Offcr:* Libn: Mr Adrian Smith
Classn: UDC *Auto Sys:* CAIRS
Staff: Libns: 1 *Other Prof:* 1 *Non-Prof:* 2

S46
Civil Service College Library
Sunningdale Pk, Larch Ave, Ascot, Berkshire, SL5 0QE (01344-634286/307; *fax:* 01344-634118)
Email: chris.mallet@college-cmps.gsi.gov.uk

Gov Body: Civil Svc Coll Directorate, part of the Cabinet Office's Centre for Mgmt & Policy Studies (CMPS) *Chief:* Coll Libn: Mr Christopher J. Mallett MA, MCLIP
Entry: written appl, ref only *Open:* Mon-Thu 0830-1700, Fri 0830-1630 (open to 2300, but not staffed)
Subj: public admin *Co-op Schemes:* BLDSC, ILL
Equip: video viewers, fax, copier, computers (incl wd-proc, internet & CD-ROM), interactive video, CD-I *Disabled:* Kurzweil *Online:* Dialog, Parliament *Svcs:* info, ref, biblio
Stock: bks/25000; periodcls/250; videos/900
Classn: LBS *Auto Sys:* Heritage
Staff: Libns: 3 *Non-Prof:* 1

S47
The Steel Construction Institute, Library
Silwood Pk, Ascot, Berkshire, SL5 7QN (01344-623345; *fax:* 01344-622944)
Email: library@steel-sci.com
Internet: http://www.steel-sci.com/

Chief: Libn: Mrs Susan Zarywacz
Entry: adv appt, non-membs ref only *Open:* Mon-Fri 0900-1700
Subj: steel construction *Co-op Schemes:* BLDSC
Equip: fax, copier, computers (incl wd-proc & CD-ROM)
Stock: bks/6000; periodcls/60
Classn: UDC *Auto Sys:* SydneyPlus
Pubns: New Steel Construction (journal, £59 pa UK, £75 pa overseas)
Staff: Other Prof: 30 *Non-Prof:* 2

Ashford

S48
Ashford Library Railway Collection
Ashford Lib, Church Rd, Ashford, Kent, TN23 1QX (01233-620649; *fax:* 01233-620295)

Type: special colln held by public lib *Gov Body:* Kent County Council (see **P67**) *Chief:* Local Studies Libn: Mrs Fiona Hukins MA
Entry: public lib, free access *Open:* Mon-Tue, Thu 0930-1800, Wed 0930-1700, Fri 0930-1900, Sat 0900-1700
Subj: local studies (railways in Kent); railway hist; social efforts of railways; railway eng; railway arch
Collns: Bks & Pamphs: relating to railways in the South East of England from Essex, London round to Southampton via Reading *Archvs:* colln of South East Railways station plans under BR copyright; number of Southern Railways/BR Southern Region diagram bks *Other:* photo collns; Channel Tunnel colln (incl Rail Link material) *Co-op Schemes:* LASER
Equip: 3 m-readers, m-printer (A4/50p), 2 fax, copier (A4/10p, A3/15p), 13 computers (incl 10 with wd-proc & 11 with internet, printouts A4/10p) *Svcs:* info, ref
Stock: bks/c10000; periodcls/12; photos/c4000; slides/200; maps/180; audios/26; videos/250
Classn: DDC *Auto Sys:* DS
Pubns: Railways in the South East (£3.50)
Staff: Libns: 1 *Non-Prof:* 1 FTE

S49
Imperial College London, Wye Campus, The Kempe Centre Library
(formerly Wye College)
High St, Wye, Ashford, Kent, TN25 5AH (020-7594-2915; *fax:* 020-7594-2929)
Email: wyelibrary@imperial.ac.uk
Internet: http://www.imperial.ac.uk/library/

Gov Body: Imperial Coll London (see **S1180**)
Chief: Campus Lib Mgr: Miss E.S. Phelps MA, MLib (s.phelps@imperial.ac.uk) *Dep:* Dep Campus Lib Mgr: Mrs K.M. Knight BA(Hons), MA (k.m.knight@imperial.ac.uk)
Entry: ref only *Open:* term: Mon-Fri 0900-2145, Sat-Sun 1200-1745; hrs may be reduced during Coll vacs
Subj: social sci; econ; development studies; sci; agric; hortic; environment *Collns: Bks & Pamphs:* historical colln of early agric & hortic bks; EDC (selective) *Co-op Schemes:* BLDSC, Canterbury Circle of Libs
Equip: 4 m-readers, m-printer, fax, 3 video viewers, 5 copiers, computers (incl 3 with CD-ROM & 6 OPACs) *Online:* Dialog (Coll membs only)
Svcs: ref
Stock: bks/55000; periodcls/750
Classn: UDC *Auto Sys:* Unicorn
Staff: Libns: 3 *Non-Prof:* 2.5

S50
William Harvey Hospital, Education Centre Library
Kennington Rd, Willesborough, Ashford, Kent, TN24 0LZ (0233-616695; *fax:* 0233-613597)
Email: philip.hall@ekht.nhs.uk

Gov Body: East Kent Hosps NHS Trust *Chief:* Libn: Mr Philip Hall BA(Hons), PGDipLIS *Dep:* Lib & Info Offcr: Mrs E. Strachan
Assoc Libs: CLINICAL STUDIES LIB, Queen Elizabeth The Queen Mother Hosp (see **S1538**); LINACRE LIB, Kent & Canterbury Hosp (see **S408**); DOVER POSTGRAD MEDICAL CENTRE LIB, Buckland Hosp, Coombe Valley Rd, Dover, Kent, CT17 0HD, Postgrad Administrator: Mrs S. Dawson
Entry: employees of East Kent Hosps NHS Trust; NHS Acute & NHS Community staff working at the hosp or in the area; membs of Kent ambulance svc; others by prior appt *Open:* Mon-Thu 0900-1700, Fri 0900-1630
Subj: social sci; sci; tech; medicine; nursing; midwifery; healthcare mgmt *Collns: Bks & Pamphs:* William Harvey Historical Colln

---

Co-op Schemes: BLDSC, STRLIS, BMA, NULJ
Equip: copier, 9 computers (all with wd-proc, internet & CD-ROM) *Online:* various databases via KA24/Athens *Officer-in-Charge:* Knowledge Svcs Mgr: Mrs Rhiannon Cox
Stock: bks/c5000; periodcls/120 *Acqs Offcr:* Libn, as above
Classn: NLM *Auto Sys:* Librarian
Staff: Libns: 1 *Non-Prof:* 1.5

Ashington

S51

Northumberland College, Learning Resource Centre

College Rd, Ashington, Northumberland, NE63 9RG (01670-841200; *fax:* 01670-841201)
Email: fiona.middlemist@northland.ac.uk
Internet: http://www.northland.ac.uk/

Chief: Libn: Miss Fiona E. Middlemist BA, MSc(Econ), MCLIP
Assoc Libs: NORTHUMBERLAND COLL AT KIRKLEY HALL LRC
Entry: ref for genl public; students & staff of Coll have borrowing rights *Open:* term: Mon-Tue & Thu 0900-2100, Wed 0900-1700, Fri 0900-1600; vac: Mon-Thu 0900-1630, Fri 0900-1600
Subj: all subjs; genl; GCSE; A level; undergrad; vocational *Co-op Schemes:* BLDSC, NEMLAC, NRLB
Equip: m-reader, m-printer, 2 video viewers, 3 copiers, clr copier, 42 computers (incl 41 with wd-proc, 41 with internet & 41 with CD-ROM) *Svcs:* info, ref, biblio
Stock: bks/26000; periodcls/150; audios/200; videos/750; CD-ROMs/50
Classn: DDC *Auto Sys:* Heritage
Staff: Libns: 1 *Non-Prof:* 4.5 *Exp:* £40000 (1999-2000)

S52 ✚

Wansbeck Hospital Library

Edu Centre, Wansbeck Hosp, Woodhorn Ln, Ashington, Northumberland, NE63 9JJ (01670-521212; *fax:* 01670-529665)
Email: sarah.abernethy@ncl.ac.uk

Gov Body: Northumbria Healthcare NHS Trust
Chief: Libn: Ms Sarah Abernethy BA, DipLib, MCLIP
Assoc Libs: other Trust libs: HEXHAM GENL HOSP, RYDER POSTGRAD MEDICAL CENTRE LIB (see **S809**); NORTH TYNESIDE EDU CENTRE LIB (see **S1607**); NORTHUMBERLAND HEALTHCARE TRUST LIB (see **S1559**)
Entry: Northumbria Healthcare NHS Trust staff only *Open:* Mon-Fri 0900-1700
Subj: medicine *Co-op Schemes:* HLN, BLDSC
Equip: fax, copier (5p per pg), 5 computers (incl wd-proc, internet & CD-ROM) *Online:* CINAHL, Medline, Cochrane *Svcs:* info, ref
Stock: bks/4000; periodcls/90
Classn: DDC *Auto Sys:* SydneyPlus
Staff: Libns: 1 *Non-Prof:* 1

Ashton-under-Lyme

S53

Tameside College Library

Beaufort Rd, Ashton-under-Lyme, Lancashire, OL6 6NX (0161-908-6662)
Email: caroline.axon@tameside.ac.uk
Internet: http://www.tameside.ac.uk/lib/

Chief: Lib, Learning & Print Svcs Mgr: Miss Caroline Axon BA, MCLIP *Dep:* Libn: Miss Helen Winningham BA, MCLIP
Assoc Libs: ASHTON CENTRE LIB, contact details as above; HYDE CENTRE LIB, Stockport Rd, Hyde, Cheshire, SK14 5EZ (0161-908-6840)

Entry: enrolled students & coll staff; ref only for membs of public *Open:* Mon-Thu 0845-1900, Fri 0845-1500, Sat 0900-1200; vac: Mon-Thu 0845-1600, Fri 0845-1500
Subj: all subjs; GCSE; A level; vocational *Co-op Schemes:* BLDSC
Equip: copier, (5p per pg), 30 computers (incl wd-proc, internet & CD-ROM) *Online:* KnowEurope, KnowUK, LION, Emerald FullText, Infotrac, Ingenta Journals, Zetoc *Svcs:* info, ref
Stock: bks/45000; periodcls/200; videos/300
Classn: DDC *Auto Sys:* Trax
Staff: Libns: 4 *Other Prof:* 2 *Non-Prof:* 5.5

S54 ✚

University of Manchester, Tameside Nursing and Midwifery Library

Tameside Genl Hosp, Fountain St, Ashton-under-Lyme, Lancashire, OL6 9RW (0161-331-6662; *fax:* 0161-331-6456)
Email: agould@fs1.li.man.ac.uk
Internet: http://rylibweb.man.ac.uk/guides/tameside.html

Gov Body: Univ of Manchester School of Nursing, Midwifery & Health Visiting *Chief:* Snr Lib Asst: Mrs Anita Gould *Other Snr Staff:* Lib Assts Mrs S. Higginson & Mrs D. Green
Assoc Libs: JOHN RYLANDS LIB (see **S1512**); GATEWAY NURSING & MIDWIFERY LIB, 4th Floor, Gateway House, Piccadilly South, Manchester, M60 7LP (0161-237 2352; *fax:* 0161-236-2445)
Entry: membs of the Univ of Manchester; restricted access for employees of Tameside & Glossop NHS Trusts *Open:* Mon-Thu 0830-1230, 1330-1630, Fri 0830-1230, 1330-1600
Equip: copier, computers (incl wd-proc & internet) *Online:* access to all databases via Univ network
Classn: RCN *Staff:* 3 in total

Aylesbury

S55

Aylesbury College Learning Resources Centre

Oxford Rd, Aylesbury, Buckinghamshire, HP21 8PD (01296-588534; *fax:* 01296-588589)
Internet: http://www.aylesbury.ac.uk/

Chief: LRC Mgr: Mrs Barbara Miller BA(Hons), AALIA (bmiller@aylesbury.ac.uk) *Dep:* LRC Co-ordinator: Mrs Diane Brandon (dbrandon@aylesbury.ac.uk)
Open: term: Mon-Fri 0900-2000, Sat 0900-0100; vac: Mon-Fri 0900-1500
Subj: all subjs; GCSE; A level; undergrad; vocational
Equip: copier, clr copier (A3/50p), 16 computers (all with wd-proc, internet & CD-ROM) *Svcs:* info, ref
Stock: bks/13000; periodcls/120; videos/200 *Acqs Offcr:* LRC Mgr, as above
Classn: DDC *Auto Sys:* AutoLib
Staff: Libns: 0.8 *Non-Prof:* 3.5 *Exp:* £30000 (1999-2000); £34000 (2000-01)

S56

Buckinghamshire Archaeological Society Library

County Museum, Church St, Aylesbury, Buckinghamshire, HP20 2QP (01296-678114 – Wed only)
Internet: http://www.buckscc.gov.uk/museum/services/bas.stm

Chief: Hon Libn: Mrs Diana Gulland MCLIP
Open: open to public: Wed 1000-1600; open to membs during museum opening hrs: Mon-Sat 1000-1700

Subj: Buckinghamshire: all aspects of county hist, incl: archaeo; arch; industrial hist; nat hist
Stock: bks/1000; periodcls/15; illusts/300 topographical prints; pamphs/760; maps/20; archvs/15 m
Pubns: Records of Buckinghamshire (1 pa, £13); Newsletter (2 pa)
Staff: Libns: 1

S57 ✚

Buckinghamshire Health Authority Library

Verney House, Gatehouse Rd, Aylesbury, Buckinghamshire, HP19 3ET (01296-318604; *fax:* 01296-310121)
Email: library@bha.powernet.co.uk

Chief: Knowledge Offcr: Ms Deirdre MacGuigan
Entry: staff of Buckinghamshire Health Authority; ref only for other NHS staff *Open:* Mon-Fri 0900-1700
Subj: health; health admin
Equip: copier, computers (incl internet & CD-ROM) *Online:* BNI, Medline, Cochrane, HMIC, ASSIA for Health, CINAHL
Stock: bks/2650; periodcls/30
Classn: NLM *Staff:* Libns: 1 *Non-Prof:* 2

S58 ✚

Buckinghamshire Mental Health NHS Trust, Tindal Centre Library

Tindal Centre, Bierton Rd, Aylesbury, Buckinghamshire, HP20 1HU (01296-504549; *fax:* 01296-399332)

Gov Body: Buckinghamshire Mental Health NHS Trust *Chief:* Libn: Mrs Valerie Cahill MCLIP (Valerie.Cahill@bmh-tr.nhs.uk) *Dep:* Lib Asst: Mr Douglas Potter (Douglas.Potter@bmh-tr.nhs.uk)
Assoc Libs: MANOR HOUSE LIB, contact details as above
Entry: membs only; ref only by adv appt for others *Open:* Mon-Fri 0900-1345
Subj: psychiatry; psy; mental health; learning disabilities *Co-op Schemes:* BLDSC, ILL
Equip: m-form reader/printer, copier, clr copier, 2 computers (both with wd-proc, internet & CD-ROM) *Svcs:* info, ref, biblio
Stock: bks/3000; periodcls/90 *Acqs Offcr:* Libn, as above
Classn: NLM *Auto Sys:* DBTextworks
Pubns: Library News (free monthly current awareness svc)
Staff: Libns: 1 *Non-Prof:* 1

S59 ✚

Stoke Mandeville Hospital NHS Trust, Wilfred Stokes Library

Postgrad Medical Centre, Stoke Mandeville Hosp, Mandeville Rd, Aylesbury, Buckinghamshire, HP21 8AL (01296-315428; *fax:* 01296-315437)
Email: jkelson@dial.pipex.com

Chief: Lib Svcs Mgr: Ms Jennie Kelson *Dep:* Asst Libn: Ms Belinda Hylton
Entry: ref only, adv appt *Open:* Mon-Fri 0830-1700
Subj: medicine; nursing; surgery; spinal cord injury *Co-op Schemes:* BLDSC
Equip: copier (A4/5p), computers (incl wd-proc, internet & CD-ROM) *Online:* Medline, CINAHL, Cochrane, HMIC, AMED, Best Evidence (available to staff only)
Stock: bks/3000; periodcls/150
Classn: NLM *Auto Sys:* DBTextworks
Staff: Libns: 2

Special Libraries

Aylesbury ▼ Bangor

S60 ✚
University of Luton, Health Care Learning Resources Centre, Aylesbury
Nuffield Rsrch Centre, Stoke Mandeville Hosp, Aylesbury, Buckinghamshire, HP21 8AL (01296-315900)

Gov Body: Univ of Luton (see **S1492**) *Chief:* Libn: Mrs Anne Rowlands
Entry: staff only *Open:* Mon-Thu 0900-1800; Sat 0900-1700
Subj: nursing; midwifery; social sci; health
Equip: video viewer, copier (5p), computers (incl wd-proc, internet & CD-ROM) *Svcs:* info, ref
Stock: bks/c7800; periodcls/150; videos/200
Classn: WRLN *Auto Sys:* Libertas
Staff: Libns: 2 *Non-Prof:* 4

S61 ♟
Waddesdon Manor (National Trust), Library
Waddesdon, Aylesbury, Buckinghamshire, HP18 0JH (01296-653203; *fax:* 01296-653212)

Type: Natl Trust property *Gov Body:* The Natl Trust (see **S1305**) *Chief:* Academic Dir: Mrs P. Glanville
Entry: adv appt *Open:* see 'Natl Trust Properties Open' for house open hrs; lib only by prior appt
Collns: Bks & Pamphs: 750 17C & 18C bks distinguished by their binding, provenance & illusts (chiefly French)

Ayr

S62 ✚
Ayr Hospital, MacDonald Education Centre Library
Dalmellington Rd, Ayr, Ayrshire, KA6 6DX (01292-610555 x4119; *fax:* 01292-288952)
Email: janice.grant@aaaht.scot.nhs.uk

Gov Body: Ayrshire & Arran Acute Hosps NHS Trust *Chief:* Libn: Mrs Janice Grant MA, BA, DipLib, MCLIP
Entry: ref only if not staff *Open:* Mon-Thu 0900-1700, Fri: 0900-1630
Subj: medicine; nursing *Collns: Archvs:* archv material from hosps in area that have now closed
Co-op Schemes: BLDSC, SHINE
Equip: 3 video viewers, copier, 6 computers (all with wd-proc, internet & CD-ROM), 5 rooms for hire
Online: Internet (staff only) *Svcs:* info, ref, biblio
Stock: bks/4000; periodcls/140
Classn: NLM *Auto Sys:* Heritage
Staff: Libns: 1 *Non-Prof:* 1 PT

S63 ♟ ⛫
Burns Cottage Trustees Library
Burns Cottage, Alloway, Ayr, Ayrshire, KA7 4PY (01292-441215; *fax:* 01292-441750)
Email: elinor@burnsheritagepark.com
Internet: http://www.burnsheritagepark.com

Chief: Curator: Miss Eleanor Clarke
Entry: by adv appt

Subj: life & works of Robert Burns *Collns: Other:* Scottish music
Svcs: info, ref *Stock:* bks/3000

S64 ♟
Hannah Research Institute Library
St Quivox, Ayr, Ayrshire, KA6 5HL (01292-674000; *fax:* 01292-671004)
Email: Barboure@hri.sari.ac.uk
Internet: http://www.hri.sari.ac.uk/

Gov Body: Council of the Hannah Rsrch Inst
Chief: Libn: Mrs E. Barbour BSc(Hons)
Entry: apply to Libn *Open:* Mon-Fri 0850-1700
Subj: dairy sci; agric; food sci; biochem; physiology; chem; nutrition; microbiology *Collns: Bks & Pamphs:* pamph colln on agric topics *Co-op Schemes:* BLDSC, SALG
Equip: m-reader, copier, computer (incl wd-proc & CD-ROM)
Stock: bks/9000; periodcls/150; photos/500; pamphs/1000
Classn: DDC

S65 🎓
Scottish Agricultural College, W.J. Thomson Library
Donald Hendrie Bldg, SAC Ayr, Ayr, Ayrshire, KA6 5HW (01292-525209; *fax:* 01292-525211)
Email: library@au.sac.ac.uk
Internet: http://www.sac.ac.uk/corporate/libraries.asp

Chief: Snr Libn: Ms Elaine Muir MA, DipLib, MCLIP
Assoc Libs: SCOTTISH AGRICULTURAL COLL LIB, Edinburgh (see **S625**)
Entry: staff & students of Coll; public ref only
Open: term: Mon-Fri 0845-2045, Sat-Sun 1000-1700; vac: Mon-Thu 0845-1715, Fri 0845-1645
Subj: undergrad; postgrad; tourism; leisure; countryside rec; agric; hortic; food sci; poultry husbandry; sport rec *Collns: Archvs:* historical colln (agric, hortic, nat hist) *Co-op Schemes:* SALG, BLDSC, ALF
Equip: m-form reader/printer, 2 video viewers, fax, copier, clr copier, 34 computers (all with wd-proc, internet & CD-ROM, access by password) *Online:* World of Science, CAB, Mintel
Stock: bks/30000; periodcls/300; pamphs/10000; maps/500; videos/360
Classn: DDC *Auto Sys:* Talis
Staff: Libns: 1 *Non-Prof:* 3 *Exp:* £70000 (1999-2000); £70000 (2000-01)

S66 🎓
University of Paisley, Ayr Campus Library
Beech Grove, Ayr, Ayrshire, KA8 0SR (01292-886345; *fax:* 01292-886288)
Email: stew-li0@paisley.ac.uk
Internet: http://library.paisley.ac.uk/

Gov Body: Univ of Paisley (see **S1782**) *Chief:* Asst Libn: Miss Margo Stewart MA, DipLib
Entry: staff & students; ref for others; external borrowers at discretion of Univ Libn; full public access to Scottish Poetry Lib & Ayrshire Sound Archv *Open:* term: Mon-Thu 0900-2100, Fri-Sat 0900-1700; vac: Mon-Fri 0900-1700
Subj: all subjs; undergrad; edu; nursing; midwifery *Collns: Bks & Pamphs:* Scottish Poetry Lib (branch) *Archvs:* Ayrshire Sound Archv (local hist)
Equip: m-readers, m-printer, copiers, computers (incl wd-proc & CD-ROM) *Svcs:* info, ref, biblio
Stock: bks/54700; periodcls/360; slides/100; illusts/5000; m-forms/600; audios/350; videos/100; archvs/144 sound tapes
Classn: DDC *Auto Sys:* Talis
Staff: Libns: 3 *Non-Prof:* 10 FTE

Bakewell

S67 ♟
Chatsworth Library
Chatsworth, Bakewell, Derbyshire, DE45 1PP (01246-582204; *fax:* 01246-565375)
Email: collection@chatsworth.org
Internet: http://www.chatsworth-house.co.uk/

Type: antiquarian bk colln within historic house
Gov Body: The Duke of Devonshire & Chatsworth Settlement Trustees *Chief:* Libn & Keeper of Collns: Mr P.J. Day MA *Dep:* Mr C.P.N. Noble LVO
Entry: by written appt; daily reading fee *Open:* Mon-Fri 0900-1700 (Apr-Oct)
Subj: printed bks 15C-19C: genl; phil; religion; sci; arts; lit; geog; hist *Collns: Bks & Pamphs:* c40000 vols of printed bks & 325 bnd vols of pamphs (17C-19C) *Archvs:* extensive estate papers (Derbyshire, Yorkshire, Sussex & Ireland); MSS of Thomas Hobbes; MSS of Henry Cavendish; correspondence of Earls & Dukes of Devonshire & family; correspondence of Joseph Paxton
Equip: copier *Svcs:* info
Stock: bks/40000; pamphs/325 bnd vols; maps/1000; archvs/500 cubic m
Classn: alphabetical by author, based on 1879 publ catalogue; other indiv lists & calendars
Pubns: 1879 Lib Catalogue, by J. Lacaita; Great Flower Bks at Chatsworth; Fine Bird Bks at Chatsworth
Staff: Other Prof: 2.5 *Non-Prof:* 0.5

Banbury

S68 🍷♪
Alcan International Ltd, Technical Information Centre
Banbury Laboratory, Southam Rd, Banbury, Oxfordshire, OX16 2SP (01295-452626; *fax:* 01295-452808)
Email: Banbury.Techinfo@alcan.com
Internet: http://www.research.alcan.com/

Chief: Info Offcr: Mrs Catherine Carr BSc, MCLIP (cathy.carr@alcan.com) *Dep:* Mrs Margaret Dean (margaret.dean@alcan.com)
Assoc Libs: ALCAN INTERNATL LTD, TECHNICAL INFO CENTRE, Kingston Rsrch & Development Centre, PO Box 8400, Princess St, Kingston, Ontario Canada, K76 5L9, Info Offcr: Mr Brian Chenoweth (+1-613-541-2400; *fax:* +1-613-541-2134; *email:* brian.chenoweth@alcan.com)
Entry: Alcan employees only
Subj: sci; tech; metallurgy *Collns: Bks & Pamphs:* Aluminium Assoc pubns *Archvs:* historical materials relating to aluminium *Other:* patents; standards *Co-op Schemes:* BLDSC, ILL
Equip: 2 m-printers, fax, 3 computers (all with wd-proc, internet & CD-ROM) *Online:* Dialog, CSA etc
Svcs: info, ref, biblio, indexing
Stock: bks/7000; periodcls/200; m-forms/10000; audios/30; videos/150; CD-ROMs/50; theses/300; standards/2000; grey lit/3000 items
Classn: DDC, UDC *Staff:* Libns: 1 *Non-Prof:* 0.5

S69 ✚
Horton Hospital Library and Education Centre
(formerly Terence Mortimer Postgrad Edu Centre Lib)
Horton Hosp, Oxford Rd, Banbury, Oxfordshire, OX16 9AL (01295-229316; *fax:* 01295-229324)
Email: library.horton@orh.nhs.uk
Internet: http://www.library-horton.demon.co.uk/

Gov Body: Oxford Radcliffe Trusts *Chief:* Lib Svcs Mgr: Mrs Carol Mortimer AIMLS (carol.mortimer@orh.nhs.uk) *Dep:* Lib Asst: Ms Bridget Lucas

Entry: open to all NHS employees, others by appt **Open:** Mon-Fri 0900-1700
Subj: medicine; nursing; health **Co-op Schemes:** BLDSC, Oxford & Anglia ILL Scheme, NULJ
Equip: copier (5p), 6 computers (all with wd-proc & CD-ROM, 4 with CD-ROM) **Officer-in-Charge:** Lib Svcs Mgr, as above **Svcs:** info, ref, biblio
Stock: bks/7000; periodcls/75; audios/19; videos/139; CD-ROMs/34 **Acqs Offcr:** Lib Svcs Mgr, as above
Classn: NLM **Auto Sys:** DBTextworks
Staff: Libns: 0.86 Non-Prof: 0.74 **Exp:** £28145 (1999-2000); £28175 (2000-01)

S70

North Oxfordshire College and School of Art Library

Broughton Rd, Banbury, Oxfordshire, OX16 9QA (01295-252221 x316; *fax:* 01295-250381)
Email: library@northox.ac.uk
Internet: http://www.northox.ac.uk/

Chief: Central Learning Resources Mgr: Ms Karen Acham BSc, DipIS, MCLIP **Dep:** Mrs Christina Hirons BSc, MSc
Assoc Libs: DE MONTFORT UNIV LIB (see **S921**)
Entry: open access **Open:** *Lib:* term: Mon-Thu 0845-1900, Fri 0845-1700, Sat 1000-1300; vac: by appt; *Study Centre:* Mon-Fri 0900-1700
Subj: all subjs; genl; GCSE; A level; undergrad **Co-op Schemes:** BLDSC, ILL, De Montfort Univ
Equip: video viewer, copier, 28 computers (all with wd-proc, internet & CD-ROM) **Svcs:** info, ref, biblio
Stock: bks/21500; periodcls/225; slides/5500; pamphs/various; videos/1000
Classn: DDC **Auto Sys:** EOSi
Staff: Libns: 1.47 Non-Prof: 2.4 **Exp:** £30510 (1999-2000)

Banchory

S71

Centre for Ecology and Hydrology, Banchory Library

Hill of Brathens, Glassel, Banchory, Aberdeenshire, AB31 4BW (01330-826300)
Email: bllib@wpo.nerc.ac.uk
Internet: http://library.ceh.ac.uk/

Gov Body: Nat Environment Rsrch Council (NERC); part of CEH Lib Svcs (see **S1786**) **Chief:** Libn: Ms Fiona Robertson
Entry: external rsrchers by adv appt **Open:** Mon-Fri 0830-1330
Subj: plant & animal ecology; animal behaviour; population ecology; ornithology; entomology; forests & forestry; conservation (esp in Scotland)
Stock: bks/1800; periodcls/200
Auto Sys: Unicorn

Bangor, *Gwynedd*

S72

Centre for Ecology and Hydrology, Bangor Library

Orton Bldg, Deiniol Rd, Bangor, Gwynedd, LL57 2UP (01248-370045; *fax:* 01248-355365)
Email: jrco@ceh.ac.uk
Internet: http://library.ceh.ac.uk/

Gov Body: Nat Environment Rsrch Council (NERC); part of CEH Lib Svcs (see **S1786**) **Chief:** Libn: Ms Jackie Cooper
Entry: bona fide rsrchers may use the Lib's facilities on appl to Reception **Open:** staffed: Mon-Thu 0845-1230, Fri 0845 -1215; access during normal working hrs on appl

Subj: ecology; forestry; soils; pollution; conservation **Collns:** Bks & Pamphs: colln of reports from the Countryside Council for Wales
Stock: bks/1800, incl reports; periodcls/150
Auto Sys: Unicorn

S73

Coleg Menai Library

Ffriddoedd Rd, Bangor, Gwynedd, LL57 2TP (01248-383329; *fax:* 01248-370052)
Email: library@menai.ac.uk
Internet: http://www.menai.ac.uk/

Gov Body: ELWA **Chief:** Libn: Mr Aled D.W. Rees BA, MCLIP
Assoc Libs: LLANGEFNI SITE LIB, Penrallt, Llangefni, Ynys Môn, LL77 7HY, Libn: Ms Jo Stroud; PARC MENAI SITE LIB, Parc Menai, Bangor, Gwynedd, Lib Asst: Mrs Siân Roberts
Entry: those associated with Coleg Menai; ref only to others **Open:** *Bangor:* term: Mon-Thu 0845-1930, Fri 0845-1630; vac: Mon-Fri office hrs; *Llangefni:* term: Mon, Thu 0845-1700, Tue-Wed 0845-1730, Fri 0845-1630; vac: closed; *Parc Menai:* term: Mon-Fri 0845-1630; vac: closed
Subj: psy; social sci; tech; arts **Co-op Schemes:** BLDSC
Equip: 2 video viewers, 3 copiers, clr copier, 100 computers (all with wd-proc & internet, 50 with CD-ROM) **Online:** Infotrac, KnowUK, KnowEurope, LION, Technical Indexes & others **Svcs:** info, ref
Stock: bks/66385; periodcls/200; slides/205; audios/74; videos/718; CD-ROMs/208; software packages/168
Classn: DDC **Auto Sys:** Heritage IV
Staff: Libns: 3 Other Prof: 1 Non-Prof: 9 **Exp:** £57800 (1999-2000); £83500 (2000-01)

S74

Countryside Council for Wales (Cyngor Cefn Gwlad Cymru), Library

Hafod Elfyn, Penrhos Rd, Bangor, Gwynedd, LL57 2LQ (01248-385522; *fax:* 01248-385510)
Email: library@ccw.gov.uk
Internet: http://www.ccw.gov.uk/

Chief: Libn: Ms D. Lloyd BA(Hons), MCLIP
Entry: ref only; prior appt essential **Open:** Mon-Thu 0830-1700, Fri 0830-1630
Subj: local study (Wales): flora & fauna; plant & animal ecology; nature conservation; forestry; agric; wildlife mgmt; planning; land use; rec; Welsh hist & geog; marine & coastal environment; countryside access, landscape & geol **Co-op Schemes:** BLDSC
Equip: m-reader, m-printer, copier, 2 computers (both with internet, 1 with CD-ROM) **Online:** Dialog, various online databases & CD-ROMs (internal users only) **Svcs:** info, ref
Stock: bks/19000; periodcls/c240
Classn: UDC **Auto Sys:** Olib
Staff: Libns: 2 Other Prof: 1 Non-Prof: 1

S75

Institute of European Finance, Research Library

Univ of Wales Bangor, Bangor, Gwynedd, LL57 2DG (01248-382277; *fax:* 01248-364760)
Email: ief@bangor.ac.uk

Gov Body: Univ of Wales **Chief:** Dirs: Prof E. Gardener & Prof P. Molyneux **Dep:** Info Offcr: Mrs Christine Owen BSocSc(Hons)
Entry: adv appt **Open:** Mon-Fri 0900-1700
Subj: banking; finance **Collns:** Bks & Pamphs: serials or periodcls in banking & financial instns **Co-op Schemes:** ILL
Equip: m-reader, fax, copier, computers (incl CD-ROM) **Online:** Datastream **Svcs:** info, ref, biblio, abstracting

Pubns: World Banking Abstracts (£660 pa); Rsrch Papers in Banking & Finance (various prices); Rsrch Monographs in Banking & Finance (various prices)
Staff: Libns: 1 Other Prof: 1 Non-Prof: 1

S76

University of Wales Bangor, Prif Lyfrgell / Main Library

Top College Bldgs, College Rd, Bangor, Gwynedd, LL57 2DG (01248-382983; *fax:* 01248-382979)
Email: library@bangor.ac.uk
Internet: http://www.bangor.ac.uk/is/library/

Gov Body: Univ of Wales **Chief:** Head of Lib Svcs: Mr Nigel S. Soane
Assoc Libs: DEAN ST LIB (see **S77**); DEINIOL RD LIB (see **S78**); FRON HEULOG (HEALTH STUDIES) LIB (see **S79**); MUSIC LIB (see **S80**); NORMAL SITE LIB (see **S81**); WOLFSON (OCEAN SCIS) LIB (see **S83**); WREXHAM (HEALTH STUDIES) LIB (see **S2156**); WELSH LIB, at Main Lib (see **S82**); DEPT OF ARCHVS & MSS, at Main Lib (01248-382966)
Entry: membs of Univ; others ref free, fees for borrowing **Open:** term: Mon-Thu 0900-2200, Fri 0900-2000, Sat-Sun 1200-1700; vac: Mon-Thu 0900-2200, Fri 0900-2000
Subj: undergrad; postgrad; arts; humanities; social sci **Collns:** Bks & Pamphs: Humanities Rsrch Collns; Sir Frank Brangwyn Art Colln; Telfourd-Jones Colln (botany, zoology); Cathedral Lib Colln Archvs: early records of the Univ Other: video colln (film studies & psy); postgrad theses **Co-op Schemes:** SCONUL, WRLS, UK Libs Plus
Equip: m-readers, m-printers, 4 copiers, computers **Disabled:** wheelchair access, induction loops, equip for visually-impaired **Online:** OCLC FirstSearch, ASSIA, INSPEC, ERIC, CSA, Web of Science, BIOSIS, BHI, BNB, CAB Abstracts, Lawtel, Medline, Cochrane & others
Stock: bks/c400000; periodcls/c3000; audios/c5000; MSS/450000; various incunabula
Classn: LC **Auto Sys:** Innopac
Staff: 41 lib & IT staff

S77

University of Wales Bangor, Dean Street Library

Rooms 201-203, School of Informatics, Dean St, Bangor, Gwynedd, LL57 1UT (01248-382986)
Email: s.t.harling@bangor.ac.uk
Internet: http://www.bangor.ac.uk/is/library/

Gov Body: Univ of Wales Bangor (see **S76**)
Chief: Subj Libn: Mr Stephen Harling (based at Deiniol Lib) **Other Snr Staff:** Lib Assts: Ms Mari Kelso & Ms Mair Richardson (based at Dean St Lib)
Assoc Libs: DEINIOL LIB (main sci collns, see **S78**)
Entry: staff & students of Univ; ref only for others **Open:** staffed: Mon-Fri 0900-1230, 1330-1700
Subj: elec eng; computer sci; maths **Co-op Schemes:** ILL
Equip: copier, computers **Online:** INSPEC, Web of Science
Classn: LC **Staff:** Libns: 1 Non-Prof: 2

S78

University of Wales Bangor, Deiniol Library

Adeilad Deiniol, Univ of Wales Bangor, Ffordd Deiniol, Bangor, Gwynedd, LL57 2UX (01248-382984)
Email: s.t.harling@bangor.ac.uk
Internet: http://www.bangor.ac.uk/is/library/

Gov Body: Univ of Wales Bangor (see **S76**)
Chief: Subj Libn: Mr Stephen Harling

Special Libraries

Bangor
▼
Bath

(Univ of Wales Bangor, Deiniol Lib cont)
Entry: staff & students of Univ; ref only from non-membs **Open:** term: Mon-Thu 0800-2200, Fri 0800-2000, Sat-Sun 0900-1700; vac: varies **Subj:** sci; agric; biochem; botany; chem; environmental sci; forestry; life sci; maths; soil sci; ocean sci; wood sci; zoology **Collns:** *Other:* map colln **Equip:** copiers, computers (incl wd-proc, internet & CD-ROM) **Svcs:** info, ref, biblio, indexing, abstracting **Classn:** LC **Auto Sys:** Innopac

S79 🎓 ✚
University of Wales Bangor, Fron Heulog (Health Studies) Library
Health Faculty Bldg, Ffriddoedd Rd, Bangor, Gwynedd, LL57 2EF (01248-383173)
Email: iss070@bangor.ac.uk
Internet: http://www.bangor.ac.uk/is/library/

Gov Body: Univ of Wales Bangor (see **S76**)
Chief: Health Studies Libn: Ms Marion Poulton
Dep: Snr Lib Asst: Ms Jenny Greene
Assoc Libs: WREXHAM HEALTH STUDIES LIB (see **S2156**)
Entry: ref only for non-membs of Univ **Open:** term & vac: Mon-Thu 0845-2000, Fri 0845-1700, Sat 0900-1300
Subj: medicine; anatomy; physiology; nursing; midwifery; health; psy; social sci
Equip: copier, computer **Online:** CINAHL, BNI, Medline, Cochrane
Classn: NLM, LC

S80 🎓
University of Wales Bangor, Music Library
Dept of Music, College Rd, Bangor, Gwynedd, LL57 2DG (01248-382187)
Email: iss100@bangor.ac.uk
Internet: http://www.bangor.ac.uk/is/library/

Gov Body: Univ of Wales Bangor (see **S76**)
Chief: Lib Asst: Mrs Catherine Evans BA, DipEd
Entry: staff & students of UWB; outside borrowers pay an annual fee **Open:** term: Mon-Fri 0900-1700 (closed 1300-1400 on Fri); vac: Mon-Fri 1400-1700
Subj: music **Collns:** *Bks & Pamphs:* small ref colln (bks on music are in Main Lib) *Other:* orchestral scores; vocal scores; instrumental music; songs; chamber music parts; music periodcls; recordings on LP & CD
Equip: m-reader, video viewer, 3 computers (incl 1 with internet), 6 LP players, 2 cassette players, 8 CD players **Svcs:** info, ref, biblio
Stock: bks/2000; periodcls/c50; audios/3000 LPs, 3000 CDs; videos/80; scores & music sets/c22000
Acqs Offcr: Lib Asst, as above
Classn: LC
Staff: *Non-Prof:* 2 (1 FTE) **Exp:** £12000 (1999-2000); £13000 (2000-01)

S81 🎓
University of Wales Bangor, Normal Site Library
School of Edu, Holyhead Rd, Bangor, Gwynedd, LL57 2PX (01248-383048)
Email: b.w.jones@bangor.ac.uk
Internet: http://www.bangor.ac.uk/is/library/

Gov Body: Univ of Wales Bangor (see **S76**)
Chief: Subj Libn: Mrs Bethan Wyn Jones BA, MCLIP
Entry: ref only if not local student **Open:** term: Mon-Thu 0900-2100, Fri 0900-2000, Sat-Sun 1200-1700; vac: varies
Subj: edu (incl primary & secondary); sport; health; physical edu **Co-op Schemes:** ILL
Equip: 2 copiers, computers (with wd-proc, internet & CD-ROM)
Classn: LC **Auto Sys:** Innopac
Staff: *Libns:* 1 *Non-Prof:* 3

S82 🎓
University of Wales Bangor, The Welsh Library
Main Lib, College Rd, Bangor, Gwynedd, LL57 2DG (01248-382913)
Email: e.p.williams@bangor.ac.uk
Internet: http://www.bangor.ac.uk/is/library/

Gov Body: Univ of Wales Bangor (see **S76**)
Chief: Welsh Libn: Ms Ellen Parry Williams **Dep:** Snr Asst: Mrs Shan Robinson
Entry: membs of Univ, others ref only; adv appt for consultation of rare bk material **Open:** for open access material: term: Mon-Thu 0900-2200, Fri 0900-2000, Sat-Sun 1200-1700; vac: contact lib; for closed access material & assistance: Mon-Thu 0930-1600, Fri 0930-1330
Subj: all subjs; Wales; Welsh lang, lit & hist; Celtic studies **Collns:** *Bks & Pamphs:* Rare Bks Colln; Welsh slate industry; local hist & topography; material publ in & about Patagonia; Welsh lang material publ in USA *Other:* Welsh periodcls & newspapers
Equip: m-reader, m-printer, 2 video viewers, 3 copiers, computer (with CD-ROM); all available in Main Lib **Online:** online catalogue **Svcs:** info, ref, biblio
Classn: own, partially based on LC
Staff: *Libns:* 0.3 *Non-Prof:* 0.65

S83 🎓
University of Wales Bangor, Wolfson Library
School of Ocean Sciences, Askew St, Menai Bridge, Bangor, Gwynedd, LL59 5EY (01248-382985)
Email: p.rolfe@bangor.ac.uk
Internet: http://www.bangor.ac.uk/is/library/

Gov Body: Univ of Wales Bangor (see **S76**)
Chief: Subj Libn: Mr Paul Rolfe
Entry: staff & students of Univ; ref only for others **Open:** term: Mon-Fri 0900-2000, Sat-Sun 1200-1700; vac: Mon-Fri 0900-1700
Subj: marine sci; marine biology; marine chem; geol; oceanography; fisheries; aquaculture
Collns: *Other:* maps, atlases & maritime charts; meteorological data; offprints
Equip: copiers, computers (incl internet & CD-ROM)
Staff: *Libns:* 1 *Non-Prof:* 2

Barking

S84 ✚
Barking and Dagenham Primary Care Trust, Clock House Library
The Clock House, East St, Barking, Essex, IG11 8EY
Email: eunice.harrison@bdpct.nhs.uk
Internet: http://www.libnel.nhs.uk/

Gov Body: Barking & Dagenham Health Authority
Chief: Lib Info Mgr: Ms Eunice Harrison
Entry: staff of Health Authority or local PCGs; membs of North East London Health Community can also apply to use the lib **Open:** Mon-Wed 1000-1800, Thu-Fri 0800-1600

Subj: public health medicine
Equip: computers (with internet) **Online:** AMED, BNI, CancerLit, CINAHL, Cochrane, Embase, HMIC, Medline, PsycInfo

Barnet

S85 ✚
Barnet and Chase Farm Hospitals NHS Trust, Barnet Medical Library
Postgrad Medical Centre, Barnet Hosp, Barnet, Hertfordshire, EN5 3DJ (020-8216-4834; *fax:* 020-8216-4678)
Email: guy@barnet2.demon.co.uk

Gov Body: Barnet & Chase Farm Hosps NHS Trust **Chief:** Info Systems Libn: Mr Guy A. Robinson BA, DipLib, MCLIP **Dep:** Asst Libn: Ms Deborah Mogg
Entry: Trust employees only **Open:** Mon-Fri 0900-1700
Subj: medicine **Co-op Schemes:** BLDSC, NTRLIS
Equip: copier, fax, computers (incl 2 wd-proc, 1 internet & 3 CD-ROM) **Svcs:** info, ref, biblio
Stock: bks/6000; periodcls/150; videos/50
Classn: NLM **Auto Sys:** InMagic
Staff: *Libns:* 1 *Non-Prof:* 1

S86 🎓
Barnet College, Independent Learning Centre
Wood St, Barnet, Hertfordshire, EN5 4AZ (020-8440-6321; *fax:* 020-8441-5236)
Internet: http://www.barnet.ac.uk/

Gov Body: Barnet Coll Corp **Chief:** Centre Mgr: Ms Marie Adams BA, MA, MCLIP
Assoc Libs: RUSSELL LN INDEPENDENT LEARNING CENTRE, Russell Ln, Whetstone, London, N20 0AX, Site/Tutor Libn: Mrs Angela Dimond DipArc, DipLib, MCLIP (020-8361-5101; *fax:* 020-8368-6426)
Entry: staff & students of the Coll; genl public: ref only, on appl **Open:** term: Mon-Thu 0845-2000, Fri 0845-1700; vac: Mon-Fri 0900-1230, 1330-1700
Subj: all subjs; GCSE; A level **Co-op Schemes:** BLDSC, ILL
Equip: m-readers, video viewers, copiers, 100 computers (incl internet & CD-ROM)
Stock: bks/35847; periodcls/200; AVs/3233
Classn: DDC **Auto Sys:** Horizon
Staff: *Libns:* 6 *Non-Prof:* 6

Barnsley

S87 ✚
Barnsley District General Hospital NHS Trust, Staff Library
Edu Centre, Barnsley Dist Genl Hosp, Gawber Rd, Barnsley, S Yorkshire, S75 2EP (01226-777973; *fax:* 01226-206774)
Email: library@bdgh-tr.trent.nhs.uk

Gov Body: Barnsley Dist Genl Hosp NHS Trust
Chief: Libn: Miss Ruth C. Merrill BA, MCLIP (ruth.merrill@bdgh-tr.trent.nhs.uk) **Dep:** Asst Libn: Mrs Eleanor Barker MSc
Entry: staff of Barnsley Community & Priority Svcs NHS Trust & Barnsley Dist Genl Hosp NHS Trust; ref only by adv appt for non-staff **Open:** Mon, Wed-Thu 0830-2000, Tue, Fri 0830-1700
Subj: medicine; nursing; midwifery; health svc mgmt; health promotion; mental health; community care **Co-op Schemes:** BLDSC, YLI
Equip: m-reader, copier (5p per sheet), video viewer, 9 computers (all with wd-proc, CD-ROM & internet) **Online:** Medline, CINAHL, Cochrane, BNI
Svcs: info, ref, biblio

Stock: bks/10000; periodcls/c150; videos/153
Classn: NLM *Auto Sys:* Heritage
Staff: Libns: 2 Other Prof: 1 Non-Prof: 2.5

Barnstaple

S88

The North Devon Athenaeum, Library

Tuly St, Barnstaple, Devon, EX31 1EL (01271-342174)

Chief: Libn: Mr L.A. Franklin
Entry: ref only *Open:* Mon-Tue, Thu-Fri 0930-1700, Wed 0930-1300
Subj: local study (Devon); social hist; political hist; biography; military hist; maritime studies; travel
Collns: Archvs: some archv material *Other:* local newspapers; maps; parish register transcripts; census returns *Co-op Schemes:* joint participation in Local Studies Centre with Devon County Council (see **P37**)
Stock: bks/14000; photos/400; slides/200; pamphs/2000; maps/400
Staff: Non-Prof: 2

S89

North Devon College Library

Old Sticklepath Hill, Barnstaple, Devon, EX31 2BQ (01271-388150; *fax:* 01271-388121)
Internet: http://www.ndevon.ac.uk/

Chief: Learning Resources Mgr: Ms Michele Taborn BA, MLS (mtaborn@ndevon.ac.uk) *Dep:* Libn: Mrs H.N. Skinner BLS, MCLIP (hskinner@ndevon.ac.uk)
Entry: public admitted for ref only *Open:* term: Mon-Thu 0845-1900, Fri 0845-1630; vac: Mon-Fri 0900-1300
Subj: all subjs; GCSE; A level *Co-op Schemes:* BLDSC
Equip: video viewer, copier, computers (incl wd-proc & CD-ROM) *Disabled:* CC Reader *Svcs:* info, ref, biblio
Stock: bks/18000; periodcls/150; videos/250
Classn: DDC *Staff:* Libns: 2 Non-Prof: 2.1

S90 ✚

Northern Devon Healthcare NHS Trust Library

North Devon Dist Hosp, Raleigh Pk, Barnstaple, Devon, EX31 4JB (01271-322363; *fax:* 01271-322692)
Email: library@ndevon.swest.nhs.uk

Gov Body: Northern Devon Healthcare NHS Trust *Chief:* Libn: Mrs Alison Housley BA, DipLib
Entry: Trust staff & other registered users *Open:* staffed: Mon-Fri 0830-1730; 24 hr access for membs
Subj: medicine; nursing *Co-op Schemes:* BLDSC, BMA, SWRLS
Equip: m-reader, copier (A4/5p, A3/10p), computers (incl wd-proc, internet & CD-ROM) *Online:* AMED, ASSIA, Medline, CINAHL, BNI, Cochrane, PsycInfo *Svcs:* info, ref, lit searches, database training
Classn: NLM *Staff:* Libns: 1 Non-Prof: 2

Barrow-in-Furness

S91

Furness College Learning Resource Centre

Channel Side, Barrow-in-Furness, Cumbria, LA14 2PJ (01229-825017; *fax:* 01229-870964)
Internet: http://www.furness.ac.uk/

Gov Body: Corp of Coll *Chief:* Head of Learning Resources: Mr Tim Lomas BA, MSc, MCLIP
Entry: ref only for genl public *Open:* Mon-Fri 0800-2100, Sat 1000-1200
Subj: all subjs *Co-op Schemes:* BLDSC, Cumbria County
Equip: m-reader, fax, video viewers, copiers, clr copier, computers (with wd-proc, internet & CD-ROM) *Svcs:* info, ref
Stock: bks/28500; periodcls/340; CD-ROMs/100+
Classn: DDC *Auto Sys:* Limes
Staff: Libns: 1 Non-Prof: 3.4

Barry

S92

Barry College, Learning Resource Centre

Colcot Rd, Barry, S Glamorgan, CF62 8YJ (01446-743519; *fax:* 01446-732667)
Email: enquires@barry.ac.uk
Internet: http://www.barry.ac.uk/

Gov Body: Barry Coll *Chief:* Learning Resources Mgr: Mrs Rachel White BLib
Entry: free access to staff & students; public ref only *Open:* term: Mon-Thu 0900-2000, Fri 0900-1645; vac: Mon-Fri 0900-1630
Subj: all subjs; genl; GCSE; A level; undergrad
Co-op Schemes: BLDSC
Equip: video viewer, copier, computers (with wd-proc & internet), binding & laminating machine, digital cameras
Stock: bks/20000; periodcls/70
Classn: DDC *Auto Sys:* Alice
Staff: Libns: 1 Non-Prof: 3

Basildon

S93 ✚

Basildon Healthcare Library

Robert Brown Postgrad Centre, Basildon Hosp, Nethermayne, Basildon, Essex, SS16 5NL (01268-593594; *fax:* 01268-593988)
Email: library@btgh-tr.nthames.nhs.uk

Chief: Genl Mgr (Lib & Knowledge Svcs): Mrs Christine Coley MLib, MCLIP (christine.coley@btgh-tr.nthames.nhs.uk) *Dep:* Libn: Ms Sarah Perthon BLS, MCLIP *Other Snr Staff:* Info Specialist: Ms Dawn Bradley
Entry: NHS employees *Open:* Mon-Fri 0900-1830, Sat 0900-1200
Subj: medicine; health *Co-op Schemes:* NTRLIS
Equip: copier (10p), 6 computers (all with wd-proc, internet & CD-ROM) *Svcs:* info, ref, biblio
Stock: bks/2500; periodcls/150
Classn: NLM *Auto Sys:* 2020
Staff: Libns: 3 Non-Prof: 7

S94 🕰🏛

The Motorboat Museum, Library and Archives

(formerly Natl Motorboat Museum)
Wat Tyler Country Pk, Pitsea Lall Ln, Basildon, Essex, SS14 4UH (01268-550077/88; *fax:* 01268-584207)

Gov Body: Basildon Dist Council *Chief:* Snr Museum Asst: Mrs Julie Graham
Entry: museum free, lib by appt only *Open:* Mon, Thu-Sun 1000-1630, closed Tue-Wed
Subj: maritime; motor boats *Collns: Archvs:* Ailsa Craig Archvs; Carstairs Colln; Charlie Sheppard Colln
Equip: copier, computer (with wd-proc) *Svcs:* info, ref
Pubns: Museum Guides; Hist of White Lady; BPB Recollections
Staff: Libns: 2 Other Prof: 1 Non-Prof: 1

Basingstoke

S95

Basingstoke College of Technology, Learning Resource Centre

Worting Rd, Basingstoke, Hampshire, RG21 8TN (01256-306383; *fax:* 01256-306444)
Email: learning.resources@bcot.ac.uk

Gov Body: Board of Governors of Basingstoke Coll of Tech *Chief:* Learning Resources Mgr: Ms Melanie Maloney BA(Lib) (melanie.maloney@bcot.ac.uk) *Dep:* Dep Learning Resources Mgr: Mrs Julie Yates BEd(Hons), PGDipIM (julie.yates@bcot.ac.uk)
Entry: students & staff full access; ref only to visitors (must sign in) *Open:* term: Mon, Wed 0900-1900, Tue, Thu 0900-1700, Fri 0900-1600; vac: Mon-Thu 0900-1700, Fri 0900-1600
Subj: all subjs; genl; GCSE; A level *Co-op Schemes:* SWRLS, HATRICS
Equip: copier, 40 computers (all with wd-proc, internet & CD-ROM)
Stock: bks/24000; periodcls/100; pamphs/600; videos/1500; AVs/700
Classn: DDC *Auto Sys:* Heritage
Staff: Libns: 2 Non-Prof: 2.6

S96 ✚

North Hampshire Hospital, Healthcare Library

Aldermaston Rd, Basingstoke, Hampshire, RG24 9NA (01256-313169; *fax:* 01256-461129)
Email: library@nhht.nhs.uk
Internet: http://healthcarelibrary.org.uk/

Gov Body: North Hampshire Hosps NHS Trust *Chief:* Lib Mgr: Ms Catherine Cade BA, DipLIS, MCLIP *Dep:* Svc Development Libn: Mr Paul Bradley BA(Econ), MCLIP
Entry: NHS employees or PCT employees in Basingstoke area; others ref only, by adv appt *Open:* Mon, Wed-Thu 0830-1700, Tue 0830-1900, Fri 0830-1630
Subj: medicine *Co-op Schemes:* SWRLIN, BLDSC, HATRICS, BMA
Equip: m-reader, video viewer, copier, computer (incl wd-proc, internet & CD-ROM) *Online:* BNI, Medline, PsycInfo, CINAHL, AMED, Embase, Cochrane & others *Svcs:* info, ref, biblio
Stock: bks/11000+, incl reports & leaflets; periodcls/100+
Classn: NLM *Staff:* Libns: 2 Non-Prof: 4

Bath

S97 🏛

American Museum in Britain Library

Claverton Manor, Bath, Somerset, BA2 7BD (01225-460503; *fax:* 01225-480726)

Gov Body: Trustees of the American Museum in Britain *Chief:* Libn/Editor: Mrs A.M. Armitage BA
Entry: ref only, adv appt *Open:* summer: Mon-Fri 0930-1730; winter: Mon-Fri 0930-1700
Subj: religion (Amish, Shakers, Penitentes); hortic; cooking; cartography; American decorative arts; arch; painting; US geog & hist; Native Americans; renaissance maps *Collns: Bks & Pamphs:* Dallas Pratt Colln (pubns on early printed maps); Antiques Magazine (complete run); incomplete files of American Heritage, Winterthur Portfolio & Maryland Historical Magazine
Equip: copier, video viewer
Stock: bks/10000; periodcls/46; photos/200; slides/400; pamphs/1000; audios/60; videos/30
Classn: DDC
Pubns: Newsletter (biannual); Journal (annual); full list of pubns available
Exp: £1000 (1999-2000)

Special Libraries

Bath ▼ Bedford

S98

Bath Royal Literary and Scientific Institution Library

16-18 Queen Sq, Bath, Somerset (01225-312084; *fax:* 01225-429452)
Email: exxbrlsi@bath.ac.uk
Internet: www.bath.ac.uk

Chief: Collns Chairman: Mr Robert Randall
Open: Mon-Fri 0930-1700
Subj: local studies (Bath & Somerset); sci; nat hist; archaeo; antiquities; geol; geog; religion; theology; church hist; lang; biography *Collns: Bks & Pamphs:* Rev Leonard Jenyns Colln (sci & nat hist, 17C-19C); Christopher Edmund Broome Colln (botany & mycology, 17C-19C); Bath Nat Hist & Antiquarian Field Club Lib; Somerset Archaeological & Nat Hist Soc (Bath Dist) Lib; Parliamentary Colln (c370 vols), incl House of Commons & House of Lords Journals; transactions of various learned socs; altases *Archvs:* Bath Royal Literary & Scientific Instn Archvs; Bath Nat Hist & Antiquarian Field Club Archvs; Jenyns Correspondence (between Leonard Jenyns & various 19C scientists incl Darwin & Henslow); various MS catalogues & maps *Other:* Photo Colln, incl Francis Lockey Colln (early calotypes); nat hist & archaeo drawings & illusts *Co-op Schemes:* AIL
Stock: bks/7000+

S99

Bath Spa University College Library

Newton Pk, Newton St Low, Bath, Somerset, BA2 9BN (01225-875490/30; *fax:* 01225-875493)
Email: j.parry@bathspa.ac.uk
Internet: http://www.bathspa.ac.uk/library/

Chief: Head of Lib & Info Svcs: Ms Julie Parry MLib, MCLIP
Assoc Libs: SION HILL LIB, 1st Floor, 8 Somerset Pl, Bath, BA1 5SF (01225-875763; *fax:* 01225-427080)
Entry: ref only by adv appt for non-membs, borrowing available for a fee *Open: Newton Park:* term: Mon, Wed 0900-2015, Tue, Thu 0900-2130, Fri 0930-2015, Sat 0930-1730, Sun 1300-1730; vac: Mon-Fri 0900-1300; *Sion Hill:* term: Mon-Thu 0900-2000, Fri 0930-2000, Sat 0930-1730, Sun 1300-1730; vac: varies
Subj: all subjs; undergrad; postgrad; local study (Bath) *Collns: Other:* Slide Lib (at Sion Hill Campus)
Equip: m-reader, m-printer, 5 video viewers, 5 copiers (5p per pg), clr copier (50p per pg), 60 computers (incl wd-proc, internet & CD-ROM)
Online: IDEAL, IBSS Online, ERIC, BEI; various CD-ROMs *Svcs:* ref, info
Stock: bks/175000; periodcls/1000; slides/40000; audios/900; AVs/4000
Classn: DDC *Auto Sys:* Olib *Staff:* 28

S100

City of Bath College, Open Learning Centre

Avon St, Bath, Somerset, BA1 1UP (01225-312191; *fax:* 01225-444213)
Email: hinchleyp@olc.citybathcoll.ac.uk
Internet: http://www.citybathcoll.ac.uk/

Chief: Learning Centre Mgr: Mr Peter Hinchley BA, MCLIP *Dep:* Learning Resources Co-ordinator: Ms Lesley Hall BA, MCLIP
Entry: ref only if not current student or staff
Open: Mon-Thu 0845-2030, Fri 0845-1630, Sat 0930-1230
Subj: all subjs; GCSE; A level; undergrad *Co-op Schemes:* SWRLS, BLDSC
Equip: 2 video viewers, 2 copiers, clr copier, computers (incl internet & 8 CD-ROM) *Svcs:* info, ref
Stock: bks/33000; periodcls/130; videos/1500
Classn: DDC *Auto Sys:* Heritage
Staff: Libns: 2 *Non-Prof:* 7 *Exp:* £35000 (1999-2000); £35000 (2000-01)

S101

Downside Abbey Library

Stratton-on-the-Fosse, Bath, Somerset, BA3 4RH (01761-232295 x155; *fax:* 01761-232973)

Gov Body: The Abbot of Downside *Chief:* Libn: The Rev (Dom) Daniel Rees MA, STL *Dep:* Archivist: Very Rev (Dom) Philip Jebb MA
Entry: adv appt plus letter of introduction *Open:* by arrangement
Subj: South West England; monastic hist; theology; liturgy; Byzantine studies; patristics, incl periodcls & bks from most of Western Europe *Collns: Bks & Pamphs:* English Catholic Recusant bks *Archvs:* records of English Benedictine Congregation
Equip: m-reader, fax, copier, computer (with wd-proc)
Stock: bks/150000; periodcls/200; photos/10000; pamphs/15000; maps/500; archvs/300 cubic yards; topographical postcards/40000
Pubns: Downside Review (quarterly, £22 pa, £6 for single copies)
Staff: Other Prof: 2 *Non-Prof:* 0.5

S102

Holburne Museum of Art, The Tanner Library and Archive

Gt Pulteney St, Bath, Somerset, BA2 4DB (01225-466669; *fax:* 01225-333121)
Email: a.m.e.wright@bath.ac.uk

Gov Body: Trustees of the Holburne Museum
Chief: Curator of Fine Art: Miss Amina Wright MA, DipAGMS *Dep:* Curator of Decorative Art: Lady E.J. White MA, FSA *Other Snr Staff:* Dir: Mr Christopher Woodward MA
Entry: adv appt, ref only *Open:* Mon-Fri 1100-1700; closed 15 Dec 2002-18 Feb 2003
Subj: fine arts; applied arts; decorative arts; arch; local hist (Bath) *Collns: Bks & Pamphs:* Ernest E. Cook Colln; T. Holburne Colln; Barbara Robertson Archv of Artists
Equip: copier, computer (with wd-proc, internet & CD-ROM) *Disabled:* lift access *Svcs:* ref
Stock: bks/3000; periodcls/2; slides/1000; pamphs/2
Staff: Non-Prof: 1 PT

S103

Museum of Costume, Library and Archives

(formerly Fashion Rsrch Centre)
4 Circus, Bath, Somerset, BA1 2EW (01225-477754; *fax:* 01225-444793)
Email: costume_enquiries@bathnes.gov.uk
Internet: http://www.museumofcostume.co.uk/

Type: local authority *Gov Body:* Bath & NE Somerset Council (see **P7**) *Chief:* Keeper of Collns: Ms Rosemary Harden BA, AMA
Entry: reading spaces must be booked in adv
Open: Thu-Fri 1000-1230, 1400-1630

Subj: arts; costume; hist of dress & fashion; accessories; textiles *Collns: Bks & Pamphs:* commercial fashion catalogues; fashion magazines *Archvs:* records of fashion firms, incl: Worth Archv; Paquin Archv; Mattli Archv; Sarah Dallas Knitwear Archv; personal archvs of costume historians, incl: Elizabeth Ewing Archv; Nancy Bradfield Archv *Other:* fashion plates; fashion photos; knitting patterns; dress-making patterns; misc works on paper
Equip: m-reader, copier (30p per pg), clr copier (£1.30 per pg) *Svcs:* info, ref
Stock: bks/3500; periodcls/5; photos/3500; slides/3000; illusts/10000; pamphs/500; archvs/c30 linear m; other materials/c150 linear m
Classn: own *Staff: Other Prof:* 2 *Non-Prof:* 1

S104

The Royal Photographic Society, Library

The Octagon, Milsom St, Bath, Somerset, BA1 1DN (01225-462841; *fax:* 01225-448688)
Email: pam@collections.rps.org
Internet: http://www.rps.org/book/bklib.html

Chief: Curator: Mrs Pamela Roberts BA(Hons), DipLib, FRSA
Entry: ref only, by appt one wk in adv; free access for membs of RPS, school children & 1st degree students *Open:* Tue Thu 1000 1300, 1400 1700
Subj: photography; hist of photography *Collns: Bks & Pamphs:* 18C pre-photography treatises; early writings on the invention & progress of photography; Du Mont Colln of photographically illustrated 19C bks *Archvs:* letters, catalogues etc relating to hist of RPS; Hurter & Driffield notebks; correspondence of photographers *Co-op Schemes:* BLDSC, ILL (photocopies only)
Equip: copier
Stock: bks/13000 + 13000 vols of bnd periodcls; periodcls/120; pamphs/2000; videos/100
Classn: own

S105

Royal United Hospital NHS Trust, Postgraduate Centre Library

Royal United Hosp, Bath, Somerset, BA1 3NG (01225-824897/8; *fax:* 01536-316575)
Email: library@ruh-bath.swest.nhs.uk

Chief: Head of Lib Svcs: Mr David Rumsey
Entry: NHS staff in the Bath area; adv appt for others *Open:* Mon-Fri 0900-1700; 24 hr access for membs
Subj: medicine; health *Co-op Schemes:* ILL
Equip: copier (A4/10p), 6 computers (incl wd-proc, internet & CD-ROM) *Online:* AMED, ASSIA for Health, BNI, CINAHL, Cochrane, DH-Data, Embase, Martindale, Medline, PsycInfo, Proquest, Zetoc *Svcs:* info, ref, biblio, lit searches
Stock: bks/14250; periodcls/305

S106

University of Bath, Library and Learning Centre

Bath, Somerset, BA2 7AY (01225-826835; *fax:* 01225-826229)
Email: library@bath.ac.uk
Internet: http://www.bath.ac.uk/library/

Gov Body: Univ of Bath *Chief:* Univ Libn: Mr H.D. Nicholson *Dep:* Dep Libn: Mr G.A. Rea
Entry: lending only after appl & payment of fee
Open: term, Xmas & Easter vacs: normally open 24 hrs, except closed Sun 0000-1000; summer vac: Mon-Fri 0900-2400, Sun 0900-1700
Subj: all subjs *Collns: Bks & Pamphs:* BSI; EDC; Pitman Colln (shorthand sys); Bath & West Soc Lib (agric, historical colln) *Co-op Schemes:* BLDSC, SWRLS

Equip: m-readers, m-camera, m-printers, video viewers, fax, copiers, clr copier, computer (with CD-ROM) *Online:* access restrict to Univ membs only *Stock:* bks/430000; periodcls/2100; maps/150; m-forms/1000; videos/150
Classn: UDC *Auto Sys:* Unicorn *Staff:* Libns: 20 *Non-Prof:* 50 *Exp:* £1075000 (1999-2000)

S107
Wessex Water Library
Claverton Down Rd, Claverton Down, Bath, Somerset, BA2 7WW (01225-526000; *fax:* 01225-528000)
Email: library@wessexwater.co.uk
Internet: http://www.wessexwater.co.uk/

Chief: Libn: Mr Ian Goodridge MA, BSc
Entry: ref only, by appt *Open:* Mon-Fri 0930-1630
Subj: sci; tech; water *Collns: Bks & Pamphs:* BSI; SI; CIRIA, WRC; WIR *Co-op Schemes:* SWRLS, BLDSC, Water Industry Lib Group
Stock: bks/14000; periodcls/150; pamphs/various; maps/various
Classn: DDC *Auto Sys:* Glas *Staff:* Libns: 2

Beamish

S108
BEAMISH, The North of England Open Air Museum, Regional Resource Centre
Beamish, Co Durham, DH9 0RG (0191-370-4000; *fax:* 0191-370-4001)
Email: museum@beamish.org.uk
Internet: http://www.beamish.org.uk/

Gov Body: Joint Cttee for BEAMISH, The North of England Open Air Museum *Chief:* Snr Keeper: Miss Rosemary E. Allan BA, AMA *Dep:* Keeper (Resource Colln): Mr Jim Lawson BSc
Entry: ref only, by adv appt *Open:* Mon-Fri 0900-1700
Subj: all subjs; local study (NE England); generalities; social & regional hist; agric; industry; religion; tech; arts; geog; hist *Collns: Bks & Pamphs:* large colln of printed trade catalogues from all over Gt Britain *Archvs:* printed ephemera *Other:* large photographic archv on computerised laser-disk sys; colln of oral recordings
Equip: copier, fax, video viewer, 3 computers (in search room), room for hire *Svcs:* info, ref
Stock: bks/70000; slides/100000; illusts/100000; maps/200; audios/250
Classn: DDC *Auto Sys:* Beamish System
Staff: Other Prof: 7 curators

Beckenham

S109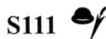
Bethlem Royal Hospital, Multidisciplinary Library
Bishopsgate Centre, Bethlem Royal Hosp, Monks Orchard Rd, Beckenham, Kent, BR3 3BX (020-8776-4817/8; *fax:* 020-8776-4819)

Gov Body: South London & Maudsley NHS Trust & King's Coll London (see **S1227**) *Chief:* Lib Mgr: Ms Claire Gabriel
Entry: staff of South London & Maudsley NHS Trust; staff of Community Health South London; staff & students of King's Coll London *Open:* Mon-Fri 0900-1700
Subj: mental health; psychiatry; psychiatric care; psy; sociology; health care mgmt; health policy
Co-op Schemes: ILL
Equip: m-fiche reader, video viewer, copier, 2 computers (incl internet), scanner, overhead projector *Online:* CINAHL, ChildData, Medline, PsycInfo *Svcs:* info, ref, lit searches

Stock: bks/6000; periodcls/40
Staff: Libns: 2

Mander and Mitchenson Theatre Collection
See TRINITY COLL OF MUSIC, JERWOOD LIB OF PERFORMING ARTS (**S1428**)

S110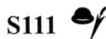
Postal History Society Library
c/o CBD Rsrch Ltd, 15 Wickham Rd, Beckenham, Kent, BR3 5JS (020-8650-9844)

Chief: Hon Libn: Mrs S.P.A. Henderson
Entry: private Soc lib open to membs only, by appt
Subj: postal hist; communications world-wide
Svcs: info, ref
Stock: bks/various bks, periodcls, pamphs & maps
Classn: A-Z author & subj *Staff:* 1 Hon Libn

Bedford

S111
Aircraft Research Association Ltd, Library
Manton Ln, Bedford, MK41 7PF (01234-350681; *fax:* 01234-328584)
Email: ara@ara.co.uk
Internet: http://www.ara.co.uk/

Chief: Libn: F.M. Guinevan
Entry: adv appt only
Subj: tech; aerospace eng; aerodynamics; wind tunnel eng
Stock: bks/3000; periodcls/20; m-forms/1000; aerospace reports/30000

S112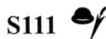
Bedford School Library
de Parys Ave, Bedford, MK40 2TU (01234-362200; *fax:* 01234-362283)
Email: library@bedfordschool.org.uk
Internet: http://www.bedfordschool.org.uk/info/schlib.htm

Chief: Libn: Mrs Janet Baxter BSc(Hons) *Dep:* Mrs Frances Litchfield *Other Snr Staff:* Archivist: Mr R.G. Miller (01234-362200); Old Bedfordian: Mr John Sharman (01234-362262)
Assoc Libs: each academic dept of the school also has its own lib
Open: Mon-Fri 0845-1700, Sat 0845-1230
Subj: all subjs; genl; GCSE & A-level; vocational
Collns: Bks & Pamphs: univ & careers info *Archvs:* records of Bedford School (1760-1945), incl: registers & other administrative records; material concerning the school, its pupils & staff; papers & memorabilia of old boys *Other:* audio & video colln *Co-op Schemes:* BLDSC
Equip: copier, 9 computers (incl wd-proc, internet & CD-ROM), printing, laminating & binding facilities *Online:* New Scientist, Newsbank, Oxford Reference Suite *Svcs:* info, ref, biblio
Stock: bks/14000; periodcls/45; audios/50; videos/300; CD-ROMs/40; DVDs/40
Classn: DDC *Auto Sys:* Autolib
Proj: new lib opening in Sep 2003

S113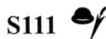
Cranfield University Library
Cranfield, Bedford, MK43 0AL (01234-754444; *fax:* 01234-752391)
Email: h.woodward@cranfield.ac.uk
Internet: http://www.cranfield.ac.uk/

Gov Body: Cranfield Univ *Chief:* Univ Libn: Dr Hazel Woodward BA, MCLIP

Assoc Libs: ROYAL MILITARY COLL OF SCI LIB (see **S2021**); SILSOE CAMPUS LIB (see **S114**)
Open: Mon-Fri 0830-1830, Sat 0930-1830
Subj: applied sci; tech; mgmt & social policy, incl aerospace; mechanical eng; materials; manufacturing; biotech; mgmt, transport; logistics
Collns: Bks & Pamphs: major colln of aerospace reports incl NASA, AGARD, AIAA, RAE, ARC (formerly part of the Aeronautic Rsrch Council colln) *Co-op Schemes:* BLDSC, UK Libs Plus, SCONUL Rsrch Extra, Milton Keynes Learning City Lib Network
Equip: m-reader, 3 copiers, computer (with CD-ROM), room for hire *Online:* Dialtech, Dialog, Orbit, STN, Datastar
Stock: bks/200000; periodcls/800
Classn: UDC *Auto Sys:* Libertas
Pubns: Cranfield Univ Press pubns
Staff: Libns: 21.8 *Non-Prof:* 28.2

S114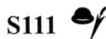
Cranfield University, Silsoe Campus Library
Barton Rd, Silsoe, Bedford, MK45 4DT (01525-863000; *fax:* 01525-863001)
Email: Silsoe-Library@cranfield.ac.uk
Internet: http://www.silsoe.cranfield.ac.uk/library/

Gov Body: Cranfield Univ (see **S113**) *Chief:* Libn: Mr C.J. Napper BA, DipLib, MCLIP
Assoc Libs: also acts as the official lib of the Inst of Agricultural Engineers
Entry: by arrangement *Open:* term: Mon-Fri 0900-2100, Sat 0900-1245; vac: Mon-Fri 0900-1730
Subj: agric; nat resource mgmt; eng; agric eng; mgmt; marketing; environmental sci; development studies; info tech; forestry; food sci; food tech; geog
Collns: Bks & Pamphs: Conservation Trust Colln (conservation & environment) *Co-op Schemes:* BLDSC, ALLCU
Equip: m-reader, m-printer, video viewer, fax, copiers, clr copier, 27 computers (incl internet & CD-ROM) *Online:* Dialog
Stock: bks/65000 (incl pamphs & reports); periodcls/425; slides/3805; maps/1540; m-forms/25000; audios/14; videos/53
Classn: UDC *Auto Sys:* Unicorn

S115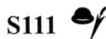
De Montfort University, Bedford Library
Polhill Ave, Bedford, MK41 9EA (01234-793077; *fax:* 01234-793209)
Internet: http://www.library.dmu.ac.uk/

Gov Body: De Montfort Univ (see **S921**) *Chief:* Lib Svcs Mgr: Ms Diana Saulsbury (ds@dmu.ac.uk) *Dep:* Snr Asst Libn: Ms Margaret Griffith (mg@dmu.ac.uk)
Entry: ref only for non-staff/students *Open:* term: Mon-Thu 0845-2100; Fri 0845-1700, Sat 1000-1545, Sun 1100-1645; vac: Mon-Fri 0900-1700
Subj: undergrad; postgrad; social sci; sociology; business studies; leisure studies; sports studies; adventure rec; dance; theatre; edu; physical edu; environmental studies; lit; hist; geog *Collns: Bks & Pamphs:* Hockcliffe Colln (early ch's bks, c1000 items, 1760-1840); historical colln of early physical edu bks *Co-op Schemes:* BLDSC, ILL, UK Libs Plus
Equip: m-form reader/printer, copiers, video viewers, 137 computers (incl wd-proc, internet & CD-ROM) *Online:* range of elec databases via ATHENS *Svcs:* info, ref
Stock: bks/c140000; periodcls/720
Classn: DDC *Auto Sys:* Talis
Staff: Libns: 8

Special Libraries

Bedford ▼ Belfast

S116 🐾 🏛 🎓

John Bunyan Museum and Library

Bunyan Meeting Free Church, 55 Mill St, Bedford, MK40 3EU *(tel & fax:* 01234-213722)
Email: pathurry@fsmail.net

Type: charity *Gov Body:* Trustees of Bunyan Meeting Free Church *Chief:* Libn: Miss Patricia Hurry MA, MCLIP
Entry: open throughout the year for groups/school parties by prior arrangement *Open:* from 1st Tue in March to last Sat in October: Tue-Sat 1100-1600 (last entry 1545)
Subj: local studies; lang; lit; religion; John Bunyan; nonconformist records *Collns: Bks & Pamphs:* John Bunyan's works & material associated with 17C *Archvs:* church records; records of nonconformist hist relaying to Bunyan Meeting *Other:* 17C-20C artefacts relating to Bunyan & the Church
Equip: fax, copier, computer (with wd-proc & CD-ROM); small fee for use of equip *Disabled:* access ramp, platform lift *Svcs:* info, ref
Stock: bks/1510; pamphs/140
Auto Sys: in-house sys
Pubns: full Catalogue of Bk Colln (£10)
Staff: Libns: 1 *Non-Prof:* 26 volunteer stewards
Proj: updating Souvenir Guide & Catalogue of Bks

S117 🏰 🎓

Silsoe Research Institute Library

Wrest Pk, Silsoe, Bedford, MK45 4HS (01525-860000; *fax:* 01525-860156)
Internet: http://www.sri.bbsrc.ac.uk/

Gov Body: BBSRC *Chief:* Head of Info Svcs: Mrs Anne Jarvis BSc, MSc, MCLIP (anne.jarvis@bbsrc.ac.uk) *Dep:* Lib Mgr: Mrs Margaret Arch BA (margaret.arch@bbsrc.ac.uk)
Entry: ref only, adv appt *Open:* Mon-Thu 0830-1700, Fri 0830-1630
Subj: physical scis: applications in agric, food & biotech; agric eng *Collns: Other:* tractor test reports *Co-op Schemes:* BLDSC
Equip: m-reader, m-printer, copier, computer (with wd-proc, internet & CD-ROM) *Svcs:* info, ref, biblio
Stock: bks/20000; periodcls/370 *Acqs Offcr:* Lib Mgr, as above
Classn: UDC
Pubns: Biennial Report (free)
Staff: Libns: 2 *Non-Prof:* 1 *Exp:* £58000 (1999-2000); £60000 (2000-01)

S118 🍂

Supply Chain Knowledge Centre

Centre for Logistics & Transportation, Cranfield Univ School of Mgmt, Cranfield, Bedford, MK43 0AL (01234-754931; *fax:* 01234-754930)
Email: sckc@cranfield.ac.uk
Internet: http://www.sckc.info/

Gov Body: Cranfield Univ (see **S113**) *Chief:* Knowledge Mgr: Ms Hilary Keeble
Entry: by appt; corporate membs free; non-membs are invited to request an introductory visit *Open:* Mon-Fri 0900-1730
Subj: logistics; supply chain mgmt
Equip: fax, copier, computers (incl internet) *Svcs:* info, ref, biblio, indexing, abstracting

Stock: bks/5000 incl reports; periodcls/120; slides/3000
Classn: in-house by subj *Auto Sys:* DBTextworks
Pubns: Internatl Logistics Abstracts (£175 UK, £215 overseas airmail); Supply Chain Practice (quarterly journal, £365 pa)
Staff: Libns: 1 *Non-Prof:* 1

Belfast

S119 🔑

Bar Library

PO Box 414, Royal Courts of Justice, Chichester St, Belfast, BT1 3JP (028-9024-1523; *fax:* 028-9023-1850)
Email: enquiries@barlibrary.com
Internet: http://www.barlibrary.com/

Gov Body: Inn of Court of Northern Ireland *Chief:* Libn: Mrs Niamh Doran LLB, MSc(Econ)
Entry: membs only *Open:* Mon-Fri 0830-1730
Subj: law; Northern Irish materials *Co-op Schemes:* Northern Ireland Legal Info Forum, BIALL
Equip: fax, video viewer, copiers, computers (incl wd-proc, internet & CD-ROM) *Online:* Lexis-Nexis
Svcs: info, ref, biblio, indexing
Stock: bks/40000, incl pamphs; periodcls/80
Classn: MOYS *Auto Sys:* Olib
Pubns: Bar Lib News (monthly); Annual Report (both for membs only)
Staff: Libns: 2 *Non-Prof:* 5

S120 🍂

Belfast Institute of Further and Higher Education, Library and Learning Resources

College Sq East, Belfast, BT1 6DJ (028-9026-5017; *fax:* 028-9026-5001)
Email: frobb@belfastinstitute.ac.uk
Internet: http://www.belfastinstitute.ac.uk/

Chief: Learning Resources Mgr: Mr Fred Robb
Assoc Libs: COLLEGE SQ LIB, addr as above, Centre Mgr: Mr Jim Hanna (028-9026-5072); COLLEGE SQ RESOURCE CENTRE, addr as above, Centre Mgr: Mr Stephen Murray (028-9026-5000 x3003); BRUNSWICK ST LRC, Brunswick St, Belfast, BT2 7GX, Centre Mgr: Mr Thomas McArdle (028-9026-5138; *fax:* 028-9026-5101); MILLFIELD LRC, 125-153 Millfield, Belfast, BT1 1HS, Centre Mgr: Ms Gerri Mitchell (028-9026-5434; *fax:* 028-9026-5401); TOWER ST LIB RESOURCE CENTRE, Tower St, Belfast, BT5 4FH, Centre Mgr: Ms Mary O'Kane-Walls (028-9026-5226; *fax:* 028-9026-5201); WHITEROCK LIB RESOURCE CENTRE, Whiterock Rd, Belfast, BT12 7PH, Centre Mgr: Mr David Fenton (028-9026-5363; *fax:* 028-9026-5351)
Open: Mon-Thu 0900-2000, Fri 0900-1630
Subj: all subjs; GCSE & A-level; undergrad
Equip: video viewer, copier, computers (incl internet & CD-ROM), laminating & binding facilities
Stock: bks/c67000; periodcls/c200; videos/c1300

S121 🔑

Belfast Library and Society for Promoting Knowledge (The Linen Hall Library)

17 Donegall Sq North, Belfast, BT1 5GB (028-9032-1707; *fax:* 028-9043-8586)
Email: info@linenhall.com
Internet: http://www.linenhall.com/

Chief: Libn: Mr John Gray BA, DipLIS *Dep:* Dep Libn: Mr John Killen MA, MLIS *Other Snr Staff:* Irish & Ref Libn: Mr Gerry Healey; Systems Libn: Ms Monica McErlane; Libn, Northern Ireland Political Colln: Ms Yvonne Murphy

Entry: borrowing for membs; others ref only
Open: Mon-Fri 0930-1730, Sat 0930-1600
Subj: all subjs; Ireland; Irish studies (particular strength); generalities; phil; psy; religion; social sci; lang; sci; tech; arts; lit; geog; hist *Collns: Bks & Pamphs:* Irish Hist Colln; Langs of Ulster Colln; Burns & Burnsiana Colln; Northern Ireland Political Colln; Genealogy Colln *Archvs:* Linen Hall Lib Archvs (1788 onwards); Clifton House Archv; MSS of local writers *Other:* Blackwood Pedigrees (Ulster family trees); Belfast Newsletter Births, Marriages & Deaths Index (1737-1863) *Co-op Schemes:* BLDSC, ILL
Equip: 3 m-readers, 3 m-printers, video viewer, fax, 3 copiers, 3 computers (all with internet & 1 with CD-ROM, internet £2 per hr), 2+ rooms for hire *Disabled:* lift access, specially designed desks
Svcs: info, ref
Stock: bks/140000; periodcls/220; photos/2500; slides/1000; pamphs/14000; maps/2000; m-forms/950; archvs/1000 vols
Classn: DDC (mod for local hist materials) *Auto Sys:* Talis
Pubns: A Hist of the Linen Hall Lib (£10); The Stage in Ulster from the 18th Century (£4.95); State of Play (£7.50); Images & Reflections (£5); Troubled Images (£12.95, £25 with CD-ROM); Ice Cream & Aliens (£9.95); Bunting's Ancient Irish Music (£22.50); William McCready of Whiteabbey (£1); An Uncommon Bookman (£5); The Heritage of the Harp (£2.50); The United Irishmen & the Govt of Ireland 1791-1801 (£2.50); The People's Panic (£2.50)
Staff: Libns: 5 *Other Prof:* 8 *Non-Prof:* 16 *Exp:* £49586 (1999-2000); £42151 (2000-01)

S122 🔑

Community Relations Council Reference Library

6 Murray St, Belfast, BT1 6DN (028-9022-7500; *fax:* 028-9022-7551)
Email: info@community-relations.org.uk
Internet: http://www.community-relations.org.uk/

Gov Body: Community Relations Council (registered charity) *Chief:* Dir of Communications: Mr Ray Mullan
Entry: open to rsrchers; ref only *Open:* Mon-Fri 0930-1645
Subj: community relations in Northern Ireland; cross-community relations; conflict resolution; cultural diversity; peace edu; reconciliation; sectarianism
Stock: bks/2200, incl reports & periodcls
Exp: majority of stock is publ in-house by local voluntary orgs

S123 🏰

Department of Agriculture and Rural Development (Northern Ireland), Library

Room 615, Upper Newtownards Rd, Dundonald House, Upper Newtownards Rd, Belfast, BT4 3SB (028-9052-4401; *fax:* 028-9052-5546)
Email: library@dardni.gov.uk
Internet: http://www.dardni.gov.uk/

Chief: Dir: Mr Noel Menary MCLIP *Dep:* Mrs Janice Ewing BLib, MCLIP
Entry: adv appt *Open:* Mon-Fri 0900-1700
Subj: public admin; environment; agric; hortic; forestry; fisheries; food sci; rural development *Co-op Schemes:* BLDSC, ILL
Equip: m-reader, m-printer, video viewer, fax, copier, computers (incl wd-proc, internet & CD-ROM), binder *Online:* Dialog *Svcs:* info, ref, biblio
Stock: bks/60000 (incl pamphs); periodcls/722; maps/590; m-forms/5138; audios/136; videos/104
Classn: DDC *Auto Sys:* C2
Staff: Libns: 3 *Non-Prof:* 5

S124 🏛

Department of Enterprise, Trade and Investment (Northern Ireland) Library

(formerly Dept of Economic Development Northern Ireland)
Netherleigh, Massey Ave, Belfast, BT4 2JP (028-9052-9555; *fax:* 028-9052-9286)
Email: library@deteni.gov.uk

Chief: Libn: Ms Ruth Menary DipLS, MCLIP (ruth.menary@deteni.gov.uk) *Other Snr Staff:* Libn: Ms June Jordan MCLIP
Entry: membs only
Subj: econ; economic development; mgmt; tech
Co-op Schemes: BLDSC, ILL
Stock: bks/16500; periodcls/200 *Acqs Offcr:* Libn, as above
Classn: DDC *Auto Sys:* Heritage
Staff: Libns: 2 *Non-Prof:* 2

S125 🏛

Department of Finance and Personnel, Northern Ireland, Construction Service Library

Room 1408, Churchill House, Victoria Sq, Belfast, BT1 4QW (028-9025-0338; *fax:* 028-9025-0100)
Email: info.cs@dfpni.gov.uk
Internet: http://www.dfpni.gov.uk/constructionservice/

Chief: Libn: Mrs A. Clarke
Open: Mon-Fri 0900-1700
Subj: quantity surveying; arch; bldg; civil, structural, mechanical eng; elec eng; bldg legislation; fire & safety; bldg products *Collns: Bks & Pamphs:* BSI (bldg legislation); agrément certificates; govt pubns; technical info; trade lit; Barbour (environment, mgmt, health & safety); microfiles; technical indexes
Equip: copier
Stock: bks/7000; periodcls/100

S126 ✚

Eastern Area Health Promotion, Communication Resource and Information Service

12-22 Linenhall St, Belfast, BT2 8BS (028-9032-1313; *fax:* 028-9055-3707)
Email: info@eahealthpro.org
Internet: http://www.eahealthpro.org/

Gov Body: South & East Belfast Health & Social Svcs Trust *Chief:* Resources Mgr: Ms Maureen Stephen BA, DipEurStudies (maureen.stephen@sebt.n-i.nhs.uk)
Entry: those working or studying within the Eastern Health & Social Svcs Board area *Open:* Mon-Thu 0930-1630, Fri 0930-1600
Subj: health promotion; health edu; sexual health; maternal & child health; community health; lifestyle; behavioural sci *Collns: Other:* range of leaflet/poster materials held for distribution to GPs, hosps, health centres, schools, colls, voluntary orgs etc
Equip: video viewer, 2 copiers (10p per copy), computer (with internet & CD-ROM, charge for printouts) *Online:* Medline, CancerLit *Officer-in-Charge:* Head of Communication: Mr D. McCabe
Svcs: info, ref
Stock: bks/c3000; periodcls/25; audios/25; videos/420; CD-ROMs/20 *Acqs Offcr:* Resources Mgr, as above
Classn: own *Auto Sys:* HPLIB 2000
Pubns: Catalogue of Resources Held in the Lib (CD-ROM, free)
Staff: Other Prof: 4 *Non-Prof:* 5 *Exp:* £60000 (1999-2000); £65000 (2000-01); incl exp on leaflets & publicity materials

S127 🎓 🙏 ♟

Edgehill Theological College Library

9 Lennoxvale, Belfast, BT9 5BY (028-9066-5870; *fax:* 028-9068-7204)
Email: office.edgehill@netmatters.co.uk
Internet: http://www.edgehilltheologicalcollege.org/

Gov Body: Methodist Church in Ireland *Chief:* Libn: Rev Donald Ker BA, BD, MTh
Entry: adv appt, ref only *Open:* Mon-Fri 0900-2100
Subj: religion; theology *Collns: Bks & Pamphs:* early Methodist bks & pamphs
Equip: copier, 5 computers *Svcs:* info
Stock: bks/18000; periodcls/12; videos/5
Classn: own *Staff: Non-Prof:* 1 PT *Exp:* £2000 (1999-2000); £2000 (2000-01)
Proj: new lib opened Nov 2002

S128 🏛

Geological Survey of Northern Ireland, Library and Information Service

20 College Gdns, Belfast, BT9 6BS (028-9066-6595; *fax:* 028-9066-2835)
Email: gsni@bgs.ac.uk

Gov Body: Dept of Enterprise, Trade & Investment for Northern Ireland *Chief:* Dir: Mr Garth Earls
Entry: adv appt; enqs accepted by phone, fax or email
Subj: geol; earth sci; surveying *Collns: Archvs:* Geological Survey of Northern Ireland records (1947-80); Geological Survey of Ireland records (1860-1921); extensive archv of geological data gathered from mid-19C onwards

S129 🏛

Invest Northern Ireland, Business Information Services and Euro Information Centre

(formerly Local Enterprise Development Unit)
Knowledge Mgmt Div, Upper Galwally, Belfast, BT8 4TB (028-9049-0486; *fax:* 028-9049-0490)
Email: bis@investni.com or eic@investni.com
Internet: http://www.investni.com/

Chief: Info Offcr: Ms Claire Gadd
Open: Mon-Fri 0900-1700
Subj: business info
Equip: fax, computers (incl CD-ROM)
Stock: bks/5000; periodcls/230
Staff: Libns: 3 *Other Prof:* 1 *Non-Prof:* 2

S130 ♟

Law Society of Northern Ireland Library

98 Victoria St, Belfast, BT1 3JZ (028-9023-1614; *fax:* 028-9023-2606)
Email: library@lawsoc-ni.org
Internet: http://www.lawsoc-ni.org/

Type: legal *Chief:* Libn: Mrs Heather Semple (hsemple@lawsoc-ni.org)
Entry: ref only; membs only *Open:* Mon-Fri 0900-1700
Subj: law; legislation (covering the jurisdictions of Northern Ireland, Republic of Ireland, UK & EU)
Collns: Bks & Pamphs: law reports
Equip: fax, copier, computer (with internet)
Online: Lexis, Justis *Svcs:* info, ref, biblio, indexing, abstracting, lit searching, current awareness, document delivery
Stock: bks/8000; periodcls/80
Classn: MOYS *Staff: Libns:* 2 *Non-Prof:* 2

S131 🎓

Methodist College, Library

1 Malone Rd, Belfast, BT6 6BY (028-9020-5205)
Email: ep@mcb.rmplc.co.uk
Internet: http://www.methody.org/library/library.html

Chief: Libn: Miss Elaine Patterson BA(Hons), DipLIS
Open: term: Mon-Fri 0830-1600; vac: closed July/August
Subj: all subjs; genl; GCSE; A level; local study (Belfast, local hist, geog & lit) *Collns: Archvs:* magazines, bks, leaflets about the school itself
Equip: computers (incl 3 internet, 3 CD-ROM, 1 computerised catalogue)
Stock: bks/18774; periodcls/17
Classn: DDC *Auto Sys:* Alice *Staff: Libns:* 1

S132 🏛

Northern Ireland Assembly Library

Parliament Bldgs, Stormont, Belfast, BT4 3XX (028-9052-1250; *fax:* 028-9052-1923)
Email: issuedesk.library@niassembly.gov.uk

Chief: Libn: vacant *Dep:* Reader Svcs Libn: Mr G.D. Woodman BA, DipLib, MCLIP
Entry: membs & staff of Northern Ireland Assembly; access for other Northern Ireland civil servants; postal & tel inquiries answered or referred elsewhere *Open:* Mon-Fri 0900-1700; remains open until one half hr after Assembly rises if this is later than 1630
Subj: religion & politics; church hist; politics; govt; public admin; law; dictionaries; Irish art & arch; British, Irish & Northern Irish hist *Collns: Bks & Pamphs:* parliamentary debates & hists; Northern Irish official pubns & legislation; 18C bks on Irish hist & travel; journals, votes etc, of pre-1800 Irish parliament *Co-op Schemes:* ILL
Equip: m-reader, copier, fax, 3 computers (all with wd-proc & internet, 2 with CD-ROM)
Stock: bks/25000+; periodcls/120+; pamphs/450; maps/100; m-forms/7500; official pubns/100000+
Classn: DDC *Auto Sys:* Heritage
Staff: Libns: 4 *Other Prof:* 9 *Non-Prof:* 3

S133 ♟

Northern Ireland Council for Voluntary Action, Reference Library

61 Duncairn Gdns, Belfast, BT15 2GB (028-9087-7777; *fax:* 028-9087-7799)
Email: info@nicva.org
Internet: http://www.nicva.org/

Type: community/voluntary sector *Chief:* Info Offcr: Ms Elaine Campbell
Entry: open to anyone with an interest in the voluntary sector; ref only, adv appt *Open:* Mon-Thu 0900-1700, Fri 0930-1640
Subj: social policy; community development; organisational development; local study (Northern Ireland) *Collns: Bks & Pamphs:* Scope Magazine (social affairs, publ by NICVA); annual reports of voluntary & community orgs *Other:* community development material
Equip: copier (12p per pg), 3 computers (all with wd-proc, internet & CD-ROM) *Svcs:* info, ref, biblio, indexing
Stock: bks/3000; periodcls/30; pamphs/2000; videos/12
Classn: community classn sys *Auto Sys:* BIBL
Pubns: Annual Report (free); current list available on request
Staff: Non-Prof: 1

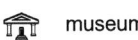

Special Libraries

Belfast
▼
Beverley

S134

Northern Ireland Museums Council, Library and Information Service

66 Donegal Pass, Belfast, Northern Ireland, BT7 1BU (028-9055-0215; *fax:* 028-9055-0216)
Email: info@nimc.co.uk
Internet: http://www.nimc.co.uk/

Type: non-departmental body *Chief:* Development Offcr: Mrs Heather McGuicken MA(Museum Studies)
Entry: ref only, adv appt *Open:* Mon-Fri 0900-1700; closed public hols
Subj: museology; conservation; other matters relating to museums, incl collns care, edu & access
Equip: copier *Svcs:* info, ref
Stock: bks/3800 bks, reports, journals & pamphs
Classn: by subj *Auto Sys:* MS Access
Staff: Other Prof. 1

S135

Northern Ireland Tourist Board, Research Library

St Anne's Ct, 59 North St, Belfast, BT1 1NB (028-9023-1221; *fax:* 028-9024-0960)
Email: researchlibrary@nitb.com
Internet: http://www.nitb.com/ (see also http://www.staruk.org.uk/)

Gov Body: Dept of Enterprise, Trade & Investment (Northern Ireland) *Chief:* Libn: Ms Lucia King
Dep: Rsrch Asst & Libn: Ms Heather Coyle
Assoc Libs: PHOTO LIB, at above addr
Entry: ref only, adv appt necessary *Open:* Mon 0930-1300, Tue, Thu 0930-1700, Wed 0930-1500
Subj: tourism (statistics & genl)
Equip: copier, computer (with wd-proc, internet & CD-ROM) *Svcs:* info, ref
Stock: bks/6000, incl pamphs; periodcls/60
Classn: own *Auto Sys:* TinLib
Pubns: Northern Ireland Tourist Board publishes a wide variety of consumer lit & corporate reports; the Rsrch Dept's statistical reports on Northern Ireland tourism are all available from the Lib
Staff: Libns: 1 PT

S136

Ordnance Survey of Northern Ireland, Map Library

Colby House, Stranmillis Ct, Belfast, BT9 5BJ (028-9025-5743; *fax:* 028-9025-5700)
Email: oldmaps@osni.gov.uk
Internet: http://www.osni.gov.uk/

Gov Body: Dept of the Environment for Northern Ireland *Chief:* Map Libn: Mr Ronnie McCausland
Entry: open to genl public; no appt required
Open: Mon-Fri 0915-1630; closed public hols
Subj: cartography; surveying; aerial photography
Collns: Bks & Pamphs: OS County Series bnd in large ref vols (complete, 1830-1900) *Other:* comprehensive coverage of Northern Ireland at all scales
Svcs: photocopying & reprographic svcs
Stock: bks/c16000
Pubns: official survey maps & plans of Northern Ireland

S137

The Police Museum, Library and Archives

PSNI HQ, 'Brooklyn', 65 Knock Rd, Belfast, BT5 6LE (028-9065-0222)
Email: museum@psni.police.uk
Internet: http://www.psni.police.uk/museum/

Gov Body: Police Svc of Northern Ireland *Chief:* Curator: Mr Hugh Forrester
Subj: law & order; crime; policing in Ireland & N Ireland; police records *Collns: Bks & Pamphs:* ref colln *Archvs:* records of Police Svc of N Ireland & predecessor bodies (early 19C onwards), esp Royal Ulster Constabulary; m-film copies of Royal Irish Constabulary svc records (1822-1922) *Other:* photographic colln
Svcs: ref, search svc (£15 per search)
Pubns: A Historical Guide to the RUC Museum (£5 + £1 p&p); The Women in Green (£4 + £1 p&p)

S138

Presbyterian Historical Society, Library and Archives

Church House, Fisherwick Pl, Belfast, BT1 6DW (028-9032-2248)

Gov Body: Presbyterian Church in Ireland *Chief:* Asst Sec: Mr Alan K. McMillan BA, MA
Entry: adv appt preferred *Open:* Mon-Fri 1000-1230, also open Wed 1315-1530
Subj: religion; local study (Ireland) *Collns: Archvs:* records of Presbyterian Congregations (mainly on m-film)
Equip: m-reader, copier *Svcs:* info, ref
Stock: bks/c4000; various photos, pamphs & archival materials
Classn: own
Staff: Other Prof: 1 *Exp:* £200 (1999-2000)

S139

The Queen's University of Belfast Library

Univ Rd, Belfast, BT7 1LS (028-9033-5020; *fax:* 028-9032-3340)
Email: n.russell.@qub.ac.uk
Internet: http://www.qub.ac.uk/lib/

Gov Body: Queen's Univ of Belfast *Chief:* Dir of Info Svcs: Mr Norman J. Russell BA, MPhil, MCLIP
Dep: Asst Dir (Rsrch Support): Mrs Elizabeth Traynor BA, MA; Asst Dir (Resources Mgmt): Mr Trevor A. Lyttle BSc, DipLS
Assoc Libs: AGRIC & FOOD SCIS LIB (see **S141**); ALTNAGELVIN LIB, Altnagelvin Area Hosp (see **S1475**); ARMAGH CAMPUS LIB (see **S42**); BIOMEDICAL LIB (see **S142**); MEDICAL LIB (see **S140**); SCI LIB, Lennoxvale, Belfast, BT9 5EQ, Libn: Miss S. Landy BA, DipLS (028-9033-5441; *fax:* 028-9038-2636; *email:* s.library@qub.ac.uk); SEAMUS HEANEY LIB, Botanic Ave, Belfast, BT7 1NN (028-9027-3966; *fax:* 028-9032-3340); VETERINARY SCIS LIB, Stoney Rd, Stormont, Belfast BT4 3SD, Libn: Ms Maxine Sprevak (028-9052-5622; *fax:* 028-9052-5773)
Entry: ref only unless a memb or associate memb; adv appt for Special Collns *Open:* term: Mon-Fri 0900-2200, Sat 0900-1230; vac: Mon-Fri 0900-1730, Sat 0900-1230
Subj: all subjs; genl; undergrad; postgrad; rsrch; local study (Ireland, all aspects) *Collns: Bks & Pamphs:* EDC; Hibernica Colln (Ireland & Celtic Studies); Simms Colln (early bks about Ireland/by Irishmen printed abroad); Gibson Colln (Thomas Moore); Savory Colln (Huguenot material); Ross-Rosenzweig Colln (Jewish theology/Dead Sea Scrolls); Macdouall Colln (genl lit, Sanskrit & comparative philology); historical colln of economic theory (incl part of lib of Adam Smith); Thomas Percy Lib (18C lib, reflecting tastes of English literary scholar, emphasis on ballad poetry &

romances); Antrim Presbytery Lib (16C-18C tech, phil & lit); plus genl colln of bks printed before 1801; first & limited eds, fine bindings & illustrated bks published post-1800; misc Western & Oriental MSS *Archvs:* Univ archv *Co-op Schemes:* BLDSC, ILL, BLCMP, SCONUL Rsrch Extra
Equip: 6 m-readers, 2 m-printers, 4 video viewers, 16 copiers, 350 computers *Online:* range of online svcs (free to staff & students; fees to others)
Stock: bks/1000000; periodcls/8000; slides/5000; pamphs/10000; maps/250; m-forms/5000; videos/2000, incl DVDs
Classn: LC *Auto Sys:* Talis
Pubns: Lib Guides (free)
Staff: Libns: 30 *Non-Prof:* 90 *Exp:* £1 mln (2000-01)

S140

Queen's University Medical Library

(incorporating the Northern Ireland Health & Social Svcs Lib)
Mulhouse Bldg, Mulhouse Rd, Belfast, BT12 6DP (028-9026-3377; *fax:* 028-9026-3221)
Email: med.info@qub.ac.uk
Internet: http://www.qub.ac.uk/lib/LibraryGuide/med/home.htm

Gov Body: Queen's Univ of Belfast (see **S139**)
Chief: Medical & Healthcare Libn: Mrs Gaynor Creighton BA, DipLS (g.creighton@qub.ac.uk)
Dep: Faculty Libn (Medicine & Health Scis): Mr Diarmuid Kennedy (d.g.kennedy@qub.ac.uk)
Assoc Libs: BIOMEDICAL LIB (see **S142**)
Entry: membs of the Univ; Health & Personal Social Svcs staff & Public Safety staff in Northern Ireland; associate membership available to others (annual subscription) *Open:* term: Mon-Fri 0830-2130, Sat 0900-1230; vac: Mon-Fri 0830-1730, Sat 0900-1230
Subj: medicine; dentistry; health; nursing; midwifery; clinical psy; social work; health mgmt & admin; professions allied to medicine *Collns: Bks & Pamphs:* 18C-19C medical works, incl Simms Colln; material of Northern Irish interest related to medicine *Co-op Schemes:* BLDSC, ILL
Equip: 4 copiers (£1 per 20 copies), 45 computers (incl wd-proc & internet) *Online:* BNI, CINAHL, Cochrane, HMIC, Medline, Web of Science, etc

S141

Queen's University of Belfast, Agriculture and Food Science Library

Agric & Food Science Centre, Newforge Ln, Belfast, BT9 5PX (028-9025-5227; *fax:* 028-9025-5400)
Email: k.latimer@qub.ac.uk
Internet: http://www.qub.ac.uk/lib/

Gov Body: Queen's Univ of Belfast (see **S139**)
Chief: Libn: Mrs Karen Latimer MA, DipLib
Assoc Libs: VETERINARY SCIS LIB, Stoney Rd, Stormont, Belfast BT4 3SD, Libn: Ms Maxine Sprevak (028-9052-5622; *fax:* 028-9052-5773)
Entry: ref only *Open:* term: Mon-Thu 0900-2130, Fri 0900-2100; vac: Mon-Fri 0900-1700
Subj: agric; food sci *Co-op Schemes:* BLDSC
Equip: video viewer, copier, 10 computers (incl 3 internet & 3 CD-ROM)
Stock: bks/30000; periodcls/400; videos/100
Classn: LC *Auto Sys:* Talis
Staff: Libns: 2 *Non-Prof:* 2 FTE

S142

Queen's University of Belfast, Biomedical Library

Univ Floor, Tower Block, Belfast City Hosp, Belfast, BT9 7AB (028-9026-3913; *fax:* 028-9031-5560)
Email: b.a.allen@qub.ac.uk
Internet: http://www.qub.ac.uk/lib/

Gov Body: Queen's Univ of Belfast (see **S139**)
Chief: User Svcs Libn: Ms Brenda Allen BA, DipLIS
Entry: QUB staff/students & DHSS staff; ref only for genl public unless registered as associate membs *Open:* term: Mon-Fri 0900-2100, Sat 0900-1230; vac: Mon-Fri 0900-1700, Sat 0900-1230
Subj: biomedical sci; medicine; pharmacy
Equip: 2 copiers (5p per pg), 8 computers (incl 4 with internet) *Online:* BNI, CINAHL, Cochrane, Medline *Svcs:* info, ref, biblio
Stock: bks/11500; periodcls/120
Classn: LC *Auto Sys:* Talis
Staff: Libns: 1 *Non-Prof:* 3.5

S143 ✚
Royal Belfast Hospital for Sick Children, Allen Memorial Reading Room

180 Falls Rd, Belfast, BT12 6BE (028-9024-0503 x3514)
Email: allen.room@royalhospitals.n-i.nhs.uk

Chief: Lib Asst in Charge: Ms Katharine Kinney BA(Hons)
Entry: postgrad & hosp staff, ref only *Open:* staffed 1 morning per wk; out of hrs access to hosp staff
Subj: medicine; paediatrics; neonatology
Equip: computer (with wd-proc, internet & CD-ROM) *Online:* Medline *Svcs:* info, ref, internet tutoring
Stock: bks/400; periodcls/20
Classn: NLM
Staff: Non-Prof: 1 PT
Further Info: The Allen Memorial Reading Room is a small specialist paediatric postgrad lib; for any queries please contact the Northern Ireland Health & Social Svcs Lib, Castle Bldgs, Stormont, Belfast, BT4 3SJ

S144 🎓
St Mary's University College Library

191 Falls Rd, Belfast, BT12 6FE (028-9032-7678; *fax:* 028-9033-3719)
Internet: http://www.stmarys-belfast.ac.uk/

Gov Body: constituted as a Univ Coll of Queen's Univ of Belfast (see **S139**), but is independent in financial matters *Chief:* Libn: Mr John Morrissey BA, DipLS (j.morrissey@stmarys-belfast.ac.uk)
Dep: Asst Libn: Ms Felicity Jones BA, DipLS (f.jones@stmarys-belfast.ac.uk) *Other Snr Staff:* Mr Ciaran Crossey MSc, BSSc (c.crossey@stmarys-belfast.ac.uk)
Entry: ref only unless registered as an external reader; must seek permission at Issue Desk & sign in *Open:* term: Mon-Thu 0900-2100, Fri 0900-1700, Sat 0900-1300; vac: Mon-Fri 0900-1700
Subj: all subjs; undergrad; postgrad; strong collns in: Irish lang; edu; religious studies; ch's lit; business studies; finance; econ; politics; European studies; human development *Collns:* Bks & Pamphs: Magee Colln (bks & other materials on Irish hist, lit & edu); Irish Medium Colln (Irish lang)
Co-op Schemes: BLDSC
Equip: m-reader, 2 copiers (5p), 2 video viewers, 30 computers (all with wd-proc, internet & CD-ROM), 2 rooms for hire *Online:* various databases *Officer-in-Charge:* Dr D. Maley (d.maley@stmarys-belfast.ac.uk)
Stock: bks/c100000; periodcls/300; large colln of AV materials *Acqs Offcr:* Acqs Libn: Mr Ciaran Crossey MSc, BSSc (c.crossey@stmarys-belfast.ac.uk)
Classn: DDC *Auto Sys:* Talis
Staff: Libns: 3 *Other Prof:* 2 *Non-Prof:* 4

S145 🎓
Stranmillis University College Library

Stranmillis Rd, Belfast, Northern Ireland, BT9 5DY (028-9038-4312; *fax:* 028-9066-3682)
Email: library@stran.ac.uk
Internet: http://www.stran-ni.ac.uk/

Gov Body: Queen's Univ of Belfast (see **S139**)
Chief: Libn & Head of Learning Support Svcs: Mr E.J.W. McCann (w.mccann@stran.ac.uk) *Dep:* Dep Libn: Miss C.E. Doherty (c.doherty@stran.ac.uk)
Open: term: Mon-Thu 0900-2100, Fri 0900-1630, Sat 0900-1300; vac: Mon-Thu 0900-1230, 1330-1700, Fri 0900-1230, 1330-1630
Subj: all subjs; undergrad; postgrad *Co-op Schemes:* ILL
Equip: Online: BIDS, BioMed, CAB Online, Cambridge Scientific Abstracts, ChildData, CINAHL, EconLit, ERIC, Geobase, IBSS, Ingenta Journals, Inspec, OCLC FirstSearch, SciDirect, Web of Science, Zetoc & others
Stock: bks/120000; periodcls/500; m-forms/5000; audios/1000; videos/200; multimedia packs/200
Acqs Offcr: Asst Libn (Acqs): Mrs L.B. Dean (l.dean@stran.ac.uk)

S146 🔑 🏛
Ulster Museum Library

Botanic Gdns, Belfast, BT9 5AB (028-9038-3000; *fax:* 028-9038-3003)
Email: history.um@nics.gov.uk

Gov Body: Natl Museums & Galleries of Northern Ireland
Assoc Libs: PICTURE LIB, addr as above (028-9038-3113; *fax:* 028-9038-3103)
Entry: ref, by prior appt *Open:* Mon-Fri 1000-1230, 1400-1630
Subj: archaeo (incl ethnography); art (fine & applied); botany; conservation; design; geol (incl mineralogy & palaeontology); industrial archaeo; local hist; museology; numismatics; photography; zoology *Collns:* Bks & Pamphs: Belfast printed bks (c200 items, 1700-1850) *Other:* R.J. Welch Photo Colln (5000 negs, 1874-1935); A.R. Hogg Photo Colln (6000-7000 negs, lantern slides & prints, 1895-1940)
Equip: copier (10p per sheet)
Stock: bks/35000; periodcls/200; photos/15000; slides/10000; pamphs/250; maps/200
Pubns: List of the Photographs in the R.J. Welch Colln in the Ulster Museum, Vol I: Topography & Hist; Vol II: Botany, Geol & Zoology

S147 🎓 🙏
Union Theological College, Gamble Library

108 Botanic Ave, Belfast, BT7 1JT (028-9020-5093; *fax:* 028-9058-0040)
Email: librarian@union.ac.uk

Gov Body: Presbyterian Church in Ireland *Chief:* Libn: Mr Stephen Gregory
Entry: adv appt preferred; membership may be available on payment of subscription *Open:* Mon-Thu 0900-1700, Fri 0900-1630
Subj: theology; religion *Collns:* Bks & Pamphs: early printed bks *Archvs:* principally related to the Presbyterian Church in Ireland
Equip: m-reader, copier, 5 computers (incl 4 wd-proc & 4 CD-ROM) *Svcs:* info, ref, biblio
Stock: bks/48000; periodcls/85; pamphs/18000; m-forms/4; audios/230; videos/90; CD-ROMs/10; theses/180
Classn: LC, own *Auto Sys:* Heritage

Staff: Libns: 1 *Exp:* £20000 (1999-2000); £20000 (2000-01)
Proj: lib refurbishment & extension (2002-03)

Belvedere

S148 🎓
Bexley College Learning Centre

Tower Rd, Belvedere, Kent, DA17 6JA (01322-442331; *fax:* 01322-448403)
Email: enquiries@bexley.ac.uk
Internet: http://www.bexley.ac.uk/

Gov Body: Bexley Coll *Chief:* Head of Learning Resources: Mr R.M. Thompson BA(Hons), MA, MCLIP
Assoc Libs: ST JOSEPH'S CAMPUS LIB, Woolwich Rd, Abbey Wood, London, SE2 0AR; ERITH RD CAMPUS LIB, Erith Rd, Belvedere, Kent, DA17 6HF
Entry: full membs to students, others by special arrangement *Open:* Mon-Thu 0900-1900, Fri 0900-1700; vac: Mon-Fri 1000-1600
Subj: genl; GCSE; A level; vocational *Co-op Schemes:* ILL
Equip: video viewers, 3 copiers, computers (incl wd-proc, internet & CD-ROM) *Online:* Reuters Online *Svcs:* info, ref, biblio
Stock: bks/c28000; periodcls/150; videos/700
Classn: DDC *Auto Sys:* AutoLib
Staff: Libns: 2 *Non-Prof:* 7

Berkhamsted

S149 🎓 ✒
Ashridge Learning Resource Centre

Ashridge, Berkhamsted, Hertfordshire, HP4 1NS (01442-841170; *fax:* 01442-841209)
Email: sue.portch@ashridge.org.uk
Internet: http://www.ashridge.org.uk/services/lrc.html

Gov Body: Ashridge Trust *Chief:* Dir of Learning Resources: Ms Sue Portch
Open: 24 hrs a day, 7 days a wk
Subj: business; mgmt; training *Collns:* Other: mgmt training videos *Co-op Schemes:* ILL, HERTIS, EBSLG, UKOLUG, BBSLG
Equip: 50 computers (incl wd-proc, internet & CD-ROM) *Online:* ABI Inform, Dun & Bradstreet, Reuters & others
Stock: bks/15000; periodcls/500; videos/300; AVs/159
Pubns: catalogue available on request

Beverley

S150 🎓
Bishop Burton College, Library and Information Centre

Bishop Burton, Beverley, E Yorkshire, HU17 8QG (01964-553103; *fax:* 01964-553101)

Chief: Coll Libn: Mrs Janice Godwin
Entry: staff & students *Open:* term: Mon 0900-2100, Tue-Fri 0900-2000, Sat 1000-1200, 1230-1600
Subj: genl; undergrad; vocational; social sci; mgmt; agric; hortic; arts; interior design *Co-op Schemes:* ILL
Equip: m-reader, video viewer, copier, computers (incl wd-proc, internet & CD-ROM)
Stock: bks/20000; periodcls/260; pamphs/7500; videos/300; CD-ROMs/50; student projects/1000
Classn: DDC *Auto Sys:* Heritage
Pubns: Lib Guide (free)
Staff: Libns: 1 *Non-Prof:* 4

Special Libraries
Bexhill-on-Sea ▼ Birmingham

Bexhill-on-Sea

S151 🔑🏛
Bexhill Museum Library
Egerton Rd, Bexhill-on-Sea, E Sussex, TN39 3HL
(*tel & fax*: 01424-787950)
Email: museum@rother.gov.uk
Internet: http://www.bexhillmuseum.co.uk/

Gov Body: Bexhill Museum Assoc *Chief:* Libn:
Mrs Margaret Ellis BSc *Other Snr Staff:* Curator:
Mr Julian Porter; Administrator: Mr Don Phillips
Entry: ref only, adv appt *Open:* Mon-Fri 1000-
1700; closed Xmas & Jan
Subj: local studies (Bexhill & Rother Dist) *Collns:*
Archvs: archv of documents & maps relating to the
Bexhill area
Equip: m-reader, copier (30p-50p), video viewer, 3
computers (all with wd-proc & CD-ROM), room for
hire (£6 per hr) *Officer-in-Charge:* Administrator,
as above *Svcs:* info, ref
Stock: bks/2500+; videos/12; various periodcls,
photos, pamphs & maps *Acqs Offcr:* Curator, as
above
Classn: DDC
Pubns: various bklets on aspects of local hist, incl:
Wartime Food (£2.50); Churches Together in
Bexhill (£3); Our Second Pilgrimage: Tales of Old
Bexhill (£1.99); 100 Years of Bexhill Motor Buses
(£1.99); Bexhill's Maharajah (£1.99)
Staff: Libns: 0.5 *Other Prof:* 2

Biggar

S152 🔑🏛
Leadhills Miners Library
15 Main St, Leadhills, Biggar, Lanarkshire, ML12
6XP (01659-74326)
Internet: http://www.lowtherhills.fsnet.co.uk/

Gov Body: Leadhills Heritage Trust *Chief:*
Chairman of Trust: Mr H. Shaw *Dep:* Vice-Chair:
Mrs M. Hamilton
Open: May-Oct: Wed, Sat-Sun 1400-1600; adv
appt required outside hrs
Subj: local study (Biggar, mining); phil (pre-1850);
religion; lit; hist; geog *Collns: Archvs:* Gibson
family correspondence *Other:* photos of local area
Svcs: info *Staff: Non-Prof:* 9

Birmingham

S153 🔑
**Aluminium Federation, Library and
Information Service**
Broadway House, Calthorpe Rd, Five Ways,
Birmingham, B15 1TN (0121-456-6100; *fax:* 0121-
456-2274)
Email: ais@alfed.org.uk
Internet: http://www.alfed.org.uk/

Type: trade assoc *Chief:* Info Mgr: Mr David J.
Keevil MCLIP (d_keevil@alfed.org.uk)
Entry: sustaining memb companies of ALFED;
bona fide students of UK establishments by adv
appt; an annual subscription svc AIS (Aluminium
Info Svc) allows access for non-membs of ALFED
(see web site or contact the Info Mgr) *Open:* Mon-
Fri 0930-1700

Subj: aluminium & its alloys *Collns: Bks &
Pamphs:* trade lit; reports *Co-op Schemes:*
BLDSC
Equip: copiers, computers *Svcs:* info, ref,
databases searches
Stock: bks/2000+; periodcls/200; pamphs/15000
Classn: DDC *Staff: Libns:* 1

S154 🎓
**Aston University, Library and
Information Services**
Aston Triangle, Birmingham, B4 7ET (0121-359-
3611; *fax:* 0121-359-7358)
Email: library@aston.ac.uk
Internet: http://www.aston.ac.uk/lis/

Chief: Dir: Dr Nick Smith PhD, MSc, MCLIP
Entry: ref only; elec info svcs & computing
facilities for staff & students of Aston Univ only
Open: term & vac: Mon-Tue, Thu-Fri 0900-2200,
Wed 1000-2200, Sat 1000-1700, Sun 1300-1700
Subj: undergrad; postgrad; rsrch; lang; tech; mgmt
Co-op Schemes: BLDSC, Access West Midlands,
SCONUL Vac Access Scheme, UK Libs Plus, BIN,
MidMAN (West Midlands HE & FE data network)
Equip: m-readers, 2 m-printers (A4/10p), 4 video
viewers, 10 copiers (A4/5p), 35 computers (incl 20
with wd-proc, 34 with internet & 4 with CD-ROM), 3
rooms for hire (incl computer suite) *Disabled:*
CCTV based magnification sys, closed caption
video reader *Online:* BIDS IBSS, Web of Science
ISF, Inspec, Compendex, Medline, Proquest Direct,
FT Discovery (staff & students only)
Stock: bks/326978; periodcls/3511; videos/570
Classn: DDC, UDC *Auto Sys:* DS
Pubns: Annual Report on web site
Staff: Libns: 9 *Other Prof:* 4 *Non-Prof:* 25 *Exp:*
£652000 (1999-2000); £683000 (2000-01)

S155 🎓🏛
**Barber Institute of Fine Arts
Library**
Univ of Birmingham, Edgbaston, Birmingham, B15
2TS (0121-414-7334; *fax:* 0121-414-5853)
Email: d.pulford@bham.ac.uk
Internet: http://www.is.bham.ac.uk/barberart/
about.htm

Gov Body: Univ of Birmingham Info Svcs (see
S179) *Chief:* Fine Art Libn: Mr David Pulford
BA(Hons), DipLib, MCLIP
Open: term: Mon-Thu 0900-1900, Fri 0900-1700,
Sat 0900-1300; vac: Mon-Fri 0900-1700
Subj: arts; fine art *Collns: Other:* sales
catalogues
Equip: m-reader, copier, 2 computers (both with
internet, 1 with CD-ROM) *Online:* BIDS, EDINA
Svcs: info, ref, biblio
Stock: bks/50000, incl pamphs & m-forms;
periodcls/115; videos/6; CD-ROMs/13
Classn: LC *Auto Sys:* Talis
Staff: Libns: 1 *Non-Prof:* 2 *Exp:* £21910 (1999-
2000)

S156 🔑
**Birmingham and Midland Institute
Library**
9 Margaret St, Birmingham, B3 3BS (0121-236-
3591; *fax:* 0121-212-4577)
Email: admin@bmi.org.uk
Internet: http://www.bmi.org.uk/

Gov Body: BMI Council *Chief:* Administrator: Mr
Philip St Fisher
Entry: membs of BMI only *Open:* Mon-Fri 1000-
1800
Subj: local studies (Birmingham & Midlands);
generalities; phil; psy; religion; social sci; sci;
maths; arts; lit; geog; hist; travel; fiction; biography

Collns: Bks & Pamphs: Joseph Priestley Colln;
Housman Colln; Francis Brett Young Colln;
Dickens Colln; pamph colln (18C-19C) *Archvs:*
minutes & other records of the Birmingham &
Midland Inst *Other:* music lib (classical LPs &
CDs) *Co-op Schemes:* AIL
Equip: fax, copier, rooms for hire (various prices)
Stock: bks/c100000; pamphs/3000; audios/8000
Classn: own

S157 ➕
**Birmingham Children's Hospital
NHS Trust, Library**
Birmingham Children's Hosp, Steelhouse Ln,
Birmingham, B4 6NH (0121-333-8642; *fax:* 0121-
333-8641)
Email: ursula.ison@bhamchildrens.wmids.nhs.uk

Gov Body: Birmingham Children's Hosp NHS
Trust *Chief:* Trust Libn: Mrs Ursula J. Ison BSc,
DipLib, MCLIP
Entry: Trust staff; ref only for genl public, by appt
Open: Mon-Fri 0900-1700
Subj: medicine; paediatrics *Co-op Schemes:*
BLDSC, WMHLN, NULJ
Equip: m-reader, copiers (A4/5p, A3/10p), 6
computers (with wd-proc, internet & CD-ROM)
Online: Medline, CINAHL, Cochrane, AMED,
PsycInfo, Embase (on Trust network) *Svcs:* info,
ref
Stock: bks/4000; periodcls/160; videos/15
Classn: LC *Auto Sys:* Heritage
Staff: Libns: 1 *Non-Prof:* 1.5

S158 🎓
**Birmingham Conservatoire, Library
Services**
Paradise Pl, Birmingham, B3 3HG (0121-331-
5914; *fax:* 0121-331-5906)
Email: conservatoire.library@uce.ac.uk
Internet: http://www.uce.ac.uk/library/public/

Gov Body: Univ of Central England (see **S183**)
Chief: Faculty Libn: Mr R.V. Allan
Subj: music *Collns: Other:* Granville Bantock
Colln (printed music); Birmingham Flute Soc Colln
(printed music) *Co-op Schemes:* ILL, IAML
Stock: bks/7300; periodcls/66; m-forms/15;
audios/100700; videos/125; MSS/25; theses/60;
printed music/100000 sheets
Classn: DDC

S159 ➕
**Birmingham Heartlands Hospital
Library**
Edu Centre, Bordesley Green East, Birmingham,
B9 5SS (0121-424-2583; *fax:* 0121-424-0584)
Email: lesley.allen@heartsol.wmids.nhs.uk

Gov Body: Birmingham Heartlands & Solihull NHS
Trust *Chief:* Lib Mgr: Miss Lesley Allen BA(Hons)
Assoc Libs: SOLIHULL HOSP LIB (see **S1931**)
Entry: Trust staff; others at discretion of Lib Mgr
Open: Mon-Fri 0900-1930; 24 hr access with
swipe card for registered users
Subj: multidisciplinary: medicine; nursing; related
professions *Co-op Schemes:* BLDSC
Equip: video viewer, copier, computers (incl wd-
proc, internet & CD-ROM) *Svcs:* info, ref, biblio
Stock: bks/3500; periodcls/145; videos/25
Classn: LC *Staff: Libns:* 1 *Non-Prof:* 4

S160 🎓
**Birmingham Institute of Art and
Design Library**
Corporation St, Gosta Green, Birmingham, B4 7DX
(0121-331-5860)
Internet: http://library.uce.ac.uk/

Gov Body: Univ of Central England (see **S183**)
Chief: Faculty Libn: Mr John Ridgway
(john.ridgway@uce.ac.uk) *Dep:* Subj Libn: Ms
Ruth Showler (ruth.showler@uce.ac.uk)
Assoc Libs: COLL OF ART LIB, Margaret St,
Birmingham, B3 3BX (0121-331-5977); BOURN-
VILLE COLL OF ART LIB, Linden Rd, Bournville,
Birmingham, B30 1JX (0121-331-5756); SCHOOL
OF JEWELLERY LIB, Vittoria St, Hockley,
Birmingham, B1 3PA (0121-331-6470)
Open: term: Mon-Thu 0900-2000, Fri 0900-1700;
vac: Mon-Thu 0900-1300, 1400-1700, Fri 0900-
1300, 1400-1600
Subj: Inst of Art & Design: art; design; hist of art;
hist of design; visual communication; fashion;
textiles; 3D design; *Coll of Art:* fine art; art edu;
Bournville: genl art & design; *School of Jewellery:*
jewellery; horology; silversmithing *Collns:* Bks &
Pamphs: bks on indiv artists & photographers
Other: slide colln *Co-op Schemes:* BLDSC, UK
Libs Plus
Equip: 2 m-readers, video viewer, 2 copiers, clr
copier, 18 computers (incl 14 with internet & 2 with
CD-ROM), DVD player *Svcs:* info, ref, biblio
Acqs Offcr: Faculty Libn, as above
Classn: DDC *Auto Sys:* Talis
Staff: Libns: 5 *Non-Prof:* 16

S161

Birmingham Law Society Library

8 Temple St, Birmingham, B2 5BT (0121-643-
9116; *fax:* 0121-633-3507)
Email: lib1@birminghamlawsociety.co.uk

Type: legal, prof soc *Gov Body:* Birmingham Law
Soc *Chief:* Head of Lib Svcs: Ms Hilary Boucher
MLS, MCLIP *Other Snr Staff:* Asst Libn: Mr
Richard Field MA, BA
Entry: membs; law students (ref only, on
production of student card); others discretionary, by
adv appt only *Open:* Mon-Fri 0900-1700
Subj: law; practitioners' lib primarily, but some
texts & periodcls for common & undergraduate/
postgrad study
Equip: copier (A4/10p, A3/20p), 4 computers (all
with wd-proc & CD-ROM, 2 with internet) *Online:*
Lawtel, Westlaw, some Butterworth Direct svcs;
printouts 20p *Svcs:* info, ref, biblio, indexing
Stock: bks/40000+; periodcls/various
Classn: Moys *Auto Sys:* LIMES
Staff: Libns: 2 *Non-Prof:* 2

S162 ✚

Birmingham Women's Hospital NHS Trust, Trust Library and Information Service

Edu Resource Centre, Metchley Park Ln,
Edgbaston, Birmingham, B15 2TG (0121-472-
1377; *fax:* 0121-623-6922)

Gov Body: Birmingham Women's Hosp NHS
Trust *Chief:* Trust Clinical Libn: Mrs Mary
Publicover (Mary.Publicover@bham-womens.
thenhs.com) *Dep:* Asst Libn: Mr Derick Yates
(derek.yates@bham-womens.thenhs.com)
Entry: Trust staff & students on attachment; others
by appt only *Open:* Mon-Fri 0900-1700
Subj: medicine; women's health
Equip: copier, 7 computers (all with internet, 6 with
wd-proc & 6 with CD-ROM) *Disabled:* indiv needs
of Trust staff catered for *Online:* Medline, CINAHL,
AMED, Embase, Psychiatric, PreMedline, PsycInfo,
full-text journal colln (Trust staff only) *Officer-in-
Charge:* Trust Clinical Libn, as above *Svcs:* info,
ref
Stock: bks/1171, plus c500 vols of bnd periodcls;
periodcls/54; pamphs/11; videos/6 *Acqs Offcr:*
Asst Libn, as above
Classn: NLM *Staff:* Libns: 1.5

S163

Bournville College of Further Education, Library Resources Centre

Bristol Rd South, Northfield, Birmingham, B31 2AJ
(0121-483-1012; *fax:* 0121-411-2231)
Email: info@bournville.ac.uk
Internet: http://www.bournville.ac.uk/

Gov Body: Bournville Coll Corp *Chief:* Lib
Resources Mgr: Mrs Angela Daniels BEd, MPhil,
PGDipLib, ALCM *Dep:* Tutor Libn: Mr Sarinder Pal
Singh BA, MA, DipLib
Entry: membs of Coll; registered external users
Open: term: Mon-Thu 0900-1930, Fri 0900-1530,
Sat 1030-1230; vac: Mon-Fri 0900-1600
Subj: all subjs; genl; GCSE; A level; vocational;
local studies (Birmingham)
Equip: copier, 14 computers (all with wd-proc &
internet, 2 with CD-ROM) *Disabled:* CCTV *Svcs:*
info, ref, biblio
Stock: bks/18700; periodcls/44; audios/185;
videos/162; CD-ROMs/85 *Acqs Offcr:* Lib
Resources Mgr, as above
Classn: DDC *Auto Sys:* Heritage
Staff: Libns: 2 *Non-Prof:* 2

S164 ✑

Cadbury Trebor Bassett, Library and Information Service

Bournville, Birmingham, B30 2LU (0121-458-2000;
fax: 0121-451-4333)
Email: sarah.foden@csplc.com

Chief: Info Mgr: Miss S. Foden BA(Hons)
Subj: chocolate scis; chocolate tech; business
records *Collns:* Bks & Pamphs: William Cadbury
Colln (hist of cocoa & of South America) *Archvs:*
records of Cadbury Ltd, Cadbury Schweppes Ltd &
subsidiaries (19C-20C); records of British Cocoa &
Chocolate Co Ltd (1919-1958); sales & publicity
records of Chivers & Sons Ltd (jam manufacturers,
1882-1976); records of J.S. Fry & Sons Ltd
(chocolate manufacturers, 19C-20C); records of
R.M. Holborn & Sons Ltd (tea, coffee & cocoa
dealers, 1936-41); minutes & accounts of Meriden
Tea Co Ltd (1947-67); records of James Pascall
Ltd (confectionary manufacturers, 1866-1969);
records of Typhoo Tea Ltd (1905-75) *Co-op
Schemes:* ILL
Equip: *Online:* Chocolate Science & Technology
Stock: bks/7000; periodcls/250; m-forms/1000;
films/25

S165 ✑

The Castings Development Centre, Library and Information Services

Bordesley Hall, The Holloway, Alvechurch,
Birmingham, B48 7BQ (01527-66414; *fax:* 01527-
585070)
Email: j.goundry@castingstechnology.com
Internet: http://www.castingsdev.com/

Chief: Head of Lib & Info Svcs: Ms Jan Goundry
Entry: membs only, by adv appt *Open:* Mon-Fri
0900-1700
Subj: sci; tech; cast metals tech; ironfounding;
metallurgy *Collns:* Bks & Pamphs: patents &
standards; reports *Co-op Schemes:* BLDSC
Equip: computers (incl wd-proc, internet & CD-
ROM) *Svcs:* info, ref, biblio, abstracting, lit
searches, current awareness
Stock: bks/15000; periodcls/40; photos/100000;
illusts/10000; pamphs/3000; standards/20000;
patents/30000
Classn: own *Auto Sys:* DBTextworks
Pubns: list of pubns available on web site
Staff: Libns: 1 *Non-Prof:* 2

S166

City College Birmingham, Learning Resource Service

The Council House, Soho Rd, Handsworth,
Birmingham, B21 9DP (0121-256-1050; *fax:* 0121-
523-4447)
Email: cwest@citycol.ac.uk
Internet: http://www.citycol.ac.uk/

Gov Body: City Coll, Birmingham *Chief:*
Learning Resources Mgr: Mrs Carol West
BA(Hons), MA, MCLIP *Other Snr Staff:* Snr
Resource Offcrs: Mrs Lydia Buaben BA, MCLIP
(lamoah@citycol.ac.uk); Mrs Kath Collman BLib,
MA, MCLIP (kcollman@citycol.ac.uk); Ms Diane
Gant (dgant@citycol.ac.uk); Ms Gloria Hunt
(ghunt@citycol.ac.uk)
Assoc Libs: HANDSWORTH CAMPUS LIB, addr
as above; CITY TECHNOLOGY CAMPUS LRC,
Amington Rd, Tyseley, Birmingham, B25 8EP
(0121-706-5522); EAST BIRMINGHAM CAMPUS
LRC, Garretts Green Ln, Birmingham, B33 0TS
(0121-743-4471 x 2257); ST GEORGE'S 6TH
FORM CAMPUS LRC, Gt Hampton Row,
Birmingham, B19 3JG (0121-233-1433); several
smaller local learning centres *Open:* term: Mon-
Fri 0900-2000 at main sites; vac: reduced opening
hrs decided on a site-by-site basis
Subj: all subjs; genl; GCSE; A level; undergrad;
supported learning; ESOL
Equip: video viewer, 5 copiers (A4/5p, A4/10p), 60
computers (all with wd-proc, internet & CD-ROM)
Online: Guardian/Observer Online Archv, Infotrac,
KnowEurope, KnowUK, LION, Oxford Reference,
Resource Discovery Network, SYBWorld, Zetoc
(free to users) *Officer-in-Charge:* all Snr Resource
Offcrs *Svcs:* info, ref
Stock: bks/15000; periodcls/140; slides/500;
videos/500 *Acqs Offcr:* all Snr Resource Offcrs
Classn: DDC *Auto Sys:* Heritage
Staff: Libns: 5 *Other Prof:* 1 *Non-Prof:* 20 *Exp:*
£72000 (1999-2000); £72000 (2000-01)

S167 ✚

City Hospital NHS Trust, Bevan Multidisciplinary Library

Dudley Rd, Birmingham, B18 7QH (0121-507-
4491; *fax:* 0121-507-4602)
Email: Bevan.Library@cityhspbham.wmids.
nhs.uk

Gov Body: City Hosp NHS Trust *Chief:* Libn: Mrs
Karen Bowen DipRSA, MCLIP (karen.bowen@
cityhspbham.wmids.nhs.uk) *Dep:* Asst Libn: Ms
Sally Barley (sally.barley@cityhspbham.wmids.
nhs.uk)
Entry: ref only to non-Trust staff *Open:* staffed:
Mon-Fri 0830-1700; 24 access for staff via
swipecard
Subj: medicine; nursing *Co-op Schemes:*
WMHLN, BMA
Equip: fax, 2 copiers (5p per pg), 6 video viewers,
16 computers (all with internet & CD-ROM, 14 with
wd-proc), 4 rooms for hire *Online:* Medline &
others *Svcs:* info, ref, biblio
Stock: bks/c10000; periodcls/210; CD-ROMs/8
Acqs Offcr: Libn, as above
Classn: LC *Auto Sys:* Heritage IV
Staff: Libns: 1 *Non-Prof:* 2

S168

College of Law, Birmingham Library

133 Gt Hampton St, Birmingham, B18 6AQ (0121-
697-8041)
Email: library.brm@lawcol.co.uk
Internet: http://www.college-of-law.co.uk/

Special Libraries

Birmingham ▼ Birmingham

(Coll of Law, Birmingham Lib cont)
Gov Body: Coll of Law **Chief:** Branch Libn: Ms Lindsey Withecombe (lindsey.withecombe@ lawcol.co.uk) **Dep:** Snr Lib Asst: Ms Jacqueline Hartwell (jacqueline.hartwell@lawcol.co.uk) **Assoc Libs:** CHESTER LIB (see **S458**); GUILD-FORD LIB (see **S769**); LONDON LIB (see **S1090**); YORK LIB (see **S2161**)
Entry: only open to certain categories of external user; tel for appt **Open:** term: Mon-Thu 0830-2000; Fri 0830-1800, Sat-Sun 1200-1700; vac: Mon-Fri 0900-1700
Subj: law
Equip: 2 copiers (5p per copy), 55 computers (incl wd-proc, internet & CD-ROM) **Online:** Butterworths Direct, Lexis-Nexis, Justis, Lawtel, Westlaw **Svcs:** info, ref

S169 📖 ✚

Health Services Management Centre and NHS Executive (West Midlands), Library and Information Service
Park House, 40 Edgbaston Park Rd, Birmingham, B15 2RT (0121-414-3672/7060; fax: 0121-414-7051)
Email: library-hsmc@bham.ac.uk
Internet: http://www.bham.ac.uk/hsmc/library/

Gov Body: Univ of Birmingham (see **S179**)
Chief: Lib & Info Svc Mgr: Ms Rachel Posaner (R.D.Posaner@bham.ac.uk) **Dep:** Libns: Mrs Pat Metcalfe MCLIP (P.A.Metcalfe@bham.ac.uk)
Other Snr Staff: Snr Lib Asst: Ms Sally Harbison (S.A.Harbison@bham.ac.uk)
Assoc Libs: NHS EXEC (W MIDLANDS) LIB, Bartholomew House, 142 Hagley Rd, Birmingham, B16 9PA
Entry: ref only, adv appt for external visitors **Open:** term: Mon-Thu 0900-1900, Fri 0900-1700; vac: Mon-Fri 0900-1700
Subj: non-clinical aspects of health care **Co-op Schemes:** BLDSC, WMHLN
Equip: copier, computers (incl wd-proc, internet & CD-ROM) **Online:** Medline, HealthStar, Embase, CINAHL, ASSIA, ABI Inform, Cochrane, HMIC
Svcs: info, ref, biblio
Stock: bks/c10000 (incl pamphs); periodcls/200; videos/30
Classn: based on NLM **Auto Sys:** DBTextworks

S170 📖

Matthew Boulton College of Further and Higher Education, Library
Sherlock St, Birmingham, B5 7DB (0121-446-4545; fax: 0121-446-4699)
Email: pdolman@matthew-boulton.ac.uk
Internet: http://www.matthew-boulton.ac.uk/

Gov Body: Matthew Boulton Corp **Chief:** Chief Libn: Mr Paul Dolman BA(Hons), MCLIP
Open: term: Mon, Wed 0900-1700, Tue, Thu 0900-1945, Fri 0900-1600; vac: Mon-Fri 1000-1500
Subj: all subjs; genl; GCSE; A level; undergrad
Collns: Bks & Pamphs: BSI (small colln, mainly tech); colln of dental & podiatry bks; podiatry dissertations **Co-op Schemes:** BLDSC
Equip: copier (5p), computers (incl 8 internet, 6 CD-ROM & 2 OPACs) **Svcs:** info, ref, some current awareness

Stock: bks/24000; periodcls/60; audios/100; videos/350; CD-ROMs/100 **Acqs Offcr:** Chief Libn, as above
Classn: DDC **Auto Sys:** Heritage IV
Staff: Libns: 1 Non-Prof: 3 **Exp:** £40000 (1999-2000); £40000 (2000-01); incl stock & other exp

S171 📖

Newman College of Higher Education Library
Genners Ln, Bartley Green, Birmingham, B32 3NT (0121-476-1181 x2208; fax: 0121-476-1196)
Email: library@newman.ac.uk
Internet: http://www.newman.ac.uk/

Chief: Dir of Lib & Learning Support: Mrs Janice Bell MA, MCLIP **Dep:** Ms Alison Huggan
Entry: ref only; borrowing on registration as external borrower **Open:** term: Mon-Thu 0845-2000, Fri 0845-1715, Sat 1000-1500; vac: Mon-Fri 0900-1700
Subj: all subjs; undergrad; local study (West Midlands) **Collns:** Bks & Pamphs: West Midlands Local Hist Colln; J.H. Newman Colln **Co-op Schemes:** ILL, SCONUL, UK Libs Plus, Access West Midlands
Equip: m-printer, 2 video viewers, 2 copiers, 43 computers (all with internet & CD-ROM)
Stock: bks/80000; periodcls/270; slides/19000; pamphs/1000
Classn: DDC **Auto Sys:** Talis
Staff: Libns: 4 Non-Prof: 5 **Exp:** £45000 (1999-2000)

S172 🏛

Office of Water Services (OFWAT) Library
Centre City Tower, 7 Hill St, Birmingham, B5 4UA (0121-625-1361; fax: 0121-625-1362)
Email: enquiries@ofwat.gsi.gov.uk
Internet: http://www.ofwat.gov.uk/

Chief: Libn: Miss J.W. Fisher BSc, MCLIP **Dep:** Dep Libn: Mrs J.S.J. Cranmer BSc, MLS, MCLIP
Other Snr Staff: Asst Libn: Mrs Holly Brown MSc
Entry: ref only; tel in adv **Open:** Mon-Fri 0930-1630
Subj: water industry; economic regulation; privatisation; consumer protection **Collns:** Other: Dir Genl's Register
Stock: bks/10000 incl pamphs; periodcls/100
Classn: DDC **Auto Sys:** TinLib
Pubns: OFWAT Annual Reports 1989-2001 (£6.70-£13.50 each); Dear MD/RD Letters (single copies free, subscription £215 pa); Rsrch Papers (£3.20 each); Regulatory Accounting Guidelines; Reports on Water Companies; ONCC pubns; consultation papers; rsrch papers; info notes; leaflets; press notices; numerous others, full list available from OFWAT
Staff: Libns: 2.9 Non-Prof: 2.5

S173 📖 🙏

Queen's Foundation for Ecumenical Theological Education Library
(formerly Queen's Coll Lib)
Somerset Rd, Edgbaston, Birmingham, B15 2QH (0121-452-2621)
Email: library@queens.ac.uk

Gov Body: Queen's Foundation **Chief:** Libn: Mr Michael Gale BA(Oxon), MLib, MCLIP
Entry: adv appt advisable **Open:** term: Mon-Fri 0900-1700; vac: tel in adv
Subj: phil; religion; social sci; hist **Collns:** Bks & Pamphs: 16C-18C Anglican & Methodist early writings, hist & theology
Equip: computers (with catalogue & CD-ROM)

Stock: bks/48000; periodcls/62; pamphs/1000; videos/50
Classn: DDC (mod in religion) **Auto Sys:** Cardbox Plus (for catalogue only)
Staff: Libns: 1 **Exp:** £16000 (2000-01)

S174 ✚

Royal Orthopaedic Hospital NHS Trust, Cadbury Medical Library
Rsrch & Teaching Centre, Woodlands, Northfield, Birmingham, B31 2AP (0121-685-4029; fax: 0121-685-4030)
Email: librarian@roh.ndirect.co.uk

Gov Body: Royal Orthopaedic Hosp NHS Trust
Chief: Libn: Mrs Judith Dawson LLB, MCLIP
Entry: non-membs adv appt, ref only **Open:** Mon-Fri 0800-1900
Subj: medicine; orthopaedics; nursing; physiotherapy **Collns:** Archvs: archv colln relating to the hist of hosp now held at Birmingham Central Lib (see **P9**) **Co-op Schemes:** BLDSC, WMRHLN, BMA, RCSE
Equip: 4 video viewers, fax, copier (5p per pg), 6 computers (all with wd-proc & CD-ROM, 4 with internet), scanner, room for hire **Online:** available to membs only **Svcs:** info, ref, biblio
Stock: bks/1500; periodcls/76; CD-ROMs/18
Acqs Offcr: Libn, as above
Classn: NLM **Auto Sys:** in-house **Staff:** Libns: 1

S175 🔑

Royal Society for the Prevention of Accidents, Library and Information Services
Edgbaston Pk, 353 Bristol Rd, Birmingham, B5 7ST (0121-248-2000; fax: 0121-248-2001)
Email: infocentre@rospa.org.uk
Internet: http://www.rospa.org.uk/

Chief: Info Svcs Mgr: Mrs Lisa Lawson BSocSc, MA
Entry: adv appt **Open:** Mon-Fri 0900-1630
Subj: health & safety (road, occupational, home, leisure); accident prevention **Collns:** Bks & Pamphs: BSI standards (safety only) **Archvs:** 70 years of safety related materials
Equip: copier, clr copier, computer (with CD-ROM) **Online:** Dialog, EINS (membs only) **Svcs:** info, ref, biblio, indexing, abstracting
Stock: bks/20000, incl pamphs; periodcls/230
Classn: CIS **Auto Sys:** Sydney Plus
Staff: Libns: 3 Non-Prof: 1 **Exp:** £25000 (1999-2000)

S176 ✚

Smallwood Clinical Library
Moseley Hall Hosp, Alcester Rd, Birmingham, B13 8JL (0121-442-4321 x3479; fax: 0121-442-3573)

Gov Body: South Birmingham Primary Care Trust
Chief: Libn: Mrs Alison Pope BA(Hons), MA (alison.pope@southbirminghampct.nhs.uk) **Dep:** Asst Libn: Ms Lesley Huss (lesley.huss@ southbirminghampct.nhs.uk) **Other Snr Staff:** Lib Skills Trainer: Ms Kate Jones (kate.jones@ southbirminghampct.nhs.uk)
Entry: employees & students on placement from any of the Birmingham Primary Care Trusts **Open:** Mon-Fri 0900-1700
Subj: clinical medicine **Co-op Schemes:** BLDSC, ILL regional scheme
Equip: fax, copier, 7 computers (all with wd-proc, internet & CD-ROM), 4 rooms for hire, scanner
Online: Medline, CINAHL, Cochrane **Svcs:** info, ref
Stock: bks/1500; periodcls/37; audios/11; videos/39; CD-ROMs/10
Classn: NLM **Auto Sys:** Heritage
Staff: Libns: 2.2 Non-Prof: 0.5

S177
South Birmingham College Library Services
Cole Bank Rd, Hall Green, Birmingham, B28 8ES (0121-694-5056; *fax:* 0121-694-5007)
Email: info@sbirmc.ac.uk
Internet: http://www.sbirmc.ac.uk/

Chief: Coll Libn: Miss Jacqui Duffus BA(Hons)
Assoc Libs: HALL GREEN CAMPUS LIB, addr as above; ST PHILIP'S 6TH FORM CENTRE LIB, Hagley Rd, Birmingham, B16 8UF, Libn: Ms Eleanor Langston; DIGBETH CENTRE FOR ARTS & DIGITAL MEDIA LIB, Floodgate St, Birmingham, B5 5SU, Libn: Mr Paul Kemp; TECH CENTRE LIB, Welby Rd, Hall Green, Birmingham, B28 8HY, Libn: Ms Jean Fletcher
Entry: ref only to public *Open:* term: Mon-Wed 0900-1900, Thu 0900-1830, Fri 0900-1430; vac: Mon-Thu 0900-1700, Fri 1000-1600
Subj: all subjs; GCSE; A level; 1st year undergrad
Co-op Schemes: BLDSC, ILL
Equip: m-reader, video viewer, copiers, computers
Disabled: text magnifier *Svcs:* info, ref
Stock: bks/39000; periodcls/200; audios/100; videos/1500
Classn: DDC *Auto Sys:* Heritage
Staff: Libns: 2 *Non-Prof:* 6

S178 ✚
University Hospital Birmingham NHS Trust Library
Nuffield House, Queen Elizabeth Hosp, Edgbaston, Birmingham, B15 2TH (0121-697-8266; *fax:* 0121-697-8300)
Email: qelibrary@uhb.nhs.uk

Gov Body: Univ Hosp Birmingham NHS Trust
Chief: Trust Lib Mgr: Mrs Ursula Ison BSc, DipLib, MCLIP (ursula.ison@uhb.nhs.uk) *Dep:* Resources Libn: Miss Diane Pritchatt BLS(Hons), DipLib, MCLIP (diane.pritchatt@uhb.nhs.uk) *Other Snr Staff:* Reader Svcs Libn: Mrs Helen Farquharson BA(Hons) (helen.farquharson@uhb.nhs.uk); Training Libn: Mrs Jagdish Pamma BA (jagdish.pamma@uhb.nhs.uk); Clinical Libn (Primary Care): Mrs Jackie Oliver BA, MA, MCLIP (jackie.oliver@uhb.nhs.uk)
Assoc Libs: EDU CENTRE LIB, Selly Oak Hosp, Raddlebarn Rd, Selly Oak, Birmingham, B29 6JD
Entry: NHS staff *Open:* Queen Elizabeth Hosp: Mon 0930-1700, Tue-Wed 0900-1800, Thu-Fri 0900-1700; Selly Oak Hosp: Mon-Wed, Fri 0900-1700, Thu 0900-1800
Subj: medical; nursing; therapies; NHS mgmt *Co-op Schemes:* BLDSC, regional scheme
Equip: 2 copiers, 1 clr copier, fax (50p-£1), 19 computers (all with wd-proc, CD-ROM & internet)
Online: Medline, CINAHL (OVID) *Svcs:* info, ref, biblio
Stock: bks/7871; periodcls/235; AVs/131
Classn: NLM *Auto Sys:* Horizon
Pubns: Lib Info leaflets
Staff: Libns: 6 *Non-Prof:* 2.4

S179
University of Birmingham, University Library
Edgbaston, Birmingham, B15 2TT (0121-414-5817; *fax:* 0121-471-4691)
Email: library@bham.ac.uk
Internet: http://www.is.bham.ac.uk/

Gov Body: Univ of Birmingham *Chief:* Univ Libn & Dir of Info Svcs: Ms Michele Shoebridge MA, PGDipLib
Assoc Libs: BARBER FINE ART & MUSIC LIBS, Barber Inst of Fine Art, Univ of Birmingham, Edgbaston, Birmingham, B15 2TT, Fine Art Libn: Mr David Pulford (0121-414-7334; *fax:* 0121-414-5853), Music Libn: post vacant (0121-414-5852; *fax:* 0121-414-5853), see **S155** for Fine Arts Lib;

EUROPEAN RESOURCE CENTRE (incorporating the BAYKOV LIB), 52 Pritchatts Rd, Univ of Birmingham, Edgbaston, Birmingham, B15 2TT, Baykov Libn: Graham Dix (0121-414-3614; *email:* g.a.dix@bham.ac.uk); BARNES LIB, Univ of Birmingham Medical School (see **S182**); EDU LIB, School of Edu, Univ of Birmingham, Edgbaston, Birmingham, B15 2TT, Edu Libn: Ms Dorothy Vuong (0121-414-4869; *email:* edlib@bham.ac.uk); ELEC & ELECTRICAL ENG LIB, Gisbert Kapp Bldg, Pritchatts Rd, Univ of Birmingham, Edgbaston, Birmingham, B15 2TT, Site Libn: Ms Paula Anne Beasley (0121-414-4321; *email:* eleceng@bham.ac.uk); GARNER CHEMICAL ENG LIB, School of Chemical Eng, Univ of Birmingham, Edgbaston, Birmingham, B15 2TT, Site Libn: Ms Paula Anne Beasley (0121-414-5321; *email:* garner@bham.ac.uk); HARDING LAW LIB, Faculty of Law, Univ of Birmingham, Edgbaston, Birmingham, B15 2TT, Harding Law Libn: Mr Gerald Watkins (0141-414-5865; *email:* harding@bham.ac.uk); LANG & MEDIA RESOURCE CENTRE, Muirhead Tower, Univ of Birmingham, Edgbaston, Birmingham, B15 2TT, Libn: Ms Lydia Gibbs (0121-414-5960/2; *email:* lclib@bham.ac.uk); RONALD COHEN DENTAL LIB (see **S181**); SHAKESPEARE INST LIB (see **S1997**); ORCHARD LRC (see **S180**)
Open: term: Mon-Thu 0830-2230, Fri 0830-1900, Sat-Sun 1000-1800; vac: Mon-Fri 0900-1900, Sat 1000-1400, except Easter vac: when term times apply; access for membs only after 1700; associate libs & Special Collns opening times vary; see web site for full details
Subj: all subjs; undergrad, postgrad, rsrch
Collns: Bks & Pamphs: printed bks from 1471: local hist; British economic hist; Russian & Soviet hist; hist of sci, printing & medicine; theology; church hist; Heslop Colln (pre-1850 & other rare bks & pamphs, c25000 vols); Hensleigh Wedgwood Lib (philology); Cannock Chase Colliery Lending Lib; Hugh Selbourne Lib (on deposit); Berington Family of Little Malvern Court Lib (on deposit); Centre for Sports Sci & Hist (incl Sports Council papers & Natl Centre for Athletics Lit Colln); RC church hist (3000 vols); 16C-18C legal treatises; 17C-19C edu & ch's lit (at Edu Lib); private press bks; EDC; official pubns (UK, Canadian & internatl); numerous others *Archvs:* Univ Archvs; numerous other collns, incl: Chamberlain Papers (Joseph, Austen & Neville); Lord Avon Papers; Harriet Martineau Papers; Jerningham Letters; Shaw Letters; Cadbury Papers; Bishop Barnes Papers; Church Missionary Soc Archv; Young Men's Christian Assoc Archv; Alma-Tadema Colln; numerous MSS vols; misc colln of autograph letters (incl Dickens, Darwin, Coleridge, Wordsworth & others); Shaw Helier Colln (18C music scores, at Barber Music Lib) *Other:* incunabula *Co-op Schemes:* BLDSC, ILL, WMRLS, SCONUL, WMHEALG, CURL, UK Libs Plus
Equip: m-readers, m-printers, video viewer, fax, copiers, computers (incl wd-proc, internet & CD-ROM) *Disabled:* resource room *Online:* BIDS, numerous CD-ROMs incl: CINAHL, ERIC, Extel, EU Infodisk, Kompass, Medline, Mintel, PsycInfo, Volnet *Svcs:* info, ref, photographic
Stock: bks/2000000; periodcls/7500; archvs/3000000 items; rare bks/60000
Classn: LC *Auto Sys:* Talis
Pubns: lib guides; IS Bulletin
Staff: Libns: 60 *Non-Prof:* 100 *Exp:* £8399000 (2000-01); incl exp for all central libs & info centres

S180
University of Birmingham, Orchard Learning Resources Centre
Hamilton Dr, Weoley Park Rd, Selly Oak, Birmingham, B29 6QW (0121-415-2255; *fax:* 0121-415-2273)
Email: olrc@bham.ac.uk
Internet: http://www.olrc.bham.ac.uk/

Gov Body: Univ of Birmingham (see **S179**)
Chief: Resource Centre Mgr: Ms Dorothy Vuong (d.n.vuong@bham.ac.uk) *Other Snr Staff:* Liaison Libn: Ms Louise Woodcock (l.a.woodcock@bham.ac.uk)
Assoc Libs: COLL OF THE ASCENSION LIB, Weoley Park Rd, Selly Oak, Birmingham; CROWTHER HALL LIB, Hamilton Dr, Selly Oak, Birmingham; FIRCROFT COLL LIB, Bristol Rd, Selly Oak, Birmingham; ST ANDREW'S HALL LIB, Weoley Park Rd, Selly Oak, Birmingham; SPRINGDALE COLL LIB, Weoley Park Rd, Selly Oak, Birmingham; WOODBROOKE LIB (see **S185**)
Entry: appl by letter *Open:* term: Mon-Thu 0900-2200, Fri 0900-1900, Sat-Sun 1000-1800; vac: Mon-Thu 0900-1900, Fri 1000-1900, Sat 1000-1400
Subj: psy; phil; religion; religious studies; comparative religion; world religions (esp Christianity, Islam, Judaism, Hinduism & Buddhism); Christian theology; Biblical studies & missiology; sociology; social work; gender studies; community studies; counselling; econ; development studies; law; internatl relations; youth work; edu; humanities; sci; arts; sports studies; hist; geog; lang; lit *Collns: Bks & Pamphs:* Mingana Colln of Arabic & Syriac MSS (c3000 items); Harold Turner Colln (new religious movements, 26000+ items); Religious Edu Resources Colln *Archvs:* archvs of several missionary & Christian edu orgs; some personal papers *Other:* theses; AV colln; Birmingham Black Oral Hist Proj Archv *Co-op Schemes:* BLDSC, ABTAPL, SCOLMA
Equip: m-readers, fax, video viewer, copier, computers (incl wd-proc, internet & CD-ROM), rooms for hire *Disabled:* CCTV magnifier, hearing loops, infrared sys
Stock: bks/200000; periodcls/400, plus 1000 no longer current; slides/744 sets; illusts/7018; audios/1235; videos/624; archvs/513 linear m; MSS/3000; papyri/500
Classn: DDC *Auto Sys:* Olib

S181
University of Birmingham, Ronald Cohen Dental Library
Birmingham Dental Hosp, St Chad's Queensway, Birmingham, B4 6NN (0121-237-2860)
Email: dllib@bham.ac.uk
Internet: http://www.is.bham.ac.uk/dental/

Chief: Snr Info Asst: Mr Jules Gray *Dep:* Info Asst: Ms Clare Harris
Entry: staff & students *Open:* term: Mon-Thu 0830-2030, Fri 0830-1930; summer vac (Jul-Sep): Mon-Fri 0900-1700
Subj: dentistry; biomaterials *Collns: Other:* theses; AV colln
Equip: copier, 4 computers (incl internet & CD-ROM)
Stock: bks/5000; periodcls/80

S182
University of Birmingham Medical School, Barnes Library
Vincent Dr, Edgbaston, Birmingham, B15 2TT (0121-414-3567; *fax:* 0121-414-5855)
Email: ba-lib@bham.ac.uk
Internet: http://www.is.bham.ac.uk/barnes/

Gov Body: Univ of Birmingham (see **S179**)
Chief: Barnes Libn: Ms Jean Scott
Entry: free access to membs of Univ, others ref only *Open:* term: Mon-Thu 0845-2100, Fri 0845-1900, Sat-Sun 1000-1800; vac: Mon-Fri 0900-1900, Sat 0900-1300, Sun closed
Subj: medicine; health sci; life sci *Collns: Bks & Pamphs:* c4000 historical items in reserve colln on subj of medicine; special colln on the Plague; Birmingham Medical Inst Colln (on deposit); Midlands Inst of Otology Colln (on deposit) ☛

Birmingham
▼
Bootle

Special Libraries

(Univ of Birmingham Medical School cont)
Co-op Schemes: BLDSC, ILL
Equip: m-reader, 6 copiers, 17 computers (incl CD-ROM) *Svcs:* info, ref
Stock: bks/115800; periodcls/800
Classn: LC *Auto Sys:* Talis
Staff: Libns: 1 *Non-Prof:* 7

S183 🎓
University of Central England, William Kenrick Library

Franchise St, Perry Barr, Birmingham, B42 2SU (0121-331-5289/6373/6374)
Email: judith.andrews@uce.ac.uk
Internet: http://www.uce.ac.uk/library/public/

Chief: Dir of Lib Svcs: Ms Judith Andrews
Assoc Libs: BIRMINGHAM CONSERVATOIRE LIB (see **S158**); NURSING LIB (see **S184**); BIRMINGHAM INST OF ART & DESIGN LIB (see **S160**); other BIAD Libs: COLL OF ART LIB, Margaret St, Birmingham, B3 3BX (0121-331-5977); BOURNVILLE COLL OF ART LIB, Linden Rd, Bournville, Birmingham, B30 1JX (0121-331-5756); SCHOOL OF JEWELLERY LIB, Vittoria St, Hockley, Birmingham, B1 3PA (0121-331-6470)
Open: Kenrick Lib: term: Mon-Thu 0830-2200, Fri 0830-1900, Sat-Sun 1000-1700; vac: Mon-Thu 0900-1700, Fri 0900-1600, Sat 1000-1700
Subj: all subjs; undergrad; postgrad *Co-op Schemes:* BLDSC, SCONUL, UK Libs Plus, Access West Midlands
Equip: copiers, 60+ computers (incl wd-proc)
Online: ABI Inform, ASSIA, BIDS, BHI, CINAHL, Cochrane, Emerald, ERIC, FAME, Infotrac, INSPEC, Westlaw, Mintel, UnCover, Web of Science & others; 2300 e-journals
Stock: bks/300000; periodcls/c1200; m-forms/8000
Classn: DDC *Auto Sys:* Talis

S184 🎓 ➕
University of Central England, Nursing Library

Butler Bldg, Westbourne Rd, Birmingham, B15 3TN (0121-331-6012)
Email: nursing.reference.library@uce.ac.uk
Internet: http://www.uce.ac.uk/library/public/

Gov Body: Univ of Central England (see **S183**)
Chief: Faculty Libn: Ms Jane Richards (jane.richards@uce.ac.uk) *Dep:* Subj Libn: Mr Peter Ebrey (peter.ebrey@uce.ac.uk)
Entry: staff & students *Open:* term: Mon-Thu 0830-2100, Fri 0830-1700, Sat 1000-1400 (Ref Lib -1700); vac: Mon-Thu 0900-1700, Fri 0900-1600
Subj: medicine; nursing; midwifery *Collns: Bks & Pamphs:* medical statistics colln
Equip: copiers, computers *Online:* CINAHL, ASSIA, Embase, Cochrane, Medline, Web of Sci
Stock: bks/231
Classn: DDC *Auto Sys:* Talis *Staff:* 9 in total

S185 🔑 🙏
Woodbrooke Library

1046 Bristol Rd, Birmingham, B29 6LJ (0121-472-5171; *fax:* 0121-472-5173)
Email: library@woodbrooke.org.uk
Internet: http://www.woodbrooke.org.uk/

Gov Body: Woodbrooke Trustees *Chief:* Libn: Mr Ian C. Jackson MA, DipLib
Entry: adv appt & ref only *Open:* varies, usually Tue-Fri 0900-1600; please ring for info
Subj: religion; Quakerism; peace studies; social justice *Collns: Bks & Pamphs:* Bevan-Naish Colln (17C-18C Quaker materials); Powicke Colln (Richard Baxter & Cambridge Platonists); Rendel Harris Colln of Greek New Testaments *Co-op Schemes:* BLDSC
Equip: copier
Stock: bks/42000; periodcls/150; pamphs/2000; m-forms/3000; videos/30
Classn: DDC, own for Quaker colln *Auto Sys:* Heritage IV *Staff:* Libns: 1

Bishop Auckland

S186 🎓
Bishop Auckland College Library

Woodhouse Ln, Bishop Auckland, Co Durham, DL14 6JZ (01388-443000)
Internet: http://www.bacoll.ac.uk/

Chief: Learning Resources Mgr: Mrs Helen Ashton
Open: term: Mon-Thu 0900-1930, Fri 1000-1600, Sat 0930-1230; vac: Mon-Thu 0900-1630, Fri 1000-1600
Subj: all subjs; GCSE; A level; undergrad; local study (Co Durham)
Equip: copier (5p per pg), 25 computers (with wd-proc & internet) *Svcs:* info, ref
Stock: bks/12000; periodcls/40; videos/2000; CD-ROMs/40
Classn: DDC *Auto Sys:* in-house
Staff: Libns: 1 *Non-Prof:* 4

S187 ➕
Bishop Auckland General Hospital Library

Postgrad Medical Edu Centre, The Genl Hosp, Bishop Auckland, Co Durham, DL14 6AD (01388-455668; *fax:* 01388-455669)
Email: merrywet@smtp.sdhc-tr.northy.nhs.uk

Gov Body: South Durham Healthcare NHS Trust
Chief: Libn: Ms Tina Merryweather DipLRCM, MCLIP
Assoc Libs: DARLINGTON MEMORIAL HOSP LIB (see **S520**)
Entry: Trust staff; membership to others on appl
Open: staffed: Mon-Thu 0830-1700, Fri 0830-1630; 24 hr access to Trust staff
Subj: medicine; nursing; health & health-related
Co-op Schemes: BLDSC, BMA, HLN, NULJ
Equip: fax, copier (A4/5p), 9 computers (all with wd-proc, internet & CD-ROM) *Online:* Medline & others via OVID *Svcs:* info, ref
Stock: bks/4000; periodcls/80 *Acqs Offcr:* Libn, as above
Classn: DDC *Auto Sys:* Libero
Staff: Libns: 1 *Non-Prof:* 0.4

Blackburn

S188 🎓
Blackburn College Library

Feilden St, Blackburn, Lancashire, BB2 1LH (01254-292566; *fax:* 01254-695265)
Email: c.rogers@blackburn.ac.uk
Internet: http://www.blackburn.ac.uk/

Gov Body: Blackburn Coll Corp Board *Chief:* Head of Learning Resources: Mrs Cecily Rogers PGDip, MCLIP
Entry: ref only for non-students of the Coll *Open:* term: Mon-Thu 0845-2000, Fri 0845-1500; vac: Mon-Fri 0845-1630
Subj: all subjs; GCSE; A level; undergrad; postgrad; vocational *Co-op Schemes:* ILL

Equip: video viewer, 4 copiers (5p per copy), 174 computers (all with wd-proc, internet & CD-ROM), 2 rooms for hire *Disabled:* Horizon reader *Svcs:* info, ref, biblio
Stock: bks/58000; periodcls/c200; audios/500; videos/1700
Classn: DDC *Auto Sys:* Heritage IV
Staff: Libns: 3 *Non-Prof:* 16 *Exp:* £70000 (2000-01)

S189 🏛️ 🏛️
Blackburn Museum and Art Gallery

Museum St, Blackburn, Lancashire, BB1 7AJ (01254-667130; *fax:* 01254-695370)
Internet: http://council.blackburnworld.com/services/museum/

Gov Body: Blackburn with Darwen Borough Council (see **P10**) *Chief:* Museum Mgr & Curator: post vacant
Entry: adv appt to consult stored material *Open:* Tue-Sat 1000-1645
Subj: local studies (Blackburn) *Collns: Bks & Pamphs:* Hart Colln (early printed bks & medieval MSS) *Archvs:* Kathleen Ferrier Archv (opera singer) *Other:* extensive photographic archv
Svcs: info, ref
Stock: bks/500; photos/2500
Classn: Modes, SHIC
Pubns: Turner, The Origins of Genius (£3)
Staff: Other Prof: 3.5 *Non-Prof:* 9

S190 🔑 🍷 🦴
North West Museums Service, Information Service

Griffin Lodge, Cavendish Pl, Blackburn, Lancashire, BB2 2PN (01254-670211; *fax:* 01254-681995)
Email: office@nwmuseums.co.uk
Internet: http://www.nwmuseums.co.uk/

Type: registered charity *Gov Body:* Trustees of North West Museums Svc *Chief:* Asst Dir (Edu & Training): Mr Paul Parry BA(Hons), PGDip
Entry: open to membs of North West Museums Svc *Open:* Mon-Fri 0900-1700; closed bank/public hols
Subj: North West England: museums; cultural activ; economic & social data; arts *Collns: Other:* numerous specialist pubns relating to cultural activ
Equip: copier, room for hire *Svcs:* info, ref, provides advice, grant aid & lib svc to museums in North West England
Stock: bks/250+; videos/20
Auto Sys: Access
Staff: Other Prof: 10 *Non-Prof:* 8

S191 🎓 🙏
Stonyhurst College House Library

Blackburn, Lancashire, BB7 9PZ (01254-86345; *fax:* 01254-86732)

Gov Body: Stonyhurst Coll Governors *Chief:* Libn: Mrs Shona C. Wademan BSc *Other Snr Staff:* Archivist: Mr David Knight
Entry: private lib; for permission to consult lib a personal, written appl must be submitted *Open:* by private arrangement
Subj: local study (Lancashire); religion; Roman Catholicism; recusancy; hist of Jesuits *Collns: Bks & Pamphs:* mostly on Catholicism *Archvs:* hist of Coll; connected with Soc of Jesus; hist of the Catholic Church in England (1550-1900)
Stock: bks/50000; photos/200; pamphs/400
Proj: extensive redevelopment programme

Blackpool

S192 🎓

Blackpool and the Fylde College, Learning Resource Centre

Ashfield Rd, Bispham, Blackpool, Lancashire, FY2 0HB (01253-352352 x4289; *fax:* 01253-356127) *Internet:* http://www.blackpool.ac.uk/

Gov Body: Blackpool & Fylde Coll *Chief:* Head of Learning Resources: Mrs C. McAllister BA, MCLIP, CertEd (cmcd@blackpool.ac.uk) *Dep:* Dep Head of Learning Resources: Mrs E. Norris BA, PGDipLib, CertEd (en@blackpool.ac.uk) *Assoc Libs:* ANSDELL RESOURCE CENTRE, Church Rd, Ansdell, Lytham St Annes, Lancashire, FY8 4AP (01253-352352 x4635); CENTRAL BLACKPOOL RESOURCE CENTRE, Palatine Rd, Blackpool, Lancashire, FY1 4DW (01253-352352 x4414); FLEETWOOD RESOURCE CENTRE (see **S685**); SOUTH BLDG RESOURCE CENTRE, Bennett Ave, Blackpool, Lancashire, FY1 4EE (01253-352352 x4505) *Entry:* lending to own students; others ref only *Open:* varies from site to site *Subj:* all subjs; GCSE; A level; undergrad; vocational *Collns: Other:* Maritime Colln (at Fleetwood Campus) *Co-op Schemes:* BLDSC, ILL, Libs Northwest *Equip:* video viewer, copiers, clr copiers, 150 computers (all with wd-proc, internet & CD-ROM) *Onlino:* via ATHENS (staff & students only) *Stock:* bks/50000; periodcls/500; slides/200; pamphs/300; maps/400; audios/100; videos/400 *Classn:* DDC *Auto Sys:* Dynix *Staff: Libns:* 3 *Non-Prof:* 17 *Proj:* introduction of virtual learning environment

S193 ✚

Blackpool, Fylde and Wyre Health Library

(formerly Blackpool Health Professionals' Lib) Health Professionals' Edu Centre, Victoria Hosp, Whinney Heys Rd, Blackpool, Lancashire, FY3 8NR (01253-303831; *fax:* 01253-303818) *Email:* norma.blackburn@exch.bvh-tr. nwest.nhs.uk

Gov Body: Blackpool, Fylde & Wyre Hosps NHS Trust *Chief:* Lib Svcs Mgr: Mrs Norma Blackburn BA, MA, MCLIP *Dep:* Dep Lib Svcs Mgr: Mrs Lorraine Fazakerley *Entry:* staff & students on placement from NHS Trusts; nursing students from UCLAN; medical students from Manchester Univ *Open:* Mon-Fri 0845-1800 *Subj:* medicine; nursing; allied health professions; health admin; midwifery; nursing; psychiatry *Co-op Schemes:* BLDSC, BMA, LIHNN, NULJ, partnership with Univ of Manchester (see **S1512**) & Univ of Central Lancashire (see **S1840**) *Equip:* m-reader, 2 copiers, 26 computers (all with wd-proc, internet & CD-ROM) *Online:* Aditus *Svcs:* info, ref, biblio *Stock:* bks/8900; periodcls/120; audios/some; videos/378; CD-ROMs/some *Classn:* DDC *Auto Sys:* Talis, Heritage *Staff: Libns:* 2 *Non-Prof:* 3

Blairgowrie

S194 🔑

Kindrogan Field Centre Library

Enochdhu, Blairgowrie, Perthshire, PH10 7PG (01250-881286; *fax:* 01250-881433) *Email:* Kindrogan@btinternet.com *Internet:* http://www.kindrogan.com/

Type: charity *Gov Body:* Scottish Field Studies Assoc *Chief:* Sec: N. Johnson BSc, PGCE

Entry: ref only *Open:* tel in adv, but open 24 hrs *Subj:* geog; ecology; nat hist; Scottish local hist *Equip:* copier, fax *Stock:* bks/3500; periodcls/12 *Classn:* own *Pubns:* 1945-1983 SFSA Pubns *Staff: Non-Prof:* 1

Blandford Forum

S195 🏛🏛

Royal Signals Museum, Library and Archive

Blandford Camp, Blandford Forum, Dorset, DT11 8RH (01258-482413; *fax:* 01258-482084) *Email:* royalsignalsmuseum@army.mod.uk *Internet:* http://www.royalsignals.army.org.uk/

Gov Body: Royal Signals Museum Trustees *Chief:* Dir: Col C.J. Walters (Rtd) *Dep:* Asst Archivist: T. Stankus *Entry:* ref only to archv, by appt *Open:* Mon-Fri 1000-1700 *Subj:* hist of military signalling; hist of Royal Corps of Signals *Collns: Bks & Pamphs:* handbks of military radios; military training handbks *Archvs:* historical records of Royal Signals Units; personal records of Royal Signals personnel *Equip:* copier *Stock:* bks/2400; photos/35000; slides/3000; maps/300; audios/30; videos/50; archvs/12 cubic m *Classn:* own *Auto Sys:* MODES Plus *Staff: Other Prof:* 1 *Non-Prof:* 1

Blantyre

S196 🔑🏛

David Livingstone Centre, Library

165 Station Rd, Blantyre, Lanarkshire, G72 9BT (01698-823140; *fax:* 01698-821424) *Email:* kcarruhters@nts.org.uk

Gov Body: Scottish Natl Memorial to David Livingstone Trust & Natl Trust for Scotland *Chief:* Property Mgr: Ms Karen Carruthers MA *Entry:* ref only, adv appt *Open: Museum:* Mon-Sat 1000-1700, Sun 1230-1700 *Subj:* David Livingstone; African exploration & missionary work *Collns: Bks & Pamphs:* bks by David Livingstone & bks relating to his life & times *Archvs:* Livingstone's journals & letters; materials relating to the Scottish Natl Memorial to David Livingstone Trust *Other:* photos & memorabilia connected with Livingstone *Svcs:* info, ref *Stock:* bks/c800 *Acqs Offcr:* Property Mgr, as above *Classn:* own

Bolton

S197 🎓

Bolton Community College, Learning Centres and Libraries

Manchester Rd Centre, Manchester Rd, Bolton, Lancashire, BL2 1ER (01204-453460; *fax:* 01204-453321) *Internet:* http://www.bolton-community-college. ac.uk/

Gov Body: Bolton Community Coll *Chief:* Learning Centres Mgr: Mrs Sheila Summerscales BA, MCLIP (sheila.summerscales@bolton-community-college.ac.uk) *Dep:* Asst Libn: Mrs Mary Carter BA, MCLIP (mary.carter@bolton-community-college.ac.uk) *Assoc Libs:* HORWICH LIB, Victoria Rd, Horwich, Bolton, Lancashire, BL6 6ED; CLARENCE ST CENTRE STUDY LIB, Clarence St, Bolton, Lancashire, BL1 2ET; WESTHOUGHTON STUDY LIB, Central Dr, Westhoughton, Bolton, Lancashire, BL5 3DS

Entry: students of the coll *Open:* term: Mon-Thu 0900-2000, Fri 0900-1700; vac: Mon-Fri 0900-1630 *Subj:* all subjs; GCSE; A level; Further Edu *Co-op Schemes:* BLDSC *Equip:* 2 copiers, 2 video viewer, 50 computers (all with wd-proc & internet, 3 with CD-ROM) *Disabled:* Kurzweil *Officer-in-Charge:* Learning Centres Mgr, as above *Svcs:* info, ref *Stock:* bks/22000; periodcls/60; maps/50; audios/20; videos/150; CD-ROMs/200 *Acqs Offcr:* Learning Centres Mgr, as above *Classn:* DDC *Auto Sys:* Heritage *Staff: Libns:* 2 *Other Prof:* 4 *Non-Prof:* 4 *Exp:* £35000 (1999-2000); £35000 (2000-01) *Proj:* extension of Learning Centres

S198 🎓

Bolton Institute of Higher Education, Learning Support Services

Deane Rd, Bolton, Lancashire, BL3 5AB (01204-903563) *Email:* learning-infodesk@bolton.ac.uk *Internet:* http://www.bolton.ac.uk/learning/

Gov Body: Bolton Inst of Higher Edu *Chief:* Learning Support & Development Mgr: Mrs Karen Snr BA, MLib, MCLIP *Entry:* memb of inst; UK Libs Plus, SCONUL & other access schemes in operation for non-membs *Open:* term: Mon-Thu 0845-2100, Fri 0845-1700, Sat 0930-1230; vac: Mon-Fri 0930-1700 *Subj:* all subjs; undergrad; postgrad; phil; psy; social scis; tech; arts; lit; geog; hist *Co-op Schemes:* BLDSC, Libs Northwest, UK Libs Plus, SCONUL *Equip:* m-readers, m-printers, video viewers, copiers, clr copier, computers (with wd-proc, internet & CD-ROM) *Disabled:* extensive facilities incl Kurzweil *Svcs:* info, ref, biblio *Stock:* bks/17000; periodcls/1200; slides/595; illusts/120; maps/3; videos/5300 *Classn:* DDC *Auto Sys:* Geac *Staff: Libns:* 13 *Other Prof:* 14 *Non-Prof:* 39

S199 🎓

Bolton School, Boys' Division, Chained Library

Chorley New Rd, Bolton, Lancashire, BL1 4PA (01204-840201; *fax:* 01204-849477)

Type: independent school *Chief:* Headmaster: Mr M.E.W. Brooker BSc *Entry:* by appt *Collns: Bks & Pamphs:* Chained Lib: Oak Press dated 1694; 56 items chained, dated 1608-1823 (mostly theology, some classical works)

Bootle

S200 🏛

Health and Safety Executive Information Services

Magdalen House, Trinity Rd, Bootle, Merseyside, L20 3QZ (0151-951-4382; *fax:* 0151-951-3674) *Email:* sandie.brown@hse.gsi.gov.uk *Internet:* http://www.hse.gov.uk/

Chief: Head of Info Svcs: Ms S. Brown *Dep:* Site Mgr (Info Centre): Mrs S. Cornwell *Assoc Libs:* HEALTH & SAFETY EXEC INFO CENTRE, Rose Ct, 2 Southwark Bridge, London, SE1 9HS, Site Mgr: Mr D. Taft (020-7717-6104; *fax:* 020-7717-6134); HEALTH & SAFETY EXEC INFO CENTRE, Broad Ln, Sheffield, S3 7HQ, Site Mgr: Mrs L. Parker (0114-289-2330; *fax:* 0114-289-2333); HEALTH & SAFETY EXEC INFO CENTRE, NUCLEAR SAFETY DIV (see **S201**)

Special Libraries

Bootle
▼
Bradford

(Health & Safety Exec Info Svcs cont)
Entry: adv appt (all sites) *Open:* Mon-Fri 0900-1700 (at all sites)
Subj: all aspects of health & safety at work *Co-op Schemes:* BLDSC, LADSIRLAC, HSE is the UK natl centre for the ILO CIS, which has its HQ in Geneva; it is also a contact pt for EC memb states
Equip: m-reader, m-printer, copier, computer (incl CD-ROM)
Classn: UDC *Auto Sys:* Unicorn
Staff: Libns: 16 *Non-Prof:* 8
Further Info: genl enqs for info on health & safety at work should be directed to: HSE Info Svcs, Caerphilly Business Park, Caerphilly, CF83 3GG (Infoline: 08701-545500; *fax:* 029-2085-9260; *email:* hseinformationservices@natbrit.com)

S201

Health and Safety Executive, Nuclear Safety Division, Information Centre
St Peter's House, Balliol Rd, Bootle, Merseyside, L20 3LZ (0151-951-4042; *fax:* 0151-951-4004)
Email: nsd.infocentre@hse.gov.uk
Internet: http://www.hse.gov.uk/

Gov Body: HSE Info Svcs (see **S200**) *Chief:* Site Mgr: Mrs Kate McNichol MA(Hons), MA, MCLIP
Entry: adv appt *Open:* Mon-Fri 0900-1700
Subj: nuclear power safety *Collns: Other:* daily transcripts & supporting technical documents for all public inquiries held in the UK concerning nuclear power *Co-op Schemes:* BLDSC, LADSIRLAC
Equip: m-reader, m-printer, copier, computer (incl CD-ROM) *Online:* not available to public *Svcs:* info, ref
Stock: bks/25000; periodcls/140
Classn: UDC *Auto Sys:* Unicorn
Pubns: Bibliography of Work Relevant to the Nuclear Industry Published by Membs of Staff of HM Nuclear Installations Inspectorate & the Health & Safety Executive 1962-1992 (free); The Work of HSE's Nuclear Installations Inspectorate (free)
Staff: Libns: 3 *Non-Prof:* 1

S202 ☙

Hugh Baird College Library
Balliol Rd, Bootle, Merseyside, L20 7EW (0161-353-4454)
Internet: http://www.hughbaird.ac.uk/

Chief: Libn & Learning Resource Mgr: Ms Karen Myatt *Dep:* Asst Learning Resources Mgr: Ms Micaela Chandler
Entry: registered student or staff of coll; ref only for others *Open:* term: Mon-Thu 0900-2000, Fri 0900-1600
Subj: all subjs; GCSE; A level; local studies (Liverpool & Sefton); politics; sociology; econ; catering; hairdressing; business studies; design; foundation art *Co-op Schemes:* LADSIRLAC, VALNOW
Equip: video viewers, copier, computers (incl internet & CD-ROM) *Disabled:* CCTV
Stock: bks/20000; periodcls/120; slides/200; videos/75
Classn: DDC *Auto Sys:* Heritage
Staff: Libns: 2 *Other Prof:* 1 *Non-Prof:* 8

Boston

S203 ☙

Boston College, Learning Resource Centre
Skirbeck Rd, Boston, Lincolnshire, PE21 6JF (01205-365701; *fax:* 01205-313252)
Email: david-c@boston.ac.uk
Internet: http://www.boston.ac.uk

Chief: Tutor-Libn: Mr David Cunniffe BA(Hons), DipLib, MCLIP *Dep:* Dep Libn: Mrs Christine Lyon BA, MCLIP
Assoc Libs: DE MONTFORT SITE LIB
Entry: guest membership available for borrowing
Open: term: Mon-Fri 0830-2030; vac: Mon-Fri 0900-1700
Subj: all subjs; genl; GCSE; A level; undergrad; vocational; local studies (Boston & Lincolnshire)
Collns: Other: large colln of music scores & recordings (vinyl, cassettes & CDs) *Co-op Schemes:* LISN, BLDSC, De Montfort Univ
Equip: 2 video viewers, 3 copiers, clr copier, 50 computers (all with wd-proc, internet & CD-ROM)
Disabled: CCTV unit *Online:* De Montfort Univ databases *Svcs:* info, ref, biblio
Stock: bks/30000; periodcls/150; slides/1500; audios/500; videos/2000
Classn: DDC *Auto Sys:* Autolib
Staff: Libns: 2 *Non-Prof:* 6 *Exp:* £18000 (1999-2000)

S204 ✚

Pilgrim Hospital Staff Library
Edu Centre, Sibsey Rd, Boston, Lincolnshire, PE21 9QS (01205-364801 x2272)
Email: library.pilgrim@ulh.nhs.uk
Internet: http://www.hello.nhs.uk/

Gov Body: United Lincolnshire Hosps NHS Trust
Chief: Hosp Libn: Mrs Ann Darling MCLIP
Assoc Libs: GRANTHAM & DIST HOSP, STAFF LIB (see **S757**); LINCOLN COUNTY HOSP, PROF LIB (see **S954**); LOUTH COUNTY HOSP MEDICAL LIB (see **S1486**)
Entry: staff of United Lincolnshire Hosps NHS Trust; staff of Lincolnshire Partnership NHS Trust; health students at Univ of Nottingham, School of Nursing & Midwifery & Univ of Leicester *Open:* Mon-Fri 0900-1700; 24 hr access also available to registered users
Subj: psy; social welfare; health care; medicine; nursing; midwifery; mgmt
Equip: copier (5p per sheet), 10 computers
Online: Medline, CINAHL, BNI, PsycInfo *Svcs:* info, ref, lit searches, database training
Stock: bks/12800; periodcls/241
Classn: DDC *Staff: Libns:* 1 *Non-Prof:* 5

Bournemouth

S205 ☙ ✚

Anglo-European College of Chiropractic, Vilhelm Krause Memorial Library
13-15 Parkwood Rd, Bournemouth, Dorset, BH5 2DF (01202-436306; *fax:* 01202-436308)
Email: library@aecc.ac.uk
Internet: http://www.aecc.ac.uk/lib/intro.htm

Chief: Head of Learning Resources: Mr David O'Neill MCLIP
Assoc Libs: associate coll of UNIV OF PLYMOUTH (see **S1812**)
Entry: ref only; adv appt *Open:* term: Mon-Fri 0845-1900, Sat 0930-1230; vac: Mon-Fri 0845-1700
Subj: medicine; chiropractic *Co-op Schemes:* BLDSC, BMA, HATRICS

Equip: m-reader, m-printer, 2 copiers, 2 video viewers, 16 computers (all with wd-proc, internet & CD-ROM, priority given to students of Coll), slide viewers, x-ray view box *Online:* range of medical & complementary medical databases *Svcs:* info, ref
Stock: bks/10500; periodcls/165; slides/2000; CD-ROMs/50; AVs/800; X-rays/1000+
Classn: DDC *Auto Sys:* Alice *Staff: Libns:* 3 *Other Prof:* 1 computer offcr *Non-Prof:* 3

Bowes

S206 🏛

The Bowes Museum, Reference Library and Archives
Barnard Castle, Bowes, Co Durham, DL12 8NP (01833-690606; *fax:* 01833-637163)
Email: info@bowesmuseum.org.uk
Internet: http://www.bowesmuseum.org.uk/

Gov Body: Trustees of the Bowes Museum
Chief: contact the Dir
Entry: specialist working lib available only by adv appt *Open: Museum:* Mon-Fri 1100-1700
Subj: local studies (Teesdale); European fine & decorative arts (1500-1900) *Collns: Bks & Pamphs:* 19C lib from Ridley Hall, Northumberland; French bks & pamphs belonging to John & Josephine Bowes *Archvs:* material relating to John & Josephine Bowes (19C)
Svcs: ref
Stock: bks/c10000; periodcls/c50
Classn: DDC
Pubns: The Bowes Museum, by E. Conran (£7.95)
Staff: Other Prof: 3 curatorial staff *Exp:* approx £200 (1999-2000)

Boxley

S207 ☙ ✚

European School of Osteopathy Library
Boxley House, Boxley, Kent, ME14 3DZ (01622-671558; *fax:* 01622-662165)
Email: raysmith@eso.ac.uk
Internet: http://www.eso.ac.uk/

Chief: Libn: Mr Ray Smith MCLIP
Entry: ref only by adv appt to non-ESO staff/students *Open:* term: Mon-Fri 0830-1930, Sat 0900-1300; vac: Mon-Fri 0900-1700
Subj: complementary medicine; osteopathy *Co-op Schemes:* HLN
Equip: copier (A4/10p), video viewer, 9 computers (all with wd-proc, internet & CD-ROM, printouts A4/5p) *Online:* Datastar (ESO membs only) *Officer-in-Charge:* Libn, as above *Svcs:* ref
Stock: bks/3000; periodcls/55; pamphs/1000; videos/250 *Acqs Offcr:* Libn, as above
Classn: in-house *Auto Sys:* Alice
Staff: Libns: 1 *Non-Prof:* 1 *Exp:* £30000 (1999-2000); £30000 (2000-01)

Bracknell

S208 ☙

Bracknell and Wokingham College, Learning Resources Centre
Church Rd, Bracknell, Berkshire, RG12 1DJ (01344-460200; *fax:* 01344-460360)
Email: lrc@bracknell.ac.uk
Internet: http://www.bracknell.ac.uk/

Chief: Learning Resources Mgr: Ms Sheila Powles MCLIP
Assoc Libs: CHURCH RD LEARNING CENTRE, addr as above; WICK HILL LEARNING CENTRE, Wick Hill, Sandy Ln, Bracknell, RG12 2JG, Centre Mgr: Mr Mike Ponting; 2 other small, unstaffed Learning Centres

Entry: ref only for non-students *Open:* term: Mon-Thu 0900-1945, Fri 0900-1500
Subj: all subjs; mainly at A level or vocational level; *Church Rd:* arts; design; photography; media; communications; film studies; performing arts; business studies; leisure; tourism; public svc; langs; eng; computing; info tech; *Wick Hill:* health; social care; child care; nursing; humanities; social sci; edu; computing; accountancy; mgmt; human resources; marketing *Co-op Schemes:* BLDSC
Equip: copier, video viewer, 38 computers (incl wd-proc & internet), scanner *Svcs:* info, ref, biblio
Stock: bks/17000
Classn: DDC *Auto Sys:* Genesis
Staff: Libns: 1 *Other Prof:* 1 *Non-Prof:* 6

S209

Building Services Research and Information Association, Library

Old Bracknell Ln West, Bracknell, Berkshire, RG12 7AH (01344-426511; *fax:* 01344-487575)
Email: Information@bsria.co.uk
Internet: http://www.bsria.co.uk

Type: rsrch assoc *Chief:* Head of Info: Mr S.R. Loyd MCLIP
Entry: adv appt *Open:* Mon-Thu 0900-1730, Fri 0900-1700
Subj: construction *Co-op Schemes:* BLDSC, BLIP, BLG
Equip: m-reader, m-printer, fax, copier, computers (incl wd-proc & CD-ROM) *Online:* Dialtech (fees)
Stock: bks/9500; periodcls/200; pamphs/20000
Classn: UDC
Pubns: Internatl Bldg Svcs Abstracts (£95 pa); Bldg Svcs Thesaurus (£25)
Staff: Libns: 1 *Other Prof:* 1 *Non-Prof:* 4 *Exp:* £15000 (2000-01)

S210

National Meteorological Library

London Rd, Bracknell, Berkshire, RG12 2SZ (01344-854841; *fax:* 01344-854840)
Email: metlib@metoffice.com
Internet: http://www.metoffice.com/corporate/library/

Gov Body: Met Office *Chief: Libn:* Ms Jill Claiden
Dep: Lib Info Mgr: Mr Graham Bartlett
Assoc Libs: NATL METEOROLOGICAL ARCHV (see **A61**)
Entry: open to public, adv notice preferred; both Lib & Archv are in govt bldgs & proof of ID may be requested on entry; visitors with disabilities recommended to contact Lib before visiting; loans available upon registration (proof of ID required)
Open: Mon-Thu 0830-1630, Fri 0830-1615
Subj: meteorology *Collns: Bks & Pamphs:* historical & rare meteorological lit, some dating from 16C, maintained in co-operation with the Royal Meteorological Soc *Other:* visual image lib (30000+ slides, prints, videos & films) *Co-op Schemes:* ILL
Equip: m-fiche reader, m-fiche printer, video viewer, copier (10p per pg)
Stock: bks/250000; periodcls/400; photos/25000; slides/30000; pamphs/50000; maps/2 mln; m-forms/3500; audios/30; videos/200; archvs/5 km
Classn: UDC *Auto Sys:* Sirsi Unicorn
Pubns: Monthly Accessions List
Staff: Other Prof: 5 *Non-Prof:* 11

Bradford

S211

Bradford Cathedral Chapter Library

Church Bank, Bradford, W Yorkshire, BD1 4EH (01274-777720)

Gov Body: Cathedral Chapter *Chief:* Chapter Libn: Miss C.E. Priestley
Assoc Libs: CATHEDRAL ARCHVS, held in separate room; some registers etc deposited in BRADFORD CITY ARCHVS DEPT (see **A62**)
Entry: adv appt only *Open:* Mon-Fri 0900-1730
Subj: religion; local hist (Bradford & Dist); hist of Cathedral
Equip: fax, copier, computer (incl wd-proc) *Svcs:* info, ref
Stock: bks/2230; photos/100; pamphs/50
Classn: DDC *Staff: Non-Prof:* 1

S212

Bradford College Library Services, Grove Library

Gt Horton Rd, Bradford, W Yorkshire, BD5 0NG (01274-755152; *fax:* 01274-394810)
Email: library@bilk.ac.uk
Internet: http://www.bilk.ac.uk/

Gov Body: Bradford Coll Corp *Chief:* Mgr, Coll Lib Svcs: Ms Margaret Chapman MA, CertEd, FCLIP (m.chapman@bilk.ac.uk) *Dep:* Dep Mgr: Mr David Crozier BA, MSc(Econ) (d.crozier@bilk.ac.uk)
Entry: Coll staff & students; written appl for external users (subscription scheme, ref only)
Open: term: Mon-Thu 0900-2000, Fri 0900-1700, Sat 0900-1700; vac: varies
Subj: all subjs; genl; GCSE; A level; undergrad; postgrad; vocational *Collns: Bks & Pamphs:* multicultural ref colln; law lib; teaching practice lib
Co-op Schemes: BLDSC
Equip: 4 video viewers, 8 copiers, clr copier, 10 computers (all with internet & CD-ROM), 5 group study rooms, WebOPAC *Disabled:* large VDUs, CCTV, minicom *Online:* numerous svcs *Svcs:* info, ref
Stock: bks/181000; periodcls/1300; slides/65000; audios/200; videos/500; CD-ROM & internet databases/40 *Acqs Offcr:* Acqs Libn: Mr Chris Martin (chrism@bilk.ac.uk)
Classn: DDC *Auto Sys:* Talis
Staff: Libns: 10 *Other Prof:* systems team *Non-Prof:* 29 *Exp:* £244000 (2001-02); £300000 (2002-03)

S213

Bradford Hospitals NHS Trust, Medical and Healthcare Library and Information Services

Bradford Royal Infirmary, Duckworth Ln, Bradford, W Yorkshire, BD9 6RJ (01274-364130; *fax:* 01274-364704)
Email: medical.library@bradfordhospitals.nhs.uk

Chief: Snr Libn: Mr I.P.G. King BA, MCLIP *Dep:* Dep Libn: Mr Michael Reid BSc(Hons), MA, MA, MCLIP, FRGS
Entry: open to those working or studying for NHS in Bradford; membs of public by appt *Open:* Mon, Wed 0830-1800, Tue 0830-2000, Thu 0830-1900, Fri 0830-1600
Subj: medicine & all related disciplines *Co-op Schemes:* BLDSC, YHJLS
Equip: m-reader, video viewer, 2 copiers, 10 computers (all with wd-proc, internet & CD-ROM) *Online:* Medline, CINAHL, AMED, Cochrane, Best Evidence, DARE, PsycInfo; on WebSPIRS: BNI Plus, HMIC *Svcs:* info, ref, biblio, indexing
Stock: bks/20000; periodcls/285; videos/75
Classn: NLM *Auto Sys:* Heritage, InMagic
Pubns: Ethnic Minorities Health: A Current Awareness Bulletin (£45, 2002)
Staff: Libns: 2 *Non-Prof:* 0.8 *Exp:* £70000 (2000-01)
Proj: new Edu Centre, incl Lib, under PFI initiative

S214

Bradford Mechanics' Institute Library

1st Floor, 76 Kirkgate, Bradford, W Yorkshire, BD1 1SZ (01274-722857)
Email: brenda@library33.freeserve.co.uk

Chief: Lib Administrator: Mrs Brenda Barnett
Entry: membership open to all for a small fee
Open: Mon-Fri 0900-1630, Sat 0900-1300
Subj: all subjs; genl; local studies (Bradford); lit; fiction *Collns: Other:* audios & videos *Co-op Schemes:* AIL

S215

National Museum of Photography, Film and Television, Collections and Research Centre (Insight)

Pictureville, Bradford, W Yorkshire, BD1 1NQ (01274-202030; *fax:* 01274-723155)
Email: talk.nmpft@nmsi.ac.uk
Internet: http://www.nmpft.org.uk/

Type: natl museum *Gov Body:* Natl Museum of Sci & Industry (see **S1387**) *Chief:* Head of Museum: Dr Amanda Nevill (a.nevill@nmsi.ac.uk)
Dep: Dep Head of Museum: Mr Anthony Sweeney (a.sweeney@nmsi.ac.uk) *Other Snr Staff:* Head of Insight & Collns Mgmt: Mr Paul Goodman (p.goodman@nmsi.ac.uk)
Entry: Museum: free; *Collns:* adv appt *Open: Museum:* Tue-Sun 1000-1800; open bank hols; *Collns:* Tue-Sun 1000-1230, 1400-1600
Subj: arts; hist of photography, film & television
Collns: Bks & Pamphs: bks & periodcls relating to the hist of photography, film & television; rare 19C photo-illustrated bks; television technical handbks & operating manuals; Andor Kraszna-Krausz Colln (photography); Roy Fowler Cinema Bk Colln *Archvs:* MSS & correspondence, incl those of W.H.F. Talbot *Other:* photo collns by 19C & 20C photographers in various formats, incl cartes-de-visite, cabinet & stereo cards, prison portraits, topographic albums & itinerant photo-graphy; important photographic holdings incl: W.H.F. Talbot Colln (early photography, 1830s-40s); Howard & Jane Ricketts Colln (19C prints & albums); work by Anna Atkins, Hill & Adamson, Roger Fenton, Henri Regnault, Lewis Carroll, George Washington Wilson & many others; Kodak Colln (popular photography, c200000 items); PYE Photographic Archv (television manufacturers); Daily Herald Photograph Archv (3 mln items, 1911-60s); other collns incl: Indian Film Cinema (Bollywood) Colln (posters & ephemera); W.E. Berry Poster Colln; colln of television commercials; film stills; posters; ephemera; animation drawings; cartoons
Equip: m-reader, copier *Disabled:* wheelchair access *Svcs:* info, ref,
Stock: films, stills & videos/3 mln items
Further Info: The museum does not currently offer a lib svc; however, its significant holdings of printed material & ephemera can be accessed through Insight: Collns & Rsrch Centre

S216

The Society of Dyers and Colourists, The Colour Museum, Library

Perkin House, PO Box 244, 82 Grattan Rd, Bradford, W Yorkshire, BD1 2JB (01274-390955; *fax:* 01274-392888)
Email: museum@sdc.org.uk
Internet: http://www.sdc.org.uk/

Gov Body: The Soc of Dyers & Colourists *Chief:* Museum & Archvs Offcr: Miss S. Burge BA(Hons), MA
Entry: by appt only *Open: Museum:* Tue-Sat 1000-1600; *Reserve Collns:* Tue-Fri 1000-1600 by appt ☞

Special Libraries

Bradford
▼
Brighton

(Soc of Dyers & Colourists, Colour Museum cont)
Subj: all aspects of clr & coloration, esp dyeing & textile printing *Collns: Other:* large colln of pattern cards relating to dyeing & textile printing *Co-op Schemes:* ILL
Equip: copier (10p per sheet) *Svcs:* info, ref
Stock: bks/25000; photos/100; slides/2500 *Acqs Offcr:* Museum & Archvs Offcr, as above
Classn: SHIC
Pubns: The Clr Museum Visitors Guide (£1)
Staff: Other Prof: 1 *Non-Prof:* 2.5
Proj: amounting to £15000

S217 🎓

University of Bradford, J.B. Priestley Library
Richmond Rd, Bradford, W Yorkshire, BD7 1DP (01274-233301; *fax:* 01274-233398)
Email: reception@bradford.ac.uk
Internet: http://www.bradford.ac.uk/lss/library/

Gov Body: Univ of Bradford *Chief:* Univ Libn (Academic Svcs): Mr John J. Horton MA, MPhil, DipLib, MCLIP (j.j.horton@bradford.ac.uk) *Other Snr Staff:* Univ Libn (Resources Mgmt): Mr Peter M. Ketley (p.m.ketley@bradford.ac.uk)
Assoc Libs: YVETTE JACOBSEN LIB, School of Mgmt, Emm Ln, Bradford, BD9 4JL (01274-234401; *fax:* 01274-234398; *email:* library@bradford.ac.uk); HEALTH STUDIES LIB, Unity Bldg, Trinity Rd, Bradford, BD5 0BB (01274-236374; *fax:* 01274-236470; *email:* hsl@bradford.ac.uk)
Entry: ref only on appl to Libn *Open:* term: Mon-Fri 0800-2400, Sat-Sun 0845-2100; vac: Mon-Fri 0845-2100
Subj: all subjs; undergrad; postgrad *Collns: Bks & Pamphs:* Commonweal Colln (non-violent social change, 11000 vols); Development Colln (development studies); Mitrinovic Lib (4500 vols); Hist of Pharmacy Colln; Dyeing Colln (textile dyeing); Waddington-Feather Colln (lit, esp Yorkshire dialect); Yorkshire Naturalists' Union Colln; Elizabeth & Arthur Raistrick Colln (industrial archaeo); Fraser Colln on Nuclear Disarmament; English Domestic Politics Colln *Archvs:* Univ of Bradford Archv; Bradford Inst of Tech Archv; Bradford Technical Coll Archv; J.B. Priestley Archv; Bradford Dyers' Assoc Archv; Constance Willis Peace Archv; Joel Martin Halpern Balkan Archv; Kennally Northern Ireland Archv; Peart-Binns Christian Socialist Archv; Ludwig Baruch Internment Archv (WW2); Archv of the Medical Assoc for the Prevention of War; papers of Sir Isaac Holden & family; Revis Barber Papers; Denis Bellamy Papers; W.R. Mitchell Archv (Yorkshire Dales); Anthrax Papers *Co-op Schemes:* BLDSC, YLI, RIDING, SCONUL, UK Libs Plus
Equip: m-readers, m-printers, video viewers, copiers, clr copier, computers (incl internet & CD-ROM) *Online:* Web of Science, Medline, Compendex, BIDS & others
Stock: bks/500000; periodcls/2400; maps/600; m-forms/25000; audios/100; videos/100; archvs/200 m
Classn: DDC, UDC *Auto Sys:* Dynix
Staff: Libns: 17.6 *Non-Prof:* 31

S218 ☕🖋

Yorkshire Water Library
PO Box 500, Western House, Western Way, Halifax Rd, Bradford, W Yorkshire, BD6 2LZ (01274-692376/518; *fax:* 01274-692706)
Email: paul_foxcroft@yorkshirewater.plc.uk
Internet: http://www.yorkshirewater.com/

Chief: Librarian/Info Scientist: Mr Paul Foxcroft BSc, DIS, MCLIP *Dep:* Asst Librarian/Info Scientist: Miss Caroline Atkins BA, PGDip, MA
Entry: ref only by adv appt *Open:* Mon-Fri 0900-1600; may vary
Subj: all subjs with ref to water
Equip: m-printer, computer (incl internet & CD-ROM) *Online:* Dialog *Svcs:* info, ref, biblio
Stock: bks/44000; various periodcls, pamphs, maps, m-forms & videos
Classn: UDC *Auto Sys:* Calm 2000
Pubns: Periodicals Holdings List
Staff: Libns: 2

Braintree

S219 🎓

Braintree College Library
Church Ln, Braintree, Essex, CM7 5SN (01376-321711; *fax:* 01376-340799)
Email: kjoslin@braintree.ac.uk
Internet: http://www.braintree.ac.uk/

Chief: Team Leader: Mrs Karen Joslin *Other Snr Staff:* Learning Advisor: Mr Michael Murcott
Entry: ref only; adv appt *Open:* term: Mon-Thu 0830-1930, Fri 0830-1700; vac: Mon-Fri 0900-1700
Subj: all subjs; GCSE; A level; vocational *Collns: Bks & Pamphs:* careers colln; Further Edu Staff Development Colln *Co-op Schemes:* BLDSC, ILL
Equip: video viewer, copier, 11 computers (all with wd-proc, internet & CD-ROM) *Svcs:* info, ref
Stock: bks/21000; periodcls/100; maps/23; audios/10; videos/850; CD-ROMs/50 *Acqs Offcr:* Team Leader, as above
Classn: DDC *Auto Sys:* Heritage
Staff: Libns: 1 *Other Prof:* 1 *Non-Prof:* 4 *Exp:* £21000 (1999-2000); £21500 (2000-01)

S220 🕐🏛

Braintree District Museum, Reference Library
c/o Town Hall Centre, Market Sq, Braintree, Essex, CM7 3YG (01376-325266; *fax:* 01376-344345)
Email: robert@bdcmuseum.demon.co.uk
Internet: http://www.braintree.gov.uk/leisure/9.4.htm

Type: local govt *Gov Body:* Braintree Dist Council & Braintree Dist Museum Trust *Chief:* Head of Cultural Svcs: Mrs Jean Grice *Dep:* Collns Mgr: Mr Robert Rose BA, MA, AMA
Entry: adv appt *Open:* Mon-Sat 1000-1700
Subj: Dist of Braintree: local hist; social hist; archaeo; genl hist & geog *Collns: Bks & Pamphs:* material relating to human hist of the Dist of Braintree *Other:* photographic archv; video colln; collns of objects relating to hist of Dist of Braintree, esp local textile industry
Equip: copier (A4/10p, A3/20p), 4 rooms for hire (varies) *Svcs:* info, ref
Stock: photos/4500; slides/200; maps/20; audios/50; videos/800; museum colln of 20000 objects
Staff: Other Prof: 3
Further Info: Primarily a museums svc with a ref lib of material relating to local hist

Brentford

S221 ☕🖋

GlaxoSmithKline, GSK Library
(formerly SmithKline Beecham Pharmaceuticals Lib)
980 Gt West Rd, Brentford, Middlesex, TW8 9GS (020-8047-2277; *fax:* 020-8047-0582)
Email: alan.j.williams@gsk.com

Chief: Lib Mgr: Mr Alan J. Williams MCLIP
Entry: adv appt accompanied by GSK host; not open to membs of the public *Open:* Mon-Fri 0900-1700
Subj: life sci; medicine; pharmaceuticals; business *Collns: Bks & Pamphs:* Office of Health Econ; Royal Soc of Medicine; World Health Reports *Co-op Schemes:* BLDSC
Equip: copier, fax, 8 computers *Online:* access to over 1500 e-journals *Officer-in-Charge:* Lib Mgr, as above
Stock: bks/3000+; periodcls/90+; some maps & videos *Acqs Offcr:* Lib Mgr, as above
Classn: UDC
Staff: Libns: 1 *Exp:* approx £27000 pa

Brentwood

S222 ➕

South Essex Health Authority, Library and Information Service
Warley Hill Business Pk, Gt Warley, Brentwood, Essex, CM13 3BE (01277-755200; *fax:* 01277-755201)
Email: corneliaturpin@sessex-ha.nthames.nhs.uk

Type: Health Authority *Chief:* Libn: Ms Cornelia Turpin MA
Entry: Health Authority staff only *Open:* Mon-Fri 0930-1700
Subj: social welfare; medical sci; drug info
Collns: Archvs: Health Authority agendas, minutes, procedures & policies *Co-op Schemes:* ILL
Equip: copiers, computers (incl wd-proc, internet & CD-ROM) *Svcs:* info, ref, biblio, indexing
Stock: bks/2000; periodcls/60
Classn: Bliss *Auto Sys:* DBTextworks
Staff: Libns: 1

Bridgend

S223 🎓

Bridgend College Library
Cowbridge Rd, Bridgend, Mid Glamorgan, CF31 3DF (01656-302262; *fax:* 01656-663912)
Internet: http://www.bridgend.ac.uk/

Gov Body: Bridgend Coll Corp *Chief:* Head of Lib: Mr M.E. Branford BA, DipLib, MCLIP, PGCE (mbranford@bridgend.ac.uk) *Dep:* Asst Libn: Miss E. Sanders BA, PGDipLIS, PGCE (esanders@bridgend.ac.uk)
Assoc Libs: PENCOED COLL LIB, Pencoed, Mid-Glamorgan, CF35 5LG, Libn: Mrs V. Jones BSc
Entry: lending to enrolled students & staff only (incl community edu students); ID card issued on enrolment *Open:* term: Mon-Thu 0845-2000, Fri 0845-1630, Sat 0900-1300; vac: Mon-Thu 0845-1700, Fri 0845-1600; Pencoed Coll Lib: term: Mon-Fri 0845-1700; vac: closed
Subj: all subjs; GCSE; A level; undergrad (1st year level); vocational *Co-op Schemes:* BLDSC, AWHL
Equip: 3 video viewers, 2 copiers (card operated), 56 computers (all with wd-proc & CD-ROM, 50 with internet) *Disabled:* large screen PC, height adjustable table *Svcs:* info, ref, biblio
Stock: bks/19000; periodcls/174; maps/20; audios/50; videos/100
Classn: DDC *Auto Sys:* Autolib

Staff: Libns: 3 *Non-Prof:* 1 *Exp:* £60000 (1999-2000); £60000 (2000-01)

S224 ✚
Bridgend Postgraduate Centre Library
Princess of Wales Hosp, Coity Rd, Bridgend, Mid Glamorgan, CF31 1RQ *(tel & fax:* 01656-752532) *Email:* bpaullada@hotmail.com

Gov Body: Bro Morgannwg NHS Trust *Chief:* Snr Libn: Mrs Barbara L. Paullada MCLIP *Dep:* Libn: Mr Phillip Rawle DipLib
Entry: multidisciplinary; open to all Trust employees & local GPs *Open:* Mon-Fri 0830-1700; closed bank hols; access after hrs to designated groups by log-in & numbered lock
Subj: medicine & related topics; psy; social sci; law; mgmt *Co-op Schemes:* BLDSC, AWHILES, PLCS, NULJ
Equip: video viewer, fax, copier, computers (incl wd-proc, internet & CD-ROM), room for hire
Online: Medline, CINAHL, Cochrane, HealthStar, AMED, CancerLit *Svcs:* info, ref, biblio
Stock: bks/5000; periodcls/160; videos/100; CD-ROMs/various
Classn: DDC *Staff: Libns:* 1.75 *Non-Prof:* 2

Bridgwater

S225 🎓
Bridgwater College, Learning Resources Centre
Bath Rd, Bridgwater, Somerset, TA6 4PZ (01278-455464; *fax:* 01278-441300)
Internet: http://www.bridgwater.ac.uk/

Chief: LRC Mgr: Ms Susan Lynn MCLIP
Entry: students & staff; ref & community membership for local people & teachers in Somerset *Open:* term: Mon-Thu 0830-2030, Fri 0830-1630; vac: Mon-Fri 0900-1630
Subj: genl; GCSE; A level; undergrad; postgrad; vocational *Collns: Bks & Pamphs:* careers lib; local hist colln; company reports; Young Adult & Children's Collns *Other:* slide colln (furniture, art & design) *Co-op Schemes:* BLDSC, SWRLS
Equip: m-reader, video viewer, copier, clr copier, 25 computers (incl 4 internet & 7 multimedia)
Stock: bks/42000; periodcls/350; videos/7000; CD-ROMs/100; learning packages/2000
Classn: DDC *Auto Sys:* Heritage
Staff: 20, incl 6 Resource Based Learning Co-ordinators
Proj: lib expansion

S226 🎓
Cannington College, Brookfield Library
Cannington, Bridgwater, Somerset, TA5 2LS (01258-655123)
Email: enquiries@cannington.ac.uk
Internet: http://www.cannington.ac.uk/

Chief: Lib Supervisor: Ms Alison Ronicle BA
Entry: adv notice preferred from non-Coll membs
Open: term: Mon-Tue, Thu 0845-2000, Wed, Fri 0845-1700, Sat 1000-1300; vac: Mon-Fri 0900-1230
Subj: food chem; biology; ecology; agric; hortic; food tech; equestrian; landscape gardening & design; floristry; turf mgmt *Collns: Bks & Pamphs:* natl floras *Archvs:* substantial archv colln *Co-op Schemes:* BLDSC
Equip: m-reader, m-printer, 2 video viewers, copier, 3 computers (incl 1 internet, 1 CD-ROM & 2 OPACs) *Svcs:* info, ref
Stock: bks/20000; periodcls/120; videos/300
Classn: DDC *Auto Sys:* Heritage

Brierley Hill

S227 🍵𝒑
Black Country Chamber and Business Link
(formerly Business Link Wolverhampton)
Dudley Court South, Waterfront East, Brierley Hill, W Midlands, DY5 1XN (0845-113-1234; *fax:* 01384-360560)
Email: info@bccbl.com
Internet: http://www.bccbl.com/

Gov Body: Black Country Chamber of Commerce *Chief:* Head of Info: Mr Stephen Taylor BA(Hons)
Entry: membs of Chamber of Commerce or SME businesses in the Black Country; ref only, adv appt
Open: Mon-Thu 0830-1730, Fri 0830-1700
Subj: business info; company info; product info; business & employment law
Equip: copier, computer (with wd-proc, internet & CD-ROM) *Online:* Dialog Profound, FAME (fees)
Svcs: info
Stock: bks/200; CD-ROMs/30
Classn: own (based on DDC)
Pubns: Prosper (free to local companies); Alert (free to membs); Black Country Chamber Membership Directory (£90)
Staff: Libns: 1 *Other Prof:* 1 *Non-Prof:* 6

Brigg

S228 ✚
South Humber Primary Care Resource Centre
Health Pl, Wrawby Rd, Brigg, N Lincolnshire, DN20 8GS (01652-601217; *fax:* 01652-601160)
Email: resource.centre@nelpct.nhs.uk
Internet: http://www.sherpa.nhs.uk/Libs/html_files/3libs.htm

Gov Body: North Lincolnshire Primary Care Trust & North East Lincolnshire Primary Care Trust
Chief: e-Libn: Ms Kate Fleming (Kate.Fleming@nelpct.nhs.uk) *Other Snr Staff:* Knowledge & Lib Svcs Trainer: Ms Caroline Smith (Caroline.Smith@nelpct.nhs.uk)
Entry: all primary care staff & NHS staff in the South Humber area; adv appt advised *Open:* Mon-Fri 0900-1700
Subj: health; medicine *Co-op Schemes:* ILL
Equip: copier, computers (with internet) *Online:* Medline, Embase, HMIC, Cochrane & others *Svcs:* info, ref, biblio
Stock: bks/1000; periodcls/100
Classn: DDC *Auto Sys:* Soutron InMagic/DBTextworks
Pubns: list available on appl
Staff: Libns: 2 *Non-Prof:* 1

Brighton

S229 🎪🏛
Booth Museum of Natural History Library
194 Dyke Rd, Brighton, E Sussex, BN1 5AA (01273-292777; *fax:* 01273-292778)
Email: boothmus@pavilion.co.uk

Gov Body: Brighton & Hove Council (see **P17**)
Chief: Keeper of Booth Museum: Mr John A. Cooper BSc, AMA, FGS
Entry: ref only, adv appt *Open:* Mon-Wed, Fri 1000-1700
Subj: sci; nat hist *Collns: Bks & Pamphs:* E.T. Booth Lib; Brighton & Hove Nat Hist Soc Lib *Archvs:* E.T. Booth MSS Colln; many other collns (see Bridson, Phillips & Harvey 1980, Nat Hist MSS Resources in the BI) *Other:* OS & geol maps

Equip: m-fiche reader, fax, copier, computer (incl wd-proc); use of equip by arrangement only
Stock: bks/15000; periodcls/10; maps/200; archvs/10 m
Classn: own (in-house catalogue)
Pubns: Unnatural Hist of an English County; The Wildlife of Hollingbury; The Booth Museum of Nat Hist, Centenary Guide Bk; The Habitats & Vegetation of Sussex; A Hist of Sussex Wild Plants; Atlas of Sussex Mosses, Liverworts & Lichens; A Revised Hist of the Butterflies & Moths of Sussex (CD-ROM, £30)
Staff: Other Prof: 3

S230 🎓
The British Library for Development Studies
Inst of Development Studies, Univ of Sussex, Falmer, Brighton, E Sussex, BN1 9RE (01273-678263; *fax:* 01273-621202/647)
Email: blds@ids.ac.uk
Internet: http://www.ids.ac.uk/blds/

Gov Body: Univ of Sussex (see **S239**) *Chief:* Head of Lib: Mr Michael Bloom BA DipLib, MCLIP (m.g.bloom@ids.ac.uk) *Dep:* Asst Libn: Ms Helen Rehin (h.m.n.rehin@ids.ac.uk)
Entry: ref only for external users; adv appt preferred *Open:* Mon-Fri 0930-1700
Subj: development studies (economic & social rsrch); environment; poverty; governance; edu; participation; globalisation; gender; politics; health; trade; rural development *Collns: Bks & Pamphs:* United Nations Deposit Lib; pubns of internatl bodies & NGOs *Co-op Schemes:* BLDSC
Equip: m-readers, m-printer, video viewer, copier, computers (incl CD-ROM) *Online:* various statistical & biblio databases, full-text sources & directories *Svcs:* info, ref, biblio
Stock: bks/80000, incl reports & working papers; periodcls/1000; m-forms/10000
Classn: own *Auto Sys:* C2 (Contec/Soutron)
Staff: Libns: 2 *Non-Prof:* 7

S231 🎓
City College Brighton and Hove, Library and Learning Resources
(formerly Brighton Coll of Tech)
Pelham St, Brighton, E Sussex, BN1 4FA (01273-667788; *fax:* 01273-667728)
Email: info@ccb.ac.uk
Internet: http://www.ccb.ac.uk/

Chief: Coll Libn: Ms Jane Evans BA, DipLib, MCLIP *Dep:* Dep Coll Libn: Ms Phyllis McDonald BA, MCLIP
Entry: ref only *Open:* Mon-Tue, Thu 0900-2000, Wed 0900-1800, Fri 0900-1700
Subj: all subjs; GCSE; A level; vocational; computing; psy *Co-op Schemes:* SASLIC, BLDSC
Equip: video viewers, copiers, computers (with wd-proc, internet & CD-ROM), audio facilities *Disabled:* 2 Teletext TVs *Online:* Infotrac, Technical Indexes, World Hospitality & Tourism Trends
Stock: bks/40000+; periodcls/315; slides/300; illusts/500; audios/780; videos/2000
Classn: DDC *Auto Sys:* Olib 7
Staff: Libns: 4.5 *Non-Prof:* 2

S232 🍵𝒑
Mott MacDonald Ltd, Library
Victory House, Trafalgar Pl, Brighton, E Sussex, BN1 4FY (01273-365000; *fax:* 01273-365100)
Email: brighton@mottmac.com
Internet: http://www.mottmac.com/

Chief: Libn: Mr Ian MacDonald BA, MCLIP
Entry: by appt, ref only *Open:* Mon-Fri 0830-1700
Subj: sci; maths; tech; eng ☞

(Mott MacDonald Ltd, Lib cont)
Collns: Bks & Pamphs: BSI; IEC Standards; selected American & European standards; company eng reports *Archvs:* company info *Other:* staff technical papers *Co-op Schemes:* BLDSC, SASLIC
Equip: m-reader, m-printer, copier, computer (with wd-proc, internet & CD-ROM) *Online:* Datastar, EINS, Kompass *Svcs:* info, ref, biblio, indexing
Stock: bks/1500; periodcls/176; maps/700; m-forms/700; archvs/10 m
Classn: UDC *Staff: Libns:* 1

S233 ⚷

National Society for Clean Air and Environmental Protection, Library

44 Grand Parade, Brighton, E Sussex, BN2 9QA (01273-878770; *fax:* 01273-606626)
Email: admin@nsca.org.uk
Internet: http://www.nsca.org.uk/

Chief: Proj Mgr: Ms Mary Stevens (mstevens@ nsca.org.uk)
Entry: outsiders need permit *Open:* Mon-Fri 0900-1700
Subj: air pollution; legislation; environmental issues *Collns: Bks & Pamphs:* Coal Smoke Abatement Soc Colln; Smoke Abatement League of Great Britain Colln; Natl Smoke Abatement Soc Colln
Equip: copier
Stock: periodcls/65; papers & documents/12000

S234 ⚷

One World Education Library

Brighton Peace & Environment Centre, 43 Gardner St, Brighton, E Sussex, BN1 1UN (01273-692880/620125; *fax:* 01273-689444)
Email: bripeace@pavilion.co.uk

Type: charitable *Gov Body:* Give Peace A Chance Trust *Chief:* Ms Natash Sharma
Entry: annual subscription for borrowing, otherwise ref only *Open:* Mon-Sat 1000-1730
Subj: social sci; environment; development; peace; human rights; animal rights; sexual politics; global issues; geog; hist
Equip: fax, video viewer, copier (A4/5p-9p), 5 computers (incl wd-proc & internet), room for hire
Svcs: info, ref
Stock: bks/5500; periodcls/40; photos/20 packs; slides/10 packs; pamphs/2000; maps/10; audios/20; videos/500
Classn: own
Pubns: Brighton's One World News (bi-monthly newsletter)
Staff: Non-Prof: 20 volunteers

S235 🎓

SPRU (Science and Technology Policy Research) Library

Mantell Bldg, Univ of Sussex, Falmer, Brighton, E Sussex, BN1 9RF (01273-678066; *fax:* 01273-685865)
Email: spru_library@sussex.ac.uk
Internet: http://www.sussex.ac.uk/spru/library/ or http://sprulib.central.sussex.ac.uk/ (catalogue)

Gov Body: Univ of Sussex (see **S239**) *Chief: Libn:* Ms B. Merchant BSc, MCLIP *Dep:* Ms M. Winder BA, MSc, MCLIP
Entry: adv appt *Open:* Mon-Fri 0900-1300, 1500-1730
Subj: sci, tech & innovation policy *Co-op Schemes:* BLDSC
Equip: m-reader, copier, computers (incl internet & CD-ROM) *Online:* FT Profile, OCLC FirstSearch, BIDS, MIMAS, EDINA etc *Svcs:* info, ref, biblio, indexing
Stock: bks/37000, excl bnd periodcls; periodcls/300
Classn: own *Auto Sys:* Heritage
Staff: Libns: 2 *Non-Prof:* 1 *Exp:* £32800 (1999-2000); £25500 (2000-01)
Proj: new bldg

S236 ✚

Sussex Postgraduate Medical Centre, Library

Brighton Genl Hosp, Elm Grove, Brighton, E Sussex, BN2 3EW (01273-242186; *fax:* 01273-690032)
Email: judy.lehmann@bsuh.nhs.uk
Internet: http://www.brighton-healthcare.nhs.uk/library/

Gov Body: Brighton & Sussex Univ Hosps NHS Trust *Chief:* Head of Lib Svcs: Mrs Judith Lehmann BA, DipLib, MCLIP *Dep:* Dep Head of Lib Svcs: Miss Sharon Springham BA(Hons), MCLIP *Other Snr Staff:* Associate Lib Svc Mgr: Ms Amanda Lackey BA(Hons), PGCE, DMS
Assoc Libs: BRANCH LIB, Rosaz House, 2-4 Bristol Gate, Brighton, BN2 5BD, Branch Libn: Ms Jil Fairclough BA(Hons) (01273-664948; *fax:* 01273-664949; *email:* Jil.Fairclough@bsuh. nhs.uk); PRINCESS ROYAL HOSP, HEALTH SCIS LIB (see **S795**)
Entry: Trust staff & students *Open:* Mon, Fri 0830-1700, Tue-Thu 0830-2000, key available at all other times
Subj: medicine; nursing; all aspects of health care
Collns: Bks & Pamphs: Sussex Medico-Chirurgical Soc Colln (hist of medicine) *Co-op Schemes:* BLDSC, Psychiatric Co-op, NULJ, HLN (South Thames)
Equip: m-reader, video viewer, fax, copier, computers (incl 16 with wd-proc, 13 with CD-ROM & 12 with internet), room for hire *Online:* Datastar, NHSNet *Svcs:* info, ref, biblio
Stock: bks/31000; periodcls/450; slides/2000; videos/50; CD-ROMs/90
Classn: NLM *Auto Sys:* Librarian
Pubns: Guide to Lib; Elec Journals Guide
Staff: Libns: 5.5 *Non-Prof:* 5.5 *Exp:* £480000 (total exp, 2000-01)

S237 🎓

University of Brighton, Information Services

1st Floor, Watts Bldg, Moulsecoomb, Brighton, E Sussex, BN2 4GJ (01273-642640; *fax:* 01273-642666)
Internet: http://www.brighton.ac.uk/is/

Gov Body: Univ of Brighton *Chief:* Dir of Info Svcs: Mr Mark Toole (M.P.Toole@brighton.ac.uk)
Dep: Dep Dir of Info Svcs: Mr Martin Hayden BA (M.Hayden@brighton.ac.uk)
Assoc Libs: Brighton Libs: ALDRICH LIB, Cockcroft Bldg, Moulsecoomb, Brighton, E Sussex, BN2 4GJ, Info Svcs Mgr: Ms Lyn Turpin MA, MCLIP (01273-642760; *fax:* 01273-642988; *email:* AskAldrich@brighton.ac.uk); FALMER LIB, Falmer, Brighton, E Sussex, BN1 9PH, Info Svcs Mgr: Mr Keith Baxter BA (01273-643569; *fax:* 01273-643560; *email:* AskFalmer@brighton.ac.uk); ST PETER'S HOUSE LIB (see **S238**); *Eastbourne Libs:* QUEENWOOD LIB (see **S584**); HEALTH SCIS LIB, Eastbourne Dist Genl Hosp (see **S583**)

Entry: ref only *Open: Aldrich Lib:* term: Mon-Thu 0830-2100, Fri 0830-1900, Sat-Sun 1300-1700; vac: Mon-Fri 0900-1730, Sun (except in Aug) 1300-1700; contact other libs for their opening hrs
Subj: all subjs; undergrad; postgrad; significant colln in art & design *Co-op Schemes:* BLDSC, SASLIC
Equip: m-readers, m-printers, video viewers, copiers, clr copier, computers (incl wd-proc & CD-ROM)
Stock: bks/560000; periodcls/3800; slides/150000; m-forms/5000; audios/5000; videos/17000
Classn: DDC *Auto Sys:* Talis
Staff: Libns: 30 *Non-Prof:* 40

S238 🎓

University of Brighton, St Peter's House Library

16-18 Richmond Pl, Brighton, E Sussex, BN2 9NA (01273-643221; *fax:* 01273-607532)
Email: AskSPH@brighton.ac.uk
Internet: http://www.brighton.ac.uk/is/

Gov Body: Univ of Brighton (see **S237**) *Chief:* Info Svcs Mgr: Ms Louise Tucker BA, MCLIP
Open: term: Mon-Thu 0900-2000, Fri 0900-1800, Sat 1300-1600; vac: Mon-Fri 0900-1700
Subj: humanities; phil; psy; religion; social sci; arts; decorative arts; design; lit; hist *Co-op Schemes:* ILL, ARLIS, UK Libs Plus
Equip: m-form reader/printer (£2 per card), 3 copiers (£2 per card), clr copier (A4/50p), 6 video viewers (Univ personnel only), 9 computers (Univ personnel only) *Disabled:* Kurzweil *Svcs:* info, ref
Stock: bks/100000; periodcls/300; m-forms/1000; audios/600; videos/2500
Classn: DDC *Auto Sys:* Talis
Staff: Libns: 3.5 *Non-Prof:* 3 full-rime, 6 PT

S239 🎓

University of Sussex Library

Lewes Rd, Falmer, Brighton, E Sussex, BN1 9QL (01273-678163; *fax:* 01273-678441)
Email: library@sussex.ac.uk
Internet: http://www.sussex.ac.uk/library/

Gov Body: Univ of Sussex at Brighton *Chief:* The Libn: Mrs D.C. Shorley BA(Hons) *Dep:* Dep Libn: Mrs M.M. Fieldhouse BA(Hons), MSc (m.m.fieldhouse@sussex.ac.uk) *Other Snr Staff:* Support Svcs Mgr: Mr William Alexander BSc, MSc, DipLib (w.alexander@sussex.ac.uk); Head of Special Collns: Mrs Dorothy Sheridan BA, MA, MBE (d.e.sheridan@sussex.ac.uk); E-Strategy Leader: Mr Ben Wynne BA, DMS, DipLIS (b.b.l.wynne@sussex.ac.uk)
Assoc Libs: SPECIAL COLLNS, addr as above (01273-687157; *fax:* 01273-678441; *email:* library.specialcoll@sussex.ac.uk)
Entry: membs of the Univ; visitors by prior arrangement; external borrowing at discretion of the Libn; access to Special Collns by appt only *Open: Main Lib:* term: Mon-Thu 0900-2130, Fri 0900-1930, Sat-Sun 1230-1830; vac: Mon, Wed-Fri 0900-1730, Tue 0900-1930; *Special Collns:* Mon-Thu 0915-1700
Subj: Main Lib: all subjs; genl; GCSE & A-level; undergrad; postgrad; *Special Collns:* family papers; personal papers; political papers; records of parent org; literary papers; scientific papers *Collns: Bks & Pamphs:* EDC; British Govt Pubns; Chester Music Colln of sheet music (c1850-1914); Eugene W. Schulkind Commune Colln (Paris Commune of 1871, c2500 items); Travers Colln (hist of printing, 350 titles); Baker Bks (18C-19C bks, 180 titles); Caffyn Bks (relating to the poet Percy Shelley); Gilbert Foyle Dickens Colln; UK social & political pamphs; pubns of British pressure groups *Archvs:* archv of the Univ of Sussex, incl official & unofficial records, pubns, maps & arch plans, personal papers of staff, photos & student materials;

Mass-Observation Archv (see **A70**); 70+ MS Collns (mainly 20C); literary papers incl: Geoffrey Gorer papers; Rudyard Kipling papers (on deposit from Natl Trust); Charles Madge papers; Kingsley Martin papers; Nigel Nicholson papers; Edith Sitwell papers; Leonard Woolf papers; Virginia Woolf papers; scientific papers incl: J.G. Crowther papers; Sir Richard Gregory papers; records of political & other orgs, incl: papers of the Common Wealth Party; New Statesman Archv (1943-88) *Other:* Reginald Phillips Philatelic Colln *Co-op Schemes:* BLDSC, SASLIC, SCONUL
Equip: 10 m-readers, 3 m-printers, 14 video viewers, 12 copiers, 2 clr copiers, 98 computers (all with internet & CD-ROM, 73 with wd-proc) *Disabled:* Kurzweil, CCTV enlarger, Aladdin Rainbow reader, other assistive tech *Online:* Dialog (no charge) *Svcs:* info, ref, biblio
Stock: bks/813721; periodcls/3949; AVs/11985; archvs/1426 linear m *Acqs Offcr:* Lib Resources Mgr: Mr Adrian Hale (a.hale@sussex.ac.uk)
Classn: LC for lib holdings, ISAD(G) & in-house for archvs *Auto Sys:* Talis
Pubns: Annual Report; catalogues of special collns, incl: Travers Colln; Baker Colln; Eugene W. Schulkind Paris Commune 1871 Colln
Staff: Libns: 17.5 *Non-Prof:* 74.2 *Exp:* £1118205 (2000-01)
Proj: evaluation of rare & fragile bk collns

S240 🎓
University of Sussex, Biological Sciences Library
School of Biological Sciences, Univ of Sussex, Falmer, Brighton, E Sussex, BN1 9QG (01273-606755; *fax:* 01273-678433)
Email: d.j.t.lamb@sussex.ac.uk

Gov Body: Univ of Sussex (see **S239**) *Chief:* Biology Libn: Miss Dorothy Lamb BA
Entry: ref only *Open:* term & vac: Mon-Fri 0830-1700
Subj: biology; biochem; some psy
Equip: 3 copiers (5p per copy), computer *Online:* Web of Science, access to main lib catalogue
Svcs: info, ref
Stock: periodcls/300 (current & previous year)
Classn: alphabetical *Staff: Libns:* 1

Bristol

S241 🏛
Audit Commission Information Service
Nicholson House, Lime Kiln Cl, Stoke Gifford, Bristol, BS34 8SU (0117-975-7865; *fax:* 0117-979-0552)
Email: d-witherden@audit-commission.gov.uk
Internet: http://www.audit-commission.gov.uk/

Chief: Info Svcs Mgr: Mr Grant Patterson *Dep:* Info Offcr: Miss Dawn Witherden BA(Hons) MCLIP
Entry: very limited access to genl enqs *Open:* Mon-Fri 0900-1700
Subj: genl; computing; law; local govt; maths; statistics; health studies; accountancy; auditing; mgmt *Co-op Schemes:* BLDSC, SWRLIN
Equip: copier *Online:* Datastar *Svcs:* info, ref
Stock: bks/8000; periodcls/50
Classn: own *Auto Sys:* Heritage IV
Pubns: about 30 pubns pa: many available from TWOTEN (tel: 0800-502030), pubns list available
Staff: Libns: 1 *Other Prof:* 1 *Non-Prof:* 2

S242 ✚
Avon and Western Wiltshire Mental Healthcare NHS Trust, Staff Library
Barrow Hosp, Barrow Gurney, Bristol, BS48 3SG (0117-928-6528; *fax:* 0117-928-6650)

Gov Body: Avon & Western Wiltshire Mental Healthcare NHS Trust *Chief:* Postgrad Sec: Mrs J. Johnson
Entry: Trust employees; others ref only *Open:* Mon-Fri 0830-1630
Subj: psychiatry *Collns: Archvs:* hist of psychiatry
Co-op Schemes: SWEHSLinC, PLCS
Equip: fax (Trust staff only), copier, computer (with CD-ROM)
Stock: bks/1636; periodcls/13; videos/70
Classn: NLM *Staff: Non-Prof:* 1

S243 ✚
Blackberry Hill Hospital Library
Manor Rd, Fishponds, Bristol, BS16 2EW (0117-975-4883)
Email: Joan.Sparke@north-bristol.swest.nhs.uk

Gov Body: North Bristol NHS Trust *Chief:* Libn: Ms Joan Sparke
Assoc Libs: FRENCHAY LIB & INFO SVC (see **S252**); KING SQUARE HOUSE LIB (see **S255**); NATL BLOOD SVC (BRISTOL CENTRE) & IBGRL LIB (see **S254**); SOUTHMEAD LIB & INFO SVC (see **S257**)
Entry: Trust staff *Open:* Mon 1100-1600, Tue-Wed, Fri 1000-1600, Thu 1000-1500
Subj: medicine; nursing; health *Classn:* NLM

S244 🎓 🕮
Bristol Baptist College Library
The Promenade, Clifton Down, Clifton, Bristol, BS8 3NJ (0117-946-7050; *fax:* 0117-946-7787)
Email: Library@bristol-baptist.ac.uk
Internet: http://www.bristol-baptist.ac.uk/

Gov Body: Bristol Edu Soc *Chief:* Libn: Mrs Shirley Shire BSc, DipLib, MCLIP
Entry: adv appt, ref only *Open:* Mon, Thu 0930-1500, Wed 1030-1700
Subj: local study (Bristol); phil; religion; hist of religion; social sci *Collns: Bks & Pamphs:* separate collns of 17C-19C material on Baptist hist; bibles & hymn bks *Archvs:* related to the Coll & to some local churches
Equip: m-reader, fax, copier, 6 computers (incl wd-proc, internet & CD-ROM) *Svcs:* info, ref
Stock: bks/17000; periodcls/40; videos/32; archvs/ not measured
Classn: own *Auto Sys:* Heritage
Staff: Libns: 1 *Non-Prof:* 2

S245 🖋
Bristol Chamber of Commerce and Initiative, Library and Information Service
16 Clifton Pk, Bristol, BS8 3BY (0117-973-7373; *fax:* 0117-923-8024)
Email: enquiries@bcci.westec.co.uk

Gov Body: Bristol Chamber of Commerce & Initiative *Chief:* contact the Info Svcs Mgr
Entry: charges made to non-membs *Open:* Mon-Fri 0900-1700
Subj: business; trade; marketing *Collns: Other:* EC legislation; company & market info (UK & worldwide)
Svcs: ref, online searches
Pubns: Directory of Membs

S246 🏛 🏛
Bristol City Museums and Art Gallery, Library and Archives
Queen's Rd, Bristol, BS8 1RL (0117-9223571; *fax:* 0117-9222047)
Email: general_museum@bristol-city.gov.uk
Internet: http://www.bristol-city.gov.uk/museums/

Type: local authority *Gov Body:* Bristol City Council (see **P18**) *Chief:* Head of Museums: Mr Stephen Price
Assoc Libs: BRISTOL INDUSTRIAL MUSEUM, Princes Wharf, Wapping Rd, Bristol, BS1 4RN (0117-925-1470); BLAISE CASTLE HOUSE MUSEUM, Henbury, Bristol, BS10 7QS (0117-903-9818)
Entry: access to specialist libs & archv collns through curator of relevant discipline, preferably via adv appt; ref only *Open:* Mon-Fri 1000-1700
Subj: local study (Bristol region): geol; archaeo; social, agric & industrial hist; tech; applied art; fine art; other geol; nat hist; Oriental art; archaeo
Collns: Archvs: records relating to origin, hist & use of colln, & the people involved *Other:* photo collns esp strong in local social & industrial hist; topographic prints covering Bristol hist
Equip: m-reader, fax, copier; use of all equip is by special arrangement
Stock: bks/several 10000s; periodcls/100; photos/ several 100000s; slides/several 10000s; illusts/ several 10000s; pamphs/several 1000s; maps/a few 1000s; archvs/100 cubic m
Classn: each subj has own method
Staff: Other Prof: 16 curators & conservators

S247 🎓
Bristol Grammar School Library
Univ Rd, Bristol, BS8 1SR (0117-973-6006; *fax:* 0117-946-7485)

Gov Body: Governors of Bristol Grammar School
Chief: Libn: Mrs M. Lane BA, MCLIP *Dep:* Mrs L. Shepherd BEd
Assoc Libs: CALDICOTT CLASSICAL LIB, Libn: Mrs D. Goodhew BA; SCHOOL ARCHVS, Archivist: Mrs A. Bradley MA
Entry: ref only, adv appt for non-school visitors
Open: term: Mon-Fri 0900-1730
Subj: all subjs; GCSE; A level; local study (Bristol, Somerset, Gloucestershire: nat hist, hist & archaeo) *Collns: Bks & Pamphs:* Local Colln; Garrett Shakespeare Lib *Archvs:* relating to school & former membs of school
Equip: copier, 11 computers (all with wd-proc, internet & CD-ROM)
Stock: bks/38000; periodcls/20; audios/350; videos/400; archvs/233 linear ft
Classn: DDC *Auto Sys:* Heritage
Staff: Libns: 1 *Other Prof:* 2

S248 🎓 🏛
British Empire and Commonwealth Museum, Library and Archives
Clock Tower Yard, Temple Meads, Bristol, BS1 6QH (0117-925-4980 x230; *fax:* 0117-925-4983)
Email: collections2@empiremuseum.co.uk
Internet: http://www.www.empiremuseum.co.uk/

Chief: Libn & Archivist: Ms Pippa Griffiths
Assoc Libs: all at above addr: FILM ARCHV, Film Archivist: Ms Jan Vaughan (0117-925-4980 x217; *email:* film@empiremuseum.co.uk); PHOTO ARCHV, Photo Archivist: Ms Joanna Hopkins (0117-925-4980 x216; *email:* photo@ empiremuseum.co.uk); ORAL HIST ARCHV, Oral Hist Archivists: Ms Mary Ingoldby & Ms Hannah Watkins (0117-925-4980 x220/228; *email:* oral.history@empiremuseum.co.uk)
Entry: admission fee; *Ref Lib:* open to public for ref only; *Special Collns & Archvs:* adv appt *Open:* *Ref Lib:* Mon-Fri 1300-1700; *Film Archv:* normally available Wed-Fri
Subj: all aspects of British Empire & Common-wealth, incl: culture; tradition; hist; maritime hist; military hist; tech; industry; arts; craft; leisure; everyday life; racism; economic exploitation; imperialism; slavery

☛

Special Libraries

Bristol
▼
Bristol

(British Empire & Commonwealth Museum cont)
Collns: Bks & Pamphs: original bks (19C-20C) on hist of the Empire & Commonwealth; collns of Commonwealth Inst Resource Centre (c15000 printed & AV items) **Archvs:** unique colln of primary sources, incl original correspondence, notes, ephemera, newspapers & reports relating to Empire & Commonwealth hist (19C-20C); selection of House of Commons & Command Papers (1830-1965) **Other:** several 1000 images in Photo Archv (c1880-date), incl prints, albums, slides, negs, postcards, transparencies & digital images; c850 titles (300+ hrs of footage) in Film Archv (1920s onwards), incl amateur film, govt info films, documentaries, news film, television material & videos of interviews; 1000+ oral hist recordings in Oral Hist Archv, covering experiences of people who lived & worked in the former Empire & Commonwealth; British & Foreign State Papers (170 vols on m-film, 1812-1968)
Pubns: Voices & Echoes: A Catalogue of Oral Hist Holdings of the British Empire & Commonwealth Museum (£12); various historical pubns
Proj: Lit Lending Lib based on Commonwealth Inst collns opening Sep 2003

S249 🔑

Burges Salmon, Solicitors, Library
Narrow Quay House, Narrow Quay, Bristol, BS1 4AH (0117-939-2000; fax: 0117-902-4400)
Email: pat.walker@burges-salmon.com

Type: law firm **Chief:** Head of Info Svcs: Mrs P.H. Walker BA, DipLib, MCLIP **Dep:** Mrs J.E. Hollands BA, DipILS
Entry: ref only, prior appt **Open:** open to membs of firm 24 hrs; manned Mon-Fri 0915-1715
Subj: law **Co-op Schemes:** BLDSC, BRILL
Equip: copier, 8 computers **Online:** Lexis-Nexis, Factiva, Westlaw, Butterworths Online, PLC, Justis, Companies House Direct **Svcs:** info, ref, biblio, indexing, abstracting
Stock: bks/20000; periodcls/330
Classn: MOYS **Auto Sys:** DBTextworks
Staff: Libns: 2 Non-Prof: 4

S250 🎓

City of Bristol College, Learning Resources Centres
College Green, George's Rd, Bristol, BS1 5UA (0117-904-2719)
Email: lrc@cityofbristol.ac.uk
Internet: http://www.cityofbristol.ac.uk/

Gov Body: Brunel Coll of Arts & Tech **Other Snr Staff:** LRC Mgr (Hartcliffe, Bedminster & Lawrence Weston): Ms Maria Bennet (0117-904-5473); LRC Mgr (Brunel & Acqs Unit): Mr Lee Bryant (0117-904-5104); LRC Mgr (Coll Green): Ms Sue Cepom (0117-907-2727); LRC Mgr (Soundwell & Parkway): vacant
Assoc Libs: BEDMINSTER LRC, Marksbury Rd, Bristol, BS3 5JL; BRUNEL LRC, Ashley Down Rd, Bristol, BS7 9BU; COLLEGE GREEN CENTRE, St George's Rd, Bristol, BS1 5UA; HARTCLIFFE LRC, Bishport Ave, Hartcliffe, Bristol, BS13 0RJ; LAWRENCE WESTON LRC, Broadlands Rd, Bristol, BS11 0NT; PARKWAY LRC, New Rd, Stoke Gifford, Bristol, BS34 8SF; SOUNDWELL LRC, St Stephen's Rd, Soundwell, Bristol, BS16 4RL

Entry: staff & students of the coll; LearnDirect students; ref only for public, by adv appt **Open:** varies from site to site; core hrs: Mon-Fri 0930-1700 with evening opening at most sites; reduced hrs during vac
Subj: all subjs; genl; GCSE; A level; undergrad; local hist **Collns:** Bks & Pamphs: local hist colln (at Brunel Site), incl: George Muller Colln (bks on the founder of Muller Soc Orphanages) **Co-op Schemes:** links with Plymouth Univ (see **S1812**), Univ of Bristol (see **S260**), Univ of West of England (see **S263**) & Lawrence Weston Public Lib
Equip: 7 copiers (5p per sheet), 6 fax (free), 45 computers (incl wd-procs, internet & CD-ROM, access free) **Disabled:** Supernova **Online:** Infotrac, Guardian & Observer Online, Know UK, Know Europe, OED, Literature Online, Oxford Reference Centre **Svcs:** info
Stock: bks/36000 bks & videos **Acqs Offcr:** Acqs Libn: Mrs Sherrilea Rickwood (sherrilea.rickwood@cityofbristol.ac.uk)
Classn: DDC **Auto Sys:** DS
Staff: Libns: 6 Non-Prof: 28
Proj: development of Brunel Centre

S251 🎓

Filton College Learning Resources Services, The Library
Filton Ave, Filton, Bristol, BS34 7AT (0117-931-2224; fax: 0117-931-2233)
Email: info@filton.ac.uk
Internet: http://www.filton.ac.uk/

Gov Body: Filton Coll Further Edu Corp **Chief:** Libn: Ms Linda Taylor BA(Hons), MCLIP **Dep:** Asst Libn: Mr Roger Gardiner BEd(Hons)
Assoc Libs: FILTON COLL SCHOOL OF ART & DESIGN LIB, Queens Rd, Clifton, Bristol, BS8 1PX
Entry: staff & students of coll **Open:** Mon-Thu 0900-2000, Fri 0900-1700
Subj: all subjs; GCSE; A level; vocational; local studies (Bristol) **Collns:** Bks & Pamphs: Bristol Area Local Colln **Co-op Schemes:** ILL, BLDSC, SWRLS
Equip: video viewers, copiers, 500 computers (incl wd-proc, internet & CD-ROM) **Online:** Infotrac, Global Market Info Database, Europe in the Round **Svcs:** info, ref, biblio
Stock: bks/24000; periodcls/200; slides/500; maps/250; audios/100; videos/500
Classn: DDC **Auto Sys:** Olib
Staff: Libns: 2 Other Prof: 2 Non-Prof: 10

S252 ✚

Frenchay Library and Information Service
North Bristol NHS Trust, Frenchay Hosp, Frenchay Park Rd, Bristol, BS16 1LE (0117-918-6570; fax: 0117-970-1691)
Email: library@north-bristol.swest.nhs.uk
Internet: http://www.northbristol.nhs.uk/depts/ ClinicalGovernance/Library/

Gov Body: North Bristol NHS Trust **Chief:** Lib Mgr: Ms Jane Villa BA, MCLIP (Jane.Villa@north-bristol.swest.nhs.uk) **Dep:** Snr Lib Asst: Ms Vicky Clayton (Vicky.Clayton@north-bristol.swest.nhs.uk)
Assoc Libs: SOUTHMEAD LIB & INFO SVC (see **S257**); KING SQUARE HOUSE LIB (see **S255**); BLACKBERRY HILL HOSP LIB (see **S243**); ELIZABETH BLACKWELL LIB, Govt Office of the South West, 2 Rivergate, Temple Quay, Bristol, BS1 6ED, Libn: Ms Jean Newman (0117-984-1844; email: Jean.Newman@doh.gsi.gov.uk); NATL BLOOD SVC (BRISTOL CENTRE) & IBGRL LIB (see **S254**)
Entry: membs of North Bristol NHS Trust **Open:** staffed Mon 0800-1900, Tue-Thu 0800-1700, Fri 0800-1630; 24 hr access to membs via swipe-card
Subj: medicine; health; nursing **Co-op Schemes:** ILL

Equip: copier, fax, 11 computers (incl wd-proc & internet) **Online:** Medline, BNI, AMED, Embase, CINAHL, ASSIA, HMIC, PsycInfo
Stock: periodcls/200
Classn: NLM **Auto Sys:** CAIRS **Staff:** 5 in total

S253 🏛

Higher Education Funding Council for England, Knowledge Centre
Northavon House, Coldharbour Ln, Bristol, BS16 1QD (0117-931-7438; fax: 0117-931-7463)
Email: knowledgecentre@hefce.ac.uk
Internet: http://www.hefce.ac.uk/

Chief: Knowledge Centre Mgr: Mrs Pat Davey BA, MCLIP
Entry: ref only, appt necessary **Open:** Mon-Fri 0900-1700
Subj: higher edu
Equip: fax, copier, computer (with internet & CD-ROM) **Svcs:** info, ref
Stock: bks/1000; periodcls/30
Classn: DDC
Pubns: full list available on web site
Staff: Libns: 2 Non-Prof: 2 **Exp:** £30000 (1999-2000)

S254 ✚

National Blood Service (Bristol Centre) and IBGRL Library
Room 3B11, NBS Bristol Centre, Southmead Rd, Bristol, BS16 1LE (0117-991-2152)
Email: lesley.greig@nbs.nhs.uk

Type: Internatl Blood Group Ref Laboratory **Gov Body:** North Bristol NHS Trust **Chief:** Lib Mgr: Ms Lesley Greig MCLIP
Assoc Libs: BLACKBERRY HILL HOSP LIB (see **S243**); FRENCHAY LIB & INFO SVC (see **S252**); KING SQUARE HOUSE LIB (see **S255**); NATL BLOOD SVC (BRISTOL CENTRE) & IBGRL LIB (see **S254**); SOUTHMEAD LIB & INFO SVC (see **S257**)
Entry: Natl Blood Svc & Internatl Blood Group Ref Laboratory employees **Open:** staffed Mon, Wed & Fri 1100-1300; open 24 hrs to membs
Subj: blood products; blood transfusion
Classn: NLM

S255 ✚

North Bristol NHS Trust, King Square House Library
King Sq House, King Sq, Bristol, BS2 8EE (0117-900-2684; fax: 0117-900-2571)
Email: Anne.Mossman@aimtc.nhs.uk

Gov Body: North Bristol NHS Trust **Chief:** Libn: Ms Anne Mossman
Assoc Libs: BLACKBERRY HILL HOSP LIB (see **S243**); FRENCHAY LIB & INFO SVC (see **S252**); KING SQUARE HOUSE LIB (see **S255**); NATL BLOOD SVC (BRISTOL CENTRE) & IBGRL LIB (see **S254**); SOUTHMEAD LIB & INFO SVC (see **S257**)
Entry: staff of Trust **Open:** Mon 0930-1630, Tue-Thu 0830-1630, Fri 0840-1600
Subj: medicine; health **Classn:** NLM

S256 🏛

Planning Inspectorate, Library and Information Centre
G/06, Temple Quay House, 2 The Square, Temple Quay, Bristol, BS1 6PN (0117-372-8677; fax: 0117-372-8970)
Email: gary.morter@planning-inspectorate.gsi. gov.uk

Gov Body: Planning Inspectorate **Chief:** Libn: Mr Gary Morter BA(Hons), MSc **Dep:** post vacant **Entry:** adv appt; only open for consultation of material not available elsewhere **Open:** Mon-Fri 0830-1700
Subj: planning; the countryside; wildlife **Collns: Other:** structure & local plans **Co-op Schemes:** BLDSC
Svcs: info, ref
Stock: bks/7500; periodcls/50
Classn: LC **Auto Sys:** Sirsi
Staff: Libns: 1 **Non-Prof:** 1.5 **Exp:** £84000 (1999-2000); £84000 (2000-01)

S257

Southmead Library and Information Service

North Bristol NHS Trust, Southmead Hosp, Westbury-on-Trym, Bristol, BS10 5NB (0117-959-5333; fax: 0117-959-5529)
Email: southmead_library@yahoo.com
Internet: http://www.northbristol.nhs.uk/depts/ClinicalGovernance/Library/

Gov Body: North Bristol NHS Trust **Chief:** Knowledge Svcs Mgr: Ms Caroline Plaice BLib, MCLIP, CertMan (cplaice.southmead@dial.pipex.com) **Dep:** Lib Mgr: Mrs Lesley Greig MCLIP (lrggreig@hotmail.com)
Assoc Libs: FRENCHAY LIB & INFO SVC (see **S252**); KING SQUARE HOUSE LIB (see **S255**); BLACKBERRY HILL HOSP LIB (see **S243**); ELIZABETH BLACKWELL LIB, Govt Office of the South West, 2 Rivergate, Temple Quay, Bristol, BS1 6ED, Libn: Ms Jean Newman (0117-984-1844; email: Jean.Newman@doh.gsi.gov.uk); NATL BLOOD SVC (BRISTOL CENTRE) & IBGRL LIB (see **S254**)
Entry: open to all Trust staff; ref only for others **Open:** staffed: Mon, Wed, Fri 0800-1730, Tue, Thu 0800-1900; 24 hr access for membs
Subj: health care mgmt; medicine; nursing; paramedicine **Collns: Bks & Pamphs:** large colln of bnd journals (c200 titles) covering all aspects of health care **Co-op Schemes:** BLDSC, ILL, BMA, SWRLIN, Bristol Univ
Equip: m-reader, video viewer, fax, copier, 7 computers (incl wd-proc, internet & CD-ROM) **Online:** Medline, BNI, AMED, Embase, CINAHL, ASSIA for Health, HMIC, PsycInfo
Stock: bks/11000+, excl bnd journals; periodcls/300; videos/40
Classn: NLM **Auto Sys:** CAIRS
Pubns: Lib Guide (free)
Staff: Libns: 4 **Non-Prof:** 5

S258

Trinity Theological College Bristol, Library

Stoke Hill, Stoke Bishop, Bristol, BS9 1JP (0117-968-2803; fax: 0117-968-7470)
Internet: http://www.trinity-bris.ac.uk/

Gov Body: Trinity Coll Council **Chief:** Libn: Ms Susan L. Brown BA, PGDipLS
Entry: ref only to non-membs, upon appl to the Libn; fee payable **Open:** Mon-Fri 0900-1700 (non-membs)
Subj: undergrad; postgrad; phil; psy; religion; social sci; lang; arts; lit; rhetoric; geog; hist **Co-op Schemes:** BLDSC
Equip: 2 m-readers, m-printer, copier, 3 computers
Stock: bks/38054; periodcls/180; pamphs/2899; m-forms/116; audios/70; videos/169
Classn: LC (mod) **Auto Sys:** Heritage
Staff: Libns: 1

S259

United Bristol Healthcare NHS Trust, Learning Resource Centre

Level 5, UBHT Edu Centre, Marlborough St, Bristol, BS2 8AE (0117-342-0105; fax: 0117-342-0128)
Email: learningresourcecentre@hotmail.com
Internet: http://www.ubht.nhs.uk/library/

Gov Body: United Bristol Healthcare NHS Trust **Chief:** Learning Resource Mgr: Ms Julie C. Smith **Dep:** Asst Learning Resource Mgrs: Mr Jason Ovens & Ms Helen March **Other Snr Staff:** Lib Assts: Ms Philomena Jeffroy & Ms Joanna Kent
Assoc Libs: BRISTOL GENL HOSP LIB, Guinea St, Bristol, BS1 6SY; BRISTOL ONCOLOGY CENTRE LIB, Horfield Rd, Bristol, BS2 8ED; ST MICHAEL'S HOSP LIB, St Michael's Hill, Bristol, BS2 8BG; BRISTOL EYE HOSP LIB, Lower Maudlin St, Bristol, BS1 2LX; STAFF DEVELOPMENT LIB, Barrow Gurney, Bristol, BS19 2NT; BRISTOL CHILDREN'S HOSP LIB, St Michael's Hill, Bristol, BS2 8BG
Entry: UBHT staff **Open:** Mon-Fri 0830-1700
Subj: medicine; oncology; ophthalmology; mgmt
Co-op Schemes: BLDSC, SWRLIN, BMA
Equip: m-reader, fax, video viewer, copier, 4 computers (incl internet) **Online:** various databases & e-journals **Svcs:** info, ref, biblio, lit searches
Stock: bks/3190 (incl pamphs, but excl bnd periodcls); periodcls/124; videos/32
Classn: NLM
Pubns: Guides for users; various flyers aimed at target audiences; business plans
Staff: 5 in total

S260

University of Bristol Information Services

Tyndall Ave, Bristol, BS8 1TJ (0117-928-8000; fax: 0117-925-5334)
Email: library@bris.ac.uk
Internet: http://www.bristol.ac.uk/is/

Gov Body: Univ of Bristol **Chief:** Dir of Info Svcs & Univ Libn: Mr Geoffrey Ford BSc, MSc, MCLIP
Dep: Dep Dir: Ms Cathryn Gallagher BA, MLS, DMS **Other Snr Staff:** Dr Peter King MA, PhD, MCLIP
Assoc Libs: 13 branch libs: ARTS & SOCIAL SCIS LIB, addr as above (0117-928-8017); BIOLOGICAL SCIS LIB, School of Biological Scis, Woodland Rd, Bristol, BS8 1UG (0117-928-7943); WORSLEY CHEMICAL LIB, School of Chem, Cantock's Cl, Bristol, BS8 1TS (0117-928-8984); CONTINUING EDU LIB, Dept for Continuing Edu, 8-10 Berkeley Sq, Bristol, BS8 1HH (0117-928-7177); DENTAL LIB (see **S261**); EDU LIB, Grad School of Edu, 35 Berkeley Sq, Bristol, BS8 1JA (0117-928-7070; fax: 0117-930-0763); GEOGRAPHICAL SCIS LIB, School for Geographical Scis, Univ Rd, Bristol, BS8 1SS (0117-928-8116); MEDICAL LIB, School of Medical Scis, Univ Walk, Bristol, BS8 1TD (0117-928-7945); MARIA MERCER PHYSICS LIB, H.H. Wills Physics Laboratory, Tyndall Ave, Bristol, BS8 1TL (0117-928-9000 x7960); QUEEN'S BLDG LIB, Queen's Bldg, Univ Walk, Bristol, BS8 1TR (0117-928-7628); SOCIAL MEDICINE LIB, Dept of Social Medicine, Canynge Hall, Whiteladies Rd, Bristol, BS8 2PR (0117-928-7366); VETERINARY SCI LIB (see **S262**); WILLS MEMORIAL LIB, Wills Memorial Bldg, Queen's Rd, Bristol, BS8 1RJ (0117-954-5398)
Entry: written appl to Univ Libn **Open:** term: Mon-Thu 0845-2300, Fri-Sat 0845-1800, Sun 1400-2000; vac (Christmas & Easter) Mon-Thu 0845-1900, Fri 0845-1645; (Summer) Mon-Fri 0845-1645, Sat 0845-1300
Subj: all subjs; undergrad; postgrad; rsrch

Collns: Bks & Pamphs: EDC; Sir Allen Lane Colln of Penguin Bks; rare botany bks; Wiglesworth Ornithological Colln; Parliamentary Election addresses; early novels colln; garden hist; business hists; early medical & geol bks **Archvs:** I.K. Brunel papers & sketch bks; papers of Pinney family; Addington Symonds papers; editorial archvs of Penguin bks, 1935-60; Natl Liberal Club papers **Co-op Schemes:** SWRLS, BLDSC, EDC, AULIC, CURL
Equip: 30 m-readers, 2 m-printers, 34 copiers, computers (incl wd-proc & CD-ROM) **Disabled:** workstation for visually impaired (incl scanner) **Online:** Dialog, Datastar, BIDS, Medline, EDINA, BLAISE, ESA-IRS, STN **Svcs:** info, ref, biblio
Stock: bks/1305854; periodcls/5000; m-forms/139000; archvs/700 m
Classn: LC **Auto Sys:** Aleph
Staff: Libns: 39.47 **Other Prof:** 5 **Non-Prof:** 58 **Exp:** £1678451 (1999-2000); £1786227 (2000-01)

S261

University of Bristol, Dental Library

Dental Hosp, Lower Maudlin St, Bristol, BS1 2LY (0117-928-4419)
Email: a.farrell@bristol.ac.uk
Internet: http://www.bristol.ac.uk/is/locations/dentlibrary/

Gov Body: Univ of Bristol (see **S260**) **Chief:** Branch Supervisor: Ms Alana Farrell **Dep:** Lib Asst: Ms Sonia McCabe
Entry: open to non-membs only during vac **Open:** term: Mon-Wed 0900-1815, Thu 0945-1815, Fri 0900-1745; vac: Mon-Wed 0900-1800, Thu 0945-1800, Fri 0900-1745
Subj: dentistry **Collns: Other:** MSc theses in Dentistry since 1991
Equip: video viewer, copier, computers (incl internet & CD-ROM), tape-slide machine **Online:** available to students only **Svcs:** ref
Stock: bks/400; periodcls/50; videos/20; AVs/10
Classn: by subj classmark **Auto Sys:** Aleph
Staff: Non-Prof: 2

S262

University of Bristol, Veterinary Sciences Library

School of Veterinary Science, Churchill Bldg, Langford, Bristol, BS40 5DU (0117-928-9205)
Email: lib-vet@bristol.ac.uk

Gov Body: Univ of Bristol (see **S260**) **Chief:** Branch Supervisor: Ms Val Warriss
Entry: staff, students & registered external users only **Open:** term: Mon-Tue 0845-1800, Wed, Fri 0845-1700, Thu 0945-1800 (reduced svcs after 1700)
Subj: veterinary medicine **Collns: Other:** MSc Meat Sci theses (1979-date); a few PhD theses
Equip: copier, computers (incl CD-ROM)
Classn: LC

S263

University of the West of England, Library Services

Bolland Lib, Univ of the West of England, Frenchay Campus, Coldharbour Ln, Bristol, BS16 1QY (0117-344-2404; fax: 0117-344-2407)
Email: lmt-admin@uwe.ac.uk
Internet: http://www.uwe.ac.uk/library/

Gov Body: Univ of the West of England **Chief:** Acting Head of Lib Svcs: Ms Cathy Carpmael **Dep:** Lib Administrator: Ms Tina Williams **Other Snr Staff:** Dep Libns: Ms Anne Lawrence & Ms Jackie Chelin
Assoc Libs: BATH CAMPUS LIB, Edu Centre, Royal United Hosp, Bath, BA1 3NG, Campus Libn: Ms Nicky Morrison (01225-824255; fax: 01225-824256; email: Nicola.Morrison@uwe.ac.uk); ☞

Special Libraries

Bristol ▼ Bury

(Univ of West of England, Lib Svcs cont)
Assoc Libs (cont): BOWER ASHTON LIB, Kennel Lodge Rd, off Clanage Rd, Bristol, BS3 2JT, Faculty/Campus Libn: Mr Geoff Cole (0117-344 4750; *fax:* 0117-344-4745; *email:* library.amd@ uwe.ac.uk); FRENCHAY LIB, addr as above (0117-344-2277; *fax:* 0117-344-2407); GLENSIDE LIB, Blackberry Hill, Stapleton, Bristol, BS16 1DD, Faculty Libns: Mr Jason Briddon & Mr Malcolm McEachran (0117-344-8404; *fax:* 0117-344-8402; *email:* library.hsc@uwe.ac.uk); HARTPURY LIB, Frank Parkinson LRC, Hartpury Campus, Hartpury, Gloucester, GL19 3BE, Faculty/Campus Libn: Ms Helena Taylor (01452-702160; *fax:* 01452-702161; *email:* Helena.Taylor@uwe.ac.uk); ST MATTHIAS LIB, Oldbury Court Rd, Fishponds, Bristol, BS16 2JP, Faculty/Campus Libn: Ms Amanda Salter (0117-344-4472; *email:* library.hums@uwe.ac.uk or library.ess@uwe.ac.uk); SWINDON LIB, Marlowe Ave, Walcot, Swindon, SN3 3JR, Campus Libn: Ms Nicola Ranger (01793-328835; *fax:* 01793-690955; *email:* Nicola.Ranger@uwe.ac.uk)
Entry: free for ref only; borrowing charge for non-membs of UWE ***Open:*** Bolland Lib: term: Mon-Thu 0800-2200, Fri 0800-1900, Sat 1000-1600, Sun 1000-1600 (ref only); vac: opening times vary; other libs: opening times vary
Subj: all subjs; undergrad; postgrad; *Bath Campus, Glenside & Swindon Libs:* nursing; health; social care; subjs allied to medicine; *Bower Ashton Lib:* arts; media; design; *Frenchay Lib:* applied sci; arch; built environment; business; computing; econ; eng; European studies; law; maths; social sci; *Hartpury Lib:* land-based studies; agric; animal husbandry & welfare; equine sci; veterinary nursing; countryside mgmt; health; nursing; *St Matthias Lib:* health; subjs allied to medicine; humanities; hist; culture; lit; music therapy; psy; social sci ***Collns:*** *Bks & Pamphs:* Gloucestershire Beekeepers Assoc Lib; Gloucestershire Naturalists Soc Lib (both at Hartpury); George Budden Music Colln (at Frenchay) *Other:* Arts & Design Audio-visual & Slide Collns (at Bower Ashton) ***Co-op Schemes:*** BLDSC, SWRLS, SWRLIN, AULIC, SCONUL, UK Libs Plus, Gloucestershire Learning Network, UPDATE (a svc co-ordinated by the Univ of Wales)
Equip: m-readers, m-printers, video viewers, copiers, clr copier, computers (each with access to various elec resources, incl networked CD-ROMs, internet, online databases, the lib catalogue & the ResIDe elec lib svc) *Disabled:* PCs with scanner, Kurzweil 3000, Jaws for Windows & ZoomText Xtra Level 2, braille printer & A3 size printing facilities, closed caption decoders, CCTV for text magnification, videophone with British Sign Lang interpreter support *Online:* FirstSearch, Web of Science, OVID, ERIC, EDINA, Eurolaw, Technical Indexes, CHEST & others; numerous e-journals
Stock: bks/c700000; periodcls/c4000; slides/ c5500; AVs/20000+, incl audios & videos
Classn: DDC ***Auto Sys:*** Sirsi Unicorn
Staff: Libns: 51 *Non-Prof:* 81.1

S264

Wesley College Library
College Park Dr, Henbury Rd, Westbury-on-Trym, Bristol, BS10 7QD (0117-959-1200; *fax:* 0117-950-1277)
Email: librarian@wesley-college-bristol.ac.uk

Gov Body: Methodist Church ***Chief:*** Libn: Mrs Janet Henderson BA(Hons), email as above ***Dep:*** Asst Libn: Mr Michael Brealey (mike.brealey@ wesley-college-bristol.ac.uk)
Assoc Libs: METHODIST CHURCH MUSIC SOC LIB, Libn: Mrs Janet Henderson BA(Hons)
Entry: ref only if not associated with Coll or Church; adv appt essential ***Open:*** unsupervised access within secure Coll bldg
Subj: local study: Methodist local hists; phil; psy; religion; social sci; religious music, mainly hymnody; church art & arch; lit; genl hist; church hist; overseas missions ***Collns:*** *Bks & Pamphs:* 58 STC bks; 27 foreign bks publ pre-1640 & c3000 publ pre-1851; the collns are strong in tracts & pamphs, largely devoted to Methodist divisions & controversies (incl anti-Methodist material) *Archvs:* particularly rich in Wesley MS material; other material relating to early hist of Methodism; archvs of other Methodist Colls now closed ***Co-op Schemes:*** local group of theological libs, ABTAPL
Equip: 2 m-readers, computers (incl wd-proc)
Stock: bks/28000; periodcls/60; m-forms/some fiche; archvs/11.2 m
Classn: own ***Auto Sys:*** Heritage IV
Pubns: Manuscripts & Other Collns at Wesley Coll, Bristol: A Catalogue 1984 (£10); Methodist Church Music Soc Lib: Catalogue 1991 (£10); Lib Guide (current year)
Staff: Libns: 1 *Non-Prof:* 8 PT student helpers
Exp: £11000 (1999-2000)

Broadstairs

S265

Thanet College Library
Ramsgate Rd, Broadstairs, Kent, CT10 1PN (01843-865111; *fax:* 01843-860482)
Email: library@thanet.ac.uk
Internet: http://www.thanet.ac.uk/

Chief: Head of Resource-Based Learning: Mrs Carolyn Flanagan BA, MCLIP ***Dep:*** Asst Libn: Mrs Sarah Marsh BA, MCLIP
Entry: ref only ***Open:*** term: Mon-Thu 0830-1930, Fri 0830-1630; vac: Mon-Fri 0830-1630
Subj: all subjs ***Co-op Schemes:*** BLDSC, ILL
Equip: 4 video viewers, copier, computers (incl wd-procs, internet & CD-ROM) ***Svcs:*** info, ref, biblio, indexing
Stock: bks/34000; periodcls/284; slides/30; pamphs/890; maps/300; audios/64; videos/600
Classn: DDC ***Auto Sys:*** Heritage
Staff: Libns: 2 *Other Prof:* 0 *Non-Prof:* 9 *Exp:* £30500 (1999-2000)

Brockenhurst

S266

The National Motor Museum, Library of Motoring
John Montagu Bldg, Beaulieu, Brockenhurst, Hampshire, SO42 7ZN (01590-614652; *fax:* 01590-612655)
Email: motoring.library@beaulieu.co.uk
Internet: http://www.beaulieu.co.uk/

Gov Body: Natl Motor Museum Trust ***Chief:*** Ref Libn: Mrs Lynda Springate
Assoc Libs: MOTORING PICTURE LIB, addr as above (01590-614656; *fax:* 01590-612655; *email:* motoring.pictures@beaulieu.co.uk); MOTORING FILM & VIDEO LIB, addr as above (01590-614664; *fax:* 01590-612655; *email:* filmandvideo@beaulieu. co.uk)
Entry: fees charged for personal callers: £5 + VAT per morning/afternoon (or part thereof) or £10 + VAT per whole day; discounts for students & Friends of the Museum ***Open:*** Mon-Sat 1000-1230, 1400-1700; closed bank hols & between Xmas & New Year

Subj: all aspects of transport, incl: automotive eng; automobiles; commercial vehicles; motorcycles & motorcycling; motor sport ***Collns:*** *Bks & Pamphs:* St John Nixon Colln; workshop manuals & handbks; manufacturers' sales catalogues *Archvs:* Sparshatt Archv; Montague Graham-White Archv *Other:* held in Motoring Picture Lib: 80000 clr transparencies & c1 mln b&w images (1885-date); held in Film & Video Colln: corporate visual archvs from Ford, Vauxhall, Rootes, Peugeot Talbot, Dunlop, Metropolitan Police, Automobile Assoc & Royal Automobile Club; also held at the Lib of Motoring is the Shell Art Colln (commercial art, posters, postcards, press advertisements etc, 1920s-60s)
Equip: copier (15p) ***Svcs:*** info, ref, Motoring Archv Rsrch Svc
Stock: bks/c12000 + 5000 bnd periodcls; periodcls/450+; maps/c250; manuals & handbks/ c16000; sales catalogues/c50000
Classn: own

Bromley

S267

Bromley College of Further and Higher Education, Library
Rookery Ln, Bromley, BR2 8HE (020-8295-7024; *fax:* 020-8295-7099)
Internet: http://www.bromley.ac.uk/

Chief: Coll Libn: Mrs Judith Murdoch MA, MCLIP ***Dep:*** Dep Libn: Mrs Alison Wilson MA, DipLib
Assoc Libs: OLD TOWN HALL SITE LIB, Old Town Hall Site, Tweedy Rd, Bromley, Kent, BR1 3PP (020-8295-7091)
Entry: ref only, adv appt ***Open:*** Rookery Lane Site: term: Mon-Tue 0830-2000, Wed-Thu 0830-1800, Fri 0830-1700, Sat 0900-1300; vac: Mon-Fri 0900-1700; Old Town Hall Site: term: Mon-Tue 1000-1800, Wed-Thu 1000-2030, Fri 1000-1645; vac: Wed 1000-1400
Subj: social work; French; German; Italian; Spanish; electrical; mechanical; computer eng; travel & tourism; business studies; life scis ***Co-op Schemes:*** BLDSC, LASER, SEAL
Equip: 2 copiers, clr copier, 18 computers (incl 16 wd-proc, 15 internet & 3 CD-ROM) ***Svcs:*** info, ref, biblio
Stock: bks/30000; periodcls/240; videos/129
Classn: DDC ***Auto Sys:*** Heritage
Staff: Libns: 2 *Other Prof:* 1 *Non-Prof:* 8

Bromsgrove

S268

Avoncroft Museum of Historic Buildings, Library
Stoke Heath, Bromsgrove, Worcestershire, B60 4JR (01527-831363; *fax:* 01527-876934)
Email: avoncroft@compuserve.com
Internet: http://www.avoncroft.org.uk/

Chief: Dir: Dr Simon Penn PhD ***Dep:*** Edu Offcr: Miss S. Hadley BA(Hons), MA
Entry: adv appt only
Subj: geog; hist; arch; crafts; traditional bldg methods; woodland mgmt
Svcs: ref
Stock: bks/100+; photos/1000+; slides/1000+; maps/10+
Classn: own

S269

North East Worcestershire College, Learning Resources Centres
Blackwood Rd, Bromsgrove, Worcestershire, B60 1PQ (01527-572518/9; *fax:* 01527-572560)
Internet: http://www.ne-worcs.ac.uk/

Gov Body: North East Worcestershire Coll Corp
Chief: Learning Resources Mgr: Mrs Carol Duncan BA, MCLIP **Dep:** Asst Learning Resources Mgr: Ms Eileen McMahan BA
Assoc Libs: REDDITCH CAMPUS LRC, Peakman St, Redditch, Worcestershire, B98 8DW
Entry: staff & students of Coll; ref only for others
Open: term: Mon-Thu 0900-2000, Fri 0830-2000; vac: hrs reduced
Subj: all subjs; GCSE; A level; undergrad; generalities; phil; psy; social psy; lang; sci; maths; tech; arts; lit; geog; hist **Co-op Schemes:** BLDSC
Equip: fax, copiers, 100+ multimedia computers (incl wd-proc, internet & CD-ROM) **Svcs:** info, ref
Stock: bks/34000+; periodcls/300+; videos/900+
Classn: DDC **Auto Sys:** TRAX
Staff: Libns: 2 Non-Prof: 16

Broxburn

S270
Oatridge College Library

Ecclesmachan, Broxburn, W Lothian, EH52 6NH (01506-854387; fax: 01506-853373)
Email: lreade@oatridge.ac.uk
Internet: http://www.oatridge.ac.uk/

Chief: Libn: Mrs Lesley Reade (lreade@oatridge.ac.uk) **Dep:** Libn: Mrs Christel Young (cyoung@oatridge.ac.uk)
Entry: open to students; public by appt **Open:** term: Mon-Thu 0840-2000, Fri 0840-1630; vac: Mon-Fri 0830-1600
Subj: computing; environment; sci; farming; veterinary sci; equine studies; small animal care; arts; geog
Equip: video viewer, copier (£1 for 60 copies), 18 computers (all with wd-proc, internet & CD-ROM) **Officer-in-Charge:** Mrs P. Skett (pskett@oatridge.ac.uk) **Svcs:** info, ref, biblio, indexing
Stock: bks/13000; periodcls/100; maps/30; videos/150; CD-ROMs/30 **Acqs Offcr:** Libn, as above
Classn: DDC **Auto Sys:** Limes
Staff: Libns: 2 Non-Prof: 1

Buckingham

S271
University of Buckingham Library

Hunter St, Buckingham, MK18 1EG (01280-820266; fax: 01280-820312)
Email: library@buckingham.ac.uk
Internet: http://www.buck.ac.uk/

Gov Body: Univ of Buckingham **Chief:** Libn: Mrs Joan Holah BA, MLib, MCLIP
Assoc Libs: HUNTER ST LIB, addr as above, Business & Humanities Libn: Mrs Swee Har Newell BA, DipLIB, LLB (01280-820218; email: sweehar.newell@buckinham.ac.uk); FRANCISCAN LIB, Verney Pk, London Rd, Buckingham, Law & Sci Libn: Miss Louise Hammond BSc, MCLIP (01280-828267; email: louise.hammond@buckingham.ac.uk); DENNING LAW LIB, at Franciscan Lib (see **S272**)
Entry: ref only for external readers **Open:** term: Mon-Thu 0900-2200, Fri 0900-2100, Sat 1200-2200, Sun 1100-2200; vac: Mon-Fri 0900-1700
Subj: undergrad; postgrad; media; journalism; psy; social sci; politics; law; econ; internatl studies; lang (English, French & Spanish); sci; maths; statistics; business; mgmt; accounting; English lit; hist
Collns: Archvs: Univ of Buckingham Archv; Beloff Archv **Co-op Schemes:** BLDSC, ILL
Equip: 2 m-readers, 2 fax, 5 copiers, clr copier, 26 computers (all with wd-proc, internet & CD-ROM)
Online: various, not available to external users
Officer-in-Charge: Libn, as above **Svcs:** info, ref
Stock: bks/90000; periodcls/400; audios/20; videos/150; CD-ROMs/100; archvs/10 linear m
Acqs Offcr: Site Libns, as above

Classn: DDC **Auto Sys:** Unicorn
Staff: Libns: 3 Non-Prof: 6 **Exp:** £131554 (1999-2000); £133024 (2000-01)

S272
University of Buckingham, Denning Law Library

Franciscan Lib, Hunter St, Buckingham, MK18 1EG (01280-814080; fax: 01280-828288)
Email: louise.hammond@buckingham.ac.uk
Internet: http://www.buckingham.ac.uk/library/

Gov Body: Univ of Buckingham (see **S271**)
Chief: Chief Libn (Univ of Buckingham Lib): Mrs Joan Holah BA, MLib, MCLIP **Dep:** Libn (Law): Miss L. Hammond BSc, MCLIP
Entry: ref only, must sign in external visitors bk
Open: term: Mon-Thu 0900-2200, Fri 0900-1900, Sat-Sun 1100-2200
Subj: law; psy **Co-op Schemes:** ILL, BIALL
Equip: 3 copiers, computers (incl 1 with CD-ROM)
Online: Lexis, Westlaw; not available to external users **Svcs:** ref
Stock: bks/25000; periodcls/200; videos/3
Classn: DDC **Auto Sys:** Sirsi Unicorn
Pubns: Denning Law Journal
Staff: Libns: 1 Non-Prof: 1.2

Budleigh Salterton

S273
Bicton College Library

East Budleigh, Budleigh Salterton, Devon, EX9 7BY (01395-562341; fax: 01395-562340)
Email: JMGardner@bicton.ac.uk

Chief: Libn: Miss J.M. Gardner
Entry: external readers by prior appt **Open:** term: Mon-Fri 0845-2000; Sat-Sun 1000-1630; vac: Mon-Fri 0900-1700
Subj: social sci; sci; rural studies; leisure studies; equine studies; veterinary nursing; animal care; agric; hortic; countryside mgmt; floristry; game-keeping; fish farming; arboriculture **Collns:** Other: County Beekeeping Colln
Equip: copier, fax, video viewer, 2 computers (both with CD-ROM), room for hire **Disabled:** lift access to all floors
Stock: bks/14000; periodcls/161; slides/134 sets; pamphs/2000; videos/210; CD-ROMs/50 **Acqs Offcr:** Libn, as above
Classn: DDC **Auto Sys:** Heritage

Burnley

S274 ✚
Burnley General Hospital, Mackenzie Medical Centre Library

Burnley Healthcare NHS Trust, Burnley Genl Hosp, Casterton Ave, Burnley, Lancashire, BB10 2PQ (01282-474720; fax: 01282-474254)

Gov Body: Burnley Healthcare NHS Trust **Chief:** Libn: Mrs Rosemary Turner BA(Hons), HDipLib
Entry: Burnley Healthcare Trust employees & membs of Mackenzie Medical Centre Charity
Open: Mon-Fri 0900-1700
Subj: medicine; nursing; palliative care **Collns:** Bks & Pamphs: very small colln of Governors' reports & command papers **Co-op Schemes:** BLDSC, RCS, BMA, John Rylands Univ of Manchester
Equip: copier, computers (incl wd-proc, internet & CD-ROM) **Online:** Medline, Cochrane **Svcs:** info, ref, biblio
Stock: bks/2805, incl pamphs etc; periodcls/128; audios/69; videos/43; CD-ROMs/6
Classn: NLM **Auto Sys:** InMagic (Soutron)
Staff: Libns: 1 Non-Prof: 1 PT

S275 🔑 🏛
Towneley Hall Art Gallery and Museums Library

Towneley Holmes Rd, Burnley, Lancashire, BB11 3RQ (01282-424213; fax: 01282-436138)
Email: towneleyhall@burnley.gov.uk
Internet: http://www.burnley.gov.uk/towneley/

Chief: Keeper of Art: Miss F. Salvesen
Entry: ref only **Open:** Mon-Fri 1000-1700
Subj: religion; arts; local study (Burnley & Lancashire) **Collns:** Other: photos of local scenes (1880-1920)
Equip: fax, copier (10p per copy), room for hire (on request) **Svcs:** ref
Stock: bks/3000; maps/5
Staff: Other Prof: 6 Non-Prof: 9

Burton-on-Trent

S276 ✚
Burton Graduate Medical Centre Library

Queen's Hosp, Belvedere Rd, Burton-on-Trent, Staffordshire, DE13 0RB (01283-566333 x2104; fax: 01283-510347)
Email: bgmc.lib@dial.pipex.com

Gov Body: Burton NHS Hosp Trust **Chief:** Medical Libn: Mrs Liza Alderman BA(Hons), DipLIS, MCLIP
Entry: ref only, written appl **Open:** Mon, Fri 0900-1700 Tue-Thu 0900-2000
Subj: clinical medicine; public health; genl practice **Co-op Schemes:** RCS, BLDSC, BMA, WMRHLN
Equip: m-reader, m-printer, video viewer, fax, copier, 4 computers (incl wd-proc, internet & CD-ROM)
Stock: bks/3154; periodcls/120; videos/70
Classn: LC **Auto Sys:** Heritage
Staff: Libns: 1 Non-Prof: 0.85

S277 ✚
University of Wolverhampton, Burton Campus Learning Centre

Queens Hosp, Belvedere Rd, Burton-on-Trent, Staffordshire, DE13 0RB (01283-566333 x2217)
Email: in5549@wlv.ac.uk

Gov Body: Wolverhampton Univ (see **S2141**)
Chief: Resource Libn: Ms Liz Watson BA, Dip
Assoc Libs: School of Nursing Learning Centres at: NEW CROSS (see **S2142**); RUSSELL HALL; MANOR (see **S2078**)
Entry: students & staff of Wolverhampton Univ; nursing staff from Burton Hosps Trust receive a restricted svc; charges for other external users
Open: Mon 0900-2000, Tue-Fri 0900-1700
Subj: nursing **Co-op Schemes:** WRLS
Equip: m-reader, copier, computers (incl wd-proc & internet) **Svcs:** info, ref
Stock: bks/12000; periodcls/90
Classn: LC **Auto Sys:** Talis
Staff: Libns: 1 Non-Prof: 3 PT

Bury

S278
Bury College Library

Millennium Centre, Market St, Bury, Lancashire, BL9 0DB (0161-280-8446)
Internet: http://www.burycollege.ac.uk/

Chief: Coll Libn: Mrs Angela Walker BA(Hons), MCLIP **Other Snr Staff:** Mrs Fiona Nightingale DipLib, MCLIP; Mrs Christine Monks BA(Hons), DipLib, MCLIP
Assoc Libs: BURY COLL LIB, Woodbury Centre, Market St, Bury, Lancashire, BL9 0BG ☞

Special Libraries

Bury ▼ Cambridge

(Bury Coll Lib cont)

Entry: coll staff & students *Open:* term: Mon-Fri 0845-2000; vac: closed
Subj: all subjs; genl; GCSE; A level; undergrad; vocational *Co-op Schemes:* BLDSC, ILL, Empowering the Learning Community
Equip: 3 m-readers, 3 video viewers, 3 copiers (5p per sheet), 14 computers (incl wd-proc, internet & CD-ROM) *Svcs:* info, ref, biblio, indexing
Stock: bks/23000; periodcls/45; audios/120; videos/200
Classn: DDC *Auto Sys:* Autolib
Staff: Libns: 2 *Other Prof:* 2 *Non-Prof:* 5 *Exp:* £6000 (1999-2000)

S279 ✚

Fairfield General Hospital Library

Pennine Acute Hosps NHS Trust, Fairfield Genl Hosp, Bury, Lancashire, BL9 7TD (0161-778-2422; *fax:* 0161-778-2421)
Email: burylibrary@yahoo.co.uk

Gov Body: Pennine Acute Hosps NHS Trust
Chief: Lib Svcs Mgr: Miss Sue Locke BSc(Hons), MA, MCLIP
Entry: ref only; adv appt *Open:* Mon-Thu 0845-1700, Fri 0845-1630
Subj: medicine *Co-op Schemes:* BLDSC, LIHNN, PLCS, NULJ
Equip: copier (5p per pg), computers (incl 5 with wd-proc & 4 with internet, printouts 5p per pg)
Officer-in-Charge: Lib Svcs Mgr, as above
Stock: bks/c3000; periodcls/100; videos/30 *Acqs Offcr:* Lib Svcs Mgr, as above
Classn: NLM *Auto Sys:* Heritage
Staff: Libns: 1 *Non-Prof:* 0.4 *Exp:* £33000 (2000-01)

Bury St Edmunds

S280 🎓 🏛

Broom's Barn Research Station Library

(formerly Inst of Arable Crops Rsrch, Broom's Barn Lib)
Higham, Bury St Edmunds, Suffolk, IP28 6NP (01284-812200; *fax:* 01284-811191)
Email: karen.hales@bbsrc.ac.uk
Internet: http://www.iacr.bbsrc.ac.uk/broom/

Gov Body: div of Rothamsted Rsrch *Chief:* Liaison Asst: Mrs Karen Hales
Assoc Libs: ROTHAMSTED RSRCH LIB (see **S786**)
Entry: adv appt; ref only; genl enquirers should contact Rothamsted Rsrch Lib, unless the enq specifically relates to sugar beet *Open:* Mon-Thu 0830-1300, 1400-1700, Fri 0830-1300, 1400-1630
Subj: agric; sugar beet *Collns: Bks & Pamphs:* materials related to sugar beet cultivation
Equip: copier (use negotiable) *Svcs:* info, ref
Classn: UDC

S281 🎓

West Suffolk College, Learning Resource Centre

Out Risbygate, Bury St Edmunds, Suffolk, IP33 3RL (01284-716267/16; *fax:* 01284-750501)
Email: library@westsuffolk.ac.uk

Gov Body: West Suffolk Coll *Chief:* LRC Mgr: Mrs Sarah-Louise Neesam BA(Hons) *Dep:* Libns: Mrs Julia Lale BLib, MCLIP; Mrs Hilary Sanders BA(Lib); Mrs Paula King BA(Lib), MCLIP
Entry: students at Coll; external membership £20 pa *Open:* term: Mon-Thu 0830-1900, Fri 0830-1700; vac: Mon-Fri 0900-1300
Subj: all subjs; genl; GCSE; A level (some subjs); undergrad (some subjs); vocational *Co-op Schemes:* ANGLES, BLDSC
Equip: m-reader, copier (A4/10p), clr copier (A4/£1), 54 computers (all with wd-proc, 10 with internet & 4 with CD-ROM), laminator, binder
Disabled: print enlarger *Svcs:* info, ref, biblio
Stock: bks/30000; periodcls/200, plus 100 e-journals; slides/10 sets; maps/several sets; videos/2500; CD-ROMs/90
Classn: DDC *Auto Sys:* Heritage
Staff: Libns: 3 *Other Prof:* 1 mgr *Non-Prof:* 6

S282 ✚

West Suffolk Hospital, Education Centre and Library

Hardwick Ln, Bury St Edmunds, Suffolk, IP33 2QZ (01284-713343; *fax:* 01284-713113)
Email: joan.hunter@wsufftrust.org.uk
Internet: http://www.wsufftrust.org.uk/library/

Gov Body: West Suffolk Hosps NHS Trust *Chief:* Libn: Mrs Joan Hunter MA, MCLIP *Dep:* Asst Libn: Mrs Lynette Last
Entry: NHS staff in West Suffolk; £20 pa subscription for non-NHS membs *Open:* Mon, Wed 0830-1700, Tue, Fri 0830-1600, Thu 0830-2100
Subj: medicine; nursing; health *Co-op Schemes:* BLDSC, Eastern Confederations Lib & Knowledge Svcs Alliance
Equip: copier, 26 computers (incl wd-proc, internet & CD-ROM) *Online:* Medline, Cochrane & others
Svcs: info, ref, biblio, indexing
Stock: bks/16000; periodcls/200; pamphs/1000; videos/100
Classn: NLM *Auto Sys:* MS Access
Staff: Libns: 1 *Non-Prof:* 5

Buxton

S283 🏛 🏛

Buxton Museum and Art Gallery

Terrace Rd, Buxton, Derbyshire, SK17 6DA (01298-24658; *fax:* 01298-79394)
Email: buxton.museum@derbyshire.gov.uk

Type: local authority *Gov Body:* Derbyshire County Council (see **P36**) *Chief:* Derbyshire Museums Mgr: Mrs R. Westwood MA, AMA *Dep:* Asst Museums Mgr: Mrs S. Palmer MA, AMA
Entry: ref only; adv appt; restricted copying except m-fiche *Open:* Tue-Fri 0930-1730, Sat 0930-1700; lib closed Mon & Sun; museum also open Sun & banks hols 1030-1700 over summer
Subj: local study (Peak Dist); archaeo; geol; local art & hist; arts *Collns: Archvs:* W.M. Boyd-Dawkins & J.W. Jackson (early cave & geol excavations) *Co-op Schemes:* Historical MSS Commission
Equip: m-reader, m-printer, video viewer, copier
Disabled: wheelchair access *Svcs:* info, ref
Stock: bks/100; photos/1000; slides/500; illusts/100; maps/50; audios/500; videos/200
Pubns: The Cave Hunters (£1.50p)
Staff: Other Prof: 4 Non-Prof: 3

S284 🎓

University of Derby College, Buxton, Learning Centre

(formerly Univ of Derby, High Peak Coll)
Harpur Hill, Buxton, Derbyshire, SK17 9JZ (*tel & fax:* 01298-28385)
Internet: http://lib.derby.ac.uk/library/

Gov Body: Univ of Derby (see **S528**) *Chief:* Learning & IT Svcs Mgr: Ms Maria Bennett BA(Hons) (M.A.Bennett@derby.ac.uk) *Dep:* Learning Centre Supervisor: Ms Yvonne Smith (Y.Smith@derby.ac.uk)
Open: term: Mon-Thu 0900-2100, Fri 0900-1600; vac: Mon-Thu 0900-1700, Fri 0900-1600
Subj: all subjs; genl; GCSE; A level; undergrad; vocational *Co-op Schemes:* BLDSC, EMUA, UK Libs Plus, CONARLS
Equip: 4 video viewers, 2 copiers, 70 computers (all with wd-proc, internet & CD-ROM) *Online:* various *Svcs:* info, ref, biblio
Stock: bks/30000; periodcls/110; maps/300; audios/100; videos/400
Classn: DDC *Auto Sys:* Talis
Staff: Libns: 2 *Non-Prof:* 11

Caerphilly

S285 ✚

Gwent Healthcare Postgraduate Library

Caerphilly Dist Miners Hosp, St Martins Rd, Caerphilly, Mid Glamorgan, CF83 2WW (029-2080-7014; *fax:* 029-2080-7101)
Email: claire.powell@gwent.wales.nhs.uk

Gov Body: Gwent Healthcare NHS Trust *Chief:* Libn: Mrs Clare Powell
Entry: Trust staff; NHS staff in Gwent area *Open:* Mon-Thu 0830-1700, Fri 0830-1630; weekend access by prior arrangement
Subj: medicine; nursing *Co-op Schemes:* BLDSC, AWHILES
Equip: copier (5p per pg), computers (incl internet) *Online:* CINAHL, Medline, AMED, PubMed
Classn: DDC

S286 🎓

Ystrad Mynach College Library

Twyn Rd, Ystrad Mynach, Caerphilly, Mid Glamorgan, CF82 7XR (01443-816888 x253 or 294; *fax:* 01443-816973)
Email: gthomas@ystrad-mynach.ac.uk
Internet: http://www.ystradmynachcollege.co.uk/

Chief: Coll Libn: Miss Gillian Thomas MLib, BA, DipLib, MCLIP
Entry: staff & students *Open:* term: Mon-Thu 0830-2000, Fri 0830-1630; vac: Mon-Fri 0830-1630
Subj: all subjs; genl; GCSE; A level; undergrad; postgrad; vocational *Co-op Schemes:* BLDSC, ILL
Equip: copier, clr copier, computers (with wd-proc, internet & CD-ROM) *Svcs:* info, ref, biblio
Stock: bks/20000; videos/c200; CD-ROMs/100
Classn: DDC *Auto Sys:* EASL
Staff: Libns: 1 *Non-Prof:* 3

Callington

S287 🎓

Duchy College Learning Centre

Stoke Climsland, Callington, Cornwall, PL17 8PB (01579-372222; *fax:* 01579-372200)
Internet: http://www.duchy.ac.uk/stoke/

Gov Body: part of the Cornwall Coll Group (see **S1856**) *Chief:* contact the Libn
Assoc Libs: DUCHY COLL, ROSEWARNE LEARNING CENTRE, Camborne, Cornwall, TR14 0AB
Entry: staff & students *Open: Stoke Climsland:* term: Mon, Wed 0830-1730, Tue, Thu 0830-2000, Fri 0830-1700, Sat 0900-1200; *Rosewarne:* term: Mon-Wed 0900-1700, Thu 0900-1900, Fri 0900-1630; vac (both sites): varies

Subj: agric; hortic; countryside care; equine studies; sport; leisure *Collns: Bks & Pamphs:* hortic & agric reports & statistics (1950s onwards) *Co-op Schemes:* ALLCU *Equip:* copier, 20 computers (incl internet), binding & laminating facilities *Online:* various databases *Stock:* bks/c11500 printed & AV items; periodcls/ c130; figs are for both sites

Camberley

S288

Frimley Park Hospital NHS Trust, Health Sciences Library

Portsmouth Rd, Frimley, Camberley, Surrey, GU16 5UJ (01276-604168; *fax:* 01276-604278) *Email:* fph_library@hotmail.com

Chief: Lib Svcs Mgr: Mrs Suzy Thompson BA(Hons), MSc, MCLIP (suzy.thompson@fph-tr.nhs.uk) *Dep:* Snr Lib Asst: Mrs Rosemary Thomas BA(Hons) *Entry:* employees of Frimley Park Hosp or NHS staff working within the West Surrey & north & mid Hampshire health communities *Open:* Mon-Thu 0900-1800, Fri 0900-1700 *Subj:* social sci; medicine; nursing *Co-op Schemes:* HLN, BMA, NULJ, BLDSC *Equip:* copier (A4/10p, A3/15p), fax (50p per sheet), 9 computers (incl 6 with wd-proc, 2 with CD-ROM & 5 with internet) *Officer-in-Charge:* Lib Svcs Mgr, as above *Svcs:* info, ref, biblio, current awareness, training *Stock:* bks/9000; periodcls/140; maps/2; videos/ 10; CD-ROMs/27 *Acqs Offcr:* Lib Svcs Mgr, as above *Classn:* NLM *Auto Sys:* Heritage *Staff: Libns:* 1 *Non-Prof:* 2.52 FTE

S289

Royal Military Academy Sandhurst, Library and Archives

Sandhurst, Camberley, Surrey, GU15 4PQ (01276-63344; *fax:* 01276-412359) *Email:* aaorgill@aol.com

Chief: Libn: Mr Andrew Orgill MA, DipLib, MCLIP *Assoc Libs:* ROYAL MILITARY ACADEMY ARCHVS, at same addr, Archivist: Mrs M. de Lee (01276-412503; *fax:* 01276-412595) *Entry:* strictly by adv appt only *Subj:* military hist; defence; internatl affairs; personal papers; records of parent org *Collns: Archvs:* records of the Academy & predecessors (Royal Military Academy, Woolwich & the Royal Military Coll, Sandhurst); papers of various military & political figs, incl: Genl J.G. Le Marchant (1766-1812); papers of Field Marshal William Harcourt (1743-1830); papers of Lord Grenville (1753-1813); papers of Michael Faraday (1791-1867) *Co-op Schemes:* ILL *Stock:* bks/150000; periodcls/300 *Classn:* UDC *Auto Sys:* CAIRS

Cambridge

S290

Ancient India and Iran Trust Library

23 Brooklands Ave, Cambridge, CB2 2BG (01223-702095; *fax:* 01223-361125) *Email:* wiesiekinc@yahoo.com *Internet:* http://www.indiran.co.uk/

Gov Body: Ancient India & Iran Trust; part of Univ of Cambridge (see L5) *Chief:* Libn: Mr Wieslaw Mical *Entry:* ref only, adv appt by tel or letter *Open:* Mon-Fri 1000-1730

Subj: ancient heritage of India, Iran & Central Asia; Indo-Iranian langs & philology; art & archaeo of Central, South & South East Asia *Collns: Bks & Pamphs:* Sir Harold Bailey Lib (ancient langs & lit, mainly Indo-Iranian); van Lohuizen Lib (art hist of South & South East Asia); Allchin Lib (archaeo of Central & South Asia) *Archvs:* Sir Harold Bailey MS Colln (MSS in Indo-Iranian langs) *Other:* Offprint Colln (c20000 items); Slide & Photo Collns *Co-op Schemes:* CULS *Staff:* 1 *Proj:* computer cataloguing

S291

The Babraham Institute Library

Babraham Hall, Babraham, Cambridge, CB2 4AT (01223-496000; *fax:* 01223-496020) *Email:* babraham.library@bbsrc.ac.uk *Internet:* http://www.babraham.ac.uk/

Type: scientific rsrch inst *Gov Body:* Boards of Dirs *Chief:* Libn: Miss Jennifer R. Maddock BA, DipLib, MCLIP *Entry:* membs of staff only *Subj:* post-doctoral; molecular biology; immunology; physiology *Co-op Schemes:* ILL, serials consortium *Equip:* m-reader, 2 copiers, computer *Online:* available only to membs of staff *Stock:* bks/2000; periodcls/225 + 275 closed titles *Auto Sys:* SBSM *Staff: Libns:* 1 *Non-Prof:* 1.5

S292

Birdlife International, Library

Wellbrook Ct, Girton Rd, Cambridge, CB3 0NA (01223-277318; *fax:* 01223-277200) *Email:* birdlife@birdlife.org.uk *Internet:* http://www.birdlife.net/

Gov Body: Birdlife Internatl *Chief:* Libn: Ms Janet Chow BA(Hons) (janet.chow@birdlife.org.uk) *Dep:* Lib Asst: Ms Christine Alder *Entry:* adv appt *Open:* Mon-Fri 0930-1700 *Subj:* ornithology; conservation *Equip:* 2 copiers (5p per pg) *Svcs:* info, ref, biblio *Stock:* bks/6000; periodcls/300; reprints/50000 *Classn:* in-house *Staff: Libns:* 1 *Non-Prof:* 1

S293

Blackfriars Cambridge Library

Blackfriars, Buckingham Rd, Cambridge, CB3 0DD (01223-741251)

Gov Body: Dominican Order of Friars Preachers *Chief:* contact the Father Libn *Entry:* apply to the Father Libn *Open:* Mon-Fri 0900-1800 *Subj:* religion; theology; phil; mainly Roman Catholic *Co-op Schemes:* CULS *Stock:* bks/c7000

S294

British Antarctic Survey Library

High Cross, Madingley Rd, Cambridge, CB3 0ET (01223-221617; *fax:* 01223-362616) *Email:* c.phillips@bas.ac.uk *Internet:* http://www.antarctica.ac.uk/Resources/ Library/

Gov Body: NERC *Chief:* Libn: Miss Christine Phillips MA, MCLIP *Entry:* bona fide rsrch workers, by arrangement with libn *Open:* Mon-Thu 0900-1730, Fri 0900-1700 *Subj:* geol; geophysics; glaciology; meteorology; climatology; upper atmosphere physics; biology; zoology; botany (all with emphasis on Antarctic studies) *Co-op Schemes:* ILL *Equip:* m-reader, copier, computer (incl CD-ROM)

Stock: bks/8500; periodcls/330, plus 200 no longer current; m-forms/250; offprints/18000; maps, photos, slides are held off site *Classn:* UDC *Staff: Libns:* 1 *Non-Prof:* 1

S295

Cambridge Refrigeration Technology Library

140 Newmarket Rd, Cambridge, CB5 8HE (01223-461352; *fax:* 01223-461522) *Email:* d.goddard@crtech.demon.co.uk *Internet:* http://www.crtech.co.uk/

Type: rsrch assoc *Chief:* Libn & Info Offcr: Mrs D. Goddard *Entry:* membs only *Open:* Mon-Fri 0900-1700 *Subj:* sci & maths (heat transfer, statistics); tech (refrigeration, shipping, food, fruit physiology); geog (maps) *Collns: Bks & Pamphs:* 28000 ref bks, journals, photos, films & videos on the carriage of perishable products *Archvs:* c5000 early refrigeration bks & manuals; early meat trades *Co-op Schemes:* BL, BSRIA, Leatherhead Food Rsrch Assoc *Equip:* m-reader, m-printer, video viewer, fax, copier, clr copier, computers (incl wd-proc & CD-ROM) *Online:* FRIDOC, CABi, ASHRAE, BHT (rate negotiated per search) *Officer-in-Charge:* Libn & Info Offcr, as above *Svcs:* info, ref, biblio, indexing, abstracting *Stock:* bks/11000; periodcls/106; photos/2000; slides/1000; pamphs/19000; maps/100; m-forms/ 100; videos/50 *Acqs Offcr:* Libn & Info Offcr, as above *Classn:* UDC *Pubns:* Cargo Companion Set (3 vols): Dry Cargo, Controlled Atmosphere, Perishable Products; RTIS Databases (CD-ROM); Remote Monitoring Symposium (CD-ROM) *Staff: Libns:* 1

S296

Cambridge Regional College, Learning Resource Centre

Kings Hedges Rd, Cambridge, CB4 2QT (01223-418216; *fax:* 01223-426425) *Internet:* http://www.camre.ac.uk/learning/

Chief: Head of Centre for Learning: Ms Penny King BA, FCLIP (pking@mail.camre.ac.uk) *Dep:* Svc Mgr: Mr Paul Chapman BA, DipLib, MCLIP (pchapman@mail.camre.ac.uk) *Other Snr Staff:* Learning Resources Advisor: Ms Karen Spencer BA, MA, DipLib, MCLIP (kspencer@mail.camre. ac.uk) *Assoc Libs:* KINGS HEDGES RD LRC, addr as above; NEWMARKET RD LRC, Newmarket Rd, Cambridge, CB5 8EG (01223-532238) *Entry:* ref only *Open: Kings Hedges:* term: Mon-Thu 0830-1900, Fri 0830-1700; vac: Mon-Thu 0830-1700, Fri 0830-1630; *Newmarket Rd:* term: Mon-Thu 0830-1800, Fri 0830-1700; vac: by arrangement only *Subj:* all subjs; GCSE; A level; vocational; psy; social sci; lang; sci; maths; tech; arts; lit; geog; hist *Equip:* 2 video viewers, copier, 13 computers (all with internet) *Svcs:* info, ref, biblio *Stock:* bks/c40000; periodcls/200; slides/1000; videos/500 *Classn:* DDC *Auto Sys:* Heritage *Staff: Libns:* 4 *Non-Prof:* 18

S297

Cambridge Union Society, Keynes Library

9a Bridge St, Cambridge, CB2 1UB (01223-568439; *fax:* 01223-566444) *Email:* ncc25@cam.ac.uk *Internet:* http://www.cus.org/

Special Libraries

Cambridge ▼ Cambridge

(Cambridge Union Soc, Keynes Lib cont)

Chief: Hon Snr Libn: Ms P. Aske MA *Dep:* Asst Libn: Mr N. Cutler BSc(Hons), MA
Entry: membs of Soc; adv appt for non-membs
Open: term: Mon-Fri 1030-1800; vac: varies
Subj: all subjs; A level; undergrad; local study (Cambridge & Cambridgeshire); particularly strong in: lit; biography; travel; other subjs incl: phil; psy; religion; social sci; lang; sci; maths; arts; geog; hist; fiction; humour; sport *Collns:* Bks & Pamphs: Erkine Allon Colln of Musical Scores (18C-20C); Fairfax Rhodes Colln of Rare Bks (c1760-1920) *Archvs:* colln of tape-recordings of Union Soc debates (1965-97, almost complete from 1972); Union Soc Archvs (incl debates) on deposit at the Univ Lib, Cambridge (see **L5**) *Co-op Schemes:* CUC
Svcs: info, ref
Stock: bks/33000; periodcls/7; audios/700; videos/30
Classn: DDC, in-house sys for older stock
Pubns: guides to collns
Staff: Libns: 1 *Exp:* £1200 (2000-01)

Cambridge University Library
See **L5**

S298 🎓
Cambridge University, African Studies Centre Library
Free School Ln, Cambridge, CB2 3RQ (01223-334398; *fax:* 01223-334396)
Email: si106@cam.ac.uk
Internet: http://www.african.cam.ac.uk/library/

Gov Body: Univ of Cambridge (see **L5**) *Chief:* Libn: Mrs Sarah Irons BA(Hons), DipIS *Dep:* Lib Asst: Ms Claudette Henry
Entry: open to membs of Univ, others by arrangement with libn *Open:* Mon-Fri 0900-1730; shortened hrs during summer vac
Subj: interdisciplinary rsrch & teaching in modern African studies *Co-op Schemes:* CAMP
Equip: m-reader, video viewer, copier (A4/7p, A3/10p), 3 computers (incl internet & CD-ROM)
Online: Internet *Svcs:* info, ref, biblio
Stock: bks/29000; periodcls/141; videos/361
Classn: UDC *Auto Sys:* CUC Systems
Pubns: Cambridge African Monographs Series
Staff: Libns: 1 Non-Prof: 1 PT *Exp:* £8115 (1999-2000)

S299 🎓
Cambridge University, Botanic Garden (Cory) Library
Cory Lodge, Bateman St, Cambridge, CB2 1JF (01223-336265; *fax:* 01223-336278)
Email: enquiries@botanic.cam.ac.uk
Internet: http://www.botanic.cam.ac.uk/

Gov Body: Univ of Cambridge (see **L5**), sub-dept of the Dept of Plant Scis (see **S317**) *Chief:* post vacant
Entry: adv appt *Open:* Mon-Fri 0900-1700
Subj: local study (Cambridgeshire); local flora; botany; hortic; hist of botany *Collns:* Archvs: Nurserymen's Catalogues *Other:* slide colln (plants); indexed colln of living plants *Co-op Schemes:* ILL

Equip: m-reader, copier
Stock: bks/6528; periodcls/64; pamphs/3068; videos/3; CD-ROMs/2
Staff: Other Prof: 0.33 *Exp:* approx £5000 (1999-2000)

Cambridge University, Centre of International Studies and Development Studies Library
See CAMBRIDGE UNIV, MILL LANE LIB (**S336**)

Cambridge University, Centre of Latin American Studies Library
See CAMBRIDGE UNIV, MILL LANE LIB (**S336**)

S300 🎓
Cambridge University, Centre of South Asian Studies, Library and Archives
Laundress Ln, Cambridge, CB2 1SD (01223-338094; *fax:* 01223-316913)
Internet: http://www.s-asian.cam.ac.uk/

Gov Body: Univ of Cambridge (see **L5**) *Chief:* Smuts Libn in South Asian & Commonwealth Studies: Ms Rachel M. Rowe (rmr29@cam.ac.uk)
Dep: Centre Administrator & Archivist: Dr Kevin Greenbank
Entry: ref only, open to students or those with letter of introduction *Open:* term: Mon-Fri 0930-1300, 1400-1730; vac: Mon-Fri 0930-1300, 1300-1700
Subj: South & South East Asia: religion; social sci; geog; hist *Collns:* Archvs: Cambridge South Asian Archv: 600 collns of MSS, incl personal papers of Europeans in India *Other:* large film & photo archv *Co-op Schemes:* BLDSC, ILL
Equip: 8 m-readers, m-form reader-printer, copier (5p), 2 computers (both with internet & CD-ROM), DVD viewer for films (transfer to DVD ongoing)
Online: Cambridge Univ Lib catalogue, OPAC
Svcs: info, ref
Stock: bks/30000; periodcls/180; photos/80000; pamphs/5000; maps/800; m-forms/10600; audios/275; archvs/600 collns; films/350
Classn: UDC *Auto Sys:* Voyager
Pubns: Centre of South Asian Studies Annual Report (free); Brief Guide to Principal Collns in the Cambridge South Asian Archv (free); Cambridge South Asian Archv (Vols 1-5, prices vary); Occasional Paper series (price on appl)
Staff: Libns: 1 Non-Prof: 2 *Exp:* £15500 (1999-2000)

S301 🎓
Cambridge University, Computer Laboratory Library
William Gates Bldg, J.J. Thomson Ave, Cambridge, CB3 0FD (01223-334648; *fax:* 01223-334678)
Email: lkt@cl.cam.ac.uk
Internet: http://www.cl.cam.ac.uk/Library/

Gov Body: Univ of Cambridge (see **L5**) *Chief:* Libn: Mr Lewis Tiffany MA
Entry: internal staff & students; users of the computing svc; others on appl *Open:* Mon-Fri 0900-1230, 1330-1700
Subj: computing; hardware; software; operating systems; LANs; maths *Co-op Schemes:* ILL, CULS
Equip: copier, m-reader *Svcs:* ref, biblio
Stock: bks/4250; periodcls/135; technical reports/13550
Classn: ACM Computing Classn System
Staff: Libns: 1

S302 🎓
Cambridge University, Department of Applied Economics Library
Sidgwick Ave, Cambridge, CB3 9DE (01223-335256; *fax:* 01223-335299)

Gov Body: Univ of Cambridge (see **L5**) *Chief:* Libn: Ms Bella Campbell-Stewart
Entry: ref only; staff & postgrad students; visitors by appt *Open:* staff at any time; postgrads Mon-Fri 0900-1815
Subj: social sci; applied econ *Co-op Schemes:* BLDSC, ILL, CULS
Equip: copier, computers *Svcs:* ref, biblio
Stock: bks/5505; periodcls/416; pamphs/40000
Classn: own *Staff:* Libns: 1 Non-Prof: 1

Cambridge University, Department of Applied Mathematics and Theoretical Physics Library
See CAMBRIDGE UNIV LIB, BETTY & GORDON MOORE LIB (**L5**)

S303 🎓
Cambridge University, Department of Biochemistry, Colman Library
Downing Site, Tennis Ct Rd, Cambridge, CB2 1QW (01223-333613; *fax:* 01223-333345)
Email: librarian@bioc.cam.ac.uk
Internet: http://www.bio.cam.ac.uk/dept/biochem/ColmanLibrary/

Gov Body: Univ of Cambridge (see **L5**) *Chief:* Colman Libn: Prof Richard Perham ScD, FRS
Dep: Asst Libn: Ms Hazel Zheng
Entry: univ staff, undergrads studying biochemistry & related subjs; others by appt with permission of libn *Open:* Mon-Fri 0800-1700
Subj: undergrad; postgrad; sci; maths; rsrch; biochem *Collns:* Bks & Pamphs: dept pubns (copies of papers publ by dept membs are collected & bnd by year, 1913-date) *Archvs:* assortment of archvs relating to the dept incl bks, pamphs, photos etc *Co-op Schemes:* BLDSC, ILL
Equip: copier (5p per sheet), 8 computers (incl wd-proc & internet) *Online:* BIDS, Medline, OCLC, IDEAL *Svcs:* info ref, biblio
Stock: bks/c11000; periodcls/113; photos/some; archvs/8 linear m
Classn: own
Pubns: Departmental Annual Report
Staff: Other Prof: 1 Non-Prof: 1

S304 🎓
Cambridge University, Department of Chemical Engineering Library
Pembroke St, Cambridge, CB2 3RA (01223-334777; *fax:* 01223-334796)

Gov Body: Univ of Cambridge (see **L5**) *Chief:* Libn: Dr J.W. Thompson PhD *Dep:* Asst Libns: Mrs H. Stevens Smith (helen@cheng.cam.ac.uk) & Miss S. Percival (samantha@cheng.cam.ac.uk)
Entry: permission from libn, ref only *Open:* Mon-Fri 1000-1330, 1500-1730
Subj: chemical eng
Equip: m-reader, copier *Svcs:* info, ref
Stock: bks/5000; periodcls/39
Classn: own *Staff:* Libns: 2

S305 🎓
Cambridge University, Department of Chemistry Library
Lensfield Rd, Cambridge, CB2 1EW (01223-336329; *fax:* 01223-336362)
Email: cc103@cam.ac.uk
Internet: http://www.ch.cam.ac.uk/library.html

Gov Body: Univ of Cambridge (see **L5**) *Chief:* Libn: Mrs C.M. Cook
Entry: membs of Univ *Open:* Mon-Fri 0830-1700, Sat 0830-1300
Subj: postgrad; chem *Co-op Schemes:* BLDSC
Equip: copier, 24 computers (all with wd-proc & internet) *Svcs:* info, ref, biblio
Stock: bks/29000; periodcls/151
Classn: own *Staff: Libns:* 2

S306
Cambridge University, Department of Clinical Veterinary Medicine Library
Madingley Rd, Cambridge, CB3 0ES (01223-337600 x7633; *fax:* 01223-337610)
Email: lel1000@cam.ac.uk
Internet: http://www.vet.cam.ac.uk/library/library.html

Gov Body: Univ of Cambridge (see **L5**) *Chief:* Libn: Mrs L.E. Leonard BSc(Econ)
Entry: local vets & associated rsrchers, with permission of libn *Open:* Mon-Fri 0845-1715
Subj: veterinary medicine & rsrch *Collns: Bks & Pamphs:* Sir John Hammond Colln (nutrition); some 18C/19C works related to domestic animals/agric *Co-op Schemes:* BLDSC, ILL
Equip: copier, computer *Online:* Web of Science, Medline, VETCD, BEASTCD, CUC
Stock: bks/3100; periodcls/189 + 162 no longer current
Classn: Barnard *Staff: Non-Prof:* 1

S307
Cambridge University, Department of Earth Sciences Library
Downing St, Cambridge, CB2 3EQ (01223-333429; *fax:* 01223-333420)
Email: libraryhelp@esc.cam.ac.uk
Internet: http://www.esc.cam.ac.uk/

Gov Body: Univ of Cambridge (see **L5**) *Chief:* Libn: Mrs Elizabeth Tilley MA (eatilley@esc.cam.ac.uk)
Assoc Libs: BULLARD LABORATORIES LIB, Madingley Rise, Madingley Rd, Cambridge, CB3 0EZ, Libn: as above
Entry: staff & postgrads in Dept have full borrowing rights; others may apply to Libn *Open: Earth Scis Lib:* Mon-Fri 0845-1700, Sat (in full term only) 0900-1300; keyholders have 24 hr access; *Bullard Lib:* by appt with Libn
Subj: postgrad; earth sci; geog; geol; geochem; mineralogy; petrology; palaeontology; glaciology; climatology *Collns: Bks & Pamphs:* personal collns of: A. Sedgwick; O.M.B. Bulman; T. McKenny Hughes; N.F. Hughes; W.A. Macfadyen; W. Black; H. Jeffreys; O. Fisher; A. Harker; E. Bullard; H. Godwin; R.G. West *Archvs:* historical offprint collns of membs of dept *Other:* historic colln of geological maps; map memoirs *Co-op Schemes:* BLDSC, ILL
Equip: 2 copiers, 8 computers (all with internet) *Disabled:* wheelchair access *Officer-in-Charge:* Libn, as above *Svcs:* info, ref, biblio
Stock: bks/148000; periodcls/1360; pamphs/40000+ *Acqs Offcr:* Libn, as above
Classn: own *Auto Sys:* Voyager
Staff: Libns: 1 *Other Prof:* 1

S308
Cambridge University, Department of Experimental Psychology Library
Downing St, Cambridge, CB2 3EB (01223-333554; *fax:* 01223-333564)
Email: library@psychol.cam.ac.uk

Gov Body: Univ of Cambridge (see **L5**) *Chief:* Hon Libn: Dr J. Russell *Dep:* Asst Libn: Mrs Maureen Wainwright

Entry: all membs of Cambridge Univ, others by appt *Open:* term: Mon-Fri 1000-1730; vac: varies
Subj: phil; psy; sci applicable to psy *Collns: Bks & Pamphs:* MacCurdy Psychopathology Lib (clinical psy) *Co-op Schemes:* ILL (membs of Dept only)
Equip: copier (10p per pg) *Online:* CUC
Stock: bks/20000+; periodcls/114
Classn: own *Staff: Libns:* 1

S309
Cambridge University, Department of Genetics Library
Downing St, Cambridge, CB2 3EH (01223-333973; *fax:* 01223-333992)
Email: Library@gen.cam.ac.uk
Internet: http://www.gen.cam.ac.uk/Library/

Gov Body: Univ of Cambridge (see **L5**) *Chief:* Libn: Mrs Christine Alexander
Entry: staff & students of Univ; others ref only at discretion of libn *Open:* Mon-Fri 0900-1700
Subj: genetics; ecology; cytology; cell biology; development *Collns: Other:* Drosophilia offprint colln (not housed in Lib, but available on appl) *Co-op Schemes:* BLDSC, ILL, CULS
Equip: copier (5p), computers (incl internet & CD-ROM) *Online:* World of Science, Medline & all major bioscience databases *Svcs:* info, ref, biblio
Stock: bks/8583; periodcls/105; offprints/10000
Classn: Bliss (mod)
Pubns: Lib Guide (free)
Staff: Libns: 1 *Exp:* £35000 (1999-2000); £40000 (2000-01)

S310
Cambridge University, Department of Geography Library
Downing Pl, Cambridge, CB2 3EN (01223-333391; *fax:* 01223-333392)
Email: library@geog.cam.ac.uk
Internet: http://www.geog.cam.ac.uk/library/

Gov Body: Univ of Cambridge (see **L5**) *Chief:* Libn: Miss Jane Robinson LLB, MA (jr108@hermes.cam.ac.uk) *Dep:* Lib Asst: Mr Colin MacLennan MA
Entry: open to dept staff & students; all others by arrangement with libn *Open:* term: Mon-Fri 0845-1800, Sat 0845-1245; vac: Mon-Thu 0900-1300, 1400-1630, Fri 0900-1300, 1400-1530
Subj: phil of geog; sociology; social theory; development; econ; planning; geomorphology; geol; soil sci; ecology; environmental sci; cartography; computing; geog info sys; remote sensing; historical geog of Britain, France, North America; regional geog of: Britain, Europe, former Soviet Union, South Asia, Pacific Islands, North & South America *Collns: Bks & Pamphs:* colln of chiefly 18C & 19C bks on travel & exploration (Clark Colln; access only by prior appt) *Other:* separate map lib *Co-op Schemes:* BLDSC, CUC
Equip: m-reader, copiers (5p per pg), 5 computers *Online:* BIDS, CUC *Svcs:* info, ref
Stock: bks/17000; periodcls/450, current & no longer current; m-forms/40; videos/30; offprints & reports/10000
Classn: Cambridge Geog Classn
Staff: Libns: 1 *Non-Prof:* 1

S311
Cambridge University, Department of History and Philosophy of Science, Whipple Library
Free School Ln, Cambridge, CB2 3RH (01223-334547; *fax:* 01223-334554)
Email: hps-lib@hermes.cam.ac.uk
Internet: http://www.hps.cam.ac.uk/

Gov Body: Univ of Cambridge (see **L5**) *Chief:* Libn: Ms Jill Whitelock MA, MPhil, PhD, MA, MCLIP

Entry: Cambridge Univ membs: borrowing, others: ref only, apply to libn *Open:* term: Mon-Fri 0930-1730; vac: Mon-Fri 0930-1700
Subj: hist & phil of sci & medicine *Collns: Bks & Pamphs:* R.S. Whipple Colln (17C-19C bks on scientific instruments, astronomy & maths); Sir Michael Foster Pamph Colln (physiology); Robert Boyle Colln; phrenology colln
Equip: m-reader, copier, 5 computers *Online:* CUC *Svcs:* info, ref, biblio
Stock: bks/21750; periodcls/100; pamphs/6715
Classn: own *Auto Sys:* Voyager
Pubns: Lib Guide (free); Instruments in Print: Bks from the Whipple Colln, by Silvia de Renzi; Whipple Museum of the Hist of Sci (£8 + p&p)
Staff: Libns: 1 *Non-Prof:* 1

Cambridge University, Department of Land Economy Library
See CAMBRIDGE UNIV, MILL LANE LIB (**S336**)

S312
Cambridge University, Department of Materials Science and Metallurgy Library
Pembroke St, Cambridge, CB2 3QZ (01223-334318; *fax:* 01223-334567)
Email: library@msm.cam.ac.uk
Internet: http://www.msm.cam.ac.uk/library/

Gov Body: Univ of Cambridge (see **L5**) *Chief:* Academic Libn: Dr K.M. Knowles *Dep:* Libn: Ms M. Glanfield
Entry: open at all times to staff, students & associated rsrch workers in Dept; membs of other Univ depts at discretion of Libn during opening hrs below *Open:* term: Mon-Fri 0900-1300, 1400-1600; vac: 0900-1300, 1400-1600
Subj: materials sci; metallurgy
Equip: copier, 2 computers *Online:* Web of Science, Zetoc, e-journals, Cambridge Scientific Abstracts etc *Svcs:* info, ref, biblio
Stock: bks/10700, plus various bnd vols of other materials; periodcls/67
Classn: own *Auto Sys:* Endeavor Voyager
Staff: Other Prof: 1 *Non-Prof:* 1

S313
Cambridge University, Department of Pathology, Kanthack and Nuttall Library
Tennis Court Rd, Cambridge, CB2 1QP (01223-333698; *fax:* 01223-333346/698)
Email: kmb27@cam.ac.uk
Internet: http://www.path.cam.ac.uk/~library/

Gov Body: Univ of Cambridge (see **L5**) *Chief:* Academic Libn: Dr T.D.K. Brown *Dep:* Asst Libn: Mrs I. Krasodomska MSc, DipLib
Entry: open to membs of univ; others on appl *Open:* Mon-Fri 0900-1700
Subj: pathology; immunology; microbiology; parasitology; virology; cell biology; oncology; genetics *Co-op Schemes:* BLDSC, ILL
Equip: m-reader, 3 copiers, computers (incl internet & 2 CD-ROM) *Online:* Medline, BIDS, IDEAL *Svcs:* ref
Stock: bks/9368; periodcls/85
Classn: NLM
Staff: Libns: 1 *Exp:* £33000 (1999-2000)

S314
Cambridge University, Department of Pharmacology Library
Tennis Court Rd, Cambridge, CB2 2QJ (01223-334000; *fax:* 01223-334040)

Gov Body: Univ of Cambridge (see **L5**) *Chief:* Academic Libn: Dr J.M. Edwardson ☞

S
Cambridge
▼
Cambridge
pecial Libraries

(Cambridge Univ, Dept of Pharmacology Lib cont)
Entry: staff & students of dept *Open:* term: Mon-Fri 1330-1600
Subj: pharmacology *Co-op Schemes:* CULS
Equip: computers *Online:* BIDS, Medline

S315 🎓

Cambridge University, Department of Physics, Rayleigh Library

Cavendish Laboratory, Madingley Rd, Cambridge, CB3 0HE (01223-337414; *fax:* 01223-363263)
Email: librarian@phy.cam.ac.uk
Internet: http://www.phy.cam.ac.uk/cavendish/library/

Gov Body: Univ of Cambridge (see **L5**) *Chief:* Academic Libn: Dr R. Ansorge MA, PhD *Dep:* Snr Lib Asst: Ms G. Wotherspoon BA(Hons), MSc, MCLIP
Assoc Libs: NAPIER SHAW LIB (meteorology), at same addr
Entry: use by outsiders is restricted, appl to Libn
Open: Mon-Fri 0900-1700
Subj: physics; maths; mechanics; electronics; computing; quantum mechanics *Co-op Schemes:* ILL, CULS
Equip: 2 copiers (A4/3p), 4 computers (all with internet & CD-ROM) *Svcs:* ref, biblio
Stock: bks/20000; periodcls/150; CD-ROMs/50
Classn: own *Auto Sys:* Endeavour
Staff: Libns: 1 *Non-Prof:* 1

S316 🎓

Cambridge University, Department of Physiology Library

Downing St, Cambridge, CB2 3EG (01223-333821; *fax:* 01223-333840)
Email: librarian@physiol.cam.ac.uk
Internet: http://www.physiol.cam.ac.uk/Library/Library.htm

Gov Body: Univ of Cambridge (see **L5**) *Chief:* Libn: Mrs Christine Ratcliff BSc(Econ), CertEd (cer34@cam.ac.uk)
Entry: ref only; membs & students of dept; others by arrangement *Open:* Mon-Fri 0830-1730
Subj: sci; physiology *Collns: Archvs:* archival materials on the hist of physiology *Co-op Schemes:* BLDSC, ILL, CULS
Equip: copiers (cards £2 or £5), 10 computers (all with wd-proc, internet & CD-ROM) *Svcs:* ref, biblio
Stock: bks/c4000; periodcls/118; photos/127; archvs/76 m
Classn: own *Auto Sys:* LibBASE *Staff: Libns:* 1

S317 🎓

Cambridge University, Department of Plant Sciences Library

Downing St, Cambridge, CB2 3EA (01223-333930; *fax:* 01223-333953)
Email: Library@plantsci.cam.ac.uk

Gov Body: Univ of Cambridge (see **L5**) *Chief:* Academic Libn: Dr David Coomes PhD *Dep:* Asst Libn: Mr Richard Savage BSc, MCLIP
Assoc Libs: CORY LIB (see **S299**)
Entry: open to membs of Cambridge Univ; visitors welcome for ref only, with adv appt preferred

Open: Mon-Fri 0830-1700
Subj: plant sci; ecology *Collns: Bks & Pamphs:* Simpson colln of local British floras *Archvs:* some material relating to past membs of dept *Co-op Schemes:* BLDSC
Equip: m-reader, 12 computers (all with wd-proc & internet, 6 with CD-ROM) *Online:* Athens, BIDS, JSTOR
Stock: bks/37000; periodcls/284; maps/300; archvs/4 linear m
Classn: Bliss
Staff: Libns: 1 *Exp:* £41000 (1999-2000); £42000 (2000-01)

Cambridge University, Department of Pure Mathematics and Mathematical Statistics Library

See CAMBRIDGE UNIV LIB, BETTY & GORDON MOORE LIB (**L5**)

S318 🎓

Cambridge University, Department of Social Anthropology Library

Free School Ln, Cambridge, CB2 3RF (01223-334599; *fax:* 01223-335993)
Email: socanth-admin@lists.cam.ac.uk
Internet: http://www.socanth.cam.ac.uk/

Gov Body: Univ of Cambridge (see **L5**) *Chief:* Libn: post vacant *Other Snr Staff:* Technician: Mr Paul Caldwell (pfc21@cam.ac.uk)
Assoc Libs: HADDON LIB, Faculty of Archaeo & Anthro (see **S323**)
Entry: membs of dept; others by adv appt *Open:* Mon-Fri 0900-1700
Subj: social anthro *Co-op Schemes:* CULS
Equip: m-reader, 4 video viewers, 2 copiers (5p per copy), 6 computers (all with wd-proc, internet & CD-ROM, charge for printing) *Officer-in-Charge:* Technician, as above *Svcs:* info, ref
Stock: bks/1297; maps/70; videos/1069; CD-ROMs/4 *Acqs Offcr:* Technician, as above
Classn: alphabetical by author

S319 🎓

Cambridge University, Department of Zoology, Balfour and Newton Libraries

Downing St, Cambridge, CB2 3EJ (01223-336648; *fax:* 01223-336676)
Email: library@zoo.cam.ac.uk
Internet: http://www.zoo.cam.ac.uk/library/

Gov Body: Univ of Cambridge (see **L5**) *Chief:* Academic Libn: Dr J.R. Flowerdew *Dep:* Libn: Ms C.M. Castle BA, MCLIP (cmc32@cam.ac.uk)
Other Snr Staff: Lib Asst: Miss J. Acred
Entry: membs of Cambridge Univ or by written appl to libn *Open:* Mon-Fri 0830-1700, Sat (term only) 0915-1230
Subj: zoology *Collns: Bks & Pamphs:* Newton Colln (ornithology & nat hist); Norman Reprint Colln *Co-op Schemes:* BLDSC
Equip: m-reader, copier (5p per sheet), computer *Online:* BIDS (membs of dept only)
Stock: bks/c40000; periodcls/189, plus 551 no longer current; pamphs/104915
Classn: Bliss (mod) *Staff: Libns:* 2

S320 🎓 ✍

Cambridge University, Divinity Faculty Library

West Rd, Cambridge, CB3 9BS (01223-763040)
Email: divlib@hermes.cam.ac.uk
Internet: http://www.divinity.cam.ac.uk/faculty/library/

Gov Body: Univ of Cambridge (see **L5**) *Chief:* Libn: Dr Peta Dunstan MA, PhD
Entry: open to theology students at Cambridge & snr membs of Univ; other scholars/students may do so by prior appl to the libn for permission
Open: term: Mon-Fri 0900-1700; vac: Mon-Fri 0900-1245, 1400-1630
Subj: phil & psy of religion; Biblical studies; theology; Judaism; Islam; Hinduism; Buddhism; social sci where concerns religious practice & ethics; Biblical langs; science-religion questions; ecclesiastical arch, music, painting, icons; novels etc concerned with religion; Church hist; hymnology
Collns: Bks & Pamphs: Bishop J.B. Lightfoot's Lib; Feltoe Colln (liturgy & liturgical studies); prayer bks; Bibles *Co-op Schemes:* ILL
Equip: copier *Online:* CUC
Stock: bks/50000; periodcls/40; pamphs/2000
Classn: own *Staff: Libns:* 2

S321 🎓

Cambridge University, Engineering Faculty Library

Trumpington St, Cambridge, CB2 1PZ (01223-332630; *fax:* 01223-332662)
Email: cued-library@eng.cam.ac.uk
Internet: http://www-lib.eng.cam.ac.uk/

Gov Body: Univ of Cambridge (see **L5**) *Chief:* Libn: Mrs H.M. McOwat BSc, MA, ARCS, MCLIP
Entry: membs of dept; others ref use only, by prior appl to libn *Open:* Mon-Fri 0900-1300, 1400-1700 for non-membs of dept
Subj: acoustics; electrical eng; mechanics; thermodynamics; aerodynamics; automatic control; soil mechanics; heat engines; materials sci; manufacturing eng; structures *Collns: Bks & Pamphs:* BSI (eng); NASA (selected) *Co-op Schemes:* BLDSC, CULS
Equip: m-readers, copier, computer *Online:* Compendex, Inspec, Web of Science, Cambridge Scientific Abstracts, OCLC FirstSearch, Dissertation Abstracts & others *Svcs:* ref, biblio, printing, photographic
Stock: bks/20000; periodcls/450
Classn: own *Staff: Libns:* 2 *Other Prof:* 2

S322 🎓

Cambridge University, English Faculty Library

Raised Faculty Bldg, Sidgwick Ave, Cambridge, CB3 9DA (01223-335077)
Email: efllib@hermes.cam.ac.uk

Gov Body: Univ of Cambridge (see **L5**) *Chief:* Libn: Miss Sandra Cromey MA(Oxon), MA(London), DipLib, MCLIP *Dep:* Asst Libn: Miss Shyani Siriwardene
Assoc Libs: also houses the ANGLO-SAXON, NORSE & CELTIC DEPT LIB
Entry: membs of English Faculty; ref only for other undergrads *Open:* term: Mon-Fri 0930-1900 (-2100 1st 5 wks of Easter term), Sat 0930-1700; vac: Mon-Fri 0930-1700
Subj: lang; English lit; genl literary studies; literary theory; American lit; foreign lit; internatl lit in English; folklore; media studies; women's studies; gender studies; linguistics; biblio *Collns: Bks & Pamphs:* Early English Text Soc Colln; 10 years of back issues of TLS, London Review of Bks & New York Review of Bks *Other:* audio & video collns
Equip: copier, computers (incl catalogue access, internet & CD-ROM) *Online:* on CD-ROM: OED, English Poetry Full-Text Database, Dr Johnson's Dictionary, Chaucer's Wife of Bath's prologue
Stock: bks/70000 *Classn:* own
Staff: Libns: 2 *Non-Prof:* 2 *Exp:* £21141 (2000-01)

S323

Cambridge University, Faculty of Archaeology and Anthropology, Haddon Library

Downing St, Cambridge, CB2 3DZ (01223-333505; *fax:* 01223-333503)
Email: haddon-library@lists.cam.ac.uk
Internet: http://www.archanth.cam.ac.uk/library/

Gov Body: Univ of Cambridge (see **L5**) *Chief:* Haddon Libn: Mr Aidan Baker MA, MCLIP
Entry: open to membs of Univ & Cambridge Antiquarian Soc; others at Libn's discretion *Open:* term: Mon-Fri 0845-1715 (Easter term -1900), Sat 0900-1700; vac: Mon-Fri 0900-1700
Subj: phil; psy; religion; social sci; social anthro; biological anthro; social archaeo; geog; hist
Collns: Bks & Pamphs: rare bk colln (c600 vols); Miles Burkitt Bequest (archaeo); G.H.S. Bushnell Bequest (archaeo); J.M. de Navarro Bequest (archaeo); Charles McBurney Bequest (archaeo); Grahame Clark Bequest (archaeo); A.H. Pitt-Rivers Gift (archaeo); James Frazer Colln (anthro); Alfred Haddon Colln (anthro); Cambridge Antiquarian Soc Colln *Co-op Schemes:* BLDSC, CULS
Equip: m-reader, copier (A4/5p, A3/10p), computers (incl CD-ROM) *Online:* BIDS, OCLC, COPAC, Newton (Cambridge Univ libs' integrated catalogue) *Svcs:* info, ref
Stock: bks/30000; periodcls/1564; pamphs/17000; maps/86; audios/5
Classn: Bliss *Auto Sys:* Endeavour Voyager
Pubns: Haddon Lib Guide (free)
Staff: Libns: 1 *Non-Prof:* 3 *Exp:* £29770 (1999-2000); £26020 (2000-01)

S324

Cambridge University, Faculty of Architecture and History of Art Library

1 Scroope Ter, Cambridge, CB2 1PX (01223-332953; *fax:* 01223-332960)
Email: mb151@cam.ac.uk
Internet: http://arct.cam.ac.uk/coursebase/resources/lib/

Gov Body: Univ of Cambridge (see **L5**) *Chief:* Libn: Mrs Madeleine Brown
Assoc Libs: MARTIN CENTRE, 6 Chaucer Rd, Cambridge, CB2 2GB, Rsrch Associate: Ms Samantha Newton
Entry: visitors by arrangement *Open:* term: Mon-Fri 0915-1730; vac: times vary
Subj: undergrad; postgrad; arch; hist of art
Collns: Bks & Pamphs: 18-19C French & English arch pubns; 19-20C journals on arch & fine & decorative arts *Co-op Schemes:* ILL (as backup to Cambridge Univ Lib)
Equip: m-reader, copiers, computers *Online:* Newton Lib Catalogue *Svcs:* info, ref, biblio
Stock: bks/30000; periodcls/106; slides/94000
Classn: own *Auto Sys:* LibBASE
Pubns: Lib Guides (free)
Staff: Other Prof: 4

S325

Cambridge University, Faculty of Classics and Museum of Classical Archaeology Library

Sidgwick Ave, Cambridge, CB3 9DA (01223-335154; *fax:* 01223-335409)
Email: library@classics.cam.ac.uk
Internet: http://www.classics.cam.ac.uk/library/library.html

Gov Body: Univ of Cambridge (see **L5**) *Chief:* Libn: Miss L.K. Bailey MLib, MCLIP *Dep:* Mr S. Howe MA
Entry: ref only for non-Univ membs

Open: term: Mon-Fri 0900-1845, Sat 0900-1800; vac: Mon-Fri 0900-1300, 1415-1700
Subj: ancient phil; ancient religion; Greek & Latin langs; arts; classical archaeo; ancient lit & rhetoric; ancient geog & hist *Collns: Bks & Pamphs:* Leake Colln; Sandys Colln; Owen Colln *Other:* large collns of photos, slides & maps; some m-forms & AV materials *Co-op Schemes:* ILL (back-up for Cambridge Univ Lib)
Equip: m-reader, copier, computer (incl wd-proc)
Svcs: info, ref, biblio
Stock: bks/50000; periodcls/270; pamphs/4380
Classn: Unique *Auto Sys:* Endeavour Voyager
Pubns: Museum Guide (£4)
Staff: Libns: 2 *Non-Prof:* 2

S326

Cambridge University, Faculty of Education, Library and Information Service

Shaftesbury Rd, Cambridge, CB2 2BX (01223-369631; *fax:* 01223-324421)
Email: library@educ.cam.ac.uk
Internet: http://www.educ.cam.ac.uk/library/

Gov Body: Univ of Cambridge (see **L5**) *Chief:* Chief Libn: Ms Angela Cutts BA, DipLib, MCLIP
Dep: Dep Libn: Ms Emma-Jane Batchelor BA, DipILS, MCLIP
Assoc Libs: BROOKSIDE SITE LIB, 17 Brookside, Cambridge, CB2 1JG
Entry: ref only *Open:* term: Mon-Tue, Thu 0930-1800, Wed 0930-1930, Fri 0930-1700, Sat 0930-1300; vac: Mon-Fri 1000-1700
Subj: all subjs; undergrad; postgrad; phil; psy; edu; sociology *Collns: Bks & Pamphs:* school textbks & bks on teaching methods; modern ch's bks (15000 vols, at Brookside Site) *Co-op Schemes:* LISE, BLDSC, ILL
Equip: m-reader, 3 video viewers, 2 copiers, computers (incl internet & CD-ROM) *Online:* BIDS, Medline (School of Education membs only) *Svcs:* info, ref, biblio
Stock: bks/85000; periodcls/240; videos/1600; stock figs incl both sites
Classn: DDC (mod) *Auto Sys:* Voyager Endeavour
Staff: Libns: 3 FT, 1 PT *Non-Prof:* 4 FT, 1 PT

S327

Cambridge University, Faculty of Modern and Medieval Languages Library

Sidgwick Ave, Cambridge, CB3 9DA (01223-335041; *fax:* 01223-335062)
Internet: http://www.mml.cam.ac.uk/libguide.html

Gov Body: Univ of Cambridge (see **L5**) *Chief:* Libn: Dr A.E. Cobby MA, PhD, DipLib
Assoc Libs: BEIT LIB (German rsrch lib, shares same bldg & staff)
Entry: apply to libn *Open:* full term: Mon-Fri 0900-1900 (-2100 for 5 wks of exam term), Sat 0900-1600; vac: Mon-Fri 0900-1700
Subj: Continental langs, lit & thought; hist; linguistics; philology; some art & topography
Collns: Bks & Pamphs: large Slavonic colln (incl hist, art, all Slavonic langs); large holdings of less studied European langs (incl Dutch, Portuguese, Hungarian); Latin American hist; 19C travel *Co-op Schemes:* ILL, only as back-up to Cambridge Univ Lib
Equip: OPAC, 18 computers (incl 12 with internet & 12 with CD-ROM) *Online:* CUC, Internet
Stock: bks/110000; periodcls/165; pamphs/1000; audios/500; videos/250
Classn: own *Auto Sys:* Endeavour Voyager
Pubns: Readers' Guide & Annual Report (free)
Staff: Libns: 1 *Other Prof:* 3 *Non-Prof:* 1 *Exp:* £28800 (1999-2000)

S328

Cambridge University, Faculty of Oriental Studies Library

Sidgwick Ave, Cambridge, CB3 9DA (01223-335111/2; *fax:* 01223-335110)
Email: library@oriental.cam.ac.uk
Internet: http://www.oriental.cam.ac.uk/guide1.html

Gov Body: Univ of Cambridge (see **L5**) *Chief:* Libn: Mrs C.A. Ansorge MA, MCLIP
Entry: membs of the univ, others with permission of Chairman of Faculty *Open:* term: Mon-Fri 0845-1730, Sat 0930-1300; vac: Mon-Fri 0900-1300, 1400-1700
Subj: undergrad; postgrad; Middle East; Indian subcontinent; China; Japan; phil; religion; social sci; lang; arts; lit; geog; hist *Collns: Bks & Pamphs:* Centre for Middle Eastern & Islamic Studies Colln (6000 monographs on the modern Middle East); Lattimore Colln of monographs (formerly the lib of Owen Lattimore on Mongolia & Central Asia); Abrahams Colln (Hebrew studies, 16C-19C); Queens' Colln (Ancient Near East, on permanent loan from Queens' Coll) *Archvs:* papers of I.B. Horner (Pali scholar); papers of Bertram Thomas (traveller in Arabia) *Other:* map colln (mainly post-1930); photographic collns (mainly South Asian archaeo sites & monuments), incl: Sir John Marshall Colln (Indian archaeo, c5000 items)
Equip: 4 m-readers, copier, 7 computers (all with internet & 2 with CD-ROM) *Svcs:* info, ref
Stock: bks/56000; periodcls/150; photos/6000; slides/500; maps/450; videos/50; archvs/6 m
Classn: own *Auto Sys:* Newton
Staff: Libns: 1 *Non-Prof:* 2 *Exp:* £29000 (1999-2000); £32000 (2000-01)

S329

Cambridge University, Faculty of Philosophy, Casimir Lewy Library

Raised Faculty Bldg, Sidgwick Ave, Cambridge, CB3 9DA (01223-762939; *fax:* 01223-335091)
Email: philib@hermes.cam.ac.uk
Internet: http://www.phil.cam.ac.uk/_Library/links.html

Gov Body: Univ of Cambridge (see **L5**) *Chief:* Libn: Mrs M. Pellegrino DipLib, MCLIP
Entry: membs of Univ *Open:* term: Mon-Fri 1000-1800, Sat 1000-1400; vac: Mon-Fri 0930-1730
Subj: all aspects of phil, excl oriental phil; phil of social sci; phil of maths
Equip: copier, 5 computers (all with internet, 1 with CD-ROM) *Online:* Athena *Svcs:* ref, biblio
Stock: bks/11500; periodcls/27; offprints/c300
Classn: own *Auto Sys:* Voyager
Staff: Libns: 1 *Non-Prof:* 3 *Exp:* £9000 pa

S330

Cambridge University, Faculty of Social and Political Sciences Library

Free School Ln, Cambridge, CB2 3RQ (01223-334522; *fax:* 01223-34550)
Email: sps-library@lists.cam.ac.uk
Internet: http://www.sps.cam.ac.uk/library/

Gov Body: Univ of Cambridge (see **L5**) *Chief:* Libn: Miss J. Nicholas *Dep:* Dep Libn: Mrs I. Chilvers
Entry: membs of univ, others on appl *Open:* Mon-Fri 0915-1900; vac: Mon-Fri 0930-1700
Subj: undergrad; postgrad; phil; psy; religion; social sci; geog; hist *Co-op Schemes:* BLDSC
Equip: m-reader, copier, 10 computers (incl 8 internet) *Online:* BIDS (SPS Dept only), other online svcs from Cambridge Univ Lib
Stock: bks/26000; periodcls/76
Classn: own *Auto Sys:* Endeavour Voyager
Staff: Libns: 1 *Other Prof:* 1 *Non-Prof:* 2 *Exp:* £27000 (1999-2000)

S pecial Libraries

Cambridge
▼
Cambridge

S331 🎓

Cambridge University, Institute of Astronomy Library

The Observatories, Madingley Rd, Cambridge, CB3 0HA (01223-337537; *fax:* 01223-337501)
Email: ioalib@ast.cam.ac.uk
Internet: http://www.ast.cam.ac.uk/IOA/

Gov Body: Univ of Cambridge (see **L5**)
Entry: adv appt *Open:* Mon-Fri 0900-1230, 1400-1700
Subj: astrophysics; astronomy; optics *Co-op Schemes:* BLDSC
Equip: m-reader, copier, 3 computers (incl internet & CD-ROM) *Online:* CUC (free)
Stock: bks/18000; periodcls/247; photos/300; slides/4628; pamphs/8700; maps/some; m-forms/various
Classn: Dewhirst *Auto Sys:* Unicorn
Pubns: Annual Report of the Inst (on web site)
Staff: Libns: 2 *Non-Prof:* 1

S332 🎓

Cambridge University, Institute of Continuing Education Library

Madingley Hall, Madingley, Cambridge, CB3 8AQ (01954-280206; *fax:* 01954-280200)
Internet: http://www.cont-ed.cam.ac.uk/

Gov Body: Univ of Cambridge (see **L5**) *Chief:*
Libn: Miss B. Pemberton
Entry: ref only; open to membs of the Board's Courses; membs of Univ by special arrangement
Open: Mon-Fri 0845-1300, 1330-1630
Subj: generalities; phil; psy; religion; social sci; lang; sci; maths; arts; lit; hist; geog *Collns:*
Archvs: Madingley Hall Archv
Equip: copier
Stock: bks/53675; slides/8825; maps/30; videos/167; CD-ROMs/2; archvs/12.76 linear m
Classn: DDC *Staff: Libns:* 1

S333 🎓

Cambridge University, Institute of Criminology, Radzinowicz Library

7 West Rd, Cambridge, CB3 9DT (01223-335386; *fax:* 01223-335356)

Gov Body: Univ of Cambridge (see **L5**) *Chief:*
Libn: Mrs Helen Krarup BA, MSc *Dep:* Asst Libn: Mrs Mary Gower MCLIP
Entry: open to those with serious rsrch interest in criminology *Open:* term: Mon-Fri 0900-1900, Sat 0900-1300; vac: Mon-Fri 0900-1300, 1400-1700
Subj: criminology *Co-op Schemes:* ILL
Equip: copier, computers (incl 6 with internet)
Stock: bks/46000; periodcls/250
Classn: Bliss *Auto Sys:* Endeavour
Pubns: Cropwood Series
Staff: Libns: 1 *Other Prof:* 1 *Non-Prof:* 1

S334 🎓

Cambridge University, Language Centre Library

Lecture Block A, Sidgwick Ave, Cambridge, CB3 9DA (01223-335058)
Email: library@langcen.cam.ac.uk
Internet: http://www.langcen.cam.ac.uk/

Gov Body: Univ of Cambridge (see **L5**) *Chief:*
Libn: Ms Lisa Cleary MA, DipLib, MCLIP (rlc1@cus.cam.ac.uk)
Entry: membs of Univ; others by appt only *Open:*
term: Mon-Thu 0900-1900, Fri 0900-1700, Sat 1000-1400; vac: Mon-Fri 1000-1600
Subj: lang: learning materials in 140 langs *Co-op Schemes:* CULS
Equip: video viewers, audio listening equip, computers (incl wd-proc & CD-ROM), satellite TV
Svcs: ref, biblio
Stock: c28500 items, incl bks, periodcls, AVs, CD-ROMs etc
Staff: Libns: 1 *Non-Prof:* 5

S335 🎓

Cambridge University, Marshall Library of Economics

Sidgwick Ave, Cambridge, CB3 9DB (01223-335217; *fax:* 01223-335475)
Email: marshlib@econ.cam.ac.uk
Internet: http://www.econ.cam.ac.uk/marshlib/

Gov Body: Univ of Cambridge (see **L5**) *Chief:*
Libn: Mr Rowland Thomas BA, MCLIP *Dep:* Dep Libn: Mr Simon Frost BA, MA
Entry: membs of Univ registered with the Univ Lib; archv collns open to bona fide scholars by appt
Open: term: Mon-Fri 0830-2100, Sat 0900-1300; vac: Mon-Fri 0900-1700
Subj: econ *Collns: Archvs:* archvs of various 19C-20C economists, incl: Alfred & Mary Marshall; Henry Fawcett; John Neville Keynes; Herbert Somerton Foxwell; Austin Robinson & others; archvs of Marshall Soc; archvs of Cambridge Economic Club; Lib's own records *Co-op Schemes:* ILL
Equip: m-reader, copier *Online:* Social Science Citation Index, IBSS, JSTOR, Ingenta Journals, IDEAL, Catchword
Stock: bks/35000; periodcls/350 current titles, plus 25000 vols no longer current
Staff: 7 in total

Cambridge University, Medical Library

See CAMBRIDGE UNIV LIB (**L5**)

S336 🎓

Cambridge University, Mill Lane Library

(formerly Cambridge Univ, Dept of Land Economy Lib)
Mill Ln Lecture Rooms, Mill Ln, Cambridge, CB2 1RX (01223-337110; *fax:* 01223-337130)
Internet: http://www.landecon.cam.ac.uk/library/library.htm

Gov Body: Univ of Cambridge (see **L5**); provides lib facilities for the Dept of Land Economy, Centre of Latin American Studies & Centre of Internatl Studies & Development Studies *Chief:* Libn: Ms Wendy Thurley BA, MCLIP (wt10000@cam.ac.uk)
Other Snr Staff: Libn: Mrs Marion Clarkestone BA, DipLib (mjc52@cam.ac.uk)
Assoc Libs: LAND ECONOMY LIB, Libn: Ms Wendy Thurley, as above; LATIN AMERICAN STUDIES LIB, Libn: Ms Julie Coimbra (mornings: 01223-335398; afternoons: 01223-337110; email: jac46@cam.ac.uk)
Entry: membs of Univ; others by appt *Open:*
term: Mon, Wed-Fri 0900-1700, Tue 0900-1900; vac: Mon-Fri 1000-1700
Subj: Land Economy Lib: econ; law; land valuation; housing; agric econ; statistics; forestry; environment; *Latin American Studies Lib:* undergrad; postgrad; Latin America; religion; social sci; lang; lit; hist; geog; strengths incl: Andean, Brazilian & Mexican materials; contemporary politics & sociology; *Internatl Studies Lib:* internatl studies; development studies

Collns: Bks & Pamphs: Land Economy colln of law reports *Other:* theses & dissertations on land economy *Co-op Schemes:* BLDSC, ILL
Equip: m-reader, 2 copiers, 6 computers (incl internet & CD-ROM) *Online:* BIDS *Officer-in-Charge:* Libn: Ms Wendy Thurley, as above
Stock: Land Economy Lib: bks/c20000; periodcls/200; *Latin American Studies Lib:* bks/c11000; periodcls/25; *Internatl Studies Lib:* bks/1000 *Acqs Offcr:* Libn: Ms Wendy Thurley, as above (Land Economy); Libn: Ms Julie Coimbra, as above (Latin American Studies)
Classn: own *Auto Sys:* Endeavor Voyager/Newton *Staff: Libns:* 2 *Other Prof:* 1 *Non-Prof:* 1

S337 🎓

Cambridge University, Pendlebury Library of Music

Univ Music School, West Rd, Cambridge, CB3 9DP (01223-335182; *fax:* 01223-335183)
Internet: http://www.mus.cam.ac.uk/external/pendlebury/pendlebury.html

Gov Body: Univ of Cambridge (see **L5**) *Chief:*
Libn: Mr Andrew Bennett BA, MLitt, DipLib
Entry: open to membs of the Univ, others by adv appt (ref only) *Open:* term: Mon-Fri 0930-1730, Sat 0930-1245; vac: Mon-Fri 0930-1315
Subj: music *Collns: Bks & Pamphs:* Picken Colln (early Bach eds) *Other:* Walter Emery Colln (Bach MSS on m-form); Ferguson Colln (Schubert piano music m-forms & facsimiles) *Co-op Schemes:* ILL
Equip: m-reader, m-printer, copier, computer *Online:* CUC
Stock: bks/55000; periodcls/54; pamphs/1800; m-forms/1400; audios/15000; videos/150
Classn: BCM *Auto Sys:* Voyager
Staff: Libns: 1 *Non-Prof:* 2

S338 🎓

Cambridge University, School of Anatomy Library

Downing St, Cambridge, CB2 3DY (01223-333780; *fax:* 01223-333786)
Email: Library@anat.cam.ac.uk
Internet: http://www.bio.cam.ac.uk/dept/anatomy/pages/lindex.html

Gov Body: Univ of Cambridge (see **L5**) *Chief:*
Libn: Mrs Fotini Papantoniou BSc, MSc
Assoc Libs: VETERINARY ANATOMY (LOVATON) LIB, at same addr, Libn: as above
Entry: Univ teaching offcrs, medical students & asst staff; others on appl *Open:* term: Mon-Fri 0900-1300, 1400-1700; 24 hr access to staff & students
Subj: anatomy *Collns: Other:* Boyd Historical Colln (slides) *Co-op Schemes:* ILL (for Dept membs only), CUC, CULS
Equip: m-reader, copier (A4/10p), computers (incl internet & CD-ROM)
Stock: Anatomy Lib: bks/1550; periodcls/40; *Veterinary Anatomy Lib:* bks/996; periodcls/2
Classn: LC *Staff: Libns:* 1

S339 🎓

Cambridge University, Scott Polar Research Institute Library

Lensfield Rd, Cambridge, CB2 1ER (01223-336552; *fax:* 01223-336549)
Email: library@spri.cam.ac.uk
Internet: http://www.spri.cam.ac.uk/library/

Gov Body: Univ of Cambridge (see **L5**) *Chief:*
Libn & Keeper of Collns: Mr W. Mills MA, MCLIP (wjm13@cam.ac.uk)
Assoc Libs: SHACKLETON MEMORIAL LIB, at same addr
Entry: adv appt *Open:* Mon-Fri 0900-1300, 1400-1730

Subj: all subjs relating to polar regions; Arctic & Antarctica; glaciology *Collns: Bks & Pamphs:* world's largest colln of bks & pamphs relating to Polar regions & to ice & snow throughout the world *Archvs:* major collns relating to hist of exploration of the Arctic & Antarctic, incl: Thomas H. Manning Polar Archvs *Other:* SPRI Picture Lib *Co-op Schemes:* BLDSC, Polar Libs Colloquy
Equip: m-reader, fax, copier, computer (incl CD-ROM) *Online:* SPRILIB (in-house database) *Svcs:* info, ref, biblio, indexing, abstracting, translation
Stock: bks/142000, incl bnd periodcls; periodcls/1000; photos/50000; slides/5000; illusts/many; pamphs/40363; maps/23872; m-forms/many; AVs/some; archvs/extensive
Classn: UDC *Auto Sys:* MUSCAT
Pubns: Polar & Glaciological Abstracts (£122 for insts, £73 for indivs)
Staff: Libns: 2.5 *Other Prof:* 2.5 *Non-Prof:* 1.5
Exp: £19043 (2000-01)

S340
Cambridge University, Seeley Historical Library
West Rd, Cambridge, CB3 9EF (01223-335335/40; *fax:* 01223-335968)
Email: seeley@hist.cam.ac.uk
Internet: http://www.hist.cam.ac.uk/

Gov Body: Univ of Cambridge (see **L5**) *Chief:* Seeley Libn: Dr L. Washington MA, PhD, DipLib, MCLIP *Dep:* Dep Libn: Miss C.J. Carty MA, MPhil
Entry: membs of the Univ; others by adv appt
Open: term: Mon-Fri 0900-1915 (Easter term - 2000), Sat 0900-1800; vac: Mon-Fri 0900-1700
Subj: phil; psy; religion; social sci; arts; lit; geog; hist *Collns: Bks & Pamphs:* Hadley Colln (French Revolution & Napoleonic era); Whitney Colln (Church hist) *Archvs:* Cabinet papers *Co-op Schemes:* CULS
Equip: m-form reader/printers, copier, computers *Online:* CUC *Svcs:* ref, biblio
Stock: bks/64104; periodcls/6114 (incl those no longer current); pamphs/5258; m-forms & AVs/5022
Classn: own *Staff: Libns:* 2 *Non-Prof:* 3

S341
Cambridge University, University Collection of Air Photographs
The Mond Bldg, Free School Ln, Cambridge, CB2 3RF (01223-334578; *fax:* 01223-763300)
Email: aerial-photography@lists.cam.ac.uk

Gov Body: Univ of Cambridge (see **L5**) *Chief:* Dir: Dr B. Devereux MA, PhD
Entry: ref only, no tourist parties *Open:* Mon-Thu 0900-1300, 1400-1700, Fri 0900-1300, 1400-1600
Subj: ecology; soil sci; nature conservation; agric; forestry; aerial survey; archaeo; quaternary studies; physiography; planning & development control
Collns: Other: aerial photos of British Isles (UK & Eire), Denmark, France & Netherlands
Equip: available to staff only *Svcs:* info, ref, indexing
Stock: bks/512; periodcls/282; photos/500000 aerial
Staff: Libns: 2 *Other Prof:* 8

S342
CASP Library
181a Huntingdon Rd, Cambridge, CB3 0DH (01223-377100; *fax:* 01223-276604)
Email: enquiries@casp.cam.ac.uk
Internet: http://www.casp.cam.ac.uk/

Gov Body: Cambridge Arctic Shelf Programme, part of the Univ of Cambridge (see **L5**) *Chief:* Info Svcs Co-ordinator: Mrs Eda L. Lesk BA, MEd (ell0006@cam.ac.uk)

Assoc Libs: EARTH SCIS LIB (see **S307**)
Entry: adv appt; fee payable by non-academic users *Open:* Mon, Wed, Fri 0800-1300
Subj: geol; Arctic geol; Central Asian geol
Collns: Bks & Pamphs: Russian & Chinese geological lit, incl maps & stratigraphic columns; Russian geological translations *Archvs:* relating to Arctic & Chinese geol
Svcs: info, ref, biblio
Stock: bks/3000; periodcls/c20; maps/250
Classn: Endnote
Pubns: contributes Arctic data to the Arctic & Antarctic Regions Database, publ by NISC
Staff: Other Prof: 1 *Exp:* approx £6000 pa

S343
Centre for Jewish-Christian Relations Library
Wesley House, Jesus Ln, Cambridge, CB5 8BQ (01223-741048)
Email: wesley-cjcr@lists.cam.ac.uk

Chief: Libn: Dr Melanie Wright
Entry: Cambridge Theological Federation membs; others adv appt only *Open:* Coll hrs during Mon-Thu, Fri 0900-1200
Subj: religion; Jewish-Christian relations
Equip: copier, computers (with wd-proc & internet)
Stock: bks/2500; periodcls/9; videos/50
Classn: LC

S344
Christ's College Library
Cambridge, CB2 3BU (01223-334950)
Internet: http://www.christs.cam.ac.uk/library/

Gov Body: Christ's Coll, Cambridge *Chief:* Fellow Libn: Dr Douglas Ferguson PhD (drf1000@cam.ac.uk) *Dep:* Sub-Libn: Miss Candace Guite MA, LTCL, MCLIP (cjeg2@cam.ac.uk) *Other Snr Staff:* Dep Sub-Libns: Mrs Pat Hall & Mrs Ann Keith
Entry: visitors by appt *Open:* Mon-Fri 0915-1700, Sat (term only) 0915-1300
Subj: most academic subjs *Collns: Bks & Pamphs:* Robertson Smith Oriental Colln; John Milton Colln (early eds); Wratislaw Slavonic Colln; Charles Lesingham Smith Colln (early scientific bks) *Archvs:* Charles Darwin letters; Henry More letters *Co-op Schemes:* BLDSC
Equip: 4 m-readers, copier, computers, skeleton (for medical students)
Stock: bks/100000; periodcls/36
Classn: LC *Auto Sys:* Heritage
Staff: Libns: 1 *Non-Prof:* 4 *Exp:* £20000 (1999-2000); £22000 (2000-01)

S345
Churchill College Library
Storey's Way, Cambridge, CB3 0DS (01223-336138; *fax:* 01223-336160)
Email: librarian@chu.cam.ac.uk
Internet: http://www.chu.cam.ac.uk/members/library/

Chief: Libn: Ms Mary Kendall MA, MCLIP
Entry: Coll membs only, otherwise adv appt
Open: Lib Office: Mon-Fri 0900-1730; 24 hrs to Coll membs
Subj: all subjs; undergrad *Collns: Bks & Pamphs:* Sir Winston Churchill's colln of bks & pamphs on Napoleon; Maisoneuve Colln (French civilisation & culture); Roskill Colln (20C hist, WW2); Powys Colln
Equip: m-reader, m-printer, copier, fax, computers (incl wd-proc, internet & CD-ROM) *Online:* CUC
Stock: bks/53000; periodcls/38; m-forms/6; audios/15; videos/9
Classn: DDC *Auto Sys:* LibBASE
Staff: Libns: 1 *Non-Prof:* 0.5
See also CHURCHILL ARCHVS CENTRE (**A88**)

S346
Clare College, Forbes Mellon Library
Memorial Ct, Clare Coll, Cambridge, CB3 9AJ (01223-333202; *fax:* 01223-765560)
Email: clarelib@hermes.cam.ac.uk
Internet: http://www.clare.cam.ac.uk/academic/library.html

Gov Body: Clare Coll *Chief:* Forbes Mellon Libn: Mrs Anne Hughes MA (ach25@cus.cam.ac.uk)
Dep: Dep Libn: Mrs Jennifer Webb MLS (jmw85@cam.ac.uk)
Assoc Libs: LIPSTEIN LAW READING ROOM, addr as above
Entry: current membership of Clare Coll *Open:* Michaelmas & Lent term: Mon-Sun 0700-2400; Easter term: Mon-Sun 0700-0200; vac: Mon-Fri 0900-1700
Subj: all subjs; undergrad; some postgrad
Collns: Archvs: colln of Cecil Sharp MSS
Equip: m-reader, fax, copier, 12 computers (all with wd-proc, internet & CD-ROM) *Online:* all those available via Cambridge Univ Lib (see **L5**)
Stock: bks/30000; periodcls/14; CD-ROMs/12
Classn: DDC *Auto Sys:* Heritage
Staff: Libns: 2 *Other Prof:* 2.5

S347
Clare Hall, The Ashby Library
Herschel Rd, Cambridge, CB3 9AL (01223-332360; *fax:* 01223-332333)
Email: RMLIO@cam.ac.uk

Gov Body: President & Fellows of Clare Hall
Chief: Libn: Dr Rosemary M. Luff PhD
Entry: membs of coll; non-membs by appt *Open:* access for membs 24 hrs a day; other by appt only
Subj: all subjs; undergrad; postgrad; rsrch; arts; sci *Collns: Bks & Pamphs:* bks written by Coll membs
Stock: bks/1500
Further Info: This is a small lib comprising bks donated since the late 1960s by Fellows of Clare Hall (Official, Rsrch & Visiting)

S348
College of West Anglia, Faculty of Land-Based Studies Library
Landbeach Rd, Milton, Cambridge, CB4 6DB (01223-860701)
Internet: http://www.col-westanglia.ac.uk/

Gov Body: Further Edu Funding Council *Chief:* Learning Centre Mgr: Ms Teresa Wicklen BEd
Dep: Lib & Info Offcr: Mr John Ross BA
Assoc Libs: COLL OF WEST ANGLIA LIB, King's Lynn (see **S864**)
Entry: ref free to membs of public; borrowing by arrangement with Libn *Open:* term: Mon-Fri 0900-1630
Subj: countryside mgmt; conservation; botany; zoology; ecology; agric; hortic; horses; small animal care; veterinary sci *Co-op Schemes:* BLDSC, ANGLES
Equip: 2 video viewers, 2 copiers, computers (incl 30 wd-proc, 30 internet & 2 CD-ROM) *Svcs:* info, ref
Stock: bks/7000; periodcls/100; videos/500
Classn: DDC *Auto Sys:* Dynix
Staff: Libns: 1 *Non-Prof:* 2

S349
Corpus Christi College, Parker Library
Trumpington St, Cambridge, CB2 1RH (01223-338025; *fax:* 01223-338041)
Email: parker-library@corpus.cam.ac.uk
Internet: http://www.corpus.cam.ac.uk/about/library.htm

Special Libraries

Cambridge ▼ Cambridge

(Corpus Christi Coll, Parker Lib cont)
Gov Body: Master & Fellows of Coll *Chief:*
Fellow Libn: Dr Christopher de Hamel *Dep:*
Parker Sub-Libn: Ms Gill Cannell
Assoc Libs: BUTLER LIB (undergrad lib), at same
addr, Butler Sub-Libn: Ms Iwona Krasodomska-
Jones (01223-338052; *email:* ik205@cam.ac.uk)
Entry: by written appl to libn, letter of ref required,
entry strictly by appt *Open:* term: Mon-Fri 0900-
1245, 1400-1615
Subj: Medieval & Renaissance MSS & early
printed bks *Collns: Bks & Pamphs:* over 600
MSS, particularly Anglo-Saxon, later medieval
Reformation; 600+ printed bks bequeathed by
Matthew Parker in 1575; 142 incunabula; 196
printed bks, 1501-20; Stokes Colln (bks on
Judaism, particularly in England); Perowne Colln
(Knights of Malta)
Equip: m-reader, m-printer, copier, computer (incl
CD-ROM)
Stock: bks/15000; periodcls/20; photos/500;
slides/2000; m-forms/400

S350 🎓
Darwin College Library
Silver St, Cambridge, CB3 9EU (01223-763547)
Email: librarian@dar.cam.ac.uk
Internet: http://www.dar.cam.ac.uk/library/

Gov Body: Darwin Coll, Univ of Cambridge (see
L5) *Chief:* Fellow Libn: Dr David MacKay MA,
PhD *Other Snr Staff:* Coll Archivist: Dr Elizabeth
Leedham-Green
Entry: Coll membs *Open:* permanently open to
membs
Subj: all subjs; postgrad *Collns: Bks & Pamphs:*
Finley Colln (ancient hist) *Co-op Schemes:* CULS
Stock: bks/5000; periodcls/4
Classn: DDC *Staff:* Non-Prof: 2 PT

S351 🎓
Downing College, Maitland Robinson Library
Regent St, Cambridge, CB2 1DQ (01223-334829/
5352; *fax:* 01223-363852)
Email: librarian@dow.cam.ac.uk
Internet: http://www.dow.cam.ac.uk/

Chief: Libn: Dr Peter Duffet-Smith *Dep:* Acting
Coll Libn: Ms Karen Lubarr *Other Snr Staff:*
Archivist: Ms Elizabeth Stratton; Lib Asst: Mrs Jill
Young
Entry: membs of Downing Coll & academic
visitors; others by appt *Open:* term: 0830-2330;
vac: 0830-1730
Subj: all subjs; undergrad; postgrad *Collns: Bks
& Pamphs:* Richmond Naval Colln; Bowtell Colln
(Cambridge); colln of 17C printed material; some
early printed material *Archvs:* Downing Coll Archvs
Co-op Schemes: Cambridge Coll Lib
Conservation Consortium
Equip: 2 m-readers, copier, 8 computers (all with
CD-ROM, 4 with wd-proc & 4 with internet)
Disabled: wheelchair access *Svcs:* info, ref, biblio
Stock: bks/46000 + 3000 rare vols; periodcls/40
Acqs Offcr: Acting Coll Libn, as above
Classn: own *Auto Sys:* Heritage
Staff: Libns: 1 *Other Prof:* 1 *Non-Prof:* 1

S352
East England Arts, Information Centre
(formerly Eastern Arts Board)
Eden House, 48-49 Bateman St, Cambridge, CB2
1LR (01223-454400; *fax:* 0870-242-1271)
Email: info@eearts.co.uk
Internet: http://www.eastenglandarts.co.uk/

Type: arts funding & development agency *Gov
Body:* Arts Council of England *Chief:* Regional
Exec Dir: Ms Andrea Stark
Open: Helpdesk: Mon-Fri 0900-1700; *Offices:*
Mon-Thu 0900-1730, Fri 0900-1700
Subj: arts
Svcs: info, ref, funding opportunities & advice
Pubns: Eye (bimonthly newsletter, free); East Life
(arts magazine, £1.75 from newsagents); other
listings available, contact Helpdesk as above
Staff: Other Prof: 42

S353 🎓
Emmanuel College Library
St Andrew's St, Cambridge, CB2 3AP (01223-
334233)
Email: library@emma.cam.ac.uk

Chief: Coll Libn: Dr H.C. Carron BA, MA, MPhil,
PhD, MCLIP, FSA *Dep:* Asst Libn: Mrs P. Bonfield
BA
Assoc Libs: EMMANUEL COLL ARCHVS, addr
as above, Asst Archivist: Mrs J. Morris (*email:*
archives@emma.cam.ac.uk)
Entry: membs only except for special collns
(visitors by adv appt) *Open:* Mon-Sun 0900-1730
Subj: all subjs; undergrad; postgrad *Collns: Bks
& Pamphs:* William Sancroft Colln; Graham
Watson Colln (18C & 19C clr plate bks)
Equip: m-readers, copier, 4 computers *Svcs:* info,
ref
Stock: bks/60000; periodcls/70; pamphs/2200
Acqs Offcr: Coll Libn, as above
Classn: DDC *Auto Sys:* Adlib
Pubns: A Brief Hist of Emmanuel Coll Lib (£1)
Staff: Libns: 1 *Non-Prof:* 2

S354 🎓
Fitzwilliam College Library
Huntingdon Rd, Cambridge, CB3 0DG (01223-
332042; *fax:* 01223-464162)
Email: librarian@fitz.cam.ac.uk
Internet: http://www.fitz.cam.ac.uk/library/

Chief: Libn: Miss M.A. MacLeod MA, DipLib
Entry: membs of Coll, others at discretion of libn
Open: term: Mon-Sun 0830-2400; vac: Mon-Sun
0830-1700
Subj: all subjs; undergrad *Co-op Schemes:* CUC
Equip: m-reader *Online:* Univ Lib catalogues
Stock: bks/37000; periodcls/70
Classn: Bliss *Auto Sys:* LibBASE
Staff: Libns: 1 *Non-Prof:* 1 *Exp:* £29000 (1999-
2000)

S355 🎓 🏛
Fitzwilliam Museum, Department of Manuscripts and Printed Books
Trumpington St, Cambridge, CB2 1RB (01223-
332900; *fax:* 01223-332923)
Email: fwm1@ula.cam.ac.uk
Internet: http://www.fitzmuseum.cam.ac.uk/

Gov Body: Univ of Cambridge (see **L5**) *Chief:*
Asst Keeper: Dr Stella Panayotova (sdp@cam.
ac.uk) *Other Snr Staff:* Snr Lib Assts: Miss
Elizabeth Fielden MA (emo1001@cam.ac.uk) & Mr
Nicholas Robinson MA, MCLIP (nrr212cu@cam.
ac.uk)
Entry: ref only; adv appt & letter of recommend-
ation required for access to curatorial materials

Open: due to a major bldg proj at the museum, the
lib is closed to the public until around Easter 2004
Subj: arts & hist of art, in widest sense; near-
Eastern archaeo *Collns: Bks & Pamphs:*
Founder's Lib; private press bks; early printed bks
Archvs: Raymond Lister archv; Blunt papers;
Hassall archv; John Linnell Archv; illuminated
MSS; music MSS; autograph letters; literary MSS
Other: printed music *Co-op Schemes:* CUC
Equip: 2 m-readers, 2 m-printers, copier, 2
computers (both with internet, 1 with CD-ROM)
Stock: bks/c250000; periodcls/c500
Classn: LC *Staff: Libns:* 1 *Non-Prof:* 2

S356 ➕
Fulbourn Hospital, Professional Medical Library
PO Box 342, Fulbourn Hosp, Cambridge, CB1 5EF
(01223-218630; *fax:* 01223-218708)
Email: janet.chow@addenbrookes.nhs.uk

Gov Body: Cambridgeshire & Peterborough
Mental Health Partnership NHS Trust *Chief:* Libn:
Ms Janet Chow
Assoc Libs: DEVELOPMENTAL PSY / CHILD &
FAMILY PSYCHIATRY LIB, Douglas House, 18b
Trumpington Rd, Cambridge, CB2 2AH; DEPT OF
PSYCHOTHERAPY LIB, Box 190, Addenbrooke's
Hosp, Hills Rd, Cambridge, CB2 2QQ; LEARNING
DISABILITIES LIB, Admin Dept, Ida Darwin Hosp,
Cambridge, CB1 5EE
Entry: NHS, Trust, Cambridge Health Authority &
East Anglian Regional Health Authority employees
or on appl to the libn *Open:* Mon, Wed 0900-1630,
Tue, Thu 0900-1700, Fri 0900-1600; staffed Mon &
Thu (all day), Wed to 1230
Subj: psychiatry; neurology; psy; psychotherapy;
child & family psychiatry; mental handicap;
addiction; creative therapies *Collns: Bks &
Pamphs:* colln of papers, reports, theses, etc
written by Cambridge Health Authority employees
based at Fulbourn etc (on psychiatry & related
subjs) *Co-op Schemes:* BLDSC, PLCS
Equip: 2 video viewers, fax, copier, 3 computers
Online: Medline
Stock: bks/1500; periodcls/35
Classn: NLM
Pubns: occasional Medical Lib Bulletin; Pubn Lists
Staff: Libns: 1 PT

S357 🎓
Girton College Library
Cambridge, CB3 0JG (01223-338970; *fax:* 01223-
339890)
Email: library@girton.cam.ac.uk
Internet: http://www-lib.girton.cam.ac.uk/

Chief: Fellow & Libn: Ms Frances Gandy BA, MA,
MCLIP *Dep:* Asst Libn: Mrs Jenny Blackhurst
MA(Hons), MA, MCLIP *Other Snr Staff:*
Archivist: Ms Kate Perry
Assoc Libs: WOLFSON CT LIB, Clarkson Rd,
Cambridge
Entry: membs of Coll only, bona fide scholars by
appt with libn, appl in writing *Open:* term: Mon-Fri
0900-2300, Sat 1000-1800, Sun 1000-2300;
visitors & vac: Mon-Fri only 0900-1700
Subj: all subjs; undergrad; postgrad *Collns: Bks
& Pamphs:* Frere Colln of Hebrew MSS; Blackburn
Colln of women's rights materials; Crews Colln of
Judaeo-Spanish material; Somerville Colln
(maths); Newall Colln (Scandinavian material);
Bibas Colln (18C French works) *Archvs:* Coll
papers from 1870: primary material on hist of
women's higher edu, suffrage, women & labour;
personal papers of: Emily Davies; Barbara
Bodichon; Bessie Parkes & others
Equip: m-reader, copier, 6 computers (incl 5 with
wd-proc, 5 with internet & 1 with CD-ROM)
Stock: bks/90000; periodcls/150
Classn: DDC *Auto Sys:* Heritage
Staff: Libns: 2 *Other Prof:* 1 *Non-Prof:* 3

S358

Gonville and Caius College Library

Cambridge, CB2 1TA (01223-332419; *fax:* 01223-332430)
Email: library@cai.cam.ac.uk
Internet: http://www.cai.cam.ac.uk/college/library/

Chief: Libn: Mr J.H. Prynne MA *Dep:* Sub-Libn: Mr Mark Statham MA, MCLIP
Entry: Working Lib: membs of Coll only; *Rare Bks Lib:* by appt *Open: Working Lib:* Mon-Sun 0700-0000; *Rare Bks Lib:* Mon-Fri 0900-1700
Subj: all subjs; undergrad; postgrad; local study (Cambridgeshire, Norfolk, Suffolk) *Collns: Bks & Pamphs:* rare & early printed bks (18000 vols) *Archvs:* MS collns (c900 items); C.M. Doughty papers; Charles Wood papers; John Venn papers
Equip: 2 m-readers, copier, 3 computers
Stock: bks/60000; periodcls/70
Classn: DDC *Auto Sys:* Endeavour Voyager
Staff: Libns: 3.6 *Other Prof:* 0.75 *Non-Prof:* 0.5
Exp: £90000 (1999-2000)

S359

Hamilton Kerr Institute Library

Mill Ln, Whittlesford, Cambridge, CB2 4NE (01223-832040)
Email: hki-admin@lists.cam.ac.uk

Gov Body: dept of the Fitzwilliam Museum (see **S355**) *Chief:* Libn: Dr R. Woudhuysen
Entry: on appl to the Dir of the Inst *Open:* Mon-Fri 0900-1700
Subj: art conservation *Collns: Archvs:* relating to conservation practice & artists' techniques, incl: Roberson Archv (19C artist's colourman) *Co-op Schemes:* CULS

S360

Henry Martyn Centre for the Study of Mission and World Christianity, Library

Westminster Coll, Madingley Rd, Cambridge, CB3 0AA (01223-741088)
Email: library@martynmission.cam.ac.uk
Internet: http://www.martynmission.cam.ac.uk/

Chief: Libn: Mrs Jane Gregory BA, DipLib *Dep:* Asst Libn: Isobel Fox BA, DipLib
Assoc Libs: HENRY MARTYN ARCHVS, at same addr, Archivist: Dr Sue Sutton BA, PhD (archive@martynmission.cam.ac.uk)
Entry: membs of Univ & Cambridge Theological Federation; others by appt only *Open:* Mon-Fri 0830-1630
Subj: religion; mission; theology; cultural studies; mission hist; mission biography *Collns: Archvs:* Henry Marytn Trust Archvs; Cambridge Cttee for Christian Work in Delhi Archvs; Murray Titus papers; A.G. Hogg papers; Peter Hinchliff papers; Ralph Leech papers; J.S. Philips papers; R.A. Minter papers; Roy Billington papers; Handley Hooper papers; Alan Macleod papers; papers relating to the 1910 Edinburgh Conference on World Mission
Equip: m-reader, copier, 2 computers (both with internet)
Stock: bks/7500; periodcls/40; pamphs/c300
Classn: DDC *Auto Sys:* Voyager *Staff:* Libns: 2 *Other Prof:* 1 *Exp:* £4000 (2000-01)

S361

Homerton College Library

Hills Rd, Cambridge, CB2 2PH (01223-507259)
Email: gm10009@cam.ac.uk
Internet: http://www.homerton.cam.ac.uk/college_library.htm

Chief: Libn: Mr Geoffrey Mizen MA, BEd(Hons), DipLib *Dep:* Asst Libn: Mrs R. Surtees BA(Hons), DipLib

Entry: ref only for non-staff/student *Open:* term: Mon-Thu 0830-2000, Fri 0900-1800, Sat 0930-1230, Sun 1330-1730; vac: Mon-Fri 0900-1700
Subj: all subjs; undergrad; postgrad; local study (Cambridgeshire, Fens) *Collns: Bks & Pamphs:* local colln; ch's fiction facsimiles; rare bks *Archvs:* Homerton Coll archv, incl bks, photos, letters, clothing, furniture etc *Co-op Schemes:* CUC
Equip: m-reader, copier, 5 computers
Stock: bks/65000; periodcls/120
Classn: DDC *Auto Sys:* Heritage IV
Staff: Libns: 1 *Other Prof:* 4

S362

Hughes Hall College Library

Mortimer Rd, Cambridge, CB1 2EW (01223-763908)
Email: library@hughes.cam.ac.uk

Gov Body: Hughes Hall *Chief:* Under-Libn: Mrs Karen Begg (keb36@hermes.cam.ac.uk) *Other Snr Staff:* Snr Lib Asst: Mrs Lorraine Scanwell
Entry: membs of Coll only *Open:* 24 hr access
Subj: all subjs; undergrad; postgrad *Collns: Archvs:* Hughes Hall archvs
Equip: m-reader, copier, computer (with wd-proc, internet & CD-ROM) *Svcs:* info, ref
Stock: bks/2500; periodcls/some law journals
Acqs Offcr: Under-Libn, as above
Classn: DDC 21 *Auto Sys:* Voyager
Staff: Libns: 1 PT *Non-Prof:* 1 PT

S363

Institute for Orthodox Christian Studies Library

Wesley House, Jesus Ln, Cambridge, CB5 8BQ (01223-741037)
Email: info@iocs.cam.ac.uk
Internet: http://www.iocs.cam.ac.uk/

Chief: Libn: Mrs Carole Reekie MSc(Hons), MCLIP
Assoc Libs: WESLEY HOUSE LIB, at same addr (see **S398**)
Entry: ref only; membs of Univ & Cambridge Theological Federation; others by appt with Libn
Subj: religion; Orthodox Church; theology; biblical studies *Co-op Schemes:* CULS
Stock: bks/1500; periodcls/6 *Staff:* Libns: 1

S364

International Extension College Resource Centre

Michael Young Centre, Purbeck Rd, Cambridge, CB2 2DS (01223-414760; *fax:* 01223-414762)
Email: iec@iec.ac.uk
Internet: http://www.iec.ac.uk/

Entry: ref only, adv appt *Open:* Mon-Fri 0900-1700; closed bank hols & subsequent Tue
Subj: distance edu; online learning; development; non-formal edu; globalisation *Collns: Archvs:* pre-1980 materials
Equip: fax, copier, computer *Svcs:* info, ref
Stock: bks/6000; periodcls/100; videos/15; CD-ROMs/20
Classn: London Inst of Edu System
Pubns: IEC News (2 pa); Edu at the Margins (IEC conference proceedings, £4.50, incl p&p); range of manuals & case studies on distance edu
Staff: Other Prof: 10 (no lib staff at present)

S365

Isaac Newton Institute for Mathematical Sciences, Library

20 Clarkson Rd, Cambridge, CB3 0EH (01223-335983; *fax:* 01223-330508)
Email: library@newton.cam.ac.uk
Internet: http://www.newton.cam.ac.uk/lib/

Gov Body: Newton Inst; part of Univ of Cambridge (see **L5**) *Chief:* Info Offcr: Ms Sarah Wilkinson
Entry: open into participants of the Inst, membs of Univ & visiting scholars; others by appt *Open:* Mon-Fri 0900-1800
Subj: maths *Co-op Schemes:* CULS
Equip: copier
Stock: bks/5000; periodcls/40

S366

Jesus College, Quincentenary Library

Cambridge, CB5 8BL (01223-339451; *fax:* 01223-324910)
Email: rkw10@cus.cam.ac.uk
Internet: http://www.jesus.cam.ac.uk/

Gov Body: Jesus Coll *Chief:* Fellow Libn: Dr A. Tooze *Dep:* Quincentenary Libn: Miss R.K. Watson BA(Hons), DipLib, MCLIP
Assoc Libs: OLD LIB, addr as above, Keeper of the Old Lib: Mr Peter Glazebrook MA; COLL ARCHVS, addr as above, Archivist: Dr F. Willmoth
Entry: adv appt, membs of Coll only *Open:* 24 hrs a day
Subj: all subjs; undergrad *Collns: Bks & Pamphs:* medieval, early modern & some modern bks held in Old Lib (apply to the Keeper) *Archvs:* archvs of the Coll (apply to Archivist)
Equip: video viewer, copier, 28 computers (all with wd-proc, internet & CD-ROM) *Svcs:* info
Stock: bks/38000; periodcls/90; videos/90
Classn: Bliss *Auto Sys:* Heritage
Staff: Libns: 2 *Non-Prof:* 1

S367

Judge Institute of Management, Library

Trumpington St, Cambridge, CB2 1AG (01223-339599; *fax:* 01223-339701)
Email: library@jims.cam.ac.uk
Internet: http://www.jims.cam.ac.uk/library/library.html

Gov Body: Univ of Cambridge (see **L5**) *Chief:* Libn: Miss S.J. Milburn MA, MCLIP
Entry: membs of Univ, others ref only by appt
Open: term: Mon-Fri 0845-1900, Sat 1000-1300; vac: Mon-Fri 0900-1700
Subj: business; mgmt (textbks only)
Equip: copier (A4/5p), computers
Staff: Libns: 1 *Non-Prof:* 5

S368

Kettle's Yard Museum and Art Gallery, Library and Archives

Castle St, Cambridge, CB3 0AQ (01223-352124)
Email: mail@kettlesyard.cam.ac.uk
Internet: http://www.kettlesyard.co.uk/

Gov Body: Univ of Cambridge (see **L5**) *Chief:* Curator: Mr Sebastiano Barassi
Entry: bona fide scholars by adv appt with the Curator *Open:* summer: Tue-Sun 1330-1630; winter: Tue-Sun 1400-1600; also open Mon Bank Hols; closed Xmas, New Year & Good Fri
Subj: visual arts; modern art; poetry; religion; phil; personal papers *Collns: Bks & Pamphs:* Harold Stanley Ede Lib (core colln) *Archvs:* Harold Stanley Ede papers (artist & critic, 1895-1990), along with correspondence from various artistic & literary figs, incl: Ian Finlay; David Jones; T.E. Lawrence; Ben Nicholson; Alfred Wallis; sketchbks & papers of Henri Gaudier-Brzeska (sculptor, 1891-1915); sketchbks & papers of Christopher Wood (painter, 1901-1930)
Equip: Disabled: wheelchair access

Special Libraries

Cambridge ▼ Cambridge

S369 🎓
King's College Library

Cambridge, CB2 1ST (01223-331232; *fax:* 01223-331891)
Email: library@kings.cam.ac.uk
Internet: http://www.kings.cam.ac.uk/library/

Gov Body: King's Coll *Chief:* Libn: Mr P.M. Jones MA *Dep:* Asst Libn: Mrs W. Kirkpatrick MA
Assoc Libs: ROWE MUSIC LIB, contact details as above; ARCHV CENTRE, at same addr, Archivist: Dr R. Moad (01223-331444; *fax:* 01223-331891; *email:* archivist@kings.cam.ac.uk)
Entry: by appt only, giving at least one wk's notice in writing *Open:* Mon-Fri 0930-1715
Subj: all subjs *Collns: Bks & Pamphs:* Mann Music Lib (pre-1850 printed music); J.M. Keynes Lib (hist of European thought); Pamph Colln *Archvs:* archvs of King's Coll; medieval MSS; papers of: J.M. Keynes; E.M. Forster; T.S. Eliot; Rupert Brooke; C.R. Ashbee; Roger Fry; Isaac Newton; Alan Turing
Equip: m-reader
Stock: bks/150000; periodcls/100
Classn: Bliss *Staff: Libns:* 3 *Non-Prof:* 2

S370 🎓
Lauterpacht Research Centre for International Law, Library

5 Cranmer Rd, Cambridge, CB3 9BL (01223-335358; *fax:* 01223-300406)
Email: als33@cam.ac.uk
Internet: http://www.lrcil.org/

Gov Body: Univ of Cambridge (see **L5**) *Chief:* contact the Libn
Entry: resident fellows, visiting scholars & faculty membs belonging to the centre; others by appt only
Subj: internatl law *Collns: Bks & Pamphs:* unique colln of pleadings *Co-op Schemes:* CULS
Stock: bks/c5000

S371 🎓
Lucy Cavendish College Library

Lady Margaret Rd, Cambridge, CB3 0BU (01223-332183; *fax:* 01223-332178)
Email: library@lucy-cav.cam.ac.uk
Internet: http://www.lucy-cav.cam.ac.uk/library/

Gov Body: part of Univ of Cambridge (see **L5**)
Chief: Libn: Ms Catherine Reid BSc, MSc, MCLIP *Dep:* Asst Libn: Mrs Joan Harris BA *Other Snr Staff:* Lib Asst: Mrs P.R. Granger MA
Assoc Libs: COLL ARCHVS, at same addr, Archivist: Mrs Karen Davies MA (01223-339009; *fax:* 01223-332178; *email:* archivist@lucy-cav.cam. ac.uk)
Entry: Coll membs only
Subj: all subjs; undergrad
Stock: bks/20000; periodcls/20; archvs/60 linear m
Classn: DDC *Staff: Libns:* 1 *Non-Prof:* 2

S372 🎓
Magdalene College Library

Cambridge, CB3 0AG (01223-332125)
Email: magd-lib@lists.cam.ac.uk

Gov Body: Master & Fellows of Magdalene Coll
Chief: Coll Libn: Dr N.G. Jones MA, PhD *Dep:* Asst Libn: Mrs A. Fitzsimons

Assoc Libs: PEPYS LIB, at same addr (see **S372**); COLL ARCHVS, at same addr, Coll Archivist: Dr R. Hyam LittD
Entry: staff & students of Coll
Subj: all subjs; undergrad *Co-op Schemes:* CULS, CUC

S373 🎓
Magdalene College, The Pepys Library

Cambridge, CB3 0AG (01223-332115; *fax:* 01223-332187)
Email: pepyslibrary@magd.cam.ac.uk
Internet: http://www.magd.cam.ac.uk/pepys/

Gov Body: The Master & Fellows of Magdalene Coll *Chief:* Pepys Libn: Dr R. Luckett MA, PhD
Dep: Asst Libn: Mrs A. Fitzsimons
Assoc Libs: COLL LIB, at same addr (see **S372**)
Entry: ref only, by written appl – must be specific, in adv & backed by appropriate credentials *Open:* Oct-Mar: Mon-Sat 1430-1530; Apr-Aug: Mon-Sat 1130-1230, 1430-1530
Subj: the navy; music; maps; calligraphy; prints; lit; ballads (all prior to 1703) *Collns: Bks & Pamphs:* Samuel Pepys private colln, incl MSS
Stock: bks/3000 vols, 7500 titles
Pubns: Pepys Lib Guide (£1 + p&p); postcards (interior & exterior, 25p each); a complete catalogue to the Pepys Lib (11 vols, 1980-93, genl editor R.C. Latham) is published by Boydell & Brewer, Woodbridge, Suffolk; all enqs regarding the catalogue should be directed to the publisher & not the Lib
Staff: Other Prof: 1 PT

S374 🙏 🎓
Margaret Beaufort Institute of Theology, Library

12 Grange Rd, Cambridge, CB3 9DX (01223-741039)
Email: btt20@cam.ac.uk

Chief: Federation Libn: Mrs Carole Reekie MSc(Econ), MCLIP (cr248@cam.ac.uk)
Entry: membs of Cambridge Theological Federation *Open:* Mon-Fri during Coll hrs
Subj: religion; theology; some Catholic materials

S375 🏛 🎓 ✚
Medical Research Council, Dunn Human Nutrition Unit Library

Wellcome Trust/MRC Bldg, Hills Rd, Cambridge, CB2 2XY (01223-252730; *fax:* 01223-252715)
Email: james.parke@mrc-dunn.cam.ac.uk
Internet: http://www.mrc-dunn.cam.ac.uk/

Gov Body: Medical Rsrch Council (see **S536**)
Chief: Informatics Co-ordinator: Mr James Parke BA(Hons), DipLib
Entry: membs of Unit only *Open:* open 24 hrs a day to Unit membs
Subj: biochem; molecular biology; nutrition *Co-op Schemes:* BLDSC, ILL
Svcs: info, ref
Stock: bks/350; periodcls/43
Classn: own *Staff: Libns:* 1

S376 🏛 ✚ 🎓
Medical Research Council, Human Nutrition Research Library

Elsie Widdowson Laboratory, Fulbourn Rd, Cambridge, CB1 9NL (01223-427519; *fax:* 01223-437515)
Email: librarian@mrc-hnr.cam.ac.uk
Internet: http://www.mrc-hnr.cam.ac.uk/

Gov Body: Medical Rsrch Council (see **S536**)
Chief: Libn: Mrs Susan Jones BSc, MA (Susan.Jones@mrc-hnr.cam.ac.uk)
Entry: staff, rsrch workers & students; others by appt on appl to the Libn *Open:* available for enqs Mon-Fri 1000-1500
Subj: biochem; chem; medicine; physiology; nutrition; dietetics *Collns: Bks & Pamphs:* historical colln on vitamins; pubns of Dr Elsie May Widdowson (1906-2000); reprint collns, incl Dame Harriette Chick Colln; numerous reports & pamphs
Co-op Schemes: BLDSC, ILL, CULS, MRC Union List of Journals
Equip: copier, computers (incl internet & CD-ROM) *Online:* various *Svcs:* info, ref, biblio
Stock: bks/3000; periodcls/155
Classn: DDC (mod)

S377 🏛 🎓 ✚
Medical Research Council, Laboratory of Molecular Biology Library

New Addenbrooke's Hosp, Hills Rd, Cambridge, CB2 2QH (01223-248011; *fax:* 01223-213556)
Email: wanda@mrc-lmb.cam.ac.uk

Type: rsrch *Gov Body:* Medical Rsrch Council (see **S536**) *Chief:* Lib Asst in Charge: Mrs W.A. Bullock
Entry: staff & local rsrch workers; others by adv appt only *Open:* Mon-Fri 0900-1700
Subj: molecular biology *Co-op Schemes:* CULS, ILL (available for membs of Laboratory only)
Equip: copier (7p per pg)
Stock: bks/3500; periodcls/130

S378 🎓
Needham Research Institute, East Asian History of Science Library

8 Sylvester Rd, Cambridge, CB3 9AF (01223-311545; *fax:* 01223-362703)
Email: jm10019@cus.cam.ac.uk

Gov Body: East Asian Hist of Sci Trust *Chief:* Libn & Curator: Mr John P.C. Moffett MA, DipLib
Entry: adv appt *Open:* Mon-Fri 1100-1600
Subj: hist of East Asian sci, tech; medicine
Collns: Bks & Pamphs: large offprint colln as well as notes, photos, maps etc on above subj collected by Dr Joseph Needham & Dr Lu Gwei-Djen; bks, offprints, personal notes & writings on South East Asian maritime hist collected by Dr J.V. Mills *Archvs:* large archv relating to composition of multi-vol 'Sci & Civilization in China' by Dr Needham et al *Co-op Schemes:* BLDSC (photocopies of articles only)
Equip: m-reader, video viewer, fax, copier, computer (incl wd-proc) *Online:* BIDS, JANET, Internet, CUC
Stock: bks/30000; periodcls/150; photos/15000; pamphs/20000; maps/100; videos/10; archvs/12 filing cabinets
Classn: own *Auto Sys:* CATS
Pubns: Newsletter (irregular)
Staff: Libns: 1 *Non-Prof:* 4

S379 🎓
New Hall College, Rosemary Murray Library

Huntingdon Rd, Cambridge, CB3 0DF (01223-762202; *fax:* 01223-763110)
Email: library@newhall.cam.ac.uk
Internet: http://www.newhall.cam.ac.uk/

Gov Body: New Hall *Chief:* Libn: Ms Alison Wilson BA, MLitt, MSc, MCLIP *Dep:* Asst Libn: Mrs Jan Waller
Entry: adv appt (usually Coll membs only) *Open:* 24 hrs for Coll membs; other enqs Mon-Fri 0930-1730

Subj: all subjs; undergrad; postgrad *Collns: Bks & Pamphs:* Rawson Bequest (Roman hist & classics); Duse Colln (Italian lit, bks belonging formerly to the Italian actress Eleonora Duse); Rilke Colln; collns on women & feminism *Archvs:* hist of New Hall (higher edu for women)
Equip: m-reader, copier, 26 computers (incl 23 with wd-proc, 23 with internet & 23 with CD-ROM) *Online:* as Univ Lib *Svcs:* info, ref, biblio
Stock: bks/55000; periodcls/50; videos/90; CD-ROMs/40
Classn: DDC *Auto Sys:* Heritage
Staff: Libns: 1 *Non-Prof:* 1.7

S380
Newnham College Library
Sidgwick Ave, Cambridge, CB3 9DF (01223-335740)
Email: library@newn.cam.ac.uk
Internet: http://www.newn.cam.ac.uk/library/

Chief: Coll Libn: Ms D. Hodder MA, MCLIP *Dep:* Snr Lib Asst: Mrs Jo Roos BA *Other Snr Staff:* Lib Asst & Clerk to the Archvs: Ms Anne Thomson BA
Assoc Libs: SKILLITER CENTRE FOR OTTOMAN STUDIES, at same addr, Curator: Dr Kate Fleet BA(Hons), PhD (01223-335804; *fax:* 01223-357898; *email:* khf11@cus.cam.ac.uk)
Entry: bona fide scholars, adv written appl to libn, ref only; archvs by written appl to Clerk to the Archvs *Open:* Mon-Fri 0900-1700
Subj: all subjs; undergrad *Collns: Bks & Pamphs:* Skilliter Colln of Ottoman Studies (Ottoman hist & travel, 4000 vols, 16C onwards); rare bk colln (c6000 items) *Archvs:* documents & material relating to the setting up of the Coll & its hist, incl letters, photographs, minutes & diaries
Co-op Schemes: CUC *Equip:* m-reader
Stock: bks/90000; periodcls/77
Classn: DDC (mod) *Auto Sys:* LibBASE
Staff: Libns: 1 *Non-Prof:* 2

S381
NIAB Library
Huntingdon Rd, Cambridge, CB3 0LE (01223-276381; *fax:* 01223-277602)
Email: liz.murfitt@niab.com

Gov Body: Natl Inst of Agricultural Botany (NIAB)
Chief: Libn: E.J. Murfitt
Entry: ref only, adv appt *Open:* Mon-Thu 0845-1715, Fri 0845-1645
Subj: agric botany; seed tech; plant pathology
Collns: Archvs: seed catalogues; floras; small antiquarian colln
Equip: m-reader, copier, computer (incl wd-proc)
Stock: bks/7000; periodcls/650; pamphs/5000; maps/50
Classn: UDC
Pubns: Selective Index to Periodicals; Accessions List
Staff: Other Prof: 1

S382
Pembroke College Library
Cambridge, CB2 1RF (01223-338100; *fax:* 01223-338163)
Email: lib@pem.cam.ac.uk

Gov Body: Master & Fellows of Coll *Chief:* Fellow Libn: Mr T.R.S. Allan MA, BCL *Dep:* Asst Libn: Ms P. Aske MA
Entry: ref only, at discretion of libn, by appt *Open:* Mon-Fri 0900-1700
Subj: phil; psy; religion; social sci; lang; sci; maths; arts; lit; geog; hist *Collns: Archvs:* T. Gray MSS; C. Smart MSS; papers of Sir R. Storrs
Equip: m-reader *Online:* CUC
Stock: bks/48000; periodcls/38
Classn: own *Staff: Libns:* 1

S383
Peterhouse, The Perne Library
Trumpington St, Cambridge, CB2 1RD (01223-338200; *fax:* 01223-337578)
Internet: http://www.pet.cam.ac.uk/

Gov Body: Master & Fellows of Peterhouse, Cambridge *Chief:* Perne Libn: Dr R.W. Lovatt MA, DPhil, FRHistS *Dep:* Associate Perne Libn: Miss M. Pamplin MA
Assoc Libs: THE WARD LIB (undergrad working lib), at same addr (see **S384**)
Entry: adv appt in writing
Subj: phil; religion; arts; lit; geog; hist *Collns: Bks & Pamphs:* 16C-18C academic texts
Equip: 2 m-readers, copier *Svcs:* info, ref, biblio
Stock: bks/5000
Classn: own *Staff: Libns:* 1

S384
Peterhouse, The Ward Library
Trumpington St, Cambridge, CB2 1RD (01223-338218)
Email: lib@pet.cam.ac.uk
Internet: http://www.pet.cam.ac.uk/

Chief: Ward Libn: Mr Martin Golding *Dep:* Asst Libn: Ms Erica McDonald
Assoc Libs: PERNE LIB, at same addr (see **S383**)
Entry: membs of coll only *Open:* term: Mon-Fri 0900-2300, Sat 1000-2300, Sun 1200-2300
Subj: all subjs; undergrad *Collns: Bks & Pamphs:* Sir Adolphus Ward Colln (hist & English lit, c5000 items) *Co-op Schemes:* CULS
Stock: bks/c40000

S385
Queens' College Library
Cambridge, CB3 9ET (01223-335549; *fax:* 01223-335522)
Email: jmw49@hermes.cam.ac.uk
Internet: http://www.lib.cam.ac.uk/University/CollLibs/Queens.html

Chief: Libn: Mr Martin Williams BA *Dep:* Fellow Libn & Keeper of the Old Lib: Dr Ian Patterson MA, PhD *Other Snr Staff:* Archivist: Dr R.A.W. Rex PhD
Entry: War Memorial Lib: open only to Coll membs; *Old Lib:* by appt only *Open:* 24 hr access to membs of Coll
Subj: all subjs; undergrad; postgrad *Collns: Bks & Pamphs:* Old Lib (pre-1800 MSS & early printed bks), incl: Thomas Smith Colln (Renaissance humanism); John Smith Colln (17C maths); Isaac Milner Bequest (18C French maths); most works of Erasmus; other collns incl: Cohen Colln (mainly Latin America); Local Collns (relating to the town, Univ & Coll); Membs' Archv (works by fellows & past membs of Coll) *Archvs:* Coll estate archvs from 15C (housed & administered by Cambridge Univ Lib; addr all enqs to Univ Lib – see **L5**) *Co-op Schemes:* CUC, Cambridge Colls Conservation Consortium
Equip: m-reader, copier, 2 computers (incl wd-proc & CD-ROM) *Online:* CUC
Stock: bks/35000; periodcls/50; pamphs/5000; rare bks/40000
Classn: Bliss *Auto Sys:* CATS
Pubns: User Guide (free to membs); Hist of Queen's Coll Lib (£1 + p&p); Catalogue of the Lib 1827 (o/p)
Staff: Libns: 1 *Non-Prof:* 0.5 *Exp:* £19150 (1999-2000)

S386
Ridley Hall Library
Ridley Hall Rd, Cambridge, CB3 9HG (01223-741080; *fax:* 01223-741081)
Email: cr248@cus.cam.ac.uk

Gov Body: Ridley Hall Council, Univ of Cambridge (see **L5**) *Chief:* Libn: Rev. Dr Michael Thompson *Dep:* Federation Libn: Mrs Carole Reekie MSc(Econ), MCLIP *Other Snr Staff:* Lib Asst: Ms Magda Fletcher
Entry: open to membs of Cambridge Theological Federation; others by appt *Open:* term: Mon-Fri during Coll hrs; vac: closed
Subj: theology & related subjs *Collns: Bks & Pamphs:* Cecil Colln (18C bks & pamphs) *Archvs:* Charles Simeon Papers (evangelical leader, 1759-1836); correspondence of Henry Martyn; correspondence between John Newton & John Thornton (1773-1778) *Co-op Schemes:* ILL (photocopies only)
Equip: m-reader, copier, computer (with wd-proc)
Stock: bks/15000; periodcls/53, incl 28 current; pamphs/650
Classn: own
Staff: Libns: 1 *Other Prof:* 0.25 *Non-Prof:* 1

S387
Robinson College Library
Cambridge, CB3 9AN (01223-339124; *fax:* 01223-351794)
Internet: http://www.robinson.cam.ac.uk/

Gov Body: Robinson Coll *Chief:* Fellow Libn: Dr D.S. McKie MA, PhD *Dep:* Coll Libn: Miss L.A. Read MA, MCLIP
Entry: membs of Robinson Coll only *Open:* term: 0900-2400; vac: 0900-1300, 1400-1700
Subj: all subjs; undergrad
Equip: 4 m-readers, copier
Stock: bks/55000
Classn: DDC *Staff: Libns:* 1 *Non-Prof:* 2

S388
Selwyn College Library
Grange Rd, Cambridge, CB3 9DQ (01223-335880; *fax:* 01223-335837 – in College)
Email: lib@sel.cam.ac.uk
Internet: http://www.sel.cam.ac.uk/library_and_archive/lib_index.shtml

Gov Body: Selwyn Coll *Chief:* Coll Libn: Mrs Sarah Taylor BA(Hons), MA *Dep:* Asst Libn: Mr Michael Wilson BA(Hons), MA
Assoc Libs: COLL ARCHVS, at same addr, Coll Archivist: Sophie Bridges (archivist@sel.cam.ac.uk)
Entry: non-Coll membs by appt only; Coll membs have access during term opening hrs *Open:* Coll membs: term: 0700-0130; vac: 0700-1400; non-membs: by appt only between 0930-1630
Subj: all subjs; undergrad *Collns: Bks & Pamphs:* theology (16C-19C); rare bks; some incunabula housed at Univ Lib (see **L5**) *Archvs:* Bishop Selwyn Archvs; Coll archvs
Equip: 2 m-readers, copier, 5 computers (incl CD-ROM) *Online:* NISS *Svcs:* info, ref
Stock: bks/38000; periodcls/60; m-forms/100; archvs/90 linear m
Classn: DDC *Auto Sys:* LibBASE
Staff: Libns: 2 *Non-Prof:* 1 *Exp:* £20000 (1999-2000)

S389
Sidney Sussex College Library
Sidney St, Cambridge, CB2 3HU (01223-338852; *fax:* 01223-338884)
Email: librarian@sid.cam.ac.uk
Internet: http://www.sid.cam.ac.uk/indepth/lib/library.html

Chief: Libn: Mrs H.E. Lane MA, DipLib, MCLIP *Dep:* Mrs K.E. Begg BSc(Econ), DipCrim *Assoc Libs:* MUNIMENT ROOM (01223-338824, e-mail: njr1002@cam.ac.uk), Archivist: Mr N. Rogers MA, MLitt, admission by appt only

 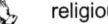

Special Libraries

Cambridge
▼
Canterbury

(Sidney Sussex Coll Lib cont)

Entry: membs of Coll only *Open:* 24 hr access; lib office Mon-Fri 0845-1600
Subj: all subjs; undergrad; postgrad *Collns: Bks & Pamphs:* 8000 early printed bks *Archvs:* Coll archvs; estate papers *Other:* 119 MSS
Equip: 3 m-readers, copier, 20 computers (all with wd-proc, internet & CD-ROM) *Online:* BIDS, EDINA, EEVL, Medline *Svcs:* info, ref, biblio, indexing, abstracting
Stock: bks/36000; periodcls/57; CD-ROMs/25
Classn: Bliss Bibliographic (2nd ed) *Auto Sys:* Heritage
Staff: Libns: 1 *Other Prof:* 1 *Non-Prof:* 1

S390 🎓

St Catharine's College Library

Cambridge, CB2 1RL (01223-338343; *fax:* 01223-338340)
Email: assistant.librarian@caths.cam.ac.uk
Internet: http://www.caths.cam.ac.uk/library/

Chief: Fellow Libn: J.R. Shakeshaft MA, PhD
Dep: Asst Libn: Mrs Suzan Griffiths MA, DipLib, MCLIP
Entry: Coll membs; or written appl to Fellow Libn for ref use only *Open:* Coll membs: Mon-Sun 24 hrs; others: Mon-Fri 0930-1500
Subj: all subjs; undergrad *Collns: Bks & Pamphs:* 25000 antiquarian bks; Addenbrooke's Colln; Chaytor Colln (Romance langs); Jarrett Colln (Biblical) *Archvs:* separate colln *Co-op Schemes:* CUC
Equip: copier, 5 computers (all with internet & 4 with CD-ROM)
Stock: bks/44900; periodcls/50; audios/1000; videos/177; CD-ROMs/6; DVDs/4
Classn: DDC *Auto Sys:* LibBASE
Pubns: Lib Guide for All New Students; Lib Guide & Lib Hist on web site
Staff: Libns: 1 *Other Prof:* 1 *Non-Prof:* 0.5 *Exp:* £28000 (1999-2000); excl exp on binding

S391 🎓

St Edmund's College, 15th Duke of Norfolk Memorial Library

Mount Pleasant, Cambridge, CB3 0BN (Coll enqs: 01223-336250)
Email: librarian@st-edmunds.cam.ac.uk
Internet: http://www.st-edmunds.cam.ac.uk/

Gov Body: St Edmund's Coll *Chief:* Libn: Dr Petà Dunstan
Entry: on appl by post to Libn *Open:* closed to visitors
Subj: all subjs; undergrad; religion; RC theology, esp English Catholics; Catholic hist
Equip: computer
Stock: bks/3500
Classn: DDC *Staff: Other Prof:* 1 *Non-Prof:* 0.2

S392 🎓

St John's College Library

Cambridge, CB2 1TD (01223-338662; *fax:* 01223-337035)
Email: library@joh.cam.ac.uk
Internet: http://www.joh.cam.ac.uk/Library/

Gov Body: St John's Coll *Chief:* Libn: Dr Mark Nicholls MA, PhD *Dep:* Sub-Libn: Mrs Kathryn McKee BA, MSc, MCLIP

Entry: membs of Coll & bona fide scholars by appt only *Open:* 24 hr access, all year round
Subj: all subjs; undergrad *Collns: Bks & Pamphs:* early printed bks; incunabula *Archvs:* medieval & modern MSS *Other:* prints & drawings; photos *Co-op Schemes:* CUC
Equip: 6 m-readers, 3 copiers, clr copier, 2 video viewers, 50 computers (all with wd-proc, internet & CD-ROM)
Stock: bks/150000; periodcls/200; photos/c5000; illusts/many; pamphs/many; maps/1000+; m-forms/ some; audios/1000; videos/500
Classn: LC *Auto Sys:* Endeavour Voyager
Staff: Libns: 6 *Non-Prof:* 5

S393 🎓

Trinity College Library

Cambridge, CB2 1TQ (01223-338488; *fax:* 01223-338532)
Email: trin-lib@lists.cam.ac.uk
Internet: http://www-lib.trin.cam.ac.uk/

Gov Body: The Master & Fellows of Trinity Coll
Chief: Libn: D.J. McKitterick LittD, FBA *Dep:* Sub-Libn: Mrs J. Ball BA, MA, MCLIP
Assoc Libs: WREN LIB, contact details as above; MODERN MSS & COLL ARCHV, addr as above, Manuscript Cataloguer: J. Smith BA, MArAd (01223-338579; *email:* js10027@cus.cam.ac.uk)
Entry: Student Lib: membs of Coll only; *Wren Lib:* by appt in writing *Open: Wren Lib:* readers: Mon-Fri 0900-1700; visitors: Mon-Fri 1200-1400, Sats in Full Term 1030-1230
Subj: all subjs; undergrad; postgrad *Collns: Bks & Pamphs:* 750 incunabula; special collns of printed bks incl: colln of Canon Law & Bibles; Julius Hare Colln (German theology, lit & phil); Rothschild Lib of 18C English Lit; French & Italian bks; classical pamphs; 19C mathematical bks; 800 vols from the lib of Isaac Newton; Civil War tracts; large colln of 18C & 19C English bks; Sraffa Colln (hist of econ) *Archvs:* Western MSS colln incl: 138 Greek MSS; medieval MSS incl 10C Gospels, Canterbury Psalter & the Apocalypse; large number of literary MSS incl: Milton's shorter poems; Tennyson's poetical drafts; works by Thackeray, Fitzgerald, Macaulay, A.E. Housman; Capell Colln of Shakespeareana; numerous MSS of Bentley, Whewell & Houghton; letters & MSS of the 17C, 18C, 19C & 20C incl: papers of the Babington family; Tennyson & Wittgenstein notebks; Munby Colln (19C photos); Coll archvs
Equip: 2 m-readers, m-printer, 2 copiers, numerous computers (incl internet & 2 CD-ROM)
Online: many databases accessible via internet
Svcs: info, ref, biblio
Stock: bks/300000; periodcls/260; photos/6000; archvs/400
Classn: own *Auto Sys:* Innopac
Pubns: Trinity Coll Lib: the first 150 years (£30)
Staff: Libns: 7.5 *Other Prof:* 1 *Non-Prof:* 7

S394 🎓

Trinity Hall, The Jerwood Library

Cambridge, CB2 1TJ (01223-332546)

Gov Body: Master & Fellows of Trinity Hall *Chief:* Fellow Libn: Dr P. Hutchinson PhD *Dep:* Coll Libn: Dr Andrew Lacey PhD (acl28@cam.ac.uk) & Mrs Alison Hunt, BA(Hons), MCLIP (amh55@cam.ac.uk)
Entry: strictly by appt, written appl to libn *Open:* term only: Mon-Fri 1000-1600
Subj: all subjs covered by Univ tripos *Collns: Bks & Pamphs:* canon & civil law; Larman Colln (medieval & modern English local & church hist, genealogy & heraldry); 16C theology; please note that access to these collns is restricted
Stock: bks/20000; periodcls/29
Classn: own
Pubns: Hist of Trinity Hall, 1350-1992

S395 🔑

TWI Library Service

Granta Pk, Gt Abington, Cambridge, CB1 6AL (01223-891162; *fax:* 01223-892588)
Email: library@twi.co.uk
Internet: http://www.twi.co.uk/

Gov Body: TWI *Chief:* Mgr, Info Svcs: Miss Linda Dumper BA, MCLIP *Dep:* Dep Libn: Mrs Helen Wilson BA, MA, MCLIP
Entry: full lib svc for membs only *Open:* Mon-Thu 0830-1700, Fri 0830-1615
Subj: welding & other joining techniques, & associated materials sci & eng *Collns: Bks & Pamphs:* trade lit on welding equip & consumables; conference proceedings; company info; reports *Archvs:* historical colln of bks on welding *Co-op Schemes:* BLDSC
Equip: m-reader, m-printer, fax, copier, computers (incl wd-proc & CD-ROM) *Svcs:* info, ref
Stock: bks/15000; periodcls/400, plus 200 no longer current; archvs/13 linear m; standards/10000+
Classn: own *Auto Sys:* Olib
Pubns: Welding Abstracts (monthly)
Staff: Libns: 1.5 *Non-Prof:* 1

S396 🔑 🎓 🙏

Tyndale House Library

36 Selwyn Gdns, Cambridge, CB3 9BA (01223-566604; *fax:* 01223-566608)
Email: librarian@tyndale.cam.ac.uk
Internet: http://www.tyndale.cam.ac.uk/

Type: rsrch *Gov Body:* Tyndale Council *Chief:* Libn: Dr E. Magba PhD, MA, MCLIP
Entry: ref only, adv appt *Open:* Mon-Fri 0830-1700
Subj: religion; biblical studies *Co-op Schemes:* BLDSC, CUC
Equip: m-reader, fax, 2 copiers, computers (incl 3 with CD-ROM) *Online:* JANET
Stock: bks/37000; periodcls/200; maps/50
Classn: DDC *Auto Sys:* in-house sys
Pubns: Tyndale Bulletin (semi-annual, £5.95 per issue)
Staff: Libns: 1

S397 🔑 🙏

United Reformed Church History Society Library

Westminster Coll, Madingley Rd, Cambridge, CB3 0AA (01223-741300; *fax:* 01223-300765)
Email: mt212@cam.ac.uk

Gov Body: United Reformed Church *Chief:* Administrator: Mrs M. Thompson BA (not in lib on Wed)
Entry: by appt only *Open:* Fri 1000-1530
Subj: hist of Presbyterian C of E & Congregational Church *Collns: Bks & Pamphs:* 17C religious pamphs *Archvs:* natl archvs of Presbyterian C of E
Equip: copier
Stock: bks/7000; photos/500; pamphs/2000; archvs/100 ft
Classn: LC
Pubns: Journal, United Reformed Church Hist Soc (2 pa, £7.50 per issue)
Staff: Libns: 1 *Exp:* stock additions usually by gift

S398 🎓 🙏

Wesley House Library

Jesus Ln, Cambridge, CB5 8BJ (01223-741033)
Email: cr248@cus.cam.ac.uk

Gov Body: Univ of Cambridge (see L5) *Chief:* Libn: Revd Dr Philip Luscombe *Dep:* Federation Libn: Mrs Carole Reekie MSc(Hons), MCLIP (cr248@cam.ac.uk) *Other Snr Staff:* Lib Asst: Ms Magda Fletcher (maf36@cam.ac.uk)

Entry: membs of the Cambridge Theological Federation & others by permission of libn *Open:* Mon-Fri during Coll opening hrs *Subj:* religion *Collns: Bks & Pamphs:* Methodist Colln *Co-op Schemes:* ILL, BLDSC (photocopies) *Equip:* m-reader, computer *Online:* CUC *Stock:* bks/19400; periodcls/28 *Classn:* own *Auto Sys:* CATS *Staff: Libns:* 0.25

S399
Westcott House Library
Jesus Ln, Cambridge, CB5 8BP (01223-741000)
Email: cr248@cus.cam.ac.uk

Gov Body: Univ of Cambridge (see **L5**) *Chief:* Libn: Dr Andrew Mein PhD *Dep:* Federation Libn: Mrs Carole Reekie MSc(Econ), MCLIP (cr248@cam.ac.uk) *Other Snr Staff:* Lib Asst: Ms Magda Fletcher (maf36@cam.ac.uk) *Entry:* membs of Cambridge Theological Federation; others by permission of libn *Open:* Mon-Fri during Coll opening hrs *Subj:* religion *Collns: Bks & Pamphs:* Brooke Foss Westcott Colln; B.K. Cunningham Colln *Co-op Schemes:* ILL, BLDSC (photocopies only) *Equip:* computer *Online:* CUC *Stock:* bks/15500; periodcls/35 *Classn:* own *Auto Sys:* CATS *Staff: Libns:* 0.25

S400
Westfield House Library
30 Huntingdon Rd, Cambridge, CB3 0HH (01223-354331; *fax:* 01223-355265)
Email: westfield.house@ntlworld.com
Internet: http://homepage.ntlworld.com/westfield.house/

Gov Body: Evangelical Lutheran Church of England *Chief:* Libn: Dr Glen Zweck DD (glen.zweck@ntlworld.com *Dep:* Tutor: Dr Tom Winger ThD (t.winger@ntlword.com) *Other Snr Staff:* Preceptor: Revd Reg Quirk MPhil (r.quirk@ntlworld.com) *Entry:* adv appt *Subj:* religion; theology; specialising in Luther & the Reformation *Co-op Schemes:* CULS *Equip:* copier (3p per sheet), computers (incl 3 with wd-proc, 3 with CD-ROM & 1 with internet) *Officer-in-Charge:* Preceptor, as above *Svcs:* info *Stock:* bks/12000; periodcls/12 *Acqs Offcr:* Libn, as above *Classn:* Union Theological Seminary sys *Auto Sys:* Filemaker *Staff: Libns:* 0.5 *Exp:* £1400 (1999-2000); £1400 (2000-01)

S401
Westminster College Library
Madingley Rd, Cambridge, CB3 0AA (01223-741084)
Email: cr248@cus.cam.ac.uk

Gov Body: Board of Governors *Chief:* Libn: Rev Dr Peter McEnhill *Dep:* Federation Libn: Mrs Carole Reekie MSc(Econ), MCLIP (cr248@cam.ac.uk) *Other Snr Staff:* Lib Asst: Ms Magda Fletcher (maf36@cam.ac.uk) *Entry:* membs of Coll & of Cambridge Theological Federation; ministers of the United Reformed Church; others by permission of libn *Open:* Mon-Fri during Coll opening hrs *Subj:* religion *Collns: Bks & Pamphs:* Elias Lib (hymnology); United Reformed Church Hist Soc Lib (see **S397**); Cheshunt Colln *Archvs:* United Reformed Church History Soc Archv; letters of Selina, Countess of Huntingdon *Other:* Hebrew fragments from Cairo Genizeh bought & given to Coll by Mrs Lewis & Mrs Gibson *Co-op Schemes:* ILL, BLDSC *Equip:* m-reader, copier, computer *Online:* CUC *Stock:* bks/40000; periodcls/55

Classn: LC *Auto Sys:* CATS *Staff: Libns:* 0.25
See also HENRY MARTYN CENTRE FOR THE STUDY OF MISSION & WORLD CHRISTIANITY LIB (**S360**)

S402
Wolfson College, The Lee Library
Cambridge, CB3 9BB (01223-335965; *fax:* 01223-335908)
Email: library@wolfson.cam.ac.uk

Gov Body: Wolfson Coll *Chief:* Lee Libn: Ms Hilary Pattison MA, MA *Entry:* membs of Coll; others only by appt *Open:* 24 hrs to Coll membs *Subj:* all subjs; undergrad; postgrad *Equip:* m-reader, copier (5p per copy), 3 computers (all with internet & CD-ROM) *Officer-in-Charge:* Lee Libn, as above *Svcs:* info, biblio *Stock:* bks/17000; periodcls/33 *Acqs Offcr:* Lee Libn, as above *Classn:* DDC *Auto Sys:* Voyager *Staff: Libns:* 1

Canonbie

S403
Royal Scottish Forestry Society Library
Hagg-on-Esk, Canonbie, Dumfries-shire, DG14 0XE (01387-371518; *fax:* 01387-371418)
Email: rsts@ednet.co.uk
Internet: http://www.rsfs.org/

Type: educational charity *Gov Body:* Council of the Royal Scottish Forestry Soc *Chief:* Dir: Mr A.G. Little *Dep:* Editor: Miss Adean Lutton MSc *Entry:* by adv appt only *Subj:* forestry *Collns: Bks & Pamphs:* Scottish Forestry journals (1854-date) *Svcs:* info *Stock:* bks/160 bnd vols *Classn:* by vol number *Pubns:* Scottish Forestry (£50 pa in UK, £67 pa overseas) *Staff: Other Prof:* 0.5

Canterbury

S404
Canterbury Cathedral Library
Cathedral House, The Precincts, Canterbury, Kent, CT1 2EH (01227-865287; *fax:* 01227-865222)
Email: library@canterbury-cathedral.org
Internet: http://www.canterbury-cathedral.org/

Gov Body: Dean & Chapter of Canterbury Cathedral *Chief:* Cathedral Libn: Mr Keith M.C. O'Sullivan MA, MSc(Econ), MCLIP (keitho@canterbury-cathedral.org) *Dep:* Dep Libn: Mrs Sarah A.L. Grey (sarahg@canterbury-cathedral.org) *Assoc Libs:* CATHEDRAL ARCHVS (see **A90**); ST AUGUSTINE'S LIB, Bulgate House, The Precincts, Canterbury, Kent, CT1 2EH *Entry:* ref only, by appt only *Open:* Mon-Thu 0900-1700, Fri by special arrangement *Subj:* Canterbury, esp the Cathedral; religion (pre-1900 bks); sci & maths (some pre-1900 bks); geog & hist (pre-1900 & 20C, particularly medieval hist) *Collns: Bks & Pamphs:* St Augustine's Lib of Theology (23000 vols, 18C-date); Howley-Harrison Colln, incl ecclesiastical hist, theology (up to 1850), political pamphs, esp slavery; Preston Parish Lib; Elham Parish Lib; Mendham Colln (owned by the Law Soc) of anti-Catholic lit incl 80 incunabula & a large colln of official Roman Catholic pubns of 16C & 17C *Archvs:* managed separately *Equip:* m-reader, m-printer, copier, computer (all except m-reader accessed via staff for readers) *Stock:* bks/65000; periodcls/6; photos/200; maps/50; m-forms/100 *Classn:* DDC, LC *Auto Sys:* own

Pubns: Slavery: A Bibliography of the Colln in Canterbury Cathedral Lib (£3.50); The Oxford Movement: Nineteenth Century Bks & Pamphs in Canterbury Cathedral Lib (Canterbury Sources 1) (£8); In Foreign Parts: Bks & Pamphs on the World Beyond Western Europe Printed Before 1900 in Canterbury Cathedral Lib (Canterbury Sources 2); The Slave Trade (Canterbury Sources 3) *Staff: Libns:* 2 *Other Prof:* 1 *Non-Prof:* 2 *Exp:* £5000 (1999-2000)

S405
Canterbury Christ Church University College, Library Services
North Holmes Rd, Canterbury, Kent, CT1 1QU (01227-782352; *fax:* 01227-767530)
Email: lib1@cant.ac.uk
Internet: http://www.cant.ac.uk/library/

Chief: Dir of Lib Svcs: Dr Angela Conyers MA, PhD, MCLIP *Dep:* Asst Dir of Lib Svcs (Support Svcs): Mr Paul Ryan BA, MCLIP; Asst Dir of Lib Svcs (Systems): Mrs Ruth Lewis MCLIP *Assoc Libs:* THANET LEARNING CENTRE, Northwood Rd, Broadstairs, Kent, CT10 2WA (01843-609103; *fax:* 01843-609130; *email:* thanetlc@cant.ac.uk); HAYLOFT LIB, Runcie Ct, David Salomons Est, Broomhill Rd, Tunbridge Wells, Kent, TN3 0TG (01892-507514; *fax:* 01892-507501; *email:* hayloftlibrary@cant.ac.uk); MANSION LIB, The Mansion, David Salomons Est, Broomhill Rd, Tunbridge Wells, Kent, TN3 0TG (01892-507717; *fax:* 01892-507719; *email:* salomons_library@cant.ac.uk) *Entry:* by appl to lib staff *Open:* term: Mon 0930-2130, Tue-Thu 0830-2130, Fri 0830-1900, Sat 1000-1700, Sun 1400-1900; vac: Mon 0930-1900, Tue-Thu 0830-1900, Fri 0830-1700, Sat 1000-1300 *Subj:* all subjs; undergrad; postgrad *Collns: Bks & Pamphs:* Elizabeth Gaskell Colln; historical colln of ch's bks *Archvs:* hist of Coll *Co-op Schemes:* BLDSC, SETRHA, Canterbury Circle of Libns *Equip:* m-form reader/printer, 7 video viewers, 3 copiers, clr copier, fax, 112 computers *Disabled:* 3 height adjustable desks for PC & study, enlarging facilities on copiers, scanner in Open Access Computing area, wheelchair access *Stock:* bks/250000; periodcls/2500; various m-forms, videos, cassettes, CDs, CD-ROMs & software *Acqs Offcr:* Academic Svcs Libn: Mrs Kath Smith *Classn:* DDC *Auto Sys:* Aleph *Staff: Libns:* 14.5 *Other Prof:* 3 *Non-Prof:* 23

S406
Canterbury College, The Carey Learning Resources Centre
New Dover Rd, Canterbury, Kent, CT1 3AJ (01227-811166; *fax:* 01227-811340)
Internet: http://www.cant-col.ac.uk/

Chief: Libn: Ms Sue Bennett BA (s.bennett@cant-col.ac.uk) *Dep:* Team Leader: Mrs Margaret Cameron MCLIP (m.cameron@cant-col.ac.uk) *Assoc Libs:* SHEPPEY COLL LRC, Bridge Rd, Sheerness, Kent, ME13 1HL, Snr Learning Resources Offcr: Ms Margaret Ellen MCLIP (01795-582510; *fax:* 01795-582500; *email:* m.ellen@cant-col.ac.uk) *Entry:* ref only for non-student/staff *Open:* term: Mon-Thu 0900-1930, Fri 1000-1630; vac: Mon-Thu 0900-1230, 1330-1700, Fri 0900-1230, 1330-1630 *Subj:* all subjs; local study (Canterbury & Kent) *Collns: Bks & Pamphs:* John Millest Colln (art); local studies colln *Co-op Schemes:* ILL *Equip:* copier (10p per copy), fax (fees vary), 2 video viewers, 84 computers (incl wd-proc, internet & CD-ROM), room for hire *Disabled:* text enlarger *Officer-in-Charge:* Learning Resources Asst: Mr Mark Revby (m.revby@cant-col.ac.uk) *Svcs:* info, ref, biblio

Special Libraries

Canterbury ▼ Cardiff

(Canterbury Coll, The Carey LRC cont)
Stock: bks/40095; periodcls/171; maps/63 charts; audios/351; videos/1395; CD-ROMs/21; DVDs/36
Acqs Offcr: Learning Resources Asst: Mr Philip Le Roy
Classn: DDC **Auto Sys:** Olib
Staff: Libns: 2 Non-Prof: 7

S407 ⚷
Institute of Heraldic and Genealogical Studies, Library
79-82 Northgate, Canterbury, Kent, CT1 1BA (01227-768664; *fax:* 01227-765617)
Email: librarian@ighs.ac.uk
Internet: http://www.ihgs.ac.uk/

Chief: Libn: Miss S.J. Bulson MA
Entry: adv appt, fee payable by non-membs
Open: Mon, Wed, Fri 1000-1630
Subj: genealogy; heraldry; hist of the family
Collns: *Bks & Pamphs:* British & European Armorial & Heraldic ref genealogical texts, manuals & printed finding aids, incl: parish register transcriptions; census indexes; marriage indexes; biographical src materials; extensive colln of '19C & 20C trade directories *Archvs:* recent (post 1945) genealogical case studies of some 2000 family hists undertaken over 30 years (indexed by surname & place, closed access) *Other:* IGI; Old Parish Registers Index; Genl personal Name Index; Catholic Marriage Index; Tylor Colln (genealogical material relating to East Kent); Sussex Colln (East Sussex baptisms 1700-1812, Index to Noncon-formist Registers, register transcripts, Settlement Papers & Heraldic Monuments of Sussex churches); Andrews Index (obituaries); Culletons Heraldic Index; Boyds Marriage Index (on fiche); Australian Civil Registration Indexes; Index to New South Wales Convicts; Griffiths Valuation of Ireland & Tithe Applotment Bks; Armorial Index; Pallot Marriage Index (London 1780-1837); Missing Person Index (1903-66); 1881 Census for England, Scotland & Wales; County genealogical src materials; biographical ref material
Equip: 4 m-readers, m-camera (staff only), m-printer (staff only), video viewer, fax (staff only), copier, computer (with wd-proc, staff only)
Stock: bks/20000; periodcls/150, plus c100 no longer current; maps/300; m-forms/20000
Pubns: Guide to Lib & Collns of the Inst of Heraldic & Genealogical Studies (SAE); bookshop catalogue also available
Staff: Libns: 1 Non-Prof: 2

S408 ✚
Kent Postgraduate Medical Centre, Linacre Library
Kent & Canterbury Hosp, Ethelbert Rd, Canterbury, Kent, CT1 3NG (01227-766877 x74851; *fax:* 01227-864154)
Email: sue.cover@kch-tr.sthames.nhs.uk

Gov Body: East Kent Hosps NHS Trust **Chief:** Libn: Mrs Susan Cover MCLIP
Assoc Libs: CLINICAL STUDIES LIB, Queen Elizabeth The Queen Mother Hosp (see **S1538**); WILLIAM HARVEY HOSP, EDU CENTRE LIB (see **S50**)
Entry: ref for non-membs at discretion of the Libn
Open: Mon-Fri 0900-1700

Subj: medicine; dentistry; veterinary medicine; hist of medicine; nursing; community health **Collns:** *Archvs:* hosp archvs from 1793 (not complete)
Equip: fax, copier, computers (incl wd-proc & internet) *Online:* Medline, BNI & related databases networked across Trust **Svcs:** info, ref
Stock: bks/7000; periodcls/150; videos/150
Classn: NLM **Auto Sys:** Librarian
Staff: Libns: 1 Non-Prof: 1

S409 🎓
The King's School Library
St Augustine's Abbey, Monastery St, Canterbury, Kent, CT1 1NN (01227-595608)
Email: kjh@kings-school.co.uk
Internet: http://www.kings-school.co.uk/

Gov Body: The King's School **Chief:** Libn: Mrs Kay J. Hoar MCLIP **Other Snr Staff:** Walpole Libn: Mr P.G. Henderson BA (in charge of Walpole Colln of English Literary MSS)
Entry: ref only, adv appt for bona fide scholars
Open: term: Mon-Fri 0900-2200, Sat 0900-1800, Sun 1100-2200
Subj: all subjs; GCSE; A level **Collns:** *Bks & Pamphs:* Hugh Walpole Colln (fine printed bks & English literary MSS); Maugham Lib (bks & pamphs of William Somerset Maugham) *Archvs:* school archvs
Equip: copier, computers **Svcs:** info, ref, biblio
Stock: bks/25000; periodcls/20; videos/200
Classn: DDC **Auto Sys:** Heritage
Staff: Libns: 2 Other Prof: 1 Non-Prof: 2 **Exp:** £19000 (1999-2000); £19000 (2000-01); figs incl all exp

S410 🎓
University of Kent at Canterbury, Templeman Library
Canterbury, Kent, CT2 7NU (01227-823570; *fax:* 01227-823984)
Email: library-enquiry@kent.ac.uk
Internet: http://library.kent.ac.uk/library/

Gov Body: Univ of Kent at Canterbury **Chief:** Libn & Dir of Info Svcs: Ms Margaret Coutts MA(Glas), MA(Shef), MCLIP (m.m.coutts@kent. ac.uk) **Other Snr Staff:** Planning & Projs Mgr: Ms Carole Pickaver (c.e.pickaver@kent.ac.uk); Head of Lib Info Svcs: Mr Steve Holland (r.s.holland@ kent.ac.uk); Head of Technical Svcs: Mr Colin Gerrard (j.c.gerrard@kent.ac.uk); Head of Lib Systems: Mr Stewart Brownrigg (s.j.brownrigg@ kent.ac.uk); Head of Lending Svcs: Ms Eva Newman (e.f.newman@kent.ac.uk)
Assoc Libs: CANTERBURY CATHEDRAL LIB (see **S404**)
Entry: public access for ref only **Open:** term: Mon-Fri 0845-2200, Sat-Sun 1200-1900; vac: Mon-Fri 0900-1900, Sat 1200-1900
Subj: undergrad; postgrad; rsrch **Collns:** *Bks & Pamphs:* EDC; SCOLMA: Madagascar; British govt pubns; Conflict & Peace Rsrch Colln; Maddison Colln (hist of sci & tech, 17C-19C); Crow Collns (ballads, bibliographies & dictionaries, English Renaissance authors); Blake Facsimiles Colln; T.S. Eliot Colln; Lloyd George Colln (1000 vols); Farquharson Colln (Greek & Roman Classics, c1000 vols); Modern 1st Eds Colln; Kent local hist; ch's lit; early printed bks; 18C bks; Victorian popular fiction; Penguin Colln (Penguin Bks) *Archvs:* Bernard Weatherill Papers; John Crow Papers; Hewlett Johnson Papers; R.E.W. Maddison Papers; E.M. Tenison Papers; Melville Colln (theatre); Pettingell Colln (theatre); Reading Raynor Theatre Colln; Playbill Colln; Boucicault Colln (theatre); C.P. Davies Wind & Watermill Colln; John Holman Colln of Mill Memorabilia; UKC pubns *Other:* Linfield Lib of Humour & Smith Colln of Cartoon & Caricature Bks (administered by Centre for the Study of Cartoons & Caricature – see **A91**); Muggeridge Collns (photos of English windmills); Kent theses & dissertations

Co-op Schemes: BLDSC, ILL, Canterbury Circle, SCONUL vac scheme
Equip: m-readers, m-printer, m-camera (Univ membs only), video viewers, copiers, clr copier (Univ membs only), computers (incl CD-ROM, Univ membs only) *Disabled:* Kurzweil (in Computing Laboratory) *Online:* ABI Inform, ASSIA, BIDS, British Humanities Index, Cochrane, EBSCO, EDINA, ERIC, ESTC, IBSS, Index to Theses, Medline, Philosopher's Index, PsycInfo, UKOP, Web of Science, Zetoc & others **Svcs:** ref, document delivery
Stock: bks/720000 incl pamphs; periodcls/3200; slides/132000; illusts/c80000 cartoons; maps/2000; m-forms/52486; audios/2389 cassettes, 543 CDs; videos/2387; CD-ROMs/c100 databases
Classn: LC, some DDC
Pubns: Special Collns (2nd ed); guides & leaflets
Staff: Libns: 15 Other Prof: 4 Non-Prof: 51

Cardiff

S411 🎓 ✚
Cancer Research Wales Library
Velindre NHS Trust, Whitchurch, Cardiff, CF14 2TL (029-2031-6291; *fax:* 029-2031-6927)
Email: library@velindre-tr.wales.nhs.uk

Gov Body: Univ of Wales Coll of Medicine (see **S427**) **Chief:** Libn: Mrs Bernadette Coles BSc(Hons), MSc (bernadette.coles@velindre-tr. wales.nhs.uk)
Entry: membs only **Open:** Mon-Fri 0830-1630
Subj: medicine; nursing; oncology; subjs related to oncology & cancer rsrch **Co-op Schemes:** BLDSC, AWHILES
Equip: fax, copier, 3 clr copiers, 8 computers (all with wd-proc & CD-ROM, 5 with internet) *Online:* CymruWeb & NHSWeb access **Svcs:** info, ref, biblio
Stock: bks/1500; periodcls/54; videos/12 **Acqs Offcr:** Libn, as above
Classn: DDC **Auto Sys:** Voyager
Staff: Libns: 1 Non-Prof: 0.75 **Exp:** £28000 (1999-2000); £30000 (2000-01)

S412 ⚷
Cardiff Naturalists' Society Library
Natl Museum of Wales, Cathays Pk, Cardiff, CF10 3NP (029-2057-3202; *fax:* 029-2057-3216)
Email: john.kenyon@nmgw.ac.uk

Gov Body: Cardiff Naturalists' Soc **Chief:** Hon Libn: Mr John Kenyon BA, MCLIP, FSA, FRHistS
Entry: ref only, adv appt **Open:** Tue-Fri 1000-1700
Subj: sci; nat hist **Collns:** *Archvs:* Morrey Salmon photo archv (ornithology) **Co-op Schemes:** BLDSC
Equip: 2 m-readers, copier
Stock: bks/9900; periodcls/80
Pubns: Cardiff's Wildlife: Six Wildlife Walks in the City (£3.50); Wildlife around Cardiff: Six Further Wildlife Walks
See also NATL MUSEUMS & GALLERIES OF WALES LIB (**S422**)

S413 🎓
Cardiff University Information Services
PO Box 430, Colum Dr, Cardiff, CF1 3XQ (029-2087-4795; *fax:* 029-2037-1921)
Email: library@cardiff.ac.uk
Internet: http://www.cardiff.ac.uk/uwcc/infos/

Gov Body: Univ of Wales, Coll of Cardiff **Chief:** Dir of Info Svcs: Mr Phillip Martin **Dep:** Dep Dir: Mr A. Jenkins
Assoc Libs: contact addr for all libs same as Univ Info Svcs, as above; ABERCONWY LIB, Mgr: Ms Sally Earney (029-2087-4770; *fax:* 029-2087-4575;

 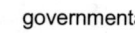

email: abcyliby@cardiff.ac.uk); ARCH LIB (029-2087-5975; *fax*: 029-2087-4926; *email*: archliby@cardiff.ac.uk); ART & SOCIAL STUDIES LIB, Operational Svcs Mgr: Ms Anne Jones (029-2087-4818; 029-2037-1921; *email*: asslliby@cardiff.ac.uk); BIOMEDICAL SCIS LIB (029-2087-4090; *email*: biomedliby@cardiff.ac.uk); BUTE LIB, Site Mgr: Ms Alison Charles (029-2087-4611; *fax*: 029-2087-4192; *email*: buteliby@cardiff.ac.uk); LAW LIB (029-2084-4791; *fax*: 029-2037-1921; *email*: lawliby@cardiff.ac.uk); LEGAL RESOURCE UNIT (029-2087-4942; *email*: lru@cardiff.ac.uk); MUSIC LIB, Music Libn: Ms Gill Jones (029-2087-4387; *fax*: 029-2037-1921; *email*: musicliby@cardiff.ac.uk); SCI LIB (029-2087-4085; *fax*: 029-2087-4995; *email*: sciliby@cardiff.ac.uk); SENGHENNYDD LIB (029-2087-4158; *fax*: 029-2087-4746; *email*: sengliby@cardiff.ac.uk); TREVITHICK LIB, Site Mgr: Ms Liz Nash (029-2087-4586; *fax*: 029-2087-4209; *email*: trevliby@cardiff.ac.uk)
Entry: Univ membs, mutual facilities arrangements with some local Higher Edu insts, other external borrowers on payment of appropriate fee
Open: term: Mon-Fri 0845-2130, Sat 1000-1730; vac: Mon-Fri 0845-1700
Subj: undergrad; postgrad; all subjs *Collns: Bks & Pamphs*: EDC; Salisbury Lib (Welsh & Celtic); BSI; Tennyson Colln (eds); Aylmer Colln (music); Victorian ch's lit *Archvs*: Welsh Music Info Centre; Edward Thomas Colln *Other*: company info svc; Wales Euro Info Centre; Welsh Economy Press Cuttings *Co-op Schemes*: BLDSC, WRLS, SCONUL, Welsh Academic Libs
Equip: 10 m-readers, 4 m-printers, video viewer, fax, 52 copiers, 4 clr copiers, 300 computers (incl wd-proc, internet & CD-ROM), 3 rooms for hire *Online*: c80 svcs, most for Univ membs only
Stock: bks/1000000; periodcls/9000; m-forms/100000; archvs/5000
Classn: DDC, LC *Auto Sys*: Voyager
Pubns: see web site
Staff: Libns: 30 *Other Prof*: 44 *Non-Prof*: 200
Exp: £2.6 mln (1999-2000)

S414
Coleg Glan Hafren, Learning Centre
Trowbridge Rd, Cardiff, CF3 8XZ (029-2025-0250; *fax*: 029-2025-0339)
Internet: http://www.glan-hafren.ac.uk/

Chief: Dir of Learning Svcs: Mrs Pamela M. Evans BA, PGCE(FE), MCLIP (evans_p@glan-hafren.ac.uk) *Dep*: Learning Centre Co-ordinator: Miss Amanda Phillips (phillips_a@glan-hafren.ac.uk)
Assoc Libs: PARADE CENTRE, Coleg Glan Hafren, 24-27 The Parade, Cardiff, CF2 3AB
Open: term: Mon-Thu 0845-1845, Fri 0930-1615; vac: Mon-Fri 1000-1600, depending on staffing
Subj: all subjs; genl; GCSE; A level; undergrad; vocational *Co-op Schemes*: BLDSC, CWLIS
Equip: 2 video viewers, 2 copiers, 134 computers (all with wd-proc & CD-ROM, 39 with internet)
Disabled: Kurzweil, TextHelp *Online*: Infotrac, EMOL, Europe in the Round, Census Data, Ingenta Journals, MIMAS Landmap *Svcs*: info, ref, biblio, IT training, basic skills support, study skills, reprographic svcs, AV technical support
Stock: bks/21500; periodcls/207; pamphs/1300; maps/70; audios/180; videos/1590; CD-ROMs/160
Classn: CLCI *Auto Sys*: Heritage
Staff: Libns: 2 *Other Prof*: 4 *Non-Prof*: 14
Proj: refurbishment of Parade Site LRC

S415
Drama Association of Wales Library
The Old Lib, Singleton Rd, Splott, Cardiff, CF24 2ET (029-2045-2200; *fax*: 029-2045-2277)
Email: aled.daw@virgin.net

Type: membership org *Gov Body*: Arts Council of Wales *Chief*: Memb Svcs Offcr: Ms Teresa Hennessy *Dep*: Memb Svcs Asst: Mr Leon Searle

Entry: membs only *Open*: Mon 1400-1645, Tue-Fri 0945-1300, 1400-1645
Subj: playtexts; biography; criticism; theatre related arts *Collns: Archvs*: Playsets Colln & Lending Colln of the one time British Theatre Assoc *Co-op Schemes*: ILL
Equip: fax, copier, computer (incl wd-proc) *Svcs*: info, ref, printing, script reading, theatre drape hire
Stock: bks/300000; various periodcls, audios & archvs
Pubns: numerous new plays published on regular basis; full details & price list from DAW

S416
The Eva Crane IBRA Library
18 North Rd, Cardiff, CF10 3DT (029-2037-2409; *fax*: 029-2066-5522)
Email: info@ibra.org.uk
Internet: http://www.ibra.org.uk/

Gov Body: Internatl Bee Rsrch Assoc *Chief*: Journals Editor: Dr Pamela Munn BSc, PhD *Other Snr Staff*: Miss Barbara Chick
Entry: membs of the IBRA only; some info searching & photocopying via post also available to non-membs *Open*: Mon-Fri 1000-1630
Subj: bees; apiculture; beekeeping; bee sci; hist of beekeeping; bees in hist *Collns: Other*: extensive colln of abstracts of bee lit (plus original sources & documents where possible) since 1949 *Co-op Schemes*: some ILL
Equip: video viewer, copier (50p per sheet), fax (£1 per sheet), computer (with wd-proc, internet & CD-ROM) *Disabled*: access extremely difficult *Officer-in-Charge*: Finance Mgr: Mr Tony Gruba (agruba@ibra.org.uk) *Svcs*: info, ref, biblio, abstracting
Stock: bks/7500; periodcls/200; CD-ROMs/some; scientific reprints/60000
Classn: IBRA sys *Auto Sys*: ProCite
Pubns: Apicultural Abstracts (journal, 4 pa); Bee World (4 pa); leaflets
Staff: Other Prof: 4 *Non-Prof*: 2

S417
Health Promotion Wales (HybuIechyd Cymru), Library
Ffynnon-Las, Ty Glas Ave, Llanishen, Cardiff, CF14 5EZ (029-2068-1239; *fax*: 029-2075-6000)
Email: hplibrary@wales.gsi.gov.uk
Internet: http://www.hpw.wales.gov.uk/English/library/

Gov Body: Natl Assembly for Wales *Chief*: Libn: Ms Sue Thomas *Dep*: Snr Lib Asst: Ms Sarah Davies
Entry: membership available to anyone in Wales *Open*: Mon-Tue, Thu-Fri 0900-1700, Wed 0900-2000
Subj: health promotion; coronary heart disease; alcoholism; smoking; drug abuse; women's health; schools & young people; epidemiology; public health; health statistics
Equip: copier, computers (incl CD-ROM) *Online*: ASSIA, CINAHL, Cochrane, ERIC, Health for All, HEBS, Medline, PsycInfo *Svcs*: info, ref, training
Stock: bks/5000 (incl reports); periodcls/135
Classn: NLM
Pubns: Lib News (newsletter); Rsrch Bulletins; New Bks Bulletins; Annual Report
Staff: Libns: 1 *Non-Prof*: 2

S418
HTV Cymru Wales, Current Affairs Library
Culverhouse Cross, Cardiff, CF5 6XJ (029-2059-0175; *fax*: 029-2059-0308)
Email: info@htv.co.uk
Internet: http://www.htv.co.uk/

Gov Body: HTV Cymru Wales *Chief*: contact the Libn
Entry: adv appt only *Open*: Mon-Fri 0930-1730
Subj: all subjs; genl; current affairs
Equip: m-reader, m-printer, video viewer (facilities for VHS, Umatic, Betacam), copier, fax, computers (incl wd-proc & CD-ROM) *Online*: FT Profile (charge payable) *Svcs*: info, ref, indexing, translation
Stock: bks/1000; periodcls/75; videos/1500
Staff: Libns: 1 *Other Prof*: 1 *Non-Prof*: 6
See also HTV CYMRU WALES, TELEVISION ARCHV (**A95**)

S419
Museum of Welsh Life Library (Llyfrgell Amgueddfa Werin Cymru)
St Fagans, Cardiff, CF5 6XB (029-2057-3446; *fax*: 029-2057-3490)
Email: post@nmgw.ac.uk
Internet: http://www.nmgw.ac.uk/mwl/

Gov Body: Natl Museum of Wales (Welsh Folk Museum)/Amgueddfol Genedlaethol Cymru (Amgueddfa Werin Cymru) *Chief*: Librarian/Llyfrgellydd: Mr N.L. Walker MA, DipLib, MCLIP
Other Snr Staff: Archivist: Ms Meinwen Ruddock
Assoc Libs: NATL MUSEUMS & GALLERIES OF WALES LIB (see **S422**); small lib at MUSEUM OF THE WELSH WOOLLEN INDUSTRY, Dre-Fach Felindre, Llanysul, Dyfed, SA44 5UP
Entry: ref only, adv appt *Open*: Mon-Fri 0930-1300, 1345-1630, closed weekends & natl hols
Subj: Wales (plus some coverage of wider British & European context): religion (social aspects); sociology; politics; natl ID; migration; economic hist; crime & punishment; edu; commerce; transport; folk customs; folk lore; folk tales; ch's lore; proverbs; sociolinguistics; dialectology; tech; medicine; farming; rural life; cooking & keeping house; crafts; manufacture; bldgs; vernacular arch; folk music; song & dance; the Eisteddfod; leisure activ; geog; topography; biography; genealogy; place-names & personal names; heraldry; Welsh hist; musical instruments; artefacts; clocks; weapons; furniture; textiles; dress & accessories *Collns: Archvs*: large colln of MS & photographic material *Other*: colln of audio & AV recordings, both commercial & generated by the Museum, incl major oral hist colln of c9000 tapes *Co-op Schemes*: BLDSC, CC-IW
Equip: 2 m-readers, copier, computers (incl 1 internet & 1 CD-ROM), audio & AV equip *Svcs*: info, ref, biblio
Stock: bks/35000; periodcls/320; photos/130000; slides/12000; maps/400; audios/9000; videos/300; archvs/110 linear m; various pamphs, m-forms & AVs
Classn: DDC, MMA *Auto Sys*: Adlib Lib
Pubns: catalogue of museum pubns available
Staff: Libns: 1 *Non-Prof*: 0.5

S420
National Assembly for Wales Library
New Crown Bldgs, Cathays Pk, Cardiff, CF10 3NQ (029-2082-3362; *fax*: 029-2082-3122)

Chief: Chief Libn: Ms Rebecca Davies
Assoc Libs: CENTRAL REGISTER OF AIR PHOTOGRAPHY OF WALES (see **S421**)
Entry: ref only, by appt *Open*: Mon-Thu 0830-1700, Fri 0830-1630
Subj: public admin in Wales; industry; planning; transport; health; edu; agric *Collns: Bks & Pamphs*: Parliamentary papers (1880-date); Assembly pubns

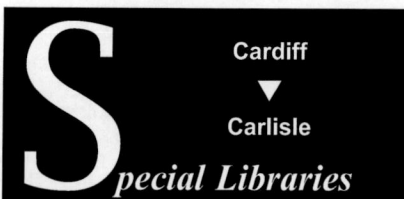

Special Libraries

Cardiff
▼
Carlisle

(Natl Assembly for Wales Lib cont)
Equip: 2 m-readers, m-printer, copier, computers (incl wd-proc & CD-ROM) *Online:* Dialog, BLAISE, POLIS, Datastar, Dialtech, PFDS, Dun & Bradstreet
Stock: bks/80000; periodcls/1100; pamphs/50000; m-forms/30000
Classn: LC *Auto Sys:* Unicorn
Pubns: annual & monthly Assembly pubns list; 7 current awareness monthly bulletins
Staff: Libns: 4 *Non-Prof:* 6

S421
National Assembly for Wales, Central Register of Air Photography of Wales
Planning Div, Room G003, Crown Offices, Cathays Pk, Cardiff, CF10 3NQ (029-2082-3819; *fax:* 029-2082-3080)
Email: Air_Photo_Officer@Wales.gsi.gov.uk

Gov Body: Natl Assembly for Wales (see **S420**)
Chief: Contact: Mr Derek Elliott
Entry: by appt only; please note that hand luggage will be searched *Open:* Mon-Fri by appt
Subj: The Central Register indexes all vertical air survey cover of Wales flown by the RAF, Ordnance Survey, commercial air survey companies & other air survey orgs. The Central Register is the only comprehensive src about air photography of Wales & advises all interested users. The Office holds an extensive colln of aerial photos covering Wales from 1940 at various scales. The base of the colln is the RAF natl survey flown predominantly between Mar-Jul, at 1:10000 scale from 1945-52. To this has been added other RAF cover such as: (i) 1940-45 obliques of South Wales towns & Welsh coastal regions from RAF Medmenham; (ii) 1945-52 & 1959-61 obliques of the Welsh coastline; (iii) natl survey of 1969 at 1:60/62000 scales flown July-Aug; (iv) natl survey of 1981 at 1:50000 scale flown Apr, Jul-Aug; (v) pre-1996 OS 1:7000-1:24000 scales (incl some infra-red from the 1960s tide resurveys at 1:20.25000 scales); (vi) Meridian Airmaps Ltd, Welsh cover 1963-84 at scales from 1:3000 to 1:15000. The Office has continued to update the colln, which now incl extensive cover of Wales flown by: RAF (1988-93 1:25/27000 b/w); CUCAP (1991-92 1:10000 clr); GEONEX (1991-92 1:5/10000 clr & 1996-97 1:25000 clr); BKS (1995 1:20000 b/w); ADAS (1990 1:20000 b/w); J.A. STORY (1983-84 1:10000 clr); Cartographical Svcs (1993 1:6000 clr) & OS (1996 1:8/9000 b/w); Getmapping (1999-2000 1:10000 clr, entirety of Wales, on computer) *Co-op Schemes:* NAPLIB
Equip: stereoscopic viewers, CCTV enlarger
Stock: photos/200000
Pubns: contact prints & enlargements from pre-1979 OS, Meridian Airmaps Ltd. (Welsh cover 1952-84) & RAF films obtainable on prepayment

S422
National Museums and Galleries of Wales, Library
Natl Museum & Gallery Cardiff, Cathays Pk, Cardiff, CF10 3NP (029-2057-3202; *fax:* 029-2057-3216)
Internet: http://www.nmgw.ac.uk/library/

Gov Body: Natl Museums & Galleries of Wales
Chief: Libn: Mr John Kenyon BA, MCLIP, FSA, FRHistS (john.kenyon@nmgw.ac.uk) *Dep:* Asst Libn: Miss Louise Carey BA, DipLib (louise.carey@nmgw.ac.uk)
Assoc Libs: NATL MUSEUMS & GALLERIES OF WALES, DEPT OF INDUSTRY COLLNS CENTRE (see **S2051**); MUSEUM OF WELSH LIFE LIB (see **S419**); small libs at: MUSEUM OF THE WELSH WOOLLEN INDUSTRY, Dre-fach Felindre, Llandysul, Dyfed, SA44 5UP (01559-370929; *fax:* 01559-371592); ROMAN LEGIONARY MUSEUM LIB, High St, Caerleon, Gwent, NP6 1AE (01633-423134; *fax:* 01633-422869); WELSH SLATE MUSEUM (AMGUEDDFA LECHI CYMRU), Llanberis, Gwynedd, LL55 4TY (01286-870630; *fax:* 01286-871906; *email:* slate@nmgw.ac.uk); dept libs (all at above addr): DEPT OF ARCHAEO & NUMISMATICS LIB (029-2057-3229; *fax:* 029-2066-7320); DEPT OF ART LIB (029-2057-3232; *fax:* 029-2057-2351; *email:* art_dept@nmgw.ac.uk); DEPT OF BIODIVERSITY & SYSTEMATIC BIOLOGY (BIOSYB) LIB (029-2057-3344; *fax:* 029-2023-9829; *email:* BioSyB@nmgw.ac.uk); DEPT OF GEOL LIB (029-2057-3213; *fax:* 029-2066-7332)
Entry: ref only, adv appt preferable *Open:* Tue-Fri 1000-1700
Subj: religion (Roman, Celtic etc); botany; geol; zoology; fine & decorative arts; arch; archaeo; numismatics; industrial archaeo; industrial hist; museology; conservation *Collns: Bks & Pamphs:* Willoughby Gardner Lib (early nat hist bks); Gregynog Press Colln; Tomlin Lib (Molluscan rare bks etc); Vaynor Colln (16C-17C astronomy); Welsh Topographical Bks Colln; Cardiff Naturalists' Soc Lib (see **S412**); Cambrian Archaeological Assoc Lib; Monmouthshire Antiquarian Assoc Lib (at Roman Legionary Museum); Vachell Colln (British flowering plants, at BioSyB Lib) *Archvs:* held in depts, not lib, incl: Sowerby letters (zoology); Sir Henry Thomas de la Beche Papers (geol) *Co-op Schemes:* BLDSC, ILL
Equip: 2 m-readers, copier
Stock: bks/185000; periodcls/1200
Classn: DDC
Pubns: Willoughby Gardner Lib (£4.50); Catalogue of the Lib, vol 1: Bks Printed Before 1701 (currently o/p)
Staff: Libns: 2 *Non-Prof:* 2

S423
Queens Dragoon Guards Museum, Library and Archives
The Castle, Cardiff, CF1 2RB (029-2022-2253; *fax:* 029-2022-7611)
Email: curator@qdg.org.uk
Internet: http://www.qdg.org.uk/

Chief: contact the Curator
Entry: ref only *Open:* Mar-Oct: Mon-Thu, Sat-Sun 1000-1800; Nov-Feb: 1000-1630; closed Fri
Subj: military hist; cavalry regiments; regimental hist; regimental records *Collns: Archvs:* records of 1st King's Dragoon Guards & The Queen's Bays/2nd Dragoon Guards (1685-1959); records of 1st The Queen's Dragoon Guards (1959 onwards); correspondence of Field Marshal George Townshend (1724-1807)
Svcs: ref, online rsrch (fees), photographic reproduction (fees)

S424
Royal Welsh College of Music and Drama Library
Castle Grounds, Cathays Pk, Cardiff, CF10 3ER (029-2039-1330; *fax:* 029-2039-1304)
Email: agusjm@rwcmd.ac.uk
Internet: http://library.rwcmd.ac.uk/

Chief: Libn: Mrs Judith Agus BA, BMus, MCLIP
Entry: staff & students *Open:* term: Mon-Thu 0830-2000, Fri 0830-1800, Sat 1000-1400; vac: Mon-Thu 0900-1700, Fri 0900-1600 (vac hrs may vary)
Subj: arts; art hist; music; drama *Co-op Schemes:* ILL
Stock: bks/20000; periodcls/90; audios/5000; videos/300; music scores/24000

S425
South Wales Institute of Engineers, Library
2nd Floor, Empire House, Mount Stuart Sq, Cardiff, CF10 5FN (029-2048-1726; *fax:* 029-2045-1953)
Email: info@swie.org.uk
Internet: http://www.swie.org.uk/

Entry: adv appt *Open:* Tue-Thu 1000-1300, Fri 1000-1300
Subj: eng *Equip:* copier
Pubns: Proceedings of the South Wales Inst of Engineers
Staff: Non-Prof: 2 PT

S426
St Michael's College, Archdeacon Gordon James Library
54 Cardiff Rd, Llandaff, Cardiff, CP5 2YJ (029-2056-3379; *fax:* 029-2057-6377)
Email: info@stmichaels.ac.uk
Internet: http://www.stmichaels.ac.uk/

Chief: Coll Libn: Ms Anna Williams
Entry: by adv appt for non-membs, ref only
Subj: religion; theology; personal papers *Collns: Archvs:* correspondence, diaries & sermon notes of Edward Copleston & Alfred Ollivant (former Bishops of Llandaff)
Equip: copier, computers (incl wd-proc & internet)
Stock: bks/c12000

S427
University of Wales College of Medicine, Sir Herbert Duthrie Library
Heath Pk, Cardiff, CF14 4XN (029-2074-2875; *fax:* 029-2074-3651)
Email: duthrielib@cf.ac.uk
Internet: http://www.uwcm.ac.uk/

Gov Body: Univ of Wales Coll of Medicine *Chief:* Dir of Info Svcs: Mr S.J. Pritchard *Dep:* Dep Dir of Info Svcs: Dr A. Weightman
Assoc Libs: BRIAN COOKE DENTAL LIB (see **S428**); COCHRANE LIB (see **S1785**); NURSING & HEALTHCARE STUDIES LIB (see **S429**); SCHOOL OF NURSING STUDIES LIB (see **S1598**); CANCER RSRCH WALES LIB (see **S411**)
Entry: staff & students of UWCM; NHS staff, GPs & other primary & community health care staff working in Greater Cardiff area; staff & students of other Higher Edu instns may be granted membership on appl; others may apply to Libn for external membership (annual fee) *Open:* Oct-July: Mon-Fri 0900-2100, Sat 0900-1700; Aug-Sept: Mon-Fri 0900-1900, Sat 0900-1230
Subj: medicine; nursing; medical sci; life sci; social sci; subjs allied to medicine *Collns: Bks & Pamphs:* Historical Colln, incl Lloyd-Roberts Colln (hist of medicine, obstetrics, 2000 vols); Health & Safety Colln; UWCM theses; LIS Colln *Co-op Schemes:* ILL, WALIA, CROESO, AWHILES
Equip: video viewer, copier, fax, computers (incl wd-proc & CD-ROM), binding & laminating machines, document scanner, tape-slide viewer, cassette player *Disabled:* Kurzweil, Duels, TextHelp, Dragon Dictate, ZoomText, CCTV

Online: AMED, Cochrane, ERIC, ClinPsyc, Medline, CINAHL, Healthstar, Web of Science, Embase, CancerLit, Health Reference & others *Svcs:* info, ref, biblio
Stock: bks/72000; periodcls/720; maps/46; m-forms/9; AVs/642, incl audios & videos
Classn: DDC *Auto Sys:* Voyager
Staff: Libns: 7 *Non-Prof:* 15

S428
University of Wales College of Medicine, Brian Cooke Dental Library
Dental School, Heath Pk, Cardiff, CF14 4XY (029-2074-2525; *fax:* 029-2074-3834)
Email: DentLib@cf.ac.uk
Internet: http://www.uwcm.ac.uk/

Gov Body: Univ of Wales Coll of Medicine (see **S427**) *Chief:* Dental Libn: Ms Julia Stevens BA, MCLIP *Other Snr Staff:* Lib Assts: Mrs Olwen Kemp, Mrs Anne Clee & Mr Andrew Blackmore
Entry: registered UWCM staff & students; NHS staff employed in Cardiff area *Open:* term: Mon, Thu 0900-2100, Tue, Fri 0900-1730, Wed 0900-1800; vac: Mon, Wed 0900-1800, Tue, Thu-Fri 0900-1730
Subj: dentistry; medicine *Collns: Bks & Pamphs:* UWCM Dental School theses; reports *Archvs:* small historical colln *Co-op Schemes:* AWHILES
Equip: 2 m-readers, fax, video viewer, 2 copiers, 40 computers (all with wd-proc, internet & CD-ROM), 2 binding machines, laminating machine, scanner *Online:* Medline *Svcs:* info, ref, biblio
Stock: bks/6000; periodcls/140; m-forms/40; videos/130; CD-ROMs/30 *Acqs Offcr:* Dental Libn, as above
Classn: own *Auto Sys:* Voyager
Pubns: Core List of Dental Bks Recommended for Purchase by Postgrad Libs (included in Bks for Primary Health Care, £3.95)
Staff: Libns: 1 *Non-Prof:* 3 (1 FT, 2 PT)

S429
University of Wales College of Medicine, Nursing and Healthcare Studies Library
Ty Dewi Sant Bldg, Heath Pk, Cardiff, CF14 4XN (029-2074-2387; *fax:* 029-2075-6431)
Email: HealthcLib@cf.ac.uk
Internet: http://www.uwcm.ac.uk/

Gov Body: Univ of Wales Coll of Medicine (see **S427**) *Chief:* Nursing & Healthcare Studies Libn: Miss Meg Gorman BA, DipLib (gormanm@cf.ac.uk) *Dep:* Asst Site Libn: Ms Elizabeth Morgan (morganec1@cf.ac.uk)
Entry: ref only *Open:* Oct-Jul: Mon-Thu 0845-2000, Fri 0845-1700, Sat 0900-1230; Aug-Sep: Mon-Fri 0845-1700
Subj: undergrad; psy; social sci; nursing; physiotherapy; occupational therapy; radiography; operating dept practice; medical photography *Co-op Schemes:* BLDSC, AWHL
Equip: m-reader, m-printer, fax, video viewer, copiers, computers (incl CD-ROM) *Online:* CINAHL, ASSIA, BNI, Medline, AMED *Svcs:* info, ref
Stock: bks/c18000; periodcls/120; videos/100
Classn: DDC *Auto Sys:* Libertas
Staff: Libns: 2 *Non-Prof:* 4

S430
University of Wales Institute Cardiff, Library and Information Services
Western Ave, Cardiff, CF5 2YB (029-2041-6240; *fax:* 029-2041-6908)
Internet: http://www.uwic.ac.uk/library/

Gov Body: Univ of Wales *Chief:* Head of Lib Div: Mr Paul Riley (priley@uwic.ac.uk) *Dep:* Lib Administrator: Ms Claire Dutfield (cldutfield@uwic.ac.uk)
Assoc (Campus) Libs: COLCHESTER AVE LIB, Colchester Ave, Cardiff, CF23 9XR, Libn: Ms Jenny Welsh (029-2041-6241; *email:* jmwelsh@uwic.ac.uk); CYNCOED LIB, Cyncoed Rd, Cardiff, CF23 6XD, Libn: Mr Stephen Gregory (029-2041-6242; *email:* sgregory@uwic.ac.uk); HOWARD GDNS LIB, Howard Gdns, Cardiff, CF24 1SP, Libn: Ms Arwen Thomas (029-2041-6243; *email:* ajthomas@uwic.ac.uk); LLANDAFF LIB, addr as above, Libn: Rev Jennifer Welsh (029-2041-6244; *email:* jwelsh@uwic.ac.uk)
Entry: student or staff of UWIC, memb of WALIA Scheme, external membership on payment of annual fee, ref only for non-membs *Open:* Colchester Avenue Lib: Mon-Thu 0900-2100, Fri 0900-1700, Sat 0900-1300; Cyncoed Lib: Mon-Thu 0845-2015, Fri 0845-1700, Sat 0900-1300; Howard Gardens Lib: Mon-Thu 0900-2030, Fri 0900-1700, Sat 0900-1300; Llandaff Lib: Mon-Thu 0845-2100, Fri 0845-1700, Sat 0900-1300; vac: opening hrs vary
Subj: undergrad; postgrad; Colchester Avenue Lib: business; computing; food sci; food tech; tourism & hospitality; Cyncoed Lib: edu; art edu; physical edu; human movement; sport studies; Howard Gardens Lib: art; design; Llandaff Lib: applied sci; health; social sci; art; design; product design; eng design *Co-op Schemes:* BLDSC, WALIA, Interlending Wales, UK Libs Plus, SCONUL
Equip: m-reader, m-printer, video viewer, copier, computers (incl wd-proc & CD-ROM) *Online:* EBSCO Masterfile, OVID, BIDS-ISI, IBSS, Journals Online, Uncover, IDEAL, Mintel, Pollution Abstracts, ISI Web of Science, EDINA Arts Abstracts *Svcs:* info, ref
Stock: bks/280000; periodcls/1200; slides/88000; AVs/various, incl audios & videos
Classn: DDC *Auto Sys:* Talis
Staff: Libns: 14 *Non-Prof:* 16

S431
Welsh Development Agency, Library and Information Unit
Principality House, The Friary, Cardiff, CF10 3FE (029-2082-8720; *fax:* 029-2082-8775)
Internet: http://www.wda.co.uk/

Chief: Lib & Info Svcs Mgr: post vacant *Dep:* Info Offcr: Ms Nia Francis
Assoc Libs: ARCHVS DEPT, QED Centre, Treforest Industrial Est, Pontypridd, Mid Glamorgan, CF37 5YR; NORTH WALES LIB, Unit 7, Ffordd Richard Davies, St Asaph Business Pk, St Asaph, Clwyd, LL17 0LJ; MID WALES LIB, Ladywell House, Newtown, Powys, SY16 1JB; LEGAL LIB, addr as above; LAND DIV LIB, addr as above
Entry: ref only, adv appt *Open:* Mon-Fri 0900-1700
Subj: Wales: econ; business *Co-op Schemes:* ILL
Equip: fax, copiers, clr copier, computers (incl wd-proc, internet & CD-ROM) *Online:* Dialog, Lexis, Kompass, Dun & Bradstreet, XLS, Profound, FT Profile, ICC, Onesource *Svcs:* info, ref, biblio, indexing
Stock: bks/9000; periodcls/500; videos/200; CD-ROMs/20
Classn: own *Auto Sys:* Heritage *Staff: Libns:* 2

S432
Welsh Music Information Centre
Ty Cerdd, 15 Mount Stuart Sq, Cardiff (029-2046-5700; *fax:* 029-2046-2733)
Email: wmic@tycerdd.org
Internet: http://www.tycerdd.org/

Gov Body: funded by the Arts Council of Wales; part of the Ty Cerdd (Music Centre Wales) network *Chief:* contact the Info Offcr
Entry: adv appt *Open:* Mon-Fri 1000-1600
Subj: music; Welsh music; Welsh composers
Collns: Other: scores by Welsh composers & other sheet music of Welsh interest; audio recordings
Equip: copier

Carlisle

S433
Carlisle Cathedral Library
7 The Abbey, Carlisle, Cumbria, CA3 8TZ (01228-548151; *fax:* 01228-547049)
Email: office@carlislecathedral.org.uk
Internet: http://www.carlislecathedral.org.uk/

Gov Body: The Chapter of Carlisle Cathedral
Chief: Canon Libn: The Revd Canon David Weston PhD
Assoc Libs: DEAN & CHAPTER ARCHVS, held at Cumbria Record Office, Carlisle (see **A98**)
Entry: by appt
Subj: local study (Cumbria, ecclesiastical & topographical); religion; Christian theology; Greek & Latin authors; some sci; some English lit; ecclesiastical hist *Collns: Bks & Pamphs:* English Caroline Divines; phil & sci (17C-18C, incl early pubns of the Royal Soc); British hist & antiquities; ecclesiastical & secular hist of Cumbria; transactions of Cumberland & Westmorland Antiquarian & Archaeological Soc; Crosby Ravensworth Parish Lib; Burgh-by-Sands Parish Lib *Co-op Schemes:* BLDSC, ILL
Equip: copier
Stock: bks/8200 *Acqs Offcr:* Canon Libn, as above
Classn: author catalogue in MSS (1966, locally compiled); STC Catalogue (Cathedral Libs Scheme); Shelf Lists (1995 onwards, locally compiled)
Staff: Non-Prof: 1 *Exp:* £350 (1999-2000); £500 (2000-01)

S434
Carlisle College Library
Victoria Pl, Carlisle, Cumbria, CA1 1HS (01228-822760)
Email: library@carlisle.ac.uk
Internet: http://www.carlisle.ac.uk/

Chief: Lib Mgr: Ms Sally Frost (sfrost@carlisle.ac.uk) *Dep:* Asst Libn: vacant
Entry: ref only; external users can also use computer facilities for a fee *Open:* term: Mon-Thu 0845-2000, Fri 0845-1600, Sat 0900-1200
Subj: all subjs; genl; GCSE; A level; undergrad; vocational *Collns: Bks & Pamphs:* BSI (incomplete) *Co-op Schemes:* BLDSC
Equip: copier (5p), 36 computers *Online:* Infotrac Onefile & Newspapers, Citymutual GNVQ databases, GMID, Britannica *Officer-in-Charge:* Lib Mgr, as above *Svcs:* info, ref, biblio
Stock: bks/16000; periodcls/80; maps/20; videos/600; CD-ROMs/15 *Acqs Offcr:* Lib Mgr, as above
Classn: DDC *Auto Sys:* CAIRS
Pubns: Lib Guide; various subj guides
Staff: Libns: 2 *Non-Prof:* 4

S435
Cumberland Infirmary, Education Centre Library
Cumberland Infirmary, Carlisle, Cumbria, CA2 7HY (01228-814879; *fax:* 01228-814843)
Email: library@ncumbria-acute.nhs.uk
Internet: http://www.northcumbriahealth.nhs.uk/

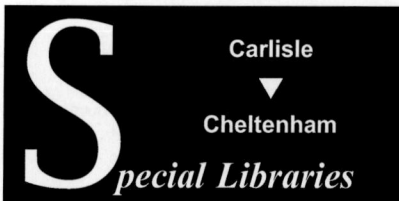

Special Libraries

Carlisle ▼ Cheltenham

(Cumberland Infirmary, Edu Centre Lib cont)
Gov Body: North Cumbria Acute Hosps NHS
Trust *Chief:* Lib Svcs Mgr: Mrs Sheila Marsh
Entry: all NHS staff; others by arrangement
Open: Mon-Thu 0900-1700, Fri 0900-1630
Subj: medicine; nursing; surgery; healthcare; genl
practice *Co-op Schemes:* BLDSC, BMA, HLN,
LIHNN, NULJ
Equip: m-reader, fax, copier, 14 computers (incl 5
wd-proc, 5 internet & 4 CD-ROM) *Online:* NHSNet
access to Medline, CINAHL, Embase, Martindale,
e-journals etc *Svcs:* info, ref, biblio
Stock: bks/10300; periodcls/200; videos/104; CD-
ROMs/35
Classn: NLM *Auto Sys:* EOSi T-Series
Pubns: Lib Users Guide; Journal Holdings List;
Medline Searching; CINAHL Searching (all free)
Staff: Libns: 0.94 *Non-Prof:* 2.35

S436
**Cumbria Institute of the Arts
Library**
(formerly Cumbria Coll of Art & Design)
Brampton Rd, Carlisle, Cumbria, CA3 9AY (01228-
400312; *fax:* 01228-514491)
Email: info@cumbria.ac.uk
Internet: http://www.cumbriacad.ac.uk/

Chief: Libn: Ms Clare Daniel MA, MCLIP
Entry: students & staff of Coll; ref only for others,
with no access to elec sources *Open:* term: Mon-
Thu 0900-2000, Fri 0900-1600, Sat 0900-1300;
vac: Mon-Fri 0900-1600
Subj: phil; psy; social sci; lang; tech; arts; lit; geog;
hist; archaeo; local hist *Collns: Bks & Pamphs:*
Cumberland & Westmorland Antiquarian &
Archaeo Soc Collns (from 19C, c6000 vols) *Other:*
AV colln *Co-op Schemes:* BLDSC, CHELPS,
LINC
Equip: video viewers, copier, computers (incl
internet & CD-ROM) *Online:* BHI, Design &
Applied Arts Index, EDINA Art Abstracts, Ingenta,
IBSS, Zetoc *Svcs:* ref
Stock: bks/20000; periodcls/200; slides/33000;
audios/100; videos/600
Classn: DDC *Auto Sys:* Talis
Staff: Libns: 1 *Other Prof:* 2 *Non-Prof:* 1

S437 ✚
**North Lakeland Healthcare NHS
Trust Library**
Geltwood House, The Carleton Clinic, Carlisle,
Cumbria, CA1 3SX (01228-602107; *fax:* 01228-
602017)
Email: val.bye@nlhc-tr.northy.nhs.uk

Gov Body: North Lakeland Healthcare NHS Trust
Chief: Libn: Mrs Valerie Bye BA, MCLIP
Entry: staff of Trust *Open:* staffed: Mon, Thu
0945-1600, Tue 0945-1245, Fri 0945-1445; access
for membs at other times
Subj: social sci; community care; counselling;
psychiatry; psy; mgmt *Co-op Schemes:* BLDSC,
HLN, PLCS
Equip: copier & clr copier (not in lib), computer
(with wd-proc, internet & CD-ROM) *Svcs:* info, ref,
biblio
Stock: bks/1000; periodcls/50
Classn: DDC *Staff: Libns:* 0.5

S438 🎓
St Martin's College, Carlisle Library
Fusehill St, Carlisle, Cumbria, CA1 2HG (01228-
616218; *fax:* 01228-616263)
Email: info.services@ucsm.ac.uk
Internet: http://www.ucsm.ac.uk/library/

Gov Body: St Martin's Coll *Chief:* Snr Info Offcr:
Ms Shirley Green (sh.green@ucsm.ac.uk) *Other
Snr Staff:* Info Offcr (Media Svcs): Mr Bob
Finlayson (b.finlayson@ucsm.ac.uk); Info Offcr
(Lib): Ms Irene Morris (i.morris@ucsm.ac.uk)
Assoc Libs: AMBLESIDE SITE LIB (see **S33**);
HAROLD BRIDGES LIB (main lib, see **S886**)
Entry: students of St Martin's Coll; external
borrowing on payment of annual subscription
Open: term: Mon-Thu 0830-1745, Fri 0830-1645,
Sat 1300-1645; vac: Mon-Fri 0900-1645
Subj: edu; teaching; health; nursing; applied social
scis; humanities *Collns: Bks & Pamphs:* Teaching
Practice Colln
Equip: video viewer, copier, computers, binding &
laminating facilities
Classn: Bliss *Auto Sys:* Talis
Staff: Libns: 3 *Non-Prof:* 12

Carmarthen

S439 🏛️🏛️
**Carmarthenshire County Museum
Library**
Abergwili, Carmarthen, SA31 2JG (01267-231691;
fax: 01267-223830)
Email: cdelaney@carmarthenshire.gov.uk
Internet: http://www.carmarthenshire.gov.uk/

Gov Body: Carmarthenshire County Council (see
P25) *Chief:* Heritage Mgr: Mr C. Delaney BSc,
FMA *Dep:* Snr Museums Offcr: Ms A. Dorsett BA,
AMA
Entry: by appt *Open:* Mon-Sat 1000-1630
Subj: Carmarthenshire: local hist; archaeo;
museology *Collns: Bks & Pamphs:* former colln of
the Carmarthenshire Antiquarian Soc *Other:* photo
& slide colln
Equip: fax, copier *Svcs:* info
Stock: bks/7000; photos/3000; slides/2000
Classn: author index

S440 🎓
**Trinity College Carmarthen,
Library**
College Rd, Carmarthen, SA31 3EP (01267-
676780; *fax:* 01267-676766)
Email: library@trinity-cm.ac.uk
Internet: http://www.trinity-cm.ac.uk/english/
library/

Gov Body: Coleg y Drindod Caerfyrddin/Trinity
Coll Carmarthen *Chief:* Learning & Info
Resources Mgr: Ms Elinor Le Bourdon
(e.lebourdon@trinity-cm.ac.uk) *Dep:* Snr Learning
Resources Adviser: Ms Sally Wilkinson
(s.a.wilkinson@trinity-cm.ac.uk)
Entry: staff & students; external borrowing
available *Open: Lib:* term: Mon-Thu 0845-2100,
Fri 0845-1800, Sun 1500-2000; vac: Mon-Thu
0900-1700, Fri 0900-1630; *Teaching Resources
Centre:* term: Mon-Thu 0845-2100, Fri 0845-2000,
Sat 1200-1600; vac: Mon-Thu 0900-1700, Fri
0900-1630
Subj: all subjs; undergrad; postgrad *Co-op
Schemes:* BLDSC, WALIA, CROESO, SCONUL
vac scheme, UK Libs Plus
Equip: m-readers, video viewer, copier, clr copier,
computers (incl internet & CD-ROM) *Online:*
various CD-ROMs; network svcs via JANET &
Internet
Stock: bks/110000
Classn: DDC *Auto Sys:* Dynix

Carshalton

S441 ✚
St Helier Hospital, Hirson Library
Wrythe Ln, Carshalton, Surrey, SM5 1AA (020-
8296-2430; *fax:* 020-8641-9417)

Gov Body: Epsom & St Helier NHS Trust *Chief:*
Lib Svcs Mgr: Mr Edward George MA(Cantab),
MA(Sheffield), MCLIP (egeorge@sthelier.sghms.
ac.uk) *Dep:* Dep Lib Svcs Mgr: Mr Gordon Smith
BA, MCLIP (gsmith@sthelier.sghms.ac.uk) *Other
Snr Staff:* Projs & Development Libn: Mr Morco
Isetta MA, PGDip, MCLIP (misetta@sthelier.
sghms.ac.uk)
Assoc Libs: EPSOM HOSP, THE SALLY
HOWELL LIB (see **S658**)
Entry: ref only by written appl for non-membs
Open: Mon-Fri 0830-1830
Subj: medicine (esp renal medicine); nursing;
health admin *Co-op Schemes:* BLDSC, BMA,
NULJ
Equip: copier, fax, computers (incl wd-proc & CD-
ROM), scanner *Online:* Medline, CINAHL & others
Stock: bks/2000; periodcls/200; videos/90
Classn: NLM (mod) *Staff: Libns:* 2 *Non-Prof:* 0.7

Chalfont St Giles

S442 🔑
Milton's Cottage Library
Deanway, Chalfont St Giles, Buckinghamshire,
HP8 4JH (01494-872313)
Email: info@miltonscottage.org
Internet: http://www.miltonscottage.org/

Gov Body: Milton Cottage Trust *Chief:* Libn: Miss
M. Hailey LLB, MCLIP *Dep:* Curator: E.A. Dawson
Entry: adv appt *Open:* Mar-Oct: Tue-Fri 1000-
1300, 1400-1800; vac: Nov-Feb
Subj: genl; GCSE; A level; undergrad; postgrad;
religion; social sci; lang; arts; lit; geog; hist; politics
Collns: Bks & Pamphs: 17C Milton 1st eds; early
& recent Milton eds; foreign translations of Milton's
works *Archvs:* Milton Papers
Stock: bks/400; periodcls/100; photos/40; illusts/
various; pamphs/various; maps/15
Pubns: Eden Renewed (£12); Life of John Milton
(£12.50); Collected Poems (£6.99); Poetry
Selection (£1); Paradise Lost (£4.99); Milton & The
English Revolution (£14.99)
Staff: Libns: 1 *Other Prof:* 1

Chatham

S443 🎓
**Mid-Kent College of Higher and
Further Education, Library and
Information Centres**
Horsted, Maidstone Rd, Chatham, Kent, ME5 9UQ
(01634-830633; *fax:* 01634-830224)
Email: library@midkent.ac.uk
Internet: http://www.midkent.ac.uk/

Chief: Info & Resources Mgr: Mr David Stanley
Other Snr Staff: Coll Libn: Mr Andrew Bryan
Assoc Libs: CITY WAY LIB & INFO CENTRE, City
Way, Rochester, Kent, ME1 2AD, Site Libn: Mrs
Angela Jones MCLIP (01634-830644); OAKWOOD
PK LIB & INFO CENTRE, Tonbridge Rd, Maidstone, Kent, ME16 8AQ (01622-691555)
Entry: students must produce proof that they are
studying at the coll; public welcome to use facilities
for ref only, no appt necessary *Open:* Mon-Thu
0830-2000, Fri 0830-1800; vac: Mon-Fri 0900-1600
Subj: genl; GCSE; A level; undergrad; phil; psy;
social scis; lang; sci; maths; tech; arts; lit; geog;
hist *Collns: Other:* BSI
Equip: m-reader, m-printer, 3 video viewers, fax
(staff only), copier, clr copier (reprographics: staff &
students only) *Online:* EBSCO, CAS Online

Stock: bks/65000; periodcls/300; videos/500; CD-ROMs/30; archvs/200 titles
Classn: UDC Auto Sys: AutoLib
Staff: Libns: 3 Non-Prof: 17

Natural Resources Institute, Library and Information Service
See UNIV OF GREENWICH, INFO & LIB SVCS (**S1439**)

S444
Royal Engineers Library
Brompton Barracks, Chatham, Kent, ME4 4UX (01634-822416; fax: 01634-822419)

Gov Body: Instn of Royal Engineers Chief: Libn: Col J.E. Nowers BSc, FIMgt Dep: Acting Lib Curator: Ms Lindsey Roxburgh
Entry: adv appt Open: Mon, Wed, Fri 0900-1230, 1330-1700
Subj: generalities; military eng; military hist (hist of Royal Engineers & military eng worldwide); fortifications; bridging; local study (Medway Towns)
Collns: Bks & Pamphs: large Peninsular War section; military eng pamphs Archvs: archvs & hist of Corps of Royal Engineers, incl: Garrison letter bks (18C-19C); WW1 diaries of most Royal Engineers units; some personal papers of personnel; MS papers of T.W.J. Connolly (historian) Other: large colln of photos (1855 onwards) of local area & military eng worldwide, incl work by Royal Engineers photographers Fentons & Robertsons; map & plan colln
Equip: copier (25p per sheet) Svcs: info, ref
Stock: bks/30000; photos/c200000; pamphs/500; maps/500; archvs/50 linear m Acqs Offcr: Acting Lib Curator, as above
Classn: UDC Staff: Non-Prof: 2
See also ROYAL ENGINEERS MUSEUM, LIB & ARCHVS (**S445**) & TECHNICAL INFO CENTRE ROYAL ENGINEERS (**S1646**)

S445
Royal Engineers Museum, Library and Archives
c/o Brompton Barracks, Chatham, Kent, ME4 4UX (01634-406397; fax: 01634-822371)

Chief: Curator: Dr John Rhodes
Assoc Libs: museum is at Prince Arthur Rd, Gillingham, Kent; use above addr for correspondence
Subj: military hist; regimental hist; military eng; personal papers Collns: Archvs: papers of serving & former serving offcrs of Royal Engineer Corps, incl Genl Sir John Burgoyne papers; Genl Sir John Hawkins papers; Genl Sir Edward Stanton papers; Major Genl Sir Elliot Wood papers; papers, notebks & correspondence of Major Genl Gordon; diaries, journals & papers of offcrs & other ranks (18C-20C) Other: plans, maps, surveys etc relating to the work of the Royal Engineer Corps & predecessors
See also ROYAL ENGINEERS LIB (**S444**) & TECHNICAL INFO CENTRE ROYAL ENGINEERS (**S1646**)

S446
World Naval Base – Chatham Historic Dockyard Trust Library
The Historic Dockyard Trust, Chatham Dockyard, Chatham, Kent, ME4 4TZ (01634-823800; fax: 01634-823801)
Email: info@chdt.org.uk
Internet: http://www.chdt.org.uk/

Gov Body: Chatham Historic Dockyard Trust
Chief: Libn: Mr John Chambers

Assoc Libs: TRUST ARCHVS, contact as above; CHATHAM DOCKYARD HISTORICAL SOC LIB & ARCHVS, contact as above
Entry: adv appt
Subj: Royal Navy; maritime hist; naval hist
Collns: Bks & Pamphs: Chatham Dockyard Historical Soc Colln Archvs: Chatham Dockyard Archvs (to 1985); Trust papers (since 1985); Chatham Dockyard Historical Soc Archvs Other: Chatham Dockyard arch plans & drawings; photo colln (Chatham Dockyard Historical Soc)
Equip: m-reader, copier, video viewer Svcs: info, ref
Stock: bks/15000; photos/2000
Classn: by subj Staff: Libns: 1

Chelmsford

S447
Broomfield Hospital, Warner Library
Court Rd, Chelmsford, Essex, CM1 7ET (01245-443651; fax: 01245-442140)

Gov Body: Mid Essex Hosps Health Svc Trust
Chief: Medical Libn: Ms Carol Roberts BSc, MCLIP
Assoc Libs: small study lib at St Johns Hosp (not separately staffed)
Entry: Trust employees; other health personnel ref only by appt Open: Mon-Fri 0900-1730
Subj: medicine & related areas
Equip: m-reader, fax, copier, computers (incl wd-proc & internet) Online: Dialog
Stock: bks/3000; periodcls/100
Classn: NLM Auto Sys: DBTextworks 2020
Staff: Libns: 1 Non-Prof: 2.5

S448
Chelmsford Cathedral Library
The Cathedral Office, Guy Harlings, New St, Chelmsford, Essex, CM1 1TY (01245-263660; fax: 01245-294499)

Gov Body: The Dean & Chapter of Chelmsford Cathedral Chief: Canon Theologian & Cathedral Libn: Revd Canon Andrew Knowles Dep: Cathedral Libn & Archivist: Dr Pachomias (Robert) Penkett
Entry: Lending Lib: unconditional access; Rsrch Lib: adv appt Open: Rsrch Lib (Essex bks, pamphs, archvs & Knightbridge Theological Lib) open by appt
Subj: ethics (moral phil); religion; arch; music
Collns: Bks & Pamphs: The Knightbridge Lib (mainly Puritan theology & patristics, c600 works, 16C-18C); Essex Colln (mainly Church hist of Chelmsford diocese) Archvs: correspondence relating to the Cathedral Co-op Schemes: informal liaison with Essex County Libs (see **P51**), e.g., inclusion in their Union List of Serials
Equip: copier, computer (with wd-proc)
Stock: bks/6500; periodcls/24; photos/1000; pamphs/1600; maps/12; prints & plans/500
Classn: DDC

S449
Writtle College Library
Lordship Rd, Writtle, Chelmsford, Essex, CM1 3RR (01245-424245; fax: 01245-420456)
Email: library@writtle.ac.uk
Internet: http://www.writtle.ac.uk/library/

Gov Body: Writtle Coll Chief: Head of Learning Info Svcs: Ms Rachel Hewings BSc, DipLib, MCLIP, DMS
Entry: ref free for public, external borrowing £20 pa; other students via UK Libs Plus access scheme Open: term: Mon-Thu 0830-2030, Fri 0830-2130, Sat 0930-1600, Sun 1330-1800; vac: Mon-Fri 0830-1630

Subj: agric; hortic; land-based industries Co-op Schemes: UK Libs Plus
Equip: copiers, computers (incl internet)
Disabled: CCTV scanner Online: Agricola, AHIS, BIDS, BNet, CCTA, COPAC, EEVL, Harper Adams Agricultural Resources, IDEAL, Medline Plus, NISS, SOSIG, Web of Science Svcs: ref, careers info
Stock: bks/50000; periodcls/500; maps/250; CD-ROMs/6; theses/200
Staff: Libns: 4 Non-Prof: 6

Cheltenham

S450
Bristol and Gloucestershire Archaeological Society Library
Univ of Gloucestershire, Francis Close Hall, Swindon Rd, Cheltenham, Gloucestershire, GL50 4AZ (01242-543496)
Email: archives@glos.ac.uk
Internet: http://home.freeuk.com/bgas/library.htm

Gov Body: Bristol & Gloucestershire Archaeological Soc Chief: Hon Libn: Mr Steve Bailey BA(Hons), MA(Dist)
Entry: ref only for non-membs Open: Mon-Fri 0900-1645; non-membs may have access only when the Libn is present
Subj: local studies (Avon & Gloucestershire); local hist; archaeo; county hists; arch; geog
Equip: m-reader, copier, clr copier, computers
Stock: bks/c6000; periodcls/77; pamphs/c1000; maps/c50
Classn: DDC Auto Sys: Unicorn
Pubns: Transactions of the BGAS (free to membs); Gloucestershire Record Series (£30 per vol)
Staff: Other Prof: 1

S451
Cheltenham Art Gallery and Museum, Library and Archive Collections
Clarence St, Cheltenham, Gloucestershire, GL50 3JT (01242-237431; fax: 01242-262334)
Email: artgallery@cheltenham.gov.uk
Internet: http://www.cheltenhammuseum.org.uk/

Type: local govt Gov Body: Cheltenham Borough Council Chief: Museum & Collns Mgr: Dr S. Blake
Entry: archv collns by appt only Open: Mon-Sat 1000-1720, Sun 1400-1620; closed Bank Hols & Easter Sun
Subj: local hist (Cheltenham & Gloucestershire); social hist; archaeo; nat hist; ethnography; decorative arts Collns: Archvs: Holst Archv (see also **A103**); Arts & Crafts Movement Archv Other: theatre playbills (c3400, 1791-1920)
Equip: copier Disabled: wheelchair access Svcs: reprographic svcs

S452
Countryside Agency Library
John Dower House, Crescent Pl, Cheltenham, Gloucestershire, GL50 3RA (01242-521381; fax: 01242-584270)
Email: info@countryside.gov.uk
Internet: http://www.countryside.gov.uk/

Chief: Libn: Miss J.V. Bacon MSc, MCLIP
Entry: currently unavailable to public
Subj: countryside conservation; informal countryside rec; town & country planning; agric; forestry; tourism; rural econ; rural social conditions
Co-op Schemes: ILL
Equip: copier
Stock: bks/20000; periodcls/250
Classn: LC Staff: Libns: 3 Non-Prof: 3

Special Libraries

Cheltenham ▼ Chichester

S453 ✚

Gloucestershire Hospitals NHS Trust Staff Library
(formerly East Gloucestershire NHS Trust Staff Lib)
Alexandra House, Cheltenham Genl Hosp, Sandford Rd, Cheltenham, Gloucestershire, GL51 7AN (01242-273036; *fax:* 01242-273060)
Email: dorothy.curtis@egnhst.org.uk

Gov Body: Gloucestershire Hosps NHS Trust
Chief: Libn: Mrs Dorothy Curtis BA, DipRSA, MCLIP
Entry: ref only, adv appt *Open:* Mon-Fri 0800-1700 (staff access 24 hrs)
Subj: postgrad; medicine; nursing; professions allied to medicine *Co-op Schemes:* BLDSC, SWRLIN, NULJ
Equip: m-reader, video viewer, fax, copier, computers (incl 4 internet & 4 CD-ROM) *Online:* Swice (membs only) *Svcs:* info (membs only)
Stock: bks/3500; periodcls/172; slides/20 sets; videos/60
Classn: NLM *Auto Sys:* Headfast
Staff: Libns: 2 *Non-Prof:* 0.9

S454 🎓

University of Gloucestershire, Learning Centres
Park Learning Centre, Park Campus, The Park, Cheltenham, Gloucestershire, GL50 2QF (01242-543458; *fax:* 01242-543492)
Email: lcinfopark@glos.ac.uk
Internet: http://www.glos.ac.uk/

Chief: Head of Learning Centres: Ms Ann Mathie BA, MPhil, MCLIP (amathie@glos.ac.uk) *Dep:* User Svcs Team Mgr: Mr Terry Smith (tsmith@glos. ac.uk) *Other Snr Staff:* Info Svcs Team Leader: Mrs Ann Cummings (acummings@glos.ac.uk); Info Svcs Team Leader (ICT): Mr Scott Jordan (sjordan@glos.ac.uk)
Assoc Libs: PARK LEARNING CENTRE, addr as above; FRANCIS CLOSE HALL LEARNING CENTRE, Swindon Rd, Cheltenham, Gloucester-shire, GL50 4AZ; PITTVILLE LEARNING CENTRE, Albert Rd, Cheltenham, Gloucestershire, GL52 3JG; OXSTALLS LEARNING CENTRE, Oxstalls Ln, Gloucester, GL2 9HW; UNIV ARCHVS, Francis Close Hall, Swindon Rd, Cheltenham, Gloucestershire, GL50 4AZ (01242-543496; *email:* archives@glos.ac.uk)
Entry: ref only, unless by prior appt & on payment of fee *Open:* term: Mon, Wed-Thu 0845-2100, Tue 1000-2100, Fri 0845-2000, Sat 0900-1600, Sun 1200-1600; vac: Mon, Wed-Fri 0900-1700, Tue 1000-1700; hrs vary at other Learning Centres; *Archvs:* Mon, Wed-Fri 0900-1645, Tue 1030-1645
Subj: all subjs; undergrad; postgrad; generalities; local studies (Gloucestershire, Cotswolds, Avon)
Collns: Bks & Pamphs: Bristol & Gloucestershire Archaeological Soc Lib (see **S450**); Cherrington Colln (edu & psy journals); Dymock Poets Colln; James Elroy Flecker Colln; Whittington Press Colln; Artists' Bks Colln *Archvs:* Univ Archvs, incl records of the Coll of St Paul & St Mary & other predecessors; Dymock Poets Archv *Co-op Schemes:* BLDSC, UK Libs Plus, Gloucestershire Learning Network, SWHELS
Equip: 2 m-readers, 2 m-printers, 8 copiers, 2 clr copiers, 6 video viewers, 330 computers (all with wd-proc, internet & CD-ROM) *Disabled:* ZoomText, Inspiration, TextHelp Read & Write, Kurzweil 3000

Officer-in-Charge: User Svcs Team Mgr, as above
Svcs: info, ref, biblio
Stock: bks/239416; periodcls/3364; slides/95000; m-forms/2900; videos/2500; CD-ROMs/15 *Acqs Offcr:* Info Svcs Team Leader, as above
Classn: DDC *Auto Sys:* Sirsi
Staff: Libns: 13.25 *Other Prof:* 1 *Non-Prof:* 45.49
Exp: £480000 (2000-01)

Chertsey

S455 ✚

Ashford and St Peter's Hospitals NHS Trust, Health Sciences Library
Postgrad Edu Centre, St Peter's Hosp, Guildford Rd, Chertsey, Surrey, KT16 0PZ (01932-723213; *fax:* 01932-723197)
Internet: http://stlis.thenhs.com/hln/surrey/ascy.htm

Gov Body: Ashford & St Peter's Hosps NHS Trust
Chief: Lib & Knowledge Svcs Mgr: Mrs Sylvia Stafford MCLIP (sylvia.stafford@asph.nhs.uk)
Dep: Asst Libn: Rosemary Herring BA, MA, DipLib (rosemary.herring@asph.nhs.uk) *Other Snr Staff:* Ms Sandy Komiliados BA, DipLib (sandy.komiliados@asph.nhs.uk)
Assoc Libs: ASHFORD HOSP HEALTH SVCS LIB, Edu Centre, Ashford Hosp, London Rd, Ashford, Middlesex, TW15 3AA (01784-884314; *fax:* 01784-884588)
Entry: membership open to staff of: Ashford & St Peter's NHS Trust; North West Surrey Mental Health Partnership NHS Trust; North Surrey PCT; Woking Area PCT; Surrey Ambulance Svc NHS Trust; Surrey & Sussex Strategic Health Authority
Open: Mon-Fri 0900-1700
Subj: medicine; nursing; health care; health mgmt; NHS *Co-op Schemes:* BLDSC, ILL, NULJ, HLN, PLCS
Equip: m video viewer, copier, fax, computers (incl wd-proc, internet & CD-ROM) *Svcs:* info, ref, biblio, alerting svcs, lit searching, info skills training
Stock: bks/16000; periodcls/230; videos/various; CD-ROMs/various
Classn: NLM *Auto Sys:* Heritage & DBTextworks
Staff: Libns: 3 *Non-Prof:* 2.5

Chester

S456 🔑 🖐

Chester Cathedral Library
c/o Cathedral Office, 12 Abbey Sq, Chester, Cheshire, CH1 2HU (01244-324756; *fax:* 01244-341110)
Email: office@chestercathedral.org.uk
Internet: http://www.chestercathedral.org.uk/

Gov Body: The Cathedral Chapter *Chief:* Cathedral Libn: The Revd Canon L. Roy Barker MA
Entry: bona fide rsrchers may apply to Cathedral Libn *Open:* closed for continuing conservation programme until 2004; open by appt
Subj: Chester & Cheshire; phil; psy; religion; sci; maths; lit; geog; hist *Collns: Bks & Pamphs:* Sanders Colln; Bishop Pearson Colln; Bishop Jacobson Colln; Bishop Wilson Colln
Equip: copier, computer
Stock: bks/c10000
Staff: 4 retired (voluntary) profs + c20 trained voluntary non-profs *Exp:* variable
Proj: extension to 2 medieval rooms in 2003

S457 🎓

Chester College, Learning Resources
Parkgate Rd, Chester, Cheshire, CH1 4BJ (01244-375444; *fax:* 01244-392820)
Email: library.enquiries@chester.ac.uk
Internet: http://www.chester.ac.uk/lr/

Gov Body: Chester Coll of Higher Edu *Chief:* Dir of Learning Resources: Mrs Christine Stockton BA, MBA, MCLIP
Assoc Libs: SCHOOL OF NURSING & MID-WIFERY LIB, Arrowe Park Hosp (see **S2134**); SCHOOL OF NURSING & MIDWIFERY LIB, Countess of Chester Hosp (see **S459**); LEIGHTON HOSP, JOINT EDU & TRAINING LIB (see **S506**)
Entry: ref only *Open:* term: Mon-Thu 0900-2100, Fri 0900-1730, Sat-Sun 1200-1800; vac: Mon-Tue, Thu-Fri 0900-1700, Wed 0900-2000
Subj: all subjs; undergrad; postgrad *Collns: Bks & Pamphs:* School Practice Colln; ch's lit *Archvs:* Chester Mystery Plays Performance Archv (productions 1951-date)
Equip: 2 m-readers, m-printer, 3 video viewers, 5 copiers, clr copier, 80 computers (all with wd-proc & internet), 2 rooms for hire *Disabled:* scanner, speech synthesiser *Svcs:* ref
Stock: bks/200000; periodcls/700; audios/500; videos/4000; CD-ROMs/30
Classn: DDC *Auto Sys:* Innopac
Staff: Libns: 12 *Other Prof:* 3 *Non-Prof:* 30 *Exp:* £270000 (1999-2000)

S458 🎓

College of Law, Chester Library
Christleton Hall, Christleton, Chester, Cheshire, CH3 7AB (01244-333225)
Email: library.chester@lawcol.co.uk
Internet: http://www.college-of-law.co.uk/

Gov Body: Coll of Law *Chief:* Branch Libn: Ms Marianne Barber (marianne.barber@lawcol.co.uk)
Assoc Libs: BIRMINGHAM LIB (see **S168**); GUILDFORD LIB (see **S769**); LONDON LIB (see **S1090**); YORK LIB (see **S2161**)
Entry: only open to certain categories of external user, by adv appt *Open:* term: Mon-Thu 0845-2100, Fri 0845-1800, Sat-Sun 1200-1600
Subj: law
Equip: 3 copiers, 70 computers (incl wd-proc, internet & CD-ROM) *Disabled:* disabled access
Online: Butterworths, Justis, Lexis, Lawtel, Westlaw UK *Svcs:* info, ref
Staff: Libns: 1 *Non-Prof:* 3

S459 🎓 ✚

Countess of Chester Hospital, School of Nursing and Midwifery Library
Countess of Chester Hosp, Liverpool Rd, Chester, Cheshire, CH2 1UL (*tel & fax:* 01244-364664)
Email: lr.countess@chester.ac.uk
Internet: http://www.chester.ac.uk/lr/

Gov Body: Chester Coll (see **S457**) *Chief:* Lib Mgr: Mrs T. Gibson
Assoc Libs: SCHOOL OF NURSING & MID-WIFERY LIB, Arrowe Park Hosp (see **S2134**); LEIGHTON HOSP, JOINT EDU & TRAINING LIB (see **S506**)
Entry: staff & students of Chester Coll; staff of Wirral & West Cheshire Community NHS Trust & Grosvenor Nuffield Hosp; membership arrange-ments also exist for staff of Countess of Chester NHS Trust *Open:* Mon-Thu 0830-1630, Fri 0830-1600
Subj: nursing
Equip: copier, computers (incl internet)

S460 ⚙

Shell Global Solutions (UK), The Information Centre
Cheshire Innovation Pk, Chester, Cheshire, CH1 3SH (0151-373-5900; *fax:* 0151-373-5230)
Email: infocentre@opc.shell.com
Internet: http://www.shellglobalsolutions.com/

Gov Body: Shell Global Solutions *Chief:* Libn & Archivist: Mr Richard Selfe BA(Hons), DipSAM, MCLIP (Rick.Selfe@shell.com)

Dep: Info Scientist: Mr Eddie Carter BSc(Hons), MCLIP (eddie.carter@shell.com)
Entry: Shell staff world-wide, visits by adv appt; in-house facility only, no svcs to non-Shell employees
Open: Mon-Fri 0800-1700
Subj: tech *Collns: Archvs:* archvs of Shell Global Solutions (oil industry rsrch & development) *Co-op Schemes:* ILL
Equip: m-reader, m-printer, copier, 4 computers (incl 2 with wd-proc, 1 with internet & 1 with CD-ROM) *Online:* Dialog, Datastar, Profound, Alacra, STN, Neraq, Questel-Orbit, EINS, Equifax-Infocheck *Officer-in-Charge:* Libn & Archivist, as above *Svcs:* info, ref, biblio, translation, document supply, ILLs, document mgmt
Stock: bks/7500; periodcls/300; CD-ROMs/14; archvs/1500 linear m *Acqs Offcr:* Info Scientist, as above
Classn: in-house *Auto Sys:* Livelink
Staff: Libns: 1 *Other Prof:* 2 *Non-Prof:* 3

S461

West Cheshire College, Library and Learning Centre

Eaton Rd, Handbridge, Chester, Cheshire, CH4 7ER (01244-670574; *fax:* 01244-670584)
Email: library@west-cheshire.ac.uk
Internet: http://www.west-cheshire.ac.uk/library/

Chief: Lib & Learning Resources Mgr: Mrs Catriona Martin BSc, DipLib (c.martin@west-cheshire.ac.uk) *Other Snr Staff:* Asst Libn & Learning Centre Mgr: Mrs Sharon Hitchmough BSc, DipLib; Asst Libn & Learning Centre Mgr: Mrs Kate Hobson BA, MA, DipLib; Internet & Systems Libn: Mr Anthony Beal BA
Assoc Libs: ELLESMERE PORT CAMPUS LEARNING CENTRE, Regent St, Ellesmere Port, Cheshire, CH65 8EJ, Learning Centre Mgr: Mrs Kath Pacey BA, MCLIP (01244-670348; *email:* k.pacey@west-cheshire.ac.uk); CAPENHURST CAMPUS LEARNING CENTRE, Capenhurst Ln, Capenhurst, Chester, CH1 6ER, Learning Centre Mgr: Mrs Sharon Hitchmough, as above (01244-670451; *email:* s.hitchmough@west-cheshire.ac.uk)
Entry: community membership available to external users, otherwise ref only; co-op arrangements with local libs *Open:* term: Mon-Thu 0830-2100, Fri 0830-1630, Sat 0900-1300; vac: Mon-Fri 0900-1700
Subj: GCSE; A level; undergrad; postgrad; vocational *Co-op Schemes:* BLDSC, ILL
Equip: 5 video viewers, 4 copiers (£1 for 15 copies), 2 fax (£1), 200 computers (all with wd-proc, internet & CD-ROM), 6 rooms for hire
Stock: bks/40000; periodcls/250; slides/2000; audios/300; videos/1000; CD-ROMs/200 *Acqs Offcr:* Lib & Learning Resources Mgr, as above
Classn: DDC *Auto Sys:* Heritage
Staff: Libns: 4.6 *Non-Prof:* 7.6, plus 5.5 in IT Support & 3 AV technicians
Proj: new bldg at Ellesmere Port opening 2003

S462 ✚

West Cheshire Postgraduate Medical Centre Library

Countess of Chester Hosp, Liverpool Rd, Chester, Cheshire, CH2 1UL (01244-364734; *fax:* 01244-364722)
Email: librarian@coch.nhs.uk

Gov Body: Postgrad Dean, Univ of Liverpool
Chief: Libn: Miss Samantha West MLIS
Entry: medical staff & students only *Open:* Mon-Fri 0900-2000
Subj: medicine; psychiatry *Co-op Schemes:* BLDSC, BMA, RCS, Univ of Liverpool
Equip: fax, copier, 6 computers (all with wd-proc & CD-ROM, 5 with internet) *Online:* via ADITUS: Medline, Embase & others *Officer-in-Charge:* Libn, as above *Svcs:* info, ref, biblio, database training

Stock: bks/3500; periodcls/91; videos/68; CD-ROMs/20 *Acqs Offcr:* Libn, as above
Classn: LC *Auto Sys:* Heritage
Staff: Libns: 1 *Non-Prof:* 0.5 *Exp:* £23000 (1999-2000); £25500 (2000-01)

Chesterfield

S463 ✚

Chesterfield and North Derbyshire Royal Hospital, Education Centre Library

Chesterfield & North Derbyshire Royal Hosp, Calow, Chesterfield, Derbyshire, S44 5BL (01246-277271 x3086; *fax:* 01246-234628)
Email: medical.library@cndrh-tr.trent.nhs.uk
Internet: http://www.cndrh-tr.trent.nhs.uk/

Gov Body: Chesterfield & North Derbyshire Royal Hosp NHS Trust *Chief:* Lib Svcs Mgr: Mrs Julia Nicholson MA (julia.nicholson@cndrh-tr.trent.nhs.uk) *Dep:* Asst Lib Svcs Mgr: Mr Jonathan Phillips BLib (jonathan.phillips@cndrh-tr.trent.nhs.uk)
Entry: NHS staff in North Derbyshire; affiliates such as students on placement & staff of Primary Care Trusts; ref only for non-membs *Open:* Mon-Thu 0830-1830, Fri 0830-1700
Subj: medicine; nursing; multidisciplinary health; some health mgmt *Co-op Schemes:* SINTO
Equip: copier (5p per pg), 5 computers (incl 2 with internet & 2 with CD-ROM) *Officer-in-Charge:* Lib Svcs Mgr, as above *Svcs:* info, ref, lit searches, current awareness
Stock: bks/9000; periodcls/104; videos/250; CD-ROMs/12 *Acqs Offcr:* Lib Svcs Mgr, as above
Classn: NLM *Auto Sys:* Heritage
Pubns: Lib Guide (free); BioMed Guide (free); Knowledge on the Net (internet guide, free)
Staff: Libns: 2 *Non-Prof:* 2 *Exp:* £146000 (2000-01); fig is for all purchases & staffing

S464

Chesterfield College Library

Infirmary Rd, Chesterfield, Derbyshire, S41 7NG (01246-500550; *fax:* 01246-500587)
Email: podmorej@chesterfield.ac.uk
Internet: http://www.chesterfield.ac.uk/

Chief: Head of Learning Resources: Ms Jane Podmore BA(Hons), MCLIP
Entry: ref only *Open:* contact svc for details
Subj: all subjs; GCSE; A level *Co-op Schemes:* EMRLS
Equip: 4 video viewers, 2 copiers, 72 computers (all with wd-proc, internet & CD-ROM) *Disabled:* Telemole
Stock: bks/30000; periodcls/181; slides/178; audios/684; videos/2418; CD-ROMs/20
Classn: UDC *Auto Sys:* Dynix
Staff: Libns: 5 *Non-Prof:* 9 *Exp:* £60000 (1999-2000); £62000 (2000-01); incl stock, equip & consumables

S465 ☕🖊

North Derbyshire Chamber of Commerce and Industry, Business Information and Research Service

Commerce Centre, Canal Wharf, Chesterfield, Derbyshire, S41 7NA (01246-207207; *fax:* 01246-203173)
Internet: http://www.derbyshire.org/

Gov Body: North Derbyshire Chamber of Commerce & Industry *Chief:* Info & Rsrch Offcr: Mrs Helen Carter BA(Hons), MCLIP
Entry: membs & others by appt *Open:* Mon-Fri 0900-1700; please phone in adv
Subj: business info *Svcs:* info, ref

Stock: various bks, periodcls, pamphs & CD-ROMs
Classn: own
Pubns: Business Voice (free to membs, £24 pa to others, available electronically as e-Business Voice)
Staff: Libns: 3 *Non-Prof:* 1

Chichester

S466 ⚷ 🙏

Chichester Cathedral Library

c/o The Royal Chantry, Cathedral Cloisters, Chichester, W Sussex, PO19 1PX (01243-782959)

Gov Body: The Dean & Chapter, Chichester Cathedral *Chief:* Canon Libn: The Revd Canon Peter Atkinson MA *Dep:* Hon Libn: vacant
Entry: by appt
Subj: theology (chiefly 16C-19C); church hist; Bibles & Prayer Bks; arch; church music; numismology; heraldry; bibliography; Sussex church hist & topography *Collns: Bks & Pamphs:* King Lib (17C); Hannah Colln (19C tracts) *Archvs:* held at West Sussex Record Office (see **A106**)
Equip: copier, computer catalogue
Stock: bks/5000; periodcls/3
Classn: own
Pubns: Chichester Cathedral Lib (£1.50); A Postscript by Mary Hobbs (30p, p&p extra); Chichester Cathedral: An Historical Survey, ed M. Hobbs (1992, £40)
Staff: Non-Prof: 4
Proj: computerising catalogue

S467 🏛

Pallant House Gallery Library

9 North Pallant, Chichester, W Sussex, PO19 1TJ (01243-774557; *fax:* 01243-536038)
Email: library@pallant.co.uk
Internet: http://www.pallanthousegallery.com/

Gov Body: Trustees of the Pallant House Gallery
Chief: Libn: Ms Pat Saunders (p.saunders@pallant.co.uk) *Other Snr Staff:* Dir: Mr Stephan van Raay; Curator: Miss Frances Guy (f.guy@pallant.co.uk); House Manager/Corporate Svcs: Mr Matthew Weewes
Entry: adv appt; ref only *Open: Gallery:* Tue-Sat 1000-1700, Sun & Bank Holidays 1200-1700
Subj: arts, esp British 20th century art; art hist; design; theatre & stage design *Collns: Bks & Pamphs:* some art magazines *Other:* cuttings; preview cards on a number of artists
Equip: copier (A4/5p, A3/10p) *Disabled:* wheelchair access limited *Svcs:* ref
Stock: bks/117500; periodcls/3+; videos/40 *Acqs Offcr:* Curator, as above
Exp: varies; many bks acquired by donation
Further Info: closed Aug 2003 to Spring 2004

S468 🔔 🏛

Royal Military Police Museum Library

Roussillon Barracks, Chichester, W Sussex, PO19 4BN (01243-534225; *fax:* 01243-534288)
Email: museum@rhqrmp.freeserve.co.uk
Internet: http://www.rhqrmp.freeserve.co.uk/

Gov Body: RMP Museum Trustees *Chief:* Lt Col (Rtd) P.H.M. Squier *Dep:* Mrs S.A. Lines
Entry: prior appt advisable *Open:* Tue-Fri 1030-1230, 1330-1630, Sat-Sun (Apr-Sep only) 1400-1700; closed Jan
Subj: military hist; military police *Collns: Archvs:* Corps Order Bks (1855-1919); soldier svc details
Equip: copier
Stock: bks/500; periodcls/300; photos/1000
Pubns: The Journal of the Military Police
Staff: Other Prof: 2

Special Libraries

Chichester ▼ Coleraine

S469 📖

University College Chichester, Information Services

Bishop Otter Campus, College Ln, Chichester, W Sussex, PO19 6PE (01243-816089; *fax:* 01243-816080)
Internet: http://www.ucc.ac.uk/

Chief: Dir of Info Svcs: Mr Terry Hanson BA, DipLib *Dep:* Head of Lib Svcs: Mr Scott Robertson MA, MEd, DipLib, MCLIP
Assoc Libs: BOGNOR CAMPUS LIB, Upper Bognor Rd, Bognor Regis, W Sussex, PO21 1HR, Campus Libn: Ms Norma Leigh BLib, MA, MCLIP (01243-816099)
Entry: ref only; associate membership available for annual fee *Open:* term: Mon-Thu 0845-2145, Fri 0845-1700, Sat 1300-1700, Sun 1300-1700; vac: Mon-Fri 0900-1700; some variations for Bognor Campus Lib
Subj: undergrad; postgrad; *Bishop Otter Campus:* art; dance; environmental sci; health; hist; lit; business studies; mgmt; media studies; music; nursing; religion; theology; sci; social sci; social work; sport sci; women's studies; *Bognor Campus:* edu; geog; maths; lang *Collns: Bks & Pamphs:* theological rsrch colln (incl former Chichester Theological Colln); Gerard Young Colln (Sussex local hist); 19C Parliamentary Papers; Hansard (1943-89); Historical Assoc Pamphs Colln *Archvs:* Ted Walker Archv (Sussex poet, incl MSS & correspondence) *Other:* fine art slides; dance videos *Co-op Schemes:* BLDSC, BLCMP, LENSE
Equip: m-reader, video viewer, copiers, clr copier, computers (incl wd-proc, internet & CD-ROM)
Disabled: Magnalink video reader, Smart Viewer, Supernova, Cipher *Svcs:* info, ref, biblio
Stock: bks/254000; periodcls/800; slides/6000
Classn: DDC *Auto Sys:* Talis
Staff: Libns: 7.2 *Non-Prof:* 11.5 *Exp:* £200000 (2000-01)

S470 🏛

Weald and Downland Open Air Museum, Armstrong Library

Singleton, Chichester, W Sussex, PO18 0EU (01243-811363; *fax:* 01243-811475)
Email: rharris@wealddown.co.uk
Internet: http://www.wealddown.co.uk/

Chief: Libn: Mr R. Harris MA
Entry: adv appt, ref only
Subj: local studies; vernacular arch; museums (esp folk & open-air); bldg materials, techniques & trades *Collns: Bks & Pamphs:* Worshipful Company of Plumbers Colln (plumbing & lead work) *Other:* J.R. Armstrong Photo Colln
Svcs: info, ref
Stock: bks/c9000; periodcls/c40; photos/c3000; slides/c100000; pamphs/c1000; maps/c500
Classn: proprietary *Staff: Other Prof:* 1

Chigwell

S471 📖

Chigwell School, Swallow Library

High Rd, Chigwell, Essex, IG7 6QF (020-8501-5757; *fax:* 020-8500-6232)
Email: sgower@chigwell-school.org
Internet: http://www.chigwell-school.org/

Gov Body: Governors of Chigwell School *Chief:* Swallow Libn: Mrs Sarah Gower BA, ACII
Assoc Libs: CHIGWELL SCHOOL ARCHVS, addr as above, Archivist: Ms Marian Delfgou MCLIP
Entry: current staff & pupils; others ref only by appt *Open:* term: Mon-Sat 0800-1800, some Sats 0930-1200; vac: closed
Subj: all subjs; genl; GCSE; A level; local study (Essex hist) *Collns: Bks & Pamphs:* Falklands War Colln; William Penn Colln (selection of bks by or about other old boys & staff); Essex hist *Archvs:* school archvs administered separately *Other:* census transcripts: parishes of Chigwell, Chigwell Row & Buckhurst Hill 1841-1891 (indexed)
Stock: bks/9500; periodcls/18; pamphs/60; maps/20 *Classn:* DDC *Staff: Other Prof:* 1

Chippenham

S472 📖

Wiltshire College, Chippenham Library

(formerly Chippenham Coll)
Cocklebury Rd, Chippenham, Wiltshire, SN15 3QD (01249-465217; *fax:* 01249-465326)
Email: masobc@wiltscoll.ac.uk
Internet: http://www.wiltscoll.ac.uk/

Chief: Libn: Ms B.C. Mason BA(Hons), MCLIP
Assoc Libs: LACKHAM LIB (see **S473**); TROWBRIDGE LIB (see **S2053**)
Entry: ref only, but external membership available
Open: term: Mon-Wed 0845-2000, Thu 1000-2000, Fri 0845-1700; vac: hrs vary
Subj: all subjs; genl; GCSE; A level; undergrad; vocational *Collns: Bks & Pamphs:* archaeo colln; dyslexia specialism *Co-op Schemes:* BLDSC, SWRLS, WILCO
Equip: copiers, clr copier, video viewer, 100 computers (all with wd-proc, internet & CD-ROM, students only) *Svcs:* info, ref, biblio
Stock: bks/19500; periodcls/143; maps/10; m-forms/1; audios/112; videos/70
Classn: DDC *Auto Sys:* Olib
Staff: Libns: 1 *Non-Prof:* 10

S473 📖

Wiltshire College, Lackham Library

Lacock, Chippenham, Wiltshire, SN15 2NY (01249-466814; *fax:* 01249-444474)
Email: vainsm@wiltscoll.ac.uk
Internet: http://www.wiltscoll.ac.uk/

Gov Body: Wiltshire Coll *Chief:* Lib & Learning Resources Mgr: Mrs Stella M. Vain MCLIP
Assoc Libs: CHIPPENHAM LIB (see **S472**); TROWBRIDGE LIB (see **S2053**)
Entry: membs only *Open:* Mon-Thu 0830-2000, Fri 0830-1700
Subj: sci; tech; agric; hortic; agric eng; subjs related to land-based industries *Co-op Schemes:* BLDSC, WILCO, SWRLS
Equip: 2 video viewers, 2 copiers, clr copier, 40 computers (all with wd-proc, internet & CD-ROM)
Svcs: info, ref
Stock: bks/23000; periodcls/220; slides/40 sets; videos/700; CD-ROMs/30
Classn: DDC *Auto Sys:* Olib *Staff: Libns:* 1 *Non-Prof:* 4 *Exp:* £23000 (2000-01)

Chislehurst

S474 📖

Ravensbourne College of Design and Communication, Learning Resource Centre

Walden Rd, Chislehurst, Kent, BR7 5SN (020-8289-4900; *fax:* 020-8325-8320)
Email: library@rave.ac.uk
Internet: http://www.rave.ac.uk/

Chief: Libn: Ms Sharon Fowler BA, MA(Ed), MCLIP *Dep:* Mrs Esther Okwok BA
Entry: adv appt, ref only *Open:* visitors hrs: Mon-Fri 0900-1700
Subj: undergrad; arts; fashion; 3D design; photography; digital media; broadcasting; film theory; fine art; graphic design *Co-op Schemes:* BLDSC
Equip: m-reader, m-printer, 10 video viewers, 2 copiers, clr copier, 30 computers (all with wd-proc, internet & CD-ROM), DVD reader, digital projection equip *Svcs:* info, ref
Stock: bks/32000; periodcls/120; slides/30000; videos/10000 hrs of recordings
Classn: DDC *Auto Sys:* Horizon
Staff: Libns: 2 *Other Prof:* 1 *Non-Prof:* 3

Chorley

S475 ✚

Lancashire Teaching Hospitals NHS Trust, Postgraduate Education Centre Library

(formerly Chorley & South Ribble NHS Trust Lib)
Preston Rd, Chorley, Lancashire, PR7 1PP (01257-245607; *fax:* 01257-245623)
Email: kathleenturtle@hotmail.com

Type: multidisciplinary *Gov Body:* Lancashire Teaching Hosps NHS Trust *Chief:* Libn: Mrs Kathleen M. Turtle MSc, BA(Hons), MCLIP
Assoc Libs: ROYAL PRESTON HOSP LIB (see **S1835**)
Entry: ref only for non-NHS, at Libn's discretion
Open: Mon, Wed-Fri 0900-1700, Tue 0900-1800
Subj: psy; counselling; health svcs structure & mgmt; biology; statistics; medical sci *Collns: Bks & Pamphs:* NVQ studies colln (health related) *Co-op Schemes:* BLDSC, BMA, RCS, LIHNN
Equip: copier, 7 computers (all with wd-proc & CD-ROM, 4 with internet) *Online:* Aditus (regional database portal giving access to a range of databases & other e-resources) *Svcs:* info, ref
Stock: bks/c4000; periodcls/87; videos/20; CD-ROMs/5
Classn: DDC *Auto Sys:* Talis
Staff: Non-Prof: 2 PT (1 FTE)

Cirencester

S476 📖

Royal Agricultural College, Hosier Library

Cirencester, Gloucestershire, GL7 6JS (01285-652531; *fax:* 01285-650219)
Email: library@royagcol.ac.uk
Internet: http://www.royagcol.ac.uk/

Chief: Head of Lib Svcs: Mrs Sarah Howie BA, MPhil, DipLib, MCLIP *Dep:* Snr Asst Libn: Mr Peter Brooks BA, PGCE, MA
Entry: membs of Coll; external membership available *Open:* term: Mon-Thu 0900-2000,Fri 0900-1800, Sat 0900-1600, Sun 1300-1800; vac: Mon, Wed-Fri 0900-1700, Tue 1000-1700
Subj: agric; agribusiness; equine; forestry; rural land use; law; taxation; internatl business; mgmt; planning; life sci; environment *Collns: Bks & Pamphs:* historical colln (agric, land mgmt & related subjs, 16C-19C) *Archvs:* all pubns by or about membs of Coll *Co-op Schemes:* BLDSC, SWRLS, EDINA UPDATE (bibliography of land-based lit)
Equip: 2 video viewers, fax, 3 copiers, 13 computers (all with internet, 7 with wd-proc & 2 with CD-ROM) *Svcs:* info, ref, biblio, indexing
Stock: bks/32000; periodcls/450; maps/50; audios/200; videos/600; CD-ROMs/25
Classn: DDC *Auto Sys:* Olib
Staff: Libns: 3 *Non-Prof:* 4

Coalville

S477

Stephenson College Learning Centre

Bridge Rd, Coalville, Leicestershire, LE67 3PW
(01530-836136; *fax:* 01530-814253)
Email: deniser@stephensoncoll.ac.uk
Internet: http://www.stephensoncoll.ac.uk/

Gov Body: Stephenson Coll *Chief:* Learning
Centre Mgr: Mrs D. Rossell BA(Hons), MA, MCLIP
Entry: students, local community *Open:* term:
Mon-Thu 0830-2000, Fri 0830-1700; vac: Mon-Fri
0830-1700
Subj: all subjs; genl; GCSE; A level; undergrad;
vocational; local study (Leicestershire) *Collns:*
Bks & Pamphs: hist of Leicestershire (esp
Coalville) *Co-op Schemes:* BLDSC, EMRLS
Equip: copier (5p per pg), 45 computers (all with
wd-proc, internet & CD-ROM, access free)
Disabled: large monitor screen, large print bks,
magnifiers, wheelchair lift *Officer-in-Charge:*
Learning Centre Mgr, as above *Svcs:* info, ref,
biblio
Stock: bks/25000; periodcls/128; pamphs/160;
maps/50; videos/180 *Acqs Offcr:* Learning
Centre Mgr, as above
Classn: DDC *Auto Sys:* Heritage
Staff: Libns: 1 *Other Prof:* 1 *Non-Prof:* 3 *Exp:*
£29000 (1999-2000); £31000 (2000-01)

Colchester

S478

Colchester Institute, Learning Resources, Information and Student Services

Sheepen Rd, Colchester, Essex, CO3 3LL (01206-518642; *fax:* 01206-518643)
Email: info@colch-inst.ac.uk
Internet: http://www.colch-inst.ac.uk/

Chief: Head of Learning Resources & Student
Svcs: Mrs Cilla Summers BSc(Hons), CertEd,
DipLib *Dep:* Dep Head of Learning Resources:
Mrs Barbara Purvis BA(Hons), DipIS
Assoc Libs: COLCHESTER SITE LIB, addr as
above, Site Libn: Mr Ian McMeekan MA, FCLIP,
FRSA; CLACTON SITE LIB, Colchester Inst,
Marine Parade East, Clacton-on-Sea, LO15 6JQ,
Site Libn: Mr Carl Slator MCLIP
Entry: ref only; external membs pay annual fee for
lending rights *Open:* term: Mon-Thu 0830-2000,
Fri 0830-1700; vac: Mon-Fri 0900-1700
Subj: all subjs; genl; GCSE; A level; undergrad;
postgrad (some subjs); vocational; social sci;
health studies; childhood studies; occupational
therapy; physiotherapy; lang; sci; maths; tech;
catering; business; mgmt; arts; music; performing
arts; lit; humanities; geog; hist; environment; auto
eng; info tech; computing *Co-op Schemes:*
BLDSC, NULJ, Essex County Lib Svc (see **P51**),
NTRHLN
Equip: m-reader, m-printer, 2 fax, 5 copiers, clr
copier, 95 computers (incl 80 wd-proc, 13 internet,
30 CD-ROM) *Svcs:* info, ref, biblio
Stock: bks/c70000; periodcls/500; slides/150 sets;
audios/475, plus 10600 music recordings; videos/
3500; AVs/50; music scores/20000
Classn: DDC *Auto Sys:* Olib
Staff: Libns: 6 *Other Prof:* 3 *Non-Prof:* 11.5

S479

Essex Society for Archaeology and History Library

c/o Albert Sloman Lib, Univ of Essex, Wivenhoe
Pk, Colchester, Essex, CO4 3SQ (01206-873188;
fax: 01206-873598)

Gov Body: Council *Chief:* Hon Libn: Mr Andrew
Phillips BA, CertEd (contact addr: 19 Victoria Rd,
Colchester, CO3 3NT) *Dep:* Dep Hon Libn: Mrs J.
Blowers
Entry: membs only; other bona fide rsrchers on
appl *Open:* term: Mon-Fri 0800-2200, Sat 0900-
1800, Sun 1400-1900; vac: Mon-Fri 0900-1730
Subj: geog; hist; archaeo *Collns: Bks & Pamphs:*
archaeo journals; bks & pamphs on Essex hist
Archvs: some ephemera *Co-op Schemes:* ILL
Equip: m-reader
Stock: bks/15000; periodcls/51 *Classn:* DDC
Pubns: Essex Archaeo & Hist (£14)
Exp: £1000 (1999-2000); £1000 (2000-01)

S480

North Essex Hospitals' Library and Information Service

Colchester Genl Hosp, Turner Rd, Colchester,
Essex, CO4 5JL (01206-742146; *fax:* 01206-
742107)
Email: library.service@essexrivers.nhs.uk

Gov Body: Essex Rivers Healthcare NHS Trust
Chief: Lib Svcs Mgr: Mrs S. Stock BA(Hons),
DipLib, MCLIP
Entry: must be employed by or working with NHS
Open: Mon-Thu 0900-1900, Fri 0900-1630
Subj: medicine; health care; health mgmt; mental
health *Co-op Schemes:* BLDSC, Regional NHS
scheme, PLCS
Equip: fax, copier, 6 computers (all with wd-proc,
internet & CD-ROM) *Online:* Medline, CINAHL,
HMIC, PsycInfo, Cochrane, NRR *Svcs:* info, ref
Stock: bks/c6000; periodcls/c180
Classn: NLM *Auto Sys:* DBTextworks
Staff: Libns: 2 *Non-Prof:* 2

S481

St Helena Hospice, Millie Hare Library

Edu Centre, Barncroft Cl, Highwoods, Colchester,
Essex, CO4 4JU (01206-851560; *fax:* 01206-
845969)
Email: cwelch@sthelenahospice.org.uk
Internet: http://www.londonlinks.ac.uk/mhec/
library/libhome.htm

Chief: Lib Mgr: Ms Candy Welch NVQ3(Lib & Info)
Entry: ref only; hospice staff; membership for
others available by subscription *Open:* Mon 0830-
1630, Tue-Fri 0830-1600
Subj: palliative care *Co-op Schemes:* ILL
(articles only, not bks)
Equip: copier (10p per side), video viewer, 2
computers (both with wd-proc, internet & CD-ROM)
Svcs: info, ref
Stock: bks/5000+; periodcls/17 specialist, various
others; pamphs/various; videos/295; CD-ROMs/6
Classn: own
Pubns: various staff papers
Staff: Non-Prof: 17 PT *Exp:* £2000 (2000-01)

S482

University of Essex, The Albert Sloman Library

Wivenhoe Pk, Colchester, Essex, CO4 3SQ
(01206-873188; *fax:* 01206-873598)
Email: lib_enq@essex.ac.uk
Internet: http://www.essex.ac.uk/

Gov Body: Univ of Essex *Chief:* Libn: Mr R.
Butler MSc
Entry: ref only, written appl to libn *Open:* term:
Mon-Fri 0800-2200, Sat 0900-1800, Sun 1400-
1900; vac: Mon-Fri 0900-1730
Subj: undergrad; postgrad; genl; psy; accounting;
art; biology; computer sci; econ; elec eng; sci; govt;
hist; lang & linguistics; law; lit; maths; health scis;

phil; physics; sociology; major rsrch collns relating
to Latin America, the former Soviet Union & the
USA *Collns: Bks & Pamphs:* Bensusan Colln;
John Hassall Colln; Bassingbourn Parish Lib; EDC;
Champion Branfill Russell Lib; Bean Memorial
Colln (William Blake facsimiles); Essex Soc for
Archaeo & Hist Lib (see **S479**); Historical Colln of
the Royal Statistical Soc; Harsnett Lib *Archvs:* Soc
of Friends (Colchester & Coggeshall meetings);
Rowhedge Ironworks archvs; Gaudier-Brzeska
papers; Social Democratic Party (SDP) Archvs;
Sieghart Human Rights Archv; Tawney Soc archvs;
SCOPE papers (Scientific Cttee on Problems of
the Environment); NVALA Archvs (Natl Viewers &
Listeners' Assoc); Lord Alport Papers (1925-92);
Lord Brimelow Papers (1944-88); Boundary
Commission Papers (England & Wales, 1988-95);
papers & pubns of Cttee on Standards in Public
Life (Nolan Cttee); Sigmund Freud Colln; Enid
Balint Papers; Windscale 1977 Public Enquiry
papers *Co-op Schemes:* BLDSC, EULOS
Equip: m-reader, m-printer, fax, copier, computers
(incl wd-proc & CD-ROM) *Online:* various
Stock: bks/676000; pamphs/38000; m-forms/
141000
Classn: LC *Auto Sys:* Innopac
Pubns: various Lib Guides
Staff: 41.8 in total (incl 9 snr staff)

Coleford

S483

Royal Forest of Dean College, Study Centre Library

Five Acres Campus, Berry Hill, Coleford,
Gloucestershire, GL6 7JT (01594-838522; *fax:*
01594-837497)
Internet: http://www.rfdc.ac.uk/

Gov Body: Governors of the Royal Forest of Dean
Coll *Chief:* Learner Svcs Mgr: Ms Kris Ventris-
Field (kris-vf@rfdc.ac.uk) *Dep:* Lib Mgr: Mrs Judy
Offord (judy-o@rfdc.ac.uk)
Entry: adv appt *Open:* term: Mon-Thu 0830-
1900, Fri 0830-1630; vac: Mon-Fri 0930-1500
Subj: all subjs; genl; GCSE; A level; vocational;
local study (Forest of Dean) *Collns: Bks &*
Pamphs: local hist colln *Archvs:* some motor
vehicle archvs *Co-op Schemes:* SWRLS (ILL),
BLDSC
Equip: 4 video viewers, 2 copiers, 8 computers
(all with wd-proc & internet, 4 with CD-ROM),
laminator, binder *Disabled:* magnifier *Online:*
Infotrac Onefile *Officer-in-Charge:* Learner Svcs
Mgr, as above *Svcs:* info, ref, biblio
Stock: bks/17000; periodcls/66; slides/600; various
slides, videos & CD-ROMs *Acqs Offcr:* Lib Mgr,
as above
Classn: DDC *Auto Sys:* Heritage
Staff: Other Prof: 2 *Non-Prof:* 4

Coleraine

S484

University of Ulster Library

Cromore Rd, Coleraine, Co Londonderry, BT52
1SA (028-7032-4245; *fax:* 028-7032-4928)
Internet: http://www.ulst.ac.uk/library/

Gov Body: Univ of Ulster *Chief:* Dir of Info Svcs:
Mr Nigel Macartney (N.Macartney@ulster.ac.uk)
Dep: Asst Dir, Lib: Ms Elaine Urquhart
(EE.Urquhart@ulster.ac.uk)
Assoc Libs: COLERAINE CAMPUS LIB, addr as
above, Campus Lib Mgr: Mr David McClure (028-
7032-4345; *fax:* 028-7032-4928; email:
DJ.McClure@ulster.ac.uk); BELFAST CAMPUS
LIB, York St, Belfast, BT15 1ED, Campus Lib Mgr:
Ms Marion Khorshidian (028-9026-7268; *fax:* 028-
9026-7278; email: M.Korshidian@ulster.ac.uk);

(Univ of Ulster Lib cont)
JORDANSTOWN LIB, Shore Rd, Jordanstown, Co Antrim, BT37 0QB, Campus Lib Mgr: Ms Mary McCullough (028-9036-6964; *email:* (M.McCullough@ulster.ac.uk); MAGEE LIB, Northland Rd, Londonderry, BT48 7JL, Campus Lib Mgr: Ms Stephanie McMullan (028-7137-5264; *fax:* 028-7137-5626; *email:* SA.McMullan@ulster.ac.uk)
Entry: staff & students of univ; others on appl to site libn *Open:* Coleraine: term: Mon-Fri 0900-2200, Sat 1000-1700; vac: Mon-Fri 0900-1700; *Belfast:* term: Mon-Thu 0900-2200, Fri 0900-1800, Sat 1000-1700; vac: Mon-Thu 0900-1700, Fri 0900-1630; *Jordanstown:* term: Mon-Fri 0900-2200, Sat 1000-1700; vac: Mon-Thu 0900-1700, Fri 0900-1600; *Magee:* term: Mon-Fri 0900-2100, Sat 0900-1700; vac: Mon-Thu 0900-1700, Fri 0900-1600; these times are subj to change – visitors should check in adv
Subj: all subjs; undergrad; postgrad *Collns: Bks & Pamphs:* at Coleraine: Henry Davis Colln (early printed bks); Headlam-Morley Colln (World War I); Paul Ricard Colln (World War II); Henry Morris Colln (Irish material); Stelfox Colln (nat hist); John Hewitt Lib (Ulster poetry); EDC; Carruthers Colln (nat hist); George Shiels Colln (playwright); Denis Johnston Colln (playwright & journalist); Francis Stuart Colln (lit & literary MSS); at Jordanstown: Irish Travellers Colln; at Magee Coll: Irish Colln; 18C Colln (5000 vols, incl Irish printing) *Other:* large slide colln (at Belfast) *Co-op Schemes:* BLDSC, ILL
Equip: m-readers, m-printers, video viewers, copiers, computers *Disabled:* Kurzweil, TextHelp, CCTV, induction loop, Brailling facilities *Online:* ABI Inform, ALTIS, AMED, ANTE, ASSIA, Barbour Index, BHI, BIDS, BNI, Celex, CINAHL, Cochrane, Compendex, EEVL, Emerald, ERIC, FirstSearch, Ingenta, Lexis-Nexis, LION, Medline, Omni, OVID Online, Philosophers Index, PsycInfo, SciDirect, Sport Discus, Web of Science, Zetoc & others (free to staff & students of univ)
Stock: bks/600000; periodcls/5000; slides/95000; audios/5000; videos/1700; (figs are for all 4 sites)
Classn: DDC, LC *Auto Sys:* Talis
Staff: Libns: 28 *Non-Prof:* 60 (figs are for all 4 sites)

Colwyn Bay

S485 🎓
Llandrillo College Library
Llandudno Rd, Colwyn Bay, Clwyd, LL28 4HZ (01492-54666 x423; *fax:* 01492-543052)
Internet: http://www.llandrillo.ac.uk/

Chief: Libn: A.D. Eynon
Assoc Libs: RHYL COLL LIB, Cefndy Rd, Rhyl, Denbighshire, LL18 2HG; DENBIGH COMMUNITY COLL LIB, Crown Ln, Denbigh, LL16 3SY
Entry: staff & students, ref only for public *Open:* term: Mon, Wed 0845-1845, Tue, Thu 0845-2045, Fri 0930-1600
Subj: all subjs; Further Edu
Equip: 4 video viewers, 2 copiers, 14 computers (all with wd-proc & internet, 1 with CD-ROM)
Stock: bks/20000; periodcls/300; audios/100; videos/200
Classn: DDC *Auto Sys:* Alice
Staff: Libns: 5 *Non-Prof:* 4

Consett

S486 🎓
Derwentside College, Learning Resource Centre
Front St, Consett, Co Durham, DH8 5EE (01207-585900; *fax:* 01207-585991)
Internet: http://www.derwentside.ac.uk/

Gov Body: Derwentside Coll Board of Corp
Chief: LRC Team Leader: Mrs Bernadette Brown BSc(Hons) (bernadette_brown@derwentside. ac.uk) *Other Snr Staff:* Ms Maureen Peacock (maureen_peacock@derwentside.ac.uk)
Assoc Libs: LANCHESTER COLL LRC, The Green, Durham Rd, Lanchester, Co Durham, DH7 0LG; STANLEY COLL LRC, Front St, Stanley, Co Durham, DH9 0TE
Entry: staff & students have borrowing rights; ref only to membs of public *Open:* term: Mon-Thu 0845-2100, Fri 0845-1700; vac: Mon-Fri 0900-1600
Subj: all subjs; genl; GCSE; A level; undergrad; vocational (HND)
Equip: m-reader, copier (5p per copy), clr copier (A4/30p), 5 video viewers, 25 computers (all with wd-proc & internet, free to students, others £1 per hr, £3 per hr for internet), desktop video conferencing available *Disabled:* specialist keyboards & mice, braille printer *Online:* Infotrac, City Mutual (health) *Officer-in-Charge:* LRC Team Leader, as above *Svcs:* info, ref
Stock: bks/14326; periodcls/26; audios/48; videos/406; CD-ROMs/15 *Acqs Offcr:* LRC Team Leader, as above
Classn: DDC *Auto Sys:* GLAS
Staff: Libns: 1 *Other Prof:* 2 *Non-Prof:* 2 *Exp:* £15000 (1999-2000); £1500 (2000-01)

Conwy

S487 🔑 🏛
Royal Cambrian Academy of Art Library
Crown Ln, Conwy, LL32 8AN (01492-593413; *fax:* 01492-593413)
Email: rca@rcaconwy.org
Internet: http://www.rcaconwy.org/

Gov Body: Royal Cambrian Academy of Art
Chief: Curator: Ms Gwyneth Jones *Dep:* Asst Curator: Ms Gill Burtwell
Entry: adv appt during busy periods; please phone before visiting *Open:* Tue-Fri 1100-1700
Subj: exhib catalogues & info on the Royal Cambrian Academy *Collns: Archvs:* catalogues since 1882 of RCA Annual Summer Exhib
Equip: copier (10p per copy) *Staff: Other Prof:* 3

Cookstown

S488 🏛 🎓
Loughry College Library
Cookstown, Co Tyrone, Northern Ireland, BT80 9AA (028-8676-8111; *fax:* 028-8676-1043)
Email: loughry.library@dardni.gov.uk

Gov Body: Dept of Agric & Rural Development (N Ireland) *Chief:* Libn: Ms Stephanie McCloskey
Assoc Libs: DEPT OF AGRIC & RURAL DEVELOPMENT LIB (see **S123**)
Entry: adv appt *Open:* term: Mon-Fri 0930-2130; vac: Mon-Fri 0930-1700
Subj: communications; food tech *Co-op Schemes:* BLDSC, informal arrangements with DARDNI HQ Lib & QUB Newforge, Belfast
Equip: copier, video viewer, computers (with internet & CD-ROM) *Svcs:* info, ref, biblio
Stock: bks/11000; periodcls/100; videos/100
Classn: LC *Auto Sys:* C2
Staff: Libns: 1 *Non-Prof:* 2

Corby

S489 🔑
Chartered Management Institute, Management Information Centre
(formerly Inst of Mgmt)
Mgmt House, Cottingham Rd, Corby, Northamptonshire, NN17 1TT (01536-204222; *fax:* 01536-401013)
Email: mic.enquiries@managers.org.uk
Internet: http://www.managers.org.uk/

Type: prof body *Gov Body:* Chartered Mgmt Inst; also provides lib svcs to the Inst of Mgmt Svcs
Chief: Memb Svcs Mgr: Mr Bob Norton BA, FCLIP, MIMgt
Entry: ref only for non-membs *Open:* Mon-Fri 0900-1700
Subj: mgmt skills & techniques; org theory & practice *Co-op Schemes:* BLDSC back-up lib for mgmt topics
Equip: 2 computers (both with CD-ROM, 1 with internet) *Online:* for membs only: IM Management Info Databases (MICLib), Infotrac Custom & Prompt on CD-ROM & online *Svcs:* info, ref, biblio
Stock: bks/40000; periodcls/100
Classn: UDC (mod) *Auto Sys:* Assassin
Pubns: Mgmt Thesaurus; Mgmt Checklists; Mgmt Thinkers; Mgmt Sources
Staff: Libns: 10 *Non-Prof:* 4 *Exp:* £50000 (1999-2000)
Proj: development of databases of mgmt sources, definitions, orgs & web sites

S490 🏛
Corby Borough Council, County Reference Library
Grosvenor House, George St, Corby, Northamptonshire, NN17 1QB (01536-402551; *fax:* 01536-464109)
Internet: http://www.corby.gov.uk/

Gov Body: Corby Borough Council *Chief:* Info Asst: Mrs Sue Crawford
Entry: staff only *Open:* Mon-Fri 0840-1700
Subj: social sci; local govt
Stock: bks/2000 *Classn:* DDC *Staff: Non-Prof:* 1

S491 🔑 🎓
Institute of Transport and Logistics, John Williams Library
PO Box 5787, Corby, Northamptonshire, NN17 4XQ (01536-740112; *fax:* 01536-740102)
Internet: http://www.iolt.org.uk/

Type: prof inst *Gov Body:* Inst of Transport & Logistics *Chief:* Libns (Corby): Mr Peter Huggins (phuggins@iolt.org.uk) & Ms Lynn Mayhew (lmayhew@iolt.org.uk)
Assoc Libs: LONDON READING ROOM, 11-12 Buckingham Gate, London, SW1E 6LB, Libn: Ms Claire Mowat (01536-740100; *fax:* 020-7592-3111; *email:* enquiry@iolt.org.uk)
Entry: entry is a benefit of Inst membership; ref only fee-paid entry for non-membs (student rate available on production of student ID) *Open: both libs:* Mon-Fri 0900-1645; it is advisable to check in adv as occasionally libs are closed in staff absence
Subj: John Williams Lib: logistics; supply chain mgmt; manufacturing; materials handling; storage systems; quality mgmt; packaging; info tech; *London Reading Room:* transport; mgmt; econ; statistical theory; marketing *Collns (John Williams Lib):* Bks & Pamphs: directories; some company annual reports *Collns (London Reading Room): Bks & Pamphs:* govt & other official pubns; colln of bnd historic journals, incl a complete run of CIT journals from 1920
Equip: John Williams Lib: copier, audio & video players, computers (incl internet & CD-ROM);

London Reading Room: copier, computers (incl internet) *Online:* Lexis-Nexis *Svcs:* info, ref, biblio, enq svc (fee based for non-membs)
Stock: bks/c30000 items
Classn: own *Auto Sys:* Alice
Pubns: list available on request

Corwen

S492
ASTIC Research Associates Library
Hendre Bach, Cerrigydrudion, Corwen, Clwyd, LL21 9TB (01490-420560)

Gov Body: ASTIC *Chief:* Dir of Rsrch & Documentation: Dr H.G.A. Hughes MA, DPhil, CSc, FCLIP, FRAI
Entry: open to affiliated or subscribing orgs only
Open: Mon-Fri 0700-1600
Subj: Spain, Portugal, Latin America; Eastern Europe; South Africa; Pacific Islands; Wales; anthro; linguistics; sociology; missions; humanities; social sci; social work; family hist *Collns: Bks & Pamphs:* Micronesia (esp Kiribati, RMI, FSM); Spain & Portugal; Latin America; Welsh lang *Archvs:* Welsh genealogy
Equip: m-reader, video viewer, fax, copier, clr copier, computers (incl wd-proc, CD-ROM & DVD), 10 cassette players/recorders, 2 reel-to-reel tape recorders
Stock: bks/20000; periodcls/40, plus 10 no longer current; photos/3200; slides/120; illusts/1000; pamphs/2000; maps/300; m-forms/2000; audios/3000; videos/300; archvs/100 m; wallcharts/50
Classn: DDC, UDC, LC
Pubns: m-fiche & CD-ROMs only; others with Gwasg Gwenffrwd imprint
Staff: Libns: 1 *Other Prof:* 2 *Non-Prof:* 11

Coventry

S493
The Chartered Institute of Housing Library
Octavia House, Westwood Way, Coventry, W Midlands, CV4 8JP (024-7669-4433; *fax:* 024-7669-5110)

Type: charity *Chief:* Policy Info Offcr: Ms Julie Wagstaff BA(Hons), PGDipLIS
Entry: ref only, mainly for internal use but membs of the Inst can visit by prior appt *Open:* Mon-Fri 0900-1600
Subj: housing; crime; community care; welfare state
Equip: fax, copier *Svcs:* info, ref, biblio
Stock: bks/9000; periodcls/60; videos/30; AVs/30
Classn: in-house sys *Auto Sys:* CALM 2000
Pubns: variety of titles in the following series: Good Practice Guides; Good Practice Briefings; Policy & Rsrch Reports; Professional Practice Svcs Housing Policy & Practice Bks; CIH/Joseph Rowntree Foundation Housing Mgmt Series; Good Practice Manuals; Legal Guides; Natl Housing Forum Titles; Scottish & Welsh Series; full list & prices available
Staff: Libns: 1

S494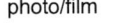
City College Coventry Library
The Butts, Coventry, W Midlands, CV1 3JD (024-7652-6700; *fax:* 024-7652-6789)
Email: r.toms@staff.covcollege.ac.uk
Internet: http://www.covcollege.ac.uk/

Chief: Mgr of Coll Libs: Mrs Rosemary Toms BA, PGCE, MA, DipLIS, MCLIP *Other Snr Staff:* Dep Mgr (Butts Centre): Ms Teresa Gazey; Dep Mgr (Tile Hill Centre): Ms Christine Okure

Assoc Libs: TILL HILL CENTRE LIB, Tile Hill Ln, Coventry, W Midlands, CV4 9SU (024-7679-1000; *fax:* 024-7646-4903)
Entry: ref only for non-staff/students *Open:* term: Mon-Thu 0840-1930, Fri 0940-1630; vac: Mon-Fri 0900-1630
Subj: all subjs; genl; GCSE; A level; undergrad; vocational *Co-op Schemes:* ILL
Equip: 2 copiers (A4/5p), 5 video viewers, 24 computers (incl wd-proc, internet & CD-ROM) *Disabled:* various facilities for visually handicapped *Officer-in-Charge:* Mgr of Coll Libs, as above
Svcs: info, ref, biblio
Stock: bks/43000; periodcls/150; pamphs/50; videos/250 *Acqs Offcr:* Mgr of Coll Libs, as above
Classn: DDC *Auto Sys:* Heritage
Staff: Libns: 3 *Non-Prof:* 10

S495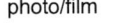
Coventry University, Lanchester Library
Fredrick Lanchester Bldg, Gosford St, Coventry, W Midlands, CV1 5DD (024-7688-7575)
Email: p.noon@coventry.ac.uk
Internet: http://www.leafrancis.coventry.ac.uk/

Gov Body: Coventry Univ *Chief:* Univ Libn: Mr Patrick Noon *Dep:* Dep Libn: Mrs Caroline Rock
Entry: open to the public with a day pass on production of official ID *Open:* term: Mon-Thu 0815-2100, Fri 0815-1915, Sat 1000-1700, Sun 1300-1700; vac: Mon-Fri 0900-1715
Subj: undergrad; postgrad; social sci; health sci; French; German; Russian; Spanish; Italian; sci; maths; eng; art; design *Collns: Bks & Pamphs:* EDC; Patent Colln (only academic colln in UK)
Archvs: papers & sketchbks of F.W. Lanchester (1895-1950) *Co-op Schemes:* BLDSC
Equip: m-readers, m-printers, video viewers, copiers, computers
Stock: bks/350000; periodcls/2200; slides/10000; audios/1000; videos/4000; archvs/200
Classn: DDC
Staff: Libns: 30 *Non-Prof:* 80

S496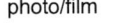
Coventry University Nursing and Midwifery Library
Walsgrave Hosp, Clifford Bridge Rd, Walsgrave, Coventry, W Midlands, CV2 2DX (024-7660-2020 x8366; *fax:* 024-7653-8838)
Email: D.Guest@coventry.ac.uk

Gov Body: Coventry Univ (see **S495**) *Chief:* Site Libn: Mr David A. Guest BA(Hons)
Entry: apply to libn *Open:* Mon-Thu 0800-2000, Fri 0800-1600, Sat 0900-1600
Subj: undergrad; postgrad; nursing; midwifery; paramedical
Equip: m-reader, m-printer, video viewer, copier, wd-proc, CD-ROM reader
Stock: bks/18000; periodcls/120; videos/600; 50 tape/slide
Classn: RCN (mod) *Staff: Libns:* 2 *Non-Prof:* 1.5

S497
National Grid Company plc, Information Learning Centre
Natl Grid House, Kirby Corner Rd, Coventry, W Midlands, CV4 8JY (024-7642-3680; *fax:* 024-7642-3681)
Email: david.parry@uk.ngrid.com
Internet: http://www.nationalgrid.com/

Chief: Info Offcr: Mr David Parry
Entry: adv appt *Open:* Mon-Fri 0830-1700
Subj: all subjs; genl; postgrad; electricity industry
Co-op Schemes: BLDSC, WMRLS, CADIG

Equip: fax, copier, computer (incl internet & CD-ROM) *Online:* Dialog, FT Profile, FT Discovery, Reuters, OXERA
Stock: bks/2500; periodcls/400; maps/280
Classn: DDC *Auto Sys:* SydneyPlus
Staff: Non-Prof: 1

S498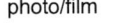
University of Warwick Library
Gibbet Hill Rd, Coventry, W Midlands, CV4 7AL (024-7652-3033; *fax:* 024-7652-4211)
Email: library@warwick.ac.uk
Internet: http://www.warwick.ac.uk/services/library/library.html

Gov Body: Univ of Warwick *Chief:* Univ Libn: Ms Anne Bell (a.bell.2@warwick.ac.uk) *Other Snr Staff:* Head of Info Svcs: Mr Robin Green (Robin.Green@warwick.ac.uk); Head of Technical Svcs: Ms Janet Gardner (Janet.Gardner@warwick.ac.uk)
Assoc Libs: MICHAEL LOVEITT BIOMEDICAL LIB, Univ of Warwick, Coventry, CV4 7AL, Info Asst: Ms Dee King (024-7657-2629; *fax:* 024-7652-3568; *email:* Dee.King@warwick.ac.uk); MATHS INST LIB, Univ of Warwick, Coventry, CV4 7AL, Libn: Ms Ros Barber (024-7652-2687; *fax:* 024-7652-4182; *email:* library@maths.warwick.ac.uk)
Entry: ref only *Open:* term: Mon-Fri 0830-2400, Sat-Sun 1000-2400; vac: Mon-Fri 0830-1930, Sat-Sun 1400-1800
Subj: all subjs; undergrad; postgrad; humanities; sci; social sci *Collns: Bks & Pamphs:* BSI; EDC; Company Reports; UK & internatl statistics; 20C German lit; industrial relations *Archvs:* see Modern Records Centre (**A114**) *Co-op Schemes:* BLDSC, ILL, CURL, RLG, Access West Midlands scheme, SCONUL
Equip: m-reader, m-printer, fax, copier, 266 computers (incl wd-proc & CD-ROM) *Online:* Web of Science & others
Stock: bks/c1 mln; periodcls/5800; maps/1600; m-forms/160000; archvs/7000 linear m
Classn: LC (mod), DDC *Auto Sys:* Talis
Pubns: numerous
Staff: Libns: 22 *Other Prof:* 10 *Non-Prof:* 58

S499
Walsgrave Health Sciences Library
Walsgrave Hosp, Clifford Bridge Rd, Coventry, W Midlands, CV2 2DX (024-7653-8755; *fax:* 024-7653-5143)
Email: library@wh-tr.wmids.nhs.uk

Gov Body: Univ Hosps Coventry & Warwickshire NHS Trust *Chief:* Proj Mgr, Knowledge Svcs: Dr Humphrey Dunn (humphrey.dunn@wh-tr.wmids.nhs.uk) *Dep:* Health Scis Libn: Mrs Denise King BA(Hons), MCLIP (denise.king@wh-tr.wmids.nhs.uk) *Other Snr Staff:* Info Svcs Libn: Mrs Petra Meeson BA(Hons), MCLIP (petra.meeson@wh-tr.wmids.nhs.uk)
Assoc Libs: SIR JOHN BLACK LIB, Warwickshire PGMC, Stoney Stanton Rd, Coventry, CV1 4FG; EDYVEAN-WALKER MEDICAL LIB (see **S1876**)
Entry: health-related personnel only *Open:* Mon-Fri 0900-2000; 24 hr access for membs
Subj: medicine; surgery; allied health *Co-op Schemes:* BLDSC, NULJ, WMRLHN
Equip: m-reader, 3 copiers, 3 fax, video viewer, 18 computers (incl 16 with internet & 3 with CD-ROM) *Officer-in-Charge:* Proj Mgr, Knowledge Svcs, as above
Stock: bks/5500; periodcls/260; pamphs/200; videos/100; CD-ROMs/50 *Acqs Offcr:* Health Scis Libn, as above
Classn: DDC *Auto Sys:* Heritage
Staff: Libns: 2.75 *Non-Prof:* 5.75

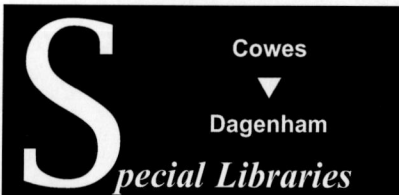

Special Libraries

Cowes ▼ Dagenham

Cowes

S500 Cowes Library and Maritime Museum

Beckford Rd, Cowes, Isle of Wight, PO31 7SG (*tel & fax:* 01983-293341)

Gov Body: Isle of Wight Council (see **P66**) *Chief:* Head of Libs (Isle of Wight Libs): Mr Tim Blackmore MCLIP *Dep:* Museum Curator (on site): Mr Tony Butler
Entry: adv appt for meeting Museum Curator
Open: Mon-Wed, Fri 0930-1800, Sat 0930-1630, closed Thu & Sun
Subj: Isle of Wight: maritime hist; all subjs (public branch lib) *Collns: Bks & Pamphs:* 7000 maritime bks & periodcls *Archvs:* ledgers & trials records *Other:* photos; ship & boat plans *Co-op Schemes:* ILL, BLDSC & South East Region
Equip: fax, copier (10p) *Svcs:* info, ref
Stock: bks/7000; periodcls/35; photos/10000; videos/25; archvs/30 m
Classn: DDC *Staff: Other Prof:* 1 *Non-Prof:* 4

Craigavon

S501 Craigavon Healthcare Library

68 Lurgan Rd, Portadown, Craigavon, Co Armagh, BT63 5QQ (028-3861-2273; *fax:* 028-3833-7600)
Email: healthcare-library@cahgt.n-i.nhs.uk

Gov Body: Queen's Univ of Belfast (see **S139**)
Chief: Asst Libn: Mrs H. Neale BLib, MCLIP (h.neale@qub.ac.uk)
Entry: DHSS employees & QUB students/staff
Open: term: Mon, Wed 0900-1700, Tue, Thu 0900-1900, Fri 0900-1630; vac: Mon-Thu 0900-1700, Fri 0900-1630; closed 1300-1330 daily
Subj: nursing; medicine
Equip: m-reader, copier (£1 per 20 copies), 3 computers (all with internet, 2 with CD-ROM), seminar room *Online:* Medline, CINAHL, BNI, Cochrane *Svcs:* info, ref
Classn: LC *Auto Sys:* Talis
Staff: Libns: 1 *Non-Prof:* 0.5

S502 Craigavon Museum Services, The Philip B. Wilson Library

Heritage Bldg, 2 Tullygally Rd, Craigavon, Co Armagh, BT65 5BY (028-3834-1635; *fax:* 028-3834-1331)
Email: museum@craigavon.gov.uk
Internet: http://www.craigavonmuseum.com/

Type: local authority *Gov Body:* Craigavon Borough Council *Chief:* Curator: Ms Susan Mannion
Entry: ref only *Open:* Mon-Fri 1000-1300, 1400-1600; closed bank hols
Subj: Co Armagh: local studies; social hist; religion; Quakerism; church hist; agric; archaeo; Irish military hist; transportation; arch *Collns: Bks & Pamphs:* Ulster Quarterly Meeting of the Religious Soc of Friends Colln (Quakerism, 17C-20C, 700 vols) *Other:* map colln (incl early 19C Ordnance Survey); photographic lib

---

Equip: copier, computers (with internet, require booking in adv) *Disabled:* wheelchair access
Stock: bks/2000+; photos/15000, incl slides

Cranfield

S503 BHR Group Ltd, Library

The Fluid Eng Centre, Cranfield, Bedfordshire, MK43 0AJ (01234-750422; *fax:* 01234-750075)
Email: nguy@bhrgroup.co.uk
Internet: http://www.bhrgroup.co.uk/

Chief: Info Svc Mgr: Mr N.G. Guy MA, MCLIP
Entry: full svcs to membs of BHRA; others ref only
Open: Mon-Fri 0900-1715, closed public hols
Subj: sci; maths, esp fluid mechanics; tech, esp fluid eng & computing *Co-op Schemes:* BLDSC
Equip: m-reader, computer (with internet) *Online:* Dialog, EINS (free to membs, prices on request for others)
Stock: bks/2500; periodcls/200
Classn: UDC *Auto Sys:* in-house
Pubns: BHR Group News (free)
Staff: Libns: 1

Crawley

S504 Crawley College, Learning Resource Centre

College Rd, Crawley, W Sussex, RH10 1NR (01293-442281; *fax:* 01293-442399)
Email: lrc_staff@crawleycollege.ac.uk

Gov Body: Crawley Coll Corp *Chief:* Learning Svcs Mgr: Mrs Janine Morgan-James BA(Hons) (jmorgan-james@crawleycollege.ac.uk) *Other Snr Staff:* Systems Libn: Mrs Sylvia Handy BA(Hons), MCLIP (shandy@crawleycollege.ac.uk)
Assoc Libs: ARUN HOUSE LRC, Horsham, Mgr: Mrs Lynne Cundey; WEST GREEN LRC, West Green Annexe, Snr Lib Asst: Mr Frank Halliday
Entry: ref only *Open:* term: Mon-Thu 0900-2100, Fri 0900-1700; vac: Mon-Thu 0900-1700, Fri 0900-1630
Subj: all subjs; genl; GCSE; A level; undergrad; careers *Collns: Bks & Pamphs:* EFL (English as a Foreign Lang) Colln; Educational Development Colln; Primary Edu Resources for teaching degree; various satellite resource centres for svc industries, incl: hair & beauty; leisure & tourism; hotel & catering; health & social care; construction *Co-op Schemes:* BLDSC
Equip: 3 video viewers, 4 copiers (A4/5p, A3/10p), 41 computers (all with wd-proc & internet, 32 with CD-ROM, £3 per hr for visitors) *Disabled:* ergonomic keyboards, lift access *Svcs:* info, ref, biblio, abstracting
Stock: bks/38287; periodcls/167; audios/646; videos/387; CD-ROMs/84
Classn: DDC *Auto Sys:* Unicorn
Staff: Libns: 3.64 *Non-Prof:* 9.66 *Exp:* £19300 (1999-2000); £14900 (2000-01)
Proj: upgrading lib sys to increase user access on-site & off-site using the internet

S505 Crawley Hospital, Library and Information Service

Postgrad Medical Centre, Crawley Hosp, West Green Dr, Crawley, W Sussex, RH11 7DH (01293-600368; *fax:* 01293-600317)
Email: chhslib@dsk.co.uk

Gov Body: Surrey & Sussex Healthcare NHS Trust *Chief:* Lib & Info Svcs Mgr: Mrs Rachel Cooke BA, MLib, MCLIP (based at East Surrey Hosp) *Dep:* Clinical Support Libn: Ms Katie R. Street BA (on site)

Assoc Libs: SURREY & SUSSEX HEALTHCARE NHS TRUST, LIB & INFO SVC (see **S1855**)
Entry: all Trust staff, others by arrangement
Open: Mon-Fri 0900-1700; 24 hr access available
Subj: social sci; sci; tech; nursing; medicine; psychiatry *Co-op Schemes:* STRLIS (ILL), BLDSC, BMA, NULJ, PLCS
Equip: copier, wd-proc, computers (incl wd-proc, internet & CD-ROM), multimedia training packages, MCQ simulator *Svcs:* info, ref, biblio
Stock: bks/c4350; periodcls/107 *Acqs Offcr:* Dep LIS Mgr: Mrs Freda Knight (at East Surrey Hosp)
Classn: NLM *Staff: Non-Prof:* 2

Crewe

S506 Leighton Hospital, Joint Education and Training Library

Middlewich Rd, Crewe, Cheshire, CW1 4QJ (01270-255141 x2705; *fax:* 01270-252611)

Gov Body: JET Lib Steering Cttee *Chief:* Medical Libn: Ms J.L. Beard BA(Hons), DipILM, MCLIP *Dep:* Lib Mgr: Mrs S. Bate C&G
Assoc Libs: CHESTER COLL LIB (see **S457**); SCHOOL OF NURSING & MIDWIFERY LIB, Arrowe Park Hosp (see **S2134**); SCHOOL OF NURSING & MIDWIFERY LIB, Countess of Chester Hosp (see **S459**)
Entry: membs of Chester Coll, PGMC, MCHT, CCHT *Open:* Mon-Fri 0830-1700
Subj: generalities; psy; social sci; medicine; nursing *Co-op Schemes:* BLDSC, BMA, LIHNN
Equip: 2 video viewers, fax, copier, 5 computers (all with wd-proc & internet) *Svcs:* info, ref, biblio
Stock: bks/14000; periodcls/105; videos/200
Classn: DDC *Auto Sys:* Innopac
Staff: Libns: 1 *Non-Prof:* 1 FTE

S507 South Cheshire College Library

Dane Bank Ave, Crewe, Cheshire, CW2 8AB (01270-654658; *fax:* 01270-651515)
Email: info@s-cheshire.ac.uk
Internet: http://www.s-cheshire.ac.uk/

Chief: Coll Libn: Ms Susan Whiteside BA, MCLIP
Entry: ref only *Open:* term: Mon, Fri 0845-1700, Tue-Thu 0845-1900; vac: Mon-Fri 0845-1630
Subj: all subjs; GCSE; A level *Co-op Schemes:* BLDSC, Libs North West
Equip: video viewers, copiers, computers (with wd-proc, internet & CD-ROM) *Disabled:* print enlarger; voice activated IT *Svcs:* info, ref
Stock: bks/20000; periodcls/70; videos/300
Classn: DDC *Auto Sys:* Genesis
Staff: Libns: 2 *Non-Prof:* 4

Criccieth

S508 The Lloyd George Museum, Reference Library

Llanystumdwy, Criccieth, Gwynedd, LL52 0SH (*tel & fax:* 01766-522071)
Email: amgueddfeydd-museums@gwynedd. gov.uk
Internet: http://www.gwynedd.gov.uk/museums/

Gov Body: Gwynedd Council (see **P58**) *Chief:* Museums & Galleries Offcr: Mrs N. Thomas BA, DipAA
Entry: ref lib by appt *Open:* Mon-Fri 1030-1700; also open Sat-Sun (Easter & Jul-Sep); Oct: Mon-Fri 1100-1600; other times by appt
Subj: materials relating David Lloyd George (statesman, 1863-1945) & his times; social hist; political hist *Collns: Archvs:* David Lloyd George papers *Other:* photos & memorabilia related to David Lloyd George

---

Equip: computer (with internet, access free, charge for printouts), room for hire (lecture theatre, £30 per session) *Stock:* bks/c400

Crieff

S509

Innerpeffray Library
Innerpeffray, near Crieff, Perthshire, PH7 (01764-652819)

Type: oldest free lending lib in the country, founded c1680 *Chief:* Keeper: Mr Ted Powell *Entry:* ref only *Open:* Mon-Wed, Fri 1000-1245, 1400-1645 *Subj:* hist; lit; nat hist; religion; theology; bibles *Collns: Bks & Pamphs:* c3000 pre-1800 bks (incl some dating back to the early 16C) & c1400 post-1800 titles; notable collns incl: Bible Colln (incl a copy of the so called "Treacle Bible" & a bible carried by the Marquis of Montrose); Lib of Archbishop Hay Drummond *Co-op Schemes:* AIL *Stock:* bks/c4400

Crowthorne

S510 🔑

British Cement Association, Centre for Concrete Information
Century House, Telford Ave, Crowthorne, Berkshire, RG45 6YS (01344-725703; *fax:* 01344-727202)
Email: etrout@bca.org.uk
Internet: http://www.bca.org.uk/services/library.html

Type: trade assoc *Chief:* Head of Centre for Concrete Info: Mr Edwin Trout DipLib *Entry:* open to membs; to non-membs on a commercial basis *Open:* Mon-Fri 0900-1700 *Subj:* cement & concrete materials; construction *Collns: Bks & Pamphs:* technical reports; conference proceedings; UK & internatl standards & regulations; trade lit *Other:* photo archv *Co-op Schemes:* ILL, exchange with similar libs overseas *Equip:* m-reader, m-printer, fax, copier, computers (incl wd-proc, internet & CD-ROM) *Svcs:* info, ref *Stock:* bks/9000; periodcls/400; photos/19000; slides/1000; pamphs/4100; videos/155 *Classn:* UDC *Auto Sys:* CAIRS *Staff: Libns:* 7

S511 🔑

The British Institute of Jazz Studies, Library
17 The Chase, Crowthorne, Berkshire, RG45 6HT (01344-775669; *fax:* 01344-780947)

Chief: Sec & Libn: Mr Graham Langley *Entry:* adv appt only *Open:* access evenings/weekends by appt *Subj:* Jazz/Blues & related music *Collns: Bks & Pamphs:* probably the largest colln of written material on Jazz/Blues & related music in the UK *Other:* ephemera & memorabilia (incl posters, handbills, postage stamps, badges etc) *Stock:* bks/3000; periodcls/20000; brochures/1000

S512 🔑

TRL Ltd Library Services
Transport Rsrch Laboratory, Old Wokingham Rd, Crowthorne, Berkshire, RG45 6AU (01344-770203; *fax:* 01344-770356)
Email: info@trl.co.uk
Internet: http://www.trl.co.uk

Gov Body: Transport Rsrch Foundation Group *Chief:* Libn: Mr Colin Howard

Entry: membership by subscription *Subj:* transport *Collns: Bks & Pamphs:* UK & internatl pubns on transport rsrch *Other:* own reports; staff papers *Co-op Schemes:* ILL *Equip:* copier, computers *Online:* various transport rsrch databases *Stock:* bks/c30000; periodcls/400; maps/350 *Pubns:* TRL News (quarterly); numerous reports

Croydon

S513 🎓

Croydon College Library
College Rd, Fairfield, Croydon, Surrey, CR9 1DX (020-8760-5849; *fax:* 020-8760-5956)
Email: kerrl@croydon.ac.uk
Internet: http://www.croydon.ac.uk/

Chief: Head of Learning Resources: Ms Linda Kerr MA, DipLib, MCLIP, FAETC *Dep:* Lib Operations Mgr: Mrs Kathy Treagus *Entry:* Croydon Coll security pass; visitors by special arrangement only *Open:* term: Mon-Tue, Thu 0900-2030, Wed 1000-2030, Fri 0900-1700, Sat 0930-1300; vac: Mon-Fri 0930-1630 *Subj:* all subjs; genl; GCSE; A level; undergrad; postgrad; vocational *Co-op Schemes:* BLDSC, Croydon Public Lib – Geac sys partner *Equip:* m-reader, m-printer, 20 video viewers, 2 copiers, clr copier, 110 computers (incl 80 with wd-proc, 20 with internet & 16 with CD-ROM) *Disabled:* 2 Kurzweil, range of software *Online:* Lawtel, Infotrac *Svcs:* info, ref, biblio, training & support svcs *Stock:* bks/81000; periodcls/401; pamphs/20000; m-forms/10; audios/175; videos/3750; CD-ROMs/70 *Classn:* DDC *Auto Sys:* Geac *Pubns:* range of leaflets for users, incl: Svcs Available in Student Support; Lib Svcs for Staff; IT Workshop; Media Svcs; Flexible Learning; various others *Staff: Libns:* 7 *Other Prof:* 30 *Further Info:* Croydon Coll Lib is an integrated Learning Centre, providing info svcs, support & training along with an IT Area, a Flexible Learning Area & Media Svcs Area

S514 ✚

Croydon Primary Care Library
(formerly Croydon Health Promotion Lib)
Croydon Primary Care Trust, 12-18 Leonard Rd, Croydon, Surrey, CR9 2RS (020-8680-2008 x256; *fax:* 020-8666-0495 – marked Attn Library)
Email: janet.mclean@croydonpct.nhs.uk

Gov Body: Croydon Primary Care Trust *Chief:* Libn: Miss Janet McLean MCLIP *Other Snr Staff:* Snr Lib Asst: Mrs Lin Hunt *Entry:* Croydon health profs; ref only for others *Open:* Mon-Thu 1000-1600 *Subj:* health; health promotion; social issues related to health *Co-op Schemes:* Kent, Surrey & Sussex Health Libs, London Health Libs, NULJ *Equip:* copier (A4/5p), 2 computers (both with internet, 1 with CD-ROM) *Svcs:* info, ref, indexing *Stock:* bks/c4500; periodcls/75 *Classn:* NLM *Auto Sys:* in-house based on DBTextworks *Staff: Libns:* 0.66 *Non-Prof:* 0.43 *Exp:* £12000 (1999-2000); £12000 (2000-01)

Cupar

S515 🎓

Elmwood College Library
Carslogie Rd, Cupar, Fife, KY15 4JB (01334-658810; *fax:* 01334-658888)
Email: Learning-Resources@elmwood.ac.uk
Internet: http://www.elmwood.ac.uk/

Chief: Libn: Mrs Christine Barclay MLib, MCLIP *Entry:* membs of coll; limited borrowing for local public; ref only for others *Open:* term: Mon, Wed 0845-1700, Tue, Thu 0845-2000; Fri 0845-1630 *Subj:* psy; social sci; sci; maths; lit; greenkeeping; conservation; leisure; mgmt; motor eng; agric; hortic; food studies *Co-op Schemes:* BLDSC, local ILL *Equip:* m-reader, copier, video viewer, 27 computers (incl wd-proc, internet & CD-ROM) *Svcs:* info, ref *Stock:* bks/145000; periodcls/115; slides/150; pamphs/2000; maps/200; videos/350 *Classn:* DDC *Auto Sys:* EASL *Pubns:* Lib Bulletins (5 pa, free); Lib Guide (annual, free) *Staff: Libns:* 1 *Non-Prof:* 1

S516 🏛🏛

Laing Museum, Reference Library
c/o Fife Council Museums East, County Bldgs, St Catherine St, Cupar, Fife, KY15 4TA (01334-412933; *fax:* 01334-413214)
Email: museums.east@fife.gov.uk

Gov Body: Fife Council (see **P53**) *Chief:* Museums Access Co-ordinator: Ms Lin Collis MA, AMA (lincollis@fife.gov.uk) *Dep:* Asst Curator: Ms Marion Wood MA, AMA *Entry:* ref only *Open:* Mon-Fri 1200-1700 during Apr-Sep; other times by appt *Subj:* local study (Fife); Scottish hist; heraldry; family hist *Collns: Bks & Pamphs:* Lib of Alexander Laing *Archvs:* Scottish parish records *Stock:* bks/2500 *Acqs Offcr:* Museums Access Co-ordinator, as above *Classn:* DDC *Staff: Other Prof:* 2 *Non-Prof:* 8 *Further Info:* The street addr for the Laing Museum is: Laing Museum, High St, Newburgh, Fife; the addr above is for correspondence

Dagenham

S517 🎓

University of East London, Learning Support Services
Longbridge Rd, Dagenham, Essex, RM8 2AS (020-8223-2707; *fax:* 020-8223-2804)
Internet: http://www.uel.ac.uk/library/lss/

Gov Body: Univ of East London *Chief:* Univ Libn & Head of Learning Support Svcs: Mrs Mary Davies (m.davies@uel.ac.uk) *Assoc Libs:* BARKING LRC, addr as above; STRATFORD LRC, Romford Rd, London, E15 4LZ, Campus Mgr: Mr Paul Chopra (chopra@uel.ac.uk); DOCKLANDS CAMPUS LIB, Royal Albert Way, London, E16 2QJ, Campus Mgr: Ms Judith Preece (judith3@uel.ac.uk); DUNCAN HOUSE LRC, High St, Stratford, London E15 2JB, Site Mgr: Ms Maureen Azubike (maureen1@uel.ac.uk); HOLBROOK LRC, Holbrook Rd, London, E15 3EA *Entry:* ref only for public *Open:* term: Mon-Fri 0900-2100, Sat-Sun 1000-1700; vac: Mon, Wed 0900-1900, Tue, Thu-Fri 0900-1700 *Subj:* all subjs; undergrad; postgrad *Co-op Schemes:* ILL, UK Libs Plus, M25 Consortium, SCONUL *Equip:* m-reader, m-printer, video viewers, copiers, clr copier, computers (incl wd-proc, internet & CD-ROM) *Disabled:* reading edge, scanner *Online:* various online databases & full-text journals *Svcs:* info, ref *Classn:* DDC *Auto Sys:* Talis *Staff:* 50 in total

Special Libraries

Dalkeith ▼ Dewsbury

Dalkeith

S518 ✏️

Midlothian Chamber of Commerce, Business Information Service
29 Eskbank Rd, Dalkeith, Midlothian, EH22 1HJ (0131-654-1234; *fax:* 0131-660-4057)
Email: info@met.org.uk
Internet: http://www.midlothianchamber.com/

Gov Body: Midlothian Enterprise Trust **Chief:** Business Info Offcr: Mrs Kerry Cringan (kerry@met.org.uk) **Dep:** Administrator: Miss Laura Thomson (laura@met.org.uk)
Open: Mon-Thu 0900-1900, Fri 0900-1700, Sat 0900-1200
Subj: business *Svcs:* info, ref
Stock: bks/c100; pamphs/c200; CD-ROMs/c20
Classn: by broad subj headings
Staff: Libns: 1 *Non-Prof:* 1

Darlington

S519 🎓

Darlington College of Technology, Information and Learning Technologies Centre
Cleveland Ave, Darlington, Co Durham, DL3 7BB (01325-503165; *fax:* 01325-503000)
Email: mdack@darlington.ac.uk
Internet: http://www.darlington.ac.uk/

Chief: Learning Resources Mgr: Ms Michelle Dack BA(Hons), DipMS
Open: term: Mon-Thu 0830-2100, Fri 0830-1630, Sat 0900-1200; vac: Mon-Thu 0830-1700, Fri 0830-1630, Sat 0900-1200
Subj: all subjs; genl; GCSE; A level *Co-op Schemes:* BLDSC, NEMLAC
Equip: copier (A4/£1 for 20), 24 computers (incl CD-ROM) *Disabled:* Supernova software *Online:* KnowUK, KnowEurope, Infotrac *Svcs:* info, ref
Stock: bks/14000; periodcls/144; videos/276; CD-ROMs/148
Classn: DDC *Auto Sys:* Genesis
Staff: Libns: 1 *Non-Prof:* 7

S520 ✚

Darlington Memorial Hospital Library
Postgrad Medical Edu Centre, Hollyhurst Rd, Darlington, Co Durham, DL3 6HX (*tel & fax:* 01325-743222)
Email: librarydmh@hotmail.com

Gov Body: South Durham Healthcare NHS Trust
Chief: Libns: Mrs Carol Houghton MA, DipLib & Miss Claire Masterman BA
Assoc Libs: BISHOP AUCKLAND GENL HOSP LIB (see **S187**)
Entry: employees of South Durham Healthcare Trust *Open:* Mon-Fri 0845-1730; 24 hr access with key
Subj: medicine; psychiatry *Co-op Schemes:* BLDSC, PLCS, BMA, RCS
Equip: m-fiche reader, video viewer, fax, 2 copiers (5p per sheet for personal use), computers (incl wd-proc, internet & CD-ROM) *Svcs:* info, ref, biblio, lit searches

Stock: bks/6000; periodcls/90; pamphs/500; videos/50
Classn: DDC *Staff: Libns:* 2

Dartford

S521 ✚

Dartford and Gravesham NHS Trust Library
Philip Farrant Study Centre, Darent Valley Hosp, Darenth Wood Rd, Dartford, Kent, DA8 8DA (01322-428549; *fax:* 01322-428547)
Email: carole.smith@dag-tr.sthames.nhs.uk

Gov Body: Dartford & Gravesham NHS Trust
Chief: Lib Mgr: Mrs C.A. Smith BA(Hons) **Dep:** Asst Libn: Mrs J.L. Fox BA(Hons)
Assoc Libs: STONE HOUSE HOSP MEDICAL LIB, Dartford, Asst Libn: Mrs S.J. Smith
Entry: NHS Trust staff & GPs: full svc; medical students: limited svc; student nurses: ref only; non-NHS staff: ref only, by adv appt *Open:* Mon, Wed 0830-1700, Tue, Thu 0830-2000, Fri 0830-1630
Subj: health scis *Co-op Schemes:* BLDSC, BMA, Inst of Psychiatry, RCSE, RSM, RCGP, STLIS ILL
Equip: video viewer, copier (A4/7p), computers (incl wd-proc, internet & CD-ROM) *Online:* CINAHL, BNI, Medline, Cochrane *Svcs:* info, ref, biblio
Stock: bks/11500; periodcls/100; pamphs/2000; videos/60
Classn: NLM *Auto Sys:* Librarian
Pubns: Lib Guide; Current Awareness Bulletin for medical staff; Health Svc circulars & pubns (all free)
Staff: Libns: 1 *Non-Prof:* 3.33
Further Info: This is the lib svc for a new acute hosp replacing the Joyce Green Hosp & Gravesend & North Kent Hosp in the Dartford area

Deeside

S522 🎓

Deeside College, Multimedia Learning Centre
Kelsterton Rd, Connam's Quay, Deeside, Flintshire, CH5 4BR (01244-834516; *fax:* 01244-814305)
Email: forresl@deeside.ac.uk
Internet: http://www.deeside.ac.uk/

Gov Body: Deeside Coll Corp *Chief:* Libn: Miss Lynn Forrester BA(Hons), MCLIP
Assoc Libs: MOLD LEARNING CENTRE, Terrig House, Chester St, Mold, Flintshire, CH7 1HB (01352-750670)
Entry: valid user ID card *Open:* term: Mon-Thu 0900-1930, Fri 0900-1630; vac: Mon-Fri 0900-1600
Subj: all subjs; genl; GCSE; A level; vocational
Co-op Schemes: BLDSC, LADSIRLAC, IW-CC
Equip: m-reader, video viewer, fax, copier, clr copier, 70 computers (incl wd-proc, internet & CD-ROM), off-air recording facilities *Disabled:* enlargers, voice teletext, large display PCs, braille printer *Svcs:* info, ref
Stock: bks/13000; periodcls/230; maps/380; audios/350; videos/170; CD-ROMs/110
Classn: UDC *Auto Sys:* Trax
Staff: Libns: 1 *Non-Prof:* 8

S523 📚

St Deiniol's Residential Library
The Highway, Hawarden, Deeside, Flintshire, CH5 3DF (01244-532350; *fax:* 01244-520643)
Email: deiniol.librarian@btinternet.com

Gov Body: The Trustees: St Deiniol's Lib (a company limited by guarantee) *Chief:* Warden: The Revd P.B. Francis MTh **Dep:** Libn: Miss P.J. Williams BA, DipLib

Entry: testimonial required from all residential & external readers, who should apply in writing to warden; ref only, no lending facilities *Open:* residential readers: Mon-Sun 0900-2200; external readers: Mon-Sat 0900-1830
Subj: genl; undergrad; postgrad; phil; psy; religion; theology; church hist; Biblical studies; ethics; pastoralia; comparative religion; edu; social & economic hist; politics; lang; painting; arch; music; ecclesiastical art; English lit (esp medieval, 16C & 19C); classics; European lit; British & European hist (esp 19C, Tudor/Stuart period) *Collns:* Bks & Pamphs: Gladstoniana (large colln relating to W.E. Gladstone, plus his personal lib of 30000 vols); Glynne Lib (16C-19C rare bks); Benson Judaica Colln; French Spirituality Colln (17C-20C); Bishop Moorman Franciscan Lib *Archvs:* Glynne-Gladstone MSS; Sir Stephen Glynne's church notes; Archbishop Green MSS; Newcastle Trust Papers; Bishop Moorman Franciscan papers
Equip: m-reader, video viewer (groups only), copier
Stock: bks/200000; periodcls/150; pamphs/50000; m-forms/400; archvs/250000 items
Classn: own *Auto Sys:* Heritage
Pubns: Gladstone: A Bibliography of Material Held at St Deiniol's Lib (£5); Wales: A Bibliography of Lit in Welsh & about Wales, Held at St Deiniol's Lib (£2); British Politics, 1800-1930: A Bibliography of Pamphs Held at St Deiniol's Lib (£2); numerous other bibliographies of the collns
Staff: Libns: 1 *Non-Prof:* 4

Derby

S524 ✚

Derby City General Hospital, Library and Knowledge Service
Uttoxeter Rd, Derby, DE22 7LE (01332-340131 x5192; *fax:* 01332-200318)
Email: david.watson@sdah-tr.trent.nhs.uk

Gov Body: Southern Derbyshire Acute Hosps NHS Trust *Chief:* Site Libn: Mr David Watson BA, MCLIP
Assoc Libs: DERBYSHIRE ROYAL INFIRMARY, LIB & INFO SVC (see **S527**)
Entry: open access to employees of Southern Derbyshire Acute Hosps NHS Trust & GPs employed in Southern Derbyshire; adv appt for external users, ref only *Open:* Mon-Fri 0800-1800
Subj: medicine; nursing *Co-op Schemes:* BLDSC, EMRLS
Equip: m-reader, copier, computers (incl wd-proc & CD-ROM) *Svcs:* info, ref, biblio
Stock: bks/3500; periodcls/107
Classn: NLM *Auto Sys:* Heritage
Staff: Libns: 1 *Non-Prof:* 1

S525 🎓

Derby College, Library and Learning Resources
Pride Parkway, Derby, DE24 8UG (01332-757570; *fax:* 01332-573149)
Email: glyn.williams@derby-college.ac.uk
Internet: http://www.derby-college.ac.uk/DClibrary/

Chief: Mgr, Info Resource Svc: Mr G.L. Williams BA(Lib), MCLIP
Assoc Libs: BROOMFIELD HALL LIB & LEARNING RESOURCES, Morley, Ilkeston, Derbyshire, DE7 6DN (01332-836600); PRINCE CHARLES AVE LIB & LEARNING RESOURCES, Prince Charles Ave, Mackworth, Derby, DE22 4LR (01332-519951); PRIDE PARKWAY LIB & LEARNING RESOURCES, addr as above
Entry: ref only if not registered Coll student; visitors should check in at reception on arrival
Open: Broomfield: Mon-Thu 0900-1530, Fri 0900-1700; Prince Charles Avenue: Mon-Thu 0830-1700, Fri 0830-1630; Pride Parkway: Mon-Thu 0845-1530, Fri 0845-1530

🎓 academic   ✏️ corporate   **- 262 -**   governmental   ✚ medical

Subj: all subjs; genl; GCSE; A level; *Prince Charles Avenue & Pride Parkway:* health; social care; arts; childcare; business studies; computing; sci; social scis; lang; humanities; catering; *Broomfield Hall:* land-based studies; agric; hortic; animal care; environmental studies; countryside care; floristry *Co-op Schemes:* BLDSC
Equip: for all 3 sites: 4 copiers (5p-6p per sheet), 81 computers (incl wd-proc, internet & CD-ROM) *Online:* Update, ECCTIS, Infotrac *Svcs:* info, ref
Stock: bks/c40000
Classn: DDC *Auto Sys:* Olib

S526

Rolls-Royce Derby FM, Library Services

PO Box 31, Victory Rd, Derby, DE24 8BJ (01332-249120; *fax:* 01332-247886)

Gov Body: OCÉ (UK) Ltd *Chief:* Central Site Svcs Mgr: Miss M.L. Parkin *Dep:* Snr Lib Asst: Mrs A. Woolley
Entry: no public entry *Open:* Mon-Fri 0800-1600
Subj: eng; fluid mechanics; aeronautics; aviation
Co-op Schemes: BLDSC
Equip: 2 m-readers, m-camera, m-printer, video viewer, fax, copier, computer (incl wd-proc) *Online:* Dialtech, Dialog, Datastar, FT Profile (only available to R-R employees)
Stock: bks/40000; periodcls/400; m-forms/100000
Classn: UDC
Pubns: Rolls-Royce Heritage Trust Series, incl. No 1: Rolls-Royce: The Formative Years 1906-1939 (£5) & others
Staff: Other Prof: 1 Non-Prof: 3

S527 ✚

Southern Derbyshire Acute Hospitals NHS Trust, Library and Knowledge Service

Devonshire House, Derbyshire Royal Infirmary, London Rd, Derby, DE1 2QY (01332-254788; *fax:* 01332-254608)

Gov Body: Southern Derbyshire Acute Hosps NHS Trust *Chief:* Lib & Knowledge Svc Mgr: Mrs Maxine Lathbury BA, MCLIP, MLS (maxine.lathbury@sdah-tr.trent.nhs.uk) *Dep:* Asst Lib & Knowledge Svc Mgr: Mr David Watson BA, MCLIP (david.watson@sdah-tr.trent.nhs.uk)
Assoc Libs: DERBY CITY GENL HOSP, LIB & KNOWLEDGE SVC (see **S524**)
Entry: ref only for non-Trust visitors *Open:* Mon-Fri 0800-1630, Sat 0900-1230
Subj: medicine; nursing; health care *Co-op Schemes:* BLDSC, BMA, DIG
Equip: 2 fax, 2 copiers, 30 computers (all with wd-proc, internet & CD-ROM), 2 scanners
Stock: bks/13600; periodcls/180; videos/40; CD-ROMs/100; various bnd periodcls
Classn: NLM *Auto Sys:* Heritage
Pubns: Newsletter
Staff: Libns: 2 Non-Prof: 8

S528 🎓

University of Derby Library

Kedleston Rd, Derby, DE22 1GB (01332-591205/6; *fax:* 01332-622767)
Internet: http://lib.derby.ac.uk/library/homelib.html

Gov Body: Univ of Derby *Chief:* Head of Lib & Learning Resources: Mr Gordon Brewer BA, MA, MCLIP (g.brewer@derby.ac.uk) *Dep:* Dep Head (Reader Svcs): Mr Richard Finch MA, DipLib, DMS, MCLIP (R.J.Finch@derby.ac.uk); Dep Head (Central Svcs): Mr David Potter BA, DipLib, MCLIP (D.J.Potter@derby.ac.uk)
Assoc Libs: KEDLESTON RD LEARNING CENTRE, addr as above; BRITANNIA MILL LEARNING CENTRE, Mackworth Rd, DE22 3BL,

Learning Centre Mgr: Ms Heather Watkins (01332-622222 x4050); CEDARS LEARNING CENTRE, The Cedars, Whitaker Rd, Derby, DE3 6AP, Snr Lib Asst: Ms Clare Bullock (01332-594246); HIGH PEAK LEARNING CENTRE, Harpur Hill, Buxton, Derbyshire, SK17 9JZ, Learning Centre Supervisor: Ms Yvonne Smith (01298-71100 x4720); MICKLEOVER LEARNING CENTRE, Univ of Derby, Western Rd, Mickleover, Derby, DE3 5GX, Learning Centre Mgr: Mr Dave Hiscock (01332-622234)
Entry: ref only for non-membs of the univ (annual fee for approved external borrowers) *Open:* term: Mon-Thu 0845-2230, Fri 0845-1900, Sat 1000-1700, Sun 1300-1700
Subj: all subjs; undergrad; selected areas at postgrad level *Collns: Bks & Pamphs:* local colln on Derbyshire & East Midlands; 19C ch's bks; Fitzmaurice Colln (internatl law) *Archvs:* univ archv *Other:* BSI (m-fiche); slide & video collns *Co-op Schemes:* BLDSC, SCONUL, UK Libs Plus, DIG, EMUA
Equip: m-readers, m-printers, video viewers, copiers, clr copier, computers (not available to external users) *Online:* access to all major on-line hosts (not available to external users)
Stock: bks/300000; periodcls/2220; slides/100000; videos/6000 *Acqs Offcr:* Acqs & Database Mgr: Ms Valerie Wilkins (V.A.Wilkins@ derby.ac.uk)
Classn: DDC *Auto Sys:* Talis
Pubns: various lib guides
Staff: Libns: 21 Non-Prof: 54

Dereham

S529 🗝

Norfolk Heraldry Society Library

13 Quebec Rd, Dereham, Norfolk, NR19 2DR
Internet: http://www.norfolkheraldry.co.uk/

Type: charity *Gov Body:* Norfolk Heraldry Soc Cttee *Chief:* Libn: Dr K.A. Mourin
Entry: membership only
Subj: heraldry
Stock: bks/160; slides/c100; m-forms/1; videos/1

Devizes

S530 🗝 🎓 🏛

Wiltshire Archaeological and Natural History Society Library

41 Long St, Devizes, Wiltshire, SN10 5JH (01380-727369; *fax:* 01380-722150)
Email: wanhs@wiltshireheritage.org.uk
Internet: http://www.wiltshireheritage.org.uk/

Gov Body: Wiltshire Archaeological & Nat Hist Soc *Chief:* Libn: Dr Lorna Haycock BA, PhD, DipELH, CertEd
Entry: ref only, adv appt *Open:* Tue-Sat 1000-1700, closed Mon & 1st Sat of each month
Subj: Wiltshire: local hist; arts; archaeo; industrial archaeo; topography; genealogy; geol; nat hist; geog; hist *Collns: Bks & Pamphs:* antiquarian, topographical, biographical & nat hist collns relating to Wiltshire; bks by Wiltshire authors; strong on local hist, archaeo & genealogy *Archvs:* Sir Richard Colt Hoare, works & MSS; William Cunnington, works & MSS; John Aubrey MSS; John Britton MSS; T.H. Baker MSS; letters diaries, business & personal papers *Other:* local newspapers; maps; rsrch notes on local hist & genealogy; sale catalogues; cuttings; photos; pedigrees; ephemera; extensive colln of watercolours, prints & drawings relating to Wiltshire; strong periodcl colln on local hist, archaeo & industrial archaeo
Equip: m-fiche reader, copier (15p per sheet), computer (with wd-proc), room for hire *Svcs:* info, ref

Stock: bks/10000; periodcls/500; photos/4000; slides/600; illusts/10000 prints & drawings; pamphs/1000; maps/2000; archvs/350 archival boxes
Classn: fixed location
Pubns: Wiltshire Archaeological Magazine (annual); annual report; biannual newsletter; local hist titles; archaeo monographs
Staff: Libns: 1 *Exp:* £2000 (1999-2000)

Dewsbury

S531 🎓

Dewsbury College Library

Halifax Rd, Dewsbury, W Yorkshire, WF13 2AS (01924-465916; *fax:* 01924-457047)
Email: abismillah@dewsbury.ac.uk
Internet: http://www.dewsbury.ac.uk/

Chief: Learning Resources Mgr: Mr Abbas Bismillah *Other Snr Staff:* Coll Libn: Mr Tim Arnold; Coll Libn (Arts): Ms Irene Rowley
Entry: ref only *Open:* term: Mon-Thu 0900-1830, Fri 1000-1600; vac: Mon-Fri 0900-1700
Subj: all subjs; GCSE; A level; undergrad; vocational
Equip: video viewer, fax, copier, 48 computers (all with wd-proc, internet & CD-ROM), room for hire *Online:* KnowEurope, KnowUK, Infotrac, XReferPlus, Newsbank, MAD, British Education Index, S-Cool, Grove Art, VADs, AXIS *Svcs:* info, ref, indexing, abstracting
Stock: bks/30000; periodcls/70; slides/6500; illusts/1300; videos/750; CD-ROMs/40
Classn: DDC *Auto Sys:* Limes
Staff: Libns: 3 *Exp:* £40000 (1999-2000)

S532 ✚

Mid-Yorkshire Hospitals NHS Trust, Library and Knowledge Services

(formerly Dewsbury Health Care NHS Trust, Staff Lib)
Oakwell Centre, Dewsbury & Dist Hosp, Halifax Rd, Dewsbury, W Yorkshire, WF13 4HS (01924-816073; *fax:* 01924-816127)
Email: library@dhc-tr.northy.nhs.uk

Gov Body: Dewsbury Health Care NHS Trust *Chief:* Libn: Ms Francesca Pendino BA(Hons)
Entry: ref only, adv appt *Open:* Mon, Wed 0930-1700, Tue, Thu 0900-1830, Fri 0900-1630
Subj: medicine; nursing; professions allied to medicine *Co-op Schemes:* JHLS interlending
Equip: m-reader, copier, fax, video viewer, 8 computers (all with wd-proc & internet, 4 with CD-ROM) *Svcs:* info, ref, biblio
Stock: bks/14000; periodcls/180; slides/200; videos/200; CD-ROMs/25
Classn: NLM *Auto Sys:* Heritage
Staff: Libns: 1 Non-Prof: 2

S533 🏛

Yorkshire Arts, Information Service

21 Bond St, Dewsbury, W Yorkshire, WF13 1AX (01924-455555; *fax:* 01924-466522)
Email: info@yarts.co.uk
Internet: http://www.arts.org.uk/

Type: regional arts board *Chief:* Info Administrator: Ms Anne Brown
Entry: ref only; adv appt *Open:* Mon-Fri 1000-1630
Subj: arts
Equip: copier (5p per copy) *Svcs:* info, ref
Stock: c6000 items, many of which are reports, pamphs & other ephemeral print items
Classn: based on North West Arts System *Auto Sys:* Access 97
Pubns: 160 info sheets (available free); these are listed in Arts Info: Guide to Info Svcs at Yorkshire Arts (publ annually in April/May)

Special Libraries

Didcot
▼
Dumfries

Didcot

S534

Baptist Missionary Society Library

Baptist House, 129 Broadway, Didcot, Oxfordshire, OX11 8XA (01235-517700; *fax:* 01235-517601)
Internet: http://www.bmsworldmission.org/

Chief: Genl Sec: Revd R.G.S. Harvey *Other Snr Staff:* Libn (PT): Mr D.S. Dancy CPhys, MInstP, MCLIP
Assoc Libs: BMS ARCHVS, located at Regent's Park Coll (see **S1760**)
Entry: strictly by appt & with permission
Subj: mission & related subjs
Equip: m-reader, m-printer, copier, computer (with wd-proc)
Stock: bks/5000
Classn: DDC *Staff: Other Prof:* 1

S535

Council for the Central Laboratory of the Research Councils, Rutherford Appleton Laboratory Library

Chilton, Didcot, Oxfordshire, OX11 0QX (01235-446668; *fax:* 01235-446403)
Email: library@rl.ac.uk
Internet: http://www.cclrc.ac.uk/

Gov Body: CCLRC *Chief:* Snr Libn: Mrs Su Lockley BSc, MSc(Econ), MCLIP
Assoc Libs: CHADWICK LIB, Daresbury (see **S2087**)
Entry: adv appt *Open:* open 24 hrs to CCLRC staff; external users 0900-1700
Subj: particle physics; nuclear physics; condensed matter physics; astronomy; astrophysics; geophysics; lasers; computing; electronics; eng; space sci; maths *Collns: Bks & Pamphs:* natl repository for European Space Agency Reports
Co-op Schemes: BLDSC, back-up lib for European Space Agency reports
Equip: m-form reader/printers, copier *Online:* Dialog
Stock: bks/25000; periodcls/350; m-forms/50 fiche; videos/5; reports/30000
Classn: UDC *Auto Sys:* Unicorn
Staff: Libns: 4 FT, 3 PT *Non-Prof:* 5 FT

S536

Medical Research Council Library

Harwell, Didcot, Oxfordshire, OX11 0RD (01235-834393; *fax:* 01235-834776)
Email: mbulman@har.mrc.ac.uk
Internet: http://www.har.mrc.ac.uk/

Gov Body: MRC *Chief:* Libn: Mrs M.J. Bulman MA, MCLIP
Entry: adv appt *Open:* Mon-Fri 0830-1700
Subj: rsrch; postgrad; radiobiology; genetics *Co-op Schemes:* BLDSC, MRC, ILL
Equip: copier, computer (incl CD-ROM) *Online:* Web of Science
Stock: bks/10000; periodcls/100
Classn: UDC *Auto Sys:* Heritage IV
Staff: Libns: 1

S537

National Radiological Protection Board Library

Chilton, Didcot, Oxfordshire, OX11 0RQ (01235-822649; *fax:* 01235-833891)
Email: david.perry@nrpb.org
Internet: http://www.nrpb.org/

Chief: Libn: Mr David Perry BA, MCLIP
Entry: adv appt *Open:* Mon-Fri 0815-1700
Subj: radiology; radiation protection *Collns: Bks & Pamphs:* series from internatl orgs e.g., Internatl Atomic Energy Agency Safety Series; US Natl Council on Radiation Protection & Measurement Report Series; Internatl Commission on Radiological Protection Pubns Series; Internatl Commission on Radiation Units & Measurements reports
Equip: m-reader, copier, computer (incl CD-ROM)
Svcs: info, ref, biblio
Stock: bks/20000; periodcls/300
Classn: UDC
Pubns: Annual Report 1997-98; Documents of the NRPB, Vols 1-10 (each vol consists of 1 or more documents individually priced, £5-£20); Guidance Notes (£4-£10); Software packages (£50-£299, p&p & VAT extra); Schools Info Pack (£4); At-a-Glance Series (single copies free); Radiation at Work Series (single copies free); various others; full text of most pubns available on web site
Staff: Libns: 1

Dingwall

S538

Highland Theological College Library

High St, Dingwall, Ross-shire, IV15 9HA (01349-867600; *fax:* 01349-867555)
Email: htc@uhi.ac.uk
Internet: http://www.htc.uhi.ac.uk/lib.html

Gov Body: Univ of the Highlands & Islands (UHI)
Chief: Coll Libn: Mr Martin Cameron
Entry: staff & students of UHI *Open:* term & vac: Mon-Thu 0845-2000, Fri 0845-1630
Subj: religion; theology; preaching; church hist; phil *Collns: Bks & Pamphs:* theological section of the Fort Augustus Benedictine Monastery Lib; part of the William Temple Colln *Co-op Schemes:* BLDSC, UHI Millennium Inst inter-lending
Equip: copier (3p per sheet), computer (with CD-ROM)
Stock: bks/35000+; periodcls/39 current, 50 no longer current; audios/200

Dollar

S539

Dollar Academy Library

Dollar, Clackmannanshire, FK14 7DU (01259-742511; *fax:* 01259-742867)
Internet: http://www.dollaracademy.org.uk/

Type: independent school *Chief:* Libn: Mrs C. Gough MA, MCLIP
Open: open to public during school term: Mon-Fri 1530-1630
Subj: all subjs; genl; standard grade & higher
Equip: computer (incl CD-ROM)
Stock: bks/12000; periodcls/12

Doncaster

S540

Doncaster College, Learning Resource Centres

Waterdale, Doncaster, S Yorkshire, DN1 3EX (01302-553553; *fax:* 01302-553559)
Internet: http://www.don.ac.uk/

Chief: Head of Learning Resources: Ms Ann Hill MA, MCLIP *Dep:* Site Libn: Mrs Lorraine Maddock BA(Hons), MCLIP
Assoc Libs: WATERDALE LRC, addr as above, Site Libn: Mrs Lorraine Maddock as above (01302-553713); HIGH MELTON LRC, High Melton, Doncaster, DN5 7SZ, Site Libn: Ms Sarah Crossland (01302-553722); CHURCH VIEW LRC, Church View, Doncaster, DN1 1RF, Site Libn: Ms Janet East (01302-553816)
Entry: ref only *Open:* term: Mon-Thu 0845-2000, Fri 0845-1645, Sat 1200-1600 (High Melton only); vac: Mon-Fri 0845-1230, 1330-1645
Subj: all subjs; phil; psy; social sci; lang; sci; maths; tech; arts; lit; geog; hist *Collns: Bks & Pamphs:* mining; careers; tutorial; resource based learning (FENC) *Archvs:* archvs of Doncaster Coll
Co-op Schemes: BLDSC, SINTO
Equip: 5 m-readers, m-printer, fax, 8 video viewers, 4 DVD players, 8 copiers, clr copier, 100 computers (incl wd-proc, internet & CD-ROM) *Online:* various e-resources *Svcs:* info, ref
Stock: bks/99958; periodcls/604; slides/11231; videos/3753; CD-ROMs/35
Classn: DDC *Auto Sys:* Genesis
Staff: Libns: 6.6 *Non-Prof:* 13.25 *Exp:* £170000 (2000-01)

S541

Doncaster Museum and Art Gallery, Library and Archives

Chequer Rd, Doncaster, S Yorkshire, DN1 2AE (01302-734293; *fax:* 01302-735409)
Email: museum@doncaster.gov.uk

Gov Body: Doncaster Metropolitan Borough Council (see **P38**) *Chief:* Head of Museums & Galleries: Mr G. Preece BA, MA, FMA
Entry: prior appt to consult ref material *Open:* Mon-Sat 1000-1700, Sun 1400-1700
Subj: local study (Doncaster & South Yorkshire); sci; arts; geog; hist
Equip: fax, video viewer, copier, room for hire
Stock: bks/various bks, pamphs, photos & slides, maps & archvs
Pubns: The Don Pottery 1801-1893, by John D. Griffin (2001, £30); Unceasing War: The 6th Svc Battalion King's Own Yorkshire Light Infantry During the Great War 1914-1918, by Malcolm K. Johnston (2000, £10)
Staff: Other Prof: 15 *Non-Prof:* 10 *Exp:* £1000 (1999-2000)
Proj: ongoing museum refurbishment to be completed in 2003

S542

Doncaster Royal Infirmary, Medical and Professional Library

Armthorpe Rd, Doncaster, S Yorkshire, DN2 5LT (01302-553118; *fax:* 01302-553250)
Email: doncaster.medicallibrary@dbh.nhs.uk

Gov Body: Doncaster & Bassetlaw Hosps NHS Trust *Chief:* Principal Lib Mgr (Medical/Healthcare Svcs): Miss Margaret Evans MCLIP *Dep:* Asst Lib Mgr (Medical/Nursing Svcs): Miss Janet Sampson BA, MCLIP
Assoc Libs: NURSING LIB, C Block, Doncaster Royal Infirmary, Armthorpe Rd, Doncaster, S Yorkshire, DN2 5LT (01302-366666 x3003; *email:* doncaster.nursinglibrary@dbh.nhs.uk); PATIENTS' & STAFF LIB, Doncaster Royal Infirmary, Armthorpe Rd, Doncaster, S Yorkshire, DN2 5LT (01302-553233; *email:* doncaster.patientslibrary@dbh.nhs.uk)
Entry: full access available to Trust employees & those on attachment; ref only to others, adv appt needed *Open:* Mon-Fri 0900-1700
Subj: multidisciplinary medicine; nursing; midwifery; allied health care *Collns: Bks & Pamphs:* patient info colln (with special interest in child health)

Equip: m-reader, copier, computers (incl wd-proc, internet & CD-ROM) *Online:* AMED, BNI, CINAHL, Cochrane, Embase, EDMR, HMIC, Pre-Medline, PsycInfo
Stock: bks/1700; periodcls/210
Classn: DDC (Patient Lib), NLM (Medical & Nursing Libs) *Auto Sys:* Heritage
Staff: Libns: 4 *Non-Prof:* 3

Dorchester

S543

Centre for Ecology and Hydrology, Dorset Library

Winfrith Tech Centre, Dorchester, Dorset, DT2 8ZD (01305-213500)
Internet: http://library.ceh.ac.uk/

Gov Body: Nat Environment Rsrch Council (NERC); part of CEH Lib Svcs (see **S1786**) *Chief:* Libn: Ms Stephanie Smith (ssmi@ceh.ac.uk) *Dep:* Ms Margaret Langran (mlan@ceh.ac.uk)
Entry: bona fide rsrchers by prior appt *Open:* Mon-Thu 0900-1700, Fri 0900-1630
Subj: freshwater ecology; pollution; aquaculture; fisheries mgmt; hydrology; sediment & water chem; coastal zone ecology; genetics; molecular ecology; biodiversity; conservation mgmt *Collns: Archvs:* Cyril Diver Colln; Ronald Good Botanical Archv
Equip: copier (fees)
Stock: bks/c5000; periodcls/500
Auto Sys: Unicorn

S544 ✚

Dorset County Hospital Library

Thomas Sydenham Edu Centre, Dorset County Hosp, Williams Ave, Dorchester, Dorset, DT1 2JY (01305-255248; *fax:* 01305-254690)
Email: library.managers@wdgh.nhs.uk

Gov Body: West Dorset Genl Hosp NHS Trust
Chief: Dist Staff Libn: Mrs A.M. Rampersad BA, MCLIP, AMBPS, LMIPP, RHS Gen Cert *Dep:* Asst Libn: Ms Patricia Graham BA(Hons), DipLib, MCLIP
Assoc Libs: STAFF LIB, Forston Clinic, Herrison, Dorchester, Dorset; various other smaller libs staffed on a rota basis
Entry: any readers other than local NHS staff should contact libn for permission *Open:* Mon-Thu 0845-1700, Fri 0845-1630
Subj: medicine; nursing; hosp admin *Co-op Schemes:* SWRLIN, NULJ
Equip: copier, 9 computers (incl wd-proc & internet) *Disabled:* hearing loop *Online:* Medline, CINAHL etc
Stock: bks/6000; periodcls/125
Classn: NLM (Wessex) *Auto Sys:* Heritage
Staff: Libns: 2 *Non-Prof:* 0.5

S545 ✿ 🗝 🏛

Dorset Natural History and Archaeological Society Library

Dorset County Museum, High West St, Dorchester, Dorset, DT1 1XA (01305-262735; *fax:* 01305-257180)
Internet: http://www.dor-mus.demon.co.uk/ or http://www.dorsetcountymuseum.org/

Gov Body: Dorset Nat Hist & Archaeological Soc
Chief: Curator & Sec: Mr R.M. De Peyer AMA
Dep: Dep Curator: Miss C. Hebditch BSc, AMA
Entry: by appt only *Open:* Mon-Sat 1000-1700
Subj: anything to do with Dorset, incl: geol; nat hist; archaeo; local hist; lit; social hist; biography; arts *Collns: Bks & Pamphs:* Thomas Hardy Memorial Colln; other literary collns concerned with: William Barnes; Sylvia Townsend Warner;

Valentine Ackland; the Powys Brothers; Elizabeth & Hope Muntz *Archvs:* nat hist records *Other:* Dorset Archaeo Collns & paper records; Dinosaur Trackways Collns
Equip: m-reader, copier
Stock: bks/35000; periodcls/80, plus 60 no longer current; photos/140000; slides/6000; pamphs/12000; maps/1000; audios/50; videos/20; wallcharts & posters/500
Classn: own
Pubns: Proceedings of the Dorset Nat Hist & Archaeological Soc (annual, £15 per vol); numerous others
Staff: Other Prof: 4 *Non-Prof:* 6

Dorking

S546 🗝 🖋

Royal School of Church Music, Colles Library

Cleveland Lodge, Westhumble St, Westhumble, Dorking, Surrey, RH5 6BW (01306-872811; *fax:* 01306-887260)
Email: library@rscm.com
Internet: http://www.rscm.com/

Chief: Hon Libn: Dr John Henderson MA, ARSCM
Entry: ref only, by appt *Open:* Mon-Fri 0900-1700
Subj: religion; arts; music (mainly choral, church & organ) *Collns: Bks & Pamphs:* church music (anthems & hymn bks); sacred music (classical & modern); organ music; bks on church music & liturgy *Archvs:* Maurice Frost Colln of Hymnody; some MSS of well-known English church composers, incl: Standford; Harwood; S. Wesley; Walmisley; & others *Other:* uncatalogued photos
Equip: 2 copiers
Stock: bks/30000, incl music; periodcls/5; photos/many
Classn: own
Pubns: RSCM publishes a wide range of church music & teaching materials for choirs & organists
Staff: Non-Prof: 0.5

Dudley

S547 ✿

Dudley College of Technology Library

The Broadway, Dudley, W Midlands, DY1 4AS (01384-363353; *fax:* 01384-363311)
Internet: http://www.dudleycol.ac.uk/

Gov Body: Dudley Coll of Tech *Chief:* Libn: Mrs Jean Edwards MCLIP *Other Snr Staff:* Snr Asst Libn: Miss Elizabeth Tromans
Assoc Libs: MONS HILL SITE LIB, 111 Mons Hill, Wrens Hill Rd, Dudley, DY1 3SB, Site Libn: Mr Charles Engola (01384-363169); CENTRE FOR LEARNING LIB, Bristol Rd South, Longbridge, Birmingham, B31 2XD, Site Libn: Miss Dena Lewis (0121-482-6101)
Entry: adv appt; fees for non-students £5 pa for ref, £25 pa for lending *Open:* term: Mon-Thu 0900-2100, Fri 0900-1630; vac: Mon-Thu 0900-1700, Fri 0900-1630
Subj: all subjs; GCSE; A level; vocational; undergrad
Equip: 2 m-readers, 2 copiers, 10 computers (all with wd-proc & CD-ROM, 2 with internet) *Online:* Athens, Lexis-Nexis, Mintel, Construction Info Svc, New Scientist *Officer-in-Charge:* Libn, as above
Svcs: info, ref, biblio
Stock: bks/55000; periodcls/200; illusts/c500; videos/150, incl DVDs; CD-ROMs/100 *Acqs*
Offcr: Asst Libn: Mrs Christine Davies
Classn: DDC *Auto Sys:* Fretwell Downing
Staff: Libns: 6 *Non-Prof:* 9

S548 ✿ ✚

Dudley Group of Hospitals NHS Trust, Clinical Library Service

Russells Hall Hosp, Dudley, W Midlands, DY1 2HQ (01384-244213; *fax:* 01384-244253)
Email: rhmlib@dial.pipex.com

Gov Body: Dudley Group of Hosps NHS Trust
Chief: Lib Mgr: Mrs Barbara Bolton BA, PGDip, MSc, MCLIP (barbara.bolton@dudleygoh-tr.wmids.nhs.uk) *Dep:* Asst Libn: Mrs Susan Hume BA(Hons), based at Corbett Medical Lib
Assoc Libs: CORBETT HOSP MEDICAL LIB (see **S1994**)
Entry: Dudley Group NHS Trust employees
Open: Mon-Tue, Thu-Fri 0830-1700, Wed 0830-1900
Subj: medicine; surgery; anaesthesia; ophthalmology; nursing; medical specialities
Collns: Other: audio & video colln *Co-op Schemes:* BLDSC, BMA, West Midlands Info Svc for Health
Equip: m-reader, video viewer, fax, copier, computers (incl wd-proc & CD-ROM) *Svcs:* info, ref, biblio
Stock: bks/7000; periodcls/112; slides/12 vols; pamphs/some; audios/66; videos/85; AVs/some
Classn: NLM *Auto Sys:* CALM 2000 Plus
Pubns: Clinical Matters Newsletter
Staff: Libns: 2 *Other Prof:* 0.5 *Non-Prof:* 1.5

S549 ✚

Dudley Health Authority Library

12 Bull St, Dudley, W Midlands, DY1 2DD (01384-239376; *fax:* 01384-455068)
Email: david.law@dudley-ha.wmids.nhs.uk

Gov Body: Dudley Health Authority *Chief:* Health Intelligence Libn: Mr David Law BA(Hons)
Entry: visits by prior arrangement *Open:* Mon-Fri 0830-1600
Subj: public health medicine; health svc mgmt; health care purchasing *Co-op Schemes:* WMHLN
Equip: copier, fax, computer (incl wd-proc, internet & CD-ROM) *Online:* Medline, Cochrane, CINAHL, AMED, Embase etc *Svcs:* info, ref, biblio
Stock: bks/2500; periodcls/40; videos/50
Classn: South West Thames Regional Lib Svc Subj Cataloguing Guide (4th ed)
Staff: Libns: 1

Dumfries

S550 ✿ ✚

Bell College of Technology, Dumfries Campus Library

Crichton Hall, Glencaple Rd, Dumfries, DG1 4SG (01387-244306; *fax:* 01387-265938)
Email: J.Anderson@bell.ac.uk
Internet: http://www.bell.ac.uk/bell2000nav/library/

Type: nursing *Gov Body:* Bell Coll *Chief:* Campus Libn: Miss Judith Anderson MA, DipHWU, MCLIP
Assoc Libs: HAMILTON CAMPUS LIB, Almada St, Hamilton, Lanarkshire, ML3 0JB (see **S780**)
Entry: students & staff of Bell Coll are given full membership; other types of membership for nurses in area & Dumfries & Galloway NHS Trusts & Health Board staff *Open:* Mon-Fri 0830-1930
Subj: social sci; tech; nursing; midwifery & allied health subjs *Co-op Schemes:* BLDSC, SHINE, NULJ
Equip: video viewer, copier, computers (incl 15 wd-proc, 4 internet & 3 CD-ROM)
Stock: bks/8000; periodcls/79; videos/500; tape-slide sets/5
Classn: DDC *Auto Sys:* CALM 2000 Plus
Staff: Libns: 2 *Non-Prof:* 1.5

Special Libraries

Dumfries ▼ Durham

S551 🎓

Dumfries and Galloway College, Clerk Maxwell Learning Resource Centre

Heathhall, Dumfries, DG1 3QZ (01387-243826; *fax:* 01387-250006)
Email: guthriea@dumgal.ac.uk

Chief: LRC Mgr: Ms Anette Guthrie MA, BSc
Assoc Libs: STRANRAER CAMPUS LRC, Lewis St, Stranraer, DG9 7AL
Entry: coll membs; genl public ref only (borrowing membership for a fee) *Open:* Mon, Wed, Fri 0830-1700, Tue, Thu 0830-1900
Subj: all subjs; SQA Higher & HNC/D levels *Co-op Schemes:* BLDSC
Equip: copier, 12 computers (all with wd-proc & CD-ROM, 7 with internet) *Svcs:* info, ref, biblio
Stock: bks/20000; periodcls/80; pamphs/1000; maps/200; m-forms/6000; audios/100; videos/350
Classn: DDC *Auto Sys:* Limes
Staff: Libns: 2 *Non-Prof:* 3

S552 🏛️🏛️

Dumfries Museum, Library and Archives

The Observatory, Dumfries, DG2 7SW (01387-253374; *fax:* 01387-265081)
Email: dumfriesmuseum@dumgal.gov.uk
Internet: http://www.dumgal.gov.uk/museums/

Type: local authority *Gov Body:* Dumfries & Galloway Council (see **P41**) *Chief:* Museums Offcr: Ms Siobhan Ratchford AMA, MLitt, FSAScot (SiobhanR@dumgal.gov.uk)
Entry: ref only, adv appt essential *Open:* by appt, tel during office hrs
Subj: Dumfries & Galloway: nat hist; hist
Equip: m-reader, m-printer, copier
Stock: bks/5000; periodcls/50; photos/10000; slides/1000; pamphs/1000
Staff: Other Prof: 5 (4 AMA, 1 conservator)

Dunblane

S553 🔑

Leighton Library

c/o Tho. & J.W. Barty, Solicitors, 61 High St, Dunblane, Perthshire, FK15 0EH (01786-822296; *fax:* 01786-824249)
Email: mail@bartys.co.uk
Internet: http://www.bartys.co.uk/

Gov Body: Leighton Lib Trustees *Chief:* Hon Custodian: Ms Mary Birch
Assoc Libs: access to the Lib is primarily through UNIV OF STIRLING LIB (see **S1978**)
Entry: no study facilities available on site; bks may be consulted in the Univ of Stirling Lib by adv appt; also open to public for limited hrs May-Oct; consult Barty's office as above for current info
Subj: mainly Christian theology; also: travel (incl America); law; phil; medicine; hist; Classics; examples of early printing in Greek & Hebrew
Collns: Archvs: some MSS held at Univ of Stirling
Stock: bks/c4000
Pubns: Catalogue of Manuscripts, Leighton Lib, by Gordon Willis (Univ of Stirling Bibliographical Soc, 1981); leaflets for visitors (free)

Staff: staffed by volunteers *Exp:* no exp on stock; lib is a complete entity from 1684
Further Info: The bks are catalogued & accessible online through the catalogue of the Univ of Stirling Lib

Dundee

S554 🎓

Duncan of Jordanstone College of Art Library

Matthew Bldg, 13 Perth Rd, Dundee, DD1 4HT (01382-345255; *fax:* 01382-229283)
Email: doj-library@dundee.ac.uk
Internet: http://www.dundee.ac.uk/library/

Gov Body: Univ of Dundee (see **S561**) *Chief:* Coll Libn: Miss Marie Simmons BA, MCLIP
Entry: Univ staff & students; annual fee for outside membership *Open:* term: Mon-Thu 0900-2030, Fri 0900-1700, Sat 1200-1700; vac: Mon-Fri 0900-1700
Subj: undergrad; postgrad; fine art; design; arch; planning; mgmt & consumer studies; TV & elec imaging *Co-op Schemes:* BLDSC, ILL
Equip: m-reader, video viewers, copiers, clr copier, computers (incl internet & CD-ROM)
Online: AMICO, Art Bibliographies Modern, Avery Index, Design & Applied Arts Index, European Visual Art Info, SCRAN; numerous e-journals
Stock: bks/60000; periodcls/205; slides/65000; illusts/500; maps/500; m-forms/12; audios/200; videos/500
Classn: DDC (mod) *Auto Sys:* Dynix
Staff: Libns: 4.5 *Non-Prof:* 8.5

S555 🎓

Dundee College Library

30 Constitution Rd, Dundee, DD3 6TB (01382-834834; *fax:* 01382-223299)
Email: library@dundeecoll.ac.uk
Internet: http://www.dundeecoll.ac.uk/library/

Gov Body: Dundee Coll *Chief:* Learning Resources Mgr: Ms Carole Gray MA, MPhil, MCLIP
Assoc Libs: CONSTITUTION RD LIB, addr as above; MELROSE CAMPUS LIB, Melrose Ter, Dundee, DD3 7QX; KINGSWAY CAMPUS LEARNING CENTRE, Old Glamis Rd, Dundee, DD3 8LE
Open: term: Mon-Thu 0845-2000, Fri 0845-1630; vac: Mon-Fri 0900-1700
Subj: all subjs; genl; GCSE; A level; vocational
Co-op Schemes: BLDSC
Equip: m-printers, video viewers, copiers, 100 computers (incl wd-proc, internet & CD-ROM)
Online: Infotrac, KnowUK, Euromonitor Global Marketing *Svcs:* info, ref, biblio
Stock: bks/50000; periodcls/200; slides/20 packs; maps/75; audios/200; videos/3000
Classn: DDC *Auto Sys:* Horizon
Staff: Libns: 1 *Non-Prof:* 10

S556 🏛️🏛️

The Mills Observatory Library

Balgay Pk, Glamis Rd, Dundee, DD2 2UB (01382-435846; *fax:* 01382-435962)
Email: mills.observatory@dundeecity.gov.uk
Internet: http://www.dundeecity.gov.uk/mills/

Gov Body: Dundee City Council (see **P42**) *Chief:* Heritage Offcr: Dr Bill Samson BSc, MSc, PhD (bill.samson@dundeecity.gov.uk)
Assoc Libs: DUNDEE ASTRONOMICAL SOC LIB, contact details as above
Entry: ref only, by appt *Open:* Apr-Sep: Tue-Fri 1100-1700; Oct-Mar: Mon-Fri 1600-2200
Subj: astronomy
Equip: Officer-in-Charge: Heritage Offcr, as above
Svcs: info, ref

Stock: bks/2500; periodcls/1; photos/100; slides/4000 *Acqs Offcr:* Heritage Offcr, as above
Pubns: The Night Sky This Month (leaflet)
Staff: Other Prof: 1 *Non-Prof:* 2

S557 ✚

Roxburghe House Library, Dundee

Royal Victoria Hosp, Jedburgh Rd, Dundee, DD2 1SP (01382-423170; *fax:* 01382-423156)
Email: marionmclagan@tpct.scot.nhs.uk

Gov Body: Tayside Primary Care NHS Trust
Chief: Consultant in Palliative Medicine: Dr Martin Leiper MB, CLB, FRCP *Dep:* MacMillan Day Care Team Leader: Mrs Marion McLagan RCN, BA, SPQ
Assoc Libs: CARSEVIEW CENTRE LIB (see **S559**); STALKER LIB, Murray Royal Hosp (see **S1790**)
Entry: open to staff of this & associate hosps; students by arrangement *Open:* Mon-Fri 0830-1630; other times by arrangement
Subj: palliative care; cancer nursing & related subjs; bereavement
Equip: copier, video viewer computer (with wd-proc, internet & CD-ROM) *Officer-in-Charge:* Day Care Team Leader, as above *Svcs:* ref
Stock: bks/372; periodcls/5; videos/81 *Acqs Offcr:* Day Care Team Leader, as above
Staff: 1 voluntary (hrs variable) *Exp:* variable

S558 🏛️

Scottish Crop Research Institute Library

Invergowrie, Dundee, DD2 5DA (01382-562731 x2013; *fax:* 01382-562426)
Email: s.stephens@scri.sari.ac.uk
Internet: http://www.scri.sari.ac.uk/

Gov Body: SCRI *Chief:* Libn: Ms Sarah E. Stephens BSc, MA, MCLIP *Dep:* Asst Libn: Miss U.M. McKean MA, DipLib
Entry: ref only, by appt *Open:* Mon-Fri 0900-1700
Subj: biological & plant sci & biotech *Collns:* Bks & Pamphs: SCRI Raspberry Lit Colln (index); Pettybridge Colln (potato lit, no index) *Co-op Schemes:* BLDSC, SALG
Equip: m-reader, fax, copier, 2 computers (both with CD-ROM), on-line catalogue terminal
Stock: bks/various; periodcls/380; slides/20000
Classn: UDC *Auto Sys:* SydneyPlus
Staff: Libns: 2 *Exp:* £83000 (1999-2000)

S559 ✚

Tayside Primary Care NHS Trust Library

Carseview Centre, 4 Tom McDonald Ave, Medipark, Dundee, DD2 1NH (01382-878735/6; *fax:* 01382-878744)
Email: kate.harrison@tpct.scot.nhs.uk

Gov Body: Tayside Primary Care NHS Trust
Chief: Libn: Mrs K.J. Harrison MA, MCLIP
Assoc Libs: STALKER LIB, Murray Royal Hosp (see **S1790**); ROXBURGHE HOUSE LIB, Royal Victoria Hosp (see **S557**)
Entry: all TPCT staff; students working within the Trust; others by appt *Open:* Mon-Thu 0845-1645, Fri 0845-1600
Subj: psy; social sci relating to medicine; psychiatry; geriatrics; primary care; community care; nursing *Co-op Schemes:* BLDSC, SHINE, PLCS
Equip: fax, copier, 6 computers (incl 1 with wd-proc & 4 with internet) *Svcs:* info, ref, biblio
Stock: bks/6480; periodcls/106
Classn: DDC, NLM (mod) *Auto Sys:* Heritage
Staff: Libns: 1 *Non-Prof:* 0.5

S560
University of Abertay Dundee, Information Services
Bell St, Dundee, DD1 1HG (01382-308866; *fax:* 01382-308880)
Email: libdesk@abertay.ac.uk
Internet: http://iserv.tay.ac.uk/

Gov Body: Univ of Abertay Dundee *Chief:* Head of Info Svcs: Mr Ivor G. Lloyd BA, DipLib, MLib, MCLIP *Other Snr Staff:* Mr Jim Huntingford MA, MSc; Ms Shirley Millar BSc, DipLib, MCLIP, DipHE *Entry:* staff & students; external & corporate membership available by subscription *Open:* term: Mon-Thu 0830-2200, Fri 0830-1700, Sat-Sun 1000-1700; vac: Mon-Fri 0845-1700
Subj: all subjs; undergrad *Co-op Schemes:* BLDSC, local reciprocal agreements, UK Libs Plus *Equip:* fax, 7 video viewers, 2 DVD players, 6 copiers, 312 computers (all with wd-proc, internet & CD-ROM), room for hire *Disabled:* WordSmith, induction loops, Aladdin Reader *Online:* STN, ESAIRS for mediated searches, 40 web/CD-ROM network databases for use by students & staff *Svcs:* info, ref, biblio, indexing, abstracting *Stock:* bks/125000; periodcls/700, plus 1915 e-journals; pamphs/13000; maps/900; CD-ROMs/1685; AVs/1500 audios & videos; archvs/13 linear m + 0.7 cubic m *Acqs Offcr:* Snr Info Offcr: Mrs Jenny Park (j.park@abertay.ac.uk)
Classn: DDC (mod for local use) *Auto Sys:* Dynix *Staff: Libns:* 4 *Other Prof:* 9 *Non-Prof:* 16 *Exp:* £367000 (1999-2000); £400847 (2000-01)

S561
University of Dundee Library
Smalls Wynd, Dundee, DD1 4HN (01382-344087; *fax:* 01382-229190)
Email: library@dundee.ac.uk
Internet: http://www.dundee.ac.uk/library/welcome.htm

Gov Body: Univ of Dundee *Chief:* Univ Libn: Mr John Bagnall *Dep:* Dep Libn: Mr Ellis Armstrong *Assoc Libs:* GARDYNE RD CAMPUS LIB, Gardyne Rd, Dundee, DD5 1NY, Campus Libn, Mr John McCaffery (01382-464267; *fax:* 01382-464255; *email:* gardyne-library@dundee.ac.uk); LAW LIB, Scrymgeour Bldg, Dundee, DD1 4HN, Law Libn, Mr David Hart (01382-344758; *fax:* 01382-228669; *email:* law-library@dundee.ac.uk); DUNCAN OF JORDANSTONE COLL OF ART LIB (see **S554**); NINEWELLS HOSP & MEDICAL SCHOOL LIB, Dundee, DD1 9SY, Medical Libn: Mr Donald Orrock (01392-632519; *fax:* 01382-566179; *email:* ninewells-medical-library@dundee.ac.uk); TAYSIDE SCHOOL OF NURSING & MIDWIFERY LIB (see **S562**); FIFE SCHOOL OF NURSING & MIDWIFERY LIB (see **S875**); UNIV ARCHVS (see **A137**); CONSERVATION UNIT, at Main Lib (01382-344094; *fax:* 01382-345614; *email:* conservation@dundee.ac.uk)
Entry: ref only; special collns require an appt in adv *Open: Main Lib:* term: Mon-Fri 0900-2200 (0900-2400 in terms 2 & 3), Sat 1200-1700, Sun 1200-1900; vac: Mon-Fri 0900-1700 (-2000 Mon-Thu during Easter & Tue & Thu during summer), Sat 1200-1700 (Easter only), Sun 1200-1900 (Easter only)
Subj: all subjs; undergrad; postgrad; arts; social sci; environmental studies; law; dentistry; sci; eng; applied sci; arch; medicine; nursing; midwifery *Collns: Bks & Pamphs:* EDC (in Law Lib); Brechin Diocesan Lib (theology, c10000 items); Nichol Colln (art & art hist); Leng Colln of Scottish Phil; Thoms Mineralogy Colln; Kinnear Local Colln; Allan Ramsey Colln; Joan Auld Memorial Colln (labour hist, mainly Scottish); Law Lib Special Collns; H Sequence (hist of medicine, at Medical Lib); U Sequence (pre-1821 bks); William Lyon Mackenzie Canadiana Colln; most special collns must be consulted in the Univ Archvs or in secure areas of the Law or Medical Libs *Co-op Schemes:* BLDSC

Equip: m-readers, video viewer, copiers, computers (incl wd-proc, internet & CD-ROM) *Online:* MIMAS Web of Science, BIDS, OCLC FirstSearch, Journal Citation Reports, numerous e-journals *Svcs:* info, ref, biblio *Stock:* bks/500000; periodcls/4500; AVs/80000 *Acqs Offcr:* Acqs Libns: Ms Chris Backler & Mrs Sandra Charles *Auto Sys:* Dynix

S562 ✚
University of Dundee, Tayside Nursing and Midwifery Library
Ninewells Hosp & Medical School, Dundee, DD1 9SY (01382-632012; *fax:* 01382-640877)
Email: snm-tayside-library@dundee.ac.uk
Internet: http://www.dundee.ac.uk/library/

Gov Body: Univ of Dundee (see **S561**) *Chief:* Learning Resources Mgr: Mr Andrew Jackson BA(Hons), MCLIP *Dep:* Libn: Mr Norrie Sandeman MA(Hons), DipLib, MCLIP *Assoc Libs:* FIFE CAMPUS LIB (see **S875**); GILLINGHAM LIB, Perth Royal Infirmary, Perth, PH1 1NX, Libn: Mrs Cathy Forbes (01738-473262); STRACATHRO HOSP LIB, Brechin, Angus, DD9 7QA
Entry: ref only; external borrowing for an annual fee *Open:* Mon-Thu 0845-2200, Fri 0845-1700, Sat 1200-1600; times vary at associated sites, please ring for details
Subj: psy; ethics; psychiatry; sociology; social welfare; social policy; nursing; medicine; mgmt *Co-op Schemes:* BLDSC, SHINE, BMA *Equip:* m-reader, video viewer, copiers, computers (incl wd-proc & CD-ROM) *Svcs:* info, ref, biblio *Stock:* bks/c32000; periodcls/250; videos/1000 *Acqs Offcr:* Acqs Libn: Miss Yvonne McKenzie *Classn:* DDC *Auto Sys:* Dynix *Pubns:* various Lib Guides *Staff: Libns:* 4 *Non-Prof:* 3

Dunfermline

S563
Lauder College Library
Halbeath, Dunfermline, Fife, KY11 5DY (01383-726201; *fax:* 01383-621109)
Internet: http://www.lauder.ac.uk/

Chief: Coll Libn: Mr Tom MacMaster MA(Hons), DipLib, MCLIP *Assoc Libs:* BABCOCK ROSYTH CAMPUS LIB, Babcock Lauder Technology, Wood Rd, Rosyth Dockyard, Rosyth, Fife *Open:* Mon-Thu 0830-1900, Fri 0830-1700, Sat 1000-1300; *Babcock Rosyth Campus:* Mon-Thu 0930-1630
Subj: all subjs; GSCE & A level; vocational *Collns: Bks & Pamphs:* genl Further Edu related materials *Equip:* copier, 2 video viewers, 14 computers (all with wd-proc, internet & CD-ROM) *Online:* Infotrac *Svcs:* info, ref, biblio *Stock:* bks/22000; periodcls/40; pamphs/300 boxed; audios/40; videos/200 *Classn:* DDC *Auto Sys:* Heritage *Staff: Libns:* 1 *Non-Prof:* 4.5 *Exp:* £36000 (2000-01)

S564 ✚
Queen Margaret Hospital NHS Trust, Education Centre Library
Whitefield Rd, Dunfermline, Fife, KY12 0SU (01383-623623 x2546; *fax:* 01383-627026)
Email: marie.smith@faht.scot.nhs.uk

Gov Body: Fife Acute Hosps NHS Trust *Chief:* Libn: Ms Marie Smith BA, MCLIP *Dep:* Centre Mgr: Mrs Isobel Cowan

Assoc Libs: POSTGRAD MEDICAL LIB, Victoria Hosp (see **S873**)
Open: 24 hr access for staff
Subj: medicine *Co-op Schemes:* BLDSC, BMA, SHINE
Equip: copier, 3 computers (all with internet, 2 with wd-proc & 1 with CD-ROM), 6 rooms for hire *Svcs:* info, ref, biblio
Stock: bks/1000; periodcls/50
Classn: NLM *Auto Sys:* Heritage
Staff: Libns: 0.5 *Non-Prof:* 1

Dunstable

S565
Dunstable College Library
Kingsway, Dunstable, Bedfordshire, LU5 4HG (01582-477776; *fax:* 01582-478801)
Email: melder@dunstable.ac.uk
Internet: http://www.dunstable.ac.uk/

Gov Body: Dunstable Coll Corp *Chief:* Libn: Mr Malcolm Elder BA(Hons), DipILS *Entry:* contact lib in adv *Open:* term: Mon-Thu 0900-2000, Fri 0900-1500, Sat 1000-1300; vac: variable
Subj: vocational; generalities; psy; religion; social sci; lang; sci; maths; tech; arts; lit; geog; hist; business; health; social care; child care *Co-op Schemes:* BLDSC
Equip: 2 video viewers, copiers (A4/6p), 13 computers (all with wd-proc, internet & CD-ROM) *Disabled:* Aladdin Rainbow Magnifier, Magnice, Lookout, BigKeysPlus *Online:* Infotrac Onefile, Custom Newspapers (no fees) *Officer-in-Charge:* Libn, as above *Svcs:* info, ref, biblio *Stock:* bks/27000; periodcls/90; pamphs/100; maps/100; audios/30; videos/1500; CD-ROMs/70 *Acqs Offcr:* Libn, as above *Classn:* DDC, CLCI *Auto Sys:* Heritage *Staff: Libns:* 1 *Non-Prof:* 4

S566
Strict Baptist Historical Society Library
c/o 38 Frenchs Ave, Dunstable, Bedfordshire, LU6 1BH (01582-602242)
Email: kdix@sbhs.freeserve.co.uk

Gov Body: Strict Baptist Historical Soc *Chief:* Libn: Mr D.J. Woodruff
Entry: adv appt *Open:* as arranged
Subj: religion; church hist *Equip:* copier *Svcs:* info, ref *Stock:* bks/5000+; periodcls/6 *Classn:* own *Pubns:* Annual Bulletin (£1); Newsletter (free) *Staff: Non-Prof:* 1 *Exp:* stock acquired by donation

Durham

S567
Archdeacon Sharp Library
The College, Durham, DH1 3EH (0191-386-2489)
Email: enquiries@durhamcathedral.co.uk

Gov Body: Trustees of Lord Crewe's Charities *Chief:* Libn: Canon Prof Dr David Brown *Assoc Libs:* DURHAM CHAPTER LIB (see **S569**); MEISSEN LIB (see **S573**); contact details for both same as above
Entry: open to all clergy & students of theology in Northumbria *Open:* Mon-Fri 0900-1300, 1415-1700; closed Aug
Subj: modern theology in English
Stock: bks/8000 *Classn:* DDC
Pubns: leaflet (free)
Staff: Libns: 1 *Other Prof:* 1

Special Libraries

Durham
▼
Eastleigh

S568 ✚ 🎓
County Durham and Darlington Primary Care Trust, Shared Services Library

Appleton House, Lanchester Rd, Durham, DH1 5XZ (0191-333-3395; *fax:* 0191-333-3398)
Email: linda.snowdon@cdd.nhs.uk

Chief: Lib Mgr: Ms Linda Snowson BA, MCLIP
Entry: NHS staff in Co Durham & Darlington
Open: Mon-Thu 0900-1700, Fri 0900-1630
Subj: health; health mgmt *Co-op Schemes:* BLDSC, regional ILL scheme
Equip: copier, 2 computers (both with wd-proc, internet & CD-ROM) *Svcs:* info, ref
Stock: bks/4000; periodcls/40; videos/10
Classn: own *Auto Sys:* Libero
Staff: Libns: 0.8 Non-Prof: 1

S569 🔑 🖐
Durham Chapter Library

The College, Durham, DH1 3EH (0191-386-2489)
Email: enquiries@durhamcathedral.co.uk

Gov Body: The Dean & Chapter of Durham
Chief: Chapter Libn: The Revd Canon Prof D.W. Brown PhD, DPhil
Assoc Libs: ARCHDEACON SHARP LIB (see **S567**); MEISSEN LIB (see **S573**); contact details for both same as above
Entry: new readers should write at least a fortnight before their intended visit; for use of historic collns a letter of recommendation & proof of ID is required
Open: Mon-Fri 0900-1300, 1415-1700; closed Aug
Subj: bibliography; palaeography; religion; monasticism; local hist; early printed bks *Collns: Archvs:* personal papers of Bishops H.H. Henson, J.B. Lightfoot & I.T. Ramsey; antiquarian historical MSS of County Durham; Saxon & medieval MSS of Durham Priory; 17C & 18C European univ theses *Other:* 17C & 18C music (MS & printed; sacred & secular)
Stock: bks/60000; periodcls/20; photos/2500
Classn: DDC, Press Mark
Pubns: Lib Guide (free)
Staff: Libns: 1 Non-Prof: 1

S570 🏛 🏛
Durham Light Infantry Museum and Durham Art Gallery Library

Aykley Heads, Durham, DH1 5TU (0191-384-2214; *fax:* 0191-386-1770)
Email: dli@durham.gov.uk
Internet: http://www.durham.gov.uk/

Type: local authority *Gov Body:* Durham County Council (see **P43**) *Chief:* Mgr: Mr Stephen D. Shannon
Assoc Libs: REGIMENTAL ARCHV, now held at Durham County Record Office (see **A141**)
Entry: ref only; adv appt required *Open:* Mon-Fri 1000-1600
Subj: regimental hist; military hist *Collns: Bks & Pamphs:* regimental & divisional hists of the Durham Light Infantry (1758-1968), incl Durham Militia, Durham Volunteers, Home Guard etc
Equip: copier (10p per pg) *Svcs:* info, ref

S571 🎓
Durham University Library

Stockton Rd, Durham, DH1 3LY (0191-374-2968; *fax:* 0191-374-2971)
Email: main.library@durham.ac.uk
Internet: http://www.dur.ac.uk/library/

Gov Body: Univ of Durham *Chief:* Univ Libn: Dr John Hall BA, PhD (j.t.d.hall@durham.ac.uk) *Dep:* Dep Libn: Ms Clare Powne (clare.powne@durham.ac.uk) *Other Snr Staff:* Sub-Libn (Academic Svcs & Systems): Ms Ros Pan (r.c.pan@durham.ac.uk); Sub-Libn (Special Collns): Ms Sheila Hingley (s.m.hingley@durham.ac.uk); Sub-Libn (Colln Mgmt): Mr Eric Watchman (e.c.watchman@durham.ac.uk)
Assoc Libs: EDU SECTION, Leazes Rd, Durham, DH1 1TA (0191-334-8137; *fax:* 0191-334-8311; *email:* educ.library@durham.ac.uk); PALACE GREEN LIB, Palace Green, Durham, DH1 3RN (0191-334-2932; *fax:* 0191-334-2942; *email:* pg.library@durham.ac.uk); QUEEN'S CAMPUS LIB (see **S1982**); DURHAM UNIV BUSINESS SCHOOL LIB (see **S572**)
Entry: ref only, limited subscription borrowing
Open: term: Mon-Thu 0830-2400, Fri 0830-2200, Sat 0900-1700, Sun 1400-2200; vac: Mon-Thu 0900-2000, Fri 0900-1700, Sat 1000-1300, Sun 1400-1800; *Edu Lib:* term: Mon-Thu 0900-2100, Fri 0900-1700, Sat 0900-1300; vac: Mon-Fri 0900-1700, Sat 0900-1300; *Palace Green Lib:* term: Mon-Thu 0900-2100, Fri-Sat 0900-1700, Sun 1400-2100; vac: Mon-Sat 0900-1700; *Archvs & Special Collns at Palace Green:* term: Mon, Fri 0900-1700, Tue 0900-2000, Wed-Thu 0900-1800, Sat 1000-1300; vac: Mon-Fri 0900-1700
Subj: all academic subjs, excl arch & medicine; *Palace Green Lib:* law; music; archvs & special collns *Collns: Bks & Pamphs:* Middle East Documentation Unit; East Asian collns; older printed bks; local material; BSI; EDC; British Official pubns; SCOLMA (Sudan) *Archvs:* Univ of Durham Archvs; Durham Cathedral Archvs; Durham diocesan & private records; Palatinate of Durham records; Sudan Archv; antiquarian collns; architects' papers; ecclesiastical papers; family papers; literary MSS; manorial records; oriental MSS; political papers; papers of scholars; scientific papers; solicitors' papers; & others *Other:* music MSS; maps & enclosure records; photo colln; prints & drawings; British Council Poetry Reading Tapes; Durham Palatinate Mint Coin Colln *Co-op Schemes:* BLDSC, SCOLMA, UK Libs Plus, SCONUL
Equip: m-reader, m-printer, video viewer, copiers, computers (incl internet & CD-ROM) *Online:* BIDS, UnCover, FirstSearch, BUBL & others *Svcs:* info, ref
Stock: bks/1095000; periodcls/3500; archvs/3067 linear m
Classn: DDC, Bliss (Edu section), LC (mod, Middle East & Asian collns) *Auto Sys:* TinLib
Pubns: lib guides & info sheets; annual reports; handlists & guides to archvs & special collns
Staff: Libns: 17 Non-Prof: 46.2

S572 🎓
Durham University, Business School Library

Mill Hill Ln, Durham, DH1 3LB (0191-334-5213; *fax:* 0191-334-5201)
Email: Colin.Theakston@durham.ac.uk
Internet: http://www.durham.ac.uk/dubs/

Gov Body: Durham Univ (see **S571**) *Chief:* Departmental Libn: Mr Colin Theakston BA, MPhil, PGCE, DipLib, MCLIP *Dep:* Lib Asst: Mrs Debbie Corner
Entry: non-Business School students may use lib for ref only *Open:* term: Mon-Fri 0845-2130, Sat 0845-1330; vac: Mon-Thu 0845-1700, Fri 0845-2000, Sat 0845-1330

Subj: business; mgmt *Collns: Bks & Pamphs:* company reports; working papers *Co-op Schemes:* ILL
Equip: m-reader, copier, computers (incl wd-proc, internet & CD-ROM) *Online:* Searchbank, Emerald, EBSCO, FAME, Mintel, Web of Science, OCLC FirstSearch, Lexis-Nexis, Reuter's Business Insight, Euromonitor GMID, Datastream
Stock: bks/60000; periodcls/400
Classn: LBC *Auto Sys:* Innopac
Staff: Libns: 1 Non-Prof: 2

S573 🎓 🖐
Meissen Library

The College, Durham, DH1 3EH (0191-386-2489)

Gov Body: The Dean & Chapter of Durham
Chief: Libn: The Revd Canon Prof D.W. Brown PhD, DPhil
Assoc Libs: ARCHDEACON SHARP LIB (see **S567**); DURHAM DEAN & CHAPTER LIB (see **S569**); contact details for both same as above
Entry: to bona fide students of religion *Open:* Mon-Fri 0900-1300, 1415-1700, closed Aug
Subj: religion; German Protestantism in the German lang
Stock: bks/14000 *Staff:* Libns: 1

S574 🎓
New College Durham, Library Services

Neville's Cross Centre, Darlington Rd, Durham, DH1 4SY (0191-375-4375; *fax:* 0191-375-4223)
Email: nxc.library@newdur.ac.uk
Internet: http://www.newdur.ac.uk/

Gov Body: New Coll Durham Corp *Chief:* Head of Lib Svcs: Mr R.W. Harvey MA, MCLIP *Dep:* Academic Libn: Mrs Denise Heslop BA, MCLIP
Assoc Libs: FRAMWELLGATE MOOR CENTRE LIB, Framwellgate Moor, Durham, DH1 5ES, Snr Libn: Mrs Theresa Lawrence BA, MCLIP
Entry: ref only *Open:* term: Mon-Thu 0845-2045, Fri 0845-1645, Sat 0845-1245; vac: Mon-Thu 0845-1645, Fri 0845-1615
Subj: all subjs; GCSE; A level; undergrad; postgrad; vocational *Co-op Schemes:* BLDSC
Equip: 2 m-readers, 2 m-printers, 2 copiers, computers (incl 12 with wd-proc & 10 with CD-ROM) *Svcs:* info, ref
Stock: bks/100000; periodcls/500
Classn: DDC *Auto Sys:* Soft Link (Alice)
Staff: Libns: 5 Non-Prof: 12.9 *Exp:* £157448 (1999-2000); £152448 (2000-01)

S575 🎓 🖐
St John's College Library

3 South Bailey, Durham, DH1 3RJ (0191-374-3572; *fax:* 0191-374-3573)
Internet: http://www.dur.ac.uk/st-johns.college/

Gov Body: St John's Coll Council *Chief:* Libn: Dr Mark Bonnington *Dep:* Asst Libn: Mrs Fay Slinn
Entry: membs of St John's Coll & subscribers
Open: open 24 hrs to key holders
Subj: religion
Equip: 3 computers (all with internet)
Stock: bks/35000; periodcls/100; videos/40
Classn: DDC (mod) *Auto Sys:* AutoLib
Staff: Non-Prof: 2 *Exp:* £12850 (1999-2000)

S576 🎓
Teikyo University of Japan in Durham, The Library

Lafcadio Hearn Cultural Centre, Mill Hill Ln, Durham, DH1 3YB (0191-334-5848; *fax:* 0191-334-5123)
Email: mikiko.davies@durham.ac.uk
Internet: http://www.dur.ac.uk/~dot0www/

Gov Body: Teikyo Univ, Japan **Chief:** Libn: Mrs Mikiko Davies
Entry: borrowing for staff & students of Durham Univ; ref only for public **Open:** Mon, Wed 0900-1200, Tue, Thu-Fri 0900-1600
Subj: all subjs; undergrad; postgrad; humanities; arts; social scis; Japanese hist; Japanese lit; holdings are mainly in Japanese, with a small colln of English lang bks on Japan **Collns:** Other: on m-film: Gordon W. Prange Colln; Asahi Shimbun (Meiji 21-); Nihon Kezai Shimbun (Meiji 9-)
Equip: m-reader, m-printer, video viewer, copier, computers (with wd-proc, internet & CD-ROM, for use of membs only) **Svcs:** info, ref
Stock: bks/c35000; periodcls/25; photos/50; maps/25; audios/50; videos/400
Classn: NDC (Nippon Decimal Classn) **Auto Sys:** Innopac **Staff:** Libns: 1 Non-Prof: 1

S577 🎓 🕊️
Ushaw College Library
Durham, DH7 9RH (0191-373-8516/2)
Email: alistair.macgregor@ushaw.ac.uk

Chief: Libn: Dr A.J. MacGregor BA, DipEd, PhD
Entry: by adv written appt during term
Subj: rsrch; postgrad; particular strength in theology; scripture; liturgy; spirituality; church hist; European hist; genl Further Edu; fine arts; early sci **Collns:** Bks & Pamphs: early printed bks up to 1700 (c2500 vols); pamphs; periodcls **Archvs:** Coll archvs; Lisbon Coll Archvs; correspondence re 18C-19C Catholic hist **Other:** Lisbon Coll Colln
Equip: copier (limited availability)
Stock: bks/60000; periodcls/60; photos/1000; pamphs/5000; archvs/2 cubic m
Classn: DDC
Pubns: Ushaw Coll Lib (1994, pamph); In Illo Tempore (lib bulletin, ongoing, Nos 1-21 available); A Hist of Ushaw Coll; Lisbon Coll Register 1628-1813 (Vol 72, Catholic Record Soc)
Staff: Libns: 1

East Dereham

S578 🏛️ 🏛️
Norfolk Rural Life Museum and Union Farm, Library
Beech House, Gressenhall, East Dereham, Norfolk, NR20 4DR (01362-869266; fax: 01362-860385)
Email: gressenhall.museum@norfolk.gov.uk

Gov Body: Norfolk County Council (see **P123**)
Chief: Collns Offcr: Ms Frances Collinson (frances.collinson@norfolk.gov.uk)
Entry: adv appt **Open:** Mon-Fri 1000-1300, 1400-1600
Subj: local study (Norfolk & East Anglia): rural life; topography; village life; farming; rural trades & crafts; agric; geog; hist **Collns:** Bks & Pamphs: Plowright Colln (ironmongers' catalogues, printed advertisements etc) **Other:** photo collns (10000 historic photos of all listed subjs); over 5000 printed ephemera collns of all subjs; the Museum's artefact collns are available if they complement rsrch
Equip: copier, light box for slides & glass negs etc
Stock: bks/3000; periodcls/6; photos/20000; slides/1000; pamphs/10000
Classn: SHIC **Staff:** Other Prof: 3 Non-Prof: 10

East Grinstead

S579 ✚
Queen Victoria Hospital NHS Trust, Clinical Library
Holtye Rd, East Grinstead, W Sussex, RH19 3DZ (01342-410210 x266; fax: 01342-301953)
Email: library@qvh.nhs.uk

Gov Body: NHS Trust **Chief:** Lib Svcs Mgr: Mrs Patricia Rey
Entry: adv appt; ref only **Open:** open 24 hrs a day; staffed: Mon-Wed 0900-1700, Thu-Fri 0930-1300
Subj: medicine & nursing; esp: plastic surgery; maxillo-facial surgery; corneo-plastic surgery **Co-op Schemes:** HLN, NULJ
Equip: m-reader, copier (5p per sheet), fax (receipt only), 8 computers (all with wd-proc & CD-ROM) **Online:** via KA24 (access through staff): Medline, PsycInfo, AMED, CINAHL, BNI, HMIC **Officer-in-Charge:** Lib Svcs Mgr, as above **Svcs:** info, ref, biblio
Stock: bks/c4000; periodcls/60; videos/30; CD-ROMs/5 **Acqs Offcr:** Lib Svcs Mgr, as above
Classn: NLM **Staff:** Libns: 0.65
Proj: extension to lib

East Kilbride

S580 🏛️
DFID Library
Dept for Internatl Development, Abercrombie House, Eaglesham Rd, East Kilbride, Glasgow, G75 8EA (01355-843880; fax: 01355-843632)
Email: library@dfid.gov.uk
Internet: http://www.dfid.gov.uk/

Gov Body: Dept for Internatl Development **Chief:** Lib Mgr: Miss Sharon Skelton **Dep:** Asst Lib Mgr: Mr Robert Martin
Entry: ref only, by adv appt only **Open:** Mon-Fri 0900-1700
Subj: internatl development; economic development; overseas aid policy **Co-op Schemes:** ILL
Stock: bks/50000; periodcls/600
Classn: LC **Auto Sys:** Unicorn
Staff: Libns: 1 Other Prof: 1 Non-Prof: 1

S581 🍵
Scottish Nuclear Ltd, Library
3 Redwood Cres, Peel Pk, East Kilbride, Glasgow, G74 5PR (01355-262000; fax: 01355-262626)
Email: evelyn.hutchinson@british-energy.com
Internet: http://www.british-energy.com/

Gov Body: British Energy **Chief:** Libn: Mrs Evelyn Hutchison
Entry: admission by appt; bona fide rsrchers
Open: Mon-Fri 0830-1630
Subj: UK & worldwide nuclear generating industry; conventional power generation; energy policy; environment; business; finance; sci; tech **Co-op Schemes:** BLDSC, ILL
Equip: video viewer, 8 computers (incl 1 with wd-proc, 1 with CD-ROM & 2 with internet) **Online:** BSI, ProFound & Technical Indexes **Svcs:** info, ref, biblio, indexing, abstracting
Stock: bks/11000; periodcls/500; technical reports/25000
Classn: UDC **Auto Sys:** CAIRS
Staff: Libns: 1 Non-Prof: 1

Eastbourne

S582 🎓
Sussex Downs College, Eastbourne Learning Centre
(formerly Eastbourne Coll of Arts & Tech)
Cross Levels Way, Eastbourne, E Sussex, BN21 2UF (01323-637261; fax: 01323-637472)
Email: lrc@sussexdowns.ac.uk
Internet: http://www.sussexdowns.ac.uk/

Chief: Learning Resources Mgr: Mr David Futter BA(Hons), CertEd, MCLIP **Dep:** Lib Assts: Ms Frances Lynn, Ms Debbie Williams

Assoc Libs: LEWES CAMPUS LRC (see **S942**)
Entry: for Coll students; others ref only & by appt on payment of a fee **Open:** term: Mon-Thu 0900-1900, Fri 0900-1700
Subj: all subjs; genl Further Edu
Equip: video viewer, fax, copier, computers (incl wd-proc & CD-ROM)
Stock: bks/27000; periodcls/200; audios/100; videos/500
Classn: DDC **Auto Sys:** Heritage IV
Staff: Libns: 6 Non-Prof: 1

S583 🎓 ✚
University of Brighton, Health Sciences Library
Dist Genl Hosp, King's Dr, Eastbourne, E Sussex, BN21 2UD (01323-417400 x4048; fax: 01323-435740)
Email: AskDGH@brighton.ac.uk

Chief: Medical Libn: Mr Michael Sibson BA(Hons), LLB, MCLIP (m.f.d.sibson@bton.ac.uk)
Entry: lib membership available to membs of Brighton Univ, Eastbourne Hosps Trust & Eastbourne & County Healthcare Trust **Open:** Mon, Wed 0830-2000, Tue, Thu-Fri 0830-1700
Subj: nursing; midwifery; medicine; psychiatry **Co-op Schemes:** BLDSC
Equip: video viewer, copier, computers (incl wd-proc, internet & CD-ROM)
Stock: bks/15000; periodcls/150
Classn: NLM **Auto Sys:** Talis

S584 🎓
University of Brighton, Queenwood Library
Darley Rd, Eastbourne, E Sussex, BN20 7UN (01273-600900; fax: 01273-643825)
Email: AskQueenwood@brighton.ac.uk
Internet: http://www.brighton.ac.uk/is/

Gov Body: Univ of Brighton (see **S237**) **Chief:** Info Svcs Mgr: Mr Michael Ainscough BA, MCLIP
Assoc Libs: other Univ of Brighton Libs
Entry: ref only to non-membs of Univ **Open:** term: Mon-Thu 0845-2000, Fri 0845-1700, Sat-Sun 1300-1700; vac: Mon-Fri 0900-1700
Subj: undergrad; postgrad; sport; exercise sci; physical edu; leisure policy; occupational therapy; physiotherapy; podiatry; leisure; tourism; mgmt **Collns:** Archvs: Chelsea School Archv **Co-op Schemes:** ILL
Equip: 4 video viewers, 5 copiers, 14 computers **Online:** BIDS **Svcs:** info, ref
Stock: bks/80000; periodcls/500; maps/25
Classn: DDC **Auto Sys:** Talis
Staff: Libns: 5 Non-Prof: 10

Eastleigh

S585 🎓
Eastleigh College Learning Centre
Chestnut Ave, Eastleigh, Hampshire, SO5 5HT (023-8091-1026; fax: 023-8032-2133)
Internet: http://www.eastleigh.ac.uk/

Chief: Libn: Ms Sheila Tomkins
Entry: students & staff of the Coll **Open:** term: Mon-Thu 0845-1900, Fri 0840-1630, Sat 0900-1230
Subj: all subjs; GCSE; A level **Co-op Schemes:** BLDSC, HATRICS
Equip: video viewers, copiers, 50+ computers (incl wd-proc & internet), scanners
Stock: bks/20000; periodcls/175

Edinburgh

S586 ⚷
Advocates Library

Faculty of Advocates, Parliament House, Edinburgh, EH1 1RF (0131-260-5683; *fax:* 0131-260-5663)

Gov Body: Faculty of Advocates *Chief:* Snr Libn: Ms Andrea Longson BSc, DipLib (andrea. longson@advocates.org.uk) *Dep:* Libn, Reader Svcs: Ms Maria Gunn (marian.gunn@advocates. org.uk)
Assoc Libs: small working collns in GLASGOW HIGH COURT, Saltmarket, Glasgow; COURT OF JUSTICIARY, Lawnmarket, Edinburgh; HOUSE OF LORDS LIB, London (see **S1167**); also has responsibility for WALTER SCOTT LIB, Abbotsford, Melrose
Entry: strictly membs of the faculty only; any bona fide rsrchers should write to the Keeper of the Lib requesting access; there may be a fee *Open:* 24 hr access; staffed: Mon-Fri 0900-1700
Subj: law & related subjs (extensive colln)
Collns: Bks & Pamphs: sizeable collns of Sessions Papers (mostly unindexed); Roman-Dutch Colln; select collns of legislative materials from other Commonwealth countries *Archvs:* some faculty records; caricatures & photos; jurisdictions *Co-op Schemes:* the Advocates Lib, a copyright lib since 1711, retains the copyright privilege for legal materials in Scotland; copyright material can be consulted via the Natl Lib of Scotland; the Advocates Lib catalogue can be consulted in the NLS (enquire at the NLS – see **L2**)
Equip: m-reader, fax, 3 copiers, video viewer, computers (incl wd-procs, internet & CD-ROM)
Online: Lexis *Svcs:* info, ref, biblio
Stock: bks/200000; periodcls/1550; some photos, m-forms & archvs
Classn: LC *Auto Sys:* Endeavour Voyager
Staff: Libns: 6 *Other Prof:* 1 *Non-Prof:* 8 + 4 PT

S587 ⚷
Age Concern Scotland Library

113 Rose St, Edinburgh, EH2 3DT (0131-220-3345; *fax:* 0131-220-2772)
Email: library@acscot.org.uk
Internet: http://www.ageconcernscotland.org.uk/

Type: charity *Chief:* Lib Svcs Offcr: Mr John Urquhart MA *Other Snr Staff:* Info Mgr: Ms Jenni Campbell
Entry: adv appt *Open:* Mon-Fri 1000-1600
Subj: social sci; older people & issues affecting them
Equip: copier (10p per sheet), video viewer, computer (with wd-proc, internet & CD-ROM)
Officer-in-Charge: Lib Svcs Offcr, as above *Svcs:* info, ref, biblio
Stock: bks/7000; periodcls/50; videos/100 *Acqs Offcr:* Lib Svcs Offcr, as above
Classn: Age Concern Scotland scheme *Auto Sys:* CAIRS
Pubns: list available
Staff: Libns: 3 *Non-Prof:* 2 *Exp:* £7400 (1999-2000)

S588
City of Edinburgh Council, City Development Library

329 High St, Edinburgh, EH1 1PN (0131-529-4911; *fax:* 0131-529-7467)
Email: elspeth.third@edinburgh.gov.uk

Gov Body: City of Edinburgh Council (see **P50**)
Chief: Libn: Mrs Elspeth Third BSc
Entry: ref only *Open:* Mon-Fri 0900-1600
Subj: local study (Edinburgh); arts; tech; construction; transport *Collns: Bks & Pamphs:* BSI (related to construction & transport) *Other:* photos of Edinburgh *Co-op Schemes:* BLDSC
Equip: copier, 2 computers (incl wd-proc, internet & CD-ROM) *Svcs:* info, ref
Stock: various bks, photos & trade lit
Classn: CI/SfB *Auto Sys:* InMagic DBTextworks
Staff: Non-Prof: 2

S589 ✚ 🏛
Common Services Agency, Information and Statistics Division Library

NHS in Scotland, Trinity Park House, South Trinity Rd, Edinburgh, EH5 3SQ (0131-551-8087; *fax:* 0131-551-8495)
Email: isdlib@isd.csa.scot.nhs.uk

Gov Body: Info & Statistics Div of the Common Svcs Agency for the NHS in Scotland *Chief:* Health Info Scientist: Mr A.H. Jamieson MA, DipLib, MCLIP
Entry: adv appt *Open:* Mon-Fri 0900-1700
Subj: health & population statistics *Collns: Archvs:* NHS in Scotland circulars (e.g., MELs, GENs) *Co-op Schemes:* SHINE, BLDSC, Edinburgh Univ Union List, CSA Lib Staff Forum
Equip: m-reader, m-printer, copier, computers (with wd-proc, internet & CD-ROM), scanner *Svcs:* info, ref, biblio, indexing, abstracting
Stock: bks/12500; periodcls/130
Classn: Bliss *Auto Sys:* BASISplus
Pubns: Lib guide; Journals Lists; Indiv SDIs
Staff: Libns: 1 *Non-Prof:* 1.68

S590 🏛
Crown Office Library

25 Chambers St, Edinburgh, EH1 1LA (0131-226-2626)
Internet: http://www.crownoffice.gov.uk/

Chief: Knowledge Mgr: Ms Susan Sandeman
Entry: membs of the Procurator Fiscal Svc only
Subj: social sci; arts
Equip: copier, computer (incl wd-proc & internet)
Svcs: info, ref, biblio
Classn: in-house sys *Staff: Libns:* 1

S591 🎓
Edinburgh College of Art Library

Lauriston Pl, Edinburgh, EH3 9DF (0131-221-6034; *fax:* 0131-221-6033)
Internet: http://www.lib.eca.ac.uk/

Chief: Chief Libn: Mr Wilson Smith MA(Hons), DipLib (w.smith@eca.ac.uk) *Other Snr Staff:* Technical Svcs Libn: Mr Gordon Andrew (g.andrew@eca.ac.uk)
Assoc Libs: LAURISTON LIB, addr as above; GRASSMARKET LIB, 79 Grassmarket, Edinburgh, EH1 2HJ, Faculty Libn: Ms Pamela Masters (0131-221-6180; *fax:* 0131-221-6293; *email:* p.masters@ eca.ac.uk)
Entry: ref only for public *Open:* term: Mon-Thu 0915-2030, Fri 1000-1700; vac: Mon-Thu 0915-1600, Fri 1000-1600

Subj: planning; arch; landscape arch; design; construction; fine arts; painting; sculpture; interior design; photography; topography; film studies; theatre studies; social sci; cultural studies *Co-op Schemes:* BLDSC, Planning Exchange, UCABLIS
Equip: m-readers, m-printer, video viewers, copiers, computers (incl internet & CD-ROM)
Disabled: stairlift, workstations for disabled, CCD magnifying machine *Online:* AMICO Lib, Art Abstracts, Avery Index, BHA, Construction & Bldg Abstracts, Design & Applied Arts Index, Digital Dissertations, IBSS, Index to Theses, Ingenta, Web of Science, RIBA, SCRAN, Zetoc & others
Stock: bks/c80000; periodcls/c400; slides/150000; illusts/500; maps/c4000; some audios, videos, DVDs & CD-ROMs
Classn: UDC *Auto Sys:* Urica
Staff: Libns: 4 *Non-Prof:* 13

S592 ⚷ 🎓
Edinburgh Geological Society Library

Robertson Science & Eng Lib, King's Bldgs, Edinburgh (*Libn:* 0131-650-0239; *Robertson Lib:* 0131-650-5666)
Email: librarian@edinburghgeolsoc.org
Internet: http://www.edinburghgeolsoc.org/

Gov Body: administered by Edinburgh Univ Lib (see **S593**) on behalf of Edinburgh Geological Soc
Chief: Libn: Mr Bob McIntosh, c/o British Geological Survey, Murchison House, West Mains Rd, Edinburgh EH9 3LA
Entry: membs of Soc; membs of Edinburgh Univ Lib *Open:* term: Mon-Fri 0900-2200, Sat 0900-1700, Sun 1200-1700; vac: Mon-Fri 0900-1700
Subj: earth sci; geol; palaeontology
Equip: copier, computers *Online:* Robertson Lib has access to Geobase, GeoRef & other sci databases
Stock: bks/c200

S593 🎓
Edinburgh University Library

George Sq, Edinburgh, EH8 9LJ (0131-650-3384/3409; *fax:* 0131-667-9780)
Email: Library@ed.ac.uk
Internet: http://www.lib.ed.ac.uk/

Chief: Univ Libn: Mr Ian R.M. Mowat MA, BPhil, FCILIP, FRSA, FRSE (ian.mowat@ed.ac.uk) *Dep:* Dep Libn: Ms Sheila Cannell MA, MCLIP (sheila. cannell@ed.ac.uk)
Assoc Libs: MAIN LIB (arts & social sci), addr as above; CENTRE OF TROPICAL VETERINARY MEDICINE LIB, Royal (Dick) School of Veterinary Studies, Easter Bush, Roslin, Midlothian, EH25 9RG (0131-650-6410; *email:* CTVM.Library@ ed.ac.uk); CHEM LIB, Joseph Black Chem Bldg, King's Bldgs, West Mains Rd, Edinburgh, EH9 3JJ (0131-650-4777; *fax:* 0131-650-6702; *email:* Nancy.Sprague@ed.ac.uk); DARWIN LIB (life sci), Darwin Bldg, King's Bldgs, West Mains Rd, Edinburgh, EH9 3JJ (0131-650-5784; *fax:* 0131-650-6702; *email:* D.Carroll@ed.ac.uk); DRUMMOND LIB (geog & archaeo), Surgeons' Sq, High School Yards, Edinburgh, EH1 1LZ (0131-650-9058; *email:* K.P.Watt@ed.ac.uk); EASTER BUSH VETERINARY CENTRE LIB, Royal (Dick) School of Veterinary Studies, Easter Bush, Roslin, Midlothian, EH25 9RG (0131-650-6405; *fax:* 0131-650-6594; *email:* ebvc.library@ed.ac.uk); ERSKINE MEDICAL LIB (see **S595**); JAMES CLERK MAXWELL LIB (physics, maths & computing), King's Bldgs, Mayfield Rd, Edinburgh, EH9 3JZ (0131-650-5206; *fax:* 0131-650-6702; *email:* James.Clerk.Maxwell.Library@ed.ac.uk); LAW & EUROPA LIB, Old Coll, South Bridge, Edinburgh, EH8 9YL (0131-650-2046; *email:* Law.Europa.Library@ed.ac.uk); MORAY HOUSE

INST OF EDU LIB (see **S609**); NEW COLL LIB (divinity, see **S596**); PSYCHIATRY LIB, Royal Edinburgh Hosp, Kennedy Tower, Morningside Pk, Edinburgh, EH10 5HF (0131-537-6285; *email:* Wendy.Mill@ed.ac.uk); REID MUSIC LIB (see **S597**); ROBERTSON ENG & SCI LIB, KB Centre, The King's Bldgs, West Mains Rd, Edinburgh, EH9 3JF (0131-650-5666; *fax:* 0131-650-6702; *email:* Robertson.Library@ed.ac.uk); ROYAL HOSP FOR SICK CHILDREN LIB (see **S619**); ROYAL INFIRMARY OF EDINBURGH LIB (see **S620**); SCOTTISH STUDIES LIB (see **S598**); VETERIN-ARY LIB, Royal (Dick) School of Veterinary Studies, Summerhall, Edinburgh, EH9 1QH (0131-650-6176; *fax:* 0131-650-6593; *email:* dick.vetlib@ ed.ac.uk); WESTERN GENL HOSP LIB (see **S648**)
Entry: non-membs of Univ may register as external users for ref; borrowing on payment of subscription fee *Open:* term: Mon-Thu 0830-2200, Fri 0830-1700, Sat 0900-1700, Sun 1200-1700; vac: Mon-Fri 0900-1700
Subj: humanities; religion; law; medicine; music; sci; maths; eng; social sci; veterinary medicine; European studies; African studies; Canadian studies; Chinese & East Asian studies; Islamic & Middle East studies; New Zealand studies; Scottish studies *Collns: Bks & Pamphs:* BSI; EDC; SCOLMA (Malawi & Zambia); New Zealand Studies Colln (formerly New Zealand House Lib); backgrnd materials (1700-1709); Clement Litill Bequest (theology); William Drummond Colln (16C-17C lit); James Nairn Bequest (mainly theology); Halliwell-Phillips Collns (16C-17C drama); Adam Smith Colln; Dugald Stewart Colln; Corson Colln (Sir Walter Scott); W.B. Hodgson Colln (econ); W. Alexander Cameron Colln (Celtic studies); Aeneas J.G. Mackay Bequest (Scots hist, lit & law); Donald Mackinnon Colln (Celtic studies & Scottish theology); James Geikie Colln (geol); William Speirs Bruce Colln (oceanography & polar exploration); Lord Abercromby Bequest (archaeo, ethnology & linguistics); Lewis Grassic Gibbon Colln (lit); Arthur Berriedale Keith Colln (British Empire, Indian lit & hist); Sigfus Blondal Colln (Icelandic studies); Arthur Koestler Colln; W.H. Auden Colln; A.H. Campbell Colln (English lit); C.M. Grieve Colln (Hugh MacDairmid); Edinburgh Univ Press Colln; Penguin Colln (bks publ by Penguin); Laing Colln & MSS; Tovey Colln; numerous others *Archvs:* various MS collns, incl: Africa Papers; Laing Colln; Tovey Colln; medieval MSS; oriental MSS *Other:* BBC Press Cuttings Colln (c10 mln cuttings); arch drawings *Co-op Schemes:* SCONUL, BLDSC, CURL
Equip: m-reader, m-camera, m-printer, video viewer, copier, computers, Caramate tape-slide viewer *Online:* all available commercial & academic hosts sys & databases (fees charged) *Svcs:* info, ref, binding
Stock: bks/1681000; periodcls/11600; slides/410000; videos/1741; maps & m-forms/99400; uncounted photos & wallcharts
Classn: DDC (mod), UDC, NLM, Barnard, Pettee, own
Pubns: list available on appl

S594

Edinburgh University, Architecture Library
School of Arts, Culture & Environment, 20 Chambers St, Edinburgh, EH1 1JZ (0131-650-2310)
Email: a.crossland@ed.ac.uk
Internet: http://www.caad.ed.ac.uk/Library/

Gov Body: Edinburgh Univ (see **S593**) *Chief:* Libn: Ms Alice Crossland *Dep:* Lib Asst: Ms Tracy Stredwick
Entry: staff & students *Open:* term: Mon-Fri 0900-1730; vac: Mon-Fri 0900-1300, 1345-1700
Subj: arch; arch hist; construction; planning; urban design; landscape arch *Collns: Bks & Pamphs:* govt pubns *Archvs:* archival colln on 20C urban

design & planning *Other:* maps & plans (mainly of Edinburgh); slide colln; video colln; student dissertations
Equip: copier, computers (incl internet & CD-ROM) *Online:* Architectural Pubns Index, Avery Index, Art Abstracts; numerous CD-ROMs
Stock: bks/c15000; slides/100000
Staff: Libns: 1 *Non-Prof:* 1

S595 ✚

Edinburgh University, Erskine Medical Library
Hugh Robson Bldg, George Sq, Edinburgh, EH8 9XE (0131-650-3684; *fax:* 0131-650-6841)
Email: eml@uk.ac.edinburgh
Internet: http://www.lib.ed.ac.uk/sites/emlm.shtml

Gov Body: Edinburgh Univ (see **S593**) *Chief:* Libn, Coll of Medicine & Veterinary Medicine: Ms Irene McGowan BA, MCLIP (i.mcgowan@ed.ac.uk) *Entry:* staff & students of Edinburgh Univ & NHS staff in Lothian; others by arrangement or payment *Open:* term: Mon-Thu 0900-2200, Fri-Sat 0900-1700, Sun 1200-1700; vac: Mon-Thu 0900-1900, Fri 0900-1700, Sat 1000-1300
Subj: medicine *Collns: Bks & Pamphs:* official pubns *Other:* AV colln *Co-op Schemes:* BLDSC, ILL
Equip: 3 copiers, video viewer, 50 computers, 4 rooms for hire (free to Univ staff & students) *Online:* Medline & other databases *Svcs:* info, ref, biblio
Stock: bks/45000; periodcls/729 titles, plus 60000 issues no longer current
Staff: Libns: 2.5 *Other Prof:* 2 *Non-Prof:* 7

S596 🙏

Edinburgh University, New College Library
Mound Pl, Edinburgh, EH1 2LU (0131-650-8957; *fax:* 0131-650-7952)
Email: newcoll@ed.ac.uk

Gov Body: Edinburgh Univ (see **S593**) *Chief:* Libn: Mrs Eileen E. Dickson MA, MCLIP *Dep:* Sites & Svcs Supervisor: Miss Sheila Dunn
Open: term: Mon-Thu 0900-2130, Fri 0900-1700, Sat 0900-1230 (under review); vac: Mon-Fri 0900-1700
Subj: religion; theology; biblical studies; liturgy; ecclesiastical hist; homiletics; hymnology *Collns: Archvs:* Thomas Chalmers papers; archvs of the Centre for the Study of Christianity in the non-Western World *Co-op Schemes:* ILL, ABTAPL, ATLA, Hebraica Lib Group
Equip: 2 m-readers, 2 copiers, 4 computers (incl 1 with internet) *Online:* FirstSearch, Web of Science; many others via Edinburgh Univ network *Svcs:* info, ref, biblio
Stock: bks/239000; periodcls/343; m-forms/various; archvs/70300 MSS; incunabula/100
Classn: LC *Auto Sys:* Voyager (Endeavour)
Staff: Libns: 1 *Non-Prof:* 4 *Exp:* £48400 (1999-2000)

S597

Edinburgh University, Reid Music Library
Alison House, Nicholson Sq, Edinburgh, EH8 9DF (0131-650-2436; *fax:* 0131-650-2425)
Email: Reid.Library@ed.ac.uk

Gov Body: Edinburgh Univ (see **S593**) *Chief:* Site & Svcs Supervisor: Ms Teresa Jones (teresa.jones@ed.ac.uk) *Dep:* Snr Lib Asst: Ms Kathy Penfold (kathy.penfold@ed.ac.uk)
Entry: staff & students; external membership available *Open:* Mon-Fri 090 -1730, Sat 0930-1230

Subj: Western art music; world music; Scottish traditional music *Collns: Bks & Pamphs:* Weiss Colln of Beethoven lit; Professor Sir Donald Tovey Music Lib; 18C-19C bks on music theory; printed music 1st eds *Archvs:* Kenneth Leighton Archv; music MSS (c100 items)
Equip: copier, computers (incl CD-ROM) *Online:* RILM Abstracts of Music Literature, Music Index on CD-ROM
Staff: 3 in total

S598

Edinburgh University, School of Scottish Studies Library
27-29 George Sq, Edinburgh, EH8 9LD (0131-650-3060; *fax:* 0131-650-4163)
Internet: http://www.celtscot.ed.ac.uk/

Gov Body: Univ of Edinburgh (see **S593**) *Chief:* Libn: Mr Arnot McDonald (arnot.mcdonald@ ed.ac.uk) *Other Snr Staff:* Archvs Asst: Dr Cathlin Macaulay (cathlin.macaulay@ed.ac.uk) *Assoc Libs:* JOHN LEVY ARCHV, addr as above, Curator: Dr Mark Trewin (0131-650-3057/8248; *email:* mark.trewin@ed.ac.uk); PHOTOGRAPHIC ARCHV, addr as above, Photographer: Mr Ian MacKenzie (0131-650-4168; *email:* i.mack@ ed.ac.uk); SOUND ARCHV, addr as above, contact the Archvs Asst
Entry: staff & students; ref only for others; adv appt required for archv collns *Open:* Mon-Fri 0900-1230, 1400-1700
Subj: Scottish studies; Scottish hist, culture & music *Collns: Archvs:* various MSS *Other:* Photographic Archv (c10000 images); John Levy Colln (Asiatic & European ethnomusicological recordings); other Sound Archv collns incl: Peter Cooke Colln of African Music; Will Forest Colln (Scottish music recordings); Edgar Ashton colln (folk music) *Co-op Schemes:* ILL
Stock: bks/8000; periodcls/250; audios/10000

S599

Faculty of Actuaries, The Ross Library
Maclaurin House, 18 Dublin St, Edinburgh, EH1 3PP (0131-240-1311; *fax:* 0131-240-1313)
Email: libraries@actuaries.org.uk
Internet: http://www.actuaries.org.uk/

Type: prof body *Gov Body:* part of joint lib svc of Faculty & Inst of Actuaries *Chief:* Libn: Mrs Christine Morgan BA, DipLib, MCLIP (chrism@ actuaries.org.uk) *Other Snr Staff:* Hon Libn: Prof A.S. MacDonald BSc, PhD, FPA
Assoc Libs: INST OF ACTUARIES HISTORICAL COLLNS (see **S1188**); INST OF ACTUARIES, THE NORWICH LIB (see **S1679**)
Entry: open to membs, actuarial students, membs of overseas actuarial bodies & others undertaking rsrch on actuarial topics *Open:* Mon-Fri 0900-1700
Subj: actuarial sci; pensions; life assurance; investment; demography; mortality; probability; statistics *Collns: Bks & Pamphs:* small antiquarian colln (c200 vols); pamphs colln (77 bnd vols, 18C-20C); actuarial journals, incl full set of Transactions of the Internatl Congress of Actuaries (1895-date); ACTED course materials & examination papers *Archvs:* early archvs of Faculty of Actuaries & Assoc of Scottish Life Offices, incl minute bks, Rolls of Students, Rolls of Fellows & account bks *Other:* photos & biographical files *Co-op Schemes:* ILL
Equip: fax, copier (A4/20p), computer (with internet) *Svcs:* info, ref
Stock: bks/6000; periodcls/100
Classn: STET *Auto Sys:* DBTextworks 4
Pubns: Monthly List of Selected Lib Additions (on web site)
Staff: Libns: 1

Special Libraries

Edinburgh
▼
Edinburgh

S600

Free Church of Scotland College Library

The Mound, Edinburgh, EH1 2LS (0131-226-5286; *fax:* 0131-220-0597)
Email: DMacleod@freescotcoll.ac.uk

Gov Body: Free Church of Scotland *Chief:* Hon Libn: Rev Prof Donald Macleod MA *Dep:* Asst Libn: Miss A.J. MacInnes
Entry: adv appt *Open:* Mon-Fri 0900-1730
Subj: religion; Reformed & Puritan lit; ecclesiastical hist; biography *Collns: Bks & Pamphs:* Free Church Heritage Colln; Gaelic pubns; 17C theology (English, Scottish, Latin); Victorian pamphs *Archvs:* Free Church of Scotland Archvs *Co-op Schemes:* BLDSC, ILL
Equip: copier, 2 computers *Disabled:* lift for wheelchair users
Stock: bks/30000; periodcls/30; pamphs/20000+
Classn: own *Staff: Non-Prof:* 1

S601

Gillis Centre Library

Gillis Centre, 113 Whitehouse Ln, Edinburgh, EH9 1BB (0131-447-1992; *fax:* 0131-623-8899)
Email: chancery@stanerd.org.uk

Chief: Libn: Rev Philip J. Kerr PhB, STL *Dep:* Dr Margaret Addly
Open: Tue, Thu 1400-1600; other times by arrangement
Subj: phil; psy; religion *Co-op Schemes:* ABTAPL
Equip: copier (5p per copy) *Svcs:* info, ref, indexing, abstracting
Stock: bks/20000; periodcls/18
Classn: own
Staff: Non-Prof: 8 *Exp:* £2000 (1999-2000); £2500 (2000-01)

S602 ⚷

Grand Lodge of Scotland Library

Freemasons' Hall, 96 George St, Edinburgh, EH2 3DM (0131-225-5304; *fax:* 0131-225-3953)
Email: thecurator@blueyonder.co.uk
Internet: http://www.grandlodgescotland.com/

Gov Body: The Grand Lodge of Antient Free & Accepted Masons of Scotland *Chief:* Grand Sec: C. Martin McGibbon ASCA *Dep:* Curator: Mr Robert L.D. Cooper BA, FSA(Scot)
Entry: ref only, adv arrangement recommended
Open: Mon-Fri 0930-1630
Subj: all aspects of freemasonry; Scottish hist (very small holding) *Collns: Bks & Pamphs:* Morison Colln (2000+ vols relating to hist of Freemasonry in Europe, esp France; 90% of vols are in French, some are in MS form)
Svcs: info, ref, biblio
Stock: bks/7000+
Classn: by geographic location
Pubns: The Yearbook of the Grand Lodge of Scotland (£10, membs only); The Ashlar (magazine, £2.50); The Lodge Master (£5); The First Freemasons (£14.95); An Account of the Chapel of Roslin 1778 (£5); Historical Sketch 1736-1986 (£2); The Genealogies of the Saintclaires of Rosslyn (£17.99); A Winter with Robert Burns (£12.95)

S603 ✚

Health Promotion Library, Scotland

Health Edu Board for Scotland, The Priory, Canaan Ln, Edinburgh, EH10 4SG (0845-912-5442; *fax:* 0131-536-5502)
Email: library.enquiries@hebs.scot.nhs.uk
Internet: http://www.hebs.com/library/

Type: NHS *Gov Body:* Health Edu Board for Scotland *Chief:* Libn: Mrs Margaret Forrest MA(Hons), MSc, DipLib, FCLIP, FSA(Scot) *Dep:* Asst Libn: Ms Katie McGlew MA(Hons), MSc
Entry: those who live and/or work in Scotland
Open: Mon-Thu 0900-1630, Fri 0900-1600
Subj: social sci; behavioural sci; health svcs; tech; health promotion *Co-op Schemes:* BLDSC, SHINE
Equip: m-reader, copier, 5 computers (incl 4 CD-ROM) *Disabled:* text phone access for disabled *Online:* OVID, Datastar (no charge) *Svcs:* info, ref, biblio
Stock: bks/12000; periodcls/350; over 25000 journal articles held on database (also accessible on-line via lib web site)
Classn: UDC *Auto Sys:* Olib 7
Pubns: Lib Bulletin (bimonthly, free)
Staff: Libns: 2 *Non-Prof:* 3 *Exp:* £79000 (1999-2000)

S604

Heriot-Watt University Library

Riccarton, Edinburgh, EH14 4AS (0131-451-3582; *fax:* 0131-451-3164)
Email: libhelp@hw.ac.uk
Internet: http://www.hw.ac.uk/library/

Chief: Libn: Mr Michael Breaks BA, DipLib *Dep:* Dep Libn: Mr Derek Stephen
Assoc Libs: MARTINDALE LIB, Scottish Borders Campus (see **S689**); INTERNATL CENTRE FOR ISLAND TECH LIB, Orkney Campus, Old Academy, Back Rd, Stromness, Orkney Islands, KW16 3AW, Libn: Ms Effy Everiss (01856-850605; *fax:* 01856-851349; *email:* E.Everiss@hw.ac.uk)
Entry: staff & students; others ref only, external borrowing membership available (fees for some categories) *Open:* term: Mon-Fri 0900-2145, Sat-Sun 1000-2000; vac: Mon-Thu 0915-2000, Fri 0915-1700
Subj: undergrad; postgrad; social sci; sci; maths; tech *Collns: Other:* BSI *Co-op Schemes:* BLDSC, SCONUL
Equip: m-reader, m-printer, video viewer, copier, computers (incl wd-proc & CD-ROM) *Disabled:* Kurzweil *Online:* Dialog, STN (cost of search plus £20)
Stock: bks/100000; periodcls/1000
Classn: DDC *Auto Sys:* Geac Adv
Pubns: various guides (free)
Staff: Libns: 6 *Other Prof:* 2 *Non-Prof:* 25 *Exp:* £750000 (1999-2000); £800000 (2000-01)

S605  🏛

Institut Français d'Ecosse Library

13 Randolph Cres, Edinburgh, EH3 7TT (0131-225-5366; *fax:* 0131-220-0648)
Email: library@ifecosse.org.uk

Gov Body: French Govt *Chief:* Libn: Mrs Anne-Marie Usher
Open: Mon-Fri 0930-1300, 1400-1830, 1st Sat of each month 0930-1330
Subj: French lang; French culture *Collns: Other:* French newspapers & magazines; French music & spkn wd *Co-op Schemes:* ILL
Equip: copier, 3 computers (incl 2 with internet & 1 with CD-ROM) *Svcs:* info, ref, biblio
Stock: bks/20000; periodcls/50; audios/1675; videos/1172; CD-ROMs/173; DVDs/142
Classn: DDC *Auto Sys:* BCDI (French sys)
Staff: Non-Prof: 2

S606 ⚷ ✚

Institute of Occupational Medicine Library

8 Roxburgh Pl, Edinburgh, EH8 9SU (0131-667-5131; *fax:* 0131-667-0136)
Email: ken.dixon@iomhq.org.uk
Internet: http://www.iom-world.org/

Chief: Scientific Info Offcr: Mr Ken Dixon MA(Hons), MA, MCLIP
Entry: adv appt, fee payable *Open:* Mon-Fri 0900-1700
Subj: sci; tech; occupational medicine *Collns: Bks & Pamphs:* large colln of papers on asbestos
Co-op Schemes: BLDSC
Equip: 2 m-readers, copier, 2 computers (incl CD-ROM) *Online:* Datastar, Dialog, Dialtech (some fees) *Svcs:* info, ref
Stock: bks/6000; periodcls/40; m-forms/300
Classn: UDC *Auto Sys:* Heritage
Pubns: various Reports & Guidance Bklets; papers covering areas of Health & Safety, hygiene, occupational medicine, environmental health, toxicology & ergonomics
Staff: Libns: 1

S607 ✚

Lothian NHS Board Library and Resource Centre

Deaconess House, 148 Pleasance, Edinburgh, EH8 9RS (0131-536-9541/2/3; *fax:* 0131-536-9246)
Email: library@lhb.scot.nhs.uk

Chief: Libn: Mr Phil Horne LLB(Hons), DipLIS
Entry: borrowing facilities for those living or working in Lothian *Open:* Mon 1300-1630, Tue-Wed 0930-1630, Thu 0930-1830, Fri 0930-1300
Subj: health *Co-op Schemes:* SHINE
Stock: bks/13000; periodcls/90

S608 🏛 ✚

Medical Research Council, Human Genetics Unit Library

Western Genl Hosp, Crewe Rd, Edinburgh, EH4 2XU (0131-467-8420; *fax:* 0131-343-2620)
Email: library@hgu.mrc.ac.uk
Internet: http://www.hgu.mrc.ac.uk/

Gov Body: Medical Rsrch Council (see **S536**)
Chief: Unit Libn: Miss Siobhan Marron (Siobhan.Marron@hgu.mrc.ac.uk)
Entry: adv appt *Open:* Mon-Fri 0830-1645
Subj: biological sci; biochem; human genetics; cryogenetics; molecular genetics; genes; neurology; ophthalmology; computers *Collns: Bks & Pamphs:* MRC Human Genetics Unit Reprints (1948-date) *Co-op Schemes:* BLDSC, SUC, MRC Union List of Periodicals, EU List of Current Serials
Equip: m-reader, copier, computers (incl wd-proc & CD-ROM) *Svcs:* info, ref, biblio
Stock: bks/6507; periodcls/94; m-forms/10 sets; videos/3
Classn: NLM *Auto Sys:* own
Pubns: Lib News; Lib Annual Report; Guide to Lib Facilities
Staff: Non-Prof: 1

S609

Moray House Institute of Education, Library

Dalhousie Land Bldg, St John St, Edinburgh, EH8 8AQ (0131-651-6193; *fax:* 0131-557-3458)
Email: morayhse@srv4.lib.ed.ac.uk
Internet: http://www.lib.ed.ac.uk/sites/mhh.shtml

Gov Body: Univ of Edinburgh (see **S593**) *Chief:* Site & Svcs Supervisor: Mr David Fairgrieve (David.Fairgrieve@ed.ac.uk)

Entry: faculty, students & authorised persons; others ref only (daily fee) or subscription (depends on status) *Open:* term: Mon-Thu 0900-2200, Fri 0900-1700, Sat 0900-1230; vac: Mon-Fri 0900-1700
Subj: edu; psy; sociology; English as a 2nd lang; mgmt; social work; counselling; community edu; ch's bks; physical edu; recreation & leisure mgmt
Collns: Other: AV colln; wall charts
Equip: copier, computers (incl internet & CD-ROM) *Online:* various e-journals & databases, incl the main internatl edu & sports-related indexes
Stock: bks/101000; periodcls/630; slides/1761; illusts/3850 pictures, 3230 wallcharts & posters; audios/3039; videos/955
Classn: DDC, LC *Auto Sys:* Voyager
Staff: Libns: 1 *Non-Prof:* 2 FT, 6 PT

S610

Napier University Learning Information Services

Sighthill Campus, Sighthill Ct, Edinburgh, EH11 4BN (0131-455-3426; *fax:* 0131-455-3428)
Internet: http://nulis.napier.ac.uk/

Chief: Dir of Learning Info Svcs: Mr C.J. Pinder BA, DipLib, MLib, MCLIP *Dep:* Dep Dir: Miss M. Lobhan MA, MCLIP, PGDipEdTech
Assoc Libs: Campus Learning Centres: CANAAN LN LEARNING CENTRE, 74 Canaan Ln, Edinburgh, EH10 4TB, Learning Centre Mgr: Ms Margaret Gill (0131-455-5616; *fax:* 0131-455-5608; *email:* CanaanLaneLC@napier.ac.uk); COMELY BANK LEARNING CENTRE, Comely Bank Campus, 13 Crewe Rd South, Edinburgh, EH4 2LD, Learning Centre Mgr: Ms Helen Steele (0131-455-5319; *fax:* 0131-455-5358; *email:* ComelyBankLC@napier.ac.uk); CRAIGHOUSE LEARNING CENTRE, Craighouse Rd, Edinburgh, EH10 5LG, Learning Centre Mgr: Ms Catherine Walker (0131-455-6020; *fax:* 0131-455-6022; *email:* CraighouseLC@napier.ac.uk); CRAIG-LOCKHART LEARNING CENTRE, 219 Colinton Rd, Edinburgh, EH14 1DJ (0131-455-4383; *email:* CraiglockhartLC@napier.ac.uk); LIVINGSTON LEARNING CENTRE, St John's Hosp, Howden Rd West, Livingston, EH54 6PP (01506-422831; *fax:* 01506-422833; *email:* LivingstonLC@napier.ac.uk); MELROSE LEARNING CENTRE, Borders Genl Hosp, Melrose, TD6 9BD, Learning Centre Mgr: Ms Jennifer MacLaine (01896-661632; *fax:* 01896-823869; *email:* MelroseLC@napier.ac.uk); MERCHISTON LEARNING CENTRE, 10 Colinton Rd, Edinburgh, EH10 5DT, Learning Centre Mgr: Ms Sheila Barcroft (0131-455-2582; *fax:* 0131-455-2377; *email:* MerchistonLC@napier.ac.uk); SIGHTHILL LEARNING CENTRE, Sighthill Ct, Edinburgh, EH11 4BN, Learning Centre Mgr: Ms Barbara Breaks (0131-455-3426; *fax:* 0131-455-3428; *email:* SighthillLC@napier.ac.uk)
Entry: ref only unless registered external memb (fee based) *Open:* Mon-Thu 0845-2100, Fri 0845-1700, Sat-Sun 1000-1600; vac: Mon, Wed, Fri 0845-1700, Tue, Thu 0845-1900, Sat 1000-1600; vac: times may vary, best to check in adv
Subj: all subjs; undergrad; postgrad; *Canaan Lane:* nursing; midwifery; health; *Comely Bank:* midwifery; child nursing; psychiatric nursing; music; politics; *Craighouse:* marketing; print media; publishing; communication; hospitality; tourism; music; *Craiglockhart:* computing; elec eng; maths; edu; *Livingston:* postgrad medicine; nursing; *Melrose:* medicine; nursing; mental health; subjs allied to health; *Merchiston:* sci; eng; psy; social sci; media; design; *Sighthill:* business; finance; law; econ; lang; music; politics *Collns: Bks & Pamphs:* Edward Clark Colln (bks relating to hist & development of printing & publishing); RIBA Colln of Trade Lit (both at Merchiston); War Poets Colln (printed material relating to poetry & other aspects of WW1); Taylor Colln (games & simulation); Univ Theses (all at Craiglockhart); company reports;

Legal Materials Colln (both at Sighthill) *Co-op Schemes:* BLDSC, SHINE
Equip: m-reader, m-printer, video viewer, copiers, c100 computers (networked, multipurpose, incl wd-proc, internet & CD-ROM), 2 overhead projectors *Disabled:* scanner, braille printer, PC with MasterTouch software *Online:* Dialog, Dialtech, BLAISE, Lawtel, Mintel
Stock: bks/390000; periodcls/4600; audios/1000; videos/3000
Classn: DDC *Auto Sys:* Dynix
Pubns: Lib Guides & study skills bklets (free); genl pubns available on web pages
Staff: Libns: 18 *Non-Prof:* 49.18

S611

National Gallery of Scotland Library

The Mound, Edinburgh, EH2 2EL (0131-624-6501; *fax:* 0131-220-0917)
Email: pcarter@nationalgalleries.org
Internet: http://www.nationalgalleries.org/

Gov Body: Natl Galleries of Scotland *Chief:* Libn: Miss Penelope Carter BD, MA, MSc, MCLIP
Assoc Libs: SCOTTISH NATL PORTRAIT GALLERY LIB (see **S634**); SCOTTISH NATL GALLERY OF MODERN ART LIB (see **S633**)
Entry: ref only, adv appt *Open:* Mon-Fri 1000-1230, 1400-1630
Subj: arts; fine art; Scottish art; art hist (1300-1900) *Collns: Bks & Pamphs:* auction & exhib catalogues; guide bks; dictionaries *Archvs:* relating to hist of the Gallery *Other:* info files relating to each work of art in the collns (2000+) *Co-op Schemes:* UCABLIS, SVAG, ILL
Stock: bks/45000; periodcls/50; photos/10000; slides/10000; archvs/24 linear m
Classn: own *Auto Sys:* DS
Pubns: Bulletin (monthly); Gallery exhib catalogues; catalogues of permanent collns
Staff: Libns: 1

S612

National Museums of Scotland, Library and Archives

Chambers St, Edinburgh, EH1 1JF (0131-247-4137; *fax:* 0131-247-4311)
Email: library@nms.ac.uk
Internet: http://www.nms.ac.uk/

Type: non-departmental public body *Gov Body:* Trustees of the Natl Museums of Scotland *Chief:* Head of Lib: Ms Elize Rowan MSc *Dep:* Mr Andrew Martin MA, DipLib & Ms Clare Whittaker MA
Assoc Libs: NATL WAR MUSEUM OF SCOTLAND (see **S613**)
Entry: ref only; adv appt advised but not essential *Open:* Mon-Fri 1000-1300, 1400-1700
Subj: archaeo; hist; museology; conservation; social hist; military hist (esp Scottish); ethnography; Egyptology; hist of sci & tech; geol; biology; zoology; decorative arts of the World; exploration & travel *Collns: Bks & Pamphs:* numismatics; archaeo (esp Scottish); zoological taxonomy *Archvs:* Harvie-Brown papers; W.S. Bruce papers; Jardine papers; J.M. Sweet papers; Soc of Antiquaries papers *Other:* incl the collns of the former Museum of Antiquities Lib (founded as the Lib of the Soc of Antiquaries of Scotland) *Co-op Schemes:* BLDSC, SALSER, SUC, UCABLIS
Equip: m-reader, m-printer, copier, computer (with CD-ROM) *Svcs:* ref, biblio
Stock: bks/300000; periodcls/800
Classn: UDC (mod), LC (mod) *Auto Sys:* Dynix
Staff: Libns: 5.5 *Non-Prof:* 4

S613

National War Museum of Scotland, Library and Archives

Edinburgh Castle, Edinburgh, EH1 2NG (0131-225-7534 x2204; *fax:* 0131-225-3848)
Email: e.philip@nms.ac.uk
Internet: http://www.nms.ac.uk/services/

Gov Body: Natl Museums of Scotland *Chief:* Asst Curator (Lib & Archvs): Ms Edith Philip
Assoc Libs: NATL MUSEUMS OF SCOTLAND LIB (parent lib, see **S612**)
Entry: ref only, adv appt *Open:* Mon-Fri 0930-1300, 1400-1700
Subj: military hist of Scotland & the Scots *Collns: Archvs:* numerous collns, varying from single letters & diaries to large collns of official & semi-official papers; important collns incl: Genl Sir David Baird papers (Napoleonic Wars); Admiral Viscount Duncan papers (Napoleonic Wars); records of Wilson of Bannockburn (19C tartan manufacturer) *Other:* photo colln
Svcs: info, ref
Stock: bks/14000; periodcls/50; photos/c6000; archvs/7000+ items
Classn: UDC, War Office Lib Special Classn System *Staff:* Other Prof: 1

S614

Queen Margaret University College Library

Clerwood Ter, Edinburgh, EH12 8TS (0131-317-3301; *fax:* 0131-339-7057)
Email: paitken@qmuc.ac.uk
Internet: http://www.qmuc.ac.uk/

Chief: Univ Coll Libn: Mrs Penny Aitken BA, AALIA *Dep:* Dep Libn: Miss Barbara Smith BSc, MCLIP, ILTM
Assoc Libs: LEITH CAMPUS LIB, Duke St, Edinburgh, EH6 8HF, Libn: Ms Vicki Cormie MSc, MCLIP (0131-317-3308)
Entry: ref only *Open:* term: Mon-Wed 0900-2100, Thu 1000-2100, Fri 0900-1700, Sat-Sun 1300-1700; vac: Mon-Thu 0900-1700, Fri 0900-1630
Subj: nursing; physiotherapy; occupational therapy; speech therapy; hospitality studies; food & nutrition; consumer studies; retailing; drama; communication studies; info mgmt *Co-op Schemes:* BLDSC, NLS
Equip: 4 m-readers, m-printer, 8 copiers, 3 video viewers, 30 computers (incl 28 internet & 2 CD-ROM) *Disabled:* JAWS, ZoomText, Kurzweil, Inspiration, CCTV
Stock: bks/120000; periodcls/1000, plus 495 no longer current; many maps, slides, m-forms
Classn: DDC *Auto Sys:* Sirsi (Unicorn)
Staff: Libns: 8.56 *Non-Prof:* 11.39 *Exp:* £245000 (1999-2000)

S615

Royal Botanic Garden Edinburgh, Library

20a Inverleith Row, Edinburgh, EH3 5LR (0131-552-7171; *fax:* 0131-552-0382)
Email: library@rbge.org.uk
Internet: http://www.rbge.org.uk

Gov Body: Trustees of the Royal Botanic Garden *Chief:* Chief Libn: Mrs Jane Hutcheon BA, MCLIP *Dep:* Serials Libn: Mr Graham Hardy BA, DipLib
Entry: ref only *Open:* Mon-Thu 0930-1630, Fri 0930-1600
Subj: genl; undergrad; postgrad; botany; hortic; forestry *Co-op Schemes:* BLDSC, EBHL
Equip: m-reader, copier *Svcs:* ref
Stock: bks/85000; periodcls/1700; photos/50000; slides/50000; illusts/50000; maps/1500; m-forms/2000; archvs/42 linear m

Special Libraries

Edinburgh
▼
Edinburgh

(Royal Botanic Gdn Edinburgh Lib cont)
Classn: Bliss *Auto Sys:* Bibliotech Pro
Staff: Libns: 4 *Other Prof:* 1.5 para-profs *Exp:*
£110000 (2000-01)

S616 🗝️ ✚

Royal College of Physicians of Edinburgh Library

9 Queen St, Edinburgh, EH2 1JQ (0131-225-7324;
fax: 0131-220-3939)
Email: library@rcpe.ac.uk
Internet: http://www.rcpe.ac.uk/

Chief: Libn: Mr Iain Milne MLib, MCLIP (i.milne@
rcpe.ac.uk) *Other Snr Staff:* Rare Bks Libn: Mr
John Dallas (j.dallas@rcpe.ac.uk); Info Libn: Ms
Emily Simpson (e.simpson@rcpe.ac.uk)
Entry: ref only; adv appt *Open:* Mon-Fri 0900-
1700
Subj: medicine; hist of medicine; early medicine;
sci; nat hist *Collns: Bks & Pamphs:* J.Y. Simpson
Colln (obstetrics & gynaecology); J.W. Ballantyne
Colln (foetal pathology); pamphs; early medical bks
& MSS (from 15C) *Archvs:* Coll correspondence,
accounts etc; William Cullen (correspondence);
J.Y. Simpson (lecture notes); 18C Edinburgh
Medical School (lecture notes) *Co-op Schemes:*
BLDSC, NLSLS, SUC, ILL
Svcs: info, ref, biblio & ref checking, current
awareness, photocopying, internet support
Stock: bks/50000; periodcls/100; slides/400;
illusts/300; pamphs/large colln; m-forms/a few;
audios/a few; archvs/180 ft
Classn: NLM
Pubns: Coll Brochure; Catalogue of 16th Century
Medical Bks in Edinburgh Libs (£45)
Staff: Libns: 4 *Non-Prof:* 2

S617 🗝️ ✚

Royal College of Surgeons of Edinburgh, The College Library and Archives

Nicolson St, Edinburgh, EH8 9DW (0131-527-
1630/1/2; *fax:* 0131-557-6406)
Email: library@rcsed.ac.uk
Internet: http://www.rcsed.ac.uk/

Gov Body: Council of the Royal Coll of Surgeons
Chief: Coll Libn: Ms M.A. Smith MCLIP
Entry: apply to Coll Libn for permission *Open:*
Mon-Fri 0900-1700
Subj: surgery; hist of medicine (esp in Scotland);
dentistry; medical biography *Collns: Bks &
Pamphs:* many interesting & rare bks on surgery
(1460-date) *Archvs:* Coll Archvs (1530s-date);
various collns of private papers, incl: John Robert
Hume Papers; Joseph Lister Papers; Odonto-
Chirurgical Soc Papers; Sir Henry Wade Papers;
Sir Douglas Guthrie Papers; William James Stuart
Papers; Prof John Chiene Papers; James Duncan
Papers; Sir Walter Mercer Papers; James Methuen
Graham Papers; Joseph Bell Papers; John Smith
Papers; Sir John Struthers Papers; George
Mackay Papers *Other:* illusts; slides; newscuttings
Co-op Schemes: BLDSC
Equip: 10 computers (incl internet), available at
Surgeons' Internet café *Online:* Medline, Cochrane
Svcs: info, ref, biblio, enqs (fee for non-membs)
Stock: bks/34000; periodcls/130
Classn: NLM *Staff:* Libns: 3

S618 🗝️ 🎓

The Royal Highland and Agricultural Society of Scotland Library

Royal Highland Centre, Ingliston, Edinburgh, EH28
8NF (0131-335-6277; *fax:* 0131-333-5236)
Email: library@rhass.org.uk
Internet: http://www.rhass.org.uk/

Gov Body: lib is the responsibility of the Sec of the
Soc by its Charter *Chief:* Libn: W.T. Johnston
Entry: ref only, by appt *Open:* Tue, Thu 0930-
1600 (by arrangement)
Subj: Scottish agric; hist of agric; all agric subjs
Collns: Bks & Pamphs: Jardine's Naturalist's Lib;
historic agric bks (1595 onwards); materials
relating to Friendly Socs; Gaelic bks; animal
portraits; periodcls incl: Transactions of the Soc
(1799-1968, with indexes); Farmer's Magazine;
Quarterly Journal of Agric; Journal of Agric;
Country Gentleman's Magazine etc *Archvs:*
Sederunt Bks; Letter Bks; genl records of Soc from
1784, incl the running of its Shows & competitions
Other: subj files for rsrch & ref on agric & other
topics, covering biographies, bibliographies,
breeds, Gaelic collns, MS indexes & transcripts,
drainage, weeds etc; MSS, maps & models on
permanent loan to the Royal Museum of Scotland,
Scottish Agric Museum, Natl Lib of Scotland & Natl
Trust for Scotland
Equip: copier
Stock: bks/3000; periodcls/75; photos/100;
pamphs/1000; maps/50; MSS/1000
Classn: Index
Pubns: The Review (bi-annual, free to membs,
sponsors etc); Annual Show Catalogue;
Programme; Prize List; Lib Catalogue; the Lib has
also prepared computerised material on indivs
prominent in the hist of the Soc, or others for whom
the Soc possesses bks & papers of especial value;
copies of subj files can also be made available;
ARK (Agricultural Resource & Knowledge, CD-
ROM); Historic Agricultural Texts (CD-ROM)
Staff: 1

S619 ✚ 🎓

Royal Hospital for Sick Children Library

Sciennes Rd, Edinburgh, EH9 1LF (0131-536-
0839; *fax:* 0131-536-0839)
Email: sick.childrens.library@ed.ac.uk

Gov Body: Edinburgh Univ (see **S593**) *Chief:*
Libn: Ms Anne Donnelly (anne.donnelly@ed.ac.uk)
Entry: membs of hosp staff & staff of the Univ of
Edinburgh & students in training; all other access
at the discretion of the Libn *Open:* Mon-Fri 0900-
1730; swipecard access outside these hrs upon
appl to the Libn
Subj: at undergrad, postgrad & prof levels:
medicine; paediatrics *Co-op Schemes:* SHINE,
BLDSC (via Edinburgh Univ)
Equip: copier (£1.18 per 12 copies), 6 computers
(all with wd-proc, internet & CD-ROM), printers,
scanner *Online:* Medline CINAHL & other health-
related databases on CD-ROM *Officer-in-Charge:*
Libn, as above *Svcs:* info, ref
Stock: bks/1200; periodcls/58; CD-ROMs/10
Acqs Offcr: Libn, as above
Classn: NLM *Auto Sys:* Endeavour Voyager
Staff: Libns: 1 *Exp:* £8000 (1999-2000); £8000
(2000-01)

S620 🎓 ✚

Royal Infirmary of Edinburgh Library

The Chancellor's Bldg, 49 Little France Cres,
Edinburgh, EH16 4SB (0131-242-6340)
Internet: http://www.lib.ed.ac.uk/sites/ril.shtml

Gov Body: Edinburgh Univ (see **S593**) *Chief:*
Liaison Libns: Ms Sheila Fisken (Sheila.L.Fisken@
ed.ac.uk) & Susan Lyle (Susan.Lyle@ed.ac.uk)
Assoc Libs: CENTRE FOR REPRODUCTIVE
BIOLOGY LIB, temporarily held at above addr
Entry: staff & students of Univ of Edinburgh; staff
of Lothian NHS Trusts *Open:* Mon-Fri 0900-1700
Subj: medicine
Equip: copier, 42 computers (incl internet)

S621 🏛️ 🎓

Royal Observatory Library

Blackford Hill, Edinburgh, EH9 3HJ (0131-668-
8397; *fax:* 0131-662-1668)
Email: library@roe.ac.uk
Internet: http://www.roe.ac.uk/atc/library/

Chief: Libn: Ms Karen Moran MA, PGDip (ksm@
roe.ac.uk)
Open: Mon-Fri 0930-1730
Subj: sci; maths; tech; astronomy; hist of
astronomy; physics; electronics; computing
Collns: Bks & Pamphs: Crawford Lib (historical
colln, 12C-19C, c15000 items) *Archvs:*
Observatory Archvs, incl: Astronomical Inst of
Edinburgh papers; papers of Astronomers Royal
for Scotland; 26th Earl of Crawford papers *Co-op
Schemes:* ILL
Svcs: info, ref, biblio
Stock: bks/50000; periodcls/650
Classn: UDC *Auto Sys:* Endeavour Voyager
Staff: Libns: 1 *Exp:* £61000 (1999-2000); £55000
(2000-01)

S622 🗝️

Royal Pharmaceutical Society of Great Britain, Scottish Department Library

36 York Pl, Edinburgh, EH1 3HU (0131-556-4386;
fax: 0131-558-8850)
Email: info@rpsis.com

Chief: Libn: Mrs C.V. Thompson
Assoc Libs: ROYAL PHARMACEUTICAL SOC
OF GT BRITAIN LIB (see **S1376**)
Subj: pharmaceuticals; pharmacy; herbalism;
botany *Collns: Other:* early Herbals & botanical
illusts *Co-op Schemes:* ILL, NLS
Stock: bks/3000; periodcls/25

S623 🗝️

Royal Scottish Academy, Library and Archive

The Dean Gallery, 73 Bedford Rd, Edinburgh, EH4
3DS (0131-624-6277; *fax:* 0131-225-2349)
Email: jsoden@nationalgalleries.org

Chief: Hon Libn: Mr Peter Collins RSA *Dep:* Asst
Librarian/Keeper: Mrs Joanna Soden MA,
DipAGMS
Entry: adv appt *Open:* Mon-Fri 1000-1300, 1400-
1630
Subj: Scotland: fine art; arch; painting; sculpture;
printmaking; some decorative arts *Collns: Bks &
Pamphs:* printed records of the Royal Scottish
Academy, incl full sets of Annual Reports & Annual
Exhib catalogues & assorted hists *Archvs:* RSA
letter colln (1825-94); complete sets of Minute Bks
etc (from 1826); RSA sales records (from 1860);
RSA Life Class registers (1843-53, 1866-1901);
files on living & certain deceased membs of the
RSA *Other:* W.G. Gillies RSA Bequest (vast colln
of paintings & drawings, also letters, photos, press
cuttings, bks & catalogues, memorabilia & assorted
contents of studio)
Equip: fax (staff use only), copier, computer (with
wd-proc)
Stock: bks/5000; photos/300; slides/2000;
pamphs/300; archvs/2 cubic m

 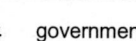

Pubns: The Royal Scottish Academy 1826-1976 (£18.50); The Making of the Royal Scottish Academy (£4.95) *Staff:* Other Prof: 1 *Exp:* £200 (1999-2000)

S624
Scottish Accountancy Research Trust Library
(formerly the Inst of Chartered Accountants of Scotland Lib)
CA House, 21 Haymarket Yards, Edinburgh, EH12 5BH (0131-247-4801; *fax:* 0131-225-3813)
Email: edinburgh-library@icas.org.uk

Type: prof body *Gov Body:* maintained by Scottish Accountancy Rsrch Trust (charitable trust) on behalf of the Inst of Chartered Accountants of Scotland *Chief:* Libn: Mrs Dorothy F. Hogg *Entry:* open to membs & students of ICAS, with access for ref only to interested parties *Open:* Mon-Fri 0900-1700
Subj: generalities; taxation; company law; accountancy; auditing *Collns:* Bks & Pamphs: antiquarian colln 1494-1930 (maintained by ICAS but deposited in Natl Lib of Scotland) *Archvs:* historical archvs of ICAS held in the Natl Archvs of Scotland (see **A150**) *Co-op Schemes:* BLDSC, ILL
Equip: m-reader, fax (50p-£1 per pg), copier (10p per pg), computers (incl 3 with wd-proc, 3 with internet & 3 with CD-ROM, printouts 10p per pg) *Online:* various abstracting & indexing databases on CD-ROM, financial & technical svc on CD-ROM *Svcs:* info, ref, biblio, abstracting
Stock: bks/10000; periodcls/150; pamphs/1000
Classn: UDC *Auto Sys:* EOSi
Staff: Libns: 1 Other Prof: 1

S625
Scottish Agricultural College Library
West Mains Rd, Edinburgh, EH9 2JG (0131-535-4116/7; *fax:* 0131-667-2601)
Email: m.mullay@ed.sac.ac.uk

Chief: Libn: Mrs Marilyn Mullay MA, MCLIP *Dep:* Asst Libn: Mr Andrew Martin BA, MSc, MCLIP *Assoc Libs:* SCOTTISH AGRICULTURAL COLL, W.J. THOMSON LIB (see **S65**)
Entry: public access available for consultation only *Open:* term: Mon-Thu 0845-2100, Fri 0845-1700, Sat-Sun 1000-1700; vac: Mon-Fri 0845-1700
Subj: agric *Co-op Schemes:* SALG
Equip: copier, 10 computers (incl CD-ROM) *Online:* various networked CD-ROMs & web-based databases
Stock: bks/15000; periodcls/310; pamphs/12000
Classn: UDC *Auto Sys:* Voyager
Staff: Libns: 2 Non-Prof: 1

S626
Scottish Agricultural Science Agency Library
82 Craigs Rd, East Craigs, Edinburgh, EH12 8NJ (0131-244-8873 (enquiries); *fax:* 0131-244-8940)
Email: library@sasa.gsi.gov.uk
Internet: http://www.sasa.gov.uk/

Gov Body: Scottish Exec Environment & Rural Affairs Dept *Chief:* Libn: Mrs Lynda J. Clark BA, MCLIP (Lynda.Clark@sasa.gsi.gov.uk)
Entry: adv appt necessary *Open:* Mon-Fri 0830-1700
Subj: chem; biology; botany; zoology; agric; seed sci; phytopathology; pesticides *Co-op Schemes:* SALG, ILL
Equip: 2 m-readers, copier, 3 computers (all with wd-proc & internet, 1 with CD-ROM) *Disabled:* large-screen monitor, text-enhancing software

Online: Dialog (SASA staff only, charged out to users) *Svcs:* info, ref, biblio, translation, loans, current awareness (contents pages of journals, official legislation), circulation of journals
Stock: various bks, periodcls, pamphs & maps (OS Scotland)
Classn: UDC *Auto Sys:* Horizon
Pubns: SASA Annual Report (free on request)
Staff: Libns: 1 Non-Prof: 1

S627
Scottish Beekeepers' Association, Moir Library
c/o Fountainbridge Lib, Dundee St, Edinburgh, EH1 1BG (0131-529-5616; *fax:* 0131-225-8783)
Internet: http://www.scottishbeekeepers.org.uk/

Type: assoc lib maintained by a public lib *Gov Body:* Lib Cttee of the Scottish Beekeepers' Assoc *Chief:* Hon Libn: Mrs. Margaret Sharp *Dep:* Assoc Libn (PT): Miss Frances Scott
Entry: assoc membs; adv appt advised *Open:* Mon, Wed 1300-2000, Tue, Thu-Fri 1000-1700, Sat 0900-1300
Subj: apiculture; beekeeping; hymenoptera
Svcs: info, ref, reading room
Stock: bks/6794; periodcls/40

S628
Scottish Executive, Library and Information Service
K Spur, Saughton House, Broomfield House, Edinburgh, EH11 1XD (0131-244-4565; *fax:* 0131-244-4545)
Email: sh.library@scotland.gov.uk
Internet: http://www.scotland.gov.uk/

Gov Body: Scottish Exec *Chief:* Head of Info Unit: Ms Jane Mackenzie MA, BA, MCLIP (jane.mackenzie@scotland.gsi.gov.uk)
Entry: ref only, by adv appt, at discretion of Libn *Open:* Mon-Thu 0830-1700, Fri 0830-1630
Subj: public admin; political sci; mgmt; edu; econ; sociology; environment; health; social work; agric; built environment; physical planning; industrial development; geog & hist of Scotland *Collns:* Bks & Pamphs: Scottish Executive/Scottish Office pubns; Environmental Impact Assessment; North Sea oil; all public & genl Acts *Co-op Schemes:* BLDSC, SHINE
Equip: m-reader, m-printer, fax, copier, 2 computers (both with wd-proc, internet & CD-ROM) *Online:* BLAISE, Dialog, Datastar, Justis, Newsline, Planex, Parliament, internet (all for Scottish Exec staff only) *Svcs:* info, ref, biblio, translation
Stock: bks/8000; periodcls/460; pamphs/21000; maps/500; govt pubns/35000
Classn: UDC *Auto Sys:* Horizon
Pubns: Lib Accessions Bulletin (monthly); Scottish Exec Pubns List (annual); Scottish Exec pubns are sold by The Stationery Office Bookshop, Edinburgh
Staff: Libns: 8 Non-Prof: 10.5 *Exp:* £150000 (2000-01)

S629
Scottish Health Service Centre, Health Management Library
Crewe Rd South, Edinburgh, EH4 2LF (0131-623-2535; *fax:* 0131-315-2369)
Email: library@shsc.csa.scot.nhs.uk

Gov Body: Common Svcs Agency for NHS Scotland (see **S589**) *Chief:* Libn: Miss Gill Hewitt
Open: Mon-Thu 0830-1700, Fri 0830-1630
Subj: health; health mgmt; health policy; mgmt info *Co-op Schemes:* ILL
Svcs: info, ref, biblio, indexing
Stock: bks/16000; periodcls/150
Auto Sys: Heritage *Staff:* Libns: 2 Non-Prof: 1

S630
Scottish Law Commission Library
140 Causewayside, Edinburgh, EH9 1PR (0131-668-2131; *fax:* 0131-662-4900)
Email: nick.brotchie@scotlawcom.gov.uk
Internet: http://www.scotlawcom.gov.uk/

Chief: Libn: Mr N.G.T. Brotchie MA, DipLib, MCLIP
Entry: bona fide rsrchers may be granted access for ref only, upon written appl *Open:* Mon-Thu 0900-1700, Fri 0900-1630
Subj: Scottish law; English & Commonwealth law; law reform; comparative law *Co-op Schemes:* BLDSC
Equip: m-reader, computer *Online:* Lexis
Stock: bks/20000; periodcls/100
Classn: own *Auto Sys:* CAIRS IMS
Staff: Libns: 1 Non-Prof: 1

S631
Scottish Museums Council Information Service
County House, 20-22 Torphichen St, Edinburgh, EH3 8JB (0131-229-7465; *fax:* 0131-229-2728)
Email: inform@scottishmuseums.org.uk
Internet: http://www.scottishmuseums.org.uk/

Chief: Info Mgr: Ms Heather Doherty BA(Hons) *Dep:* Info Offcr: Mrs Lesley Castell
Entry: ref only, membs of Scottish Museums Council only *Open:* Mon-Fri 1000-1200, 1400-1600
Subj: museology; Scottish museums; heritage; culture
Equip: video viewer *Svcs:* info, ref
Stock: bks/1500; periodcls/120; videos/50
Classn: own (based on DDC) *Auto Sys:* MS Access
Pubns: Tak Tent (monthly newsletter, membs only)
Staff: Libns: 1

S632
Scottish National Blood Transfusion Service, Protein Fractionation Centre, Library
21 Ellen's Glen Rd, Edinburgh, EH17 7QT (0131-536-5751/6; *fax:* 0131-536-5758)
Internet: http://www.snbts-pfc.co.uk/

Gov Body: Common Svcs Agency of the Scottish Health Svc (see **S589**) *Chief:* Libn: Ms Druscilla T. Rodger
Entry: adv appt, specialist enqs only *Open:* Mon-Fri 0930-1700
Subj: medical tech, specifically: blood products; protein pharmaceuticals; blood transfusion
Collns: Bks & Pamphs: BSI; Govt Acts; EC directives; regulatory affairs documents; patents
Equip: m-readers, m-printer, copiers, fax, video viewer, computers (incl wd-proc, internet & CD-ROM) *Svcs:* info
Stock: bks/3000; scientific papers/25000; various photos, slides, pamphs, maps & videos
Classn: own *Staff:* Libns: 1

S633
Scottish National Gallery of Modern Art Library
Dean Gallery, Belford Rd, Edinburgh, EH4 3DS (0131-624-6252; *fax:* 0131-623-7126)
Email: library@natgalscot.ac.uk
Internet: http://www.natgalscot.ac.uk/

Gov Body: Natl Galleries of Scotland *Chief:* Snr Curator (Archv & Lib): Mrs Ann Simpson (asimpson@nationalgalleries.org) *Dep:* Libn: Miss Jane Furness (jfurness@nationalgalleries.org)

Special Libraries

Edinburgh ▼ Elgin

(Scottish Natl Gallery of Modern Art Lib cont)
Assoc Libs: NATL GALLERY OF SCOTLAND LIB (see **S611**); SCOTTISH NATL PORTRAIT GALLERY LIB (see **S634**)
Entry: adv appt *Open:* Mon-Fri 1000-1300, 1400-1630
Subj: modern art, esp Scottish *Collns: Archvs:* Roland Penrose Archv; Gabrielle Keiller Archv; Richard Demarco Archv; Ashley Havinden Archv; other holdings concerning Scottish art & artists, Dada & Surrealism *Co-op Schemes:* ARLIS
Stock: bks/58000; periodcls/27; archvs/3000 MSS
Classn: in-house classn scheme *Auto Sys:* DS
Staff: Libns: 1 *Other Prof:* 2

S634 🔑🏛

Scottish National Portrait Gallery Library

1 Queen St, Edinburgh, EH2 1JD (0131-624-6420; *fax:* 0131-558-3691)
Email: hwatsonlib@nationalgalleries.org
Internet: http://www.nationalgalleries.org/

Gov Body: Natl Galleries of Scotland *Chief:* Libn: Ms Helen Watson BA
Assoc Libs: NATL GALLERY OF SCOTLAND LIB (see **S611**); SCOTTISH NATL GALLERY OF MODERN ART LIB (see **S633**)
Entry: ref only, by adv appt *Open: Gallery:* Mon-Sat 1000-1700, Sun 1400-1600; *Lib:* by appt on weekdays only
Subj: arts; Scottish portraiture; photography
Collns: Other: ref colln of photos
Stock: bks/16000+; periodcls/c20; photos/30000
Auto Sys: CALM 2000 Plus
Staff: Libns: 1
Proj: ongoing automation of lib records

S635 🏛

Scottish Natural Heritage, Information and Library Services

2 Anderson Pl, Edinburgh, EH6 5NP (0131-446-2479/2478; *fax:* 0131-446-2405)
Email: library@snh.gov.uk

Chief: Lib Mgr: Ms Alwyn Coupe MCLIP
Entry: ref only, consultation by appt *Open:* Mon-Thu 0830-1700, Fri 08300-1630
Subj: all aspects of nature & landscape conservation; land use & recreation esp in relation to Scotland's nat heritage *Co-op Schemes:* ILL
Equip: copier (staff only), computers (incl internet, staff only) *Online:* internal database (staff only)
Stock: bks/15000; periodcls/800
Classn: UDC *Auto Sys:* Adlib, Olib
Staff: Libns: 4 *Non-Prof:* 3

S636 🔑 🎓

Scottish Poetry Library

5 Crichton's Cl, Cannongate, Edinburgh, EH8 8DT (0131-557-2876; *fax:* 0131-557-8393)
Email: enquiries@spl.org.uk
Internet: http://www.spl.org.uk/

Type: voluntary sector, open to public *Gov Body:* Mgmt Cttee *Chief:* Dir: Dr Robyn Marsack *Dep:* Libn: Mr Iain Young MA

Assoc Libs: small branches throughout Scotland in: Ayr; Elgin; Glasgow; Grangemouth; Paisley; Scottish Borders; Ullapool; Inverness; Shetland; Renfrew; contact Edinburgh Lib for details
Entry: open to public, free *Open:* Mon-Fri 1100-1800, Sat 1200-1600
Subj: Scottish & internatl poetry (mainly 20C)
Collns: Archvs: Scottish Poetry Lib Archv *Other:* small braille poetry colln *Co-op Schemes:* SUC
Equip: m-reader, video viewer, copier, computer (incl CD-ROM), sound recording & listening equip, TV *Svcs:* info, ref, biblio, indexing
Stock: bks/18000; periodcls/50; pamphs/1000; audios/1000; videos/50; cuttings & photos/4000
Classn: DDC (mod) *Auto Sys:* own
Pubns: Scottish Poetry Index: An Index to Poetry & Poetry-Related Material in Scottish Literary Magazines 1952- (Vols 1-8 publ, £15-£25 each); Makar's Walk: Walks in the Old Town of Edinburgh (£6.95); The Jewel Box: Contemporary Scottish Poems (audio CD, £8.99)
Staff: Libns: 2 *Other Prof:* 4 *Non-Prof:* 2

S637 🔑

Scottish Society for Prevention of Cruelty to Animals, Library

603 Queensferry Rd, Braehead Mains, Edinburgh, EH4 6EA (0131-339-0222; *fax:* 0131-339-4777)
Email: enquiries@scottishspca.org
Internet: http://www.scottishspca.org/

Chief: Chief Exec: Mr James Morris CBE, BSc
Dep: Dir of Support Svcs: Mr Ronald Mochrie
Entry: adv appt; ref only; tel enqs accepted
Open: Mon-Fri 0900-1700
Subj: animals; veterinary sci; work of the SSPCA
Stock: bks/150; photos/500; slides/4000
Pubns: Annual Report; SSPCA News (ad membership magazine); Animal Express (jnr membership magazine)

S638 🏛

Sea Fish Industry Authority, Headquarters Library

18 Logie Mill, Logie Green Rd, Edinburgh, EH7 4HG (0131-558-3331; *fax:* 0131-558-1442)
Email: g_buck@seafish.co.uk

Type: primarily statutory body serving an industry sector *Chief:* Libn: Mr Graeme Buck BSc(Hons), DipLIS
Assoc Libs: SEAFISH TECH LIB, St Andrew's Dock, Hull, HU3 4QE, Libn: Mrs Deborah Dalton (01482-327837; *fax:* 01482-223310; *email:* d_dalton@seafish.co.uk); SEAFISH AQUA-CULTURE LIB, Ardtoe, Acharacle, Argyll, PH36 4LD, Libn: Mrs Judy O'Rourke (01397-875000; *fax:* 01397-875001; *email:* j_orourke@seafish.co.uk)
Entry: adv appt, photocopying available to personal callers (circumstances allowing), direct ILL possible *Open:* Mon-Fri 0900-1700
Subj: fishery econ; fishery mgmt; stock assessment; food tech (fish processing, handling, nutritional value); *Seafish Tech Lib:* fishing methods; fishing gear tech; safety at sea; marine electronics; port development; finfish & shellfish processing; industry training; *Seafish Aquaculture Lib:* marine aquaculture; halibut; shellfish (culture)
Collns: Bks & Pamphs: Fishery Statistical Colln (statistics from European & North American countries on fish landings & fish trade); statistical pubns from internatl bodies (ICES, OECD) *Co-op Schemes:* BLDSC
Equip: video viewer, fax, copier, computer (incl wd-proc)
Stock: bks/5000; periodcls/24
Classn: own
Pubns: Sea Fish Industry Authority Pubns Guide (free)
Staff: Libns: 1 *Non-Prof:* 2 *Exp:* £3000 (1999-2000); £3500 (2000-01)

S639 🔑

Signet Library

Parliament Sq, Edinburgh, EH1 1RF (0131-225-4923; *fax:* 0131-220-4016)
Email: library@wssociety.co.uk
Internet: http://www.signetlibrary.co.uk/

Gov Body: Soc of Writers to Her Majesty's Signet
Chief: Libn: Ms Audrey Walker BA, MCLIP *Dep:* Snr Asst Libn: Mrs Kate Corbett LLB
Entry: written appl only *Open:* Mon-Fri 0930-1630
Subj: law; Scottish hist, topography & genealogy
Collns: Bks & Pamphs: Session Papers 1713-1820 (2500 vols pertaining to Scottish Civil cases); Roughead Colln (trials, 500 vols)
Equip: fax, copier, 4 computers (incl wd-proc, internet & CD-ROM) *Svcs:* info, ref
Stock: bks/75000; periodcls/60
Classn: UDC *Auto Sys:* Endeavour
Staff: Libns: 3 *Non-Prof:* 2

S640 🔑

Society of Solicitors in the Supreme Court of Scotland (SSC) Library

11 Parliament Sq, Edinburgh, EH1 1RF (0131-225-6268; *fax:* 0131-225-2270)
Email: enquiries@ssclibrary.co.uk
Internet: http://www.ssclibrary.co.uk/

Chief: Keeper of the Lib: Mrs Christine Wilcox BA(Hons), MCLIP
Entry: SSC membs only; ref only rsrch by special arrangement *Open:* court term: Mon-Fri 0930-1600; court vac: Mon-Fri 1000-1600
Subj: Scots law (all aspects); UK law where it is common to Scotland & England
Equip: fax, copier, computers (incl wd-proc & internet), 2 rooms for hire (on appl) *Svcs:* info, ref
Stock: bks/15000; periodcls/80
Classn: legal subj headings adapted from current law
Pubns: The SSC Story 1784-1984 (£15)
Staff: Libns: 1 *Other Prof:* 0.5 *Non-Prof:* 0.5

S641 🏛

Sportscotland, Library

Caledonia House, South Gyle, Edinburgh, EH12 9DQ (0131-317-7200; *fax:* 0131-317-7202)
Email: library@sportscotland.org.uk
Internet: http://www.sportscotland.org.uk/

Chief: Info Offcr: Ms E. Maxwell BA, DipLib
Entry: ref only, adv appt
Subj: statistics; econ; legislation; leisure; sport; sports medicine; sports sci; sports planning; sports bldg design; indiv sports; training; coaching; sport for people with disabilities; women & sport; young people & sport *Collns: Bks & Pamphs:* Coaching Resource Centre
Equip: 2 copiers (via staff), computer *Svcs:* info, ref, biblio
Stock: bks/7000+; periodcls/160; videos/50
Classn: UDC *Auto Sys:* EOSi
Staff: Libns: 1 *Exp:* £17000 (1999-2000); £25000 (2000-01); figs represent whole lib budget

S642 ✚

St Columba's Hospice, Clinical Library

Challenger Lodge, Boswall Rd, Edinburgh, EH5 3RW (0131-551-2517)
Email: m.gill@napier.ac.uk

Chief: Libn: Ms Margaret Gill BA, DipLib
Entry: staff *Open:* Mon-Fri 0830-2000
Subj: palliative care
Equip: copier (£1 per 12 copies) *Svcs:* info, indexing

Stock: bks/c2000; periodcls/15; videos/40
Classn: Strathcarron Scheme for Palliative Care
Staff: Libns: 0.2

S643 🎓
The Stair Society Library
Saltire Ct, 20 Castle Ter, Edinburgh, EH1 2ET
(0131-473-5248; fax: 0131-228-1222)
Email: mail.desk@shepwedd.co.uk
Internet: http://www.stairsociety.org/

Chief: Sec & Treasurer: Mr Thomas Drysdale
Dep: Trust Administrator: Mrs Janine Christie
Subj: hist of Scots law **Collns:** Bks & Pamphs: vols publ by the Stair Soc, incl old & discontinued vols
Stock: periodcls/70; stock of own pubns
Pubns: numerous pubns, incl: The Practicks of Sir James Balfour of Pittendreich, Vol 2 (membs £15, non-membs £30); The Justiciary Records of Argyll & the Isles 1664-1742 (membs £15, non-membs £30); The Minute Bk of the Faculty of Advocates, Vol 1: 1661-1712, Vol 2: 1713-1750 (membs £15 each, non-membs £30 each); Perpetuities in Scots Law (membs £15, non-membs £30); The Stair Tercentenary Studies (membs £15, non-membs £30); Formulary of Old Scots Legal Documents (membs £15, non-membs £30); Selkirk Protocol Bks 1511-1547 (membs £15, non-membs £30); many others, list available from the Stair Soc

S644 🎓
Stevenson College Edinburgh, Library
Bankhead Ave, Sighthill, Edinburgh, EH11 4DE
(0131-535-4600; fax: 0131-535-4666)
Internet: http://www.stevenson.ac.uk/

Chief: Lib & Study Centre Mgr: Miss Alma Wardrope BA(Hons)
Entry: matriculated students & staff of Coll, lending & ref; others ref only **Open:** term: Mon, Fri 0845-1645, Tue-Thu 0845-2100; vac: Mon-Fri 0845-1230, 1330-1645
Subj: all subjs; genl; GCSE; A level; vocational
Co-op Schemes: ILL, SUC
Equip: m-reader, video viewer, copier, 13 computers (incl 7 with wd-proc, 5 with internet & 3 with CD-ROM) **Svcs:** info, ref
Stock: bks/20000; periodcls/150; audios/5; videos/50; CD-ROMs/60
Classn: DDC **Auto Sys:** Heritage
Staff: Libns: 1 Non-Prof: 5 **Exp:** £18000 (1999-2000); £18000 (2000-01)

S645 🍷 📷
The Still Moving Picture Company, Library
157 Broughton Rd, Edinburgh, EH7 4JJ (0131-557-9697; fax: 0131-557-9699)
Email: info@stillmovingpictures.com
Internet: http://www.stillmovingpictures.com/

Type: commercial picture agency **Chief:** Dir: Mr John Hutchinson
Entry: please ring for appt **Open:** Mon-Fri 0845-1800
Subj: photos of Scotland, the country, its businesses & its people, & other parts of the world; special emphasis on sport & travel; early hist of Scottish football; Scottish life (1990-date) **Collns:** Other: Wade Cooper Colln; AEA tech; Allsport (for which SMPC is Scottish Agent)
Equip: fax, computer (with wd-proc), light boxes, viewing glasses
Stock: slides/150000
Pubns: Subj List & Brochure (free)
Staff: Libns: 2

S646 🎓 🙏
The United SCOC Library
Old Coates House, 32 Manor Pl, Edinburgh, EH3 7EB (0131-225-4911; fax: 0131-220-2294)
Email: scoclibrary@britishlibrary.net
Internet: http://pages.britishlibrary.net/~scoclibrary/

Gov Body: Scottish Churches Open Coll (SCOC)
Chief: Libn: Mr Michael Buck MSc, DipLib, BD, MCLIP
Subj: religion **Svcs:** info, ref
Stock: bks/c22000; periodcls/90
Classn: DDC **Auto Sys:** DBTextbase
Staff: Libns: 0.7 **Exp:** £8000 (1999-2000); £8000 (2000-01)

S647 🎓
Waddington Environment Library
John Muir Bldg, The King's Bldgs, Mayfield Rd, Edinburgh, EH9 3JK (0131-650-4866; fax: 0131-650-7214)
Email: cecs-office@ed.ac.uk
Internet: http://www.cecs.ed.ac.uk/

Gov Body: Centre for the Study of Environmental Change & Sustainability (CECS), part of Edinburgh Univ (see **S593**) **Chief:** contact the Libn
Entry: by appt only
Subj: environment; sustainable resources
Stock: bks/2000

S648 ✚ 🎓
Western General Hospital Library
Crewe Rd South, Edinburgh, EH4 2XU (0131-537-2299; fax: 0131-537-1144)
Email: Western.General.Library@ed.ac.uk
Internet: http://www.ed.ac.uk/

Gov Body: Univ of Edinburgh (see **S593**) **Chief:** Libn: Mrs Claire Leach
Entry: hosp staff; staff & students of Univ **Open:** Mon-Thu 0900-2100, Fri 0900-1700
Subj: medicine; oncology; gastroenterology; neuroscience; surgery **Co-op Schemes:** BLDSC, SHINE
Equip: m-fiche reader, copier, video viewer, 7 computers (incl 3 with wd-proc, 3 with CD-ROM & 6 with internet) **Online:** Medline
Stock: bks/3700; periodcls/167 + 81 no longer current
Classn: NLM **Auto Sys:** Voyager

Egham

S649 🍷 🍴
CABi Bioscience Library
Bakeham Ln, Egham, Surrey, TW20 9TY (01784-470111; fax: 01784-470909)
Email: bioscience@cabi.org
Internet: http://www.cabi.org/

Type: rsrch **Chief:** Snr Libn: Mrs L.A. Regab BA, MCLIP
Entry: written appl to Libn
Subj: bioscience; mycology; pest control; ecology
Equip: m-reader, copier **Svcs:** charged document delivery svc
Stock: bks/15000; periodcls/500
Classn: own **Auto Sys:** TechLib Plus
Pubns: list available on request
Staff: Libns: 1
See also CABi INFO FOR DEVELOPMENT (**O91**)

S650 🍷 🏛
Egham Museum Library
High St, Egham, Surrey, TW20 9EW (01344-843047)

Gov Body: Egham Museum Trust **Chief:** Hon Curator: Mr John Mills BSc
Open: Tue, Thu, Sat 1000-1230, 1400-1630
Subj: local study (Egham); geog; hist **Collns:** Bks & Pamphs: bks & pamphs connected with Egham & dist's hist **Archvs:** Egham & local hist in newspapers, magazines, photos, objects etc
Equip: m-reader
Stock: bks/1200; periodcls/5; photos/4500; slides/2000; maps/500; audios/10; videos/2; documents/4000 **Acqs Offcr:** Hon Curator, as above
Classn: by subj **Auto Sys:** Museums Documentation Assoc System
Pubns: Egham Picture Bk (£5.95); Virginia Water Picture Bk (£5.95); Englefield Green Picture Bk (£5.95); Thorpe Picture Bk (£5.95); Runnymede Pictorial Hist (£6.95)
Staff: Non-Prof: 30 volunteers

S651 🎓
Royal Holloway University of London Library
Egham Hill, Egham, Surrey, TW20 0EX (01784-443823; fax: 01784-447670)
Email: library@rhul.ac.uk
Internet: http://web.rhul.ac.uk/Information-Services/

Gov Body: Univ of London (see **S1440**) **Chief:** Dir of Info Svcs: Mr David Sweeney (d.sweeney@rhul.ac.uk) **Dep:** Libn & Dep Dir of Info Svcs: Mrs Sarah Gerrard BA, DipLib, MCLIP (s.gerrard@rhul.ac.uk)
Assoc Libs: FOUNDER'S LIB (01784-443321); MUSIC LIB (01784-443560); ARCHV SVC, addr as above, Coll Archivist: Ms Nicky Sugar (01784-443814; email: archives@rhul.ac.uk)
Entry: ref only for non-membs; borrowing rights on payment of annual fee **Open:** term: Mon-Thu 0900-2100, Fri 0900-1900, Sat 1100-1700, Sun 1300-1800; vac: Mon-Fri 0900-1700
Subj: all subjs; undergrad; postgrad **Collns:** Bks & Pamphs: Oliver Colln (local hist & topography); A.V. Coton Colln (dance); Anselm Hughes Lib (early music) **Archvs:** Coll archvs (with special interest in edu of women), incl predecessors: Bedford Coll Archvs (1849-1985); Royal Holloway Coll Archvs (1876-1985); personal papers, incl: Robert Simpson Archv; Sir Alfred Sherman papers; theatre company archvs, incl: records of Theatre Proj Consultants Ltd; Gay Sweatshop Theatre Company Archv (1974-1995); Half Moon Theatre Company Archv (1972-1990); some estate papers
Co-op Schemes: BLDSC, M25, SASLIC, UK Libs Plus
Equip: m-readers, m-printer, video viewers, copiers, clr copier, computers (all with wd-proc, internet & CD-ROM) **Online:** Dialog, Datastar, Orbit, BRS, BIDS (charged to depts; outside readers at cost) **Svcs:** info, ref
Stock: bks/548815; periodcls/1759; slides/153; m-forms/351; AVs/6050 (audios & videos); archvs/900 linear m; elec media/49 items
Classn: DDC **Auto Sys:** Libertas
Staff: Libns: 11.8 Other Prof: 7.9 Non-Prof: 15.4

Elgin

S652 🍷 🏛
Elgin Museum – Moray Society, Library
1 High St, Elgin, Moray, IV30 1EQ (01343-543675; fax: 01343-543675)

Gov Body: Moray Soc **Chief:** Curator: Ms Susan Bennett BSc(Hons)
Entry: ref only, used mainly by Moray Soc membs
Open: Apr-Oct: Mon-Fri 1000-1700, Sat 1100-1600, Sun 1400-1700; winter: by appt
Subj: Morayshire: sci; geog; hist **Collns:** Bks & Pamphs: small specialist colln with a few rare bks
Archvs: some archv holdings ☛

Elgin
▼
Exeter

Special Libraries

(Elgin Museum - Moray Soc, Lib cont)

Svcs: info
Stock: bks/15 m; archvs/10 m
Staff: Other Prof: 1 *Non-Prof:* 2 custodians, 50 volunteers *Exp:* no budget for stock; acqs are by donation

S653
Moray College Learning Resource Centre

Moray St, Elgin, Moray, IV30 1JJ (01343-576206; *fax:* 01343-576000)
Email: angie.mackenzie@moray.uhi.ac.uk
Internet: http://www.moray.ac.uk/

Gov Body: part of the Univ of the Highlands & Islands *Chief:* LRC Offcr: Mrs Angela MacKenzie BA, DipLib, DipEdTech, MCLIP
Entry: external membs fee £10 pa *Open:* term: Mon-Thu 0845-2000, Fri 0845-1630; vac: Mon-Thu 0845-1645, Fri 0845-1630
Subj: all subjs; genl; undergrad; postgrad; vocational *Collns: Bks & Pamphs:* health & safety *Other:* Natl Coaching Foundation Colln *Co-op Schemes:* Grampian Info, BLDSC, UHI inter-site lending scheme
Equip: 4 video viewers, copier, 65 computers (all with wd-proc, internet & CD-ROM) *Disabled:* Supernova, Dragon, TextHelp, Inspiration, magnifier, personal hearing loop, study support room & qualified staff *Online:* online journals databases *Officer-in-Charge:* LRC Offcr, as above
Svcs: info, ref, biblio
Stock: bks/25000; periodcls/95; audios/40; videos/780; CD-ROMs/25 *Acqs Offcr:* LRC Offcr, as above
Classn: DDC *Auto Sys:* Olib
Staff: Libns: 1 *Non-Prof:* 4
Proj: new LRC opened Sep 2002

Enfield

S654
Capel Manor College, Frances Perry Library

Bullsmoor Ln, Enfield, Middlesex, EN1 4RQ (020-8366-4442; *fax:* 01992-717544)
Email: info@capel.ac.uk
Internet: http://www.connected.co.uk/get/capelmanor/

Gov Body: Capel Manor Coll *Chief:* Lib Administrative Offcr: Mrs Elaine Holtam (elaine.holtam@capel.ac.uk) *Dep:* Lib Administrative Asst: Ms Lea Spicer (lea.spicer@capel.ac.uk)
Open: term: Mon-Tue, Thu 0830-1930, Wed 0830-1830, Fri 0900-1730; vac: Mon-Fri 0930-1700
Subj: environmental conservation; ecology; botany; agric; hortic; landscape design; leisure mgmt *Collns: Bks & Pamphs:* some BSI; Working Lib of the late Frances Perry *Co-op Schemes:* BLDSC
Equip: copier, video viewer, 43 computers (all with wd-proc & internet, 12 with CD-ROM) *Svcs:* info, ref, biblio, indexing
Stock: bks/7000; periodcls/107; maps/6; AVs/20
Classn: DDC *Auto Sys:* LIMES
Staff: Libns: 1 *Other Prof:* 0.5 *Non-Prof:* 1.5

S655 ✚
Chase Health Information Centre

Block C4, Chase Farm Hosp, The Ridgeway, Enfield, Middlesex, EN2 8JL (020-8967-5982; *fax:* 020-8367-4561)
Email: libcf1@mdx.ac.uk

Gov Body: Middlesex Univ (see **S1282**) *Chief:* Libn: Ms Linda Farley BA, MCLIP
Entry: open to staff of North London Consortium & staff & students of Middlesex Univ *Open:* Mon, Fri 0930-1700, Tue-Thu 0930-1900
Subj: medicine; nursing *Co-op Schemes:* BLDSC, BMA, NTRLS
Equip: copier, computers (incl wd-proc & internet), scanners *Online:* OVID *Svcs:* info, ref, biblio
Stock: bks/5500; periodcls/100
Classn: NLM *Auto Sys:* Horizon
Pubns: Lib Guide
Staff: Libns: 1.6 *Non-Prof:* 1.4

S656 🔑
Occupational and Environmental Diseases Association, Library

Mitre House, 66 Abbey Rd, Bush Hill Pk, Enfield, Middlesex, EN1 2QH (020-8360-8490)
Internet: http://www.oeda.demon.co.uk/

Type: registered charity *Chief:* Info Offcr: Dr Nancy Tait MBE
Entry: rsrchers welcome, by adv appt *Open:* Mon-Fri 0930-1730
Subj: industrial diseases, esp asbestosis; occupational & environmental hazards *Collns: Bks & Pamphs:* early papers on risks of asbestos
Pubns: OEDA Newsletter (4 pa, subscription £10); Asbestos Facts

Enniskillen

S657
Fermanagh College of Further Education Library

Fairview, 1 Dublin Rd, Enniskillen, Co Fermanagh, BT74 6AE (028-6634-2216; *fax:* 028-6632-6357)
Email: oneillj@fermanaghcoll.ac.uk
Internet: http://www.fermanaghcoll.ac.uk/

Gov Body: Fermanagh Coll *Chief:* Coll Libn: Ms Janet O'Neill BLS, MLS, MCLIP
Entry: staff & students of the Coll *Open:* term: Mon-Thu 0845-2100, Fri 0845-1700
Subj: all subjs; genl; GCSE; A level; vocational; business (at undergrad level)
Equip: copier, computers (with wd-proc, internet & CD-ROM) *Svcs:* info
Stock: bks/10500; periodcls/25; CD-ROMs/some
Classn: DDC *Staff: Libns:* 1 *Non-Prof:* 2

Epsom

S658 ✚
Epsom Hospital, The Sally Howell Library

Dorking Rd, Epsom, Surrey, KT18 7EG (01372-735688; *fax:* 01372-735687)

Gov Body: Epsom & St Helier NHS Trust *Chief:* Libn: Mr Gordon Smith BA, MCLIP (gsmith@sthelier.sghms.ac.uk) *Dep:* Asst Libn: Mrs Marion Morrison MA, DipLib, MCLIP (mmorrison@sthelier.sghms.ac.uk)
Assoc Libs: ST HELIER HOSP, HIRSON LIB (see **S441**)
Entry: NHS staff only *Open:* Mon-Fri 0830-1830
Subj: medicine; psychiatry *Co-op Schemes:* BLDSC, BMA, NULJ
Equip: copier, computers *Online:* Medline, CINAHL & others *Svcs:* info, ref, biblio

Stock: bks/3600 incl pamphs; periodcls/115
Classn: NLM *Staff: Libns:* 2.55

S659
North East Surrey College of Technology (NESCOT) Library

Reigate Rd, Ewell, Epsom, Surrey, KT17 3DS (020-8394-3174; *fax:* 020-8394-3030)
Internet: http://www.nescot.ac.uk/

Chief: Libn: Mr Graeme Hodge BLib(Hons), MCLIP
Entry: ref only for outside users *Open:* term: Mon-Thu 0830-2000, Fri 0830-1700, Sat 1000-1400; vac: Mon-Fri 0900-1700
Subj: all subjs; GCSE; A level; undergrad; postgrad; vocational *Co-op Schemes:* ILL
Equip: m-reader, m-printer (10p per pg), fax (in Coll), 4 video viewers, 3 copiers (4p per pg), clr copier (in Coll), 60 computers (all with wd-proc, 55 with internet), video & digital editing suite *Disabled:* text enlarger, minicoms, HAL voice synthesiser, adjustable tables *Online:* Medline, BNI & others *Svcs:* info, ref, biblio
Stock: bks/45000; periodcls/350; videos/1500
Classn: DDC *Auto Sys:* Dynix
Staff: Libns: 5 *Non-Prof:* 5

Esher

S660 ✚
The Princess Alice Hospice Education Library

West End Ln, Esher, Surrey, KT10 8NA (01372-461843)
Email: library@princess-alice-hospice.org.uk

Chief: Libn: Mrs Jan Brooman BA, MCLIP (janbrooman@princess-alice-hospice.org.uk)
Entry: registered membs (hospice staff/students); ref only for others *Open:* Mon-Fri 0900-1700
Subj: palliative care *Co-op Schemes:* BLDSC, HLN
Equip: copier (5p per sheet), 2 computers (both with wd-proc, internet & CD-ROM) *Online:* via KA24 *Officer-in-Charge:* Libn, as above *Svcs:* info, ref, biblio
Stock: bks/2000; periodcls/38; videos/50 *Acqs Offcr:* Libn, as above
Classn: own *Auto Sys:* LIMES
Staff: Libns: 1 *Non-Prof:* 5 volunteers *Exp:* £12000 (2000-01)

Exeter

S661 🏛
Bill Douglas Centre for the History of Cinema and Popular Culture, Library and Archive

Univ of Exeter, Old Lib, Prince of Wales Rd, Exeter, Devon, EX4 4PT (01392-264321; *fax:* 01392-263871)
Email: bdc@exeter.ac.uk
Internet: http://www.billdouglas.org/

Gov Body: Univ of Exeter (see **S482**) *Chief:* Curator: Dr Hester Higton PhD (h.k.higton@ex.ac.uk)
Entry: ref only, membership required for non-Univ users *Open: Museum:* Mon-Fri 1000-1600; *Reading Room:* Mon-Fri 1000-1300, 1400-1700
Subj: arts; cinema; film; hist of cinema; popular culture *Collns: Bks & Pamphs:* bks & periodcls relating to film, the cinema & their pre-hist; 1st eds of major works on hist of cinema *Other:* photos, postcards, cigarette cards, posters, programmes, handbills & other ephemera relating to film; magic lantern slides; toys, instruments, records etc relating to cinema & its pre-hist
Equip: computer (with wd-proc) *Svcs:* info, ref

---

 academic   corporate

🏛 governmental   ✚ medical

Stock: bks/18000; periodcls/5000; photos/4000; slides/500; pamphs/5000; audios/500; archvs/4000 items
Classn: DDC
Staff: Other Prof: 1 *Non-Prof:* 0.5
Further Info: most of the bks & archv materials come as gifts from the major donor to the Centre, Mr Peter Jewell

S662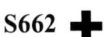

Dean Clarke House NHS Library

Dean Clarke House, Southernhay East, Exeter, Devon, EX1 1PQ (01392-207372)
Email: jeff.skinner@eastdevon-pct.nhs.uk
Internet: http://www.ex.ac.uk/library/eml/ nedhalib.html

Gov Body: North & East Devon Health Care Community *Chief:* Libn: Mr Jeff Skinner, BA, MCLIP
Entry: staff of North, Mid & East Devon Primary Care Trusts; other NHS employees; external rsrchers by adv appt *Open:* term: Mon-Tue, Thu 0900-1500, Fri 0900-1230, closed Wed; vac: Mon-Tue 0900-1700, Fri 0900-1230, closed Wed-Thu
Subj: health care; health svc policy & planning; health svcs mgmt; public health; health improvement; epidemiology; evidence-based medicine; clinical governance; health statistics
Collns: Other: grey lit colln *Co-op Schemes:* SWRLIN, Exeter Health Libs Group
Equip: Online: Medline, Cochrane & others
Staff: Libns: 1

S663 🗝

Devon and Exeter Institution, Library and Reading Rooms

7 Cathedral Cl, Exeter, Devon, EX1 1EZ (01392-251017; *fax:* 01392-263871)
Email: info@devonandexeterinstitution.org.uk
Internet: http://www.devonandexeterinstitution. org.uk/

Gov Body: Lib is independent but admin undertaken by Univ of Exeter (see **S671**) *Chief:* Librarian-in-Charge: Dr Jessica Gardner PhD
Entry: membership lib, but short-term facilities possible for non-membs by prior arrangement
Open: Mon-Fri 0900-1700
Subj: hist; local study (the South West, all aspects) *Collns: Bks & Pamphs:* pamphs (c200 bnd vols, 19C) *Archvs:* local newspapers (from 18C); newspaper cuttings (mainly local); minute bks of Instn *Other:* maps (OS 25" etc); F.W.L. Stockdale Papers (incl MS Hist of Devon) *Co-op Schemes:* AIL
Equip: m-fiche reader, copier, 4 computers (incl 1 wd-proc, 3 internet & 1 CD-ROM), overhead projector, 2 rooms for hire *Online:* as for Univ of Exeter Lib (fees on appl) *Svcs:* info, ref, biblio
Stock: bks36000; periodcls/40; photos/500; illusts/1500; pamphs/3000; maps/3500; m-forms/1000; archvs/20 linear m
Classn: DDC (mod in-house)
Pubns: The Devon & Exeter Instn 1813-1988 (£2); postcards (20p each)
Staff: Libns: 0.3 *Non-Prof:* 0.9, incl volunteers

S664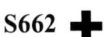

Devon Partnership NHS Trust, Wonford House Hospital Library

Dryden Rd, Exeter, Devon, EX2 5AF (01392-403449)
Email: Mary.Smith@devonptnrs.nhs.uk
Internet: http://www.ex.ac.uk/library/eml/whh.html

Gov Body: Devon Partnership NHS Trust *Chief:* Libn: Mrs Mary Smith BA, MCLIP
Entry: Trust staff *Open:* 24 hr access for cardholders; staffed: Mon 0830-1630, Tue 1230-1630, Wed 0900-1300, Thu 0900-1600, Fri 0830-1430

Subj: medicine; psychiatry; mental health *Co-op Schemes:* Exeter Health Libs Group
Equip: Online: Medline, CINAHL, BNI, Cochrane, Embase; various e-journals
Staff: Libns: 1

S665 🗝 🙏

Exeter Cathedral Library

Old Bishop's Palace, Diocesan House, Palace Gate, Exeter, Devon, EX1 1HX (01392-272894)
Email: library@exeter-cathedral.org.uk
Internet: http://www.exeter-cathedral.org.uk/ Admin/Library.html

Gov Body: Dean & Chapter of Exeter *Chief:* Cathedral Libn: Mr P.W. Thomas MA, DipLib
Assoc Libs: EXETER CATHEDRAL ARCHVS, at same addr (see **A163**); archvs administered separately from lib by Exeter Cathedral & Devon Record Office (see **A161**)
Entry: borrowing (of modern non-ref works only) restricted to clergy & to staff & postgrads of Univ of Exeter *Open:* Mon-Fri 1400-1700
Subj: the South West, particularly Exeter & Devon: hist; religious hist; genl; Christianity, particularly C of E (much early printed material); church hist; British hist; lang; sci; maths *Collns: Bks & Pamphs:* Medical & Scientific Colln (15C-early 20C, comprising Thomas Glass Bequest & other material, plus Exeter Medical Lib pre-1901 items); Cook Colln (incl early linguistics); Harington Colln (16C-19C); Civil War tracts *Other:* medieval & later MS bks
Equip: copier, computer
Stock: bks/20000; periodcls/8; photos/1000; slides/800; illusts/500; pamphs/3000; maps/150; m-forms/50; audios/1; archvs/60000 items
Classn: own *Auto Sys:* Heritage
Pubns: The Lib of Exeter Cathedral (£1)
Staff: Libns: 1 *Non-Prof:* 20 PT

S666 🎓

Exeter College, Library Resources

Hele Rd, Exeter, Devon, EX4 4JS (01392-205466; *fax:* 01392-205511)
Email: bfortnam@exe-coll.ac.uk
Internet: http://www.exe-coll.ac.uk/

Chief: Head of Learning Resources: Mrs Bobby Fortnam MCLIP
Assoc Libs: HELE RD LIB, addr as above; BRITANNY HOUSE LIB, Exeter Coll, New North Rd, Exeter, Devon, EX4 4EP (01392-205527); EPISCOPAL CENTRE LIB, Dinham Rd, Exeter, EX4 4EE (01392-205575); BISHOP BLACKALL LIB, Pennsylvania Rd, Exeter, Devon, EX4 6BB (01392-205536); MARSH BARTON LIB (01392-205673); VICTORIA HOUSE LIB, 33-36 Queen St, Exeter, Devon, EX4 3SR (01392-205310)
Entry: staff & students; associate membership available to membs of public *Open:* term: Mon 0830-1700, Tue-Thu 0830-1900, Fri 0930-1700; vac: Mon-Fri 1200-1600
Subj: all subjs; genl; GCSE; A level; undergrad; vocational *Co-op Schemes:* BLDSC
Equip: m-reader, copiers, clr copier, video viewers, 6 computers (incl wd-proc, internet & CD-ROM) *Svcs:* info, ref
Stock: bks/55000; periodcls/300; audios/100; videos/5000
Classn: DDC *Auto Sys:* Heritage
Staff: Libns: 3 *Non-Prof:* 14

S667 🗝

Exeter Law Library Society

The Lodge, The Castle, Exeter, Devon, EX4 3PF (01392-411585; *fax:* 01392-431511)

Chief: Chair: Miss S. Parnell
Entry: membs only (annual subscription) *Open:* Mon-Fri 0900-1730

Subj: law (reports only)
Stock: bks/5000 vols of law reports
Classn: by year

S668 🎓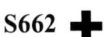

Exeter Medical Library

Exeter Postgrad Medical Centre, Barrack Rd, Exeter, Devon, EX2 5DW (01392-403002)
Email: MedLib@ex.ac.uk
Internet: http://www.ex.ac.uk/library/eml/

Gov Body: Univ of Exeter (see **S671**) *Chief:* Libn: Miss Virginia Newton BSc, DipLib, MCLIP (V.B.Newton@exeter.ac.uk) *Dep:* Snr Lib Asst: Mrs Jill Maxted MCLIP (J.Maxted@exeter.ac.uk)
Entry: local NHS staff & students; Univ of Exeter SPMHS staff & postgrad students; others may use the Lib for ref only at the discretion of Lib staff
Open: Mon-Fri 0900-1730
Subj: medicine *Co-op Schemes:* SWRLIN, Exeter Health Libs Group
Equip: copier (10p per copy), 5 computers (with internet) *Svcs:* info, ref
Stock: bks/c8000; periodcls/c250; videos/36
Classn: NLM *Auto Sys:* Innopac
Staff: Libns: 2.5 *Non-Prof:* 2 *Exp:* £40000 (1999-2000)

S669

South West Water Ltd, Headquarters Library

Peninsula House, Rydon Ln, Exeter, Devon, EX2 7HR (01392-446688; *fax:* 01392-434966)
Internet: http://www.swwater.co.uk/

Chief: Libn: Mrs Sue Alcock BA, DipLib, MSLS, MCLIP *Dep:* Lib Asst: Miss Chris Martin BA, DPS
Entry: staff of company & its subsidiaries; others by appt *Open:* Mon-Fri 0830-1700
Subj: local study; sci; maths; tech (esp water related); geog; hist *Collns: Bks & Pamphs:* legal; Commercial Info System *Archvs:* internally produced documents *Co-op Schemes:* BLDSC, Water Company Inter-Lib Co-operation
Equip: video viewer, fax, copier, computers (incl wd-proc, internet & CD-ROM) *Online:* Aqualine
Stock: bks/2000; periodcls/150; m-forms/7; videos/50; archvs/1000
Classn: DDC *Auto Sys:* Calm
Staff: Libns: 1 *Non-Prof:* 1

S670 🎓

St Loye's School of Health Studies Library

Millbrook House, Millbrook Ln, Topsham Rd, Exeter, Devon, EX2 6ES (01392-219774; *fax:* 01392-435357)
Email: g.barber@exeter.ac.uk
Internet: http://www.ex.ac.uk/Affiliate/stloyes/

Gov Body: St Loye's Foundation *Chief:* Head of Academic Svcs: Mr Graeme Barber BA, MSc, DipLib, MCLIP *Dep:* Asst Libn: Mrs Rosemary Warren BA, DipLib, MCLIP
Entry: full access to students & staff of St Loye's; ref only access provided to membs of health care professions at discretion of Libn *Open:* term: Mon-Thu 0900-1730, Fri 0900-1700; vac: variable
Subj: undergrad; postgrad; occupational therapy; phil & psy; social sci; medicine; health care *Co-op Schemes:* BLDSC, SWRLIN, NULJ
Equip: video viewer, copier, CD-ROM reader
Stock: bks/13000; periodcls/115; slides/210; pamphs/200; videos/315
Classn: NLM *Auto Sys:* Trax
Pubns: Info Guides incl: Academic Svcs Guide, Searching the Journal Lit, Occupational Therapy Info Sources (free)
Staff: Libns: 2 *Non-Prof:* 1

S671 🎓
University of Exeter Library
Stocker Rd, Exeter, Devon, EX4 4PT (01392-263263; *fax:* 01392-263871)
Email: library@exeter.ac.uk
Internet: http://www.ex.ac.uk/library/

Chief: Libn: Mr Alasdair T. Paterson MA, ALAI
Dep: Dep Libn: Mr Martin Myhill MA, MCLIP
Assoc Libs: EXETER MEDICAL LIB (see **S668**); SCHOOL OF EDU LIB, St Luke's Campus, Heavitree Rd, Exeter, Devon, EX1 2LU, Site Libn: Mr Roy Davies (01392-264785; *fax:* 01392-264784; *email:* roy.davies@exeter.ac.uk); LAW LIB, Amory Bldg, Rennes Dr, Exeter, Devon, EX4 4RJ, Libn: Mr Paul Kershaw (01392-263356; *fax:* 01392-263871); OLD LIB, Prince of Wales Rd, Exeter, Devon, EX4 4PX, Site Libn: Mr Paul Auchterlonie (01392-264052; *fax:* 01392-263871; *email:* j.p.c.auchterlonie@exeter.ac.uk); ARAB WORLD DOCUMENTATION UNIT (see **S672**); CAMBORNE SCHOOL OF MINES LIB (see **S1857**); RODNEY FRY MAP LIB, Amory Bldg, Rennes Dr, Exeter, Devon, EX4 4RJ, Map Curator: Mr Terry Bacon (01392-263361; *fax:* 01392-263342; *email:* T.J.Bacon@exeter.ac.uk); EXETER CATHEDRAL LIB (see **S665**); DEVON & EXETER INSTN LIB (see **S663**)
Entry: apply to Libn *Open:* term: Mon-Fri 0900-2200, Sat 0900-1700, Sun 1400-2000; vac: Mon-Fri 0900-1730 or 1800
Subj: most univ subjs *Collns:* *Bks & Pamphs:* EDC (at Law Lib); SCOLMA (Ghana); Arabic & Islamic Colln; Hypatia Colln of Women's Hist; Syon Abbey Lib; John Betjeman's working lib; A.L. Rowse Colln; Henry Williamson Colln; Jack Clemo Colln; local parish libs *Archvs:* numerous MS collns, incl: Exeter Cathedral Lib Collns; papers of local authors (Henry Williamson, Charles Causley & others) *Other:* Schnitzler Press-Cuttings Archv
Co-op Schemes: ILL, SCOLMA, SWRLS, SUPC
Equip: m-reader, m-camera, m-printer, fax, 20 video viewers, 8 copiers, 100 computers *Online:* various host sys, various databases (at cost)
Stock: bks/1000000; periodcls/3500; slides/120000; m-forms/8000; audios/7500; videos/7000
Classn: DDC *Auto Sys:* Innopac
Pubns: various guides for internal Univ use (free)
Staff: Libns: 17 Other Prof: 12.2 Non-Prof: 41
Proj: restructuring of special collns space

S672 🎓
University of Exeter, Arab World Documentation Unit
Inst of Arab & Islamic Studies, Stocker Rd, Exeter, Devon, EX4 4ND (01392-264041; *fax:* 01392-263871)
Email: awdu@ex.ac.uk
Internet: http://www.ex.ac.uk/awdu/

Gov Body: Univ of Exeter (see **S482**) *Chief:* Site Libn: Mr Ahmed Abu Zayed
Entry: adv appt *Open:* Mon-Fri 0900-1700
Subj: Arab studies; Islamic studies; Gulf studies; econ; Middle East soc & culture; politics & hist of the Middle East; hist of the Gulf Wars; Arab-Israeli conflict; hist of British & internatl involvement in the region (18C-date) *Collns:* *Bks & Pamphs:* Uri Davis Colln (Arab-Israeli Conflict); periodcls; media reports; govt reports; statistical data; development plans & reports; official gazettes *Other:* several collns of press cuttings, incl the Council for the Advancement of Arab-British Understanding Colln; newspaper colln; video colln
Equip: m-readers, copier
Stock: bks/1000+ linear m of bks & printed materials; periodcls/c250 *Staff:* 3

S673 🎓
University of Plymouth, Exeter Campus Library
Veysey Bldg, Earl Richards Rd, Exeter, Devon, EX2 6AS (01392-475049; *fax:* 01392-475053)
Internet: http://www.plymouth.ac.uk/library/

Gov Body: Univ of Plymouth (see **S1812**) *Chief:* Snr Subj Libn (Art): Ms Vicki Maguire (v.maguire@plymouth.ac.uk) *Other Snr Staff:* Subj Libn (Health): Ms Anne Henderson (anne.henderson@plymouth.ac.uk); Subj Libn (Design): Ms Anne Davey (anne.davey@plymouth.ac.uk)
Entry: staff & students; ref only for membs of the public *Open:* term: Mon-Thu 0845-2100, Fri 0845-1800, Sat 1200-1600; vac: Mon-Fri 0900-1700
Subj: arts; art hist; fine arts; visual arts; design; edu; health; nursing; midwifery
Equip: copiers, computers (incl internet)

Exmouth

S674 🎓
University of Plymouth, Exmouth Campus Library
Douglas Ave, Exmouth, Devon, EX8 2AT (01395-255331; *fax:* 01395-255337)
Email: stella.pearson@plymouth.ac.uk
Internet: http://www.plymouth.ac.uk/library/

Gov Body: Univ of Plymouth (see **S1812**) *Chief:* Snr Subj Libn: Ms Stella Pearson
Entry: staff & students of Univ; ref only for public *Open:* term: Mon-Thu 0845-2100, Fri 0845-1900, Sat 1000-1600, Sun 1400-1700; vac: Mon-Fri 0930-1630
Subj: arts; edu *Collns:* *Bks & Pamphs:* School Practice Colln (ch's bks & proj packs)
Equip: copier, computers

Falkirk

S675 🎓
Falkirk College of Further and Higher Education Library
Grangemouth Rd, Falkirk, Stirlingshire, FK2 9AD (01324-403047; *fax:* 01324-403046)
Email: library@falkirkcollege.ac.uk
Chief: Coll Libn: Ms Sheila I. Cameron BSc, DipLib, MCLIP
Open: term: Mon-Thu 0830-1900, Fri 0830-1645; vac: Mon-Fri 0845-1645
Subj: GCSE; A level; undergrad; business studies; technical subjs; health care; social sci; computing; art & design; catering *Collns:* *Bks & Pamphs:* BSI (complete) *Co-op Schemes:* BLDSC, NLS
Equip: 2 video viewers, 2 copiers, clr copier, 11 computers (incl 8 wd-proc, 6 internet & 8 CD-ROM)
Disabled: HAL 95 *Svcs:* info, ref, biblio
Stock: bks/20000; periodcls/120; maps/100; videos/600; AVs/250
Classn: DDC *Auto Sys:* EOSi
Staff: Libns: 4 Non-Prof: 3 *Exp:* £40000 (1999-2000)

S676 🏛 🎓
Scottish Prison Service College, Learning Resource Centre
Newlands Rd, Brightons, Falkirk, Stirlingshire, FK2 0DE (01324-710467/8; *fax:* 01324-710471)
Email: angela.mcinnes@sps.gov.uk

Gov Body: Scottish Prison Svc *Chief:* Info Specialist: Ms Angela McInnes MA(Hons), DipILS, MCLIP *Dep:* Info Assts: Mrs Lindsay Hendry & Mrs Lisa Stanners
Entry: SPS staff only; adv appt, ref only *Open:* Mon-Thu 0830-1700, Fri 0830-1600
Subj: rsrch methods; psy; counselling; social sci; human rights; law; edu; health; business; personnel mgmt; exec mgmt; biography; criminology; penology *Co-op Schemes:* BLDSC, IPD, govt libs
Equip: fax, copier *Online:* SPIN (Scottish Prison Info Network) *Svcs:* info, ref, biblio, indexing, abstracting
Stock: bks/5000; periodcls/25; AVs/100
Classn: DDC *Auto Sys:* GLAS
Staff: Libns: 1 Other Prof: 1

Falmouth

S677 🎓
Falmouth College of Arts, Library and Information Services
Woodlane, Falmouth, Cornwall, TR11 4RH (01326-213815; *fax:* 01326-213827)
Email: library@falmouth.ac.uk
Internet: http://www.falmouth.ac.uk/library/

Chief: Head of Lib & Info Svcs: Mr Roger Towe BA, DipLib
Assoc Libs: TREMOUGH CAMPUS LRC, Treliever Rd, Penryn, Cornwall, TR10 9EZ (01326-370441; *fax:* 01326-370437)
Entry: current staff & students; external membership available at the discretion of the Head of Lib & Info Svc *Open:* term: Mon-Tue, Thu 0900-2000, Wed 0930-2000, Fri 0900-1700, Sat 1000-1300; vac: office hrs: Mon-Thu 0900-1730, Fri 0900-1700
Subj: all subjs; undergrad; postgrad; local studies (Cornwall); arts; design; humanities; media; culture; literary studies; hist *Collns:* *Bks & Pamphs:* Cornwall artists; artist's bks; contemporary artists; exhib catalogues *Other:* Slide Colln *Co-op Schemes:* BLDSC, Cornwall County Cataloguing Scheme, ILL, ARLIS
Equip: m-reader, m-printer, video viewer, copier, computers (incl wd-proc, internet & CD-ROM)
Online: Art Bibliographies Modern, Design & Applied Arts Index, MLA Database, Edina Art Abstracts & Art Index Retrospective, Zetoc, IBSS, Ingenta & others
Stock: bks/36000; periodcls/250, plus c100 non current; photos/100; slides/56000; illusts/6000; audios/1000; videos/1000
Classn: DDC *Auto Sys:* Geac
Staff: Libns: 4 Non-Prof: 8

Fareham

S678 🎓
Fareham College, Library and Information Centre
Bishopsfield Rd, Fareham, Hampshire, PO14 1NH (01329-815200; *fax:* 01329-822483)
Internet: http://www.fareham.ac.uk

Gov Body: Fareham Coll *Chief:* Coll Libn: Mrs M. Newman MA, MCLIP, DipRSA (meg.newman@fareham.ac.uk) *Dep:* Asst Libn: Miss H. Constance MCLIP (heather.constance@fareham.ac.uk)
Entry: open to public for ref; £5 pa for non-student borrowers *Open:* term: Mon-Thu 0830-1900, Fri 0830-1630; vac: Mon-Fri 0900-1700
Subj: all subjs; genl; GCSE; A level; vocational
Co-op Schemes: HATRICS
Equip: m-reader, 2 video viewers, copier (A4/5p), 50 computers (all with wd-proc, 25 with internet & 4 with CD-ROM) *Disabled:* CCTV *Online:* Infotrac *Officer-in-Charge:* Coll Libn, as above *Svcs:* info, ref, biblio

Stock: bks/21700; periodcls/80; audios/240; videos/100; CD-ROMs/10 *Acqs Offcr:* Coll Libn, as above
Classn: DDC *Auto Sys:* Adlib
Staff: Libns: 1.8 *Non-Prof:* 1.7 *Exp:* £16840 (1999-2000); £12682 (2000-01)

S679
Ravenswood House Library and Resource Centre
Medium Secure Unit, Knowle, Fareham, Hampshire, PO17 5NA (01329-836115; *fax:* 01329-836194)
Email: library.ravenswood@wht.nhs.uk

Gov Body: West Hampshire NHS Trust *Chief:* Libn: Mrs D.M. Campbell-Lendrum BA
Entry: ref only, adv appt *Open:* Mon, Wed 0830-1345, Tue 1330-1700; closed vacs
Subj: forensic psychiatry *Co-op Schemes:* SWRLIN, STLIS, PLCS, HLN
Equip: copier, fax, 4 computers (all with wd-proc, internet & CD-ROM)
Stock: bks/500; periodcls/20; CD-ROMs/2 *Acqs Offcr:* Libn, as above
Classn: NLM *Auto Sys:* Heritage
Staff: Non-Prof: 1

S680
Royal Armouries Library Fort Nelson
Royal Armouries Museum of Artillery, Fort Nelson, Down End Rd, Fareham, Hampshire, PO17 6AN (01329-233734; *fax:* 01329-822092)
Email: phil.magrath@armouries.org.uk
Internet: http://www.armouries.org.uk/

Gov Body: Board & Trustees/Dept of Culture, Media & Sport *Chief:* Snr Curator: Mr Philip Magrath MA *Other Snr Staff:* Keeper of Artillery: Mr Nicholas Hall
Assoc Libs: ROYAL ARMOURIES LIB (main lib, see **S913**); ROYAL ARMOURIES (LONDON), HM Tower of London, Tower Hill, London, EC3N 4AB, Snr Curator: Ms Bridget Clifford (020-7480-6358x30; *email:* bridget.clifford@armouries.org.uk)
Entry: adv appt *Open:* Mon-Fri 0900-1700
Subj: genl; local studies (nat hist of Fort Nelson & surroundings); hist; military hist; artillery; fortification *Collns: Bks & Pamphs:* rare bks (17C-19C); various artillery journals (19C-20C) *Archvs:* rare late 19C-early 20C gun registers; Bailey Pegg Archv of gun drawings (19C)
Equip: m-reader, m-printer, copier, fax *Svcs:* info
Auto Sys: STAR

Farnborough

S681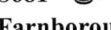
Farnborough College of Technology Library
Boundary Rd, Farnborough, Hampshire, GU14 6SB (01252-407445; *fax:* 01252-407071)
Email: library@farn-ct.ac.uk

Gov Body: Coll of Tech Corp *Chief:* Coll Libn: Mrs A. Coburn BSc, DipLib, MCLIP
Entry: ref only unless memb of Coll *Open:* Mon-Thu 0830-2000, Fri 0830-1630, Sat 1000-1600; vac: Mon-Thu 0900-1700, Fri 0900-1600
Subj: social scis; sci; maths; tech *Co-op Schemes:* BLDSC, ILL, HATRICS, local schools
Equip: fax, 3 video viewers, 3 copiers, clr copier, 15 computers (all with internet, 1 with CD-ROM) *Online:* BIDS, BRAD, British Standards Online, Emerald, ENDS Report, Infotrac, IBSS, Web of Science, LION, Sport Discus, Weekly Law Reports, Zetoc & others *Svcs:* info, ref, biblio
Stock: bks/40000; periodcls/300; slides/70; audios/100; videos/1000

Classn: DDC *Auto Sys:* Heritage
Staff: Libns: 5 *Non-Prof:* 9

Farnham

S682
Forestry Commission Library
Forest Rsrch Station, Alice Holt Lodge, Wrecclesham, Farnham, Surrey, GU10 4LH (01420-22255; *fax:* 01420-23653)
Email: library@forestrygsi..gov.uk
Internet: http://www.forestry.gov.uk/

Chief: Head of Lib & Info Section: Miss C.A. Oldham BA, MA, DipLib, MCLIP *Dep:* Asst Libn: Mrs E.M. Harland MA
Assoc Libs: NORTHERN RSRCH STATION LIB, Roslin, Midlothian, EH25 9SY (0131-445-2176; *fax:* 0131-445-5124)
Entry: by appt *Open:* Mon-Fri 0900-1630
Subj: forestry; arboriculture; ecology; plant scis; environmental scis *Co-op Schemes:* BLDSC, HATRICS
Equip: m-reader, m-printer, copier, computer (with CD-ROM) *Online:* Tree CD *Svcs:* info, ref
Stock: bks/20000; periodcls/300; videos/60
Classn: UDC, FDC (forestry bks) *Auto Sys:* CAIRS *Staff: Libns:* 2 *Non-Prof:* 2

S683
Surrey Institute of Art and Design Library
Farnham Campus, Falkner Rd, Farnham, Surrey, GU9 7DS (01252-732249)
Internet: http://www.surrart.ac.uk/

Chief: Learning Resources Mgr: Mrs Rosemary Lynch BA, MA, MCLIP *Dep:* Ms Gwynneth Wilkey
Assoc Libs: EPSOM CAMPUS LIB, Ashley Rd, Epsom, Surrey, KT18 5BE, Libn: Ms Jan Seabourne
Entry: ref only *Open:* term: Mon, Tue, Thu 0900-1930, Wed 1000-1930, Fri 0900-1730; vac: Mon-Tue, Thu-Fri 0900-1700, Wed 1000-1700
Subj: arts *Co-op Schemes:* BLDSC, ILL
Equip: m-reader, copier, clr copier, video viewer, computers (incl wd-proc & CD-ROM) *Svcs:* ref
Stock: bks/86000+; periodcls/400; slides/250000+; videos/9000+
Classn: DDC *Auto Sys:* Talis

Feltham

S684
Defence Geographic and Imagery Intelligence Agency, Library and Information Centre
Clarke Bldg, Elmwood Ave, Feltham, Middlesex, TW13 7AH (020-8818-2227)

Gov Body: Ministry of Defence (see **S1284**)
Chief: Libn: Mr S.R. Miles
Entry: internal lib; staff only
Subj: geodesy; land survey; maths; cartography; photogrammetry; geophysics; computer sci
Collns: Archvs: survey records
Stock: bks/70000

Fleetwood

S685
Blackpool and the Fylde College, Nautical Campus Learning Resource Centre
Broadwater, Fleetwood, Lancashire, FY7 8JZ (01253-352352 x4714; *fax:* 01253-773014)
Internet: http://www.blackpool.ac.uk/

Gov Body: Blackpool & The Fylde Coll (see **S192**)
Chief: Head of Learning Resources: Mrs Christine McAllister BA, CertEd, MCLIP
Entry: ref only *Open:* Mon-Thu 0845-1930, Fri 1000-1700
Subj: maritime studies *Co-op Schemes:* BLDSC, ILL
Equip: copier, video viewer, 6 computers (all with wd-proc & internet, 1 with CD-ROM)
Stock: bks/12000; periodcls/100; AVs/2000; bnd documents/1000
Classn: DDC *Auto Sys:* Dynix

Folkestone

S686
South Kent College Library
Shorncliffe Rd, Folkestone, Kent, CT20 2NA (01303-850061; *fax:* 01303-220354)
Email: paul.north@southkent.ac.uk
Internet: http://www.southkent.ac.uk/

Chief: Coll Learning Resources Co-ordinator: Mr P.M. North BA, MCLIP
Assoc Libs: ASHFORD LRC, Jemmett Rd, Ashford, Kent, TN23 2RJ, Site Learning Resources Co-ordinator: Mrs C. Brailsford MCLIP (claire.brailsford@southkent.ac.uk); DOVER LRC, Maison Dieu Rd, Dover, Kent, CT16 1DH, Site Learning Resources Co-ordinator: Ms R. Gabr (ros.gabr@southkent.ac.uk)
Entry: ref only *Open:* term: Mon-Thu 0830-2100, Fri 0830-1630; vac: Mon-Thu 0830-1700, Fri 0830-1630
Subj: all subjs; genl; GCSE; A level *Co-op Schemes:* BLDSC, ILL
Equip: 5 video viewers, 3 copiers, 2 clr copiers, 240 computers (incl wd-proc & CD-ROM), flatbed scanner *Online:* Internet *Svcs:* info, ref, biblio
Stock: bks/55000; periodcls/200; audios/250; videos/450
Classn: DDC *Auto Sys:* Liberty
Staff: Libns: 3 *Non-Prof:* 12 *Exp:* £48000 (1999-2000); £60000 (2000-01)

Forres

S687
Brodie Castle Library
Brodie, Forres, Morayshire, IV36 0TE (01309-641371; *fax:* 01309-641600)

Type: historic house *Gov Body:* Natl Trust for Scotland *Chief:* Property Mgr: Dr Stephanie Blackden MA(Hons), PhD
Entry: adv appt necessary, ref only *Open:* during Castle opening hrs: 1 Apr-30 Sep, Mon-Sat 1100-1730
Subj: local study (Nairn & Moray); generalities; phil; religion; arts; lit; geog; hist; gardening; travel; novels; poetry *Collns: Bks & Pamphs:* The Scots Magazine (1739-89); Blackwood's Magazine (1824-1960) Annual Register; Illustrated London News; other bnd periodcls
Stock: bks/6000 *Classn:* NTS Recording System

Fortrose

S688
Groam House Museum, Library and Archives
High St, Rosemarkie, Fortrose, Ross-shire, IV10 8UF (01381-620961; *fax:* 01381-621730)
Email: groamhouse@ecosse.net
Internet: http://www.cali.co.uk/highexp/fortrose/groam.htm

Type: independent *Gov Body:* Groam House Museum Trust *Chief:* Curator: Ms Susan Seright DipMGS

Special Libraries

Fortrose
▼
Glasgow

(Groam House Museum, Lib & Archvs cont)
Entry: ref only **Open:** May-Sep: Mon-Sat 1000-1700, Sun 1400-1630; Oct-Apr: Sat-Sun 1400-1600 or by appt
Subj: Highlands of Scotland: hist & folklore; Pictish era; Celtic religion; Gaelic lang; Celtic art; geog; local hist; Picto/Celtic hist; archaeo of Dark Ages; folklore of Highlands **Collns:** *Bks & Pamphs:* small ref lib specialising on Pictish bks & papers; local hist, incl the Black Isle & Ross-shire *Archvs:* Stent Rolls (1731-1802, 1802-1833); Register of poor persons of Rosemarkie parish; Burgh Court Bks; Council minutes of Fortrose; Rosemarkie Town Council (1647-1658, 1674-1710); original Celtic artwork by George Bain (1881-1968) & associated archv *Other:* 6 albums of photos of Pictish stones in Scotland; 2 albums of local photos from 1885
Stock: bks/150; periodcls/50; photos/8 vols; slides/150; pamphs/6 Pictish & Museum leaflets; maps/8; audios/12; videos/3; Pictish & local papers/15 files
Pubns: Perceptions of the Picts: from Eumenius to John Buchan, by Anna Ritchie (£4.50); Earl & Mormaer, Norse-Pictish relationships in Northern Scotland, by Barbara Crawford (£4.50); The Picts & their Place Names, by W.F.H. Nicolaisen (£4.50); A Persona for the Northern Picts, by John Hunter (£4.50); Recording Early Christian Monuments in Scotland, by J.N. Graham Ritchie (£4.50); The Dream of the Rood, by I.L. Gordon (£1.75); prices incl p&p
Staff: Other Prof: 1

Galashiels

S689 🎓
Heriot-Watt University, Martindale Library
Scottish Borders Campus, Netherdale, Galashiels, Scottish Borders, TD1 3HF (01896-892185; *fax:* 01896-758965)
Email: libhelp@sbc.hw.ac.uk
Internet: http://www.hw.ac.uk/sbc/library/

Gov Body: Heriot-Watt Univ (see **S604**) **Chief:** Mgr, Lib & Info Systems: Mr Peter Sandison (P.E.C.Sandison@hw.ac.uk) **Dep:** Asst Libn: Ms Jan McIntyre (J.M.C.McIntyre@hw.ac.uk)
Entry: staff & students of Univ; ref only for others, external borrowing membership available (fees for some categories) **Open:** term: Mon-Thu 0830-2145, Fri 0830-1645, Sat 1000-1545; vac: Mon-Fri 0900-1645
Subj: undergrad; postgrad; art; design; business **Collns:** *Bks & Pamphs:* historic textile bks; company annual reports; small patents colln *Other:* art, fashion & design files; company files; org files; slide colln; theses colln
Equip: m-form reader/printer, copiers, clr copier, video viewers, computers (incl wd-proc, internet & CD-ROM), scanners *Online:* ADAM, ARIAD, Arts & Humanities Citations Index, Design & Applied Arts Index, EconLit, Emerald, Ingenta, Index to Theses, Medline, MINTEL Reports, Profound, Proquest, SciDirect, SOSIG, Web of Science, World Textiles, Zetoc & others
Stock: bks/16000; periodcls/150
Staff: Libns: 2 Non-Prof: 6

Gateshead

S690
Gateshead College Centre4... Knowledge
Durham Rd, Gateshead, Tyne & Wear, NE5 9BN (0191-490-2248; *fax:* 0191-490-2313)
Email: jen.black@gateshead.ac.uk
Internet: http://www.gateshead.ac.uk/

Type: Coll of Further Edu **Gov Body:** Gateshead Coll Board of Governors **Chief:** Learning Resources Mgr: Mrs Jennifer Black BA, DipLib, MCLIP
Entry: enrolled students **Open:** Mon-Thu 0845-2100; Fri 1000-1630; Sat 0900-1300
Subj: most subjs; GCSE; A level; some undergrad courses **Co-op Schemes:** BLDSC, NEMLAC, TWIRL
Equip: copier (£3 per card), clr copier (70p per pg), 14 computers (all with wd-proc, internet & CD-ROM)
Stock: bks/28000; periodcls/89 **Acqs Offcr:** Learning Resources Mgr, as above
Classn: DDC **Auto Sys:** EOSi
Staff: Libns: 1 Other Prof: 6

Gatwick

S691 🏛
Civil Aviation Authority, Library and Information Centre
Aviation House, Gatwick Airport South, Gatwick, W Sussex, RH6 0YR (01293-573725; *fax:* 01293-573181)
Email: library-enquiries@srg.caa.co.uk
Internet: http://www.caa.co.uk/library/

Chief: Mgr: Mr Stephen Moore BA, MCLIP (stephen.moore@srg.caa.co.uk)
Entry: ref only **Open:** Mon-Fri 0930-1630; 1000-1630 on 1st Wed of month
Subj: aviation; electronics; computers; medicine; airports; air traffic control; econ **Collns:** *Bks & Pamphs:* past & present CAA pubns; reports issued by CAA, NASA, FAA, AAIB, ICAO & other orgs; aircraft & engine manuals; Acts of Parliament & Statutory Instruments **Co-op Schemes:** BLDSC
Equip: m-form reader/printers, copier, computers (incl wd-proc & CD-ROM)
Stock: bks/50000; periodcls/600
Classn: UDC **Auto Sys:** CAIRS
Pubns: Lib Bulletin (monthly)
Staff: Libns: 5 Non-Prof: 5

Gillingham

S692 ✚
Medway NHS Trust Library
Windmill Rd, Gillingham, Kent, ME7 5NY (01634-833849; *fax:* 01634-407820)

Gov Body: Medway NHS Trust **Chief:** Libn: Mrs Rhiannon Cox BSc, DipLib, MCLIP **Dep:** Dep Libn: Miss Julie Stoppani BA
Entry: health profs employed by NHS & designated students **Open:** Mon-Fri 0830-2100
Subj: health care **Co-op Schemes:** BLDSC, STRLIS, RCSE, BMA
Equip: video viewer, fax, copier, clr copier, computers (incl wd-proc, internet & CD-ROM) *Online:* Datastar **Svcs:** info, ref, biblio
Stock: bks/11000; periodcls/200; videos/250
Classn: NLM **Auto Sys:** Librarian
Staff: Libns: 2 Non-Prof: 4

Glasgow

S693 🎓
Anniesland College, The Metro
19 Hatfield Dr, Glasgow, G12 0YE (0141-357-6065)
Email: metro@anniesland.ac.uk

Chief: Head of Metro: Mr Eric Simpson DipEdTech, MCLIP **Dep:** Lib & Info Mgr: Mr Tom Kelly BA(Hons), MSc, MCLIP (T_Kelly@anniesland.ac.uk) **Other Snr Staff:** Snr Resource Centre Asst: Miss Elisabet Minkova MA(Hons), DipLib (E_Minkova@anniesland.ac.uk)
Assoc Libs: BALSHAGRAY CAMPUS METRO, 27 Broomhill Ave, Glasgow, G11 7AB
Entry: full membership for students; off-peak membership for local residents & ex-students
Open: term: Mon-Thu 0900-2100, Fri 0930-1645, Sat 0930-1230; vac: Mon-Fri 0930-1630
Subj: all subjs; genl **Co-op Schemes:** part of Glasgow Colls Group, LearnDirect Centre with SUfI
Equip: 3 video viewers, copier, computers (incl 50 with wd-proc, 50 with CD-ROM & 47 with internet)
Disabled: ZoomText software, JAWS **Svcs:** info, ref
Classn: DDC **Auto Sys:** EASL
Staff: Libns: 4 Non-Prof: 6 **Exp:** £42000 (1999-2000)

S694 ✚
Beatson Oncology Centre Library
Western Infirmary, Glasgow, G11 6NT (0141-211-1917; *fax:* 0141-211-6356)
Email: kirsty.coltart@northglasgow.scot.nhs.uk
Internet: http://www.northglashealthinfo.org.uk/

Gov Body: North Glasgow Univ Hosps NHS Trust
Chief: Clinical Libn: Ms Kirsty Coltart **Dep:** Asst Libn: Ms Alison McEwan
Assoc Libs: GLASGOW ROYAL INFIRMARY LIB (see **S706**); GARTNAVEL GENL HOSP STAFF LIB (see **S700**); STOBHILL HOSP LIB (see **S722**); WESTERN INFIRMARY LIB (see **S742**)
Entry: Trust staff; other NHS employees **Open:** Mon-Fri 0900-1700
Subj: medicine; oncology; non-surgical cancer care **Co-op Schemes:** BLDSC, SHINE
Equip: copier (5p per copy), 3 computers *Online:* Medline, CINAHL, Cochrane, AMED, HMIC, PsycInfo, BNI & others, 400+ e-journals **Svcs:** info, ref, current awareness, lit searching, training sessions
Staff: Libns: 1 Non-Prof: 1

S695 🗝✚
British Homoeopathic Library, Glasgow
Faculty of Homoeopathy, Glasgow Homoeopathic Hosp, 1053 Gt Western Rd, Glasgow, G12 0XQ (0141-211-1617; *fax:* 0141-211-1610)
Email: hom-inform@dial.pipex.com
Internet: http://www.hom-inform.org/

Gov Body: Faculty of Homoeopathy, Academic Depts Glasgow Homoeopathic Hosp **Chief:** Libn: Mrs Mary Gooch BSc, MCLIP **Dep:** Asst Libn: Ms Candida Fenton BA, MSc, MCLIP
Entry: ref only, adv appt **Open:** Mon-Fri 0900-1700
Subj: homoeopathy; complementary medicine
Co-op Schemes: BLDSC, ILL, SHINE
Equip: fax, copier, computers (incl wd-proc, internet & CD-ROM) *Online:* Hom-Inform Info Svc
Svcs: info, ref, biblio, indexing, abstracting
Stock: bks/2400; periodcls/50; audios/600
Classn: UDC, own
Pubns: Hom-Inform database searchable online (free)
Staff: Libns: 2 Non-Prof: 0.5

S696 ✚
Cancer Research UK, Beatson Laboratory Library
Garscube Est, Switchback Rd, Bearsden, Glasgow, G61 1BD (0141-330-4801; *fax:* 0141-942-6521)
Email: library@beatson.gla.org.uk

Type: rsrch org, charity funded *Gov Body:* Cancer Rsrch UK *Chief:* Libn: Mrs Elizabeth Gordon BSc, DipLib, MCLIP
Assoc Libs: CANCER RSRCH UK, LIB & INFO SVC (see **S1054**)
Entry: ref only for visitors *Open:* Mon-Fri 0900-1700, closed bank hols
Subj: oncology; cancer rsrch *Co-op Schemes:* SHINE
Equip: copier *Svcs:* ref
Stock: bks/500; periodcls/100; CD-ROMs/6
Classn: NLM
Pubns: Cancer Rsrch UK Beatson Laboratories Scientific Report (annual)
Staff: Libns: 1

S697 🎓
Cardonald College Library
690 Mosspark Dr, Glasgow, G52 3AY (0141-272-3323; *fax:* 0141-272-3444)
Internet: http://www.cardonald.ac.uk/

Chief: Head Libn: Miss Loraine Forde BA, DipLib, MCLIP (lforde@cardonald.ac.uk) *Other Snr Staff:* Libn: Ms Mary Gallacher BSc, MSc (mgallacher@cardonald.ac.uk)
Entry: students & staff; ref only for public *Open:* term: Mon, Fri 0815-1700, Tue-Thu 0815-2000; vac: Mon-Fri 1000-1600
Subj: all subjs; GCSE; A level; undergrad; vocational *Co-op Schemes:* BLDSC
Equip: 2 video viewers, 3 copiers, clr copier, 8 computers (all with internet & CD-ROM) *Online:* Infotrac, SCRAN, KnowUK *Svcs:* info, ref, biblio
Stock: bks/18000; periodcls/100; maps/50; audios/100; videos/500; CD-ROMs/25
Classn: DDC *Auto Sys:* Alice
Staff: Libns: 2 *Non-Prof:* 2.5 *Exp:* £50000 (2000-01)

S698 🎓
Central College of Commerce Library
Charles Oakley Bldg, Central Business Learning Zone, 190 Cathedral St, Glasgow, G4 0NO (0141-552-3941; *fax:* 0141-552-5514)
Email: library@central-glasgow.ac.uk/
Internet: http://www.centralcollege.ac.uk/

Gov Body: Central Coll of Commerce Board of Mgmt *Chief:* Head of Lib Svcs: Mrs Kirsteen Dowie MA(Hons), DipLib, MCLIP *Dep:* Libn: Mrs Jackie Barry BA(Hons), MCLIP
Entry: membership available to staff & students of Coll *Open:* term: Mon-Thu 0900-2000, Fri 1000-1645, Sat 0900-1230; vac: Mon-Fri 0900-1645
Subj: all subjs; A level; undergrad; vocational; generalities; phil; psy; social sci; lang; tech; arts; lit; geog; hist *Collns: Archvs:* pertaining to Coll (photos, prospectuses & genl pubns) *Co-op Schemes:* ILL, Glasgow Telecolleges Network
Equip: video viewers, copiers, computers (incl wd-proc, internet & CD-ROM) *Svcs:* info, ref, biblio
Stock: bks/15000; periodcls/90
Classn: DDC *Auto Sys:* Olib 7
Staff: Libns: 2 *Non-Prof:* 3.5

S699 ✚
Forrester Cockburn Centre for Education and Learning, Library
Royal Hosp for Sick Children, Yorkhill NHS Trust, Glasgow, G3 8SJ (0141-201-0794)
Email: yorlib@yahoo.co.uk

Gov Body: Yorkhill Trust *Chief:* Libn: Mrs Frances Anderson FLA *Dep:* Asst Libn: Mr Ron Carrick BA, DipLIS
Assoc Libs: ARCHVS, held separately at same addr, Archivist: Ms Alma Topen (PT)
Entry: Yorkhill Trust staff, students & parents of patients; NHS Scotland ID holders *Open:* Mon-Thu 0900-1800, Fri 0900-1700
Subj: all aspects of paediatric medicine *Co-op Schemes:* BLDSC, SHINE, BMA
Equip: m-reader, 2 video viewers, copier, 9 computers (incl 3 with wd-proc, 5 with internet & 1 with CD-ROM) *Online:* Dialog, CHEST (via ATHENS) *Svcs:* info, ref, biblio, indexing, abstracting
Stock: bks/3700; periodcls/108; slides/some; pamphs/some; videos/138
Classn: DDC *Auto Sys:* CAWS *Staff: Libns:* 2

S700 ✚
Gartnavel General Hospital, Staff Library
1053 Gt Western Rd, Glasgow, G12 0YN (0141-211-3013; *fax:* 0141-211-0178)
Internet: http://www.northglashealthinfo.org.uk/

Gov Body: North Glasgow Univ Hosps NHS Trust *Chief:* Divisional Lib Svcs Mgr (Medicine): Ms Amanda Wright (Amanda.Wright@northglasgow.scot.nhs.uk) *Dep:* Asst Libn: Ms Louise Black (Louise.Black@northglasgow.scot.nhs.uk)
Assoc Libs: BEATSON ONCOLOGY CENTRE LIB (see **S694**); GLASGOW ROYAL INFIRMARY LIB (see **S706**); STOBHILL HOSP LIB (see **S722**); WESTERN INFIRMARY LIB (see **S742**)
Entry: Trust staff & students; ref only for others, at Libn's discretion (adv appt required); external membership available for a fee *Open:* Mon-Fri 0900-1700
Subj: medicine *Co-op Schemes:* BLDSC, SHINE
Equip: Online: Medline, CINAHL, Cochrane, AMED, HMIC, PsycInfo, BNI & others, 400+ e-journals

S701 🎓
Glasgow Caledonian University, Library and Information Centre
Cowcaddens Rd, Glasgow, G4 0BA (0141-331-3000; *fax:* 0141-331-3005)
Email: library@gcal.ac.uk
Internet: http://www.gcal.ac.uk/

Gov Body: Glasgow Caledonian Univ *Chief:* Chief Libn: post vacant
Assoc Libs: GLASGOW CALEDONIAN UNIV ARCHVS, at same addr, Univ Archivist: Ms Carole McCallum (0141-331-3199; *fax:* 0141-331-3005; *email:* C.McCallum@gcal.ac.uk)
Entry: staff & students; external membs have restricted access for a fee; archvs open to all rsrchers, adv appt for external users *Open:* term: Mon-Thu 0830-2100, Fri 0830-1700, Sat 1000-1800, Sun 1100-1600; vac: Mon-Fri 0900-1700; *Archvs:* Mon-Thu 0900-1700, Fri 0900-1600
Subj: generalities; phil; psy; social sci; lang; sci; tech; eng; econ; mgmt; paramedicine; consumer studies; hospitality *Collns: Bks & Pamphs:* Norman & Janey Buchan Colln; Queen's Coll Colln (19C & 20C domestic sci bks, c600 vols); Ophthalmic Optics Colln; Bulk Solids Handling Colln; Scottish & Northern Bk Distribution Centre Colln *Archvs:* Glasgow Caledonian Univ Institutional Archv (records of Univ & parent instns), incl the records of: Glasgow School of Cookery; West End School of Cookery; Glasgow & West of Scotland Coll of Domestic Sci; Queen's Coll Glasgow; Glasgow Coll of Tech; Glasgow Coll; Glasgow Polytechnic; other collns incl: Anti-Apartheid Movement in Scotland Archv (early 1970s-1994); Communist Party of Great Britain Scottish Cttee Archv (1960s onwards); RSSPCC

Children First Archvs (20000 case records, mainly 1940-76); Scottish Council for Unmarried Mothers Archv; Social Democratic Party (Scotland) Archv; Scottish Trade Union Congress Archv (1897-date)
Co-op Schemes: BLDSC, ILL
Equip: 3 video viewers, 15 copiers, computers *Disabled:* visual impairment unit *Online:* Dialog, Datastar; see also – http://www.gcal.ac.uk/services/database.htm
Stock: bks/350630; periodcls/5815; videos/3858; archvs/251 linear m
Classn: DDC *Auto Sys:* Ameritech
Pubns: Lib Guide; External users' Guide; Lib Regulations; Guide to Bibliographic Citations; Video Introduction to the Lib; various leaflets
Staff: Libns: 25 *Non-Prof:* 45

S702 🎓
Glasgow College of Building and Printing, Laird Library
60 North Hanover St, Glasgow, G1 2BP (0141-566-4132; *fax:* 0141-332-5170)
Internet: http://www.gcbp.ac.uk/library/

Chief: Dir of Lib & Learning Svcs: Ms Catherine Kearney (catherine.kearney@gcbp.ac.uk) *Other Snr Staff:* Libn: Ms Caroline Cochrane (caroline.cochrane@gcbp.ac.uk); IT Libn: Mr Andrew Jackson (andrew.jackson@gcbp.ac.uk)
Entry: ref to students & staff of other academic instns; visitors should report to issue desk *Open:* term: Mon, Fri 0900-1700; Tue-Thu 0900-1930; vac: Mon-Fri 1000-1200, 1400-1600
Subj: all subjs; undergrad; vocational; tech; construction; printing; graphic design; photography; interior design *Collns: Bks & Pamphs:* RIBA trade lit
Equip: 3 copiers, video viewers, 23 computers (incl wd-proc, internet & CD-ROM), 11 scanners, room for hire *Disabled:* Kurzweil 3000, ZoomText Xtra, Wordsmith TextHelp, text magnifier *Online:* Technical Indexes, OHSIS, KnowUK, X-refer Plus, SCRAN, Ingenta Journals *Svcs:* info, ref, biblio
Stock: bks/15000; periodcls/160; videos/250; CD-ROMs/120
Classn: DDC *Auto Sys:* Unicorn
Staff: Libns: 3 *Other Prof:* 1 *Non-Prof:* 4

S703 🎓
Glasgow College of Food Technology, Library
230 Cathedral St, Glasgow, G1 2TG (0141-271-5264)
Internet: http://www.gcft.ac.uk/

Chief: Librarian-in-Charge: Mr Tony Donnelly BSc, MA, DipLib, MCLIP (tony.donnelly@gcft.ac.uk) *Dep:* Snr Lib Asst: Mrs Mary Dignam HNC (mary.dignam@gcft.ac.uk) *Other Snr Staff:* Lib Systems Offcr: Mr George Hawkins
Assoc Libs: other libs in Glasgow Colls Lib Group
Entry: ref use by appt *Open:* term: Mon-Wed 0800-2000, Thu 0800-1700, Fri 0800-1600; vac: Mon-Fri 0900-1630
Subj: all subjs; undergrad; postgrad; vocational; food sci; food tech *Co-op Schemes:* BLDSC, Glasgow Colls Lib Group
Equip: video viewer, copier (£2 per 30 copies), 40 computers (incl 25 with wd-proc, 31 with internet & 2 with CD-ROM) *Online:* Dialog Newsline, Technical Indexes: Food & Drink, Health & Safety, Environmental Management (free) *Officer-in-Charge:* MIS Mgr: Mr Kemp Andrewson (kemp.andrewson@gcft.ac.uk) *Svcs:* info, ref, biblio
Stock: bks/12500; periodcls/60; videos/37; CD-ROMs/75 *Acqs Offcr:* Librarian-in-Charge, as above
Classn: DDC *Auto Sys:* EASL 7
Staff: Libns: 1 *Other Prof:* 1 *Non-Prof:* 1 *Exp:* £30000 (2000-01)

S704 🎓

Glasgow College of Nautical Studies Library

21 Thistle St, Glasgow, G5 9XB (0141-565-2582; *fax:* 0141-565-2599)
Email: resources@gcns.ac.uk
Internet: http://www.gcns.ac.uk/

Chief: Libn: Ms Margaret Scalpello MA, DipLib, MCLIP
Entry: open to students & staff, all other users ref only *Open:* term: Mon-Tue, Thu 0830-1930, Wed 0830-1800, Fri 0830-1700; vac: Mon-Fri 0830-1630
Subj: all subjs; genl; vocational; maritime studies
Collns & Pamphs: maritime hist colln *Co-op Schemes:* BLDSC, ILL
Equip: copier, 53 computers (all with wd-proc, internet & CD-ROM) *Svcs:* info, ref, biblio
Stock: bks/15500; periodcls/160; maps/60; videos/20
Classn: DDC *Auto Sys:* EASL
Staff: Libns: 1 *Non-Prof:* 5

S705 🏛🏛

Glasgow Museums, Library and Information Centre

Art Gallery & Museum, Kelvingrove, Glasgow, G3 8AG (0141-287-2640; *fax:* 0141-287-2690)

Gov Body: Glasgow City Council (see **P56**)
Chief: no post designated currently
Entry: not open to public at present
Subj: bibliography; museology; nat hist; transport; fine arts; decorative arts; conservation; social hist; hist *Collns & Pamphs:* some private collns held with Depts
Stock: bks/50000; periodcls/200
Classn: LC
Exp: £10500 (1999-2000); £10500 (2000-01)

S706 ✚

Glasgow Royal Infirmary, Library and Learning Centre

10 Alexandra Parade, Glasgow, G31 2ER (0141-211-5975; *fax:* 0141-211-4802)
Email: ann.wales@northglasgow.scot.nhs.uk
Internet: http://www.northglashealthinfo.org.uk/

Gov Body: North Glasgow Univ Hosps NHS Trust
Chief: Libn: post vacant *Other Snr Staff:* Asst Libn: Ms Lesley Robertson (Lesley.Robertson@northglasgow.scot.nhs.uk); Divisional Lib Svcs Mgr, Trauma Div: Ms Liz Garrity (Liz.Garrity@northglasgow.scot.nhs.uk)
Assoc Libs: BEATSON ONCOLOGY CENTRE LIB (see **S694**); GARTNAVEL GENL HOSP STAFF LIB (see **S700**); STOBHILL HOSP LIB (see **S722**); WESTERN INFIRMARY LIB (see **S742**)
Entry: Trust staff & students on placement within the Trust; membs of public ref only by adv appt; external membership available on subscription basis *Open:* Mon-Fri 0830-1700
Subj: medicine *Collns & Pamphs:* T.F. Elias-Jones Colln (bacteriology, public health & hygiene)
Co-op Schemes: SHINE, BLDSC
Equip: copier, computers, scanner *Online:* Medline, CINAHL, Cochrane, AMED, HMIC, PsycInfo, BNI & others, 400+ e-journals etc (NHS staff only) *Svcs:* info, ref, lit searches
Stock: bks/4200; periodcls/200

Classn: NLM *Auto Sys:* Heritage
Staff: 6 FT (2 with Trust-wide responsibilities), 4 PT

S707 🎓

Glasgow School of Art Library

167 Renfrew St, Glasgow, G3 6RQ (0141-353-4551; *fax:* 0141-353-4670)
Internet: http://www.gsa.ac.uk/

Gov Body: Glasgow School of Art *Chief:* Head of Info Svcs: Mr John McKay MA, DipLib, MCLIP
Entry: free ref if referred from other libs, or by appt
Open: term: Mon-Thu 0930-2000, Fri 0930-1700; vac: Mon-Fri 0930-1700
Subj: arts; fine art; design; arch *Collns: Archvs:* Glasgow School of Art Archvs; bks, exhib catalogues, newspaper cuttings & other documents relating to hist of the school, its staff & students
Other: Hill & Adamson Colln of calotypes & carbon prints *Co-op Schemes:* BLDSC
Equip: m-reader, 2 video viewers, 3 copiers, 50 computers
Stock: bks/60000; periodcls/300; photos/1400; slides/61000; illusts/14 albums; videos/1200
Classn: DDC *Auto Sys:* Talis
Staff: Libns: 4 *Non-Prof:* 6.5

S708 🔑

Glasgow Women's Library

109 Trongate, Glasgow, G1 5HD (0141-552-8345; *fax:* 0141-552-8345)
Email: gwl@womens-library.org.uk
Internet: http://www.womens-library.org.uk/

Chief: Co-ordinator: Ms Sue John
Assoc Libs: LESBIAN ARCHV & INFO CENTRE, at same addr
Entry: women only *Open:* Tue-Fri 1300-1800, Sat 1400-1700
Subj: women's studies; feminism
Svcs: info, ref, rsrch consultancy, cuttings svc
Pubns: newsletter

S709 🔑

Goethe-Institut Library

3 Park Circus, Glasgow, G3 6AX (0141-332-2555; *fax:* 0141-333-1630)
Email: library@glasgow.goethe.org
Internet: http://www.goethe.de/gr/gla/enibib.htm

Chief: Libn: Ms Gisela Moohan *Dep:* Lib Asst: Ms Christiane Voss-Riehle
Assoc Libs: GOETHE-INSTITUT INTER NATIONES LIB, London (see **S1147**); GOETHE-INSTITUT LIB, Dublin (see **IS80**)
Entry: open to public; proof of addr for membership; from Apr-Sep membership fees will apply
Open: term: Mon, Wed 1300-1900, Tue 1400-1900, Thu 1400-2000, Fri closed, 1st Sat of month 1000-1330; vac: Mon-Thu 1300-1800
Subj: Germany; German lit; arts; social sci; lang
Co-op Schemes: ILL
Equip: video viewer, copier, computer (with CD-ROM), audio equip, DVD player
Stock: bks/9300; periodcls/48; audios/1501; videos/577
Classn: UDC
Pubns: Video Catalogue (£2); Cassette/CD Catalogue (£2)
Staff: Libns: 1 *Non-Prof:* 1

S710 🔑

Grand Orange Lodge of Scotland, Cameron Library

Olympia House, 13 Olympia St, Glasgow, G40 3TA (0141-414-1418; *fax:* 0141-414-1419)
Email: info@gols.org.uk
Internet: http://www.gols.org.uk

Gov Body: Grand Orange Lodge of Scotland
Chief: Exec Offcr: Mr Robert McLean
Entry: ref only; adv appt *Open:* Mon-Fri 1000-1500
Subj: religion; hist; Orange Order
Equip: photocopying & computer facilities

S711 ✚

Greater Glasgow Primary Care NHS Trust, Maria Henderson Library

Trust HQ, Gartnavel Royal Hosp, 1055 Gt Western Rd, Glasgow, G12 0XH (0141-211-3913; *fax:* 0141-211-0348)
Email: catriona.denoon@gartnavel.glacomen.scot.nhs.uk
Internet: http://www.ggpctlibrary.org.uk/

Gov Body: Greater Glasgow Primary Care NHS Trust *Chief:* Lib Svcs Mgr: Ms Catriona Denoon MA(Hons), DipLib, MCLIP *Dep:* Sector Libn: Mr David Burns BA(Hons), DipILS
Entry: open to Trust employees & to staff & students of Glasgow Univ Dept of Psychological Medicine; external borrowing rights available for a fee; ref only for others *Open:* Mon-Tue, Thu-Fri 0900-1700, Thu 0900-1900
Subj: clinical psy; behavioural sci; psychiatry; multidisciplinary medicine *Co-op Schemes:* SHINE
Equip: copiers (A4/5p, A3/10p), computers (incl wd-proc & internet) *Online:* Medline, ClinPsyc, PsycInfo, OVID, CINAHL, Best Evidence, Cochrane, Embase, SwetsNet & others
Stock: bks/3000; periodcls/60
Staff: Libns: 2 *Non-Prof:* 1

S712 🎓🏛

Heatherbank Museum of Social Work, Library and Archives

Glasgow Caledonian Univ, City Campus, Cowcaddens Rd, Glasgow, G4 0BA (0141-331-8637; *fax:* 0141-331-3005)
Email: A.Ramage@gcal.ac.uk
Internet: http://www.lib.gcal.ac.uk/heatherbank/

Gov Body: Glasgow Caledonian Univ *Chief:* Curator: Rev Alastair Ramage BA, MA, ADB, CertEd *Dep:* Museum Asst: Ms Marlene Macowan BA
Assoc Libs: ARCHV OF THE DIRS OF SOCIAL WORK, addr as above, Univ Archivist: Ms Carol McCallum (0141-331-3199; *email:* c.mccallum@gcal.ac.uk)
Entry: access to archvs is limited to approved rsrchers *Open:* Mon-Fri 0900-1430; closed public hols
Subj: social work; hist of social work; biography; child care law; crime; religion; health care; housing
Collns & Pamphs: School Histories Colln (hists & pupil lists of schools in UK); Biography Colln (c700 vols); Church Social Work Colln; Govt reports & acts; Heatherbank Press Colln; various bnd journals, incl the full set of The Poor Law Magazine (1859-1929) & The British Workman (1855-1892) *Archvs:* Assoc of Dirs of Social Work (ADSW) Archv (1969 onwards); various small collns covering poor houses, admin of poor law, former hosps & instns, former prisoner support agencies *Other:* Picture Lib (7000 prints, negs & slides); Audiovisual Lib; Ephemera Lib (incl poetry by Poorhouse residents)
Equip: 2 copiers (20p per copy), clr copier (50p per copy), computer (with wd-proc) *Disabled:* wheelchair access
Stock: bks/2000; photos/6000; slides/500; videos/12; archvs/30 linear m
Auto Sys: Dynix
Pubns: Factsheets
Staff: Other Prof: 1 *Non-Prof:* 1

S713

Kelvinside Academy Library

33 Kirklee Rd, Glasgow, G12 0SW (0141-357-3376; *fax:* 0141-357-5401)
Internet: http://www.kelvinsideacademy.org.uk/

Type: school *Gov Body:* Kelvinside Academy Memorial Trust *Chief:* Libn: Mrs Ann Boyle MA, DipLib, MCLIP
Open: term: 0900-1630; vac: closed
Subj: local study (Glasgow & Scotland); generalities; phil; psy; religion; social sci; lang; sci; maths; tech; arts; lit; geog; hist
Equip: copier, video viewer, computers (incl wd-proc, internet & CD-ROM) *Svcs:* info, ref, biblio
Stock: bks/10000; periodcls/6; audios/30; videos/30
Classn: DDC *Auto Sys:* ALS, Alice
Staff: Libns: 1

S714

Langside College, The Litehouse

50 Prospecthill Rd, Glasgow, G42 9LB (0141-272-3679; *fax:* 0141-632-5252)
Email: library@perseus.langside.ac.uk
Internet: http://www.litehouse.org.uk/

Gov Body: Board of Mgmt *Chief:* Litehouse Mgr: Mr Donald Morrison MA(Hons), DipLib (donald@perseus.langside.ac.uk)
Entry: students of Coll; ref only for non-students
Open: tcrm: Mon Thu 0900-2000, Fri 1000-1700, Sat 1000-1400; vac: Mon-Fri 0930-1630
Subj: all subjs; genl; GCSE; A level; undergrad
Collns: Archvs: Langside Coll archvs *Co-op Schemes:* ILL
Equip: copier (A4/5p), clr copier (A4/70p), 26 computers (incl 24 with wd-proc, 24 with internet & 24 with CD-ROM) *Disabled:* CCTV for visually impaired *Online:* Infotrac, KnowUK, KnowEurope, LION, Tips & Advice Internet (all free) *Officer-in-Charge:* Litehouse Mgr, as above *Svcs:* info, ref, biblio
Stock: bks/20000; periodcls/93; pamphs/500; audios/700; videos/1000; CD-ROMs/60 *Acqs Offcr:* Litehouse Mgr, as above
Classn: DDC *Auto Sys:* EASL
Pubns: Langside Line (free); various lib leaflets
Staff: Libns: 1 *Non-Prof:* 2.5 *Exp:* £37250 (1999-2000); £42500 (2000-01); incl all exp except staff costs

S715

Learning and Teaching Scotland, Glasgow Library

(formerly Scottish Council for Educational Tech Lib)
74 Victoria Crescent Rd, Glasgow, G12 9JN (0141-337-5071; *fax:* 0141-337-5070)
Email: j.mackecknie@scet.org.uk
Internet: http://www.ltscotland.com/

Gov Body: Board of Governors *Chief:* Info Specialist: Mr Jim MacKecknie MA(Hons), DipLib, MCLIP
Entry: ref only to non-SCET staff *Open:* Mon-Fri 0900-1630
Subj: edu
Equip: computer (with wd-proc & internet)
Stock: bks/3000; periodcls/103
Classn: DDC *Auto Sys:* Lib Pro
Staff: Libns: 1 *Exp:* £20540 (1999-2000)

S716

Mediateque de l'Alliance Française de Glasgow

7 Bowmont Gdns, Glasgow, G12 9LR (0141-339-4281; *fax:* 0141-339-4224)
Email: biblio@afglasgow.org.uk
Internet: http://www.afglasgow.org.uk/

Chief: Libn: Miss Carole Jacquet *Other Snr Staff:* Miss Karen Marquardsen
Entry: open to students of the Alliance Française; membership scheme for others (subscription fees vary) *Open:* Mon-Wed 1200-1830, Thu 1200-2030, Fri 1100-1300, Sat 0930-1330; group visits by arrangement
Subj: all subjs (in French); France; French lang, lit, hist, art & culture *Collns: Bks & Pamphs:* ref colln; French periodcls *Other:* audios, videos, DVDs & CD-ROMs *Co-op Schemes:* ILL
Equip: copier (10p per sheet), computer (with internet & CD-ROM), television *Officer-in-Charge:* Dir of the Alliance Française: Mr Patrick Girard
Stock: bks/5000; periodcls/35; maps/50; audios/820; videos/860; CD-ROMs/150; posters/100 *Acqs Offcr:* Libn, as above
Classn: DDC *Auto Sys:* BCDI *Staff:* Libns: 2

S717   +

Medical Research Council, Social and Public Health Sciences Unit, Library

4 Lilybank Gdns, Glasgow, G12 8RZ (0141-357-3949; *fax:* 0141-337-2389)
Email: library@msoc.mrc.gla.ac.uk
Internet: http://www.msoc-mrc.gla.ac.uk/

Gov Body: Medical Rsrch Council (see **S536**)
Chief: Libn: Mrs Mary Robins HNC
Assoc Libs: other MRC Unit Libs
Entry: adv appt by phone or by letter; the bldg is not suitable for disabled visitors *Open:* Mon-Fri 1000-1700
Subj: social sci; medical sociology; social policy; family; ethnicity; health statistics; medical rsrch methods; public health *Collns: Other:* copies of Unit working & occasional papers *Co-op Schemes:* SHINE
Stock: bks/3500; periodcls/65
Classn: own *Auto Sys:* CALM 2000
Pubns: Annual Report & some occasional papers available on web site
Staff: Non-Prof: 1

S718

Museum of Education, Scotland Street School

225 Scotland St, Glasgow, G5 8QB (0141-287-0500; *fax:* 0141-420-3292)

Type: local authority *Gov Body:* Glasgow City Council (see **P56**) *Chief:* Curator Mgr: Ms D. Stewart MA, DipEd
Entry: ref only, adv appt *Open:* Mon-Thu, Sat 1000-1700, Fri, Sun 1100-1700
Subj: edu
Equip: Disabled: wheelchair access
Stock: bks/8000; photos/1000; maps/100
Classn: MDA
Pubns: Six of the Best (£7.50p)

S719 +

National Centre for Training and Education in Prosthetics and Orthotics, Information Centre

Univ of Strathclyde, Curran Bldg, 131 St James' Rd, Glasgow, G4 0LS (0141-548-3814; *fax:* 0141-552-1283)
Email: h.smart@strath.ac.uk

Gov Body: Univ of Strathclyde (see **S741**) *Chief:* Info Offcr: Mrs Heather Smart BA(Hons), MCLIP
Entry: adv appt *Open:* Mon-Fri 0900-1700
Subj: undergrad; postgrad; rehabilitation professions; prosthetics; orthotics; rehabilitation eng *Co-op Schemes:* BLDSC, SHINE
Equip: copier, computer
Stock: bks/20000; periodcls/150 *Classn:* NLM

Pubns: RECAL Current Awareness (NHS £50, indivs £60 UK, £85 overseas, libs, instns & companies £85 UK, £100 overseas); RECAL Thesaurus (£60); RECAL Bibliographic Database (CD-ROM £550 initial purchase + £350 pa subscription; Internet £60 pa subscription)
Staff: Libns: 1.5 *Non-Prof:* 1.5

S720

North Glasgow College, Barmulloch Campus Library

186 Rye Rd, Barmulloch, Glasgow, G21 3JY (0141-558-9001; *fax:* 0141-558-9744)
Email: library@ngcb.n-net.com
Internet: http://www.north-gla.ac.uk/

Gov Body: North Glasgow Coll *Chief:* Libn: Mr Chris Rogers BA, DipLib, MCLIP
Assoc Libs: SPRINGBURN CAMPUS LIB (see **S721**)
Entry: ref only if not staff or student *Open:* term: Mon-Fri 0845-1630; vac: variable
Subj: all subjs; GCSE; A level; vocational *Co-op Schemes:* Glasgow Community Colls Group
Equip: video viewer, copier, computers (incl wd-proc, internet & CD-ROM) *Svcs:* info, ref
Stock: bks/12000; periodcls/50; audios/120; videos/600; CD-ROMs/26
Classn: DDC *Auto Sys:* Heritage
Staff: Libns: 2 *Non-Prof:* 3

S721

North Glasgow College, Springburn Campus Library

110 Flemington St, Glasgow, G21 4BX (0141-558-9001; *fax:* 0141-558-9905)
Email: F.Paris@north_gla.ac.uk
Internet: http://www.north-gla.ac.uk/

Chief: Libn: Ms Fiona Paris BA, MCLIP
Assoc Libs: BARMULLOCH CAMPUS LIB (see **S720**)
Entry: open to staff & students; community for ref only *Open:* term: Mon, Fri 0845-1630, Tue, Thu 0845-2000, Wed 0845-1800; vac: varies
Subj: all subjs; GCSE; A level; undergrad *Co-op Schemes:* BLDSC
Equip: video viewer, fax, copier, computers (incl wd-proc, internet & CD-ROM)
Stock: bks/25000; periodcls/65; slides/40 packs; maps/15; audios/20; videos/150
Classn: DDC *Auto Sys:* Heritage
Staff: Libns: 4 *Non-Prof:* 2.5

S722 +

North Glasgow University Hospitals NHS Trust, Stobhill Hospital Library

133 Balornock Rd, Glasgow, G21 3UW (0141-201-3357; *fax:* 0141-201-3957)
Internet: http://www.northglashealthinfo.org.uk/

Gov Body: North Glasgow Univ Hosps NHS Trust *Chief:* Medical Libn: Ms Chloe Stewart MA, MCLIP
Dep: Dep Libn: Ms Shona MacLeod MA, MCLIP
Assoc Libs: BEATSON ONCOLOGY CENTRE LIB (see **S694**); GLASGOW ROYAL INFIRMARY LIB (see **S706**); GARTNAVEL GENL HOSP STAFF LIB (see **S700**); WESTERN INFIRMARY LIB (see **S742**)
Entry: adv appt for non-Trust staff *Open:* Mon-Tue, Thu-Fri 0900-1700, Wed 0900-1930
Subj: medicine; nursing; health *Co-op Schemes:* BLDSC, SHINE, NULJ
Equip: copier, 7 computers (incl 6 with internet) *Online:* Medline, CINAHL, Cochrane, AMED, HMIC, PsycInfo, BNI & others, 400+ e-journals
Svcs: info, ref, biblio
Stock: bks/5000; periodcls/120; audios/100; videos/50 *Auto Sys:* Heritage *Staff:* Libns: 2

S723 🗝

The Planning Exchange Information Unit

Tontine House, 8 Gordon St, Glasgow, G1 3PL (0141-248-9441; *fax:* 0141-248-9433)
Email: iu@planex.co.uk
Internet: http://www.planex.co.uk/

Chief: Info Unit Mgr: Mrs Christine Johnston MA, MSc, DipLib, CertEd, MCLIP *Dep:* Mr Alan Gillies MA, DipLib
Entry: subscription-paying membership *Open:* Mon-Fri 0900-1700
Subj: social sci; planning; housing; local economic development; local govt; transport; environment; social work; edu; training *Collns: Bks & Pamphs:* 83000 bks, reports & articles, all abstracted on PLANEX database & available to membs on the Web *Co-op Schemes:* BLDSC
Equip: Online: PLANEX on the Web (in-house database) *Svcs:* info, abstracting
Stock: bks/c41000 vols & 42000 articles; periodcls/c500
Auto Sys: own
Pubns: Economic Development Today (monthly journal, £140 pa); Scottish Planning & Environmental Law (bi-monthly, £110 pa); Journal of Lifelong Learning Initiatives (bi-monthly, £75 pa)
Staff: Libns: 8 *Non-Prof:* 6
See also **O318**

S724 🎓 🗝 ✚

Royal College of Physicians and Surgeons of Glasgow Library

232-242 St Vincent St, Glasgow, G2 5RJ (0141-227-3204; *fax:* 0141-221-1804)
Email: library@rcpsglasg.ac.uk
Internet: http://www.rcpsglasg.ac.uk/

Chief: Libn: Mr James Beaton MA, DipLib, MCLIP, FSA(Scot) (james.beaton@rcpsglasg.ac.uk)
Other Snr Staff: Info Resources Libn: Mrs Valerie McClure MA, MSc (valerie.mcclure@rcpsglasg. ac.uk); Archivist: Mrs Carol Parry BA, DipAA (carol.parry@rcpsglasg.ac.uk)
Entry: outsiders need authorisation; contact the Libn *Open:* Mon-Fri 0900-1700
Subj: medicine; surgery; hist of medicine; local studies (Glasgow & West of Scotland) *Collns: Bks & Pamphs:* Historical Colln (15C-20C); Dr William Mackenzie Lib (ophthalmology); colln of historical journals *Archvs:* records of the Coll (1602-date); records of other medical orgs, incl: Glasgow Medical Soc (1814-1924); Glasgow Odontological Soc (1902-2002); Glasgow Southern Medical Soc (1844-1998); Royal Medico-Chirurgical Soc of Glasgow (1844-1987); papers of indivs incl: Ronald Ross Papers (tropical medicine); William Macewan Papers (surgery); Joseph Lister Papers (surgery & antisepsis); Young Family Papers *Other:* large archival photo colln
Co-op Schemes: BLDSC, SHINE, SUSCAG
Equip: m-reader, copier (A4/20p), 2 computers (both with wd-proc, internet & CD-ROM) *Officer-in-Charge:* Libn, as above
Stock: bks/35000; periodcls/40; photos/2000; slides/400; pamphs/10000; m-forms/10 *Acqs Offcr:* Libn, as above
Classn: NLM *Auto Sys:* Alice
Pubns: Treasures of the Coll (£35)
Staff: Libns: 2 *Other Prof:* 1 *Non-Prof:* 1

S725 🗝

Royal Faculty of Procurators Library

12 Nelson Mandela Pl, Glasgow, G2 1BT (0141-332-3593; *fax:* 0141-333-9104)
Email: library@rfpg.org
Internet: http://www.rfpg.org/

Chief: Snr Libn: Mr John McKenzie LLB(Hons), DipLIS (jmackenzie@rfpg.org) *Dep: Asst Libn:* Ms Marjory Stewart
Assoc Libs: ROYAL FACULTY OF PROCURATORS LIB, Sheriff Ct, 1 Carlton Pl, Glasgow, G5 9DA
Entry: open to membs, entry to rsrchers is for ref only & by appt; written appl should be made to the Clerk of the RFP *Open:* Mon-Thu 0900-2100, Fri 0900-1700, Sat 0900-1300, Sun 1300-1700
Subj: law *Collns: Bks & Pamphs:* Dr William Henry Hill Colln (1600 bks & MSS relating to Glasgow & its citizens)
Equip: fax, 2 copiers, 3 computers (all with wd-proc & CD-ROM, 1 with internet, internet access £1 per hr), 6 rooms for hire *Online:* CCH Elec, CLI (current Legal Info), EIN (Elec Immigration Network) *Svcs:* info, ref, biblio, indexing
Stock: bks/20000; periodcls/250; maps/36
Auto Sys: Heritage
Pubns: A List of Legal Firms in the City of Glasgow etc (Supplement), extending from January 1953 to December 1994 (£5)
Staff: Libns: 1 *Other Prof:* 2 *Non-Prof:* 2

S726 🎓

Royal Scottish Academy of Music and Drama, The Whittaker Library

100 Renfrew St, Glasgow, G2 3DB (0141-270-8268; *fax:* 0141-270-8353)
Email: library@samd.ac.uk
Internet: http://www.samd.ac.uk/

Chief: Head of Info Svcs: Mr Gordon Hunt *Other Snr Staff:* Music & Academic Svcs Libn: Mrs Karen McAuley; Drama Libn: Mr Alan Jones; Drama Libn: Ms Marian Fordom
Entry: open to public for ref only *Open:* term: Mon-Thu 0900-2030, Fri 0900-1700, Sat 1000-1600; vac: Mon-Fri 0900-1700; times may vary; contact lib in adv of visit
Subj: drama; music; music hist; musicology
Collns: Bks & Pamphs: choral & orchestral scores *Other:* performance music colln; Scottish Musical Studies Colln *Co-op Schemes:* BLDSC, ILL, NLSLS, Music Libs Online
Equip: m-reader, copier, fax, 4 video viewers, 6 computers (incl 1 with internet) *Online:* Grove Music *Svcs:* info, ref, biblio
Stock: bks/19000; periodcls/96; audios/9500; videos/950; CD-ROMs/20; music scores/45500; orchestral sets/1240; choral sets/798
Classn: LC, own *Auto Sys:* Dynix
Staff: Libns: 3 *Other Prof:* 1 *Non-Prof:* 5

S727 🎓 🗝

Royal Scottish Geographical Society Library

Curran Bldg, 101 St James Rd, Glasgow, G4 0NS (*Soc:* 0141-552-3330; *Lib:* 0141-552-4400 x4607)
Email: R.S.G.S@strath.ac.uk
Internet: http://www.lib.strath.ac.uk/RSGS/ or http://www.geo.ed.ac.uk/~rsgs/

Gov Body: RSGS & Univ of Strathclyde *Chief:* Dir of Lib Svcs: Mr K.R. Davis BA, DipLib (k.r.davis@strath.ac.uk) *Dep: Depute Libn:* Dr K.J. Cameron MA, PhD, DipLib (k.j.cameron@strath. ac.uk) *Other Snr Staff:* Subj Libn: Mrs Janet Davidson

Assoc Libs: part of UNIV OF STRATHCLYDE, ANDERSONIAN LIB at same addr (see **S741**); the Soc also holds additional materials at its HQ: Royal Scottish Geographical Soc, Graham Hills Bldg, 40 George St, Glasgow, G1 1QE (0141-552-3330)
Entry: membs of Soc & Univ; bona fide rsrchers by appt *Open:* term: Mon-Fri 0900-2200, Sat 0900-1200; vac: Mon-Fri 0900-1700, Sat 0900-1200; additional opening hrs as advertised
Subj: geog; cartography; travel; exploration; topography *Collns: Archvs:* RSGS Archv, incl records of past expeditions (1884-date) *Other:* extensive map colln; slide colln (20000 clr slides & 5000 antique glass lantern slides); historic photo colln *Co-op Schemes:* ILL
Equip: computer
Stock: bks/15000; periodcls/200; slides/25000; maps/15000; bnd periodcls/3000 vols
Classn: DDC *Auto Sys:* Endeavour

S728 ✚

Scottish Centre for Infection and Environmental Health, SCIEH Library

Clifton House, Clifton Pl, Glasgow, G3 7LN (0141-300-1129; *fax:* 0141-300-1170)
Email: SCIEH.library@scieh.csa.scot.nhs.uk

Gov Body: Common Svcs Agency for the NHS in Scotland (see **S589**) *Chief: Libn:* Mr Norman McDonald BA, DipLib (norman.mcdonald@scieh.csa.scot.nhs.uk)
Entry: ref only for non-membs, by adv appt (please tel for access) *Open:* Mon-Fri 0930-1700
Subj: medicine; communicable diseases; environmental health *Co-op Schemes:* BLDSC, SHINE
Equip: m-reader, m-printer, copier, computers (incl wd-proc & CD-ROM) *Online:* Benenson, Environmental Health, Justis, Medline etc *Svcs:* info, ref, biblio, current awareness
Stock: bks/3000; periodcls/100; pamphs/500; m-forms/4000; audios/10; videos/30
Classn: NLM (mod) *Auto Sys:* LibraryPac
Staff: Libns: 1 *Non-Prof:* 1

S729 🏛 ☕

Scottish Enterprise, Business Information Centre

5 Atlantic Quay, 150 Broomielaw, Glasgow, G2 8LU (0141-248-2700; *fax:* 0141-221-3217)
Email: Gail.Rogers@scotent.co.uk
Internet: http://www.scottish-enterprise.com/

Chief: Mgr: Ms Gail Rogers MA(Hons), DipLib *Dep:* Business Info Exec: Ms Karen Perkington
Entry: Scottish Enterprise staff only *Open:* Mon-Fri 0900-1700
Subj: company, market & economic info *Collns: Archvs:* Scottish Enterprise reports
Equip: copier *Online:* Dialog, Datastar, Maid, ICC, Dun & Bradstreet, Nomis, Profile, Kompass, Mintel, Reuters Business Briefing
Stock: bks/10000; periodcls/400
Classn: own *Auto Sys:* CAIRS
Staff: Libns: 3 *Non-Prof:* 2

S730 🗝

Scottish Music Information Centre Ltd

1 Bowmont Gdns, Glasgow, G12 9LR (0141-334-6393; *fax:* 0141-337-1161)
Email: info@smic.dircon.co.uk
Internet: http://www.smic.org.uk/

Type: natl music archv, resource & info centre
Gov Body: Board of Dirs *Chief:* Info Mgr: Mr Alasdair Pettinger

Open: Mon-Fri 0930-1730 excl public hols (other times possible by arrangement)
Subj: Scottish music *Collns: Archvs:* holographs of scores of compositions by a number of 20C Scottish or Scotland-based composers *Other:* comprehensive colln of scores by contemporary Scottish or Scotland-based composers, both commercially publ works & unpublished (photocopies of MSS)
Equip: fax, 2 copiers, listening facilities (LP, cassette, CD) *Online:* catalogue of ref lib holdings (printouts 15p per pg) *Svcs:* info, ref, biblio, indexing
Stock: bks/1000; periodcls/45; photos/100; pamphs/100; audios/6000; videos/10; music scores/7000 for ref, 800 for hire
Classn: own *Auto Sys:* Cardbox
Pubns: Music Current (quarterly newsletter, £5 pa, £10 overseas); monthly email newsletter (printed version on request)
Staff: 5 in total

S731

Scottish Screen, Information Service
249 West George St, Glasgow, G2 4QE (0141-302-1730; *fax:* 0141-302-1711)
Email: info@scottishscreen.com
Internet: http://www.scottishscreen.com/

Gov Body: Scottish Screen *Chief:* Info Mgr: Ms Isabella Edgar BA, PGDipLIS (isabella.edgar@scottishscreen.com) *Dep:* Info Asst: Ms Kirsten Stewart BA, PGDipLIS (kirsten.stewart@scottishscreen.com)
Assoc Libs: SCOTTISH SCREEN ARCHV (see A181)
Entry: open to public, ref only *Open:* Mon-Thu 0900-1730, Fri 0900-1700
Subj: moving image in Scotland; film; cinema; television; film industry, esp Scottish *Collns: Bks & Pamphs:* Shiach Lib (shooting scripts); film industry trade directories; film industry reports (esp Scottish) *Other:* Scottish VHS Colln; Lindsay Anderson's Private VHS Colln; EIFF VHS Colln; stills from Scottish films & television programmes; press cuttings; newsletters
Equip: video viewer, DVD viewer *Online:* Scottish Film & Television Database *Svcs:* ref, info
Stock: bks/1000+; photos/300+; videos/3000+
Acqs Offcr: Info Mgr, as above
Classn: in-house
Pubns: Roughcuts (newsletter)
Staff: Libns: 2 *Other Prof:* 1

S732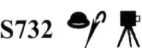

Scottish Television Library Services
Scottish Television, 200 Renfield St, Glasgow, G2 3PR (0141-300-3000; *fax:* 0141-300-3030)

Gov Body: Scottish Media Group *Chief:* Head of Lib Svcs: Mr John Rushton BA(Hons), DipLib, MCLIP (john.rushton@smg.plc.uk) *Dep:* Dep Head of Lib Svcs: Mrs Fiona Gunn BA(Hons) (fiona.gunn@smg.plc.uk) *Other Snr Staff:* Footage Sales: Ms Francesca Scott (0141-300-3122; *email:* francesca.scott@smg.plc.uk)
Assoc Libs: GRAMPIAN TELEVISION LIB, Queens Cross, Aberdeen, AB15 3XJ, Lib Supervisor: Mr Bill Moir
Entry: adv appt only *Open:* Mon-Fri 0900-1830, Sat 0900-1700
Subj: all subjs; genl; local studies (Scotland)
Equip: 4 video viewers *Online:* Scottish Media Newspapers *Svcs:* info, ref
Stock: videos/c300000 items
Classn: Strix Free-Text Database *Auto Sys:* ProLib
Staff: Libns: 8 *Non-Prof:* 1

S733

Scottish Universities Research and Reactor Centre, Library
Scottish Enterprise & Technology Pk, East Kilbride, Glasgow, G75 0QU (01355-223332; *fax:* 01355-229898)
Email: r.ellam@surrc.gla.ac.uk
Internet: http://www.gla.ac.uk/centres/surrc/

Gov Body: Scottish Univs RRC Consortium
Chief: Reader & Libn: Dr R.M. Ellam BSc, PhD
Entry: by appt *Open:* Mon-Fri 0900-1700
Subj: sci; nuclear sci; earth sci; environmental sci
Co-op Schemes: ILL
Equip: m-reader, copier, clr copier (by arrangement), fax, computer (with CD-ROM, by arrangement) *Online:* BIDS
Stock: bks/4000; periodcls/30
Classn: DDC
Staff: Other Prof: 7 *Non-Prof:* 40 *Exp:* £10000 (1999-2000); £10000 (2000-01)

S734 ✚

South Glasgow University Hospitals NHS Trust, Central Library
Govan Rd, Glasgow, G51 4TF (0141-201-2163; *fax:* 0141-201-2133)
Email: gcl095@clinmed.gla.ac.uk

Gov Body: South Glasgow Univ Hosps NHS Trust
Chief: Libn: Miss Charlotte Boulnois BA(Hons), MCLIP
Assoc Libs: JAMES BRIDIE LIB, Victoria Infirmary (see S735)
Entry: Trust staff; ref only to other health profs
Open: Mon-Thu 0900-1900, Fri 0900-1700
Subj: medicine; nursing; allied healthcare; health care mgmt *Co-op Schemes:* BLDSC, SHINE, PLCS, NULJ, BMA, RCSE
Equip: fax, copier, computers (incl wd-proc, internet & CD-ROM) *Online:* OVID, Medline, CINAHL, Cochrane, HEBS
Stock: bks/5500; periodcls/127
Classn: DDC *Auto Sys:* DS
Pubns: List of Journals Holdings (free), Guide to Lib (free)
Staff: Libns: 2 *Other Prof:* 1

S735 ✚

South Glasgow University Hospitals NHS Trust, The James Bridie Library
Victoria Infirmary, Langside Rd, Glasgow, G42 9TY (0141-201-5760; *fax:* 0141-201-5759)
Email: library@gvic.scot.nhs.uk

Gov Body: South Glasgow Univ Hosps NHS Trust
Chief: Asst Libn: Ms Shona MacNeilage BA(Hons)
Assoc Libs: SOUTH GLASGOW UNIV HOSPS NHS TRUST, CENTRAL LIB (see S734)
Entry: open to all Trust staff & students; ref only for students *Open:* term: Mon 0900-1700, Tue, Thu 0900-1900, Wed, Fri 0900-1700; vac: Mon-Fri 0900-1700
Subj: medicine; health sci *Co-op Schemes:* BLDSC, SHINE, NULJ
Equip: copier, fax, 5 computers (all with wd-proc, 4 with internet & 4 with CD-ROM) *Svcs:* info, ref, biblio
Stock: bks/8500; periodcls/150
Classn: DDC *Auto Sys:* CALM 2000
Staff: Libns: 1 *Non-Prof:* 0.4

S736

Stow College Library
43 Shamrock St, Glasgow, G34 9LD (0141-564-7292; *fax:* 0141-332-5207)
Email: lvaughan@stow.ac.uk
Internet: http://www.stow.ac.uk/

Gov Body: Scottish Exec (see S628) *Chief:* Libn: Mrs Linda A. Vaughan MA(Hons), DipLIS
Entry: ref only *Open:* term: Mon, Fri 0900-1645, Tue-Thu 0900-1830; vac: closed
Subj: all subjs; genl; GCSE & A-level equivalents; vocational (HNC/D, NQ, Access) *Co-op Schemes:* ILL, SLIC, Glasgow Coll Group
Equip: copier (£1 for 16 copies), 6 computers (all with wd-proc, internet & CD-ROM) *Officer-in-Charge:* Info & Learning Svcs Mgr: Mrs Margaret Cairns (mcairns@stow.ac.uk) *Svcs:* info, ref, biblio
Stock: bks/17000; periodcls/80; pamphs/500; CD-ROMs/70; offprints/700 *Acqs Offcr:* Libn, as above
Classn: DDC *Auto Sys:* EASL
Staff: Libns: 1 *Non-Prof:* 2 *Exp:* £30000 (1999-2000); £20000 (2000-01)
Further Info: lib is part of ILS (Info & Learning Svcs); AV materials, video viewers & clr printing are provided by FLEX, a complementary part of the svc; further computing facilities provided by FLEX & SUPERFLEX (all part of ILS)

S737

Strathclyde Graduate Business School, Business Information Service
199 Cathedral St, Glasgow, G4 0QU (0141-553-6026; *fax:* 0141-553-6137)
Email: bis@gsb.strath.ac.uk
Internet: http://www.sgsb.strath.ac.uk/

Gov Body: Univ of Strathclyde (see S741) *Chief:* Mgr: Miss Christine Reid BA, MA, MCLIP (c.rcid@gsb.strath.ac.uk)
Entry: adv appt in writing *Open:* term: Mon-Thu 0900-2000, Fri 0900-1700, Sat 1100-1700; vac: Mon-Fri 0900-1700, Sat 1100-1700
Subj: postgrad; business; mgmt *Collns: Other:* company reports
Equip: Online: Amadeus, FAME, Dow Jones, Reuters & others
Stock: bks/5000; periodcls/700
Auto Sys: CAIRS *Staff: Libns:* 1 *Non-Prof:* 2

S738

University of Glasgow, Library
Hillhead St, Glasgow, G12 8QE (0141-330-6704; *fax:* 0141-330-4952)
Email: library@lib.gla.ac.uk
Internet: http://www.gla.ac.uk/Library/

Chief: Dir of Lib Svcs & Keeper of the Hunterian Bks & MSS: Mrs Chris Bailey
Assoc Libs: CHEM BRANCH LIB, Joseph Black Bldg, Univ Pl, Glasgow, G12 8QH, Libn: Mrs Denise Currie (0141-330-0502; *fax:* 141-330-4888; *email:* d.currie@library.gla.ac.uk); JAMES HERRIOT LIB, Veterinary Hosp Bldg, Faculty of Veterinary Medicine, Bearsden Rd, Bearsden, Glasgow, G61 1QH, Libn: Mrs Maureen McGovern (0141-330-5708; *fax:* 0141-942-7215; *email:* vetlib@udcf.gla.ac.uk); JAMES IRELAND MEMORIAL LIB (see S740); ADAM SMITH LIB (see S739); GLASGOW UNIV ARCHV SVCS (see A176)
Entry: membs of Univ & UK grads, others apply to Libn; external membership available *Open:* term: Mon-Fri 0800-2300, Sat 0900-1930, Sun 1330-2130; vac: Mon-Fri 0900-1700, Sat 0900-1230
Subj: most subjs; undergrad; postgrad; strengths incl: artists (painters, sculptors); biography; bible; bibliography; Celtic lit; hist of Eastern Europe & former Soviet Union; hist of medicine; music; music hist; musicology; oriental & Asian hist; oriental lit; phil; local hist; Scottish hist *Collns: Bks & Pamphs:* Euing Collns of the Bible & music; Farmer Music Colln; Fergusson Colln (hist of chem, alchemy, occultism, 7500 vols); Hamilton Colln (phil); Hunterian Bks & MSS; Spencer Darien Scheme (17C Scottish colony in Panama); David Murray Colln (regional hist); Edwin Morgan Papers; Trotsky Colln; UK official pubns; EU documentation ☞

Special Libraries

Glasgow ▼ Gosport

(Univ of Glasgow Lib cont)

Collns: Archvs: Fergusson, Laver, McColl & Wright Papers (fine art); J.M. Whistler archv; Scottish Theatre Archv *Other:* Map Colln *Co-op Schemes:* SCONUL, CURL, SCURL, BLDSC *Equip:* m-reader, m-printer, video viewers, copiers, 357 computers (incl CD-ROM) *Online:* BIDS, OCLC FirstSearch, EDINA, LION, ISI, NISS *Svcs:* info, ref
Stock: bks/1650000 incl pamphs; periodcls/8250; MSS/100000+
Classn: own *Auto Sys:* Innopac
Staff: Libns: 34 *Other Prof:* 4 *Non-Prof:* 148

S739 🎓

University of Glasgow, Adam Smith Library

1st Floor, Adam Smith Bldg, Bute Gdns, Glasgow, G12 8RT (0141-330-5648)
Email: adamsmith@lib.gla.ac.uk
Internet: http://www.lib.gla.ac.uk/AboutLibrary/adam.html

Gov Body: Univ of Glasgow (see **S738**) *Chief:* Libn: Mr Kerr Ross (k.ross@lib.gla.ac.uk)
Entry: membs of Univ, others by appt *Open:* term: Mon-Thu 0900-2100, Fri 0900-1700; vac: Mon-Fri 0900-1700
Subj: undergrad; econ; politics; psy; social sci; economic hist; social hist; urban studies
Pubns: How to Use the Adam Smith Lib
Staff: Libns: 1 *Non-Prof:* 1 FT, 3 PT

S740 🎓 ✚

University of Glasgow, James Ireland Memorial Library

Dental Hosp & School, 378 Sauchiehall St, Glasgow, G2 3JZ (0141-211-9705; *fax:* 0141-331-2798)
Email: library@dental.gla.ac.uk
Internet: http://www.lib.gla.ac.uk/

Gov Body: Univ of Glasgow (see **S738**) *Chief:* Libn: Miss Beverley Rankin (b.rankin@lib.gla.ac.uk) *Other Snr Staff:* Subj Libn (based at Glasgow Univ Lib): Dr Helen S. Marlborough (h.marlborough@lib.gla.ac.uk)
Entry: registered membs of Univ; other by appt
Open: term: Mon-Thu 0900-2100, Fri 0900-1700; vac: Mon-Fri 0900-1700
Subj: dentistry *Collns: Bks & Pamphs:* hist of dentistry *Co-op Schemes:* ILL
Equip: copier, video viewer, 11 computers (all with internet, 7 with wd-proc, 1 with CD-ROM) *Online:* OVID Online, World of Science, OCLC, Edina *Svcs:* info, ref
Stock: bks/7000; periodcls/153; pamphs/543; videos/85; CD-ROMs/10; EU theses/187
Classn: NLM (mod) *Auto Sys:* III (Innovative Interfaces Inc) *Staff: Libns:* 1 *Non-Prof:* 2

S741 🎓

University of Strathclyde, The Andersonian Library

Curran Bldg, 101 St James Rd, Glasgow, G4 0NS (0141-548-3701; *fax:* 0141-552-3304)
Email: library@strath.ac.uk
Internet: http://www.lib.strath.ac.uk/

Gov Body: Univ of Strathclyde *Chief:* Univ Libn & Head of Info Resources: Prof Derek G. Law *Other Snr Staff:* Dir of Lib Svcs: Mr Keith R. Davis BA, DipLib; Depute Libn (Bibliographical Svcs): Dr Kenneth J. Cameron MA, PhD, DipLib *Assoc Libs:* LAW LIB, Stenhouse Bldg, 173 Cathedral St, Glasgow, G4 0QR, Officer-in-Charge: Mrs Christina MacSween MA, DipLib; JORDAN-HILL LIB, 76 Southbrae Dr, Glasgow, G13 1PP, Officer-in-Charge: Mrs M. Harrison MA, MCLIP; ROYAL SCOTTISH GEOGRAPHICAL SOC LIB (see **S727**)
Entry: non-membs for ref only on appl to Libn
Open: term: Mon-Fri 0900-2100 (reading 0850-2200), Sat 0900-1700, Sun 1100-1700; vac: Mon-Fri 0900-1700 (reading 0850-2200 during Easter), Sat 0900-1200
Subj: undergrad; postgrad; local studies (Scotland); generalities; phil; psy; religion; social sci; lang; sci; maths; tech; arts; lit; geog; hist; business studies *Collns: Bks & Pamphs:* Anderson Colln (Founder's Lib: various subjs, pre-19C); Young Colln (rare bks on alchemy); Strathclyde Colln (staff & official pubns relating to univ); Laing Colln (18C & 19C maths); Robertson Colln (Glasgow, West of Scotland); company reports; govt pubns *Archvs:* univ archvs; Internatl Union of Food Sci Archv; Meehan Papers; Sir Patrick Geddes papers *Other:* media colln (at Jordanhill Lib); BSI standards (on Level 4, Andersonian Lib)
Equip: m-readers, m-printer, video viewers, copiers, computers (incl CD-ROM), audio-visual equip *Disabled:* chairlift for wheelchair users, magnifiers, Magnilink CCTV, braille embosser, Kurzweil scanner, Calera Wordscan software, dyslexia software *Online:* various datahosts available incl STN, Datastar, Dialog, BLAISE, EPIC (cost from datahosts passed on to lib users) *Svcs:* info, ref, biblio
Stock: bks/930000; periodcls/5400; maps/2500; m-forms/193000; audios/4200; videos/3000; AVs/12000; MSS/2500; company reports/4000; software/1600 packages
Classn: DDC, UDC (older stock) *Auto Sys:* Endeavor Voyager
Pubns: variety of lib guides & reports, incl: Past & Present (£1); Reader's Guide; Direction Finder; Annual Report
Staff: Libns: 26 *Non-Prof:* 63 *Exp:* £1484849 (1999-2000); £1520747 (2000-01); figs cover all acqs, elec svcs, ILLs & document delivery

S742 ✚

Western Infirmary Library and eLearning Centre

Western Infirmary, Dumbarton Rd, Glasgow, G11 6NT (0141-211-2472; *fax:* 0141-211-1975)
Email: shona.mcquistan.wg@northglasgow.scot.nhs.uk
Internet: http://www.northglashealthinfo.org.uk/

Gov Body: North Glasgow Univ Hosps NHS Trust
Chief: Divisional Libn: Ms Shona McQuistan BSc(Hons), MSc
Assoc Libs: BEATSON ONCOLOGY CENTRE LIB (see **S694**); GLASGOW ROYAL INFIRMARY LIB (see **S706**); GARTNAVEL GENL HOSP STAFF LIB (see **S700**); STOBHILL HOSP LIB (see **S722**)
Entry: trust staff & students; membs of NHS Glasgow; all others require adv appt *Open:* Mon-Fri 0900-1700
Subj: medicine; nursing; health promotion *Co-op Schemes:* SHINE, RCSE, BMA, BLDSC
Equip: copier (£1 per 14 pgs), video viewer, 25 computers (all with wd-proc, internet & CD-ROM) *Online:* various databases, e-journals, e-textbks & web site *Officer-in-Charge:* Divisional Libn, as above *Svcs:* info, ref, biblio
Stock: bks/4000; periodcls/124; audios/15; videos/30; CD-ROMs/30 *Acqs Offcr:* Divisional Libn, as above

Classn: NLM *Auto Sys:* Heritage
Staff: Libns: 2 *Exp:* £3000 (1999-2000); £5000 (2000-01)

Glastonbury

S743 🍷

The Library of Avalon

2-4 High St, Glastonbury, Somerset, BA6 9DY (01458-832759)
Email: staff@libraryofavalon.co.uk
Internet: http://www.libraryofavalon.co.uk/

Gov Body: Avalon Lib Assoc
Entry: paid membership only (£25 pa, £18 concession) *Open:* Mon, Wed-Fri 1000-1700, Tue 1000-1900, Sat 100-1600
Subj: local study (Glastonbury, Somerset, West Country); Arthurian mythology; Grail Quest; phil; psy; religion; social sci; lang; arts; lit; hist; occult & esoteric discussion; paganism; "alternative" & complementary healing; astrology; "Earth Mysteries"
Equip: room for hire *Svcs:* info, ref
Stock: bks/10000; pamphs/500+; audios/250+; videos/40
Classn: own *Staff: Non-Prof:* 15 volunteers

Glenrothes

S744 🎓

Glenrothes College Learning Resource Service, Learner Development Centre

Stenton Rd, Glenrothes, Fife, KY6 2RA (01592-568038; *fax:* 01592-568094)
Email: jpriestley@glenrothes.ac.uk
Internet: http://www.glenrothes-college.ac.uk/

Chief: Libn: Mrs Jean Priestley BA, MCLIP
Open: term: Mon-Thu 0830-2100, Fri 0830-1645; vac: varies as required
Subj: subjs to cater for courses offered by Coll *Co-op Schemes:* BLDSC
Equip: m-reader, copier, fax, video viewer, 24 computers (all with wd-proc, 16 with internet & 10 with CD-ROM), 5 lang labs, comb binding machine *Disabled:* image enhancer *Online:* fees charged for external users
Stock: bks/17000; periodcls/34; maps/230; audios/67; videos/60; CD-ROMs/35
Classn: DDC *Auto Sys:* Heritage
Staff: Libns: 1 *Non-Prof:* 2 *Exp:* £6700 (1999-2000); £5050 (2000-01)

Gloucester

S745 🍷

British Energy plc Corporate Library

Barnett Way, Barnwood, Gloucester, GL4 3RS (01452-654163; *fax:* 01452-654163)
Email: evelyn.hutchison@british-energy.com
Internet: http://www.british-energy.com/

Chief: Libn: Mrs Evelyn Hutchison BSc(Econ)
Entry: adv appt *Open:* Mon-Fri 0830-1630
Subj: tech; nuclear eng; mechanical eng; electrical eng; mgmt; health & safety
Equip: m-reader, m-printer, 2 video viewers, computers (incl 2 with internet & 2 with CD-ROM) *Svcs:* info, ref
Stock: bks/5000+; periodcls/46; CD-ROMs/25
Classn: UDC *Auto Sys:* EOSi GLAS
Staff: Libns: 1 *Other Prof:* 1 relief libn *Non-Prof:* 1

---

 academic   corporate   **- 288 -**   governmental   ✚ medical

S746 🔑 🙏

Gloucester Cathedral Library

2 College Green, Gloucester, GL1 2LR (01452-528095; *fax:* 01452-300469)

Gov Body: Dean & Chapter of Gloucester *Chief:* Cathedral Libn: Mr L. Maddison MA, MMus *Entry:* adv appt for rsrch only, at discretion of Libn *Open:* Tue 1400-1700, Wed & Fri 1015-1700 *Subj:* hist & arch of Gloucester Cathedral; church music; Greek & Latin lit; English hist *Collns: Bks & Pamphs:* Selden Colln of 17C bks; Wheeler Colln of 18C bks *Archvs:* archvs of the Three Choirs Festival (1721-date) *Other:* medieval deeds of St Peter's Abbey, Gloucester (1134-1539) *Equip:* 2 m-readers, m-printer, copier *Stock:* bks/6630; periodcls/2; photos/417; slides/235; pamphs/180; maps/45; m-forms/10; videos/4 *Pubns:* Catalogue of Gloucester Cathedral Lib (£5.25); Three Choirs: A Hist of the Festival (£20) *Staff: Libns:* 1

S747 🎓

Gloucestershire College of Arts and Technology, Brunswick Campus Learning Centre

Brunswick Rd, Gloucester, GL1 1HU (01452-426530; *fax:* 01452-426852) *Email:* hallj07@gloscat.ac.uk *Internet:* http://www.gloscat.ac.uk/

Gov Body: Gloucestershire Coll of Arts & Tech (Gloscat) *Chief:* Centre Mgr: Ms Jill Hall BA, DipLIS *Dep:* Prof Support Staff: Ms Jan Rose BSc, DipLIS, CertEd *Assoc Libs:* CHELTENHAM CAMPUS LEARNING CENTRE, Princess Elizabeth Way, Cheltenham, Gloucestershire, GL51 7SJ *Entry:* Gloscat student ID or ref only *Open:* term: Mon-Thu 0830-2000, Fri 0830-1700; vac: varies *Subj:* all subjs; GCSE; A-level; undergrad; arts; tech *Collns: Archvs:* media stock *Equip:* video viewers, copier, computers (incl wd-proc, internet & CD-ROM), scanner, video editing *Stock:* bks/20000; periodcls/90; videos/400 *Classn:* DDC *Auto Sys:* Heritage IV *Staff: Libns:* 2 *Non-Prof:* 11

S748 ✚

Gloucestershire Royal Hospital Library

Redwood Edu Centre, Gt Western Rd, Gloucester, GL1 3NN (01452-394495; *fax:* 01452-394170) *Email:* library@gloucr-tr.swest.nhs.uk *Internet:* http://www.grhlib.demon.co.uk/

Gov Body: Gloucestershire Royal NHS Trust *Chief:* Libn: Miss Claire Harman BA(Hons), MCLIP (claire.harman@gloucr-tr.swest.nhs.uk) *Entry:* NHS staff in Gloucestershire *Open:* Mon-Thu 0830-1700, Fri 0900-1600; 24 hr access for membs by arrangement with lib staff *Subj:* medicine; health sci *Co-op Schemes:* BLDSC, SWRLIN, NULJ *Equip:* fax, video viewer, copier (5p), 8 computers (all with wd-proc, 7 with internet) *Online:* Medline, CINAHL, Cochrane etc *Svcs:* info, ref *Stock:* bks/3900; periodcls/150; CD-ROMs/various *Classn:* NLM (Wessex) *Auto Sys:* WebCat *Staff: Libns:* 1 *Non-Prof:* 1.2

S749 🔑 🏛

The National Waterways Museum, Library

Llanthony Warehouse, Gloucester Docks, Gloucester, GL1 2EH (01452-318200; *fax:* 01452-318202) *Email:* tony.conder@thewaterwaystrust.org *Internet:* http://www.nwm.org.uk/

Type: charitable trust *Chief:* Curator: Mr A.J. Conder BSc, AMA *Dep:* Keeper of Collns: Mr D.L. McDougall BSc, AMA *Assoc Libs:* BRITISH WATERWAYS ARCHVS (see **A183**); DAVID OWEN WATERWAYS ARCHV (see **A159**) *Entry:* ref only, adv appt *Open:* Mon-Fri 1000-1700 *Subj:* inland waterways; hist of inland waterways; geog *Collns: Other:* bks & archvs relating to inland waterways *Equip:* copier (10p per sheet at staff discretion) *Svcs:* info, ref *Stock:* bks/500-600; audios/c20 *Classn:* own *Staff: Other Prof:* 3

S750 ✚

Severn NHS Trust, Wotton Lawn Library

Wotton Lawn, Horton Rd, Gloucester, GL1 3WL (01452-891518) *Email:* library@wottlawn.demon.co.uk

Chief: Libn: Ms Jackie Webb BA(Hons), DipLib, MSc, MCLIP *Dep:* Lib Asst: Ms Chris Howarth *Entry:* NHS employees *Open:* Mon-Thu 0830-1600, Fri 0930-1430 *Subj:* mental health; psychiatry *Co-op Schemes:* BLDSC, PLCS, SWRLIN *Equip:* copier, 2 computers (both with wd-proc & internet, 1 with CD-ROM) *Svcs:* info, ref *Stock:* bks/2000; periodcls/25 *Classn:* NLM *Staff: Libns:* 2 *Non-Prof:* 2

S751 🎓 🔑

The Traditions Library and Ethnic Resources Archive

16 Brunswick Sq, Gloucester, GL1 1UG (01452-415110; *fax:* 01452-503643) *Email:* peter@folktrax.freeserve.co.uk *Internet:* http://www.folktrax.org/

Chief: Dirs: Mr Peter D. Kennedy & Mrs Beryl L. Kennedy *Entry:* adv appt *Subj:* worldwide: traditions; anthro; ethnomusicology; Gaelic lang; Welsh lang; Cornish lang; Gammon lang; Norman-French dialect; lowland Scots dialect; Norn dialect; instrumental & vocal music; balladry; storytelling *Collns: Bks & Pamphs:* children's lore; folk music; mummers; customs; dialect *Archvs:* relating to: folk music; dialect & customs of Britain & internatl; ch's games; Travellers' traditions *Other:* oral traditions colln *Equip:* fax, 2 video viewers, copier, clr copier, 2 computers (incl 1 with internet & 1 with CD-ROM), studio for hire, audio equip *Stock:* bks/3000; periodcls/200; photos/500; slides/50; illusts/50; pamphs/100; maps/40; audios/3000; videos/50 *Classn:* own *Pubns:* Folksongs of Britain & Ireland (£25); Fiddlers Tune Bks (£10) *Staff: Non-Prof:* 2 *Exp:* £1500 (1999-2000)

Godalming

S752  🎓

Barclays University Library

Bell House, Moss Ln, Godalming, Surrey, GU7 1EF (01483-704757/99; *fax:* 01483-704750) *Email:* bu.library@barclays.co.uk *Internet:* http://www.barclays-university.com/

Chief: Mgr: Mrs Alison Footitt BSc, MSc, MCLIP (alison.footitt@barclays.co.uk) *Dep:* Team Leader: Mrs Mary Page CIPD (mary.page@barclays.co.uk) *Entry:* Barclays employees only *Open:* Mon-Fri 0830-1630

Subj: mgmt; business *Equip:* video viewer, fax, copier, 3 computers (all with wd-proc, internet & CD-ROM) *Online:* Barclays Business Intelligence Gateway (on intranet) *Officer-in-Charge:* Mgr, as above *Svcs:* ref *Stock:* 9000+ bks, videos, audios & CD-ROMs *Acqs Offcr:* Mgr, as above *Classn:* own *Staff: Libns:* 1

Gosport

S753 🏛 🎓 ✚

Defence Medical Training Library

(formerly Royal Defence Medical Coll Lib)
Horton Block, Fort Blockhouse, Gosport, Hampshire, PO12 2AB (023-9276-5899; *fax:* 023-9276-5747) *Email:* interlib.loans@fbigs.mod.uk

Gov Body: Ministry of Defence (see **S1284**) *Chief:* Medical Libn: Ms Paula Younger BA(Hons), PGCE, MA (head.librarian@fbigs.mod.uk) *Dep:* Interlibrary Loans/IT Offcr: Mrs Deborah Watts & Miss Anne Buchanan (job share), email as above *Entry:* MoD staff only; other visitors must make appl in writing *Open:* Mon-Thu 0800-1630, Fri 0800-1530 *Subj:* medicine; military; allied health (mainly primary care) *Co-op Schemes:* SWRLIN ILL, HATRICS *Equip:* copier, video viewer, 8 computers (incl 4 with wd-proc, 4 with internet & 1 with CD-ROM) *Online:* Dialog (via Libn, MoD staff only) *Stock:* bks/9000; periodcls/150; slides/200; videos/450; CD-ROMs/100 *Acqs Offcr:* Medical Libn, as above *Classn:* NLM *Auto Sys:* Heritage *Pubns:* internal pubns only *Staff: Libns:* 1 *Non-Prof:* 1.5 *Exp:* £30000 (1999-2000); £25000 (2000-01)

S754 ✚ 🏛

Royal Hospital Haslar, Sir William Burnett Library

Haslar, Gosport, Hampshire, PO12 2AA (*tel & fax:* 023-9276-2053) *Email:* office@haslib.demon.co.uk

Gov Body: Ministry of Defence (see **S1284**) *Chief:* Libn: Mr Michael Rowe BA(Hons) *Entry:* Ministry of Defence staff only *Open:* Mon-Thu 0830-1700, Fri 0830-1630 *Subj:* medicine; military medicine *Co-op Schemes:* SWRLIN ILLs *Equip:* copier, computers (incl wd-proc, internet & CD-ROM) *Online:* Medline, Dialog (via staff) *Svcs:* info, ref, translation, lit searches *Classn:* NLM *Staff: Libns:* 2 *Non-Prof:* 1.5

S755 🎓 🏛

Royal Navy School of Marine and Air Engineering, HMS Sultan Library

HMS Sultan, Military Rd, Gosport, Hampshire, PO12 3BY (023-9254-2678; *fax:* 023-9254-2555) *Email:* sultanlibrary@gtnet.gov.uk

Gov Body: Ministry of Defence (Navy) *Chief:* Libn: Mr J.R.C. Quibell BA, MCLIP *Assoc Libs:* all other Ministry of Defence Libs *Entry:* adv appt *Open:* Mon-Thu 0815-1645, Fri 0815-1615 *Subj:* sci; maths; tech; marine eng; aerospace eng *Collns: Bks & Pamphs:* hist of naval eng *Archvs:* historical archvs of Royal Naval Eng Branch *Co-op Schemes:* BLDSC

☛

Gosport
▼
Guildford

Special Libraries

(RN School of Marine & Air Eng cont)
Equip: 2 m-readers, m-printer, 5 computers (incl 4 wd-proc, 1 internet & 4 CD-ROM) **Svcs:** info, ref, biblio
Stock: bks/30000; periodcls/70; m-forms/2000; videos/200
Classn: DDC **Auto Sys:** Heritage
Staff: Libns: 1 Non-Prof: 1

Grange over Sands

S756

Centre for Ecology and Hydrology, Merlewood Library
Windermere Rd, Grange over Sands, Cumbria, LA11 6JU (01539-532264)
Internet: http://library.ceh.ac.uk/

Gov Body: Nat Environment Rsrch Council (NERC); part of CEH Lib Svcs (see **S1786**) **Chief:** Libn: Ms Celia Cook (ccc@ceh.ac.uk) **Dep:** Ms Jeanette Coward (jcowa@ceh.ac.uk)
Entry: external visitors by adv appt **Open:** Mon-Fri 0900-1630
Subj: land use; environmental change; analytical chem; botany; mycology; soil ecology; radio-ecology; environmental effects of radiation **Collns:** **Archvs:** archv of pubns produced by staff of Nature Conservancy & former Inst of Terrestrial Ecology
Stock: bks/c5000; periodcls/300
Auto Sys: Unicorn

Grantham

S757 ✚

Grantham and District Hospital, Staff Library
101 Manthorpe Rd, Grantham, Lincolnshire, NG31 8DG (01476-565232 x4321; *fax:* 01476-590441)
Internet: http://www.hello.nhs.uk/

Gov Body: United Lincolnshire Hosps NHS Trust
Chief: Asst Libn: Mrs S.M. Stevens BA, MA, DipLib, MCLIP
Assoc Libs: LINCOLN COUNTY HOSP, PROF LIB (see **S954**); LOUTH COUNTY HOSP MEDICAL LIB (see **S1486**); PILGRIM HOSP LIB (see **S204**)
Entry: ref only, by prior appt **Open:** Mon-Fri 0900-1700
Subj: psy; social sci; tech; health; welfare; medicine; nursing; psychiatry; mgmt; statistics
Equip: copier, computers **Svcs:** info, ref, biblio
Stock: bks/c6000; periodcls/100
Classn: DDC
Staff: Libns: 1 PT Non-Prof: 1 FT, 3 PT

Grays

S758

Thurrock and Basildon College, Learning Resource Centre
(formed by the merger of Thurrock Coll & Basildon Coll)
Woodview Campus, Grays, Essex, RM16 2YR (01375-362691; *fax:* 01375-373356)
Email: lawrence.barker@tab.ac.uk
Internet: http://www.tab.ac.uk/

Gov Body: The Corp of Thurrock & Basildon Coll
Chief: Learning Resources Mgr: Mr Lawrence A. Barker BA(Hons), PGCE, DipLib, DMS
Assoc Libs: NETHERMAYNE CAMPUS LRC, Nethermayne, Basildon, Essex, SS16 5NN (01268-461614)
Entry: apply to Learning Resources Mgr if not a coll memb **Open:** term: Mon-Thu 0845-1900, Fri 0845-1600; vac: Mon-Thu 0900-1700, Fri 0900-1600 (Nethermayne Campus closed Aug)
Subj: all subjs; GCSE; A level; vocational **Co-op Schemes:** Essex Libs (ELAN)
Equip: video viewer, 2 copiers (4p per copy), 30 computers (all with internet, coll membs only)
Online: Infotrac Onefile, OCLC FirstSearch (coll membs only)
Stock: bks/30000; periodcls/170; slides/21000
Classn: DDC **Auto Sys:** Olib
Staff: Libns: 1 Non-Prof: 9 **Exp:** £100000 (2000-01)

Great Grimsby

S759

National Fisheries Research Centre
c/o Natl Fishing Heritage Centre, Alexandra Dock, Great Grimsby, NE Lincolnshire, DN32 1UZ (01472-323345; *fax:* 01472-323555)
Email: craig.lazenby@nelincs.gov.uk

Gov Body: North East Lincolnshire Council (see **P125**) **Chief:** Museums Historian: Dr Craig Lazenby BA, PhD **Dep:** Rsrch Asst: Mr Roy Roberts
Entry: ref only **Open:** Mon-Fri 0900-1700
Subj: hist of UK fisheries & dependent comm-unities **Collns:** **Archvs:** current holdings incl: Mission to Seamen Archvs; Royal Natl Mission to Deep Sea Fishermen Archvs **Other:** Natl Fisheries Sound Archv
Equip: m-reader, fax, video viewer, copier, computers (incl wd-proc & CD-ROM) **Svcs:** ref
Stock: bks/12000; periodcls/3; photos/26000; slides/600; pamphs/4000; maps/300; audios/300; videos/90; CD-ROMs/45
Classn: DDC
Pubns: Deep Sea Voices: The Role of Women in Our Distant Water Fishing Communities, by Craig & Jenny Lazenby (Tempus, £9.99)
Staff: Libns: 1 Other Prof: 1 Non-Prof: 2

Great Malvern

S760

QinetiQ, Malvern Library and Information Centre
(formerly Defence Evaluation & Rsrch Agency, Malvern Lib)
St Andrews Rd, Great Malvern, Worcestershire, WR14 3PS (01684-894969; *fax:* 01684-894148)
Email: malvernic@qinetiq.com

Gov Body: QinetiQ Info Resources **Chief:** Info Specialist: Ms Carol Minter MCLIP (cminter@qinetiq.com)
Entry: official policy is that only Qinetiq staff have access; special arrangements may be made to loan documents to other libs
Subj: maths; programming; tech; electronics; radar; electro-optics; signal processing; microwaves **Co-op Schemes:** BLDSC
Stock: bks/40000; periodcls/300 **Acqs Offcr:** Info Specialist, as above
Classn: UDC **Auto Sys:** Unicorn/Sirsi
Staff: Libns: 3 Other Prof: 3 Non-Prof: 4

Great Yarmouth

S761 ✚

Sir James Paget Library
James Paget Healthcare NHS Trust, Lowestoft Rd, Gorleston, Great Yarmouth, Norfolk, NR31 6LA (01493-452811; *fax:* 01493-452878)
Email: chris.thompson@jpaget.nhs.uk

Gov Body: James Paget Healthcare NHS Trust
Chief: Lib Mgr: Mrs Christine Thompson CertEd, MCLIP **Dep:** Asst Libn: D. Reade
Assoc Libs: NORTHGATE HOSP LIB (psychiatric), Gt Yarmouth (also administered by Mrs Thompson)
Entry: staff only **Open:** Mon, Wed-Thu 0800-1730, Tue 0800-1930, Fri 0800-1700, Sat 0900-1400
Subj: medicine; nursing **Co-op Schemes:** BLDSC, ANGLES, East Anglian Medical Libs, East Anglian Health Care Libs, SCOLIS
Equip: fax, copier, computers (incl wd-proc & internet) **Online:** Medline, CINAHL, AMED, Cochrane, eBNF **Svcs:** info, ref, biblio, indexing, abstracting, translation
Stock: bks/7000; periodcls/120
Classn: NLM **Staff:** Libns: 1 Non-Prof: 4

Greenhithe

S762

LaFarge Cement UK, Quality Support Laboratory Library
(formerly Blue Circle Industries, Technical Centre Lib)
305 London Rd, Greenhithe, Kent, DA9 9JQ (01322-382244; *fax:* 01322-382266)
Email: ian.bailey@lafargecement.co.uk

Gov Body: Blue Circle Industries plc **Chief:** Technical Administrator: Mr Ian Bailey MSc, FRMets, MCLIP
Entry: adv appt **Open:** Mon-Fri 1000-1600
Subj: cement manufacture; tech **Co-op Schemes:** BLDSC, British Cement Assoc
Equip: m-reader, m-form printer/digitiser, copier, computer (with CD-ROM)
Stock: bks/500; periodcls/100; pamphs/20000; maps/100; m-forms/1000
Classn: UDC **Auto Sys:** CAIRS
Staff: Libns: 1 **Exp:** £50000 (2000-01)

Greenock

S763 ✚

Inverclyde Royal Hospital, Robert Lamb Library
Larkfield Rd, Greenock, Renfrewshire, PA16 0XN (01475-656011; *fax:* 01475-635810)
Email: mhwright@irh.scot.nhs.uk

Gov Body: Argyll & Clyde Acute Hosps NHS Trust
Chief: Lib Svcs Mgr: Mrs M.H. Wright
Entry: open to all Acute Trust staff; others by arrangement **Open:** Mon-Thu 0830-1700, Fri 0830-1630; extended access with security card (£5) 0800-2300 daily, incl weekends & hols
Subj: medicine; surgery; nursing; paramedicine; health svc mgmt **Co-op Schemes:** BLDSC, SHINE
Equip: m-reader, 4 video viewers, fax (costs vary), 2 copiers (7p or 10p per page), 14 computers (all with internet, 12 with wd-proc & 12 with CD-ROM), 4 rooms for hire **Online:** via NHS Scotland e-Lib: Medline, CINAHL, Embase, PsycInfo, BNI, AHMED, EBM Reviews, Sports Discus, Wilson Social Sciences Abstracts **Officer-in-Charge:** Lib Svcs Mgr, as above **Svcs:** info, ref, biblio, lending, lit searching, current awareness, user edu

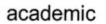 

Stock: bks/c6500; periodcls/123; slides/c400; audios/17; videos/96; CD-ROMs/50 *Acqs Offcr:* Lib Svcs Mgr, as above
Classn: DDC *Auto Sys:* CALM
Pubns: Lib Guide; Periodicals List; Database Searching Guide
Staff: Other Prof: 1 *Non-Prof:* 1.5 *Exp:* £32842 (1999-2000); £44000 (2000-01); figs incl stock, stationery, subscriptions & equip

S764
James Watt College of Further and Higher Education Library
Finnart Campus, Finnart St, Greenock, Renfrewshire, PA16 8HF (01475-724433; *fax:* 01475-888079)
Email: almc@jameswatt.ac.uk
Internet: http://www.jameswatt.ac.uk/

Gov Body: Board of Mgmt *Chief:* Tutor Libn: Mr Alistair McIntyre BSc, DipLib, MCLIP
Assoc Libs: NORTH AYRSHIRE CAMPUS LIB, Lauchlan Way, Kilwinning, Ayrshire, KA13 6DE, Librarian-in-Charge: Ms Catriona Fisher MA(Hons), DipLib; WATERFRONT CAMPUS LIB, Custom House Way, Greenock, Renfrewshire, PA15 1EN, Lib Assistant-in-Charge: Ms Catherine McGrory; LARGS CAMPUS LIB, Scottish School of Sport, Burnside Rd, Largs, Ayrshire, KA30 8RW, Officers-in-Charge: Ms Helen Fulton & Ms Denise Butler
Entry: staff & registered students; others by appt only *Open:* term: Mon, Wed, Fri 0850-1650, Tue, Thu 0850-2000; vac: Mon-Fri 0850-1650
Subj: all subjs; SQA level; undergrad *Collns: Bks & Pamphs:* some material on James Watt *Archvs:* some material relating to hist of Coll *Co-op Schemes:* BLDSC
Equip: 8 video viewers, 4 copiers (10p per pg), 50 computers (incl 42 with wd-proc & 45 with internet & CD-ROM) *Svcs:* info, ref, biblio, IT support
Stock: bks/45000; periodcls/350; slides/600; pamphs/5000; maps/500; audios/300; videos/800; CD-ROMs/160
Classn: DDC *Auto Sys:* Custom Software Systems
Staff: Libns: 2 *Non-Prof:* 7 *Exp:* £80000 (1999-2000); £160000 (2000-01); incl all stock, equip & supplies; fig for 2000-01 also incl £80000 for establishment of new lib at Kilwinning

Grimsby

S765
Diana Princess of Wales Hospital, Trust Library
Scartho Rd, Grimsby, NE Lincolnshire, DN33 2BA (01472-874111 x7706; *fax:* 01452-875329)
Email: pgrecp@nlg.nhs.uk

Chief: Lib Mgr: Mrs Jo Thomas MSc (Jo.Thomas@nlg.nhs.uk)
Entry: membs only *Open:* Mon-Tue 0830-1700, Wed-Thu 0830-2000, Fri 0830-1630, alternate Sats 1000-1300
Subj: medicine; nursing; healthcare; social sci
Co-op Schemes: BLDSC, NULJ
Equip: video viewer, copier (5p per sheet), 6 computers (all with internet & CD-ROM) *Online:* selection of OVID BioMed databases & online journals *Officer-in-Charge:* Lib Mgr, as above
Svcs: info, ref, biblio
Stock: bks/6000; periodcls/155; videos/16; 80 tape/slides *Acqs Offcr:* Lib Mgr, as above
Classn: NLM *Auto Sys:* Heritage
Staff: Libns: 1.4 *Non-Prof:* 1.2

S766
Grimsby College Library
Nuns Corner, Laceby Rd, Grimsby, NE Lincoln-shire, DN34 5BQ (01472-311213; *fax:* 01472-879924)

Chief: Coll Libn: Ms K.L. Knight BA(Hons), MA (knightkl@grimsby.ac.uk)
Assoc Libs: 3 Libs in sys: FURTHER EDU LIB & HIGHER EDU LIB, both on main campus (as above); ART & DESIGN LIB, Westward Ho, Grimsby
Entry: ref only *Open:* term: Mon, Wed-Thu 0845-1945, Tue 1000-1945, Fri 0845-1700, Sat 0900-1200 (HE Lib only); vac: Mon-Thu 0900-1700, Fri 0900-1630
Subj: all subjs *Collns: Other:* collns of periodcl articles arranged by topic to support a variety of degree & HND courses *Co-op Schemes:* BLDSC, LISN, GRIP
Equip: 2 video viewers, 3 copiers (5p), clr copier (45p), 65 computers (all with wd-proc, internet & CD-ROM) *Disabled:* Kurzweil, braille printer etc in Visually Impaired Unit *Online:* various databases (Lib membs only) *Officer-in-Charge:* Coll Libn, as above & Computer Svcs Mgr: Mr B. Clarkson
Stock: bks/70000; periodcls/120, plus 5000 e-journals; slides/6000; videos/1000 *Acqs Offcr:* Acqs Libn: Mrs D. Hediger
Classn: DDC *Auto Sys:* Heritage
Staff: Libns: 2 *Other Prof:* 1 *Non-Prof:* 11 *Exp:* £84500 (1999-2000); £74685 (2000-01); exp on stock & online resources

Guildford

S767
The Associated Examining Board, Library
Stag Hill House, Guildford, Surrey, GU2 7XJ (01483-506506; *fax:* 01483-300152)
Internet: http://www.aeb.org.uk/

Chief: Officer-in-Charge: Mrs Emma Parker
Subj: GCE & GCSE subjs
Equip: copier, computers (incl wd-proc, internet & CD-ROM) *Svcs:* info, ref, biblio
Stock: bks/6000

S768
Borax Europe Ltd, Library and Information Department
1a Guildford Business Pk, Guildford, Surrey, GU2 8XG (01483-242000; *fax:* 01483-242001)

Chief: Libn: C. Krishnaswamy
Subj: boron chem; industrial chem *Co-op Schemes:* RSC
Stock: bks/2500; periodcls/140; m-forms/1500; CD-ROMs/20; theses/65; films/300

S769
College of Law, Guildford Library
Braboeuf Manor, St Catherine's, Portsmouth Rd, Guildford, Surrey, GU3 1HA (01483-460317; *fax:* 01483-460305)
Internet: http://www.college-of-law.co.uk/

Gov Body: Coll of Law *Chief:* Branch Libn: Ms Mary Draffin BA(Hons), DipLib, MCLIP (mary.draffin@lawcol.co.uk) *Dep:* Asst Libn: Ms Catherine Hammond BSc(Hons), MSc (catherine.hammond@lawcol.co.uk)
Assoc Libs: BIRMINGHAM LIB (see **S168**); CHESTER LIB (see **S458**); LONDON LIB (see **S1090**); YORK LIB (see **S2161**)
Entry: only open to certain categories of external user; tel for appt *Open:* term: Mon-Fri 0830-2100, Sat-Sun 1200-1700; vac: Mon-Fri 0900-1700
Subj: law
Equip: 3 copiers (5p per sheet), 48 computers (all with wd-proc, internet & CD-ROM) *Disabled:* CCTV Aladdin Genie Pro for visually impaired
Svcs: info, ref
Stock: bks/60000; periodcls/218; videos/300; CD-ROMs/23

Classn: local *Auto Sys:* Heritage
Staff: Libns: 2 *Non-Prof:* 1 FT, 2 PT *Exp:* £126000 (1999-2000)

S770
Guildford College of Further and Higher Education, Learning Resource Centre
Stoke Pk, Guildford, Surrey, GU1 1EZ (01483-448611; *fax:* 01483-448606)
Email: library@guildford.ac.uk
Internet: http://www.guildford.ac.uk/library/welcome.htm

Chief: Coll Libn: Ms Diana Marshall MEd, MCLIP
Dep: Dep Coll Libn: Ms Carolyn Wheeler MA, MCLIP
Open: term: Mon-Thu 0830-2000, Fri 0830-1700, Sat 1000-1300; vac: Mon-Fri 1000-1630
Subj: all subjs; genl; GCSE; A level; undergrad; construction; catering; tourism; hairdressing *Co-op Schemes:* BLDSC, SASLIC
Equip: 3 video viewers, 2 copiers, clr copier, 57 computers (all with internet & 2 with CD-ROM), 4 rooms for hire *Svcs:* info, ref
Stock: bks/35000; periodcls/300; audios/450; videos/800
Classn: DDC *Auto Sys:* Heritage IV
Staff: Libns: 4 *Non-Prof:* 6 *Exp:* £60000 (1999-2000)

S771
The Guildford Institute of The University of Surrey Library
Ward St, Guildford, Surrey, GU1 4LH (01483-562142; *fax:* 01483-451034)
Email: guildford-institute@surrey.ac.uk

Gov Body: Univ of Surrey (see **S776**) & membership *Chief:* Libn: Mrs Anne Milton-Worssell BA(Hons), MCLIP
Entry: ref only, unless a memb *Open:* Tue-Fri 1000-1500; other times by appt with the Libn
Subj: all subjs at public lib level; lit; travel; biography; local studies (Surrey) *Collns: Bks & Pamphs:* Victorian lit; Illustrated London News (from 1843); bnd vols of Punch *Archvs:* many prints & photos relating to Guildford & surrounding area *Co-op Schemes:* AIL
Equip: copier, computer *Svcs:* info, ref
Stock: bks/13000; photos/3000+; illusts/8000+
Classn: DDC *Auto Sys:* Oracle
Pubns: The Keep (termly, £1 per issue)
Staff: Libns: 1

S772
Merrist Wood College, Learning Resource Centre
Worplesdon, Guildford, Surrey, GU3 3PE (01483-884022; *fax:* 01483-884021)
Email: mtarron@merristwood.ac.uk
Internet: http://www.merristwood.ac.uk/

Chief: LRC Team Leader: Mrs Miriam Tarron BA, DipLIS
Open: term: Mon-Thu 0830-2000, Fri 0830-1700, Sat 1200-1500; vac: Mon-Fri 0930-1600; closed for extended Xmas & Easter
Subj: conservation; botany; ecology; agric; hortic; landscaping & garden design; golf studies; equine studies; small animal care; arboriculture; floristry; greenkeeping *Collns: Bks & Pamphs:* agric, hortic & forestry historical colln *Co-op Schemes:* BLDSC, UPDATE
Equip: 5 video viewers, copier, fax, 17 computers (all with wd-proc & internet, 1 with CD-ROM), scanner *Online:* Update, Zetoc, Ingenta *Officer-in-Charge:* LRC Team Leader, as above

Special Libraries

Guildford
▼
Harrow

(Merrist Wood College LRC cont)
Stock: bks/21000; periodcls/170; slides/168 sets; maps/110; videos/420; CD-ROMs/20 **Acqs Offcr:** LRC Team Leader, as above
Classn: DDC **Auto Sys:** Heritage
Staff: Libns: 1 Non-Prof: 4 **Exp:** £17000 on lib stock, with £6500 on AVs (2000-01)

S773 🎓
Royal Grammar School, The Chained Library
High St, Guildford, Surrey, GU1 3BB (01483-880608; *fax:* 01483-306127)
Email: bwright@mail.rgs-guildford.ac.uk

Chief: Headmaster's Sec: Ms Barbara M. Wright
Entry: adv appt (limited to school hols), ref only
Open: by appt, mostly during school hols
Collns: Bks & Pamphs: mainly the Parkhurst Bequest of 1573: Reformation theological texts in Latin, incl works by Brentius, Bullinger, Calvin, Zwingli; additions up to 18C
Stock: bks/400
Exp: historical lib; no exp on stock; some exp on maintenance & conservation

S774 ✚
Royal Surrey County Hospital, Education Centre Library
Egerton Rd, Guildford, Surrey, GU2 7XX (01483-464137; *fax:* 01483-576240)
Email: jonathan.hutchins@royalsurrey.nhs.uk
Internet: http://www.royalsurreylibrary.org.uk/

Gov Body: Royal Surrey County Hosp **Chief:** Dist Libn: Mr Jonathan V.P. Hutchins MA, DipLib, MCLIP **Dep:** Asst Libn: post vacant
Assoc Libs: WEST SURREY HEALTH AUTHORITY LIB, The Ridgewood Centre, Old Bisley Rd, Frimley, Camberley, Surrey, GU16 5QE
Entry: all facilities open to NHS staff working within West Surrey Dist; others ref only or external membership **Open:** Mon-Thu 0900-2000, Fri 0900-1700
Subj: medicine; nursing; NHS mgmt **Co-op Schemes:** STLIS, BLDSC, NULJ
Equip: copier, computer (incl internet & CD-ROM)
Online: Medline on CD-ROM, Datastar (no fees to bona fide users)
Stock: bks/8000; periodcls/200; videos/20
Classn: NLM **Auto Sys:** InMagic
Staff: Libns: 2 Non-Prof: 2

S775 🗝
Surrey Archaeological Society, Library and Archive
Castle Arch, Guildford, Surrey, GU1 3SX (01483-532454; *fax:* 01483-532454)
Email: surreyarch@compuserve.com
Internet: http://surreyarchaeology.org.uk/

Chief: Hon Libn: Miss G.M. Drew BA, MCLIP
Dep: Asst Libn: Mrs S.K. Ashcroft MCLIP
Entry: adv appt for non-membs or for membs wishing to consult rsrch material **Open:** Mon, Wed 0930-1630, Tue 0930-1330, first Sat in month 0930-1330; membs may use lib at any time Mon-Sat 0900-1700

Subj: Surrey: archaeo; local hist; industrial archaeo; domestic & ecclesiastical arch; genealogy
Collns: Archvs: soc archvs Other: maps; drawings/prints; glass plates **Co-op Schemes:** BLDSC
Equip: m-reader, fax, copier, computer network
Stock: bks/9000; periodcls/92; slides/150; pamphs/1400; maps/2500
Classn: Inst of Archaeo (mod)
Pubns: Surrey Archaeological Soc Collns (free to membs, prices vary for non-membs); Rsrch Vols I-II (prices vary); The Archaeo of Surrey to 1540 (£10); Early Medieval Surrey (£10); Hidden Depths (£12.95); Shere (£5)
Staff: Libns: 1
Proj: computerisation of rsrch colln under way
See also **O396**

S776 🎓
University of Surrey, University Library
Guildford, Surrey, GU2 7XH (01483-689232 (library office); *fax:* 01483-689500)
Email: library-enquiries@surrey.ac.uk
Internet: http://www.surrey.ac.uk/library/

Gov Body: Univ of Surrey **Chief:** Dir of Info Svcs & Libn: Mr T.J.A. Crawshaw BEng, DipLIS **Dep:** Head of Lib Svcs: Mr Robert B. Hall BA, MA, MCLIP (R.Hall@surrey.ac.uk) **Other Snr Staff:** Dep Head of Lib Svcs & Academic Svcs Mgr: Mrs Jennifer A. Nordon MSc, MCLIP; Resources Mgr: Mrs Kirsty S. Green BSc, DipLib; Public Svcs & Systems Mgr: Ms Jennifer J. Treherne BA
Entry: ref only; borrowing rights for a fee **Open:** semester: Mon 1000-2200, Tue-Fri 0900-2200, Sat 1300-1800, Sun 1400-1800; out of semester: Mon-Fri 0900-2000, Sat 1300-1800
Subj: undergrad; postgrad; phil; psy; social sci; sociology; econ; edu; law; lang (French, German, Russian, Swedish, Spanish); linguistics; sci; maths; physics; chem; life scis; tech; eng; mgmt; tourism; hospitality; nursing; music; dance; lit; hist **Collns:** Bks & Pamphs: EDC; statistics; Goodale Colln (cinema) Archvs: Univ of Surrey & Battersea Polytechnic archvs Other: Natl Resource Centre for Dance (archvs & info svcs); E.H. Shepard Archv (original drawings & letters); BSI **Co-op Schemes:** BLDSC, SASLIC, SCONUL, UK Libs Plus, M25 Consortium
Equip: 4 m-readers, m-printer, 4 video viewers, 14 copiers, 60 Univ networked computer terminals, 25 catalogue terminals, 6 public access internet computers (no fee) **Online:** Dialog, Datastar, Lexis
Stock: bks/403000, incl bnd periodcls; periodcls/c7000 (print & elec); maps/200; m-forms/9000; AVs/930 audios & videos; Special Collns/2300 items
Classn: DDC **Auto Sys:** Talis
Pubns: various genl & subj guides (free); Articles in Hospitality & Tourism (jointly with Oxford Brookes Univ)
Staff: Libns: 14.7 Non-Prof: 36 **Exp:** £1091640 (1999-2000); £1135994 (2000-01)

Halesowen

S777 🎓
Halesowen College Library and Learning Centre
Whittingham Rd, Halesowen, W Midlands, B63 3NA (0121-602-7777; *fax:* 0121-585-0369)
Email: info@halesowen.ac.uk
Internet: http://www.halesowen.ac.uk/

Gov Body: Halesowen Coll Corp **Chief:** Lib Svcs Mgr: Miss Deborah Adams BA(Hons) (dadams@halesowen.ac.uk) **Dep:** Learning Svcs Mgr: Mr Adam Bailey BA(Hons) (abailey@halesowen.ac.uk) **Other Snr Staff:** Snr Lib Asst: Ms Averil Pearson (apearson@halesowen.ac.uk)

Entry: open to Coll students with valid ID card throughout year; ref only to genl public **Open:** term (Sep-Jun): Mon-Thu 0830-1930, Fri 0830-1600, Sat 0930-1230; vacs (Jul-Aug): Mon-Fri 0900-1700
Subj: all subjs; genl; GCSE; A level; undergrad; vocational **Co-op Schemes:** BLDSC
Equip: m-reader, copier, 50 computers (all with wd-proc, internet & CD-ROM) **Online:** Infotrac Onefile (online full-text newspaper & journal) **Svcs:** info, ref
Stock: bks/28000; periodcls/130; slides/3000; pamphs/2800; videos/700; CD-ROMs/45 **Acqs Offcr:** Lib Svcs Mgr, as above
Classn: DDC **Auto Sys:** Olib
Staff: Libns: 1 Other Prof: 1 Non-Prof: 7 **Exp:** £32000 (2000-01)
Proj: development of curriculum-based resource centres where students can access both print & elec resources

Halifax

S778 ✚
Calderdale and Huddersfield NHS Trust, Library and Information Service
Learning & Development Centre, The Calderdale Royal Hosp, Godfrey Rd, Halifax, W Yorkshire, HX3 0PW (01422-224191; *fax:* 01422-224185)
Email: library@calderdale.nhs.uk

Gov Body: Calderdale & Huddersfield NHS Trust **Chief:** Libns: Ms Helen Curtis BA, MCLIP & Mrs Chris Jackson BA, MCLIP (job-share) **Other Snr Staff:** Lib Assts: Ms Pam Whippey & Ms Viv Benbow-Browne
Entry: Trust employees only; paid membership available for other users **Open:** Mon-Thu 0830-1700, Fri 0830-1630, Sat 0830-1300
Subj: medicine (multidisciplinary); health **Collns:** Other: small video colln **Co-op Schemes:** BLDSC
Equip: video viewer, copier, computers (incl wd-proc, internet & CD-ROM), scanner, CD copier
Online: AMED, BNI, CareData, CINAHL, EBMR, Cochrane, HMIC, HSWE, Martindale, BNF, Medline, PEDro, PsycInfo
Stock: bks/6000+; periodcls/150+
Classn: NLM (Wessex) **Auto Sys:** Heritage IV
Staff: Libns: 1.9 Non-Prof: 2

S779 🎓
Calderdale Colleges Corporation, Campus Library and Learning Centre
Francis St, Halifax, W Yorkshire, HX1 3UZ (01422-399312; *fax:* 01422-399320)
Email: kenp@calderdale.ac.uk
Internet: http://www.calderdale.ac.uk/

Gov Body: Calderdale Colls Corp **Chief:** Resource-Based Learning Mgr: Mr Kenneth Poole MA(Lib) **Dep:** Mrs Alison Harling LLB(Hons), MSc
Entry: ref only by agreement **Open:** term: Mon-Thu 0845-2045, Fri 0845-1800; vac: Mon-Fri 0900-1600
Subj: all subjs; genl; GCSE; A level; undergrad; vocational **Co-op Schemes:** BLDSC
Equip: video viewer, copier, 45 computers (all with wd-proc & internet, 19 with CD-ROM) **Disabled:** Kurzweil, 2 Trackballs, 1 joystick, braille printer, JAWS, ZoomText **Svcs:** info, ref
Stock: bks/40000+; periodcls/100; pamphs/2500; audios/100; videos/2000
Classn: DDC **Auto Sys:** Heritage
Pubns: CLLC Guide (free)
Staff: Libns: 6 Other Prof: 9

Hamilton

S780 🎓
Bell College of Technology, Hamilton Campus Library
Almada St, Hamilton, Lanarkshire, ML3 0JB (01698-894424; *fax:* 01698-286856) *Internet:* http://www.bell.ac.uk/bell2000nav/library/

Chief: Coll Libn: Ms Barbara Catt (b.catt@bell.ac.uk) *Dep:* Depute Libn: Mr John Burke (j.burke@bell.ac.uk)
Assoc Libs: DUMFRIES CAMPUS LIB (see **S550**)
Entry: ref only for genl public; external visitors may borrow at cost of £15 pa *Open:* term: Mon-Thu 0830-2100, Fri 0830-1630, Sat 0900-1300; vac: Mon, Thu-Fri 0830-1630, Tue-Wed 0830-1900
Subj: all subjs; undergrad; postgrad; vocational; tech; sci; eng; sci; environment; mgmt; business
Co-op Schemes: ILL
Equip: copiers, computers (incl internet) *Online:* ASSIA, BHI, BIDS, Emerald, Ingenta, Cochrane, CINAHL, OVID, Zetoc & others *Svcs:* info, ref, enq svc, BECTIS (Coll industrial info svc)
Stock: all items/90000
Classn: DDC *Auto Sys:* Dynix *Staff:* 15 in total

S781 ✚
Lanarkshire Health Board, James B.P. Ferguson Library
14 Beckford St, Hamilton, Lanarkshire, ML3 0TA (01698-281313; *fax:* 01698-423134)
Email: malcolm.dobson@lanarkshirehb.scot.nhs.uk

Gov Body: Lanarkshire Health Board *Chief:* Libn: Mr Malcolm Dobson MCLIP
Entry: Health Board staff only, not open to public
Subj: health svc mgmt; medicine *Co-op Schemes:* SHINE
Equip: computer (with internet & CD-ROM)
Online: BLAISE, Datastar *Svcs:* info, ref, biblio
Stock: bks/c1500, incl pamphs; periodcls/90; CD-ROMs/10
Classn: DDC *Auto Sys:* Adlib *Staff:* Libns: 0.6

Harefield

S782 ✚
Harefield Hospital Library
Harefield Hosp, Hill End Rd, Harefield, Middlesex, UB9 6JH (01895-828947; *fax:* 01895-828993)
Email: deptlibraryharefield@rbh.nthames.nhs.uk

Gov Body: Royal Brompton & Harefield NHS Trust
Chief: Lib Mgr: Ms Michelle Hutton
Assoc Libs: NATL HEART & LUNG INST LIB (see **S1181**)
Entry: Trust staff; ref only for visitors *Open:* Mon-Fri 0900-1700
Subj: medicine; nursing; surgery; cardiology; cardiothoracic medicine; respiratory medicine
Equip: copier, computers (incl wd-proc & internet)
Online: Medline, CINAHL, BNI, Cochrane, AMED, PsycInfo, Embase, Web of Science
Stock: bks/several 1000; periodcls/120

Harlow

S783 🎓
Harlow College Library
Velizy Ave, Town Centre, Harlow, Essex, CM20 3LH (01279-868000; *fax:* 01279-868260)

Chief: Coll Libn: Mr David Monk BA(Hons), MA, MCLIP
Entry: ref only for non-Harlow Coll students
Open: term: Mon-Thu 0845-2000, Fri 0845-1700; vac: Mon-Fri 0900-1630

Subj: all subjs; genl; GCSE; A level; undergrad; vocational *Co-op Schemes:* Essex ILL Scheme
Equip: video viewer, copier (A4/5p), clr copier (A4/£1), 8 computers (all with wd-proc, internet & CD-ROM) *Online:* virtual learning environment
Stock: bks/40000; periodcls/200; audios/300; videos/500; CD-ROMs/50
Classn: DDC *Auto Sys:* Olib
Pubns: User Survey Report 1996 (£15)
Staff: Libns: 2 *Other Prof:* 1 *Non-Prof:* 5 *Exp:* £35000 (1999-2000)
Proj: new LRC completed Jul 2003

S784 📷
Merck Sharp and Dohme Research Laboratories, Research Library
Neuroscience Rsrch Centre, Terlings Pk, Eastwick Rd, Harlow, Essex, CM20 2QR (01279-440131; *fax:* 01279-440667)

Chief: Libn: Mrs J. Bilson BA, MCLIP & Mrs J. Chambers BA(Hons), MCLIP (job-share) *Dep:* Ms Emma Wood BA(Hons)
Entry: company employees only *Open:* Mon-Fri 0845-1700
Subj: undergrad; postgrad; organic chem; biochem; pharmacology; central nervous sys
Equip: m-reader, 2 copiers, 2 computers (incl CD-ROM) *Online:* Dialog, Datastar
Stock: bks/2500; periodcls/220
Classn: NLM, LC *Auto Sys:* Horizon Epixtech
Staff: Libns: 2

S785 ✚
Princess Alexandra Hospital NHS Trust Medical Library
Parndon Hall, Hamstel Rd, Harlow, Essex, CM20 1QX (01279-827021; *fax:* 01279-445101)
Email: lib.desk@pah.nhs.uk

Gov Body: Princess Alexandra Hosp NHS Trust
Chief: Libn: Mrs Jane Leary BSc, DipIS, MCLIP
Entry: Trust & other local NHS staff; health profs & others by arrangement *Open:* Mon-Thu 0900-1730, Fri 0900-1700
Subj: medicine; nursing; allied healthcare; health policy; health mgmt *Co-op Schemes:* BLDSC, BMA, EULOS
Equip: fax, copier (5p per pg), computers (incl wd-proc, internet & CD-ROM) *Svcs:* info, ref, lit searches, training, current awareness, document delivery
Stock: bks/4000; periodcls/172; pamphs/1000
Classn: NLM *Staff:* Libns: 3 *Non-Prof:* 6

Harpenden

S786 🏛
Rothamsted Research Library
(formerly Inst of Arable Crops Rsrch, Rothamsted Experimental Station)
Rothamsted, Harpenden, Hertfordshire, AL5 2JQ (01582-763133; *fax:* 01582-760891)
Email: liz.allsopp@bbsrc.ac.uk
Internet: http://www.res.bbsrc.ac.uk/

Gov Body: BBSRC *Chief:* Inst Libn: Mrs S.E. Allsopp BA(Hons), MCLIP *Dep:* Dep Libn: Mrs A.M.R. Arnold BSc, DipIS
Assoc Libs: BROOM'S BARN LIB, Bury St Edmunds (see **S280**)
Entry: ref only by arrangement with libn *Open:* Mon-Thu 0900-1730, Fri 0900-1700
Subj: statistics; plant sci; entomology; pesticide sci; soil sci; agronomy *Collns: Bks & Pamphs:* c2500 early agric bks *Archvs:* colln relating to the early years of Rothamsted *Other:* c200 livestock prints & paintings *Co-op Schemes:* BLDSC
Equip: m-reader, m-printer, fax, copier, computer (incl CD-ROM) *Online:* Dialog (by arrangement)

Stock: bks/100000; periodcls/1500
Staff: Libns: 2.5 *Non-Prof:* 6

Harrogate

S787 🎓 ✚
University of York Health Studies, Library and Information Service
Strayside Edu Centre, Harrogate Dist Hosp, Lancaster Park Rd, Harrogate, N Yorkshire, HG2 7SX (01423-553104; *fax:* 01423-553234)
Email: hslibhg@.york.ac.uk

Gov Body: Univ of York (see **S2168**) *Chief:* Lib & Info Svc Mgr: Ms Gillian Jarrett BA(Hons) (gj7@york.ac.uk)
Entry: ref only for non-Univ & non-Trust users
Open: Mon-Thu 0830-1930, Fri 0830-1630, Sat 0930-1230
Subj: medicine; nursing; mgmt; psy; sociology
Equip: m-reader, copier, 6 computers (incl 4 with wd-proc, 5 with internet & 2 with CD-ROM) *Officer-in-Charge:* Lib & Info Svc Mgr, as above *Svcs:* info, ref
Stock: bks/6500; periodcls/120 *Acqs Offcr:* Lib & Info Svc Mgr, as above
Classn: DDC *Auto Sys:* Aleph
Staff: Libns: 1 *Non-Prof:* 1.68

Harrow

S788 🎓
Harrow School, The Vaughan Library
High St, Harrow, Middlesex, HA1 3HT (020-8872-8278; *fax:* 020-8423-3112)
Internet: http://www.harrowschool.org.uk/

Gov Body: The Keepers & Governors of Harrow School *Chief:* Libn: Mrs Margaret Knight MCLIP (mek@harrowschool.org.uk) *Dep:* Dep Libn: Mrs Elizabeth Webber (ew@harrowschool.org.uk)
Other Snr Staff: Assts: Ms Karen Storms BA & Mr Andrew Newton MA; Archivist: Mrs Rita Gibbs
Entry: adv appt *Open:* term: Mon-Fri 0830-1830, Sat 0830-1230, 1400-1700, Sun 1400-1700; vac: closed
Subj: all subjs; genl; GCSE; A level; undergrad; local studies (Harrow); phil; psy; religion; social sci; lang; sci; maths; tech; arts; lit; classics; geog; hist; travel *Collns: Bks & Pamphs:* Aldine Colln (160 vols) *Archvs:* School Archvs (from 1572); Byron MSS; Sheridan MSS; Churchill MSS *Co-op Schemes:* ILL, London Borough of Harrow Class Sector Lib Group
Equip: video viewer, copier (5p per sheet), 31 computers (all with wd-proc & internet, 1 with CD-ROM), clr printer *Online:* Grove Art, Grove Music, Economist, ECCTIS, Encyclopedia of Astronomy, Encyclopedia of Life Sciences, Oxford Reference, Scientific American *Officer-in-Charge:* Libn, as above *Svcs:* info, ref
Stock: bks/27000; periodcls/40; photos/5000; maps/250; audios/200; videos/400; CD-ROMs/20; archvs/extensive; extensive archvs & other holdings *Acqs Offcr:* Libn, as above
Classn: DDC *Auto Sys:* DS
Staff: Libns: 3 *Non-Prof:* 1 *Exp:* £20000 (1999-2000); £20000 (2000-01)
Proj: newly refurbished (Listed Grade II)

S789 ✚
John Squire Library
Northwick Park & St Mark's Hosps, Watford Rd, Harrow, Middlesex, HA1 3UJ (020-8869-3322; *fax:* 020-8869-3326)
Email: jslib@clara.net
Internet: http://www.jslib.clara.net/

(John Squire Lib cont)
Gov Body: North West London Hosps NHS Trust
Chief: Head Libn: Mr Mike Kendall BA(Hons), DipLib (mkendall@jslib.clara.net) **Dep:** Elec Info Libn: Mr Jason Curtis BSc(Hons), DipIM
Assoc Libs: CENTRAL MIDDLESEX HOSP LIB (see **S1058**)
Entry: ref only **Open:** Mon-Fri 0900-1800, Sat (in term time only) 1000-1600
Subj: medicine; clinical sci; nursing
Equip: copier (10p per copy), computers (incl 5 with CD-ROM, £1 per hr); other equip available for use of membs only **Online:** available to membs only **Officer-in-Charge:** Head Libn, as above
Stock: bks/c50000; periodcls/c290; photos/some; pamphs/750; CD-ROMs/c80 **Acqs Offcr:** Elec Info Libn, as above
Classn: NLM **Auto Sys:** DBTextworks
Staff: Libns: 4 Non-Prof: 0.5

Hartlepool

S790 ✚

University Hospital of Hartlepool, Medical Library
(formerly Hartlepool Genl Hosp Medical Lib)
Univ Hosp of Hartlepool, Holdforth Rd, Hartlepool, Cleveland, TS24 9AH (01429-266654; *fax:* 01429-522632)
Email: hartmedlib@hotmail.com

Gov Body: North Tees & Hartlepool NHS Trust
Chief: Libn: Mr Andrew Davison BA, DipLib
Other Snr Staff: Lib Assts: Miss Paula Carney & Ms Kath Chapman BA
Assoc Libs: UNIV HOSP OF NORTH TEES MEDICAL LIB (see **S1984**)
Entry: Trusts employees plus staff & students of the Univ of Teesside **Open:** Mon-Fri 0900-1700
Subj: psy; medical ethics; social sci; sociology; law; nursing; medicine; health mgmt **Co-op Schemes:** BLDSC, BMA, RCN, NULJ
Equip: fax, copier (10p per sheet), 5 computers (all with wd-proc, internet & CD-ROM)
Stock: bks/6000; periodcls/100; videos/200
Classn: DDC **Auto Sys:** Libero
Staff: Libns: 1 Non-Prof: 2

Hatfield

S791 🎓

University of Hertfordshire, Learning and Information Services
College Ln, Hatfield, Hertfordshire, AL10 9AB (01707-284678; *fax:* 01707-284666)
Email: lisadmin@herts.ac.uk
Internet: http://www.herts.ac.uk/lis/

Gov Body: Univ of Hertfordshire Board of Governors **Chief:** Dir of Learning & Info Svcs: Ms D. Martin MA, MCLIP, MCIPD **Dep:** Dep Dir: Mr D. Piper BA, MCLIP
Assoc Libs: HATFIELD CAMPUS LIB, addr as above, LIS Mgr: Ms C. Parr; HERTFORD CAMPUS LIB, Mangrove Rd, Hertford, Hertfordshire, SG13 8QF, LIS Mgr: Mr A. Wroot; ST ALBANS CAMPUS LIB, 7 Hatfield Rd, St Albans, Hertfordshire, AL1 3RS, LIS Mgr: Ms K. Thompson; WATFORD CAMPUS LIB, Aldenham Rd, Watford, Hertfordshire, WD2 8AT, LIS Mgr: Ms J. Arthur

Entry: ref only **Open:** term: Mon-Sat 0830-2300, Sun 1100-2300
Subj: all subjs; undergrad; postgrad **Co-op Schemes:** SCONUL, UK Libs Plus, M25 Consortium of Higher Edu Libs
Equip: video viewers, copiers, clr copier, computers (incl wd-proc, internet & CD-ROM) **Online:** various
Stock: bks/c500000; periodcls/c6000
Classn: DDC **Auto Sys:** Voyager
Pubns: Univ of Hertfordshire Press pubns

Havant

S792 🎓

South Downs College, Learning Resources Centre
College Rd, Havant, Hampshire, PO7 8AA (023-92797976; *fax:* 023-92797940)
Email: sreed@staff.southdowns.ac.uk
Internet: http://www.southdowns.ac.uk/

Chief: Learning Resources Mgr: Ms Sarah Reed BA(Hons), MCLIP **Dep:** Dep Learning Resources Mgr: Ms Carolyne Sheppard BA(Ed)
Entry: all students, ref only for public **Open:** term: Mon-Thu 0830-2000, Fri 0830-1800, Sat 0930-1200; vac: Mon-Fri 0845-1300
Subj: all subjs; GCSE; A level; vocational **Co-op Schemes:** HATRICS
Equip: video viewer, 2 copiers, 30+ networked computers (incl wd-proc & CD-ROM) **Online:** Internet **Svcs:** info, ref, biblio
Stock: bks/28000; periodcls/230; videos/3000
Classn: DDC **Auto Sys:** Olib
Staff: Libns: 1 Non-Prof: 9

Haverfordwest

S793 🎓

Pembrokeshire College Library
Haverfordwest, Pembrokeshire, SA61 1SZ (01437-765247; *fax:* 01437-767279)
Email: ma.thomas@pembrokeshire.ac.uk
Internet: http://www.pembrokeshire.ac.uk/

Chief: Learning Svcs Mgr: Ms Maxine Thomas BA(Hons), MLib, DipLib, PGCE **Dep:** Asst Lib Mgr: Ms Stasia Danks BEd
Open: term: Mon-Thu 0800-2000, Fri 0800-1700, Sat 0900-1600, Sun (May/Jun) 1100-1500; vac: Mon-Fri 0845-1700
Subj: all subjs; genl; GCSE; A level; undergrad; postgrad **Co-op Schemes:** BLDSC
Equip: m-reader, m-printer, video viewer, copier, clr copier, computers (incl wd-proc, internet & CD-ROM), room for hire **Svcs:** info, ref, biblio, indexing, abstracting
Stock: bks/63000; periodcls/500; videos/5000
Classn: DDC **Auto Sys:** Alice
Staff: Libns: 1 Other Prof: 3 Non-Prof: 3

S794 ✚

Withybush General Hospital, Library Services
Withybush Genl Hosp, Fishguard Rd, Haverfordwest, Pembrokeshire, SA61 2PZ (01437-773730; *fax:* 01437-773729)

Gov Body: Pembrokeshire & Derwen NHS Trust
Chief: Lib Svcs Mgr: Mrs Andrea Thomas MSc (andrea.thomas@pdt-tr.wales.nhs.uk) **Dep:** Snr Lib Asst: Miss Angela Laws (angie.laws@pdt-tr.wales.nhs.uk)
Entry: membs of Trust & students on placement; external membership for health profs by appt
Open: staffed: Mon-Thu 0900-1800, Fri 0900-1730; 24 hr access for membs of staff
Subj: medicine; psy; social sci **Collns:** Archvs: journals held as co-op scheme **Other:** video colln

Co-op Schemes: BLDSC, AWHILES, AWHL, NULJ
Equip: copier (A4/5p), 14 computers (all with wd-proc, internet & CD-ROM), clr printer **Online:** Medline, CINAHL, CancerLit, HealthStar, Cochrane, Natl Rsrch Register **Officer-in-Charge:** Lib Svcs Mgr, as above **Svcs:** info, ref, biblio
Stock: bks/7000; periodcls/80; videos/100; CD-ROMs/20 **Acqs Offcr:** Lib Svcs Mgr, as above
Classn: NLM **Auto Sys:** Voyager
Staff: Libns: 1 Non-Prof: 1

Haywards Heath

S795 ✚

Princess Royal Hospital, Health Sciences Library
Princess Royal Hosp, Lewes Rd, Haywards Heath, W Sussex, RH16 4EX (01444-441881 x4463; *fax:* 01444-443228)
Email: amanda.lackey@mid-sussex.sthames.nhs.uk
Internet: http://www.brighton-healthcare.nhs.uk/library/

Gov Body: Brighton & Sussex Univ Hosps NHS Trust **Chief:** Associate Lib Svc Mgr: Ms Amanda Lackey BA(Hons), PGCE, DMS **Dep:** Snr Lib Asst: Mrs Diane Roberts
Entry: all NHS staff **Open:** Mon 0900-1900, Tue-Fri 0900-1700
Subj: medicine; health care **Co-op Schemes:** BLDSC, HLN
Equip: copier, computers (with internet) **Online:** Medline, BNI, CINAHL, Cochrane, PsycInfo **Svcs:** info, ref, current awareness, lit searches, database & internet training
Classn: NLM **Staff:** Libns: 1 Non-Prof: 2

Hebburn

S796 🎓

South Tyneside College, Hebburn Library
Mill Ln, Hebburn, Tyne & Wear, NE31 2ER (0191-427-3614; *fax:* 0191-427-3535)
Email: pamela.robinson@stc.ac.uk

Gov Body: South Tyneside Coll **Chief:** Libn: Mrs Pamela Robinson MCLIP **Other Snr Staff:** Asst Libns: Ms Jacqueline Devine MCLIP, Mr Michael Dann BA(Hons) & Ms Catherine Walmsley BA(Hons)
Assoc Libs: SOUTH TYNESIDE COLL LIB (see **S1935**)
Entry: enrollment on a Coll course for borrowing; others ref only **Open:** term: Mon, Wed 0900-2000, Tue, Thu 0900-1700, Fri 0900-1630; vac: closed
Subj: vocational; counselling; health & social care; childcare; welding; fabrication; business mgmt; health & safety mgmt; sports studies; leisure; tourism; performing arts
Equip: video viewer, copier, 4 computers (incl 3 with CD-ROM) **Svcs:** info, ref, biblio, indexing
Stock: bks/8986; periodcls/32; CD-ROMs/21
Classn: DDC **Auto Sys:** Heritage
Staff: Libns: 1 Non-Prof: 1

Helensburgh

S797 🔑

The Hill House Library of Blackie Books
Upper Colquhoun St, Helensburgh, Strathclyde, G84 9AJ (01436-673900; *fax:* 01436-674685)
Email: crostek@nts.org.uk
Internet: http://www.nts.org.uk/

Type: historic house *Gov Body:* Natl Trust for Scotland *Chief:* Property Mgr & Curator: Ms Charlotte Rostek MA
Entry: adv appt for study, ref only *Open:* Apr-Oct: Mon-Sun 1330-1730; closed Nov-Mar
Collns: Bks & Pamphs: colln of Walter Blackie bks (bks publ by Blackie & Son)
Staff: Other Prof: 1 *Non-Prof:* 20

Hemel Hempstead

S798 ✚
Hemel Hempstead Hospital Library
Hillside Rd, Hemel Hempstead, Hertfordshire, HP2 4AD (01442-287185; *fax:* 01442-287992)
Email: library.hemel@whht.nhs.uk

Gov Body: West Hertfordshire Hosps NHS Trust
Chief: Lib Development Mgr: Ms Diane Levey
Assoc Libs: LES CANNON MEMORIAL LIB (see **S1620**); ST ALBANS CITY HOSP, STAFF LIB & INFO SVC (see **S1962**); WATFORD GENL HOSP LIB (see **S2092**)
Entry: Trust staff *Open:* Mon-Fri 0900-1700
Subj: medicine; nursing
Equip: copier (5p per pg), computers (incl internet) *Online:* CINAHL, Medline, BNI, HMIC
Classn: NLM

S799 🎓
West Hertfordshire College (Dacorum Campus), Teaching and Learning Resources Service
Marlowes, Hemel Hempstead, Hertfordshire, HP1 1HD (01442-221580; *fax:* 01442-221586)
Email: cherylc@westherts.ac.uk
Internet: http://www.westherts.ac.uk/

Chief: Team Leader (Dacorum Campus): Mrs Cheryl Coveney BA(Hons), DipLib, MCLIP
Assoc Libs: CASSIO CAMPUS LIB (see **S2093**); LEGATTS CAMPUS LIB, Leggatts Way, Watford, Hertfordshire, Team Leader: Mrs Pam Acreman (01923-814898); WATFORD CAMPUS LIB (see **S2094**)
Entry: students & staff of coll; external membership available, otherwise ref only *Open:* term: Mon 0845-1700, Tue-Thu 0845-1930, Fri 0845-1630
Subj: all subjs; GCSE & A-level; undergrad; vocational *Co-op Schemes:* ILL
Equip: copier (A4/5p), 3 video viewers, 65 computers (all with wd-proc & internet, 10 with CD-ROM) *Disabled:* large screens, ZoomText *Officer-in-Charge:* Team Leader, as above *Svcs:* info
Stock: bks/10000; periodcls/50; videos/350; CD-ROMs/20 *Acqs Offcr:* Team Leader, as above
Classn: DDC *Auto Sys:* Voyager
Staff: Libns: 1 *Non-Prof:* 6

Henley-on-Thames

S800 🎓
Henley Management College, PowerGen Library
Greenlands, Henley-on-Thames, Oxfordshire, RG9 3AU (01491-418823; *fax:* 01491-418896)
Email: Library@henleymc.ac.uk
Internet: http://www.henleymc.ac.uk/env/pglib.htm

Chief: Info Svc Mgr: Mrs Jane Goldsmith (Jane.Goldsmith@henleymc.ac.uk)
Entry: Coll staff, students, alumni & rsrchers; students from other univs with letter of introduction admitted for consultation only *Open:* Mon-Fri 0845-2130, Sat 0900-1700, Sun 1300-1700
Subj: mgmt; business *Collns: Archvs:* papers of Col Lyndall Urwick *Other:* Economist Intelligence Unit Reports; Top 200 FTSE company reports;

working papers; theses; AV colln, incl mgmt videos
Co-op Schemes: BLDSC
Equip: m-reader, fax, 2 video viewers, copier (A4/5p, A3/10p), 9 computer (incl wd-proc, internet & CD-ROM) *Disabled:* lift access *Online:* Infotrac, Proquest, Mintel, Reuters, Fame, Amadeus, Osiris
Stock: bks/10000; periodcls/400
Classn: London Business School *Auto Sys:* Heritage *Staff: Libns:* 3 *Other Prof:* 5

Hereford

S801 🔑 🐾
Hereford Cathedral Library
The Cathedral, Hereford, HR1 2NG (01432-374225/6/7; *fax:* 01432-374220)
Email: library@herefordcathedral.co.uk
Internet: http://www.herefordcathedral.co.uk/

Gov Body: The Dean & Chapter of Hereford Cathedral & the Hereford Mappa Mundi Trust
Chief: Chancellor: The Revd Canon Val Hamer BA *Dep:* Libn: Miss J. Williams BA, MPhil, MCLIP
Assoc Libs: HEREFORD CATHEDRAL ARCHVS, at above addr, Archivist: Mrs Rosalind Caird BA, DipAA
Entry: none for modern lib during opening hrs; adv appt advised for all historical materials (refs sometimes required); £6 pa subscription for borrowers *Open:* Tue-Thu 1000-1600, 1st Sat in month 1000-1230
Subj: Hereford Cathedral & Diocese: church hist; hist; bibliography; theology; Christian church; church music *Collns: Bks & Pamphs:* c3000 early printed bks (1800 or earlier), incl 50 incunabula, of which c1230 vols are chained to 17C bk presses (subjs chiefly theology, canon law); c250 vols church music (18C-19C) *Archvs:* records of the Dean & Chapter of Hereford (c30000 items, 12C onwards) *Other:* 227 medieval MSS chained to 17C bk presses
Equip: m-reader, fax (staff only, not on site), copier (staff only, copies can be made for readers on demand), computer (with wd-proc, staff only) *Svcs:* info, talks, exhibs
Stock: bks/14000; periodcls/4; photos/2500; slides/1000; illusts/500; pamphs/3000; maps/50; m-forms/200; audios/30; archvs/200 linear m
Classn: DDC
Staff: Libns: 1 *Other Prof:* 0.6 *Non-Prof:* 0.6
Exp: £2700 (1999-2000); £2800 (2000-01)

S802 ✚
Herefordshire Clinical Library
(formerly John Ross Postgrad Medical Lib)
Postgrad Medical Centre, Hereford County Hosp, Hereford, HR1 2ER (01432-355444 x5840; *fax:* 01432-355265)
Email: her.library@hh-tr.wmids.nhs.uk

Gov Body: Hereford County Hosp *Chief:* Lead Health Libn: Miss Lindsey Baker BA(Hons), MCLIP
Other Snr Staff: Asst Info Libn: Ms Elise Collins BSc(Hons)
Assoc Libs: NURSE EDU CENTRE LIB, at same addr (staff to be appointed)
Entry: NHS staff throughout Herefordshire *Open:* Mon-Fri 0900-1700; 24 hr access via swipecard
Subj: medicine; health *Co-op Schemes:* BLDSC, BMA, WMRHLN, Barnes Lib (see **S182**)
Equip: fax, copier, 5 computers (all with wd-proc & CD-ROM, 3 with internet) *Svcs:* info, ref
Stock: bks/2600, excl bnd periodcls; periodcls/75; pamphs/70; videos/50; CD-ROMs/25
Classn: NLM (Wessex) *Auto Sys:* Heritage, moving to Sirsi
Staff: Libns: 3 *Non-Prof:* 1 *Exp:* £20000 (2000-01)

S803 🎓
Herefordshire College of Art and Design Library
Folly Ln, Hereford, HR1 1LT (01432-273359; *fax:* 01432-341099)
Email: hcad@hereford-art-coll.ac.uk
Internet: http://www.hereford-art-coll.ac.uk/

Gov Body: Herefordshire Coll of Art & Design
Chief: Coll Libn: Ms Joanne Lacy BA(Hons), DipLib (j.lacy@hereford-art-coll.ac.uk) *Dep:* Snr Lib Asst: Mr Ashley Nunn BA(Hons)
Assoc Libs: HEREFORDSHIRE COLL OF TECH LIB (see **S804**); the 2 Colls share the same LRC, with Art & Design a separate section, separately staffed
Entry: ref only *Open:* term: Mon-Thu 0840-2100, Fri 0945-1645; vac: Mon-Fri 0900-1300
Subj: arts; design *Co-op Schemes:* ILL
Equip: 2 copiers, 2 clr copiers, 6 computers (incl wd-proc, internet & CD-ROM) *Svcs:* info, ref
Stock: bks/c14000; periodcls/54; videos/100; CD-ROMs/25
Classn: DDC *Auto Sys:* Talis
Staff: Libns: 1 *Non-Prof:* 2 *Exp:* £25000 (2000-01)

S804 🎓
Herefordshire College of Technology, Learning Resources Centre
Folly Ln, Hereford, HR1 1LS (01432-352235 x270; *fax:* 01432-353449)
Email: enquiries@herefordtech.co.uk
Internet: http://www.hereford-tech.ac.uk/

Gov Body: independent coll *Chief:* Learning Resources Mgr: Mrs Rosemary Wootton BA, MCLIP *Dep:* Asst Libns: Dr Jane Foster BSc, PhD, DipILS & Mrs Catherine Wrathall BA
Assoc Libs: HEREFORDSHIRE COLL OF ART & DESIGN LIB (see **S803**)
Entry: ref only for public *Open:* term: Mon-Thu 0840-2100, Fri 0945-1645; vac: Mon-Fri 0900-1300
Subj: all subjs; GCSE; A level; undergrad; postgrad; vocational *Co-op Schemes:* BLDSC
Equip: video viewer, copiers, computers (with wd-proc, internet & CD-ROM)
Stock: bks/c21000; periodcls/150; slides/2000; audios/200; videos/1000
Classn: DDC *Auto Sys:* Talis
Staff: Libns: 2 *Non-Prof:* 7

S805 🎓
Holme Lacy College, Learning Resource Centre
Holme Lacy, Hereford, HR2 6LL (01432-870316; *fax:* 01432-870566)
Email: hlc-library@hotmail.com
Internet: http://www.pershore.ac.uk/

Gov Body: Pershore Group of Colls *Chief:* Learning Resources Mgr: Mrs Mary Hilder
Assoc Libs: PERSHORE COLL LIB, Avonbank, Pershore, Worcestershire, WR10 3JP
Entry: ref only, adv appt *Open:* term: Mon-Fri 0900-1700; vac: reduced hrs, as advertised
Subj: sci; agric; animal care; equine studies; hortic; forestry; floristry; leisure; outdoor pursuits; sports; environment *Collns: Bks & Pamphs:* Workman Colln (forestry) *Co-op Schemes:* ILL
Equip: video viewer, copier, 10 computers (all with wd-proc, internet & CD-ROM), scanner *Svcs:* info, ref
Stock: bks/7300, incl pamphs; periodcls/180; slides/a few; maps/50; audios/a few; videos/315; multimedia/12
Classn: DDC *Auto Sys:* Heritage
Staff: Libns: 1 *Non-Prof:* 1 FTE

Special Libraries

Hereford ▼ Huddersfield

S806 ✚ 🎓

University College Worcester, Faculty of Health and Exercise Sciences, Hereford Library

Hereford County Hosp, Union Walk, Hereford, HR1 2ER (01432-357777; fax: 01432-341619)
Internet: http://www.worc.ac.uk/services/library/about/Hereford/library.htm

Gov Body: Univ Coll Worcester *Chief:* Lead Health Libn: Miss Lindsey Baker BA(Hons), MCLIP (lind_sey07@hotmail.com) *Dep:* Faculty Libn: Mrs Janice Bell BEd, DipLIS, MCLIP (j.bell@worc.ac.uk)
Entry: ref only except for UCW students *Open:* term: Mon 0900-1630, Tue-Thu 0900-2000, Fri 0900-1600; vac: Mon-Thu 0900-1630, Fri 0900-1600
Subj: nursing *Co-op Schemes:* BLDSC, West Midlands Scheme, NULJ
Equip: copier, computer (with internet) *Online:* CSA, CINAHL *Svcs:* info, ref
Stock: bks/9000; periodcls/30 *Classn:* DDC
Staff: Non-Prof: 1.5 *Exp:* £3600 (1999-2000)

S807 🔑

Woolhope Naturalists' Field Club Library

Hereford Lib, Broad St, Hereford, HR4 9AU (01432-272456; fax: 01432-359668)

Chief: Lib Sub-Cttee
Entry: membs only
Subj: archaeo; antiquities; folklore; geol; nat hist; genealogy *Collns: Bks & Pamphs:* Marshall Bequest (bks & graphic material on archaeo) *Co-op Schemes:* BLDSC, exchange of pubns with other learned socs, both local & natl
Equip: m-reader, copier *Stock:* bks/3500
Pubns: Annual Transactions (for membs)
Exp: stock not acquired through purchase

Hertford

S808 🔑

Tun Abdul Razak Research Centre Library

Brickendonbury, Hertford, SG13 8NL (01992-584966; fax: 01992-554837)

Gov Body: Malaysian Rubber Rsrch & Development Board, Kuala Lumpur *Chief:* Head, Info Group: Ms K. Lawson MCLIP
Entry: adv appt *Open:* Mon-Fri 0900-1700
Subj: polymers; rubber *Co-op Schemes:* BLDSC, RSC, HERTIS
Equip: m-reader, m-camera, m-printer, video viewer, fax, copier, computers (incl wd-proc & CD-ROM) *Online:* Dialog etc
Stock: bks/10000; periodcls/100; photos/10000; slides/1000; m-forms/200; Morphs database/ 100000+ items
Classn: UDC, Morphs *Staff: Libns:* 1 *Non-Prof:* 1

Hexham

S809 ✚

Hexham General Hospital, Ryder Postgraduate Medical Centre Library

Hexham Genl Hosp, Hexham, Northumberland, NE46 1QJ (tel & fax: 01434-655048)
Email: susanne.ellingham@northumbria-healthcare.nhs.uk

Gov Body: Northumbria Healthcare NHS Trust
Chief: Libn: Mrs Susanne Ellingham
Assoc Libs: other Trust libs: NORTH TYNESIDE EDU CENTRE LIB (see **S1607**); NORTHUMBER-LAND HEALTHCARE TRUST LIB (see **S1559**); WANSBECK HOSP LIB (see **S52**)
Entry: membs only; open to Trust staff & students, local NHS & RCN membs *Open:* Mon-Fri 0900-1630
Subj: medicine; nursing *Co-op Schemes:* BLDSC (borrowing from only), HLN
Equip: video viewer, copier, 3 computers (incl 3 with wd-proc, 2 with internet & 2 with CD-ROM, access to internet restricted) *Online:* OVID (online) & various CD-ROMs
Stock: bks/900 bks; periodcls/48 + 130 bnd vols; videos/40 *Acqs Offcr:* Libn, as above
Classn: DDC *Auto Sys:* SydneyPlus
Staff: Libns: 1 *Exp:* £12000 (2000-01)

High Wycombe

S810 🎓

Buckinghamshire Chilterns University College, Library

Queen Alexandra Rd, High Wycombe, Buckinghamshire, HP11 2JZ (01494-522141; fax: 01494-450774)
Email: hwlib@bcuc.ac.uk
Internet: http://www.bcuc.ac.uk/

Chief: Head of Lib & Media Svcs: Ms Lizanne Thackray
Assoc Libs: HIGH WYCOMBE CAMPUS LIB, addr as above; CHALFONT CAMPUS LIB, Gorelands Ln, Chalfont St Giles, Buckinghamshire, HP8 4AD (01494-605135; email: challib@bcuc.ac.uk); WELLESBOURNE CAMPUS LIB, Kingshill Rd, High Wycombe, Buckinghamshire, HP13 5BB (email: wellib@bcuc.ac.uk)
Entry: ref only except for staff & students *Open: High Wycombe & Chalfont Campuses:* term: Mon-Thu 0830-2400, Fri 0830-2100, Sat 1000-1700, Sun 1200-1900; vac: varies; *Wellesbourne Campus:* Mon-Wed 0900-1630, Thu 0900-1800, Fri 0900-1600; vac: closed
Subj: all subjs; undergrad; postgrad; phil; psy; social sci; lang; sci; maths; tech; art; design; health studies; leisure; tourism; business studies; mgmt; computing; bldg; forestry *Collns: Bks & Pamphs:* European Ref Colln; Wood Info Lib (incl Timber Rsrch & Development Assoc Lib)
Equip: m-reader, m-printer, video viewer, fax, copiers (A4/5p, A3/10p), clr copiers (A4/£1, A3/ £1.25), computers (incl internet & CD-ROM) *Online:* BIDS, Web of Science, IBSS, EDINA, ABI Inform, SCAD, Penal Lexicon, NISS, CareData, ChildData, PsycInfo, Mintel, Wilson Art Index etc
Stock: bks/200000; periodcls/1800
Classn: DDC *Auto Sys:* Sirsi
Staff: Libns: 6.5 *Non-Prof:* 27.21

S811 ✚

Chiltern Medical Library

Chiltern Postgrad Medical Centre, Wycombe Hosp, High Wycombe, Buckinghamshire, HP11 2TT (01494-426368; fax: 01494-426376)
Email: lesley.martyn@wyclib.demon.co.uk
Internet: http://www.wyclib.demon.co.uk/

Gov Body: South Buckinghamshire NHS Trust
Chief: Trust Libn: Mrs Leslie Martyn CertLib *Dep:* Snr Lib Asst: Mrs June Kendell
Assoc Libs: AMERSHAM HOSP STAFF LIB (see **S35**)
Entry: staff & students of South Buckinghamshire NHS Trust & Buckinghamshire Mental Health Trust; primary care staff in the area; adv appt for membs of public *Open:* Mon-Fri 0900-1730
Subj: health svc mgmt; medicine *Co-op Schemes:* BLDSC, HeLIN, BMA
Equip: copier, computers (incl wd-proc, internet & CD-ROM) *Online:* Medline, Cochrane, CINAHL, AMED, HMIC, BNI, NRR, Embase & others *Svcs:* info, ref, lit searches
Stock: bks/5500; periodcls/100; audios/35; videos/ 107
Classn: NLM *Auto Sys:* InMagic
Pubns: Lib Guide; Dist Union List of Periodicals
Staff: Libns: 1 *Non-Prof:* 1

S812 🔑 🏛

Hughenden Manor Library

Hughenden Valley, High Wycombe, Buckingham-shire, HP14 4LA (01494-755573; fax: 01494-474284)

Gov Body: The Natl Trust *Chief:* Property Mgr: Mr Charles Pugh *Dep:* House & Visitor Svcs Mgr: Mrs Roslyn Lee
Entry: by special arrangement to specialist rsrchers only *Open:* by arrangement
Subj: colln of Benjamin Disraeli
Stock: bks/3000 *Staff: Non-Prof:* 2

Hitchin

S813 🏛 🎓 🏛

Museum Resource Centre, Hitchin

Bury Mead Rd, Hitchin, Hertfordshire, SG5 1RT (01462-435197; fax: 01462-434883)

Gov Body: North Hertfordshire Dist Council
Chief: Keeper: Mr Brian Sawford BSc(Hons), AMA
Entry: ref only, adv appt *Open:* Mon-Fri: 0930-1630
Subj: local study (North Hertfordshire): sci; geog; hist
Equip: copier, study room
Stock: bks/6000; periodcls/50; photos/6000; slides/4000; maps/500
Classn: DDC
Staff: Other Prof: 1 *Exp:* £1000 (1999-2000)

S814 🎓

North Hertfordshire College, Hitchin Learning Resource Centre

Cambridge Rd, Hitchin, Hertfordshire, SG4 0JD (01462-424331)
Email: lrc@nhc.ac.uk
Internet: http://www.nhc.ac.uk/

Gov Body: North Hertfordshire Coll *Chief:* Distribution Learning Mgr: Mrs Sally Dawson (sdawson@nhc.ac.uk) *Dep:* Learning Centre Mgr: Mr Karl Scott (kscott@nhc.ac.uk) *Other Snr Staff:* Lib Systems Mgr: Mrs Nora Evans (nevans@nhc.ac.uk)
Assoc Libs: STEVENAGE LRC (see **S1975**)
Entry: coll staff & students; associate membership available *Open:* term: Mon-Thu 0845-2045, Fri 0845-1600
Subj: all subjs; genl; GCSE; A level; undergrad; vocational *Co-op Schemes:* ILL with associated colls in Hertfordshire & with Univ of Hertfordshire (see **S791**)
Equip: 2 copiers (A4/7p, A3/10p), 2 clr copiers (A4/50p, A3/£1), video viewer, 43 computers (all with wd-proc, internet & CD-ROM) *Disabled:* Dragon Naturally Speaking, Wd Bar, TextHelp

Read & Write, Inspiration *Online:* Infotrac, Britannica, AdBrands, ECGIS, KnowUK, KnowEurope, City Mutual (all free to membs) *Officer-in-Charge:* Libn, as above *Svcs:* info, ref *Stock:* bks/22000; periodcls/108 *Acqs Offcr:* Lib Systems Mgr, as above *Classn:* DDC *Auto Sys:* Voyager *Staff:* Libns: 0.5 *Non-Prof:* 6

Holywood

S815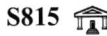
Ulster Folk and Transport Museum, Library and Archives
Cultra, Holywood, Co Down, BT18 0EU (028-9042-8428; *fax:* 028-9042-8728)
Email: dixonroger@talk21.com
Internet: http://www.uftm.org.uk/

Chief: Libn: Mr Roger Dixon *Dep:* Asst Libn: Ms Sally Skilling *Other Snr Staff:* Archv Mgr: Ms Anne Smyth; Head of Photographic Archv: Mr Kenneth Anderson; Audio Technical Offcr (contact for Sound Archv): Mr Peter Carson
Entry: ref only; adv appt *Open:* Mon-Fri 0900-1700
Subj: Ulster: local studies; industry; transport; shipbuilding; costume; business records *Collns: Archvs:* Ulster Dialect & Linguistic Diversity Archv; BBC Northern Ireland Archv (see **A205**); JH Capper & Co Ltd records (linen goods manufacturers, 1870-1916); Harland & Wolff Ltd records (shipbuilders, c1913-c1951), incl shipbuilding plans for the Titanic & other vessels; Whiteabbey Flax Spinning Co records (flax spinners, c1872); Workman, Clark & Co Ltd records (shipbuilders, 1928-34) *Other:* Still & Moving Images Archv (1860s-date), incl: W.A. Green Colln; Titanic Colln; Sound Archv, incl oral hist colln; maps & plans
Stock: bks/c25000

Hook

S816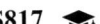
National Police Library
Centrex Bramshill, Bramshill House, Bramshill, Hook, Hampshire, RG27 0JW (01252-602650; *fax:* 01252-602285)
Email: library@centrex.pnn.police.uk
Internet: http://www.centrex.police.uk/

Chief: Libn: Mrs S.E. King MCLIP *Dep:* Miss J. Mussell BA(Hons), DipLib, MCLIP
Entry: police offcrs; govt officials; rsrchers by arrangement
Subj: crime; criminal law; penology; police; mgmt
Collns: Bks & Pamphs: HM Inspectors of Constabulary: annual reports (from 1858); Police Review (from 1893); Police & Constabulary Almanac (from 1858) *Co-op Schemes:* BLDSC
Equip: m-reader, m-printer, 2 copiers, 5 computers (all with wd-proc, plus CD-ROM) *Svcs:* info, ref, document delivery
Stock: bks/65000; periodcls/250; m-forms/20; theses/1320
Classn: DDC, own *Auto Sys:* CAIRS Total Lib
Pubns: Natl Police Lib Catalogue on CD-ROM
Staff: Libns: 6 *Non-Prof:* 5

Hornchurch

S817
Havering College of Further and Higher Education Library
Ardleigh Green Rd, Hornchurch, Essex, RM11 2LL (01708-455011 x2040; *fax:* 01708-462788)
Internet: http://www.havering-college.ac.uk/

Gov Body: Coll Board of Governors *Chief:* Learning Resources Mgr: Mrs Audrey Stranders BA(Hons), MA, MCLIP *Dep:* Libn: Mrs Ann Stevart BA(Hons), DipLib, MCLIP
Assoc Libs: QUARLES CAMPUS LRC, Tring Gdns, Harold Hill, Romford, Essex, Libn: Mrs Judith Forsythe BA, DipLib, MCLIP; HARROW LODGE LRC, Hyland Way, Hornchurch, Essex, Libn: Mrs A. Stevart
Entry: staff or students of Coll only *Open: Ardleigh Green LRC:* Mon-Thu 0900-2100, Fri 1000-1700; *Quarles LRC:* Mon-Thu 0900-2000, Fri 0900-1700; *Harrow Lodge LRC:* Mon-Thu 0900-1830, Fri 0930-1700
Subj: all subjs; genl; GCSE; A level; undergrad; postgrad; vocational *Co-op Schemes:* BLDSC, EULOS
Equip: 3 copiers, 5 video viewers, 66 computers (all with wd-proc, internet & CD-ROM) *Disabled:* 2 CCTVs, variable height desks
Stock: bks/45242; periodcls/291; illusts/156; pamphs/524; audios/148; videos/1402; CD-ROMs/165; DVDs/21
Classn: DDC *Auto Sys:* Dynix
Staff: Libns: 3 *Non-Prof:* 11

S818 ✚
St George's Hospital, Aubrey Keep Library
The Link Centre, St George's Hosp, Sutton's Ln, Hornchurch, Essex, RM12 6RS (01708-465530/29; *fax:* 01708-465410)
Email: Maureen.Rouse@bhbchc-tr.nthames.nhs.uk
Internet: http://www.libnel.nhs.uk/

Chief: Trust Libn: Ms Maureen Rouse *Dep:* Lib Asst: Mr Chris Stephens
Entry: NHS staff in North East London *Open:* Mon-Fri 0800-1700
Subj: health; community health; community nursing; mental health; Learning Disabilities; physiotherapy; occupational therapy; speech therapy; podiatry; dietetics *Co-op Schemes:* ILL
Equip: computers (incl internet & CD-ROM)
Online: AMED, BNI, CancerLit, CINAHL, Cochrane, Embase, HMIC, Medline, PsycInfo
Svcs: info, ref, mediated search svc

Horsham

S819
Horsham Museum Society Library
Horsham Museum, Causeway House, 9 The Causeway, Horsham, W Sussex, RH12 1HE (01403-254959)
Email: museum@horsham.gov.uk

Chief: Libn: Ms Elizabeth Vaughan
Assoc Libs: both at above addr: HORSHAM MUSEUM, SHELLEY LIB; HORSHAM MUSEUM ARCHVS
Open: Mon-Sat 1000-1700
Subj: Horsham: local hist & geog
Stock: bks/1000
Exp: £500 (1999-2000); £500 (2000-01); incl conservation

S820
Royal Society for the Prevention of Cruelty to Animals, Headquarters Library
RSPCA HQ, Wilberforce Way, Horsham, W Sussex, RH13 9RS (0870-754-0188; *fax:* 0870-753-0188)
Email: creed@rspca.org.uk
Internet: http://www.rspca.org.uk/

Type: charity *Chief:* Info Offcr: Mr Chris Reed *Dep:* Info Asst: Mrs Pat Squire
Entry: adv appt *Open:* Mon-Fri 0900-1700
Subj: animal welfare; hist of animal welfare; works on animal rights; parliamentary & technical reports (with relevance to animal welfare) *Collns: Bks & Pamphs:* Soc's Minute bks, Annual Reports & Journals (1824 onwards)
Equip: fax, copier, computer (incl wd-proc)
Online: Dialog *Svcs:* info, ref
Stock: bks/5000; periodcls/150
Classn: DDC (mod) *Staff:* Other Prof: 1

Huddersfield

S821 ✚
Huddersfield Royal Infirmary, Learning Centre Library
(formerly Huddersfield NHS Trust Lib Svc)
Lindley, Huddersfield, W Yorkshire, HD3 3EA (01484-342869; *fax:* 01484-347085)
Email: richard.heywood@cht.nhs.uk

Gov Body: Calderdale & Huddersfield NHS Trust
Chief: Libn: Mr R.W. Heywood BA, MCLIP
Entry: non-employees ref only *Open:* Mon-Fri 0900-1700
Subj: medicine; healthcare; nursing; health svc admin *Co-op Schemes:* BLDSC, ILL, N&YRLAS
Equip: fax, copier, 3 computers (incl wd-proc, internet & CD-ROM) *Online:* OVID, NCN (fees negotiable)
Stock: bks/8000; periodcls/180
Classn: NLM *Auto Sys:* Heritage
Pubns: various guides & resources lists (free)
Staff: Libns: 1 *Non-Prof:* 1 *Exp:* £37000 (1999-2000)

S822
Huddersfield Technical College Library
New North Rd, Huddersfield, W Yorkshire, HD1 5NN (01484-536521; *fax:* 01484-511885)
Email: libraryenquiries@huddcoll.ac.uk
Internet: http://www.huddcoll.ac.uk/

Gov Body: Huddersfield Technical Coll Corp
Chief: Libn: Ms Alicja Zalewska BA(Hons), CertEd, MCLIP *Dep:* Ms Samantha Emmott BA
Entry: ref only for membs of public *Open:* term: Mon-Thu 0845-2000, Fri 0845-1600; vac: reduced opening hrs
Subj: all subjs; genl; GCSE; A level; vocational
Co-op Schemes: BLDSC, ILL (local)
Equip: video viewers, copiers, clr copier, computers (incl wd-proc, internet & CD-ROM)
Disabled: Supernova scanner, voice recognition software, speech synthesiser, CCTV magnifier
Svcs: info, ref *Stock:* bks/45000; periodcls/160; videos/700
Classn: UDC *Auto Sys:* Heritage
Pubns: Lib Guides (free); Subj Guides (free)
Staff: Libns: 3 *Non-Prof:* 6

S823
Tolson Memorial Museum Library
Ravensknowle Pk, Wakefield Rd, Huddersfield, W Yorkshire, HD5 8DJ (01484-223830; *fax:* 01484-223843)

Gov Body: Kirklees Metropolitan Council (see **P69**) *Chief:* Museums Offcr: Ms Jenny Salton BA, MusDip
Entry: ref only, adv appt *Open:* Mon-Fri 1100-1700, Sat-Sun 1200-1700
Subj: local study (Huddersfield); hist; local hist; social hist; costume
Equip: copier *Svcs:* ref *Stock:* bks/5000

S824

University of Huddersfield, Computing and Library Services
Queensgate, Huddersfield, W Yorkshire, HD1 3DH
(01484-473888; *fax:* 01484-516151)
Email: lc@hud.ac.uk
Internet: http://wwwcls.hud.ac.uk/

Gov Body: Univ of Huddersfield *Chief:* Dir of
Computing & Lib Svcs: Mr Phil Sykes BA, MCLIP
Dep: Asst Head of Lib Svcs: Mrs Susan White
Assoc Libs: MUSIC LIB, Queensgate, Huddersfield, HD1 3DH (01484-472009; *email:* library.mh@
hud.ac.uk); UNIV OF HUDDERSFIELD ARCHVS,
addr as above, Univ Archivist, Mrs E.A. Hilary
Haigh BA, MPhil, DipAA (01484-473168; *fax:*
01484-517987; *email:* archives@hud.ac.uk)
Entry: ref only for public *Open:* term: Mon-Thu
0845-2100, Fri 0845-1700, Sat 0930-1700, Sun
1230-1700; vac: Mon-Fri 0845-1700
Subj: undergrad; postgrad; arts; sci; eng; law;
business *Collns: Bks & Pamphs:* BSI (complete
set); Rare Bks Colln (incl original Lib of
Huddersfield Mechanics' Instn); local hist colln;
G.H. Wood Colln (econ, social & women's issues);
Yudkin Colln (diet & nutrition, 1645-1938);
Huddersfield Foreign Lib Soc Colln (1851-70)
Archvs: archvs of: Huddersfield Mechanics Instn
(1843-84); Huddersfield Female Educational Inst
(1846-83); Huddersfield Technical School &
Mechanics' Instn (1884-96); Huddersfield Literary &
Scientific Soc (1857-82); Huddersfield Fine Art &
Industrial Exhib (1882-84); Colne Valley Labour
Party (1891-1970); Huddersfield Labour Party
(1918-date) *Other:* historic colln of newspapers &
journals *Co-op Schemes:* BLDSC, YHJLS
Equip: m-readers, m-printers, video viewer,
copier, clr copier, computers (incl wd-proc & CD-
ROM) *Disabled:* minicom, CCTV *Online:* wide
variety of databases, incl: BHINet, BIDS, CINAHL,
Eurolaw, Medline, Mintel, PsycInfo, Web of
Science, Zetoc
Stock: bks/400000; periodcls/1800
Classn: DDC *Auto Sys:* Dynix Horizon
Staff: Libns: 24 *Non-Prof:* 45

Hull

S825

Croda Universal Ltd, Library
Oak Rd, Clough Rd, Hull, Humberside, HU6 7PH
(01482-443181; *fax:* 01482-341792)
Email: jhutty@croda-universal.com

Chief: Libn: Mrs Jenny Hutty BA *Dep:* Clerical
Asst: Ms Jill Embley
Entry: by appt *Open:* Mon-Fri 0900-1630
Subj: sci; tech; chem; polymer chem; nat product
chem *Collns: Other:* Chemical Abstracts (1919-
74) *Co-op Schemes:* HULTIS
Equip: m-reader, video viewer, fax, copier,
computer (incl CD-ROM) *Online:* STN, Datastar
(staff only, no charge)
Stock: bks/3000; periodcls/50
Classn: UDC
Pubns: Essential Fatty Acids: A Review... (£45)
Staff: Libns: 1 *Non-Prof:* 1

S826

Hull and East Yorkshire Hospital NHS Trust, ERMEC Library
East Riding Medical Edu Centre, Anlaby Rd, Hull,
Humberside, HU3 2JZ (01482-674337; *fax:* 01482-
674342)
Email: Jacqui.Smales@hey.nhs.uk

Gov Body: Hull & East Yorkshire Hosp NHS Trust
Chief: Mgr of Lib & Knowledge Development
Svcs: Mrs Jacqui Smales BA(Hons), PGCE
Assoc Libs: CASTLE HILL HOSP LIB, Entrance 2,
Castle Rd, Cottingham, HU16 5JQ
Entry: NHS employees & various others as
approved *Open:* Mon-Fri 0830-1800; 24 hr access
to both sites
Subj: medicine; health care *Collns: Bks &
Pamphs:* hist of medicine colln (c200 vols) *Co-op
Schemes:* BLDSC, NULJ, PCLS, Recall, regional
schemes
Equip: 2 video viewers, 2 copiers (5p per sheet),
clr copier, 2 fax, 16 computers (all with wd-proc,
internet & CD-ROM) *Online:* Dialog, Proquest,
various e-journals *Officer-in-Charge:* Mgr, as
above *Svcs:* info, ref, biblio, indexing, abstracting
Stock: bks/20000; periodcls/200; videos/260 *Acqs
Offcr:* Mgr, as above
Classn: DDC *Auto Sys:* Heritage
Staff: Libns: 2 *Non-Prof:* 6

S827

Hull College, The Library
Queen's Gdns, Hull, Humberside, HU1 3DG
(01482-329943 x2925; *fax:* 01482-219079)

Gov Body: Learning & Skills Council *Chief:* Snr
Coll Libn: Ms Emily Armstrong BA(Hons), MCLIP
Dep: Asst Libn: Mrs A.D. Thompson BA(Hons),
MCLIP
Assoc Libs: RILEY CENTRE LIB, Parkfield Dr,
Anlaby Rd, Hull, HU3 6TE; PARK ST CENTRE
LIB, Park St, Hull, HU2 8RR
Entry: membs of Coll only *Open:* term: Mon-Thu
0845-2000, Fri 0845-1630; vac: Mon-Thu 0900-
1630, Fri 0900-1600
Subj: all subjs
Equip: 2 video viewers, 2 copiers, 8 computers
(all with wd-proc, internet & CD-ROM) *Disabled:*
print enlarger *Svcs:* binding svc
Stock: bks/36606; periodcls/121; videos/816
Classn: DDC *Auto Sys:* Heritage IV
Staff: Libns: 3 *Non-Prof:* 14

S828

University of Hull, Brynmor Jones Library
Cottingham Rd, Hull, Humberside, HU6 7RX
(01482-466581; *fax:* 01482-466205)
Email: libhelp@acs.hull.ac.uk
Internet: http://www.acsweb.hull.ac.uk/lib/

Chief: Lib Mgr: Ms Sue Geale (S.E.Geale@hull.
ac.uk)
Assoc Libs: MAP ROOM, Cohen Bldg, Hull
Campus, Cottingham Rd, Hull, HU6 7RX (01482-
465551); KEITH DONALDSON LIB (see **S1899**);
UNIV ARCHVS, addr as above (01482-465265;
fax: 01482-466205; *email:* archives@hull.ac.uk)
Entry: adv appt *Open:* term: Mon-Thu 0900-
2200, Fri 0900-1730, Sat 0900-2100, Sun 1300-
2100; vac: reduced opening hrs
Subj: all subjs; undergrad; postgrad; labour hist;
South East Asian studies; political papers; family
papers; estate archvs; literary papers *Collns: Bks
& Pamphs:* EDC; South East Asian Colln *Archvs:*
modern political papers & archvs of pressure
groups: Natl Council for Civil Liberties; Women's
Co-op Guild; Union of Democratic Control; Socialist
Medical Assoc; family & estate papers: Beaumont
of Carlton, Hotham of South Dalton, Maxwell-
Constable of Everingham, Sykes of Sledmere;

modern literary MSS: Philip Larkin; George
Bernard Shaw; John Ruskin & others; business
records; religious archvs; manorial records *Other:*
Record Lib; Audio Visual Colln; Map Colln (at Map
Room) *Co-op Schemes:* BLDSC, SCONUL,
YHJLS, UK Libs Plus
Equip: m-readers, m-printer, video viewer, fax,
copiers, clr copier, computers (incl wd-proc,
internet & CD-ROM) *Online:* 50+ indexing,
abstracting & full-text databases & c5000 e-
journals *Svcs:* info, ref
Stock: bks/936176; periodcls/3857; maps/65000;
m-forms/13039; archvs/4205 linear m
Classn: LC *Auto Sys:* Innopac
Staff: Libns: 15 *Non-Prof:* 49.5

Huntingdon

S829

Anglia Support Partnership, Knowledge Library Services
(formerly Cambridgeshire Health Authority Lib)
Kingfisher House, Kingfisher Way, Hinchingbrooke
Business Pk, Huntingdon, Cambridgeshire, PE29
6FH (01480-398622; *fax:* 01480-398501)
Email: hilary.jackson@asp.nhs.uk

Chief: Libn: Ms Hilary Jackson BSc, MCLIP
Entry: adv appt, loans only to libs *Open:* Mon-Fri
0900-1700
Subj: health svc mgmt
Equip: computer (incl CD-ROM, internal users
only)
Stock: bks/500; periodcls/40; pamphs/10000
Classn: own *Auto Sys:* DBTextworks
Staff: Libns: 3 *Non-Prof:* 1

S830

Anglian Water plc, Library
Anglian House, Ambury Rd, Huntingdon,
Cambridgeshire, PE18 6NZ (01480-326973; *fax:*
01480-326987)

Chief: Libn: Mrs Dorothy Kackhoven
Open: Mon-Fri 0930-1700
Subj: water; waste water; environmental eng
Equip: video viewer, fax, clr copier, computer (incl
CD-ROM) *Svcs:* info, ref
Classn: DDC *Auto Sys:* DS

S831

Centre for Ecology and Hydrology, Monks Wood Library
Abbots Ripton, Huntingdon, Cambridgeshire, PE17
2LS (01487-772400)
Internet: http://library.ceh.ac.uk/

Gov Body: Nat Environment Rsrch Council
(NERC); part of CEH Lib Svcs (see **S1786**) *Chief:*
Libn: Ms Pam Moorhouse (pmo@ceh.ac.uk) *Dep:*
Ms Helen Suddaby (hsu@ceh.ac.uk)
Entry: adv appt for bona fide rsrchers *Open:*
Mon-Thu 0845-1715, Fri 0845-1645
Subj: botany; zoology; floras; ecology; soil sci;
pollution; land use; remote sensing; statistics
Stock: bks/5000, incl reports; periodcls/350+
Auto Sys: Unicorn

S832

Hinchingbrooke Health Care NHS Trust, Education Centre Library
Hinchingbrooke Hosp, Huntingdon, Cambridge-
shire, PE18 8NT (01480-416114; *fax:* 01480-
416299)

Chief: Lib Svcs Mgr: Mrs K. Herbert
Entry: adv appt if not a memb of staff *Open:*
Mon-Fri 0900-1700; 24 hr access for hosp staff

Subj: medicine; nursing; health care *Co-op Schemes:* Anglian Health Care Libs
Equip: m-reader, copier, computers (incl internet & CD-ROM) *Svcs:* info, ref
Stock: bks/5000; periodcls/164 *Classn:* NLM
Pubns: Lib Guide
Staff: Libns: 1 *Non-Prof:* 1.24

S833

Homerton School of Health Studies, Huntingdon Library

Community Unit, Primrose Ln, Huntingdon, Cambridgeshire, PE18 6SE (01480-415267; *fax:* 01480-415212)

Gov Body: Homerton Coll, Cambridge (see **S361**)
Chief: Libn: Mr Graham Haldane BD(Hons), DipLib, MCLIP
Assoc Libs: PETERBOROUGH LIB (see **S1795**); PAPWORTH EVERARD LIB, St. Peter's Edu Centre, Church Ln, Papworth Everard, Cambridgeshire, CB3 8QT (01480-830541; *fax:* 01480-831154)
Entry: lending to students/staff of coll & trained nursing/midwifery staff in Cambridgeshire *Open:* Mon-Fri 0845-1800
Subj: nursing; medicine *Co-op Schemes:* BLDSC, BMA, East Anglia Health Care Libs
Equip: video viewers, copiers, computers (incl wd-proc & CD-ROM)
Stock: bks/12000; periodcls/137; videos/100
Classn: NLM, RCN *Staff: Libns:* 1 *Non-Prof:* 1.9

S834

Huntingdonshire Regional College Library

California Rd, Huntingdon, Cambridgeshire, PE29 1BL (01480-379100; *fax:* 01480-379127)
Internet: http://www.huntingdon.ac.uk/

Chief: Libn: W.A. Vigor
Entry: staff & students *Open:* term: Mon-Thu 0900-1930, Fri 0900-1700; vac: varies
Subj: genl; GCSE & A-level; vocational; leisure; health care; social care; art; sci; eng; business; photography; lit; hist *Co-op Schemes:* ILL
Equip: copier, computers (incl wd-proc, internet & CD-ROM, available to membs only)
Stock: bks/20000; periodcls/110; maps/400; audios/400; videos/1000; CD-ROMs/60

Ilford

S835 🝙

Barnardo's Library

Tanners Ln, Barkingside, Ilford, Essex, IG6 1QG (020-8550-8822; *fax:* 020-8551-6870)
Email: library@barnardos.org.uk
Internet: http://www.barnardos.org.uk/

Gov Body: Barnardo's Council *Chief: Libn:* Mr Christopher Reeve BA, MSc, MCLIP *Dep:* Dep Libn: Mrs H.D. Mackin BA(Hons), DipLib
Entry: ref only, adv appt *Open:* Mon-Fri 0930-1630
Subj: psy; social welfare; edu; law; health; mgmt
Collns: Archvs: MSS of Thomas J. Barnardo & of Barnardo's (1866-present); child care & admin files (held by Liverpool Univ on our behalf; applications for access to the Libn, Barnardo's)
Equip: m-reader, fax, video viewer, copier, computers (incl internet & CD-ROM) *Online:* Datastar
Stock: bks/20000; periodcls/200; photos/500000; slides/15000; pamphs/4000; m-forms/30; audios/50; videos/200
Classn: Bliss *Auto Sys:* Olib
Pubns: Lib Bulletin (£15 pa)
Staff: Libns: 2.5 *Non-Prof:* 2.5 *Exp:* £13500 (1999-2000)

S836 ✚

James Fawcett Education Centre, Goldberg Library

King George Hosp, Barley Ln, Goodmayes, Ilford, Essex, IG3 8YB (020-8970-8239; *fax:* 020-8970-8237)
Email: james.moore@bhrhospitals.nhs.uk
Internet: http://www.libnel.nhs.uk/

Type: multidisciplinary health *Gov Body:* North East London Workforce Development Confederation *Chief: Libn:* Mr Jim Moore BSc(Hons), DipCLST, DipLib
Entry: NHS staff in the Borough of Redbridge; others ref only, by adv appt *Open:* Mon, Fri 0900-1700, Tue, Thu 0900-1800, Wed 0900-1900
Subj: medicine; health care; psychiatry; psy *Co-op Schemes:* BLDSC, NTRLS
Equip: copier (5p per sheet), fax, 13 computers (incl 12 with wd-proc, 7 with internet & 3 with CD-ROM), room for hire *Svcs:* info, ref, biblio, lit searches, info searches, training
Stock: bks/c6500; periodcls/170
Classn: NLM *Auto Sys:* DBTextworks
Staff: Libns: 1 *Non-Prof:* 2.5

S837 ✚

Redbridge and Waltham Forest Health Authority, Beckett's House Library

Beckett's House, 2-14 Ilford Hill, Ilford, Essex, IG1 2QX (020-8926-5123; *fax:* 020-8926-5001)
Email: chriss@ha.rwf-ha.nthames.nhs.uk
Internet: http://www.libnel.nhs.uk/

Gov Body: Redbridge & Waltham Forest Health Authority *Chief: Lib & Info Svc Mgr:* Mr Chris Sheriffs *Dep:* Lib Asst: Mr Roger Slazenger
Entry: Health Authority staff & membs of North East London Health Community *Open:* staffed Mon-Fri 0900-1700
Subj: health; health promotion; health mgmt
Collns: Other: health promotion teaching packs & videos *Co-op Schemes:* ILL
Equip: computers (with internet & CD-ROM)
Online: AMED, BNI, CancerLit, CINAHL, Cochrane, Embase, HMIC, Medline, PsycInfo; on CD-ROM: Best Evidence *Svcs:* info, ref, mediated searches, current awareness

Ilkeston

S838

South East Derbyshire College Library

Field Rd, Ilkeston, Derbyshire, DE7 5RS (0115-849-2049; *fax:* 0115-849-2121)
Email: h.gascoyne@sedc.ac.uk
Internet: http://www.sedc.ac.uk/

Chief: Learning Centre Mgr: Ms Hazel Gascoyne MLS, MCLIP, CertEd *Dep: Learning Centre Co-ordinator:* Mr Keith Wakerley MCLIP
Assoc Libs: MUNDY ST LEARNING CENTRE, Mundy St, Heanor, Derbyshire, DE75 7DZ, Learning Centre Co-ordinator: Ms Dorothy Mingay (01773-785217)
Entry: ref use, loans at discretion of libn *Open:* term: Mon-Thu 0845-1900, Fri 0845-1630
Subj: GCSE; A level; psy; sociology; caring; edu; English; French; German; sci; motor vehicle; childcare; construction; design; art; performing arts; music; sport; English lit; geog; hist *Co-op Schemes:* BLDSC, EMRLS
Equip: 2 m-readers, 2 copiers, 60 computers (all with CD-ROM, 54 with internet) *Online:* Internet
Stock: bks/27000; periodcls/165; slides/100; pamphs/2000; maps/160; m-forms/15; audios/650; videos/720
Classn: DDC *Auto Sys:* Alice
Pubns: various lib guides (free)

Staff: Libns: 3 *Non-Prof:* 6 *Exp:* £50000 (1999-2000); £47000 (2000-01)

Inverness

S839  ✚

Highland Health Sciences Library

Highland Campus, Univ of Stirling, Old Perth Rd, Inverness, IV2 3FG (01463-705269; *fax:* 01463-713471)
Email: hhsl-inverness@stir.ac.uk
Internet: http://www.nm.stir.ac.uk/HHSL/HHSLibrary.htm

Gov Body: Univ of Stirling (see **S1978**) *Chief: Campus Libn:* Mrs Anne Gillespie BA, DipLib, MCLIP (ag5@stir.ac.uk) *Other Snr Staff:* Asst Info Offcrs: Mr Rob Polson MA(Hons), DipLib, MCLIP, MSc, FSA(Scot) (robert.polson@stir.ac.uk) & Ms Kathleen Irvine BSc, DipLib, MCLIP, DipEdTech (k.y.irvine@stir.ac.uk)
Assoc Libs: BELFORD HOSP LIB, Fort William; CAITHNESS GENL HOSP LIB, Wick; NEW CRAIGS HOSP LIB, Inverness; HIGHLAND HEALTH BOARD LIB, Assynt House, Beechwood Pk, Inverness (all administered from Highland Health Scis Lib)
Entry: ref only for public, by adv appt; Health Board employees in the Highlands; all free excl photocopying & ILL journal req *Open:* Mon-Fri 0900-2100, Sat 1000-1700
Subj: medicine & its specialities; paramedicine; nursing; psy; social sci; mgmt; edu; computer sci; laboratory sci; health svc admin *Collns: Bks & Pamphs:* colln of the Social Work Dept of Highland Council *Archvs:* Highland Health Board Archvs *Other:* video colln *Co-op Schemes:* BLDSC, SHINE, PLCS, Grampian Info, BMA
Equip: copiers, computers (incl wd-proc & CD-ROM) *Online:* Medline, CINAHL, BNI, Cochrane, HEBS, BIDS (Stirling Univ staff only) *Svcs:* ref, lit searches, current awareness
Stock: bks/20000; periodcls/300; pamphs/1000; audios/200; videos/300
Classn: LC, NLM *Auto Sys:* Dynix
Pubns: various lib guides
Staff: Libns: 3 *Non-Prof:* 5

S840

Inverness College, Learning Resource Centre

3 Longman Rd, Inverness, IV1 1SA (01463-273248; *fax:* 01463-711977)
Email: margaret.butteris@inverness.uhi.ac.uk
Internet: http://www.inverness.uhi.ac.uk/

Gov Body: Univ of the Highlands & Islands (UHI) *Chief: LRC Mgr:* Miss Margaret Butteriss MCLIP
Entry: staff & students; ref only for public *Open:* Mon-Thu 0830-1900, Fri 0830-1700, Sat 0900-1600; vac: Mon-Fri 0900-1700
Subj: genl; GCSE; A level; undergrad; local studies (Highlands) *Collns: Bks & Pamphs:* Natl Coaching Foundation Resource Colln; special collns on forestry & aquaculture *Co-op Schemes:* BLDSC, UHI Millennium Inst inter-lending scheme
Equip: video viewers, copiers, 80 computers (incl wd-procs & CD-ROM)
Stock: bks/20000; periodcls/250; maps/50; videos/70
Classn: DDC *Auto Sys:* Calm
Staff: Libns: 3 *Non-Prof:* 2

Ipswich

S841

BT Library

Adastral Pk, Martlesham Heath, Ipswich, Suffolk, IP5 3RE (01473-643337; *fax:* 01473-606638)
Email: library@bt.com

(BT Lib cont)
Gov Body: BT **Chief:** Libn: Mr David Alsmeyer
Subj: tech; telecommunications; mgmt
Svcs: info, ref, translation, document delivery
Stock: bks/c6000; periodcls/800

S842 ✚

Ipswich Medical Library

Edu Centre, Ipswich Hosp, Heath Rd, Ipswich, Suffolk, IP4 5PD (01473-702544; *fax:* 01473-702548)
Email: medical.library@ipsh-tr.anglox.nhs.uk

Gov Body: Ipswich Hosp NHS Trust **Chief:** Asst Libn: Ms Tanya McLaven
Entry: Trust staff; others ref only, by appt **Open:** Mon-Thu 0900-1700, Fri 0900-1630; 24 hr access for membs
Subj: medicine **Co-op Schemes:** BLDSC, Regional Lib Scheme, PLCS
Equip: copier, computers **Online:** Medline, CINAHL, Cochrane **Svcs:** info, ref, database training
Stock: bks/7383; periodcls/308; videos/30
Classn: NLM **Auto Sys:** Cardbox
Pubns: East Anglian Healthcare Libs Union List
Staff: Libns: 1 Non-Prof: 2

S843 ✚

Ipswich Primary Care Trust, Suffolk Knowledge Services

(formerly Suffolk Health Lib)
Suffolk Public Health Network, Recreation Hall, St Clements Main Bldg, Foxhall Rd, Ipswich, Suffolk, IP3 8LS (01473-329418; *fax:* 01473-329077)

Type: health svc mgmt **Gov Body:** Ipswich Primary Care Trust **Chief:** Librarian/Rsrch Offcr: Mrs Wendy Marsh BA(Hons), PGDipLIS, MCLIP (wendy.marsh@lhp.nhs.uk) **Dep:** Snr Lib Asst: Ms Lynn Scannell (lynn.scannell@lhp.nhs.uk)
Entry: health care staff in Suffolk; ref only for public, by adv appt **Open:** Mon-Fri 0830-1630
Subj: health svc mgmt; public health; primary care; health statistics for Suffolk **Co-op Schemes:** BLDSC, BMA, Regional ILLs
Equip: copier, computer (incl CD-ROM) **Online:** info, ref
Stock: bks/5000; periodcls/18
Classn: own **Auto Sys:** Heritage
Staff: Libns: 1 Non-Prof: 0.6 **Exp:** £15000 (1999-2000); £16000 (2000-01)

S844 🎓

Otley College Library

Otley, Ipswich, Suffolk, IP6 9EY (01473-784114; *fax:* 01473-785353)
Email: library@otleycollege.ac.uk
Internet: http://www.otleycollege.ac.uk/

Chief: Learning Resources Co-ordinator: Ms Kaljinder Dhanda BA(Hons), MSc (kdhanda@otleycollege.ac.uk)
Entry: loans for staff & students; ref only for others **Open:** term: Mon-Wed 0845-1700, Thu 0845-1915, Fri 0845-1645; vac: Mon-Fri 0845-1645
Subj: all subjs; computers; ethics; ecology; conservation; Health & Safety; surveying; geol; biology; bio-diversity; botany; arboriculture;

zoology; eng; food tech; agric; gamekeeping; hortic; animal care; mgmt; construction; garden design; interior design; floristry; fashion; hist of countryside; careers **Collns:** *Bks & Pamphs:* Frank Knight Memorial Lib; hist of agric & hortic **Co-op Schemes:** ANGLES, Univ of East Anglia Federation
Equip: video viewer, 2 copiers, 70 computers (all with wd-proc, internet & CD-ROM), scanners, white boards **Online:** Update, Inside Web, CAB Abstracts (EDINA) **Svcs:** info, ref, biblio
Stock: bks/1600; periodcls/114; slides/2 sets; pamphs/several 1000; maps/25; videos/c450; CD-ROMs/45; archvs/1 linear m
Classn: DDC **Auto Sys:** Aleph
Staff: Libns: 1 Non-Prof: 3

S845 🖋

Suffolk Chamber of Commerce, Library and Information Service

Felaw Maltings, South Kiln, 42 Felaw St, Ipswich, Suffolk, IP2 8SQ (01473-694800; *fax:* 01473-603888)
Email: ken@suffolkchamber.co.uk
Internet: http://www.suffolknetwork.co.uk/

Chief: Business Info Mgr: Mr Ken Stone
Entry: adv appt **Open:** Mon-Fri 0900-1700
Subj: genl; business info
Equip: 2 rooms for hire (by arrangement) **Svcs:** info, ref
Stock: c6000 genl business pubns
Staff: Non-Prof: 1

S846 🎓

Suffolk College Library

Rope Walk, Ipswich, Suffolk, IP4 1LT (01473-296585; *fax:* 01473-230054)
Email: deirdre.griffin@suffolk.ac.uk
Internet: http://www.suffolk.ac.uk/

Gov Body: Suffolk Coll Corp **Chief:** Head of Lib Svcs: Mrs Deirdre Griffin MA, DipLib, DMS, MCLIP **Other Snr Staff:** Snr Asst Libns: Ms K. Holmes BA, MA, MCLIP & Ms L. Walker BA, MA **Assoc Libs:** SUFFOLK COLL HEALTH LIB (see **S847**)
Entry: ref only **Open:** term: Mon-Thu 0830-2130, Fri 0815-1700, Sat 0900-1200
Subj: all subjs; GCSE; A level; undergrad; postgrad **Co-op Schemes:** ANGLES, BLDSC
Equip: m-fiche reader, 5 video viewers, 3 copiers, networked computers **Disabled:** Kurzweil **Online:** available for coll membs only **Svcs:** info, ref, biblio
Stock: bks/83000; periodcls/500; slides/190; audios/214; videos/8500
Classn: DDC **Auto Sys:** Aleph
Pubns: Suffolk Union List of Serials (£10); Lib Guide (free)
Staff: Libns: 3.4 Non-Prof: 8 **Exp:** £113000 (1999-2000); £111000 (2000-01)
Proj: installation of new computer sys

S847 🎓 ✚

Suffolk College Health Library

Edu Centre, Ipswich Hosp, Heath Rd, Ipswich, Suffolk, IP4 5PD (01473-702547; *fax:* 01473-710757)
Internet: http://www.suffolk.ac.uk/

Gov Body: Suffolk Coll (see **S846**) **Chief:** Libn: Ms Margaret Moss
Entry: ref only to non-Coll or affiliated membs
Open: term: Mon-Thu 0830-1900, Fri 0830-1600; vac: Mon-Thu 0830-1630, Fri 0830-1600
Subj: psy; social sci (as applied to health); nursing; midwifery; radiography **Co-op Schemes:** BLDSC, HeLIN
Equip: m-form reader/printer, video viewer, copier (5p per pg), computers (incl internet & CD-ROM)

Online: Datastar (Coll membs only) **Svcs:** info, ref, biblio
Stock: bks/11000; periodcls/60; pamphs/c1000; videos/c300
Classn: NLM, LC **Auto Sys:** Dynix
Staff: Libns: 1 Non-Prof: 2

S848 🖋

TXU Europe Group plc, Information Service

PO Box 40, Wherstead Pk, Ipswich, Suffolk, IP9 2AQ (01473-553205; *fax:* 01473-553251)

Chief: Info Mgr: Ms Fiona Parkinson BLS(Hons), MCLIP **Dep:** Miss Claire Fahy BLib
Entry: adv appt **Open:** Mon-Fri 0830-1700
Subj: energy; business info **Co-op Schemes:** BLDSC, Suffolk Coll
Equip: copier, fax, computers (incl internet & CD-ROM) **Online:** FT Profile, Datastar, Dun & Bradstreet, Lexis-Nexis **Svcs:** info, ref, biblio
Stock: bks/1500; periodcls/100
Classn: UDC **Auto Sys:** DBTextworks
Staff: Libns: 3

Isle of Cumbrae

S849 🎓

University Marine Biological Station Library

Millport, Isle of Cumbrae, KA28 0EG (01475-530581/2; *fax:* 01475-530601)
Email: kathryn.stevenson@millport.gla.ac.uk
Internet: http://www.gla.ac.uk/Acad/Marine/

Gov Body: Univ of London (see **S1440**) in assoc with Univ of Glasgow (see **S738**) **Chief:** Libn: Mrs Kathryn Stevenson BSc, MSc
Entry: adv appt **Open:** Mon-Fri 0900-1500
Subj: marine biology; oceanography; hydrography; geol; palaeontology; aquaculture; fisheries; marine microbiology **Collns:** *Other:* extensive colln of charts & maps
Stock: numerous bks; maps & charts; large colln of journals, reprints & papers
Classn: LC **Auto Sys:** AutoLib **Staff:** Libns: 1 PT

Isleworth

S850 ✚

West Middlesex University Hospital NHS Trust, Library and Information Service

Twickenham Rd, Isleworth, Middlesex, TW7 6AF (020-8565-5968; *fax:* 020-8565-5408)
Email: library@wmuh-tr.nthames.nhs.uk
Internet: http://www.wmuhnhst.demon.co.uk/

Type: nursing **Gov Body:** NHS **Chief:** Libn: Mrs P.A. Bowen MCLIP **Dep:** Systems Libn: Mrs M. Badhe **Other Snr Staff:** Asst Libns: Miss L. Wann & Mr M. Walne
Entry: staff of West Middlesex Univ Hosp NHS Trust, Hounslow Primary Care Trust & West London Mental Health Trust; students on attachment; local NHS staff **Open:** Mon, Wed, Fri 0930-1700, Tue, Thu 0930-1900
Subj: medicine; nursing; health
Equip: video viewer, copier, 8 computers (with wd-proc, internet & CD-ROM) **Online:** Medline, CINAHL, Embase, PsycInfo, BNI, AMED, HMIC, CancerLit, OVID **Svcs:** info, ref, current awareness
Stock: bks/c7000; periodcls/233
Classn: NLM **Auto Sys:** DBTextworks
Staff: Libns: 3 Non-Prof: 0.5

S851 🎓

West Thames College, The Learning Resources Centre
London Rd, Isleworth, Middlesex, TW7 4HS (020-8326-2308)
Internet: http://www.west-thames.ac.uk/

Chief: Head of Lib Svcs: Mrs Karen Bewen-Chappell BA(Hons) *Dep:* Dep Libn: Miss Karen Kelly MA *Other Snr Staff:* Circulation Libn: Mr Robert Eastwood; Acqs Libn: Mr Thomas Butler
Entry: full access for staff & students (ID card required for borrowing), ref only for non-membs of Coll *Open:* Mon 0845-1800, Tue-Thu 0845-2100, Fri 0930-1600
Subj: all subjs; genl; GCSE; A level; local study (Middlesex, esp Hounslow, Feltham etc, local hist & geog) *Collns:* Archvs: Joseph Banks & Pears House Colln (hist, pamphs, artwork, drawings & displays) *Other:* newspaper cuttings *Co-op Schemes:* BLDSC
Equip: copier, video viewer, 11 computers (incl 10 with internet & 1 with CD-ROM) *Disabled:* lift access *Svcs:* info, ref
Stock: bks/50000; periodcls/120; slides/10000; audios/200; videos/1200 *Acqs Offcr:* Acqs Libn, as above
Classn: DDC *Auto Sys:* Heritage
Staff: Libns: 4 *Non-Prof:* 3

Keighley

S852 ✚

Airedale NHS Trust Library Information Service
Edu Centre, Airedale Genl Hosp, Steeton, Keighley, W Yorkshire, BD20 6TD (01535-294412; *fax:* 01535-292196)
Email: airedale.library@anhst.nhs.uk

Chief: Libn & Edu Centre Mgr: Mrs Anne Troth BA(Hons), PGCE *Dep:* Libn: Ms Becky Williams
Entry: ref only, adv appt *Open:* Mon-Thu 0830-1900, Fri 0830-1600
Subj: medicine; biomedicine; surgery; nursing; related health care fields
Equip: copier, computers (incl internet & CD-ROM), room for hire *Online:* Medline, CINAHL, Cochrane, Best Evidence, BNI *Svcs:* info, ref
Stock: bks/10000; periodcls/230; pamphs/50 boxes; videos/c50
Classn: NLM *Auto Sys:* SydneyPlus
Staff: Libns: 1.5 *Non-Prof:* 2

S853 🔑 🏛

Brontë Parsonage Museum Library
Church St, Haworth, Keighley, W Yorkshire, BD22 8DR (01535-642323; *fax:* 01535-647131)
Email: ann.dinsdale@bronte.org.uk
Internet: http://www.bronte.org.uk/

Gov Body: The Brontë Soc *Chief:* Libn: Ms Ann Dinsdale
Entry: access by prior written appt only; academic ref required for study of MSS material *Open:* Mon-Fri 1000-1630 excl bank hols
Subj: life & work of the Brontë family *Collns:* Other: MSS; paintings & drawings; Brontë Soc Colln; Bonnell Colln; Seton-Gordon Colln; Grolier Colln
Equip: copier (via staff)
Stock: bks/4000; photos/1000
Classn: MDA sys (museum objects), own (others)
Pubns: The Brontë Parsonage Museum: A Souvenir Guide (£3.95); Early Visitors to Haworth (£4.95); Classics of Brontë Scholarship (£5); A Brief Guide to Jane Eyre (50p); A Brief Guide to Wuthering Heights (50p); A Brief Guide to Shirley (50p)
Staff: Non-Prof: 1

Kendal

S854 🍷 📷 🎥

Eric Whitehead Photography
(incorporating the Cumbria Picture Lib)
PO Box 33, Sedbergh, Kendal, Cumbria, LA10 4SU (01539-448894; *fax:* 01539-448294)
Email: info@ewphotography.com
Internet: http://www.ewphotography.com/ or http://www.snookerimages.co.uk/

Type: commercial picture agency *Chief:* Proprietor: Mr Eric Whitehead
Entry: no personal access; enqs by phone, fax, email or in writing *Open:* Mon-Fri 0900-1700
Subj: people & places of Cumbria & the Lake Dist; snooker *Collns:* Other: world's premier specialist lib on snooker photography
Stock: photos/30000

S855 🎓

Kendal College, Learning Resource Centre
Milnthorpe Rd, Kendal, Cumbria, LA9 5AY (01538-814750)
Email: lrc@kendal.ac.uk
Internet: http://www.kendal.ac.uk/

Gov Body: Kendal Coll *Chief:* Resources Centre Mgr: Mrs Michelle Smart *Dep:* Ms Alison Rigden
Entry: borrowing to registered students & staff; public access for ref only *Open:* term: Mon-Thu 0830-2100, Fri 0830-1600; vac: Mon-Fri 1000-1600
Subj: psy; social sci; lang; tech; arts; lit; expressive arts *Co-op Schemes:* ILL with Univ of Central Lancashire
Equip: 4 video viewers, copier, 102 computers (all with wd-proc, internet & CD-ROM) *Online:* BIDS, Emerald, Athens, Ingenta Journals *Svcs:* info, ref
Stock: bks/15000; periodcls/70; videos/600
Classn: DDC *Auto Sys:* Heritage
Staff: Libns: 1 *Non-Prof:* 4

S856 ✚

Westmorland General Hospital, Education Centre Library
Burton Rd, Kendal, Cumbria, LA9 7RG (01539-795234; *fax:* 01539-795308)
Email: wgh.library@wgh.mbht.nhs.uk

Gov Body: Morecambe Bay Hosps NHS Trust
Chief: Libn: Mr Sam Burgess BA(Hons) MCLIP
Entry: Trust staff & students of St Martins Coll
Open: Mon-Fri 0900-1700; out of hrs access by arrangement with Libn
Subj: psy; social sci; medicine *Collns:* Archvs: Westmorland County Hosp medical records *Co-op Schemes:* BLDSC, BMA, LIHNN
Equip: copier, computer (incl internet & CD-ROM)
Svcs: info, ref, biblio, indexing, abstracting
Stock: bks/2685; periodcls/34; videos/32
Classn: NLM *Auto Sys:* InMagic
Staff: Libns: 1 *Non-Prof:* 1

Kenilworth

S857 🏛

Lantra Library
Lantra House, Natl Agricultural Centre, Kenilworth, Warwickshire, CV8 2LG (024-7669-6996; *fax:* 024-7669-6732)
Email: connect@lantra.co.uk
Internet: http://www.lantra.co.uk/

Chief: Libn: A.M. Sealy
Subj: agric; livestock; hortic; training skills; mgmt; health & safety; agric statistics *Co-op Schemes:* ILL, IAALD, BIM, IPM
Stock: bks/7000; periodcls/150

Keswick

S858 🏛 🏛

Keswick Museum and Art Gallery Library
Fitz Pk, Station Rd, Keswick, Cumbria, CA12 4NF (017687-73263; *fax:* 017687-80390)
Email: hazel.davison@allerdale.gov.uk

Type: local authority *Gov Body:* Allerdale Borough Council *Chief:* Curator: Miss Hazel Davison BA(Hons), MA
Entry: adv appt *Open:* Mon-Fri 1000-1600
Subj: Keswick & Northern Lakes: local hist; Lake poets & writers, esp Southey & Walpole; sci; geol *Collns:* Archvs: original MSS of works, letters etc of Robert Southey & Hugh Walpole
Equip: Disabled: wheelchair access *Svcs:* info
Stock: bks/500; photos/100; pamphs/150; archvs/3000 items
Staff: Other Prof: 1 *Exp:* £80 (1999-2000)

S859 🔑

Mirehouse Library
Mirehouse, Keswick, Cumbria, CA12 4QE (01768-772287; *fax:* 01768-772287)

Gov Body: private house *Chief:* Owner: Mr John Spedding
Entry: adv appt only
Subj: local study (Lake Dist, lit & genl); phil; psy; religion; lang; sci; maths; arts; lit; geog; hist
Collns: Bks & Pamphs: English literary MSS & bks (c1600-1900) *Archvs:* kept at The Wordsworth Trust Lib (see **S34**), except for MSS on display in house
Stock: bks/3000; uncounted photos, pamphs & maps
Pubns: Mirehouse Guidebook (£1.50 incl p&p)

Kidderminster

S860 🔑

British Institute of Learning Disabilities, Information and Resource Centre
Campion House, Green St, Kidderminster, Worcestershire, DY10 1JL (01562-723010; *fax:* 01562-723029)
Email: bild@bild.demon.co.uk
Internet: http://www.bild.org.uk

Chief: Info Offcr: Ms Nesta Muller
Entry: appt only *Open:* Mon-Fri 0900-1300, 1400-1630
Subj: learning disabilities & multiple handicap *Co-op Schemes:* BLDSC, PLCS, WMLCS
Equip: video viewer, copier, computer *Online:* own on-site database (30000 refs on learning disability from 1985; £3 membs, £12 non-membs)
Stock: bks/3000; periodcls/120; videos/100
Classn: own
Pubns: Current Awareness Svc (monthly, £38 pa); Bulletin (quarterly, £33.50 pa)
Staff: Non-Prof: 0.25

S861 ✚

Lea Castle Centre Library
North Warwickshire NHS Trust, Wolverley, Kidderminster, Worcestershire, DY10 3PP (01562-850461; *fax:* 01562-859010)
Email: janette.hill@nw-pct.nhs.uk

Gov Body: North Warwickshire NHS Primary Care Trust *Chief:* Libn: Mrs J. Hill
Entry: adv appt for non-registered users *Open:* Mon-Tue, Fri 1000-1400, Wed-Thu 0900-1715
Subj: psychiatry; learning disabilities; nursing *Co-op Schemes:* BLDSC, WMRHLN, PLCS ☛

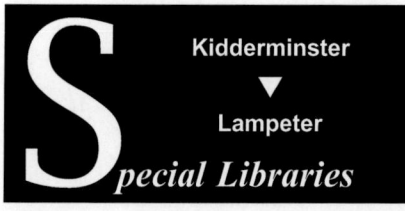

Kidderminster ▼ Lampeter

Special Libraries

(Lea Castle Centre Lib cont)
Equip: fax, copier, computers (incl internet & CD-ROM) *Svcs:* info, ref
Stock: bks/3000; periodcls/50; videos/25
Classn: NLM (Wessex) *Staff:* Libns: 1

S862 ✚

Worcestershire Acute Hospitals NHS Trust, Kidderminster Hospital Library
(formerly Kidderminster Acute NHS Trust)
Kidderminster Hosp, Bewdley Rd, Kidderminster, Worcestershire, DY11 6RJ (01562-823424 x3295; *fax:* 01562-825733)
Email: jan.brown@worcsacute.wmids.nhs.uk
Internet: http://www.worcestershireknowledgeportal. co.uk/

Chief: Site Libn: Mrs Jan Brown BLib, MCLIP
Assoc Libs: ALEXANDRA HOSP LIB (see **S1852**); WORCESTER ROYAL HOSP, ROWLANDS LIB (see **S2149**)
Entry: Worcestershire health staff *Open:* Mon-Tue, 0900-1700, Wed-Thu 0900-1630; closed Fri
Subj: medicine; nursing; allied health; health svc mgmt *Co-op Schemes:* BLDSC, WMRHLN, Worcestershire Health Libs
Equip: 2 copiers, 8 computers (all with wd-proc, CD-ROM & internet), 2 scanners *Svcs:* info, ref, biblio
Stock: bks/c2200; periodcls/56; audios/20; videos/40 *Acqs Offcr:* Site Libn, as above
Classn: NLM (Wessex) *Auto Sys:* Sirsi Unicorn
Staff: Libns: 0.5 *Non-Prof:* 0.4

Kilbarchan

S863 ⚷

Scottish Natural History Library
Foremount House, Kilbarchan, Renfrewshire, PA10 2EZ (01505-702419)

Chief: Libn: Dr J.A. Gibson
Entry: adv appt essential
Subj: Scottish nat hist *Collns: Bks & Pamphs:* Royal Physical Soc of Edinburgh Lib; Royal Soc of Edinburgh Nat Hist Lib; Scottish Soc for the Protection of Birds Lib; Kintyre Nat Hist Soc Lib (partial); Perthshire Nat Hist Soc Lib (partial); Renfrewshire Nat Hist Soc Lib (partial); A. Rodger Waterston Colln; Duncan Colville Colln; F.J. Ramsay Colln; H.F. Witherby Colln; H.J. Egglishaw Colln; J.A. Gibson Colln; J.M. McWilliam Colln; J.P. Ritchie Colln; James Anderson Colln; James Lumsden Colln *Archvs:* Royal Scottish Forestry Soc Archv
Svcs: ref, biblio
Stock: bks/c120000; periodcls/500
Pubns: Scottish Naturalist (3 pa, annual subscription £30)

King's Lynn

S864 🎓

College of West Anglia Library
Tennyson Ave, King's Lynn, Norfolk, PE30 2QW (01553-761144; *fax:* 01553-770388)
Internet: http://www.col-westanglia.ac.uk/

Gov Body: Norfolk Edu Authority *Chief:* Learning Centre Mgr: Mrs Teresa Wicklen *Dep:* Lib & Info Offcr: Mr John Ross BA
Assoc Libs: FACULTY OF LAND-BASED STUDIES LIB (see **S348**); WISBECH LIB, Newcommon Bridge, Wisbech, Cambridgeshire, PE13 2SJ (01945-581024)
Entry: ref only *Open:* term: Mon-Thu 0830-2000, Fri 0830-1600; vac: Mon-Fri 0900-1600
Subj: all subjs *Co-op Schemes:* ANGLES
Equip: m-reader, m-printer, video viewer, fax, copier, computers (incl wd-proc & CD-ROM) *Svcs:* info, ref, biblio
Stock: bks/50000; periodcls/120; videos/500
Classn: DDC *Auto Sys:* Dynix
Staff: Libns: 2 *Other Prof:* 1 *Non-Prof:* 8

S865 ⚷

Construction Industry Training Board, Information Centre
Bircham Newton, King's Lynn, Norfolk, PE31 6RH (01485-577682; *fax:* 01485-577684)
Email: information.centre@citb.co.uk
Internet: http://www.citb.co.uk/

Gov Body: CITB *Chief:* Centre Mgr
Entry: ref only, adv appt (except for CITB staff)
Open: Mon-Thu 0845-1700, Fri 0900-1600
Subj: construction; bldg; bldg svcs; civil eng; computing; edu; mgmt; marketing; safety; training
Collns: Bks & Pamphs: BSI relevant to construction; complete colln of CITB pubns; pamph colln *Other:* video colln *Co-op Schemes:* BLDSC, ANGLES
Equip: m-reader, fax, 2 video viewers, copier, computer (with internet & CD-ROM), room for hire
Svcs: info, ref
Stock: bks/3500; periodcls/200; pamphs/8000; videos/500
Classn: own
Pubns: Resource Centre Brief Guide
Staff: Libns: 1 *Non-Prof:* 1

S866 🏛 🎓

King's Lynn Museum, Library
Market St, King's Lynn, Norfolk, PE30 1NL (01553-775001)
Email: lynn.museum@norfolk.gov.uk

Gov Body: Norfolk Museums & Archaeo Svc
Chief: Area Museums Offcr: Dr Robin Hanley
Dep: Curator: Mr Tim Thorpe AMA
Assoc Libs: TOWN HOUSE MUSEUM LIB, 46 Queen St, Kings Lynn, Norfolk, PE30 3DQ
Entry: ref only, adv appt *Open:* Tue-Sat 1000-1700
Subj: all subjs; genl; local hist; arts; geog; hist
Equip: copier
Pubns: Norfolk Museums pubns
Staff: Other Prof: 4 *Non-Prof:* 7

S867 🎓 ✚

University of East Anglia, School of Nursing and Midwifery Library (King's Lynn)
Queen Elizabeth Hosp, Gayton Rd, King's Lynn, Norfolk, PE30 4ET (01553-613959; *fax:* 01603-259490)
Internet: http://www.lib.uea.ac.uk/

Gov Body: Univ of East Anglia (see **S1631**) & Queen Elizabeth Hosp NHS Trust *Chief:* Trust Libn: Ms Ann Osborne *Dep:* Lib Assts: Ms Alison Castleton & Ms Karen Lupton (PT)
Entry: membs of Univ *Open:* Mon, Fri 0900-1700, Tue-Thu 0900-1800
Subj: health; medicine; nursing
Equip: copier (A4/5p), computers (incl internet)

Online: CINAHL, Medline, PsycInfo, Cochrane
Classn: LC *Auto Sys:* Aleph *Staff:* 3

Kingston upon Thames

S868 🎓

Kingston College, Learning Resources Centre
Kingston Hall Rd, Kingston upon Thames, Surrey, KT1 2AQ (020-8268-3051; *fax:* 020-8268-2900)
Email: info@kingston-college.ac.uk
Internet: http://www.kingston-college.ac.uk/

Gov Body: Further Edu Funding Council *Chief:* Head of Learning Resources: Mrs Linda Foster PGDipIS *Dep:* Mrs Helen Davies
Assoc Libs: SCHOOL OF ART & DESIGN LIB
Entry: adv appt *Open:* term: Mon-Thu 0845-2000, Fri 0845-1600; vac: variable
Subj: all subjs; GCSE; A level *Co-op Schemes:* BLDSC, ILL
Equip: m-reader, 3 video viewers, 2 copiers, 50 computers *Disabled:* Kurzweil, laptops *Svcs:* info, ref
Stock: bks/40000; periodcls/200; slides/2000; videos/2000
Classn: DDC *Auto Sys:* Heritage
Staff: Libns: 8 *Non-Prof:* 1.2

S869 🎓

Kingston University Library Services
Penrhyn Rd, Kingston upon Thames, Surrey, KT1 2EE (020-8547-7101; *fax:* 020-8547-7111)
Email: library@kingston.ac.uk
Internet: http://www.king.ac.uk/library_media/

Gov Body: Kingston Univ *Chief:* Dir of Lib Svcs: Mr Graham Bulpitt *Other Snr Staff:* Head of Learning & Rsrch Support: Ms Jane Savidge; Head of E-Strategy & Colln Mgmt: Ms Elizabeth Malone; Head of Planning, Finance & Resources: Mr Simon Mackie
Assoc Libs: PENRHYN RD LIB, addr as above; KINGSTON HILL LIB, Kingston Hill, Kingston upon Thames, Surrey, KT2 7LB (020-8547-7380; *fax:* 020-8547-7312; *email:* Khlibrary-info@kingston. ac.uk); KNIGHTS PK LIB (see **S870**); ROE-HAMPTON VALE LIB, Friars Ave, London, SW15 3DW (020-8547-7903; *fax:* 020-547-7800)
Entry: ref only *Open:* *Penrhyn Rd:* term: Mon-Thu 0845-2100, Fri 1000-1730, Sat-Sun 1015-1545; *Kingston Hill:* term: Mon-Thu 0845-2100, Fri 1000-2100, Sat-Sun 1015-1545; *Roehampton Vale:* term: Mon-Thu 0845-1800, Fri 0830-1700; vac: hrs vary
Subj: all subjs; undergrad; postgrad; *Penrhyn Rd:* computing; psy; social sci; lang; sci; maths; tech; hist; geog; politics; civil eng; electronics; women's studies; econ; lit; *Kingston Hill:* business; healthcare; nursing; midwifery; music; law; edu; *Roehampton Vale:* mechanical eng; aeronautical eng; production eng *Collns: Bks & Pamphs:* Mineralogical Soc Lib (at Penrhyn Rd) *Co-op Schemes:* BLDSC
Equip: m-readers, m-printer, video viewers, 14 copiers (A4/6p, A3/12p), 3 clr copiers (A4/£1, A3/£1.50), computers (incl wd-proc & CD-ROM)
Online: ABI Inform, Cambridge Scientific Abstracts, ASSIA, BHI, ChildData, CINAHL, Design & Applied Arts Index, EBSCO, EconLit, EEVL, Emerald, ERIC, Eurolaw, FAME, IBSS, Ingenta Journals, Inspec, Lawtel, Lexis, Medline, Mintel, OHSIS, SciDirect, Web of Science, Westlaw, XreferPlus, Zetoc & others
Stock: bks/320000; periodcls/2000
Classn: DDC *Auto Sys:* Talis
Staff: Libns: 18 *Non-Prof:* 25

S870

Kingston University, Knights Park Library

Knights Pk, Kingston upon Thames, Surrey, KY1 2QJ (020-8547-7057; *fax:* 020-8547-7011)
Email: j.savidge@kingston.ac.uk
Internet: http://www.king.ac.uk/library_media/

Gov Body: Kingston Univ (see **S869**) *Chief:* Libn: Ms Jane Savidge MA, MCLIP
Entry: open access to students; membs of public ref only *Open:* Mon-Thu 0900-2100, Fri 1000-1700, Sat 1015-1545
Subj: social sci; arts; design; hist of art; fashion
Collns: Bks & Pamphs: rare & antiquarian bks (c2000 titles); portfolios; postcard-type pubns (1930s); 19C exhib catalogues (trade fairs); 3000 manufacturers' trade catalogues *Other:* slide colln
Co-op Schemes: ILL, M25, ARLIS, IFLA, COPOL, UK Libs Plus
Equip: m-reader, m-printer, video viewer, copier, clr copier, 25 computers (incl wd-proc, internet & 5 CD-ROM), guillotines, spiral binder, room for hire
Svcs: info, ref, biblio
Stock: bks/100000; periodcls/270; slides/180000; illusts/17000; maps/1000; m-forms/4600; audios/3100; videos/1200
Classn: DDC *Auto Sys:* Talis
Pubns: in-house instruction leaflets; lib guide; journals list; termly newsletter
Staff: Libns: 3 *Non-Prof:* 11

S871 🔑

Mineralogical Society of Great Britain and Ireland Library

c/o Kingston Univ Lib, Penrhyn Rd, Kingston upon Thames, Surrey, KT1 2EE (020-8547-2000 x62119)
Email: n.dowson@kingston.ac.uk

Chief: Info Libn (Earth Scis & Geog): Miss Nicola Dowson
Entry: soc membs, ref only *Open:* term: Mon-Thu 0845-2100, Fri 1000-1730, Sat-Sun 1015-1545; vac: Mon-Fri 0900-1730
Subj: various bks & periodcls in the earth scis
Equip: m-reader, copier, computer (incl CD-ROM)
Svcs: info, ref

Kinross

S872 🔑 🏛

Michael Bruce Cottage Museum

The Cobbles, Kinnesswood, Kinross, Tayside, KY13 9HL

Gov Body: Michael Bruce Memorial Trust *Chief:* Chairman: Dr David M. Munro BSc, PhD, FSA(Scot) *Dep:* Vice Chairman: Mr Thomas Buchan
Entry: adv appt for ref *Open:* Mon-Fri 0900-1700
Subj: local study (Kinross-shire & local hist of Portmoak parish); life & works of the poet Michael Bruce (1746-67) *Collns: Bks & Pamphs:* biographies & poetic works of Michael Bruce
Stock: bks/120
Pubns: The Life & Works of Michael Bruce (£10); collns of poems submitted to Michael Bruce Trust Poetry Competitions: Time Returning (1991, £3); A Mindin' (1993, £3); Grace (1995, £3)
Staff: administered by local volunteers

Kirkcaldy

S873 ✚

Fife Acute Hospitals NHS Trust, Postgraduate Library

Victoria Hosp, Hayfield Rd, Kirkcaldy, Fife, KY2 5AH (01592-643355 x8790; *fax:* 01592-204599)

Gov Body: Fife Acute Hosps NHS Trust *Chief:* Libn: Ms Dorothy McGinley BSc, MSc, MCLIP (dorothy.mcginley@faht.scot.nhs.uk) *Dep:* Postgrad Centre Mgr: Mrs Ann Sheach HNC (ann.sheach@faht.scot.nhs.uk)
Assoc Libs: EDU CENTRE LIB, Queen Margaret Hosp (see **S564**)
Entry: open to Trust staff & grad doctors *Open:* 24 hr access
Subj: medicine *Co-op Schemes:* BLDSC, SHINE, BMA
Equip: copier, video viewer, 4 computers (all with wd-proc, CD-ROM & internet) *Online:* NHS Scotland eLibrary *Svcs:* info, ref, biblio
Stock: bks/1500; periodcls/60; videos/40
Classn: NLM *Auto Sys:* Heritage
Staff: Libns: 0.54 *Non-Prof:* 1

S874

Fife College of Further and Higher Education Library

St Brycedale Ave, Kirkcaldy, Fife, KY1 1EX (01592-268591)
Internet: http://www.fife.ac.uk/support/studentsrvs/library/

Chief: Libn: Mr Sandy Stevenson *Dep:* Asst Libn: Mrs Lesley Jackson
Entry: students & staff of Coll; ref only for public
Open: term: Mon-Wed, Fri 0850-2100, Thu 0850-1700; vac: Mon-Fri 0900-1700
Subj: all subjs; genl; GCSE; A level; undergrad; postgrad; vocational
Equip: video viewer, copier, 51 computers (all with wd-proc, internet & CD-ROM), LCT scanner
Stock: bks/14000; periodcls/12; videos/150
Classn: DDC *Auto Sys:* Heritage
Staff: Libns: 1 *Non-Prof:* 4

S875 ✚

University of Dundee, School of Nursing and Midwifery, Fife Campus Library

Forth Ave, Kirkcaldy, Fife, KY2 5YS (01382-345930; *fax:* 01382-345931)
Email: snm-fife-library@dundee.ac.uk
Internet: http://www.dundee.ac.uk/library/

Gov Body: Univ of Dundee (see **S561**) *Chief:* Libn: Ms Alison Aiton MA, DipLib, MCLIP *Dep:* Asst Libn: Mrs Donna Duff MA(Hons)
Entry: for use by Dundee Univ students & staff; others on payment of annual fee *Open:* Mon-Thu 0845-2100, Fri 0845-1700 Sat 1000-1400
Subj: nursing; midwifery; psy; social sci; psychiatry; mental health *Co-op Schemes:* BLDSC, SHINE, NULJ, BMA
Equip: video viewer, copier, computers *Online:* CINAHL, Medline, BNI, ASSIA, Cochrane & others; large colln of e-journals *Svcs:* info, ref, biblio
Classn: DDC *Auto Sys:* Dynix
Pubns: in-house guides & lit (free to registered membs)
Staff: Libns: 2 *Non-Prof:* 8

Kirkcudbright

S876 🔑

E.A. Hornel Library

Broughton House, 12 High St, Kirkcudbright, Dumfries & Galloway, DG6 4JX (01557-330437)
Email: broughtonhouse@nts.org.uk

Gov Body: Natl Trust for Scotland *Chief:* Libn: Mr James Allan
Entry: adv appt preferred *Open:* Mon-Fri 1000-1300, 1400-1700
Subj: local study (Dumfries & Galloway); Scottish religion; tech pertaining to Dumfries & Galloway;

Scottish art ('Glasgow Boys'); local authors; mainly Scottish geog & hist *Collns: Bks & Pamphs:* Robert Burns Colln (2500 items); Thomas Carlyle Colln; Covenanters Colln; James M. Barrie Colln; John Paul Jones Colln *Archvs:* literary & artistic MSS; local hist material (records, diaries, account bks, letters); Childe Ballads Colln *Other:* photos (Japan c1890 & Ceylon 1907)
Equip: m-reader, copier (fees vary), clr copier (fees vary)
Stock: bks/20000; photos/1600; illusts/500; maps/100; archvs/40 m
Classn: own
Staff: Libns: 1 *Exp:* £500 (1999-2000); £1000 (2000-01)

Knebworth

S877 🔑

Knebworth House, Library and Archive

Knebworth, Hertfordshire, SG3 6PY (01438-812661; *fax:* 01438-811908)
Email: info@knebworthhouse.com
Internet: http://www.knebworthhouse.com/

Chief: Archivist: Mrs C.E. Fleck MA, AMA
Entry: by appt, ref only
Subj: generalities; phil; sci; maths; lit; geog; hist
Collns: Bks & Pamphs: static colln largely collected in 19C by Sir Edward Bulwer Lytton, 1st Lord Lytton (1803-1873) *Archvs:* relating to Lytton family & Knebworth Estate
Equip: copier *Svcs:* info, ref
Stock: bks/5000 *Staff: Non-Prof:* 1

Laindon

S878

Ford Motor Company, Dunton Technical Centre Library

GB15/2A-PO4, Dunton, Laindon, Essex, SS15 6EE (01268-403020; *fax:* 01268-401110)
Email: sdraper2@ford.com

Chief: Libn: Ms Sue Draper
Entry: company staff; lib staff of other orgs *Open:* Mon-Fri 0815-1630
Subj: automotive eng, design & development
Equip: m-reader, fax, copier, 2 computers (both with internet & CD-ROM) *Svcs:* info, ref, abstracting
Stock: bks/2000; periodcls/96
Classn: DDC
Staff: Libns: 1 *Exp:* £45000 (1999-2000); £37500 (2000-01)

Lampeter

S879

University of Wales Lampeter, Library

College St, Lampeter, Ceredigion, SA48 7ED (01570-422351; *fax:* 01570-423875)
Internet: http://www.lamp.ac.uk/library/

Gov Body: Univ of Wales *Chief:* Libn: Ms Miriam Perrett MA, DipLib (m.perrett@lamp.ac.uk) *Other Snr Staff:* Administrator: Ms Jennie Bracher (j.bracher@lamp.ac.uk)
Assoc Libs: FOUNDERS' LIB, addr as above (see **S880**); UNIV OF WALES LAMPETER ARCHVS, addr as above, Archivist: Dr John Morgan-Guy (01570-424772; *email:* founderslibrary@lamp.ac.uk)
Entry: membs of univ only, ref only for public
Open: term: Mon-Fri 0900-2145, Sat 0900-1545, Sun 1400-1645; vac: Mon-Fri 0900-1645 ☛

Special Libraries

Lampeter ▼ Lee on Solent

(Univ of Wales Lampeter, Lib cont)
Subj: undergrad; postgrad; generalities; phil; psy; religion; social sci; lang; arts; lit; geog; hist *Collns: Archvs:* archvs of the Univ of Wales Lampeter & predecessors (1822 onwards); Alister Hardy Archv of Religious Experience, incl the papers of Sir Alistair Hardy FRS; Welsh Religious Hist Soc Records; Ystrad Meurig Grammar School (St John's Coll) Archv; papers of scholars associated with the Univ, incl: Alfred Edwin Morris papers (Archbishop of Wales); G.O. Williams papers (Archbishop of Wales); Thomas Wood papers; Dom Illtyd Evans papers *Co-op Schemes:* ILL, SCONUL, WALIA, Croeso Scheme, UK Libs Plus *Equip:* m-readers, copiers, computers *Online:* Aslib Index to Theses, COPAC, OCLC FirstSearch, Routledge Encyclopedia of Phil, Zetoc
Stock: bks/160000; periodcls/950; some pamphs, m-forms, sound recordings, videos & archvs *Acqs Offcr:* Acqs Libn: Ms Jan Thomas (jan.thomas@ lamp.ac.uk)
Classn: DDC *Auto Sys:* Libertas
Staff: Libns: 5.5 *Non-Prof:* 6

S880

University of Wales Lampeter, Founders' Library

Lampeter, Ceredigion, SA48 7ED (01570-424716/ 72; *fax:* 01570-423875)
Email: founderslibrary@lamp.ac.uk
Internet: http://www.lamp.ac.uk/founders_library/

Gov Body: Univ of Wales *Chief:* Conservator: Rev David Selwyn MA(Cantab), MA(Oxon) (selwyn@lamp.ac.uk)
Assoc Libs: UNIV OF WALES LAMPETER LIB (see **S879**); UNIV OF WALES LAMPETER ARCHVS, addr as above, Archivist: Dr John Morgan Guy (01570-424772; *email:* as above)
Entry: staff & students of Univ; bona fide scholars by written arrangement with Conservator, normally giving 3 wks notice, stating the nature of their rsrch & supplying evidence of their position within their respective instn *Open:* term: Mon-Fri 1400-1630; vac: Mon-Thu 1400-1630
Subj: religion; theology; biblical studies; church hist (to 19C); world religions; lang; biblical langs; linguistics; eng; arts; arch; music; painting; theatre; lit; hist (economic, political & social); geog; travel; exploration *Collns: Bks & Pamphs:* Foundation Colln, formed & donated by Thomas Burgess & Thomas Phillips; Tract Colln (11450 items in 832 vols, c1520-1843), incl Bowdler Family Colln (9000 items, 1638-1787); Cenarth Colln (early Welsh bibles, prayer bks, hymnals, catechisms & sermons, 500 vols); Ystrad Meurig Colln (615 vols); Welsh Ballad Colln (700 items); Welsh Hymn Colln (300 vols); Isaac Williams Colln (215 vols); Harford Colln (185 vols); Thomas Wood Colln (2000 vols); Brinkley Colln (1500 vols); 16C-17C continental printing (c1800 vols); 67 incunabula *Archvs:* 110 MSS & 3 scrolls (incl 8 medieval MSS & 1 medieval scroll); records of the Lib, incl: donors & acqs registers (1827-95); MS catalogue of Bowdler Tract Colln (1787); provenance index; notebks & correspondence relating to the collns; exhib catalogues etc *Other:* photographic archv (mid 19C-date)
Equip: computer (with wd-proc, internet & CD-ROM)
Stock: bks/28000; slides/4000; pamphs/11400; maps/c50 atlases; CD-ROMs/14; archvs/8 linear m
Classn: none (fixed location) *Auto Sys:* Voyager

Pubns: The Founders' Lib, Univ of Wales, Lampeter: Bibliographical & Contextual Studies, ed William Marx (1997, £15); Éditions Françaises du XVIe siècle conservées dans le fonds ancien de la Bibliothèque de Saint David's Univ Coll, Lampeter, by Trevor Peach (1992, £5); Catalogues des Ouvrages du Fonds Français 1601-1850 conservés dans la Founders' Lib Université Du Pays de Galles, Lampeter, by D.J. Culpin (1996)
Staff: Libns: 1.5

Lanark

S881

Lanark State Hospital, Staff Library

Carstairs Junction, Lanark, ML11 8RP (01555-840293 x578)
Email: gerry.maclean@tsh.scot.nhs.uk

Chief: Libn: Ms Gerry Maclean BA, MEd, MCLIP
Entry: all hosp staff; external users by prior arrangement *Open:* Mon-Thu 0900-1700, Fri 0900-1600
Subj: psy; psychiatry; forensic psychiatry; nursing; mental health nursing; mental health svcs; social work; criminology *Co-op Schemes:* PLCS, SHINE, NULJ
Equip: copier, computers (incl internet) *Online:* Medline, CINAHL, Cochrane, PsycInfo, Embase
Svcs: info, ref, biblio
Stock: bks/c3000; periodcls/36; offprints/c6000
Classn: Royal Coll of Psychiatrists
Staff: Libns: 1

Lancaster

S882

Lancaster and Morecambe College Library

Morecambe Rd, Lancaster, LA1 2TY (01524-66215; *fax:* 01524-843078)
Internet: http://www.lanmore.ac.uk/

Chief: Libn: Mrs Andrea Wilson BSc, CertEd, MCLIP
Assoc Libs: HEYSHAM LEARNING CENTRE, 406 Heysham Rd, Heysham, Lancashire, LA3 2BJ (01524-850830; *fax:* 01524-858889); MORE-CAMBE LEARNING CENTRE, 66-68 Euston Rd, Morecambe, Lancashire, LA4 5DG (01524-410365); RIDGE ONLINE LEARNING CENTRE, 1 Ridge Sq, Lancaster, Lancashire, LA1 3HR (01524-67881)
Entry: students of coll; ref only for others *Open:* term: Mon-Thu 0845-2000, Fri 0845-1700; vac: Mon-Fri 0900-1600
Subj: all subjs; genl
Equip: video viewer, copier, computers (incl wd-proc & internet) *Svcs:* info, ref, biblio
Stock: bks/20000; periodcls/50
Classn: DDC *Auto Sys:* Heritage
Staff: Libns: 1 *Non-Prof:* 3.5

S883

Lancaster University Library

Bailrigg, Lancaster, LA1 4YH (01524-592535; *fax:* 01524-63806)
Email: library@lancs.ac.uk
Internet: http://www.lancs.ac.uk/

Chief: Univ Libn: Ms Jacqueline Whiteside MA, MCLIP *Dep: Dep Libn:* Mr David Summers *Other Snr Staff:* Curator of Rare Bks: Ms Helen Clish
Assoc Libs: RUSKIN LIB (see **S885**)
Entry: written appl to libn *Open:* term: Mon-Tue, Thu-Fri 0845-2200, Wed 0930-2200, Sat 1000-1700, Sun 1400-1900 (not open evenings & Sun in vacs)
Subj: all subjs, excl medicine; undergrad; postgrad; local study (North West England)

Collns: Bks & Pamphs: EDC; British official pubns; Quaker Colln; Business Hist Colln; Legal Hist Colln; Socialist Colln; Ford Railway Colln; Wordsworth Colln; H.F. Redlich Colln; rare bks collns; historic collns on deposit incl: Beetham Parish Lib; Burnley Grammar School Lib; Ribchester Porch Lib; Thomas Preston Lib *Archvs:* Jack Hylton Archv (bandleader) *Other:* Map Colln; Slide Colln *Co-op Schemes:* BLDSC, Libs North West, UK Libs Plus
Equip: m-reader, m-printers, video viewers, fax, 14 copiers, clr copier, computers (with wd-proc, internet & CD-ROM) *Disabled:* Kurzweil, Tieman text enlarger, large monitor PC *Online:* BIDS, EDINA, Web of Science, Lexis-Nexis, Westlaw UK, OCLC First Search (all for Univ membs only)
Svcs: info, ref, biblio
Stock: bks/c1 mln, incl pamphs; periodcls/3000; photos/3800; slides/75000; maps/5600; m-forms/50000 vols (equivalent); audios/7300; videos/2160; archvs/16 linear m
Classn: Bliss (mod) *Auto Sys:* own
Pubns: Report of the Libn (annual); Guide to the Lib; c50 guides to indiv collns & svcs
Staff: Libns: 18.5 *Non-Prof:* 37.8

S884

Royal Lancaster Infirmary, Education Centre Library

Morecambe Bay Hosps NHS Trust, Ashton Rd, Lancaster, LA1 4RR (01524-583954; *fax:* 01524-848289)

Gov Body: Morecambe Bay Hosps NHS Trust
Chief: Site Libn: Mr Paul Longbottom
Entry: open to all NHS employees in the Morecambe Bay patch; full borrowing rights to membs of hosp & Primary Care Trust
Subj: medicine; health disciplines *Co-op Schemes:* stock is a co-op shared colln with Kendal & Barrow Hosps
Equip: copier *Stock:* bks/2000; periodcls/60
Classn: DDC *Staff: Libns:* 1 *Non-Prof:* 0.81

S885

The Ruskin Library

Lancaster Univ, Lancaster, LA1 4YH (01524-593587; *fax:* 01524-593580)
Email: ruskin.library@lancs.ac.uk
Internet: http://www.lancs.ac.uk/users/ruskinlib/

Gov Body: Lancaster Univ *Chief:* Curator: Mr Stephen Wildman MA *Dep:* Dep Curator: Mrs Rebecca Patterson
Assoc Libs: LANCASTER UNIV LIB (see **S883**)
Entry: ref only, by appt *Open:* Mon-Fri 1000-1600
Subj: John Ruskin: arts; lit *Collns: Bks & Pamphs:* works by & pertaining to John Ruskin (1819-1900) *Archvs:* MSS (diaries, letters etc) by & pertaining to John Ruskin *Other:* 1500 water-colours & drawings, chiefly by John Ruskin *Co-op Schemes:* see under Univ Lib entry
Equip: m-reader, m-printer, computer (with internet & CD-ROM), access to Univ Lib facilities *Disabled:* bldg fully accessible *Online:* access to networked Univ Lib svcs *Svcs:* info, ref, biblio
Stock: bks/5000; photos/1500; archvs/200 MSS & 8000 letters; transcripts/150
Classn: own *Auto Sys:* JBase, with web interface
Staff: Libns: 1 *Other Prof:* 1 *Non-Prof:* 1 *Exp:* £250 (1999-2000)
Further Info: Exhib galleries are open throughout the year

S886

St Martin's College, Harold Bridges Library

Bowerham Rd, Lancaster, LA1 3JD (01524-384243; *fax:* 01524-384588)
Email: library@uscm.ac.uk
Internet: http://www.ucsm.ac.uk/library/

Gov Body: St Martin's Coll **Chief:** Coll Libn: Mr David Brown BA, MA, MCLIP **Dep:** Dep Libn: Ms Judy Dyer MA, MCLIP
Assoc Libs: AMBLESIDE SITE LIB (see **S33**); CARLISLE SITE LIB (see **S438**)
Entry: ref only for non-staff/students; external borrowing for a fee **Open:** term: Mon-Fri 0845-2100; vac: Mon-Fri 0900-1700
Subj: all subjs; undergrad; postgrad; local study (Lancashire & Cumbria) **Co-op Schemes:** BLDSC, North West Health Libs, ALLIS, UK Libs Plus, SCONUL Vac Scheme
Equip: 2 m-readers, fax, 3 video viewers, 7 copiers, 80 computers (incl CD-ROM) **Online:** JANET, CINAHL, Sport Discus & many others
Officer-in-Charge: Acqs Libn: Mrs Helen Jones (helen.jones@ucsm.ac.uk) **Svcs:** ref
Stock: bks/234000; periodcls/800; slides/4000; illusts/4000; maps/200; m-forms/500; audios/300; videos/400 **Acqs Offcr:** Acqs Libn, as above
Classn: DDC, Bliss **Auto Sys:** Talis
Staff: Libns: 14 Other Prof: 4 Non-Prof: 31 **Exp:** £345000 (1999-2000); £332600 (2000-01)
Proj: new Charlotte Mason Lib at Ambleside (completed Jan 2003)

Lancing

S887 🎓

Lancing College Library
Lancing, W Sussex, BN15 0RW (01273-452213)

Gov Body: Lancing Coll **Chief:** Libn: Mrs S.M. Gwilliam BLS, MCLIP
Entry: adv appt **Open:** term: Mon-Fri 0830-2100, Sat 0830-1230; closed during school hols
Subj: all subjs; genl; GCSE; A level **Collns:** Archvs: complete set of Coll magazines, No 1 (June 1877) to present day; all other Coll archv material held by archivist
Equip: 25 computers (all with wd-proc, internet & CD-ROM)
Stock: bks/9500; periodcls/50
Classn: DDC **Auto Sys:** Limes
Staff: Libns: 1 **Exp:** £20000 (1999-2000)

Langholm

S888 🔑

Langholm Library
Lib Bldgs, High St, Langholm, Dumfries & Galloway, DG13 0JH

Gov Body: Langholm Lib Trust
Entry: ref only
Collns: Bks & Pamphs: bks, mainly of Victorian era (largely in poor state of repair) **Co-op Schemes:** AIL
Equip: m-reader **Svcs:** ref
Stock: bks/c5000 **Staff:** run by volunteers

Leamington Spa

S889 🍴✒

Ashorne Hill Management College Library
Ashorne Hill, Leamington Spa, Warwickshire, CV33 9PY (01926-488095; fax: 01926-488005)

Gov Body: Corus **Chief:** Librarian/Info Offcrs: Ms Margaret Brittin BA, MCLIP & Ms Christine Crabtree MCLIP
Entry: access to public at discretion of libn & Coll only **Open:** Mon-Thu 0900-1630, Fri 0900-1300
Subj: mgmt; steel industry (not technical info) **Co-op Schemes:** BLDSC
Equip: computer (incl CD-ROM)
Stock: bks/20000; periodcls/200; videos/100
Classn: UDC **Auto Sys:** CAIRS
Staff: Libns: 0.75

S890 🔑 🐾

Coventry Diocesan Readers Library
Offa House, Diocesan Retreat House & Conference Centre, Offchurch, Leamington Spa, Warwickshire, CV33 9AS (0192-423309)

Type: C of E training resource **Gov Body:** Coventry Diocesan Readers Board **Chief:** Libn: Mr Rupert Allen BA(Hons)
Entry: primarily for Readers, Readers-in-training, tutors for Readers' course **Open:** lib is housed at the Diocesan Retreat House & is open as far as the use of the House allows
Subj: religion **Svcs:** info, ref, biblio
Stock: bks/2500; periodcls/1 **Classn:** DDC
Pubns: Lib Catalogue (£5)
Staff: Non-Prof: 1

Leatherhead

S891 🍴✒

ERA Technology Ltd, Information Centre
Cleeve Rd, Leatherhead, Surrey, KT22 7SA (01372-367007; fax: 01372-367009)
Email: info@era.co.uk
Internet: http://www.era.co.uk/

Gov Body: ERA Tech Ltd **Chief:** Info Svcs Group Mgr: Mrs Judith H. Potter BSc, MCLIP
Entry: not open for public access **Open:** Mon-Fri 0845-1715
Subj: tech **Collns:** Bks & Pamphs: technical standards & specifications **Co-op Schemes:** SASLIC, BLDSC
Equip: m-reader, fax, 6 computers (all with wd-proc, internet & CD-ROM) **Online:** Dialog, GEM, STN (cost of search + hourly rate) **Svcs:** info, biblio, indexing
Stock: bks/50000; periodcls/300
Classn: UDC **Auto Sys:** SydneyPlus
Staff: Libns: 1 Other Prof: 4

S892 🍴✒

ExxonMobil, Information and Library Services
(formerly Esso Petroleum Company Ltd)
ExxonMobil House, Ermyn Way, Leatherhead, Surrey, KT22 8UX (01372-222519; fax: 01372-222622)
Internet: http://www.exxonmobil.co.uk/

Chief: Info & Lib Svcs Dir: Miss Lindsay Parrish BSc, MCLIP
Entry: company staff; external enqs accepted where lib is sole src of info; appl by tel, fax or letter
Subj: econ; energy industry; mgmt; oil & petroleum industry; environment; health & safety; oil industry hist **Co-op Schemes:** BLDSC
Equip: m-reader, m-printer, copier **Online:** Orbit, FT Profile, CCN, Reuters, Dialog, Datastar, PFDS
Svcs: info, ref, biblio
Stock: bks/5000; periodcls/150; govt documents/5500
Classn: UDC **Auto Sys:** OpenRSO
Staff: Libns: 1 Non-Prof: 10

S893 🍴✒

Kellogg Brown and Root Ltd, Information Resource Centre
(formerly Brown & Root Ltd)
Hill Park Ct, Springfield Rise, Leatherhead, Surrey, KT22 7NL (01372-863143; fax: 01372-863180)
Email: caitriona.macneill@halliburton.com
Internet: http://www.halliburton.com/

Chief: Info Resource Centre Mgr: Ms Caitriona MacNeill MA(Hons), DipIS

Entry: adv appt **Open:** Mon 1000-1730, Tue-Fri 0900-1730
Subj: sci; maths; tech **Co-op Schemes:** BLDSC, LASER
Equip: copier, computers (incl internet) **Online:** Dialog, Dun & Bradstreet, Newsline, Lexis-Nexis, Datastar **Svcs:** info, ref, biblio, indexing, abstracting, translation
Stock: bks/20000; periodcls/200; maps/500; CD-ROMs/70
Classn: UDC **Auto Sys:** Sydney Plus
Staff: Libns: 3

S894 🔑

Leatherhead Food International, Library
Randalls Rd, Leatherhead, Surrey, KT22 7RY (01372-822280; fax: 01372-822268)
Email: gford@leatherheadfood.com
Internet: http://www.leatherheadfood.com/

Type: rsrch assoc **Chief:** Libn: Mr G.R. Ford MCLIP **Dep:** Asst Libn: Ms S.L. Coe BA(Hons)
Entry: membs only **Open:** Mon-Fri 0830-1730
Subj: food sci & tech **Co-op Schemes:** SASLIC, BLDSC
Equip: m-reader, m-printer, fax, 2 copiers, clr copier, computers (incl wd-proc, internet & CD-ROM) **Online:** Dialog, Echo, Dialtech
Stock: bks/16000; periodcls/750
Classn: UDC **Auto Sys:** CAIRS
Pubns: Acqs List (membs only); Periodicals Holdings List (membs only)
Staff: Libns: 2 Non-Prof: 2

S895 🔑

PIRA International, Information Centre
Randalls Rd, Leatherhead, Surrey, KT22 7RU (01372-802050; fax: 01372-802239)
Email: infocentre@pira.co.uk
Internet: http://www.piranet.com/

Type: rsrch assoc **Chief:** Info Scientist: Miss Mairead MacKenzie
Entry: membs only, by appt **Open:** Mon-Fri 0900-1700
Subj: paper; packaging; printing; publishing; non-wovens **Collns:** Bks & Pamphs: standards colln relating to paper, print & packaging (BSI, TAPPI, SCAN-TEST) **Co-op Schemes:** BLDSC
Equip: m-reader, m-printer, fax, copier, computer (incl CD-ROM) **Online:** PIRA database (available on CD-ROM, Dialog, Datastar, STN, Orbit & on PIRA web site; fees on appl)
Stock: bks/7000; periodcls/1000; pamphs/30000
Classn: UDC **Auto Sys:** Calm
Pubns: wide variety of pubns on mgmt, environment, packaging, printing, publishing, pulp & paper; catalogue on appl, or can be viewed on the PIRA web site

Lee on Solent

S896 🔑 🏛

Hovercraft Museum Trust Library
c/o HMS Daedalus, Chark Ln, Lee on Solent, Hampshire, PO13 9NY (tel & fax: 023-9255-2090)
Internet: http://www.hovercraft-museum.org/

Type: charitable trust **Gov Body:** The Hovercraft Soc & Hovercraft Museum Trust **Chief:** Mgr: Mr Brian Russell
Entry: membs; rsrchers on appl
Subj: hovercraft hist (past, present & future development); all types of hovering craft worldwide
Collns: Archvs: original papers relating to the development of the hovercraft **Other:** plans, logs & photos ☞

Lee on Solent ▼ **Leeds**

Special Libraries

(Hovercraft Museum Trust Lib cont)
Equip: copier, fax, video viewer, computers (incl internet & CD-ROM), slide & cine projectors *Svcs:* info, ref
Stock: bks/1000; periodcls/200, plus 500 no longer current; photos/1000; slides/600; pamphs/250; maps/300; m-forms/100; audios/500; videos/2000; wallcharts & posters/70
Classn: own
Pubns: Hovercraft Bulletin (quarterly, £25)
Staff: Non-Prof: 5 *Exp:* £1000 (1999-2000); £1000 (2000-01)

Leeds

S897 🎓 ✚

Centre for the Development of Nursing Policy and Practice, Knowledge and Information Resources
Room 4.12, Baines Wing, School of Healthcare Studies, Univ of Leeds, Leeds, W Yorkshire, LS2 9UT (0113-233-1381; *fax:* 0113-233-1378)
Email: temp-rc@healthcare.leeds.ac.uk

Gov Body: Univ of Leeds (see **S918**) *Chief:* Knowledge Mgr: Mr Roger Cowell BA, RN
Entry: staff of School of Healthcare Studies & associates of the Centre *Open:* Mon-Thu 0930-1700, Fri 0930-1600
Subj: nursing; healthcare mgmt; healthcare leadership *Co-op Schemes:* ILL
Equip: copier
Stock: bks/120; periodcls/16, plus 49 no longer current *Acqs Offcr:* Knowledge Mgr, as above
Staff: Other Prof: 0.4 *Exp:* £2372 (1999-2000); £1400 (2000-01)

S898 ✚

Chapel Allerton Hospital NHS Staff Library
Admin Corridor, Chapel Allerton Hosp, Chapeltown Rd, Leeds, W Yorkshire, LS7 4SA (*tel & fax:* 0113-392-4662)
Email: dominic.gilroy@leedsth.nhs.uk

Gov Body: Leeds Teaching Hosps NHS Trust
Chief: Libn: Mr Dominic Gilroy BA, MA, MA
Assoc Libs: COOKRIDGE HOSP NHS STAFF LIB (see **S899**); LEEDS GENL INFIRMARY, POSTGRAD MEDICAL LIB (see **S905**); SEACROFT HOSP NHS STAFF LIB (see **S914**); WHARFEDALE GENL HOSP, POSTGRAD MEDICAL CENTRE LIB (sees **S1662**)
Entry: NHS staff or students on placement *Open:* staffed: Tue 0900-1300, Thu 0900-1700, Fri 1330-1700; open to membs 24 hrs via coded door entry sys
Subj: medicine; health *Co-op Schemes:* Northern & Yorkshire Regional Libns ILL photocopy scheme
Equip: copier, computer (with wd-proc, internet & CD-ROM) *Online:* CINAHL, Medline & associated medical lit searching databases *Officer-in-Charge:* Libn, as above *Svcs:* info, ref
Stock: bks/1300; periodcls/18 *Acqs Offcr:* Libn, as above
Classn: NLM
Staff: Libns: 0.4 *Exp:* £10500 (2000-01)

S899 ✚

Cookridge Hospital NHS Staff Library
Cookridge Hosp, Hospital Ln, Leeds, W Yorkshire, LS16 6QD (*tel & fax:* 0113-392-4293)
Email: cookridge.library@leedsth.nhs.uk

Gov Body: Leeds Teaching Hosps NHS Trust
Chief: Libn: Mr Dominic Gilroy BA, MA
Assoc Libs: CHAPEL ALLERTON HOSP NHS STAFF LIB (see **S898**); LEEDS GENL INFIRMARY, POSTGRAD MEDICAL LIB (see **S905**); SEACROFT HOSP NHS STAFF LIB (see **S914**); WHARFEDALE GENL HOSP, POSTGRAD MEDICAL CENTRE LIB (sees **S1662**)
Entry: Trust staff only; other NHS staff by arrangement *Open:* 24 hr opening for membs
Subj: medicine; nursing; psy; allied health *Collns: Bks & Pamphs:* small historical colln of medical texts *Co-op Schemes:* BLDSC, ILL, HLN/ Yorkshire Health Libs Scheme
Equip: copier (A4/10p), 4 computers (all with wd-proc, internet & CD-ROM) *Online:* CINAHL, Cochrane, Medline *Officer-in-Charge:* Libn, as above *Svcs:* info, ref, lit searches, training
Stock: bks/3000; periodcls/39; videos/2; CD-ROMs/5 *Acqs Offcr:* Libn, as above
Classn: NLM *Auto Sys:* Access
Staff: Libns: 0.4

S900 🔑

The Henry Moore Institute Library
74 The Headrow, Leeds, W Yorkshire, LS1 3AH (0113-246-9469; *fax:* 0113-246-1481)
Email: library@henry-moore.ac.uk
Internet: http://www.henry-moore-fdn.co.uk/site/thesite/institutep/

Type: rsrch inst *Gov Body:* Leeds Museums & Galleries & The Henry Moore Foundation *Chief:* Libn: Miss Denise Raine BA(Hons) (Denise@henry-moore.ac.uk) *Other Snr Staff:* Audiovisual Libn: Miss Christine Kay (Chris@henry-moore.ac.uk)
Assoc Libs: HENRY MOORE INST ARCHVS, addr as above, Archivist: Ms Victoria Worsley (Victoria@henry-moore.ac.uk); HENRY MOORE FOUNDATION LIB & ARCHV (see **S1562**)
Entry: Lib: ref only, no appt necessary; *Archv:* open to rsrchers by adv appt only, proof of ID required *Open: Lib:* Mon-Tue, Thu-Sun 1000-1730, Wed 1000-2100; *Archv:* Mon-Fri 1000-1300, 1400-1700; closed bank hols
Subj: arts; sculpture *Collns: Bks & Pamphs:* current & back issues of Christies' & Sotheby's catalogues *Archvs:* over 50 collns relating to sculptors working in 18C-20C, incl personal papers & correspondence, sketchbks, photos, diaries, drawings, notes & catalogues *Other:* ephemera relating to sculpture, incl private view cards & press cuttings *Co-op Schemes:* LALIC
Equip: copier, 3 computers (incl internet & CD-ROM) *Online:* Grove Dictionary of Art Online, ARTbibliographies Modern *Svcs:* info, ref
Stock: bks/7000; periodcls/20; photos/4000; slides/30000; illusts/1000; pamphs/7000; m-forms/2 collns; audios/200; videos/200; archvs/12 cubic m
Classn: DDC *Auto Sys:* Alice
Staff: Libns: 2 *Other Prof:* 1

S901 🎓

Leeds College of Art and Design Library
Vernon St, Leeds, W Yorkshire, LS2 8PH (0113-202-8095; *fax:* 0113-202-8150)
Email: info@leeds-art.ac.uk
Internet: http://www.leeds-art.ac.uk/

Chief: Lib Mgr: Mr Christopher Graham BA, MA, MSc (chrisg@leeds-art.ac.uk)

Entry: ref only *Open:* term: Mon, Wed 0830-1845, Tue, Thu 0830-2000, Fri 0915-1630; vac: varies
Subj: undergrad; arts; textiles; woodwork; product design *Collns: Archvs:* Coll archv *Other:* slide colln; illusts colln (1940s-50s graphics)
Equip: video viewers, copier, clr copier, computers (incl wd-proc, internet & CD-ROM) *Svcs:* ref
Stock: bks/18000; periodcls/90; slides/25000; illusts/8000; videos/500
Classn: DDC *Auto Sys:* Alice
Staff: Libns: 1 *Non-Prof:* 4.5

S902

Leeds College of Building Library
North St, Leeds, W Yorkshire, LS2 7QT (0113-222-6098; *fax:* 0113-222-6001)
Email: info@lcb.ac.uk
Internet: http://www.lcb.ac.uk/

Chief: Libn: Mrs P.N. Duckett BSc, MA, MSc, MCLIP *Dep:* Asst Libn: Mrs H. Weir BSc
Entry: ref only *Open:* term: Mon-Thu 0830-2030, Fri 0830-1700; vac: Mon-Fri 0830-1700
Subj: construction & related subjs
Equip: 2 video viewers, 21 computers
Stock: bks/c20000; periodcls/150; slides/120; videos/450
Classn: DDC *Auto Sys:* Heritage IV
Staff: Libns: 1.6 *Non-Prof:* 1.5 *Exp:* £25000 (1999-2000)

S903 🎓

Leeds College of Music Library
3 Quarry Hill, Leeds, W Yorkshire, LS2 7PD (0113-222-3458)
Email: C.Marsh@lcm.ac.uk
Internet: http://www.lcm.ac.uk/library/

Chief: Head of Lib & Learning Resources: Mrs Jay Glasby BA, MCLIP *Dep:* Libn: Ms Claire Marsh
Open: term: Mon-Wed 0900-1930, Thu 0900-2000, Fri 0900-1700, Sat 0900-1300; vac: Mon-Fri 0900-1700
Subj: music *Collns: Archvs:* Jazz Archv (MSS, sound recordings, periodcls & ephemera) *Other:* large colln of uncatalogued music *Co-op Schemes:* Music Libs Online, ILL
Equip: m-reader, 2 video viewers, copier, computers (with wd-proc, internet & CD-ROM), audio players *Disabled:* magnifier/reader for partially sighted *Online:* BHI, Internatl Index to Music Periodicals, MUSE, NISC DISCover & others
Stock: bks/5000+; periodcls/45; audios/0; videos/159; CD-ROMs/15; sheet music & scores/c1000
Classn: DDC *Auto Sys:* Olib
Staff: Libns: 2 *Non-Prof:* 4

S904 🎓

Leeds College of Technology Library
Cookridge St, Leeds, W Yorkshire, LS2 8BL (0113-297-6300; *fax:* 0113-297-6301)
Email: library@leeds-lcot.ac.uk
Internet: http://www.lct.ac.uk/

Gov Body: Corp of Leeds Coll of Tech *Chief:* Coll Libn: Mr John Metcalfe BA(Hons), PGCE(FE) *Dep:* Ms Abigail Reed DipHE
Assoc Libs: OPEN LRC, Westland Rd, Leeds, LS11 5SB; LEARNING BASE, East Bank Centre, East St, Leeds, LS9 4DP
Entry: lending to staff & students, ref only to genl public *Open:* term: Mon-Wed 0830-2030, Wed 0930-2030, Fri 0830-1630; vac: reduced hrs
Subj: generalities; social sci; sci; maths; tech; arts; lit *Co-op Schemes:* BLDSC, Leeds Further Edu Libns, Leeds Libns Exchange
Equip: m-reader, fax, video viewer, copier, computers (incl wd-proc, internet & CD-ROM), lap top computers *Disabled:* Spellmasters *Online:* access to selected internet resources via Alice; Croner's H&S online svc *Svcs:* info, ref, biblio

Stock: bks/17000; periodcls/40; slides/1003; illusts/23; pamphs/2000; maps/10; audios/40; videos/300
Classn: DDC *Auto Sys:* Alice for Windows
Staff: Libns: 1 *Non-Prof:* 2 *Exp:* £20000 (1999-2000); £21000 (2000-01)

S905 ✚
Leeds General Infirmary, Postgraduate Medical Library
Gt George St, Leeds, W Yorkshire, LS1 3EX (0113-292-6445; *fax:* 0113-292-2930)

Gov Body: Leeds Teaching Hosps NHS Trust
Chief: Libn: Mrs Sheila Leadbeater *Dep:* Lib Administrator: Ms Angie Bramma
Assoc Libs: CHAPEL ALLERTON HOSP NHS STAFF LIB (see **S898**); COOKRIDGE HOSP NHS STAFF LIB (see **S899**); SEACROFT HOSP NHS STAFF LIB (see **S914**); WHARFEDALE GENL HOSP, POSTGRAD MEDICAL CENTRE LIB (see **S1662**)
Entry: Trust staff *Open:* Mon-Thu 0900-1700, Fri 0900-1630
Subj: medicine; health *Equip:* copier, computers
Classn: NLM

S906 🎓
Leeds Grammar School, The Lawson Library
Alwoodly Gates, Harrogate Rd, Leeds, W Yorkshire, LS17 8GS

Gov Body: Governors of Leeds Grammar School
Chief: Head of Learning Resources: Mrs Hana Oldman MA (ho@lgs.leeds.sch.uk) *Dep:* Lib Svcs Mgr: Ms Stephanie Roberts BA(Lib) (sr@lgs.leeds.sch.uk) *Other Snr Staff:* Lawson Libn: Mr John Neill Hargreaves BA (jnh@lgs.leeds.sch.uk)
Assoc Libs: SCHOOL ARCHVS, at same addr, School Archivist & Historian: Mr John Davies
Entry: adv appt *Open:* term: Mon-Fri 0800-1730; vac: Mon-Fri 0900-1700
Subj: all subjs; GCSE; A level; undergrad; pre-GCSE age 10-14 *Collns: Bks & Pamphs:* original Lawson Lib from old grammar school c1685 onwards, incl at least five 15C vols & c300 pre-1820 vols *Archvs:* material relating to the hist of the school *Other:* full colln of "The Leodiensian" dating from c1820; complete set of OS 1:50000
Equip: m-reader, copier, 28 wd-procs, 30 computers (all with wd-proc & CD-ROM, 27 with internet)
Stock: bks/25000; periodcls/55; pamphs/200; audios/400; archvs/2 cubic m
Classn: DDC *Auto Sys:* Alice
Staff: Libns: 2 *Other Prof:* 1 *Non-Prof:* 1

S907 🗝
The Leeds Library
18 Commercial St, Leeds, W Yorkshire, LS1 6AL (0113-245-3071; *fax:* 0113-243-8218)
Email: enquiries@leedslibrary.co.uk

Gov Body: Trustees & Cttee *Chief:* Libn: Mr Geoffrey Forster BA, MA, MCLIP *Dep:* Dep Libn: Mr Stephen Potten
Entry: membs: borrowing & ref; others by appt, ref only *Open:* Mon-Fri 0900-1700
Subj: genl; Leeds & Yorkshire: biography; hist; lit; travel; arts *Collns: Bks & Pamphs:* Civil War tracts; Reformation tracts *Archvs:* Wilson MSS Pedigrees; Leeds Lib Archvs *Other:* local newspapers *Co-op Schemes:* AIL
Equip: copiers, computers
Stock: bks/135000
Pubns: The Dial (newsletter, free); The Leeds Lib 1768-1990 (£7); The Leeds Lib: A Checklist of Pubns Relating to its Hist (£3.50); occasional pubns (various prices)
Staff: Libns: 1 *Non-Prof:* 7

S908 🎓
Leeds Metropolitan University Library
City Campus, Leeds, W Yorkshire, LS1 3HF (0113-283-2600; *fax:* 0113-283-3123)
Internet: http://www.lmu.ac.uk/lis/

Chief: Head of Learning Support Svcs: Mr Philip Payne BA, MCLIP (p.payne@lmu.ac.uk)
Assoc Libs: CITY CAMPUS LEARNING CENTRE, addr as above, Mgr: Ms Meg Message BA, MCLIP (0113-283-7467; *email:* m.message@lmu.ac.uk); BECKETT PK LEARNING CENTRE, James Graham Bldg, Leeds Metropolitan Univ, Leeds, W Yorkshire, LS6 3QS, Mgr: Mrs Norma Thompson MA(Lib) (0113-283-5968; *email:* n.thompson@lmu.ac.uk); HARROGATE COLL LEARNING CENTRE, Hornbeam Pk, Harrogate, North Yorkshire, HG2 8QT, Mgr: Mr Arthur Sargeant BA(Hons), MA(Lib), CertFE (01423-878213; *email:* a.sargeant@lmu.ac.uk)
Entry: ref use only, borrowing by subscription
Open: term: Mon-Thu 0830-2300, Fri 0830-1900, Sat 1000-1600, Sun 1000-1800
Subj: all subjs; undergrad; postgrad *Collns: Bks & Pamphs:* EDC; school practice *Other:* slide colln; illusts; audio & video tapes *Co-op Schemes:* BLDSC, UK Libs Plus
Equip: m-reader/printer, video viewer, printer/copier, clr copier, computers, audio facilities
Disabled: Kurzweil, PC facilities for disabled students *Online:* Inside Info & ISI databases (via BIDS), Lexis, Lawtel, EBSCO Masterfile
Stock: bks/400000; periodcls/3000; slides/165000; AVs/13000
Classn: DDC *Auto Sys:* Sirsi Unicorn
Staff: Libns: 47.8 *Non-Prof:* 62.6 *Exp:* £3783755 (2000-01)

S909 🏛
Leeds Museum Resource Centre
Moorfield Industrial Est, Moorfield Rd, Yeadon, Leeds, W Yorkshire, LS19 7BN (0113-214-6526; *fax:* 0113-214-6539)
Email: antonia.lovelace@leeds.gov.uk
Internet: http://www.leeds.gov.uk/

Type: local govt *Gov Body:* Leeds City Council (see **P72**); part of Leeds Museums & Galleries
Chief: Curator: Ms Antonia Lovelace
Entry: adv appt *Open:* Mon-Thu 1000-1600, Fri 1000-1500
Subj: local studies (Leeds); nat hist; geol; archaeo; world cultures; hist; warfare; numismatics *Collns: Bks & Pamphs:* relating to the museum collns
Equip: Disabled: wheelchair access

S910 🎓 🏛
Museum of the History of Education Library
Univ of Leeds, Parkinson Ct, Leeds, W Yorkshire, LS2 9JT (0113-233-4665)
Email: museum@education.leeds.ac.uk

Gov Body: Univ of Leeds (see **S918**) *Chief:* Libn: Dr Elizabeth J. Foster BA, PhD, PGCE
Entry: ref only, adv appt advisable for confirmation of opening times *Open:* Mon, Wed-Fri 1400-1630, Tue closed
Subj: Yorkshire: schools & edu; religion; social sci; lang; sci; maths; tech; arts; geog; hist; hist of edu; edu admin; school subjs (infant-A level); teacher training *Collns: Bks & Pamphs:* museum colln of text bks & teacher texts (1700-date, but mainly 19C-20C) *Archvs:* teacher training records; pupil exercise bks; school logs bks
Equip: m-reader, m-printer, video viewer, copier
Stock: bks/8500; bnd periodcls/3250
Pubns: Journal of Educational Admin & Hist (2 pa); Museum Catalogue
Staff: Other Prof: 2

S911 🏛 ✚
NHS Estates Information Centre
1 Trevelyan Sq, Boar Ln, Leeds, W Yorkshire, LS1 6AE (0113-254-7070; *fax:* 0113-254-7167)
Email: nhs.estates@doh.gov.uk
Internet: http://www.nhsestates.gov.uk/

Gov Body: Dept of Health *Chief:* Libn: Ms Lesley Vickers BA(Hons) *Dep:* Asst Libn: Ms Clare Drury BA(Hons)
Entry: ref only for non-Dept of Health staff; adv appt required *Open:* Mon-Fri 0900-1700
Subj: health bldgs *Collns: Bks & Pamphs:* Barbour Index: Health & Safety Microfile; Bldg Law Microfile; all NHSE pubns, new & archival; BSI *Archvs:* archival BSIs; archival Dept of Health records; Health Bldgs Lib pubns *Co-op Schemes:* BLDSC, loans to other govt libs
Equip: m-printer, fax, copier, computer (with wd-proc, internet & CD-ROM) *Svcs:* info
Stock: bks/13000; periodcls/30; photos/200; slides/300; maps/some
Classn: Bliss *Auto Sys:* Unicorn
Pubns: see pubns list on web site
Staff: Libns: 2 *Non-Prof:* 1

S912 🎓
Park Lane College Library
Park Ln, Leeds, W Yorkshire, LS3 1AA (0113-216-2046; *fax:* 0113-216-2020)
Email: j.warner@mail.parklanecoll.ac.uk
Internet: http://www.parklanecoll.ac.uk/

Chief: Lib Svcs Mgr: Mrs Janet Warner BA, MCLIP
Assoc Libs: HORSFORTH CENTRE LIB, Calverey Ln, Hosforth, Leeds, LS18 4RQ, Libn: Ms Janice White BA(Hons) (0113-216-2440); VICAR LN HOUSE WORKSHOP, Templar St, Leeds, LS2 7NU, Libn: Ms Nicola Bachelor (0113-216-2265)
Entry: ref only *Open:* term: Mon-Thu 0830-2030, Fri 1000-1600; vac: Mon-Thu 0900-1630, Fri 1000-1600
Subj: all subjs; genl; GCSE; A level; vocational
Co-op Schemes: BLDSC
Equip: m-reader, 2 video viewers, 2 copiers, clr copier, computers (incl 20 internet & 22 CD-ROM)
Disabled: magnifying screens, other facilities available in Coll *Svcs:* info, ref
Stock: bks/30000; periodcls/87; pamphs/1000; audios/200; videos/1500
Classn: DDC *Auto Sys:* AutoLib
Staff: Libns: 7 *Non-Prof:* 7.5 *Exp:* £49450 (1999-2000); £40000 (2000-01); incl all exp except staffing & furniture

S913 🏛
Royal Armouries Library
Royal Armouries Museum, Armouries Dr, Leeds, W Yorkshire, LS10 1LT (0113-220-1832; *fax:* 0113-220-1934)
Email: enquiries@armouries.org.uk
Internet: http://www.armouries.org.uk/

Gov Body: Board & Trustees/Dept of Culture, Media & Sport *Chief:* Libn: Mr Philip Abbott BA, PGDipLib, MCLIP (philip.abbott@armouries.org)
Dep: Asst Libn: Mr Danny Millum MSc (daniel.millum@armouries.org) *Other Snr Staff:* Picture Libn: Ms Charlotte Chipchase BSc (charlotte.chipchase@armouries.org)
Assoc Libs: FORT NELSON LIB (see **S680**); ROYAL ARMOURIES (LONDON), HM Tower of London, Tower Hill, London, EC3N 4AB, Snr Curator: Ms Bridget Clifford (020-7480-6358x30; *email:* bridget.clifford@armouries.org.uk)
Entry: ref only, no appt necessary *Open:* Mon-Fri 1000-1630; closed Xmas & New Year
Subj: warfare; military weapons; arms & armour ☛

Special Libraries

Leeds
▼
Leicester

(Royal Armouries Lib cont)

Collns: Bks & Pamphs: early fencing bks; early bks on military sci; auction sales catalogues *Archvs:* archvs of the Royal Armouries Museum, Leeds; archvs of various scholars & historians of arms & armour *Other:* photo lib (b&w prints, clr transparencies, 35mm slides & films/videos produced by Royal Armouries)
Equip: m-form reader/printer, video viewer, copier
Svcs: info, ref, biblio
Stock: bks/20000, incl pamphs; periodcls/70; photos/40000; slides/15000; videos/200; archvs/ 200 linear m
Classn: own *Auto Sys:* Star
Pubns: contact the Head of Pubns at above addr
Staff: Libns: 2 *Other Prof:* 1 *Exp:* £17500 (1999-2000); £20000 (2000-01)

S914 ✚

Seacroft Hospital NHS Staff Library

Edu Centre, York Rd, Leeds, W Yorkshire, LS14 6UH (0113-206-3675; *fax:* 0113-206-3325)
Email: library.seacroft@leedsth.nhs.uk
Internet: http://www.leedsteachinghospitals.com/

Gov Body: Leeds Teaching Hosps NHS Trust
Chief: Libn: Mrs Christine Reid BA, MCLIP
Assoc Libs: CHAPEL ALLERTON HOSP NHS STAFF LIB (see **S898**); COOKRIDGE HOSP NHS STAFF LIB (see **S899**); LEEDS GENL INFIRMARY, POSTGRAD MEDICAL LIB (see **S905**); WHARFEDALE GENL HOSP, POSTGRAD MEDICAL CENTRE LIB (see **S1662**)
Entry: all NHS staff *Open:* Mon-Thu 0900-1700, Fri 0900-1630
Subj: medicine *Co-op Schemes:* BLDSC, regional ILLs
Equip: copier, fax, 3 computers (all with wd-proc & CD-ROM, 2 with internet), room for hire *Online:* Medline, CINAHL, Cochrane, PsycInfo etc *Svcs:* info, ref, biblio
Stock: bks/2500; periodcls/50; videos/35; CD-ROMs/10 *Acqs Offcr:* Libn, as above
Classn: NLM *Auto Sys:* InMagic Plus
Staff: Libns: 1 *Exp:* £12000 (1999-2000); £13000 (2000-01)

S915 🎓

Thomas Danby College, Learning Centre Library

Roundhay Rd, Sheepscar, Leeds, W Yorkshire, LS7 3BG (0113-284-6306; *fax:* 0113-240-1967)
Email: info@thomasdanby.ac.uk
Internet: http://www.thomasdanby.ac.uk/

Chief: Head of Lib Svcs: Ms Margery Ellis
Entry: ref only *Open:* term: Mon-Thu 0830-2000, Fri 0830-1530, Sat 0900-1345; vac: Mon-Thu 0830-1700, Fri 0830-1530
Subj: hair & beauty; media & performing arts; hospitality mgmt & catering; leisure; social care; child care; meat/bakery; business studies; health studies *Collns: Bks & Pamphs:* European Colln; Concord Multi-Faith Colln *Co-op Schemes:* BLDSC, ILL
Equip: video viewer, fax, copier, computers (incl internet & CD-ROM)
Stock: bks/30000; periodcls/100; videos/200
Classn: DDC *Auto Sys:* Heritage
Staff: Libns: 4 *Non-Prof:* 3

S916 🔑

Thoresby Society Library

Claremont, 23 Clarendon Rd, Leeds, W Yorkshire, LS2 9NZ
Internet: http://www.thoresby.org.uk/

Gov Body: Thoresby Soc *Chief:* Hon Libn: Mrs J.M.D. Forster MA, DipLib
Entry: adv appt *Open:* Tue, Thu 1000-1400
Subj: local studies (Leeds & dist) *Collns: Bks & Pamphs:* directories of Leeds; biographies of Leeds' people *Other:* 18C-19C newspapers; map colln; pictures
Equip: copier
Stock: bks/4000; periodcls/20
Pubns: Pubns of the Thoresby Soc (annually since 1891, £20, price list on appl)
Staff: Libns: 1 plus occasional helpers

S917 🎓

Trinity and All Saints' College Library

Brownberrie Ln, Horsforth, Leeds, W Yorkshire, LS18 5HD (0113-283-7100; *fax:* 0113-283-7200)
Internet: http://www.tasc.ac.uk/

Gov Body: Univ of Leeds (see **S918**) *Chief:* Dir of Info Support Svc: Mr Edward Brush BA *Dep:* Coll Libn: Ms Elizabeth Murphy MA, MCLIP
Entry: limited borrowing for non-Coll membs
Open: term: Mon-Thu 0900-2045, Fri 0900-1745, Sat 1300-1645, Sun 1400-2045; vac: Mon-Fri 0915-1645
Subj: all subjs; undergrad; vocational; local study (Yorkshire); media studies; edu; business mgmt
Co-op Schemes: BLDSC, UK Libs Plus, SCONUL Rsrch Extra, NEYAL Purchasing Consortium
Equip: 24 m-readers, 3 video viewers, 3 copiers, 133 computers (incl 120 with wd-proc, 130 with internet & 1 with CD-ROM) *Disabled:* sound loops, large font OPAC terminal
Stock: bks/132500; periodcls/560; videos/1500; CD-ROMs/25; archvs/12 linear m
Classn: DDC *Auto Sys:* Geac
Staff: Libns: 4.1 *Non-Prof:* 9.1

S918 🎓

University of Leeds Library

Leeds, W Yorkshire, LS2 9JT (0113-233-6383; *fax:* 0113-233-5561)
Email: library@library.leeds.ac.uk
Internet: http://www.leeds.ac.uk/library/

Gov Body: Univ of Leeds *Chief:* Univ Libn & Keeper of the Brotherton Colln: Ms Janet Wilkinson BA, DipLib, DMS, CNAA, FCLIP, FRSA (j.wilkinson@leeds.ac.uk) *Other Snr Staff:* Head of Learning & Rsrch Support: Mr Brian E. Clifford, BA, MA, CNAA, MCLIP, HonFCLIP (b.e.clifford@ leeds.ac.uk); Head of Resources & Financial Svcs: Mrs Angela Byram, ACCA (a.byram@leeds.ac.uk); Head of e-Strategy & Development: Ms Tracey Stanley. BA, MSc (t.s.stanley@leeds.ac.uk); Head of Special Collns: Mr Christopher Sheppard, BA, MA (c.d.w.sheppard@leeds.ac.uk)
Assoc Libs: BROTHERTON LIB (also houses Special Collns), addr & contact details as above; EDWARD BOYLE LIB (also houses Student Lib), addr as above (0113-343-5540; *fax:* 0113-343-5539); HEALTH SCIS LIB, addr as above (0113-343-5549; *fax:* 0113-343-4381); BRETTON HALL CAMPUS LIB, West Bretton, Wakefield, W Yorkshire, WF4 4LG (0113-343-9134; *fax:* 0113-343-9136); ST JAMES'S UNIV HOSP LIB, Level 3, Clinical Scis Bldg, St James's Univ Hosp, Beckett St, Leeds, LS9 7TF (0113-206-5638; *fax:* 0113-206-4682); WAKEFIELD CAMPUS LIB, Manygates Ln, Wakefield, WF1 5NS (0113-343-9413; *fax:* 0113-343-9409); LEEDS UNIV ARCHV, Baines Wing, Univ of Leeds, Leeds, LS2 9JT (0113-343-5061)

Entry: membs of the univ; others by written appl, at discretion of libn *Open:* term: Mon-Fri 0830-0000, Sat 1000-1700, Sun 1200-1900; vac: Mon-Fri 0900-2100, Sat 0900-1300
Subj: all subjs; undergrad; postgrad; *Brotherton Lib:* arts; social scis; law; *Edward Boyle Lib:* sci; eng; *Health Scis Lib:* medicine; dentistry; health; *Bretton Hall Campus Lib:* fine art; hist of art; music; cultural studies; edu; *Archvs:* records of parent org
Collns: Bks & Pamphs: BSI; EDC; Brotherton Colln (rare bks & MSS, esp 17C-18C England); Leeds Philosophical & Literary Soc Lib; Icelandic Colln; Anglo-French Colln; William Blake Colln; Chaston Chapman Colln (early sci, alchemy, hermeticism, 17C-18C); Mattison Colln (early socialism); Roth Colln (rare Hebrew bks & MSS); Birkbeck Lib (Quakerism); Leeds Friends Old Lib (Quakerism); Ripon Cathedral Lib; Romany Colln (gypsy life & culture); Blanche Leigh Colln (cookery); Preston Colln (cookery); Whitaker Colln (maps & atlases); Civil War Pamphs; Yorkshire Colln; early travel bks; numerous other printed collns *Archvs:* records of the Univ; numerous collns, incl: Liddle Colln (WW1 personal papers); Ripon Cathedral Archvs; Quaker Archvs (Yorkshire area); Woollen & Textile Industry Archvs; Lancashire Cotton Districts Relief Fund records (1860s); Leeds Russian Archv; Leeds Local Edu Authority Archv; Assoc of Edu Committees Archv; Assoc for Sci Edu Archv; Eshton Hall Estate Papers; Wentworth of Woolley Hall Papers; John Wilson of Broomhead Papers; Marrick Priory Papers; Chevalier D'Eon Colln; Ernest John Tinsley Archv (theology); MS & papers of literary figs (17C-20C) incl A.C. Swinburne, Lord Byron, Charles Dickens, Sir Walter Scott, Sir Edmund Gosse, the Brontës, the Rossettis & others; Medieval MSS; Arabic MSS *Co-op Schemes:* CURL, NEYAL, RLG
Equip: m-reader, m-printer, video viewer, copiers, clr copier, computers (incl CD-ROM) *Online:* Dialog, BLAISE, STN, Datastar etc (at cost)
Stock: bks/2600000; periodcls/9000; pamphs/ 400000; m-forms/320000
Classn: own *Auto Sys:* III
Pubns: Brotherton Colln Review; numerous others

S919 🔑

Yorkshire Archaeological Society Library

'Claremont', 23 Clarendon Rd, Leeds, W Yorkshire, LS2 9NZ (0113-245-7910; *fax:* 0113-244-1979)
Email: j.heron@shef.ac.uk

Type: learned soc *Gov Body:* Yorkshire Archaeological Soc Council *Chief:* Libn: Mr Robert Frost BA, DipAA *Dep:* Mrs Janet Teague
Assoc Libs: YORKSHIRE ARCHAEOLOGICAL SOC ARCHVS, administered in conjunction with West Yorkshire Archvs Svc, Leeds (see **A226**)
Entry: ref only; entrance fee of £4 for non-membs; adv appt for archvs & use of m-fiche *Open:* Tue-Wed 1400-2030, Thu-Fri 1000-1730, Sat 0930-1700, limited archvs svc on Sat
Subj: local study (Yorkshire); hist; archaeo; topography; estate archvs; family papers *Collns: Bks & Pamphs:* local hist & archaeo of Yorkshire (pre-1974 boundaries) *Archvs:* mainly estate papers, family collns & manorial records (Yorkshire, pre-1974 boundaries) *Other:* prints & photos; glass slides; aerial photos
Equip: 8 m-readers, m-printer, fax, 2 copiers, room for hire
Stock: bks/45000; periodcls/200; slides/1000; archvs/3000 linear ft; large colln of pamphs, glass slides, photos, maps & m-fiche
Classn: fixed location lib; dictionary catalogue by subj, place, author etc
Pubns: Yorkshire Archaeological Journal; Journal Offprints; Wakefield Court Rolls (Vols 2-13); Record Series; Parish Registers Series; Parish Registers on Microfiche Series; Yorkshire Archaeological Reports; various others

Staff: Libns: 1 *Other Prof:* 2 *Exp:* £4000 (1999-2000); £4000 (2000-01)

Leek

S920

Leek College of Further Education, Learning Resource Centre

Stockwell St, Leek, Staffordshire, ST13 6DP (01538-398866; *fax:* 01538-399506)
Internet: http://www.leek.ac.uk/

Chief: LRC Mgr: Mrs Berni Williams BA, MA (bwilliams@leek.ac.uk) *Dep:* LRC Asst: Mrs Cathy Challand BA (cchalland@leek.ac.uk)
Entry: staff & students; ref only for others *Open:* term: Mon-Thu 0845-1930, Fri 0845-1700; vac: Mon-Fri 0845-1700
Subj: all subjs; GCSE; A level; vocational
Equip: copier, 14 computers (all with wd-proc, internet & CD-ROM) *Svcs:* info, ref
Stock: bks/12000; periodcls/50; videos/200
Classn: DDC *Auto Sys:* Heritage
Staff: Libns: 1 *Non-Prof:* 1 PT *Exp:* £26000 (1999-2000); £35000 (2000-01)

Leicester

S921

De Montfort University Library

The Gateway, Leicester, LE1 9BH (0116-257-7042; *fax:* 0116-257-7046)
Internet: http://www.library.dmu.ac.uk/

Gov Body: De Montfort Univ *Chief:* Head of Lib Svcs: Mrs Kathryn Arnold (karnold@dmu.ac.uk)
Other Snr Staff: Lib Svcs Mgr (Leicester): Mr Eric Loveridge; Lib Svcs Mgr (Bedford): Ms Diana Saulsbury; Staff & Quality Development Mgr: Ms Margaret Oldroyd
Assoc Libs: KIMBERLIN LIB, addr as above; BEDFORD LIB (see **S115**); CHARLES FREARS LIB (see **S922**); MILTON KEYNES INFO CENTRE (see **S1550**); SCRAPTOFT LIB (see **S923**)
Entry: ref only for non-staff/students; external borrowing membership available on payment of annual subscription *Open: Kimberlin Lib:* term: Mon-Fri 0845-2200, Sat 0900-1600, Sun 1200-1600; vac: varies
Subj: all subjs; undergrad; postgrad *Co-op Schemes:* BLDSC, EMUA, EMRLS, LAILLAR, UK Libs Plus
Equip: m-readers, m-printers, video viewers, copiers, clr copier, computer facilities (registered DMU membs only) *Disabled:* 4 PCs with specialist software *Svcs:* info, ref
Classn: DDC *Auto Sys:* Talis *Staff: Libns:* 10

S922 ✚

De Montfort University, Charles Frears Library

266 London Rd, Leicester, LE2 1RQ (0116-201-3904; *fax:* 0116-201-3822)
Internet: http://www.library.dmu.ac.uk/

Gov Body: De Montfort Univ (see **S921**) *Chief:* Libn: Ms Barbara Freeman (bfreeman@dmu.ac.uk)
Dep: Snr Asst Libn: Ms Beryl Welding (bwelding@dmu.ac.uk)
Entry: staff or student of Univ; external borrowing for an annual fee *Open:* term: Mon-Thu 0830-2000, Fri 0830-1700; vac: Mon-Thu 0830-1800, Fri 0830-1700
Subj: health; nursing; midwifery *Co-op Schemes:* BLDSC, UK Libs Plus
Equip: copiers (£1 per 20 copies), 28 computers (incl wd-proc & internet) *Svcs:* info, ref
Classn: DDC *Auto Sys:* Talis *Staff: Libns:* 4

S923

De Montfort University, Scraptoft Library

Scraptoft Campus, Scraptoft, Leicester, LE7 9SU (0116-257-7867; *fax:* 0116-257-7866)
Internet: http://www.library.dmu.ac.uk/

Gov Body: De Montfort Univ (see **S921**) *Chief:* Site Libn: Miss Olwyn Reynard (mor@dmu.ac.uk)
Dep: Snr Asst Libn: Ms Sally Luxton (sluxton@dmu.ac.uk)
Entry: staff or student of Univ; ref only for others; external borrowing available *Open:* term: Mon-Thu 0845-2100, Fri 0900-1700, Sat 1000-1600, Sun 12001600; vac: varies
Subj: undergrad; postgrad; psy; biology; health; nursing; midwifery; social sci; social work; human communication; speech & lang therapy; public policy; dance; youth studies; community studies
Co-op Schemes: BLDSC, ILL, UK Libs Plus
Equip: copiers, computers (incl wd-proc, internet & CD-ROM) *Svcs:* info, ref
Stock: bks/80000; periodcls/600; m-forms/200; AVs/2000
Classn: DDC *Auto Sys:* Talis *Staff: Libns:* 3

S924

Fullhurst Community College Library

Imperial Ave, Leicester, LE3 1AH (0116-282-4326)

Type: secondary school *Gov Body:* Leicester City Council (see **P73**) *Chief:* Coll Libn: Ms P.J. Wilson BA(Hons)
Open: term: Mon-Fri 0830-1615; vac: closed
Subj: all subjs; GCSE; local study (Leicestershire)
Collns: Bks & Pamphs: large print colln for the elderly etc
Equip: clr copier, video viewer, 15 computers (all with wd-proc, internet & CD-ROM) *Svcs:* info, ref
Stock: bks/11500
Classn: DDC *Auto Sys:* LIMES *Staff: Libns:* 1

S925 ✚

Glenfield Hospital NHS Trust, Medical Library

Groby Rd, Leicester, LE3 9QP (0116-256-3672; *fax:* 0116-256-3334)
Email: library@earthling.net
Internet: http://www.glenlib.demon.co.uk/

Gov Body: Univ Hosps of Leicester *Chief:* Lib Svcs Mgr: Mrs Jacqueline Verschvere BSc, MCLIP
Dep: Dep Libn: Mr Nigel Brook BA(Hons), PGDip, MCLIP
Assoc Libs: LEICESTER FRITH MEDICAL LIB, contact details as above
Entry: adv appt *Open:* Mon-Thu 0830-1900, Fri 0830-1800, Sat 0900-1300
Subj: medicine; nursing; psychiatry *Co-op Schemes:* BLDSC, BMA, PLCS, NULJ
Equip: 2 m-readers, m-printer, copier, video viewer, 10 computers (all with wd-proc & CD-ROM, 8 with internet), 4 rooms for hire *Online:* Datastar
Svcs: info, ref
Stock: bks/1500; periodcls/190; videos/100
Classn: NLM *Auto Sys:* Heritage
Pubns: Nursing Union List of Journals (£50 pa)
Staff: Libns: 2 *Non-Prof:* 1.5

S926

Leicester College Library

Aylestone Rd, Leicester, LE2 7LW (0116-224-2046; *fax:* 0116-224-2091)
Internet: http://www.leicestercollege.ac.uk/

Gov Body: Further Edu Funding Council *Chief:* Acting Lib Svcs Mgr: Ms Karen Sylvester

Assoc Libs: ABBEY PARK CAMPUS LIB, Painter St, Leicester, LE1 3WA; BEDE ISLAND CAMPUS LIB, Narborough Rd, Leicester, LE3 0BT; FREEMEN'S PARK CAMPUS LIB, Aylestone Rd, Leicester, LE2 7LW; ST MARGARETS CAMPUS LIB, Grafton Pl, St John St, Leicester, LE1 3WL
Entry: registration as student *Open:* term: Mon-Thu 0900-1700, Fri 0900-1630; vac: Mon-Fri 0900-1630
Subj: all subjs *Co-op Schemes:* EMRLS, ILL
Equip: 3 video viewers, 4 copiers, computers (incl wd-proc, internet & CD-ROM), binding & laminating facilities *Online:* Infotrac, KnowUK, KnowEurope, TI Onestop *Svcs:* info, ref, biblio
Stock: bks/68000; periodcls/350; videos/1000
Classn: DDC *Auto Sys:* Heritage IV
Staff: Libns: 6.5 *Non-Prof:* 16

S927 🏛

Leicester Museum and Art Gallery

New Walk, Leicester, LE1 7EA (0116-255-4100; *fax:* 0116-247-3005)
Internet: http://www.leicestermuseums.ac.uk/

Gov Body: Leicester City Council, Arts & Leisure (see **P73**) *Chief:* Managing Curator: Mr Nick Gordon
Entry: limited facilities; outside rsrchers ref only, strictly by appt *Open:* Apr-Oct: Mon-Sat 1000-1700, Sun 1400-1700; Nov-Mar: Mon-Sat 1000-1630, Sun 1400-1630
Subj: Leicestershire: geol; biology; arts; generalities; sci; arts
Equip: copier, computer (with wd-proc) *Svcs:* info, ref
Stock: bks/10000 *Classn:* UDC

S928 ✚

Leicester, Leicestershire and Rutland Health Promotion Agency Library

Regent House, 92 Regents Rd, Leicester, LE1 7PE (0116-258-8885; *fax:* 0116-258-8852)
Email: sandie.nicholson@llr-hpa.nhs.uk
Internet: http://www.healthpromotion.org.uk/

Chief: Knowledge & Info Svcs Mgr: Ms Sandie Nicholson
Entry: ref only, no appt required *Open:* Mon-Thu 0845-1700, Fri 0845-1600
Subj: health; health promotion; health edu
Equip: Online: various health databases (via staff)
Svcs: info, enq svc
Stock: 9000+ bks, videos, teaching packs, leaflets & journals

S929

Leicestershire Archaeological and Historical Society, Library

The Guildhall, Leicester, LE1 5FQ
Internet: http://www.le.ac.uk/archaeology/lahs/lahs.html

Gov Body: Cttee of the Soc *Chief:* Hon Libn: Mr A.W. Stevenson MCLIP
Entry: open to membs of the soc
Subj: Leicestershire: archaeo; hist *Collns: Archvs:* records of the soc
Stock: various bks, periodcls, photos, illusts, pamphs & maps
Pubns: Leicestershire Archaeological & Historical Soc Transactions; Leicestershire Historian; Leicestershire Archaeological & Historical Soc newsletter; offprints (prices vary); other occasional pubns

Special Libraries

Leicester ▼ Lichfield

S930

Mount St Bernard Abbey Library
Coalville, Leicester, LE67 5UL (01530-833298/2022; fax: 01530-814608)

Gov Body: Mount St Bernard Abbey Trustees (Registered) **Chief:** Libn: Rev Fr Ambrose Southey **Dep:** Asst Libn: Rev Fr Paul Diemer **Entry:** prior arrangement with Libn **Subj:** phil; religion **Collns:** Bks & Pamphs: 500+ bks printed during Reformation period (16C-18C) **Archvs:** Cistercian Archvs **Co-op Schemes:** ILL **Equip:** fax, copier, computer (with wd-proc) **Stock:** bks/30000; periodcls/50 **Classn:** DDC (mod) **Exp:** £6000 (1999-2000)

S931

National Institute of Adult Continuing Education, Library
21 De Montfort St, Leicester, LE1 7GE (0116-255-4200; fax: 0116-285-4514)
Email: helen.kruse@niace.org.uk
Internet: http://www.niace.org.uk/

Chief: Libn: Mrs Helen Kruse BA(Hons), MCLIP **Entry:** adv appt, ref only **Open:** Mon-Fri 0930-1700 **Subj:** social sci; edu **Collns:** Archvs: Adult Edu Colln **Equip:** copier, computer **Svcs:** info, ref **Stock:** bks/10000; periodcls/170; archvs/1500 **Auto Sys:** Heritage **Pubns:** Yearbook of Adult Continuing Edu 2002-03 (£18.95) **Staff:** Libns: 2 Non-Prof: 2.5

S932

National Youth Agency Library
17-23 Albion St, Leicester, LE1 6GD (0116-285-3792; fax: 0116-285-3775)
Email: dutydesk@nya.org.uk
Internet: http://www.nya.org.uk/

Type: voluntary **Chief:** Libn: Ms Jo Poultney BA **Entry:** open to all who work with young people, by appt **Open:** Mon-Fri 0930-1700 **Subj:** social sci; young people, youth svc & youth affairs **Collns:** Archvs: natl archv on the Youth Svc & youth affairs **Co-op Schemes:** BLDSC **Equip:** video viewer, copier, computer **Disabled:** minicom **Stock:** bks/6000; periodcls/250; pamphs/8000; videos/80 **Classn:** Thesaurus on Youth **Auto Sys:** DBTextworks **Pubns:** catalogue available on request **Staff:** Libns: 1 Other Prof: 5 Non-Prof: 2 **Exp:** £10000 (1999-2000)

S933

University Hospitals of Leicester NHS Trust, Leicester General Hospital Education Centre Library
Gwendolen Rd, Leicester, LE5 4PW (0116-258-8124; fax: 0116-258-8078)
Email: cjh17@le.ac.uk
Internet: http://www.le.ac.uk/li/lgh/library.htm

Type: multidisciplinary **Gov Body:** Univ Hosps of Leicester NHS Trust **Chief:** Chief Libn: Ms Claire Honeybourne MSc **Dep:** Dep Libn: Ms Jane Tatlow **Other Snr Staff:** Clinical Libn: Mrs Linda Ward MSc **Open:** 24 hrs a day; staffed: Mon-Fri 0830-1700, Sat 0900-1300 **Subj:** medicine; nursing; health; professions allied to medicine **Co-op Schemes:** BLDSC, NULJ, PLCS **Equip:** m-reader, copier, fax, 2 video viewers, 12 computers (all with wd-proc, internet & CD-ROM), room for hire **Online:** Medline, CINAHL, AMED, HMIC, BNI, Embase **Svcs:** info, ref, biblio **Stock:** bks/5000; periodcls/140; videos/50 **Classn:** NLM **Auto Sys:** Heritage **Staff:** Libns: 3 Non-Prof: 2.3

S934

University of Leicester, University Library
PO Box 248, Univ Rd, Leicester, LE1 9QD (0116-252-2043; fax: 0116-252-2066)
Email: libdesk@le.ac.uk
Internet: http://www.le.ac.uk/li/

Chief: Univ Libn: Ms Christine Fyfe (c.fyfe@le.ac.uk) **Other Snr Staff:** Special Collns Libn: Dr A.C. Lacey (acl9@le.ac.uk) **Assoc Libs:** CLINICAL SCIS LIB (see **S935**); EDU LIB (see **S936**) **Entry:** non-membs of univ should apply for permission to use lib; a charge may be made **Open:** term: Mon-Fri 0830-2400, Sat 0900-1800, Sun 1200-2100; vac: Mon-Fri 0900-1750; Special Collns: Mon-Fri 0900-1700 **Subj:** all subjs (excl religion); undergrad; postgrad; rsrch **Collns:** Bks & Pamphs: EDC; Challis Colln (Beat lit); English Local Hist Colln; French Memoirs Colln; Hatton Colln (English topography & county hists); Higson Colln (early ch's bks); Inst for the Study of Terrorism Colln; Leicester Medical Soc Colln; Leicester Univ Press Colln; Lewis Lilley Colln (music bks & scores); Majut Colln (German lang & lit); Mathematical Assoc Lib; Multi-Faith Colln; Museum Studies Colln; Pamph Colln (16C-18C, c800 items); Physical Soc Colln (hist of physics); Robjohns Colln (early printed Bibles & medieval MSS); Neuberg Colln (religion & free-thought); Transport Colln; incunabula **Archvs:** Diplomatic Archv (1950s-60s); Internatl Labour Office Colln; Joe Orton Papers; Gorrie Colln (socialism in Leicester, c1889-1909); correspond-ence of Laura Riding (American poet & critic); Thomas Ford Papers; misc 12C-20C MSS **Other:** Fairclough Colln (17C portrait prints & illusts) **Co-op Schemes:** BLDSC, links with other medical libs in region, Leicestershire LIP, SCONUL, UK Libs Plus, LAILLAR Access Scheme **Equip:** m-readers, m-printers, video viewers, fax, 7 copiers, clr copier, computers (incl wd-proc, internet & CD-ROM), room hire to univ groups (no charge) **Online:** BIDS, EDINA, OCLC FirstSearch, Medline, MIMAS, Web of Science (no charge unless very expensive, univ membs only) **Stock:** bks/989335; periodcls/5000; non-bk items/68575 **Classn:** DDC **Auto Sys:** Unicorn **Staff:** Libns: 16.8 Non-Prof: 64.89

S935

University of Leicester, Clinical Sciences Library
Leicester Royal Infirmary, PO Box 65, Leicester, LE2 7LX (0116-252-3104; fax: 0116-252-3107)
Email: clinlib@le.ac.uk
Internet: http://www.le.ac.uk/li/clinical/clinlib.htm

Gov Body: Univ of Leicester (see **S934**) **Chief:** Clinical Scis Libn: Ms Joanne Dunham (jd1@le.ac.uk) **Other Snr Staff:** Clinical Libn: Ms Sarah Sutton (sas27@le.ac.uk)

Entry: staff & students of the Univ of Leicester, Leicester Warwick Medical School & NHS employees in Leicestershire **Open:** Mon-Fri 0900-2200, Sat 0900-1800, Sun 1400-2100 **Subj:** medicine; clinical sci **Collns:** Bks & Pamphs: Leicester Medical Soc Historical Colln **Equip:** 2 copiers, video viewer, computers (incl wd-proc, internet & CD-ROM) **Online:** all major medical & health databases **Svcs:** info, ref, biblio **Stock:** bks/18000; periodcls/500; slides/10000; videos/300 **Classn:** NLM **Auto Sys:** Unicorn (Sirsi) **Staff:** Libns: 7 Non-Prof: 22

S936

University of Leicester, Education Library
21 Univ Rd, Leicester, LE1 7RF (0116-252-3738; fax: 0116-252-5798)
Email: edlib@le.ac.uk
Internet: http://www.le.ac.uk/li/education/ed.html

Gov Body: Univ of Leicester (see **S934**) **Chief:** Edu Libn: Mr Roy Kirk BA, MCLIP (rwk3@le.ac.uk) **Entry:** staff & students of the School of Edu; external borrowing membership available **Open:** term: Mon-Thu 0900-2100, Fri-Sat 0900-1700; vac: Mon-Fri 0900-1730 **Subj:** edu **Collns:** Bks & Pamphs: 19C ch's lit, incl parts of the Higson Colln; hist of edu src materials; education/industry resource colln **Equip:** m-reader, video viewer, copier, computers (incl internet & CD-ROM), audio players, scanner, laminating facilities, TV **Stock:** bks/90000; periodcls/140 **Classn:** Bliss **Auto Sys:** Unicorn

Letchworth

S937

First Garden City Heritage Museum
296 Norton Way South, Letchworth, Hertfordshire, SG6 1SU (01462-482710; fax: 01462-486056)
Email: fgchm@letchworth.com

Gov Body: Letchworth Garden City Heritage Foundation **Chief:** Curator: Mr Robert Lancaster BA(Hons) **Dep:** Asst Curator: Miss Victoria Rawlings BA(Hons), PGDip **Entry:** reserve collns by appt only **Open:** Public Display Area: Mon-Sat 1000-1700; Office: Mon-Fri 0900-1700 **Subj:** Letchworth, Hertfordshire: arch; geog; hist **Collns:** Bks & Pamphs: extensive colln on Garden City Movement; co-op housing; development of Letchworth Garden City **Archvs:** records of Garden City Pioneer Company; First Garden City Ltd; Letchworth Garden City Corp; local industry **Other:** Barry Parker Colln (arch drawings); Bennet & Bidwell Colln (arch drawings) **Equip:** m-reader, m-printer, copier **Stock:** bks/2000; photos/40000; slides/1000; pamphs/1000; maps/500; m-forms/45 reels; audios/50; videos/20

Leven

S938

Fife Primary Care NHS Trust Health Promotion Department, Information and Resources Centre
Haig House, Cameron Hosp, Leven, Fife, KY8 5RA (01592-712812; fax: 01592-716858)
Email: info@fife-hpd.demon.co.uk
Internet: http://www.fife-hpd.demon.co.uk/

Chief: Resources Offcr: Mrs Evelyn Moodie (EvelynMoodie@fife-pct.scot.nhs.uk) **Dep:** Resources Offcr (PT): Ms Donna Palmer (DonnaPalmer@fife-pct.scot.nhs.uk)

---

academic   corporate   governmental   medical

Entry: open to all who live & work in Fife; appt advisable but not essential **Open:** Mon-Thu 0900-1700, Fri 0900-1630
Subj: health promotion **Co-op Schemes:** SHINE
Equip: 2 computers (incl 1 with wd-proc, 1 with internet & 1 with CD-ROM) **Officer-in-Charge:** Office & Financial Co-ordinator: Mrs Roberta Simpson (RobertaSimpson@fife-pct.scot.nhs.uk)
Svcs: info, ref
Stock: bks/4469; periodcls/52; pamphs/276 leaflets & posters; videos/925, incl teaching kits; CD-ROMs/various **Acqs Offcr:** Office & Financial Co-ordinator, as above
Classn: DHSS Thesaurus **Auto Sys:** Heritage
Staff: Non-Prof: 3

Lewes

S939

East Sussex, Brighton and Hove Health Authority, Lewes Library
36-38 Friars Walk, Lewes, E Sussex, BN7 2PB (tel & fax: 01273-403508)
Email: elizabeth.pierce@esbh.nhs.uk

Gov Body: East Sussex, Brighton & Hove Health Authority **Chief:** Lib Asst: Ms Elizabeth Pierce
Entry: employees of & health profs under contract to East Sussex, Brighton & Hove Health Authority; other health profs by appt only **Open:** Thu-Fri 0830-1630; key available to membs 24 hrs a day
Subj: NHS; UK health policy; health delivery & planning; social aspects of health; primary care
Collns: Bks & Pamphs: Dept of Health circulars (1980 onwards) **Co-op Schemes:** BLDSC
Equip: copier, computers (with internet) **Online:** Medline, Cochrane, ASSIA for Health, Health CD, SIGLE, HMIC (Health Management Info Consortium)

S940 🎓

Plumpton College Library
Ditchling Rd, Lewes, E Sussex, BN7 3AE (01273-890454; fax: 01273-890071)
Email: enquiries@plumpton.ac.uk
Internet: http://www.plumpton.ac.uk/

Chief: Resources Centre Mgr: Mrs A. Boryer
Entry: adv appt **Open:** Mon-Thu 0900-2200, Fri 0830-1700
Subj: hortic; agric; equestrian; wine studies; business studies; small animal care; veterinary nursing; environmental sci; forestry
Equip: copier, 50 computers (all with internet)
Stock: bks/7000; periodcls/1004; slides/14000; videos/150
Classn: DDC **Staff:** Non-Prof: 1

S941 🔑

Sussex Archaeological Society Library
Barbican House, 169 High St, Lewes, E Sussex, BN7 1YE (01273-405738)
Email: library@sussexpast.co.uk
Internet: http://www.sussexpast.co.uk/

Gov Body: Sussex Archaeological Soc **Chief:** Hon Libn: Miss E. Evans BA, MCLIP
Entry: ref only; free access to membs; non-membs by appt only (Mon-Fri) **Open:** membs: Mon-Sat 1000-1700, Sun & most public hols 1100-1700
Subj: Sussex: archaeo; arch; local hist; topography **Collns: Other:** reports of excavations & sites of archaeo interest; index of Sussex clergy; archaeo, arch, ecclesiastical & domestic plans of sites & bldgs; brass rubbings; engravings
Equip: m-reader, copier (A4/5p, A3/10p) **Svcs:** ref
Stock: bks/40000; periodcls/130; incunabula/40
Acqs Offcr: Hon Libn, as above

Classn: DDC **Staff:** Libns: 3 Other Prof: 1 Non-Prof: 17 all volunteers **Exp:** £1000 (1999-2000); £1000 (2000-01)

S942 🎓

Sussex Downs College, Lewes Campus Learning Resource Centre
(formerly Lewes Tertiary Coll)
Mountfield Rd, Lewes, E Sussex, BN7 2XH (01273-402264; fax: 01273-478561)
Email: lrc@sussexdowns.ac.uk
Internet: http://www.sussexdowns.ac.uk/

Chief: Learning Resources Mgr: Mr Andrew Mowbray BA, MCLIP (andrew.mobray@sussexdowns.ac.uk) **Dep:** LRC Administrator: Mrs Tina Smith CertEd
Assoc Libs: EASTBOURNE LEARNING CENTRE (see **S582**)
Entry: ref available to all, lending to membs of Coll only **Open:** term: Mon-Thu 0830-2000, Fri 0830-1700; vac: normally Mon-Fri 1230-1630
Subj: all subjs; GCSE; A level; vocational; local study (East Sussex) **Co-op Schemes:** BLDSC, SASLIC
Equip: 4 video viewers, 2 copiers, 20 computers (all with wd-proc & internet, 8 with CD-ROM) **Svcs:** info, ref, biblio, abstracting
Stock: bks/22000; periodcls/120; pamphs/100; maps/30; audios/50; videos/1300; CD-ROMs/30
Classn: DDC **Auto Sys:** Heritage
Staff: Libns: 2 Non-Prof: 10 Exp: £24000 (1999-2000); £25000 (2000-01)

Leyland

S943 🎓

Runshaw College Library
Langdale Rd, Leyland, Lancashire, PR25 2DQ (01772-622677; fax: 01772-642009)
Email: phillips.m@runshaw.ac.uk
Internet: http://www.runshaw.ac.uk/

Chief: Learning Resources Unit Manager/Coll Libn: Mrs Margaret Phillips BA(Lib & Info Studies)
Open: term: Mon, Fri 0845-1645, Tue-Thu 0845-1945; vac: Mon-Fri 0900-1600
Subj: all subjs; GCSE; A level; undergrad **Co-op Schemes:** BLDSC, ILL
Equip: video viewer, copier, computers (incl wd-proc, internet & CD-ROM) **Svcs:** info, ref, biblio, indexing, abstracting
Stock: bks/25000; periodcls/140; slides/100; audios/100; videos/50; CD-ROMs/100
Classn: DDC **Auto Sys:** Heritage
Staff: Libns: 2 Non-Prof: 6

Lichfield

S944 🔑

Institute of Leadership and Management, Library and Information Service
(formerly the Inst for Supervision & Mgmt)
Stowe House, Netherstowe, Lichfield, Staffordshire, WS13 6TJ (01543-251346; fax: 01543-266811)
Internet: http://www.i-l-m.com/

Type: educational charity **Chief:** Info Svcs Mgr: Valerie J. Nurcombe
Entry: adv appt only **Open:** Mon-Fri 1000-1600
Subj: mgmt; leadership; supervision
Equip: room for hire **Online:** charged at cost
Svcs: info, ref, biblio, indexing
Stock: bks/3000+; periodcls/c30
Classn: DDC **Auto Sys:** own **Staff:** Libns: 1
Further Info: This is a small, new Info Svc

S945 🔑 🎓

Lichfield Cathedral Library
19a The Close, Lichfield, Staffordshire, WS13 7LD (01543-306100; fax: 01543-306109)
Email: inquiries@lichfield-cathedral.org
Internet: http://www.lichfield-cathedral.org/

Gov Body: The Chapter of the Cathedral **Chief:** Canon Chancellor: Canon A.N. Barnard **Dep:** Asst Libn: Mrs Pat Bancroft
Assoc Libs: DEAN SAVAGE LIB, contact details as above
Entry: by appt only
Subj: local study (Staffordshire); phil; religion; theology; ecclesiastical hist; music
Equip: computer (with internet) **Svcs:** info, ref
Stock: bks/c8000 **Classn:** DDC
Staff: Libns: 1 Non-Prof: 1 **Exp:** £700 (1999-2000)

S946 🔑 🏛

Museum of the Staffordshire Regiment, Regimental Library and Archives
RHQ Staffords, Whittington Barracks, Lichfield, Staffordshire, WS14 9PY (0121-311-3225; fax: 0121-311-3205)
Email: museum@rhqstaffords.fsnet.co.uk

Gov Body: Trustees of the Regiment Museum
Chief: Curator: Major R.D.W. McLean **Dep:** Mrs A.S. Elsom
Entry: by appt for the Butler Room **Open:** Mon-Fri 0930-1630
Subj: military hist; regimental hist; regimental records; personal papers **Collns: Bks & Pamphs:** bks relating to the South & North Staffordshire Regiments & the Staffordshire Regiment **Archvs:** records of the South & North Staffordshire Regiments & the Staffordshire Regiment; records of associated Militia, Volunteer & Home Guard units; papers of Sir Charles Tucker; diaries of Sir Edward Alan Holdich
Equip: copier **Disabled:** wheelchair access
Stock: videos/5; large colln of photos & maps
Staff: Non-Prof: 1
Proj: ongoing archv conservation proj (began 1996)

S947 🏛 🏛

Samuel Johnson Birthplace Museum Library
Breadmarket St, Lichfield, Staffordshire, WS13 6LG (01543-264972; fax: 01543-414779)
Email: sjmuseum@lichfield.gov.uk
Internet: http://www.lichfield.gov.uk/sjmuseum/

Type: local authority **Gov Body:** Lichfield City Council **Chief:** Museums & Heritage Offcr: Miss A.M. French
Entry: rsrch enqs welcome by prior appt **Open:** Apr-Sep: Mon-Sun 1030-1630; Oct-Mar: Mon-Sun 1200-1630; rsrch enqs Mon-Fri only
Subj: Samuel Johnson; 18C studies; Lichfield local hist **Collns: Bks & Pamphs:** items associated with Johnson, Boswell & Hester Piozzi (Thrale)
Equip: computer (with wd-proc)
Stock: bks/4000 **Staff:** Other Prof: 1

S948

South Staffordshire Healthcare NHS Trust, Library Services
(formerly Premier Health NHS Trust)
St Michael's Hosp, Trent Valley Rd, Lichfield, Staffordshire, WS13 6EF (01543-414555 x2131; fax: 01543-442031)
Email: library_stm@hotmail.com
Internet: http://www.sshlf.nhs.uk/ ☞

Special Libraries

Lichfield
▼
Liverpool

(South Staffs Healthcare NHS Trust, Lib Svcs cont)
Chief: Lib Svcs Team Leader: Mrs Rosalyn Pitt
Dep: Asst Libn: Ms Philippa Rimmington
Assoc Libs: LIB SVCS – STAFFORD SITE (see
S1972)
Entry: employees of Trust; others ref use only
Open: Mon-Fri 0900-1700
Subj: mental health; community health; allied
specialities **Co-op Schemes:** BLDSC, WMRHLN,
PLCS
Equip: fax, copier, 4 computers (all with wd-proc,
internet & CD-ROM) *Online:* Medline, CINAHL,
AMED, Cochrane, Embase, Best Evidence **Svcs:**
info, ref, biblio, lit searching, current awareness
Stock: bks/1500; periodcls/40; audios/6; videos/30
Classn: NLM (Wessex) **Auto Sys:** Heritage
Pubns: Guide to Lib Svcs (free)
Staff: Libns: 2 Other Prof: 1 Non-Prof: 1.69

Limavady

S949

Limavady College of Further and Higher Education, Library

Main St, Limavady, Co Londonderry, BT49 0EX
(028-7776-2334; *fax:* 028-7776-1018)
Email: jmoore@limavady.ac.uk
Internet: http://www.limavady.ac.uk/

Gov Body: Board of Governors of Limavady Coll
of Further Edu **Chief:** Libn: Mr Jonathan Moore
BA, MLib
Entry: interview/appt **Open:** term: Mon-Thu 0845-
1700 (plus Thu 1800-2030), Fri 0845-1500; vac:
closed
Subj: all subjs; vocational **Collns:** *Other:* info &
clippings files
Equip: copier, 38 computers (all with wd-proc,
internet & CD-ROM) **Svcs:** info, ref
Stock: bks/500; periodcls/25; pamphs/500 **Acqs**
Offcr: Libn, as above
Classn: DDC **Auto Sys:** Heritage **Staff:** Libns: 1

Lincoln

S950

Bishop Grosseteste College, Sibthorp Library

Newport, Lincoln, LN1 3DY (01522-530771; *fax:*
01522-530243)
Internet: http://www.bgc.ac.uk/

Gov Body: Bishop Grosseteste Coll **Chief:** Libn:
Mr J.C. Child BA, MCLIP (c.child@bgc.ac.uk)
Dep: Asst Libn: Mrs Karin McBride BA
(k.e.mcbride@bgc.ac.uk)
Entry: ref for all; borrowing for Coll membs &
membs of UK Libs Plus scheme; otherwise
borrowing fee of £50 pa **Open:** term: Mon-Thu
0845-2030, Fri 0845-1700, Sat 1000-1600, Sun
1330-1700; vac: Mon-Fri 0900-1700
Subj: undergrad; local study (Lincolnshire); phil;
psy; religion; social sci; arts; lit; geog; hist; archaeo;
teaching studies; ch's bks **Collns:** *Archvs:* Coll
Archvs (1862-date); Tom Baker Colln of Local Hist
Co-op Schemes: BLDSC, ILL, LISN, EMUA
Equip: m-reader, video viewer, 4 copiers, clr
copier, 25 computers (all with wd-proc & Internet, 1
with CD-ROM) *Online:* Web of Science, Infotrac,
BEI, BHI, Grove's Music, Libweb, Newsbank **Svcs:**
info, ref, biblio

Stock: bks/143000; periodcls/240; m-forms/470;
audios/1303; videos/704; archvs/160 linear m
Classn: Bliss **Auto Sys:** Olib 7.1
Pubns: Introduction to the Coll Lib Resources;
Papers of Robin Tanner HMI 1904-1989: A
Summary List; various Bibliographies & Holding
Lists
Staff: Libns: 2.5 Non-Prof: 3.5 **Exp:** £50000
(1999-2000); £55000 (2000-01)

S951

The Foster Library

St Rumbold St, Lincoln, LN2 5AB (01522-526204)
Email: lincolnshire.archive@lincolnshire.gov.uk
Internet: http://lincolnshire.gov.uk/archives/

Gov Body: Lincolnshire Archvs (see **A233**)
Chief: Libn: Mrs C. Mitchell BSc, MCLIP
Entry: ref only, adv appt **Open:** Mon 1300-1900
(1100-1700 during Nov-Feb), Tue-Fri 0900-1700,
Sat 0900-1600
Subj: hist; local hist; ecclesiastical hist; genealogy
Svcs: info, ref, biblio, indexing
Stock: bks/c30000; periodcls/55 **Classn:** DDC
Staff: Libns: 0.5 **Exp:** £1214 (1999-2000); £1119
(2000-01)

S952

Lincoln Cathedral Library

The Cathedral, Lincoln, LN2 1PZ (01522-544544;
fax: 01522-511307)
Email: librarian@lincolncathedral.com

Gov Body: The Dean & Chapter of Lincoln **Chief:**
Vice-Chancellor & Libn: Dr Nicholas Bennett MA,
DPhil
Assoc Libs: LINCOLNSHIRE ARCHVS (see
A233)
Entry: adv appt only **Open:** (normally) Tue & Thu
0930-1230, 1400-1630 (closed in Aug)
Subj: Lincolnshire & the Ancient Diocese of
Lincoln: church hist; bibliography; church art &
arch; church music **Collns:** *Bks & Pamphs:* Wren
Lib (pre-1801 printed bks on all scholarly subjs);
John Wilson Lib (17C-19C theological works); tract
colln (19C theology) *Archvs:* MSS (17C-20C);
music MSS (17C-19C)
Svcs: annual exhib of bks & MSS in Medieval Lib
(May-Aug)
Stock: bks/17000; periodcls/9; photos/1500;
slides/200; illusts/300; archvs/10 linear m
Classn: DDC
Staff: Libns: 1 Other Prof: 0.4 **Exp:** £4800 (1999-
2000); £3300 (2000-01)
Proj: heating & humidity control in Wren &
Medieval Libs (£80000)

S953

Lincoln College, Library and Learning Resources Unit

(formerly North Lincolnshire Coll)
Lincoln Centre, Monks Rd, Lincoln, LN2 5HQ
(01522-876231/2/4; *fax:* 01522-876200)
Email: enquiries@lincolncollege.ac.uk
Internet: http://www.lincolncollege.ac.uk/

Gov Body: The Coll Corp **Chief:** Lib & Learning
Resources Mgr: Ms Laraine Cooper MPhil, MCLIP
Dep: Co-ordinator of Lib & Flexible Learning Svcs:
Mrs Andrea Tanner BSc
Assoc Libs: GAINSBOROUGH LRC, Acland St,
Gainsborough, DN21 2SU, Libn: Ms Fiona Cowan
(01427-617471 x829); LOUTH LRC, Riverhead Rd,
Louth, Lincolnshire, LN11 7AH, Libn: Ms Fiona
Cowan (01507-601041); FLEXIBLE LEARNING
CENTRE, addr as above, Flexible & Open
Learning Liaison Offcr: Ms Linda Richardson
(01522-876234)
Entry: free borrowing rights only to enrolled
students & membs of staff; ref only to membs of
public, with some chargeable svcs

Open: *Lib:* term: Mon-Thu 0845-1945, Fri 0845-
1615; vac: Mon-Fri 0915-1545; *Flexible Learning
Centre:* term: Mon-Thu 0830-2045, Fri 0830-1630;
vac: Mon-Thu 0830-1645, Fri 0830-1630
Subj: all subjs; genl; GCSE; A level; undergrad;
vocational; BTEC; HND; other academic subjs
Collns: *Bks & Pamphs:* bnd dissertations prepared
for Dip in Mgmt Studies & BSc in Sports Sci **Co-
op Schemes:** BLDSC, Univ of Birmingham Centre
for Sports Sci & Hist, LISN, EMRLS
Equip: m-fiche printer, 3 video viewers, 2 copiers,
clr copier, 60 computers (incl 55 internet & 6 CD-
ROM), flatbed scanner, laminator, thermal binder,
spiral binder *Disabled:* braille embosser, CCTV,
height-adjustable table, 2 large screen PCs
Online: Infotrac, Internatl Newsbank, Olib
Webview; CD-ROM resources incl Further Edu
Natl Consortium (FENC) elec packages **Svcs:**
info, ref, biblio
Stock: bks/30000; periodcls/120; maps/150 (OS);
CD-ROMs/70; audios & videos/2300; range of lang
resources in various formats
Classn: DDC **Auto Sys:** Olib
Pubns: Guide to Your Coll Lib & Learning
Resource Svcs; Getting the Most out of Learning
Resources; Learning Resources bookmarks;
variety of resources lists & user guides
Staff: Libns: 1 Other Prof: 3 Non-Prof: 8 **Exp:**
£65000 (1999-2000)
Proj: new bldg to combine Lib & Flexible Learning
facilities in one area, commenced Nov 2002

S954

Lincoln County Hospital, Professional Library

Edu Centre, Greetwell Rd, Lincoln, LN2 5QY
(01522-573954; *fax:* 01522-573940)
Internet: http://www.hello.nhs.uk/

Gov Body: United Lincolnshire Hosps NHS Trust,
Lincolnshire County Council (see **P75**) & Univ of
Nottingham (see **S1647**) **Chief:** Acting Libns: Ms
Ruth Rimen (ruth.rimen@ulh.nhs.uk) & Ms Celia
Unsworth (celia.unsworth@ulh.nhs.uk)
Assoc Libs: GRANTHAM & DIST HOSP, STAFF
LIB (see **S757**); LOUTH COUNTY HOSP
MEDICAL LIB (see **S1486**); PILGRIM HOSP LIB
(see **S204**)
Entry: staff of United Lincolnshire Hosp NHS Trust
& students on placement with the Trust; staff &
students of Univ of Nottingham School of Nursing
& Academic Div of Midwifery; staff of Lincolnshire
NHS Trusts **Open:** Mon-Thu 0845-2100, Fri 0845-
1700, Sat 1000-1700, Sun 1200-1700
Subj: medicine; nursing; health care; mgmt **Co-
op Schemes:** BLDSC, NULJ
Equip: m-reader, 2 copiers, 10 computers (incl 8
with wd-proc, 7 with internet & 6 with CD-ROM)
Online: via OVID BioMed: Medline, CINAHL,
Embase, PsycInfo, Evidence Based Medicine
Reviews, AMED, BNI **Svcs:** info, ref, biblio,
indexing
Stock: bks/18000; periodcls/120; m-forms/5
Classn: DDC **Auto Sys:** Galaxy
Staff: Non-Prof: 4

S955

Museum of Lincolnshire Life, Library and Archives

Burton Rd, Lincoln, LN1 3LY (01522-528448; *fax:*
01522-521264)
Email: lincolnshirelife_museum@lincolnshire.
gov.uk
Internet: http://www.lincolnshire.gov.uk/

Gov Body: Lincolnshire County Council (see **P75**)
Chief: Principal Keeper: Miss Janet Edmond
(janet.edmond@lincolnshire.gov.uk) **Other Snr
Staff:** Keeper of Collns Mgmt: Miss Sara Basquill;
Keeper of Visitor & Community Svcs: Ms Kate
Howard

---

 academic corporate - 312 - governmental medical

Entry: appt required for access to ref collections/ archvs *Open:* Mon-Fri 1000-1730
Subj: old County of Lincolnshire: local/social hist
Collns: Bks & Pamphs: Lincolnshire: social, industrial; arch; agric; community hist; large colln of industrial firm catalogues particularly Robey of Lincoln *Archvs:* Lincolnshire Regiment Archvs (see **A234**); Lincolnshire Windmill Archv; some material non-Lincolnshire
Equip: m-reader, copier
Stock: bks & m-forms/various; photos/20000; slides/30000
Classn: MERL *Staff: Other Prof:* 3

S956

Society for Lincolnshire History and Archaeology, Library

Jews' Ct, Steep Hill, Lincoln, LN2 1LS *(tel & fax:* 01522-521337)
Email: slha@lincolnshirepast.org.uk
Internet: http://www.lincolnshirepast.org.uk/

Gov Body: Soc for Lincolnshire Hist & Archaeo
Chief: Administrator: Mr Rodney Callow
Entry: by appt *Open:* daily 1000-1600, excl Bank Hols
Subj: Lincolnshire: local hist; archaeo; industrial archaeo; allied subjs
Equip: room for hire (£10 per hr), slide projector, overhead projector *Svcs:* info
Classn: DDC (mod)
Pubns: Past & Present (4 pa, £1.60); Lincolnshire Hist & Archaeo Annual Journal (£10)
Exp: stock mostly from donations
See also **O353**

S957

University of Lincoln, Learning Resource Centres

(formerly Univ of Lincolnshire & Humberside)
Brayford Pool, Lincoln, LN6 7TS (01522-886222; *fax:* 01522-886047)
Internet: http://www.lincoln.ac.uk/ls/

Chief: Head of Learning Resources: Ms Michelle Anderson BA(Hons), MA (manderson@lincoln. ac.uk) *Other Snr Staff:* Resources Mgr: Ms Lys Ann Bale (lbale@lincoln.ac.uk); Support Mgr: Ms Philippa Dyson (pdyson@lincoln.ac.uk)
Assoc Libs: BRAYFORD POOL LRC, addr as above; CATHEDRAL CAMPUS LRC (see **S958**); RISEHOLME LIB (see **S959**); CITY CAMPUS LRC, Hooper Bldg, Guildhall Rd, Kingston-upon-Hull, HU1 1HT (01482-462312; *fax:* 01482-462315)
Entry: staff & students of Univ; associate membership available (fees for some categories)
Open: term: Mon-Thu 0900-2100, Fri 1000-1700; Sat 1100-1700; vac: Mon-Tue, Thu-Fri 1000-1700, Wed 1200-1900, Sat 1100-1400
Subj: all subjs; undergrad; postgrad *Collns: Archvs:* Remould Theatre Archv *Other:* Art & Design Slide Colln *Co-op Schemes:* ILL, SCONUL, UK Libs Plus
Equip: m-readers, copiers, clr copiers, computers (incl internet & CD-ROM), printers, video viewers, sound & video editing equip *Online:* BLAISE, SDC, Dialog, Datastar, DialTechnology, TextLine, InfoLine, Datastream, Lexis
Stock: bks/250000; periodcls/1000; m-forms/2500; audios/500; films/100

S958

University of Lincoln, Cathedral Campus Learning Resource Centre

(formerly De Montfort Univ Lincoln)
Chad Varah House, Wordsworth St, Lincoln, LN1 3BP (01522-895080; *fax:* 01522-895019)
Email: chadlib@lincoln.ac.uk
Internet: http://www.lincoln.ac.uk/ls/

Gov Body: Univ of Lincoln (see **S957**) *Chief:* Lib Team Leader: Mrs Janet Maughan (jmaughan@ lincoln.ac.uk) *Other Snr Staff:* Lib Offcr: Mrs Paula Hill BA, MCLIP
Entry: staff & students of Univ; associate membership available to others *Open:* term: Mon-Thu 0830-1900, Fri 0830-1700, sat 0900-1600; vac: Mon-Fri 0900-1300, 1400-1600
Subj: arts; design *Co-op Schemes:* BLDSC, ILL, SCONUL, UK Libs Plus
Equip: copier (A4/5p), video viewer, 14 computers (all with wd-proc & internet, 2 with CD-ROM)
Online: Art Abstracts, Proquest, Design & Applied Arts Index, Arts Index, some e-journals *Svcs:* info, ref
Stock: bks/15000; periodcls/100; videos/250
Classn: DDC *Auto Sys:* Horizon
Staff: Libns: 1.5 *Non-Prof:* 2 *Exp:* £35000 (1999-2000); £12000 (2000-01)

S959

University of Lincoln, Riseholme Library

School of Agric, Riseholm Hall, Riseholm, Lincoln, LN2 2LG (01522-895310; *fax:* 01522-895414)
Internet: http://www.lincoln.ac.uk/ls/

Gov Body: Univ of Lincoln (see **S957**) *Chief:* Lib Team Leader: Mrs Janet Maughan (jmaughan@ lincoln.ac.uk)
Entry: adv appt, must report to reception *Open:* term: Mon-Thu 0900-2000, Fri 0900 1700, Sat-Sun 1400-1700; vac: Mon-Fri 0900-1230, 1330-1700 (advisable to phone prior to visit)
Subj: genl; undergrad; computing; info tech; psy; ethics; lang (dictionaries); chem; biology; physics; ecology; statistics; animal care; veterinary medicine; agric; hortic; floristry; study aids *Co-op Schemes:* BLDSC, ILL, UK Libs Plus, SCONUL
Equip: m-reader, m-printer, video viewer, fax, 2 copiers, 60 computers (incl wd-proc, internet & CD-ROM) *Svcs:* info, ref
Stock: bks/15000; periodcls/110; pamphs/500; maps/50; videos/300
Classn: DDC *Auto Sys:* Horizon
Pubns: Guide to Lib; Subj Guides to Dewey System; Lit Searching (all free)
Staff: Libns: 2 *Non-Prof:* 2

Lisburn

S960

Irish Linen Centre and Lisburn Museum, Library and Archives

Market Sq, Lisburn, Co Antrim, BT28 1AG (028-9266-3377; *fax:* 028-9267-2624)
Email: brenda.collins@lisburn.gov.uk

Gov Body: Lisburn Borough Council *Chief:* Curator: Mr Brian J. Mackey BA *Dep:* Rsrch Offcr: Mrs Brenda Collins BSocSc, MPhil, DipMan
Entry: ref only, adv appt preferred *Open:* Mon-Fri 0900-1700
Subj: local study (Lisburn & the Lagan Valley); local hist; fine arts; textiles; Irish linen industry
Collns: Bks & Pamphs: complete lib of former Linen Industrial Rsrch Assoc (access strictly by prior appt) *Archvs:* archv of the former Linen Industry Rsrch Assoc, currently being catalogued
Equip: m-reader, m-printer, fax, copier, computer (with wd-proc) *Svcs:* info, ref, biblio
Stock: bks/5000; periodcls/25
Classn: DDC & in-house scheme *Auto Sys:* Status
Pubns: Flax to Fabric: The Story of Irish Linen (£4.50)
Staff: Libns: 1 *Other Prof:* 7
Proj: computer cataloguing & conservation of LIRA colln

S961

Religious Society of Friends, Lisburn Preparative Meeting Library

c/o 22 Whitla Rd, Lisburn, Co Antrim, BT28 3PD (028-9260-1864)
Email: jscott22@fish.co.uk

Gov Body: Lisburn Preparative Meeting of the Religious Soc of Friends *Chief:* Libn: Mr John Scott
Assoc Libs: Lib is held at Friends Meeting House, Magheralave Rd, Lisburn, BT28 3BH, but all correspondence should be addressed to the Libn at the above addr; ARCHVS, also held at Friends Meeting House, Lisburn, Archivist: Ms J. Muriel Cameron
Entry: by adv appt only; contact the Libn as above
Subj: religion; Quaker & Christian lit (excl genealogical material)
Stock: bks/500 *Staff: Non-Prof:* 1 volunteer

Liverpool

S962

Aintree Library and Information Resource Centre

1st Floor, Clinical Sciences Centre, Univ Hosp Aintree, Lower Ln, Liverpool, L9 7AL (0151-529-5851; *fax:* 0151-529-5856)
Internet: http://www.edgehill.ac.uk/ims/

Gov Body: svc managed by Edge Hill Coll (see **S1655**) *Chief:* LIRC Mgr: Miss Rachel Bury BA(Hons), MCLIP (buryr@edgehill.ac.uk) *Dep:* Learner Support Advisor & Resources Mgr: Mr Leo Appleton BA(Hons), MA (appletol@edgehill.ac.uk)
Assoc Libs: MERSEY CARE NHS TRUST, GABBY KEARNEY LIB (see **S1951**); ROYAL LIVERPOOL CHILDREN'S NHS TRUST, ALDER HEY EDU CENTRE LIB, Alder Hey Hosp, Eaton Rd, Liverpool, L12 2AP (tel & fax: 0151-252-5476); SOUTHPORT & ORMSKIRK NHS TRUST, THE HANLEY LIB (see **S1952**); STOCKPORT NHS TRUST, EDU CENTRE LIB (see **S1981**)
Entry: staff & students of Edge Hill Coll; staff of Aintree Hosps NHS Trust; staff of Walton Centre for Neurology & Neurosurgery NHS; Univ of Liverpool medical students on placement at Aintree site *Open:* Mon-Thu 0830-2000, Fri 0830-1700
Subj: medicine; nursing; psy *Co-op Schemes:* BLDSC, LIHNN
Equip: 2 copiers (card operated), 42 computer terminals (all with wd-proc, internet & CD-ROM facilities), 2 OPACs *Online:* full access to various online databases *Svcs:* info, ref
Stock: bks/25000; periodcls/300; CD-ROMs/20
Acqs Offcr: Resources Mgr, as above
Classn: NLM *Auto Sys:* Geac
Staff: Libns: 2 *Non-Prof:* 6

S963

The Athenaeum, Liverpool, Library

Church Alley, Liverpool, L1 3DD (0151-709-7770; *fax:* 0151-709-0418)
Email: library@athena.force9.net
Internet: http://www.athena.force9.co.uk/

Gov Body: Cttee of the club *Chief:* Libn: Mr E.H. Seagroatt FCLIP *Dep:* Libn: Mr J.D. Rogers BA, FCLIP
Entry: ref only & adv appt for non-membs *Open:* Mon-Tue 0930-1600, Wed-Fri 0930-2100
Subj: all subjs; Liverpool & Merseyside incl Wirral; early law bks; classical lit & foreign Liverpool directories (1766-1970); Eshelby (Yorkshire hist, topography & genealogy); William Roscoe Colln (Italian & classical); Blanco White Colln (South American & Spanish); Jackson Colln (mid 19C economic pamphs); misc pamphs; Play Colln (18C English); Liverpool playbills; ☛

Special Libraries

Liverpool ▼ Livingston

(The Athenaeum, Liverpool, Lib cont)
Collns (cont): Bks & Pamphs: Robert Gladstone Colln (law, local: bks & MSS); Norris Colln (civil & canon law) *Other:* local maps **Co-op Schemes:** AIL
Equip: m-reader, copier, room for hire **Svcs:** biblio
Stock: bks/70000; periodcls/40; pamphs/5000 (300 bnd vols); maps/500
Classn: DDC
Pubns: The Athenaeum Liverpool, 1797-1997 (£10, pf £11.75)
Staff: Libns: 2 PT

S964 ✚

Broadgreen Hospital, Education Centre Library

Thomas Dr, Liverpool, L14 3LB (0151-282-6447; fax: 0151-282-6988)

Gov Body: Royal Liverpool Univ Hosps – Broadgreen & Liverpool NHS Trust **Chief:** Libn: Miss Julie McKie BA(Hons)
Assoc Libs: ROYAL LIVERPOOL UNIV HOSP, RAYMOND HELSBY STAFF LIB (see **S976**)
Entry: full membership for Trust staff; ref only for other NHS staff **Open:** Mon-Thu 0830-1700, Fri 0830-1630
Subj: medicine; surgery; health care; nursing
Collns: Bks & Pamphs: UKCC & RCN pamphs
Co-op Schemes: BLDSC, LIHNN
Equip: m-reader, video viewer, copier (A4/5p), 3 computers (all with wd-proc, internet & CD-ROM), slide projector, scanner **Online:** Medline, CINAHL etc **Officer-in-Charge:** Snr Libn, as above **Svcs:** info, ref, biblio
Stock: bks/4000; periodcls/80; pamphs/various; maps/10; audios/20; videos/85; CD-ROMs/10
Acqs Offcr: Snr Libn & Libn, both as above
Classn: NLM **Auto Sys:** Alice **Staff:** Libns: 1

S965 🎓

Institute of Popular Music, Library and Archives

Roxby Bldg, Liverpool, L69 3BX (0151-794-3101; fax: 0151-794-2566)
Email: ipm@liverpool.ac.uk
Internet: http://www.liv.ac.uk/ipm/main.htm

Gov Body: Univ of Liverpool (see **S972**)
Assoc Libs: VINYL LIB, contact details as above
Entry: staff of the Univ of Liverpool; approved external readers on written appl; *Vinyl Lib:* membership fee of £7.50 pa **Open:** *Vinyl Lib:* Tue & Thu 1100-1600
Subj: music industry; music policy; popular music, incl: jazz; folk country music (UK, Irish & American); British R&B; rock'n'roll; rockabilly; Cajun; soul; funk; disco; stage & screen; World Music (Brazilian, Latin American, African etc); reggae **Collns:** Archvs: Robert Shelton Archv (writer on popular music, rsrch notes, papers etc); Mikis Theodorakis Colln (Greek composer & political activist) *Other:* Radio City FM Colln (singles); Robert Pring-Mill Colln (Latin American song); Sylvia Patterson Jazz Colln; Philip Snell Colln; Roger Hill Tapes Colln
Stock: bks/c1000, incl journals; audios/15000 LPs, 10000 singles; numerous CDs, audio tapes & videos
Pubns: The Black Book: The Merseyside Music Industry Directory

S966 ♟🙏

Liverpool Cathedral, Radcliffe Library

St James Mount, Liverpool, L1 7AZ (0151-709-6271; fax: 0151-702-7292)
Internet: http://www.liverpoolcathedral.org.uk/

Gov Body: Liverpool Cathedral, Dean & Chapter
Chief: Canon Chancellor: Canon David Hutton MA
Dep: Hon Libn: Mr J.E. Vaughan MA, FSA, FRSA
Entry: membs & others for ref after adv appt
Open: by appt
Subj: undergrad; postgrad; liturgy; theology, church hist; art; arch **Collns:** Bks & Pamphs: incl former Liverpool Church House Lib & Lib of St Aidan's Theological Coll, Birkenhead (now closed); early printed bks & medieval MSS are deposited in Special Collns Dept, Sydney Jones Lib, Univ of Liverpool (see **S972**)
Equip: copier
Stock: bks/20000; periodcls/7
Pubns: Short Title Catalogue of Bks Printed Before 1801 (£5 incl postage)
Staff: staffed by volunteers

S967 ☕✒

Liverpool Chamber of Commerce and Industry, Business Information Service

Old Hall St, Liverpool, L3 9HG (0151-227-1234; fax: 0151-236-0121)
Email: information@liverpoolchamber.org.uk
Internet: http://www.liverpoolchamber.org.uk/

Chief: Info Mgr: Ms Carole Crosby
Entry: primarily for membs of Liverpool & Knowsley Chamber, but svc available to wider business community on request **Open:** Mon-Fri 0900-1700
Subj: business info **Collns:** Bks & Pamphs: range of DTI pubns
Equip: fax, copier (both via staff, at a charge)
Stock: bks/various pamphs, videos & CD-ROMs
Classn: own
Pubns: various info packs, incl Merseyside China Link
Staff: Other Prof: 1 Non-Prof: 4

S968 🎓

Liverpool Hope University College, Sheppard-Worlock Library

PO Box 95, Hope Pk, Liverpool, L16 9LB (0151-291-2000 (enquiries); 0151-291-2001 (administration); fax: 0151-291-2037)
Email: taylorl@hope.ac.uk
Internet: http://www.hope.ac.uk/lib/lrd.htm

Gov Body: Liverpool Hope Univ Coll **Chief:** Dir of Learning Resources: Ms Linda Taylor MEd, BA, MCLIP **Dep:** Ms Susan Murray MA, BSc, MCLIP
Entry: by written appl to the Dir of Learning Resources; visitor status with ref rights is offered to serving teachers & clergy in the locality **Open:** term: Mon-Thu 0900-0700, Fri 0900-2200, Sun 1400-1700; vac: see web site for latest details
Subj: all subjs; undergrad; postgrad; American studies; art; ch's lit; design; drama; edu; English lit; environmental studies; French lit; geog; hist; maths; music; physical edu; religion; psy; sociology; theology; women's studies; info tech; business; mgmt **Collns:** Bks & Pamphs: Gradwell Colln (theology, previously housed at St Joseph's Coll, Upholland); former lib of the Natl Soc's Religious Edu Centre **Co-op Schemes:** BLDSC, Libs Together: Liverpool Learning Partnership
Equip: m-readers, m-printer, video viewers, copiers, clr copier, computers, video editing facilities, rooms for hire **Disabled:** RNIB kit, CCTV
Svcs: ref

Stock: bks/250000; periodcls/1000; slides/12000; audios/1000; videos/300; AVs/66000; dissertations/250; govt documents/3000; music scores/7000; films/220
Classn: DDC **Auto Sys:** Talis
Staff: Libns: 8.5 Non-Prof: 26 total **Exp:** £193288 (1999-2000)

S969 🎓

Liverpool John Moores University, Learning and Information Services

Aldham Robarts LRC, Mount Pleasant, Liverpool, L3 5UZ (0151-231-3544; fax: 0151-231-3113)
Internet: http://www.livjm.ac.uk/

Gov Body: Univ Governing Body **Chief:** Dir of Learning & Info Svcs: Ms Maxine Melling BA, MLib, MCLIP (m.melling@livjm.ac.uk) **Dep:** Head of User Svcs: Mr Graham Chan
Assoc Libs: ALDHAM ROBARTS LRC, addr as above, LRC Mgr: Mr Ken Graham (0151-231-3634/3701; fax: 0151-707-1307; email: k.r.graham@livjm.ac.uk); AVRIL ROBARTS LRC, 79 Tithebarn St, Liverpool, L2 2ER, LRC Mgr: Mr Jim Ainsworth (0151-231-4022; fax: 0151-231-4479; email: j.w.ainsworth@livjm.ac.uk); I.M. MARSH CAMPUS LRC, Barkhill Rd, Aigburth, Liverpool, L17 6BD, LRC Mgr: Ms Brigid Badger (0151-231-5216; fax: 0151-729-0165; email: b.j.badger@livjm.ac.uk)
Entry: genl public: ref only or external membership for limited use; proof of ID required **Open:** term: Mon-Thu 0900-2300, Fri 0930-2100, Sat-Sun 1000-1600 (Aldham Robarts LRC open 24 hrs to Univ card holders); vac: as advertised
Subj: undergrad; postgrad; generalities; phil; psy; social sci; lang; sci; maths; tech; arts; lit; geog; hist; *Aldham Robarts LRC:* accountancy; arch; business studies; construction; lang; law; librarianship; mgmt; social work; surveying; art; design; drama; lit; media studies; cultural studies; *Avril Robarts LRC:* sci; sports sci; elec eng; mechanical eng; marine eng; maritime studies; maths; computing; health care; nursing; politics; social sci; econ; *I.M. Marsh Campus:* edu; home econ; physical edu; dance; teaching practice **Collns:** Bks & Pamphs: Liddell Hart Colln (fashion); Stafford Beer Colln on automation; Commission for New Towns Colln; Art Exhib Catalogues **Archvs:** Univ Cttee papers; requisitions; England's Dreaming Punk Archv *Other:* Barbour fiche (construction industry) **Co-op Schemes:** Libs Together: The Liverpool Learning Partnership
Equip: 10 m-readers, 10 m-printers, video viewers, 2 fax, 20 copiers, clr copier, computers (incl wd-proc & CD-ROM) **Online:** various **Svcs:** info, ref, biblio
Stock: bks/65000; periodcls/2600; slides/71000; illusts/3000; maps/5000; m-forms/60000; videos/6000
Classn: DDC **Auto Sys:** Dynix
Staff: Libns: 35.9 Non-Prof: 78

S970 🎓✚

Liverpool Medical Institution Library

114 Mount Pleasant, Liverpool, L3 5SR (0151-709-9125; fax: 0151-707-2810)
Email: library@lmi.org.uk
Internet: http://www.lmi.org.uk/library.html

Gov Body: Liverpool Medical Instn **Chief:** Libn: Mrs M. Pierce Moulton **Dep:** Asst Libn: Ms L. Crane
Entry: ref only, adv appt, must be introduced by memb **Open:** Mon-Fri 0930-1800, Sat 0930-1230
Subj: clinical medicine **Co-op Schemes:** BLDSC, BMA
Equip: video viewer, fax, copier, computers (incl wd-proc, internet & CD-ROM), room for hire
Stock: bks/35000; periodcls/167; archvs/3000 items
Classn: Barnard

Pubns: A Hist of the Liverpool Medical Instn (£6.50)
Staff: Libns: 2 *Other Prof:* 2 *Non-Prof:* 1

S971

Liverpool School of Tropical Medicine, The Donald Mason Library

Pembroke Pl, Liverpool, L3 5QA (0151-708-9393 x2221; *fax:* 0151-708-8733)
Email: cmdcar1@liverpool.ac.uk
Internet: http://www.liv.ac.uk/lstm/libr/libr1.htm

Chief: Head of Lib & Info Svcs: Dr C.M. Deering BA, PhD, DipLib, MCLIP
Entry: open to staff & students; others by appt
Open: Mon-Fri 0900-1700
Subj: tropical medicine *Collns: Archvs:* School of Tropical Medicine Archvs
Equip: Online: BIDS, Web of Science, Medline, Grateful Med
Stock: bks/45000; periodcls/250; slides/200 sets; videos/100
Classn: Barnard *Auto Sys:* Dobis *Staff: Libns:* 1

S972

Liverpool University Library

PO Box 123, Liverpool, L69 3DA (0151-794-2674; *fax:* 0151-794-2681)
Email: library@liverpool.ac.uk
Internet: http://www.liv.ac.uk/library/libhomep.html

Gov Body: Univ of Liverpool *Chief:* Univ Libn: Ms Frances Thomson MA, BLitt (thomson@liverpool.ac.uk) *Other Snr Staff:* Head of Academic Liaison: Mr Stan Davies (qlis17@liv.ac.uk); Head of Systems: Mr David Backham (d.backham@liv.ac.uk); Head of Technical Svcs: Mr Phil Cohen (p.cohen@liv.ac.uk); Head of User Svcs: Mr Ian Jackson (i.b.jackson@liv.ac.uk); Head of Special Collns & Archvs: Ms Maureen Watry (mwatry@liv.ac.uk)
Assoc Libs: SYDNEY JONES LIB, Chatham St, Liverpool, L69 3DA (0151-794-2679; *fax:* 0151-794-2681); HAROLD COHEN LIB, Ashton St, Liverpool, L69 3DA (0151-794-5411; *fax:* 0151-794-5417); *Departmental Libs:* ARCHAEO LIB, 14 Abercromby Sq, Liverpool (0151-794-2474); CHEM LIB (0151-794-3597); CIVIC DESIGN LIB, Dept of Civic Design, 74 Bedford St South, Liverpool, L69 7ZQ (0151-794-3127); CONTINUING EDU LIB, 126 Mount Pleasant, Liverpool, L69 3GR (0151-794-3285); EDU LIB, 19 Abercromby Sq, Liverpool, L69 3DA (0151-794-2575); LAW LIB, Liverpool Law School, Chatham St, Liverpool, L69 7ZS (0151-794-2832); MUSIC LIB, Dept of Music, Univ of Liverpool, Liverpool, L69 3BX (0151-794-3105); PHYSICS LIB, Dept of Physics, Oxford St, Liverpool, L69 7ZE (0151-794-3470); MARINE BIOLOGY LIB, Marine Biological Station, Port Erin, Isle of Man, IM9 6JA (01625-831031); VETERINARY FIELD STATION LIB, Chester High Rd, Neston, Wirral, CH64 7TE (0151-794-6006)
Entry: ref on appl to libn, adv appt required for archvs & special collns *Open:* term: Mon-Fri 0830-2130, Sat 0900-1700, Sun 1200-1700; vac: Mon-Fri 0900-1700, Sat 0900-1300
Subj: all subjs; undergrad; postgrad; *Sydney Jones Lib:* arts; humanities; social sci; environmental studies; Latin American studies; special collns; *Harold Cohen Lib:* sci; medicine; eng; veterinary sci; dental sci *Collns: Bks & Pamphs:* Radcliffe Lib of Liverpool Cathedral; Liverpool School of Tropical Medicine Colln; Natl Museums & Galleries on Merseyside Colln; Early Children's Bks (17C-19C, c10000 items); Blake Colln; Comte Colln; Fraser Colln (tobacco); Merseyside Poets Colln; Edgar Allison Peers Colln (Spanish Civil War); Sci Fiction Foundation Colln (see **S973**); Scott Macfie Gypsy Colln; 17C pamphs; 19C private presses *Archvs:* records of the Univ (1834-date); Gypsy Lore Soc Archv; Cunard Steam-Ship

---

Co Archvs (1840-c1976); Univs' Athletic Union Archvs (1919-1994); English Table Tennis Assoc Archvs (1919-1986); Physical Edu Assoc Archvs (1910-1986); Royal Soc for the Prevention of Accidents Archvs (1917-1994); records of certain social work orgs, incl: Barnardos Archv (1867-c1996); Natl Children's Home Archv (1867-c1996); Fairbridge Soc Archv (1912-1991); Simon Community Archv (1964-c.1990); personal & literary papers, incl: Joseph Blanco White papers; John & Katharine Bruce Glasier papers; Josephine Butler papers; Adrian Henri papers; Rathbone family papers; papers of former membs of the univ, incl: Sir Cyril Burt papers (psychologist); Lord Holford papers (civic designer); Sir Charles Reilly papers (architect); Prof Gordon Stephenson papers (town planner); Lord David Owen papers *Other:* Ronald Fraser Oral Hist Colln (Spanish Civil War)
Co-op Schemes: BLDSC, ILL, Liverpool Learning Partnership, CURL, RLG
Equip: m-readers, m-printers, video & DVD players, copiers, clr copier, computers (incl wd-proc, internet & CD-ROM), room for hire *Online:* Dialog, BLAISE, Dialtech, Orbit, STN (£10 + cost)
Svcs: info, ref, biblio
Stock: bks/1.5 mln; periodcls/4500; photos/30000; slides/200; pamphs/6000; maps/90; m-forms/5800; audios/80; videos/600; archvs/4000 linear m *Acqs Offcr: Acqs Offcr:* Mr Keith Hinds (khinds@liv.ac.uk)
Classn: LC, DDC, UDC *Auto Sys:* Innopac
Pubns: User Guides to Main Libs (free); Guide to Special Collns (free); Guide to the Manuscript Collns in Liverpool Univ Lib (free)
Staff: Libns: 35.26 *Non-Prof:* 48.91

S973

Liverpool University, Sydney Jones Library, Science Fiction Foundation Collection

PO Box 123, Liverpool, L69 3DA (0151-794-2733/2696; *fax:* 0151-794-2681)
Email: asawyer@liverpool.ac.uk.

Gov Body: Sci Fiction Foundation & Univ of Liverpool (see **S972**) *Chief:* Librarian/Administrator, Sci Fiction Foundation Colln: Mr Andy Sawyer BA, MPhil, MCLIP
Entry: adv appt *Open:* Mon-Fri 0900-1300, 1400-1700
Subj: sci fiction; fantasy lit; criticism *Collns: Bks & Pamphs:* Myers Colln of Russian sci fiction; J. Michael Rosenblum Fanzine Colln; sci fiction magazines from 1930s onwards *Archvs:* archvs of the Flat Earth Soc; Eric Frank Russell Archv; John Brunner Archv
Stock: bks/25000; periodcls/2000; m-forms/21; audios/90; archvs/18 m
Classn: LC
Pubns: Foundation: The Review of Sci Fiction (£6.95 single issue, £19.50 pa for 3 issues)
Staff: Libns: 1

S974

Modern Churchpeople's Union, Library and Archives

MCU Office, 9 Westward View, Aigburth, Liverpool, L17 7EE (0151-726-9730)
Email: modchurchunion@btinternet.com
Internet: http://www.modchurchunion.org/

Gov Body: Genl Council *Chief:* Genl Sec: The Revd J.R. Clatworthy
Assoc Libs: LAMBETH PALACE LIB (see **S1234**)
Entry: adv appt *Open:* mornings only
Subj: religion *Svcs:* info, ref
Pubns: Modern Believing (journal, £6 per issue); The Contemporary Challenge of Modernist Theology (membs £9.99, non-membs £12.99); The New Liberalism: Faith for the Third Millennium (membs £5.99, non-membs £10); Engineering:

Mechanical or Moral Sci (membs £4, non-membs £7.70); Melodious Truth (membs £5.99, non-membs £8.99); Hastings Rashdall: Bibliography of the Publ Writings (membs £5, non-membs £10); Jesus of Nazareth: A New Look (membs £5.99, non-membs £7.95)
Staff: Non-Prof: 1

S975

North West Health Library and Information Service

Central Liverpool Primary Care Trust, Hamilton House, 24 Pall Mall, Liverpool, L3 6AL (0151-285-2010; *fax:* 0151-285-2264)
Email: library.services@fade.nhs.uk

Gov Body: Central Liverpool Primary Care Trust *Chief:* Lib Svcs Mgr: Mr Kieran Lamb BA(Hons), DipLib, MA (kieran.lamb@fade.nhs.uk) *Dep:* Asst Libn: Ms Maureen Horrigan BA(Hons) (maureen.horrigan@fade.nhs.uk) *Other Snr Staff:* Ms Tracy Dickinson & Mr Michael Heaton
Entry: ref only, adv appt *Open:* Mon-Thu 0900-1700, Fri 0900-1630
Subj: health promotion; medicine; public health; mgmt *Collns: Bks & Pamphs:* Dept of Health & NHS grey lit; NHS circulars (1948-date) *Co-op Schemes:* LIHNN
Equip: fax, 3 copiers (20p per pg), 2 computers (both with wd-proc, internet & CD-ROM) *Online:* Aditus (no fees) *Officer-in-Charge:* Lib Svcs Mgr, as above *Svcs:* info, ref, biblio, indexing, abstracting
Stock: bks/10000, incl pamphs; periodcls/75 *Acqs Offcr:* Lib Svcs Mgr, as above
Classn: Bliss *Auto Sys:* CAIRS Total Lib
Pubns: Lib Bulletin (monthly); Abstracts of NHS Circulars; Grey Lit Bulletin (all free)
Staff: Libns: 3.5 *Non-Prof:* 1

S976

Royal Liverpool University Hospital, Raymond Helsby Staff Library

Edu Centre, Royal Liverpool Univ Hosp, Prescot St, Liverpool, L7 8XP (0151-706-2248; *fax:* 0151-706-2249)
Email: angela.hall@rlbuh-tr.nwest.nhs.uk

Gov Body: Royal Liverpool Univ Hosps – Broadgreen & Liverpool NHS Trust *Chief:* Lib mgr: Ms Angela Hall BA(Hons) *Dep:* Lib Asst: Mrs Helen Blackburn BA(Hons)
Assoc Libs: BROADGREEN HOSP, EDU CENTRE LIB (see **S964**)
Entry: staff & students of Royal Liverpool Univ Hosps *Open:* Mon-Fri 0830-1800; after hrs access by proximity card
Subj: medicine; nursing; professions allied to medicine *Co-op Schemes:* BLDSC, BMA, RCS, NULJ, LIHNN
Equip: 2 m-readers, fax, 2 video viewers, copier, 15 computers (all with wd-proc, internet & CD-ROM) *Online:* Medline, CINAHL, BNI, Cochrane, Natl Rsrch Register *Svcs:* info, ref, indexing
Stock: bks/7000; periodcls/111; videos/115
Classn: NLM *Auto Sys:* Alice
Staff: Libns: 2 *Other Prof:* 1 *Non-Prof:* 2 *Exp:* £35000 (1999-2000); £35000 (2000-01)

Livingston

S977

West Lothian College Library

Student Development Centre, Almondvale Cres, Livingston, W Lothian, EH54 7EP (01506-427601; *fax:* 01506-409980)
Email: lhartley@west-lothian.ac.uk
Internet: http://www.west-lothian.ac.uk/

Gov Body: West Lothian Coll *Chief:* Libn: Ms Linda Hartley BA, MCLIP

Livingston ▼ London

Special Libraries

(West Lothian Coll Lib cont)
Other Snr Staff: Student Development Centre Mgr: Mrs Elizabeth Bathgate BA
Entry: ref only *Open:* term: Mon-Thu 0800-2100, Fri 0800-1630, Sat 0900-1600; vac: Mon-Thu 0830-1800, Fri 0830-1630
Subj: all subjs; vocational *Co-op Schemes:* BLDSC
Equip: networked copiers, 60 computers (incl wd-proc, internet & CD-ROM) *Disabled:* 2 special need machines *Svcs:* info, ref
Stock: bks/12000; periodcls/100; audios/20; videos/50; CD-ROMs/30 *Acqs Offcr:* Libn, as above
Classn: DDC *Auto Sys:* Dynix
Staff: Libns: 1 *Other Prof:* 1 *Non-Prof:* 5
Further Info: provides ref lib facilities in partnership with West Lothian Council Public Libs (see **P197**)

Llanelli

S978 ✚

Prince Philip Hospital, Multidisciplinary Library
Carmarthenshire NHS Trust, Prince Philip Hosp, Llanelli, Carmarthenshire, SA14 8QF (*tel & fax:* 01554-749301)
Email: annlee@princephilip.demon.co.uk

Gov Body: Carmarthenshire NHS Trust *Chief:* Libn: Ms Ann Leeuwerke MCLIP *Dep:* Asst Libn: Ms Sarah Bruch BSc
Assoc Libs: UNIV OF WALES COLL OF MEDICINE (see **S427**)
Entry: employees of Carmarthenshire NHS Trust & fee-paying external readers *Open:* Mon-Tue, Thu 0830-1730, Wed 0830-2000, Fri 0830-1700
Subj: medicine; health; allied subjs *Co-op Schemes:* BLDSC, AWHILES, AWHL, NULJ, BMA, RCSE
Equip: fax, video viewer, copier, 10 computers (incl wd-proc, internet & CD-ROM) *Online:* Medline, PsycInfo, Embase, CINAHL, CancerLit, AMED, ASSIA, HMIC, BNI
Stock: bks/9000; periodcls/c90; pamphs/600; videos/90
Classn: NLM *Auto Sys:* Libertas
Staff: Libns: 1 *Non-Prof:* 1.5

Llantrisant

S979 ✚

Royal Glamorgan Hospital Library
Ynysmaerdy, Llantrisant, Mid Glamorgan, CF72 8XR (01443-443443; *fax:* 01443-443242)
Email: jan.hooper@pr-tr.wales.nhs.uk

Gov Body: Pontypridd & Rhondda NHS Trust
Chief: Libn: Mrs Janet M. Hooper BA(Hons), MA, MCLIP
Entry: ref only for external users *Open:* Mon-Thu 0830-1900, Fri 0830-1700
Subj: medicine; nursing; health *Co-op Schemes:* BLDSC, AWHILES Interlending Network
Equip: copier (A4/10p), fax, 2 video viewers, 14 computers (all with wd-proc & internet, 8 with CD-ROM) *Online:* Medline, CINAHL, Cochrane etc
Svcs: info, ref, biblio
Stock: bks/6000; periodcls/70; videos/30 *Acqs Offcr:* Libn, as above

---

Classn: DDC *Auto Sys:* Voyager
Staff: Libns: 2 *Non-Prof:* 4

Lochgilphead

S980 🏛

Kilmartin House Trust, The Marion Campbell Library
Kilmartin House, Kilmartin, Lochgilphead, Argyll, PA31 8RQ (01546-510278; *fax:* 01546-510330)
Email: museum@kilmartin.org
Internet: http://www.kilmartin.org/

Gov Body: Kilmartin House Trust *Chief:* Dir of Finance & Admin: Mr Richard Adair LLB, MIAT (richard@kilmartin.org) *Dep:* Dir of Marketing: Mr David Adams McGilp MCIM, FSAS (djam@kilmartin.org) *Other Snr Staff:* Marketing Dir: Mr Colin Schafer BSc (colin@kilmartin.org); Dir of Edu: Ms Georgia Crook BA (georgia@kilmartin.org)
Assoc Libs: NAT HIST & ANTIQUARIAN SOC OF MID-ARGYLL LIB
Entry: adv appt *Open:* Mon-Fri 1000-1730
Subj: local study (Mid-Argyll); Scottish archaeo & hist *Collns: Other:* photographic slides of Kilmartin landscape & monuments
Equip: m-reader, copier (10p per sheet), fax (50p per call), 2 computers (both with wd-proc, internet & CD-ROM, internet £1 per hr), room for hire (£10 per hr) *Disabled:* full disabled access *Officer-in-Charge:* Dir of Finance & Admin, as above *Svcs:* info
Stock: bks/2000; periodcls/12; photos/3000; slides/10000; illusts/200; pamphs/200; maps/100; m-forms/32; audios/3; videos/3 *Acqs Offcr:* Dir of Finance & Admin, as above
Classn: DDC
Pubns: The Kilmartin Sessions: The Sounds of Ancient Scotland (£14.50); Kilmartin Prehistoric & Early Historic Monuments (£12.50); Kilmartin: An Introduction & Guide to Scotland's Richest Prehistoric Landscape (£10); Argyll: The Enduring Heartland (£10); The Horsieman (£10)
Staff: Other Prof: 5 *Non-Prof:* 5

London

S981 ⚷ 📷

01 Photolibrary
67 Connaught Gdns, London, N10 3LG (020-8444-1888; *fax:* 020-8444-1888)
Email: contact@andrew-holt.com
Internet: http://www.andrew-holt.com/

Chief: Proprietor: Mr Andrew Holt BSc, DipM, FRGS
Entry: adv appt *Open:* Mon-Fri 0800-2200
Subj: broad range of genl image stock
Stock: photos/50000 *Staff: Other Prof:* 1

S982 🏛

ACAS Information Centre
180 Borough High St, London, SE1 1LW (020-7210-3911; *fax:* 020-7210-3615)
Email: library@acas.org.uk
Internet: http://www.acas.org.uk/

Gov Body: Advisory, Conciliation & Arbitration Svc *Chief:* Info Centre Mgr: Ms Alison Matthews MA(Cantab) *Dep:* Info Specialist: Mr Richard Wilsher
Entry: primarily for ACAS employees; others by appt for ref only *Open:* Mon-Fri 0930-1630
Subj: social sci; employment relations; employment law; industrial relations; quality of working life; employment; conciliation; mediation; trade unions; personnel mgmt *Collns: Archvs:* ACAS annual reports (1974-date) *Co-op Schemes:* ILLs with other govt depts

---

Equip: available to ACAS staff only: copier, fax, video viewer, 3 computers (all with CD-ROM & internet, 2 with wd-proc) *Online:* Lexis-Nexis, Dialog (ACAS staff only) *Svcs:* info, ref, biblio, abstracting
Stock: bks/c8000; periodcls/c200; pamphs/c2000; audios/c70; videos/c150; CD-ROMs/c20
Classn: DDC *Auto Sys:* Adlib for catalogue & circulation; GLAS for serials
Pubns: current awareness bulletins, contents pages, press cuttings (for ACAS use only)
Staff: Libns: 2 *Non-Prof:* 2

S983 ⚷ 📷

Ace Stock
Satellite House, 2 Salisbury Rd, Wimbledon, London, SW19 4EZ (020-8944-9944; *fax:* 020-8944-9940)
Email: info@acestock.com
Internet: http://www.acestock.com/

Type: stock photo agency *Gov Body:* BAPLA
Chief: Managing Dir: Mr John Panton
Open: Mon-Fri 0930-1800
Subj: genl modern stock lib, incl business; lifestyles; industry; sports; animals; travel
Stock: photos/250000, incl illusts; 25000 images online
Pubns: various catalogues (free) plus CD
Staff: Other Prof: 11

S984 ⚷

Action for Blind People, Information and Advice Centre
14-16 Verney Rd, London, SE16 3DZ (020-7635-4800; *fax:* 020-7635-4829)
Email: info@afbp.org
Internet: http://www.afbp.org/

Chief: Info & Advice Svcs Mgr: Ms Sandra Hanafin
Assoc Libs: MOBILE INFO & ADVICE SVC (based at Verney Rd), Mobile Svcs Mgr: Mr Bob Welsh
Entry: ref only, adv appt *Open:* Mon-Fri 0900-1700
Subj: svc provision & other matters relevant to visual impairment *Co-op Schemes:* participation in VISUGATE Proj to provide a gateway to digital info for visually impaired; the Centre's role is to digitise leaflets published by various local socs
Equip: copier *Disabled:* CCTV, braille embosser
Stock: bks/230; periodcls/89, plus 5300 journal articles; pamphs/5000
Classn: DISS
Pubns: various brochures & factsheets
Staff: Libns: 1 *Other Prof:* 1 *Non-Prof:* 2 *Exp:* £3400 (2000-01)

S985 ⚷ 📷

Action Images Ltd
Image House, Station Rd, London, N17 9LR (020-8885-3000; *fax:* 020-8267-2035)
Email: info@actionimages.com
Internet: http://www.actionimages.com/

Type: commercial photo agency *Chief:* Lib Mgr: Mr Gavin Clay
Open: Mon-Fri 0800-1900
Subj: sport
Equip: copier, computers, photo transmission & reception facilities
Stock: slides/1000000

S986 🎓

Acton and West London College, Acton Learning Centre
Mill Hill Rd, Acton, London, W3 8UX (020-8931-6000; *fax:* 020-8993-2725)

Gov Body: Ealing, Hammersmith & West London Coll *Chief:* LRC Mgr: Ms A. Ray MA, MCLIP, DMS *Assoc Libs:* EALING & WEST LONDON COLL, EALING LEARNING CENTRE, The Green, Ealing, London, W5 5EW; HAMMERSMITH & WEST LONDON COLL, HAMMERSMITH LEARNING CENTRE (see **S1156**); HAMMERSMITH & WEST LONDON COLL, LIME GROVE LEARNING CENTRE, Lime Grove, London, W12 8EA; SOUTHALL & WEST LONDON COLL, SOUTHALL LEARNING CENTRE (see **S1937**) *Entry:* ref only for non-staff or students *Open:* term: Mon-Fri 0845-1930; vac: 1000-1600 *Subj:* all subjs; GCSE; A level; social sci; lang; sci; maths; tech; geog; hist *Co-op Schemes:* BLDSC, ILL *Equip:* video viewer, fax, copier, clr copier, computers (incl wd-proc, internet & CD-ROM), room for hire *Svcs:* info, ref, biblio *Stock:* bks/70000; periodcls/200; slides/1200; audios/1500; videos/3000 *Classn:* DDC *Auto Sys:* Unicorn *Staff:* Libns: 12 *Non-Prof:* 15

S987

The Advertising Archives

45 Lyndale Ave, London, NW2 2QB (020-7435-6540; *fax:* 020-7794-6584)
Email: suzanne@advertisingarchives.co.uk
Internet: http://www.advertisingarchives.co.uk/

Type: commercial picture agency *Chief:* Managing Dir: Mrs Suzanne Viner BA(Hons) *Dep:* Dir: Mr Larry Viner *Other Snr Staff:* Snr Picture Rsrcher: Ms Ann Stephenson
Entry: visiting by appt only; searches available by phone, fax or email *Open:* Mon-Fri 0900-1800, weekends by arrangement
Subj: 20C advertising & illustration
Equip: copier, clr copier, fax, 4 computers (all with wd-proc, internet & CD-ROM) *Online:* image database (keyworded for easy access) *Svcs:* ref *Stock:* bks/500; slides/50000; illusts/1 mln; 20000 images on database *Acqs Offcr:* Dir, as above
Pubns: brochure (free)
Staff: Libns: 3

S988

The Advertising Association Information Centre

Abford House, 15 Wilton Rd, London, SW1V 1NJ (*genl enqs:* 020-7828-4831; *business enqs:* 020-7828-2771; *fax:* 020-7931-0376)
Email: ic@adassoc.org.uk
Internet: http://www.adassoc.org.uk/

Chief: Head of Info Svcs: Mr Philip Spink BA, MCLIP *Dep:* Info Offcr: to be appointed
Entry: ref only, non-membs (business or public) by appt only *Open:* membs: Mon-Fri 0930-1300, 1400-1700; non-membs: Tue-Thu 1400-1600; tel enqs: Mon-Thu 0930-1300, 1400-1700 for businesses, Tue-Thu 1400-1600 for other non-membs
Subj: advertising; marketing; sales promotion; media; public relations *Collns: Bks & Pamphs:* ref bks relating to advertising, mainly in the UK *Other:* extensive statistics colln; press cuttings relating to advertising (300+ files)
Equip: copier (A4/10p), computers (incl internet, printouts A4/50p) *Online:* World Advertising Rsrch Centre database (costs on appl)
Stock: bks/3000; periodcls/150
Classn: own
Pubns: Advertising Assoc: An Introduction (free); Advertising Assoc Annual Review (free); Advertising Assoc List of Constituent Orgs (£5, free to membs); numerous other Advertising Assoc pubns
Staff: Other Prof: 1

S989

Al-Furqan Islamic Heritage Foundation Library

Eagle House, High St, Wimbledon, London, SW19 5EF (020-8944-1233; *fax:* 020-8944-1633)
Email: info@al-furqan.com
Internet: http://www.al-furqan.com/

Entry: open to students of Islamic heritage & scholars with a particular interest in Islamic MSS
Subj: Islamic studies; Islamic phil; sci; Islamic hist; Islamic art; Sufism; Arabic lang; Arabic lit; Arab & Muslim biography; bibliography *Collns: Bks & Pamphs:* catalogues of MS collns in some 90 countries *Other:* several 1000 MSS on m-film
Stock: bks/c14000; periodcls/20
See also **O9**

S990

Alpine Club Library

55 Charlotte Rd, London, EC2A 3QF (020-7613-0745; *fax:* 020-7613-0755)
Email: lib@alpine-club.org.uk
Internet: http://www.alpine-club.org.uk/

Chief: Libn: Mrs M.J. Ecclestone BA, DipLib, MCLIP
Entry: adv appt, ref only *Open:* Wed-Fri 1400-1700
Subj: mountaineering world-wide; hist of mountaineering; ski mountaineering; walking; high altitude medicine *Collns: Bks & Pamphs:* mountaineering bks & journals world-wide (historical & current); expedition reports *Archvs:* mountaineering diaries; correspondence; newspaper cuttings (1891-date) *Other:* mountaineering photos
Equip: copier *Svcs:* info
Stock: bks/30000; periodcls/100; photos/3000; pamphs/5000; archvs/100 linear ft
Classn: in-house sys *Auto Sys:* Adlib
Pubns: Alpine Club Lib Catalogue (£7 + p&p); Index to the Ladies' Alpine Club Yearbooks, 1910-1975 (£10 + p&p)
Staff: Libns: 1

S991

Alzheimer's Society, Ann Brown Memorial Library

Gordon House, 10 Greencoat Pl, London, SW1P 1PH (020-7306-0606; *fax:* 020-7306-0808)
Email: info@alzheimers.org.uk
Internet: http://www.alzheimers.org.uk/

Chief: Libn: Ms Lesley A. MacKinnon DipILS (lmackinnon@alzheimers.org.uk)
Entry: adv appt only *Open:* Mon-Fri 0900-1700
Subj: health & social care of dementia *Co-op Schemes:* BLDSC, CHILL
Svcs: info, ref, biblio, lit searches (free of charge)
Stock: bks/5000; periodcls/70; videos/30
Classn: in-house *Auto Sys:* DBTextworks
Staff: Libns: 1 *Exp:* £15000 (2002-03)

S992

Amnesty International, Information Resources Program

1 Easton Rd, London, WC1X 0DW (020-7413-5589; *fax:* 020-7956-1157)
Email: amnestyis@amnesty.org
Internet: http://www.amnesty.org/

Type: NGO *Chief:* Dir of Info Resources: Ms Chris Catton
Entry: by appt only; apply in writing to the Dir of Info Resources
Subj: human rights
Classn: own *Auto Sys:* Heritage, Lotus Notes

S993

Architectural Association Library

36 Bedford Sq, London, WC1B 3ES (020-7887-4036; *fax:* 020-7414-0782)
Email: hsklar@aaschool.ac.uk
Internet: http://www.aaschool.ac.uk/library/

Gov Body: Architectural Assoc (AA) *Chief:* Libn: Ms Hinda F. Sklar BA, MLS *Dep:* Dep to the Libn: Miss Aileen Smith
Entry: AA students/membs only *Open:* term: Mon-Fri 1000-2000, Sat 1100-1500; vac: Mon-Fri 1000-1700
Subj: at undergrad & postgrad level: arch; art; planning; landscapes *Collns: Bks & Pamphs:* rare bk colln; 19C colln; internatl exhibs; AA theses *Archvs:* AA colln & AA archv *Co-op Schemes:* BLDSC
Equip: copier, computer (with CD-ROM)
Stock: bks/30000; periodcls/150; maps/1102
Classn: UDC *Auto Sys:* Sirsi
Pubns: Guide to the Architectural Assoc Lib (annual); Architectural Assoc Lib Bibliographies (new series); theses & essays; periodcls & serials
Staff: Libns: 2 *Non-Prof:* 2 *Exp:* £20000 (2000-01)

S994

Archway Healthcare Library

Holborn Union Bldg, Archway Campus, Highgate Hill, London, N19 5LW (020-7288-3580; *fax:* 020-7288-3571)
Email: AHL@mdx.ac.uk
Internet: http://www.archway.ac.uk/AHL/

Gov Body: run by Middlesex Univ (see **S1282**) on behalf of: Royal Free & Univ Coll Medical School (see **S1360**), Whittington Hosp NHS Trust, Camden & Islington Primary Care Trusts & Camden & Islington Mental Health Trust *Chief:* Lib & Info Mgr: Ms Beverley Chapman (b.chapman@mdx.ac.uk) *Other Snr Staff:* Health Info Libn: Mr Richard Peacock (r.peacock@mdx.ac.uk)
Entry: open to all membs of partner orgs & to membs of North Central London Workforce Development Confederation; others by arrangement or fee *Open:* Mon, Fri 0900-1700, Tue-Thu 0900-2000, Sat 1000-1430
Subj: medicine; health related; nursing; some psychiatry *Co-op Schemes:* BLL, LAMDA, RCSE, UK Libs Plus, M25 Consortium, North London Edu Consortium
Equip: 2 video viewers, 3 copiers (card-operated), 50 computers (incl 31 with wd-proc, 31 with internet & 3 with CD-ROM), training room for hire (£150 pd) *Online:* Medline, CINAHL, PsycInfo; wide range of elec journals *Officer-in-Charge:* Lib & Info Mgr, as above *Svcs:* info, ref
Stock: bks/20000; periodcls/162; videos/30; CD-ROMs/200 *Acqs Offcr:* Trainee Prof Libn: Ms Sarah Castle (s.castle@mdx.ac.uk)
Classn: NLM *Auto Sys:* Horizon
Staff: Libns: 3.8 *Non-Prof:* 3.2 *Exp:* £100500 (1999-2000)

S995

Army Library Service, Services Central Library

Royal Military Academy, Red Lion Ln, Woolwich, London, SE18 4JJ (020-8781-5917; *fax:* 020-8781-5931)
Email: ets.scl@gtnet.gov.uk

Gov Body: Ministry of Defence (see **S1284**)
Assoc Libs: LIB HQ (2, 3, 4 & 5 Divs), Ward Barracks, Bulford Camp, Salisbury, Wiltshire, SP4 9NG (01980-672267; *fax:* 01980-672149; *email:* hq.lib@gtnet.gov.uk); PRINCE CONSORT'S LIB (see **S26**); numerous local Army Libs throughout the UK & overseas ➡

(Army Lib Svc, Svcs Central Lib cont)
Entry: all UK military personnel, their families, MoD civilians & employees of MoD agencies
Open: Mon-Fri 0900-1630
Subj: all subjs; mgmt; law; computing; eng; edu; sociology; fiction *Co-op Schemes:* BLDSC, MoD ILLs
Equip: computers (incl internet & CD-ROM)
Online: various resources via DELOS *Svcs:* info, ref, lit searches
Stock: bks/30000 *Acqs Offcr:* contact the Acqs Section (ets.las@gtnet.gov.uk)

S996 🗝

Art Workers Guild Library

6 Queen Sq, London, WC1 3AR (020-7713-0966; *fax:* 020-7713-0967)
Internet: http://www.artworkersguild.org/

Gov Body: The Cttee *Chief:* Hon Libn: Mr John Shaw *Other Snr Staff:* Hon Archivist: Mr Alan Powers
Entry: membs of the Guild; students & rsrchers by appt only *Open:* by arrangement
Subj: arts; crafts; restoration; preservation; arch; the Arts & Crafts Movement *Collns: Bks & Pamphs:* works by & about membs of the Guild *Archvs:* Art Workers Guild Archvs (1884-date), incl minutes of meetings & lectures, correspondence with membs, designs & records of various exhibs, masques etc *Other:* arch drawings by guild membs & others
Stock: bks/c5000; photos/c500 *Staff: Non-Prof:* 1

S997 🏛

Arts Council England Library

14 Gt Peter St, London, SW1P 3NQ (0845-300-6200; *fax:* 020-7973-6590)
Email: enquiries@artscouncil.org.uk
Internet: http://www.artscouncil.org.uk/

Gov Body: Arts Council of England *Chief:* contact the Info Offcr
Entry: ref only, adv appt
Subj: cultural policy (UK & overseas); arts mgmt, policy & funding; arts marketing & market rsrch *Collns: Archvs:* Arts Council Colln of publ material *Other:* Market Rsrch Index for the Arts *Co-op Schemes:* BLDSC
Equip: copier *Svcs:* info, ref, biblio
Stock: bks/25000; periodcls/300; pamphs/2000
Classn: own *Auto Sys:* Heritage
Pubns: factsheets on cultural policy, fundraising, sponsorship, arts mgmt, marketing (all free)
Staff: Libns: 4

S998 🗝

Arup Library and Information Services

13 Fitzroy St, London, W1P 4BQ (020-7755-3271; *fax:* 020-7755-2126)
Email: arup.library@arup.com
Internet: http://www.arup.com/

Chief: Snr Libn: Ms Andrea Beddard MCLIP (andrea.beddard@arup.com)
Assoc Libs: all at the above addr: PHOTO LIB, contact: Ms Pauline Shirley (020-7755-3081; *email:* pauline.shirley@arup.com); MAP LIB, contact: Mr

John Henry (020-7755-2079; *email:* john.henry@arup.com); ARCHV, contact: Mr Ian Patrick (020-7755-2582; *email:* ian.patrick@arup.com)
Open: Mon-Fri 0830-1800
Subj: arch; construction; eng (civil, electrical, industrial, mechanical) *Collns: Other:* photo colln; map colln; aerial photo colln
Equip: m-reader, fax, 2 copiers (10p per pg), 2 computers (all with wd-proc, internet & CD-ROM)
Svcs: info, ref, biblio, indexing, abstracting
Stock: bks/20000; periodcls/250; pamphs/50000
Acqs Offcr: Snr Libn: Ms Heide Pirwitz (heide.pirwitz@arup.com)
Classn: UDC *Auto Sys:* Heritage
Pubns: ARUP Journal (4 pa, distributed to approved recipients); ARUP Focus
Staff: Libns: 9

S999

Aspect Picture Library

40 Rostrevor Rd, London, SW6 5AD (020-7736-1998; *fax:* 020-7731-7362)
Email: aspect.ldn@btinternet.com

Type: commercial photo agency *Chief:* Chief Libn: Ms Angela Bush
Open: Mon-Fri 0930-1800
Subj: all subjs; genl *Stock:* photos/250000
Staff: Libns: 2 *Non-Prof:* 2

S1000 🖋

Associated Newspapers Ltd, Reference Library

Northcliffe House, 2 Derry St, Kensington, London, W8 5TT (020-7938-6300; *fax:* 020-7584-1095)

Chief: Lib Editor: Mr Steve Torrington *Dep:* Ref Lib Mgr: Mr Richard Jones
Open: open 24 hrs a day
Collns: Bks & Pamphs: Hansard; White Papers *Other:* Associated Newspapers cuttings since 1896
Equip: m-reader, m-printer, copier, computers (incl wd-proc, internet & CD-ROM)
Stock: bks/1000+; m-forms/various

S1001 🗝 🎓

Association of Anaesthetists of Great Britain and Ireland, Library and Archives

(incorporating the British Journal of Anaesthesia Lib)
21 Portland Pl, London, W1B 1PY (020-7631-1650; *Archivist:* 020-7631-8806; *fax:* 020-7631-4352)
Email: trishwillis@aagbi.org
Internet: http://www.aagbi.org/

Type: prof body *Gov Body:* Assoc of Anaesthetists of Great Britain & Ireland *Chief:* Hon Libn: Dr C. Neil Adams *Dep:* Archivist: Mrs Patricia Willis
Assoc Libs: CHARLES KING COLLN OF HISTORIC ANAESTHETIC APPARATUS, housed in British Oxygen Company Museum in same bldg *Entry:* bona fide rsrchers into the hist of anaesthesia, by prior appt only *Open:* Mon-Fri 0930-1630
Subj: hist of medicine, esp the hist of anaesthesia *Collns: Bks & Pamphs:* Charles King Colln (288 vols); Dr K. Bryn Thomas Colln (91 vols); Dr J. Alfred Lee Colln (140 vols); complete sets of Anaesthesia & The British Journal of Anaesthesia; technical lit *Archvs:* archvs of Assoc of Anaesthetists of Great Britain & Ireland (1932 onwards), incl minute bks, annual reports, correspondence files, pubns & publicity material; some deposited archvs, incl records of the Intensive Care Soc *Other:* historic colln of photos & AV materials relating to anaesthesia

S1002 🗝

Association of British Theatre Technicians, Library and Archives

47 Bermondsey St, London, SE1 3XT (020-7403-3778; *fax:* 020-7378-6170)
Email: office@abtt.org.uk
Internet: http://www.abtt.org.uk/

Gov Body: ABTT
Entry: not open to genl public; membs should contact the office for access
Subj: arts; theatre tech; theatre design *Collns: Archvs:* theatre plans
Svcs: info, ref *Staff: Other Prof:* 2

S1003 🗝 🎓

Association of Commonwealth Universities, Reference Library

John Foster House, 36 Gordon Sq, London, WC1H 0PF (020-7380-6700; *fax:* 020-7387-2655)
Email: info@acu.ac.uk
Internet: http://www.acu.ac.uk

Type: inter-univ assoc *Gov Body:* Assoc of Commonwealth Univs *Chief:* Libn: Mr Nick Mulhern
Entry: ref only *Open:* Mon-Fri 0930-1300, 1400-1730
Subj: Higher Edu in the Commonwealth *Collns: Bks & Pamphs:* course guides; award guides; univ calendars; prospectuses; reports
Equip: copier *Svcs:* info, ref
Stock: bks/18500; periodcls/1000
Classn: UDC *Auto Sys:* CAIRS
Staff: Other Prof: 1

S1004 🖋 ✚

Association of the British Pharmaceutical Industry Library

12 Whitehall, London, SW1A 2DY (020-7930-3477; *fax:* 020-7747-1447)
Email: ccoomber@abpi.org.uk
Internet: http://www.abpi.org.uk/

Gov Body: Assoc of the British Pharmaceutical Industry *Chief:* Libn: Ms Caroline Coomber BA(Hons)
Entry: not open to public, but enqs welcome from other libs *Open:* Mon-Fri 0930-1630
Subj: health; pharmaceuticals; pharmaceutical industry *Co-op Schemes:* ILL
Equip: copier *Svcs:* info
Stock: bks/2000; periodcls/200
Classn: DDC *Auto Sys:* Heritage *Staff: Libns:* 1

S1005 🗝

The Athenaeum, Library

107 Pall Mall, London, SW1Y 5ER (020-7930-4843)

Gov Body: The Athenaeum *Chief:* Libn: Ms Kay Walters BA, MCLIP *Other Snr Staff:* Keeper of Archvs, Bks & Collns: Ms Sarah Douglas MA, MCLIP
Entry: membs only; applications from non-membs by letter only (access granted only for study of unique materials not available elsewhere) *Open:* Mon-Fri 0930-1730; closed Aug
Subj: all subjs (eclectic) *Collns: Bks & Pamphs:* Morton Pitt Colln; Basil Hall Colln; Boer War Colln
Svcs: ref
Stock: bks/70000 *Acqs Offcr:* Libn, as above
Classn: LC
Pubns: The Athenaeum Colln, ed Tait & Walker (£45); Armchair Athenians (£20)
Staff: Libns: 2 *Other Prof:* 20 *Non-Prof:* 30

S1006
Austrian Cultural Forum London, Library
28 Rutland Gate, London, SW7 1PQ (020-7548-8653; *fax:* 020-7225-0470)
Email: culture@austria.org.uk
Internet: http://www.austria.org.uk/culture/

Chief: Libn & Proj Mgr: Ms Andrea Rauter (andrea.rauter@bmaa.gv.at)
Entry: open to public *Open:* Mon-Fri 0900-1300, 1500-1700
Subj: subjs relating to Austria: generalities; phil; arts; lit; geog; hist
Equip: copier, computer (with wd-proc, internet & CD-ROM) *Svcs:* ref
Stock: bks/8000; some audios & videos
Staff: Non-Prof: 1

S1007
The Aviation Picture Library
116 The Avenue, St Stephen's, West Ealing, London, W13 8JX (020-8566-7712; *fax:* 020-8566-7714)
Email: avpix@aol.com
Internet: http://www.aviationpictures.com/

Chief: Owner: Capt Austin J. Brown LBIPP
Entry: adv appt *Open:* Mon-Fri 1030-1645 or by arrangement
Subj: aerospace; aviation; arch; travel; aerial photography (oblique) *Collns: Archvs:* John Stroud Colln (aviation photos)
Equip: fax, copier, computer (with wd-proc, internet & CD-ROM) *Svcs:* info, ref, translation & editing (to German)
Stock: photos/35000; slides/500000; illusts/few; videos/some, incl aviation video clips
Auto Sys: Capture *Staff:* Other Prof: 1 PT

S1008
Bank of England, Information Centre
Threadneedle St, London, EC2R 8AH (020-7601-4846/4715; *fax:* 020-7601-4356)
Email: InfoCentre@bankofengland.co.uk
Internet: http://www.bankofengland.co.uk/

Gov Body: Court of Dirs of the Bank of England
Chief: Libn: Ms P.A. Hope BA, MA, MSc, DipLib, MCLIP *Dep:* Dep Libn: Mr H.A. Picton BA, MCLIP
Assoc Libs: BANK OF ENGLAND ARCHV (see **A253**)
Entry: ref only for rsrchers, adv appt required
Open: Mon-Fri 0930-1730
Subj: econ; banking; finance *Collns: Bks & Pamphs:* 17C-19C economic tracts & govt reports on banking & finance *Co-op Schemes:* ILL
Equip: m-reader, m-printer, copier (10p) *Online:* not available to public *Svcs:* info, ref, biblio
Stock: bks/75000; periodcls/2000
Classn: DDC *Auto Sys:* Olib
Staff: Libns: 7 Non-Prof: 2

S1009
BBC Information and Archives
BBC Rsrch Central, Bush House LG 26 CB, PO Box 76, Strand, London, WC2B 4PH (020-7557-2425; *fax:* 020-7557-2728)
Email: research-central@bbc.co.uk
Internet: http://www.bbcresearchcentral.com/

Gov Body: British Broadcasting Corp *Chief:* contact the Rsrch Team
Entry: adv appt for personal visits, 24 hrs notice required; access is subj to copyright & contractual restrictions; licensing of material is arranged through BBC Worldwide Lib Sales *Open:* Rsrch Centre: Mon-Fri 0930-1800

Subj: all subjs *Collns: Bks & Pamphs:* covering: art & design; broadcasting; business; industrial affairs; defence; foreign affairs; entertainment; European Union info; govt pubns; music; politics; social affairs; sci; medicine *Archvs:* in addition to programme archvs, the BBC has guardianship of the documents which are part of the corporation's hist, dating back to the BBC's inception *Other:* films; videos; stills
Svcs: info, rsrch (minimum charge £36 + VAT, payment by Visa, Delta, Mastercard or Switch)
Stock: bks/120000; photos/4 mln; film & video/1.5 mln items; document files/550000; press cuttings/26 mln
Staff: c500 in total
Further Info: BBC Info & Archvs comprises the BBC's regional & natl libs, programme archvs & rsrch centres, & has a wealth of resources which stretch back over seventy years of broadcasting. Collns cover programme archvs, photographs, music (both sheet & recorded), sound material, sound effects & document archvs. BBC I&A has several rsrch centres where our svcs & resources can be accessed. It is the largest svc of its kind in the UK & the most extensive in the world.
See also BBC PHOTOGRAPH LIB (**S1010**), BBC SHEET MUSIC LIB (**S1011**) & BBC WRITTEN ARCHVS (**A428**)

S1010
BBC Photograph Library
Room B116, Television Centre, Wood Ln, London, W12 7RJ (020-8225-7193; *fax:* 020-8576-7020)

Gov Body: BBC Info & Archvs (see **S1009**)
Chief: Mgr, BBC Photo Lib: Ms Kathryn Meldrum BA, DipLib
Entry: adv appt *Open:* Mon-Fri 0930-1730
Subj: radio & television broadcasting *Collns: Archvs:* BBC's unique colln of images relating to output on radio & television since 1924, continually updated
Equip: fax, copier *Svcs:* translation, rsrch svc (fee payable)
Stock: photos/4000000, incl slides
Staff: Libns: 4 Other Prof: 6

S1011
BBC Sheet Music Library
Unit 7, Ariel Way, London, W12 7SL (020-8576-0208; *fax:* 020-8225-9984)
Email: peter.linnitt@bbc.co.uk

Gov Body: British Broadcasting Corp *Chief:* Mgr: Mr Peter Linnitt
Entry: BBC employees only *Open:* Mon-Fri 0930-1800
Subj: music (sheet music only)
Stock: sheet music/c4.5 mln items, incl c300000 titles
Classn: LC *Auto Sys:* Sirsi Unicorn
Staff: Libns: 12 Non-Prof: 3

S1012
Bechtel Ltd Library
245 Hammersmith Rd, London, W6 8DP (020-8846-4144; *fax:* 020-8846-5544)
Email: hxpandya@bechtel.com

Chief: Libn: Mrs Hilary Pandya BA(Hons)
Entry: staff only
Subj: tech; eng *Collns: Other:* British & European Eng Standards (BSI, ASME, API, IEC etc) *Co-op Schemes:* BLDSC, BSI, IChemE, Inst of Petroleum etc
Equip: m-reader, computers (incl internet & CD-ROM) *Online:* various databases *Svcs:* info, ref
Stock: bks/750; periodcls/30; maps/180; m-forms/2000
Classn: DDC *Auto Sys:* Adlib

S1013
BFI National Library
British Film Inst, 21 Stephen St, London, W1P 2LN (020-7255-1444; *fax:* 020-7436-2388)
Email: library@bfi.org.uk
Internet: http://www.bfi.org.uk/nationallibrary/

Gov Body: Board of Governors *Chief:* Head of BFI Natl Lib: Mr Ray Templeton BA, MCLIP, FRSA
Dep: Dep Head (User Svcs): Mr David Sharp BA, MCLIP; Dep Head (Technical Svcs): Mr Stephen Pearson BA, MCLIP
Assoc Libs: NATL FILM & TELEVISION ARCHV (incorporating BFI Stills, Posters & Designs Collns)
Entry: ref only, annual pass, limited day passes available; adv appt required for Special Collns
Open: Mon, Fri 1030-1730, Tue, Thu 1030-2000, Wed 1300-2000
Subj: film; television *Collns: Bks & Pamphs:* collns of former Independent Television Commission Lib; extensive runs of many film journals; publicity materials, incl press & campaign bks & festival catalogues *Archvs:* Special Collns incl over 100 major collns relating to indivs, orgs & companies involved in film & television production, in Britain & abroad, since c1919; colln of cinema programmes & ephemera, incl: British Board of Film Censors; ACTT; Trevor Griffiths; Carol Reed; Michael Balcon; Joseph Losey; Ivor Montague; Southern Television Archv (c1894-date); unpublished scripts (19000+) *Other:* newspaper cuttings (2 mln, mostly on m-fiche); 100 interviews with film-makers on audio from Natl Film Theatre (1962-92); oral hist colln (organised by BECTU); misc m-form, multimedia & CD-ROM resources
Co-op Schemes: BLDSC
Equip: 7 m-readers, 7 m-printers, 3 copiers (clr copying svc also available), computers (incl 3 CD-ROM) *Online:* Profile, Baseline, Dialog (quotations for rsrch on appl) *Svcs:* info, ref, biblio
Stock: bks/45000, incl pamphs; periodcls/5000; m-forms/200000; audios/200
Classn: UDC *Auto Sys:* Olib (Fretwell Downing)
Pubns: lib guide (leaflet); study guides; bibliographies; web pubns; see web site for catalogue
Staff: Libns: 22 Other Prof: 6 Non-Prof: 10
Proj: acq & integration of Independent Television Commission Lib collns (2002-03)

S1014
Bhavan's Centre – Institute of Indian Art and Culture, Library and Archives
Bhavan's Inst, 4a Castletown Rd, West Kensington, London, W14 9HQ (020-7381-3086; *fax:* 020-7381-8758)
Email: info@bhavan.net
Internet: http://www.bhavan.net/

Type: cultural, performing arts *Gov Body:* Bhavan's Exec Cttee *Chief:* Exec Dir: Dr Nanda Kumar *Other Snr Staff:* Libn: to be appointed
Entry: all welcome *Open:* Mon-Sun 1000-1700
Subj: all subjs: generalities; phil; world religions; biography; arts; Indian music & performing arts; Indian lit; biography *Collns: Other:* AV colln (Indian Classical music & dance)
Equip: copier (20p per pg), fax (£1 per pg), 5 rooms for hire *Disabled:* no disabled facilities
Svcs: info, ref, translation (Indian langs)
Stock: bks/3000
Pubns: Bhavan's Journal (fortnightly digest)
Proj: development of archival & AV collns

S1015
Birkbeck College Library
Malet St, London, WC1E 7HX (020-7631-6239; *fax:* 020-7631-6066)
Email: library-help@bbk.ac.uk
Internet: http://www.bbk.ac.uk/lib/

London
▼
London

Special Libraries

(Birkbeck Coll Lib cont)
Gov Body: Univ of London (see **S1440**) **Chief: Libn:** Ms Philippa Dolphin **Dep: Dep Libn:** Mr Robert Atkinson
Assoc Libs: GRESSE ST LIB, Birkbeck Coll, 7-15 Gresse St, London, W1P 1PA (020-7631-6492; *fax:* 020-7631-6435); CONTINUING EDU LIB, Birkbeck Coll, 26 Russell Sq, London, WC1B 5DQ, Libn: Ms Elizabeth Charles (020-7631-6168; *fax:* 020-7631-6163)
Entry: various membership schemes; check web site for details **Open:** *Malet St Lib:* term: Mon-Thu 1000-2230, Fri 1100-2230, Sat -Sun 1000-2000; Easter vac: Mon-Thu 1000-2100, Fri 1100-2100, Sat-Sun 1000-2000; Xmas & Summer vac: Mon-Thu 1000-2000, Fri 1100-2000, Sat 1200-1700; *Gresse St Lib:* Mon-Thu 1000-2130, Fri 1100-2130, Sat 1000-1700; vac: Mon-Thu 1000-2000, Fri 1100-2000, Sat (Easter only) 1000-1700
Subj: generalities; phil; psy; social sci; lang; sci; maths; arts; lit; geog; hist **Collns:** *Archvs:* records of Coll & its predecessors (London Mechanics' Inst, Birkbeck Literary & Scientific Inst), 1823-date; papers of Sir John Lockwood (1903-65), Master of Birkbeck 1951-65 (incl material relating to his work for the Inter-Univ Council for Higher Edu Overseas); papers of David Bohn (Physicist); J.D. Bernal papers are on permanent loan to Cambridge Univ Lib (see **L5**) **Co-op Schemes:** M25 Consortium
Equip: 3 m-form reader/printers, 4 video viewers, 9 copiers, 50 computers **Online:** large number of online databases, e-journals & e-bks **Svcs:** info, ref, biblio
Stock: bks & videos/350000; periodcls/2500+
Classn: DDC, Bliss **Auto Sys:** Horizon
Staff: 41 FTE **Exp:** £535000 (2000-01)

S1016 🔑
Bishopsgate Institute Library
230 Bishopsgate, London, EC2M 4QH (020-7247-6198; *fax:* 020-7247-6318)
Email: library@bishopsgate.org.uk
Internet: http://www.bishopsgate.org.uk/

Type: charity **Gov Body:** The Bishopsgate Inst **Chief: Chief Libn:** Ms Alice Mackay MA, MCLIP (amackay@bishopsgate.org.uk) **Dep: Dep Libn:** Mr Jeff Abbott BA(Hons) (jabbot@bishopsgate. org.uk)
Entry: ref only **Open:** Mon-Tue, Thu-Fri 1000-1730, Wed 1000-2000
Subj: all subjs; genl; hist of London (City & Inner London, 16C-date); religion; social sci; arts; geog; hist; political hist; labour hist; co-op movement
Collns: *Bks & Pamphs:* Howell Colln (labour & trade union hist, 1830-1914), incl minute bk of First Internatl Working Men's Assoc (1866-70); Holyoake Colln (Co-op & Secular Movements, 1840-1900); Natl Secular Soc Lib, incl Charles Bradlaugh Colln of MSS; Freedom Press Lib (anarchist movement 1870-date, incl Spanish Civil War) *Archvs:* Co-op Soc Archvs (mainly London & Home Counties, 1928-date), incl minutes bks of Co-op Women's Guild; Bishopsgate Inst Archvs (1894-date); Raphael Samuel Working Papers (limited access)
Equip: 4 m-readers, m-printer, copier, computers
Svcs: info, ref
Stock: bks/100000; periodcls/150; photos/500; slides/3000; pamphs/6000; maps/500; m-forms/3000

Classn: DDC, own (London Colln)
Pubns: Bishopsgate Foundation Centenary Hist (£2.50)
Staff: *Libns:* 2 *Non-Prof:* 2 **Exp:** £27000 (1999-2000)
Proj: computer suite opening Apr 2003

S1017 ✚
Bloomsbury Healthcare Library
52 Gower St, London, WC1E 6EA (020-7380-9097; *fax:* 020-7436-5111)
Email: ILL@bhllib.demon.co.uk
Internet: http://www.bhllib.demon.co.uk/

Chief: Lib & Resources Mgr: Miss Jane Williamson BA, MPhil
Entry: local hosp & NHS Community staff, full svc; others by appt **Open:** Mon, Wed, Fri 0900-1700, Tue, Thu 0900-1900
Subj: social sci; medicine; healthcare **Co-op Schemes:** BLDSC, NTRLN
Equip: m-reader, m-printer, video viewer, copier, fax, computers (incl wd-proc, internet & CD-ROM)
Online: Medline, CINAHL, BNI, AMED, Embase, CancerLit, HMIC (all via KA24 network svc) **Svcs:** info, ref, biblio, abstracting
Stock: bks/15000; periodcls/220; m-forms/30; videos/300
Classn: NLM **Auto Sys:** Adlib
Staff: *Libns:* 2.8 *Non-Prof:* 2.6

S1018 🔭
The Bridgeman Art Library
17-19 Garway Rd, London, W2 4PH (020-7727-4065; *fax:* 020-7792-8509)
Email: info@bridgeman.co.uk
Internet: http://www.bridgeman.co.uk/

Type: commercial photo agency **Chief: Dir:** Viscountess Bridgeman **Dep: Genl Mgr:** Ms Sarah Rice
Assoc Libs: BRIDGEMAN ART LIB INTERNATL, 65 East 93rd St, New York, NY 10128, USA, contact: Ed Whitley; BRIDGEMAN ART LIB (PARIS), 31 Rue des Bourdonnais, 75001 Paris, France, contact: Didier Lénart
Entry: adv appt **Open:** Mon-Fri 0930-1730
Subj: images: phil; psy; religion; social sci; arts; design; lit; geog; hist **Collns:** *Other:* leading src of fine art images from museums, private collns & artists throughout the world, available as both transparencies & digital files
Equip: fax, copier, clr copier, computer (with CD-ROM) **Online:** seachable web catalogue **Svcs:** info, ref, image licensing
Stock: transparencies & digital files/c750000; some bks, photos & slides
Classn: by subj **Auto Sys:** own
Staff: *Other Prof:* 30

S1019 🔑
British Architectural Library
Royal Inst of British Architects, 66 Portland Pl, London, W1B 1AD (020-7580-5533; *fax:* 020-7631-1802)
Email: info@inst.riba.org
Internet: http://www.architecture.com/

Gov Body: Royal Inst of British Architects **Chief: Dir:** Ms R.H. Kamen BA, MAT, MLS, MCLIP, FRSA
Assoc Libs: BAL DRAWINGS COLLN, addr as above (020-7307-3653/28); moving to V&A in 2004
Entry: free to RIBA membs for ref only, charges for loan & for non-membs; special collns by appt only; *Drawings Colln:* adv appt (some material may not be available pending move to V&A) **Open:** Tue 1000-2000, Wed-Fri 1000-1700, Sat 1000-1330; *Drawings Colln:* Mon 1400-1700 only
Subj: arch **Collns:** *Bks & Pamphs:* Handley-Read Colln (Victorian decorative arts); Modern Movement Colln (1920s & 30s arch); early imprints colln

---

(4000 bks on arch & related subjs published before 1841) *Archvs:* MSS & archvs colln (17C-date, incl the RIBA's administrative archv) *Other:* drawings (15C-date); photos **Co-op Schemes:** BLDSC, ILL
Equip: m-printer, 2 copiers, clr copier, computer
Stock: bks/135000; periodcls/700; photos/600000+; illusts/450000 drawings; pamphs/20000; m-forms/400; audios/200; videos/30+; archvs/700 linear m
Classn: UDC
Pubns: Architectural Periodicals Index (quarterly); Architectural Keywords (£45); Catalogue of RIBA Drawings; RIBA: A Guide to its Archvs & Hist (£32.50); Early Printed Bks: Catalogue of the British Architectural Lib Early Imprints Colln; Arch Database (Dialog, file 179); APId (Architectural Pubns Index on disc); list of pubns available
Staff: *Libns:* 13 *Other Prof:* 8 *Non-Prof:* 3

S1020 🎓 🔑
British Astronomical Association Library
Burlington House, Piccadilly, London, W1J 0DU (020-7734-4145; *fax:* 020-7439-4629)
Internet: http://www.ast.cam.ac.uk/~baa/

Gov Body: BAA **Chief: Hon Libn:** Mr Anthony Kinder BA(Hons), MSc, PGCE, FRAS
Entry: adv appt required **Open:** staffed: Wed 1300-1645; visits at other times by prior arrangement with office staff
Subj: astronomy & related subjs, incl: hist of astronomy; astronautics; optics; astro-photography & imaging **Collns:** *Bks & Pamphs:* incl: 3rd ed of Newton's 'Principia' & Flamsteed's 'Atlas Coelestis'; works by George Adams, Ferguson, W. & J. Herschel & others *Archvs:* mostly relating to hist of Assoc; autograph letters of: Flamsteed; C. Darwin; C. Huyghens; & others
Equip: copier **Svcs:** info, ref, postal loan svc (membs only)
Stock: bks/c4000; periodcls/100+; archvs/2 cabinets; various pamphs, slides & videos; some photos & CD-ROMs
Classn: own modified alphanumerical
Pubns: Catalogues (available in print, on floppy disk or CD-ROM)
Staff: *Non-Prof:* 1 FT, 1 PT

British Beer and Pub Association Library
See NATL BREWING LIB (**S1694**)

S1021 🎓 ✚
British College of Osteopathic Medicine Library
Frazer House, 6 Netherhall Gdns, London, NW3 5RR (020-7431-8859)
Email: pf@bcom.ac.uk
Internet: http://www.bcom.ac.uk/

Chief: Libn: Mr P. Folly BA, DipLib
Entry: Coll membs only **Open:** term: Mon-Thu 0830-1830, Fri 0830-1730; vac: Mon-Fri 0900-1730
Subj: medicine; osteopathy **Collns:** *Bks & Pamphs:* historical alternative medicine bks
Equip: copier, computers (incl internet & CD-ROM) **Online:** Medline **Svcs:** info, ref
Classn: in-house **Auto Sys:** Heritage
Staff: *Libns:* 1 *Non-Prof:* 1

S1022 🔑 ✚
British Dental Association Information Centre
64 Wimpole St, London, W1M 8AL (020-7935-0875; *fax:* 020-7935-6492)
Email: InfoCentre@bda-dentistry.org.uk
Internet: http://www.bda-dentistry.org.uk/

Type: prof assoc *Chief:* Mgr: Mr Roger Farbey BA, DipLib, MCLIP
Assoc Libs: BRITISH DENTAL ASSOC MUSEUM ARCHVS, addr as above, Curator: Ms Roxanne Fea (020-7563-4549)
Entry: adv appt only *Open:* Mon-Fri 0900-1800
Subj: dentistry *Collns: Bks & Pamphs:* rare bk colln *Co-op Schemes:* BLDSC (photocopies only)
Equip: video viewer, copier, computers (with wd-procs & CD-ROM, membs only) *Online:* Medline, Cochrane *Svcs:* info, ref, postal lib svc for membs
Stock: bks/13000; periodcls/250; pamphs/3200; videos/200
Classn: NLM, Black *Auto Sys:* CALM 2000
Staff: Libns: 3 *Non-Prof:* 1

S1023

British Geological Survey, London Information Office

Nat Hist Museum Earth Galleries, Exhib Rd, London, SW7 2DE (020-7589-4090; *fax:* 020-7584-8270)
Email: bgslondon@bgs.ac.uk

Chief: Mgr: Miss Sylvia J. Brackell
Assoc Libs: BGS LIB & INFO SVC, Nottingham (see **S1636**)
Entry: ref & sale collns, no appt necessary *Open:* Mon-Fri 1000-1700
Subj: earth sci *Collns: Bks & Pamphs:* British Geological Survey publ & unpublished material incl memoirs, rsrch reports *Other:* MS geological maps of British Isles (1:10000/1:10560); some overseas geological maps; photos; sale colln of BGS & other pubns
Equip: fax, copier, computer *Online:* British Geological Survey in-house databases incl Geoscience Data Index
Stock: bks/12000; periodcls/140; photos/9000; maps/17000
Classn: UDC *Auto Sys:* Geolib
Pubns: Guide to the London Office; many pubns too numerous to list – catalogue available
Staff: 2

S1024 🗝

British Institute of International and Comparative Law, Grotius Library

Charles Clore House, 17 Russell Sq, London, WC1B 5JP (020-7862-5151/68; *fax:* 020-7862-5152)
Email: e.wintle@biicl.org
Internet: http://www.biicl.org/

Type: prof assoc *Chief:* Libn: Ms E.M. Wintle LLB, DipLib, MCLIP
Assoc Libs: HUMAN RIGHTS DEPOSITORY, at same addr
Entry: ref only for non-membs, adv appt *Open:* Mon-Fri 0930-1730
Subj: law; internatl law; comparative law; European law; human rights law *Co-op Schemes:* ILL (photocopies only), EC/Court of Human Rights photocopy & fax svc (charge made)
Svcs: info, ref *Stock:* bks/4500; periodcls/20
Staff: Libns: 0.8

S1025 🗝➕

British Institute of Radiology, Library and Information Service

36 Portland Pl, London, W1B 1 AT (020-7307-1405; *fax:* 020-7307-1414)
Email: infocentre@bir.org.uk
Internet: http://www.bir.org.uk/

Type: charitable prof body *Gov Body:* British Inst of Radiology; also provides info svcs for the Coll of Radiographers, the Royal Coll of Radiologists & the British Medical Ultrasound Soc *Chief:* Lib & Info System Mgr: Ms Kate Sanders BA, MCLIP

Entry: ref only, adv appt preferred *Open:* Mon, Wed, Fri 0900-1700, Tue, Thu 1000-1800
Subj: radiology & allied disciplines *Collns: Archvs:* records of British Inst of Radiology, incl minute bks, financial records & photos *Other:* K.C. Clark Slide Colln (c500 glass slides) *Co-op Schemes:* back-up lib for BLDSC
Equip: copier, computer (with CD-ROM), room for hire *Online:* on CD-ROM: Excerpta Medica (Radiology & nuclear medicine); Knowledge Finder: Radline, Healthstar, Medline *Svcs:* info, ref, lit search, photocopying
Stock: bks/5000; periodcls/80; photos/numerous; archvs/various holdings
Classn: own *Auto Sys:* Dynix (Horizon)
Pubns: leaflet; BIR itself publishes a number of pubns, incl British Journal of Radiology
Staff: Libns: 1 *Exp:* £16000 (1999-2000)

S1026 🗝

British Interplanetary Society, L.J. Carter Library

27-29 South Lambeth Rd, London, SW8 1SZ (020-7735-3160; *fax:* 020-7820-1504)
Email: mail@bis-spaceflight.com
Internet: http://www.bis-spaceflight.com/

Chief: Libn: Mrs Suszann Parry
Entry: membs only *Open:* Mon-Fri 1030-1530; 1st Wed of each month (except Aug) 1730-1850
Subj: tech; astronautics; space exploration; astronomy *Collns: Other:* space medallions; space first day covers
Equip: copier (10p per pg), computer (with wd-proc)
Stock: bks/4000; periodcls/20; maps/60; various audios, films & technical reports

S1027 🗝➕

British Medical Association Library

Tavistock Sq, London, WC1H 9JP (020-7383-6625; *fax:* 020-7388-2544)
Email: bma-library@bma.org.uk
Internet: http://www.bma.org.uk/library/

Gov Body: The BMA *Chief:* Chief Libn: Mr T. McSeán MCLIP *Dep:* Dep Libn: Ms Jane Smith
Entry: personal & indiv membs only; non-memb access via internet only *Open:* Mon-Fri 0900-1800; closed statutory/natl hols
Subj: medicine & related subjs; medical ethics
Collns: Bks & Pamphs: Sir Charles Hastings Colln
Co-op Schemes: BLDSC
Equip: m-reader; copier, 2 video viewers, 9 computers (incl wd-proc, internet & CD-ROM)
Svcs: info, ref, biblio
Stock: bks/60500; periodcls/1200; pamphs/30000; videos/4000, incl films
Classn: NLM *Auto Sys:* Dynix
Pubns: Lib Bulletin (free to membs)
Staff: Libns: 12 *Other Prof:* 2 *Non-Prof:* 9

S1028

British Museum, Department of Libraries and Archives

Gt Russell St, Bloomsbury, London, WC1B 3DG (020-7323-8118)
Email: libraries@thebritishmuseum.ac.uk
Internet: http://www.thebritishmuseum.ac.uk/libraries/

Gov Body: Trustees of the British Museum
Chief: The David Eccles Libn
Assoc Libs: all at above addr: CENTRAL LIB, Central Libn: Ms Joanna Bowring (020-7323-8491); PAUL HAMLYN LIB, Fleming Libn: Ms Pam Smith (020-7323-8907); BRITISH MUSEUM ARCHVS (see **A259**); also see separate entries for the following libs of indiv depts: DEPT OF COINS & MEDALS LIB (see **S1029**); DEPT OF GREEK &

ROMAN ANTIQUITIES LIB (see **S1030**); DEPT OF PREHISTORY & EUROPE LIB (see **S1031**); DEPT OF PRINTS & DRAWINGS LIB (see **S1032**); DEPT OF THE ANCIENT NEAR EAST LIB (see **S1033**); BRITISH MUSEUM ANTHRO LIB (see **S1034**)
Entry: Central Lib: Museum staff; membs of public by special arrangement only; *Paul Hamlyn Lib:* open to public, ref only *Open: Paul Hamlyn Lib:* Mon-Wed, Sat-Sun 1230-1730, Thu-Fri 1230-2030
Subj: Central Lib: museology; collecting; archaeo; antiquities; arts; conservation; hist of the British Museum; *Paul Hamlyn Lib:* archaeo; hist; arts; arch
Collns: Bks & Pamphs: British Museum pubns (Central Lib) *Other:* British Museum posters & postcards (Central Lib)
Equip: copiers, 50 COMPASS terminals in Paul Hamlyn Lib *Online:* COMPASS (Collns Multimedia Public Access System)
Stock: bks/c350000 bks, offprints, pamphs & periodcls (total for all Museum libs)
Classn: DDC
Proj: centralisation of Central Lib collns in the former Sanskrit Lib (2002); acq of House of Commons Old Lib, to be housed in the King's Lib (2003)

S1029

British Museum, Department of Coins and Medals Library

Gt Russell St, Bloomsbury, London, WC1B 3DG (020-7323 8607; *fax:* 020-7323-8171)
Email: coins@thebritishmuseum.ac.uk
Internet: http://www.thebritishmuseum.ac.uk/cm/cmhome.html

Type: natl museum *Gov Body:* Trustees of the British Museum *Chief:* Departmental Libn: Ms Mary Hinton (mhinton@thebritishmuseum.ac.uk)
Entry: ref only; adv appt; study space limited
Open: Study Room: Mon-Tue, Thu-Fri 1000-1300, 1415-1600, Wed 1415-1600
Subj: numismatics; hist of the development & use of money world-wide *Collns: Bks & Pamphs:* UK's leading specialist numismatic lib: bks, periodcls & sales catalogues relating to all aspects of numismatics *Archvs:* numismatic studies; casework for Treasure Trove & Treasure Act (1996) coin finds
Equip: copier (A4/10p) *Svcs:* info, ref, biblio

S1030

British Museum, Department of Greek and Roman Antiquities Library

Gt Russell St, Bloomsbury, London, WC1B 3DG (020-7323-8321; *fax:* 020-7323-8355)
Email: greekandroman@thebritishmuseum.ac.uk
Internet: http://www.thebritishmuseum.ac.uk/gr/grhome.html

Type: natl museum *Gov Body:* Trustees of the British Museum *Chief:* Departmental Libn
Entry: by appt only; proof of ID required *Open: Study Room:* Mon-Fri 1000-1300, 1415-1600
Subj: classical archaeo (Bronze Age-4C); Greek archaeo; Roman archaeo; Cycladic archaeo; Minoan archaeo; Mycenaean archaeo

S1031

British Museum, Department of Prehistory and Europe Library

Gt Russell St, Bloomsbury, London, WC1B 3DG (020-7323-8629)
Email: prehistoryandeurope@thebritishmuseum.ac.uk
Internet: http://www.thebritishmuseum.ac.uk/pe/pehome.html

☛

London ▼ London
Special Libraries

(British Museum, Dept of Prehistory & Europe Lib cont)

Type: natl museum **Gov Body:** Trustees of the British Museum **Chief:** contact the Departmental Libn
Assoc Libs: HOROLOGICAL STUDY ROOM, addr as above (020-7323-8395; *email:* horological@thebritishmuseum.ac.uk); PALAEOLITHIC & MESOLITHIC COLLNS, Franks House, 56 Orsman Rd, London, N1 5QJ (020-7323-8454; *email:* quat@thebritishmuseum.ac.uk)
Entry: adv appt only; proof of ID required **Open:** all Study Rooms: Mon-Fri 1000-1300, 1400-1630
Subj: archaeo; prehistory; palaeoanthropology; Palaeolithic, Neolithic, Bronze Age & Iron Age archaeo; Roman Britain; European art & archaeo (4C-20C); medieval antiquities; ceramics; horology; scientific instruments; modern design **Collns:** *Bks & Pamphs:* directories of clockmakers; complete runs of horological & related journals
Equip: *Online:* EPACT (digital catalogue of pre-1600 European scientific instruments)

S1032 British Museum, Department of Prints and Drawings Library

Gt Russell St, Bloomsbury, London, WC1B 3DG (020-7323-8408; *fax:* 020-7323-8999)
Email: prints@thebritishmuseum.ac.uk
Internet: http://www.thebritishmuseum.ac.uk/pd/pdhome.html

Type: natl museum **Gov Body:** Trustees of the British Museum **Chief:** Departmental Libn: Mr Richard Perfitt
Assoc Libs: less frequently used bks are held at: Dept of Prints & Drawings, Blythe House, 23 Blythe Rd, London W14 0QF
Entry: *Study Room (Bloomsbury):* ref only; no appt required, but proof of ID must be shown; *Blythe House:* by adv appt only (bookings must be made by Mon morning for access on Tue) **Open:** *Study Room (Bloomsbury):* Mon-Fri 1000-1300, 1415-1600, 1st Sat of each month 1000-1300; *Blythe House:* Tue 1000-1300
Subj: arts; fine arts; Western prints & drawings; illustration; printmaking **Collns:** *Bks & Pamphs:* ref works (mainly from 19C onwards); rare illustrated bks, incl Robin de Beaumont Colln (German Renaissance bks & British bks of the 1860s); printmakers' catalogues; British & foreign art auction catalogues (early 18C-date); extensive runs of most major art periodcls *Other:* prints & drawings from the collns can also be viewed in the Study Room; collns incl: works by Dürer, Michelangelo, Raphael, Rembrandt, Goya & others; historical, satirical & topographical prints; printed ephemera (incl trade & visiting cards, fans & playing cards)
Equip: m-reader **Svcs:** ref
Stock: bks/50000, incl periodcls; illusts/50000 drawings, 2 mln prints; m-forms/270
Pubns: The Dept of Prints & Drawings in the British Museum: User's Guide, by A. Griffiths & R. Williams (1987); A Catalogue of German Bks before 1800 in the Dept of Prints & Drawings, by D. Paisey (2002)
Exp: £20500 (1999-2000); £22500 (2000-01)

S1033 British Museum, Department of the Ancient Near East Library

Gt Russell St, Bloomsbury, London, WC1B 3DG (020-7323-8308; *fax:* 020-7323-8489)
Email: ancientneareast@thebritishmuseum.ac.uk
Internet: http://www.thebritishmuseum.ac.uk/ane/anehome.html

Type: natl museum **Gov Body:** Trustees of the British Museum **Chief:** Asst Keeper (Levant Collns, with responsibility for lib & archvs): Ms Sarah Collins
Entry: by adv appt; letter of recommendation & proof of ID required **Open:** Mon-Fri 1000-1300, 1400-1630
Subj: art & archaeo of the Ancient Near East, incl that of: Mesopotamia; Iran; the Levant; Anatolia; Arabia; Central Asia; the Caucasus

S1034 British Museum Anthropology Library

(incorporating the former Lib of the Royal Anthropological Inst)
Gt Russell St, Bloomsbury, London, WC1B 3DG (020-7323-8041)
Email: AnthropologyLibrary@thebritishmuseum.ac.uk
Internet: http://www.thebritishmuseum.ac.uk/

Gov Body: Trustees of the British Museum
Chief: Snr Libn: Mrs Sheila A. Mackie BA, DipLib, MCLIP (smackie@thebritishmuseum.ac.uk) **Dep:** Lib Reading Room Svcs Offcr: Ms Renée Evans
Other Snr Staff: RAI Lib Offcr: Mrs Janice Archer BSc (jarcher@thebritishmuseum.ac.uk)
Entry: ticket holders & fellows of the RAI only; other readers by appt **Open:** Mon-Fri 1000-1645; closed public hols & last 2 wks of Sep
Subj: anthro; ethnography; ethnic art; archaeo
Collns: *Bks & Pamphs:* entire former Royal Anthropological Inst Lib; Sir Eric Thomas Lib (Mesoamerican arch, with emphasis on the Maya); Christy Lib (19C antiquarian & travel); ethnographic bibliographies *Archvs:* Royal Anthropological Inst Archvs (to be housed elsewhere by RAI in late 2003 – see **A328**); MSS, fieldnotes etc *Other:* c15 linear m of MSS & typescripts, incl theses
Equip: m-reader, video viewer (in Edu Dept)
Svcs: info, ref, biblio, indexing, photocopying svc, lending facilities for Fellows of RAI
Stock: bks/120000, incl pamphs; periodcls/4000, incl 1460 current; photos/150000; illusts/some; maps/500; m-forms/700; audios/some; videos/some; AVs/some
Classn: Bliss (mod)
Pubns: Museum of Mankind Lib catalogues (1989, 763 m-fiche); Anthropological Index to Current Periodicals in the Museum of Mankind Lib (publ by RAI to 1994, now on Internet)
Staff: *Libns:* 3 *Non-Prof:* 4
Proj: closed Sep 2003 to Apr 2004 following relocation to Bloomsbury

S1035 British Music Information Centre

10 Stratford Pl, London, W1N 9AE (020-7499-8567; *fax:* 020-7499-4795)
Email: info@bmic.co.uk
Internet: http://www.bmic.co.uk/

Chief: Info Mgr: Mr Daniel Goven
Entry: ref only, adv appt to view video recordings
Open: Mon-Fri 1200-1700
Subj: 20C British classical music **Collns:** *Other:* over 31000 works by more than 2600 composers; scores (publ & unpublished, incl copies of composers' MSS); recordings; videos; programme notes; press clippings; publishers lists; photos

Equip: video viewer, fax, copier, listening room, room hire (for concerts) *Online:* entire BMIC database now available online **Svcs:** enqs, repertoire searches
Stock: bks/100; photos/100; audios/12000; some videos
Classn: own
Pubns: info pack (£5, incl p&p); leaflets; Counterpoints (6 pa, subscription £15); New Voices: Scores by 25 Young Composers
Staff: *Other Prof:* 3

S1036 British National Space Centre, Library and Information Unit

151 Buckingham Palace Rd, London, SW1W 9SS (020-7215-0901; *fax:* 020-7215-0936)
Internet: http://www.bnsc.gov.uk/

Gov Body: BNSC **Chief:** Head of Info Unit: Mr Steven Warren (Steven.Warren@bnsc.gsi.gov.uk)
Dep: Lib Mgr: Mr Stuart Grayson (stuart.grayson@bnsc.gsi.gov.uk)
Entry: ref only, open to public by appt only
Subj: space; space sci; space tech; remote sensing **Collns:** *Bks & Pamphs:* European Space Agency pubns **Co-op Schemes:** BLDSC, ILL
Svcs: info, ref
Classn: UDC **Auto Sys:** CAIRS
Pubns: BNSC Space News; UK Space Index; UK Space Activs (all free)
Staff: 5 in total

S1037 British Optical Association Library

Coll of Optometrists, 42 Craven St, London, WC2N 5NG (020-7839-6000; *fax:* 020-7839-6800)
Email: library@college-optometrists.org
Internet: http://www.college-optometrists.org/college/library.htm

Chief: Libn: Mrs Jan Ayres BA, DipLib, MCLIP
Entry: membs & associate membs of Coll of Optometrists; public may join on a subscription basis; adv appt required for historical materials
Open: Mon-Fri 0930-1300, 1400-1700
Subj: optics; optometry; eye-testing **Collns:** *Bks & Pamphs:* historical optics & optometry colln (16C-20C); Keith Clifford Hall Lib (held & administered for the British Contact Lens Assoc, ref only) *Other:* AV Colln (slides, videos & audios)
Co-op Schemes: BLDSC
Equip: copier (10p per pg), clr copier (50p per pg)
Online: Medline **Svcs:** info, ref, biblio, enqs (by tel or letter)
Stock: bks/10000, incl pamphs
Classn: DDC **Auto Sys:** Libero **Staff:** *Libns:* 1

S1038 British Orthodox Church Library

10 Heathwood Gdns, Charlton, London, SE7 8EP (020-8854-3090; *fax:* 020-8244-7888)
Email: boc@nildram.co.uk

Gov Body: Trustees of the British Orthodox Church **Chief:** Hon Libn: Fr Gregory Tillett
Entry: by appt only, with letter of introduction
Open: by appt: Mon-Fri 1000-1700
Subj: genl theology; liturgy (Eastern & Western)
Collns: *Bks & Pamphs:* Eastern & Oriental Orthodox Churches; restored apostles (Irvingite); independent Episcopal Churches
Equip: m-reader, fax
Stock: bks/10000; periodcls/15; photos/2500; pamphs/5000; audios/50; videos/15
Pubns: Glastonbury Review (3 pa, annual subscription £8.50)
Staff: *Non-Prof:* 2 **Exp:** £3000 (1999-2000); £3000 (2000-01)

S1039 🔑

British Psycho-Analytical Society Library

Inst of Psycho-Analysis, Byron House, 114 Shirland Rd, London, W9 2EQ (020-7563-5008; *fax:* 020-7563-5001)
Email: 106027.3376@compuserve.com
Internet: http://www.psychoanalysis.org.uk/

Gov Body: British Psycho-Analysis Soc *Chief:* Exec Offcr, Lib: Ms Andrea Chandler
Assoc Libs: BRITISH PSYCHO-ANALYTICAL SOC ARCHVS, addr as above
Entry: Lib: open to all, on payment of a fee (range of charges, £10 pd, £5 for students); *Archvs:* permission of Hon Archivist required in adv of visit, fee £12 pd *Open:* Mon-Thu 1200-2100
Subj: psychoanalysis *Collns: Archvs:* archvs of the Soc; Ernest Jones Archvs (see access conditions above) *Co-op Schemes:* ILL
Equip: copier, computer (incl CD-ROM & internet)
Svcs: info, ref, biblio
Stock: bks/60000; periodcls/65
Classn: own *Auto Sys:* CALM *Staff: Libns:* 1

S1040 🎓

British Psychological Society Collection

c/o Psy Lib, Univ of London Lib, Senate House, Malet St, London, WC1E 7HU (020-7862-8451/61; *fax:* 020-7862-8480)
Email: ull@ull.ac.uk
Internet: http://www.ull.ac.uk/

Gov Body: Univ of London (see **S1440**) *Chief:* Psy Libn, Univ of London Lib: Mrs Susan Tarrant BA, MCLIP
Entry: charges (day tickets/annual membership)
Open: term: Mon-Thu 0900-2100, Fri 0900-1830, Sat 0930-1730; vac: Mon-Fri 0900-1800, Sat 0930-1730
Subj: psy
Equip: m-reader, m-printer, 6 copiers, computers (incl 4 CD-ROM)
Stock: bks/35000; periodcls/250; incl Univ of London Psy holdings
Classn: Bliss *Auto Sys:* Innopac
Staff: Libns: 1

S1041 🎓 ✚

British School of Osteopathy Library

275-287 Borough High St, Southwark, London, SE1 1JE (*clinic:* 020-7930-9254; *switchboard:* 020-7407-0222; *fax:* 020-7089-5300)
Email: admin@bso.ac.uk
Internet: http://www.bso.ac.uk/

Chief: Chief Libn: Mr Will Podmore MA, DipLib, MCLIP (willp@bso.ac.uk) *Dep:* Asst Libn: Ms Marianna Emmanouel (mariannae@bso.ac.uk)
Entry: ref only for non-BSO students *Open:* term: Mon-Tue 0900-1930, Wed-Thu 0900-2130, Fri 0900-1700; vac: Mon-Fri 0900-1700
Subj: medicine; osteopathy *Collns: Bks & Pamphs:* osteopathic classics *Co-op Schemes:* BLDSC, LASER
Equip: 2 video viewers, copier, computers (incl 20 with wd-proc & CD-ROM) *Online:* Medline (1990-date)
Stock: bks/9000; periodcls/44; slides/2000; audios/20; videos/200
Classn: DDC *Auto Sys:* Autolib
Pubns: BOJ Indexes: New Series & Old Series; Spinal Manipulation: Outcome Studies; Study Methods; Palpation: A Bibliography; How to do Rsrch; Cranial Osteopathy: A Bibliography
Staff: Libns: 2

S1042 📷

British Standards Institution Library

389 Chiswick High Rd, London, W4 4AL (020-8996-7004; *fax:* 020-8996-7005)
Email: library@bsi-global.com
Internet: http://www.bsi-global.com/

Chief: Lib Mgr: Mrs M.E. Yates BSc, DipLib (mary.yates@bsi-global.com)
Entry: free to BSI membs, charge for non-membs
Open: Mon-Fri 0900-1700
Subj: standards on all subjs *Collns: Bks & Pamphs:* British, foreign & internatl standards & technical regulations from around the world; EU legislation; codes of practice; technical legislation *Archvs:* withdrawn British Standards *Co-op Schemes:* BLDSC
Equip: m-reader, m-printer, copier, 3 computers (incl 1 wd-proc, 2 internet & 2 CD-ROM) *Online:* Eurobases (search svc provided by staff for fee)
Svcs: info, ref, loans, bk shop
Stock: bks/600000; periodcls/250; maps/100; m-forms/10000
Classn: own *Auto Sys:* Olib
Pubns: see web site for BSI pubns
Staff: Libns: 3 *Other Prof:* 1 *Non-Prof:* 2
Proj: automation of lib using Olib sys
See also **O85**

S1043 🎓 🔑 📷

British Universities Film and Video Council, Information Service

77 Wells St, London, W1P 3RE (020-7393-1500; *fax:* 020-7393-1554)
Email: ask@bufvc.ac.uk
Internet: http://www.bufvc.ac.uk/

Gov Body: British Univs Film & Video Council
Chief: Head of Info: Mr Luke McKernan BA, DipLib (luke@bufvc.ac.uk) *Dep:* Lib & Database Mgr: Mr Sergio Angelini MA, LLB (sergio@bufvc.ac.uk)
Entry: membs of BUFVC *Open:* Mon-Fri 0930-1730
Subj: all subjs; undergrad; postgrad; sci & the media; media tech; arts; film & TV studies; film & hist (incl propaganda); drama & film *Collns: Bks & Pamphs:* British newsreel documentation; catalogues of British & foreign film & video distributors; bk lib of the British Kinematograph Sound & Television Soc *Archvs:* Scientific Film Assoc papers; Channel 4 press releases
Equip: m-reader, 2 copiers, fax, video viewer, film projector, video projector, DVD player, computer (with wd-proc, internet & CD-ROM), room for hire *Online:* HERMES, Researcher's Guide Online (RGO), Moving Image Gateway (MIG), British Univs Newsreel Database (BUND), Television & Radio Index for Learning & Teaching (TRILT)
Svcs: info, ref
Stock: bks/4300; periodcls/84; audios/100; videos/2000; catalogues/6600; small collns of slides, CD-ROMs, audiotapes, DVDs *Acqs Offcr:* Lib & Database Mgr, as above
Classn: UDC
Pubns: Viewfinder (journal, 4 pa); Researcher's Guide: Film, Television, Radio & Related Documentation Collns in the UK; BUFVC Handbook; Filming Hist: The Memoirs of John Turner, Newsreel Cameraman; British Cinema Newsreel Reader
Staff: Libns: 2 *Non-Prof:* 6

S1044 📷

British-Israel Chamber of Commerce, Library

PO Box 4268, London, W1A 7WH (020-7224-3212; *fax:* 020-7486-7877)
Email: mail@b-icc.org.uk
Internet: http://www.b-icc.org.uk/

Chief: Exec Offcr: Ms Denise Arden
Entry: by appt *Open:* office hrs
Subj: Israeli foreign & bilateral trade & investment with the UK; commerce; business

S1045 📷 🔑 📷

Bubbles Photo Library

16 Ramsgate St, London, E8 2NA (020-7249-6879; *fax:* 020-7249-4349)
Email: info@bubblesphotolibrary.co.uk
Internet: http://www.bubblesphotolibrary.co.uk/

Type: commercial photo agency *Chief:* Partner: Ms Sarah Robinson BA *Dep:* Partner: Ms Loisjoy Thurstun BA
Entry: 100 shots submission *Open:* Mon-Fri 0930-1800
Subj: pregnancy; baby & child development; teenagers; couples; women's health; old age
Stock: photos/various *Staff: Libns:* 2

S1046 🔑 🕉

The Buddhist Society Library

58 Eccleston Sq, London, SW1V 1PH (020-7834-5858)
Email: info@thebuddhistsociety.org.uk
Internet: http://www.thebuddhistsociety.org.uk/

Gov Body: The Buddhist Soc *Chief:* Libn: Dr R.B. Parsons MA, PhD *Dep:* Mrs R. Goonesena
Entry: ref only for non-membs, lending for membs
Open: Mon-Fri 1400-1800, Sat 1400-1700
Subj: materials relating to Buddhist practice & belief, particularly in the UK & at the present time *Collns: Archvs:* archvs of The Buddhist Soc (founded 1924) incorporating those of The Buddhist Soc of Great Britain & Ireland (1907-1914)
Equip: copier *Online:* lib catalogue now available on the internet via web site
Stock: bks/3400
Classn: own (bespoke) *Auto Sys:* Cardbox (catalogue only)
Staff: Libns: 1 (2 PT) *Exp:* £1750 (1999-2000); £1750 (2000-01); incl binding & supplies

S1047 🎓

Burntwood Foundation School Library

Burntwood Ln, London, SW17 0AQ (020-8946-6201; *fax:* 020-8944-6592)
Email: wallace_alison@hotmail.com
Internet: http://www.burntwoodschool.com/

Chief: School Libn: Ms Alison Wallace BEd, DipIS, MCLIP
Entry: adv appt *Open:* term: Mon-Fri 0800-1630; vac: closed
Subj: all subjs; genl; GCSE; A level; GNVQ
Equip: copier, computers (incl wd-proc, internet & CD-ROM) *Svcs:* info, ref, biblio, indexing
Stock: bks/16000; periodcls/47; photos/30; slides/50; pamphs/130; maps/20; audios/20; videos/20
Classn: DDC *Auto Sys:* Alice
Staff: Libns: 1 *Non-Prof:* 1.5

S1048 🔑

Business Archives Council, Business History Library

3rd-4th Floors, 101 Whitechapel High St, London, E1 7RE (*tel & fax:* 020-7247-0024)
Internet: http://www.archives.gla.ac.uk/bac/

Chief: contact W.S. Quinn-Robinson
Entry: adv appt *Open:* Mon-Wed, Fri 0930-1700
Subj: business hists only *Collns: Bks & Pamphs:* pamphs (mainly own pubns) *Archvs:* none, only index of archvs with which the Council has contact
Equip: copier *Svcs:* info ☛

 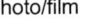

(Business Archvs Council, Business Hist Lib cont)
Stock: bks/6000; periodcls/50; pamphs/1000
Classn: SIC
Pubns: numerous
Staff: Other Prof: 3 Non-Prof: 2 **Exp:** no budget for stock; bks acquired by donation
See also **O89**

S1049 🎓

Byam Shaw School of Art, Library

2 Elthorne Rd, London, N19 4AG (020-7281-4111)
Internet: http://www.byam-shaw.ac.uk/

Chief: Libn: Ms Margaret Agnew BA(Hons), MA, DipIST **Dep:** Lib Asst: Mr Oliver Ronca
Entry: adv appt **Open:** term: Mon-Fri 1000-1800; vac: closed
Subj: fine art **Collns:** Bks & Pamphs: fine art monographs, periodcls & exhib catalogues
Equip: video viewer, copier, computer (with wd-proc)
Stock: bks/10000; periodcls/30; slides/10000
Classn: DDC
Staff: Libns: 1 Non-Prof: 1 **Exp:** £10000 pa

S1050 🎓

Camberwell College of Arts, Library and Learning Resources

Peckham Rd, Camberwell, London, SE5 8UF
(020-7514-6349; fax: 020-7514-6324)
Email: l.kerr@camb.linst.ac.uk
Internet: http://www.camb.linst.ac.uk/

Gov Body: London Inst **Chief:** Head of Lib & Learning Resources: Ms Liz Kerr
Entry: ref only, adv appt **Open:** term: Mon, Fri 1000-1930, Tue, Thu 1000-2000, Fri 1000-1700; vac: Mon-Fri 1000-1600
Subj: tech; arts; art hist; ceramics; conservation; film; fine art; graphics; illustration; metalwork; photography; printmaking; silversmithing; textiles
Collns: Bks & Pamphs: Thorold Dickinson Cinema Colln (c3000 items); Walter Crane Colln (c150 items); Poster Lit Colln (500+ items) **Co-op Schemes:** BLDSC, M25 Consortium
Equip: m-reader, video viewers, copiers, clr copier, computers (incl wd-proc, internet & CD-ROM) **Disabled:** hearing loop, wheelchair access
Online: Conservation Info Network, Art Abstracts, Mintel, Guardian **Svcs:** info, ref, biblio
Stock: bks/40000; periodcls/200; slides/100000; videos/1000
Classn: DDC **Auto Sys:** Talis
Staff: Libns: 4 Other Prof: 3 Non-Prof: 2

S1051 ✚

Camden and Islington Primary Care Trusts, Library and Information Service

3rd Floor, West Wing, St Pancras Hosp, 4 St Pancras Way, London, NW1 0PE (020-7530-3910; fax: 020-7530-3904)
Email: hp.library@cichs-tr.nthames.nhs.uk
Internet: http://www.candihps.org.uk/library/ or http://www.islingtonpct.nhs.uk/

Gov Body: serves Islington Primary Care Trust, Camden Primary Care Trust & Camden & Islington Mental Health Svcs Trust

Chief: Lib & Info Mgrs: Mrs Mandy Guest & Mrs Sarah Panzetta **Dep:** Ms Lyn Coventry
Assoc Libs: ST PANCRAS SITE LIB, contact details as above; INSULL WING SITE LIB, Ground Floor, Insull Wing, 110 Hampstead Rd, London, NW1 2LJ (020-7853-5395; fax: 020-7853-5355; email: mandy.guest@islingtonpct.nhs.uk)
Entry: open to everyone over 18 working to improve health & social care in Camden or Islington; appt advised for Insull Wing Site **Open:** St Pancras: Mon 0900-1800, Tue, Thu-Fri 0900-1630, Wed 0900-1200; Insull Wing: Mon-Thu 0900-1500, Fri 1000-1400
Subj: health care policy; health care mgmt; health promotion; public health **Co-op Schemes:** ILL
Equip: copier, clr copier, video viewer (at St Pancras), 7 computers (all with wd-proc & CD-ROM, 6 with internet) **Online:** Medline, CINAHL, Cochrane, PsycInfo & others
Stock: bks/4000+; periodcls/150+; videos/1000, incl teaching packs
Pubns: leaflets & posters
Staff: Libns: 3 Non-Prof: 4 **Exp:** £200000 (2000-01)
Proj: planned move of Islington Primary Care Trust & eventual merger of the two libs

S1052 🔑

Campaign for Nuclear Disarmament Library

162 Holloway Rd, London, N7 8DQ (020-7700-2393; fax: 020-7700-2357)
Email: enquiries@cnduk.org

Entry: ref only by special appt **Open:** Mon-Fri 1000-1600, by appt
Subj: all subjs related to nuclear weapons, warfare & disarmament, incl hist of the peace movement
Collns: Archvs: colln of archv papers dating back to 1950 kept at LSE (see **S1241**) & at British Lib (see **L1**)
Stock: bks/1000; periodcls/20; photos/various; slides/50; illusts/various; pamphs/50; m-forms/50 reels; videos/500

S1053 🏛

Canada House Library

Trafalgar Sq, London, SW1Y 5BJ (020-7258-6493; fax: 020-7258-6434)
Email: dorian.hayes@dfait-maeci.gc.ca
Internet: http://lib-bib.dfait-maeci.gc.ca/

Gov Body: Dept of Foreign Affairs & Internatl Trade (DFAIT), Canada **Chief:** Mission Libn: Mr Dorian Hayes PhD
Entry: ref only **Open:** Mon-Tue 1000-1800, Wed 1000-1300
Subj: relating to Canada: generalities; social sci; lang; Canadian French; sci; tech; arts; lit; geog; hist; political hist; Canadian Francophone culture
Collns: Bks & Pamphs: large political hist colln; large & exclusive colln of Canadian playscripts from Playwrights Union of Canada; "Makers of Canada" Series Archvs: Hudson's Bay Company records; Champlain Soc records **Co-op Schemes:** ILL with Natl Lib of Canada & DFAIT HQ Lib, Ottawa
Equip: copier, computers (incl 6 with internet & 1 with CD-ROM) **Disabled:** wheelchair access
Online: DFAIT OPAC, access to Canadian govt web sites **Officer-in-Charge:** Mission Libn, as above **Svcs:** info, ref, biblio
Stock: bks/50000; some photos, maps & CD-ROMs **Acqs Offcr:** Mission Libn, as above
Classn: LC **Auto Sys:** Canadian Govt OPAC
Staff: Other Prof: 1
Proj: several lib displays relating to current holdings & recent acqs

S1054 🔑✚

Cancer Research UK, Library and Information Services

(formerly Imperial Cancer Rsrch Fund)
61 Lincoln's Inn Fields, London, WC2A 3PX (020-7269-3602; fax: 020-7269-3644)
Email: j.chester@cancer.org.uk
Internet: http://science.cancerresearchuk.org/

Gov Body: Cancer Rsrch UK **Chief:** Head of Lib & Info Svcs: Ms Julia Chester BA(Hons), DipLib, MCLIP
Assoc Libs: CLARE HALL LABORATORIES LIB, South Mimms, Potters Bar, Hertfordshire, EN6 3LD; BEATSON LABORATORY LIB (see **S696**); CANCER EPIDEMIOLOGY UNIT LIB (see **S1668**)
Entry: staff only; possible access for others by adv appt, ref only **Open:** Mon-Fri 0900-1700
Subj: oncology; cancer rsrch; biomedicine
Collns: Bks & Pamphs: Imperial Cancer Rsrch Fund annual scientific reports (1902-2001); staff pubns **Co-op Schemes:** BLDSC, CHILL
Equip: fax, copiers, clr copier, computers (with wd-proc, internet & CD-ROM), digital scanner/printer
Online: PubMed, SciSearch, Web of Science
Svcs: info, ref **Stock:** bks/5000; periodcls/210
Classn: NLM
Pubns: Annual Scientific Report; Rsrch Prospectus
Staff: Libns: 7 Non-Prof: 6

S1055 🔑🎓

Canning House Library

2 Belgrave Sq, London, SW1X 8PJ (020-7235-2303; fax: 020-7235-3587)
Email: enquiries.library@canninghouse.com
Internet: http://www.canninghouse.com/

Gov Body: Hispanic & Luso-Brazilian Council
Chief: Libn: Ms Carmen Suárez MA(Hispanic Studies), Diplomatura en Biblioteconomía y Documentación
Entry: open to public for ref, borrowing facilities for membs **Open:** Mon 1400-1830, Tue-Fri 0930-1300, 1400-1730
Subj: Latin America; Caribbean; Portugal; Spain; Iberian studies **Collns:** Bks & Pamphs: W.H. Hudson Colln; R.B. Cunninghame-Graham Colln; George Canning Colln **Co-op Schemes:** BLDSC, SALALM, ACLAIIR
Equip: copier, computers (Including wd-proc & CD-ROM)
Stock: bks/50000; periodcls/100
Classn: LC **Auto Sys:** Horizon
Pubns: British Bulletin of Pubns on Latin America, the Caribbean, Portugal & Spain (biennial, £20 pa)
Staff: Libns: 2 **Exp:** £9000 (1999-2000)

S1056 🔑🏛

Carlyle's House

24 Cheyne Row, Chelsea, London, SW3 5HL (020-7352-7087; fax: 020-7352-5108)
Email: carlyleshouse@ntrust.org.uk

Type: historic house & museum **Gov Body:** Natl Trust **Chief:** Custodian: Mrs Uta Thompson
Entry: Natl Trust membs or admission charge
Open: Apr-Oct: Wed-Fri 1400-1700, Sat-Sun 100-1700
Collns: Bks & Pamphs: Thomas Carlyle's colln of ref bks & works by him
Equip: copier **Svcs:** ref

S1057 🔑🖐

Catholic Central Library

Lancing St, London, NW1 1ND (020-7383-4333; fax: 020-7388-6675)
Email: librarian@catholic-library.org.uk
Internet: http://www.catholic-library.org.uk/

Gov Body: Board of Trustees *Chief:* Libn: Ms Joan Bond
Entry: open to public, no appt necessary; no fee for single visit, £10 for several visits; £25 pa for borrowing rights (proof of addr required) *Open:* Mon-Tue, Thu-Fri 1030-1700, Wed 1030-1900; closed Sat, public hols, Holy Wk & Xmas-New Year
Subj: religion; Roman Catholicism; hist of Roman Catholicism in England; scripture; theology; moral theology; spirituality; pastoral care; liturgy; sacraments; Church hist; religious orders; ecumenism; Church Fathers; comparative religion; religious edu; Church arch; Catholic lit; biography (saints, popes & leading lay people of all denominations); religious fiction *Collns: Bks & Pamphs:* 19C pamphs & tracts; Papal documents *Co-op Schemes:* ILL, ABTAPL
Stock: bks/55000; periodcls/150+; pamphs/several 1000

S1058 ✚
Central Middlesex Hospital Library
Avery Jones Postgrad Medical Centre, Central Middlesex Hosp, Acton Ln, London, NW10 7NS (020-8453-2504; *fax:* 020-8453-2503)
Internet: http://www.cmhlib.demon.co.uk/

Gov Body: North West London Hosps NHS Trust *Chief:* Lib Mgr: Mr Alan Fricker (alan.fricker@ nwlh.nhs.uk) *Other Snr Staff:* Asst Libns: Ms Marina Rossi (marina@cmhlib.demon.co.uk) & Ms Linda Liu (linda@cmhllb.demon.co.uk)
Entry: staff of North West London Hosps NHS Trust & Central & North West London Mental Health Trust; health personnel & other orgs in the area making contributions to the lib budget; others ref only on appl to the Lib Mgr *Open:* Mon, Thu-Fri 0900-1700, Tue-Wed 0900-1900
Subj: medicine; psychiatry; child & adolescent psychiatry; psychotherapy; genl practice *Co-op Schemes:* NTRLS, BLDSC
Equip: copier, computers (incl internet & CD-ROM) *Online:* Medline, CINAHL, Embase, BNI, Clinical Evidence, Cochrane *Svcs:* info, ref, biblio
Stock: bks/3500; periodcls/130
Classn: NLM *Auto Sys:* DBTextworks
Staff: Libns: 3

S1059 👨‍🎓
Central School of Speech and Drama, Learning and Information Services
64 Eton Ave, London, NW3 3HY (020-7559-3942; *fax:* 020-7722-4132)
Email: library@cssd.ac.uk
Internet: http://www.cssd.ac.uk/

Gov Body: Higher Edu Funding Council (England) *Chief:* Head of Learning & Info Svcs: Mr J. Adam Edwards BA, MSc, MCLIP *Dep:* Systems Mgr & Dep Head: Mr Brian Harry BA *Other Snr Staff:* Lib Svcs Mgr: Mr Peter Collett BA, PGDip, MCLIP
Entry: ref only, adv appt *Open:* term: Mon-Thu 0915-1945, Fri 0915-1645, Sat 1315-1645; vac: Mon-Fri 1100-1645, please phone to confirm
Subj: at undergrad & postgrad levels: generalities; psy; social sci; lang; arts; lit; hist; edu; linguistics; speech therapy; drama; musical theatre; design; voice *Collns: Archvs:* small archv concerned with hist of the school *Co-op Schemes:* BLDSC, UK Libs Plus
Equip: m-reader, m-printer, 4 video viewers, copier, clr copier, 30 computers (all with wd-proc, internet & CD-ROM) *Svcs:* info, ref
Stock: bks/31000; periodcls/70; audios/890; videos/890
Classn: DDC *Auto Sys:* Heritage IV
Pubns: various bibliographies & info sheets (free)
Staff: Libns: 2.5 *Other Prof:* 3 *Non-Prof:* 2.9
Exp: £24000 (1999-2000); £25000 (2000-01)

S1060 📚
Central St Martin's College of Art and Design, Learning Resources
Southampton Row, London, WC1B 4AP (020-7514-7037; *fax:* 020-7514-7033)
Email: p.christie@csm.linst.ac.uk
Internet: http://www.linst.ac.uk/library/libinf/csm.htm

Gov Body: The London Inst *Chief:* Head of Learning Resources: Ms Pat Christie
Assoc Libs: CHARING CROSS RD LIB, 107 Charing Cross Rd, London, WC2H 0DU (020-7514-7191); DRAMA CENTRE LONDON LIB, 176 Chalk Farm Rd, London, NW5 3PT (020-7428-2077)
Entry: staff & students; others may apply in writing for ref access to materials not available elsewhere *Open: Southampton Row & Charing Cross Rd:* term: Mon-Thu 0930-2000, Fri 1000-1900; vac: Mon-Fri 1230-1630; *Drama Centre London:* term: Mon-Tue, Thu 1100-1600, Fri 1300-1600; vac: closed
Subj: arts; fine art; design; product design; ceramics; film; graphics; illustration; metalwork; photography; printmaking; jewellery; textiles
Collns: Bks & Pamphs: Trade & Technical Lit Colln (at Southampton Row) *Other:* Fashion Files Colln (at Charing Cross Rd); Slide Lib (at Southampton Row) *Co-op Schemes:* ILL, ARLIS, SCONUL
Stock: bks/80000; periodcls/120; videos/1000
Auto Sys: Talis

S1061 📚
Centre for Information on Language Teaching and Research, Resources Library
20 Bedfordbury, Covent Gdn, London, WC2N 4LB (020-7379-5110)
Email: library@cilt.org.uk
Internet: http://www.cilt.org.uk/

Type: educational charity *Gov Body:* Board of Governors *Chief:* Contact: Mr J. Hawkins BA, MCLIP
Entry: ref only, open to all those professionally concerned with langs & lang teaching *Open:* school term time: Mon-Tue, Thu-Fri 1030-1700, Wed 1030-2000, Sat 1000-1300; vac: Mon-Fri 1030-1700
Subj: lang teaching; langs; linguistics
Equip: 2 video viewers, copier, 8 computers (incl 6 with internet & 6 with CD-ROM), satellite TV, audio players, Lang Master *Svcs:* info, ref
Stock: bks/10000; periodcls/260; audios/3000; videos/300; CD-ROMs/220; teaching materials/3700 titles
Classn: own *Auto Sys:* EOSi, GLAS
Pubns: Conferences List; materials publ on web site
Staff: Libns: 2 *Other Prof:* 5 *Non-Prof:* 1

S1062 🔑
Centre for Policy on Ageing, Library and Information Service
19-23 Ironmonger Row, London, EC1V 3QP (020-7553-6500; *fax:* 020-7553-6501)
Email: cpa@cpa.org.uk
Internet: http://www.cpa.org.uk/

Type: charity, independent policy & info unit *Gov Body:* CPA Board of Governors *Chief:* Dir & Head of Info: Ms Gillian Crosby BA, MCLIP (gcrosby@cpa.org.uk) *Dep:* Lib & Info Offcr: Ms Ruth Hayes (rhayes@cpa.org.uk)
Entry: by appt only
Subj: gerontology; social, behavioural & health aspects of ageing

Equip: copier, computer (incl CD-ROM) *Svcs:* info, ref, biblio, lit searches
Stock: bks/40000; periodcls/400
Pubns: New Lit on Old Age (6 pa, £25); AgeInfo CD-ROM (quarterly updates, 3 databases, annual subscription for single user/network license); various bibliographies/reading lists; leaflet
Staff: Other Prof: 2 *Non-Prof:* 2

S1063 🏛
Charity Commission Information Centre
Harmsworth House, 13-15 Bouverie St, London, EC4Y 8DP (020-7210-2409)
Email: joyce.watkins@charitycommission.gsi.gov.uk
Internet: http://www.charitycommission.gov.uk/

Chief: Libn: Ms Sarah Whiting *Other Snr Staff:* Info Centre Mgr: Mrs Joyce Watkins (based at Taunton Centre)
Assoc Libs: CHARITY COMMISSION INFO CENTRE, 2nd Floor, 20 Kings Parade, Queens Dock, Liverpool, L3 4DQ (0151-703-1634); CHARITY COMMISSION INFO CENTRE, Woodfield House, Tangier, Taunton, TA1 4BL (01823-345160)
Entry: adv appt, ref only *Open:* Mon-Fri 1000-1600
Subj: law; charity law; admin; mgmt *Collns: Bks & Pamphs:* 19C reports of the Commissioners for inquiries concerning charities; unreported vols concerning charities (mid 19C-1947) *Co-op Schemes:* ILL
Equip: m-readers, m-printers (30p per sheet), copiers (30p per sheet) *Svcs:* info, ref
Acqs Offcr: Info Centre Mgr, as above
Classn: DDC, MOYS *Auto Sys:* TinLib
Staff: Other Prof: 1 *Non-Prof:* 2.5

S1064 👨‍🎓 🔑
The Charles Lamb Society Library
The Guildhall Lib, Aldermanbury, London, EC2P 2EJ

Chief: Principal Ref Libn: Mr Andrew Harper
Entry: adv appt (48 hrs); apply to the Principal Ref Libn
Subj: lit; works by & about Charles Lamb
Stock: bks/c2000
Pubns: The Charles Lamb Bulletin; A Handlist to the Charles Lamb Soc Colln at Guildhall Lib; for details of pubns contact The Charles Lamb Soc, BM ELIA, London, WC1N 3XX
Exp: no budget, but review copies & gifts added to colln
For full contact details see Corp of London Libs (**P99**)

S1065 🔑
Chartered Institute of Environmental Health, Library
Chadwick Ct, 15 Hatfields, London, SE1 8DJ (020-7827-5821; *fax:* 020-7827-5866)
Email: information@cieh.org
Internet: http://www.cieh.org/

Chief: Info & Communications Mgr: Ms Tina Garrity BA(Hons), MA
Entry: ref only, adv appt *Open:* Mon-Fri 1400-1700, excl bank hols
Subj: environmental health *Co-op Schemes:* BLDSC
Equip: m-reader, copier *Svcs:* info, ref
Stock: bks/800; periodcls/70
Classn: stock not yet classified
Staff: Other Prof: 2

London ▼ London

Special Libraries

S1066 ⚷

Chartered Institute of Library and Information Professionals, Information Centre

7 Ridgmount St, London, WC1E 7AE (020-7255-0620; *fax:* 020-7255-0501)
Email: info@cilip.org.uk
Internet: http://www.cilip.org.uk/info/
   infocentre.html

Type: prof body *Gov Body:* Chartered Inst of Lib & Info Profs (CILIP) *Chief:* Info Mgr: Ms Caroline Nolan
Assoc Libs: membs of CILIP also have access to the former BLISS Lib collns at the British Lib (see **L1**)
Entry: ref only; membs of CILIP; bona fide rsrchers by appt only *Open:* Mon-Fri 0900-1700
Subj: librarianship; lib & info sci; lib hist; conservation; info mgmt; collns mgmt *Collns: Bks & Pamphs:* complete sets of CILIP pubns, incl guidelines, leaflets & journals; other lib & info prof journals *Co-op Schemes:* BLDSC
Equip: copier, computers (with internet & CD-ROM) *Online:* various web-based databases incl Lib & Info Abstracts (LISA) *Svcs:* info, ref, enq svc, current awareness, search svc (membs only)
Auto Sys: Heritage
See also **O110**

S1067 ⚷

Chartered Institute of Management Accountants, Library and Information Service

26 Chapter St, London, SW1P 4NP (020-7663-5441; *fax:* 020-7663-5442)
Internet: http://www.cimaglobal.com/

Type: prof inst *Chief:* Libn & Info Offcr: Miss Soot Hong Ng BSc, MA, MCLIP
Entry: membs & students of the Inst *Open:* Mon-Fri 1000-1700
Subj: mgmt accountancy *Collns: Archvs:* records of the Inst, incl minutes (1919-date)
Equip: copier, computer (incl internet & CD-ROM)
Svcs: info, ref, biblio, indexing, abstracting
Stock: bks/8000; periodcls/175
Classn: UDC *Auto Sys:* CALM 2000
Staff: Libns: 2 *Non-Prof:* 2

S1068 ⚷

Chartered Institute of Patent Agents, Library

95 Chancery Ln, London, WC2A 1DT (020-7405-9450; *fax:* 020-7430-0471)
Email: mail@cipa.org.uk
Internet: http://www.cipa.org.uk/

Type: prof body *Chief:* Sec & Registrar: Mr Michael C. Ralph
Entry: adv appt only
Subj: intellectual property *Collns: Archvs:* archvs of the Chartered Inst of Patent Agents
Svcs: info, ref

S1069 ⚷

Chartered Institute of Personnel and Development, Library and Information Service

CIPD House, 35 Camp Rd, London, SW19 4UX (020-8263-3355; *fax:* 020-8263-3400)
Email: lis@cipd.co.uk
Internet: http://www.cipd.co.uk/

Chief: Head of Lib & Info Svcs: Mrs Barbara Salmon BA, MCLIP
Entry: non-membs: ref only, admission charge £50 pd; no appt necessary *Open:* Mon-Fri 0915-1700; closed between Xmas & New Year
Subj: personnel mgmt; industrial relations; training; industrial psy; employment law; salaries & benefits (incl internatl coverage)
Equip: fax, copier, computer
Stock: bks/16000; periodcls/200
Classn: LCBS *Auto Sys:* Ivor
Pubns: Quick Facts on various topics on web site
Staff: Libns: 9.6 *Other Prof:* 2 *Non-Prof:* 10.5

S1070 ⚷

Chartered Institution of Building Services Engineers, Library

Delta House, 222 Balham High Rd, London, SW12 9BS (020-8675-5211; *fax:* 020-8675-5449)
Email: enquiries@cibse.org
Internet: http://www.cibse.org/

Type: prof body *Chief:* Policy Mgr: Mr Richard Howard
Entry: by appt *Open:* Mon-Fri 0900-1300, 1400-1700
Subj: bldg svcs eng; heating, ventilation, air conditioning, water supply, fire protection, sanitation, electrical power supply, acoustics, refrigeration & heat rejection, lifts, paternosters & escalators, interior & exterior lighting; energy use of bldgs; plant commissioning
Equip: copier

S1071 ⚷

Chartered Institution of Water and Environmental Management, Library

15 John St, London, WC1N 2EB (020-7831-3110; *fax:* 020-7405-4967)
Email: admin@ciwem.org.uk
Internet: http://www.ciwem.org.uk/

Type: prof body *Chief:* Hon Libn: Dr I.E. Alexiou
Entry: adv appt; fee for non-membs *Open:* Mon-Fri 0930-1700 (if Libn is available)
Subj: water; waste water; waste; environmental mgmt *Collns: Bks & Pamphs:* 40+ magazines & periodcls of water & environment industry *Archvs:* archvs of CIWEM & predecessors
Equip: copier (charges), fax (charges), computer (with wd-proc, internet & CD-ROM) *Svcs:* info, ref, biblio, indexing
Stock: bks/4500+ items; periodcls/40+; photos/300+; videos/20
Classn: Dataflex
Pubns: Journal of Water & Environmental Mgmt (6 pa); Water & Environmental Mgr (magazine, 6 pa); various specialist pubns
Staff: Non-Prof: 1 volunteer

S1072 ⚷

Chartered Insurance Institute Library

20 Aldermanbury, London, EC2V 7HY (020-7417-4415; *fax:* 020-7972-0110)
Email: library@cii.co.uk
Internet: http://www.ciilo.org/

Chief: Libn: Mr Robert Cunnew BA, FCLIP *Dep:* Asst Libn: Ms Samantha Crown BSc
Entry: membs: ref & lending; non-membs: ref only (charges); other libs: ref & lending (charges)
Open: Mon-Fri 0900-1700
Subj: insurance; financial svcs; risk *Collns: Bks & Pamphs:* historical colln of insurance publishing; directories; company annual reports; course bks & other study materials; legal materials, incl statutes, statutory instruments, law reports, directives & rule bks *Archvs:* unique colln of policy documents & other ephemera
Equip: m-reader, copier, fax, 3 computers (all with internet & CD-ROM) *Online:* All England Law Reports, Current Legal Info, Insurance Database, Axco Insurance Market Reports *Svcs:* info, ref, biblio, indexing, full-text info resources on web site
Stock: bks/20000 incl reports & pamphs; periodcls/c1000; m-forms/10; audios/31; videos/85
Classn: own *Auto Sys:* Unicorn
Pubns: Journal
Staff: Libns: 3 *Non-Prof:* 3

S1073 ⚷

Chartered Society of Designers, Information Service

5 Bermondsey Exchange, 179-181 Bermondsey St, London, SE1 3UW (020-7357-8088; *fax:* 020-7407-9878)
Email: csd@csd.org.uk
Internet: http://www.csd.org.uk/

Chief: Head of Info & Prof Svcs: Miss L. De Bay
Dep: Asst, Info Svcs: Miss Yvonne Hunt
Entry: membs only *Open:* Mon-Tue, Thu-Fri 0930-1730, Wed 0930-1900
Subj: design (UK only)
Equip: fax, copier, room for hire
Stock: bks/500, plus 1000 bnd journals; periodcls/20
Staff: Other Prof: 2

S1074 🎓 ✚

Chartered Society of Physiotherapy, Library and Information Services

14 Bedford Row, London, WC1R 4ED (020-7306-6155; *fax:* 020-7306-6629)
Email: lis@csphysio.org.uk
Internet: http://www.csp.org.uk/

Type: prof body *Chief:* Lib & Info Svcs Mgr: Miss Andrea Peace BA, MA (peacea@csphysio.org.uk)
Other Snr Staff: Snr Info Offcr: Miss Anna Sewerniak (sewerniaka@csphysio.org.uk)
Entry: ref only, adv appt *Open:* Mon-Fri 0900-1700
Subj: physiotherapy & allied subjs *Collns: Bks & Pamphs:* Grey Lit Colln *Other:* CSP specific interest group lit; membs' theses & dissertations; English & foreign lang physiotherapy journals *Co-op Schemes:* BLDSC, BMA lib
Equip: fax, copier, computers (incl 3 with internet & 3 with CD-ROM) *Disabled:* scanner, speech synthesiser, text enlarger, CCTV *Online:* Medline, CINAHL, Embase *Officer-in-Charge:* Snr Info Offcr, as above *Svcs:* info, ref, biblio, enqs
Stock: bks/450; periodcls/140 *Acqs Offcr:* Snr Info Offcr, as above
Classn: NLM (Wessex) *Auto Sys:* EOSi
Pubns: pubns list available
Staff: Libns: 3 *Non-Prof:* 1

S1075 🎓

Chelsea College of Art and Design Library

Manresa Rd, London, SW3 3LS (020-7514-7773; *fax:* 020-7514-7785)
Email: mr-lib@linst.ac.uk
Internet: http://www.linst.ac.uk/library/

Gov Body: The London Inst *Chief:* Head of Learning Resources: Ms Liz Ward BA, MA, DipLib, MCLIP
Assoc Libs: HUGON RD LIB, Hugon Rd, London, SW6 3ES (020-7514-7901); LIME GROVE LIB, Lime Grove, London, W12 8EA (020-7514-7833)
Entry: adv appt (wk in adv), ref only *Open:* term: Mon-Tue, Thu 0900-1800, Wed 0900-1900, Fri 0900-1700; vac: Mon-Fri 0930-1300, 1400-1700
Subj: arts; fine art; art hist; design; arch; public art
Collns: Bks & Pamphs: artists' bks; rare bks; exhib catalogues Archvs: Coll Archvs; African-Caribbean, Asian & African Art in Britain Archv; Green Textiles Archv; Inventory Archv; Mariko Mori Archv; Public Art Archv; Jean Spencer Archv; Womens Internatl Art Club Archv; Ian Hamilton Finlay Archv; Kurt Schwitters Colln & Archv; Stephen Willats Archv Other: Contemporary Art Slide Scheme Archv; facsimile sketchbks *Co-op Schemes:* BLDSC, ILL, ARLIS, M25 Consortium
Equip: m-reader, video viewer, copier, computers (incl internet) *Svcs:* info, ref, biblio, indexing
Stock: bks/74000; periodcls/291; photos/3000; slides/160000; illusts/5000; pamphs/42000; m-forms/500; audios/200; videos/100; archvs/25 linear m
Classn: DDC, Doran-Philpot-Bury *Auto Sys:* Talis
Pubns: Recordings: A Select Bibliography of Contemporary African, Afro-Caribbean & Asian British Art (£9.99)
Staff: Libns: 6 Non-Prof: 3 *Exp:* £43000 (1999-2000)

S1076 🎓 ✚

The Chelsea Physic Garden, Library

66 Royal Hosp Rd, London, SW3 4HS (020-7352-5646 x6; *fax:* 020-7376-3910)
Email: enquiries@cpgarden.demon.co.uk

Type: charity, botanic garden *Gov Body:* Chelsea Physic Garden Co *Chief:* Curator: Ms Rosie Atkins
Entry: available only as a lib of last resort; adv appt required; ref only *Open:* Mon-Tue 0900-1600
Subj: sci; hortic *Collns:* Bks & Pamphs: 18C Working Lib of Apothecaries; bks on herbs, medicinal plants, herbal medicine etc; bks on hist of Chelsea Physic Garden Archvs: small colln of material relating to hist of garden Other: historical herbarium colln *Co-op Schemes:* EBHL
Equip: copier *Svcs:* ref
Stock: bks/2000; periodcls/30; archvs/6 linear m
Classn: UDC (mod)
Pubns: Seed List (free to botanic gardens); Guide Bks (£1.50); series on past curators (£3); Plants in Medicine (50p); & others
Staff: currently staffed by volunteers
Further Info: Other parts of the Lib of Soc of Apothecaries held at: Black Friars Lane, London, EC4V 6JE (see **A346**)

S1077 🎓

Child Accident Prevention Trust, Library and Resource Centre

4th Floor, Clerk's Ct, 18-20 Farringdon Ln, London, EC1R 3HA (020-7608-3828; *fax:* 020-7608-3674)
Email: safe@capt.org.uk
Internet: http://www.capt.org.uk/

Entry: adv appt *Open:* Mon-Fri 0900-1600
Subj: accident prevention; child safety; child health
Equip: copier *Svcs:* info, ref
Stock: bks/10000

S1078 🎓

The Children's Society Library

Edward Rudolf House, Margery St, London, WC1X 0JL (020-7841-4400; *fax:* 020-7841-4500)
Email: info@childrenssociety.org.uk
Internet: http://www.the-childrens-society.org.uk/

Type: charity *Chief:* Libns: Mrs Sue Peisley MCLIP & Ms Denise Tinant BA, MCLIP
Assoc Libs: CHILDREN'S SOC RECORDS & ARCHV CENTRE (see **A264**)
Entry: ref only *Open:* Mon-Fri 0930-1700
Subj: social sci; voluntary sector childcare; fundraising; social welfare *Collns:* Archvs: held at Records & Archv Centre: historic & modern records reflecting all aspects of the work of The Children's Soc
Equip: computer (with internet & CD-ROM) *Svcs:* info, ref, biblio, abstracting
Stock: bks/12000; periodcls/100; photos/2000
Classn: Bliss *Auto Sys:* CAIRS
Pubns: Lib Accessions List (monthly); Subj Reading Lists; Lib Guide
Staff: Libns: 5 Other Prof: 3 Non-Prof: 1

S1079 🏛

China-Britain Business Council Library

Abford House, 15 Wilton Rd, London, SW1V 1LT (020-7828-5176; *fax:* 020-7630-5780)
Email: enquiries@cbbc.org
Internet: http://www.cbbc.org/library/overview.html

Gov Body: China-Britain Business Council *Chief:* Info Offcr: Mr Leo X. Liu BA, MA(China Academy of Cultures)
Entry: ref only, adv appt *Open:* Mon 1030-1300, 1400-1730, Tue-Fri 0930-1300, 1400-1730
Subj: People's Republic of China: business, economy & trade
Equip: copier *Svcs:* info, ref
Stock: bks/450; periodcls/40 *Classn:* own
Pubns: China-Britain Trade Review (monthly, £150 pa)
Staff: Other Prof: 0.2

S1080 🎓 🙏

Christian Research Association Library

Vision Bldg, 4 Footscray Rd, Eltham, London, SE9 2TZ (020-8294-1989; *fax:* 020-8294-0014)
Email: admin@christian-research.org.uk

Gov Body: Board of Trustees *Chief:* Editor & Info Offcr: Miss Heather Wraight MTh *Other Snr Staff:* Exec Dir: Dr Peter Brierley BSc, DipTh
Entry: adv appt please *Open:* Mon-Fri 0930-1230, 1330-1630
Subj: religion (esp quantitative & European aspects) *Collns:* Bks & Pamphs: Christian handbks (European, African, Asian etc)
Equip: fax, copier, computers (with internet)
Stock: bks/500; periodcls/120; archvs/225 linear ft
Classn: own, with computerised search facility
Pubns: UK Christian Handbook (£28); World Churches Handbook (£30); Religious Trends (£20); Quadrant (bi-monthly to membs)
Staff: Non-Prof: 3

S1081 🎓

City and Islington College Learning Resources

Spring House, 8-38 Holloway Rd, London, N7 7JL (020-7697-3492)
Internet: http://www.candi.ac.uk/

Chief: Head of Learning Resources: Mrs Catherine Harland BSc, MCLIP (tharla@candi.ac.uk) *Other Snr Staff:* Learning Resources Mgrs: Ms Sylvia Whitehouse BA, MCLIP (switehous@candi.ac.uk) & Ms Larua Simmons BSc, MA, MCLIP (lsimmons@candi.ac.uk)
Assoc Libs: 6th Form Centres: ANNETTE RD CENTRE (020-7697-9805); BENWELL RD CENTRE (020-7700-5596); MARLBOROUGH BLDG CENTRE (020-7700-9283); CAMDEN RD VOCATIONAL CENTRE (020-7700-8642);

SPRING HOUSE CENTRE (020-7697-3429); WILLEN HOUSE CENTRE (020-7614-0304)
Entry: adv appt *Open:* may vary from site to site; ring for details
Subj: all subjs; genl; GCSE & A-level; vocational; some local studies (London) *Collns:* Bks & Pamphs: text bks supporting the curriculum; extensive ref & fiction collns; journals; careers materials; univ & Coll prospectuses Other: audio & videos *Co-op Schemes:* BLDSC
Equip: copiers, clr copiers (some sites), video viewers, computers (incl wd-proc, internet & CD-ROM), laser printers *Online:* EBSCO, Infotrac, Athens, Oxford Reference Online; various networked CD-ROMs *Officer-in-Charge:* Learning Resources Mgrs, as above *Svcs:* ref, biblio
Stock: bks/81334
Classn: DDC *Auto Sys:* Heritage
Staff: Libns: 17.6 Non-Prof: 12.2 *Exp:* £122000 (1999-2000); £118117 (2000-01)

S1082 🎓

City Literary Institute (The City Lit), Learning Centre

16 Stukeley St, Drury Ln, London, WC2B 5LJ (020-7242-9872; *fax:* 020-7405-3347)
Internet: http://www.citylit.ac.uk/

Gov Body: The City Lit *Chief:* Head of Learning Centre: Mr John Hywel Williams BA(Hons), DipLib, MCLIP, CertEd (j.williams@citylit.ac.uk) *Dep:* Asst Head of Learning Centre: Mrs Pat Grant MCLIP (p.grant@citylit.ac.uk) *Other Snr Staff:* E-Learning Programme Co-ordinator: Ms Linda Partridge; E-Learning Facilitator: Ms Chantal Cracy; E-Learning Facilitator: Ms Liz Procter
Entry: City Lit students *Open:* term: Mon 1200-2000, Tue-Fri 1030-2000, Sat 1200-1600; vac: closed
Subj: computing; counselling; drama; edu; training; hist; lang; lit; phil; psy; sociology; social sci; some local hist; music; visual arts; deaf awareness; sign lang; health
Equip: 6 video viewers, copier, 30 computers (incl wd-proc, internet, CD-ROM & DVD) *Disabled:* Kurzweil, JAWS, TextBridge, ZoomText etc *Online:* Oxford Reference Online, XreferPlus etc *Officer-in-Charge:* Head of Learning Centre: Mr John Hywel Williams *Svcs:* info, ref, UK Online Centre, LearnDirect Centre
Stock: bks/c30000; periodcls/50; videos/400; CD-ROMs/100; DVDs/100 *Acqs Offcr:* Acqs Offcr: Ms Pat Grant
Classn: DDC *Auto Sys:* Heritage
Staff: Libns: 3 Other Prof: 3 Non-Prof: 10
Proj: new coll bldg & learning centre (2003-04)

S1083 🎓

City of Westminster College, Paddington Learning Centre

25 Paddington Green, London, W2 1NB (020-7258-8826; *fax:* 020-7258-2700)
Internet: http://www.cwc.ac.uk/

Chief: Dir of Learner Development: Ms Colette Xavier *Dep:* Head of School, Learning Svcs: Mrs Linda Sargent
Assoc Libs: MAIDA VALE LEARNING CENTRE, Elgin Ave, London, W9 2NR (020-7258-2830; *fax:* 020-7258-2842); QUEENS PK LEARNING CENTRE, Saltnam Cres, London, W9 3HW (020-7258-2812; *fax:* 020-7258-2826)
Entry: ref only, adv appt *Open:* term: Mon-Thu 0900-2000, Fri 1030-1700
Subj: all subjs; genl; GCSE; A level; vocational *Co-op Schemes:* BLDSC
Equip: video viewers, copiers, computers (with wd-proc, internet & CD-ROM) *Svcs:* info, ref
Stock: bks/35000; periodcls/200; videos/200
Classn: DDC *Auto Sys:* Talis
Staff: Libns: 7 Other Prof: 3 Non-Prof: 5

Special Libraries

London ▼ London

S1084 🎓

City University London, Information Services

Northampton Sq, London, EC1V 0HB (020-7040-8191; *fax:* 020-7040-8194)
Email: library@city.ac.uk
Internet: http://www.city.ac.uk/library/

Chief: Dir of Lib Info Svcs: Mr Brendan Casey (b.m.casey@city.ac.uk) *Other Snr Staff:* Associate Dirs of Lib Info Svcs: Ms Liz Harris (e.d.harris@city.ac.uk); Mr Lesley Baldwin (l.r.baldwin@city.ac.uk); Ms Sandy Leitch (s.o.leitch@city.ac.uk); Ms Diane Beckett (d.m.beckett@city.ac.uk)
Assoc Libs: CYRIL KLEINWORT LIB, Frobisher Cres, Barbican Centre, London, EC2Y 8HB (020-7040-8787); WEST SMITHFIELD LIB (see **S1086**); WHITECHAPEL LIB (see **S1087**); DEPT OF RADIOGRAPHY LIB, Charterhouse Sq, Rutland Pl, London, EC1M 6PA; DEPT OF ARTS POLICY & MGMT RESOURCE CENTRE (see **S1085**)
Entry: non-membs of Univ via M25 Access Scheme or fee-based membership (casual ref by appt) *Open:* term: Mon-Thu 0900-2100, Fri 0900-2000, Sat 1200-1800; vac: Mon-Fri 0900-1700
Subj: generalities; psy; computing; social sci; sci; maths; tech *Collns:* Bks & Pamphs: Kipling Soc Lib *Archvs:* internal records *Co-op Schemes:* BLDSC, M25 Access Scheme
Equip: m-reader, m-printer, fax, video viewer, 21 copiers (A4/5p), 36 computer (all with wd-proc & internet, registered users only) *Online:* various (some charges)
Stock: bks/290000; periodcls/1500; slides/500; maps/130; m-forms/1600; audios/1000; videos/1300
Classn: DDC *Auto Sys:* Innopac
Staff: Libns: 12 *Other Prof:* 14 *Non-Prof:* 23

S1085 🎓

City University London, Department of Arts Policy and Management Resource Centre

Level 7, Frobisher Cres, Barbican, London, EC2Y 8HB (020-7477-8752; *fax:* 020-7477-8887)
Email: artspol@city.ac.uk
Internet: http://www.city.ac.uk/artspolicy/

Gov Body: City Univ London (see **S1084**) *Chief:* contact the Resource Centre Libn
Entry: ref only, postgrad students by adv appt *Open:* term: Mon-Fri 0930-1730; vac: Mon-Fri 0900-1700
Subj: arts; museums
Equip: copier, computer (incl CD-ROM) *Svcs:* ref
Stock: bks/5500; periodcls/90; pamphs/5000; MA theses/900
Classn: own
Staff: Libns: 1 PT *Non-Prof:* 1 FT asst

S1086 🎓 ✚

City University London, St Bartholomew School of Nursing and Midwifery, West Smithfield Library

20 Bartholomew Cl, London, EC1A 7QN (020-7505-5744; *fax:* 020-7040-5762)
Email: sonmlibraries@city.ac.uk
Internet: http://www.city.ac.uk/library/

Gov Body: City Univ London (see **S1084**) *Chief:* Associate Dir: Ms Sandy Leitch (S.O.Leitch@city.ac.uk) *Dep:* Dep Site Mgr: post vacant
Assoc Libs: WHITECHAPEL LIB (see **S1087**)
Entry: ref only; adv appt *Open:* Mon-Thu 0830-1900, Fri 0830-1800
Subj: nursing; midwifery; medicine *Co-op Schemes:* NULJ, North Thames Union List of Serials, LAMDA
Equip: video viewer, 4 copiers (A4/5p), 8 computers (incl 6 with internet & 6 with CD-ROM)
Stock: bks/20000; periodcls/125; videos/50 *Acqs Offcr:* Snr Info Asst (Acqs): Ms Jane Clark
Classn: NLM *Auto Sys:* Innopac
Staff: Libns: 4 *Non-Prof:* 4

S1087 🎓 ✚

City University London, St Bartholomew School of Nursing and Midwifery, Whitechapel Library

Philpott St, London, E1 2EA (020-7040-5878; *fax:* 020-7040-5858)
Email: sonmlibraries@city.ac.uk
Internet: http://www.city.ac.uk/library/

Gov Body: City Univ London (see **S1084**) *Chief:* Associate Dir: Ms Diane Beckett (D.M.Beckett@city.ac.uk) *Dep:* Dep Site Mgr: Mr Steve O'Driscoll
Other Snr Staff: Snr Info Asst (Cataloguing): Ms Alison Raffan
Assoc Libs: WEST SMITHFIELD LIB (see **S1086**)
Entry: ref only; adv appt *Open:* Mon-Thu 0830-1900, Fri 0830-1800
Subj: nursing; midwifery; medicine *Co-op Schemes:* North Thames Union List of Serials, NULJ, LAMDA
Equip: 2 copiers (A4/5p), video viewer, 12 computers (incl 8 with internet & 8 with CD-ROM)
Stock: bks/20000; periodcls/125; videos/100 *Acqs Offcr:* Snr Info Asst (Acqs): Ms Jane Clark
Classn: NLM *Auto Sys:* Innopac
Staff: Libns: 4 *Non-Prof:* 4

S1088 🔑

Civic Trust Library

17 Carlton House Ter, London, SW1Y 5AW (020-7930-0914; *fax:* 020-7321-0180)
Internet: http://www.civictrust.org.uk/

Gov Body: Trustees *Chief:* Libn: Ms Saskia Hallam
Entry: ref, adv appt *Open:* Mon-Fri 0900-1700
Subj: regeneration; conservation of built environment *Collns: Archvs:* Civic Soc pubns
Equip: copier
Stock: bks/2000; periodcls/40; slides/30000
Classn: own

S1089 🔑 📷

Collections Picture Library

13 Woodberry Cres, London, N10 1PJ (020-8883-0083; *fax:* 020-8883-9215)
Email: collections@btinternet.com
Internet: http://www.collectionspicturelibrary.com/

Type: commercial photo agency *Chief:* Mr Brian Shuel *Dep:* Mr Simon Shuel
Entry: adv appt; fees are charged at all times *Open:* 24 hrs (within reason)
Subj: British Isles: topography & people
Stock: slides/500000+
Staff: Other Prof: 4 *Non-Prof:* 1

S1090 🎓

College of Law, London Library

14 Store St, London, WC1E 7DE (020-7291-1295)
Email: library.ss@lawcol.co.uk
Internet: http://www.college-of-law.co.uk/

Gov Body: Coll of Law *Chief:* Asst Libns: Ms Dunia Garcia-Ontiveros (dunia.garcia-ontiveros@lawcol.co.uk) & Ms Michelle Cotton (michelle.cotton@lawcol.co.uk)
Assoc Libs: BIRMINGHAM LIB (see **S168**); CHESTER LIB (see **S458**); GUILDFORD LIB (see **S769**); YORK LIB (see **S2161**)
Entry: access for certain categories of external user, by adv appt only *Open:* term: Mon-Thu 0900-2200, Fri 0900-1800, Sat-Sun 1100-1700
Subj: law
Equip: 3 copiers (5p per pg), computers (with wd-proc & internet) *Svcs:* info, ref
Staff: Libns: 2 *Non-Prof:* 8

S1091 🎓

College of North East London, Centenary Learning Centre

High Rd, Tottenham, London, N15 4RU (020-8442-3014)
Internet: http://www.conel.ac.uk/

Chief: Learning Resources Team Leader: Ms Jan Dunster BA(Hons), MCLIP
Entry: enrolled students only *Open:* Mon-Thu 0900-2000, Fri-Sat 0900-1630
Subj: all subjs; genl; GCSE; A level; vocational
Co-op Schemes: BLDSC
Equip: 3 video viewers, 3 copiers (£1 per 30 copies), clr copier (50p per pg), computers (incl 40 with wd-proc, 40 with CD-ROM & 18 with internet)
Svcs: info, ref
Stock: bks/45000; periodcls/200; videos/300
Classn: DDC *Auto Sys:* Olib
Staff: Libns: 3 *Exp:* £56000 (1999-2000); £60000 (2000-01)

S1092 🔑

College of Occupational Therapists Library

106-114 Borough High St, Southwark, London, SE1 1LB (020-7450-2316; *fax:* 020-7450-2364)
Email: library@cot.co.uk
Internet: http://www.cot.co.uk/

Gov Body: British Assoc of Occupational Therapists *Chief:* Libn: Ms Ann Mason (ann.mason@cot.co.uk) *Dep:* Dep Libn: Ms Stephanie Picton *Other Snr Staff:* Asst Libn: Mr Tim Judkins
Assoc Libs: archvs of the British Assoc of Occupational Therapists are held at: ARCHVS & MSS, Wellcome Lib for the Hist of Medicine (see **S1457**), Archivist: Mrs Annie Lindsay (020-7611-7293; *fax:* 020-7611-8703; *email:* a.lindsay@wellcome.ac.uk)
Entry: membs & those with a legitimate interest in occupational therapy *Open:* Mon-Fri 0900-1700
Subj: all aspects of occupational therapy, mainly at postgrad & vocational levels *Collns: Other:* occupational therapy theses *Co-op Schemes:* LOPS
Equip: copier (10p per pg), video viewer (UK & US formats), 3 computers (all with wd-proc, internet & CD-ROM) *Svcs:* info, ref, biblio
Stock: bks/6000; periodcls/70; videos/20
Classn: DDC *Auto Sys:* Limes
Staff: Libns: 2 *Non-Prof:* 0.5

S1093 🏛

Commission for Racial Equality Library

St Dunstans House, 201-211 Borough High St, London, SE1 1GZ (020-7828-7022; *fax:* 020-7630-7605)
Email: ppinto@cre.gov.uk
Internet: http://www.cre.gov.uk/

Type: quango *Chief:* Libn: Mr Philip Pinto BA, MSc, DipLib, MCLIP

Entry: ref only, adv appt *Open:* Mon-Fri 1000-1600 (ring in adv)
Subj: race relations in UK & Europe *Collns: Other:* race relations in Britain news cuttings
Equip: m-reader, copier (10p per sheet), computer
Svcs: info, ref
Stock: bks/20000; periodcls/17000+ indiv issues
Classn: own *Auto Sys:* SydneyPlus
Staff: Libns: 1

S1094

Commission of the European Communities, London Library

8 Storey's Gate, London, SW1P 3AT (020-7973-1900/10; *fax:* 020-7973-1992)

Chief: Libn: Marguerite-Marie Brenchley
Entry: no public access; enqs may only be referred to the Lib via a recognised European Public Info Centre (EPIC); details of the nearest EPIC can be obtained from public libs
Subj: all EC related subjs *Collns: Bks & Pamphs:* official Journal; Eurostat Bulletins & all EC pubns
Equip: m-reader, m-printer, copier
Stock: 30000 items in total
Classn: UDC *Staff: Other Prof:* 1

Commonwealth Resource Centre

See BRITISH EMPIRE & COMMONWEALTH MUSEUM (**S248**)

S1095 🔑

Commonwealth Secretariat Library

Marlborough House, Pall Mall, London, SW1Y 5HX (020-7747-6164; *fax:* 020-7747-6168)
Email: d.blake@commonwealth.int
Internet: http://www.thecommonwealth.org/

Type: internatl *Gov Body:* Commonwealth Secretariat *Chief:* Libn: Mr David Blake BA, MSc, DipLib, MCLIP
Entry: adv appt *Open:* Mon-Fri 0915-1700
Subj: Commonwealth; Africa; Asia; Caribbean; econ; politics; edu; gender; youth *Collns: Bks & Pamphs:* Commonwealth Secretariat pubns *Archvs:* archvs of Commonwealth Secretariat (under 30 year rule), shared records
Equip: m-reader, 2 copiers, computer (with wd-proc, internet & CD-ROM) *Svcs:* info, ref, biblio
Stock: bks/20000; periodcls/4000; pamphs/25000
Acqs Offcr: Libn, as above
Classn: UNBIS *Auto Sys:* CDS/ISIS
Staff: Libns: 1 *Other Prof:* 1 *Non-Prof:* 2 *Exp:* £80000 (2000-01)

S1096 🔑 ✚

Community Practitioners and Health Visitors' Association, Information Resources and Library

40 Bermondsey St, London, SE1 3UD (020-7939-7000; *fax:* 020-7403-2976)
Email: indi.munasinghe@amicus-m.org
Internet: http://www.msfcphva.org/

Type: prof assoc *Gov Body:* Exec Cttee *Chief:* Info Offcr: Mrs Indi Munasinghe BA, MCLIP
Entry: adv appt for non-membs, ref only *Open:* Mon-Fri 0900-1700
Subj: social sci; tech; info on health & social care, relating mainly to health visiting, nursing, community nursing & practice nursing *Collns: Bks & Pamphs:* printed bks; reports; Dept of Health pubns; journals *Archvs:* CPHVA archvs are held at Wellcome Inst *Co-op Schemes:* ILL
Equip: copier, computers (incl wd-proc & CD-ROM) *Online:* in-house databases: biblio, rsrch projs, clinical audit *Svcs:* info, ref, biblio, indexing, abstracting
Stock: bks/2000; periodcls/104

Classn: NLM *Auto Sys:* DBTextworks
Pubns: Health Visitor (journal circulated to membs & other orgs)
Staff: Libns: 1 *Non-Prof:* 1

S1097 🏛

Competition Commission, Library and Information Centre

New Ct, 48 Carey St, London, WC2A 2JT (020-7271-0243; *fax:* 020-7271-0367)
Email: info@competition-commission.gsi.gov.uk
Internet: http://www.competition-commission.org.uk/

Gov Body: part of DTI Lib & Info Svc *Chief:* Info Centre Mgr: Miss L.J. Fisher MA, MCLIP
Entry: normally restricted to Commission staff & membs; staff of govt depts admitted by appt
Open: Mon-Thu 0900-1715, Fri 0900-1700
Subj: monopolies; competition; industrial econ
Co-op Schemes: DTI Info & Lib Svcs
Equip: m-reader, m-printer, fax, copier, computers (incl internet) *Online:* Dialog, Datastar, Lexis-Nexis
Svcs: info, ref
Classn: DDC *Auto Sys:* DBTextworks
Pubns: info pack on Commission; Annual Review
Staff: Libns: 3 *Non-Prof:* 2

S1098 🔑

Confederation of British Industry Information Centre

Centre Pt, 103 New Oxford St, London, WC1A 1DU (020-7395-8247; *fax:* 020-7240-1578)
Email: enquiry.desk@cbi.org.uk
Internet: http://www.cbi.org.uk/

Chief: Info Centre Mgr: Miss Emma Houston
Entry: to membs & to co-operating libs; others by arrangement *Open:* Mon-Fri 0930-1730
Subj: industry & govt relations; parliamentary affairs; economic policy; statistics; industrial relations; wages & conditions of employment; industrial & company law; energy & nat resource policy; training & skills; competitiveness & benchmarking; small & medium-sized enterprises policy; tech policy; European & wider internatl aspects of business policy; environmental mgmt policy; health & safety policy *Collns: Archvs:* CBI's predecessor orgs to 1965, on permanent loan to the Modern Records Centre (see **A114**)
Equip: Online: various svcs, incl FAME, IMID & Eurolaw
Auto Sys: DBTextworks
Pubns: Economic Situation Report; Industrial Trends Survey; numerous others
Staff: Libns: 3 *Non-Prof:* 3

S1099 🔑 🙏

The Congregational Library

15 Gordon Sq, London, WC1H 0AG

Gov Body: Congregational Memorial Hall Trust Ltd; lib is administered by Dr Williams' Trust (see **S1116**); all enqs should be directed via Dr Williams' Lib *Chief:* Libn: Dr David L. Wykes
Open: Mon, Wed, Fri 1000-1700, Tue & Thu 1000-1830; closed Xmas & Easter
Subj: religion *Staff: Libns:* 2

S1100 🔑

Conservative Party Library

Conservative Central Office, 32 Smith Sq, London, SW1P 3HH (020-7984-8203; *fax:* 020-7222-1135)

Gov Body: Conservative Party *Chief:* Libn: Miss Emma Watts
Assoc Libs: CONSERVATIVE PARTY ARCHVS, Bodleian Lib, Archivist: Ms Jill Davidson (see **L4**)

Entry: adv appt; lib is generally for internal use only; info can be provided over the phone & photocopies by post
Subj: politics *Svcs:* info, ref

S1101 🔑

Copyright Tribunal Library

Harmsworth House, 13-15 Bouverie St, London, EC4Y 8DP (020-7596-6510; minicom: 0845-922-2250; *fax:* 020-7596-6526)
Email: copyright.tribunal@patent.gov.uk
Internet: http://www.patent.gov.uk/copy/tribunal/

Type: independent *Chief:* Tribunal Sec: Ms Jill Durdin
Entry: adv appt
Subj: copyright *Collns: Other:* copies of decisions of the Copyright Tribunal & evidence relating to hearings
Svcs: ref

S1102 🔑 🙏

Council for the Care of Churches Library

Fielden House, 13 Little College St, London, SW1P 3NZ (020-7898-1866; *fax:* 020-7898-1881)
Email: enquiries@ccc.c-of-e.org.uk
Internet: http://www.churchcare.co.uk/ccc/

Gov Body: Genl Synod of the C of E *Chief:* Libn: Miss Janet Seeley MCLIP
Entry: ref only, adv appt *Open:* Mon-Fri 0930-1300, 1400-1630
Subj: religion; arts; arch; geog; hist (esp of Anglican Church); heraldry; conservation *Collns: Bks & Pamphs:* Canon B.F.L. Clarke Colln (church bldg & restoration, 18C-19C); Canon J.L. Cartwright Colln (ecclesiastical heraldry); Gordon Barnes Bequest (Victorian church arch); Canon P.G. Binnall Colln (stained glass) *Archvs:* Natl Survey of Churches (c15000 files containing correspondence, photos, guidebks, etc)
Equip: copier
Stock: bks/12000; periodcls/120; photos/15000; slides/c12000; m-forms/30; archvs/50 4-drawer filing cabinets; dissertations & theses/30
Classn: own *Staff: Libns:* 1

S1103 🔑

Council for the Protection of Rural England (CPRE) Library

128 Southwark St, London, SE1 0SW (020-7976-6433; *fax:* 020-7976-6373)
Email: info@cpre.org.uk
Internet: http://www.cpre.org.uk/

Type: charity *Chief:* Head of Lib & Info: Ms Hilary Moriss BA, MCLIP (hilarym@cpre.org.uk) *Dep:* Lib & Info Offcr: Mrs Estelle Lipworth BA, DipEd, DipLIS (estelle-lip@cpre.org.uk) *Other Snr Staff:* Lib Asst: Mr Oliver Hilliam BA (oliverh@cpre.org.uk)
Entry: adv appt; lending for membs only *Open:* Mon-Fri 0930-1730
Collns: Bks & Pamphs: ecology; environment; govt environmental planning policy; rural affairs; nat resources *Archvs:* CPRE pubns *Other:* CPRE Archvs (archvs also held at the Rural Hist Centre, Univ of Reading – see **S1850**)
Equip: copier *Svcs:* info, biblio
Stock: bks/16354, incl reports; periodcls/150; pamphs/1000; archvs/228 holdings
Classn: Faceted (in-house) *Auto Sys:* SydneyPlus
Pubns: CPRE Voice (magazine, 3 pa); Annual Report; reports; campaigners' guides; leaflets
Staff: Libns: 2 *Non-Prof:* 1

S1104 🎓

Courtauld Institute of Art Library

Somerset House, Strand, London, WC2R 0RN
(020-7873-2701; *fax:* 020-7873-2887)
Email: booklib@courtauld.ac.uk
Internet: http://www.courtauld.ac.uk/

Gov Body: Courtauld Inst of Art (independent coll funded by HEFCE) *Chief:* Bk Libn: Mr Timothy Davies BA, MSc, MCLIP *Dep:* Dep Bk Libn: Ms Ann Sproat BA, MA, MCLIP
Entry: ref only, as lib of last resort, adv appt
Open: term: Mon-Fri 0930-1900; vac: as announced
Subj: hist of art
Equip: 3 m-readers, m-printer, 2 copiers, computers (incl internet & 3 CD-ROM) *Svcs:* ref
Stock: bks/140000; periodcls/c300
Classn: LC *Auto Sys:* Aleph

S1105 🔑 🎓

Crafts Council Resource Centre

44a Pentonville Rd, Islington, London, N1 9BY
(020-7806-2501; *fax:* 020-7833-4479)
Email: reference@craftscouncil.org.uk
Internet: http://www.craftscouncil.org.uk/

Type: independent arts org *Chief:* Ref Mgr: Ms Ursula Everett BA, MA (u.everett@craftscouncil. org.uk) *Dep:* Ref Offcr: Ms Sally Freeman BA (s.freeman@craftscouncil.org.uk) *Other Snr Staff:* Photostore & Prof Development Mgr: Mr Stewart Drew (s.drew@craftscouncil.org.uk)
Entry: ref only, appt required for group visits but not indivs *Open:* Tue-Sat 1100-1745, Sun 1400-1745; closed Mon
Subj: contemporary & applied arts & crafts, all aspects; automata; basketry; bookbinding; ceramics; fashion accessories; furniture; glass; jewellery; leather; lettering; metalwork; mosaic; musical instruments; paper; stone; textiles; toys; wood *Collns: Archvs:* archv craft exhib catalogues *Other:* Photostore (visual database of contemporary British crafts); Natl Register of Contemporary Craftsmakers (4500+ designers & makers living & working in Britain)
Equip: video viewer, fax, copier (A4/10p, A3/20p), computer (with internet & CD-ROM) *Svcs:* info, ref, biblio
Stock: bks/6000+; periodcls/130+; slides/45000+ (in Photostore); videos/70; CD-ROMs/20; archvs/5.5 linear m
Pubns: Crafts Magazine (6 pa, £29 indiv UK subscription); Makers' News (2 pa, free to Natl Register makers); Running A Workshop (£15 + p&p); various exhib catalogues (further details from Crafts Council)
Staff: Libns: 1 *Other Prof:* 3 *Non-Prof:* 1

S1106 🔑

Cruising Association, Library and Information Centre

CA House, 1 Northey St, Limehouse Basin, London, E14 8BT (020-7536-2828; *fax:* 020-7537-2266)
Email: library@cruising.org.uk
Internet: http://www.cruising.org.uk/

Gov Body: Cruising Assoc *Chief:* Libn: Mr Michael Howe

Entry: membs of the Assoc *Open:* Mon 1030-1800, Tue 1030-2000, Wed-Thu 1030-1900, Fri 1030-1545, Sat 1000-1500 (tel to confirm)
Subj: sci; ship bldg; seamanship; navigation; maritime hist; voyages & exploration; cruises & cruising; sport; lit; biography; inland waterways; geog; social hist *Collns: Bks & Pamphs:* ref colln of pilot bks *Other:* chart colln; regional file colln (info sent in by membs); video colln
Equip: copier, video viewer, computer (incl internet & CD-ROM) *Online:* various CD-ROMs *Svcs:* info, ref, enq svc for membs
Stock: bks/15000+; maps/3000 charts
Classn: own *Staff: Libns:* 1

S1107 🖌️ 📷

David Hoffman Photo Library

c/o BAPLA, 18 Vine Hill, London, EC1R 5DZ (020-8981-5041; *fax:* 020-8980-2041)
Email: lib@hoffmanphotos.com
Internet: http://www.hoffmanphotos.com/

Type: commercial photo lib *Chief:* Principal: Mr David Hoffman DipAd
Entry: adv appt for personal calls, but supply is usually by post, digital delivery or bike *Open:* Mon-Fri 0900-1800 but often available out of hrs
Subj: genl; clr & b/w lib, specialising in social issues (drugs & drug use, policing, disorder, riots, major strikes & protest, race issues, housing & homelessness); ecology, environmental issues & pollution; current affairs; some specialist files (e.g. leisure cycling, local authority svcs) *Co-op Schemes:* BAPLA
Stock: photos/c50000; slides/c50000
Classn: own *Staff: Other Prof:* 1 *Non-Prof:* 1

S1108 🏛️

Department for Culture, Media and Sport, Information Centre

2-4 Cockspur St, London, SW1Y 5DH (020-7211-6200; *fax:* 020-7211-6032)
Email: enquiries@culture.gov.uk
Internet: http://www.culture.gov.uk/

Chief: Libn: Ms Felicitas Montgomery BEd(Hons), DipLib, MCLIP *Dep:* Asst Libn: Ms Abigail Humber BA(Hons), MA, MCLIP (abigail.humber@culture. gsi.gov.uk)
Entry: for non-Dept staff, adv appt as lib of last resort *Open:* Mon-Fri 0900-1730
Subj: govt policy on the arts; sport; the Natl Lottery; libs; museums & galleries; broadcasting; film; press freedom & regulation; the historic environment; tourism; the creative industries; royal parks; the Govt Art Colln *Collns: Archvs:* departmental pubns; bill papers for broadcasting, Natl Heritage, the Natl Lottery & television; Acts of Parliament *Co-op Schemes:* BLDSC, ILL
Equip: fax (Dept staff), copier (Dept staff), computer (with internet & CD-ROM, IC staff only)
Online: Datastar, Dialog, Lexis-Nexis Professional, Parlianet (IC staff only) *Svcs:* info, ref, biblio, translation, Open Learning Centre
Stock: bks/4000; periodcls/300; maps/25; archvs/6 shelves of Departmental pubns
Classn: DDC *Auto Sys:* Unicorn
Staff: Libns: 2 *Non-Prof:* 3
Further Info: provides info & lib svcs to the Dept for Culture, Media & Sport, incl dealing with public enqs to the Dept

S1109 🏛️

Department for Education and Skills, Library and Information Service

LG.01, Sanctuary Bldgs, Gt Smith St, London, SW1P 3BT (020-7925-5040; *fax:* 020-7925-5085)
Email: enquiries.library@dfes.gsi.gov.uk

Gov Body: Dept for Edu & Skills *Chief:* Chief Libn: post vacant *Dep:* Libn: Ms Julia Reed
Assoc Libs: LIB & INFO SVC, Room E3, Moorfoot, Sheffield, S1 4PQ (0114-259-3338; *fax:* 0114-259-3564)
Entry: adv appt only to see material not readily available through another src or lent via ILL *Open:* Mon-Fri 0900-1700
Subj: all subjs; edu; politics; govt *Collns: Archvs:* pubns by dept & its predecessors, incl HMI
Equip: fax, copier *Auto Sys:* Horizon

S1110 🏛️

Department for Environment, Food and Rural Affairs, Nobel House Library

(formerly the Ministry of Agric, Fisheries & Food)
Nobel House, 17 Smith Sq, London, SW1P 3JR
(020-7238-6575; *fax:* 020-7238-6609)
Email: defra.library@defra.gsi.gov.uk
Internet: http://www.defra.gov.uk/

Gov Body: DEFRA *Chief:* Chief Libn: Mr Peter McShane BA, MA, MCLIP (Peter.C.Mcshane@ defra.gsi.gov.uk) *Dep:* Dep Chief Libn: Mr Kevin Jackson BSc, MCLIP (kevin.jackson@ defra.gsi.gov.uk) *Other Snr Staff:* Libn: Mrs Jenny Carpenter BA, MCLIP (Jenny.Carpenter@ defra.gsi. gov.uk); Libn: Mr Cliff van Dort (Clifford.J.VanDort@defra.gsi.gov.uk)
Entry: ref only by adv appt *Open:* Mon-Fri 0900-1700
Subj: agric; hortic; sci; animal health; animal welfare; fisheries; food production; food eng; food processing; environmental protection; wildlife; conservation; sustainable development *Collns: Archvs:* materials publ by DEFRA & predecessor ministries (MAFF, Ministry of Food, Ministry of Agric) *Co-op Schemes:* BLDSC, ILL, AGLINET
Equip: m-reader, m-printer, copier (A4/14p), fax, 4 computers (incl 2 with wd-proc, 1 with internet & 1 with CD-ROM) *Online:* Dialog, Factiva, ENDS, Web of Science *Officer-in-Charge:* Dep Chief Libn, as above *Svcs:* info, ref, biblio, indexing, translation
Acqs Offcr: Acqs Libn: Ms Maggie McDonald (Margaret.Mcdonald@defra.gsi.gov.uk)
Classn: DDC *Auto Sys:* Unicorn
Pubns: reading lists; bibliographies
Staff: Libns: 8 *Other Prof:* 3 *Non-Prof:* 7 *Exp:* £217000 (1999-2000); £253000 (2000-01)

S1111 🏛️ ✚

Department of Health Library and Information Services

Skipton House, 80 London Rd, London, SE1 6LH
(020-7972-6541; *fax:* 020-7972-5976)
Email: Pek_Lan.Bower@doh.gsi.gov.uk

Gov Body: Dept of Health *Chief:* Head of Lib & Info Svcs: Mrs Pek Lan Bower BA, DipLib, MCLIP
Assoc Libs: DEPT OF HEALTH LIB, Quarry House, Quarry Hill, Leeds, W Yorkshire, LS2 7UE, Snr Libn: Ms Kerry Hanson (0113-254-5071; *fax:* 0113-254-5084; *email:* kerry.hanson@doh.gsi. gov.uk); DEPARTMENTAL RECORD OFFICE, Dept of Health, Premier Bldgs, Brunswick St, Nelson, Lancashire, BB9 0HU, Departmental Records Mgr: Mrs Annette Greenwood
Entry: ref only to bona fide rsrchers seeking materials not available elsewhere; adv appt only
Open: Mon-Fri 0900-1700
Subj: health; personal social svcs; health policy; health mgmt; health admin *Collns: Archvs:* pubns of Dept of Health & its predecessors
Svcs: info, ref, biblio, indexing, abstracting, translation
Stock: bks/200000; periodcls/2000
Classn: Bliss *Auto Sys:* Unicorn

S1112

Department of Work and Pensions, Information Centre

(formerly Dept of Social Security)
Room 114 Adelphi, 1-11 John Adam St, London,
WC2N 6HT (020-7712-2500; *fax:* 020-7962-8491)
Email: library@dwp.gsi.gov.uk
Internet: http://www.dwp.gov.uk/

Chief: Info Centre Team Leader: Ms Melanie
Harris BA, DipLib, MCLIP (melanie.harris@
dwp.gsi.gov.uk) *Dep:* Info Centre Mgr: Mrs Angela
Tailby BA(Hons) (angela.tailby@dwp.gsi.gov.uk)
Other Snr Staff: Industrial Injuries Advisory
Council Rsrch Libn: Mrs Andria Lannon BA, MA,
DipLib, MCLIP
Assoc Libs: DEPT OF WORK & PENSIONS
LEGAL INFO CENTRE, 4th Floor, New Ct, Carey
St, London, WC2A 2LS, Legal Info Centre Mgr: Ms
Liz Murray (020-7412-1333; *fax:* 020-7412-1324;
email: liz.murray@dwp.gsi.gov.uk); DEPT OF
WORK & PENSIONS PSY LIB, Occupational Psy
Div, B3 Porterbrooke House, Pear St, Sheffield,
S11 8JF, Info Mgr: Ms Karen Gommersall (0114-
259-6082; 0114-259-7901; *email:* karen.
gommersall@dwp.gsi.gov.uk)
Entry: ref only by appt *Open:* Mon-Fri 0900-1700
Subj: all subjs; genl; social sci; social policy; social
security; poverty; taxation; distribution of income;
public admin; mgmt; company pension scheme
Co-op Schemes: BLDSC
Equip: m-reader, m-printer, m-form camera,
copier, fax, video viewer, 2 computers (both with
wd-proc, internet & CD-ROM) *Online:* Dialog/
Datastar *Svcs:* info, ref, biblio, abstracting
Stock: bks/40000; periodcls/330; m-forms/1700;
videos/50; CD-ROMs/15 *Acqs Offcr:* Acqs Libn:
Mr Philip Warnock (philip.warnock@dwp.gsi.
gov.uk)
Classn: DDC, own *Auto Sys:* Unicorn
Staff: Libns: 10 *Other Prof:* 1 *Non-Prof:* 8 *Exp:*
£150000 (1999-2000); £250000 (2000-01)

S1113

The Dickens House Museum, Library

48 Doughty St, London, WC1N 2LF (020-7405-
2127; *fax:* 020-7831-5175)
Email: dhmuseum@rmplc.co.uk
Internet: http://www.dickensmuseum.com/

Gov Body: Trustees of the Dickens House *Chief:*
Curator: Mr Andrew Xavier MA *Dep:* Asst Curator:
Mr Florian Schweizer MA
Entry: adv appt *Open:* Mon-Sat 1000-1700, Sun
1100-1700; rsrch facilities not available on Sat or
Sun
Subj: life & works of Charles Dickens *Collns:*
Archvs: numerous MSS, incl ALS Dickens letters
(600 items)
Equip: copier
Stock: bks/7000; periodcls/4, plus 2 no longer
current; photos/9000; slides/600; illusts/100;
pamphs/various; maps/a few; AVs/a few; archvs/
c2000 MSS
Classn: Bliss (mod)
Pubns: The Dickensian (3 pa, £3)
Staff: Other Prof: 2 *Non-Prof:* 4.5

S1114

Docklands Library and Archive

No 1 Warehouse, West India Quay, Hertsmere Rd,
London, E14 4AL (020-7001-9825; *fax:* 020-7001-
9801)
Email: raspinal@museumoflondon.org.uk

Gov Body: Museum of London (see **S1288**)
Chief: Libn & Archivist: Mr Robert Roy Aspinall
BA(Hons), DipArch

Entry: strictly by prior tel appt *Open:* Mon-Fri
1100-1800
Subj: local study (London Docklands & the Port of
London): regeneration; cargoes; hist & development; business records; comprises the largest colln
of port-related materials in the world *Collns: Bks
& Pamphs:* bks covering: the River Thames;
shipping companies using the Port of London;
industries based in the Port of London; the
regeneration of the Docklands since 1981 *Archvs:*
minute bks of the private dock companies (1799-
1900); minute bks of the Corp of London River
Cttee (1770-1857); minute bks of the Thames
Conservancy (1857-1909); minute bks of the Port
of London Authority (1909 onwards); records of the
Docklands Forum; some records of the London
Docklands Development Corp; misc records
relating to the Port of London & Docklands *Other:*
substantial photo & slide colln; map colln
Equip: fax, copier *Svcs:* info, photographic & film
svc
Stock: bks/5000; photos/40000; slides/10000;
pamphs/2500; maps/500; audios/350; videos/20;
archvs/4000 sq ft
Pubns: Docklands Life, 1860-1970 (£20);
London's Riverscape, Lost & Found (£15); City of
Ships (video, £12); Waters of Time (video, £12)
Staff: Libns: 1 *Exp:* £2600 (1999-2000)

S1115

Dr Johnson's House, Library

17 Gough Sq, London, EC4A 3DE (*tel & fax:* 020-
7353-3745)
Email: curator@drjh.dircon.co.uk

Type: charity *Chief:* Curator of House: Mrs
Natasha McEnroe
Entry: ref only, adv appt *Open:* Mon-Sat 1100-
1730 (-1700 Oct-April); closed bank hols
Subj: lang; arts; lit; hist *Collns: Bks & Pamphs:*
1st eds of Dr Johnson's Dictionary *Other:* letters &
prints
Stock: bks/1200

S1116

Dr Williams' Library

14 Gordon Sq, London, WC1H 0AG (020-7387-
3727; *fax:* 020-7388-1142)
Email: enquiries@dwlib.co.uk

Gov Body: Dr Williams' Trust *Chief:* Dir: Dr
David L. Wykes
Assoc Libs: also administers the
CONGREGATIONAL LIB (see **S1099**)
Entry: ref only for non-membs; adv appt advised,
proof of ID required *Open:* Mon1000-1700, Wed,
Fri 1000-1730, Tue, Thu 1000-1830; closed Xmas
& Easter
Subj: at postgrad level: religion; theology; hist;
ecclesiastical hist; phil; lit *Collns: Bks & Pamphs:*
Norman Baynes Colln (Byzantine hist & culture);
pre-19C works relating to English nonconformity
Archvs: MSS relating to the hist of nonconformity in
England
Equip: m-reader, copier
Pubns: numerous lists of accessions; occasional
papers, lectures etc
Staff: Libns: 4

S1117

Dulwich College, Wodehouse Library

London, SE21 7LD (020-8299-9244; *fax:* 020-
8299-9245)
Email: library@dulwich.org.uk
Internet: http://library.dulwich.org.uk/

Gov Body: Governors of Dulwich Coll (Alleyn's
Coll of God's Gift) *Chief:* Head of Lib: Ms A.M.
Bradnock BA, DipLib, MCLIP

Assoc Libs: JNR SCHOOL LIB, Libn: Mrs A.E.
Dawson DipLib, MCLIP; LOWER SCHOOL LIB,
Libn: Mrs L. Ellis-Brrett BA, MSc; MASTER'S LIB;
DULWICH COLL ARCHVS, Archivist: Dr J.R.
Piggott (all at above addr)
Entry: adv appt for Archvs; school time for others
Open: term: Mon-Fri 0815-1730
Subj: all subjs; GCSE; A level; all subjs relating to
boys' edu, age 7 years upwards *Collns: Archvs:*
Edward Alleyn (Founder of Dulwich Coll); P.G.
Wodehouse; Sir Ernest Shackleton (photos & other
memorabilia: his whaler, James Caird, is on display
in West Cloister); Barry Phelps Colln; Elizabethan
theatre; documents relating to the Manor of
Dulwich *Co-op Schemes:* BLDSC
Equip: video viewer, fax, copier, clr copier, 22
computers (all with wd-proc, internet & CD-ROM),
2 TVs, 1 CD player
Stock: bks/37541; periodcls/115; pamphs/327;
audios/1041; videos/1038, incl DVDs
Classn: DDC *Auto Sys:* ALICS (own)
Staff: Libns: 3 *Non-Prof:* 1.7

S1118 +

Eastman Dental Institute for Oral Healthcare Sciences, Library and Information Centre

256 Gray's Inn Rd, London, WC1X 8LD (020-
7915-1045/1262; *fax:* 020-7915-1147)
Email: IC@eastman.ucl.ac.uk
Internet: http://www.eastman.ucl.ac.uk/

Gov Body: Univ of London (see **S1440**) *Chief:*
Libn: Ms Heather Lodge BLib, MSc, MCLIP *Dep:*
Lib Assts: Mrs Sally Jacobs & Mr John Evans BSc,
MLib
Entry: membs only; ref use only for others on
payment of £10 pd *Open:* Mon-Thu 0800-2000,
Fri 0800-1730, Sat 1100-1500 (-1900 in May, Jun &
Sep)
Subj: dentistry; oral medicine *Co-op Schemes:*
BLDSC, reciprocal arrangements with UCL libs
Equip: m-reader, copier, computers (incl wd-proc
& CD-ROM) *Online:* Datastar, Medline, Embase
Svcs: info, ref, biblio, indexing, abstracting
Stock: bks/2500; periodcls/100; pamphs/600; m-
forms/50; videos/30
Classn: own
Pubns: Lib Update Newsletter (free)
Staff: Libns: 2 *Non-Prof:* 1

S1119

The Egypt Exploration Society Library

3 Doughty Mews, London, WC1N 2PG (020-7242-
2266; *fax:* 020-7404-6118)
Email: eeslibrary@talk21.com
Internet: http://www.ees.ac.uk/

Gov Body: Egypt Exploration Soc *Chief:* Libn: Mr
Chris Naunton BA, MPhil *Dep:* Sec: Dr Patricia
Spencer
Assoc Libs: EGYPT EXPLORATION SOC
EXCAVATIONS ARCHVS, at same addr, contact
Dr Patricia Spencer (020-7242-1880)
Entry: membs during opening hrs, non-membs
with permission of governing body; membership is
open to anyone with an interest in ancient Egypt
(contact Soc for subscription details); special Lib
Membership also available for academic instns
Open: Mon-Fri 1030-1245, 1415-1630
Subj: Egyptology; Graeco-Roman Egypt; Christian
Egypt
Equip: copier (10p) *Svcs:* info, ref
Stock: bks/c11000; slides/4000
Staff: Libns: 1 *Non-Prof:* 2 *Exp:* £2000 (1999-
2000)

S1120
Embassy of Finland, Press and Information Office
38 Chesham Pl, London, SW1X 8HN (020-7838-6200; *fax:* 020-7235-3680)
Internet: http://www.finemb.org.uk/

Gov Body: Ministry for Foreign Affairs, Finland
Chief: Press & Info Offcrs: Ms P. Pellinen & Mrs L. Linnoila
Open: Mon-Fri 0830-1630
Subj: Finland: generalities; religion; Finnish lang; tech; Finnish arts; Finnish lit; Finnish hist; Finnish geog *Collns: Bks & Pamphs:* bks & leaflets related to Finland
Svcs: info
Stock: bks/some bks, photos, slides, pamphs, maps, audios, videos & CD-ROMs

S1121 ♀
Engineering Employers' Federation Library
Broadway House, Tothill St, London, SW1H 9NQ (020-7654-1572/4; *fax:* 020-7222-2782)
Internet: http://www.eef.org.uk/

Chief: Libn: Ms Jean Bennett (jbennett@eef-fed.org.uk) *Other Snr Staff:* Ms Catherine Rochester (crochester@eef-fed.org.uk) & Ms Debbie Howard (dhoward@eef-fed.org.uk)
Subj: eng; industry; employment affairs; business; mgmt; health & safety; industrial relations; company info
Equip: copier *Svcs:* info, ref, current awareness
Stock: bks/c15000; periodcls/c250
Pubns: elec newsletter (9 pa)
Staff: 3 in total

S1122 ♔
English Heritage Library
Room B1, 23 Savile Row, London, W1X 1AB (020-7973-3031; *fax:* 020-7973-3001)
Email: library@english-heritage.org.uk
Internet: http://www.english-heritage.org.uk/

Chief: Libn: Ms Catherine Phillpotts BA, MCLIP
Dep: Asst Libn: Ms Sally England MA
Assoc Libs: ENGLISH HERITAGE PHOTO LIB, at same addr, contact Ms Celia Sterne (020-7973-3338/9; *fax:* 020-7973-3027; *email:* celia.sterne@english-heritage.org.uk); NATL MONUMENTS RECORD CENTRE LIB (see **A483**)
Entry: adv appt necessary, bona fide rsrchers only
Open: Mon-Tue, Thu-Fri 0900-1700, Wed 1000-1700
Subj: museology; curatorship; civil eng; bldg; fine art; arch; interiors; design; planning; gardens; archaeo; hist; conservation
Equip: 2 m-readers, 2 m-printers, 6 computers (incl 3 with wd-proc, 4 with internet & 3 with CD-ROM) *Svcs:* ref
Stock: bks/43000; periodcls/500; illusts/3000; maps/30; m-forms/500; videos/200 *Acqs Offcr:* Libn, as above
Classn: UDC *Auto Sys:* Adlib
Staff: Libns: 2 *Non-Prof:* 1 *Exp:* £81000 (1999-2000)

S1123 ♀
English-Speaking Union, Page Memorial Library
Dartmouth House, 37 Charles St, London, W1J 5ED (020-7529-1550; *fax:* 020-7495-6108)
Email: esu@esu.org
Internet: http://www.esu.org/

Chief: Librarian/Info Offcr: Ms Andrea K. Wathern BA(Hons), DipLib
Entry: genl public by appt for ref only, borrowing restricted to membs, ILL & Schools Loans Scheme
Open: Mon-Fri 1000-1700
Subj: social sci; English lang; arts; lit; hist (emphasis is on the USA which accounts for approx 80% of the stock; some Commonwealth material, esp from New Zealand) *Collns: Bks & Pamphs:* Adlai Stevenson Colln *Archvs:* archvs of the ESU from 1918 onwards *Co-op Schemes:* BLDSC, ILL, Books-Across-The-Sea
Equip: copier, room for hire *Svcs:* info, ref
Stock: bks/12000; periodcls/30; videos/40
Classn: DDC *Auto Sys:* in-house sys
Pubns: Quarterly Accessions List (free); annotated reading guides on subjs in stock (free)
Staff: Libns: 1 *Exp:* £2000 (1999-2000)

S1124 ♔
European Parliament, Library
2 Queen Anne's Gate, London, SW1H 9AA (020-7227-4300; *fax:* 020-7227-4301)
Email: eplondon@europarl.eu.int
Internet: http://www.europarl.org.uk/

Type: EC *Chief:* Libn: Mrs Avis Furness
Entry: open to public; adv appt for complicated queries *Open:* Mon-Fri 1000-1300, 1400-1700
Subj: European Parliament *Collns: Other:* reports, debates & minutes of European Parliament from 1973
Equip: m-reader, copier, computer (with internet); all at discretion of libn
Stock: bks/150; periodcls/2
Pubns: free info pubns on European Parliament
Staff: Non-Prof: 1

S1125 ♀🙏
The Evangelical Library Ltd
78a Chiltern St, London, W1U 5HB (020-7935-6997)
Email: stlibrary@aol.com
Internet: http://evangelical-library.org.uk/

Chief: Libn: S.J. Taylor BA, DipLib
Entry: ref only for non-membs, borrowing restricted to membs *Open:* Mon-Sat 1000-1700
Subj: Christian lit; biography; doctrine; church hist etc
Equip: copier *Svcs:* info, ref, biblio
Stock: bks/80000; periodcls/120; photos/2000, incl illusts; slides/23 sets; audios/50
Classn: Sayer
Pubns: In Writing (magazine, free to membs); Lib Catalogues (15p-70p); Annual Lectures (15p-£1.99); Classn Scheme (25p); Lib Hist (30p)
Staff: Libns: 1 *Non-Prof:* 3

S1126 ♀🏛
The Fan Museum Library
12 Grooms Hill, Greenwich, London, SE10 8ER (020-8305-1441; *fax:* 020-8293-1889)
Email: admin@fan-museum.org

Type: charitable trust *Gov Body:* The Fan Museum Trust *Chief:* Curator & Dir: Mrs Helène Alexander FRSA
Entry: adv appt only *Open:* Mon-Fri 1100-1700
Subj: fans; hist of fans

Equip: fax, copier, clr copier, 3 computers (all with wd-proc & internet) *Svcs:* info, ref
Stock: bks/300; periodcls/1000; photos/2000; slides/550; pamphs/500 *Acqs Offcr:* Curator & Dir, as above
Pubns: Fan Directory of Great Britain (£5); Fans, by Helène Alexander (£4.50); Dictionary of Fan Painters (in preparation)
Staff: Other Prof: 4

S1127 ♀🎓
The Feminist Library and Resource Centre
5-5a Westminster Bridge Rd, Southwark, London, SE1 7XW (020-7928-7789)
Email: FeministLibrary@beeb.net

Type: registered charity *Gov Body:* Feminist Lib Mgmt Cttee *Chief:* run by volunteers
Entry: women only, membership fee (sliding scale) *Open:* Tue 1100-2000, Wed 1500-2000, Sat 1400-1700 (closed Aug)
Subj: GCSE & A-level; undergrad; postgrad; phil; psy; religion; social sci; arts; lit; women's studies; feminism *Collns: Archvs:* Women's Liberation Movement (1960s-date) *Other:* papers & dissertations on various feminist subjs; various posters & ephemera
Equip: copier *Svcs:* info, ref, biblio, indexing, readings, discussion groups, social events
Stock: bks/c10000; periodcls/1500; pamphs/1750; archvs/60 cubic m; articles/1200
Pubns: Feminist Lib Newsletter (quarterly, sliding scale for subscriptions)
Staff: Non-Prof: 6-12 volunteers

S1128 🌿/🎥
Film Images (London) Ltd
2 The Quadrant, 135 Salusbury Rd, London, NW6 6RJ (020-7624-3388; *fax:* 020-7624-3377)
Email: research@film-images.com
Internet: http://www.film-images.com/

Chief: Mgr: Ms Angela Saward BA, MA MTA
Dep: Acqs & Processing Co-ordinator: Ms Ginny Harrold BA
Assoc Libs: COI FOOTAGE FILE (Govt's AV archive/lib)
Entry: business only; public upon payment of a fee *Open:* Mon-Fri 0930-1700
Subj: all genres of film-making from 1890s-date, worldwide *Collns: Archvs:* COI Footage File (UK Govt); Overseas Film & TV Centre (Africa); historic films (newsreels, music)
Equip: 8 video viewers, 16mm & 35mm Steenbecks *Disabled:* wheelchair access *Online:* online catalogue (free) *Officer-in-Charge:* Acqs & Processing Co-ordinator, as above *Svcs:* info, ref, licensing
Stock: videos/10000 *Acqs Offcr:* Acqs & Processing Co-ordinator, as above
Classn: in-house sys *Staff: Other Prof:* 4

S1129 🌿/
Financial Times Library
1 Southwark Bridge, London, SE1 9HL (020-7873-3920; *fax:* 020-7873-4854)
Email: sara.margetts@ft.com

Chief: Lib Mgr: Ms Sara Margetts
Assoc Libs: FT READERS ENQ SVC (020-7873-4211; *fax:* 020-7873-3084)
Entry: internal staff only
Subj: finance; business statistics & biographies; companies; industries; markets; current affairs
Equip: Online: Lexis-Nexis, Factiva, Dialog, Datastar, KnowUK *Svcs:* info, ref
Stock: bks/2000; periodcls/200

S1130
Firepower – The Royal Artillery Museum, James Clavell Library

Royal Arsenal (West), Warren Ln, Woolwich, London, SE18 6ST (020-8312-7125; *fax:* 020-8855-7100)
Email: research@firepower.org.uk
Internet: http://www.firepower.org.uk/

Gov Body: administered by the museum on behalf of the Royal Artillery Historical Trust *Chief:* Libn: Mr Maurice Evans BSc *Other Snr Staff:* Historical Sec: Lt Col W.A.H. Townend RA; Rsrcher: Mr Matthew Buck MA; Administrative Offcr: Ms Jill Lindsey
Entry: adv appt with the Libn; a fee may be charged; lib closed until Nov 2003 *Open:* Wed-Thu 1000-1600; reduced svc from 1230-1330 & no svc after 1530
Subj: local study (Woolwich); military eng; artillery; warfare; tactics; training; fortification; military hist; military geog; military biography; regimental hist (Royal Artillery); regimental records; personal papers *Collns: Bks & Pamphs:* bks, periodcls & other publ works (16C-date) on artillery from the 13C onwards *Archvs:* archvs of the Regiment of Artillery (1716-date), incl unit war diaries for both World Wars; Genl Sir Robert Biddulph papers; Genl Sir Robert Gardiner papers (1781-1864); Lt Genl John Lefroy papers (1817-1890); Lt Genl Samuel Cleveland Colln; Major Genl Sir Alexander Dickson MSS (1777-1840); Major A.F. Becke papers (1871-1947); papers & diaries of indiv ex-membs of the Regiment of all ranks *Other:* Royal Artillery photo colln (incl images from Crimean War & Chinese War of 1860)
Equip: copier (A4/20p, A3/25p)
Stock: bks/5000+ collns
Auto Sys: Adlib *Staff: Libns:* 1
Further Info: The Lib is closed until Nov 2003 during Phase 2 of the Museum's expansion

S1131
The Football Association Library

25 Soho Sq, London, W1D 4FA (020-7704-4000; *fax:* 020-7402-0486)
Email: info@thefa.com
Internet: http://www.thefa.com/

Gov Body: The Football Assoc *Chief:* Libn & Historian: Mr David Barber
Entry: ref only, adv appt *Open:* Mon-Fri 0900-1700
Subj: assoc football *Equip:* copier *Svcs:* info, ref
Stock: bks/c3000

S1132
Foreign and Commonwealth Office Library

King Charles St, London, SW1A 2AL (020-7270-3925; *fax:* 020-7270-3270)
Email: library.historical@fco.gov.uk
Internet: http://www.fco.gov.uk/

Chief: Chief Libn: Mr Stephen Latham
Assoc Libs: LEGAL LIB, at same addr (see S1133)
Entry: public access by appt only *Open:* Mon-Fri 0930-1730
Subj: internatl relations; diplomacy; politics; hist; law of overseas countries *Collns: Bks & Pamphs:* British overseas territories legislation *Other:* photo colln *Co-op Schemes:* BLDSC
Equip: m-film reader, m-fiche reader, m-printer, fax, copier *Svcs:* info, ref
Stock: bks/500000; periodcls/850; photos/35000; pamphs/some; maps/some
Classn: LC *Auto Sys:* Unicorn
Staff: Libns: 26 *Non-Prof:* 14

S1133
Foreign and Commonwealth Office, Legal Library

King Charles St, London, SW1A 2AH (020-7270-3050/82; *fax:* 020-7270-4529)
Email: library.legal@fco.gov.uk

Chief: Libn: Mrs Susan Halls BA(Hons), MCLIP
Assoc Libs: FOREIGN & COMMONWEALTH OFFICE LIB, at same addr (see S1132)
Entry: by appt (only on special grounds); written & tel enqs *Open:* Mon-Fri 0930-1730
Subj: internatl & UK law; EU law; British Overseas Territories laws *Collns: Other:* treaties: bilateral & multilateral
Equip: fax, copier, computers (incl wd-proc & CD-ROM) *Online:* Lexis, Celex, Justis
Stock: bks/15000; periodcls/100; pamphs/200
Classn: Moys *Auto Sys:* Unicorn
Staff: Libns: 2 *Non-Prof:* 2

S1134
FPA Library and Information Centre

2-12 Pentonville Rd, London, N1 9FP (020-7923-5228; *fax:* 020-7837-3034)
Email: library&information@fpa.org.uk
Internet: http://www.fpa.org.uk/

Gov Body: FPA (Family Planning Assoc) *Chief:* Info & Lib Mgr: Ms Margaret McGovern BA *Other Snr Staff:* Info & Lib Offcr: Mr Paul Minter
Entry: by appt, ref only *Open:* Mon-Fri 0900-1700
Subj: family planning; sexual behaviour & relationships; contraception & reproductive tech & sexual health *Collns: Archvs:* FPA archvs are held at the Archvs & Manuscripts Dept, Wellcome Inst (see S1457)
Equip: copier
Stock: bks/2000; periodcls/100
Classn: own *Auto Sys:* Headfast
Pubns: 15 Factsheets (£1 each); Leaflet (free)
Staff: Libns: 2 *Exp:* £6000 (1999-2000)

S1135
Francis Skaryna Belarusian Library and Museum

37 Holden Rd, London, N12 8HS (*tel & fax:* 020-8445-5358)
Email: library@skaryna.org
Internet: http://www.skaryna.org/

Type: rsrch *Gov Body:* Board of Trustees *Chief:* Libn: Rev Alexander Nelson
Entry: adv appt
Subj: all aspects of Belarus; generalities; phil; psy; religion; social sci; lang; sci; arts; lit; geneography; hist; holdings are mainly in Belarusian, with some pubns in English, Russian, Polish, French & German *Collns: Archvs:* MSS relating to Belarus church hist & the Belarus Diaspora *Other:* museum collns, incl maps, coins, postage stamps, folk arts & crafts
Equip: m-readers, copier (5p per pg), fax, computer (with wd-proc, internet & CD-ROM), accommodation facilities (for limited duration) for overseas users *Svcs:* info, ref
Stock: bks/25000; periodcls/30
Classn: own *Staff: Non-Prof:* 2
Further Info: The Lib holds the largest colln of Belarusian bks & periodcls outside Belarus

S1136
French Protestant Church of London Library

8-9 Soho Sq, London, W1V 5DD (020-7437-5311; *fax:* 020-7434-4579)
Email: eglisoho@globalnet.co.uk

Gov Body: French Protestant Church of London
Entry: by adv appt only *Open:* Mon-Fri 0900-1700
Subj: Bibles & Psalters; Biblical exegesis; sermons; works of early Christian fathers & of Reformation figs; lit (esp classical authors); a few works on medicine, gardening, maths etc *Collns: Archvs:* Act bks; accounts; poor relief; membership & other records of the church (originally located in Threadneedle St, 1560-date, excl pre-1840 registers of baptisms & marriages)
Equip: m-reader (m-films of own archvs only), copier
Stock: bks/1470; periodcls/5; photos/2 vols; archvs/350 MSS, 20 boxes of loose papers, plus c40 boxes recent acqs
Pubns: Archvs of the French Protestant Church of London: A Handlist (£15, obtainable from: The Huguenot Soc, Univ Coll, London, WC1E 6BT, not from FPCL); The French Protestant Church of London & the Huguenots: From the Church's Foundation to the Present Day (£4)
Staff: Other Prof: 1

S1137
Freud Museum, Library and Archives

20 Maresfield Gdns, Hampstead, London, NW3 5SX (020-7435-2002/5167; *fax:* 020-7431-5452)
Email: freud@gn.apc.org
Internet: http://www.freud.org.uk/

Chief: Libn: Mr Keith Davies
Assoc Libs: FREUD MUSEUM PICTURE LIB, at same addr, contact Mr Michael Molnar
Entry: open to serious rsrchers, by adv appt in writing with the Libn *Open: Museum:* Wed-Sun 1200-1700
Subj: Sigmund Freud; hist of psychoanalysis
Collns: Bks & Pamphs: largest remaining part of Freud's personal lib (1600+ titles, incl offprints & journals); rsrch lib (hist, theory & culture of psychoanalysis), incl working lib bequeathed by Anna Freud & bks left by Dorothy Burlingham *Archvs:* personal papers of Sigmund Freud (mainly copies, incl correspondence); papers of Anna Freud *Other:* Freud Museum Picture Lib (commercial picture lib), incl: Archv Colln (4000+ b&w images); Museum Colln (clr transparencies of Museum & collns)

S1138
The Friends of the Children of Great Ormond Street Library

Inst of Child Health, 30 Guilford St, London, WC1N 1EH (020-7242-9789 x2424; *fax:* 020-7831-0488)
Internet: http://www.ich.ucl.ac.uk/library/

Gov Body: Univ Coll London (see S1433) *Chief:* Libn: Mr John Clarke MA, DipLib *Dep:* Asst Libn: Ms Susan Holloway BA(Hons), MA, MCLIP
Entry: not open to genl public; admittance for ref only at discretion of Libn *Open:* Mon-Fri 0900-1800
Subj: paediatrics *Collns: Bks & Pamphs:* Centre for Internatl Child Care Resource Centre: materials on internatl child health, maternal-child health, disability; TALC – Teaching Aids at Low Cost: bks publ by Friends of the Children of Great Ormond St *Co-op Schemes:* BLDSC, Univ of London
Equip: m-reader, video viewer, 2 copiers, clr copier, 8 computers (incl 7 internet & 7 CD-ROM)
Online: wide range of networked databases for registered membs
Stock: bks/15000; periodcls/230; slides/50; pamphs/1500; videos/120
Classn: NLM *Auto Sys:* Unicorn
Pubns: Teaching Aids at Low Cost (various titles)
Staff: Libns: 3 *Non-Prof:* 1

S1139 ♀

Garrick Club Library

Garrick St, London, WC2E 9AY (020-7836-1737; *fax:* 020-7379-5966)
Internet: http://www.garrickclub.co.uk/

Chief: Libn: Ms Enid Foster MBE
Entry: bona fide rsrchers only; apply in writing to Libn, stating subj of rsrch; a fee of £5 is charged; additional fee may be charged for excess use of facilities *Open:* Wed 1000-1300, 1400-1700
Subj: British drama & the theatre; particularly strong in theatrical hist of late 18C & early 19C
Collns: Archvs: letters, prints, playbills & theatre programmes (18C & 19C)
Stock: many bks & pamphs *Staff:* 1 Libn

S1140 ♀ ✍

Garry Weston Library

(formerly Southwark Diocesan Training Lib)
Millenium Bldgs, Montague Cl, London, SE1 9DA (020-7407-3708 x216)

Gov Body: Diocese of Southwark *Chief:* Libn: Canon Dr Jeffrey John
Open: Mon 0845-1230, Thu 1430-1900
Subj: religion *Stock:* bks/5000 *Classn:* DDC
Staff: Non-Prof: 1 *Exp:* £1500 (1999-2000)

S1141 🏛

Geffrye Museum, Reference Library and Archives

Kingsland Rd, London, E2 8EA (020-7739-9893; *fax:* 020-7729-5647)
Email: info@geffrye-museum.org.uk
Internet: http://www.geffrye-museum.org.uk/

Gov Body: DCMS (see **S1108**)
Entry: adv appt *Open:* Tue-Fri 1000-1700
Subj: local study (East London furniture industry); design hist; English domestic interiors; furniture
Collns: Archvs: relating to the furniture trade, incl trade catalogues; Interiors Archv
Equip: copier, room for hire *Svcs:* info, ref
Stock: bks/10000; periodcls/10; photos/1000; slides/500
Auto Sys: MODES Plus *Staff: Other Prof:* 4

S1142 ♀ ✍

The General Conference of the New Church Library

Swedenborg House, 20 Bloomsbury Way, London, WC1A 2TH (020-7229-9340)

Chief: Sec, Lib & Archvs Cttee: Mrs Frances Fisher
Assoc Libs: New Church Coll Lib, 25 Radcliffe New Rd, Radcliffe, Manchester, M26 1LE (0161-766-2521; *fax:* 0161-796-1142), Administrative Asst: Mrs Anne Cansell
Entry: for ref by appt only *Open:* lib is not normally staffed & is accessible by appt only
Subj: material related to the New Church, its hist & teachings & material by & about Emanuel Swedenborg *Collns: Archvs:* minute bks, registers etc of our various local churches & other associated insts & socs; minute bks etc of the Genl Conference

Equip: computer (with wd-proc)
Stock: bks/2000; periodcls/4; pamphs/1000; archvs/100 ft; some photos, slides, audios, videos
Staff: Non-Prof: 1 PT

S1143 ♀

The Geological Society of London Library

Burlington House, Piccadilly, London, W1J 0BG (020-7432-0999; *fax:* 020-7439-3470)
Email: library@geolsoc.org.uk
Internet: http://www.geolsoc.org.uk/

Type: learned soc *Gov Body:* Geological Soc
Chief: Chief Libn: Miss S. Meredith *Dep:* Asst Libn: Miss W.A. Cawthorne BSc(Hons), DipLib
Other Snr Staff: Archivist: Mr Andrew Mussell BA(Hons), DipAS
Entry: ref only access, by appt *Open:* Mon-Fri 0930-1730
Subj: earth scis; geol & related subjs *Collns: Archvs:* material relating to the Soc's hist & membership, incl papers of eminent 19C geologists such as R.I. Murchison & G.B. Greenough *Co-op Schemes:* BLDSC
Equip: m-reader, fax, copier, computer (with CD-ROM)
Stock: bks/300000; periodcls/800; maps/35000
Classn: UDC *Auto Sys:* C2
Pubns: Lib Guide
Staff: Libns: 4 *Other Prof:* 0.2 *Non-Prof:* 1.8

S1144 🎓

German Historical Institute Library

17 Bloomsbury Sq, London, WC1A 2NJ (020-7309-2019/22; *fax:* 020-7404-5573)
Email: library-ghil@ghil.co.uk
Internet: http://www.ghil.co.uk/

Chief: Libns: Ms Anna Maria Klauk & Mr Christoph Schönberger
Entry: ref only; passport photo & proof of addr required for reader's ticket *Open:* Mon, Thu 1000-2000, Tue-Wed, Fri 1000-1700; closed from May 2003 for renovation
Subj: German hist (Reformation-present day); English hist; historiography; Anglo-German relations; auxiliary subjs only: phil; psy; social sci
Collns: Bks & Pamphs: special colln on hist of Eastern Europe & Communism; Working Class Movement Colln
Equip: m-reader, m-printer, copier, 2 computers
Stock: bks/c60000; periodcls/180; pamphs/300; m-forms/60
Classn: own *Auto Sys:* Allegro
Pubns: Pubns of the German Historical Inst; Studies of the German Historical Inst; Bulletin; Annual Lecture; Periodicals List (as of Jul 1998, free)
Staff: Libns: 2 *Other Prof:* 1
Proj: renovation of lib, necessitating closure of lib from May 2003 until completion

S1145 ☕

German-British Chamber of Industry and Commerce, Marketing Services

Mecklenburg House, 16 Buckingham Gate, London, SW1E 6LB (020-7976-4100; *fax:* 020-7976-4101)
Email: mail@ahk-london.co.uk
Internet: http://www.ahk-london.co.uk/

Chief: Marketing Mgr: Mr Sven Riemann BA, MBA
Entry: internal staff only; no public access, but enqs accepted by phone, fax or letter *Open:* Mon-Fri 0900-1700
Subj: Anglo-German commerce *Svcs:* info
Stock: bks/220; CD-ROMs/various

Pubns: initiative (bi-monthly magazine, membs free, non-membs £20 pa); Membership Directory 1999-2000 (membs free, extra copy £15, non-membs £70); conference packs; various others, list available
Staff: Other Prof: 3

S1146 ♀

Glass and Glazing Federation, Library

44-48 Borough High St, London, SE1 1XB (020-7403-7177; *fax:* 020-7357-7458)
Email: info@ggf.org.uk
Internet: http://www.ggf.org.uk/

Chief: Head of Public Relations: Ms Catherine Hogan
Entry: membs only
Subj: subjs related to glass & glazing trade
Collns: Bks & Pamphs: GGF Info leaflets; Annual Reports; glazing manuals; data sheets
Stock: pamphs/10000
Pubns: Fire Resistant Glazing: Basic Info (55p each); Glazing With Plastics (40p each); The Strength & Safety of Toughened Glass (video, £12 each + VAT); numerous others incl data sheets, leaflets & videos
Staff: Libns: 1

S1147 ♀

Goethe-Institut Inter Nationes Library

50 Princes Gate, London, SW7 2PH (*issue desk:* 020-7596-4040; *enqs:* 020-7596-4044; *fax:* 020-7594-0230)
Email: library@london.goethe.org
Internet: http://www.goethe.de/gr/lon/enibib.htm

Chief: Chief Libn: Ms Gerlinde Buck *Dep:* Dep Libn: Ms S. Muehlen
Assoc Libs: GOETHE-INSTITUT LIB, Glasgow (see **S709**); GOETHE-INSTITUT LIB, Dublin (see **IS80**)
Entry: open to public for ref; borrowing for membs only, proof of addr required for membership (fees vary, conc available) *Open:* Mon-Thu 1200-2000, Sat 1100-1700
Subj: Germany; German lit; arts; social sci; lang
Co-op Schemes: ILL
Equip: video viewer, copier (A4/10p, A3/20p), 6 computer (with internet & CD-ROM, membs only)
Stock: bks/22000; periodcls/126; audios/600; videos/1300; CD-ROMs/175
Classn: UDC *Staff: Libns:* 2 *Non-Prof:* 3

S1148 🎓

Goldsmiths' College Library

New Cross, London, SE14 6NW (020-7919-7150; *fax:* 020-7919-7165)
Email: library@gold.ac.uk
Internet: http://libweb.gold.ac.uk/

Gov Body: Univ of London (see **S1440**) *Chief:* Dir of Info Svcs: Ms Joan G. Pateman *Dep:* Dep Libn: Mrs I.A. Shaw BSc, MPhil, MCLIP
Entry: ref only; day or vac ticket appl must be completed & ID shown at lib entrance; day tickets only issued in term time & only if good case accepted *Open:* term & Easter vac: Mon-Fri 0915-2045, Sat 0930-1700 (term only), Sun 1130-1700 (term only); vac: Mon-Fri 0915-1645
Subj: generalities; phil; psy; religion; social sci; lang; arts; lit; hist *Collns: Bks & Pamphs:* A.L. Lloyd Colln (ethnomusicology); McColl/Seeger Colln (folk music); Marlowe Soc Colln; Alan Bush Colln (music scores); Centre for Russian Music Colln; Stevens Colln (music of Monteverdi)
Archvs: Serge Prokofiev Archv (see **A344**); Natl Campaign for the Arts Archv *Co-op Schemes:* BLDSC, LAMDA, SEAL

Equip: 3 m-form reader/printers (A4/12p), 6 copiers (A4/6p), clr copier, video viewers (Coll membs only), computers (Coll membs only) *Online:* available to Coll membs only *Svcs:* ref *Stock:* bks/250000; periodcls/1400; slides/130000; maps/1199; m-forms/9500; audios/10000; videos/11000; archvs/98 linear m
Classn: DDC *Auto Sys:* Aleph
Staff: Libns: 10.8 *Non-Prof:* 22

S1149

The Goldsmiths' Company Library

Goldsmiths' Hall, Foster Ln, London, EC2V 6BN (020-7606-7010; *fax:* 020-7606-1511)
Email: the.library@thegoldsmiths.co.uk
Internet: http://www.thegoldsmiths.co.uk/

Gov Body: Worshipful Company of Goldsmiths
Chief: Libn: Mr D.A. Beasley BA, MCLIP *Dep:* Asst to the Libn: Miss Jane Bradley BA
Entry: adv appt *Open:* Mon-Fri 1000-1645
Subj: hist of assaying & hallmarking; hist of gold & silver; goldsmithing; jewellery & applied arts
Collns: Bks & Pamphs: Twining Colln (Crown jewels & regalia) *Archvs:* Worshipful Company of Goldsmiths, incl the London Assay Office
Stock: bks/7000; periodcls/68; photos/10000; slides/5000; videos/17
Classn: own *Staff:* Libns: 1 *Non-Prof:* 2

S1150

Gray's Inn Library

5 South Sq, Gray's Inn, London, WC1R 5ET (020-7458-7822; *fax:* 020-7458-7850)
Email: Library.Information@graysinn.org.uk
Internet: http://www.graysinn.org.uk/

Gov Body: The Honourable Soc of Gray's Inn
Chief: Libn: Mrs T. Thom MA, MCLIP
Entry: membs of the Bar of England & Wales; membs of Gray's Inn; other profs on payment of a fee; postgrad scholars by arrangement & at discretion of Libn *Open:* term: generally Mon-Fri 0900-2000; call or check web site for variations
Subj: English law *Collns: Bks & Pamphs:* colln on public internatl law *Archvs:* records of Gray's Inn (mid-16C onwards); papers of Lord Atkin *Co-op Schemes:* Inter-Inn Stock Specialisation Scheme, BLDSC (photocopies only)
Equip: m-reader, m-printer (8p per sheet), 3 copiers, computers (incl 8 with wd-proc, 1 with CD-ROM & 13 with internet, printouts 8p per sheet)
Online: Lawtel, Lexis, Butterworth Direct (all England law reports & EU), Justis Case Law, Statutory Material & European Law, Jordans UK Human Rights & Family Law Reports *Officer-in-Charge:* Libn, as above *Svcs:* info, ref
Stock: bks/50000; periodcls/300 *Acqs Offcr:* Libn, as above
Auto Sys: Unicorn *Staff:* Libns: 3 *Non-Prof:* 3

S1151

Greater London Authority Research Library

City Hall, The Queen's Walk, London, SE1 2AA (020-7983-4455; *fax:* 020-7983-4674)
Email: RLinfo@london.gov.uk
Internet: http://www.london.gov.uk/

Type: local govt *Chief:* Head of Rsrch Lib: Ms Annabel Davies BA(Hons), MCLIP *Dep:* Info Svcs Mgr: Mr Andy Land BA(Hons), PGDip, MCLIP
Entry: open to GLA staff & membs; also Function Body staff, London borough offcrs & councillors (by appt), Lib membs (by appt); not open to membs of the public *Open:* Mon-Fri 0900-1730
Subj: social policy; local govt; transport; environment; urban & regional planning; culture; economic development; housing; econ *Co-op Schemes:* BLDSC

Svcs: info, ref
Stock: bks/10000; periodcls/400; pamphs/70000
Classn: UDC (for ref bks) *Staff:* 17 in total

S1152

Greenwich Community College, Library and Learning Resources Centre

95 Plumstead Rd, Plumstead, London, SE18 7OQ (020-8488-4813)
Internet: http://www.gcc.ac.uk/

Chief: Learning Centres Mgr: Mrs Heather Wells BSc, MSc, MCLIP (Heatherw@gcc.ac.uk)
Entry: coll students & staff; others by prior arrangement only *Open:* term: Mon-Tue, Thu 0900-1900, Wed 0900-1700, Fri 0900-1600; vac: opening times reduced
Subj: all subjs; genl; GCSE; A level; vocational
Co-op Schemes: BLDSC
Equip: copier (5p per copy) *Disabled:* 17" computer screens, vari-height tables, voice recognition tech, Supernova software, OmniReader etc
Online: Infotrac, NLN, XRefer, Oxford Reference, City Mutual, ECTIS *Svcs:* info, ref, biblio
Stock: bks/c30000; periodcls/100; videos/200; CD-ROMs/70
Classn: DDC *Auto Sys:* Heritage
Staff: Libns: 2.2 *Non-Prof:* 9 *Exp:* £45000 (2000-01)

S1153

Guardian / Observer Research Department Library

119 Farringdon Rd, London, EC1R 3ER (020-7239-9772; *fax:* 020-7239-9532)
Email: richard.nelsson@guardian.co.uk
Internet: http://www.guardian.co.uk/

Type: media *Gov Body:* Guardian Media Group plc *Chief:* Info Mgr: Mr Richard Nelsson PGDipIM
Entry: private; Guardian Media Group employees only; no access to public
Subj: all subjs; genl
Staff: Libns: 8 *Non-Prof:* 4

S1154

Guildhall School of Music and Drama Library

Barbican, London, EC2Y 8DT (020-7382-5281; *fax:* 020-7786-9378)
Internet: http://www.gsmd.ac.uk/

Gov Body: Corp of London (see **P99**) *Chief:* Snr Libn: Mrs Kate Eaton MA, MCLIP (kate.eaton@ gsmd.ac.uk) *Dep:* Dep Libn: Mr Adrian Yardley BA(Hons), PGDip, MCLIP (adrian.yardley@ gsmd.ac.uk) *Other Snr Staff:* Orchestral Libn: Ms Miranda Cramp MA (miranda.cramp@gsmd.ac.uk)
Entry: by adv arrangement for ref only *Open:* term: Mon 0830-1900, Tue-Fri 0900-1900; vac: Mon-Fri 0930-1645 (with closure periods; please check in adv)
Subj: drama; music; theatre hist; acting; technical theatre *Collns: Archvs:* deposited at Corp of London Records Office (see **A270**) *Other:* Appleby Colln of guitar music; Goossens Colln of oboe music; Alkan Soc Colln; Harris Opera Colln *Co-op Schemes:* BLDSC
Equip: not available to public *Svcs:* info, ref
Stock: bks/30000+; periodcls/82; audios/5000+; videos/1000+; music scores/60000+
Classn: McColvin Music Classn, own drama classn *Auto Sys:* Unicorn
Pubns: series of leaflets on lib svcs
Staff: Libns: 5 *Non-Prof:* 1.6 *Exp:* £55000 (2000-01)

S1155

Hackney Community College, Library and Learning Centre

Falkirk St, London, N1 6HQ (020-7613-9282; *fax:* 020-7613-9452)
Internet: http://www.comm-coll-hackney.ac.uk/

Chief: Lib Dir: Ms Brenda Osakwe BA(Hons), MCLIP *Dep:* Libn: Ms Jan Dunster BA(Hons), MCLIP
Assoc Libs: BROOKE HOUSE LIB, Brooke House, Kenninghall Rd, London, E5 8BP, Libn: Ms Jan Dunster, as above
Entry: by appt *Open:* Mon-Thu 0845-1900; Fri 0845-1700
Subj: all subjs; genl; GCSE; A level; vocational; *Brook House:* bldg; construction; ESOL; adult basic edu *Co-op Schemes:* BLDSC
Equip: copier, video viewer, computers (incl wd-proc, internet & CD-ROM) *Svcs:* info, ref
Stock: bks/50000; periodcls/200; videos/400
Classn: DDC *Auto Sys:* LIMES *Staff:* Libns: 6

S1156

Hammersmith and West London College, Hammersmith Learning Centre

Gliddon Rd, Barons Ct, London, W14 9BL (020-8741-1688; *fax:* 020-8741-2491)
Email: cic@hwlc.ac.uk
Internet: http://www.hwlc.ac.uk/

Gov Body: Ealing, Hammersmith & West London Coll *Chief:* Lib Mgr: Ms Sue Bull BA, MCLIP *Dep:* Mr David Evans BMus, MCLIP
Assoc Libs: HAMMERSMITH & WEST LONDON COLL, LIME GROVE LEARNING CENTRE, Lime Grove, London, W12 8EA, Site Libn: Ms Sue Geddes BA, MCLIP; ACTON & WEST LONDON COLL, ACTON LEARNING CENTRE (see **S986**); EALING & WEST LONDON COLL, EALING LEARNING CENTRE, The Green, Ealing, London, W5 5EW; SOUTHALL & WEST LONDON COLL, SOUTHALL LEARNING CENTRE (see **S1937**)
Entry: students of Coll only *Open:* term: Mon-Thu 0900-2030, Fri 0900-1600, Sat 1000-1400
Subj: all subjs; GCSE; A level; vocational
Equip: 18 video viewers, 2 copiers, clr copier, 123 computers (all with wd-proc & CD-ROM, 12 with internet), 3 rooms for hire *Disabled:* print magnifier *Svcs:* info, ref, biblio
Stock: bks & videos/55000; periodcls/220
Classn: DDC *Auto Sys:* EOSi *Staff:* Libns: 6 *Non-Prof:* 12 *Exp:* £71000 (2000-01)

S1157

Health Education Authority, Health Promotion Information Centre

Trevelyan House, 30 Gt Peter St, London, SW1 2HW (020-7413-1995; *fax:* 020-7413-2605)
Email: hpic.enquiry@hea.org.uk
Internet: http://www.hea.org.uk/

Chief: Head of Health Promotion Info Svcs: Ms Catherine Herman
Entry: by adv appt, ref only for those with a prof interest in health promotion *Open:* Mon-Tue, Thu-Fri 1000-1300, 1400-1700, Wed 1400-1700
Subj: health edu & promotion; alcohol; smoking; nutrition; AIDS & sexual health
Equip: video viewer, copier, multimedia PC
Online: own databases: HealthPromis (main database), health related resources for: black & minority ethnic groups, people with learning difficulties, older people, young people, men, database of HEA rsrch pubns *Svcs:* info, ref, abstracting, database searching, current awareness
Stock: bks/16000; periodcls/400; videos/2500; article references/25000
Classn: UDC

London ▼ London
Special Libraries

(Health Edu Authority, Health Promotion Info Centre cont)

Pubns: Journal Articles of Interest to Health Educators; Health Related Resources for Black & Minority Ethnic Groups; Health Related Resources for People with Learning Difficulties; Health Related Resources for Older People

S1158 ✚
Health First Learning Centre

Mary Sheridan House, 15 St Thomas St, London, SE1 9RY (020-7955-4942; *fax:* 020-7378-6789)
Email: learningcentre@chsltr.sthames.nhs.uk
Internet: http://www.healthfirst.org.uk/

Chief: Acting Learning Svcs Mgr: Ms Heidi Fanning
Entry: open to health profs, volunteers, community workers & NHS students working in Lambeth, Southwark, Lewisham, Bexley, Bromley & Greenwich *Open:* Mon 1200-1630, Tue, Thu-Fri 0930-1630, Wed 0930-1830
Subj: health; health promotion; health mgmt
Collns: Other: large video colln
Equip: computers (incl internet) *Online:* various databases *Svcs:* info, internet & rsrch training support, leaflet & poster distribution svc

S1159 ⚷ 🎓
Hellenic and Roman Societies Joint Library and Institute of Classical Studies Library

Senate House, Malet St, London, WC1E 7HU (020-7862-8709; *fax:* 020-7862-3735)
Internet: http://www.sas.ac.uk/icls/

Gov Body: Univ of London (see **S1440**) *Chief:* Libn: Mr C.H. Annis MA, MCLIP (colin.annis@sas.ac.uk) *Dep:* Dep Libn: Mr P.L. Jackson MA, MCLIP (paul.jackson@sas.ac.uk)
Entry: membs of Inst of Classical Studies and/or Hellenic & Roman Socs; otherwise for consultation of unique material or bks not readily available elsewhere (one visit allowed per year) *Open:* term: Mon, Wed, Fri 0930-1800, Tue, Thu 0930-2000, Sat 1000-1630; vac: Mon-Fri 0930-1800, Sat 1000-1630 (Aug: closed every Sat & for last 2 weeks-early Sept to incl bank hol)
Subj: phil of Greece & Rome; religion of Greece & Rome; hist of the Early Church; anthro of Greece & Rome; sci & maths in Greek & Roman world; tech in Greek & Roman World; the arts of Greece & Rome; geog & hist of Greece & Rome; the whole field of classical antiquity, incl also archaeo, epigraphy & papyrology of the Graeco-Roman world *Collns: Bks & Pamphs:* some 20% of the bk stock was originally donated as special collns by experts in the field, such as the colln of Homeric philology belonging to Walter Leaf, the colln of works on Ancient Greek music & metre belonging to Prof R.P. Winnington-Ingram & the lib of Roman hist belonging to Prof H.H. Scullard *Archvs:* Wood Donation; Bent Diaries *Other:* Slides Lib of the Hellenic & Roman Socs; colln of antiquities bequeathed by Dr Victor Ehrenberg; rsrch materials of unpublished typescripts, papers & letters of scholars
Equip: m-reader, fax, copier, computers (incl wd-proc & CD-ROM)

Stock: bks/107255; periodcls/577; slides/6800; maps/1050, plus 50 atlases; m-forms/60m of m-film, 12 m-fiche sets; audios/50; videos/13; CD-ROMs/50; databases/25
Classn: own *Auto Sys:* Innopac
Pubns: Lib Guide
Staff: Libns: 3 *Non-Prof:* 3 *Exp:* £42802 (1999-2000); £45434 (2000-01); incl binding

S1160 🎓
Heythrop College Library

Kensington Sq, London, W8 5HQ (020-7795-4250; *fax:* 020-7795-4253)
Email: library@heythrop.ac.uk
Internet: http://www.heythrop.ac.uk/

Gov Body: Univ of London (see **S1440**) *Chief:* Libn: Fr Christopher Pedley SJ (c.pedley@heythrop.ac.uk) *Dep:* Asst Libn: Mr Michael Morgan BA, DipLib, MCLIP (m.morgan@heythrop.ac.uk) *Other Snr Staff:* Archivist: Mr Michael Walsh (mjwalsh@heythrop.ac.uk)
Entry: ref only; fees for non-academic visitors *Open:* term: Mon-Fri 0930-1900, Sat 0930-1630; vac: Mon-Fri 0930-1730
Subj: phil; psy; social sci; religion; theology; lang; lit *Co-op Schemes:* ILL, BLDSC, M25 Access Scheme
Equip: m-readers, copiers, computers (incl wd-proc, internet & CD-ROM) *Online:* Dialog, BIDS
Stock: bks/250000; periodcls/300 *Acqs Offcr:* Acqs Libn: Mr Larry Markey (l.markey@heythrop.ac.uk)
Classn: LC, LYNN *Auto Sys:* Innopac
Staff: Libns: 6 *Non-Prof:* 2
Proj: ongoing catalogue conversion proj

S1161 ⚷
Highgate Literary and Scientific Institution, Library

11 South Grove, Highgate Village, London, N6 6BS (020-8340-3343; *fax:* 020-8340-5632)
Email: admin@hlsi.demon.co.uk

Gov Body: HLSI Cttee of Mgmt *Chief:* Administrator: Jane Hill *Dep:* Dep Administrator: Ms Tasja Gardner *Other Snr Staff:* Libn: Mr Robert Walker; Archivist: Ms Gwynydd Gosling
Entry: ref only *Open:* Tue-Fri 1000-1700, Sat 1000-1600
Subj: local study (London, Highgate); arts; lit; hist *Collns: Bks & Pamphs:* local hist collns; collns on local poets (Coleridge, Betjeman & Housman) *Archvs:* relating to Highgate
Equip: copier, fax, 2 rooms for hire
Stock: bks/25000
Pubns: Hist of Highgate

S1162 🏛
HM Customs and Excise, Library and Information Service

22 Upper Ground, London, SE1 9PJ (020-7865-5668/9; *fax:* 020-7865-5670)
Email: LibraryEnquiriesNKHB@hmce.gsi.gov.uk
Internet: http://www.hmce.gov.uk/

Gov Body: HM Customs & Excise *Chief:* Chief Libn: Ms Lorna Banks BSc, MCLIP (based at Ralli Quays)
Assoc Libs: HM CUSTOMS & EXCISE, LIB & INFO SVC, Salford (see **S1883**)
Entry: authenticated rsrchers only, by appt *Open:* Mon-Fri 0830-1700
Subj: genl; taxation; criminology *Collns: Bks & Pamphs:* historical colln (material relating to hist of HM Customs & Excise) *Co-op Schemes:* BLDSC
Equip: m-reader, fax, copier, 2 computers (both with wd-proc & internet) *Online:* Reuters, Mintel, FAME, Companies House, Eurolaw, Land Registry, Butterworths Indirect Taxes

Stock: bks/10000; periodcls/80
Classn: DDC *Auto Sys:* Unicorn
Pubns: Info Alert (bulletin); bibliographies (various)
Staff: Libns: 3.5 *Non-Prof:* 1

S1163 🏛
Home Office, Library and Information Services Unit

50 Queen Anne's Gate, London, SW1H 9AT (020-7273-3398; *fax:* 020-7273-3957)

Gov Body: Home Office *Chief:* Chief Libn & Head of Unit: Mr Peter Griffiths BA, FCLIP *Other Snr Staff:* Snr Libn: Ms Karen George BA, DipLib
Entry: Home Office staff; no public access *Open:* Mon-Fri 0900-1730
Subj: social sci; criminology; policing; race relations; immigration *Collns: Bks & Pamphs:* archival colln of Home Office & Prison Svc pubns
Co-op Schemes: BLDSC
Equip: 2 m-readers, m-printer, copier, computer (incl CD-ROM) *Online:* Dialog, Dialtech, Lexis, Parliament
Stock: bks/53000; periodcls/3400; m-forms/100000
Classn: LC *Auto Sys:* Unicorn
Staff: Libns: 11 *Non-Prof:* 13

S1164 ✚
Homerton University Hospital NHS Trust, Newcomb Library

Homerton Hosp, Homerton Row, London, E9 6SR (020-8510-7751; *fax:* 020-8510-7281)
Email: newcomb.library@homerton.nhs.uk
Internet: http://www.newcomb.demon.co.uk/

Gov Body: Homerton Univ Hosp NHS Trust *Chief:* Lib Mgr: Ms Isabel Cantwell BA, MCLIP (isabel.cantwell@homerton.nhs.uk) *Other Snr Staff:* Mr Andrew Marshall (andrew.marshall@homerton.nhs.uk); Ms Heather Mills (heather.mills@homerton.nhs.uk)
Entry: letter of introduction if not staff/student *Open:* Mon 1100-2000, Tue-Fri 0900-2000 (staff availability permitting)
Subj: medicine *Co-op Schemes:* NTRLIS, NULJ, PLCS
Equip: m-reader, video viewer, copier (A4/5p), 10 computers (all with wd-proc, internet & CD-ROM, printouts 5p) *Online:* OVID, BookFind, BinleysOnline *Officer-in-Charge:* Lib Mgr, as above *Svcs:* info, ref, biblio
Stock: bks/5087, excl bnd periodcls; periodcls/148; videos/10; CD-ROMs/54 *Acqs Offcr:* Lib Mgr, as above
Classn: NLM *Auto Sys:* DBTextworks
Pubns: New Bks list
Staff: Libns: 3 *Non-Prof:* 0.4 *Exp:* £33581 (1999-2000); £37616 (2000-01)

S1165 ⚷ 🏛
The Horniman Museum Library

The Horniman Museum & Gdns, 100 London Rd, Forest Hill, London, SE23 3PQ (020-8699-1872; *fax:* 020-8291-5506)
Email: enquiry@horniman.ac.uk
Internet: http://www.horniman.ac.uk/

Gov Body: The Horniman Public Museum & Public Park Trust *Chief:* Libn: Mr D.W. Allen BSc, MCLIP *Dep:* Asst Libn: John Marriott BA, MA
Entry: ref only *Open:* Tue-Sat 1030-1730, Sun 1400-1730, closed Mon & bank hols
Subj: ethnography; musical instruments; nat hist
Collns: Archvs: Beryl De Zoete Colln (non-European dance material) *Co-op Schemes:* BLDSC, SEAL
Equip: m-reader, video viewer, copier, computer (incl CD-ROM) *Online:* Dialog (at cost)

Stock: bks/30000; periodcls/130, plus 200 no longer current; photos/2500; slides/3000; maps/300; audios/1000; videos/250
Classn: UDC *Auto Sys:* Alice (Softlink UK)
Staff: Libns: 3.5 *Exp:* £12000 (1999-2000); £13000 (2000-01)

S1166

House of Commons Library
House of Commons, Westminster, London, SW1A 0AA (020-7219-4272; *fax:* 020-7219-5839)
Email: hcinfo@parliament.uk
Internet: http://www.parliament.uk/directories/hcio.cfm

Gov Body: House of Commons Commission
Chief: Libn: Miss Priscilla Baines BLitt
Assoc Libs: HOUSE OF COMMONS INFO CENTRE (HCIO), contact details as above, Info Offcr: Mr C.M. Sear; all external enqs should be addressed via HCIO
Entry: HCIO: enqs only (tel, email, written); *Lib:* not open to public; access for MPs & their staff only
Open: HCIO: Mon-Thu 0900-1800, Fri 0900-1630; recesses: Mon-Fri 1000-1700
Subj: HCIO: info on the work, hist & membership of the House of the Commons; *Lib:* genl lib stock specialising in Parliament, politics, law *Co-op Schemes:* loans to govt dept libs only
Equip: Lib (available to MPs & their staff only): m-reader, m-printer, fax, video viewer, copiers, 210 computers (with wd-proc & CD-ROM) *Online:* POLIS database *Svcs:* info, rsrch (internal), outside enqs via HCIO
Stock: bks/150000; periodcls/1650; m-forms/150
Classn: DDC, London Lib
Pubns: House of Commons Lib Document Series (TSO); Weekly Info Bulletin (TSO); Sessional Info Digest (TSO); Parliamentary Holdings in Libs
Staff: 200 in total
See also HOUSE OF LORDS LIB (**S1167**) & RECORD OFFICE (**A286**)

S1167

House of Lords Library
Westminster, London, SW1A 0PW (020-7219-5242; *fax:* 020-7219-6396)
Email: hllibrary@parliament.uk

Gov Body: House of Lords *Chief: Libn:* Mr D.L. Jones MA *Dep:* Dep Libn: Dr P. Davis PhD
Entry: by special appl, for material not held elsewhere *Open:* Mon-Fri 0930-rising of the House; recess: Mon-Fri 0930-1630
Subj: all subjs; special emphasis on law & parliament *Collns: Bks & Pamphs:* Truro Colln of English law; Peel Colln of Irish pamphs
Equip: m-reader, m-printer, 3 copiers, computers (incl internet & CD-ROM) *Online:* POLIS, Lexis Nexis *Svcs:* info, ref, biblio
Stock: bks/120000; periodcls/500
Classn: DDC *Auto Sys:* Geac
Staff: Libns: 15 *Other Prof:* 5 *Non-Prof:* 9 *Exp:* £1538502 (2000-01); figs are for total exp
See also HOUSE OF LORDS RECORD OFFICE (**A286**)

S1168 ♈

Howard League for Penal Reform, John Howard Library
1 Ardleigh Rd, London, N1 4SH (020-7249-7373; *fax:* 020-7249-7788)
Email: howardleague@ukonline.co.uk
Internet: http://www.howardleague/co.uk

Gov Body: Howard League for Penal Reform
Chief: Administrator: Miss E. Lolomari
Entry: for ref, when staff available; always tel in adv of visit *Open:* Mon-Fri 0930-1700

Subj: criminal justice *Collns: Archvs:* own archvs
Equip: copier
Stock: bks/30 *Classn:* Bliss *Staff: Other Prof:* 8

S1169 🎓 🙏

The Huguenot Library
Univ Coll, Gower St, London, WC1E 6BT (020-7679-5199)
Email: s.massil@ucl.ac.uk
Internet: http://www.ucl.ac.uk/ucl-info/library/hugenot.htm

Type: learned soc *Gov Body:* Huguenot Soc of Great Britain & Ireland *Chief: Libn:* S.W. Massil BA, DipLib, FLA
Entry: adv appt *Open:* Mon-Wed 1000-1600
Subj: religion; lang; arts; lit; geog; hist *Collns: Other:* bks, periodcls, pamphs, genealogical tables etc on Huguenot subjs; French Churches; Bounty Papers; French Hosp Friendly Soc
Equip: m-reader, m-printer, computer *Svcs:* info, ref, biblio
Stock: bks/10000; periodcls/50; pamphs/5000; various photos, slides, illusts, maps, m-forms, videos, AVs (a few 100 in each category)
Classn: own *Auto Sys:* Ex Libris
Pubns: Huguenot Soc: Proceedings; Quarto (series)
Staff: Libns: 1 *Exp:* £1000 (1999-2000)

S1170 ♈ 📷

Hulton Archive – Getty Images
Unique House, 21-31 Woodfield Rd, London, W9 2AB (020-7266-2662; *fax:* 020-7266-0743/3154)
Email: hultonresearch@getty-images.com
Internet: http://www.hultonarchive.com/

Gov Body: Getty Images *Chief:* Rsrch Mgr: Miss Caroline Theakstone *Dep:* Dep Rsrch Mgr: Mr Luigi Di Dio *Other Snr Staff:* Curator: Ms Sarah McDonald (sarah.mcdonald@getty-images.com)
Assoc Libs: part of GETTY IMAGES, 101 Bayham St, London, NW1 0AG
Entry: ref & rsrch, by adv appt; svc fee charge for visiting clients (£25+VAT) *Open:* Mon-Fri 0915-1800
Subj: generalities; news & features; transport; social & political issues; arts; theatre; cinema; ballet; dance; war (worldwide coverage); Royalty; personalities; sport *Collns: Other:* Slim Aarons Colln (American soc & portraits, 1940s-80s); Gordon Anthony Theatre Colln (c1835-55); Erich Auerbach Colln (music, 1940s-70s); Baron Ballet & Portrait Colln (1935-56); Felice Beato Colln (Indian Mutiny, China, Japan, c1857); Central Press Colln (portraits & news, 1914-80s); W&D Downey Colln (court photos, 1860-1938); Evening Standard Colln (1939-80); Express Colln (1939-80); Foz Photos Colln (news & features, c1920s-40s); Genl Photographic Agency Colln (news & features, 1920s-46); Henry Guttman Colln (c1930); Ernst Haas Colln (travel, abstracts, motion, portraits, 1940s-86); Keystone Colln (news & features, 1910-80s); Serge Lemoine Colln (royalty, 1971-81); London Stereoscopic Colln (c1860-1910); Picture Post Colln (1938-57); Rischgitz Colln (prints, engravings & photography, c1850s-1900); Sasha London Theatre Colln (1924-40); Three Lions Colln (news & features, 1900s-57); Topical Press Colln (1900s-57); Weegee Colln (American photojournalism, 1930s-60s)
Equip: m-reader, video viewer, fax, 2 copiers, 2 computers (both with wd-proc, internet & CD-ROM) *Online:* on-line search engine & internet site *Svcs:* info, ref, image supply
Stock: bks/3000; photos/18-20 mln; slides/10 mln; illusts/50000; maps/10000; m-forms/40 reels; posters/5000
Classn: Gibbs-Smith/various
Pubns: catalogues (print & CD-ROM, free)
Staff: Libns: 10 *Other Prof:* 20 *Non-Prof:* 5

S1171 ♈ 📷

The Hutchison Library
118b Holland Park Ave, London, W11 4UA (020-7229-2743; *fax:* 020-7972-0259)
Email: library@hutchisonpic.demon.co.uk
Internet: http://www.hutchisonpictures.co.uk/

Chief: Dir: Mr Michael Lee BA
Entry: call to arrange an appt *Open:* Mon-Fri 1000-1800; closed from Christmas to end of New Year hols
Subj: genl documentary clr photo lib with world-wide coverage concentrating on geographical & anthropological subjs
Equip: fax, copier, computer (with wd-proc)
Stock: slides/500000
Staff: Libns: 2 *Other Prof:* 2
Further Info: The lib is undergoing reorganisation & may join up with another colln mid-2003

S1172 ♈

IEA The Clean Coal Centre, Library
Gemini House, 10-18 Putney Hill, London, SW15 6AA (020-8780-2111; *fax:* 020-8780-1746)
Email: library@iea-coal.org.uk
Internet: http://www.iea-coal.org.uk/

Type: internationally funded non-profit org *Gov Body:* Internatl Energy Agency *Chief:* Info Officer/Libn: Ms Anne Carpenter MSc, MCLIP *Dep:* Lib Asst: Mrs Ida Blunt
Entry: not open to the public
Subj: coal; energy

S1173 🦪 📷

Image Bank UK, Library
17 Conway St, Fitzrovia, London, W1P 6EE (020-7312-0300; *fax:* 020-7391-9111)
Email: ladams@theimagebank.com
Internet: http://www.imagebank.co.uk/

Type: commercial picture agency *Chief:* Lib Mgr: Miss Lorraine Adams BSc(Hons)
Assoc Libs: IMAGE BANK UK, 57 Melville St, Edinburgh, EH3 7HL (0131-225-1770; *fax:* 0131-225-1660); IMAGE BANK DUBLIN, 11 Upper Mount St, Dublin 2, Ireland (00-353-1-676-0872; *fax:* 00-353-1-676-0873)
Entry: adv appt *Open:* Mon-Fri 0930-1800
Subj: all subjs (excl news footage & current celebrities) *Collns: Archvs:* archv photos (based in New York); huge selection of archival imagery *Other:* Swanstock Colln (fine art)
Stock: slides/20 mln; illusts/10000; film/30000 hrs
Staff: Libns: 6 *Other Prof:* 44

S1174 🦪 📷

Imagestate Ltd Library
(formerly Images Clr Lib)
Ramillies House, 1-2 Ramillies St, London, W1F 7LN (020-7734-7344; *fax:* 020-7287-3933)
Email: esales@imagestate.co.uk
Internet: http://www.imagestate.com/

Type: commercial photo agency *Chief:* Dir: Ms Cara Williams *Dep:* Head of Lib: Mr Matthew Pope
Entry: adv appt *Open:* Mon-Fri 0900-1800
Subj: stock photography: lifestyle; nature; business; industry; travel *Collns: Other:* Charles Walker Colln (myths, magic, strange phenomena)
Stock: photos/over 1 mln
Pubns: stock photography catalogues

Special Libraries

London ▼ London

S1175 📷

Impact Photos Ltd, Photographic Library

26-27 Gt Sutton St, London, EC1V 0DS (020-7251-5091; *fax:* 020-7608-0114)
Email: library@impactphotos.demon.co.uk

Chief: Ms Sally Neal
Open: Mon-Fri 0930-1800
Subj: stock photography on all subjs
Stock: photos/1.5 mln

S1176 ☕

Imperial Chemical Industries plc, Group Headquarters Library

20 Manchester Sq, London, W1U 3AN (020-7009-5000; *fax:* 020-7009-5001)
Email: sheen_russell@ici.co.uk

Chief: Libn: Miss Sheena Russell
Entry: adv appt *Open:* Mon-Thu 0900-1715, Fri 0900-1700
Subj: all subjs; econ; law; mgmt; statistics; trade
Collns: Archvs: company archvs *Co-op Schemes:* BLDSC, ILL
Equip: m-reader, m-printer, fax, computers (incl wd-proc & CD-ROM) *Online:* Dialog, Datastar, Justis, Dun & Bradstreet *Svcs:* info, ref, biblio
Stock: bks/20000; periodcls/650; pamphs/2000; maps/100; m-forms/10000
Classn: UDC *Auto Sys:* Soutron
Staff: Libns: 1 *Non-Prof:* 2

S1177 🎓 ✚

Imperial College Faculty of Medicine, Charing Cross Campus Library

Reynolds Bldg, St Dunstan's Rd, London, W6 8RP (020-7594-0755; *fax:* 020-7594-0851)
Email: librarycx@imperial.ac.uk
Internet: http://www.imperial.ac.uk/library/

Gov Body: Imperial Coll London (see **S1180**)
Chief: Campus Libn: Mr Paul Morrell BA, MCLIP (p.morrell@imperial.ac.uk)
Assoc Libs: CHELSEA & WESTMINSTER CAMPUS LIB, Chelsea & Westminster Hosp, 369 Fulham Rd, London, SW10 9NH, Site Libn: Mr Reinhard Wentz DipLB (020-8746-8107; *fax:* 020-8746-8215)
Entry: ref access possible for bona fide rsrchers; fee for non-membs *Open:* term: Mon-Thu 0900-2100, Fri 0900-2000, Sat 0900-1200; vac: closed Sat
Subj: medicine; nursing *Collns: Bks & Pamphs:* Charing Cross Colln *Archvs:* Charing Cross Hosp archvs; Charing Cross Hosp Medical School archvs *Co-op Schemes:* Univ of London
Equip: m-reader, 4 video viewers, 4 copiers, numerous computers *Online:* Medline etc *Svcs:* info, ref, biblio
Stock: bks/20000; periodcls/400; videos/200
Classn: NLM *Auto Sys:* Unicorn
Pubns: MedIC (ICSM newsletter)
Staff: Libns: 6

S1178 🎓 ✚

Imperial College Faculty of Medicine, Hammersmith Campus, Wellcome Library

Hammersmith Hosp, Du Cane Rd, London, W12 0NN (020-8383-3246; *fax:* 020-8383-2195)
Email: lib.hamm@imperial.ac.uk
Internet: http://www.imperial.ac.uk/library/

Gov Body: Imperial Coll London (see **S1180**)
Chief: Campus Lib Mgr: Mrs Georgina Going MCLIP
Entry: ref only except for academic staff & registered rsrch students of Univ Lib & academic staff of M25 Higher Edu Consortium; non-membs of M25 are required to pay membership fee *Open:* Mon-Fri 0900-2100, Sat 0930-1230 (access after 1800 & on Sats is by ID card & PIN only)
Subj: biomedicine *Collns: Other:* small AV colln
Co-op Schemes: ILL, M25 Consortium
Equip: video viewer, 4 copiers, 18 computers, tape-slide viewer *Online:* Datastar, STN, Dialog, BLAISE-LINE, BLAISE-LINK
Stock: bks/8000; periodcls/450; slides/45; videos/50; archvs/20 m
Classn: NLM *Auto Sys:* Unicorn (Sirsi)
Staff: Libns: 1 *Other Prof:* 3 *Non-Prof:* 5

S1179 🎓 ✚

Imperial College Faculty of Medicine, St Mary's Campus Library

Norfolk Pl, Paddington, London, W2 1PG (020-7594-3692; *fax:* 020-7402-3971)
Email: sm-lib@imperial.ac.uk
Internet: http://www.imperial.ac.uk/library/

Gov Body: Imperial Coll London (see **S1180**)
Chief: Campus Lib Mgr: Miss S.E. Smith BA, MLS, MCLIP
Entry: ref access possible for bona fide rsrchers; fee for non-membs *Open:* term: Mon-Fri 0900-2100, Sat 0900-1300; vac (last 2 wks Jul & All of Aug): Mon-Fri 0900-1900
Subj: undergrad; postgrad; clinical; medicine
Collns: Other: monograph pubns by past & present staff of St Mary's Hosp Medical School
Co-op Schemes: BLDSC, NTRLIS
Equip: m-reader, copier, computer
Stock: bks/37500; periodcls/300; pamphs/350
Classn: own *Auto Sys:* Unicorn
Pubns: Lib Guide (internal circulation only); A Bibliography of Sir Alexander Fleming 1885-1955 (£4); Catalogue of Reprints & Bks, by Augustus Desire Waller
Staff: Libns: 5 *Non-Prof:* 2

S1180 🎓

Imperial College London, Central Library

Exhibition Rd, South Kensington, London, SW7 2AZ (020-7594-8820; *fax:* 020-7594-8876)
Email: libhelp@imperial.ac.uk
Internet: http://www.imperial.ac.uk/library/

Gov Body: Univ of London (see **S1440**) *Chief:* Dir of Lib Svcs: Ms Clare Jenkins BA, DipLib
Assoc Libs: Dept Libs (at South Kensington Campus, addr as above): AERONAUTICS LIB, Roderic Hill Bldg (020-7594-5069; *fax:* 020-7584-8120); CHEMICAL ENG & CHEM-ICAL TECH LIB, Room 232, Roderic Hill Bldg (020-7594-5598; *fax:* 020-7594-5604); CHEM LIB, Room 232, Chem Dept Bldg (020-7594-5736; *fax:* 020-7594-5804; *email:* chemlib@imperial.ac.uk); CIVIL & ENVIRONMENTAL ENG LIB, 4th floor, Civil Eng Dept Bldg (020-7594-6007; *fax:* 020-7225-2716; *email:* civenglib@imperial.ac.uk); COMPUTING COLLN (at Central Lib); ELECTRICAL & ELECTRICAL ENG LIB, Level 6, Electrical Eng Bldg (020-7594-6182; *fax:* 020-7823-8125); LIFE SCIS & MEDICINE COLLN (at Central Lib); MGMT & SOCIAL SCIS COLLN (at Central Lib); MATERIALS LIB, Level 4, Bessemer Bldg (020-7594-6751; *fax:* 020-7584-3194); MATHS LIB, Room 416, Huxley Bldg (020-7594-8542; *fax:* 020-7594-8517); MECHANICAL ENG LIB, Level 3, Mechanical Eng Bldg (020-7594-7166; *email:* mechenglibrary@imperial.ac.uk); PHYSICS LIB, Level 2, Blackett Laboratory (020-7594-7871; *fax:* 020-7594-7777; *email:* physics.library@imperial.ac.uk); *Faculty of Medicine Libs:* CHARING CROSS CAMPUS LIB (see **S1177**); CHELSEA & WESTMINSTER HOSP LIB, 369 Fulham Rd, London, SW10 9NH; HAMMERSMITH CAMPUS, WELLCOME LIB (see **S1178**); ST MARY'S CAMPUS LIB (see **S1179**); NATL HEART & LUNG INST LIB (see **S1181**); also part of Imperial Coll Lib: THE KEMPE CENTRE, Wye Campus (see **S49**); Central Lib also shares bldg & some collns with SCI MUSEUM LIB (see **S1387**).
Entry: ref only, at discretion of Dir *Open:* Central Lib: term: Mon-Fri 0830-2200, Sat 0930-1730; Xmas & summer vacs: Mon-Sat 0930-1730
Subj: sci, tech & medicine *Collns: Bks & Pamphs:* aeronautical eng rsrch reports; computing & control; applied geol; transport studies; Haldane Colln; Annan Colln; London Nat Hist Soc Lib (see **S1263**); Operational Rsrch Soc Lib *Archvs:* T.H. Huxley papers; archvs of the Royal Commission for the 1851 Exhib
Equip: m-reader, m-printer, video viewer, copiers, computers (incl CD-ROM) *Online:* not available to external users
Stock: bks/800000; periodcls/6000 (print & elec); audios/8000; 100000 items incl pamphs, photos (satellite images), maps, m-forms, videos; figs are for all Imperial Coll Libs
Classn: UDC *Auto Sys:* Unicorn
Pubns: various Lib Guides (free); various archv pubns: e.g., Pictorial Histories of Imperial Coll & St Mary's Hosp Medical School (£2); Catalogue of the Huxley Papers (£13)
Staff: Libns: 109 *Non-Prof:* 17 total for all Imperial Coll Libs, incl Central Lib *Exp:* £3.5 mln (2000-01); fig is for all exp on info provision

S1181 🎓 ✚

Imperial College London, National Heart and Lung Institute Library

Royal Brompton Campus, Dove House St, London, SW3 6LY (020-7351-8150; *fax:* 020-7351-8117)
Email: nhli.library@imperial.ac.uk
Internet: http://www.imperial.ac.uk/library/

Gov Body: Imperial Coll London (see **S1180**)
Chief: Campus Lib Mgr: Miss Rachel C. Shipton BA, MSc, MCLIP
Assoc Libs: HAREFIELD HOSP LIB (see **S782**)
Entry: ref only by prior appt for advanced rsrch material only unavailable elsewhere; a charge may be made *Open:* Mon-Fri 0900-2100
Subj: cardiorespiratory medicine, nursing & surgery
Stock: bks/c90000; periodcls/c200
Classn: NLM *Auto Sys:* Unicorn
Staff: Libns: 3 *Non-Prof:* 1.5

S1182 🏛 🏛

Imperial War Museum, Department of Printed Books

Lambeth Rd, London, SE1 6HZ (020-7416-5342; *fax:* 020-7416-5264)
Email: books@iwm.org.uk
Internet: http://www.iwm.org.uk/

Type: natl museum *Gov Body:* Trustees of the Imperial War Museum *Chief:* Libn: Mr Richard Golland BA, DipLib, MCLIP
Assoc Libs: DEPT OF ART (see **A288**); DEPT OF DOCUMENTS (see **A289**); FILM & VIDEO ARCHV (see **A290**); PHOTO ARCHV (see **A291**); SOUND ARCHV (see **A292**)

Entry: adv appt *Open:* Mon-Sat 1000-1700; tel enq svc also available Mon-Fri 0900-1700 *Subj:* social sci; lit; hist; military hist; warfare involving Britain & the Commonwealth since 1914; WW1; WW2; Spanish Civil War; war in Ethiopia (1930s); Korean War; Vietnam War; Middle East conflict; Falklands War; peace-keeping role of UN forces generally & British forces in particular; non-military aspects of war incl economic, literary, social & political; war poetry; pacifism; propaganda *Collns: Bks & Pamphs:* British women's activs in WW1; unit hists of British, French, German & American units, incl publ hists of armies down to battalion level, navies down to indiv ships & air forces down to squadrons *Archvs:* reports of US Strategic Bombing Survey; aerial leaflets; propaganda; army forms; ID cards; ration bks; other ephemera *Other:* map colln, incl: WW1 trench maps, situation & order of battle maps; WW2 topographic sheets of various theatres of war & some situation & order of battle maps *Co-op Schemes:* M25 Consortium of Academic Libs *Equip:* 4 m-readers, m-printer, fax, copier, computers (incl 1 with internet & 1 with CD-ROM) *Disabled:* CCTV & PC-based equip for blind & partially sighted *Svcs:* info, ref, biblio *Stock:* bks/150000; periodcls/15000; pamphs/ 25000; maps & technical drawings/15000 *Classn:* own *Auto Sys:* DBTextworks *Pubns:* numerous; catalogue available on request *Staff: Libns:* 12 *Non-Prof:* 6 *Exp:* £25000 (2000-01)

S1183

Independent Healthcare Association, Library

Westminster Tower, 3 Albert Embankment, London, SE1 7SP (020-7793-4620; *fax:* 020-7820-3738)
Email: info@iha.org.uk
Internet: http://www.iha.org.uk/

Entry: membs only *Open:* Mon-Fri 0900-1700 *Subj:* health care, particularly independent health care *Collns: Other:* press clippings, selection from the last 6 years on health care & particularly independent health care *Equip:* copier *Svcs:* info, ref *Stock:* bks/200; periodcls/100 *Staff: Non-Prof:* 8

S1184

India House Library

High Commission of India, India House, Aldwych, London, WC2B 4NA (020-7836-8484 x115; *fax:* 020-7836-2632)
Email: pnihci@compuserve.com
Internet: http://www.hcilondon.org/

Gov Body: Govt of India, Ministry of External Affairs, New Delhi *Chief:* Libn: Mr Wazir Singh Mour *Other Snr Staff:* Hon Libn: Miss M.S. Travis
Entry: closed lib for use of High Commission staff & govt servants from India only; no outside access; some photocopied material can be supplied to those who apply in writing
Subj: India; Indian phil & religion; Indian geog & hist; Indian arts; Indian langs & lit *Collns: Bks & Pamphs:* Mahatma Gandhi Colln *Other:* some maps (restricted)
Svcs: info (by written correspondence only) *Stock:* bks/c17000; periodcls/10 *Classn:* DDC
Exp: all material is received directly from the Ministry of External Affairs, New Delhi

S1185

ING Barings: Information Centre

60 London Wall, London, EC2M 5TQ (020-7767-1000; *fax:* 020-7767-7147)

Chief: Head of Info Svcs: Mr Peter Maddock
Assoc Libs: ING BARINGS ARCHVS, at same addr, Archivist: Dr J. Orbell (020-7767-1401; *fax:* 020-7767-7131)
Entry: not open to visitors outside the ING Group, although special cases may be considered
Subj: Info Centre: business; finance; banking; *Archvs:* business records; estate archvs; family papers; personal papers *Collns: Archvs:* historical archvs of Baring Brothers & Co Ltd (merchant bank, 1763-1899); H.S. Lefevre & Co records (merchant bankers) & CJ Mare & Co records (shipbuilders); family & estate papers of Baring family, Barons Northbrook (1692-1899); papers of indiv membs of the Barings family, incl correspondence to & from various political, military & cultural 18C & 19C figs: Benjamin Disraeli; Major Genl Charles Gordon; Major Genl William Napier; Gioacchino Rossini; Arthur Wellesley & others
Equip: 2 m-readers (staff only), 2 m-printers, 2 copiers *Online:* connections to several host systems & databases (staff only) *Svcs:* info, ref *Classn:* own *Auto Sys:* Unicorn
Staff: 17, incl 6 FT rsrchers

S1186

Inland Revenue Library

Room 28, New Wing, Somerset House, Strand, London, WC2R 1LB (020-7438-6648; *fax:* 020-7438-7562)
Email: library.ir.sh@gtnet.gov.uk

Chief: Libn: F. Higginson
Entry: adv appt only; req should be submitted in writing *Open:* Mon-Fri 0900-1700
Subj: taxation *Svcs:* info
Stock: bks/60000; periodcls/800

S1187

Inner Temple Library

Temple, London, EC4Y 7DA (020-7797-8217/8/9; *fax:* 020-7797-8224/7583-6030)
Email: library@innertemple.org.uk
Internet: http://www.accesstolaw.com/

Gov Body: Honourable Soc of the Inner Temple *Chief:* Libn & Keeper of MSS: Ms Margaret Clay BA, DipLib, MCLIP *Dep:* Dep Libn: Mr Adrian Blunt BA, MCLIP
Entry: ref only; open to barrister membs of the Inns of Court & to student membs of the Inner Temple; others at Libn's discretion upon written appl *Open:* student term: Mon-Thu 0900-2000, Fri 0900-1900; otherwise: Mon-Fri 0900-1900; Aug & Sep: Mon-Fri 0900-1700 (closed last 2 wks of Aug) *Subj:* law *Collns: Bks & Pamphs:* Commonwealth law *Archvs:* Petyt MSS *Co-op Schemes:* Inns of Court Specialisation Scheme *Equip:* 2 copiers, 19 computers (incl 2 with wd-proc, 10 with internet & 4 with CD-ROM) *Online:* Lexis, Lawtel, Westlaw *Svcs:* info, ref, biblio, indexing
Stock: bks/80000; periodcls/1000; pamphs/2000; maps/100
Classn: own *Auto Sys:* Unicorn
Staff: Libns: 5 *Non-Prof:* 4

Institute and Guild of Brewing, Historical Library

See NATL BREWING LIB (**S1694**)

S1188

Institute of Actuaries, Historical Library

Staple Inn Hall, High Holborn, London, WC1V 7QL (020-7632-2114; *fax:* 020-7632-2111)
Email: libraries@actuaries.org.uk
Internet: http://www.actuaries.org.uk/library/ library_welcome.html

Type: prof body *Gov Body:* part of joint lib svc of Faculty & Inst of Actuaries *Chief:* Libn: Ms Sally Grover MA, MCLIP (based at main Oxford lib)
Dep: Asst Libn & Archivist: Mr David Raymont BA (based in London)
Assoc Libs: INST OF ACTUARIES, THE NORWICH LIB, Oxford (see **S1679**); FACULTY OF ACTUARIES, ROSS LIB, Edinburgh (see **S599**)
Entry: adv appt recommended; open to Inst & Faculty membs & students, overseas actuarial soc membs, rsrchers & univ students *Open:* Mon-Fri 0900-1700; occasional late opening on meeting days
Subj: actuarial sci; social sci; demography; econ; insurance; maths; probability; statistics; records of parent org *Collns: Bks & Pamphs:* antiquarian & rare bks, incl Edwin James Farren Lib (part of personal lib of the Actuary of the Asylum Life Office, 19C); Newmarch Colln (bnd pamphs, on deposit from Royal Statistical Soc); ref colln of actuarial pubns; demographic journals; European & American actuarial journals; insurance prospectuses & promotional leaflets; mortality statistics *Archvs:* Archv of the Actuarial Profession, incl the formal records of the Inst of Actuaries (minute bks etc) & the Actuarial Club; other MSS relating to hist of actuarial sci *Other:* photo colln *Co-op Schemes:* ILIOS, incl union list of periodcl holdings
Equip: copier (A4/20p), computer (with internet)
Svcs: info, ref, biblio
Stock: bks/3000, incl c1000 rare bks & pamphs
Classn: LCBS *Auto Sys:* DBTextworks
Staff: Libns: 4 *Non-Prof:* 3

S1189

Institute of Alcohol Studies Library

Alliance House, 12 Caxton St, London, SW1H 0QS (020-7222-4001; *fax:* 020-7799-2510)
Email: librarian@ias.org.uk
Internet: http://www.ias.org.uk/

Type: charity *Gov Body:* United Kingdom Temperance Alliance (UKTA) Ltd *Chief:* Libn: Miss Judith Crowe BSc, MCLIP (judith@ias.org.uk)
Entry: adv appt *Open:* Mon-Fri 0930-1600
Subj: social sci; alcohol studies; policy & social aspects of alcohol-related harm; temperance *Collns: Archvs:* historical temperance archv *Other:* grey lit on alcohol policy; article reprints; conference documents; various ephemeral papers *Equip:* copier *Online:* Online Bulletin Board System networking alcohol-related info & orgs *Svcs:* info, ref, biblio, current awareness *Stock:* bks/5000+; reprints/c3500; stock is still being catalogued
Classn: own *Auto Sys:* EndNote
Pubns: Alcohol Aler (4 pa); The Globe (4 pa); Monthly Digest of Press Cuttings & Statistics; prices on appl
Staff: Libns: 1 *Other Prof:* 6 *Non-Prof:* 2

S1190

Institute of Biomedical Science, Library

12 Coldbath Sq, London, EC1R 5HL (020-7713-0214; *fax:* 020-7436-4946)
Email: mail@ibms.org
Internet: http://www.ibms.org/

Gov Body: Council of the Inst *Chief:* Libn: Mr. John Mercer AIBMS, ARPS, AIMI
Entry: adv appt *Open:* 0900-1700
Subj: medical laboratory scis *Collns: Other:* IBMS Fellowship theses *Co-op Schemes:* BLDSC, ILL
Equip: copier, computer (incl wd-proc)
Stock: bks/1100; periodcls/35; theses/530
Classn: own
Pubns: list of current periodcls received by lib, Catalogue of IBMS Fellowship Theses

S1191

Institute of Business Ethics, Reference Library

24 Greencoat Pl, London, SW1P 1BE (020-7798-6040; *fax:* 020-7798-6044)
Email: info@ibe.org.uk
Internet: http://www.ibe.org.uk/

Chief: Dir of Rsrch: Mr Simon Webley
Entry: by arrangement only
Subj: business ethics; business social responsibility
Equip: fax, copier, computers (incl wd-proc & internet) *Svcs:* info, ref
Stock: bks/100 *Staff:* Other Prof: 2 Non-Prof: 2

S1192

Institute of Cancer Research Library

Chester Beatty Laboratories, 237 Fulham Rd, London, SW3 6JB (020-7352-5946; *fax:* 020-7352-6283)
Email: fullib@icr.ac.uk
Internet: http://www.icr.ac.uk/

Gov Body: Council of the Inst *Chief:* Libn: to be appointed *Dep:* Lib Asst: Mrs Tina Lockley *Other Snr Staff:* Lib Sec: Mrs June Greenwood
Assoc Libs: FRANZ BERGEL LIB, 15 Cotswold Rd, Sutton, Surrey, SM2 5NG, Lib Assts: Mr Barry Jenkins & Miss Sue Rogers
Entry: ref only by prior appt *Open:* Mon-Fri 0900-1730
Subj: molecular biology; chem; oncology *Co-op Schemes:* BLDSC, BMA
Equip: m-readers, m-printers, fax, copiers, computers (incl wd-proc, internet & CD-ROM) *Online:* CINAHL, Cancer-CD *Svcs:* info, ref, lit searches
Stock: bks/10000; periodcls/550; photos/200
Classn: NLM
Pubns: Lib Guide Pack; Periodicals Holdings List (both free)
Staff: Libns: 4 Non-Prof: 2

S1193

Institute of Chartered Accountants in England and Wales Library

Chartered Accountants' Hall, PO Box 433, Moorgate Pl, London, EC2P 2BJ (020-7920-8620; *24 hr answering machine:* 020-7920-8622; *fax:* 020-7920-8621)
Email: library@icaew.co.uk
Internet: http://www.icaew.co.uk/library/

Gov Body: Chartered Accountants' Trust for Edu & Rsrch (CATER) *Chief:* Libn: Ms S.P. Moore BA(Hons), MCLIP *Dep:* Dep Libn: Ms A.J. Dennis BA, MCLIP
Entry: membs of Inst of Chartered Accountants; non-membs: bona fide rsrchers sponsored by memb or by prior arrangement with Libn (may involve fee) *Open:* Mon-Thu 0900-1730, Fri 1000-1730 (closed for 3 wks during Aug)
Subj: accounting; auditing; company law; statutes; finance & investment; mgmt; taxation; computing; company financial info *Collns: Bks & Pamphs:* early bks on bookkeeping & accounting (1494-1914) *Co-op Schemes:* BLDSC

Equip: m-reader, m-printer, video viewer, fax, copier, computers (incl internet & CD-ROM), room for hire *Online:* Lexis-Nexis *Svcs:* info, ref
Stock: bks/40000; periodcls/320 *Acqs Offcr:* Collns Mgr: Ms J. Baylis
Classn: UDC *Auto Sys:* Sirsi Unicorn
Pubns: Historical Accounting Lit (catalogue, £30); The Earliest Bks on Bookkeeping 1494-1683 (£1.50); Foreign Bks on Bookkeeping 1494-1750 (£1.50)
Staff: Libns: 9 Non-Prof: 4

S1194

Institute of Chartered Secretaries and Administrators, Information Centre

16 Park Cres, London, W1B 1AH (020-7580-4741; *fax:* 020-7323-1132)
Email: informationcentre@icsa.co.uk
Internet: http://www.icsa.org.uk/icsa/

Type: prof body *Chief:* Info Mgr: Mr Andrew Tillbrook LLB(Hons)
Entry: preference given to membs; ref only, adv appt preferred (limited space) *Open:* Mon-Fri 0930-1700
Subj: social sci; business; law; company law; mgmt; company secretarial practice; corporate governance
Equip: copier *Officer-in-Charge:* Info Mgr, as above *Svcs:* ref
Stock: bks/2000; periodcls/40 *Acqs Offcr:* Info Mgr, as above
Classn: own; subj headings *Auto Sys:* PenLib
Pubns: Best Practice Guides; Guidance Notes (see web site for details); various bk pubns (see http://www.icsapublishing.co.uk/)
Staff: Non-Prof: 1 *Exp:* £27000 (2000-01)

S1195

Institute of Contemporary History and Wiener Library

4 Devonshire St, London, W1N 2BH (020-7636-7247; *fax:* 020-7436-6428)
Email: info@wienerlibrary.co.uk
Internet: http://www.wienerlibrary.co.uk/

Gov Body: Exec Cttee *Chief:* Dir: Mr Ben Barkow MSc
Entry: letter of introduction, apply in writing to libn; membership scheme for a moderate fee *Open:* Mon-Fri 1000-1730
Subj: contemporary European & Jewish hist; the rise & fall of the Third Reich; the survival & revival of the Nazi & fascist movements, anti-Semitism, racism; the Middle East & post-war Germany
Collns: Bks & Pamphs: on Europe, Germany, the Holocaust, World War II, contemporary Germany, internatl issues (human rights, ethnic relations, refugees) *Archvs:* 8 press archvs (2 mln cuttings); documents & eye-witness accounts *Other:* photo archv (on Holocaust); video colln
Equip: m-reader, m-printer, video viewer, copier, 2 computers (incl 1 internet & CD-ROM)
Stock: bks/60000; periodcls/300; photos/10000; m-forms/6000; audios/75; videos/1500
Classn: own *Auto Sys:* Genesis
Pubns: Newsletter (3 pa)
Staff: Libns: 5 Non-Prof: 7

S1196

Institute of Directors, Business Library

116 Pall Mall, London, SW1Y 5ED (020-7451-3100; *fax:* 020-7321-0145)
Email: businessinfo@iod.com

Gov Body: Inst of Dirs *Chief:* Head of Info & Advisory Svcs: Mrs Anna Burmajster MA(Phil), MA(IM), MCLIP

Entry: ref only, strictly by appt *Open:* Mon-Fri 0830-1830
Subj: business *Collns: Bks & Pamphs:* colln of articles on dirs & boardroom practice
Equip: fax, copier, CD-ROM network *Online:* Dialog, Companies House, Datastar, Dow Jones, Dun & Bradstreet, Reuters
Stock: bks/8000; periodcls/100
Classn: DDC *Auto Sys:* Unicorn
Staff: Libns: 9 Non-Prof: 1

S1197

Institute of Financial Services, Information Service

(formerly the Chartered Inst of Bankers)
90 Bishopsgate, London, EC2N 4DQ (020-7444-7100; *fax:* 020-7444-7109)
Email: library@ifslearning.com
Internet: http://www.ifsis.org.uk/

Gov Body: Chartered Inst of Bankers *Chief:* Head of Info Svc: Ms Susana Vazquez
Entry: free to CIB membs; external membership (indiv or corporate) for a fee *Open:* Mon, Wed, Fri 0900-1700, Tue, Thu 0900-1800
Subj: banking; finance *Collns: Bks & Pamphs:* annual reports of banks; banking law reports *Archvs:* banking hist *Other:* bank note colln (housed in British Museum) *Co-op Schemes:* BLDSC, ILL
Equip: computers (incl wd-proc, internet & CD-ROM), Bloomberg TV *Online:* ABI Inform, Emerald Intelligence, Business Source Elite, Bureau Van Dyke, Bankers Almanac Online, Lexis-Nexis, FT, Corporate Profound *Svcs:* ref, rsrch
Stock: bks/30000; periodcls/200
Classn: UDC *Auto Sys:* Unicorn
Pubns: Reading Lists; bibliographies; City Contact Directory; Banks in London List; Private Banks List; Investment Banks List
Staff: Libns: 7 Non-Prof: 3

S1198

Institute of Linguists Library

Saxon House, 48 Southwark St, London, SE1 1UN (020-7359-7445; *fax:* 020-7354-0202)
Email: info@iol.org.uk
Internet: http://www.iol.org.uk/

Gov Body: Inst of Linguists *Chief:* Hon Libn: Mr Andrew Dalby
Entry: Fellows & membs of the Inst
Subj: lang; linguistics *Collns: Bks & Pamphs:* multilingual technical dictionaries; journals & papers *Co-op Schemes:* ILL
Stock: bks/3500; periodcls/60

S1199

Institute of Marine Engineering, Science and Technology, Marine Information Centre

(formerly Inst of Marine Engineers)
80 Coleman St, London, EC2R 5BJ (020-7382-2600; *fax:* 020-7382-2670)
Email: imarest@imarest.org
Internet: http://www.imarest.org/

Type: learned soc *Gov Body:* Inst of Marine Eng, Sci & Tech (IMarEST) *Chief:* Mgr of Info Centre: Mr David Bartle BA, DipLib, MCLIP *Dep:* Libn: Mrs Nuala Briody BA, DipLib
Entry: full svc for memb of Inst, ref only for non-membs *Open:* Mon-Fri 0900-1700
Subj: marine eng; offshore tech *Collns: Bks & Pamphs:* transactions & conferences of Inst; sets of transactions of Royal Instn of Naval Architects (RINA), Inst of Mechanical Engineers, North East Coast Inst of Engineers & Shipbuilders, Soc of Naval Architects & Marine Engineers (SNAME); all abstracts, from 1970-present, are computerised

Archvs: colln of late 19C eng journals & Insts' pubns *Co-op Schemes:* ILL
Equip: copier, computer (with CD-ROM) *Online:* Marine Technology Abstracts (own) *Svcs:* info, ref, biblio, abstracting
Stock: bks/51000; periodcls/100
Classn: UDC
Pubns: Calendar of Marine Events; Internatl Directory of Maritime Consultancy (online); Marine Tech Abstracts (online)
Staff: Libns: 2 *Other Prof:* 3 external abstractors

S1200

Institute of Materials, Minerals and Mining, Library and Information Services

(formerly the libs of the Instn of Mining & Metallurgy & the Inst of Materials)
1 Carlton House Ter, London, SW1Y 5DB (020-7451-7300/60; *fax:* 020-7451-7406)
Email: admin@iom3.org
Internet: http://www.iom3.org/

Type: prof/learned instn *Gov Body:* Inst of Materials, Minerals & Mining (formed from merger of Instn of Mining & Metallurgy & Inst of Materials) *Chief:* Materials Info Co-ordinator: Ms Hilda Kaune BA(Hons), DipLib (hilda.kaune@iom3.org); Mining Info Co-ordinator: Mr Mike McGarr (mike.mcgarr@iom3.org) *Other Snr Staff:* Info Asst: Ms Frances Perry (frances.perry@iom3.org)
Entry: visitors by prior appt *Open:* Mon-Fri 0930-1700; please check for availability
Subj: materials sci; sci & tech of metals, polymers, rubbers, ceramics & composites; economic geol; eng; mining; mining industry; metallurgy; minerals & mineral processing *Collns: Archvs:* several special collns, incl Sir Henry Bessemer Colln (MS material, bks & drawings of the 19C engineer & inventor); John Percy Papers (19C metallurgist); further info available on request *Co-op Schemes:* BLDSC
Equip: m-reader, fax, copier, computers (incl wd-proc, internet & CD-ROM), room for hire *Online:* IMMAGE *Svcs:* info, ref, biblio, indexing, abstracting, translation, lit searches (fees)
Stock: bks/5000+; periodcls/1000
Classn: UDC (local scheme) *Staff: Libns:* 3

S1201

Institute of Ophthalmology and Moorfields Eye Hospital, Joint Library

11-43 Bath St, London, EC1V 9EL (*tel & fax:* 020-7608-6814)
Email: ophthlib@ucl.ac.uk
Internet: http://www.ucl.ac.uk/ioo/library/

Gov Body: Univ of London (see **S1440**) *Chief:* Libn: Ms Deborah Heatlie BA
Entry: ref only; tel in adv; proof of ID required; a fee is charged *Open:* Mon, Fri 0900-1700, Tue-Thu 0900-1800
Subj: postgrad; ophthalmology; visual sci; optics; ophthalmic nursing; orthoptics *Collns: Bks & Pamphs:* historical bks colln (bnd vols of leaflets/pamphs & minor works,1566-1920, 600 items); reprint colln (1800-1997) *Archvs:* some papers/letters by E. Nettleship; assorted drawings & photos by I. Mann *Co-op Schemes:* BLDSC, UCL, North Thames Libs, ILL (photocopies only), UCL Aleph
Equip: fax, 2 copiers, 6 computers (not available to visitors) *Online:* ISI, EMBASE, Medline, PsycInfo, CINAHL, BNI (not available to visitors) *Svcs:* info, ref, biblio
Stock: bks/17600; periodcls/200; archvs/3 boxes; reprints/254000
Classn: NLM (mod) *Auto Sys:* Aleph
Staff: Libns: 2 *Non-Prof:* 1.4

S1202

Institute of Petroleum Library

61 New Cavendish St, London, W1G 7AR (020-7467-7100; *fax:* 020-7255-1472)
Email: lis@petroleum.co.uk
Internet: http://www.petroleum.co.uk/

Gov Body: Inst of Petroleum *Chief:* Head of Lib & Info Svc: Mrs Catherine M. Cosgrove BSc(Hons), BA, MCLIP, FInstPet (ccosgrove@petroleum.co.uk) *Other Snr Staff:* Snr Info Offcr: Mr Chris Baker
Entry: membs free; non-membs £30 pd, £20 per half day, students £2 pd with student ID card & letter from tutor *Open:* Mon-Fri 0915-1700, excl bank hols
Subj: petroleum industry *Collns: Bks & Pamphs:* unique colln of oil industry pubns covering sci & tech, economic & environmental affairs, market rsrch & statistics; conference proceedings; annual reports & house journals; directories; ASTM, BSI, IP & API standards relevant to the petroleum industry *Other:* press cuttings files *Co-op Schemes:* BLDSC
Equip: copier *Online:* Dialog, Factiva (£50 per hr for membs, £100 non-membs + costs) *Svcs:* info, ref, biblio, indexing, abstracting
Stock: bks/15000; periodcls/c200 *Acqs Offcr:* Head of Lib & Info Svc, as above
Classn: UREN
Pubns: IPSTAT Svc: Statistics Relevant to the Petroleum Industry (£80 UK, via internet); Educational Bklets; the Lib & Info Svc also manages & maintain the Inst's web site
Staff: Libns: 1 *Other Prof:* 2 *Non-Prof:* 1 *Exp:* £26000 (2000); £28000 (2001)

S1203

Institute of Race Relations Library

2-6 Leeke St, King's Cross Rd, London, WC1X 9HS (020-7837-0041; *fax:* 020-7278-0623)
Internet: http://www.irr.org.uk/

Type: educational charity *Gov Body:* Inst of Race Relations *Chief:* Libn: Ms Hazel Waters MA, MCLIP
Entry: ref only, adv appt at Libn's discretion *Open:* Mon-Thu 1000-1300, 1400-1700
Subj: race & minority group relations; imperialism; migration; asylum
Svcs: ref
Stock: bks/4000; periodcls/150; pamphs/3000
Classn: own (area & subj) *Staff: Libns:* 2

S1204

Institute of Revenues, Rating and Valuation Library

41 Doughty St, London, WC1N 2LF (020-7831-3505; *fax:* 020-7831-2048)
Email: enquiries@irrv.org.uk
Internet: http://www.irrv.org.uk/

Gov Body: Council of IRRV *Chief:* Pubns Offcr: Mr Sam Brierley
Entry: ref only, by adv appt; essentially a private lib for IRRV membs, but bona fide scholars may apply to use the collns *Open:* Mon-Fri 0900-1700
Subj: social sci; property valuation; revenues admin; local taxation; local benefits *Collns: Bks & Pamphs:* substantial reserve colln of old textbks in above subjs
Equip: fax, copier *Svcs:* ref
Stock: bks/1000, plus 10000 in reserve colln
Classn: Eccentric
Pubns: IRRV Pubns (annual catalogue, free on request)
Staff: Other Prof: 20

S1205

Institution of Civil Engineers, Library and Information Services

1 Gt George St, Westminster, London, SW1P 3AA (020-7665-2251; *fax:* 020-7976-7610)
Email: library@ice.org.uk
Internet: Http://www.ice.org.uk/

Type: prof instn *Gov Body:* Instn of Civil Engineers *Chief:* Libn: Mr Michael M. Chrimes BA, MLS, MCLIP *Dep:* Dep Libn: Ms Rose Marney BSc, MCLIP
Entry: membs only; non-membs by appt & on payment of fee *Open:* Mon-Fri 0915-1730
Subj: postgrad; geol; hydrology; applied physics; bldg; eng; civil eng; transport; arch; town planning; biography; hist of tech *Collns: Bks & Pamphs:* Vulliamy Horological Colln; Telford Lib; early printed eng reports *Archvs:* Inst of Civil Engineers Archvs; Inst of Municipal Engineers Archvs; Smeatonian Soc of Civil Engineers Archvs; Soc of Civil Eng Technicians Archvs; British Dam Soc Archvs; British Geotechnical Soc Archvs; Telford MSS; Rennie Reports; MacKenzie Colln; Frank Smith Colln; J.G. James Colln; Gibb Colln; Ellingen Papers *Co-op Schemes:* BLDSC, ILL
Equip: m-reader, m-printer, fax, video viewer (on request), 3 copiers, clr copier, 20 computers (incl user access to internet & CD-ROM), room for hire *Online:* Dialog (on cost recovery basis to membs only) *Svcs:* info, ref
Stock: bks/90000; periodcls/1000; slides/6000; illusts/200; pamphs/20000; videos/300; archvs/600 linear m; paintings/200; various photos, audios, maps & m-forms; total holdings amount to c3000 linear m
Classn: UDC *Auto Sys:* EuroTec
Pubns: Periodicals Catalogue (£10); Audio Visual Catalogue (£3); various Exhib Catalogues (£3-£10)
Staff: Libns: 8 *Other Prof:* 1 *Non-Prof:* 2

S1206

Institution of Electrical Engineers Library

(incorporating the British Computer Soc Lib)
Savoy Pl, London, WC2R 0BL (020-7344-5461; *fax:* 020-7497-3557)
Email: libdesk@iee.org.uk
Internet: http://www.iee.org/library/

Chief: Head of Lib Svcs: Mr John W. Coupland BA, MCLIP (jcoupland@iee.org.uk) *Dep:* Dep Libn: Ms Helen Sparks BA, MCLIP (hsparks@iee.org.uk)
Assoc Libs: BRITISH COMPUTER SOC LIB, Libn: Mr Anthony Everson MA, MEd, MA(Lib), MCLIP; INSTN OF MANUFACTURING ENGINEERS LIB; INSTN OF ELEC & RADIO ENGINEERS LIB; INSTN OF ELECTRICAL ENGINEERS ARCHVS (incl NATL ARCHV FOR ELECTRICAL SCI & TECH, see **A294**); all at above addr
Entry: public, ref only *Open:* Mon-Fri 0900-1700
Subj: tech; electrical, elec & manufacturing eng; computing; info tech; telecommunications; physics; mgmt; hist *Collns: Bks & Pamphs:* Ronald's Lib; S.P. Thompson Lib; all IEE pubns; ECMA & ITU standards *Archvs:* Michael Faraday papers; Oliver Heaviside papers *Co-op Schemes:* BLDSC, ILL
Equip: copier (A4/10p), 9 computers (all with internet, 5 with CD-ROM), video player *Online:* Dialog (min charge £50 membs, £100 non-membs) *Svcs:* info, ref, biblio, photocopying svc
Stock: bks/150000; periodcls/1100; pamphs/10000; videos/300; AVs/50
Classn: UDC *Auto Sys:* CAIRS
Staff: Libns: 5 *Other Prof:* 1 *Non-Prof:* 2 *Exp:* £200000 (1999-2000); £180000 (2000-01)

Special Libraries

London ▼ London

S1207
Institution of Gas Engineers and Managers, Library and Information Services

12 York Gate, London, NW1 4QG (020-7487-0650; *fax:* 020-7224-4762)
Email: general@igem.org.uk
Internet: http://www.igem.org.uk/

Chief: Libn: Ms A. Witten BA, MLS, MCLIP
Entry: adv appt for non-membs of Instn *Open:* 0900-1700 when Libn is present (usually Tue-Thu)
Subj: gas eng; fuel gas tech *Co-op Schemes:* ILL
Equip: photocopying svc (min charge £8) *Online:* GasLine, internet searching via Libn (fee charged)
Svcs: info, ref, biblio, rsrch (fee charged)
Stock: various bks, periodcls, photos, pamphs, CD-ROMs & archvs
Classn: Internatl Gas Union *Auto Sys:* Adlib
Staff: Libns: 0.4 *Exp:* £1500 (1999-2000)

S1208
Institution of Mechanical Engineers, Information and Library Service

1 Birdcage Walk, Westminster, London, SW1H 9JJ (020-7973-1265; *fax:* 020-7222-8762)
Email: ils@imeche.org.uk
Internet: http://www.imeche.org.uk/ils/

Type: prof body *Gov Body:* Instn of Mechanical Engineers Council *Chief:* Snr Libn & Archivist: Mr Keith Moore (k_moore@imeche.org.uk) *Dep:* Libn: Mr Mike Claxton (m_claxton@imeche.org.uk)
Entry: ref only for non-membs *Open:* Mon-Fri 0915-1730
Subj: mechanical eng; transport eng; thermo-dynamics; fluid mechanics; manufacturing; machine tools; pressure vessels; robotics *Collns: Bks & Pamphs:* IMechE pubns; eng company hists; eng standards *Archvs:* records of IMechE business meetings (1847-date); administrative papers of Instn of Automobile Engineers & Instn of Locomotive Engineers; business records of eng companies; archvs relating to the hist of mechanical eng, incl: George Stephenson papers; Robert Stephenson papers; Sir Joseph Whitworth papers; Frederick Lanchester papers; Lord Hinton papers; Sir Frank Ewart Smith papers *Other:* Brunel photos; David Joy drawings; Nasmyth drawings; Boulton & Watt drawings etc *Co-op Schemes:* BLDSC, ILL
Equip: m-reader, m-printer, video viewer, fax, copier, 10 computers (incl wd-proc & CD-ROM) *Online:* Dialog, ECCTIS, ESDU, Inside, ILI Standards Infodisk, ILI Metals Infodisk, Kompass, MIRA Abstracts & others *Svcs:* info, ref, document supply
Stock: bks/120000; periodcls/200
Classn: DDC *Auto Sys:* CAIRS
Staff: Libns: 6 *Non-Prof:* 3

S1209
Institution of Structural Engineers, Information and Library Service

11 Upper Belgrave St, London, SW1X 8BH (020-7235-4535; *fax:* 020-7201-9118)
Email: library@istructe.org.uk
Internet: http://www.istructe.org.uk/

Chief: Info & Lib Svc Mgr: Mrs Sue Claxton BSc(Hons)
Entry: student membs & non-membs should make an appt *Open:* Tue-Fri 0930-1730
Subj: tech; structural eng *Collns: Bks & Pamphs:* 19C textbks; industry reports & standards *Other:* AV colln *Co-op Schemes:* BLDSC, ILL
Equip: m-fiche reader, copier, computer (with CD-ROM) *Online:* Dialtech (cost of search + staff time)
Svcs: info, ref
Stock: bks/13000; periodcls/c160; slides/32 sets; pamphs/11000; m-forms/180; videos/85
Classn: UDC *Auto Sys:* Heritage
Pubns: Journal Holdings; Video Colln; see current IStructE pubns list for details
Staff: Libns: 2 *Non-Prof:* 1

S1210
Instituto Cervantes Library

102 Eaton Sq, London, SW1W 9AN (020-7235-0324; *fax:* 020-7235-0329)
Email: iclondre@globalnet.co.uk or biblon@cervantes.es

Gov Body: Spanish Govt *Chief:* Head Libn: Ms Consuelo Alvarez BA *Dep:* Libns: Ms Matilde Javaloyes BA & Ms Rosa Barbany BA
Assoc Libs: INSTITUTO CERVANTES LIB, 322-330 (Unit 8) Deansgate, Campfield Ave Arcade, Manchester, M3 4FN (0161-661-4210); INSTITUTO CERVANTES LIB, Dublin (see **IS92**)
Entry: ref, study & lending *Open:* Mon-Thu 1200-1830, Sat 0930-1330, closed Fri; summer: Mon-Thu 12-1830, Fri 1200-1700
Subj: Spain: law; politics; sociology; edu; lang; arts; Spain & Latin America: lit; geog; hist *Collns: Bks & Pamphs:* ref colln of dictionaries, encyclo-paedias, directories etc
Equip: video viewer, copier, computer (incl CD-ROM) *Svcs:* info, ref, biblio
Stock: bks/20000; periodcls/70; slides/240; audios/200 CDs, 2000 cassettes; videos/1200; CD-ROMs/various; AVs/300
Classn: UDC *Auto Sys:* ABSYS (BRS)
Staff: Libns: 1 *Other Prof:* 2

S1211
International Book Development Ltd, Research Library

305-307 Chiswick High Rd, London, W4 4HH (020-8742-7474; *fax:* 020-8747-8715)
Email: enquiries@ibd.uk.net

Type: consultancy for aid agencies & developing countries *Gov Body:* Centre for British Teachers (CfBT)
Entry: IBD staff; also available to donors & governments
Subj: bk development; info development
See also **O238**

S1212
International Coffee Organization Library

22 Berners St, London, W1P 4DD (020-7612-0603/10; *fax:* 020-7580-6129)
Email: library@ico.org
Internet: http://www.ico.org/libser/library.htm

Chief: Head of Lib & Public Relations: Mr Martin Wattam
Entry: ref only; adv appt
Subj: coffee; coffee industry; trade; development
Collns: Bks & Pamphs: economic & statistical data on coffee *Other:* slide colln; video colln
Stock: bks/13000; periodcls/200

S1213
International Institute for Strategic Studies, Holinger-Telegraph Library

Arundel House, 13-15 Arundel St, London, WC2R 3PX (020-7395-9122; *fax:* 020-7836-3108)
Email: library@iiss.org
Internet: http://www.iiss.org/

Chief: Chief Libn: Ms Ellen Peacock BA *Dep:* Dep Libn: Ms Emma Sullivan BA, MSc
Entry: fee payable: £5 pd (£2 conc) *Open:* Mon-Fri 1000-1700
Subj: military & political aspects of internatl relations; arms control; security; foreign countries' domestic politics & defence policies *Collns: Archvs:* press & journals articles cuttings colln (1958-date) *Co-op Schemes:* BLDSC, ILL
Equip: 2 m-readers, m-printer, copier, computers (incl internet & CD-ROM), room for hire *Online:* Lexis-Nexis (fee based) *Svcs:* info, ref, biblio
Stock: bks/10000; periodcls/90; pamphs/11000; CD-ROMs/30
Classn: own *Auto Sys:* Unicorn (SIRSI)
Staff: Libns: 3 *Non-Prof:* 1

S1214
International Labour Office, Reference Library and Information Unit

Millbank Tower, 21-24 Millbank, London, SW1P 4QP (020-7828-6401; *fax:* 020-7233-5925)
Email: evansn@ilo-london.org.uk

Type: UN agency *Chief:* Info Unit Mgr: Mr Nick Evans *Dep:* Info Offcr: Mr Carl David
Entry: ref only, by appt *Open:* Mon-Fri 1000-1300, 1400-1630
Subj: labour issues; labour law; social issues; labour hist; human rights; trades unions; employment; mgmt; women's issues; child labour; Health & Safety
Equip: m-reader, copier, computer (with CD-ROM)
Online: on CD-ROM: ILOLEX, NATLEX, LABORDOC (own databases)
Pubns: ILO pubns incl: printed materials, videos, audios & computer databases

S1215
International Planned Parenthood Federation Library

Regent's Coll, Inner Circle, Regent's Pk, London, NW1 4NS (020-7487-7855; *fax:* 020-7487-7950)
Internet: http://www.ippf.org/

Chief: Libn: Ms Rita Ward MCLIP
Entry: adv appt essential, ref only *Open:* Mon-Fri 1000-1700
Subj: social sci; medicine; family planning *Co-op Schemes:* BLDSC
Equip: m-reader, video viewer, copier, computer (with CD-ROM)
Stock: bks/6000; periodcls/90; pamphs/2000; m-forms/3500; audios/50; videos/400
Classn: own *Auto Sys:* DBTextworks
Staff: Libns: 1

S1216
Italian Cultural Institute Library

39 Belgrave Sq, London, SW1X 8NX (020-7235-1461; *fax:* 020-7235-4618)
Email: library@italcultur.org.uk
Internet: http://www.italcultur.org.uk/

Gov Body: Italian Ministry of Foreign Affairs
Chief: Libn: Mrs Riccobono Reidy
Entry: open to public for ref, but membership required for loans *Open:* Mon-Fri 1000-1300, 1400-1700

Subj: Italy: arts; lit; geog; hist *Collns: Bks & Pamphs:* Dante Alighieri section *Co-op Schemes:* BLDSC
Equip: copier (A4/10p) *Svcs:* info, ref, biblio, indexing
Stock: bks/26000; periodcls/150; videos/300
Classn: DDC *Auto Sys:* Q&A
Staff: Libns: 1 *Other Prof:* 1

S1217

The Iveagh Bequest, Kenwood, Library

Hampstead Ln, London, NW3 7JR (020-8348-1286; *fax:* 020-7973-3891)
Email: laura.houliston@english-heritage.org.uk

Gov Body: English Heritage *Chief:* Snr Curator: Ms Cathy Power *Dep:* Asst Curator: Ms Laura Houliston
Entry: adv appt, ref only (specialist lib) *Open:* Mon-Fri 1000-1600
Subj: arts; hist of art; Irish hist; Irish lit; local hist (Kenwood) *Co-op Schemes:* associated with English Heritage Lib (see **S1122**)
Equip: computer (with wd-proc)
Stock: 2500 items
Classn: UDC *Staff: Other Prof:* 3

S1218

J. Rothschild Capital Management Ltd, Library

27 St James's Pl, London, SW1A 1NR (020-7493-8111; *fax:* 020-7629-3247)

Chief: Libn: Miss Susan Riggs BSc(Hons)
Entry: staff only *Open:* Mon-Fri 0930-1730
Subj: business info
Equip: copier, fax, computer (with wd-proc, CD-ROM & internet) *Online:* Companies House *Svcs:* info, ref

S1219

Japan Foundation Library

17 Old Park Ln, London, W1Y 3LG (020-7499-4726; *fax:* 020-7495-1133)
Internet: http://www.nihongocentre.org.uk/

Chief: Libn: Ms F. Simmons MA
Entry: teachers, rsrchers & administrators in Japanese studies *Open:* Mon-Fri 1000-1300, 1400-1700
Subj: Japanese studies; Japanese lang *Co-op Schemes:* ILL
Equip: 2 video viewers, copier, 2 computers (1 PC, 1 Apple Mac, both with internet & CD-ROM)
Svcs: info, ref, loan by post for eligible membs
Stock: bks/4988; periodcls/20; audios/513; videos/460; CD-ROMs/124 *Acqs Offcr:* Libn, as above
Classn: CDC *Auto Sys:* Allegro
Staff: Libns: 1 *Exp:* £10000 (1999-2000)

S1220

Japan Information and Cultural Centre Library

Embassy of Japan, 101-104 Piccadilly, London, W1V 9FN (020-7465-6500; *fax:* 020-7491-9347)
Email: info@embjapan.org.uk
Internet: http://www.embjapan.org.uk/

Gov Body: Ministry of Foreign Affairs, Japan
Chief: Info Libn: Ms Teruko Sekiguchi (teruko.sekiguchi@jpembassy.org.jp)
Entry: open to membs of public for ref; bks may be borrowed upon presentation of some ID & introductory letter from an academic instn *Open:* Mon-Fri 0930-1245, 1430-1700; closed Japanese natl hols & British bank hols (please ring to check)

Subj: Japan, all aspects, incl: phil; psy; religion; social sci; lang; arts; lit; geog; hist *Collns: Bks & Pamphs:* unique ref bks on Noh & Kabuki theatre *Other:* Japanese govt & related pubns; Japanese Diplomatic Blue Bk; Japanese newspapers: Asahi shinbun (1986-date); Japan Times (1980-date)
Equip: 2 video viewers
Stock: bks/6000; periodcls/30; photos/2500; slides/30 sets; videos/270 *Acqs Offcr:* Info Libn, as above
Classn: NDC
Staff: Non-Prof: 1 *Exp:* £1500 (1999-2000); £2000 (2000-01)

S1221

The Japan Society Library

Swire House, 59 Buckingham Gate, London, SW1E 6AJ (020-7828-6330; *fax:* 020-7828-6331)
Email: info@japansociety.org.uk or ajhp@japansociety.org.uk
Internet: http://www.japansociety.org.uk/

Chief: Hon Libn: Mr Sebastian Dobson *Dep: Lib Asst:* Ms Clare Barclay
Entry: ref only for non-membs, appointments must be made with the asst in adv; membs of the Japan Soc may borrow a selection of bks, other bks are for ref only *Open:* Wed 1500-1800, Fri 1200-1500
Subj: Japan; Anglo-Japanese relations; Anglo-Japanese hist *Collns: Bks & Pamphs:* bks in English on Japan (1850-1930) *Archvs:* documents relating to Japan Soc's own activs since its inception in 1891, incl original 'Proceedings' & photographic materials *Other:* 19C photo albums ('souvenir'-type albums brought back by early travellers to Japan)
Equip: computer (with CD-ROM)
Stock: bks/c6000; periodcls/5; photos/c800; slides/c300; maps/40; archvs/unquantified
Classn: own
Pubns: Proceedings of the Japan Soc
Staff: 3 in total
Proj: ongoing digitisation of photographic stock; development of searchable database

S1222

The Jewish Museum, London, Library and Archives

The Strenberg Centre, 80 East End Rd, Finchley, London, N3 2SY (020-8349-1143; *fax:* 020-8343-2162)
Email: enquiries@jewishmuseum.org
Internet: http://www.jewishmuseum.org/

Type: independent museum & archv *Gov Body:* Council of the Jewish Museum *Chief: Curator:* Ms Carol Seigel MA (carol.seigel@jewishmuseum.org
Dep: Curator of Collns: Ms Sarah Jillings MA (sarah.jillings@jewishmuseum.org)
Assoc Libs: THE JEWISH MUSEUM, Raymond Burton House, 129-131 Albert St, London, NW1 7NB, Curator: Ms Jennifer Marin MA (020-7284-1997; *fax:* 020-7267-9008)
Entry: adv appt preferred *Open:* Mon-Thu 1030-1700; closed all public & Jewish hols & 24 Dec-4 Jan
Subj: Judaism; Jewish religious & social hist; hist of Jewish community in Britain, esp London; World War Two; Holocaust *Collns: Bks & Pamphs:* museum catalogue; exhib catalogues; rsrch papers *Archvs:* archvs, photos & oral hist recordings relating to Jewish social hist, esp in London
Equip: copier (10p) *Svcs:* info, ref
Stock: bks/400; photos/c10000; slides/200; audios/470; videos/25; archvs/20 cubic m
Classn: Museum Catalogue
Pubns: list available on web site
Staff: Other Prof: 7 *Non-Prof:* 1

S1223

John Lewis plc, Business Information Department

171 Victoria St, London, SW1E 5NN (020-7592-6319; *fax:* 020-7592-6333)
Email: business_information@johnlewis.co.uk

Chief: Head of Business Info: Mr Peter Allen
Entry: bona fide rsrchers by appt *Open:* Mon-Fri 0900-1730
Subj: business; retailing *Collns: Archvs:* The Gazette of the John Lewis Partnership (1918-date)
Stock: bks/7500; periodcls/750; pamphs/2000
Classn: UDC *Auto Sys:* Notebooks
Staff: Libns: 2 *Non-Prof:* 0.5

S1224

Kate Sharpley Library

BM Hurricane, London, WC1N 3XX
Email: katesharpleylibrary@hushmail.com
Internet: http://www.katesharpley.org/

Entry: adv appt
Subj: politics; anarchism; hist of anarchism, syndicalism & related political movements; political records *Collns: Archvs:* IWA (AIT/IAA) records; Anarchist Federation of Britain records (1945-50); Syndicalist Workers Federation records (1950-79); records of anarchist publishing houses, incl Cienfuegos Press & ASP *Other:* anarchist newspapers, incl: Freedom (complete); Spain & the World (complete); Direct Action (1945 onwards); Black Flag & others; tapes; videos; posters; flyers
Stock: bks/c3000; pamphs/c2700
Pubns: KSL Bulletin (quarterly); The Struggle Against the State & Other Essays, by Nestor Mahkno (1996, £7.95); The Friends of Durruti Group 1937-1939, by Augustin Guillamon (1997, £7.95); No Gods, No Masters, ed Daniel Guerin (1998, 2 vols, £11.95 each); Yiddish Anarchist Bibliography, ed John Patten (£7.50); A Contribution to an Anarchist Bibliography of Latin America, by Max Nettlau (£4); numerous pamphs

S1225

Keats Memorial Library

Keats House, Keats Grove, Hampstead, London, NW3 2RR (020-7435-2062; *fax:* 020-7431-9293)
Email: keatshouse@corpoflondon.gov.uk

Gov Body: Corp of London (see **P99**); administered by London Metropolitan Archvs (see **A304**) *Chief:* Curator: Dr Deborah G. Jenkins MA, PhD, DipAS
Entry: by appt only *Open:* April-Nov: Tue-Sun 1200-1700; Nov-Mar: Tue-Sun 1200-1600
Subj: John Keats, the poet & his circle; Romantic poetry (1792-1830) *Collns: Bks & Pamphs:* Dilke Colln (Keats's bks & relics); Buxton Forman Colln *Archvs:* MSS & letters relating to John Keats *Co-op Schemes:* ILL
Stock: bks/8000; periodcls/10; photos/500; slides/100; pamphs/1000; audios/5; videos/4; maps & m-forms/60
Classn: own
Pubns: Guide to Keats House (£1.50); Keats at Wentworth Place; Select Booklist of Keats
Staff: Other Prof: 5 *Non-Prof:* 1

S1226

Kenneth Ritchie Wimbledon Library

Wimbledon Law Tennis Museum, Church Rd, Wimbledon, London, SW19 5AE (020-8946-6131; *fax:* 020-8944-6497)
Email: asne@aeltc.com
Internet: http://www.wimbledon.org/museum/

Gov Body: All England Lawn Tennis & Croquet Club *Chief: Hon Libn:* Mr Alan Little

(Kenneth Ritchie Wimbledon Lib cont)

Entry: open to public for ref only; prior appt required (contact the Hon Libn) **Open:** Tue-Fri 1030-1700 (closed public hols & during Wimbledon Championships)
Subj: lawn tennis **Collns:** *Bks & Pamphs:* British & foreign lawn tennis bks, annuals, periodcls & programmes *Other:* cuttings, videos & photos
Equip: copier, video player *Disabled:* wheelchair access
Pubns: Lib Catalogue (£9)

S1227 🎓

King's College London, Information Services and Systems

Strand, London, WC2R 2LS (*enqs:* 020-7848-2430; *lib office:* 020-7848-2140; *fax:* 020-7848-1777)
Email: issenquiry@kcl.ac.uk
Internet: http://www.kcl.ac.uk/iss/

Gov Body: Univ of London (see **S1440**) **Chief:** Dir of Info Resources & Svcs: post vacant **Other Snr Staff:** Info Resources Mgr: Dr Astrid Wissenburg (astrid.wissenburg@kcl.ac.uk); Bibliographic Svcs Coordinator: Ms Abigail Edwards (abigail.edwards@kcl.ac.uk); Elec Resources Coordinator: Mr Russell Burke (russell.burke@kcl.ac.uk); Journals & Document Delivery Coordinator: Mr Stephen Prowse (stephen.prowse@kcl.ac.uk); Special Collns Coordinator: Ms Katie Sambrook (catherine.sambrook@kcl.ac.uk)
Assoc Libs: *Strand Campus:* MAUGHAN LIB & INFO SVCS CENTRE, Chancery Ln, London, WC1A 1LR (020-7848-2424; *fax:* 020-7848-2277); FOYLE SPECIAL COLLNS LIB, Maughan Lib, Chancery Ln, London, WC1A 1LR (020-7848-1843/5; *fax:* 020-7848-1843); KING'S COLL LONDON ARCHVS, Info Svcs & Systems, Strand, London, WC2R 2LS (020-7848-2015; *fax:* 020-7848-2760; *email:* archives@kcl.ac.uk); *Waterloo Campus:* WATERLOO INFO SVCS CENTRE, Franklin-Wilkins Bldg, 150 Stamford St, London, SE1 9NN (020-7848-4378; *fax:* 020-7848-4290); *St Thomas' Campus:* MEDICAL SCHOOL LIB, St Thomas' Hosp, Lambeth Palace Rd, London, SE1 7EH (020-7928-9292 x2367/1569; *fax:* 020-7401-3932); CALNAN LIB, Block 7, St Thomas' Hosp, Lambeth Palace Rd, London, SE1 7EH (020-7928-9292 x1313; *fax:* 020-7928-1428); *Guy's Campus:* GUY'S INFO SVCS CENTRE, Guy's Hosp, London Bridge, London, SE1 1UL (020-7848-6600; *fax:* 020-7848-6743); F.S. WARNER LIB & INFO CENTRE, 18th Floor, Guy's Tower, Guy's Hosp, London, Bridge, London, SE1 9RT (020-7955-4238; *fax:* 020-7955-4103); *Denmark Hill Campus:* DENMARK HILL INFO SVCS CENTRE, Weston Edu Centre, Cutcombe Rd, London, SE5 9PJ (020-7848-5541/2; *fax:* 020-7848-5550); INST OF PSYCHIATRY LIB (see **S1228**); BETHLEM ROYAL HOSP MULTIDISCIPLINARY LIB (see **S109**)
Entry: ref only; most bldgs are by card access only, so appt or registration in adv required **Open:** *Maughan Lib:* term: Mon-Fri 0830-2200, Sat 0930-1730, Sun 1100-1900; *Franklin-Wilkins ISC:* Mon-Fri term: 0900-2100, Sat 0930-1730; *St Thomas' Medical School Lib:* Mon-Fri 1000-1800; *Calnan Lib:* Mon-Fri 1000-1800; *New Hunt's House ISC:* term: Mon-Fri 0900-2100, Sat 0930-1730, Sun 1100-1900; *F.S. Warner Lib:* Mon-Fri 0900-1900; *Denmark Hill ISC:* term: Mon-Fri 0900-2100, Sat 1000-1330; vac: hrs vary

Subj: undergrad; postgrad; *Maughan Lib:* phil; psy; religion; social sci; lang; sci; maths; tech; arts; lit; geog; hist; *Waterloo ISC:* edu; mgmt; nursing; health; midwifery; *St Thomas' Medical School Lib:* medicine; *Calnan Lib:* dermatology; *Guy's ISC:* medicine; biomedical sci; *F.S. Warner Lib:* dentistry; *Denmark Hill ISC:* medicine; clinical sci
Collns: *Bks & Pamphs:* pre-1800 rare bks; Early Sci Colln (19C-early 20C); Marsden Colln (lib of William Marsden 1754-1836); Adam Archv (lib of Miron Grindea b1909, editor of Adam Internatl Review, 20C European lit); Box Colln (Judaica & biblical hist); Burrows Colln (Greek & Byzantine studies); Cohn Colln (European law); Coll Hist Colln (hist of Coll, Coll authors); De Beer Colln (bks by or about Charles Darwin); Enk Colln (classics); Hamilton Colln (military hist, lit); B.S. Johnson Colln (20C lit & poetry); Liddell Hart Colln (military hist); Maurice Colln (military hist); Mottram Colln (English & American lit); Rainbow Lib (Jewish & Christian liturgy); Ratcliff Lib (Christian liturgy); Relton Lib (theology, spiritualism, ecclesiastical hist); Richardson Colln (Italian lit); Ruggles Gates Colln (genetics & heredity); Sion Colln (theology, ecclesiastical hist); Skeat & Furnivall Colln (early English lang & lit); Stebbing Colln (zoology); Todd Colln (anatomy & physiology); Wheatstone Colln (19C maths & physics); Carnegie Colln of British Music *Archvs:* Coll Archvs; Liddell Hart Centre for Military Archvs (see **A298**) **Co-op Schemes:** BLDSC, SCONUL, M25 Consortium
Equip: m-readers, m-printers, fax, copiers, computers (incl internet & CD-ROM), audio equip *Online:* BIDS, EDINA, MIMAS, OCLC FirstSearch, OVID, Medline, CINAHL, Web of Science & others (Coll membs only)
Stock: bks/c990000; periodcls/c2500
Classn: LC, NLM **Auto Sys:** Aleph

S1228 🎓

King's College London, Institute of Psychiatry Library

De Crespigny Pk, London, SE5 8AF (020-7703-5411; *fax:* 020-7848-0209)
Email: spyllib@iop.kcl.ac.uk
Internet: http://www.iop.kcl.ac.uk/iop/AdminSup/Library/index.shtml

Gov Body: King's Coll London (see **S1227**)
Chief: Libn: Mr Martin Guha BA, MCLIP **Dep:** Dep Libn: Ms Clare Martin BA, MCLIP
Entry: ref by previous arrangement with libn only
Open: Mon-Fri 0900-2000, Sat 0900-1300
Subj: psy; neuroscience; psychiatry **Co-op Schemes:** PLCS
Equip: m-reader, m-printer, copiers, computer (incl CD-ROM), binding facilities *Online:* BIDS, Cochrane, ISI Citation Indexes, Medline, Embase, PsycInfo, PsycInfo, IBSS, IDEAL, NISS *Officer-in-Charge:* Libn, as above
Stock: bks/250000; periodcls/310 **Acqs Offcr:** Libn, as above
Classn: Bliss **Auto Sys:** Aleph
Staff: Libns: 3 *Non-Prof:* 4 **Exp:** £260000 (2000-01)

S1229 🗝✚

King's Fund, Library and Information Service

11-13 Cavendish Sq, London, W1G 0AN (020-7307-2568; *fax:* 020-7307-2805)
Email: library@kingsfund.org.uk

Gov Body: King Edward's Hosp Fund for London
Chief: Info & Lib Svc Mgr: Ms Lynette Cawthra MA, DipLib, MCLIP
Entry: ref only **Open:** Mon-Tue, Thu-Fri 0930-1730, Wed 1100-1730, Sat 0930-1700 (closed bank hol weekends)
Subj: health svcs; mgmt; policy; planning; community care; urban health; health & race

Collns: *Bks & Pamphs:* World Health Org Documentation Centre; strategic plans; Trust documents; public health reports *Archvs:* King's Fund Archvs (1897-date) **Co-op Schemes:** BLDSC, Health Mgmt Info Consortium, Health Mgmt Libns Forum, CHILL
Equip: m-reader, 4 copiers, 5 computers (incl 4 internet) *Disabled:* ZoomText on OPAC *Online:* Datastar etc (priced svc) *Svcs:* info, ref, biblio
Stock: bks/27000; periodcls/350
Classn: Bliss **Auto Sys:** Unicorn
Pubns: Periodicals Received in Lib; reading lists on popular topics
Staff: Libns: 7 *Non-Prof:* 3

S1230 🗝

Kipling Society Library

c/o City Univ Lib, Northampton Sq, London, EC1V 0HB

Chief: Hon Libn: Mr John Slater (020-7359-2404)
Dep: Sec of the Kipling Soc: Mrs Jane Keskar, 6 Clifton Rd, London, W9 1SS (020-7286-0194)
Entry: adv appt only **Open:** Mon-Fri 0930-1700
Subj: Kipling's life & works with associated subjs
Svcs: ref
Stock: bks/1400; periodcls/1; some photos, slides, illusts, pamphs, audios & videos
Pubns: Kipling Journal (quarterly, distributed to membs of Soc & to academic lib membs, subscription £25 pa)

S1231 🏛

La Médiatèque de L'Institut Français

17 Queensberry Pl, London, SW7 2DT (020-7073-1350; *fax:* 020-7073-1363)
Email: library@ambafrance.org.uk
Internet: http://institut.ambfrance.org.uk/

Gov Body: Ministry of Foreign Affairs (France)
Chief: Head of Libs & Info Svcs: Mme Isabel Fernandez (isabel.fernandez@ambafrance.org.uk)
Dep: Dep Head of Libs & Info Svcs: Mme Chantal Morel (chantal.morel@ambafrance.org.uk)
Assoc Libs: CHILDREN'S LIB, 32 Harrington Rd, London, SW7, Libn in Charge: Mme Josette Gerlier; INSTITUT FRANÇAIS ARCHVS, 32 Harrington Rd, London, SW7, Libn in Charge: Mme Chantal Morel, as above
Entry: free on site; to borrow, membership of Institut Français (fee payable) **Open:** *La Médiatèque:* Tue-Fri 1200-1900, Sat 1200-1800; *Children's Lib:* Tue-Sat 1200-1800; both closed bank hols, Aug & between Xmas & New Year
Subj: all subjs on France, at all levels from GCSE to postgrad **Collns:** *Bks & Pamphs:* Free French Colln (La France Libre); back copies of French periodcls, from late 19C *Archvs:* Archvs of L'Institut Français; Denis Saurat MSS *Other:* Le Monde newspaper on m-film & CD-ROM (1944 onwards); videos (French cinema, some subtitled) & video documentaries; press cuttings of French current affairs; CDs of French music; audio bks & CD-ROMs on all subjs related to France; recordings of lectures held at the Inst **Co-op Schemes:** ILL
Equip: video viewer, copier (10p per pg), computers (incl 2 with internet & 2 with CD-ROM, access free), rooms for hire *Svcs:* info, ref, biblio
Stock: bks/45000; periodcls/136; audios/3500; videos/2550; CD-ROMs/300; archvs/2 miles; various photos & m-forms
Classn: DDC **Auto Sys:** Agate
Pubns: List of Periodicals; selected bibliographies
Staff: Libns: 8 **Exp:** £33000 (1999-2000); £33100 (2000-01)
Proj: digitisation of archival material

S1232 📖

Laban Library and Archive

Laban, Creekside, London, SE8 3DZ (020-8649-9533; *fax:* 020-8691-8400)
Email: library@laban.co.uk
Internet: http://www.laban.org/

Chief: Head of Lib: Mr Ralph Cox (r.cox@laban.org) *Dep:* Reader Svcs Mgr: Mrs Freda Lodge (f.lodge@laban.org)
Entry: ref only for genl public; no appt required
Open: term: Mon, Wed-Thu 0900-2000, Tue 0900-1930, Fri 0900-1700, Sat 1030-1430; vac: Mon-Fri 0900-1700
Subj: arts; dance & related subjs *Collns: Archvs:* Laban Colln (work of Rudolph von Laban & associates in 20s & 30s); Peter Williams Colln (photos, programmes, posters etc); dance generally (1940-date); Peter Brinson Colln (incl Ballet For All archv) *Co-op Schemes:* BLDSC, SEAL, Theatre Info Group
Equip: m-reader, 7 video viewers, copier, 26 computers (all with wd-proc, internet & CD-ROM, Laban students only) *Online:* Dialog, Dance on Disc (networked CD-ROM), Dance Resources on the Net (see web site) *Officer-in-Charge:* Head of Lib, as above *Svcs:* info, ref, biblio
Stock: bks/17500; periodcls/50; photos/40000; slides/5000; pamphs/500; m-forms/150; audios/600; videos/2600; archvs/300 linear m *Acqs Offcr:* Head of Lib, as above
Classn: DDC (mod) *Auto Sys:* Softlink Europe/Alice
Pubns: Lib Bulletin; Thesis List; Periodicals List (free)
Staff: Libns: 2 *Other Prof:* 1 archivist *Non-Prof:* 4

S1233 📖

Lambeth College, Learning Resources Service

Vauxhall Centre, Wandsworth Rd, London, SW8 2JY (020-7501-5631; *fax:* 020-7501-5490)
Email: mfindlay@lambethcollege.ac.uk
Internet: http://www.lambethcollege.ac.uk/

Gov Body: Lambeth Coll *Chief:* Head of Lib Svcs: Ms Mary Findlay MA, PGLib, CertEd, MCLIP
Assoc Libs: VAUXHALL LRC, addr as above; BRIXTON LRC, 56 Brixton Hill, London, SW2 1QS; CLAPHAM LRC, 45 Clapham Common South Side, London, SW4 9BL; TOWER BRIDGE LRC, Tooley St, London, SE1 2JR
Entry: students & staff, others ref only, adv appt
Open: Mon, Wed 0900-1900, Tue, Thu 0900-1700, Fri 1000-1600
Subj: all subjs; genl; GCSE; A level
Equip: copiers, video viewers, computers (incl wd-proc, internet & CD-ROM) *Disabled:* Kurzweil
Svcs: info, ref, biblio
Stock: bks/73568; periodcls/302; slides/500; audios/200; videos/1423; CD-ROMs/136
Classn: DDC *Auto Sys:* Dynix
Staff: Libns: 10.5 *Non-Prof:* 8.8

S1234 🔑 🕊

Lambeth Palace Library and Archives

Lambeth, London, SE1 7JU (020-7898-1400; *fax:* 020-7928-7932)
Internet: http://www.lambethpalacelibrary.org/

Type: rsrch lib *Gov Body:* C of E *Chief:* Libn & Archivist: Dr R.J. Palmer BA, PhD, MCLIP
Entry: ref only, letter of introduction required
Open: Mon-Fri 1000-1700, closed bank hols & for 10 days at Christmas & Easter
Subj: hist; religion; ecclesiastical hist; hist of C of E & Anglican Communion; topography; arts (ecclesiastical); lit (early periods); bibliography; local studies (Kent, Surrey, Sussex & other counties) *Collns: Bks & Pamphs:* c3500 early printed English bks (1501-1640); c6000 early printed English bks (1641-1700); c3500 early printed foreign bks (1501-1640); c6000 early printed foreign bks (1641-1700); c200 incunabula; pamph colln (esp 16C-19C religious & political controversies) *Archvs:* extensive C of E archvs, incl: Archvs of the Archbishop (registers, modern papers, faculty office, Vicar Genl, Court of Arches); Fulham Papers (collns of Bishops of London); collns of leading churchmen & Bishops, incl Rev John Newton & Bishop Bell of Chichester; records of C of E Socs *Other:* c4000 MSS (from 9C-20C, mainly ecclesiastical); Sion Coll pre-1850 bks & MSS (c35000); large colln of plans of 19C churches *Co-op Schemes:* ILLs made but not via co-op scheme
Equip: 2 m-readers, m-printer, copier
Stock: bks/200000; periodcls/130; photos/600; illusts/4000 prints; pamphs/50000; maps/400; m-forms/several sets; archvs/unmeasured
Classn: LC (mod) *Auto Sys:* Dynix
Pubns: Annual Review, various Catalogues of MSS & Archvs (list available on request)
Staff: Libns: 3 *Other Prof:* 4 *Non-Prof:* 5
Proj: computerisation of archvs (under way); increased strong room storage (under consideration)

S1235 🔑

The Landscape Institute Library

6-8 Barnard Mews, London, SW11 1QU (020-7350-5202; *fax:* 020-7350-5201)
Email: library@l-i.org.uk
Internet: http://www.l-i.org.uk/

Type: prof assoc *Chief:* Libn: Mrs Sheila Harvey BA, MPhil, MCLIP, Hon FLI
Entry: ref only, adv appt for non-membs *Open:* Tue, Thu 0930-1700
Subj: landscape arch *Collns: Archvs:* drawings archv
Equip: copier *Svcs:* info, ref, biblio, subj searches (fee)
Stock: bks/5000; periodcls/40; slides/3000
Classn: UDC *Auto Sys:* own
Staff: Libns: 1 *Non-Prof:* 1

S1236 🏛

Law Commission Library

Conquest House, 37-38 John St, Theobalds Rd, London, WC1N 2BQ (020-7453-1241/2; *fax:* 020-7453-1296/7)
Email: library@lawcommission.gsi.gov.uk
Internet: http://www.lawcom.gov.uk/

Gov Body: Lord Chancellor's Dept *Chief:* Libn: Mr K.S. Tree (keith.tree@lawcommission.gsi.gov.uk) *Dep:* Asst Libn: Mr M. Hallissey (michael.hallissey@lawcommission.gsi.gov.uk)
Entry: by agreement with libn *Open:* Mon-Fri 0900-1700
Subj: law *Collns: Bks & Pamphs:* Law Reform in Commonwealth; colln of Local Acts *Co-op Schemes:* BLDSC, BIALL
Equip: m-reader, m-printer, copier, computer (incl CD-ROM) *Online:* Lexis, Lawtel *Svcs:* info, ref, biblio
Stock: bks/5000; periodcls/200; pamphs/large stock
Classn: MOYS 3 *Auto Sys:* MOYS 2
Pubns: Law Under Review (on web site)
Staff: Libns: 2 *Non-Prof:* 1

S1237 🔑

Law Society's Library

113 Chancery Ln, London, WC2A 1PL (0870-606-2511; *fax:* 020-7831-1687)
Email: lib-enq@lawsociety.org.uk
Internet: http://www.library.lawsociety.org.uk/

Gov Body: Law Soc *Chief:* Libn: Mr Chris Holland BA, MCLIP
Entry: membs only, ref only; non-membs at Libn's discretion on written appl (e.g., bona fide rsrchers or as lib of last resort) *Open:* Mon-Fri 0900-1700
Subj: law (UK & EU); parliamentary affairs
Collns: Bks & Pamphs: Law Soc's Mendham Colln (housed at Canterbury Cathedral Lib – see **S404**); early legal texts from 15C onwards; parliamentary papers (1870-date); European Relay Centre *Archvs:* Law Soc Archvs
Equip: 2 m-form reader/printers, video viewer, 3 copiers, 10 computers (incl 1 with wd-proc & 9 with internet & CD-ROM) *Disabled:* AM Smort Reader, ZoomText, JAWS, minicom phone, conversion of text to large print, tape or braille *Svcs:* info, ref, photocopying, document delivery (for photocopies etc)
Stock: bks/45000, incl pamphs; periodcls/400; m-forms/numerous; videos/300
Classn: own *Auto Sys:* Olib
Pubns: Legal Resources on the Internet (free via email); Law Soc Lib Journals & Law Reports (£45); various guides (free)
Staff: Libns: 9 *Non-Prof:* 7
Proj: stores refurbishment; web site development

S1238 📖 🕊

Leo Baeck College Centre for Jewish Education Library

Sternberg Centre, 80 East End Rd, London, N3 2SY (020-8349-5611; *fax:* 020-8343-2558)
Email: library@lbc.ac.uk
Internet: http://www.lbc.ac.uk/

Gov Body: Leo Baeck Coll *Chief:* Libn: Dr César Merchán Hamman MA, PhD *Dep:* Asst Libns: Ms Marian Smelik MA & Ms Philippa Claiden BA
Other Snr Staff: Archivist: Mr Ernest David
Assoc Libs: DEPT OF EDU & PROF DEVELOPMENT RESOURCE CENTRE, addr as above, contact Ms Pamela Hartog (020-8349-5622; *fax:* 020-849-5639; *email:* admin@cje.org.uk)
Entry: staff & students; others can become membs for £15 pa (or £20 pa incl borrowing rights)
Open: Sep-Jun: Mon-Thu 0900-1700, Fri 0900-1300; Jul-Aug: by appt only; closed on Jewish Festivals, bank hols & last wk of Dec
Subj: Jewish studies; religion; biblical studies; Judaism; Rabbinics; Kabbalah; Hasidism; Hebrew lang; phil & Jewish thought; Zionism; liturgy; social sci; Jewish hist; Progressive Judaism; Anglo-Judaica; lit; Holocaust; Israel *Collns: Bks & Pamphs:* Chagall Colln (illustrated bks & photos); Hochschule Lib (part of the lib of the Hochschule für die Wissenschaft des Judentums, Berlin); Lib of the United Synagogue Beth Din; Podro Colln of Judaica (bks & pamphs, 19C-early 20C); Gillinson Colln (pamphs on Israel & Zionism); Progressive Jewish Colln (European Progressive Jewish movements) *Archvs:* papers of several European rabbis, incl: Leo Baeck; Israel Mattuck; Bruno Italiener *Other:* Rabbinic dissertations (160 items); Siegward Kunath Colln (archaeo artefacts) *Co-op Schemes:* BLDSC, ILL
Equip: m-reader, copier (10p per copy), 7 computers (incl 5 with wd-proc, 6 with internet & 1 with CD-ROM) *Online:* access to Jewish search engines & lib catalogues *Svcs:* info, ref
Stock: bks/50000; periodcls/80; pamphs/10000; audios/1500; CD-ROMs/4; archvs/16 MSS
Classn: Elazar System for Jewish Libs *Auto Sys:* own
Staff: Other Prof: 2 *Exp:* £10000 (1999-2000); £10000 (2000-01)

S1239 📖

Lewisham College Learning Centre

Lewisham Way, London, SE4 1UT (020-8692-0353 x3086; *fax:* 020-8694-3272)
Email: learningcentres@lewisham.ac.uk
Internet: http://www.lewisham.ac.uk/

☛

(Lewisham Coll Learning Centre cont)
Chief: Learning Centre Mgr: Ms Frances Sweeney
Assoc Libs: DEPTFORD CAMPUS LEARNING
CENTRE, Learning Centre Mgr: Ms Ann Foreman
Entry: registered students & staff of Coll **Open:**
term: Mon, Wed-Thu 0845-1945, Tue 1000-1945,
Fri 0845-1645; vac: Mon-Fri 1000-1645
Subj: genl; GCSE; A level; undergrad
Equip: m-reader, fax, video viewers, copiers,
computers (incl wd-proc & CD-ROM) **Svcs:** info,
ref
Stock: bks/45000; periodcls/208; audios/1200;
videos/800
Classn: DDC **Auto Sys:** Alice
Staff: Libns: 3.5 Other Prof: 10 Non-Prof: 11.5

S1240 ♀ 🏛

Library and Museum of Freemasonry

Freemason's Hall, 60 Gt Queen St, London, WC2B
5AZ (020-7395-9257; *fax:* 020-7404-7418)
Internet: http://www.grandlodge-england.org/
museum.htm

Gov Body: United Grand Lodge of England
Chief: Dir: Mrs Diane Clements **Dep:** Libn: Ms
Rebecca Coombes
Entry: ref only **Open:** Mon-Fri 1000-1700
Subj: freemasonry **Collns:** *Bks & Pamphs:*
printed bks dating back to 18C *Archvs:* MSS &
archvs dating back to 18C
Equip: copier
Stock: bks/c45000; periodcls/c100; photos/
c40000, incl slides & illusts; videos/c50; archvs/
c3000 MSS
Classn: in-house
Staff: Libns: 1 Other Prof: 1 curator Non-Prof: 7

S1241 🎓

Library of the London School of Economics and Political Science (British Library of Political and Economic Science)

10 Portugal St, London, WC2A 2HD (020-7955-
7229; *fax:* 020-7955-7454)
Email: library@lse.ac.uk
Internet: http://www.library.lse.ac.uk/

Gov Body: London School of Econ & Political Sci,
Univ of London **Chief:** Libn: Ms Jean Sykes MA,
MLitt **Dep:** Dep Libn: Ms Maureen Wade BA,
DipLib, MCLIP
Entry: open for ref purposes to academic &
private rsrchers, certain conditions apply; fees
charged for commercial users; see web site for full
details **Open:** subj to change; see web site
Subj: social sci in the widest sense of the term;
particularly rich in econ; transport; statistics;
political sci; public admin; internatl law; economic
hist; political hist; social hist; internatl aspects of
hist **Collns:** *Bks & Pamphs:* UN Depository Lib;
depository lib for other intergovernmental orgs;
European Documentation Centre; selective
depository for Canadian govt pubns *Archvs:* LSE
archvs (1894-95, 3500 vols & files); Sir William
Beveridge Colln; Passfield Colln; Booth Colln;
Dalton Colln; Hall Carpenter Archvs; Liberal Party
archvs **Co-op Schemes:** BLDSC back-up lib,
Lamda, SCONUL, CURL, M25 Consortium of
Higher Edu Libs, UK Libs Plus

Equip: m-form reader/printers, video viewers,
copiers, limited computer facilities for non-LSE
users *Disabled:* access to all floors, induction
loops at svc pts, 2 video magnifying systems
(CCTV), additional assistance on request *Online:*
range of elec info resources (many available to
LSE membs only)
Stock: bks/1170000; periodcls/10500, plus 22000
no longer current
Classn: LC **Auto Sys:** Unicorn (SIRSI)
Pubns: Internatl Bibliography of the Social Scis
(annual)
Staff: Libns: 25.5 Other Prof: 6 Non-Prof: 51

S1242 ♀ 🙏

Library of the Religious Society of Friends, Britain Yearly Meeting

Friends House, Euston Rd, London, NW1 2BJ
(020-7663-1135; *fax:* 020-7663-1001)
Email: library@quaker.org.uk
Internet: http://www.quaker.org.uk/

Gov Body: Britain Yearly Meeting of the Religious
Soc of Friends **Chief:** Libn: Ms Heather Rowland
Dep: Dep Libn: Mr Josef Keith
Entry: bona fide rsrchers with letter of introduction
welcome; adv appt preferred **Open:** Mon-Tue,
Thu-Fri 1300-1700, Wed 1000-1700; usually
closed for wk in May & last wk of Nov
Subj: Quakerism; Quaker hist & supporting areas
(e.g., pacifism, anti-slavery) **Collns:** *Bks &
Pamphs:* anti-slavery; peace collns *Archvs:*
London Yearly Meeting & its central records (17C-
date); London & Middlesex Genl Meeting & its
subordinate bodies (local records, 17C-date); 50
year rule *Other:* Swarthmore MSS & other 17C
Quaker MSS; other family & personal collns **Co-
op Schemes:** BLDSC, ILL
Equip: m-reader, m-printer, copier (staff only)
Stock: bks/28000; periodcls/300; photos/20000;
slides/4000; pamphs/50000; m-forms/900; archvs/
250 linear m; MSS/250 linear m
Classn: own **Auto Sys:** Adlib
Pubns: various leaflets (for info send SAE or see
web site)
Staff: Libns: 4 Other Prof: 1 archivist

S1243 ♀ 🙏

The Library of the Theosophical Society in England

50 Gloucester Pl, London, W1v 8EA (020-7563-
9816; *fax:* 020-7935-9543)

Gov Body: The Theosophical Soc in England
Chief: Libn: Mr B. Thompson
Entry: open to membs; public may become
subscribers for 6 monthly or annual fee (2 written
refs required) **Open:** Tue-Fri 1400-1830, Sun
1600-2000 (when there is a lecture)
Subj: theosophy; religion; phil; psy; mysticism;
arts; sci; modern civilisation & culture; lit; health &
healing; folklore; mythology; yoga; ancient
civilisations; Western occultism; parapsychology;
astrology; sociology
Equip: video viewer, copier (10p)
Stock: bks/12500; audios/700; videos/125
Classn: own
Pubns: The Theosophical Journal; Insight (£1.80)

S1244 📷

Life File Photographic Library

76 Streathbourne Rd, London, SW17 8QY (020-
8767-8832; *fax:* 020-8767-8879)

Type: commercial picture agency **Chief:** Dirs: Mr
Simon Taylor BA & Miss Josie Elias
Entry: tel appt **Open:** Mon-Fri 0830-1930 (24 hr
answering machine)

Subj: photographic transparencies of people,
places & nat phenomena world-wide
Equip: copier, fax, computers (incl wd-proc & CD-
ROM) **Svcs:** search svc (small fee)
Stock: slides/300000+ **Staff:** Other Prof: 2

S1245 ♀

Lincoln's Inn Library

Lincoln's Inn, Holborn, London, WC2A 3TN (020-
7242-4371; *fax:* 020-7404-1864)
Email: library@lincolnsinn.org.uk
Internet: http://www.lincolnsinnlibrary.org.uk/

Gov Body: Honourable Soc of Lincoln's Inn
Chief: Libn: Mr Guy Holborn MA, LLB, MCLIP
Dep: Dep Libn: Mrs Catherine McArdle BA, MCLIP
Entry: by appt only **Open:** term: Mon-Fri 0900-
2000; vac: Mon-Fri 0930-1730
Subj: law **Collns:** *Bks & Pamphs:* Common-
wealth law; early legal bks & legal hist; legal & non-
legal pamphs & tracts (c2000 pre-1700) *Archvs:*
legal & non-legal MSS, incl Hale MSS (12C-19C);
Archvs of the Inn (15C-date)
Equip: m-printer, 4 copiers, 15 computers (incl 4
with wd-proc, 10 with internet & 11 with CD-ROM)
Stock: bks/150000; periodcls/450; pamphs/20000;
m-forms/100000; archvs/3000 vols
Auto Sys: Unicorn
Staff: Libns: 4.5 Other Prof: 0.5 Non-Prof: 2.5

S1246 ♀ 📷

Link Picture Library

33 Greyhound Rd, London, W6 8NH (020-7381-
2261; *fax:* 020-7385-6244)
Email: lib@linkpicturelibrary.com
Internet: http://www.linkpicturelibrary.com/

Chief: Proprietor: Mr Orde Eliason MA
Assoc Libs: liaison network in India, Brazil,
Norway, Japan, South Africa & Israel
Entry: adv appt preferred **Open:** Mon-Fri 0930-
1730
Subj: generalities; religion; social sci; arts; geog;
hist; culture; agric; industry; wildlife; environment;
ecology; tourism; development; arch; conflict
Collns: *Other:* photos & transparencies of all
aspects of South Africa & India
Equip: copier, fax, 3 computers (all with wd-proc &
CD-ROM, 2 with internet), dedicated film scanner
Online: under development **Svcs:** info
Stock: photos/2000; slides/100000; CD-ROMs/
some
Staff: Non-Prof: 1 **Exp:** £20000 (1999-2000);
£20000 (2000-01)
Proj: digitisation of stock (ongoing)

S1247 ♀

Linnean Society of London Library

Burlington House, Piccadilly, London, W1J 0BF
(020-7434-4479/4470; *fax:* 020-7287-9364)
Internet: http://www.linnean.org/

Gov Body: Linnean Soc of London **Chief:** Libn &
Archivist: Miss Gina Douglas BSc, FLS **Dep:** Asst
Libn: Ms Cathy Broad
Entry: open to the genl public by appt, for ref only
Open: Mon-Fri 1000-1700 (excl public hols)
Subj: biology; taxonomy; systematics; nat hist;
evolution; travel with nat hist component; hist of sci
Collns: *Bks & Pamphs:* Lib of Carolus Linnaeus
(1707-1778); Lib of Alfred Russel Wallace; the
James Insch Tea Lib (bks on tea cultivation & hist);
British Ornithologists Union Balfour Bequest Lib
(bird bks) *Archvs:* archvs of the Linnean Soc;
archvs of the Selborne Soc (access by permission
only); MSS of Carolus Linnaeus (1707-1778); MSS
& correspondence of past fellows of the soc, incl
Sir J.E. Smith, William Swainson & John Ellis
Other: large colln of engraved portraits of
naturalists

Equip: m-reader, copier (10p-20p per pg), room for hire
Stock: bks/100000; periodcls/900; photos/1000; pamphs/10000
Classn: UDC *Auto Sys:* Heritage
Pubns: see web site for details
Staff: Libns: 2 *Other Prof:* 1
Proj: lib automation

S1248

Listening Books
(formerly Natl Listening Lib)
12 Lant St, London, SE1 1QH (020-7407-9417; *fax:* 020-7403-1377)

Type: charity *Gov Body:* Board of Trustees
Chief: Chief Libn: Ms L. Knightsbridge
Entry: membs only (fee £50 pa) *Open:* Mon-Fri 0900-1700
Subj: generalities *Stock:* audios/3000 talking bks
Pubns: Catalogues (free to membs only)
Staff: Other Prof: 5 *Non-Prof:* 6

S1249

Lloyd's Business Intelligence Centre
1 Lime St, London, EC3M 7HA (020-7327-5448; *fax:* 020-7327-6400)
Email: lloyds-external-enquiries@lloyds.com
Internet: http://www.lloyds.com/

Chief: Chief Info Offcr: Mr Howard Knight BLib, MLib
Entry: by arrangement, a fee may be charged
Open: Mon-Fri 0930-1700
Subj: insurance; law
Equip: m-reader, m-printer, fax, copier, 5 computers (all with internet & CD-ROM) *Online:* Reuters Business Briefing (fees according to usage) *Svcs:* info, ref
Stock: bks/15000; periodcls/180; pamphs/200; maps/150; m-forms/3000; archvs/750 cubic ft
Classn: DDC *Auto Sys:* DBTextworks
Pubns: Statistics Relating to Lloyd's (CD-ROM, £115+VAT); Lloyd's Syndicates Report & Accounts (CD-ROM, £450)
Staff: Libns: 2 *Other Prof:* 1

S1250

Local Government Association, Library and Information Centre
1st Floor, Local Govt House, Smith Sq, London, SW1P 3HZ (020-7664-3131; *fax:* 020-7664-3030)
Email: info@lga.gov.uk
Internet: http://www.lga.gov.uk/

Type: local govt *Chief:* Info Offcr: Mr Nick Georgiou
Assoc Libs: RECORD OFFICE, at same addr
Entry: adv appt *Open:* Mon-Fri 0900-1700
Subj: social sci; local govt & local govt svcs; mgmt; govt; law; politics *Collns: Bks & Pamphs:* LGA pubns; parliamentary pubns; local authority pubns *Archvs:* archvs of Assoc of Dist Councils & of County & Metropolitan Authorities (merged April 1997 to form the LGA) *Co-op Schemes:* BLDSC, ILL
Equip: copier *Disabled:* wheelchair access
Online: Urbaline, IDEA *Svcs:* info, ref, biblio, enqs
Stock: bks/5000; periodcls/50; videos/25
Classn: by subj & author *Staff: Libns:* 1

S1251

London Business School Library
Regent's Pk, London, NW1 4SA (020-7262-5050; *fax:* 020-7706-1897)
Email: library@london.edu
Internet: http://www.london.edu/library/

Gov Body: Univ of London (see **S1440**) *Chief:* Head of Lib: Ms Helen Edwards BA, MCLIP *Dep:* Mrs Gillian Dwyer BA, MCLIP
Entry: open to staff, students & alumni of LBS for borrowing; ref only for academics & registered PhD students from other instns; other rsrchers should apply in writing to Head of Lib; for others: day ticket £30 (ref only), or for regular access £400+VAT pa for indivs (ref only), £1250+VAT pa for companies (incl borrowing) *Open:* Mon-Fri 0830-2200 (0900-2200 during spring & autumn vac), Sat 0900-1700, Sun 1100-1900; summer vac: Mon-Fri 0900-2100, Sat 0900-1700
Subj: business; econ; finance; law; politics; behavioural sci; mgmt; info tech; scis relevant to business *Collns: Bks & Pamphs:* company annual reports; market rsrch reports; working papers *Other:* AV colln under development *Co-op Schemes:* BLDSC, M25 Consortium, SCONUL
Equip: 2 m-form reader/printers, 3 video viewers, 5 copiers, 17 computers *Online:* 60+ databases, incl: Amadeus, Bloomberg, Company Data Direct, Datastream, EconLit, Economist, Factiva, FAME, FT, Forrester, Global Market Info Database, IBSS, IDEAL, JSTOR, KeyNote, Lexis-Nexis, Mintel, Proquest Direct (ABI/Inform), PsycInfo, Reuters, Web of Sci; fees vary; most svcs limited to certain categories of user *Svcs:* info, ref, rsrch (fee based), document delivery svc
Stock: bks/20000; periodcls/1000; m-forms/various
Classn: LCBS *Auto Sys:* Unicorn
Staff: Libns: 11 *Non-Prof:* 5

S1252

London Canal Museum Library
12-13 New Wharf Rd, King's Cross, London, N1 9RT (020-7713-0836; *fax:* 020-7713-0836)
Email: ValPinder@canalmuseum.org.uk
Internet: http://www.canalmuseum.org.uk/

Gov Body: London Canal Museum Trust *Chief:* Edu Offcr: Ms Val Pinder
Entry: ref only by appt *Open:* Tue-Sun 1000-1630
Subj: canal boats & people; canal hist; ice trade
Collns: Bks & Pamphs: pertaining to canal & waterways hist; works relating to Carlo Gatti & Gatti family (ice & ice cream merchants) *Archvs:* waterway reports & official documents *Other:* maps & photos
Equip: room for hire *Svcs:* ref
Classn: DDC *Staff: Non-Prof:* 12

S1253

London Chamber Business Information Centre
33 Queen St, London, EC4R 1AP (020-7248-4444; *fax:* 020-7489-0391)
Email: info@londonchamber.co.uk
Internet: http://www.londonchamber.co.uk/

Gov Body: London Chamber of Commerce & Industry *Chief:* Head of Info: Ms Marita Ewins
Entry: free to membs of the Chamber; non-membs £20 pd (incl VAT) *Open:* Mon-Fri 0900-1730
Subj: business; commerce; industry; enterprise; mgmt *Collns: Bks & Pamphs:* business & trade directories *Other:* govt documents; statistics; marketing data; newspapers
Equip: Online: Dialog, Lexis-Nexis, various CD-ROMs
Stock: bks/5000; periodcls/300; pamphs/250000

S1254

London College of Fashion Library
20 John Prince's St, Oxford Circus, London, W1M 0BJ (020-7514-7453/5; *fax:* 020-7514-7580)
Internet: http://www.linst.ac.uk/library/libinf/lcf.htm

Gov Body: London Inst *Chief:* Chief Libn: Mrs Diane Mansbridge MA, DipLib, MCLIP
Entry: ref only; adv appt for visitors, giving 24 hrs notice *Open:* term: Mon-Thu 0930-2015, Fri 1000-1715, Sat 1115-1700; vac: please phone for details
Subj: business; mgmt; arts; costume hist; fashion design; footwear & accessories; hairdressing; beauty therapy; clothing production; clothing tech; fashion mgmt; fashion promotion; journalism; media studies; tailoring; textiles *Collns: Bks & Pamphs:* Clothing & Footwear Inst Colln (tailoring & clothing industry, 19C-early 20C, c350 items) *Archvs:* London Coll of Fashion Archv (hist of coll)
Co-op Schemes: BLDSC
Equip: 3 video viewers, 6 copiers, clr copier, computers (incl 12 internet & 2 CD-ROM)
Stock: bks/40000; periodcls/150; photos/500; slides/19000; illusts/10000; audios/15; videos/1000
Classn: DDC *Auto Sys:* Talis
Pubns: Couture or Trade: An Early Pictorial Record of the London Coll of Fashion (£14.99)
Staff: Libns: 8 *Non-Prof:* 4

S1255

London College of Printing, Library and Learning Resources
Elephant & Castle, London, SE1 6SB (020-7514-6527; *fax:* 020-7514-6597)
Email: e.davison@lcp.linst.ac.uk
Internet: http://www.linst.ac.uk/library/

Gov Body: London Inst *Chief:* Head of Learning Resources: Ms Elizabeth Davison BA, MCLIP *Dep:* Dep Head of Learning Resources: Ms Jacky Camroux MSc, MCLIP, DipEdTech
Assoc Libs: BACK HILL LIB, Back Hill, Clerkenwell, London, EC1R 5LQ, Site Mgr: Mr Paul Mellinger (020-7514-6882)
Entry: ref only, write in adv *Open: Elephant & Castle:* term: Mon-Thu 0930-2015, Fri 0930-1745, Sat 1000-1545; vac: Mon-Fri 1000-1600; *Back Hill:* term: Mon 0930-1900, Tue-Thu 0930-2000, Fri 0930-1800; vac: Mon-Fri 1200-1600
Subj: at undergrad, postgrad & foundation levels: generalities; social sci; tech; arts; hist; geog; *Elephant & Castle:* art; design; fine art; graphic design; marketing; mgmt; printing; publishing; retail; travel; tourism; typography; visual merchandising; *Back Hill:* film & video; journalism; media; photography *Collns: Bks & Pamphs:* Printing Historical Colln (hist & development of the bk in the Western world, c5000 items); Script Colln (hist & development of publ & unpublished scripts); Pickering Colln (c2500 items); artists & private press bks *Archvs:* London Coll of Printing Archv (1894-date); C&A Ltd Archv (1922-2001); Robert Fenton Archv (printing) *Other:* London Coll of Printing Ephemera Colln (calendars, posters, cards, menus etc, 19C-20C, c4000 items), incl: Westwood Colln of Printed Ephemera (20C design, c1000 items) *Co-op Schemes:* BLDSC, UK Libs Plus, RSLP, M25, Public Libs Referral Scheme
Equip: video viewers, fax, copiers, clr copiers, computers (with wd-proc, internet & CD-ROM)
Online: Mintel, PIRA
Stock: bks/90000; periodcls/400; slides/30000; illusts/6000; videos/300
Classn: DDC *Auto Sys:* Talis
Staff: Libns: 19 *Non-Prof:* 19

S1256

London Directorate of Health and Social Care, Library Information Centre
(formerly NHS Exec, London Regional Office)
40 Eastbourne Ter, London, W2 3QR (020-7725-5400; *fax:* 020-7725-2715)

Gov Body: Dept of Health (see **S1111**) *Chief:* Head of Lib Info Centre: Mrs Susan Andrew MSc, MCLIP *Dep:* Svcs Mgr: Mrs Penny Bateman MSc

London ▼ London Special Libraries

(London Directorate of Health & Social Care cont)
Entry: ref only for non-NHS staff *Open:* Mon-Fri 0900-1700
Subj: health
Equip: fax, copier, computers (incl internet & CD-ROM) *Svcs:* info, ref
Stock: bks/c5000; periodcls/c150
Classn: Bliss *Auto Sys:* Unicorn (Sirsi)
Staff: Libns: 3 *Non-Prof:* 2

S1257

London Film School Library
24 Shelton St, Covent Gdn, London, WC2H 9UB (020-7240-0161; *fax:* 020-7497-3718)
Email: c.bright@lfs.org.uk
Internet: http://www.lfs.org.uk/

Chief: Libn: Miss Chrissy Bright
Entry: staff & students only; not open to public
Open: Mon-Fri 0945-1730
Subj: film; student in-house films & technical bks (in-house use only)
Staff: Libns: 1

S1258

London Fire Brigade Library
Room 520, Hampton House, 20 Albert Embankment, London, SE1 7SD (020-7587-6340; *fax:* 020-7587-6086)
Email: judy.seaborne@london-fire.gov.uk

Gov Body: London Fire & Emergency Planning Authority *Chief:* Brigade Libn: Ms J. Seaborne BA, MCLIP *Dep:* Visual Info System Administrator: vacant
Entry: ref only, adv appt *Open:* Mon-Fri 1000-1630
Subj: tech; fire prevention; fire safety; health & safety; mgmt; training; hist of London Fire Brigade
Collns: Archvs: fire related journals *Other:* photo colln of all photos taken by London Fire Brigade (end of 19C to date); available to rsrchers on payment of search & full reproduction rights *Co-op Schemes:* BLDSC
Equip: video viewer *Online:* Fire CD
Stock: bks/8000; periodcls/50; photos/200000; videos/300
Classn: UDC *Auto Sys:* CALM 2000 Plus
Staff: Libns: 1 *Non-Prof:* 2 *Exp:* £35000 (1999-2000)

S1259

London Foot Hospital and School of Podiatric Medicine Library
33 Fitzroy Sq, London, W1P 6AY (020-7530-4509)

Gov Body: Univ Coll London (see **S1433**) & Camden & Islington NHS Trust *Chief:* Libn: Ms Ruth Murphy
Entry: by adv appt only *Open:* Wed, Fri 0930-1645
Subj: podiatry; biomechanics; sports medicine
Co-op Schemes: BLDSC, NTRLIU
Equip: fax, copier, computers (incl wd-proc & CD-ROM)
Stock: bks/3200; periodcls/22; slides/3000; videos/30
Classn: NLM *Staff: Libns:* 0.6

S1260

The London Library
14 St James's Sq, London, SW1Y 4LG (020-7930-7705; *fax:* 020-7766-4766)
Email: membership@londonlibrary.co.uk
Internet: http://www.londonlibrary.co.uk/

Type: independent *Gov Body:* Cttee of membs
Chief: Libn: Miss Inez T.P.A. Lynn BA, MLitt, MCLIP *Dep:* Dep Libn: Mrs Alison Sposton BA, MCLIP
Entry: membs only; membership particulars on appl *Open:* Mon, Fri-Sat 0930-1730, Tue-Thu 0930-1930
Subj: genl; generalities; phil; psy; religion; social sci; lang; arts; lit; geog; hist *Collns: Bks & Pamphs:* Higginson Colln (hunting & field sports); Heron-Allen Colln (Omar Khayyám) *Co-op Schemes:* BLDSC, ILL
Equip: copiers (A4/5p), computers (incl 3 with internet & 2 with CD-ROM) *Online:* range of biblio databases, ref works & newspapers on CD-ROM
Svcs: info, ref, biblio
Stock: bks/1000000; periodcls/450; pamphs/4000
Classn: own *Auto Sys:* Dynix
Pubns: Annual Report & Accounts (unpriced)
Staff: Libns: 21 *Other Prof:* 2 *Non-Prof:* 29 *Exp:* £181000 (2000-01)

S1261

London Metropolitan University, City Campus Library Services
(formerly London Guildhall Univ)
Calcutta House, Old Castle St, London, E1 7NT (020-7320-1183; *fax:* 020-7320-1177)
Internet: http://www.lgu.ac.uk/as/library/

Gov Body: London Metropolitan Univ *Chief:* Head of Info Svcs & Learning Resources: Ms Ann Constable
Assoc Libs: CALCUTTA HOUSE LRC, contact details as above, Learning Resources Mgr: Ms Helen Dalton; COMMERCIAL RD LRC, 41-71 Commercial Rd, London, E1 1LA (020-73210-1869; *fax:* 020-7320-2831), Learning Resources Mgr: Ms Pat Christie; MOORGATE LRC, 84 Moorgate, London, EC2M 6SQ (020-7320-1567); WOMEN'S LIB (see **S1469**)
Entry: staff & students of Univ; external membership available *Open:* term: Mon 0900-2100, Tue 1015-2100, Wed-Fri 0900-1700, Sat 1100-1600 (Commercial Rd LRC closed Sat); vac: Mon-Fri 0900-1700 (may vary during summer)
Subj: Calcutta House: computing; maths; info tech; social sci; lang; politics; modern hist; psy; civil aviation; law; *Commercial Rd:* art; design; computing; fine art; applied art; furnishings; interior design; arch; restoration; conservation; communications; media studies; *Moorgate:* accountancy; banking; business studies; econ; insurance; mgmt; marketing; transport; shipping
Collns: Bks & Pamphs: Census Reports, statistics & govt survey data (at Calcutta House); Artist's Bks Colln; Technical & Trade Lit Colln (both at Commercial Rd); Annual Reports; market rsrch colln (both at Moorgate) *Other:* media, audio, video & slide collns (at Commercial Rd) *Co-op Schemes:* BLDSC, ARLIS, BIALL, SCONUL, UK Libs Plus Scheme
Equip: copiers, computers *Online:* ABC POLSCI, Geobase, PsycInfo, Social Trends, Computer Select, Le Monde (all at Calcutta House); Bloomberg, Datastream, Eurolaw, Lexis, Key Notes, Current Legal Info (all at Moorgate) *Svcs:* info, ref
Stock: bks/286396; periodcls/2500, incl standing orders; slides/80000; audios/852; videos/9640; CD-ROMs/2025
Classn: DDC *Auto Sys:* Millennium
See also LONDON METROPOLITAN UNIV, NORTH CAMPUS LIB SVCS (**S1262**)

S1262

London Metropolitan University, North Campus Library Services
(formerly Univ of North London)
236-250 Holloway Rd, London, N7 6PP (020-7753-3132; *fax:* 020-7753-7037)
Email: j.howell@unl.ac.uk
Internet: http://www.unl.ac.uk/lclh/

Chief: Dir of Info Systems & Svcs: Mr Roy Williams *Dep:* Lib Svcs Mgr: Ms Julie Howell
Assoc Libs: LADBROKE HOUSE LIB, 62-66 Highbury Grove, London, N5 2AD, Lib Mgr & Faculty Libn, Environmental & Social Studies: Ms Ann Aungie
Entry: external users by appl to the Operations Team Mgr *Open:* term: Mon-Fri 0900-2100, Sat 1100-1700, Sun 1300-1700; vac: Mon-Fri 0900-1900
Subj: undergrad; postgrad; psy; social sci; lang; sci; maths; tech; business; arts; arch; interior design; lit; hist; geog *Collns: Bks & Pamphs:* EDC; TUC Lib Collns (see **S1425**) *Archvs:* H.G. Wells Colln; as part of TUC Lib: Workers Edu Authority Archv; Gertrude Tuckwell Papers *Co-op Schemes:* UK Libs Plus, M25 Consortium
Equip: m-reader, m-printer, video viewer, copiers, computers (incl wd-proc, internet & CD-ROM), rooms for hire *Disabled:* Kurzweil etc *Online:* Web of Science, variety of web-based resources *Svcs:* info, ref
Stock: bks/539792; periodcls/5126 (print & elec); AVs/16000; archvs/181 linear m
Classn: DDC *Auto Sys:* Talis
Staff: Libns: 23 *Non-Prof:* 33.7 *Exp:* £691606 (1999-2000); £684406 (2000-01)
See also LONDON METROPOLITAN UNIV, CITY CAMPUS LIB SVCS (**S1261**)

S1263

London Natural History Society Library
c/o Central Libs, Imperial Coll London, London, SW7 2AZ (020-7589-5111; *fax:* 020-7584-3763)
Internet: http://www.users.globalnet.co.uk/~lnhsweb/

Chief: Libn: Mrs Linda Hewitt MCLIP
Entry: membs of the Soc; staff & students of Imperial Coll *Open:* term: Mon-Fri 0930-2100, Sat 0930-1730; vac: Mon-Sat 0930-1730
Subj: archaeo; botany; ecology; entomology; geol; nat hist; ornithology
Equip: computers, copier
Stock: bks/7000; periodcls/105 *Classn:* UDC

S1264

The London Oratory Library
The Oratory, Brompton Rd, London, SW7 2RP (020-7080-0900; *fax:* 020-7584-1095)

Gov Body: The Fathers of the London Oratory
Chief: Father Libn: Revd R.C. Creighton-Jobe BA, BD
Entry: adv appt, ref only
Subj: religion *Collns: Bks & Pamphs:* pamphs, produced by or for the Oratory *Archvs:* historical archvs of London Oratory
Equip: copier, fax
Stock: bks/40000; photos/various; pamphs/various; archvs/3 m

S1265

London School of Hygiene and Tropical Medicine Library
Keppel St, Gower St, London, WC1E 7HT (020-7927-2276; *fax:* 020-7927-2273)
Email: library@lshtm.ac.uk
Internet: http://www.lshtm.ac.uk/library/

Gov Body: Univ of London (see **S1440**) *Chief:* Libn & Dir of Info Svcs: Mr Brian Furner BA, MSc, MCLIP *Dep:* Dep Libn: Mr John Eyers BA, MLS, MCLIP
Assoc Libs: ARCHVS, addr as above, Archivist: Ms Victoria Killick BSocSc, MArAd (020-7927-2966; *fax:* 020-7927-2273; *email:* victoria.killick@ lshtm.ac.uk)
Entry: ref only for non-membs wishing to consult specialist lit not readily available elsewhere; ID required *Open:* Mon-Fri 0830-2025 (-2300 for staff & students), Sat 0900-1230 (-1700 for staff & students), Sun (staff & students only) 1100-1700
Subj: postgrad; public health; tropical medicine; human nutrition; demography; hist of public health & tropical medicine *Collns: Bks & Pamphs:* Reece Colln (smallpox & vaccination); Daley Colln; Manson Colln *Archvs:* administrative papers of the School; Sir Patrick Manson papers (tropical medicine specialist); Major Genl Sir Leonard Rogers papers (tropical public health physician); Sir Ronald Ross papers (malariologist) *Other:* large archival photo colln *Co-op Schemes:* BLDSC
Equip: m-reader, video viewer, 6 copiers, computers (incl CD-ROM) *Online:* African Journals Online, AgeInfo, BioMed Central, CAB Abstracts, Cochrane, Embase, HEED, HMIC, IBSS, Medline, PAHO-LILACS, Popline, PsycInfo, SIGLE, SciELO, Web of Science, Zetoc & others *Svcs:* info
Stock: bks/50000; periodcls/800; pamphs/15000; tape-slide sets/120
Classn: Barnard *Auto Sys:* Unicorn
Pubns: Catalogue of the Ross Archvs (£35)
Staff: Libns: 4 *Non-Prof:* 6 FT, 7 PT

S1266

London School of Jewish Studies, The Library
(formerly Jews' Coll)
Schaller House, Albert Rd, London, NW4 2SJ (020-8203-6427; *fax:* 020-8203-6420)
Email: enquiries@lsjs.ac.uk
Internet: http://www.brijnet.org/lsjs/library/

Gov Body: Univ of London (see **S1440**) *Chief:* Head Libn: Mr Esra Kahn *Dep:* Miss K. Roberg & Mrs E. Zimmels
Entry: ref only, fee charged *Open:* term: Mon, Tue-Thu 0900-1800, Wed 0900-2100, Fri 0900-1300, Sun 0930-1230; vac: Mon-Thu 0900-1600
Subj: at undergrad & postgrad levels, in the field of Jewish & Hebrew studies: local study (London); phil; psy; religion; theology; biblical studies; liturgy; music; social sci; lang; sci; arts; lit; hist; Zionism
Collns: Bks & Pamphs: Montefiore Colln of Hebrew MSS & printed bks; colln of rare bks *Co-op Schemes:* BLDSC, ILL
Equip: m-fiche reader/printer (£1 per copy), 2 copiers, fax, 4 computers (incl wd-proc & CD-ROM)
Svcs: info, ref, biblio
Stock: bks/90000; periodcls/100; audios/1000
Classn: Elazar *Staff: Libns:* 3

S1267

The London Society Library
Mortimer Wheeler House, 46 Eagle Wharf Rd, London, N1 7ED (020-7253-9400)
Email: londonsociety@hotmail.com
Internet: http://www.lonsoc.org.uk/lonsoc/

Gov Body: Trustees of London Soc *Chief:* Chairman: Mr Gayne Wells
Assoc Libs: lib is held at the LONDON ARCHAEOLOGICAL ARCHV & RSRCH CENTRE (see **A301**)
Entry: adv appt *Open:* Mon-Fri 1000-1700
Subj: local study (London): topography; hist; arch; traditions *Collns: Bks & Pamphs:* Survey of London (almost all vols); London Topographical record (complete); The London Journal (complete)
Archvs: misc material, in course of indexing

Equip: copier
Stock: bks/3000; periodcls/3; photos/100; slides/200; illusts/1000; pamphs/100; maps/80; archvs/2 cubic m
Pubns: The Journal of the London Soc (2 pa, subscription £6 private, £9 corporate)
Staff: Non-Prof: 2 PT volunteers

S1268

London's Transport Museum, Reference Library
39 Wellington St, Covent Gdn, London, WC2E 7BB (020-7379-6344; *fax:* 020-7497-3527)
Email: museum@londontransport.co.uk
Internet: http://www.ltmuseum.co.uk/

Gov Body: London Transport *Chief:* Lib & Info Svcs Mgr: Ms Caroline Walhurst BA(Hons), MCLIP
Assoc Libs: TRANSPORT FOR LONDON ARCHVS & RECORD MGMT, 55 Broadway, London, SW1H 0BD
Entry: adv appt, ref only *Open: Ref Lib:* Tue-Thu 1000-1700; *Museum Learning Centre:* Mon-Thu, Sat-Sun 1000-1730, Fri 1100-1730
Subj: hist of London Transport & its predecessors; relevant design & arch; technical developments in urban transport; any material having an identifiable link with the development of London's public transport *Collns: Bks & Pamphs:* 10000 bks & pamphs; 150 journal & house news-letter titles
Archvs: Frank Pick Archv; Reinohl Colln *Other:* photo archv; posters; maps; tickets & ephemera
Equip: video viewer, copier, rooms for hire *Svcs:* info, ref, biblio, abstracting
Stock: bks/11500; periodcls/120; photos/100000 (b&w); slides/5000 (clr); maps/600; audios/178; videos/25; posters/5000
Classn: own (alphanumerical) *Auto Sys:* INDEX+
Pubns: various edu packs (see web site)
Staff: Libns: 2 *Other Prof:* 2

S1269

Lord Chancellor's Department, Headquarters Library
Southside, 105 Victoria St, London, SW1E 6QT (020-7210-1979/80; *fax:* 020-7210-1981)
Email: Christine.Younger@lcdhq.gsi.gov.uk

Chief: HQ Libn: Ms Christine Younger BLib, MCLIP
Entry: staff; govt depts; public by prior appt only
Open: Mon-Fri 0930-1700
Subj: law; public admin *Svcs:* info
Stock: bks/20000 *Staff: Libns:* 2 *Non-Prof:* 1

S1270

Lubavitch Lending Library
Lubavitch House, 107-115 Stamford Hill, London, N16 5RP (020-8800-5823; *fax:* 020-8809-7324)
Internet: http://www.lubavitchuk.com/

Gov Body: Lubavitch UK *Chief:* Libn: Mr Zvi Rabin MCLIP
Subj: religion; Judaism; Jewish hist; Jewish culture; Jewish heritage
Svcs: enq svc *Stock:* bks/10000

S1271

Magnum Photos Ltd, Photo Agency and Archive
5 Old St, London, EC1V 9HL (020-7490-1771; *fax:* 020-7608-0200)
Email: magnum@magnumphotos.co.uk
Internet: http://www.magnumphotos.com/

Chief: Archv Dir: Mr Hamish Crooks (crooks@ magnumphotos.co.uk) *Dep:* Dep Archv Dir: Mr Nick Galvin (nickg@magnumphotos.co.uk)

Entry: adv appt *Open:* Mon-Fri 0930-1800
Equip: fax, video viewer, copier, 20 computers (all with wd-proc, internet & CD-ROM), computer database of digital images *Svcs:* info, ref, biblio
Stock: photos/c1000000; videos/100; CD-ROMs/200
Staff: Other Prof: 20

S1272

MAKE Resource
(formerly the Women's Art Lib)
107-109 Charing Cross Rd, London, WC2H 0DU (020-7514-8860; *fax:* 020-7514-8864)
Email: womensart.lib@ukonline.co.uk
Internet: http://web.ukonline.co.uk/womensart.lib/

Gov Body: funded by funded by London Arts, the Arts Council of England & Central St Martins Coll of Art & Design *Chief:* Dir: Ms Katrina Crookall (k.crookall@csm.linst.ac.uk) *Dep:* Rsrch & Edu Resource Offcr: Ms Althea Greenan (a.greenan@ csm.linst.ac.uk)
Entry: ref only, adv appt *Open:* Tue-Fri 1000-1700
Subj: visual arts, specifically women artists; women's studies; gender; cultural studies *Collns: Archvs:* Women Artists Slide Lib; archvs of The Women's Internatl Art Club (1900-1978); archival photos from Dame Laura Knight's private colln *Other:* presscuttings on 8000+ women artists
Equip: copier, video viewer, computer, light tables for slide viewing *Svcs:* info, ref, biblio, image supply & copyright advice, rsrch svc
Stock: bks/5000; slides/200000+; audios/100; videos/100
Classn: own
Pubns: Make Magazine (4 pa); Women's Art Lib Slide Pack
Staff: Other Prof: 3 *Exp:* no special budget; all bks & periodcls received as review copies for magazine, reciprocal subscriptions & donations
Further Info: The most comprehensive info resource on women's art in the UK, MAKE is a voluntary-aided org, constituted as an educational charity to promote the work of women artists working in any medium in any part of the world.

S1273

The Marine Society, Seafarers Libraries
202 Lambeth Rd, London, SE1 7JW (020-7261-9535; *fax:* 020-7401-2537)
Email: enq@marine-society.org.uk
Internet: http://www.marine-society.org.uk/

Gov Body: Marine Soc *Chief:* Head of Lib Svcs: Mr Brian Thomas BA(Hons), PGCE (brian@ marine-society.org.uk)
Entry: provides an exchange lib svc to ships at sea & offshore installations
Subj: all subjs
Stock: bks/500000+
Staff: Non-Prof: 6 *Exp:* £50000 (1999-2000); £45000 (2000-01)

S1274

Marx Memorial Library
Marx House, 37a Clerkenwell Green, London, EC1R 0DU (020-7253-1485; *fax:* 020-7251-6039)
Email: marx.library@britishlibrary.net
Internet: http://www.marxmemoriallibrary. sageweb.co.uk/

Type: charity, independent subscription lib *Chief:* Libn: Ms Tish Collins BA, MSc *Dep:* Ms Tina Corry
Entry: by membership subscription (£9, oaps £4, other rates for insts) *Open:* Mon-Tue, Thu 1300-1800, Wed 1300-2000, Fri closed, Sat 1000-1300; Aug closed

Special Libraries

London ▼ London

(Marx Memorial Lib cont)

Subj: arts; lit; social sci; hist; politics; Marxism; working-class movement hist **Collns: Bks & Pamphs:** John Williamson Colln (US Labour Movement 1920s-1970s); James Klugmann Colln (early radicals & Chartists); Bernal Peace Colln (natl & internatl peace movement); Internatl Brigade Lib (Spanish anti-fascist war) **Archvs:** Internatl Brigade Archv; British-Soviet Friendship Soc Archv; Marx Memorial Lib Archv; Wal Hannington Papers (activs of Natl Unemployed Workers Movement) **Other:** bnd vols of Daily Worker-Morning Star (1930-date); colln of radical, socialist & labour movement journals & pamphs
Equip: m-reader, video viewer, fax, copier, 3 computers (incl 2 CD-ROM), 2 rooms for hire
Svcs: info, ref
Stock: bks/100000; periodcls/120 current titles, 30000 filed issues; photos/various; illusts/various; pamphs/50000; m-forms/25; videos/10
Classn: own
Pubns: Marx Memorial Lib Bulletin (£1.50); Marx Memorial Lib Bulletin Index: 1933-1993
Staff: Other Prof: 1 *Non-Prof:* 1

S1275 Mary Evans Picture Library

59 Tranquil Vale, Black Heath, London, SE3 0BS (020-8318-0034; *fax:* 020-8852-7211)
Email: lib@mepl.co.uk
Internet: http://www.mepl.co.uk/

Type: commercial picture lib specialising in hist
Chief: Managing Dir: Valentine Ward Evans
Other Snr Staff: Dirs: Mary Evans, Hilary Evans & Valentine Ward Evans
Entry: by appt only *Open:* Mon-Fri 0930-1730
Subj: We are a historical picture lib with millions of pictures covering all subjs; our archv contains: illustrated bks; periodcls from many countries; original prints & engravings; cartoons; postcards; ephemera of all kinds; each depicting some aspect of the past: people, places, events, social scenes & activs **Collns: Other:** many, incl: Sigmund Freud copyrights; Fawcett Colln (women's rights); Bruce Castle Museum; Instn of Civil Engineers
Equip: copier
Stock: over 4 mln pictures on transparency
Classn: by subj
Pubns: The Picture Rsrcher's Handbook; Practical Picture Rsrch; free clr brochure about the colln
Staff: 20 *Exp:* no fixed budget

S1276 Marylebone Cricket Club Library

Lord's Cricket Ground, London, NW8 8QN (020-7289-1611; *fax:* 020-7432-1062)
Internet: http://www.mcc.org.uk/

Gov Body: MCC *Chief:* Curator: Mr Stephen Green MA, DipAA *Dep:* Asst Curator: Ms Glenys Williams BA(Hons), MPhil
Entry: ref only, adv appt preferred *Open:* normally Mon-Fri 1000-1700; open on cricket Sats & Suns
Subj: cricket & some other sports (e.g. real tennis)
Collns: Bks & Pamphs: probably the most comprehensive cricket colln in existence; incl the libs of A.L. Ford, Sir Julien Cahn & F.S. Ashley-Cooper *Archvs:* MCC minute bks *Other:* MCC, Middlesex & England scorebks

Equip: 2 computers (with wd-proc, staff use only)
Stock: bks/10000; periodcls/20; photos/8000; some sound recordings, maps & videos
Classn: own *Auto Sys:* Headfast
Pubns: Lord's Pictorial Souvenir Brochure (£2.50)
Staff: Other Prof: 2 *Non-Prof:* 1

S1277 The McDougall Library for Electoral Studies

(formerly the Lakeman Lib for Electoral Studies)
6 Chancel St, Blackfriars, London, SE1 0UX (020-7620-1080; *fax:* 020-7928-1528)
Email: admin@mcdougall.org.uk

Type: charity *Gov Body:* Trustees of the McDougall Trust (Registered Charity No. 212151)
Chief: Exec Sec: Mr Paul Wilder BA(Hons), CertVolSecMgmt, CertCharityMgmt
Entry: by appt only *Open:* Mon-Fri 0930-1730
Subj: social sci; political sci; election studies; voting systems; constitutions *Collns: Bks & Pamphs:* all UK Parliamentary Reform Acts from 1832 onwards *Archvs:* archvs of Proportional Representation/Electoral Reform Soc; papers & correspondence of Dr J.F.S. Ross & Lord Courtney of Penwith *Other:* press cuttings (dated & sourced)
Equip: fax, copier, 3 computers (all with wd-proc & CD-ROM, 1 with internet), room for hire *Svcs:* info, ref
Stock: bks/2500; periodcls/36; pamphs/2500
Acqs Offcr: Exec Sec, as above
Classn: DDC *Auto Sys:* TinLib
Pubns: Representation: Journal of Representative Democracy (quarterly, subscription for indivs UK/£25, overseas/£35, instn rates vary)
Staff: Other Prof: 1 *Exp:* £6000 (1999-2000); £7000 (2000-01)

S1278 Medical Devices Agency Library

Room 1001, Hannibal House, Elephant & Castle, London, SE1 6TQ (020-7972-8341; *fax:* 020-7972-8079)
Email: library@medical-devices.gov.uk
Internet: http://www.medical-devices.gov.uk/

Chief: Libn: Mrs Karen Morgan BSc(Hons), MSc, MCLIP (Karen.Morgan@doh.gsi.gov.uk) *Dep:* Asst Libn: Mr Jonathan Ginn BSc(Hons), MA, LCGI (Jonathan.Ginn@doh.gsi.gov.uk)
Entry: adv appt *Open:* Mon-Fri 0900-1700
Subj: medical tech
Stock: bks/4000; periodcls/160
Classn: Bliss *Auto Sys:* Sirsi Unicorn
Staff: Libns: 2 *Exp:* £80000 (1999-2000); £65000 (2000-01)

S1279 Medical Toxicology Unit Library

Guy's & St Thomas NHS Trust, Avonley Rd, New Cross, London, SE14 5ER (020-7771-5364; *fax:* 020-7771-5363)
Email: helaina.checketts@gstt.sthames.nhs.uk

Gov Body: Guy's & St Thomas' NHS Trust *Chief:* Libn: Ms Helaina Checketts BA, BSc, MLib
Entry: adv appt *Open:* Mon-Fri 1000-1745
Subj: clinical & analytical toxicology *Co-op Schemes:* BLDSC, HLN, BMA
Equip: m-reader, fax (call charge), copier (5p per sheet), 4 computers (all with internet & CD-ROM, 3 with wd-proc) *Online:* Dialog/Datastar (charged to reader) *Officer-in-Charge:* Libn, as above *Svcs:* info, ref, biblio
Stock: bks/2000; periodcls/45 *Acqs Offcr:* Libn, as above
Classn: NLM *Auto Sys:* Winchill *Staff: Libns:* 1

S1280 Medicines and Healthcare Products Regulatory Agency, Information Centre

(formerly Medicines Control Agency)
Room 1208, Market Towers, 1 Nine Elms Ln, Vauxhall, London, SW8 5NQ (020-7273-0000; *fax:* 020-7273-0353)
Email: info@mhra.gsi.gov.uk
Internet: http://www.mhra.gov.uk/

Gov Body: exec agency of the Dept of Health
Chief: Head of Lib Svcs: Mr Edward Scully BA, DipLib (edward.scully@mhra.gsi.gov.uk) *Dep:* Dep Head of Lib Svcs: Ms Susan Doherty BA, MSc, MA (susan.doherty@mhra.gsi.gov.uk)
Entry: not open to public *Open:* Mon-Fri 0900-1700
Subj: pharmaceuticals; medicine
Stock: bks/2500; periodcls/250; CD-ROMs/10
Classn: Bliss *Auto Sys:* Unicorn
Pubns: MAIL: The MCA Updating Svc; Eurodirect: The MCA's European Guidelines Svc
Staff: Libns: 2 *Non-Prof:* 2 *Exp:* £110000 (1999-2000); £120000 (2000-01)

S1281 Middle Temple Library

Middle Temple Ln, London, EC4Y 9BT (020-7427-4830; *fax:* 020-7427-4831)

Gov Body: Parliament of the Honourable Soc of the Middle Temple *Chief:* Keeper of the Lib: Miss V. Hayward BSc(Hons),MCLIP *Dep:* Dep Libn: Miss A.J. Knox BA, MCLIP *Other Snr Staff:* Snr Libn: Mr A.S. Adams BA(Hons), MA, DPhil, DipLib, MCLIP
Entry: strictly by prior appt & for ref only, with the permission of the libn, & only if no other lib has the material *Open:* term: Mon-Thu 0900-2000, Fri 0900-1830; vac: Mon-Fri 0900-1730
Subj: law (British, European & American) *Collns: Bks & Pamphs:* Robert Ashley's Colln; John Donne's Colln (part thereof); 80 incunabula *Archvs:* Middle Temple records (1501-date) *Co-op Schemes:* BIALL exchange scheme, liaison with other 3 Inn libs
Equip: m-reader, 2 fax, 4 copiers, computers (incl 2 with wd-proc & 10 with internet) *Online:* Daily Law Reports Index, Legal Journals Index
Stock: bks/200000; periodcls/250; archvs/280 linear m
Auto Sys: Unicorn
Pubns: Middle Temple Register of Admissions (5 vols, £50); Middle Temple Bench Bk (2 vols, £25); Middle Temple Minutes of Parliament (4 vols, £16)
Staff: Libns: 7 *Other Prof:* 1 *Non-Prof:* 3 *Exp:* £130000 (1999-2000)

S1282 Middlesex University, Information and Learning Resource Services

Bounds Green Rd, London, N11 2NQ (020-8411-5240; *fax:* 020-8411-6150)
Internet: http://www.ilrs.mdx.ac.uk/

Gov Body: Middlesex Univ *Chief:* Head of ILRS & Univ Libn: Mr William Marsterson MA, MCLIP (william6@mdx.ac.uk) *Dep:* Dep Heads of ILRS: Ms Gill Madden (gill1@mdx.ac.uk) & Ms Judith Cattermole (judith8@mdx.ac.uk)
Assoc Libs: CAT HILL LIB, Cat Hill, Barnet, Hertfordshire, EN4 8HT, Learning Resources Mgr: Ms Penny Dade (020-8411-5042; *fax:* 020-8411-5105; *email:* Penny11@mdx.ac.uk); ENFIELD LIB, Queensway, Enfield, Middlesex, EN3 4SA, Learning Resources Mgr: Ms Diane Coxon (020-8411-5334; *email:* diane9@mdx.ac.uk); HENDON LIB (Middlesex Univ Business School), The Burroughs, London, NW4 4BT, Learning Resource Mgr: Ms Pauline Hollis (020-8411-5852; *email:*

p.hollis@mdx.ac.uk); QUICKSILVER PL LIB, Weston Rd, London, N22 6HX (020-8411-5000 x2139; *fax:* 020-8888-6741); TOTTENHAM LIB, White Hart Ln, London, N17 8HR, Learning Resources Mgr: Ms Meg Kirk (020-8411-5165; *email:* m.kirk@mdx.ac.uk); TRENT PARK LIB, Bramley Rd, London, N14 4XS, Learning Resources Mgr: Ms Monica Glynn (020-8411-5646; *email:* tplrlib@mdx.ac.uk)
Entry: libs are open for ref to the genl public, access at peak times may be restricted *Open: Cat Hill:* term: Mon-Thu 0930-2100, Fri 0930-1700; vac: Mon-Fri 0930-1700; *Enfield:* term: Mon-Thu 0900-2100, Fri 0900-1800, Sat 1000-1700; vac: Mon-Fri 0900-1700; *Hendon:* term: Mon-Thu 0900-2300, Fri 1000-1800, Sat-Sun 1000-1600; vac: Mon-Thu 0900-1730, Fri 1000-1700; *Quicksilver Place:* term: Mon-Thu 1000-1800, Fri 1000-1730; vac: closed; *Tottenham:* term: Mon-Thu 0900-2100, Fri 0900-1800, Sat 1100-1600; vac: Mon-Thu 0900-2045, Fri 0900-1700; *Trent Park:* term: Mon-Fri 0900-2300, Sat 1000-1600; vac: Mon-Fri 0900-1700
Subj: all subjs; undergrad; postgrad; *Cat Hill:* arts; design; arch; fashion; textiles; art & design hist; graphic design; furniture; interior design; cultural theory; film studies; *Enfield:* social sci; health; geog; *Quicksilver Place:* fine art; *Hendon:* business; law; mgmt; *Tottenham:* humanities; lang; law; business; info tech; *Trent Park:* edu; performance arts; dance; drama; computing; media; cultural studies; life scis; lit; hist; music; product design & eng *Collns: Bks & Pamphs:* Hornsey Coll of Art Colln (c1200 vols, at Cat Hill) *Archvs:* Silver Studio Colln (designs for wall coverings, furnishings etc 1870-1963, with archvs of the Silvor Studio) *Other.* Lib of Historic Advertising (late 19C-1970s, at Cat Hill); Lesbian & Gay Newsmedia Archv (c80000 cuttings, at Cat Hill) *Co-op Schemes:* London Plus, ILL, BLDSC
Equip: m-reader, m-printer, video viewer, copier, clr copier, computers (incl wd-proc & CD-ROM) *Online:* BIDS, EBSCO, EDINA, Emerald, Ingenta, Lexis-Nexis, OCLC FirstSearch, OVID Online, Web of Science, Zetoc
Stock: bks/400000; periodcls/2650; m-forms/250; audios/2000; videos/12000; archvs/50000 designs etc; photos, illusts & slides/330000
Classn: DDC *Auto Sys:* Horizon
Pubns: various guides & info packs
Staff: Libns: 36.2 *Other-Prof:* 2 *Non-Prof:* 45.3
Proj: possible move of Info & Learning Resource Svcs admin in 2004, following closure of Bounds Green as a teaching campus in 2003

S1283
MIND Library
Granta House, 15-19 Broadway, Stratford, London, E15 4BQ (*office:* 020-8519-2122; *info line:* 0845-766-0163; *fax:* 020-8522-1725)
Email: info@mind.org.uk
Internet: http://www.mind.org.uk/

Type: charity
Entry: ref only *Open:* Mon-Fri 1000-1230, 1400-1630
Subj: mental health *Collns: Archvs:* relating to MIND's hist
Equip: copier, computer
Stock: bks/1000; periodcls/60
Classn: own
Pubns: numerous, incl: Understanding Series (£1 each); How to Series (£1 each); A-Z Series (£3 each); Rights Guides (£1 each); full list available
Staff: Other-Prof: 2 *Non-Prof:* 4

S1284
Ministry of Defence Headquarters, Information and Library Service
3-5 Gt Scotland Yard, Whitehall, London, SW1A 2HW (020-7218-4445; *fax:* 020-7218-5413)
Email: whitehall.lib@dgics.mod.uk

Chief: contact the Chief Libn
Assoc Libs: MINISTRY OF DEFENCE ABBEY WOOD INFO & LIB SVC, Abbey Wood, Bristol, BS34 8JH, Snr Libn: Mr C.C.W. Watson BA, MCLIP; MINISTRY OF DEFENCE LIB GLASGOW, 65 Brown St, Glasgow, G2 8EX, Libn: Ms M.J. Gair MA, MCLIP (*email:* library@khinf.demon.co.uk); MINISTRY OF DEFENCE SMALL ARMS TECHNICAL INFO CENTRE, Nottingham, NG2 1EQ, Libn: Mr R.A. Sharrock BA(Hons), MCLIP
Entry: adv appt only; apply in writing to Chief Libn
Open: visitors: Mon-Fri 0930-1230, 1330-1630
Subj: defence policy; defence forces worldwide; politics; tech; mgmt; computer sci *Collns: Bks & Pamphs:* historical collns on the 3 svcs, incl British Army regimental hists & military campaigns; official pubns (esp those related to defence) *Co-op Schemes:* BLDSC
Equip: copier (charges made for enqs & photocopies to personal visitors)
Stock: bks/150000; periodcls/800
Classn: UDC, own *Auto Sys:* C2
Pubns: various lib guides; Lib Bulletin
Staff: Libns: 24 *Non-Prof:* 20

Moorfields Eye Hospital Library
See INST OF OPHTHALMOLOGY & MOORFIELDS EYE HOSP JOINT LIB (**S1201**)

S1285
Morden College Library
19 St Germans Pl, Blackheath, London, SE3 0PW (020-8858 3365)

Type: charity *Gov Body:* Trustees of Morden Coll
Chief: Libn & Archivist: Mrs Elizabeth Wiggans MCLIP
Entry: adv appt *Open: Lib:* Tue 0900-1200; *Archvs:* Mon 0900-1700, Tue 1300-1700
Subj: all subjs; genl; classics; hist of South East London *Collns: Bks & Pamphs:* Kelsall Colln (Charles Kelsall bequeathed colln of bks, largely classics & travel on his death in 1857, together with money for bldg of lib) *Archvs:* archvs of Morden Coll, a charitable foundation (1695) for accommodation of 'decayed Turkey merchants' (admission requirements now expanded, but many with City connections)
Svcs: info, ref, biblio, indexing
Stock: bks/3075; periodcls/5; archvs/30 cubic m
Pubns: Morden Coll: A Brief Guide (1995, £2.50); The Hist of Morden Coll, by Patrick Joyce (1982, £1)
Staff: Libns: 1 PT *Exp:* no budget; occasional acqs on ad hoc basis

S1286
Morley College Library and Ursula Hyde Learning Centre
61 Westminster Bridge Rd, London, SE1 7HT (020-7450-1827/8; *fax:* 020-7928-4074)
Email: uhlc@morleycollege.ac.uk
Internet: http://www.morleycollege.ac.uk/

Chief: Lib Mgr: Ms Liz Shaughnessy
Entry: staff & students *Open:* Mon-Thu 1100-2000, Fri 1100-1900
Subj: all subjs; genl; GCSE; A level; vocational; psy; art; fashion; photography; music; lang *Co-op Schemes:* ILL
Equip: copiers, computers (incl wd-proc & internet)
Stock: bks/c30000

S1287
Museum and Library of The Order of St John
St John's Gate, St John's Ln, Clerkenwell, London, EC1M 4DA (020-7324-4070; *fax:* 020-7336-0587)
Internet: http://www.sja.org.uk/history/

Gov Body: The Order of St John (The Priory of England & The Islands) *Chief:* Libn: Prof Jonathan Riley-Smith *Dep:* Curator: Miss Pamela Willis MA
Entry: adv appt, ref only *Open:* Mon-Fri 1000-1700; closed lunchtime
Subj: religion; arts; geog; hist; military religious orders; hist of the Knights Hospitallers, Knights Templars & the Crusades; local hist (Islington & Clerkenwell); medical hist; hist of Order of St John's; St John Ambulance Brigade *Collns: Bks & Pamphs:* extensive colln of bks & MSS on the hist of the Hospitallers *Other:* photographic archv *Co-op Schemes:* ILL
Equip: m-reader, m-printer, copier (A4/20p, A3/30p), video viewer, room for hire *Svcs:* info, ref
Stock: bks/8000, incl pamphs; photos/10000; slides/2000; maps/100; videos/20; archvs/20000 items
Pubns: Hospitallers: The Hist of the Order of St John (hb/£14.95; pb/£9.95); A Brief Hist of the Order of St John (£3.25); Image of a Knight (catalogue, £5); Silver at St John's Gate: Maltese & Other Silver in the Colln of the Order of St John (£2.99); The Crusades: Cultures in Conflict (£5.95); The Order of St John & the Peasants' Revolt of 1381 (50p); The Siege of Rhodes 1480 (£1.20); The Rhodes Missal (bklet, 50p); Maps of Malta (catalogue, £3.95); The Badge of Serving Brother (50p); St John Ambulance in Victorian Britain (pack for primary schools, £1.50); Knowledge of the Order: A Training Resources Pack for Cadet Leaders (£7.95); A Century of Svc to Mankind (£4.95); St John Historical Soc Proceedings, Vols 4-7 (£3 each); The Story of the Eight-Pointed Cross (video, £15); postage in UK: £2 1st item, £4 for up to 5 items, 5+ items free
Staff: Other-Prof: 4

S1288
Museum of London, Library and Archives
150 London Wall, London, EC2Y 5HN (020-7600-3699; *fax:* 020-7600-1058)
Email: info@museumoflondon.org.uk
Internet: http://www.museumoflondon.org.uk/

Chief: Libn: Ms Sally Brooks MA
Assoc Libs: PICTURE LIB, at same addr; LONDON ARCHAEOLOGICAL ARCHV (see **A301**); DOCKLANDS LIB & ARCHVS (see **S1114**)
Entry: rsrchers only, by adv appt *Open:* Mon-Fri, times by appt
Subj: London: arts; hist; geog; archaeo *Collns: Bks & Pamphs:* W.G. Bell Colln (the Plague & the Great Fire of London); Sir Richard Tangye Colln (Cromwelliana); London & Middlesex Archaeological Soc Lib (membs only) *Archvs:* London Archaeological Archv (incl records of 2000 sites, 1908-91) *Other:* photo collns, incl: Bassano Colln; Photo Union Colln; Patrick Smith Colln; Henry Grant Colln; 20000+ photos illustrating hist of London, held at Picture Lib *Co-op Schemes:* ILL
Stock: bks/35000; periodcls/c50; maps/c300; MSS/20
Classn: in-house
Pubns: various Museum pubns in Museum Shop
Staff: Libns: 1

S1289
National Army Museum, Department of Printed Books
Royal Hosp Rd, Chelsea, London, SW3 4HT (020-7730-0717; *fax:* 020-7823-6573)
Internet: http://www.national-army-museum.ac.uk/

Chief: Head of Dept of Printed Bks: Mr Michael Ball MA, AMA
Assoc Libs: DEPT OF ARCHVS (see **A311**)
Entry: adv appl for reader's ticket, forms available from the Dept of Printed Bks ☞

(Natl Army Museum, Dept of Printed Bks cont)
Open: Tue-Sat 1000-1630; closed Sats before bank hols & last 2 wks of October
Subj: military hist; hist of British army from 1485; hist of Indian army until 1947; hist of Colonial armies (prior to independence) *Collns: Archvs:* papers of Lord Raglan, Lord Roberts, Lord Rawlinson & others
Equip: m-reader, m-camera, m-printer, copier
Stock: bks/44000; periodcls/200; photos/1500000; slides/10000; audios/2500; videos/60; maps & m-forms/2000
Classn: UDC (mod) *Auto Sys:* Filemaker Pro 5
Staff: Libns: 1

S1290 🔑 🏛
National Art Library
Victoria & Albert Museum, South Kensington, London, SW7 2RL (020-7942-2400; *fax:* 020-7942-2401)
Email: nal.enquiries@vam.ac.uk
Internet: http://www.nal.vam.ac.uk/

Gov Body: Victoria & Albert Museum *Chief:* Chief Libn & Curator of the Natl Art Lib: Ms Sue Lambert *Dep:* Dep Libn: Mr John Meriton *Assoc Libs:* ARCHV OF ART & DESIGN (see **A250**); V&A ARCHVS (see **A353**)
Entry: open to public with valid reader's ticket (separate ticket needed for Natl Art Lib special collns) *Open:* Tue-Sat 1000-1700; closed for 3 wks for stocktaking from the Sat before August Bank Hol
Subj: fine arts; decorative arts; design; arch; calligraphy; fine printing; furniture; woodwork; textiles; dress; ceramics & glass; metalwork; sculpture; art & design of Far East, India & South East Asia; art, craft & design of the bk; lit (Western Europe, some Asian) *Collns: Bks & Pamphs:* various ongoing special collns incl those of bindings, illuminated & calligraphic MSS, fine printing & illust, artists' bks & bk art; 'closed' collns incl: Clements Colln (heraldic bindings); Cole Colln (diaries, notebks, correspondence & bks of Sir Henry Cole); Collings Colln (20C Slavonic art); Dyce Colln (lit & theatre, 16C-19C); Forster Colln (lit, incl MSS of Charles Dickens); Great Exhib of 1851 Colln; Harrod Colln (19C illustrated bks); Hole Bequest (17C-18C lit); Hutton Bequest (works on fencing, swordsmanship, weapons, self-defence); Jobbing Printing Colln (1920s & 30s, some 1960s material); Jones Colln (art & manufacture, some lit); Larionov Colln (materials relating to the theatre & opera in Europe, esp Russia & France; work by Larionov & Goncharova); Liberty & Co Printed Catalogues Colln (1881-1949); Linder Bequest (Beatrix Potter drawings, watercolours, literary MSS & correspondence, held at Blythe House); Little Bequest (illustrated ch's bks, mostly European, 17C-20C); Osbert Lancaster Colln (comic art, humour); Osman-Gidal Colln of 20C magazines (1920s-1950s, showing development of photo-reportage); Pinto Colln (directories relating to London & the provinces); Piot Colln (pageantry, fetes & ceremonies, 16C-19C); Queen Mary Colln (ch's bks); Rakoff Colln of comics & graphic novels; Renier Colln of Historic & Contemporary Pubns for Children (80000 vols, 1585-1988); Weale Colln (part of working lib of W.H. Weale, Keeper of NAL 1890-99); museum & gallery exhib catalogues; trade lit (19C-date) *Archvs:* documentary MSS colln, incl letters, account bks & other records

relating to indiv artists & the production & marketing of decorative & fine art objects *Other:* prints, drawings & photos are held by the Museum's Prints, Drawings & Paintings Colln *Co-op Schemes:* BLDSC (photocopies only)
Equip: m-reader, m-printer, video viewer, fax, computers (incl internet & CD-ROM), videodisc viewer, facilities for laptop computers *Online:* OCLC, Nexis *Svcs:* info, photocopying
Stock: bks/1 mln; periodcls/1500; info files/8000; illuminated MSS/300; videodiscs/19; non-print items/1 mln
Classn: subj keywords, DDC (open ref material)
Auto Sys: Dynix
Pubns: leaflets & guides; The Reading Room (newsletter, 2 pa); Handbook to the Dyce & Forster Collns in the South Kensington Museum; Beatrix Potter: the V&A Colln; numerous others; contact Reader Svcs at the above addr for details
Staff: Libns: 41 *Other Prof:* 6 *Non-Prof:* 1

S1291 🔑 ✚
National Asthma Campaign, Library and Information Service
Providence House, Providence Pl, London, N1 0NT (020-7226-2260; *fax:* 020-7704-0740)
Internet: http://www.asthma.org.uk/

Type: voluntary sector health charity *Chief:* Head of Info & Policy: Ms H. Donohoe MSc *Dep:* Info Offcr: Ms Judith Stott BSc
Entry: no visiting facilities; tel enqs only; will help with queries from students & health profs or point them in right direction for accessing the info they require *Open:* for tel enqs only: Tue-Wed 1400-1700
Subj: asthma; respiratory conditions
Svcs: info *Stock:* bks/100; periodcls/50
Classn: NLM *Staff: Other Prof:* 3

S1292 🏛
National Audit Office Library
157-197 Buckingham Palace Rd, Victoria, London, SW1W 9SP (020-7798-7262; *fax:* 020-7798-7710)
Email: enquiries@nao.gsi.gov.uk
Internet: http://www.nao.gov.uk/

Entry: not open to public; ref svc to outside users by arrangement only *Open:* Mon-Fri 0930-1700
Subj: official pubns on a wide range of subjs, particularly: audit; accountancy; public finance
Collns: Bks & Pamphs: special colln of reports from Auditors Genl overseas
Stock: bks/3000; periodcls/120
Classn: DDC *Auto Sys:* Unicorn
Pubns: Annual Report
Staff: Libns: 3 *Non-Prof:* 5

S1293 🔑
National Autistic Society Information Centre
393 City Rd, London, EC1V 1NG (020-7833-2299; *fax:* 020-7903-3767)
Email: nas@nas.org.uk
Internet: http://www.nas.org.uk/

Type: charity *Gov Body:* Natl Autistic Soc *Chief:* Info Centre Mgr: Mr David Potter MSc, BA, MCLIP
Entry: ref only, adv appt *Open:* Mon-Fri 1000-1400
Subj: autism; Asperger Syndrome
Equip: copier (10p) *Svcs:* info, ref, biblio, abstracting
Stock: bks/3400; periodcls/48
Classn: Bliss *Auto Sys:* InMagic DBTextworks
Staff: Libns: 2.5 *Non-Prof:* 2.5 *Exp:* £7000 (1999-2000)

S1294 🔑
National Centre For Volunteering, Information Service and Library
Regents Wharf, 8 All Saints St, London, N1 9RL (020-7520-8900; *fax:* 020-7520-8910)
Email: Information@thecentre.org.uk
Internet: http://www.volunteering.org.uk/

Chief: Head of Info: Mr Michael Stuart
Entry: ref only, by appt *Open:* Mon-Fri 0900-1700
Subj: social policy; volunteering; voluntary sector; community involvement *Collns: Bks & Pamphs:* reports & dissertations; pubns of the Inst for Volunteering Rsrch & Natl Centre for Volunteering *Other:* cuttings colln
Equip: copier, computer *Online:* VOLNET UK
Stock: bks/5000; periodcls/100; audios/5; videos/62; serial articles/16000
Classn: NYB
Pubns: Working With Volunteers Handbooks (£4.50 each); Good Practice Guides (various); 1991 Natl Survey of Voluntary Activ in the UK (£15); others too numerous to mention
Staff: Other Prof: 2.5 *Non-Prof:* 1

S1295 🔑 ✚
National Childbirth Trust Library
Alexandra House, Oldham Ter, London, W3 6NH (0870-770-3236; *fax:* 0870-770-3237)
Email: library@natural-childbirth-trust.co.uk

Type: charity *Chief:* Info Offcr & Libn: Ms Linda Griffiths
Entry: by appt *Open:* Mon-Fri 0900-1730
Subj: pregnancy; childbirth; post-natal care
Svcs: info, ref, biblio *Staff: Libns:* 1

S1296 🔑
National Children's Bureau, Library and Information Service
8 Wakley St, London, EC1V 7QE (020-7843-6008; *fax:* 020-7843-6007)
Email: library@ncb.org.uk
Internet: http://www.ncb.org.uk/

Type: registered charity *Chief:* Head of Lib & Info Svc: Ms Nicola Hilliard BA, MCLIP *Dep:* Libn: Ms Jayne Parkin MCLIP
Entry: adv appt; ref only; £10 per visit for non-membs *Open:* Mon-Fri 1000-1700
Subj: social sci; childcare; child abuse; under-5s; play; child disability; child health; children in care; family breakdown *Collns: Bks & Pamphs:* govt reports; directories *Co-op Schemes:* BLDSC
Equip: fax, video viewer, copier, computers (incl wd-proc & CD-ROM), room for hire *Online:* various online databases *Svcs:* info, ref, biblio
Stock: bks/30000; periodcls/300; pamphs/20000
Classn: Bliss *Auto Sys:* InMagic
Pubns: Highlights (£2 each, complete set of 100+ titles £75); Childstats (£25 pa); Guide to Lib & Info Svc (free); Reading Lists (£5 each); Student Reading Lists (£20 complete set); Org Lists (£20 complete set); Children in the News (£175 pa); Conferences & Events (£25 pa); ChildData on CD-ROM & WWW (£705 pa, incl VAT); ChildData Abstracts (£30 pa); discount prices for membs
Staff: Libns: 4 *Non-Prof:* 2 *Exp:* £148000 (1999-2000)

S1297 🔑 🏛
National Gallery Library and Archive
Trafalgar Sq, London, WC2N 5DN (*lib:* 020-7747-2542; *archvs:* 020-7747-2831; *fax:* 020-7747-2892)
Email: lad@ng-london.org.uk
Internet: http://www.nationalgallery.org.uk/

Gov Body: Trustees of the Natl Gallery **Chief:** Head of Libs & Archvs: Miss Elspeth J. Hector MA, MCLIP **Dep:** Archivist: Mr David Carter **Entry:** Lib: primarily for Natl Gallery staff; ref only by adv appt for visiting academics, postgrad rsrch students & other scholars who cannot obtain the material they require elsewhere; Archvs: open to bona fide rsrchers by appt **Open:** Mon-Fri 0930-1730 **Subj:** hist of Western European painting (1200-1925) **Collns:** Bks & Pamphs: c2000 early src works; early guidebks; auction, exhib & colln catalogues Archvs: archvs of the Natl Gallery (1821-date), incl letters, reports, minutes, press cuttings & other material relating to the hist of the Gallery & its colln; papers of former Dirs & Keepers of the Natl Gallery, incl: Sir Charles Lock Eastlake; Sir William Boxall Papers; Sir Ralph Wornum Papers; Philip Hendy Papers **Other:** photo & slide lib **Equip:** m-reader, m-printer, copier, video viewer, computer (incl CD-ROM) **Stock:** bks/c80000; periodcls/150, plus 100 no longer current; photos/200000; slides/80000 **Classn:** own **Staff:** Libns: 3 Other Prof: 2 Non-Prof: 5

S1298 🎓📷
The National Heritage Library
313-315 Caledonian Rd, London, N1 1DR (020-7609-9639)

Chief: Founder Dir: Mr M. McNeil **Entry:** by prior appt in writing **Subj:** British Isles, esp Wales: landscape; culture; arts; social hist; religion; churches & chapels; mosques; synagogues; arts; geog; hist; welfare; public & historic bldgs; commerce; travel; industry; farming; environment; sport **Collns:** Archvs: Natl Heritage Archv of British Isles (textual & photographic) **Stock:** bks/10000; photos/100000; slides/500; illusts/2000; pamphs/140000; maps/1000 **Pubns:** The Fieldguide to Wales; photo archv to be made available on CD-ROM (both forthcoming, pending sponsorship) **Proj:** lib extension; bar-coding of collns (pending sponsorship)

S1299 🎓✚
National Information Centre for Speech-Language Therapy, Department of Human Communication Science Library
Chandler House, 2 Wakefield St, London, WC1N 1PF (020-7679-4207; fax: 020-7679-0861) **Email:** hcs.library@ucl.ac.uk **Internet:** http://library.hcs.ucl.ac.uk/

Gov Body: Univ Coll London (see **S1433**) **Chief:** Site Libn: Ms Stevie Russell BA(Hons), DipLib **Entry:** membs; visitors by arrangement **Open:** term: Mon 0915-1800, Tue-Thu 0915-1900, Fri 1000-1800; vac: Mon-Fri 0930-1700 **Subj:** psy; social sci; lang; linguistics; edu; medicine; speech sci; anatomy **Collns:** Archvs: historical colln of speech sci material **Other:** Tests/Assessments Colln relating to speech sci **Co-op Schemes:** BLDSC, PLCS, North Thames Region **Equip:** m-reader, 2 video viewers, 2 copiers, computer (with CD-ROM), video cameras, tape recorders **Online:** Medline, LLBA, PsycInfo, ERIC, Web of Science etc (£20 per search) **Svcs:** info, ref, biblio **Stock:** bks/6000; periodcls/80; pamphs/100; videos/50; AVs/15; tests/400 **Classn:** DDC **Auto Sys:** Aleph 500 **Staff:** Libns: 1 Non-Prof: 2

S1300 ✚
National Institute for Medical Research, Library and Information Service
The Ridgeway, Mill Hill, London, NW7 1AA (020-8913-8630; fax: 020-8913-8534) **Email:** library@nimr.mrc.ac.uk **Internet:** http://www.nimr.mrc.ac.uk/

Type: rsrch council **Gov Body:** Medical Rsrch Council (see **S536**) **Chief:** Libn: Mr Frank Norman BSc, MCLIP **Dep:** Dep Libn: Miss Patti Biggs BSc, MCLIP **Entry:** MRC staff; others in exceptional circumstances **Open:** Mon-Fri 0900-1700 **Subj:** basic biomedical sci; biochem; physiology; chem; microbiology; cell biology; neuroscience; genetics; virology; immunology **Collns:** Bks & Pamphs: MRC pubns **Equip:** copier, m-reader, computers (incl internet) **Online:** Medline, Beilstein Crossfire, CAS SciFinder, Web of Sci **Svcs:** info, ref, biblio **Stock:** bks/20000; periodcls/250 **Classn:** Barnard **Staff:** Libns: 3 Non-Prof: 4

S1301 🗝
National Institute for Social Work, Library and Information Service
5-7 Tavistock Pl, London, WC1H 9SN (020-7387-9681; fax: 020-7387-7968) **Email:** niswis@nisw2.org.uk **Internet:** http://www.nisw.org.uk/

Gov Body: Natl Inst for Social Work **Chief:** Head of Lib & Info Svc: Mr Mark Watson BA, MCLIP **Entry:** adv appt; no undergrad students **Open:** Mon-Fri 1000-1700 **Subj:** social sci, particularly social work **Collns:** Archvs: papers of Dame Eileen Younghusband **Equip:** copier, computer (with CD-ROM) **Svcs:** info, ref, biblio, indexing, abstracting **Stock:** bks/40000; periodcls/250 **Classn:** Bliss **Auto Sys:** CAIRS **Pubns:** CareData Abstracts Monthly (prices on request); Journals List (free) **Staff:** Libns: 5 Other Prof: 1 Non-Prof: 5

S1302 🗝
National Institute of Economic and Social Research Library
2 Dean Trench St, Smith Sq, London, SW1P 3HE (020-7654-1907; fax: 020-7654-1900) **Email:** library@niesr.ac.uk **Internet:** http://www.niesr.ac.uk/

Chief: Libn: Mrs Patricia Oliver BA(Hons), MCLIP (p.oliver@niesr.ac.uk) **Entry:** academic rsrchers only, by prior appt **Open:** Mon-Fri 0930-1730 **Subj:** social sci; econ **Co-op Schemes:** BLDSC, ILL with certain London libs **Equip:** 2 copiers, computers (with wd-proc & CD-ROM) **Online:** not available to outside users **Stock:** bks/5000; periodcls/400; pamphs/1000 **Classn:** American Econ Assoc **Auto Sys:** InMagic **Staff:** Libns: 1 **Exp:** £34000 (1999-2000); £36000 (2000-01)

S1303 🏛🏛
National Maritime Museum, Caird Library
Greenwich, London, SE10 9NF (020-8312-6673; fax: 020-8312-6722) **Email:** library@nmm.ac.uk **Internet:** http://www.nmm.ac.uk/

Type: natl museum **Gov Body:** Trustees of the Natl Maritime Museum **Chief:** Head of Lib & Manuscripts: Ms Jill Davies BSc, DipLib, MCLIP (jdavies@nmm.ac.uk) **Dep:** Snr Lib Asst: Ms Hellen Pethers BA(Hons) (hpethers@nmm.ac.uk) **Other Snr Staff:** Manuscripts Mgr: Mrs Daphne Knott BA, DipArch (dknott@nmm.ac.uk) **Assoc Libs:** MUSEUM ARCHVS, Archivist: Ms Geraldine Charles MSc, FLS, FRGS (gcharles@nmm.ac.uk) **Entry:** rsrch & ref only; apply on arrival for Reader's Ticket (ID required); Sat by prior appt only, with restricted svc **Open:** Mon-Fri 1000-1645, Sat by appt only; closed Sun, bank hols & 3rd wk of Feb **Subj:** local studies (Greenwich); all aspects of maritime & naval hist (Royal Navy & Merchant Navy); emigration; navigation; piracy; shipwrecks; biography; astronomy; horology; specialist collns in: family hist; merchant shipping; warships **Collns:** Bks & Pamphs: rare bks colln (pre-1850); Gosse Piracy Colln; MacPherson Colln of Atlases; Lloyd's Register; Lloyd's List; Navy List Archvs: Nelson letters; shipping company records, incl P&O; Masters Certificates; Lloyd's Survey (kept off-site); crew lists (selected years, kept off-site); lieutenant's logs & personal papers **Equip:** 3 m-printers, video viewer, copier (A4/25p, A3/40p), 10 computers (all with internet & CD-ROM) **Online:** Journal for Maritime Rsrch (£20), PORT Maritime Info Gateway (free), online catalogues incl Lib & MSS catalogue **Svcs:** info, ref **Stock:** bks/100000, incl 15000 pre-1850 rare bks; periodcls/200+; pamphs/20000; maps/100000+ incl charts; m-forms/200; CD-ROMs/60; archvs/3.5 linear miles of MSS **Classn:** UDC **Auto Sys:** Unicorn **Staff:** Libns: 4 Other Prof: 8 Non-Prof: 2

S1304 🗝
National Society for the Prevention of Cruelty to Children, Library and Information Service
Weston House, 42 Curtain Rd, London, EC2A 3NH (020-7825-2706; fax: 020-7825-2706) **Email:** library@nspcc.org.uk **Internet:** http://www.nspcc.org.uk/

Type: charity **Chief:** Libn: Ms Catherine Tite BA, DipLib, MCLIP & Ms Karen Childs Smith BA, MCLIP (job share) **Entry:** by appt; over 18s only **Open:** Mon-Fri 0900-1700 **Subj:** child protection; child abuse; social work; social welfare; family law; sociology; family therapy; child psy **Collns:** Bks & Pamphs: bks on hist of child abuse Archvs: NSPCC Archv (reports, pubns, photos, artefacts) **Co-op Schemes:** BLDSC **Equip:** video viewer, copier **Online:** Datastar **Stock:** bks/6000; periodcls/100, plus 50 no longer current; pamphs/1500; audios/50; videos/100 **Classn:** Bliss **Auto Sys:** Adlib **Pubns:** various bibliographies; list on appl **Staff:** Libns: 6 Other Prof: 0.5 Non-Prof: 2

S1305 🗝
The National Trust Libraries
36 Queen Anne's Gate, London, SW1H 9AS (020-7447-9251) **Email:** lhbmep@smtp.ntrust.org.uk **Internet:** http://www.ntrust.org.uk/

Type: environmental/conservation charity **Chief:** Libs Curator: Mr Mark Purcell MA, DipLib **Dep:** Asst Libs Curator: Ms Yvonne Lewis MA, DipLib **Assoc Libs:** NATL TRUST PHOTO LIB, at same addr (see **S1306**); over 150 historic house libs, ranging from houses with only 1 bk to collns of 10000+ vols

Special Libraries

London ▼ London

(The Natl Trust Libs cont)

Entry: ref only, by adv appt, according to terms laid out in NT Libs Access Policy (available on request); the collns are integral parts of the contents of the Trust's historic bldgs, & are available as resources of last resort for material that is not available elsewhere; all enqs should be directed to the Trust's Libs Curator
Subj: all subjs; rare bks & MSS (as held in historic house libs), many pre-1801
Stock: bks/c250000 (in all 150 libs)
Pubns: Treasures of the Libs of the Natl Trust
Staff: Libns: 4 *Exp:* no exp on stock; acqs only in exceptional circumstances
Proj: Appeal for Country House Libs

S1306 🍷 🎥

National Trust Photographic Library

36 Queen Anne's Gate, London, SW1H 9AS (020-7447-6788; *fax:* 020-7447-6767)
Email: photolibrary@ntrust.org.uk
Internet: http://www.nationaltrust.org.uk/photolibrary/

Gov Body: Natl Trust *Chief:* Photo Lib Mgr: Ms Maggie Gowan *Dep:* Mr Robert Morris
Assoc Libs: NATL TRUST LIBS, at same addr (see **S1305**)
Entry: adv appt *Open:* Mon-Fri 0930-1700
Subj: photos: landscape, coastline, arch, interiors, gardens, paintings etc
Stock: photos/200000
Staff: Other Prof: 5 Non-Prof: 5

S1307 🍷

National Union of Teachers, Library and Information Unit

Hamilton House, Mabledon Pl, London, WC1H 9BD (020-7380-4713; *fax:* 020-7387-8458)
Email: inf.unit@netcomuk.co.uk
Internet: http://www.teachers.org.uk/

Chief: Info Offcr: Ms Janet Friedlander BA(Hons), MCLIP
Entry: svc only available to NUT Staff & Exec, except for quick ref svc & info regarding NUT documentation (tel & letters only); adv appt *Open:* Mon-Fri 0900-1715
Subj: edu *Collns: Archvs:* archvs at Modern Records Centre, Univ of Warwick, Coventry, CV4 7AL (see **A114**) *Other:* Annual Reports (1871-date); Schoolmaster (now The Teacher) Jan 1972-date; NUT pubns *Co-op Schemes:* BLDSC
Equip: m-reader, m-printer, copier, computer (with CD-ROM)
Classn: DDC, in-house for govt pubns *Auto Sys:* Genesis (new sys to be selected)
Staff: Libns: 1 Other Prof: 0.5

S1308 🏛️ 🏛️

The Natural History Museum, Library and Archives

Cromwell Rd, London, SW7 5BD (020-7942-5460; *fax:* 020-7942-5559)
Email: library@nhm.ac.uk
Internet: http://www.nhm.ac.uk/library/

Type: natl museum *Gov Body:* Trustees of Nat Hist Museum *Chief:* Head of Lib Svcs: Mr Graham Higley BSc, DipLib, MCLIP (G.Higley@nhm.ac.uk) *Dep:* Mr Christopher Mills BA, MA, DipLib, MCLIP (C.Mills@nhm.ac.uk)
Assoc Libs: ROTHSCHILD & ORNITHOLOGY LIBS, Zoological Museum, Akeman St, Tring, Hertfordshire, HP23 6AP, Libn: Mrs Effie Warr (020-7942-6156; *email:* ornlib@nhm.ac.uk); NAT HIST MUSEUM ARCHVS, addr as above (020-7942-5507/5873; *fax:* 020-7942-5559; *email:* archives@nhm.ac.uk)
Entry: reader's ticket, adv appt *Open: both libs:* Mon-Fri 1000-1630
Subj: Lib & Archvs: nat hist; botany; entomology; mineralogy; palaeontology; geol; anthro; zoology; related areas of life & earth scis; *Rothschild & Ornithology Libs:* ornithology; early genl zoology; early travel *Collns: Bks & Pamphs:* Linnaeus Colln; Tweeddale Colln (ornithology); Rothschild Colln (ornithology & travel); nat hist MSS (many collns); Walsingham Colln (entomology); Wallace Colln; First Fleet Colln *Archvs:* Nat Hist Museum Archvs; Banks Archv *Other:* nat hist drawings & watercolours (3rd largest colln of original art & papers in the UK) *Co-op Schemes:* BLDSC
Equip: Lib & Archvs: m-reader, m-printer, copier, clr copier, computers (incl wd-proc & CD-ROM); *Rothschild & Ornithology Libs:* 5 m-readers, fax, copier, 2 computers (both with internet, 1 with wd-proc) *Svcs:* info, ref, biblio
Stock: bks/1000000; periodcls/10000; photos/65000; slides/5000; illusts/750000; maps/75000; m-forms/30000; audios/1000; videos/150
Classn: UDC (Main Lib), Woodward (Ornithology), own (Rothschild) *Auto Sys:* Unicorn
Staff: Libns: 23 Other Prof: 3 Non-Prof: 19

S1309 ✚

North Middlesex Hospital NHS Trust, David Ferriman Library

Sterling Way, Edmonton, London, N18 1QX (020-8887-2223; *fax:* 020-8887-2714)
Email: libnm1@mdx.ac.uk

Gov Body: North Middlesex Hosp Trust & Middlesex Univ (see **S1282**) *Chief:* Libn: Ms Linda Farley
Assoc Libs: provides svcs to Middlesex Univ staff & students
Entry: bona fide membs only; memb fee for all others *Open:* Mon-Tue, Thu 0900-1900, Wed 0800-1900, Fri 0900-1800, Sat 0900-1200
Subj: medicine; nursing; midwifery; professions allied to health *Co-op Schemes:* BLDSC, Regional Document Supply
Equip: copier, networked computers *Svcs:* info, ref, biblio
Stock: bks/13000; periodcls/200; pamphs/1000
Classn: NLM *Auto Sys:* Heritage
Staff: Libns: 3 Non-Prof: 2.4

S1310 🎥

Novosti Photo Library

(incorporating the former JVZ Picture Lib)
3 Rosary Gdns, London, SW7 4NW (020-7370-1873; *fax:* 020-7244-7875)
Email: photos@novosti.co.uk

Type: commercial photo agency & archv *Chief:* Lib Mgr: Ms Vaughan Melzer BA(Sociology), BA(Photography) (vaughan.melzer@novosti.co.uk)
Dep: Commercial Dir: Mr Ralph Gibson
Entry: adv appt *Open:* Mon-Fri 1000-1600
Subj: all subjs pertaining to Russia & the former Soviet Union, incl: Russian & Soviet hist; personalities (historic, cultural, political & foreign); arts; space exploration; World War Two; military; geog; various features of 'New Russia'
Stock: photos/1 mln *Staff:* Other Prof: 1

S1311 🎓 🍷 🖐️

Oak Hill College Library

Chase Side, Southgate, London, N14 4PS (020-8449-0467; *fax:* 020-8441-5996)
Email: wendyb@oakhill.ac.uk
Internet: http://www.oakhill.ac.uk/

Gov Body: Kingam Hill Trust *Chief:* Libn: Miss Wendy Bell BA(Hons), DipLib, MCLIP
Entry: ref use free, £50 pa to borrow *Open:* visitors: Mon-Fri 0900-1700; 24 hrs for residents
Subj: religion *Co-op Schemes:* BLDSC
Equip: m-reader, copier, fax, computer (with CD-ROM)
Stock: bks/40000; periodcls/200; slides/15 sets; audios/138; videos/150; AVs/40
Classn: LC *Auto Sys:* Heritage
Staff: Libns: 1 Non-Prof: 0.2

S1312 🏛️

Office for National Statistics Information and Library Service

Office for Natl Statistics, 1 Drummond Gate, Pimlico, London, SW1V 2QQ (0845-601-3034)
Email: info@statistics.gov.uk
Internet: http://www.statistics.gov.uk/

Chief: Chief Libn: Mr John Birch BLib, MCLIP
Dep: Mr Ian Bushnell BA, MCLIP (at Newport)
Assoc Libs: RSRCH LIB, addr as above, London Libn: Mr Alan Cliftlands BA(Hons), DipLib (0845-601-3034); NEWPORT Lib, Govt Bldgs, Cardiff Rd, Newport, Gwent, NP10 8XG, Libn: Mr Ian Bushnell as above (0845-601-3034)
Entry: open to public without appt, ref only *Open:* Mon-Fri 0900-1700
Subj: The Rsrch Lib, London: health; population; demographics; genl social & economic info; statistical methodology; *Newport Lib:* economic, business & financial statistics *Collns: Bks & Pamphs:* at London: Natl Statistics series from across govt; internatl statistics; methodological monographs & periodcls; ex-OPCS material; at Newport: statistical & market report data; ex-CSO material *Archvs:* at London: all census results for England & Wales from 1801; birth, marriage & death statistics from 1837 *Co-op Schemes:* govt libs, BLLD
Equip: at both libs: fax, copier, computers (incl internet & CD-ROM) *Disabled:* minicom (at London), wheelchair access (at both) *Svcs:* info, ref, biblio, enqs
Stock: bks/60000; periodcls/1000; maps/200; m-forms/200
Classn: DDC & in-house *Auto Sys:* Sirsi Unicorn
Staff: Libns: 8 Non-Prof: 9

S1313 🏛️

Office of Fair Trading (OFT), Library and Information Centre

Fleetbank House, 2-6 Salisbury Sq, London, EC4Y 8AE (020-7211-8941; *fax:* 020-7211-8940)
Internet: http://www.oft.gov.uk/

Gov Body: Office of Fair Trading *Chief:* Head of Lib & Info Svcs: Mr M.A. Shrive BA(Hon), MCLIP
Entry: OFT staff, loans to other govt depts; not open to genl public *Open:* Mon-Thu 0900-1715, Fri 0900-1700
Subj: consumer affairs; consumer credit; competition policy *Co-op Schemes:* BLDSC
Equip: copier, computers *Online:* range of mostly electronic-based info sources, most accessible from offcrs' own desktops
Stock: bks/c1000; periodcls/c380
Classn: DDC *Auto Sys:* CAIRS
Pubns: OFT pubns available free from: OFT, PO Box 266, Hayes, Middlesex, UB3 1XB (0870-606-0321), or via web site (as above)
Staff: Libns: 3 Non-Prof: 1

S1314

Office of Gas and Electricity Markets (OFGEM) Library

9 Millbank, London, SW1P 3GE (020-7901-7217; *fax:* 020-7901-7003)
Email: library@ofgem.gov.uk
Internet: http://www.ofgem.gov.uk/

Gov Body: part of DTI Lib & Info Svc
Entry: open to bona fide enquirers, by prior appt
Open: Mon-Fri 1000-1700
Subj: UK gas industry, regulation, competition, consumer aspects (e.g. fuel poverty) *Co-op Schemes:* ILL to other govt depts, BLDSC
Equip: m-reader, copier *Online:* Dialog, Dialtech, Press Assoc (internal use only)
Stock: bks/various; periodcls/75
Classn: DDC
Pubns: numerous leaflets & genl reports
Staff: Libns: 1 *Non-Prof:* 2

S1315

Office of Telecommunications (OFTEL) Library

50 Ludgate Hill, London, EC4M 7JJ (020-7634-8761; *fax:* 020-7634-8946)
Email: infocent.oftel@gtnet.gov.uk
Internet: http://www.oftel.gov.uk/

Gov Body: part of DTI Lib & Info Svc *Chief: Libn:* Ms Anne Cameron *Dep: Asst Libn:* Mrs Rachel Reeve
Entry: adv appt, public register only *Open:* Mon-Fri 0930-1200, 1330-1600
Subj: telecommunications; utilities regulation
Collns: Archvs: OFTEL pubns from creation of OFTEL in 1984 *Co-op Schemes:* BLDSC, ILL
Equip: m-reader, m-printer, copier (A4/10p+VAT)
Svcs: info
Stock: bks/1000; periodcls/150; pamphs/200
Classn: DDC
Pubns: Pubns List (free, UK only); License List (free, UK only)
Staff: Libns: 1 *Non-Prof:* 3

S1316

Office of the Deputy Prime Minister and Department for Transport, Information Services and Sources

Zone 2/H25, Ashdown House, 123 Victoria St, London, SW1E 6DE (020-8890-3039; *fax:* 020-8890-6098)
Internet: http://www.odpm.gov.uk/

Chief: Libn in Charge: Ms Sue Westcott *Dep:* Snr Libns: Mrs Anne Layton & Mrs Clare Gibson
Assoc Libs: ODPM INFO SVCS & SOURCES, Zone 1/F8, Eland House, Bressenden Rd, London, SW1E 5DU (020-8890-3199); DFT INFO SVCS & SOURCES, LG11, Gt Minster House, 76 Marsham St, London, SW1P 6DE
Entry: by adv appt, students require letter from tutor *Open:* Mon-Fri 0900-1700 (for tel enqs); Mon-Fri 1000-1630 (for external visitors)
Subj: housing; construction; regeneration; countryside; local & regional govt; planning; roads; local transport; railways; aviation *Co-op Schemes:* BLDSC, LASER
Equip: video viewer, fax, copier, computer (incl CD-ROM) *Online:* wide range of genl & environmental databases *Svcs:* info
Stock: bks/300000; periodcls/700
Classn: LC *Auto Sys:* Unicorn
Staff: Libns: 15 *Non-Prof:* 4

S1317

One Plus One, Library and Information Service

The Wells, 7-15 Rosebery Ave, London, EC1R 4SP (020-7841-3660; *fax:* 020-7841-3670)
Email: info@oneplusone.org.uk
Internet: http://www.oneplusone.org.uk/

Type: voluntary body *Chief: Info Offcr:* Ms Fiona Hovsepian
Entry: ref only, adv appt, entry fee *Open:* flexible
Subj: psy (of marriage etc); marriage; partnership; family; divorce *Collns: Bks & Pamphs:* own rsrch findings on marriage & partnership; antique marriage manuals *Archvs:* relating to the hist of One Plus One; some official statistics on marriage etc (1960s onwards, a few pre-war) *Co-op Schemes:* BLDSC
Equip: copier, video viewer, computer
Stock: bks/2000; periodcls/20; videos/a few
Classn: own *Auto Sys:* CAIRS
Pubns: Beginning of the Rest of Your Life?; Marital Breakdown & the Health of the Nation; Relationship Revolution; list available
Staff: Other Prof: 8

S1318

Operational Research Society Library

c/o Central Lib, Imperial Coll, South Kensington, London, SW7 2AZ (020-7594-8841; *fax:* 020-7594-8876)

Chief: Librarian-in-Charge: Miss S.G. Nutsford
Entry: membs for ref only *Open:* term: Mon-Fri 0830-2200, Sat 0930-1730; vac: Mon-Sat 0930-1730
Subj: operational rsrch; mgmt
Stock: bks/1600; periodcls/30
Classn: UDC *Auto Sys:* Unicorn *Staff: Libns:* 2

S1319

Overseas Development Institute Library

111 Westminster Bridge Rd, London, SE1 7JD (020-7922-0300; *fax:* 020-7922-0399)
Email: library@odi.org.uk
Internet: http://www.odi.org.uk/library.html

Chief: contact the Libn
Entry: staff & Council of the Inst
Subj: developing countries; macroeconomics; trade; finance; overseas aid; poverty; public exp; disaster relief & rehabilitation; rural resource mgmt; water resources; pastoral development; rural development; forestry; agric
Stock: c16000 printed & AV items
Auto Sys: DBTextworks

S1320

PA Photos

292 Vauxhall Bridge Rd, London, SW1V 1AE (020-7963-7990; *fax:* 020-7963-7066)
Email: paphotos.research@pa.press.net
Internet: http://www.paphotos.com/

Type: commercial photo archv *Chief: Photo Lib Mgr:* Mr Dave McCall (david.mccall@pa.press.net)
Entry: digital lib; not open to public *Open:* tel enqs: Mon-Fri 0700-2300, Sat 1200-2030
Subj: UK & internatl news & current affairs
Collns: Archvs: photographic archv of news photos covering sport, politics, current affairs, royalty, celebrity etc
Svcs: picture rsrch *Stock:* photos/7.5 mln
Auto Sys: G7, PICDAR *Staff: Non-Prof:* 25

S1321

Palestine Exploration Fund, Library and Archives

2 Hinde Mews, Marylebone Ln, London, W1M 5RR (020-7935-5379; *fax:* 020-7486-7438)
Internet: http://www.pef.org.uk/

Gov Body: Palestine Exploration Fund *Chief: Exec Sec & Libn:* Ms Rupert Chapman (ExecSec@PEF.org.uk) *Other Snr Staff:* Curator: Ms Felicity Cobbing (Curator@PEF.org.uk)
Entry: Lib: subscribers only; *Archvs:* contact the Curator in adv (refs required) *Open:* Mon-Fri 1030-1700
Subj: The Levant: archaeo; hist; nat hist; geog
Collns: Bks & Pamphs: 19C travel bks *Archvs:* archvs of Fund's rsrch in Palestine (1865 onwards) *Other:* Photographic Colln (1850s-date); original & MS maps & plans
Equip: m-reader, copier (A4/10p, A3/15p) *Svcs:* info, ref
Stock: bks/c12000
Classn: custom sys for highly specialised colln
Exp: many bks & periodcls received for review or on exchange

S1322

Partnership House Mission Studies Library

157 Waterloo Rd, London, SE1 8XA (020-7803-3215; *fax:* 020-7928-3627)
Email: phmslib@freenet.co.uk
Internet: http://phmsl.soutron.com/

Gov Body: World Mission Assoc *Chief: Libn:* Mr Colin Rowe BA, MA, MCLIP *Dep: Asst Libn:* Miss Elizabeth Williams BA, MCLIP
Assoc Libs: RHODES HOUSE LIB, Oxford (see L4)
Entry: no adv appt for ref use; borrowing: annual subscription £25 *Open:* Mon-Fri 0930-1700
Subj: religion; geog; hist; missiology; growth of the Anglican Church world-wide & its social concerns; comparative religion; ecumenical movement
Collns: Bks & Pamphs: CMS Max Warren Colln (comprises pre-1946 bks from the Church Missionary Soc Lib & copies of all CMS pubns); the United Soc for the Propagation of the Gospel's pre-1946 collns are deposited at Rhodes House Lib, Oxford; the main collns are based on the post-1945 collns of the CMS Lib & the USPG Lib, & also incl back copies of missionary journals & overseas diocesan reports
Equip: m-reader, copier
Stock: bks/25000; periodcls/410; pamphs/3500; maps/500
Classn: DDC (mod) *Auto Sys:* DBTextworks
Pubns: Lib Bulletin (monthly, incl new bks, abstracts & journal articles)
Staff: Libns: 2

S1323

Performing Arts Library

1st Floor, Production House, 25 Hackney Rd, London, E2 7NX (020-7749-4850; *fax:* 020-7749-4858)
Email: admin@performingartslibrary.com
Internet: http://www.performingartslibrary.co.uk/

Chief: Database Mgr: Ms Harriet Orr
Entry: adv appt *Open:* Mon-Fri 0930-1800
Subj: arts; opera; theatre; music; dance; performance; cureos
Svcs: sale of images
Stock: photos/800000; illusts/various
Classn: own *Staff: Libns:* 1 *Other Prof:* 2

London
▼
London

Special Libraries

S1324
Petrie Museum of Egyptian Archaeology, Library and Archives
Univ Coll London, Gower St, London, WC1E 6BT (020-7679-2884; *fax:* 020-7679-2886)
Email: petrie.museum@ucl.ac.uk
Internet: http://www.petrie.ucl.ac.uk/

Gov Body: Univ Coll London (see **S1433**) *Chief:* Asst Curator: Dr Stephen Quirke (s.quirke@ucl.ac.uk)
Entry: rsrchers by appt *Open: Museum:* Tue-Fri 1300-1700, Sat 1000-1300; *Rsrch Facilities:* Mon 0900-1700 or by appt
Subj: archaeo; Egyptology

S1325
Poetry Library
Level 5, Royal Festival Hall, South Bank Centre, London, SE1 8XX (020-7921-0943; *fax:* 020-7921-0939)
Email: info@poetrylibrary.org.uk
Internet: http://www.poetrylibrary.org.uk/

Type: independent lending & ref lib *Gov Body:* South Bank Board & Arts Council England (see **S997**) *Chief:* Libn: Ms Mary Enright
Entry: public lib open to all, membership on proof of ID & addr *Open:* Tue-Sun 1100-2000
Subj: 20C poetry in English *Collns: Bks & Pamphs:* large colln of literary magazines *Other:* press cuttings (1950-date); poster poems; poem cards; Images of Poets Colln (photos & drawings of 20C poets) *Co-op Schemes:* LASER
Equip: m-reader, copier, video viewer, computer (with CD-ROM), audio playback *Online:* in-house poetry database *Svcs:* info, ref, biblio, loans
Stock: bks/80000; periodcls/300; photos/2000; pamphs/7000; audios/75; videos/100; AVs/900
Auto Sys: SydneyPlus
Staff: Libns: 5 *Non-Prof:* 5

S1326
Polani Research Library
8th Floor, Guy's Tower, Guy's, King's & St Thomas' School of Medicine, Guy's Campus, London Bridge, London, SE1 9RT (020-7955-4135; *fax:* 020-7955-4644)
Email: lesley.exton@kcl.ac.uk

Gov Body: King's Coll London (see **S1227**)
Chief: Info Scientist: Miss Lesley S. Exton BSc, MSc, MCLIP
Entry: non-KCL Guy's Campus staff ref only, adv notice advisable *Open:* Mon-Fri 0900-1700
Subj: medical genetics; birth defects *Co-op Schemes:* BLDSC, SETRHA, ILL
Equip: copier, 2 computers (incl wd-proc) *Online:* Medline, various e-journals *Svcs:* info, ref
Stock: bks/3500; periodcls/60
Classn: Barnard (mod) *Staff: Other Prof:* 1

S1327
Polish Institute and Sikorski Museum, Reference Library
20 Princes Gate, London, SW7 1PT (020-7589-9249)

Chief: Chief Libn: Mr Aleksander Szkuta MA
Assoc Libs: MUSEUM ARCHVS, addr as above, Keeper of Archvs: Capt Waclaw Milewski
Entry: ref only *Open:* Mon-Fri 1400-1600
Subj: Poland; hist of Polish Forces, esp during WW1 & WW2 *Collns: Archvs:* records of the Polish Inst & Sikorski Museum (1966-94); records of the Assoc of Polish Prof Soldiers in Gt Britain (1946-65); correspondence & papers of Gen Wladyslaw Sikorski; papers of Gen Wladyslaw Anders; papers of Ian Colvin (relating to Katyn Massacre & Gen Sikorski's death); papers of Count Edward Raczynski; correspondence & papers of Josef Retinger
Stock: bks/12000; periodcls/11; m-forms/40000; films/800

S1328
Polish Library
238-246 King St, London, W6 0RF (020-8741-0474; *fax:* 020-8741-7724)
Email: polish.library@posk.org
Internet: http://www.posk.org/

Gov Body: The Lib Commission, Polish Social & Cultural Assoc *Chief:* Libn: Mrs Jadwiga Szmidt MA
Entry: reading room open to all readers & scholars; borrowing limited to residents of UK who comply with lib's regulations *Open:* Mon, Wed 1000-2000, Fri 1000-1700, Sat 1000-1300
Subj: Polish community in the UK; generalities; phil; psy; religion; social sci; Polish culture; arts; econ; emigration; folklore; geog; hist; lit; lang; politics; sociology; WW2 etc *Collns: Bks & Pamphs:* Anglo-Polonica; Conradiana (bks of & about Joseph Conrad); Polish Underground & Solidarity (1976-90) pubns *Archvs:* archvs of some Polish periodcls & orgs; MSS, typescripts & personal papers of various writers etc *Other:* bkplates *Co-op Schemes:* BLDSC, ILL, LASER, Public Lib Development Incentive Scheme
Equip: copier *Svcs:* info, ref, biblio
Stock: bks/150000, plus 30000 bnd periodcls; periodcls/230; photos/45500; pamphs/20000; maps/830, plus 390 atlases; audios/110; videos/20; archvs/1200 MSS; bkplates/16000+
Classn: DDC *Auto Sys:* Libpac
Pubns: Bks in Polish or Relating to Poland; A List of Bks Added to the Collns of the Polish Lib (quarterly, £21 pa); Bibliography of Bks in Polish or Relating to Poland Publ Outside Poland Since 1 Sept 1939, Vols 4-7 (£15 each); The Polish Lib 1942-79 (free); The Automation of the Catalogue at the Polish Lib to Form a Centre of Excellence as a Resource for Public Libs (£10); Biblioteka Polska w Londynie 1942-1992 (£5); Bibliography: The Joseph Conrad Soc (UK) (1992 The Polish Lib, £15); other pubns in Polish
Staff: Libns: 2 *Other Prof:* 1 *Non-Prof:* 4

S1329
Press Association News Library
292 Vauxhall Bridge Rd, London, SW1V 1AE (0870-830-6824; *fax:* 0870-830-6825)
Email: newslibrary@pa.press.net
Internet: http://www.palibrary.press.net/

Chief: Chief News Libn: Mr Eugene Weber *Dep:* Dep Chief News Libn: Mrs Katarina Shelley
Assoc Libs: PHOTO LIB, at same addr (see **S1320**)
Entry: fee charged for lib use & rsrch, discount for students *Open:* Mon-Fri 0800-2000, Sat 0800-1800, Sun 0900-1700
Subj: all subjs *Collns: Other:* presscuttings from all natl newspapers
Equip: m-reader, m-printer, copier, computers
Stock: bks/c500; press cuttings/14 mln
Classn: own *Staff: Non-Prof:* 8

S1330
Prison Service Headquarters Library
Cleland House, Page St, London, SW1P 4LN (020-7217-5548; *fax:* 020-7217-5209)

Gov Body: Prison Svc Agency *Chief:* contact Prison Svc HQ Libn
Assoc Libs: HOME OFFICE LIB (see **S1163**); PRISON SVC COLL LIB (see **S1877**)
Entry: ref only; adv appt *Open:* Mon-Fri 0930-1700
Subj: social sci; penal policy *Collns: Bks & Pamphs:* Prison Svc & Home Office pubns
Svcs: info, ref, biblio
Stock: bks/5800; periodcls/65
Classn: UDC *Auto Sys:* Sirsi
Staff: Libns: 1.5 *Non-Prof:* 1

S1331
Public Health Laboratory Service Central Library
61 Colindale Ave, London, NW9 5HT (020-8200-4400; *fax:* 020-8200-7875)
Email: mclennett@phls.nhs.uk
Internet: http://www.phls.co.uk/

Gov Body: Public Health Laboratory Svc Board *Chief:* Chief Libn: Miss Margaret A. Clennett BA, MCLIP *Dep:* Dep Libn: Mr D.J. Keech MSc, DipLib, MCLIP
Entry: ref only, phone for appt *Open:* Mon-Fri 0900-1730
Subj: postgrad; microbiology; infectious diseases; epidemiology
Equip: 2 copiers, clr copier, computers (incl 2 internet) *Svcs:* ref, biblio
Stock: bks/35000; periodcls/220
Classn: Barnard (mod) *Auto Sys:* CAIRS
Pubns: PHLS Food & Environment Bulletin (monthly, £60 pa); PHLS Hosp Infection & infection Control Bulletin (£60 pa)
Staff: Libns: 3 *Non-Prof:* 5

S1332
Queen Elizabeth Hospital NHS Trust, Knowledge Services
Queen Elizabeth Hosp, Stadium Rd, Woolwich, London, SE18 4QH (020-8836-6748; *fax:* 020-8836-6744)
Email: library.qeht@nhs.net

Gov Body: Queen Elizabeth Hosp NHS Trust
Chief: Knowledge Svcs Mgr: Mr Andy Richardson MCLIP *Dep:* Dep Libn: Ms Imrana Ghumra BA(Hons), MCLIP
Entry: NHS staff working within Greenwich, Bromley & Bexley Health Authorities; others at the discretion of the Libn *Open:* Mon, Wed-Thu 0900-1900, Tue, Fri 0900-1700
Subj: health care
Equip: copier, 12 computers (all with wd-proc & CD-ROM, 4 with internet) *Online:* via KA24: Medline, CINAHL, PsycInfo, AMED, Embase, BNI, HMIC, CancerLit, e-journals *Svcs:* info, ref
Stock: bks/150
Classn: NLM *Auto Sys:* Librarian
Staff: Libns: 2.5 *Non-Prof:* 3.5

S1333
Queen Mary, University of London, Information Services
Mile End Rd, London, E1 4NS (020-7882-3300; *fax:* 020-7981-0028)
Email: library@qmul.ac.uk
Internet: http://www.library.qmul.ac.uk/

Gov Body: Univ of London (see **S1440**) *Chief:* Dir of Info Svcs: Mr Brian Murphy BA, MCLIP (b.murphy@qmul.ac.uk) *Other Snr Staff:* Main Lib Mgr: Mr Neil Entwhistle BA, MA, MCLIP (n.w.entwhistle@qmul.ac.uk); Asst Main Lib Mgr: Ms June Hayles BA, MCLIP (j.m.hayles@qmul.ac.uk); Medical Libn: Mr Paul Hockney BSc, DipLib, MCLIP
Assoc Libs: MEDICAL LIB, St Bartholomew's & The London Queen Mary's School of Medicine & Dentistry, Medical Libn: Mr Paul Hockney, as above; sites at: WHITECHAPEL SITE LIB, Church of St Augustine, Newark St, London, E1 2AD; WEST SMITHFIELD SITE LIB, West Smithfield, London, EC1A 7BA
Entry: Main Lib: ref only to visitors, with times of entry restricted during term to Sat, Sun & weekday evenings after 5pm *Open:* term: Mon-Fri 0900-2100, Sat 1000-1600, Sun 1300-1900; Xmas & summer vacs: Mon-Fri 0900-1700; Easter vac: Mon-Fri 0900-2100
Subj: undergrad; postgrad; phil; psy; social sci; lang; sci; maths; tech; arts; lit; geog; hist; medicine; dentistry *Collns: Bks & Pamphs:* EDC; small colln on forensic medicine *Archvs:* Westfield Coll Archv; Constance Maynard Archv; Queen Mary Coll Archv (People's Palace); papers of Genl Sir Neville Lyttleton *Other:* works by ex-staff of London Hosp Medical Coll & Royal London Hosp *Co-op Schemes:* BLDSC, LAMDA, M25 Consortium *Equip:* 8 m-readers, 2 m-printers (20p per copy), 10 video viewers, 20 copiers (A4/5p, A3/10p), 2 clr photocopies (A4/50p, A3/£1), 250 computers (all with wd-proc, internet & CD-ROM, available to registered users/coll membs only) *Disabled:* Magnilink reader, braille scanner & printer, voice synthesiser *Online:* various networked databases *Svcs:* info, ref, biblio
Stock: bks/631653; periodcls/3614; slides/500; pamphs/8459; maps/33900; m-forms/318; audios/242; videos/4908; CD-ROMs/609; archvs/235 linear m *Acqs Offcr:* Acqs Libn: Mr Anselm Nye (a.c.nye@qmul.ac.uk)
Classn: NLM, LC *Auto Sys:* Unicorn
Staff: Libns: 21.7 *Non-Prof:* 53.6 *Exp:* £244388 (1999-2000); £215448 (2000-01)

S1334

Radiocommunications Agency, Information and Library Service

9th Floor, Wyndham House, 189 Marsh Wall, London, E14 9SX (020-7211-0502/5; *fax:* 020-7211-0507)
Email: library@ra.gsi.gov.uk
Internet: http://www.radio.gov.uk/

Gov Body: DTI *Chief:* Info & Publicity Mgr: Ms Julia Fraser BA(Hons), DipLib *Dep:* Libn: Ms Jenny Cann BSc, DipLib, MCLIP
Entry: ref only, by appt *Open:* Mon-Fri 0830-1730
Subj: social sci; tech; radio communications *Co-op Schemes:* BLDSC
Equip: fax, computers (incl 2 with wd-proc & 2 with internet) *Online:* Dialog, FT Profile, Datastar
Svcs: info, ref, biblio, abstracting
Classn: DDC *Auto Sys:* Adlib
Staff: Libns: 2 *Non-Prof:* 6
Further Info: Svc is part of Communications Unit which incl Press & Publicity, Internet & Intranet

S1335

Regent's College Library

Inner Circle, Regent's Pk, London, NW1 4NS (020-7487-7449; *fax:* 020-7487-7545)
Email: collinsm@regents.ac.uk
Internet: http://www.regents.ac.uk/

Gov Body: Regents Coll *Chief:* Head Libn: Ms Mary Collins MSc(Econ)
Entry: membs only; visitors by appl to Head Libn *Open:* term: Mon-Thu 0900-2300, Fri 0900-2100, Sat 1200-0600, Sun 1000-2300; vac: varies

Subj: all subjs (not extensive); main holdings are in: business; psychotherapy; counselling *Co-op Schemes:* arrangements with Univ of Westminster Libs
Equip: 2 copiers, 3 video viewers, 25 computers *Online:* Dialog, JANET, UK Company FactFinder, West European Business Intelligence, East European Business Intelligence
Stock: bks/35000; periodcls/1000; audios/200
Acqs Offcr: Head Libn, as above
Classn: DDC, Inst of Linguistics *Auto Sys:* Heritage
Staff: Libns: 2 *Non-Prof:* 10 + casual staff

S1336

The Remote Sensing and Photogrammetric Society Library

c/o Dept of Geomatic Eng, Univ Coll London, Gower St, London, EC1U 0HB (020-7504-2726; *fax:* 020-7380-0453)
Email: srobson@ge.ucl.ac.uk
Internet: http://www.rspsoc.org/

Type: learned soc *Gov Body:* Remote Sensing & Photogrammetric Soc *Chief:* Officer-in-Charge: Dr Stewart Robson BSc(Hons), PhD
Entry: by previous arrangement, at reasonable hrs, for ref only
Subj: photogrammetry
Equip: copier *Svcs:* info, ref
Stock: bks/350; periodcls/30
Pubns: The Photogrammetric Record
Staff: Other Prof: 1 *Exp:* no exp on stock; additional stock acquired mainly through exchanging journals with other socs & groups

S1337

Reuters Editorial Reference Unit

200 Grays Inn Rd, London, WC1X 8XZ (020-7542-7968; *fax:* 020-7542-8648)
Email: edref@rtlondon.co.uk

Chief: Snr Rsrcher: Mr David Cutler BA(Hons)
Dep: Rsrcher: Ms Mair Salts
Assoc Libs: REUTERS ARCHV, at same addr (see **A323**)
Entry: internal users; staff & subscribers to Reuters only *Open:* Mon-Thu 0800-2000, Fri-Sat & bank hols 1000-1800; closed Xmas day
Subj: all subjs; genl; politics; current affairs
Equip: m-reader, copier, 5 computers (incl wd-proc, internet & CD-ROM) *Online:* Factiva, Reuters Business Briefing *Svcs:* info, ref
Stock: bks/1000; periodcls/10; m-forms/1000s (stored off-site) *Acqs Offcr:* Snr Rsrcher, as above
Classn: DDC *Auto Sys:* in-house cataloguing sys based on Microsoft Access *Staff: Other Prof:* 1

S1338 🎥

Robert Harding Picture Library

58-59 Gt Marlborough St, London, W1V 1DD (020-7478-4000; *fax:* 020-7631-1070)
Email: info@robertharding.com
Internet: http://www.robertharding.com/

Chief: Marketing Mgr: Mr Oliver Hemson
Entry: searches via tel, fax, email or web; visits by appt only *Open:* Mon-Fri 0900-1800
Subj: all subjs; genl *Collns: Bks & Pamphs:* 16 full clr catalogues incl: Sci & Medical; Business & Industry; Nat World; Lifestyle; Travel; Sports *Archvs:* c30000 b&w prints covering most genl subjs, dating back to 1920s *Other:* c2 mln clr transparencies covering all genl subjs & specialising in travel
Equip: Online: online image search *Svcs:* image searching; licensing for image use
Stock: bks/16; photos/c30000; slides/2 mln+
Pubns: Catalogues (free)
Staff: Other Prof: 20 picture rsrchers

S1339 🔑

Royal Academy of Arts Library

Burlington House, Piccadilly, London, W1V 0DS (020-7300-5737; *fax:* 020-7300-5765)
Email: adamw@royalacademy.org.uk
Internet: http://www.royalacademy.org.uk/

Gov Body: Royal Academy of Arts *Chief:* Head of Lib Svcs: Mr Adam Waterton
Entry: by appt only to bona fide rsrchers *Open:* Tue-Fri 1000-1300, 1400-1700
Subj: British art, 18C-20C *Collns:* Bks & Pamphs: earliest colln in Britain of bks & engravings intended for training & inspiration of artists in all fields (1769-1920); recently formed colln of English illustrated bks, with special ref to work of Royal Academicians & Associate membs *Archvs:* papers of various British artists of 18C & 19C; Royal Academy archvs *Co-op Schemes:* BLDSC, ILL
Equip: copier
Stock: bks/35000; periodcls/9; photos/25000
Staff: Libns: 2 *Other Prof:* 2 *Non-Prof:* 2

S1340

Royal Academy of Dramatic Art Library

18 Chenies St, London, WC1E 7EX (020-7636-7076; *fax:* 020-7323-3868)
Email: library@rada.ac.uk
Internet: http://www.rada.org/

Chief: Libn: Ms Jayne Mann
Entry: ref only, external rsrchers should apply by letter *Open:* term: Mon-Fri 0930-1900
Subj: arts; drama; theatre; plays; theatre hist; theatre criticism & biographies; poetry; costume; stage fights; stage make-up; social hist *Collns: Bks & Pamphs:* Ivo Currall Colln (George Bernard Shaw, 450 vols) *Co-op Schemes:* ILL
Equip: video viewer, copier, computers (with CD-ROM) *Svcs:* info
Stock: bks/22000; periodcls/8
Classn: own *Staff: Libns:* 2

S1341

Royal Academy of Music Library

Marylebone Rd, London, NW1 5HT (020-7873-7323; *fax:* 020-7873-7322)
Email: library@ram.ac.uk
Internet: http://www.ram.ac.uk/

Gov Body: Royal Academy of Music *Chief:* Libn: Ms Kathryn Adamson BA, MA, DipLib
Entry: ref only, adv appt *Open:* term: Mon-Fri 0900-1800, Sat 0900-1200; vac: varies, please tel
Subj: music *Collns: Archvs:* Academy's student registers; concert programmes *Other:* Henry Wood Orchestral Lib; Savage-Stevens Lib of early printed music; Arthur Sullivan Colln; David Munrow's Lib; York Bowen MSS; Organ Club Lib; Robert Spencer Colln *Co-op Schemes:* BLDSC, ILL
Equip: m-reader, m-printer, copier, 11 listening stations (LP, cassette & CD)
Stock: bks/20000; periodcls/200; photos/100; m-forms/350; audios/6000; videos/120; archvs/20 m; music/100000 items
Classn: own *Auto Sys:* Unicorn
Pubns: Lib guide (in-house); Manuscripts in the RAM Lib (1650-c1930)
Staff: Libns: 3.6 *Non-Prof:* 2.6

S1342 🔑

Royal Aeronautical Society Library

4 Hamilton Pl, London, W1V 7BQ (020-7670-4362; *fax:* 020-7670-4359)
Email: brian.riddle@raes.org.uk
Internet: http://www.aerosociety.com/

Special Libraries

London ▼ London

(Royal Aeronautical Soc Lib cont)
Chief: Libn: Mr B.L. Riddle BLib
Entry: open to non-membs of the Eng Council instns on a daily fee basis **Open:** Mon-Fri 1000-1700
Subj: aerospace; aeronautics; aviation; aeronautical eng & tech, incl recent developments
Collns: *Bks & Pamphs:* Official Pubns (govt reports relating to aviation & the aircraft industry); collns of early ballooning, airships & early aeronautical material, incl: Cuthburt-Odgson Colln; Poynton Colln; Maitland Colln *Archvs:* papers relating to the hist of the Royal Aeronautical Soc; papers & MSS left by early membs of the Soc & other aeronautical pioneers, incl: Sir George Cayley (1773-1857); John Stringfellow (1799-1883); Wilbur Wright (1867-1912); Orville Wright (1871-1948); Katherine Wright (1874-1929); Lawrence Hargrave (1850-1915); Major B.F.S. Baden-Powell (1860-1937); C.G. Grey (1875-1953); design notebks of F.S. Barnwell (1880-1938) *Other:* aviation images (photos, glass lantern slides & lithographs), from the early days of ballooning to the present, incl portrait photos of aviation personalities **Co-op Schemes:** ILL
Equip: copier *Online:* database available on web site (for membs only) *Svcs:* ref, photographic
Stock: bks/27000; periodcls/300 current, 1000 in total; photos/100000; technical reports/20000
Classn: own
Pubns: Accessions List (published bimonthly in Aerospace Professional); Royal Aeronautical Soc Archv Series of CD-ROMs, incl: Early Aviation: The Pioneering Years Through to the First World War (Vol 1); Aeronautical Classics (Vol 2); Imperial Airways (Vol 3); Aircraft of the 1920s (Vol 4); CD-ROMs cost £11.44 (incl postage) & are available from: Archv Britain, Suite 407, Victory House, Somers Rd North, Portsmouth, PO1 1PJ (023-9275-6275; *email:* raes@archivebritain.com)
Staff: Libns: 1 *Other Prof:* 2 *Non-Prof:* 1

S1343
Royal Air Force Museum, Department of Research and Information Services, Library
Grahame Park Way, Hendon, London, NW9 5LL (020-8205-2266; *fax:* 020-8200-1751)
Email: info@rafmuseum.com
Internet: http://www.rafmuseum.com/

Chief: Libn: P.J.V. Elliott
Entry: by appt **Open:** Mon-Fri 1000-1700
Subj: aviation; British military aviation; Royal Air Force **Collns:** *Bks & Pamphs:* technical manuals for aircraft, engines & instruments *Archvs:* aircrew flying log bks; manufacturers' drawings; personal papers
Equip: copier, m-reader, m-printer
Stock: bks/27000; periodcls/170; m-forms/5000 fiche; bnd periodcls/15000 vols; air diagrams/8000; aeronautical maps/3000
Exp: £4000 (1999-2000)

S1344
Royal Asiatic Society Library
60 Queen's Gdns, London, W2 3AF (020-7724-4741; *fax:* 020-7706-4008)
Email: royalasiaticsociety@btinternet.com
Internet: http://www.royalasiaticsociety.co.uk/

Gov Body: Royal Asiatic Soc **Chief:** Libn: Mr M.J. Pollock MA, MCLIP
Entry: primarily for membs; other visitors by prior appt **Open:** Tue 1100-2000, Wed-Thu 1100-1700
Subj: at postgrad level: Asia (Turkey to Japan); phil; religion; lang; linguistics; arts; lit; hist; geog
Collns: *Bks & Pamphs:* Storey Colln (Persian lit); Sir Richard Francis Burton Colln (1821-90); Schrumpf Colln (Armenian lit) *Other:* prints, drawings & 2000 Oriental MSS in various collns
Co-op Schemes: ILL (if collected by other lib, no postal svc)
Equip: 2 m-readers (1 m-film, 1 m-fiche), fax (staff operated), copier (staff operated), 2 computers (staff operated)
Stock: bks/100000; periodcls/170; photos/4000; slides/200; illusts/2000; pamphs/c2500
Classn: own **Auto Sys:** CATS
Staff: Libns: 1 *Other Prof:* 1 PT conservator *Non-Prof:* 1

S1345
Royal Astronomical Society Library
Burlington House, Piccadilly, London, W1V 0NL (020-7734-4582/3307; *fax:* 020-7494-0166)
Email: info@ras.org.uk
Internet: http://www.ras.org.uk/html/ras_library.html

Chief: Libn: Mr Peter Hingley (pdh@ras.org.uk)
Dep: Asst Libn: Miss Mary Chibnall (mic@ras.org.uk)
Entry: by appt; apply in writing, tel or email to Libn **Open:** Mon-Fri 1000-1700
Subj: astronomy; geophysics; hist of astronomy & geophysics **Collns:** *Bks & Pamphs:* Grove-Hills Colln (astronomical name bks); Lib of the Spitalfields Mathematical Soc *Archvs:* archvs of the Soc; archvs of Sir William Herschel, Candice Herschel & Sir John Herschel *Other:* photographs; portraits
Equip: m-reader, m-filming, copier
Stock: bks/15000; periodcls/380; maps, m-forms & wallcharts
Classn: LC

S1346
Royal Automobile Club Library
89 Pall Mall, London, SW1Y 5HS (020-7747-3398; *fax:* 020-7451-9980)
Email: library@royalautomobileclub.co.uk
Internet: http://www.royalautomobileclub.co.uk/

Gov Body: RAC Ltd **Chief:** Clubhouse Libn: Mr T.G. Dunmore
Entry: ref only, by written appl at discretion of libn
Open: Mon-Fri 0900-1700
Subj: motoring hist; hist of motorsport & allied subjs; travel; business ref colln; genl ref colln; small local colln of bks on London **Collns:** *Bks & Pamphs:* complete sets of RAC pubns *Archvs:* RAC archv colln (letters, papers, badges, photos, memorabilia) *Other:* maps **Co-op Schemes:** BLDSC
Equip: m-reader, m-printer, fax, copier, computer *Online:* Lexis-Nexis (charge to cover costs)
Stock: bks/10000; periodcls/90; photos/5000; slides/200; pamphs/500; maps/250; videos/25
Classn: Natl Motor Museum **Auto Sys:** CALM
Staff: Libns: 1

S1347
Royal College of Art Library
Kensington Gore, London, SW7 2EU (020-7590-4224; *fax:* 020-7590-4500)
Email: library@rca.ac.uk
Internet: http://www.rca.ac.uk/

Chief: Head of Learning Svcs & Libn: Mr Peter Hassell **Dep:** Lib Mgr: Miss P. Rae **Other Snr Staff:** Asst Libns: Ms Darlene Maxwell, Ms Lucy Neville & Ms Cathy Johns

Assoc Libs: SLIDE COLLN, Slide Curator: Ms J. Murton
Entry: access for students by appt; others at discretion of Lib Mgr **Open:** term: Mon-Fri 0900-2100, Sat 1200-1700; vac: Mon-Fri 1000-1700
Subj: the arts **Collns:** *Bks & Pamphs:* Colour Ref Lib (special colln on colour)
Equip: video viewer, copier, computer (incl CD-ROM)
Stock: bks/70000; periodcls/200; slides/100000; videos/300
Classn: DDC **Auto Sys:** Dynix
Pubns: Lib Guide; Subj Guides
Staff: Libns: 3 FT, 1 PT *Non-Prof:* 1 FT, 4 PT

S1348
Royal College of General Practitioners, Geoffrey Evans Library
14 Princes Gate, Hyde Pk, London, SW7 1PU (020-7581-3232; *fax:* 020-7584-1992)
Email: library@rcgp.org.uk
Internet: http://www.rcgp.org.uk/informat/index.htm

Chief: Snr Info Mgr: Mr Gil Richardson MCLIP
Entry: membs at any time, others by appt, ref only
Open: Mon-Fri 0900-1700
Subj: medicine; all aspects of genl practice & related primary care **Collns:** *Bks & Pamphs:* genl practice *Other:* genl practice theses **Co-op Schemes:** BLDSC, NWRHS
Equip: fax, copier, computers (incl wd-proc, internet & CD-ROM) *Online:* Datastar, Dialog, in-house database *Svcs:* info, ref, biblio
Stock: bks/5500; periodcls/220; pamphs/1000; theses/200
Classn: NLM (Wessex) **Auto Sys:** DBTextworks
Staff: Libns: 2 *Other Prof:* 3 *Non-Prof:* 1

S1349
Royal College of Midwives, The Arnold Walker and Florence Mitchell Library
15 Mansfield St, London, W1M 0BE (020-7291-9220/1; *fax:* 020-7312-3536)
Email: library@rcm.org.uk
Internet: http://www.rcm.org.uk/

Chief: Libn: Ms Mary Dharma Chandran
Assoc Libs: ROYAL COLL OF MIDWIVES ARCHVS, addr as above (020-7291-9204)
Entry: ref only, adv appt **Open:** Mon-Fri 0915-1645
Subj: medicine; psy; sociology; social medicine; midwifery; edu **Collns:** *Bks & Pamphs:* specialist midwifery colln; Marion Rabl Colln *Archvs:* midwifery texts & artefacts; RCM records; papers of indiv midwives; misc memorabilia (Coll since 1881)
Co-op Schemes: BLDSC, BMA, RCN
Equip: m-reader, m-printer, copier, computer (incl CD-ROM) *Online:* Medline, PsycInfo, CINAHL, Embase, BNI, AMED, DH-Data *Svcs:* info, ref, biblio
Stock: bks/6500; periodcls/50; m-forms/5; archvs/unquantified archival materials; reports/1750
Classn: own **Auto Sys:** Olib

S1350
Royal College of Music Library
Prince Consort Rd, London, SW7 2BS (020-7591-4323; *fax:* 020-7589-7740)
Email: pthompson@rcm.ac.uk
Internet: http://www.rcm.ac.uk/

Chief: Chief Libn: Mrs Pamela Thompson BA, HonRCM **Dep:** Ref Libn: Dr Peter Horton
Assoc Libs: DEPT OF PORTRAITS & PERFORMANCE HIST, addr as above, by appt only, Keeper: Oliver Davies FRCM

Entry: ref only (except for Coll membs) *Open:* term: Mon-Thu 0930-1800, Fri 0930-1730; vac: Mon-Fri 1000-1300, 1400-1700; closed for approx 10 days at Christmas & Easter
Subj: music *Collns:* *Bks & Pamphs:* Lib of Sacred Harmonic Soc (early printed music); Lib of Concerts of Ancient Music (early printed music); Heron-Allen Colln (on string instruments); Maurice Frost Colln (on hymnology) *Other:* 20000 music MSS *Co-op Schemes:* ILL
Equip: m-form reader/printer (20p per pg), 2 video viewers, fax, 2 copiers, computers (incl wd-proc & CD-ROM, for internal membs only) *Disabled:* enlarger *Svcs:* info, ref, translation
Stock: bks/c300000, incl printed music; periodcls/102; pamphs/numerous; m-forms/c5000; audios/c20000; videos/c200; archvs/12 linear m
Classn: DDC (for bks), own (for music) *Auto Sys:* Unicorn
Pubns: Catalogue of the Manuscripts of Herbert Howell in the RCM Lib (£8.50); A Musical Directory for the Year 1794 (£6.50)
Staff: Libns: 7.2 *Exp:* £53800 (1999-2000)

S1351 🗝️ ✚
Royal College of Nursing Library and Information Services
20 Cavendish Sq, London, W1G 0RN (020-7647-3610; *fax:* 020-7647-3420)
Email: rcn.library@rcn.org.uk
Internet: http://www.rcn.org.uk/

Type: trade union *Chief:* Head of Lib & Info Svcs: Miss Jacqueline Lord BA(Hons), DipLib, MCLIP
Dep: Lib Operations Mgr: Mrs Carol Banks MA, BSc(Hons), C&G 730, DipLib, MCLIP
Assoc Libs: RCN NORTHERN IRELAND, VIRGINIA HENDERSON LIB, 17 Windsor Ave, Belfast, BT9 6EE, Libn: Ms Maureen Dwyer (028-9066-8236; *fax:* 028-9038-2188; *email:* library.belfast@rcn.org.uk); RCN SCOTLAND LIB, 42 South Oswald Rd, Edinburgh, EH9 2HH, Libn: Ms Enid Forsyth (0131-662-1010; *fax:* 0131-662-1032; *email:* scotland.library@rcn.org.uk); RCN WALES LIB, Ty Maeth, King George V Dr East, Cardiff, CF14 4XZ, Libn: Ms Karen Field (029-2075-1373; *fax:* 029-2068-0726; *email:* wales.library@rcn.org.uk); RCN ARCHVS (see **A153**)
Entry: membs only; ref access for non-membs by appt in writing, charge currently £5 pd *Open:* Mon-Tue, Thu-Fri 0830-1900, Wed 1000-1900, Sat 0900-1700
Subj: nursing; allied health *Collns:* *Bks & Pamphs:* historical colln *Other:* Steinberg Colln of Nursing Rsrch (Masters & PhD theses) *Co-op Schemes:* BLDSC, ILL
Equip: m-reader, fax, video viewer, copiers, computers (incl wd-proc, internet & CD-ROM) *Online:* BNI, WebCat lib catalogue *Svcs:* info, ref, biblio, indexing, lit searching
Stock: bks/60000; periodcls/400; videos/500
Classn: RCN Lib Classn Scheme *Auto Sys:* Unicorn
Pubns: Steinberg Catalogue 1997 (indivs £13, instns £16); RCN Lib Thesaurus of Lib Terms 1998 (£25); RCN Classn Schedules (£7.50); Subj Index to RCN Classn Scheme (£7.50)
Staff: Libns: 20 *Other Prof:* 1 *Non-Prof:* 9.5

S1352 🗝️ ✚
Royal College of Obstetricians and Gynaecologists, Markland Library and Information Service
27 Sussex Pl, Regent's Pk, London, NW1 4RG (020-7772-6309; *fax:* 020-7262-8331)
Email: library@rcog.org.uk
Internet: http://www.rcog.org.uk/

Chief: Head of Info Svcs: Ms Lucy Reid BA, MA (lreid@rcog.org.uk)

Assoc Libs: COLL ARCHVS, addr as above (020-7772-6277; *email:* archives@rcog.org.uk)
Entry: ref only, Fellows & membs only; others admitted only by adv appt *Open:* *Lib:* Mon-Fri 0900-1800; *Archvs:* Mon, Wed, Fri by appt only
Subj: postgrad; medicine; obstetrics; gynaecology & closely related subjs only *Collns:* *Bks & Pamphs:* reports & monographs; historical colln (c2000 vols, pre-1900) *Archvs:* Coll Archvs (1929-date); Gynaecological Visiting Soc Archvs (1926-43); Internatl Federation of Gynaecology & Obstetrics Archvs (1952-97); correspondence of: Eliab Harvey; Edward Jenner; Joseph Lister; Florence Nightingale; Alexander Russell Simpson; personal & prof papers of: J.M. Munro Kerr; Donald Ray; William Fletcher Shaw; William Blair Bell; Chasser Moir; Norman Jeffcote; Bethel Solomons; William Rothercam
Equip: m-printer (A4/10p), 3 copiers (A4/10p), 2 fax, 9 computers (incl 1 with wd-proc, 4 with internet & 4 with CD-ROM) *Online:* OVID *Svcs:* info, ref
Stock: bks/11000; periodcls/200
Classn: Barnard *Auto Sys:* Adlib
Pubns: Short-Title Catalogue of Bks Published Before 1851 in the RCOG Lib (£1 + p&p)
Staff: Libns: 2 *Other Prof:* 0.5 *Non-Prof:* 1.5

S1353 🗝️
Royal College of Organists Library
Holborn Circus, 7 St Andrew St, London, EC4A 3LQ (020-7936-4321; *fax:* 020-7936-3966)
Email: robinlangley@rco.org.uk
Internet: http://www.rco.org.uk/

Chief: Libn: Mr Robin Langley BMus *Dep:* Academic Co-ordinator: Mr Andrew McCrea BMus, MMus, ARCM
Entry: ref only, adv appt for non-membs (entry charge £5 pd) *Open:* Wed-Fri 1000-1700 only
Subj: arts; organ music *Collns:* *Bks & Pamphs:* bks on organ music, organists & organ builders; organ sheet music *Archvs:* misc organ-related materials; MSS (on loan to British Lib – see **L1**)
Equip: copier *Svcs:* ref, biblio
Stock: bks/c40000, incl music

S1354 ✚
Royal College of Paediatrics and Child Health, Library
50 Hallam St, London, W1W 6DE (020-7307-5634; *fax:* 020-7307-5601)
Email: mary.butler@rcpch.ac.uk
Internet: http://www.rcpch.ac.uk/

Chief: Info Mgr: Ms Mary Butler
Entry: ref only, adv appt *Open:* Mon-Fri 0900-1700
Subj: paediatrics; child health *Collns:* *Other:* archvs of Disease in Childhood (journal); Coll pubns
Svcs: info
Stock: bks/200; pamphs/500; audios/10; videos/20
Classn: alphabetical
Pubns: Archvs of Disease in Childhood (£116 pa); Coll pubns (prices vary)
Staff: Libns: 1 PT *Exp:* stock received as gifts

S1355 🗝️ ✚
Royal College of Physicians of London, Library and Information Service
11 St Andrew's Pl, London, NW1 4LE (020-7935-1174; *fax:* 020-7486-3729)
Email: info@rcplondon.ac.uk
Internet: http://www.rcplondon.ac.uk/

Chief: Mgr: Ms Caroline Moss-Gibbons BLib(Hons), PGCE *Dep:* Dep Mgr & Collns Libn: Mrs Julie Beckwith BA, MSc, MCLIP

Entry: open to Fellows, membs & bona fide rsrchers; ref only for non-membs, appt advisable for pre-1900 materials *Open:* Mon-Fri 0900-1700
Subj: UK health policy; hist of medicine; medical biography *Collns:* *Bks & Pamphs:* Lib of 1st Marquis of Dorchester (1606-80); Evan Bedford Lib of Cardiology *Archvs:* RCP Archvs; H.M. Barlow Colln of medical bkplates; papers of C.E. Brown-Sequard (1817-94), Sir James MacKenzie (1853-1925) & Lord Brain (1895-1966) *Co-op Schemes:* BLDSC, ILL
Equip: m-reader, m-printer, video viewer, copier, 3 computers (all with internet & CD-ROM) *Online:* Medline, Embase, Cochrane *Officer-in-Charge:* Mgr, as above *Svcs:* info, ref, lit searches
Stock: bks/50000; periodcls/100; photos/18000; slides/3200; pamphs/7000; m-forms/100; videos/40; archvs/430 linear m *Acqs Offcr:* Dep Mgr & Collns Libn, as above
Classn: UDC *Auto Sys:* Adlib
Pubns: Evan Bedford Lib of Cardiology Catalogue (£40); Catalogue of Engraved Portraits in the RCP (£10); The Royal Coll of Physicians of London Portraits, Vol II (£20); Lives of the Fellows (10 vols, price on appl)
Staff: Libns: 5 *Other Prof:* 2 *Non-Prof:* 1 *Exp:* £18000 (1999-2000)

S1356 🗝️
Royal College of Psychiatrists, Information Services
17 Belgrave Sq, London, SW1X 8PG (020-7235-2351; *fax:* 020-7259-6303)
Email: infoservices@rcpsych.ac.uk
Internet: http://www.rcpsych.ac.uk

Chief: Info Offcr: Ms Morwenna Davis BSc, MSc (mdavis@rcpsych.ac.uk) *Dep:* Info Administrator: Ms Laura Hulse BA (lhulse@rcpsych.ac.uk) *Other Snr Staff:* Archivist: Mrs M. Harcourt Williams BA, DipAA
Entry: membs only; ref only *Open:* Mon-Fri 0930-1630
Subj: psychiatry; mental health *Collns:* *Bks & Pamphs:* antiquarian psychiatry texts (c500 vols, 15C onwards) *Archvs:* minutes from Coll Council & Cttee meetings (1841-date); complete set of Coll reports; asylum plans; records of nursing exams *Other:* small photo colln *Co-op Schemes:* ILL scheme with British Lib, Inst of Psychiatry & BMA
Equip: copier, fax, 3 computers (all with wd-proc, internet & CD-ROM) *Online:* Medline, EMBASE, PsycInfo, Cochrane *Officer-in-Charge:* Info Offcr, as above *Svcs:* info, ref, biblio
Stock: bks/3000; periodcls/40 *Acqs Offcr:* Info Offcr, as above
Classn: own *Auto Sys:* Heritage
Staff: Libns: 3 *Non-Prof:* 1

S1357 📚 ✚
Royal College of Surgeons of England, Library and Lumley Study Centre
35-43 Lincoln's Inn Fields, London, WC2A 3PN (020-7865-6555/6; *fax:* 020-7405-4438)
Email: library@rcseng.ac.uk
Internet: http://www.rcseng.ac.uk/

Chief: Coll Libn & Head of Info Svcs: Mrs T. Knight *Dep:* Dep Coll Libn: Mrs T. Craig
Entry: free access for membs, affiliates & those registered for Coll exams & courses; academic & private rsrchers in the hist of medicine or sci have free access subj to prior appt; others (e.g., prof/commercial rsrchers etc) should contact the Lib in adv as charges may apply (see web site) *Open:* Mon-Tue, Thu-Fri 0930-1730, Wed 1000-1730
Subj: all aspects of clinical surgery, incl surgical specialities & dental surgery; anatomy; physiology; pathology; medical biography; hist of medicine ☛

Special Libraries

London ▼ London

Special Libraries

(Royal Coll of Surgeons Lib cont)
Collns: Bks & Pamphs: Hunter-Baillie Colln (1500 items); bks & MSS of John Hunter FRS & his pupils (1100 items); Lord Lister Colln (250 items); Richard Owen Colln (750 items); Arthur Keith Colln (300 items); incunabula (57 items) *Archvs:* archvs of RCS (1745-date); archvs of the London Lock Hosp (1755-1946) *Other:* engraved portraits, bkplates & medals **Co-op Schemes:** BLDSC, ILL, CHILL Serials Consortium
Equip: m-reader, 2 video viewers, 2 copiers, 9 computers (incl wd-proc, internet & CD-ROM) *Online:* Datastar, Medline, Cochrane, HMIC & others **Svcs:** info, ref, biblio, lit searches, photographic svc, genealogical svc (full details & charges on web site)
Stock: bks/60000; periodcls/300, plus 3000 no longer current; photos/2000; slides/1000; pamphs/30000; videos/240; CD-ROMs/90; archvs/200 ft; engraved portraits/3000; bkplates/1000
Classn: Barnard **Auto Sys:** Unicorn
Pubns: English Bks publ before 1701 in the Lib of the RCS; Lives of the Fellows of the Royal Coll of Surgeons; current periodcl, AV & multimedia lists
Staff: Libns: 7 Other Prof: 2 Non-Prof: 3

S1358
Royal College of Veterinary Surgeons, Library and Information Service
Belgravia House, 62-64 Horseferry Rd, London, SW1P 2AF (020-7222-2021; *fax:* 020-7222-2004)
Email: library@rcvs.org.uk
Internet: http://www.rcvs.org.uk/

Chief: Head of Lib & info Svcs: Mr Tom Roper BA, DipLib, MCLIP
Entry: membs of Royal Coll only; other bona fide rsrchers on appl **Open:** Mon-Fri 0915-1700
Subj: veterinary medicine; hist of veterinary medicine **Collns:** Bks & Pamphs: Henry Gray Colln (late 19C-early 20C ornithology) **Co-op Schemes:** BLDSC, ILL, LASER
Equip: copier, computers (incl CD-ROM) *Online:* Biosis, CAB Abstracts, Medline, Science Citation Index, Zoological Records **Svcs:** info, ref, biblio, indexing, abstracting, lit searches, document delivery
Stock: bks/25000; periodcls/300; photos/many; pamphs/many
Classn: Barnard **Auto Sys:** Unicorn
Staff: Libns: 3 Non-Prof: 2

S1359
Royal Entomological Society Library
41 Queen's Gate, London, SW7 5HR (020-7584-8361; *fax:* 020-7581-8505)
Email: lib@royensoc.co.uk
Internet: http://www.royensoc.co.uk/

Chief: Libn: Berit Pedersen BA(Hons), MCLIP
Entry: membs & Fellows of the Soc; genl public may make an appt for one-off study time **Open:** Mon-Fri 0930-1700
Subj: entomology; biology & taxonomy of insects; some material on arachnids **Collns:** Bks & Pamphs: rare bks, incl c1000 early entomological works (pre-1850) *Archvs:* very fine archv of letters & diaries eminent entomologists & naturalists, incl

original Darwin material *Other:* fine colln of photos of entomologists; Miriam Rothschild Colln of Flea Reprints **Co-op Schemes:** BLDSC, reciprocal arrangement with Zoological Soc of London Lib (see **S1474**)
Equip: 2 copiers (A4/5p-40p depending on status), 3 computers (all with wd-proc & CD-ROM, 2 with internet), 2 rooms for hire **Svcs:** info, ref, biblio, translation
Stock: bks/11000; periodcls/250, plus 500 non-current; photos/1000; reprints/c30000
Classn: own **Auto Sys:** CAIRS
Pubns: Royal Entomological Soc Journals, Handbooks & Symposia; see web site for details
Staff: Libns: 1 Non-Prof: 3

S1360
Royal Free and University College Medical School, Medical Library
Royal Free Hosp, Rowland Hill St, London, NW3 2PF (020-7794-0500; *fax:* 020-7794-3534)
Email: library@rfc.ucl.ac.uk
Internet: http://www.rfc.ucl.ac.uk/library.htm

Gov Body: Univ Coll London (see **S1433**), part of Univ of London (see **S1440**) **Chief:** Libn: Ms Betsy Anagnostelis BSc(Hons), DipLib, MSc
Assoc Libs: BOLDERO LIB (see **S1361**)
Entry: ref only, adv appt **Open:** Mon-Fri 0900-1900, Sat 0900-1300 (excl Aug)
Subj: medicine **Collns:** Bks & Pamphs: psychiatry (large part of colln of the former Friern Hosp) *Archvs:* some original material relating to early women doctors from late 19C onwards (separate dept, not under control of lib)
Equip: 3 copiers, 2 computers (incl CD-ROM), 3 OPAC *Online:* STN, DIMDI (charged) **Svcs:** info, ref, biblio, training
Stock: bks/c20000; periodcls/c400
Classn: NLM **Auto Sys:** Aleph
Staff: Libns: 5 Other Prof: 0.75 Non-Prof: 5.5

S1361
Royal Free and University College Medical School, Boldero Library
Bland Sutton Bldg, 48 Riding House St, London, W1W 7EY (020-7679-9454)
Email: bolderolib@ucl.ac.uk
Internet: http://www.ucl.ac.uk/

Gov Body: Univ Coll London (see **S1433**) **Chief:** Libn: Ms Patricia Campbell BA, DipLib
Assoc Libs: ROYAL FREE HOSP MEDICAL LIB (see **S1360**)
Entry: ref only **Open:** term: Mon-Thu 0930-2100, Fri 0930-1700; vac: Mon-Thu 0930-1900, Fri 0930-1700
Subj: clinical medicine **Collns:** Bks & Pamphs: incl former Lib of the Inst of Urology **Co-op Schemes:** BLDSC
Equip: 2 copiers (A4/5p), video viewer, 9 computers (Coll membs only) *Online:* Medline, Embase, Cochrane, etc **Svcs:** info, membs only
Stock: bks/12000; periodcls/300; videos/120
Classn: NLM **Auto Sys:** Aleph
Staff: Libns: 1 Non-Prof: 2 FTE

S1362
Royal Free Hospital Patients' Library
Royal Free Hosp, Pond St, Hampstead, London, NW3 2QG (020-7794-0500)

Type: charity **Gov Body:** St John's Ambulance Assoc **Chief:** Libn: Mrs Helen Rogers BA, DipEd
Open: Mon-Fri 1000-1500
Subj: all subjs; local study (hist of Belsize Park, Hampstead & Muswell Hill); generalities; sci; tech; arts; lit (large stock of fiction); geog; hist **Collns:** Bks & Pamphs: large print bks & talking bks

Equip: audio tape players **Officer-in-Charge:** Libn, as above **Svcs:** info, ref
Stock: bks/7000; audios/450 **Acqs Offcr:** Libn, as above
Classn: own, clr coding
Staff: Non-Prof: 19 PT volunteers **Exp:** £1500 (1999-2000); £1500 (2000-01)

S1363
Royal Geographical Society Library
(incl the Inst of British Geographers Lib)
1 Kensington Gore, London, SW7 2AR (020-7591-3044; *fax:* 020-7591-3001)
Email: library@rgs.org
Internet: http://www.rgs.org/

Chief: Libn: Mr Eugene Rae **Dep:** Dep Libn: Miss Janet Turner BA(Hons) **Other Snr Staff:** Lib Asst: Ms Julie Carrington
Assoc Libs: all at above addr: PICTURE LIB (see **S1365**); MAP ROOM (see **S1364**); ARCHVS (see **A334**); ARTEFACT COLLN
Entry: membs only; foreign academics may visit at discretion of libn, by adv appt only **Open:** Mon-Fri 1100-1700
Subj: physical geog; geog & travel; exploration
Collns: Bks & Pamphs: Feilden Colln (Arctic); Brown Colln (travel in Morocco); Gunther Colln (Italian geol & antiquities); Hotz Colln (Persia & the East); Andrews Colln (hist of cartography); Fordham Colln (17C-19C road bks); Rennell Colln (Asia, Middle East & Africa) *Archvs:* papers of Sir Clements Markham, H.M. Stanley & various Everest expeditions *Other:* audio recordings of Soc lectures
Equip: m-reader, video viewer, copier, computer (incl CD-ROM) *Disabled:* lift access **Svcs:** info
Stock: bks/150000; periodcls/800; videos/60
Classn: own **Auto Sys:** CAIRS
Pubns: The Geographical Journal; Area; Transactions of the IBG (prices vary; included in membership or can be bought separately)
Staff: Libns: 2 Non-Prof: 1
Further Info: The Lib is closed until Spring 2004 as a consequence of the Soc's 'Unlocking the Archvs' proj

S1364
Royal Geographical Society, Map Room
1 Kensington Gore, London, SW7 2AR (020-7591-3050; *fax:* 020-7591-3001)
Email: maps@rgs.org
Internet: http://www.rgs.org/

Chief: Curator of Maps: Mr Francis Herbert **Dep:** Asst Map Curator: Mr David McNeill **Other Snr Staff:** Maps & Archvs Asst: Ms Sarah Strong
Assoc Libs: MAIN RGS LIB (see **S1363**)
Entry: ref only; daily charge for non-membs of £10 (£5 unwaged or in full time edu) for access to all RGS collns, provided prior appt is made **Open:** Mon-Fri 1100-1700 (closed 2-4 wks Jun/Jul)
Subj: cartography **Collns:** Bks & Pamphs: M.C. Andrews Colln (British Isles, Ireland, portolan charts); Sir H.G. Fordham Colln (post-road bks & maps & topographies, mainly of British Isles & France); G.B. Greenough Colln (scientific mapping & charting, world-wide); George Philip Ltd Colln (geographer, cartographer, edu publisher, 1860s-1980s); carto-bibliographies; catalogues; directories *Archvs:* various archival & ref materials from Laurie & Whittle, G. Philip & from E. Stanford (incorporating the Arrowsmith firm) *Other:* gazetteers (world & natl, 18C onwards); aerial photography (1919 onwards); satellite imagery maps
Equip: m-reader, copiers, clr copier *Disabled:* wheelchair access **Svcs:** current awareness
Stock: bks/1100; pamphs/800; maps/1 mln; m-forms/200; atlases/2600; globes/40; gazetteers/700; expedition reports/4000

Classn: own
Pubns: The Fordham Colln (Roads Bks & Atlases): A Catalogue (£3); nearly 1500 maps produced for Journal of the RGS; Proceedings of the RGS; Geographical Journal; facsimiles of rare & MS maps etc (prices vary); the card catalogue is now available in the NIDS: UK & Ireland Microfiche Series (Cambridge, Chadwyck-Healey), incl the in-house MS listing of 'Indian Govt Survey' maps of 1882-1935
Staff: Libns: 2 *Other Prof:* 1
Further Info: The Map Room is closed until Spring 2004 as a consequence of the Soc's 'Unlocking the Archvs' proj

S1365

Royal Geographical Society, Picture Library

1 Kensington Gore, London, SW7 2AR (020-7591-3060; *fax:* 020-7591-3061)
Email: pictures@rgs.org
Internet: http://www.rgs.org/picturelibrary/

Chief: Curator of Photography & Picture Lib Mgr: Mrs Joanna Wright BA(Hons), MA *Dep:* Asst Picture Libn: Ms Pauline Hubner *Other Snr Staff:* Picture Lib Sales Mgr: Mr Justin Hobson
Assoc Libs: MAIN RGS LIB (see **S1363**)
Entry: adv appt *Open:* Mon-Fri 1000-1300, 1400-1700
Subj: geog *Collns: Other:* photos, transparencies & modern clr travel shots; remote areas of the world; old archival shots (1831-date); various special collns incl unique images not found elsewhere
Equip: copier, clr copier
Stock: photos/500000; slides/100000
Staff: Libns: 2 *Non-Prof:* 2

S1366

Royal Historical Society Library

Univ Coll London, Gower St, London, WC1E 6BT (*tel & fax:* 020-7387-7532)
Email: rhsinfo@rhs.ac.uk
Internet: http://www.rhs.ac.uk/

Gov Body: Council of The Royal Historical Soc
Chief: Hon Libn: Mr D.A.L. Morgan MA *Dep:* Exec Sec: Mrs J. McCarthy
Entry: adv appt with Exec Sec *Open:* Mon-Fri 0900-1700
Subj: hist (limited fields); historiography *Collns: Bks & Pamphs:* pre-1850 historical & antiquarian works; record series pubns concerning English hist *Archvs:* minute bks & papers of the Royal Historical Soc (1868 onwards); papers of the Camden Soc (1838-1897); papers of Sir George Prothero; papers of Sir Geoffrey Elton; papers of the Rev Dr Charles Rogers
Stock: bks/3000
Pubns: Texts & Calendars: An Analytical Guide
Staff: Non-Prof: 2

S1367

Royal Horticultural Society, The Lindley Library

80 Vincent Sq, London, SW1P 2PE (020-7821-3050; *fax:* 020-7828-3022)
Email: library.london@rhs.org.uk
Internet: http://www.rhs.org.uk/libraries/

Type: learned soc *Gov Body:* The Royal Horticultural Soc *Chief:* Libn: Dr Brent Elliott
Dep: Asst Libn: Miss Jennifer Vine
Assoc Libs: WISLEY LABORATORY LIB (see **S2137**); ROSEMOOR STAFF LIB, RHS Garden Rosemoor, Gt Torrington, N Devon, EX38 8PH (01805-624067); informal Garden Libs (overseen by Wisley Laboratory Lib but run by volunteers):

WISLEY GARDEN LIB, RHS Garden Wisley, Woking, Surrey, GU23 6QB (contact Wisley Laboratory Lib); HYDE HALL GARDEN LIB, RHS Garden Hyde Hall, Rettendon, Chelmsford, Essex, CM3 8ET, Volunteer Libn, Mrs Ann Dix (01245-400256; *email:* library.hydehall@rhs.org.uk); HARLOW CARR GARDEN LIB, RHS Garden Harlow Carr, Beckswithshaw, Crag Ln, Harrogate, HG3 1QB, Hon Libn: Mrs Kathryn White (01423-565418; *email:* library.harlowcarr@rhs.org.uk)
Entry: Lindley Lib: ref only, preferably by appt; membs of the RHS have borrowing privileges; *Wisley Laboratory Lib:* adv appt only; *Rosemoor Staff Lib:* staff only, no public access; *Garden Libs:* ref only for visitors *Open:* Mon-Fri 0930-1730
Subj: botany; hortic & gardening; garden design; flower arranging *Collns: Bks & Pamphs:* early hortic works (1514 onwards), incl c650 pre-Linnaean texts & 16-17C herbals; John Lindley Colln (works of 19C horticulturalist); hortic trade catalogues (mainly 1860-date); guidebks & pubns on various indiv gardens; John Bond Lib (at Hyde Hall) *Archvs:* archvs of the Royal Horticultural Soc; colln of personal papers of various gardening writers *Other:* botanical drawings *Co-op Schemes:* ILL
Equip: copier *Svcs:* info, ref
Stock: bks/50000; periodcls/300; illusts/18000
Classn: UDC *Auto Sys:* Sirsi Unicorn
Staff: Libns: 4 *Non-Prof:* 3
Proj: refurbishment of Wisley Garden Lib; development of Garden Lib at Rosemoor with full visitor access

S1368

Royal Humane Society, Library and Archives

Brettenham House, Lancaster Pl, London, WC2E 7EP (*tel & fax:* 020-7836-8155)
Email: rhs@supanet.com
Internet: http://www.royalhumane.org/

Chief: Sec: Major Genl C. Tyler MA, CB *Dep:* Asst Sec: Miss S. Sell *Other Snr Staff:* Archivist: Mrs D. Coke
Entry: ref only, adv appt *Open:* Mon-Thu 1000-1600
Subj: bravery awards; resuscitation *Collns: Bks & Pamphs:* annual reports *Archvs:* records, casebks & minutes (1774-date)
Equip: copier, 4 computers (all with wd-proc, 1 with internet & 1 with CD-ROM) *Svcs:* info
Pubns: Annual Report (£5); Short Hist of the Royal Humane Soc (£5); Medals of the Royal Humane Soc (£7.50); Saved from a Watery Grave (£10)
Staff: Non-Prof: 4

S1369

Royal Institute of International Affairs, Chatham House Library

10 St James's Sq, London, SW1Y 4LE (020-7957-5723; *fax:* 020-7957-5710)
Email: libenquire@riia.org
Internet: http://www.riia.org/

Chief: Libn: Mrs Catherine Hume MSc, BA, DipLib, MCLIP *Dep:* Dep Libn: Mrs Mary Bone BA
Entry: ref only, bona fide postgrad rsrchers should make prior written appl for reader's ticket (fee charged) *Open:* Mon-Fri 1100-1730 (closed part of Aug)
Subj: internatl & foreign affairs, with particular emphasis on internatl politics, econ & security (focus is on past 30-35 years, but extensive older primary src material continues to be held) *Collns: Archvs:* inst archvs *Other:* extensive colln of press cuttings (formerly known as the Chatham House Press Lib) *Co-op Schemes:* BLDSC, ILL
Equip: 2 m-readers, m-printer, 2 fax, copier, 4 computers *Online:* FT Profile, BLAISE, Eurobases, etc (fees: cost, plus)

Stock: bks, pamphs & maps/140000; periodcls/450; m-forms/various; newspapers/50; press cuttings/2000000
Classn: own *Auto Sys:* Unicorn
Pubns: Monthly List of Articles Indexed in the Lib; Monthly List of Bks & Periodicals Added to the Lib (for subscription details apply to libn)
Staff: Libns: 4 *Non-Prof:* 1 *Exp:* £20000 (1999-2000)

S1370

Royal Institution of Chartered Surveyors Library

12 Gt George St, Parliament Sq, London, SW1P 3AD (0870-333-1600 or 020-7222-7000; *fax:* 020-7334-3784)
Email: library@rics.org.uk
Internet: http://www.rics.org/

Chief: Head of Lib & Info Svcs: Ms Pauline Lane-Gilbert MCLIP
Assoc Libs: RICS IN SCOTLAND LIB, 9 Manor Pl, Edinburgh, EH3 7DN, Libn: Mrs Dorothy Lewis BA, MCLIP (0131-225-7078; *fax:* 0131-240-0830; *email:* edlib@rics.org.uk)
Entry: membs of RICS; non-membs by prior arrangement with Libn & on payment of £15 pd (£10 conc) *Open:* Mon-Fri 0930-1730
Subj: land & bldg econ; land, bldg & housing law; agric holdings; estate agency; planning & development; valuation; housing & property mgmt; compulsory purchase & compensation; agric; forestry; land hydrographic & mineral surveying; quantity surveying; proj mgmt; taxation & rating of land & property; landlord & tenant; statistics; commercial property *Collns: Bks & Pamphs:* historical colln on land surveying & bldg econ; Board of Agric Reports (19C); Royal Commission Reports on land use (19C) *Archvs:* RICS pubns
Co-op Schemes: BLDSC
Equip: copier, 6 computers (all with internet, 1 with CD-ROM), contact Westminster Centre for details of fax facilities & rooms for hire *Disabled:* induction loop *Svcs:* info, ref, biblio, indexing, abstracting
Stock: bks/35000; periodcls/390; pamphs/2000; audios/120; videos/200
Classn: DDC *Auto Sys:* Unicorn
Pubns: Lib Info for Subscribers, incl Abstracts & Reviews (monthly with weekly briefings)
Staff: Libns: 12 *Non-Prof:* 5 *Exp:* £120000 (1999-2000)

S1371

Royal Institution of Great Britain Library

21 Albemarle St, London, W1X 4BS (020-7409-2992; *fax:* 020-7629-3569)
Email: ril@ri.ac.uk
Internet: http://www.rigb.org/

Chief: Libn & Keeper of Collns: Dr Frank James
Entry: adv appt
Subj: sci; tech; hist of sci; hist of tech *Collns: Archvs:* MSS of 19C & 20C scientists connected with The Royal Inst, incl: C. Davy; Faraday; Tyndall; Dewar; W.H. Bragg; W.L. Bragg
Stock: bks/90000; periodcls/100

S1372

Royal Institution of Naval Architects, Denny Library

10 Upper Belgrave St, London, SW1X 8BQ (020-7253-4622; *fax:* 020-7259-5912)
Email: rsaunders@rina.org.uk
Internet: http://www.rina.org.uk/

Type: prof inst *Chief:* Libn: Mr Robert Saunders
Entry: ref only; open to membs of Instn; access by adv appt to membs of other co-operating prof instns & socs *Open:* Mon-Fri 0900-1700

London
▼
London

Special Libraries

(Royal Instn of Naval Architects, Denny Lib cont)
Subj: marine eng; marine tech; naval arch
Collns: Archvs: Lloyd's Register of Ships *Other:*
technical papers
Equip: copier *Svcs:* info
Stock: bks/6000; periodcls/42 *Staff: Libns:* 1

S1373 ♀ 🎓 ✚
Royal National Institute for Deaf People, RNID Library

The Royal Natl Throat, Nose & Ear Hosp, 330-332
Gray's Inn Rd, London, WC1X 8EE (*voice &
textphone:* 020-7915-1553; *fax:* 020-7915-1443)
Email: rnidlib@ucl.ac.uk
Internet: http://www.ucl.ac.uk/Library/RNID/

Gov Body: Royal Natl Inst for Deaf People & Univ
Coll London (see **S1433**) *Chief:* Site Libn: Ms
Mary Plackett (m.plackett@ucl.ac.uk)
Entry: open to public, ref only; borrowing available
for registered UCL Lib borrowers *Open:* Mon-Fri
1000-1300, 1400-1730
Subj: deafness; hearing loss; speech; lang; lit
Collns: Bks & Pamphs: wide range of lit on
deafness, incl: academic journals; rsrch reports;
student textbks; ch's bks; novels with deaf
characters *Archvs:* extensive historical materials
relating to deafness *Co-op Schemes:* BLDSC
Equip: copier, database terminals *Disabled:* no
wheelchair access, wheelchair users should tel for
alternative arrangements *Online:* Medline & other
databases, access to UCL catalogues *Svcs:* info,
ref, postal photocopying svc
Pubns: reading lists (free)

S1374 ♀
Royal National Institute of the Blind, Research Library

105 Judd St, London, WC1H 9NE (020-7391-
2052; *fax:* 020-7391-2210)
Email: library@rnib.org.uk
Internet: http://www.rnib.org.uk/library/research/

Gov Body: RNIB (registered charity no 226227)
Chief: Rsrch Lib Mgr: Mr Julian B. Roland BA,
DipLib, MCLIP (julian.roland@rnib.org.uk) *Dep:*
Libn (Digital Lib Svcs): Ms Eona Bell MA(Cantab),
MA(London) (eona.bell@rnib.org.uk)
Assoc Libs: ROYAL NATL INST OF THE BLIND
ARCHV, Falcon Pk, Neasden Ln, London, NW10
1TB, Archivist: Ms Elizabeth Dawson BA(Hons),
PGCE(A) (020-8438-9031; *email:* archive@
rnib.org.uk); RNIB LIB & INFO SVCS (incl Braille
Lib & Cassette Lib), PO Box 173, Peterborough,
PE2 6WS (01733-375333)
Entry: Rsrch Lib: ref only, borrowing for a fee
(membership info available on request); *Archvs:* by
appt only; *Other Libs:* enqs by post/tel only *Open:
Rsrch Lib:* Mon-Fri 0930-1700, Sat 0930-1200;
Archvs: Mon-Fri 1000-1700
Subj: visual impairment; blind welfare *Collns:
Archvs:* archvs of the RNIB & related orgs; other
material relating to the hist of provision for the blind
& visually impaired *Co-op Schemes:* BLDSC
Equip: copier, computers (incl 6 wd-proc & 2 CD-
ROM) *Disabled:* Kurzweil, JAWS, ZoomText
Svcs: info, biblio, photocopying

Stock: bks/5300; periodcls/175; pamphs/6150;
archvs/50 m; govt papers/2300; annual reports/
3600; Braille/70000 vols (at Braille Lib); cassettes/
28000 (at Cassette Lib)
Classn: RNIB Rsrch Lib Scheme *Auto Sys:* Geac
Pubns: New Lit on Sight Problems (£22.50 pa UK,
£32.50 pa EC, £37.50 outside EC); subscription
info available on request
Staff: Libns: 2 *Non-Prof:* 0.5

S1375 ♀
Royal Numismatic Society and British Numismatic Society Libraries

c/o Warburg Inst, Woburn Sq, London, WC1H 0AB

Gov Body: Royal Numismatic Soc *Chief:* Libn:
A.J. Holmes
Entry: membs of Royal Numismatic Soc & British
Numismatic Soc only
Subj: numismatics *Collns: Bks & Pamphs:*
auction catalogues & periodcls
Stock: bks/7000; periodcls/150
See also WARBURG INST LIB (**S1456**)

S1376 ♀
Royal Pharmaceutical Society of Great Britain Library

1 Lambeth High St, London, SE1 7JN (020-7735-
9141; *fax:* 020-7572-2499)
Email: infocentre@rpsgb.org.uk
Internet: http://www.rpsgb.org.uk/

Chief: Head of Info Centre: Mr Roy Allcorn *Dep:*
Libn: Mr Roddy Morrison
Assoc Libs: SCOTTISH DEPT LIB (see **S622**)
Entry: membs only, others ref only on payment of
fee *Open:* Mon-Wed, Fri 0900-1700, Thu 1000-
1745
Subj: pharmacy *Collns: Bks & Pamphs:* herbals;
pharmacopoeias *Co-op Schemes:* BLDSC
Equip: video viewer, copier, 5 computers (all with
CD-ROM, 1 with internet) *Online:* Dialog *Svcs:*
info, ref, biblio, indexing, abstracting
Stock: bks/70000; periodcls/350; pamphs/10000
Classn: UDC *Auto Sys:* Olib 7
Staff: Libns: 3 *Non-Prof:* 2

S1377 🎓 ♀
Royal Society for Asian Affairs, Library

2 Belgrave Sq, London, SW1X 8PJ (020-7724-
4741)
Email: library@rsaa.org.uk
Internet: http://www.rsaa.org.uk/library.htm

Gov Body: Royal Soc for Asian Affairs *Chief:*
Hon Libn: Mr M.J. Pollock MA, MCLIP
Entry: open for borrowing by membs of the Soc;
ref only & adv appt for non-membs; this is a small
lib with limited space *Open:* Mon-Thu 1000-1300,
1400-1600, Fri 1000-1300; closed 1030-1500 on
lecture days
Subj: Asia (Turkey to Japan, largely 20C); hist;
geog; politics; travel; biography; religion *Collns:
Archvs:* some private papers (largely
uncatalogued) *Other:* colln of glass slides &
photographs; some maps
Equip: copier (via staff) *Svcs:* ref
Stock: bks/c7000; periodcls/10; various photos,
slides, maps & archvs (mainly uncatalogued)
Classn: own (alphabetically by geographical area)
Pubns: collns in the Lib archvs are described in
Chapter 10 of the Centenary Hist of the Soc,
entitled Strolling About on the Roof of the World, by
Hugh Leach with Sue Farrington (Routledge
Curzon, 2003)
Staff: Libns: 1 *Non-Prof:* PT volunteers on
irregular basis

S1378 ♀
Royal Society for the Encouragement of Arts, Manufactures and Commerce, Library

8 John Adam St, London, WC2N 6EZ (020-7451-
6874; *fax:* 020-7839-5805)
Email: matthew.mccarthy@rsa.org.uk
Internet: http://www.rsa.org.uk/

Gov Body: RSA (founded in 1754 "to embolden
enterprise, enlarge sci, refine art, improve our
manufactures & extend our commerce") *Chief:*
Libn: Mr Matthew McCarthy
Assoc Libs: RSA ARCHVS, at same addr,
Archivist: Ms Nicola Gray (020-7451-6847; *email:*
archive@rsa.org.uk)
Entry: fellows of RSA; & rsrchers on appl *Open:*
Mon-Fri 0930-2000; closed bank hols, Xmas-New
Year & for 1 month in summer; archvs are
accessible by appt only
Subj: contemporary lending & ref colln relevant to
the Soc's current work: arts; design; edu; environment; manufacture; commerce; small ref colln to
support access to the Soc's archv *Collns: Bks &
Pamphs:* 500 pre-1830 printed bks & tracts
Archvs: minutes, transactions & other records of
the soc & its committees (1754 onwards); MSS
letters, drawings, designs, etc relating to Soc's
premium offers; minutes of Internatl Postage Assoc
(1852-54); minutes of Natl Memorial Fund (1862-
65) *Co-op Schemes:* BLDSC
Equip: copier (via staff memb), computer (with
internet & CD-ROM) *Disabled:* wheelchair access
Stock: bks/8000; periodcls/35; photos/800; slides/
400; pamphs/150; maps/12; archvs/500 linear ft
Classn: DDC
Staff: Non-Prof: 2 *Exp:* £15000 (2000-01)

S1379 ♀
The Royal Society Library

6-9 Carlton House Ter, London, SW1Y 5AG (020-
7451-2606; *fax:* 020-7930-2170)
Email: library@royalsoc.ac.uk
Internet: http://www.royalsoc.ac.uk/

Type: learned soc *Chief:* Head of Lib & Info Svcs:
Ms Karen Peters MCLIP (karen.peters@royalsoc.
ac.uk) *Dep:* Lib Mgr: Mr Rupert Baker MA
(rupert.baker@royalsoc.ac.uk) *Other Snr Staff:*
Archivist: Mrs Joanna Corden DipAA (joanna.
corden@royalsoc.ac.uk)
Entry: open to Fellows of the Soc, historians of sci
& other bona fide rsrchers; adv appt preferred
Open: Mon-Fri 1000-1700
Subj: sci; maths; tech; hist of sci; sci policy;
biography (Fellows of the Soc) *Collns: Bks &
Pamphs:* biographies of Fellows *Archvs:* Royal
Soc records (1660 onwards); papers of some
scientists *Co-op Schemes:* BLDSC, ILL
(photocopies only)
Equip: m-reader, m-printer (A4/25p), copier (A4/
20p), computer (with internet & CD-ROM) *Officer-
in-Charge:* Head of Lib & Info Svcs, as above
Svcs: info, ref
Stock: bks/200000; periodcls/500; photos/4000;
slides/200; illusts/2000; pamphs/20000; maps/500;
m-forms/100; audios/200; videos/50; CD-ROMs/20;
archvs/5000 ft *Acqs Offcr:* Lib Mgr, as above
Classn: own *Auto Sys:* CALM 2000
Pubns: Hist of the Royal Soc Lib & Archvs 1660-
1990 (free); Guide to the Archvs & Manuscripts of
the Royal Soc (free); List of Fellows of the Royal
Soc 1660-2001 (£15); Obituaries & Biographical
Memoirs of Fellows of the Royal Soc 1830-2001
(£7.50)
Staff: Libns: 3 *Other Prof:* 2 *Non-Prof:* 3 *Exp:*
£24000 (1999-2000); £24000 (2000-01)

S1380 🔑 🎓 ⚜

Royal Society of Chemistry, Library and Information Centre

Burlington House, Piccadilly, London, W1V 0BA (020-7437-8656; *fax:* 020-7437-9798)
Email: library@rsc.org
Internet: http://www.rsc.org/library/

Type: learned soc *Chief:* Mgr, Lib & Archival Svcs: Mr Nigel Lees MSc, MCLIP *Other Snr Staff:* Info Offcr: Ms Nazma Masud; Info Offcr: Mr Ronald Hudson; Snr Lib Asst: Ms Nicola Best *Entry:* membs of RSC; Lib & Info Centre corporate membs; non-membs by appt *Open:* Mon-Fri 0930-1730
Subj: chem; biochem; hist of chem *Collns: Bks & Pamphs:* colln of historical bks (300 vols); Nathan Colln (explosives & firearms, 1000 vols); Roscoe Colln (96 vols) *Archvs:* Royal Soc of Chem Archvs, incl: council & cttee minutes of RSC's constituent socs; original Victorian charters; Royal Charters; artefacts presented to the RSC; architect's plans of Burlington House in mid-19C *Other:* Image Colln (c8000 items), incl Cribb Colln (433 items, 1538-1890) *Co-op Schemes:* BLDSC, journal exchange agreement with 100 other orgs *Equip:* m-reader, m-printer, fax, 2 copiers, 7 computers *Online:* STN (£60 per hr for membs, £80 per hr for non-membs, plus online fees); 20 CD-ROM resources, incl Chemical Abstracts, Chemical Citations Index, Chemical Business Newsbase etc *Officer-in-Charge:* info, ref, biblio, document delivery
Stock: bks/25000; periodcls/630; photos/78000; CD-ROMs/20; archvs/c100 ft; some pamphs & m-forms
Classn: UDC *Auto Sys:* EOSi GLAS Series
Pubns: Periodicals Holding List (free); Chem Guide to the Internet (free)
Staff: Libns: 3 *Other Prof:* 3 *Non-Prof:* 1 *Exp:* £250000 (1999-2000); £260000 (2000-01)

S1381 🔑 ✚

Royal Society of Medicine Library

1 Wimpole St, London, W1M 8AE (020-7290-2940; *fax:* 020-7290-2939)
Email: library@rsm.ac.uk
Internet: http://www.roysocmed.ac.uk/librar/library.htm

Gov Body: Council of the RSM *Chief:* Dir of Info Svcs: Mr I. Snowley MBA, MCLIP (ian.snowley@rsm.ac.uk) *Dep:* Head of Customer Svcs: Ms S. Burton BA, MA, MCLIP (sheron.burton@rsm.ac.uk) *Assoc Libs:* ROYAL SOC OF MEDICINE ARCHVS, addr as above, Archivist & Records Mgr: Ms S. Gilbert (020-7290-2948; *email:* sally.gilbert@rsm.ac.uk)
Entry: membs & fellows of RSM; other may apply for temp membership *Open:* Mon-Fri 0900-2030, Sat 1000-1700
Subj: at postgrad level: medicine; biomedical sci; hist of medicine; medical biography; health statistics *Collns: Bks & Pamphs:* Comfort Colln of Gerontology *Archvs:* archvs of Royal Soc of Medicine & parent socs from 1805, incl: minutes; charters & bye-laws; membership papers; deed & bldg records; financial records; correspondence; conference programmes; pubns etc; archvs of RSM sections, fora & sub-committees; archvs of predecessor specialist socs incl: Soc of Anaesthetists (1893-1908); British Balneological & Climatology Soc (1895-1909); Soc for the Study of Diseases in Children (1900-1908); Dermatological Soc of London (1882-1907); Clinical Soc of London (1868-1907); British Electrotherapy Soc (1901-1907); Epidemiological Soc (1850-1907); British Gynaecological Soc (1884-1907); British Laryngological, Rhinological & Otological Assoc (1888-1907); Neurological Soc (1886-1907); Obstetrical Soc of London (1858-1907); Odontological Soc of Great Britain (1856-1907); Pathological Soc of London (1846-1907);

Therapeutical Soc (1902-1907) *Other:* historical medical colln from 1491; medical portrait colln; Diamond Colln (photos of psychiatric patients, mid-19C) *Co-op Schemes:* BLDSC
Equip: 5 copiers, 10 computers (incl wd-proc, internet & CD-ROM) *Online:* Medline, Embase, Cochrane, Cochrane Database of Systematic Reviews (CDSR), Database of Reviews of Effectiveness (DARE) *Svcs:* info, ref, biblio, in-depth searches, document delivery
Stock: bks/500000; periodcls/2000 current, 10000 in total; illusts/3000; pamphs/25000
Classn: NLM *Auto Sys:* Unicorn
Pubns: contact Pubns Dept for a full list
Staff: Libns: 14 *Other Prof:* 2 *Non-Prof:* 17
Further Info: The RSM Lib is the largest biomedical postgrad lib in Europe

S1382 🔑

Royal Television Society, Library and Archive

Holborn Hall, 100 Grays Inn Rd, London, WC1X 8AL (020-7430-1000; *fax:* 020-7430-0924)
Email: info@rts.org.uk
Internet: http://www.rts.org.uk/

Chief: Archivist: Ms Clare Colvin MA, DipAA
Entry: by written appl *Open:* by appt
Subj: television hist *Collns: Bks & Pamphs:* bks on early hist of television *Archvs:* written, photographic & AV material on early television hist & development of the soc (1927-date)
Equip: video viewer, fax, copier (fees charged for items retrieved from store)
Staff: Other Prof: 1

S1383 🪡

Royal Town Planning Institute Library

41 Botolph Ln, London, EC3R 8DL (020-7929-9452; *fax:* 020-7929-9490)
Email: library@rtpi.org.uk
Internet: http://www.rtpi.org.uk/

Chief: Libn: Ms Pam Dobby BA, MCLIP
Entry: ref only, prior appt essential *Open:* Mon-Fri 0900-1600
Subj: town planning; planning law; environmental topics
Equip: copier (via staff) *Svcs:* info, ref, indexing, enq svc
Stock: bks/2000; periodcls/100; local plans
Classn: UDC *Staff: Libns:* 1

S1384 🎓⚜

Royal Veterinary College Library

Royal College St, London, NW1 0TU (*tel & fax:* 020-7468-5162)
Email: libary@rvc.ac.uk
Internet: http://www.rvc.ac.uk/

Gov Body: Univ of London (see **S1440**) *Chief:* Coll Libn: Mr Simon Jackson MA, MCLIP *Dep:* Ms Deborah Walker BSc(Hons), MCLIP
Assoc Libs: HAWKSHEAD CAMPUS LIB, Hawkshead House, Hawkshead Ln, North Mymms, Hatfield, Hertfordshire, AL9 7TA (01707-666214)
Entry: ref only, with proof of ID & at discretion of Libn; 24 hrs notice required *Open:* Mon-Fri 0830-1800
Subj: veterinary scis; animal health *Collns: Bks & Pamphs:* 3000 monographs of early veterinary lit *Archvs:* hist of development of the RVC & the veterinary profession *Co-op Schemes:* BLDSC
Equip: m-reader, 2 copiers, computers (incl 3 CD-ROM)
Stock: bks/50000
Classn: LC *Auto Sys:* Unicorn (Sirsi)
Staff: Libns: 7 *Non-Prof:* 2

S1385 🔑 🕊

Salvation Army, Territorial Headquarters Library

101 Newington Causeway, Elephant & Castle, London, SE1 6BN (020-7367-4908; *fax:* 020-7367-4913)
Email: thq@salvationarmy.org.uk
Internet: http://www.salvationarmy.org.uk/

Gov Body: Salvation Army *Chief:* Libn: Major Fiona MacLean MA (fiona.maclean@salvationarmy.org.uk)
Assoc Libs: SALVATION ARMY INTERNATL HERITAGE CENTRE (see **A341**); WILLIAM BOOTH COLL LIB (see **S1463**)
Entry: adv appt *Open:* Mon-Fri 0900-1600
Subj: religion; Christian bks, mainly Salvation Army *Collns: Bks & Pamphs:* Salvation Army pubns *Other:* photos (wide range of Salvation Army photos incl overseas & genl photos); War Cry on m-form from 1880s *Co-op Schemes:* with Heritage Centre & Training Coll Lib
Equip: m-reader, copier, computer (with internet)
Svcs: info, ref
Stock: bks/3000; photos/10000; m-forms/50 *Acqs Offcr:* Libn, as above
Classn: DDC *Staff: Libns:* 1

S1386 🏛

Saudi Arabian Information Centre Library

Cavendish House, 18 Cavendish Sq, London, W1M 0AQ (020-7629-8803; *fax:* 020-7629-0374)
Email: sair@saudinf.com
Internet: http://www.saudinf.com/

Gov Body: Royal Embassy of Saudi Arabia
Open: Mon-Fri 0900-1600
Subj: genl; most subjs; Islamic culture & arts; Saudi writers, scholars & scientists
Equip: copier

Save the Children Fund Library

See SAVE THE CHILDREN FUND ARCHVS (**A342**)

S1387 🏛 🏛

Science Museum Library

Imperial College Rd, South Kensington, London, SW7 5NH (020-7942-4242; *fax:* 020-7942-4243)
Email: smlinfo@nmsi.ac.uk
Internet: http://www.nmsi.ac.uk/library/

Type: natl museum *Gov Body:* Natl Museum of Sci & Industry (Trustees of the Sci Museum) *Chief:* Head of Lib: Mrs Pauline O. Dingley BA, MCLIP
Assoc Libs: NATL RAILWAY MUSEUM, LIB & ARCHV (see **S2165**); NATL MUSEUM OF PHOTOGRAPHY, FILM & TELEVISION, COLLNS & RSRCH CENTRE (see **S215**); shares bldg, svcs & catalogue with IMPERIAL COLL LONDON CENTRAL LIBS (see **S1180**)
Entry: open to public for rsrch & ref *Open:* term & Easter vac: Mon-Fri 0930-2100, Sat 0930-1730; other vacs: Mon-Fri 0930-1730, Sat 0930-1730
Subj: hist & public understanding of sci & tech; scientific & technical biography *Collns: Bks & Pamphs:* rare bks colln (mainly pre-1800 scientific & technical bks & serials); 19C & 20C colln (scientific & technical bks & serials); Comben Colln (historic bks on veterinary sci & animal husbandry); trade lit colln *Archvs:* museum archv colln (material with special relevance to the museum's collns in the physical scis & industry); archv for the hist of quantum physics *Co-op Schemes:* BLDSC
Equip: 2 m-readers, m-camera, 2 m-printers, video viewer, 9 copiers ☞

(Science Museum Lib cont)
Stock: bks/600000; periodcls/2000; various pamphs, maps, m-forms & videos
Classn: UDC, LC subj headings **Auto Sys:** Unicorn
Pubns: Lib Leaflet (free); Catalogue of the Comben Colln
Staff: Libns: 9 Other Prof: 1 Non-Prof: 9 **Exp:** £169000 (1999-2000); £168000 (2000-01)

S1388

Science Photo Library Ltd
327-329 Harrow Rd, London, W9 3RB (020-7432-1100; *fax:* 020-7286-8668)
Email: info@sciencephoto.com
Internet: http://www.sciencephoto.com/

Chief: Rsrch Mgr: Mr Mark Abbott (mark.abbott@sciencephoto.com)
Entry: fees payable for loan & use of images, visits by appt only **Open:** Mon-Fri 0930-1800
Subj: sci; medicine; tech; earth; space; nature
Svcs: rsrch svc (fee payable)
Stock: photos/120000
Classn: customised **Auto Sys:** customised
Pubns: Clr Catalogue (free to commercial users)
Staff: Other Prof: 45

S1389

Serious Fraud Office, Library
Elm House, 10-16 Elm St, London, WC1X 0BJ (020-7239-7359; *fax:* 020-7833-5413)
Email: library.sfo@gtnet.gov.uk
Internet: http://www.sfo.gov.uk/

Chief: Libn: Miss Emma Lodge BLib, MCLIP
Entry: govt depts & official bodies only **Open:** Mon-Fri 0900-1730
Subj: criminal law
Equip: 2 m-readers, m-printer, copier, computers (incl internet & CD-ROM) **Svcs:** info, ref, biblio, indexing, on-line searching, multimedia learning resource centre
Stock: bks/10000; videos/50; CD-ROMs/20; archvs/20 m
Classn: Moys **Auto Sys:** Adlib
Staff: Libns: 1 Non-Prof: 1

S1390

Shakespeare's Globe Centre, Library and Archives
21 New Globe Walk, Bankside, London, SE1 9EB (020-7902-1580; *fax:* 020-7902-1401)
Email: library@shakespearesglobe.com

Chief: Libn: Ms Ros Aitken **Other Snr Staff:** Archivist: Ms Undine Concannon
Entry: ref only; adv appt in writing or by email
Open: Tue-Thu 1000-1600
Subj: theatre; drama; Elizabethan drama **Collns:** Bks & Pamphs: Gielgud Colln (bks belonging to Sir John Gielgud) **Archvs:** MSS & correspondence
Other: videos of performances; photos; promptbooks; programmes; clippings; posters; production material

S1391

Sir John Soane's House and Museum Library
13 Lincoln's Inn Fields, London, WC2A 3BP (020-7440-4251; *fax:* 020-7831-3957)
Email: library.soane1@ukgateway.net
Internet: http://www.soane.org/

Gov Body: Trustees of Sir John Soane's Museum
Chief: Archivist: Ms Susan Palmer MA, DipAA
Dep: Asst Curator (Drawings): Mr Stephen Astley BA
Entry: ref only, adv appt necessary **Open:** Tue-Fri 1000-1300, 1400-1700, Sat 1000-1300
Subj: art & arch to 1840 **Collns:** Bks & Pamphs: Soane's own lib to 1837, comprising architect's lib of bks on art & arch & gentleman's genl lib; small complementary ref lib **Archvs:** Soane's private correspondence & papers relating to his arch practice **Other:** arch drawings c1490-1837 (40000 incl c8000 by Robert Adam); drawings also available on m-film
Equip: m-reader, m-printer, copier (limited use)
Svcs: info, ref
Stock: bks & pamphs/8000
Staff: Other Prof: 1 Non-Prof: 1 **Exp:** £1000 (1999-2000); £1000 (2000-01); for Modern Ref Lib only; Main Lib is a closed colln

S1392

Ski Club of Great Britain Library
The White House, 57-63 Church Rd, Wimbledon, London, SW19 5SB (0845-458-0780; *fax:* 0845-458-0781)
Email: skiers@skiclub.co.uk
Internet: http://www.skiclub.co.uk/

Chief: Hon Libn: Ms O. Freeman **Dep:** Ms C. Whiteley
Entry: adv appt **Open:** Mon-Fri 0930-1700
Subj: specialist sport; skiing **Collns:** Bks & Pamphs: skiing, mountaineering & alpine incl old sets of club's records
Stock: bks/750+; photos/500+

S1393

Society for Co-operation in Russian and Soviet Studies, Library
320 Brixton Rd, London, SW9 6AB (020-7274-2282; *fax:* 020-7274-3230)
Email: ruslibrary@scrss.co.uk
Internet: http://www.scrss.co.uk/

Gov Body: SCR Council **Chief:** Libn & Info Offcr: Ms Jane Rosen BA(Hons), DipLib
Entry: appt required for non-membs **Open:** Mon-Fri 1000-1300, 1400-1800
Subj: all subjs (in relation to Russia & republics of the former USSR) **Collns:** Bks & Pamphs: ch's lib (bks in Russian & English); theatre section (bks & programmes etc on theatre in Russia & the former USSR); Art Ref Lib; WW2 Soviet war memoirs **Archvs:** archvs of soc since 1924 (its foundation) **Other:** photo & visual aids colln; Elsie Timbey photo colln (early Soviet photos); Cecily Osmond Colln (schools on early collective farms); music scores; newspaper cuttings lib **Co-op Schemes:** ILL
Equip: copier, slide viewer, 2 rooms for hire (£10-£20 per hr) **Svcs:** info, ref, biblio
Stock: bks/30000; periodcls/50; photos/40000; slides/20000; pamphs/1000; maps/100; audios/500; archvs/4 cubic m
Classn: Lenin Lib scheme
Pubns: SCR Russian Info Guide (annual, £5.95 + 35p p&p); SCR Info Digest (3 pa, £10 pa UK, £20 pa overseas)
Staff: Libns: 1 Non-Prof: 1

S1394

Society for Psychical Research Library
49 Marloes Rd, Kensington, London, W8 6LA (020-7937-8984; *fax:* 020-7837-8984)
Internet: http://www.spr.ac.uk/

Chief: Libn: Mrs M.W. Poynton
Assoc Libs: old bks & archv are on permanent loan at CAMBRIDGE UNIV LIB, RARE BKS DEPT (see **L5**)
Entry: Marloes Rd: free access for membs of Soc, others may make one-off visits for a fee; Cambridge: permission from Soc to have access
Open: Tue-Thu 1300-1700
Subj: psychical rsrch; parapsychology **Collns:** Bks & Pamphs: from 1882-1982 (at Cambridge); 1982-date (at Marloes Rd) **Co-op Schemes:** ILL
Equip: copier, computer
Stock: bks/7000; periodcls/53
Pubns: Journal of the Soc for Psychical Rsrch (quarterly); The Paranormal Review (quarterly)
Staff: Libns: 1 Non-Prof: 1.5

S1395

Society for Research into Higher Education, Library
76 Portland Pl, London, W1B 1NT (020-7637-2766; *fax:* 020-7637-2781)
Email: srheoffice@srhe.ac.uk
Internet: http://www.srhe.ac.uk/

Type: prof soc **Chief:** Dir: Prof Heather Eggins
Other Snr Staff: Office Mgr: Ms Betty Woessner; Finance & Administrative Offcr: Mr Franco Carta
Entry: ref only, adv appt; small lib of own pubns & small colln of other materials for Soc's own use, which may be referenced by others after contacting the office **Open:** office hrs (phone for details)
Subj: higher edu **Collns:** Bks & Pamphs: SRHE pubns, incl SRHE/Open Univ Press bks, in-house pubns & SRHE journals (Rsrch Into Higher Edu Abstracts, Studies in Higher Edu & Higher Edu Quarterly) **Archvs:** archv of SRHE admin & pubns held at Modern Records Centre (see **A114**) **Other:** small working colln of current reports & newsletters on higher edu; Higher Edu Statistics Agency (HESA) statistical reports & datapacks
Equip: photocopying by arrangement
Staff: Other Prof: 4

S1396

Society of Antiquaries of London Library
Burlington House, Piccadilly, London, W1J 0BE (020-7479-7084; *fax:* 020-7287-6967)
Email: library@sal.org.uk
Internet: http://www.sal.org.uk/

Chief: Libn: Mr E.B. Nurse MA, FSA, MCLIP
Dep: Asst Libn: A. James MA, DipLib
Entry: ref, by appt **Open:** Mon-Fri 1000-1700, closed Aug
Subj: decorative arts; medieval arts; British hist; archaeo (esp British & European); arch; hist of arch
Collns: Bks & Pamphs: broadsides & proclamations; Civil War tracts **Other:** topographical prints & drawings; seal impressions; brass rubbings **Co-op Schemes:** BLDSC
Equip: m-reader, m-printer, copier, computer
Online: BLAISE
Stock: bks/150000; periodcls/600
Auto Sys: Voyager
Pubns: Antiquaries Journal; Archaeologia
Staff: Libns: 4

S1397

Society of Chemical Industry, Library and Archive

15 Belgrave Sq, London, SW1X 8PS (020-7235-3681; *fax:* 020-7823-1698)
Email: ian.shepherd@soci.org

Type: learned soc *Chief:* Hon Libn: Mr I.D. Shepherd CEng, MIChemE
Entry: ref only; non-membs by appt, no charge
Open: Mon-Fri 0900-1700
Subj: chemical industry (SCI pubns only) *Collns: Bks & Pamphs:* journals of SCI, incl JSCI, Chem & Industry (1881-date); monographs; reports; proceedings of meetings/conferences; all publ by or on behalf of SCI *Archvs:* minutes of Council meetings (1881-date)
Svcs: info, ref, photocopying (charge to non-membs), lecture theatre for hire (prices & availability on appl to reception)
Stock: bks/32 linear m; periodcls/5; archvs/2 linear m
Classn: Random
Pubns: various journals, incl: Chem & Industry (24 pa, free to membs, subscription £360, $560 in USA, Canada & Mexico); Polymer Internatl (12 pa, annual subscription $1615); Journal of the Sci of Food & Agric (15 pa, annual subscription $2075); Pesticide Mgmt Sci (12 pa, annual subscription $1300); Journal of Chemical Tech & Biotech (12 pa, annual subscription $1410)
Staff: Non-Prof: 1 PT

S1398

Society of Genealogists Library

14 Charterhouse Bldgs, Goswell Rd, London, EC1M 7BA (020-7251-8799; *fax:* 020-7250-1800)
Email: library@sog.org.uk
Internet: http://www.sog.org.uk/

Type: learned soc *Gov Body:* Exec Cttee of the Soc of Genealogists *Chief:* Libn: Mrs Susan Gibbons BA, MCLIP *Other Snr Staff:* Genealogy Offcr: Ms Else Churchill DipLib (genealogy@sog.org.uk)
Entry: mainly ref (only membs may borrow); fees charged to non-membs; no appts necessary except for large groups & guided tours *Open:* Tue-Wed, Fri-Sat 1000-1800, Thu 1000-2000; closed 1st full wk of Feb for stocktaking
Subj: genealogy; heraldry; hist; family hist; local hist; topography; biography *Collns: Bks & Pamphs:* directories; poll bks; family hists *Archvs:* indexes to births, marriages & deaths in Scotland (1855-1920), England & Wales (1837-1925); indexes to births & marriages in Scotland (1553-1854); indexes to births, marriages & deaths in Australia & New Zealand up to c1913; Internatl Genealogical Index (400 mln worldwide baptisms & marriages up to c1875); Great Card Index (misc refs to several mln indivs); Boyd's Inhabitants of London (c60000 names); Boyd's London Burials (c250000 adult male burials in London 1538-1853); Boyd's Marriage Index (c7 mln English marriages, 1538-1837); Trinity House petitions, 1750-1890; Civil Svc Evidences of Age (1855-1939); Bank of England Wills (1717-1845); parish register copies & transcripts; lists of clergy (C of E & nonconformist); Great Western Railway stock transfer registers (1835-1932); Teachers' Registration Council registers (1902-48) *Other:* monumental inscriptions *Co-op Schemes:* BLDSC (info only)
Equip: 40 m-readers, 5 m-printers (A4/20p), 3 copiers (A4/20p), 20 computers (incl 6 with internet & 5 with CD-ROM), room for hire *Officer-in-Charge:* Libn, as above *Svcs:* info, ref
Stock: bks/c100000; periodcls/c500, plus c500 no longer current; maps/c1000; m-forms/3000000; audios/220; CD-ROMs/c200; archvs/500 linear m
Acqs Offcr: Libn, as above
Classn: own *Auto Sys:* Q Series (EOSi)

Pubns: Genealogists' Magazine; Computers in Genealogy; many others
Staff: Libns: 4.5 *Non-Prof:* 2
See also **O376**

S1399

South Africa House Library

South African High Commission, Trafalgar Sq, London, WC2N 5DP (020-7451-7299; *fax:* 020-7451-7283)

Chief: Libn: Miss Y. Baker BA(Hons), HDipLib
Entry: written enqs only (please supply postal addr for replies)
Subj: South Africa: very small genl ref colln of bks of South African interest
Classn: own, DDC
Proj: refurbishment; conversion to genl resource centre with emphasis on elec facilities

S1400

South Bank University, Learning and Information Services

250 Southwark Bridge Rd, London, SE1 6NJ (020-7815-6625; *fax:* 020-7815-6699)
Email: library@sbu.ac.uk
Internet: http://www.lisa.sbu.ac.uk/

Chief: Head of Learning & Info Svcs: Mr John Akeroyd BSc, MPhil, DipLIS, MCLIP (john.akeroyd@sbu.ac.uk) *Dep:* Dep Head of Learning & Info Svcs: Ms Christine Muller BA, MCLIP (mullerc@sbu.ac.uk)
Assoc Libs: PERRY LIB, addr as above, Acting Site Mgr: Ms Louise Hughes (020-7815-6600; *fax:* 020-7815-6699; *email:* hughescl@sbu.ac.uk); WANDSWORTH RD LIB, Faculty of the Built Environment, Wandsworth Rd, London, SW8 2JZ, Site Mgr: Ms Patricia Noble (020-7815-8320; *fax:* 020-7815-8366; *email:* noblep@sbu.ac.uk); EAST LONDON CAMPUS LIB (see **S1401**); ESSEX CAMPUS LIB (see **S1871**)
Entry: adv appt *Open: Perry Lib:* term: Mon-Wed 0830-2100, Thu 0830-2130, Fri 0830-1900, Sat-Sun 1030-1630; *Wandsworth Rd Lib:* term: Mon-Tue, Thu 0830-2100, Wed, Fri 0830-1900, Sat varies, Sun 1030-1630; vac (both sites): Mon-Fri 0900-1700
Subj: all subjs *Collns: Other:* AV collns; slide colln; OS map colln *Co-op Schemes:* BLDSC, SEAL, UK Libs Plus, SCONUL
Equip: m-reader, m-printer, video viewer, fax, copier, clr copier, computers (incl wd-proc, internet & CD-ROM) *Online:* most online svcs
Stock: bks/376994; periodcls/c2000; slides/40000; videos/11000
Classn: DDC *Auto Sys:* Dynix
Pubns: numerous
Staff: Libns: 24 *Non-Prof:* 28 *Exp:* £978572 (1999-2000); £1121538 (2000-01)

S1401

South Bank University, East London Campus Library

(formerly Redwood Coll of Health Studies Lib)
Whipps Cross Hosp, Leytonstone, London, E11 1NR (020-7815-4707; *fax:* 020-7815-4777)
Email: lisel@sbu.ac.uk
Internet: http://www.lisa.sbu.ac.uk/

Gov Body: South Bank Univ (see **S1400**) *Chief:* Lib Site Mgr: Miss D.J. Watmough MCLIP
Assoc Libs: ESSEX CAMPUS LIB (see **S1871**)
Entry: membs only *Open:* Mon-Thu 0830-1930, Fri 0830-1700, Sat 1000-1600
Subj: health; nursing *Co-op Schemes:* BLDSC, North Thames Region (NHS), NULJ
Equip: video viewer, copier (A4/5p), fax, 10 computers (all with wd-proc, internet & CD-ROM, printouts 5p per pg) *Svcs:* info, ref, biblio

Stock: bks/17500; periodcls/73; slides/5; pamphs/30; m-forms/2; audios/6; videos/276; CD-ROMs/12
Classn: DDC *Auto Sys:* Dynix
Staff: Libns: 1 *Non-Prof:* 4 FTE *Exp:* £20000 on bks & £13000 on serials (2001-02)

S1402

South London and Maudsley NHS Trust, Multidisciplinary Library

(formerly Lambeth Healthcare NHS Trust)
108 Landor Rd, Stockwell, London, SW9 9NT (020-7411-6336; *fax:* 020-7411-6301)
Email: multidisciplinary.library@slam.nhs.uk
Internet: http://stlis.thenhs.com/hln/s_london/lsw/Main/

Chief: Trust Libn: post vacant *Dep:* Reader Svcs Supervisor: Mr Paul Harrington *Other Snr Staff:* Lib Asst: Ms Jane Gleeson
Entry: Trust staff, King's Coll London medical students, Lambeth social svcs staff, local PCT staff; others by arrangement *Open:* Mon-Fri 0900-1700
Subj: health sci; psychiatry; community medicine & nursing; social welfare *Co-op Schemes:* BLDSC, BMA, PLCS, NULJ, HLN
Equip: copier, computers (incl wd-proc, internet & CD-ROM) *Online:* Datastar *Svcs:* info, ref, biblio
Stock: bks/7200; periodcls/110
Classn: NLM *Auto Sys:* Librarian
Staff: Libns: 1 *Non-Prof:* 2

S1403

South Thames College, Learning Centre

Wandsworth High St, London, SW18 2PP (020-8918-7161; *fax:* 020-8918-7136)
Email: doreenp@south-thames.ac.uk
Internet: http://www.south-thames.ac.uk/

Gov Body: South Thames Coll Corp *Chief:* Learning Centre Mgr (Wandsworth): Ms Doreen Pinfold BA(Hons), DipLib, MCLIP
Assoc Libs: PUTNEY LEARNING CENTRE, 50-52 Putney Hill, London, SW15 6QX; TOOTING LEARNING CENTRE, 71 Tooting High St, London, SW17 0TQ; ROEHAMPTON LEARNING CENTRE, Roehampton Ln, London, SW15 4HR; WANDSWORTH LEARNING CENTRE, addr as above
Entry: ref only, adv appt *Open:* term: Mon-Thu 0900-2000, Fri 1000-1600, Sat (Wandsworth only) 1000-1400
Subj: all subjs; genl; GCSE; A level; undergrad; social sci; lang; tech; arts *Co-op Schemes:* SWIFT
Equip: copiers, computers (incl internet & CD-ROM) *Svcs:* info, ref
Stock: bks/78850; periodcls/536; videos/1430; CD-ROMs/131; Open Learning packs/1000
Classn: DDC *Auto Sys:* Genesis
Staff: Libns: 9 *Non-Prof:* 18

S1404

Southgate College Library

High St, Southgate, London, N14 6BS (020-8886-6521; *fax:* 020-8982-5051)
Internet: http://www.southgate.ac.uk/

Gov Body: Southgate Coll *Chief:* Lib & Learning Resources Mgr: Ms S. Drury *Dep:* Snr Learning Resources Mgr: Mr C. Lancaster Marr
Entry: ref only, adv appt
Subj: all subjs; genl; GCSE; A level *Collns: Bks & Pamphs:* radio & television svc sheets *Co-op Schemes:* BLDSC
Equip: copiers, computers *Svcs:* ref
Stock: bks/20000; periodcls/100; slides/880 sets; pamphs/380; audios/600; videos/1000
Classn: DDC *Auto Sys:* CALM
Staff: Libns: 4 *Non-Prof:* 4.5

S1405 🐝

Southwark College Learning Centre

Waterloo Centre, The Cut, London, SE1 8LE (020-7815-1577; *fax:* 0171-928-0402)
Email: jeanh@southwark.ac.uk
Internet: http://www.southwark.ac.uk/

Chief: Head of Learning Resources: Ms Jean Helm BA
Assoc Libs: BERMONDSEY LEARNING CENTRE, Keetons Rd, London, SE16 4EE; CAMBERWELL LEARNING CENTRE, Southampton Way, London, SE5 7EW, Libn: Alan Lees BA, MCLIP; WATERLOO LEARNING CENTRE, The Cut, London, SE1 8LE, Libn: Valmai McConnell BA, MCLIP & Liz Ramsey BA, MCLIP (job share)
Entry: Coll membs & membs of SEAL *Open:* term: Mon-Thu 0930-1930, Fri 0930-1600; vac: Mon-Fri 1000-1600, when open
Subj: all subjs; genl; GCSE; A level; vocational; local study (London, South East London); computing *Co-op Schemes:* SEAL
Equip: m-readers, video viewers, copiers, clr copier, computers (with wd-proc, internet & CD-ROM) *Disabled:* VTEK magnifier *Svcs:* info, ref, biblio
Stock: bks/65000; periodcls/200; audios/300; videos/500
Classn: DDC *Auto Sys:* Datatrek
Staff: Libns: 6 *Non-Prof:* 9.5

S1406 🔑

Sport England, Information Centre

16 Upper Woburn Pl, London, WC1H 0QP (020-7273-1500; *fax:* 020-7383-5740)
Email: info@sportengland.org
Internet: http://www.sportengland.org/

Type: NGO *Chief:* Snr Info Mgr: Ms Sally Hall BA, MCLIP
Assoc Libs: nine regional offices in England with info centres attached (appt required)
Entry: ref only, adv appt; not open to school students or undergrads *Open:* Mon-Fri 1330-1630
Subj: sport; physical rec; recreation mgmt; sponsorship; sports statistics; physical edu
Collns: Bks & Pamphs: Sport England pubns
Equip: m-reader, m-printer, video viewer, copier
Svcs: info, ref, biblio, indexing, abstracting
Stock: bks/c33000, incl reports; periodcls/600; videos/100
Classn: ESC Classn Scheme *Auto Sys:* Unicorn
Pubns: SCAN (monthly bulletin); numerous others
Staff: Libns: 5 *Non-Prof:* 2

S1407 🐝🙏

Spurgeon's College Library

189 South Norwood Hill, London, SE25 6DJ (020-8653-0850; *fax:* 020-8771-0959)
Email: enquiries@spurgeons.ac.uk

Chief: Libn: Mrs Judith C. Powles BA, DipLib, MCLIP
Entry: ref only, written appl to libn *Open:* Mon-Fri 0900-1615
Subj: theology; ethics; sociology *Collns: Archvs:* relating to life & work of Charles Haddon Spurgeon (bks, pamphs, MSS letters, newspaper cuttings, portraits etc) *Co-op Schemes:* BLDSC, ILL, ABTAPL

Equip: m-reader, copier
Stock: bks/50000; periodcls/90; audios/150; videos/150
Classn: DDC *Auto Sys:* Heritage
Staff: Libns: 1 *Exp:* £15662 (1999-2000); £17879 (2000-01)

S1408 🏛

St Bride Printing Library

Bride Ln, Fleet St, London, EC4Y 8EE (020-7353-4660; *fax:* 020-7583-7073)
Email: stbride@corpoflondon.gov.uk
Internet: http://www.stbride.org/

Type: specialist public lib *Gov Body:* Corp of London (see **P99**) *Chief:* Libn: Mr James Mosley
Dep: Dep Libn: Mr Nigel A. Roche
Entry: for ref; prior appt necessary for use of special collns, archvs & MSS *Open:* Mon-Fri 0930-1730
Subj: printing & related subjs, incl: paper; binding; graphic design; typography; typefaces; calligraphy; illustration; printmaking; publishing; bkselling
Collns: Bks & Pamphs: broadsides & chapbks (18C & 19C); trade documents & lit (1785 to date); type specimens; shorthand colln; William Blades Lib (1824-90); Talbot Baines Reed (1852-93, historian of typefounding); John Southward Colln (printing tech); BSI (printing & related fields); British patents for printing & related fields (c40000)
Archvs: Taylor & Francis Archv (printer & publisher); Charles Griffin & Co Archv (publisher); m-film records of the Stationers' Company & the Cambridge Univ Press *Other:* Emery Walker Photographic Colln (William Morris & his circle); Eric Gill drawings
Equip: m-reader, copier
Stock: bks/40000; periodcls/200 + 3000 no longer current; photos/2000 negs
Classn: own
Staff: Libns: 1 *Other Prof:* 2 *Non-Prof:* 1

S1409 ✚

St Christopher's Hospice, Halley Stewart Library

51-59 Lawrie Park Rd, Sydenham, London, SE26 6DZ (020-8768-4660; *fax:* 020-8776-9345)

Chief: Libn: Ms Denise Brady MCLIP
Entry: ref only by adv appt; enqs also accepted by phone & email *Open:* Mon-Fri 0900-1700
Subj: palliative & hospice care; death; dying; bereavement *Co-op Schemes:* Health Info for London Online
Equip: copier, 2 computers (with database access) *Online:* in-house database; Medline & Cochrane on CD-ROM *Officer-in-Charge:* Libn, as above *Svcs:* info, ref, biblio
Stock: various bks & pamphs; periodcls/30 *Acqs Offcr:* Libn, as above
Classn: in-house
Staff: Libns: 1 *Non-Prof:* 5 volunteers

S1410 ✚

St George's Hospital Medical School Library

Hunter Wing, Cranmer Ter, London, SW17 0RE (020-8725-5466; *fax:* 020-8767-4696)
Email: logan@sghms.ac.uk
Internet: http://www.sghms.ac.uk/depts/is/library/

Gov Body: St George's Hosp Medical School
Chief: Lib Svcs Mgr: Ms Marina Logan-Bruce BA
Assoc Libs: ATKINSON MORLEYS HOSP MEDICAL LIB, Copse Hill, Wimbledon, London, SW20 0NE, Branch Libn: Mr Tarquin Mittermayer (020-8725-4137; *email:* tmitterm@sghms.ac.uk); BOLINGBROKE HOSP LIB, Wandsworth Common, London, SW11 6HN, Branch Libn: Ms

Kate Blackwell (020-8725-4898; *email:* kblackwell@sghms.ac.uk); QUEEN MARY'S HOSP HEALTH SVC LIB, Roehampton Ln, London, SW15 5PN, Branch Libn: Mr Mick Arber (*tel & fax:* 020-8355-2093; *email:* marber@sghms. ac.uk); SPRINGFIELD HOSP STAFF LIB, Glenburnie Rd, London, SW17 7DJ, Branch Libn: Ms Olga Rak (020-8682-6033; *email:* orak@swlstg-tr.nhs.uk); SUTTON HOSP PROF LIB, Chiltern Wing, Sutton Hosp, Cotswold Rd, Sutton, Surrey, SM2 5NF, Branch Libn: Ms Olga Rak (020-8296-4230; *fax:* 020-8770-7051; *email:* orak@swlstg-tr. nhs.uk)
Entry: staff & students of Medical School & Faculty of Health & Social Care Scis; staff of NHS Trusts connected with St George's; ref only on payment of fee for non-membs *Open:* Mon-Thu 0800-2200, Fri 0800-2100, Sat (term only) 0900-1700
Subj: undergrad; postgrad; medicine; nursing; health care scis *Co-op Schemes:* BLDSC, ILL, SWTRLS, SWIFT, EAHIL, LAMDA, M25 Access Scheme
Equip: 2 m-readers, m-printer, 7 video viewers, fax, 7 copiers, 100 networked computers (all with wd-proc, internet & CD-ROM) *Online:* Web of Science, Medline, CINAHL, Cochrane, AMED, HMIC, BNI, ASSIA *Svcs:* info, ref biblio, lit searches
Stock: bks/100000; periodcls/800; audios/100; videos/600; archvs/2000 ft
Classn: NLM *Auto Sys:* Unicorn
Pubns: Periodicals Holdings (£1); Audiovisual Holdings
Staff: Libns: 13 *Non-Prof:* 14
See also ST GEORGE'S HOSP ARCHV (**A348**)

S1411 🐝🔑🙏

St Joseph's Missionary Society, Mill Hill Library

St Joseph's Coll, Lawrence St, Mill Hill, London, NW7 4JX (020-8959-8254; *fax:* 020-8959-8493)
Email: milcom@catholic.org
Internet: http://www.millhillmissionaries.org/

Gov Body: The Genl Council – St Joseph's Missionary Soc *Chief:* Libn: Miss A. Shelley
Assoc Libs: ST JOSEPH'S MISSIONARY SOC ARCHVS, at same addr, Archivist: Fr H. Boeraaker
Entry: by appt *Open:* Mon-Fri 0900-1700
Subj: generalities; phil; religion (all areas) *Collns: Archvs:* mainly correspondence between Mill Hill & its various missions & Colleges/houses
Equip: copier (5p), computer (with internet & CD-ROM, internet charged at 1p per minute) *Officer-in-Charge:* Libn, as above *Svcs:* info, ref
Stock: bks/50000; periodcls/120 *Acqs Offcr:* Libn, as above
Classn: DDC *Staff: Non-Prof:* 1 *Exp:* £10000 (1999-2000); £10000 (2000-01)

S1412 🔑🙏

St Paul's Cathedral Library

Chapter House, St Paul's Cathedral, London, EC4M 8AD (020-7246-8345; *fax:* 020-7248-3104)
Email: library@stpaulscathedral.org.uk

Gov Body: Dean & Chapter of St Paul's *Chief:* Cathedral Libn: Mr J.J. Wisdom MA, MCLIP
Entry: by appt, please make written appl to libn *Open:* by appt
Subj: theology; councils; patristic lit; phil *Collns: Bks & Pamphs:* Paul's Cross sermons; Bishop Sumner Colln (tracts); bibles & liturgies *Archvs:* held at Guildhall Lib (see **A280**)
Equip: m-reader, copier
Stock: bks/13500; periodcls/3; photos/300; pamphs/10000
Staff: Libns: 0.5

S1413

St Paul's Girls' School Library

Brook Green, Hammersmith, London, W6 7BS
(020-7603-2288; *fax:* 020-7602-9932)
Email: sara.swann@spgs.org
Internet: http://www.spgs.org/

Chief: Libn: Miss Sara Swann BA(Hons), MCLIP
Entry: ref only, adv appt *Open:* term: Mon-Fri
0800-1750; vac: Mon-Fri 1000-1600 or as
advertised in school
Subj: all subjs; GCSE; A level; undergrad *Collns:*
Bks & Pamphs: Warburg Colln (fiction, poetry,
biography, hist & phil, bequeathed to school by Sir
Siegmund Warburg) *Archvs:* material relating to
hist of school bldgs, former & present pupils & staff
Co-op Schemes: BLDSC
Equip: copier, 8 computers (all with wd-proc,
internet & CD-ROM) *Svcs:* info, ref
Stock: bks/22783; periodcls/73; audios/115;
videos/321; CD-ROMs/23; music scores/623
Classn: DDC *Auto Sys:* Heritage
Staff: Libns: 1 *Non-Prof:* 2

S1414

St Paul's School, The Walker Library

Lonsdale Rd, London, SW13 9JT (020-8748-9162;
fax: 020-8748-9557)
Email: reception@stpaulsschool.org.uk
Internet: http://www.stpaulsschool.org.uk/

Chief: Libn: Mrs A.M. Aslett BA, MCLIP
Assoc Libs: ST PAUL'S SCHOOL ARCHVS, addr
as above, Archivist: Mr Simon May MA (020-8748-
9162; *email:* sam@stpaulsschool.org.uk)
Entry: ref only, by appt *Open:* term: Mon-Fri
0830-1630
Subj: all subjs; GCSE; A level *Collns: Bks &*
Pamphs: rare bks colln with particular appl to
school & ex-pupils; publ works by old boys of
school e.g., G.K. Chesterton, Edward Thomas, Sir
Compton MacKenzie *Archvs:* records relating to
hist of school & ex-pupils *Co-op Schemes:*
BLDSC
Equip: m-reader, video viewer, copier, computers
(incl wd-proc, internet & CD-ROM)
Stock: bks/25000; periodcls/60; pamphs/500;
videos/60; archvs/4000 items
Classn: DDC *Auto Sys:* Heritage
Staff: Libns: 1 *Non-Prof:* 0.75
Proj: lib refurbishment

S1415

St Thomas' Hospital Library

Lambeth Palace Rd, London, SE1 7EH (020-
7928-9292 x2507)
Email: fiona.letendrie@gsst.sthames.nhs.uk

Gov Body: Guy's & St Thomas' Hosp NHS Trust
Chief: Lib Mgr: Ms Fiona Letendrie BA, DipIS
Entry: in-patients & staff of Guy's & St Thomas'
Trust *Open:* Mon-Fri 0900-1600
Subj: all subjs *Collns: Bks & Pamphs:* patient
info; bks & leaflets on medical conditions
Equip: copier, computer (with CD-ROM)
Disabled: magnifiers, cassette players *Online:*
Health CD, CINAHL, Healthstar, EUTIS, Help for
Health, Patientwise
Stock: bks/16000; periodcls/34; audios/300;
videos/1000
Classn: DDC *Auto Sys:* Alice
Staff: Libns: 2 *Non-Prof:* 4

S1416

Supreme Court Library

Queen's Bldg, Royal Courts of Justice, Strand,
London, WC2A 2LL (020-7947-6587; *fax:* 020-
7947-6661)

Gov Body: Court Svc *Chief:* Supreme Court
Libn: Ms Julia Robertson MCLIP
Assoc Libs: SUPREME COURT LIB (BAR), Royal
Courts of Justice, Royal Courts of Justice, London,
WC2A 2LL (020-7947-6420)
Entry: ref only *Open:* legal term: Mon-Fri 0930-
1700; vac: Mon-Fri 0930-1630
Subj: law, mainly English but some coverage of
Commonwealth & EC law *Collns: Bks & Pamphs:*
Court of Appeal (Civil Div) transcripts (1950-date);
Immigration Appellate Authority transcripts; old eds
of textbks
Equip: m-reader
Stock: bks/450000; periodcls/300
Classn: Moys *Auto Sys:* Dynix
Staff: Libns: 2 *Non-Prof:* 6

S1417

Swedenborg Society Library

20-21 Bloomsbury Way, London, WC1A 2TH (020-
7405-7986; *fax:* 020-7831-5848)
Email: swed.soc@netmatters.co.uk
Internet: http://www.swedenborg.org.uk/

Gov Body: Elected Council of the Swedenborg
Soc *Chief:* Libn: Mrs N.S. Dawson BA *Dep:*
Asst: Mr S. McNeilly MA(Hons)
Open: Mon-Fri 0930-1700
Subj: specialist Swedenborgian & New Church lib
Collns: Bks & Pamphs: original Latin eds of
Swedenborg's works; original eds of Swedenborg's
work translated into 33 different langs; biographies
of Swedenborg; various collateral works
concerning Swedenborg's writings & their influence
Archvs: original letters, documents, rare vols,
photos etc relating to Swedenborg & his followers
Other: current journals from Swedenborgian groups
world-wide *Co-op Schemes:* BLDSC, ILL
Equip: copier, fax, computers (incl 3 wd-proc & 1
CD-ROM), 2 rooms for hire *Svcs:* info, ref
Stock: bks/7700; periodcls/30, plus 90 no longer
current; photos/500; slides/650; pamphs/4350; m-
forms/111 rolls of film; audios/30; videos/2; some
wallcharts
Classn: own, based on Hyde "Bibliography"
Pubns: Swedenborg Soc Lib Catalogue: 4 vols +
addenda (price on request)
Staff: Other Prof: 3 *Non-Prof:* 1 *Exp:* new stock
acquired largely through donations
Proj: computerised automation of lib catalogue &
archvs section

S1418

Tate Library

Hyman Kreitman Rsrch Centre, Tate Britain,
Millbank, London, SW1P 4RG (020-7887-8838;
fax: 020-7887-8901)
Email: research.centre@tate.org.uk
Internet: http://www.tate.org.uk/Collections/
ResearchServices/

Gov Body: Trustees of the Tate Gallery *Chief:*
Head of Lib & Archv: Ms Beth Houghton DipAD
(beth.houghton@tate.org.uk) *Other Snr Staff:*
Libn: Ms Meg Duff BA, DipEd, DipNZLS; Head of
Readers' Svcs: Ms Erica Foden-Lenahan BA, MA
(erica.foden-lenahan@tate.org.uk); Gallery
Records Mgr: Mr Alan Crookham
Assoc Libs: TATE ARCHV, at same addr (see
A348)
Entry: ref only; strictly by appt; reader ticket
requires letter of academic or prof ref, photographic
ID & 2 passport-sized photos *Open: Reading*
Room: Mon-Fri 1000-1700
Subj: British art from the Renaissance; modern art
from c1870; some coverage of related arts subjs,
incl: arch; design; decorative arts; applied arts;
photography; film *Collns: Bks & Pamphs:* 120000
exhib catalogues (museums & galleries world-
wide); permanent colln catalogues (museums &
private collns world-wide); museum pubns;
catalogues of fine art sales from major auction
houses; artists' bookworks (1960s onwards);
material on the hist of the Tate; Turner Prize
catalogues (1984 onwards) *Co-op Schemes:*
BLDSC (photocopies only)
Equip: 2 m-readers, m-printer (A4/20p), copier
(A4/20p, A3/40p), video viewer, 13 computers (incl
4 with internet & 4 with CD-ROM), television, video
viewer, DVD player, audio cassette players *Online:*
Wilson Art Abstracts, Art Bibliographies Modern,
Grove Dictionary of Art, Art Quest *Svcs:* info, ref,
photocopying svc, photographic reproduction for
rsrch purposes
Stock: bks/50000+; periodcls/400, plus c1600 non-
current; photos/30000; slides/c130000; illusts/2000
posters; m-forms/80; audios/c2000; videos/100;
exhib catalogues/c120000; artists' bkworks/3000
Acqs Offcr: Acqs Libn (Bks): Ms Clare Storey
(clare.storey@tate.org.uk); Acqs Libn
(Catalogues): Mr Krzysztof Cieszkowski
(krzysztof.cieszkowski@tate.org.uk)
Classn: UDC, own *Auto Sys:* Unicorn/CALM
Staff: Libns: 11 *Other Prof:* 5 *Non-Prof:* 8

S1419

Tavistock and Portman NHS Trust Library

Tavistock Centre, 120 Belsize Ln, London, NW3
5BA (020-7447-3776; *fax:* 020-7447-3434)
Email: adouglas@tavi-port.org
Internet: http://www.tavi-port.org/

Gov Body: Tavistock & Portman NHS Trust
Chief: Libn: Ms Angela Douglas BSc, MA, MCLIP
Dep: Dep Libn: Ms Angela Haselton BA, MCLIP
Entry: non-Trust membs ref only, by adv appt
Open: term: Mon-Thu 0900-2100, Fri 1000-1600;
vac: Mon-Fri 1000-1700
Subj: psy; social sci; medicine *Collns: Bks &*
Pamphs: pamph colln *Co-op Schemes:* BLDSC,
North Thames Regional Scheme, PLCS
Equip: video viewer, copier, computers (incl 10
wd-proc, 10 internet & 20 CD-ROM) *Online:*
PsycInfo, E-Psyche, Web of Science, ERIC, BEI,
CareData, ChildData (Trust membs only)
Stock: bks/28000; periodcls/140; pamphs/3000;
audios/40; videos/250
Classn: Bliss *Auto Sys:* Unicorn
Staff: Libns: 3 *Non-Prof:* 5.2 *Exp:* £75000 (1999-
2000)

S1420

Tavistock Institute Library

Tavistock House, 30 Tabernacle St, London, EC2A
4DD (020-7457-3930; *fax:* 020-7417-0568)
Email: s.halper@tavinstitute.org
Internet: http://www.tavinstitute.org/

Type: registered charity *Chief:* Lib & Resources
Mgr: Mrs Sally Halper PGDipIM
Assoc Libs: TAVISTOCK INST ARCHVS, contact
details as above (held off-site, access via Lib)
Entry: membs of Tavistock Inst & Tavistock Assoc
only *Open:* Mon-Fri 0900-1700
Subj: psy; social sci; social work; social policy;
mgmt
Equip: m-reader, fax, copier, computer (with wd-
proc, internet & CD-ROM) *Officer-in-Charge:* Lib &
Resources Mgr, as above *Svcs:* info, ref, biblio
Stock: bks/c8000; periodcls/30 *Acqs Offcr:* Lib &
Resources Mgr, as above
Classn: bespoke *Auto Sys:* Heritage
Staff: Libns: 1

S1421

Thames Valley University, Learning Resource Service

St Mary's Rd, Ealing, London, W5 5RF (020-8579-
5000; *fax:* 020-8231-2631)
Email: lrs@tvu.ac.uk
Internet: http://www.tvu.ac.uk/

Special Libraries

London ▼ London

(Thames Valley Univ, Learning Resource Svc cont)
Chief: Head of Learning Resources: Mr John Wolstenholme BA(Hons), MSc(Edu)
Assoc Libs: ST MARY'S RD LRC, addr as above; PAUL HAMLYN LRC, Wellington St, Slough, Berkshire, SL1 1YG, LRC Mgr: Mr Simon Whitby; *Faculty of Health & Human Scis Centres:* WESTEL HOUSE LRC (see **S1422**); ROYAL BERKSHIRE HOSP LRC, London Rd, Reading, Berkshire, RG1 5AN, LRC Mgr: Mr Felix Oliver-Tasker; WEXHAM PARK HOSP LRC, Slough, Berkshire, SL2 4HL, LRC Mgr: Mr Simon Whitby
Entry: students only, plus membs of UK Libs Plus & SCONUL schemes **Open:** *St Mary's Rd LRC:* term: open 24 hrs; vac: varies
Subj: at undergrad & postgrad levels: generalities; phil; psy; social sci; lang; sci; maths; tech; arts; lit; geog; hist **Collns:** *Bks & Pamphs:* European Ref Colln **Co-op Schemes:** BLDSC, ILL, M25 Scheme, SCONUL, UK Libs Plus, BIALL
Equip: 4 m-readers, 25 video viewers, 2 fax, 19 copiers, 2 clr copiers, 598 computers (incl wd-proc, internet & CD-ROM), 2 self-issue machines, 33 rooms for hire *Disabled:* Dragon Dictate, Winvision, Magnum Deluxe, Kurzweil 3000 *Online:* EDSCO, FT Profile, Datastream, Lexis, Mintel, ABI Inform, Emerald, Anbar Management Abstracts, Anbar Computing Abstracts, Profound, Cochrane, Biomedical Date Svc, Education Web Svc; plus others on CD-ROM **Svcs:** info, ref
Stock: bks/256951; periodcls/2930; slides/44793; audios/4069; videos/10371; AVs/5179
Classn: DDC, NLM **Auto Sys:** Talis
Staff: Libns: 36 Other Prof: 6 Non-Prof: 32

S1422 🎓 ✚

Thames Valley University, Westel House Learning Resource Centre

(formerly Wolfson Inst of Health Scis)
Westel House, 42 Uxbridge Rd, Ealing, London, W5 2BS (020-8280-5043; *fax:* 020-8280-5045)
Internet: http://www.wolfson.tvu.ac.uk/westellrc/page1.html

Gov Body: Thames Valley Univ (see **S1421**), Faculty of Health & Human Scis **Chief:** LRC Mgr: Mr Brent Evans (brent.evans@tvu.ac.uk) **Other Snr Staff:** Subj Libns: Mr Mark Foster (marc.forster@tvu.ac.uk) & Ms Pam Louison (pam.louison@tvu.ac.uk)
Assoc Libs: ROYAL BERKSHIRE HOSP LRC, London Rd, Reading, Berkshire, RG1 5AN, LRC Mgr: Mr Felix Oliver-Tasker; WEXHAM PARK HOSP LRC, Slough, Berkshire, SL2 4HL, LRC Mgr: Mr Simon Whitby
Entry: staff & students of Thames Valley Univ **Open:** Mon-Thu 0830-1900, Fri 1000-1700, Sat 1100-1600
Subj: medicine; nursing; midwifery; psy; surgery; women in medicine; culture; religion; maths; computing
Equip: copiers, 63 computers
Classn: NLM **Auto Sys:** Talis

S1423 🏛️ 🏛️

Theatre Museum Library

1e Tavistock St, Covent Gdn, London, WC2E 7PA (020-7943-4720; *fax:* 020-7943-4777)
Email: c.hudson@vam.ac.uk
Internet: http://www.theatremuseum.vam.ac.uk/

Gov Body: Victoria & Albert Museum **Chief:** Head of Info & Collns Mgmt Svcs: Mrs Claire Hudson BA(Hons), MCLIP
Entry: adv appt **Open:** Wed-Fri 1030-1630
Subj: all the live performing arts; theatre; drama; stage design; playtexts **Collns:** *Bks & Pamphs:* c120000 vols on the performing arts, incl monographs, periodcls, pamphs & playtexts *Archvs:* c300 discrete named archvs; core collns incl theatre programmes (over 1m), photos & press cuttings *Other:* original sets & costume designs; prints; paintings; autograph letters; posters; video recordings **Co-op Schemes:** Backstage
Equip: m-reader, video viewer, copier **Svcs:** info, ref, biblio
Stock: bks/120000 incl pamphs; periodcls/40; photos/3 mln; illusts/10000; videos/200; archvs/300 discrete collns; set designs/10000; biographical & topic files/25000
Classn: LC
Staff: Libns: 3 Other Prof: 4 curators, 1 archivist Non-Prof: 6 curatorial & archival assts
Further Info: This is the natl colln of lib & archv materials, ephemera & objects relating to the performing arts

S1424 🏛️

Trade Partners UK Information Centre

(formerly Export Market Info Centre)
Kingsgate House, 66-74 Victoria St, London, SW1E 6SW (020-7215-5444/5; *fax:* 020-7215-4231)
Internet: http://www.tradepartners.gov.uk/information-centre/

Gov Body: British Trade Internatl **Chief:** Snr Mgr: Miss Ann Hughes MA (ann.hughes@tradepartners.gov.uk) **Dep:** Mgr: Mrs Diana Mcauley (diana.mcauley@tradepartners.gov.uk)
Entry: ref only **Open:** Mon-Thu 0900-2000, Fri 0900-1725
Subj: overseas statistical, directory & market rsrch info (incl country profiles, CD-ROMs, export sales leads) **Co-op Schemes:** BLDSC
Equip: 2 m-readers, m-printer, 3 copiers (A4/15p),11 computers (incl 6 with internet & 5 with CD-ROM) *Online:* D&B Worldbase Locator, EWaO, KBE, World Trade Atlas, Global Trade Atlas, Euromonitor's GMID, Eurostat, Kompass *Officer-in-Charge:* Dep Mgr (Acqs): Miss Kay Armstrong (kay.armstrong@tradepartners.gov.uk) **Svcs:** info, ref
Stock: bks/16500; CD-ROMs/11; online databases/15 **Acqs Offcr:** Dep Mgr (Acqs): Miss Kay Armstrong (kay.armstrong@tradepartners.gov.uk)
Classn: own **Auto Sys:** Unicorn
Staff: Libns: 9 Non-Prof: 21

S1425 🎓

Trades Union Congress Library Collections

c/o London Metropolitan Univ Learning Centre, 236-250 Holloway Rd, London, N7 6PP (020-7133-2260; *fax:* 020-7133-2529)
Email: tuclib@londonmet.ac.uk
Internet: http://www.unl.ac.uk/library/tuc/

Chief: Libn: Christine Coates MA, MCLIP
Entry: rsrch only, strictly by appt **Open:** Mon-Fri 0900-1700 (visitors: 0915-1645)
Subj: industrial relations; wages & conditions of employment; trade unions; health & safety; internatl trade union activs; other areas covered by TUC policy; collns dated mainly from 1900 onwards **Collns:** *Bks & Pamphs:* trade union pubns; Workers' Educational Assoc Lib; large pamph colln *Archvs:* Gertrude Tuckwell Colln (early 20C cuttings & ephemera on working women); Workers'

Educational Assoc Archv; Marjorie Nicholson Papers (labour movement & the colonies); records of unemployed workers' centres in SE; Genl Strike 1926 Colln *Other:* various periodcls & m-forms
Equip: m-reader, m-printer, copier
Classn: LC **Auto Sys:** Talis

S1426 🏛️

Treasury and Cabinet Office Library

1 Horse Guards Rd, London, SW1A 2HQ (020-7270-5290; *fax:* 020-7270-5681)
Email: library@hm-treasury.gov.uk

Chief: Libn: Ms Jean Clayton
Subj: econ; taxation **Co-op Schemes:** ILL
Stock: bks/c54000

S1427 🏛️

Treasury Solicitor's Library Information Centre

Queen Anne's Chambers, 28 Broadway, London, SW1H 9JS (020-7210-3045; *fax:* 020-7210-3058)

Chief: Libn: Mr Paul Woods
Entry: staff only **Open:** Mon-Thu 0845-1700, Fri 0845-1645
Subj: law: English, EC, internatl, Scots & Irish **Co-op Schemes:** ILL
Equip: copier, *Online:* Lexis **Svcs:** info
Stock: bks/27500

S1428 🎓

Trinity College of Music, Jerwood Library of Performing Arts

(incorporating the Mander & Mitchenson Theatre Colln)
King Charles Ct, Old Royal Naval Coll, Greenwich, London, SE10 9JF (020-8305-3951; *fax:* 020-8305-3950)
Email: library@tcm.ac.uk
Internet: http://www.tcm.ac.uk/

Chief: Chief Libn: Dr Rosemary Firman (rfirman@tcm.ac.uk) **Other Snr Staff:** Dir, Mander & Mitchenson Theatre Colln: Mr Richard Mangan
Assoc Libs: CENTRE FOR YOUNG MUSICIANS LIB, Lib Asst: Mr Tony Lynes (020-7733-7235)
Entry: membs of coll; others by adv appt only
Open: *Jerwood Lib:* Mon-Thu 0900-1930, Fri 0900-1830, Sat 1000-1500; *Mander & Mitchenson Theatre Colln:* Mon-Fri 1100-1600
Subj: performing arts; music; music hist; musicology; theatre **Collns:** *Bks & Pamphs:* Mander & Mitchenson Theatre Colln (15000 bks & 1500 archv boxes relating to the theatre); Antonio de Almeida Colln (printed music, 5456 vols); Sir Frederick Bridge Lib (18C-19C printed music) *Archvs:* British Music Soc Archv; Filmharmonic Archv (film music); Joseph Ortiz Colln (materials relating to New York Metropolitan Opera); Margaret Purcell Colln (music & other MSS); Lionel Tertis Colln (music MSS); Christopher Wood Colln (music MSS & personal papers & memorabilia); autograph MSS of Richard Arnell, Frank Cordell, William Lovelock, Charles Procter & Kaikhosru Shapurji Sorabji *Other:* Sir John Barbirolli Colln (conducting scores); Shura Cherkassky Colln (piano music, c300 items); AV collns, incl Music Preserved (1500 archv recordings of live performances, 1930s-date, formerly the Music Performance Rsrch Centre)
Equip: copiers, computers, audio facilities *Online:* New Grove Dictionary of Music & Musicians, RILM Abstracts of Music Literature, Internatl Index to Music Periodicals, Oxford Reference Online
Stock: bks/60000+ **Staff:** 11 in total

S1429 🗝

Turkish Community Library

86 Balls Pond Rd, London, N1 4AJ (*tel & fax:* 020-7923-2095)

Type: voluntary *Gov Body:* grant given & monitored by Islington Borough Council (see **P94**)
Chief: Libn: Mr Ahmet Yener BA
Entry: lending svc to membs *Open:* Mon-Tue, Thu-Fri 1200-1900, Sat 1300-1700
Subj: Turkey: phil; psy; religion; social sci; lang; sci; maths; tech; lit; geog; hist; statistical data on Turkey
Equip: copier, fax *Svcs:* info, ref, biblio
Stock: bks/10000; archvs/1 cubic m
Classn: DDC
Pubns: Toplum Kütüphanesi'nden Haberler (free newsletter)
Staff: Libns: 1 *Non-Prof:* 1

S1430 🗝 📚

The Turner Library

Whitefield Schools Centre, Macdonald Rd, London, E17 4AZ (020-8531-8703; *fax:* 020-8527-0907)
Email: lib@whitefield.org.uk
Internet: http://www.whitefield.org.uk/

Chief: Libns: Ms Gillian Goodchild & Ms Maureen May
Entry: membership by annual subscription *Open:* term: Mon-Tue, Thu 0900-1830, Wed 0900-1700, Fri 0900-1630; vac: Mon-Fri 0900-1630 (Tue-Thu only during Aug, closed Xmas)
Subj: special educational needs; disabilities; psy; sociology; educational mgmt
Svcs: info, ref, databases searches
Pubns: Current Awareness Bulletin (bimonthly)

S1431 🏛

United Nations Information Centre, Reference Library

21st Floor, Millbank Tower, 21-24 Millbank, London, SW1P 4QH (*lib:* 020-7630-2709; *info centre:* 020-7630-1981; *fax:* 020-7976-6478)
Email: library@uniclondon.org
Internet: http://www.uniclondon.org/

Gov Body: United Nations *Chief:* Dir of Info Centre: Mr Ahmad Fawzi *Dep:* Libn: Ms Alexandra McLeod
Entry: ref only, adv appt advised *Open: Info Centre:* Mon-Fri 0900-1800; *Lib:* Mon-Thu 1000-1300, 1400-1700
Subj: United Nations & its agencies *Collns: Bks & Pamphs:* official UN reports & documents *Archvs:* official records of the major organs of the United Nations (1946 onwards); basic holdings of some of the United Nations Specialized Agencies *Other:* photo & video collns
Equip: copier (10p per pg) *Svcs:* info, ref
Stock: bks/8500

S1432 🏛

United States Embassy, Information Resource Center

American Embassy, 24 Grosvenor Sq, London, W1A 1AE (020-7499-9000; *fax:* 020-7629-8288)
Email: reflond@pd.state.gov
Internet: http://www.usembassy.org.uk/

Gov Body: US Dept of State *Chief:* Libn: Ms Kate Bateman MA, DipLib *Dep:* Ms Anna Girvan
Entry: ref only; not open to public; journalists, academics & other serious rsrchers admitted strictly by prior appt *Open:* prior arrangement only; Embassy office hrs: Mon-Fri 0830-1730, excl British & American public hols
Subj: US govt, politics, legislation; current social issues; foreign & domestic policies of the US

Collns: Other: CIS (Congressional Info Svc) complete m-fiche colln (1976-2000)
Equip: 2 m-readers, 2 m-printers, copier *Svcs:* info, ref
Stock: bks/2000 *Classn:* DDC *Staff: Libns:* 3.5

S1433 📚

University College London Library

Gower St, London, WC1E 6BT (020-7679-7700; *fax:* 020-7679-7373)
Email: library@ucl.ac.uk
Internet: http://www.ucl.ac.uk/library/

Gov Body: Univ Coll London, part of Univ of London (see **S1440**) *Chief:* Dir of Lib Svcs: Dr Paul Ayris *Dep:* Snr Sub-Libn (Planning & Resources): Ms Janet Percival
Assoc Libs: MAIN LIB, Wilkins Bldg, Gower St, London, WC1E 6BT (020-7679-7792); SCI LIB, DMS Watson Bldg, Gower St, London, WC1E 6BT (020-7679-7795; *fax:* 020-7679-7727); SPECIAL COLLNS, 140 Hampstead Rd, London, NW1 2BX (020-7679-5175; *fax:* 020-7679-5157; *email:* spec.coll@ucl.ac.uk); ENVIRONMENTAL STUDIES LIB, Wates House, 22 Gordon St, London, WC1H 0QB (020-7679-6079; *fax:* 020-7679-7373); INST OF ARCHAEO LIB, 31-34 Gordon Sq, London, WC1H 0PY (020-7679-4788); HUMAN COMMUNICATION SCI LIB, Chandler House, 2 Wakefield St, London, WC1N 2PG (020-7679-4210; *fax:* 020-7713-0861; *email:* hcs.library@ucl.ac.uk); SCHOOL OF SLAVONIC & EAST EUROPEAN STUDIES LIB (see **S1436**); *Royal Free & Univ Coll Medical School Libs:* ARCHWAY HEALTHCARE LIB (see **S994**); BOLDERO LIB (see **S1361**); CRUCIFORM LIB, Cruciform Bldg, Gower St, London, WC1E 6BT (020-7679-6079; *fax:* 020-7209-6981; *email:* clinscilib@ucl.ac.uk); EASTMAN DENTAL INST LIB (see **S1118**); INST OF CHILD HEALTH LIB, 30 Guilford St, London, WC1N 1EH (020-7242-9789 x2424; *fax:* 020-7831-0488; *email:* library@ich.ucl.ac.uk); INST OF LARYNGOLOGY & OTOLOGY LIB (see **S1434**); INST OF NEUROLOGY, ROCKEFELLER MEDICAL LIB (see **S1448**); INST OF OPHTHALMOLOGY LIB (see **S1201**); INST OF ORTHOPAEDICS LIB, Royal Natl Orthopaedic Hosp, Brockley Hill, Stanmore, Middlesex, HA7 4LP (020-8909-5351; *fax:* 020-8954-1213); LONDON FOOT HOSP & SCHOOL OF PODIATRIC MEDICINE LIB (see **S1259**); ROYAL FREE HOSP MEDICAL LIB (see **S1360**); ROYAL NATL INST FOR DEAF PEOPLE LIB (see **S1373**)
Entry: appl in adv to Admissions Offcr (020-7679-7953; *email:* library-membership@ucl.ac.uk); a fee may be charged *Open: Main & Sci Libs:* term: Mon-Thu 0845-2230, Fri 0845-1900, Sat 0930-1630; vac: Mon-Fri 0930-1845; *Special Collns:* Mon-Fri 0930- 1700 (by appt only)
Subj: undergrad; postgrad; rsrch; most academic subjs *Collns: Bks & Pamphs:* Barlow Dante Lib; Castiglione Colln; Filtration Soc Lib; Folklore Soc Lib; Gaelic Soc of London Lib; Geologist's Assoc Lib; Graves Early Sci Lib; Hertfordshire Nat Hist Soc Lib; Huguenot Soc Lib; James Joyce Colln; Jewish Historical Soc Lib; Johnstone Lavis Vulcanology Lib; Little Magazines Colln; London Mathematical Soc Lib; Malacological Soc Lib; Margaret Murray Colln; Mocatta Lib of Anglo-Judaica; Museums Assoc Lib; C.K. Ogden Lib; Philological Soc Lib; Piranesi Colln; Sir John Rotton Lib; Royal Historical Soc Lib; Royal Statistical Soc Lib; Viking Soc for Northern Rsrch Lib; Whitley Stokes Celtic Lib *Archvs:* archvs of Univ Coll London; numerous other collns, incl: Arnold Bennett papers; Jeremy Bentham Colln; 1st Lord of Brougham Papers; Sir Edwin Chadwick Papers; de Beer Papers; De Morgan Papers; Fleming Colln; Gaitskell Papers; Sir Francis Galton Papers; Dr Moses Gaster Papers; Haldane Papers; George Orwell Archv; Paget Papers; Mervyn Peake MSS; Penrose Papers; Latin American business archvs; British Maritime Law Assoc Archvs; Chadwick Trust Archvs; Shakespeare

Assoc records; Soc for the Diffusion of Useful Knowledge archvs *Co-op Schemes:* BLDSC
Equip: m-readers, m-printers, video viewers, copiers, 2 clr copiers, computers (incl wd-proc); use of some equip restricted to membs of Univ Coll
Stock: bks/1300000; periodcls/7500
Classn: NLM, Garside & others *Auto Sys:* Aleph
Pubns: various guides to special collns

S1434 📚 ✚

University College London, Institute of Laryngology and Otology Library

Royal Natl Throat, Nose & Ear Hosp, 330-332 Gray's Inn Rd, London, WC1X 8EE (020-7915-1445)
Email: ilolib@ucl.ac.uk
Internet: http://www.ucl.ac.uk/Library/ilo/

Gov Body: Univ Coll London (see **S1433**) *Chief:* Libn: Dr Alex Stagg BA, MA (a.stagg@ucl.ac.uk)
Entry: ref only for non-UCL staff & students
Open: Mon-Tue 0930-1900, Wed-Fri 0930-1730; summer vac (Jun-Sep): Mon-Fri 0930-1700
Subj: otorhinolaryngology; head & neck surgery; facial plastic surgery *Collns: Bks & Pamphs:* historical colln *Co-op Schemes:* BLDSC, ILL, NULJ, ARIEL
Equip: video viewer, copier, 4 computers (incl 2 with wd-proc, 1 with CD-ROM & 2 with internet, UCL membs only) *Online:* Medline *Svcs:* info, ref, biblio
Stock: bks/3000; periodcls/60; videos/80
Classn: NLM *Auto Sys:* Aleph
Staff: Libns: 1 *Non-Prof:* 2

S1435 📚

University College London, Observatory Library

553 Watford Way, Mill Hill Pk, London, NW7 2QS (020-8959-0421; *fax:* 020-8906-4161)
Email: sjb@star.ucl.ac.uk or mmd@star.ucl.ac.uk
Internet: http://www.ulo.ucl.ac.uk/library/

Gov Body: Univ Coll London (see **S1433**) *Chief:* Libn: Dr M.M. Dworestky PhD *Dep:* Asst Libn: Mr S.J. Boyle BSc
Entry: ref only, normally restricted to staff & students of Univ Coll London *Open:* irregular, depending on presence of asst libn
Subj: sci; maths; astronomy
Equip: fax, copier, computers (incl wd-proc & CD-ROM)
Stock: bks/5000; periodcls/30
Classn: by genl area of astronomical rsrch
Pubns: Communications from the Univ of London Observatory
Staff: Other Prof: 2

S1436 📚

University College London, School of Slavonic and East European Studies Library

Senate House, Malet St, London, WC1E 7HU (020-7862-8523; *lib enqs:* x4094; *fax:* 020-7862-8644)
Internet: http://www.ssees.ac.uk/libarch.htm

Gov Body: Univ Coll London (see **S1433**) *Chief:* Libn: Ms Lesley Pitman BA, DipLib (l.pitman@ssees.ucl.ac.uk) *Other Snr Staff:* Snr Asst Libn (Acqs): Ms Erika Panagakis BA, DipLib (e.panagakis@ssees.ucl.ac.uk); Snr Asst Libn: Ms Ursula Phillips BA, DipLib (u.phillips@ssees.ucl.ac.uk)
Entry: adv appt, initial appl in writing; recommendation & proof of ID usually required; a fee may be payable *Open:* term: Mon-Fri 0900-2100, Sat 1000-1700; Xmas & Easter vac: Mon-Thu 0900-1900, Fri 1000-1800; summer vac: Mon-Fri 1000-1800

☛

(Univ Coll London, School of Slavonic & East European Studies Lib cont)

Subj: hist, langs, lit, politics, arts, demography, ethnography, religion, econ & social conditions of: Russia/CIS; Ukraine; Belarus; Estonia; Latvia; Lithuania; Moldavia; Poland; former Czechoslovakia; former Yugoslavia; Bulgaria; Romania; Albania; Hungary; Finland **Collns: Bks & Pamphs:** Gaster Colln (Romanian lit); Ivanyi Colln (Hungarica); Russian Orthodox Church Colln (hist & doctrine) **Archvs:** School of Slavonic & East European Studies Archvs; over 190 indiv collns, incl: Sir Bernard Pares Colln (Russia & Russian studies in Britain); R.W. Seton-Watson Colln (Czechoslovakia & Yugoslavia); Manó Kónyi & Menyhért Lónyay Colln (Hungarian politics) **Co-op Schemes:** ILL via BLDSC, SCONUL Vac Access Scheme
Equip: m-readers, m-form reader/printer, video viewers (membs of School only), copiers, computers (incl wd-proc & internet, membs of School only)
Stock: bks/357000; periodcls/1100; videos/1400
Acqs Offcr: Snr Asst Libn (Acqs), as above
Classn: own **Auto Sys:** Innopac **Staff:** Libns: 5

S1437 🔑
University College School Library
Frognal, Hampstead, London, NW3 6XH (020-7435-2215; *fax:* 020-7433-2111)
Email: library@ucs.org.uk

Chief: Head of Lib: Ms Rebecca Hemmind MusB(Hons), BA, MSc (rhemming@ucs.org.uk)
Dep: Asst Libn: Mr Edward Benton BA, MA(Hons), MA (ebenton@ucs.org.uk) **Other Snr Staff:** Lib Asst: Mrs Susan Jacobs BA
Assoc Libs: UNIV COLL SCHOOL JNR BRANCH LIB, Holly Hill, London, NW3 6QN, Libn: Mrs Annette Davis BA, DipIS
Entry: school membs **Open:** term: Mon-Fri 0800-1700; vac: Mon-Fri 1000-1600
Subj: all subjs; genl; GCSE; A level
Equip: copier, video viewer, 18 computers (incl 13 with wd-proc, 13 with internet & 13 with CD-ROM)
Svcs: info, ref
Stock: bks/17000; periodcls/49; audios/18; videos/250; CD-ROMs/50
Classn: DDC **Auto Sys:** Heritage
Staff: Libns: 2 Non-Prof: 0.34

S1438 ✚
University Hospital Lewisham, Library
Lewisham High St, London, SE13 6LH (020-8333-3030 x6454; *fax:* 020-8333-3247)
Email: jane.coyte@uhl.nhs.uk

Gov Body: Lewisham Hosp NHS Trust **Chief:** Libns: Ms Jane Coyte BA, MCLIP & Ms Julia Jamieson
Entry: trust employees, others by referral only
Open: term: Mon-Thu 0900-1900, Fri 0900-1700; vac: Mon-Fri 0900-1700
Subj: health sci **Co-op Schemes:** BLDSC
Equip: m-reader, fax, copier, computer (with CD-ROM), Computer Assisted Learning room **Online:** Medline **Svcs:** info, ref
Stock: bks/3200; periodcls/224
Classn: NLM **Auto Sys:** Librarian
Staff: Libns: 2 Non-Prof: 4

S1439 🎓
University of Greenwich, Information and Library Services
Lib Admin, Riverside House, Beresford St, London, SE18 6BU (020-8331-8190; *fax:* 020-8331-9084)
Internet: http://www.gre.ac.uk/directory/library/

Chief: Dir of Info & Lib Svcs: Mr Denis Heathcote
Dep: Head of Lib Svcs: Ms Ann Murphy
Assoc Libs: AVERY HILL CAMPUS LIB, Mansion Site, Bexley Rd, Eltham, London, SE9 2PQ, Campus Libns: Ms Chris Hogg & Ms Rosemary Moon (020-8331-8484; *fax:* 020-8331-9645; *email:* C.G.Hogg@gre.ac.uk or R.M.Moon@gre.ac.uk); MARITIME GREENWICH CAMPUS, DREADNOUGHT LIB, 30 Park Row, London, SE10 9LS, Campus Libns: Mr Tim Cullen & Ms Virginia Malone (020-8331-7551; *fax:* 020 8331 7775; *email:* T.Cullen@gre.ac.uk or V.G.Malone@gre.ac.uk); MEDWAY & NATL RESOURCES INST CAMPUS LIB, Nelson Bldg, Chatham Maritime, Kent, ME4 4AW, Campus Libn & Head of NRI Lib: Mr David Mitchell (020-8331-9617; *fax:* 020-8331-9837; *email:* D.Mitchell@gre.ac.uk)
Entry: membs of Univ; other students under the terms of the SCONUL Vac Access Scheme, M25 Consortium scheme & UK Libs Plus scheme
Open: opening hrs may vary, esp on Sat & during vacs (phone for confirmation); *Avery Hill:* term: Mon-Thu 0900-2100, Fri 0900-1700, Sat 1000-1700; vac: Mon-Fri 0900-1700; *Maritime Greenwich:* term: Mon-Thu 0900-2100, Fri 0900-1700, Sat 0900-1700; vac: Mon-Fri 0900-1700; *Medway:* term: Mon-Thu 0900-2100, Fri 0900-1800, Sat 1000-1700; vac: Mon-Fri 0900-1700
Subj: all subjs; *Avery Hill:* arch; construction; econ; edu; nursing; health care; psy; sociology; sports sci; *Maritime Greenwich:* computing; law; maritime studies; maths; post-compulsory edu & training; humanities; business; *Medway:* chemical & life scis; geol; applied geochemistry; geog; geographical info systems; environmental sci; eng; civil eng; eng geol; remote sensing; nat resource mgmt **Co-op Schemes:** ILL, UK Libs Plus, SCONUL, M25 Consortium
Equip: copiers, computers
Classn: DDC **Auto Sys:** Talis

S1440 🎓
University of London Library
Senate House, Malet St, London, WC1E 7HU (020-7862-8461/2; *fax:* 020-7862-8480)
Email: enquiries@ull.ac.uk
Internet: http://www.ull.ac.uk/

Chief: Chief Libn: Mrs Emma Robinson BSc, MCLIP, FRSA **Other Snr Staff:** Snr Sub-Libn (Academic Svcs): Mr Paul McLaughlin; Sub-Libn (Admin & Resources): Ms Gail Duggett; Sub-Libn (Historic Collns): Ms Christine Wise; Sub-Libn (Info Strategy): Mr Steve Clews
Entry: Univ of London internal arrangements apply: UK univ rsrch community free ref; all other categories may apply but charge usually made
Open: term: Mon-Thu 0900-2100, Fri 0900-1830, Sat 0930-1730; vac: Mon-Fri 0900-1800, Sat 0930-1730; see web site for up-to-date opening times & opening times for Historic Collns
Subj: rsrch, but providing for wider needs of taught-course students; humanities, with most important strengths in: social sci; classics; English lit; hist; economic hist; social hist; hist of art; modern langs (primarily Romance & Germanic); geog; music; phil; psy; Latin American Studies; Caribbean studies; Commonwealth studies (strong in Australiana & Canadiana); palaeography; also significant collns in: hist of sci & tech; phil of sci; theology; edu; hist of London; etc **Collns: Bks & Pamphs:** important rsrch collns incl: Durning Lawrence Lib (mainly 16C-17C English lit, c5750 vols); Sterling Lib (early & fine eds English lit 14C-20C, c7000 vols, c100 MSS); Goldsmiths' Lib of Economic Hist (see **S1441**); British Psychological

Soc Lib (see **S1040**); Palaeography Room Colln; large colln of US Govt pubns; other special collns incl: Bright Colln (psychical rsrch, 191 vols); Bromhead Colln (hist of London, c4000 items); John Burns Colln (labour hist, 19C-20C); Carlton Shorthand Colln (16C-20C); De Morgan Colln (maths, c4500 items); Eliot-Phelips Colln (Spanish imprints, 16C-20C, c3500 items); Family Welfare Assoc Lib (social issues, 19C-20C); Francis Bacon Soc Colln (16C-17C, 1500 items); Grote Colln (mainly classics, 7500 items); Martin Colln (19C ch's lit); Malcolm Morley Lib (19C-20C stagecraft, c4000 vols); Plainsong & Medieval Music Soc Lib; Porteus Lib; Harry Price Lib of Psychical Rsrch (16C-20C, 18000 items); Prize Colln (19C Sunday School prize bks); Quick Memorial Lib (edu); Ethel M. Wood Biblical Colln; many others, incl extensive historical periodcls colln (19C & earlier) **Archvs:** Univ of London archvs **Other:** extensive map colln; Grieve Colln (original watercolours of stage designs); Fuller Colln of Seals **Co-op Schemes:** BLDSC, CURL, RLG, CERL
Equip: 5 m-readers, 2 m-printers, 2 video viewers, 7 copiers, computers (incl CD-ROM network), 2 rooms for hire **Disabled:** Kurzweil **Online:** BIDS, BLCPM, BNB, Web of Science, ERIC, IDEAL, Justis, Medline, NISS, Philosophers Index, PsycInfo & others
Stock: bks/2000000; periodcls/5500; maps/65000; m-forms/25000; archvs/840 linear m
Classn: Bliss, DDC, own **Auto Sys:** Innopac
Pubns: Catalogue of Goldsmiths Lib of Early Economic Lit; Newsletter of the Univ of London Lib
Staff: Libns: 24 Other Prof: 2 Non-Prof: 41

S1441 🎓
University of London, The Goldsmiths' Library of Economic History
Univ of London Lib, Senate House, Malet St, London, WC1E 7HU (020-7862-8470; *fax:* 020-7862-8480)
Email: historic@ull.ac.uk
Internet: http://www.ull.ac.uk/goldsmiths/

Gov Body: Univ of London (see **S1440**) **Chief:** Head of Historic Collns & Rare Bks: Ms Christine Wise
Entry: adv appt preferred; materials must be consulted in the Palaeography Reading Room
Open: term: Mon 0930-2045, Tue-Thu 0930-1845, Fri 0930-1815, Sat 0930-1300, 1400-1715; vac: Mon-Fri 0930-1645, Sat 0930-1300, 1400-1715
Subj: econ; economic hist; politics; financial policy; early English & French socialism; slavery; trade; guilds; transport; railway hist; temperance movement **Collns: Bks & Pamphs:** incl: Reform Club pamphs (360 vols, 1770-1910); Sabatier Colln (French monetary hist, c1000 items, 1651-1852); Temperance Colln (temperance movement, c500 vols); Sheffield Colln (part of colln of John Holroyd, 1st Earl of Sheffield, 320 items); Rastrick Colln (transport hist, 18C-19C); Family Welfare Assoc Lib (social issues, 19C-20C, 5000 vols)
Stock: bks/66000+ bks, pamphs, MSS, periodcls, broadsides & proclamations

S1442 🎓
University of London, Institute of Advanced Legal Studies Library
17 Russell Sq, London, WC1B 5DR (020-7862-5790; *fax:* 020-7862-5770)
Email: ials.lib@sas.ac.uk
Internet: http://www.ials.sas.ac.uk/

Gov Body: Univ of London (see **S1440**) **Chief:** Libn: Mr J.R. Winterton BA, LLB, MCLIP **Dep:** Dep Libn: Miss J. Jones MA, MCLIP **Other Snr Staff:** Reader Svcs Mgr: Mr David Gee BA, MA, DipLib, MCLIP (David.Gee@sas.ac.uk); Info Resources Mgr: Ms Lesley Young BA, DipLib, MCLIP (Lesley.Young@sas.ac.uk)

Entry: lecturers & postgrad rsrch degree students admitted without charge; barristers & solicitors may be admitted on payment of fee; apply to Lib Admin Offcr *Open:* Mon-Fri 0900-2000; Sat 1000-1730; closed 2nd 2 wks of Sep
Subj: law (postgrad & higher rsrch colln) *Collns: Bks & Pamphs:* SCOLMA (South Africa); FCO Commonwealth Law Lib (apart from material on the dependent territories) has been transferred to IALS *Archvs:* Records of Legal Edu Archvs, listed at http://ials.sas.ac.uk/archives/ *Co-op Schemes:* BLDSC, ILL, CURL, participant in COPAC
Equip: 2 m-readers, m-printer, 9 copiers (£1 for 18 copies), 34 computers (all with wd-proc, internet & CD-ROM) *Online:* Lexis, Westlaw *Officer-in-Charge:* Reader Svcs Mgr, as above *Svcs:* info, ref
Stock: bks/258436; periodcls/2982; m-forms/15000; audios/23; CD-ROMs/88; archvs/57 linear m *Acqs Offcr:* Info Resources Mgr, as above
Classn: own *Auto Sys:* Innopac
Pubns: numerous – see web site for details
Staff: Libns: 15 *Other Prof:* 1 *Non-Prof:* 7 *Exp:* £315000 (1999-2000); £318000 (2000-01)

S1443

University of London, Institute of Commonwealth Studies Library

28 Russell Sq, London, WC1B 5DS (020-7862-8842; *fax:* 020-7862-8820)
Email: icommlib@sas.ac.uk
Internet: http://www.sas.ac.uk/commonwealthstudies/

Gov Body: Univ of London School of Adv Study *Chief:* Info Resources Mgr: Ms Erika Gwynnett *Dep:* Dep Info Resources Mgr: Mr Ian Cooke *Entry:* ref only; open to academic staff & registered postgrads in Britain & abroad; others at discretion of the Inst Dir (fee payable, reductions for unwaged) *Open:* term: Mon, Wed-Fri 0930-1830, Tue 0930-1930; vac: Mon-Fri 0930-1730
Subj: Commonwealth of Nations: Africa; Asia; Caribbean; Australia; Pacific; Canada; hist from 1850; politics; econ; human rights; bibliography
Collns: Bks & Pamphs: SCOLMA (Gambia & Sierra Leone); West Indies (Lib of the West India Cttee held on permanent loan) *Archvs:* 230 archv collns, incl: West India Cttee Archv (18C-20C); C.L.R. James papers (West Indian politician & writer); Richard Jebb papers (publicist & writer); John Ferguson papers (Sri Lanka, 19C); Simon Taylor papers (18C Jamaican plantation owner); Ruth First papers (anti-apartheid activist); Castle Wemyss estate papers (Jamaica, 19C) *Other:* political parties colln (13000 pubns issued by political parties, trade unions & pressure groups)
Co-op Schemes: SCOLMA
Equip: m-readers, fax, copier, computers (incl internet & CD-ROM) *Online:* African Journals Online, IBSS, JSTOR, Web of Science, Zetoc
Stock: bks/c170000; periodcls/c800 current, 8200+ no longer current; pamphs/10000; archvs/164 linear m
Classn: LC (mod) *Auto Sys:* Innopac
Pubns: Accessions List (quarterly); Theses in Progress in Commonwealth Studies (annual, free)
Staff: Libns: 4 *Other Prof:* 1 archivist *Non-Prof:* 1

S1444

University of London, Institute of Education, Newsam Library

20 Bedford Way, London, WC1H 0AL (020-7612-6080; *fax:* 020-7612-6093)
Email: lib.enquiries@ioe.ac.uk
Internet: http://www.ioe.ac.uk/

Gov Body: Univ of London (see **S1440**) *Chief:* Libn: Ms Anne B. Peters BA
Assoc Libs: INST OF EDU ARCHVS, at above addr, Archivist: Ms Sarah Aitchison (020-7612-6983; *fax:* 020-7612-6093; *email:* s.aitchison@ioe.ac.uk)

Entry: appl to Libn; visitor's membership available for a fee (some categories only); adv appt required for Archvs *Open: Lib:* term: Mon-Thu 0930-2215, Fri 0930-2015, Sat 0930-2015, Sun 1100-1700
Subj: psy; social sci; edu *Collns: Bks & Pamphs:* curriculum resources (bks & other materials for use in schools); ILEA pubns; Official Pubns Colln (on edu); Historical Textbks Colln (c18000 items, 19C onwards); Baines Colln (c200 ch's bks, c1700-1920); Brooke Colln (c1000 printed bks, c1600-1860); Grenfell Colln (physical edu, c1880-1940); Sir Fred Clarke Colln (late 19C-mid 20C); Bernard Rainbow Colln (20C music edu); various other named collns *Archvs:* archvs of the inst; archvs of various edu orgs, incl: Schools Council; Asst Masters Assoc; Natl Union of Women Teachers; World Edu Fellowship; Coll of Preceptors; Univs Council for the Edu of Teachers; Soc of Teachers Opposed to Physical Punishment; Natl Commission on Edu; Jack Kitching Archv (Board of Edu Inspectors Assoc); London Hist Teachers Assoc; Bullock Cttee; British Comparative & Internatl Edu Soc; & others; numerous collns of personal papers of indivs associated with edu (mid-19C onwards) *Co-op Schemes:* BLDSC
Equip: m-reader, m-printer, video viewer, copier, computers (incl wd-proc & CD-ROM), audio & video recording equip *Svcs:* ref, biblio, seminars
Stock: bks/300000; periodcls/c1000
Classn: DDC (curriculum resources), London Edu Classn (main colln) *Auto Sys:* Libertas
Pubns: Edu Libs Journal (3 pa, £12); plus supplements (individually priced)
Staff: Libns: 10 *Non-Prof:* 20

S1445

University of London, Institute of Germanic Studies Library

29 Russell Sq, London, WC1B 5DP (020-7862-8967; *fax:* 020-7862-8970)
Email: igslib@sas.ac.uk
Internet: http://www.sas.ac.uk/igs/

Gov Body: Univ of London School of Advanced Study *Chief:* Libn: Mr William Abbey BA
Entry: ref only, admission criteria vary; open to all bona fide HEI rsrchers *Open:* Mon-Fri 0945-1800
Subj: German lang & lit *Collns: Bks & Pamphs:* Priebsch-Closs Colln (18C & 19C texts); English Goethe Soc Lib; German literary periodcls; Stefan George & his Kreis; contemporary Swiss & former GDR lit; Exile Colln *Archvs:* Friedrich Gundolf Archv; English Goethe Soc papers; Exile Archv; hist of German studies in the UK; indiv scholars
Equip: m-fiche reader, video viewer, copier, 3 rooms for hire *Svcs:* info, ref, biblio
Stock: bks/90000; periodcls/320; pamphs/several 1000s; m-forms/20000; archvs/many 1000s of documents
Classn: Garside (mod) *Auto Sys:* Innovative
Staff: Libns: 2 *Non-Prof:* 1 *Exp:* £30000 (1999-2000); £30000 (2000-01)

S1446

University of London, Institute of Historical Research Library

Univ of London, Senate House, Malet St, London, WC1E 7HU (020-7862-8760; *fax:* 020-7862-8762)
Email: IHR.Library@sas.ac.uk
Internet: http://www.history.ac.uk/ihrlibrary/

Gov Body: Univ of London (see **S1440**) *Chief:* Libn: Mr Robert Lyons BA, DipLib
Entry: membs only; limited ref access for those who apply in adv *Open:* Mon-Fri 0900-2045, Sat & some hols 0900-1645
Subj: hist of Western Europe & its expansion overseas: primary src materials *Collns: Bks & Pamphs:* printed Parliamentary poll bks *Co-op Schemes:* BLDSC
Equip: 6 m-readers, m-printer, 2 copiers, 20 computers (incl wd-proc & CD-ROM), 5 rooms for hire *Svcs:* info, ref

Stock: bks/165000; periodcls/300; m-forms/44000
Classn: own *Auto Sys:* Innopac
Staff: Libns: 4 *Non-Prof:* 2

S1447

University of London, Institute of Latin American Studies Library

31 Tavistock Sq, London, WC1H 9HA (020-7862-8501; *fax:* 020-7862-8971)
Email: ilas.lib@sas.ac.uk
Internet: http://www.sas.ac.uk/ilas/

Gov Body: Univ of London School of Adv Study *Chief:* Info Resources Mgr: Ms Sarah Pink BA, MA, MCLIP (Sarah.Pink@sas.ac.uk) *Other Snr Staff:* Snr Lib Asst: Ms Catherine Worth BA, MA (Catherine.Worth@sas.ac.uk)
Entry: academic staff & postgrads of the Univ of London; ref only for other bona fide rsrchers (undergrads should provide a letter of introduction) *Open:* Mon-Fri 0930-1730
Subj: humanities & social sci of Latin America *Collns: Bks & Pamphs:* bibliography & ref; news sources; British Union Catalogue of Latin Americana (to 1988, closed); special collns on human rights, internatl relations, Chilean politics, Cuban drama, Mexican anthro *Other:* rsrch papers; MA dissertations; press cuttings on Latin America (1930s-date); recent (post 1945) current affairs & political party ephemera (1960s-80s); Nissa Torrents Video Colln *Co-op Schemes:* BLDSC
Equip: m-reader, video viewer, fax, copier, computer (with CD-ROM) *Online:* BIDS/IBSS
Stock: bks/11000+; periodcls/260, plus over 1500 non-current; pamphs/c2000; maps/50; videos/c300; CD-ROMs/36; rsrch papers/c3000
Classn: DDC *Auto Sys:* Innopac
Pubns: Latin American & Caribbean Lib Resources in London: A Guide (7th ed 1997, £3)
Staff: Libns: 3 *Non-Prof:* 1

S1448

University of London, Institute of Neurology, Rockefeller Medical Library

The Natl Hosp, Queen Sq, London, WC1N 3BG (020-7829-8709; *fax:* 020-7278-1371)
Email: library@ion.ucl.ac.uk
Internet: http://www.ion.ucl.ac.uk/library/

Gov Body: Univ of London (see **S1440**) *Chief:* Libn: Ms Louise Shepherd BA(Hons) *Dep:* Dep Libn: Ms Kate Brunskill
Entry: ref only, adv appt; proof of ID required *Open:* Mon-Fri 0900-1900
Subj: neurology; neurosurgery; clinical neuro-science & allied fields *Collns: Bks & Pamphs:* bks & papers by Inst & Natl Hosp for Neurology staff; historical neurology colln (2700+ vols) *Co-op Schemes:* BLDSC, informal local arrangements
Equip: 2 copiers, computers (incl wd-proc & CD-ROM) *Online:* Web of Science, Medline, CINAHL, CancerLit, Embase, PsycInfo, Biosis, Cochrane, Biotech Abstracts, Index to Theses & others *Svcs:* ref, document delivery, current awareness, lit searches, training
Stock: bks/10000 + 14900 vols of bnd journals; periodcls/160; other materials/61.2 m
Classn: NLM *Auto Sys:* Unicorn
Staff: Libns: 2 *Non-Prof:* 2

S1449

University of London, School of Oriental and African Studies Library

Thornhaugh St, Russell Sq, London, WC1H 0XG (020-7898-4163; *fax:* 020-7898-4159)
Email: libenquiry@soas.ac.uk
Internet: http://www.soas.ac.uk/library/

(Univ of London, School of Oriental & African Studies Lib cont)

Gov Body: Univ of London (see **S1440**) **Chief:** Libn: Mr Keith G. Webster BSc, MLib, MCLIP **Dep:** Lib Mgr: Miss Anne McIlwaine BA(Oxon), MA, MPhil (am90@soas.ac.uk)
Entry: letter of introduction from person with knowledge of your rsrch interest; fees charged for both ref & borrowing use **Open:** term, Xmas & Easter vacs: Mon-Thu 0900-2045, Fri 0900-1900, Sat 0900-1700; summer vac: Mon-Fri 0900-1700, Sat 0930-170
Subj: social sci & humanities with ref to Asia, Africa & Pacific Islands, incl material in the langs of those regions **Collns:** *Bks & Pamphs:* SCOLMA (North Africa, Ethiopia, Lesotho, Swaziland, Botswana); Islamic Law Colln *Archvs:* records of Standing Conference on Lib Materials on Africa (SCOLMA, see **O393**); missionary archvs, incl Council for World Mission Archvs & Methodist Missionary Soc Archvs; business archvs; private papers; relating to China, Pacific, India, Africa, Malaysia **Co-op Schemes:** SCOLMA, BLDSC back up lib for ILL of Asian lang material **Equip:** 10 m-readers, m-printer, 5 copiers, computers (incl 2 CD-ROM) **Online:** BIDS, PCI, Ideal (SOAS students & staff only), JSTOR, BAS Online, African/South Africa Studies (lib membs only) **Svcs:** info, ref, biblio
Stock: bks/800000; periodcls/5000; photos/2500; slides/5000; pamphs/30000; maps/60000; m-forms/large colln; audios/2000
Classn: own **Auto Sys:** Innopac
Staff: Libns: 14 *Other Prof:* 1 archivist *Non-Prof:* 30

S1450 🎓 ✚
University of London, School of Pharmacy Library
29-39 Brunswick Sq, London, WC1N 1AX (020-7753-5833; *fax:* 020-7753-5947)
Email: library@ulsop.ac.uk

Gov Body: Univ of London (see **S1440**) **Chief:** Head of Lib & Info Svcs: Mrs Linda Lisgarten BA, MCLIP
Entry: ref only **Open:** term: Mon-Fri 0900-2000; vac: Mon-Fri 0900-1700
Subj: biomedical & chemical sci; tech **Co-op Schemes:** SCONUL, M25 Group of univ libs **Equip:** m-reader, copier, video viewer, CD-ROM reader (own users only) **Online:** databases for use by own readers only **Svcs:** info, ref, biblio
Stock: bks/c80000; periodcls/200; slides/50; videos/50
Classn: UDC **Auto Sys:** Unicorn
Staff: Libns: 3 *Other Prof:* 1 *Non-Prof:* 1.5

S1451 🎓
University of Surrey Roehampton, Learning Resources Centre
Harvey Bldg, Roehampton Ln, Roehampton, London, SW15 5PU (020-8392-3770; *fax:* 020-8392-3259)
Email: enquiry.desk@roehampton.ac.uk
Internet: http://www.roehampton.ac.uk/

Gov Body: Univ of Surrey (see **S776**) **Chief:** Dir of Info Svcs: Miss Susan Clegg BA, MBA, MCLIP **Dep:** Asst Dirs of Info Svcs: Mr John Mill & Mr Paul Scarsbrook

Assoc Libs: WHITELANDS LRC, Giles Gilbert Scott Bldg, West Hill, London, SW15 5SN, Svc Co-ordinator: Ms Pat Biggs
Entry: ref only, external subscription available **Open:** term: Mon-Thu 0830-2100, Fri 0830-1900, Sat-Sun 1200-1700; vac: Mon-Fri 0900-1700
Subj: all subjs; undergrad; postgrad; rsrch; edu (prof & non-prof) **Collns:** *Bks & Pamphs:* ch's lit colln **Co-op Schemes:** BLDSC, ILL, SWIFT, SETG, M25 Consortium
Equip: m-reader, m-printer, video viewer, copier, clr copiers, computers (with wd-proc, internet & CD-ROM), media & viewing suite **Online:** range of svcs (membs only) **Svcs:** info, ref
Stock: bks/420000; periodcls/1500; slides/3000; illusts/2500; maps/200; m-forms/702; videos/900; archvs/60 m; elec media/110
Classn: DDC **Auto Sys:** Talis
Staff: Libns: 20 *Other Prof:* 3 *Non-Prof:* 44

S1452 🎓
University of Westminster, Information Systems and Library Services
115 New Cavendish St, London, W1M 8JS (020-7911-5100; *fax:* 020-7911-5093)
Internet: http://www.wmin.ac.uk/library/

Chief: Dir of Info Systems & Lib Svcs: Ms Suzanne Enright BA, DipLib, MCLIP **Other Snr Staff:** Dir of Info Systems: Mr Stuart Johnston BSc, MBA
Assoc Libs: CAVENDISH CAMPUS LIB, 115 New Cavendish St, London, W1W 6UW, Lib Mgr: Ms Ann Sainsbury BA, MCLIP (020-7911-5000 x3627; *fax:* 020-7911-5093; sainsba@wmin.ac.uk); HARROW LRC, Watford Rd, Northwick Pk, Harrow, HA1 3TP, Lib Mgr: Ms Carole Symes (020-7911-5885; *fax:* 020-7911-5952; *email:* c.symes@wmin.ac.uk); MARYLEBONE CAMPUS LIB, 35 Marylebone Rd, London, NW1 5LS, Lib Mgr: Jane Harrington BA, MLib, MCLIP (020-7911-5000 x3171; *fax:* 020-7911-5058; *email:* harrinj@westminster.ac.uk); REGENT CAMPUS LIB, 4-12 Little Titchfield St, London, W1B 2UW, Lib Mgr: Ms Elaine Salter BA, MLib, MCLIP (020-7911-5000 x2537; *fax:* 020-7911-5894; *email:* e.salter@wmin.ac.uk); UNIV OF WESTMINSTER ARCHV SVCS, 4-12 Little Titchfield St, London, W1W 7UW, contact the Univ Archivist (020-7911-5000 x2524; *fax:* 020-7911-5894; *email:* archive@westminster.ac.uk)
Entry: membership of Univ of Westminster (ID card) or letter of authorisation; archvs open to public by appt only **Open:** *Cavendish:* term: Mon-Thu 0930-2100, Fri 0930-1900, Sat-Sun 1100-1700; vac: Mon-Fri 0930-1700; *Harrow:* term: Mon-Thu 0830-2100, Fri 0930-1900, Sat-Sun 1000-1700; vac: Mon-Fri 0900-1700; *Marylebone:* term: Mon-Thu 0915-2100, Fri 0915-1900, Sat-Sun 1100-1700; vac: Mon-Fri 0915-1700; *Regent:* Mon-Thu 0915-2100, Fri 0915-1900, Sat-Sun 1100-1700; vac: Mon 0915-2000, Tue-Fri 0915-1700; *Archvs:* Mon-Fri 0915-1700
Subj: all subjs; undergrad; postgrad; *Cavendish:* biomedicine; life sci; biotech; computing; eng; tech; maths; public health; nutrition; complementary medicine; *Harrow:* business; communication; arts; design; media; computing; *Marylebone:* accounting; arch; computing; construction; estate mgmt; finance; housing; law; mgmt; marketing; planning; surveying; tourism; transport; *Regent:* law; social sci; humanities; lang; community care; primary health **Collns:** *Bks & Pamphs:* BSI; official pubns; statistics; lib of the Internatl Inst of Communications (3500 vols) *Archvs:* Univ Archvs; archvs of predecessor bodies, incl: Polytechnic of Regent St Archv; Harrow Coll of Higher Edu Archv; Royal Polytechnic Instn Archv; Sidney Webb Coll Archv & others; deposited collns incl: John Turner Archv (development planner); Max Lock Archv (architect); Hogg, Sons & J B Johnstone Ltd Colln

(tailoring) *Other:* OS Maps; art slides **Co-op Schemes:** BLDSC, LAMDA, M25 Consortium, UK Libs Plus
Equip: m-reader, m-printer, video viewer, copier, clr copier, computers (incl wd-proc & CD-ROM) **Online:** BIDS, Emerald, Lexis, Lawtel & others **Svcs:** info, ref, biblio
Stock: bks/398000; periodcls/5400; photos/200; slides/30000; illusts/20000; pamphs/20000; maps/1000; audios/350; videos/12000; AVs/5000; archvs/50 linear m
Classn: DDC **Auto Sys:** Aleph 500
Staff: Libns: 32 *Non-Prof:* 32

S1453 🔑
Vaughan Williams Memorial Library, English Folk Dance and Song Society
Cecil Sharp House, 2 Regent's Park Rd, London, NW1 7AY (020-7485-2206; *fax:* 020-7284-0534)
Internet: http://www.efdss.org/

Gov Body: EFDSS **Chief:** Libn: Mr M.H. Taylor OBE, MCLIP **Dep:** Asst Libn: Ms E. Bradtke & Ms P. Webb (job-share)
Entry: non-membs of EFDSS pay a daily fee **Open:** Tue-Fri 0930-1730; also open 1st & 3rd Sat of each month
Subj: traditional dance, song, customs & drama **Collns:** *Archvs:* MS colln (Cecil Sharp, Lucy Broadwood, George Butterworth, etc) **Co-op Schemes:** BLDSC (photocopies only)
Equip: m-reader, m-printer, video viewer, fax, copier, computer (incl wd-proc), reel to reel/cassette audiotape players/readers, CD player, phonograph
Stock: bks/22000, incl pamphs; periodcls/220; photos/12000; slides/1000; audios/6000; videos/150
Classn: own (loosely based on LC)
Pubns: bklets & study guides: English Folk Song: An Introductory Bibliography; May Day in England: An Introductory Bibliography; An Introductory Bibliography on Clog & Stap Dance; A Checklist of Manuscript Songs & Tunes Collected from the Oral Tradition by Frank Kidson; periodcls (some back issues also available): Folk Music Journal; English Dance & Song; various audio cassettes & CDs; 3 study guides available on web site: English Folk Song; Sword Dancing in Britain; Introductory Bibliography on Morris Dancing
Staff: Libns: 2 *Non-Prof:* 1

S1454 🏛
VisitBritain, Thames Tower Library
(formerly the English Tourism Council & British Tourist Authority Lib)
Thames Tower, Black's Rd, Hammersmith, London, W6 9EL (020-8563-3011; *fax:* 020-8563-0302)
Internet: http://www.visitbritain.org/

Chief: Info Offcrs: Ms Gaynor Evans (Gaynor.evans@visitbritain.org) & Ms Joanne Scott (Joanne.scott@visitbritain.org)
Entry: by appt only; svc charge applies
Subj: tourism **Collns:** *Bks & Pamphs:* tourism statistics & info files covering econ, social & historical aspects of tourism, marketing & development of the tourist product *Archvs:* English Tourism Council & British Tourist Authority Archvs (1930-date) **Co-op Schemes:** ILL (only if lib of last resort & bk o/p)
Equip: m-reader, fax, copier, computers (incl wd-proc & CD-ROM) **Online:** FT Profile (staff only)
Stock: bks/17000; periodcls/250; maps/500; m-forms/300; archvs/40 linear m; info files/40
Classn: own **Auto Sys:** CALM
Staff: Libns: 1 *Other Prof:* 1

S1455

The Wallace Collection, Library and Archives

Hertford House, Manchester Sq, London, W1M 6BN (*Lib:* 020-7563-9528; *Museum:* 020-7563-9500; *fax:* 020-7224-2155)
Email: andrea.gilbert@wallacecollection.org
Internet: http://www.the-wallace-collection.org.uk/

Type: natl museum & art gallery *Gov Body:* Trustees of the Wallace Colln *Chief:* Libn & Archivist: Ms Andrea Gilbert BA, PGDipLib *Assoc Libs:* PICTURE LIB (020-7563-9534; *email:* ebaudey@the-wallace-collection.org.uk) *Entry:* ref only; adv appt; 5 days notice required for archv materials *Open: Museum:* Mon-Sat 1000-1700, Sun 1200-1700, closed public hols; *Lib & Archvs:* Tue-Fri 1000-1300, 1400-1700 by appt only
Subj: European fine & decorative arts (esp 18-19C French); arms & armour; painting; sculpture; furniture; porcelain; family papers; personal papers
Collns: Bks & Pamphs: extensive colln of early & rare pre-1850 sale catalogues (French & English) *Archvs:* MS & printed materials relating to the hist of Hertford-Wallace family, collns & museum, incl: Wallace Colln Trustees records (1897-20C); Seymour family, Marquesses of Hertford, papers (19C); correspondence of Samuel James Camp (former Keeper of the Colln, 1876-1936)
Equip: m-reader, m-printer (10p per copy), copier (A4/5p, A3/10p), computers (incl 2 with wd-proc & 2 with internet) *Officer-in-Charge:* Libn & Archivist, as above
Stock: bks/15000; periodcls/40; m-forms/c50; archvs/c300 files *Acqs Offcr:* Libn & Archivist, as above
Classn: in-house *Auto Sys:* Adlib (not available to readers)
Staff: Libns: 1 *Exp:* £13000 (1999-2000); £14000 (2000-01)

S1456

Warburg Institute Library

Woburn Sq, London, WC1H 0AB (020-7862-8935; *fax:* 020-7862-8939)
Email: Warburg.Library@sas.ac.uk
Internet: http://www.sas.ac.uk/warburg/

Gov Body: Univ of London (see **S1440**) *Chief:* Academic Libn: Dr Jill Kraye *Dep:* Dep Libn: Mr J. Perkins MA, DipLib
Assoc Libs: WARBURG INST ARCHV, at same addr, Archivist: Dr Dorothea McEwan
Entry: any postgrad student, univ teacher, or others showing good reason & with letter of recommendation, may be admitted *Open:* Mon, Fri 1000-1800, Tue-Thu 1000-2000, Sat (term only) 1000-1600; *Archv:* Mon-Fri 1000-1700
Subj: hist of classical tradition in art, religion, magic & sci; intellectual & cultural hist of Europe
Collns: Bks & Pamphs: Royal & British Numismatic Socs Libs (see **S1375**) *Archvs:* held in Inst Archv: academic & administrative records of the Inst; working materials & correspondence of Aby Warburg; papers & correspondence of Fritz Saxl, Gertrud Bing, Frances A. Yates & Alfons A. Barb; literary papers of Robert Eisler; papers relating to various other scholars *Co-op Schemes:* ILL
Equip: 3 m-readers, m-printer, 2 copiers, 3 computers (with CD-ROM)
Stock: bks/300000; periodcls/1350, plus 1300 no longer current; photos/290000; m-forms/4090
Classn: own *Auto Sys:* Innopac
Pubns: The Warburg Inst (pamph); Catalogue of the Lib of the Warburg Inst (Boston, Mass. 1967-71)
Staff: Libns: 5 *Non-Prof:* 3

S1457

Wellcome Library for the History and Understanding of Medicine

183 Euston Rd, London, NW1 2BE (020-7611-8582; *fax:* 020-7611-8369)
Email: library@wellcome.ac.uk
Internet: http://library.wellcome.ac.uk/

Gov Body: Wellcome Trust *Chief:* Libn: Mr David Pearson BA, MA, DipLib, ALS *Other Snr Staff:* Reader Svcs Mgr: Ms Sue Gold; Lib Support Svcs Mgr: Mr Simon Jones; Head of Special Collns: Ms Julia Sheppard
Assoc Libs: INFO SVC, addr as above, Info Svc Mgr: Ms Elizabeth Graham (020-7611-8722; *fax:* 020-7611-8726; *email:* infoserv@wellcome.ac.uk); ICONOGRAPHIC COLLNS, addr as above, Curator: Mr William Schupbach (020-7611-8582; *fax:* 020-7611-8726; *email:* icon@wellcome.ac.uk); ARCHVS & MSS, addr as above, Head of Archvs & MSS: Dr Richard Aspin (*email:* arch+mss@wellcome.ac.uk); MEDICAL PHOTOGRAPHIC LIB, 210 Euston Rd, London, NW1 2BE, Head of Medical Photographic Lib: Ms Catherine Draycott (020-7611-8348; *fax:* 020-7611-8577; *email:* photolib@wellcome.ac.uk); MEDICAL FILM & AUDIO COLLNS, 210 Euston Rd, London, NW1 2BE, Head of Medical Film & Audio Collns: Dr Michael Clark (020-7611-8596/7; *fax:* 020-7611-8765; *email:* mfac@wellcome.ac.uk)
Entry: ref only, proof of ID required; adv appt recommended to view Archvs (contact the Duty Archivist) *Open: Hist of Medicine Collns (incl Archvs):* Mon, Wed, Fri 0945-1715, Tue, Thu 0945-1915, Sat 0945-1300; *Info Svc (biomedical topics):* Mon-Fri 0900-1700, Sat 0900-1300; *Medical Photographic Lib:* Mon-Fri 0930-1730 (by appt); *Medical Film & Audio Collns:* Mon-Fri 0915-1730 (by appt)
Subj: hist of medicine & allied scis; social hist & anthro; biomedical scis (incl genetics & the human genome); sci policy; biomedical ethics; oriental medical topics *Collns: Bks & Pamphs:* Oriental Colln (11000 MSS & c3000 printed bks in 43 langs); Early Printed Bks Colln (c66000 vols, pre 1851); Modern Medicine Colln (c600000 vols, post 1850); Historical Colln (c50000 vols of secondary sources, post 1850) *Archvs:* the dept of Archvs & MSS is based on 2 main sections: Western MSS Colln (7000 MSS & 1000s of autograph letters in 25 different European langs, from antiquity to 20C); Contemporary Medical Archvs (20C archvs); major collns are as follows: Wellcome Archvs (papers of Sir Henry Wellcome papers, 1853-1936, & archvs of the Wellcome Inst & its predecessor bodies, notably the Wellcome Historical Medical Museum, & also of other rsrch instns he established); Wellcome Tropical Inst Collns; Royal Army Medical Corps Muniment Colln (from 17C, but mainly from 1850s onwards); Medical Soc of London MSS; major archival collns of medical orgs incl: Chartered Soc of Physiotherapy; Eugenics Soc; Family Planning Assoc; Group Analytic Soc; Health Visitors' Assoc; Lister Inst; Medical Women's Federation; Mental Aftercare Assoc; Natl Birthday Trust Fund; Physiological Soc; Queens' Nursing Inst; Strangeways Rsrch Laboratory; major collns of personal papers incl: John Bowlby Papers; Lord Moran papers; Sir Peter Medawar papers; Sir Ernst Chain papers; Sir Edward Sharpey-Schafer papers; Sir Thomas Lewis papers; Cicely Williams papers; Marie Stopes papers; Melanie Lein papers; Grantly Dick-Read papers *Other:* Iconographic Colln (over 100000 paintings, prints, drawings, photos, films etc); over 160000 photographs of medical & social hist; 17000 photos of modern clinical medicine & biomedical scis; over 1300 films, videos, TV programmes & audio-tapes *Co-op Schemes:* ILL, M25, LLiL, School of Advanced Study (Univ of London), CURL
Equip: 2 digital m-printers, video viewer, copiers (via staff), computers (incl 18 internet & CD-ROM)
Svcs: enq svc, photography svc, microfilming svc, photocopying svc, online retrieval svcs.

Stock: bks/c600000; periodcls/c500; photos/177000+; AVs/1300+; archvs/2000 linear m (c600 collns)
Classn: NLM, Barnard (mod), local *Auto Sys:* Innopac
Pubns: elec pubns: Pscicom (public engagement with sci & sci communication info); Current Work in the Hist of Medicine (monthly listing of periodcl articles on the hist of medicine & allied scis); MedHist (Gateway to hist of medicine Internet resources); printed pubns: Early Printed Bks (Vol 1: before 1641; Vol 2: 1641-1850); Western MSS; Arabic MSS; Persian MSS; American MSS; Burmese MSS; Chinese MSS; Hindi MSS; Sanskrit & Prakrit MSS; Sinhalese MSS; Tibetan MSS (prices vary); Wellcome Inst for the Hist of Medicine: A Short Hist (£5); Annual Review (free); info guides & leaflets (free); full pubns list available
Staff: Libns: 40 *Other Prof:* 17 *Non-Prof:* 12
Exp: £468000 (1999-2000)

S1458

Wesley's Chapel, John Wesley's House and the Museum of Methodism

49 City Rd, London, EC1Y 1AU (020-7253-2262; *fax:* 020-7608-3825)
Email: administration@wesleyschapel.org.uk

Gov Body: Wesley's Chapel Circuit Meeting *Chief:* Curator: Miss Noorah Al-Gailani BA, MA *Entry:* ref only, adv appt *Open:* Mon-Fri 1000-1600
Subj: religion; hist of Methodism; Wesley's Chapel; John Wesley *Collns: Bks & Pamphs:* John Wesley's Lib (personal lib; bks bear his comments); Gypsy Smith Colln *Archvs:* John Wesley's letters; other Methodist letters & papers *Other:* photographic colln of Wesley's Chapel, the Leysian Mission & other Methodist bodies
Equip: copier, video viewer, fax, room for hire
Svcs: info, ref, postal enqs accepted with charge for postage, photocopies & other expenses
Stock: not yet counted
Classn: card index (author, title & subj)
Staff: Other Prof: 1 curator
Proj: conservation of John Wesley's Lib bks & pubn of Wesley's MS letters

S1459

Westminster Abbey, Library and Muniment Room

East Cloister, Westminster Abbey, London, SW1P 3PA (020-7654-4830; *fax:* 020-7654-4827)
Email: library@westminster-abbey.org
Internet: http://www.westminster-abbey.org/

Gov Body: Dean & Chapter of Westminster *Chief:* Libn: Dr Tony Trowles DPhil *Other Snr Staff:* Keeper of the Muniments: Dr Richard Mortimer PhD, FSA, FRHistS
Entry: ref only, appt required; students are asked to provide letter of introduction *Open:* Mon-Fri 1000-1300, 1400-1645
Subj: local study (Westminster Abbey & precincts); early eds of scriptures & commentaries; sermons; ecclesiastical art & arch; hist of Westminster Abbey & related topics, incl coronations *Collns: Bks & Pamphs:* bks & pamphs from the lib of William Camden (1551-1623); printed & MS music, 16C-19C; Oldaker Binding Colln; early MSS *Archvs:* archvs of Westminster Abbey & its estates from the last nine centuries *Other:* Langley Colln of prints & drawings; photo colln
Equip: copier
Stock: bks/16000; photos/5000 negs; slides/1200; audios/70; videos/20; archvs/70000 documents
Classn: own
Pubns: Lib Info Leaflet (10p)
Staff: Libns: 1 *Other Prof:* 2

S1460 🎓

Westminster Kingsway College Library Service

Vincent Sq, London, SW1P 2PD (020-7828-1222)
Internet: http://www.westking.ac.uk/

Chief: Head of Learning Support & Development: Ms Judith Cuninghame BA, MA, MCLIP
Assoc Libs: VINCENT SQ SITE LIB, addr as above, Mgr: Ms Lesley Gaj; BATTERSEA SITE LIB, Battersea Park Rd, London, SW11 4JR, Mgr: Ms Praveen Manghane; CASTLE LN SITE LIB, Castle Ln, London, SW1E 6DR, Mgr: Mr Simon Harper; GREYS INN SITE LIB, Sidmouth St, London, WC1H 8JB, Mgr: Ms Gloria Bloomfield; PETER ST LIB, Peter St, London, W1F 0HS, Mgr: Mr Simon Harper; KENTISH TOWN SITE LIB, 87 Holmes Rd, London, NW5 3AX, Mgr: Ms Antonina Spittal; REGENTS PARK SITE LIB, Longford St, London, NW1 3HB, Mgr: Ms Antonina Spittal
Entry: ref only *Open:* term: Mon-Fri 0900-1900 (times vary according to site)
Subj: all subjs *Collns: Bks & Pamphs:* Penrose Colln (cookery bks) *Co-op Schemes:* BLDSC, SWIFT
Equip: video viewer, copier, computers (incl wd-proc, internet & CD-ROM)
Stock: bks/80000; periodcls/200; pamphs/ numerous; audios/2000; videos/1000
Classn: DDC *Auto Sys:* Horizon
Staff: Libns: 12 *Other Prof:* 9 *Non-Prof:* 15

S1461 🎓

Westminster School Library

17 Dean's Yard, London, SW1P 3PB (020-7963-1045; *fax:* 020-7963-1046)
Email: hugh.eveleigh@westminster.org.uk
Internet: http://www.westminster.org.uk/

Gov Body: Governing Body of Westminster School *Chief: Libn:* Mr F. Hugh Eveleigh
Assoc Libs: WESTMINSTER SCHOOL ARCHVS, at same addr, Archivist: Mr E. Smith (020-7963-1078; *email:* undermaster@westminster.org.uk)
Entry: adv appt *Open:* term: Mon-Fri 0830-1800, Sat 0830-1300
Subj: all subjs; GCSE; A level *Collns: Bks & Pamphs:* Busby Lib (academic bks from 16C & 17C); Greene Lib (works by old Westminsters) *Archvs:* Westminster School hist
Equip: fax, video viewer, copier, 7 computers (all with internet, 2 with CD-ROM)
Stock: bks/30000; periodcls/80; photos/2000; audios/400; videos/300; DVDs/70
Classn: DDC *Auto Sys:* bespoke sys
Staff: Libns: 2 *Non-Prof:* 2 *Exp:* £23000 (1999-2000); £25000 (2000-01)

S1462 ✚

Whipps Cross University Hospital, Multidisciplinary Library Service

Medical Edu Centre, Whipps Cross Hosp, Whipps Cross Rd, London, E11 1NR (020-8535-6973; *fax:* 020-8535-6973)
Email: library@fhcare.demon.co.uk
Internet: http://www.nthames-health.tpmde.ac.uk/ ntrl/mec/

Gov Body: North East London Workforce Development Confederation *Chief:* Trust Libn: Mrs Sue Kerslake BA(Hons), MA, DipCG, MCLIP

Dep: Asst Libn: Ms Mary Last BA(Hons), MSc
Other Snr Staff: Clinical Support Libn: Mrs Anthea Levene BA(Hons), PGDipLib, MCLIP
Entry: Trust & local NHS staff *Open:* Mon-Fri 0900-1800
Subj: at postgrad level: medicine; psy; psychiatry
Collns: Other: Eurotransmed video colln; slide colln (infectious diseases) *Co-op Schemes:* BLDSC, BMA, North Thames Co-op Scheme, PLCS
Equip: m-reader, m-printer, video viewer, fax (staff only), copier, c20 computers (all with wd-proc, internet & CD-ROM) *Online:* AMED, BNI, CancerLit, CINAHL, Cochrane, Embase, HMIC, Medline, PsycInfo
Stock: bks/5000; periodcls/150; slides/various; videos/various; CD-ROMs/c40
Classn: NLM *Auto Sys:* DBTextworks
Staff: Libns: 3 *Non-Prof:* 3

S1463 🎓 🙏

William Booth College Library

(formerly Salvation Army Training Coll Lib)
Champion Pk, Denmark Hill, London, SE5 8BQ (020-7326-2747; *fax:* 020-7326-2750)
Email: mauricefoley@salvationarmy.org.uk

Type: theological training coll *Gov Body:* Salvation Army *Chief: Libn:* Mr Maurice Foley MA, MSc, BEd, DipLib, MCLIP
Assoc Libs: SALVATION ARMY TERRITORIAL HQ LIB (see **S1385**); SALVATION ARMY INTERNATL HERITAGE CENTRE (see **A341**)
Entry: adv appt *Open:* Mon-Fri 0830-1630; closed for a few wks each summer
Subj: religion; social sci; ethics; biblical studies; Christian doctrine; spirituality; pastoral theology; mission; church & soc; church hist; Salvation Army hist; social welfare; Salvation Army social svcs; music (mostly hymns & Salvation Army music); biography *Collns: Bks & Pamphs:* Salvation Army Studies (hist, doctrine, devotional works, biography, music, theses)
Equip: copier (5p per pg), 2 computers (incl wd-proc & CD-ROM) *Svcs:* info, ref
Stock: bks/16000; periodcls/120; pamphs/400; maps/65; audios/100; videos/200; CD-ROMs/10
Classn: DDC *Auto Sys:* Alice
Staff: Libns: 1 *Non-Prof:* 1

S1464 🏛

William Morris Gallery, Reference Library and Archives

Lloyd Pk, Forest Rd, London, E17 4PP (020-8527-3782; *fax:* 020-8527-7070)
Internet: http://www.lbwf.gov.uk/wmg/

Gov Body: London Borough of Waltham Forest (see **P108**) *Chief:* Keeper: Miss N.C. Gillow MA
Dep: Dep Keeper: Mr P.D. Cormack MA, FSA
Entry: adv appt necessary, ref only *Open: Museum:* Tue-Sat 1000-1300, 1400-1700; *Library/ Archv:* adv appt
Subj: William Morris & British applied arts (c1860-1920) *Collns: Bks & Pamphs:* socialist pamphs 1880s/90s; Kelmscott Press bks (complete set); The Studio (magazine); The Century Guild Hobby Horse (magazine) *Archvs:* MS correspondence of William Morris & his circle & of Arthur H. Mackmurdo; materials re William Morris, incl printed catalogues of Morris & Company
Svcs: photocopying svc via staff
Stock: bks/4000; periodcls/5; photos/750; illusts/ 200; archvs/12 cubic m
Classn: own
Pubns: Sir Frank Brangwyn 1867-1956: Catalogue of Works in Gallery's Colln (£3); Karl Parsons 1884-1934, Stained Glass Artist (£3.50); May Morris 1862-1938 (£4); Henry Holiday 1839-1927 (£4)
Staff: Other Prof: 3 curators
See also WILLIAM MORRIS SOC LIB (**S1465**)

S1465 🎓 🏛

William Morris Society Library

Kelmscott House, 26 Upper Mall, London, W6 9TA (020-8741-3735; *fax:* 020-8748-5207)
Email: william.morris@care4free.net

Gov Body: William Morris Soc *Chief:* Chair, Lib Cttee: Mr David Rainger BA
Assoc Libs: WILLIAM MORRIS SOC ARCHV, at same addr, contact the Curator
Entry: ref only *Open:* Thu, Sat 1400-1700 only
Subj: relating to William Morris & his circle & influence today: arts; lit; politics; hist
Equip: fax, computer (with wd-proc & internet)
Svcs: info, ref
Stock: bks/2500; slides/100; pamphs/50; audios/4; videos/4; CD-ROMs/2
Classn: own, using card index & computer lists
Pubns: William Morris Soc Journal (2 pa); Kelmscott Lecture (annual)
Staff: Other Prof: 1 curator (PT) *Non-Prof:* 2 (Office Mgr & Lib Chair, both voluntary & PT)
See also WILLIAM MORRIS GALLERY (**S1464**)

S1466 🎓

Wimbledon College, Milward Learning Resources Centre

Edge Hill, Wimbledon, London, SW19 4NS (020-8946-2533; *fax:* 020-8947-6512)
Email: enquiries@wimbledoncollege.org.uk
Internet: http://www.wimbledoncollege.org.uk/

Chief: Dir of Learning Resources: Mr Albert W.L. McDonald BEd(Hons)
Assoc Libs: CAMPION LIB, Campion Centre, Grand Dr, West Wimbledon, London, SW20 9NA (020-8540-4385; *fax:* 020-8540-8314)
Entry: coll membs only *Open:* term: Mon-Fri 0800-1400
Subj: all subjs; GCSE; A level; vocational *Collns: Archvs:* Wimbledon Coll Archvs (1892-date); records of Wimbledon School (1859-92); records of Wimbledon Mission
Equip: video viewer, copier, 29 computers (all with wd-proc, internet & CD-ROM) *Disabled:* Evacuchair *Officer-in-Charge:* Dir of Learning Resources, as above *Svcs:* info, ref, archv rsrch (£25 per hr)
Stock: bks/10000; archvs/150 linear m *Acqs Offcr:* Dir of Learning Resources, as above
Classn: DDC
Staff: Other Prof: 1 *Non-Prof:* 1 *Exp:* £4000 (2000-01)
Proj: new Lib Resource Centre (£1.2 mln)

S1467 🎓

Wimbledon School of Art Library

Merton Hall Rd, London, SW19 3QA (020-8408-5057; *fax:* 020-8408-5050)
Internet: http://www.wimbledon.ac.uk/

Chief: Head of Learning Resources: Mr Peter Jennett MA, MCLIP (p.jennett@wimbledon.ac.uk)
Dep: Libn: Ms Helen Davies MA, MCLIP (hdavies@wimbledon.ac.uk)
Entry: ref only by adv appt *Open:* term: Mon-Thu 1000-2030, Fri 1000-1930; vac: Mon-Fri 1000-1700 (subj to variation)
Subj: arts; costume; theatre *Co-op Schemes:* BLDSC, ILL, UK Libs Plus
Equip: 5 video viewers, copier (A4/5p, A3/10p), clr copier (A4/50p, A3/£1), computers (all with wd-proc & internet, available only to students) *Officer-in-Charge:* Head of Learning Resources, as above
Svcs: info, ref, biblio
Stock: bks/29000; periodcls/100; slides/40000; videos/1850; CD-ROMs/4 *Acqs Offcr:* Libn, as above
Classn: DDC *Auto Sys:* Unicorn
Staff: Libns: 3 *Other Prof:* 2 *Non-Prof:* 3 *Exp:* £10000 (1999-2000); £11000 (2000-01)

S1468 ♟ 🏛
Wimbledon Society Museum Library
22 Ridgeway, Wimbledon, London, SW19 4QN (020-8296-9914)
Email: info@wimbledonmuseum.org.uk
Internet: http://www.wimbledonmuseum.org.uk/

Type: amenity soc *Gov Body:* Wimbledon Soc
Chief: Curator of Bks: Mrs Cassandra Taylor BA
Entry: free entry to membs of public *Open:* Sat-Sun 1430-1700, other times by appt
Subj: local study (Wimbledon); any subjs pertaining to the hist, geog & notables of Wimbledon; biography; nat hist
Equip: copier (25p), clr copier (25p), computer (with wd-proc, internet & CD-ROM) *Svcs:* info, ref
Stock: bks/400; photos/3000; maps/250
Classn: own
Pubns: numerous pubns; list on appl
Staff: 1 bks curator plus other voluntary staff *Exp:* £200 (1999-2000)

S1469 🎓
The Women's Library
(formerly London Guildhall Univ, Fawcett Lib)
Old Castle St, London, E1 7NT (020-7320-2222; *fax:* 020-7320-2333)
Email: moreinfo@thewomenslibrary.ac.uk
Internet: http://www.thewomenslibrary.ac.uk/

Gov Body: London Metropolitan Univ (see **S1261**)
Chief: Dir: Ms Antonia Byatt *Dep:* Head of Lib Svcs: Ms Wendy Thomas
Entry: ref only; proof of ID & deposit of £4.50 required for Reading Room pass *Open:* Tue-Wed, Fri 0930-1700, Thu 0930-2000, Sat 1000-1600
Subj: genl; A level; undergrad; postgrad; all subjs of interest/relevance to women, particularly British
Collns: Bks & Pamphs: Josephine Butler Soc Colln (prostitution, sexuality & related topics, 1870, c500 vols, pamphs, archvs, photos & artefacts); Cavendish Bentinck Colln of old & rare items; Sadd Brown Lib (Women in the Commonwealth, 1939, 300 vols, 3 serials) *Archvs:* nearly 400 collns, primarily of women's suffrage orgs & their successors; records of prominent indivs & business & campaigning groups; records of 19C female emigration socs; Emily Wilding Davison papers; Fawcett Soc archvs; Josephine Butler Soc archvs *Other:* newspaper cuttings (19C-date); photo colln; ephemera
Equip: 3 m-readers, 3 m-printers, copier, video viewer, 8 computers (incl 2 with internet) *Svcs:* info, ref
Stock: bks/62000+, incl pamphs; periodcls/2400; photos/4398; m-forms/150+ m-form, 6000+ m-fiche; audios/130; videos/150; postcards/600+; banners/50+; numerous artefacts
Classn: DDC, UDC for uncatalogued pamphs
Auto Sys: Millennium
Staff: Libns: 3 Other Prof: 4 Non-Prof: 15

S1470 ♟ ✍
The Work Foundation Information Service
(formerly the Industrial Soc)
3 Carlton House Ter, London, SW1Y 5DG (020-7479-2323; *fax:* 020-7479-2121)
Email: infoserv@theworkfoundation.com
Internet: http://www.theworkfoundation.com/

Chief: Head of Info Svc: Mr Brendan McDonagh BLS, MSLS, MPhil (bmcdonagh@theworkfoundation.com) *Dep:* Knowledge Offcr: Ms Jill Duffin (jduffin@theworkfoundation.com)
Entry: membs only; others by adv appt *Open:* Mon-Fri 0915-1715
Subj: employment; work; employment law; industrial relations
Equip: copier, room for hire *Svcs:* info, ref

Stock: bks/2000; periodcls/100; pamphs/8000
Classn: LBS *Auto Sys:* BTP
Staff: Libns: 4 *Other Prof:* 1 *Non-Prof:* 3 *Exp:* £40000 (2000-01)

S1471 ♟ 🎓
World Energy Council, Information Services
5th Floor, Regency House, 1-4 Warwick St, London, W1b 5LT (020-7734-5996; *fax:* 020-7734-5926)
Email: info@worldenergy.org
Internet: http://www.worldenergy.org/

Type: NGO *Chief:* Mgr, Info Svcs: Mr Ted Mole DipLib *Dep:* Info Svcs Asst: Ms Gry Pedersen
Entry: adv appt *Open:* Mon-Fri 0930-1630
Subj: energy: oil, gas, nuclear, wind, solar, hydro etc
Equip: copier *Svcs:* info, ref
Stock: bks/500; periodcls/100
Classn: WEC Energy Classn
Pubns: reports, surveys & others; list of pubns regularly updated on web site
Staff: Libns: 1 *Non-Prof:* 1 (both have other responsibilities in addition to Info Svcs)

S1472 ♟
Young Book Trust Library
Book House, 45 East Hill, London, SW18 2QZ (020-8516-2985; *fax:* 020-8516-2978)
Email: ed@booktrust.org.uk
Internet: http://www.booktrusted.com/

Chief: Children's Libn: Mr E. Zaghini MCLIP
Entry: adv appt *Open:* Mon-Fri 0900-1700
Subj: ch's bks: fiction; non-fiction; ref *Collns: Archvs:* journals on ch's lit *Other:* Beatrix Potter Colln (bks & drawings)
Equip: copier, fax *Svcs:* info, ref, biblio
Stock: periodcls/57 past & present
Classn: own (non-fiction by category, fiction by author) *Auto Sys:* Cardbox
Pubns: Booktrusted News (3 pa); Children's Bk Handbook (1 pa); 100 Best Bks (1 pa); Looking for an Author (1 pa)
Staff: Libns: 1 *Non-Prof:* 14

S1473 ♟
Zinc/Lead Library
42 Weymouth St, London, W1G 6NP (020-7499-8422; *fax:* 020-7493-1555)

Type: trade assoc *Gov Body:* Lead Development Assoc Internatl *Chief:* Dir: Dr D.N. Wilson
Entry: ref only *Open:* Mon-Fri 0930-1715
Subj: metallurgy; zinc; lead *Co-op Schemes:* ILL
Equip: copier *Stock:* bks/6000

S1474 ♟
Zoological Society of London Library
Regent's Pk, London, NW1 4RY (020-7499-6293; *fax:* 020-7586-5743)
Email: library@zsl.org
Internet: http://www.zsl.org/

Chief: Libn: Ms Ann Sylph BSc, MSc, MCLIP
Dep: Asst Libn & Archivist: Mr Michael Palmer
Entry: borrowing for Fellows & corporate membs of the Soc & Fellows of the Royal Entomological Soc; Lifewatch membs & Friends of Whipsnade may use the lib for ref only; others may purchase a Lib Ref Ticket for a fee *Open:* Mon-Fri 0930-1730
Subj: zoology; animal conservation *Collns: Archvs:* archvs of the Zoological Soc of London, incl materials relating to the hist & admin of the Soc, London Zoo & Whipsnade *Other:* Image Colln, incl photographs of animals formerly at

London Zoo & Whipsnade Wild Animal Park (1864 onwards) & various illusts, prints & watercolours (16C onwards) *Co-op Schemes:* BLDSC
Equip: m-reader, copier *Svcs:* postal photocopying svc
Stock: bks/200000; periodcls/1300, plus 3700 non-current; photos/30000
Classn: Bliss *Auto Sys:* EOSi
Staff: Libns: 3

Londonderry

S1475 ✚
Altnagelvin Area Hospital, Multi-Disciplinary Education Centre Library
Glenshane Rd, Londonderry, BT47 1SB (028-7134-5171 x3725; *fax:* 028-7134-9334)
Email: RDoherty-Allan@alt.n-i.nhs.uk

Gov Body: Altnagavin Hosps Trust & Queen's Univ Belfast (see **S139**) *Chief:* Trust Libn: Ms Rosina Doherty-Allan BA, MA, DipIM *Dep:* Lib & info Offcr: Mr Paul McCabe
Entry: NHS staff; QUB staff *Open:* term: Mon, Wed-Fri 0900-1700, Tue 0900-2100, Sat 0930-1300; vac: Mon-Thu 0900-1700, Fri 0900-1630
Subj: medicine; nursing; social work; sociology
Co-op Schemes: BLDSC, Northern Ireland Health & Social Svcs Lib
Equip: video viewer, fax, 2 copiers (£1 per 20 copies), 5 computers (incl 2 with internet & 2 with CD-ROM) *Disabled:* wheelchair access, disabled parking, specially designed issue desk *Online:* Medline, CINAHL, Cochrane, BNI, Web of Science, HMIC, ChildData, ERIC, CareData *Officer-in-Charge:* Trust Libn, as above *Svcs:* info, ref, indexing
Stock: bks/6000; periodcls/120; pamphs/1100; videos/50 *Acqs Offcr:* Faculty Libn, Medicine & Health Scis: Mr Diarmuid Kennedy
Classn: LC *Auto Sys:* Talis
Staff: Libns: 1 *Non-Prof:* 2

S1476 ♟
The Heritage Library (Inner City Trust)
Hegarty House, 14 Bishop St, Londonderry, BT48 6PW (028-7126-9792; *fax:* 028-7136-0921)

Chief: Libn: Ms Patricia Ann Griffin
Entry: ref only *Open:* Mon-Fri 0900-1700
Subj: local study (Londonderry): hist & heritage
Collns: Other: Oral Hist Colln (local life from 1920s onwards); past issues of: London Illustrated News; Irish Telegraph; Belfast Newsletter (c1850-1940); The Capuchin Annual (c1920-70)
Stock: bks/c5000

S1477 🎓
North West Institute for Further and Higher Education, Library and Learning Resource Centre
Strand Rd, Londonderry, BT48 7AL (028-7126-6024/6127; *fax:* 028-7126-7054)
Email: llrcstaff@nwifhe.ac.uk
Internet: http://www.nwifhe.ac.uk/library/

Gov Body: Western Edu & Lib Board (see **P136**)
Chief: Libn: Mrs Madeleine Coyle MCLIP
Entry: staff & students *Open:* term: Mon-Thu 0900-2100, Fri 0900-1630; vac: Mon-Thu 0900-1300, 1400-1700, Fri 0900-1630
Subj: all subjs; genl; GCSE; A level; vocational
Co-op Schemes: ILL
Equip: m-reader, video viewer, copier, computers (incl wd-proc, internet & CD-ROM)
Stock: bks/17000
Classn: DDC *Staff: Libns:* 1 *Non-Prof:* 8

S1478 🎺🗝🖐

St Columb's Cathedral, Chapter House Library

London St, Londonderry, BT48 6RQ (028-7126-7313/2746)
Email: dean@derry.anglican.org
Internet: http://www.stcolumbscathedral.org/

Gov Body: Dean & Chapter of the Cathedral Church of St Columb, Londonderry *Chief:* Dean: Very Rev Dr William Morton
Open: Mon-Sat 0900-1600
Subj: Londonderry: generalities; religion *Collns: Bks & Pamphs:* Heygate Colln (rare pamphs on Irish affairs); Munn Colln (bks & pamphs etc relating to Londonderry area); Tenison Grove Colln of bks relating to Londonderry & Co Londonderry; hist of Londonderry companies; bks relating to Honourable Irish Soc *Archvs:* Cathedral records (from 1642) *Other:* artefacts relating to the Siege of Londonderry (1689); genealogical material
Equip: video viewer *Staff: Non-Prof:* 2

Loughborough

S1479 ✚ 🎺

3M BeST Information Services

3M Health Care Ltd, Morley St, Loughborough, Leicestershire, LE11 1EP (01509-613302; *fax:* 01509-613164)
Email: uk-best@mmm.com

Gov Body: managed by Instant Lib Ltd *Chief:* Managing Dir: Ms Diana Edmonds BA, FCLIP (de@instant-library.com) *Dep:* Info Offcr: Mr Andrew Poole BA, DipLib, MCLIP, FETC (ajpoole@mmm.com) *Other Snr Staff:* Info Offcr: Ms Emma Young BA, MA (alyoung@mmm.com)
Assoc Libs: branch of the 3M LIB & INFO SVC at the 3M Centre, St Paul, Minnesota, USA
Entry: 3M staff only *Open:* open 24 hrs to 3M staff; staffed: Mon-Fri 0900-1730
Subj: business; manufacturing; medicine; nursing; physiology *Co-op Schemes:* BLDSC
Equip: copier, computers (with internet) *Online:* 3M ATLAS Electronic Library (via intranet)
Stock: bks/c1500; periodcls/60; maps/40; CD-ROMs/5 *Acqs Offcr:* Info Offcr, as above
Classn: LC *Auto Sys:* Voyager *Staff: Libns:* 2

S1480 🎺

AstraZeneca Research and Development Charnwood, Information Science, Library and Archives

Bakewell Rd, Loughborough, Leicestershire, LE11 5RH (01509-644120; *fax:* 01509-645570)
Email: library.charnwood1@astrazeneca.com
Internet: http://charnwood.astrazeneca.com/

Chief: Libn: Mrs Susan Cooper BA(Hons), MCLIP
Entry: staff only
Subj: sci; pharmaceuticals
Equip: m-reader, m-printer, copiers, clr copier, computers (incl wd-proc, internet & CD-ROM), 2 rooms for hire *Svcs:* info, ref, biblio, indexing, abstracting, translation
Stock: bks/6000; periodcls/350
Classn: DDC *Auto Sys:* Aleph
Staff: Libns: 2 *Other Prof:* 7 *Non-Prof:* 3

S1481 🎺

BPB Information Centre

(formerly BPB Gypsum Ltd)
Technical Centre, East Leake, Loughborough, Leicestershire, LE12 6JS (0115-945-1500; *fax:* 0115-945-1678)
Email: information.centre@bpb.com
Internet: http://www.bpb.com/

Gov Body: BPB plc *Chief:* Mgr: Miss Elsa Audouard MSc (elsa.audouard@bpb.com) *Other Snr Staff:* Snr Info Scientist: Ms Hazel Biggs MSc (hazel.biggs@bpb.com)
Entry: not open to public; external enqs will be acknowledged *Open:* Mon-Fri 0900-1700
Subj: bldg materials; chem; physics; acoustics; paper; minerals; gypsum & plaster tech *Co-op Schemes:* BLDSC
Equip: m-reader, m-printer, fax, video viewer, copier, clr copier, 3 computers (all with wd-proc & CD-ROM, 1 with internet), room for hire *Online:* Dialog, Datastar, STN, Technical Indexes, Inside Science, EINS *Svcs:* info, ref, biblio, indexing, abstracting, translation
Stock: bks/5000; periodcls/35; pamphs/3000; maps/100; CD-ROMs/15
Classn: UDC *Auto Sys:* MS Access
Staff: Libns: 2 *Non-Prof:* 1

S1482 🎓

Loughborough Grammar School Library

Burton Walks, Loughborough, Leicestershire, LE11 2DU (01509-233233; *fax:* 01509-210486)
Internet: http://www.loughgs.leics.sch.uk/

Gov Body: Loughborough Endowed Schools *Chief:* School Libn: Mrs Valerie Bunn MCLIP
Assoc Libs: SCHOOL ARCHV, at same addr, Archivist: Mr Roger Willson
Open: term: Mon-Fri 0815-1700; vac: closed
Subj: all subjs; genl; GCSE; A level; local study (Loughborough) *Collns: Archvs:* hist of Loughborough Grammar School
Equip: video viewer, copier, clr copier, 7 computers (incl 5 wd-proc, 5 internet & 6 CD-ROM), TV with teletext *Svcs:* info, ref
Stock: bks/17000; periodcls/30; audios/180; videos/180
Classn: DDC *Auto Sys:* Alice
Staff: Libns: 1 *Non-Prof:* 1

S1483 🎓

Loughborough University, Pilkington Library

Ashby Rd, Loughborough, Leicestershire, LE11 3TU (01509-222360; *fax:* 01509-223993)
Email: library@lboro.ac.uk
Internet: http://www.lboro.ac.uk/library/

Gov Body: Loughborough Univ *Chief:* Univ Libn: Mrs Mary Morley BA, DipLib, MCLIP
Assoc Libs: UNIV ARCHVS, addr as above, Univ Archivist: Ms Jenny Clark (01509-222359; *fax:* 01509-223993; *email:* J.G.Clark@lboro.ac.uk)
Entry: non-membs by prior written request to libn; personal & corporate external membership available; adv appt for Univ Archvs *Open:* term: Mon-Fri 0900-2200, Sat 0900-1730, Sun 1000-2100; vac: Mon-Fri 0900-1730
Subj: all subjs; genl; undergrad; postgrad; local study (Leicestershire) *Collns: Bks & Pamphs:* EDC *Archvs:* records of Loughborough Univ (1966-date); records of predecessors, incl: Loughborough Coll (1909-52); Loughborough Coll of Tech (1952-66); Loughborough Coll of Edu (1952-77); Loughborough Coll of Art & Design (1952-98); various collns of deposited papers, incl: F.W. Collins Papers; John Lucas Literary Colln; Dan Maskell Papers; W.E. Pegg Papers & others
Co-op Schemes: BLDSC, SCONUL, UK Libs Plus

Equip: m-readers, m-printers, fax, video viewers, 4 copiers (A4/5p, A3/10p), clr copier (A4/70p, A3/£1.40), 94 computers (all with wd-proc, internet & CD-ROM), slide viewers, audio players *Disabled:* Kurzweil, Telesensory Chroma Plus enlarger/magnifier *Online:* 100+ different databases (access normally restricted to Univ membs) *Svcs:* info, ref, biblio
Stock: bks/400000, plus 111000 vols of bnd periodcls; periodcls/4000, plus 5000 e-journals; slides/26213; pamphs/41000; maps/108; m-forms/32500; AVs/751, incl audios & videos; reports/132000
Classn: DDC *Auto Sys:* Aleph
Pubns: range of leaflets & guides for lib users
Staff: 95 in total (59 FTE)

Loughton

S1484 🎓

Epping Forest College, Learning Resources Centre

Borders Ln, Loughton, Essex, IG10 3SA (020-8508-8311; *fax:* 020-8502-0186)
Email: rbarber@epping-forest.ac.uk
Internet: http://www.epping-forest.ac.uk/

Gov Body: Epping Forest Coll Corp Board *Chief:* Head of Learning Resources: Mrs Ruth Barber MEd, MCLIP
Entry: external membership by subscription
Open: term: Mon-Thu 0845-2000, Fri 0845-1600; vac: Mon-Fri 0845-1500
Subj: all subjs; genl; GCSE; A level; vocational
Collns: Other: illusts colln *Co-op Schemes:* BLDSC, Essex Lib Svc (LIFE)
Equip: video viewers, copier, computers (incl wd-proc, internet & CD-ROM) *Online:* Infotrac *Svcs:* info, ref, biblio
Stock: bks/35041; periodcls/120; audios/129; videos/361; CD-ROMs/50
Classn: DDC *Auto Sys:* Unicorn
Staff: Libns: 3 *Other Prof:* 4.5 *Non-Prof:* 3

Louth

S1485 🎺🖐

The Churches' Fellowship for Psychical and Spiritual Studies Library

The Rural Workshop, South Rd, North Somercotes, Louth, Lincolnshire, LN11 7TT (01507-358845; *fax:* 01507-358845)
Internet: http://www.cfpss.freeserve.co.uk/

Chief: Genl Sec: Mr Julian Drewett
Entry: membs only *Open:* by arrangement
Subj: phil; psy; religion; parapsychology
Equip: copier
Stock: bks/900; periodcls/2; audios/300; videos/10
Pubns: The Christian Parapsychologist (£2 per quarter)
Staff: Other Prof: 1 *Non-Prof:* 1 *Exp:* £200 (1999-2000)

S1486 ✚

Louth County Hospital, Medical Library

Thoresby Edu Centre, Louth County Hosp, High Holme Rd, Louth, Lincolnshire, LN11 0EU (01507-600100 x1324)
Email: library.louth@ulh.nhs.uk
Internet: http://www.hello.nhs.uk/

Gov Body: United Lincolnshire Hosps NHS Trust *Chief:* Libn: Ms Gill Kettle
Assoc Libs: GRANTHAM & DIST HOSP STAFF LIB (see **S757**); LINCOLN COUNTY HOSP PROF LIB (see **S954**); PILGRIM HOSP LIB (see **S204**)

Entry: primarily for staff & students of United Lincolnshire Hosps NHS Trust; limited svcs to staff of Lincolnshire Partnership NHS Trust; ref only to other Lincolnshire health workers **Open:** Mon, Wed, Fri 1100-1700; 24 hr access for membs **Subj:** medicine; health **Co-op Schemes:** BLDSC, NULJ
Equip: copier (not in lib), computers **Online:** Medline, CINAHL, BNI, PsycInfo **Svcs:** info, ref, lit searches, database training
Staff: Libns: 1

S1487 🗝 🏛
Louth Museum, Library
4 Broadbank, Louth, Lincolnshire, LN11 0EQ (01507-601211)

Gov Body: Louth Naturalists', Antiquarian & Literary Soc **Chief:** Hon Curator: Mrs Jean Howard **Dep:** Hon Sec: Mr J.R. Barker
Entry: by prior appt **Open:** Museum: Wed 1000-1600, Fri-Sat 1400-1600 (Mar-Oct)
Subj: local studies (Lincolnshire); generalities; sci; botany etc
Svcs: info
Stock: bks/1200; photos/400; illusts/60; maps/150; videos/2
Classn: own
Pubns: Fowler of Louth (£8.50 + £1.50 p&p); The Louth Flood, 29 May 1920 (£6.99); Brackenborough: The Story of a Manor (£16.95 + £2.75 p&p); The Lincolnshire Rising 1536 (£6.50 + £1.50 p&p); Recollections of a Lincolnshire Miller (£8.50 + £2 p&p); Kidgate (£6 + £1 p&p); Lincolnshire Stuff (£6.95 + £1.05 p&p); Billy Paddison of Soloby (£7.95 + £1.45 p&p); Upon the Parish Rate: The Story of Louth Workhouse & the Paupers of East Lindsey (£6.95); William Brown & the Louth Panorama (£26.50 & £4.10 p&p)
Staff: Non-Prof: 2

Lowestoft

S1488 🏛
Centre for the Environment, Fisheries and Aquaculture Science, Records and Information Unit
Lowestoft Laboratory, Pakefield Rd, Lowestoft, Suffolk, NR33 0HT (01502-562244; fax: 01502-524525)
Email: library@cefas.co.uk
Internet: http://www.cefas.co.uk/

Gov Body: DEFRA (see **S1110**) **Chief:** Libn: Mr David Hyett BSc, DipLib, MCLIP
Assoc Libs: CEFAS BURNHAM LABORATORY LIB, Remembrance Ave, Burnham-on-Crouch, Essex, CM0 8HA, Lib Mgr: Ms Paula Jones; CEFAS WEYMOUTH LABORATORY LIB, The Nothe, Barrack Rd, Weymouth, Dorset, DT4 8UB, Libn: Ms Sue Walker
Entry: adv appt (phone/writing) **Open:** Mon-Thu 0830-1700, Fri 0830-1630
Subj: fisheries; aquaculture; environmental sci
Collns: Bks & Pamphs: Fisheries pubns of the Food & Agric Org; pubns of ICES (Internatl Council for the Exploration of the Sea); expedition reports
Co-op Schemes: ANGLES
Equip: m-reader, m-printer, video viewer, fax, copier, computer (with CD-ROM) **Online:** Dialog, ASFA IDS (CEFAS staff only) **Svcs:** info, ref
Stock: bks/20000; periodcls/1000; various pamphs, slides & videos
Classn: own **Auto Sys:** CAIRS Total Library
Pubns: Lib Guide & Accessions Lists (internal only); List of Staff Pubns (quarterly)
Staff: Libns: 1 Non-Prof: 8

S1489 🎓
Lowestoft College Library
St Peter's St, Lowestoft, Suffolk, NR32 2NB (01502-525064; fax: 01502-500031)
Email: library@lowestoft.ac.uk
Internet: http://www.lowestoft.ac.uk/

Chief: Learning Resources Group Mgr: Ms C.A. Tunstill BA, PGCE, MCLIP, MLS
Entry: staff & students; ref only for others **Open:** term: Mon-Tue, Thu 0830-2000, Wed 1000-2000, Fri 0830-1700; vac: Mon-Fri 0900-1700
Subj: all subjs; GCSE; A level; undergrad; vocational **Collns:** Bks & Pamphs: maritime colln
Co-op Schemes: ILL
Equip: video viewers, copier, computers (all with wd-proc, internet & CD-ROM) **Svcs:** info, ref
Stock: bks/40000; periodcls/246; audios/200; videos/4000
Classn: DDC **Auto Sys:** Heritage IV
Staff: Libns: 1 Non-Prof: 6

Luton

S1490 ✚
Luton and Dunstable Hospital, The Library
Lewsey Rd, Luton, Bedfordshire, LU4 0DZ (01582-497201; fax: 01582-497164)
Email: david.johnson@lah-tr.anglox.nhs.uk
Internet: http://www.ldmedics.nhs.uk/

Gov Body: Luton & Dunstable NHS Trust **Chief:** Medical Libn: Mr David Johnson BA, DipLib, MCLIP
Entry: ref only to public **Open:** Mon-Fri 0830-1800; 24 hr access to hosp staff
Subj: healthcare **Co-op Schemes:** BLDSC, North Thames ILL Scheme, Anglia/Oxford ILL Scheme
Equip: fax, copier (A4/6p), 6 computers (all with wd-proc, 4 with internet & 5 with CD-ROM) **Online:** OVID, BNI, Medline **Svcs:** info, ref
Stock: bks/2500; periodcls/120; videos/125
Classn: NLM
Staff: Libns: 1 Non-Prof: 1 **Exp:** £18945 (1999-2000)

S1491 🗼 🏛
Luton Museum and Art Gallery, Reference Library
Wardown Pk, Old Bedford Rd, Luton, Bedfordshire, LU2 7HA (01582-546725; fax: 01582-746763)
Email: adeye@luton.gov.uk

Gov Body: Luton Borough Council (see **P111**)
Chief: Keeper of Local Hist: Dr Elizabeth Adey
Entry: staff only; access by others restricted, by appt only
Subj: local study (Luton); generalities; tech; arts; geog; hist **Collns:** Bks & Pamphs: Bagshawe Colln **Other:** various materials relating to straw plait & hat trade & to the lace industry
Equip: copier **Svcs:** info, ref
Stock: bks/10000
Staff: Other Prof: 1 **Exp:** £1300 (1999-2000); £800 (2000-01)

S1492 🎓
University of Luton, Learning Resources
Park Sq, Luton, Bedfordshire, LU1 3JU (01582-734111; fax: 01582-489325)
Email: ideas@luton.ac.uk
Internet: http://www.luton.ac.uk/LR/

Gov Body: Univ of Luton **Chief:** Dir (Learning Resources): Mr Tim Stone MA, MCLIP (tim.stone@luton.ac.uk)

Assoc Libs: PARK SQ LRC, addr as above (01582-743262); MEDIA CENTRE, addr as above (01582-489260); PUTTERIDGE BURY RESOURCE CENTRE, Putteridge Bury Campus, Hitchin Rd, Luton, LU2 3JU, Libn: Audrey Stewart BA, MCLIP (01582-489079); Hosp Site Libs: HEALTH CARE LRC (LUTON & DUNSTABLE), Dept of Acute & Critical Care, Univ of Luton & Dunstable Hosp NHS Trust, Dunstable Rd, Luton, LU4 0DZ, (01582-497296); HEALTH CARE LRC (BEDFORD), Dept of Primary & Continuing Care, Univ of Luton, Britannia Rd, Bedford, MK42 9DJ (01234-792215); HEALTH CARE LRC (AYLESBURY), Stoke Mandeville Hosp (see **S60**); HEALTH CARE LRC (HIGH WYCOMBE), Univ of Luton, Lovelock-Jones Edu Centre, Barracks Rd, High Wycombe, HP1 1QN (01494-425137)
Entry: permit must be obtained for ref by public **Open:** term: Mon 1030-2200, Tue-Thu 0830-2200, Fri 0830-1800, Sat-Sun 1000-1730; vac: Mon-Fri 0900-1700
Subj: all subjs; undergrad; postgrad; medicine
Co-op Schemes: BLDSC, BBI
Equip: m-reader, m-printer, video viewer, copier, 350 computers (all with wd-proc, internet & CD-ROM) **Disabled:** Kurzweil
Stock: bks/250000; periodcls/2500; slides/8000
Acqs Offcr: Acqs Offcr: Mr Paul Naish
Classn: DDC **Auto Sys:** Millennium
Staff: Libns: 18 Other Prof: 7 Non-Prof: 45 **Exp:** £570000 (1999-2000); £680000 (2000-01)

Macclesfield

S1493 🗝
Amateur Festivals Movement, Library
Festivals House, 198 Park Ln, Macclesfield, Cheshire, SK11 6UD (01625-428297; fax: 01625-503229)
Email: info@festivals.demon.co.uk
Internet: http://www.festivals.demon.co.uk/

Gov Body: British & Internatl Federation of Festivals **Chief:** Chief Exec: Ms Liz Whitehead BA, CertEd, FSCT, FRSA **Dep:** Administrator: Mr Anthony H. Lawson BSc, BA
Entry: adv appt **Open:** Mon-Fri 0930-1730
Subj: arts; festivals **Collns:** Bks & Pamphs: bks by membs on other famous membs, e.g., Vaughan Williams (founder of Federation); all Year Bks of the Federation since 1921; ref copies of special festival pubns
Equip: copier, computers (incl wd-proc, internet & CD-ROM) **Svcs:** info, ref
Stock: bks/c200; photos/c500; pamphs/c500; audios/c200
Classn: Chrono
Pubns: Year Bk (£6); current pubns by membs (all around £12.50)
Staff: Non-Prof: 4
Proj: applying to Lottery for grant to update Lib/Archv

S1494 ✚
East Cheshire NHS Trust, Multi-Professional Health Sciences Library
Macclesfield Dist Genl Hosp, Victoria Rd, Macclesfield, Cheshire, SK10 3BL (01625-661360; fax: 01625-663145)
Email: health_science_library@echeshire-tr.nwest.nhs.uk

Gov Body: East Cheshire Assoc for Medical Edu
Chief: Trust Libn: Mrs M. Perry MCLIP
Entry: membs of East Cheshire NHS Trust & primary care staff; students on placement **Open:** Mon-Fri 0900-1700; 24 hr ref access to membs
Subj: medicine; health scis; dentistry **Co-op Schemes:** BLDSC, Mersey Region ILL scheme, BMA, NULJ

Special Libraries

Macclesfield ▼ Manchester

(East Cheshire NHS Trust cont)
Equip: copier, 2 video viewers, 8 computers (incl wd-proc, internet & CD-ROM), scanner *Online:* AMED, BNI, CINAHL, Cochrane, Embase, HMIC, Medline, PsycInfo *Svcs:* info, ref, training
Stock: bks/5000+; periodcls/140; videos/20
Classn: DDC **Staff:** Libns: 1 Non-Prof: 1

S1495 ✎
King's School in Macclesfield Library
Cumberland St, Macclesfield, Cheshire, SK10 1DA
(01625-260000; *fax:* 01625-262002)
Email: mail@kingsmac.co.uk
Internet: http://www.kingsmac.co.uk/

Type: school **Chief:** Foundation Libn: Mrs G. Parry BA, MCLIP (gparry@kingsmac.co.uk) **Dep:** School Libn: Mrs J. Laidlaw MCLIP
Assoc Libs: KING'S SCHOOL (GIRLS' DIV), INFO RESOURCE CENTRE, Fence Ave, Macclesfield, SK10 1LS
Entry: adv appt **Open:** term: Mon-Fri 0830-1630; vac: closed
Subj: all subjs; genl; GCSE; A level **Collns:** Archvs: relating to hist of school **Co-op Schemes:** BLDSC
Equip: Cumberland St: 6 video viewers, copier, 17 computers (incl wd-proc, internet & CD-ROM); Fence Ave: 2 video viewers, copier, clr copier, 14 computers (incl wd-proc, internet & CD-ROM)
Svcs: info
Stock: bks/13559 (at Cumberland St), 8313 (at Fence Ave); periodcls/40; videos/180; AVs/180
Classn: DDC **Auto Sys:** Heritage **Staff:** Libns: 2 Non-Prof: 1 PT **Exp:** £19000 (2000-01)

S1496 🔑 ✎
Macclesfield College, Learning Resource Centre
Park Ln, Macclesfield, Cheshire, SK11 8LF
(01625-410035; *fax:* 01625-410001)
Email: info@macclesfield.ac.uk
Internet: http://www.macclesfield.ac.uk/

Chief: LRC Mgr: Mrs Barbara Taylor MA, MCLIP, PGCE (btaylor@macclesfield.ac.uk)
Entry: students & staff of Coll; ref only for public
Open: term: Mon-Thu 0900-2100, Fri 0900-1600; vac: Mon-Thu 0900-1630, Fri 0900-1600
Subj: all subjs; genl; GCSE; A level; local study (Macclesfield/Cheshire) **Co-op Schemes:** BLDSC
Equip: m-reader, copier, 2 video viewers, 24 computers (all with wd-proc, internet & CD-ROM)
Disabled: Aladdin Enlarger **Officer-in-Charge:** LRC Mgr, as above **Svcs:** info, ref
Stock: bks/17000; periodcls/60; audios/100; videos/200; CD-ROMs/50 **Acqs Offcr:** LRC Mgr, as above
Classn: DDC **Auto Sys:** Alice
Staff: Libns: 1 Non-Prof: 2

S1497 🏛
Macclesfield Museums, Library and Archives
Park Ln, Macclesfield, Cheshire, SK11 6TJ
(01625-613210; *fax:* 01625-617880)
Email: silkmuseum@tiscali.org.uk
Internet: http://www.silk-macclesfield.org/

Gov Body: Macclesfield Museums Trust **Chief:** Dir: Mrs Louanne Collins BA, MCLIP, AMA
Entry: ref only, by appt **Open:** Mon-Fri 0930-1700
Subj: local study (Macclesfield); social sci; tech; arts; silk industry; textiles; costume **Collns:** Archvs: Silk Manufacturers Archv (pattern bks & some documentation for Macclesfield silk firms) Other: photo colln (c20000 local images); oral hist archv (c300 recorded interviews); map colln
Equip: fax, copier, room for hire **Svcs:** info
Classn: DDC
Pubns: Macclesfield: The Silk Industry (£3.99); Silk Museums in Macclesfield (£1.95); numerous others, incl src bks, info leaflets, postcards & document packs
Staff: Libns: 1 Other Prof: 3 Non-Prof: 9

Magherafelt

S1498 ✎
North East Institute, Magherafelt Campus Learning Resource Centre
22 Moneymore Rd, Magherafelt, Co Londonderry, BT45 6AE (028-7963-2462; *fax:* 028-7963-3501)
Internet: http://www.nei.ac.uk/

Chief: LRC Co-ordinator (job share): Mrs K. Culbertson MCLIP (k.culbertson@nei.ac.uk) & Mrs Jacqui Moore (j.moore@nei.ac.uk)
Assoc Libs: ANTRIM CAMPUS LRC, Fountain St, Antrim, Co Antrim, BT41 4AL; FARM LODGE LRC, Farm Lodge Bldg, Ballymena, Co Antrim, BT43 7BN; TROSTAN AVE LRC, Trostan Ave, Ballymena, Co Antrim, BT43 7BN
Entry: students of Coll; others by appt, fee payable (Univ of Ulster students free) **Open:** Mon-Thu 0900-1700, Fri 0900-1630
Subj: GCSE; A level; vocational (GNVQ); computing; social sci; tech; business; arts **Collns:** Other: educational videos **Co-op Schemes:** Univ of Ulster
Equip: copier, computers (with wd-proc, internet & CD-ROM), scanner **Svcs:** info, ref, biblio, indexing
Stock: bks/4018; periodcls/40; videos/250; CD-ROMs/52
Classn: DDC **Staff:** Non-Prof: 5

Maidenhead

S1499 ✎
Berkshire College of Agriculture, Learning Resources Centre
Hall Pl, Burchetts Green, Maidenhead, Berkshire, SL6 6QR (01628-827427)
Email: lrc@bca.ac.uk
Internet: http://www.bca.ac.uk/

Chief: Learning Resources Mgr: Miss Rowena Perry BA(Hons), PGDipLib, MCLIP **Dep:** Asst Learning Resources Mgr: Mrs Sarah Lear BA(Hons), PGDipLib, MCLIP
Entry: ref only for genl public; please call before visiting **Open:** term: Mon-Thu 0900-1900, Fri 0900-1700; vac: Mon-Fri 0900-1700
Subj: agric; hortic; sports turf; equine studies; animal care; sport & leisure; veterinary nursing
Equip: video viewer, clr copier, copier, computers (with wd-proc, internet & CD-ROM) **Svcs:** info, ref
Stock: bks/9000; periodcls/150; videos/500
Classn: DDC **Auto Sys:** Heritage
Staff: Libns: 2 Non-Prof: 2

S1500 🔑
Chartered Institute of Marketing, Information and Library Service
Moor Hall, Cookham, Maidenhead, Berkshire, SL6 9QH (01628-427333; *fax:* 01628-427499)
Email: library@cim.co.uk
Internet: http://www.cim.co.uk/

Type: prof body **Chief:** Info Svcs Mgr: Ms Dawn Smith DipHE, BA, MCLIP
Entry: some loan material for membs; non-membs by appt only (fee chargeable) **Open:** Mon-Fri 0900-1700
Subj: marketing; mgmt **Collns:** Bks & Pamphs: market rsrch reports; directories
Equip: m-printer, fax, copier, computers (incl internet & CD-ROM) **Online:** FT Online Svcs **Svcs:** info, ref, biblio, indexing
Stock: bks/5000; periodcls/120; pamphs/various; CD-ROMs/some
Classn: London Business Classn **Auto Sys:** DBTextworks
Staff: Libns: 4 Non-Prof: 1 FT (2 job share)

S1501 🔑 🏛
The Stanley Spencer Gallery, Library
Kings Hall, High St, Cookham, Maidenhead, Berkshire, SL6 9SJ (01628-520890)

Type: independent art gallery **Gov Body:** Trustees & Mgmt Cttee of The Stanley Spencer Gallery **Chief:** Chairman of the Trustees & Cttee of Mgmt: Mr Richard Hurley
Entry: ref only **Open:** Easter-Nov: Mon-Sun 1030-1730; Nov-Easter: Sat & Sun 1100-1700 + public hols
Subj: all material relating to Sir Stanley Spencer CBE, RA **Collns:** Bks & Pamphs: catalogues of Spencer's gallery exhibs (1962-date); scrapbks Archvs: unique colln of cuttings from magazines & newspapers; colln of out-of-print bks as well as latest pubns on Spencer; Desmond Chute correspondence
Stock: bks/65
Pubns: Stanley Spencer (£25); Stanley Spencer (£14.95); Apotheosis of Love: Barbican Catalogue (£17.95); Stanley (£4.50); Catalogue Raissonne (£25)
Staff: 32 volunteers

Maidstone

S1502 🔑
Kent Archaeological Society Library
Maidstone Museum, St Faith's St, Maidstone, Kent, ME14 1LH (01634-240015)
Email: librarian@kentarchaeology.ac
Internet: http://www.kentarchaeology.co.uk/ or http://www.kentarchaeology.ac/

Gov Body: Kent Archaeological Soc Council
Chief: Hon Libn: Dr F.H. Panton BSc, PhD, FRSC, FRArS
Entry: membs only; non-membs if accompanied by a memb, otherwise non-membs may visit on Mon, Wed & Fri afternoons by appt **Open:** during Museum opening hrs: Mon-Sun 1000-1700
Subj: local studies (Kent); hist & archaeo, esp of Kent & Kentish locations & people **Collns:** Bks & Pamphs: journals etc of other historical & archaeo socs in the UK & Europe Other: Gordon Ward Archv (historical ephemera); extensive colln of visual records, incl photographic prints & negs, glass plate slides, clr transparencies, postcards, drawings, paintings, engravings, prints & lithographs (early 18C-date)
Stock: bks/10000+; illusts/50000, incl photos
Staff: Libns: 1 (retired, PT) **Exp:** £15000 (1999-2000); £15000 (2000-01)

S1503 ✎
Kent Institute of Art and Design Library
Oakwood Pk, Maidstone, Kent, ME16 8AG
(01622-757286; *fax:* 01622-621100)
Email: librarymaid@kiad.ac.uk
Internet: http://www.kiad.ac.uk/

Chief: Head of Lib & Learning Resources: Ms Vanessa Crane BA, DipLib, MCLIP (vcrane@kiad.ac.uk) **Dep:** Dep Head: Mrs Kathleen Gudfrey MA, DipLib, MCLIP **Other Snr Staff:** Site Libn (Maidstone): Ms Annamarie McKie
Assoc Libs: CANTERBURY LIB, New Dover Rd, Canterbury, Kent, CT1 3AN, Site Libn: Mrs Kathleen Godfrey MA, DipLib, MCLIP (01227-769371; *fax:* 01622-621100; *email:* librarycant@kiad.ac.uk); ROCHESTER LIB, Fort Pitt, Rochester, Kent, ME1 1DZ, Site Libn: Mrs Pauline Sowry BA, MCLIP (01634-830022; *fax:* 01634-820300; *email:* libraryroch@kiad.ac.uk)
Entry: access for ref, contact Libn in adv; borrowing by arrangement **Open:** term: Mon-Thu 0900-1900 (Canterbury -2030, Rochester -2000), Fri 0900-1700; vac: Mon-Thu 0900-1700, Fri 0900-1630 (times may vary)
Subj: arts; applied arts; decorative arts; design; arch; fashion; photography **Collns:** *Bks & Pamphs:* Herbert Read Colln (bks by & about H. Read); some antiquarian bks **Co-op Schemes:** BLDSC, Canterbury Circle of Libs, UK Libs Plus
Equip: m-reader, 15 video viewers, 6 copiers, 2 clr copiers (at Canterbury & Rochester), 40 computers
Svcs: info, ref
Stock: bks/72000; periodcls/300; slides/100000; videos/1000
Classn: DDC, CISfb (for arch collns) **Auto Sys:** Unicorn
Staff: Libns: 10 Other Prof: 3 Non-Prof: 8

S1504 ✚
Maidstone and Tunbridge Wells NHS Trust, Maidstone Hospital Library
(formerly Mid-Kent Healthcare Trust Lib)
Postgrad Centre, Maidstone Hosp, Hermitage Ln, Maidstone, Kent, ME16 9QQ (01622-224647; *fax:* 01622-224120)
Email: maidlib@netcomuk.co.uk
Internet: http://www.netcomuk.co.uk/~maidlib/

Gov Body: Maidstone & Tunbridge Wells NHS Trust **Chief:** Lib & Info Svcs Mgr: Mr David Copsey MA, DipLib, MCLIP (dcopsey@netcomuk.co.uk) **Dep:** Asst LIS Mgr: Mrs Emma Aldrich MA, MCLIP
Assoc Libs: KENT & SUSSEX HOSP, THE MACDONALD LIB (see **S2057**); PEMBURY HOSP LIB (see **S2058**)
Entry: free membership for employees of Maidstone & Tunbridge Wells NHS Trust; West Kent NHS & Social Care Trust; local PCTs; Kent Ambulance Trust; Kent & Medway Strategic Health Authority; INAM students; access by subscription to others **Open:** Mon, Wed-Thu 0900-2100, Tue, Fri 0900-1700
Subj: medicine; psychiatry; nursing; health mgmt & info **Co-op Schemes:** KSS, BLDSC, PLCS, NULJ
Equip: copier, fax, 6 computers (all with wd-proc, internet & CD-ROM) **Online:** KA24, Medline, CINAHL, Cochrane, PsycInfo, BNI, HMIC, Datastar
Svcs: info, ref, biblio
Stock: bks/14000; periodcls/500; videos/100
Classn: NLM **Auto Sys:** Librarian
Staff: Libns: 2 Non-Prof: 3.5 **Exp:** £330000 (2000-01); figs incl all Trust libs

Maldon

S1505 ♀
Thomas Plume's Library
Market Hill, Maldon, Essex, CM9 4PL (01621-856976; *fax:* 01621-854051)

Gov Body: Thomas Plume's Trust (registered charity No. 310661) **Chief:** Thomas Plume's Libn: Mrs O.G. Earnshaw **Dep:** Asst Libn: Mrs S.R. Belsham MCLIP
Entry: ref only **Open:** Tue-Thu 1400-1600, Sat 1000-1200; other times by adv appt

Subj: 16C, 17C & 19C pubns: phil; psy; sci; maths; tech; lit; geog; hist **Collns:** *Bks & Pamphs:* large colln of bks & pamphs collected between 1650 & 1704 as the basis for selecting titles for a genl ref lib & never weeded out; many of the bks were collected by buying from early London auctions *Archvs:* notebks & commonplace notes by the Lib's founder, Archdeacon Thomas Plume; MSS sermons of Dr Plume
Equip: copier (10p) **Svcs:** info, ref, biblio
Stock: bks/8000; pamphs/1500
Classn: catalogued by author; subj catalogue in progress
Pubns: Catalogue of the Plume Lib at Maldon, Essex (1959, £10); The Intentions of Thomas Plume (1985, £1.25); The Fathers of English Heritage (exhib catalogue, 1999, 50p); postcards (20p each)
Staff: Libns: 2
Further Info: This is a charitable lib which is open to both visitors & students; the Trustees are compiling applications for access & conservation grants.

Manchester

S1506 ✚
Bolton, Salford and Trafford Mental Health Partnership, Professional Library
(formerly Mental Health Svcs of Salford NHS Trust)
Prestwich Hosp, Bury New Rd, Manchester, M25 7BL (0161-772-3618; *fax:* 0161-772-3663)
Email: jcoulshed@library.bstmhp.nhs.uk

Gov Body: Bolton, Salford & Trafford Mental Health Partnership **Chief:** Libn: Mr N.J. Coulshed BA, MSc, DipLib **Dep:** Lib Assts: Mrs Valerie Hoath & Mrs Caroline Collinge
Assoc Libs: MEADOWBROOK DEPT OF PSYCHIATRIC MEDICINE, PROF LIB, Stott Ln, Eccles, Salford (0161-772-3749), Libn & Lib Assts as above (alternate between sites)
Entry: Trust staff; students on placement; others by appt for ref use only **Open:** Mon-Thu 0900-1200, 1300-1700, Fri 0900-1200, 1300-1600 (both sites)
Subj: psychiatry; psy; medicine **Co-op Schemes:** BLDSC, LIHNN, PLCS
Equip: 2 copiers (5p per sheet), fax, 6 computers (all with internet, 4 with wd-proc & 1 with CD-ROM) **Online:** PsycInfo, Medline & CONAHL via regional ADITUS internet access organised by North West Health Care Libs Unit **Svcs:** info, ref, biblio
Stock: bks/7500; periodcls/55; slides/5; m-forms/5; videos/40; AVs/20
Classn: Royal Coll of Psychiatrists **Auto Sys:** InMagic
Pubns: 3 quarterly Current Awareness Bulletins distributed free within Trust
Staff: Libns: 1 Other Prof: 1 **Exp:** £66850 (1999-2000); £68087 (2000-01)

S1507 ♀
Chetham's Library
Long Millgate, Manchester, M3 1SB (0161-834-7961; *fax:* 0161-839-5797)
Email: librarian@chethams.org.uk
Internet: http://www.chethams.org.uk/

Gov Body: Feoffees of Chetham's Hosp & Lib **Chief:** Libn: Dr Michael Powell BD, PhD **Dep:** Asst Libn: Dr Fergus Wilde BA, MA, PhD
Entry: ref only, adv appt for MSS & archvs **Open:** Mon-Fri 0930-1630
Subj: North West of England: hist; topography **Collns:** *Bks & Pamphs:* John Byrom Lib; Halliwell-Phillipps colln of broadsides; Manchester hist; early printed bks; shorthand *Archvs:* medieval MSS; local archvs
Equip: fax, copier, computer (with wd-proc, internet & CD-ROM) **Svcs:** info, ref

Stock: bks/100000; periodcls/50; photos/3000; slides/2500; pamphs/7000; maps/500; archvs/500 linear m
Classn: own
Staff: Libns: 2.5 Other Prof: 1 Non-Prof: 1.5

S1508 ✚
Christie Hospital NHS Trust, Kostoris Medical Library
Wilmslow Rd, Withington, Manchester, M20 4BY (0161-446-3452; *fax:* 0161-446-3454)
Internet: http://www.christie.nhs.uk/

Gov Body: Christie Hosp NHS Trust **Chief:** Medical Libn: Mr Steve Glover BSc(Hons) (sglover@picr.man.ac.uk) **Dep:** Systems Libn: Mrs Jenny Allen BA (jenny.allen@picr.man.ac.uk
Entry: external NHS staff ref only; academics by appt; not open to genl public **Open:** Mon-Wed 0900-1900, Thu 0800-1730, Fri 0800-1700, Sat 0900-1300
Subj: oncology & related subjs **Co-op Schemes:** BLDSC, LIHNN
Equip: m-reader, m-printer, fax, copier, 18 computers (all with wd-proc, internet & CD-ROM)
Svcs: info, ref
Stock: bks/5000; periodcls/120; pamphs/200; CD-ROMs/20 **Acqs Offcr:** Medical Libn, as above
Classn: Barnard **Auto Sys:** Winchill
Staff: Libns: 3 Non-Prof: 1 **Exp:** £103000 (1999-2000); £110000 (2000-01)

S1509 ☜
City College Manchester, Learning Centres
Alder House, Sale Rd, Manchester, M23 0DD (0161-957-1725)
Internet: http://www.manchester-city-coll.ac.uk/

Chief: Mgr, Learning Centres: Ms Liz Collier
Assoc Libs: ARDEN LEARNING CENTRE, addr as above, Centre Co-ordinator: Ms Jude Goslyn; ABRAHAM MOSS LEARNING CENTRE, Second Floor, Crescent Rd, Crumpsall, Manchester, M8 5UF, Centre Co-ordinator: Ms Rachel Folkes (0161-908-2853/5); CITY CAMPUS LEARNING CENTRE, 34 Whitworth St, Manchester, M1 3HB, Centre Co-ordinator: Mr Chris Hall (0161-236-7261); FIELDEN LEARNING CENTRE, 141 Barlow Moor Rd, Didsbury, Manchester, M20 2PQ, Centre Co-ordinator: Ms Helen Fishwick (0161-957-1686/93); WYTHENSHAWE LEARNING CENTRE, Moor Rd, Wythenshawe, Manchester, M23 9BQ, Centre Co-ordinator: Mr Glenn Clarke (0161-957-1506)
Entry: full facilities for coll staff & students; ref for all other users **Open:** *Arden Learning Centre:* term: Mon 0845-1800, Tue-Thu 0845-2000, Fri 0845-1600; vac: Mon-Fri 0900-1600; other sites vary
Subj: all subjs; genl; GCSE; A level; undergrad **Co-op Schemes:** BLDSC
Equip: video viewers, copiers, clr copier, computers (incl wd-proc, internet & CD-ROM) **Online:** Infotrac
Stock: bks/60000; periodcls/450; videos/200
Classn: DDC **Auto Sys:** Olib 7
Staff: Libns: 6 Non-Prof: 24

Co-operative College Library
See NATL CO-OP ARCHV (**A370**)

S1510 🏛
Equal Opportunities Commission, Information Centre
Arndale House, Arndale Centre, Manchester, M4 3EQ (0161-838-8324; *fax:* 0161-834-0803)
Email: research@eoc.org.uk
Internet: http://www.eoc.org.uk/ ☛

Manchester
▼
Manchester
Special Libraries

(Equal Opportunities Commission cont)
Chief: Libn: Ms Julie Foster BA, MCLIP (julie.joster@eoc.org.uk)
Entry: adv appt only, for rsrchers requiring access to material not available elsewhere
Subj: social sci; sex discrimination; gender equality; equal opportunities **Collns:** Bks & Pamphs: Court decisions (IT, EAT, ECJ, Court of Appeal) in respect of the Sex Discrimination & Equal Pay Acts **Co-op Schemes:** BLDSC
Equip: copier **Svcs:** info, biblio
Stock: bks/10000; periodcls/200 **Acqs Offcr:** Libn, as above
Classn: DDC **Auto Sys:** Olib
Pubns: list available; see web site
Staff: Libns: 1 Non-Prof: 0.5

S1511

Greater Manchester Police Museum, Library and Archives

Newton St, Manchester, M1 1ES (0161-856-3287; fax: 0161-856-3286)
Email: police.museum@gmp.police.uk
Internet: http://www.gmp.police.uk/about_gmp/history.asp

Gov Body: Police Authority funded **Chief:** Museum Curator: Mr Duncan Broady BA, MPhil
Dep: Museum Asst: Mr David Tetlow BA, MA
Entry: by appt only **Open:** Tue 1030-1530, other wk days by appt only, some evening visits
Subj: local study; social sci; geog & hist; policing
Collns: Archvs: police records of svc (Manchester City & Salford City, from mid 19C); Chief Constable's genl orders; original papers for Watch Cttee Minutes & Chief Constable's Annual Reports (both from late 19C)
Equip: m-reader, video viewer, copier **Svcs:** info, ref
Classn: UDC (mod)
Pubns: Greater Manchester Police; The Police! 150 Years of Policing in the Manchester Area (£8.95)
Staff: Other Prof: 2 **Exp:** £7500 (1999-2000); £8200 (2000-01); figs are for total budget, excl staff & maintenance

S1512

John Rylands University Library of Manchester

250 Oxford Rd, Manchester, M13 9PP (0161-275-3751; fax: 0161-273-7488)
Email: libtalk@man.ac.uk
Internet: http://rylibweb.man.ac.uk/

Gov Body: Univ of Manchester **Chief:** Dir & Univ Libn: Mr Bill Simpson (bill.simpson@man.ac.uk)
Dep: Asst Dir & Dep Libn: Dr Diana Leitch (diana.leitch@man.ac.uk) **Other Snr Staff:** Head of Admin & Staffing: Dr John Laidlar (john.laidlar@man.ac.uk); Head of Bibliographical Data Svcs: Ms Shirley Perry (shirley.perry@man.ac.uk); Head of Cataloguing: Ms Sandra Bracegirdle (s.j.bracegirdle@man.ac.uk); Head of Circulation Svcs: Ms Cheryl Cottrell (ccottrel@fs1.li.man.ac.uk); Head of Document Supply: Mr David Orman (david.orman@man.ac.uk); Head of Periodicals & Serials: Ms Sue Bate (s.m.bate@man.ac.uk); Head of Preservation & Photography:

Mr John Woodhouse (john.woodhouse@man.ac.uk); Head of Public Svcs: Ms Jessie Kurtz (jessie.kurtz@man.ac.uk); Head of Archvs: Mr John Hodgson (john.hodgson@man.ac.uk); Head of Special Collns: Dr Stella Butler (stella.v.butler@man.ac.uk)
Assoc Libs: SPECIAL COLLNS DIV, John Rylands Lib, 150 Deansgate, Manchester, M3 3EH (0161-834-5343/6765; fax: 0161-834-5574; email: special.collections@man.ac.uk); LABOUR HIST ARCHV & STUDY CENTRE (see **A365**); *Departmental Libs:* LEWIS LIB, Faculty of Social Scis & Law, Dover St, Manchester, M13 9PL (0161-275-4757); MEDICAL FACULTY LIB (see **S1535**); KANTOROWICH LIB, Arch & Planning Bldg, Oxford Rd, Manchester, M13 9PL (0161-275-6858); GEOG DEPT LIB, School of Geog, Mansfield Cooper Bldg, Oxford Rd, Manchester, M13 9PL, Libn: Ms Michele Moffat (0161-275-3657; email: michele.moffat@man.ac.uk); MUSIC DEPT LIB, Dept of Music, Denmark Rd, Manchester (0161-275-4985; email: kdeloose@fs1.li.man.ac.uk); PHYSICS DEPT LIB, Schuster Bldg, Dept of Physics & Astronomy, Oxford Rd, Manchester, M13 9PL, Snr Lib Asst: Mrs Adele Gillibrand (0161-275-4078); GATEWAY NURSING & MIDWIFERY LIB, 4th Floor, Gateway House, Piccadilly South, Manchester, M60 7LP (0161-237-2352; fax: 0161-236-2445); TAMESIDE NURSING & MIDWIFERY LIB (see **S54**)
Entry: main lib is open to all registered students & staff of the Univ of Manchester & to membs of other instns with which reciprocal arrangements are maintained; an external membership scheme operates for which there is a charge; *John Rylands Lib, Deansgate:* this bldg is open to membs of the public, collns here can be used subj to provision of appropriate proof of ID **Open:** *Main Lib:* term & Easter vac: Mon-Fri 0830-2130; Sat 0900-1800, Sun 1300-1800; other vacs: Mon-Thu 0830-1900, Fri 0830-1730, Sat 0900-1300; *John Rylands Lib, Deansgate:* Mon-Fri 1000-1730, Sat 1000-1300
Subj: undergrad; postgrad; all academic subjs in the fields of arts, humanities, medicine, sci & social sci are covered with exception of agric & veterinary sci **Collns:** Bks & Pamphs: Hester Adrian Colln (handicapped edu); Aldine Colln (early printed bks); Brockbank Cricket Colln; G.L. Brook Colln (theatre & drama); Kenneth Brown Railway Colln; Bullock Colln (early printed bks); Celtic studies colln; Christie Colln (early printed bks); Congregational Coll Colln (nonconformity); Dante Colln; Deaf Edu Colln; EDC; T.J. Edmondson Railway Colln; Raymond English Colln (anti-slavery); Esperanto Colln; French Revolution Colln; Haskalah Colln (Judaica); Health & Safety Colln; Hilliard Colln (handicapped edu); Annie Horniman Colln (theatre & drama); Peter Huchel Colln (German studies); Kelmscott Press Colln (private press); Labour Party Colln (newscuttings & pamphs); Manchester Geographical Soc Colln; Manchester Medical Soc Colln (hist of medicine); Manchester Museum Colln; Marmion Colln (ch's lit); Marmorstein Colln (Judaica); Mazarinades Pamphs (French studies); Near Eastern Collns (esp Arabic & Persian); Allardyce Nicoll Colln (theatre & drama); Northern Baptist Coll Colln (nonconformity); Official Pubns Colln (British & internatl orgs); Partington Colln (hist of chem); H.E. Roscoe Colln (hist of chem); Vera Southgate Booth Colln (ch's lit); Spencer Colln (early printed bks); William Temple Colln (church & soc); Unitarian Coll Colln (nonconformity); Alison Uttley bks & papers (ch's lit); H.G. Wilson Pamph Colln (anti-slavery); WW1 Colln Archvs: Manchester Univ Archvs; also: Robert Adamson papers (phil); Alexis Aladin papers (Russian hist); Samual Alexander papers (phil); Auchinleck papers (military studies); Audenshaw Colln (church & soc); Bagshaw family muniments; George Bellairs MSS; Bolton Cotton Spinners archvs; Thomas Botfield & Co archvs; Bromley Davenport family muniments; Clinton papers (military studies); Cornwall-Legh family

muniments; W.P. Crozier papers (journalism); John Dalton papers (hist of chem); Basil Dean papers (theatre & drama); Ducie family muniments; Dunham Massey family muniments; E.A. Freeman papers (English historian); Elizabeth Gaskell MSS; Moses Gaster Colln (Judaica, incl Genizah Fragments); Guardian Archvs (journalism); L.P. Hartley MSS; Alastair Hetherington papers (journalism); Victor Hugo correspondence; Holman Hunt papers (Pre-Raphaelite painter); W.S. Jevons papers (political econ); Jodrell Bank Colln (hist of astronomy); Stephen Joseph papers (theatre & drama); Zdenek Kopal archv (hist of astronomy); Legh of Lyme family muniments; Bernard Lovell archv (hist of astronomy); Manchester Soc of Architects archvs; T.W. Manson papers (nonconformity); McConnel & Kennedy archvs; Methodist archvs; A.N. Monkhouse papers (theatre & drama); P.J. Monkhouse papers (journalism); C.E. Montague papers (theatre & drama); Dorman O'Gowan papers (military studies); Oldham Textile Employers archvs; Owen Owens archvs; Papyri Collns (Arabic, Coptic, Greek, Hieratic & Hieroglyphic); Thomas Raffles papers (nonconformity); John Ruskin papers (Pre-Raphaelite painter); C.P. Scott papers (journalism); Soc of Architectural Historians of Great Britain archvs; Howard Spring MSS; Tabley family muniments; James Tait papers (English historian); Thrale-Piozzi MSS; T.F. Tout papers (English historian); Warburton family muniments; Western medieval MSS (esp Latin, English & French); Cheshire, Lancashire & Derbyshire Family Muniment Collns Other: BSI (on m-fiche); Spectral Data Colln; map colln; newspaper colln **Co-op Schemes:** ASLIB, CALIM, CERL, CURL, ESTC, FIL, ISTC, Libs North West, Rsrch Libs Group, SCOLMA, SCONUL, UKOLUG, LAMDA
Equip: m-readers, m-cameras, m-printers (staff operated), video viewer, 23 copiers (A4/6p, A3/10p), clr copier (staff operated), 240 computers (all with online & CD-ROM facilities) Disabled: Kurzweil, CCTV, braille embosser Online: numerous **Svcs:** info, ref
Stock: bks/3700000; periodcls/8886; slides/21900; m-forms/341857; audios/10900; videos/285; AVs/37000; archvs/1198063 MSS & archival items
Acqs Offcr: Head of Bk Acqs: Ms Charlotte Sing (charlotte.sing@man.ac.uk)
Classn: DDC **Auto Sys:** Talis
Pubns: Bulletin of the John Rylands Univ Lib of Manchester (£60 pa, 3 issues); John Rylands Rsrch Inst Newsletter (free); John Rylands Rsrch Inst Prospectus entitled "The Riches of the Rylands" (£1.50); numerous guides & exhib catalogues
Staff: Libns: 34.75 Other Prof: 13 Non-Prof: 155.25

S1513

Lancashire and Cheshire Antiquarian Society Library

Manchester Central Ref Lib, St Peter's Sq, Manchester, M2 5PD (0161-234-1979; fax: 0161-234-1927)
Email: lsu@libraries.manchester.gov.uk

Gov Body: LCAS Council **Chief:** City Libn of Manchester **Dep:** Asst Libn: Mr Terry Wyke
Entry: borrowing for membs only; ref only for others **Open:** Mon-Thu 0900-1930, Fri-Sat 0900-1700
Subj: Lancashire & Cheshire: local studies
Stock: bks/4000; periodcls/8
Classn: DDC
Pubns: Printed Catalogue (1968, £2.50); new catalogue in preparation
Further Info: the lib is housed at Manchester Central Ref Lib & is accessed via the Local Studies Unit
See also **O247**

 academic 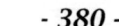 corporate

   governmental   medical

S1514
Manchester Business School, Library and Information Service
Booth St West, Manchester, M15 6PB (0161-275-6507; *fax:* 0161-275-6505)
Email: libdesk@man.mbs.ac.uk
Internet: http://www.mbs.ac.uk/studentlife/lis/

Gov Body: Univ of Manchester *Chief:* Libn & Info Svcs Mgr: Miss Kathy Kirby MA, DipLib, PGCE, MCLIP
Entry: corporate membership available for organisations/firms; info svc provided to anyone on fee-paying basis *Open:* term: Mon-Fri 0830-2030, Sat 0930-1700, Sun 1300-1700; vac: Mon-Fri 1000-1700
Subj: business *Collns: Other:* 2000 company reports; elec access to 20 mln businesses world-wide; UK & internatl market reports *Co-op Schemes:* BLDSC, Libs North West, EBSLG, LAMDA
Equip: m-reader, m-printer, copier, computers (incl wd-proc & CD-ROM)
Stock: bks/20000; periodcls/400
Classn: LBSC *Auto Sys:* Talis
Staff: Libns: 8 *Non-Prof:* 7
See also JOHN RYLANDS UNIV LIB OF MANCHESTER (**S1512**)

S1515
Manchester College of Arts and Technology, City Centre Campus Library
Lower Hardman St, Manchester, M3 3ER (0161-953-5995 x2226; *fax:* 0161-953-2259)
Internet: http://www.mancat.ac.uk/

Chief: Libn: Mrs Val Graham
Entry: authorisation required for external users
Open: Mon-Thu 0900-2000, Fri 0900-1600
Subj: genl; GCSE; A level; undergrad; vocational; business studies; mgmt; edu; furniture; bldg; construction; continuing edu
Equip: copier, m-reader, m-printer, video viewer, Alpha-vision viewer
Stock: bks/25000; periodcls/350; audios/150; videos/150
Classn: DDC

S1516
Manchester Evening News Library
164 Deansgate, Manchester, M60 2RD (0161-211-2486; *fax:* 0161-831-9467)
Email: cuttings.library@mcr-evening-news.co.uk

Gov Body: Guardian Media Group *Chief:* Libn: Mr Alan L. Ormerod *Dep:* Mrs Ann Gorry
Open: Mon-Fri 0730-1600
Subj: media *Collns: Archvs:* Manchester Evening News (m-film, from 1860s) *Other:* extensive cuttings lib (Manchester Evening News & natl newspapers); several 100 photos & slides
Equip: m-reader, m-printer, fax, copier, 2 computers (both with wd-proc & internet) *Svcs:* info, ref
Staff: Non-Prof: 6

S1517
Manchester Jewish Museum
190 Cheetham Hill Rd, Manchester, M8 8LW (0161-834-9879; *fax:* 0161-834-9801)
Email: info@manchesterjewishmuseum.com
Internet: http://www.manchesterjewishmuseum.com/

Gov Body: Trustees of Manchester Jewish Museum *Chief:* Administrator: Mr Don Rainger BEd(Hons)

Entry: adv appt *Open:* Mon-Thu 1030-1600, Sun 1030-1700; closed Jewish hols
Subj: local study (Greater Manchester): Jewish social hist; Jewish religion; Jewish lit; Jewish hist & traditions *Collns: Bks & Pamphs:* colln of pamphs: Jewish hist; Jewish women; local & natl synagogues; anti-Semitism; anti-fascism; Zionism; Palestine
Equip: fax, copier
Stock: bks/560; photos/18000; pamphs/1600
Classn: DDC
Pubns: Guide Bk (£2 + p&p)
Staff: Other Prof: 4

S1518
Manchester Literary and Philosophical Society, Library and Archives
Loxford Tower, Lower Chatham St, Manchester, M15 6BS (0161-247-6774; *fax:* 0161-247-6773)
Email: admin@manlitphil.co.uk
Internet: http://www.manlitphil.org.uk/

Chief: Hon Curator & Libn: Miss S.J. Lowe MA
Entry: adv appt, ref only *Open:* Mon-Fri 1000-1600
Subj: local studies: material by & about the Soc & its membs
Svcs: info, ref
Pubns: Manchester Memoirs & Proceedings (approx annual, publ since 1781); Index to Manchester Memoirs & Proceedings 1781-1989 (supplement 1959-99 publ in Vol 137 of Memoirs & Proceedings); John Dalton: A Biography, by A.L. Smyth (2nd ed, 1997); other occasional monographs

S1519
The Manchester Metropolitan University Library
All Saints, Manchester, M15 6BH (0161-247-6104; *fax:* 0161-247-6349)
Internet: http://www.mmu.ac.uk/services/library/

Chief: Univ Libn: Prof Colin Harris BA, MA, MLS, BPhil, PhD, FCLIP *Dep:* Dep Libn: Mrs G. Barry BA, MSc, MCLIP
Assoc (Site) Libs: AYTOUN LIB; ELIZABETH GASKELL LIB; DIDSBURY LIB; HOLLINGS LIB; CREWE LIB; ALSAGER LIB; all communications via Univ Libn
Entry: external users other than locally agreed by prior arrangement *Open:* term: Mon-Thu 0845-2045, Fri 0845-1800, Sat-Sun 1000-1600 (ref only on Sun); vac: Mon-Fri 0900-1630
Subj: all subjs; undergrad; postgrad; local study (Manchester, 20 mile radius) *Collns: Bks & Pamphs:* Assocs File; Bk Design Colln (late 18C-date); Children's Colln; Illusts Colln; Lancashire Cotton Trade Colln; Local Studies Colln; Manchester Soc of Architects Colln (18C-20C); Open Univ Colln; RIBA Lib; Statistics Colln; parliamentary papers (19C-20C); European info; exhib catalogues (all at All Saints Lib); Market Reports Colln (at Aytoun Lib); School Experience Colln (at Crewe Lib); Morten Dandy Colln; Schools Colln (all at Didsbury Lib); Statutes Colln (at Elizabeth Gaskell Lib); Home Studies Colln (at Hollings Lib) *Archvs:* Artists' Archv, incl work & correspondence of: Barnett Freedman; John Farleigh; Peter Reddick; Rigby Graham; Paul Hogarth; Simon Laurence; archv materials from Univ & predecessor Colls, incl Coll of Art & Polytechnic (official records are housed separately); all held at All Saints Lib *Other:* maps & atlases; Seddon Colln (32000 Victorian & Edwardian greetings cards); Harry Page Colln (Victorian ephemera & 20C bkplates); North West Film Archv (see **A371**) *Co-op Schemes:* BLCMP, Libs North West, CALIM, NoWAL, UK Libs Plus

Equip: wide range of equip & facilities *Online:* wide range of online svcs (CD-ROM & web-based), available only to membs of Univ
Stock: bks/833000, excl bnd periodcls; periodcls/4400
Classn: DDC *Auto Sys:* Talis
Pubns: numerous
Staff: Libns: 61.5 *Other Prof:* 3 *Non-Prof:* 98.1
Exp: £1863571 (1999-2000); £1914288 (2000-01)

S1520
Manchester Royal Infirmary, Jefferson Library
Oxford Rd, Manchester, M13 9WL (0161-276-4344; *fax:* 0161-276-6918)
Email: Jefferson.Library@cmmc.nhs.uk

Gov Body: Central Manchester & Manchester Children's Univ Hosps NHS Trust *Chief:* Trust Libn: Mrs Rini Banerjee BA, MA, MCLIP
Entry: staff of Trust *Open:* Mon-Thu 0930-2000, Fri 0930-1700
Subj: medicine; nursing; surgery *Collns: Bks & Pamphs:* Dr G. Jefferson Neurosurgical Colln *Archvs:* archvs of Manchester Royal Infirmary *Co-op Schemes:* BLDSC, LIHNN
Equip: m-reader, video viewer, fax, copier, computers (incl wd-proc, internet & CD-ROM)
Svcs: info, ref, biblio
Stock: bks/3400; periodcls/94; photos/1000; slides/500; pamphs/100; maps/200; archvs/50 shelves
Classn: NLM *Staff: Libns:* 1 *Non-Prof:* 2

S1521
Manchester School of Physiotherapy Library
Manchester Royal Infirmary, Oxford Rd, Manchester, M13 9WL (0161-276-8716; *fax:* 0161-276-8711)
Email: Colette.King@cmmc.nhs.uk
Internet: http://www.cmht.nwest.nhs.uk/sop/physiolibrary2.asp

Gov Body: Central Manchester & Manchester Children's Univ Hosps NHS Trust *Chief:* Libn: Ms Colette King MSc, BA, MCLIP *Dep:* Lib Asst: Ms Deborah Booth
Entry: adv appt for external visitors *Open:* Mon, Wed-Thu 0845-1700, Tue 0845-1900, Fri 0845-1630
Subj: medicine; physiotherapy *Co-op Schemes:* ILL
Equip: copiers (£1 per 20 copies), 17 computers (incl wd-proc & internet) *Online:* Medline, AMED, CINAHL, Cochrane

S1522
Nazarene Theological College Library
Dene Rd, Didsbury, Manchester, M20 8GU (0161-438-1922; *fax:* 0161-448-0275)
Email: library@nazarene.ac.uk
Internet: http://www.nazarene.ac.uk/

Gov Body: Coll Academic Board *Chief:* Libn: Mr Donald MacIver BSc, ThB, BD, DipILM *Other Snr Staff:* Bookshop Mgr: Mrs Heather Bell ThB, DipLib; Archivist: Dr Hugh Rae
Entry: ref required *Open:* Mon-Sat 0800-2230
Subj: phil (undergrad); religion (undergrad & postgrad); sociology of religion; Biblical studies; theology; church hist; practical & social theology; comparative religion; geog; hist (A level) *Collns: Archvs:* Church of the Nazarene in the British Isles
Co-op Schemes: BLDSC, ILL
Equip: m-reader, copier, 14 computers (incl 12 with wd-proc, 12 with CD-ROM & 12 with internet)

Special Libraries

Manchester
▼
Matlock

(Nazarene Theological Coll Lib cont)
Stock: bks/14000; periodcls/104; audios/400; archvs/20 linear m
Classn: DDC
Pubns: Lib Handbook (free to membs)
Staff: Libns: 1 *Other Prof:* 1
Proj: new library/teaching centre, starting Spring 2003

S1523
North Manchester General Hospital, Joint Education Library
Postgrad Medical Centre, Delaunays Rd, Crumpsall, Manchester, M8 6RN (0161-720-2722/18; *fax:* 0161-720-2443)
Email: Deborah.Dunton@mail.nmcnhc-tr.nwest.nhs.uk

Chief: Libn: Mrs Deborah A. Dunton BA, MCLIP
Dep: Mrs Sonia Coffey
Open: Sep-Jun: Mon-Thu 0830-2000, Fri 0830-1630; Jul-Aug: Mon-Tue, Thu 0900-1700, Wed 0900-2000, Fri 0900-1630
Subj: medicine; nursing *Co-op Schemes:* BLDSC, LIHNN
Equip: copier (A4/£1 per 14), fax, 3 computers (all with wd-proc, internet & CD-ROM) *Online:* Aditus: 9 databases incl Medline, CINAHL, Embase, AMED, PsycInfo (NHS staff only) *Svcs:* info, ref, biblio
Stock: bks/4200; periodcls/105 *Acqs Offcr:* Libn, as above
Classn: DDC *Auto Sys:* DBTextworks
Staff: Libns: 1 *Non-Prof:* 3

S1524
North Trafford College Library
Talbot Rd Centre, Stretford, Manchester, M32 0XH (0161-886-7012; *fax:* 0161-872-7921)
Email: j.temple@northtrafford.ac.uk
Internet: http://www.northtrafford.ac.uk/

Gov Body: North Trafford Corp *Chief:* Snr Libn: Mr Jim Temple BA(Hons), PGDipLIS
Assoc Libs: MOSS RD LIB, Moss Rd, Stretford, Manchester, M32 0AZ
Entry: enrolled students, others by permission of Libn *Open: Talbot Rd Lib:* Mon-Thu 0845-1900, Fri 0845-1630; *Moss Rd Lib:* Mon-Thu 0900-1900, Fri 0900-1200
Subj: GCSE; A level; vocational; generalities; social sci; lang; sci; maths; tech *Co-op Schemes:* BLDSC
Equip: m-reader, copier, computers (incl wd-proc, internet & CD-ROM) *Svcs:* info, ref, biblio
Stock: bks/20000; periodcls/200; videos/200
Classn: DDC *Staff:* Libns: 1.5 *Non-Prof:* 1.5

S1525
North West Arts Board, Library and Information Service
Manchester House, 22 Bridge St, Manchester, M3 3AB (0161-834-6644; *fax:* 0161-834-6969)
Email: info@nwarts.co.uk
Internet: http://www.arts.org.uk/

Type: regional arts board *Chief:* Libn: Ms Julie Leather (jleather@nwarts.co.uk)

Entry: ref only, adv appt *Open:* Mon-Thu 0900-1730, Fri 0900-1700
Subj: arts (all art-forms); arts admin; cultural policy
Equip: computer (with internet & CD-ROM); FunderFinder & Grantseeker software *Svcs:* info, ref
Stock: bks/6487; periodcls/90; audios/23; videos/23; CD-ROMs/32
Classn: DDC
Staff: *Other Prof:* 51 *Non-Prof:* 1 for whole of North West Arts Board *Exp:* £18400 (1999-2000); £19000 (2000-01)

S1526
Partnership for Theological Education, Luther King House Library
(formerly Northern Federation for Training in Ministry)
Brighton Grove, Rusholme, Manchester, M14 5JP (0161-224-6404; *fax:* 0161-248-8201)
Email: rachel.eichhorn@lkh.co.uk

Gov Body: Luther King House Educational Trust; provides lib svcs for Northern Baptist Coll, Northern Ordination Course, Unitarian Coll, Hartley-Victoria Coll, Northern Coll & Manchester Christian Inst
Chief: Learning Resources Tutor: Mrs Rachel Eichhorn BA, PGDip *Dep:* Learning Resources Asst: Ms Pat Anstis
Entry: open to public for ref only by appt *Open:* Mon-Fri 0930-1730
Subj: phil; religion; social sci *Collns: Archvs:* held in John Rylands Lib (see **S1512**) *Other:* community studies colln (resource materials) *Co-op Schemes:* ABTAPL, Union List of Periodicals
Equip: copier
Stock: bks/27000; periodcls/140; pamphs/400; audios/10; videos/50
Classn: DDC *Staff:* Libns: 1

S1527
The Portico Library
57 Mosley St, Manchester, M2 3HY (0161-236-6785; *fax:* 0161-236-6803)
Email: thelibrarian@theportico.org.uk
Internet: http://www.theportico.org.uk/

Gov Body: Trustees & Cttee *Chief:* Libn: Miss Emma Marigliano
Entry: membership by subscription or rsrch by appt *Open:* Mon-Fri 0930-1630
Subj: mostly 19C fiction; poetry; drama; travel; biography; hist; topography; nat hist; arch; politics & travel; temp new fiction/non-fiction *Collns: Bks & Pamphs:* Portico Colln of North West Fiction (fiction about the North West, or by local novelists) *Archvs:* archvs of the lib since its foundation in 1806, incl catalogues *Co-op Schemes:* AIL
Equip: copier, fax *Svcs:* info, ref, biblio
Stock: bks/25000; periodcls/24; slides/400; maps/50; photos & illusts/500
Classn: Fixed Shelf-Ref
Pubns: Boomtown Manchester & The Portico Colln (£9.95); Treasures from the Portico (£2.50); An Ornament to the Town: A Hist of the Portico Lib (£25); various monographs from 75p
Staff: Libns: 1 *Non-Prof:* 6
Further Info: The Portico Lib also awards the biennial North West Prize for Lit, & the Biennial Schools Exhib & Art Prize

S1528
Royal Northern College of Music Library
124 Oxford Rd, Manchester, M13 9RD (0161-907-5243; *fax:* 0161-273-7611)
Email: library@rncm.ac.uk
Internet: http://www.rncm.ac.uk/

Gov Body: RNCM plc *Chief:* Libn: Ms Anna Smart (anna.smart@rncm.ac.uk) *Dep:* Snr Asst Libns: Ms Rhiannon Jones (rhiannon.jones@rncm.ac.uk) & Mr Geoff Thomason (geoff.thomason@rncm.ac.uk)
Entry: ref only by adv appt for non-membs *Open:* term: Mon-Thu 0900-1900, Fri 0930-1700, Sat 0900-1300; vac: Mon-Fri 1000-1300, 1400-1630
Subj: music *Collns: Bks & Pamphs:* Richard Hall Colln (scores & early eds); Hansen Colln (20C Scandinavian music); Horenstein Colln (conducting); Manchester European Wind Lib (printed & MS scores); early printed & MS music *Archvs:* records of Coll & predecessors, incl: Northern School of Music archvs; Royal Manchester Coll of Music archv (1893-1973); other deposited collns incl: Alan Rawsthorne MSS; Walter & Ida Carroll Collns; John Ogdon MSS; Adolph Brodsky Archv; Philip Newman Colln; Gwydion Brooke Bassoon Colln; Gordon Green Colln (keyboard music); Sir Charles Groves Colln (contemporary scores); Halifax Colln (keyboard music); Hesketh Colln (chamber music & early 20C song); Evelyn Rothwell Colln (wind chamber music); Dame Eva Turner Colln (vocal music) *Other:* Rabenovitch Colln (opera & vocal music recordings); RNCM Colln of Historic Musical Instruments *Co-op Schemes:* BLDSC, CALIM, Manchester & Salford Music Libns' Group, Music Libs Online (JISC eLib proj), RSLP Ensemble Proj
Stock: bks/c85000; periodcls/98; audios/c20000; videos/200+
Classn: LC *Auto Sys:* Geac
Staff: Libns: 4 *Non-Prof:* 6

S1529
Salford College, Learning Resource Centres
Worsley Campus, Walkden Rd, Worsley, Manchester, M28 7QD (0161-886-5097; *fax:* 0161-886-5100)
Email: una.gillham@salford-col.ac.uk
Internet: http://www.salford-col.ac.uk/

Chief: LRC Mgr: Ms Una Gillham BA, PGCE
Assoc Libs: WORSLEY CAMPUS LRC, addr as above; CITY CAMPUS LRC, Lissadel St, Salford, Lancashire, M6 6AP
Entry: Coll staff & students *Open:* term: Mon-Thu 0830-1900, Fri 0830-1600
Subj: all subjs; vocational; generalities; phil; psy; social sci; tech; arts *Co-op Schemes:* ILL
Equip: 2 m-readers, m-printer, fax, copiers, computers (with wd-proc, internet & CD-ROM)
Svcs: info, ref, biblio, abstracting
Stock: bks/20500; periodcls/65; videos/c500; archvs/4000 items
Classn: DDC *Auto Sys:* Heritage
Staff: Libns: 1 *Other Prof:* 2 *Non-Prof:* 8

S1530
Siemens plc, Automation and Drives Library and Information Service
Sir Williams Siemens House, Princess Rd, Manchester, M20 2UR (0161-446-5708; *fax:* 0161-446-5522)
Email: jonesh@plcman.siemens.co.uk

Chief: Libn: Mrs Hilary J. Jones BA(Hons), MCLIP
Entry: company staff; external enqs by phone, fax or email as appropriate *Open:* staffed: Mon-Fri 0830-1630; open 24 hrs for staff
Subj: Siemens products; numeric controls; drives; automation; process control *Co-op Schemes:* BLDSC, ILL, certain BSI pubns
Equip: m-reader, copier, computers (with internet & CD-ROM) *Online:* company intranet *Svcs:* info, ref, biblio
Stock: bks/10500; periodcls/30; maps/some; AVs/some; technical data on CD-ROM & disk
Classn: DDC, own (specialised subj area) *Auto Sys:* Heritage IV *Staff:* Libns: 1

S1531 ✚

South Manchester University Hospitals NHS Trust, Library Services

Edu & Rsrch Centre, Wythenshawe Hosp, Southmoor Rd, Manchester, M23 9LT (0161-291-5778; *fax:* 0161-291-5780)
Email: erclibrary@fs1.with.man.ac.uk

Chief: Trust Lib Svcs Mgr: Mrs D.T. Schofield BA, DipLib
Entry: Trust membs only, or via "Passport" Scheme *Open:* Mon-Tue, Thu 0830-1900, Wed, Fri 0830-1730
Subj: health *Co-op Schemes:* BLDSC, LIHNN, PLCS, NULJ
Equip: copier, computers (with internet) *Online:* health databases via internet *Svcs:* info, ref, biblio
Stock: bks/5000; periodcls/200
Classn: NLM *Auto Sys:* Winchill
Pubns: Lib News
Staff: Libns: 3 *Non-Prof:* 2

S1532 ✚

St Mary's Medical Library

Biomedical Rsrch Centre, St Mary's Hosp, Hathersage Rd, Manchester, M13 0JH (0161-276-6467; *fax:* 0161-276-6694)

Chief: Libn: Ms Deborah Thornton
Entry: non-staff by adv appt *Open:* Mon-Thu 0900-1700, Fri 0900-1630; 24 hr access for membs
Subj: medicine; nursing; midwifery; obstetrics; paediatrics *Co-op Schemes:* BLDSC
Equip: copier, computers *Svcs:* info
Stock: bks/3732; periodcls/63
Classn: NLM *Auto Sys:* DBTextworks
Staff: Libns: 1

S1533 🗝

The Textile Institute, Lord Barnby Foundation Library

4th Floor, St James's Bldgs, Oxford St, Manchester, M1 6FQ (0161-237-1188; *fax:* 0161-236-1991)
Email: tiihq@textileinst.org.uk
Internet: http://www.texi.org/

Chief: Info Mgr: Ms Rebecca Unsworth BA(Hons), MSc (runsworth@textileinst.org.uk) *Dep:* Lib & Info Offcr: Mr Ian Calloway BA(Hons) (icalloway@textileinst.org.uk)
Entry: ref only, adv appt *Open:* Mon-Fri 0900-1700
Subj: textiles; clothing *Collns: Bks & Pamphs:* BSI; back issues of Journal of the Textile Inst *Co-op Schemes:* BLDSC, ILL
Equip: copier, fax, 11 computers (all with wd-proc, internet & CD-ROM) *Online:* Kompass *Officer-in-Charge:* Info Mgr, as above *Svcs:* info, ref, biblio, indexing, abstracting
Stock: bks/500; periodcls/1000+; CD-ROMs/4
Acqs Offcr: Info Mgr, as above
Classn: DDC
Pubns: full catalogue on appl
Staff: Libns: 2 *Exp:* £2000 (2000-01)

S1534 ✚

Trafford Healthcare NHS Trust Library

Edu Centre, Trafford Genl Hosp, Moorside Rd, Manchester, M41 5SL (0161-746-2263; *fax:* 0161-748-1260)
Email: library@traffdhc-tr.nwest.nhs.uk

Chief: Lib Mgr: post vacant *Dep:* Mrs Christin Bond *Other Snr Staff:* Mrs Patricia Brocklehurst; Mrs Helen Collantine

Open: Sep-Jun: Mon-Tue, Fri 0900-1700, Wed 0930-2000, Thu 0930-1800; Jul-Aug: Mon-Fri 0900-1700
Subj: medicine; healthcare
Equip: copier (10p), 6 computers (incl 2 with wd-proc, 5 with internet & 5 with CD-ROM) *Svcs:* info, ref
Stock: bks/6000; periodcls/100; videos/50
Classn: DDC
Staff: Non-Prof: 1.5 *Exp:* £1500 (1999-2000)

S1535 🎓 ✚

University of Manchester, Medical Faculty Library

3rd Floor, Stopford Bldg, Oxford Rd, Manchester, M13 9PT (0161-275-5539)
Email: medfacli@fs1.li.man.ac.uk
Internet: http://rylibweb.man.ac.uk/medicine/medfac.html

Gov Body: Univ of Manchester (see **S1512** for John Rylands Lib) *Chief:* Acting Faculty Libn: Ms Eleri Strittmatter (eleri.g.strittmatter@man.ac.uk)
Dep: Snr Lib Asst: Ms Sarah Rickards
Entry: staff & students of the Univ *Open:* term: Mon-Fri 0900-2000; vac: Mon-Fri 0930-1700
Subj: medicine; dentistry
Equip: 2 copiers (A4/6p, A3/10p), computers (incl internet) *Online:* Medline, Cochrane, AMED, Embase, CancerLit, BNI, PsycInfo, Zetoc, ToxLine, HMIC, Web of Science & others
Classn: DDC *Staff:* 3 in total

S1536 🎓

University of Manchester Institute of Science and Technology, Library and Information Service

PO Box 88, Sackville St, Manchester, M60 1QD (0161-200-4924; *fax:* 0161-200-4941)
Email: infodesk@umist.ac.uk
Internet: http://www2.umist.ac.uk/library/

Gov Body: UMIST *Chief:* Univ Libn: Mr Mike Day BSc, MSc (M.Day@umist.ac.uk) *Dep:* Dep Libn: Mr David Whitehurst BSc, DipLib (David.Whitehurst@umist.ac.uk) *Other Snr Staff:* Head of Cataloguing, Rare Bks & Archvs: Ms Janet Barratt (Janet.Barratt@umist.ac.uk)
Assoc Libs: JOULE LIB, contact details as above; PRECINCT LIB, Crawford House, Oxford Rd, Manchester, Site Libn: Ms Rachel Beckett (0161-200-3200; *fax:* 0161-200-3205; *email:* Rachel.Beckett@umist.ac.uk)
Entry: ref only for external readers; annual fees for borrowing *Open: Joule Lib:* term & Easter vac: Mon-Fri 0900-2045, Sat 0900-1800, Sun 1300-1800; vac: Mon-Fri 0900-1700, Sat 0900-1145; *Precinct Lib:* term & Easter vac: Mon-Fri 0900-2100, Sat 0900-1800, Sun 1300-1800; vac: Mon-Fri 0900-1700, Sat 0900-1200
Subj: sci; tech; social sci; lang; mgmt; business; accounting; econ *Collns: Bks & Pamphs:* Joule Colln (personal lib of James Prescott Joule); Shirley Inst Colln (textiles) *Archvs:* selected records of UMIST & predecessors (1824 onwards)
Co-op Schemes: BLDSC, CALIM, SCONUL
Equip: m-reader, m-printer (A4/12p), video viewer, 9 copiers (A4/6p, A3/12p), computers (incl internet), room for hire *Online:* numerous databases, incl: ABI Inform, BSI, Compendex, Datastream, EBSCO, EEVL, ESDU, Emerald, FAME, Infotrac, Inspec, Investext, Journal Citation Reports, Medline, Mintel, PsycInfo, EconLit, Reuters, Textile Technology Digest, Thomson Analytics, Web of Science & others (generally restricted to internal users) *Svcs:* info, ref
Stock: bks/303000; periodcls/2400; m-forms/2400; videos/600; CD-ROMs/805; software packages/1102
Classn: DDC *Auto Sys:* Talis
Pubns: WireLIS (lib newsletter, 2 pa)
Staff: Libns: 18.7 *Other Prof:* 1 *Non-Prof:* 24.2

Mansfield

S1537 🎓

West Nottinghamshire College, Learning Resource Centre

Derby Rd, Mansfield, Nottinghamshire, NG18 5BH (01623-627191; *fax:* 01623-623063)
Email: lrc@westnotts.ac.uk
Internet: http://www.westnotts.ac.uk/

Gov Body: Corp Board of the Coll *Chief:* Learning Resources Development Mgr: Mr Keith Mellor BA, DipLib, MCLIP (k.mellor@westnotts.ac.uk) *Dep:* LRCs Mgr: Mrs Denise Davie BA, DipLib, MCLIP (denise.davie@westnotts.ac.uk)
Entry: registered coll students; others by appt
Open: term: Mon-Thu 0830-1730, Fri 0830-1630, Sat 1000-1200
Subj: all subjs; genl; GCSE; A level *Co-op Schemes:* BLDSC
Equip: copier, 57 computers (incl 40 with wd-proc, 2 with CD-ROM & 17 with internet) *Disabled:* 21" screens, specialist software, incl Supernova, HAL, Lunar etc *Officer-in-Charge:* Learning Resources Development Mgr, as above
Stock: bks/30000; periodcls/170; videos/150; CD-ROMs/30 *Acqs Offcr:* LRCs Mgr, as above
Classn: DDC *Auto Sys:* Heritage
Staff: Libns: 4 *Non-Prof:* 9 *Exp:* £50000 (1999-2000); £70000 (2000-01)

Margate

S1538 ✚

East Kent Hospitals NHS Trust, Clinical Studies Library

(formerly Thanet Healthcare Trust Clinical Studies Lib)
Queen's Centre for Clinical Studies, Queen Elizabeth The Queen Mother Hosp, Ramsgate Rd, Margate, Kent, CT9 4AN (01843-225544 x62536; *fax:* 01843-296082)
Email: jonathan.baker@ekht.nhs.uk

Gov Body: East Kent Hosps NHS Trust *Chief:* Libn: Mr Jonathan Baker MA, DipLib, MCLIP *Dep:* Mrs Kate Macey
Assoc Libs: KENT POSTGRAD MEDICAL CENTRE, LINACRE LIB (see **S408**); WILLIAM HARVEY HOSP, EDU CENTRE LIB (see **S50**)
Entry: ref only for non-NHS staff *Open:* Mon-Thu 0900-1800, Fri 0900-1630
Subj: medicine *Co-op Schemes:* SETRHA
Equip: video viewer, fax, copier, 9 computers *Online:* Dialog
Stock: bks/2000; periodcls/60; videos/50
Classn: NLM *Staff:* Libns: 1 *Non-Prof:* 1

Matlock

S1539 🗝 🏛

National Tramway Museum, John Price Library and Archive

Crich, Matlock, Derbyshire, DE4 5DP (01773-853787; *fax:* 01773-852326)
Email: ntm_library@online.rednet.co.uk or info@tramway.co.uk
Internet: http://www.tramway.co.uk/

Gov Body: The Tramway Museum Soc *Chief:* Libn: Mrs R.E. Thacker MA, MCLIP, CertEd *Dep:* Photo Offcr: Mr G.C.G. Wilton
Entry: ref, by appt *Open:* Mon-Fri 0900-1700
Subj: tramway & light railway systems of Great Britain & world, incl new rapid transit; other road transport, operation & eng *Collns: Bks & Pamphs:* historical periodcls colln *Archvs:* Municipal Tramways & Transport Assoc archvs; Bus & Coach Council archvs; Edgar Allen archvs; British Electric Traction archvs ☞

Special Libraries

Matlock
▼
Mold

(Natl Tramway Museum cont)

Collns: *Other:* Photo & Film Archv, incl photographic collns of: H.B. Priestley; M.J. O'Connor; D.W.K. Jones; Dr H. Nicol; technical drawings, incl those of: Maley & Taunton; Glasgow Corp; EMB
Equip: m-reader, copier, computer (incl wd-proc)
Online: online catalogue, photo database, journal index
Stock: bks/20000; periodcls/60; photos/250000; slides/2000; m-forms/200; audios/25; archvs/not measured; technical drawings/7000; films/450
Classn: UDC **Auto Sys:** in-house
Staff: Libns: 1 Other Prof: 1
Proj: lib extension (2003)

Melton Mowbray

S1540 🎓

Brooksby Melton College Library

Brooksby, Melton Mowbray, Leicestershire, LE14 2LJ (01664-434291; *fax:* 01664-434572)
Email: enquiries@brooksbymelton.ac.uk
Internet: http://www.brooksbymelton.ac.uk/

Gov Body: Board of Governors **Chief:** Lib & Info Svc Mgr: Mrs J.M. Hooper BA(Hons), MA, MCLIP
Dep: Asst Libn: Mrs S. Peat
Assoc Libs: MELTON CAMPUS LIB, Asfordby Rd, Melton Mowbray, Leicester, LE13 0HJ
Entry: staff & students **Open:** term: Mon-Fri 0900-2000; vac: Mon-Fri 0900-1700
Subj: sci; agric; hortic; animal care; land-based enterprises **Collns:** *Archvs:* Inst of Fisheries Mgmt archvs; agric records **Co-op Schemes:** EMRLS, BLDSC
Equip: video viewers, copier, computers (with wd-proc, internet & CD-ROM) **Svcs:** info, ref
Stock: bks/8000; periodcls/200; videos/700
Classn: DDC **Auto Sys:** Heritage
Pubns: Lib Handbook/Newsletter; Guides to Info Sources; Guide to IT
Staff: Libns: 1 Other Prof: 1 Non-Prof: 1.5

Menstrie

S1541 ⚗️

Diageo plc, Brand Technical Centre Library

(formerly United Distillers & Vintners)
Brand Technical Centre, Glenochil, Menstrie, Clackmannanshire, FK11 7ES (01259-761481; *fax:* 01259-766893)
Email: karen.mckinnon@diageo.com

Chief: Dir: Mrs Karen McKinnan
Open: Mon-Fri 0830-1700
Subj: tech; chem; biochem; chemical eng; computer tech; info tech; microbiology; food packaging **Collns:** *Bks & Pamphs:* 250 periodcl titles, technical reports & memoranda (1945-date)
Co-op Schemes: ARTEL & ILL, both with BLDSC
Equip: video viewer, fax, copier, clr copier, computers (incl wd-proc & internet) **Online:** CBA, Dialog, Profound **Svcs:** info, ref, biblio, indexing, abstracting, translation
Stock: bks/6000; periodcls/155; slides/2000; maps/60; m-forms/50; videos/500; AVs/50
Auto Sys: CAIRS
Staff: Libns: 1 Other Prof: 1
See also DIAGEO LTD, ARCHVS **(A376)**

Merthyr Tydfil

S1542 🎓

Merthyr Tydfil College, Learning Resources Centre

Ynysfach, Merthyr Tydfil, Mid Glamorgan, CF48 1AR (01685-726005; *fax:* 01685-726100)
Email: college@merthyr.ac.uk

Gov Body: Corp of Coll **Chief:** Tutor Libn: Mrs L. Lloyd BA(Hons), DipLib, PGCE (l.lloyd@ merthyr.ac.uk) **Dep:** Snr Lib Asst: Mrs D. Snape
Entry: ref only for public **Open:** term: Mon-Thu 0900-2000, Fri 0900-1600; vac: times on appl
Subj: all subjs; GCSE; A level; vocational; generalities; local studies (Merthyr Tydfil) **Co-op Schemes:** ILL
Equip: copier, 6 computers (all with wd-proc, internet & CD-ROM) **Svcs:** info, ref, biblio
Stock: bks/12000; periodcls/100; audios/50; videos/300; CD-ROMs/30 **Acqs Offcr:** Tutor Libn, as above
Classn: DDC **Auto Sys:** EASL
Staff: Libns: 1 Non-Prof: 3

S1543 ✚

North Glamorgan NHS Trust Library

Prince Charles Hosp, Gurnos Est, Merthyr Tydfil, Mid Glamorgan, CF47 9DT (01685-721721 x8251; *fax:* 01923-721816)

Gov Body: North Glamorgan NHS Trust & Univ of Glamorgan **Chief:** Libn: Ms Felicity Armstrong
Entry: staff & students of Trust & Univ **Open:** Mon-Wed 0900-2000, Thu-Fri 0900-1700
Subj: health; medicine; nursing
Equip: copier, computer
Stock: bks/c5000 **Classn:** DDC

Middlesbrough

S1544 🎓

Cleveland College of Art and Design Library

Green Ln, Linthorpe, Middlesbrough, TS5 7RJ (01642-821441; *fax:* 01642-823467)
Internet: http://www.ccad.ac.uk/

Chief: Lib Resource Centre Mgr: Mrs Ann Kenyon
Dep: Slide & Video Libn: Mrs Andrea Godson
Assoc Libs: HARTLEPOOL SITE BRANCH LIB, Church Sq, Hartlepool, TS24 7EX
Entry: some external borrowers (e.g., local art teachers); ref only for other categories of enquirer
Open: term: Mon-Thu 0900-1900, Fri 0900-1630; vac: closed
Subj: all subjs; A level; undergrad; mainly art & design; local study (Cleveland & Yorkshire hist & geog) **Co-op Schemes:** BLDSC, partnership with Univ of Teesside (see **S1548**)
Equip: copier, clr copier, fax, 19 computers (all with wd-proc, internet & CD-ROM)
Stock: bks/30000; periodcls/150; slides/30000; illusts/500; audios/180; videos/1400; CD-ROMs/50
Classn: DDC **Staff:** Libns: 1 Non-Prof: 3.5

S1545 ⚗️

Corus Research, Teesside Technology Centre Library

PO Box 11, Grangetown, Middlesbrough, TS6 6UB (01642-467144; *fax:* 01642-460321)
Email: ttc.library@corusgroup.com

Gov Body: Corus plc **Chief:** Admin Mgr: Dr P.M. Fellows **Dep:** Lib Administrator: Mrs C. Patton
Assoc Libs: SWINDEN TECH CENTRE LIB (see **S1873**)

Entry: by prior appl to Admin Mgr **Open:** Mon-Fri 0900-1700
Subj: metallurgy (ferrous); eng; chemical eng; materials sci; control & instrumentation; chem
Collns: *Bks & Pamphs:* British Steel Reports; BSI
Co-op Schemes: BLDSC
Equip: m-readers, m-printers, copier, computer (with wd-proc)
Stock: bks/10000; pamphs/1000
Classn: UDC
Pubns: Genl guides; Acqs List; Reporting Guide; Reports Lists etc
Staff: Libns: 1 Other Prof: 1 Non-Prof: 1

S1546 🏛️

Dorman Museum Resources Room

Linthorpe Rd, Middlesbrough, TS5 6LA (01642-358101; *fax:* 01642-358100)
Email: ken_sedman@middlesbrough.gov.uk

Type: local authority museum **Gov Body:** Middlesbrough Council (see **P115**) **Chief:** Head of Museums/Galleries: Mr Godfrey Worsdale **Dep:** Snr Curator: Mr Ken Sedman
Assoc Libs: MIDDLESBROUGH ART GALLERY, 320 Linthorpe Rd, Middlesbrough, TS1 4AW (01642-247445); CAPTAIN COOK BIRTHPLACE MUSEUM, Stewart Pk, Marton, Middlesbrough TS7 6AS (01642-311211; *fax:* 01642-817419); CLEVELAND CRAFT CENTRE, 57 Gilkes St, Middlesbrough, TS1 5EL (01642-262376; *fax:* 01642-226351)
Entry: adv booking **Open:** Tue-Sat 1000-1730
Subj: Middlesbrough: local studies; sci (esp geol); archaeo; hist; social hist; industry (esp iron & steel)
Collns: *Archvs:* local archival materials *Other:* Linthorpe Art Pottery
Equip: m-reader, copier, fax, room for hire, 2 computers (both with wd-proc & CD-ROM) **Online:** colln database (also on m-fiche) **Svcs:** info, ref, biblio
Stock: bks/800; periodcls/5; photos/600; slides/1200; pamphs/500 **Acqs Offcr:** Snr Curator, as above
Staff: Other Prof: 4 Non-Prof: 5

S1547 🎓

Middlesbrough College, Learning Resources Centres

Roman Rd, Linthorpe, Middlesbrough, TS5 5PJ (01642-333276; *fax:* 01642-333200)
Internet: http://www.mbro.ac.uk/

Gov Body: Corp of Middlesbrough Coll **Chief:** Learning Resources Mgr: Mrs Cathryne Proud BA, MCLIP, Grad IPD, CertEd (cc.proud@mbro.ac.uk)
Other Snr Staff: Dep Learning Resources Mgr (ILT): Ms Paula Kilburn (pa.kilburn@mbro.ac.uk); Dep Learning Resources Mgr (Acqs): Ms Lynn Malyon
Assoc Libs: KIRBY CAMPUS LRC, addr as above; ACKLAM CAMPUS LRC, Hall Dr, Acklam, Middlesbrough, TS5 7DY; MARTON CAMPUS LRC, Marton Rd, Middlesbrough, TS4 3RZ; LONGLANDS CAMPUS LRC, Douglas St, Middlesbrough, TS4 2JW
Entry: registered students of the Coll **Open:** *Kirby Campus:* term: Mon-Thu 0845-2000, Fri 1000-1630, Sat 1000-1300; vac: Mon-Thu 0900-1700, Fri 1000-1630, Sat 0900-1200
Subj: all subjs; GCSE; A level; vocational **Co-op Schemes:** NEMLAC, BLDSC, Learning North-East
Equip: video & DVD viewers, copiers, computers (with internet & CD-ROM), scanners, clr printers
Disabled: HAL, Liberator, CCTV, large screen monitors **Online:** Infotrac **Svcs:** info, ref, biblio
Stock: bks/32000; periodcls/160; pamphs/1666; maps/24; audios/154; videos/197; AVs/253 **Acqs Offcr:** Dep Learning Resources Mgr (Acqs), as above
Classn: DDC **Auto Sys:** AutoLib
Staff: Libns: 3 Non-Prof: 8

S1548

University of Teesside, Library and Information Services

Borough Rd, Middlesbrough, TS1 3BA (01642-342100; *fax:* 01642-342190)
Internet: http://www.tees.ac.uk/lis/

Chief: Dir of Lib & Info Svcs: Mr Ian Butchart BA, MSc, MCLIP, PGCE (ian.butchart@tees.ac.uk)
Dep: Asst Dir: Mr Paul Mayes (paul.mayes@tees.ac.uk)
Entry: no charge for ref use only, categories of external membership *Open:* term: Mon-Thu 0830-2200, Fri 0830-1700, Sat 1100-1700, Sun 1100-2200; vac: Mon-Fri 0900-1700
Subj: all subjs; undergrad *Collns: Archvs:* North East Television & Film Archv (NETFA); European Green Archv *Co-op Schemes:* NEMLAC, UK Libs Plus
Equip: m-readers, m-printers A4/24p), video viewers, 9 copiers (A4/6p), 350 computers (incl wd-proc, internet & CD-ROM), TV studio, 2 video editing suites *Disabled:* large screen PC with enlarging software, speech synthesiser, Kurzweil reading edge machine, CCTV, brailler, low level copier *Online:* wide range of svcs, incl: AMED, ASSIA, British Humanities Index, BNI, ChildData, CINAHL, Design & Applied Arts Index, Digimap, EEVL, FAME, Historical Abstracts, HMIC, Inspec, Medline, MIDIRS, OMNI, PsycInfo, Reuters Business Insight, SciDirect, UnCover, Web of Science, Westlaw UK, Zetoc *Svcs:* info, ref, biblio, indexing, abstracting, translation
Stock: bks/281205; periodcls/1900; m-forms/31000; videos/430; slides & illusts/45966
Classn: DDC *Auto Sys:* Talis
Staff: Libns: 19 *Other Prof:* 20 *Non-Prof:* 32

Middleton

S1549

Hopwood Hall College, Learning Resource Centres

Spotland Bldg, Rochdale Rd, Middleton, Lancashire, M24 6XH (0161-643-7500; *fax:* 0161-643-2114)
Email: enquiries@hopwood.ac.uk
Internet: http://www.hopwood.ac.uk/

Gov Body: Hopwood Hall Coll *Chief:* LRC Mgr: Ms M. Redmond
Assoc Libs: MIDDLETON CAMPUS LRC, addr as above; ROCHDALE CAMPUS LRC, Benjamin Rudman Bldg, St Mary's Gate, Rochdale, Lancashire, OL12 6RY (01706-345346; *fax:* 01706-641426)
Entry: students & staff only *Open:* both sites: term: Mon-Tue, Thu 0900-2000, Wed 0930-2000, Fri 0900-1600; vac: Mon-Fri 0900-1200, 1300-1600
Subj: all subjs; genl; GCSE; A level; undergrad; vocational *Co-op Schemes:* BLDSC, ILL
Equip: video viewer, copier, computers (incl internet & CD-ROM), scanner *Disabled:* Kurzweil, Dragon Easyspeak, vision intensifier
Stock: bks/50000; periodcls/110; figs are for both sites
Classn: DDC *Auto Sys:* EOSi
Staff: Libns: 5 *Non-Prof:* 6.66

Milton Keynes

S1550

De Montfort University, Milton Keynes Information Centre

Hammerwood Gate, Kents Hill, Milton Keynes, Buckinghamshire, MK7 6HP (01908-834921; *fax:* 01908-834929)
Internet: http://www.library.dmu.ac.uk/

Gov Body: De Montfort Univ (see **S921**) *Chief:* Site Libn: N. Scantlebury (nscant@dmu.ac.uk)

Other Snr Staff: Asst Info Offcrs: Ms H. Kirkham (hkirkham@dmu.ac.uk) & Ms A. Warren (aswarren@dmu.ac.uk)
Entry: ref only for non-membs of Univ; external borrowing available for a fee *Open:* term: Mon, Wed-Thu 0845-2100, Tue 0845-1800, Fri 0845-1600, Sat 1000-1600; vac: varies
Subj: undergrad; postgrad; business; computing; primary edu; social sci; social work *Co-op Schemes:* BLDSC, UK Libs Plus
Equip: copiers, computers (incl wd-proc & internet) *Svcs:* info, ref
Classn: DDC *Auto Sys:* Talis *Staff: Libns:* 3

S1551

International Centre for Distance Learning, Library

Open Univ, Walton Hall, Milton Keynes, Buckinghamshire, MK7 6AA (01908-653537; *fax:* 01908-654173)
Email: icdl-enquiries@open.ac.uk
Internet: http://www-icdl.open.ac.uk/

Gov Body: Open Univ (see **S1554**) *Chief:* Dir: Dr N.C. Farnes
Entry: ref only, adv notice preferred *Open:* Mon-Fri 0900-1700
Subj: distance edu
Equip: computer (with CD-ROM) *Online:* ICDL Distance Education Database (free on web site)
Stock: bks/3000; periodcls/50; pamphs/9000
Classn: own

S1552

Milton Keynes College Learning Resources Centre

Chaffron Way, Leadenhall, Milton Keynes, Buckinghamshire, MK6 5LP (01908-684444; *fax:* 01908-684399)
Email: info@mkcollege.ac.uk
Internet: http://www.mkcollege.ac.uk/

Chief: Learning Resources Mgr: Ms Liz Annetts BA(Hons), PGCE, DipRSA, CertMgt, MCLIP
Assoc Libs: BLETCHLEY CAMPUS LRC, Sherwood Dr, Bletchley, Milton Keynes, MK3 6DR
Entry: ref only for those external to Coll *Open:* term: Mon-Thu 0900-2000, Fri 1000-1600; vac: Mon-Fri 0930-1230
Subj: GCSE; A level; undergrad; vocational; social sci; sci; maths; tech; arts; lit; geog; hist *Co-op Schemes:* BLDSC, BBI
Equip: 4 video viewers, 2 copiers, clr copier, 60 computers (all with internet) *Disabled:* Kurzweil, 4 large screen PCs *Svcs:* info, ref
Stock: bks/32000; periodcls/200; videos/1000
Classn: DDC *Auto Sys:* Heritage
Staff: Libns: 1 *Other Prof:* 1.5 *Non-Prof:* 6

S1553 ✚

Milton Keynes General NHS Trust, Staff Library

Postgrad Edu Centre, Standing Way, Milton Keynes, Buckinghamshire, MK6 5LD (01908-243077; *fax:* 01908-671977)
Email: lis@powernet.co.uk

Gov Body: Milton Keynes Genl NHS Trust *Chief:* Knowledge Mgr: Mrs Lorna R. Maguire MA, DipLib, MCLIP *Dep:* Lib Svcs Mgr: Mrs Sue Whiteley
Entry: ref only, adv appt *Open:* Mon-Fri 0900-1700
Subj: medicine; nursing; healthcare mgmt *Co-op Schemes:* BLDSC, HeLIN
Equip: fax, video viewer, copier, computers (incl internet & MS Office) *Svcs:* info, ref, biblio
Stock: bks/12000; periodcls/250; videos/100; AVs/20
Classn: NLM *Auto Sys:* Heritage IV
Staff: Libns: 2 *Non-Prof:* 3 *Exp:* £50000 (1999-2000)

S1554

The Open University Library

Walton Hall, Milton Keynes, Buckinghamshire, MK7 6AA (01908-653138; *fax:* 01908-653571)
Email: oulibrary@open.ac.uk
Internet: http://www.open.ac.uk/library/

Gov Body: The Open Univ *Chief:* Dir of Lib Svcs: Ms N. Whitsed MSc, FCLIP *Dep:* Dep Dir of Lib Svcs: Mrs Ann Davies
Entry: open to all visitors *Open:* Mon-Thu 0830-1930, Fri 0900-1700, Sat 1000-1300
Subj: all subjs; undergrad; postgrad; vocational *Collns: Archvs:* all OU course materials; Jennie Lee Papers; Betty Boothroyd Papers *Co-op Schemes:* BLDSC, FIL
Equip: 2 m-form reader/printers, 10 video viewers, 5 copiers, 33 computers (all with wd-proc, internet & CD-ROM) *Disabled:* Kurzweil 1000, JAWS screen readers, CCTV magnifier, ZoomText software, TextHelp (dyslexia software), IBM Homepage Reader for web, trackerballs, magnifying glasses, enlarged letter keyboards *Online:* wide range of online databases (list available on web site) *Svcs:* info, ref
Stock: bks/193000; periodcls/7462; slides/62000; illusts/58000; maps/200; m-forms/1820; audios/3600; videos/5800; CD-ROMs/400; archvs/79 linear m
Classn: DDC *Auto Sys:* Voyager
Staff: Libns: 42 *Non-Prof:* 32
Proj: new lib bldg completed Dec 2002

Mirfield

S1555 ♛

The Community of the Resurrection Library

The House of the Resurrection, Stocksbank Rd, Mirfield, W Yorkshire, WF14 0BW (01924-494318)
Email: community@mirfield.org.uk
Internet: http://www.mirfield.org.uk/

Chief: Libn: Fr Eric Simmons CR *Dep:* Mrs Rosie Irvine BA
Entry: not open to genl public
Subj: religion *Collns: Bks & Pamphs:* rare bks (pre-1800) & incunabula are deposited in the Mirfield room at York Univ Lib (see **S2168**); a duplicate catalogue is at Mirfield *Archvs:* held at York Univ
Equip: copier
Stock: bks/70000; periodcls/25; videos/10
Classn: own
Staff: Non-Prof: 2 *Exp:* £3500 (1999-2000)

Mold

S1556

Welsh College of Horticulture (Coleg Garddwriaeth Cymry), Learning Resources Centre

Northop, Mold, Clwyd, CH7 6AA (01352-841011; *fax:* 01352-841031)
Email: info@wcoh.ac.uk
Internet: http://www.wcoh.ac.uk/

Chief: Lib Mgr: Ms Francesca Garner MBA
Entry: ref only *Open:* term: Mon-Fri 0900-1800; vac: Mon-Fri 1000-1600
Subj: hortic
Equip: video viewers, copier, computers (with wd-proc, internet & CD-ROM), scanners
Stock: bks/8000; periodcls/50; videos/200
Classn: DDC
Staff: Libns: 1 *Other Prof:* 1 *Non-Prof:* 1

Special Libraries

Morden ▼ Newcastle upon Tyne

Morden

S1557

Merton College, Library Learning Centres

Morden Pk, London Rd, Morden, Surrey, SM4 5QX (020-8408-6499; *fax:* 020-8408-6666)
Email: library@merton.ac.uk
Internet: http://www.merton.ac.uk/

Gov Body: Merton Coll Inc *Chief:* Head of Learning Centres: Ms Brenda Keyte BA(Hons), MCLIP (bkeyte@merton.ac.uk) *Other Snr Staff:* Ms Faye Sisson BA(Hons), MA; Mr Rowan Williamson BA(Hons), MA
Entry: adv appt *Open:* term: Mon-Thu 0830-2000, Fri 0830-1630; vac: Mon-Fri 0900-1630
Subj: all subjs; GCSE; A level; undergrad; vocational; business studies; hotel & catering; eng; musical instrument tech *Collns: Bks & Pamphs:* motor cycle eng; musical instrument tech *Co-op Schemes:* SASLIC
Equip: 4 video viewers, 2 copiers (A4/5p), 60 computers (all with wd-proc & internet, 8 with CD-ROM) *Officer-in-Charge:* Head of Learning Centres, as above *Svcs:* info, ref, biblio
Stock: bks/32000; periodcls/180; pamphs/various; videos/850; CD-ROMs/25 *Acqs Offcr:* Head of Learning Centres, as above
Classn: DDC *Auto Sys:* AutoLib
Staff: Libns: 3 *Non-Prof:* 7 *Exp:* £40000 (1999-2000); £55000 (2000-01); £67000 (2001-02, incl £15000 for software)

Moreton-in-Marsh

S1558

Fire Service College, Library and Information Resource Centre

Moreton-in-Marsh, Gloucestershire, GL56 0RH (01608-812050; *fax:* 01608-812047)
Email: library@fireservicecollege.ac.uk
Internet: http://www.fireservicecollege.ac.uk/

Gov Body: Office of the Dep Prime Minister (see **S1316**) *Chief:* Coll Libn: Miss Margaret Fuller BA, MCLIP, MCMI *Other Snr Staff:* Asst Libns: Miss M. Barnes, Mrs J. Watson, Mrs D. Kiey-Thomas & Mrs A. Collicutt
Entry: non membs by appt only; charge made to commercial enterprises; enq svc by writing, phone, fax or email *Open:* Mon-Wed 0830-2100, Thu 0830-1800, Fri 0830-1530
Subj: fire prevention; fire extinction; fire-fighting etc
Collns: Bks & Pamphs: acts (13C onwards); statutes (early 1900s onwards); incident reports; fire journals dating back to 19C; many rare pubns dating back to early 1900s *Archvs:* records relating to hist of Fire Svc Colls & hist of UK Fire Svc
Other: large video colln; newspaper cuttings etc
Co-op Schemes: BLDSC, ILL
Equip: m-reader, 3 video viewers, fax (£1 per pg), copier (A4/5p), clr copier (A4/£1), 22 computers (incl 11 with wd-proc, 10 with CD-ROM & 4 with internet) *Online:* FINDS (cost of search + 10% for non-fire brigade users) *Officer-in-Charge:* Acq & Cataloguing Libn: Miss M. Barnes (mbarnes@fireservicecollege.ac.uk) *Svcs:* info, ref, biblio, indexing

Stock: bks/70000; periodcls/c300; audios/40; videos/1200; CD-ROMs/100+; various photos, slides, illusts, maps & m-forms *Acqs Offcr:* Acqs & Cataloguing Libn, as above
Classn: LC *Auto Sys:* Heritage IV
Pubns: Flash (index to fire-related journals, 10 pa, £24 pa)
Staff: Libns: 4.5 *Non-Prof:* 4 *Exp:* £50525 (1999-2000); £43500 (2000-01)
Proj: refurbishment of archv room

Morpeth

S1559 ✚

Northumberland Healthcare Trust, Library and Information Service

Merley Croft, Loansdean, Morpeth, Northumberland, NE61 2DL (01670-394400; *fax:* 01670-394501)
Email: northumberland.libraryservice@ northumberland-haz.org.uk

Gov Body: Northumbria Healthcare NHS Trust *Chief:* Libn: Ms Vasanthi Elder *Dep:* Asst Libn: Mrs Catherine Graham
Assoc Libs: HEXHAM GENL HOSP, RYDER POSTGRAD MEDICAL CENTRE LIB (see **S809**); NORTH TYNESIDE EDU CENTRE LIB (see **S1607**); WANSBECK HOSP LIB (see **S52**)
Entry: NHS staff in Northumberland *Open:* Mon-Fri 0900-1700
Subj: healthcare *Collns: Archvs:* Northumberland Health Authority documents *Co-op Schemes:* BLDSC, BMA, HLN, NULJ
Equip: copier, computer (with internet & CD-ROM)
Svcs: info, ref, lit searching
Stock: bks/6000; periodcls/100; videos/20
Classn: categorised *Staff: Libns:* 2 *Non-Prof:* 1

S1560 ✚

St George's Hospital, Mental Health Library

St George's Hosp, Morpeth, Northumberland, NE61 2NU (01670-512121 x3365; *fax:* 01670-395829)
Email: librarysgh@nmht.nhs.uk
Internet: http://www.nnt.nhs.uk/mh/library.asp

Gov Body: Newcastle, North Tyneside & Northumberland Mental Health NHS Trust *Chief:* Snr Lib Asst: Ms Lisa Jenkinson
Assoc Libs: NEWCASTLE GENL HOSP, TOMLINSON TEACHING CENTRE LIB (see **S1578**); ST NICHOLAS HOSP, MENTAL HEALTH LIB (see **S1585**)
Entry: Trust staff & students *Open:* Mon, Thu-Fri 0930-1500; Tue-Wed 0940-1630; 24 hr access for membs
Subj: psy; sociology; psychiatry; mental health nursing; occupational therapy; art therapy; mental health mgmt *Co-op Schemes:* BLDSC, ILL with Northern Region Medical Libs, ILL using NULJ
Equip: copier, 2 computers (incl wd-proc, internet & CD-ROM) *Online:* Dialog, NHSNet *Svcs:* info, ref, biblio
Stock: bks/1400; periodcls/10, plus 67 non-current; videos/20
Classn: DDC *Staff: Non-Prof:* 2

Motherwell

S1561

Motherwell College Library

Dalzell Dr, Motherwell, N Lanarkshire, ML1 2DD (01698-232308; *fax:* 01698-275430)
Email: jgoodfel@motherwell.co.uk
Internet: http://www.motherwell.ac.uk/

Gov Body: Motherwell Coll Board of Mgmt *Chief:* Coll Libn: Mrs Judith Goodfellow MCLIP *Dep:* Lib Asst: Ms Audrey Mitchell HND LibSc

Entry: ref only to non-membs *Open:* term: Mon, Fri 0930-1630, Tue-Thu 0930-1730; vac: Mon-Fri 0930-1630
Subj: all subjs; genl; GCSE & A-level; vocational
Co-op Schemes: BLDSC
Equip: copier, computers (incl wd-proc, internet & CD-ROM) *Svcs:* info, ref, biblio
Stock: bks/18973; periodcls/49; audios/32; videos/ 649; CD-ROMs/10
Classn: DDC *Auto Sys:* EASL
Staff: Libns: 1 *Non-Prof:* 1

Much Hadham

S1562 ⚷

The Henry Moore Foundation Library

Elmwood, Perry Green, Much Hadham, Hertfordshire, SG10 6EE (01279-843333; *fax:* 01279-843647)
Email: library@henry-moore-fdn.co.uk
Internet: http://www.henry-moore-fdn.co.uk/site/ thesite/pages/

Gov Body: Henry Moore Foundation *Chief:* Info Mgr: Mr Martin Davis (martin@henry-moore-fdn.co.uk) *Other Snr Staff:* Libn & Archivist: Mr Michael Phipps; Picture Archivist: Ms Emma Stower
Assoc Libs: HENRY MOORE ARCHV, contact details as above (archive@henry-moore-fdn.co.uk)
Entry: Lib: by adv appt to all bona fide rsrchers; *Archv:* by adv appt to postgrad rsrchers, references usually required
Subj: arts; sculpture; art hist; Henry Moore; personal papers *Collns: Bks & Pamphs:* bks by & about Henry Moore; sales catalogues *Archvs:* Henry Moore Archv (c40000 items, 1920s-80s), incl correspondence, MSS & ephemera *Other:* press cuttings (1920s-date); miscellanea relating to Moore's life & works
Equip: copier, 2 computers, camera stands
Stock: bks/c20000; AVs/c300 audios & videos
See also HENRY MOORE INST LIB (**S900**)

Musselburgh

S1563 ⚷

Scottish Ornithologists' Club, Waterston Library

Harbour Pt, Newhailes Rd, Musselburgh, Midlothian, EH21 6SJ (0131-653-0653; *fax:* 0131-653-0654)
Email: mail@the-soc.org.uk

Chief: Libn: J.G. Davies
Subj: nat hist; ornithology
Stock: bks/4000; periodcls/400
Further Info: the lib is temporarily in store; only limited facilities exist at present

Nantwich

S1564

Reaseheath College Library

Reaseheath, Nantwich, Cheshire, CW5 6DF (01270-625131; *fax:* 01270-625665)
Internet: http://www.reaseheath.ac.uk/

Chief: Lib Assts: Ms Ann Ferguson & Ms Alison Rafferty
Entry: students on approved Coll courses
Subj: agric; land based industries *Co-op Schemes:* ALLCU
Equip: copier, computers
Stock: bks/c27000 *Staff: Non-Prof:* 2

Neath

S1565
Neath Port Talbot College, Neath Campus Library
Dwr Y Felin Rd, Neath, W Glamorgan, SA10 7RF (01639-648071; *fax:* 01639-648009)
Email: louise.norman@nptc.ac.uk
Internet: http://www.nptc.ac.uk/

Gov Body: Academic Board *Chief:* Libn: Mrs Louise Norman MCLIP, DipMan
Assoc Libs: AFAN CAMPUS LIB (see **S1820**)
Open: term: Mon-Thu 0830-1930, Fri 0830-1630; vac: Mon-Thu 0830-1700, Fri 0830-1630
Subj: all subjs; local study (Neath area); generalities; phil; psy; religion; social sci; lang; sci; maths; tech; arts; lit; geog; hist *Co-op Schemes:* BLDSC
Equip: copier, computers (incl wd-proc, internet & CD-ROM) *Svcs:* info, ref
Stock: bks/30000; periodcls/100; videos/121
Classn: DDC *Auto Sys:* Alice
Staff: Libns: 1 *Non-Prof:* 4

Nelson

S1566
Nelson and Colne College, Learning Resource Centre
Scotland Rd, Nelson, Lancashire, BB9 7YT (01282-440200; *fax:* 01282-440274)
Email: lshaw@nelson.ac.uk

Chief: LRCs Mgr: Mrs Lesley Eve Shaw MCLIP, CertEd
Assoc Libs: BARROWFORD RD SITE LRC, Nelson & Colne Coll, Barrowford Rd, Colne, Lancashire, Officer-in-Charge: Mrs Lesley Eve Shaw (as above)
Entry: adv appt (0915-1630) *Open:* term: Mon-Thu 0900-2000, Fri 0900-1500
Subj: all subjs; genl; GCSE; A level; undergrad
Collns: Archvs: Coll archv colln: slides; newspaper cuttings; old prospectuses *Co-op Schemes:* ILL
Equip: 5 video viewers, fax, 2 copiers (card operated), 50 computers (all with wd-proc, 48 with internet & 20 with CD-ROM), 6 scanners *Disabled:* 2 large computer monitors, Read & Write software on 2 machines, 2 computer workstations & study table of adjustable height *Svcs:* info, ref, biblio
Stock: bks/12000; periodcls/120; maps/25; audios/102 cassettes; videos/410; topic files/304; some DVDs *Acqs Offcr:* LRCs Mgr, as above
Classn: DDC *Auto Sys:* Heritage
Staff: Libns: 1 *Non-Prof:* 6.5 *Exp:* £15000 (1999-2000); £17000 (2000-01); on bks, AVs & periodcls

Newark

S1567
British Horological Institute Library
Upton Hall, Upton, Newark, Nottinghamshire, NG23 5TE (01636-813795; *fax:* 01636-812258)
Email: research@bhi.co.uk
Internet: http://www.bhi.co.uk/

Chief: contact the Libn
Entry: membs only
Subj: horology; timekeeping
Stock: bks/c5000

S1568
Newark and Sherwood College Learning Centre
Friary Rd, Newark, Nottinghamshire, NG24 1PB (01636-680680; *fax:* 01636-680681)
Email: clchelpdesk@newark.ac.uk
Internet: http://www.newark.ac.uk/

Gov Body: Newark & Sherwood Coll *Chief:* Coll Learning Centre Co-ordinator: Mrs Alison Clark BA, DipLib, MCLIP
Entry: ref only for non-membs of Coll *Open:* term: Mon-Thu 0845-2100, Fri 0845-2000, Sat 0900-1300, Sun 1000-1300; vac: Mon-Fri 0900-1700
Subj: all subjs; genl; GCSE; A level; vocational; music instrument making & repair *Co-op Schemes:* BLDSC, EMRLS (ILL)
Equip: 4 video viewers, copier (A4/10p), 44 computers (all with wd-proc & internet, 5 with CD-ROM), presentation suite, media wall *Disabled:* software for blind & partially sighted (JAWS) *Svcs:* info, ref
Stock: bks/23000; periodcls/107; audios/650; videos/200
Classn: DDC *Auto Sys:* Olib
Staff: Libns: 1 *Non-Prof:* 6.75

S1569
Newark Hospital Medical Library
Newark Hosp, Boundary Ln, Newark, Nottinghamshire, NG24 4DE (01636-681681)
Email: GwennethClarke@sfh-tr.nhs.uk

Gov Body: Sherwood Forest Hosps NHS Trust *Chief:* Medical Libn: Mrs Gwenneth Clarke BA, MCLIP
Entry: NHS staff only *Open:* Tue 0900-1500, Thu 0900-1300
Subj: medicine; nursing *Co-op Schemes:* NULJ
Equip: computer (with wd-proc, internet & CD-ROM) *Online:* BioMed svcs (free) *Officer-in-Charge:* Asst Hosp Mgr: Mrs E. Cooper
Stock: bks/1500; periodcls/20; videos/10 *Acqs Offcr:* Medical Libn, as above
Classn: DDC
Staff: Libns: 1 *Exp:* £4500 (2000-01)

Newbury

S1570
Institute for Animal Health, Compton Library
Compton, Newbury, Berkshire, RG20 7NN (01635-578411; *fax:* 01635-577304)
Email: compton.library@bbsrc.ac.uk

Type: rsrch *Gov Body:* sponsored by BBSRC
Chief: Libn: Miss Diane Collins BSc, DipLib
Assoc Libs: PIRBRIGHT LABORATORY LIB (see **S2136**)
Subj: sci; animal health
Equip: Online: Dialog
Classn: UDC *Staff:* Libns: 1 *Non-Prof:* 1.5

S1571
Newbury College Learning Resource Centre
Monks Ln, Newbury, Berkshire, RG14 7TD (01635-845000)
Email: library@newbury-college.ac.uk
Internet: http://www.newbury-college.ac.uk/

Gov Body: Newbury Coll Corp *Chief:* Coll Libn: Mrs Fiona Lees BA(Hons), DipLib, MCLIP *Dep:* Asst Libn: Miss Louise Webb
Entry: ref only if not current staff or student
Open: term: Mon-Thu 0845-1900, Fri 0845-1630; vac: Mon-Fri 0930-1230, 1330-1630 (closed Xmas & Aug)
Subj: all subjs; GCSE; A level; vocational; local study (Newbury area, hist, genl info) *Co-op Schemes:* COLRIC, COFHE, BBOB
Equip: video viewer, copier, 80 computers (with wd-proc, internet & CD-ROM)
Stock: bks/27000; periodcls/250; non-bk stock/2000
Classn: DDC *Auto Sys:* Heritage
Staff: Libns: 1.25 *Non-Prof:* 2.25

Newcastle, Staffordshire

S1572
Keele University Library
Keele, Newcastle, Staffordshire, ST5 5BG (01782-583232; *fax:* 01782-711553)
Email: kis@keele.ac.uk
Internet: http://www.keele.ac.uk/

Gov Body: Keele Univ *Chief:* Dir of Info Svcs: Mr Allan Foster *Dep:* Associate Libn: Mr Bernard Finnemore
Assoc Libs: HEALTH LIB (see **S1987**)
Entry: ref only, external membership at £47 pa
Open: term: Mon-Fri 0855-2200, Sat 0930-2200, Sun 1000-2200; vac: Mon-Fri 0845-1830, Sat 0930-1700, Sun 1400-1700
Subj: all subjs; undergrad; postgrad; local study (Staffordshire, Shropshire & Cheshire, hist, geog & econ); generalities; phil; psy; religion; social sci; lang; sci; maths; arts; lit; geog; hist *Collns:* Bks & Pamphs: Blake Colln; local hist colln; Walton Colln; Reserve (antiquarian) Colln; Law Lib; EDC *Archvs:* Wedgwood Papers; Spode Papers; Sneyd Papers; Bennett Papers; Havergal Brian Papers; Raymond Richards Papers; Tamworth Court Rolls; Warrilow Photos *Co-op Schemes:* BLDSC, ILL, EDC, TLP-WM
Equip: m-reader, m-printer, video viewer, fax, copier, clr copier, computers (incl wd-proc & CD-ROM), LCD *Online:* BIDS, First Search, Biosis, JSTOR, FT Discovery, Elsevier, SciDirect, EBSCO FullText, Digimap *Svcs:* info, ref, biblio
Stock: bks/490000; periodcls/1000; photos/3000; pamphs/8000; maps/18000; m-forms/1100; audios/4000; videos/500; archvs/356 linear m
Classn: LC *Auto Sys:* Innopac Millennium
Pubns: list available on request
Staff: Libns: 10 *Other Prof:* 12 *Non-Prof:* 18
Exp: £942000 (1999-2000); £965000 (2000-01)

S1573
Newcastle-under-Lyme College, Learning Resources Centre
Liverpool Rd, Newcastle, Staffordshire, ST5 2DF (01782-254353; *fax:* 01782-717996)
Email: liz.wyman@nulc.ac.uk
Internet: http://www.nulc.ac.uk/

Chief: Learning Resources Mgr: Mrs E. Wyman BA, MA
Entry: ref only *Open:* term: Mon-Thu 0800-2100, Fri 0800-1700; vac: Mon-Fri 0900-1700
Subj: all subjs; genl; GCSE; A level; vocational *Co-op Schemes:* ILL
Equip: video viewer, copier (5p per copy), clr copier (50p per copy), 133 computers (all with wd-proc, internet & CD-ROM) *Disabled:* Supernova
Svcs: info, ref
Stock: bks/20000; periodcls/70; audios/200; videos/250; CD-ROMs/50
Classn: DDC *Auto Sys:* Heritage
Staff: Libns: 2 *Non-Prof:* 7.5

Newcastle upon Tyne

S1574
Freeman Hospital Library
Edu Centre, Freeman Hosp, Freeman Rd, Newcastle upon Tyne, NE7 7DN (0191-223-1325; *fax:* 0191-284-3783)

Gov Body: Newcastle upon Tyne Hosps NHS Trust *Chief:* Trust Libn: Mrs Margaret Valentine BA, MCLIP *Dep:* Dep Trust Libn: Ms Joanne Mullen BA *Other Snr Staff:* Elec Svcs Libn: Mr Mark Chambers BA
Assoc Libs: ROYAL VICTORIA INFIRMARY LIB (see **S1583**)
Entry: ref only for non-Trust staff *Open:* Mon-Wed 0900-1900, Thu-Fri 0900-1700, Sat 1000-1300

S
Newcastle upon Tyne
▼
Newcastle upon Tyne

pecial Libraries

(Freeman Hosp Lib cont)
Subj: psy; social sci; tech; medicine; nursing *Co-op Schemes:* HLN
Equip: m-reader, copier, 6 computers (incl 1 wd-proc, 5 internet & 5 CD-ROM) *Svcs:* info, ref, biblio
Stock: bks/12000; periodcls/180
Classn: DDC *Auto Sys:* SydneyPlus
Staff: Libns: 1 *Non-Prof:* 2.42

S1575 ♈

Literary and Philosophical Society of Newcastle upon Tyne, Library

Westgate Rd, Newcastle upon Tyne, NE1 1SE
(0191-232-0192; *fax:* 0191-261-4494)
Email: Library@litandphil.org.uk
Internet: http://www.litandphil.org.uk/

Gov Body: Cttee & Trustees of Soc *Chief:* Libn: Mrs K. Easson *Dep:* Sub-Libn: Ms A. Rudjord
Entry: open to membs; bona fide rsrchers may apply to the libn for ref facilities *Open:* Mon-Fri 0930-1900 (Tue to 2000), Sat 0930-1300
Subj: all subjs; genl; local study (Northumberland & Durham, genl coverage, esp rich in 18C & 19C material); fiction *Collns: Archvs:* records relating to the Soc; Northern Arts Literary MSS Colln; Northern Architectural Assoc records *Other:* 10000 music recordings (mainly classical) *Co-op Schemes:* BLDSC, ILL, ESTC
Equip: copier (via staff), 2 rooms for hire
Stock: bks/140000; periodcls/150; pamphs/5500; maps/100; audios/10000
Classn: DDC
Pubns: The Hist of the Literary & Philosophical Soc of Newcastle upon Tyne, Vol 2, 1896-1989 (£15)
Staff: Libns: 2.5 *Other Prof:* 3 *Non-Prof:* 3.5

S1576 ⚷

The Natural History Society of Northumbria Library

The Hancock Museum, Newcastle upon Tyne, NE2 4PT (0191-232-6386)

Gov Body: Council of the Soc *Chief:* Chairman of Lib Cttee: Mr H. Chambers *Dep:* Sec to the Soc: Mr D.C. Noble-Rollin
Entry: only by appt with Sec to the Soc *Open:* Mon-Fri 1000-1300,
Subj: nat hist; ornithology; geol; entomology; mammalogy; hist of nat hist *Collns: Other:* original drawings & watercolours by Thomas Bewick (1753-1828)
Equip: copier
Classn: DDC
Pubns: Transactions of the Nat Hist Soc of Northumbria; special pubns: Flora of Northumberland (1993); Birds on the Farne Islands (annual ornithological report); Red Data Bk for Northumberland (1998); Robson's Geol of North East England (2nd ed)
Exp: £2500 (1999-2000)

S1577 🎓

Newcastle College Library Service

Rye Hill Campus, Scotswood Rd, Newcastle upon Tyne, NE4 7SA (0191-200-4020; *fax:* 0191-200-4100)
Email: fiona.forsythe@ncl-coll.ac.uk

Chief: Dir of Libs & Learning Centres: Mrs Fiona Forsythe BA, MCLIP
Assoc Libs: PARSONS LIB (main lib), contact details as above; ART & DESIGN LIB & RESOURCE CENTRE, addr as above, Libn: Mrs Helen Charlton BA, MCLIP; MUSIC & MEDIA LIB, Libn: Mr Stephen Edwards BA, MCLIP; SANDYFORD LIB, Libn: Mrs Christine Kelly BA, MCLIP
Entry: staff, students & associate membs; public ref only *Open: Parsons Lib:* Mon, Wed-Thu 0830-1930, Tue 0930-1930, Fri 0830-1630; *Art & Design Lib:* Mon, Wed-Thu 0830-1700, Tue 0930-830, Fri 0830-1630; *Music & Media Lib:* opening hrs to be confirmed; *Sandyford Lib:* Mon, Wed-Fri 0830-1700, Tue 0930-1700, Fri 0830-1630
Subj: all subjs; genl; GCSE; A level; vocational; local study (North East England, esp Newcastle upon Tyne) *Co-op Schemes:* BLDSC, ILL, NLJWP, TWIRL
Equip: 6 video viewers, 9 copiers, computers *Disabled:* enlarger for visually impaired *Svcs:* info, ref, biblio
Stock: bks/125000, incl pamphs & maps; periodcls/300; AVs/14500, incl all slides, audios & videos
Classn: DDC *Auto Sys:* Olib
Staff: Libns: 6 *Non-Prof:* 18 *Exp:* over £100000 pa

S1578 ✚

Newcastle General Hospital, Tomlinson Teaching Centre Library

Westgate Rd, Newcastle upon Tyne, NE4 6BE
(0191-273-8811; *fax:* 0191-219-5044)
Email: nghlib@nghlib.demon.co.uk
Internet: http://www.nnt.nhs.uk/mh/library.asp

Gov Body: Newcastle, North Tyneside & Northumberland Mental Health NHS Trust *Chief:* Libn: Mrs Kati Russell BA(Hons), MCLIP (kati.russell@ncht.northy.nhs.uk)
Assoc Libs: ST GEORGE'S HOSP, MENTAL HEALTH LIB (see **S1560**); ST NICHOLAS HOSP, MENTAL HEALTH LIB (see **S1585**)
Open: Mon-Wed 0900-1800, Thu-Fri 0900-1700
Subj: medicine; nursing; paramedicine; psychiatry
Co-op Schemes: HLN
Equip: copier, fax, computers (incl wd-proc, internet & CD-ROM)
Stock: bks/6500; periodcls/150
Classn: DDC *Auto Sys:* SydneyPlus
Pubns: New Bk List; Lib Guide; Journals Holdings List
Staff: Libns: 1 *Non-Prof:* 1.6

S1579 🏛

Newcastle Law Courts Library

The Quayside, Newcastle upon Tyne, NE1 2LA
(0191-201-2028; *fax:* 0191-201-0498)
Email: hazel.eccleston@courtservice.gsi.gov.uk

Type: legal *Gov Body:* The Court Svc *Chief:* Asst Regional Libn: Mrs Hazel Eccleston BA(Hons), LLB(Hons), MCLIP
Entry: open to court staff, barristers & solicitors; others by appt only *Open:* Mon-Fri 0830-1700
Subj: law *Equip:* copier
Stock: bks/304; periodcls/4178 vols, incl law reports
Staff: Libns: 1

S1580 ♈

The North of England Institute of Mining and Mechanical Engineers Library

Neville Hall, Westgate Rd, Newcastle upon Tyne, NE1 1SE (0191-232-2201/233-2459)

Chief: Hon Sec: Mr J.S. Porthouse *Dep:* Sec: Mrs B. Harris
Entry: ref only; appt advisable *Open:* Mon-Tue, Thu 1000-1400
Subj: mining hist *Collns: Archvs:* held at Northumberland Record Office (see **A390**) *Co-op Schemes:* ILL
Equip: copier, computers (incl wd-proc), 3 rooms for hire
Staff: Other Prof: 1 *Non-Prof:* 2

S1581 🏛

Northern Arts, Library and Information Service

Central Sq, Forth St, Newcastle upon Tyne, NE2 3PJ (0191-255-8573; *fax:* 0191-255-1020)
Email: info@northernarts.org.uk
Internet: http://www.arts.org.uk/

Type: arts board *Gov Body:* Arts Council (see **S997**) *Chief:* Communications Offcr: post vacant
Dep: Communications Asst: post vacant
Entry: adv appt *Open:* Mon-Fri 0930-1630
Subj: arts *Collns: Bks & Pamphs:* locally funded bks, prints etc *Other:* locally funded or made films
Equip: copier, 2 computers (both with wd-proc, internet & CD-ROM), 3 rooms for hire *Disabled:* minicom *Online:* FunderFinder
Stock: bks/1000; periodcls/50; videos/200
Exp: £17000 (1999-2000)
Proj: new lib & info area

S1582 🎓

Northumberland College at Kirkley Hall, Uplands Learning Resource Centre

Kirkley Hall, Ponteland, Newcastle upon Tyne, NE20 0AQ (01661-841200; *fax:* 01661-860047)
Email: Rosemary.Milton@northland.ac.uk
Internet: http://www.northland.ac.uk/

Gov Body: Northumberland Coll *Chief:* Libn: Miss Fiona Middlemist BA, MA *Dep:* Lib Mgr: Ms Rosemary Milton BSc, PGCE
Entry: ref only for non-membs of Coll *Open:* term: Mon-Thu 0900-2000, Wed 0900-1630, Fri 0900-1630
Subj: GCSE; A level; undergrad; local studies (North East England, land-based); sci; agric; hortic; textile crafts
Equip: copier, video viewer, 18 computers (all with wd-proc, internet & CD-ROM) *Online:* ATHENS, Tionestop *Officer-in-Charge:* Libn, as above *Svcs:* info, ref
Stock: bks/30000; periodcls/80; pamphs/1000; maps/20; videos/300; CD-ROMs/30 *Acqs Offcr:* Lib Mgr, as above
Classn: DDC *Auto Sys:* Heritage
Staff: Libns: 1 *Other Prof:* 0.5 *Non-Prof:* 1 *Exp:* £40000 (1999-2000); £20000 (2000-01)

S1583 🎓 ✚

Royal Victoria Infirmary Library

Royal Victoria Infirmary, Queen Victoria Rd, Newcastle upon Tyne, NE1 4LP (0191-282-5208; *fax:* 0870-169-0295)
Email: library@trri.nuth.northy.nhs.uk

Gov Body: Newcastle upon Tyne Hosps NHS Trust *Chief:* Trust Libn (at Freeman Hosp): Mrs Margaret Valentine BA, MCLIP *Dep:* Dep Trust Libn (on site): Ms Joanne Mullen BA (joanne. mullen@nuth.northy.nhs.uk)
Assoc Libs: FREEMAN HOSP TEACHING CENTRE LIB (see **S1574**)
Open: Mon-Wed 0900-1800, Thu-Fri 0900-1700
Subj: psy; nursing; midwifery; health; biology; anatomy; mgmt; medical tech *Collns: Bks & Pamphs:* hist of nursing colln (for ref & lending)

Co-op Schemes: BLDSC, HLN, NULJ
Equip: fax, copier (A4/10p, A3/15p), 3 computers (all with wd-proc, internet & internet databases) *Officer-in-Charge:* Dep Trust Libn, as above *Svcs:* info, ref
Stock: bks/4000; periodcls/40 *Acqs Offcr:* Dep Trust Libn, as above
Classn: DDC *Auto Sys:* SydneyPlus
Staff: Libns: 1 *Other Prof:* 0.5 *Non-Prof:* 1

S1584

Society of Antiquaries of Newcastle upon Tyne Library

Black Gate, Newcastle upon Tyne (0191-263-2793)
Email: Socantiqs@ncl.ac.uk
Internet: http://museums.ncl.ac.uk/Socantiqs/

Type: antiquarian soc *Chief:* Libn: Mr D. Peel
Assoc Libs: archvs of Soc held at NORTHUMBERLAND RECORD OFFICE (see **A390**)
Entry: non-membs by appt only *Open:* Wed 1400-1600, Thu 1700-1900, Sat 1000-1200
Subj: Northern England: hist; antiquities; arch; archaeo *Co-op Schemes:* ILL, interlending via NEMLAC
Equip: m-reader, copier
Stock: bks/30000; periodcls/60
Pubns: Archaeologia Aeliana (hb/£10.40, pb/£7.65)
Staff: 10 PT volunteers *Exp:* £3000 (19999-2000)

S1585

St Nicolas Hospital, Mental Health Library

St Nicholas Hosp, Jubilee Rd, Gosforth, Newcastle upon Tyne, NE3 3XT (0191-213-0151 x28154; *fax:* 0191-213-0286)
Email: medlib@library.demon.co.uk
Internet: http://www.nnt.nhs.uk/mh/library.asp

Gov Body: Newcastle, North Tyneside & Northumberland Mental Health NHS Trust *Chief:* Snr Lib Asst: Miss Glenys Goodwill BA, MCLIP (glenys.goodwill@ncht.northy.nhs.uk)
Assoc Libs: NEWCASTLE GENL HOSP, TOMLINSON TEACHING CENTRE LIB (see **S1578**); ST GEORGE'S HOSP, MENTAL HEALTH LIB (see **S1560**)
Entry: Trust staff *Open:* Mon-Thu 0830-1600, Fri 0830-1400
Subj: mental health *Co-op Schemes:* BLDSC, PLCS, other local NHS libs
Equip: copier (5p per sheet), computer (with wd-proc, internet & CD-ROM) *Online:* NHS databases via HERDING *Officer-in-Charge:* Snr Lib Asst, as above *Svcs:* info, ref
Stock: bks/1000; periodcls/33; videos/c24; CD-ROMs/a few *Acqs Offcr:* Snr Lib Asst, as above
Classn: DDC *Auto Sys:* LIMES *Staff: Libns:* 1

S1586

University of Newcastle upon Tyne, University Library

Jesmond Rd West, Newcastle upon Tyne, NE2 4HQ (0191-222-7674; *fax:* 0191-222-6235)
Email: library@ncl.ac.uk
Internet: http://www.ncl.ac.uk/library/

Gov Body: Univ of Newcastle *Chief:* Univ Libn & Keeper of Pybus Colln: Dr Thomas W. Graham MA, PhD, DipLib, MCLIP *Dep:* Dep Libn: Mr Jon Purcell BA, DMS, DipLib, MCLIP
Assoc (Divisional) Libs: WALTON (MEDICAL & DENTAL) LIB (see **S1590**); LAW LIB, Univ of Newcastle upon Tyne, Newcastle Law School, 22-24 Windsor Ter, Newcastle upon Tyne NE1 7RU, Libn: Mrs Linda Kelly BA, MCLIP (0191-222-7944)

Entry: adv appt *Open:* term: Mon-Fri 0900-2200, Sat 0900-1630, Sun 1100-1730; vac: Mon-Fri 0900-1700, Sat 0900-1300
Subj: all subjs; undergrad; postgrad *Collns: Bks & Pamphs:* Catherine Cookson Colln; Pybus Colln (medicine); Merz Colln (sci, medicine); Wallis Colln (maths); Robert White Colln (hist of Northumberland) *Archvs:* Gertrude Bell Papers (politics, arch); Pybus Papers (hist of medicine); Runciman Papers (19C-20C politics); Stanford Colln (music); Trevelyan Papers (18C-20C politics) *Co-op Schemes:* BLDSC, SCONUL vac access, Newcastle/Gateshead Libs Partnership, SCONUL Rsrch Extra, UK Libs Plus
Equip: 3 m-readers, 4 m-printers, 40 copiers, 3 clr copiers, 300 computers (incl wd-proc, internet & CD-ROM) *Disabled:* Vantage CCTV reader, 2 low level copiers, 1 text playing video, 1 text phone, 2 deaf alerters, 1 PC with JAWS software *Svcs:* info, ref, biblio
Stock: bks/1140050; periodcls/6712; photos/81000; slides/9928; maps/6700; videos/984; archvs/1600 linear m *Acqs Offcr:* Acqs Libn: Mr Neil Brabban (Neil.Brabban@ncl.ac.uk)
Classn: DDC *Auto Sys:* Aleph
Pubns: Special Collns Guide (free)
Staff: Libns: 24.7 *Non-Prof:* 61.8 *Exp:* £2508683 (1999-2000); £2476865 (2000-01)

S1587

University of Newcastle upon Tyne, Centre for Lifelong Learning Library

Joseph Cowen House, St Thomas St, Univ of Newcastle, Newcastle upon Tyne, NE1 7RU (0191-222-6793; *fax:* 0191-222-7090)
Email: c.m.wride@ncl.ac.uk
Internet: http://www.ncl.ac.uk/lifelong-learning/library/

Gov Body: Univ of Newcastle (see **S1586**) *Chief:* Libn: Ms Melissa Wride BSc, MA
Entry: for use of students at the Centre only
Open: term: Mon-Thu 0945-1300, 1400-1900, Fri 0945-1300; vac: Mon-Thu 0945-1300, 1400-1600, Fri 0945-1300
Subj: all subjs; undergrad
Equip: m-reader, copier, 7 computers (all with wd-proc & internet, 5 with CD-ROM), scanner *Disabled:* video magnifiers *Svcs:* info, ref
Stock: bks/22000; periodcls/24; slides/9000; maps/55; m-forms/50; videos/100
Classn: DDC *Staff: Libns:* 1

S1588

University of Newcastle upon Tyne, Department of Archaeology, Cowen Library

Univ of Newcastle upon Tyne, Newcastle upon Tyne, NE1 7RU (0191-222-5342; *fax:* 0191-222-8561)
Email: averill.robson@ncl.ac.uk
Internet: http://historical-studies.ncl.ac.uk/info/cowen_library.htm

Gov Body: Univ of Newcastle (see **S1586**) *Chief:* Libn: Mrs Averill Robson BA(Hons)
Entry: students of archaeo/classics, rsrchers, local historians *Open:* term: Mon-Fri 1000-1700; vac: Mon-Fri 1200-1600
Subj: undergrad; postgrad; local studies (Northumberland & Durham, archaeo & related); archaeo; classics *Collns: Bks & Pamphs:* off-prints of local excavations, finds etc *Archvs:* Gertrude Bell Photo Colln *Other:* aerial photos of Northumberland & Durham
Equip: 2 copiers *Svcs:* info, ref, biblio, indexing
Stock: bks/22983; periodcls/24; photos/50000
Classn: own, based on Inst of Archaeo Scheme (geographical area – period – subj) *Staff: Libns:* 1

S1589

University of Newcastle upon Tyne, Fine Art Library

The Quadrangle, Univ of Newcastle upon Tyne, Newcastle upon Tyne, NE1 7RU (0191-222-6041; *fax:* 0191-222-6047)
Email: a.m.horn@ncl.ac.uk
Internet: http://www.ncl.ac.uk/fineart/

Gov Body: Univ of Newcastle upon Tyne (see **S1586**) *Chief:* Fine Art Libn: Ms Angela Horn
Entry: staff & students; adv appt for others
Subj: fine art; art hist
Equip: video player, projectors, seminar room
Stock: bks/c20000; periodcls/19; slides/50000; m-forms/296; clippings/15000
Staff: Libns: 1

S1590

University of Newcastle upon Tyne, Walton Library

Medical School, Framlington Pl, Newcastle upon Tyne, NE2 4HH (0191-222-7550; *fax:* 0191-222-8102)
Email: lib-walton-rs@ncl.ac.uk
Internet: http://www.ncl.ac.uk/library/medical/medindex.html

Gov Body: Univ of Newcastle upon Tyne (see **S1586**) *Chief:* Medical Libn: Ms Erika Gwynnett BA (Hons), DipLib (erika.gwynnett@ncl.ac.uk)
Entry: membs of the Univ; NHS staff of the Northern part of the Northern & Yorkshire NHS region *Open:* term: Mon-Thu 0900-2200, Fri 0900-2100, Sat 0900-1630, Sun 1100-1730; vac: Mon-Thu 0900-2000, Fri 0900-1700, Sat 0900-1300
Subj: medicine; health; dentistry; biomedical scis
Co-op Schemes: BLDSC, Northern & Yorkshire Regional Union List of Serials
Equip: 6 copiers (A4/6p, A3/12p), clr copier (A4/50p, A3/£1), 10 computers *Online:* BIOSIS (Biological Abstracts), CINAHL, Cochrane, EBMR (Evidence-Based Medicine Reviews), Embase, Health CD, HMIC, Medline, PsycInfo, Web of Science, various e-journals
Stock: bks/80000; periodcls/900; videos/numerous
Staff: Libns: 5 *Non-Prof:* 17

S1591

University of Northumbria at Newcastle, Learning Resources Department

Lib Bldg, Sandyford Rd, Newcastle upon Tyne, NE1 8ST (0191-227-4736; *fax:* 0191-227-4563)
Email: lbv2@unn.ac.uk
Internet: http://www.unn.ac.uk/central/isd/

Gov Body: Univ of Northumbria at Newcastle *Chief:* Dir of Learning Resources: Professor Jane Core (jane.core@unn.ac.uk) *Other Snr Staff:* Asst Dir (Resources): Ms Christine Willoughby (christine.willoughby@unn.ac.uk); Asst Dir (Info Svcs): Ms Carole Moreland (carole.moreland@unn.ac.uk); Asst Dir (Specialist Technical Support): Ms Jackie Eager (jackie.eager@unn.ac.uk); Asst Dir (Learning Support): Mr Ken Etherington (ken.etherington@unn.ac.uk)
Assoc Libs: CITY CAMPUS LIB, addr as above; CARLISLE CAMPUS LIB, Milbourne St, Carlisle, Cumbria, CA2 5UZ (01228-404660; *fax:* 01228-404669); COACH LN LIB, Coach Ln, Benton, Newcastle, NE7 7XA (0191-215-6540; *fax:* 0191-215-6560); LANG RESOURCES CENTRE, Room 126, Lipman Bldg, Sandyford Rd, Newcastle upon Tyne, NE1 8ST (0191-227-4930); LONGHIRST CAMPUS LIB, Longhirst Hall, Longhirst, Morpeth, Northumberland, NE61 3LL (01670-795050; *fax:* 01670-795052); SUTHERLAND LAW PRACTICE LIB, Sutherland Bldg, Northumberland Rd, Newcastle upon Tyne, NE1 8ST (0191-227-4383)

(Univ of Northumbria at Newcastle cont)
Entry: ref only for non-membs; external borrowing membership available for a fee *Open: City Campus Lib:* term: Mon-Fri 0900-2400, Fri 0900-1700, Sat 0930-1700, Sun 1100-1700, vac: Mon, Wed, Fri 0900-1700, Tue 0900-2100
Subj: all subjs; undergrad; postgrad *Collns: Bks & Pamphs:* EDC; govt pubns; CIBSE Lib *Archvs:* Visual Arts UK Archv; English Regional Arts Boards Archv; Year of the Artist Colln *Other:* Thompson Newspaper Colln (cuttings, c1900-81); Labour Hist Colln (on m-film) *Co-op Schemes:* NEMLAC, Newcastle Libs Joint Working Party, BLDSC
Equip: m-reader, 2 m-printers (A4/10p), video viewer, fax, 21 copiers (A4/6p, A3/12p), clr copier (A4/75p, A3/£1), computers (incl wd-proc & CD-ROM), room for hire *Online:* ADAM, AMED, Art Abstracts, ASSIA, BHI, BIDS, BNI, Cambridge Scientific Abstracts, Cochrane, Datastream, EBSCO, EconLit, EEVL, Emerald, ERIC, FAME, Hansard, Index to Theses, Infotrac, JSTOR, Lawtel, Lexis-Nexis, Mintel, PubMed, SciDirect, Web of Science etc
Stock: bks/500000; periodcls/3000
Classn: DDC, some UDC *Auto Sys:* Talis
Staff: Libns: 28 *Non-Prof:* 95.8

Newmarket

S1592 ⚷
Animal Health Trust Library
Lanwades Pk, Kentford, Newmarket, Suffolk, CB8 7UU (08700-502424; *fax:* 08700-502425)
Email: sandra.tatum@aht.org.uk
Internet: http://www.aht.org.uk/

Gov Body: Animal Health Trust *Chief:* Libn: Mrs Sandra J. Tatum MCLIP
Entry: please apply to libn *Open:* Mon-Fri 0900-1700
Subj: veterinary medicine; equine medicine *Co-op Schemes:* BLDSC
Equip: copier, computers (incl 3 internet) *Online:* Medline, VET-CD
Stock: bks/5000; periodcls/65, plus 50 no longer current
Classn: UDC
Pubns: Animal Health Trust Annual Review; Animal Health Trust Scientific Review
Staff: Libns: 1

S1593 ⚷ 🏛
The National Horseracing Museum, Library and Archive
99 High St, Newmarket, Suffolk, CB8 8JL (01638-667333; *fax:* 01638-655600)
Internet: http://www.nhrm.co.uk/

Type: charity *Gov Body:* Council of Mgmt of the Natl Horseracing Museum *Chief:* Dir: Ms Hilary Bracegirdle BSc, MBA *Dep:* Curator: Mr G.R. Snelling
Entry: lib & archv by appt *Open:* by appt Mon-Fri 1000-1700
Subj: local study (Newmarket); racing industry; hist of horseracing & breeding *Collns: Bks & Pamphs:* complete run of racing calendars *Archvs:* photo colln (2000+)
Svcs: info, ref

Stock: bks/800+; photos/2000+; maps/10; videos/5
Classn: MDA *Staff: Other Prof:* 2
Proj: rehousing of glass neg colln

Newport, Gwent

S1594 🎓
Coleg Gwent, Learning Resources Centre
Newport Campus, Nash Rd, Newport, Gwent, NP19 4TS (01633-466101; *fax:* 01633-466100)
Internet: http://www.coleggwent.ac.uk/

Chief: Dir of Learning Resources (Newport Campus): Mrs Anne Williams BA, MCLIP
Assoc Libs: CROSSKEYS CAMPUS LRC, Risca Rd, Crosskeys, Gwent, NP11 7ZA; EBBW VALE CAMPUS LRC, College Rd, Ebbw Vale, Gwent, NP23 6GT; PONTYPOOL CAMPUS LRC, Blaendare Rd, Pontypool, Gwent, NP4 5YE; USK CAMPUS LRC, The Rhadyr, Usk, Gwent, NP15 1XJ
Entry: staff & students *Open:* term: Mon-Thu 0900-1900, Fri 0900-1630
Subj: all subjs *Co-op Schemes:* NEWLIS
Equip: video viewer, copier, computers (incl wd-proc, internet & CD-ROM) *Svcs:* info, ref
Stock: bks/9000; periodcls/70; videos/100
Classn: DDC *Auto Sys:* Dynix
Staff: Libns: 1 *Non-Prof:* 3
Proj: new learning resource centres at Newport & Pontypool campuses

S1595 ✚
Gwent Healthcare NHS Trust Library Services
Royal Gwent Hosp, The Friars, Friars Rd, Newport, Gwent, NP20 4EZ (01633-238134/3/1; *fax:* 01633-238123)

Gov Body: Gwent Healthcare NHS Trust *Chief:* Lib Svcs Mgr: Mrs Joanna Dundon BA(Hons) (Joanna.Dundon@gwent.wales.nhs.uk) *Dep:* Asst Libn: Mrs Maureen Williams BA(Hons) (Maureen.Williams@gwent.wales.nhs.uk)
Assoc Libs: GWENT HEALTHCARE POSTGRAD LIB (see **S285**); NEVILL HALL POSTGRAD LIB, Nevill Hall Hosp, Brecon Rd, Abergavenny, Monmouthshire, NP7 7EG; ST CADOC'S PSYCHIATRIC HOSP LIB, Lodge Rd, Caerleon, Newport, S Wales, NP6 1XQ; MAINDIFF COURT LIB, Maindiff Court Hosp, Ross Rd, Abergavenny, Monmouthshire, NP7 8NF
Entry: open to Trust staff & health profs working in Gwent area; others by letter of introduction from their org libn or libn who is a memb of NEWLIS
Open: Mon-Thu 0900-1800, Fri 0900-1700
Subj: at undergrad, postgrad & vocational levels: medicine; health; nursing; professions allied to medicine; mgmt *Collns: Bks & Pamphs:* clinical effectiveness bks & journals; Trust pubns *Archvs:* historical memorabilia, minutes bks & registers of Royal Gwent Hosp & St Woolos Hosp *Co-op Schemes:* BLDSC, AWHILES, One Lib Network (formerly AWLS), NEWLIS
Equip: copier (A4/5p), video viewer, fax, 6 computers (all with wd-proc, internet & CD-ROM), thermal binder *Online:* all major knowledge bases via Homs (NHS Wales Intranet), incl: Medline, CINAHL, Embase etc *Officer-in-Charge:* Lib Svcs Mgr, as above *Svcs:* info, ref
Stock: bks/13000, plus c4000 bnd periodcls; periodcls/220; photos/200; videos/200; CD-ROMs/28; archvs/1 cubic m *Acqs Offcr:* Lib Svcs Mgr, as above
Classn: DDC *Auto Sys:* in-house based on MS Access, moving to Voyager
Pubns: Lib Guide; Current Journals Holdings; Handy Hints on Effective Searching; Handy Hints on Harvard Referencing
Staff: Libns: 2 *Non-Prof:* 1

S1596 🏛
Patent Office, Classification Library
The Patent Office, Cardiff Rd, Newport, Gwent, NP10 8QQ (01633-814000; *fax:* 01633-814410)
Internet: http://www.patent.gov.uk/

Chief: Lib Mgr: Mr Tony Davies
Entry: adv appt
Subj: patents & patenting *Collns: Archvs:* patent archv & classn material

S1597 🎓
University of Wales College Newport, Library and Information Services
Caerleon Campus, PO Box 179, Newport, Gwent, NP18 3YG (01633-432294; *fax:* 01633-632108)
Email: library@newport.ac.uk
Internet: http://lis.newport.ac.uk/library/

Gov Body: Univ of Wales *Chief:* Head of Lib & Info Svcs: Ms Janet Peters BA, MLS, MCLIP *Dep:* Dep Head of Lib & Info Svcs: Ms Lesley May BA, DipLib, PGCE, MCLIP
Assoc Libs: ALLT-YR-YN CAMPUS LIB, PO Box 180, Newport, NP20 5XR, Campus Libn: Ms Dawne Leatherdale MBA, MCLIP (01633-432310)
Open: Caerleon: term: Mon-Thu 0900-2100, Fri 0930-1700, Sat-Sun 1300-1700; *Allt-yr-yn:* term: Mon-Thu 0900-2000, Fri 0930-1700, Sat-Sun 1300-1700; reduced hrs during vacs
Subj: all subjs; undergrad; postgrad; *Caerleon:* media; art; design; teacher edu; humanities; sci; community studies; youth work; *Allt-yr-yn:* business; mgmt; computing; eng; social studies
Collns: Bks & Pamphs: at Caerleon: archaeo colln; Teaching Practice Lib (ch's bks & related media); David Hurn Colln (photography); Primrose Hockey Colln (Caerleon local hist) *Other:* at Caerleon: documentary photography colln; art slide colln; off-air video colln *Co-op Schemes:* BLDSC
Equip: copiers, computers *Online:* Infotrac, Gate Newspapers, Swetsnet Navigator, Art Abstracts, World of Science, ISTP, Design & Applied Arts Index, FAME, BEI/ERIC, ASSIA, BHI, Sports Discus, Index to Theses, Digimap, BSS, Reuters Business Insight, British Standards Online
Stock: bks/180000; periodcls/1800 printed & elec; slides/35000; videos/2500
Classn: DDC *Auto Sys:* Sirsi
Pubns: How to Study Successfully (2nd ed)
Staff: Libns: 8 *Non-Prof:* 13

S1598 🎓 ✚
University of Wales College of Medicine, School of Nursing and Midwifery Studies Library
Caerleon Edu Centre, St Cadoc's Hosp, Caerleon, Newport, Gwent, NP18 1XR (01633-436224/430919; *fax:* 01633-430717)
Email: CaerleonLib@cf.ac.uk
Internet: http://www.uwcm.ac.uk/

Gov Body: Univ of Wales Coll of Medicine (see **S427**) *Chief:* Nursing & Healthcare Studies Libn: Ms M. Gorman *Dep:* Site Libn: Ms Angela Bowyer
Entry: registered UWCM students & nurses on UWCM courses; trained nurses based in Gwent Trusts; other nurses may join for annual fee of £50+VAT *Open:* Mon-Fri 0830-1700
Subj: nursing; related subjs *Collns: Bks & Pamphs:* Health & Safety; Open Learning; UWCM theses *Co-op Schemes:* ILL
Equip: m-reader, copier, computer (incl CD-ROM) *Online:* CINAHL, ASSIA, BNI, ENB
Stock: bks/17000; periodcls/102
Classn: DDC *Auto Sys:* Voyager
Staff: Libns: 1.5 *Non-Prof:* 3

Newport, *Isle of Wight*

S1599 🔖

Isle of Wight College, Victor Stevenson Learning Resource Centre

Medina Way, Newport, Isle of Wight, PO30 5TA (01983-535201; *fax:* 01983-521707)
Email: library@iwight.ac.uk
Internet: http://www.iwightc.ac.uk/

Chief: Head of Learning Svcs: Mrs Lynne Christopher BLib, MCLIP *Dep:* Lib Co-ordinator: Mrs Karen Erskine
Entry: borrowing for staff & students; others ref only *Open:* term: Mon-Thu 0845-2000, Fri 1000-1700; vac: Mon-Fri 0900-1700 (-1300 during summer)
Subj: all subjs; GCSE; A level; undergrad; vocational; local study (Isle of Wight), covering: phil; psy; religion; social sci; lang; sci; maths; tech; arts; lit; geog; hist *Co-op Schemes:* HATRICS
Equip: video viewers, copiers, clr copier, computers (incl wd-proc, internet & CD-ROM) *Online:* Infotrac *Svcs:* info, ref
Stock: bks/c36000; periodcls/268; maps/192; audios/384; videos/3000
Classn: UDC *Auto Sys:* Heritage
Staff: Libns: 5 *Other Prof:* 7 PT *Non-Prof:* 4

S1600 ✚

Isle of Wight Healthcare NHS Trust, Oliveira Library

Edu Centre, St Mary's Hosp, Newport, Isle of Wight, PO30 5TG (01983-534519/471; *fax:* 01983-534232)
Email: postgradlibrary@iow.nhs.uk

Gov Body: Isle of Wight Healthcare NHS Trust
Chief: Lib Svcs Mgr: Mr G.K. Amos BA(Hons), MA (gary.amos@iow.nhs.uk)
Entry: contact Libn if not an NHS employee
Open: Mon-Fri 0900-1700; 24 hr access for staff
Subj: medicine; nursing; allied health; social care
Co-op Schemes: HLN, SWRLIN
Equip: copier, fax, 4 computers (incl wd-proc, internet & CD-ROM) *Svcs:* info, ref, biblio, current awareness
Stock: bks/5500; periodcls/180; videos/100
Classn: NLM *Auto Sys:* Heritage
Staff: Libns: 1 *Non-Prof:* 2

Newport, *Shropshire*

S1601 🎓

Harper Adams University College Library

Newport, Shropshire, TF10 8NB (01952-815393; *fax:* 01952-815290)
Email: libhelp@harper-adams.ac.uk
Internet: http://www.harper-adams.ac.uk/

Chief: Lib Svc Mgr: Ms Kathryn Greaves BLib(Hons), MCLIP (kgreaves@harper-adams.ac.uk) *Other Snr Staff:* Mrs Janet Parnaby BLib(Hons) (jparnaby@harper-adams.ac.uk); Ms Helen Smith BA(Hons), MA (hsmith@harper-adams.ac.uk); Mr Dermot Ryan BA(Hons), MSc(Econ) (dryan@harper-adams.ac.uk); Mrs Sue Hill BA(Hons), DipLib, MCLIP (shill@harper-adams.ac.uk)
Entry: ref only, external membership available for £25 pa (ex-students) or £100 pa (others) *Open:* term: Mon-Thu 0900-2200, Fri 0900-1700, Sat & Sun 1000-1700; vac: Mon-Fri 0900-1700
Subj: agric; livestock production; poultry; crop production; crop protection; land use; conservation; agric econ; marketing; agric eng *Collns: Bks & Pamphs:* bulk of lib of Sir Edward Brown (first

president of World's Poultry Sci Assoc); historical colln of bks on poultry *Co-op Schemes:* BLDSC, Access West Midlands, SHAIR
Equip: m-form reader/printer, fax, 3 copiers, 10 computers (all with internet & CD-ROM) *Online:* Web of Science, Update, AGDEX, Compendium, ABInform; on CD-ROM: CAB Abstracts, Agricola, FOMAD, FROSTI, EcoDisc, Financial Times
Officer-in-Charge: Lib Svc Mgr, as above
Stock: bks/34500; periodcls/975; pamphs/11300; videos/400; CD-ROMs/various *Acqs Offcr:* Lib Svc Mgr, as above
Classn: DDC *Auto Sys:* Talis
Staff: Libns: 3.26 *Non-Prof:* 4.57 *Exp:* £155000 (1999-2000); £153000 (2000-01); on bks & journals

Newry

S1602 🎓

Newry and Kilkeel Institute of Further and Higher Education Library

Patrick St, Newry, Co Down, BT35 8DN (028-3026-1071; *fax:* 028-3026-0684)
Email: institute@newry-kilkeel.ac.uk
Internet: http://www.newry-kilkeel.ac.uk/

Chief: Libn: Mrs Ursula Whyatt
Entry: adv appt for membs of public *Open:* Mon-Thu 0900-2000, Fri 0900-1700
Subj: all subjs; genl; GCSE; A level; undergrad; postgrad; vocational *Co-op Schemes:* BLDSC
Equip: copier, computers (incl 12 wd-proc, 12 internet & 12 CD-ROM) *Svcs:* info, ref, biblio
Stock: bks/21000; periodcls/40; pamphs/500; videos/400
Classn: DDC *Auto Sys:* Heritage
Staff: Libns: 1 *Non-Prof:* 3 *Exp:* £38000 (1999-2000)

Newton Abbot

S1603 🎓

University of Plymouth, Seale-Hayne Library

Newton Abbot, Devon, TQ12 6NQ (01626-325828; *fax:* 01626-325836)
Email: angela.blackman@plymouth.ac.uk
Internet: http://www.plymouth.ac.uk/library/

Gov Body: Univ of Plymouth (see **S1812**) *Chief:* Site Libn: Mrs Angela Blackman BA, MCLIP
Entry: ref only *Open:* term: Mon-Thu 0900-2100, Fri 0900-1900, Sat 0900-1300; vac: Mon-Fri 0900-1230, 1330-1700
Subj: land use; agric; food tech; rural estates mgmt; tourism; hospitality mgmt *Collns: Bks & Pamphs:* Dart Colln (amenity rsrch) *Archvs:* Barkworth Colln (microbiology) *Co-op Schemes:* BLDSC
Equip: 3 m-readers, m-printer, video viewers, copiers, clr copier, computers (incl wd-proc, internet & CD-ROM)
Stock: bks/45000; periodcls/350; videos/300
Classn: DDC *Auto Sys:* Libertas
Staff: Libns: 3 *Non-Prof:* 4.5

Newtongrange

S1604 🗝🏛

Scottish Mining Museum Library

Lady Victoria Colliery, Newtongrange, Midlothian, EH22 4QN (0131-663-7519; *fax:* 0131-654-1618)
Email: enquiries@scottishminingmuseum.org
Internet: http://www.scottishminingmuseum.com/

Gov Body: Scottish Mining Museum Trust *Chief:* Dir: Mr Fergus Waters *Dep:* Keeper: Ms Julia Stephen

Entry: adv appt, ref only *Open:* Mon-Fri 1000-1600 (all year excl Scottish public hols)
Subj: local study (Scotland); coal mining; mining communities; tech; geog; hist *Collns: Bks & Pamphs:* genl & specialised vols; HM Inspector of Mines Reports; Annual Reports of NCB/BCC/MFGB/NUM; Guides to the Coal Fields; periodcls e.g., Coal News & Colliery Eng; transactions of the Inst of Mining Engineers *Archvs:* records of the Lothian Coal Company, Natl Coal Board & Natl Union of Mineworkers (Scottish area) *Other:* some ephemera (waybills, payslips, etc)
Equip: copier (10p per sheet), video viewer, fax, 2 computers (both with CD-ROM, 1 with wd-proc), room for hire *Officer-in-Charge:* Keeper, as above
Svcs: info, ref
Stock: bks/200 linear m; photos/8000; slides/2000; maps/2000; audios/50; videos/200; archvs/50 linear m *Acqs Offcr:* Keeper, as above
Classn: UDC
Pubns: edu packs: The Story of Coal (£4.75); A Race Apart (£4.75); Operations Centre (£4.25); genl bks: Coal Mining in Scotland (50p); Mining the Lothians (£12.95)
Staff: Other Prof: 6 *Non-Prof:* 13

Newtown

S1605 🗝🏛

The Robert Owen Memorial Museum, Library

The Cross, Broad St, Newtown, Powys, SY16 2BB (01686-626345)
Email: johnd@robert-owen.midwales.com
Internet: http://robert-owen.midwales.com/

Chief: Hon Curator: Mr John Hatton Davidson BA, DIC, MSc
Entry: for items not on display: access to Owen scholars for ref only, by adv appt, preferably outside advertised opening hrs *Open: Museum:* Mon-Fri 0930-1200, 1400-1530, Sat 0930-1130
Collns: Bks & Pamphs: printed bks, pamphs, letters & cuttings by or about Robert Owen (1771-1858) & the Owenites
Equip: video viewer, copier, computer (with wd-proc)
Stock: bks/200; photos/50; illusts/50 paintings & prints; pamphs/50; videos/2
Pubns: Robert Owen: Social Reformer & Master Manufacturer (70p); Robert Owen: Industrialist, Reformer, Visionary: 4 Bicentenary Essays (£1); Robert Owen 1771-1858 (resource pack, £2)
Staff: Non-Prof: 0.2

Newtownabbey

S1606 🎓

East Antrim Institute of Further and Higher Education, College Library

400 Shore Rd, Newtownabbey, Co Antrim, BT37 9RS (028-9085-5000 x216; *fax:* 028-9086-2076)
Email: info@eaifhe.ac.uk
Internet: http://www.eaifhe.ac.uk/

Gov Body: East Antrim Inst of Further & Higher Edu *Chief:* Libn: Mrs Holly Sweeney
Entry: through enrolment on arrival at Lib & issue of Lib card *Open:* term: Mon-Thu 0900-2100, Fri 0900-1600
Subj: all subjs; genl; GCSE; A level; undergrad; vocational
Equip: copier, computers (with wd-proc, internet & CD-ROM), printers, scanners, TV & video, rooms for hire *Svcs:* info, ref, biblio
Stock: bks/14000; periodcls/10; videos/180; CD-ROMs/250
Classn: DDC *Auto Sys:* Heritage
Staff: Libns: 1 *Non-Prof:* 1 FT, 2 PT

Special Libraries

North Shields ▼ Norwich

North Shields

S1607 ✚
North Tyneside Education Centre Library

North Tyneside Genl Hosp, Rake Ln, North Shields, Tyne & Wear, NE29 8NH (0191-293-2761; *fax:* 0191-293-2763)
Email: library@northumbria-healthcare.nhs.uk
Internet: http://www.northumbria-healthcare.nhs.uk/

Gov Body: Northumbria Healthcare NHS Trust *Chief:* Libn: Ms Jackie McGuire PGDipLIM (jackie.mcguire@northumbria-healthcare.nhs.uk) *Dep:* Asst Libn: Ms Jo Gray BA(Hons) (jo.gray@northumbria-healthcare.nhs.uk)
Assoc Libs: HEXHAM GENL HOSP, RYDER POSTGRAD MEDICAL CENTRE LIB (see **S809**); NORTHUMBERLAND HEALTHCARE TRUST LIB (see **S1559**); WANSBECK HOSP LIB (see **S52**)
Entry: staff of Trust & students on placement *Open:* Mon-Thu 0900-1700, Fri 0900-1630
Subj: medicine; health; nursing
Equip: copier, video viewer, 15 computers (all with wd-proc & CD-ROM, 14 with internet)
Stock: bks/7000; periodcls/150; videos/200
Classn: DDC *Auto Sys:* SydneyPlus
Staff: Libns: 2 *Non-Prof:* 1 *Exp:* £40000 (1999-2000); £40000 (2000-01)
Proj: new security sys in 2002

Northallerton

S1608 ✚
Friarage Hospital Study Centre, District Library

Friarage Hosp, Northallerton, N Yorkshire, DL6 1JG (01609-762526; *fax:* 01609-771126)
Email: mas11@york.ac.uk

Gov Body: NHS Trust *Chief:* Libn: Mrs Meri Snowdon BA, DipLib, MCLIP *Dep:* Mrs Janet Gee
Entry: adv appt *Open:* Mon-Sun 0700-2200 (only staffed during office hrs)
Subj: medicine; health *Co-op Schemes:* BLDSC, BMA, local networks
Equip: m-reader, copier, computer (with CD-ROM)
Stock: bks/6500; periodcls/120
Classn: DDC
Pubns: Lib Guide; Journal Holdings; New Bk List
Staff: Libns: 2 *Non-Prof:* 0.81

Northampton

S1609 ✐
Carlsberg-Tetley Brewing Ltd, Central Information Services

Jacobsen House, 140 Bridge St, Northampton, NN1 1PZ (01604-668866; *fax:* 01604-234444)

Chief: Mgr, Central Info Svcs: Mrs M. Pass BSc
Entry: enqs by phone only
Subj: tech; brewing *Co-op Schemes:* BLDSC
Equip: copier
Stock: bks/2000; periodcls/1000
Classn: UDC *Staff:* Other Prof: 1

S1610 ✿
Moulton College Learning Resource Centre

West St, Moulton, Northampton, NN3 7RR (01604-491131 x222; *fax:* 01604-491127)
Email: karina@moulton.ac.uk

Gov Body: Moulton Coll *Chief:* Learning Resources Mgr: Ms Karen Arthur BSc, DipIS, MCLIP *Other Snr Staff:* Dep Libns: Ms Emma Hopley & Ms Rosie Williams
Entry: ref only for non-coll membs *Open:* term: Mon-Thu 0830-2100, Fri 0830-1700, Sat 1000-1300; vac: Mon-Fri 0900-1700
Subj: sci; maths; tech; agric; land-based industry; equine studies; animal welfare; floristry; hortic; interior design; sports studies
Equip: copier, clr copier, fax, video viewer, 96 computers (incl wd-procs, internet & CD-ROM) *Online:* various internet & CD-ROM subscriptions
Stock: bks/16000; periodcls/100; various maps, pamphs, videos & CD-ROMs
Classn: DDC *Auto Sys:* Heritage
Staff: Libns: 3 *Non-Prof:* 2.5 *Exp:* £73000 (2000-01)

S1611 ✿
Northampton College Library

Booth Ln, Northampton, NN3 3RF (01604-734020; *fax:* 01604-734207)
Internet: http://www.northamptoncollege.ac.uk/

Gov Body: Northampton Coll *Chief:* Coll Libn: Mrs Grazyna Kuczera MA, MLIS, DipEd (grazyna.kuczera@northamptoncollege.ac.uk) *Dep:* Asst Libn: Miss Lynn Haynes BA(Hons), MA (lynn.haynes@northamptoncollege.ac.uk)
Assoc Libs: MULTICULTURAL RESOURCES CENTRE, Northampton Coll, Military Rd Centre, Military Rd, Northampton, NN1 3ET (01604-734179)
Entry: ref only for non-membs of Coll *Open:* term: Mon-Tue, Thu 0845-1900, Wed 0845-2000, Fri 0845-1600; vac: Mon-Fri 1000-1600
Subj: all subjs; genl; GCSE; A level; vocational; arts; local study (Northamptonshire) *Collns:* Bks & Pamphs: Northamptonshire Local Studies Colln; European Colln; Children's Colln; Easy Readers Colln *Co-op Schemes:* ALLIN, ILL, CULN
Equip: video viewer, copier (10p per copy), 11 computers (all with wd-proc, internet & CD-ROM) *Officer-in-Charge:* Coll Libn, as above *Svcs:* info, ref
Stock: bks/25000; periodcls/200; audios/20; videos/600; CD-ROMs/50 *Acqs Offcr:* Coll Libn, as above
Classn: DDC *Auto Sys:* Talis
Staff: Libns: 2 *Non-Prof:* 5 *Exp:* £30000 (2000-01)
Proj: new furnishings

S1612 ✚
Northampton General Hospital, Cripps Library

Northampton Genl Hosp, Billing Rd, Northampton, NN1 5BD (01604-545258/9; *fax:* 01536-545803)
Email: crippslibrary@northants.nhs.uk

Gov Body: Northamptonshire Health Support Svcs *Chief:* Lib Mgr: Mrs Ann Skinner BSc, MCLIP *Dep:* Asst Libn: Ms Jane Cooper
Assoc Libs: HIGHFIELD LIB (see **S1613**); PRINCESS MARINA LIB (see **S1615**)
Entry: NHS staff within Northamptonshire *Open:* Mon-Fri 0900-1700; 24 hr access for registered users
Subj: health; medicine; nursing
Equip: copier (A4/5p), computers (incl internet & CD-ROM) *Online:* NHSNet, Medline, CINAHL, Embase, Cochrane, AMED, BNI, PsycInfo, HMIC, OVID, EBSCO *Svcs:* info, ref, biblio, current awareness, lit searches

Classn: NLM *Auto Sys:* Unicorn
Staff: Libns: 2 *Non-Prof:* 3

S1613 ✚
Northamptonshire Health Support Services, Highfield Library

Highfield, Cliftonville Rd, Northampton, NN1 5DN (01604-615266; *fax:* 01604-615149)
Email: highfieldlibrary@northants.nhs.uk

Gov Body: Northamptonshire Health Support Svcs *Chief:* Head of Knowledge Mgmt Svcs: Ms Jane Holdsworth BA, MCLIP *Dep:* Lib Mgr: Mr Gary Meades
Assoc Libs: NORTHAMPTON GENL HOSP, CRIPPS LIB (see **S1612**); PRINCESS MARINA LIB (see **S1615**)
Entry: membership restricted to NHS staff within county; others by special arrangement *Open:* Mon-Fri 0900-1600; 24 hr access to Cripps & Princess Marina Libs for membs
Subj: health strategies; health mgmt; public health; health promotion; epidemiology; health improvement *Co-op Schemes:* BLDSC, HeLIN, ALLIN
Equip: copiers (A4/5p), computers *Online:* NHSNet, Medline, CINAHL, Embase, Cochrane, AMED, BNI, PsycInfo, HMIC, OVID, EBSCO *Svcs:* info, ref, biblio, current awareness, lit searches
Stock: bks/30000, incl reports; periodcls/c500; figs are for all libs
Classn: DDC, NLM *Auto Sys:* Unicorn
Pubns: Annual Report; Gateway to the World's Healthcare Knowledge Base (info pack); training handouts to support workshops; pubns available only to membs
Staff: Libns: 2 *Non-Prof:* 2

S1614 ✐ 🎥
Popperfoto (Paul Popper Ltd)

The Old Mill, Overstone Farm, Overstone, Northampton, NN6 0AB (01604-670670; *fax:* 01604-670635)
Email: inquiries@popperfoto.com
Internet: http://www.popperfoto.com/

Chief: Sales Dir: Mr Ian Blackwell *Dep:* Asst Sales Mgr: Mrs Samantha Chamberlain
Entry: appt required *Open:* Mon-Fri 0900-1800
Subj: all subjs; sport; royalty; animals; space; humans; wars etc *Collns:* Bks & Pamphs: extensive sporting archvs; Illustrated Magazine 1940-1960; Illustrated London News (extensive 19C bnd vols) *Other:* photo library/illusts (representatives for Reuters, AFP & EPA); extensive World War II material; original glass negs by H.G. Ponting of Scott's Antarctic expedition 1910-1912 *Co-op Schemes:* BAPLA
Equip: fax, copier, computer (with CD-ROM)
Stock: bks/500; images/13 mln+
Staff: Libns: 8 *Other Prof:* 10 *Non-Prof:* 3

S1615 ✚
Princess Marina Library

Princess Marina Hosp, 3 Alexandra Cl, Upton, Northampton, NN5 6UH (01604-575266/8; *fax:* 01604-586056)
Email: pmhlibrary@northants.nhs.uk

Gov Body: Northamptonshire Health Support Svcs *Chief:* Lib Mgr: Mr Gary Meades *Other Snr Staff:* Lib Assts: Ms Kristi Smith & Ms Ruth Thurston Ward
Assoc Libs: HIGHFIELD LIB (see **S1613**); NORTHAMPTON GENL HOSP, CRIPPS LIB (see **S1612**)
Entry: ref only, adv appt *Open:* Mon-Fri 0900-1700; 24 hr access for membs
Subj: medicine; nursing; psychiatry; learning disabilities; psy; mental health; community care
Co-op Schemes: BLDSC, PLCS, ORLIN

Equip: fax, video viewer, copier (A4/5p), computers (incl wd-proc, internet & CD-ROM) *Online:* NHSNet, Medline, CINAHL, Embase, Cochrane, AMED, BNI, PsycInfo, HMIC, OVID, EBSCO *Svcs:* info, ref, biblio, current awareness, lit searches
Stock: bks/6800; periodcls/60
Classn: NLM *Auto Sys:* Unicorn
Staff: Libns: 1 *Non-Prof:* 2

S1616 ✚
St Andrew's Group of Hospitals Medical Library
St Andrew's Hosp, Billing Rd, Northampton, NN1 5DG (01604-616466; *fax:* 01604-616266)
Email: libraryassistants@standrew.co.uk
Internet: http://www.stah.org/en/1/abtothmed.html

Gov Body: independent charitable trust *Chief:* Head Libn: Ms Nicola Newman DipInf, PGCE, MCLIP (nnewman@standrews.co.uk)
Assoc Libs: ST ANDREW'S HOSP ARCHVS, addr as above, Archivist: Ms Liz Ridley (contact via reception on 01604-616000)
Entry: staff membs; public/visitors by appt; external membership £50 pa *Open:* Mon-Thu 0915-1700, Fri 0915-1630
Subj: psy; social sci; sociology; psychiatry; mental health; brain injury; learning disabilities; rehabilitation; some religion (in relation to health care) *Collns: Other:* grey lit; voice colln *Co-op Schemes:* BLDSC, PLCS, HeLIN, NULJ
Equip: fax, copier, 3 computers (all with wd-proc, 2 with internet & 1 with CD-ROM) *Officer-in-Charge:* Head Libn, as above *Svcs:* info, ref, biblio, indexing, current awareness
Stock: bks/5900; periodcls/109; pamphs/1500; videos/20; CD-ROMs/1 *Acqs Offcr:* Head Libn, as above
Classn: NLM *Auto Sys:* Heritage
Staff: Libns: 1 *Non-Prof:* 3 *Exp:* £8000 (1999-2000); £8000 (2000-01)

S1617 🎓
University College Northampton, Park Campus Library
Boughton Green Rd, Northampton, NN2 7AL (01604-735500; *fax:* 01604-718819)
Internet: http://www.northampton.ac.uk/

Chief: Chief Libn: Ms Hilary Johnson BA, MA, MCLIP (hilary.johnson@northampton.ac.uk) *Dep:* Dep Libn: Mr Andrew Martin BSc, MA, PGDM, MCLIP (andrew.martin@northampton.ac.uk)
Other Snr Staff: Learning Support Co-ordinator: Chris Powis BA, MLib, DipHE, MCLIP, ILTM (chris.powis@northampton.ac.uk); Head of Centre for Academic Practice: Sandy Gilkes CertEd (sandy.gilkes@northampton.ac.uk)
Assoc Libs: AVENUE CAMPUS LIB, Maidwell Bldg, St George's Ave, Northampton, NN2 6JD
Entry: UCN staff & students; associate membership available for a fee; UK Libs Plus membs; ref only to others *Open:* term: Mon-Thu 0830-2200, Fri 0830-1900, Sat 1000-1700, Sun 1300-1700; vac: varies
Subj: all subjs; undergrad; postgrad; local study (Northamptonshire); *Park Campus:* psy; mgmt; business; law; edu; health; humanities; social sci; sports sci; *Avenue Campus:* art; design; performance studies; music; eng; computing; info sci *Collns: Bks & Pamphs:* AEA Tech Waste Mgmt Colln; European Ref Colln; Law Colln; Northamptonshire Colln (local studies); School Experience Colln (ch's bks & resources) *Archvs:* Coll Archv (established 1997) *Other:* Illusts Colln
Co-op Schemes: BLDSC, SCONUL, local libs
Equip: 3 m-printers, 14 video viewers, 11 copiers, 2 clr copiers, 65 computers (all with internet & CD-ROM, 25 with wd proc) *Disabled:* JAWS screen reader, magnifying CCTV, Kurzweil, TextHelp, ZoomText *Svcs:* info, ref

Stock: bks/225000; periodcls/3874; slides/14000; illusts/350; pamphs/30000; maps/275; m-forms/1200; videos/6000; CD-ROMs/50; archvs/20 linear m *Acqs Offcr:* Learning Resources Mgr: Mr Philip Thornborow (philip.thornborow@northampton.ac.uk)
Classn: DDC *Auto Sys:* Talis
Staff: Libns: 15 *Non-Prof:* 30 *Exp:* £422079 (1999-2000); £391512 (2000-01)
Proj: new wing to Avenue Lib starting 2002

Northwich

S1618 🎓
Mid-Cheshire College Library
Hartford Campus, Chester Rd, Northwich, Cheshire, CW8 1LJ (01606-720646)
Email: library@midchesh.ac.uk
Internet: http://www.midchesh.ac.uk/

Gov Body: Mid-Cheshire Coll *Chief:* Coll Libn: Mrs C.M. Lunt MCLIP (klunt@midchesh.ac.uk)
Dep: Libn: Mrs S.M. Woodward BA, PGCE, MCLIP
Other Snr Staff: Libn: Mrs P. Buttrick BA, PGCE, MCLIP; Libn: Miss H. Jubb BA
Entry: staff & students of the Coll; ref only for membs of the public *Open:* term: Mon-Thu 0900-2000, Fri 0900-1615; vac: Mon-Thu 0915-1215, 1315-1645, Fri 0915-1215, 1315-1615
Subj: all subjs; genl; GCSE; A level; vocational
Equip: copier, 11 computers (all with wd-proc & CD-ROM, 10 with internet) *Officer-in-Charge:* Coll Libn, as above *Svcs:* info, ref
Stock: bks/25000; periodcls/120; maps/150; videos/300; CD-ROMs/80 *Acqs Offcr:* Coll Libn, as above
Classn: DDC *Auto Sys:* EASL
Staff: Libns: 4 *Non-Prof:* 6 *Exp:* £30000 (1999-2000); £26000 (2000-01)

Northwood

S1619 🎓 🖐
London Bible College Library
Green Ln, Northwood, Middlesex, HA6 2UW (01923-456190; *fax:* 01923-456001)
Email: library@londonbiblecollege.ac.uk
Internet: http://www.londonbiblecollege.ac.uk/

Chief: Coll Libn: Mr Alan M. Linfield BA(Hons), DipLib *Dep:* Lib Administrator: Mrs Kate Merchant
Entry: ref only; prior appt preferred, admission at Libn's discretion, fee payable *Open:* Mon-Fri 0845-1645
Subj: phil; theology; historical theology; biblical studies; comparative religion; Biblical hermeneutics & linguistics; church hist *Co-op Schemes:* BLDSC, ILL, ABTAPL
Equip: m-printer, 2 copiers, online catalogue
Stock: bks/48000; periodcls/220; audios/800; videos/200; some slides, maps, m-forms & wallcharts
Classn: own *Auto Sys:* Unicorn
Pubns: Lib Guide
Staff: Libns: 1 *Non-Prof:* 0.6

S1620 ✚
Mount Vernon Postgraduate Medical Centre, Les Cannon Memorial Library
West Hertfordshire Hosps NHS Trust, Rickmansworth Rd, Northwood, Middlesex, HA6 2RN (01923-844143; *fax:* 01923-827216)
Email: library.mvernon@whht.nhs.uk

Gov Body: West Hertfordshire Hosps NHS Trust
Chief: Asst Libn: Ms Jane McFarlane
Assoc Libs: other Trust Libs: HEMEL HEMP-STEAD HOSP LIB (see **S798**); ST ALBANS CITY HOSP, STAFF LIB & INFO SVC (see **S1962**);

WATFORD GENL HOSP LIB (see **S2092**); *other assoc libs:* HAREFIELD HOSP LIB (see **S782**); HILLINGDON HOSP NHS TRUST LIB (see **S2066**)
Entry: open to all staff & health workers in area (incl dentists); letter of appl required from other users *Open:* Mon-Tue, Thu-Fri 0900-1700, Wed 0900-1900; key access for Trust staff at other times
Subj: medicine; nursing; surgery; dentistry
Collns: Archvs: archvs of Postgrad Centre *Co-op Schemes:* NTRLIS, BLDSC, NULJ, arrangements with other medical & nursing libs
Equip: m-reader, video viewer, copier, computers (incl wd-proc, internet & CD-ROM) *Online:* OVID, Medline, CINAHL, Cochrane *Svcs:* info, ref, biblio, translation, current awareness
Stock: bks/3000; periodcls/150; videos/50
Classn: NLM (Wessex)
Pubns: Lib Guide; Journal Holdings List; Lib Bulletin
Staff: Libns: 1.8

Norwich

S1621 🔑
2nd Air Division Memorial Library
The Forum, Millennium Plain, Norwich, Norfolk, NR2 1AW (01603-774747; *fax:* 01603-774749)
Email: 2admemorial.lib@norfolk.gov.uk
Internet: http://www.2ndair.org.uk/

Gov Body: Memorial Trust of the 2nd Air Div USAAF & Norfolk County Council *Chief:* Trust Libn: Mr Derek Hills
Assoc Libs: archival materials are held at NORFOLK RECORD OFFICE (see **A400**); additional "Wing Collns" housed in Dereham, Sprowston, Long Stratton & Attleborough Libs (see **P123** for NORFOLK LIB & INFO SVC)
Entry: open to public; borrowing for membs of Norfolk Lib & Info Svc; ref only for others *Open:* Mon, Wed-Fri 0900-2000, Tue 1000-2000, Sat 0900-1700
Subj: local studies (East Anglia); WW2; air warfare; military aviation; American military hist; American hist, life & culture; Anglo-American relations *Collns: Archvs:* archv of photographs, ephemera & official records relating to 2nd Air Div USAAF in Norfolk during WW2 (mainly held at NRO) *Other:* small audio & video collns
Equip: copier, video viewer, 6 computers (incl wd-proc, internet & CD-ROM) *Svcs:* info, ref
Stock: bks/c5000
Classn: DDC *Staff:* 5 in total

S1622 🎓
Easton College Library
Easton, Norwich, Norfolk, NR9 5DX (01603-731252; *fax:* 01603-741438)
Email: library@easton-college.ac.uk
Internet: http://www.easton-college.ac.uk/

Chief: Libn: Mrs Lydia Crick MA, MCLIP (lcrick@easton-college.ac.uk)
Entry: lending for students & staff; ref only by appt for genl public *Open:* term: Mon, Wed 0900-2000, Tue, Thu 0900-1700, Fri 0900-1645
Subj: life scis; biology; botany; animal care; floristry; agric; hortic; landscape design; garden design; sport; equestrianism; conservation; public svcs *Co-op Schemes:* ALLCU, ANGLES
Equip: copier, video viewer, 2 computers (both with CD-ROM, 1 with wd-proc & 1 with internet) *Online:* KnowUK, KnowEurope, Update, AGDEX *Svcs:* info, ref
Stock: bks/8000; periodcls/200; maps/50; videos/400; CD-ROMs/75
Classn: DDC *Auto Sys:* Liberty3
Staff: Libns: 1 *Non-Prof:* 2 PT
Proj: introduction of Liberty3; move to new lib in late 2003

Special Libraries

Norwich ▼ Nottingham

S1623

Institute of Food Research, Library and Information Services

Norwich Rsrch Pk, Colney Ln, Norwich, Norfolk, NR4 7UA (01603-255223; *fax:* 01603-507723)
Email: ifr.library@bbsrc.ac.uk
Internet: http://www.ifr.bbsrc.ac.uk/

Type: rsrch council *Gov Body:* BBSRC *Chief:* Info Svcs Mgr: Ms Rebecca Rose Walton BA, BSc, MCLIP
Entry: ref only, adv appt recommended *Open:* Mon-Fri 0930-1300, 1400-1600
Subj: at postgraduate/rsrch level: psy (related to consumer sci); social sci; sci; tech; food sci *Co-op Schemes:* ILL
Equip: copiers (5p-7p per sheet), 4 computers (all with wd-proc, internet & CD-ROM) *Online:* Dialog Web (cost + 10%) *Svcs:* info, ref
Stock: bks/20000; periodcls/235
Classn: UDC *Auto Sys:* Libero
Staff: Libns: 2 Non-Prof: 1

S1624

John Innes Centre, The Library

Norwich Rsrch Pk, Colney, Norwich, Norfolk, NR4 7UH (01603-450670; *fax:* 01603-450045)
Email: jii.library@bbsrc.ac.uk
Internet: http://www.jic.bbsrc.ac.uk/

Type: rsrch inst *Gov Body:* John Innes Centre & Sainsbury Laboratory *Chief:* Libn: Mr K.T. Dick BA(Hons), PGDip, MCLIP
Assoc Libs: ARCHVS & SPECIAL COLLNS, at above addr, Archivist: Ms E.A. Stratton (jii.archives@bbsrc.ac.uk)
Entry: by prior appt (tel, fax, email or letter all acceptable) *Open:* Mon-Fri 0900-1700
Subj: plant sci; plant & microbial biotech; classical & molecular genetics; plant pathology; hist & phil of sci *Collns: Bks & Pamphs:* Modern Sci Colln (14000 vols, 1000+ serial titles); Hist of Genetics Lib (4000 vols); private lib of William Bateson (300 vols); working lib of C.D. Darlington; John Innes Reprints Colln (40000+ scientific reprints, mid 18C onwards); John Innes Foundation Colln of Rare Botanical Bks (1611 onwards) *Archvs:* John Innes Archvs (1910-date); archvs of associated orgs, incl: Plant Breeding Inst Archvs; Nitrogen Fixation Laboratory Archvs; Virus Rsrch Unit Archvs; Sainsbury Laboratory Archvs; numerous collns relating to indivs associated with hist of John Innes Centre, esp the Innes family & William Bateson (1st Dir of the John Innes Inst); other archvs incl: the Genetical Soc of Great Britain Archvs (1919-date) *Other:* photo colln; AV colln, incl oral hist material *Co-op Schemes:* BLDSC, ANGLES, BBSRC
Equip: m-reader, m-printer, 2 copiers, clr copier, 5 public access computers *Online:* Dialog, STN, internet access *Svcs:* info, ref
Stock: bks/40000; periodcls/600; m-forms/100; archvs/500 m
Classn: UDC *Auto Sys:* Unicorn
Pubns: Catalogue of Special Colln
Staff: Libns: 2 Non-Prof: 2

S1625

London Aerial Photo Library

PO Box 25, Ashwellthorpe, Norwich, Norfolk, NR16 1HL (01508-488320; *fax:* 01508-488282)
Email: info@londonaerial.co.uk
Internet: http://www.londonaerial.co.uk/

Type: commercial photo agency *Chief:* Libn: Mrs Sandy Stockwell
Entry: contact by mail, phone or fax only *Open:* Mon-Fri 0900-1800
Subj: aerial photos of all parts of Britain
Svcs: info, ref *Stock:* photos/80000
Staff: Libns: 2

S1626

Martin Kaye Library

Emmaus House, 65 The Close, Norwich, Norfolk, NR1 4DH

Gov Body: Diocese of Norwich *Chief:* Libn: Major Ewart Griffin
Entry: membs only; membership open to anyone over 16, subscription £5 pa *Open:* Mon-Fri 1000-1600; closed Aug & during Xmas & Easter
Subj: religion, esp modern theology in English
Collns: Bks & Pamphs: theological journals
Stock: bks/c5000 *Classn:* DDC

S1627

Norwich Cathedral, Dean and Chapter Library

52 The Close, Norwich, Norfolk, NR1 4EG (01603-218327)

Gov Body: Dean & Chapter of Norwich *Chief:* Libn: Archdeacon C.J. Offer BA *Dep:* Sub-Libn: Mr Tom Mollard MCLIP *Other Snr Staff:* Asst Libn: Miss B. Lemon MCLIP
Assoc Libs: CATHEDRAL ARCHVS, held at Norfolk Record Office (see **A400**); CHRISTIAN STUDY CENTRE LIB; RUNNETT MUSIC LIB (both to be incorporated into new lib)
Entry: ref only *Open:* currently closed; tel enqs: Wed 1000-1300, 1400-1700
Subj: predominantly theology; also hist; topography; classics; heraldry; law; bibliography
Collns: Bks & Pamphs: 800 pamphs on theology & politics (1625-1750)
Stock: bks/8000; slides/480
Classn: fixed location
Pubns: Norwich Cathedral Lib: Its Foundation, Destruction & Recoveries (£2)
Staff: Libns: 2 (for 1 day each)
Proj: new lib to incorporate the Dean & Chapter Lib, the Christian Study Centre Lib (c8000 vols) & the Runnett Music Lib

S1628

Norwich City College of Further and Higher Education, Library

Ipswich Rd, Norwich, Norfolk, NR2 2LJ (01603-773114; *fax:* 01603-773301)
Email: libhelp@ccn.ac.uk
Internet: http://www.ccn.ac.uk/

Chief: Head of Learning Svcs: Mr Steve Phillips BSc, MCLIP (sphillip@ccn.ac.uk) *Dep:* Lib Svcs Mgr: Ms Linda Webb MCLIP (lwebb@ccn.ac.uk)
Entry: ref only *Open:* term: Mon-Thu 0815-2000, Fri 0815-1800, Sat 0915-1300; vac: Mon-Fri 0900-1700
Subj: all subjs; genl; GCSE; A level; undergrad; vocational
Equip: 3 copier (A4/10p), clr copier (A4/50p), 20 computers
Stock: bks/70000; periodcls/400; videos/10000
Classn: DDC *Auto Sys:* Dynix
Staff: Libns: 8 Non-Prof: 8 FTE

S1629

Norwich Primary Care Trust, Eastern Support Services Library

St Andrew's House, Northside, St Andrew's Business Pk, Norwich, Norfolk, NR7 0HT (01603-307258; *fax:* 01603-307123)
Email: rosemary.stark@norfolk.nhs.uk

Chief: Lib Svcs Mgr: Mrs Rosemary Stark BA(Hons), DipLib
Entry: ref only access available to non-membs by prior arrangement with the Lib Svcs Mgr *Open:* Mon-Fri 0900-1730
Subj: social sci; public health; health policy *Co-op Schemes:* BLDSC, BMA
Equip: copier (free to membs), video viewer, computer (with wd-proc, internet & CD-ROM) *Online:* via OVID: Medline, CINAHL, BNI, Embase etc *Officer-in-Charge:* Lib Svcs Mgr, as above
Svcs: info, ref, biblio
Stock: bks/7000; periodcls/45; videos/20 *Acqs Offcr:* Lib Svcs Mgr, as above
Classn: NLM *Auto Sys:* Soutron 2020
Staff: Libns: 1 Non-Prof: 2

S1630

Norwich School of Art and Design Library

St George St, Norwich, Norfolk, NR3 1BB (01603-610561; *fax:* 01603-615728)
Email: info@nsad.ac.uk
Internet: http://www.nsad.ac.uk/

Chief: Libn: Mr Tim Giles BA, DipLib (tim.g@nsad.ac.uk) *Dep:* Asst Libn: Mrs Kitty Guiver BA, MA, MCLIP
Entry: registered students & staff; visitors ref only, with proof of ID & addr *Open:* term: Mon-Fri 0915-1900; vac: Mon-Fri 1400-1700
Subj: arts; design; social sci; lit *Collns: Bks & Pamphs:* artists' bks; illustrated bks; historical colln of 20C design journals *Co-op Schemes:* ANGLES, ARLIS
Equip: copiers, video viewers, computers (incl internet & CD-ROM) *Online:* ABM, Art Index, Design & Applied Art Index *Svcs:* info, ref
Stock: bks/37000; periodcls/100; slides/165000; videos/3600
Classn: DDC (mod between 700-799) *Auto Sys:* Dynix
Staff: Libns: 2.5 Other Prof: 1 slide libn Non-Prof: 3.2

S1631

University of East Anglia, The Library

Univ Plain, Norwich, Norfolk, NR4 7TJ (01603-456161; *fax:* 01603-259490)
Email: library@uea.ac.uk
Internet: http://www.lib.uea.ac.uk/

Chief: Libn: Ms Jean Steward
Assoc Libs: CURRICULUM & LEARNING RESOURCE CENTRE, Univ of East Anglia, Univ Plain, Norwich, NR4 7TJ (01603-592621); SCHOOL OF NURSING & MIDWIFERY LIB, Norwich (see **S1633**); SCHOOL OF NURSING & MIDWIFERY LIB, King's Lynn (see **S867**); ROBERT SAINSBURY LIB (see **S1632**)
Entry: membs of Univ & affiliated insts, others by written appl to Libn (subscription payable) *Open:* term: Mon-Fri 0900-2100, Sat 1100-1700, Sun 1100-1900; vac: Mon-Fri 0900-1800
Subj: all subjs; undergrad; postgrad; local studies (East Anglia) *Collns: Bks & Pamphs:* Special Collns incl: Abbott Colln (English lit); Ketton-Cremer Colln (local hist); Kimber Colln (local lit); illustrated bks colln; military sci colln; statistics colln; parliamentary papers; EDC *Archvs:* Univ Archvs; Holloway Colln (printed ephemera relating to arts & culture in Britain); Lord Zuckerman Archv;

Kenney Papers; Pritchard Papers (arch & design); Tinkler Colln (local theatre); Williams Colln (local theatre); Fisher Colln (local theatre); East Anglian Film Archv *Other:* CD Music Lib *Co-op Schemes:* UK Libs Plus, HeLIN, ANGLES
Equip: m-readers, m-printers (6p per sheet), copiers (6p per sheet), clr copier, video viewers, 60 computers (all with internet) *Disabled:* Kurzweil, JAWS, CCTV reader *Online:* numerous elec resources, incl EBSCO, Ingenta Journals, Web of Science, JSTOR, Zetoc, BHI, EEBO, AMED, CINAHL, Cochrane, Embase, Medline, PsycInfo, ASSIA, EconLit, ERIC, FAME, IBSS, Lexis-Nexis, Westlaw UK & others; see web site for full list
Officer-in-Charge: Central Office Mgr: Mrs Christine Christopher (c.christopher@uea.ac.uk)
Stock: bks/800000; periodcls/4500 (print & elec)
Acqs Offcr: Head of Acqs: Mrs Anne Baker (anne.baker@uea.ac.uk)
Classn: LC *Auto Sys:* Aleph
Pubns: WWII – Zuckerman Archv (£3); Zuckerman Archv (£3); Annual Report (free); Pritchard Papers (£3)
Staff: Libns: 16.5 *Non-Prof:* c42 *Exp:* £1.1 mln (1999-2000); £1.2 mln (2000-01)

S1632

University of East Anglia, Robert Sainsbury Library

Sainsbury Rsrch Unit for the Arts of Africa, Oceania & the Americas, Sainsbury Centre, Univ of East Anglia, Norwich, Norfolk, NR4 7TJ (01603-592659; *fax:* 01603-259401)
Email: sru.library@uea.ac.uk
Internet: http://www.lib.uea.ac.uk/art/sru/

Gov Body: Univ of East Anglia (see **S1631**)
Chief: Libn: Ms Pat Hewitt BA, DipLib (p.hewitt@ uea.ac.uk) *Dep:* Lib Asst: Ms Asia Gaskell (a.gaskell@uea.ac.uk)
Entry: membs of Univ; membs of public with academic interest in subj coverage on appl *Open:* term: Mon, Wed, Fri 0930-1700, Tue, Thu 0930-1900, vac: Mon-Fri 1000-1300, 1400-1700, closed part of summer vac
Subj: arts; indigenous arts & material culture of Africa, Oceania (incl Indonesia) & the Americas; related works in: anthro; archaeo; museology *Co-op Schemes:* ANGLES
Equip: m-reader, copier (A4/5p, A3/10p), computers (with internet & CD-ROM) *Svcs:* ref, biblio
Stock: bks/17000 (incl pamphs); periodcls/50, plus c90 no longer current
Classn: LC *Auto Sys:* Aleph
Pubns: Lib Guide
Staff: Libns: 1 *Non-Prof:* 1

S1633

University of East Anglia, School of Nursing and Midwifery Library (Norwich)

Peddars Centre, Hellesdon Hosp, Drayton High Rd, Norwich, Norfolk, NR6 5BE (01603-421527; *fax:* 01603-259490)
Internet: http://www.lib.uea.ac.uk/

Gov Body: Univ of East Anglia (see **S1631**)
Chief: Head of User Svcs: Ms Ruth Moore BA(Hons) (ruth.moore@uea.ac.uk) *Other Snr Staff:* Lib Assts: Ms Anne Cook (a.cook@uea. ac.uk) & Ms Christine Ramsden (c.ramsden@uea. ac.uk)
Entry: membs of Univ & affiliated insts; others on written appl to Libn (subscription payable) *Open:* Mon 0845-1700, Tue-Thu 0845-1830, Fri 0845-1630
Subj: health; nursing; midwifery *Co-op Schemes:* SCONUL Vac Access Scheme, UK Libs Plus
Equip: copier, 4 computers (all with internet)
Online: CINAHL, Medline, PsycInfo, Cochrane
Svcs: info, ref

Stock: bks/c12000; periodcls/c110
Classn: LC *Auto Sys:* Aleph
Staff: Libns: 1 *Non-Prof:* 3

Nottingham

S1634

Galleries of Justice, Wolfson Resource Centre

Shire Hall, High Pavement, Lace Market, Nottingham, NG1 1HN (0115-952-0555; *fax:* 0115-993-9828)
Email: beverleybaker@galleriesofjustice.org.uk
Internet: http://www.galleriesofjustice.org.uk/

Type: natl museum for the hist of law *Chief:* Libn & Archivist: Ms Beverley Baker
Entry: adv appt *Open:* Mon-Fri 1000-1600; closed bank hols, Xmas & New Year
Subj: hist of law; crime & punishment; English & internatl legal systems; constitutional law; administrative law; criminal law; criminology; policing; transportation; probation; private law; citizenship; crime & popular culture (fiction, film, lit, TV etc); legal papers; personal papers; police records *Collns: Bks & Pamphs:* substantial rare bk colln; police criminal identification bks (late 19C) *Archvs:* wide range of documents (15C-20C) related to all aspects of law; Rainer Foundation Archv (trials, probation & reform, 1820s-1997); Nuremburg Colln (materials compiled by Lord Justice Lawrence, President of Internatl Tribunal); papers of legal figures, incl: Sir Norman Birkett papers; Alfred Cock papers; Rufus Isaacs papers; police records incl Nottingham City police & Nottinghamshire Constabulary; records of famous trials, incl John Lee Papers (letters, statements & trial documents); legal deeds *Other:* picture & photo colln (police, prisons & legal figs, 1880s-date); newspaper clippings; videos, CD-ROMs & teaching aids
Equip: m-readers, copier *Disabled:* wheelchair access *Svcs:* enq svc, photographic reproductions
Auto Sys: Adlib

S1635

Nottinghamshire Chamber of Commerce, Information Department

309 Haydn Rd, Nottingham, NG5 1DG (0115-962-4624; *fax:* 0115-985-6612)
Email: info@nottschamber.co.uk
Internet: http://www.nottschamber.co.uk/

Chief: Head of Info: Miss E.H. Carter BA(Hons), MCLIP (ecarter@nottschamber.co.uk) *Dep:* Snr Info Offcr: Miss W. York BA(Hons) (wyork@ nottschamber.co.uk)
Entry: adv appt preferred by not essential *Open:* Mon-Fri 0845-1715
Subj: business info; local studies (Nottinghamshire business & industry); generalities; social sci; lang; geog; hist *Collns: Bks & Pamphs:* European Commission pubns
Equip: copier (10p per copy) *Svcs:* info, ref, biblio
Acqs Offcr: Head of Info, as above
Classn: own, based on Superlink
Pubns: Top 100 Companies in Nottinghamshire (from £15); Companies on Industrial Estates in Nottinghamshire (from £35)
Staff: Libns: 2 *Non-Prof:* 1

S1636

British Geological Survey Library and Archives

Kingsley Dunham Centre, Keyworth, Nottingham, NG12 5GG (0115-936-3205; *fax:* 0115-936-3200)
Email: libuser@bgs.ac.uk
Internet: http://www.bgs.ac.uk/

Chief: Chief Libn & Archivist: Mr G. McKenna MA, MCLIP (g.mckenna@bgs.ac.uk) *Dep:* Team Leader (Keyworth): Mrs J. Fileman BA, MCLIP (jf@bgs.ac.uk)
Assoc Libs: BGS EDINBURGH OFFICE, Murchison House, West Mains Rd, Edinburgh, EH9 3LA, Libn: Mr Robert McIntosh (0131-667-1000; *fax:* 0131-668-2683; *email:* mhlib@bgs.ac.uk); BGS LONDON INFO CENTRE (see **S1023**)
Entry: ref only, adv appt preferred *Open:* Mon-Thu 0900-1700, Fri 0900-1630
Subj: at postgrad level: sci; earth sci world-wide
Collns: Archvs: British Geological Survey Historical Archvs (incl material relating to BGS, Geological Survey & Museum & some Imperial Inst Overseas Geological Surveys) *Other:* extensive geological map collns (world-wide coverage); BGS Photograph Colln; BAAS Geological Photograph Colln *Co-op Schemes:* EMRLS
Equip: m-reader, m-printer, fax, 3 copiers, 4 computers (all with CD-ROM) *Online:* some svcs (some fees); OPAC available via internet *Svcs:* info, ref, biblio
Stock: bks/500000; periodcls/c2000; photos/ 100000; maps/200000; archvs/25000 items
Classn: UDC *Auto Sys:* Olib
Staff: Libns: 8 *Non-Prof:* 6.5

S1637

Bromley House Library

(also known as the Nottingham Subscription Lib)
Bromley House, Angel Row, Nottingham, NG1 6HL (0115-947-3134)
Email: nsl@bromho.freeserve.co.uk

Chief: Libn: Mrs Julia V. Wilson BA, MCLIP
Entry: non-membs or applicants should make written appl to use bks or archvs; ref only for non-membs & rsrchers *Open:* Mon-Fri 0930-1700
Subj: local study (Nottinghamshire); generalities; phil; religion; social sci; French lit; sci; arts; lit; geog; hist; poetry; 19C-20C fiction *Collns: Bks & Pamphs:* 19C works, esp in religion, local hist & arts *Archvs:* records of Lib (1820-date) *Co-op Schemes:* AIL
Equip: copier, computer
Stock: bks/35000; periodcls/15; some maps
Classn: own
Pubns: Bromley House 1752-1991: Four Essays Celebrating the 175th Anniversary of Nottingham Subscription Lib (£6)
Staff: Libns: 1 *Other Prof:* 1 *Non-Prof:* 5 *Exp:* £7000 (1999-2000); £7000 (2000-01)

S1638

New College Nottingham, Basford Hall Learning Centre

Stockhill Ln, Basford, Nottingham, NG6 0NB (0115-916-2001)
Email: julia.murden@ncn.ac.uk
Internet: http://www.ncn.ac.uk/

Chief: Libn: Ms Julia Murden MCLIP
Assoc Libs: CITY ADAMS LEARNING CENTRE, Adams Bldg, The Lace Market, Nottingham, NG1 1LJ (0115-910-4576); HUCKNALL LEARNING CENTRE, Portland Rd, Hucknall, Nottingham, NG15 7SN (0115-840-2057); BERRIDGE LEARNING CENTRE, Stanley Rd, Forest Fields, Nottingham, NG7 6HW (0115-953-1473); CLARENDON LEARNING CENTRE, Mansfield Rd, Nottingham, NG5 1AL (0115-953-4331); HIGH PAVEMENT LEARNING CENTRE, Chaucer St, Nottingham, NG1 5LP (0115-912-5512); BULWELL LEARNING CENTRE, Squires Ave, Bulwell, Nottingham, NG6 8GL (0115-916-6660); CITY BATH ST LEARNING CENTRE, Bath St, Sneinton, Nottingham, NG1 1DA (0115-912-5616)
Entry: Coll staff & enrolled students only *Open:* term: Mon, Thu 0830-1930, Tue-Wed 0830-2030, Fri 0830-1700; vac: Mon-Fri 0900-1630; opening times vary for other sites
☛

Special Libraries

Nottingham
▼
Omagh

(New Coll Nottingham, Basford Hall Learning Centre cont)

Subj: genl; GCSE; A level; vocational; local study (Nottinghamshire); child psy; child care; business studies; construction *Co-op Schemes:* BLDSC, EMRLS
Equip: copier (A4/5p), computers (incl wd-proc, internet & CD-ROM), scanners *Disabled:* ZoomText
Stock: bks/21000; periodcls/110; videos/400
Classn: DDC *Auto Sys:* Limes

S1639 ✚

Nottingham City Hospital Library
Postgrad Edu Centre, City Hosp, Hucknall Rd, Nottingham, NG5 1PB (0115-969-1169 x45736; *fax:* 0115-962-7741)

Gov Body: Nottingham City Hosp NHS Trust
Chief: Lib & Info Svcs Mgr: Dr John S. Rule BA(Hons), DPhil, DipILS (jrule@ncht.trent.nhs.uk)
Dep: Lib Info Offcr: Mrs Priscilla Morley (pmorley@ncht.trent.nhs.uk)
Entry: open to hosp staff & other NHS employees
Open: Mon-Fri 0900-1700
Subj: sci; medicine *Co-op Schemes:* BLDSC, local ILL scheme
Equip: m-reader, video viewer, fax, copier, 17 computers (all with internet, 11 with wd-proc & 8 with CD-ROM) *Disabled:* wheelchair access
Online: Cochrane, Medline, CINAHL, Embase, PsycInfo *Svcs:* info, ref, biblio
Stock: bks/6000; periodcls/150; videos/100
Classn: NLM *Auto Sys:* Heritage
Staff: Libns: 1.4 *Non-Prof:* 2.66 *Exp:* £30000 (1999-2000)

S1640 🏛

Nottingham Natural History Museum, Reference Library
Wollaton Hall, Wollaton Pk, Nottingham, NG8 2AE (0115-915-3900; *fax:* 0115-915-3932)
Email: wollaton@ncmg.demon.co.uk

Chief: Libn: Mr Graham Walley
Assoc Libs: NOTTINGHAM BIOLOGICAL RECORDS CENTRE, at same addr (0115-928-1330)
Entry: ref only *Open:* Nov-Mar: Mon-Sun 1100-1600; Apr-Oct: Mon-Sun 1100-1700
Subj: Nottinghamshire: nat hist *Co-op Schemes:* ILL
Stock: bks/3500; periodcls/9; slides/500; maps/100; m-forms/100

S1641 🎓

Nottingham Trent University, Library and Information Services
The Boots Lib, City Campus, Goldsmith St, Nottingham, NG1 5LS (0115-848-2175)
Internet: http://www.ntu.ac.uk/lis/

Gov Body: Nottingham Trent Univ *Chief:* Head of Dept: Mrs E. Lines BSc, MCLIP
Assoc Libs: BOOTS LIB, addr as above; CLIFTON CAMPUS LIB, Clifton Ln, Nottingham, NG11 8NS (0115-848-3570); BRACKENHURST LIB (see S1955)

Entry: ref only *Open:* term: Mon-Fri 0830-2100 (Fri -1900 at Clifton), Sat 0900-1700, Sun 1400-1900; vac: Mon-Fri 0830-1700
Subj: all subjs; undergrad; postgrad; *Boots Lib:* art; design; eng; environmental studies; law; business; econ; social sci; *Clifton Lib:* edu; humanities; sci; maths; *Brackenhurst Lib:* land based studies
Collns: Bks & Pamphs: law reports (at Boots Lib)
Other: Slide Colln (at Boots Lib) *Co-op Schemes:* SCONUL
Equip: m-readers, video viewers, copiers, computers (incl wd-proc, internet & CD-ROM)
Disabled: pg magnifier *Online:* Art Abstracts, ASSIA, BHI, Cochrane, Compendex, ICEA, Index to theses, Justis-Celex, Lawtel, Mintel, UnCover, Web of Science & others (internal users only)
Stock: bks/400000; periodcls/2500; slides/145000; various pamphs, maps, m-forms, audios, videos
Classn: DDC, UDC *Auto Sys:* Urica
Staff: Libns: 25.29 *Non-Prof:* 50.76

S1642 ✚

Nottinghamshire Healthcare NHS Trust, Medical Library
Duncan MacMillan House, Porchester Rd, Mapperley, Nottingham, NG3 6AA (0115-969-1300 x40760; *fax:* 0115-969-1882)
Email: library@medl.demon.co.uk

Gov Body: Nottinghamshire Healthcare NHS Trust
Chief: Libn: Mr Brian C. Spencer BA, MCLIP
Dep: Asst Libn: Mrs Kate Hudson BSc, MCLIP
Other Snr Staff: Snr Lib Asst: Mrs Diana Reed
Assoc Libs: PATIENTS' LIB
Entry: own membership; external users must make prior appt, then ref only & journal article copies *Open:* Mon 0845-1200, 1300-1700, Tue 0845-1700, Wed-Thu 0845-1800, Fri 0845-1630
Subj: psychiatry; psychiatric nursing *Collns: Archvs:* small historical archv for Mapperley Hosp
Co-op Schemes: reciprocal links with other Nottingham health libs, BLDSC, PLCS, NULJ
Equip: copier (costs vary), fax (no charge), 3 computers (all with wd-proc, internet & CD-ROM)
Disabled: wheelchair access *Online:* BioMed Registration (full internet access, £2.50 charged for mediated searches) *Officer-in-Charge:* Libn, as above *Svcs:* info, ref, biblio, lit searches, search tuition
Stock: bks/7400; periodcls/55; photos/c400 historical; audios/5; videos/19; archvs/2 cupboards
Acqs Offcr: Libn, as above
Classn: own *Auto Sys:* Heritage IV
Staff: Libns: 1.5 *Non-Prof:* 1.3 *Exp:* £18376 (2000-01)

S1643 🎓

The Peoples' College, Nottingham, Learning Resources Centres
Maid Marian Way, Nottingham, NG1 6AB (0115-912-8636; *fax:* 0115-912-8600)
Internet: http://www.peoples.ac.uk/

Chief: Learning Resources Mgr: Miss Jenni Sutcliffe BA, MCLIP
Assoc Libs: CARLTON RD CENTRE LIB, Nottingham, Asst Learning Resources Mgr: Mrs K. Hilditch
Entry: ref only for genl public *Open:* term: Mon-Thu 0900-1900, Fri 0900-1630; vac: Mon-Thu 0900-1700, Fri 0900-1630
Subj: all subjs; genl; GCSE; A level *Co-op Schemes:* BLDSC, EMRLS
Equip: 2 video viewers, 2 copiers, computers
Svcs: info, ref
Stock: bks/30000; periodcls/220; videos/750
Classn: DDC *Auto Sys:* Heritage
Staff: Libns: 2 *Non-Prof:* 10

S1644 ✑

Powergen, Power Technology Centre Library
Ratcliffe on Soar, Nottingham, NG11 0EE (0115-936-2360; *fax:* 0115-936-2711)
Email: sue.seal@powertech.co.uk
Internet: http://www.powertech.co.uk/

Chief: Libn: Mrs Susan Seal BA(Hons)
Entry: access only by adv appt *Open:* Mon-Thu 0845-1500
Subj: sci; tech; power industry *Collns: Archvs:* CEGB Archv colln; in-house reports & documents
Co-op Schemes: BLDSC
Equip: m-reader, m-printer, fax, copier, computers (incl wd-proc & CD-ROM) *Online:* Dialog, Dialtech, Datastar (internal users only), intranet lib catalogue
Svcs: ref
Stock: bks/14000; periodcls/180; photos/2000; slides/4000; pamphs/4000; maps/1200; m-forms/10000; videos/200; archvs/250 linear m; reports/70000
Classn: UDC *Auto Sys:* TechLib
Staff: Libns: 2 *Non-Prof:* 1 *Exp:* £55000 (1999-2000)

S1645 🎓

South Nottingham College Library
Greythorn Dr, West Bridgford, Nottingham, NG2 7GA (0115-914-6400; *fax:* 0115-914-6444)
Internet: http://www.south-nottingham.ac.uk/

Chief: Head of Lib, Info & Learning Resources: Mr Philip Wilson MA, DipLIS, MCLIP *Dep:* Lib Svcs Mgr: Mrs Denise Douglas (douglasd@south-nottingham.ac.uk)
Assoc Libs: CHARNWOOD CENTRE LIB, Farnborough Rd, Clifton, Nottingham, NG11 8LU
Entry: enrolled students of the coll *Open:* term: Mon-Thu 0830-1930, Fri 0830-1600; vac: Mon-Fri 0900-1600
Subj: all subjs; genl; GCSE; A level; vocational; local study (Nottingham & Nottinghamshire) *Co-op Schemes:* BLDSC
Equip: m-reader, 2 video viewers, 2 copiers, clr copier, 18 computers (all with wd-proc & internet, 7 with CD-ROM), room for hire *Disabled:* CCTV reader for visually impaired, adjustable height computer workstations for wheelchair users *Svcs:* info, ref, biblio
Stock: bks/28000; periodcls/70; slides/50; illusts/654; maps/444; audios/40; videos/4614; AVs/32
Acqs Offcr: Lib Svcs Mgr, as above
Classn: DDC *Auto Sys:* Heritage
Staff: Libns: 1 *Non-Prof:* 5.4 *Exp:* £27000 (1999-2000)

S1646 🏛

Technical Information Centre Royal Engineers
Military Works Force, Chetwynd Barracks, Chilwell, Nottingham, NG9 5AH (0115-957-2309)

Gov Body: Ministry of Defence (see **S1284**)
Chief: Libn: Miss Judith M. Seaman BA(Hons), MCLIP
Entry: by appt only *Open:* Mon-Thu 0800-1630, Fri 0800-1600
Subj: civil & military eng *Co-op Schemes:* BLDSC
Equip: m-reader, copier, computers (incl internet & CD-ROM)
Stock: bks/9000; periodcls/55; photos/4000; slides/19000; m-forms/150; videos/80; CD-ROMs/150; reports/16000 *Acqs Offcr:* Libn, as above
Classn: UDC *Auto Sys:* Calm
Staff: Libns: 1 *Non-Prof:* 1
See also ROYAL ENGINEERS LIB (**S444**) & ROYAL ENGINEERS MUSEUM, LIB & ARCHVS (**S445**)

S1647
University of Nottingham, Library Services
Univ Pk, Nottingham, NG7 2RD (0115-951-4548; *fax:* 0115-951-4558)
Email: librarians-office@nottingham.ac.uk
Internet: http://www.nottingham.ac.uk/is/

Gov Body: Univ of Nottingham *Chief:* Dir of Info Svcs: Ms Karen Stanton (karen.stanton@ nottingham.ac.uk) *Other Snr Staff:* Asst Dir (Customer Svcs): Mr Stan Smith (stan.smith@ nottingham.ac.uk); Asst Dir (Rsrch & Learning Resources): Mr Stephen Pinfield (stephen. pinfield@nottingham.ac.uk); Asst Dir (IT Systems): Ms Joyce Graves (joyce.graves@nottingham. ac.uk); Asst Dir (Planning & Quality): Ms Paula Manning (paula.manning@nottingham.ac.uk)
Assoc (Site) Libs: HALLWARD LIB, Univ Pk, Nottingham, NG7 2RD (0115-951-4557; *fax:* 0115-951-4558); DEPT OF MSS & SPECIAL COLLNS, at Hallward Lib (0115-951-4565; *fax:* 0115-951-4558); GEORGE GREEN LIB OF SCI & ENG, Univ Pk, Nottingham, NG7 2RD (0115-951-4570; *fax:* 0115-951-4578); GREENFIELD MEDICAL LIB, Queen's Medical Centre, Nottingham, NG7 2UH (0115-970-9435; *fax:* 0115-970-9449); JAMES CAMERON-GIFFORD LIB OF AGRICULTURAL & FOOD SCIS, Sutton Bonington Campus, Loughborough, Leicestershire, LE12 5RD (0115-951-6390; *fax:* 0115-951-6389); DJANOGLY LRC, Wollaton Rd, Nottingham, NG8 1FF (0115-846-6700; *fax:* 0115-846-6705); MUSIC LIB, Arts Centre, Univ Pk, Nottingham, NG7 2RD (0115-951-4596); CHEM LIB, Chem Dept, Univ Pk, Nottingham, NG7 2RD (0115-951-4574); SCHOOL OF NURSING LIB (DERBY), Derby Centre, Derbyshire Royal Infirmary, London Rd, Derby, DE1 2QY (01332-347141 x2561); SCHOOL OF NURSING LIB (MANSFIELD), Mansfield Edu Centre, Kings Mill Hosp, Mansfield Rd, Sutton-in-Ashfield, Nottinghamshire, NG17 4JL (01623-465634)
Entry: staff & students of Univ; others by appt, ref only or apply for external borrowing rights (£50 pa); appt in writing for special collns *Open: Hallward Lib, George Green Lib & Djanogly LRC:* term: Mon-Fri 0900-2145, Sat 0900-1645, Sun 0930-1645; vac: Mon-Fri 0900-1700, Sat 0900-1230; *Greenfield Medical Lib:* term: Mon-Fri 0900-2145, Sat 0900-1700, Sun 0930-1645; vac: Mon-Fri 0900-1900, Sat 0900-1230; *James Cameron-Gifford Lib:* term: Mon-Fri 0900-2145, Sat 0900-1645, Sun 0930-1645; vac: Mon-Fri 0900-2145, Sat 0900-1645; *Music Lib:* term: Mon-Fri 0900-2145, Sat 0900-1700; vac: normally Mon-Fri 0900-1230, 1345-1645; *Chem Lib:* term: Mon-Fri 0900-1700; *School of Nursing (Derby):* term & vac: Mon-Thu 0830-1700, Fri 0830-1630; *School of Nursing (Mansfield):* term & vac: Mon-Thu 0830-1630, Fri 0830-1600
Subj: all subjs; undergrad; postgrad; local studies (East Midlands) *Collns: Bks & Pamphs:* EDC; East Midlands Colln (historic counties of Derbyshire, Leicestershire, Lincolnshire, Nottinghamshire, Rutland); Porter Colln (on ornithology); F.H. Jacob Hist of Medicine Colln; Nottingham Medico-Chirurgical Soc Colln; holdings from former East German Lib (Zwiesdorf, Magdeburg); agric colln (18C-19C); early legal bks (over 500 vols); Briggs Colln (edu bks, pre-1850); Cambridge Drama Colln (English plays, 1750-1850); Cambridge Shake-speare Colln (18C-19C eds); Charles Knight Colln; H.G. Wells Colln (mainly 1st eds); D.H. Lawrence Colln (MSS & bks); Coventry Kersey Dighton Patmore Colln (bks & MSS); Parker Woodward Colln (Bacon-Shakespeare question); French Revolution Colln; Mellish Meteorological Colln; Oakham & Elston Parochial Libs *Archvs:* Archdeaconry of Nottingham & other local ecclesiastical archvs; local industrial & trade union collns; substantial collns of local family papers; records of the Severn Trent Water Authority & its forerunners (1616-1973); records of Genl Hosp & other Nottingham hosps; MS collns in Restoration verse; William of Orange & the 1688 Revolution; Jacobite Rising of 1745; American War of Independence; Peninsular War; Crimean War; British & Irish politics & foreign affairs (18C-19C); India (early 19C); British colonies (19C); hist of nonconformity; draining of the Fens; John Ray & Francis Willoughby (17C naturalists); literary papers & MSS relating to the politics, social, economic & cultural conditions in Germany (esp East Germany) 1946-1981; Waldenheim: A Commission of Enquiry: documentary rsrch material collected by Thames Television for television programme in June 1988 *Other:* Brass Rubbings Colln *Co-op Schemes:* BLDSC, SCONUL, CURL
Equip: 40 m-readers, 3 m-printers, 14 video viewers, 29 copiers, clr copier, 78 computers *Disabled:* Kurzweil, CCTV enlarger *Online:* Dialog; most databases now publicly accessible via web or CD-ROM
Stock: bks/1000000+; periodcls/5000+; archvs/2220 m
Classn: LC *Auto Sys:* Aleph
Pubns: too numerous to mention
Staff: Libns: 25 *Other Prof:* 20 *Non-Prof:* 100

Nuneaton

S1648
MIRA Ltd, Automotive Information Centre
Watling St, Nuneaton, Warwickshire, CV10 0TU (024-7635-5275; *fax:* 024-7635-5069)
Email: aic.enquiries@mira.co.uk
Internet: http://www.mira.co.uk/

Gov Body: MIRA (Motor Industry Rsrch Assoc)
Chief: Info Offcr: Mr Paul Wilcox
Entry: adv appt *Open:* Mon-Fri 0800-1600
Subj: tech; automobile eng *Co-op Schemes:* ILL, IIS
Equip: fax, copier *Online:* Dialog, INS; Virtual Automotive Info Centre available on internet
Stock: bks/3000; periodcls/200
Pubns: Automobile Abstracts (monthly); Automotive Business News (weekly)

Oban

S1649
Scottish Association for Marine Science, Dunstaffnage Marine Laboratory Library
Dunbeg, Oban, Argyll, PA37 1QA (01631-559217; *fax:* 01631-559001)
Email: ew@dml.ac.uk

Chief: Libn: Miss E.J. Walton MA
Entry: membs by adv appt *Open:* Mon-Fri 0900-1300, 1400-1700
Subj: life sci; chem; physics; marine sci; oceanography *Collns: Bks & Pamphs:* oceanographic expedition reports *Other:* expedition reports
Equip: internal facilities only *Online:* on CD-ROM: ISI, Aquatic Science & Fisheries Abstract
Stock: bks/15000; periodcls/70; m-forms/100
Classn: own
Staff: Libns: 1 *Exp:* £42000 (1999-2000); £43000 (2000-01)

Oldham

S1650
The Oldham College Library
J.T. Milton Centre, Rochdale Rd, Oldham, Lancashire, OL9 6AA (0161-785-4207; *fax:* 0161-785-4234)
Email: library@oldham.ac.uk
Internet: http://www.oldham.ac.uk/

Chief: Centre Mgr: Mrs Margaret Wood (margaret.wood@oldham. ac.uk) *Other Snr Staff:* Head of Learning Resources: Mr Roger Clegg (roger.clegg@oldham. ac.uk)
Entry: staff & students of Coll only *Open:* term: Mon-Thu 0900-2000, Fri 1000-1600, Sat 0900-1300; vac: Mon-Fri 0900-1230, 1330-1630
Subj: all subjs; genl; GCSE; A level *Co-op Schemes:* BLDSC, LNW
Equip: video viewer, copier, clr copier, 80 computers (all with wd-proc & internet, 10 with CD-ROM)
Officer-in-Charge: Head of Learning Resources, as above
Stock: bks/23800; periodcls/81; videos/600; CD-ROMs/16 *Acqs Offcr:* Centre Mgr, as above
Classn: DDC *Auto Sys:* EOS GLAS
Staff: Non-Prof: 3

S1651
Royal Oldham Hospital, Education Centre Library
Frank Lord Postgrad Medical Centre, Royal Oldham Hosp, Rochdale Rd, Oldham, Lancashire, OL1 2JH (0161-627-8462/3; *fax:* 0161-627-8463)
Email: library@oldham-tr.nwest.nhs.uk

Chief: Lib Mgr: post vacant *Dep:* Mr John Addison BA, PGDipILM (john.addison@pat.nhs.uk)
Entry: NHS staff only *Open:* Mon-Fri 0900-1800
Subj: medicine; nursing *Co-op Schemes:* BLDSC, LIHNN, PLCS, NULJ
Equip: copier (5p per pg), 15 computers (all with wd-proc, internet & CD-ROM) *Online:* Medline, Embase, CINAHL, BNI, PsycInfo, HMIC, AMED, ASSIA for Health *Svcs:* info, ref, biblio
Stock: bks/4000; periodcls/100; audios/20; videos/100
Classn: NLM *Auto Sys:* Heritage
Staff: Libns: 2 *Non-Prof:* 1.25

Olney

S1652
The Cowper and Newton Museum, Library and Archive
Orchard Side, Market Pl, Olney, Buckinghamshire, MK46 4AJ (01234-711516)
Email: cnm@mkheritage.co.uk
Internet: http://www.cowperandnewtonmuseum.org

Gov Body: Trustees of Cowper & Newton Museum *Chief:* Custodian: Mrs Joan McKillop
Entry: lib & archvs by appt only *Open: Museum:* 1 Mar-22 Dec: Tue-Sat 1000-1300, 1400-1700
Subj: local study (Olney & North Buckinghamshire); religion; arts; lit; lace & other local trades *Collns: Bks & Pamphs:* various eds of the works of William Cowper & John Newton; associated biographical works; other works by their contemporaries, esp evangelical material; John Sparrow Colln of Cowper Bks; bks relating to hand-made lace *Archvs:* MSS letters of Cowper & Newton now held at the Centre for Buckinghamshire Studies (see **A19**); Johnny Johnson MSS, Lady Heskett MSS etc & Barham Johnson Colln transferred to Centre for Buckinghamshire Studies, but copies of most retained in museum
Equip: copier *Staff: Non-Prof:* 1

Omagh

S1653
Centre for Emigration Studies at the Ulster-American Folk Park, Library
Mellon Rd, Castletown, Omagh, Co Tyrone, BT78 5QY (028-8225-6315; *fax:* 028-8224-2241)
Email: uafp@iol.ie
Internet: http://www.qub.ac.uk/cms/ or http://www.folkpark.com/

Special Libraries

Omagh
▼
Oxford

(Centre for Emigration Studies at the Ulster-American Folk Park, Lib cont)
Gov Body: Western Edu & Lib Board (see **P136**)
Chief: Principal Libn: Ms Christine McIvor BA(Hons), MSSc, MCLIP (christine_mcivor@welbni.org.uk) **Other Snr Staff:** Dir, Centre for Migration Studies: Dr Brian Lambkin; Lecturer & Development Offcr: Dr Patrick Fitzgerald
Entry: ref only, adv appt preferable **Open:** Mon-Fri 0930-1630
Subj: all subjs; museums & museum edu; religion in Ulster, Ireland, America & worldwide (18C & 19C); folk art; crafts; vernacular arch; furnishings etc; politics, family life, edu etc in Ulster, Ireland & America; industry, transport & agric in Ulster, Ireland & America; biography; emigration from Ulster & Ireland to America (18C-19C); hist of Ireland & America & Irish Diaspora worldwide (17C-20C) **Collns:** Other: Irish Emigration Database: 30000 computerised historical documents relating to Irish emigration to North America, incl emigrant letters, family papers & diaries of emigrants, shipping advertisements & newspaper reports, govt reports (accessible in person at Lib of UAFP & in local studies depts of the 5 Northern Ireland Edu & Lib Boards); Griffiths Valuation (maps for Northern Ireland) **Co-op Schemes:** ILL
Equip: m-reader, m-printer, video viewer, copier, 5 computers (all with CD-ROM, 1 with internet)
Svcs: info, ref
Stock: bks/10000; periodcls/50; various slides, photos, maps, m-forms, audios, videos & CD-ROMs **Acqs Offcr:** Principal Libn, as above
Classn: own, switching to DDC in 2003
Pubns: Atlantic Crossroads: Historical Connections Between Scotland, Ulster & North America, ed Patrick Fitzgerald & Steve Ickringill (2001, £9.99)
Staff: Libns: 1 Other Prof: 1 database mgr Non-Prof: 1.5 **Exp:** £12000 (1999-2000); £12000 (2000-01)

S1654 🎓
Omagh College of Further Education Library
Mount Joy Rd, Omagh, Co Tyrone, BT79 7AH (028-8224-5433; *fax:* 028-8224-1440)
Email: janice.owens@omagh.ac.uk
Internet: http://www.omagh.ac.uk/

Gov Body: Board of Governors of Omagh Coll
Chief: Libn: Ms Janice Owens **Dep:** Lib Asst: Mr Kevin Green
Entry: students & staff of coll or those who have been granted external reader status **Open:** term: Mon 0900-1700, Tue-Thu 0900-2000, Fri 0900-1600
Subj: GCSE; A level; undergrad; psy; social scis; arts; lang; sci; tech; lit; geog; hist; law; medicine; travel; tourism
Equip: m-reader, video viewer, copier (£2 per 20 copies), computers
Stock: bks/c12000; periodcls/35; pamphs/300; audios/30; videos/250
Classn: DDC **Staff:** Libns: 1 Non-Prof: 1

Ormskirk

S1655 🎓
Edge Hill College, Information and Media Services
St Helens Rd, Ormskirk, Lancashire, L39 4QP (01695-584298; *fax:* 01695-584592)
Email: robertss@edgehill.ac.uk
Internet: http://www.edgehill.ac.uk/ims/

Chief: Head of Info & Media Svcs: Ms Sue Roberts **Other Snr Staff:** User Svcs Mgr: Ms Coral Black; Lending Svcs Mgr: Ms Zoe Collyer-Strutt; Head of Media Svcs: Mr Ken Harrison; Learning Svcs & Development Mgr: Ms Dawn McLoughlin; Elec Resources Mgr: Ms Maureen Richardson
Assoc Libs: ORMSKIRK LRC, contact details as above; ORMSKIRK LEARNING INNOVATION CENTRE, addr as above (01695-584522; *fax:* 01695-584891); AINTREE LIB & INFO RESOURCE CENTRE (see **S962**); WOODLANDS LRC, The Woodlands Centre, Southport Rd, Chorley, Lancashire, PR7 1QR, LRC Mgr: Ms Ruth Wilson (01257-517136)
Entry: staff & students; ref only for genl public, borrowing membership for a fee **Open:** Ormskirk: term: Mon-Fri 0845-2100, Sat-Sun 1300-1700; Woodlands: term: Mon-Thu 0900-2030, Fri 0900-1700; vac: hrs vary
Subj: all subjs; undergrad; Woodlands: edu
Collns: Bks & Pamphs: ch's materials at Woodlands **Co-op Schemes:** ILL
Equip: copiers, 160+ computers (incl internet & CD-ROM), scanners, printers, video viewers, TV **Online:** 54 online databases, c4000 e-journals
Stock: bks/157000+; periodcls/c900
Staff: 55.7 FTE in total

S1656 ✚
Ormskirk Hospital, Sanderson Library
Clinical Edu Centre, Omskirk Hosp, Wigan Rd, Ormskirk, Lancashire, L39 2AZ (01695-656403; *fax:* 01695-656566)
Email: michael.mason@southportandormskirk.nhs.uk
Internet: http://www.southportandormskirk.nhs.uk/

Gov Body: Southport & Ormskirk Hosp NHS Trust
Chief: Trust Lib Mgr: Mr Michael Mason **Dep:** Lib Assts: Ms Colleen Hickling & Ms Laura Eves
Assoc Libs: SOUTHPORT HOSP, THE HANLEY LIB (see **S1952**)
Entry: membs only; others at discretion of Libn
Open: Mon, Wed, Fri 0900-1700, Tue, Thu 0900-1900
Subj: undergrad; postgrad; medicine; surgery
Collns: Archvs: small local medical hist colln **Co-op Schemes:** LIHNN, BLDSC
Equip: m-reader, fax, video viewers, copier, computers (incl wd-proc, internet & CD-ROM)
Online: Medline, BNI, Cochrane **Svcs:** info, ref, biblio, lit searching
Stock: bks/3000; periodcls/80; videos/96; CD-ROMs/20; archvs/1 cubic m
Classn: DDC **Auto Sys:** DBTextworks
Staff: Libns: 1 Non-Prof: 0.5

Orpington

S1657 ✑
Coates Lorilleux Information Department
Cray Ave, St Mary Cray, Orpington, Kent, BR5 3PP (01689-894208; *fax:* 01689-894051)
Email: barry.hermiston@coates.com

Chief: Info Dept Mgr: Mr Barry N. Hermiston BSc, BA, MPhil
Assoc Libs: COATES & LORILLEUX COMPANY ARCHVS, Officer-in-Charge: Mr Barry Hermiston, as above
Entry: by appt **Open:** Mon-Fri 0830-1700
Subj: tech **Collns:** Bks & Pamphs: printing; ink tech **Co-op Schemes:** BLDSC
Equip: 2 copiers, computer (with wd-proc, internet & CD-ROM) **Online:** Dialog, STN **Svcs:** info, ref, biblio, abstracting
Stock: bks/3000; periodcls/150
Classn: UDC
Staff: Libns: 1 Other Prof: 2 Non-Prof: 1

S1658 ✚
Farnborough Education Centre Library
(formerly West Kent Postgrad Centre Lib)
Farnborough Hosp, Farnborough Common, Orpington, Kent, BR6 8ND (01689-814306; *fax:* 01689-814307)
Email: library.assistants@bromleyhospitals.nhs.uk

Gov Body: Bromley Hosps NHS Trust **Chief:** Head of Lib Svcs: Ms Rebecca Hewitt BA (rebecca.hewitt@bromleyhospitals.nhs.uk) **Other Snr Staff:** Info Skills Training Libn: Mrs Claire Jones BSc
Assoc Libs: BROMLEY HOSP LIB, Edu Centre, Bromley Hosp, Cromwell Ave, Bromley, Kent, BR2 9AL, Lib Asst: Mrs Christina Sealy (*email:* christina.sealy@bromleyhospitals.nhs.uk); ORPINGTON HOSP LIB, Edu Centre, Orpington Hosp, Orpington, Kent, BR6 8JU, Lib Asst: Mr Michael Harney (*email:* michael.harney@bromleyh-tr.sthames.nhs.uk)
Entry: all staff working for the health of the people of Bromley **Open:** Mon-Fri 0900-1800
Subj: medicine; psychiatry; nursing; health related subjs **Co-op Schemes:** BLDSC, South Thames ILL Scheme, PLC ILL Scheme, HLN
Equip: 3 fax, 3 copier, clr copier, 173 computers (all with wd-proc & internet, 3 with CD-ROM)
Disabled: wheelchair access & facilities **Online:** KA24 (OVID) **Officer-in-Charge:** Head of Lib Svcs, as above **Svcs:** info, ref, biblio, info skills training
Stock: bks/6500; periodcls/160; videos/80; CD-ROMs/10 **Acqs Offcr:** Head of Lib Svcs, as above
Classn: NLM **Auto Sys:** Librarian
Staff: Libns: 1 Non-Prof: 9

S1659 🎓
Orpington College Library
The Walnuts, High St, Orpington, Kent, BR6 0TE (01689-899712; *fax:* 01689-877949)
Internet: http://www.orpington.ac.uk/

Gov Body: Orpington Coll **Chief:** Libn: Mrs Annamarie McKie BA(Hons), MA, MCLIP
Entry: ref only for non-membs, by adv appt with Libn **Open:** term: Mon-Thu 0900-2100, Fri 0900-1700; vac: Mon-Fri 0930-1630
Subj: all subjs; genl; GCSE; A level; local study (Bromley & Kent); generalities; phil; psy; religion; social sci; lang; sci; maths; arts; lit; geog; hist **Co-op Schemes:** BLDSC, Canterbury Christchurch Univ Coll (see **S405**)
Equip: copier, computers (incl wd-proc, internet & CD-ROM) **Disabled:** wheelchair access **Svcs:** info, ref, biblio
Stock: bks/20000; periodcls/85; videos/25; AVs/15
Classn: DDC **Auto Sys:** LIMES
Staff: Libns: 1 Non-Prof: 3

Oswestry

S1660 📖 ✚
Institute of Orthopaedics, Francis Costello Library
Robert Jones & Agnes Hunt Orthopaedic & Dist Hosp NHS Trust, Oswestry, Shropshire, SY10 7AG (01691-404388; *fax*: 01691-404071)
Email: marie.carter@rjah.nhs.uk

Gov Body: Robert Jones & Agnes Hunt Orthopaedic & Dist Hosp NHS Trust *Chief*: Health Scis Libn: Miss M.F. Carter BA, DipLib, MCLIP *Entry*: staff & students based at the hosp; others by appt *Open*: Mon-Thu 0845-1700, Fri 0845-1600
Subj: medicine; nursing *Collns: Bks & Pamphs*: orthopaedics incl historical works *Archvs*: material relating to the hist of the hosp & its founders *Co-op Schemes*: BLDSC, WMHLN, SHAIR
Equip: copier, 4 computers (incl 3 with wd-proc, 3 with internet & 1 with CD-ROM) *Svcs*: info, ref, biblio
Stock: bks/6000; periodcls/120; videos/150; AVs/100; archvs/unquantified
Classn: NLM *Auto Sys*: Heritage
Pubns: Healing & Hope: 100 Years of 'The Orthopaedic', by M. Carter (RJAH Trust, £6.50)
Staff: Libns: 2 *Non-Prof*: 1

S1661 📖
Walford and North Staffordshire College Library
Oswestry Campus, Shrewsbury Rd, Oswestry, Shropshire, SY11 4QB (01939-262156; *fax*: 01939-261112)
Internet: http://www.wnsc.ac.uk/

Chief: Learning Resources Mgr: Miss Christine Whittingham BA, MCLIP (c.whittingham@wnsc.ac.uk)
Assoc Libs: WALFORD CAMPUS LIB, Baschurch, Shrewsbury, Shropshire, SY4 2HL, Libn: Mrs Rosemarie Duxbury MCLIP (01939-262156; *fax*: 01939-261112; *email*: r.duxbury@wnsc.ac.uk)
Entry: public access preferably by prior tel appt *Open*: *Oswestry*: term: Mon-Thu 0845-2000, Fri 0845-1630; *Walford*: term: Mon-Thu 0900-1930, Fri 0900-1615
Subj: all subjs; A level; vocational *Co-op Schemes*: SHAIR
Equip: 3 video viewers, 2 copiers, 47 computers (incl wd-proc & internet) *Disabled*: adjustable tables, magnifying glasses, rollerball mouse for PCs
Stock: bks/19000; periodcls/180; various videos & CD-ROMs
Classn: DDC *Auto Sys*: Heritage
Staff: Libns: 1.7 *Non-Prof*: 4.3
Proj: new LRC at Oswestry Campus in 2002

Otley

S1662 ✚
Wharfedale General Hospital, Postgraduate Medical Centre Library
Newall Carr Rd, Otley, W Yorkshire, LS21 2LY (0113-292-6072; *fax*: 0113-392-7010)
Email: val.williams@leedsth.nhs.uk

Gov Body: Leeds Teaching Hosps NHS Trust
Chief: Libn: Mrs Val Williams BSc, MSc, PGCE
Assoc Libs: CHAPEL ALLERTON HOSP NHS STAFF LIB (see **S898**); COOKRIDGE HOSP NHS STAFF LIB (see **S899**); LEEDS GENL INFIRMARY, POSTGRAD MEDICAL LIB (see **S905**); SEACROFT HOSP NHS STAFF LIB (see **S914**)

Entry: staff, local GPs *Open*: Mon-Fri 0900-1700
Subj: medicine; nursing; allied health
Equip: video viewer, fax, copier (A4/5p), 3 computers (all with wd-proc, internet & CD-ROM) *Online*: Medline, DARE, CINAHL, AMED, Cochrane, PsycInfo *Svcs*: info, ref
Stock: bks/2000; periodcls/56; videos/20
Classn: NLM *Staff: Libns*: 0.54

Oxford

S1663 📖
All Souls College, Codrington Library
High St, Oxford, OX1 4AL (01865-279318; *fax*: 01865-279299)
Email: codrington.library@all-souls.ox.ac.uk

Gov Body: All Souls Coll *Chief*: Libn: Dr Norma Aubertin-Potter BA, PhD, MCLIP *Dep*: Asst Libn: Miss Gaye Morgan MA
Entry: letter of introduction from tutor/supervisor; adv appt required if wishing to see MSS or early printed bks *Open*: term: Mon-Fri 0930-1830; vac: Mon-Fri 0930-1630 (closed Aug & Sep)
Subj: undergrad; postgrad; religion; lit; geog; hist; law; military hist; strategic studies; social sci
Collns: Archvs: Vaughan papers *Other*: Christopher Wren Drawings Colln *Co-op Schemes*: ILL
Equip: m-reader, m-printer, copier, computer *Online*: OLIS
Stock: bks & periodcls/175000 items; photos/410; pamphs/10000; maps/80
Classn: own *Auto Sys*: OLIS
Staff: Libns: 2 *Exp*: £55000 (1999-2000)

S1664 📖
Balliol College Library
Broad St, Oxford, OX1 3BJ (01865-277709; *fax*: 01865-277803)
Email: library@balliol.oxford.ac.uk
Internet: http://web.balliol.ox.ac.uk/library/

Chief: Libn: Dr P. Bulloch MA, PhD, MCLIP *Dep*: Asst Libn: Mr A.R. Tadiello BA
Assoc Libs: BALLIOL COLL ARCHVS, Archivist: Dr J.H. Jones MA, DPhil, CChem, FRSC, FRHistS (01865-277733)
Entry: special collns open to non-membs; apply to libn, in writing
Subj: academic subjs studied at Oxford Univ
Collns: Bks & Pamphs: early printed bks; MSS *Archvs*: papers of old membs of Coll
Equip: m-reader, computer (with CD-ROM)
Stock: bks/100000; periodcls/100
Auto Sys: OLIS *Staff: Libns*: 1 *Non-Prof*: 3

S1665 📖 🙏
Blackfriars Library
Blackfriars, 64 St Giles, Oxford, OX1 3LY (01865-278435)
Internet: http://www.bfriars.ox.ac.uk/library.htm

Gov Body: private hall of the Univ of Oxford (see **L4**), run by the English Dominican Friars *Chief*: Libn: Rev Dr Richard Finn OP
Entry: ref only; adv appt for outside scholars
Open: variable
Subj: phil; religion; theology (primarily Catholic)
Equip: copier (£3 per 50 copies)
Stock: bks/35000; periodcls/54

S1666 📖
Brasenose College, Library
Radcliffe Sq, Oxford, OX1 4AJ (01865-277827; *fax*: 01865-277822)
Email: liz.kay@bnc.ox.ac.uk

Gov Body: The Fellows of the Coll *Chief*: Fellow Libn: Dr E.H. Bispham MA, DPhil *Dep*: Coll Libn: Ms Liz Kay
Assoc Libs: COLL ARCHVS, Archivist: post vacant
Entry: adv appt *Open*: term & vac: Mon-Fri 0900-1230, 1415-1700
Subj: all subjs; undergrad; postgrad *Collns: Bks & Pamphs*: bks & pamphs by past & present membs of Coll; Heberden Colln of bks on ancient music *Archvs*: documents referring to the hist of Coll; its bldgs, properties & membs; papers of former membs *Co-op Schemes*: BLDSC
Stock: bks/60000; periodcls/100 *Acqs Offcr*: Coll Libn, as above
Classn: own *Auto Sys*: OLIS
Staff: Libns: 1 *Non-Prof*: 1

S1667 📖 🙏
Campion Hall Library
Brewer St, Oxford, OX1 1QS (01865-286104; *fax*: 01865-286148)
Email: norman.tanner@campion.ox.ac.uk

Gov Body: Campion Hall *Chief*: Libn: Dr N.P. Tanner MA, DPhil *Dep*: Mr L. Weeks MA
Entry: open to membs of Campion Hall, otherwise by appt *Open*: 24 hrs for membs of Campion Hall; 0900-1900 for others
Subj: all subjs; genl; undergrad; postgrad; religion
Collns: Bks & Pamphs: Roman Catholic theology; Jesuit works *Archvs*: C.M. Hopkins MSS
Equip: copier
Stock: bks/30000; periodcls/40 current
Classn: own

S1668 📖 ✚
Cancer Research UK, Cancer Epidemiology Unit Library
Gibson Bldg, Radcliffe Infirmary, Woodstock Rd, Oxford, OX2 6EH (01865-311933; *fax*: 01865-310545)
Email: joy.hooley@cancer.org.uk

Gov Body: Cancer Rsrch UK *Chief*: Lib Asst: Ms Joy Hooley
Assoc Libs: CANCER RSRCH UK, LIB & INFO SVC (see **S1054**)
Entry: ref only, adv appt *Open*: Mon-Fri 0830-1630 or by arrangement
Subj: cancer; medicine *Collns: Bks & Pamphs*: sci journals, mainly cancer related
Equip: copier, computer (with wd-proc & CD-ROM) *Svcs*: info, ref
Stock: bks/c2000; periodcls/30 current, 78 titles in total
Classn: NLM
Staff: Other Prof: 1 *Exp*: £11000 (2000-01)

S1669 🏛 📖
Centre for Ecology and Hydrology, Oxford Library
(formerly the lib of the Inst of Virology & Environmental Microbiology)
Mansfield Rd, Oxford, OX1 3SR (01865-281630; *fax*: 01865-281696)
Email: cjw@ceh.ac.uk
Internet: http://www.nerc-oxford.ac.uk/

Gov Body: Nat Environment Rsrch Council (NERC); part of CEH Lib Svcs (see **S1786**) *Chief*: Libn: Mr Chris Wilson
Entry: bona fide rsrchers by adv appt during staffed hrs *Open*: staffed: Tue, Thu 0845-1545; open 24 hrs to CEH Oxford staff
Subj: virology; microbiology; entomology; plant scis *Collns: Bks & Pamphs*: Kenneth M. Smith Colln (virologist, personal lib & papers) *Archvs*: archival colln of staff papers ☞

Special Libraries

Oxford
▼
Oxford

(Centre for Ecology & Hydrology, Oxford Lib cont)
Equip: *Online:* access to OLIS & other databases
Stock: bks/2000, incl pamphs; periodcls/c70
Auto Sys: Unicorn

S1670 🎓
Christ Church College Library
St Aldate's, Oxford, OX1 1DP (01865-276169)
Email: library@chch.ox.ac.uk
Internet: http://www.chch.ox.ac.uk/library/

Gov Body: Christ Church, Oxford **Chief:** Libn:
Revd Prof O.M.T. O'Donovan MA, DPhil **Other
Snr Staff:** Asst Libns: Mrs J.E. McMullin MA,
MCLIP & Mr M.E. Phillips MA, MCLIP
Assoc Libs: ALLESTREE LIB, addr & offcrs as
above; COLL ARCHVS, Archivist: Mrs J.H.
Curthoys (01865-276171; *email:* archives@
chch.ox.ac.uk)
Entry: ref only, adv appt, bona fide scholars only
Open: Mon-Fri 0900-1700
Subj: all subjs; undergrad **Collns:** *Bks &
Pamphs:* early printed & MS music; parochial lib of
Wotton-under-Edge *Archvs:* MS Collns (held by
Lib, not as part of Coll Archvs): Driberg Papers;
Phillimore Papers; papers of Archbishop Wake;
MSS Colln (extensive, incl many Greek MSS);
archvs of Coll administered separately **Other:**
Brady Colln (theatrical ephemera) **Co-op
Schemes:** ESTC
Equip: m-printer **Svcs:** ref
Stock: bks/150000; periodcls/192; photos/300;
slides/60; pamphs/4000; maps/16; m-forms/200;
audios/20; videos/40; archvs/numerous MSS
Classn: own **Auto Sys:** Geac, Heritage
Pubns: Christ Church Oxford: The Portrait of a
Coll (£1.50); Edu at Christ Church 1660-1800
(£35); The Bldg Accounts of Christ Church Lib
1716-1779 (£60); The Emergence of Estate Maps,
Christ Church Oxford 1600-1840 (£60)
Staff: Libns: 3 Other Prof: 1 Non-Prof: 1

S1671 🎓 ✚
Churchill Hospital, Ruth Gibbes Library
Sir Michael Sobell House, Old Rd, Headington,
Oxford, OX3 7JL (01865-225797; *fax:* 01865-
741862)
Email: library@sobell-house.demon.co.uk

Chief: Libn: Ms Meg Roberts
Entry: staff & registered students **Open:** staffed
Tue, Thu-Fri 0900-1630
Subj: medicine; palliative care

S1672 🎓
Corpus Christi College, The Library
Merton St, Oxford, OX2 6JH (01865-276744; *fax:*
01865-276767)
Email: library.staff@ccc.ox.ac.uk
Internet: http://www.ccc.ox.ac.uk/library/library.htm

Chief: Librarian-in-Charge: Miss Joanna Snelling
BA, MA, MCLIP (joanna.snelling@ccc.ox.ac.uk)
Dep: Asst Libn: Mrs Gail Beadnell BA, MA, MCLIP
(gail.beadnell@ccc.ox.ac.uk)
Assoc Libs: COLL ARCHVS, addr as above,
Archivist: Mr Julian Reid BA, MArAd (01865-
276717; *email:* julian.reid@ccc.ox.ac.uk)

Entry: adv appt **Open:** term: Mon-Fri 0930-1300,
1400-1745; vac: Mon-Fri 0930-1300, 1400-1700
(depending on staff availability)
Subj: all subjs; undergrad; phil; lit; geog; hist; law
Collns: *Bks & Pamphs:* the genl collns are
particularly strong in Classics, hist, English, phil &
law; Rare Bk Colln, incl 8000+ early printed bks on
wide range of subjs *Archvs:* estate records of Coll,
covering land holdings in several counties;
administrative records of Coll from its foundation in
1517 to present **Other:** MSS Colln (built up since
1517): 300 items incl texts in Anglo-Saxon, Greek
& Hebrew; most MSS are listed in H.O. Cox's
Catalogue of Oxford Coll Manuscripts (publ 1852)
Co-op Schemes: OLIS
Equip: m-reader, m-printer, copier, 6 computers
(incl 5 with internet & 5 with CD-ROM) **Svcs:** info,
biblio
Stock: bks/70000; periodcls/80
Classn: DDC (mod) **Auto Sys:** Geac
Staff: Libns: 2 Non-Prof: 1

S1673 🔑 🐾
Dr Pusey Memorial Library
Pusey House, 61 St Giles', Oxford, OX1 3LZ
(01865-278415; *fax:* 01865-278416)
Email: pusey.house@ic24.com

Gov Body: The Governors of Pusey House
Chief: Custodian: The Revd William Davage
Entry: at the discretion of custodian **Open:** term:
Mon-Fri 0915-1245, 1400-1645, Sat 0915-1245;
vac: variable
Subj: theology; church hist; patristics; Christian
worship; Biblical studies; ecumenism; phil **Collns:**
Archvs: unique colln of 19C material on Oxford
Movement
Equip: copier
Stock: bks/85000; periodcls/30; photos/4000;
pamphs/100000 **Classn:** own

S1674 🎓
Exeter College Library
Turl St, Oxford, OX1 3DP (01865-279657/279600;
fax: 01865-279630)
Email: juliet.chadwick@exeter.ox.ac.uk

Gov Body: Exeter Coll **Chief:** Fellow Libn &
Archivist: Dr J.R.L. Maddicott MA, DPhil **Dep:**
Sub-Libn: Ms Juliet Chadwick
Entry: adv appt only **Open:** visitors: Mon-Fri
0830-1630
Subj: all subjs; undergrad; postgrad **Collns:**
Archvs: Exeter Coll Archvs (14C onwards) **Other:**
medieval MSS
Equip: copier
Stock: bks/65000; periodcls/120; photos/200
archival; archvs/60 linear m
Classn: Bliss **Staff:** Libns: 1 Other Prof: 1

S1675 🎓
Green College Library
Woodstock Rd, Oxford, OX2 6HG (01865-274788;
fax: 01865-274796)
Email: gill.edwards@green.ox.ac.uk

Gov Body: Univ of Oxford (see **L4**) **Chief:** Fellow
Libn: Prof D. Jewell MA, BM, BCh, DPhil, FRCP
Dep: Libn: Mrs Gill Edwards BSc(Hons)
Entry: membs of Coll only **Open:** term & vac:
Mon, Wed, Fri 1400-1730, Tue, Thu 1630-1930,
Sat 1000-1230
Subj: medicine; social sci
Equip: copier, computer **Online:** OLIS networked
databases **Officer-in-Charge:** Libn, as above
Svcs: info, ref, resource-seeking tuition
Stock: bks/7000; periodcls/29; CD-ROMs/3 **Acqs**
Offcr: Libn, as above
Classn: NLM, LC **Auto Sys:** Geac
Staff: Libns: 0.5 **Exp:** £10000 (1999-2000);
£19500 (2000-01); figs are for total budget

S1676 🎓 🐾
Greyfriars Library
Iffley Rd, Oxford, OX4 1SB (01865-243694; *fax:*
01865-727027)
Email: thomas.weinandy@greyfriars.ox.ac.uk
Internet: http://www.greyfriars.oc.ac.uk/

Gov Body: Capuchin Province of Great Britain
Chief: Warden: Dr T. Weinandy
Entry: ref only, adv appt **Open:** Mon-Fri 0900-
1800
Subj: religion; Franciscan hist
Equip: copier **Svcs:** info **Stock:** bks/6000

S1677 🎓
Harris Manchester College Library
Mansfield Rd, Oxford, OX1 3TD (01865-271016;
fax: 01865-271012)
Email: librarian@hmc.ox.ac.uk

Gov Body: The Fellows of Harris Manchester Coll
Chief: Libn: Mrs S.A. Killoran BA, DipLIS **Dep:**
Mrs Joyce Meakin MCLIP
Assoc Libs: HARRIS MANCHESTER COLL
ARCHVS, at same addr
Entry: open to membs of Coll; bona fide rsrchers
admitted (letter of recommendation & proof of ID
required) **Open:** term: Mon-Fri 0930-1300, 1330-
1630; closed Aug
Subj: undergrad; postgrad; phil; psy; religion;
social sci; lit; geog; hist **Collns:** *Bks & Pamphs:*
Carpenter Lib of Comparative Religion; Unitarian
materials; tract colln (mainly religious & political
pamphs: 17C-20C); early printed bks *Archvs:* Coll
archvs (minutes, photos, account bks etc) **Other:**
MSS; papers of prominent Unitarians (18C-20C),
incl: Martineau; Shepherd; Priestley; Blanco-White
Co-op Schemes: BLDSC, ABTAPL
Equip: copier **Online:** Oxford Univ networked CD-
ROMs, OLIS, Internet
Stock: bks/70000; periodcls/25; photos/150;
archvs/30 linear m
Classn: own **Auto Sys:** Geac
Pubns: A Catalogue of Manuscripts in Harris
Manchester Coll Oxford, by D. Porter (1998)
Staff: Libns: 1 Other Prof: 1 Fellow Libn **Exp:**
£7000 (1999-2000)

S1678 🎓
Hertford College Library
Catte St, Oxford, OX1 3BW (01865-279409; *fax:*
01865-279466)
Email: susan.griffin@hertford.ox.ac.uk

Gov Body: Hertford Coll **Chief:** Fellow Libn: Dr S.
R. West MA, DPhil, FBA **Dep:** Libn: Mrs S. Griffin
BA, PGCE, DipLib
Assoc Libs: COLL ARCHVS, Archivist: Dr T.C.
Barnard MA, DPhil (01865-279418)
Entry: ref only, by adv appt with lib staff
Subj: phil; psy; social sci; lang; sci; maths; tech;
arts; lit; geog; hist **Collns:** *Bks & Pamphs:*
Magdalen Hall Lib (forerunner of Hertford, 16C-
18C) *Archvs:* relating to hist of Coll
Equip: computer **Online:** OLIS
Stock: bks/48000; periodcls/82
Classn: own **Staff:** Libns: 1.75 Non-Prof: 3

S1679 🔑
Institute of Actuaries, The Norwich Library
Napier House, 4 Worcester St, Oxford, OX1 2AW
(01865-268206/8; *fax:* 01865-268211)
Email: libraries@actuaries.org.uk
Internet: http://www.actuaries.org.uk/library/
library_welcome.html

Type: prof body **Gov Body:** part of joint lib svc of
Faculty & Inst of Actuaries **Chief:** Libn: Ms Sally
Grover MA, MCLIP **Dep:** Dep Libn: Ms Fiona
McNeil BA, MCLIP

🎓 academic   🖋 corporate   **- 400 -**   governmental   ✚ medical

Assoc Libs: other libs in the joint svc: INST OF ACTUARIES HISTORICAL COLLN (see **S1188**); FACULTY OF ACTUARIES, THE ROSS LIB (see **S599**)
Entry: adv appt for membs of public *Open:* Mon-Fri 0900-1700
Subj: actuarial sci & its applications; demography; insurance; pensions; social security; investment; finance; law; statistics; market info *Collns: Bks & Pamphs:* actuarial journals from UK, Europe, America & Australia; extensive colln of statistics & market data (in printed & elec formats) *Co-op Schemes:* BLDSC, ILL
Equip: copier (A4/20p) *Online:* Profile *Svcs:* info, ref, enq svc, postal photocopying svc
Stock: bks/15000; periodcls/200; photos/500; pamphs/3000
Classn: LCBS *Auto Sys:* DBTextworks
Pubns: Reading Lists (list of subjs on appl)
Staff: Libns: 3 *Non-Prof:* 2

S1680 🔑 🎓
Institute of Paper Conservation, Judith Chantry Library and Resource Centre
Grove Cottage, St Cross Rd, Oxford, OX1 3TX (01865-251303)
Email: library@ipc.org.uk
Internet: http://www.lib.ox.ac.uk/ipc-chantry/

Gov Body: Inst of Paper Conservation *Chief:* Libn: Dr Cristina Neagu
Entry: open to IPC membs & non-membs; adv appt required *Open:* Mon 0900-1300, Thu 0900-1730
Subj: bk & paper conservation; paper sci; paper hist; printing; bk design; bk binding; bk hist; colln care; art hist *Collns: Bks & Pamphs:* rsrch papers & abstracts presented to various conservation annual meetings
Equip: copier, computer
Stock: bks/c1000; periodcls/several 100
Auto Sys: OLIS
See also **O236**

S1681 🎓
Jesus College Library
Turl St, Oxford, OX1 3DW (01865-279704)
Email: library@jesus.ox.ac.uk

Gov Body: Principal & Fellows, Jesus Coll *Chief:* Fellow Libn: Dr T.J. Horder MA, PhD *Dep:* Coll Libn: Miss S.A. Cobbold MA, DipLib
Assoc Libs: MEYRICKE LIB; FELLOWS' LIB; COLL ARCHVS, Archivist: Dr B. Allen (01865-279761)
Entry: Meyricke Lib: membs of Jesus Coll only; *Fellows' Lib:* open to bona fide scholars, by prior appt *Open: Meyricke Lib:* 24 hrs pd
Subj: undergrad; most academic subjs *Collns: Bks & Pamphs: Fellows' Lib:* bks on Coll & eminent membs, 17C & 18C printed bks; Celtic Colln (access by permission of the Jesus Professor of Celtic) *Archvs:* archvs relating to hist of Coll & its membs (administered separately); papers of J.R. Green (19C historian); material relating to T.E. Lawrence (Lawrence of Arabia); MSS Colln (strong Welsh assoc)
Equip: copier, computer
Stock: bks/51000; periodcls/140
Classn: own *Auto Sys:* OLIS
Staff: Libns: 1 *Non-Prof:* 0.7

S1682 🎓
Keble College Library
Parks Rd, Oxford, OX1 3PG (01865-272797)
Email: library@keb.ox.ac.uk

Gov Body: Warden & Fellows of Keble Coll
Chief: Fellow Libn: Prof Ralph Hanna MA, PhD

Dep: Libn: Mrs Margaret A. Sarosi BA, HDipLib
Entry: generally membs only
Subj: all Honours school subjs *Collns: Bks & Pamphs:* medieval MSS; Port Royale Colln *Other:* 19C correspondence
Equip: copier, computer
Stock: bks/40000; periodcls/98
Classn: own *Auto Sys:* OLIS (Geac)
Staff: Libns: 1 *Non-Prof:* 1

S1683 ✚
Kilner Library of Plastic Surgery
Dept of Plastic Surgery, Radcliffe Infirmary, Woodstock Rd, Oxford, OX2 6HE (01865-224792; *fax:* 01865-311673)
Email: tim.goodacre@uds.ox.ac.uk

Gov Body: Univ of Oxford (see **L4**) *Chief:* Hon Libn: Mr Tim Goodacre BSc, FRCS
Entry: ref only, adv arrangement *Open:* Mon-Fri 0830-1700
Subj: plastic surgery & allied subjs *Collns: Archvs:* Kilner Colln
Equip: copier, fax, computer (with internet) *Svcs:* ref
Stock: periodcls/25
Exp: £5000 (1999-2000); £5000 (2000-01)

S1684 🎓
Lady Margaret Hall Library
Norham Gdns, Oxford, OX2 6QA (01865-274361)
Email: library@lmh.ox.ac.uk

Gov Body: Lady Margaret Hall *Chief:* Libn: Ms R. Staples BA, DipLib
Assoc Libs: LADY MARGARET HALL ARCHVS, Archivist: Mrs J. Courtney
Entry: membership of LMH; non-membs of Coll should make adv appointments *Open:* 24 hrs pd for Coll membs; 0900-1700 for non-membs
Subj: all subjs; undergrad; postgrad *Collns: Bks & Pamphs:* Briggs Room (colln of antiquarian bks donated by Katherine M. Briggs)
Equip: m-reader, copier, 5 computers
Stock: bks/70000; periodcls/101
Classn: DDC *Auto Sys:* Geac
Pubns: Guide to LMH Lib
Staff: Libns: 1 *Non-Prof:* 0.5

S1685 🔑 🙏
Library of The Fellowship of St Alban and St Sergius
House of St Gregory & St Macrina, 2 Canterbury Rd, Oxford, OX2 6LU (01865-552991)
Email: gensec@sobornost.org
Internet: http://www.sobornost.org/

Gov Body: Council of the Fellowship of St Alban & St Sergius *Chief:* Genl Sec & Libn: Rev Stephen Platt
Assoc Libs: LIB OF THE HOUSE OF ST GREGORY & ST MACRINA (see **S1686**)
Entry: adv appt only
Subj: religion; hist, doctrine & worship of the Eastern Orthodox Churches
Equip: copier
Stock: bks/1500; periodcls/50 *Classn:* DDC
Pubns: Sobornost (incorporating Eastern Churches Review, £20 pa)

S1686 🔑 🙏
Library of The House of St Gregory and St Macrina
1 Canterbury Rd, Oxford, OX2 6LU (01865-552991; *fax:* 01865-316700)
Email: gensec@sobornost.org
Internet: http://www.sobornost.org/

Gov Body: Council of the House of St Gregory & St Macrina *Chief:* Genl Sec & Libn: Rev Stephen Platt *Dep:* Mr Peter Petkov
Assoc Libs: LIB OF THE FELLOWSHIP OF ST ALBAN & ST SERGIUS (see **S1685**)
Entry: adv appt only *Open:* term: Wed 1400-1700 or by appt
Subj: religion; hist, doctrine & worship of the Eastern Orthodox Churches *Collns: Archvs:* Chitty Archv (MS dealing mainly with 4C-5C Christian monasticism)
Equip: copier
Stock: bks/2500 *Classn:* own

S1687 🎓
Linacre College Library
St Cross Rd, Oxford, OX1 3JA (01865-271661; *fax:* 01865-271668)
Email: library@linacre.ox.ac.uk
Internet: http://www.linacre.ox.ac.uk/college/library/

Gov Body: Principal & Fellows of the Coll *Chief:* Fellow Libn: Ms Margaret Robb BS, MLS, MCLIP
Dep: Asst Libn: Ms Louise Trevelyan BA, MA
Entry: Coll membs only *Open:* 24 hr access for coll membs
Subj: all subjs; undergrad; postgrad
Equip: copier, computers, clr printer, scanner
Stock: bks/12000

S1688 🎓
Lincoln College Library
Turl St, Oxford, OX1 3DR (01865-279831)
Email: library@lincoln.ox.ac.uk

Chief: Fellow Libn & Archivist: Dr P.E. McCullough PhD *Dep:* Libn: Mrs F.M. Piddock BA, DipLib
Entry: for membs of Lincoln Coll only *Open:* term: Mon-Sun 0830-2330
Subj: all subjs; undergrad
Equip: copier, computers *Online:* various major databases via Univ info network
Classn: DDC *Auto Sys:* Geac
Staff: Libns: 1 *Non-Prof:* 1

S1689 🎓
Magdalen College Library
High St, Oxford, OX1 4AU (01865-276045; *fax:* 01865-276057)
Email: sally.speirs@magdalen.ox.ac.uk

Gov Body: President & Fellows of Magdalen Coll *Chief:* Fellow Libn: Dr C.Y. Ferdinand MA, DPhil *Dep:* Asst Libn: Ms K.S. Speirs MA, MLIS
Assoc Libs: COLL ARCHVS, Archivist: Dr R.A. Darwall-Smith MA, DPhil, MArAd (01865-276088; *email:* robin.darwall-smith@magdalen.ox.ac.uk)
Entry: Coll membs only, others by adv appt
Subj: all subjs; undergrad; some postgrad
Collns: Archvs: Coll related material *Co-op Schemes:* OLIS
Stock: bks/100000; videos/1000
Classn: DDC *Auto Sys:* OLIS
Pubns: Magdalen Coll Occasional papers (series); Magdalen Poets: 5 Centuries of Poetry from Magdalen Coll Oxford
Staff: Libns: 2 *Other Prof:* 1 archivist *Non-Prof:* 1

S1690 🎓 🏛
Maison Française D'Oxford Library
37 Norham Rd, Oxford, OX2 6SE (01865-274224; *fax:* 01865-274225)
Email: maison@herald.ox.ac.uk

Gov Body: French Ministry of Foreign Affairs & Univ of Oxford (see **L4**) *Chief:* Bibliothécaire: Mrs Anna Rosenchild-Paulin

☞

S Oxford ▼ Oxford
pecial Libraries

(Maison Française D'Oxford Lib cont)
Entry: open to everyone interested in French culture; free membership except for video loans (£20 pa) **Open:** Tue-Fri 1000-1800, Sat 1000-1300 (closed in Aug, Xmas & Easter vacs)
Subj: French lit; French hist; social sci; also petaining to France: phil; psy; arts; geog
Equip: m-form reader/printer, fax, copier, 3 computers (incl wd-proc, internet & CD-ROM)
Online: OLIS, OXLIP
Stock: bks/43000, excl bnd periodcls; periodcls/100; audios/3550; videos/300
Classn: DDC **Auto Sys:** Geac **Staff:** Libns: 2

S1691 🎓
Mansfield College Library
Mansfield Rd, Oxford, OX1 3TF (01865-270975; *fax:* 01865-270970)
Email: alma.jenner@mansfield.ox.ac.uk
Internet: http://www.mansfield.ox.ac.uk/study/resources.htm

Chief: Libn: Ms Alma Jenner **Dep:** Asst Libn: Ms Sheila Glen
Entry: primarily for students of Coll; external readers should send letter of introduction to Principal of Coll **Open:** students 24 hr access; for external readers Mon-Fri 0900-1600
Subj: all subjs; undergrad; postgrad **Collns:** Bks & Pamphs: inheritance of 18C & 19C theology (incl a colln of sermons) from Spring Hill Coll Lib, Birmingham
Equip: fax, copier, computer **Online:** OLIS, Internet & others (through new computing room adjacent to lib)
Stock: bks/28000
Classn: own **Auto Sys:** Inheritance
Pubns: Guide to Mansfield Coll Lib (free)
Staff: Libns: 2

S1692 🎓
Merton College Library
Merton St, Oxford, OX1 4JD (01865-276380; *fax:* 01865-276361)
Email: library@admin.merton.ox.ac.uk (not to be used for unsolicited commercial correspondence)

Gov Body: Merton Coll **Chief:** Fellow Libn: Dr Julia Walworth MA, PhD **Dep:** Asst Libn: Ms Catherine Ross BA, PGDipILM, MCLIP **Other Snr Staff:** Archivist: Mr Julian Reid
Entry: to consult unique material: written appl with proof of ID **Open:** Mon-Fri 0900-1230, 1330-1700
Subj: undergrad; most academic subjs **Collns:** Bks & Pamphs: Max Beerbohm Colln; F.H. Bradley Colln; T.F. Brenchley Colln (publ works by T.S. Eliot); medieval MSS; early printed bks **Archvs:** Coll Archvs **Co-op Schemes:** BLDSC
Equip: m-reader, copier, computers (Coll membs only) **Online:** svcs provided by Oxford Univ
Officer-in-Charge: Fellow Libn, as above **Svcs:** info, ref, biblio
Stock: bks/80000; periodcls/200; photos/1000; pamphs/500; m-forms/300; audios/20; videos/3
Acqs Offcr: Fellow Libn, as above
Classn: Bliss **Auto Sys:** Geac
Staff: Libns: 2 Other Prof: 1 archivist Non-Prof: 2
Proj: automated cataloguing of early printed bks & archvs

S1693
Modern Art Oxford
(formerly the Lib & Museum of Modern Art, Oxford)
30 Pembroke St, Oxford, OX1 1BP (01865-813822; *fax:* 01865-722573)
Email: becky.simms@moma.org.uk
Internet: http://www.moma.org.uk

Gov Body: Council of Mgmt **Chief:** Programme Administrator: Miss Becky Simms BA(Hons) Oxon
Entry: adv appt only, by calling or emailing the Programme Administrator 2 wks in adv **Open:** Thu-Fri 0930-1730
Subj: modern art; contemporary art; art theory
Collns: Bks & Pamphs: artist's bks; rare art periodcls/catalogues **Archvs:** administrative & visual records of past exhibs, incl: letters, photos, slides & associated material **Co-op Schemes:** catalogue exchange scheme with museums & galleries worldwide – currently on hold due to sale of lib to Oxford Brookes Univ
Equip: copier **Svcs:** info, ref
Stock: bks/2000; various photos, slides, illusts, pamphs, audios, videos, CD-ROMs & archvs
Pubns: MOMA pubns are listed on web site (see URL above), & in the Cornerhouse Catalogue (from Cornerhouse Pubns, Manchester)
Staff: no dedicated lib staff
Further Info: The former Lib has been sold to Oxford Brookes Univ. However, we still have rare bks & artists bks, & the archv. Access to the colln at Oxford Brookes can be arranged by calling the Programme Administrator at Modern Art Oxford.

S1694 🎓 🗝
The National Brewing Library
(combining the former libs of the Inst of Brewing, the Internatl Brewers' Guild & the Brewers & Licensed Retailers Assoc)
Oxford Brookes Univ Lib, Gipsy Ln, Oxford, OX3 0BP (01865-483136; *fax:* 01865-483998)
Email: dmarshall@brookes.ac.uk
Internet: http://www.brookes.ac.uk/services/library/

Gov Body: Mgmt Cttee representing the Inst & Guild of Brewing Lib & Archv Group, The British Beer & Pub Assoc, Oxford Brookes Univ Lib (see **S1700**) & the Brewing Rsrch Group **Chief:** Librarian-in-Charge & Subj Team Leader (Chem): Mr Donald Marshall
Entry: ref only; membs of the Inst & Guild of Brewing & membs of Oxford Brookes Univ; bona fide rsrchers & scholars by prior appt; some rare material can only be accessed under supervision **Open:** term: Mon-Thu 0900-2200, Fri 0900-2000, Sat-Sun 1000-1600; vac: Mon-Fri 0900-1700
Subj: beer; fermentation; brewing; trades & industries related to brewing; alcoholic beverages; hist of public houses & licensed trade; temperance; alcoholism; alcohol & health **Collns:** Bks & Pamphs: English lang brewing bks (18C-date); bks from the former Whitbread Brewing Archv; company hists & pubns; technical brewing journals **Other:** ephemera relating to the social & technical hist of the brewing industry
Equip: photocopying only available with permission
Stock: bks/c3000

S1695 🎓
New College Library
New College Ln, Oxford, OX1 3BN (01865-279580; *fax:* 01865-279590)
Email: library@new.ox.ac.uk
Internet: http://www.new.ox.ac.uk/

Gov Body: Warden & Fellows of New Coll **Chief:** Libn: Mrs Naomi van Loo MA, BA, MCLIP (naomi.vanloo@new.ox.ac.uk) **Other Snr Staff:** Fellow Libn: Prof A.D. Nuttall

Assoc Libs: COLL ARCHVS, Archivist: Mrs C. Dalton MA (01865-279581)
Entry: membs of Coll, visiting scholars by prior arrangement **Open:** term: Mon-Sun 0900-2400; vac: Mon-Fri 0900-1700
Subj: undergrad; postgrad; most academic subjs
Collns: Bks & Pamphs: early printed bks **Archvs:** medieval-recent; Sydney Smith letters; C.W.M.C. Cox Colln; New Coll muniments **Other:** Seton Watson Colln; Milner Colln
Equip: 3 computers
Stock: bks/100000; periodcls/162
Classn: own **Auto Sys:** Geac (OLIS)
Staff: Libns: 1 Non-Prof: 2.5 **Exp:** £36000 (1999-2000)

S1696 🎓
Nuffield College Library
New Rd, Oxford, OX1 1NF (01865-278550; *fax:* 01865-278621)
Email: library-enquiries@nuf.ox.ac.uk
Internet: http://www.nuff.ox.ac.uk/library/

Gov Body: The Warden & Fellows of Nuffield Coll **Chief:** Libn: Ms Elizabeth Martin MA, DipLib, MCLIP (librarian@nuf.ox.ac.uk)
Assoc Libs: COLL ARCHVS (01865-278549; *email:* library-archives@nuf.ox.ac.uk)
Entry: printed material: grad rsrch workers; MSS: pre-booking & letter of introduction required **Open:** Mon-Fri 0930-1730; summer (mid-Jul to mid-Sep): Mon-Fri 1400-1730
Subj: postgrad; social sci **Collns:** Archvs: modern socio-political papers **Co-op Schemes:** ILL
Equip: m-reader, m-printer (10p per sheet), copier (cost varies), 7 computers (incl 5 with CD-ROM)
Online: OLIS
Stock: periodcls/1000; archvs/1244 ft; total items/190000
Classn: LC **Auto Sys:** Geac
Staff: Libns: 5 Other Prof: 1 Non-Prof: 3

S1697 🎓 ✚
Nuffield Laboratory of Ophthalmology Library
Walton St, Oxford, OX2 6AW (01865-248996; *fax:* 01865-794508)
Email: john.tiffany@eye.ox.ac.uk

Gov Body: Univ of Oxford (see **L4**) **Chief:** Hon Libn: Dr John M. Tiffany PhD, MA
Entry: ref only; all membs of Univ & Oxford Eye Hosp; others by arrangement **Open:** accessible 24 hrs to anyone with access to bldg (locked 1800-0830)
Subj: ophthalmology (clinical scis, surgery, basic sci); biochem, physical sci & pharmacology as applied to eye rsrch
Equip: copier (staff only)
Stock: bks/3480; periodcls/36
Exp: £6500 (1999-2000)

S1698 🎓 ✚
Nuffield Orthopaedic Centre NHS Trust, Girdlestone Memorial Library
Windmill Rd, Headington, Oxford, OX3 7LD (01865-227361; *fax:* 01865-227362)
Email: eve.hollis@ndos.ox.ac.uk

Gov Body: Univ of Oxford, Nuffield Dept of Orthopaedic Surgery; also serves the Nuffield Orthopaedic Centre NHS Trust, Oxford Orthopaedic Eng Centre, Oxford Centre for Musculoskeletal Rsrch, Natl Orthotics Rsrch Eng, Mary Marlborough Centre & Oxford Centre for Enablement **Chief:** Lib Svcs Mgr: Mrs Eve Hollis BSc **Dep:** Lib Asst: Mr Derek Godwin

Entry: ref only for non-membs *Open:* Mon-Fri 0800-1800; 24 access for membs via swipecard *Subj:* clinical psy; medicine; rehabilitation; neurological rehabilitation; musculoskeletal diseases & disorders; orthopaedics; rheumatology; orthotics; prosthetics; orthopaedic nursing *Collns: Archvs:* relating to hist of orthopaedics; meeting papers of BOA & Girdlestone Orthopaedic Soc *Co-op Schemes:* BLDSC, STLIS *Equip:* m-reader, copier (A4/8p), 7 computers (all with wd-proc, internet & CD-ROM) *Online:* KA24 via Oxford Univ Lib Svcs: Medline, CINAHL, PsycInfo, EMBASE, SIGLE & others *Officer-in-Charge:* Lib Svcs Mgr, as above *Svcs:* info, ref, biblio, teaching *Stock:* bks/c4000; periodcls/80; pamphs/c400; audios/10; videos/35; CD-ROMs/26; archvs/1 m *Acqs Offcr:* Lib Svcs Mgr, as above *Classn:* NLM *Auto Sys:* DBTextworks *Pubns:* Lib Guide; Welcome Leaflet; Journal List; Acqs List *Staff: Libns:* 1 *Non-Prof:* 0.4

S1699 ✿

Oriel College Library

Oriel Sq, Oxford, OX1 4EW (01865-276558)
Email: library@oriel.ox.ac.uk
Internet: http://www.oriel.ox.ac.uk/library/

Gov Body: Oriel Coll *Chief:* Fellow Libn: Dr A. Volfing MA, DPhil *Dep:* Libn: Mrs Marjory Szurko BA, DipLib, MRes, MCLIP
Assoc Libs: COLL ARCHVS, addr as above, Archivist: post vacant
Entry: visiting scholars on appl by letter *Open:* term: Mon-Fri 0900-1700; vac: Mon-Fri 0930-1700 *Subj:* all subjs; undergrad; postgrad *Collns: Bks & Pamphs:* colln of bks by old membs; colln of bks pre-1800 *Archvs:* material from Coll records & relating to old membs (particularly those connected with Oxford Movement) *Co-op Schemes:* ILL *Equip:* computer *Stock:* bks/100000; periodcls/200 *Classn:* own *Auto Sys:* OLIS *Staff: Libns:* 1 *Non-Prof:* 1 PT

S1700 ✿

Oxford Brookes University Library

Gipsy Ln Campus, Headington, Oxford, OX3 0BP (01865-483133; *fax:* 01865-483998)
Email: library@brookes.ac.uk
Internet: http://www.brookes.ac.uk/services/library/

Chief: Dir of Learning Resources & Univ Libn: Dr Helen M. Workman PhD, MCLIP
Assoc Libs: WHEATLEY LIB, Wheatley Campus, Wheatley, Oxford, OX9 1HX (01865-485869; *fax:* 01865-485750), Dep Libn: Ms C.M. Jeffery BSc, DipLib, MCLIP; DORSET HOUSE LIB, 58 London Rd, Headington, Oxford, OX3 7PE (01865-485261), Subj Libn: Ms H. Rothera MA, MCLIP; HARCOURT HILL LIB (formerly Westminster Coll Lib), Harcourt Hill, Oxford, OX2 9AT (01865-488222; *fax:* 01865-488224), Dep Libn: Ms C.M. Jeffery BSc, DipLib, MCLIP
Entry: access for ref purposes on proof of ID & addr; institutional membership scheme; external membership scheme for Higher Edu students; reciprocal arrangements within UK Libs Plus Scheme *Open: Gipsy Lane:* term: Mon-Thu 0900-2200, Fri 0900-2000, Sat-Sun 1000-1600; vac: Mon-Fri 0900-1700; *Wheatley:* term: Mon-Thu 0900-2100, Fri 0900-1800, Sat-Sun 1000-1600; vac: Mon-Fri 0900-1700; *Dorset House:* term: Mon-Fri 0900-1900, Sat 0900-1200, Sun 1000-1300; vac: Mon-Fri 0900-1500; *Harcourt Hill:* term: Mon-Thu 0845-2100, Fri 0845-1800, Sat-Sun 1200-1800; vac: Mon-Fri 0900-1700 *Subj:* all subjs; undergrad; postgrad; *Gipsy Lane:* arch; humanities; tourism; nursing; planning; social sci; eng; *Wheatley:* business; mgmt; *Dorset House:* occupational therapy; *Harcourt Hill:* edu; theology

Collns: Bks & Pamphs: Fuller Colln of bks on hospitality & catering (7000 vols) *Co-op Schemes:* BLDSC, ORLIN
Stock: bks/413000; periodcls/2700
Classn: DDC *Auto Sys:* Talis
Pubns: Lit Guides & Periodicals Lists (all subjs); Guides to Svcs (all free)
Staff: Libns: 33 *Non-Prof:* 44

S1701 ✿

Oxford Centre for Hebrew and Jewish Studies, Leopold Muller Memorial Library

Yarnton Manor, Yarnton, Oxford, OX5 1PY (01865-377946; *fax:* 01865-375079)
Email: muller.library@ochjs.ac.uk
Internet: http://users.ox.ac.uk/~ochjs/library/

Gov Body: Board of Governors *Chief:* Head Libn: Dr Piet W. van Boxel PhD *Dep:* Asst Libn: Ms Zosia Sochanska MA
Entry: free access to fellows, visiting scholars & students of Centre; others bona fide students & scholars require letter of introduction from academic instn; annual membership fee £30 *Open:* term: Mon -Thu 0930-2100, Fri 0930-1600, Sat 1000-1500; vac: Mon-Fri 1000-1600 *Subj:* Hebrew lit; Jewish hist; Israel & Zionism; Holocaust; biography; Hebrew & Jewish bibliography *Collns: Bks & Pamphs:* Elkoshi Colln (Hebrew lit, 19C-20C, 17000 vols); Kressel Colln (Jewish hist & Hebrew lit, 19C-20C, 25000 bks & pamphs); Yizkor Bks Colln (European Jewish communities, 450 vols) *Archvs:* Kressel Archv (Israeli & Jewish biography, incl newscuttings, newspapers & journals, rare pamphs & private papers) *Co-op Schemes:* informal assoc with Oxford Univ & Bodleian, Oriental Inst etc *Equip:* digital m-film reader, copier, computers (with internet) *Stock:* bks/42000+; periodcls/70; pamphs/500; m-forms/25000 fiche, 400 reels of film *Classn:* DDC *Staff:* 4 in total

S1702 ✿

Oxford Centre for the Environment, Ethics and Society, William Robbins Library

Mansfield Coll, Mansfield Rd, Oxford, OX1 3TF (*tel & fax:* 01865-270886)
Email: ocees@mansfield.ox.ac.uk

Gov Body: Univ of Oxford (see **L4**) *Chief:* Libn: Ms Anne Maclachlan
Entry: ref only; membs of Univ & academic visitors *Open:* term: Mon-Fri 0900-1200, 1400-1700; vac: contact lib *Subj:* environment; social sci; phil; ethics; theology; sociology; politics; econ; law; policy; geog; hist *Collns: Bks & Pamphs:* William Robbins Colln *Equip:* copier, computer *Online:* BIDS, OCLC FirstSearch

S1703 ✿

Oxford College of Further Education, The Olive Gibbs Centre

Oxpens Rd, Oxford, OX1 1SA (01865-235871; *fax:* 01865-248871)
Email: Enquiries@oxfordcollege.ac.uk
Internet: http://www.oxfordcollege.ac.uk/

Chief: Lib & Info Resources Administrator: Ms G. Southgate MCLIP
Assoc Libs: BLACKBIRD LEYS PRECINCT LIB, Cuddesdon Way, Blackbird Leys, Oxford
Entry: ref only *Open:* term: Mon-Fri 0900-2000; vac: Mon-Fri 0900-1700
Subj: genl; GCSE; A level

Equip: video viewer, 2 copiers, computers (incl CD-ROM) *Svcs:* info, ref
Stock: bks/30000; periodcls/200; videos/500
Classn: DDC *Auto Sys:* Heritage
Staff: Libns: 1.5 *Non-Prof:* 4 *Exp:* £20000 (2000-01)

S1704 ✿

Oxford Institute for Energy Studies, Library

57 Woodstock Rd, Oxford, OX2 6FA (01865-311377; *fax:* 01865-510327)
Email: lavinia.brandon@oxfordenergy.org
Internet: http://www.oxfordenergy.org/

Gov Body: Oxford Inst for Energy Studies (self-governing) *Chief:* Libn: Ms Lavinia Brandon
Entry: adv appt *Open:* Mon-Fri 0900-1700 *Subj:* energy; econ; politics
Stock: bks/5000; periodcls/100; pamphs/1000
Classn: own

S1705 🎞 🎥

Oxford Picture Library

Unit 15, Curtis Yard, North Hinksey Ln, Oxford, OX2 0LX (01865-723404; *fax:* 01865-725294)
Email: chris.andrewa1@btclick.com
Internet: http://www.cap-ox.co.uk/

Type: commercial picture agency *Chief:* Partner: Mr Christopher Andrews *Dep:* Miss Annabel Webb
Entry: visits by appt only; phone/postal enqs preferred *Open:* Mon-Fri 0900-1700 *Subj:* contemporary images of Oxford City & Univ; the Cotswolds, Thames, Chilterns & Channel Islands *Collns: Bks & Pamphs:* pictorial guidebks of Oxford, Cotswolds & Chilterns *Stock:* bks/6; slides/25000+; maps/1 *Staff: Other Prof:* 2 *Exp:* £120000 (1999-2000); £100000 (2000-01)

S1706 🔑 ✿

Oxford Union Society Library

Oxford Union Soc, Frewin Ct, Oxford, OX1 3BJ (01865-241353; *fax:* 01865-250092)
Email: library@oxford-union.org
Internet: http://www.oxford-union.org/Library/

Gov Body: Oxford Union Soc *Chief:* Libn-in-Charge: Dr David Johnson MA, DPhil (librarian-in-charge@oxford-union.org) *Dep:* Snr Lib Asst: Mr Niels Sampath MPhil *Other Snr Staff:* Cataloguer: Mrs Sophie Floate MA (cataloguer@oxford-union.org)
Assoc Libs: administrative records of the Oxford Union Soc are held at OXFORDSHIRE RECORD OFFICE (see **A412**)
Entry: membs of Soc; bona fide rsrchers with special permission *Open:* term: Mon-Sat 0930-1900; vac: Mon-Fri 1000-1700 *Subj:* all subjs; undergrad; postgrad; local study (Oxford Univ) *Collns: Bks & Pamphs:* Edward VII Colln (bks owned by future Edward VII when at Oxford); Pamph Colln (19C) *Equip:* copier (4p), rooms for hire *Officer-in-Charge:* Libn-in-Charge, as above *Svcs:* info, ref *Stock:* bks/c90000; periodcls/c45; pamphs/2500 *Acqs Offcr:* Libn-in-Charge, as above *Classn:* DDC *Auto Sys:* Geac *Staff: Libns:* 2 *Non-Prof:* 3 *Exp:* £25000 pa

Oxford University, The Bodleian Library

See **L4**

S1707 🎓

Oxford University, Botanic Garden Library

Rose Ln, Oxford, OX1 4AZ (01865-286690; *fax:* 01865-286693)
Email: postmaster@botanic-garden.ox.ac.uk
Internet: http://www.botanic-garden.ox.ac.uk/

Gov Body: Univ of Oxford (see **L4**) *Chief:* Offcr in Charge: Mr Timothy Walker
Entry: adv appt essential *Open:* Mon-Fri 0900-1300, 1400-1600
Subj: hortic (small eclectic colln) *Svcs:* ref
Stock: bks/c2500; periodcls/4 *Staff: Non-Prof:* 1

S1708 ✚

Oxford University, The Cairns Library, Radcliffe Infirmary Branch

Radcliffe Infirmary, Woodstock Rd, Oxford, OX2 6HE (01865-224478; *fax:* 01865-224789)
Email: library@cairns-library.ox.ac.uk
Internet: http://www.medicine.ox.ac.uk/cairns/

Gov Body: Univ of Oxford, School of Clinical Medicine *Chief:* Site Libn: Mr Neal Thurley BA, MA (neal.thurley@cairns-library.ox.ac.uk) *Dep:* Lib Asst: Ms Jolanta Wasowicz-Labbad (jolanta. wasowicz-labbad@cairns-library.ox.ac.uk)
Assoc Libs: branch of CAIRNS LIB, John Radcliffe Hosp (see **S1749**); GEORGE WIERNIK LIB (see **S1729**)
Entry: staff & students of Faculty of Clinical Medicine, staff of Oxford Radcliffe Trust, primary care workers & doctors in training in Oxfordshire
Open: staffed Mon-Fri 0900-1700; 24 hrs access to registered users
Subj: medicine; health; gerontology; neuroscience; diabetes rsrch
Equip: copier, computers *Online:* numerous, incl AMED, ASSIA, BNI, CINAHL, Cochrane, Embase, HealthStar, Medline, PsycInfo, Web of Science
Stock: bks/4000; periodcls/110

S1709 🎓

Oxford University, Careers Service Library

56 Banbury Rd, Oxford, OX2 6PA (01865-274646; *fax:* 01865-274653)
Email: postmaster@cas.ox.ac.uk
Internet: http://www.careers.ox.ac.uk/

Gov Body: Univ of Oxford (see **L4**) *Chief:* Info Room Mgr: Ms Kay Heard BA, MCLIP *Dep:* Info Room Supervisor: Ms Judith Charlton BEd
Entry: ref only; restricted to current students & recent grads of Oxford Univ
Open: term: Mon-Fri 1000-1700, Sat 1000-1300; vac: Mon-Fri 1000-1300, 1400-1700
Subj: careers info; work experience; work & study abroad; grad recruiters; postgrad study *Co-op Schemes:* Assoc of Grad Careers Advisory Svcs, mutual aid scheme for recent grads of UK univs
Equip: video viewers, copiers, computers (incl internet) *Disabled:* wheelchair lift (access to ground floor & basement) *Online:* local databases
Svcs: info, ref
Stock: bks/200; periodcls/30; pamphs/many 1000s; videos/50
Classn: AGCAS Classn

Pubns: Careers Svc Guide (membs only); Annual Report (free); The Bridge Vacancy Bulletin (price on appl)
Staff: Libns: 2 *Other Prof:* 10 *Non-Prof:* 18

S1710 🎓

Oxford University, Centre for Criminological Research Library

12 Bevington Rd, Oxford, OX2 6LH (01865-274448; *fax:* 01865-274445)
Email: library@crim.ox.ac.uk
Internet: http://www.crim.ox.ac.uk/

Gov Body: Univ of Oxford (see **L4**) *Chief:* Libn: Ms Elizabeth Wells
Entry: open to those with Bodleian readership; ref only *Open:* term & vac: Mon-Fri 0900-1630 (closed 1300-1400 Mon, Thu-Fri)
Subj: social sci; criminology; criminal justice; criminal law *Collns: Bks & Pamphs:* specialised colln for Probation Studies Unit under development
Equip: copier, computer (with wd-proc, internet & CD-ROM) *Online:* all Univ of Oxford networked databases, free *Svcs:* info, ref, indexing
Stock: bks/4000; periodcls/25
Classn: local sys *Auto Sys:* Geac
Pubns: the Centre's pubns are listed on OLIS, the Univ's online catalogue
Staff: 1 PT

S1711 🎓

Oxford University, Centre for Socio-Legal Studies, Neill Library

Wolfson Coll, Oxford, OX2 6UD (01865-284220; *fax:* 01865-284221)
Email: ruth.schroeder@csls.ox.ac.uk

Gov Body: Univ of Oxford (see **L4**) *Chief:* Libn: Ms Ruth Schroeder
Entry: academic staff & students of univ; others by adv appt only *Open:* term: Mon-Fri 0900-1700; vac: varies
Subj: social sci & law, incl: medicine; psy; criminology; environment; family law
Equip: copier, computer (incl CD-ROM) *Svcs:* info, ref
Stock: bks/2000; periodcls/30
Classn: own *Auto Sys:* Geac *Staff: Libns:* 1 PT

S1712 🎓

Oxford University, Clarendon Laboratory Library

Parks Rd, Oxford, OX1 3PU (01865-272265; *fax:* 01865-272400)
Email: library@physics.ox.ac.uk
Internet: http://www2.physics.ox.ac.uk/library/

Gov Body: Univ of Oxford (see **L4**) *Chief:* Libn: Miss Amey Sherlock BA
Assoc Libs: NUCLEAR & ASTROPHYSICS LIB (see **S1740**)
Entry: postgrads & staff of Physics Dept; others at Libn's discretion only *Open:* Mon-Fri 0830-1300 (24 hr access to physics membs)
Subj: physics; atomic & laser physics; condensed matter physics; theoretical physics *Collns: Archvs:* Clarendon Laboratory Archv
Equip: m-reader, copier, computer (incl wd-proc & CD-ROM) *Online:* Internet *Svcs:* info, ref, biblio
Stock: bks/12500; periodcls/68
Classn: own *Auto Sys:* Geac *Staff: Libns:* 1

S1713 🎓

Oxford University, Computing Laboratory Library

Wolfson Bldg, Parks Rd, Oxford, OX1 3QD (01865-273837; *fax:* 01865-273839)
Email: library@comlab.ox.ac.uk

Gov Body: Univ of Oxford (see **L4**) *Chief:* Libn: Mr Gordon Riddell MA, DipLib
Entry: ref only, adv appt for non-Oxford membs
Open: Mon-Fri 0900-1300, 1400-1700
Subj: computer sci; maths *Co-op Schemes:* BLDSC
Equip: copier, computers
Stock: bks/6000; periodcls/70; pamphs/10000
Auto Sys: Geac *Staff: Libns:* 1

S1714 🎓

Oxford University, Department for Continuing Education Library

Rewley House, 1 Wellington Sq, Oxford, OX1 2JA (01865-270454; *fax:* 01865-270309)
Email: library@conted.ox.ac.uk
Internet: http://www.conted.ox.ac.uk/facilities/library.asp

Gov Body: Univ of Oxford (see **L4**) *Chief:* Libn: Mrs Ann Rees CertEd *Dep:* Associate Libn (PT): Mr Peter Jackson
Entry: dept membs; ref only for non-membs
Open: term: Mon-Thu 0900-2000, Fri 0900-1700, Sat 0900-1300; vac: Mon-Fri 0900-1700
Subj: undergrad; postgrad; most academic subjs
Collns: Bks & Pamphs: local studies colln *Archvs:* Rewley House Archvs *Other:* AV colln *Co-op Schemes:* BLDSC
Equip: m-reader, video viewer, copier (A4/5p, A3/10p), computers (incl CD-ROM) *Online:* OLIS OPAC, OXLIP, e-journals *Svcs:* info, ref, biblio, bk supply for external classes
Stock: bks/80000; periodcls/139; slides/8600; maps/50; m-forms/1; audios/450; videos/757
Classn: DDC & subj classn *Auto Sys:* Geac
Staff: Libns: 2 *Non-Prof:* 3

S1715 🎓

Oxford University, Department of Earth Sciences Library

Parks Rd, Oxford, OX1 3PR (01865-272050; *fax:* 01865-272072)
Email: jennyc@earth.ox.ac.uk

Gov Body: Univ of Oxford (see **L4**) *Chief:* Libn: Ms Jenny Colls MCLIP
Entry: ref only, apply in writing to libn *Open:* term: Mon-Thu 0900-1300, 1400-1730, Fri 0900-1300, 1400-1630; vac: Mon-Wed 0900-1300, 1400-1730, Thu 0900-1300, 1400-1645
Subj: earth sci; geol; mineralogy
Equip: m-reader, copier
Classn: own
Pubns: list of articles published by membs of Dept; Accessions List
Staff: Libns: 1

S1716 🎓

Oxford University, Department of Educational Studies Library

15 Norham Gdns, Oxford, OX2 6PY (01865-274028; *fax:* 01865-274027)
Email: judy.reading@edstud.ox.ac.uk
Internet: http://www.edstud.ox.ac.uk/Library/webpage_main.htm

Gov Body: Univ of Oxford (see **L4**) *Chief:* Libn: Ms Judy Reading MA, MCLIP (judy.reading@edstud.ox.ac.uk) *Dep:* Asst Libn: Mr Nick Watts MA (nick.watts@edstud.ox.ac.uk)
Entry: ref only, except for certain categories
Open: term: Mon-Thu 0900-1900, Fri 0900-1700, Sat 1200-1600; vac: Mon-Thu 0900-1730, Fri 0900-1700
Subj: genl; social sci; edu; sci; maths; tech; geog; hist *Collns: Bks & Pamphs:* pre-1918 govt pubns & other historical src material (e.g., hists of indiv schools) *Co-op Schemes:* ILL, LISE

Equip: 2 m-readers, 2 m-printers, 4 video viewers, 2 copiers, 9 computers (all with wd-proc, internet & CD-ROM) *Online:* Dialog, BIDS, Connect *Stock:* bks/40000; periodcls/350; videos/300 *Classn:* DDC *Auto Sys:* Geac *Staff:* 8 in total

S1717
Oxford University, Department of Engineering Science Library
Parks Rd, Oxford, OX1 3PJ (01865-273193; *fax:* 01865-273010)
Email: library@eng.ac.ox.uk
Internet: http://www.eng.ox.ac.uk/

Gov Body: Univ of Oxford (see **L4**) *Chief:* Libn: Miss A.C. Greig MCLIP
Entry: membs of dept; adv appt for others; non-membs of Univ may require letter of introduction
Open: term & vac: Mon-Fri 0900-1300, 1400-1700
Subj: eng *Co-op Schemes:* BLDSC, OLIS
Equip: m-reader, m-printer, copier
Stock: bks/25000; periodcls/200
Classn: own *Auto Sys:* Dobis/Libis
Staff: Libns: 1 *Non-Prof:* 0.5

S1718
Oxford University, Department of Experimental Psychology Library
South Parks Rd, Oxford, OX1 3UD (01865-271312; *fax:* 01865-310447)
Email: library@psy.ox.ac.uk
Internet: http://www.psych.ox.ac.uk/

Gov Body: Univ of Oxford (see **L4**) *Chief:* Libn: Mrs Rebecca Dalton *Dep:* Lib Asst: Mrs Grace Sewell
Entry: membs of Univ; others by appt, ref only
Open: term: Mon-Fri 0900-1700; vac: Mon-Fri 0900-1300, 1400-1700
Subj: psy; experimental psy

S1719
Oxford University, Department of Human Anatomy and Genetics Library
South Parks Rd, Oxford, OX1 3QX (01865-272157; *fax:* 01865-272420)

Gov Body: Univ of Oxford (see **L4**) *Chief:* Offcr responsible: Dr S.J. Ward BSc, DPhil *Dep:* Libn: Mrs Philippa Franks
Entry: staff & grad students of the dept; other univ staff on appl to the Libn *Open:* term & vac: Mon-Fri 0900-1700
Subj: anatomy; genetics *Collns:* Bks & Pamphs: colln of reprints
Stock: bks/6000; periodcls/47; theses/30

S1720
Oxford University, Department of Materials, Materials Science Library
Hume-Rothery Bldg, Parks Rd, Oxford, OX1 3PH (01865-273697; *fax:* 01865-273789)
Email: library@materials.ox.ac.uk
Internet: http://www.materials.ox.ac.uk/research/

Gov Body: Univ of Oxford (see **L4**) *Chief:* Academic Libn: Dr David Bucknall BSc, PhD, DIC *Dep:* Libn: Mrs Mel Eyeons BTh (melanie.eyeons@materials.ox.ac.uk)
Entry: ref only, adv appt *Open:* term & vac: Mon-Fri 0900-1700 (Libn available 0900-1300)
Subj: materials sci; metallurgy
Equip: copier, 3 computers (all with wd-proc & internet) *Svcs:* Info, ref
Stock: bks/5000; periodcls/40; videos/85 *Acqs Offcr:* Academic Libn, as above
Classn: own *Auto Sys:* Geac *Staff:* Libns: 0.5

S1721
Oxford University, Department of Plant Sciences Library and Information Service
(incorporating the CAB International-Oxford Forestry Inst Info Svc)
Dept of Plant Sciences, South Parks Rd, Oxford, OX1 3RB (01865-275087; *fax:* 01865-275095)
Email: enquiries@plantlib.ox.ac.uk
Internet: http://www.plantlib.ox.ac.uk

Gov Body: Univ of Oxford (see **L4**) *Chief:* Head, Lib & Info Svc: Mr R.A. Mills MA, MCLIP *Other Snr Staff:* Reader Svcs Libn: Mrs J.B.D. Pinfold BA, DipLib; Special Collns Libn & Archivist: Mrs A.M. Townsend BSc, ARCS, MSc
Entry: open to the public for ref only *Open:* term & vac: Mon-Fri 0900-1730
Subj: plant biology; plant taxonomy; botany; forestry *Collns:* Bks & Pamphs: Sherard Colln (plant taxonomy) *Co-op Schemes:* BLDSC
Equip: m-readers, m-printers, copiers, computers (incl CD-ROM), scanner *Online:* AGRIS, Forestry Compendium, Index Kewensis, Prospect, Tree-CD (forestry colln catalogue & abstracts)
Stock: bks/70000; periodcls/2000
Classn: UDC *Auto Sys:* Dobis
Staff: Libns: 3 *Non-Prof:* 3

S1722
Oxford University, Department of Social Policy and Social Work Library
Barnett House, Wellington Sq, Oxford, OX1 2ER (01865-270322; *fax:* 01865-270324)
Email: library@socres.ox.ac.uk
Internet: http://www.ssl.ox.ac.uk/

Gov Body: Univ of Oxford (see **L4**) *Chief:* Libn: Ms Margaret Robb
Entry: membs of the Univ; others ref only with permission of Libn *Open:* term: Mon-Fri 0915-1645; vac: Mon-Fri 0930-1230, 1330-1630
Subj: psy; social sci; criminology; demography; health & welfare; social policy; social work
Equip: copier, 2 computers *Online:* various databases & e-journals via OXLIP *Svcs:* info, ref, biblio
Stock: bks/13000; periodcls/45
Classn: LC *Staff:* Libns: 1
Proj: lib to merge with other social sci libs in 2004

Oxford University, Department of the History of Art Library
See THE SACKLER LIB (**S1747**)

S1723
Oxford University, Department of Zoology Library
South Parks Rd, Oxford, OX1 3PS (01865-271141; *fax:* 01865-310447)
Email: zoolib@zoo.ox.ac.uk
Internet: http://users.ox.ac.uk/~zoolib/

Gov Body: Univ of Oxford (see **L4**) *Chief:* Departmental Libn: Dr M.L. Birch BSc, PhD (linda.birch@zoo.ox.ac.uk) *Dep:* Reader Svcs Libn: Ms N.L. Behmer (naomi.behmer@ zoo.ox.ac.uk)
Assoc Libs: ELTON LIB, contact details as above; EDWARD GREY INST OF FIELD ORNITHOLOGY, ALEXANDER LIB, also at above addr (see **S1725**)
Entry: membs of Univ's life scis depts; others ref only, adv appt *Open:* term & vac: Mon-Fri 0830-1700
Subj: Main Lib: zoology; Elton Lib: animal ecology
Collns: Archvs: small archv of rsrch notes & other materials by membs of Dept (late 19C-early 20C), incl photo albums of Challenger Expedition (1872-76) *Other:* rsrch papers & theses

Equip: m-reader, copier (5p per pg), 8 computers (all with internet & CD-ROM, 1 with wd-proc)
Officer-in-Charge: Departmental Libn, as above
Stock: bks/5700; periodcls/100; pamphs/39000
Acqs Offcr: Departmental Libn, as above
Staff: Libns: 1 *Other Prof:* 1

S1724
Oxford University, Economics Library
Manor Rd Bldg, Manor Rd, Oxford, OX1 3UQ (01865-271071; *fax:* 01865-271072)
Email: library@economics.ox.ac.uk
Internet: http://www.ssl.ox.ac.uk/

Gov Body: Univ of Oxford (see **L4**), Social Studies Faculty *Chief:* Libn: Ms M.G. Robb BS, MLS, MCLIP *Dep:* Dep Libn: Mrs Louise Clarke BA, MA, MCLIP
Entry: membs of Univ; others by appl to libn
Open: term: Mon-Thu 0900-2200, Fri 0900-1800, Sat 0930-1700; vac: Mon-Fri 0900-1800
Subj: social sci; econ; basic statistics *Collns:* Bks & Pamphs: working papers in econ *Co-op Schemes:* BLDSC, ILL
Equip: 2 m-readers, fax, 2 copiers, 12 computers (all with internet & CD-ROM, 4 with wd-proc)
Online: Dialog (at cost) *Svcs:* info, ref, biblio
Stock: bks/120000; periodcls/1700, plus 400 no longer current; pamphs/6000; m-forms/300
Classn: LC *Auto Sys:* Geac
Staff: Libns: 3 *Non-Prof:* 5 *Exp:* £400000 (1999-2000)

S1725
Oxford University, Edward Grey Institute of Field Ornithology, Alexander Library
South Parks Rd, Oxford, OX1 3PS (01865-271143; *fax:* 01865-310447)
Internet: http://users.oc.ac.uk/~zoolib/

Gov Body: Univ of Oxford (see **L4**), Dept of Zoology *Chief:* Libn: Dr M.L. Birch BSc, PhD (linda.birch@zoo.ox.ac.uk) *Dep:* Reader Svcs Libn: Ms N.L. Behmer (naomi.behmer@ zoo.ox.ac.uk)
Assoc Libs: DEPT OF ZOOLOGY MAIN LIB (see **S1723**); ELTON LIB; both at above addr
Entry: Univ, BOU & BTO membs, ornithology students & rsrchers for ref only, adv appt *Open:* Mon-Fri 0830-1700
Subj: ornithology *Collns:* Bks & Pamphs: British Ornithologists Union Lib; British Falconers' Club Lib *Archvs:* ornithological notebks of eminent ornithologists (mostly British) *Co-op Schemes:* BLDSC backup lib (photocopies only)
Equip: m-reader, copier, computer (incl CD-ROM) *Online:* available
Stock: bks/10200; periodcls/580, plus 1300 no longer current; m-forms/250; audios/100; archvs/40 linear m; reprints/83000; theses/430 *Acqs Offcr:* Libn, as above
Classn: own *Auto Sys:* Geac
Staff: Other Prof: 1

S1726
Oxford University, English Faculty Library
St Cross Bldg, Manor Rd, Oxford, OX1 3UQ (01865-271050; *fax:* 01865-271054)
Email: enquiries@efl.ox.ac.uk
Internet: http://users.ox.ac.uk/~enginfo/

Gov Body: Univ of Oxford (see **L4**) *Chief:* Libn: Ms Susan Usher BA(Hons), DipLib, MCLIP (susan.usher@efl.ox.ac.uk) *Dep:* Dep Libn: Ms Vanya Murray BA(Hons), MA, MCLIP (vanya. murray@efl.ox.ac.uk)

Special Libraries

Oxford
▼
Oxford

(Oxford Univ, English Faculty Lib cont)
Entry: open to faculty & students; others by appl
Open: term: Mon-Fri 0930-1900, Sat 0930-1230;
vac: Mon-Fri 0930-1700
Subj: English lang; English lit **Collns:** Bks &
Pamphs: c4000 pre-1800 bks; Icelandic & Old
Norse Collns; Wilfred Owen Lib **Archvs:** Wilfred
Owen MSS; E.H.W. Meyerstein MSS; A.S. Napier
MSS
Equip: m-reader, m-printer, 7 video viewers, fax, 2
copiers **Online:** various networked databases
Stock: bks/97000; periodcls/200; audios/500;
videos/4000
Classn: own **Auto Sys:** Geac Adv
Staff: Libns: 1 Other Prof: 3 Non-Prof: 1.79

S1727 🎓

Oxford University, Faculty of Modern Languages Library

Taylor Instn, St Giles', Oxford, OX1 3NA (01865-278152; *Libn:* 01865-278155)
Email: library@mlfl.ox.ac.uk

Gov Body: Univ of Oxford (see **L4**) **Chief:** Libn:
Mr G.L. Robson MA, DipLib **Dep:** Dep Libn: Mr
R.J. Shilcock BA
Entry: resident membs of Univ; others only if
sponsored by faculty memb **Open:** term: Mon-Fri
0900-1800, Sat 0900-1300; vac: Mon-Fri 0900-
1300, 1400-1730 (-1700 Jul-Sep)
Subj: Western European langs & lit; linguistics
Equip: m-reader, 2 copiers
Stock: bks/67000; periodcls/48; pamphs/100;
audios/1200; videos/2000
Classn: ML **Auto Sys:** Geac
Staff: Libns: 1 Non-Prof: 4 **Exp:** £29000 (1999-
2000)

S1728 🎓

Oxford University, Faculty of Music Library

St Aldate's, Oxford, OX1 1DB (01865-276146; *fax:*
01865-286260)
Internet: http://www.music.ox.ac.uk/library/

Gov Body: Univ of Oxford (see **L4**) **Chief:** Libn:
Mr John Wagstaff BA, MMus, MCLIP (john.
wagstaff@music.ox.ac.uk) **Dep:** Dep Libn: Ms
Julie Crawley MMus, MS (julie.crawley@music.ox.
ac.uk)
Entry: ref only to genl public; items loaned only to
membs of Univ **Open:** term: Mon-Fri 0930-1730,
Sat 1000-1300; vac: varies, generally Mon-Fri
1000-1300, 1400-1630
Subj: the arts, esp music **Collns:** Bks & Pamphs:
Sir Hugh Allen Colln (core colln); Oxford Univ
Music Soc Colln; Egon Wellesz Colln (Byzantine
music); Frank Howes Colln (folk song); various
other bequests **Co-op Schemes:** ILL
Equip: m-printer, video viewer, 2 copiers,
computer, 10 CD players, 5 record players,
cassette player **Online:** OCLC/RLIN
Stock: bks/36000; periodcls/90; pamphs/600; m-
forms/200; audios/12500 LPs, 3500 CDs; videos/
120 **Acqs Offcr:** Libn, as above
Classn: LC **Auto Sys:** Geac
Pubns: Lib Guide (free)
Staff: Libns: 2 Non-Prof: 0.88 **Exp:** £20975
(2000-01); £23593 (2001-02)

S1729 🎓

Oxford University, George Wiernik Library

Rsrch Inst, The Churchill Hosp, Headington,
Oxford, OX3 7LJ (01865-225815; *fax:* 01865-
225834)
Email: library@cairns-library.ox.ac.uk
Internet: http://www.medicine.ox.ac.uk/cairns/

Gov Body: Univ of Oxford, School of Clinical
Medicine **Chief:** Site Libn: Mrs Claire Abbott
(clare.abbott@cairns-library.ox.ac.uk) **Dep:** Lib
Asst: Ms Trish Howkins (trish.howkins@cairns-
library.ox.ac.uk)
Assoc Libs: branch of CAIRNS LIB, John Radcliffe
Hosp (see **S1749**); CAIRNS LIB, Radcliffe Infirmary
(see **S1708**)
Entry: membs of the Faculty of Clinical Medicine
& students of Oxford Medical School **Open:** term
& vac: Mon-Fri 0900-1730; staffed: Mon-Tue, Thu-
Fri 0900-1700, Wed 0930-1700
Subj: medicine; health; oncology; radiotherapy
Equip: copier, computers **Online:** numerous, incl
AMED, ASSIA, BNI, CINAHL, Cochrane, Embase,
HealthStar, Medline, PsycInfo, Web of Science
Stock: bks/1000; periodcls/28

S1730 🎓

Oxford University, History Faculty Library

Broad St, Oxford, OX1 3BD (01865-277262)
Email: library@history.ox.ac.uk
Internet: http://www.history.ox.ac.uk/libraryit/faclib/

Gov Body: Univ of Oxford (see **L4**) **Chief:** Hist
Libn: Dr Christopher Skelton-Foord MA, MLitt, MA,
PhD **Dep:** Dep Libn: Ms Valerie Lawrence BA,
DipLib, MCLIP **Other Snr Staff:** Principal Lib Asst
(Collns): Ms Suzanne Eckersley BSc(Econ);
Principal Lib Asst (Reader Svcs): Mr Simon Phillips
BA
Entry: current membs of Univ; others need to
register (forms available from lib) **Open:** term:
Mon-Fri 0900-1900, Sat 0900-1230; vac: Mon-Fri
0900-1730
Subj: modern hist; medieval hist; historiography;
hist of sci; hist of art; palaeography **Collns:** Bks &
Pamphs: strong collns in medieval sources &
palaeography
Equip: m-reader, copier, video viewer, 16
computers (incl 1 multimedia & 4 dedicated OLIS
terminals) **Online:** various online resources via
OXLIP
Stock: bks/73500; periodcls/60+; videos/36; CD-
ROMs/7
Staff: 7 in total

S1731 🎓 ✚

Oxford University, Institute of Health Sciences Library

Old Rd, Headington, Oxford, OX3 7LF (01865-
226688; *fax:* 01865-226619)
Email: library.enquiries@ihs.ox.ac.uk
Internet: http://www.ihs.ox.ac.uk/library/
homepage.htm

Gov Body: Univ of Oxford (see **L4**) **Chief:** Info
Svcs Mgr: Ms Nicola Bexon
Entry: membs of Inst only **Open:** Mon-Fri 0900-
1700
Subj: health policy; health mgmt; public health;
primary care **Co-op Schemes:** BLDSC, HeLIN
Equip: m-reader, m-printer, copier, 3 computers
(all with wd-proc, internet & CD-ROM) **Online:** Univ
networked resources **Svcs:** info, ref, biblio
Stock: bks/7000; periodcls/60
Classn: NLM **Auto Sys:** OLIS
Staff: Libns: 1 Non-Prof: 2

S1732 🎓

Oxford University, Institute of Social and Cultural Anthropology, Tylor Library

51 Banbury Rd, Oxford, OX2 6PE (01865-274687;
fax: 01865-274630)
Email: scalibrary@anthro.ox.ac.uk
Internet: http://www.rsl.ox.ac.uk/isca/

Gov Body: Univ of Oxford (see **L4**) **Chief:** Libn:
Mr Mike Morris BA, MA, DipLib, MCLIP
(mike.morris@anthro.ox.ac.uk)
Entry: ref only; rsrchers admitted by
recommendation/special permission **Open:** term:
Mon-Fri 0900-1245, 1415-1730, Sat 0930-1230;
vac: Mon-Fri 0900-1245, 1415-1700 (closed Aug)
Subj: anthro **Equip:** Online: OLIS

S1733 🎓

Oxford University, International Development Centre Library

Queen Elizabeth House, 21 St Giles, Oxford, OX1
3LA (01865-273629; *fax:* 01865-273607)
Email: library@qeh.ox.ac.uk
Internet: http://www.qeh.ox.ac.uk/library/

Gov Body: Univ of Oxford (see **L4**) **Chief:** Libn &
Info Svcs Mgr: Mrs Sheila L. Allcock BSc
(sheila.allcock@qeh.ox.ac.uk) **Dep:** Dep Libn: Ms
G.M. Short BEd
Assoc Libs: REFUGEE STUDIES CENTRE LIB
(see **S1744**)
Entry: ref only, adv appt by letter or tel; IDC Lib
lends to membs of Oxford Univ only **Open:** term:
Mon-Fri 0900-1800; vac: Mon-Fri 0900-1700
Subj: social sci; geog; hist; development studies;
agric econ **Collns:** Other: news cuttings of
developing countries (closed colln, 1950-95) **Co-
op Schemes:** ILL, document delivery for CABi
Equip: m-reader, copier **Disabled:** wheelchair
access to computers **Online:** OLIS **Officer-in-
Charge:** Libn & Info Svcs Mgr, as above **Svcs:**
info, ref, biblio
Stock: bks/60000; periodcls/600
Classn: classn for development studies **Auto
Sys:** Geac
Staff: Libns: 1 Non-Prof: 2.5 **Exp:** £24000 (1999-
2000); incl exp on binding

S1734 🎓

Oxford University, Language Centre, Library

12 Woodstock Rd, Oxford, OX2 6HT (01865-
283362; *fax:* 01865-283366)
Email: taube.marks@lang.ox.ac.uk
Internet: http://www.lang.ox.ac.uk/library.html

Gov Body: Univ of Oxford (see **L4**) **Chief:** Libn:
Ms Heidi T. Marks BA
Entry: ref only; membs of Univ, employees of Univ
depts & Colls; external users at discretion of dept &
on payment of fee **Open:** term: Mon-Thu 0930-
2000, Fri 0930-1830, Sat 1000-1300; wks 0 & 9:
Mon-Fri 0930-1830; vac (Xmas & Easter): Mon-Fri
0930-1300, 1400-1730; vac (summer): Mon-Fri
0830-1630
Subj: lang; linguistics; phonetics **Collns:** Bks &
Pamphs: lang learning materials; mono & bilingual
dictionaries; grammars; vocabulary texts **Archvs:**
audio & video cassettes of lang learning materials
Other: CALL programs
Equip: video viewer, copier, computers (incl
internet & CD-ROM) **Disabled:** audio-sound
recording-listening machines, computer-aided lang
learning **Svcs:** info, ref, biblio
Stock: bks/6000; periodcls/11; audios/15000;
videos/1800; CD-ROMs/175 **Acqs Offcr:** Libn, as
above
Classn: own
Pubns: language video materials
Staff: Libns: 1 Non-Prof: 5

 academic   corporate   **- 406 -**   governmental   medical

S1735 🎓

Oxford University, Latin American Centre Library

St Antony's Coll, Woodstock Rd, Oxford, OX2 6JF (01865-274483; *fax:* 01865-274489)
Email: ruth.hodges@lac.ox.ac.uk
Internet: http://www.lac.ox.ac.uk/

Gov Body: Univ of Oxford (see **L4**) *Chief:* Libn: Mrs Ruth C. Hodges MA, DipLib *Dep:* Asst Libn: Mrs Laura Salinas Wainwright BA, Dip Mgmt of Historic Archvs (Spain)
Assoc Libs: ST ANTONY'S COLL LIB (see **S1764**)
Entry: normally univ membs only, others in exceptional circumstances with refs *Open:* Mon-Fri 0900-1245, 1400-1700 (excl hols)
Subj: undergrad; postgrad; Latin America: hist; politics; econ; agric *Collns: Bks & Pamphs:* extensive boxed colln of pamphs on Latin America
Co-op Schemes: ILL
Equip: m-reader, fax, 2 computers *Online:* OLIS
Stock: bks/c9000; periodcls/36; pamphs/220 file boxes; m-forms/375
Classn: LC *Auto Sys:* OLIS *Staff: Libns:* 2

S1736 🎓

Oxford University, Mathematical Institute, Whitehead Library

24-29 St Giles, Oxford, OX1 3LB (01865-273559; *fax:* 01865-27353)
Email: cathy@maths.ox.ac.uk
Internet: http://www.maths.ox.ac.uk/

Gov Body: Univ of Oxford (see **L4**) *Chief:* Whitehead Libn: Prof F.C. Kirwan MA, DPhil, FRS
Dep: Asst Libn: Mrs Cathy Hunt BA, MSc
Entry: adv appt; open only to academic & postgrad membs of Maths Faculty & to certain membs of other Univ Depts *Open:* term & vac: Mon-Fri 0900-1700
Subj: maths (at postgrad level)

S1737 🎓

Oxford University, Middle East Centre Library and Archives

St Antony's Coll, 68 Woodstock Rd, Oxford, OX2 6JF (01865-284764; *fax:* 01865-311475)
Email: mastan.ebtehaj@sant.ox.ac.uk
Internet: http://www.sant.ox.ac.uk/areastudies/middle-east-library.shtml

Gov Body: Univ of Oxford (see **L4**) *Chief:* Libn: Mrs Mastan Ebtehaj
Assoc Libs: MIDDLE EAST CENTRE ARCHVS, at same addr, Archivist: Miss Debbie Usher (01865-284706; *fax:* 01865-311475; *email:* debbie.usher@sant.ox.ac.uk)
Entry: Lib: staff & grads of the Univ, ref access for undergrads reading Oriental Studies & other scholars & rsrchers holding a Bodleian Reader's Card (admission fee for outside users); *Archvs:* adv appt; membs of Univ & approved readers with letter of introduction *Open: Lib:* Mon-Fri 0930-1715; *Archvs:* Mon-Fri 0945-1300, 1400-1715
Subj: Middle East studies; Middle Eastern hist; Islam; Arabic lit; Ottoman Empire *Collns: Bks & Pamphs:* pamph colln; rare bks *Archvs:* Private Papers Colln (350+ collns of personal & official papers of indivs who served in Middle East, 18C-date); Photographic Archv (60000 images covering all areas of the Middle East, 1850s-1960s); both collns held in MEC Archvs *Other:* Arabic & other newspapers & weeklies on m-film, incl: Al-Ahram; Jerusalem Post; Umm al-Qura
Equip: copier
Stock: bks/35000; photos/60000; archvs/350+ collns

S1738 🎓 🏛

Oxford University, Museum of Natural History, The Hope Library

Parks Rd, Oxford, OX1 3PW (01865-272950/82; *fax:* 01865-272970)
Email: stella.brecknell@oum.ox.ac.uk
Internet: http://www.oum.ox.ac.uk/library.htm

Gov Body: Univ of Oxford (see **L4**) *Chief:* Libn: Ms S.M. Brecknell BA, DipLib, MCLIP
Assoc Libs: ARKELL LIB OF JURASSIC GEOL, addr as above, Libn: as above
Entry: anyone requiring rsrch-level taxonomic material, at the discretion of the Dir of the Museum; letter of recommendation from supervisor or recognised academic instn required for access to MSS *Open:* Mon-Fri 0900-1300, 1400-1700
Subj: nat hist; entomology; geol; palaeontology; mineralogy; zoology (mainly taxonomy) *Collns: Bks & Pamphs:* Arkell Lib & other geological collns; major entomological collns incl: Rev F.W. Hope Colln; J.O. Westwood Colln; Pickard-Cambridge Lib; F.P. Pascoe Lib; L.G. Higgins Lib *Archvs:* 19-20C entomological & geological MSS (diaries, letters, field notebks, lecture notes etc of eminent practitioners), incl: Rev F.W. Hope (entomology); William Smith papers (geol); William Buckland papers (geol); John Phillips papers (geol) *Other:* photos illustrating hist of museum etc *Co-op Schemes:* BLDSC
Equip: m-reader, copier, computer *Online:* online: Web of Science, COPAC,OCLC First Search; via CD-ROM: Zoological Record, Biological Abstracts, GeoRef, Geobase
Stock: bks/21000; periodcls/150, plus 180 no longer current
Classn: UDC, own *Staff: Libns:* 1

S1739 🎓 🏛

Oxford University, Museum of the History of Science Library

Old Ashmolean Bldg, Broad St, Oxford, OX1 3AZ (01865-277278; *fax:* 01865-277288)
Email: library@mhs.ox.ac.uk
Internet: http://www.mhs.ox.ac.uk/

Gov Body: Univ of Oxford (see **L4**) *Chief:* Libn: Ms Shona Marran MA(Hons), MSc (shona.marroan@mhs.ox.ac.uk)
Assoc Libs: MUSEUM OF THE HIST OF SCI ARCHVS, addr as above, Archivist: Mr A.V. Simcock (01865-87241; *email:* tony.simcock@mhs.ox.ac.uk)
Entry: by appt, ref only *Open:* Mon-Fri 0900-1300, 1400-1700; Archivist available Mon-Tue only
Subj: hist of scientific instruments; hist of sci; hist of maths; hist of tech
Equip: m-reader, copier, 2 computers
Stock: bks/18000; periodcls/15; various photos, illusts, pamphs, m-forms, CD-ROMs & archvs
Staff: Libns: 1

S1740 🎓

Oxford University, Nuclear and Astrophysics Library

Nuclear & Astrophysics Laboratory, Keble Rd, Oxford, OX1 3RH (01865-273421; *fax:* 01865-273418)
Email: library@physics.ox.ac.uk
Internet: http://www2.physics.ox.ac.uk/library/

Gov Body: Univ of Oxford (see **L4**), Dept of Physics *Chief:* Libn: Miss Amey Sherlock BA
Assoc Libs: CLARENDON LABORATORY LIB (see **S1712**)
Entry: admission to staff & grad students of Physics Dept only *Open:* term & vac: Mon-Fri 1400-1700; 24 hr access for those entitled to admission
Subj: particle & nuclear physics; astronomy; astrophysics

Equip: m-reader, fax (Dept), copier, 2 computers
Stock: bks/28000; periodcls/133; slides/1600; m-forms/3000
Classn: own *Auto Sys:* OLIS (Geac)
Staff: Libns: 1

S1741 🎓

Oxford University, Pauling Centre for Human Sciences Library

58 Banbury Rd, Oxford, OX2 6QS (01865-274702; *fax:* 01865-274699)
Email: ros.odling-smee@human-sciences.ox.ac.uk
Internet: http://www.human-sciences.ox.ac.uk/

Gov Body: Univ of Oxford (see **L4**) *Chief:* Libn: Mrs Ros Odling-Smee
Entry: staff & students in Human Scis; others ref only by appt *Open:* term: Mon-Fri 0900-1300, 1400-1630; vac: open 1st & last wks of long vac, otherwise closed
Subj: biology; evolution; human evolution; ecology; human sci; biological anthro; social anthro; genetics; zoology; social sci; demography; population studies

S1742 🎓 🏛

Oxford University, Pitt Rivers Museum, Balfour Library

School of Anthro & Museum of Ethnography, South Parks Rd, Oxford, OX1 3PP (01865-270939; *fax:* 01865-270943)
Email: mark.dickerson@prm.ox.ac.uk
Internet: http://www.prm.ox.ac.uk/balfour.html

Gov Body: Univ of Oxford (see **L4**) *Chief:* Libn: Mr Mark Dickerson MA, DipIM
Entry: adv appt *Open:* Oxford term: Mon-Fri 0900-1700; vac: Mon-Fri 0900-1230, 1400-1600 (closed Aug)
Subj: anthro; ethnomusicology; archaeo; material culture; ethnography
Equip: copier
Stock: bks/30000; periodcls/50
Classn: Bliss *Staff: Libns:* 1 *Non-Prof:* 0.5

S1743 🎓

Oxford University, Politics, International Relations and Sociology Library

Dept of Politics & Internatl Relations, George St, Oxford, OX1 2RL (01865-278710; *fax:* 01865-278711)
Email: library@socstud.ox.ac.uk
Internet: http://www.ssl.ox.ac.uk/

Gov Body: Univ of Oxford (see **L4**) *Chief:* Libn: Ms Margaret Robb BS, MLS, MCLIP (margaret.robb@ssl.ox.ac.uk) *Dep:* Dep Libn: Mrs Louise Clarke BA, MA, MCLIP (louise.clarke@ssl.ox.ac.uk)
Entry: membs of Univ *Open:* term: Mon-Fri 0900-1900, Sat 0930-1300; vac: Mon-Fri 0900-1700
Subj: social sci; politics; internatl relations; sociology
Equip: 2 copiers, 9 computers (incl 2 CD-ROM)
Online: local networked databases
Stock: bks/46000; periodcls/90
Classn: LC (mod) *Auto Sys:* Geac
Staff: Libns: 2 *Non-Prof:* 3

S1744 🎓

Oxford University, Refugee Studies Centre Library

Queen Elizabeth House, 21 St Giles, Oxford, OX1 3LA (01865-270298; *fax:* 01865-270721)
Email: rspdoc@ermine.ox.ac.uk
Internet: http://www.qeh.ox.ac.uk/rsp/

☞

Special Libraries

Oxford ▼ Oxford

Special Libraries

(Oxford Univ, Refugee Studies Centre Lib cont)
Gov Body: independent lib within Univ of Oxford (see **L4**) **Chief:** Libn: Ms Sarah Rhodes BA, DipLib, MA **Dep:** Ms Joanna Soedring BSc **Entry:** ref only for external readers; Refugee Studies Centre & Queen Elizabeth House postgrads may borrow **Open:** term: Mon-Fri 0900-1800; vac: Mon-Fri 0900-1700 **Subj:** social sci; refugee studies; forced migration; internal displacement **Collns:** *Bks & Pamphs:* unique grey lit colln on refugee issues (28000 items) *Archvs:* Paul Weis personal papers; Tristam Betts Africa Colln; Major Derek Cooper's personal papers (Middle East) **Equip:** m-form reader/printer, fax, video viewer, copier, 6 computers (all with internet, 3 with wd-proc, 3 with CD-ROM) **Online:** large selection as provided by OXLIP (Oxford Univ Libs Info Platform) **Svcs:** info ref, biblio, abstracting **Stock:** bks/5000; periodcls/240; AVs/310; archvs/35 linear m; grey lit/28000 items **Classn:** in-house **Auto Sys:** Geac, CardBox **Staff:** Libns: 1 Non-Prof: 1.5 **Exp:** £4500 (1999-2000)

S1745 🎓

Oxford University, Ruskin School of Drawing and Fine Art, Library

74 High St, Oxford, OX1 2BG (01865-276940; *fax:* 01865-276949)
Email: anne.gregory@ruskin-school.ox.ac.uk
Internet: http://www.ruskin-sch.ox.ac.uk

Gov Body: Univ of Oxford (see **L4**) **Chief:** Libn: Mrs Anne Gregory **Entry:** membs of univ reading Fine Art; others on appl (with recommendation) **Open:** term: Mon-Fri 0900-1700; vac: closed **Subj:** arts; fine art; art hist; art theory; human anatomy; art technique **Equip:** copier, computer (with wd-proc & internet) **Online:** OLIS (free) **Staff:** Libns: 1 Other Prof: 1 Non-Prof: 1

S1746 🎓

Oxford University, Russian and East European Centre Library

St Antony's Coll, 68 Woodstock Rd, Oxford, OX2 6JF (01865-284728; *fax:* 01865-310518)
Email: jackie.willcox@sant.ox.ac.uk
Internet: http://www.sant.ox.ac.uk/russian/

Gov Body: Univ of Oxford (see **L4**) **Chief:** Libn: Ms Jackie Willcox **Entry:** academic staff & postgrad students of the Univ; ref only for membs of other academic instns (letter of introduction required) **Open:** term & vac: Mon-Tue, Thu-Fri 0900-1700, Wed 0900-1300 **Subj:** Russian & East European studies; special strengths in Russian & Soviet politics, hist & lit **Stock:** bks/c24000 **Staff:** Non-Prof: 1

S1747 🎓

Oxford University, Sackler Library

(incorporating the former Ashmolean Lib, Griffith Inst Lib, Western Art Lib, Classics Lending Lib, Hist of Art Lib & Eastern Art Lib)
1 St John St, Oxford, OX1 2LG (01865-278088; *fax:* 01865-278098)
Internet: http://www.saclib.ox.ac.uk/

Gov Body: Univ of Oxford (see **L4**) **Chief:** Libn: Mr James Legg (james.legg@saclib.ox.ac.uk) **Dep:** Dep Libn: Dr Graham Piddock MA, DPhil (graham.piddock@saclib.ox.ac.uk) **Assoc Libs:** HEBERDEN COIN ROOM LIB (accessible via the Ashmolean Museum); the Sackler Lib also incorporates THE GRIFFITH INST LIB & ARCHVS **Entry:** adv appt, ref only **Open:** *Main Lib:* Mon-Fri 0900-2200, Sat 1000-1700; *Heberden Coin Room Lib:* Tue-Fri 1000-1645, Sat 1000-1300; *Griffith Inst Archvs:* Mon-Fri 0915-1645 **Subj:** arch; prehistoric archaeo; classics; classical archaeo; European archaeo; classical art; fine art; Byzantine art; ancient hist; epigraphy; classical langs; classical lit; papyrology; Egyptology; cuneiform langs; numismatics; Western art hist (9C-date); Ancient Near Eastern studies **Collns:** *Bks & Pamphs:* Griffith Inst Lib (Egyptology, Coptic & Ancient Near Eastern studies, 30000 titles); Oxford Architectural & Historical Soc Lib; Grenfell & Hunt Papyrological Lib; Haskell Colln; Wind Colln (iconography & iconology); Hope Colln of early illustrated bks (primarily portraiture & topography); French Salon Criticism (important 19C colln) *Archvs:* Griffith Inst Archvs (Egyptology); Haverfield Archv; notebks & papers of Sir Ian Richmond *Other:* photographic archv (on m-fiche) of the Deutsches Archäologisches Institut in Rome **Equip:** *Online:* OLIS **Stock:** bks/256000; periodcls/2270; maps/700 **Staff:** 16 in total

S1748 🎓

Oxford University, Said Business School, Sainsbury Library

Said Business School, Park End St, Oxford, OX1 1HP (01865-288880)
Email: gslibrary@sbs.ox.ac.uk
Internet: http://www.sbs.ox.ac.uk/

Gov Body: Univ of Oxford (see **L4**) **Chief:** Lib Svcs Mgr: Ms Fiona Richardson BA, MSc, MCLIP **Other Snr Staff:** Snr Info Offcr: Mr Andy Priestner (andy.priestner@sbs.ox.ac.uk); Snr Info Offcr: Ms Sharon Cure (sharon.cure@sbs.ox.ac.uk) **Entry:** Oxford Univ membs & visiting academics (by prior appt) **Open:** staffed hrs: Mon-Fri 0900-1900, Sat 1100-1700 **Subj:** business; mgmt studies; business admin **Equip:** 2 copiers (5p), 30 computers (all with wd-proc, CD-ROM & internet) **Online:** Virtual Lib carries databases & reading lists (membs of the school only) **Svcs:** info, ref **Classn:** London Business School (LCBS) **Auto Sys:** Geac **Staff:** Libns: 3 Non-Prof: 4

S1749 🎓 ➕

Oxford University, School of Clinical Medicine, The Cairns Library

John Radcliffe Hosp, Headington, Oxford, OX3 9DU (01865-221936; *fax:* 01865-221941)
Email: library@cairns-library.ox.ac.uk
Internet: http://www.medicine.ox.ac.uk/cairns/

Gov Body: Univ of Oxford (see **L4**) **Chief:** Head of Health Care Libs: Mr Steven Rose BA(Hons), MSc, DipLib (steve.rose@cairns-library.ox.ac.uk) **Other Snr Staff:** Reader Svcs Mgr: Ms Helen Carter (helen.carter@cairns-library.ox.ac.uk); Lib Administrator: Ms Anne-Marie Cawasjee (anne-marie.cawasjee@cairns-library.ox.ac.uk) **Assoc Libs:** GEORGE WIERNIK LIB (see **S1729**); CAIRNS LIB (see **S1708**); INST OF HEALTH SCIS LIB (see **S1731**) **Entry:** ref only **Open:** *John Radcliffe Hosp:* open 24 hrs (access control sys); staffed in term: Mon-Fri 0900-2100; vac: Mon-Fri 0900-1700, opens 0930 Wed, term & vac **Subj:** medicine; clinical sci **Collns:** *Archvs:* newspaper cuttings **Co-op Schemes:** HeLIN

Equip: video viewer, 6 copiers, 22 computers (all with internet & CD-ROM), 2 rooms for hire **Online:** Datastar, BIOS, ASSIA, CINAHL, Cochrane, EMBASE, Medline, Best Evidence & others **Svcs:** info, ref, biblio **Stock:** bks/12000; periodcls/450 **Classn:** NLM **Auto Sys:** Geac **Staff:** Libns: 9 Other Prof: 3 Non-Prof: 10

S1750 🎓

Oxford University, School of Geography and the Environment Library

Mansfield Rd, Oxford, OX1 3TB (01865-271912; *fax:* 01865-271929)
Email: linda.atkinson@geog.ox.ac.uk
Internet: http://www.geog.ox.ac.uk/facilities/library/

Gov Body: Univ of Oxford (see **L4**) **Chief:** Libn: Mrs Linda Atkinson BSc, MSc, MCLIP **Assoc Libs:** OXFORD MOUNTAINEERING LIB, contact: Mrs S.L. Atkinson & Oxford Univ Mountaineering Club **Entry:** ref only, prefer adv appt **Open:** term: Mon-Fri 0930-1800, Sat 1000-1300; vac: Mon-Fri 0900-1300, 1400-1700 **Subj:** geog; meteorology; environmental change **Collns:** *Bks & Pamphs:* Oxford Mountaineering Lib (1800-date); mountaineering journals; atlases *Archvs:* Halford-Mackinder Archv *Other:* maps **Co-op Schemes:** BLDSC, ILL **Equip:** 3 m-readers, m-printer, 2 copiers, 15 computers (incl 5 with wd-proc, 6 with internet & 6 with CD-ROM, wd-procs for dept membs only) **Online:** OCLC FirstSearch, RLIN, MIMAS WOS, COPAC (Univ membs only) **Officer-in-Charge:** Libn, as above **Svcs:** info, ref, biblio **Stock:** bks/60000; periodcls/190; photos/4000; slides/3500; pamphs/12000; maps/60000; m-forms/500; archvs/2 linear m **Acqs Offcr:** Libn, as above **Classn:** own **Auto Sys:** Geac **Staff:** Libns: 2 Non-Prof: 2 **Exp:** £30000 (1999-2000); £30000 (2000-01) **Further Info:** The School, incl the lib, will be relocating to a new site in summer 2004

S1751 🎓

Oxford University, Taylor Institution Library

Univ of Oxford, St Giles', Oxford, OX1 3NA (01865-278158; *fax:* 01865-278165)
Email: enquiries@taylib.ox.ac.uk
Internet: http://www.taylib.ox.ac.uk/

Type: rsrch **Gov Body:** Univ of Oxford (see **L4**) **Chief:** Libn: Ms E.A. Chapman BA, MA, DipLib, FCLIP **Dep:** Dep Libn: Ms A.J. Peters BA, MA, DipLib **Assoc Libs:** TAYLOR INSTN, SLAVONIC & GREEK LIB, Univ of Oxford, 47 Wellington Sq, Oxford, OX1 2HF (01865-270464; *fax:* 01865-270469) **Entry:** rsrch level; apply in writing to the Libn **Open:** 1 Oct-30 Jun: Mon-Fri 0900-1900, Sat 0900-1300; 1st July-30 Sept: Mon-Fri 0900-1300, 1400-1700, Sat 1000-1300 **Subj:** modern continental European langs & lit, incl those of Latin America, Canada & North & sub-Saharan Africa; linguistics; *Slavonic & Greek Lib:* Russian & other Slavonic langs; modern Greek **Collns:** *Bks & Pamphs:* Voltaire & the French Enlightenment; Latin American, Yiddish, Francophone African, Canadian, North & sub-Saharan African & Celtic lit; lit of the former GDR; bks on Anglo-German relations & Goethezeit; Luther Flugschriften & the Fiedler Colln; Dante & futurist holdings; Golden Age lit; Strachan Colln (livres d'artistes); Slavonic & modern Greek collns; Morfill Colln (Russian); Nevill Forves Colln (Russian); Dawkins Colln (Greek); Hasluck Colln (Albanian) **Co-op Schemes:** BLDSC, ILL

🎓 academic   corporate   **- 408 -**   governmental   ➕ medical

Equip: m-reader, m-printer, copiers, computers (with CD-ROM), scanner *Officer-in-Charge:* Dep Libn, as above
Stock: bks/c510000; periodcls/1334 *Acqs Offcr:* Dep Libn, as above
Classn: own *Auto Sys:* Geac, OLIS
Pubns: A Checklist of Eds of Major French Authors in Oxford Libs 1526-1800
Staff: Libns: 2 *Other Prof:* 7

S1752

Oxford University, Theology Faculty Library

41 St Giles, Oxford, OX1 3LW (01865-270731; *fax:* 01865-270796)
Email: library@theology.ox.ac.uk
Internet: http://www.theology.ox.ac.uk/

Gov Body: Univ of Oxford (see **L4**) *Chief:* Libn: Miss Kate Alderson-Smith BA, MA *Dep:* Dep Libn: Miss Ruth Harris
Entry: matriculated & official visitors to Univ; others by appl to Libn as lib of last resort within Oxford *Open:* term: Mon-Fri 0930-1700, Sat 0930-1300; vac: Mon-Fri 1000-1300,1400-1700
Subj: religion; theology; biblical studies; Christian doctrine; church hist; patristics; liturgy; psy, sociology & phil of religion; sci & religion
Equip: copier, computers (incl wd-proc, internet & CD-ROM) *Online:* ATLA Religion Database, FRANCIS, Philosophers Index, Index Islamicus, Internatl Medieval Bibliography, Old Testament Abstracts, New Testament Abstracts

S1753

Oxford University, Transport Studies Unit Library

11 Bevington Rd, Oxford, OX2 6NB (01865-274715; *fax:* 01865-515194)
Email: sylvia.boyce@tsu.ox.ac.uk
Internet: http://www.tsu.ox.ac.uk/

Gov Body: Univ of Oxford (see **L4**) *Chief:* Administrator: Mrs Sylvia Boyce
Entry: ref only; adv appt *Open:* Mon-Fri 1000-1400, otherwise by appt
Subj: transport
Equip: copier, computer (with wd-proc & internet) *Officer-in-Charge:* Administrator, as above *Svcs:* ref
Stock: bks/c3050; periodcls/14 *Acqs Offcr:* Administrator, as above
Classn: own *Staff: Non-Prof:* 1 PT

S1754

Oxford University, University Laboratory of Physiology Library

(incorporating the Sherrington Room Lib for the Hist of Neuroscience)
Univ Laboratory of Physiology, Parks Rd, Oxford, OX1 3PT (01865-272524; *fax:* 01865-272469)
Email: library@physiol.ox.ac.uk
Internet: http://www.physiol.ox.ac.uk/Library/

Gov Body: Univ of Oxford (see **L4**) *Chief:* Libn: Mrs Sophie Wilcox BSc(Hons), MA
Entry: on appl to libn for ref only *Open:* Mon-Thu 0800-1600
Subj: undergrad; postgrad; psy; physiology; neuroscience *Collns: Bks & Pamphs:* Sherrington Room Lib (hist of neuroscience & related subjs); material relating to Sir Charles Sherrington *Archvs:* colln of letters & photos & other memorabilia relating to Charles Sherrington
Equip: m-reader, 2 copiers (5p per pg), 3 computers (all with internet & CD-ROM), scanner *Online:* variety of on-line svcs available via OXLIP
Svcs: info, ref, biblio
Stock: bks/15626; periodcls/93; photos/200; CD-ROMs/14; archvs/10 linear m

Classn: own *Auto Sys:* Geac
Pubns: Bi-annual Report of the Sherrington Room (free)
Staff: Libns: 0.6 *Non-Prof:* 0.4 *Exp:* £52400 (1999-2000)

S1755

Oxford University, Wellcome Unit for the History of Medicine Library

45-47 Banbury Rd, Oxford, OX2 6PE (01865-274604; *fax:* 01865-274605)
Email: library@wuhmo.ox.ac.uk
Internet: http://www.wuhmo.ox.ac.uk/library/

Gov Body: Univ of Oxford (see **L4**) *Chief:* Libn: Miss Suzanne Eckersley BSc(Econ) (suzanne. eckersley@history-library.ox.ac.uk) *Dep:* Lib Asst: Mrs Jane Phipps
Entry: ref only, adv appt *Open:* libn present only for limited hrs; please check web site for opening times
Subj: hist of medicine; particular strengths in: natl & local public health admin; UK hosps & hosp movements; infectious diseases; tropical medicine; pharmacology; biography
Equip: copier (A4/10p, A3/20p), clr copier (A4/15p, A3/30p), computers (incl 3 with CD-ROM & 3 with internet)
Stock: bks/c15000, incl periodcls
Classn: NLM *Auto Sys:* Geac
Staff: Libns: 1 PT *Non-Prof:* 1 PT

S1756

Pembroke College, McGowin Library

Pembroke Sq, Oxford, OX1 1DW (01865-276409; *fax:* 01865-276418)
Email: library@pembroke.oxford.ac.uk
Internet: http://www.pmb.ox.ac.uk/Library/library.html

Gov Body: Pembroke Coll *Chief:* Fellow Libn: Dr C. Melchert BA, MA, PhD *Dep:* Libn & Archivist: Miss E.J. Pike MA, MSc
Entry: adv appt *Open:* term: Mon-Sun 0900-2400; vac: Mon-Fri 0900-1700
Subj: all subjs; undergrad *Collns: Bks & Pamphs:* Samuel Johnson; Aristotle *Archvs:* Coll Archvs
Equip: m-reader, 5 computers (incl 4 internet & 1 CD-ROM)
Stock: bks/40000; periodcls/100; photos/c1000; slides/c100; pamphs/some; videos/some; archvs/150 linear m
Classn: own *Staff: Libns:* 1 *Non-Prof:* 0.5

S1757

Plater College Library

Pullens Ln, Oxford, OX3 0DT (01865-740516; *fax:* 01865-740510)
Email: cgibbins@plater.ac.uk

Chief: Libn: Mrs C. Gibbins BA, MCLIP
Entry: Plater Coll students, others ref only *Open:* Mon-Sun 0830-2300
Subj: genl; A level; undergrad; generalities; phil; psy; religion; social sci; hist *Collns: Bks & Pamphs:* materials pertaining to Catholic Social Guild
Equip: video viewer, copier, 2 computers (both with wd-proc, internet & CD-ROM)
Stock: bks/12500; periodcls/50; audios/50; videos/50
Classn: DDC, own *Auto Sys:* Heritage
Staff: Libns: 1 *Exp:* £10000 (1999-2000); £7500 (2000-01)

S1758

Plunkett Foundation Reference Library and Information Centre

23 Hanborough Business Pk, Long Hanborough, Oxford, OX29 8SG (01993-883636; *fax:* 01993-883576)
Email: info@plunkett.co.uk
Internet: http://www.plunkett.co.uk/

Chief: Info Svcs Mgr: Mrs Elodie Nallomme
Entry: adv appt, ref only *Open:* Mon-Fri 0900-1700
Subj: social sci; hist; co-operatives & co-op movement (all aspects, 1860s-date), incl: agric; banking; business; econ; edu; finance; gender issues; health care; housing; insurance; law; mgmt; marketing; political & economic phil; rural development; training; worker-owned businesses
Collns: Archvs: diaries & letters of Horace Plunkett (1881-1932); documents relating to IAOS; SAOS; Irish Recess Cttee (1896); Irish Convention (1917-18) *Co-op Schemes:* ILL
Equip: copier (10p per copy), computer (with wd-proc, internet & CD-ROM), room for hire *Online:* catalogue available online at web site *Svcs:* info, ref, biblio, abstracting
Stock: bks/10000; periodcls/100; pamphs/5000
Classn: DDC *Auto Sys:* Reference Manager
Pubns: The World of Co-op Enterprise; Directory of Agricultural Co-operatives; Facts & Figures About Farmer Controlled Business
Staff: Libns: 1 *Non-Prof:* 8

S1759

The Queen's College Library

High St, Oxford, OX1 4AW (01865-279130; *fax:* 01865-790819)
Email: library@queens.ox.ac.uk
Internet: http://www.queens.ox.ac.uk/library/

Gov Body: The Provost & Fellows of Queen's Coll Oxford *Chief:* Libn: Ms Amanda Saville MA(Cantab), MA(Sheffield), MCLIP (amanda. saville@queens.ox.ac.uk) *Dep:* Asst Libn (Admin): Ms Tessa Shaw BA, DipLib (tessa.shaw@ queens.ox.ac.uk) *Other Snr Staff:* Asst Libn (Cataloguing): Mrs Veronika Vernier BA, PGDip *Assoc Libs:* PEET OF EGYPTOLOGY, contact details & staff as above; COLL ARCHVS, addr as above, Archivist: Mr Michael Riordan (michael.riordan@queens.ox.ac.uk)
Entry: lending to membs only; ref only by adv appt for others *Open:* term: varies, contact lib for details; vac: Mon-Fri 0930-1630
Subj: all subjs; undergrad; postgrad *Collns: Bks & Pamphs:* rare & antique bks; historical collns (particularly strong in classics, phil, theology & church hist, tracts & proclamations, ecclesiastical law, early medicine & British regional hist) *Archvs:* 500 medieval & post-medieval MSS; Coll Archvs are administered separately *Co-op Schemes:* ILL, OLIS
Equip: m-reader, m-printer, copier, 5 computers (all with wd-proc, internet & CD-ROM) *Online:* OXLIP, OLIS *Officer-in-Charge:* Asst Libn (Admin), as above *Svcs:* info, ref, biblio
Stock: bks/150000; periodcls/120; videos/2; CD-ROMs/100; archvs/c500 MSS *Acqs Offcr:* Asst Libn (Admin), as above
Classn: own *Auto Sys:* Geac
Pubns: Treasures of the Queen's Coll Lib (£3)
Staff: Libns: 2 *Other Prof:* 1 *Non-Prof:* 1 *Exp:* £36000 (1999-2000); £38000 (2000-01)

S1760

Regent's Park College Library

Pusey St, Oxford, OX1 2LB (01865-288127/42; *fax:* 01865-288121)
Email: sue.mills@regents.ox.ac.uk

(Regent's Park Coll Lib cont)

Gov Body: Regent's Park Coll **Chief:** Libn: Mrs Susan J. Mills MA, MA, MCLIP **Dep:** Lib Asst: Mrs. Sheila Wood
Assoc Libs: THE ANGUS LIB, addr as above (01865-288142); COLL ARCHVS, Archivist: Mrs Jennifer Thorp BA (01865-288142; *email:* jennifer.thorp@regents.ox.ac.uk)
Entry: Coll Lib: Coll membs only; Angus Lib: adv appt, with written refs **Open:** Coll Lib: 24 hrs to RPC students; Angus Lib: Mon-Fri 0930-1600
Subj: phil; psy; religion; social sci; lang; arts; lit; geog; hist **Collns:** Bks & Pamphs: The Angus Lib (c70000 items, Baptist hist & Baptist authors, 17C-20C, other nonconformist authors, 16C-19C, incorporates former Baptist Union & Baptist Historical Soc Libs); David Nicholls Colln (church & state, political theology, Caribbean, esp Haiti) **Archvs:** Baptist Missionary Soc Archvs on deposit; Baptist church records; Coll archvs; Baptist Union & other Baptist orgs & assocs minute bks **Other:** many misc MSS from prominent Baptists; good runs of most 19C Baptist periodcls **Co-op Schemes:** OLIS, RSLP projs
Equip: m-readers, m-printer, copier **Online:** OLIS & svcs networked within Oxford Univ **Svcs:** info, ref
Stock: bks/50000; periodcls/150; pamphs/10000; m-forms/200; archvs/400 m; BMS Archvs: photos/25000; slides/7000; maps/10 drawers
Classn: DDC (Coll lib)
Pubns: Sources for the Study of Baptist Hist (offprint from Baptist Quarterly April 1992, £2); From Stepney to St Giles (£2.50)
Staff: Libns: 1 Other Prof: 1 archivist Non-Prof: 1

S1761
Ruskin College Library
Walton St, Oxford, OX1 2HE (01865-554331; *fax:* 01865-554372)
Email: library@ruskin.ac.uk

Chief: Libn: Mr D.F.M. Horsfield MA, DipLib **Dep:** Asst Libn: Mrs C. Keable BA, MCLIP
Entry: ref only, by special arrangement (prior appt necessary) **Open:** term: Mon-Fri 0900-1700; vac: by arrangement
Subj: social studies; industrial relations; social work; community work; lit in English; hist; women's studies **Collns:** Archvs: 20C British Labour movement & working class hist; James & Lucy Middleton papers; Ewan Maccoll/Peggy Seeger Archv **Co-op Schemes:** BLDSC
Equip: m-reader, video viewer, copier, 12 computers (all with wd-proc, internet & CD-ROM), reel-to-reel tape recorder, cassette player
Stock: bks/35000; periodcls/150; photos/300; pamphs/7000; audios/50; videos/85; archvs/200 ft
Classn: DDC **Auto Sys:** Alice
Staff: Libns: 2 Non-Prof: 1

S1762
Somerville College Library
Woodstock Rd, Oxford, OX2 6HD (01865-270694; *fax:* 01865-270620)
Email: library@somerville.oxford.ac.uk

Gov Body: Somerville Coll **Chief:** Libn & Fellow in Charge: Miss Pauline Adams BLitt, MA, DipLib (pauline.adams@somerville.ox.ac.uk) **Dep:** Asst Libn: Miss Susan Purver MA, DipLIS

Entry: open to membs of Coll only; accredited scholars may, by prior arrangement with libn, consult special collns **Open:** term: Mon-Fri 0900-1800, Sat 0900-1300; vac: Mon-Fri 0900-1700
Subj: all subjs; undergrad; postgrad **Collns:** Bks & Pamphs: John Stuart Mill Lib; Amelia B. Edwards Lib **Archvs:** Amelia B. Edwards MSS; Vernon Lee MSS; Percy Withers MSS; Margaret Kennedy MSS; Vera Brittain MSS
Equip: m-reader
Stock: bks/120000; periodcls/122; pamphs/3000
Classn: DDC (mod) **Staff:** Libns: 2 Non-Prof: 1

S1763
St Anne's College Library
Woodstock Rd, Oxford, OX2 6RL (01865-274811; *fax:* 01865-274899)
Email: david.smith@st-annes.oxford.ac.uk

Gov Body: St Anne's Coll **Chief:** Libn: Dr David F. Smith MA, DPhil, MCLIP **Dep:** Asst Libn: Mrs A.S. Corley MA, CertEd
Entry: by written appl to libn
Subj: all subjs; undergrad **Collns:** Bks & Pamphs: Handover Bequest (hist of printing) **Archvs:** material on hist of the Coll & of women's edu at Oxford **Co-op Schemes:** OLIS
Equip: 2 m-readers, copier, 3 computers
Stock: bks/105000; periodcls/220; photos/50; pamphs/5000; archvs/10 linear m
Classn: DDC **Auto Sys:** Geac
Staff: Libns: 2 Non-Prof: 2 Exp: £44580 (1999-2000)

S1764
St Antony's College Library
62 Woodstock Rd, Oxford, OX2 6JF (01865-284700; *fax:* 01865-301518)
Email: rosamund.campbell@sant.ox.ac.uk

Gov Body: St Antony's Coll **Chief:** Lib Fellow: Dr R.J. Svc MA, PhD **Dep:** Libn: Ms R. Campbell MA
Assoc Libs: MIDDLE EAST CENTRE LIB (see **S1737**); LATIN AMERICAN CENTRE LIB (see **S1735**); RUSSIAN & EAST EUROPEAN CENTRE LIB (see **S1746**)
Entry: non-membs may be admitted, under special circumstances; by written appl only, to the Lib Fellow, giving reasons for use **Open:** term: Mon-Fri 0900-1700; vac: variable
Subj: modern hist; politics; econ; internatl affairs
Collns: Archvs: 20C archvs (incl Genl Sir Neill Malcolm papers & Sir John Wheeler-Bennett papers) **Co-op Schemes:** BLDSC
Equip: m-reader, copier **Online:** OLIS
Stock: bks/100000; periodcls/250

S1765
St Catherine's College Library
Manor Rd, Oxford, OX1 3UJ (01865-271707)
Email: library@stcatz.ox.ac.uk

Chief: Fellow Libn: Dr A.G. Rosser MA, PhD
Dep: Asst Libn: Mrs S. Collins
Entry: membs of Coll only; not available to public
Open: Mon-Fri 0830-0000, Sat-Sun 0900-0000
Subj: all subjs; undergrad
Equip: copier, computers (incl internet)
Stock: bks & periodcls/50000

S1766
St Cross College Library
St Giles, Oxford, OX1 3LZ (01865-278481; *fax:* 01865-311765)
Email: librarian@stx.ox.ac.uk
Internet: http://www.stx.ox.ac.uk/

Gov Body: Univ of Oxford (see **L4**) **Chief:** Libn: Ms Sheila L. Allcock BSc(Hons)
Assoc Libs: COLL ARCHVS, Archivist: Dr A.E. Coates MA, DPhil, DipLib

Entry: membs of Coll only; others by adv appt **Open:** 24 hrs to Coll membs
Subj: all subjs; postgrad **Co-op Schemes:** cataloguing on to OLIS (Oxford Lib System)
Equip: computers (with access to CD-ROM network & access to internet via OXLIP) **Svcs:** info, ref, biblio, lending to Coll membs
Stock: bks/3000
Classn: DDC **Auto Sys:** Geac **Staff:** Libns: 0.33

S1767
St Edmund Hall Library
Queen's Ln, Oxford, OX1 4AR (01865-279000; *fax:* 01865-279062)
Email: deborah.eaton@seh.ox.ac.uk

Gov Body: St Edmund Hall **Chief:** Libn: Miss Deborah Eaton BA, MA **Dep:** Asst to the Libn: Mrs Ailsa Crofts
Assoc Libs: OLD LIB, Libn: as above; ST EDMUND HALL ARCHVS, Archivist: Dr R. Crampton MA, PhD (01865-279015)
Entry: adv appt **Open:** term: Mon-Fri 0830-0100; vac: Mon-Fri 0830-2245
Subj: phil; psy; social sci; lang; arts; sci; maths; tech; lit; geog; hist **Collns:** Bks & Pamphs: Emden Colln (military hist); Hearne Colln (works by Thomas Hearne); definitive colln of works concerning early Evangelical Movement in Britain
Equip: 2 m-readers, copier, 11 computers (all with internet & CD-ROM, 7 with wd-proc), microscope, molecular models, skeleton **Online:** OLIS **Svcs:** info, ref
Stock: bks/50000; periodcls/150; videos/50; CD-ROMs/25
Classn: Sui Generis **Auto Sys:** Geac
Staff: Libns: 1 Other Prof: 1 Non-Prof: 1
Proj: redecoration & refurnishing; laptop carrels

S1768
St Hilda's College Library
Cowley Pl, Oxford, OX4 1DY (01865-276848)
Email: maria.croghan@st-hildas.ox.ac.uk

Gov Body: St Hilda's Coll **Chief:** Libn: Miss M.F.J. Croghan MA, MCLIP **Dep:** Asst Libn: Mr T. Kirtley BA, MA
Assoc Libs: COLL ARCHVS, Archivist: Mrs E. Boardman BA, DipAA (01865-276882)
Entry: adv appt, ref only **Open:** term: Mon-Fri 0830-1800; vac: Mon-Fri 0930-1700
Subj: undergrad; most academic subjs **Collns:** Archvs: Coll archvs; early hist of univ edu for women **Other:** music MSS of Elizabeth Maconchy
Equip: copier **Online:** BIDS, OLIS
Stock: bks/60000; periodcls/132; audios/200; videos/1
Classn: DDC (mod) **Auto Sys:** Heritage
Pubns: The Centenary Hist of St Hilda's Coll, Oxford (£10.95)
Staff: Libns: 2 Non-Prof: 1

S1769
St Hugh's College Library
St Margaret's Rd, Oxford, OX2 6LE (01865-274938; *fax:* 01865-274912)
Email: library@st-hughs.ox.ac.uk
Internet: http://www.st-hughs.ox.ac.uk/

Gov Body: St Hugh's Coll **Chief:** Libn & Archivist: Miss Deborah Quare BA, MLitt, MCLIP
Entry: membs of St Hugh's Coll; others by adv appt with Libn
Subj: all subjs; undergrad; postgrad **Collns:** Bks & Pamphs: Oxford Movement Colln; Nat Hist & Ornithology Colln **Archvs:** St Hugh's Coll Archvs; medical records from the WW2 when the Coll was requisitioned as a Military Hosp for Head Injuries
Co-op Schemes: OLIS
Stock: bks/95342; periodcls/94
Classn: DDC **Auto Sys:** Geac
Staff: Libns: 1 Non-Prof: 2

S1770

St John's College, Library

St Giles', Oxford, OX1 3JP (01865-277330/1; *fax:* 01865-277435)
Email: library@sjc.ox.ac.uk
Internet: http://www.sjc.ox.ac.uk/college/library/ library.html

Chief: Fellow Libn: Dr P.M.S. Hacker MA, DPhil
Dep: Libn: Mrs Catherine Hilliard MA, MLIS (catherine.hilliard@sjc.ox.ac.uk) *Other Snr Staff:* Lib Administrator: Mrs Ruth Ogden BA, DipLib (ruth.ogden@sjc.ox.ac.uk)
Assoc Libs: COLL ARCHVS, addr as above, contact Keeper of Muniments: Dr. M.G.A. Vale or Asst Archivist: Mr. M.K. Riordan (e-mail: archives@ sjc.ox.ac.uk).
Entry: membs of Coll only; others by arrangement *Open:* term: Mon-Sat 0900-2300, Sun 1000-2300; vac: hrs vary, closed several wks in summer
Subj: all subjs; undergrad; local study (Oxfordshire) *Collns: Bks & Pamphs:* Bulmer-Thomas Colln (hist of maths & sci) *Archvs:* Coll archvs, incl papers & estate maps (administered separately) *Co-op Schemes:* occasional ILL (not theses – available from Bodleian Lib or BLDSC)
Equip: m-reader, m-printer, copier, 2 computers (incl wd-proc, internet & CD-ROM) *Disabled:* Kurzweil (available in Coll, not lib) *Online:* access to Univ of Oxford, Bodleian & remote databases
Svcs: ref
Stock: bks/c80000; periodcls/190; videos/50 *Acqs Offcr:* Libn, as above
Classn: own *Auto Sys:* Geac
Pubns: St John's Coll Lib: a brief guide (free)
Staff: Libns: 3.5 *Non-Prof:* PT team of grad students for evening/weekend cover & shelving
Exp: £55000 (2000-01)

S1771

St Peter's College Library

New Inn Hall St, Oxford, OX1 2DL (01865-278882; *fax:* 01865-277885)
Email: alistair.ricketts@st-peters.ox.ac.uk

Chief: Libn: Mr Alistair Ricketts
Entry: membs of Coll; others by appt only
Subj: all subjs; undergrad
Equip: computers
Stock: bks & periodcls/c40000

S1772

Templeton College, Information Centre

Kennington, Oxford, OX1 5NY (01865-422564; *fax:* 01865-422501)
Email: infocent@templeton.ox.ac.uk
Internet: http://www.templeton.ox.ac.uk/

Gov Body: Univ of Oxford (see **L4**) *Chief:* Info Centre Team Leader: Ms Michele Walker BA, DipIML, AALIA *Dep:* Info & Rsrch Offcr: Mr Stephan Gant
Entry: restricted access; tel or write in adv *Open:* term & vac: Mon-Fri 0830-1700
Subj: social sci; business; mgmt; retail mgmt; industrial relations; human resource mgmt; info mgmt; company info *Collns: Other:* company reports & accounts *Co-op Schemes:* BLDSC, EBSLG
Equip: copier, computers (incl wd-proc, internet & CD-ROM) *Online:* Amadeus, Dashboard, Datastream, FAME, Hoovers, Investext Plus, Reuters Business Insight, Thomson Analytics; e-journals via: Infotrac, Proquest, TDNet
Stock: bks/c20000; periodcls/150; videos/100
Classn: LBS *Auto Sys:* CAIRS *Staff:* 4 in total

S1773

Trinity College Library

Broad St, Oxford, OX1 3BH (01865-279863; *fax:* 01865-279902)
Email: jan.martin@trinity.ox.ac.uk

Gov Body: The Coll of the Holy & Undivided Trinity in the Univ of Oxford of the Foundation of Sir Thomas Pope, Knight *Chief:* Libn: Ms Jan Martin MA
Assoc Libs: COLL ARCHVS, Archivist: Mrs C. Hopkins (01865-279861; *fax:* 01865-279902; *email:* archive@tri.ox.ac.uk)
Entry: Coll membs only; archvs & special collns by appt *Open:* term time: 24 hrs pd, 7 days per wk
Subj: all subjs; undergrad *Collns: Bks & Pamphs:* Old Lib (classics, theology & topology, 15C-19C); 18C-19C topography; all to be consulted in situ, by appt *Archvs:* Trinity Coll archvs (1555-date); Sir Arthur Quiller-Couch papers; undergrad ephemera
Equip: copier, computers, scanner, printer
Stock: bks/80000 *Auto Sys:* OLIS

S1774

University College Library

High St, Oxford, OX1 4BH (01865-276621; *fax:* 01865-276987)
Email: library@univ.ox.ac.uk

Gov Body: Univ Coll *Chief:* Fellow Libn: Dr T.W. Child MA, BPhil, DPhil *Dep:* Libn: Miss C.M. Ritchie MA, DipLib, MCLIP
Assoc Libs: UNIV COLL ARCHVS, Archivist: Dr R.H. Darwall-Smith MA, DPhil, MArAd (01865-276952; *email:* robin.darwall-smith@magd.ox. ac.uk)
Entry: no admittance without prior arrangement *Open:* term: 24 hrs pd; vac: Mon-Sun 0815-2400
Subj: all subjs; undergrad *Co-op Schemes:* ILL (via Bodleian Lib)
Equip: video viewer, computers (incl CD-ROM & 4 with internet)
Stock: bks/50000; periodcls/55; videos/63
Classn: Bliss *Auto Sys:* Heritage
Staff: Libns: 1 *Non-Prof:* 1 (not incl Fellow Libn)

S1775

Wadham College Library

Parks Rd, Oxford, OX1 3PN (01865-277914; *fax:* 01865-277937)
Email: sandra.bailey@wadh.ox.ac.uk

Chief: Fellow Libn: R.H. Robbins MA, DPhil *Dep:* Libn: S.C. Bailey BA, MA
Assoc Libs: WADHAM COLL ARCHVS, addr as above, contact Keeper of the Coll Archvs
Entry: by adv appt for non-Coll membs *Open:* Mon-Fri 0900-1700
Subj: all subjs; undergrad
Equip: copier, 3 computers with internet *Online:* OLIS
Stock: bks/40000; periodcls/100
Classn: Cheltenham Ladies Coll *Auto Sys:* Geac
Staff: Libns: 1 *Non-Prof:* 0.5 *Exp:* £22000 (1999-2000); £23000 (2000-01)

S1776

Wesley and Methodist Studies Centre, Library and Archive

Westminster Inst of Edu, Oxford Brookes Univ, Harcourt Hill, Oxford, OX2 9AT (01865-488319; *fax:* 01865-488317)
Email: wmsc@brookes.ac.uk
Internet: http://www.brookes.ac.uk/wmsc/

Chief: Libn, Archivist & Curator: Mr Peter Forsaith (pforsaith@brookes.ac.uk) *Dep:* Hon Libn, Wesley Historical Soc: Mr John Lenton MPhil (jclenton@cablenet.co.uk)
Entry: adv appt *Open:* Mon-Fri 0900-1700
Subj: religion; Methodist hist; Wesleyan theology
Collns: Bks & Pamphs: Wesley Historical Soc Lib; Garlick Colln *Archvs:* Westminster Coll Oxford Archvs; Wesley Historical Soc Archv; AVEC Archvs; Bletchley Park/Lady Spencer Churchill Coll Archv; Donald English Archv *Other:* Methodist Colln of Modern Christian Art; Smetham Colln (art works by James Smetham, 1821-89)
Equip: m-reader, copier, computer (with wd-proc, internet & CD-ROM), room for hire *Svcs:* info, ref
Stock: bks/c8500; periodcls/6; photos/c1500; pamphs/c4000; maps/1; m-forms/200; archvs/150 linear m *Acqs Offcr:* Libn, as above
Classn: DDC (mod) *Auto Sys:* Talis
Pubns: Westminster Wesley Series
Staff: Other Prof: 1 *Exp:* £500 (1999-2000); £500 (2000-01)

S1777

Wolfson College Library

Linton Rd, Oxford, OX2 6UD (01865-274076; *fax:* 01865-274125)
Email: library@wolfson.ox.ac.uk

Gov Body: constituent Coll of Univ of Oxford (see **L4**) *Chief:* Libn: Mrs Fiona E. Wilkes BA, MA, DipLib, MCLIP (fiona.wilkes@wolfson.ox.ac.uk)
Assoc Libs: WOLFSON COLL ARCHVS, addr as above, Archivist: Dr Jane Potter (jane.potter@ wolfson.ox.ac.uk)
Entry: membs of Coll only; materials not available elsewhere by be viewed only by appt *Open:* 24 hrs
Subj: all subjs; genl; undergrad; postgrad *Co-op Schemes:* BLDSC
Equip: m-reader, copier, 8 computers (incl 4 with internet) *Online:* OLIS OPAC, OXLIP (Oxford Libs Info Platform, giving access to internet & other hosted svcs) *Officer-in-Charge:* The Coll Bursar: Major Alan Gordon *Svcs:* info, ref, biblio
Stock: bks/28930; periodcls/3 *Acqs Offcr:* Libn, as above
Classn: UDC *Auto Sys:* Geac
Staff: Libns: 1 *Non-Prof:* 2 grad student assts
Exp: £11280 (2000-01)

S1778

Worcester College Library

Worcester St, Oxford, OX1 2HB (01865-278354; *fax:* 01865-278387)
Email: joanna.parker@worc.ox.ac.uk
Internet: http://www.worcester.ox.ac.uk/

Gov Body: Worcester Coll *Chief:* Libn: Dr Joanna Parker MA, DPhil *Dep:* Asst Libn: Dr Natalia Perevezentseva DPhil *Other Snr Staff:* Lib Asst: Mrs Shelley Bruce BA
Entry: accredited scholars with a need to use special collns by appt; ID/letter of recommendation required *Open:* for non-membs of coll: Mon-Fri 0900-1300, 1400-1700
Subj: all subjs; undergrad *Collns: Bks & Pamphs:* 17C-19C pamphs; 16C-17C plays; 17C-18C bks (lit, arch, travel etc) *Archvs:* Coll archvs *Other:* Clarke papers (Civil War MSS); arch drawings; 17C & 18C prints; misc MSS
Equip: copier, 3 computers (incl 1 with CD-ROM)
Stock: bks/120000; pamphs/30000
Classn: own *Staff: Libns:* 2 *Non-Prof:* 1

S1779

Wycliffe Hall, Library

54 Banbury Rd, Oxford, OX2 6PW (01865-274204; *fax:* 01865-274215)
Email: library@wycliffe.ox.ac.uk
Internet: http://www.wycliffe.ox.ac.uk/

Gov Body: Univ of Oxford (see **L4**) *Chief:* Libn: Mr Chris Leftley BA, BSc, MCLIP
Entry: current students & faculty only; others by appt *Open:* 0700-2300 all year round

(Wycliffe Hall Lib cont)

Subj: religion *Collns: Archvs:* archvs of photos, logs, yearbks etc of the Coll
Equip: 2 copiers (5p), 7 computers (incl wd-proc, internet & CD-ROM) *Svcs:* info, ref, biblio
Stock: bks/13000; periodcls/95; photos/3000; audios/200; videos/70; CD-ROMs/5
Classn: DDC *Auto Sys:* Geac (for Univ System), Heritage *Staff: Libns:* 1 *Exp:* £9300 (1999-2000)

Paignton

S1780 ♀

Whitley Wildlife Conservation Trust Library

Totnes Rd, Paignton, Devon, TQ4 7EU (01803-697500; *fax:* 01803-697513)
Email: tmechell@paigntonzoo.org.uk

Chief: Libn: Mrs Tina Mechell
Entry: ref only, adv appt; admitted at our discretion
Open: 0915-1300, 1330-1500
Subj: sci; wildlife; conservation
Equip: copier
Stock: bks/3500; periodcls/13 *Classn:* DDC
Pubns: various pubns relating to wildlife conservation & zoos
Staff: Non-Prof: 1 *Exp:* £1800 (1999-2000)

Paisley

S1781 🎓🙏

Scottish Baptist College Library

Univ Lib, Paisley Univ, High St, Paisley, Strathclyde, PA1 2BE (0141-849-4116; *fax:* 0141-887-0812)
Email: library@paisley.ac.uk
Internet: http://www.scottishbaptistcollege.co.uk/

Chief: Scottish Baptist Coll Libn: Mrs Wilma Wilson BA, MCLIP (wils-li3@paisley.ac.uk)
Entry: ref only; external borrowers at discretion of libn *Open:* term: Mon-Thu 0900-2100, Fri-Sat 0900-1700; vac: Mon-Fri 0900-1700
Subj: religion; theology *Co-op Schemes:* ABTAPL
Equip: m-readers, m-printer, fax, copiers, computers (incl internet & CD-ROM) *Svcs:* info, ref
Stock: bks/13000; periodcls/100
Classn: DDC *Auto Sys:* Talis
Staff: Libns: 1
Further Info: The Lib is now fully integrated into the Univ of Paisley Lib (see **S1782**), while continuing its primary function as the lib for the staff & students of the Scottish Baptist Coll.

S1782 🎓

University of Paisley, Robertson Trust Library and Learning Resource Centre

High St, Paisley, Strathclyde, PA1 2BE (0141-848-3758; *fax:* 0141-887-0812)
Email: library@paisley.ac.uk
Internet: http://library.paisley.ac.uk/

Gov Body: Univ of Paisley *Chief:* Univ Libn: Mr Stuart James BA, FCLIP, FRSA *Dep:* Dep Libns: Mr G. McCrae & Ms T. Gilbery

Assoc Libs: UNDERGRAD READING ROOM, Paisley; AYR CAMPUS LIB (see **S66**); ROYAL ALEXANDRA HOSP LIB (see **S1783**)
Entry: ref access; external borrowers at discretion of libn *Open: Main Lib:* term: Mon-Thu 0900-2100, Fri-Sat 0900-1700; vac: Mon-Fri 0900-1700; *Undergrad Reading Room:* term: Mon-Fri 0900-2200, Sat 0900-1700, Sun 1200-1600
Subj: all subjs; undergrad; postgrad *Collns: Bks & Pamphs:* UK govt pubns; EC official documents (selection); aeronautical hist; local hist *Archvs:* L.F. Richardson papers; Norman Buchan MP Parliamentary papers; Paisley Coll Archv; West of Scotland Community Relations Council Archvs *Other:* railway maps *Co-op Schemes:* BLDSC, SALCTG, SCURL, SCONUL, NLS, ALF
Equip: 4 m-readers, m-printer, fax, 4 copiers, computers (incl internet & 30 CD-ROM) *Online:* Chest, Dialog, STN, Dialtech, Datastar (some fees)
Stock: bks/320000; periodcls/3800; pamphs/10000; maps/2000; m-forms/1000; videos/750; archvs/30 linear m *Acqs Offcr:* Dep Libn: Mr G. McCrae (Gordon.McCrae@paisley.ac.uk)
Classn: DDC *Auto Sys:* Talis
Staff: Libns: 15 *Non-Prof:* 48 *Exp:* £493100 (1999-2000); £495034 (2000-01)

S1783 🎓✚

University of Paisley, Royal Alexandra Hospital Library

Corsebar Rd, Paisley, Strathclyde, PA2 9PN (0141-580-4757; *fax:* 0141-887-4962)
Email: ruth.robinson@paisley.ac.uk
Internet: http://library.paisley.ac.uk/index.htm

Gov Body: Univ of Paisley (see **S1782**) *Chief:* Sub-Libn (Health): Ms Ruth Robinson BA, MCLIP
Dep: Asst Libn: Ms Katrina Dalziel BA, MCLIP
Entry: ref access to printed materials only for non-membs *Open:* Mon-Thu 0830-1630, Fri 0830-1600
Subj: psy; sociology; medicine; nursing; health studies *Co-op Schemes:* BLDSC, SHINE
Equip: m-reader, copier (card operated), 6 computers (all with wd-proc, internet & CD-ROM)
Svcs: info, ref
Stock: bks/5000; periodcls/180
Classn: DDC *Auto Sys:* Talis
Staff: Libns: 2 *Non-Prof:* 5

Papworth Everard

S1784 ✚

Papworth Hospital NHS Trust, Clinical Library Service

Papworth Everard, Cambridgeshire, CB3 8RE (01480-830541)
Email: lyn.edmonds@papworth-tr.anglox.nhs.uk

Chief: Clinical Lib Mgr: Mrs L. Edmonds BA, MCLIP
Entry: staff only, others by adv appt *Open:* Mon-Fri 0900-1700
Subj: medicine; nursing; health care
Equip: copier, 3 computers (all with CD-ROM, 2 with internet) *Svcs:* info, ref, biblio
Stock: periodcls/92
Classn: NLM
Pubns: Lib Guide; Current Journals List; Journal Holdings List; Newsletter
Staff: Libns: 1.53 *Non-Prof:* 1 FTE

Penarth

S1785 🎓✚

Llandough Hospital NHS Trust, Cochrane Library

Llandough Hosp, Penarth, S Glamorgan, CF64 2XX (029-2071-5497; *fax:* 029-2070-8973)
Email: cochranelib@cf.ac.uk
Internet: http://www.uwcm.ac.uk/libraries/librarysites/cochrane/

Gov Body: Univ of Wales Coll of Medicine (see **S427**) *Chief:* Hosps Libn: Ms Rosemary Soper BA, DipLib, MCLIP (soper@ cf.ac.uk) *Dep:* Lib Assts: Ms MariAnn Hilliar (hilliarm@cf.ac.uk) & Ms Beatrice Nichol (nicholbl@cf.ac.uk)
Entry: registered UWCM staff & students; NHS staff employed in Cardiff area *Open:* Mon-Fri 0900-1700
Subj: medicine; obstetrics; gynaecology; evidence-based healthcare *Collns: Archvs:* Cochrane Archv (memorabilia relating to the life & work of Prof Archie Cochrane) *Co-op Schemes:* ILL
Equip: copier, computers (incl wd-proc, internet & CD-ROM) *Online:* Cochrane, Medline, CINAHL, CancerLit, HealthStar, access to UWCM computer network & CymruWeb (NHS Wales Intranet)
Staff: Libns: 1 *Non-Prof:* 3

Penicuik

S1786 🏛🎓

Centre for Ecology and Hydrology, Library Service

Edinburgh Rsrch Station, Bush Est, Penicuik, Midlothian, EH26 0QB (0131-445-8512; *fax:* 0131-445-3943)
Email: ssco@ceh.ac.uk
Internet: http://library.ceh.ac.uk/

Gov Body: Nat Environment Rsrch Council (NERC) *Chief:* Head of Lib Svcs: Ms Sheila Scobie *Dep:* Deputy/Collns Libn: Mrs Sue Wharton *Other Snr Staff:* Libn (Edinburgh): Ms Linda Dickson
Assoc (Site) Libs: CEH BANCHORY LIB (see **S71**); CEH BANGOR LIB (see **S72**); CEH DORSET LIB (see **S543**); CEH EDINBURGH LIB, addr as above; CEH MERLEWOOD LIB (see **S756**); CEH MONKS WOOD LIB (see **S831**); CEH OXFORD LIB (see **S1669**); CEH WALLINGFORD LIB (see **S2072**); CEH WINDERMERE LIB (joint svc with Freshwater Biological Assoc – see **S32**)
Entry: ref only upon appt for bona fide rsrchers
Open: Edinburgh: Mon-Wed 0830-1700, Thu-Fri 0830-1645; other sites vary
Subj: Lib Svcs: rsrch; sci; maths; geog; biology; ecology; hydrology; land use within terrestrial & aquatic environments; *Edinburgh Lib:* trace gases; air pollution; climatology; ecosystem process modelling; tropical forestry; freshwater ecology
Collns: Archvs: held at various sites: Cyril Diver Colln; Fritsch Colln of Algal Illusts; Ronald Good Botanical Archv; Hurst Colln of Nile Hydrology; Rofe Colln; Leesdale Colln *Co-op Schemes:* BLDSC, RESCOLINC, SALG, WLG, BIASLIC, IAMSLIC
Equip: 9 m-readers, 2 m-printers, 9 copiers, 10 computers (all with wd-proc, CD-ROM & internet) *Online:* Dialog, STN, Web of Science, Zetoc *Svcs:* info, ref, biblio, indexing, abstracting
Stock: bks/c4000; periodcls/550; figs are for Edinburgh Lib only
Classn: UDC, in-house *Auto Sys:* Unicorn
Staff: Libns: 8 *Non-Prof:* 9

S1787
Moredun Research Institute Library
Pentlands Science Pk, Bush Loan, Penicuik, Midlothian, EH26 0PZ (0131-445-6157; *fax:* 0131-445-6235)
Email: library@mri.sari.ac.uk
Internet: http://www.mri.sari.ac.uk/

Chief: Libn: Ms Diane S. Donaldson BSc, MSc, MCLIP
Entry: adv appt required *Open:* Mon-Fri 0850-1715
Subj: veterinary sci; microbiology; immunology; virology *Co-op Schemes:* SALG, BLDSC, BRISC, RESCOLINC
Equip: copier, 6 computers (all with wd-proc, internet & CD-ROM) *Online:* Dialog, STN
Stock: bks/3000; periodcls/120
Classn: LC *Auto Sys:* DBTextworks
Staff: Libns: 1 *Non-Prof:* 1

Penrith

S1788
University of Central Lancashire, Cumbria Campus Library
Newton Rigg, Penrith, Cumbria, CA11 0AH (01768-894200; *fax:* 01768-894991)
Email: clibrary@uclan.ac.uk
Internet: http://www.uclan.ac.uk/ or http://www.newtonrigg.ac.uk/

Gov Body: Univ of Central Lancashire (see **S1840**) *Chief:* Campus Libn: Mr D. Singleton BSc(Hons), MA, DipLib, MCLIP
Entry: ref only to genl public; external membership available *Open:* term: Mon-Fri 0830-2100, Sat 1000-1600; vac: Mon-Fri 0900-1700
Subj: all subjs; undergrad; postgrad; vocational; computing; info tech; social sci; social care; childhood studies; agric; forestry; hortic; environmental studies; outdoor edu *Collns: Bks & Pamphs:* forestry colln *Co-op Schemes:* BLDSC, LNW, CHELPS
Equip: m-reader, video viewer, fax, copier, 80 computers (all with internet), 8 rooms for hire
Online: available to staff & students of the instn
Svcs: info, ref
Stock: bks/30000; periodcls/200; maps/200; videos/200
Classn: DDC, UDC *Auto Sys:* Talis
Pubns: Seeds of Change (hist of Newton Rigg Coll, £8.50)
Staff: Libns: 3.5 *Non-Prof:* 7 *Exp:* £38000 (1999-2000); £40000 (2000-01)
Proj: £3.5 mln lib bldg

Penzance

S1789
Morrab Library
Morrab Gdns, Penzance, Cornwall, TR18 4DA (*tel & fax:* 01736-364474)
Internet: http://www.morrablibrary.co.uk/

Type: independent subscription lib
Entry: lending to membs (£20 pa); prospective membs welcome to visit first; daily fee for rsrch use by non-membs *Open:* Tue-Fri 1000-1600, Sat 1000-1300
Subj: local studies (West Cornwall); lit; fiction; ch's lit; hist; biography; antiquities; topography; travel; religion; Celtic studies *Collns: Bks & Pamphs:* Cornish Colln; Celtic Studies Colln; pre-1801 bks (2750 vols); extensive runs of 18C & 19C periodcls; Parliamentary Reports (17C-18C); Blue Bks (19C) *Other:* Photographic Archv (life in West Cornwall, 1870-1970); Nat Hist Illusts Colln; Dawson Colln (illusts), comprising two collns: Napoleonic Colln (c3000 illusts, 1770-1840); British Aristocracy Colln (23 vols of prints, 1500-1850)

Co-op Schemes: AIL
Svcs: ref, lending, lectures
Stock: bks/40000+; photos/10000, plus 15000 transparencies
Pubns: newsletter
Proj: planned lib extension

Perth

S1790
Murray Royal Hospital, Stalker Library
Murray Royal Hosp, Perth, Tayside, PH2 7BH (01738-621151 x2247; *fax:* 01738-440431)
Email: dianne.mitchell@tpct.scot.nhs.uk

Gov Body: Tayside Primary Care NHS Trust
Chief: Libn: Ms Dianne Mitchell BA(Hons), DipLib
Assoc Libs: CARSEVIEW CENTRE LIB (see **S559**); ROXBURGHE HOUSE LIB (see **S557**)
Entry: lending facilities for Trust staff & students; ref only by adv appt for genl public *Open:* Tue, Thu 0915-1315
Subj: psychiatry *Co-op Schemes:* BLDSC, SHINE
Equip: computers (incl wd-proc & internet)
Online: Cochrane, Medline, limited on-line journals; for staff & students only *Svcs:* info, ref
Stock: bks/1500; periodcls/17
Classn: DDC *Staff:* Libns: 1

S1791
Perth College, Learning Resources Centre
Creiff Rd, Perth, Tayside, PH1 2NX (01738-877721; *fax:* 01738-877009)
Email: pc.lrcdesk@perth.uhi.ac.uk
Internet: http://www.perth.ac.uk/

Gov Body: part of the Univ of the Highlands & Islands (UHI) *Chief:* Learning Resources Mgr: Mrs Jennifer Louden (jennifer.louden@perth.uhi.ac.uk) *Dep:* Learning Resources Supervisor: Miss Ishbel Leggat MA, PGDipLIS (ishbel.leggat@perth.uhi.ac.uk)
Entry: membership automatic to all students (FT, PT, Open Learning etc); membs of other academic insts by appl to Learning Resources Mgr *Open:* term: Mon-Thu 0900-2100, Fri 0900-1645; vac: Mon-Fri 0900-1645
Subj: all subjs; genl; undergrad; postgrad; vocational; SQA Highers; NQ; HNC; HND *Co-op Schemes:* BLDSC, SILLR (NLSLS), ILL, UHI Millennium Inst (inter-site loan scheme)
Equip: video viewer, copier (£1 per 15 copies), 30 computers (all with wd-proc, internet & CD-ROM), clr printer, laminating & binding facilities *Disabled:* height-adjustable desks for wheelchair users
Officer-in-Charge: Learning Resources Administrator: Miss Helen Cairns (helen.cairns@perth.uhi.ac.uk) *Svcs:* info, ref, biblio
Stock: bks/21065; periodcls/122; maps/207; audios/66; videos/549; CD-ROMs/219 *Acqs Offcr:* Learning Resources Mgr, as above
Classn: DDC *Auto Sys:* Olib 7.1
Staff: Libns: 3 *Other Prof:* 1 *Non-Prof:* 4

S1792
Perth Museum and Art Gallery
George St, Perth, Tayside, PH1 5LB (01738-632488; *fax:* 01738-443505)
Email: museum@pkc.gov.uk
Internet: http://www.pkc.gov.uk/ah/

Type: local authority *Gov Body:* Perth & Kinross Council (see **P144**) *Chief:* Head of Arts & Heritage: Mr Michael A. Taylor BSc(Hons), AMA, FMA
Entry: by appt, ref only *Open:* Mon-Fri 1000-1700

Subj: local study; sci
Equip: copier
Stock: bks/5000; periodcls/20
Staff: Other Prof: 9 *Exp:* £2000 (1999-2000); £2000 (2000-01)

Peterborough

S1793
British Sugar Business Information Centre
(formerly BSTC Lib & Info Svcs)
Oundle Rd, Peterborough, Cambridgeshire, PE2 9QU (01603-422434; *fax:* 01603-422418)
Email: hwilson@britishsugar.org.uk
Internet: http://www.britishsugar.org.uk/

Chief: Scientific Libn: Ms Helen Wilson BSc
Entry: company staff only; provides enq svc only for public on subj of sugar *Open:* Mon-Tue, Thu-Fri 1000-1500
Subj: sugar; sugar beet; agric; food industry
Equip: copier, computers (incl wd-proc, internet & CD-ROM) *Svcs:* info, ref, abstracting, translation
Stock: bks/2000; periodcls/40; various patents, standards & abstracts *Acqs Offcr:* Scientific Libn, as above
Classn: UDC *Staff:* Other Prof: 0.5

S1794
English Nature, Information and Library Services
Northminster House, Peterborough, Cambridgeshire, PE1 1UA (01733-455094; *fax:* 01733-68834)
Internet: http://www.english-nature.org.uk/

Gov Body: DEFRA (see **S1110**) *Chief:* Lib, Enq & Records Mgr: Ms I. Chivers BA(Hons), DipLib, MCLIP (isabel.chivers@english-nature.org) *Dep:* Libn: Mrs B. Newland (brigid.newland@english-nature.org.uk)
Entry: adv appt *Open:* Mon-Thu 1000-1600
Subj: nature conservation; planning; land use; botany; zoology *Collns: Bks & Pamphs:* English county floras (ref only) *Co-op Schemes:* BLDSC
Equip: m-reader, copier, computer (with CD-ROM)
Svcs: ref
Stock: bks/25000; periodcls/1800 *Acqs Offcr:* Libn, as above
Classn: UDC *Auto Sys:* Unicorn
Staff: Libns: 5 *Non-Prof:* 5 *Exp:* £80000 (2000-01)

S1795
Homerton School of Health Studies, Peterborough Library
Peterborough Dist Hosp, Gable Dr, Thorpe Rd, Peterborough, Cambridgeshire, PE3 6DA (01733-874766)

Gov Body: Homerton Coll, Cambridge (see **S361**)
Chief: Libn: Mr Graham Haldane BD(Hons), DipLib, MCLIP
Assoc Libs: HUNTINGDON LIB (see **S833**); PAPWORTH EVERARD LIB, St. Peter's Edu Centre, Church Ln, Papworth Everard, Cambridgeshire, CB3 8QT (01480-830541; *fax:* 01480-831154)
Entry: local Trust nursing staff & Homerton Coll students *Open:* Mon, Fri 0830-1200, 1230-1700, Tue-Thu 0830-1830
Subj: nursing; medicine *Co-op Schemes:* BLDSC, Anglia HeLIN
Stock: bks/6000; periodcls/110
Classn: NLM *Auto Sys:* Heritage
Staff: Libns: 2 *Non-Prof:* 2

Special Libraries

Peterborough ▼ Plymouth

S1796 ✚
John Fawcett Postgraduate Medical Centre, The Laxton Library
Peterborough Dist Hosp, Thorpe Rd, Peterborough, Cambridgeshire, PE3 6DA (01733-874662; *fax:* 01733-347142)
Email: laxton.library@pbh-tr.nhs.uk

Gov Body: Peterborough Hosp NHS Trust *Chief:* Lib Info Svcs Mgr: Ms Dorothy Husband
Entry: all local NHS staff may use lib's svcs, although with varying conditions; others at Libn's discretion *Open:* 24 hr access available to registered users with digital PIN; usually staffed: Mon-Thu 0900-1700, Fri 0900-1600
Subj: medicine; health related subjs *Co-op Schemes:* Anglia & Oxford ILL
Equip: copier, 6 computers (all with internet, registered users only) *Svcs:* info, ref
Stock: bks/3500; periodcls/c100
Classn: NLM *Auto Sys:* DBTextworks
Staff: Libns: 1 *Non-Prof:* 1 FTE

S1797 🔑
National Operatic and Dramatic Association, The NODA Library
58-60 Lincoln Rd, Peterborough, Cambridgeshire, PE1 2RZ (0870-770-2480; *fax:* 0870-770-2490)
Email: everyone@noda.org.uk
Internet: http://www.noda.org.uk/

Chief: contact the Hon Libn
Entry: membs of NODA; ref only *Open:* Mon-Fri 0900-1700
Subj: theatre; drama; light opera; musicals
Collns: Bks & Pamphs: ref lib of theatrical texts, ref bks etc *Other:* scores & libretti

S1798 🔑 🙏
Peterborough Cathedral Library
Minster Precincts, Peterborough, Cambridgeshire, PE1 1XS (01733-562125; *fax:* 01733-552465)

Gov Body: Dean & Chapter of Peterborough
Chief: Canon Libn: Canon J. Higham MA, STM
Assoc Libs: pre-1800 bks are deposited at CAMBRIDGE UNIV LIB (see **L5**)
Entry: by prior arrangement with Canon Libn
Open: Mon-Fri 1000-1600
Subj: religion; Benedictine Order; C of E; ecclesiastical hist; liturgy; Peterborough local hist & topography *Collns: Bks & Pamphs:* hist of Peterborough Abbey & Cathedral; Northamptonshire Record Soc Lib; Lincolnshire Record Soc Lib; Rolls Series *Archvs:* Peterborough Dean & Chapter Archvs
Equip: m-reader, copier, computer (with wd-proc), room for hire
Stock: bks/3000; periodcls/4; photos/500; pamphs/500; maps/50
Classn: own
Pubns: Friends of Peterborough Cathedral (annual, £2.50)
Staff: Libns: 1
Proj: new catalogue in progress

S1799 🕍 🏛
Peterborough Museum and Art Gallery, Library and Archives
Priestgate, Peterborough, Cambridgeshire, PE1 1LF (01733-343329; *fax:* 01733-341928)
Email: museum@peterborough.gov.uk
Internet: http://www.peterboroughheritage.org.uk/

Type: local authority *Gov Body:* Peterborough City Council (see **P145**) *Chief:* Heritage Collns Mgr: Ms Glenys Wass
Entry: adv appt *Open:* lib not open to public; *Museum:* Tue-Fri 1200-1700, Sat 1000-1700, Sun 1200-1600
Subj: local study (Peterborough); sci; geog; hist
Collns: Archvs: John Clare Poetry Colln (150 items); John Thompson Colln (plans, 2000 items); 5000 other documents & MSS
Equip: copier, room for hire
Stock: bks/10000; photos/30000, plus 2500 glass negs; slides/8000; illusts/1000 prints; pamphs/5000; maps/1500; audios/20; ephemera/15000 items
Classn: own
Staff: Libns: 1 *Other Prof:* 6 *Non-Prof:* 6

S1800 🎓
Peterborough Regional College, Learning Resources and Library Centre
Park Cres, Peterborough, Cambridgeshire, PE1 4DZ (01733-762137)
Email: claire.chinnery@peterborough.ac.uk
Internet: http://www.peterborough.ac.uk/

Chief: Libn: Ms Claire Chinnery
Assoc Libs: FORWARD HOUSE LIB, Shrewbury Ave, Woodston, Peterborough, PE2 7BX (01733-762302)
Open: term: Mon-Wed 0845-1930, Thu 0845-2015, Fri 0845-1630, Sat 0930-1230; vac: Mon-Thu 0845-1300, 1400-1645, Fri 0845-1300, 1400-1615; *Forward House Lib:* term: Mon-Thu 1030-1415, 1445-1830; vac: closed
Subj: all subjs; GCSE; A level; undergrad; local studies (Peterborough); sci; tech; accounting; mgmt; law *Collns: Bks & Pamphs:* BSI; company reports; Local Hist Colln *Other:* maps
Equip: copier, 30 computers (incl wd-proc, internet & CD-ROM)
Stock: bks/40000; periodcls/100; videos/2500

Peterlee

S1801 🎓
East Durham and Houghall Community College, Learner Services Centre
Burnhope Way, Peterlee, Co Durham, SR8 1NU (0191-518-2000)
Email: libraryservices@eastdurham.ac.uk

Gov Body: Coll Corp *Chief:* Learner Svcs Centre Mgr: Mrs Jenete Gilling MA, DipMgmt *Dep:* Dep Mgr: Ms Denise Kirkbride
Assoc Libs: HOUGHALL LEARNER SVCS CENTRE, Houghall, Co Durham, DH1 3SG
Entry: ref only for public *Open:* Mon-Thu 0830-2000, Fri 0830-1630
Subj: all subjs *Collns: Bks & Pamphs:* agric & hortic ref lib *Co-op Schemes:* BLDSC
Equip: m-form camera, fax, video viewer, copier, clr copier, computers (incl wd-proc, internet & CD-ROM), room for hire *Svcs:* info, ref
Stock: bks/30000; periodcls/70; slides/20; various photos, maps, audios, videos & CD-ROMs *Acqs Offcr:* Learner Svcs Centre Mgr, as above
Classn: DDC *Auto Sys:* GLAS
Staff: Libns: 1 *Other Prof:* 2 *Non-Prof:* 10 *Exp:* £30000 (1999-2000); £45000 (2000-01)

Petersfield

S1802 🎓
Bedales Memorial Library
Bedales School, Steep, Petersfield, Hampshire, GU32 2DW (01730-300100; *fax:* 01730-300500)

Gov Body: Bedales School *Chief:* Libn: Mrs Anne Archer BSc, MCLIP
Entry: adv appt *Open:* term: Mon-Fri 0845-2100, Sat 0845-1300; vac: by arrangement
Subj: undergrad; lit; hist; fiction *Collns: Bks & Pamphs:* school pubns, incl hists *Archvs:* broad range of documents & photos relating to the school since founding in 1893
Stock: bks/35000; photos/500; archvs/3 cubic m
Classn: DDC *Staff: Libns:* 1

Pitlochry

S1803 🕍
Fisheries Research Services, Freshwater Fisheries Laboratory Library
Fisheries Rsrch Svcs, Faskally, Pitlochry, Perthshire, PH16 5LB (01796-472060; *fax:* 01796-473523)
Email: j.robbins@marlab.ac.uk
Internet: http://www.marlab.ac.uk/

Chief: Head Libn (Marine Laboratory, Aberdeen): Ms Sarah P. Heath BA(Hons) *Dep:* Asst Libn (Freshwater Fisheries Laboratory, Pitlochry): Miss Jane Robins BA(Hons)
Assoc Libs: MARINE LABORATORY LIB (parent lib, see **S8**)
Entry: ref only *Open:* Mon-Fri 0830-1700
Subj: freshwater fisheries; freshwater biology; environmental sci *Co-op Schemes:* ILL (staff only)
Equip: m-reader, copier, computer (with CD-ROM) *Online:* Dialog, CORDIS, ASFA
Stock: bks/4000; periodcls/200
Classn: UDC *Auto Sys:* Sydney Plus
Staff: Libns: 1 *Non-Prof:* 0.5

Plymouth

S1804 🎓
College of St Mark and St John Library
(formerly Univ Coll of St Mark & St John)
Derriford Rd, Plymouth, Devon, PL6 8BH (01752-636700; *fax:* 01752-636712)
Email: fclements@marjon.ac.uk
Internet: http://www.marjon.ac.uk/

Chief: Dir of Info Svcs: Mr Frank A. Clements FCLIP *Dep:* Libn: Mrs Alison Bidgood MCLIP
Entry: ref only, appl in writing *Open:* term: Mon-Fri 0830-2000, Sat-Sun 1000-1645; vac: Mon-Fri 0900-1900
Subj: local studies (South West England, geog & hist); computer sci; phil in genl; phil & psy of edu; comparative religion; Anglicanism; religious edu; social sci; development studies; English; French; English as a Foreign Lang; primary & secondary sci; environmental sci; design & tech; art in edu; pottery; crafts; English & American lit; Europe; Asia; North & South America; Australasia; media studies *Collns: Bks & Pamphs:* Lang Lib; teaching practice material *Archvs:* Coll archvs from 1850 *Co-op Schemes:* BLDSC
Equip: m-readers, m-camera (staff only), m-printers, video viewers, copiers, clr copier, computers (incl wd-proc, internet & CD-ROM)
Stock: bks/137000; periodcls/1100; photos/500; slides/2500; illusts/700; maps/500; m-forms/250; audios/1300; videos/2750; archvs/148 m
Classn: DDC, Lang Teaching Classn (Lang Lib)

🎓 academic   🖋 corporate   **- 414 -**   🕍 governmental   ✚ medical

Auto Sys: Dynix
Staff: Libns: 5 *Non-Prof:* 11.8 *Exp:* £230000
(2000-01)

S1805

National Marine Biological Library

Citadel Hill, Plymouth, Devon, PL1 2PB (01752-
633266; *fax:* 01752-633102)
Email: nmbl@pml.ac.uk
Internet: http://www.mba.ac.uk/nmbl/

Gov Body: NERC; provides lib svcs for Plymouth
Marine Laboratory, Marine Biological Assoc & Sir
Alister Hardy Foundation for Ocean Sci *Chief:*
Head of Lib & Info Svcs: Ms Linda Noble BSc,
MCLIP
Assoc Libs: MARINE POLLUTION INFO
CENTRE, at same addr; WEST HOE LIB, West
Hoe, Plymouth, Devon, PL1 3DH
Entry: by appt *Open:* Mon-Fri 0900-1700
Subj: aquatic sci; marine biology; chem;
oceanography; fisheries; pollution; ecology
Collns: Bks & Pamphs: deposited collns of
monographs & reprints: Bidder Lib; Browne Lib;
Harmer Lib; Lebour Lib; Young Lib *Archvs:* relating
to hist of Marine Biological Assoc & the Laboratory;
personal & scientific papers of marine biologists,
incl letters, notebks, documents, illusts & photos
Other: marine pollution info (c60000 documents,
held at Marine Pollution Info Centre); charts &
maps *Co-op Schemes:* ASFIS, EURASLIC,
IAMSLIC
Equip: m-reader, m-printer, copier, computer (incl
CD-ROM) *Online:* Biosis, Science Citation Index,
RSC databases & others *Svcs:* info, ref, biblio,
indexing, abstracting
Stock: bks/13000; periodcls/1061, plus 3435 no
longer current; photos/500; slides/500; maps/1250;
m-forms/2100; reprints/80000
Pubns: Marine Pollution Rsrch Titles (monthly
bibliography); Estuaries & Coastal Waters of the
British Isles (annual bibliography)
Staff: Libns: 4 *Non-Prof:* 3

S1806

Plymouth Athenaeum Library

Derry's Cross, Plymouth, Devon, PL1 2SW
(01752-266079)
Email: athenaeum_theatre@hotmail.com

Type: lecture soc *Gov Body:* Council of the
Plymouth Athenaeum *Chief:* Hon Libn: Mrs Muriel
Halfacree
Assoc Libs: reciprocal membership with
PLYMOUTH PROPRIETARY LIB (see **S1811**)
Entry: membs of the Plymouth Athenaeum; others
admitted only in company of a cttee memb *Open:*
Mon-Fri 1000-1630
Subj: local studies (South West England);
generalities; phil; psy; religion; social sci; sci; tech;
arts; lit; geog; hist *Collns: Bks & Pamphs:*
Proceedings of the Plymouth Instn (subsequently
the Plymouth Athenaeum); Proceedings of the
Devonshire Assoc; full colln of Doidges Annual
(1903-53, some earlier vols); Western Antiquary
Colln; local journals, incl: Devon & Cornwall Notes
& Queries; Devon Historian; Tamar – Journal of the
Friends of Morwelham; various pamphs *Other:*
newspaper cuttings; old photographs; theatre
programmes
Equip: copier (5p), video viewer, 3 rooms for hire
Svcs: info, ref
Stock: bks/3550; periodcls/9
Classn: DDC
Staff: Non-Prof: 3 run by a cttee of membs on a
voluntary basis *Exp:* £300 (1999-2000); £300
(2000-01)

S1807

Plymouth College of Art and Design Library

Tavistock Pl, Plymouth, Devon, PL4 8AT (01752-
203412; *fax:* 01752-203444)
Email: LHarding@pcad.ac.uk
Internet: http://www.pcad-web.org/

Gov Body: Plymouth Coll of Art & Design *Chief:*
Libn: Ms Linda Harding MA, MCLIP
Entry: ref only *Open:* term: Mon-Thu 0845-1930,
Fri 0845-1700; vac: Mon-Fri 1000-1600
Subj: social sci; arts; lit *Co-op Schemes:*
SWRLS, Devon Coll Libns, Learning Through Libs
in Plymouth
Equip: 3 video viewers, copier, 50 computers (all
with wd-proc, internet & CD-ROM) *Svcs:* info, ref
Stock: bks/20000; periodcls/120; maps/110; m-
forms/13 sets; audios/20; videos/200
Classn: DDC *Auto Sys:* Innopac
Pubns: Student Study Guide (£3)
Staff: Libns: 1 *Other Prof:* 1 *Non-Prof:* 3 *Exp:*
£26000 (1999-2000); £26000 (2000-01); figs incl
stock & addl exp

S1808

Plymouth College of Further Education, Library and Learning Resources Service

Kings Rd, Devonport, Plymouth, Devon, PL1 5QG
(01752-385378; *fax:* 01752-385300)
Internet: http://www.pcfe.ac.uk/

Gov Body: The Coll Corp *Chief:* Head of Lib &
Learning Resources: Ms H.A. Rees BA(Hons),
DipLib, MEd, MCLIP *Dep:* Coll Libn: Ms A.
Gandon BA, MCLIP
Assoc Libs: GOSCHEN CENTRE LIB, Saltash
Rd, Plymouth, Devon, PL2 2DP (01752-305074)
Entry: ref only, adv appt *Open:* term: Mon-Thu
0830-1900, Fri 0930-1700 (1000-1700 at Groschen
Centre); vac: varies
Subj: all subjs; genl; GCSE; A level; undergrad;
postgrad *Collns: Bks & Pamphs:* chiropody colln;
catering colln; podiatry colln *Co-op Schemes:*
BLDSC, SWRLS
Equip: video viewers, copiers, computers (with
wd-proc, CD-ROM & internet), audio players
Disabled: Kurzweil *Svcs:* info, ref, biblio
Stock: bks/40000; periodcls/419; videos/2000
Classn: DDC *Auto Sys:* CAIRS
Staff: Libns: 5.81 *Non-Prof:* 7.75

S1809

Plymouth Hospitals NHS Trust Staff Library

Level 7, Derriford Hosp, Derriford Rd, Plymouth,
Devon, PL6 8DH (01752-792265; *fax:* 01752-
792314)
Email: library@phnt.swest.nhs.uk
Internet: http://www.sdhl.nhs.uk/

Gov Body: Plymouth Hosps NHS Trust *Chief:*
contact the Libn
Assoc Libs: SOUTH DEVON HEALTHCARE NHS
TRUST LIB (see **S2048**)
Entry: all NHS & primary health care staff working
within South & West Devon *Open:* Mon-Thu
0830-1900, Fri 0830-1700; out of hrs access
available to membs
Subj: medicine; nursing *Co-op Schemes:* South
Devon Health Libs
Equip: copier, computers (incl internet) *Online:*
CancerLit, BNI, CINAHL, DHData, Medline,
Embase, PsycInfo, AMED, MIDIRS, Pedro *Svcs:*
info, ref, biblio
Classn: NLM

S1810

Plymouth Museum and Art Gallery

(incorporating the Cottonian Colln Lib & Archvs)
Drake Circus, Plymouth, Devon, PL4 8AJ (01752-
304774; *fax:* 01752-304775)
Email: plymouthmuseum@plymouth.gov.uk
Internet: http://www.plymouthmuseum.gov.uk/ or
http://www.cottoniancollection.org.uk/

Type: local authority *Gov Body:* Plymouth City
Council (see **P146**) *Chief:* Curator of Museums &
Heritage: Ms Nicola Moyle MA *Dep:* Dep Curator:
Mr Mark Tosdevin *Other Snr Staff:* Keeper of Art:
Miss Maureen Attrill (m.attrill@cottoniancollection.
org.uk), responsible for Cottonian Colln
Entry: Museum & Art Gallery: free to public;
Cottonian Colln Lib & Archvs: adv appt *Open:*
Tue-Fri 1000-1730, Sat & Bank Hol Mons 1000-
1700; other times by appt
Subj: genl; art *Collns: Bks & Pamphs:* Cottonian
Colln Lib (mainly art, 17C-19C) *Archvs:* Cottonian
Colln Archvs (accounts, correspondence etc
relating to the acq & the development of the colln,
18C-19C) *Other:* prints & drawings
Equip: m-reader
Stock: bks/c2000; illusts/c7000
Staff: Other Prof: 1

S1811

Plymouth Proprietary Library

Alton Ter, 111 North Hill, Plymouth, Devon, PL4
8JY (01752-660515)

Gov Body: Elected Mgmt Cttee of Subscribers
Chief: Libn: Mr John R. Smith *Dep:* Dep Libn:
Miss A. Prizeman
Entry: ref only for non-membs *Open:* Mon-Tue,
Thu-Fri 0930-1730, Wed 0930-1400, Sat 0930-
1230
Subj: genl; Devon & Cornwall; small sections of
most subjs; lit; geog; hist *Collns: Bks & Pamphs:*
Cottonian Colln of bks, prints & drawings now
administered by Plymouth City Council & housed in
Plymouth City Museum *Co-op Schemes:* BLDSC
Equip: room hire could be considered
Stock: bks/17000; periodcls/14
Classn: DDC
Staff: Other Prof: 2 *Non-Prof:* 1 all PT *Exp:*
£2100 (1999-2000)

S1812

University of Plymouth, Information & Learning Services

Drake Circus, Plymouth, Devon, PL4 8AA (01752-
232307; *fax:* 01752-232340)
Email: libraryservices@plymouth.ac.uk
Internet: http://www.plymouth.ac.uk/library/

Gov Body: Univ of Plymouth *Chief:* Head of Info
& Learning Svcs: Mr Bob Sharpe BSc, MSc, DMS
Dep: Head of Customer Svcs: Miss Penny Holland
BA, DipLib, MCLIP; Head of Learning & Rsrch
Support: Miss Jane Gosling BSc, MCLIP
Assoc Libs: PLYMOUTH SITE LIB, addr as above;
SEALE-HAYNE SITE LIB (see **S1603**); EXETER
CAMPUS LIB (see **S673**); EXMOUTH CAMPUS
LIB (see **S674**)
Entry: ref only *Open: Plymouth:* term: Mon-Fri
0830-2200, Sat 0900-1700, Sun (ref only) 1000-
1800; vac: Mon-Fri 0830-1700, Sat 0900-1700,
Sun (ref only) 1000-1800, closed Sat-Sun during
summer; hrs may vary at other sites
Subj: all subjs; undergrad; postgrad; vocational
Co-op Schemes: Learning Through Libs in
Plymouth, UK Libs Plus, SCONUL Vac Scheme
Equip: 3 m-readers, m-printer, 4 video viewers, 12
copiers (A4/5p), clr copier, 55 computers (incl wd-
proc & CD-ROM, access limited) *Disabled:* CCTV

Special Libraries

Plymouth
▼
Portsmouth

(Univ of Plymouth, Info & Learning Svcs cont)
Equip: *Online:* EBSCO, IDEAL, EDINA, ASSIA, BHI, CINAHL, Medline, NISS, PsycInfo, Index to Theses, Web of Science, Ingenta, Business Source Premier & others (for membs of Univ only)
Svcs: ref
Stock: bks/502185, incl AVs; periodcls/2874
Classn: DDC **Auto Sys:** Libertas
Staff: Libns: 25 Other Prof: 22 Non-Prof: 41 (incl media svcs staff)

Pontefract

S1813 ✚
Pontefract General Infirmary, Health Library
Pontefract Genl Infirmary, Friarwood Ln, Pontefract, W Yorkshire, WF8 1PL *(tel & fax:* 01977-606638)
Email: health-library.pgi@panp-tr.northy.nhs.uk

Gov Body: Mid Yorkshire Hosps NHS Trust
Chief: Libn: Miss Jane Smethurst BA, MCLIP
Entry: adv appt for non-Trust staff **Open:** Mon, Wed-Thu 0830-1700, Tue 0830-1900, Fri 0830-1630
Subj: medicine; healthcare **Co-op Schemes:** Northern & Yorkshire Health Libs, JHLS, BLDSC
Equip: copier (5p per pg), 4 computers (all with wd-proc, internet & CD-ROM) **Svcs:** info, ref, biblio
Stock: bks/4000; periodcls/100
Classn: NLM (Wessex) **Auto Sys:** DBTextworks
Staff: Libns: 1 Non-Prof: 1

Pontypridd

S1814 🎓
Pontypridd College Learning Centre
Ynys Ter, Rhydyfelin, Pontypridd, Rhondda Cynon Taff, CF37 5RN (01443-663005; *fax:* 01443-663028)
Email: d.mitchell@pontypridd.ac.uk
Internet: http://www.pontypridd.ac.uk/

Chief: Libn: Mr Donald Mitchell BA(Hons), MA, MCLIP
Assoc Libs: ABERDARE CAMPUS LEARNING CENTRE, Cwmdare Rd, Aberdare, Rhondda Cynon Taff, CF44 8BR; GLAMORGAN CENTRE FOR ART & DESIGN TECH LEARNING CENTRE, Glyntaff Rd, Glyntaff, Pontypridd, Rhondda Cynon Taff, CF37 4AT; RHONDDA CAMPUS LEARNING CENTRE, Llwynypia, Tonypandy, Rhondda Cynon Taff, CF40 2TQ
Entry: open to all Coll staff & students, ref access only for public **Open:** term: Mon-Thu 0830-1900, Fri 0830-1600; vac: may vary, 0900-1600 on days when open, tel in adv to confirm
Subj: all subjs; genl; GCSE; A level; undergrad; vocational; prof **Co-op Schemes:** BLDSC
Equip: m-reader, m-printer, video viewer, copier, computers (incl wd-proc, internet & CD-ROM), tape/slide viewer, audio-cassette player **Svcs:** info, ref, biblio
Stock: bks/18400 titles (c37000 vols incl bnd periodcls); periodcls/291; slides/160; pamphs/1570; maps/85; m-forms/2 databases; audios/50; videos/551; CD-ROMs/134
Classn: DDC, CLCI (for careers material) **Auto Sys:** Trax
Staff: Libns: 1 Other Prof: 2 Non-Prof: 3

S1815 🎓
University of Glamorgan, Learning Resources Centre
Treforest, Pontypridd, Rhondda Cynon Taff, CF37 1DL (01443-482625; *fax:* 01443-482629)
Email: smorgan1@glam.ac.uk
Internet: http://www.glam.ac.uk/lrc/

Chief: Head of the LRC: Mr Jeremy Atkinson BSc, MPhil, DipLib, MCLIP **Dep:** Dep Head of the LRC: Mr Steve Morgan BA, MEd, MBA, FCLIP
Assoc Libs: GLYNTAFF LRC, Cemetry Rd, Glyntaff, Pontypridd, CF37 4BL (01443-483153; *fax:* 01443-483150); *Hosp Libs:* PRINCE CHARLES HOSP LIB (see **S1543**); PRINCESS OF WALES HOSP POSTGRAD LIB (see **S224**); ROYAL GLAMORGAN HOSP LIB (see **S979**)
Entry: ref access for external users; corporate & external membership available (details on request)
Open: term: 7 days a wk; vac: 5 days a wk (precise opening hrs in LRC guide)
Subj: all subjs; undergrad; postgrad **Collns:** Bks & Pamphs: Centre for the Study of Welsh Writing in English **Co-op Schemes:** UK Libs Plus, WALIA, CROESO
Equip: m-readers, m-printers, video viewers, copiers, computers (incl wd-proc, internet & CD-ROM), slide viewers, digital cameras, audio cassette players, room for hire, laptops for loan **Disabled:** Kurzweil **Online:** Dialog **Svcs:** info, ref, biblio, indexing, abstracting
Stock: bks/250000; periodcls/c6000; slides/8537; m-forms/20763; AVs/7752
Classn: DDC **Auto Sys:** Talis
Pubns: LRC Guide; other specialist guides
Staff: Libns: 20.5 Non-Prof: 46.5, incl media svcs staff

Poole

S1816 🎓
The Bournemouth and Poole College, Learning Resources Centre
North Rd, Parkstone, Poole, Dorset, BH14 0LS (01202-205804; *fax:* 01202-205477)
Internet: http://www.thecollege.co.uk/

Chief: Head of Learning Resource Svcs: Mr Quinton O'Kane MA(Hons), MCLIP **Dep:** Mgr of Coll LRCs: Ms Rosemary Beal BLib, MCLIP
Assoc Libs: NORTH RD LRC, addr as above; CONSTITUTION HILL LRC, Parkstone, Poole, Dorset, BH14 0QS; LANSDOWNE LRC, The Lansdowne, Bournemouth, Dorset, BH1 3JJ; POOLE LRC, Parkstone, Poole, Dorset, BH14 0LS
Entry: ref only (must register as external student)
Open: term: Mon-Thu 0845-2100, Fri 0845-1700, Sat 0900-1300; vac: Mon-Fri 0900-1700
Subj: North Rd LRC: eng; construction; computing; business studies; social studies; health care; arts; humanities; mgmt; prof studies; Constitution Hill LRC: GCSE; A level; music & drama; Lansdowne LRC: GCSE; A level; social care; health care; counselling; edu; hairdressing; beauty therapy; business studies; catering; tourism; hotel mgmt; sci; maths; computing **Co-op Schemes:** BLDSC, HATRICS
Equip: m-reader, m-printer, video viewers, copiers (A4/5p), computers (incl internet, students only)
Svcs: info, ref
Stock: bks/69865; periodcls/311; videos/3692; AVs/2452
Classn: DDC **Auto Sys:** COLS
Staff: Libns: 8 Non-Prof: 13

S1817 🎓
Bournemouth University Library
Talbot Campus, Fern Barrow, Poole, Dorset, BH12 5BB (01202-595044; *fax:* 01202-595475)
Email: jascott@bournemouth.ac.uk
Internet: http://www.bournemouth.ac.uk/library/

Gov Body: Bournemouth Univ **Chief:** Associate Head of Academic Svcs (Univ Libn): Mr David Ball MA(Oxon), DipLib, MLitt, MIMgt, FCLIP (dball@bournemouth.ac.uk) **Dep:** Dep Univ Libn: Mrs Jill Beard BA, MCLIP **Other Snr Staff:** Lib Procurement & Systems Development Mgr: Mr Chris Spencer BSc, DipLib, MCLIP (cspencer@bournemouth.ac.uk)
Assoc Libs: BOURNEMOUTH HOUSE LIB, 19 Christchurch Rd, Bournemouth, BH1 3LH
Entry: non-membs by appt **Open:** term: Mon-Thu 0900-2100, Fri 0915-1715, Sat 0930-1800, Sun 1000-1700; vac: Mon-Fri 0900-1700 (see web site for opening hrs on selected weekends)
Subj: all subjs; undergrad; postgrad **Collns:** Bks & Pamphs: Wedlake & Greening Colln (archaeo); Dorset Colln; CHIDE Colln (Centre for Hist of Defence Electronics, radar & related war-time documents); Media Hist Colln **Co-op Schemes:** BLDSC, Southern Univs Purchasing Consortium, Wessex Libs PC, HATRICS, SCONUL, SWRLS
Equip: m-reader, 3 m-printers (5p per sheet), 13 video viewers, 15 copiers (A4/5p), 2 clr copiers (A4/50p, A3/£1), 250 computers (incl wd-proc & CD-ROM), 4 rooms for hire **Disabled:** Kurzweil on 2 PCs, 5 PCs & 4 scanners with range of software for dyslexics, hearing impaired & visually impaired
Stock: bks/257538; periodcls/2700 + 3100 e-journals; slides/6 sets; pamphs/some; videos/5000; CD-ROMs/1000 **Acqs Offcr:** Lib Procurement & Systems Development Mgr, as above
Classn: DDC **Auto Sys:** Talis
Pubns: BUOPOLIS 1 – Routes to Quality: Proceedings of Conference BULISC 95 (£17.70); BUOPOLIS 2 – New Tricks? Staff Development for the Elec Lib: Proceedings of Conference BULISC 96 (£17.50); British Nursing Index (annual, £130, also available on CD-ROM & via internet); Nursing & Midwifery Index (1994, 1995, 1996, £105 each)
Staff: Libns: 19.4 Other Prof: 1 Non-Prof: 25.5 + 9.2 ancillary posts **Exp:** £844060 (2000-01); £903558 (2001-02); exp on total info provision, incl stock, serials, binding, elec resources & ILL transactions

S1818 🔑 🏛
Dorset Provincial Museum and Library
Masonic Hall, 57 Ashley Rd, Parkstone, Poole, Dorset, BH14 9BT (01202-736323)
Internet: http://ourworld.compuserve.com/homepages/PGL_Dorset/museum.htm

Chief: Curator: Mr Peter Marks **Other Snr Staff:** Asst Curator: Mr Fred Poate; Libn: Mr Ron Adlem
Entry: membs of the Province of Dorset **Open:** Tue-Wed, Fri 0930-1230; other times by appt
Subj: freemasonry **Collns:** Bks & Pamphs: Lodge hists & refs, incl some early eds
Stock: bks/c1000

S1819 🔑
Royal National Lifeboat Institute Library
West Quay Rd, Poole, Dorset, BH15 1HZ (01202-663000; *fax:* 01202-663189)
Email: info@rnli.org.uk
Internet: http://www.rnli.org.uk/

Type: lifeboat charity **Chief:** Hon Libn: Mr Barry Cox
Entry: by appt **Open:** Mon-Fri 0930-1630
Subj: lifeboats **Collns:** Archvs: RNLI minute bks from 1824; RNLI annual reports from 1824; RNLI journals from 1852
Equip: copier, fax **Disabled:** wheelchair access & lift **Svcs:** info, ref
Stock: bks/500
Staff: Non-Prof: 1 **Exp:** stock acquired mainly in form of gifts

Port Talbot

S1820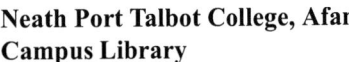
Neath Port Talbot College, Afan Campus Library

Margam, Port Talbot, W Glamorgan, SA13 2AL (01639-648000)
Email: lynne.evans@nptc.ac.uk
Internet: http://www.nptc.ac.uk/

Gov Body: Corp Coll *Chief:* Lib & Learning Resources Mgr: Miss Lynne Evans BA, MA
Assoc Libs: NEATH CAMPUS LIB (see **S1565**)
Entry: ref only for non-Coll students & teaching/support staff *Open:* term: Mon-Thu 0830-1915, Fri 0830-1615; vac: Mon-Fri 0845-1645
Subj: all subjs; GCSE; A level; vocational *Collns: Bks & Pamphs:* European Info Colln; Further Edu Staff Info Colln *Co-op Schemes:* BLDSC
Equip: copier, 24 computers (incl 21 with wd-proc, 21 with internet & 3 with CD-ROM) *Svcs:* info, ref, biblio
Stock: bks/15000; periodcls/65; audios/100
Classn: DDC *Auto Sys:* Alice
Pubns: Recent Acqs Listing (3 pa, free); Lib & Info Skills Training Aids (free)
Staff: Libns: 1 *Non-Prof:* 2.5

S1821 ✚
Neath Port Talbot Hospital, Education Library

Edu Centre, Neath Port Talbot Hosp, Baglan Way, Port Talbot, W Glamorgan, SA12 7BX (01639-862369; *fax:* 01639-862548)
Email: sarah.george@bromor-tr.wales.nhs.uk

Gov Body: Bro Morgannwg NHS Trust *Chief:* Health Libn: Miss Sarah M. George *Dep:* Lib Asst: Mrs Susan J. Lewis
Entry: all staff within Bro Morgannwg NHS Trust; genl medical & health practitioners in the Trust area *Open:* Mon-Fri 0830-1630
Subj: medicine; allied health sci; primary care *Co-op Schemes:* regional: AWHL, AWHILES; natl: BLDSC, BMA, RCS
Equip: m-fiche reader, copier, 4 computers (all with wd-proc & CD-ROM, 3 with internet), flatbed scanner *Svcs:* info, ref, biblio
Stock: bks/4000; periodcls/60; videos/100
Classn: NLM (Wessex) *Auto Sys:* Voyager
Pubns: Lib Svc Guide; Lit Searching Guide (both for NHS staff only)
Staff: Libns: 1 *Non-Prof:* 0.6 *Exp:* £5000 (2000-01)

Portsmouth

S1822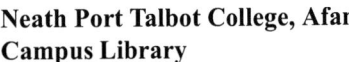
Centre for Economics and Management of Aquatic Resources, Reading Room

Univ of Portsmouth, Locksway Rd, Portsmouth, Hampshire, PO4 8JF (023-9284-4082; *fax:* 023-9284-4614)
Email: christopher.martin@port.ac.uk
Internet: http://web.port.ac.uk/departments/economics/cemare/

Gov Body: Univ of Portsmouth (see **S1829**)
Chief: Technical Asst: Mr Christopher Martin BSc(Hons)
Entry: staff & students of Univ; ref only for others (regular external visitors must register as external users with the Univ Lib) *Open:* term: Mon-Fri 0900-1300, 1400-1700; vac: Mon-Fri 0900-1300, 1400-1600
Subj: undergrad; postgrad; social sci; sci; tech; econ; mgmt & development of aquatic resources; fisheries; aquaculture; coastal zone mgmt;

environmental mgmt *Collns: Bks & Pamphs:* extensive reprint colln; major colln of reports, bulletins & other documents; FAO Colln (pubns of the Food & Agric Org of the United Nations) *Other:* maps & charts *Co-op Schemes:* BLDSC, EURASLIC, IAMSLIC, IAALD
Equip: m-reader, m-printer, copier *Online:* own specialised databases: FISHECON, CEMARE Serials, TROPFISH; other databases incl: Aquatic Sciences & Fisheries Abstracts, ABI Inform Global, Applied Science & Technology Index, BHI, Biological & Agricultural Index, BNB, EconLit, GeoRef, Geobase
Stock: bks/12000; periodcls/80, plus c320 no longer current; m-forms/800
Classn: DDC *Auto Sys:* Talis
Pubns: CEMARE misc pubns; CEMARE rsrch papers (free); CEMARE reports
Staff: Non-Prof: 1

S1823 🏛️ 🏛️
Charles Dickens Birthplace Museum

393 Old Commercial Rd, Portsmouth, Hampshire, PO1 4QL (023-92827261; *fax:* 023-92875276)
Internet: http://ourworld.compuserve.com/homepages/portmus/

Type: local authority *Gov Body:* Portsmouth City Council (see **P148**) *Chief:* Collns Offcr: Rosalinda Handiman BA, DipAGMS, AMA
Entry: ref only, adv appt *Open: Museum:* Apr-Oct: Mon-Fri 1000-1630; *Reserve Collns:* strictly by appt
Subj: lit: solely relating to Charles Dickens
Collns: Bks & Pamphs: publ refs to Charles Dickens *Archvs:* a few autograph letters, notes, paper items signed by Charles Dickens
Equip: fax, copier (main museum only) *Disabled:* not accessible to disabled *Svcs:* ref
Stock: bks/30; photos/50; slides/100; illusts/150; pamphs/10-15; 120 other items
Pubns: Guide to Museum (£1); postcards (20p-60p)
Staff: Other Prof: 1 *Non-Prof:* 2

S1824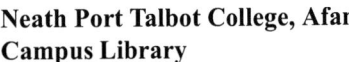
Highbury College Portsmouth, Library

Dovercourt Rd, Cosham, Portsmouth, Hampshire, PO6 2SA (023-9228-3213; *fax:* 023-9232-5551)
Email: info@highbury.ac.uk
Internet: http://www.highbury.ac.uk/

Chief: Coll Libn: Mrs S. Stevenson BA, CertEd, MCLIP
Assoc Libs: UNICORN LIB, Unicorn Rd, Portsmouth, Hampshire, PO1 4AU (023-9285-6610; *email:* unicorn.library@highbury.ac.uk)
Open: Cosham Lib: term: Mon-Thu 0830-2100, Fri 0830-1800, Sat 1000-1600; vac: Mon-Thu 0900-1700, Fri 0900-1630; *Unicorn Lib:* term: Mon, Thu 0830-1900, Tue 0830-1730, Wed, Fri 0830-1700
Subj: all those supporting courses offered by the Coll, incl: bldg; civil eng; business; mgmt studies; electrical eng; elec eng; mechanical eng; media studies; hotel & catering (particularly strong) *Co-op Schemes:* BLDSC, SWRLS, HATRICS
Equip: video viewer, copier, clr copier, 100 computers (incl wd-proc, internet & CD-ROM), cassette player *Online:* Campus 2000 *Svcs:* info, ref
Stock: bks/55000; periodcls/300
Classn: DDC *Auto Sys:* Heritage IV
Staff: Libns: 5 *Non-Prof:* 13

S1825 ✚
Portsmouth Hospitals NHS Trust Library Service

Edu Centre, St Mary's Hosp, Milton Rd, Portsmouth, Hampshire, PO3 6AD (023-9228-6000 x4856; *fax:* 023-9286-6847)
Email: Library.smh@porthosp.nhs.uk
Internet: http://www.portshosp.org.uk/text/library/

Chief: Lib Svcs Mgr: Miss H.E. Bingham MSc, MCLIP *Other Snr Staff:* Svc Development Libn: Ms Pauline Blagden
Assoc Libs: QUEEN ALEXANDRA HOSP LIB (see **S1826**)
Entry: Hampshire health or social care staff & students; others adv appt, ref only *Open:* Mon-Fri 0830-1700
Subj: medicine; nursing; midwifery; mental health; biomedical sci; health care mgmt *Co-op Schemes:* BLDSC, SWRLIN, HATRICS, HLN, PLCS, NULJ
Equip: video viewers, copiers, computers (incl wd-proc & internet), scanners *Online:* AMED, BNI, CINAHL, Cochrane, Embase, HMIC, Medline, PsycInfo, Zetoc & others *Svcs:* info, ref
Stock: bks/14000; periodcls/400
Classn: NLM (Wessex) *Auto Sys:* Heritage
Staff: Libns: 3.81 *Non-Prof:* 4.95

S1826 ✚
Queen Alexandra Hospital Library

The QuAD Centre, Queen Alexandra Hosp, Cosham, Portsmouth, Hampshire, PO6 3LY (023-9228-6039; *fax:* 023-9228-6880)
Email: Library.qah@porthosp.nhs.uk

Gov Body: Portsmouth Hosps NHS Trust *Chief:* Lib Svcs Mgr: Miss Helen Bingham MSc, MCLIP
Assoc Libs: ST MARY'S HOSP LIB (see **S1825**)
Entry: Hampshire health/social care staff & students; adv appt, ref only for others *Open:* Mon-Fri 0830-1700
Subj: medicine; nursing; midwifery; mental health; biomedical sci; health care mgmt *Co-op Schemes:* BLDSC, SWRLIN, HATRICS, HLN, PLCS, NULJ
Equip: copier, computers (incl wd-proc & internet) *Online:* AMED, BNI, CINAHL, Cochrane, Embase, HMIC, Medline, PsycInfo, Zetoc & others *Svcs:* info, ref
Classn: NLM (Wessex) *Auto Sys:* Heritage

S1827 🏛️ 🏛️
Royal Naval Museum Library

HM Naval Base (PP66), Portsmouth, Hampshire, PO1 3NH (023-9272-3795; *fax:* 023-9272-3942)
Email: library@royalnavalmuseum.org
Internet: http://www.royalnavalmuseum.org/

Gov Body: Trustees of The Royal Navy Museum *Chief:* Libn & Head of Info Svcs: Mrs A.D. Wareham BA(Hons), MCLIP *Dep:* Asst Libn: Miss H. Downer MA, MCLIP
Assoc Libs: ROYAL NAVAL MUSEUM ARCHV, at same addr, Curator of MSS: Mr M. Sheldon
Entry: prior appt only *Open:* Mon-Fri 1000-1600
Subj: Royal Navy in social & maritime hist; naval sci; naval law; naval biography; naval hist (esp WW1 & WW2) *Collns: Bks & Pamphs:* Admiralty Lib (c60000 vols); large journal colln of British & foreign titles; Navy Records Soc Colln; selected parliamentary papers *Archvs:* Admiralty Lib MSS; Admiral John Fisher papers; personal documentary & ephemeral material relating aspects of the social hist of Royal Navy *Other:* charts & atlases
Equip: m-reader, copier *Svcs:* info, ref, biblio, indexing
Stock: bks/70000; periodcls/30
Classn: LC (mod) *Auto Sys:* SydneyPlus
Staff: Libns: 2 *Other Prof:* 1 *Exp:* £3000 (1999-2000)

S1828 🎓

University of Portsmouth, Eldon Library

Eldon Bldg, Winston Churchill Ave, Portsmouth, Hampshire, PO1 2DJ (023-9282-6437; *fax:* 023-9275-6152)
Internet: http://www.port.ac.uk/

Gov Body: Univ of Portsmouth (see **S1829**)
Chief: Subj Libn: Ms Jane Paine *Dep:* Site Libn: Mr Chris Martin
Entry: membs of Univ *Open:* term: Mon-Thu 0830-1830, Fri 0830-1630; vac: Mon-Thu 0830-1700, Fri 0830-1630
Subj: art; design *Collns: Bks & Pamphs:* careers colln *Other:* AV Colln; posters; sound effects; newspaper cuttings *Co-op Schemes:* ILL, ARLIS
Equip: video viewers, copier, computers (incl wd-proc, internet & CD-ROM) *Online:* Art Abstracts, Design & Applied Arts Index, Art Bibliographies Modern, BHI, BFI Film Index Internatl
Stock: bks/24000; periodcls/260; slides/c30000 + 40 tape-slide sets; audios/450; videos/1796
Staff: Libns: 2 *Non-Prof:* 4

S1829 🎓

University of Portsmouth, Frewen Library

Cambridge Rd, Portsmouth, Hampshire, PO1 2ST (023-9287-6543; *fax:* 023-9284-3233)
Email: library@port.ac.uk
Internet: http://www.libr.port.ac.uk/

Chief: Univ Libn: Mr Ian Bonar BSc, MCLIP
Assoc Libs: ELDON LIB (see **S1828**); GOLD-SMITH LEARNING CENTRE, Goldsmith Bldg, Univ of Portsmouth, Portsmouth, Hampshire (023-9284-4048)
Entry: ref only; for external borrowing membership, appl to Libn *Open:* term: Mon-Sun 0800-2400; vac: Mon-Fri 0900-1730, Sat 1000-1600
Subj: undergrad; postgrad; academic subjs *Co-op Schemes:* BLDSC, HATRICS
Equip: m-reader, m-printer, video viewer, copiers, computers
Stock: bks/500000; periodcls/3000
Auto Sys: Talis
Staff: Libns: 18 *Other Prof:* 48 *Non-Prof:* 4 *Exp:* £910000 (1999-2000); £928000 (2000-01)

Potters Bar

S1830 🏛

National Institute for Biological Standards and Control, Library

Blanche Ln, South Mimms, Potters Bar, Hertfordshire, EN6 3QG (01707-654753; *fax:* 01707-646845)
Email: library@nibsc.ac.uk
Internet: http://www.nibsc.ac.uk/

Gov Body: Natl Biological Standards Board
Chief: Lib Dir: Mrs Anita Brewer BSc, DipIS, MCLIP *Dep:* Dep Libn: Mr Jeremy Evans BSc, MSc, MCLIP
Entry: ref only, adv appt *Open:* Mon-Fri 0900-1700
Subj: antibiotics; biology; blood coagulation factors; hormones; immunology; biomedical rsrch; bacteriology; haematology; virology; medicine;

antisera vaccines; immunobiology; endocrinology; blood products; enzymes; AIDS; biochem; chem; vaccines; endovirology; microbiology; electron microscopy; computing; statistics
Equip: copier, m-reader, computers (incl CD-ROM) *Online:* ISI Web of Science, STN Easy
Stock: bks/5000; periodcls/175; m-forms/30; AVs/20; theses/30; govt documents/1100
Classn: NLM *Auto Sys:* Sirsi Unicorn
Staff: Libns: 1 *Other Prof:* 1

S1831 🔑

Radio Society of Great Britain, National Amateur Radio Library

Lambda House, Cranbourne Rd, Potters Bar, Hertfordshire, EN6 3JE (0870-904-7373; *fax:* 0870-904-7374)
Internet: http://www.rsgb.org/

Chief: Libn: Mr J. Crabbe
Entry: ref for membs & staff *Open:* Mon-Fri 1000-1600
Subj: radio; electronics; am radio; television
Collns: Bks & Pamphs: RADCOM Soc journals from foreign countries *Archvs:* amateur radio & soc hist from 1894
Equip: fax, computer (with wd-proc) *Svcs:* info, ref
Stock: bks/1100; periodcls/50; photos/50; audios/20; videos/5
Staff: Non-Prof: 1 *Exp:* £500 (1999-2000)

Prenton

S1832 🏛

Proudman Oceanographic Laboratory Library

Bidston Observatory, Bidston Hill, Prenton, Merseyside, CH43 7RA (0151-653-8633; *fax:* 0151-653-6269)
Email: jul@pol.ac.uk

Type: rsrch *Gov Body:* NERC *Chief:* Libn: Ms Julia Martin BA, MSc, MCLIP
Entry: bona fide rsrchers by prior appt only
Open: Mon-Fri 0900-1700
Subj: physical oceanography; marine sci *Co-op Schemes:* BLDSC, ILL
Equip: m-reader, copier, 2 computers (both with internet & CD-ROM) *Svcs:* info, ref, indexing
Stock: bks/5000; periodcls/79
Classn: LC *Auto Sys:* Olib
Staff: Libns: 2 *Non-Prof:* 1 temp

Presteigne

S1833 🔑

Radnorshire Society Library

Pool House, Discoyd, Presteigne, Powys, LD8 2NW (01547-560318)

Chief: Hon Libns: Mr J. Barker & Mr G. Ridyard
Entry: membs of Soc only *Open:* as required
Subj: Radnorshire: local hist & geog
Svcs: ref

Preston

S1834 ✎

Central and West Lancashire Chamber of Commerce, Library and Information Service

9-10 Eastway Business Village, Olivers Pl, Fulwood, Preston, Lancashire, PR2 9WT (01772-653000; *fax:* 01772-655544)
Email: info@lancschamber.co.uk
Internet: http://www.lancschamber.co.uk/

Chief: Info Offcr: Mr Mark Whittle *Dep:* Mr Mark Hodson
Entry: adv appt preferred *Open:* Mon-Fri 0900-1300, 1400-1700
Subj: business
Equip: 2 copiers, fax, video viewer, 20 computers (all with wd-proc, internet & CD-ROM), room for hire *Online:* ICC, Experian, Kompass (on appl)
Svcs: info, ref
Stock: bks/1000; CD-ROMs/30
Staff: Other Prof: 2 *Non-Prof:* 2

S1835 🎓 ✚

Lancashire Teaching Hospitals NHS Trust, Library and Information Service

(formerly Royal Preston Hosp, Acute Lib)
Royal Preston Hosp, Sharoe Green Ln, Fulwood, Preston, Lancashire, PR4 9HT (01772-522763; *fax:* 01772-788472)
Email: mandy.beaumont@lthtr.nhs.uk

Type: multiprofessional *Gov Body:* Lancashire Teaching Hosps NHS Trust *Chief:* Lib Mgr: Mrs Amanda Beaumont BA, MSc
Assoc Libs: CHORLEY LIB (see **S475**)
Entry: Trust employees, students on placement & community staff *Open:* Mon, Wed-Fri 0900-1700, Tue 0900-1900
Subj: medicine (all aspects); health svc mgmt & admin; nursing *Co-op Schemes:* BLDSC, BMA, John Rylands Univ, RCS
Equip: m-reader, copier, video viewer, 8 computers (incl wd-proc & internet) *Svcs:* info, ref, biblio, training
Classn: NLM *Auto Sys:* Heritage
Pubns: Guide to the Lib; Guide to Using Databases; database info handout
Staff: Libns: 1 *Non-Prof:* 2

S1836 🔑

Library of Light-Orchestral Music

Lancaster Farm, Chipping Ln, Longridge, Preston, Lancashire, PR3 2NB (01772-783646; *fax:* 01772-786026)

Gov Body: Light Music Soc *Chief:* Chairman: Mr Ernest Tomlinson MusB, FRCO, FRMCM *Dep:* Sec: Mrs Hilary Ashton BA, DipABRSM
Entry: adv appt by mail, fax or phone *Open:* phone: Mon-Fri 0930-2000
Subj: light-orchestral music *Collns: Other:* performing material (available for hire, sale); preservation
Equip: copier, computer (staff only), music proc (staff only)
Stock: orchestral sets/30000
Classn: alphanumeric
Pubns: Quarterly Newsletter (Soc membs only, membership £15 pa)
Staff: Other Prof: 3 PT

S1837 🎓

Myerscough College Library

Myerscough Hall, Bilsborrow, Preston, Lancashire, PR3 0RY (01995-642122; *fax:* 01995-642333)
Email: mailbox@myerscough.ac.uk
Internet: http://www.myerscough.ac.uk/

Chief: Coll Libn: Mr J.R. Humfrey BA(Hons), MA, DipLIS, DipEdMan, MCLIP
Entry: ref only *Open:* term: Mon-Thu 0900-2000, Fri 0900-1700, Sat 1000-1700, Sun 1000-1600; vac: Mon-Fri 0900-1700
Subj: local study (Lancashire); land-based industries; leisure mgmt; generalities; social sci; sci; tech; equine sci; veterinary nursing *Collns: Archvs:* coll hist, incl photos & record bks *Other:* specialist agric & hortic colln *Co-op Schemes:* BLDSC, LINNET, ILL, VALNOW

Equip: m-reader, video viewer, copier, clr copier, computers (incl wd-proc & CD-ROM network), audio-cassette player *Online:* link to UCLAN lib (see **S1840**)
Stock: bks/25000; periodcls/175; photos/250; slides/3000; pamphs/7250; maps/385; videos/200; charts/60
Classn: DDC *Auto Sys:* Talis (via LINNET)
Staff: Libns: 1 *Non-Prof:* 6

S1838

Preston College, The William Tuson Library

St Vincent's Rd, Fulwood, Preston, Lancashire, PR2 4UR (01772-225310; *fax:* 01772-225314)
Email: ejones@prestoncoll.ac.uk
Internet: http://www.prestoncoll.ac.uk/

Chief: Lib Mgr: Mrs E. Jones
Entry: membs of Coll *Open:* term: Mon-Thu 0845-2100, Fri 0930-1700; vac: Mon-Fri 0900-1700
Subj: all subjs; genl; GCSE; A level; vocational
Collns: Bks & Pamphs: local hist colln *Co-op Schemes:* BLDSC, VALNOW, LALNET
Equip: 6 video viewers, 2 copiers, clr copier, 8 computers (all with internet & CD-ROM) *Disabled:* Smartview *Svcs:* info, ref, biblio
Stock: bks/c30000; periodcls/250; CD-ROMs/30
Classn: DDC *Auto Sys:* Heritage
Staff: Libns: 4 *Non-Prof:* 4 FTE

S1839

Talbot Library

(incorporating the RC Diocese of Lancashire Archvs)
St Walburges, Weston St, Preston, Lancashire, PR2 2QE (01772-760186)
Email: mdolan@blueyonder.co.uk

Gov Body: RC Diocese of Lancaster *Chief:* Libn: Rev Michael Dolan MA, FCLIP *Other Snr Staff:* Mr Charles Miller; Ms Judith Swarbrick BA
Entry: ref only *Open:* Mon, Wed, Fri 1000-1600
Subj: local studies (Lancashire & Cumbria); phil; religion; geog; hist; Irish studies; diocesan records
Collns: Bks & Pamphs: Irish Studies Colln; G.K. Chesterton Colln; H. Belloc Colln *Archvs:* RC Diocese of Lancaster Archv
Equip: copier (5p per copy) *Officer-in-Charge:* Libn, as above *Svcs:* info, ref, biblio, rsrch
Stock: bks/60000; periodcls/12; pamphs/1000
Acqs Offcr: Libn, as above
Classn: local scheme
Staff: Libns: 2 *Non-Prof:* 4 *Exp:* £3000 (2000-01)

S1840

University of Central Lancashire, Library and Learning Resource Services

Preston, Lancashire, PR1 2HE (01772-892261; *fax:* 01772-892937)
Email: k.r.ellard@uclan.ac.uk
Internet: http://www.uclan.ac.uk/

Chief: Head of Lib & Learning Resource Svcs: Mr Kevin Ellard BA, MA, DMS, MCLIP *Dep:* Head of Info Svcs: Mr Jeremy Andrew BSc
Assoc Libs: CUMBRIA CAMPUS LIB (see **S1788**); *Clinical Site Libs:* BLACKBURN CLINICAL LIB, Edu Centre, Blackburn Royal Infirmary, Bolton Rd, Blackburn, Lancashire, BB2 3LR (01254-294312; *fax:* 01254-294318; *email:* lblackburn1@uclan.ac.uk); BLACKPOOL CLINICAL LIB (see **S193**); BURNLEY CLINICAL LIB, Edu Centre, Burnley Genl Hosp, Casterton Ave, Burnley, Lancashire, BB10 2PQ (01282-474699; *fax:* 01282-474701; *email:* lburnley@uclan.ac.uk); CHORLEY CLINICAL LIB (see **S475**); ORMSKIRK CLINICAL LIB, LRC, Southport & Ormskirk Dist Genl Hosp, Wigan Rd, Ormskirk, Lancashire, L39 2AZ (01695-656790; *fax:* 01695-575359; *email:* lormskirk@

uclan.ac.uk); WIGAN CLINICAL LIB, Bernard Surgeon Suite, Wigan Edu Centre, RAE Infirmary, Wigan Ln, Wigan, WN1 2NN (01942-822162; *fax:* 01942-822444; *email:* lwigan@uclan.ac.uk)
Entry: staff & students of Univ; ready access for Lancashire County Lib cardholders or cardholders of other University/Coll libs; others by appt only
Open: term: Mon-Thu 0800-0200, Fri 0845-2200, Sat -Sun 0800-2000, vac: Mon-Sun 0800-2000
Subj: all subjs; undergrad; postgrad; vocational
Collns: Bks & Pamphs: local colln (Preston area); illustrated bks colln (18C-20C); Wainright Colln (late 19C political texts); 19C scientific, technical & travel bks *Archvs:* Univ Archvs (incl archvs of original Harris Inst, from 1900s); Shepherd St Mission Colln (homeless accommodation, emigration of children); Livesey Colln (temperance movement); Woodruff Colln *Other:* Design Colln; Charnley Colln of photographs & postcards *Co-op Schemes:* SCONUL, BLDSC, ILL, reciprocal arrangement with Lancaster Univ Lib (see **S883**)
Equip: m-form reader/printer, fax, video viewers, copiers, clr copier, 300 computers (all with wd-proc, internet & CD-ROM), room for hire *Disabled:* equip for deaf, blind & partially sighted *Online:* IDEAL, BIDS, Lexis, Mintel, Profile, CAB, Dissertation Abstracts *Svcs:* info, ref
Stock: bks/450000; periodcls/2100; videos/3000
Classn: DDC *Auto Sys:* Talis
Pubns: info leaflets
Staff: Libns: 28 *Other Prof:* 26 *Non-Prof:* 51

Radlett

S1841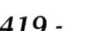

Hertfordshire Partnership NHS Trust, Harperbury Library Services

(formerly Horizon NHS Trust)
Harperbury Hosp, Harper Ln, Shenley, Radlett, Hertfordshire, WD7 9HQ (01923-427205; *fax:* 01923-427390)
Email: helen.bond@hpt.nhs.uk

Gov Body: Horizon NHS Trust *Chief:* Lib Mgr: Mrs D. Levey *Dep:* Snr Lib Asst: Mrs H. Bond
Entry: medical & NHS staff; public by appt *Open:* Mon-Fri 0915-1645
Subj: postgrad; medicine; psychiatry; learning disabilities *Collns: Bks & Pamphs:* special colln on learning disabilities *Other:* training material (videos, tape slides etc on learning disabilities)
Co-op Schemes: PLCS, NWTRLIS, BLDSC
Equip: fax, copier (5p per copy), 4 computers (incl 2 with wd-proc, 3 with CD-ROM & 1 with internet)
Svcs: room hire
Classn: NLM *Staff: Libns:* 1 *Non-Prof:* 2

Reading

S1842

Atomic Weapons Establishment Library

Aldermaston, Reading, Berkshire, RG7 4PR (01734-814111; *fax:* 01734-815320)
Internet: http://www.awe.co.uk/

Gov Body: AWE Mgmt Ltd *Chief:* Mgr, Lib & Info Svcs: Mr A.E.G. Willson *Dep:* Info Section Mgr: Dr J. Brock
Entry: not generally available for use by the public *Open:* Mon-Fri 0830-1600
Subj: at postgrad level: sci; maths; tech; nuclear physics *Co-op Schemes:* BLDSC
Equip: 10 m-readers, m-printer, video viewer, copier, computers (incl 4 CD-ROM) *Online:* Dialog, Datastar, Dialtech, STN, BLAISE LINE *Svcs:* info, ref
Stock: bks/22000; periodcls/450; maps/500; m-forms/250000; technical reports/20000
Classn: UDC *Auto Sys:* EOSi System T
Staff: Libns: 2 *Other Prof:* 2 *Non-Prof:* 7

S1843

British Dyslexia Association Library

98 London Rd, Reading, Berkshire, RG1 5AU (0118-966-2677; *fax:* 0118-935-1927)
Email: admin@bda-dyslexia.demon.co.uk
Internet: http://www.bda-dyslexia.org.uk/

Entry: adv appt
Subj: dyslexia; psy; lang
Stock: bks/600
Pubns: various computer bklets (£3.50 each); various introductory computer leaflets (20p-40p each); Dyslexia: Your Questions Answered (£1.95); The Dyslexia Handbook 2000 (£7 + p&p); Day to Day Dyslexia in the Classroom (£12.99); Winning with Dyslexia (£4.50); numerous others, p&p extra
Proj: lib facilities currently being updated

S1844

Council for Environmental Education, Library and Resource Centre

94 London St, Reading, Berkshire, RG1 4SJ (0118-950-2550; *fax:* 0118-959-1955)
Email: enquiries@cee.org.uk
Internet: http://www.cee.org.uk/

Type: charity *Chief:* Head of Info: Ms Christine Midgley BA, MA, MCLIP
Entry: adv appt *Open:* Mon-Fri 0930-1700
Subj: environmental edu
Equip: video viewer, copier, computer (incl CD-ROM) *Online:* access to own database (fees vary)
Svcs: info, ref, biblio
Stock: bks/5000; periodcls/230; pamphs/1000; videos/100; CD-ROMs/30
Classn: CEE Classn Scheme for Environmental Edu
Pubns: CEEview (4 pa, part of membs' subscription); CEEmail (£15 pa)
Staff: Libns: 1 *Non-Prof:* 1 *Exp:* most items received are review/complementary copies

S1845

Institute of Leisure and Amenity Management, Information Centre

ILAM House, Lower Basildon, Reading, Berkshire, RG8 9NE (01491-874800; *fax:* 01491-874801)
Internet: http://www.ilam.co.uk/

Chief: Snr Info Offcr: Ms L. Roper *Dep:* Libn: Ms S.C. Broughton
Entry: adv appt, ref only (charge to non-membs)
Open: Tue-Fri 0900-1700
Subj: leisure; genl activs; tourism, parks & open spaces; sport; play; contracting; genl mgmt
Equip: copier (25p), computer (with wd-proc, internet & CD-ROM) *Svcs:* info, ref
Stock: bks/10000; periodcls/200; CD-ROMs/12
Classn: own *Auto Sys:* CAIRS
Pubns: 101 Ways Series (Best Value, Cultural Strategies, Children's Holiday Activs, Sports Development, Disability Discrimination Act), £15 + p&p membs, £18.75 + p&p non-membs; various parks titles; genl leisure titles; see web site for details
Staff: Libns: 1 *Other Prof:* 2 *Exp:* £6800 (1999-2000); £6800 (2000-01)

S1846

Queen Anne's School Library

6 Henley Rd, Caversham, Reading, Berkshire, RG4 6DX (0118-918-7338; *fax:* 0118-918-7310)
Email: brandh@queenannes.reading.sch.uk

Chief: School Libn: Dr Heather Brand BA(Hons), MA, PhD, DipLib
Entry: those associated with school *Open:* term: Mon-Fri 0800-1830; vac: closed

Special Libraries

Reading ▼ Richmond

(Queen Anne's School Lib cont)
Subj: all subjs; genl; GCSE; A level **Collns:**
Archvs: school archvs (1894-date)
Equip: copier, 11 computers (incl 6 with wd-proc, 6 with internet & 2 with CD-ROM)
Stock: bks/20000; periodcls/30; archvs/1 cubic m
Classn: DDC **Auto Sys:** Alice for Windows
Staff: Libns: 1 *Other Prof:* 2 (1 FTE) *Non-Prof:* 1 (0.5 FTE)

S1847 🎓
Reading College and School of Art and Design, Learning Resource Centres
Crescent Rd, Reading, Berkshire, RG1 5RQ (0118-967-5060; *fax:* 0118-967-5063)
Email: lrckr@reading-college.ac.uk
Internet: http://www.reading-college.ac.uk/

Chief: Learning Resources Mgr: Mr A.R. Turner BA(Hons), MCLIP (turnera@reading-college.ac.uk)
Assoc Libs: CRESENT RD LRC, addr as above, Libn: Mrs Delia Turner BA, MCLIP (0118-967-5360; *fax:* 0118-967-5301; *email:* lrccr@reading-college.ac.uk); KINGS RD LRC, Kings Rd, Reading, Berkshire, RG1 4HJ, Centre Mgr: Mrs Helen Williams BA(Hons), MCLIP (0118-967-5060; *fax:* 0118-967-5063; *email:* lrckr@reading-college.ac.uk)
Entry: non-Coll membs ref only, appt preferred **Open:** term: Mon-Fri 0845-2000, Fri 0930-1630, Sat 1030-1330 (King's Rd only); vac: normally Mon-Fri 0900-1630
Subj: all subjs; genl; GCSE; A level; undergrad; vocational; arts **Co-op Schemes:** BLDSC
Equip: 3 video viewers, 3 copiers A4/4p), 22 computers (all with wd-proc, internet & CD-ROM)
Online: wide range of online subscriptions, incl BS Online, Grove Art & Music, Emerald (coll membs only) **Svcs:** info, ref
Stock: bks/65000; periodcls/250; slides/10000; audios/50; videos/3000; CD-ROMs/100
Classn: DDC **Auto Sys:** Heritage
Staff: Libns: 5 *Non-Prof:* 4.89 **Exp:** £52000 (1999-2000)
Proj: enlarged & refurbished centre at Kings Rd

S1848 🎓
Reading University Library
PO Box 223, Whiteknights, Reading, Berkshire, RG6 6AE (0118-931-8770; *fax:* 0118-931-6636)
Email: Library@reading.ac.uk
Internet: http://www.library.rgd.uk/

Gov Body: The Univ of Reading **Chief:** Univ Libn: Mrs Julia Munro BSc, ARCS, MSc, MBA, MCLIP **Dep:** Dep Libn: Miss Celia Ayres
Assoc Libs: BULMERSHE LIB, Woodlands Ave, Reading, RG6 1HY, Bulmershe Libn: Mr Gordon Connell MA, MSc, MCLIP; MUSIC LIB, 35 Upper Redlands Rd, Reading, RG1 5JE, Music Liaison Libn: Mr Christopher B. Cipkin BA, MA, ARCO, MCLIP
Entry: free access for ref; adv appt for special collns; borrowing privileges available to certain applicants on payment **Open:** Main Whiteknights Lib: term: Mon-Thu 0900-2215, Fri 0900-1900, Sat-Sun 1100-1700; vac: Mon-Fri 0900-1700; contact site libs for opening hrs

Subj: undergrad; postgrad; lang & lit; fine art; planning; law; hist; econ; sci; food studies; agric; edu; music **Collns:** *Bks & Pamphs:* EDC; Cole Lib of Zoology & Hist of Medicine; colln on printing hist; ch's bks colln; Samuel Beckett Colln *Archvs:* farm records; Archv of British Publishing **Co-op Schemes:** HATRICS, ILL
Equip: m-reader, 2 m-printers, video viewer, 12 copiers, clr copier, computers (incl wd-proc, internet & CD-ROM, for membs of Univ only)
Disabled: minicom, CCTV text enlarger **Online:** various **Svcs:** info, ref
Stock: bks/c1000000; periodcls/3700; slides/2100; illusts/1500; pamphs/89018; maps/600; audios/3000; videos/2300; archvs/9000+
Classn: DDC **Auto Sys:** Unicorn
Pubns: The Cole Lib of Early Medicine & Zoology, Part 1 (£15), Part 2 (£10); The Finzi Bk Room at the Univ of Reading: A Catalogue (£15); Catalogue of the Colln of Children's Bks: 1617-1939 (£28); Historical Farm Records (£7.50); Beckett's Dream Notebook (£25); The Samuel Beckett Colln: A Catalogue (£5, £20 with supplements); & others
Staff: Libns: 31.2 *Other Prof:* 1 *Non-Prof:* 42.8
Exp: £1094000 (1999-2000)

S1849 ✚
Royal Berkshire and Battle Hospitals NHS Trust, Trust Library
Trust Edu Centre, Royal Berkshire Hosp, London Rd, Reading, Berkshire, RG1 5AN (0118-987-7848/9; *fax:* 0118-987-7032)
Email: Trustlibrary.enquiries@rbbh-tr.nhs.uk

Chief: Lib Svcs Mgr: Ms Marie Hickman (marie.hickman@rbbh-tr.nhs.uk) **Other Snr Staff:** Asst Libns: Mrs Jill Duncan & Mrs Lucy Gilham
Entry: ref only for non membs **Open:** staffed: 0900-1700; 24 hr access available for Trust staff only
Subj: health; medicine **Collns:** *Bks & Pamphs:* Hamilton Fairley Colln (tropical medicine, 200 vols); Keith Lyle Colln (ophthalmology, 100 vols); Bryn Thomas Colln (hist of medicine & anaesthesia, 400 vols)
Equip: m-reader, copier, clr copier, 9 computers (all with wd-proc, 8 with internet & 8 with CD-ROM)
Online: OVID databases: AMED, Medline, CINAHL, PsycInfo **Svcs:** info, ref
Stock: bks/4000; periodcls/300; CD-ROMs/25
Classn: NLM **Auto Sys:** Heritage, Winchill
Staff: Libns: 2.2 *Non-Prof:* 1.3

S1850 🔑 🎓
Rural History Centre
Univ of Reading, Whiteknights, PO Box 229, Reading, Berkshire, RG6 6AG (0118-931-8660; *fax:* 0118-975-1264)
Email: j.s.creasey@reading.ac.uk
Internet: http://www.ruralhistory.org/

Gov Body: Univ of Reading (see **S1848**) **Chief:** Libn & Info Offcr: Mr John S. Creasey BA, MA(Lib)
Entry: ref only, appt needed for specific rsrch **Open:** Mon-Fri 1000-1630
Subj: genl; undergrad; postgrad; economic & agrarian hist; land & environment; agric; agric tech; livestock husbandry; food hist; craft industries; farm & rural bldgs; local hist; rural life & soc **Collns:** *Bks & Pamphs:* Edgar Thomas Colln (agric econ); Nuptown House Colln (early agric lit); historic dairying; milling & baking *Archvs:* agric eng industry; agric assocs; unions & co-op socs; countryside amenity orgs **Co-op Schemes:** ILL
Equip: m-reader, video viewer, fax, copier, computers (incl wd-proc & CD-ROM) **Online:** Rural Hist Database (via WWW)
Stock: bks/40000; periodcls/80 + 500 no longer current; photos/500000; slides/2000; pamphs/7000; maps/500; m-forms/100; audios/300; videos/50

Classn: RHC **Auto Sys:** Olib
Pubns: Lib Procedure & Classn (£1)
Staff: Libns: 1 *Other Prof:* 0.25 *Non-Prof:* 0.5
Exp: £3000 (1999-2000)

S1851 🎓
Witan Hall Library
London Rd, Reading, Berkshire, RG1 5AQ (0118-920-9321)
Email: sharrocks@gyosei.ac.uk
Internet: http://www.gyosei.ac.uk/en/facilities/library.html

Gov Body: Witan Hall, incorporating Gyosei Internatl Coll in the UK **Chief:** Libn: Mr Mike Sharrocks BA, MCLIP **Dep:** Asst Libn: Ms Naoko Furuichi **Other Snr Staff:** Lib Asst: Ms Naomi Inglis
Entry: staff & students of Coll; ref only for others at the discretion of the Libn **Open:** term: Mon, Wed 0900-2000, Tue, Thu-Fri 0900-1800, Sat 1000-1300
Subj: business; mgmt; cultural studies; lit; hist; Japan; Japanese lang; Japanese culture
Equip: copier, video viewer, computers (incl internet & CD-ROM) **Online:** various CD-ROM databases & online info resources
Stock: bks/45000 (32000 in Japanese, 13000 in English)

Redditch

S1852 ✚
Worcestershire Acute Hospitals NHS Trust, Alexandra Hospital Library
Woodrow Dr, Redditch, Worcestershire, B98 7UB (01527-503030; *fax:* 01527-518489)
Email: pgmc.library@worcsacute.wmids.nhs.uk
Internet: http://www.worcestershireknowledgeportal.co.uk/

Gov Body: Worcestershire Acute Hosps NHS Trust **Chief:** Site Libn: Ms Samantha Lloyd BA, MCLIP (sam.lloyd@worcsacute.wmids.nhs.uk)
Assoc Libs: KIDDERMINSTER HOSP LIB (see **S862**); WORCESTER ROYAL HOSP, ROWLANDS LIB (see **S2149**)
Entry: Worcestershire health staff **Open:** Mon-Fri 0830-1700
Subj: medicine **Co-op Schemes:** BLDSC, WMRHLN, Worcestershire Health Libs
Equip: copier, computers
Classn: NLM **Auto Sys:** Unicorn

Redhill

S1853 🎓
East Surrey College, Learner Centres
Claremont Rd, Gatton Pt North, Redhill, Surrey, RH1 2JX (01737-772611; *fax:* 01737-768641)
Internet: http://www.esc.org.uk/

Gov Body: East Surrey Coll Corp **Chief:** Head of Libs: Mrs Fina Harries BA(Hons) **Dep:** Mrs Sarah Costelloe BSc(Hons)
Entry: ref only for membs of public, or payment of annual fee for limited membership **Open:** term: Mon-Thu 0845-1950, Fri 0845-1650, Sat 1000-1400; vac: Mon-Fri 0900-1650
Subj: all subjs; genl; GCSE; A level; vocational **Collns:** *Bks & Pamphs:* art colln **Co-op Schemes:** ILL, SASLIC
Equip: 2 video viewers, 2 copiers, 80 computers (incl 75 with wd-proc, 70 with internet & 70 with CD-ROM) **Svcs:** info, ref
Stock: bks/40000; periodcls/350; videos/600
Classn: DDC **Auto Sys:** Heritage
Staff: Libns: 2 *Non-Prof:* 5

S1854

Philips Research Laboratories, Information Centre
Cross Oak Ln, Redhill, Surrey, RH1 5HA (01293-815432; *fax:* 01293-815500)
Email: helen.elliott@philips.com

Chief: Info Centre Libn: Mrs Helen Elliott BA, DipLib, MCLIP
Entry: at discretion of Info Centre Libn *Open:* Mon-Fri 0830-1630
Subj: sci (excl life scis); maths; electronics; computer sci *Collns: Archvs:* some Philips Technical Press bks *Co-op Schemes:* BLDSC, SASLIC
Equip: m-form reader/printer, copier, computer (with wd-proc, internet & CD-ROM)
Stock: bks/10000; periodcls/400
Classn: DDC, UDC *Auto Sys:* Unicorn
Staff: Libns: 1 *Non-Prof:* 0.5

S1855 ✚

Surrey and Sussex Healthcare NHS Trust, Library and Information Service
Maple House, East Surrey Hosp, Canada Ave, Redhill, Surrey, RH1 5RH (01737-768511 x6056/7; *fax:* 01737-231790)
Email: library.esh@sysx.tr.eshcare-tr.sthames. nhs.uk

Gov Body: Surrey & Sussex Healthcare NHS Trust *Chief:* Lib & Info Svcs Mgr: Mrs Rachel Cooke BA, MLib, MCLIP *Dep:* Dep Lib & Info Svcs Mgr: Mrs Freda Knight MCLIP
Assoc Libs: CRAWLEY HOSP LIB & INFO SVC (see **S505**)
Entry: membs 24 hr access on appl; non-membs ref only *Open:* Mon, Thu-Fri 0900-1700, Tue-Wed 0900-1900
Subj: undergrad; postgrad; vocational; generalities; phil; psy; religion; social sci; sci; tech; health care *Collns: Bks & Pamphs:* medicine; nursing; mental health; learning disabilities *Co-op Schemes:* BLDSC, PLCS, NULJ, BMA, Inst of Psychiatry
Equip: copier, fax, 13 computers (all with wd-proc, 11 with internet & 1 with CD-ROM) *Officer-in-Charge:* LIS Mgr, as above *Svcs:* info, ref, biblio
Stock: bks/c11000; periodcls/230; videos/140
Acqs Offcr: Dep LIS Mgr, as above
Classn: NLM *Auto Sys:* DBTextworks
Staff: Libns: 3 *Non-Prof:* 2.6 *Exp:* £55000 (1999-2000); £70000 (2000-01); figs are approx

Redruth

S1856

Cornwall College, Learning Services
Camborne Pool Redruth Coll, Trevenson Rd, Pool, Redruth, Cornwall, TR15 3RD (01209-616183; *fax:* 01209-616184)
Email: enquiries@cornwall.ac.uk
Internet: http://www.cornwall.ac.uk/

Gov Body: part of the Cornwall Coll Group *Chief:* Lib Svcs Mgr: Ms S.J. Halstead BA, DipLib, CertEd, DMS, MCLIP
Assoc Libs: CAMBORNE POOL REDRUTH COLL LEARNING CENTRE, addr as above; DUCHY COLL, STOKE CLIMSLAND LEARNING CENTRE (see **S287**); DUCHY COLL, ROSEWARNE LEARNING CENTRE, Camborne, Cornwall, TR14 OAB; SALTASH COLL LEARNING CENTRE, Church Rd, Saltash, Cornwall, PL12 4AE; ST AUSTELL COLL LIB (see **S1965**); THE COLL OF FALMOUTH LEARNING CENTRE, Killigrew St, Falmouth, Cornwall, TR11 3QS

Entry: ref only for those who are not staff or students of the Coll; annual membership fee payable for those requiring loans *Open:* term: Mon-Thu 0830-2100, Fri 0830-1700, Sat 1000-1600; vac: varies
Subj: all subjs; genl; GCSE; A level; undergrad; postgrad; vocational *Co-op Schemes:* ILL, SWRLS
Equip: m-reader, m-printer, video viewers, copiers, 400 computers (incl wd-proc, internet & CD-ROM) *Online:* various databases
Stock: bks/64000 bks, pamphs, maps & AVs; periodcls/200
Classn: DDC *Auto Sys:* Trax
Pubns: genl & subj guides
Staff: Libns: 4.34 *Non-Prof:* 7.86

S1857

University of Exeter, Camborne School of Mines Library
Pool, Redruth, Cornwall, TR15 3SE (01209-714866; *fax:* 01209-716977)
Email: libcsm@csm.ex.ac.uk
Internet: http://www.ex.ac.uk/library/csm/

Gov Body: Univ of Exeter (see **S671**) *Chief:* Libn: Ms Jay Foote (jfoote@csm.ex.ac.uk) *Dep:* Asst Libn: Mr Stephen Atkinson
Open: Mon-Thu 0915-2045, Fri 0915-1700
Subj: earth sci; mining; mineral processing; metallurgy; industrial geol; surveying; mineral resource mgmt; environmental mgmt; mined land rehabilitation; industrial heritage mgmt. *Co-op Schemes:* ILL
Equip: copier (8p-10p per copy), computers *Online:* IMMAGE, Environmental Mgmt, Raw Materials Database, various other databases & e-journals
Stock: bks/c30000; periodcls/c250; maps/c1500; m-forms/1000

Retford

S1858 ✚

Rampton Hospital, Staff Education Centre Library
Retford, Nottinghamshire, DN22 0PD (01777-247229; *fax:* 01777-247563)

Gov Body: Nottinghamshire Healthcare NHS Trust *Chief:* Tutor Libn: Mr John Clark BA(Hons), DipLib, MCLIP, MBA *Dep:* Hosp Libn: Miss Maureen Thomas BA(Hons), CertEd, MCLIP *Other Snr Staff:* Lib Asst: Ms Jean Taylor
Entry: for employees & students at hosp *Open:* Mon-Thu 0900-1700, Fri 0900-1630
Subj: psy; social sci; medicine; psychiatry
Equip: m-reader, fax, copier, computers (incl 4 CD-ROM) *Online:* PsycInfo, Medline, CareData
Svcs: info, ref, biblio, indexing, abstracting
Stock: bks/15000; periodcls/80
Classn: DDC *Auto Sys:* SoftLink
Pubns: Current Awareness in Forensic Mental Health (6 pa, free to hosp staff, £80 pa to others)
Staff: Libns: 1.5 *Non-Prof:* 0.5

Rhyl

S1859 ✚

Glan Clwyd Hospital Library
Bodelwyddan, Rhyl, Denbighshire, LL18 5UJ (01745-534882; *fax:* 01745-534731)
Email: MainPC.Library@cd-tr.wales.nhs.uk

Gov Body: Conwy & Denbighshire NHS Trust *Chief:* Snr Libn: Mrs Eryl M. Smith BA, MCLIP
Entry: NHS personnel from North Wales *Open:* Mon, Wed 0900-1900, Tue, Thu-Fri 0900-1700
Subj: health scis *Co-op Schemes:* BLDSC, AWHILES, NULJ, PLCS

Equip: copier (A4/7p), clr copier (A4/50p), 10 computers (incl 5 with wd-proc, 1 with CD-ROM & 4 with internet), scanner *Svcs:* info, ref
Stock: bks/16000; periodcls/287; videos/200
Classn: NLM *Auto Sys:* Voyager
Pubns: Lib Guide; Newsletter
Staff: Libns: 3 *Non-Prof:* 4

Richmond

S1860

British Mycological Society Library and Archives
c/o The Herbarium, Royal Botanic Gdns, Kew, Richmond, Surrey, TW9 3AE (01784-259198)
Email: v.barkham@rbgkew.org.uk or g.p.sharples@livjm.ac.uk
Internet: http://www.britmycolsoc.org.uk/

Type: learned soc *Gov Body:* British Mycological Soc *Chief:* Hon Libn: Mrs Valerie Barkham
Entry: adv appt only
Subj: mycology *Collns: Archvs:* photos & letters relating to 100 years of the British Mycological Soc, incl photos of past presidents
Equip: copier *Officer-in-Charge:* Hon Libn, as above *Svcs:* info, abstracting, photocopying svc
Stock: bks/1000; periodcls/50; photos/c500; pamphs/13 boxes; archvs/0.5 cubic m *Acqs Offcr:* Hon Libn, as above
Pubns: numerous mycological pubns, list available
Staff: 1 Hon Libn

S1861

Richmond: The American International University in London, Cyril Parker Library
Queens Rd, Richmond, Surrey, TW10 6JP (020-8332-8210; *fax:* 020-8332-3050)
Email: Richmond.Library@richmond.ac.uk
Internet: http://www.richmond.ac.uk/

Chief: Dean of Lib & Tech Svcs: Mr David Nutty *Dep:* Snr Libn: Mr Frank Trew (trewf@richmond. ac.uk)
Assoc Libs: KENSINGTON CAMPUS LIB, 1 St Albans Grove, Kensington, London, W8 5PN (020-7368-8410)
Open: term: Mon-Thu 0900-2300, Fri 0900-1700, Sat 1300-1700, Sun 1300-2300; vac: varies
Subj: all subjs; undergrad; postgrad *Collns: Bks & Pamphs:* Asa Briggs Colln (at Richmond); Harvard Core Business Colln (at Kensington) *Co-op Schemes:* BLDSC, ILL
Equip: m-reader, m-printer, video viewer, copier, 55 computers (all with wd-proc, internet & CD-ROM), printers *Svcs:* info, ref
Stock: bks/60000; periodcls/250; pamphs/80 files; videos/1500
Classn: DDC *Auto Sys:* Voyager
Staff: Libns: 8 *Non-Prof:* 10 *Exp:* £80000 (1999-2000)

S1862

Royal Botanic Gardens, Kew, Library and Archives
Kew, Richmond, Surrey, TW9 3AE (020-8332-5414; *fax:* 020-8332-5430)
Email: librarian@rbgkew.org.uk
Internet: http://www.rbgkew.org.uk/collections/

Gov Body: Board of Trustees of the Royal Botanic Gardens, Kew *Chief:* Head of Lib & Archvs: Mr John Flanagan MCLIP
Entry: to bona fide rsrchers for ref only, adv written appl *Open:* Mon-Fri 0900-1700
Subj: plant & fungal taxonomy, distribution & conservation; hortic; systematic botany; economic botany; plant anatomy; genetics; biochem; tropical botany ☛

Special Libraries

Richmond ▼ Runcorn

(Royal Botanic Gdns, Kew, Lib & Archvs cont)
Collns: Bks & Pamphs: pre-Linnean botany; Linnean Colln *Archvs:* Sir Joseph Banks; Sir William & Sir Joseph Hooker; George Bentham; Lovell Reeve (publishers); approved place of deposit for Kew's own records *Other:* botanical prints & drawings (175000) incl Ann Lee, Tankerville & Curtis's Botanical Magazine & Margaret Mee drawings
Equip: 2 m-readers, m-printer, video viewer, fax, copier, 6 computers
Stock: bks/165000; periodcls/1600 + 2400 no longer current; illusts/175000; pamphs/140000; maps/11000; m-forms/10000; archvs/250000 letters
Classn: UDC, own *Auto Sys:* Unicorn
Pubns: Kew Record of Taxonomic Lit, 1971-; full catalogue available on request
Staff: Libns: 5 *Other Prof:* 3 *Non-Prof:* 5 + 3 trainees

Ripon

S1863 🔑 🤲
Ripon Cathedral Library
Ripon Cathedral, Ripon, N Yorkshire, HG4 1QS (01765-604108)
Internet: http://www.riponcathedral.org.uk/

Gov Body: Dean & Chapter of Ripon Cathedral *Chief:* Chief Libn: The Revd Canon Keith Punshon TD, MA, JP *Dep:* Dep Libn: Mrs Joy Calvert *Assoc Libs:* HIGGINS LIB, at Brotherton Lib, Univ of Leeds (see **S918**)
Entry: ref only *Open:* Mon-Fri 1000-1700
Subj: religion; New Testament; Church hist (esp modernist movement); personalities of the Church; classics *Collns: Archvs:* parish registers
Classn: BLS
Staff: Libns: 2 *Other Prof:* 1 *Non-Prof:* 5

Roby

S1864 🎓
Knowsley Community College, Roby Centre Library
Rupert Rd, Roby, Liverpool, L36 9TD (0151-477-5810; *fax:* 0151-477-5810)
Internet: http://www.knowsleycollege.ac.uk/

Chief: Dep Dir: Mr Tom Rowbottom BSc, MCLIP, CertEd (trowbottom@knowsleycollege.ac.uk)
Dep: Learning Centres Co-ordinator: Mrs Amanda Ducker (aducker@knowsleycollege.ac.uk)
Assoc Libs: KIRKBY LEARNING CENTRE, Cherryfield Dr, Kirkby, L32 8SF (*tel & fax:* 0151-477-5815)
Entry: registered student *Open: Roby:* term: Mon-Tue 0845-1700, Wed-Thu 0845-1900, Fri 0845-1500; *Kirkby:* term: Mon-Tue 0845-1900, Wed-Fri 0845-1700
Subj: all subjs; genl; GCSE; A level; undergrad
Co-op Schemes: LADSIRLAC, BLDSC
Equip: 2 fax, 4 copiers, 150 computers (multi-media) *Disabled:* ZoomText, large monitor, magnifier, JAWS, brailler, variety of software packages for dyslexia etc
Stock: bks/22000; periodcls/140
Classn: DDC
Staff: Libns: 4.5 *Other Prof:* 10 *Non-Prof:* 5 *Exp:* £36000 (1999-2000); £40000 (2000-01)

Rochdale

S1865 ✚
Pennine Acute Hospitals NHS Trust, Jack Taylor Library
Rochdale Edu Centre, Rochdale Infirmary, Whitehall St, Rochdale, Lancashire, OL12 0NB (01706-517058; *fax:* 01706-517772)
Email: rochdale.library@pat.nhs.uk

Type: multidisciplinary health care *Gov Body:* Pennine Acute Hosps NHS Trust *Chief:* Lib Svcs Mgr: Mr Graham Titley BA(Hons), MCLIP (graham.titley@pat.nhs.uk)
Entry: non-Trust staff require adv appt *Open:* Mon-Fri 0900-1700 (24 hr access for Trust staff)
Subj: health; medicine (mainly at postgrad level)
Co-op Schemes: BLDSC, LIHNN
Equip: fax (20p per pg to send, 10p per pg to receive), copier (A4/5p), clr copier (A4/25p), 2 video viewers (subj to room use), 6 computers (all with wd-proc, internet & CD-ROM), 4 rooms for hire
Svcs: info, ref, biblio
Stock: bks/11000; periodcls/120; videos/100
Classn: DDC *Auto Sys:* Heritage
Staff: Libns: 1 *Non-Prof:* 1.2 *Exp:* £27000 (1999-2000); £34000 (2000-01)

Rochester

S1866 🔑 🤲
Rochester Cathedral Library
Cathedral Office, The Precinct, Rochester, Kent, ME1 1SX (01634-843366)
Email: phdlock@ukonline.co.uk

Gov Body: Rochester Cathedral Chapter *Chief:* Canon Libn: The Ven Peter Lock
Entry: membership *Open:* Mon-Fri 0900-1700
Subj: religion; local hist; ecclesiastical biography
Collns: Bks & Pamphs: Phyllis Ireland Colln (Norman England with special ref to Battle Abbey & associated topics)
Stock: bks/7000; periodcls/6; photos/500; slides/100
Classn: DDC *Exp:* £250 (2000-01)

Romford

S1867 🎓
Barking College Library and Information Service
Dagenham Rd, Romford, Essex, RM7 0XU (01708-770100; *fax:* 01708-731067)
Internet: http://www.barkingcollege.ac.uk/

Gov Body: Barking Coll Corp *Chief:* Learning Resources Svc Mgr: Mr H. Stannard BA(Hons) (stannardh@barking-coll.ac.uk) *Dep:* Dep Lib & Info Svc Mgr: Mr John Blake BLib, MCLIP (blakej@barking-coll.ac.uk) *Other Snr Staff:* Systems Libn & Workshops Co-ordinator: Mr Norman Boyd BA(Hons), MCLIP; Online Materials Developer: Mr Paul Moore
Entry: ref only *Open:* term: Mon-Thu 0845-1915, Fri 0845-1700, Sat 0845-1245; vac: Mon-Thu 0845-1700, Fri 0845-1530
Subj: all subjs; genl; A level; vocational *Collns: Archvs:* Barking Coll Archvs, incl press cuttings, photos, minutes, pubns etc *Co-op Schemes:* BLDSC
Equip: 2 video viewers, 2 copiers, clr copier, 50 computers (incl 46 with internet) *Svcs:* info, ref
Stock: bks/25000; periodcls/126; audios/50; videos/855; CD-ROMs/50
Classn: DDC, CLCI *Auto Sys:* Unicorn
Pubns: Lib Guides etc
Staff: Libns: 3 *Other Prof:* 1 *Non-Prof:* 8 *Exp:* £22500 (2000-01)

S1868 ✚
Harold Wood Hospital, Multidisciplinary Library and Information Service
Academic Centre, Harold Wood Hosp, Gubbins Ln, Romford, Essex, RM3 0BE (*tel & fax:* 01708-708113)
Email: jackie@haroldwoodhospital.freeserve.co.uk
Internet: http://www.libnel.nhs.uk/

Gov Body: North East London Workforce Development Confederation *Chief:* Lib Mgr: Miss Jackie Blanks BA(Hons), DipLIS, MCLIP *Other Snr Staff:* Lib Assts: Mrs Diane Marke & Mrs Carmen Pauling
Assoc Libs: OLDCHURCH HOSP LIB & INFO SVC (see **S1869**)
Entry: NHS staff *Open:* 24 hrs access, 7 days a wk; staffed: Mon-Fri 0900-1700
Subj: medicine, all specialities *Co-op Schemes:* BLDSC, BMA, NTRHLN
Equip: copier (2p per copy), clr copier, fax (50p per pg), 6 computers (all with wd-proc, internet & CD-ROM, printouts 3p per pg) *Online:* via KA24 Database: AMED, BNI, CancerLit, CINAHL, Cochrane, Embase, HMIC, Medline, PsycInfo *Officer-in-Charge:* Lib Mgr, as above *Svcs:* info, ref, biblio
Stock: bks/2228, excl bnd periodcls; periodcls/70; audios/22; videos/42; CD-ROMs/50 *Acqs Offcr:* Lib Mgr, as above
Classn: NLM *Auto Sys:* DBTextworks
Staff: Libns: 2 *Non-Prof:* 2

S1869 ✚
Oldchurch Hospital Library and Information Service
Academic Centre, Oldchurch Hosp, Waterloo Rd, Romford, Essex, RM7 0BE (*tel & fax:* 01708-708397)
Email: karen@oldchurchhospital.freeserve.co.uk
Internet: http://www.libnel.nhs.uk/

Gov Body: BHR Hosps NHS Trust *Chief:* Asst Libn: Ms Karen Johnston *Dep:* Lib Asst: Mr Roger Sutherland
Assoc Libs: HAROLD WOOD HOSP, MULTIDISCIPLINARY LIB & INFO SVC (see **S1868**)
Entry: Trust employees *Open:* 24 hrs access, 7 days a wk; staffed: Mon-Fri 0900-1700
Subj: medicine; health; nursing; professions allied to medicine
Equip: copier, 11 computers (all with wd-proc, internet & CD-ROM) *Online:* via KA24 Database: AMED, BNI, CancerLit, CINAHL, Cochrane, Embase, HMIC, Medline, PsycInfo *Svcs:* info, ref
Stock: bks/3000; periodcls/60; videos/50; CD-ROMs/20
Classn: NLM *Auto Sys:* DBTextworks
Staff: Libns: 1 *Non-Prof:* 1

S1870 🎓
Redbridge College, Learning Resource Centre
Little Heath, Romford, Essex, RM6 4XT (020-8599-5231; *fax:* 020-8599-8224)
Email: info@redbridge-college.ac.uk
Internet: http://www.redbridge-college.ac.uk/

Gov Body: Coll Corp *Chief:* LRC Mgr: Mrs Ruth Gold MCLIP (rgold@redbridge-college.ac.uk)
Dep: Dep Mgr: Ms A. van Welzen
Entry: registers student at Coll or staff *Open:* Mon-Thu 0900-2015, Fri 1000-1530
Subj: all subjs
Equip: video viewer, copier, computers (incl internet & CD-ROM), clr printer, scanner *Svcs:* info, ref, user edu

Stock: bks/25000; periodcls/100; videos/600; CD-ROMs/50
Classn: DDC *Auto Sys:* Heritage
Staff: Libns: 2 *Non-Prof:* 4 *Exp:* £29000 (1999-2000)

S1871
South Bank University, Essex Campus Library

Harold Wood Hosp, Gubbins Ln, Romford, Essex, RM3 0BE (020-7815-5982; *fax:* 020-7815-4786)
Email: lisex@sbu.ac.uk
Internet: http://www.lisa.sbu.ac.uk/

Gov Body: South Bank Univ (see **S1399**) *Chief:* Lib Site Mgr: post vacant
Assoc Libs: EAST LONDON CAMPUS LIB (see **S1400**)
Entry: students & staff of Univ & associated NHS membs; membs of UK Libs Plus scheme *Open:* Mon-Thu 0830-1930, Fri 0830-1700, Sat 1000-1600
Subj: nursing & allied health *Co-op Schemes:* BLDSC, North Thames Region (NHS), NULJ, UK Libs Plus
Equip: m-reader, 2 video viewers, copier, fax, 20 computers (all with wd-proc, internet & CD-ROM)
Svcs: info, ref, biblio
Stock: bks/36000; periodcls/78; slides/91; audios/120; videos/510
Classn: DDC *Auto Sys:* Dynix
Staff: Libns: 1 *Non-Prof:* 3.5

Roslin

S1872 🏛
Roslin Institute, Library and Information Service

Roslin BioCentre, Roslin, Midlothian, EH25 9PS (0131-527-4260; *fax:* 0131-440-0434)
Email: roslin.library@bbsrc.ac.uk
Internet: http://www.ri.bbsrc.ac.uk/

Type: rsrch inst *Gov Body:* Roslin Inst *Chief:* Libn & Info Offcr: Mr Mike McKeen DMS, MCLIP
Entry: at discretion of libn *Open:* Mon-Fri 0900-1700
Subj: at postgrad level: animal breeding; genetics; physiology; endocrinology; nutrition; poultry husbandry; ethology; immunogenetics; animal production *Co-op Schemes:* BLDSC, BRIL, SALG
Equip: m-reader, m-printer, copier, computers (with wd-proc, internet & CD-ROM) *Online:* Dialog, BIDS, Edina, MIMAS
Stock: bks/8000; periodcls/200; bnd periodcls/6000
Classn: DDC *Staff: Libns:* 1 *Non-Prof:* 1.5

Rotherham

S1873 ✒
Corus Research, Swinden Technology Centre Library

Moorgate, Rotherham, S Yorkshire, S60 3AR (01709-820166; *fax:* 01709-825337)
Email: stc.library@corusgroup.com

Gov Body: Corus plc *Chief:* Libn: Ms Christine Rawson
Assoc Libs: TEESSIDE TECH CENTRE (see **S1545**)
Entry: adv appt only
Subj: steel industry; metallurgy; eng *Co-op Schemes:* ILL, SINTO
Stock: bks/20000; periodcls/400; pamphs/27000
Classn: UDC

S1874 🎓
Rotherham College of Arts and Technology, Library Learning Centre

Clifton Bldg, Eastwood Ln, Rotherham, S Yorkshire, S65 1EG (01709-722741; *fax:* 01709-360765)
Email: ctaylor@rotherham.ac.uk
Internet: http://www.rotherham.ac.uk/

Chief: Head of Learning Centre: Mr Colin Taylor
Assoc Libs: IT LEARNING CENTRE, at same addr
Entry: students only (ID with student card); adv appt for membs of public *Open:* term: Mon, Wed 0845-1800, Tue, Thu 0845-2000, Fri 0900-1700; vac: Mon-Thu 0900-1700, Fri 1000-1630
Subj: all subjs; GCSE; A level; undergrad; vocational; tech; arts *Co-op Schemes:* BLDSC, SINTO, CLEAR
Equip: 2 video viewers, copier (A4/5p), video viewer, 78 computers (all with wd-proc & internet, 39 with CD-ROM) *Disabled:* Kurzweil, Jaws & others *Online:* InfoTrac *Svcs:* info, ref, biblio
Stock: bks/25000; periodcls/60 + 6000 e-journals; videos/500; AVs/40 *Acqs Offcr:* Faculty teams
Classn: DDC *Auto Sys:* Heritage
Pubns: Learning Centre Guide
Staff: Libns: 4 *Non-Prof:* 1

S1875 ✚
Rotherham Health Care Library and Information Service

Rotherham Dist Genl Hosp, Moorgate Rd, Rotherham, S Yorkshire, S60 2UD (01709-304525; *fax:* 01709-373948)
Email: library.healthcare@rothgen.nhs.uk

Gov Body: Rotherham Metropolitan Borough Council (see **P155**) & Rotherham Genl Hosps Trust *Chief:* Principal Libn: Mr Graham Matthews MCLIP
Entry: staff of Rotherham Genl Hosp NHS Trust, Rotherham Priority Health Svcs NHS Trust, Rotherham Hospice NHS Trust, Rotherham Health Authority & Rotherham CHC; healthcare personnel living or working in Rotherham; others ref only, by appt *Open:* Mon 1030-2000, Tue, Fri 0900-1730, Wed-Thu 0900-2000, Sat 0930-1300
Subj: medicine; nursing; healthcare *Co-op Schemes:* BLDSC, SINTO 2000
Equip: m-reader, video viewers, copier (7p per pg), computers (incl internet & CD-ROM) *Disabled:* access to Kurzweil (offsite), magnifiers & other reading aids *Online:* Medline, CINAHL, ASSIA, Cochrane, HMIC, CareData, BNI *Svcs:* info, ref, database training
Stock: bks/12000; periodcls/200; slides/6000
Classn: NLM (Wessex) *Staff:* 8 in total

Rugby

S1876 ✚
Edyvean-Walker Medical Library

Hosp of St Cross, Barby Rd, Rugby, Warwickshire, CV22 5PX (01788-572831 x2470; *fax:* 01788-545274)
Email: library@wh-tr.wmids.nhs.uk

Gov Body: Univ Hosps Coventry & Warwickshire NHS Trust *Chief:* Medical Libn: Mrs Petra Meeson BA(Hons), MCLIP
Assoc Libs: WALSGRAVE HEALTH SCIS LIB (see **S499**); SIR JOHN BLACK LIB, Warwickshire PGMC, Stoney Stanton Rd, Coventry, CV1 4FG
Entry: by appt, ref only *Open:* Mon-Fri 0900-1700
Subj: medicine; health
Equip: copier, computer *Online:* Medline (staff only) *Svcs:* info, ref
Stock: bks/1000; periodcls/35
Classn: DDC *Auto Sys:* Heritage *Staff: Libns:* 1

S1877 🏛 🎓
Prison Service College Library

PSC Newbold Revel, Rugby, Warwickshire, CV23 0TH (01788-834119; *fax:* 01788-834114)
Email: cath@newbold4.demon.co.uk

Gov Body: HM Prison Svc *Chief:* Libn: Miss Catherine Fell BA(Hons), DipLib
Entry: open to membs of the Prison Svc & membs of Boards of Visitors; facilities available to bona fide rsrchers on written request *Open:* Mon 1000-1730, Tue-Thu 0830-1730, Fri 0830-1400
Subj: social sci; criminology; penology; mgmt; training; psy *Collns: Archvs:* historical colln incl complete set of official reports on prisons, crime, transportation to Australia etc (1835-date) *Co-op Schemes:* will loan to other libs upon request
Equip: fax, video viewer, copier, computers (incl 2 wd-proc, internet & 2 CD-ROM)
Stock: bks/20000; periodcls/70; archvs/300 items
Classn: UDC *Auto Sys:* Alice
Pubns: Accessions List (monthly); Journals Bulletin (monthly); Subj Reading Lists can be prepared on request
Staff: Libns: 1 *Non-Prof:* 1

S1878 🎓
Rugby College, Learning Resource Centre

Lower Hillmorton Rd, Rugby, Warwickshire, CV21 3QS (01788-338800; *fax:* 01788-338575)

Gov Body: Governing Board of Coll *Chief:* Coll Libn: Ms Tracy Dale BA(Hons), MPhil, MCLIP
Entry: enrolment on a Coll course *Open:* term: Mon-Thu 0845-2100, Fri 0845-1700; vac: Mon-Fri 0845-1630
Subj: all subjs; genl; GCSE; A level; vocational *Co-op Schemes:* BLDSC
Equip: copier, video viewer, 50 computers (networked, with access to CD-ROM) *Online:* Internet
Stock: bks/25000; periodcls/150; audios/50; videos/200; CD-ROMs/100
Classn: DDC *Auto Sys:* AutoLib
Staff: Libns: 1 *Non-Prof:* 4

S1879 🎓
Rugby School, Temple Reading Room

Barby Rd, Rugby, Warwickshire, CV22 5DW (01788-556227; *fax:* 01788-556228)
Email: dsrm@rugby-school.warwks.sch.uk

Type: public school *Chief:* Libn: Mr D.S.R. Maclean
Entry: staff & pupils; adv appt for others *Open:* term: Mon-Fri 0900-1600
Subj: all subjs; genl; GCSE; A level *Collns: Archvs:* records of Rugby School & its properties (1670s-date, mainly from 1750 onwards); papers & correspondence of former headmasters, teachers & pupils, incl: Thomas Arnold Papers (headmaster & historian, 1795-1842)
Staff: Libns: 3

Runcorn

S1880 🔑 🏛
The Norton Priory Museum Trust Library

Norton Priory Museum & Gdns, Tudor Rd, Manor Pk, Runcorn, Cheshire, WA7 1SX (01928-569895)
Email: info@nortonpriory.org
Internet: http://www.nortonpriory.org/

Gov Body: The Norton Priory Museum Trust *Chief:* Snr Keeper: Mr D.J. Marrow MA *Dep:* Ms Kay Hoare

Special Libraries

Runcorn
▼
Sandy

(Norton Priory Museum Trust Lib cont)
Entry: adv appt, ref only *Open:* Apr-Oct: Mon-Fri 1200-1700, Sat-Sun 1200-1800; Nov-Mar: Mon-Sun 1200-1600
Subj: medieval & post-medieval archaeo & hist; monasticism
Equip: copier (on enq) *Disabled:* wheelchair access, induction loops
Staff: Other Prof: 4 *Non-Prof:* 10

S1881
SOG Ltd, The Heath Library
The Heath, PO Box 13, Runcorn, Cheshire, WA7 4QF (*tel & fax:* 01928-513334)
Email: heath_library@sog.ltd.uk
Internet: http://www.sog.ltd.uk/library/

Chief: Libn: Mrs Silvana Briers BA, MCLIP
Entry: subscription by business only *Open:* Mon-Fri 0830-1630
Subj: generalities; sci; tech *Co-op Schemes:* BLDSC
Equip: 2 m-readers, 2 m-printers, copier, 3 computers (incl internet & CD-ROM) *Svcs:* info, ref, translation, patent ordering
Stock: bks/c50000; periodcls/12; m-forms/c1000; a few pamphs, maps & CD-ROMs
Classn: UDC *Auto Sys:* Heritage *Staff: Libns:* 1

Rushden

Random House Library
See RANDOM HOUSE GROUP ARCHV & LIB (**A440**)

Ruthin

S1882
Llysfasi College of Agriculture Library
Pentrecelyn, Ruthin, Denbighshire, LL15 2LB (01978-790263)
Internet: http://www.llysfasi.ac.uk/

Chief: Libn: Miss Jayne Lewis (jlewis@llysfasi.ac.uk) *Dep: Lib Asst:* Ms Eirian Evans (eevans@llysfasi.ac.uk)
Entry: staff & students; external membership available to public (ID required) *Open:* term: Mon-Thu 0845-1900, Fri 0845-1700; vac: Mon-Fri 0845-1700, times may vary
Subj: agric; animal care; environment; accounting; conservation; land admin; soil sci; forestry; langs; Welsh lang; business; info tech; health; social care
Equip: video viewer, copier (A4/5p, A3/8p), 12 computers (incl wd-proc, internet & CD-ROM)
Classn: DDC *Auto Sys:* Eclipse
Staff: Libns: 1 *Non-Prof:* 1

Salford

S1883
HM Customs and Excise, Library and Information Service
1st Floor, East Ralli Quays, 3 Stanley St, Salford, Lancashire, M60 9LA (0161-827-0450; *fax:* 0161-827-0491)

Gov Body: HM Customs & Excise *Chief:* Chief Libn: Ms Lorna Banks BSc, MCLIP *Dep:* Dep Libn: Ms Fiona Stewart
Assoc Libs: LIB & INFO SVC, London (see **S1162**)
Entry: open to authenticated rsrchers by written appl *Open:* Mon-Fri 0900-1700
Subj: GCSE; A level; undergrad; revenue trades & techniques; business; taxation; govt; admin *Co-op Schemes:* BLDSC
Equip: m-printer, video viewer, fax, copier, 3 computers *Online:* Dialog, BLAISE, Echo, Eurobases, FirstSearch, Reuters
Stock: bks/5000; periodcls/40; maps/315; videos/190
Classn: DDC *Auto Sys:* Unicorn
Staff: Libns: 6.5 *Non-Prof:* 3

S1884
Hope Hospital Medical Library
Salford Royal Hosps NHS Trust, Stott Ln, Salford, Lancashire, M6 8HD (0161-787-5405; *fax:* 0161-787-5409)
Email: libmail@fs1.ho.man.ac.uk
Internet: http://www.hop.man.ac.uk/academic/library1/

Gov Body: Salford Royal Hosps NHS Trust
Chief: Libn: Mrs Valerie Haigh BA(Hons), MCLIP
Other Snr Staff: Asst Libn: Mrs Rhona Dalton BA(Hons); Asst Libn (Technical Support): Mr Andrew Norfolk BA(Hons), MSc
Entry: Trust staff; univ staff & students based at hosp site; health & social svc workers based in Salford *Open:* Mon-Fri 0915-2000
Subj: medicine *Co-op Schemes:* ILL
Equip: m-reader, copier, 6 computers (incl internet & CD-ROM) *Svcs:* info, ref, lit searches, current awareness
Stock: bks/5000+; periodcls/180
Classn: NLM *Auto Sys:* DBTextworks
Staff: Libns: 3 *Non-Prof:* 2

S1885
Lancashire Mining Museum, Salford, Reference Library
Buile Hill Pk, Eccles Old Rd, Salford, Lancashire, M6 8GL (0161-736-1832)

Type: local authority *Gov Body:* City of Salford Metropolitan Council (see **P157**) *Chief:* Museum Offcr: Mr Alan Davies BA(Hons)
Entry: ref, adv appt *Open:* lib only open on request Mon-Fri 1000-1230, 1330-1630
Subj: coalmining; other types of mining also covered world-wide to a lesser degree *Collns: Bks & Pamphs:* coalmining; metalliferous mining; quarrying; opencast (1548-date, c15000 vols); mining manufacturers' catalogues/pamphs (c1900-date); bulk of former Wigan Mining Lib *Archvs:* archvs relating to former Lancashire coalfield (c1790-date) *Other:* maps/plans mineworkings, mainly North West
Equip: video viewer, copier, wd-proc, room hire
Stock: bks/15000; photos/5000; slides/1000; illusts/1000; pamphs/2000; maps/1000; archvs/120 ft
Classn: own
Pubns: Coalmining (75p); Museum Guidebook (25p)
Staff: Other Prof: 1 *Non-Prof:* 4

S1886
University of Salford, Information Services Division
Clifford Whitworth Bldg, The Crescent, Salford, Lancashire, M5 4WT (0161-295-2444; *fax:* 0161-295-5888)
Email: advisor@salford.ac.uk
Internet: http://www.salford.ac.uk/

Gov Body: Univ of Salford *Chief:* Dir of Info Svcs: Mr A.M. Lewis BA(Hons), MSc, MICE, MIWEM, CEng (a.m.lewis@salford.ac.uk) *Dep:* Dep Dir of Info Svcs: Mrs M. Duncan BA(Hons), MCLIP (m.duncan@salford.ac.uk) *Other Snr Staff:* Head of Liaison & Planning: Ms Julie Berry BA(Hons) (j.berry@salford.ac.uk); Head of Customer Svcs: Ms Elizabeth Jolly BA(Hons) (e.c.jolly@salford.ac.uk); Head of Learning Resources: Ms Wendy Carley BA(Hons), MA (w.j.carley@salford.ac.uk)
Assoc Libs: ADELPHI CAMPUS LIB, Peru St, Salford, Lancashire, M3 6EQ (0161-295-6185); ECCLES CAMPUS LIB, Peel House, Albert St, Eccles, Lancashire, M30 0NJ (0161-295-2747); FREDERICK RD CAMPUS LIB, Allerton Bldg, Frederick Rd, Salford, Lancashire, M6 6PU (0161-295-2448); IRWELL VALLEY CAMPUS LIB, Blandford Rd, Salford, Lancashire, M6 6BN (0161-295-2633)
Entry: by prior arrangement *Open: Clifford Whitworth:* term: Mon-Fri 0900-2100, Sat-Sun 1000-1600; *Frederick Rd:* Mon-Thu 0855-2000, Fri 0855-1700, Sat 1000-1600; no weekend openings at other libs; vac: Mon-Fri 0855-1700
Subj: undergrad; postgrad; rsrch; generalities; phil; psy; social scis; lang; sci; maths; tech; arts; lit; geog; hist *Collns: Bks & Pamphs:* EDC; Govt Pubns Colln *Archvs:* Walter Greenwood Colln; Canal Duke Colln (Duke of Bridgewater Archv); Bridgewater Estate Archv; Revans Colln for Action Learning *Other:* BSI (m-fiche) *Co-op Schemes:* BLDSC, CALIM
Equip: 6 m-readers, 2 m-printers, 16 copiers, 4 clr copiers, 800 computers (incl wd-proc, internet & CD-ROM) *Disabled:* Kurzweil, ZoomText, Inspiration *Online:* Dialog, STN (free to univ membs) *Svcs:* info, ref
Stock: bks/650000; periodcls/2270, incl e-journals; photos/40000; maps/600; m-forms/189 linear m; videos/1500 *Acqs Offcr:* Data Centre Mgr: Mrs Rose Kenyon (r.kenyon@salford.ac.uk)
Classn: DDC *Auto Sys:* Talis
Pubns: various lib leaflets (free)
Staff: 130 FTE in Lib & Computing Svc *Exp:* £1320000 (1999-2000); £1348000 (2000-01); figs incl exp on e-resources

S1887
Working Class Movement Library
Jubilee House, 51 The Crescent, Salford, Lancashire, M5 4WX (0161-736-3601; *fax:* 0161-737-4115)
Email: enquiries@wcml.org.uk
Internet: http://www.wcml.org.uk/

Gov Body: charitable trust, financed & administered by City of Salford Metropolitan Council (see **P157**) *Chief: Libn:* Mr Alain Cahan BA, MCLIP
Entry: adv appt *Open:* Tue, Thu-Fri 1000-1700, Wed 1000-1900, Sun (alternate wks) 1400-1700
Subj: labour movement; socialism; Marxism; anarchism; labour hist; politics; political hist; political movements & parties; Chartism; trade unions; co-op movement; women's suffrage; econ; economic hist; manufacture; agric; govt; public admin; law; housing; internatl relations; edu; environment; phil; religion; phil of sci; social sci; arts; leisure; lit; drama; cinema; biography; personal papers; political papers; trade union records *Collns: Bks & Pamphs:* Irish Colln (incl private libs of C. Desmond Greaves & T.A. Jackson); Thomas Paine Colln; Internatl Colln (incl sections on USA, India, Europe, former USSR); British regional hist; trade union hists; mining industry *Archvs:* extensive trade union archvs, incl: Amalgamated Eng Union (AEU); Genl, Municipal & Boilermakers & Allied Trades Union (GMBATU); Silk Workers Archvs; also: Benny Rothman Archvs; Temperance & Friendly Soc records; John Wilkes correspondence; Angela Tuckett papers

Other: various microfilms, photos, audios, posters & ephemera
Equip: m-reader, fax, copier, computer *Online:* full catalogue available on the internet at above URL
Svcs: info, ref
Stock: bks/25000; photos/2000; slides/c500; pamphs/20000; m-forms/70 titles; archvs/10000 vols; posters/3000; Objects/1500 (incl banners, badges, trade union emblems, plaques, crockery)
Classn: DDC *Auto Sys:* Talis
Pubns: Working Class Movement Lib Bulletin (1 pa, Nos 1-13 available, £1.50 each); North West Labour Hist Group Bulletin (1 pa, £5.95); The Early Trade Unions (edu pack, £1.50); The Genl Strike (edu pack, £1.50); Eddie Frow: Making of an Anarchist; Chartism in Manchester & Salford; pamphs & reprints of historical pamphs; numerous other pubns; postcards & posters; all available from above addr
Staff: Libns: 2 Non-Prof: 1
Further Info: Friends Group (volunteers) £5 to join

Salisbury

S1888
Centre for Applied Microbiology and Research Library
Porton Down, Salisbury, Wiltshire, SP4 0JG (01980-612711; *fax:* 01980-612818)
Email: library@camr.org.uk
Internet: http://www.camr.org.uk/

Gov Body: Health Protection Agency *Chief:* Libn: Mrs S. Goddard BLib
Entry: CAMR employees; not open to outsiders
Open: Mon-Fri 0900-1700
Subj: microbiology; biotech *Co-op Schemes:* WILCO, BLDSC, ILL
Equip: m-reader, copier, 5 computers (incl internet & CD-ROM) *Online:* Dialog (searches charged)
Svcs: info, ref
Stock: bks/2000, excl bnd periodcls; periodcls/112
Classn: UDC *Staff:* Libns: 1 Non-Prof: 1.5
Exp: £100500 (1999-2000); £98400 (2000-01)

S1889
The John Creasey Museum, Salisbury Library
Market Pl, Salisbury, Wiltshire, SP1 1BL (01722-324145; *fax:* 01722-413214)

Gov Body: Trustees & Mgmt Cttee *Chief:* Art Curator: Mr Peter Riley
Entry: no conditions during opening hrs; otherwise adv appt *Open:* Mon 1000-1900, Tue-Wed, Fri 0900-1900, Thu, Sat 0900-1700
Subj: arts; lit *Collns: Bks & Pamphs:* works of novelist John Creasey *Other:* artefacts; colln of contemporary art; awards; scrapbks; jacket designs
Equip: 8 m-readers, m-printer, video viewer, fax, 3 copiers, 3 rooms for hire
Stock: bks/3000; photos/200; audios/2; videos/6; archvs/300 *Staff:* Libns: 1 Non-Prof: 1

S1890
Salisbury and South Wiltshire Museum, Stevens Memorial Library
The King's House, 65 The Close, Salisbury, Wiltshire, SP1 2EN (01722-332151; *fax:* 01722-325611)
Email: museum@salisburymuseum.org.uk
Internet: http://www.salisburymuseum.org.uk/

Gov Body: Salisbury & South Wiltshire Museum Trust *Chief:* Dir: Mr P.R. Saunders BA, FSA, FMA, FRSA *Dep:* Hon Libn: Mrs M. Broad BA

Entry: by adv appt through curatorial staff *Open:* Mon-Fri 1000-1700
Subj: Salisbury & South Wiltshire: local hist; archaeo *Collns: Archvs:* papers of Genl A.L.F. Pitt Rivers *Co-op Schemes:* ILL
Equip: m-reader, copier, room for hire (£13.50 per hr) *Officer-in-Charge:* Office Mgr: Mrs Pam Barton
Svcs: info
Stock: bks/3500; periodcls/20; photos/4000; pamphs/1200; maps/200 *Acqs Offcr:* Dir, as above
Staff: Non-Prof: 1

S1891
Salisbury Cathedral Library
Salisbury, Wiltshire, SP1 2EN (01722-555160)

Gov Body: Dean & Chapter of Salisbury *Chief:* Libn & Keeper of Muniments: Miss Suzanne Eward MA, FSA, FRHistS, MCLIP
Entry: by prior written appt only (refs may be asked for) *Open:* Mon-Fri 1000-1230, 1415-1600
Collns: Bks & Pamphs: from the 15C onward; the subjs of the bks reflect the interests of those who gave them in the past *Archvs:* from the 12C onwards *Other:* medieval MSS, from the 9C onwards
Stock: bks/c16000; MSS/224
Classn: own *Staff:* Libns: 1

S1892
Salisbury College Library
Southampton Rd, Salisbury, Wiltshire, SP5 3SH (01722-344325; *fax:* 01722-344345)
Email: Library@salisbury.ac.uk
Internet: http://www.salisbury.ac.uk/

Chief: Learning Resources Mgr: Mrs Janet Beauchamp BA(Hons) (janet.beauchamp@salisbury.ac.uk)
Entry: registered student membs; ref only to genl public & visitors *Open:* term: Mon 0830-1730, Tue-Thu 0830-1945, Fri 1000-1615; vacs: varies
Subj: all subjs; genl; GCSE; A level; undergrad; postgrad; vocational; local hist (Salisbury) *Co-op Schemes:* ILL, Univ for Swindon & Wiltshire Proj Partner, SWRLS, WILCO
Equip: 3 video viewers, 2 copiers (5p per sheet), clr copier (80p per sheet), 20 computers (all with wd-proc, internet & CD-ROM), 3 rooms for hire
Disabled: full wheelchair access, Supernova, BSL Communicator, CCTV *Officer-in-Charge:* Learning Resources Mgr, as above
Stock: bks/20000; periodcls/100; slides/4000; videos/600; CD-ROMs/100+ *Acqs Offcr:* Learning Resources Mgr, as above
Classn: DDC *Auto Sys:* Heritage
Staff: Libns: 1 Non-Prof: 6
Proj: VLE implementation; online learning

S1893
Salisbury Health Care NHS Trust, Staff Library
Edu Centre, Salisbury Dist Hosp, Salisbury, Wiltshire, SP2 8BJ (01722-336262 x4433; *fax:* 01722-339690)
Email: Library.Office@shc-tr.swest.nhs.uk

Gov Body: Salisbury Health Care NHS Trust *Chief:* Head Libn: Mrs J.C. Lang BA, DipLib, MCLIP (Jenny.Lang@salisbury.nhs.uk) *Other Snr Staff:* Asst Libn: Ms Katherine Barker MA, MSc (Katherine.Barker@salibury.nhs.uk); Asst Libn: Ms Janet Guy MCLIP (Janet.Guy@salisbury.nhs.uk)
Assoc Libs: OLD MANOR HOSP LIB, Salisbury
Entry: ref use to non-membs *Open:* Mon-Fri 0900-1700
Subj: at undergrad, postgrad & vocational levels: social sci; medicine; nursing; psychiatry; midwifery; professions allied to medicine *Co-op Schemes:* BLDSC, BMA, NULJ, SWRLIN, PsychLib

Equip: 2 copiers, video viewer, 11 computers (all with wd-proc, 8 with CD-ROM, 7 with internet, membs only), room for hire (membs only) *Online:* available to membs only: AMED, BNI, CINAHL, Embase, HMIC, Medline, PsycInfo, ASSIA, Serfile
Stock: bks/22000; periodcls/290; videos/110
Classn: NLM *Auto Sys:* Heritage
Staff: Libns: 3 Non-Prof: 3

S1894
Sarum College Library
19 The Close, Salisbury, Wiltshire, SP1 2EE (01722-424803; *fax:* 01722-338508)
Email: library@sarum.ac.uk
Internet: http://www.sarum.ac.uk/

Gov Body: Sarum Coll Trust (Registered Charity 309501) *Chief:* Coll Libn: Ms Jennifer Davis BLib, MCLIP
Entry: subscription-based arrangement (daily, monthly or annually) *Open:* Mon-Fri 0900-1700
Subj: theology; phil of religion; comparative religion; religious edu; church hist; social studies; psy *Collns: Bks & Pamphs:* Bishop Hamilton's Colln; Markham Bequest (292 vols of bnd pamphs, mainly 19C) *Co-op Schemes:* SWRLS, BLDSC
Equip: m-reader, copier, computer (with wd-proc, internet & CD-ROM, internet charged at £5 per hr)
Stock: bks/40000; periodcls/60, plus 12 no longer current
Classn: DDC (mod) *Auto Sys:* Heritage IV
Staff: Libns: 1 Non-Prof: 1.5 *Exp:* £10000 (1999-2000); £10000 (2000-01)

Sand Hutton

S1895
Central Science Laboratory, Information Centre
Central Science Laboratory, Sand Hutton, N Yorkshire, YO41 1LZ (01904-462000; *fax:* 01904-462111)
Email: science@csl.gov.uk
Internet: http://www.csl.gov.uk/

Chief: Info Centre Mgr: Mr Anthony Michael Cassels MA, MSc, MCLIP
Entry: adv appt, ref only *Open:* Mon-Fri 0930-1700
Subj: sci; maths; tech; pesticides; plant pathology; food safety; conservation; entomology
Equip: m-reader, m-printer, copier, video viewer, computers (incl wd-proc & CD-ROM) *Online:* available for a fee *Svcs:* info, ref, biblio
Stock: bks/60000; periodcls/600; pamphs/10000; m-forms/2000; videos/200
Classn: UDC *Auto Sys:* Dynix
Pubns: CSL Sci Review; CSL Annual Report & Accounts (both available from Stationery Office)
Staff: Libns: 3 Non-Prof: 8

Sandy

S1896
Royal Society for the Protection of Birds Library
The Lodge, Sandy, Bedfordshire, SG19 2DL (01767-680551; *fax:* 01767-692365)
Email: ian.dawson@rspb.org.uk
Internet: http://www.rspb.org.uk/

Chief: Snr Libn: Mr I. Dawson BA, DipLib
Entry: ref only; tel or write for appt to visit (this also applies to RSPB membs); lib is mainly a staff facility *Open:* Mon-Fri 0900-1245, 1330-1715
Subj: ornithology (world); nat hist (British); nature conservation *Collns: Archvs:* W.H. Hudson Archv
Co-op Schemes: BLDSC, BBI
Equip: m-reader, copier *Online:* Dialog (staff only)

Special Libraries

Sandy ▼ Sheffield

(Royal Soc for the Protection of Birds Lib cont)
Stock: bks/9000; periodcls/200; archvs/15 m; some pamphs, maps, m-forms & sound recordings **Classn:** UDC (mod) **Auto Sys:** Heritage IV **Staff:** Libns: 1 Non-Prof: 1

Saxilby

S1897 ✚

Lincolnshire Knowledge and Resource Service
2 Highfield Rd, Saxilby, Lincolnshire, LN1 2QJ (01522-704635; *fax:* 01522-704627)
Email: library.LKRS@lht.nhs.uk
Internet: http://www.hello.nhs.uk/

Chief: Libn: Ms Alison Price **Dep:** Primary Care Libn: Mr Richard Holmes
Entry: all NHS staff working in the primary care, genl practice & community care sectors in Lincolnshire **Open:** Mon-Fri 0900-1700
Subj: evidence-based medicine; primary health care; health promotion **Co-op Schemes:** ILL
Equip: copiers (2p per sheet), computers **Online:** Medline, CINAHL, BNI, PsycInfo **Svcs:** info, ref, lit searching, database training, health promotion
Staff: 4 in total

Scalloway

S1898 🎓

North Atlantic Fisheries College Library
Port Arthur, Scalloway, Shetland, ZE1 0UN (01595-772350; *fax:* 01595-880549)
Email: cathy.brompton@nafc.uhi.ac.uk
Internet: http://www.nafc.ac.uk/

Gov Body: Univ of the Highlands & Islands (UHI)
Chief: Libn: Ms Cathy Brompton
Entry: staff & students of Coll **Open:** term & vac: Mon-Fri 0900-1700
Subj: fish biology; aquaculture; marine biology; fisheries; nautical studies; marine eng; quality control; oceanography; fish processing; business; computing; yachting; boating **Collns:** Bks & Pamphs: Raymond Beverton Colln (fisheries); Braer Shipping Incident Colln **Co-op Schemes:** UHI Millennium Inst inter-lending
Equip: copier, computers (incl internet & CD-ROM)

Scarborough

S1899

University of Hull, Keith Donaldson Library
Scarborough Campus, Filey Rd, Scarborough, N Yorkshire, YO11 3AZ (01723-357277; *fax:* 01723-357328)
Email: libhelp-scar@hull.ac.uk
Internet: http://www.acsweb.hull.ac.uk/lib/

Gov Body: Univ of Hull (see **S828**) **Chief:** Team Leader: Ms Juliet Crowther (J.Crowther@hull. ac.uk)
Entry: ref only **Open:** term: Mon-Thu 0900-2100, Fri 0900-1700, Sat 0900-1200; vac: Mon-Fri 0900-1700

Subj: all subjs; undergrad; postgrad **Collns:** Bks & Pamphs: ch's lit; teaching practice materials **Other:** AV colln
Equip: m-reader, m-printer, copier, video viewer, 40 computers (incl internet & CD-ROM) **Svcs:** info, ref, biblio
Stock: bks/c80000; periodcls/360; maps/220; m-forms/380; videos/1250
Classn: DDC

Scunthorpe

S1900 🏛🏛

North Lincolnshire Museum, Library and Archives
Oswald Rd, Scunthorpe, N Lincolnshire (01724-843533; *fax:* 01724-270474)
Email: joannemayall@northlincs.gov.uk
Internet: http://www.northlincs.gov.uk/museums/

Gov Body: North Lincolnshire Council (see **P127**)
Chief: Local Hist Asst: Mr D.J. Taylor BSc, AMA (david.taylor@northlincs.gov.uk)
Entry: ref only; adv appt preferred but not essential **Open:** Tue-Fri 1000-1600
Subj: North Lincolnshire: local hist; social hist; archaeo; sci; fine & decorative art; museology
Collns: Archvs: primary archvs & printed ephemera, some held at museum, other material on special deposit at North East Lincolnshire Archvs (see **A191**) **Other:** large photo archv, recently digitised
Equip: copier, computerised image archv of local photos **Svcs:** info, ref
Stock: bks/c20000; other holdings unquantified
Acqs Offcr: Local Hist Asst, as above
Pubns: several pubns mainly of local interest publ by the Museum
Staff: Other Prof: 1 museum asst

S1901 🎓

North Lindsey College Library
Kingsway, Scunthorpe, N Lincolnshire, DN17 1AJ (01724-294164; *fax:* 01724-294020)
Internet: http://www.northlindsey.ac.uk/nlclr.htm

Chief: Learning Resources Mgr: Mrs Belinda Allen (belinda.allen@northlindsey.ac.uk) **Dep:** Lib Supervisor: Mrs Carolyn Blanchard (carolyn. blanchard@northlindsey.ac.uk)
Entry: membs of coll only **Open:** term: Mon-Wed 0845-2000, Thu 0845-1630, Fri 0845-1600; vac: Mon-Fri 0900-1300
Subj: all subjs; local studies (North Lincolnshire)
Equip: 2 video viewers, fax, 2 copiers, 68 computers (incl wd-proc, internet & CD-ROM)
Stock: bks/20000; periodcls/150; audios/500; videos/3500
Classn: DDC **Auto Sys:** Heritage
Staff: Other Prof: 1 Non-Prof: 8

S1902 ✚

Scunthorpe and Goole NHS Hospital Trust, Healthcare Library
Butterwick House, Scunthorpe Genl Hosp, Church Ln, Scunthorpe, N Lincolnshire, DN15 7BH (01724-290472; *fax:* 01724-387829)
Email: Healthcare.Library@nlg.nhs.uk

Chief: Libn: Mrs Vere Conolly BSc(Econ) (Vere.Conolly@nlg.nhs.uk)
Entry: Trust staff **Open:** Mon-Thu 0830-1730, Fri 0830-1700
Subj: psy; social sci; medicine **Co-op Schemes:** BLDSC, NULJ
Equip: copier (5p per pg), video viewer, 5 computers (all with wd-proc & internet, 4 with CD-ROM) **Online:** OVID **Svcs:** info, ref
Stock: bks/8000; periodcls/140; videos/200; CD-ROMs/20 **Acqs Offcr:** Libn, as above

Classn: NLM **Auto Sys:** Heritage
Staff: Libns: 2 Non-Prof: 1.6 **Exp:** £41781 (1999-2000); £43325 (2000-01)

Sevenoaks

S1903 🎓

Sevenoaks School, Johnson Library
Sevenoaks School, High St, Sevenoaks, Kent, TN13 1HU (01732-467720; *fax:* 01732-461862)
Email: Brit-Lib@soaks.org
Internet: http://www.soaks.kent.sch.uk/

Chief: Head Libn: Mrs Patricia Kino BA, CertEd, DipLib (pk@soaks.org) **Dep:** Snr Lib Asst: Miss Chrissa Woodhouse BA (cw@soaks.org)
Entry: adv appt or membership **Open:** term: Mon-Fri 0800-2030, Sat 0800-1600
Subj: all subjs; genl; GCSE; A level; local study (Kent & Sevenoaks); particularly strong on hist
Collns: Bks & Pamphs: materials relating to Sevenoaks & Kent; South Africa Colln (apartheid era) **Archvs:** archvs of Sevenoaks School **Co-op Schemes:** BLDSC
Equip: fax, copier, 20 computers (all with wd-proc, internet & CD-ROM) **Online:** Factiva, Britannica, New Scientist, Economist **Officer-in-Charge:** Head Libn, as above **Svcs:** info, ref, biblio
Stock: bks/27000; periodcls/70; videos/100 **Acqs Offcr:** Head Libn, as above
Classn: DDC **Auto Sys:** Heritage
Staff: Libns: 2 Other Prof: 1 Non-Prof: 1

Sheffield

S1904 🔑

British Glass Library
Northumberland Rd, Sheffield, S10 2UA (0114-2686201; *fax:* 0114-2681073)
Internet: http://www.britglass.co.uk/

Chief: Info Offcr: T.L. Green
Entry: open to membs & SINTO membs **Open:** Mon-Fri 0830-1730
Subj: glass tech **Co-op Schemes:** Bliss, SINTO
Equip: copier, computer
Stock: bks/3000; periodcls/30+
Classn: computerised sys
Pubns: British Glass Digest of Info & Patent Review (£100 pa)
Staff: Other Prof: 1 Non-Prof: 1

S1905 🏛

Kelham Island Museum, Library and Archives
Alma St, Sheffield, S3 8RY (0114-272-2106; *fax:* 0114-275-7847)
Email: postmaster@simt.co.uk
Internet: http://www.simt.co.uk/

Gov Body: Sheffield Industrial Museums Trust
Chief: Collns & Access Offcr: Ms Catherine Hamilton MA (c.hamilton@simt.co.uk)
Entry: adv appt; ref only **Open:** Mon-Thu 1000-1600
Subj: local study (Sheffield industries); tech; metallurgy; steel industry; business records
Collns: Bks & Pamphs: many bks originally from libs of Sheffield steel firms; metallurgical & technical bks **Archvs:** collns of documents relating to Sheffield companies (not a comprehensive colln; most of these are housed at Sheffield Archvs – see **A452**) **Other:** Firth Brown Photographic Colln; historic photos relating to industrial Sheffield
Equip: copier, video viewer, 2 rooms for hire
Svcs: info
Stock: bks/8000; photos/40000; slides/400; audios/20; videos/250; archvs/80 cubic m **Acqs Offcr:** Collns & Access Offcr, as above
Classn: in-house **Staff:** Other Prof: 3 museum profs, 2 educational **Non-Prof:** 10

S1906 📖
Rother Valley College Learning Centre
Doe Quarry Ln, Dinnington, Sheffield, S25 2NF (01909-559281; *fax:* 01909-559003) *Internet:* http://www.rothervalley.ac.uk/

Gov Body: Rotherham Metropolitan Borough Council (see **P155**) *Chief:* Libn: Mrs Anne Sarah Lee BA(Hons), PGDip *Other Snr Staff:* Asst Libns: Mrs Nickie Roome BA, MCLIP & Mrs Elizabeth Vick BA, DipLib, MCLIP
Entry: open to public *Open:* term: Mon-Thu 0900-2000, Fri 0900-1630, Sat 0900-1200; vac: Mon-Fri 0900-1630
Subj: all subjs; genl; GCSE; A level; undergrad; postgrad; vocational *Co-op Schemes:* BLDSC, SINTO
Equip: 3 m-form reader/printers, 2 video viewers, copier (10p per pg), clr copier, 73 computers (all with wd-proc, internet & CD-ROM) *Disabled:* JAWS, flatscreen monitor, Dragon Dictate, Kurzweil, lift chair *Online:* City Mutual, FENC, NetLogic, Europe in the Round, THES *Svcs:* info, ref, biblio
Stock: bks/18000; periodcls/115; slides/70; maps/25; audios/50; videos/700
Classn: DDC, CLCI *Auto Sys:* Olib
Staff: Libns: 2 FTE *Non-Prof:* 2.36 *Exp:* £30000 (2000-01)

S1907 🏛
Ruskin Gallery Library
Millennium Galleries, Arundel Gate, Sheffield, S1 2PP (0114-278-2600; *fax:* 0114-273-4705) *Internet:* http://www.sheffieldgalleries.org.uk/

Gov Body: Sheffield Galleries & Museums Trust *Chief:* Curator: Ms Dorian Church BA, MA (dorian.church@sheffieldgalleries.org.uk) *Dep:* Asst Curator: Ms Rachel Woodruff MA, BACS (rachel.woodruff@sheffieldgalleries.org.uk)
Entry: adv appt, ref only *Open:* by appt only
Subj: social sci; sci; maths; arts; lit *Collns: Bks & Pamphs:* vols gathered by John Ruskin associated with his museum collns; subsequent additions relate to Ruskin or his concerns *Archvs:* some MS letters
Equip: copier
Stock: bks/2500; photos/1000; slides/1000; videos/40
Pubns: Ruskin & Sheffield; lists of other pubns (mainly connected to temp exhibs) available on request
Staff: Non-Prof: 2

S1908 ✚
Sheffield Children's NHS Trust, Illingworth Library
Floor F, Stephenson Wing, Sheffield Children's Hosp, Western Bank, Sheffield, S10 2TH (0114-271-7347; *fax:* 0114-271-7185) *Email:* s.j.massey@shef.ac.uk

Gov Body: Sheffield Children's NHS Trust *Chief:* Libn: Mrs Sarah Massey BLib, MCLIP
Entry: open access; for borrowing current Univ card & lib ticket from Sheffield Univ required
Open: Mon, Thu 0900-1900, Tue-Wed 0830-1900, Fri 0900-1700
Subj: genl medicine; paediatrics
Equip: m-reader, fax, copier, 6 computers (all with wd-proc & CD-ROM, 4 with internet), 2 rooms for hire *Online:* Medline, Cochrane *Svcs:* info, ref, biblio
Stock: bks/3720; periodcls/30; videos/25
Classn: NLM
Staff: Libns: 1 *Non-Prof:* 0.7 *Exp:* £19000 (1999-2000)

S1909 📖
Sheffield College, Norton Learning Resource Centre
Dyche Ln, Sheffield, S8 8BR (0114-260-2334; *fax:* 0114-260-2301)

Chief: LRC Mgr (job-share): Ms Lynda Josse PGCE, MCLIP (lynda.josse@sheffield.ac.uk) & Ms Ruth Johnson BA, MSc (ruth.johnson@sheffield.ac.uk)
Entry: students & staff; ref only for public; external borrower ticket available *Open:* term: Mon, Thu 0845-1700, Tue-Wed 0845-1830, Fri 0845-1515; vac: some opening, phone for details
Subj: all subjs; genl; GCSE; A level *Collns: Other:* art & design hist slide colln; orchestral scores *Co-op Schemes:* SINTO, SYALL
Equip: m-reader, 3 video readers, 2 copiers (5p per copy), 79 computers (all with wd-proc & internet, 3 with CD-ROM, for student use only), lightbox, digital camera, Alphasmarts, clr printers *Disabled:* large screen computer, wheelchair access *Officer-in-Charge:* LRC Mgr, as above
Svcs: info, ref, biblio
Stock: bks/28000; periodcls/214; slides/4700; maps/50; audios/367; videos/1437; CD-ROMs/93
Acqs Offcr: LRC Mgr, as above
Classn: DDC *Auto Sys:* Dynix Epixtech
Staff: Libns: 1 *Non-Prof:* 8.4 *Exp:* £52757 (1999-2000); £44843 (2000-01)
Further Info: LRC incorporates lib, ICT facilities & key skills support

S1910 📖
Sheffield College, Parson Cross Learning Resource Centres
Remington Rd, Parson Cross, Sheffield, S5 9PB (0114-260-2556; *fax:* 0114-260-2501) *Internet:* http://www.sheffield.co.uk/

Gov Body: Sheffield Coll *Chief:* LRC Mgr: Miss Jo Waller MA (jo.waller@sheffcol.ac.uk) *Dep:* Asst LRC Mgr: Ms Brenda Desmond MA (brenda.desmond@sheffcol.ac.uk)
Assoc Libs: 2 LRCs at Parson Cross: REMINGTON RD SITE LRC, as above; MORRALL RD SITE LRC, Morrall Rd, Parson Cross, Sheffield
Entry: membs of the Sheffield Colls; membs of SINTO; limited external borrowing *Open: Remington Rd Site:* Mon-Tue, Thu 0900-1700, Wed 0945-1700, Fri 0900-1515; *Morrall Rd Site:* Mon-Tue 0900-1800, Wed 0945-1900, Thu 0900-1900, Fri 0900-1515
Subj: all subjs; genl; GCSE; A level; undergrad; vocational; some Higher Edu *Co-op Schemes:* BLDSC, SINTO, SYALL Access Scheme
Equip: 2 copiers (card operated), 2 video viewers, 34 computers (all with wd-proc, internet & CD-ROM) *Online:* Keynotes, Lawtel, EBSCO *Officer-in-Charge:* LRC Mgr, as above *Svcs:* info, ref
Stock: bks/60; CD-ROMs/40; 20000 bks, maps, audios & videos
Classn: DDC *Auto Sys:* Dynix
Staff: Libns: 2 *Non-Prof:* 8 *Exp:* £37000 (1999-2000); £20000 (2000-01)

S1911 📖
Sheffield Hallam University, Learning Centre
City Campus, Pond St, Sheffield, S1 1WB (0114-225-2109; *fax:* 0114-225-3859) *Email:* learning.centre@shu.ac.uk *Internet:* http://www.shu.ac.uk/services/lc/

Chief: Dir & Univ Libn: Mr Graham Bulpitt MA, MCLIP *Dep:* Head of Technical Svcs & Development: Mr E. Oyston; Head of Academic Svcs & Development: Ms B. Fisher; Head of Learning & Teaching Inst: Dr D. Mowthorpe
Assoc Libs: ADSETTS LEARNING CENTRE, contact details as above; COLLEGIATE LEARNING CENTRE, Collegiate Cres, Sheffield, S10 2BP, Info Specialist: Ms K. Moore (0114-253-2474; *fax:* 0114-253-2476); PSALTER LN LEARNING CENTRE, Psalter Ln, Sheffield, S11 8UZ, Info Specialist: Ms C. Abson (0114-253-2721; *fax:* 0114-253-2717)
Entry: open to SHU staff & students; public for ref only; subscription membership available to indivs & orgs *Open:* term: Mon-Thu 0845-2100, Fri 0845-1800, Sat 1000-1700, Sun 1000-1700 (1300-2000 at Psalter Lane Centre); vac: Mon-Fri 0900-1700, Sat (Adsetts & Collegiate Centres only) 1000-1700
Subj: undergrad; computing; social studies; law; communication; edu; sci; eng; construction; business; health; planning; hospitality; art; design; film; English; hist *Collns: Bks & Pamphs:* EDC; BSI *Co-op Schemes:* SINTO
Equip: 3 m-form readers/printers, 60 video presenters/viewers, 20 copiers, clr copier, 520 computers *Online:* over 200 elec info svcs, internet-based on Univ network
Stock: bks/494319; periodcls/2330 subscriptions; AVs/25469
Classn: DDC *Auto Sys:* Innopac
Pubns: various Source Guides (free)
Staff: Prof: 50.45 *Non-Prof:* 45.11 *Exp:* £1231349 (2000-01); fig incl subscriptions, binding, e-resources & ILLs

S1912 📖
The University of Sheffield Library
Western Bank, Sheffield, S10 2TN (0114-222-7200; *fax:* 0114-222-7290) *Email:* library@sheffield.ac.uk *Internet:* http://www.shef.ac.uk/library/

Gov Body: Univ of Sheffield *Chief:* Dir of Lib Svcs & Univ Libn: Mr M.J. Lewis MA, MCLIP *Other Snr Staff:* Asst Dirs: Mr David Jones BA(Econ), MA, MCLIP; Mr P.H. Stubley BSc(Hons), DipLib, MCLIP; Mrs K O'Donovan, BA MCLIP; Mr John Van Loo BA, DMS, MCLIP
Assoc Libs: CROOKESMOOR LIB, Crookesmoor Bldg, Conduit Rd, Sheffield, S10 1FL (0114-222-7340; *fax:* 0114-275-4620; *email:* lib-cml@sheffield.ac.uk); GEOG, PLANNING & LANDSCAPE LIB, Geog Bldg, Winter St, Sheffield S3 7ND (0114-222-7335; *email:* gpl-lib@sheffield.ac.uk); HEALTH SCIS LIB, Royal Hallamshire Hosp (see **S1913**); MUSIC LIB, Dept of Music, 38 Taptonville Rd, Sheffield, S10 5BR (0114-222-7330; *fax:* 0114-266-8053; *email:* t.mccanna@sheffield.ac.uk); PORTOBELLO LIB, Inst for Lifelong Learning, 196-198 West St, Sheffield, S1 4ET (0114-222-7070; *fax:* 0114-222-7001; *email:* portobello.lib@sheffield.ac.uk); ST GEORGE'S LIB, Mappin St, Sheffield, S1 4DT (0114-222-7301; *fax:* 0114-279-6406; *email:* sgl@sheffield.ac.uk)
Entry: for ref, on appl to Libn; borrowing allowed only in special circumstances *Open: Main Lib:* term: Mon-Thu 0900-2130, Fri-Sat 0900-1700, Sun 1400-1800; vac: Mon-Fri 0900-1700, Sat 0900-1230
Subj: Main Lib: arts; sci; social sci; arch; edu; *Crookesmoor Lib:* law; *Geog, Planning & Landscape Lib:* environment; geog; town & regional planning; urban studies; landscape arch; developing countries; *Music Lib:* music; *Portobello Lib:* social scis; women's studies; sci; earth sci; hist; archaeo; lit; film studies; photography; *St George's Lib:* eng; mgmt; business; computer sci; info studies; leisure mgmt *Collns: Bks & Pamphs:* major collns incl: Rare Bks Colln (pre-1851, c26000 vols); Sir Hans Krebs Lib (life scis, c900 items); Firth Ballad Colln; Kennedy Colln (Japan & Far East, c350 vols); Lazar Zaidman Lib (mid 20C politics, econ & Judaism, c330 vols); Tattersall Colln (concrete eng, c1000 items); Wheat Colln (17C-19C law, c245 vols); Left Bk Club Colln (c200 vols); Left Pamph Colln (20C politics, 400+ items); Fascism in Great Britain & Europe Collns; Inst of Edu Historical Colln; Soc of Glass Tech (journals & printed sources, at St George's Lib)

☞

Special Libraries

Sheffield ▼ Slough

(Univ of Sheffield Lib cont)
Collns: *Archvs:* numerous archival & MS collns, incl: correspondence & papers of Samuel Hartlib (1600-1662); papers of Sir Hans Krebs (1900-1982); Natl Union of Mineworkers Energy Rsrch Archv (1970s-90s); Natl Fairground Archv (see **A451**) *Other:* Sheffield Newspapers Colln (late 18C-early 19C); BSI on m-fiche (at St George's Lib); Natl Medical Slidebank on videodisc (at Health Scis Lib) **Co-op Schemes:** BLDSC, SINTO, RIDING, CURL, RLG
Equip: m-readers, m-printers, video & DVD players, fax, copiers, open access PCs (stand-alone & networked, incl wd-proc & CD-ROM facilities) *Online:* wide range of databases & e-journals, usually accessible by Univ membs only **Stock:** bks/1200000; photos/6450; pamphs/46000; *St George's Lib:* bks/66000; periodcls/800; videos/100; *Health Scis Lib:* bks/55000; periodcls/700; videos/250
Classn: DDC, NLM (Health Scis Lib) **Auto Sys:** Talis **Staff:** 170 in total

S1913 🎓 ✚
University of Sheffield, Health Sciences Library
Royal Hallamshire Hosp, Glossop Rd, Sheffield, S10 2JF (0114-271-2030; *fax:* 0114-278-0923)
Email: hsl.rhh@sheffield.ac.uk
Internet: http://www.shef.ac.uk/library/libsites/ hslindex.html

Gov Body: Univ of Sheffield (see **S1912**) **Chief:** Health Scis Libn: Mr John van Loo **Dep:** Site Libn: Ms Fionna Macgillivray
Assoc Libs: NORTHERN GENL HOSP LIB, Samuel Fox House, Herries Rd, Sheffield, S5 7AU, Site Libns: Ms Vicky Grant & Ms Alison Little (0114-226-6800; *fax:* 0114-226-6804; *email:* hsl.ngh@ sheffield.ac.uk); MANVERS CAMPUS LIB, Humphry Davy House, Golden Smithies Ln, Rotherham, S63 7ER, Site Libn: Ms Lyn Parker (0114-222-7390; *fax:* 0114-222-7399; *email:* hsl.mc@sheffield.ac.uk)
Entry: borrowing for registered users only **Open:** *Royal Hallamshire Hosp:* term: Mon-Thu 0900-2130, Fri 0900-1700, Sat 0900-1300; vac: Mon-Thu 0900-1900, Fri 0900-1700, Sat 0900-1230; *Northern Genl Hosp:* term: Mon-Thu 0900-2000, Fri 0900-1700, Sat 0900-1300; vac: Mon-Thu 0900-1900, Fri 0900-1700, Sat 0900-1300; *Manvers Campus:* term & vac: Mon-Thu 0900-1800, Fri 0900-1700
Subj: medicine; nursing
Equip: copier, videos viewers, computers (with wd-proc, internet & CD-ROM, registered users only), room for hire *Online:* Medline, CINAHL & others **Svcs:** info, ref, biblio
Stock: bks/11600; periodcls/421
Classn: NLM **Auto Sys:** Talis

S1914 ✚
Weston Park Hospital, Barnard Library
Whitham Rd, Sheffield, S10 2SJ (0114-226-5216)

Gov Body: Weston Park Hosp NHS Trust **Chief:** Hon Libn: Dr D. Levy MB, BS, BSc, MRCP, FRCR **Dep:** Libn: Mr D. Sunderland BA, FRSA, MCLIP **Open:** Mon-Fri 0830-1700; 24 hr access by key **Subj:** oncology; medicine; medical physics

Equip: video viewer, copier, computers (incl wd-proc & CD-ROM)
Stock: bks/3000; periodcls/25; videos/30
Classn: LC **Staff:** Libns: 1

Sherborne

S1915 🎓
Sherborne School Library
Abbey Rd, Sherborne, Dorset, DT9 3AP (01935-810559; *fax:* 01935-816628)
Internet: http://www.sherborne.org/

Chief: School Libn: Mrs Victoria A. Clayton BA, MCLIP (vac@sherborne.org) **Dep:** Lib Asst: Mrs Clare Dough C&G (ced@sherborne.org) **Other Snr Staff:** Lib Assts: Mrs Helen Foote & Mrs Nikki Cornell
Assoc Libs: various dept libs, managed by subj depts with material purchased by school lib
Entry: written appl to Libn **Open:** term: Mon-Fri 0830-1800, Sat 0830-1300; vac: closed
Subj: GCSE; A level; most academic subjs; local studies (Wessex) **Collns:** *Bks & Pamphs:* old school lib of c900 vols *Archvs:* most now in Dorset Archvs Svc (see **A125**) **Co-op Schemes:** BLDSC, ILL
Equip: m-reader, copier, clr copier, 11 computers (all with wd-proc, internet & CD-ROM), 2 rooms for hire **Svcs:** info, ref, biblio
Stock: bks/42000; periodcls/80
Classn: DDC **Auto Sys:** ALS
Pubns: Lib Guide; Periodicals List; Lib Catalogues
Staff: Libns: 1 *Non-Prof:* 3

Shipley

S1916 ✚
Bradford Health Informatics Service Library
New Mill, Victoria Rd, Saltaire, Shipley, W Yorkshire, BD18 3LD (01274-366051; *fax:* 01274-366024)
Email: kwhite@bradford.nhs.uk
Internet: http://www.bradford.nhs.uk/

Gov Body: NHS **Chief:** Lib Svcs Mgr: Mrs Kim White BA, MCLIP
Entry: NHS staff only **Open:** Mon-Fri 0830-1700
Subj: health; health policy; public health; genl practice; primary care; clinical governance
Equip: copier, fax, computers *Online:* all major medical databases **Officer-in-Charge:** Lib Svcs Mgr, as above **Svcs:** info, ref, biblio, indexing, abstracting
Stock: bks/4000; periodcls/30 **Acqs Offcr:** Lib Svcs Mgr, as above
Classn: NLM **Auto Sys:** Heritage
Staff: Libns: 1 *Other Prof:* 2 *Non-Prof:* 1 **Exp:** £11000 (1999-2000); £11000 (2000-01)

Shoreham

S1917 🔑 📷
Eye Ubiquitous, Picture Library
65 Brighton Rd, Shoreham, W Sussex, BN43 6RE (01273-440113; *fax:* 01273-440166)
Email: library@eyeubiquitous.com
Internet: http://www.eyeubiquitous.com/

Chief: Libn: Mr Stephen Rafferty
Entry: adv appt **Open:** Mon-Fri 0930-1800
Subj: generalities; religion; social sci; tech; geog; hist; travel; wildlife **Collns:** *Archvs:* photos of Tim Page
Equip: fax, copier, computers (incl wd-proc, internet & CD-ROM)
Stock: slides/800000
Pubns: Catalogue (free)
Staff: Libns: 2 *Non-Prof:* 2

Shrewsbury

S1918 🔑
RAPRA Technology Ltd, Porritt and Dawson Library
Shawbury, Shrewsbury, Shropshire, SY4 4NR (01939-252458; *fax:* 01939-251118)
Email: jmccarthy@rapra.net
Internet: http://www.rapra.net/

Chief: Libn: Mrs J. McCarthy BA(Hons), DipLIS
Entry: membs only **Open:** Mon-Fri 0900-1700
Subj: tech; rubber; plastics; polymers **Co-op Schemes:** ILL
Equip: computer (with internet & CD-ROM) *Online:* Dialog, STN, Orbit, Datastar, Dialtech, RAPRA Abstracts
Stock: bks/20500; periodcls/400; maps/120; m-forms/200; database references/500000 **Acqs Offcr:** Libn, as above
Classn: own **Auto Sys:** CAIRS
Pubns: Rapra Abstracts & Rapra Adhesive Abstracts (both available in print, online & on CD-ROM); various technical journals & polymer pubns
Staff: Libns: 1 *Other Prof:* 3 *Non-Prof:* 1

S1919 🎓
Shrewsbury College of Arts and Technology, Learning Resource Centres
London Rd, Shrewsbury, Shropshire, SY2 6PR (01743-342350; *fax:* 01743-342342)
Email: g.taylor@shrewsbury.ac.uk
Internet: http://www.s-cat.ac.uk/

Chief: LRC Mgr: Mrs G.S. Taylor MCLIP **Dep:** Asst LRC Mgr: Mrs C. Thornton BA, MCLIP
Assoc Libs: RADBROOK COLL LRC, Radbrook Rd, Shrewsbury, Shropshire, SY3 9BL, Snr LRC Asst: Mrs H. Brown; BRIDGNORTH COLL LRC, Stourbridge Rd, Bridgnorth, Shropshire, WV15 6AL, Snr LRC Asst: Mrs R. Cunningham
Entry: Coll students free; membs of public ref only; external membership on appl **Open:** term: Mon-Thu 0800-2000, Fri 0800-1700; vac: Mon-Fri 0800-1700
Subj: all subjs; genl; GCSE; A level; undergrad; vocational; local hist (Shropshire) **Collns:** *Bks & Pamphs:* Art Lib *Other:* technical indexes (construction & eng) **Co-op Schemes:** BLDSC, SHAIR, NILTA, BOLDU Ltd
Equip: m-reader, fax, video viewer, fax, copier, clr copier, computers (incl wd-proc, internet & CD-ROM), room for hire **Disabled:** specialised computers & software *Online:* Emerald Intelligence, OVID **Svcs:** info, ref, biblio, careers info, Open Learning
Stock: bks/42000; periodcls/300; slides/2000; pamphs/3000; audios/250; videos/800; CD-ROMs/120
Classn: DDC **Staff:** Libns: 4 *Non-Prof:* 17 **Exp:** £45000 (1999-2000)

S1920 🎓
Shrewsbury School, Taylor Library and Archives
The Schools, Shrewsbury, Shropshire, SY3 7BA (01743-280595; *fax:* 01743-243107)
Email: archivist@shrewsbury.org.uk

Type: independent school **Gov Body:** Chairman & Governors of Shrewsbury School **Chief:** Taylor Libn & Archivist: Mr J.B. Lawson MA
Entry: accredited scholars by appt in writing **Open:** by appt only, preferably in term
Subj: genl; GCSE; A level **Collns:** *Bks & Pamphs:* Taylor Lib Collns: ancient lib of the school, founded in 1606, with c7500 vols, primarily of 15C-18C bks of English & European origin, also incl medieval MSS, incunabula, fine bk bindings, modern private press bks etc; Darwiniana Colln

---

Archvs: School Archvs (1552-date) *Other:* Moser Colln of 19C Watercolours; photo archvs (c1860-date); Shropshire Local Hist Colln; memorabilia
Equip: copier
Classn: MS Catalogues for Taylor Lib
Pubns: Shrewsbury School Lib Bindings: Catalogue Raisonné (this is not a school pubn but available via bksellers)

S1921 🎓 ✚
Staffordshire University, School of Health Library
Royal Shrewsbury Hosps NHS Trust, Mytton Oak Rd, Shrewsbury, Shropshire, SY3 8XQ (01743-261440; *fax:* 01743-261061)
Email: s.kennedy@staffs.ac.uk

Gov Body: Staffordshire Univ (see **S1989**) *Chief:* Site Operations Mgr: Ms Shirley Kennedy
Entry: staff & students of Staffordshire Univ; employees of Shropshire HA *Open:* Mon, Wed-Fri 0830-1700; Tue 0830-1900
Subj: nursing; midwifery; mental health; NHS mgmt *Co-op Schemes:* BLDSC, WMHLN, NULJ
Equip: copier, 8 computers *Svcs:* info, ref
Stock: bks/11000; periodcls/65; videos/50; AVs/20
Classn: NLM *Auto Sys:* Horizon
Staff: Libns: 1 *Non-Prof:* 3

Sidcup

S1922 ✚
Queen Mary's Hospital, Charnley Library
Queen Mary's Hosp, Sidcup, Kent, DA14 6LT (020-8302-2504; *fax:* 020-8308-9384)
Email: val.jennings@qms-tr.sthames.nhs.uk

Type: multidisciplinary postgrad health *Gov Body:* Queen Mary's Sidcup NHS Trust *Chief:* Lib Svc Mgr: Mrs V.J. Jennings MCLIP *Dep:* Snr Lib Asst: Mrs S. Pateman
Entry: 24 hr access to resident prof staff; other NHS employees welcome during opening hrs, non-NHS staff at Libn's discretion for ref purposes only *Open:* Mon-Fri 0830-1800
Subj: medicine; health care; health svc mgmt
Collns: Archvs: hist of hosp; Gillies Archv (plastic surgery from WW1 – see **A454**) *Co-op Schemes:* BLDSC, Bexley London Borough, ILL between NHS WDC libs in London
Equip: m-reader, fax (50p per pg UK, £1 abroad), copier (A4/5p), video viewer, 12 computers (all with wd-proc, 1 with internet & 9 with CD-ROM), laser printer, clr inkjet printer *Online:* 8 health databases + e-journals, via NHSNet (free with NHS password)
Officer-in-Charge: Lib Svc Mgr, as above *Svcs:* info, ref, biblio
Stock: bks/3025; periodcls/127; slides/2500; videos/100; archvs/4.9 cubic m *Acqs Offcr:* Lib Svc Mgr, as above
Classn: NLM *Auto Sys:* Librarian
Pubns: Lib Guide; Annual Report; Recent Acqs; Journal Holdings; News Bulletins (all on hosp intranet)
Staff: Libns: 1 *Non-Prof:* 1 *Exp:* £34942 (1999-2000); £35854 (2000-01); incl exp on elec svcs & databases, ILLs etc

S1923 🎓
Rose Bruford College, Learning Resources Centre
Lamorbey Pk, Sidcup, Kent, DA15 9DF (020-8308-2626)
Internet: http://www.bruford.ac.uk/library/

Chief: Coll Libn: Mr John Collis BA, ARCM, MCLIP (john@bruford.ac.uk) *Dep:* Asst Libn: Ms Elinor Skedgell BA (elinor@bruford.ac.uk)
Entry: ref only, adv appt preferred *Open:* Mon-Fri 0900-1700

Subj: arts (esp theatre); lit (esp dramatic works)
Co-op Schemes: BLDSC, Libpac
Equip: 2 m-readers, 3 video viewers, 2 copiers, 16 computers (all with wd-proc, 9 with internet & 7 with CD-ROM) *Officer-in-Charge:* Coll Libn, as above
Svcs: info, ref, biblio, indexing
Stock: bks/38874; periodcls/85; slides/6000; m-forms/50; audios/1900; videos/1919 *Acqs Offcr:* Coll Libn, as above
Classn: DDC *Auto Sys:* Dynix
Staff: Libns: 2 *Non-Prof:* 1.3 *Exp:* £14901 (1999-2000); £20153 (2000-01)

Sindlesham

S1924 🔑 🏛
Berkshire Masonic Library and Museum
Berkshire Masonic Centre, Mole Rd, Sindlesham, Berkshire, RG41 5DB (0118-979-5104; *fax:* 0118-977-3571)
Email: robin@berkspgl.demon.co.uk
Internet: http://www.berkspgl.demon.co.uk/library.htm

Gov Body: Berkshire Provincial Grand Lodge
Chief: Libn: Mr Robin White
Entry: membs of the Province of Berkshire may borrow; membs of other provinces & genl public ref only, by appt *Open:* Mon-Sat 1400-2230
Subj: freemasonry *Stock:* bks/13500

Sleaford

S1925 🏛 🎓
Royal Air Force College Library
Cranwell, Sleaford, Lincolnshire, NG34 8HB (01400-261201 x6329; *fax:* 01400-261201 x6266)
Internet: http://www.cranwell.raf.mod.uk/

Gov Body: Ministry of Defence (see **S1284**)
Chief: Libn & Archivist: Miss Mary Guy BA(Hons), DipLib, MCLIP
Assoc Libs: TRENCHARD HALL LIB, Trenchard Hall, RAF Coll Cranwell, Sleaford, Lincolnshire, NG34 8HB, Technical Libn: Miss S.A. Burrows BA, MCLIP
Entry: not open to public; written permission may be given to bona fide rsrchers & students *Open:* Mon, Tue & Thu 0815-1700, Wed & Fri 0815-1600
Subj: genl; military sci & hist; air power; RAF hist; defence studies; current affairs; warfare; air warfare; computer sci; maths; aeronautics; mgmt sci; eng (mechanical, electrical, elec, materials, aerospace); logistics; weapons; British hist
Collns: Bks & Pamphs: T.E. Lawrence colln of bks, pamphs & clippings *Archvs:* RAF Coll hist & archvs (1915-date) *Co-op Schemes:* BLDSC, Ministry of Defence
Equip: 20 m-readers, 4 m-printers, 2 video viewers, 2 copiers, clr copier, 30 computers (incl wd-proc & CD-ROM) *Online:* Dialtech
Stock: bks/116000; periodcls/332; photos/7050; slides/3200; m-forms/22000; audios/3; videos/90; archvs/3000 bks & pamphs
Classn: DDC, UDC *Auto Sys:* TinLib
Pubns: internal use only: Monthly Booklist; Subj Bibliographies
Staff: Libns: 4 *Non-Prof:* 8

Sleat

S1926 🎓
Leabharlann An t-Sabhail Mhòir (Sabhal Mòr Ostaig Library)
An Teanga, Sleat, Isle of Skye, Scotland, IV44 8RQ (01471-888431; *fax:* 01471-888000)
Email: leabharlann@smo.uhi.ac.uk
Internet: http://www.smo.uhi.ac.uk/leabharlann/

Gov Body: Sabhal Mòr Ostaig; part of the Univ of the Highlands & Islands (UHI) *Chief:* Libn: Ms C. Cain MA, MSc (sm00cfc@groupwise.uhi.ac.uk)
Dep: Lib Asst: Mrs S. NicRàth
Entry: students & staff of Sabhal Mòr Ostaig & Univ of the Highlands & Islands Millennium Inst; ref only for public *Open:* Mon-Fri 0900-1700; addl evening hrs: Mon 1730-1930, Tue 1800-2030, Thu 1730-2030
Subj: undergrad; postgrad; ethnography; politics & economy of the Scottish Highlands & North Atlantic margin; Scottish Gaelic lang; other Celtic langs, incl Irish & Welsh; Scottish Gaelic lit; Celtic lit; hist of the Scottish Highlands & North Atlantic margin; Celtic studies *Collns: Bks & Pamphs:* Celtica Colln (antiquarian colln of Celtic studies materials); MacCormick Colln (rare early printed Gaelic materials & Highland related) *Co-op Schemes:* ILL, UHI Millennium Inst inter-site lending
Equip: copier, 15 computers (all with wd-proc, internet & CD-ROM) *Online:* ISI (Web of Sci), Index to Theses, CAB Abstracts, EBSCO, Ingenta Journals *Svcs:* info, ref, biblio
Stock: bks/10000; audios/70; videos/250; CD-ROMs/60
Classn: DDC *Auto Sys:* Olib
Staff: Libns: 1 *Non-Prof:* 1

Slough

S1927 ✚
Heatherwood and Wexham Parks Hospitals NHS Trust, John Jamison Library
c/o Wexham Park Hosp, Slough, Berkshire, SL2 4HL (01753-634857; *fax:* 01753-634189)
Email: wxlibrary@hwph-tr.nhs.uk
Internet: http://www.hwph-tr.nhs.uk/

Chief: Lib Mgr: Ms Sarah Pallot
Assoc Libs: HEATHERWOOD HOSP LIB, London Rd, Ascot, Berkshire, SL5 8AA
Entry: open to NHS staff & subscribers (ID required); others may also use svc for ref purposes only *Open:* Mon, Wed, Fri 0900-1730, Tue, Thu 0900-2000
Subj: medicine; health care; nursing; mgmt *Co-op Schemes:* HeLIN, BLIP
Equip: 2 m-readers, m-printer (5p per pg), video viewer, 2 fax (varies), 2 copiers (5p per pg), 9 computers (all with wd-proc, internet & CD-ROM, printing 5p per sheet) *Online:* Datastar, Medline, PubMed, CINAHL, Cochrane *Svcs:* info, ref, biblio, short training courses in searching for health info
Stock: bks/c6000; periodcls/c150; various slides, audios, videos & CD-ROMs
Classn: NLM *Auto Sys:* Heritage
Pubns: lib leaflet
Staff: Libns: 2 *Non-Prof:* 1.89
Proj: merger of two libs on site; lib extension

S1928 ☕🎞
ICI Paints Library
Wexham Rd, Slough, Berkshire, SL2 5DS (01753-877599; *fax:* 01753-539855)
Email: paul_hollins@ici.com
Internet: http://www.dulux.com/

Chief: Business Info Specialist: Mr Paul Hollins BLib
Entry: adv appt *Open:* Mon-Fri 0830-1700
Subj: organic chem; polymer sci; colloidal chem; paint tech *Collns: Archvs:* clr cards; hist of Dulux
Co-op Schemes: BLDSC, BLIP, Paint Rsrch Assoc
Equip: m-reader, m-printer, copier, fax, computers (incl wd-proc & CD-ROM) *Online:* for staff only
Svcs: info, ref
Stock: bks/10000; periodcls/35; m-forms/20000; videos/550; archvs/12 m
Classn: UDC *Auto Sys:* Soutron
Staff: Libns: 1 *Non-Prof:* 0.2

S1929 ♈ ⚷

National Foundation for Educational Research, Library and Information Services

The Mere, Upton Pk, Slough, Berkshire, SL1 2DQ (01753-574123; *fax:* 01753-691632)
Email: enquiries@nfer.ac.uk
Internet: http://www.nfer.ac.uk/

Type: independent rsrch org *Chief:* Head of Lib & Info Svcs: Mrs Janet May-Bowles BA, MCLIP
Dep: Dep Libn: Mrs Pauline Benfield BA(Hons), MCLIP
Entry: ref only, adv appt preferred *Open:* Mon-Fri 0915-1715
Subj: social sci; edu *Collns: Bks & Pamphs:* statistics; legislation relating to edu; annual reports; bks written by membs of staff *Archvs:* incomplete records of APU (Assessment of Performance Unit) *Other:* educational tests (not for loan)
Equip: m-reader, m-printer, copier, fax, computer (incl wd-proc & CD-ROM) *Online:* Current Educational Rsrch in the UK, ProCite, ASSIA, BOPCAS, British Education Index, CBCA FullText Education, ERIC, Social Rsrch Methodology & others *Svcs:* info, ref, biblio, lit searches (fees), training
Stock: bks/24000; periodcls/350; pamphs/2000
Classn: Bliss *Auto Sys:* CAIRS
Pubns: Current Awareness Bulletin (monthly); New Bks List (monthly); Periodical Holdings List; Statistical Info Guide; NFER also publ a wide range of titles; full catalogue available from NFER
Staff: Libns: 5 *Non-Prof:* 5

Solihull

S1930 🎓 ✚

Marie Curie Centre – Warren Pearl, Library

Edu Dept, 911-913 Warwick Rd, Solihull, W Midlands, B91 3ER (0121-254-7832; *fax:* 0121-254-7840)

Chief: Libn: Mrs J. Reuben
Open: Mon-Fri 1000-1400
Subj: palliative care
Equip: video viewer, fax, copier, computer (with wd-proc, internet & CD-ROM), room for hire *Svcs:* info, ref
Stock: bks/400; periodcls/9; videos/15
Auto Sys: LIMES *Staff: Non-Prof:* 1

S1931 ✚

Solihull Hospital Library

Edu Centre, Lode Ln, Solihull, W Midlands, B91 2JL (0121-424-5196; *fax:* 0121-424-4194)

Gov Body: Birmingham Heartlands & Solihull NHS Trust *Chief:* Lib Mgr: Ms Elizabeth Preston (elizabeth.preston@heartsol.wmids.nhs.uk) & Ms Ann Button (ann.button@heartsol.wmids.nhs.uk)
Assoc Libs: BIRMINGHAM HEARTLANDS HOSP LIB (see **S159**)
Entry: staff of Trust *Open:* Mon-Fri 0900-1700; 24 hr access to membs
Subj: medicine; psy; psychiatry
Staff: Libns: 2 *Non-Prof:* 2

South Brent

S1932 ♈ ✋

Syon Abbey Library

Marley, South Brent, Devon, TQ10 9JX (01364-72256)

Gov Body: Syon Abbey Community *Chief:* none, please contact Mother Abbess
Entry: ref only, by special appt, arranged with Mother Abbess
Subj: mainly spirituality & devotional works
Collns: Bks & Pamphs: Bridgettine hist *Archvs:* community archvs (in preparation)
Stock: bks/9000; periodcls/15 *Classn:* own

South Croydon

S1933 ♈

Croydon Natural History and Scientific Society Ltd, Library

96a Brighton Rd, South Croydon, Surrey, CR2 6AD (020-8688-4539)
Email: john@greig51.freeserve.co.uk
Internet: http://www.greig51.freeserve.co.uk/cnhss/

Chief: Libn: Mr Paul W. Sowan *Other Snr Staff:* Museum Curator: Mr John Greig
Entry: ref only for non-membs, by written appt
Subj: local studies (Croydon); archaeo; industrial archaeo; nat hist; geog; geol; meteorology; transport; conservation; planning *Collns: Other:* maps & plans (c800 items), incl C.C. Fagg Colln (unpublished land use surveys, 1920s)
Pubns: CNHSS Bulletin (3 pa); Croydon Bibliographies for Regional Survey (irregular); A Croydon Backcloth: Some Little Known Estate Maps in Lambeth Palace Lib

South Queensferry

S1934 ⚱🖋

Aligent Technologies UK plc, Research and Development Library and Information Service

Station Rd, South Queensferry, W Lothian, EH30 9TG (0131-331-7318; *fax:* 0131-331-6757)
Email: christine_macleod@aligent.com

Chief: Libn & Info Offcr: Mrs Christine Macleod MA(Hons), DipLib, MCLIP *Dep:* Mrs Mayumi N. Hepburn BLib
Entry: not open to public; tel or letter enqs only
Open: Mon-Thu 0800-1700, Fri 0800-1600
Subj: tech; telecommunications; computing
Collns: Bks & Pamphs: Bellcore Standards; ITU-T Standards *Co-op Schemes:* BLDSC
Equip: m-reader, m-printer, copier, computers (incl wd-proc & CD-ROM) *Online:* Dialog *Svcs:* info, ref, biblio, indexing
Stock: bks/3000; periodcls/150; videos/200
Classn: UDC *Auto Sys:* Sirsi
Staff: Libns: 2 *Exp:* £13000 (1999-2000)

South Shields

S1935 🎓

South Tyneside College Library

St George's Ave, South Shields, Tyne & Wear, NE34 6ET (0191-427-3604; *fax:* 0191-427-3643)
Email: pamela.robinson@stc.ac.uk

Gov Body: South Tyneside Coll *Chief:* Libn: Mrs Pamela Robinson MCLIP *Other Snr Staff:* Asst Libns: Ms Jacqueline Devine MCLIP, Mr Michael Dann BA(Hons) & Ms Catherine Walmsley BA(Hons)

Assoc Libs: HEBBURN LIB (see **S796**)
Entry: students enrolled on Coll courses; others may use for ref only *Open:* term: Mon, Tue-Thu 0845-2000, Wed 0900-2000, Fri 0845-1630; vac: Mon-Thu 0900-1700, Fri 0900-1630
Subj: all subjs; genl; GCSE; A level; undergrad; local study (South Tyneside, hist & geog) *Collns: Bks & Pamphs:* large marine eng colln *Co-op Schemes:* BLDSC, NEMLAC
Equip: m-reader, video viewer, copier, 7 computers (incl 2 with wd-proc, 3 with CD-ROM & 2 with internet) *Svcs:* info, ref, biblio
Stock: bks/32450; periodcls/103; CD-ROMs/35
Classn: DDC
Staff: Libns: 4 *Non-Prof:* 5 *Exp:* £47000 (2000-01); fig is for both sites

S1936 ✚

South Tyneside Healthcare NHS Trust, Education Centre Library

South Tyneside Dist Hosp, Harton Ln, South Shields, Tyne & Wear, NE34 0PL (0191-454-8888 x2572; *fax:* 0191-427-0096)

Gov Body: South Tyneside Healthcare NHS Trust
Chief: Libn: Mrs Maureen Duffy BA, MCLIP (Maureen.Duffy@sthct.nhs.uk) *Other Snr Staff:* Lib Asst: Ms Claire Leng BA (Claire.Leng@sthct.nhs.uk)
Entry: Trust employees; medical & dental practitioners in Trust area *Open:* Mon-Thu 0830-1700, Fri 0830-1630
Subj: medicine & related subjs (at undergrad & postgrad level) *Co-op Schemes:* BLDSC, Health Libs North, BMA
Equip: m-reader, fax, video viewer, 2 copiers, 8 computers (all with wd-proc, internet & CD-ROM)
Officer-in-Charge: Libn, as above
Stock: bks/5000; periodcls/110; slides/54 sets; audios/23; videos/170; CD-ROMs/50 *Acqs Offcr:* Libn, as above
Classn: DDC *Auto Sys:* SydneyPlus
Staff: Libns: 1 *Non-Prof:* 0.5

Southall

S1937 🎓

Southall and West London College, Southall Learning Centre

Beaconsfield Rd, Southall, Middlesex, UB1 1DP (020-8231-6141; *fax:* 020-8574-2460)
Email: linaw@wcl.ac.uk

Gov Body: Ealing, Hammersmith & West London Coll *Chief:* Learning Centre Mgr: Mrs Linda Wilde MCLIP
Assoc Libs: ACTON & WEST LONDON COLL, ACTON LEARNING CENTRE (see **S986**); EALING & WEST LONDON COLL, EALING LEARNING CENTRE, The Green, Ealing, London, W5 5EW; HAMMERSMITH & WEST LONDON COLL, HAMMERSMITH LEARNING CENTRE (see **S1156**); HAMMERSMITH & WEST LONDON COLL, LIME GROVE LEARNING CENTRE, Lime Grove, London, W12 8EA
Entry: adv appt for membs of public *Open:* term: Mon, Thu 0830-1900, Tue-Wed 0830-1700, Fri 0830-1930; vac: Mon-Fri 1000-1500
Subj: all subjs; genl; GCSE; A level; vocational; ESOL; Access courses
Equip: copier, clr copier, 2 video viewers, 42 computers (all with wd-proc & internet, 10 with CD-ROM) *Svcs:* info, ref, biblio
Stock: bks/24000; periodcls/70; videos/900 *Acqs Offcr:* Learning Centre Mgr, as above
Classn: DDC *Auto Sys:* Unicorn
Staff: Libns: 1 *Non-Prof:* 6
Proj: new Learning Centre in Sep 2003, to incl provision for 6th Form Coll on same site

Southampton

S1938

British-American Tobacco Information Centre

Regents Park Rd, Millbrook, Southampton, Hampshire, SO15 8TL (023-8079-3603; *fax:* 023-8079-3800)
Email: val_rice@britamtob.com
Internet: http://www.bat.com/

Chief: Snr Info Scientist: Mrs V.L. Rice MCLIP
Entry: ref only, adv appt *Open:* Mon-Fri 0830-1700
Subj: tech related to the tobacco industry *Collns: Bks & Pamphs:* some pubns on the hist of tobacco
Co-op Schemes: BLDSC, HATRICS
Equip: m-reader, fax, copier, 7 computers (incl 1 internet & 1 CD-ROM) *Online:* Dialog, Datastar, STN *Svcs:* info, ref, indexing, abstracting
Stock: bks/18000; periodcls/80
Classn: UDC *Auto Sys:* Basis Plus
Staff: Libns: 1 *Non-Prof:* 2

S1939

Maritime and Coastguard Agency, Marine Information Centre

Spring Pl, 105 Commercial Rd, Southampton, Hampshire, SO15 1EG (023-8032-9297; *fax:* 023-8032-9298)
Internet: http://www.mcagency.org.uk/

Gov Body: Dept for Transport *Chief:* Head of Marine Info Centre: Miss S. De Marco
Entry: ref only, by appt *Open:* Mon-Fri 0900-1700
Subj: maritime law; shipping; ship sci & tech
Collns: Bks & Pamphs: merchant shipping legislation *Co-op Schemes:* BLDSC, HATRICS, Maritime Info Assoc
Equip: copier *Svcs:* info, ref
Stock: bks/10000; periodcls/150
Classn: DDC *Staff: Non-Prof:* 3

S1940

Ordnance Survey Library

Room C128, Romsey Rd, Southampton, Hampshire, SO16 4GU (023-8079-2691; *fax:* 023-8079-2888)
Internet: http://www.ordsvy.gov.uk/

Chief: Libn: Mrs S.J. Caine BSc, MCLIP *Dep:* Asst Libn: Ms C. Layton BSc(Econ) (clayton@ordsvy.gov.uk)
Entry: ref only, adv appt *Open:* Mon-Fri 0930-1530
Subj: generalities; land use; surveying; cartography; remote sensing; photogrammetry; computer sci; geog; GIS; mgmt; marketing *Co-op Schemes:* BLDSC, HATRICS
Equip: m-reader, fax, video viewer, copier, 4 computers (all with wd-proc & CD-ROM, 3 with internet) *Online:* EINS (OS employees only)
Stock: bks/10000; periodcls/300; photos/2000; slides/10000; pamphs/40000; m-forms/200; audios/30; videos/200
Classn: UDC, Keyword *Auto Sys:* CALM 2000
Pubns: Accessions List; Current Awareness Bulletin (on intranet)
Staff: Libns: 2 *Non-Prof:* 2

S1941

Royal South Hants Hospital, Staff Library

Dept of Psychiatry, Brintons Ter, Southampton, Hampshire, SO14 0YG (023-8082-5714; *fax:* 023-8023-4020)
Email: library.rsh@suht.swest.nhs.uk

Gov Body: West Hampshire NHS Trust *Chief:* Dist Libn: Ms R. Noyes BA, DipLib (bobby.noyes@wht.nhs.uk) *Dep:* Asst Libn: post vacant *Other Snr Staff:* Libn: Mrs Alex Coley BA, DipLib, MCLIP *Assoc Libs:* HAMPSHIRE & ISLE OF WIGHT STRATEGIC HEALTH AUTHORITY LIB, Oakley Rd, Southampton, SO16 4GX, Libn: Dr Derek Jenkins PhD, FRSC, MCLIP (023-8072-5440; *fax:* 023-8072-5565; *email:* derekjenkins@sswh-ha.nhs.uk); STAFF LIB, Rufus Lodge, Tatchbury Mount, Calmore, Southampton, SO40 2RZ (023-8087-4231; *fax:* 023-8087-4225; *email:* library.tatchbury@wht.nhs.uk); STAFF LIB, Hawthorn Lodge, Moorgreen Hosp, Southampton, SO30 2JB, Libn: Mrs Francis Little MCLIP (023-8047-5154; *fax:* 023-8047-5155; *email:* library.moorgreen@wht.nhs.uk); STAFF LIB, Ashurst Centre, Southampton, SO40 7AR (023-8074-2360; *fax:* 023-8074-2361); RAVENSWOOD HOUSE LIB & RESOURCE CENTRE (see **S679**)
Entry: NHS staff & students *Open:* Mon-Fri 0900-1730
Subj: medicine; psy; psychiatry *Co-op Schemes:* SWRLIN, STLIS, HATRICS, BLDSC
Equip: copier (10p per pg), 5 computers (incl 4 with wd-proc, 4 with internet & 1 with CD-ROM) *Online:* KAZ4 *Svcs:* info, ref, biblio
Stock: bks/8500; periodcls/160; videos/25; CD-ROMs/4
Classn: NLM (local variation) *Auto Sys:* Heritage
Staff: Libns: 4.69 *Non-Prof:* 4.02

S1942

Southampton City College Library

St Mary St, Southampton, Hampshire, SO14 1AR (023-8057-7437; *fax:* 023-8057-7473)
Email: jo.webb@southampton-city.ac.uk
Internet: http://www.southampton-city.ac.uk/

Gov Body: Corp of Coll *Chief:* Libn: Mrs J.M. Webb BA, MCLIP *Dep:* Miss Charlotte Everitt BA
Open: term: Mon-Thu 0830-2000, Fri 1000-1700; vac: Mon-Fri 0900-1230, 1330-1645
Subj: all subjs; generalities; phil; psy; religion; social sci; lang; sci; maths; tech; arts; lit; geog; hist
Co-op Schemes: HATRICS, SLIC
Equip: video viewer, copier, computers (incl wd-proc, internet & CD-ROM) *Svcs:* info, ref
Stock: bks/25000; periodcls/200; videos/4000; CD-ROMs/200
Classn: DDC *Auto Sys:* Heritage
Staff: Libns: 3 *Non-Prof:* 9

S1943

Southampton City Cultural Services, Collections Management Centre

Unit 31, City Industrial Pk, Southern Rd, Southampton, Hampshire, SO15 1HG (023-8023-7584; *fax:* 023-8021-2048)
Email: a.arnott@southampton.gov.uk
Internet: http://www.southampton.gov.uk/

Gov Body: Southampton City Council (see **P171**) *Chief:* Curator of Local Collns: A.T. Arnott BA, BSc, MA, CertEd
Entry: ref only, adv appt required *Open:* Mon-Fri 0800-1630
Subj: local study (Southampton, incl docks); museology; shipping; shipbuilding; port records *Collns: Bks & Pamphs:* shipping registers (Lloyds from 1875 & continental registers); yacht registers (from 1879); Southampton Shipping Guide; journals & periodcls, incl: Motor Ship, Blue Peter, Yachting World, Yachting Monthly, Yachts & Yachting, Shipbuilding & Shipping Record, Syren, Shipbuilder, Ports *Archvs:* Harbour Board minutes; Furness Withy archv *Other:* Associated British Ports Photo Archv; British Power Boat Co (drawings, photos & ephemera); Thorneycroft & Day, Summers (shipbuilding drawings); OS maps; dock company/shipping company ephemera; topographical & ship photos

Svcs: info, ref, photographic svc
Stock: bks/8000; periodcls/5; photos/40000; slides/3000; illusts/2000; maps/250; audios/2000; videos/50; eng drawings/9000
Classn: own *Auto Sys:* Library Manager
Pubns: Titanic Voices; Images of Southampton; Dream Palaces; Southampton & D-Day; Maritime Southampton
Staff: Other Prof: 3 (2 FTE) *Non-Prof:* 5 volunteers *Exp:* £600 pa, but materials purchased as necessary & also received by request

S1944

Southampton Institute, Mountbatten Library

East Park Ter, Southampton, Hampshire, SO14 0YN (023-8031-9248; *fax:* 023-8031-9697)
Email: robert.burrell@solent.ac.uk
Internet: http://www.solent.ac.uk/library/

Gov Body: Southampton Inst *Chief:* Head of Learning Support: post vacant *Other Snr Staff:* Info Svcs Mgr: Mr Robert Burrell BSc(Econ), MCLIP; User Svcs Mgr: Ms Elizabeth Selby MCLIP *Assoc Libs:* MOUNTBATTEN LIB, Newtown Rd, Warsash, Southampton, SO31 9ZL
Entry: open access for ref only *Open:* term: Mon-Thu 0830-2100, Fri 0830-1800, Sat 0900-1700, Sun 1300-1700; vac: Mon-Thu 0830-1700, Fri 0830-1630
Subj: all subjs; undergrad; postgrad; phil; psy; social sci; tech; arts; lit; antiques; fine art valuation; maritime hist; marine tech; marine eng; oceanography; marine sci; marine law; navigation
Collns: Archvs: Godden Colln (auction house catalogues, 1930s onwards); Ken Russell Colln (MSS & photos of the film-maker); Rome Colln (documents on Sizewell B & Hinkley Pt) *Co-op Schemes:* BLDSC, HATRICS, SWRLS
Equip: 2 m-form reader/printers, 22 video viewers, 16 copiers, 2 clr copiers, 60 computers (incl wd-proc, internet & CD-ROM) *Disabled:* Kurzweil, Inspiration, Dragon Dictate, ZoomText software, CCTV screen magnifiers, voice synthesisers, braille facilities *Online:* Dialog, BLAISE, Datastar, BRS, BCIS, Lexis *Officer-in-Charge:* Asst Libn: Mr G. Burridge *Svcs:* info, ref, biblio
Stock: bks/227000; periodcls/5482; photos/200; slides/59000; maps/87; m-forms/469; audios/1854; videos/9072; archvs/90 linear m
Classn: DDC *Auto Sys:* DDE
Pubns: Yacht & Boat Design: Select List of Refs (£15)
Staff: Libns: 16 *Non-Prof:* 30

S1945

Southampton Oceanography Centre, National Oceanographic Library

European Way, Southampton, Hampshire, SO14 3ZH (023-8059-6111; *fax:* 023-8059-6115)
Email: nol@soc.soton.ac.uk

Gov Body: NERC & Univ of Southampton (see **S1946**) *Chief:* Head of Info Svcs: Mrs Pauline Simpson BA, MCLIP
Entry: open for bona fide rsrch workers, by appt
Open: term: Mon-Fri 0830-2030, Sat-Sun 1200-1700; vac: Mon-Fri 0830-1730; open to visitors: Mon-Fri 0930-1630 only
Subj: all disciplines of marine sci; marine biology; marine chem; marine eng; marine physics; marine geol & geophysics; computing & geol *Collns: Bks & Pamphs:* Challenger Soc; Intergovernmental Oceanographic Commission Depository *Archvs:* Deacon Archvs; Discovery Investigation Archvs *Co-op Schemes:* BLDSC, IAMSLIC, EURASLIC, HATRICS
Equip: 4 m-readers, m-printer, 4 copiers, 11 computers (incl 9 CD-ROM) *Online:* OCEANIS; the Centre also offers its unique info svc, MIAS, providing info, data & advice to orgs with interests in the marine environment, via a two-level subscription svc; full details from the Centre ☛

Southampton

▼

St Albans

Special Libraries

(Southampton Oceonography Centre cont)
Svcs: info, ref, biblio, indexing
Stock: bks/18000; periodcls/1000; slides/2000;
pamphs/200000; maps/5000
Classn: own *Auto Sys:* Olib
Pubns: Lib leaflet; MIAS leaflet; Lib Guide; Serial
Holdings; OCEANIS User Guide
Staff: Libns: 3 Non-Prof: 6

S1946 🎓

University of Southampton, Hartley Library

Highfield, Southampton, Hampshire, SO17 1BJ
(023-8059-2180; *fax:* 023-8059-3007)
Email: libenquiries@soton.ac.uk
Internet: http://www.soton.ac.uk/~library/

Gov Body: Univ of Southampton *Chief:* Univ
Libn: Dr M.L. Brown BA, PhD, DipLib, MCLIP
Dep: Dep Libn: Mr R.L. Wake MA, MA, CertMgmt,
MCLIP
Assoc Libs: AVENUE CAMPUS LIB, Avenue
Campus, Highfield Rd, Southampton, Hampshire,
SO17 1BF (023-8059-5405; *email:* alenqs@
soton.ac.uk); BIOMEDICAL SCI LIB (see **S1947**);
HEALTH SVCS LIB (see **S1948**); NATL
OCEANOGRAPHIC LIB (see **S1945**);
SOUTHAMPTON UNIV NEW COLL LIB (see
S1949); WINCHESTER SCHOOL OF ART LIB
(see **S2127**)
Entry: formal appl to libn *Open:* term: Mon-Fri
0900-1800, Sat 0900-1700, Sun 1200-2100; vac:
some reductions in hrs, closed Sun
Subj: all subjs; undergrad; postgrad; rsrch; local
studies (Hampshire & Isle of Wight, hist &
topography) *Collns: Bks & Pamphs:* UK official
pubns; EDC; Bullar Colln (theology, hist & lit); Cope
Colln (hist & topography of Hampshire & the Isle of
Wight); Hampshire Field Club Lib (British hist &
archaeo); Hampshire Gardens Trust Lib;
Hampshire Ornithological Soc Lib; Hartley Colln
(hist & lit, 17C-19C); Oates Colln (slavery in West
Indies); Parkes Lib (Jewish/non-Jewish relations);
Perkins Agricultural Lib; Spanish Drama Colln;
Univ Colln; Wellington Pamphs; parish libs *Archvs:*
archvs of Univ & predecessors; Univ Coll of
Southampton & Hartley Instn); papers of earlier
Southampton instns, incl: Southampton Medical
Reading Club; Southampton School of Art; papers
of indivs associated with the Univ; Natl Assoc of
Divisional Executives in Edu Archv; Jewish Archvs
(Anglo-Judaism, 550 collns of indivs & orgs, 18C-
20C); Wellington Papers; Pamerston Papers;
Mountbatten Papers; Shaftesbury Papers; William
Lamb Papers; Sir Ernest Cassel Papers;
Battenburg Family Papers; literary MSS, incl:
Edmund Blunden MSS; E.M. Almedingen MSS;
Norman Crisp MSS; Bournemouth Poetry Soc
papers; extensive estate archvs (Ireland &
Hampshire, 16C-20C) *Co-op Schemes:* BLDSC,
SWRLS, HATRICS, SCONUL, CURL, RLG, UK
Libs Plus
Equip: 15 m-readers, m-printer, video viewer, 11
copiers, computers (incl 6 CD-ROM) *Svcs:* info,
ref, biblio
Stock: bks/150000; periodcls/6500; photos/5000;
m-forms/100000; archvs/250 cubic m
Classn: LC *Auto Sys:* Unicorn
Pubns: occasional papers (variously titled &
priced)
Staff: Libns: 35 Other Prof: 2 Non-Prof: 63
Proj: extension (2002-03)

S1947 🎓 ✚

University of Southampton, Biomedical Sciences Library

Biomedical Sciences Bldg, Bassett Cres East,
Southampton, Hampshire, SO16 7PX (023-8059-
4215; *fax:* 023-8059-3251)
Email: bslenqs@soton.ac.uk
Internet: http://www.library.soton.ac.uk/bsl/

Gov Body: Univ of Southampton (see **S1946**)
Chief: Site Libn: Ms Adrienne Norman BA, DipLib,
MCLIP
Entry: staff & students; others by appl to the Libn
Open: term: Mon-Fri 0900-2200, Sat 0900-1700,
Sun 1200-2100; vac: Mon-Fri 0900-1800, Sat
0900-1300
Subj: medicine; biology; occupational therapy;
physiotherapy *Co-op Schemes:* ILL
Equip: 2 copiers, computers (incl internet & CD-
ROM) *Online:* Biosis, CAB Abstracts, Medline,
Web of Science
Stock: bks/60000; periodcls/500; m-forms/200

S1948 🎓 ✚

University of Southampton, Health Services Library

Southampton Genl Hosp, Tremona Rd,
Southampton, Hampshire, SO16 6YD (023-8079-
6547; *fax:* 023-8079-8939)
Email: hslib@soton.ac.uk
Internet: http://www.library.soton.ac.uk/hsl/

Gov Body: Univ of Southampton (see **S1946**)
Chief: Site Libn: Mr Chris Fowler BSc, MCLIP
Entry: Univ staff & students; employees of
Southampton Univ Hosps Trust *Open:* term: Mon-
Thu 0900-2100, Fri 0900-1800, Sat 0900-1700,
Sun 1400-1800
Subj: medicine; nursing; health sci
Equip: copiers, computers (incl wd-proc &
internet) *Online:* AMED, ASSIA, Biosis, BNI, CAB
Abstracts, Cambridge Scientific Abstracts,
CancerLit, CINAHL, Cochrane, Embase, HMIC,
Index to Theses, Medline, PsycInfo, Web of
Science, Zetoc
Stock: bks/86000; periodcls/1250

S1949 🎓

University of Southampton, New College Library

The Avenue, Southampton, Hampshire, SO17 1BG
(023-8059-7220; *fax:* 023-8059-7339)
Email: nclib@soton.ac.uk
Internet: http://www.library.soton.ac.uk/ncl/

Gov Body: Univ of Southampton (see **S1946**)
Chief: Site Libn: Ms Elizabeth Upson BA, MCLIP
Entry: staff & students; others by appl to the Libn
Open: term: Mon-Thu 0900-2100, Fri 0900-1830,
Sat 0900-1600, Sun 0900-1700
Subj: undergrad; postgrad; psy; counselling;
mgmt; arts; English lit; hist; social sci; archaeo;
anthro; criminology; podiatry; sports sci; edu
Collns: Bks & Pamphs: teaching practice lib (ch's
bks); Southampton Primary Curriculum Centre
(edu materials) *Co-op Schemes:* ILL
Equip: m-readers, m-printer, 3 copiers, 40
computers
Stock: bks/400+ *Staff:* Libns: 4

Southend-on-Sea

S1950 🎓

South East Essex College, The Study Centre

(formerly Southend Coll of Tech)
Carnarvon Rd, Southend-on-Sea, Essex, SS2 6LS
(01702-220400)
Internet: http://www.southend.ac.uk/

Chief: Study Centre Mgr: Ms Penny Thacker
Subj: all subjs; genl; A level; undergrad; vocational
Co-op Schemes: ILL
Stock: bks/52000; periodcls/290; videos/2000
Classn: DDC

Southport

S1951 🎓 ✚

Mersey Care NHS Trust, Gabby Kearney Library

(formerly the Hesketh Centre Lib)
Hesketh Centre, 51-55 Albert Rd, Southport,
Merseyside, PR9 0LT (01704-383177; *fax:* 01704-
502014)
Email: Graeme.Ford@nswl-tr.nwest.nhs.uk
Internet: http://www.southportandformbypct.
nhs.uk/

Chief: Lib Asst: Mr Graeme Ford
Assoc Libs: AINTREE LIB & INFO RESOURCE
CENTRE (see **S962**); ROYAL LIVERPOOL
CHILDREN'S NHS TRUST, ALDER HEY EDU
CENTRE LIB, Alder Hey Hosp, Eaton Rd,
Liverpool, L12 2AP (*tel & fax:* 0151-252-5476);
SOUTHPORT & ORMSKIRK NHS TRUST, THE
HANLEY LIB (see **S1952**); STOCKPORT NHS
TRUST, EDU CENTRE LIB (see **S1981**)
Entry: staff of Mersey Care NHS Trust &
Southport & Formby Primary Care Trust; student
nurses from Edge Hill Coll on placement at the
Hesketh Centre *Open:* Mon-Fri 1200-1500
Subj: psychiatry; nursing; medicine *Collns: Bks &
Pamphs:* medical journals *Co-op Schemes:*
BLDSC, North West Libs Group
Equip: copier, 3 computers (all with wd-proc &
internet) *Online:* AMED, Embase, PsycInfo,
Cochrane, CINAHL *Svcs:* info, ref, lit searches
Stock: bks/2500
Classn: NLM *Auto Sys:* Heritage IV
Staff: Non-Prof: 1

S1952 ✚

Southport and Ormskirk Hospital NHS Trust, The Hanley Library

Southport Hosp, Town Ln, Southport, Merseyside,
PR8 6PN (01704-704202; *fax:* 01704-704454)
Email: michael.mason@southportandormskirk.
nhs.uk
Internet: http://www.southportandormskirk.nhs.uk/

Chief: Trust Lib Mgr: Mr Michael Mason *Dep:* Lib
Asst: Ms Sandy Hick
Assoc Libs: other Trust Libs: ORMSKIRK HOSP,
SANDERSON LIB (see **S1656**); *other assoc libs:*
AINTREE LIB & INFO RESOURCE CENTRE (see
S962); MERSEY CARE NHS TRUST, GABBY
KEARNEY LIB (see **S1951**); ROYAL LIVERPOOL
CHILDREN'S NHS TRUST, ALDER HEY EDU
CENTRE LIB, Alder Hey Hosp, Eaton Rd,
Liverpool, L12 2AP (*tel & fax:* 0151-252-5476);
STOCKPORT NHS TRUST, EDU CENTRE LIB
(see **S1981**)
Entry: employees of Trust *Open:* Mon-Thu 0830-
1700, Fri 0830-1630; 24 hr access for medical staff
Subj: social sci; medicine; nursing; subjs allied to
health *Co-op Schemes:* BLDSC, BMA, ILL
Equip: video viewer, fax, copier, computers (incl
wd-proc, internet & CD-ROM) *Online:* CINAHL,
Medline, BNI, Cochrane *Svcs:* info, ref
Stock: bks/9000; periodcls/62; videos/45
Classn: UDC *Auto Sys:* ALS
Staff: Libns: 1 Non-Prof: 1 PT

S1953 🎓

Southport College Library

Mornington Rd, Southport, Merseyside, PR9 0TT
(01704-392651; *fax:* 01704-546240)
Email: library@southport-college.ac.uk
Internet: http://www.southport-college.ac.uk/

 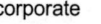

Chief: Coll Libn: Mrs Susan Haydock MCLIP (haydocks@southport-college.ac.uk) **Dep:** Dep Libn: Mrs S.J. Nelson BA(Hons), DipILM (nelsons@southport-college.ac.uk)
Entry: enrolled Coll students only **Open:** term: Mon-Wed 0845-1900, Thu 0845-1700, Fri 0845-1600; vac: hrs dependent on staff availability
Subj: all subjs; genl; GCSE; A level; undergrad; vocational **Co-op Schemes:** BLDSC
Equip: fax, 2 video viewers, copier (5p per pg), 12 computers (all with wd-proc, internet & CD-ROM)
Disabled: adjustable height table, teletext **Online:** Infotrac **Svcs:** info, ref, biblio
Stock: bks/23000; periodcls/130; slides/12000; pamphs/3440; maps/100; audios/670; videos/465; CD-ROMs/73; some DVDs
Classn: DDC **Auto Sys:** Heritage
Staff: Libns: 2 Non-Prof: 4 **Exp:** £26105 (1999-2000); £27237 (2000-01)

Southsea

S1954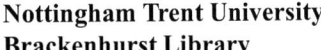

Royal Marines Museum, Historical Reference Library
Southsea, Hampshire, PO4 9PX (023-9281-9385 x224; fax: 023-9283-8420)
Email: info@royalmarinesmuseum.co.uk
Internet: http://www.royalmarinesmuseum.co.uk/

Chief: Archivist & Libn: Mr Matthew G. Little
Entry: ref only, prior appt (minimum 24 hrs)
Open: Mon-Fri 1000-1630 (excl bank hols)
Subj: all subjs; genl; GCSE; A level; undergrad; postgrad; local study (Hampshire, Medway, Kent, Devon), incl: naval & military hist; naval & military biographies **Collns:** Bks & Pamphs: naval & military hist (1648-present), incl Royal Marines Corps hist, weapons, uniforms, unit hists, social conditions, terms of employment, locations, campaigns, prisoners of war, medals, exploration; Navy Lists (from 1783); Marine Offcrs Lists (from 1755) Archvs: relating to the Royal Marines: letters; diaries; operational reports; deployments; svc records; divisional admin; maps; prints Other: photo colln (1860s onwards); tape & video colln
Equip: m-reader, m-printer, 2 video viewers, fax, copier
Stock: bks/11000; periodcls/1000; photos/300000; illusts/400; pamphs/250; maps/350; audios/55; videos/220; archvs/15 m
Classn: Museum Kalamazoo
Pubns: Royal Marines Museum (£1.50); Royal Marines Victoria Crosses (£1); From Trench & Turret (£3.50); Royal Marines Barracks Eastney (£9.99)
Staff: Other Prof: 1
Further Info: Archv & Lib have "place of deposit" status (Public Record Office)

Southwell

S1955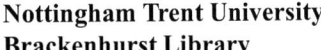

Nottingham Trent University, Brackenhurst Library
School of Land-based Studies, Brackenhurst, Southwell, Nottinghamshire, NG25 0QF (01636-817049)
Email: beth.gibbs@ntu.ac.uk
Internet: http://www.ntu.ac.uk/lis/

Gov Body: Nottingham Trent Univ (see **S1641**)
Chief: Libn & Info Specialist: Ms Beth Gibbs BEng(Hons), MSc(Econ), MCLIP
Open: term: Mon-Thu 0830-1900, Fri 0830-1730, Sat 1000-1400; vac: Mon-Fri 0900-1300, 1400-1700
Subj: basic sci & maths relevant to land-based industries; agric; animal care; countryside & conservation; equine studies; floristry; food tech; hortic **Co-op Schemes:** BLDSC, EMRLS, UK Libs Plus, SCONUL

Equip: m-reader, video viewer, fax, copier, computers (incl wd-proc & CD-ROM)
Stock: bks/10000; periodcls/100; videos/300
Classn: DDC **Staff:** Libns: 1 Non-Prof: 0.5

S1956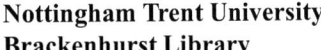

Southwell Minster Library
Minster Office, Bishop's Dr, Southwell, Nottinghamshire, NG26 0JP (01636-812649; fax: 01636-815904)
Internet: http://www.southwellminster.org.uk/

Gov Body: Chapter of Southwell Minster **Chief:** Hon Libn: Mr Laurence Craik
Entry: by appt, ref only **Open:** as required
Subj: religion **Collns:** Archvs: Minster Chapter Decree bks & minutes; Nottinghamshire Bishops' Transcripts
Stock: bks/1300; photos/300; archvs/25 linear m
Staff: Libns: 1

St Albans

S1957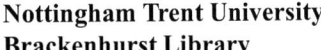

Cimtech Ltd, Library
45 Grosvenor Rd, St Albans, Hertfordshire, AL1 3AW (01727-813651; fax: 01727-813649)
Email: c.cimtech@herts.ac.uk

Gov Body: Univ of Hertfordshire (see **S791**)
Chief: Info Offcr: Ms Anne Grimshaw MA, FCLIP
Entry: only to membs of CIMTECH **Open:** Mon-Fri 0900-1700
Subj: info tech **Collns:** Bks & Pamphs: bks (c100) & journals on info tech; document/record mgmt; optical disks etc
Stock: bks/108; periodcls/40
Pubns: Content & Document Mgmt 2002 – Guide & Directory (annual); Info Mgmt & Tech (bi-monthly journal)
Staff: Libns: 2 Other Prof: 3 Non-Prof: 3

S1958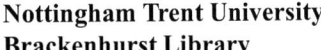

Hudson Memorial Library
Cathedral & Abbey Church of St Alban, St Albans, Hertfordshire, AL1 1BY (01727-830576)

Type: church **Gov Body:** Trustees of Hudson Memorial Lib **Chief:** Canon Libn: Canon Iain Lane
Dep: Asst Libn: Ms Helen Fordham BSc, MCLIP
Open: Mon-Fri 1000-1430, Sat 1000-1300, Sun 1030-1100
Subj: local hist (The Abbey, St Albans); theology; church hist; comparative religion **Collns:** Bks & Pamphs: Local Hist Colln (ref only, left to Abbey by local donor)
Equip: copier **Disabled:** access difficult (1st floor, no lift) **Svcs:** info, ref, lending (membs only)
Stock: bks/15000+; periodcls/4 **Acqs Offcr:** Asst Libn, as above
Classn: LC
Staff: Libns: 0.5 Non-Prof: volunteers

S1959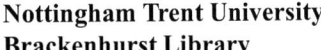

Institute of Acoustics Library
77a St Peter's St, St Albans, Hertfordshire, AL1 3BN (01727-848195; fax: 01727-850553)
Email: ioa@ioa.org.uk
Internet: http://www.ioa.org.uk/

Type: prof body **Gov Body:** Inst of Acoustics
Chief: Lib Administrator: post vacant
Entry: ref only, adv appt advisable **Open:** Mon-Fri 0900-1700
Subj: sci; maths; tech; acoustics **Collns:** Bks & Pamphs: Proceedings of the Inst of Acoustics
Equip: 2 copiers **Svcs:** ref
Stock: bks/350; periodcls/35; pamphs/350; videos/3

Classn: own (BEPAC) **Auto Sys:** own database
Pubns: Proceedings of the Inst of Acoustics (ProcIoA, prices vary); Acoustics Bulletin (6 pa, £110 pa)
Staff: Other Prof: 1

S1960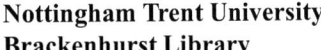

Oaklands College, Smallford Campus Library
Hatfield Rd, St Albans, Hertfordshire, AL4 0JA (01727-737717; fax: 01727-737752)
Internet: http://www.oaklands.ac.uk/

Gov Body: Oaklands Corp **Chief:** ICLT Mgr: Mr Richard Everett **Dep:** Learning Resources Supervisor: Ms Gill Hall MCLIP (Gill.Hall@oaklands.ac.uk)
Assoc Libs: BOREHAMWOOD CAMPUS LIB, Elstree Way, Borehamwood, Hertfordshire, WD6 1JZ, Learning Centre Mgr: Ms Gill Hall, as above (01727-737418); WELWYN GARDEN CITY CAMPUS LIB, The Campus, Welwyn Garden City, Hertfordshire, AL8 6AH, Learning Centre Mgr: Mrs Louise Lichfield (01727-737511)
Entry: ref only **Open:** term: Mon-Thu 0900-2000, Fri 1000-1630; vac: Mon-Thu 0900-1700, Fri 0900-1630
Subj: land-based industries **Collns:** Archvs: Barley Colln (antiquarian, finely illustrated, mostly botanical) **Co-op Schemes:** BLDSC
Equip: copier (5p per sheet), video viewer, 28 computers (all with wd-proc & internet, 4 with CD-ROM, not available to external users) **Officer-in-Charge:** ICLT Mgr, as above
Stock: bks/9500; periodcls/50; pamphs/1000; videos/100; CD-ROMs/20 **Acqs Offcr:** Learning Resources Supervisor, as above
Classn: DDC **Auto Sys:** Voyager
Staff: Libns: 1 Non-Prof: 2.5

S1961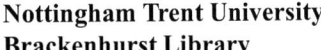

The Royal National Rose Society, Library and Archive
Chiswell Green, St Albans, Hertfordshire, AL2 3NR (01727-850461; fax: 01727-850360)
Email: mail@rnrs.org.uk

Chief: contact the Sec
Entry: adv appt **Open:** Mon-Fri 0900-1700
Subj: hortic; floristry, esp roses; records of parent org **Collns:** Archvs: records of the Royal Natl Rose Soc; records of rose nurseries & rose trials
Equip: copier
Stock: archvs/10 cubic m
Pubns: How to Grow Roses (£5); Roses to Enjoy (£5); Judging Roses (£4)
Staff: Non-Prof: 0.5

S1962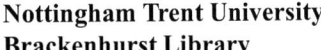

St Albans City Hospital, Staff Library and Information Service
Waverley Rd, St Albans, Hertfordshire, AL3 5PN (01727-897347; fax: 01727-897246)
Email: library.stalbans@whht.nhs.uk

Gov Body: West Hertfordshire Hosps NHS Trust
Chief: Lib Development Mgr: Ms Diane Levey
Assoc Libs: LES CANNON MEMORIAL LIB (see **S1620**); HEMEL HEMPSTEAD HOSP LIB (see **S798**); WATFORD GENL HOSP LIB (see **S2092**)
Entry: Trust staff; ref only for non-membs **Open:** Mon-Fri 0900-1700
Subj: medicine; nursing
Equip: copier (5p per pg), computers (incl internet) **Online:** CINAHL, Medline, BNI, HMIC
Classn: NLM

S1963

St Albans Museums Library

Verulamium Museum, St Michael's, St Albans, Hertfordshire, AL3 4SW (01727-751824; *fax:* 01727-859919)

Type: local authority **Gov Body:** City & Dist of St Albans **Chief:** Keeper of Archaeo: Mr David Thorold (d.thorold@stalbans.gov.uk) **Dep:** Asst Keeper of Archaeo: Miss Clare Thornton (c.thornton@stalbans.gov.uk)
Assoc Libs: MUSEUM OF ST ALBANS, Hatfield Rd, St Albans, Hertfordshire, Keeper of Social Hist: Anne Wheeler; holds similar material for post-medieval period **Entry:** ref only, by prior appt **Open:** Mon-Fri 1000-1700
Subj: genl; local study (St Albans & Hertfordshire), esp: Iron Age & Roman archaeo; tools & trade hist
Collns: Archvs: archv of the City of St Albans & predecessor authorities; Verulamium excavation archvs, incl those of the excavations of Sir Mortimer Wheeler (1930s) & Sheppard Frere (1950s-60s)
Equip: copier
Stock: bks/1800; periodcls/15; slides/5000

St Andrews

S1964

University of St Andrews, Library and Information Services

North St, St Andrews, Fife, KY16 9TR (01334-462281; *fax:* 01334-462282)
Email: lis.library@st-and.ac.uk
Internet: http://www-library.st-andrews.ac.uk/

Gov Body: Univ of St Andrews **Chief:** Dir of Lib & Info Svcs: Dr Louis Lee (lcyl@st-and.ac.uk) **Other Snr Staff:** Head of Ref & Info Svcs: Ms Jean Young (jmy@st-and.ac.uk); Head of Special Collns & Rare Bks: Mrs Christine Gascoigne (cmg@st-and.ac.uk)
Assoc Libs: SPECIAL COLLNS READING ROOM, addr as above (01334-462339; *email:* speccoll@st-and.ac.uk); MODERN/SCOTTISH HIST LIB, Room 3, St Katherine's Lodge, The Scores, St Andrews, Fife, Libn: Mrs Maureen Kidd (01334-462912; *email:* msk@st-and.ac.uk); PHIL LIB, Room 107, Edgecliffe, St Andrews, Fife, Libn: Ms Gillian Read (01334-462472); PHYSICS/MATHS LIB, Physics Bldg, North Haugh, St Andrews, Fife, KY16 9SS, Libn: Ms Karen Innes (01334-463231; *email:* kk8@st-and.ac.uk); PURDIE LIB, Purdie Bldg, North Haugh, St Andrews, Fife, KY16 9ST, Libn: Mrs Hilary Ritchie (01334-463775; *email:* hr6@st-and.ac.uk); SOUTH ST LIB, St Mary's Coll, South St, St Andrews, Fife, KY16 9JU, Libn: Mr Colin Bovaird (01334-462855; *email:* cab@st-and.ac.uk)
Entry: faculty & students; ref only for others; external borrowing membership available for a fee
Open: term: Mon-Thu 0845-2200, Fri 0845-1800, Sat 0900-1700, Sun 1300-1900; vac: Mon-Fri 0900-1700, Sat (Sep, Easter & May) 0900-1300
Subj: all subjs; undergrad; postgrad **Collns:** *Bks & Pamphs:* Alchemy Colln (pre-1851, c350 items); Anderson Colln (phil, edu hist, c1000 vols); Beveridge Colln (Norway, Esperanto & apiculture, c1600 vols); Bible Colln (16C-20C, c1600 vols); Buchanan Colln (250 vols by & about George

Buchanan); Crombie Colln (19C theology, c5000 vols); Donaldson Colln (classics & edu, c10000 vols); Finzi Colln (18C music, c700 vols); Fleeman Johnson Colln (c500 vols by & about Samuel Johnson); G.H. Forbes Colln (17C-19C theology & liturgy, c4000 vols); J.D. Forbes Colln (sci, 16C-19C, c1350 vols); Gillespie & Scott Colln (arch hist & design, c450 vols); Hay Fleming Ref Lib (Scottish hist, mainly 19C-early 20C, c13000 vols); Andrew Lang Colln (c6500 vols); Low Colln (pre-1851 theology, c750 vols); MacGillivray Colln (Scottish lit & hist, 18C-20C, c1250 vols); Mackenzie Colln (genl, c2500 vols); William Moore Colln (16C-17C theology, c250 vols); St Andrews Colln (bks & pamphs relating to town & univ); St Andrews Univ Missionary Soc Colln (19C, c175 vols); Shewan Colln (19C Homeric studies, c5000 pamphs); James Simson Colln (16C-18C medicine, 200+ vols); Von Hügel Colln (theology & phil, c5000 vols); Wightman Pamph Colln (archaeo & ancient hist); Typographical Colln (c4000 early printed bks); 200 incunabula **Archvs:** St Andrews Univ Archvs; records of the former North-East Fife Burghs; Presbytery & Kirk Session Records of the former Presbyteries of Cupar & St Andrews; family & estate papers incl: Cheape of Rossie Papers; Hay of Leyes Papers; personal papers incl: D'Arcy Wentworth Thompson Papers; David Hay Fleming Papers; papers relating to the Roman Catholic Modernist Movement; the Univ Lib is the official repository for North East Fife
Equip: m-readers, m-printers, video viewers, copiers, clr copier, computers (incl wd-proc, internet & CD-ROM) *Online:* LION, Web of Science, FirstSearch, EDINA **Svcs:** info, ref
Stock: bks/880000; periodcls/2800; photos/350000; pamphs/14000; maps/3500; videos/250; archvs/2000 linear m **Acqs Offcr:** Acqs Libn: Mrs Jennifer Evetts (jse@st-and.ac.uk)
Classn: LC **Auto Sys:** Innopac
Pubns: The Univ of St Andrews, by R.G. Cant (£12.50); St Andrew & Scotland, by Ursula Hall (£14.95); Living in St Andrews, by Catherine Forrest (£19.95)
Staff: Libns: 12 *Non-Prof:* 33

St Austell

S1965

St Austell College Library

Trevarthian Rd, St Austell, Cornwall, PL25 4BU (01726-226626; *fax:* 01726-226627)
Email: info@st-austell.ac.uk
Internet: http://www.st-austell.ac.uk/

Gov Body: part of the Cornwall Coll Group (see **S1856**) **Chief:** Snr Libn: Miss Sarah Thorneycroft BA, MCLIP
Entry: public, ref only **Open:** term: Mon 0830-1700, Tue-Thu 0830-1900, Fri 0830-1630; vac: Mon-Thu 0900-1700, Fri 0900-1630
Subj: all subjs; genl; GCSE; A level; undergrad; vocational; local study (Cornwall)
Equip: m-reader, video viewers, copier, computers (incl internet & CD-ROM), audio players **Svcs:** info, ref, biblio
Stock: bks/25000; periodcls/150; illusts/200; pamphs/2100; videos/1700; AVs/100
Classn: DDC **Auto Sys:** Heritage
Staff: Libns: 1 *Non-Prof:* 4

St Helens

S1966

St Helens College, SmithKline Beecham Library

Brook St, St Helens, Merseyside, WA10 1PZ (01744-623225; *fax:* 01744-623007)
Email: library@sthelens.ac.uk
Internet: http://www.sthelens.ac.uk/

Chief: Head of Learning Resources: Mr Barry Jones

Assoc Libs: NEWTON COLL CAMPUS LIB, Crow Ln East, Newton-le-Willows, Merseyside, WA12 9TT (01744-623756); TECH CENTRE LIB, Waterside Campus, Pocket Nook St, St Helens, Merseyside, WA9 1TT (01744-623552)
Entry: staff & students; others at libn's discretion
Open: term: Mon-Thu 0845-2000, Fri 0845-1630, Sat 1000-1500, Sun 1000-1400; vac: varies
Subj: arts; humanities; business & mgmt; construction; tech; sci **Co-op Schemes:** BLDSC, LADSIRLAC
Equip: m-reader, video viewer, fax, copiers, computers (incl wd-proc, internet & CD-ROM)
Online: Infotrac, KnowUK, Know Europe, FAME, LION, BIDS, Emerald etc
Stock: bks/50000; periodcls/500; videos/1200
Classn: DDC **Auto Sys:** Geac
Staff: Libns: 4 *Non-Prof:* 6

St Ives, Cambridgeshire

S1967

Norris Library and Museum

The Broadway, St Ives, Cambridgeshire, PE17 5BX (01480-497314; *fax:* 01480-493177)
Email: norris.st-ives-tc@co-net.com

Gov Body: St Ives Town Council **Chief:** Curator: Mr R.I. Burn-Murdoch MA
Entry: adv appt advisable **Open:** Tue-Fri 1000-1300, 1400-1600
Subj: Huntingdonshire: local hist; archaeo; palaeontology **Collns:** *Other:* newspaper cuttings; maps; prints & drawings
Stock: bks/5000; photos/3000; maps/350; archvs/20 linear m
Staff: Other Prof: 1 **Exp:** £1000 (1999-2000)

St Leonards-on-Sea

S1968

Hastings and Rother NHS Trust, Rosewell Library

Edu Centre, Conquest Hosp, The Ridge, St Leonards-on-Sea, E Sussex, TN37 7RD (01424-758148; *fax:* 01424-758010)
Email: rosewell.library@mail.har-tr.sthames.nhs.uk

Chief: Libn: Ms Jenny Turner BA, DipLib, MCLIP
Dep: Dep Libn: Mrs Margaret Ellis BSc
Entry: staff, students & health care workers attached to Trust **Open:** Mon-Thu 0830-2000, Fri 0830-1700, Sat 1000-1600
Subj: medicine; nursing; hosp mgmt & related topics **Co-op Schemes:** BLDSC, STRLIS
Equip: copier, computers (incl wd-proc & internet)
Online: access to major online health databases, incl Medline & Embase
Stock: bks/5000; periodcls/130; videos/50
Classn: NLM **Auto Sys:** Librarian
Staff: Libns: 2 *Non-Prof:* 3

S1969

Hastings College of Arts and Technology Library

Archery Rd, St Leonards-on-Sea, E Sussex, TN38 0HX (01424-442222; *fax:* 01424-721763)
Internet: http://www.hastings.ac.uk/

Gov Body: Coll Corp **Chief:** Libn: Mrs Sarah Eatwell PGDip, CertEd (seatwell@hastings.ac.uk)
Other Snr Staff: E-Learning Mgr: Mr Nica Benson (nbenson@hastings.ac.uk)
Assoc Libs: 16-19 CENTRE LIB, addr as above
Entry: prior arrangement with Libn **Open:** Main Lib: term: Mon-Wed 0830-1900, Thu 1000-1900, Fri 0830-1700; vac: Mon-Fri 0930-1630; *16-19 Centre:* term: Mon-Thu 0900-1700, Fri 0900-1630; vac: closed

Subj: all subjs; genl; GCSE; A level; undergrad; vocational; art & design; business studies; construction; eng; sci; hotel catering & beauty; ad & community edu; teacher edu *Co-op Schemes:* ILL via SASLIC & British Lib
Equip: 2 video viewers, copier, clr copier, 30 computers (all with wd-proc, internet & CD-ROM), laminator *Officer-in-Charge:* E-Learning Mgr, as above *Svcs:* info, ref
Stock: bks/2500; periodcls/150; audios/600; videos/3500; CD-ROMs/100 *Acqs Offcr:* Libn, as above
Classn: DDC *Auto Sys:* LIMES
Pubns: lib guides; curriculum specialist induction packs
Staff: Libns: 1 *Non-Prof:* 4

Stafford

S1970 ✚
Mid Staffordshire General Hospitals NHS Trust, Postgraduate Medical Library
Weston Rd, Stafford, ST16 3SA (01785-230638; *fax:* 01785-230625)
Email: lyn_brain@hotmail.com

Gov Body: Mid Staffordshire Genl Hosps NHS Trust *Chief:* Libn: Ms Lynda Brain *Dep:* Lib Asst: Ms Ruth Finister
Entry: employees of Trust *Open:* any time; staffed: Mon-Fri 0930-1730
Subj: medicine; surgery; health admin *Collns: Bks & Pamphs:* Dental Ref Lib *Co-op Schemes:* BLDSC, regional ILL, BMA, RCS, WMRLS, RCGP
Equip: copier (5p per pg), computers (incl wd-proc, internet & CD-ROM) *Online:* Medline, CINAHL, AMED
Stock: bks/2300; periodcls/150; slides/80; videos/60
Classn: NLM
Pubns: Lib Guide; Periodicals Lists
Staff: Libns: 1 *Non-Prof:* 1

S1971 ☛
Rodbaston College, Library and Learning Resources
Rodbaston, Penkridge, Stafford, ST19 5PH (01785-712209; *fax:* 01785-715701)
Email: library1@rodbaston.ac.uk
Internet: http://www.rodbaston.com/

Chief: Libn: Ms P. Dalby BA(Hons)
Entry: ref only unless a student of the Coll *Open:* term: Mon-Thu 0830-2000, Fri 0830-1630; vac: Mon-Fri 0900-1630
Subj: vocational; social sci; sci; tech; agric; animal care; countryside mgmt; equine studies; fisheries; hortic; floristry; veterinary nursing *Co-op Schemes:* ALLCU, Staffordshire Regional Elec Resources Sharing & Co-operation
Equip: video viewer, copier, computers (with wd-proc, internet & CD-ROM), video editing facilities
Svcs: info, ref
Stock: bks/12000; periodcls/125; slides/200; pamphs/500; audios/50; videos/400
Classn: DDC *Auto Sys:* Lexicon
Staff: Libns: 1 *Non-Prof:* 2

S1972 ✚
South Staffordshire Healthcare NHS Trust, Library Services – Stafford Site
Edu & Training Centre, St George's Hosp, Corp St, Stafford, ST16 3AG (01785-221584; *fax:* 01785-221367)
Email: library_sta@yahoo.co.uk
Internet: http://www.sshlf.nhs.uk/

Gov Body: South Staffordshire Healthcare NHS Trust *Chief:* Site Libn: Mrs Fiona Rees BLib(Hons), MCLIP
Assoc Libs: SOUTH STAFFORDSHIRE HEALTHCARE NHS TRUST LIB SVCS (see **S948**)
Entry: Trust employees; others ref only *Open:* Mon-Fri 0900-1700
Subj: health care
Equip: fax, copier, 4 computers (all with wd-proc, internet & CD-ROM) *Online:* Medline, CINAHL, AMED, Cochrane, Embase, Best Evidence
Classn: NLM (Wessex) *Auto Sys:* Heritage
Staff: Libns: 1

Stanmore

S1973 ☛
Stanmore College Learning Centre
Elm Pk, Stanmore, Middlesex, HA7 4BQ (020-8420-7700; *fax:* 020-8420-6502)
Email: enquiry@magic.stanmore.ac.uk
Internet: http://www.stanmore.ac.uk/

Gov Body: Stanmore Coll Further Edu Corp
Chief: Dir of Learning Centre: Mr D.M. Cook BA, MA, PGDip, MCLIP (m.cook@stanmore.ac.uk)
Entry: membs only *Open:* term: Mon-Thu 0850-1930, Fri 0850-1700; vac: hrs vary
Subj: all subjs; genl; A level; vocational
Equip: copier (10p per sheet), 65 computers (all with wd-proc, internet & CD-ROM) *Disabled:* desks & PC desks for wheelchair users *Svcs:* info, ref
Stock: bks/c17000; periodcls/c30; audios/c100; videos/c100; CD-ROMs/c15
Classn: DDC *Auto Sys:* Autolib
Staff: Libns: 1 *Non-Prof:* 7 FTE
Proj: merging of Lib & Learning Resources to form new Learning Centre

Stevenage

S1974 ✚
Lister Hospital Library
East & North Hertfordshire NHS Trust, Corey's Mill Ln, Stevenage, Hertfordshire, SG1 4AB (01438-781092; *freephone:* 0800-665544; *fax:* 01438-312498)
Email: sallyk@sklister.demon.co.uk

Gov Body: East & North Hertfordshire NHS Trust
Chief: Libn: Mrs Sally Knight MPhil, FCLIP, MIMgt
Assoc Libs: NURSES LIB, at same addr; *other Trust Libs:* QUEEN ELIZABETH II HOSP LIB (see **S2099**)
Open: Mon-Thu 0900-1700, Fri 0900-1630
Subj: medicine & allied disciplines *Collns: Bks & Pamphs:* health info *Co-op Schemes:* BLDSC
Equip: copier, computers (incl wd-proc, internet & CD-ROM)
Stock: bks/2000; periodcls/150
Classn: NLM *Staff:* Libns: 1 *Non-Prof:* 3

S1975 ☛
North Hertfordshire College, Learning Resources
Monkswood Way, Stevenage, Hertfordshire, SG1 1LA (01462-443079; *fax:* 01462-443054)
Email: lrc@nhc.ac.uk
Internet: http://www.nhc.ac.uk/

Gov Body: North Hertfordshire Coll *Chief:* Distribution Learning Mgr: Mrs Sally Dawson (sdawson@nhc.ac.uk) *Dep:* Learning Centre Mgr: Mr Karl Scott (kscott@nhc.ac.uk) *Other Snr Staff:* LRC Lib Systems Mgr: Ms Nora Evans (nevans@nhc.ac.uk)
Assoc Libs: HITCHIN LRC (see **S814**)
Entry: Coll staff & learners; associate membership & ref for others (fee based) *Open:* term: Mon-Thu 0845-2000, Fri 0845-1600

Subj: all subjs; genl; GCSE; A level; undergrad
Co-op Schemes: BLDSC, ILL, LASER, Hertfordshire Lib Agreement
Equip: video viewers, 2 fax, 4 copiers, 2 clr copiers, 100 computers (all with wd-proc & internet, 10 with CD-ROM) *Disabled:* JAWS, Dragon
Officer-in-Charge: Distribution Learning Mgr, as above *Svcs:* info, ref
Stock: bks/40000; periodcls/200+; videos/1000
Acqs Offcr: LRC Lib Systems Mgr, as above
Classn: DDC *Auto Sys:* Voyager
Staff: Libns: 2 *Non-Prof:* 12

S1976
Stevenage Museum Library
St George's Way, Stevenage, Hertfordshire, SG1 1XX (01438-218881; *fax:* 01438-218882)
Email: museum@stevenage.gov.uk

Gov Body: Stevenage Borough Council *Chief:* Cultural Svcs Mgr: Ms Jo Ward & Ms Maggie Appleton (job-share) *Dep:* Curator: Ms Sally Ackroyd BA, MA
Entry: adv appt, ref only *Open:* Mon-Sat 1000-1700, Sun 1400-1700; excl bank hols
Subj: local study (Stevenage & Hertfordshire); social sci; sci; geog; hist *Collns: Other:* material on setting up of New Towns; some original plans
Equip: copier (10p per sheet)
Stock: photos/15000; objects/10000
Classn: SHIC *Staff:* Other Prof: 4 *Non-Prof:* 3

Stirling

S1977 ✚
Forth Valley NHS Health Board, Library
33 Spittal St, Stirling, FK8 1DX (01786-457294; *fax:* 01786-451474)
Email: gwen.condon@fvhb.scot.nhs.uk
Internet: http://www.show.scot.nhs.uk/fvhb/index.htm

Gov Body: Forth Valley NHS Health Board *Chief:* Libn: Mrs Gwen Condon BA
Open: Thu-Fri 0900-1600
Subj: medicinal based lit & reports *Co-op Schemes:* SHINE ILL network (periodcls only)
Equip: fax, 2 copiers, 2 computers *Disabled:* wheelchair access *Svcs:* info, ref
Stock: bks/100; periodcls/50; pamphs/500; videos/20; CD-ROMs/50
Classn: DDC
Staff: Non-Prof: 1 *Exp:* stock acquired by indiv depts, then stored in lib

S1978 ☛
University of Stirling Library
Stirling, FK9 4LA (01786-467235; *fax:* 01786-466866)
Email: infocentre@stir.ac.uk
Internet: http://www.library.stir.ac.uk/

Gov Body: Univ of Stirling *Chief:* Dir of Info Svc & Univ Libn: Dr Peter Kemp (pk2@stir.ac.uk) *Dep:* Dep Dir: Mr Robin Davis BA, DipLib *Other Snr Staff:* Associate Dir (Academic): Mrs Carolyn Rowlinson MA, DipLS; Associate Dir (Business): Mr Tony Osborne
Assoc Libs: PATHFOOT RESOURCES CENTRE, Pathfoot Bldg, Univ of Stirling, Stirling, FK9 4LA (01786-673171 x7635); HIGHLAND HEALTH SCIS LIB (see **S839**)
Entry: public are welcome for ref only; external membership for borrowing £30 pa (£15 pa for grads of Univ, no charge for 6th year pupils)
Open: term: Mon-Thu 0900-2200, Fri 0900-1900, Sat 1100-1600, Sun 1200-1800; vac: Mon-Thu 0900-1900, Fri 0900-1700, Sat 0900-1230

☛

Special Libraries

Stirling ▼ Stornoway

(Univ of Stirling Lib cont)

Subj: most academic subjs at undergrad & postgrad level (excl medicine); publishing; anthro; phil; social sci; politics; edu; mgmt; sociology; social policy; econ; sports; sci; maths; physics; biology; earth sci; chem; astronomy; tech; computing; nursing; midwifery; arts; fine art; music; media; lit; English lit; Scottish lit; French lit; Spanish lit; Japanese lit; hist; geog *Collns: Bks & Pamphs:* British bks publ 1843-46 acquired by lib as result of the Joint Standing Cttee on Lib Co-operation (Drummond Colln (religious tracts); Horden Colln (scripts & alphabets); Tait Colln (left wing political pamphs); Watson Colln (left wing politics & labour hist); Scott Colln (Walter Scott first eds & other contemporary with Scott); MacLeod Colln (Scottish theatrical hist); Richie-Calder Colln (popular sci texts) *Archvs:* Univ Archvs; Lindsay Anderson Archv (film-maker); John Grierson Archv (documentary film maker); Howietoun Fish Farm Archv; MSS Colln (incl papers & correspondence of James Hogg) *Other:* access to Leighton Lib, Dunblane: 4000 vols + MSS from the personal lib of Archbishop Robert Leighton (1611-1684) *Co-op Schemes:* BLDSC, ILL, SHINE, NLSLS, SLIC, SCONUL, CAIRNS, access to Leighton Lib, Dunblane, through Stirling Univ Lib
Equip: 6 m-readers, m-printer, fax, video viewers, copiers, computers (incl CD-ROM) *Online:* Biosis, Web of Science, CINAHL, EconLit, MLA, PsycInfo, Emerald & others *Svcs:* info, ref
Stock: bks/c500000; periodcls/5000; videos/c500; various slides, pamphs, maps & m-forms *Acqs Offcr:* Bibliographic Svcs Mgr: Mr Colin Sinclair (c.a.sinclair@stir.ac.uk)
Classn: in-house *Auto Sys:* Dynix
Pubns: John Grierson Archv: List of Contents; Tait Pamph Colln: A Checklist; Checklist of News-papers in the Tait & Watson Collns; Index to Stirling Journal & Advertiser, 1820-1970 (3 vols); Map of Stirlingshire, 1725
Staff: Libns: 14 *Other Prof:* 2 *Non-Prof:* 26.6

Stockport

S1979 🔑

National Library for the Blind

Far Cromwell Rd, Bredbury, Stockport, Cheshire, SK6 2SG (0161-355-2000; *fax:* 0161-355-2098)
Email: enquiries@nlbuk.org
Internet: http://www.nlbuk.org/

Chief: Chief Exec: Ms Helen Brazier
Entry: membership open to anyone who needs to use the svcs (e.g., visually impaired, teachers, libns, parents etc); no fees *Open:* Mon-Fri 0830-1600; answerphone available outside these hrs
Subj: generalities; arts; lit; geog; hist; music
Collns: Bks & Pamphs: large print bks colln; ch's & yng people's colln; two-ways (print/braille) bks; Moon print bks *Archvs:* colln of early tactile bks *Other:* braille music scores
Equip: Disabled: various facilities for visually impaired, wheelchair access *Online:* elec bks & ref material; Fiction Café (discussion/info svc for young people) *Svcs:* info, ref, biblio, world-wide postal lending svc
Stock: bks/5000
Classn: DDC *Auto Sys:* ALS
Pubns: Read On (membs magazine, 4 pa); Focus (supporters' newsletter, 4 pa); New Reading

(catalogue of additions to stock, 4 pa); SoapBox (NLB Campaigners' Network newsletter); Rsrch Bulletin (2 pa); Annual Report; all pubns available in print/braille & free of charge
Staff: Libns: 5 *Non-Prof:* 69

S1980

Stockport College of Further and Higher Education, Library and Learning Centre

Wellington Rd South, Stockport, Cheshire, SK1 3UQ (0161-958-3471; *fax:* 0161-958-3469)
Internet: http://www.stockport.ac.uk/

Type: integrated dept for lib, IT & media svcs *Gov Body:* Stockport Coll of Further & Higher Edu
Chief: Lib & Learning Centres Mgr: Mrs Roshanara Nair *Dep:* Lib Resources Mgr: Ms Deborah Ryan BA(Hons), MCLIP
Assoc Libs: DAVENPORT CENTRE LIB & LEARNING CENTRE, Highfield Cl, Davenport, Stockport, SK3 8UA
Entry: public: free for ref only, fee for borrowing; students: must be enrolled on course *Open:* term: Mon-Thu 0850-2000, Fri 0850-1700; vac: Mon-Fri 0900-1700
Subj: most academic subjs *Collns: Other:* illusts colln *Co-op Schemes:* BLDSC, Libs North West
Equip: m-form reader/printer, video viewers, 3 copiers, 78 computers (with wd-proc, internet & CD-ROM), audio players, slide projectors
Disabled: Kurzweil, minicom, CCTV, ZoomText
Stock: bks/35000; periodcls/200; illusts/500; maps/150; audios/250; videos/2000
Classn: DDC *Auto Sys:* Olib
Staff: Libns: 4 *Non-Prof:* 7

S1981 ✚

Stockport NHS Trust, Education Centre Library

Pinewood House, Stepping Hill Hosp, Poplar Grove, Stockport, Cheshire, SK2 7JE (0161-419-4690; *fax:* 0161-419-5696)
Email: library.enquiries@stockport-tr.nwest.nhs.uk
Internet: http://www.stockport.nhs.uk/education/

Gov Body: Stockport NHS Trust *Chief:* Lib Mgr: Ms Gwenda Mynott BA(Hons), MCLIP (gwenda.mynott@stockport-tr.nwest.nhs.uk) *Dep:* Asst Libn: Ms Lucy Anderson
Assoc Libs: AINTREE LIB & INFO RESOURCE CENTRE (see **S962**); MERSEY CARE NHS TRUST, GABBY KEARNEY LIB (see **S1951**); ROYAL LIVERPOOL CHILDREN'S NHS TRUST, ALDER HEY EDU CENTRE LIB, Alder Hey Hosp, Eaton Rd, Liverpool, L12 2AP (*tel & fax:* 0151-252-5476); SOUTHPORT & ORMSKIRK NHS TRUST, THE HANLEY LIB (see **S1952**)
Entry: employees of Trust *Open:* Mon-Thu 0830-1800, Fri 0830-1630; out-of-hrs access for membs by appl to Lib Mgr
Subj: medicine; health; nursing
Equip: copier (5p per pg), computers (incl internet) *Online:* AMED, BNI, CINAHL, Embase, DH-Data, Medline, PsycInfo
Staff: Libns: 2 *Non-Prof:* 1

Stockton-on-Tees

S1982

Durham University, Queen's Campus Library

Ebsworth Bldg, Univ Blvd, Thornaby, Stockton-on-Tees, TS17 6BH (0191-334-0270; *fax:* 0191-334-0271)
Email: stockton.library@durham.ac.uk
Internet: http://www.durham.ac.uk/library/

Gov Body: Univ of Durham (see **S571**) *Chief:* Univ Libn: Dr John Hall BA, PhD *Dep:* Campus Libn: Mrs C.W. Purcell MTheol, MA, MCLIP, ILTM (c.w.purcell@durham.ac.uk) *Other Snr Staff:* Ms Heather Metcalf & Ms Jane Hodgson
Entry: membs of Univ; ref only for others *Open:* term: Mon-Thu 0845-2200, Fri 0845-1700, Sat-Sun 1300-1700; vac: Mon-Fri 0900-1700
Subj: at undergrad level: applied psy; social sci; sociology; anthro; European studies; edu; lang (French, German, Spanish); environmental scis; medicine; physiology; sport; health & exercise; geog; European hist *Collns: Archvs:* Cleveland Social Survey archvs *Co-op Schemes:* ILL svc
Equip: m-reader, 3 copiers (6p per sheet), 3 video viewers, 73 computers (for membs of Univ only, incl 70 with wd-proc & internet) *Disabled:* Kurzweil, JAWS, Aladdin CCTV (registered Univ membs only) *Svcs:* info, ref, biblio
Stock: bks/28000; periodcls/250; audios/190; videos/300
Classn: DDC *Auto Sys:* Innopac
Staff: Libns: 3 *Non-Prof:* 3

S1983

Stockton Riverside College, Learning Resource Centre

(formerly Stockton & Billingham Coll of Further Edu)
Harvard Ave, Thornsby, Stockton-on-Tees, TS17 6FB (01642-865472)
Internet: http://www.stockbill.ac.uk/

Chief: LRC Mgr: Mr John Casey (john.casey@stockton.ac.uk) *Dep:* Snr LRC Asst: Mrs Julia Stephen (julia.stephen@stockton.ac.uk)
Entry: restricted *Open:* term: Mon-Thu 0800-2045; Fri 0800-1615; vac: Mon-Thu 0900-1645, Fri 0900-1615
Subj: undergrad; vocational; psy; social sci; lang; sci; maths; tech; arts; lit; edu *Collns: Bks & Pamphs:* BSI (partial) *Co-op Schemes:* ILL
Equip: copier, 2 video viewers, 67 computers (all with wd-proc, internet & CD-ROM), 14 rooms for hire *Officer-in-Charge:* LRC Mgr, as above *Svcs:* info, ref
Stock: bks/22200; periodcls/125; maps/200 OS; audios/450; videos/430 *Acqs Offcr:* LRC Mgr, as above
Classn: DDC *Auto Sys:* Heritage
Staff: Libns: 1 *Other Prof:* 1 *Non-Prof:* 4
Proj: move to new premises at end of 2002

S1984 ✚

University Hospital of North Tees, Medical Library

(formerly North Tees Medical Lib)
Univ Hosp of North Tees, Stockton-on-Tees, TS19 8PE (01642-624789)
Email: medicallibrary@nth.nhs.uk

Gov Body: North Tees & Hartlepool NHS Trust
Chief: Lead Libn: Mr John Blenkinsopp BA(Hons), MCLIP (Jblenkinsopp@hotmail.com)
Assoc Libs: UNIV HOSP OF HARTLEPOOL MEDICAL LIB (see **S790**)
Entry: membs of Trust; ref only for non-membs
Open: Mon-Wed, Fri 0900-1700, Thu 0900-2000
Subj: medicine; sci relating to medicine; medical tech *Co-op Schemes:* BLDSC, NULJ
Equip: m-reader, copier (10p per sheet), 9 computers (all with wd-proc & internet, 5 with CD-ROM) *Officer-in-Charge:* Lead Libn, as above
Svcs: info, ref, biblio, indexing, abstracting
Stock: bks/16000; periodcls/200; videos/20; CD-ROMs/15 *Acqs Offcr:* Lead Libn, as above
Classn: DDC *Auto Sys:* Libero
Staff: Libns: 1 *Non-Prof:* 2 *Exp:* £92000 (1999-2000); £94000 (2000-01)

 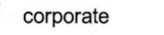

Stoke-on-Trent

S1985 🔑
Ceram Research Ltd Library
Queens Rd, Penkhull, Stoke-on-Trent, ST4 7LQ
(01782-764444; *fax:* 01782-412331)
Email: enquiries@ceram.com
Internet: http://www.ceram.co.uk/

Chief: Chief Exec: Dr N.E. Sanderson *Dep:* Info
Svcs Mgr: Mrs Ann Pace
Entry: membs; rsrchers *Open:* Mon-Thu 0845-
1715, Fri 0845-1645
Subj: ceramic raw materials; bldg ceramics;
whitewares (tiles, sanitaryware, tableware);
refractories; technical ceramics or electrical & eng
applications; glass; vitreous enamels; porcelain
Collns: Bks & Pamphs: Mellor Memorial Lib;
Graves Lib (bricks, bldg) *Co-op Schemes:* ILL
Equip: Online: World Ceramics Abstracts *Svcs:*
info, ref, biblio, indexing, abstracting, translation,
document supply, on-line searching
Stock: bks/12000; periodcls/300; slides/5500;
pamphs/50000
Classn: UDC
Pubns: World Ceramics Abstracts (12 issues pa,
subscription £345 UK & Europe, £385 elsewhere)

S1986 🔑
Esperanto Association of Britain, Butler Library
Esperanto House, Wedgwood Memorial Coll,
Barlaston, Stoke-on-Trent, ST12 9DE (01782-
372141; *fax:* 01782-372393)
Email: eab@esperanto-gb.org
Internet: http://www.esperanto-gb.org/

Gov Body: Esperanto Assoc of Britain/Esperanto-
Asocio de Britujo *Chief:* Hon Libn: Mr Geoffrey
King
Subj: lang; Esperanto *Collns: Bks & Pamphs:*
bks publ in Esperanto *Co-op Schemes:* ILL
Stock: bks/20000; periodcls/150; audios/100

S1987 🎓 ✚
Keele University, Health Library
Nurse Edu Centre, City Genl Hosp, Newcastle Rd,
Stoke-on-Trent, ST4 6QG (01782-552949; *fax:*
01782-712941)

Gov Body: Keele Univ (see **S1572**) *Chief:* Health
Faculty Libn: Mr David Bird MA (nsa17@keele.
ac.uk) *Dep:* Snr Lib Asst: Mrs Mariet Bailey
(nsa15@keele.ac.uk)
Entry: ref only for genl public *Open:* Mon-Thu
0845-1930, Fri 0845-1645, Sat 1000-1400
Subj: at undergrad, postgrad & vocational levels:
psy; social sci; medical sci; medicine; nursing;
health *Co-op Schemes:* BLDSC
Equip: 2 video viewers, 2 copiers, 3 computers
(all with internet) *Online:* BIDS, FirstSearch etc
Stock: bks/24000; periodcls/250; videos/100
Classn: LC *Auto Sys:* Innopac
Staff: Libns: 2 *Non-Prof:* 6

S1988 ✚
North Staffordshire Medical Institute, Library
Hartshill Rd, Hartshill, Stoke-on-Trent, ST4 7NY
(01782-554198; *fax:* 01782-554258)
Email: nsmilib@dial.pipex.com
Internet: http://www.nsmilib.dial.pipex.com/

Chief: Lib Svcs Mgr: Mrs Irene Fenton *Dep:* Asst
Libn: Ms Alison Thornley *Other Snr Staff:*
Clinical Effectiveness Libn: Mr David Rogers
Open: Mon, Fri 0830-1800, Tue-Thu 0830-2030,
Sat 0930-1300
Subj: medicine; health *Co-op Schemes:*
WMHLN, PLCS, ILL

Equip: copier, 8 computers (incl wd-proc, internet
& CD-ROM) *Online:* Medline, CINAHL, AMED,
Embase, BNI, DH-Data, PsycInfo *Svcs:* info, ref
Stock: bks/4000; periodcls/310
Classn: LC *Auto Sys:* Heritage
Staff: Libns: 5 *Non-Prof:* 4

S1989 🎓
Staffordshire University, Library and Learning Resources Service
PO Box 664, College Rd, Stoke-on-Trent, ST4 2XS
(01782-294443; *fax:* 01782-295799)
Email: LLRS@staffs.ac.uk
Internet: http://www.staffs.ac.uk/

Gov Body: Staffordshire Univ *Chief:* Dir of Info
Svcs: Mrs Liz Hart BA, DipLib, FCLIP
Assoc Libs: THOMPSON LIB, College Rd, Stoke-
on-Trent, Staffordshire, ST4 2DE, Site Operations
Mgr: Ms Janice Broad (01782-294771; *fax:* 01782-
295799; *email:* as above); NELSON LIB,
Beaconside, Stafford, ST18 0DP, Site Operations
Mgr: Ms Gill Edwards (01785-353604; *email:*
Nelson@staffs.ac.uk); LAW LIB, Leek Rd, Stoke-
on-Trent, ST4 2DF, Site Operations Mgr: Ms Nicky
Adams (01782-294921; *email:* n.adams@staffs.
ac.uk); SCHOOL OF HEALTH LIB (see **S1921**);
FRANCIS COSTELLO LIB (see **S1660**); HEALTH
LIB (see **S2034**)
Entry: ref only *Open: Thompson Lib:* term: Mon-
Thu 0900-0300, Fri 0900-2000, Sat 1300-1800,
Sun 9000-0300; vac: Mon-Fri 0900-1700
Subj: all subjs; undergrad; postgrad *Collns: Bks
& Pamphs:* Dorothy Thompson Colln (Chartist hists
& rsrch notes); Centre for the Hist of Psy &
Eysenck Colln; ROAPE Colln (African Studies);
Riley Colln (development studies); Badminton
Colln (sports) *Archvs:* Mining Archv (bks, journals,
pamphs, maps, surveys, photos & ceramics
catalogues, mainly UK & Midlands mining issues,
some internatl); Iris Strange Colln (war widow
archv of letters, diaries, photos & press cuttings);
Arts Archv (parliamentary papers, govt papers &
political journals); Film Archv (relating to hist of the
Potteries & the County); British Psychological Soc,
rsrch papers & ephemera *Co-op Schemes:* ILL,
UK Libs Plus
Equip: m-form reader/printers, fax, video viewers,
video viewers, copiers, clr copiers, computers (incl
wd-proc, internet & CD-ROM) *Online:* BIDS, Web
of Science, Mintel, CINAHL, Sport Discus, FAME,
Art Abstracts, numerous others *Svcs:* info, ref
Stock: bks/325000; periodcls/1750; slides/190000;
pamphs/7370; maps/300; m-forms/250; audios/
610; videos/3700; archvs/c500 linear m (at Stoke);
exhib catalogues/2000
Classn: DDC *Auto Sys:* Horizon
Staff: Libns: 23 *Other Prof:* 100 *Exp:* £750000
(1999-2000)

S1990 🎓
Stoke-on-Trent College, Learning Resources Centre
New Lib Bldg, Cauldon Campus, Stoke Rd,
Shelton, Stoke-on-Trent, ST4 2DG (01782-
603566; *fax:* 01782-603601)
Email: lharv1sc@stokecoll.ac.uk
Internet: http://www.stokecoll.ac.uk/

Chief: LRCs Mgr: Mrs Lesley Harvey BA(Hons),
MCLIP
Assoc Libs: BURSLEM LRC, Burslem Campus,
Moorland Rd, Burslem, Stoke-on-Trent, ST6 1JJ
Entry: students of Coll; others by adv appt *Open:*
term: Mon-Thu 0830-2100, Fri 0830-1800, Sat
0900-1300; vac: Mon-Thu 0830-1630, Fri 0830-
1600, Sat 0900-1300
Subj: all subjs; genl; GCSE; A level; local study
(Stoke-on-Trent) *Co-op Schemes:* BLDSC
Equip: 2 video viewers, 3 copiers (5p per sheet),
70 computers (all with wd-proc, internet & CD-
ROM) *Disabled:* ZoomText *Svcs:* info, ref, biblio

Stock: bks/66170; periodcls/318; pamphs/127;
maps/418; audios/1556; videos/2466 *Acqs Offcr:*
Snr LRC Asst: Mrs Fiona Thomas
Classn: DDC *Auto Sys:* Heritage IV
Staff: Libns: 4 *Non-Prof:* 14.5

Stoneleigh Park

S1991 🔑 🎓
Royal Agricultural Society of England Library
Natl Agricultural Centre, Stoneleigh Park,
Warwickshire, CV8 2LZ (024-7685-8262; *fax:* 024-
7669-6900)
Email: phillips@rase.org.uk
Internet: http://www.rase.org.uk/

Chief: Hon Libn: Mr Phillip C. Sheppy MBE,
FRAGS
Entry: ref only, adv appt to visit, enqs by phone/
fax/email/internet *Open:* Tue, Thu 0900-1700
Subj: agric; rural development; land-based
industries *Collns: Bks & Pamphs:* rare pre-1700
bks; Gibley Pamphs (colln of 170 vols of pamphs
late 1700s-early 1900s, mostly on agric/rural
development); RASE pubns *Archvs:* RASE archvs
Svcs: info, ref
Stock: bks/9000; pamphs/1200
Classn: DDC *Staff: Non-Prof:* 1

Stornoway

S1992 🎓
Lews Castle College Library
Stornoway, Isle of Lewis, PA86 0XR (01851-
770409; *fax:* 01851-770007)
Email: erica.mcload@lews.uhi.ac.uk
Internet: http://www.lews.uhi.ac.uk/

Gov Body: Lews Castle Coll Board of Mgmt; part
of the Univ of the Highlands & Islands (UHI)
Chief: Libn: Mrs Erica G. MacLeod *Other Snr
Staff:* Libn: Mrs Jessie Murray
Entry: current students & staff *Open:* Mon-Tue,
Thu -Fri 0900-1700, Wed 0900-1900
Subj: genl; undergrad; postgrad; local studies
(Western Isles) *Collns: Bks & Pamphs:* Francis
G. Thompson Colln (hist of Highlands & Islands);
Shawbost Colln (Scottish nat hist) *Co-op
Schemes:* BLDSC
Equip: copier, 35 computers *Officer-in-Charge:* IT
Systems Mgr: Mr I. Macaulay *Svcs:* info, ref, biblio,
indexing, abstracting
Stock: bks/9000; periodcls/35 *Acqs Offcr:* Libn,
as above
Classn: DDC *Auto Sys:* Olib 7.1
Staff: Libns: 1 *Non-Prof:* 2

S1993 ✚
Western Isles Hospital Library
Macaulay Rd, Stornoway, Isle of Lewis, PA87 2AF
(01851-708236; *fax:* 01857-706070)
Email: lynnchipperfield@hotmail.com

Gov Body: Western Isles Health Unit & Univ of
Stirling (see **S1978**) *Chief:* Libn: Ms Lynn
Chipperfield
Entry: all NHS staff in the Western Isles; staff &
students of Univ of Stirling *Open:* lib staffed: Mon-
Tue, Thu-Fri 0945-1445; access available to
membs at other times
Subj: medicine; nursing; psy; sociology; social
svcs; mgmt; social welfare; health care delivery
Co-op Schemes: BLDSC, SHINE, Grampian Info
Equip: copier, computers
Stock: bks/2000; periodcls/60; videos/30; Open
Univ packs/50; tape-slide packages/200 sets; info
folders/40
Classn: NLM, LC *Staff: Libns:* 1 *Non-Prof:* 1
(both PT)

Stourbridge

S1994 ✚

Dudley Group of Hospitals NHS Trust, Corbett Hospital Medical Library

Corbett Hosp, Vicarage Rd, Stourbridge, W Midlands, DY8 4JB (01384-456111 x4819; *fax:* 01384-443631)
Email: Cor.library@dudleyph-tr.wmids.nhs.uk

Chief: Asst Libn: Ms Grace Boyle
Assoc Libs: CLINICAL LIB SVC, Russells Hall Hosp (see **S548**)
Entry: ref only, adv appt *Open:* Mon-Thu 0930-1600
Subj: medicine; dermatology; othopaedics; paediatrics; rheumatology *Collns: Bks & Pamphs:* GPVTS Colln; extensive colln of GP journals *Co-op Schemes:* BLDSC, BMA, West Midlands Info Svc for Health
Equip: copier, fax, video viewer, computers (with wd-proc, internet & CD-ROM) *Online:* Medline, Cochrane *Svcs:* info, ref, biblio, translation
Stock: bks/1500; periodcls/55; videos/69
Classn: NLM *Auto Sys:* CALM *Staff:* Libns: 0.5

S1995 🎓

King Edward VI College, Library and Learning Resources Centre

Lower High St, Stourbridge, W Midlands, DY8 1TD (01384-398100; *fax:* 01384-398123)
Email: library@kedst.ac.uk
Internet: http://www.kedst.ac.uk/

Chief: Head of Lib: Mrs Kim Bell BSc, MA *Dep:* Asst Libn: Mrs Menna Sanderson C&G
Assoc Libs: SCHOOL & COLL ARCHVS, at same addr, Coll Archivist: J.T. Greany
Entry: Lib: membs of Coll 'Open House' during Coll term time; no public access, but enqs about the Coll will be answered where possible; *Archvs:* request to view archvs must be made to the Chairman of the Foundation Trustees, c/o the Archivist *Open:* term: Mon-Fri 0800-1655
Subj: all subjs; A level *Collns: Archvs:* archvs of the School (founded 1552) & of Chantry School on same site before that date; collns consist of records of staff & governors; clerical, finance & property records; pictures etc (see entry conditions above for access) *Other:* newspaper & magazine cuttings lib
Equip: 4 video viewers, copier, clr copier, 80 computers (all with MS Office 2000, CD-ROM & internet) *Online:* New Scientist *Svcs:* info, ref, biblio
Stock: bks/c24000; periodcls/41; maps/157; videos/624; CD-ROMs/90; AVs/350
Classn: DDC *Auto Sys:* DS
Staff: Libns: 1 Non-Prof: 3

Stratford-upon-Avon

S1996 🔑

Shakespeare Centre Library

Henley St, Stratford-upon-Avon, Warwickshire, CV37 6QW (01789-204016; *fax:* 01789-296083)
Email: library@shakespeare.org.uk
Internet: http://www.shakespeare.org.uk/

Gov Body: Shakespeare Birthplace Trust *Chief:* Head of Lib & Info Resources: Dr Susan Brock BA, PhD, DipAA *Dep:* Dep Head of Lib & RSC Libn: Mrs Sylvia Morris BA, MCL
Assoc Libs: SHAKESPEARE BIRTHPLACE TRUST RECORDS OFFICE (see **A476**)
Entry: ref only; tickets for reading room issued to bona fide readers upon appl *Open:* Mon-Fri 1000-1700, Sat 0930-1230
Subj: Shakespeare; theatre hist; drama; English lit; Elizabethan & Jacobean life; Warwickshire local hist *Collns: Bks & Pamphs:* RSC Colln; Bram Stoker Colln (Henry Irving); Alan Dent Colln; Wheler & Saunders Collns (Warwickshire documents & drawings); Bloom Colln (local genealogy); Tom Holte Theatre Photo Colln (RST 1961-80); Joe Cocks Studio Colln (RSC theatre photos, 1962-90) *Archvs:* Shakespeare Memorial Theatre (1879-1960); Royal Shakespeare Co (1961-date) *Other:* Reg Wilson Colln (RSC photos, 1963-98)
Equip: m-reader, m-printer (A4/40p, A3/60p), 3 video viewers (£3 per half day), copier (A4/15/p, A3/20p), 2 computers (incl 1 with CD-ROM for public use) *Online:* database of RSC productions & personnel (1879-date) *Officer-in-Charge:* Head of Lib & Info Resources, as above
Stock: bks/55000; periodcls/45; photos/244000; slides/32000; illusts/20000; audios/600; videos/750; archvs/206 cubic m; maps & m-forms/200
Acqs Offcr: Head of Lib & Info Resources, as above
Classn: own *Auto Sys:* Talis
Staff: Libns: 4 FTE Non-Prof: 2
Proj: OPACs (Talis for printed bks since Sep 2001 & CALM for archvs) to be available on internet during 2003

S1997 🎓

Shakespeare Institute Library

Church St, Stratford-upon-Avon, Warwickshire, CV37 6HP (01789-293384; *fax:* 01789-292021)
Email: silib@bham.ac.uk
Internet: http://www.is.bham.ac.uk/shapespeare/

Gov Body: Univ of Birmingham (see **S179**)
Chief: Inst Libn: Mr Jim Shaw (J.A.Shaw@ bham.ac.uk) *Dep:* Info Asst: Ms Kate Welch (K.J.Welch@bham.ac.uk)
Entry: registered readers of Univ Lib, others may apply for readership (various arrangements)
Open: term: Mon-Thu 0900-2000, Fri-Sat 0900-1700, Sun 1000-1700
Subj: English lit, 16C-17C; English drama & theatre before the Restoration; life & works of William Shakespeare *Collns: Bks & Pamphs:* Renaissance Theatre Co prompt bks *Archvs:* newspaper reviews of Renaissance plays (from 1964); New Shakespeare Co theatrical archvs (1962 onwards) *Other:* extensive m-film collns; video colln; press cuttings
Equip: m-readers, m-printers, copier, 7 computers (incl 6 with internet & 1 with CD-ROM), slide viewers, audio listening facilities *Disabled:* hand-held magnifiers *Online:* various CD-ROMs, incl: Complete Works of William Shakespeare, World Shakespeare Bibliography, OED, English Drama, English Poetry, London Theatre Record 1981-1990 *Svcs:* info, ref *Staff:* 2

S1998 🎓

Stratford-upon-Avon College Library

The Willows North, Alcester Rd, Stratford-upon-Avon, Warwickshire, CV37 9QR (01789-266245; *fax:* 01789-267524)
Internet: http://www.strat-avon.ac.uk/

Gov Body: Stratford-upon-Avon Coll Corp *Chief:* Coll Libn: Mrs J. Davies BA, MCLIP
Entry: ref only *Open:* term: Mon-Thu 0845-1730, Fri 0845-1630, Sat 0920-1130; half terms: Mon-Fri 0900-1300

Subj: most academic subjs; genl; GCSE; A level; undergrad; vocational; additional needs *Co-op Schemes:* CADIG, BLDSC
Equip: m-reader, 2 video viewers, copier, clr copier, computers (incl internet & CD-ROM)
Stock: bks/28700; periodcls/201; pamphs/200; audios/816; videos/870
Classn: DDC *Auto Sys:* EOSi
Staff: Libns: 1.6 Non-Prof: 2.25

Stromness

S1999 🔑 🏛

Pier Arts Centre, Archive Library

Victoria St, Stromness, Isle of Orkney, KW16 3AA (01856-850209; *fax:* 01856-851462)
Email: info@piersartcentre.com

Gov Body: Pier Arts Centre Trust *Chief:* Dir: Mr Neil Firth DA *Dep:* Administrator: Mrs Maureen Gray BA; Exhibs Offcr: Mr Andrew Parkinson BA
Entry: ref only, permission from staff *Open:* Tue-Sat 1030-1230, 1330-1700
Subj: arts
Equip: copier, computer, room for hire
Stock: bks/2000; periodcls/3; slides/24
Staff: Other Prof: 3

Stroud

S2000 🔑

Biodynamic Agricultural Association, Library

Painswick Inn Project, Gloucester St, Stroud, Gloucestershire, GL5 1QG (01453-759501; *fax:* 01453-759501)
Email: bdaa@biodynamic.freeserve.co.uk
Internet: http://www.anth.org.uk/biodynamic/

Gov Body: Council of Mgmt *Chief:* Libn: Miss Jessica Standing
Entry: lending for membs, others ref only *Open:* Mon-Fri 0900-1300
Subj: phil of ecology; anthroposophy; biology; botany; astronomy; soil sci; agric; hortic; veterinary medicine *Collns: Other:* scientific rsrch papers on biodynamic & organic agric & related subjs
Stock: bks/c600
Pubns: Star & Furrow (2 pa, £3 each)

Sudbury

S2001 🔑 🏛

Gainsborough's House Society, Library and Archive

46 Gainsborough St, Sudbury, Suffolk, CO10 2EU (01787-372958; *fax:* 01787-376991)
Email: mail@gainsborough.org
Internet: http://www.gainsborough.org/

Gov Body: private charitable trust *Chief:* Curator: Mr Hugh Belsey BA, MLitt *Dep:* Asst Curator: Mr Andrew Hunter MA
Entry: ref only, by adv appt *Open:* Mon-Sat 1000-1700, Sun & bank hols 1400-1700
Subj: local study (Sudbury & Suffolk); arts
Collns: Bks & Pamphs: 18C art *Archvs:* relating to Thomas Gainsborough (1727-88) & family
Equip: m-printer, fax, copier (10p) *Svcs:* info, biblio
Stock: bks/1000; periodcls/4; photos/1000; pamphs/100; m-forms/50; archvs/150 documents
Classn: based on London Lib scheme
Pubns: Gainsborough's House Review (annual, £5.95)
Staff: Other Prof: 2

Sunbury upon Thames

S2002

BP Exploration Operating Co Ltd, Map Library

Chertsey Rd, Sunbury upon Thames, Middlesex, TW16 7LN (01932-762000)
Email: greenwok@bp.com

Chief: Map Libn: Mr Keith Greenwood
Entry: not open to the public, but bona fide enqs will be answered as far as possible
Subj: cartography *Collns:* Other: extensive world-wide geological, topographic, hydrologic & thematic coverage related hydrocarbon exploration
Stock: c55000 maps & 200 atlases

Sunderland

S2003

City of Sunderland College Learning Centres

Tunstall Centre, Sea View Rd West, Sunderland, Tyne & Wear, SR2 9LH (0191-511-6000; *fax:* 0191-511-6589)
Internet: http://www.citysun.ac.uk/

Gov Body: FE Funding Council *Chief:* Learning Resources Development Mgr: Mrs Jean Hornsey BA(Hons) MCLIP *Dep:* Dep Learning Resources Development Mgr: Mrs Annette Knowlson MCLIP
Assoc Libs: BEDE LEARNING CENTRE, Durham Rd, Sunderland, Tyne & Wear, SR3 4AH; HYLTON LEARNING CENTRE, North Hylton Rd, Sunderland, Tyne & Wear, SR5 5DB; SHINEY ROW LEARNING CENTRE, Success Rd, Philadelphia, Houghton-le-Spring, Tyne & Wear, DH4 4TL
Entry: enrolled students of the coll; ref only for membs of the public *Open:* term: Mon-Thu 0815-2100, Fri 0815-1700, Sat 1000-1300; vac: Mon-Fri 0900-1200, 1300-1600
Subj: all subjs; genl; GCSE; A level; undergrad; vocational *Co-op Schemes:* BLDSC, ILL, NEMLAC, LASH
Equip: m-readers, video viewers, copiers (A4/5p, A3/10p), clr copier, 450 computers (incl wd-proc, internet & CD-ROM) *Online:* Infotrac *Svcs:* info, ref
Stock: bks/125000
Classn: DDC *Auto Sys:* Heritage
Staff: Libns: 7 Other Prof: 3

S2004

University of Sunderland, Information Services

Murray Lib, Chester Rd, Sunderland, Tyne & Wear, SR1 3SD (0191-515-2900; *fax:* 0191-515-2904)
Email: libenquiry@sunderland.ac.uk
Internet: http://www.library.sunderland.ac.uk/

Gov Body: Univ of Sunderland *Chief:* Dir of Info Svcs: Prof Andrew C. McDonald BSc, FCLIP (andrew.mcdonald@sunderland.ac.uk) *Dep:* Asst Dir (Systems): Ms Kirsten Black (kirsten.black@sunderland.ac.uk); Asst Dir (Svcs): Mr Oliver Pritchard (oliver.pritchard@sunderland.ac.uk)
Assoc Libs: ASHBURNE LIB, Ashburne House, Backhouse Pk, Ryhope Rd, Sunderland, SR2 7EF (0191-515-2119; *fax:* 0191-515-3166); MURRAY LIB, addr as above; ST PETER'S LIB, The Prospect Bldg, St Peter's Campus, St Peter's Way, Sunderland, SR6 0DD (0191-515-3059; *fax:* 0191-515-3061)
Open: Murray & St Peters Libs: term: Mon-Thu 0830-2200, Fri 0830-2100, Sat 0945-1800, Sun 0945-1800 (Murray Lib 24 hr access during term); Ashburne Lib: term: Mon-Tue 0900-2100, Wed-Thu 0900-2000, Fri 0900-1700, Sat 1000-1300; vac (all libs): Mon-Fri 0900-1700

Subj: all subjs; undergrad; postgrad; *Ashburne Lib:* hist of art; ceramics; glass; graphics; illustration; painting; photography; print making; sculpture; *Murray Lib:* communication; media studies; edu; lang; lit; hist; phil; social sci; politics; religion; internatl studies; eng; tech; environment; health sci; *St Peters Lib:* accountancy; business; computing; econ; EU; law; mgmt; marketing; maths; psy; statistics *Collns: Bks & Pamphs:* NACODS Colln; Pollard Colln; Quaker Colln (all at Murray Lib) *Archvs:* Quaker Archv (at Murray Lib) *Other:* Art Slide Colln (at Ashburne Lib) *Co-op Schemes:* BLDSC, British Lib Fast Track Scheme, ILL, Libs Access Sunderland Scheme, UK Libs Plus, Riding Plus, SCONUL Rsrch Extra, Tyne & Wear Info Resources for Learning Partnership
Equip: m-form reader/printers, video viewers, copiers, computers (incl wd-proc, internet & CD-ROM) *Disabled:* TextHelp, Supernova, Office 97 Pro *Online:* range of online biblio databases & e-journals *Svcs:* info, ref, biblio
Stock: bks/460000; periodcls/7212; slides/c65000; maps/c1000
Classn: DDC *Auto Sys:* Talis
Pubns: Self Svc in Academic Libs – Future or Fallacy?: proceedings of a conference organised by Info Svcs in conjunction with SCONUL, held at St Peter's Campus, Univ of Sunderland 24-26 June 1996 (£30)
Staff: Libns: 28.2 Non-Prof: 40.3

Sutton

S2005

Hotel and Catering International Management Association, Information and Technical Services

Trinity Ct, 34 West St, Sutton, Surrey, SM1 1SH (020-8661-4900; *fax:* 020-8661-4901)
Email: library@hcima.org.uk
Internet: http://www.hcima.org.uk/

Type: prof body *Chief:* Dir (Info & Technical Svcs): Ms Kelly Saini Badwal BA(Hons) (kellyb@hcima.co.uk) *Other Snr Staff:* Info Asst: Mr Nana Nyarko MSc (nanan@hcima.co.uk)
Entry: primarily a membs' lib by appt only; non-membs by prior arrangement (fee payable); contact the lib svc for details *Open:* Mon-Fri 1000-1600, excl bank hols & Xmas/New Year period
Subj: hotel mgmt; hospitality; catering; tourism; leisure *Collns: Bks & Pamphs:* colln of Trade journals dating back to 1970 (e.g., Caterer & Hotelkeeper)
Equip: copier (A4/10p), fax (£1 1st pg, 50p per additional), video viewer, computer (with wd-proc, internet & CD-ROM), room for hire *Officer-in-Charge:* Dir (Info & Technical Svcs), as above
Svcs: info, ref, biblio, indexing, abstracting, lit searches (for membs)
Stock: bks/8000; periodcls/60; photos/100; videos/100; CD-ROMs/10 *Acqs Offcr:* Dir (Info & Technical Svcs), as above
Classn: DDC
Pubns: WHATT database; variety of pubns available, see web site for details
Staff: Libns: 2 Other Prof: 1 Non-Prof: 1 *Exp:* £100000 (1999-2000); £90000 (2000-01)

Sutton Coldfield

S2006

Good Hope Hospital NHS Trust, Education Centre Library

Rectory Rd, Sutton Coldfield, W Midlands, B75 7RR (0121-378-2211; *fax:* 0121-378-6039)
Email: library@goodhope.nhs.uk

Gov Body: Good Hope Hosp NHS Trust *Chief:* Trust Lib Svcs Mgr: Mrs Gwen Giles MLib, BA, DipLib, MCLIP (gwen.giles@goodhope.nhs.uk)

Dep: Trust Libn (Edu & Training): Ms Sue Peacock BA, DipLib, MCLIP (sue.peacock@goodhope.nhs.uk)
Entry: NHS staff only *Open:* Mon-Fri 0830-1700
Subj: health; medicine *Co-op Schemes:* BLDSC, WMRHLN
Equip: video viewer, fax, copier (5p per pg), 18 computers (all with CD-ROM, 16 with wd-proc & 16 with internet) *Online:* Dialog *Officer-in-Charge:* Trust Lib Svcs Mgr, as above *Svcs:* info, ref
Stock: bks/5500 + 3000 vols of bnd periodcls; periodcls/130; videos/130; CD-ROMs/22
Classn: NLM *Auto Sys:* Heritage
Pubns: Bulletin; Lib Guide
Staff: Libns: 3.5 Non-Prof: 1

Sutton-in-Ashfield

S2007

King's Mill Hospital Medical Library

Mansfield Rd, Sutton-in-Ashfield, Nottinghamshire, NG17 4JL (01623-622515 x4009/4010; *fax:* 01623-625449)
Email: Madeline.Cox@sfh-tr.nhs.uk

Gov Body: Sherwood Forest Hosps NHS Trust *Chief:* Libn: Miss Madeline Cox BA, MCLIP *Dep:* Asst Libn: Mrs M.H. Hallam
Entry: hosp staff & employees of Nottinghamshire Healthcare NHS Trust in the Ashfield & Mansfield areas; open to other medical staff who can show a need to use *Open:* Mon-Fri 0900-1800
Subj: genl; postgrad; medicine; nursing *Co-op Schemes:* ILL, local schemes, NULJ
Equip: fax, copier (A4/5p, A3/10p), computers (incl wd-proc, internet & CD-ROM) *Online:* Medline, Cochrane, Embase, CINAHL, PsycInfo
Stock: bks/8000; periodcls/c70; videos/30
Classn: NLM *Auto Sys:* Heritage
Staff: Libns: 1.5 Non-Prof: 0.5

S2008

University of Nottingham, School of Nursing Library

Dukeries Centre, Kings Mill Hosp, Mansfield Rd, Sutton-in-Ashfield, Nottinghamshire, NG17 4JL (01623-465634; *fax:* 01623-465601)
Email: sarah.carlile@nottingham.ac.uk

Gov Body: Univ of Nottingham (see **S1647**) *Chief:* Libn: Ms Sarah Carlile BA(Hons), MCLIP *Dep:* Lib Asst: Miss Louise Crossley
Entry: ref only for non-Univ students or staff *Open:* Mon-Thu 0830-1630, Fri 0830-1600
Subj: primary psy; sociology; edu; nursing; midwifery; some medicine *Co-op Schemes:* BLDSC, NULJ, Nottingham Univ Libs
Equip: copier, 7 computers (all with wd-proc & internet) *Svcs:* info, ref, biblio
Stock: bks/12000; periodcls/52
Classn: DDC, NLM *Staff:* Libns: 1 Non-Prof: 1 *Exp:* £18500 (1999-2000)

Swaffham

S2009

Swaffham Museum Library

Town Hall, London St, Swaffham, Norfolk, PE37 7DQ (01760-721230; *fax:* 01760-720469)
Email: swaffhammuseum@ic24.net

Type: local authority *Gov Body:* Swaffham Town Council *Chief:* Museum Mgr: Mrs Patricia Finch *Dep:* Asst: Ms Barbara Gathercole
Open: April-Oct: Tue-Sat 1100-1300, 1400-1600
Subj: all subjs; genl; local study (Swaffham & surrounding villages); family hist; genealogy

Swaffam
▼
Tamworth

Special Libraries

(Swaffam Museum Lib cont)
Collns: *Bks & Pamphs:* Howard Carter Colln; Admiral Knyvet Wilson Colln *Other:* local newspapers; extensive photo colln; illusts; press cuttings **Equip:** copier, computers (incl wd-proc), 2 rooms for hire **Svcs:** info, ref, genealogical rsrch **Stock:** bks/1000; photos/4000+; slides/2000+; pamphs/1000; maps/500 **Classn:** in-house **Pubns:** various pubns on local topics (50p-£2) **Staff:** *Non-Prof:* 2 **Proj:** public rooms relocating to ground floor

Swansea

S2010 🏛
Driver and Vehicle Licensing Agency, Open Resource Centre
Room D1/N, DVLA, Longview Rd, Morriston, Swansea, W Glamorgan, SA6 7JL (01792-782712; *fax:* 01792-782760)
Internet: http://www.dvla.gov.uk/

Gov Body: Exec Agency of the Dept for Transport (see **S1316**) **Chief:** Mgr & Exec Offcr: Mr Matt Bounds **Dep:** Admin Offcr: Mr Ian Lewis **Entry:** adv appt, ref only **Open:** Mon-Fri 0830-1700 **Subj:** mgmt; health & safety; transport; social sci; sci; tech **Co-op Schemes:** ILL **Equip:** m-reader, fax, video viewers, copier, computers (incl wd-proc, internet & CD-ROM) **Svcs:** info, ref, translation (contracted out) **Stock:** bks/5000; periodcls/150; pamphs/1000; maps/30; videos/50 **Classn:** LC **Auto Sys:** Lybreeze **Pubns:** DVLA Lib Bulletin (free) **Staff:** *Non-Prof:* 4

S2011 ✚
Morriston Hospital Staff Library
Postgrad Centre, Morriston Hosp, Swansea, W Glamorgan, SA6 6NL (01792-703131; *fax:* 01792-701007)
Email: edcent@hotmail.com

Gov Body: Swansea NHS Trust **Chief:** Dep Dist Libn: Mrs Anne Powell BA, DipLib, MCLIP **Assoc Libs:** SINGLETON HOSP STAFF LIB (see **S2012**); SWANSEA PSYCHIATRIC EDU CENTRE LIB (see **S2014**) **Entry:** Trust staff **Open:** Mon-Thu 0830-1700, Fri 0830-1630 **Subj:** medicine; nursing; professions allied to medicine **Collns:** *Bks & Pamphs:* Burns & Plastics Lib, previously housed at St Lawrence Hosp, Chepstow *Archvs:* various archv materials **Co-op Schemes:** AWHILES, BLDSC, BMA, SBHILS, NULJ **Equip:** copier (5p per pg), fax, video viewer, computers (incl wd-proc, internet & CD-ROM), binding machine **Online:** Cochrane, Medline, CINAHL, PsycInfo, Embase, MOCIS (Morriston Online Clinical Info System, own networked info resource) **Svcs:** info, ref, biblio, database training **Stock:** bks/11000; periodcls/130; videos/150; AVs/30 **Classn:** NLM **Auto Sys:** Libertas **Pubns:** various lib & database guides **Staff:** *Libns:* 1 *Non-Prof:* 2

S2012 ✚
Singleton Hospital Staff Library
Singleton Hosp, Sketty Ln, Swansea, W Glamorgan, SA2 8QA (01792-205666 x5281; *fax:* 01792-297207)
Email: staff.library@swansea-tr.wales.nhs.uk

Gov Body: Swansea NHS Trust **Chief:** Lib Svcs Mgr: Mr Colin Engel BA, DipLib, MCLIP **Assoc Libs:** MORRISTON HOSP STAFF LIB (see **S2011**); SWANSEA PSYCHIATRIC EDU CENTRE LIB (see **S2014**) **Entry:** employees of Swansea NHS Trust, Bro Morgannwg Trust, Primary Care Swansea Bay & Iechyd Morgannwg Health **Open:** Mon-Fri 0900-1700 **Subj:** health care **Co-op Schemes:** AWHILES, AWHL, PLCS, BMA, RCS, BLDSC **Equip:** 2 m-readers, 3 video viewers, 4 fax, 4 copiers, 10 computers (incl wd-proc, internet & CD-ROM), room for hire **Svcs:** info, ref, biblio, SDIs **Stock:** bks/30000; periodcls/450; pamphs/10; videos/300; CD-ROMs/30 **Classn:** NLM **Auto Sys:** Soutron **Pubns:** various free lib site orientation & info skills training guides, regularly updated **Staff:** *Libns:* 5 *Non-Prof:* 6

S2013 🎓
Swansea Institute of Higher Education, Library and Learning Support Services
Townhill Rd, Swansea, W Glamorgan, SA2 0UT (01792-481000; *fax:* 01792-298017)
Email: t.lamb@sihe.ac.uk
Internet: http://www.sihe.ac.uk/

Gov Body: Swansea Inst of Higher Edu **Chief:** Head of Lib & Learning Support: Mr J.A. Lamb BA, CertEd, MCLIP **Dep:** Libn: Miss Anne Harvey LIB, DipLib **Assoc Libs:** MOUNT PLEASANT CAMPUS LIBS: OWEN LIB, Mount Pleasant, Swansea, W Glamorgan, SA1 6ED (01792-481000 x4221; *fax:* 01792-644076); THOMPSON LIB, Mount Pleasant, Swansea, W Glamorgan, SA1 6ED (01792-481000 x4141) **Entry:** ref only **Open:** term: Mon-Thu 0845-2100, Fri 0845-1630, Sat 1000-1600, Sun 1100-1600; vac: Mon-Thu 0845-1700, Fri 0845-1630 **Subj:** all subjs; *Owen Lib:* business; *Thompson Lib:* eng **Co-op Schemes:** BLDSC, Interlending Wales, UK Libs Plus, ATLIS, WALIA, CROESO **Equip:** 2 fax, 5 copiers, clr copier, computers (incl wd-proc, internet & CD-ROM) **Stock:** bks/180000; periodcls/1000+ **Classn:** DDC **Auto Sys:** Talis **Staff:** *Libns:* 8 *Non-Prof:* 23 **Exp:** £28000 (1999-2000); £29000 (2000-01)

S2014 ✚
Swansea Psychiatric Education Centre Library
Cefn Coed Hosp, Cockett, Swansea, W Glamorgan, SA2 0GH (01792-516546; *fax:* 01792-516607)
Email: library.ccoed@swansea-tr.wales.nhs.uk

Gov Body: Swansea NHS Trust & Swansea Clinical School **Chief:** Centre Mgr & Mental Health Unit Libn: Mrs Emma Jones BA(Hons), MCLIP (emma.jones@swansea-tr.wales.nhs.uk) **Dep:** Lib Asst: Mrs Rachel Jones (rachel.jones@swansea-tr.wales.nhs.uk) **Assoc Libs:** MORRISTON HOSP STAFF LIB (see **S2011**); SINGLETON HOSP STAFF LIB (see **S2012**) **Entry:** Swansea NHS Trust staff or other identified readers; ref only for others **Open:** Mon-Thu 0830-1700, Fri 0830-1630; 24 hr access to certain categories of users

Subj: medicine; psychiatry; psychotherapy; nursing; health svc mgmt **Co-op Schemes:** PLCS, NULJ, AWHL **Equip:** copier (5p per sheet), fax (10p per fax), 2 video viewers, 14 computers (all with wd-proc, internet & CD-ROM), room for hire **Disabled:** disabled access **Online:** via Health of Wales Info Svc, incl ClinPsych & Embase Psychiatry **Officer-in-Charge:** Centre Mgr, as above **Svcs:** info, ref, biblio **Stock:** bks/2500; periodcls/38; pamphs/300; audios/40; videos/150; CD-ROMs/25 **Acqs Offcr:** Centre Mgr, as above **Classn:** NLM (Wessex) **Auto Sys:** Voyager **Staff:** *Libns:* 1 *Non-Prof:* 2 **Exp:** £25000 (2000-01)

S2015 🎓
University of Wales Swansea, Library and Information Services
Singleton Pk, Swansea, W Glamorgan, SA2 8PP (01792-295697; *fax:* 01792-295851)
Email: library@swan.ac.uk
Internet: http://www.swan.ac.uk/lis/

Gov Body: Univ of Wales Swansea **Chief:** Dir of Lib & Info Svcs: Mr Christopher West **Dep:** Dep Dir (Human Resources): Ms Sara Marsh; Dep Dir (ICT Svcs): Mr Tony Ollier **Assoc Libs:** NAT SCIS LIB, Nat Scis Bldg West, Singleton Pk, Swansea, W Glamorgan, SA2 8PP, Asst Libn: Mr Alasdair Montgomery (01792-295024; *fax:* 01792-295851; *email:* nslcirc@swan.ac.uk); EDU LIB, Hendrefoelan Campus, Swansea, W Glamorgan, SA2 7NB, Asst Libn: Ms Madeleine Rogerson (01792-518659; *fax:* 01792-290219; *email:* edmail@swan.ac.uk); NURSING LIB, Morriston Hosp, Swansea, W Glamorgan, SA6 6NL, Site Libn: Mr Stephen Storey (01792-703767; *email:* s.m.storey@swan.ac.uk); SOUTH WALES MINERS' LIB, Hendrefoelan Campus, Swansea, W Glamorgan, SA2 7NB, Asst Libn: Ms Siân Williams (01792-518603/93; *fax:* 01792-518694; *email:* miners@swan.ac.uk) **Entry:** full access to all staff & students of the univ; for non-membs: ref access for over-18s; borrowing £50 pa (but no charge for WALIA & UK Libs Plus); no access to computing facilities for non-membs of the univ **Open:** term: Mon-Fri 0845-2200, Sat 0900-1700, Sun 1200-2000; vac: Mon 0900-2200, Tue-Sat 0900-1700; shorter hrs in branch libs **Subj:** undergrad; postgrad; full range of academic subjs to support university's teaching & rsrch **Collns:** *Bks & Pamphs:* strong collns in Celtic studies & maths; modest colln of rare bks *Archvs:* Local Archv Colln, incl: estate records; business records (esp metallurgical industries & Mumbles Railway); Methodist records; RC records; South Wales Coalfield Colln; Univ of Wales Swansea archvs (minutes & correspondence (1920 onwards) *Other:* AV Colln **Co-op Schemes:** BLDSC, SCONUL, WALIA Reciprocal Access Scheme, UK Libs Plus **Equip:** 8 m-readers, m-printer, 12 video viewers, 12 copiers, 420 computers (all with internet, wd processing & CD-ROMs, for use by UWS membs only), further 30 computers with limited internet only for genl use, 2 dedicated CD-ROM readers **Disabled:** recording, photocopying & braille svcs **Online:** for UWS membs only: Web of Science, Science Direct, Early English Bks Online; BSI, IEL; usual range of Higher Edu networked info svcs & elec journals **Svcs:** info, ref for non-membs **Stock:** bks/800000 (incl periodcls); periodcls/3200; videos/2000; archvs/600 m **Classn:** DDC, LC **Auto Sys:** Voyager **Pubns:** Inform (termly newsletter); guide to local archv colln; usual info leaflets **Staff:** *Libns:* 28 *Other Prof:* 1 archivist *Non-Prof:* 44 **Exp:** £1144000 (1999-2000); £1169000 (2000-01)

S2016
University of Wales Swansea, Egypt Centre Library
Univ of Wales Swansea, Singleton Pk, Swansea, W Glamorgan, SA2 8PP (01792-295960)
Internet: http://www.swansea.ac.uk/egypt/

Gov Body: Univ of Wales Swansea (see **S2015**)
Chief: Curator: Ms C.A. Graves-Brown BA(Hons), AMA (c.a.graves-brown@swansea.ac.uk) *Dep:* Asst Curator: Ms W.R. Goodridge MA (w.r.goodridge@swansea.ac.uk)
Entry: ref, adv appt *Open:* Tue-Sat 1000-1600
Subj: Egyptology; archaeo *Collns: Bks & Pamphs:* Egyptology bks relating to the Centre's collns
Equip: copier (5p per sheet) *Svcs:* info, ref
Stock: bks/c483; photos/c2000; slides/c500 *Acqs Offcr:* Curator, as above
Auto Sys: Excel *Staff: Other Prof:* 2 curators
Non-Prof: 2 *Exp:* £1000 (1999-2000)

Swindon

S2017
Innogy plc Information Centre
(formerly Natl Power plc Info Centre)
Windmill Hill Business Pk, Whitehill Way, Swindon, Wiltshire, SN5 6PB (01793-892565; *fax:* 01973-892001)
Internet: http://www.lnnogy.com/

Chief: Info Administrator: Miss Suzanne Vines BSc(Hons)
Entry: adv appt essential *Open:* Mon-Thu 0830-1700, Fri 0830-1600
Subj: genl ref; econ; lang (dictionaries); electricity industry: technical & commercial aspects, UK & worldwide *Collns: Bks & Pamphs:* reports of former Central Electricity Generating Board (CEGB) *Other:* some historical material on UK electricity industry, incl files on current & former power stations & sites *Co-op Schemes:* WILCO
Equip: m-reader, m-printer, copier, fax, 7 computers (incl 3 wd-proc, & 1 CD-ROM), scanner *Online:* First Call, BS, IHSERC Online, RIBA, FIS Online, construction info svc *Svcs:* info, ref, translation
Stock: bks/14000; periodcls/300; maps/200; CD-ROMs/12
Classn: UDC *Auto Sys:* CAIRS
Staff: Non-Prof: 1
Further Info: This has become a self-svc info centre, with staff also using svcs of instant lib based in Loughborough

S2018
Joint Services Command and Staff College Library
Faringdon Rd, Watchfield, Swindon, Wiltshire, SN6 8TS (01793-788000)
Email: chobson@jscsc.org
Internet: http://www.jscsc.org.uk/

Gov Body: Ministry of Defence (see **S1284**)
Chief: Head of Lib Svcs: Mr Chris Hobson MCLIP
Entry: adv appt *Open:* Mon-Fri 0830-1700
Subj: social sci; tech; geog; hist *Collns: Bks & Pamphs:* air power papers *Other:* audio-visual aids (35mm transparencies, video tapes) *Co-op Schemes:* BLDSC
Equip: m-reader, m-printer, video viewers, copier, computers (incl wd-proc & CD-ROM) *Svcs:* info, ref
Stock: bks/150000; periodcls/350; slides/50000; pamphs/60000; m-forms/5000; audios/50; videos/2000
Classn: UDC *Auto Sys:* CAIRS
Staff: Libns: 8 *Non-Prof:* 5

S2019
New College Library
Helston Rd, Park North, Swindon, Wiltshire, SN3 2LA (01793-611470; *fax:* 01793-436437)
Email: ncjeanhi@newcollege.co.uk

Gov Body: New Coll Corp *Chief:* Libn: Mrs J. Hillier BA(Hons), MCLIP *Dep:* Ms L. Lea BA, MSc
Entry: ref only *Open:* term: Mon-Wed 0815-1830, Thu-Fri 0815-1630
Subj: all subjs; genl; GCSE & AS level; undergrad; local study (Swindon); railway studies *Collns: Bks & Pamphs:* ch's lit (19C-early 20C, on loan from Wiltshire Lib & Museum Svc) *Co-op Schemes:* BLDSC, SWRLS, WILCO
Equip: video viewer, copier, computers (incl wd-proc, internet & CD-ROM) *Svcs:* info, ref, biblio
Stock: bks/c21000; periodcls/100; photos/10; slides/150; pamphs/500; maps/20; videos/200
Classn: DDC *Auto Sys:* DS
Staff: Libns: 2 *Non-Prof:* 2 *Exp:* £37000 (2000-01)

S2020
The Research Councils, Joint Information and Library Service
Polaris House, North Star Ave, Swindon, Wiltshire, SN2 1SZ (01793-442103; *fax:* 01793-442042)
Email: library@pparc.ac.uk

Gov Body: provides joint svc for: Particle Physics & Astronomy Rsrch Council (PPARC); Biotech & Biological Scis Rsrch Council (BBSRC); Eng & Physical Scis Rsrch Council (EPSRC); Nat Environment Rsrch Council (NERC) *Chief:* Snr Libn: Ms Ingrid Howard BA, DipLib
Assoc Libs: institutional libs of the 4 rsrch councils
Entry: primarily for staff & bona fide rsrchers; others by adv appt only *Open:* Mon-Fri 0900-1700
Subj: generalities; social sci; sci; maths; tech *Co-op Schemes:* BLDSC, WILCO, RESCOLINC
Equip: fax, video viewer, copier, computers (incl wd-proc, internet & CD-ROM) *Online:* FT Profile, Dialog *Svcs:* info, ref, abstracting, translation
Stock: bks/15000; periodcls/200; pamphs/5000; maps/150; videos/20
Classn: local *Auto Sys:* Microsoft
Pubns: Current Awareness Bulletin
Staff: Libns: 1 *Non-Prof:* 3

S2021
Royal Military College of Science Library
Shrivenham, Swindon, Wiltshire, SN6 8LA (01793-785743; *fax:* 01793-785555)
Email: library2@rmcs.cranfield.ac.uk
Internet: http://www.rmcs.cranfield.ac.uk/infoserv/

Gov Body: Cranfield Univ (see **S113**) *Chief:* Dir of Info Svcs: Mr Stephen Town MA, FCLIP, BIM (J.S.Town@rmcs.cranfield.ac.uk) *Dep:* Dep Dir of Info Svcs: Ms Marcia Harrison (M.A.Harrison@rmcs.cranfield.ac.uk)
Assoc Libs: REPORTS SECTION, addr as above (01793-785486; *email:* reports@rmcs.cranfield.ac.uk)
Entry: ref only, by prior appt *Open: Lib:* Michaelmas & Spring terms: Mon-Thu 0830-2100, Fri 0830-1700, Sat 1000-1300; Summer term: as before except Sat 1000-1600, Sun (May-June) & late May Bank Hol 1100-1700; vac: Mon-Fri 0830-1700; *Reports Section:* all year: Mon, Thu 0830-1800, Tue-Wed, Fri 0830-1700
Subj: defence mgmt; defence studies; internatl relations; radiography; military sci & tech; electrical, mechanical & civil eng; materials sci *Collns: Bks & Pamphs:* BSI; Defence Standards; STANAGE; AGARD Reports *Archvs:* all RMCS dissertations at undergrad, postgrad & MPhil level *Co-op Schemes:* BLDSC, SWRLS, WILCO, HeLIN, SCONUL, UK Libs Plus

Equip: m-readers, m-printer, video viewers, 2 copiers (A4/5p, A3/10p), computers (with wd-proc, internet & CD-ROM) *Online:* ABI Inform, BIDS, BNB, BUBL, COPAC, EBSCO, Index to Theses, Ingenta, XreferPlus, Zetoc; numerous specialist military & technical e-resources *Svcs:* info, ref, biblio, indexing, abstracting, translation
Stock: bks/200000; periodcls/1000; maps/250; videos/900
Classn: UDC *Auto Sys:* Unicorn
Pubns: Military Sci Index (free); Defence News (free)
Staff: Libns: 9 *Non-Prof:* 9

S2022
Water Research Centre Swindon, Library
WRC plc, Frankland Rd, Blagrove, Swindon, Wiltshire, SN5 8YF (01793-865154; *fax:* 01793-865001)
Email: morrisroe_s@wrcplc.co.uk
Internet: http://www.wrcplc.co.uk/

Chief: Libn: Miss S. Morrisroe BSc(Hons), DipLib, MLib
Entry: restricted to WRC staff only *Open:* Mon-Fri 0930-1700
Subj: water & wastewater treatment processes; sewerage; water supply; instrumentation *Co-op Schemes:* BLDSC, WILCO
Equip: m-reader, m-printer, copier, computer (with CD-ROM) *Online:* Dialog
Stock: bks/8500; periodcls/260; maps/250
Classn: UDC *Auto Sys:* Heritage *Staff: Libns:* 1

Tain

S2023
Scottish Highland Photo Library
The Croft Studio, Croft Roy, Crammond Brae, Tain, Ross-shire, IV19 1JG (01862-892298; *fax:* 01862-892968)
Email: info@shpl.co.uk
Internet: http://stockscotland.com/

Type: commercial photo agency *Chief:* Photo Libn: Mr Hugh Webster
Entry: adv appt *Open:* Mon-Fri 0900-1700
Subj: photos: Scottish Highlands & Islands *Co-op Schemes:* BAPLA
Equip: computer (with CD-ROM) *Svcs:* reproduction of stock photos
Classn: own
Pubns: CD-ROM Catalogue
Staff: 1 photo libn

Tamworth

S2024
Tamworth and Lichfield College, John McDermott Library and Learning Resources Centre
(formerly Tamworth Coll Lib)
Croft St, Upper Gungate, Tamworth, Staffordshire, B79 8AE (01827-310202; *fax:* 01827-59437)
Email: library@tamworth.ac.uk
Internet: http://www.tlc.ac.uk/

Gov Body: Tamworth & Lichfield Coll *Chief:* Learning Resources Mgr: Mrs Joanne Rowley BA(Hons), MCLIP (jo.rowley@tamworth.ac.uk)
Dep: LRC Supervisor: Mrs Kay Atkinson (kay.atkinson@tamworth.ac.uk)
Assoc Libs: LICHFIELD LIB, The Friary, Lichfield, Staffordshire, WS13 6QG (01543-301100; *fax:* 01543-301103)
Entry: ref only for non-students *Open:* term: Mon-Fri 0845-2100, Sat 1000-1300; vac: Mon-Fri 0900-1630

Special Libraries

Tamworth ▼ Thurso

(Tamworth & Lichfield Coll cont)
Subj: all subjs; genl; GCSE & A-level; undergrad; vocational **Co-op Schemes:** Staffordshire Univ Regional Federation
Equip: copier (A4/5p, A3/10p), video viewer, 20 computers (all with wd-proc, internet & CD-ROM)
Disabled: HAL readers **Svcs:** info
Stock: bks/16000; periodcls/100; maps/204; videos/500 **Acqs Offcr:** Learning Resources Mgr: Mrs Joanne Rowley
Classn: DDC **Auto Sys:** Heritage
Staff: Libns: 2 Non-Prof: 5 **Exp:** £26000 (1999-2000); £58000 (2000-01)
Proj: new LRC under construction

Taunton

S2025 ⚷

Somerset Archaeological and Natural History Society Library
Paul St, Taunton, Somerset, TA1 3XZ (01823-340300; *fax:* 01823-340301)
Internet: http://www.sanhs.org/

Gov Body: Somerset Archaeological & Nat Hist Soc **Chief:** Hon Libn: Mr D. Bromwich MA, MCLIP
Entry: non-membs are denied personal access to lib, but bks may be fetched for them to consult in Somerset Studies Lib (see **A488**) **Open:** Mon-Tue, Thu 0930-1730, Wed, Fri 0930-1700, Sat 0930-1600
Subj: Somerset (pre-1974 boundaries): archaeo; hist; lit; nat hist **Collns:** Bks & Pamphs: Charles Tite Colln (Somerset bks) Archvs: Soc's archv colln is deposited in Somerset Record Office (see **A487**) Other: Pigott & Braikenridge Collns of Somerset drawings
Equip: 3 m-readers, m-printer, 2 copiers
Stock: bks/40000; periodcls/90; photos/6000 glass negs; slides/4000 glass slides; illusts/10000
Exp: £1000 (1999-2000); £1250 (2000-01)

S2026 🎓•

Somerset College of Arts and Technology Library
Wellington Rd, Taunton, Somerset, TA1 5AX (01823-366454; *fax:* 01823-366411)
Email: ngp@somerset.ac.uk
Internet: http://www.somerset.ac.uk/

Chief: Dir of Learning Resources: Mr N.G. Pickles BA(Hons), MSc, PGCE, MCLIP
Entry: ref only, or apply for associate membership in writing **Open:** term: Mon-Thu 0830-2030, Fri 0830-1700, Sat 0930-1230; vac: Mon-Fri 0830-1630
Subj: all subjs; genl; GCSE; A level; undergrad **Co-op Schemes:** BLDSC, SWRLS, Univ of Plymouth Partnership Link
Equip: 3 copiers, clr copier, fax, video viewer, 240 computers (incl all with wd-proc, internet & CD-ROM) **Svcs:** info, ref, biblio
Stock: bks/60000; periodcls/450; slides/40000; videos/6500; CD-ROMs/120
Classn: DDC **Auto Sys:** Olib
Staff: Libns: 9 Non-Prof: 20

S2027 ✚

Somerset Postgraduate Centre Medical Library
Taunton & Somerset Hosp, Musgrove Pk, Taunton, Somerset, TA1 5DA (01823-342433; *fax:* 01823-342434)
Email: 106616.441@compuserve.com

Gov Body: Taunton & Somerset NHS Trust
Chief: Libn: Mrs Susan McEnroe MCLIP **Dep:** Lib Asst: Mrs Marjorie Borthwick
Entry: membs of Taunton & Somerset NHS Trust
Open: Mon-Fri 0900-1730; 24 hr access for membs
Subj: postgrad; medicine; nursing; allied health
Co-op Schemes: BLDSC, ILL, SWRLIN
Equip: fax, copier, computers (incl wd-proc, internet & CD-ROM) **Online:** Medline, Embase, PsycInfo, ASSIA, CINAHL, BNI **Svcs:** info, ref, biblio
Stock: bks/1600; periodcls/100
Classn: NLM **Staff:** Libns: 1 Non-Prof: 0.4

S2028 🎓 ✚

University of Plymouth, Institute of Health Studies Learning Resources Service
Somerset Coll of Arts & Tech, Wellington Rd, Taunton, Somerset, TA1 5AX (01823-366389; *fax:* 01823-366411)
Email: lxc@somerset.ac.uk

Type: nurse edu **Gov Body:** Univ of Plymouth (see **S1812**) **Chief:** Libn: Miss Lyn Crecy BA(Hons), DipLib
Entry: enrolled students only; ref access possible for membs of public **Open:** Mon-Thu 0900-1700, Fri 0900-1630
Subj: nursing & health related; psy; social sci **Co-op Schemes:** BLDSC, SWRLIN
Equip: video viewer, fax, copier, clr copier (A4/90p), 30 computers (incl wd-proc, internet & CD-ROM, students only) **Online:** via OVID: AMED, BioMed; via BIDS: PsycInfo, ERIC **Svcs:** info, ref, biblio
Stock: bks/10000; periodcls/100; audios/30+; videos/100+; CD-ROMs/6
Classn: DDC **Auto Sys:** Olib
Staff: Libns: 1 Non-Prof: 1.57 **Exp:** £8000 (1999-2000); £8000 (2000-01)

Tavistock

S2029 ⚷

Tavistock Subscription Library
Court Gate, Guildhall Sq, Tavistock, Devon, PL19 0AE

Chief: Hon Secretary/Treasurer: Mr John M. Gale TD, BEd(Hons) (john.gale@longash.co.uk) **Dep:** Hon Libn: Mrs Phoebe Henning
Entry: ref only, on appl **Open:** 24 hrs pd, by personal key (available to membs)
Subj: local studies (Tavistock, West Devon & East Cornwall): local hist; geog; arch; lit etc **Collns:** Bks & Pamphs: some fiction works by local 19C authors; some ref bks on the Bedford family (Dukes of Bedford, Woburn Abbey); local parish magazines (1940-50) Archvs: some minute & account bks dating back to 1799
Stock: bks/c900; periodcls/5; pamphs/some **Acqs Offcr:** Hon Libn, as above
Classn: printed catalogue (alphabetical by author & subj)
Pubns: pamph on hist of lib
Exp: £2000 (1999-2000); £2500 (2000-01); bks bought when funds allow, with stock usually augmented by gifts from membs

Teddington

S2030 ⚷ ☕⚷

British Maritime Technology Library
Orlando House, 1 Waldegrave Rd, Teddington, Middlesex, TW11 8LZ (020-8943-5544; *fax:* 020-8943-5347)
Email: dgriffiths@bmtmail.com
Internet: http://www.bmt.org/

Chief: Libn: Mr D.J. Griffiths BA, MA
Assoc Libs: BRITISH MARITIME TECH, WALLSEND RSRCH STATION LIB (see **S2073**)
Entry: not normally open to public; loans to other libs **Open:** Mon-Fri 0830-1700
Subj: fluid mechanics; naval arch; ocean eng
Collns: Bks & Pamphs: transactions of Royal Instn of Naval Architects & Soc of Naval Architects & Marine Engineers Archvs: reports of Natl Physical Laboratory Ship, Aero & Maritime Sci Divs **Co-op Schemes:** BLDSC
Stock: bks/2000; periodcls/100
Classn: UDC
Pubns: BMT Focus (free); Technical Reports (£20 UK, £25 overseas); BMT Abstracts (monthly, £220 pa UK + £18 overseas); Marine Tech Abstracts (jointly with Inst of Marine Engineers, available online)
Staff: Libns: 1

S2031 🏛

National Physical Laboratory Library
Bldg 27, Queens Rd, Teddington, Middlesex, TW11 0LW (020-8943-6417; *fax:* 020-8943-6458)
Email: library@npl.co.uk

Chief: Libn: Ms B.M. Sanger
Subj: sci; tech; physics; eng **Co-op Schemes:** ILL
Stock: bks/65000; periodcls/500

S2032 ⚷ ☕⚷

Paint Research Association Library
8 Waldegrave Rd, Teddington, Middlesex, TW11 8LD (020-8614-4800; *fax:* 020-8943-4705)
Email: library@pra.org.uk
Internet: http://www.pra.org.uk/library/

Type: rsrch assoc **Chief:** Libn: S.C. Haworth
Entry: free to PRA membs, fee payable by non-membs (varies)
Subj: paint tech **Collns:** Bks & Pamphs: patents; standards; govt reports; legislation; market reports; conference proceedings **Co-op Schemes:** ILL
Equip: Online: WSCA **Svcs:** ref, info, enq svc, document delivery
Stock: bks/7000; periodcls/350
Pubns: Paint Titles (weekly journal, available as hard copy, disk or by email); WSCA (annual summaries & abstracts compilation, available as hard copy, disk or online); Coatings Comet (regular compilation of market statistics etc)

Telford

S2033 ⚷ 🏛

Ironbridge Gorge Museum Trust Library
Ironbridge, Telford, Shropshire, TF8 7AW (01952-432141; *fax:* 01952-435937)
Email: library@ironbridge.org.uk
Internet: http://www.ironbridge.org.uk/

Chief: Libn & Info Offcr: J. Powell BA, MCLIP
Entry: adv appt only **Open:** Mon-Fri 0900-1700
Subj: local study (East Shropshire); religion (nonconformist); industrial hist; hist of tech; eng;

metallurgy; decorative arts; hist & geog of East Shropshire; museology **Collns:** *Bks & Pamphs:* Elton Colln (hist of the Industrial Revolution); Telford Colln (life & works of Thomas Telford, hist of civil eng) *Archvs:* records of Coalbrookdale Company; records of Lilleshall Company; records of Maw & Co
Equip: m-reader, video viewer, fax, copier, computer (incl wd-proc), room for hire
Stock: bks/50000; periodcls/100; photos/5000; slides/1000; pamphs/1000; maps/200; m-forms/200
Classn: UDC **Staff:** *Libns:* 1.5 *Other Prof:* 1

S2034 ✚
Princess Royal Hospital NHS Trust Library
Edu Centre, Princess Royal Hosp, Apley Castle, Leegomery, Telford, Shropshire, TF6 6TF (01952-641222; *fax:* 01952-243405)
Email: allan.davies@prh-tr.wmids.nhs.uk

Gov Body: Princess Royal Hosp NHS Trust
Chief: Libn: Mr Allan Davies BA, DipILM **Dep:** Miss Louise Stevens
Entry: hosp staff, local health profs & Staffordshire Univ School of Health staff & students **Open:** Mon-Thu 0830-1900, Fri 0830-1630, Sat 0830-1230
Subj: medicine; nursing; health **Co-op Schemes:** BLDSC, WMRHLN, SHAIR
Equip: m-reader, copier, 14 computers (incl 13 with wd-proc, 13 with internet & 13 with CD-ROM)
Online: Medline, CINAHL, Cochrane **Svcs:** info, ref
Stock: bks/7000; periodcls/90; pamphs/3000; videos/70; CD-ROMs/50
Classn: NLM **Auto Sys:** Heritage
Staff: *Libns:* 1 *Non-Prof:* 3.5 *Exp:* £23000 (1999-2000); £27000 (2000-01)

S2035 🎓
Telford College of Arts and Technology, Learning Resource Centre
Haybridge Rd, Wellington, Telford, Shropshire, TF1 2NP (01952-642200; *fax:* 01952-642263)
Email: sheila.etherington@tcat.ac.uk
Internet: http://www.tcat.ac.uk/

Chief: LRC Mgr: Ms Sheila Etherington
Entry: staff & students, loan facilities; others, ref
Open: term: Mon-Thu 0830-2100, Fri 0900-1630, Sat 0900-1300; vac: generally Mon-Fri 0900-1700
Subj: all subjs; GCSE; A level; undergrad **Co-op Schemes:** BLDSC
Equip: copier, computers (incl internet & CD-ROM)
Stock: bks/27000; periodcls/120; videos/100
Classn: DDC **Auto Sys:** Heritage IV
Staff: *Libns:* 2 *Other Prof:* 7 *Non-Prof:* 2

Tenby

S2036 🔑 🎓 🏛
Tenby Museum and Art Gallery, Library and Archives
Castle Hill, Tenby, Pembrokeshire, SA70 7BP (*tel & fax:* 01834-842809)
Email: tenbymuseum@hotmail.com
Internet: http://www.tenbymuseum.free-online.co.uk/

Gov Body: Trustees of Tenby Museum & Art Gallery **Chief:** Hon Libn & Trustee: Mrs Susan V. Baldwin **Other Snr Staff:** Hon Curator: Mr John Beynon BA; Asst Curator: Mr Mark Lewis BA
Entry: ref only, adv appt **Open:** *Museum:* Mon-Sun 1000-1700 (Mon-Fri only Nov-Easter); *Rsrch Room:* Tue-Fri 1000-1230, 1400-1630

Subj: local studies (Pembrokeshire); nat hist; generalities; religion; Celtic saints; monastic hist (Caldey Island); social sci; sci; maths; arts; local artists; lit; geog; social hist (Tenby); archaeo; geol
Collns: *Bks & Pamphs:* local guide bks (19C onwards); local nat hist; Augustus & Gwen John Colln (artists) *Archvs:* Tenby Borough Archvs (17C onwards) *Other:* local newspapers (1853-date); postcards & photos of Tenby area
Equip: m-reader, video viewer, copier (10p-20p), fax *Disabled:* hearing loop, wheelchair access
Officer-in-Charge: Hon Libn, as above **Svcs:** info, ref, abstracting
Stock: bks/4000; periodcls/500; photos/5600; slides/150; illusts/1000; pamphs/1000; maps/1000; m-forms/300; audios/20; videos/90 **Acqs Offcr:** Hon Libn, as above
Classn: DDC
Pubns: The Story of Tenby (£1.50); Fair & Fashionable Tenby (£4.50); A Brief Hist of Tenby Harbour & Surrounding Area (£1); The Prehistory of Caldey Island (£1); Tenby Local Museum 1878 (£1); Caldey Monastic Island (£1); In Praise of Tenby (£1); Nina Hamnett 1890-1956 (£1); Edward J. Head (£1); The Shell Colln of Arthur Goodwin Stubbs (£1); The Ridsdale Geol Colln at Tenby Museum (£1); Tenby in Camera: A Hist of Photography & Tenby Photographers (£1); Let's Look at Tenby Harbour & Beaches (£1.50); Victorian Naturalists in Tenby (£1)
Staff: *Other Prof:* 2 *Non-Prof:* 5
Further Info: Tenby Museum & Art Gallery is the oldest independent museum in Wales, celebrating its 125th anniversary in Jul 2003

Tenterden

S2037 🔑 🏛
The Ellen Terry Memorial Museum Library
Smallhythe Pl, Smallhythe, Tenterden, Kent, TN30 7NG (01580-762334; *fax:* 01580-762334)
Email: smallhytheplace@ntrust.org.uk

Gov Body: The Natl Trust **Chief:** contact the Custodian
Entry: ref only, adv appt **Open:** Mon-Fri (Nov-Mar only) 1000-1730, by arrangement
Subj: theatre **Collns:** *Bks & Pamphs:* Ellen Terry's annotated scripts & related bks; Edward Gordon Craig Colln *Archvs:* Edith Craig archv; letters to & from Ellen Terry & Edith Craig; suffrage material *Other:* theatre programmes; playbills
Equip: copier
Stock: bks/2000; photos/5000; scripts/100; letters/3000
Pubns: Catalogue of Ellen Terry's Working Lib (£5)
Proj: elec cataloguing of archvs

Thame

S2038 🎓
Rycotewood College, Learning Resources Centre
Priest End, Thame, Oxfordshire, OX9 2AF (01844-212501; *fax:* 01844-218809)
Email: enquiries_rycote@oxfe.ac.uk
Internet: http://www.hill.dircon.co.uk/rycotewood/

Chief: Coll Libn: Mr Robert Collier BSc
Entry: ref only **Open:** term: Mon 0900-1700, Tue-Wed 0900-1730, Thu 0900-2000, Fri 0830-1630; vac: Mon-Thu 0900-1230, 1330-1700, Fri 0900-1230, 1330-1630
Subj: generalities; sci; maths; tech; arts **Collns:** *Bks & Pamphs:* Frederick Oughton (woodworking, 400 vols); BSI (311)
Equip: m-reader, m-printer, 2 video viewers, copier, 7 computers (all with wd-proc, internet & CD-ROM) *Disabled:* wheelchair access **Svcs:** info, ref, biblio, indexing

Stock: bks/12587; periodcls/105
Classn: DDC **Auto Sys:** Heritage
Staff: *Non-Prof:* 2 *Exp:* £5500 (1999-2000)

Thirsk

S2039 🔑 🏛
Thirsk Museum, Library
14-16 Kirkgate, Thirsk, N Yorkshire, YO7 1PQ (01845-527707)
Email: thirskmuseum@supanet.com
Internet: http://www.thirskmuseum.org/

Gov Body: Thirsk Museum Soc **Chief:** Curator: Mr Cooper Harding
Entry: ref only; adv appt **Open:** Easter-end Oct: Mon-Wed, Fri-Sat 1000-1600; closed Thu & Sun
Subj: Thirsk & dist: local life & hist
Svcs: ref, rsrch
Stock: bks/80; photos/600+; pamphs/50; maps/25; audios/1; videos/1
Classn: SHIC
Pubns: Outlines of Thirsk & Sowerby (pamph, 15p); Around Thirsk (Britain in Old Photographs, publ by Sutton, £7.99)

Thornton Heath

S2040 ✚
Croydon Health Sciences Library
Mayday Univ Hosp, London Rd, Thornton Heath, Surrey, CR7 7YE (020-8401-3197; *fax:* 020-8401-3883)

Gov Body: Mayday Univ Hosp NHS Trust **Chief:** Lib Svc Mgr: Mr Ray Phillips (ray.phillips@mayday.nhs.uk) **Dep:** Associate Libn: Ms Arpita Banerjee BA, DipLib, MCLIP (arpita.banerjee@mayday.nhs.uk) **Other Snr Staff:** Associate Libn: Mr David Hayes BA, DipLib (david.hayes@mayday.nhs.uk); Info Skills Libn: Mr San Fun Chu BSc, DipILM (san.chu@mayday.nhs.uk)
Entry: Croydon NHS staff; ref access for genl public by appt only **Open:** Mon-Fri 0900-1700; after hrs access by arrangment
Subj: medicine; nursing **Co-op Schemes:** BLDSC, BMA, STLIS
Equip: 2 copiers (5p per sheet), clr copier (staff only), 9 computers (all with wd-proc & CD-ROM, 8 with internet) **Online:** via KA24 & Dialog **Officer-in-Charge:** Lib Svc Mgr, as above **Svcs:** info, ref, biblio
Stock: bks/600; periodcls/112 **Acqs Offcr:** Lib Svc Mgr, as above
Classn: NLM **Auto Sys:** DBTextworks
Staff: *Libns:* 4 *Non-Prof:* 2 *Exp:* £47000 (1999-2000); £49000 (2000-01)

Thurso

S2041 🎓
North Highland College Library
Ormlie Rd, Thurso, Caithness, KW14 7EE (01847-889292/3; *fax:* 01847-889001)
Internet: http://www.nhcscotland.com/

Gov Body: Univ of the Highlands & Islands (UHI)
Chief: Libn: Mrs Rhona Mason BA, MLib, MCLIP (rhona.mason@thurso.uhi.ac.uk) **Dep:** Asst Libn: Ms Heather Stewart BA, DipLib (heather.stewart@thurso.uhi.ac.uk)
Entry: day visitors can use facilities; regular day visitors can enroll as external membs for a year at a time **Open:** term: Mon-Fri 0830-1630; longer opening hrs may be reinstated in future
Subj: all subjs; Further Edu; local studies (Highlands of Scotland) **Collns:** *Bks & Pamphs:* Highland Colln (local hist) **Co-op Schemes:** BLDSC, UHI Millennium Inst Lib

☞

(North Highland Coll Lib cont)
Equip: m-form reader/printer, 2 video viewers, copier, 8 computers (all with wd-proc & internet, 4 with CD-ROM), slide viewers; 70 computers, all with wd-proc, internet & CD-ROM, also available at main computing suite neaby *Disabled:* available in Support Section *Officer-in-Charge:* Libn, as above *Svcs:* info, ref, biblio
Stock: bks/13000; periodcls/200; slides/400; maps/50; audios/50; videos/250; CD-ROMs/200
Acqs Offcr: Libn, as above
Classn: DDC, own *Auto Sys:* Olib
Staff: Libns: 2 *Exp:* £18000 (2000-01)

Tiverton

S2042 🎓

Blundell's School, Amory Library
Blundells Rd, Tiverton, Devon, EX16 4DN (01884-252543; *fax:* 01884-243232)
Email: info@blundells.org

Chief: Libn: Mrs J. Gordon BA, BEd, DSE *Dep:* Mrs P. Deighton-Gibson
Entry: all pupils/staff *Open:* term: Mon-Fri 0800-2100, Sat 0800-1200, Sun 1400-1700; vac: closed
Subj: all subjs; genl; GCSE; A level; vocational; local studies (South West England); generalities; phil; psy; religion; social sci; lang; sci; maths; tech; arts; lit; geog; hist *Collns: Bks & Pamphs:* related to hist of Blundell's School & of Tiverton
Equip: fax, copier, computers (incl wd-proc, internet & CD-ROM)
Stock: bks/15000; periodcls/30
Classn: DDC *Staff:* Libns: 1 *Other Prof:* 1

S2043 🎓

East Devon College, Library and Learning Resources Centre
Bolham Rd, Tiverton, Devon, EX16 6SH (01884-235234; *fax:* 01884-235262)
Email: library@admin.eastdevon.ac.uk
Internet: http://www.edc.ac.uk/lrc/

Chief: Libn: L.E. Boyce
Entry: ref; subscriptionfor non-membs to borrow
Open: term: Mon 0845-1800, Tue & Thu 0845-1900, Wed 0900-1900, Fri 0845-1645; vac: varies
Subj: all subjs; genl; GCSE; A level; undergrad *Collns: Archvs:* small colln relating to hist of Coll & edu in Tiverton *Co-op Schemes:* SWRLS, BLDSC
Equip: m-readers, m-printer, video viewers, copiers, computers (with internet & CD-ROM)
Online: BIDS, Infotrac, Ingenta Journals *Svcs:* info, ref, biblio
Stock: bks/22000; periodcls/100; maps/200; m-forms/200; audios/100; videos/100; archvs/200 MSS; clippings/400
Classn: DDC *Staff:* Libns: 1 *Non-Prof:* 3 FTE

Tobermory

S2044 🔑 🏛

Mull Museum, Reference Library and Archive
Columba Bldgs, Main St, Tobermory, Isle of Mull, PA75 6NY (01688-302208)
Email: wclegg@ukonline.co.uk

Gov Body: Isle of Mull Museum Trust *Chief:* Curator: Mr W.H. Clegg *Dep:* Libn: Mr Bruce B. Whittaker OBE, MA, FRICS
Entry: membership of Isle of Mull Museum Assoc; ref only *Open:* Easter-mid Oct: Mon-Fri 1000-1600, Sat 1000-1300; adv appt at other times
Subj: Mull, adjacent islands & Morven: archaeo; local hist; nat hist; genealogy *Collns: Archvs:* 19C legal documents; letter bks; account bks *Other:* photographic lib (19C-date)
Equip: photographic copies may be ordered; commercial copier nearby
Stock: bks/320; periodcls/3; photos/2000; maps/50; archvs/131 boxes of MSS & documents
Pubns: Isle of Mull Museum Archv List (£7.50)
Staff: Non-Prof: volunteers

Tonbridge

S2045 🎓

Hadlow College Library
Hadlow, Tonbridge, Kent, TN11 0AL (01732-850551; *fax:* 01732-853207)
Email: library@hadlow.ac.uk
Internet: http://www.hadlow.ac.uk/

Chief: Head of Lib Svcs: Mrs Melanie Fisher MCLIP (librarian@hadlow.ac.uk)
Entry: adv appt (phone call sufficient) *Open:* term: Mon-Thu 0830-2030, Fri 0830-1700, Sat 1000-1300; vac: Mon-Fri 0900-1600
Subj: local study (Hadlow & Kent); sci; biology; plant scis; genetics; biotech; animal scis; tech; agric; machinery; hortic; gardening; animal care; veterinary nursing; equine studies; business; arts; landscape design; landscape mgmt; garden design; floristry; sport sci; conservation; countryside mgmt; fisheries mgmt *Co-op Schemes:* BLDSC, ILL with Univ of Greenwich & various local libs
Equip: copier, video viewer, 15 computers (all with wd-proc, internet & CD-ROM) *Svcs:* info, ref, biblio
Stock: bks/9000; periodcls/50; slides/1000; maps/25; videos/425; CD-ROMs/25 *Acqs Offcr:* Head of Lib Svcs, as above
Classn: DDC *Auto Sys:* Limes
Staff: Libns: 1 *Non-Prof:* 2.5

S2046 🎓

West Kent College, Library Services
Brook St, Tonbridge, Kent, TN9 2PW (01732-358101; *fax:* 01732-771415)
Internet: http://www.wkc.ac.uk/

Gov Body: West Kent Coll *Chief:* Head of Lib Svcs: Mrs E. Scott BA(Hons), CertEd, DipLib, CMS, MCLIP *Dep:* Libn: post vacant
Assoc Libs: 3 satellite Learning Centres on same site serving faculty areas
Entry: ref only for non-enrolled users *Open:* term: Mon-Thu 0830-1900, Fri 0930-1630; vac: Mon-Thu 0900-1630, Fri 0900-1600
Subj: genl; GCSE; A level; undergrad; postgrad; vocational; communication studies; psy; sociology; statistics; politics; law; lang (English & foreign); maths; chem; physics; biology; eng; medicine; auto eng; computing; environmental studies; business; construction; arts; lit; geog; hist *Co-op Schemes:* BLDSC, ILL
Equip: 3 video viewers, copier, 35 computers (all with wd-proc & internet, 1 with CD-ROM), binding equip *Disabled:* enlarger, lift for access *Svcs:* info, ref, biblio, indexing, abstracting
Stock: bks/34000; periodcls/240; slides/75000; maps/200; videos/500; CD-ROMs/50+
Classn: UDC *Auto Sys:* Autolib
Staff: Libns: 2 *Non-Prof:* 6 FTE *Exp:* £46000 (1999-2000); £52000 (2000-01)

Torquay

S2047 🎓

South Devon College Learning Centre
Newton Rd, Torquay, Devon, TQ2 5BY (01803-406451)
Email: karen.brazier@southdevon.ac.uk

Chief: Learning Resources Co-ordinator: Miss Karen Brazier
Entry: open to public for ref only *Open:* term: Mon-Fri 0845-1700
Subj: all subjs; local study (Torquay & Devon) *Co-op Schemes:* Plymouth Univ ILL
Equip: m-reader, 3 copiers, clr copier, 2 video viewers, 47 computers (incl 45 with wd-proc, 45 with internet & 2 with CD-ROM, membs of Coll only) *Online:* not available to non-membs of Coll *Officer-in-Charge:* Learning Resources Co-ordinator, as above *Svcs:* info, ref
Stock: bks/c60000; periodcls/c150; audios/c100; videos/c100; CD-ROMs/c250 *Acqs Offcr:* Learning Resources Co-ordinator, as above
Classn: DDC *Auto Sys:* Heritage
Staff: Libns: 1 *Other Prof:* 4.6 *Non-Prof:* 1.3

S2048 ✚

South Devon Healthcare NHS Trust Library
Medical Centre, Torbay Hosp, Lawes Bridge, Torquay, Devon, TQ2 7AA (01803-654704; *fax:* 01803-616395)
Email: library@sdevonhc-tr.swest.nhs.uk
Internet: http://www.sdhl.nhs.uk/

Gov Body: South Devon Healthcare NHS Trust *Chief:* Trust Libn: Mrs Susan Martin BSc(Hons), DipLib, MCLIP
Assoc Libs: PLYMOUTH HOSPS NHS TRUST STAFF LIB (see **S1809**)
Entry: full access to all NHS & primary health care staff working in South & West Devon; ref only to membs of public *Open:* staffed: Mon-Fri 0830-1700; out of hrs access available
Subj: medicine; health *Co-op Schemes:* BLDSC, BMA, RCSE, SWRLIN, South Devon Health Libs
Equip: fax, video viewer, copier, computers (all with wd-proc, internet & CD-ROM) *Online:* CancerLit, BNI, CINAHL, DHData, Medline, Embase, PsycInfo, AMED, MIDIRS, Pedro *Svcs:* info, ref, biblio
Stock: bks/15000; periodcls/150
Classn: NLM *Auto Sys:* DBTextworks
Staff: Libns: 1 *Other Prof:* 1 *Non-Prof:* 4

S2049 🔑 🏛

Torquay Natural History Society Library and Torquay Museum Pictorial Records Archive
The Museum, 529 Babbacombe Rd, Torquay, Devon, TQ1 1HG (01803-293975)

Gov Body: Torquay Nat Hist Soc *Chief:* Libn: Miss Lorna Smith MCLIP
Entry: Local Studies Centre: open to public Tue-Wed, TNHS membs during Museum opening hrs; *Pictorial Records Archv:* adv appt only *Open: Local Studies Centre:* Tue-Wed 1000-1300, 1400-1700; *Museum:* Mon-Sat 1000-1700, Sun (Apr-Oct) 1330-1700
Subj: all subjs; genl; undergrad; postgrad; local studies (Torbay, Devon); generalities; religion; sci; maths; tech; arts; lit; geog; hist; archaeo; ethnography; geol; nat hist; palaeontology *Collns: Bks & Pamphs:* 16C verse & prose (by Spenser, Green, Nashe, Dekker); various 17C-18C pubns *Archvs:* The Hester Pengelly (Forbes-Julian) letter & autograph colln; Pengelly diaries & other info

relating to Kents Cavern Excavation; Hansford-Worth photos of Dartmoor etc *Other:* prints, postcards, bklets, newspapers, letters etc linked to Devon; large colln of glass negs; London Illustrated News; Torquay Directory
Equip: copier
Stock: bks/15000
Classn: in-house
Pubns: Transactions of Torquay Nat Hist Soc (annual); Dartmoor Granite & Its Uses (£1.25); Beatrix Potter (£1.95); Bruness in Torbay (£1.25); William Pengelly's Techniques of Archaeological Excavation (£1)
Staff: Libns: 1 *Other Prof:* 1 *Non-Prof:* 14 *Exp:* £250 (1999-2000); £200 (2000-01)

Totnes

S2050 📖

Dartington College of Arts, Library and Learning Resources Centre
Totnes, Devon, TQ9 6EJ (01803-861652; *fax:* 01803-863569)
Email: library@dartington.ac.uk
Internet: http://www.dartington.ac.uk/

Gov Body: Dartington Coll of Arts *Chief:* Dir of Academic Svcs: Ms Dorothy Faulkner BA, MA, DipLib, MCLIP *Dep:* Mr Richard Taylor BA(Hons), DipLib, MCLIP
Entry: ref only unless registered *Open:* term: Mon-Thu 0900-2100, Fri 0900-1800, Sat-Sun 1330-1730; vac: Mon-Fri 0900-1700 (closed 2 wks at Xmas)
Subj: all subjs; genl; undergrad; postgrad; arts (main bulk of colln) *Co-op Schemes:* BLDSC
Equip: m-reader, 2 video viewers, 2 copiers, 34 computer workstations (incl CD-ROM); equip available to Coll students & staff only *Svcs:* info, ref
Stock: bks/c48000, incl pamphs; periodcls/170; slides/8000; m-forms/10 vols; audios/c4500; videos/c300
Classn: DDC *Auto Sys:* Heritage
Staff: Libns: 2 *Non-Prof:* 2.27 *Exp:* £36700 (1999-2000)

Trefforest

S2051 🔔 🏛️

National Museums and Galleries of Wales, Department of Industry Reference Library
(formerly the Welsh Industrial & Maritime Museum)
The Collns Centre, Heol Crochendy, Parc Nantgarw, Trefforest, CF15 7QT (029-2039-7951; *fax:* 029-2057-3561)
Email: industry@nmgw.ac.uk
Internet: http://www.nmgw.ac.uk/industry/

Type: natl museum *Gov Body:* Natl Museums & Galleries of Wales (see **S422**) *Chief:* contact the relevant Curator
Assoc Libs: PHOTOGRAPHIC COLLNS, at same addr, Curator: Mr Peter Bennett
Entry: adv appt with the Curator responsible for the relevant section of the Lib; proof of ID required; ref only *Open:* Mon-Fri 0930-1600 (closed natl hols)
Subj: Welsh industrial, transport & maritime hist; business records *Collns: Bks & Pamphs:* Industrial Histories Colln; various industrial technical & instructional works; Lloyds Registers (selected vols 1764-1832, full set 1836-date); Shipwrecks Colln; HMSO Annual List of Mines (1850s-date); HM Inspectors of Mines Reports; Coal Mining Colln (c8000 bnd vols & pamphs) *Archvs:* various industrial & maritime collns, incl: Evan Thomas Radcliffe & Co records (shipowners);

Melingriffith Co Ltd records (tinplate manufacturers, 1779-1934); Nantyglo & Blaina Ironworks Co Ltd records (19C & early 20C); Pentyrch Ironworks records (1822-79); Rhymney Valley & Tirphil Land & Workman's Cottage Co Ltd records (1889-1978) *Other:* Photographic Collns: Tempest Colln (25000 aerial photographs, 1950-70); Hansen Colln (4560 images of ships in & around Cardiff Docks, 1920-75); J.E. Martin Colln (transport, post-war to c1970, 575 negs); A.C. Mitchell Colln (South Wales, 258 negs); Associated British Ports Colln (South Wales docks, c2000 negs) *Co-op Schemes:* ILL
Svcs: ref, photographic reproduction (list of fees available)
Stock: bks/20000, incl periodcls; periodcls/40; photos/100000

Tring

S2052 🔑

Royal Forestry Society of England, Wales and Northern Ireland Library
102 High St, Tring, Hertfordshire, HP23 4AF (01442-822028; *fax:* 01442-890395)
Email: rfshq@rfs.org.uk
Internet: http://www.rfs.org.uk/

Type: educational charity
Entry: prior appt only *Open:* Mon-Fri 0930-1630
Subj: forestry & related topics *Collns: Other:* slide colln
Equip: copior, fax *Svcs:* info, rcf, biblio, abstracting
Pubns: Quarterly Journal of Forestry
Staff: Non-Prof: 2

Trowbridge

S2053 📖

Wiltshire College, Trowbridge Library
(formerly Trowbridge Coll)
Edington Bldg, College Rd, Trowbridge, Wiltshire, BA14 0ES (01225-766241; *fax:* 01225-777148)
Internet: http://www.wiltscoll.ac.uk/

Chief: Libn: Mrs G. Thomas
Assoc Libs: CHIPPENHAM LIB (see **S472**); LACKHAM LIB (see **S473**)
Entry: membs of Coll; others ref only *Open:* Mon, Wed-Thu 0845-2000, Tue 1000-2000, Fri 0845-1700
Subj: all subjs; genl; GCSE; A level; undergrad *Co-op Schemes:* ILL
Equip: copiers, clr copier, networked computers
Stock: bks/18000; periodcls/150
Auto Sys: Olib 7

Truro

S2054 🐚

Bishop Phillpotts Library
Diocesan House, Kenwyn, Truro, Cornwall, TR1 1JQ (01872-262228)
Email: philpott.library@ukonline.co.uk

Gov Body: Diocese of Truro *Chief: Libn:* Ms Wynona Wright BA, BEd, BLS, MCLIP
Entry: adv appt useful *Open:* Mon-Fri 0900-1700
Subj: religion; theology *Co-op Schemes:* Theology South-West
Equip: computer (with wd-proc & CD-ROM), room for hire
Stock: bks/c15000; periodcls/12
Classn: DDC *Auto Sys:* Heritage
Staff: Libns: 1 PT *Exp:* £5000 (1999-2000); £4000 (2000-01)

S2055 ✚

Cornwall Postgraduate Centre Medical Library
Royal Cornwall Hosps Trust, Truro, Cornwall, TR1 3LJ (01872-252610; *fax:* 01872-222838)
Email: medical.library@rcht.swest.nhs.uk

Chief: Libn: Mrs P.W. Kitch *Dep:* Ms Sue ApThomas & Ms Trica Ellis
Open: staffed: Mon-Fri 0830-1730
Subj: medicine; health *Collns: Bks & Pamphs:* genl practice colln (300 vols) *Co-op Schemes:* SWRLIN
Equip: copier, fax, computers (incl 4 internet & 4 CD-ROM) *Online:* Datastar
Stock: bks/5000; periodcls/300
Classn: NLM *Auto Sys:* Winchill

S2056 🔑

Royal Institution of Cornwall, The Courtney Library and Cornish History Research Centre
River St, Truro, Cornwall, TR1 2SJ (01872-272205; *fax:* 01872-240514)
Email: RIC@royal-cornwall-museum.freeserve.co.uk
Internet: http://www.cornwall-online.co.uk/ric/

Gov Body: The Royal Instn of Cornwall *Chief: Libn:* Miss Angela Broome *Dep:* Hon Archivist: Mr H.L. Douch DA (Fri only)
Entry: private membs' lib, but public access to study area for ref; appt advised for use of m-readers & MSS collns *Open:* Mon-Sat 1000-1300, 1400-1700 excl bank hols
Subj: genl; Cornwall; all aspects of Cornish hist; Methodist Church in Cornwall; Cornish & Celtic langs; arts; geog; hist; maritime hist *Collns: Bks & Pamphs:* J.T. Dunn Colln (Rev R.S. Hawker's works); John Sparrow Colln (Rev R. Polwhele's works); Doble Colln (Celtic hagiography); Staal Colln (fine arts); Shaw Colln (Cornish Methodism, incl some MSS); Rex Hall Colln (c300 maritime vols); local directories; guidebks *Archvs:* Henderson Colln (Cornish estate documents 13C-19C plus articles/notes etc); Enys Autograph Colln (MSS 16C-20C, natl significance); Lloyd's Registers (from 1790, some gaps); Lloyd's Registers of Yachts (from 1887); Lloyd's Captains Register (1869, on m-fiche); parish registers (m-film) & transcripts *Other:* Lloyd Dunn Colln (Cornish shipwrecks 18C-20C); Cyril Noall Colln (fishing, lifeboats, lighthouses, shipwrecks, smuggling); Philbrick Colln (Cornish Packet Service/Postal & turnpike records); Nance Colln (Cornish lang, lit, folklore); photo colln (incl prints & negs); Cornish Ship-Bldg database (1786-1914); Phillimore Marriage Register Index (Cornwall); IGI (Devon & Cornwall); local newspapers (from 1798); maps & engravings (from 17C); posters (mainly mid-19C)
Equip: 5 m-readers, m-printer (staff operated), copier (staff operated), 3 computers *Disabled:* wheelchair access *Svcs:* info, ref, abstracting, translation
Stock: bks/c32000; periodcls/55; photos/35000; slides/150; illusts/500 engravings; pamphs/500; maps/400; m-forms/790; audios/43; videos/2; archvs/30000 items
Classn: UDC
Pubns: Journal of the Royal Instn of Cornwall & Newsletter of the Royal Instn of Cornwall (free to membs, £6 to non-membs); Copyright & Copying from Bks & Manuscripts in the Courtney Lib (20p); List of Cornish Parish Registers on Microfilm in Courtney Lib (20p); List of Cornish Parish Register Transcripts in Courtney Lib (20p); Sources for Maritime Rsrch (20p)
Staff: Libns: 1.2 *Other Prof:* 0.2

Tunbridge Wells

S2057 ✚

Kent and Sussex Postgraduate Medical Centre, The MacDonald Library

Kent & Sussex Hosp, Tunbridge Wells, Kent, TN4 8AT (01892-526111 x2384; *fax:* 01892-531975)

Gov Body: Maidstone & Tunbridge Wells NHS Trust *Chief:* Lib & Info Svcs Mgr: Mr David Copsey MA, DipLib, MCLIP (dcopsey@netcomuk. co.uk) *Dep:* Asst LIS Mgr: Mrs Jane Beeley BA, MCLIP
Assoc Libs: MAIDSTONE & TUNBRIDGE WELLS NHS TRUST, LIB & INFO SVCS (see **S1504**); PEMBURY HOSP LIB (see **S2058**)
Entry: free membership for employees of Maidstone & Tunbridge Wells NHS Trust; West Kent NHS & Social Care Trust; local PCTs; Kent Ambulance Trust; Kent & Medway Strategic Health Authority; INAM students; access by subscription to others *Open:* Mon-Fri 0900-1700
Subj: medicine; nursing *Co-op Schemes:* KSS, BLDSC, PLCS, NULJ
Equip: copier, fax, 4 computers (all with wd-proc, internet & CD-ROM) *Online:* KA24, Medline, CINAHL, Cochrane, PsycInfo, BNI, HMIC, Datastar, NHS Net *Svcs:* info, ref, biblio
Stock: bks/2950; periodcls/105
Classn: NLM *Auto Sys:* Librarian
Staff: Libns: 1 *Non-Prof:* 2 *Exp:* £330000 (2000-01); figs incl all Trust libs

S2058 ✚

Maidstone and Tunbridge Wells NHS Trust, Pembury Hospital Library

Edu Centre, Pembury, Tunbridge Wells, Kent, TN2 4QJ (01892-823535)

Gov Body: Maidstone & Tunbridge Wells NHS Trust *Chief:* Lib & Info Svcs Mgr: Mr David Copsey MA, DipLib, MCLIP (dcopsey@netcomuk. co.uk) *Dep:* Dep LIS Mgr: Mrs Jan Hurst BA, MCLIP *Other Snr Staff:* Clinical Outreach Support Libn: Miss Alison Paul BA
Assoc Libs: MAIDSTONE & TUNBRIDGE WELLS NHS TRUST, LIB & INFO SVCS (see **S1504**); KENT & SUSSEX HOSP, THE MACDONALD LIB (see **S2057**)
Entry: free membership for employees of Maidstone & Tunbridge Wells NHS Trust; West Kent NHS & Social Care Trust; local PCTs; Kent Ambulance Trust; Kent & Medway Strategic Health Authority; INAM students; access by subscription to others *Open:* Mon-Thu 0900-1700, Fri 0900-1600
Subj: medicine; nursing; psychiatry *Co-op Schemes:* KSS, PLCS, STRLIS, NULJ
Equip: copier, fax, 2 computers (both with wd-proc, internet & CD-ROM) *Online:* KA24, Medline, CINAHL, Cochrane, PsycInfo, BNI, HMIC, Datastar, NHS Net
Stock: bks/5000; periodcls/60
Classn: NLM *Auto Sys:* Librarian
Staff: Libns: 1 *Non-Prof:* 2 *Exp:* £330000 (2000-01); figs incl all Trust libs

S2059 🏛🏛

Tunbridge Wells Museum and Art Gallery, Library and Archives

Civic Centre, Mount Pleasant, Tunbridge Wells, Kent, TN1 1JN (01892-554171; *fax:* 01892-534227)
Email: museum@tunbridgewells.gov.uk
Internet: http://www.tunbridgewells.gov.uk/ museum/

Type: local govt *Gov Body:* Tunbridge Wells Borough Council *Chief:* Museum Technical Offcr: Dr Ian Beavis MSc, PhD *Dep:* Audience Development Offcr: Ms Susan Potter BA(Hons), PGCE
Entry: adv appt *Open:* Mon-Fri 0930-1700; closed Bank Holidays
Subj: local studies (Tunbridge Wells); sci; arts; geog; hist *Collns: Archvs:* materials pertaining to the hist of Royal Tunbridge Wells & Council
Equip: copier, clr copier, fax *Disabled:* limited disabled access *Officer-in-Charge:* Museum Technical Offcr, as above *Svcs:* info, ref, biblio, indexing
Acqs Offcr: Museum Technical Offcr, as above
Pubns: various, pertaining to hist & nat hist of the area
Staff: Other Prof: 3 *Non-Prof:* 2
Proj: refurbishment of museum & art gallery

Twickenham

S2060 🔑🏛

Museum of Rugby, Library

Rugby Football Union, Rugby Rd, Twickenham, Middlesex, TW17 0RX (020-8892-8877; *fax:* 020-8892-2817)
Email: museum@rfu.com
Internet: http://www.rfu.com/

Gov Body: Rugby Football Union *Chief:* Lib Offcr: Mr Ross Hamilton MA (rosshamilton@ rfu.com)
Entry: ref only, adv appt as space is limited *Open:* Mon-Fri 1030-1600
Subj: hist of rugby football & associated subjs
Collns: Bks & Pamphs: bks relating to all aspects of rugby football hist *Other:* team photographs; match programmes
Equip: copier (A4/5p, A3/10p), fax *Svcs:* info, ref
Stock: bks/4000; periodcls/500; photos/3000; videos/50; match programmes/5000
Pubns: The Power & the Beauty (£4)
Staff: Libns: 1 *Other Prof:* 3

S2061 🎓

Richmond Adult Community College Library

Clifden Rd, Twickenham, Middlesex, TW1 4LT (020-8891-5907; *fax:* 020-8332-6560)
Email: info@racc.ac.uk
Internet: http://www.racc.ac.uk/

Gov Body: Richmond upon Thames LEA *Chief:* Coll Libn: Ms Renee Anderson BSocSc, BA, MCLIP
Assoc Libs: PARKSHOT SITE LIB, Parkshot, Richmond, Surrey, TW9 2RE
Entry: staff & students of Coll & membs of designated community groups may borrow; others ref only *Open: Clifden:* term: Mon-Thu 0900-2000, Fri 0900-1700; *Parkshot:* term: Mon-Thu 0900-1900, Fri 0900-1600
Subj: all subjs; genl; GCSE; A level; undergrad; vocational; arts *Co-op Schemes:* BLDSC
Equip: video viewer, copier, computers (with CD-ROM)
Stock: bks/9408; periodcls/70; slides/800; audios/182; videos/280; figs cover both sites
Classn: DDC *Auto Sys:* Heritage
Staff: Libns: 3 *Non-Prof:* 3

S2062 🎓🖋

Richmond upon Thames College, Library and Learning Resource Centre

Egerton Rd, Twickenham, Middlesex, TW2 7SJ (020-8607-8356)
Email: library@richmond-utcoll.ac.uk

Chief: Coll Libn: Mrs Jane Stauch BA, MCLIP
Dep: Dep Libn: Ms Jane Winspear MA, MCLIP
Entry: adv appt for non-coll membs *Open:* term: Mon-Thu 0830-2000, Fri 0830-1600; vac: Mon-Fri 0930-1630
Subj: all academic subjs; GCSE; A level *Collns: Bks & Pamphs:* company reports *Other:* map colln; AV colln *Co-op Schemes:* BLDSC
Equip: video viewers, copier, clr copier, computers (incl 25 with wd-proc & 40 with internet)
Stock: bks/60000; periodcls/200; slides/35000; illusts/3000; maps/300; m-forms/168; audios/200; videos/200
Classn: DDC *Auto Sys:* DS Galaxy 2000
Staff: Libns: 5 *Non-Prof:* 5

S2063 🏛🎓🖋

Royal Military School of Music, Reference Library

Kneller Hall, Kneller Rd, Twickenham, Middlesex, TW2 7DU (020-8898-5533 x39; *fax:* 020-8898-7906)

Gov Body: Ministry of Defence (Army) *Chief:* Ref Librarian/Orchestra Leader: SSgt F. Leprince DipHSchuleMusikFrankfurt, MISM *Dep:* Asst Libn: Mr Nigel Grubb
Assoc Libs: ROYAL MILITARY SCHOOL OF MUSIC ARCHVS, addr as above, Archivist: Major Gordon Turner MBE
Entry: ref & study; adv appt for membs of public *Open:* Mon-Fri 0830-1645, except during official leave periods
Subj: music (at undergrad, postgrad & vocational levels); military music; military hist *Collns: Bks & Pamphs:* rare bks on military music hist, incl: Memoirs on the Royal Artillery Band (Henry George Farmer) & Military Bands & Their Uniforms (J. Cassin-Scott) *Archvs:* rare printed music & original compositions by: C. Zavertal; Holst; Vaughn-Williams; others *Other:* recordings on CD, tape & vinyl; all types of music scores (for study & academic purposes), incl piano, orchestral, instrumental, chamber, wind, vocal (opera, operetta, lieder, choral etc)
Equip: fax, copier, clr copier, computers (incl wd-proc, internet & CD-ROM), audio players *Svcs:* info, ref, rsrch (on military music/band interests by request from public, subj to availability of experts or specialists)
Stock: bks/3935; periodcls/51; photos/800; slides/200; pamphs/various; audios/1212 CDs, 4223 LPs; videos/20; CD-ROMs/30
Classn: DDC, internal numbering code
Pubns: Fanfare Magazine (£1)
Staff: Libns: 1 *Non-Prof:* 1

S2064 🎓

St Mary's College, Information Services and Systems

Waldegrave Rd, Strawberry Hill, Twickenham, Middlesex, TW1 4SX (020-8240-4097; *fax:* 020-8240-4270)
Email: enquiry@smuc.ac.uk
Internet: http://www.smuc.ac.uk/

Chief: Dir of Info Svcs & Systems: Ms Máire Lanigan (laniganm@smuc.ac.uk) *Other Snr Staff:* Asst Dir (IT Svcs) Ms Moeen Muzaffar (moeen@smuc.ac.uk); Asst Dir (Teaching & Learning Support): Mr Martin Scarrott (scarrotm@ smuc.ac.uk)

Entry: for ref only *Open:* term: Mon-Fri 0830-2100, Sat 1100-1700; vac: Mon-Fri 0900-1700
Subj: religion; social sci; lang; arts; lit; geog; hist; sports sci; Irish studies *Co-op Schemes:* BLDSC, Surrey Univ, M25 Consortium, UK Libs Plus, SWELTEC, LAMDA
Equip: m-reader, m-printer, video viewers, fax, copiers (5p per pg), clr copiers (40p per pg), computers (incl wd-proc, internet & CD-ROM), scanner, rooms for hire *Online:* BIDS, EBSCO, Ingenta, Lexis-Nexis, Literature Online, Medline, PsycInfo, Sport Discus, Web of Science & others
Svcs: info, ref, biblio, indexing
Stock: bks/146000; periodcls/500; pamphs/2066; m-forms/100; audios/141; videos/191
Classn: DDC *Auto Sys:* Innopac
Staff: Libns: 9 Non-Prof: 6

Uxbridge

S2065

Brunel University Library

Cleveland Rd, Uxbridge, Middlesex, UB8 3PH (01895-274000; *fax:* 01895-203263)
Email: library@brunel.ac.uk
Internet: http://www.brunel.ac.uk/

Gov Body: Brunel Univ *Chief:* Head of Lib Svcs: Mr. Nick Bevan MSc(Econ), MSc, MCLIP
Assoc Libs: OSTERLEY CAMPUS LIB, Borough Rd, Isleworth, Middlesex, TW7 5DU (020-8847-1514); RUNNYMEDE CAMPUS LIB, Coopers Hill, Englefield Green, Egham, Surrey, TW20 0JZ (01784-470342); TWICKENHAM CAMPUS LIB, 300 St Margarets Rd, Twickenham, Middlesex, TW1 1PT (020-8891-8240)
Entry: ref only; borrowing facilities available on payment of £25 or £60 fee *Open:* term: Mon-Thu 0900-2100, Fri 0900-1900, Sat 0930-1300, Sun 1400-1900; vac: Mon-Fri 0900-1700 (with variations)
Subj: all subjs; genl; undergrad; postgrad *Collns: Bks & Pamphs:* Clinker Colln (railway hist); Garnet Colln (railway hist); Working Class Autobiographies
Co-op Schemes: M25 Consortium
Equip: m-readers, m-printers, video viewers, copiers, computers (incl CD-ROM)
Stock: bks/434000; periodcls/4000; videos/1000
Classn: LC *Auto Sys:* SIRSI Unicorn
Staff: Libns: 12 Non-Prof: 47

S2066

Hillingdon Hospital NHS Trust Library

Postgrad Medical Centre, Hillingdon Hosp, Pield Heath Rd, Uxbridge, Middlesex, UB8 3NN (01895-279250; *fax:* 01895-234150)
Email: library@hillib.demon.co.uk

Gov Body: Hillingdon Hosp NHS Trust *Chief:* Libn: Mr James Riste
Entry: Trust staff; local GPs *Open:* Mon-Fri 0900-1700
Subj: health; medicine *Equip:* copier
Stock: bks/2500; periodcls/90 *Classn:* NLM

S2067

Uxbridge College Learning Centre

Park Rd, Uxbridge, Middlesex, UB8 1NQ (01895-853300; *fax:* 01895-853377)
Internet: http://www.uxbridge.ac.uk/

Chief: Learning Resources Mgr: Ms Anne Harris BLib, MCLIP
Assoc Libs: UXBRIDGE LEARNING CENTRE, addr as above; HAYES COMMUNITY CAMPUS LEARNING CENTRE, Coldharbour Ln, Hayes, Middlesex, UB3 2BB
Entry: ref only *Open:* term: Mon-Fri 0900-2000; vac: Mon-Fri 1000-1600

Subj: GCSE; A level; GNVQ; NVQ; generalities; religion; social sci; lang; sci; maths; tech; arts; lit; geog; hist *Co-op Schemes:* BLDSC
Equip: copier, computers (incl wd-proc, internet & CD-ROM) *Svcs:* info, ref
Stock: bks/50000; periodcls/100; maps/100; videos/400
Classn: DDC *Auto Sys:* Geac
Staff: Libns: 2.5 Non-Prof: 20

Wakefield

S2068

National Coal Mining Museum for England Library

Cap House Colliery, New Rd, Overton, Wakefield, W Yorkshire, WF4 4RH (01924-848806; *fax:* 01924-840694)
Email: curatorial.librarian@ncm.org.uk
Internet: http://www.ncm.org.uk/

Chief: Libn: Ms Alison Henesey BA, MCLIP
Entry: ref only; adv appt for main rsrch colln; study colln open to public without appt at weekends
Open: Study Colln: 1st full weekend of every month Sat-Sun 1000-1600; *Rsrch Colln:* by appt
Subj: all aspects of coal mining in England; mining hist; social hist of mining life; biography; lit; industrial relations; working conditions; health & safety; coal mining tech; geol *Collns: Bks & Pamphs:* fiction & poetry related to coal industry; trade catalogues of coal machinery; early printed material on coal production (18C onwards); mining textbks; Inspectors of Mines reports; Royal Commission reports; Natl Coal Board pubns; union pubns; coal & mining journals (incl Colliery Guardian, Mining Journal etc); transactions of socs, e.g., Instn of Mining Engineers *Other:* the museum also holds a large colln of art & photography relating to coal mining
Equip: copier (10p per sheet) *Svcs:* info, ref
Stock: bks/c5000; periodcls/20
Classn: UDC *Auto Sys:* Alice *Staff:* Libns: 1

S2069

South West Yorkshire Mental Health NHS Trust, Fieldhead Hospital Library

The Edu Centre, Fieldhead Hosp, Ouchthorpe Ln, Wakefield, W Yorkshire, WF1 3SP (01924-328608; *fax:* 01924-328616)
Email: michael.morley@swyt.nhs.uk

Gov Body: South West Yorkshire Mental Health NHS Trust *Chief:* Libn: Mr Michael Morley
Entry: Trust staff only *Open:* Mon-Thu 0845-1645, Fri 0845-1615
Subj: health; psychiatry; health mgmt; psy; clinical effectiveness; occupational therapy; psychotherapy; schizophrenia; health promotion; nursing; physiotherapy *Co-op Schemes:* ILL
Equip: computers (incl wd-proc, internet & CD-ROM) *Online:* via Dialog: Medline, PsycInfo, CINAHL, Embase, BNI, AMED, DH-Data; via Proquest: 840 full-text e-journals *Svcs:* info, internet training
Stock: bks/c5000; periodcls/c50; pamphs/c1000; videos/20; CD-ROMs/10
Classn: NLM (Wessex) *Staff:* Non-Prof: 1

S2070

Stephen Beaumont Museum of Mental Health, Printed Collections

Fieldhead Hosp, Ouchthorpe Ln, Wakefield, W Yorkshire, WF1 3SP (01924-328654)

Gov Body: Wakefield & Pontefract Community Health Trust

Entry: adv appt *Open:* term: Wed 1000-1300, 1330-1600
Subj: psychiatric hist *Collns: Bks & Pamphs:* texts etc from original Asylum Medical Lib *Archvs:* the bulk of the Museum's records have been taken over by the Archvs Svc of Wakefield Metropolitan Council (see **A497**); remaining archival colln consists of records or copies in display cabinets
Equip: copier, fax, computer (with wd-proc) *Svcs:* info, ref
Stock: bks/100
Pubns: Stanley Royd: 150 Years: A Hist (£2.50 incl p&p)
Staff: Non-Prof: 1 PT

S2071

Wakefield College Learning Centres

Margaret St, Wakefield, W Yorkshire, WF1 2DH (01924-789220; *fax:* 01924-789340)
Email: wakelrc@wakcoll.ac.uk
Internet: http://www.wakcoll.ac.uk/

Chief: Snr Learning Centre Mgr: Mrs Helen Sherwood BA(Hons), PGCE, PGDipLIS (h.sherwood@wakcoll.ac.uk) *Other Snr Staff:* Learning Centre Mgrs: Ms Janet Lingwood MSc, Ms Margaret Lowham & Mr John Rhodes
Assoc Libs: THORNES PK CENTRE LIB, Horbury Rd, Wakefield, W Yorkshire, WF2 8QZ; WHITWOOD CENTRE LIB, Four Ln Ends, Castleford, W Yorkshire, WF10 5NF
Entry: students & staff at Wakefield Coll *Open:* term: Mon-Wed 0830-2000, Thu 0830-1700, Fri 0830-1630; vac: Mon-Fri 0830-1630, Sat 0900-1230
Subj: all academic subjs *Co-op Schemes:* BLDSC, local authority ILL
Equip: copier, 24 computers (all with wd-proc, internet & CD-ROM) *Disabled:* HAL speech recognition software *Svcs:* info, ref
Stock: bks/45000; periodcls/150; audios/50; videos/1000; CD-ROMs/50
Classn: DDC *Auto Sys:* Heritage
Staff: Libns: 3 Non-Prof: 7 *Exp:* £65000 (1999-2000); £65000 (2000-01)

Wallingford

S2072

Centre for Ecology and Hydrology, Wallingford Library

Maclean Bldg, Crowmarsh Gifford, Wallingford, Oxfordshire, OX10 8BB (01491-692266; *fax:* 01491-692424)
Email: wllibrary@ceh.ac.uk
Internet: http://library.ceh.ac.uk/wallingford.htm

Gov Body: Nat Environment Rsrch Council (NERC); part of CEH Lib Svcs (see **S1786**); provides lib svcs for both CEH Wallingford & British Geological Survey Wallingford (Groundwater Systems & Water Quality Programme) *Chief:* Libn: Mrs Sue Wharton BA, MCLIP *Dep:* Ms Fiona Sutherland
Entry: bona fide rsrchers by prior arrangement *Open:* Mon-Fri 0900-1700
Subj: all aspects of hydrological sci; maths; physical & applied hydrology; meteorology; climatology; geomorphology; soil sci; agric hydrology; water resources; water quality; ecology; environment *Collns: Bks & Pamphs:* Hurst Colln (Nile hydrology); Rofe Colln (water legislation); small colln of bks belonging to the British Geological Survey *Co-op Schemes:* BLDSC, ILL
Equip: copier, computer (incl CD-ROM) *Online:* variety of databases for staff use only
Stock: bks/15000; periodcls/400
Classn: own *Auto Sys:* Unicorn
Pubns: Lib Guide; Staff Pubns List (both free)
Staff: Libns: 2 Non-Prof: 1

Special Libraries

Wallsend ▼ Warwick

Wallsend

S2073 British Maritime Technology, Wallsend Research Station Library

Wallsend Rsrch Station, Wallsend, Tyne & Wear, NE28 6UY (0191-262-5242; *fax:* 0191-263-8754)
Email: gsmith@bmtshipdes.demon.co.uk
Internet: http://www.bmt.org/

Chief: Libn: Ms Gillian Smith
Assoc Libs: BRITISH MARITIME TECH LIB (see **S2030**)
Subj: marine tech; naval eng *Collns: Archvs:* reports & other pubns of British Ship Rsrch Assoc (BSRA) *Co-op Schemes:* BLDSC, ILL
Equip: m-reader, copier
Stock: bks/5000; periodcls/250; m-forms/3000
Pubns: BMT Focus (free); Technical Reports (£40-£100); misc technical pubns; BMT Abstracts (monthly, £270 pa in UK + £20 p&p overseas)

S2074 North Tyneside College, Learning Resource Centre

Embleton Ave, Wallsend, Tyne & Wear, NE28 9NJ (0191-229-5243; *fax:* 0191-229-5243)
Email: gillian.rutherford@ntyneside.ac.uk
Internet: http://www.ntyneside.ac.uk/

Chief: LRC Mgr: Ms Gillian Rutherford BA(Hons), PGDipLRCM *Dep:* Dep Coll Libn: Mr Mark Callan MLitt
Assoc Libs: RIVERSIDE LRC, Riverside Centre, Minton Ln, North Shields, Tyne & Wear, NE29 6DQ, Learning Resource Offcr: Ms Linda Merritt BA(Hons) (0181-200-5219)
Entry: full access for Coll staff & students; others ref only *Open: Wallsend LRC:* term: Mon-Thu 0900-2000, Fri 0900-1600, Sat 1000-1300; vac: Mon-Fri 0900-1600; *Riverside LRC:* term: Mon-Thu 0900-2100, Fri 0900-1600, Sat 1000-1300
Subj: all subjs; GCSE; A level; undergrad; vocational; Higher Nationals *Co-op Schemes:* NRLB, BLDSC
Equip: video viewer, copier, 7 computers (all with wd-proc, 6 with internet & 1 with CD-ROM)
Disabled: text magnifier, teletext *Online:* Infotrac Onefile (free) *Svcs:* info, ref, biblio
Stock: bks/18000; periodcls/55; audios/100; videos/570; CD-ROMs/15; info files/300
Classn: DDC *Auto Sys:* Olib
Staff: Libns: 3 *Other Prof:* 1 *Non-Prof:* 6 (for both LRCs)

Walsall

S2075 Manor Hospital Postgraduate Medical Centre Library

Manor Hosp, Moat Rd, Walsall, W Midlands, WS2 9PS (01922-656628; *fax:* 01922-656612)
Email: duffusj@wht.walsallh-tr.wmids.nhs.uk

Gov Body: Walsall Hosps NHS Trust *Chief:* Libn: Mrs J. Duffus BA(Hons)
Entry: medical staff of Trust only; others by adv appt for ref only *Open:* Mon-Fri 0900-1700
Subj: medicine *Co-op Schemes:* WMHLN

Equip: copier, 5 computers (incl 4 internet)
Online: Medline, Cochrane *Svcs:* info, ref
Stock: bks/c5500; periodcls/130; slides/5 sets; audios/9; videos/80
Classn: NLM *Auto Sys:* Heritage
Staff: Libns: 1 *Non-Prof:* 0.81

S2076 The New Art Gallery Walsall, Art Library

(formerly Walsall Museum & Art Gallery)
Gallery Sq, Walsall, W Midlands, WS2 8LG (01922-654400/19; *fax:* 01922-654401)
Email: info@artatwalsall.org.uk
Internet: http://www.artatwalsall.org.uk/

Type: local authority *Gov Body:* Walsall Metropolitan Borough Council (see **P192**) *Chief:* Interpretation Curator: Mr Oliver Buckley *Other Snr Staff:* Collns Curator: Ms Jo Digger
Entry: ref only, adv appt advised; appt required for Archvs (contact Collns Curator on 01922-654428)
Open: Tue 1000-1600 (term only), Thu 1000-1500 (all year); other times by prior appt
Subj: arts; contemporary art; historic art; arch; world cultures; museum & gallery edu *Collns: Bks & Pamphs:* bks, art journals & catalogues comprising Walsall's only specialist art lib; bks relating to Garman Ryan Art Colln *Archvs:* materials relating to Garman Ryan Art Colln & to the life of Jacob Epstein (sculptor)
Equip: copier, 8 computers (all with wd-proc, internet & CD-ROM) *Officer-in-Charge:* Interpretation Curator, as above *Svcs:* info, ref
Stock: bks/50 linear m; periodcls/12; photos/500; some pamphs, videos, CD-ROMs & archvs *Acqs Offcr:* Interpretation Curator, as above
Classn: DDC
Pubns: Just Like Drawing in your Dinner – 3-5 Year Olds (£15); The People's Shows – Collns by Local People (£5); Brenda & Other Stories – HIV-ART & You; START – 3-5 year Olds' Interactive Exhib (£5)
Staff: Other Prof: 20 *Non-Prof:* 20

S2077 Staffordshire Archaeological and Historical Society, Library

c/o 6 Lawson Cl, Aldridge, Walsall, W Midlands, WS9 0RX

Type: learned soc *Gov Body:* Staffordshire Archaeological & Historical Soc
Subj: local study (Staffordshire hist & archaeo)
Collns: Bks & Pamphs: colln of own pubn (Annual Transactions) & transactions of other similar socs with whom copies are exchanged; the Soc's own pubns are held at the above addr, exchange copies are held at Lichfield Lib
Svcs: info, ref
Stock: bks/c100
Pubns: Transactions (1 pa, free to membs); back issues available (£1-£5 mostly); Index to Vols I-XXXIV (£3 incl p&p)

S2078 University of Wolverhampton, Manor Campus Library

Edu & Training Centre, Manor Hosp, Pleck Rd, Walsall, W Midlands, WS2 9PS (01922-721172 x7181; *fax:* 01922-649008)
Email: m.nicholls@wlv.ac.uk
Internet: http://www.wlv.ac.uk/snm/

Gov Body: Univ of Wolverhampton (see **S2141**)
Chief: Resource Libn: Miss Marie Nicholls
Assoc Libs: other Nursing & Midwifery Libs: NEWCROSS LIB (see **S2142**); RUSSELLS HALL LIB, Dudley, W Midlands; plus all Univ of Wolverhampton Libs

Entry: full borrowing rights for Univ of Wolverhampton students & nursing & midwifery students; external rights for Trust staff *Open:* Mon, Wed-Fri 0900-1700, Tue 0900-2000
Subj: nursing; midwifery *Co-op Schemes:* BLDSC, WMRHLN
Equip: fax, video viewer, copier, 5 computers (incl 3 wd-proc, 2 internet & 1 CD-ROM) *Online:* Medline, CINAHL, CancerLit, Mental Health Colln, BL OPAC 97, BUBL, NISS, online OPAC *Svcs:* info, ref, biblio, indexing
Stock: bks/13000; periodcls/108; videos/80
Classn: LC *Auto Sys:* Talis
Staff: Libns: 1 *Non-Prof:* 4 PT

S2079 Walsall College of Arts and Technology, European Design Centre Library

St Paul's St, Walsall, W Midlands, WS1 1XN (01922-657078; *fax:* 01922-657083)
Email: pearson@walcat.ac.uk
Internet: http://www.walcat.ac.uk/

Chief: Libn: Mrs Janet Pearson
Entry: adv appt *Open:* term: Mon-Thu 0900-2000, Fri 0945-1230, 1300-1630; vac: Mon-Thu 0900-1630, Fri 0945-1630
Subj: all subjs; genl; GCSE; A level; undergrad; postgrad; vocational; local studies (Walsall); hair & beauty care; business; mgmt; computing; hospitality mgmt; catering; teacher training
Collns: Bks & Pamphs: some BSI *Co-op Schemes:* BLDSC, ILL
Equip: copiers, video viewer, 200 computers (all with wd-proc, internet & networked CD-ROM), 3 additional stand-alone CD-ROM readers
Stock: bks/30000+; periodcls/100+; slides/500; audios/200; videos/2000
Classn: DDC *Auto Sys:* Olib 7
Staff: Libns: 3 *Non-Prof:* 7

S2080 Walsall Health Authority District Library

Lichfield House, Lichfield St, Walsall, W Midlands, WS1 1TE (01922-720255; *fax:* 01922-656000)

Chief: Sec to the Authority: Mrs K.J. Sharpe
Entry: Health Authority staff only *Open:* Mon-Fri 0900-1700
Subj: generalities; psy; social sci; tech; health
Collns: Bks & Pamphs: mainly in-house reports & pubns
Equip: Online: Dialog, DIMDI, Datastar
Stock: bks/300
Classn: DDC *Staff: Non-Prof:* 0.2

Ware

S2081 All Nations Christian College Library

Easneye, Ware, Hertfordshire, SG12 8LX (01920-461243; *fax:* 01920-462997)
Email: library@allnations.ac.uk
Internet: http://www.allnations.ac.uk/

Gov Body: All Nations Christian Coll *Chief:* Libn: Mr R.S. Bruce MA(Hons), BD(Hons), DipLib (s.bruce@allnations.ac.uk)
Entry: staff & students of the Coll, external users may apply in person or in writing *Open:* term: Mon-Sat 0800-2200; vac: Mon-Fri 0900-1700; only open to external users Mon-Fri 0900-1700 (year round)
Subj: theology; missiology; Christianity & other religions *Collns: Archvs:* All Nations Missionary Union Archvs; All Nations Bible Coll Archvs; All Nations Missionary Coll Archvs; All Nations

Christian Coll Archvs; Mount Hermon Missionary Training Coll Archvs; Ridgelands Bible Coll Archvs; The Missionary Training Colony Archvs; Buxton Family papers *Co-op Schemes:* ABTAPL *Equip:* 3 m-readers, video viewer, 2 copiers, 5 networked computers, stand-alone computer (with internet & CD-ROM) *Svcs:* ref, biblio, indexing *Stock:* bks/37750; periodcls/180; maps/200; m-forms/350; audios/2480; videos/630; CD-ROMs/44; archvs/10 linear m *Acqs Offcr:* Libn, as above *Classn:* DDC *Auto Sys:* own *Pubns:* Lib Guide (free) *Staff: Libns:* 1 *Non-Prof:* 1 *Exp:* £21000 (1999-2000); £23000 (2000-01)

S2082
Hertford Regional College, Library and Learning Resources
Scotts Rd, Ware, Hertfordshire, SG12 0BB (01992-411977; *fax:* 01992-411978) *Internet:* http://www.hertreg.ac.uk/

Chief: Head of Lib & Learning Resources: Mr Ian Radcliffe BSc(Econ), PGCE, DipLib, MCLIP, DPSE *Assoc Libs:* WARE CENTRE LIB, addr as above; BROXBOURNE CENTRE LIB, Turnford, Broxbourne, Hertfordshire, EN10 6AF (01992-411565) *Entry:* ref only, at Libn's discretion, for non-staff/students of Coll *Open: Ware:* term: Mon-Thu 0900-1930, Fri 0900-1600; vac: Mon-Fri 1000-1300, 1400-1600; *Broxbourne:* term: Mon-Thu 0845-2000, Fri 0845-1645; vac: Mon-Fri 1000-1300, 1400-1600 *Subj:* all subjs; GCSE; A level; undergrad *Co-op Schemes:* BLDSC, ILL between all Hertfordshire Colls & Univ of Hertfordshire *Equip:* video viewers, fax, copier, computers (with wd-proc, internet, CD-ROM) *Disabled:* image enlarger (at Broxbourne) *Stock:* bks/50000; periodcls/200; slides/2000; videos/4000; figs are for both sites *Classn:* DDC *Auto Sys:* Voyager *Staff: Libns:* 4 *Other Prof:* 1 *Non-Prof:* 5

Wareham

S2083
Butterfly Conservation, Library
Manor Yard, East Lulworth, Wareham, Dorset, BH20 5QP (0870-774-4309; *fax:* 01929-400210) *Email:* info@butterfly-conservation.org *Internet:* http://www.butterfly-conservation.org/

Gov Body: Natl Exec Cttee *Chief:* staffed by volunteers *Entry:* by correspondence *Subj:* entomology (lepidoptera), ecology & conservation *Stock:* bks/366; periodcls/some

S2084
The Tank Museum, Reference Library and Archive
Bovington Camp, Wareham, Dorset, BH20 6JG (01929-405096; *fax:* 01929-462410) *Email:* librarian@tankmuseum.co.uk *Internet:* http://www.tankmuseum.co.uk/

Gov Body: The Trustees of the Tank Museum *Chief:* Libn: Mrs Janice Tait MA, MCLIP, DMS (JaniceT@tankmuseum.co.uk) *Other Snr Staff:* Historian: Mr David Fletcher (DavidF@tankmuseum.co.uk) *Entry:* by adv appt *Open:* Mon-Fri 1000-1630 *Subj:* design & development of tanks & armoured vehicles; military hist; hist of mechanised armoured & warfare *Collns: Bks & Pamphs:* large colln of pubns on armoured warfare & associated subjs, incl: textbks on tank design; popular monographs;

British & internatl armoured regimental hists; biographies of most of the pioneers of British tank design; bks related to uniforms & weapons *Archvs:* document archv incl: handbks, technical manuals & historical documents; documents on training, tactics & techniques of armoured warfare; reports on captured equip; Genl J.F.C. Fuller's Great War diary; MSS of Colonel Sir Albert Stern's unpublished bk on Great War tank design & his scrapbk; the most significant part of the colln is the Archv of War Diaries covering virtually every armoured regiment of both world wars *Other:* extensive colln of photos & technical drawings covering fighting vehicle design; growing colln of personal hists *Equip:* m-reader, copier, clr copier, fax, video viewer, computers (incl 1 wd-proc, 1 CD-ROM & 1 internet) *Officer-in-Charge:* Libn, as above *Stock:* bks/6000; periodcls/150; photos/250000; slides/15000; maps/5 m shelving; audios/150; videos/5050; archvs/490 m shelving *Acqs Offcr:* Libn, as above *Classn:* UDC *Auto Sys:* MUSIMS *Staff: Libns:* 1 *Non-Prof:* 2.5 *Exp:* £3000 (2000-01); most materials acquired through donation

Warley

S2085
Sandwell College, Smethwick Campus Learning Centre
Crocketts Ln, Smethwick, Warley, W Midlands, B66 3BU (0121-253-6203; *fax:* 0121-253-6322) *Internet:* http://www.sandwell.ac.uk/

Chief: Learning Centre Mgr: Mrs Barbara Thompson BA *Assoc Libs:* WEDNESBURY CAMPUS LEARNING CENTRE (see **S2095**); WEST BROMWICH CAMPUS LEARNING CENTRE (see **S2103**) *Entry:* students, lecturers & support staff; outside users ref only *Open:* Mon-Thu 0830-2000, Fri 1000-1500 *Subj:* all subjs; genl; GCSE; A level; undergrad; vocational *Collns: Bks & Pamphs:* Die-Casting Soc Colln *Co-op Schemes:* ILL, catalogue shared with Sandwell Public Libs (see **P158**) *Equip:* 2 m-readers, m-printer, 4 video viewers, copier, 40 computers (all with wd-proc, internet & CD-ROM), room for hire, LCD projector, AV equip *Disabled:* Kurzweil, Aladdin *Online:* Infotrac & others via JISC *Svcs:* info, ref *Stock:* bks/24000; periodcls/100; audios/200; videos/1000 *Classn:* DDC *Auto Sys:* Genesis *Staff: Libns:* 1 *Other Prof:* 2 *Non-Prof:* 4 *Exp:* £40000 (1999-2000)

Warminster

S2086
Longleat House, Library and Archives
Estate Office, Warminster, Wiltshire, BA12 7NW (01985-845434; *fax:* 01985-844885) *Email:* longleatlibrary@btinternet.com *Internet:* http://www.longleat.co.uk/

Gov Body: The Most Honorable the Marquess of Bath *Chief:* Libn & Archivist: Dr Kate Harris MA, DPhil *Entry:* open to established scholars by appt only *Open:* Mon-Fri 1000-1300, 1415-1615 *Collns: Bks & Pamphs:* medieval MSS; incunabula; late 17C-early 18C pamphs; French Revolution pamphs; Balkan affairs; nat hist; Lib of Beriah Botfield *Archvs:* Thynne, Dudley, Devereux, Seymour, Talbot, Whitelocke & Portland papers; Carteret & Granville papers; Botfield papers; records of Glastonbury Abbey; estate papers & maps (chiefly Wiltshire & Somerset)

Equip: m-reader, copier, computer (with wd-proc, staff only) *Stock:* bks/40000; archvs/2040 linear ft *Pubns:* Longleat Lib; Glastonbury Abbey Records at Longleat House: A Summary List; Catalogues to Thynne, Dudley, Devereux etc papers, included in Microform (Wakefield) Limited Edition; Descriptive Catalogue of Mediaeval MSS (in preparation); Computer Catalogue of Estate Papers & 2nd series of Thynne Papers (in preparation) *Staff: Libns:* 1 *Other Prof:* 2

Warrington

S2087
Council for the Central Laboratory of the Research Councils, Daresbury Laboratory, Chadwick Library
Keckwick Ln, Daresbury, Warrington, Cheshire, WA4 4AD (01925-603397; *fax:* 01925-603779) *Email:* library@dl.ac.uk *Internet:* http://www.cclrc.ac.uk/

Gov Body: Office of Sci & Tech *Chief:* Libn: Mrs Debbie Franks BSc, MCLIP *Assoc Libs:* CCLRC RUTHERFORD APPLETON LABORATORY LIB (see **S535**) *Entry:* tel libn in adv to arrange access *Open:* access 24 hrs; staffed: Mon-Thu 0830-1700, Fri 0830-1600 *Subj:* atomic, molecular & solid state physics; nuclear physics; biophysics; biochem; chem; metallurgy; surface sci; computing & computational sci; eng; accelerator physics; synchrotron radiation *Co-op Schemes:* BLDSC *Equip:* m-reader, m-printer, copier *Online:* Web of Science, Inspec, Info4education *Stock:* bks/23000; periodcls/160 *Classn:* UDC *Auto Sys:* Unicorn *Staff: Libns:* 2 *Non-Prof:* 1 *Exp:* £122500 (1999-2000); £130500 (2000-01)

S2088
Warrington Collegiate Institute, Learning Resource Centre
Winwick Rd, Warrington, Cheshire, WA2 8QA (*tel & fax:* 01925-494422) *Email:* learner.services@warr.ac.uk *Internet:* http://www.warr.ac.uk/

Gov Body: Warrington Collegiate Inst *Chief:* LRC Mgr: Ms Ellen Cassidy (e.cassidy@warr.ac.uk) *Entry:* full access to those enrolled on a course at WCI; ref only for membs of public *Open:* term: Mon-Thu 0845-2000, Fri 0845-1630, Sat 0900-1300; vac: Mon-Fri 0900-1600 *Subj:* all subjs; genl; GCSE; A level; undergrad; vocational *Co-op Schemes:* BLDSC *Equip:* copier, fax, 3 video viewers, 54 computers (all with wd-proc & internet, 2 with CD-ROM) *Online:* Infotrac Onefile & Newspaper Database, Emerald Management Journals, Literature Online, JANET *Svcs:* info, ref, biblio, AV svcs, stationery shop *Stock:* bks/25000; periodcls/100; audios/50; videos/500; CD-ROMs/20 *Acqs Offcr:* LRC Mgr, as above *Classn:* DDC *Auto Sys:* Heritage *Staff: Libns:* 2 *Non-Prof:* 3

Warwick

S2089
Horticulture Research International, Wellesbourne Library
Wellesbourne, Warwick, CV35 9EF (01789-470382; *fax:* 01789-470552) *Internet:* http://www2.hri.ac.uk/

Special Libraries

Warwick ▼ West Malling

(Hortic Rsrch Internatl, Wellesbourne Lib cont)
Type: rsrch **Gov Body:** Exec Cttee (under independent chairman) reporting to Minister of Agric **Chief:** Libn: Ms Claire Singleton BA, MA **Assoc Libs:** HRI EAST MALLING LIB (see **S2107**) **Entry:** ref only at Libn's discretion, adv appt necessary **Open:** Mon-Thu 0900-1700, Fri 0900-1600
Subj: plant sci; entomology; hortic **Collns:** Bks & Pamphs: small colln of rare 18C & 19C gardening bks **Co-op Schemes:** BLDSC
Equip: m-reader, copier, computer (incl CD-ROM) **Online:** Dialog (fees by arrangement) **Svcs:** info, ref
Stock: bks/40000; periodcls/400
Classn: UDC
Pubns: Annual Report of HRI (£15)
Staff: Libns: 1 Non-Prof: 1.5

S2090 ✚
South Warwickshire Medical Education Centre Library
John Turner Bldg, Warwick Hosp, Lakin Rd, Warwick, CV34 5BW (01926-495321; *fax:* 01926-400895)
Email: veronica.mitchell@swh.nhs.uk

Chief: Lib Svcs Mgr: Ms Veronica Mitchell **Dep:** Libn: Mr Nicholas Harden
Entry: NHS staff only **Open:** Mon, Wed 0845-1700, Tue, Thu 0845-2000, Fri 0845-1645
Subj: health; medicine **Co-op Schemes:** ILL, PLCS
Equip: copier (A4/5p, A3/10p), fax, 6 computers (all with wd-proc, internet & CD-ROM) **Online:** OVID biomedical databases **Svcs:** info, ref
Stock: bks/6500; periodcls/122; videos/110
Classn: NLM **Auto Sys:** Autolib
Staff: Libns: 2 Non-Prof: 1

S2091 🏛️🏛️
Warwickshire Museum, Library
Market Pl, Warwick, CV34 4SA (01926-412500; *fax:* 01926-419840)
Email: museum@warwickshire.gov.uk
Internet: http://www.warwickshire.gov.uk/

Type: local authority **Gov Body:** Warwickshire County Council (see **P194**) **Chief:** County Museum Curator: Dr W.C. Allan BSc, PhD, FMA
Assoc Libs: WARWICKSHIRE SITES & MONUMENTS RECORD, Museum Field Svcs, The Butts, Warwick, CV34 4SS (01926-412734; *fax:* 01926-412974; *email:* sitesandmonuments@warwickshire.gov.uk)
Entry: access to lib by arrangement only **Open:** Mon-Fri 1000-1700
Subj: Warwickshire: local hist; archaeo; biology; geol; sci & maths; geog & hist; museology
Equip: copier, room hire **Staff:** Other Prof: 8

Watford

S2092 ✚
Watford General Hospital Library
Postgrad Medical Centre, Watford Genl Hosp, Vicarage Rd, Watford, Hertfordshire, WD1 8HB (01923-217437; *fax:* 01923-217909)
Email: library.watford@whht.nhs.uk

Gov Body: West Hertfordshire Hosps NHS Trust **Chief:** Libn: Miss Janet Reynolds BA, MSc, CertEd, DipLib, MCLIP (janet.reynolds@whht.nhs.uk)
Assoc Libs: LES CANNON MEMORIAL LIB (see **S1620**); HEMEL HEMPSTEAD HOSP LIB (see **S798**); ST ALBANS CITY HOSP, STAFF LIB & INFO SVC (see **S1962**)
Entry: genl public, ref only by adv appt **Open:** Mon-Fri 0900-1700 (24 hr access for medical staff)
Subj: medicine; health care **Co-op Schemes:** NTRLIS, BLDSC, NULJ
Equip: photocopier(5p-10p per pg), computers (incl wd-proc, internet & CD-ROM) **Online:** Medline, CINAHL, Cochrane, AMED, ClinPsych
Stock: bks/3700; periodcls/100; videos/100
Classn: NLM
Pubns: Lib Bulletin; Audit Bulletin
Staff: Libns: 1 Non-Prof: 0.95

S2093 🎓
West Hertfordshire College (Cassio Campus), Teaching and Learning Resources Service
Cassio Campus, Langley Rd, Watford, Hertfordshire, WD1 3RH (01923-812200; *fax:* 01923-812232)
Email: marilynw@cwestherts.ac.uk
Internet: http://www.westherts.ac.uk/

Chief: Team Leader (Cassio Campus): Mrs Marilyn Williams BA, MCLIP
Assoc Libs: DACORUM CAMPUS LIB (see **S799**); LEGATTS CAMPUS LIB, Leggatts Way, Watford, Hertfordshire, Team Leader: Mrs Pam Acreman (01923-814898); WATFORD CAMPUS LIB (see **S2094**)
Entry: adv appt, ref only, external borrowing possible **Open:** term: Mon 0845-1700, Tue-Thu 0845-2000, Fri 0845-1630; vac: Mon-Thu 0900-1230, 1330-1700, Fri 100-1230, 1330-1630
Subj: GCSE; A level; vocational; social sci; lang; arts; lit; hist; geog; catering; hairdressing; leisure; tourism; retail **Co-op Schemes:** ILL
Equip: video viewer, fax, copier (5p), clr copier (75p), 11 computers (all with wd-proc & internet, 1 with CD-ROM), digital camera, video camera **Online:** Dialog, Profile (free) **Svcs:** info, ref, biblio
Stock: bks/17000; periodcls/80; audios/120; videos/350; CD-ROMs/46 **Acqs Offcr:** Team Leader, as above
Classn: DDC **Auto Sys:** Voyager
Staff: Libns: 1.5 Other Prof: 1 Non-Prof: 5

S2094 🎓
West Hertfordshire College (Watford Campus), Teaching and Learning Resources Service
Watford Campus, Hempstead Rd, Watford, Hertfordshire, WD1 3EZ (01923-812554)
Internet: http://www.westherts.ac.uk/

Chief: Team Leader (Watford Campus): Ms Anne Russell
Assoc Libs: CASSIO CAMPUS LIB (see **S2093**); DACORUM CAMPUS LIB (see **S799**); LEGGATTS CAMPUS LIB, Leggatts Way, Watford, Hertfordshire, Team Leader: Mrs Pam Acreman (01923-814898)
Entry: students & staff of coll; external membership available; ref only for non-membs **Open:** term: Mon-Fri 0845-2100; vac: Mon-Fri 0900-1230, 1330-1700
Subj: business; mgmt; accountancy; office skills; leisure; eng; photography; art; maths; sci; computing; advertising; design; marketing; printing; leisure; graphic arts; tech **Collns:** Bks & Pamphs: printing & packaging colln
Equip: video viewer, copier, m-reader, m-printer
Stock: bks/52800; periodcls/396; slides/2500; pamphs/2900; audios/440; videos/150; AVs/2750
Classn: DDC **Auto Sys:** Voyager

Wednesbury

S2095 🎓
Sandwell College, Wednesbury Campus Learning Centre
Woden Rd South, Wednesbury, W Midlands, WS10 0PE (0121-253-6003; *fax:* 0121-253-6104)
Email: eleanor.cook@sandwell.ac.uk
Internet: http://www.sandwell.ac.uk/

Chief: Lib Mgr: Mrs Anne Hughes **Dep:** Dep Mgr: Mrs E. Cook
Assoc Libs: SMETHWICK CAMPUS LRC (see **S2085**); WEST BROMWICH CAMPUS LRC (see **S2103**)
Entry: ref only **Open:** term: Mon-Thu 0830-2000, Fri 0830-1600
Subj: social sci; sci; maths; tech; arts; lit; mgmt; accountancy **Collns:** Bks & Pamphs: all England law reports; current statutes (1946-date); govt statistics **Co-op Schemes:** WMRLB, BLDSC, Sandwell Public Lib
Equip: m-reader, 2 video viewers, 2 copiers, 32 computers (all with wd-proc, 15 with internet & 20 with CD-ROM, £3 per session), 2 scanners **Disabled:** Kurzweil **Online:** Encyclopaedia Britannica **Svcs:** info, ref, IT, BBC Webwise
Stock: bks/20079; periodcls/149; maps/60; audios/20; videos/320
Classn: DDC **Auto Sys:** Genesis
Staff: Libns: 1 Non-Prof: 5

Wells

S2096 🔑🖐️
Wells Cathedral Library
West Cloister, Wells, Somerset, BA5 2PA (01749-674483; *fax:* 01749-832210)
Email: library@wellscathedral.uk.net

Gov Body: Chapter of Wells Cathedral **Chief:** Chancellor of Wells Cathedral: The Revd Canon M.W. Matthews MA, AKC **Dep:** Cathedral Archivist: Miss Anne Crawford MPhil, FRHistS **Other Snr Staff:** Libns: Miss Jane Swinyard MCLIP & Mrs Pam Burrough MCLIP
Entry: *Reading Room:* by annual subscription; *Old Lib (pre-1800 bks):* by written appt for postgrads (as lib of last resort) **Open:** *Reading Room (subscribers only):* Mon-Thu 1000-1200, 1400-1600; *Reading Room (visitors):* Fri-Sat 1430-1630
Subj: religion; phil; arts; geog; hist **Collns:** Bks & Pamphs: colln of theological, patristic & other lit of interest to 17C & 18C clerics **Archvs:** archvs of the Dean & Chapter (11C-date) **Co-op Schemes:** UWE proj
Equip: computer (with internet) **Svcs:** info, ref, biblio
Classn: DDC, 18C press marks for pre-1800 materials
Pubns: Wells Cathedral Lib (£1); postcards (10p)
Staff: Libns: 2 PT Other Prof: 1 PT archivist

S2097 🔑🏛️
Wells Museum Library
8 Cathedral Green, Wells, Somerset, BA5 2UE (01749-673477; *fax:* 01749-675337)

Gov Body: Trustees & Mgrs of Wells Museum **Chief:** Hon Libn: Mr Graeme Osborn
Entry: ref only, adv appt desirable but not necessary **Open:** Nov-Mar: Mon, Wed-Fri 1100-1600; Apr-Oct: Mon-Fri 1100-1600
Subj: local study (South of the Mendip Hills, City of Wells & Wells Cathedral); local caves; prehistory & scis of Somerset **Collns:** Bks & Pamphs: Somerset Archaeological & Nat Hist Soc, full set (1849-date); Notes & Queries for Somerset & Dorset, full set (1890-date) **Other:** Platten Bequest (spelaeological bks & periodcls); Reid Bequest (local material); large scale local maps

Equip: m-reader, copier, computer (with wd-proc), 2 rooms for hire, light table
Stock: bks/2000; periodcls/5, plus 15 no longer current; slides/various, included in Museum stock; illusts/650, incl photos; pamphs/600; maps/80
Classn: own
Staff: Non-Prof: 8 *Exp:* £130 (1999-2000); £210 (2000-01)

Welwyn Garden City

S2098 ✚
Bedfordshire and Hertfordshire Health Library
(formerly East & North Hertfordshire Health Authority, Medical Lib)
Charter House, Parkway, Welwyn Garden City, Hertfordshire, AL8 6JL (01707-361264; *fax:* 01707-390864)
Email: patti.bristow@his-herts.nhs.uk

Gov Body: Royston, Buntington & Bishops Stortford Primary Care Trust *Chief:* Libn: Mrs Patti Bristow MCLIP
Assoc Libs: ST ALBANS LIB, Tonman House, Victoria St, St Albans, Hertfordshire, AL1 3ER (01727-792925); BEDFORD LIB, Bedford Heights, Manton Ln, Bedford, MK41 7PA (01234-315776); Libn (both sites): Mrs Patti Bristow as above
Entry: external users by prior appt *Open:* Mon-Fri 0900-1700
Subj: health; medicine; allied subjs *Co-op Schemes:* BLDSC, ILL with local NHS Trusts (Health Libs Alliance)
Equip: copier, computer (for database searches)
Svcs: info, ref, biblio
Auto Sys: InMagic DBTextworks v4.01
Staff: Libns: 1 *Non-Prof:* 4

S2099 ✚
Queen Elizabeth II Hospital Library
Howlands, Welwyn Garden City, Hertfordshire, AL7 4HQ (01707-328111 x4565; *fax:* 01707-390425)
Gov Body: East & North Hertfordshire NHS Trust
Chief: Libn: Ms J.M. Lomas BA, DipIS, MCLIP (joan.lomas@qeii.enherts-tr.nhs.uk) *Dep:* Mrs Gill Jones BA, MA, MCLIP (gill.jones@britishlibrary.net)
Assoc Libs: NURSING LIB; PATIENTS' LIB (both at same addr); *other Trust Libs:* LISTER HOSP LIB (see **S1974**)
Entry: NHS staff & students; *Open:* Mon-Thu 0930-1715, Fri 0930-1600
Subj: medicine; nursing *Co-op Schemes:* BLDSC, BMA
Equip: 2 fax (varies), 2 copiers (5p), 10 computers (all with wd-proc & CD-ROM, 7 with internet)
Online: networked databases *Svcs:* info, ref, biblio
Stock: bks/8500; periodcls/152
Classn: NLM (Wessex) *Auto Sys:* InMagic
Staff: Libns: 2 *Non-Prof:* 3

Wembley

S2100 🏛
International Rubber Study Group, Library
Heron House, 109-115 Wembley Hill Rd, Wembley, Middlesex, HA9 8DA (020-8903-7727; *fax:* 020-8903-2848)
Email: irsg@rubberstudy.com
Internet: http://www.rubberstudy.com/

Type: inter-governmental *Gov Body:* Heads of Delegation of the IRSG *Chief:* Secretary-Genl: Dr A.F.S. Budiman *Other Snr Staff:* Statistician: Mr Darren Cooper (statistics@rubberstudy.com)
Entry: by appt, ref only *Open:* Mon-Fri 1000-1600
Subj: economic & statistical info on nat & synthetic rubber & associated products

Equip: m-reader, copier (with permission) *Svcs:* ref
Stock: bks/100; periodcls/150; m-forms/1000; specialist pubns/1256
Pubns: over 100 IRSG pubns for sale

West Bromwich

S2101 🔑
Institute of Cast Metals Engineers, Library
(formerly the Inst of British Foundrymen)
Natl Metalforming Centre, 47 Birmingham Rd, West Bromwich, W Midlands, B70 6PY (0121-601-6979; *fax:* 0121-601-6981)
Email: info@icme.org.uk
Internet: http://www.icme.org.uk/

Gov Body: Genl Council *Chief:* Technical/Training Offcr: Dr P.A. Murrell
Entry: ref only, adv appt *Open:* Mon-Thu 0900-1700, Fri 0900-1330
Subj: tech; cast metal tech; pattern making tech
Collns: Bks & Pamphs: BSI (foundry/casting related, metal related); ESTU pubns *Archvs:* The Foundryman (Inst of British Foundrymen Journal, bnd copies from 1908)
Equip: fax, copier, room for hire (fees for all on appl) *Svcs:* info
Stock: bks/c1200; periodcls/10; videos/30
Classn: DDC
Pubns: The Foundryman (subscription UK £110 pa, internatl £130 pa); Lib List now available on computer disk
Staff: Other Prof: 2

S2102 ✚
Sandwell and West Birmingham Hospitals NHS Trust, Sandwell Clinical Library
(formerly Sandwell Healthcare NHS Trust)
Lyndon, West Bromwich, W Midlands, B71 4HJ (0121-607-3551; *fax:* 0121-607-3315)
Email: sanlib@dial.pipex.com

Chief: Lib Svcs Mgr: post vacant *Dep:* Asst Lib Mgr: Mrs Sue Caldicott *Other Snr Staff:* Asst Libns: Ms Jessica Cooke, Ms Anita Phul & Ms Rachel Lewis
Assoc Libs: INFO KIOSK, Hallam St Site, West Bromwich
Entry: staff of Trust & of Black Country Mental Health Trust *Open:* Mon 0930-1930, Tue-Thu 0830-1930, Fri 0830-1800, Sat 0900-1300
Subj: medicine *Co-op Schemes:* BLDSC, BMA
Equip: copier, 9 computers (all with wd-proc, 7 with internet & 7 with CD-ROM), *Online:* Medline on CD-ROM *Svcs:* info, ref
Stock: bks/c10000; periodcls/120; pamphs/250; videos/50
Classn: NLM *Auto Sys:* Heritage IV
Staff: Libns: 3 *Other Prof:* 1 *Non-Prof:* 2

S2103 🎓
Sandwell College, West Bromwich Campus Learning Centre
High St, West Bromwich, W Midlands, B70 8DW (0121-556-6000; *fax:* 0121-556-6601)
Email: ann.hughes@sandwell.ac.uk
Internet: http://www.sandwell.ac.uk/

Chief: Mgr: Mrs Ann Hughes *Dep:* Dep Mgr: Mrs Barbara Thompson BA
Assoc Libs: SMETHWICK CAMPUS LRC (see **S2085**); WEDNESBURY CAMPUS LRC (see **S2095**)
Entry: ref only *Open:* Mon-Thu 0830-2000; Fri 1000-1600
Subj: accounting & finance; art & design; arch; bldg studies; business; catering; chem; computing;

fashion; electronics; eng; English; fashion & beauty; health & social care; lang; law; mgmt; manufacturing; marketing; media studies; music; sci; sport; leisure; teaching; tech; travel; tourism
Co-op Schemes: BLDSC, WMRLS
Equip: 3 m-readers, m-printer, 3 video viewers, 3 copiers, 115 computers (all with wd-proc, 70 with internet & incl CD-ROM network server) *Online:* Internet (staff & students only) *Svcs:* info, ref
Stock: bks/c80000; periodcls/350; videos/500
Classn: DDC *Auto Sys:* Genesis
Staff: Libns: 3 *Non-Prof:* 18

S2104 ✚
Sandwell Primary Care Trusts Library
Kingston House, 438 High St, West Bromwich, W Midlands, B70 9LD (0121-500-1500; *fax:* 0121-500-1501)
Email: maureen.jones@os-pct.nhs.uk

Gov Body: Oldbury & Smethwick Primary Care Trust *Chief:* Info Resource Offcr: Mrs Maureen Jones
Entry: adv appt *Open:* Mon-Thu 0900-1200, 1400-1630, Fri 0900-1200, 1400-1530
Subj: public health; health promotion materials
Co-op Schemes: BLDSC, BMA, ILL
Equip: computer (with internet & CD-ROM)
Online: CINAHL, West Midlands database *Svcs:* info, ref
Stock: bks/5800 (incl pamphs); periodcls/40; videos/30 *Acqs Offcr:* Info Resource Offcr, as above
Classn: own
Staff: Non-Prof: 1 FT *Exp:* £7847 (2000-01)

West Drayton

S2105 ⚕✚
Merck Pharmaceuticals Library
Harrier House, High St, Yiewsley, West Drayton, Middlesex, UB7 7QG (01895-452325; *fax:* 01895-452296)
Email: hkorjonen-close@merckpharma.co.uk

Gov Body: Merck Pharmaceuticals (UK) *Chief:* Company Libn & Medical Info Offcr: Mrs Helena Korjonen-Close BSc(Hons), MA
Entry: staff only; product info enqs should be directed to Medical Info *Open:* Mon-Fri 0900-1700
Subj: medicine; pharmaceuticals *Collns: Other:* data files on company products; clinical papers
Svcs: info (via Medical info), abstracting
Stock: bks/5000; periodcls/50 *Acqs Offcr:* Company Libn, as above
Classn: NLM *Auto Sys:* Reference Manager
Staff: Libns: 1 *Non-Prof:* 1 *Exp:* part of overall medical budget

West Malling

S2106 ⚕✚
Aventis Pharma UK, Library
Aventis House, 50 Kings Hill Ave, West Malling, Kent, ME19 4AH (01732-584000; *fax:* 01732-584080)
Internet: http://www.aventispharma.co.uk/

Chief: Lib Mgr: Ms Claire Cooper BA(Hons)
Entry: ref only, adv appt *Open:* Mon-Fri 0900-1730; excl bank hols, closed Xmas-New Year
Subj: medicine; pharmaceuticals *Co-op Schemes:* BLDSC
Equip: m-reader, m-printer, copier, fax, computers (incl wd-proc, internet & CD-ROM) *Online:* Embase, Dialog *Svcs:* info, ref
Stock: bks/1000; periodcls/112
Classn: UDC *Auto Sys:* Lotus Notes
Staff: Libns: 1 *Non-Prof:* 1

Special Libraries

West Malling
▼
Winchester

S2107

Horticulture Research International, East Malling Library

East Malling, West Malling, Kent, ME19 6BJ (01732-843833; *fax:* 01732-849067)
Email: malling.library@hri.ac.uk
Internet: http://www.hri.ac.uk/

Chief: Libn: Miss Sarah Loat BA(Hons), MCLIP (sarah.loat@hri.ac.uk)
Assoc Libs: HRI WELLESBOURNE LIB (see **S2089**)
Entry: prior appt *Open:* Mon-Fri 0900-1700
Subj: hortic; temperate fruit crops; farm & woodland mgmt; plant sci; biotech *Co-op Schemes:* BLDSC, BBSRC Libs (BRISC & BRIL), KILN
Equip: 2 m-readers, copier, 5 computers (incl CD-ROM) *Online:* Dialog, Datastar (fees on appl)
Svcs: info, ref
Stock: bks/20000; periodcls/200; CD-ROMs/20
Acqs Offcr: Libn, as above
Classn: own *Auto Sys:* BRS Search
Pubns: HRI Annual Report
Staff: Libns: 1

Westcliff-on-Sea

S2108

Southend Hospital, Education Centre Library

Prittlewell Chase, Westcliff-on-Sea, Essex, SS0 0RY (01702-435555 x2620; *fax:* 01702-221081)
Email: library@southend.nhs.uk

Gov Body: Southend Hosp NHS Trust *Chief:* Lib Mgr: Mr Ian Mather BA, MCLIP (imather@southend.nhs.uk) *Other Snr Staff:* Asst Libn: Mrs Elizabeth Thres
Entry: registered membs only *Open:* Mon-Thu 0830-1800, Fri 0830-1700; 24 hr study room available
Subj: medicine; health *Co-op Schemes:* BLDSC, ILL, BMA
Equip: copier (A4/5p, A3/10p), video viewer, 14 computers (all with wd-proc & internet, 8 with CD-ROM) *Online:* Cochrane, Best Evidence etc; various full-text journals *Svcs:* info, ref, biblio
Stock: bks/6000; periodcls/120; AVs/90 *Acqs Offcr:* Asst Libn, as above
Classn: NLM *Auto Sys:* 2020/DBTextworks
Pubns: Lib Guide; Journal Holdings List
Staff: Libns: 1 *Other Prof:* 1.33 *Non-Prof:* 2.14

Weston-super-Mare

S2109

Weston College Library

Knightstone Rd, Weston-super-Mare, N Somerset, BS23 2AL (01934-411411; *fax:* 01934-411410)
Email: lrc@weston.ac.uk
Internet: http://www.weston.ac.uk/lrc/

Chief: Libn: Miss Jenny Welsh BA, DMS, MCLIP
Assoc Libs: WESTON 6TH FORM COLL LIB, Loxton Rd, Weston-super-Mare, N Somerset, BS23 4QU
Entry: staff & students; ref only for membs of public *Open:* term: Mon-Thu 0845-2100, Fri 0845-1615; vac: Mon-Thu 0900-1700, Fri 0900-1630

Subj: all subjs; GCSE; A level; undergrad *Co-op Schemes:* SWRLS
Equip: copier, clr copier, 20 computers (incl wd-proc, internet & CD-ROM)
Stock: bks/22000; periodcls/110; videos/150; CD-ROMs/51
Classn: DDC *Auto Sys:* Heritage
Staff: Libns: 2 *Non-Prof:* 2

Weymouth

S2110

Weymouth College Library

Cranford Ave, Weymouth, Dorset, DT4 7LQ (01305-208820; *fax:* 01305-208912)
Email: library@weymouth.ac.uk
Internet: http://www.weycoll.ac.uk/

Chief: Libn: Mr Peter Vowles MLS, MA, CertEd, MCLIP (peter.vowles@weymouth.ac.uk) *Dep:* Asst Libn: Mrs Liz Hayman BA (liz.hayman@weymouth.ac.uk)
Entry: open to public *Open:* term: Mon-Thu 0845-2100, Fri 0845-1730, Sat 0930-1600; vac: Mon-Fri 0845-1700
Subj: all subjs; genl; GCSE; A level; undergrad; vocational *Co-op Schemes:* BLDSC, HATRICS
Equip: video viewer, fax, 3 copiers, clr copier, computers (incl 84 with wd-proc, 90 with internet & 90 with CD-ROM) *Disabled:* Kurzweil
Stock: bks/50000; periodcls/300; slides/2000; pamphs/4000; maps/100; videos/1500; CD-ROMs/100
Classn: DDC *Auto Sys:* Dorset County Council
Pubns: Resource Lists (unpriced); Lib Guides
Staff: Libns: 2 *Non-Prof:* 5

Whitchurch

S2111

Skishoot-Offshoot Picture Library

Hall Pl, Upper Woodcott, Whitchurch, Hampshire, RG28 7PY (01635-255527; *fax:* 01635-255528)
Email: skishootsnow@aol.com
Internet: http://www.skishoot.co.uk/

Type: commercial picture agency *Chief:* Felice & Peter Hardy *Dep:* Kate Parker & Jo Crossley
Assoc Libs: OFFSHOOT-FRANCE, specialist French picture lib, Officers-in-Charge: Kate Parker & Jo Crossley
Entry: adv appt *Open:* Mon-Fri 0930-1830
Subj: skiing in Europe, North America & world-wide; non-skiing material from France & Australia
Collns: Other: transparencies of skiing & snow-boarding
Equip: fax, copier, 5 computers (all with wd-proc & CD-ROM, 4 with internet) *Svcs:* info, ref
Stock: slides/400000
Staff: Libns: 2 *Other Prof:* 2

Whiteley

S2112

Kvaerner Engineering and Construction (UK), Information Services

4500 Parkway, Solent Business Pk, Whiteley, Hampshire, PO15 7AY (01489-614480; *fax:* 01489-614243)
Email: claire.holder@kvaerner.com
Internet: http://www.kvaerner.com/

Chief: Libn: Miss Claire Holder BA(Hons) *Dep:* Asst Libn: Miss Marie Kybett
Entry: adv appt *Open:* Mon-Thu 0830-1630, Fri 0830-1530
Subj: tech; eng; construction *Co-op Schemes:* BLDSC, HATRICS

Equip: computer (incl CD-ROM) *Svcs:* info, ref, biblio, indexing
Stock: bks/12000; periodcls/9; videos/300
Classn: UDC *Auto Sys:* Soutron *Staff:* Libns: 1

Whitley Bay

S2113

Library of Japanese Science and Technology

24 Duke St, Whitley Bay, Tyne & Wear, NE26 3PP (0191-253-3479/222-6693; *fax:* 0191-253-3479)

Chief: Director/Libn: Mr Robert Phillifent BSc, MA
Entry: staff/students of Univ of Newcastle, others by adv appt *Open:* Mon-Fri 0900-1700
Subj: undergrad; postgrad; rsrch; lib sci; biblio; econ; business; sociology; edu; sci; maths; tech; physical & economic geog *Collns: Bks & Pamphs:* located at Porter Bldg (BI), Univ of Newcastle, Newcastle upon Tyne, NE1 7RU: Japanese sci & tech generally; very strong holdings of periodcls issued by Japanese Colls & Univs; also biomedical periodcls; annual reports/profiles of Japanese companies; Japanese business hists *Other:* Patent Abstracts of Japan on CD-ROM *Co-op Schemes:* ILL, Japan Lib Group
Equip: m-reader, copier, fax *Svcs:* info, ref, current awareness, lit searching (all charged svcs)
Stock: periodcls/3700; unrecorded numbers of bks, pamphs & m-forms *Acqs Offcr:* Libn, as above
Classn: own
Pubns: Lib Bulletin (free to selected mailing list); List of Annual Reports/Profiles of Japanese Companies Held in the Lib (£2.50+p&p)
Staff: Other Prof: 1

Widnes

S2114

Halton College, Widnes, Library

Kingsway, Widnes, Cheshire, WA8 7QQ (0151-423-1391; *fax:* 0151-420-2408)
Email: learningcentre@haltoncollege.ac.uk
Internet: http://www.haltoncollege.ac.uk/

Chief: Libn: Mrs Christine Hopkins BA(Hons)
Assoc Libs: RUNCORN CAMPUS LIB, Campus Dr, off Picow Form Rd, Runcorn, Cheshire, WA7 4RE
Entry: ref only for public; external borrowing for small annual fee *Open:* term: Mon-Thu 0900-2100, Fri 0900-1700; vac: Mon-Fri 0900-1700
Subj: all subjs *Co-op Schemes:* BLDSC
Equip: copier, computers (with wd-proc, internet & CD-ROM)
Stock: bks/c17000; periodcls/c100
Classn: DDC *Auto Sys:* Heritage
Staff: Libns: 1 *Other Prof:* 1 *Non-Prof:* 10

Wigan

S2115

Wigan and Leigh College, Learning Resources and Library Services

PO Box 53, Parsons Walk, Wigan, Lancashire, WN1 1RS (01942-761508; *fax:* 01942-761569)
Email: j.richler@wigan-leigh.ac.uk
Internet: http://www.wigan-leigh.ac.uk/

Gov Body: Wigan & Leigh Coll *Chief:* Head of Learning Resources: Ms Jo Richler BA, CertEd, FITT, MSc *Other Snr Staff:* Curriculum Advisor (Learning Resources): Ms Hazel Hales
Assoc Libs: Wigan Campus Libs: PAGEFIELD LIB, Wigan (01942-761893); *Leigh Campus Libs:* MARSHALL ST LIB, Marshall St, Leigh (01942-761449); RAILWAY RD LIB, Railway Rd, Leigh (01942-761750)

Entry: student of Coll; community access **Open:** term: Mon 1000-2030, Tue-Thu 0830-2030, Fri 0830-1700, Sat 0930-1230; vac: Mon-Fri 1000-1600
Subj: all subjs; genl; GCSE; A level; undergrad; local study (Wigan, mining) **Collns:** Archvs: Coll archvs & local hist **Other:** mining colln; Barbour on m-form **Co-op Schemes:** ILL
Equip: m-reader, m-printer, 4 fax, 4 video viewers, 4 copiers, 30 computers (all with wd-proc, internet & CD-ROM) **Disabled:** specialised equip available
Svcs: info, ref, biblio, indexing, abstracting
Stock: bks/60000; periodcls/300
Classn: DDC **Auto Sys:** EOSi **Staff:** Libns: 9
Other Prof: 10 **Exp:** £66000 (1999-2000)
Proj: rebuilding of Crawford Lib; refurbishment of Pagefield & Railway Rd Libs

S2116 ✚
Wigan and Leigh Medical Institute, Library
Royal Albert Edward Infirmary, Wigan, Lancashire, WN1 2NN (01942-822508; *fax:* 01942-822355)
Email: library@wiganlhs-tr.nwest.nhs.uk

Chief: Lib Svcs Mgr: Miss Cheryl Housley BSc, MA (cheryl.housley@wiganlhs-tr.nwest.nhs.uk)
Entry: medical staff only **Open:** Mon-Thu 0900-1700, Fri 0900-1630
Subj: medicine; healthcare **Co-op Schemes:** BLDSC, ILL
Equip: copier, 8 computers (all with wd-proc, 7 with internet & 7 with CD-ROM) **Online:** Dialog, Medline, CINAHL, PsycInfo (Aditus Portal)
Stock: bks/3200; periodcls/65; videos/40
Classn: LC **Auto Sys:** DBTextworks
Staff: Libns: 1 Non-Prof: 2

Wigston

S2117 ☛
South Leicestershire College, Learning Resources Centre
(formerly Wigston Coll of Further Edu)
Station Rd, Wigston, Leicestershire, LE18 2DW (0116-288-5051 x2102; *fax:* 0116-288-0823)
Email: beth@wigston-college.ac.uk
Internet: http://www.wigston-college.ac.uk/

Chief: Learning Resources Svcs Mgr: Miss E.A. McHugh MA(Hons), DipILS, MCLIP, NDipM **Entry:** registered Coll students & approved students only **Open:** term: Mon-Thu 0845-2000, Fri 0845-1700, Sat 0900-1230; vac: Mon-Fri 1000-1600
Subj: all subjs; genl; GCSE; A level; vocational
Collns: Other: Press Cuttings Bulletin **Co-op Schemes:** ILL
Equip: copier (5p per sheet), clr copier, 23 computers (incl 20 with wd-proc, 22 with internet & 1 with CD-ROM) **Disabled:** scanning equip
Officer-in-Charge: Learning Resources Svcs Mgr, as above **Svcs:** info, ref, biblio
Stock: bks/14000; periodcls/200; slides/1500; pamphs/500; audios/400; videos/4000 **Acqs**
Offcr: Learning Resources Svcs Mgr, as above
Classn: DDC **Auto Sys:** Heritage
Staff: Libns: 1 Non-Prof: 4 **Exp:** £28000 (1999-2000); £28000 (2000-01)

Wigton

S2118 ☝ 🎥
Chris Bonington Picture Library
Badger Hill, Nether Row, Hesket Newmarket, Wigton, Cumbria, CA7 8LA (016974-78286; *fax:* 016974-78238)
Email: frances@bonington.com
Internet: http://www.bonington.com/

Gov Body: Chris Bonington Ltd **Chief:** Picture Lib Mgr: Frances Daltrey
Entry: adv appt **Open:** Mon-Fri 1000-1730; answerphone (all hrs) otherwise
Subj: mountains; mountaineers; mountaineering & related topics; ethnic people, villages, occupations
Collns: Archvs: Pete Boardman Colln; Joe Tasker Colln; Doug Scott Colln
Stock: slides/170000 **Staff:** Libns: 1

Wimborne Minster

S2119 ☝ ☛ 🖐
Wimborne Minster Chained Library
c/o Parish Office, Church House, High St, Wimborne Minster, Dorset, BH21 1HT (01202-384753)

Gov Body: Wimborne Minster Church of St Cuthberga **Chief:** Chief Libn: Mrs Judith L. Monds
Dep: Libn: Mr Frank Tandy Esq
Entry: open to public from Easter Monday until end of Oct; small donation requested (ad 50p, ch of school age free); out-of-hrs groups charged £1 per head, as lib must be specially staffed for these visits **Open:** Mon-Thu 1000-1200, 1400-1600; Fri 1000-1200; open most Sat mornings (weddings permitting)
Subj: most subjs, esp: religion; ancient langs; hist; early English music; the lib was set up in 1686 as a public lib for the town & contains quite a lot of genl info **Collns:** Bks & Pamphs: bnd vols of early English church music **Archvs:** Charles I Charter; Tudor Achievement
Equip: room hire (by donations accompanied by lib guide) **Disabled:** the lib is up a 26-step spiral staircase & regrettably unsuitable for the disabled
Stock: bks/413, incl 23 vols of music
Staff: Non-Prof: 32 volunteers **Exp:** no exp on stock purchases; some on restoration & repairs
Proj: downstairs display planned for 2004

Winchester

S2120 ☝ 🖐
Diocese of Winchester, Thorold and Lyttleton Library
The Basement, 11 The Close, Winchester, Hampshire, SO23 9LS (01962-870605)
Email: tandl.library@ukgateway.net

Gov Body: The Lib Mgmt Cttee **Chief:** Hon Libn: Dr Stella Rogers BSc, PhD **Dep:** Mr Alan Thorns
Entry: by adv appt for non-membs **Open:** as per Cathedral Close
Subj: religion (all areas); some social sci; some sci; some art & arch; some lit; hist (genl BC & AD English hist); church hist; English church hist
Collns: Bks & Pamphs: Lockton Liturgy Bequest
Equip: copier, computer (for enqs only) **Svcs:** info, ref
Stock: bks/14000; periodcls/3
Classn: own shelfmark codes **Auto Sys:** Heritage
Staff: Non-Prof: 7 **Exp:** £1750 (1999-2000); £2000 (2000-01)

S2121 🖐
IBM UK Ltd Technical Library
MP 149, Hursley Pk, Winchester, Hampshire, SO21 2JN (01962-815641; *fax:* 01962-818199)
Email: library@uk.ibm.com

Chief: Libn: Ms Jayne Downey MA, DipLib (jayne_downey@uk.ibm.com) **Dep:** Asst Libn: Mrs Jan Ward (jan_ward@uk.ibm.com)
Entry: ref only, by appt **Open:** Mon-Fri 0830-1700
Subj: computer sci **Collns:** Bks & Pamphs: IBM technical reports & standards **Co-op Schemes:** BLDSC, HATRICS

Equip: copier, fax, 4 computers (all with wd-proc, internet & CD-ROM) **Online:** for internal use only: Dialog, Datastar, Dow Jones Interactive, OneSource, IEEEXplore, ACM Digital Lib **Svcs:** info, ref, biblio, indexing
Stock: bks/2500; periodcls/65; pamphs/500; CD-ROMs/100; e-books/250; e-journals/10
Classn: own **Auto Sys:** Horizon
Staff: Libns: 1 Non-Prof: 1

S2122 ☛
King Alfred's College, Martial Rose Library
Sparkford Rd, Winchester, Hampshire, SO22 4NR (01962-827306; *fax:* 01962-827443)
Email: d.farley@wkac.ac.uk
Internet: http://www.lrc.wkac.ac.uk/

Chief: Libn: Mr David Farley BA, DipLib, MCLIP
Dep: Dep Libn: Mrs Liz Fletcher BA, DipLib
Entry: ref only **Open:** Mon-Fri 0900-1600; extended hrs during Coll term
Subj: local study (Hampshire); phil; psy; religion; social sci; arts; lit; geog; hist **Co-op Schemes:** BLDSC, HATRICS, SWRLS
Equip: 3 m-reader, 6 video viewers, 6 copiers, 150 computers (incl 144 with wd-proc, 3 with internet & 3 with CD-ROM) **Online:** Dialog
Stock: bks/180000; periodcls/600; audios/500; videos/12500
Classn: DDC **Auto Sys:** Talis
Pubns: Guide to Martial Rose Lib
Staff: Libns: 7 Non-Prof: 8.6

S2123 ☛
Sparsholt College Hampshire, Library and Information Centre
Sparsholt, Winchester, Hampshire, SO21 2NF (01962-797232; *fax:* 01962-776587)
Email: library@sparsholt.ac.uk
Internet: http://www.sparsholt.ac.uk/

Chief: Libn: Ms Nicola Swainson BA(Hons), DipLib, MCLIP **Dep:** Ms Joanna Austin BA(Hons)
Entry: ref only for non-membs of coll, adv appt preferred **Open:** term: Mon-Thu 0830-2000, Fri 0830-1730, Sat 0900-1700; vac: times vary
Subj: agric; hortic; animal care; aquaculture **Co-op Schemes:** HATRICS, BLDSC
Equip: m-reader, video viewer, copier, computers (incl wd-proc & internet) **Online:** not available to public **Svcs:** info, ref
Stock: bks/15000; periodcls/275; videos/c400
Classn: UDC **Auto Sys:** Inheritance
Staff: Libns: 2 Other Prof: 2

S2124 ✚
Winchester and Eastleigh Health-care NHS Trust, Healthcare Library
Royal Hampshire County Hosp, Romsey Rd, Winchester, Hampshire, SO22 5DG (01962-824680/420; *fax:* 01962-824659)
Email: library@weht.swest.nhs.uk
Internet: http://www.hants.org.uk/weht/

Chief: Libn & Info Svcs Mgr: Miss B.M. Goddard CertHSM, MIHM, MCLIP (brenda.goddard@weht.swest.nhs.uk) **Dep:** Dep Libn: Mrs S.V. Stephenson MCLIP
Entry: all NHS staff on registering; ref only for non-NHS (fees) **Open:** Mon-Fri 0830-1730
Subj: medicine; nursing; health sci **Collns:** Archvs: relating to hist of Royal Hampshire County Hosp **Co-op Schemes:** BLDSC, HLN, SWRLIN, HATRICS
Equip: fax, video viewer, copier (5p per sheet), 12 computers (with internet, membs only) **Officer-in-Charge:** Libn & Info Svcs Mgr, as above **Svcs:** info, ref

☛

Special Libraries

Winchester ▼ Wolverhampton

(Winchester & Eastleigh Healthcare NHS Trust, Healthcare Lib cont)
Stock: bks/15000; periodcls/350; videos/100 *Acqs*
Offcr: Libn & Info Svcs Mgr, as above
Classn: NLM (mod) *Auto Sys:* Heritage
Pubns: Guide to the Lib & Info Svcs; Statistics; Medline User Guide; CINAHL User Guide (free)
Staff: Libns: 3.29 *Non-Prof:* 2.81 *Exp:* £50000 (1999-2000); £50000 (2000-01)

S2125 🎓
Winchester College, Warden and Fellows' Library
College St, Winchester, Hampshire, SO23 9NA (*school office:* 01962-621100; *fax:* 01962-621106)
Internet: http://www.winchestercollege.org/

Gov Body: Warden & Fellows of Winchester Coll
Chief: Fellows' Libn: R.D.H. Custance MA, DPhil
Assoc Libs: SCHOOL ARCHVS, at same addr (se **A511**)
Entry: by written appt only, refs may be required
Subj: religion; sci; maths; lit; geog; hist; classics
Collns: *Bks & Pamphs:* Turner Colln (rare & early bibles); 18C Wykehamical authors; Reformation & Counter-Reformation lit
Stock: bks/10000; MSS/200; incunabula/50
Staff: Non-Prof: 1

S2126 🏰🏛️
Winchester Museums Service, Historical Resources Centre
75 Hyde St, Winchester, Hampshire, SO23 7DW (01962-848269; *fax:* 01962-848299)
Email: museums@winchester.gov.uk

Type: local authority **Gov Body:** Winchester City Council **Chief:** Curator: Mr K. Qualmann MA, AMA **Dep:** Keeper of Local Records: Miss K. Parker BA, AMA
Entry: adv appt **Open:** Mon-Thu 0900-1230, 1400-1630, Fri 0900-1230, 1400-1600
Subj: local study (Winchester & dist, archaeo & local hist); archaeo; social hist; museology **Collns:** *Archvs:* archaeo records (Winchester & dist)
Other: photos, prints, drawings & paintings (Winchester & dist)
Equip: m-reader, video viewer, copier
Stock: bks/13051; photos/36000
Auto Sys: Modes for Windows
Pubns: Glimpses of Hampshire History... (£4.95); Winchester Excavations 1949-1960, Vol 1 (£2.50), Vol 2 (£5); Medieval Hall Houses of the Winchester Area (£12.95); The Brooks, Winchester: Preliminary Reports (£10); The Brooks, Winchester: 1987-88 – The Roman Structural Remains, by J.M. Zant; Winchester Museums Svc Archaeo Report 2
Staff: Other Prof: 6

S2127 🎓
Winchester School of Art Library
Park Ave, Winchester, Hampshire, SO23 8DL (023-8059-6900)
Email: wsaenqs@soton.ac.uk
Internet: http://www.library.soton.ac.uk/wsal/

Gov Body: Univ of Southampton (see **S1946**)
Chief: Libn: Ms Linda Newington BA, PGDip

Entry: ref only, adv appt **Open:** term: Mon-Fri 0900-1900, Sat 1000-1600; vac: Mon-Fri 0900-1700
Subj: art; design; textile conservation **Collns:** *Bks & Pamphs:* design hist study colln (primary sources c1800-1960); artists' bks
Equip: 6 video viewers (students only), 2 copiers, 12 computers (students only) **Online:** Internet
Stock: bks/30000; periodcls/160; slides/100000; videos/5000
Classn: DDC **Auto Sys:** Unicorn
Staff: Libns: 3 **Exp:** £52100 (2000-01)

Windlesham

S2128 ✍️
Eli Lilly & Co Ltd, Information Centre
Erl Wood Manor, Sunninghill Rd, Windlesham, Surrey, GU20 6PH (01276-483344; *fax:* 01276-483901)
Email: wickenden@lilly.com

Gov Body: Lilly Industries Ltd **Chief:** Biomedical Info Scientist: Mr John Wickenden MCLIP
Entry: apply in writing **Open:** Mon-Fri 0830-1630
Subj: organic & analytical chem; pharmacology; pharmaceutical chem **Co-op Schemes:** HATRICS, SASLIC
Equip: m-readers, m-printers, fax, copier, computers (incl wd-proc & CD-ROM) **Svcs:** document delivery
Stock: bks/5000; periodcls/320
Classn: UDC **Auto Sys:** Sirsi Unicorn
Staff: Libns: 1 **Other Prof:** 1

Windsor

S2129 🎓
East Berkshire College Windsor, Learning Centre
Claremont Rd, Windsor, Berkshire, SL4 3AZ (01753-793121; *fax:* 01753-793119)
Email: howard.stone@eastberks.ac.uk
Internet: http://www.eastberks.ac.uk/

Gov Body: East Berkshire FE Corp **Chief:** Learning Centre Co-ordinator: Mr Howard Stone BA, MCLIP
Entry: open to all FT & PT students of Coll; others ref only **Open:** term: Mon-Thu 1900-2000, Fri 1000-1630
Subj: all subjs; genl; GCSE; A level
Equip: copier, clr copiers, 12 computers (all with wd-procs, internet & CD-ROM) **Svcs:** info, ref
Stock: bks/13000; periodcls/30
Classn: DDC **Auto Sys:** Olib
Pubns: Lib Introductory Leaflet; Accessions List (3 pa); Periodicals List (all free)
Staff: Libns: 1 **Non-Prof:** 5 **Exp:** £31000 (2000-01)

S2130 🎓
Eton College Library
Eton, Windsor, Berkshire, SL4 6DB (01753-671221; *fax:* 01753-801570)
Email: collections@etoncollege.org.uk

Gov Body: The Provost & Fellows of Eton Coll
Chief: Coll Libn: Mr M.C. Meredith MA **Dep:** Archivist: Mrs P. Hatfield MA, DAA
Entry: adv appt in writing **Open:** Mon-Fri 0930-1700 (closed 24 Dec-2 Jan & bank hols)
Subj: classics; theology; English lit; Italian & French lit; genl sci; arts; geog; hist **Collns:** *Bks & Pamphs:* Topham Colln of Drawings & Prints after the Antique; Storer Colln of Elizabethan & Stuart plays; Parikian Armenian Colln; Classical Schoolbk Colln; Thomas Hardy Colln; Robert & Elizabeth Barrett Browning Colln *Archvs:* large colln relating

to the hist of Eton Coll *Other:* Edward Gordon Craig Colln of prints, drawings, MSS & printed bks; 19C & 20C autograph letters
Equip: video viewer, fax, copier, computer (incl wd-proc & CD-ROM) **Svcs:** info
Stock: bks/75000; periodcls/15; photos/10000; maps/500; audios/100; videos/100
Auto Sys: forthcoming
Pubns: A Hist of Eton Coll Lib, by Robert Birley (£1); Treasures of Eton Coll Lib, 500 Years of Collecting, ed. P.R. Quarrie (£15); Eton 1440-1990 (essays on the collns, £5); 100 Bks, Manuscripts & Pictures 1800-1996 in the Eton Coll Lib, ed M.C. Meredith (£5)
Staff: Libns: 2 **Other Prof:** 3 **Non-Prof:** 1

S2131 🏰🏛️
Household Cavalry Museum, Regimental Library and Archives
Combermere Barracks, St Leonards Rd, Windsor, Berkshire, SL4 3DN (*tel & fax:* 01753-755112)
Internet: http://www.householdcavalry.co.uk/ museum.htm

Gov Body: Trustees **Chief:** Curator: Lt Col S.F. Sibley MBE **Dep:** Asst Curator: Mr K.C. Hughes
Entry: adv appt **Open:** Mon-Fri 1000-1230, 1400-1630
Subj: regimental hist; regimental records **Collns:** *Archvs:* Household Cavalry Regimental records (late 17C-date), incl historical records of: The Life Guard; The Royal Horse Guards; The Royal Dragoons; army svc records of listed men (1801-date); private letters; war diaries; marriage & birth registers; records of state occasions *Other:* photographic records (mid-19C onwards)
Equip: computer (with wd-proc)
Stock: bks/3000; photos/5000; maps & m-films/3000
Staff: Other Prof: 2

S2132 🔑📿
St George's Chapel, The Chapter Library
The Vicars' Hall Undercroft, The Cloisters, Windsor Castle, Windsor, Berkshire, SL4 1NJ (01753-848725; *fax:* 01753-848763)
Email: archives@stgeorges-windsor.org

Gov Body: The Dean & Canons of Windsor
Chief: Chapter Libn & Archivist: Dr Eileen Scarff
Entry: by appt **Open:** Mon-Fri 0930-1645
Subj: hist & topography of Windsor Castle & surroundings; phil; religion; hist **Collns:** *Archvs:* Chapter Archvs (early 12C-date) *Other:* music MSS & on m-film
Equip: 2 m-readers, 2 computers (incl internet & CD-ROM) **Disabled:** chairlift
Stock: bks/5749; archvs/340 linear m
Auto Sys: CALM 2000 Plus
Pubns: A Catalogue of Printed Bks in the Lib of St George's Chapel (£23)
Staff: Other Prof: 2 **Non-Prof:** 1

Wirral

S2133 ✚
Arrowe Park Hospital, McArdle Postgraduate Medical Library
Arrowe Park Rd, Upton, Wirral, Merseyside, CH49 5PE (*tel & fax:* 0151-604-7223)
Email: mcardlelibrary@hotmail.com

Gov Body: Wirral Hosp NHS Trust **Chief:** Head of Trust Lib Svcs: Ms A. Elkerton
Assoc Libs: CLATTERBRIDGE HOSP, JOHN A. AITKEN LIB (see **S2135**)
Entry: NHS staff & students on placement **Open:** Mon-Fri 0900-1700

Subj: medicine; health; nursing; paediatrics; orthopaedics; rheumatology
Equip: copier (A4/5p), 5 computers (all with internet) *Online:* CINAHL, Medline, HMIC, AMED, BNI, PsycInfo, Cochrane, Embase *Svcs:* info, ref, database training
Stock: bks/5000; periodcls/120
Classn: DDC *Auto Sys:* Heritage
Staff: Libns: 1 *Non-Prof:* 0.8

S2134
Chester College, School of Nursing and Midwifery Library
Arrowe Park Hosp, Upton, Wirral, Merseyside, CH49 5PE (0151-609-7291; *fax:* 0151-678-5322)
Email: lr.arrowe@chester.ac.uk
Internet: http://www.chester.ac.uk/lr/

Gov Body: Chester Coll (see **S457**) *Chief:* Asst Dir, Nursing & Midwifery Lib Svcs (based at Chester Coll): Mrs Wendy Fiander BA, MA, MCLIP
Dep: Libn (based at Arrowe Park): Ms Christine Holly BSc, PGDipInf (c.holly@chester.ac.uk)
Assoc Libs: SCHOOL OF NURSING & MIDWIFERY LIB, Countess of Chester Hosp (see **S459**); LEIGHTON HOSP, JOINT EDU & TRAINING LIB (see **S506**)
Entry: borrowing: nurses on Chester Coll School of Nursing courses, Wirral Hosp Trust & Wirral Community Trust nurses, Wirral practice nurses, Murrayfield Private Hosp nurses; others ref only *Open:* Mon 0830-1630, Tue-Thu 0830-1730, Fri 0830-1600; closed Xmas-New Year & Easter
Subj: psy; social sci; edu; medicine; nursing; mgmt
Co-op Schemes: BLDSC, LIHNN
Equip: m-reader, fax (40p per pg, overseas £1), copier (5p per sheet), 5 computers (all with wd-proc, internet & CD-ROM) *Svcs:* info, ref
Stock: bks/19000; periodcls/35
Classn: DDC *Auto Sys:* Innopac
Staff: Libns: 1 *Non-Prof:* 4

S2135
Clatterbridge Hospital, John A. Aitken Library
Bebington, Wirral, Merseyside, CH63 4JY (*tel & fax:* 0151-482-7849)
Email: library@ccotrust.nhs.uk

Gov Body: Wirral Hosp NHS Trust & Clatterbridge Centre for Oncology Trust *Chief:* Libn: Mrs Joan Richardson BA(Hons)
Assoc Libs: ARROWE PARK HOSP, MCARDLE POSTGRAD MEDICAL LIB (see **S2133**)
Entry: postgrads & medical & allied profs, others ref only *Open:* Mon-Fri 0900-1630
Subj: postgrad; medicine; psychiatry; dentistry; dermatology; oncology *Co-op Schemes:* ILL, BLDSC, BMA, Regional Hosps (NW)
Equip: m-reader, fax, copier, 6 computers (incl wd-proc, internet & CD-ROM), room for hire *Online:* Medline, Embase etc *Svcs:* info, ref, biblio
Stock: bks/3000; periodcls/100
Classn: DDC *Auto Sys:* Heritage
Staff: Libns: 1 *Non-Prof:* 1 PT

Woking

S2136
Institute for Animal Health, Pirbright Laboratory Library
Ash Rd, Pirbright, Woking, Surrey, GU24 0NF (01483-232441; *fax:* 01483-232448)
Email: sheila.shrigley@bbsrc.ac.uk
Internet: http://www.iah.bbsrc.ac.uk/

Chief: Libn: Mrs S. Shrigley FCLIP
Assoc Libs: COMPTON LIB (see **S1570**)
Entry: prior permission of head of laboratory
Open: Mon-Thu 0900-1700, Fri 0900-1630

Subj: virology; immunology; molecular biology
Collns: Other: refs on foot-&-mouth disease *Co-op Schemes:* BLDSC, BBSRC
Equip: m-reader, m-printer, copier, computer (with wd-proc) *Online:* Web of Science, Biosis, CABi
Svcs: info, ref, biblio
Stock: bks/3000; periodcls/100
Classn: UDC *Auto Sys:* BRS
Staff: Libns: 1 *Non-Prof:* 1

S2137
Royal Horticultural Society, Wisley Laboratory Library
RHS Gdn Wisley, Woking, Surrey, GU23 6QB (01483-212428; *fax:* 01483-479727)
Email: library.wisley@rhs.org.uk
Internet: http://www.rhs.org.uk/libraries/

Type: learned soc *Chief:* Libn: Ms Barbara Collecott *Other Snr Staff:* Bibliographic Svcs Libn: Ms Valerie Brooke
Assoc Libs: LINDLEY LIB (see **S1367**); ROSEMOOR STAFF LIB, RHS Garden Rosemoor, Gt Torrington, N Devon, EX38 8PH (01805-624067); the Wisley Laboratory Lib is also responsible for the RHS Garden Libs: WISLEY GARDEN LIB, contact details as above; HYDE HALL GARDEN LIB, RHS Garden Hyde Hall, Rettendon, Chelmsford, Essex, CM3 8ET, Volunteer Libn, Mrs Ann Dix (01245-400256; *email:* library.hydehall@rhs.org.uk); HARLOW CARR GARDEN LIB, RHS Garden Harlow Carr, Beckswithshaw, Crag Ln, Harrogate, HG3 1QB, Hon Libn: Mrs Kathryn White (01423-565418; *email:* library.harlowcarr@rhs.org.uk)
Entry: RHS staff; visitors by prior appt only *Open:* Mon-Fri 1100-1600
Subj: botany; hortic; fruit; prof gardening; entomology; plant pathology; soil sci
Svcs: info, ref, limited lit searches
Stock: bks/20000; periodcls/400
Staff: Libns: 2 *Non-Prof:* 2
Proj: refurbishment of Wisley Garden Lib; development of Garden Lib at Rosemoor with full visitor access

Wokingham

S2138
Soil Mechanics Library
Glossop House, Hogwood Ln, Finchampstead, Wokingham, Berkshire, RG40 4QW (0118-932-8888; *fax:* 0118-932-8383)
Email: peter.eldred@esgl.co.uk

Chief: Associate Libn: Mr P.J.L. Eldred *Dep:* Asst Libn: Ms Andrea Capon
Entry: adv appt only *Open:* Mon-Fri 0845-1700
Subj: geol; soil mechanics; civil eng *Collns: Archvs:* in-house report colln, incl site investigation data for most of UK & some overseas *Co-op Schemes:* BLDSC, ILL
Equip: m-reader, m-printer, fax, copier, computer (with wd-proc) *Online:* ESA-IRS (fees charged)
Stock: bks/500; periodcls/10; slides/2000; pamphs/20000; maps/500; m-forms/50, plus 14000 company reports stored on fiche; videos/20
Classn: own *Staff: Libns:* 0.5 *Other Prof:* 0.1
Exp: £3500 (1999-2000)

Wolverhampton

S2139
ADAS Information Services
ADAS Wolverhampton, Woodthorne, Wolverhampton, W Midlands, WV6 8TQ (01902-693123; *fax:* 01902-693159)
Email: ariadne.plant@adas.co.uk
Internet: http://www.adas.co.uk/

Chief: Libn: Ms Ariadne Plant BA(Hons)
Entry: ADAS staff only; not available to external visitors *Open:* Mon-Fri 0830-1700, excl public hols
Subj: environmental sci; agric; livestock; land-based industries & related subjs *Collns: Bks & Pamphs:* ADAS pamphs & leaflets *Co-op Schemes:* BLDSC, WMRLS, FIRST, MIDAIG
Equip: m-reader, copier, computers *Svcs:* info, ref
Stock: bks/2500; periodcls/650; pamphs/2500; m-forms/12 series *Acqs Offcr:* Libn, as above
Classn: DDC *Staff: Libns:* 1 *Non-Prof:* 0.5

S2140
City of Wolverhampton College, Learning Centre Services
(formerly Wolverhampton Coll)
Bilston Campus, Wellington Rd, Bilston, Wolverhampton, W Midlands, WV14 6BT (01902-821054; *fax:* 01902-821101)
Email: pardoea@wolverhampton.ac.uk
Internet: http://www.wolverhamptoncollege.ac.uk/

Chief: Learning Resources Mgr: Mrs V.R. Bigford BA (Hons), MSc, MCLIP *Dep:* Learning Centres Co-ordinator: Mrs Alison Pardoe MA, DipLib, MCLIP *Other Snr Staff:* Learning Resources Offcr: Mrs Rosemary Roberts BA(Hons), MCLIP
Assoc Libs: WULFRUN CAMPUS LEARNING CENTRE, Paget Rd, Wolverhampton, WV6 0DU
Entry: ref only or by enrolment *Open:* term: Mon-Thu 0900-2100, Fri 1015-1700, Sat 0900-1300; vac: Mon-Thu 0900-1700, Fri 1015-1630
Subj: all subjs; genl; GCSE; A level; undergrad; vocational *Collns: Bks & Pamphs:* Salter/Slater Colln (rsrch material on post-16 edu & training); Trade Union Edu Centre (all aspects of labour law, health & safety etc) *Co-op Schemes:* BLDSC, UKOnline, LearnDirect
Equip: 2 video viewers, 2 copiers, 70 computers (all with wd-proc, internet & CD-ROM), room for hire *Disabled:* HAL reader *Svcs:* info, ref
Stock: bks/60000; periodcls/200; photos/c50; maps/165; videos/2400; CD-ROMs/20; archvs/4 bays of shelving
Classn: DDC *Auto Sys:* Genesis
Staff: Libns: 5 FTE *Non-Prof:* 9 FTE *Exp:* £150000 (2000-01)

S2141
University of Wolverhampton, Learning Resources
St Peter's Sq, Wolverhampton, W Midlands, WV1 1RH (01902-322802; *fax:* 01902-322668)
Internet: http://www.wlv.ac.uk/lib/

Chief: Dir of Learning Resources: Ms Mary Heaney *Dep:* Mr C. Evans
Assoc Libs: HARRISON LEARNING CENTRE, addr as above (01902-322305; *fax:* 01902-322668); BURTON LEARNING CENTRE (see **S277**); COMPTON LEARNING CENTRE, Compton Rd West, Wolverhampton, WV3 9DX (01902-323642; *fax:* 01902-323702); MANOR LEARNING CENTRE (see **S2078**); NEW CROSS LEARNING CENTRE (see **S2142**); RUSSELL'S HALL LEARNING CENTRE, Esk House, Russell's Hall Hosp, Dudley, W Midlands, DY1 2HQ (01384-456111 x2594); TELFORD LEARNING CENTRE, Priorslee Hall, Priorslee, Telford, TF2 9NT (01902-323983; *fax:* 01902-323985); WALSALL LEARNING CENTRE, Gorway, Walsall, W Midlands, WS1 3BD (01902-323158; *fax:* 01902-323079)
Open: Harrison Learning Centre: term: Mon-Thu 0900-2200, Fri 0900-1900, Sat-Sun 1330-1730; vac: Mon-Fri 0900-1700
Subj: all subjs; undergrad; postgrad; local hist (West Midlands, Shropshire, Staffordshire, Worcestershire & Hereford); edu; computing; bldg construction *Collns: Other:* BSI *Co-op Schemes:* BLDSC, WMRLS, BCLIP, BLCMP, SCONUL

(Univ of Wolverhampton, Learning Resources cont)
Equip: m-reader, m-printer, video viewer, copier, computers (incl wd-proc & CD-ROM) *Disabled:* video enlarger *Online:* Dialog, Pergamon Infoline *Stock:* bks/572008; periodcls/4588; slides/115000; maps/2503; AVs/3179 audios & videos
Classn: DDC *Auto Sys:* Talis
Pubns: Lib Guide & Guides to Subj Resources
Staff: Libns: 60 *Other Prof:* 3 *Non-Prof:* 118

S2142 🎓 ✚
University of Wolverhampton, New Cross Learning Centre

Edu Centre, New Cross Hosp, Wolverhampton, W Midlands, WV10 0QP (01902-644805; *fax:* 01902-306072)
Internet: http://www.wlv.ac.uk/lib/

Gov Body: Univ of Wolverhampton (see **S2141**)
Chief: Learning Centre Mgr: Mrs P. Collins BA(Hons) *Dep:* Resource Libn: Mrs K. Ewart MCLIP
Assoc Libs: BURTON LEARNING CENTRE (see **S277**); MANOR LEARNING CENTRE (see **S2078**); RUSSELL'S HALL LEARNING CENTRE, Esk House, Russell's Hall Hosp, Dudley, W Midlands, DY1 2HQ
Entry: ref only, or external membership £35 pa
Open: Mon-Wed, Fri 0900-1700, Thu 0900-2000
Subj: nursing; midwifery *Co-op Schemes:* WMRHLN, NULJ
Equip: video viewer, copier, 11 computers (univ membs only) *Online:* OVID, Medline, CINAHL, CancerLit, BNI, AMED, ChildData *Svcs:* info, ref
Stock: bks/30000; periodcls/150; audios/4; videos/230; CD-ROMs/2
Classn: LC *Auto Sys:* Talis *Staff:* Libns: 2

S2143 ✚
Wolverhampton Medical Institute, The Bell Library

New Cross Hosp, Wolverhampton, W Midlands, WV10 0QP (01902-643109; *fax:* 01902-723037)
Email: David.Law@rwh-tr.nhs.uk

Gov Body: Royal Wolverhampton Hosps NHS Trust *Chief:* Lib & Info Svcs Mgr: Mr David Law
Entry: staff of Royal Wolverhampton Hosps NHS Trust, Wolverhampton Health Authority & Wolverhampton Health Care Trust; local GPs, dentists & paramedics; visiting students *Open:* Mon, Wed 0830-1700, Tue, Thu 0830-1900, Fri 0830-1630
Subj: medicine; nursing; health
Equip: copier (4p-10p per pg), 14 computers

Worcester

S2144 🔑 🏛
The Museum of Worcester Porcelain, Library and Archives

Severn St, Worcester, WR1 2NE (01905-746000; *fax:* 01905-617807)
Email: museum@royal-worcester.co.uk

Gov Body: The Dyson Perrins Museum Trust
Chief: Curator: Mrs Wendy Cook BA(Hons)
Entry: ref only, by adv appt *Open:* Mon-Fri 0930-1630

Subj: local study (Worcester ceramic industry); ceramic manufacture; arts *Collns:* Bks & Pamphs: Worcester Royal Porcelain Co Design Lib *Archvs:* Worcester Royal Porcelain Co Archvs *Stock:* various bks, periodcls, photos, slides, illusts, archvs, drawings & designs
Classn: Victorian numbering sys (under review)
Staff: Other Prof: 1

S2145 🎓
Royal National Institute of the Blind, New College Library

Whittington Rd, Worcester, WR5 2JX (01905-763933; *fax:* 01905-763277)
Email: wright@rnibcw.demon.co.uk

Gov Body: The Coll Governors *Chief:* Libn: Mrs C.M. Wright BA(Hons), PGCE, MCLIP
Entry: Coll student or staff *Open:* Mon, Wed 1100-1900, Tue, Thu-Fri 0900-1700; students have access Mon-Sun 0900-2000
Subj: GCSE; A level; vocational; Key Stage 3.4; generalities; religion; social sci; lang; sci; maths; tech; arts; lit; geog; hist; fiction *Collns:* Bks & Pamphs: small specialist colln for prof development of teachers of visually-impaired children; braille range (fiction & some non-fiction) *Co-op Schemes:* contributing to Union Catalogue of material available in various formats
Equip: 16 computers (all with internet) *Disabled:* CCTV, Speech Synthesiser, speech/magnification software on all computers, 4 Braille strips *Online:* Global Newsbank *Svcs:* info, ref
Stock: bks/500 print, c500 braille; periodcls/20; audios/300 story tapes
Classn: DDC *Auto Sys:* Heritage IV
Staff: Libns: 1 *Exp:* £4500 (2000-01)

S2146 🎓
University College Worcester, Peirson Library

Henwick Grove, Worcester, WR2 6AJ (01905-855346)
Internet: http://www.worc.ac.uk/services/library/libhp.html

Chief: Head of Lib Svcs: Ms Anne Hannaford (a.hannaford@worc.ac.uk) *Other Snr Staff:* Customer Svcs Mgr: Ms Gina Walford (g.walford@worc.ac.uk); Technical Svcs Libn: Ms Judy Reed (j.reed@worc.ac.uk); Learning & Info Systems Mgr: Mr Roger Fairman (r.fairman@worc.ac.uk)
Entry: ref only, external membs may borrow for a fee *Open:* term: Mon-Thu 0845-2230, Fri 0845-2100, Sat 1000-2100, Sun 1300-2100; vac: Mon-Fri 0900-1700
Subj: all subjs; genl; GCSE; A level; undergrad *Co-op Schemes:* ILL
Equip: m-reader, 2 copiers (A4/5p, A3/10p), clr copier (A4/45p, A3/90p), computers (incl wd-proc, internet & CD-ROM) *Online:* British Education Index, BHI, Cambridge Scientific Abstracts, CINAHL, Cochrane, Emerald, Europe Intelligence Wire, Historical Abstracts, PsycInfo, Sport Discus & others
Stock: bks/100000; periodcls/550; m-forms/900; audios/600
Pubns: lib guides & newsletters; guides to info resources; periodcls lists

S2147 🔑 ✍
Worcester Cathedral Library

c/o Chapter Office, 10a College Green, Worcester, WR1 2LH (01905-28854; *fax:* 01905-611139)
Email: DavidMorrison@worchestercathedral.org.uk

Gov Body: The Chapter of Worcester Cathedral
Chief: Canon Libn: The Revd Canon Dr Alvyn Pettersen *Dep:* Libn & Archivist: Dr David Morrison

Entry: only by written appl to the Canon Libn
Open: by appt
Subj: phil; psy; religion; lang; sci; maths; arts; lit; geog; hist *Collns:* Bks & Pamphs: Lib of John Prideaux (Bishop of Worcester 1641-50) *Archvs:* monastic rolls, treasurers' accounts, Chapter Acts etc (9C-date) *Other:* 285 monastic MSS (10C-15C) *Co-op Schemes:* certain bks listed in STC, WING & Cathedral Libs Catalogue
Equip: copier *Officer-in-Charge:* Libn & Archivist, as above *Svcs:* info, ref, m-filming by arrangement with Birmingham Univ Lib (see **S179**)
Stock: bks/5600; photos/1400; slides/400; illusts/500; pamphs/1200; maps/428; audios/100; videos/4; AVs/3; 285 m-fiches of MSS & certain archv vols available at Birmingham Univ Lib *Acqs Offcr:* Libn & Archivist, as above
Classn: Worcester Cathedral Classn
Staff: Libns: 1 *Other Prof:* 1 *Non-Prof:* 22
Proj: continuing conservation of medieval MSS & printed bks

S2148 🎓
Worcester College of Technology Library

Deansway, Worcester, WR1 2JF (01905-725576; *fax:* 01905-28906)
Email: Library@wortech.ac.uk
Internet: http://www.wortech.ac.uk/

Chief: Lib & LRC Mgr: Mrs K.M. Gardner BA, MLib, MCLIP *Dep:* Snr Learning Resources Libn: Mrs J. Whitworth BA, MCLIP
Assoc Libs: RAFFLES ART & DESIGN LIB, Worcester Coll of Tech, School of Art & Design, Barbourne, Worcester, WR1 1RT, Libn: Mrs L. Lane BA
Entry: ref only *Open:* term: Mon-Thu 0830-1930, Fri 0830-1645; vac: please enquire
Subj: GCSE; A level; undergrad; genl edu; caring; art & design; business & prof studies; lang; construction; eng *Co-op Schemes:* BLDSC
Equip: video viewer, copier, computers (incl wd-proc & CD-ROM)
Stock: bks/20000; periodcls/300
Classn: DDC *Auto Sys:* Heritage
Staff: Libns: 4 *Other Prof:* 1 *Non-Prof:* 6 *Exp:* £65000 (1999-2000)

S2149 ✚
Worcester Royal Hospital, Rowlands Library

Charles Hastings Postgrad Medical Centre, Worcestershire Royal Hosp, Charles Hastings Way, Worcester, WR5 1DD (01905-760601; *fax:* 01905-760866)
Email: rowlands.enquiries@worsacute.wmids.nhs.uk
Internet: http://www.worcestershireknowledgeportal.co.uk/

Gov Body: Worcestershire Acute Hosps NHS Trust *Chief:* Site Libn & Team Leader: Mrs Margaret Rowley BSc, MA, MCLIP, DMS (margaret.rowley@worsacute.wmids.nhs.uk) *Dep:* User Svcs Libn: Mr Richard Brook BA, MCLIP (richard.brook@worsacute.wmids.nhs.uk) *Other Snr Staff:* Info Svcs Libn: Ms Lucy Wright BA, DipLib (lucy.wright@worsacute.wmids.nhs.uk)
Assoc Libs: ALEXANDRA HOSP LIB (see **S1852**); KIDDERMINSTER HOSP LIB (see **S862**)
Entry: medical staff only, ref only *Open:* Mon-Fri 0830-1700
Subj: medicine; medical sci; nursing; social care; psy *Collns:* Bks & Pamphs: Royal Coll of Nursing Resource Colln *Co-op Schemes:* BLDSC, WMRHLN, Worcestershire Health Libs
Equip: copier, computers (incl wd-proc, 2 internet & CD-ROM) *Online:* Medline & others (available to NHS employees only) *Officer-in-Charge:* Site Libn, as above *Svcs:* info, ref

Stock: bks/5000; periodcls/200; videos/100; CD-ROMs/30 **Acqs Offcr:** Site Libn, as above
Classn: NLM **Auto Sys:** Unicorn
Staff: Libns: 3 Non-Prof: 2

S2150

Worcestershire Archaeological Society, Library and Archives

The Commandery, Sidbury, Worcester, WR1 2HU (01905-361821; fax: 01905-361822)

Gov Body: Worcestershire Archaeo Soc & Worcester City Museum **Chief:** Hon Libn: Miss B. Ronchetti MA, MCLIP **Dep:** Keeper of Collns (Worcester City Museum): Mr T. Bridges MA, Dip Museums
Entry: ref only, adv appt **Open:** Mon-Fri 1000-1700
Subj: local studies (Worcestershire); religion; arts; geog; hist; archaeo **Collns:** Bks & Pamphs: Hore Colln; large colln of guidebks **Archvs:** Worcestershire Archaeo Soc Archvs **Other:** slides & photos; postcards; engravings
Equip: copier (5p per sheet) **Officer-in-Charge:** Keeper of Collns (Worcester City Museum), as above **Svcs:** info, ref, biblio
Stock: bks/9000+, incl pamphs **Acqs Offcr:** Hon Libn, as above
Classn: DDC
Pubns: Transactions of the Worcestershire Archaeological Soc (biennial); Worcestershire Archaeological Soc Recorder (2 pa)
Staff: Libns: 1 (voluntary, PT) **Exp:** £500 (1999-2000); £400 (2000-01)

Workington

S2151

Lakes College – West Cumbria, Library

(formerly West Cumbria Coll)
Hallwood Rd, Lillyhall Business Pk, Workington, Cumbria, CA14 4JN (01946-839300; fax: 01946-839301)
Email: asklib@lcwc.ac.uk
Internet: http://www.lcwc.ac.uk/

Type: Further Edu Coll **Chief:** Libn: Mrs G.A. Ingram BA, MCLIP **Dep:** Mrs L.M. Mansell
Entry: free to students & staff of coll; external membs scheme for limited loan & computer use
Open: term: Mon 1000-2045, Tue-Thu 0845-2045, Fri 0845-1645; vac: Mon 1000-1645, Tue-Thu 0900-1645, Fri 0900-1630
Subj: all subjs; GCSE; A level; undergrad; vocational **Collns:** Bks & Pamphs: law colln **Co-op Schemes:** BLDSC
Equip: copier (£2 per 80 copies), 2 video viewers, 90 computers (all with wd-proc, internet & CD-ROM) **Disabled:** Kurzweil, tracker balls **Svcs:** info, ref
Stock: bks/25000; periodcls/150; videos/500
Classn: DDC **Auto Sys:** Heritage
Staff: Libns: 1.3 Other Prof: 4 Non-Prof: 2 FTE **Exp:** £52000 (2000-01)

Worksop

S2152

Bassetlaw Hospital, Staff Library

Postgrad Centre, Bassetlaw Hosp, Worksop, Nottinghamshire, SB1 0BD (01909-500990 x2917; fax: 01709-502885)
Email: hazel.croucher@bhcs-tr.trent.nhs.uk

Gov Body: Bassetlaw Hosp & Community NHS Trust **Chief:** Libn: Mrs Hazel Croucher **Dep:** Asst Libn: Mr Chris Fone
Entry: staff of Trust **Open:** Mon-Fri 0900-1700, Sat 0930-1200

Subj: medicine; nursing
Equip: copier (5p-10p per copy), computers (incl internet & CD-ROM) **Online:** Medline, CINAHL, ASSIA, Cochrane **Svcs:** info, ref, lit searches
Stock: bks/2100; periodcls/65
Classn: NLM **Staff:** Libns: 2 Non-Prof: 2

Worthing

S2153

Northbrook College Sussex, Library and Information Services

6 Littlehampton Rd, Goring by Sea, Worthing, W Sussex, BN12 6NU (01903-606213; fax: 01903-606007)
Email: enquiries@nbcol.ac.uk
Internet: http://www.northbrook.ac.uk/

Chief: Head of Lib & Info Svcs: Mr Alastair Torley **Assoc Libs:** BROADWATER LIB, Broadwater Rd, Worthing, W Sussex, BN14 8HJ; SHOREHAM LIB, Shoreham Airport, Shoreham, W Sussex, BN43 5FJ; HORSHAM LIB, 90 Hurst Rd, Horsham, W Sussex, RH12 2DT; WEST DURRINGTON LIB, addr as above
Entry: ref only, adv appt **Open:** term: Mon-Thu 0900-1930, Fri 0900-1700; vac: Mon-Fri 0900-1700
Subj: all subjs; undergrad **Co-op Schemes:** BLDSC, West Sussex County Lib ILL scheme, SASLIC
Equip: video viewers, copiers, computers (incl wd-proc, internet & CD-ROM) **Svcs:** info, ref, biblio
Stock: bks/50000; periodcls/200; slides/5000; audios/100; videos/600
Classn: DDC **Auto Sys:** Olib 7
Staff: Libns: 5 Other Prof: 4

S2154

Worthing and Southlands Hospitals NHS Trust, Worthing Health Libraries

Worthing Postgrad Centre, Park Ave, Worthing, W Sussex, BN11 2HR (01903-285025; fax: 01903-285125)
Email: sue.merriot@wash-tr.sthames.nhs.uk

Chief: Lib Svcs Mgr: Ms Sue Merriott MCH, RSHom, MCLIP **Dep:** Dep Lib Svcs Mgr: Mrs Margaret Calver MCLIP
Entry: NHS staff only, others on appl to Lib Svcs Mgr **Open:** Mon-Fri 0900-1700; access out of hrs via security swipe card sys
Subj: health scis **Co-op Schemes:** PLCS, NULJ, Kent, Surrey & Sussex Workforce Development Confederation
Equip: fax, 2 video viewers, copier, 12 computers (incl 3 wd-proc, 4 internet & 4 CD-ROM) **Online:** Dialog **Svcs:** info, ref, biblio, indexing
Stock: bks/14000, incl pamphs; periodcls/250; videos/300
Classn: NLM **Auto Sys:** DBTextworks
Staff: Libns: 2 Non-Prof: 3

Wrexham

S2155

North East Wales Institute of Higher Education LibraryInformation and Student Services

Edward Llwyd Bldg, Plas Coch, Mold Rd, Wrexham, Clwyd, LL11 2AW (01978-293237)
Email: a.hughes@newi.ac.uk
Internet: http://www.newi.ac.uk/library/library.htm

Chief: User Svcs Mgr: Mr Paul Jeorrett (p.jeorrett@newi.ac.uk)
Assoc Libs: HEALTH PROMOTION LIB, addr as above, Resource Offcr: Mr Eilian Jones (01978-293265; email: jonesge@newi.ac.uk)

Entry: staff & students of the Inst; external borrowing for a fee **Open:** term: Mon-Thu 0845-1900, Fri 0845-1700, Sat 1000-1700; vac: varies
Subj: all subjs; genl; GCSE; A level; undergrad
Co-op Schemes: BLDSC, WALIA
Equip: copiers, computers **Online:** BIDS, OCLC FirstSearch, Web of Science, Infotrac, Barbour Index, Design & Applied Arts Index & others
Stock: bks/c100000; periodcls/400; videos/350
Acqs Offcr: Acqs Offcr: Ms Fran Isherwood (f.isherwood@newi.ac.uk)

S2156

University of Wales Bangor, Health Studies Library

Archimedes Centre, Wrexham Tech Pk, Wrexham, Clwyd, LL13 7YP (01978-316370)
Email: iss059@bangor.ac.uk
Internet: http://www.bangor.ac.uk/is/library/

Gov Body: Univ of Wales Bangor (see **S76**)
Chief: Health Studies Libn: Ms Gwyneth Haylock
Dep: Snr Lib Asst: Mrs Samantha Dodd
Assoc Libs: FRON HEULOG (HEALTH STUDIES) LIB (see **S79**)
Entry: staff & students of Univ; others ref only **Open:** term & vac: Mon-Thu 0845-2000, Fri 0845-1700, Sat 0900-1300 (closed public hols)
Subj: health; medicine; physiology; nursing; midwifery; radiography; psy; social sci **Co-op Schemes:** BLDSC, LAMDA, NULJ, GALW
Equip: m-reader, video viewer, 2 copiers, 38 computers (all with internet & CD-ROM, 34 with wd-proc) **Online:** CINAHL, Medline, BNI, Cochrane, ASSIA
Acqs Offcr: Health Studies Libn, as above
Classn: NLM, LC **Auto Sys:** Innopac
Staff: Libns: 1 Non-Prof: 1 computer support offcr, 3.5 lib assts

S2157

Wrexham Medical Institute, John Spalding Library

Croesnewydd Rd, Wrexham, Clwyd, LL13 7YP (01978-727456; fax: 01978-727466)

Chief: Snr Libn: Mr Richard Bailey BA(Hons), MLib, MCLIP (richard.bailey@new-tr.wales.nhs.uk)
Other Snr Staff: Snr Lib Asst: Ms Jane Baker (jane.baker@new-tr.wales.nhs.uk)
Entry: membs only **Open:** daily 0800-2400; staffed: Mon-Thu 0830-1700, Fri 0830-1630
Subj: medicine; dentistry; professions allied to medicine **Collns:** Other: video colln **Co-op Schemes:** BLDSC, BMA, AWHILES
Equip: m-reader, copier, fax, video viewer, computers (incl 8 with wd-proc, 8 with internet & 8 with CD-ROM), 2 laptop computers **Online:** HOWIS (Health of Wales Info Svc), incl Medline, Embase, PsycInfo, CINAHL, AMED, CancerLit & Cochrane **Svcs:** info, ref, biblio, lit searching, careers info
Stock: bks/4100; periodcls/205; pamphs/1000; videos/370; CD-ROMs/20
Classn: NLM **Auto Sys:** Voyager
Pubns: Wrexham Journal of Healthcare
Staff: Libns: 1 Non-Prof: 3

Yeovil

S2158

East Somerset NHS Trust Library Service

Marsh Jackson Edu Centre, Yeovil Dist Hosp, Higher Kingston, Yeovil, Somerset, BA21 4AT (01935-384495; fax: 01935-384495)
Email: hillj@est.nhs.uk

Type: multiprof **Chief:** Medical Libn: Mrs Jean Hill MCLIP **Dep:** Mrs Linda Foote MCLIP

(East Somerset NHS Trust Lib Svc cont)
Entry: NHS staff in Somerset, Devon & Cornwall WDC area & students on placement; others by appt, ref only *Open:* 24 hr access to staff *Subj:* medicine; nursing; sociology; health care *Co-op Schemes:* SWRLIN, BLDSC, BMA *Equip:* m-fiche reader, fax, copier, 14 computers (incl CD-ROM, all with wd-proc & internet) *Online:* SWICE databases e-journals *Svcs:* info, ref *Stock:* bks/6000+; periodcls/150+; videos/50; CD-ROMs/50 *Classn:* NLM (Wessex) *Auto Sys:* DBTextworks *Pubns:* YDH: The Story of Yeovil Dist Hosp, by John R. Guy (£2 incl p&p) *Staff: Libns:* 2 *Non-Prof:* 0.6

S2159 ☙

Yeovil College, The Study Centre

Mudford Rd, Yeovil, Somerset, BA21 4DR (01935-423921; *fax:* 01935-429962)
Email: info@yeovil-college.ac.uk
Internet: http://www.yeovil-college.ac.uk/

Gov Body: Yeovil Coll *Chief:* Learning Svcs Mgr: Mrs Elizabeth Berry MA, DipLib, MCLIP (lizb@yeovil-college.ac.uk) *Dep:* Info Svcs Mgr: Mrs Christine Irwin (chrisi@yeovil-college.ac.uk) *Entry:* on production of Coll ID card *Open:* term: Mon-Thu 0830-2030, Fri 0830-1700, Sat 0900-1300; vac: Mon-Fri 0900-1300 *Subj:* all subjs; genl; GCSE; A level; undergrad; vocational *Co-op Schemes:* BLDSC, HATRICS, ILL, inter-campus loan with partner univs *Equip:* m-reader, 2 video viewers, 2 copiers (5p per copy), 62 computers (all with wd-proc, internet & CD-ROM), room for hire *Officer-in-Charge:* Learning Svcs Mgr, as above *Svcs:* info, ref, biblio, indexing, Support for Learning *Stock:* bks/24000; periodcls/240; pamphs/98; audios/54; videos/1952; CD-ROMs/97 *Acqs Offcr:* Bibliographic Svcs Team Leader: Mr Kern Vickers (kernv@yeovil-college.ac.uk) *Classn:* DDC *Auto Sys:* Olib *Staff: Libns:* 6 *Other Prof:* 1 *Non-Prof:* 9 FT *Exp:* £46110 (1999-2000); £48750 (2000-01)

York

S2160 ☙

Askham Bryan College Library

Askham Bryan, York, YO23 3FR (01904-772234; *fax:* 01904-772287)
Email: julie.amery@askham-bryan.ac.uk
Internet: http://www.askham-bryan.ac.uk/

Chief: Learning Resources Mgr: Miss Julie Amery BSc(Hons), DipILM, MCLIP
Entry: ref only *Open:* term: Mon-Thu 0845-2100, Fri 0845-1900, Sat-Sun 1245-1630; vac: Mon-Fri 0900-1700
Subj: social sci; environment; law; life sci; animal life; health & safety; eng; planning; landscape arch; agric; hortic; livestock; business; mgmt *Collns: Bks & Pamphs:* MAFF pubns; Forestry Commission pubns *Co-op Schemes:* York Biosciences Initiative Lib & Info Svcs *Equip:* fax, copier, 6 video viewers, copier, 39 computers (incl 35 with wd-proc & internet, 2 with CD-ROM), 32 other computers for teaching purposes (incl CD-ROM), scanner, ink-jet printer, light box *Svcs:* info, ref

Stock: bks/c30000, incl pamphs; periodcls/300; slides/600; maps/440; videos/650; learning & lang packs/650; student projects/2800 *Classn:* DDC *Auto Sys:* AutoLib *Pubns:* Farming in Yorkshire (£15) *Staff: Libns:* 1.5 *Non-Prof:* 3.5 *Exp:* £25000 (2000-01)

S2161 ☙

College of Law, York Library

Bishopthorpe Rd, York, YO23 2GA (01904-682054)
Email: library.york@lawcol.co.uk
Internet: http://www.college-of-law.co.uk/

Gov Body: Coll of Law *Chief:* Branch Libn: Mr Tony Simmonds (tony.simmonds@lawcol.co.uk) *Dep:* Snr Lib Asst: Ms Karen Baker *Assoc Libs:* BIRMINGHAM LIB (see **S168**); CHESTER LIB (see **S458**); GUILDFORD LIB (see **S769**); LONDON LIB (see **S1090**) *Open:* term: Mon-Thu 0900-2100, Fri 0900-1800, Sat-Sun 1200-1700 *Subj:* law *Equip:* copiers (A4/5p), computers (incl wd-procs, internet & CD-ROM) *Svcs:* info, ref *Staff: Libns:* 1 *Non-Prof:* 1 FT, 2 PT

S2162 ☙

Council for British Archaeology Library

Bowes Morrell House, 111 Walmgate, York, YO1 9WA (01904-671417; *fax:* 01904-671384)
Email: info@britarch.ac.uk
Internet: http://www.britarch.ac.uk/

Chief: Dep Dir: Dr Mike Heyworth BA, MA, PhD, MIFA, FSA
Entry: small, very specialised lib primarily for own use; others ref only, by adv appt *Open:* Mon-Fri 0930-1630
Subj: British archaeo

S2163 🏛

Emergency Planning College Library

The Hawkhills, Easingwold, York, YO61 3EG (01347-825007; *fax:* 01347-822575)
Email: john.parkinson@cabinet-office.x.gsi.gov.uk
Internet: http://www.ukresilience.info/college/

Gov Body: Cabinet Office *Chief:* Libn: Mr John Parkinson BA(Hons), MCLIP
Entry: emergency planning personnel & rsrchers by appt *Open:* Mon-Thu 0830-1730, Fri 0830-1500
Subj: emergency planning; disasters; civil defence *Collns: Other:* emergency plans; newspaper clippings; videos & news footage *Co-op Schemes:* BLDSC
Equip: video viewers, copier, room for hire *Stock:* bks/1000; periodcls/71; slides/2000; videos/128; archvs/14 m *Classn:* DDC *Auto Sys:* CAIRS *Staff: Libns:* 1 *Non-Prof:* 1

S2164 ☙

Joseph Rowntree Foundation, Library

The Homestead, 40 Water End, York, YO30 6WP (01904-629241; *fax:* 01904-620072)
Email: info@jrf.org.uk
Internet: http://www.jrf.org.uk/

Type: rsrch foundation *Chief:* Lib & Info Svcs Mgr: Mr Vaughan Birbeck BA, MA, MPhil, MCLIP *Entry:* ref, adv appt *Open:* Mon-Fri 0900-1700

Subj: social scis *Collns: Bks & Pamphs:* Joseph Rowntree Foundation pubns, incl: Hist of Rowntree Trusts; Garden Village of New Earswick; Joseph Rowntree Life & Work; Seebohm Rowntree Life & Work; JRF-funded rsrch *Equip:* m-reader, m-printer, video viewer, computers (with internet & CD-ROM) *Svcs:* info, ref, biblio *Stock:* bks/7000; periodcls/150; photos/3000, incl slides *Classn:* own *Auto Sys:* Paradox *Staff: Libns:* 1 *Non-Prof:* 1 PT *Exp:* £18500 (1999-2000)

S2165 🏛🏛

National Railway Museum, Library and Archive

Leeman Rd, York, YO26 4XJ (01904-686235; *fax:* 01904-631319)
Email: nrm.library@nmsi.ac.uk
Internet: http://www.nrm.org.uk/

Type: natl museum *Gov Body:* Natl Museum of Sci & Industry (The Sci Museum – see **S1387**) *Chief:* Head of Dept (Lib & Archv Collns): Mr Dieter Hopkin BA, MA, FMA *Dep:* Libn: Mr Philip Atkins BSc *Other Snr Staff:* Curator (Archvs): Mr Richard Taylor; Curator (Photographic & Film Collns): Mr Ed Bartholomew BA; Curator (Pictorial Collns): Ms Beverley Cole BA *Entry:* ref only, adv appt *Open:* Mon-Fri 1000-1700 *Subj:* rail transport, esp in British Isles *Collns: Bks & Pamphs:* govt pubns, incl: Board of Trade Railway Returns & other statistics; accident reports from 1855; Railway Clearing House pubns *Archvs:* technical records of railway companies & bodies associated with the industry, incl: Locomotive Manufactures Assoc; North East Railway Station Masters & Agents Assoc; Wiltshire, Somerset & Waymouth Railway Co; personal papers of indivs in the industry, incl: John Click Papers (locomotive engineer); E.S. Cox Papers (locomotive engineer); G.P. Neele Diaries *Other:* photo collns (180 collns, 1850s-date); eng drawings (1 mln+, 1820-date); pictorial collns, incl paintings, prints & engravings (1825 onwards); poster, notice & handbill colln (early 19C-date); timetables (1840s-date) *Equip:* m-reader, copier, touch screen Image Access Terminal (provides access to c20000 digitised photos) *Svcs:* info, ref, sales of photographs, prints & copy drawings *Stock:* bks/14000; periodcls/800; photos/1.4 mln; maps/500; m-forms/35000 *Acqs Offcr:* Head of Dept, Libn or Curator of relevant colln *Classn:* Ottley (mod) *Auto Sys:* Aleph *Pubns:* Readers' Guide (£6.50 incl p&p) *Staff: Other Prof:* 5

S2166 ☙

Nestec York Ltd, Technical Information Services

Nestec York Ltd, PO Box 201, York, YO91 1XY (01904-602421; *fax:* 01904-604887)
Email: maxine-keeping@rdyo.nestle.com

Chief: Info Offcr: Mrs Maxine Keeping *Entry:* adv appt *Open:* Mon-Fri 0830-1800 *Subj:* food sci; food tech *Collns: Other:* journals on m-form *Co-op Schemes:* ILL, York Bioscience Inst *Equip:* m-reader, m-printer, fax, copier, clr copier, computer (with internet & CD-ROM) *Online:* Dialog, Datastar, Foodline *Svcs:* info, ref, biblio *Stock:* bks/3000; periodcls/400; pamphs/2000; maps/40; videos/30; patents/1500 *Classn:* DDC *Auto Sys:* TechLib Opentext *Staff: Non-Prof:* 2

S2167

Shandy Hall, Library

Coxwold, York, YO61 4AD (01347-868465)

Type: historic house *Gov Body:* The Laurence Sterne Trust *Chief:* Hon Curator: Mrs Julia Monkman
Entry: admission fee *Open:* May-Sep: Wed 1400-1630, Sun 1430-1630; at other times by appt only
Subj: lit *Collns: Bks & Pamphs:* mainly works of Laurence Sterne

S2168

University of York, J.B. Morrell Library

Heslington, York, YO10 5DD (01904-433865; *fax:* 01904-433866)
Email: lib-enquiry@york.ac.uk
Internet: http://www.york.ac.uk/

Gov Body: Univ of York *Chief:* Univ Libn: Ms A.E.M. Heaps BA, MA, DipLib, MCLIP
Assoc Libs: HEALTH STUDIES LIB (see **S787**); KING'S MANOR LIB, King's Manor, Exhib Sq, York, YO1 7EP (01904-433969; *email:* lib-km@lists.york.ac.uk); WHINFIELD LIB, Chem Dept, Univ of York, Heslington, York, YO1 5DD; BORTHWICK INST OF HISTORICAL RSRCH, LIB & ARCHVS (see **A522**)
Entry: ref only except with permission of libn
Open: term: Mon-Fri 0900-2200, Sat -Sun 1100-1800; vac: times vary
Subj: all subjs; undergrad; postgrad; generalities; phil; psy; religion; social sci; edu; lang; sci; maths; tech; computer sci; electronics; arts; lit; geog; hist
Collns: Bks & Pamphs: held at the J.B. Morrell Lib: Cooper Abbs Colln (18C family lib, mainly lit, hist, sci & theology); Copland Colln (157 scores by Aaron Copland); Dyson Colln (17C-19C poetry, c1500 vols); Eliot Colln (English lit, 20C 1st eds); Halifax Parish Lib Colln (mainly theology & lit, 17C onwards); Milner-White Colln (English detective fiction, c800 vols); Milnes Walker Colln (early medical bks); Mirfield Colln (lib of Community of the Resurrection at Mirfield, mainly pre-1800); Peggy Janiurek Colln (ch's lit); Poetry Soc Lib (poetry, c11000 vols); Slaithwaite Parish Lib Colln (mainly 17C-18C theology); Smith Colln (British printing & engraving, 18C-19C); Special Colln (misc rare bks); Thesis Colln; Toynbee Colln (lib of Arnold Toynbee); Vickers Colln (scientific instrument manufacture); held at King's Manor Lib: Newbold Colln (fine arts); Newton Colln (medieval art); Wormald Colln (medieval art, lit & hist)
Archvs: held at Borthwick Inst of Historical Rsrch
Co-op Schemes: BLDSC, ILL, Yorkshire Univs, Riding Plus, UK Libs Plus, NEYAL
Equip: 8 m-readers, m-camera, 2 m-printers, 3 video viewers, 7 copiers, 45 computers (incl 15 wd-proc, 15 with CD-ROM & 15 with internet)
Disabled: Kurzweil *Online:* access to the internet & a range of subscription databases, plus 3500 e-journals (membs only) *Svcs:* info, ref
Stock: bks/800000; periodcls/3200; slides/800000; maps/380; m-forms/13000; videos/1000; CD-ROMs/various; e-journals/3500
Classn: DDC (mod) *Auto Sys:* Aleph
Pubns: 100+ lib guides on all subjs & svcs
Staff: Libns: 14 *Non-Prof:* 33.5
Proj: bldg of Humanities Rsrch Lib

S2169

York Archaeological Trust Library

Cromwell House, 13 Ogleforth, York, YO1 7FG (01904-663000; *fax:* 01904-663024)
Email: ckyriacou@yorkarchaeology.co.uk
Internet: http://www.yorkarchaeology.co.uk

Gov Body: York Archae Trust for Excavation & Rsrch Ltd *Chief:* Libn: Mrs C. Kyriacou BA, DipLib
Entry: adv appt *Open:* Mon-Fri 0900-1700

Subj: local study (York); arts; hist; archaeo
Collns: Archvs: York Archaeo Trust excavation records & photos (1972-date)
Equip: m-reader, fax, copier, clr copier, computer (with wd-proc, internet & CD-ROM) *Online:* Gazetteer of YAT Excavations *Svcs:* info
Pubns: Archaeo of York Series (50+ pubns to date, £1.50-£39); Yorkshire Archaeo Today (£1.95)
Staff: Libns: 1 PT

S2170

York Castle Museum, Library and Archives

Tower St, York, YO1 1RY (01904-650333)
Email: castle.museum@ymt.org.uk
Internet: http://www.yorkcastlemuseum.org.uk/

Gov Body: City of York Council (see **P208**)
Chief: Acting Curator: Mr Keith Matthews
Entry: adv appt for access to Lib & Archv materials
Subj: York & Yorkshire: local hist; social hist; military hist; costume & textile hist *Collns: Bks & Pamphs:* trade catalogues *Other:* photos of local subjs; ephemera
Svcs: museum artefact related enq svc
Stock: bks/3000
Staff: Other Prof: 6 *Non-Prof:* 50

S2171

York City Art Gallery Library

Exhibition Sq, York, YO1 7EW (01904-551861; *fax:* 01904-551866)
Email: art.gallery@york.gov.uk

Gov Body: York Museums Trust *Chief:* Curatorial Asst: Miss Allison Sharpe MA(Hons), MA(Museum Studies)
Entry: ref only; adv appt
Subj: arts; art hist *Collns: Other:* drawings, watercolours & prints, incl: Evelyn Colln of Topographical Works; Tillotson-Hyde Colln of Illusts
Svcs: info, ref
Stock: bks/8000; periodcls/10
Classn: by country & medium
Pubns: York City Art Gallery: An Illustrated Guide (1991); York Through the Eyes of the Artist (1990)
Staff: Other Prof: 1

S2172

York College of Further and Higher Education, Learning Resources Centre

Dringhouses, Tadcaster Rd, York, YO24 1UA (01904-770406; *fax:* 01904-770499)
Internet: http://www.yorkcollege.ac.uk/

Chief: Lib Svcs Mgr: Mr Chris Ryan BA(Hons), DipLib
Assoc Libs: 6TH FORM COLL LRC, Sim Balk Ln, Tadcaster Rd, York, YO23 2UD (01904-770858)
Entry: ref only if not student *Open:* term: Mon-Thu 0845-2100, Fri 0845-1800, Sat 0900-1300
Subj: all subjs; genl; GCSE; A level; undergrad; local studies (York) *Co-op Schemes:* BLDSC, ILL
Equip: fax, copier, clr copier, 200 computers (incl wd-proc, internet & CD-ROM) *Disabled:* CCTV, link with RNIB Lib Svc *Online:* Infotrac
Stock: bks/50000; periodcls/300; videos/500
Classn: DDC *Staff: Libns:* 1 *Non-Prof:* 7.5

S2173

York District Hospital, Library and Information Service

3rd Floor, Admin Block, York Dist Hosp, Wigginton Rd, York, YO31 8HE (01904-726712; *fax:* 01904-675583)
Email: hslibydh@york.ac.uk

Chief: Lib Mgr: Mrs H. Brownhill BA(Hons), DipIM, MCLIP
Assoc Libs: BOOTHAM PARK HOSP LIB
Entry: staff & students of York Health Trust & Univ of York only; all others by appl to Lib Mgr *Open:* Mon-Thu 0900-2000, Fri 0900-1700, Sat 0900-1200
Subj: social sci; all aspects of health care *Collns: Archvs:* York Health Trust Archvs (please contact Lib for further info) *Co-op Schemes:* YRLS, DoH Studies Group
Equip: m-reader, copier, 4 computers (all with wd-proc & internet) *Svcs:* info, biblio
Stock: bks/20000 excl bnd periodcls; periodcls/400; videos/80
Classn: Barnard *Auto Sys:* Aleph
Staff: Libns: 2.55 *Non-Prof:* 2.35

S2174

York Minster Library

Dean's Pk, York, YO1 7JQ (01904-625308; *fax:* 01904-611119)
Email: d.mortimer@yorkminsterlibrary.org.uk
Internet: http://www.yorkminster.org/

Type: cathedral lib *Gov Body:* The Dean & Chapter of York *Dep:* Libn: Mrs D.M. Mortimer BA(Hons), MA, DipLib, MCLIP
Assoc Libs: YORK MINSTER ARCHVS, at same addr, Archivist: Mr Peter Young (01904-611118; *fax:* 01904-611119; *email:* archives@yorkminster.org)
Entry: adv appt *Open:* Mon-Thu 0900-1700, Fri 0900-1200; closed Xmas & Easter
Subj: undergrad; postgrad; rsrch; Yorkshire: pre-20C hist; lit; topography; biography; printing; religion (Anglican); church hist; Cathedral & Diocese of York; ecclesiastical art & arch; English lit; English hist *Collns: Bks & Pamphs:* York (Minster, city & county); Yorkshire Civil War tracts; early printed bks; music; parish lib deposits
Archvs: administered separately: archvs of Dean & Chapter; Vicars Choral; Hailstone Colln; music; photos & sound recs; papers of Deans & Canons; medieval MSS *Other:* Yorkshire topographical prints; early Yorkshire newspapers; Yorkshire playbills
Equip: m-form reader/printer, fax, copier, 7 computers, UV lamp (use restricted), room for hire (£100 pd + VAT) *Disabled:* illuminated magnifier *Online:* computer catalogue provides access to other designated lib catalogues *Officer-in-Charge:* Libn, as above *Svcs:* info, ref, biblio, photographic
Stock: bks/120000 incl pamphs; periodcls/30; m-forms/200; Stock (archvs): archvs/1000 linear m; photos/12000; slides/8000; illusts/1000; maps/100; audios/50; AVs/100; medieval MSS/101 *Acqs Offcr:* Libn, as above
Classn: Univ of York special scheme *Auto Sys:* Aleph
Pubns: Catalogue of Printed Music to 1850 (£2.50); Catalogue of Music MSS (£15); The Beautifullest Church: York Minster 1472-1972 (exhib catalogue, £1); A Candidate for Praise: William Mason (exhib catalogue, £1); York Minster Lib (historical account, £1.95)
Staff: Libns: 3 *Other Prof:* 0.5 + 1 archivist *Non-Prof:* 1

S2175

York St John College, Library and Information Services

Lord Mayor's Walk, York, YO3 7EX (01904-716700; *fax:* 01904-612512)
Email: library@yorksj.ac.uk
Internet: http://www.yorksj.ac.uk/library/

Chief: Coll Libn: Mr Tony Chalcraft BA, MA, MCLIP (a.chalcraft@yorksj.ac.uk) *Dep:* Principal Asst Libn: Ms Helen Westmancoat BA, MCLIP (h.westmancoat@yorksj.ac.uk)
Entry: open access for ref, borrowing for fee

(York St John Coll, Lib & Info Svcs cont)
Open: term: Mon-Thu 0845-2130, Fri 0845-1900, Sat 0900-1700, Sun 1400-1900; vac: Mon-Fri 0900-1700
Subj: all subjs; undergrad **Collns:** Bks & Pamphs: York Religious Edu Centre; Victorian ch's bks; Comenius Centre (lang teaching) **Archvs:** Coll Archvs; Yorkshire Film Archv **Co-op Schemes:** BLDSC, UK Libs Plus, RIDING
Equip: 3 m-readers, m-printer, 6 video viewers, 6 copiers, 45 computers (all with wd-proc, internet & CD-ROM) **Online:** FirstSearch, OVID (selected databases), Newsbank **Svcs:** info, ref, biblio
Stock: bks/190000; periodcls/800; slides/500 sets; maps/750; audios/2000; videos/900; CD-ROMs/100; archvs/40 linear m **Acqs Offcr:** Snr Asst Libn: Mr Bryan Jones (b.jones@yorksj.ac.uk)
Classn: DDC **Auto Sys:** Sirsi Unicorn
Staff: Libns: 6 Non-Prof: 17 **Exp:** £249000 (2000-01); incl bks, periodcls & e-resources
Proj: new learning centre for completion in 2003

S2176 🏛
Yorkshire Museum, Library
Museum Gdns, York, YO1 7FR (01904-629745; *fax:* 01904-651221)
Email: yorkshire.museum@york.gov.uk
Internet: http://www.york.gov.uk/

Gov Body: York Museums Trust **Chief:** Registrar: Ms Melanie Baldwin BA(Hons)
Entry: ref only, adv appt required
Subj: York & Yorkshire: archaeo; biology; geol; numismatics; decorative art; sci; arts; geog; hist
Equip: m-reader, copier
Stock: various bks, periodcls & photos

ISLE OF MAN
Castletown

S2177 🎓
King William's College, The Dr Scholl Library
Castletown, Isle of Man, IM9 1TP (01624-820480; *fax:* 01624-824990)
Email: glanda.murphy@kwc.sch.im
Internet: http://www.kwc.sch.im/

Gov Body: King William's Coll **Chief:** Libn: Mrs G.R. Murphy DipLib, MCLIP
Assoc Libs: THE CUBBON LIB, The Buchan School, Castletown, Isle of Man
Entry: adv appt **Open:** Mon-Fri 0845-1645, 1930-2130
Subj: all subjs; genl; GCSE; local studies
Equip: copier, 6 computers (all with wd-proc, internet & CD-ROM) **Svcs:** info, ref
Stock: bks/15000; periodcls/15; audios/250
Classn: DDC **Auto Sys:** Heritage **Staff:** Libns: 1

Douglas

S2178 🎓 ✚
Isle of Man Centre for Nurse Education, Library
7th Floor, Victory House, Prospect Hill, Douglas, Isle of Man, IM1 1EQ (01624-642993; *fax:* 01624-642997)
Email: library@nurseed.dhss.gov.im

Gov Body: Isle of Man Govt, Isle of Man Health Svcs Div **Chief:** Lib Co-ordinator: Miss Jacquie Lesley BEd, CertEd, RNT, RMN, SRN **Dep:** Lib Assts: Mrs Joyce Barber & Mrs Rose Lunt
Assoc Libs: NOBLE'S ISLE OF MAN HOSP, POSTGRAD MEDICAL LIB, Westmoreland Rd, Douglas, Isle of Man, IM1 4QA, Libn: Ms Christine Sudgen (01624-642377)
Entry: health svc employees & authorised others
Open: Mon-Fri 0900-1700
Subj: nursing (undergrad & postgrad); phil; psy; social sci; sci **Co-op Schemes:** BLDSC, LIHNN
Equip: video viewers, fax, copier (A4/5p, A3/10p), computers (incl wd-proc, internet & CD-ROM) **Online:** AMED, ASSIA for Health, BNI, CINAHL, Embase, HMIC, Medline, PsycInfo **Svcs:** info, ref, biblio
Stock: bks/4210; periodcls/52; pamphs/various; audios/12; videos/306
Classn: by subj **Auto Sys:** Heritage
Staff: Other Prof: 1 Non-Prof: 1
Proj: merger with Noble's Isle of Man Hosp Postgrad Medical Lib in 2003

S2179 🎓
Isle of Man College Library
Homefield Rd, Douglas, Isle of Man, IM2 6RB (01624-648207; *fax:* 01624-663675)
Internet: http://www.iomcollege.ac.im/

Gov Body: Isle of Man Dept of Edu **Chief:** Snr Libn: Miss Carole Graham BA(Hons), MSc, MCLIP (carole.graham@iomcollege.ac.im) **Dep:** Coll Libn: Mr Timothy L.G. Kenyon BA(Hons), MCLIP (tim.kenyon@iomcollege.ac.im) **Other Snr Staff:** Libn: Mrs Susan Holden (susan.holden@iomcollege.ac.im)
Entry: public lib open to anyone **Open:** term: Mon-Thu 0900-2100, Fri 0900-1700, Sat 0900-1145; vac: Mon-Thu 0900-1700, Fri 0900-1630
Subj: all subjs; genl; GCSE; A level; undergrad; postgrad; vocational; special needs; local study (all aspects of Isle of Man & Manx culture); generalities; social sci; sci; maths; tech; arts; lit; geog; hist **Co-op Schemes:** BLDSC

Equip: video viewers, copier, clr copiers, computers (incl wd-proc, internet & CD-ROM)
Svcs: info, ref, biblio
Stock: bks/26000; periodcls/150; audios/245; videos/1200; CD-ROMs/150
Classn: DDC **Auto Sys:** Heritage IV
Staff: Libns: 3 Non-Prof: 2

S2180 🏛
Isle of Man Department of Education, Noble's Library
Noble's Hall, Westmoreland Rd, Douglas, Isle of Man, IM1 1RL (01624-673123; *fax:* 01624-671043)
Internet: http://www.gov.im/education/

Gov Body: Isle of Man Govt, Dept of Edu **Chief:** Librarian-in-Charge (Mobile Lib): Mrs Sandra Henderson MCLIP; Librarian-in-Charge (Jnr Lib): Ms Mary Cousins BS(Hons) **Dep:** Asst Libn: Mrs L. Strickett
Open: Mobile Lib: Mon-Fri 0900-1700; Jnr Lib: Tue-Fri 1000-1230, 1330-1700, Sat 1030-1600
Subj: all subjs; genl
Equip: m-reader, copier **Officer-in-Charge:** Librarian-in-Charge (Jnr Lib), as above
Stock: bks/30000; audios/500; videos/500; CD-ROMs/100 **Acqs Offcr:** Libns, as above
Classn: DDC **Auto Sys:** Heritage (used only for videos at present)
Staff: Libns: 1 Other Prof: 1 Non-Prof: 2

S2181 🏛
Isle of Man Government, Tynwald Library
Isle of Man Govt Offices, Legislative Bldgs, Buck's Rd, Douglas, Isle of Man, IM1 3PW (01624-685520; *fax:* 01624-685522)
Email: library@tynwald.org.im

Gov Body: The Tynwald (Parliament of the Isle of Man) **Chief:** Libn: Mr Geoff Haywood
Entry: membs & offcrs of the Tynwald, others by subscription **Open:** office hrs Mon-Fri
Subj: laws & legislation (Isle of Man) **Collns:** Bks & Pamphs: copies of recent lit produced by the various govt depts
Equip: copier

S2182 🎓
Isle of Man International Business School Library
The Nunnery, Old Castletown Rd, Douglas, Isle of Man, IM2 1QB (01624-693727)
Email: P.Weatherall@ibs.ac.im
Internet: http://www.ibs.ac.im/

Chief: Learning Resources Mgr: Mr Paul Weatherall
Entry: staff & students of School; ref only for others, by arrangement with the Learning Resources Mgr; external borrowing membership available for a fee **Open:** term: Mon-Thu 0900-2100, Fri 0900-1700, Sat 0900-1300; vac: Mon-Fri 0900-1700
Subj: business; finance; admin; accountancy **Co-op Schemes:** ILL
Equip: copier, computers **Svcs:** info, ref

CHANNEL ISLANDS

Alderney

S2183 🎵🏛
The Alderney Society Museum Library
High St, Alderney, Channel Islands, GY9 3TG (01481-823222; *fax*: 01481-824979)
Email: info@alderneymuseum.org
Internet: http://www.alderneysociety.org/

Gov Body: Alderney Soc *Chief*: Administrator: Mr Peter Arnold
Entry: ref only, preferably by appt *Open*: Mon-Fri 1000-1200, 1400-1600
Subj: Alderney, Channel Islands: all subjs at genl level; local hist; archaeo; nat hist *Collns*: Bks & Pamphs: Alderney Soc Bulletin (annual reports of the Soc etc); Société Guernesiaise Transactions; Société Jersiaise Bulletin *Archvs*: Ewen Archv (mainly hist); Harbour Journals (1862-65, 1868-71); Alderney Public School Log Bks (1862-1907)
Equip: 10 m-readers, copier (10p per pg), fax (50p per pg), 2 computers (all with wd-proc, internet & CD-ROM) *Officer-in-Charge*: Administrator, as above *Svcs*: ref
Stock: bks/500; periodcls/4; photos/4000; slides/ 100; maps/110; audios/20; videos/2; CD-ROMs/10
Acqs Offcr: Administrator, as above
Auto Sys: Modes for Windows
Pubns: Alderney Annals (£4.95); The Alderney Story (£2.95); Bird & Plant Lists; notes on hist & geol
Staff: Non-Prof: 1

Guernsey

S2184 🎓
Guernsey College of Further Education Library
Rue de Coutanchez, St Peter Port, Guernsey, Channel Islands, GY1 2TT (01481-737508; *fax*: 01481-714152)
Email: Library@cfe.edu.gg
Internet: http://www.cfe.edu.gg/

Gov Body: States of Guernsey Edu Council
Chief: Snr Lib Asst: Mrs Jill Cameron HNC(LIS) (JillCamercon@cfe.edu.gg)
Open: term: Mon-Thu 0845-2100, Fri 0845-1700; vac: only by special arrangement
Subj: all subjs; genl; GCSE; A level; undergrad; vocational; local study (Channel Islands) *Collns*: Bks & Pamphs: small careers lib *Other*: BSI (limited colln); local study resources, incl: Billets d'Etat (1987-date); Orders in Council (incomplete sequence); resource boxes & files *Co-op Schemes*: BLCMP
Equip: m-reader, video viewer, copier, 6 computers (all with wd-proc & internet) *Online*: various CD-ROMs *Svcs*: info, ref
Stock: bks/15000; periodcls/48; pamphs/ numerous; videos/200
Classn: DDC *Auto Sys*: Talis *Staff*: Non-Prof: 3

S2185 🎓 ✚
Guernsey Institute of Health Studies Library
Princess Elizabeth Hosp, Le Vauquiedor, St Andrews, Guernsey, Channel Islands, GY4 6UU (01481-707329; *fax*: 01481-700938)

Gov Body: States of Guernsey Board of Health
Chief: Libn: Miss Jodie Knight BSc(Hons), MCLIP (JKnight@health.gov.gg) *Dep*: Lib Asst: Mrs Penny Mann (PMann@health.gov.gg)
Entry: employees of Board of Health; others ref only, or purchase of membership by annual subscription of £25 *Open*: Mon-Fri 0900-1600

Subj: medicine; health studies; nursing *Co-op Schemes*: SWRLIN, BLDSC, NULJ
Equip: fax (20p per pg), video viewer, copier (10p per pg), 13 computers (incl 10 with wd-proc, 9 with internet & 1 with CD-ROM) *Online*: Medline, CINAHL, Cochrane *Svcs*: info, ref, biblio, current awareness, training
Stock: bks/8000; periodcls/48; videos/300; CD-ROMs/10
Classn: NLM (Wessex) *Auto Sys*: Talis
Staff: Libns: 1 Non-Prof: 0.5 *Exp*: £10000 (1999-2000); £10400 (2000-01)

S2186 🏰🏛
Guernsey Museum and Art Gallery, Library and Archives
Candie Gdns, St Peter Port, Guernsey, Channel Islands, GY1 1UG (01481-726518; *fax*: 01481-715177)
Internet: http://www.museum.guernsey.net/

Gov Body: Guernsey Museums Svc *Chief*: Museum Dir: Mr Peter Sarl
Entry: admission charge for Museum *Open*: Museum: Mon-Fri 1000-1700 (-1600 Nov-Mar); closed Xmas & New Year
Subj: Guernsey: nat hist; local hist; archaeo; geol *Collns*: Archvs: Lukis MS Colln on local archaeo sites; also holds the Sites & Monuments Record for Guernsey

S2187 🎵
La Société Guernesiaise, Library
Candie Gdns, St Peter Port, Guernsey, Channel Islands, GY1 1UG (01481-725093; *fax*: 01481-726248)
Internet: http://www.societe.org.gg/

Chief: Libns: Mr Gavin Sampson & Mrs Jean Sampson
Entry: adv appt *Open*: Tue, Thu Sat 1000-1130; or by appt
Subj: Bailiwick of Guernsey: archaeo; botany; marine biology; geog; geol; ornithology; entomology; hist; family hist; conservation
Equip: copier
Stock: bks/1000; slides/2000
Pubns: Report & Transactions (annual)
Staff: Non-Prof: 2

Jersey

S2188 ✚
Harvey Besterman Education Centre Library
Jersey Genl Hosp, St Helier, Jersey, Channel Islands, JE1 3QS (01534-622664; *fax*: 01534-622510)
Email: s.alberici@gov.je
Internet: http://www.health.gov.je/

Gov Body: States of Jersey Health & Social Svcs Dept *Chief*: Info & Lib Svcs Mgr: Mr Simon Alberici BA(Hons)
Open: Mon-Fri 0900-1700
Subj: medicine; health care *Co-op Schemes*: SWRLIN, BLDSC, NULJ
Equip: m-reader, m-printer, copier (10p per copy), 7 computers (all with wd-proc, internet & CD-ROM) *Online*: Medline, CINAHL, BNI, Cochrane (all on CD-ROM) *Svcs*: info, ref, biblio
Stock: bks/6000; periodcls/150; AVs/some, incl videos
Classn: NLM *Staff*: Libns: 1 Non-Prof: 1 *Exp*: £30000 (1999-2000); £30000 (2000-01)
Proj: automation of catalogue

S2189 🎓
Highlands College Learning Resource Centre and Eric Young Memorial Library
PO Box 1000, St Saviour, Jersey, Channel Islands, JE4 9QA (01534-608590; *fax*: 01534-608600)
Email: library@highlands.ac.uk
Internet: http://www.highlands.ac.uk/

Gov Body: Highlands Coll *Chief*: Head of Learning Resource: Miss Sandra Harris BA(Hons), CertEd, MCLIP (sandra.harris@highlands.ac.uk)
Dep: Lib Mgr: Ms Kate Hall (kate.hall@ highlands.ac.uk)
Entry: students & staff of Coll; ref only for non-membs, distance learning, OU & UK-based students *Open*: term: Mon-Thu 0900-1930, Fri 0900-1700; vac: Mon-Fri 0900-1600
Subj: all subjs; genl; undergrad; postgrad; vocational *Collns*: Bks & Pamphs: BSI *Co-op Schemes*: BLDSC, SWRLS, BLCMP, local scheme with Jersey Lib
Equip: copier, clr copier, video viewer, fax, 35 computers (all with wd-proc, internet & CD-ROM) *Disabled*: 2 computer workstations designed for wheelchairs *Svcs*: info, ref, biblio, indexing, info skills programmes, Open Learning access to network
Stock: bks/22100; periodcls/85; slides/2400; videos/352
Classn: DDC *Auto Sys*: Talis
Staff: Libns: 1 Non-Prof: 4 *Exp*: £25000 (1999-2000)

S2190 🎵
Société Jersiaise, Lord Coutanche Library
7 Pier Rd, St Helier, Jersey, Channel Islands, JE2 4UW (01534-730538; *fax*: 01534-888262)
Email: library@societe-jersiaise.org
Internet: http://www.societe-jersiaise.org/

Gov Body: Société Jersiaise *Chief*: Libn: Mrs Angela Underwood BA, DipLib, MCLIP *Dep*: Asst Libn & Edu Offcr: Mrs Anna Baghiani MA, CertEd
Entry: ref only to non-membs *Open*: Mon- Fri 0900-1700
Subj: Channel Islands (esp Jersey): hist; archaeo; geol; genealogy; family papers; business records; personal papers *Collns*: Bks & Pamphs: guide bks (French & English, from 1826); almanacs (from 1785); attempts to collect all written material on Channel Islands, particularly Jersey *Archvs*: Jersey newspapers (1784-1959); parish church records (1590-1842); Jersey Merchant Seamen's Benefit Soc Registers (c1830s-1880s, fragile); misc documents relating to the German occupation (1940-45), incl Jersey Evening Post, bks & ephemera; family papers & correspondence, incl: Amy of Patier; Trinity Manor; Pipon; Vavasseur dit Durell; authors' MSS & notes, incl: Philip Ahier; William Davies; E.T. Nicholle; Joan Stevens; Marguerite Syvret; ancient MSS (e.g., Chevalier's diary, 1643-51, incl translation) *Other*: map colln (from 14C); prints
Equip: 2 m-readers, m-printer (A4/50p), copier (A4/20p, A3/40p), fax, video viewer, 4 computers (all with wd-proc, internet & CD-ROM), 2 rooms for hire *Officer-in-Charge*: Libn, as above
Stock: bks/20000; periodcls/25; photos/40000; illusts/550; pamphs/3000; maps/400; m-forms/50; audios/100; videos/10; archvs/500 m *Acqs Offcr*: Libn, as above
Classn: DDC *Auto Sys*: Filemaker Pro
Pubns: Balleine's Hist of Jersey (£25); Birds in Jersey (£1.50); numerous others in English, French & German; list available on appl
Staff: Libns: 1 Non-Prof: 2 + volunteers
Proj: lib refurbishment

SECTION 5 – UK LIBRARY AND INFORMATION ORGANISATIONS

Entries are arranged alphabetically under organisation names. Organisations listed include professional societies and associations such as CILIP, Aslib and the Society of Archivists (along with branches and special interest groups), co-ordinating bodies, pressure groups, specialist information services, bibliographic and record societies, local and family history societies, and library and information studies departments of universities and colleges.

The section also includes some Irish organisations that are based in Northern Ireland.

While every effort is made to ensure that addresses and other contact details are accurate and up-to-date, it should be noted that a number of the following organisations can only be contacted via their senior officers, and that contact details may change following any turnover in these positions.

To telephone organisations within the United Kingdom from outside the country, dial 00-44 followed by the number, minus the initial 0.

Entries are based on the organisations' responses to the following questions:

	1.	**a) Official name of organisation**
		b) Acronym of organisation
	2.	**Full postal address** *(incl. postcode)*
		Tel & Fax *(incl. STD code)*
Email:		Electronic Mail
Internet:		Internet address
Type:	3.	**Type of Organisation**
		(see key to Symbols below)
Gov Body:	4.	**Governing body** *(if any)*
Chief:	5.	**Chief Officer** *(incl. name, designation & email)*
Other Snr Offcrs:	6.	**Other Senior Officers** *(incl. name, designation & email)*
Membs:	7.	**Members** *(if any)*
indivs		**a)** individual
instns		**b)** institutional
Memb Req:		**Membership Requirements** *(if applicable, incl. subscription fees)*
Branches & Groups:	8.	**Branch Organisations/Special Interest Groups** *(if any; give contact details & name & designation of officer in charge)*
Activs:	9.	**Main activities/services of organisation**
Pubns:	10.	**Publications** *(give Titles, Terms of issue, Prices)*
Further Info:	11.	**Further Information**

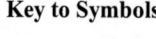

Key to Symbols

 Academic/Educational   Corporate/Business   Governmental (incl local)   Medical/Health

 Museum/Gallery   Photo/Film   Private   Religious

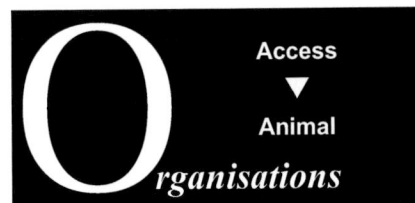

Access ▼ Animal Organisations

O1 🗝 ✚

Access Network
(formerly the Community Care Network)
c/o Ms Linda Butler, Birmingham Central Lib, Chamberlain Sq, Birmingham, B3 3HG (0121-303-4402)
Email: linda.butler@birmingham.gov.uk
Internet: http://www.cilip.org.uk/interests/oils/an/

Chief: Chair: Ms Linda Butler, as above
Membs: 84 indivs; 4 instns *Memb Req:* subscription: indivs £8 (concessions £4), instns £12
Activs: An independent organisation bringing together all those interested in library or information services to people with disabilities, those who are housebound or in residential care, carers and people in hospital. Organises seminars and an annual conference.
Pubns: Network News (2 pa); Making the Link: Key Contacts in Public Libs (2002, £15)
Further Info: The Access Network is an Org in Liaison with CILIP (see **O110**)

O2 🏛

Access to Archives [A2A]
Natl Archvs, Kew, Richmond, Surrey, TW9 4DU (020-8487-9211)
Email: a2a@nationalarchives.gov.uk
Internet: http://www.pro.gov.uk/archives/A2A/

Gov Body: Steering Group *Chief:* Programme Mgr: Ms Louise Craven
Activs: As part of the national archives network, A2A aims to provide a database of catalogue descriptions for archives held throughout England, and to make this documentary heritage more easily available to the public.
Further Info: The A2A database is available online at: http://www.a2a.pro.gov.uk/

O3 🗝

Access to Learning Libraries Information in Northamptonshire [ALLIN]
c/o Mr Andrew Martin, Univ Coll Northampton, Park Campus Lib, Boughton Green Rd, Northampton, NN2 7AL (01604-735500; *fax:* 01604-718819)
Email: andrew.martin@northampton.ac.uk
Internet: http://oldweb.northampton.ac.uk/lrs/allin/

Type: co-op *Chief:* Chair: Mr Eric Wright (ewright@northamptonshire.gov.uk) *Other Snr Offcrs:* Sec: Mr Andrew Martin, as above
Memb Req: info providers in Northamptonshire
Activs: Aims to promote co-operation between information providers in Northamptonshire and to increase public access to information resources for lifelong learning.

O4 🗝

Accessing Lancashire Library and Information Services [ALLIS]
c/o Ms Karen Haddon, Univ of Central Lancashire Lib, Preston, Lancashire, PR1 2HE (01772-892105)
Email: kshaddon@uclan.ac.uk
Internet: http://www.allis.org.uk/

Type: co-op *Chief:* contact Ms Karen Haddon
Membs: 19 instns *Memb Req:* Higher Edu, Further Edu, health & public libs in Lancashire
Activs: Exists to facilitate improved access to library and information resources in Lancashire to all who may benefit from them.

O5 🗝

ADSET
Britannia House, 29 Station Rd, Kettering, Northamptonshire, NN15 7HJ (01536-410500; *fax:* 01536-414274)
Email: info@adset.org.uk
Internet: http://www.adset.org.uk/

Chief: Genl Mgr: Mrs Hazel Edmunds
Membs: 85 instns *Memb Req:* open to orgs involved in info provision in the training, careers & employment fields; subscription: £105-£325 pa depending on size of company
Activs: Aims to improve the quality, management, use and usefulness of information in areas of training, lifelong learning, careers and employment; activities and services include the provision of standards for recording information in these areas; meetings and seminars; consultancy services; business advice; members' library; enquiry service.
Pubns: Careers Software News (termly); Membs' Update (free to membs); Opportunity (directory of sources, £40); Directory of Guidance Provision for Adults in the UK (CD-ROM, £39.50); non-membs charged p&p at 10% of price of order

O6 🏛

Advisory Council on Libraries [ACL]
c/o Libs Div, Dept of Culture, Media and Sport, 2-4 Cockspur St, London, SW1Y 5DH (020-7211-6124; *fax:* 020-7211-6130)

Chief: Chairman: Mr Bill Macnaught
Membs: 12 indivs
Activs: To advise the Secretary of State for Culture, Media and Sport on English public library issues for which he or she has responsibility under the 1964 Public Libraries Act.

O7 🗝

Affiliation of Local Government Information Specialists [ALGIS]
c/o Ms Mandy Wickham, Room 1.59/1.60, Sessions House, County Hall, Maidstone, Kent, ME14 1XQ
Internet: http://www.laria.gov.uk/algis_f.htm

Type: prof *Gov Body:* LARIA (Local Authorities Rsrch & Intelligence Assoc) *Chief:* Chair: Ms Jane Inman, Warwickshire Lib & Info Svc *Other Snr Offcrs:* Sec: Ms Mandy Wickham, as above
Membs: 120 indivs *Memb Req:* subscription: £11 pa
Activs: Aims to represent the interests and concerns of information specialists working in local government; organises events and visits and other activities designed to raise awareness of the potential and actual benefits of the work of information specialists within local government.
Pubns: ALGIS Newsletter (4 pa to membs)

O8 🗝

African Caribbean Library Association [ACLA]
ACLA Project Office, c/o 52 Burgundy House, 9 Bedale Rd, Enfield, Middlesex, EN2 0NZ (*tel & fax:* 01992-620239)
Email: acla_uk@yahoo.co.uk
Internet: http://www.la-hq.org.uk/groups/acla/acla.html

Chief: Chair: Ms Ann Thompson, Waltham Forest Central Lib (020-8520-3031; *email:* libraryannie@yahoo.co.uk) *Other Snr Offcrs:* Sec: Ms Evadne Hill, addr as above
Memb Req: open to libns, lib workers, info & IT specialists, lib edu specialists, writers, artists & publishers of African or Caribbean origin
Activs: Works to represent the interests of librarians and others in the library and information fields of African or Caribbean origin. ACLA is committed to the full implementation of race equality principles and policies throughout librarianship, and confronts racism in publications, recruitment, training and workplace practice. Organises training events, seminars and conferences, provides consultancy, and is represented at recruitment fairs, bookfairs and festivals.
Further Info: ACLA is an Org in Liaison with CILIP (see **O110**)

O9 🗝 🙏

Al-Furqan Islamic Heritage Foundation
Eagle House, High St, Wimbledon, London, SW19 5EF (020-8944-1233; *fax:* 020-8944-1633)
Email: info@al-furqan.com
Internet: http://www.al-furqan.com/

Gov Body: Board of Dirs *Chief:* Chairman: Sheikh Ahmed Zaki Yamani
Activs: Aims to promote and facilitate the documentation and preservation of the Islamic written heritage, through its work in surveying, cataloguing, editing and publishing Islamic manuscripts. The Foundation provides a specialist post-graduate course in cataloguing and preservation, and organises conferences, symposia, lectures and discussions.
Pubns: various surveys, catalogues, proceedings, monographs & others; see web site for details
See also **S989**

O10 🗝 🎓 ✚

All Wales Health Information and Library Extension Services [AWHILES]
c/o Mr Steve Pritchard, Univ of Wales Coll of Medicine Lib Svcs, Heath Pk, Cardiff, CF14 4XN (029-2074-2876; *fax:* 029-2074-3651)
Email: Pritchard@cf.ac.uk

Type: co-op *Chief:* Sec: Mr Steve Pritchard, as above *Other Snr Offcrs:* Dr Alison Weightman (weightmanal@cf.ac.uk)
Membs: 26 indivs; 26 instns *Memb Req:* all NHS Trust libs in Wales in Postgrad or Edu Centres
Activs: AWHILES is a collaboration between the University of Wales College of Medicine and Cardiff and Vale NHS Trust Libraries with all libraries in Postgraduate and/or Education Centres in Welsh NHS Trusts. The collaboration includes: a shared library catalogue; a rapid and economic inter-library loans service; news dissemination and communication including an email discussion list; liaison with the Postgraduate and Undergraduate Deans; a wide range of professional development activities including an annual conference, training events, library accreditation and support.

O11 🗝

Animal Health Information Specialists (UK and Ireland) [AHIS]
c/o Ms Fiona Brown, Royal (Dick) School of Veterinary Studies, Summerhall, Edinburgh, EH9 1QH (0131-650-6175; *fax:* 0131-650-6593)
Email: f.brown@edinburgh.ac.uk
Internet: http://www.ahis.org/

☛

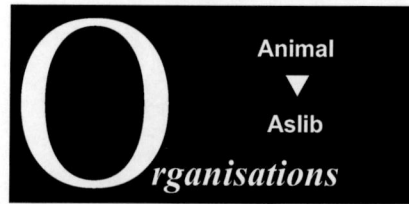

Organisations

Animal
▼
Aslib

(Animal Health Info Specialists cont)
Type: prof **Chief:** Hon Sec: Ms Fiona Brown, as above
Memb Req: open to anyone involved or interested in the dissemination of animal health info; subscription: £20 pa
Activs: Aims to foster co-operation and resource sharing in the field of animal health information and to stimulate interest in these and related areas; organises meetings, discussions and an Annual Conference; collects and disseminates information of interest to members.
Pubns: newsletter (2 pa, free to membs); Membership Directory (free to membs)

O12 ♀

Architecture Librarians Group [ARCLIB]
c/o Ms Hinda F. Sklar, Architectural Assoc School of Arch, 34-36 Bedford Sq, London, WC1B 3ES (020-7887-4035; *fax:* 020-7414-0782)
Email: hsklar@aaschool.ac.uk
Internet: http://cwis.livjm.ac.uk/lea/misc/arcweb.htm

Type: prof **Chief:** Chairperson: Ms Kathleen Godfrey, Kent Inst of Art & Design (01227-817514; kgodfrey@kiad.ac.uk) **Other Snr Offcrs:** Sec: Ms Hinda F. Sklar, as above
Membs: 37 full, 9 associate **Memb Req:** full membership: £15 pa (open to representatives of instns offering RIBA-approved courses in the UK & Ireland); associate membership: £20 pa (open to any indiv with an interest in architectural libnship)
Activs: An independent co-operative group which aims: to promote the sharing of good practice and co-operation amongst architecture librarians; to provide a forum for the exchange of experience, ideas and information; to act as a pressure group for architecture information providers; to promote an awareness of libraries as information sources for architectural education and training; to support the activities of, and co-operate with, organisations with similar objectives. Organises meetings and an Annual Conference
Pubns: ARCLIB Bulletin (1 pa, published electronically)

O13 ♀

Archives Council Wales (Cyngor Archifau Cymru) [ACW/CAC]
c/o Mr Gwyn Jenkins, Keeper of Manuscripts and Records, Natl Lib of Wales, Aberystwyth, Ceredigion, SY23 3BU (01970-632802; *fax:* 01970-632883)
Email: gwyn.jenkins@llgc.org.uk
Internet: http://www.llgc.org.uk/cac/

Gov Body: Council **Chief:** Sec: Mr Gwyn Jenkins, addr as above
Membs: 17 instns; 3 observers
Activs: Aims to bring together institutions and organisations involved with the administration of archives in Wales and to provide a forum for the regular exchange of views; to influence policy on archives in Wales; to bring matters of concern to the attention of the public, government or relevant institutions; to provide a focus for collaborative projects in the field of Welsh archives; meets at least 3 times per year.

Pubns: Annual Report (in elec format only, available on web site)

O14 ♀

Archivists in Independent Television
c/o Mr Barrie MacDonald, Independent Television Commission Lib, 33 Foley St, London, W1P 7LB (020-7306-7766; *fax:* 020-7306-7750)
Email: library@itc.org.uk

Chief: Chairman: Mr Barrie MacDonald, as above
Memb Req: open to those involved in records mgmt or archvs in the commercial television sector, or in television documentation in associated archvs, museums or other orgs
Branches & Groups: affiliated to the SOC OF ARCHIVISTS, SPECIALIST REPOSITORIES GROUP (see **O369**)
Activs: An informal, voluntary group established to provide a forum for the exchange of ideas and information amongst workers involved in the field of television documentation; organises regular meetings and visits.
Pubns: Guidelines for Managing Television Written Archvs (1995)

O15 ♀ 🎓

ARLIS UK and Ireland: The Art Libraries Society [ARLIS]
18 College Rd, Bromsgrove, Worcestershire, B60 2NE (*tel & fax:* 01527-579298)
Email: sfrench@arlis.demon.co.uk
Internet: http://www.arlis.org.uk/

Type: prof **Gov Body:** Council **Chief:** Chair: Ms Margaret Young, Newington Lib, Edinburgh (margaret.young@edinburgh.gov.uk) **Other Snr Offcrs:** Administrator: Ms Sonia French, addr as above
Membs: 158 indivs; 189 instns; 356 overseas membs **Memb Req:** open to all those involved in the documentation of the visual arts, incl arch & design; subscription fees vary
Branches & Groups: various committees & working groups, covering: cataloguing & classn; natl co-ordination of art lib resources; edu & prof development; pubns; visual resources; visual archvs
Activs: Promotion of art librarianship through education and co-operation both nationally and internationally. Improvement of access to visual arts information, documentation and materials. Advancement of public education in, and the appreciation and understanding of, the visual arts.
Pubns: Art Libs Journal (4 pa); ARLIS News-sheet (bi-monthly); ARLIS UK & Ireland Directory (free to membs, £45 to non-membs); Union List of Art, Arch & Design Serials; various guidelines & resource guides; contact ARLIS for details
Further Info: ARLIS UK & Ireland is an Org in Liaison with CILIP (see **O110**)

O16 ♀ 🎓

Army Records Society [ARS]
c/o Natl Army Museum, Royal Hosp Rd, Chelsea, London, SW3 4HT

Chief: Pres: Genl Sir Anthony Farrar-Hockley GBE, KCB, DSO, MC, BLitt **Other Snr Offcrs:** Hon Sec: Dr William Philpott MA, DPhil, FRHistS, Dept of War Studies, King's Coll London (william.philpott@kcl.ac.uk)
Membs: 500 indivs; 40 instns **Memb Req:** open to anyone interested in British military hist; subscription: indivs £25 pa; instns & overseas indivs £35 pa; contact Membership Admin, Heritage House, PO Box 21, Baldock, Hertfordshire, SG7 5SH (01462-896688; *fax:* 01462-896677)
Activs: Founded in 1984 with the aim of publishing documents relating to the military history of Britain.

Pubns: 1 vol pa, incl in membs' subscription; recent vols incl: John Peebles: A Scottish Grenadier in America, 1776-1782 (1997); The Maratha War Papers of Arthur Wellesley, January to December 1803 (1998); The Papers of Charles À Court Repington, Military Correspondent of the Times 1903-18 (1999); Sir Hugh Rose & the Central India Campaign, 1858 (2000); Lord Roberts & the War in South Africa 1899-1902 (2001); ARS pubns also available from Sutton Publishing

O17 ♀

Asian Librarians and Advisors Group [ALAG]
c/o Mr Kalyan K. Dutt, Lib Support Centre, Ealing Central Sports Ground, Horsenden Ln South, Greenford, Middlesex, UB6 8AP (020-8810-7650; *fax:* 020-8810-7651)
Email: KDutt@ealing.gov.uk
Internet: http://www.la-hq.org.uk/groups/alag/alag.html

Type: prof, co-op **Chief:** Chair: Mrs Gulshan Iqbal (0845-456-2899; gulshan-iqbal@cip.org.uk) **Other Snr Offcrs:** Sec: Mr Kalyan K. Dutt MA, MCLIP, as above; Treasurer: Mrs Monna Rizvi (monnar@sloughlibrary.org.uk)
Activs: Promotes the use of library and leisure services in, and to raise awareness of the needs of and to maintain service provision to, Asian communities in particular and the community at large in general; promotes racial equality in the library field; promotes Asian languages, history, culture and heritage through library and information services; provides a forum for Asian librarians and workers from similar fields. Provides regular meetings and a yearly AGM.
Pubns: Asian Periodicals: An Annotated list of South Asian Newspapers & Periodicals
Further Info: ALAG is an Org in Liaison with CILIP (see **O110**)

O18 ♀

Aslib, The Association for Information Management [ASLIB]
Temple Chambers, 3-7 Temple Ave, London, EC4Y 0HP (020-7583-8900; *fax:* 020-7583-8401)
Email: aslib@aslib.com
Internet: http://www.aslib.co.uk/aslib/

Type: prof **Chief:** Chief Exec: Mr Roger Bowes
Membs: c1700 instns **Memb Req:** Corporate Membership: varies on size of instn; Affiliate Membership: £47 pa; Student Membership: £20 pa; contact Membership Dept (020-7583-8900; email: members@aslib.com)
Branches & Groups: Regional Branches: MIDLANDS BRANCH (see **O26**); NORTHERN BRANCH (see **O28**); SCOTTISH BRANCH (see **O305**); Special Interest Groups: BIOSCIENCES GROUP (see **O19**); CHARITABLE INFO GROUP (see **O20**); ECON & BUSINESS INFO GROUP (see **O21**); ENG GROUP (see **O22**); EUROPEAN BUSINESS OPPORTUNITIES SVC (see **O23**); IT & COMMUNICATIONS GROUP (see **O24**); KNOWLEDGE & INFO MGMT NETWORK (see **O25**); MULTIMEDIA GROUP (see **O27**); ONE MAN BANDS GROUP (see **O29**); SOCIAL SCIS INFO GROUP & NETWORK (see **O31**); TECHNICAL TRANSLATION GROUP (see **O32**)
Activs: Founded in 1924, Aslib is a world class corporate membership organisation with over 2000 members in some 70 countries. Actively promotes best practice in the management of information resources, and represents its members and lobbies on all aspects of the management of and legislation concerning information at local, national and international levels. Aslib provides consultancy and information services, training, conferences, specialist recruitment and the Aslib Internet programme, and supports many specialist interest groups.

Pubns: Aslib Directory of Info Sources in the UK (12th ed, membs £268, non-membs £335, also available on CD-ROM); Managing Info (10 pa, subscription £75/$99/€99 pa); over 100 titles currently available, see web site for details

O19
Aslib Biosciences Group [ABG]

c/o Ms Andrea Reid, British Lib, 96 Euston Rd, London, NW1 2DB (020-7412-7038; *fax:* 020-7412-7217)
Email: andrea.reid@bl.uk
Internet: http://www.aslib.co.uk/sigs/biosciences/

Type: prof **Gov Body:** Aslib (see **O18**) **Chief:** Chair: Ms Carol Gokce, Nat Hist Museum Lib (c.gokce@nhm.ac.uk) **Other Snr Offcrs:** Sec: Ms Andrea Reid, as above
Memb Req: Aslib Corporate Membs £29 pa; Affiliate Membership (for non-memb orgs) £47 pa
Activs: Promotes the exchange of information in the fields of biology, agriculture, medicine and the environment, and works actively with other similar specialised groups in the UK and elsewhere; organises regular meetings, seminars, conferences and visits designed to provide instruction and training, as well as stimulate the analysis of techniques and management of information in the field of biosciences.

O20
Aslib Charitable Information Group [CIG]

c/o Aslib, Temple Chambers, 3-7 Temple Ave, London, EC4Y 0HP (020-7583-8900; *fax:* 020-7583-8401)
Email: aslib@aslib.com
Internet: http://www.aslib.co.uk/

Type: prof **Gov Body:** Aslib (see **O18**) **Chief:** contact the Group Liaison Offcr
Memb Req: Aslib Corporate Membs £29 pa; Affiliate Membership (for non-memb orgs) £47 pa
Activs: Provides a support network for information professionals working or otherwise involved in the charity sector.

O21
Aslib Economics and Business Information Group [AEBIG]

c/o Aslib, Temple Chambers, 3-7 Temple Ave, London, EC4Y 0HP (020-7583-8900; *fax:* 020-7583-8401)
Email: aslib@aslib.com
Internet: http://www.aslib.co.uk/sigs/aebig/

Type: prof **Gov Body:** Aslib (see **O18**) **Chief:** contact the Group Liaison Offcr
Memb Req: Aslib Corporate Membs £29 pa; Affiliate Membership (for non-memb orgs) £47 pa
Activs: The largest of Aslib's special interest groups, providing a leading forum for information professionals involved or interested in business information; organises seminars and workshops on products, applications and developments in the business information field, and arranges visits to business information centres.

O22
Aslib Engineering Group [AEG]

c/o Ms Andrea Beddard, Libn, Arup, 13 Fitzroy St, London, W1P 6BQ (020-7465-2128; *fax:* 020-7465-2126)
Email: andrea.beddard@arup.com
Internet: http://www.aslib.co.uk/sigs/engineering/

Type: prof **Gov Body:** Aslib (see **O18**) **Chief:** Chair: Mr John Harrington, Cranfield Univ Info & Lib Svc (j.harrington@cranfield.ac.uk) **Other Snr Offcrs:** Group Sec: Ms Andrea Beddard, as above
Memb Req: Aslib Corporate Membs £29 pa; Affiliate Membership (for non-memb orgs) £47 pa
Activs: Aims to bring practising engineers and information professionals together, to exchange views and needs; organises whole-day and afternoon workshops, and a spring and autumn programme of visits to research centres, industrial companies and professional institutions. Also provides a contact list of information professionals throughout the field through the Engineering Group Membership List.

O23
Aslib European Business Opportunities Service

c/o Aslib, Temple Chambers, 3-7 Temple Ave, London, EC4Y 0HP (020-7583-8900; *fax:* 020-7583-8401)
Email: peter.matthews@aslib.co.uk
Internet: http://www.aslib.co.uk/sigs/ebos/

Type: prof **Gov Body:** Aslib (see **O18**) **Chief:** European Union Co-ordinator: Mr Peter Matthews, at above addr
Memb Req: Aslib Corporate Membs £29 pa; Affiliate Membership (for non-memb orgs) £47 pa
Activs: A new service under development for Aslib members; aims to advise and assist members to find relevant information leading to business opportunities, concentrating on sources within the European Commission and the World Bank; plans to offer sponsored trips to these institutions and to organise workshops.
Pubns: Newsletter; guide bk to European Commission dept offices, functions & grant funding programmes

O24
Aslib IT and Communications Group [ACG]

(formed by the merger of the Aslib Computer & Electronics Groups)
c/o Mr John Coupland, IEE, Savoy Pl, London, WC2R 0BL (020-7344-5451; *fax:* 020-7497-3557)
Email: jcoupland@iee.org.uk
Internet: http://www.aslib.com/sigs/itc/

Type: prof **Gov Body:** Aslib (see **O18**) **Chief:** Chairman: Mrs Julia MacGregor (julia.macgregor@btinternet.com) **Other Snr Offcrs:** Hon Sec: Mr John W. Coupland, addr as above
Membs: 10 indivs; 240 instns; figs are approx
Memb Req: Aslib Corporate Membs £29 pa; Affiliate Membership (for non-memb orgs) £47 pa
Activs: The group represent the interests of information professionals in the IT, electronics, communications and engineering sectors. Organises an annual conference, presentations and educational meetings (approximately 6 meetings per year) to discuss IT issues of concern to library and information professionals, especially those working in special libraries. The group also hosts practical demonstrations and assessments of new products in the market place.

O25
Aslib Knowledge and Information Management Network [KIMNET]

(formerly Aslib Info Resources Mgmt Network)
c/o Aslib, Temple Chambers, 3-7 Temple Ave, London, EC4Y 0HP (020-7583-8900; *fax:* 020-7583-8401)
Email: aslib@.aslib.com
Internet: http://www.irm.org.uk/

Type: prof **Gov Body:** Aslib (see **O18**) **Chief:** Chair: Ms Susan Montgomery
Memb Req: subscription £80 pa; non-membs of Aslib may join as affiliates
Activs: To initiate and encourage the development of IRM concepts and practices within organisations; to promote awareness and understanding of IRM among senior managers and information professionals by providing a forum for discussion and exchange of experience; to support the adoption of IRM policies as sound business practice. Offers: a forum to meet experts who lead the field in IRM; innovative IRM concepts and practices for the workplace; professional development in a critical sphere of management; a regular meeting programme; networking with other practitioners and academics specialising in the subject; an opportunity for personal involvement in research and information gathering.

O26
Aslib Midlands Branch

c/o Ms Linda Norbury, Univ of Birmingham Lib, Edgbaston, Birmingham, B15 2TT (0121-414-5817)
Email: l.norbury@bham.ac.uk
Internet: http://www.aslib.co.uk/sigs/midlands/

Type: prof **Gov Body:** Aslib (see **O18**) **Chief:** Acting Chair: Mr Harry Drummond (H.Drummond@wlv.ac.uk) **Other Snr Offcrs:** Sec: Ms Linda Norbury, as above
Memb Req: all Aslib membs in the Midlands region are automatically membs
Activs: Aims to support Aslib members in the Midlands by providing a forum for professional communication, training and development. Arranges a wide-ranging programme of seminars, meetings and visits. These events cover topics of universal appeal as well as addressing areas of specific interest to members in the region, and provide an opportunity to update professional knowledge, to network and make contacts.
Pubns: Newsletter

O27
Aslib Multimedia Group [AMG]

c/o Aslib, Temple Chambers, 3-7 Temple Ave, London, EC4Y 0HP (020-7583-8900; *fax:* 020-7583-8401)
Email: aslib@aslib.com
Internet: http://www.aslib.co.uk/sigs/multimedia/

Type: prof **Gov Body:** Aslib (see **O18**) **Chief:** contact the Group Liaison Offcr
Membs: 100 instns **Memb Req:** subscription: Aslib Corporate Membs £29 pa; Affiliate Membership (for non-memb orgs) £47 pa
Activs: Co-ordinating interests of information professionals involved in the storage, retrieval and effective use of all forms of audiovisual data, from World Wide Web materials to overhead projectors; membership includes media librarians, information officers, archivists, AVM producers, technicians, networkers, software experts, publishers, distributors of multimedia and educators; keeps members informed of developments in multimedia through conferences, workshops and demonstrations throughout the year.
Pubns: Audiovisual Libn (quarterly journal)

O28
Aslib Northern Branch

c/o Mr Ian McCulloch, CEH Windermere, Ferry House, Far Sawrey, Ambleside, Cumbria, LA22 0LP (01539-487716; *fax:* 01539-446914)
Email: idm@ceh.ac.uk
Internet: http://www.aslib.co.uk/sigs/northern/ ☞

Organisations

Aslib ▼ **Association**

(Aslib Northern Branch cont)
Type: prof *Gov Body:* Aslib (see **O18**) *Chief:* Chair: Mrs Pam Keen, LADSIRLAC, Liverpool Central Libs (0151-207-1937; pamela.keen@ liverpool.gov.uk) *Other Snr Offcrs:* Hon Treasurer: Mrs Debbie Franks, Daresbury Laboratory Lib (d.franks@dl.ac.uk); Minutes Sec: Mr Ian McCulloch, addr as above (idm@ceh.ac.uk)
Memb Req: automatic membership for all membs of Aslib in the region
Activs: Promotes the work of Aslib in the North, and encourages networking between information professionals within the region. Arranges talks and an Annual General Meeting.

O29 ⚷

Aslib One Man Bands Group
c/o Aslib, Temple Chambers, 3-7 Temple Ave, London, EC4Y 0HP (020-7583-8900; *fax:* 020-7583-8401)
Email: aslib@aslib.com
Internet: http://www.aslib.co.uk/

Type: prof *Gov Body:* Aslib (see **O18**) *Chief:* contact the Group Liaison Offcr
Memb Req: Aslib Corporate Membs £29 pa; Affiliate Membership (for non-memb orgs) £47 pa
Activs: Aims to promote the interests of individuals in all areas of the information industry who work alone, or with no assistance other than clerical. The group's activities reflect the special needs of its members for management, promotional, organisational and presentational skills at an early stage of their careers, and at a more specialised level than their counterparts in larger organisations.
Pubns: Newsletter (quarterly)

O30 ⚷

Aslib Scottish Branch
c/o Ms Kirsty Crawford, BBC Scotland Info & Archvs, Room G121, Broadcasting House, Queen Margaret Dr, Glasgow, G12 8DG (0141-338-3030; *fax:* 0141-338-3640)
Email: kirsty.crawford@bbc.co.uk
Internet: http://www.aslib.co.uk/sigs/scottish/

Type: prof *Gov Body:* Aslib (see **O18**) *Chief:* Chair: Ms Elize Rowan, Natl Museums of Scotland, Chambers St, Edinburgh, EHi 1JF (0131-247-4153; *fax:* 0131-247-4311; *email:* e.rowan@nms.ac.uk) *Other Snr Offcrs:* Sec: Ms Kirsty Crawford, as above
Memb Req: automatic membership for all membs of Aslib in Scotland
Activs: Promotes the work of Aslib in Scotland, and encourages networking between information professionals within the region. Arranges seminars, visits, presentations and workshops.

O31 ⚷

Aslib Social Sciences Information Group and Network [ASSIGN]
c/o Ms Heather Dawson, British Lib of Political & Economical Sci, 10 Portugal St, London, EC3A 7PB (020-7955-6806)
Email: h.dawson@lse.ac.uk
Internet: http://www.aslib.co.uk/

Type: prof *Gov Body:* Aslib (see **O18**) *Chief:* Sec: Ms Heather Dawson, as above
Membs: 165 indiv & institutional membs *Memb Req:* subscription: Aslib Corporate Membs £29 pa; Affiliate Membership (for non-memb orgs) £47 pa
Activs: Forum for information professionals (academic, public, voluntary etc.) within social sciences; promotes information handling skills and information management in the field; activities include conferences, seminars and visits throughout the year.
Pubns: ASSIGnation (quarterly journal, £40 pa, £30 to membs)

O32 ⚷

Aslib Technical Translation Group [TTG]
c/o Aslib, Temple Chambers, 3-7 Temple Ave, London, EC4Y 0HP (020-7583-8900; *fax:* 020-7583-8401)
Email: aslib@aslib.com
Internet: http://www.aslib.co.uk/sigs/ttg/

Type: prof *Gov Body:* Aslib (see **O18**) *Chief:* contact the Group Liaison Offcr
Memb Req: Aslib Corporate Membs £29 pa; Affiliate Membership (for non-memb orgs) £47 pa
Activs: An international forum for technical and specialised freelance and staff translators; organises the "Translating and the Computer" annual conference in association with the Institute of Translation and Interpreting, as well as meetings and visits to places of interest to translators.
Pubns: Newsletter

O33 ⚷

Association for Geographic Information [AGI]
Block C, 4th Floor, Morelands, 5-23 Old St, London, EC1V 9HL (020-7017-8496)
Email: info@agi.org.uk
Internet: http://www.agi.org.uk/

Gov Body: elected council *Chief:* Dir: Mr Mark Linehan (mark@agi.org.uk) *Other Snr Offcrs:* Dep Dir: Ms Sallie Payne (sallie@agi.org.uk)
Membs: 183 instns *Memb Req:* open to indivs & orgs involved in the analysis or supply of geographical info; subscription fees vary according to category
Branches & Groups: Regional Groups: AGI NORTHERN IRELAND (northernireland@ agi.org.uk); AGI SCOTLAND (see **O34**); AGI CYMRU (cymru@agi.org.uk); *Special Interest Groups:* LOCAL GOVT SIG; HEALTH SIG; MARINE & COASTAL ZONE SIG; ENVIRON-MENT SIG; CRIME & DISORDER SIG; SCHOOL SIG; EUROPEAN SIG; ADDR GEOG SIG
Activs: Aims to maximise the use of geographic information for the benefit of the citizen, good governance and commerce, and to formulate and implement standards related to geographic information provision. Activities include lobbying, publications, specialist meetings and seminars throughout the country, as well as an annual conference and trade exhibition.
Pubns: AGI Newsletter (4 pa)

O34 ⚷

Association for Geographic Information in Scotland [AGIS]
9 Manor Pl, Edinburgh, EH3 7DN (0800-015-4423; *fax:* 020-7278-0266)
Email: scotland@agi.org.uk
Internet: http://www.geo.ed.ac.uk/agiscot/

Gov Body: regional group of the Assoc for Geographic Info (see **O33**) *Chief:* Chair: Mr Mike Traynor (mike.traynor@ros.gov.uk)

Memb Req: open to membs of AGI working or living in Scotland
Activs: Aims to promote standards in the provision of geographical information and to support the aims and objectives of the association in Scotland.

O35 ⚷ 🤲

Association of British Theological and Philosophical Libraries [ABTAPL]
c/o Mr Colin Clarke, Dr Williams's Lib, 14 Gordon Sq, London, WC1H 0AR (020-7387-3727)
Email: colin.clarke@dwlib.co.uk
Internet: http://www.abtapl.org.uk/

Chief: Chair: Mrs Judith Powles, Spurgeon's Coll Lib (j.powles@spurgeons.ac.uk) *Other Snr Offcrs:* Hon Sec: Mr Colin Clarke, as above
Membs: 300 indivs & instns *Memb Req:* open to anyone interested in the bibliography, libnship or mgmt of our specialist subjs
Activs: An organisation formed to help those working in libraries containing theological, philosophical and related materials by sharing information and experience; produces a guide to religious bibliographies in serial literature, and a guide to theological collections in libraries in the United Kingdom and Ireland; organises two meetings a year and also provides for its members an informal network for consultation, advice and support in both individual and continuing professional problems.
Pubns: Bulletin of ABTAPL (3 pa, £15 pa, £25 pa for instns); Union List of Periodicals (2000 ed, £12 + £2.50 p&p)
Further Info: ABTAPL is an Org in Liaison with CILIP (see **O110**)

O36 ⚷

Association of Chief Archivists in Local Government [ACALG]
c/o East Sussex Record Office, The Maltings, Castle Precincts, Lewes, East Sussex, BN7 1YT (01273-482349; *fax:* 01273-482341)
Email: archives@eastsussexcc.gov.uk

Type: prof *Chief:* Chairman: Mr Bruce Jackson, County Archivist, Lancashire Record Office (01772-533039) *Other Snr Offcrs:* Sec: Mrs Elizabeth Hughes, East Sussex County Archivist, addr as above
Membs: 88 indivs
Activs: To represent local government archive services on issues of urgency and importance and to provide a forum for the exchange of views on common issues.

O37 ⚷

Association of Genealogists and Researchers in Archives [AGRA]
(formerly Assoc of Genealogists & Record Agents)
c/o 29 Badgers Cl, Horsham, West Sussex, RH12 5RU
Email: agra@agra.org.uk
Internet: http://www.agra.org.uk/

Type: prof *Chief:* Chairman: Dr S.W. Taylor *Other Snr Offcrs:* contact the Joint Secretaries at the above addr
Membs: 90 indivs; 15 affiliates *Memb Req:* prospective membs should have at least 2 years full-time experience in genealogy & a high standard of competence; subscription: £65 pa
Activs: Aims to promote and maintain high standards of professional conduct and expertise within the spheres of genealogy, heraldry and record searching, and to safeguard the interests of members and clients. Administers a Code of Practice for members.
Pubns: Membs List (£2 + 50p p&p)

O38 ♟

Association of Independent Libraries [AIL]

c/o The Leeds Lib, 18 Commercial St, Leeds, LS1 6AL (0113-245-3071)
Internet: http://www.independentlibraries.co.uk/

Gov Body: elected cttee *Chief:* Chairman: Mr Geoffrey Forster MCLIP
Membs: 24 instns
Activs: The members of the Association of Independent Libraries are all subscription libraries, founded between 1768 and 1841, before the creation of our public library service. They combine care of their historic collections and beautiful buildings with the supply of the latest books and periodicals, and a personal service to their members. Unlike most libraries they are not controlled or financed by outside bodies, and many of them are still owned collectively by their members. The Association has been formed to further the advancement, conservation and restoration of a little known but important living portion of our cultural heritage.
Pubns: occasional newsletter

O39 ♟

Association of Information Officers in The Pharmaceutical Industry [AIOPI]

PO Box 297, Slough PDO, Slough, Berkshire, SL1 7XT
Email: aiopi@aiopi.org.uk
Internet: http://www.aiopi.org.uk/

Type: prof *Chief:* Pres: Mrs Christine Cameron
Membs: 650+ indivs *Memb Req:* 3 membership categories: full (open to info workers in the pharmaceutical industry; associate (open to other info workers); affiliate (open to those with a commercial interest in info work in the industry); subscription: UK £30 pa, overseas £35 pa
Branches & Groups: SPECIAL INTEREST GROUP ON ADVERSE REACTIONS (SIGAR) (*email:* sigar@aiopi.org.uk); ONE MAN BANDERS (OMB); INTERNET WORKING PARTY (IWP); STANDARDS WORKING PARTY (SWP); DIPLOMA WORKING PARTY (DWP)
Activs: Provides a forum for the exchange of experience and the advancement of all aspects of medical, scientific and technical information handling relating to the pharmaceutical industry; facilitates communication between those with a special interest in the subject; encourages the maintenance and development of professional standards in all aspects of information work in the industry; encourages and facilitates the development of relevant skills and their application to information work within the pharmaceutical industry. Organises meetings and an annual conference.
Pubns: AIOPI Newsletter (6 pa)

O40 ♟

Association of Law Librarians in Central England [ALLICE]

c/o Ms Lianne Johns, Eversheds, 115 Colmore Row, Birmingham, B3 3AL (0121-232-1558; *fax:* 0121-232-1929)
Email: liannejohns@eversheds.com
Internet: http://www.allice.org.uk/ (under construction)

Type: prof, legal *Chief:* Sec: Ms Lianne Johns, as above
Membs: 45 *Memb Req:* open to info profs working with legal info in Central England
Activs: Provides a forum for legal information professionals within the region; meets four times a year in central Birmingham and organises incidental meetings, product demonstrations, seminars and courses as well as social events.

O41 ♟ ☕ ✎

Association of Learned and Professional Society Publishers [ALPSP]

South House, The Street, Clapham, Worthing, West Sussex, BN13 3UU (01903-871686; *fax:* 01903-871457)
Email: sec-gen@alpsp.org
Internet: http://www.alpsp.org/

Type: trade assoc *Gov Body:* Council *Chief:* Chair: Ms Andrea Powell (a.powell@cabi.org)
Other Snr Offcrs: Sec Genl: Mrs Sally Morris
Membs: 240 instns *Memb Req:* open to non-commercial publishers of all kinds, such as learned socs, prof instns & assocs, univ presses & charities; subscription rates depend on memb's annual turnover
Activs: Represents the community of not-for-profit publishers and those who work with them to disseminate academic and professional information. The Association monitors national and international issues and represents members' interests to the wider world. It offers an extensive programme of education, training and development, including a full programme of seminars on issues of current concern and a series of training courses. Also provides information and advice to members, both individually and via email discussion lists and its web site.
Pubns: Learned Publishing (journal, 4 pa, free to membs, subscription to non-membs varies); ALPSP Alert (elec newsletter, free to membs)

O42 🎓

Association of Librarians in Land-based Colleges and Universities [ALLCU]

c/o Ms Stella Vain, Wiltshire Coll, Lackham Lib, Lacock, Chippenham, Wiltshire, SN15 2NY (01249-466814)
Email: vainsm@wiltscoll.ac.uk

Type: prof *Chief:* Chairperson: Ms Stella Vain MCLIP, as above *Other Snr Offcrs:* Sec: Ms Christine Barclay MCLIP
Membs: c40 indivs *Memb Req:* open to lib & info workers in academic instns within the agricultural & land-based industry sector; subscription: £5 pa
Activs: To provide mutual support and encouragement to library staff; to encourage co-operation between member libraries; where appropriate, to negotiate on behalf of the association with publishers, suppliers etc.
Pubns: ALLCU directory (1 pa, free to membs); ALLCU newsletter (1 pa, free to membs)
Further Info: ALLCU is an Org in Liaison with CILIP (see **O110**)

O43 ♟ 🎓

Association of Local History Tutors [ALHT]

c/o Mrs Joan Dils, 47 Ramsbury Dr, Earley, Reading, Berkshire, RG6 7RT (0118-926-4729)
Email: ray.dils@lineone.net

Chief: Hon Sec: Mrs Joan Dils, as above
Membs: c80 indivs *Memb Req:* open to those involved in the teaching of local hist, whether in schools, univs, adult edu or in occasional lectures to groups; subscription £8 pa
Activs: Aims to promote local history and to support its teaching and research; organises an annual conference and disseminates useful information to members.
Pubns: Bulletin (3pa, membs only)

O44 ♟

Association of London Chief Librarians [ALCL]

c/o Ms Karen Tyerman, London Borough of Brent, Chesterfield House, 9 Park Ln, Wembley, Middlesex, HA9 7RW (020-8937-3146; *fax:* 020-8937-3023)
Email: karen.tyerman@brent.gov.uk

Chief: Chair: Mr Martin Molloy, Derbyshire Libs & Heritage *Other Snr Offcrs:* Hon Sec: Ms Karen Tyerman BA(Hons), DipLib, MCLIP, as above
Membs: 33 indivs; 4 instns
Activs: The ALCL is the senior professional manager group representing London Public Library authorities. The ALCL was formed in 1965 following the formation of the London boroughs and seeks to maintain and improve the quality of public library and information services for the people of London. Its objectives are: to promote and facilitate discussion and exchange of views on policies affecting London Public Libraries so that professional advice may be given to appropriate bodies; to promote the better management and administration of London Public Libraries and enable opportunities to be provided for members of the Association to develop and apply their own management and professional skills; to promote and encourage co-operation between, and co-ordination of, London Public Libraries; and co-operation with other appropriate bodies.

O45 🏛

Association of Northern Ireland Education and Library Boards [ANIELB]

40 Academy St, Belfast, BT1 2HQ (028-9056-4031; *fax:* 028-9033-1715)
Email: michaelp@belb.co.uk

Chief: Hon Sec: Mr Michael Prichard
Membs: 38 indivs; 5 instns
Activs: Aims to achieve and maintain the highest standards in the provision of library, education and youth services in Northern Ireland.

O46 ♟ 🎓

Association of Northumberland Local History Societies

c/o Dr C.M. Fraser, Centre for Lifelong Learning, Univ of Newcastle upon Tyne, Newcastle upon Tyne, NE1 7RU (0191-222-5680)

Chief: Genl Sec: Dr C.M. Fraser, as above
Membs: 120 indivs; 56 instns
Activs: Promotion of interest in local history in Northumberland and Tyne and Wear by advising local history societies, organising lectures, one day conferences and excursions, and directing projects. The Association also provides information about sources available locally for the study of the history of the area.
Pubns: Tyne & Tweed (1 pa, £3 to non-membs)

O47 ♟

Association of Scottish Genealogists and Record Agents [ASGRA]

51/3 Mortonhall Rd, Edinburgh, EH9 2HN
Internet: http://www.asgra.co.uk/

Type: prof *Chief:* Chairman: Mr Alan MacLeod FSA(Scot) *Other Snr Offcrs:* Publicity Sec: Mr Norman Thompson ☛

(Assoc of Scottish Genealogists & Record Agents cont)
Memb Req: open to experienced & well-qualified prof searchers working personally in Scotland
Activs: Aims to encourage and maintain high standards for professional genealogical, family history and archival research through a Code of Practice for members; provides a point of contact for its members and potential clients.

O48 ♀
Association of Senior Children's and Education Librarians [ASCEL]
c/o Ms Nicola Parker, Manchester Central Lib, St Peter's Sq, Manchester, M2 5PD (0161-234-1936; *fax:* 0161-234-1963)
Email: nicolap@libraries.manchester.gov.uk
Internet: http://www.ascel.org.uk/

Gov Body: ASCEL Cttee **Chief:** contact Ms Nicola Parker, as above
Membs: c200 indivs **Memb Req:** open to libns with snr-mgmt responsibility for providing lib svcs to ch & yng people in England & Wales
Activs: The Association provides a strong voice to reflect the needs and concerns of children's public and educational library services. The Association is a pro-active forum to stimulate developments and share good practice, and provides a single united response to initiatives both from within the profession and externally.
Pubns: ASCEL Directory (1 pa, £25)

O49 ♀
Association of UK Media Librarians [AUKML]
c/o Ms Sara Margetts, FT Ref Lib, 1 Southwark Bridge, London, SE1 9HL (020-7873-3920)
Email: Sara.Margetts@ft.com
Internet: http://www.aukml.org.uk/

Chief: Chair: Ms Jill Tulip, IPC (Jill_Tulip@ipcmedia.com) **Other Snr Offcrs:** Membership Sec: Ms Sara Margetts, as above
Membs: 147 indivs; 70 instns **Memb Req:** full membership (open to those directly employed in the print & broadcasting industries): £25 pa; associate membership (open to other interested parties): £20 pa; student/unwaged: £15
Activs: Aims to create links, both formal and social, between people engaged in similar work in the UK and abroad; to increase the status of the information profession in text-based information services in the broadcasting and print news media; organises regular meetings and demonstrations of new online products, visits to members' libraries and an annual conference; maintains a Directory of Members.
Pubns: Deadline (quarterly, free to membs)

O50 ♀
Authors' Licensing and Collecting Society [ALCS]
Marlborough Ct, 14-18 Holborn, London, EC1N 2LE (020-7395-0600; *fax:* 020-7395-0660)
Email: alcs@alcs.co.uk
Internet: http://www.alcs.co.uk/

Type: non-profit collecting soc **Chief:** Acting Chief Exec: Mr Owen Atkinson
Membs: represents 35000+ membs & associates
Memb Req: open to all writers & successors to their estates; subscription: full membs £7.50 pa (£10 outside Europe), no annual fee for associate membs, but small handling fee & commission charged on royalties
Activs: Established to enable writers to receive fees that are uniquely or more effectively handled collectively. It administers rights in the UK, and has reciprocal arrangements with foreign collecting societies. Its aims are to campaign for collective rights schemes by statute and voluntary agreement, and to ensure that writers receive a just share from all such collective rights schemes. Along with the Publishers Licensing Society, it administers the Copyright Licensing Agency (see **O174**).
Pubns: See web site or contact office for details

O51 ♀ 🎓
Avon Local History Association
c/o Ms Barbara Tuttiet, 4 Dalkeith Ave, Kingswood, Bristol, BS15 1HH (0117-967-1362)

Type: registered charity **Chief:** Hon Sec: Ms Barbara Tuttiet, as above
Membs: 20 indivs; 60 instns
Activs: Encourages the study of local history in Bristol, Bath, South Gloucestershire and North Somerset; funds research; organises an Annual Study Day and summer walks; awards Schools Local History Prizes.
Pubns: Newsletter (4 pa, £3)

O52 ♀ 🎓
Avon University Libraries in Co-operation [AULIC]
c/o Mr Alastair Sleat, Univ of the West of England Lib Svcs, Frenchay Campus, Coldharbour Ln, Bristol, BS16 1QY (0117-344-2277; *fax:* 0117-344-2407)
Email: Alastair.Sleat@uwe.ac.uk
Internet: http://www.uwe.ac.uk/library/info/aulic.htm

Type: co-op **Gov Body:** AULIC Cttee **Chief:** Sec to the Cttee: Mr Alastair Sleat, as above
Membs: 4 instns
Activs: Co-operative access scheme for academic libraries in the Avon region. The AULIC Committee also meets termly to discuss current issues affecting academic libraries and co-operation between the institutions.

O53 ♀
Banking Information Group
c/o Mr Jim Basker, 107 Festing Grove, Southsea, Hampshire, PO4 9QE (*tel & fax:* 023-9273-4224)

Type: prof **Chief:** Sec: Mr Jim Basker, as above
Activs: Provides a forum for those involved or interested in the provision of financial services information.

O54 ♀
Bedfordshire Historical Record Society
c/o Mr Richard Smart, 48 St Augustine's Rd, Bedford, Bedfordshire, MK40 2ND (01234-309548)
Email: rsmart@dmu.ac.uk
Internet: http://www.bedfordshirehrs.org.uk/

Gov Body: Council **Chief:** Chairman: Mr A.M. Lawrence **Other Snr Offcrs:** Hon Sec: Mr Richard Smart, as above

Membs: c200 indivs; c100 instns **Memb Req:** subscription: indivs £12 pa, orgs £16 pa; add £3 for overseas subscriptions
Activs: Promotes access to Bedfordshire County history, especially from archival sources, through the publication of an annual volume of source material, along with monographs on aspects of the County's history.
Pubns: 1 vol pa; recent vols incl: Vol 75: Bedfordshire Chapels and Meeting Houses: Official Registration 1672-1901 (1996, £15); Vol 76: Bedfordshire Wills 1484-1533 (1997, £15); Vol 77: Bedfordshire Churches in the Nineteenth Century, Vol 2 (1998, £15); Vol 78: Strawopolis: Luton Transformed 1840-1876 (1999, £15); Bedfordshire Churches in the Nineteenth Century, Vol 3 (2000, £15); Bedfordshire Churches in the Nineteenth Century, Vol 4 (2001, £15); Episcopal Visitations in Bedfordshire 1706-1720 (2002, £25); also: Supplements to A Bedfordshire Bibliography 1961-65, 1966-70 & 1971-75 (£3.50 each)

O55 ♀ 🎓
Bedfordshire Local History Association [BLHA]
c/o Mrs E.M. Field, 29 George St, Maulden, Bedford, MK45 2DF (01525-633029)

Chief: Sec: Mrs E.M. Field, as above
Membs: 42 indivs; 9 instns; 25 local hist socs
Memb Req: subscription: £5 pa for indivs, £10 pa for socs & instns
Activs: Acts as a liaison body for all parties in the county interested in local history, and acts as a channel of communication between them. Organises joints activities, lectures and visits.
Pubns: Hist in Bedfordshire (newsletter, 3-4 pa, free to membs)

O56 ♀
Beds and Bucks Information [BBi]
c/o Ms Nicky Whitsed, Open Univ Lib, Walton Hall, Milton Keynes, Buckinghamshire, MK7 6AA (01908-652669; *fax:* 01908-653571)
Email: n.whitsed@open.ac.uk
Internet: http://www.bbinfo.org.uk/

Chief: Chair: Ms Nicky Whitsed MSc, FCLIP, as above **Other Snr Offcrs:** Sec: Ms Diana Saulsbury, Lib Svcs Mgr, De Montfort Univ, Polhill Campus, Bedford (ds@dmu.ac.uk)
Membs: 2 indivs; 22 instns **Memb Req:** info providers in Bedfordshire & Buckinghamshire
Branches & Groups: BUSINESS & INDUSTRY GROUP; EDU GROUP, Convenor: Ms Josephine Burt (01908-659121; *email:* jburt@dunstable.ac.uk); HEALTH GROUP, Convenor: Ms Judy Thomas (01908-659103; *email:* j.m.thomas@open.ac.uk)
Activs: BBi is the information development agency for Bedfordshire and Buckinghamshire; promotes and organises co-operative ventures between librarians and information providers, including seminars, workshops, exhibitions, visits and training events.

O57 ♀
Berkshire Library and Information Partnership [BLIP]
c/o Ms Lisa Westmorland, Wokingham Lib, Denmark St, Wokingham, Berkshire, RG40 2BB (0118-979-3474; *fax:* 0118-989-1214)
Email: lisa.westmorland@wokingham.gov.uk
Internet: http://www.blipweb.org.uk/

Type: co-op **Chief:** Interim Chairman: Mr Norman Briggs (nwbriggs@pcintell.co.uk) **Other Snr Offcrs:** Sec: Ms Lisa Westmorland, as above; Treasurer: Mr Mike Sharrocks (sharrocks@gyosei.ac.uk)

Memb Req: open to all libs & info providers in the Berkshire area; subscription: £25 pa
Branches & Groups: EDU INFO NETWORK, contact Ms Pam King (0118-967-5461); 5 local area groups
Activs: Aims to promote co-operation between library services and other information providers in Berkshire; encourages the sharing of information resources and professional expertise; provides support and assistance for professional development; offers a means for local participation in the planning of library and information services at national level; organises various events, including seminars, group visits, staff exchanges and meetings.
Pubns: BLIP Newsletter (2 pa); BLIP Directory (free to membs, extra copies £7.50 each)

O58 🗝

Berkshire Local History Association [BLHA]

c/o Dr Margaret Yates, Univ of Reading School of Hist, Whiteknights, Reading, Berkshire, RG6 6AA (0118-378-8147; *fax:* 0118-378-6440)
Email: secretary@blha.org.uk
Internet: http://www.blha.org.uk/

Type: voluntary body *Chief:* Chairman: Mr Peter Johnson (chairman@blha.org.uk) *Other Snr Offcrs:* Hon Sec: Dr Margaret Yates, as above
Membs: 80+ indivs; 40+ instns *Memb Req:* open to indivs & socs interested in local & family hist & archaeo of the old county of Berkshire (pre-1974 boundaries); subscription: indiv £7 pa, family £9 pa, corporate £14 pa
Activs: Encourages local history research and interest in the county, both pre- and post the 1974 boundary changes. It provides a common meeting ground for individual members, the various local history societies and groups within the county, and the professionals who work in archives, libraries, museums and education.
Pubns: Berkshire Old & New (1 pa, £3.50, free to membs); Newsletter (3 pa, membs only)

O59 🗝 🎓

Berkshire Record Society

c/o Berkshire Record Office, 9 Colen Ave, Reading, Berkshire, RG1 6AF (0118-901-5132; *fax:* 0118-901-5131)
Email: arch@reading.gov.uk

Chief: Chairman: Prof Ralph Houlbrooke *Other Snr Offcrs:* Genl Editor: Dr Peter Durrant, as above (and to whom all enq should be addressed)
Membs: 160 indivs; 50 instns
Activs: Berkshire Record Society is an educational charity whose purpose is to publish scholarly editions of records relating to the historic county of Berkshire, for the encouragement of research into the county's history.
Pubns: recent published vols (£25 each + £2.50 p&p) incl: Correspondence of the Foundling Hosp Inspectors in Berkshire 1757-1768 (1994); Berkshire Glebe Terriers 1634 (1995); Berkshire Oversees' Papers 1654-1834 (1997); Berkshire Probate Accounts 1583-1712 (1999); also: An Historical Atlas of Berkshire (1998, £14.95 + £2 p&p)

O60 🗝

Bibliographical Society

c/o Inst of English Studies, Room 304, Senate House, Malet St, London, NW1 2BE (020-7862-8675; *fax:* 020-7862-8720)
Email: secretary@bibsoc.org.uk
Internet: http://www.bibsoc.org.uk/

Gov Body: Council of the Soc *Chief:* Hon Sec: Ms Margaret Ford, at above addr

Membs: 800 indivs; 300 instns *Memb Req:* open to anyone interested in the study of bibliography; subscription: £33 pa (students & over-65s £25 pa)
Activs: To promote the study of bibliography and the history of books; to publish the fruits of research in those fields; to hold meetings; to award grants and bursaries for bibliographical research.
Pubns: The Library (4 pa); numerous monographs & ref works

O61 📚

BIDS: Bath Information and Data Services

PO Box 3077, Bath, BA2 3EF (01225-361022; *fax:* 01225-361152)
Email: svcs: bidshelp@bids.ac.uk; *other queries:* arashid@ingenta.com
Internet: http://www.bids.ac.uk/

Gov Body: funded by Joint Info Systems Cttee (JISC) (see **O242**) *Chief:* contact Ayesha Rashid at the above addr
Activs: Provides bibliographic services and electronic access to scholarly publications and research data to academic institutions and their members within the UK.
Pubns: BIDS academic databases, incl: CAB Abstracts; EMBASE; INSPEC; Internatl Bibliography of the Social Scis (IBSS); PsycInfo; ERIC; British Edu Index

O62 🗝 🎓

Birmingham and District Local History Association [BDLHA]

c/o Mrs Joan Davies, 112 Brandworth Rd, Kings Heath, Birmingham, B14 6BX (0121-444-7470)
Email: contact@bdlha.org
Internet: http://www.bdlha.org/

Chief: Chairman: Mr Peter Leather *Other Snr Offcrs:* Vice-Chairman: Mrs Joan Davies, as above
Membs: c200 indivs
Activs: Provides an umbrella group for local history societies in and around the city; organises local history fairs; provides assistance to members where necessary.
Pubns: The Birmingham Historian (2 pa, £4 each); Newsletter (4 pa, membs only); A Brief Hist of Birmingham (£4.95); Images of England – Quinton (£11.99)

O63 🗝

Black Country Local History Consortium

c/o The Black Country Living Museum, Tipton Rd, Dudley, W Midlands, DY1 4SQ

Chief: Sec: Ms Gay Hill, at above addr
Activs: Umbrella organisation for local and family history groups and others interested in the local heritage of the four Black County Boroughs; aims to promote and safeguard the interests of local and family history in the region and to disseminate information about local heritage activities; organises regular meetings.
Pubns: The Brolley (newsletter, £2 per issue)

O64 🗝 🎓

Bliss Classification Association [BCA]

c/o Mrs Heather Lane, Libn, Sidney Sussex Coll Lib, Cambridge, CB2 3HU (01223-338852; *fax:* 01223-338884)
Email: librarian@sid.cam.ac.uk
Internet: http://www.sid.cam.ac.uk/bca/bcahome.htm

Type: prof *Gov Body:* elected cttee *Chief:* BCA Chair (ex officio): Mr Jack Mills *Other Snr Offcrs:* Sec: Mrs Heather Lane, as above
Memb Req: open to all orgs & indivs interested in or using the Classn; subscription £15 pa
Activs: A non-profit making organisation of users and supporters of the Bliss Bibliographic Classification scheme. Promotes the development and use of the classification, publishes official amendments, provides a forum for users to keep in touch and exchange experience, and to give users a say in the future development of the scheme. Organises lectures and visits to libraries, and an AGM each November.
Pubns: Bliss Classn Bulletin (1 pa, free to membs); Bliss Bibliographic Classn schedules
Further Info: BCA is an Org in Liaison with CILIP (see **O110**)

O65 🗝

Book Aid International

39-41 Coldharbour Ln, Camberwell, London, SE5 9NR (020-7733-3577; *fax:* 020-7978-8006)
Email: info@bookaid.org
Internet: http://www.bookaid.org/

Type: charity *Chief:* Dir: Mrs Sara Harrity
Activs: Book Aid International is the major UK support for libraries in sub-Saharan Africa. It is a cost effective agency that believes in people's potential for self-development and transformation through learning, and that the development of human capacity is essential for escaping poverty. Support for the long term development of the local book trade is a high priority. The aim is that locally produced and culturally relevant books should be made available for readers in Africa and beyond. Carefully selected materials are made available to these organisations in around 50 developing countries – 85% of resources are targeted in 13 countries in sub-Saharan Africa; other programmes focus on the Middle East and South East Asia.
Pubns: BookMark (UK supporter newsletter); BookLinks (bk trade networking newsletter)

O66 🗝

Book Industry Communications [BIC]

39-41 North Rd, London, N7 9DP (020-7607-0021; *fax:* 020-7607-0415)
Email: brian@bic.org.uk
Internet: http://www.bic.org.uk/

Gov Body: BIC Board *Chief:* Managing Agent: Mr Brian Green
Membs: 150 instns *Memb Req:* open to publishers, distributors & other org involved in the bk industry
Branches & Groups: EDItEUR (bk & serials industries' internatl standards org); SUPPLY CHAIN GROUP, Chair: Mr David Young; PRODUCT METADATA GROUP, Chair: Mr Stuart Ede; EDI IMPLEMENTATION CLINIC, Chair: Mr Brian Green
Activs: BIC exists to facilitate the provision and communication of information throughout the book industry, particularly in electronic form, and to be responsible for the development and promotion of standards for the format and transmission of bibliographical information, commercial messages and other information designed to increase efficiency and effectiveness in trading and supply within the industry.
Pubns: Data Elements for Book Trade Product Info (£10); The Use of Mgmt Data in Public & Academic Libs: Four Case Studies (£20); Standards for Elec Security Tagging: A Feasibility Study (£10); INA Directory of UK Networked Svcs (£10); Elec Tables of Contents for Serials: Standards for Structure & Transmission (free); EDI The Future of Lib Supply – Conference Papers (£20); among others; contact BIC for details

Organisations
Book ▼ British

O67 ⚷
Book Trust
Book House, 45 East Hill, Wandsworth, London, SW18 2QZ (020-8516-2977; *fax:* 020-8516-2978)
Internet: http://www.booktrust.org.uk/

Type: charity *Chief:* Exec Dir: Mr Chris Meade
Membs: 250 indivs; also many subscribers to Young Bk Trust
Activs: Promotion of books and reading through prize administration (including the Smarties Children's Book Award), and information provision for both children and adults. Organises a number of projects and programmes, including Bookstart, the national books for babies programme.
Pubns: Booktrusted News; 100 Best Books; The Children's Book Handbook; Looking For an Author; Parent's Pack; Families Just Like Us: The One Parent Families Good Book Guide; Pop-Ups! A Guide to Novelty Books; Celebrate a Book: A DIY Guide to Planning a Book Event; Natl Children's Book Week materials (posters, sticker, postcards & bkmarks); see http://www.booktrusted.com/booktrust/publications.html
See also S1472

O68 ⚷
The Booksellers Association of the United Kingdom and Ireland Ltd
Minster House, 272-274 Vauxhall Bridge Rd, London, SW1V 1BA (020-7802-0802; *fax:* 020-7802-0803)
Email: mail@booksellers.org.uk
Internet: http://www.booksellers.org.uk/

Type: trade assoc *Gov Body:* The BA Council
Chief: Chief Exec: Mr Tim Godfray (tim.godfray@booksellers.org.uk) *Other Snr Offcrs:* Office Administrator: Mr Chris Tolley (chris.tolley@booksellers.org.uk)
Membs: 3250 instns *Memb Req:* open to booksellers in the UK & Ireland
Branches & Groups: LIB BOOKSELLERS GROUP, addr as above (see O262)
Activs: Represents the book trade in the UK and Ireland; promotes retail bookselling to Government and outside bodies; provides training, marketing aids, professional services and trade advice.
Pubns: Bookselling (4 pa free to membs); Directory of BA Membs (£28); Directory of Publishers, Wholesalers & Distributors (£55)

O69 ⚷
Bristol Law Librarians Group
c/o Ms Christina Moneta, Veale Wasbrough, Orchard Ct, Bristol, BS1 5WS (0117-925-2020; *fax:* 0117-925-2025)
Email: cmoneta@vwl.co.uk

Type: prof, legal *Chief:* Christina Moneta
Membs: 30 indivs *Memb Req:* open to law libns in Bristol & surrounding area
Activs: Networking and information sharing amongst members; meets twice yearly.
Pubns: Union List of Journal Holdings; Union List of Law Report Holdings

O70 ⚷ 🎓
Britain and Ireland Association of Aquatic Sciences Libraries and Information Centres [BIASLIC]
c/o Ms Sarah Carter, CEFAS Lowestoft Laboratory, Pakefield Rd, Lowestoft, Suffolk, NR33 0HT (01502-562244; *fax:* 01502-513865)
Email: S.L.Carter@cefas.co.uk
Internet: http://www.ife.ac.uk/biaslic/

Type: special interest group *Chief:* Chair: Mr Ian McCulloch, Centre for Ecology and Hydrology, Windermere (idm@ceh.ac.uk) *Other Snr Offcrs:* Sec: Ms Sarah Carter, as above
Memb Req: membership free; open to all persons in Britain & Ireland working in lib, data & info svcs applied to the aquatic scis
Activs: Provides a forum for the exchange of information and the discussion of issues relevant to aquatic science librarianship and to librarianship as a whole. Organises annual conferences in members' libraries with reports on activities and developments in BIASLIC libraries, demonstrations of new information products, and discussions with colleagues from other organisations.
Pubns: Directory of Marine & Freshwater Scientists & Rsrch Engineers in the United Kingdom; Union Serials lists; also provides data for the Aquatic Scis & Fisheries Abstracts database

O71 🎓
British and Irish Archaeological Bibliography [BIAB]
c/o The British Academy, 10 Carlton House Ter, London, SW1Y 5AH (020-7969-5223/5444; *fax:* 020-7969-5300)
Email: info@biab.ac.uk
Internet: http://www.britarch.ac.uk/biab/

Gov Body: Council for British Archaeo *Chief:* contact Ms Isabel Holroyd (iholroyd@biab.ac.uk) or Mr Robert Bath (robbath@biab.ac.uk)
Activs: Provides bibliographical resources for archaeology, historic buildings, maritime and industrial archaeology, environmental history and the conservation of material culture, with a geographical focus on the UK and Republic of Ireland. Publishes printed guides and maintains an Internet-mounted database referencing materials published from 1695-1991.
Pubns: British & Irish Archaeological Bibliography (6 monthly printed guide); Internet database

O72 ⚷
British and Irish Association of Law Librarians [BIALL]
26 Myton Cres, Warwick, CV34 6QA (*tel & fax:* 01926-491717)
Email: susanfrost@compuserve.com
Internet: http://www.biall.org.uk/

Type: prof, legal *Gov Body:* Council of the Assoc
Chief: Chair: Ms Victoria Jannetta (victoria_jannetta@hotmail.com) *Other Snr Offcrs:* Sec: Ms Catherine McArdle (catherine.mcardle@lincolnsinn.org.uk); Administrator: Mrs Susan Frost, as above
Membs: 547 indivs; 196 instns *Memb Req:* open to persons & instns engaged in the provision or exploitation of legal lit and info; associate membership open to others who support the aims of the Assoc; subscriptions: indivs £54 pa (student/retired/unemployed £15 pa), instns £90 pa
Branches & Groups: IRISH GROUP (see IO3); FREELANCERS GROUP, contact: Ms Jennie Yeomans (020-7404-0606; *email:* jyeomans@goodmanderrick.co.uk); ONE MAN BANDS GROUP, contact: Ms Susan Parker (020-7242-7363; *email:* susan.parker@collyerbristow.com); various regional affiliate groups

Activs: To support the objectives of the Association to benefit members, enhancing the status of the legal information profession and promoting better administration and exploitation of law libraries and legal information units nationwide. Offers publications, courses and Annual Conference to members.
Pubns: Legal Info Mgmt (formerly the Law Libn, 4 pa); Newsletter (4 pa, free to membs); Directory of British & Irish Law Libs (7th ed, membs £50, non-membs £70)

O73 ⚷ 🎓
British Association for Information and Library Education and Research [BAILER]
c/o Dr Judith Broady-Preston, Dept of Lib & Info Studies, Univ of Wales Aberystwyth, Landadarn Fawr, Aberystwyth, Ceredigion, SY23 3AS (01970-622188; *fax:* 01970-622190)
Email: jbp@aber.ac.uk
Internet: http://www.bailer.ac.uk/

Type: prof *Chief:* Chair: Ms Linda Ashcroft, Liverpool John Moores Univ (l.s.ashcroft@livjm.ac.uk) *Other Snr Offcrs:* Sec: Dr Judith Broady-Preston, addr as above
Membs: 18 instns; open to all teaching & rsrch staff in depts or teaching teams in the UK & Ireland with HE programmes in info or lib studies
Activs: Exists to reflect and to help focus the evolution of the field of information studies through: bringing together those involved in teaching, learning and research to exchange ideas and practice; acting as a forum within the UK for matters relating to information education and research; maintaining contact with organisations outside the UK concerned with information education and research.
Pubns: Directory of Courses in Lib & Info Studies in the UK (published annually in Dec, free)

O74 ⚷
British Association for Local History [BALH]
PO Box 1576, Salisbury, Wiltshire, SP2 8EY (01722-332158; *fax:* 01722-413242)
Email: info@balh.co.uk
Internet: http://www.balh.co.uk/

Gov Body: Trustees *Chief:* Genl Sec: Mr Michael Cowan, at above addr
Membs: 2000 indivs; 1000 instns *Memb Req:* open to all indivs & socs interested in local & family hist; subscriptions: indivs £25 pa (students on local hist courses £18), local socs or groups £52 pa, instns £38 pa
Activs: National charity promoting local history and serving local historians; publishes books and pamphlets on local history; organises regular visits, seminars and conferences; commissions the annual Phillimore Lecture; offers an insurance scheme to local societies.
Pubns: The Local Historian (journal, 4pa, back-issues £8 each); Local Hist News (magazine, 4 pa); Local Hist catalogue (free); numerous others relating to the local historian's sources, methods & need for backgrnd knowledge

O75 ⚷
British Association of Paper Historians [BAPH]
c/o Ms Joan Marchant, 47 Ellesmere Rd, Chiswick, London, W4 3EA
Email: baph@fsmail.net
Internet: http://www.baph.freeserve.co.uk/

Chief: Chairman: Mr Phil Crocket *Other Snr Offcrs:* Sec: Ms Joan Marchant, as above

---

 academic   corporate   **- 470 -**   governmental   medical

Membs: 173 indivs; 48 instns; corporate membs incl PITA, NAPM, IPH, IPC, the British Lib & Deutche Bücherie. *Memb Req:* open to indivs, companies & instns with an interest in paper hist; subscription: indivs £29 pa (£38 overseas), orgs & instns £52 pa (£60 overseas), UK students £12 pa *Activs:* Brings together those interested in all aspects of the history of paper, its uses, its production and the people and mills involved since it was first produced in Britain over 500 years ago. Organises several meetings and visits each year and holds a 2-3 day summer conference.
Pubns: BAPH News (newsletter, 4 pa); The Quarterly (journal, 4 pa, free to membs); The Quarterly Index (£5.50 to membs, £6.50 + p&p to non-membs); The Oxford Papers: Studies in British Paper Hist Vol 1 (membs £12 + p&p, non-membs £16 + p&p); The Exeter Papers: Studies in British Paper Hist Vol 2 (£25 + p&p); The Taxation of Paper in Gt Britain 1643-1861: A Hist & Document-ation, by H. Dagnall (£27.50 + p&p)

O76
British Association of Picture Libraries and Agencies [BAPLA]
18 Vine Hill, London, EC1R 5DZ (020-7713-1780; *fax:* 020-7713-1211)
Email: enquiries@bapla.org.uk
Internet: http://www.bapla.org.uk/

Type: trade assoc *Gov Body:* Exec Cttee *Chief:* Chief Exec: Ms Linda Royles *Other Snr Offcrs:* Assoc Administrator: Ms Sharron Preston
Membs: 400+ instns *Memb Req:* open to commercial UK picture libs & agencies, subj to approval by the Exec Cttee; subscription fees vary
Branches & Groups: various committees, covering key issues of importance to the industry, such as tech, copyright, industry rsrch, marketing, industry networking & socials, pubns & careers
Activs: Established in 1975, BAPLA is a non-profit making organisation whose remit is to promote and safeguard the interests of the picture library industry. The largest organisation of its kind in the world, BAPLA represents over 400 picture libraries and agencies, and collectively promotes the work of over 20000 photographers. BAPLA works in such diverse areas as marketing, industry surveys, industry statistics, lobbying and setting standards in such areas as business practice and technology. BAPLA operates a free referral service to assist picture researchers in locating the best source of photographic images, as well as a job seekers' register for a career in picture libraries. BAPLA also organises the Annual Picture Buyers Fair.
Pubns: BAPLA Directory of Membs (1 pa, non-membs £20 for 1 year, £30 for 2 years); The ABCD of UK Photographic Copyright (£5.50); prices incl p&p within the UK

O77
British Business Schools Librarians' Group [BBSLG]
c/o Mr David Clare, Univ of Wolverhampton, Telford Learning Centre, Priorslee Hall, Priorslee, Telford, West Midlands, TF2 9NT (01902-323906; *fax:* 01902-323985)
Email: D.Clare@wlv.ac.uk
Internet: http://www.bbslg.org/

Chief: Chair: Mr Chris Martindale, Univ of Derby *Other Snr Offcrs:* Sec: Mr David Clare, as above
Membs: 78 indivs; 78 instns *Memb Req:* open to libns involved in business info provision & instns offering postgrad edu in business & mgmt
Activs: Acts as a forum for discussion and exchange of ideas and information on topics of interest to members; encourages co-operation among members and provides a vehicle for the co-operation of members in co-operational projects; organises training and an annual conference.

O78
British Cartographic Society, Map Curators Group [MCG]
c/o Mrs Ann Sutherland, 61 Alnwickhill Rd, Liberton, Edinburgh, EH16 6NJ
Email: Ann.M.Sutherland@talk21.com
Internet: http://www.cartography.org.uk/Pages/Curators.html

Gov Body: The British Cartographic Soc *Chief:* Convenor: Mrs Ann Sutherland MA, FBCartS, as above
Membs: 170 indivs; 36 instns *Memb Req:* open to membs of the BCS involved with map libs, also to map collectors & historians
Activs: The national body for map curators, map librarians, map archivists, etc. MCG is the contact for all involved in the care of maps and for those providing access to information in the broadest sense both nationally and internationally. MCG runs a map curators' workshop annually in conjunction with the British Cartographic Society's Annual Technical Symposium.
Pubns: Cartographiti (4 pa, BCS membs free, non-membs £6 pa, £10 for airmail); UK Directory of Map Collns (4th ed)
Further Info: MCG is an org in Liaison with CILIP (see **O110**); The British Cartographic Soc Lib is held at the Natl Lib of Scotland, Map Lib (see **L2**)

O79
British Copyright Council [BCC]
29-33 Berners St, London, W1T 3AB (01986-788122; *fax:* 01986-788847)
Email: copyright@bcc2.demon.co.uk
Internet: http://www.editor.net/bcc/aboutbcc.htm

Chief: Chairman: Prof Gerald Dworkin *Other Snr Offcrs:* Sec: Ms Janet Ibbotson
Membs: 28 instns
Activs: An umbrella organisation bringing together societies representing all those who create, or hold rights in, literary, dramatic, musical and artistic works and those who perform such works; performs an advisory function; works for harmonis-ation of British and European copyright laws.
Pubns: The BCC's Guide to Copyright & Rights in Performances, by Denis de Freitas (2nd ed 1998, £14.95)

O80 ✚
British Medical Informatics Society [BMiS]
c/o Ms Sheila Price, Loughborough Univ Dept of Info Sci, Ashby Rd, Loughborough, Leicestershire, LE11 3TU (01509-223074)
Email: s.price@lboro.ac.uk
Internet: http://www.bmis.org/

Chief: Chair: Mr Colin Gordon (c.gordon@rbh.nthames.nhs.uk) *Other Snr Offcrs:* Hon Sec: Ms Sheila Price, as above
Membs: c260 indivs *Memb Req:* open to all, prof or otherwise, who share the Soc's concerns & objectives; subscription: indivs £45 pa (students & retired £25), instns £65 pa
Activs: Brings together healthcare professionals and scientists, information professionals and academic researchers and educators to advance the knowledge and application of medical and health informatics. Aims to develop and serve an informed, interdisciplinary medical and health informatics community; to promote research and development within that community; to provide a forum for discussion and debate; to influence the formation of information policies and strategies in the national health services; to advance the quality and provision of medical and health informatics education and training.
Pubns: BMIT: Biomedical Informatics Today (newsletter, 4 pa)

O81 🎓
British Official Publications Collaborative Reader Information Service [BOPCRIS]
Ford Colln of British Official Pubns, Hartley Lib, Univ of Southampton, Southampton, SO17 1BJ (023-8059-4249; *fax:* 023-8059-5451)
Email: bopcris@soton.ac.uk
Internet: http://www.bopcris.ac.uk/

Chief: Proj Mgr: Mr Simon Brackenbury
Activs: Aims to overcome shared problems in 18C-20C British Official Publications Collections, such as under-utilisation or difficulty of access, through a shared reader information service. Works to develop online bibliographic databases of British Official Publications, and to create a national directory of British Official Publications holdings in the UK.

O82 🎓
British Official Publications Current Awareness Service [BOPCAS]
Ford Colln of British Official Pubns, Univ of Southampton, Hartley Lib, Highfield, Southampton, SO17 1BJ (023-8059-2370; *fax:* 023-8059-3007)
Email: bopcas@soton.ac.uk
Internet: http://www.bopcas.com/

Gov Body: joint venture between Aslib (see **O18**) & Univ of Southampton (see also **S1946**) *Chief:* contact the Chief Libn: Mr Bernard Naylor
Activs: Promotes current awareness of and access to official publications in Britain; maintains and develops a database registry of official publications based on data from the Ford Collection of British Official Publications at Southampton University; access to database and other services is by annual site license subscription (free trials are available on request).

O83
British Records Association [BRA]
London Metropolitan Archvs, 40 Northampton Rd, London, EC1R 0HB (020-7833-0428; *fax:* 020-7833-0416)
Email: britrecassoc@hotmail.com
Internet: http://www.hmc.gov.uk/bra/

Type: charity *Chief:* Hon Sec: Mrs Elizabeth Hughes
Membs: 400 indivs; 350 instns; plus 80 in other categories *Memb Req:* open to everyone with an interest in archvs; full membership: indivs £25 pa (retired/student/unwaged £15), instns £55 pa; affiliate membership (instns only): £20 pa
Activs: Founded in 1932, the British Records Association aims to encourage and assist with the preservation, care, use and publication of records. The BRA is the only organisation which provides a forum for everyone with an interest in archives. Members include historians and other researchers, owners of records, archivists, librarians and others responsible for keeping archives. This breadth of support ensures that the BRA has a strong voice in promoting the interests of archives and archive users at a national level. Undertaking a major part in the work of the BRA, the Records Preservation Section acts as a clearing house and rescue body for historic documents. Solicitors and other bodies are encouraged to contact the BRA in order to discover where they should send documents which are no longer required.
Pubns: Archives (journal, 2 pa, free to membs, £50 pa for instns); Newsletter (2 pa, free to membs); Archives & The User series (prices vary, discounts for BRA membs); archival guidelines leaflets (free on receipt of SAE)

British ▼ Catholic *Organisations*

O84

British Records Society Ltd

c/o Coll of Arms, Queen Victoria St, London, EC4V 4BT (020-7236-9612)
Internet: http://members.lycos.co.uk/ carolyn_busfield/brshome.html

Gov Body: governing council *Chief:* Hon Sec: Mr P.L. Dickinson MA, Richmond Herald, at above addr *Other Snr Offcrs:* Hon Treasurer: Ms Carolyn Busfield, Stone Barn Farm, Sutherland Rd, Longsdon, Stoke-on-Trent, Staffordshire, ST9 9QD (01538-385024; carolynbusfield@hotmail.com)
Membs: c350 indivs & instns
Activs: Publication of historical records, including Indexes to Wills etc.

O85

British Standards Institution [BSI]

389 Chiswick High Rd, London, W4 4AL (020-8996-9000; *fax:* 020-8996-7001)
Email: cservices@bsi-global.com
Internet: http://www.bsi-global.com/

Gov Body: Incorporated by Royal Charter *Chief:* Chief Operating Offcr: Mr Kevin Wilson
Membs: Subscribing: 25000; Cttee: 22000
Activs: National standards organisation of UK; UK member of CEN, CENELEC, ISO and IEC; Product testing, systems assessment, product certification, training services.
Pubns: Business Standards & Standards Update (monthly); Catalogue (annual)
See also **S1042**

O86

BUBL Information Service

Centre for Digital Lib Rsrch, Strathclyde Univ, 101 St James Rd, Glasgow, G4 0NS (0141-548-4752; *fax:* 0141-552-3304)
Email: bubl@bubl.ac.uk
Internet: http://www.bubl.ac.uk/

Gov Body: funded by Joint Info Systems Cttee (JISC) *Chief:* Dir: Mr Dennis Nicholson (d.m.nicholson@strath.ac.uk) *Other Snr Offcrs:* Info Offcr: Mr Andrew Williamson (a.williamson@ strath.ac.uk)
Membs: 3 staff
Activs: A national information service for the higher education community in the UK, BUBL acts to provide access to Internet resources and services of academic, research and professional significance. Also provides BUBL Journals, a journals current awareness service for the library and information science community, and Lis-link, the UK's major library and information science mailing list.
Pubns: Annual Report; poster (free); leaflet (free)

O87

Buckinghamshire Record Society

c/o Centre for Buckinghamshire Studies, County Hall, Aylesbury, Buckinghamshire, HP20 1UU (01296-382771)
Email: archives@buckscc.gov.uk
Internet: http://www.buckscc.gov.uk/archives/ publications/brs.stm

Gov Body: Exec Cttee *Chief:* Hon Sec: Mr H.A. Hanley, addr as above
Membs: 150 indivs *Memb Req:* subscription: £15 pa
Activs: Publication of historical texts relating to the historic county of Buckinghamshire.
Pubns: 32 vols, of which 12, 15, 16, 18, 19 and 23-31 are currently in print; recent vols incl: Vol 28: Buckinghamshire Dissent and Parish Life, 1669-1712 (membs £16, non-membs £20); Vol 29: Buckinghamshire Inquests and Indictments from later 14th Century Buckinghamshire (membs £20, non-membs £25); Vol 30: Buckinghamshire Glebe Terriers, 1578-1640 (membs £20, non-membs £25); Vol 31: Recollections of 19th Century Buckinghamshire (hardback: membs £20, non-membs £25; paperback: membs £7, non-membs £7.50); Vol 32: Index to Probate Records in the Archdeaconry Court of Buckingham, 1483-1660, & of the Buckinghamshire Peculiars, 1420-1660 (membs £22, non-membs £30); prices excl p&p; o/p vols also available on m-fiche; full list of pubns available

O88

Business and Legal Information Network [BLINE]

c/o Ms Wendy Rochester, Ward Hadaway, Sandgate House, 102 Quayside, Newcastle upon Tyne, NE1 3DX
Email: wendy.rochester@wardhadaway.com

Type: prof, legal *Chief:* Sec: Ms Wendy Rochester
Membs: 20 indivs *Memb Req:* open to business & legal info profs working within small libs & info units in the North of England
Activs: Provides a forum for debate on topical issues affecting members; meets four times a year; runs seminars and courses for members.
Pubns: Membership Directory; Union List of Law Reports & Periodicals (1996)

O89

Business Archives Council [BAC]

c/o Ms Fiona Maccoll, Rio Tinto plc, 6 St James's Sq, London, SW1Y 4LD (020-7753-2338; *fax:* 020-7753-2211)
Email: fiona.maccoll@riotinto.com
Internet: http://www.archives.gla.ac.uk/bac/

Type: charity *Gov Body:* Trustees/Exec Cttee
Chief: contact Ms Fiona Maccoll as above
Membs: 200 indivs; 180 instns; 160 corps *Memb Req:* open to indivs & orgs involved in the mgmt & preservation of business records
Activs: Aims to encourage the preservation of British business records; to advise on the administration and management of archives and current records; to promote the use of business records. Provides training and publications on business records and archives; organises visits; works to rescue records at risk; maintains a large business history library containing books and pamphlets about individual firms (see **S1048**).
Pubns: Business Archvs (journal, 2 pa), comprising Principles & Practice (1 pa, £15 to non-membs) & Sources & Hist (1 pa, £15 to non-membs); Newsletter (4 pa, £3 to non-membs); Conference Proceedings (1 pa, £15 to non-membs); Annual Report (£6 to non-membs); Insights (leaflets series, £3.50 to membs, £5 to non-membs); Record Aids (leaflets series, £2.50 to membs, £3.50 to non-membs); Directory of Corporate Archvs (4th ed, £10 to membs, £15 to non-membs)

O90

Business Archives Council of Scotland [BACS]

Glasgow Univ Archv Svcs, 77-87 Dumbarton Rd, Glasgow, G11 6PW (0141-330-4159; *fax:* 0141-330-4158)
Email: bacs@archives.gla.ac.uk
Internet: http://www.archives.gla.ac.uk/bacs/

Gov Body: Council *Chief:* contact the BACS Surveying Offcr
Membs: 200 indivs & insts *Memb Req:* open to anyone concerned with the use & preservation of business archvs & the control of modern records; subscription: indiv £10 pa, institutional £20 pa, corporate £50 pa
Activs: Independent archive body concerned with the active preservation of Scottish business records, and the promotion of their study; locates and surveys records of historical interest; rescues records in danger of destruction; offers an advisory service on the establishment of records management policies and archives systems.
Pubns: Scottish Industrial Hist Journal

O91

CABI Information for Development

Nosworthy Way, Wallingford, Oxfordshire, OX10 8DE (01491-832111; *fax:* 01491-833508)
Email: development@cabi.org
Internet: http://www.cabi.org/

Gov Body: CAB Internatl
Activs: Programme aiming to assist developing countries in the acquisition and management of scientific information, including: the design and planning of sustainable library and information systems; training in information and biological sciences; facilitating the transition to new media formats such as the Internet; delivering information content in new formats.
Pubns: Crop Protection Compendium; Forestry Compendium; Animal Health & Production Compendium; all available on CD-ROM

O92

Caernarvonshire Historical Society

c/o Gwynedd Archvs, County Offices, Caernarfon, Gwynedd, LL55 1SH (01286-679088)
Email: caernarvonshirehistoricalsociety@ btinternet.com
Internet: http://www.caernarvonshirehistoricalsociety. btinternet.co.uk/

Membs: 350+ indivs *Memb Req:* open to anyone interested in the hist of Caernarvonshire; subscription: £7.50 pa (joint membership £9 pa)
Activs: Promotes the study of the history of Caernarvonshire and North West Wales; organises three meetings a year, lectures and other events.
Pubns: Transactions (1 pa)

O93

Cambridge Bibliographical Society

c/o Mr Nicholas Smith, Cambridge Univ Lib, West Rd, Cambridge, CB3 9DR (01223-333123; *fax:* 01223-333160)
Email: cbs@ula.cam.ac.uk

Chief: Pres: Mr David McKitterick *Other Snr Offcrs:* Hon Sec: Mr Nicholas Smith (nas1000@ cam.ac.uk), addr as above
Membs: 200 indivs; 250 instns *Memb Req:* open to all who are interested in the hist of bks & bk production
Activs: Organises lectures and visits; publishes journal.
Pubns: Transactions (1 pa); occasional monographs

O94 🗝️ 🎓

Cambridgeshire Local History Society [CLHS]

c/o Mrs Gillian Rushworth, 1a Archers Cl, Swaffham Bulbeck, Cambridge, CB5 0NG (01223-811703)
Internet: http://www.cambridgeshirehistory.com/societies/clhs/aboutclhs.html

Chief: Chair: Mr Michael Farrar *Other Snr Offcrs:* Sec: Mrs Gillian Rushworth, as above
Membs: 122 indivs; 14 instns *Memb Req:* open to anyone interested in the hist of old county of Cambridgeshire and the Isle of Ely; subscription: indiv membership £8 pa, joint membership £10 pa, corporate membership £10 pa
Branches & Groups: COLLECTORS/BYGONES INTEREST GROUP, c/o Mrs L. Delaney, 1 Wilton Gdns, Mepal, Ely, Cambridgeshire, CB6 3BP
Activs: Formed in 1951 to encourage the study of local history of the Cambridgeshire area. There are regular lectures during the autumn and winter, held on Saturday afternoons, some devoted to collectors/bygones interests. There are outdoor visits during spring and summer. Members are encouraged to transcribe records and carry out research, and to make their results known through the Review or elsewhere.
Pubns: Review: Journal of the Cambridgeshire Local Hist Soc (1 pa every autumn, free to membs, £2 to non-membs); newsletter
Further Info: Archival material collected by the Soc is held at the Cambridgeshire Record Office (see **A87**) & in the Cambridge Colln at Cambridge Central Lib (see **P23**)

O95 🗝️

Cambridgeshire Records Society [CRS]

c/o Mrs Francesca Ashburner, 5 Bateman St, Cambridge, CB2 1NB
Email: francesca@bateman5.demon.co.uk
Internet: http://www.cambridgeshirehistory.com/Societies/crs/

Chief: Pres: Prof Margaret Spufford *Other Snr Offcrs:* Sec: Mrs Francesca Ashburner, as above
Membs: c75 indivs; c25 instns *Memb Req:* subscription: £14 pa
Activs: Publishing editions of material relating to the historic counties of Cambridgeshire and Huntingdonshire; documenting records from newspapers, archive listings and other areas of historical interest.
Pubns: recent vols incl: A Cambridgeshire Lieutenancy Letterbook 1595-1605 (membs £13, non-membs £19.50); Baker's Map of the Town & Univ of Cambridge 1830 (membs £5, non-membs £7.50); Romilly's Cambridge Diary 1848-1864 (membs £16, non-membs £24); Cambridgeshire Hearth Tax Assessments 1662-1664 (membs £25, non-membs £35)

O96 🗝️

Campaign for Freedom of Information [CFOI]

Suite 102, 16 Baldwin Gdns, London, EC1N 7RJ (020-7831-7477; *fax:* 020-7831-7461)
Email: admin@cfoi.demon.co.uk
Internet: http://www.cfoi.org.uk/

Type: non-governmental org *Chief:* Dir: Mr Maurice Frankel
Membs: 900 indivs; 85 instns
Branches & Groups: CAMPAIGN FOR FREEDOM OF INFO IN SCOTLAND, contact: Mr David Goldberg (deegee_98@hotmail.com) or Ms Carole Ewart (Carole@ewartcc.com)
Activs: The CFOI aims to obtain a Freedom of Information Act which would eliminate unnecessary official secrecy and to give people legal rights to information which affects their lives, or which they need in order to hold public authorities properly accountable, by creating a general right of access to official records subject to exemptions where disclosure would create real harm to essential interests such as defence, law enforcement and privacy. This includes rights of access for individuals to personal files that hold data about themselves. The CFOI also campaigns for a public interest defence under the Official Secrets Act, and seeks disclosure in the private sector on issues of public interest. The Campaign is an all-party body and has over 80 national supporting and observer organisations in addition to individual supporters. It has promoted a series of successful private members bills, which give people the right to see their medical, social work and housing records, and information concerning environmental and safety hazards. It has promoted other private member bills to give protection to those disclosing information in the public interest as well as amendments to government legislation to disclose more information voluntarily.
Pubns: Secrets Newspaper (£1 per issue, back copies available); numerous briefings, papers & other pubns; full list from CFOI

O97 🎓

Canolfan Y Llyfr - Aberystwyth Centre for the Book

c/o Natl Lib of Wales, Aberystwyth, Ceredigion, SY23 3BU (01970-632801; *fax:* 01970-632882)
Email: wrg@llgc.org.uk

Chief: contact Dr Rhidian Griffiths at above addr
Membs: 3 instns
Activs: A co-operative venture by the Welsh Book Council, the National Library of Wales and the University of Wales Aberystwyth, to foster interest in the book in Wales. It supports fellowships and issues an annual journal of book studies, and organises the biennial Sir John Williams Lecture.
Pubns: Y Llyfr Yng Nghymru – Welsh Book Studies (annual journal, £7.95); Llyfrau Plant – Children's Books in Welsh, 1900-1991 (bibliography, 1997, £30); A Nation and Its Books: A Hist of the Book in Wales (joint pubn with the Natl Lib of Wales, 1998, £35)

O98 🗝️

Canterbury Circle of Libraries

c/o Miss Sarah Bulson, Inst of Heraldic & Genealogical Studies, 79-82 Northgate, Canterbury, Kent, CT1 1BA (01227-768664)
Email: librarian@ighs.ac.uk
Internet: http://www.lib.circle.cant.ac.uk/

Type: co-op *Chief:* Chair: Dr Angela Conyers, Canterbury Christ Church Univ Coll Lib Svcs
Other Snr Offcrs: Sec: Miss Sarah Bulson, as above
Membs: 17 instns *Memb Req:* open to libs in the Canterbury area
Activs: Meets twice a year to exchange information and promote collaboration between libraries in the area; organises visits to member libraries, shared training events and other joint activities; co-ordinates a system of inter-lending between members.

O99 🎓 🙏

Cathedral Libraries and Archives Association

c/o Dr Tony Trowles, Westminster Abbey Lib, London, SW1 3PA (020-7654-4826; *fax:* 020-7654-4827)
Email: tony.trowles@westminster-abbey.org

Chief: Chairman: Very Rev Dr Wyn Evans *Other Snr Offcrs:* Hon Sec: Dr Tony Trowles, as above
Membs: 5 indivs; 30 instns *Memb Req:* orgs £20 pa, associate membership for indivs £10 pa
Activs: Brings together those working in the libraries and archives held by Anglican cathedrals in the UK and Republic of Ireland; shares information with regard to the care and upkeep of cathedral libraries; organises meetings and conferences.

O100 🗝️ 🙏

Catholic Archives Society

Innyngs House, Hatfield Pk, Hatfield, Hertfordshire, AL9 5PL
Internet: http://www.catholic-history.org.uk/catharch/

Chief: Chairman: Mr Graham Foster
Membs: 200 indivs *Memb Req:* open to any indiv interested in the objectives of the Soc; subscription: £15 pa
Activs: Promotes the care and preservation of records of dioceses, religious foundations, institutions and societies of the Roman Catholic Church in the UK and Ireland so that they may be of administrative use to the organisations they concern and may become accessible for academic research and cultural purposes; to this end it promotes the identification and listing of Catholic records, by providing those responsible for such records with information, technical advice and training opportunities; also organises an annual conference.
Pubns: Catholic Archives (yearly periodical, incl in membership fee, subscription £5 to non-membs); Directory of Catholic Archives (4th ed, free to membs); Church Archives (pamph); Bulletin (1 pa)

O101 🗝️ 🙏

Catholic Family History Society [CFHS]

c/o Terry & Judith Goggin, 45 Gates Green Rd, West Wickham, Kent, BR4 9DE
Internet: http://www.catholic-history.org.uk/cfhs/

Chief: Chairman: Mr Michael Gandy *Other Snr Offcrs:* Joint Secs: Terry & Judith Goggin, as above
Memb Req: subscription: £10 pa + £1 for each addl memb at same addr; overseas: £14 pa
Activs: To promote and facilitate the study of Catholic family history in the UK; holds regular meetings; maintains a number of indexes which can be searched for members (some searches are free, others require payment). The Society's Register Transcripts are on open access at the Catholic Central Library (see **S1057**).
Pubns: Catholic Ancestor (3 pa, free to membs, back issues £1.50 each incl p&p); list of pubns available from the Joint Secs

O102 🗝️ 🙏

Catholic Record Society [CRS]

12 Melbourne Pl, Wolsingham, Co Durham, DL13 3EH (01388-527747)
Internet: http://www.catholic-history.org.uk/crs/

Chief: contact the Hon Sec as above
Memb Req: subscription: £20 pa (overseas £25 or US$45)
Activs: CRS is the premier Catholic historical society in the UK, and is devoted to the study of Roman Catholicism in the British Isles from the Reformation to the present day. Its main activity is the publication of articles and collections of records and historical materials. It also organises yearly conferences, including an international 3-day conference at Plater College, Oxford, and administers the David Rogers Research Fund and the CRS Oxford Conference Bursary.
Pubns: Recusant Hist (journal); Monograph Series; Records Series; Occasional Pubns Series

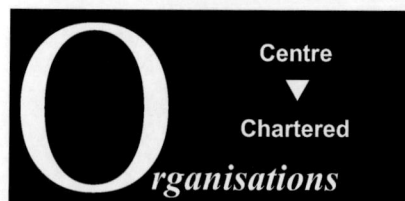

Centre ▼ Chartered Organisations

O103

Centre for Digital Library Research
Dept of Computer & Info Scis, Univ of Strathclyde, 26 Richmond St, Glasgow, G1 1XH (0141-548-2102; *fax:* 0141-552-5330)
Email: cdlr@strath.ac.uk
Internet: http://cdlr.strath.ac.uk/

Gov Body: Univ of Strathclyde, Dept of Computer & Info Scis (see **O420**) *Chief:* Dir: Mr Dennis Nicholson
Membs: 16 staff
Activs: Acts as a centre for research on digital libraries issues, including information policy, information retrieval, document storage technologies and standards.

O104

Centre for Health Information Management Research [CHIMR]
Dept of Info Studies, Univ of Sheffield, Western Bank, Sheffield, South Yorkshire, S10 2TN (0114-222-2636)
Email: P.A.Bath@sheffield.ac.uk
Internet: http://www.shef.ac.uk/~is/research/chimr/chimr.html

Gov Body: Univ of Sheffield, Dept of Info Studies (see **O419**) *Chief:* Dir: Dr Barry Eaglestone (b.eaglestone@sheffield.ac.uk) *Other Snr Offcrs:* Dep Dir: Miss Paula Procter (p.procter@sheffield.ac.uk); Sec: Dr Peter Bath
Activs: The aims of the Centre are: to undertake high-quality research to improve the management of health information; to facilitate the dissemination of research in the above area to the international community; to provide research-led education in health information management and informatics as part of professional development of workers in healthcare; to liaise with healthcare policy makers, providers of services, professional organisations and academic groups; to inform, advise and collaborate in the utilisation of the results of health information management research.

O105

Centre for Information Quality Management [CIQM]
Info Automation Ltd, Penbryn, Bronant, Aberystwyth, Ceredigion, SY23 4TJ (01974-251302; *fax:* 01974-251441)
Email: lisqual@cix.co.uk
Internet: http://www.i-a-l.co.uk/ciqm_index.html

Gov Body: administered by Info Automation Ltd on behalf of CILIP (see **O110**) & UKOLUG (see **O409**)
Chief: Managing Dir: Mr C.J. Armstrong
Activs: Monitors the quality of database and Internet resources, and aims to ease the means by which users can report quality concerns to information providers and vendors.
Pubns: db Qual (e-journal available from web site); incidental papers & documents

O106

Centre for Research in Library and Information Management [CERLIM]
c/o Dept of Info & Communications, Manchester Metropolitan Univ, Geoffrey Manton Bldg, Rosamund St West, Manchester, M15 6LL (0161-247-6142; *fax:* 0161-247-6979)
Email: cerlim@mmu.ac.uk
Internet: http://www.mmu.ac.uk/h-ss/cerlim/

Gov Body: Manchester Metropolitan Univ (see **S1519**) *Chief:* Dir: Prof Peter Brophy (p.brophy@mmu.ac.uk)
Activs: Undertakes research with a practical focus to support operational work in all kinds of library and information services; performs consultancy work in the UK and overseas; contributes to postgraduate programmes of Manchester Metropolitan University's Department of Information and Communications; hosts the Libraries Without Walls conferences.
Pubns: rsrch reports

O107

Centre for the History of the Book [CHS]
Inst for Advanced Studies in the Humanities, Univ of Edinburgh, Hope Park Sq, Edinburgh, EH8 9LN (0131-650-4671)
Email: chb@ed.ac.uk
Internet: http://www.arts.ed.ac.uk/chb/

Gov Body: Univ of Edinburgh (see **S593**) *Chief:* Co-Dirs: Mr Bill Bell & Mr Jonquil Bevan
Branches & Groups: BOOK HIST READING GROUP
Activs: Research centre dedicated to the study and promotion of bibliography and book history; areas of study include literacy and reading practices, relations among publishers, authors, and readers, and media production technology. Organises conferences, seminars and the CHB Lecture.
Pubns: Across Boundaries: The Book in Culture & Commerce (£25); Nineteenth-Century Media & The Construction of Identities (£45)

O108

Centre for the Public Library in the Information Society [CPLIS]
Dept of Info Studies, Univ of Sheffield, Western Bank, Sheffield, South Yorkshire, S10 2TN (0114-222-2635)
Email: r.usherwood@sheffield.ac.uk
Internet: http://panizzi.shef.ac.uk/cplis/

Gov Body: Univ of Sheffield, Dept of Info Studies (see **O419**) *Chief:* Dir: Prof Bob Usherwood
Membs: 5 staff
Activs: Research and postgraduate education specialising in the public library sector. The Centre also provides consultancy services for public library services, and for other information and advice agencies in the public and voluntary sectors, as well as for government and professional bodies in this country and overseas.
Pubns: various rsrch reports

O109

Charity Archivists and Records Managers Group [CHARM]
c/o Mr Mark Pomeroy, Royal Academy of Arts, Piccadilly, London, W1V 0DS (020-7300-5737)
Email: mark.pomeroy@royalacademy.org.uk

Chief: Sec: Mr Mark Pomeroy, as above
Membs: 50+ indivs *Memb Req:* open to those who either work with charity records, or are employed by an org registered with the Charity Commissioners

Branches & Groups: affiliated to the SPECIALIST REPOSITORIES GROUP OF THE SOC OF ARCHIVISTS (see **O369**)
Activs: Provides a forum for archivists, records managers and others responsible for the management of charity records and archives. Aims to promote the importance of charity records and archives, to raise the profile of archivists and records managers working in the charity sector, and to provide a support network for those in this field. CHARM holds four half-day meetings a year. It also has a private email discussion group and web site to aid communication between members.

O110

Chartered Institute of Library and Information Professionals [CILIP]
(formed by the merger of the Lib Assoc & the Inst of Info Scientists)
7 Ridgmount St, London, WC1E 7AE (020-7255-0500; *textphone:* 020-7255-0505; *fax:* 020-7255-0501)
Email: info@cilip.org.uk
Internet: http://www.cilip.org.uk/

Type: chartered prof body *Gov Body:* CILIP Council *Chief:* Dir: Dr Bob McKee PhD, MCLIP, FRSA *Other Snr Offcrs:* Dir of Memb Svcs: Ms Sue Brown MCLIP; Dir of CILIP Enterprises: Ms Janet Liebster BA
Membs: c23000 indivs; 637 instns
Branches & Groups: Regional Branches: BERKSHIRE, BUCKINGHAMSHIRE & OXFORDSHIRE (see **O113**); EASTERN LIB & INFO PROFS PARTNERSHIP (see **O189**); EAST MIDLANDS (see **O121**); CILIP IN IRELAND (see **O150**); LONDON & HOME COUNTIES (see **O131**); NORTH EASTERN (see **O133**); NORTH WESTERN (see **O134**); CILIP IN SCOTLAND (see **O151**); SOUTH WESTERN (see **O143**); CILIP WALES (see **O152**); WEST MIDLANDS (see **O147**); YORKSHIRE & HUMBERSIDE (see **O148**); *Special Interest Groups:* BRANCH & MOBILE LIBS GROUP (see **O114**); CAREER DEVELOPMENT GROUP (see **O115**); CATALOGUING & INDEXING GROUP (see **O116**); COLLS OF FURTHER & HIGHER EDU (see **O118**); COMMUNITY SVCS GROUP (see **O120**); EDU LIBNS GROUP (see **O122**); GOVT LIBS GROUP (see **O123**); HEALTH LIBS GROUP (see **O124**); INDUSTRIAL & COMMERCIAL LIBS GROUP (see **O125**); INFO SVCS GROUP (see **O126**); INTERNATL LIB & INFO GROUP (see **O127**); LIB & INFO RSRCH GROUP (see **O128**); LIB HIST GROUP (see **O129**); LOCAL STUDIES GROUP (see **O130**); MULTIMEDIA INFO & TECH GROUP (see **O132**); PATENT & TRADE MARK GROUP (see **O135**); PERSONNEL, TRAINING & EDU GROUP (see **O136**); PRISON LIBS GROUP (see **O137**); PUBLIC LIBS GROUP (see **O138**); PUBLICITY & PUBLIC RELATIONS GROUP (see **O139**); RARE BKS GROUP (see **O140**); SCHOOL LIBS GROUP (see **O142**); UNIV, COLL & RSRCH GROUP (see **O144**); YOUTH LIBS GROUP (see **O149**); other groups incl: AFFILIATED MEMBS GROUP (see **O112**); RETIRED MEMBS GUILD (see **O1414**)
Activs: CILIP was formed in April 2002 from the merger of the Library Association and the Institute of Information Scientists. It is committed to enabling its members to achieve and maintain the highest professional standards, and encourages and supports them in the delivery and promotion of high quality library and information services. CILIP's members work in all sectors of the information community, including business and industry, further and higher education, schools, prisons, local and central government departments and agencies, the health service, the voluntary sector, and national and public libraries. The Institute's Royal Charter enables it to award Chartered status to members fulfilling the professional criteria for Membership (MCLIP) and Fellowship (FCLIP). CILIP actively campaigns to secure a healthy, well-

resourced library network. It also offers expert information and advice on library and information services, support for personal professional development (short courses, briefings, conferences), professional publishing in library and information science, a monthly journal and members' fortnightly appointments bulletin, and a recruitment agency (INFOmatch).
Pubns: Lib & Info Update (12 pa, free to membs, subscription for non-membs: £79.50, overseas except North America £98, North America $180); Buyers' Guide (quarterly supplement); Lib & Info Appointments (twice-monthly supplement); Annual Yearbook; other titles (over 200 in print) published by CILIP's own imprint: Facet Publishing, 7 Ridgmount St, London, WC1E 7AE (020-7255-0590; *fax:* 020-7255-0591; *email:* info@facetpublishing.co.uk); catalogue available at: http://www.facetpublishing.co.uk/
See also **S1066**

O111

Chartered Institute of Library and Information Professionals, Aerospace and Defence Librarians Group [ADLG]

c/o Mr Rory Souter, Swets Blackwell, Abingdon Business Pk, Abingdon, Oxfordshire, OX14 1UQ (01235-857708)
Email: rsouter@uk.swetsblackwell.com
Internet: http://www.adlg.org.uk/

Type: prof *Gov Body:* CILIP Industrial & Commercial Libs Group (see **O125**) *Chief:* Chair: Ms Jill Halford, Charles Taylor & Co Ltd (jill.halford@ctcplc.com) *Other Snr Offcrs:* Sec: Mr Rory Souter, as above
Activs: Brings together librarians working in the aerospace and defence sectors; provides an active seminar and course programme; organises visits.
Pubns: ADLG Newsletter

O112

Chartered Institute of Library and Information Professionals, Affiliated Members Group

c/o Ms Gerdette Doyle, Antrim Group Lib HQ, Ballcraugy, Bracken Ave, Antrim, BT41 1PU
Email: gerdettedotle@hotmail.com
Internet: http://www.cilip.org.uk/groups/amnc/amnc.html

Type: prof *Gov Body:* CILIP (see **O110**) *Chief:* Chair: Mr Jim Jackson, Law Lib, Univ of Exeter, Rennes Dr, Exeter, EX4 4RJ (01392-263356; *email:* J.G.Jackson@exeter.ac.uk) *Other Snr Offcrs:* Sec: Ms Gerdette Doyle, as above
Memb Req: Affiliated Membership of CILIP is open to non-prof or para-prof staff within the lib & info sector, incl lib assts & administrative staff
Activs: Provides a forum for Affiliated Members of CILIP; awards the Robinson Medal for innovation in library administration to recognise excellence in administration and administrative procedures.
Pubns: Frontline (newsletter)

O113

Chartered Institute of Library and Information Professionals, Berkshire, Buckinghamshire and Oxfordshire Branch [BBOB]

c/o Mrs Catherine Lidbetter, Univ of Reading, Bulmershe Lib, Woodlands Ave, Earley, Reading, Berkshire, RG6 1HY (0118-931-8652; *fax:* 0118-931-8651)
Email: c.s.lidbetter@rdg.ac.uk
Internet: http://www.cilip.org.uk/interests/branches/bbob/

Type: prof *Gov Body:* CILIP (see **O110**) *Chief:* Chair: Mrs Vicky Hibberd (Vicky_Hibberd@oxera.co.uk) *Other Snr Offcrs:* Hon Sec: Mrs Catherine Lidbetter BA (Hons), MA, as above
Memb Req: open to membs of CILIP in the Berkshire, Buckinghamshire & Oxfordshire area
Activs: To promote the aims and objectives of CILIP at local level. Objectives are: 1) to recruit new members and actively involve them in the branch. 2) to publish a regular branch newsletter for all members. 3) to promote and support continuing education in librarianship at all levels through visits, courses and meetings. 4) to report to CILIP's council and committees on all matters affecting members views and to report back to members about developments. 5) to respond to and raise awareness of change within the library profession on behalf of members. 6) to promote and support international links within the library/book profession.
Pubns: BBOB News (4 pa)

O114

Chartered Institute of Library and Information Professionals, Branch and Mobile Libraries Group [BMLG]

c/o Ms Vivien Warren, 145 Queens Park Rd, Brighton, East Sussex, BN2 0GH (01273-697229)
Email: vivw@aol.com
Internet: http://www.cilip.org.uk/groups/bmlg/

Type: prof *Gov Body:* CILIP (see **O110**) *Chief:* Chairman: Mr Mike Brook (mbrook@westberks.gov.uk) *Other Snr Offcrs:* Hon Sec: Ms Vivien Warren BA, MCLIP, addr as above
Activs: Acts as a forum for staff working in smaller libraries in all types of public library services, especially those working on or with mobile libraries; organises training courses and two major annual events: the Weekend Study School, and the National Mobilemeet.
Pubns: Servicepoint (periodical, 3 pa, free to membs); active pubns programme covers a range of practical subjs relevant to needs & interest of membs

O115

Chartered Institute of Library and Information Professionals, Career Development Group

c/o 7 Ridgmount St, London, WC1E 7AE (020-7255-0500; *fax:* 020-7255-0501)
Internet: http://www.careerdevelopmentgroup.org.uk/

Type: prof *Gov Body:* CILIP (see **O110**) *Chief:* Pres: Mr Ayub Khan (ayub.khan@birmingham.gov.uk) *Other Snr Offcrs:* Hon Sec: Ms Lorna Robertson (Lorna.Robertson@mms.co.uk)
Membs: 6335 indivs
Branches & Groups: 15 geographical divs within the UK (see web site for contact details)
Activs: Aims to support, represent and promote the development of new, existing, and student library and information workers; provides a range of practical lifelong learning opportunities; provides support through the chartership process; stimulates new ideas, debates and developments; creates and expands local development and networking opportunities; ensures that the views and concerns of members are effectively represented; holds an annual National Conference and National Student Conference, and organises courses and meetings at divisional level. The Group is also active internationally, organising study tours abroad and raising money to support VSO and library projects in the Third World.

Pubns: Impact (journal, free to membs, 10 pa); Counterpoint Series; Fiction Index; Sequels Index; Picture Bk Index; various introductory texts & works on topical issues

O116

Chartered Institute of Library and Information Professionals, Cataloguing and Indexing Group [CIG]

c/o Ms Emma Bull, Central Lib, Imperial Coll of Sci, Tech & Medicine, Exhib Rd, South Kensington, London, SW7 2AZ (020-7594-8883; *fax:* 020-7594-8876)
Email: e.bull@ic.ac.uk
Internet: http://www.cilip.org.uk/groups/cig/cig.html

Type: prof *Gov Body:* CILIP (see **O110**) *Chief:* Hon Chair: Mr Alan Danskin, British Lib (alan.danskin@bl.uk) *Other Snr Offcrs:* Hon Sec: Ms Emma Bull, as above
Membs: 2500 indivs
Branches & Groups: CATALOGUING & INDEXING GROUP IN SCOTLAND (see **O117**)
Activs: Meetings and promotion of education and training within the field of library catalogues and database management, and information storage and retrieval; representation in relevant committees; maintenance of current bibliographic standards; advice to CILIP and members on matters concerning bibliographic control.
Pubns: Catalogue & Index (quarterly, free to membs, £13.50 pa to others); AACR, DDC, MARC and Friends (1993, £31); Annual Report; Report to Membership Svcs Cttee

O117

Chartered Institute of Library and Information Professionals, Cataloguing and Indexing Group in Scotland [CIGS]

c/o Ms Penny Robertson, 1st Floor, Bldg C, Brandon Gate, Leechlee Rd, Hamilton, Lanark-shire, ML3 6AU (01698-458888; *fax:* 01698-283170)
Email: penny_mr@yahoo.co.uk
Internet: http://www.slainte.org.uk/cilips/cigs/

Type: prof *Gov Body:* CILIP Cataloguing & Indexing Group (see **O116**) *Chief:* Chair: Mr Gordon Dunsire (g.dunsire@napier.ac.uk) *Other Snr Offcrs:* Sec: Ms Penny Robertson, as above
Activs: Represents the interests of CILIP Scotland members engaged or interested in the use of library catalogues, databases, systems or networks, information storage and retrieval, and the production and use of indexes and bibliographic tools. Aims to develop and encourage standards of practice, as well as training and professional development, within these areas, and provides a forum for disseminating information about current standards and innovations. Organises courses, seminars and workshops.
Pubns: Annual Reports

O118

Chartered Institute of Library and Information Professionals, Colleges of Further and Higher Education [CoFHE]

c/o Ms Helen Ashton, Bishop Auckland Coll, Woodhouse Ln, Bishop Auckland, Co Durham, CF23 6XD (01388-443018; *fax:* 01388-609294)
Email: helen.ashton@bacoll.ac.uk
Internet: http://www.cilip.org.uk/groups/cofhe/cofhe.html

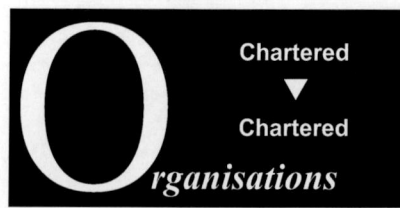

Chartered ▼ Chartered
Organisations

(CILIP Colls of Further & Higher Edu cont)
Type: prof *Gov Body:* CILIP (see **O110**) *Chief:* Chair: Mr Chris Kelland (chris.kelland@becta. org.uk) *Other Snr Offcrs:* Sec: Ms Helen Ashton, as above
Membs: 2000 indivs
Branches & Groups: 16 local circles, incl CoFHE SCOTLAND (see **O119**)
Activs: Provides services to library staff within further and higher education colleges and the university sector; promotes the interests of library staff and libraries in further and higher education within CILIP and in the world of education; supports college library staff in their jobs and provides a professionally and socially stimulating environment for the exchange of ideas and for meeting colleagues; organises and annual conference and a country-wide programme of seminars and workshops.
Pubns: CoFHE Bulletin (3 pa); Annual Report; Guidelines for Learning Resource Svcs in Further & Higher Edu (6th ed, £15.95); conference proceedings; other occasional pubns

O119 🔑 🎓

Chartered Institute of Library and Information Professionals, Colleges of Further and Higher Education (Scotland) [CoFHE Scotland]
c/o Ms Jennifer Louden, Perth Coll Learning Resources, Crieff Rd, Perth, Tayside, PH1 2NX (01738-877639)
Email: jennifer.louden@perth.uhi.ac.uk

Type: prof *Gov Body:* Colls of Further & Higher Edu Group (see **O118**) of CILIP (see **O110**) *Chief:* Chair: Ms Carole Gray *Other Snr Offcrs:* Sec: Ms Jennifer Louden, as above; Cttee Membs: Ms Cleo Jones & Ms Anne Hogg
Membs: c200 indivs; within overall membership of CILIP
Activs: Provides services to library staff within further and higher education colleges and the university sector in Scotland; promotes the interests of library staff and libraries in further and higher education; supports college library staff and provides an environment for the exchange of ideas and for meeting colleagues; organises an annual conference, seminars and workshops.
Pubns: CoFHE Bulletin (3 pa)

O120 🔑

Chartered Institute of Library and Information Professionals, Community Services Group [CSG]
c/o Mr Philip Wark, Midlothian Council Libs, 2 Clerk St, Loanhead, Midlothian, EH20 9DR (0131-271-3980; *fax:* 0131-440-4635)
Email: philip.wark@midlothian.gov.uk
Internet: http://www.cilip.org.uk/groups/csg/ csg.html

Type: prof *Gov Body:* CILIP (see **O110**) *Chief:* Chair: Mr Philip Wark MCLIP, as above
Membs: 1595 indivs
Activs: Promotes equal access to library and information services for all communities; provides training, publications and information to help library

and information workers combat disadvantages for users and to get involved in community development; organised conferences, seminars and workshops, and administers Community Initiative Award, which commends examples of good practice in community library and information work.
Pubns: Community Libn (newsletter, 3 pa, free to membs); catalogue of pubns available

O121 🔑

Chartered Institute of Library and Information Professionals, East Midlands Branch
c/o Mr Rob McInroy, Lincolnshire County Council, Council Offices, Newland, Lincoln, LN1 1YL (01522-553352)
Email: rob.mcinroy@lincolnshire.gov.uk
Internet: http://www.cilip.org.uk/interests/ branches/em/

Type: prof *Gov Body:* CILIP (see **O110**) *Chief:* Pres: Ms Kath Owen BA, MCLIP, Nottingham-shire Libs (01623-653551; kath.owen@nottscc. gov.uk) *Other Snr Offcrs:* Hon Sec: Mr Rob McInroy, as above
Membs: 1450 indivs *Memb Req:* open to CILIP membs living or working in the East Midlands area (Derbyshire, Leicestershire, Lincolnshire, Northamptonshire, Nottinghamshire & Rutland)
Activs: To promote the library services of the East Midlands, and to provide information and training for members; organises meetings; operates the Solo Professional Network (administered on behalf of the Branch by SINTO – see **O352**), for people in the region working on their own in library and information services, including independent consultants.
Pubns: East Midlands Bibliography (annual, £15); NEMCOM (newsletter 4 pa, free to membs, £10 to non-membs)

O122 🔑 🎓

Chartered Institute of Library and Information Professionals, Education Librarians Group [ELG]
c/o Ms Clare Swanson, Genl Teaching Council for England, 344-354 Gray's Inn Rd, London, WC1X 8BP
Email: clare.swanson@gtce.org.uk
Internet: http://www.cilip.org.uk/groups/elg/

Type: prof *Gov Body:* CILIP (see **O110**) *Chief:* Chair: Ms Judy Reading MA, MCLIP, Dept of Educational Studies, Oxford Univ *Other Snr Offcrs:* Hon Sec: Ms Clare Swanson MA, MCLIP, as above
Membs: 1500 indivs
Activs: Aims to represent members of the library and information profession involved in education and lifelong learning. Provides fora where issues can be discussed and disseminated, supports professional development, produces a newsletter and hosts an email discussion group. ELG is keen to develop an international perspective.
Pubns: ELG News (published termly); LIS-EDUC (open email list – Mailbase ListServ)

O123 🔑

Chartered Institute of Library and Information Professionals, Government Libraries Group [GLG]
c/o Mr David Taylor, Dept for Work & Pensions, Room 2/E22, Quarry House, Quarry Hill, Leeds, LS2 7UA (0113-232-4237; *fax:* 0113-232-4209)
Email: david.taylor2@dwp.gsi.gov.uk
Internet: http://www.cilip.org.uk/groups/glg/

Type: prof *Gov Body:* CILIP (see **O110**) *Chief:* Chair: Ms Suzanne Burge BA, FCLIP, Lib & Info Svc, Ombudsman's Office, 15th Floor, Millbank Tower, Millbank, London, SW1P 4QP (Suzanne.Burge@ombudsman.gsi.gov.uk) *Other Snr Offcrs:* Hon Sec: Mr David Taylor BA, MCLIP, as above; Journal Editor: Ms Karen George BA, PGDipLib, Snr Libn, Home Office Info Svcs Unit, 50 Queen Anne's Gate, London, SW1H 9AT (karen.george@homeoffice.gsi.gov.uk)
Activs: Aims to represents the professional interests of librarians in government, parliamentary and national libraries; organises training on topical subjects, including freedom of information, mentoring, electronic publishing and information handling; organises visits and social activities.
Pubns: Govt Libs Journal (3 pa)

O124 🔑 ✚

Chartered Institute of Library and Information Professionals, Health Libraries Group [HLG]
c/o Mr James Beaton, Royal Coll of Physicians & Surgeons of Glasgow Lib, 232-242 St Vincent St, Glasgow, G2 5RJ (0141-227-3204)
Email: james.beaton@rcpsglasg.ac.uk
Internet: http://www.cilip.org.uk/groups/hlg/

Type: prof *Gov Body:* CILIP (see **O110**) *Chief:* Chair: Ms Jackie Lord BA, MCLIP, Head of Lib and Info Svcs, Royal Coll of Nursing (jackie.lord@rcn. org.uk) *Other Snr Offcrs:* Hon Sec: Mr James Beaton MA, DipLib, MCLIP, FSA(Scot), as above
Membs: 2157 indivs
Branches & Groups: Subj Groups: INFO FOR THE MGMT OF HEALTHCARE (see **O233**); LIBS FOR NURSING (see **O254**)
Activs: Represents the interests of those working or interested in libraries and information services for the medical, nursing and allied health professions; supports professional interests of members and upholds standards of service provision; runs study days, workshops, seminars and a national conference.
Pubns: Newsletter; Health Info & Libs Journal (subscription £37 pa for membs); Directory of Health Lib & Info Svcs in the United Kingdom & the Republic of Ireland (£39.50, 2001)

O125 🔑

Chartered Institute of Library and Information Professionals, Industrial and Commercial Libraries Group [ICLG]
c/o Mrs Dawn Taylor-Williams, Olswang, 90 High Holborn, London, WC1V 6XX (020-7267-3120; *fax:* 020-7267-3999)
Email: dawn.taylor-williams@olswang.com
Internet: http://www.iclg.org.uk

Type: prof *Gov Body:* CILIP (see **O110**) *Chief:* Acting Chair: Ms Jill Halford (jill.halford@ctcplc. com) *Other Snr Offcrs:* Sec: Mrs Dawn Taylor-Williams, as above
Branches & Groups: AEROSPACE & DEFENCE LIBNS GROUP (see **O111**); various informal regional groups
Activs: ICLG promotes and supports the professional interests of all members involved in special libraries, especially those practising in the workplace sector. It has an active programme designed to facilitate professional development, encourages and supports activity in the regions, and provides a voice for the workplace sector by offering comment on national and topical issues.
Pubns: ICLG Newsletter (4 pa)

O126 ♀

Chartered Institute of Library and Information Professionals, Information Services Group [ISG]

c/o Ms Diana Herman, Main Lib, Univ Coll London, Gower St, London, WC1E 6BT (020-7679-2612; *fax:* 020-7679-7373)
Email: d.herman@ucl.ac.uk
Internet: http://www.cilip.org.uk/groups/isg/isg.html

Type: prof *Gov Body:* CILIP (see **O110**) *Chief:* Chair: Mrs Valerie Nurcombe (nurcombe@cix.co.uk) *Other Snr Offcrs:* Hon Sec: Ms Diana Herman, at above addr
Branches & Groups: Regional Sections: EAST ANGLIAN SECTION, c/o Ms Janet Hughes (Sec), Dormer Cottage, Beck St, Hepworth, Diss, Suffolk, IP22 2PN (01359-250539, 9am-3pm only; *email:* janet.hughes@btinternet.com); NORTH EAST SECTION, c/o Ms Sheila Moffatt (Hon Sec), 23 Victoria Rd, Wooler, Northumberland, NE71 6DX (01668-283051; *email:* raistrick.cj@pg.com); SOUTH EAST SECTION, c/o Mr John Proctor (Hon Sec), 46 Lawn Ter, Blackheath, London, SE3 9LP (020-8852-4530); SOUTH WEST SECTION, c/o Ms Gloria Curtis (Sec), Gloucester Central Lib, Brunswick Rd, Gloucester, GL1 1HT (01452-426930; *fax:* 01452-521468; *email:* gcurtis@gloscc.gov.uk); INFO SVCS GROUP SCOTLAND, c/o Ms Frances Foster (Sec), Dundee City Council, Mitchell St Centre, Mitchell St, Dundee, DD2 2LJ (01382-435803; *fax:* 01382-435805; *email:* frances.foster@dundeecity.gov.uk); INFO SVCS GROUP WALES
Activs: Unites members with interest in all branches of the information profession; promotes activities that improve the effectiveness of information provision in all sectors of society; organises one-day meetings and visits; branches provide training on reference work and supporting materials; two Standing Committees, SCOOP (see **O392**) and SCOBI (see **O391**), are concerned with official publications and business information respectively.
Pubns: Refer (3 pa, free to membs, subscription for non-membs £18 UK, £21 overseas); Basic Ref Stock for the Public Lib (£10, £7.50 to membs); Future Roles: Info Quality Not Quantity (£16, £12 to membs); The Virtual Lib (£5, £4 to membs); many others; contact Chair for details

O127 ♀

Chartered Institute of Library and Information Professionals, International Library and Information Group [ILIG]

c/o Ms Kathleen Ladizesky, Glantrisant, Trisant, Aberystwyth, Ceredigion, SY23 4RL (01974-282411)
Email: ladizesky@yahoo.com
Internet: http://www.cilip.org.uk/groups/ilig/introduction.html

Type: prof *Gov Body:* CILIP (see **O110**) *Chief:* Chairman: Dr Paul Sturges, Dept of Info & Lib Studies, Loughborough Univ *Other Snr Offcrs:* Sec: Ms Diana Rosenberg, Roadways, The Ridge, Bussage, Stroud, Gloucestershire, GL6 8BB (*tel & fax:* 01453-887214; *email:* drosenberg@gn.apc.org); Treasurer: Ms Kathleen Ladizesky, at above addr
Membs: 1300 indivs; 200 instns
Activs: To serve the interests of international library and information work worldwide; to foster good international relations within the profession; to lessen professional isolation; encourage closer international understanding; to contribute to the development of library and information services overseas. Organises meetings and seminars; administers the Anthony Thompson Award (enables overseas librarians to visit UK libraries for the first time); also participates in the LIBEX scheme (bureau for international staff exchange, administered by CILIP since March 2003) which offers long or short term job exchanges in many countries.
Pubns: Focus on Internatl Lib & Info Work (3 pa, free to membs, subscription to non-membs £22); Emerging Democracies & Freedom of Info (conference proceedings, £25.95); Disaster & After: The Practicalities of Info Svc in Times of War & Other Catastrophes (conference proceedings, £25); Nothing to Read? The Crisis of Document Provision in the Third World (conference proceedings, £15); From Hackney to Havana: Breaking the Info Blockade (£7.50); Libs & Info in East and Southern Africa: A Bibliography (£12.50); various others

O128 ♀ 🎓

Chartered Institute of Library and Information Professionals, Library and Information Research Group [LIRG]

c/o Ms Biddy Fisher, Academic Svcs & Development Learning Centre, Sheffield Hallam Univ, Howard St, Sheffield, South Yorkshire, S1 1WB (0114-225-2104; *fax:* 0114-225-3859)
Email: b.m.fisher@shu.ac.uk
Internet: http://www.lirg.org.uk/

Type: prof *Gov Body:* CILIP (see **O110**) *Chief:* Chair: Ms Biddy Fisher, as above *Other Snr Offcrs:* Sec: Ms Carolynn Rankin, Leeds Metropolitan Univ (0113-283-2600 x5125; c.rankin@lmu.ac.uk)
Membs: 120 indivs; 130 instns; figs incl subscribers to LIRN (see pubns below) *Memb Req:* open to rsrchers, students & academic teaching staff involved in lib & info rsrch; subscription: £25 pa (students & unwaged £7.50 pa)
Activs: An independent professional group to bring together all those who are interested in library and information research and its application; organises seminars, courses, local meetings, and residential conferences; offers research awards and student research prizes.
Pubns: Lib & Info Rsrch News (3 pa, free to membs, subscription £45 pa, £50 overseas); various vols of conference papers (with CILIP)

O129 ♀

Chartered Institute of Library and Information Professionals, Library History Group [LHG]

c/o Dr Jean Everitt, Broncastell, Devils Bridge, Aberystwyth, Ceredigion, SY23 34QU (01970-890615)
Email: jean@jeveritt.fsnet.co.uk
Internet: http://www.cilip.org.uk/groups/lhg/welcome.html

Type: prof *Gov Body:* CILIP (see **O110**) *Chief:* Chair: Dr John Crawford BA, MA, PhD, FCLIP, FSA(Scot), Glasgow Caledonian Univ (jcr@gcal.ac.uk) *Other Snr Offcrs:* Vice-Chair: Mr Bob Duckett (bobduckett@biskit.yorks.com); Hon Sec: Dr Jean Everitt BLib, PhD, at above addr
Membs: c900 indiv & institutional membs
Activs: The Library History Group (LHG) is the only group in the UK specifically devoted to the history of libraries and librarianship. The LHG organises seminars, conferences, and visits, and seeks to support action for the preservation of library records, artefacts and buildings. Indeed it is often said that the LHG represents the historical conscience of librarianship. The LHG's main aim is to encourage the growth of knowledge about the history of libraries.

Pubns: Library History (3 pa, £34 pa for indivs, £49 for instns); Library History Newsletter (3 pa, free to membs)

O130 ♀

Chartered Institute of Library and Information Professionals, Local Studies Group [LSG]

c/o Ms Diana Dixon, 10 Kent Dr, Oadby, Leicester, LE2 4PN (0116-271-3796)
Email: diana.dixon@cilip.org.uk
Internet: http://www.cilip.org.uk/groups/lsg/

Type: prof *Gov Body:* CILIP (see **O110**) *Chief:* Chairman: Mr Ian Maxted MA, MCLIP, County Local Studies Libn, Exeter Central Lib (imaxted@devon.gov.uk) *Other Snr Offcrs:* Hon Sec: Ms Diana Dixon BA, MPhil, DipLib, MCLIP, addr as above
Membs: 1664 indivs; 131 instns
Branches & Groups: sub-groups in London & Home Counties, Midlands & Anglia, North West, Northern Ireland, Scotland, Wales
Activs: Aims to bring together all those engaged or interested in local studies librarianship, and to improve public and professional awareness of local studies libraries and their role in the community. A wide range of meetings, one-day school visits and conferences are organised by members of the various sub-groups, with national committee members taking responsibility for organising events in other parts of the country. The group's annual Dorothy McCulla Award recognises outstanding contributions to local studies librarianship.
Pubns: Local Studies Librarian (2 pa, free to membs); LOCSCOT (newsletter for Scottish membs); newsletters produced by other regional sub-groups; Guidelines for Local Studies Svc

O131 ♀

Chartered Institute of Library and Information Professionals, London and Home Counties Branch

7 Ridgmount St, London, WC1E 7AE (020-7255-0648; *fax:* 020-7255-0501)
Email: Eric.Winter@cilip.org.uk
Internet: http://www.cilip.org.uk/interests/branches/lhc/

Type: prof *Gov Body:* CILIP (see **O110**) *Chief:* Exec Sec: Mr Eric Winter BA, FCLIP, HonFCLIP
Membs: 7600 indivs *Memb Req:* open to membs of CILIP in Bedfordshire, Essex, Hertfordshire, Kent, London, Surrey, East Sussex & West Sussex
Branches & Groups: KENT SUB-BRANCH, c/o Ms Georgia Wyver (Sec), Kent Inst of Art & Design, Rochester Site, Fort Pitt, Rochester, Kent, ME1 1DZ (01634-820334; *email:* gwyver@kiad.ac.uk)
Activs: Providing a local presence for CILIP (via sub-branches) in all of the Home Counties and Central London; running and developing CILIP's relations with France and Germany; professional publishing.
Pubns: Kent Bibliography; Kent maps & plans; Public Libs of Greater London; conference proceedings on a wide range of topics; etc

O132 ♀

Chartered Institute of Library and Information Professionals, Multimedia Information and Technology Group [MmIT]

c/o Mr A.W. Brewerton, Oxford Brookes Univ Lib, Headington Campus, Headington, Oxford, OX3 0BP (01865-483139; *fax:* 01865-483998)
Email: awbrewerton@brookes.ac.uk
Internet: http://www.mmit.org.uk/ ☞

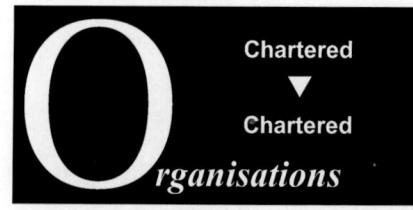

Chartered ▼ Chartered
Organisations

(CILIP Multimedia Info & Tech Group cont)
Type: prof *Gov Body:* CILIP (see **O110**) *Chief:* Chair: Ms Tina Theis BSc, MA, MCLIP, Lib Consultant, 1 Highfield Pk, Heaton Mersey, Stockport, Cheshire, SK4 3HD (tina@tinatheis. com) *Other Snr Offcrs:* Hon Sec: Mr A. W. Brewerton MA, DipLib, FCLIP, addr as above
Membs: 5750 indivs
Branches & Groups: MULTIMEDIA INFO & TECH GROUP SCOTLAND (MmITS), Sec: Ms Paulette Hill (0131-668-8651; email: Paulette.Hill@ scotland.gsi.gov.uk)
Activs: Exists to represent librarians and information staff interested in multimedia information and technologies and to provide advice via publications, events, and electronic and personal support networks.
Pubns: MmIT: Multimedia Info & Tech (4 pa)

O133 ♀
Chartered Institute of Library and Information Professionals, North East Branch
c/o Ms Pamela Dodds, Robinson Lib, Univ of Newcastle upon Tyne, Newcastle upon Tyne, Tyne & Wear, NE2 4HQ (0191-222-5143; fax: 0191-222-6235)
Email: pamela.dodds@newcastle.ac.uk
Internet: http://www.cilip.org.uk/interests/ branches/northern/

Type: prof *Gov Body:* CILIP (see **O110**) *Chief:* Chair: Ms Jane Hall BA, MCLIP, Sunderland City Lib & Arts Centre (jane.hall@edcom.sunderland. gov.uk) *Other Snr Offcrs:* Sec: Ms Pamela Dodds BA(Hons), MCLIP, as above
Membs: 1000 indivs *Memb Req:* open to membs of CILIP in the North East of England (Cumbria, Durham, Northumberland, those parts of Yorkshire within the Darlington & Teesside postal areas, Newcastle upon Tyne, Gateshead, Hartlepool, Middlesborough, Redcar & Stockton-on-Tees)
Activs: Represents regional membership to CILIP and acts locally for CILIP's secretariat; co-ordinates regional groups, encouraging informal and formal support networks; acts as a contact point for regional CILIP members, facilitating communication; holds meetings to encourage and enable debate on professional issues; promotes an active and positive relationship with the Division of Information and Communication Studies at the University of Northumbria (see **O417**).
Pubns: Northern Librarian (bi-monthly, £10 pa)

O134 ♀
Chartered Institute of Library and Information Professionals, North West Branch
c/o Mr Albert Hartley, 2 Solway Cl, Cinnamon Brow, Warrington, Cheshire, WA2 0UP (0161-247-5012; fax: 0161-247-6807)
Email: albert_hartley@hotmail.com
Internet: http://www.cilip.org.uk/interests/ branches/nw/

Type: prof *Gov Body:* CILIP (see **O110**) *Chief:* Chair: Ms Clare Connor (c.connor@chester.ac.uk) *Other Snr Offcrs:* Sec: Mr Albert Hartley, as above

Membs: 2095 indivs *Memb Req:* open to CILIP membs in Lancashire, Cheshire, Merseyside, Manchester & the Isle of Man
Branches & Groups: CAREER DEVELOPMENT GROUP; LOCAL STUDIES GROUP; INFO TECH GROUP; YOUTH LIBS GROUP; COLLS OF FURTHER & HIGHER EDU GROUP
Activs: Represents the interests of CILIP members in the region; organises talks & meetings.
Pubns: North West News

O135 ♀
Chartered Institute of Library and Information Professionals, Patent and Trade Mark Group [PATMG]
c/o 7 Ridgmount St, London, WC1E 7AE (020-7255-0500; fax: 020-7255-0501)
Internet: http://www.patmg.org.uk/

Type: prof *Gov Body:* CILIP (see **O110**) *Chief:* Chair: Mr Bob Stembridge (bob.stembridge@ derwent.co.uk) *Other Snr Offcrs:* Sec: Ms Anne Chapman (achapman@minesoft.com)
Memb Req: open to anyone involved or interested in info provision in the patents industry; subscription: £18 pa for non-CILIP membs
Activs: Acts as a collective voice for members involved in patent and trade mark searching and other related information matters in dealing with government and other official bodies, both national and international; organises patent information workshops, training courses on online retrieval and lectures on various aspects of patent and trade mark law.
Pubns: Searcher (newsletter, 4 pa)

O136 ♀
Chartered Institute of Library and Information Professionals, Personnel, Training and Education Group [PTEG]
c/o Ms Anne Poulson, School of Oriental & African Studies Lib, Thornhaugh St, London, WC1H 0XG (020-7898-4161)
Email: ap45@soas.ac.uk
Internet: http://www.cilip.org.uk/groups/pteg/

Type: prof *Gov Body:* CILIP (see **O110**) *Chief:* Chair: Mr Tony Durcan BA, MCLIP, Gateshead Central Lib *Other Snr Offcrs:* Hon Sec: Ms Anne Poulson, as above
Activs: Represents the interests of all the Institute's members with an interest in personnel management, training or education, and works to promote and support excellence in the management and development of human resources throughout the library and information community. Provides a support network, current awareness meetings and a wide variety of training and development programmes.
Pubns: Personnel, Training & Edu (journal, 3 pa, free to membs, subscription to non-membs £45 in UK, £50 overseas); Directory of Trainers and Personnel Offcrs in the UK

O137 ♀
Chartered Institute of Library and Information Professionals, Prison Libraries Group [PrLG]
c/o Mrs Carole Bowe, HM Prison Gloucester, Barrack Sq, Gloucester, Gloucestershire, GL1 2JN (01452-529551; fax: 01452-310302)
Email: CBowe@gloscc.gov.uk
Internet: http://www.cilip.org.uk/groups/prlg/ prislg.html

Type: prof *Gov Body:* CILIP (see **O110**) *Chief:* Chair: Ms Cathy Evans (CEvans@ worcestershire. gov.uk) *Other Snr Offcrs:* Sec: Mrs Carole Bowe, as above
Activs: Aims to improve standards of library provision in penal institutions, and so provides a forum for contact between library authorities and prisons, librarians, home office and education staff. Provides regular residential Study Schools and one-day seminars, and maintains a close working relationship with the Prison Service Agency. Runs the Inside Books Project, a project to establish reading groups in prisons.
Pubns: Prison Libs Journal (3 pa); Guidelines for Prison Libs; Directory of Prison Libns; Prison Libs Training Pack

O138 ♀
Chartered Institute of Library and Information Professionals, Public Libraries Group [PLG]
c/o Mrs Anne Kelsall, Morecambe Lib, Central Dr, Morecambe, Lancashire, LA4 5DL (01524-402100)
Email: anne.kelsall@lcl.lancscc.gov.uk
Internet: http://www.cilip.org.uk/groups/plg/ plg.html

Type: prof *Gov Body:* CILIP (see **O110**) *Chief:* Chair: Ms Jacquie Campbell BA, MCLIP (js-campbell@auditcommission.gov.uk) *Other Snr Offcrs:* Hon Sec: Mrs Anne Kelsall
Membs: 6500 indivs
Activs: Promotes the interests of public librarians and public libraries; organises Weekend School (biennial), courses and seminars, and the annual Public Library Authorities Conference; offers travel bursaries for librarians wishing to visit libraries in Europe for study or research; promotes the library symbol; organises regional networks of librarians to comment on professional issues, each network maintained by a member of the committee.
Pubns: Public Lib Journal (quarterly, free to membs, Europe £54, outside Europe £60)

O139 ♀
Chartered Institute of Library and Information Professionals, Publicity and Public Relations Group [PPRG]
c/o Ms Linda Smith, Nottingham Trent Univ Lib, Dryden St, Nottingham, NG1 4FZ (0115-848-2256)
Email: linda.smith@ntu.ac.uk
Internet: http://www.cilip.org.uk/groups/pprg/

Type: prof *Gov Body:* CILIP (see **O110**) *Chief:* Chair: Ms Linda Smith, as above *Other Snr Offcrs:* Hon Sec: post vacant
Membs: 1100 indivs
Activs: To promote planned and professional public relations, publicity and marketing within the library and information services world. Annual conference held at Grasmere in November; day courses held twice a year. Involved in the organisation and planning of CILIP's Public Relations and Publicity Awards.
Pubns: Public Eye (4 pa, free to membs); Creating a Web Site (£9.95 + p&p); Manipulating the Media (£7.95 + p&p); Effective Copy Writing for Libns (£10.95 + p&p)

O140 ♀
Chartered Institute of Library and Information Professionals, Rare Books Group [RBG]
c/o Ms Yvonne Lewis, 1 Earle Croft, Warfield, Berkshire, RG42 2QY (tel & fax: 01344-304459)
Email: yvonne.lewis@nationaltrust.org.uk
Internet: http://www.cilip.org.uk/groups/rbg/

Type: prof *Gov Body:* CILIP (see **O110**) *Chief:* Chair: Ms Sarah Dodgson, Keeper of Archvs, Bks & Collns, The Athenaeum, The Athenaeum, 107 Pall Mall, London, SW1Y 5ER (sarahd@hellenist. org.uk) *Other Snr Offcrs:* Hon Sec: Ms Yvonne Lewis, as above
Membs: 1200 indivs
Activs: To cater for the interests and concerns of rare book librarians, and to represent them where appropriate; to promote the importance and study of rare books and special collections; to foster awareness of preservation and conservation issues involved in the maintenance and display of such collections; to gather and disseminate information about rare book holdings and current acquisitions policies; to monitor and contribute to new developments in the field of rare book librarianship; to promote good relations with the book trade in the interest of rare book libraries and librarians. Organises talks, exhibitions, visits and an annual residential study conference.
Pubns: Rare Books Newsletter (3 pa, £16 in UK & Europe, £22 overseas, free to membs); Directory of Rare Books & Special Collns, ed by B. Bloomfield (LAPL 1997, £90); Guideline for the Cataloguing of Rare Books, ed by Hillyard & Pearson (RBG, 1997)

O141

Chartered Institute of Library and Information Professionals, Retired Members Guild [RMG]

c/o Ms Jean Plaister, 3 St Regis Cl, London, N10 2DE (*tel & fax:* 020-8444-8860)
Email: plaister@dircon.co.uk
Internet: http://www.la-hq.org.uk/groups/rmg/ rmg1.html

Type: prof *Gov Body:* CILIP (see **O110**) *Chief:* Chair: Mr Tom Featherstone (the.featherstones@ which.net) *Other Snr Offcrs:* Hon Sec: Ms Jean Plaister OBE, BSc, FCLIP, as above
Membs: c700 indivs *Memb Req:* open to all membs of CILIP, whether retired or not; former membs of the Book & Lib Equip trade may join as affiliated membs; subscription: £8 pa
Activs: Aims to enable retired librarians to keep in touch with each other and to continue to participate in the library and information field. Activities include meetings and visits to libraries and other places of interest to librarians both at home and overseas. The Guild also provides advice on additional financial and other benefits available for retired and older people, helps CILIP and its Branches and Groups to organise and conserve their records and archives and assists CILIP and Library Campaign to maintain and improve library services. It also responds to requests from voluntary societies and charities for assistance with their library services where this complies with CILIP's Guidelines for voluntary work
Pubns: Post Lib (periodical/newsletter, 4 pa)

O142

Chartered Institute of Library and Information Professionals, School Libraries Group [SLG]

c/o Ms Anne-Marie Tarter, Ripon Grammar School, Clotherholme Rd, Ripon, North Yorkshire, HG4 2DG (01765-602647; *fax:* 01765-606388)
Email: library@ripon-grammar.n-yorks.sch.uk
Internet: http://www.cilip.org.uk/groups/slg/ slg.html

Type: prof *Gov Body:* CILIP (see **O110**) *Chief:* Sec: Ms Anne-Marie Tarter, addr as above
Membs: 3500 indivs
Branches & Groups: LONDON & HOME COUNTIES BRANCH, c/o Ms Sue Hyland (Sec), County Lib HQ, Walton St, Aylesbury, Buckinghamshire, HP20 1UU (01296-383161; *fax:* 01296-382122; *email:* shyland@buckscc.gov.uk)

Activs: Providing a forum for discussion and debate for all members including annual weekend school; working through its national and branch committees and working parties to raise awareness of school libraries and to support the work of librarians in schools.
Pubns: School Libs in View (2 pa free to membs, £15 pa to non-membs)

O143

Chartered Institute of Library and Information Professionals, South Western Branch

c/o Mr Andrew Davey, Exeter Central Lib, Castle St, Exeter, Devon, EX4 3PQ (01392-384255; *fax:* 01392-384228)
Email: Ajdavey@devon.gov.uk
Internet: http://www.cilip.org.uk/interests/ branches/sw/

Type: prof *Gov Body:* CILIP (see **O110**) *Chief:* Chair: Ms Sarah Dobson (sarahdobson@ kingsturge.co.uk) *Other Snr Offcrs:* Hon Sec: Mr Andrew Davey BSc, MCLIP, as above
Memb Req: open to CILIP membs in South West England (west of & incl Gloucestershire, Wiltshire, Hampshire, Isle of Wight & the Channel Islands)
Activs: Aims to provide professional contact and activities for CILIP members in the region; to promote their interests and to represent and promote professional ideals and the social standing of librarianship locally. Activities include meetings, social events, training courses, sponsorship, publicity and the promotion of European links.
Pubns: South Western News (4 pa)

O144

Chartered Institute of Library and Information Professionals, University, College and Research Group [UC&R]

c/o Ms Jo Webb, De Montfort Univ, Kimberlin Lib, The Gateway, Leicester, LE1 9BH (0116-207-8046; *fax:* 0116-257-7046)
Email: jwebb@dmu.ac.uk
Internet: http://www.ucrg.org.uk/

Type: prof *Gov Body:* CILIP (see **O110**) *Chief:* Chair: Mr Andrew Martin, Univ Coll Northampton Lib (andrew.martin@northampton.ac.uk) *Other Snr Offcrs:* Hon Sec: Ms Jo Webb, addr as above; Vice-Chair: Ms Mary Pickstone, Manchester Metropolitan Univ (m.pickstone@mmu.ac.uk); Hon Treasurer: Mr Jon Purcell, Robinson Lib, Univ of Newcastle upon Tyne (j.purcell@ncl.ac.uk)
Membs: 5000 indivs
Branches & Groups: Regional Sections: SCOTTISH SECTION (see **O145**); WELSH SECTION (see **O146**); BERKSHIRE, BUCKING-HAMSHIRE & OXFORDSHIRE SECTION, c/o Ms Sue Egleton (Sec), Reading Univ Lib, White-knights, PO Box 223, Reading, RG6 6AE (0118-931-8779; *email:* s.l.egleton@ reading.ac.uk); EAST MIDLANDS SECTION, c/o Ms Philippa Dyson (Sec), Univ of Lincoln Learning Resources, Brayford Pool, Lincoln, LN6 7TS; LONDON SECTION, c/o Mr David Clover (Sec), Inst of Edu Lib, 20 Bedford Way, London, WC1H 0AL (020-7612-6086; *email:* D.clover@ioe.ac.uk); NORTHERN SECTION, c/o Ms Jackie Oliver (Sec), Lib & Info Svcs, Univ of Teesside, Middles-brough, TS1 3BA (01642-342189; *email:* j.oliver@ tees.ac.uk); NORTH-WEST SECTION, c/o Dr Philip Cohen, Didsbury Site Lib, Manchester Metropolitan Univ, 799 Wilmslow Rd, Didsbury, Manchester, M20 2RR (0161-247-6120; *email:* p.cohen@mmu.ac.uk); SOUTH-WEST SECTION, c/o Ms Diane Workman (Sec), Univ of Exeter Lib, Stocker Rd, Exeter, EX1 2SR (01392-263768; *email:* d.workman@exeter.ac.uk);

WEST MIDLANDS SECTION, c/o Ms Judith Hegenbarth (Sec), Info Svcs, Univ of Birmingham, Birmingham, B15 2TT (0121-414-5854; *email:* J.Hegenbarth@bham.ac.uk); YORKSHIRE & HUMBERSIDE SECTION, c/o Mr Gareth Johnson (Sec), J.B. Morrell Lib, Univ of York, Heslington, York, YO10 5DD
Activs: Unites and represents the interests of librarians in national, research, university and higher education libraries; prepares policy documents on current topics affecting these sectors of the profession; at a national level organises an Annual Study Conference and international meetings; the regional sections organise their own programme of meetings, weekend schools and visits.
Pubns: Relay (3 pa); Annual Reports; occasional papers

O145

Chartered Institute of Library and Information Professionals, University, College and Research Group (Scottish Section) [UC&R]

c/o Mr Malcolm Jones, Napier Univ Learning Centre, Sighthill Ct, Edinburgh, EH11 4BN (0131-455-2693; *fax:* 0131-455-2377)

Type: prof *Gov Body:* CILIP Univ, Coll & Rsrch Group (see **O144**) *Chief:* Hon Sec: Mr Malcolm Jones, as above
Activs: Unites and represents the interests of librarians in national, research, university and higher education libraries in Scotland; organises weekend schools and visits.
Pubns: UC&R Newsletter (3 pa); Relay (2 pa)

O146

Chartered Institute of Library and Information Professionals, University, College and Research Group (Welsh Section) [UC&R]

c/o Ms Clare Boucher, Lib & Info Centre, Univ of Wales Swansea, Singleton Pk, Swansea, West Glamorgan, SA2 8PP (01792-295040)
Email: c.boucher@swan.ac.uk
Internet: http://www.swan.ac.uk/lis/ucrwales/

Type: prof *Gov Body:* CILIP Univ, Coll & Rsrch Group (see **O144**) *Chief:* Chair: Mr Paul Jeorrett, North East Wales Inst (jeorrettp@newi.ac.uk)
Other Snr Offcrs: Sec: Ms Carol Edwards, Public Svcs Dept, Natl Lib of Wales, Aberystwyth, Ceredigion, SY23 3BU (01970 632881; *email:* cce@llgc.org.uk); Meetings Sec: Ms Clare Boucher, as above
Activs: Provides a forum for professional librarians working in higher education and research libraries in Wales; organises visits, training events, seminars and social events, open to CILIP members and non-members alike; provides a network for members to make contact with colleagues outside their own workplaces; provides a voice for librarians working in Welsh HE and research institutions; liaises with other professional bodies in Wales, including WLA, CoFHE and other CILIP groups.

O147

Chartered Institute of Library and Information Professionals, West Midlands Branch [CILIP]

c/o Ms Kate Millin, Dudley Central Lib, St James's St, Dudley, West Midlands, DY1 1HR (01384-814745)
Email: kate.millin@dudley.gov.uk
Internet: http://www.cilip.org.uk/interests/ branches/wm/

(CILIP West Midlands Branch cont)
Type: prof *Gov Body:* CILIP (see **O110**) *Chief:*
Chair: Ms Kate Millin, as above
Membs: 1750 indivs; 22 instns *Memb Req:* open
to membs of CILIP working or residing in the West
Midlands area (also incl Staffordshire, Shropshire,
Herefordshire, Worcestershire & Warwickshire)
Activs: Aims to raise represent the interests of its
members and enhance the expertise of library and
information workers in the region; provides
professional contacts and support networks;
organises activities in relation to libraries and
information, including meetings and training
events.
Pubns: Open Access Journal (4 pa, free to
membs, £7 pa to others)

O148 ♀

Chartered Institute of Library and Information Professionals, Yorkshire and Humberside Branch [CILIP]

c/o Ms Alison Jobey, 161 Manchester Rd, Deepcar,
Sheffield, South Yorkshire, S36 2QY
Internet: http://www.cilip.org.uk/

Type: prof *Gov Body:* CILIP (see **O110**) *Chief:*
Chair: Mr Ronan O'Beirne BA(Hons)
(ronan@openline.go-legend.net) *Other Snr
Offcrs:* Hon Sec: Ms Alison Jobey, as above
Memb Req: open to CILIP membs in the
Yorkshire/Humberside area
Activs: Regional group of CILIP. Provides training
courses, meetings, visits, information sharing and
co-ordination of activities. Also operates a
Research Study and Development Fund (details
from Hon Sec).
Pubns: Yorkshire Lib News (quarterly, free to
membs)

O149 ♀

Chartered Institute of Library and Information Professionals, Youth Libraries Group [YLG]

c/o Ms Susan Roe, Bebington Central Lib, Civic
Way, Bebington, Wirral, Merseyside, CH63 7PN
(0151-643-7223; *fax:* 0151-643-7231)
Email: susanroe4@aol.com
Internet: http://www.cilip.org.uk/groups/ylg/

Type: prof *Gov Body:* CILIP (see **O110**) *Chief:*
Chair: Ms Anne Marley (anne.marley@hants.
gov.uk) *Other Snr Offcrs:* Hon Sec: Ms Susan
Roe, as above
Membs: 3500 indivs
Activs: YLG aims to influence the provision of
quality literature and library services for children
and young people in a variety of ways, including
training courses, an annual weekend conference,
the award of the Carnegie and Kate Greenaway
Medals, publications and promotional materials.
Pubns: Youth Lib Review (2 pa); other YLG pubns
are available only from The Norfolk Children's Bk
Centre, Alby, Norfolk, NR11 7HB (01263-761402;
fax: 01263-768167; *email:* ncbc@argonet.co.uk);
pubns incl: All Our Children (£7.50, £6 for CILIP
membs); Bridging the Digital Divide: ICT in
Children's Libs (£5, £4 for CILIP membs); Take
Them to the Lib: Early Years Provision in Libs

(£6, £5 for CILIP membs); Read Smarter Not
Harder: Reading Promotions in Children's Libs (£5,
£4 for CILIP membs); The Best of Carnegie
(leaflet, sold in packs of 50); The Best of Kate
Greenaway (leaflet, sold in packs of 50)

O150 ♀

Chartered Institute of Library and Information Professionals in Ireland [CILIP in Ireland]

c/o Ms Elga Logue, Central Lib, 35 Foyle St,
Londonderry, BT48 6AL (028-7127-2307; *fax:* 028-
7126-1374)
Email: elgal@belb.co.uk
Internet: http://www.cilip.org.uk/interests/
  branches/ireland/

Type: prof *Gov Body:* CILIP (see **O110**) *Chief:*
Chairperson: Mr John Graham (john.graham@NI-
Libraries.net) *Other Snr Offcrs:* Exec Offcr: Ms
Elga Logue, as above; Hon Sec & Affiliated
Representative: Ms Gerdette Doyle (dgerdette@
yahoo.com)
Membs: 347 indivs
Activs: To keep members informed of all current
issues directly affecting libraries; organises
courses, conferences and training programmes
throughout the year.
Pubns: Branch Newsletter; Annual Report; An
Leabharlann (in co-operation with the Lib Assoc of
Ireland – see **IO26**)

O151 ♀

Chartered Institute of Library and Information Professionals in Scotland [CILIPS]

(formerly the Scottish Lib Assoc)
1st Floor, Bldg C, Brandon Gate, Leechlee Rd,
Hamilton, Lanarkshire, ML3 6AU (01698-458888;
fax: 01698-458899)
Email: cilips@slainte.org.uk
Internet: http://www.slainte.org.uk/CILIPS/
  clpshome.htm

Type: prof *Gov Body:* CILIP (see **O110**) *Chief:*
Dir: Ms Elaine Fulton BA, MCLIP (e.fulton@slainte.
org.uk) *Other Snr Offcrs:* Asst Dir: Ms Rhona
Arthur BA, FCLIP (r.arthur@slainte.org.uk)
Membs: 2500 indivs
Branches & Groups: Sub-Groups: CAREER
DEVELOPMENT GROUP; CATALOGUING &
INDEXING GROUP; COLLS OF FURTHER &
HIGHER EDU SCOTLAND (see **O119**);
COMMUNITY SVCS GROUP; INFO SVCS
GROUP; INDUSTRIAL GROUP; LOCAL STUDIES
GROUP; SCHOOL LIBS GROUP; UNIVS &
COLLS GROUP (see **O145**); YOUTH LIBS
GROUP
Activs: Professional organisation for librarians in
Scotland; co-sponsor of SLAINTE (Scottish
Libraries Across the INTErnet), along with the
Scottish Library and Information Council (see
O343).
Pubns: Scottish Lib & Info Resources (annual,
£15); Scottish Libs (bi-monthly journal, £36)

O152 ♀

Chartered Institute of Library and Information Professionals Wales [CILIP Wales]

(formerly the Welsh Lib Assoc)
c/o Dept of Info Svcs, Univ of Wales Aberystwyth,
Llanbadarn Fawr, Aberystwyth, Ceredigion, SY23
3AS (01970-622174; *fax:* 01970-622190)
Email: hle@aber.ac.uk
Internet: http://users.aber.ac.uk/hle/

Chief: Pres: Mr Andrew Green, Libn, Natl Lib of
Wales *Other Snr Offcrs:* Chair: Dr Rhidian
Griffiths, Dir, Dept of Public Svcs, Natl Lib of
Wales, Aberystwyth, Ceredigion, SY23 3BU; Exec
Offcr: Mr Huw Llywelyn Evans, as above
Membs: 900 indivs
Activs: Provides and disseminates information to
its members, promotes their professional development and represents their views; promotes the
development of library and information services
nationally and internationally; advocates the vital
role of high quality library and information services;
seeks to influence the development of policies on
the provision of information and library services at
local and national level; supports the development
of guidelines for the provision of services; advises
on the development of library and information
services.
Pubns: various bks & journals

O153 ♀ 🎓

Cheshire Local History Association

c/o Cheshire Record Office, Duke St, Chester,
Cheshire, CH1 1RL (01244-602559; *fax:* 01244-
603812)
Internet: http://www.cheshirehistory.org.uk/

Chief: Chairman: Mr Doug Haynes (chairman@
cheshirehistory.org.uk) *Other Snr Offcrs:* Hon
Sec: Mr A.J. Bostock (ab@cheshirehistory.org.uk)
Membs: 130 indivs; 45 instns *Memb Req:* open
to all those with an interest in the preservation &
wider understanding of the hist of the ancient
County Palatine; subscription: £20 pa
Activs: The Association is a gathering of history
societies, academic institutions, record
depositories and local authority supporters
concerned with the local history of the County.
Organises quarterly meetings, an annual Cheshire
History Day, and provides advice to members on
local history projects and publishing.
Pubns: Cheshire History (1 pa, £5.25 incl p&p)

O154 ♀

Children's Book Circle [CBC]

c/o Ms Susan Barry, Orchard Bks, 96 Leonard St,
London, EC2A 4RH (020-7739-2929; *fax:* 020-
7739-2318)
Email: susan.barry@wattspub.co.uk

Chief: Chair: Ms Susan Barry, as above
Membs: 350 indivs *Memb Req:* open to anyone
connected with, or interested in, ch's bks (incl
authors, illustrators, publishers, bksellers, libns,
teachers & agents)
Activs: The Children's Book Circle is a voluntary
organisation comprised of people in the children's
book world. We hold monthly evening meetings in
London to discuss a wide range of issues to do
with children's books. We organise the annual
Patrick Hardy lecture and are responsible for
awarding the Eleanor Farjeon Award.

O155 ♀

Children's Books History Society [CBHS]

c/o Mrs Pat Garrett, 25 Field Way, Hoddeston,
Hertfordshire, EN11 0QN (*tel & fax:* 01922-
464885)
Email: cbhs@abcgarrett.demon.co.uk

Chief: Chairman: Mrs Morna Daniels *Other Snr
Offcrs:* Sec: Mrs Pat Garrett, at above addr;
Treasurer: Ms Sarah Jardine-Willoughby;
Newsletter Editors: Mr Brian Alderson & Mrs Pat
Garrett
Membs: 310 indivs; 10 instns
Activs: The CBHS exists to promote an
appreciation of children's books in their literary,
historical and bibliographical aspects, and to

encourage the distribution and exchange of information on children's literature. Meetings and talks are held in London four to six times a year with occasional provincial meetings. Visits to collections are also arranged.
Pubns: Newsletter (3 pa); Occasional Papers (1 pa, £4 each), incl: 1) Early Alphabets: After Henry; 2) The Neverland: Two Flights Over the Territory; 3) Chapbooks; 4) Children's Illustration in the 1860s
Further Info: CBHS is an Org in Liaison with CILIP (see **O110**)

O156 ♟
China Library Group [CLG]
c/o Mr John Moffett, Needham Rsrch Inst, 8 Sylvester Rd, Cambridge, CB3 9AF (01223-311545)
Email: jm10019@cus.cam.ac.uk

Type: prof *Chief:* Convenor: Mr John Moffett, as above
Memb Req: open to libns in the field of Chinese studies in the UK
Activs: Aims to foster co-operation between China collections in the UK and with similar collections abroad.

O157 🎓 🙏
Church of England Record Society [COERS]
c/o Lambeth Palace Lib, London, SE1 7JU (020-8699-0820)
Email: mbarber@coers.org
Internet: http://www.coers.org/

Gov Body: Council *Chief:* Pres: Prof Diarmaid MacCulloch *Other Snr Offcrs:* Exec Sec: Miss Melanie Barber, as above; Genl Editor: Dr Stephen Taylor, Dept of Hist, Univ of Reading
Membs: 360 indivs; 90 instns *Memb Req:* open to all those interested in Anglican church hist; subscription: indivs £21 pa (full-time students £10), instns £30 pa, life membership for over-65s £200
Activs: Promotes interest in and knowledge of the Church of England from the 16C onwards; publishes primary material of significance for the history of the Church of England, such as letters, diaries, specula, visitation articles and other documents; publishes one volume per year; organises an annual lecture.
Pubns: published vols incl in membs' sub-scriptions, retail cost £40+ per vol; currently available vols incl: Visitation Articles & Injunctions of the Early Stuart Church (2 vols); The Speculum of Archbishop Thomas Secker; The Early Letters of Bishop Richard Hurd 1739-1762; Brethren in Adversity; The Anglican Canons 1529-1947; From Cranmer to Davidson: A Church of England Miscellany; Tudor Church Reform; The Community of All Saints; Elizabethan Conferences: Pedham & Bury St Edmunds 1582-90

O158 🎓 📽
Cimtech Ltd
Innovation Centre, Univ of Hertfordshire, College Ln, Hatfield, Hertfordshire, AL10 9AB (01707-281060; *fax:* 01707-281061)
Email: c.cimtech@herts.ac.uk
Internet: http://www.cimtech.co.uk/

Gov Body: Univ of Hertfordshire (see **S791**)
Chief: Managing Dir: Mr Tony Hendley
Membs: 1000+ instns *Memb Req:* corporate membership: £200+VAT pa
Activs: Advice and consultancy services in the field of information management; carries out strategy studies, helping users to define their information management requirements and procure the most cost-effective solutions; arranges conference and exhibitions; provides short courses

on document and record management, including image processing and workflow.
Pubns: Info Mgmt & Tech (6 pa, £95 pa to non-membs in UK); Content & Document Mgmt Guide & Directory (13th ed, £30 to membs, £45 to non-membs; also available on CD-ROM: £35 to membs, £50 to non-membs)

O159 ♟
Circle of Officers of National and Regional Library Systems [CONARLS]
c/o Ms Kate Holliday, Lib HQ, Balne Ln, Wakefield, West Yorkshire, WF2 0DQ (01924-302210; *fax:* 01924-302245)
Email: kholliday@wakefield.gov.uk
Internet: http://thenortheast.com/conarls/

Chief: Chair (2002): Ms Kate Holliday, as above
Membs: 13 instns; representatives from each of the English regions, the natl libs, Resource & FIL
Activs: To facilitate the interlending of books and other materials; to facilitate the organisation of the efficient delivery of books and other library materials by transport schemes or electronic transmission; to publish standards and information on interlending and library co-operation and arrange seminars; to provide training.
Pubns: CONARLS leaflet; Interlibrary Lending – Common Standards for Best Practice; Guide to the Joint Fiction Reserves (2nd ed); The Lib Regions in Profile (2nd ed); Why Requests Fail (rsrch report)

O160 ♟
Circle of State Librarians [CSL]
c/o Ms Lynda Cooper, Home Office, ISU Resources, Room 1004, Queen Anne's Gate, London, SW1H 9AT (020-7273-4463; *fax:* 020-7273-3957)
Email: Lynda.Cooper@homeoffice.gsi.gov.uk
Internet: http://www.circleofstatelibrarians.co.uk/

Chief: Chairman: Mr Paul Woods, Treasury Solicitor's Lib (PWoods@treasury-solicitor.gsi.gov.uk) *Other Snr Offcrs:* Sec: Ms Lynda Cooper, as above
Membs: 520 indivs *Memb Req:* open to libns & info workers (at all grades & levels) from govt depts, agencies & related orgs; subscription £7.50 pa
Activs: Semi-formal, non-profit making organisation bringing together workers in the government library sector. Provides training courses; annual conference; publishing; social events; visits to libraries; networking.
Pubns: State Libn (2 pa)

O161 ♟ 📽
City Information [CiG]
(formerly City Info Group, a special interest group of the Inst of Info Scientists)
PO Box 13297, London, SW19 8GH (020-8543-7339)
Email: admin@cityinformation.org.uk
Internet: http://www.cityinformation.org.uk/

Type: prof *Chief:* Administrator: Ms Phillipa Mills
Membs: 800 indivs *Memb Req:* open to anyone involved with or interested in the provision or use of business & financial info; subscription £38 pa
Activs: To stimulate communication and the exchange of knowledge, experience and ideas between specialists in the financial and business information sector and represent members on issues of importance; organises monthly seminars on topical subjects and regular social events.
Pubns: CIGLET (newsletter, 4pa, free to membs); CiG Yearbook (1 pa, free to membs)

O162 ♟
City Legal Information Group [CLIG]
(formerly the City Law Libns Group)
c/o Ms Jas Sembhi, DJ Freeman, 43 Fetter Ln, London, EC4A 1JU (020-7556-4147; *fax:* 020-7556-4690)
Email: JasSembhi@djfreeman.com
Internet: http://www.clig.org/

Type: legal, prof *Chief:* Chair: Ms Claire Fox, Eversheds (020-7919-0635; *email:* foxc@eversheds.com) *Other Snr Offcrs:* Vice Chair: Ms Charlotte Russell-Hargreaves, Reuters Limited (Charlotte.russell-hargreaves@reuters.com); Membership Sec: Ms Jas Sembhi, as above
Membs: c300
Activs: Aims to promote the role of legal information professionals working in the London area, to provide them with opportunities for professional development and to provide a friendly forum and network for mutual support and the exchange of information. Organises a wide range of events throughout the year, from talks and seminars on professional and legal issues, to practical sessions on management or Intranet development, to visits to leading libraries, to networking breakfasts and other social occasions. An AGM is held around March each year.
Pubns: CLIG Newsletter; occasional reports & special pubns

O163 🎓
City University School of Informatics, Department of Information Science
Northampton Sq, London, EC1V 0HB (020-7040-8381; *fax:* 020-7040-8584)
Internet: http://www.soi.city.ac.uk/organisation/is/

Gov Body: City Univ London (see **S1084**) *Chief:* Head of Dept: David Nicholas (nicky@soi.city.ac.uk)
Membs: 18 staff
Branches & Groups: rsrch groups incl: DIGITAL HEALTH RSRCH UNIT (DHRU); CENTRE FOR INTERACTIVE SYSTEMS RSRCH (CISR); KNOWLEDGE & INFO MGMT GROUP (KIMG); INTERNET STUDIES RSRCH GROUP (ISRG); HEALTH SCIS INFO GROUP (HSIG); GEOGRAPHIC INFO SCI GROUP (GISG); INFO POLICY RSRCH GROUP (IPRG)
Activs: Postgraduate education and research in the field of Information Science.

O164 ♟
Cleveland and Teesside Local History Society
c/o Mr Geoff Braddy, 150 Oxford Rd, Linthorpe, Middlesbrough, Teesside, TS5 5EL (01642-816903)
Email: ctlhs@freenetname.co.uk
Internet: http://www.ctlhs.org.uk/

Chief: Chairperson: Ms Carol Cook *Other Snr Offcrs:* Hon Sec: Mr Geoff Braddy, as above (geoff.s.braddy@virgin.net)
Membs: c270 indivs *Memb Req:* open to all those interested in the local hist of the region; subscription: indivs £10 pa (students, under-18s & unemployed £5, oaps £7), households £12 pa, oap couples £8 pa, instns (schools, colls, libs etc) £12 pa; surcharge of £3 for overseas membs
Activs: Promotes various projects in local history; provides advice and regular talks and occasional all-day meetings with invited speakers; organises guides walks and visits to places of historical interest; maintains links with local archives, libraries, museums and other groups connected with archaeology, family history and industrial archaeology. ☛

Organisations

Cleveland ▼ Dugdale

(Cleveland & Teesside Local Hist Soc cont)
Pubns: Cleveland Hist (2 pa, £3, free to membs); regular newsletter for membs; Historic Reflections across the Tees (£4 + 60p p&p); Tomorrow's Hist (CD-ROM, £5 + 80p p&p); postcards (20p each, £1.50 for set of 8, 25p p&p)

O165 ♀

Co-East

10a Princes St, Huntingdon, Cambridgeshire, PE29 3PH (01480-376041; *fax:* 01480-376039)
Email: linda.berube@cambridgeshire.gov.uk
Internet: http://www.co-east.net/

Type: co-op, consortium **Chief:** Regional Mgr: Ms Linda Berube
Membs: consortium of 10 public lib authorities operating in the East of England
Activs: Aims to establish ICT solutions to enable members of the public to easily obtain resources from libraries across the region, either via computers in libraries or over the Internet. Runs the web-based information service Ask a Librarian (http://www.ask-a-librarian.org.uk) and the online directory of family history resources Familia (http://www.familia.org.uk).

O166 ♀

The Combined Regions

c/o Somerset Libs, Arts & info, Lib HQ, Mount St, Bridgwater, Somerset, TA6 3ES (01278-451201; *fax:* 01278-452787)
Email: bpowell@swrls.org.uk
Internet: http://www.thecombinedregions.com/

Type: co-op **Gov Body:** Council **Chief:** Chairman: Mr Robert Froud (rnfroud@somerset.gov.uk) **Other Snr Offcrs:** Vice-Chair: Mr Robert Gent (robert.gent@derbyshire.gov.uk); Hon Treasurer: Ms Patricia McKenzie (p.mckenzie@nls.uk)
Membs: 10 instns **Memb Req:** regional lib orgs in the UK & Ireland
Activs: Aims to encourage and assist the development of interlending and co-operation within and between the regional and national library organisations and their member libraries in the UK and Ireland; supports library resource sharing by enabling the creation and maintenance of a union catalogue together with an inter-library loan requesting system; has a contractual partnership with Talis Information Ltd (see **O400**) to develop and operate the union catalogue and requesting system UnityWeb.
Pubns: RAPPORT (occasional newsletter)

O167 ♀ 🎓

Concerted Action on Management Information for Libraries in Europe [CAMILE]

c/o Mr Ian Bloor, De Montfort Univ Lib, The Gateway, Leicester, LE1 9BH (0116-250-6041)
Email: ipb@dmu.ac.uk
Internet: http://www.dmu.ac.uk/~camile/

Chief: Proj Mgr: Mr Ian Bloor
Activs: Aims to use European expertise and experience to advance the research and application of library management techniques

throughout the library community in Europe. Its main goal is to disseminate and promote the common results of four EC-supported projects – DECIDE, DECIMAL, EQLIPSE and MINSTREL – which develop models and tools to support decision making in libraries throughout Europe.
Pubns: various papers

O168 ♀ 🎓

Conference of Regional and Local Historians [CORAL]

c/o Dr Winifred Stokes, 18 King Edward Rd, Tynemouth, Tyne & Wear, NE30 2RP (0191-257-5918)
Email: treasurer@coral-historians.org.uk
Internet: http://www.coral-historians.org.uk/

Chief: Chair: Dr. Geoff Timmins, Dept of Historical & Critical Studies, Univ of Central Lancashire (j.g.timmins@uclan.ac.uk) **Other Snr Offcrs:** Treasurer: Dr Winifred Stokes, as above
Membs: c100 indivs
Activs: Promotes local history studies in the UK; organises conferences and meetings.
Pubns: Journal of Regional & Local Studies (2 pa, subscription £14.00)

O169 🎓

Consortium of University Research Libraries [CURL]

12th Floor, Muirhead Tower, Univ of Birmingham, Edgbaston, Birmingham, B15 2TT (0121-415-8109)
Email: m.detraz@bham.ac.uk
Internet: http://www.curl.ac.uk/

Gov Body: Board of Dirs **Chief:** Chairman: Dr Tom Graham, Univ Libn, Robinson Lib, Univ of Newcastle (t.w.graham@ncl.ac.uk) **Other Snr Offcrs:** Exec Sec: Dr Marie-Pierre Détraz, at Birmingham addr; Dep Exec Sec & Database Offcr: Dr Mike Mertens, at Birmingham address
Membs: 25 full membs, 1 associate memb & 1 partner **Memb Req:** univ & legal deposit libs in the UK & Ireland which support a broad range of high-quality rsrch at a natl level
Branches & Groups: CURL DATABASE, hosted by: Manchester Computing, Univ of Manchester, Oxford Rd, Manchester, M13 9PL, contact the CURL Database Offcr: Dr Mike Mertens (0121-415-8107; *email:* m.j.mertens@bham.ac.uk); COPAC, at same addr (0161-275-6037; *fax:* 0161-275-6040; *email:* copac@mimas.ac.uk)
Activs: The promotion and maintenance of library resources for research in universities by cost-effective co-operation across the whole range of research library activities. Sponsors COPAC, a union catalogue giving free access to the merged online catalogues of Consortium members.
Pubns: Curlnews (newsletter); Guide to the Rsrch Collns of Memb Libs (1996)

O170 ♀

Consortium of Welsh Library and Information Services [CWLIS]

c/o Ms Linda Tomos, Dept of Info Studies, Univ of Wales Aberystwyth, Aberystwyth, Ceredigion, SY23 3AS (01970-622155)
Email: elt@aber.ac.uk
Internet: http://www.dils.aber.ac.uk/holi/cwlis/cwlis.htm

Type: co-op (info sector) **Gov Body:** Council of Membs **Chief:** Hon Chairman: Sir Donald Walters **Other Snr Offcrs:** Projs Dir: Ms Linda Tomos, as above
Membs: 53 instns
Activs: Operational forum for library and information services in Wales. CWLIS aims to: facilitate the development of library and information

services; instigate research and innovation in the sector; respond to reports and initiatives; propose new initiatives; influence policy; lobby on behalf of the library and information sector.
Pubns: Gwybodaeth Cymru/Info Wales (3 pa, free to membs)

O171 ♀

Construction Industry Information Group [CIIG]

c/o The Bldg Centre, Store St, London, WC1E 7BT (020-7222-7000)
Email: ciigsecretary@yahoo.co.uk
Internet: http://www.ciig.org.uk/

Chief: Chair: Mr Malcolm Weston **Other Snr Offcrs:** Sec: Mr Robin Viner, as above; Treasurer: Mr Ted Hastings
Memb Req: open to indivs & orgs involved or interested in info provision in the construction industry; indiv membership: £25 pa (students £5); corporate membership: £75 pa; affiliate membership: £150 pa
Activs: Brings together professionals concerned with the provision, dissemination and use of information in the construction industry. Promotes good practice in construction libraries and information services; aims to improve liaison and co-operation between members; provides a forum for the airing of common problems; helps members keep abreast of current developments; arranges meetings, visits, conferences, workshops and social gatherings.
Pubns: CIIG News (monthly, free to membs); CIIG Review (occasional pubn, free to membs)
Further Info: CIIG is an Org in Liaison with CILIP (see **O110**)

O172 ♀ ➕

Consumer Health Information Consortium [CHIC]

c/o Ms Elizabeth Eastwood, Arthritis Care, 18 Stephenson Way, London, NW1 2HD (020-7380-6500; *fax:* 020-7380-6505)
Email: lizziee@arthritiscare.org.uk
Internet: http://omni.ac.uk/CHIC/

Chief: contact Ms Elizabeth Eastwood, as above
Memb Req: open to any indiv or org interested in the provision of health info to the public; subscriptions: indivs £15.00 (conc £5); instns £40 (with less than 4 staff) or £60 (with 4 or more staff)
Activs: Autonomous support organisation for those interested in the provision of health information to the public; provides training; encourages good practice; participates in various national policy forums; promotes the principle of free, open access to health information for all.
Pubns: CHIC Update (3 pa, free to membs)
Further Info: CHIC is an Org in Liaison with CILIP (see **O110**)

O173 ♀

Conurbation Library and Information Plan [CLIP]

c/o Mr David Ball, Bournemouth Univ, Dorset House Lib, Fern Barrow, Poole, Dorset, BH12 5BB (01202-595044; *fax:* 01202-595475)
Email: dball@bournemouth.ac.uk

Type: co-op **Chief:** Sec: Mr David Ball
Activs: The Conurbation Library and Information Plan covers the conurbation centred on Bournemouth, Poole and Christchurch. The broad aims of CLIP are: to review and rationalise information provision in the area; to support regional and national initiatives; to make the best use of public and programme funding to serve the conurbation's communities; to maximise managed access to information resources and expertise.

O174 ♟

Copyright Licensing Agency Ltd [CLA]

90 Tottenham Court Rd, London, W1P 4LP (020-7631-5555; *fax:* 020-7631-5500)
Email: cla@cla.co.uk
Internet: http://www.cla.co.uk/

Gov Body: owned by and run on behalf of the Authors' Licensing & Collecting Soc (see **O50**) & the Publishers' Licensing Soc (see **O322**) *Chief:* Chief Exec: Mr Peter Shepherd (peter.shepherd@cla.co.uk)
Branches & Groups: CLA SCOTLAND, contact: Mr Jim MacNeilage, Business Development Mgr Scotland, CBC House, 24 Canning St, Edinburgh, EH3 8EG (0131-272-2711; *fax:* 0131-272-2811; *email:* clascotland@cla.co.uk)
Activs: The CLA is the UK's reproduction rights organisation, and is responsible for looking after the interests of rights owners in copying from books, journals and periodicals. It aims to encourage respect for copyright, licenses users for copying extracts from books, journals and periodicals, collects fees for such copying and pays authors and publishers (via ALCS and PLS) their shares of the fees collected, and institutes legal proceedings, if necessary, to enforce the rights entrusted to it. Maintains CLARCS, the CLA's Rapid Clearance Service.
Pubns: CLArion (magazine, 2 pa); Annual Report; various pubns for licence holders & on genl copyright issues

O175 ♟

Council for Learning Resources in Colleges [CoLRiC]

122 Preston New Rd, Blackburn, Lancashire, BB2 6BU (01254-662923; *fax:* 01254-610979)
Email: colric@colric.org.uk
Internet: http://www.colric.org.uk/

Chief: Exec Dir: Mr Jeff Cooper MA, FCLIP
Membs: 250+ instns *Memb Req:* open to learning resources svcs within FE (incl 6th Form) coll in the UK & Ireland; staff of memb instns may also join as indivs; subscriptions: instns £15-£220 pa depending on budget, indivs £15 pa
Activs: Aims to enhance and maintain the quality of learning resources services in colleges throughout the UK and Ireland. Offers accreditation and certification of college learning resources services and libraries; publishes guidelines to raise the quality and profile of service provision; initiates research and development in the Council's area of interest; awards the CoLRiC Beacon Award every year.
Pubns: Newsletter (3 pa); Annual Report; Working Papers series (9 published to date, £5 each to membs, £30 for the set, non-membs £7.50 each, £45 for the set); Quality Assurance for Learning Resources Svcs (free to membs); Guidelines for Self-Assessment (free to membs); Involvement in the Coll Curriculum (free to membs); various guidelines & policy papers
Further Info: CoLRiC is an Org in Liaison with CILIP (see **O110**)

O176 ♟ 🎓

Council for Slavonic and East European Library and Information Services [COSEELIS]

c/o Ms Janet Zmroczek, British Lib, Slavonic & East European Collns, 96 Euston Rd, London, NW1 2DB (020-7412-7586; *fax:* 020-7412-7781)
Email: Janet.Zmroczek@bl.uk
Internet: http://www.gla.ac.uk/Library/COSEELIS/

Chief: Chair: Ms Lesley Pitman, School of Slavonic & East European Studies *Other Snr Offcrs:* Sec: Ms Janet Zmroczek, as above
Memb Req: indiv & institutional membership is open to all those interested in info provision for Slavonic & East European Studies
Activs: Represents the interests of those working in libraries and other information organisations in the field of Slavonic and East European Studies. Group interests are furthered through publications, co-operative activities, collective representation, and the exchange of views and ideas at conferences.
Pubns: Newsletter (2 pa); Solanus; European Bibliography of Slavic & East European Studies; Register of Slavonic & East European Src Materials in Microforms; Microform Material from the FSU & Central & Eastern Europe in UK Libs; Union List of Slavonic & East European Newspapers in British Libs; Union List of Serials on Soviet Edu

O177 🏛

Cultural Heritage National Training Organisation

1st Floor, Glyde House, Glydegate, Bradford, BD5 0UP (01274-391056; *fax:* 01274-394890)
Email: mail@chnto.co.uk
Internet: http://www.chnto.co.uk/

Chief: Dir: Mr David Wears (david@chnto.co.uk)
Activs: Aims to provide up-to-date information, advice and practical support on all aspects of training and development of interest to the cultural heritage sector.

O178 ♟

Cumbria Local History Federation [CLHFED]

Oakwood, The Stripes, Cumwhinton, Cumbria, CA4 0AP (01228-561143)
Email: lir@respop.globalnet.co.uk
Internet: http://www.cumbrialocalhistory.org.uk/

Chief: Chair & sec: Mrs Jill Wishart, at above addr
Membs: 1500 through affiliated socs & indivs
Activs: Aims to encourage interest in the local history of Cumbria through research and publication; provides a forum where local history societies and individuals can exchange information and expertise; arranges an annual conference.
Pubns: Bulletin; Diary (both 3 pa, £5 pa)

O179 ♟

Derbyshire Local History Societies Network

c/o Ms Margaret O'Sullivan, Derbyshire Record Office, County Hall, Matlock, Derbyshire, DE4 3AG (01629-580000 x35201; *fax:* 01629-576110)

Chief: Co-ordinator: Ms Margaret O'Sullivan
Membs: c80 indivs
Activs: Umbrella group for local history organisations in the County of Derbyshire; promotes Derbyshire local studies and organises meetings.
Pubns: Network News (4 pa)

O180 ♟

Design and Artists Copyright Society Ltd [DACS]

Parchment House, 13 Northburgh St, London, EC1V 0JP (020-7336-8811; *fax:* 020-7336-8822)
Email: Info@dacs.org.uk
Internet: http://www.dacs.org.uk/

Type: collecting soc *Gov Body:* Council of Mgmt
Chief: Chief Exec: Ms Joanna Cave

Membs: 36000+ internationally *Memb Req:* open to all artists irrespective of the artistic discipline in which they practise, or whether they are famous or commercially successful; subscription: single life membership fee of £25
Activs: established in 1983 as a not-for-profit membership organisation, DACS exists to protect and promote the copyright of visual artists in the UK and worldwide, representing 36000 fine artists and 16000 commercial artists. Where rights are administered collectively under blanket licences, DACS collects a share of revenue on behalf of artists and distributes it through annual Payback campaigns.

O181 ♟

Devon and Cornwall Record Society [D&CRS]

c/o 7 The Close, Exeter, Devon, EX1 1EZ
Internet: http://www.cs.ncl.ac.uk/genuki/DEV/DCRS/

Type: registered charity *Chief:* Hon Sec: J.D. Brunton
Memb Req: subscriptions (UK): indiv £12.50 pa, joint £16.50 pa, instns £15.50 pa; higher rates apply outside UK; prof record agents £25 pa; temp membership for use of lib only is available for £5 for 3 months
Activs: Founded in 1904 for the publication of local records and the promotion of historical and genealogical research. A large collection of source material, mainly copies of Devon and Cornwall parish registers, is held at the Westcountry Studies Library, Exeter (see **A164**), for the use of members.
Pubns: 1 vol published pa, which membs receive as part of subscription; past pubns are available, mostly at £15 per vol in the UK, £20 overseas; Shelflist of the Soc's Collns (£2.50 UK, £3.50 overseas)

O182 ♟

Devon History Society

c/o Mr D.L.B. Thomas, 112 Topsham Rd, Exeter, Devon, EX2 4RW
Internet: http://www.devonhistorysociety.org.uk/

Chief: Membership Sec: Mr D.L.B. Thomas, as above
Membs: c600 indivs *Memb Req:* open to anyone interested in the local hist of Devon; subscription: indivs £10 pa, families £15 pa, affiliated socs £10 pa, corporate membership £15 pa; life membership £100
Activs: Founded in 1969 to further the knowledge and study of the county's history. Two conferences are held each year in various parts of Devon, and in addition papers are presented at the annual general meeting held in Exeter.
Pubns: Devon Historian (2pa, £10); In Pursuit of Devon's Hist (£1 to new membs)

O183 ♟

The Dugdale Society

c/o The Shakespeare Centre, Henley St, Stratford-upon-Avon, Warwickshire, CV37 6QW (01789-204016; *fax:* 01789-296083)
Email: records@shakespeare.org.uk
Internet: http://www.shakespeare.org.uk/main/3/37/

Gov Body: Council of the Dugdale Soc *Chief:* Chairman: Dr Levi Fox OBE, MA, FSA, FRSL, DL *Other Snr Offcrs:* Hon Sec: Mrs Cathy Millwood, at above addr
Membs: c216 indivs; c113 instns
Activs: The Dugdale Society exists to publish historical records of the County of Warwick and generally to encourage interest in the original historical sources for Warwickshire history. Two meetings of members are held each year. ☛

Organisations

Dugdale ▼ Forum

(Dugdale Soc cont)

Pubns: Since its inauguration in 1920, 38 main vols of edited historical records, together with 39 Occasional Papers dealing with a wide range of historical subj matter have been publ; details are available from the Sec & copies are available for sale to non-membs

O184 ♀

Durham County Local History Society [DCLHS]

c/o Dr John Banham, 21 St Mary's Grove, Tudhoe Village, Spennymoor, Co Durham, DL16 6LR
Email: jdbanham@lineone.net
Internet: http://www.durhamweb.org.uk/dclhs/

Gov Body: Council **Chief:** Chair: Dr Winifred Stokes **Other Snr Offcrs:** Sec: Dr John Banham, as above: Editor & Sales Organiser: Emeritus Prof Gordon Batho
Membs: 250 indivs; 40 instns **Memb Req:** open to all those interested in the hist of Co Durham; subscription: ordinary membs £10 pa (students £5), joint membership £12.50 pa, instns £20 pa
Activs: Formed in 1964 to encourage and promote interest in the study of the history of County Durham; arranges lectures, day and weekend schools, excursions and occasional social functions.
Pubns: Bulletin (2 pa, free to membs, £3.50 + £1 p&p to non-membs); Newsletter (4 pa, membs only); Documentary Series (free to membs); Occasional Papers Series (various prices, reduced rates for membs)

O185 🏛🏛

East Midlands Museums, Libraries and Archives Council [EMMLAC]

56 King St, Leicester, LE1 6RL (0116-285-1350)
Email: info@emmlac.org.uk
Internet: http://www.emmlac.org.uk/

Type: strategic agency **Chief:** Chief Exec: Mr Tim Hobbs (thobbs@emmlac.org.uk) **Other Snr Offcrs:** Administrative Mgr: Ms Julie Robinson (jrobinson@emmlac.org.uk)
Activs: Provides strategic leadership for museums, libraries and archives in the East Midlands; aims to enable museums, libraries and archives to provide a better service to the public and to play a full role in the social, educational, cultural and economic life of the East Midlands; encourages co-operation both within and across the three domains; organised training programmes and provides grants to publicly accessible museums, libraries and archives in the region.

O186 🏛

East Midlands Regional Archive Council [EMRAC]

c/o Mr Carl Harrison, Record Office for Leicester-shire, Leicester & Rutland, Long St, Wigston Magna, Leicester, LE18 2AH (0116-257-1080)
Email: charrison@leics.gov.uk
Internet: http://www.eastmidlandsarchives.org.uk/

Chief: Chair: Mr Carl Harrison, as above
Activs: Aims to promote the effective preservation of, and foster access to, archives in the East Midlands; works with other regional and national agencies and organisations with similar interests, to enhance the value and utility of archival and heritage resources.

O187 ♀

East Midlands Regional Library System [EMRLS]

c/o Alfreton Lib, Severn Sq, Alfreton, Derbyshire, DE4 3AG (01773-835064; *fax:* 01773-521020)
Email: emrls@derbyshire.gov.uk
Internet: http://www.emrls.org.uk/

Type: co-op **Gov Body:** Regional Council **Chief:** Chair: Mr Brian Ashley (brian.ashley@ nottinghamcity.gov.uk) **Other Snr Offcrs:** Regional Libn: Ms Lynn Hodgkins, as above; Vice-Chair: Mr Roy Knight (rknight@rutland.gov.uk); Hon Sec: Mr Eric Loveridge (esl@dmu.ac.uk); Hon Treasurer: Mr Robert Gent (robert.gent@ derbyshire.gov.uk)
Membs: 40 instns **Memb Req:** full membership available to any LIS org within the East Midlands; associate membership open to all other LIS org
Branches & Groups: *Strategic Groups:* LEARNING & ACCESS; RSRCH & INFO; TRAINING & DEVELOPMENT; RESOURCE SHARING & CO-OPERATION; *Special Interest Groups:* LOCAL STUDIES FORUM; MUSIC LIBNS; EAST MIDLANDS & EAST OF ENGLAND NEWSPLAN GROUP; all groups may be contacted via the Regional Libn at the above addr
Activs: EMRLS is the strategic body for the library and information services domain in the East Midlands. It encourages and supports resource sharing and co-operation between member organisations. EMRLS works closely with the East Midlands Museums, Libraries and Archives Council (EMMLAC – see **O185**) and with domain-specific bodies for museums and archives within the region.
Pubns: Sharing the Future: A Strategy for Lib & Info Svcs in the East Midlands (2002)

O188 ⚷

East of England Libraries and Information Services Development Agency [ELISA]

c/o Regional Svcs Unit, Suffolk County Council Libs & Heritage, Northgate St, Ipswich, Suffolk, IP1 3DE (01473-583719; *fax:* 01473-583700)
Email: regional.services@libher.suffolkcc.gov.uk
Internet: http://www.elisa.org.uk/

Type: strategic agency **Chief:** Chair: Mr Barry George, Bedfordshire Libs **Other Snr Offcrs:** contact the Regional Svcs Unit as above
Membs: 32 instns **Memb Req:** open to instns, orgs & bodies who deliver lib & info svcs in the East of England; subscription: £50-£1000 pa (depending on revenue budget)
Activs: Strategic planning body for library and information services in the East of England. Aims include: to develop a strategy to support the regional cultural and economic strategies in the region; to offer advice as a focus of expertise for the library and information service communities; to promote collaboration and co-operation; to enable the library and information service sector to support the East of England as a world-class economy, support the development of a competitive infra-structure, and the development of jobs and skills within the region; to identify the need for new operational services and facilitate their establish-ment; to advise and provide representation to regional bodies as appropriate; to develop relations with the museums and archives sectors at regional level.

O189 ♀

Eastern Library and Information Professionals Partnership [ELIPP]

(formerly East Anglian Libns Consultative Cttee)
c/o Ms Jacky Offord, Central Lib, Clapham Rd South, Lowestoft, Suffolk, NR32 1DR (01502-405335; *fax:* 01502-405350)
Email: jacky.offord@libher.suffolkcc.gov.uk
Internet: http://www.elipp.org.uk/

Type: prof **Gov Body:** ELIPP comprises the Eastern Branch of CILIP (see **O110**), along with local representation from several of CILIP's special interest groups **Chief:** Chair: Ms Jenny Salisbury, Cambridge Central Lib (jenny.salisbury@ cambridgeshire.gov.uk) **Other Snr Offcrs:** Sec: Ms Jacky Offord, as above
Memb Req: open to membs of CILIP in the Cambridgeshire, Norfolk, Suffolk & Peterborough area
Branches & Groups: CONTINUING EDU WORKING GROUP; PUBNS & PROF LIAISON WORKING GROUP
Activs: Represents the interests of all CILIP members in the Eastern region. It promotes professional matters and runs a varied programme of events, courses and meetings.
Pubns: Easterner (quarterly, free to membs Eastern Branch); East Anglian Bibliography (quarterly, £30 pa)

O190 🏛

Eastern Regional Archive Council [ERAC]

c/o Ms Elizabeth Stazicker, Cambridgeshire County Record Office, Shire Hall, Castle Hill, Cambridge, CB3 0AP (01223-718131/3; *fax:* 01223-362425)
Email: Liz.Stazicker@libraries.camcnty.gov.uk
Internet: http://nca.archives.org.uk/race.htm

Chief: Chair: Ms Elizabeth Stazicker, as above
Activs: Acts as a strategic body for archives in the East of England; aims to improve access and to promote standards through co-operative projects.

O191 🎓

The Eccles Centre for American Studies

The British Lib, 96 Euston Rd, London, NW1 2DB (020-7412-7551/7757; *fax:* 020-7412-7792)
Email: philip.davies@bl.uk
Internet: http://www.bl.uk/services/information/ american.html

Chief: Dir: Prof Philip Davies
Activs: Aims to promote the British Library's North American materials, and to support American Studies in schools and universities. In support of these aims the Centre produces an on-going series of bibliographical guides to the Library's collections; hosts the Douglas W. Bryant Annual Lecture; provides bibliographic training for post-graduate students; collaborates with the British Association for American Studies; participates in a BL/UCL History Summer School programme for 6th form students; supports the British Library's exhibition programme.
Pubns: American Studies in the United Kingdom: Undergrad & Postgrad Courses; biblio guides; annual lecture series (available on web site as PDF)

O192 ♀

Edinburgh Bibliographical Society

c/o Dept of Special Collns, Edinburgh Univ Lib, George Sq, Edinburgh, EH8 9LJ (0131-650-3412; *fax:* 0131-650-6863)
Email: p.freshwater@ed.ac.uk
Internet: http://www.edbibsoc.lib.ed.ac.uk/

Chief: Pres: Dr Murray Simpson *Other Snr Offcrs:* Acting Hon Sec: Dr Warren McDougall, 53 Ladysmith Rd, Edinburgh, EH9 3EY (warrenmcdougall@aol.com); Hon Treasurer: Mr Peter Freshwater, as above
Membs: 95 indivs; 105 instns *Memb Req:* open to all indivs & orgs who support the aims & objectives of the Soc; subscription: indiv £10 pa (students £5), corporate £15 pa
Activs: Promotes bibliography, especially Scottish, and knowledge of the book and of libraries.
Pubns: Transactions (biennial, free to membs); occasional pubns (prices vary)

O193 ✚

Electronic Knowledge Access Team [eKAT]

(successor to the former London Lib & Info Development Unit)
20 Guilford St, London, WC1N 1DZ (020-7692-3389; *fax:* 020-7692-3393)
Email: ctwomey@llidu.ac.uk
Internet: http://www.londonlinks.ac.uk/

Chief: Team Leader & Co-ordinator: Dr Cheryl Twomey
Activs: From April 2003, the Electronic Knowledge Access Team will be working for and with the NHS Workforce Development Confederations across London as part of Library, Information and Knowledge Services. The Team will develop and deliver electronic services and products to health and social care staff in London, and will aim to improve access to knowledge in support of delivering the NHS plan for modernised patient-centred services.

O194 ♟

Ephemera Society [EPHSOC]

PO Box 112, Northwood, Middlesex, HA6 2WT (01923-829079; *fax:* 01923-825207)
Email: info@ephemera-society.org.uk
Internet: http://www.ephemera-society.org.uk/

Gov Body: Council *Chief:* Chairman: Ms Sally de Beaumont *Other Snr Offcrs:* Sec: Mr Graham Hudson
Membs: 700 indivs; 75 instns *Memb Req:* open to indivs & instns interested in the conservation & study of printed & hand-written ephemera; subscriptions: indivs £20 pa (£15 if living over 100 miles from London), dealers/institutions/corps £25 pa; higher rates for overseas membs
Activs: The Ephemera Society is a non-profit body concerned with the preservation, study, presentation and educational uses of printed and hand-written ephemera – the "minor transient documents of everyday life". The Society organises numerous Fairs each year, as well as a programme of lectures and other meetings.
Pubns: The Ephemerist (4 pa, for membs); Ephemera Soc Handbook (membs only)

O195 ♟

Essex Archaeological and Historical Congress

c/o Mrs Nicola Thomas, 6 Heathgate, Wickham Bishops, Witham, Essex, CM8 3NZ (01621-891592; *fax:* 01621-890868)
Email: EssexAHC@aol.com
Internet: http://www.essexhistory.net/ EssexCongress.htm

Chief: Hon Chairman: Mrs Dorothy Lockwood *Other Snr Offcrs:* Hon Sec: Mrs Nicola Thomas, as above
Membs: c100 instns *Memb Req:* open to orgs in Essex interested in archaeo, local hist & family hist
Activs: Promotes the study of the local history and archaeology of the County of Essex. Organises an annual general meeting and two symposia – one for archaeological topics and the other for local and family history – each year.
Pubns: Newsletter (4pa, free to membs); Essex Journal (co-pubn, 2pa); various others

O196 🗝

European Information Association [EIA]

c/o Central Lib, St Peter's Sq, Manchester, M2 5PD (0161-228-3691; *fax:* 0161-228-6547)
Email: eia@libraries.manchester.gov.uk
Internet: http://www.eia.org.uk/

Gov Body: annually elected cttee *Chief:* Mgr: Ms Catherine Webb, as above
Membs: 40 indivs; 460 instns *Memb Req:* open to libns & info offcrs specialising in EU material; subscription: indivs £40+VAT pa, commercial orgs £120+VAT pa, non-profit orgs £90+VAT pa
Activs: Non-profit making international body of information specialists whose aim is to develop, co-ordinate and improve access to EU information. Organises training courses and events; administers the EIA Awards to encourage better quality printed and electronic sources.
Pubns: Focus (monthly); EIA Update (monthly newsletter); EIA Quick Guides (membs £4.50, non-membs £5.50); European Union Info: An Introduction (membs £10, non-membs £15); full list available from EIA

O197 ♟ 🎓

Federation of Family History Societies [FFHS]

PO Box 2425, Coventry, West Midlands, CV5 6YX
Email: info@ffhs.org.uk
Internet: http://www.ffhs.org.uk/

Gov Body: Exec Cttee *Chief:* Chairman: Mr A. Tritton
Membs: 230 memb socs *Memb Req:* full membership is open to UK family hist socs, associate membership to overseas socs & UK socs to whom family hist is a secondary interest; applicants must have been in existence for at least 1 year, must have an agreed constitution, at least 40 membs & a regularly published journal; full membership: 30p per memb pa (minimum £30, maximum £600); associate membership: £40 pa
Activs: Formed in 1974 with the aim of co-ordinating and assisting the work of societies or other bodies interested in family history, genealogy and heraldry, and to foster mutual co-operation and regional projects in these subjects. Organises conferences nationally in conjunction with member bodies; represents the interest of members to official bodies affecting the study of family history and related topics; maintains close links with national organisations with related interests.
Pubns: Family Hist News & Digest (2 pa); numerous guides & handbooks relating to sources & methods for family hist rsrch, incl: Basic Series (£1.50 each); Introduction To Series (£2.50-£3); Gibson Guides (£2.50-£4.50); British Genealogical Lib Guides Series (incl genealogical county bibliographies, various prices); My Ancestor Series (£2.95-£5.50); numerous others; available from FFHS Pubns Ltd, Units 15-16, Chesham Industrial Centre, Oram St, Bury, Lancashire, BL9 6EN (0161-797-3843; *fax:* 0161-797-3846; *email:* orders@ffhs.co.uk); for details see web site at http://www.familyhistorybooks.co.uk/

O198 🗝

Federation of Ulster Local Studies

18 May St, Belfast, BT1 4NL (029-9023-5254; *fax:* 028-9043-4086)
Email: FULSTD@aol.com
Internet: http://www.ulsterlocalhistory.org/

Chief: Chairman: Mr W. John Bradley *Other Snr Offcrs:* Admin Offcr: Ms Janet Lundy (JanLundy12@aol.com)
Membs: c100 instns *Memb Req:* Ulster local hist orgs
Activs: Aims to promote the study and recording of the history, antiquities and folk-life of Ulster; to encourage the provision of the necessary services for the furtherance of those local historical studies in Ulster; to develop communication and co-operation between voluntary organisations and statutory bodies.; to encourage cross-community and cross-border activities in the field of local studies. Organises a regular programme of educational workshops and seminars; acts as a lobby on behalf of the heritage sector; operates a lost cost insurance scheme for member societies.
Pubns: Due North (2 pa); Ulster Local Studies (former quarterly journal, some back issues still available)

O199 ♟ 🎥

Film Archive Forum [FAF]

c/o British Univs Film & Video Council, 77 Wells St, London, W1T 3QJ (020-7393-1508; *fax:* 020-7393-1555)
Email: faf@bufvc.ac.uk
Internet: http://www.bufvc.ac.uk/faf/faf.htm

Chief: Chair: Mr Luke McKernan, British Univs Film & Video Council (luke@bufvc.ac.uk)
Membs: 11 instns; 3 observing membs
Activs: Provides an informal network of British moving image archives, aiming to represent the best practice in UK film and moving image archiving, and to act as an advisor on national archive policy. It has particular interest in the preservation of nitrate film, acetate film and videotape, in the training of archivists, acquisitions policy, standards for archives, copyright, co-operation with film laboratories and contacts with foreign archives.

O200 🗝

Fire Information Group (UK) [FIG UK]

c/o Mrs Pam Evans, Forensic Sci Svc Info Section, 10 Albert Embankment, London, SE1 7SP (020-7840-2966; *fax:* 020-7840-2971)
Email: pam.evans@fss.pnn.police.uk
Internet: http://www.figuk.org.uk/

Type: co-op *Chief:* Sec: Mrs Pam Evans, as above
Membs: 3 indivs; 22 instns *Memb Req:* open to info mgrs, info offcrs, libns, rsrchers & other indivs & orgs involved in the field of fire & loss prevention; subscription £30 pa
Activs: FIG is an information exchange co-operative in the fire and loss prevention fields. It holds twice yearly meetings to discuss new developments in members' areas of expertise.

O201 ♟

Forum for Interlending [FIL]

c/o Mr Neil Dalley, Reading Univ Lib, PO Box 223, Reading, RG6 6AE (0118-378-8786; *fax:* 0118-378-8049)
Email: n.m.dalley@reading.ac.uk
Internet: http://www.cilip.org.uk/groups/fil/ introf.html

Chief: Chair: Ms Jennifer Cox, Bibliographical Svcs, Bromley Central Lib (jennifer.cox@ bromley.gov.uk) *Other Snr Offcrs:* Sec: Mr Neil Dalley, as above
Membs: 5 indivs; 244 instns *Memb Req:* open to anyone involved in inter-lib loans & document supply; subscription: £30 pa

☛

Organisations

Forum
▼
Heraldry

(Forum for Interlending cont)

Activs: Established to enable library and inform-ation workers in the field of interlibrary loans and document supply to exchange ideas and views and also to raise the profile of this area of work nationally and internationally. Organises an annual conference, workshops and seminars; liaises with regional and national organisations (e.g., BLDSC and LINC) and is represented on national bodies (e.g., CONARLS); publishes a newsletter, reports and surveys; facilitates expression of views and ideas on interlibrary loans and document supply.
Pubns: FIL Newsletter; Annual Conference Proceedings; Theses Interlending in the UK (FIL, 1993); Charging for Inter-Lib Loans: Results of a Survey (FIL, 1994); Report on Document Supply Svcs & Projs (FIL, 1995)

O202 🔑

The Four Parishes Research Group

c/o Mrs P. Hill, 14 Hockenhull Ln, Tarvin, Chester, Cheshire, CH3 8LA (01829-740343)

Chief: Sec: Mrs P. Hill, as above
Membs: 19 indivs
Activs: Transcription, research and publication of wills and inventories of the four parishes Christleton, Tarvin, Tattenhall and Waverton from the mid-16C to the mid-17C.
Pubns: Wills & Inventories with Related Documents for Christleton, Tarvin, Tattenhall & Waverton (Vol 1, 1546-1650, £10 per copy + £3 p&p) Vol 2 in preparation

O203 🎓 🏛

Friends of The National Libraries [FNL]

c/o Dept of Manuscripts, The British Lib, 96 Euston Rd, London, NW1 2DB (020-7412-7559)

Type: voluntary org **Gov Body:** Exec Cttee
Chief: Chairman: Lord Egremont **Other Snr Offcrs:** Hon Sec: Mr Michael Borrie; Hon Treasurer: Mr Charles Sebag-Montefiore
Membs: 700 indivs; 120 instns
Activs: To help acquire for the nation printed books, manuscripts and archives by making grants towards purchase by libraries and record offices, by eliciting and channelling benefactions and by organising appeals and publicity.
Pubns: Annual Report

O204 🔑

Gloucestershire Local History Committee

c/o Mrs Elizabeth Bourne, Gloucestershire Rural Community Council, Community House, 15 College Green, Gloucester, GL1 2LZ (01452-309783)
Email: info@cpreglos.fsnet.co.uk
Internet: http://home.freeuk.com/gloshistory/

Gov Body: Gloucestershire Rural Community Council Ltd **Chief:** Chairman: Mr John Loosley (John@loosleyj.freeserve.co.uk) **Other Snr Offcrs:** Sec: Mrs Elizabeth Bourne, as above
Membs: 40+ instns **Memb Req:** open to socs & indivs interested in Gloucestershire local hist; membership of GRCC: indivs £20 pa, socs £25 pa

Activs: Meets quarterly to discuss matters relating to local history in Gloucestershire; encourages the study of local history in the county by local history societies and individuals within Gloucestershire, by organising meetings and through publications.
Pubns: Gloucestershire Hist & Newsletter (1 pa, £3.99); annual local hist newsletter

O205 🔑

Grampian Information

PO Box 11786, Peterhead, Aberdeenshire, AB42 5YH (01771-624855; *fax:* 01771-624755)
Email: info@grampianinfo.co.uk
Internet: http://www.grampianinfo.co.uk/

Gov Body: Grampian Info **Chief:** Development Offcr: Ms Elspeth Scott, as above
Memb Req: open to all information-providing orgs in public, private & voluntary sectors; full, associate or affiliate membership available
Branches & Groups: BUSINESS GROUP (see O206); HEALTH & COMMUNITY GROUP (see O207); LOCAL STUDIES & ARCHVS GROUP (see O208); OIL GROUP (see O209); SCI RSRCH GROUP (see O210)
Activs: Provides opportunities for regular contact and networking amongst information providers in North East Scotland. Aims to encourage the development of coherent and co-operative information strategies; to facilitate the sharing of resources and expertise; to act as a forum for information providers; to ensure that all potential users of library and information services are aware of the services available to them; to identify problems and opportunities which should be dealt with locally. Organises seminars, training events and conferences, and provides an interlibrary photocopying scheme, Union List of Journals, and a Directory of Resources.
Pubns: GI News

O206 🔑 ✂

Grampian Information, Business Group

c/o Scottish Enterprise Grampian, 27 Albyn Pl, Aberdeen, AB10 1DB (01224-575100; *fax:* 01224-580055)
Email: celia.hukins@scotent.co.uk
Internet: http://www.grampianinfo.co.uk/business.htm

Gov Body: Grampian Info (see O205) **Chief:** Chair: Ms Celia Hukins, as above
Membs: 12 instns
Activs: Aims to improve and co-ordinate business information services in the Grampian region; to support a Grampian business information network; to facilitate the efficient exchange of business information; to support members in establishing and maintaining high standards of information provision.

O207 🔑 ✚

Grampian Information, Health and Community Group

c/o Grampian Info, PO Box 11786, Peterhead, Aberdeenshire, AB42 5YH (01771-624855; *fax:* 01771-624755)
Email: info@grampianinfo.co.uk
Internet: http://www.grampianinfo.co.uk/health.htm

Gov Body: Grampian Info (see O205) **Chief:** Co-Chairs: Ms Audrey Bell & Ms Jacqui Mackay
Activs: Aims to promote better information services in Aberdeen, Aberdeenshire and Moray in the field of health and community information; to encourage mutual support between the different organisations involved in health and community

information provision; to promote a greater awareness of the range of health and community information resources in the region; to identify and address training needs; to develop a Grampian Health and Community Information referral and sign-posting network for members and users. Activities include meetings, presentations and visits

O208 🔑

Grampian Information, Local Studies and Archives Group

c/o Northern Health Svc Archvs, Aberdeen Royal Infirmary, Woolmanhill, Aberdeen, AB25 1LD (01224-555562)
Internet: http://www.grampianinfo.co.uk/history.htm

Gov Body: Grampian Info (see O205) **Chief:** Chair: Ms Eleanor Rowe (El.Rowe@legal.aberdeen.net.uk) **Other Snr Offcrs:** Convenor: Miss Fiona Watson, as above
Membs: 15 indivs
Activs: Aims to encourage the retention and documentation of historical records in private hands; to press for adequate resourcing of archival centres in order to safeguard endangered materials; to promote co-ordinated policies for the acquisition, conservation and reproduction of local studies material; to encourage the dissemination of local studies knowledge and practice. Supports the establishment of a regional conservation workshop for local studies materials at risk, and projects for the automatic cataloguing and indexing of local studies materials in the region. Promotes the continued development of the Regional Newsplan to conserve local newspaper files, and is engaged in an ongoing project to produce a Directory of Local Studies Sources in Grampian. Also organises conferences and exhibition displays.
Pubns: Railways in the North-East (bklet accompanying exhib, £1.50); contact Convenor as above

O209 🔑

Grampian Information, Oil Group

c/o Ms Rosie Mackay, Marathon Oil (UK) Ltd, Rubislaw Hill, Anderson Dr, Aberdeen, AB15 6FZ
Email: ramackay@marathonoil.com
Internet: http://www.grampianinfo.co.uk/oil.htm

Gov Body: Grampian Info (see O205) **Chief:** Chair: Ms Rosie Mackay, as above
Membs: 17 instns
Activs: Consists of representatives from the Information Services/Libraries of oil operators and contractors. Meets quarterly to discuss topics of shared interest, provide an opportunity for networking with colleagues and to provide a forum for speakers to give relevant presentations.

O210 🔑 🎓

Grampian Information, Science Research Group

c/o Mrs Lorraine Robertson, Macaulay Land Use Rsrch Inst, Craigiebuckler, Aberdeen, AB15 8HQ (01224-318611; *fax:* 01224-311556)
Email: l.robertson@macaulay.ac.uk
Internet: http://www.grampianinfo.co.uk/science.htm

Gov Body: Grampian Info (see O205) **Chief:** Group Chairperson: Ms Mary W. Mowat BA, MLib, MCLIP, Rowett Rsrch Inst, Reid Lib (m.mowat@rri.sari.ac.uk) **Other Snr Offcrs:** Group Sec: Mrs Lorraine Robertson BA, DipEd, at above addr
Membs: 10 instns
Activs: The Science Research Group exists to facilitate and promote excellence in information

service provision amongst libraries serving the scientific research community in North East Scotland. Holds twice yearly meetings to promote networking and share information.

O211 🗝
The Guild of One-Name Studies
Box G, 14 Charterhouse Bldgs, Goswell Rd, London, EC1M 7BA
Email: guild@one-name.org
Internet: http://www.one-name.org/

Type: rsrch *Chief:* Hon Sec: Mr James Isard (secretary@one-name.org)
Memb Req: open to all who have an interest in one-name studies; subscription: £12 pa
Activs: Exists to promote and facilitate the researching of individual surnames, their frequency and distribution; acts as a forum and contact point for those engaged or interested in such research; provides a register of surnames being researched by members and an email discussion group; holds regular speaker meetings throughout Britain.
Pubns: Journal of One-Name Studies (4 pa to membs)

O212 🗝
Gwent Local History Council
c/o Mr Byron Grubb, 8 Pentonville, Newport, Gwent, NP20 5XH (01633-213229; *fax:* 01633-221812)
Email: byron.grubb@gavowales.org.uk

Chief: Sec: Mr Byron Grubb
Membs: c250 indivs
Branches & Groups: GWENT COUNTY HIST ASSOC, Sec: Ms Gwenllian Jones, 1 Brunel Ave, High Cross, Newport, Gwent, NP10 0DN
Activs: Exists to promote the study of the history of the County of Gwent; has established the Gwent County History Association to promote and publish a new county history in five volumes.
Pubns: Gwent Local Hist Journal (2 pa, £4 pa); Gwent Local Hist News (2 pa, free with Journal)

O213 🗝
The Hakluyt Society
c/o The Map Lib, The British Lib, 96 Euston Rd, London, NW1 2DB (01428-641850; *fax:* 01428-641933)
Email: office@hakluyt.com
Internet: http://www.hakluyt.com/

Type: charity *Chief:* Pres: Prof R.C. Bridges
Other Snr Offcrs: Administrator: Mr Richard Bateman, as above
Membs: 1800 indivs; 600 instns *Memb Req:* open to everyone interested in the hist of exploration & travel; subscription: £35 pa
Activs: Publishers of scholarly books, historical geography, travel and maritime history for the advancement of postgraduate education; 366 volumes published to date.
Pubns: Third Series vols, free with membership (3 pa); occasional other vols not in Third Series; list of pubns available from the Soc

O214 🗝
The Harleian Society
c/o Coll of Arms, Queen Victoria St, London, EC4V 4BT (020-7236-7728; *fax:* 020-7248-6448)

Gov Body: Council of the Harleian Soc *Chief:* Hon Sec: Mr T.H.S. Duke
Membs: 150 indivs; 180 instns *Memb Req:* subscription: indivs £20, instns £25
Activs: Founded in 1869 for the purpose of transcribing, printing and publishing MSS relating to genealogy, family history and heraldry.

Pubns: pubns can be either obtained through membership, or purchased at £35 each incl p&p; a list of titles is available from the Hon Sec

O215 🗝
Hatrics: The Southern Information Network
81 North Walls, Winchester, Hampshire, SO23 8BY (01962-826650; *fax:* 01962-856615)
Email: hatricshq@hants.gov.uk
Internet: http://www.hants.gov.uk/hatrics/

Gov Body: Exec Cttee *Chief:* Chair: Ms C. Holder BA *Other Snr Offcrs:* Vice-Chair: Mr I. Bonar BSc, MCLIP; Hon Sec: Mr H.A. Richards BA, MCLIP, City Libn, Southampton City Libs; Asst Hon Sec: Mr N. Fox BA, FCLIP
Membs: 250 instns *Memb Req:* open to libs, industrial & commercial firms & other bodies in the southern area of the UK
Activs: Aims to make information resources more widely available through co-operation between member organisations. Organises courses, visits and provides professional advice.
Pubns: Directory of Resources (free to membs); Bulletin (4 pa, free to membs); Periodical List (for membs only)

O216 🗝✚
Health Archives Group [HAG]
c/o Ms Libby Adams, UCL Hosps NHS Trust Archvs, Vezey Strong Wing, 112 Hampstead Rd, London, NW1 2LT (020-7387-9300 x3717)
Email: libby.adams@uclh.org

Type: prof *Chief:* Sec: Ms Libby Adams
Memb Req: open to archivists and records mgrs involved in the care & admin of health archvs
Activs: Aims to encourage and support the professional management of archives and records throughout the health sector and to provide a network for those working with health archives to exchange ideas, experiences and expertise.

O217 🗝✚
Health Libraries and Information Confederation [HeLICon]
(formerly LINC Health Panel)
c/o Ms Sue Thomas, Health Promotion Wales Lib, Ty Glas Ave, Llanishen, Cardiff, CF14 5EZ (01222-681245)
Email: Susan.Thomas@wales.gsi.gov.uk
Internet: http://www.helicon-info.com/

Type: co-op *Chief:* Chairman: Mr Bruce Madge (bruce.madge@bl.uk) *Other Snr Offcrs:* Sec: Ms Sue Thomas, as above
Membs: 6 foundation membs, 34 subscribing membs *Memb Req:* open to any org or network of libs or info svcs concerned to improve the provision of health care info; foundation membership: £500 pa; subscribing membership: £215 pa; corresponding membership: £50 pa
Branches & Groups: various task groups
Activs: Aims to improve the availability and quality of health information and to improve patient care by increasing the effectiveness of UK health library, information and knowledge services.
Pubns: Lib & Info Svcs for the Nursing Profession: Methods of Funding & Delivery; Accreditation of Lib & Info Svcs in the Health Sector: A Check-list to Support Assessment; Accreditation of Lib & Info Svcs the Health Sector: Implementation Guide & Toolkit for Libs in the NHS; for further details contact: the Pubns Administrator, Ms Linda Dorrington, c/o Imperial Coll Central Lib, South Kensington, London, SW7 2AZ (020-7594-8842; *fax:* 020-7584-3736; *email:* l.dorrington@ic.ac.uk)

O218 ✚
Health Libraries Network [HLN]
(formerly South Thames Regional Lib & Info Svc)
c/o Lib and Knowledge Svcs Team, Edu Centre, Royal Surrey County Hosp, Egerton Rd, Guildford, GU2 5XX (01483-464082; *fax:* 01483-455888)
Email: twilson@royalsurrey.org.uk
Internet: http://stlis.thenhs.com/hln/index1.htm

Chief: Knowledge Svcs Development Mgr: Mrs Tina Wilson
Activs: HLN is a collaborative network of NHS and other health and social care libraries within south east England and south London. The Network infrastructure is supported by the Library and Knowledge Services Team of the Surrey & Sussex and Kent & Medway Workforce Development Confederations. HLN aims to contribute to the quality of patient care by facilitating access to shared knowledge resources which support the learning, teaching, practice and research needs of all health and social care staff. Activities include: integrating and organising information about resources available to through NHS library services; promoting 24/7 access to electronic knowledge resources via the web site; managing a web based directory of resource sharing libraries; working with NHS librarians and other co-operating partners to share best practice, provide opportunities for CPD and lifelong learning, raise standards and develop improved and cost effective services.
Pubns: see web site

O219 🗝
Hebraica Libraries Group [HLG]
c/o Mr Stephen Massil, Sir John Soane's Museum Lib, 113 Lincoln's Inn Fields, London, WC2A 3BP (020-7440-4253)
Email: cat@soane.org.uk
Internet: http://www.lib.cam.ac.uk/hebraica/ hebraicam2.htm

Chief: Convenor: Mr Stephen Massil, as above
Membs: 12 instns *Memb Req:* open to specialist libns in academic libs, specialists in public or private instns, as well as scholars & rsrchers with an interest in the Hebrew bk
Activs: Provides a joint forum of Judaica and Hebraica Libraries in the UK; enables librarians and other specialists working with Hebraica to share their views and experiences, to discuss current developments as well as future projects, and to co-ordinate their activities; meets at least once a year.

O220 🗝
The Heraldry Society of Scotland
36 Anson Ave, Falkirk, Stirlingshire, FK1 5JB (01324-625610)
Email: scottishphilately@hotmail.com
Internet: http://www.heraldry-scotland.co.uk/

Chief: Pres: Sir Malcolm Innes of Edingight, Orkney Herald Extraordinary *Other Snr Offcrs:* Sec: Mr Alan Watson
Memb Req: open to any person or org interested in the study & practice of heraldry & allied subjs in Scotland; subscription: £25 pa (jnr membs £10)
Activs: Aims to promote the study of heraldry and encourage its correct use in Scotland; meets several times during the year for lectures or visits to places of historic and heraldic interest, both in Scotland and in other countries; organises the Saint Andrew Lecture in November
Pubns: The Double Tressure (annual journal); Tak Tent (newsletter, 4 pa); numerous illustrated bklets on heraldic & related matters

Organisations
Hertfordshire ▼ International

O221 ♀ 🎓

Hertfordshire Association for Local History

c/o Dr Gillian Gear, Nicholls Farmhouse, Lybury Ln, Redbourn, Hertfordshire, AL3 7JH (01582-792603)
Email: gillian@m-gear.demon.co.uk

Chief: Chair: Dr Gillian Gear, as above *Other Snr Offcrs:* Sec: Mrs Clare Ellis
Membs: 150 indivs; 30 instns
Activs: Acts as a forum and umbrella group for the study of local history in the county of Hertfordshire; organises an annual symposium in November, a Spring Meeting in May, and an annual garden party in June/July; represents local historians' views at a county level; runs a Recorder Scheme to assist in the collection of modern material for future historians.
Pubns: Hertfordshire's Past (2 pa); Newsletter

O222 ♀ 🎓

Hertfordshire Record Society [HRS]

c/o Mrs Heather Falvey, 119 Winton Dr, Coxley Green, Rickmansworth, Hertfordshire, WD3 3QS (01923-248581)
Email: info@hrsociety.org.uk
Internet: http://www.hrsociety.org.uk/

Chief: Chairman: Mr A. Ruston *Other Snr Offcrs:* Sec: Mrs Heather Falvey, as above
Membs: c150 in total
Activs: The object of the Society is to publish selections from Hertfordshire's abundant historical records. The documents thus published are held in various repositories and are not necessarily readily available to members of the public for consultation. The Society's regular series of volumes are not only of interest to the general reader, but also a stimulus and aid to further research into the county's local history.
Pubns: Newsletter (1 pa, free to membs); recently published vols incl: Vol XIV: Lay Subsidy Rolls for Hertfordshire 1307-8 & 1334 (£18.50 + p&p); Vol XV: Observations of Weather: The Weather Diary of Sir John Wittewronge of Rothamsted 1648-89 (£19 + p&p); Vol XVI: Survey of the Royal Manor of Hitchin 1676 (£18.75 + p&p); Vol XVII: Garden-Making & the Freeman Family: A Memoir of Hamels (£18.75 + p&p); prices given are for non-membs; membs receive current vol as part of subscription, and may purchase earlier vols at reduced cost

O223 ♀

Historic Houses Archivists Group [HHAG]

c/o Mrs J. Thorp, Highclare Castle, Newbury, Berkshire, RG20 9RN (01635-253210; *fax:* 01635-255066)
Email: jennifer.thorp@regents-park.oxford.ac.uk

Chief: Sec: Mrs J. Thorp, as above
Memb Req: open to archivists working in country houses & landed estates throughout the UK
Branches & Groups: affiliated to the SOC OF ARCHIVISTS, SPECIALIST REPOSITORIES GROUP (see **O369**)

Activs: Encourages the best possible maintenance and administration of privately-owned archives; provides a forum for discussion for those responsible for privately-owned archives; maintains links with other interested organisations within the UK and Europe; meets twice a year.
Pubns: Newsletter (2 pa); Guide to the Retention of Modern Records on Landed Estates (1992)

O224 ♀

Historic Libraries Forum [HLF]

c/o Mr Peter Hoare, 21 Oundle Dr, Nottingham, NG8 1BN (*tel & fax:* 0115-978-5297)
Email: p.hoare@virgin.net

Chief: Chairman: Mr P. Hoare MA, DipLib, FSA, HonFCLIP, as above
Memb Req: open to anyone interested in the historic libs of Gt Britain
Activs: Informal group dedicated to raising awareness of libraries of historical significance and issues relating to them; organises talks and seminars.
Further Info: HLF is an Org in Liaison with CILIP (see **O110**)

O225 ♀

The Historical Association

59a Kennington Park Rd, London, SE11 4JH (020-7735-3901; *fax:* 020-7582-4989)
Email: enquiry@history.org.uk
Internet: http://www.history.org.uk/

Chief: Chief Exec Offcr: Ms Madeline Stiles
Membs: 6000 *Memb Req:* open to all; subscription rates vary according to journals taken
Branches & Groups: c70 branches countrywide
Activs: Acts as the voice for history both locally and nationally; brings together and represents people who share an interest in history; aims to further the study, teaching and enjoyment of history at all levels: teacher, students, amateur and professional; holds an annual general meeting, conferences and other regular events.
Pubns: The Historian (4 pa, £62 pa for non-membs); Teaching History (4 pa, £80 pa for non-membs); Primary History (4 pa, £45 pa to non-membs); the three main journals are available to membs as part of their subscription, prices depend on subscription category; History (4 pa, indiv membs £21, schools £24); Annual Bulletin of Historical Lit (1 pa, indiv membs £25, schools £31); History & the Annual Bulletin are available together to non-membs for £188 pa; various pamphs & resources packs

O226 🕰️

Historical Manuscripts Commission

National Archives, Kew, Richmond, Surrey, TW9 4DU (020-8876-3444)
Email: enquiry@nationalarchives.gov.uk
Internet: http://www.hmc.gov.uk/

Gov Body: part of the Natl Archvs (formerly Public Record Office – see **A432**) *Chief:* Sec to the Commission: Dr C.J. Kitching PhD
Activs: The Commission locates, reports and disseminates information about British historical papers outside the public records. It maintains the National Register of Archives, which includes over 43000 unpublished catalogues indexed by person, family, company & organisation, and the Manorial Documents Register, which gives details of the location of manorial documents.
Pubns: Annual Review 2001-02 (£6); Record Repositories in Gt Britain (11th ed, £4.99); Archv Bldgs in the United Kingdom 1977-1992 (£17.95); Surveys of Historical Manuscripts in the United Kingdom: A Select Bibliography, 3rd ed (£3); Archvs at the Millennium: The Twenty-Eighth Report to the Crown (£9.50); Reports & Calendars

Series (several in print, prices vary); Prime Minister's Papers Series (several in print, prices vary); Guides to Sources for British Hist Series (several in print, prices vary)
Further Info: Merged with the Public Record Office on 1st Apr 2003 to form The Natl Archvs. *See also* **A285**

O227 ♀

ICIA Europe

c/o Mr Geoff Turner, 'Minstrels', 2 Higham Gdns, Tonbridge, Kent, TN10 4HZ (*tel & fax:* 01732-771658)
Email: gturner@infocomm.org
Internet: http://www.infocomm.org/

Gov Body: Internatl Communications Industries Assoc Inc, based at Fairfax, Virginia, USA *Chief:* contact Mr Geoff Turner as above
Membs: 2700 companies & indivs worldwide
Activs: Acts as a spokesman for the digital information and communication industry in both the UK and in Europe; provides a network for information providers, service developers and integrators, telecommunications operators, hardware and software developers, and all other players in the arena of electronic publishing; holds regular meetings; sponsors exhibitions and seminars.

O228 ♀ 🖋️

Independent Publishers Guild [IPG]

PO Box 93, Royston, Bedfordshire, SG8 5GH (01763-247014; *fax:* 01763-246293)
Email: info@ipg.uk.com
Internet: http://www.ipg.uk.com/

Chief: Sec: Ms Sheila Bounford (sheila@ipg.uk.com)
Membs: 330 companies *Memb Req:* open to independent publishers & their suppliers; subscription: £85+VAT pa
Activs: Founded in 1962, the IPG aims to promote knowledge about publishing and to provide a forum for the exchange of ideas and information for independent publishing companies. It organises a Spring Conference, four Open Meetings per year, and a shared stand at both the London and Frankfurt Book Fairs.
Pubns: Bulletin (quarterly, membs only)

O229 🏛️

Information Committee

House of Commons, London, SW1A 0AA (020-7219-3275; *fax:* 020-7219-2622)
Email: infcom@parliament.uk
Internet: http://www.parliament.uk/commons/selcom/infohome.htm

Chief: Chairman: Mr Michael Fabricant MP; all enq should be addressed to the Clerk of the Cttee: Mr Gordon Clarke (clarkeg@parliament.uk)
Membs: 9 indivs
Activs: To consider the services provided by the House of Commons in regard to information.
Pubns: The reports and evidence of the Cttee are published by The Stationery Office; all pubns (incl press notices) can be found on the web site

O230 ♀ ✚

Information Focus for Allied Health [InFAH]

c/o Ms Clare Burnham, Royal Coll of Speech & Lang Therapists Lib, 2 White Hart Yard, London, SE1 1NX (020-7378-1200; *fax:* 020-7403-7254)
Email: clare.burnham@rcslt.org

Chief: Sec: Ms Clare Burnham, as above
Memb Req: open to indivs & orgs with an interest in info issues affecting the allied health professions;

subscriptions: indivs £7 pa, instns £20 pa
Activs: Aims to identify relevant sources of information in health and social care; improve access to information for the allied health professions; provide mutual support and debate; to work to improve standards. Holds quarterly meetings, study days and an Annual General Meeting.
Pubns: InFAH Bulletin (4 pa); InFAH membs also contribute to the allied health sections of the Core Colln of Medical Bks & Journals.
Further Info: InFAH is an Org in Liaison with CILIP (see **O110**)

O231
Information for Energy Group [IFEG]
c/o Inst of Petroleum, 61 New Cavendish St, London, W1G 7AR (020-7467-7111; *fax:* 020-7255-1472)
Email: ifeg@petroleum.co.uk
Internet: http://www.petroleum.co.uk/

Gov Body: under the auspices of the Inst of Petroleum (see **S1202**) *Chief:* Sec: Ms Sally Ball, as above
Membs: 150 indivs *Memb Req:* open to anyone concerned with any aspect of info within the energy industry as a whole; subscription: £20 pa (£5 for full-time students)
Activs: Provides a forum for those interested in the provision, evaluation and dissemination of information relating to all aspects of the energy industries. Holds conferences, evening meetings and arranges visits.
Pubns: Membs Directory (only available to membs of IFEG)

O232
Information for Social Change
c/o John Pateman, 32 Petten Grove, Orpington, Kent, BR5 4PU (01689-872586)
Internet: http://libr.org/ISC/

Gov Body: Editorial Board *Chief:* Sec: Mr John Pateman BA, DipLib, MBA, FCLIP
Activs: Aims to address issues of freedom of information and censorship as they affect library and information work; promotes alternatives to mainstream library and information provision; provides a forum to exchange radical views on library and information issues and to debate ethics and freedom within the profession.
Pubns: Info for Social Change (journal, 2 pa; subscription: £5 indiv, £15 instn, free to exchanging journals)
Further Info: Info for Social Change is an Org in Liaison with CILIP (see **O110**)

O233
Information for the Management of Healthcare [IFMH]
PO Box 539, York, YO24 4XA (01904-433496)
Email: jmg1@york.ac.uk
Internet: http://www1.york.ac.uk/inst/crd/ifmh/

Type: prof *Gov Body:* CILIP Health Libs Group (see **O124**) *Chief:* Chair: Ms Maria J. Grant (m.j.grant@salford.ac.uk) *Other Snr Offcrs:* Sec: Mr Steve Rose, Cairns Lib (steve.rose@cairns-library.ox.ac.uk); Treasurer: Ms Julie Glanville, as above
Memb Req: subscription: indivs £20 pa, instns £40; internatl £55
Activs: Aims to improve the provision of information, both text-based and statistical, to health care managers and other professionals. Through various activities, including at least two study days every year and an email discussion list, IFM Healthcare allows subscribers to keep up to date on issues related to the management and

delivery of healthcare. IFM Healthcare is also one of the sponsors of the HeLICon ResearcHoS Research in the Workplace Award.
Pubns: IFMH Inform (newsletter, free to membs); Not Collected Centrally: Problems of Finding and Using Health Statistics (£12, £8.50 to IFMH membs); A Guide to Health Care Abbreviations & Acronyms (£10, £8 to IFMH membs)

O234
Information Services National Training Organisation [ISNTO]
Suite 303, Parkgate House, Parkgate, Bradford, BD1 5BS (01274-391773; *fax:* 01274-391828)
Email: alix@isnto1.fsnet.co.uk
Internet: http://www.isnto.org.uk/

Chief: Chief Exec: Mr John Pluse *Other Snr Offcrs:* Proj & Admin Mgr: Ms Alix Craven
Activs: National Training Organisation for and library and information services, archives and records management; aims include: assisting sector leaders to articulate future directions; formulating plans to supply and maintain the skills needed; improving access to effective and innovative learning; promoting collaboration among stakeholders to optimise service provision.

Institute of Information Scientists
See CHARTERED INST OF LIB & INFO PROFS (**O110**)

O235
Institute for Scientific Information [ISI]
14 Gt Queen St, London, WC2B 5DF, UB8 3PQ (020-7344-2800; *fax:* 020-7344-2900)
Email: uksales@isinet.com
Internet: http://www.isinet.com/

Gov Body: Thomson Corp
Activs: The ISI, headquartered in Philadelphia, USA, produces information databases for researchers and information specialists in all fields of research. ISI captures and presents bibliographic data from published books, journals and proceedings. What distinguishes the ISI Web of Science from other databases is that it facilitates cited reference searching as it includes all the cited references (footnotes and bibliographies) published with each item in the literature that ISI covers. The Institute also provides a number of current awareness products, including Current Contents, a journal-based current awareness database that is available on the web via Current Contents Connect.
Pubns: databases incl: ISI Web of Knowledge; ISI Web of Science (web access to ISI citation indexes: Science Citation Index, Social Sciences Citation Index & Arts & Humanities Citation Index); ISI Chemistry; Derwent Innovations Index (web access to the Derwent World Patents Index & Derwent Patents Citation Index); Current Contents Connect (current awareness table of contents database)

O236
Institute of Paper Conservation [IPC]
Bridge House, Waterside, Upton-upon-Severn, Worcestershire, WR8 0HG (01684-591150; *fax:* 01684-592380)
Email: information@ipc.org.uk
Internet: http://www.ipc.org.uk/

Chief: Chairman: Ms Kate Colleran *Other Snr Offcrs:* Administrator: Ms Tina Marshall
Membs: 950 indivs; 550 instns *Memb Req:* subscription rates (UK): accredited membs

£105.84 pa, grad & associate membs £50 pa, corporate membs £93 pa, student membs £25 pa
Activs: The leading international organisation devoted solely to the conservation of paper, books and related materials. Its members include conservators, scientists and collectors as well as experts in related fields such as librarians, archivists, artists and papermakers. IPC exists to advance paper conservation and to inform and educate the general public. It organises international conferences and seminars on the latest techniques and developments in paper conservation, and provides advice on how to contact paper conservators, geographically or by specialisation.
Pubns: The Paper Conservator (journal, 1 pa); Paper Conservation News (4 pa); Conference Papers (various prices); leaflets for the public on the care & conservation of paper
See also **S1680**

O237
International Association of Music Libraries, Archives and Documentation Centres (UK) [IAML(UK)]
c/o Mr Peter Baxter, Music Lib, Edinburgh City Libs, 9 George IV Bridge, Edinburgh, EH1 1EG (0131-242-8053; *fax:* 0131-242-8009)
Email: pbbaxter@hotmail.com
Internet: http://www.iaml-uk-irl.org/

Gov Body: IAML (UK) Exec Cttee *Chief:* Pres: Ms Susi Woodhouse (susi@fortissimo.demon.co.uk) *Other Snr Offcrs:* Genl Sec: Mr Peter Baxter BMus, DipLib, MCLIP, as above
Membs: 150 indivs; 110 instns *Memb Req:* open to music libs & libns & to anyone working with music; subscription: indivs £35 pa (students, retired, unemployed £11 pa); instns £47 pa
Activs: Represent the interests of music libraries and librarians through out the world, and promotes co-operation between them. Aims to keep music librarians and those in the music trade abreast of current developments; organises an annual study weekend, meetings and day training courses; plays a key role in the development of a Music Library and Information Plan for the UK and Republic of Ireland.
Pubns: Brio (journal, 2 pa, free to membs); Newsletter (2 pa, free to membs); Annual Report (free to membs); Annual Survey of Music Libs (£13); Lib & Info Plan for Music (£10); Music Sets Survey (£5); British Union Catalogue of Music Periodicals (2nd ed, £60, not available direct from IAML)
Further Info: IAML(UK) is an Org in Liaison with CILIP (see **O110**)

O238
International Book Development Ltd [IBD]
305-307 Chiswick High Rd, London, W4 4HH (020-8742-7474; *fax:* 020-8747-8715)
Email: enquiries@ibd.uk.net

Type: consultancy for aid agencies & developing countries *Gov Body:* owned by Centre for British Teachers (CfBT), Reading *Chief:* Managing Dir: Mr Tony Read
Activs: Consultancy, research and policy development work for aid agencies and governments in developing countries in all aspects of instructional materials supply, publishing, reading and information development for educational projects. IBD works with many international and bilateral organisations including the World Bank, Ascan Development Bank, UN agencies (e.g., UNICEF), DANIDA (Denmark), Department for International Development (UK), CIDA (Canada) etc.

International Libraries Organisations

(Internatl Book Development Ltd cont)
Pubns: IBD's directors have written or contributed to various pubns in the field of book development, incl: Content Analysis of Reading and Maths Books in Fifteen Developing Countries (1989); Analysis of Rsrch on Textbook Availability & Quality in Developing Countries (1989); African Book Sector Studies: Summary Report (1991); Publishing & The Book Trade in Central and Eastern Europe (1992)

O239
Irish Science Librarians' Group [ISLG]

c/o The Sci Libn, Queen's Univ Sci Lib, Lennoxvale, Belfast, BT9 5EQ (028-9033-5441; fax: 028-9038-2636)
Email: s.landy@qub.ac.uk
Internet: http://www.heanet.ie/ISLG/

Chief: Chairperson: Ms Sheila Landy, Sci Libn, Queen's Univ of Belfast (at above addr)
Membs: 17 indivs
Activs: Provides a forum for science librarians throughout the island of Ireland; aims to discuss matters of common interest particularly as they relate to science and technology, to share relevant information on topics of mutual interest, and to liaise and co-operate wherever relevant.

O240
The John Campbell Trust

c/o Mr Stephen Robertson, Microsoft Rsrch Ltd, 7 J.J. Thomson Ave, Cambridge, CB3 0FB (01223-479774; fax: 01223-479999)
Email: ser@microsoft.com
Internet: http://www.cilip.org.uk/jct/

Type: charity **Gov Body:** Trustees **Chief:** Chair: Mr Stephen Robertson, as above
Activs: An independent charitable trust which acts to further the education and development of information professionals through grants, scholarships, research or travel awards. The John Campbell Conference/Travel Bursary is intended to help an information professional to attend a conference or undertake a programme of travel, while the John Campbell Dissertation Bursary is intended to help a student on a course in information or library studies to undertake a particular project.

O241
Joint Academic Network User Group for Libraries [JUGL]

c/o Ms Caroline Williams, All Saints Lib, Manchester Metropolitan Univ, Manchester, M15 6BH (0161-247-6659; fax: 0161-247-6349)
Email: c.a.williams@mmu.ac.uk
Internet: http://www.bubl.ac.uk/org/jugl/

Gov Body: subcommittee of the Joint Academic Network Natl User Group (JNUG) **Chief:** Chair: Dr Andrew Dalgleish (ajdalgle@glam.ac.uk) **Other Snr Offcrs:** Sec: Ms Caroline Williams, as above
Membs: 100 instns
Activs: Represent interests of librarians in institutions connected to the Joint Academic Network (JANET). Activities include: providing a forum for the exchange of information; meetings and seminars; liaison with UKERNA and other networking organisations.
Pubns: Newsletter

O242
Joint Information Systems Committee [JISC]

JISC Exec, Northavon House, Coldharbour Ln, Bristol, BS16 1QD (0117-931-7403; fax: 0117-931-7255)
Email: assist@jisc.ac.uk
Internet: http://www.jisc.ac.uk/

Chief: Chair: Prof Maxwell Irvine **Other Snr Offcrs:** Exec Sec: Dr Malcolm Read (m.read@jisc.ac.uk)
Branches & Groups: Regional Support Centres: JISC RSC EAST MIDLANDS, Loughborough Coll, Radmoor Rd, Loughborough, Leicestershire, LE11 3BT (01509-618110; email: support@rsc-east-midlands.ac.uk); JISC RSC EASTERN, Anglia Polytechnic Univ, Benfleet Campus, Kiln Rd, Benfleet, Essex, SS7 1PZ (01268-638606; email: support@rsc-eastern.ac.uk); JISC RSC LONDON, City & Islington Coll, 8-26 Bath St, London, EC1V 9PL (020-7614-0393; email: support@rsc-london.ac.uk); JISC RSC NORTH WEST, Blackpool & The Fylde Coll, Ashfield Rd, Bispham, Blackpool, Lancashire, FY2 0HB (01253-504070; email: support@rsc-northwest.ac.uk); JISC RSC NORTHERN, The Gardener's Lodge, Neville's Cross Centre, Darlington Rd, Durham, DH1 4SY (0191-375-4993; email: support@rsc-north.ac.uk); JISC RSC SOUTH EAST, Computing Centre, Univ of Kent at Canterbury, Canterbury, Kent, CT2 7NF (0118-967-5050; email: support@rsc-southeast.ac.uk); JISC RSC SOUTH WEST, Babbage 316, Univ of Plymouth, Drake Circus, Plymouth, PL4 8AA (01752-233899; email: support@rsc-south-west.ac.uk); JISC RSC WEST MIDLANDS, IT Svcs, Univ of Wolverhampton, Wulfruna St, Wolverhampton, West Midlands, WV1 1SB (01902-322001; email: support@rsc-westmidlands.ac.uk); JISC RSC YORKSHIRE & HUMBER, Beech Grove House, Univ of Leeds, Leeds, West Yorkshire, LS2 9JT (0113-343-1000; email: support@rsc-yh.ac.uk); JISC RSC NORTHERN IRELAND, Queen's Univ of Belfast, 6 College Pk East, Belfast, BT7 1LQ (028-9027-3884; email: support@rsc-ni.ac.uk); JISC RSC SCOTLAND NORTH & EAST, Telford Coll, Crewe Toll, Edinburgh, EH4 2NZ (0131-315-7674; email: support@rsc-ne-scotland.ac.uk); JISC RSC SCOTLAND SOUTH & WEST, North Glasgow Coll, 110 Flemington St, Glasgow, G21 4BX (0141-558-9001 x292; email: support@rsc-sw-scotland.ac.uk); JISC RSC WALES, Lib & Info Svcs, Univ of Wales Swansea, Singleton Pk, Swansea, SA2 8PP (01792-295959; email: support@rsc-wales.ac.uk)
Activs: Exists to stimulate and enable the cost effective exploitation of information systems and to provide a national network infrastructure for the higher education and research council communities in the UK. Arranges conferences and seminars, and funds projects within further and higher education institutions to trial, pilot, develop or evaluate new technologies and techniques.
Pubns: JISC Inform (newsletter, formerly JISC News); various other newsletters, policy documents, guidance documents, reports & circulars

O243
Kent History Federation

c/o Mrs F.I. Percival, 14 Valliers Wood Rd, Sidcup, Kent, DA15 8HE (020-8300-3830)

Chief: Chairman: Mrs P. Winzar **Other Snr Offcrs:** Hon Sec: Mrs F.I. Percival, at above addr
Membs: 95 affiliated socs
Activs: Umbrella organisation for local history societies in Kent; organises four quarterly meetings at County Hall, Maidstone, each year.
Pubns: Journal of Kent Hist (2 pa, £6 for 4 issues)

O244
Kent Information and Library Network [KILN]

c/o Ms Sarah Loat, Horticulture Rsrch Internatl, East Malling, West Malling, Kent, ME19 6BJ (01732-843833)
Email: info@kiln.org.uk
Internet: http://www.kiln.org.uk/

Type: co-op **Chief:** Chair: Ms Helen Leech, Chatham Lib (helen.leech@medway.gov.uk) **Other Snr Offcrs:** Sec: Ms Jan Rudolph (jan.rudolph@kent.gov.uk); Membership Sec: Ms Sarah Loat, as above (sarah.loat@hri.ac.uk)
Membs: 29 instns **Memb Req:** open to lib, info, advisory & related orgs in Kent; subscriptions vary according to nature of org
Activs: Aims to support the provision of high quality library, information and advice services through collaboration and networking; provides a framework for the dissemination of information about the activities, services and resources of its members. Offers professional support and development, networking opportunities, training, seminars, meetings, visits and an online discussion forum.
Pubns: KILN Newsletter; Directory of Membs

O245
Korea Library Group [KLG]

c/o Mrs Beth McKillop, British Lib Oriental & India Office Collns, 96 Euston Rd, London, NW1 2DB (020-7412-7873; fax: 020-7412-7641)
Email: beth.mckillop@bl.uk

Chief: Convenor: Mrs Beth McKillop, as above
Membs: 9 instns **Memb Req:** open to libs & related instns with significant amounts of Korea-related materials
Activs: Promotes co-operation in professional matters relating to library provision for Korean Studies in the UK.

O246
Labour Heritage

c/o Mr Sean Creighton, 18 Ridge Rd, Mitcham, Surrey, CR4 2ET (tel & fax: 020-8640-2014)
Email: sean.creighton@btopenworld.com

Gov Body: Exec Cttee **Chief:** Chair: Mr Stan Newens **Other Snr Offcrs:** Sec: Mr Sean Creighton, as above: Treasurer: Ms Irene Wagner
Membs: 100+ indivs **Memb Req:** open to all those with an interest in labour hist & who support the soc's aims
Activs: Aims to promote the study of the history of the labour movement; organises conferences and meetings; publishes a regular bulletin and pamphlets on labour history topics.
Pubns: Labour Heritage Bulletin (3 pa, 70p incl p&p); In the Face of Poverty (Women's Rsrch Cttee Bulletin, 1966, £1.20 incl p&p); Doing Hist (Women's Rsrch Cttee Bulletin, 1990, £1.20 incl p&p); The Roots of Labour in a West London Suburb, by Barbara Humphries (2002, £1.75 incl p&p)

O247
Lancashire and Cheshire Antiquarian Society [LCAS]

c/o Mr J.S. Matthews, 7 Riddings Rd, Hale, Altrincham, Cheshire, WA15 9DS (0161-928-7908)

Gov Body: LCAS Council **Chief:** Hon Treasurer & Membership Sec: Mr J.S. Matthews, as above
Memb Req: open to all indivs & orgs interested in the various historical aspects of the two counties Palatine; subscriptions: indivs £15 pa (students £7), joint membership £21 pa, instns 18 pa
Activs: Promotes the study of the history of Lancashire and Cheshire, including archaeology (both traditional and industrial), social history, trade and trades, architecture and the arts, the history of institutions and local government, and the customs and traditions of the two counties. Organises a programme, which runs from September to July, which includes lectures, visits and at least one Day School. Joint meetings are sometimes held with other Societies. The Society also makes representations concerning the conservation of the region's heritage to the appropriate authorities, and is represented on the Manchester Areas Historic Buildings Panel and other local and regional organisations.
Pubns: Transactions (1 pa, free to membs); offprints of selected recent papers
See also **S1513**

O248 🔑 🎓
Lancashire Local History Federation [LLHF]
c/o Mr Mark Pearson, 101 Todmorden Rd, Little-borough, Lancashire, OL15 9EB (01706-379949)
Email: secretary@lancashirehistory.co.uk
Internet: http://www.lancashirehistory.co.uk/

Gov Body: Exec Cttee **Chief:** Chairman: Mr John Wilson **Other Snr Offcrs:** Membership Sec: Mr Mark Pearson, as above
Membs: 48 indivs; 80 instns **Memb Req:** open to all those interested in the hist of Lancashire; subscription: indivs £5 pa, socs £8 pa
Activs: Co-ordinating body for local history in the county palatine of Lancaster, and umbrella group for local history, family history and industrial archaeology groups. Provides a point of exchange for information relevant to affiliated societies in the pre-1974 county of Lancashire; seeks to represent the views of affiliated societies when called upon at regional government level; furthers the interest in and study of local history, family history and industrial archaeology in the county.
Pubns: Lancashire Local Historian (1 pa, £5.75 incl p&p); Newsletter (4 pa, free to membs)

O249 🔑
LASER Foundation
(successor body to the London and South Eastern Lib Region)
c/o Martin House Farm, Whittle-le-Woods, Chorley, Lancashire, PR6 7QR (01257-274833; *fax:* 01257-266488)
Email: laser@laserfoundation.org.uk
Internet: http://www.bl.uk/concord/laser-about.html

Type: grant making foundation for public libs **Gov Body:** Board of Trustees **Chief:** Chair: Mr Bernard Naylor **Other Snr Offcrs:** Company Sec: Ms Frances Hendrix JP, BA, MBA, MCLIP, MInstD (frances@laserfoundation.org.uk)
Activs: Aims to improve library facilities available to the public through the awarding of grants to public library authorities. The Foundation has been set up to continue to support the end users of public libraries, by co-operative activity and in the same manner as the precursor body LASER (London and South Eastern Library Region). In particular this will be to promote co-operative activity, which benefits end users of public libraries, both in the former region of LASER and in the public libraries beyond that former region.

Further Info: Awards from the Laser Foundation are administered by the British Library's Co-operation & Partnership Programme; contact the Awards Administrator, c/o British Lib Co-operation & Partnership Programme, 96 Euston Rd, London, NW1 2DB (co-operation@bl.uk)

O250 🎓
Leeds Metropolitan University, School of Information Management
The Grange, Beckett Pk, Leeds, LS6 3QS (0113-283-2600; *fax:* 0113-283-3182)
Email: j.blake@lmu.ac.uk
Internet: http://www.lmu.ac.uk/ies/im/

Gov Body: Leeds Metropolitan Univ (see also **S908**) **Chief:** Head of School: Mr John Blake
Membs: 66 staff; 1000 undergrad & 200 postgrad students
Activs: Information and Library Management education and training, focusing on the management of information as a strategic resource to meet the needs of individuals, groups, and organisations primarily though the understanding, design and exploitation of computing systems and applications.

O251 🔑 🐾
Librarians' Christian Fellowship [LCF]
c/o Mr Graham Hedges, 34 Thurlestone Ave, Seven Kings, Ilford, Essex, IG3 9DU (020-8599-1310)
Email: secretary@librarianscf.org.uk
Internet: http://www.librarianscf.org.uk/

Gov Body: Exec Cttee **Chief:** Pres: Mr Gordon Harris, Univ of Birmingham (galexharris@netscape.net) **Other Snr Offcrs:** Chair: Ms Kirsty Robinson (Kirsty.Robinson@hants.gov.uk); Sec: Mr Graham Hedges MCLIP, as above
Membs: 340 indivs; 30 instns **Memb Req:** open to Christians employed in lib, archv & info svcs of all kinds; associate membership is available to interested indivs in other professions
Branches & Groups: CTTEE FOR OVERSEAS LIB DEVELOPMENT (COLD), contact the Overseas Sec: Ms Winette Field (overseas@librarianscf.org.uk); WORKING PARTY ON ISSUES IN LIB MGMT; WORKING PARTY ON TRENDS IN CHILDREN'S & YNG PEOPLE'S LIT
Activs: Organising events and publications helping Christian librarians to relate their faith to their work; expressing a Christian viewpoint on current issues in library and information work; making the skills of librarians available to the wider Christian and library communities; maintains a cassette library for members.
Pubns: Christian Libn (annual, free to membs, £2.50 to non-membs); Libn's Christian Fellowship Newsletter (3 pa, free to membs); Issues in Librarianship: The Christian Dimension (75p); Issues in Librarianship 2: The Debate Continues (£3)
Further Info: LCF is an Org in Liaison with CILIP (see **O110**)

O252 🔑
Libraries and Archives Copyright Alliance [LACA]
c/o CILIP, 7 Ridgmount St, London, WC1E 7AE (020-7255-0500; *fax:* 020-7255-0501)
Email: info@cilip.org.uk
Internet: http://www.cilip.org.uk/committees/laca/laca.html

Type: prof **Chief:** Chair: Mr Denis Heathcote, Univ of Greenwich Lib **Other Snr Offcrs:** Sec: Ms Barbara Stratton, as above
Membs: 21 indiv membs representing 11 orgs

Activs: Aims to monitor and lobby the Government and the EU on all aspects to do with copyright on behalf of UK libraries, archives and information services and their users; to encourage dialogue on copyright issues within the library, information and archive profession at large.

O253 🔑
Libraries for Life for Londoners
31 Milton Pk, London, N6 5QB (020-7607-2665)
Email: mail@librarylondon.org
Internet: http://www.librarylondon.org/

Type: lib support network **Chief:** Chair: Mr Alan Templeton **Other Snr Offcrs:** Vice-Chair: Ms Susan Chinn; Treasurer: Mr Peter Richardson
Activs: Umbrella organisation for local library support groups and their supporters in the London area; promotes a comprehensive, high quality, well-managed and accessible library service for all Londoners; co-ordinates activities of member groups; organises meetings and workshops.

O254 🔑 🎓 ✚
Libraries for Nursing [LfN]
c/o Ms Jane Shelley, Univ Lib, Anglia Polytechnic Univ, Chelmsford, Essex, CM1 1SQ (01245-493131 x3760; *fax:* 01245-495920)
Email: j.shelley@apu.ac.uk
Internet: http://www.cilip.org.uk/groups/hlg/lfn/

Gov Body: CILIP Health Libs Group (see **O124**) **Chief:** Chair: Ms Vickie Orton (vo2@york.ac.uk)
Memb Req: subscription £15 pa
Activs: Sub-group of CILIP's Health Libraries Group, bringing together those interested in library and information provision for nurses and those allied to the nursing profession. Keeps members informed of current developments through its quarterly Bulletin; arranges regional events and twice yearly national study days; liaises with the Heath Libraries Group and NHS Library Advisor on relevant issues; is involved in the LIS-NURSING mailing list.
Pubns: LfN Bulletin (4 pa)

O255 🔑
Libraries North West [LNW]
(successor body to the North West Regional Lib System)
Chester Coll, Parkgate Rd, Chester, Cheshire, CH1 4BJ (01244-220362)
Internet: http://www.lnw.org.uk/

Chief: Dir: Ms Clare Connor (c.connor@chester.ac.uk) **Other Snr Offcrs:** Admin Asst: Ms Jane Graham (jane.graham@chester.ac.uk)
Membs: 42 instns
Branches & Groups: LNW BUSINESS UNIT, Bk Deliveries, Bowran St, Preston, Lancashire, PR1 2UX, Business Unit Supervisor: Ms Gillian Wilson (01772-264047; *fax:* 01772-264002; *email:* gillian.wilson@lcl.lancscc.gov.uk)
Activs: Aims to raise the profile and status of libraries in the region through advocacy, marketing and planning; to ensure that funding opportunities are fully exploited; to provide knowledge of, and access to, library services in the North West; to harness the learning, cultural and information capacity of libraries in the region through effective cross sector working; to contribute to and actively promote libraries' cultural role in the region; to facilitate the delivery of appropriate operational services for the benefit of all library sectors in the region; to ensure the library domain is pro-active and fully effective in cross-domain work with archives and museums; to provide inter-lending services to members through the LNW Inter-Library Loan Business Unit.
Pubns: Newsletter

Libraries
▼
Manchester
Organisations

O256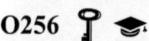

Libraries of Institutes and Schools of Education [LISE]

c/o Mr Alan Bradwell, Anglia Polytechnic Univ, Rivermead Campus Lib, Bishop Hall Ln, Chelmsford, Essex, CM1 1SQ (01245-493131 x3597)
Email: a.bradwell@anglia.ac.uk
Internet: http://www.educ.cam.ac.uk/lise/

Chief: Chair: Ms Judith Stewart (judith.stewart@uwe.ac.uk) *Other Snr Offcrs:* Sec: Mr Alan Bradwell, as above
Membs: 63 instns *Memb Req:* open to edu libs at univs & insts in England, Wales & Northern Ireland
Activs: Encourages and sustains the provision of books and services in support of study and research in education; serves the information needs of the teaching profession, its co-workers and the public at large.
Pubns: Education Libraries Journal (3 pa); Acronyms & Initialisms in Edu (6th ed, £5); Guide to British Educational Journals (£5); Teaching Resources Collns: An Essential Tool in the Training of Teachers (£5); wide range of other titles incl bibliographies & guides to various aspects of educational & ch's lit

The Libraries Partnership - West Midlands

See MLA WEST MIDLANDS (**O281**)

O257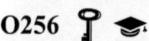

Libraries Together: Liverpool Learning Partnership [LTLLP]

(formerly Liverpool Libs Group)
c/o Learning Svcs, Liverpool Hope Univ Coll, Hope Pk, Liverpool, L16 9JD (0151-291-3582; *fax:* 0151-291-2037)
Email: taylorl@hope.ac.uk
Internet: http://www.liv.ac.uk/Library/llgroup/llg.html

Type: co-op *Chief:* Chair (2002-02): Miss Linda Taylor, addr as above *Other Snr Offcrs:* Chair is rotated annually among the dirs of memb libs
Membs: 6 instns
Activs: LTLLP is a partnership of the major public, HE and FE libraries in Liverpool. Its aims are to co-operate to develop access for customers, advance the use of ICT, support the delivery of lifelong learning and organise joint training seminars. The partnership maintains a web site at http://www.merseylibraries.org, which gives access to the union catalogue of four of its partner libraries. It is planned to expand this to include all members, the archive holdings of the Liverpool Record Office, and other libraries in the region. An annual conference is held on a topic of current interest.

O258

Library + Information Show

2 Forge House, Summerley Rd, Princes Risborough, Buckinghamshire, HP27 9DT (01844-342894; *fax:* 01844-346354)
Internet: http://www.lishow.co.uk/

Activs: Organises the annual Library + information Show, bringing together all sectors of the library and information world together to share the key industry developments, the latest technology, exchange ideas and opinions and debate current issues.

O259

Library and Information Services Council (Northern Ireland) [LISC(NI)]

PO Box 1231, Belfast, BT8 6AL (028-9070-5441; *fax:* 028-9040-1180)
Email: mairead@liscni.freeserve.co.uk
Internet: http://www.liscni.co.uk/

Type: co-ordinating body *Gov Body:* Exec Cttee
Chief: Chairperson: Mrs Linda Houston (linda.houston@ni-libraries.net) *Other Snr Offcrs:* Exec Offcr: Ms Mairead Gilheany, addr as above
Activs: Aims to maintain and enhance the standard of library and information services in Northern Ireland by providing advice and consultation to government departments, representing the views of the library and information sector and by acting as a catalyst for progress and development in all areas of library and information provision.

O260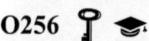

Library and Information Statistics Unit [LISU]

Loughborough Univ, Loughborough, Leicestershire, LE11 3TU (01509-223071; *fax:* 01509-223072)
Email: lisu@lboro.ac.uk
Internet: http://www.lboro.ac.uk/departments/dis/lisu/lisuhp.html

Gov Body: Loughborough Univ (see **S1483**)
Chief: Dir: Dr J.E. Davies
Activs: Aims to be the authoritative national centre for the collection and dissemination of statistical data to support the management of UK library and information services, and to be the major UK provider of expert advice on the effective use of such data. Specific goals include: to provide data for the advocacy of library and information services with government and the media; to increase the understanding and use of statistics by library and information service managers; to maintain data-bases for key library and information service sectors, and to make data available in print and/or electronic formats; to encourage benchmarking in the field, and to provide benchmarking services; to provide objective advice to library and information service managers, linked to interpretation of local data; to underpin UK research into library and information services, through databases and through advice in statistical analysis; to undertake research into the development and use of valid data for the sector; to make constructive use of data across the different library and information service sectors.
Pubns: LISU Annual Lib Statistics (£35); Average Prices of British/American Academic Books (both 2 pa, £15 each or £25 together); Public Lib Materials Fund & Budget Survey (1 pa, £30); A Survey of Lib Svcs to Schools & Children in the UK (1 pa, £30); Lib & Info Statistics Tables (1 pa, free on receipt of SAE); Who Else Writes Like ...?: A Readers' Guide to Fiction Authors (£17.99); Who Next? A Guide to Children's Authors (£11.99); other occasional pubns

Library Association

See CHARTERED INST OF LIB & INFO PROFS (**O110**)

O261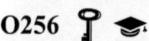

Library Association of Ireland, Irish Language Group (Meitheál Oibre na Leabharlainnthe)

c/o Mrs Mary Delargy, Aberfoyle House, Magee Campus, Univ of Ulster, Londonderry, Northern Ireland, BT48 9JF (028-7137-5569)
Email: m.delargy@ulster.ac.uk

Type: prof *Gov Body:* Lib Assoc of Ireland (see **IO26**) *Chief:* Chairperson: Mrs Mary Delargy, as above
Activs: Promotes library and information services to the Irish speaking community; holds seminars and provides a network to advise on problems in cataloguing and bibliographic searching.
Further Info: The group has been in abeyance, but intends to restart in 2003

O262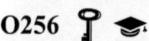

Library Booksellers Group of the Booksellers Association

Minster House, 272 Vauxhall Bridge Rd, London, SW1V 1BA (020-7802-0813; *fax:* 020-7802-0803)
Email: mail@booksellers.org.uk
Internet: http://www.booksellers.org.uk/

Gov Body: The Council of the Booksellers Assoc
Chief: contact Mr John Parke (john.parke@booksellers.org.uk)
Membs: 75 instns
Activs: Supplying public and academic libraries.

O263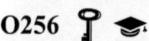

The Library Campaign

22 Upper Woburn Pl, London, WC1H 0TB (0870-770-7946; *fax:* 0870-770-7947)
Email: Librarycam@aol.com
Internet: http://www.librarycampaign.co.uk/

Gov Body: The Steering Group *Chief:* Campaign Dir: Ms Jill Wight *Other Snr Offcrs:* Hon Pres: Mr Ron Surridge (rgs@statacom.net); Natl Sec: Mr Andrew Coburn (andrew.coburn@essexcc.gov.uk)
Membs: 600 indivs; 150 instns
Branches & Groups: various local lib support groups (UK wide); contact Campaign Dir
Activs: An independent body that represents the interests of library users and workers; co-ordinates local campaigns and campaigns nationally against cuts in publicly funded libraries; promotes library services; organises conferences on library issues.
Pubns: The Lib Campaigner (3 pa, free to membs); Starter Pack for Setting Up a Local Group (£5 for non-membs); leaflets & posters

O264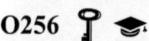

Library Services Trust [LST]

c/o CILIP, 7 Ridgmount St, London, WC1E 7AE (020-7255-0648; *fax:* 020-7255-0501)
Email: Eric.Winter@cilip.org.uk

Gov Body: Board of Trustees, part of CILIP (see **O110**) *Chief:* Exec Sec: Mr Eric Winter
Activs: Grant-making trust to CILIP members for travel, research etc. Also has a range of awards: International Librarian of the Year, and for local history publishing by libraries.

O265

Liverpool and District Scientific Industrial and Research Library Advisory Council [LADSIRLAC]

c/o Central Libs, William Brown St, Liverpool, Merseyside, L3 8EW (0151-207-1937; *fax:* 0151-233-5886)

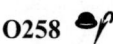 academic   corporate   governmental   + medical

Gov Body: Liverpool City Council (see **P76**)
Membs: 180+ instns
Activs: Subscription based information service for industry and commerce, offering document delivery, computer and other information searches, fax, copying and current awareness services.
Pubns: Annual Report

O266

Liverpool John Moores University, Centre for Information and Library Management [CILM]

School of Business Info, John Foster Bldg, 98 Mount Pleasant, Liverpool, L3 5UZ (0151-231-3801; *fax:* 0151-707-0423)
Email: a.j.farrow@livjm.ac.uk
Internet: http://cwis.livjm.ac.uk/bus/cilm/

Gov Body: Liverpool John Moores Univ (see also **S969**) **Chief:** Team Leader: Ms Janet Farrow
Membs: 10 staff
Activs: Provides teaching, research and consult-ancy in Information and Library Management. Courses include BA(Hons) in Business and Information, BSc(Hons) in e-Business Communications and MA in Information and Library Management.
Pubns: various rsrch reports

O267

London Libraries Development Agency [LLDA]

35 St Martin's St, London, WC2H 7HP (*tel & fax:* 020-7641-5266)
Email: contact@llda.org.uk
Internet: http://www.llda.org.uk/

Type: development agency **Gov Body:** LLDA Advisory Board **Chief:** Dir: Mr David Murray
Membs: 40 instns **Memb Req:** open to London Boroughs maintaining public lib svcs, academic instns with lib & learning facilities, other public svcs with an interest in working in partnership with libs & orgs that represent or bring together other sectors or sections of govt; subscription: lib parent orgs (local govt & academic): £3,000 + VAT pa; other public svcs: £100 + VAT pa
Activs: The LLDA has been created to develop a co-ordinated strategic vision for library and information services across London. The LLDA acts as a single entry point for those interested in working with or through libraries, and as the first point of contact for information or suggestions for London's libraries; develops evidence and advocacy materials to make clear the contribution libraries can make to London; forges partnerships with a wide range of major London organisations.
Pubns: Bulletin (2 pa); strategy documents

O268

London Metropolitan University, Department of Applied Social Science [SLGIM]

(formerly Univ of North London, School of Law, Governance & Info Mgmt)
Ladbroke House, 62-66 Highbury Grove, London, N5 2AD (020-7753-5031; *fax:* 020-7753-5763)
Internet: http://www.londonmet.ac.uk/dass/

Gov Body: London Metropolitan Univ (see **S1262**)
Chief: Head of Dept: Ms Sue Pike (s.pike@londonmet.ac.uk) **Other Snr Offcrs:** Info Mgmt Team Leader: Mr Tony Beard
Membs: 90+ permanent staff (7 in Info Mgmt)
Activs: Provides postgraduate (masters) courses in Librarianship, Knowledge Management and Information Management. Founded in 1946 the school is one of Britain's oldest library schools. Besides postgraduate degrees in this field the

school also offers research for MPhil and PhD qualifications. The school has links with similar schools in numerous other countries.
Pubns: Prospectus

O269

London Record Society [LRS]

c/o Inst of Historical Rsrch, Senate House, Malet St, London, WC1E 7HU (020-7862-8798; *fax:* 020-7862-8793)
Email: heather.creaton@sas.ac.uk
Internet: http://www.history.ac.uk/cmh/

Gov Body: Council of the Soc **Chief:** Chairman: Mr H.S. Cobb MA, FSA, FRHS **Other Snr Offcrs:** Hon Sec: Miss H.J. Creaton BA, MPhil
Membs: 144 indivs; 197 instns **Memb Req:** subscription: £12 pa for indivs, £18 pa for instns
Activs: Founded in 1964 to publish transcripts, abstracts and lists of primary sources for the history of London, and generally to stimulate interest in archives relating to London; aims to publish one volume of such material per year; holds a lecture and AGM in November.
Pubns: published vols are available to membs as part of the annual subscription, with previous vols available for same sums, £20 per vol for non-membs. Recent pubns incl: London Debating Socs 1776-99 (1994); London Bridge, Selected Accounts & Rentals 1381-1547 (1995); London Consistory Court Depositions 1586-1611 (1997); The Settlement & Bastardy Examinations of St Luke, Chelsea 1730-66 (1999); Records of St Andrew Hubbard 1454-1560 (1999); a full list is available from the LRS.

O270

London Regional Archive Council [LRAC]

c/o Mr David Mander, Hackney Archvs Dept, 43 De Beauvoir Rd, London, N1 5SQ (0207-241-2477/2886; *fax:* 0207-241-6688)
Email: dmander@gw.hackney.gov.uk
Internet: http://www.lmn.net.uk/larc/

Chief: Chair: Mr David Mander, as above **Other Snr Offcrs:** Sec: Ms Janet Percival, Univ Coll London Lib (020-7679-7791; *email:* ucyljan@ucl.ac.uk)
Activs: Strategic organisation for London's archives; aims to promote the care, use and development of archives in the nation's capital; works with the London Museums Agency and the London Libraries Development Agency (see **O267**) to improve cross-sector co-operation and to develop joint initiatives.

O271

London's Museums, Archives and Libraries [LMAL]

c/o London Museums Agency, Cloister Ct, 22-26 Farringdon Ln, London, EC1R 3AJ (020-7549-1712; *fax:* 020-7490-5225)
Email: steve.slack@londonmuseums.org
Internet: http://www.lmal.org.uk/

Type: prof **Gov Body:** partnership of the agencies representing the three domains in London: London Regional Archv Council (see **O270**); London Libs Development Agency (see **O267**); London Museums Agency (LMA) **Chief:** Strategic Development Offcr: Ms Jemima Johnstone (jemima.johnstone@londonmuseums.org) **Other Snr Offcrs:** Head of Learning & Access: Ms Sophie Perkins (sophie.perkins@llda.org.uk); Administrative Offcr: Mr Steve Slack, as above
Membs: 12 board membs
Activs: Aims to promote effective co-operation between the capital's museums, archives and

libraries and to support their development through joint strategic planning. Organises various events and meetings in support of these aims, and is currently drawing up a proposal for a new, strategic cross-domain agency for museums, archives and libraries in London.

O272

Loughborough University, Department of Information Science [DIS]

Ashby Rd, Loughborough, Leicestershire, LE11 3TU (01509-223052; *fax:* 01509-223053)
Email: dis@lboro.ac.uk
Internet: http://www.lboro.ac.uk/departments/dis/

Gov Body: Loughborough Univ (see also **S1483**)
Chief: Head of Dept: Prof Ron Summers (r.summers@lboro.ac.uk)
Membs: 31 staff; 330 students
Branches & Groups: Dept incl two externally funded rsrch units: LIB & INFO STATISTICS UNIT (see **O260**); LEARNING & TEACHING SUPPORT NETWORK (LTSN)
Activs: Education and research in information and library studies and related subjects.
Pubns: Annual Report; DIS Newsletter; DIS Briefing; Undergrad Programmes Guide; Postgrad Programmes Guide; Rsrch Guide

O273

M25 Consortium of Academic Libraries

c/o Ms Suzanne Enright, Univ of Westminster, Cavendish Campus, 115 New Cavendish St, London, W1W 6UW (020-7911-5095; *fax:* 020-7911-5093)
Email: s.enright@westminster.ac.uk
Internet: http://www.M25lib.ac.uk/

Chief: Chair (2002-03): Ms Anne Bell, Info Systems & Svcs, King's Coll London (anne.bell@kcl.ac.uk) **Other Snr Offcrs:** Sec (2002-03): Ms Suzanne Enright, as above
Membs: 39 instns **Memb Req:** open to Higher Edu & related libs in the Greater London area as defined by the M25 motorway; subscription-based
Branches & Groups: ACCESS WORKING GROUP; ADVOCACY WORKING GROUP; CPD25: TRAINING & DEVELOPMENT FOR HE LIBS IN THE LONDON REGION; CREATIVE ARTS GROUP; DISASTER MGMT GROUP; RESOURCE DISCOVERY WORKING GROUP; WORKING GROUP ON DISABLED & SPECIAL NEEDS SUPPORT
Activs: Aims to foster co-operation amongst member libraries. Interests include staff development, improving access to collections and resources, disaster and business continuity planning and co-operative purchasing. Also provides the virtual catalogue InforM25.

O274

Manchester Legal Information Group [MLIG]

c/o Miss Lisa Smith, Head of Info Svcs, DWF, Harvester House, 37 Peter St, Manchester, M2 5GB (0161-228-3702; *fax:* 0161-835-2407)
Email: lisa.smith@dwf.co.uk

Type: prof, legal **Chief:** Sec: Miss Lisa Smith, as above
Membs: 30 indivs **Memb Req:** open to legal info profs in the Manchester area
Activs: Provides a forum for members; meets four times a year; holds lunches where a guest speaker is invited, or new products are demonstrated.
Pubns: Union List of Law Reports & Periodicals; List of CD-ROMs (forthcoming)

O275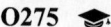

Manchester Metropolitan University, Department of Information and Communications

Geoffrey Manton Bldg, Rosamund St West, off Oxford Rd, Manchester, M15 6LL (0161-247-6144; *fax:* 0161-247-6351)
Email: infcomms-hums@mmu.ac.uk
Internet: http://www.mmu.ac.uk/h-ss/dic/

Gov Body: Manchester Metropolitan Univ (see **S1519**) *Chief:* Head of Dept: Prof Dick Hartley (r.j.hartley@mmu.ac.uk)
Membs: 47 staff
Branches & Groups: CERLIM (Centre for Rsrch in Lib & Info Mgmt, see **O106**)
Activs: Education and research; undergraduate and postgraduate courses, include: BA(Hons) in Information and Library Management; BSc(Hons) in Information Management; MA in Information and Library Management; MSc Information Management.

O276 ♀

Manorial Society of Great Britain [MSGB]

104 Kennington Rd, London, SE11 6RE (020-7735-6633; *fax:* 020-7582-7022)
Email: msgb1906@msgb.co.uk
Internet: http://www.msgb.co.uk/

Gov Body: Council of the Soc *Chief:* Exec Chairman: Mr Robert A. Smith BA, OStJ
Membs: 1600 indivs
Activs: Aims to promote the study of English history and traditions, especially the monarchy and British parliamentary institutions and to promote the preservation of manorial records. Activities include the sale of Manorial Lordships and Feudal Baronies in British Isles; publishing; social events; historical research.
Pubns: Annual Bulletin; periodic pubns: Royal Armada (1988); The House of Lords (1993); The House of Commons (1996); The Monarchy (1997)

O277 ♀

Maritime Information Association [MIA]

c/o Mr Stephen Grace, Southampton Ref Lib, Civic Centre, Southampton, SI15 3HN (023-8083-2205; *fax:* 023-8033-6305)
Email: stephen.grace@libraries.southampton. gov.uk

Chief: Chair: Mr Michael Naxton *Other Snr Offcrs:* Sec: Mr Stephen Grace, as above; Membership Sec: Ms Desma Goddard (dgoddard@crtech.demon.co.uk)
Memb Req: open to libns & info workers & others working or having an interest in the maritime world; contact Membership Sec for details
Activs: Promotes contact and co-operation between marine and maritime librarians and information workers. Aims to develop an body of professional expertise relevant to the literature and other information sources in maritime activities. Organises an annual conference, with lectures and speakers, and arranges visits to places and events of maritime interest.

Pubns: Newsletter (4 pa); Maritime Info: A Guide to Libs & Sources of Info

O278 ♀

Merseyside Archives Liaison Group

c/o Merseyside Record Office, Central Lib, William Brown St, Liverpool, L3 8EW (0151-233-5817)
Email: david.stoker@liverpool.gov.uk

Chief: Chairman: Mr David Stoker
Membs: 9 instns
Activs: Brings together archivists and local studies librarians in Merseyside, representing local government, business and academic archives. Activities include a series of projects to make archival resources on Merseyside more accessible.
Pubns: Archives on Merseyside (1992); Public Health on Merseyside: A Guide to Local Sources (1991); Edu on Merseyside: A Guide to Local Sources (1992); annual combined accessions lists for memb instns (1990-94); copies obtainable from Merseyside Record Office (small charge for pubns & for postage)

O279 ♀

Middle East Libraries Committee [MELCOM]

c/o Mr Peter Colvin, The Lib, School of Oriental and African Studies, Thornhaugh St, London, WC1H 0XG (020-7898-4152; *fax:* 020-7898-4159)
Email: pc7@soas.ac.uk
Internet: http://www.ex.ac.uk/MELCOM/

Chief: Chair: Mr Paul Auchterlonie, Exeter Univ Lib (j.p.c.auchterlonie@exeter.ac.uk) *Other Snr Offcrs:* Sec: Mr Peter Colvin, at above addr
Membs: 36 instns *Memb Req:* open to all those interested in the provision of info on the Middle East; no membership fee
Activs: To establish contacts between individuals in the UK concerned with collecting, organising and making available materials on the Middle East; to provide a forum for the exchange of information and ideas between institutions and persons in the UK involved in the foregoing activities; to facilitate and encourage the co-ordination of acquisitions of materials on and from the Middle East by UK libraries; to compile and publish bibliographical handbooks in the field of Middle Eastern studies; to encourage the proper use and cultivation of Middle Eastern bibliography as a tool of teaching and research and as a field of scholarly enquiry; organises twice yearly meetings and occasional conferences.
Pubns: Official Pubns on the Middle East: A Selective Guide to the Statistical Sources (£5.25); Union Catalogue of Persian Serials & Newspapers in British Libs (£20); Books from the Arab World: A Guide to Selection & Acquisition (£6.25); Middle Eastern Photographic Collns in the United Kingdom (£25); Introductory Guide to Middle Eastern & Islamic Bibliography (£9.50); Periodicals in Turkish & Turkic Langs: A Union List of Holdings in UK Libs (£20); The Intifada, The Palestinian Uprising in the West Bank & Gaza Strip: A Bibliography of Books & Articles 1987-1992 (£25); many others; all available through: Joppa Bks Ltd, 68 High Rd, Byfleet, Surrey, KT14 7QL (01392-336777; *fax:* 01392-348881; *email:* joppa@dial. pipex.com)

O280 ♀

Milton Keynes Learning City Libraries Network [MKLCLN]

c/o The Lib, The Open Univ, Walton Hall, Milton Keynes, Buckinghamshire, MK7 6AA (01908-653254; *fax:* 01908-653571)
Email: nwhitsed@open.ac.uk
Internet: http://www.mklclibraries.org/

Type: co-op *Chief:* Convenor: Ms Nicky Whitsed MSc, FCLIP, at above addr
Membs: public, univ, coll & health libs
Activs: Aims to encourage the use of all the libraries in the network by all the people who live, work or study in Milton Keynes; to improve public access to libraries and their facilities; to provide opportunities for comment and feedback for library users.

O281 ⛪ 🏛

MLA West Midlands: The Regional Council for Museums, Libraries and Archives

2nd Floor, Grosvenor House, 14 Bennetts Hill, Birmingham, B2 5RS (0121-631-5800; *fax:* 0121-631-5825)
Email: info@mlawestmidlands.org.uk
Internet: http://www.mlawestmidlands.org.uk/

Chief: Chief Exec: Ms Kathryn Gee (kathy.gee@ mlawestmidlands.org.uk) *Other Snr Offcrs:* Development Dir: Mr Geoff Warren; Development Mgr (Libs & learning): Ms Linda Saunders; Development Mgr (Museums & Access): Ms Lesley Ann Kerr; Development Mgr (Archvs & Knowledge Mgmt): Ms Heather Williamson
Membs: 22 instns
Activs: To provide strategic leadership and advocacy for museums, libraries and archives in the West Midlands.
Further Info: formed in Apr 2003 to replace The Libs Partnership – West Midlands (TLP-WM), The West Midlands Regional Archvs Council (WMRAC) & The West Midlands Regional Museums Council (WMRMC)

O282 ♀ 🏛

Museums Association [MA]

24 Calvin St, London, E1 6NW (020-7426-6970; *fax:* 020-7426-6961)
Email: info@museumsassociation.org
Internet: http://www.museumsassociation.org/

Gov Body: Council of the MA *Chief:* Dir: Mr Mark Taylor (mark@museumsassociation.org)
Membs: 4647 indivs; 611 instns; 246 corporate membs *Memb Req:* open to anyone involved in or interested in museums & galleries, incl full-time employees, volunteers, students & freelance workers; subscriptions vary according to indiv income or institutional exp
Activs: Independent professional body representing museums and galleries in the UK. Aims to improve professional standards through information and advice, and to raise awareness of key issues affecting museums; represents members on many other bodies and has strong links with other European museums organisations; maintains an active publishing and research programme and an extensive library of museological materials based at City University London; provides courses and training; awards the AMA, a formal professional qualification qualifying recipients for Associateship of the Museums Association.
Pubns: Museums Journal (monthly, free to membs); Museums & Galleries Yearbook (2 vols, £100); Museums Practice (3 pa, subscription £120); advisory bklets; many other pubns on museum work; discounts for membs

O283 ♀

Music Publishers Association [MPA]

3rd Floor, Strandgate, 18-20 York Bldgs, London, WC2N 6JU (020-7839-7779; *fax:* 020-7839-7776)
Email: info@mpaonline.org.uk
Internet: http://www.mpaonline.org.uk/

Chief: Chief Exec: Ms Sarah Faulder
Memb Req: music publishers in the UK
Activs: Promotes and protects the mutual interests of music publishers; provides information for good publishing practice; organises training events and seminars; produces the Catalogue of Printed Music on CD-ROM. The MPA also owns the Mechanical Copyright Protection Society Ltd (MCPS).
Pubns: Music Copyright Matters (4 pa, free)

O284 ♀

National Acquisitions Group [NAG]
12 Holm Oak Dr, Madeley, Crewe, Cheshire, CW3 9HR (*tel & fax:* 01782-750462)
Email: nag@psilink.co.uk
Internet: http://www.nag.org.uk/

Gov Body: Exec Cttee *Chief:* Chair: Mrs Jo Grocott (jo.grocott@staffordshire.gov.uk) *Other Snr Offcrs:* Sec: Mr Chris Hall (chris.hall@ corpoflondon.gov.uk); Treasurer: Mr Michael Fortune (michael.fortune@first-edition.co.uk); Administrator: Ms Diane Roberts, as above
Membs: 9 indivs; 475 instns *Memb Req:* open to all orgs involved in the acq process, incl libs & info providers, publishers, booksellers & lib systems suppl; subscription: £61 pa
Activs: Established in 1986, NAG is a broadly based organisation which stimulates, co-ordinates and publicises developments in acquisitions and the book trade. The membership includes individuals and organisations within publishing, bookselling and systems supply, as well as librarians from academic, public, national, government and special institutions. The group has two main aims: to bring together those concerned with library acquisitions as a whole or in part, to assist them in exchanging information and comment, and by so doing to promote understanding and good practice between them; to seek to influence other organisations and individuals to adopt its opinions and standards when promulgated.
Pubns: NAG Newsletter (quarterly, free to membs); Taking Stock (journal, 2 pa, May & Nov, free to membs, £20 pa to non-membs); Directory of Acquisitions Libns (membs £45, non-membs £55); Public Lib Stock Mgmt (membs £39, non-membs £43); Tendering for Lib Supply (membs £47.50, non-membs £52); The Value to Libs of Special Svcs provided by Lib Suppliers (membs £35, non-membs £39); Standards for Book Servicing (membs £21, non-membs £28)

O285 ♀ 📷

National Association of Aerial Photographic Libraries [NAPLIB]
Landsdown House, Breton Cl, Toftwood, East Dereham, Norfolk, NR19 1JH (01362-695835)
Email: dae@aerialarchaeology.freeserve.co.uk
Internet: http://www.naplib.org.uk/

Gov Body: Exec Cttee *Chief:* Chairman: Mr Christopher J. Going (chrisg@crworld.co.uk)
Other Snr Offcrs: Hon Sec: Mr Kevin McLaren (kevinm@rcahms.gov.uk)
Membs: 51 indivs; 27 instns
Activs: Aims to promote the use and preservation of collections of aerial photography; to increase public awareness of collections of aerial photo-graphy and to facilitate access to them; to encourage the exchange of ideas and expertise and, in particular, to develop appropriate indexing and storage procedures. Organises an annual conference and field trips.
Pubns: The Flyer (quarterly newsletter); NAPLIB Directory of Aerial Photographic Collns in the United Kingdom (2nd ed, £20 incl p&p); The Care and Preservation of Photographs: Recommend-ations for Good Practice (UK £5 incl p&p, overseas £5.50 incl p&p)

O286 ♀

National Association of Literature Development
PO Box 140, Ilkley, W Yorkshire, LS29 6RH (01943-872546)
Email: steve@nald.org
Internet: http://www.nald.org/

Type: prof *Chief:* Co-ordinator: Mr Steve Dearden
Membs: 184 indivs
Activs: A membership network organisation that was formed to provide literature development specialists with a forum for networking, information exchange and specialist training.

O287 🎓

National Cataloguing Unit for the Archives of Contemporary Scientists [NCUACS]
c/o The Lib, Univ of Bath, Claverton Down, Bath, BA2 7AY (01225-323522; *fax:* 01225-826229)
Email: ncuacs@bath.ac.uk
Internet: http://www.bath.ac.uk/Centres/NCUACS/

Gov Body: Advisory Cttee *Chief:* Dir: Mr Peter Harper BA, MA
Membs: 4 membs of staff
Activs: Successor to the Contemporary Scientific Archives Centre at Oxford, NCUACS was established in 1987 to locate, sort, index and catalogue the MS papers of distinguished contemporary scientists and engineers in Britain, including: correspondence, professional and technical documents such as laboratory notebooks, experimental drawings and calculations, lecture notes, engagement diaries and travel journals. The processed collections are then deposited in an appropriate national or university repository in accordance with the wishes of the donors.
Pubns: Progress Reports (2 pa, free); Lists of CSAC and NCUACS Catalogues; Guide to the Manuscript Papers of British Scientists Catalogued by the CSAC & NCUACS 1973-1993; Preserving Scientific Src Materials: A Guide for Owners (bklet)

O288 ♀

National Council on Archives [NCA]
c/o Ms Margaret Turner, 26 Cruise Rd, Sheffield, South Yorkshire, S11 7EF (0114-230-4772)
Email: turnermargaret@hotmail.com
Internet: http://nca.archives.org.uk/

Chief: Chairman: Mr Nicholas Kingsley, Gloucestershire Record Office *Other Snr Offcrs:* Sec: Ms Margaret Turner, as above; Vice-Chairman: Dr E. Hallam-Smith, Public Record Office (e-hallam-smith@pro.gov.uk); Policy & Development Offcr: Ms Katie Norgrove, Public Record Office (katie.norgrove@pro.gov.uk)
Membs: 16 instns
Branches & Groups: NATL ARCHVS NETWORK USER RSRCH GROUP (NANURG)
Activs: To provide a forum for the regular exchange of views between the major bodies and organisations concerned with archives; to bring matters of current concern in the field of archives to the attention of the public and government; to encourage public education in archive matters; to encourage the improved funding of repositories and to pursue the definition of standards for archive repositories; to examine current archive acquisition policies and to draw attention to such gaps or shortcomings as may be perceived; to encourage collaborative or regional initiatives to improve or advance the cause of archive services.

Pubns: Local Authorities Archive Svcs 1992 (HMSO, 1993); Archives: The Very Essence of Our Heritage (Phillimore, 1996); A Natl Archives Policy for the United Kingdom (1996); Archives On-line (1998); Natl Name Authority File (1998); Rules for the Construction of Personal, Corporate & Place Names (1997); An Introduction to Fundraising for Archives (1999); British Archives: The Way Forward (1999); Survey of Recruitment of Archivists, Conservators & Records Mgrs (2000); Annual Report (2000-01); Archives in the Regions: An Overview of the English Regional Archive Strategies (2002)

O289 🎓

National Council on Orientalist Library Resources [NCOLR]
c/o Dr Colin Baker, British Lib Oriental & India Office Collns, 96 Euston Rd, London, NW1 2DB (020-7412-7873; *fax:* 020-7412-7641)
Email: Colin.Baker@bl.uk
Internet: http://www.bodley.ox.ac.uk/users/gae/ NCOLR/NCOLRWEB.htm

Chief: Chairman: Mr Graham Shaw, Dir, Oriental & India Office Collns, British Lib (Graham.Shaw@ bl.uk) *Other Snr Offcrs:* Sec: Dr Colin Baker, as above
Membs: 110 indivs *Memb Req:* open to instns actively acquiring orientalist lib materials & other bodies & indivs interested in the aims of the org; no subscription fee
Activs: Aims to provide a general forum for librarians, archivists and scholars involved in the collection of library resources for Asian and Hebraic studies; to promote projects to improve access to these resources; to liase with and encourage co-operation between library groups concerned with particular regions of Asia, with a view to developing common policies on library and bibliographical matters, and to promote contacts with similar bodies overseas; organises an annual general meeting and conference.

O290 ♀

National Forum for Information Planning and Co-operation [NFIP]
c/o SINTO, The Learning Centre, Sheffield Hallam Univ, Collegiate Cres, Sheffield, South Yorkshire, S10 2BP (0114-225-5739)
Email: sinto@shu.ac.uk
Internet: http://www.bl.uk/concord/linc/nfip.html

Type: co-op *Chief:* Chair: Mr Carl Clayton, at above addr
Membs: 25 instns *Memb Req:* lib & info planning orgs in the UK & Ireland
Activs: Acts as a forum for organisations involved in the practical implementation of information planning. It actively promotes the Library and Information Plan (LIP) concept: intra-sectoral, cross-sectoral and cross-domain library and information planning on a geographical or subject basis at local, regional and national levels. It provides exchanges of experience, advice and support, and is an active contributor to the policy debate on the development of a national information plan.
Pubns: NFIP Directory of Membs

O291 ♀ 🎓

The National Literacy Trust [NLT]
Swire House, 59 Buckingham Gate, London, SW1E 6AJ (020-7828-2435; *fax:* 020-7931-9986)
Email: contact@literacytrust.org.uk
Internet: http://www.literacytrust.org.uk/

Type: educational charity *Chief:* Dir: Mr Neil McClelland ☛

National ▾ Open Organisations

(Natl Literacy Trust cont)

Activs: Aims to contribute to the creation of a society in which all can enjoy the appropriate skills, confidence and pleasures of literacy to support their educational, economic, social and cultural goals. Provides information and support, including an extensive web site; runs the National Reading Campaign and Reading is Fundamental (UK); promotes and facilitates literacy partnerships; organises courses, seminars and conferences for literacy practitioners and key policy makers; encourages and supports the involvement of the business sector in promoting literacy.
Pubns: Literacy Today (quarterly, £18 pa); The Natl Literacy Trust's Internatl Annotated Bibliography of Books on Literacy, by Ann Finlay & Jo Weinberger (eds)

O292
National Preservation Office
The British Lib, 96 Euston Rd, London, NW1 2DB (020-7412-7612; *fax:* 020-7412-7796)
Email: npo@bl.uk
Internet: http://www.bl.uk/services/preservation/national.html

Gov Body: Mgmt Cttee *Chief:* Dir: Dr Vanessa Marshall
Activs: Aims to provide an independent focus to ensure the preservation and continued accessibility of library and archival material in the UK and Ireland; to develop and co-ordinate a national preservation strategy, utilising both traditional and electronic media; to provide an information and referral service; to promote good practice through education and training; to co-ordinate and initiate research. The NPO also administers grants from the National Manuscripts Conservation Trust.
Pubns: NPO Journal (2 pa, £20 pa); other pubns incl: Preservation Guidance Leaflets (free); Natl Preservation Office Seminar Papers (£9.95 each); Preservation Training Pack (£60); Microforms in Libs: The Untapped Resource (£11.50); Guide to Preservation Microfilming (£25); Security in Academic and Rsrch Libs (£15); Natl Preservation Office Conference Reports Colln (£35); videos; posters; bookmarks; prices incl p&p

O293
Navy Records Society [NRS]
c/o Dr A.D. Lambert, King's Coll London, Dept of War Studies, Strand, London, WC2R 2LF
Internet: http://www.navyrecordssociety.com/

Gov Body: Council of the NRS *Chief:* Hon Sec: Dr A.D. Lambert PhD, FRHistS, as above
Membs: 700 indivs; 150 instns *Memb Req:* open to all those interested in the study of naval hist; subscription: £30 pa
Activs: Publication of Royal Naval historical and archival materials to provide a basis for the development of policy and doctrine; acts as pressure group and opinion former; promotes naval history as a professional historical discipline.
Pubns: over 130 vols published to date; 1-2 vols published pa (incl in membership fee); other vols in print can be ordered by membs from the Membership Sec (Mrs A. Gould, 5 Goodwood Cl, Midhurst, West Sussex, GU29 9JG); some of the most recent vols incl: Naval Admin 1715-1750, ed

by Prof D.A. Baugh; The Royal Navy in the Mediterranean 1915-1918, ed by Prof Paul G. Halpern; Anglo-American Naval Relations 1917-1919, ed by Dr Michael Simpson; British Naval Documents 1204-1960, ed by Prof J.B. Hattendorf et al; Samuel Pepys & The Second Dutch War, ed by R. Latham; The Royal Navy in the River Plate 1806-1807, ed by John D. Grainger

O294
The Network: Tackling Social Exclusion in Libraries, Museums, Archives and Galleries [SEAPN]
c/o Mr John Vincent, Wisteria Cottage, Nadderwatter, Exeter, Devon, EX4 2JQ (*tel & fax:* 01392-256045)
Email: john@nadder.org.uk
Internet: http://www.seapn.org.uk/

Type: co-op *Chief:* Networker: Mr John Vincent, as above
Membs: 12 indivs; 97 instns *Memb Req:* subscription: varies from £19.80 pa for indivs to £198 pa for lib authorities with population of 500000+
Activs: Promotes social inclusion in the provision of library, archive and museum services; acts as an information exchange on issues relating to social exclusion within these domains; organises training courses and conferences; works with Resource (see **O328**) and other agencies to develop strategies to tackle social exclusion.
Pubns: Newsletter (monthly); Public Lib Svcs for Refugees & Asylum Seekers: The Results of the "Words Without Frontiers" Survey (2002, free); Social & Racial Exclusion Handbook for Libs, Archvs, Museums & Galleries (2001, £7.50 to membs, £10 to non-membs)

O295
The Newspaper Society
Bloomsbury House, 74-77 Gt Russell St, London, WC1B 3DA (020-7636-7014; *fax:* 020-7631-5119)
Email: ns@newspapersoc.org.uk
Internet: http://www.newspapersoc.org.uk/

Gov Body: Council *Chief:* Chief Exec: Mr David Newell (david_newell@newspapersoc.org.uk)
Membs: 1300+ regional & local newspapers
Memb Req: open to newspaper companies within the UK; subscription: £700 pa minimum
Activs: The Society represents and promotes the interests of Britain's regional press, nationally and in Europe. It provides advice on advertising control, legal and technical matters, and careers and training. It promotes the medium to national advertisers and maintains an extensive media and marketing database of the industry.
Pubns: NS News (newsletter, monthly); Headlines (magazine, 6 pa); Annual Review & Accounts; numerous reports & guides

O296
NEWSPLAN Panel
c/o Mr Edmund King, British Lib Newspaper Lib, Colindale Ave, London, NW9 5HE (020-7412-7362; *fax:* 020-7412-7386)
Email: ed.king@bl.uk
Internet: http://www.bl.uk/concord/linc/newsplan.html

Type: co-op *Chief:* Sec: Mr Edmund King, as above
Activs: Co-operative programme for the micro-filming and preservation of local newspapers and for making them accessible to users. It involves public, academic and national libraries, archives, and the newspaper industry.
Pubns: NEWSPLAN News

O297
NHS Library and Knowledge Development Network [NHS LKDN]
(formerly NHS Regional Libns Group)
c/o Lib & Knowledge Svcs Team, Edu Centre, Royal Surrey County Hosp, Egerton Rd, Guildford, Surrey, GU2 5XX (01483-464082; *fax:* 01483-455888)
Internet: http://www.lkdn.nhs.uk/

Chief: Chair: Mrs Tina Wilson, Knowledge Svcs Development Mgr, Kent, Surrey & Sussex Workforce Development Confederation (twilson@ royalsurrey.nhs.uk) *Other Snr Offcrs:* Chair Elect: Ms Sharon Dobbins, Knowledge Svcs Mgr, Co Durham & Tees Valley Workforce Development Confederation (library.alliance@virgin.net)
Memb Req: membs incl Library/Knowledge Svc representatives from each of the English Workforce Development Confederations, Northern Ireland, Scotland & Wales, plus partners in health & social care knowledge svcs and initiatives
Activs: Aims to support, work, plan and campaign for the excellence of healthcare through evidence-based practice and lifelong learning, by developing and providing high quality knowledge, information and library services. LKDN replaces the former Regional Librarians Group (RLG) in order to reflect the new NHS structures introduced by 'Shifting the Balance of Power'.
Pubns: various surveys & reports

O298
North American Studies Group [NASG]
c/o Dr Kevin Halliwell, Natl Lib of Scotland, George IV Bridge, Edinburgh, EH1 1EW (0131-226-4531)
Email: k.halliwell@nls.uk
Internet: http://scurl.ac.uk/about/nasg/nasg.html

Gov Body: affiliate group of the Scottish Confederation of Univ & Rsrch Libs (see **O338**) *Chief:* Convenor: Dr Tony Parker, Univ of Dundee (a.w.parker@dundee.ac.uk) *Other Snr Offcrs:* Sec: Dr Kevin Halliwell, as above
Membs: Scottish univ libs with significant holdings in North American Studies, the Natl Lib of Scotland & the Mitchell Lib, Glasgow
Activs: Promotes the research resources available on North America in Scottish libraries, especially through the use of new technology and the co-ordination of acquisition and the sharing of resources; communicates and liaises with other groups in the field; maintains a Union List of US and Canadian Newspapers in Scottish Libraries and is engaged in developing an online Bibliography of Scottish Emigration to North America. Meets three or four times a year.

O299
North East Museums, Libraries and Archives Council [NEMLAC]
House of Recovery, Bath Ln, Newcastle upon Tyne, NE4 5SQ (0191-222-1661; *fax:* 0191-261-4725)
Email: nemlac@nemlac.co.uk
Internet: http://www.nemlac.co.uk/

Type: regional agency *Gov Body:* funded by Resource (see **O328**) *Chief:* Chief Exec: Ms Sue Underwood (sue.underwood@nemlac.co.uk)
Other Snr Offcrs: Dep Chief Exec: Ms Penny Wilkinson (penny.wilkinson@nemlac.co.uk)
Membs: 87 instns
Activs: NEMLAC is the regional strategic body and development agency for museum, library and archive organisations in the North East region of England. Promotes socially inclusive services and wider access to resources; encourages high professional and operational standards in

collections management and other areas; provides advice on funding and assists members to prepare funding applications; hosts training sessions.

O300 North East Regional Archive Council [NERAC]

c/o Ms Liz Rees, Tyne & Wear Archv Svc, Blandford House, Blandford Sq, Newcastle upon Tyne, NE1 4JA (0191-232-6789; *fax:* 0191-230-2614)
Email: lizrees@gateshead.gov.uk
Internet: http://nca.archives.org.uk/racne.htm

Type: regional strategic body *Chief:* Chair: Ms Liz Rees, as above
Membs: 26 nominees of represented bodies
Activs: Co-ordinating and strategic body aiming to promote the advancement of archives in the North East of England. Acts in co-operation with NEMLAC (see **O299**).
Pubns: An Archive Strategy for the North East of England (2001, free); copies are available online at http://www.thenortheast.com/archives/ and http://www.nemlac.co.uk/

O301 North West Academic Libraries [NoWAL]

(formerly Consortium of Academic Libs in Manchester)
Minshull House, Manchester Metropolitan Univ, 47-49 Chorlton St, Manchester, M1 3EU (0161-247-6673; *fax:* 0161-247-6846)
Email: P.Wynne@mmu.ac.uk
Internet: http://www.calim.ac.uk/

Gov Body: NoWAL Board *Chief:* Sec: Mr Peter Wynne, addr as above *Other Snr Offcrs:* Support Offcr: Mrs Gil Young (g.young@mmu.ac.uk)
Membs: 8 instns *Memb Req:* univ & other academic libs in North West England
Branches & Groups: OPERATIONS GROUP; STAFF TRAINING & DEVELOPMENT GROUP; ACCESS & BORROWING GROUP; EQUAL OPPORTUNITIES GROUP; contact via NoWAL Office at above addr
Activs: Aims to enhance the delivery of library services to the Higher Education community in the North West Region by: developing collaborative and innovative approaches to the delivery of library services and processes; sharing information and experience; pursuing collaborative procurement of products and services; engaging in staff training and development; influencing policy in professional/government areas; liaising as appropriate with regional bodies; the promotion of cross-domain and cross-sectoral collaboration.

O302 North West Museums, Libraries and Archives Council [NWMLAC]

Griffin Lodge, Cavendish Pl, Blackburn, Lancashire, BB2 2PN (01254-670211; *fax:* 01254-681995)
Email: info@nwmlac.org.uk
Internet: http://www.nwmlac.org.uk/

Type: strategic agency *Chief:* Chief Exec: Ms Clare Connor (clare.connor@nwmlac.org.uk)
Activs: Regional Agency for museums, archives and libraries in the North West of England. Aims to advance the education of the public and to further the establishment, maintenance, operation and development of museums, art galleries, libraries and archives, and related services and activities. Works to ensure that: museums, archives and libraries are recognised within and effectively integrated into local regional social, cultural and

economic frameworks; they offer improved levels of, and increased access to, services through implementation of agreed standards; user and learning needs are mapped, analysed and worked towards on a regional basis; a strengthened and sustainable regional funding base is established.

O303 North West Regional Archive Council [NWRAC]

c/o NWMLAC, Griffin Lodge, Cavendish Pl, Blackburn, Lancashire, BB2 2PN (01254-670211; *fax:* 01254-681995)
Email: janice.taylor@nwmlac.org.uk
Internet: http://www.northwestarchives.org.uk/

Chief: Chair: Mr Jim Grisenthwaite (jim.grisenthwaite@cumbriacc.gov.uk) *Other Snr Offcrs:* Regional Archv Development Offcr: Ms Janice Taylor, as above
Activs: Acts as a co-ordinating strategic body for the archive community for Cumbria, Lancashire, Merseyside, Greater Manchester and Cheshire. Aims to improve the provision of services and enhance the experience of archive users throughout the North West; organises various projects and surveys towards this end.

O304 Northamptonshire Association for Local History

c/o Ms Diana Dalton, 143 Clophill Rd, Maulden, Bedfordshire, MK45 2AF
Email: diana.dalton@virgin.net
Internet: http://www.northants-history.org.uk/

Chief: Hon Sec: Ms Diana Dalton
Memb Req: open to Northamptonshire local hist socs & other orgs or indivs with allied interests; subscription: £10 pa
Activs: Promotes and supports interest in local history and related subjects in Northamptonshire; provides a forum for the encouragement of local history societies, and lines of communication and information for individual members; provides advice and support for work and activities related to local history in the county. Organises two meetings a year, an AGM held at Northampton Record Office in May and an Autumn History Day in October, and maintains a register of Northamptonshire local history resources.
Pubns: Hindsight – Northamptonshire Local Hist Magazine (2 pa, free to membs, £3.50 per issue to non-membs)

O305 Northamptonshire Record Society

c/o Wootton Hall Pk, Northampton, NN4 8BQ (01604-762297)

Gov Body: Council of the Soc *Chief:* Sec: Ms Leslie C. Skelton MA
Membs: c1000 indivs; 10 instns
Activs: Promotes the study and publication of documents relating to the history of Northamptonshire; organises two lectures per year in the Spring and Autumn; publishes a regular journal; maintains a library covering most aspects of county life.
Pubns: Northamptonshire Past & Present (1 pa); 40 vols have been printed since inception

O306 Northern Chief Librarians Group [NCL]

c/o Mrs Jane Hall, Sunderland City Lib & Arts Centre, Fawcett St, Sunderland, Tyne & Wear, SR1 1RE (0191-514-1235)
Email: jane.f.hall@edcom.sunderland.gov.uk

Type: prof *Chief:* Sec: Mrs Jane Hall, as above
Memb Req: chief lib offcrs in local authorities in the North of England
Branches & Groups: various specialist sub-groups, incl: LOCAL HIST LIBNS; PEOPLE'S NETWORK ICT CONTENT GROUP
Activs: Facilitates and promotes co-operative ventures between public library authorities in the region; provides training; manages reading schemes and the Northern Children's Book Festival.

O307 Nottinghamshire Local History Association [NLHA]

c/o Mr D. Walker, Cratley, Back Ln, Eakring, Newark, Nottinghamshire, NG22 0DJ
Email: dwalker@cratley.freeserve.co.uk
Internet: http://www.local-history.co.uk/nlha/

Gov Body: Exec Cttee & the Trustees *Chief:* contact the Membership Sec: Mr D. Walker
Membs: 160 indivs; 52 local hist socs & groups
Memb Req: open to all those interested in the hist of Nottinghamshire; subscription: £6 pa
Activs: The designated umbrella organisation for the association of groups and societies interested in the history of the County of Nottinghamshire. Co-ordinates and disseminates information and organises day schools (seminars/lectures open to members and non-members alike).
Pubns: Nottinghamshire Historian (2 pa, £2.50 each)

O308 Office of the Information Commissioner

(formerly Office of the Data Protection Commissioner)
Wycliffe House, Water Ln, Wilmslow, Cheshire, SK9 5AF (01625-545700; *fax:* 01625-524510)
Email: data@dataprotection.gov.uk
Internet: http://www.dataprotection.gov.uk/

Chief: Info Commissioner: Mr Richard Thomas
Activs: The Information Commissioner enforces and oversees the Data Protection Act 1998 and the Freedom of Information Act 2000. The Commissioner is a UK independent supervisory authority reporting directly to the UK Parliament and has an international role as well as a national one. In the UK the Commissioner has a range of duties including the promotion of good information handling and the encouragement of codes of practice for data controllers, that is, anyone who decides how and why personal data (information about identifiable, living individuals) are processed.
Pubns: various codes of practice, guides, reports, tribunal decisions, policy documents & other papers; see web site for further details

O309 Open and Distance Learning Quality Council [ODLQC]

16 Park Cres, London, W1B 1AH (020-7612-7090; *fax:* 020-7612-7092)
Email: info@odlqc.org.uk
Internet: http://www.odlqc.org.uk/

Chief: Chief Exec: Dr David Morley
Membs: c50 instns
Activs: Independent body working to enhance quality in education and training, and to protect the interests of learners, through the accreditation of open and distance learning providers.
Pubns: newsletter (quarterly); Courses Offered by Accredited Providers (1 pa); A Buyer's Guide to Distance Learning

Opening ▼ Resource Organisations

O310 🔑 ✐
Opening the Book Ltd
181 Carleton Rd, Pontefract, W Yorkshire, WF8 3NH (01977-602188/988; *fax:* 01977-690621)
Email: info@openingthebook.com
Internet: http://www.openingthebook.com/

Chief: Dir: Ms Rachel Van Riel (rachel@openingthebook.com) *Other Snr Offcrs:* Administrator: Ms Jill Brook (jill@openingthebook.com)
Activs: Creates resources for readers and provides courses, training and consultancy services to all the professions who work with readers – librarians, booksellers, publishers, arts organisations and government departments.

O311 🔑 🎓
Oral History Society
British Lib Sound Archv, 96 Euston Rd, London, NW1 2DB (020-7412-7405; *fax:* 020-7412-7441)
Email: rob.perks@bl.uk
Internet: http://www.oralhistory.org.uk/

Type: prof *Chief:* Sec: Dr Robert Perks, at above addr
Membs: 400 indivs; 600 instns
Branches & Groups: ORAL HIST SOC NETWORK (over 40 local representatives throughout the UK), see web site for details
Activs: National and international organisation dedicated to the collection and preservation of oral history. Offers practical advice and support those interested in recording oral history material; organises conferences.
Pubns: Oral History Journal (2 pa, £5); other pubns incl: Oral Hist: Talking About the Past; Talking in Class: Oral History & the Natl Curriculum; Copyright, Ethics & Oral History

O312 🔑 🎓
Oxford Bibliographical Society
c/o Dr Julia Walworth, Merton Coll, Merton St, Oxford, OX1 4JD
Email: secretary@oxbibsoc.org.uk
Internet: http://www.oxbibsoc.org.uk/

Chief: Pres: Prof Nigel Palmer, St Edmund Hall *Other Snr Offcrs:* Hon Sec: Dr Julia Walworth, as above; Hon Treasurer: Mr David Thomas, Taylor Instn Lib (treasurer@oxbibsoc.org.uk)
Memb Req: open to all those interested in MSS, printed bks & the arts & trades connected with them; subscription: £20 pa (students £10)
Activs: Founded in 1922 to encourage bibliographic research. Organises lectures and visits; holds an Annual General Meeting.
Pubns: numerous, incl: The Buildwas Books: Book Production, Acquisition & Use at an English Cistercian Monastery 1165-c1400 (1997); Oxford Bookbinding 1500-1640 (2000 for 1998-99); Fragments of Medieval Manuscripts (reprint, 2003); The Library of Anthony Wood (2002)

O313 🔑 🎓
Oxfordshire Local History Association [OLHA]
12 Meadow View, Witney, Oxfordshire, OX28 3TY (01993-778345)

Type: voluntary assoc *Chief:* Joint Secretaries: Mr John Davey & Mrs Janet Davey, at above addr
Membs: 150 indivs; 63 local hist socs instns
Memb Req: open to anyone interested in the hist of Oxfordshire; subscription: £9 pa
Activs: Promotes the study of local history in Oxfordshire; encourages links between amateur local historians and with academic and professional bodies involved in local history; organises twice-yearly meetings or day schools.
Pubns: Newsletter (4 pa, free to membs); Oxfordshire Local Hist (2 pa, free to membs); back issues available on application to Newsletter Editor

O314 🔑 🎓
Oxfordshire Record Society
c/o Bodleian Lib, Oxford, OX1 3BG (01865-277164; *fax:* 01865-277182)

Gov Body: Council *Chief:* Hon Sec: Mr Steven Tomlinson
Membs: 220 indivs; 140 instns
Activs: Publication of documents relating to the history of Oxfordshire; holds an Annual General Meeting.
Pubns: recent vols incl: Woodstock Chamberlain's Accounts; Oxfordshire & North Berkshire Protestation Returns & Tax Assessments 1641-42; Oxfordshire Muster Rolls 1538-42; Index to the Probate Records of Oxfordshire 1733-1857; Brightwell Parish Diaries 1774-1892

O315 🔑
Parliamentary and Political Parties Archive Group [PPPAG]
c/o Mr Stephen Bird, Labour Hist Archvs & Study Centre, 103 Princess St, Manchester, M1 6DD (0161-228-7212; *fax:* 0161-237-5965)
Email: sbird@fs1.li.man.ac.uk
Internet: http://www.bodley.ox.ac.uk/pppag.htm

Type: prof *Chief:* Sec: Mr Stephen Bird, as above
Memb Req: open to those working in the admin & care of party political & parliamentary archvs & records
Branches & Groups: affiliated to the SOC OF ARCHIVISTS, SPECIALIST REPOSITORIES GROUP (see O369)
Activs: Promotes professional co-operation and communication between the archivists and archives holding papers of political parties and of parliaments; encourages standardised practice between such specialist repositories; acts as a forum through which knowledge and concerns can be shared; acts to raise the identity of political collections both nationally and internationally; holds two meetings a year.

O316 🔑 ✐
Periodical Publishers Association [PPA]
Queens House, 28 Kingsway, London, WC2B 6JR (020-7404-4166; *fax:* 020-7404-4167)
Email: info1@ppa.co.uk
Internet: http://www.ppa.co.uk/

Chief: Chief Exec: Mr Ian Locks *Other Snr Offcrs:* Company Sec: Mr Brian Williamson (brian.williamson@ppa.co.uk)
Membs: 400 instns *Memb Req:* open to magazine & periodical publishers & their suppl in the UK; subscription: publishers £720+VAT or higher based on company turnover; suppl £2250+VAT; an initial application fee is also charged
Branches & Groups: PPA SCOTLAND, Exec Sec: Ms Carolyn Roulston (01620-895195; *email:* cazza@globalnet.co.uk); PPA IRELAND, Exec Sec: Ms Grace Aungier (00-353-1-668-2056; *email:* gaungier@indigo.ie)

Activs: To promote and protect the interests of magazine publishing; maintains a small members-only library. The PPA umbrella also includes the Periodical Training Council (PTC) and the Association of Publishing Agencies (APA).
Pubns: wide range of pubns on magazine publishing-related topics; list available from the PPA

O317 🔑 🎓
Pipe Roll Society
c/o Dr D. Crook, Public Record Office, Kew, Richmond, Surrey, TW9 4DU

Gov Body: Council *Chief:* Pres: Prof Sir James Holt *Other Snr Offcrs:* Sec: Dr D. Crook, as above
Membs: 200 indivs; 100 instns
Activs: Aims to enlarge public knowledge of medieval English History by the publication of Pipe Rolls and the associated records of medieval English government and of other manuscripts of national importance prior to the year 1250.
Pubns: 90 vols issued since 1884 to subscribers; prices available on application

O318 🔑 ✐
The Planning Exchange (Idox Information Services)
Tontine House, 8 Gordon St, Glasgow, G1 3PL (0141-574-1900; *fax:* 0141-248-8277)
Email: iv@i-documentsystems.com
Internet: http://www.planex.co.uk/

Chief: Managing Dir: Mr Tony Burton OBE *Other Snr Offcrs:* Info Svcs Mgr: Ms Christine Johnston (christine.johnston@i-documentsystems.com)
Membs: 286 instns *Memb Req:* by annual subscription
Activs: Information service which includes current awareness, enquiries and searches, and document supply on all topics relating to economic development, planning, housing, environment, transport, leisure, tourism, education, training and social work. Organises seminars and conferences on the above subjects and undertakes consultancy work.
Pubns: Info Svc Bulletin (weekly, membs only); Scottish Planning & Environmental Law (6 pa, £110 pa); Economic Development Today (monthly, £130 pa, £140 to non-membs); Journal of Lifelong Learning Initiatives (6 pa, £75 pa); Housing Info Digest (monthly, £65); Urban Regeneration in Britain Directory of Contacts 2002 (£50); Scottish Planning Appeal Decisions (online databases, £500+VAT pa); Briefing Papers (occasional series); The Planning Exchange also maintains 2 web-based info networks, one on regeneration (http://www.regen.net/), and one on Lifelong Learning (http://www.life-learning.net/)
See also S723

O319 🔑
Private Libraries Association [PLA]
c/o Mr James Brown, 49 Hamilton Park West, London, N5 1AE (020-7503-9827)
Email: jb@illuminata.co.uk
Internet: http://www.the-old-school.demon.co.uk/pla.htm

Chief: Hon Sec: Mr James Brown, as above
Membs: 800 indivs; 200 instns *Memb Req:* open to anyone interested in bk collecting; subscription: £25 pa, student rates available
Activs: An international society of book collectors. It aims to promote the awareness of the benefits of book ownership, and the study of books and their production. It promotes works concerned with these aims and arranges lectures which are open to non-members.

Pubns: The Private Lib (quarterly); Newsletter & Exchange List (quarterly); Private Press Books (annual); Membs' Handbook; Membs' vols, on some specialised aspect of bibliophily (every year or so); all free to membs (some copies also for sale to non-membs); previously published vols also available (discounts for membs)
Further Info: PLA is an Org in Liaison with CILIP (see **O110**)

O320 🏛️ 🔔

Public Lending Right [PLR]
Richard House, Sorbonne Cl, Stockton-on-Tees, TS17 6DA (01642-604699; *fax:* 01642-615641)
Email: corporateservices@plr.uk.com
Internet: http://www.plr.uk.com/

Chief: Registrar: Dr James Parker (jim.parker@plr.uk.com)
Activs: Government body making annual payments to authors on basis of loans of their books from public libraries; payments are calculated on the basis of loans data from a representative sample of UK libraries which is changed each year.
Pubns: Report on the Public Lending Right Scheme (annual, £2.80); Whose Loan is it Anyway?: Essays in Celebration of PLR's 20th Anniversary (£4.50); both available from PLR office

O321 🔑 ☕🎨

Publishers Association [PA]
29b Montague St, London, WC1B 5BH (020-7691-9191; *fax:* 020-7691-9199)
Email: mail@publishers.org.uk
Internet: http://www.publishers.org.uk/

Type: trade assoc **Gov Body:** PA Council **Chief:** Chief Exec: Mr Ronnie Williams
Membs: 180 instns **Memb Req:** open to bona fide publishers operating within the UK; subscription rates are based on company turnover, varying from £250 pa to £31505 pa upwards
Branches & Groups: Main Divisional Councils: BK DEVELOPMENT COUNCIL INTERNATL (BDCI); COUNCIL OF ACADEMIC & PROF PUBLISHERS (CAPP); EDUCATIONAL PUBLISHERS COUNCIL (EPC); GENL BKS COUNCIL (GBC); ELEC PUBLISHERS FORUM (EPF)
Activs: Acts as a focal point for all book, journal and electronic publishers in the UK, formulates policy and campaigns to ensure a secure trading environment for the industry. Provides information and advice to members; assists companies exhibiting at trade fairs; organises educational exhibitions, overseas trade delegations and seminars; promotes trade initiatives such as World Book Day.
Pubns: Book Trade Yearbook; How to Assess Your School's Book Needs (free); School Book Buying Survey (free to membs, else £95); EPC Statistics (4 pa, free); Books for a Better Edu (free); many others, contact the PA for a full list

O322 🔑

Publishers Licensing Society Ltd [PLS]
37-41 Gower St, London, WC1E 6HH (020-7299-7730; *fax:* 020-7299-7780)
Internet: http://www.pls.org.uk/

Gov Body: Publishers Assoc (see **O321**), the Periodical Publishers Assoc (see **O316**) & the Assoc of Learned & Prof Soc Publishers (see **O41**)
Chief: Chairman: Mr Robert Kiernan **Other Snr Offcrs:** Chief Exec: Mr Jens Bammel
Membs: 1600+ publishers
Memb Req: no subscription (administrative costs deducted from licence income)

Activs: Exists to protect the interests of publishers on copyright issues, to provide collective licensing arrangements on behalf of its members, and to ensure that fees generated by those licenses are distributed fairly. It also acts to promote the understanding of publishing and the role of collective licensing. With the Authors' Licensing and Collecting Society (see **O50**), it administers the Copyright Licensing Agency (see **O174**).
Pubns: Newsletter

O323 🎓

Queen's University of Belfast, School of Management and Economics
25 Univ Sq, Belfast, Northern Ireland, BT7 1NN (028-9033-5010; *fax:* 028-9033-5156)
Email: sme@qub.ac.uk
Internet: http://www.qub.ac.uk/mgt/

Gov Body: Queen's Univ of Belfast (see also **S139**) **Chief:** Head of School: Mr James Bradley
Other Snr Offcrs: Professor of Mgmt & Info Systems: Prof George Philip
Membs: 24 staff
Activs: Undergraduate and postgraduate teaching and research in management, accounting, finance, economics and information management.

O324 🔑

The Reading Agency for Libraries Ltd [TRA]
PO Box 96, St Albans, Hertfordshire, AL1 3WP (0871-750-1200; *fax:* 0871-750-1201)
Email: info@readingagency.org.uk
Internet: http://www.readingagency.org.uk/

Type: lib development agency **Gov Body:** funded by the Arts Council (see **S997**), Southern & South East Arts & CILIP (see **O110**) **Chief:** Dir: Ms Miranda McKearney **Other Snr Offcrs:** Head of resources: Ms Penny Shapland (penny.shapland@readingagency.org.uk)
Activs: Library and reader development organisation aiming to inspire and support libraries in creating the best access to reading for children, young people and adults. Develops pilot models for working, national programmes and partnerships; provides advocacy, research and training; works closely with national library networks and organisations to achieve these aims.
Pubns: rsrch reports

O325 🔑 🎓

Record Society of Lancashire and Cheshire
c/o Dept of Hist, Liverpool Hope Univ, Liverpool, L16 9JD (0151-291-3115)
Email: rslc@lineone.net
Internet: http://www.gmcro.co.uk/guides/record_society/record_society.htm

Other Snr Offcrs: Dr Fiona Pogson, at above addr; Mrs Maureen Barber, at above email
Memb Req: subscription: indiv £15 pa (£20 overseas), instns £20 pa (£25 overseas)
Activs: Transcribes and publishes original documents relating to the counties of Lancashire and Cheshire; aims to publish a volume per year.
Pubns: contact Soc for details of available vols

O326 🔑

Records Management Society of Great Britain [RMS]
Woodside, Coleheath Bottom, Speen, Princes Risborough, Buckinghamshire, HP27 0SZ (01494-488599; *fax:* 01494-488590)
Email: rms@rms-gb.org.uk
Internet: http://www.rms-gb.org.uk/

Type: prof **Chief:** Chairman: Ms Ceri Hughes (Ceri.Hughes@KPMG.co.uk) **Other Snr Offcrs:** Exec Sec: Mr Alan Masters (am@instant-library.com); Administrative Sec: Mrs Jude Awdry, email as above
Membs: 550 indivs; 120 instns **Memb Req:** open to those working in or interested in the fields of records & info mgmt; indiv membership: £60 pa; corporate membership: £250 pa; student membership: £12 pa (full-time students only); retired membership: £30 pa
Branches & Groups: LOCAL GOVT GROUP, contact Ms Samantha Ryan (samantha.ryan@staffordshire.gov.uk); LONDON CIRCLE, contact Ms Ceri Hughes, as above; SPECIAL INTEREST GROUP ON LEGAL RECORDS, contact Ms Susan Mansfield (susan.s.mansfield@si.shell.com)
Activs: Brings together those interested in all aspects of records management; promotes the highest professional standards; holds regular meetings and seminars; organises training programmes.
Pubns: Records Mgmt Bulletin (bi-monthly, free to membs)

O327 🔑 🙏

Religious Archivists Group [RAG]
c/o Ms Sarah Duffield, Natl Soc Archivist, C of E Record Centre, 15 Galleywall Rd, South Bermondsey, London, SE16 3PB (020-7898-1033)
Email: sarah.duffield@c-of-e.org.uk

Type: prof **Chief:** contact: Mr Ian Wakeling, Children's Soc Records Centre or Ms Sarah Duffield, as above
Memb Req: open to archivists, libns & others working in or interested in religious archvs in the UK; no subscription
Branches & Groups: affiliated to the SOC OF ARCHIVISTS, SPECIALIST REPOSITORIES GROUP (see **O369**)
Activs: An informal group bringing together those interested in the administration and care of religious records of all faiths; provides a forum for the exchange of views and expertise; organises an annual conference and maintains a group mailing list.

O328 🏛️ 🎓 🏛️

Resource: Council for Museums, Archives and Libraries
16 Queen Anne's Gate, London, SW1H 9AA (020-7273-1444; *fax:* 020-7273-1404)
Email: info@resource.gov.uk
Internet: http://www.resource.gov.uk/

Chief: Acting Chief Exec: Mr Chris Batt (chris.batt@resource.gov.uk) **Other Snr Offcrs:** Dir of Strategy & Planning: Mr Stuart Davies (stuart.davies@resource.gov.uk); Dir of Libs & Info Soc Team: Mr Chris Batt, as above; Dir of Learning & Access: Ms Sue Wilkinson (sue.wilkinson@resource.gov.uk)
Activs: Strategic agency working with museums, libraries and archives across the UK. It aims to providing strategic leadership and act as an advocate for the sector, to promote innovation and change, to encourage the development of accessible and inclusive collections, and to develop the organisational and funding infra-structure that will support the sector's future development.
Pubns: Resource News (4 pa); Manifesto; numerous reports; Resource also maintains a backlist of the pubns of its predecessor orgs: the Museums & Galleries Commission (MGC) & the Lib & Info Commission (LIC)

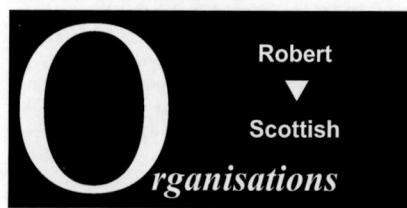

Organisations

Robert ▼ Scottish

O329 🎓

The Robert Gordon University, Department of Information Management

Aberdeen Business School, Garthdee Rd, Aberdeen, AB10 7QE (01224-263901; fax: 01224-263553)
Email: aberdeen.business.school@rgu.ac.uk
Internet: http://www.rgu.ac.uk/abs/

Gov Body: Robert Gordon Univ (see **S12**) *Chief:* Associate Head of Dept: Dr Robert Newton (r.newton@rgu.ac.uk) *Other Snr Offcrs:* Rsrch Co-ordinator: Prof Dorothy Williams (d.williams@ rgu.ac.uk)
Membs: 40+ staff; 480+ students
Activs: Education, training, research and consultancy in information and libraries studies and related disciplines.

O330 🔑 🎓

Royal Society of Literature [RSL]

Somerset House, Strand, London, WC2R 0RN (020-7845-4676; fax: 020-7845-4679)
Email: info@rslit.org
Internet: http://www.rslit.org/

Chief: Chairman of Council: Mr Ronald Harwood CBE *Other Snr Offcrs:* Sec: Ms Maggie Fergusson
Membs: 880 indivs; 10 instns *Memb Req:* open to all those with an interest in lit; subscription: £30 pa
Activs: Aims to sustain and encourage the best in English letters, whether traditional or experimental, and to promote a wider appreciation of literature; organises monthly lectures, discussions and readings; awards 3 annual prizes – the W.H. Heinemann Award, the Winifred Holtby Memorial Prize (for regional fiction) and the V.S. Pritchett Memorial Prize (for unpublished short stories); runs a writers' retreat. The Society is also empowered to confer the honour of Companion of Literature on writers of conspicuous attainment.
Pubns: The Royal Soc of Lit: A Portrait (2000, £7, available from the RSL)

O331 🔑 🎓

Rutland Local History and Record Society [RLHRS]

c/o Rutland County Museum, Catmos St, Oakham, Rutland, LE15 6HW (01572-758440)
Internet: http://www.rutnet.co.uk/rlhrs/

Gov Body: Exec Cttee *Chief:* Chairman: Mrs Auriol Thomson *Other Snr Offcrs:* Hon Sec: Mrs Sue Howlett (sue@suehowlett.freeserve.co.uk); Hon Editor: Mr Tim Clough
Membs: 224 indivs; 40 instns *Memb Req:* open to those interested in the local & family hist of Rutland; indivs £7 pa, families £8 pa, instns £8 pa; overseas membs add £1 to cover addl postage
Branches & Groups: ARCHAEO GROUP, contact: Mrs Kate Don, 2 Cordle Way, Market Overton, Oakham, Rutland, LE15 7PU
Activs: Promotion of history and archaeology of Rutland through research and publication; organises lectures and excursions.

Pubns: Rutland Record (1 pa); Rutland Record Series (various prices); Rsrch Reports; Occasional Pubns; for further details contact the Hon Editor at the above addr

O332 🔑

Saffron Walden Archive Society [SWAS]

c/o Mr Sean Brady, 16 Lambert Cross, Saffron Walden, Essex (0199-527212)
Email: sean.brady1@ntlworld.com

Chief: Chairman: Mr Sean Brady, as above
Membs: 27 indivs; 3 instns *Memb Req:* subscription: £7 pa
Activs: Aims to raise awareness and assist in the preservation and cataloguing of archive materials in the Saffron Walden area; holds monthly meetings from September to April; currently engaged in cataloguing the town archive.

O333 🔑 🎓

School Library Association [SLA]

Unit 2, Lotmead Business Village, Lotmead Farm, Wanborough, Swindon, Wiltshire, SN4 0UY (01793-791787; fax: 01793-791786)
Email: info@sla.org.uk
Internet: http://www.sla.org.uk/

Type: membership assoc *Gov Body:* Exec Cttee (elected offcrs & membs) *Chief:* Chief Exec: Ms Kathy Lemaire BA, DipLib, MCLIP, FRSA
Membs: 3500 indivs & instns *Memb Req:* open to indivs & orgs involved in the provision of school lib svcs; subscription: £45 pa
Branches & Groups: 15 regional branches: CAMBRIDGESHIRE; HAMPSHIRE; NORTHERN IRELAND; REPUBLIC OF IRELAND; LANCA-SHIRE; NORTH EAST ENGLAND; MERSEYSIDE; OXFORDSHIRE; SCOTLAND (see **O334**); SOMERSET; SOUTH EAST WALES; SOUTH WEST WALES; STAFFORDSHIRE; SURREY; WEST OF ENGLAND; contact via SLA office
Activs: Promotes the development and use of school libraries; supports and encourages those working in school libraries; campaigns at regional and national level to ensure appropriate provision for school libraries and School Library Services; provides advisory information service; publishes guidelines and quarterly journal; mounts regular training courses.
Pubns: The School Libn (4 pa); regular newsletters; SLA Guidelines Series; Bks to Enjoy; fiction booklists; numerous others, contact SLA for details

O334 🔑 🎓

School Library Association in Scotland [SLA(S)]

c/o Ms Alison MacPhail, James Hamilton Academy, Sutherland Dr, Kilmarnock, E Ayrshire, KA3 7DF (01563-533221)
Email: Alison.McPhail@east-ayrshire.gov.uk

Gov Body: regional group of the School Lib Assoc (see **O333**) *Chief:* Convenor: Miss Elspeth Scott *Other Snr Offcrs:* Sec: Ms Alison MacPhail, as above
Membs: 200 indivs
Activs: The SLA(S) exists to support and encourage those working in school libraries in Scotland, raising awareness and promoting good practice through an effective training and publications programme. The Association provides an advisory/information service for national and international enquiries, a quarterly journal and reduced rates for all publications and training courses.
Pubns: The School Libn (quarterly journal)

O335 🔑

Scottish Academic Libraries Co-operative Training Group [SALCTG]

c/o Mrs Anabel Marsh, Univ of Strathclyde, Jordanhill Campus, 76 Southbrae Dr, Glasgow, G13 1PP (0141-950-3555; fax: 0141-950-3150)
Email: a.c.marsh@strath.ac.uk
Internet: http://www.jiscmail.ac.uk/files/LIS-SALCTG/welcome.html

Type: co-op *Chief:* Convenor: Ms Eileen Ulas (e.ulas@vms.strath.ac.uk) *Other Snr Offcrs:* Sec: Ms Anabel Marsh, as above; Treasurer: Ms Elaine Miur (e.muir@au.sac.ac.uk)
Membs: 27 instns *Memb Req:* academic libs, primarily those in Scotland; subscription: £10 pa
Activs: Co-operative group specialising in the provision of workshops and training courses, both practical and managerial, appropriate to the needs of academic libraries in Scotland.

O336 🔑 🎓

Scottish Book Trust

Scottish Book Centre, 137 Dundee St, Edinburgh, EH11 1BG (0131-229-3663; fax: 0131-228-4293)
Email: info@scottishbooktrust.com
Internet: http://www.scottishbooktrust.com/

Chief: Exec Dir: Mr Marc Lambert
Activs: An independent organisation promoting books, reading and writers in Scotland. Provides a Book Information Service; administers the Writers in Scotland Scheme; co-ordinates National Poetry Day in Scotland.
Pubns: Beginning with Books; Radical Reading; Pointers: Poetry; A Book of Books & Writers; Writing Scotland's Future; The Writers in Scotland Scheme Handbook; literary guides; posters

O337 🎓

Scottish Centre for the Book [SCOB]

Napier Univ, Craighouse Rd, Edinburgh, EH10 5LG (0131-455-6150; fax: 0131-455-6193)
Email: scob@napier.ac.uk
Internet: http://www.scob.org.uk/

Gov Body: Napier Univ (see also **S610**) *Chief:* contact Prof Alistair McCleery (a.mccleery@napier. ac.uk)
Membs: 6 staff
Activs: Acts as a focus for research into, scholar-ship in, and teaching of print culture and the sociology of texts. Hosts seminars and con-ferences, including the Edward Clarke Seminar Series, and the annual Macmillan Lecture in the Sociology of the Text; is involved in the provision of visiting fellowships; issues publications relating to the past, present and future of the printed word, its creation, diffusion and reception.
Pubns: Bibliotheck (1 pa, £15)

O338 🔑 🎓

Scottish Confederation of University and Research Libraries [SCURL]

c/o Ms Cate Newton, Natl Lib of Scotland, George IV Bridge, Edinburgh, EH1 1EW (0131-226-4531; fax: 0131-220-6662)
Email: c.newton@nls.uk
Internet: http://scurl.ac.uk/

Type: co-op *Gov Body:* Board of Trustees of the Natl Lib of Scotland *Chief:* Chair: Mr Stuart James, Univ of Paisley Lib (stuart.james@paisley. ac.uk) *Other Snr Offcrs:* Sec: Ms Cate Newton, as above; Development Dir: Mrs Catherine Nicholson, Glasgow Caledonian Univ Lib (c.nicholson@gcal.ac.uk)

Membs: 25 + 4 observers instns
Branches & Groups: affiliated groups incl: SCOTTISH UNIVS SPECIAL COLLNS & ARCHVS GROUP (see **O346**); SCOTTISH WORKING GROUP ON OFFICIAL PUBNS (see **O348**); SCOTTISH HIGHER EDU & RSRCH ACQUISITIONS LIBNS (see **O341**); SCOTTISH VISUAL ARTS GROUP (see **O347**); NORTH AMERICAN STUDIES GROUP (see **O298**)
Activs: The principal association of research libraries in Scotland. Exists to improve services for users and maximise resource through collaborative action; to work with other organisations, sectors and domains towards the creation of a co-operative library infrastructure in Scotland; to lobby funding and planning bodies on matters of shared interest; to provide mutual support for members.

O339 🔑
Scottish Genealogy Society
15 Victoria Ter, Edinburgh, EH1 2JL (*tel & fax:* 0131-220-3677)
Email: info@scotsgenealogy.com
Internet: http://www.scotsgenealogy.com/

Chief: Hon Pres: Sir Malcolm Innes of Edingight KCVO, WS *Other Snr Offcrs:* Acting Hon Sec: Miss Joan Ferguson MBE, MA, MCLIP, FRCP(Edin)
Memb Req: open to those interested in Scottish family hist; subscription: £16 pa
Activs: Aims to promote research into Scottish family history, and to undertake the collection, exchange and publication of information and material relating to Scottish genealogy by means of meetings, lectures and other events. Maintains a Library and Family History Centre (see **A156**) to facilitate genealogical research.
Pubns: Scottish Genealogist (4 pa); numerous other pubns available on web site

O340 ✚
Scottish Health Information Network [SHINE]
c/o Ms Katrina Dalziel, School of Nursing, Midwifery and Health Lib, Royal Alexandra Hosp, Paisley, PA2 9PN (0141-580-4757; *fax:* 0141-887-4962)
Email: katrina.dalziel@paisley.ac.uk
Internet: http://www.shinelib.org.uk/

Type: co-op *Gov Body:* Cttee *Chief:* Chair: Ms Margaret Forrest, Fife Campus, Univ of Dundee (m.e.s.forrest@dundee.ac.uk) *Other Snr Offcrs:* Sec: Ms Katrina Dalziel, as above
Memb Req: open to indivs & instns involved in the provision of health care info in Scotland
Activs: Aims to ensure the best possible access to health care information through supporting activities and developments in library and inform-ation services in Scotland; seeks to inform and influence policy-making and funding bodies on issues relating to health care libraries and inform-ation services; promotes recognised guidelines and standards and encourages collaboration and partnership; acts as a forum for the exchange of views and information.
Pubns: Interim (newsletter, 3 pa); Shine Union Directory

O341 🔑 🎓
Scottish Higher Education and Research Acquisitions Librarians [SHERAL]
c/o Mr Collin Galloway, Glasgow Univ Lib, Hillhead St, Glasgow, G12 8QE (0141-330-6775; *fax:* 0141-330-4198)
Email: c.galloway@lib.gla.ac.uk
Internet: http://scurl.ac.uk/about/sheral.html

Gov Body: specialist group of the Scottish Confederation of Univ & Rsrch Libs (see **O338**)
Chief: contact Mr Collin Galloway, Head of Acquisitions (Bks), Glasgow Univ Lib, addr as above *Other Snr Offcrs:* Mr Tony Kidd, Serial Libn, Glasgow Univ Lib (t.kidd@lib.gla.ac.uk)
Membs: 22 instns; serials & acqs libns from the libs of the Scottish univs, Natl Lib of Scotland, Edinburgh City Libs, the Mitchell Lib & other SHEFC-funded higher edu instns
Activs: Provides a forum for serials and acquisitions librarians in the academic sector in Scotland where topics relevant to members' departments and interests can be discussed; meets twice yearly; monitors suppliers' services to ensure that consortium purchasing contracts are adhered to.

O342 🔑
Scottish Law Librarians Group [SLLG]
c/o Ms Andrea Longson, Advocates Lib, Parliament House, Edinburgh, EH1 1RF (0131-260-5637)
Email: andrea.longson@advocates.org.uk

Type: prof, legal *Chief:* Convenor: Mr Roddy Waldhelm, Solicitors Office Lib, Edinburgh (roddy.waldhelm@scotland.gsi.gov.uk) *Other Snr Offcrs:* Sec: Ms Andrea Longson, as above
Membs: 88 indivs *Memb Req:* open to legal info profs in Scotland
Activs: Provides a forum for Scottish legal librarians and information workers; meets 3 times a year; organises visits and training courses.
Pubns: Newsletter; Union List of Overseas Materials (1994); Directory of Legal Libs in Scotland (2nd ed, 1995); Union List of Serials (forthcoming)

O343 🔑
Scottish Library and Information Council [SLIC]
1st Floor, Bldg C, Brandon Gate, Leechlee Rd, Hamilton, Lanarkshire, ML3 6AU (01698-458888; *fax:* 01698-458899)
Email: slic@slainte.org.uk
Internet: http://www.slainte.org.uk/Slic/slichome.htm

Chief: Dir: Ms Elaine Fulton BA, MCLIP (e.fulton@slainte.org.uk) *Other Snr Offcrs:* Asst Dir: Ms Rhona Arthur BA, FCLIP (r.arthur@slainte.org.uk)
Membs: 140 instns
Activs: i) To promote development of all types of library and information services in Scotland; ii) To act as a link between library/information services in Scotland and the Secretary of State; iii) To provide grant aid for library and information service projects; iv) To undertake research and consult-ancy work; v) To monitor library and information services standards in Scotland. Co-sponsor of SLAINTE (Scottish Libraries Across the INTErnet), along with CILIP Scotland (see **O151**)
Pubns: Public Libs & Adult Edu in Scotland, May 1993 (£10); Libs & The Arts: Report of a Working Group (£10); Libs in Scottish Further Edu Colls (£10); numerous others

O344 🔑
Scottish Record Society [SRS]
c/o Prof James Kirk, Dept of Scottish Hist, Univ of Glasgow, Glasgow, Strathclyde, G12 8QQ (0141-330-5682)

Gov Body: Council *Chief:* Hon Sec: Prof James Kirk MA, PhD, DLitt, FRSE
Membs: 300 total *Memb Req:* open to anyone interested in historical records in Scotland
Activs: Founded in 1897, the SRS publishes numerous volumes of calendars and indices of

public records and private muniments relating to Scotland which are of particular value to historians and genealogists. The society does not undertake research on behalf of members.
Pubns: annual pubn, subscription covers cost

O345 🔑
Scottish Records Association [SRA]
c/o Mrs Carol Parry, Royal Coll of Physicians & Surgeons of Glasgow, 232-242 St Vincent St, Glasgow, G2 5RJ (0141-227-3234; *fax:* 0141-221-1804)
Email: carol.parry@rcpsglasg.ac.uk
Internet: http://www.scottishrecordsassociation.org/

Gov Body: Council *Chief:* Sec: Mrs Carol Parry, as above
Membs: 294 indivs; 70 instns *Memb Req:* open to anyone involved or interested in the preservation & use of historical records in Scotland.
Activs: Provides a forum where users, owners and custodians of records can discuss matters relating to their custody, conservation and accessibility; organises conferences on Scottish archival and historical subjects; arranges visits to archives.
Pubns: Scottish Archvs (journal, 1 pa); Newsletter (2 pa); Scottish Handwriting 1500-1700: A Self Help Pack

O346 🔑 🎓
Scottish University Special Collections and Archives Group [SUSCAG]
c/o Ms Johanna King, Univ of Stirling, Stirling, FK9 4LA (01786-466670; *fax:* 01786-466653)
Email: j.l.king@stir.ac.uk
Internet: http://www.archives.gla.ac.uk/suscag/

Gov Body: affiliate group of the Scottish Confederation of Univ & Rsrch Libs (see **O338**)
Chief: Convenor: Ms Ann Jones *Other Snr Offcrs:* Sec: Ms Johanna King, as above
Membs: 20 instns
Activs: Aims to foster closer co-operation between University Archives and Special Collections departments and to consider issues of common concern; promotes the development of collective level description that can be accessed across the internet, and of University information strategies and related records management policies; meets three times a year to consider policy and explore new developments.
Pubns: SUSCAG Brochure; conference proceedings

O347 🔑 🎓
Scottish Visual Arts Group [SVAG]
c/o Ms Jane Furness, Scottish Natl Gallery of Modern Art, Belford Rd, Edinburgh, EH4 3DS (0131-624-6253; *fax:* 0131-343-2802)
Email: jfurness@nationalgalleries.org
Internet: http://scurl.ac.uk/about/svag.html

Gov Body: affiliate group of the Scottish Confederation of Univ & Rsrch Libs (see **O338**)
Chief: contact Ms Jane Furness, as above
Membs: 24 full membs; 7 corresponding membs
Memb Req: open to libns & info providers from academic & public libs, museums, galleries & other instns concerned with the promotion & docu-mentation of the visual arts in Scotland
Activs: Professional support and research group committed to the dissemination of art information and the exchange of ideas. Its aims are: to maximise opportunities for co-operation in Scottish institutions; to promote collections and services; to act as a lobbying body; to heighten awareness of visual arts documentation; to link activities of local and UK wide initiatives. Meets twice a year.

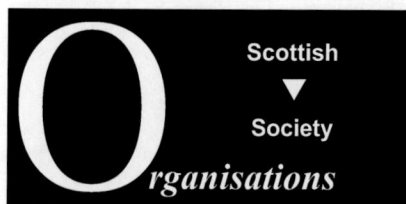

Scottish ▼ Society

Organisations

O348 🔑 🎓
Scottish Working Group on Official Publications [SWOP]

c/o Ms Paulette Hill, Historic Scotland, Longmore House, Salisbury Pl, Edinburgh, EH9 1SH (0131-668-8600)
Email: paulette.hill@scotland.gsi.gov.uk
Internet: http://scurl.ac.uk/about/swop.html

Gov Body: affiliated to the Scottish Confederation of Univ & Rsrch Libs (see **O338**) *Chief:* Sec: Ms Paulette Hill
Membs: incl representatives from Scotland's univ libs, the two major public ref libs in Glasgow & Edinburgh, the Natl Lib of Scotland, special libs & other bodies concerned with official material
Activs: Aims to improve access to official publications in Scotland; maintains a Directory of the main repositories of official information in Scotland.
Pubns: Directory of Official Pubns in Scotland (available online)

O349 🔑 🎓
Sexuality Issues in Libraries Group [SILG]

(formerly Burning Issues Group)
c/o Mr John Vincent, Wisteria Cottage, Nadderwater, Exeter, EX4 2QJ (01392-256045)
Email: john@nadder.org.uk
Internet: http://www.silg.org.uk/

Chief: Chair: Mr John Vincent, as above
Membs: 40 instns
Activs: An independent group of public and academic librarians working to improve library services to lesbians, gay men, bisexuals and transgendered individuals. It also acts as an informal support network for lesbians, gay men and bisexuals working in the library and information field; works in partnership with relevant agencies to develop strategies and policies for service development and training; shares and encourages best practice.
Further Info: SILG is an Org in Liaison with CILIP (see **O110**)

O350 🔑
Share the Vision (Libraries) Ltd [STV]

Natl Lib for the Blind, Far Cromwell Rd, Bredbury, Stockport, Cheshire, ME14 2LH (0161-355-2079/88; *fax:* 0161-355-2098)
Email: sharethevision@nlbuk.org

Gov Body: charitable company ltd by guarantee
Chief: Exec Dir: Mr David Owen
Membs: 11 instns
Activs: Promoting library and information services for visually impaired and other print handicapped people, via partnership working between publicly funded libraries and voluntary sector agencies.
Pubns: Lib Svcs for Visually Impaired People: A Manual of Best Practice, ed by L. Hopans (2000, revised 2002)

O351 🔑
Shropshire Access to Information Resources [SHAIR]

c/o Ms Elaine Moss, Shrewsbury Lib, 1 Castle Gates, Shrewsbury, Shropshire, SY1 2AS (01743-255385)
Email: elaine.moss@shropshire-cc.gov.uk

Type: co-op *Chief:* Ms Elaine Moss, as above
Memb Req: open to info providers in Shropshire
Branches & Groups: SHROPSHIRE ACCESS TO INFO FOR LEARNING (SAIL)
Activs: Acts as a forum in which member organisations can share expertise, training and access to information. Organises meetings, visits and training opportunities.
Pubns: Resource Directory

O352 🔑
SINTO: The Information Partnership for South Yorkshire and North Derbyshire

The Learning Centre, Sheffield Hallam Univ, Collegiate Cres, Sheffield, South Yorkshire, S10 2BP (0114-225-5739/40; *fax:* 0114-225-2476)
Email: sinto@shu.ac.uk
Internet: http://www.shu.ac.uk/sinto/

Type: co-op *Gov Body:* Exec Board *Chief:* Dir: Mr Carl Clayton BA, MCLIP, DMS
Membs: 40 instns *Memb Req:* open to all orgs involved with or interested in the provision of info in the region of Sheffield, South Yorkshire, North Derbyshire & surrounding areas; subscription rates vary
Branches & Groups: SOUTH YORKSHIRE ACCESS TO LIBS FOR LEARNING (SYALL); BUSINESS INFO GROUP; INTERLENDING & DOCUMENT SUPPLY GROUP; LEGAL INFO GROUP; SPORTS & HEALTH INFO GROUP; TRAINING GROUP; SMALL BUSINESSES GROUP
Activs: Co-operative organisation for library and information organisations in South Yorkshire and North Derbyshire (Library and Information Plan for the area); aims to promote and develop the use of information through co-operation, planning and partnership; encourages investment in information provision and resources in the region; represents the library and information services sector within local, regional and national forums.
Pubns: SINTO Newsletter (available to membs); various leaflets

O353 🔑
Society for Lincolnshire History and Archaeology

c/o Miss Pearl Wheatley, Jews' Ct, 2-3 Steep Hill, Lincoln, LN2 1LS (*tel & fax:* 01522-521337)
Email: slha@lincolnshirepast.org.uk
Internet: http://www.lincolnshirepast.org.uk/

Chief: Chairman: Miss Pearl Wheatley, as above
Other Snr Offcrs: Administrator: Mr Rod Gallow
Memb Req: open to anyone interested in the hist of Lincolnshire; subscription: indivs £17 pa (under-21s £9, overseas £21), families £18 pa, instns £18 pa (overseas £22)
Activs: Aims to create a greater awareness and knowledge of the history and heritage of Lincolnshire and assist the discovery and recording of new and relevant information; arranges lectures, conferences, local history fairs and site visits; runs a bookshop; facilitates research and field investigation; works with affiliated groups throughout the county.
Pubns: Lincolnshire Past & Present (magazine, 4 pa); Lincolnshire Hist & Archaeo (journal, 1 pa); Bulletin (4 pa)
See also **S956**

O354 🔑
Society for Name Studies in Britain and Ireland

c/o Miss Jennifer Scherr, Univ of Bristol Medical Lib, Univ Walk, Bristol, BS8 1TD
Internet: http://www.snsbi.org/

Chief: Pres: Mr Ian Fraser *Other Snr Offcrs:* Hon Sec: Miss Jennifer M. Scherr, as above
Membs: 202 indivs *Memb Req:* open to all those interested in the study of proper names; subscription: indivs £15 pa (students £5), families £20 pa, instns £15 pa
Activs: Promotes the study of proper names, including place names, personal names & surnames; organises conferences and day schools.
Pubns: Nomina (journal, 1 pa); newsletters

O355 🔑
Society of Archivists

Prioryfield House, 20 Canon St, Taunton, Somerset, TA1 1SW (01823-327030; *fax:* 01823-271719)
Email: societyofarchivists@archives.org.uk
Internet: http://www.archives.org.uk/

Type: prof *Gov Body:* Council *Chief:* Chair: Ms Aideen Ireland, Natl Archvs of Ireland *Other Snr Offcrs:* Hon Sec: Mr Mark Weaver, AstraZeneca R&D Charnwood; Exec Sec: Mr Patrick Cleary
Membs: 1730 indivs; 122 instns *Memb Req:* open to workers in archvs & records mgmt in the UK & Ireland; subscription rates vary
Branches & Groups: Regional Groups: EASTERN REGION (see **O360**); EAST MIDLANDS REGION (see **O359**); IRISH REGION (see **IO42**); LONDON REGION (see **O362**); NORTHERN REGION (see **O364**); NORTH WEST REGION (see **O363**); SCOTTISH REGION (see **O371**); SOUTH EAST REGION (see **O367**); SOUTH WEST REGION (see **O368**); WELSH REGION (see **O372**); WEST MIDLANDS REGION (see **O370**); Special Interest Groups: ARCHVS FOR EDU & LEARNING GROUP (see **O356**); BUSINESS RECORDS GROUP (see **O357**); EAD/DATA EXCHANGE GROUP (see **O358**); FILM & SOUND GROUP (see **O361**); PRESERVATION & CONSERVATION GROUP (see **O365**); RECORDS MGMT GROUP (see **O366**); SPECIALIST REPOSITORIES GROUP (see **O369**)
Activs: Professional body in the United Kingdom and the Republic of Ireland for archivists, archive conservators and records managers. Aims to promote the care and preservation of archives and the better administration of archive repositories; to advance the training and professional development of its members; to encourage relevant research and publication; to develop standards in the field; to represent the views and interests of archivists to any official body that seeks advice or whose activities affect archives. Organises training events, conferences and seminars.
Pubns: Journal of the Soc of Archivists (2 pa, subscription £52); ARC: Archives Records Mgmt & Conservation (monthly newsletter, membs only); ARC Recruitment & ARC Recruitment Plus (free to membs with ARC); other pubns incl: modules from British Archival Practice, the Soc's Archv Diploma training manual; info leaflets; Best Practice Guidelines; seminar proceedings & occasional papers

O356 🔑 🎓
Society of Archivists, Archives for Education and Learning Group [AfELG]

c/o Ms Jenny Moran, Nottinghamshire Archvs, County House, Castle Meadow Rd, Nottingham, NG2 1AG (0115-950-4524; *fax:* 0115-941-3997)
Email: kerr.avon@virgin.net
Internet: http://www.archives.org.uk/

Type: prof *Gov Body:* Soc of Archivists (see **O355**) *Chief:* Chairman: Ms Eileen Wallace (rgw@brooked. freeserve.co.uk) *Other Snr Offcrs:* Sec: Ms Jenny Moran, as above *Membs:* 470 indivs *Memb Req:* open to membs of the Soc interested in the educational use of archvs
Branches & Groups: 4 regional self-help groups
Activs: Aims to promote the use of archives for formal education purposes and for lifelong learners; to provide a forum for those working in archives and education; to enhance awareness within the archive, teaching and research professions of the potential role of archives in education; to foster links with government and heritage organisations including museums and libraries and to contribute and respond to policy documents where appropriate. Organises training and publications for archivists, teachers and other information professionals.
Pubns: Newsletter; Annual Report; Best Practice Guidelines on Archv Edu Svcs (1998)

O357

Society of Archivists, Business Records Group [BRG]

c/o Ms Teresa Doherty, Archivist, The Welcome Lib for the Hist & Understanding of Medicine, 183 Euston Rd, London, NW1 2BE (020-7611-7340)
Email: t.doherty@wellcome.ac.uk
Internet: http://www.archives.org.uk/BRG/

Type: prof *Gov Body:* Soc of Archivists (see **O355**) *Chief:* Chairman: Ms Teresa Doherty, as above *Other Snr Offcrs:* Joint Secretaries: Ms Sarah Emmerson (sarah.emmerson@diaego.com) & Ms Rachel Jarvis (rachel.jarvis@diaego.com)
Memb Req: open to membs of the Soc of Archivists involved or interested in business records
Activs: Aims to be the professional body of choice for archivists and records managers working with business records; provides a focused and informed group representing the interests of business records within the Society; act as a forum for advice, support and the promotion of best practice in the field; organises speaker meetings and training events; liaises closely with the Business Archives Council (see **O89**).
Pubns: speaker papers (available on web site)

O358

Society of Archivists, EAD/Data Exchange Group

c/o Soc of Archivists, Prioryfield House, 20 Canon St, Taunton, Somerset, TA1 1SW (01823-327030; *fax:* 01823-271719)
Email: societyofarchivists@archives.org.uk
Internet: http://www.archives.org.uk/

Type: prof *Gov Body:* Soc of Archivists (see **O355**) *Chief:* Chair: Ms Meg Sweet *Other Snr Offcrs:* Sec: Mr Robert Baxter
Membs: 205 indivs; 111 instns *Memb Req:* institutional or indiv membs of the Soc
Activs: Aims to represent the Society in international discussions and decisions on data exchange; to promote and co-ordinate UK and Irish archival contributions to international developments in data exchange; to contribute to international decisions on data content and data structure standards in regard to archival collections; to endeavour to ensure mutual compatibility across different sectors of the archival community in the implementation of standards; to strive to promote best practice and to liaise with the Society's Training Officer in providing training in EAD and metadata standards; to contribute to all of the above by regular meetings, presentations and training events for members.

O359

Society of Archivists, East Midlands Region

c/o Mr James Stevenson, Lincolnshire Archvs, St Rumbold St, Lincoln, LN2 5AB (01522-526204; *fax:* 01522-530047)
Email: James.Stevenson@lincolnshire.gov.uk
Internet: http://www.archives.org.uk/regions/ eastmidlands.asp

Type: prof *Gov Body:* Soc of Archivists (see **O355**) *Chief:* Chair: Ms Jenny Moran, Nottinghamshire Archvs (kerr.avon@virgin. net) *Other Snr Offcrs:* Sec: Mr James Stevenson, as above; Training Offcr: Mr Mark Jones (archives@ nottscc.gov.uk)
Memb Req: automatic membership for Soc of Archivists membs in the East Midlands (Derby-shire, Leicestershire, Lincolnshire, Northampton-shire & Nottinghamshire)
Activs: Acts as a focal point for Society activities in the East Midlands; organises meetings and training events; represents the interests and concerns of the region's archivists on the Society's Committee for the Regions.

O360

Society of Archivists, Eastern Region

c/o Ms Kate Thompson, 152 Kristiansand Way, Letchworth, SG6 1TY (01462-621248)
Email: kathryn.thompson@ntlworld.com
Internet: http://www.archives.org.uk/regions/ eastern.asp

Type: prof *Gov Body:* regional group of the Soc of Archivists (see **O355**) *Chief:* Chair: Ms Kate Thompson, as above
Memb Req: membership is automatic for membs of the Soc of Archivists living or working in Bedfordshire, Cambridgeshire, Essex, Hertford-shire, Norfolk & Suffolk
Activs: Provides a point of contact for Society members in the region; acts to promote professional development and to the care of the region's archives; provides meetings and training events; represents the regional membership on the Society's Committee for the Regions.

O361

Society of Archivists, Film and Sound Group [FSG]

c/o Ms Lorraine Finch, 87 St Georges Rd, Great Yarmouth, Norfolk, NR20 2JR (01493-854395)
Email: lorraine.finch@paperconservation.fsnet. co.uk
Internet: http://www.pettarchiv.org.uk/fsg/

Type: prof *Gov Body:* Soc of Archivists (see **O355**) *Chief:* Chair: Mrs Jane Alvey, East Anglia Film Archv (eafa@ uea.ac.uk) *Other Snr Offcrs:* Sec: Ms Lorraine Finch, as above
Membs: 310 *Memb Req:* open to membs of the Soc interested in audiovisual archvs
Activs: Established to develop the exchange of views and information and the encouragement of good practice amongst those concerned with the acquisition, preservation and arrangement of film and sound archives. Maintains links with related outside groups; encourages education and research through publications and training; provides a helpline for members. The group is also actively involved in recording the memories and thoughts of archive professionals and para-professionals in order to build up a resource bank for research and information about archive work and the profession.
Pubns: Film & Sound Group News (2 pa); Annual Report; Film & Sound Archv Sourcebook

O362

Society of Archivists, London Region

c/o Mr Rob Baker, Historical Manuscripts Commission, Quality Ct, Chancery Ln, London, WC2A 1HP (020-7242-1198; *fax:* 020-7831-3550)
Email: robertb@hmc.gov.uk
Internet: http://www.archives.org.uk/regions/ london.asp

Type: prof *Gov Body:* Soc of Archivists (see **O355**) *Chief:* Chairman: Mr Matthew Stephenson, London School of Econ (m.stephenson@lse.ac.uk) *Other Snr Offcrs:* Sec: Mr Rob Baker, as above
Memb Req: Soc of Archivists membs living or working in Greater London
Activs: Promotes the Society's aims and objectives in the London area; organises talks and other events; provides training opportunities; represents local members on the Society's Committee for the Regions.

O363

Society of Archivists, North West Region

c/o Ms Emily Burningham, Greater Manchester Record Office, 56 Marshall St, Manchester, M4 5FU (0161-832-5284; *fax:* 0161-839-3808)
Email: EBurningham@gmcro.co.uk
Internet: http://www.archives.org.uk/regions/ northwest.asp

Type: prof *Gov Body:* Soc of Archivists (see **O355**) *Chief:* Chair: Mr Vincent McKernan, Greater Manchester Record Office (vm@gmcro. co.uk) *Other Snr Offcrs:* Sec: Ms Emily Burningham, as above
Membs: 140 indivs; 10-20 instns *Memb Req:* subscribed membs of the Soc of Archivists in Cheshire, Cumbria, Lancashire, Greater Manchester, Merseyside & the Isle of Man; subscription fee varies according to salary
Activs: Promotes the care of archives and records in the region's repositories; represents local members on the Society's Committee for the Regions; organises training events, talks and a regional Annual General Meeting.

O364

Society of Archivists, Northern Region

c/o Mr Andrew George, WYAS Bradford, 15 Canal Rd, Bradford, W Yorkshire, DB1 4AT (01274-731931; *fax:* 01274-734013)
Email: ageorge@wyjs.gov.uk
Internet: http://www.archives.org.uk/regions/ northern.asp

Type: prof *Gov Body:* Soc of Archivists (see **O355**) *Chief:* Chairman: Mr Andrew George, as above
Memb Req: Soc of Archivists membs in North East England (Cleveland, Durham, North Lincoln-shire, Northumberland, Tyne & Wear, Yorkshire)
Activs: Acts to advance the Society's aims in the region; promotes standards and the care of archives; organises events for members locally; represents the regional membership on the Society's Committee for the Regions.

O365

Society of Archivists, Preservation and Conservation Group [PCG]

c/o Mr Mark Hingley, Norfolk Record Office, Anglia Sq, Upper Green Ln, Norwich, NR3 1AX (01603-761349; *fax:* 01603-761885)
Email: mark.hingley.nro@norfolk.gov.uk
Internet: http://www.archives.org.uk/ preservationandconservation/ ☛

Society ▼ South Organisations

(Soc of Archivists, Preservation & Conservation Group cont)
Type: prof *Gov Body:* special interest group of the Soc of Archivists (see **O355**) *Chief:* Chairman: Mr Richard Nichols, Staffordshire Record Office *Other Snr Offcrs:* Sec: Mr Mark Hingley, as above
Memb Req: open to conservators & other Soc membs interested in the preservation & conservation of records
Branches & Groups: various Regional Groups of Conservators
Activs: Aims to promote the exchange of information and to facilitate contacts between members of the Society with a special interest in the field of preservation and conservation; to advise on training matters and to provide support at events; to encourage research into the nature of archival materials and the causes of deterioration; to monitor developments elsewhere and to co-operate with other organisations with similar aims; organises workshops on preservation themes.
Pubns: Annual Report; Directory of Suppliers

O366 🔑
Society of Archivists, Records Management Group [RMG]
c/o Ms Fiona Cairns, Glasgow Univ Archv Svcs, 77-87 Dumbarton Rd, Glasgow, G11 6PW (0141-330-4543; *fax:* 0141-330-4158)
Email: F.Cairns@archives.gla.ac.uk
Internet: http://www.archives.org.uk/rmg/

Type: prof *Gov Body:* special interest group of the Soc of Archivists (see **O355**) *Chief:* Chairman: Mr Kelvin Smith, Public Record Office (kelvin.smith@pro.gov.uk) *Other Snr Offcrs:* Sec: Ms Fiona Cairns, as above
Membs: 520+ indivs *Memb Req:* open to membs of the Soc involved or with a particular interest in records mgmt
Activs: Provides a forum to assist in the exchange of information and facilitate contacts between members of the Society interested in the field of records management; promotes records management and undertakes outreach work to those outside the Society with responsibilities in this area; organises meetings, including an AGM, training and other events.
Pubns: Annual Report

O367 🔑
Society of Archivists, South East Region
c/o Ms Cerys Russell, East Kent Archvs Centre, Honeywood Rd, Whitfield, Dover, Kent, CT16 3EH (01304-829306; *fax:* 01304-820783)
Email: cerys.russell@kent.gov.uk
Internet: http://www.archives.org.uk/regions/southeast.asp

Type: prof *Gov Body:* regional group of the Soc of Archivists (see **O355**) *Chief:* Chairman: Mr Richard Smout, Isle of Wight Record Office (record.office@iow.gov.uk) *Other Snr Offcrs:* Sec: Ms Cerys Russell, as above
Memb Req: automatic membership for Soc of Archivists membs in Berkshire, Buckinghamshire, Kent, Oxfordshire, Surrey, Sussex, Hampshire & the Isle of Wight

Activs: Acts as a focal point for the Society's activities in South East England; organises meetings and training events; provides representation for the regional membership on the Society's Committee for the Regions.

O368 🔑
Society of Archivists, South West Region
c/o Ms Lucy Jefferis, Bath Record Office, Guildhall, High St, Bath, BA1 5AW (01225-477420)
Email: lucy_jefferis@bathnes.gov.uk
Internet: http://www.archives.org.uk/regions/southwest.asp

Type: prof *Gov Body:* regional group of the Soc of Archivists (see **O355**) *Chief:* Chair: Mr Paul Brough, Cornwall Record Office (pbrough@cornwall.gov.uk) *Other Snr Offcrs:* Sec: Ms Lucy Jefferis, as above
Memb Req: membs of the Soc living or working in Avon, Channel Islands, Cornwall, Devon, Dorset, Gloucestershire, Somerset & Wiltshire
Activs: Acts to support the objectives of the Society locally; provides meetings and training opportunities; represents members on the Society's Committee for the Regions.

O369 🔑
Society of Archivists, Specialist Repositories Group [SRG]
c/o Ms Susan Scott, Archivist, The Savoy Group, 1 Savoy Hill, London, WC2R 0BP (020-7307-5624)
Email: sfescott@savoy-group.co.uk
Internet: http://www.archives.org.uk/srg/

Type: prof *Gov Body:* special interest group of the Soc of Archivists (see **O355**) *Chief:* Chair: Ms Susan Scott, as above
Membs: 350+ indivs *Memb Req:* open to membs of the soc working outside local authority record offices, esp those in higher edu, business, museums, schools etc, and archivists working in small archv svcs
Branches & Groups: Affiliated Groups: ARCHIVISTS IN INDEPENDENT TELEVISION (see **O14**); CHARITY ARCHIVISTS & RECORDS MGRS GROUP (see **O109**); HEALTH ARCHVS GROUP (see **O216**); HISTORIC HOUSES ARCHIVISTS GROUP (see **O223**); PARLIA-MENTARY & POLITICAL PARTIES ARCHV GROUP (see **O315**); RELIGIOUS ARCHIVISTS GROUP (see **O327**)
Activs: Originally founded as the Universities and Colleges group, the SRG provides a forum for non-local government archivists; participates in the development of archival description standards and methods of listing for a wide range of records; encourages non-Society of Archivists members responsible for the preservation and conservation of records to join the Society; organises meetings and training events; operates a helpline for members.
Pubns: SRG News (2 pa); Annual Report

O370 🔑
Society of Archivists, West Midlands Region
c/o Ms Joanna Terry, Modern Records Unit, County Hall, Spetchley Rd, Worcester, WR5 2NP (01905-766694; *fax:* 01905-766698)
Email: JTerry@worcestershire.gov.uk
Internet: http://www.archives.org.uk/regions/westmidlands.asp

Type: prof *Gov Body:* regional group of the Soc of Archivists (see **O355**) *Chief:* Chair: Ms Mary Mckenzie, Shropshire Records & Rsrch Centre (mary.mckenzie@shropshire-cc.gov.uk) *Other Snr Offcrs:* Sec: Ms Joanna Terry, as above

Memb Req: automatic membership for Soc membs in Herefordshire, Shropshire, Staffordshire, Warwickshire, the West Midlands & Worcestershire
Activs: Promotes the aims of the Society in the West Midlands; organises meetings and training sessions; represents the regional membership on the Society's Committee for the Regions.

O371 🔑
Society of Archivists Scotland
c/o Ms Helen Taylor, Archv, Records Mgmt & Museum Svc, Heriot-Watt Univ, Edinburgh, EH14 4AS (0131-451-3638; *fax:* 0131-451-3164)
Email: h.e.taylor@hw.ac.uk
Internet: http://www.archives.org.uk/regions/scotland.asp

Type: prof *Gov Body:* regional group of the Soc of Archivists (see **O355**) *Chief:* Chairperson: Dr Irene O'Brien, Glasgow City Archvs (irene.o'brien@cls.glasgow.gov.uk) *Other Snr Offcrs:* Sec: Ms Helen Taylor, as above
Membs: 168 indivs *Memb Req:* membs of the Soc working in Scotland
Activs: Promotes the care and conservation of Scottish archives and the professional develop-ment of archive workers in Scotland; represents the interests of members on the Society's Committee of the Regions; organises regular talks, meetings and training events.
Pubns: Annual Report

O372 🔑
Society of Archivists Wales
c/o Ms Rosemary Boyns, The Council of Museums of Wales, The Courtyard, Letty St, Cardiff, CF24 4EL (029-2022-5432; *fax:* 029-2066-8516)
Email: BoynsRE@cardiff.ac.uk
Internet: http://www.archives.org.uk/regions/wales.asp

Type: prof *Gov Body:* regional group of the Soc of Archivists (see **O355**) *Chief:* Chairman: Mr Rowland Williams, Flintshire Record Office (Rowland_Williams@flintshire.gov.uk) *Other Snr Offcrs:* Sec: Ms Rosemary Boyns, as above
Memb Req: membs of the Soc of Archivists working in repositories in Wales
Branches & Groups: ARCHVS IN EDU (WALES)
Activs: Acts to advance the aims and objectives of the Society in Wales; organises meetings and training sessions; represents the Welsh member-ship on the Society's Committee of the Regions.
Pubns: Annual Report

O373 🔑
Society of Authors
84 Drayton Gdns, London, SW10 9SB (020-7373-6642; *fax:* 020-7373-5768)
Email: info@societyofauthors.org
Internet: http://www.societyofauthors.org/

Gov Body: Mgmt Cttee *Chief:* Genl Sec: Mr Mark Le Fanu
Membs: 7000 indivs *Memb Req:* subscription: £80 pa
Branches & Groups: Regional Groups: SOC OF AUTHORS IN SCOTLAND; *Specialist Groups:* THE TRANSLATORS ASSOC; ACADEMIC WRITERS GROUP; BROADCASTING GROUP; CHILDREN'S WRITERS & ILLUSTRATORS GROUP; EDUCATIONAL WRITERS GROUP; MEDICAL WRITERS GROUP; contact the Soc for further details
Activs: Trade union representing the interests of authors; offers advice to members on all business aspects of writing, including the vetting of contracts; campaigns for improved terms and changes in legislation, such as copyright and libel laws.

Pubns: The Author (quarterly, free to membs, £30 pa to non-membs); Quick Guides & Occasional Papers (£1-£10, free to membs); for A Guide to Membership & a complementary copy of The Author, contact the Soc

O374   🗝
Society of Chief Librarians in England and Wales [SCL]
c/o Ms Catherine Blanshard, Leeds Lib & Info Svc, The Town Hall, The Headrow, Leeds, LS1 3AB (0113-247-8330; *fax:* 0113-247-8331)
Email: catherine.blanshard@leeds.gov.uk
Internet: http://www.chieflib.org/

Type: prof   *Gov Body:* Natl Exec Cttee   *Chief:* Hon Sec: Ms Catherine Blanshard, as above
Membs: 122 indivs   *Memb Req:* open to Chief Libns of each lib authority in England & Wales
Activs: Aims to influence the statutory, financial and other decisions which relate to the effective-ness of public library services and take a leading role in the national development of public library services. Represents the views of its members to governmental departments and other public bodies.
Pubns: Annual Report

O375   🗝
Society of College, National and University Libraries [SCONUL]
(formerly Standing Conference of Natl & Univ Libs)
102 Euston St, London, NW1 2HA (020-7387-0317; *fax:* 020-7383-3197)
Email: info@sconul.ac.uk
Internet: http://www.sconul.ac.uk/

Type: prof   *Chief:* Chair: Mr Andrew Green, Natl Lib of Wales   *Other Snr Offcrs:* Sec: Mr Toby Bainton; Asst Sec: Ms Gail Downe; both at above addr
Membs: 160 instns   *Memb Req:* open to natl, univ & higher edu libs of the UK & Ireland
Activs: Aims to promote and advance the science and practice of librarianship; to improve the quality and extend the influence of library services in higher education and the national libraries; to represent the interests of its member libraries. Organises meetings and conferences; encourages and facilitates professional development; promotes and develops policy initiatives; provides information and advice in both national and international fora. Runs a number of co-operative schemes, including SCONUL Vacation Access scheme.
Pubns: Newsletter (3 pa, subscription £20 pa); Annual Lib Statistics (£35); Annual Review (free); SCONUL Directory (£25); Working Papers Series; Briefing Papers Series; other occasional pubns

O376   🗝 🎓
Society of Genealogists
14 Charterhouse Bldgs, Goswell Rd, London, EC1M 7BA (020-7251-8799; *fax:* 020-7250-1800)
Internet: http://www.sog.org.uk/

Type: learned soc, educational charity   *Gov Body:* Exec Cttee   *Chief:* Acting Dir: Ms June Perrin (asstdir@sog.org.uk)   *Other Snr Offcrs:* Genea-logy Offcr: Miss Else Churchill (genealogy@sog. org.uk); Libn: Mrs Sue Gibbons (librarian@sog. org.uk)
Memb Req: open to anyone with an interest in family & social hist; subscription: £43 pa (£40 by direct debit) + £7.50 joining fee for new membs
Activs: Exists to promote and encourage the study, science and knowledge of genealogy; organises a wide range of lectures and courses; maintains an extensive bookshop and the foremost genealogical library in the British Isles (see **S1398**).

Pubns: Genealogists' Magazine (4 pa, free to membs, £1.85 each to non-membs); Computers in Genealogy (4 pa, subscription £8 pa to membs, £10 to non-membs); numerous other genealogical pubns

O377   🗝
Society of Indexers
Blades Enterprise Centre, John St, Sheffield, S Yorkshire, S2 4SU (0114-292-2350; *fax:* 0114-292-2351)
Email: admin@indexers.org.uk
Internet: http://www.socind.demon.co.uk/

Type: prof   *Chief:* Chair: Ms Michèle Clarke
Other Snr Offcrs: Vice-Chair: Ms Sue Lightfoot; Sec: Ms Ann Kingdom; Treasurer: Mr Frank Merrett
Membs: 950 indivs; 20 instns
Branches & Groups: Regional Groups: SCOTLAND (see **O378**); IRELAND (see **IO43**); LONDON; KENT; NORTH EAST; NORTH WEST; HAMPSHIRE; SUSSEX; THREE CHOIRS (Worcestershire, Herefordshire & Gloucestershire); YORKSHIRE; EAST ANGLIA; CORNWALL & DEVON; *Special Interest Groups:* ARCHAEO GROUP, contact: Ms Cherry Lavell, 67 Brighton Rd, Cheltenham, Gloucestershire, GL52 6BA (01242-517096); EARTH SCI GROUP, contact: Ms Ann Griffiths, 26 Presthope Rd, Selly Oak, Birmingham, B29 4NJ (0121-475-4469; *email:* angharad@lloydgriffiths.freeserve.co.uk); GENEALOGY GROUP, contact: Mr Colin Mills, 70 Chestnut Ln, Amersham, Buckinghamshire, HP6 6EH (01494-726103); LAW GROUP, contact: Moira Greenhalgh, 38 Manton Hollow, Manton, Marlborough, Wiltshire, SN8 1RR (01672-513862; *fax:* 01672-515595; *email:* moira@m-greenhalgh. co.uk); MEDICAL INDEXING GROUP, contact: Ms Jill Dormon, Bryn Derw, Cymau, Wrexham, Flintshire, LL11 5ER (01978-761453; *email:* jilldormon@classicfm.net)
Activs: Guidance and support on professional and technical indexing matters for members, publishers and authors; improvement of standards in indexing; training course in indexing.
Pubns: SIdelights (newsletter, 4 pa, free, available to membs only); The Indexer (journal, 2 pa, free to membs, subscription £40 pa to non-membs); Indexers Available (distributed free to publishers annually); Training in Indexing (5 module course: Units A-D £30 each, Unit E £40); Anthology for the Millennium (£5 + p&p to membs, £6 to non-membs); Occasional Papers, incl: Indexing Biographies & Other Stories of Human Lives (£11 + p&p); Indexing Legal Materials (£9.50 + p&p); Indexing the Medical & Biological Scis (£12 + p&p); Indexing Newspapers, Magazines & Other Periodicals (£12 + p&p); Indexing Children's Books (£12 + p&p); various leaflets & bklets
Further Info: The Soc is an Org in Liaison with CILIP (see **O110**)

O378   🗝
Society of Indexers, Scottish Group
c/o Ms Anne McCarthy, Bentfield, Gullane, East Lothian, EH31 2AY (*tel & fax:* 01620-842247)
Email: annemccarthy@btinternet.com
Internet: http://www.socind.demon.co.uk/localsig/ scot.htm

Type: prof   *Gov Body:* Soc of Indexers (see **O377**)   *Chief:* Sec: Ms Anne McCarthy, as above
Memb Req: membs of the Soc of Indexers living or working in Scotland
Activs: Organises meetings, workshops and seminars, and acts to promote the Society and its objectives in Scotland.

O379
Society of Public Information Networks [SPIN]
PO Box 2306, Chippenham, Wiltshire, SN14 7WA (0771-700-8158)
Email: info@spin.org.uk
Internet: http://www.spin.org.uk/

Chief: SPIN Chair: Mr Danny Budzak (chair@spin. org.uk)   *Other Snr Offcrs:* Sec: Ms Lin O'Keeffe, addr as above
Membs: 300+ instns   *Memb Req:* open to orgs involved in public info provision; subscription rates vary according to type of org
Activs: Brings together local authorities, health agencies, libraries, museums, government departments, voluntary organisations and private sector companies involved in the dissemination or exchange of information with the public. Represents the interests of public information network providers in the UK; provides a forum for ideas and advice; encourages the advance of electronic public information services and technologies; holds regular meetings, including an annual conference and exhibition.
Pubns: Electronic Public Information (quarterly journal, free to membs, subscription rates vary for non-membs)

O380   🗝
Somerset Record Society
c/o Mr David Bromwich, Somerset Studies Lib, Paul St, Taunton, Somerset, TA1 3XZ (01823-340300; *fax:* 01823-340301)
Internet: http://www.westcountrygenealogy.com/ somerset/somrecsoc.htm

Chief: Hon Sec: Mr David Bromwich
Membs: c250 indivs   *Memb Req:* open to all those interested in the hist of Somerset; subscription: full membership £10 pa, associate membership (open to others in a full memb's household) £1 pa
Activs: Exists to make record sources for the study of Somerset history available in printed form, and has issued 88 volumes since 1886. Holds an annual meeting in October which includes a lecture and/or a visit to a place of interest.
Pubns: recent vols incl: Sir Stephen Glynne's Church Notes for Somerset (£35); Wookey Manor & Parish 1544-1841 (£27); Bishop's Still's Visitation, 1594, etc (£15); Forde Abbey Cartulary (£15); John Allen Giles' Diary & Memoirs (£21); Wells Corp Properties (£15); Tudor Subsidies (£15)

O381   🎓
South Asia Archive and Library Group [SAALG]
(formerly South Asia Lib Group)
c/o Ms Antonia Moon, British Lib Asia, Pacific & Africa Collns, 96 Euston Rd, London, NW1 2DB (020-7412-7842; *fax:* 020-7412-7858)
Email: antonia.moon@bl.uk
Internet: http://www.bodley.ox.ac.uk/users/gae/ NCOLR/salg1.htm

Chief: Chairman. Ms Catherine Pickett (catherine. pickett@bl.uk)   *Other Snr Offcrs:* Sec: Ms Antonia Moon, as above
Membs: 163 indivs   *Memb Req:* open to representatives of libs, archvs & other instns in the UK with some degree of specialisation in South Asian Studies
Activs: Concerned with the acquisition and use of books and MSS in the field of South Asian Studies, co-operative bibliographical projects and other matters which can be resolved by common consultation. The group meets twice annually.
Pubns: SAALG Newsletter (annual)

Organisations

O382 🏛🏛
South East Museum, Library and Archive Council [SEMLAC]
15 City Business Centre, Hyde St, Winchester, Hampshire, SO23 7TA (01962-858844; *fax:* 01962-878439)
Email: info@semlac.org.uk
Internet: http://www.semlac.org.uk/

Type: government-funded strategic regional agency *Chief:* Chief Exec: Ms Helen Jackson (helenj@semlac.org.uk)
Activs: Regional development agency for museum, library and archive activity in the South East of England. Aims to improve the quality of museum, library and archive provision in the region; to extend participation in and access to the region's museums, libraries and archives; to promote standards in preservation and management; to maximise access to resources and funding.

O383 🏛
South East Regional Archive Council [SERAC]
c/o Mr Richard Childs, West Sussex Record Office, County Hall, Chichester, W Sussex, PO19 1RN (01243-753600; *fax:* 01243-533959)
Email: richard.childs@westsussex.gov.uk
Internet: http://nca.archives.org.uk/racse.htm

Chief: Chair: Mr Richard Childs, as above
Activs: Co-ordinating body for archives in South East England; aims to promote the preservation of, and access to, archival materials in the region.

O384 🔑 🎓
South East University Librarians [SEUL]
c/o Ms Nicky Whitsed, Open Univ Lib Svcs, Walton Hall, Milton Keynes, Buckinghamshire, MK7 6AA (01908-653138; *fax:* 01908-653571)
Email: n.whitsed@open.ac.uk
Internet: http://seul.open.ac.uk/

Type: co-op *Chief:* Convenor: Ms Nicky Whitsed MSc, FCLIP, as above
Membs: 25 instns *Memb Req:* open to libs in the South East of England
Activs: Exists to aid communication about regional topics including collaboration, co-operation and partnership initiatives, and to represent the views of the higher education libraries of the region to the South East Museum, Library and Archive Council (SEMLAC, see **O382**), SCONUL (see **O375**) and other appropriate organisations.

O385 🏛🏛
South West Museums, Libraries and Archives Council [SWMLAC]
Creech Castle, Bathpool, Taunton, Somerset, TA1 2DX (01823-259696; *fax:* 01823-270933)
Email: general@swmlac.org.uk
Internet: http://www.swmlac.org.uk/

Type: strategic development agency *Chief:* Chief Exec: Mr Sam Hunt (samhunt@swmlac.org.uk)

Memb Req: associate membership open to museums, libs, archvs & supporting orgs in the South West (no subscription); subscription for local authorities based on a svc level agreement
Activs: SWMLAC is the regional development agency for museums, libraries and archives, covering the counties of Bristol, Cornwall, Devon, Dorset, Gloucestershire, Somerset and Wiltshire, the Isles of Scilly and the Channel Islands. Provides strategic leadership and acts as an advocate for museums, libraries and archives in the South West; encourages the best possible service provision to the public; aims to develop skill sharing, knowledge management, learning, access and stewardship of collections; advises on funding and development; supports research and continuous improvement; provides an information service to the sector, a grant aid scheme and organises awareness-raising events.

O386 🏛
South West Regional Archive Council [SWRAC]
c/o Mr Paul Brough, Cornwall Record Office, County Hall, Truro, Cornwall, TR1 3AY (01872-323125; *fax:* 01872-270340)
Email: dtritton@cornwall.gov.uk
Internet: http://www.southwestarchives.org/

Chief: Chair: Mr Paul Brough, as above
Activs: Exists to support and advocate for archives in the South West of England. It aims to help develop the region's archives through improving access and standards of care, promoting learning, and through advocacy and partnership, especially with regional museum and libraries bodies.

O387 🔑
South Western Regional Library System [SWRLS]
c/o Somerset Libs, Arts & info, Lib HQ, Mount St, Bridgwater, Somerset, TA6 3ES (01278-451201; *fax:* 01278-452787)
Email: swrls@swrls.org.uk
Internet: http://www.swrls.org.uk/

Type: co-op *Gov Body:* Regional Council & Mgmt Cttee *Chief:* Chairman: Mr Robert Froud (rnfroud@somerset.gov.uk)
Membs: 61 instns *Memb Req:* subscription svc for lib & info svcs in the South West of England
Branches & Groups: OPERATIONAL INTER-LENDING BUSINESS UNIT, c/o Central Lib, Coll Green, Bristol, BS1 5TL (0117-927-3962; *fax:* 0117-923-0216; *email:* as above)
Activs: Aims to encourage co-operation and inter-library lending between member libraries and libraries in the rest of UK and Ireland; provides workshops, training and demonstrations; facilitates other projects agreed by the Regional Council or Management Committee.
Pubns: Annual Report (free)

O388 🔑
Special Libraries Association (European Chapter)
c/o Ms Celia Jackson, Spencer Stuart & Associates Ltd, 16 Connaught Pl, London, W2 2ED (020-7298-3333)
Email: cjackson@spencerstuart.com
Internet: http://www.sla-europe.org/

Chief: European Pres: Mr Neil Infield, Business Info Svcs, Hermes Pensions Mgmt (n.infield@Hermes.co.uk) *Other Snr Offcrs:* Sec: Ms Rosemary Winkworth, as above
Activs: European branch of the US-based Special Libraries Association; acts as a forum for information specialists and special librarians across Europe; runs regular meetings and social events.

Pubns: Chapter Newsletter; Info Outlook (monthly); Membership Directory

O389 🔑 🐌
SPRIG: Promoting Information in Leisure, Tourism and Sport [SPRIG]
c/o Mr Daniel Park, Sport England, 4th Floor, Minerva House, East Parade, Leeds, LS1 5PS (0113-205-3319)
Email: info@sprig.org.uk
Internet: http://www.sprig.org.uk/

Type: prof *Chief:* Chair: Mr Martin Scarrott (chair@sprig.org.uk) *Other Snr Offcrs:* Hon Sec: Mr Peter Drake, Birmingham Central Lib (0121-303-4220; *email:* secretary@sprig.org.uk); Publicity Offcr: Mr Daniel Park, as above
Membs: 25 indivs; 85 instns
Activs: Promotes information sources in leisure, tourism and sport. Its aims are: to act as a special interest group for those involved in disseminating and managing information; to disseminate information to users with an interest in leisure, tourism and sport; to lobby information providers for better co-ordination in provision and to identify gaps in provision; to improve awareness of leisure, tourism and sport information sources. Holds an annual seminar and organises regular visits and courses.
Pubns: Bulletin (2 pa); guides to biblio sources; proceedings of various seminars
Further Info: SPRIG is an Org in Liaison with CILIP (see **O110**)

O390 🔑
Staffordshire Record Society
c/o William Salt Lib, 19 Eastgate St, Stafford, ST16 2LZ (01785-278372)

Chief: Hon Sec: Mr D.A. Johnson
Memb Req: open to anyone interested in Staffordshire local hist; subscription: £10 pa
Activs: Publication of material relating to the history of the county of Staffordshire.
Pubns: Collns for a Hist of Staffordshire (free to membs, non-membs contact Soc for prices)

O391 🔑 🐌
Standing Committee on Business Information [SCOBI]
c/o Ms Ann Hughes, Trade Partners UK Info Centre, Kingsgate House, 66-74 Victoria St, London, SW1E 6SW (020-7215-4782)
Email: ann.hughes@tradepartners.gov.uk
Internet: http://www.cilip.org.uk/groups/isg/scobi.html

Gov Body: CILIP Info Svcs Group (see **O126**)
Chief: Chair: Mr Tony Eves (edmonton.green.library@enfield.gov.uk) *Other Snr Offcrs:* Hon Sec: Ms Ann Hughes, as above
Memb Req: open to libs & other orgs involved in business info provision
Activs: Provides a discussion forum for libraries offering business information; organises regular meetings and seminars; identifies and proposes solutions to problems in the provision of access to business information publications.

O392 🔑
Standing Committee on Official Publications [SCOOP]
c/o Mr Howard Picton, Dep Mgr, Bank of England Info Centre, Threadneedle St, London, EC2R 8AH (020-7601-4715; *fax:* 020-7601-4356)
Email: howard.picton@bankofengland.co.uk
Internet: http://www.cilip.org.uk/groups/isg/scoop.html

🐌 academic   🐌 corporate   **- 506 -**   🏛 governmental   ✚ medical

Gov Body: CILIP Info Svcs Group (see **O126**)
Chief: Chairman: Mr Alastair Allan, Univ of Sheffield Lib (a.allan@sheffield.ac.uk) *Other Snr Offcrs:* Sec: Mr Howard Picton, as above
Membs: representatives of groups within CILIP & other info orgs
Activs: Aims to improve access to and availability of UK official publications; to identify and propose solutions to problems in the provision of access to such publications, in particular their bibliographical control and distribution; to provide a mechanism for the exchange of views on matters of common interest to the library community concerning UK official publications; to provide a forum with The Stationary Office for the constructive discussion of services provided by The Stationary Office for the library community; and to keep the library community informed of their deliberations. Organises meetings and seminars.
Pubns: Directory of British Official Publishing, ed by S. Richard (Mansell, 2nd ed 1986); seminar brochures

O393 🔑 🎓

Standing Conference on Library Materials on Africa [SCOLMA]

c/o Mr David Blake, Commonwealth Secretariat Lib, Marlborough House, Pall Mall, London, SW1Y 5HX (020-7747-6164; *fax:* 020-7747-6168)
Email: scolma@hotmail.com
Internet: http://www.soas.ac.uk/scolma/

Chief: Chairman: Ms Sheila Allcock, Internatl Development Centre Lib, Queen Elizabeth House, 22 St Giles, Oxford, OX1 3LA (01865-273629; *email:* sheila.allcock@qeh.ox.ac.uk) *Other Snr Offcrs:* Sec: Mr David Blake, as above
Membs: 63 indivs & instns *Memb Req:* open to instns & libs concerned with lib materials on Africa; subscription: £23 pa (incl receipt of journal by surface mail) or £30 pa (incl receipt of journal by airmail)
Activs: Forum for libraries and others concerned with the provision of materials for African Studies in the UK, and increasingly in Europe. Publishes bibliographical and other reference works, organises meetings and consultations on African bibliographical and library topics.
Pubns: African Rsrch & Documentation (3 pa, £20 surface mail, £27 airmail); SCOLMA Directory of Libs & Special Collns on Africa in the UK & Europe (5th ed, 1993, £52, 6th ed in preparation); African Population Census Reports: A Bibliography & Checklist (1985, £9); African Studies: Papers Presented at a Colloquium in January 1985 (1986, £14.95); New Directions in African Bibliography (1988, £3.75); Maps & Mapping of Africa (1988, £2.50); Theses on Africa 1976-1988 (1993, £58); Images of Africa: The Pictorial Record (1994, £7.50); Writings on African Archvs (1996, £55)

O394 🔑 🎓

Suffolk Local History Council

2 Wharfedale Rd, Ipswich, Suffolk, IP1 4JP (01473-242500)
Email: admin@suffolklocalhistorycouncil.org.uk
Internet: http://www.suffolklocalhistorycouncil.org.uk/

Type: registered charity (No 294270) *Chief:* Hon Chairman: Dr Philip Pantelis *Other Snr Offcrs:* Hon Sec: Mr Jonathan Abson
Membs: 300+ indivs; 95 instns *Memb Req:* open to socs, groups & indivs interested in the local hist of Suffolk; subscription: indiv £7.50 pa, joint, soc or overseas £10 pa
Branches & Groups: SUFFOLK LOCAL HIST RECORDER SCHEME, Hon Recorders' Sec: Mrs Daphne Lloyd, at the above addr
Activs: Encourages and assists Suffolk local history; supports and advises members, local history groups and societies; organises a system of

Local History recorders; arranges day meetings of interest to local historians; co-operates in the running of an annual residential history course; organises exhibitions and encourages school history projects; assists with publishing through the Gwen Dyke Project Fund.
Pubns: Suffolk Review (2 pa, membs only); Newsletter (2 pa, membs only); Calendar of Events; Register of Speakers

O395 🔑

Surrey and Sussex Libraries in Co-operation [SASLIC]

c/o Mr Stephen Bowman, Park Coll Lib, King's Dr, Eastbourne, East Sussex, BN21 2UN (01323-503475)
Email: sb@park-college.ac.uk
Internet: http://www.sussex.ac.uk/saslic/

Type: co-op *Chief:* Chair: Ms Irene Campbell, Head of Info Svcs, West Sussex Libs (irene.campbell@westsussex.gov.uk) *Other Snr Offcrs:* Sec: Mr Stephen Bowman BA(Hons), MCLIP, as above
Memb Req: open to libs of all kinds throughout Surrey & Sussex; subscription: £20 pa for orgs with up to 3 sites, £4 pa per addl site
Activs: Aims to promote co-operation and the sharing of information and resources between member libraries. Organises training courses, meetings and visits.
Pubns: Newsflash (regular newsletter); Annual Report; Broadsheet Series; Location Key to British & Foreign Standards

O396 🔑 🎓

Surrey Archaeological Society, Local History Committee

(formerly Surrey Local Hist Council)
c/o Castle Arch, Guildford, Surrey, GU1 3SX (01372-812831)
Internet: http://www.surreyarchaeology.org.uk/lhc/

Chief: Chairman: Prof Alan Crocker (surreyarch@compuserve.com) *Other Snr Offcrs:* Hon Sec: Mrs A.E. Milton-Worssell (milton-worsell@msn.com)
Membs: 150 indivs *Memb Req:* Surrey Archaeological Soc subscriptions: indivs £25 pa (students £12.50), instns £30 pa (overseas £40)
Activs: Exists to foster an interest in the history of Surrey, both directly and in co-operation with other bodies; encourages local history societies and individuals within the County; organises a half-day Spring Meeting and an annual one-day Symposium in November, with a series of speakers on a topic of interest and an exhibition.
Pubns: Newsletter (3 pa, membs only); Surrey Hist (1 pa, £4); former Surrey Local Hist Council pubns incl: Pastors, Parishes & People in Surrey, by David Robinson (£2.95, 1989); Old Surrey Receipts & Food for Thought, by Daphne Grimm (£3.95, 1991); The Sheriffs of Surrey, by David Burns (£4.95, 1992); Two Hundred Years of Aeronautics & Aviation in Surrey 1785-1985, by Sir Peter Masefield (£3.95, 1993)
See also **S775**

O397 🔑 🎓

Surrey Record Society

c/o Surrey Hist Centre, 130 Goldsworth Rd, Woking, Surrey, GU21 1ND (01483-594603; *fax:* 01483-594595)
Internet: http://www.surreycc.gov.uk/surreyhistoryservice/

Chief: Hon Sec: Ms Margaret Vaughan-Lewis
Membs: c200 indivs *Memb Req:* open to all those interested in the study of Surrey hist & genealogy; subscription: indivs & instns £5 pa

Activs: The Society exists to publish records relating to the historic county of Surrey, so that manuscript sources held in repositories in and outside the county are made more readily available and comprehensive to students, scholars and amateur historians. Please note that no research can be undertaken by officers of the Society.

O398 🔑

Sussex Local History Forum

c/o Dr R. Jones, Barbican House, High St, Lewes, E Sussex, BN7 1YE (01273-504736; *fax:* 01273-486990)
Email: research@sussexpast.co.uk
Internet: http://www.sussexpast.co.uk/

Chief: Convenor: Dr Richard Jones
Membs: c70 instns
Activs: Acts as a forum for the study of the history of the county of Sussex, by bringing together local history societies and individuals.
Pubns: Foreign Country (5-6 pa, membs only)

O399 🔑 🎓

Sussex Record Society

c/o Mr P.M. Wilkinson, West Sussex Record Office, County Hall, Chichester, W Sussex, PO19 1RN (01243-753600; *fax:* 01243-533911)
Email: peter.wilkinson@westsussex.gov.uk

Chief: Hon Sec: Mr P.M. Wilkinson, as above
Membs: 250 indivs; 100 instns
Activs: Publishes editions of historical texts relating to the county of Sussex.
Pubns: recent vols incl: Vol 77: East Sussex Land Tax 1785 (membs £16, non-membs £24); Vol 78: Chichester Diocesan Surveys 1686 & 1724 (membs £19.33, non-membs £29); Vol 80: The Ashdown Forest Dispute 1876-1882 (membs £15, non-membs £18.50); Vol 81: Sussex Schools in the 18th Century (membs £15, non-membs £25)

O400 🔑 ✒️

Talis Information Ltd

Birmingham Rsrch Pk, Vincent Dr, Edgbaston, Birmingham, B15 2SQ (0121-471-1179; *fax:* 0121-472-0298)
Email: info@talis.com
Internet: http://www.talis.com/

Type: lib info systems *Chief:* Managing Dir: Mr Stephen Gray (s.m.gray@talis.com) *Other Snr Offcrs:* Sales Dir: Mr Ken Chad; Technical Dir: Mr Neal Clements; Financial Dir: Mr Nick Williams
Membs: over 110 major public, univ, coll & special libs; 140+ UnityWeb users
Activs: Talis Information Ltd is the leading Library Management System company supplying software services and solutions to libraries in the UK and Ireland. Services include not only an advanced Library Management System but also a cross-domain resource discovery portal (TalisPrism), compre-hensive reading/course list management (TalisList), guided resource access (Talis Signpost), a compre-hensive cataloguing database, a managed EDI service, state-of-the-art manage-ment information and e-journal management (TD-Net). Talis also provides solutions for local digital content (inVisage) and, in partnership with the Combined Regions (see **O166**), a nationwide inter-library loan database and ILL client (UnityWeb).

O401 🎓

Thames Valley University, Centre for Information Management

Faculty of Business & Mgmt, St Mary's Rd, Ealing, London, W5 5RF (020-8579-5000; *fax:* 020-8566-1353)
Internet: http://www.tvu.ac.uk/ ☛

Organisations
Thames ▼ University

(Thames Valley Univ, Centre for Info Mgmt cont)
Gov Body: Thames Valley Univ (see **S1421**)
Chief: Head of Academic Rsrch Programmes & Pathway Leader: Mr Colin Askew BA, MSc, DipEd, DipLib, MCLIP
Membs: c270 students
Activs: Undergraduate and postgraduate education in Information Management; research in library and information services, communications, publishing and related disciplines.

O402 ⚷
Theatre Information Group [TIG]
c/o Theatre Museum, 1e Tavistock St, London, WC2E 7PA (020-7943-4720; *fax:* 020-7943-4777)

Type: prof **Chief:** Sec: Mr John Collis, Rose Bruford Coll (john@bruford.ac.uk)
Memb Req: open to libns, archivists & curators in the field of theatre info
Activs: Provides a forum and meeting point for professionals within the subject area; organises meetings and seminars.
Further Info: The group is the UK Affiliate of SIBMAS, the Internatl Assoc of Libs & Museums of the Performing Arts

O403 ⚷
The Thoroton Society of Nottinghamshire
c/o Mr Keith Goodman, 59 Briar Gate, Long Eaton, Nottingham, NG10 4BQ (0115-972-6590)
Email: thoroton@keithgoodman.com
Internet: http://www.thorotonsociety.org.uk/

Chief: Chairman: Prof John Beckett, Dept of Hist, Nottingham Univ **Other Snr Offcrs:** Hon Sec: Mrs Barbara Cast; Treasurer & Membership Sec: Mr Keith Goodman, as above
Branches & Groups: RECORD SECTION, contact: Mr Adrian Henstock, Nottinghamshire Archvs, Castle Meadow Rd, Nottingham, NG2 1AG (adrian.henstock@nottscc.gov.uk)
Activs: The county historical and archaeological society for Nottinghamshire. Arranges monthly lectures and summer excursions; maintains a Record Section, whose volumes hold records relating to Nottinghamshire which have merited publication. The Society's printed collections are held on deposit as part of the East Midlands Collection at Nottingham University Library (see **S1647**), and its MS and record collections are held at Nottinghamshire Archives Office (see **A407**).
Pubns: Transactions (1 pa, membs only); newsletter (4 pa membs only); Record Series vols

O404 ⚷ 🎓 ✍
UK Libraries Plus [UKLP]
c/o Mr Adam Edwards, Whitelands Coll Learning Resource Centre, West Hill, London, SW15 3SN (020-8392-3551)
Email: adam.edwards@roehampton.ac.uk
Internet: http://www.uklibrariesplus.ac.uk/

Type: co-op **Gov Body:** Steering Group **Chief:** Chair: Mr Philip Payne (p.payne@lmu.ac.uk)
Other Snr Offcrs: Convenor: Mr Adam Edwards, as above

Membs: 121 instns **Memb Req:** open to any UK public sector Higher Edu lib, subj to approval by the Steering Group
Activs: Co-operative venture between higher education libraries, enabling part-time, distance and placement students to borrow material from member libraries nearer to home or to work, and for staff and full-time students to use other member libraries for reference.
Pubns: Statistics of Use (free, available from the Convenor at above addr)

O405 🏛
UKOLN: The Office for Library and Information Networking
Univ of Bath Lib, Bath, BA2 7AY (01225-826580; *fax:* 01225-826838)
Email: ukoln@ukoln.ac.uk
Internet: http://www.ukoln.ac.uk/

Chief: Dir: Ms Liz Lyon (e.j.lyon@ukoln.ac.uk)
Membs: 30 staff
Activs: UKOLN is a national centre for information management. It provides services to the library, information and cultural heritage communities. Its goals are: to influence policy and to inform practice; to advance the state of the art and to contribute to knowledge; to build useful and innovative distributed systems and services; to promote community building and consensus-making through awareness and events services. UKOLN is funded by Resource (see **O328**) and the Joint Information Systems Committee (JISC – see **O242**) of the Higher Education Funding Councils, as well as receiving project funding from JISC and the European Union. UKOLN also receives support from the University of Bath where it is based.
Pubns: UKOLN Newsletters (2 pa, free); Annual Report; rsrch reports; details of pubns can be found on UKOLN web site & in the UKOLN newsletters

O406 ⚷
Ulster Genealogical and Historical Guild
Balmoral Bldgs, 12 Coll Sq East, Belfast, BT1 6DD (028-9033-2288; *fax:* 028-9023-9885)
Email: enquiry@uhf.org.uk
Internet: http://www.ancestryireland.co.uk/

Gov Body: Ulster Historical Foundation (see **A43**)
Chief: Exec Dir: Mr Fintan Mullan BSSc, MSSc
Membs: 7000+ indivs **Memb Req:** subscription: £17-£33 pa (rates vary according to pubns received & method of dispatch)
Activs: Research co-operative for those interested in the history and genealogy of Ireland, especially the North. Aims to prevent duplication of research effort and to facilitate contacts between people with similar interests.
Pubns: Familia – Ulster Genealogical Review (annual, incl in membs' subscription, £5.95 non-membs); Directory of Irish Family Hist Rsrch (annual, incl in membs subscription, £6.95 non-membs); Irish Roots (4 pa, £8 pa to membs); Researching Irish Australians: Directory of Rsrch with Will Abstracts & Gravestone Inscriptions, ed by Brian Trainor (1998, £5.50)

O407 ⚷ ✍
Unitarian Historical Society [UHS]
c/o Rev Andrew Hill, 6 Ventnor Ter, Edinburgh, EH9 2BL (0131-667-4360)
Email: andrew@unitarian.ednet.co.uk
Internet: http://www.theopenmind.org.uk/heritage/UHS.html

Chief: Sec: Rev Andrew Hill, as above
Activs: Encourages and supports the study of Unitarian history and that of its cognate

nonconformist traditions. Organises an annual meeting and lecture and operates a research enquiry service about Unitarian history. The Society also keeps on file information about the records and archives of most Unitarian congregations and organisations in the British Isles and the Commonwealth.
Pubns: Transactions (annual, free to membs)

O408 🎓
United Kingdom Education and Research Networking Association [UKERNA]
Atlas Centre, Chilton, Didcot, Oxfordshire, OX11 0QS (01235-822200; *fax:* 01235-822399)
Email: R.Arak@ukerna.ac.uk
Internet: http://www.ukerna.ac.uk/

Chief: Chief Exec: Mr Robin Arak
Activs: Manages the operation and development of the JANET network, the networking programme of the UK education and research community, and researches, develops and provides advanced electronic communication facilities for use in that community and in industry.

O409 ⚷
United Kingdom Online User Group [UKOLUG]
The Old Chapel, Walden, West Burton, Leyburn, North Yorkshire, DL8 4LE (*tel & fax:* 01969-663749)
Email: cabaker@ukolug.org.uk
Internet: http://www.ukolug.org.uk/

Type: prof **Gov Body:** Mgmt Cttee; Special Interest Group of CILIP (see **O110**) **Chief:** Chair: Mr Chris Armstrong (lisqual@cix.co.uk) **Other Snr Offcrs:** Hon Sec: Ms Karen Blakeman (Karen.Blakeman@rba.co.uk); Administrator: Ms Christine Baker, as above
Membs: 1050 indivs; 130 instns **Memb Req:** open to users & developers of elec info resources; subscriptions: indivs £20 pa (£5 students), instns £90 pa
Activs: National user group for online, CD-ROM and Internet searchers. It aims to act as a user forum and as a consumer group to represent users' interests within the information industry. Produces a newsletter and occasional books; arranges conferences, seminars and training; and provides informal advice. It maintains close links with online hosts, database producers, CD-ROM distributors and telecommunications services.
Pubns: UKOLUG Newsletter (6 pa, free to membs, £50 pa to non-membs)

O410 ⚷
United Kingdom Serials Group [UKSG]
PO Box 5594, Newbury, Berkshire, RG20 0YD (01635-254292; *fax:* 01635-253826)
Email: uksg.admin@dial.pipex.com
Internet: http://www.uksg.org/

Chief: Chair: Mr Keith Courtney, Taylor & Francis (keith.courtney@tandf.co.uk) **Other Snr Offcrs:** Sec: Ms Lesley Crawshaw, Univ of Hertfordshire (l.a.crawshaw@herts.ac.uk); UKSG Business Mgr: Ms Alison Whitehorn, addr as above
Membs: 18 cttee membs indivs; c600 instns
Activs: The UK Serials Group exists to encourage the exchange and promotion of ideas on printed and electronic serials, and the process of scholarly communication. An autonomous, non-profit making, national and international interest group, it is the only body spanning the wide range of interest and activity between serials producers and readers.

Pubns: Serials: The Journal of the Serials Community (3 pa, membs only); The Serials Mgmt Handbook; conference papers

O411

Universities and Colleges Information Systems Association [UCISA]

Univ of Oxford, 13 Banbury Rd, Oxford, OX2 6NN (01865-283425; *fax:* 01865-283426)
Email: admin@ucisa.ac.uk
Internet: http://www.ucisa.ac.uk/

Gov Body: Exec Cttee *Chief:* Administrator: Ms Sue Peacock
Membs: 140 full membs; 25 affiliate membs; 26 corporate membs *Memb Req:* open to Higher & Further Edu instns & orgs; full membership: £975 pa; affiliate membership: £500 pa; corporate membership: £1500 pa
Branches & Groups: HARDWARE GROUP (UCISA-HG); MGMT INFO SYSTEMS GROUP (UCISA-MISG); NETWORKING GROUP (UCISA-NG); SOFTWARE GROUP (UCISA-SG); STAFF DEVELOPMENT GROUP (UCISA-SDG); TEACHING, LEARNING AND INFO GROUP (UCISA-TLIG)
Activs: Promotes the application of information systems and services in support of teaching, learning, research and administration in Higher Education; promotes and supports collaboration between institutions; promotes research and development; informs and supports policy making bodies on the cost effective application of information systems and services; organises conferences, seminars and workshops.
Pubns: newsletters; meeting reports; press releases

O412

University College London, School of Library, Archive and Information Studies [SLAIS]

Gower St, London, WC1E 6BT (020-7679-7204; *fax:* 020-7383-0557)
Email: o.manager@ucl.ac.uk
Internet: http://www.ucl.ac.uk/SLAIS/

Gov Body: Univ Coll London (see also **S1433**)
Chief: Dir: Prof Susan Hockey
Membs: 15 full-time staff; 257 students
Activs: Provides postgraduate courses in library and information studies, archives and records management, information science, and electronic communication and publishing. Also provides undergraduate course in Information Management.

O413

University Medical School Librarians Group [UMSLG]

c/o Ms Betsy Anagnostelis, Royal Free & Univ Coll Medical School Lib, Rowland Hill St, London, NW3 2PF (020-7794-0500 x4996; *fax:* 020-7794-3534)
Email: ucylbet@ucl.ac.uk
Internet: http://www.umslg.ac.uk/umslg.html

Type: prof *Chief:* Chair: Ms Linda Dorrington, Imperial Coll Central Lib (l.dorrington@ic.ac.uk)
Other Snr Offcrs: Sec: Ms Betsy Anagnostelis, as above
Membs: 48 indivs *Memb Req:* open to libns in undergrad & postgrad medical schools in the UK and Ireland
Activs: Aims to improve communication and co-operation between medical school libraries, to represent its members interests both nationally and internationally and to develop links with other library organisations; organises regular meetings and other events.

O414

University of Brighton, School of Computing, Mathematical and Information Sciences [CMIS]

Watts Bldg, Lewes Rd, Moulsecoomb, Brighton, BN2 4GJ (01273-642428; *fax:* 01273-642405)
Email: CMISAdmissions@Brighton.ac.uk
Internet: http://www.cmis.brighton.ac.uk/

Gov Body: Univ of Brighton (see also **S237**)
Chief: Head of School: Dr John Taylor (John.Taylor@brighton.ac.uk) *Other Snr Offcrs:* Head of Rsrch & Professor of Info Sci: Prof Peter Enser (P.G.B.Enser@brighton.ac.uk)
Activs: Teaching, research and consultancy in media and communications, librarianship and information management, computing and information systems and mathematical sciences. The school offers a comprehensive range of HND, foundation degree, honours degree and masters degree programmes.

O415

University of Bristol, Information and Library Management Programme

Grad School of Edu, 8-10 Berkeley Sq, Bristol, BS8 1HH (0117-928-7147; *fax:* 0117-925-4975)
Email: Cathy.Badley@bris.ac.uk
Internet: http://www.bris.ac.uk/education/ilm/

Gov Body: Univ of Bristol (see **S260**) *Chief:* Programme Sec: Mrs Cathy Badley
Activs: Full-time and part-time education leading to MSc in Information and Library Management, delivered in co-operation with the information and library services of the Bristol area.

O416

University of Central England, School of Information Studies

Franchise St, Perry Barr, Birmingham, B42 2SU (0121-331-5625; *fax:* 0121-331-5675)
Email: sis@uce.ac.uk
Internet: http://www.cie.uce.ac.uk/

Gov Body: Univ of Central England (see also **S183**) *Chief:* Head of School: Mr William Foster (william.foster@uce.ac.uk)
Membs: 273 students
Activs: Professional education, continuing professional development, research and consultancy in the field of Information Studies.

O417

University of Northumbria at Newcastle, Division of Information and Communication Studies

Room 005, Lipman Bldg, Univ of Northumbria, Newcastle upon Tyne, NE1 8ST (0191-227-4917; *fax:* 0191-227-3671)
Email: il.admin@northumbria.ac.uk
Internet: http://northumbria.ac.uk/sd/academic/soi/

Gov Body: Univ of Northumbria at Newcastle (see also **S1591**) *Chief:* Head of Subj Div: Ms Shona McTavish (shona.mctavish@northumbria.ac.uk)
Membs: 26 staff; 280 full-time students, 122 part-time
Branches & Groups: INFO MGMT RSRCH INST (IMRI, see **O418**)
Activs: Undergraduate and postgraduate teaching and research in Information Studies, Library Management, Communications Management and Records Management.

O418

University of Northumbria at Newcastle, Information Management Research Institute [IMRI]

School of Informatics, Univ of Northumbria, Ellison Pl, Newcastle upon Tyne, NE1 8ST (0191-227-3222; *fax:* 0191-227-3671)

Gov Body: Univ of Northumbria at Newcastle (see **S1591**) *Chief:* Dir: Dr Linda Banwell (linda.banwell@northumbria.ac.uk) *Other Snr Offcrs:* Asst Dir (Strategy): Mr Graham Walton (graham.walton@northumbria.ac.uk); Administrator: Ms Maureen Dickson (maureen.dickson@northumbria.ac.uk)
Membs: 16 staff; 13 doctoral students
Activs: Research and degree supervision in Information Management, E-Learning, Health Information and Records Management.

O419

University of Sheffield, Department of Information Studies [DIS]

Western Bank, Sheffield, S Yorkshire, S10 2TN (0114-222-2630; *fax:* 0114-278-0300)
Email: dis@sheffield.ac.uk
Internet: http://www.shef.ac.uk/~is/

Gov Body: Univ of Sheffield (see also **S1912**)
Chief: Head of Dept: Prof Peter Willett
Membs: 18 full-time academic staff; 12 technical/admin staff; 16 rsrch staff
Branches & Groups: CENTRE FOR HEALTH INFO MGMT RSRCH (see **O104**); CENTRE FOR THE PUBLIC LIB IN THE INFO SOC (see **O108**)
Activs: The Department offers a number of taught degree programmes both at graduate (MA/MSc) and undergraduate (BA/BSc) levels in the areas of Librarianship, Information Management, Information Systems, Health Informatics and Chemoinformatics. In addition, the Department has an internationally renowned research profile within which two main research groups operate: Computational Informatics and Library and Information Management. At any one time, a number of externally funded research projects within the remit of each of these research groups are being undertaken. The Department also offers higher research degree opportunities at MPhil and PhD levels.
Pubns: Annual Report; Occasional Pubns Series (£4.50-£20); departmental brochures

O420

University of Strathclyde, Department of Computing and Information Sciences

Livingstone Tower, 26 Richmond St, Glasgow, G1 1XH (0141-548-3700; *fax:* 0141-553-1393)
Email: enquiries@cis.strath.ac.uk
Internet: http://www.cis.strath.ac.uk/

Gov Body: Univ of Strathclyde (see also **S741**)
Chief: Head of Dept: Prof Andrew McGettrick
Other Snr Offcrs: Dep Head of Dept (Info Sci): Prof Forbes Gibb BA, FCLIP
Branches & Groups: CENTRE FOR DIGITAL LIBS RSRCH (see **O103**)
Activs: Instructional postgraduate courses in computing, information management and information and library studies. Research and consultancy in information management, information systems and technology.

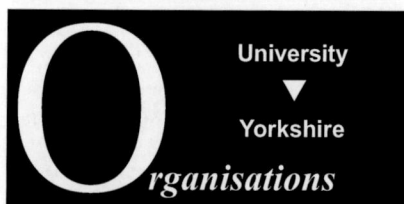

Organisations

O421
University of Wales Aberystwyth, Department of Information Studies [DIS]
Llanbadarn Fawr, Aberystwyth, Ceredigion, SY23 3AS (01970-622188; *fax:* 01970-622190)
Email: dils@aber.ac.uk
Internet: http://www.dil.aber.ac.uk/

Gov Body: Univ of Wales Aberystwyth (see also **S18**) *Chief:* Head of Dept: Mr Gwilym Huws BA, MCLIP (gwh@aber.ac.uk)
Membs: 17 staff; c700 full-time & part-time students
Activs: Research, consultancy and teaching at undergraduate and postgraduate levels in the fields of archives, information and library studies and records management.

O422
University Science and Technology Librarians Group [USTLG]
c/o Ms Moira Bent, Univ of Newcastle Lib, Jesmond Rd West, Newcastle upon Tyne, NE2 4HQ
Email: Moira.Bent@newcastle.ac.uk
Internet: http://www.leeds.ac.uk/library/ustlg/

Chief: contact Ms Moira Bent, as above
Activs: An informal group meeting two or three times a year to discuss topics of interest and to promote contacts between librarians involved in engineering, science or technology information provision in university libraries. Runs lis-scitech, an email discussion list for librarians in the fields of science and technology.

O423
US Law Firms in London Librarians Group
c/o Ms Julie Keys, Alder Castle, 10 Noble St, London, EC2V 7QJ (020-7645-2400)
Email: keys@bdh.com

Type: prof, legal *Chief:* contact Ms Julie Keys, as above *Other Snr Offcrs:* Ms Sue Doe (sdoe@sidley.com)
Memb Req: open to law libns & info mgrs of US law firms in London
Activs: Provides a forum for the exchange information and ideas.

O424
Wales Higher Education Libraries Forum [WHELF]
c/o Mr Nigel Soane, Univ of Wales Bangor Lib Svcs, Coll Rd, Bangor, Gwynedd, LL57 2DG (01248-382983; *fax:* 01248-382979)
Email: n.s.soane@bangor.ac.uk
Internet: http://library.newport.ac.uk/whelf/

Type: co-op *Chief:* Chair: Mr Andrew Green, Natl Lib of Wales (ang@llgc.org.uk) *Other Snr Offcrs:* Sec: Mr Nigel Soane, as above
Membs: 14 instns; Chief Libns & Dirs of Info Svcs of the Natl Lib of Wales & the 13 higher edu instns in Wales

Activs: Exists to promote library and information services co-operation, to encourage the exchange of ideas, to provide a forum for mutual support and to help facilitate new initiatives in library and information service provision. Meets twice a year.

O425
Warwickshire Local History Society
c/o Dr H. Phythian-Adams, 9 Willes Ter, Leamington Spa, Warwickshire, CV31 1DL (01926-429671)

Type: registered charity *Gov Body:* Exec Cttee
Chief: Hon Sec: Dr H. Phythian-Adams, as above
Membs: 152 indivs; 29 instns; Families: 34; Jnr: 1
Activs: Founded in 1965 to promote the study of local history in Warwickshire. Holds meetings with talks approximately every month; arranges visits and historical walks and social events at historical buildings; produces various regular and occasional publications.
Pubns: Warwickshire Hist (2 pa); Bulletin (2 pa, membs only); occasional pubns incl: Women's Capabilities: Light on the Lives of the Women of Stratford-upon-Avon (40p); The Making of the Warwickshire Country House 1500-1650 (£2.25); An Eighteenth Century Warwickshire Village: Snitterfield (£2.25)

O426
West Midlands Regional Archive Forum [WMRAR]
(formerly West Midlands Regional Archv Council)
c/o Mr Roger Vaughan, Herbert Art Gallery & Museum, Jordan Well, Coventry, West Midlands, CV1 5QP (024-7683-2375; *fax:* 024-7683-2141)
Email: roger.vaughan@coventry.gov.uk
Internet: http://www.westmidlandsarchives.org.uk/

Chief: Chair: Mr Roger Vaughan, as above
Membs: comprises representatives of prof bodies, users, funding bodies, regional museum & lib bodies & natl archv orgs
Activs: Exists to promote the care, use and development of archives in the West Midlands, as well as to encourage co-operative working between archives, museums and libraries and between archives and other regional agencies in the West Midlands.

O427
West Sussex Archives Society [WSAS]
c/o West Sussex Record Office, County Hall, Chichester, West Sussex, PO19 1EN (01243-533911; *fax:* 01243-533959)
Email: recordsoffice@westsussex.gov.uk
Internet: http://www.westsussex.gov.uk/librariesandarchives/recordoffice/friends/wsas/

Chief: Chairman: Mrs Brenda Fox *Other Snr Offcrs:* Sec: Ms Norma Weir
Membs: 310 indivs; 23 instns *Memb Req:* subscription: single £7 pa; joint £9 pa; institutional £10 pa; life membership £100
Activs: To arouse and stimulate interest in historical records and increase awareness of the need for their preservation; to assist in the work of the West Sussex Record Office by fund-raising, working parties or any other means; to seek out material of historical interest and persuade owners to ensure its preservation; to arrange outings, lectures and other activities to further interest in the history of West Sussex.
Pubns: West Sussex Hist (2 pa, £2 per issue); WSAS Newsletter (4 pa, free to membs)

O428
WILCO: Wiltshire Libraries in Co-operation
Central Lib, Regent Circus, Swindon, Wiltshire, SN1 1QG (01793-463240; *fax:* 01793-541319)
Email: reference.library@swindon.gov.uk
Internet: http://www.rmcs.cranfield.ac.uk/wilco/

Type: co-op *Gov Body:* Cttee of Membs *Chief:* Secretary/Treasurer: R.J. Trayhurn
Membs: 62 instns *Memb Req:* open to libs, info svcs & related orgs in Wiltshire; full membership is open to orgs with lib or info svc staff & which can contribute to WILCO's svcs; associate membership is open to orgs without specialist staff (subscription £25 pa)
Activs: Promotes and facilitates the free flow of information and documents between member libraries; provides an enquiry service, training seminars, bi-monthly business updates, a directory of member's specialist sources, and a journals listing.
Pubns: Directory of Membs (free to membs); WILCO News (bi-monthly, free to membs)

O429
Wiltshire Local History Forum [WLHF]
c/o Ms Ruth Newman, Tanglewood, Laverstock Pk, Salisbury, Wiltshire, SP1 1QJ (01722-328922)

Chief: Chairman: Ms Ruth Newman
Membs: 90 indivs; 50 instns *Memb Req:* open to anyone interested in the hist of Wiltshire; subscription: £7 pa
Activs: Operates as an umbrella organisation promoting local history in Wiltshire and giving local societies and individuals the opportunity to come together for mutual benefit. Organises an AGM and 2 day conferences each year: April Day School (practical emphasis on sources and methods); October Day Conference (4 talks on a particular theme on Wiltshire local history).
Pubns: WLHF Newsletter (3 pa, incl in membership, otherwise £1.50 each); Wiltshire Newspapers: A Guide (2002, £2.50 + 50p p&p)

O430
Wiltshire Record Society
c/o Wiltshire & Swindon Record Office, Lib HQ, Bythesen Rd, Trowbridge, Wiltshire, BA14 8BS (01225-713136; *fax:* 01225-713515)

Chief: Hon Sec: Mr John d'Arcy, at above addr
Other Snr Offcrs: Editor: Dr J. Chandler
Membs: 187 indivs; 121 instns
Activs: The publication of documents illustrating Wiltshire history.
Pubns: over 50 vols of historical records, new vols approx 1 pa; currently available vols incl: Calendar of Antrobus Deeds before 1625 (1947); Wiltshire Quarter Sessions & Assizes 1736 (1955, reprinted 1972); The Rolls of Highworth Hundred 1275-1287 (1966, 1968); Wiltshire Coroners' Bills 1752-1796 (1981); Wiltshire Dissenters' Meeting House Certificates & Registrations 1689-1852 (1985); Early Trade Directories of Wiltshire (1992); The Apprentice Registers of the Wiltshire Soc 1817-1922 (1997); other vols in preparation; all vols £15 to membs, £20 + p&p to non-membs

O431
Worcestershire Local History Forum
c/o Mr Bob Field, 45 Moreland Rd, Droitwich Spa, Worcestershire, WR9 8RN (01905-773420)

Chief: Chairman: Mr Robin Whittaker *Other Snr Offcrs:* Sec: Mr Bob Field, as above; Treasurer: Ms Theresa Nixon

Membs: 6 indivs; 39 instns *Memb Req:* subscriptions: indivs £3 pa, orgs £6 pa
Activs: Umbrella organisation covering local, family and community history throughout Worcestershire for the exchange of information on associated topics, e.g., projects, day schools, newsletters, exhibitions and meetings.
Pubns: Quarterly Newsletter (membs only); Speakers Directory 2002 (free to membs, £3 to non-membs)

O432
Working Group Against Racism in Children's Resources [WGARCR]
460 Wandsworth Rd, London, SW8 3LX (*tel & fax:* 020-7627-4594)
Email: wgarc.r@virgin.net
Internet: http://freespace.virgin.net/wgarc.r/

Type: social welfare, anti-racist ch's svcs *Gov Body:* WGARCR Mgmt Cttee *Chief:* Chair: Ms Marcia Tatham
Membs: 12 indivs
Branches & Groups: BKS SUB-GROUP; CHILD DEVELOPMENT SUB-GROUP; TOYS SUB-GROUP
Activs: To raise awareness amongst all those caring for young children that racism is damaging and hurtful to them and to all the children they care for; to identify racism in the resources that influence the lives of young children and to define and adopt strategies for its removal; to encourage the production and use of anti-racist resources and to develop techniques for their most effective use; to provide advice, counselling, support, representation and training services aimed at combating school exclusions.
Pubns: Guidelines for the Evaluation & Selection of Toys (£5); Guidelines and More Selected Titles (£7); Anti-Racist Resource Bklet (£3); Student Info Pack (£2.50); Kwanzaa (£4); Guidelines for the Evaluation & Selection of Child Development Bks (£3); Schools Exclusion: Wasteful, Destructive, Discriminatory (£5); poster set (£4); Dragons Teeth (magazine published by NCRCB, £1)

O433
WORKWELL: Workplace and Welsh Law Librarians Group
c/o Ms Ann Hemming, Hugh James Solicitors, Arlbee House, Greyfriars Rd, Cardiff, CF10 3QB (029-2022-4871; *fax:* 029-2038-8222)
Internet: http://www.workwellgroup.org.uk/

Type: prof *Chief:* Sec: Ms Ann Hemming, as above
Memb Req: open to anyone involved or concerned with the info provision in the workplace in Wales; no subscription
Branches & Groups: WORKWELL NORTH (regional group); WORKWELL LAW (specialist legal group, affiliated to BIALL – see O72)
Activs: Aims to provide an informal networking group for information workers, especially solo librarians in Wales, regardless of qualifications or CILIP membership; holds about nine meetings a year; provides discussion groups and e-mail newsgroups; organises presentations, training, product demonstrations; encourages self-help and the exchange of views and information.

O434
Wrekin Local Studies Forum [WLSF]
c/o Madeley Lib, Russell Sq, Madeley, Telford, TF7 5BB (01952-586575; *fax:* 01952-587105)
Email: wlsf@hotmail.com
Internet: http://www.library.madeley.org.uk/

Chief: Chair: Mrs Marilyn Higson
Membs: 24 instns
Activs: Brings together all the societies and organisations with an interest in local studies operating in the Wrekin district of Shropshire. Membership includes libraries, museums, archives, FE colleges, local history societies, family history societies and reminiscence groups. The Forum meets four times per year to exchange information and ideas, and organises an annual event at which all member organisations can display their interests and achievements.
Pubns: Events Calendar (2 pa); indiv memb orgs have their own pubns programmes

O435
Writers' Guild of Great Britain
15 Britannia St, London, WC1X 9JN (020-7833-0777; *fax:* 020-7833-4777)
Email: admin@writersguild.org.uk
Internet: http://www.writersguild.org.uk/

Type: trade union *Chief:* Genl Sec: Mr Bernie Corbett
Memb Req: open to all writers working in television, radio, film, theatre, bks & multimedia; subscription: full membs £125 pa + 1% of earnings from writing over £12500, to a maximum of £1250 pa, candidate membs £75 pa, affiliate membs £225 pa
Activs: Trade union for professional writers in all media, dedicated to ensuring that writers are properly paid and credited. Organises various professional, cultural and social activities, and provides insurance and pension schemes for members.
Pubns: Writers' Bulletin (6 pa, free to membs, £25 pa to non-membs)

O436
Writers, Artists and their Copyright Holders [WATCH]
c/o Univ of Reading Lib, PO Box 223, Whiteknights, Reading, Berkshire, RG6 6AE (0118-931-8783; *fax:* 0118-931-6636)
Email: D.C.Sutton@reading.ac.uk
Internet: http://www.watch-file.com/

Gov Body: Univ of Reading (see S1848) & Univ of Texas at Austin *Chief:* UK Dir: Dr David Sutton
Activs: The successor to the location register project, WATCH provides an on-line database of literary copyright holders; the database is available free of charge on the internet and the world wide web.

O437
York Bibliographical Society
c/o Mr Chris Weston, 'Asher-Beth', 8 Low Green, Copmanthorpe, York, YO2 3SB (01904-708570)
Internet: http://www-users.york.ac.uk/~pml1/ybs.htm

Chief: Hon Sec: Mr Chris Weston, as above
Other Snr Offcrs: Hon Treasurer: Mr Peter Lee, Wentworth Coll, Univ of York, Heslington, York, YO10 5DD (01904-433014; *fax:* 01904-433019; *email:* pml1@york.ac.uk)
Memb Req: open to all those interested in the hist, production, illustration, dissemination, ownership and reading of bks
Activs: Provides a point of contact for all those who love books, and who would like to share their enthusiasm and knowledge with others; holds monthly meetings and six annual lectures, and organises visits to libraries.

O438
Yorkshire Archaeological Society, Local History Section
Claremont, 23 Clarendon Rd, Leeds, W Yorkshire, LS2 9NZ (0113-245-7910; *fax:* 0113-244-1979)
Email: secretary@yas.org.uk

Gov Body: Yorkshire Archaeological Soc *Chief:* contact the Section via the Sec of the Soc at the above addr
Membs: 170 indivs
Activs: Informal group aiming to promote the study of local history in Yorkshire through the pooling of knowledge and experience, meetings, lectures, excursions and day schools – all on a wide variety of topics.
Pubns: Bulletin (£1 per issue)
See also S919

O439
Yorkshire Archives Council [YAC]
c/o Mrs Louise Hampson, Church House, 10-14 Ogleforth, York, YO1 7JN (01904-557239; *fax:* 01904-557215)
Email: louiseh@yorkminster.org
Internet: http://www.yarc.org.uk/

Chief: Chair: Mrs Louise Hampson, as above
Other Snr Offcrs: Archvs Offcr: Ms Claire Dyson (clare@yhmc.org.uk)
Membs: elected or co-opted as cross-section of prof & user bodies in the region
Activs: Strategic body for archives in the Yorkshire region; aims to enhance communication and co-ordination across all archives in the region and to improve access and standards through co-operative projects. Acts as an advisory body to the Yorkshire Museum, Library and Archives Council.
Pubns: Yorkshire Archvs Forward: Regional Strategic Framework for Archvs in Yorkshire 2001-2005

O440
Yorkshire Libraries and Information [YLI]
c/o Lib HQ, Balne Ln, Wakefield, W Yorkshire, WF2 0DQ (01924-302210; *fax:* 01924-302245)
Email: kholliday@wakefield.gov.uk
Internet: http://www.yli.org.uk/

Type: co-op *Chief:* Hon Sec: Mr Rob Warburton
Membs: 29 instns; open to any org engaged in the provision of lib or info svcs which has its HQ or centre of operations within the region
Activs: Brings together libraries and information providers in the Yorkshire area in order to create a comprehensive regional community of library and information interests; aims to assist library and information providers in the region to offer cost-effective quality services through co-operative effort and interlending; operates a delivery and exchange service between libraries and information providers and to form a link with other regions in the country.

SECTION 6 – IRISH LEGAL DEPOSIT LIBRARIES

This section consists of the two main legal deposit or copyright libraries entitled to receive copies of all materials published in the Republic of Ireland:

National Libraries
IL1 The National Library of Ireland

University Libraries
IL2 Trinity College Library Dublin

Each entry has the following general format:

An introductory paragraph, including a brief history of the Library.

General Information – including address and contact details; opening hours (if applicable to the Library as a whole); names of chief officers; staff numbers; general financial figures; stock and holdings; admissions policy; any other general points of relevance.

Structure of the Library – lists the main departments or divisions of the Library, including (where appropriate): address and contact details; opening hours; names of chief officers; a description of the functions of the department; details of stock and special collections; details of any other organisations or services for which the department is responsible.

Special Collections – if not covered by entries for individual departments. Please note that only major collections are included.

Electronic Information Resources – if not covered by entries for individual departments. Includes details of major resources available, such as online databases and CD-ROMs.

Dependent or Branch Libraries – including address and contact details; opening hours; names of chief officers; subjects covered; details of stock and special collections; details of services provided and online resources available.

Other Services – such as exhibitions and publications, if not covered by entries for individual departments.

Telephone and fax numbers are given in the form of area dialling codes within the Republic of Ireland. To telephone the Irish Republic from outside the country, dial 00-353 followed by the number, minus the initial 0.

IL1 - NATIONAL LIBRARY OF IRELAND
(Leabharlann Náisiúnta na h-Éireann)

THE NATIONAL LIBRARY OF IRELAND derives its origins from the Library of the Royal Dublin Society, founded in 1731. In 1877 a substantial portion of the Royal Dublin Society library was purchased by the State and the new National Library of Ireland was established. An agreement of 1881 provided that the Library should operate under the superintendence of a Council of Trustees, eight of whom are appointed by the Royal Dublin Society and four by the Government. The National Library of Ireland aims to collect, preserve and make accessible materials on or relating to Ireland, whether published in Ireland or abroad, together with a supporting reference collection.

GENERAL INFORMATION

National Library of Ireland, 2-3 Kildare Street, Dublin 2, Ireland (01-603-0200; *fax:* 01-676-6690)
Email: info@nli.ie
Internet: http://www.nli.ie/

Director (and Chief Herald of Ireland): Mr Brendan O Donogue
Keeper: Ms Catherine Fahy
Keeper of Collections: Mr Dónall Ó Luanaigh
Keeper of Systems: Mr Brian McKenna
Keeper of Manuscripts: Mr Gerald Lynn
Keeper, Genealogical Office: Mr Fergus Mac Giolla Easpaig
Keeper, Administration: Mr Aongus Ó hAonghusa
Total staff: 103
Holdings: c6 million items
Admission: Genealogy (microfilms)/Newspaper research: passes, which may be obtained in the main Library building, are required. Other readers must apply for a Readers Ticket (for which proof of identity and two passport photos are necessary). To view manuscripts, a supplementary Manuscripts Readers Ticket, issued by the Duty Librarian, is required.

The Reader's Ticket Office is open during the following hours: Mon-Wed 1000-1230, 1400-1700, Thu-Fri 1000-1230, 1400-1630, Sat 1000-1200.

STRUCTURE OF THE LIBRARY

The main Library building was opened in 1890. Over the years the Library has extended to adjacent premises in Kildare Street and moved its photographic collections to the National Photographic Archive in the Temple Bar area of Dublin. Further expansion is underway, with a phased building programme scheduled for completion in 2004. Expanded facilities at the Kildare Street premises will include new specialist reading rooms, a new exhibition area, state of the art storage and a new administrative centre.

Printed books, pamphlets and newspapers may be consulted in the main Reading Room. Microforms are viewed in the adjacent Microform Reading Room. The Library's manuscript collections are made available in the Manuscripts Reading Room, while the photographic collections may be consulted in the Reading Room at the National Photographic Archive.

MAIN READING ROOM AND MICROFILM READING ROOM
Open: Mon-Wed 1000-2100, Thu-Fri 1000-1700, Sat 1000-1300

MANUSCRIPTS READING ROOM
Open: Mon-Wed 1000-2030, Thu-Fri 1000-1630, Sat 1000-1230

READING ROOM, NATIONAL PHOTOGRAPHIC ARCHIVE
Open: Mon-Fri 1000-1700

The main departments of the Library are:

PRINTED BOOKS AND PAMPHLETS
Acquisitions Librarian: Mr Gerard Long
Collections comprise approximately 1 million titles, with extensive general coverage of the humanities. The emphasis, particularly as regards current acquisitions policy, is on material relating to Ireland and the Irish people.

Holdings, with certain exceptions, are listed on the Library's OPAC.

SPECIAL COLLECTIONS
Foundation collections: Royal Dublin Society Library Collection (mainly science and technology, 70,000 vols); Joly Collection (Irish materials and rare editions, 25,000 vols); other major collections include: Dix Collection (printing in Ireland, 18C-19C, 8,000 vols); Lough Fea Pamphlets (17C, 300 items); William O'Brien Collection (republican and socialist pamphlets, 19C-20C, c1000 items); O'Kelly

Collection (religion in Ireland, 18C-20C, 946 titles); Swift Collection (early editions by Jonathan Swift, 500 vols); Alexander Thom Collection (general interest, 3,900 vols); Thorpe Pamphlets (Irish politics, 18C-19C, 300 items).

MANUSCRIPTS

Comprising some 750,000 items, the earliest dating from the 12C, the main components of the manuscripts collection are Gaelic manuscripts, landed estate archives, maps, political material and literary papers.

There are four parts to the manuscripts catalogue: *Manuscript Sources for the History of Irish Civilisation* (items catalogued pre-1965), the *Supplement* to *Manuscript Sources for the History of Irish Civilisation* (items catalogued 1965-75), Manuscripts card catalogue (items catalogued 1976-90), and on OPAC (items catalogued post-1990).

SPECIAL COLLECTIONS
Gaelic MSS Collection (earliest dating from 14C, 1,236 vols); extensive collections of estate papers (mostly 17C-20C), among the more notable of which are: Balfour; Bellew; Castletown; Clements; Clonbrock; Conyngham; Coolattin; De Freyne; De Vesci; Doneraile; Farnham; Fingall; Ffrench; Headford; Inchiquin; Lismore; Louth; Mahon; Mansfield; Monteagle; O'Hara; Ormond; Powerscourt; Prior-Wandesford; Sarsfield; Wicklow; Wynne; papers of Irish political figures, 18C onwards, including: Wolfe Tone; Daniel O'Connell; William Smith O'Brien; James Fintan Lalor; T.C. Harrington; T.P. Gill; William O'Brien; J.F.X. O'Brien; John Redmond; Piarais Béaslaí; Sir Roger Casement; Erskine Childers; Thomas MacDonagh; Bulmer Hobson; Eoin McNeill; Seán T. O'Kelly; Patrick Pearse; Thomas Johnston; papers of Irish writers, including: William Butler Yeats; James Joyce (including the James Joyce/Paul Léon Papers); Maria Edgeworth; Canon Sheehan; Richard Brinsley Sheridan; George Moore; John Millington Synge; George Bernard Shaw; Seán O'Casey; Patrick Kavanagh; Brendan Behan; Benedict Kiely; James Plunkett; Hugh Leonard; Michael Hartnett; Tom MacIntyre.

The Gaelic manuscripts in the collections are being made available online in digital format through the ongoing Irish Script on Screen project.

NEWSPAPERS AND PERIODICALS
Assistant Keeper (Newspapers & Periodicals): Ms Colette O'Daly
Consists mainly of material of Irish interest and includes complete files of a high percentage of the several hundred titles which have been published from late 17C to the present day. The Library receives about 300 titles annually. These include national, provincial and local titles and also Irish newspapers published abroad.

Newspaper holdings are listed in the Library's Newspaper Index and in the published *Report of the NEWSPLAN Project in Ireland* (revised 1998). Periodicals are listed on the Library's OPAC, and particular articles of Irish interest are listed in *Sources for the History of Irish Civilisation: Articles in Irish Periodicals*, available in the main Reading Room.

MAJOR TITLES
Include: An Account of the Chief Occurrences in Ireland (Ireland's first newspaper, 1660s); Belfast Newsletter (from 1737); Limerick Chronicle (from 1766); The Pilot; The Nation; The Freeman's Journal; Nationality; Fáinne an Lae.

OFFICIAL PUBLICATIONS
Consists of Irish governmental and other official materials dating from the 17C, including acts, statutes, proclamations, departmental reports and statistics. British material relating to Ireland is also held. The collection includes many official publications of international bodies

such as the EU, the UN and its agencies, GATT, the Council of Europe, OECD. The library also holds good collections of publications and reports of Irish semi-state bodies such as Bord Fáilte, CIE, Aer Lingus and others, although these are not catalogued as official publications.

SPECIAL COLLECTIONS
Include: Irish Statutes (pre-1801); Irish House of Commons Journal (pre-1801); Blue Books (British Parliamentary Papers, post-1801, 7,000 vols); Acts of an tOireachtas (1922 onwards); debates of Dáil Éireann and Seanad Éireann (1922 onwards).

PRINTS AND DRAWINGS
Curator (Prints & Drawings): Ms Joanna Finegan
Open: Mon-Fri 1000-1700 by appointment
Collections comprise some 100,000 items, many of them acquired with the Royal Dublin Society and Joly Collections. Materials include topographical and antiquarian drawings, architectural drawings (including many by major 19C architects) and some 20,000 portraits. There are important illustrations, watercolours, engravings and cartoons recording the political, social and economic history of Ireland, and a growing collection of works by 20C Irish illustrators and artists.

SPECIAL COLLECTIONS
Include: Joseph Holloway Collection (drawings relating to Irish literary and theatrical society, 19C-20C); Ray Collection (cartoons and portraits of Daniel O'Connell)

Holdings are listed in various sources including the published *Catalogue of Irish Topographical Prints* and the *Catalogue of Engraved Irish Portraits*. A card index of architectural drawings in available in the Catalogue Room. A number of collections have been selected for digitisation and these images may be viewed via their respective catalogue entries on the OPAC. An appointment is required to view original materials.

MAPS
Keeper (MS Maps): Ms Elizabeth Kirwan
Keeper (Printed Maps): Ms Joanna Finegan
Collections comprise some 150,000 maps and include cartographic materials ranging from a 12C coloured sketch map of Europe to the most recent Ordnance Survey maps.

SPECIAL COLLECTIONS
Down Survey maps (18C copies of 17C originals); 18C estate maps including the collection of surveyors Brownrigg, Longfield and Murray; maps commissioned by the County Grand Juries (late 18C-19C) and Ordnance Survey maps (1830s onwards).

Pre-1990 printed and MS maps are listed in the Map Catalogue, a card index located in the Catalogue Room. Maps catalogued since 1990 are listed on the Library's OPAC. MS maps are also listed in the various MSS catalogues.

NATIONAL PHOTOGRAPHIC ARCHIVE
Meeting House Square, Temple Bar, Dublin 2, Ireland (01-603-0371; fax: 01-677-7451)
Email: photoarchive@nli.ie
Open: Mon-Fri 1000-1700, Sat (exhibition space only) 1000-1400; an appointment may be required to view some unsorted or fragile materials.
Curator: Ms Gráinne MacLochlainn

Comprising some 300,000 items, the Library's photographic collections are held at the National Photographic Archive, a purpose-built facility in the Temple Bar area of Dublin.

Subjects: historical photography in Ireland, mainly topographical, but also including studio portraits, early tourist photos and photographic coverage of political & social events; some contemporary material.
Stock: 180 sq m of archives, 300,000 photos
Collections: numerous collections of negatives, photo albums and photo prints, including: Cardall Collection (postcard photography,

5,000 negatives, 1950s-60s); Clonbrock Collection (landed estate life, 3,500 glass plates, 1860-1930); Eason Collection (postcard photography, 4,000 negatives, 1900-40); Eblana Collection (early photography, 3,000 glass plates); Keogh Collection (political figures and events, 330 glass plates, 1915-30); Lawrence Collection (commercial photography, 40,000 glass negatives, 1870-1914); Morgan Collection (aerial photography, 1950s); O'Dea Collection (Irish railway transport, 5,350 prints, 1937-66); Poole Collection (commercial photography, 60,000 glass plates, 1884-1945); Valentine Collection (topographical images, 3,000 negatives, 1900-60); Wiltshire Collection (Dublin life, 1,000 negatives, 300 prints, 1951-71); Wynne Collection (social life in Co Mayo, 8,000 glass negatives, 1867-1960); the Archive also maintains a small reference collection. Indexes and catalogues to most of the collections are available in the Archive's Reading Room.
Services: microform readers, photocopying, reprographic service, exhibitions, shop.
Publications: Into the Light: An Illustrated Research Guide to the Photographic Collection of the National Library of Ireland
Staff: 9

GENEALOGICAL OFFICE (OFFICE OF THE CHIEF HERALD OF IRELAND)
2 Kildare Street, Dublin 2, Ireland (01-603-0311; fax: 01-662-1062)
Email: herald@nli.ie

The Genealogical Office, which incorporates the Office of the Chief Herald of Ireland, has functioned as a branch of the Library since 1943 and the Director of the Library also acts as Chief Herald. The Chief Herald is the heraldic authority for Ireland, the State authority responsible for the devising and granting of arms.

Subjects: heraldry and genealogy. Archives of the Office can be read in the Library's Manuscripts Reading Room. Book collections are used mainly by staff, and are available only by appointment.
Collections: Registers of Arms; Registers of Pedigrees; funeral entries; archives from 1552.
Services: granting of arms to corporate bodies and individuals; limited genealogical searches within the records of the Office, on a fee basis.

HERALDIC MUSEUM
Open: Mon-Wed 1000-2030, Thu-Fri 1000-1630, Sat 1000-1230
A permanent exhibition illustrating the history, use and development of heraldy in Ireland and Europe. Admission is free.

LIBRARY SERVICES

FAMILY HISTORY RESEARCH
Open: Mon-Fri 1000-1645, Sat 1000-1230
The Library's Genealogy Service is freely available to all personal callers to the Library. The Service is intended to assist those who wish to carry out their own research but who require advice on relevant records and research procedure.

Sources held by Library which are of particular interest to genealogists include: Catholic parish registers (up to 1880); Tithe Applotment Books (1823-38); Griffith's Valuation (1848-64); trade and social directories (18C to date); newspapers; rentals, surveys and other records of the former landed estates (18-19C).

REPROGRAPHIC SERVICES
Subject to copyright provisions and conservation requirements, photocopying services, microfilming services and photo reproduction are all available.

EXHIBITIONS AND PUBLICATIONS
Exhibitions are held in both the main Library building and in the National Photographic Archive. The Library also publishes a wide range of materials including books and guides, reports, booklets, document facsimile folders, CD-ROMS, calendars and postcards. These are available in the Library shop.

IL2 - TRINITY COLLEGE LIBRARY DUBLIN

TRINITY COLLEGE LIBRARY DUBLIN is located in five buildings on the College Campus, one branch library and the Book Repository. The collection has been built up from the late 16th century and is now the largest library in Ireland. It became a legal deposit library in 1801, and continues to receive copies of materials published in Ireland and the United Kingdom. The Library fulfils a triple role: as the central information resource for the University, as a legal deposit library for both Ireland and the United Kingdom and as a major research resource.

GENERAL INFORMATION

Trinity College Library Dublin, College St, Dublin 2, Ireland (01-677-2941; *fax:* 01-671-9003)
Internet: http://www.tcd.ie/Library/

Librarian: Robin Adams BA, DipLib (radams@tcd.ie)
Deputy Librarian: post vacant
Total staff: 150
Holdings: 4.25 million volumes; 30,000 periodical titles
Expenditure: €8,700,000 (2001-02)
Admission: on production of a current College identity card; academic staff and doctoral students from institutions participating in the ALCID scheme (Academic Libraries Co-operating in Ireland); other users should apply in writing to the Librarian, specifying the nature of their research and the special collections which they need to consult. It would be advisable to contact the Keeper of Readers' Services (see below) about current admission arrangements prior to visiting the Library.

Open: see individual departments; the Library closes completely for 2 weeks during summer for stocktaking and maintenance.

STRUCTURE OF THE LIBRARY

The Library has four major operational units:

1. READERS' SERVICES

Keeper: Trevor Peare (trevor.peare@tcd.ie)
Reader Services are provided from three Reading Rooms and from the Santry Book Repository. The Reading Rooms have access to the Library's on-line catalogue and to a wide range of electronic databases. Circulation and reference services are provided to students and staff and to over 10,000 external readers per year. The main Reading Rooms are:

Open: Berkeley Ussher Lecky Library Complex and Hamilton Library: term: Mon-Fri 0900-2200, Sat 0930-1600; vac: Mon-Wed, Fri 0930-1700, Thu 0930-2100 (Hamilton -1700), Sat 0930-1300; hours on Sat during term may vary after 1300 according to staffing levels.

THE BERKELEY/LECKY/USSHER LIBRARY

(01-608-1127/1125/1461)
Open: term: Mon-Fri 0900-2200, Sat 0930-1600
Houses the central reference collections and research material in Arts (Humanities), Arts (Letters), Business, Economics and Social Studies, Geography, Geology and Nursing. Details for the special collections in Maps, Music, Official Publications and the Research Area, also located in this Library, are given below:

MUSIC LIBRARY

1st Floor, Berkeley (01-608-1156)
Music Librarian: Roy Stanley (rstanley@tcd.ie)
Houses the main collections of printed music and music literature. The collection of music literature comprises books, periodicals, reference works and bibliographies (some now in electronic format). The open access holdings of printed music include collected editions of the works of major composers, anthologies, manuscript facsimiles, and other individual works and editions. The more substantial closed access collection contains diverse items received under legal deposit since the early 20C. Early printed music is held in the Department of Early Printed books, and MS material in the Department of Manuscripts.

OFFICIAL PUBLICATIONS

1st Floor, Berkeley (01-608-2342)
Official Publications Librarian: John Goodwillie (john.goodwillie@tcd.ie)
The collection includes Irish, UK and Northern Ireland publications. The Library has been a European Documentation Centre since 1973, and receives most publications of the European Union. Full or partial collections are also held of the publications of the UN and associated organisations (e.g., World Bank, International Labour Organisation, World Health Organization and International Monetary Fund), European Free Trade Association, Organisation for Economic Co-operation and Development, Commonwealth of Nations, Council of Europe, North Atlantic Treaty Organization, Pan American Union and Western European Union.

RESEARCH AREA

2nd Floor, Berkeley (01-608-1666)
Assistant Librarian: Anne Walsh (walsha@tcd.ie)
Houses printed sources and reference materials primarily in the fields of medieval and modern history. Also holds British and Irish historical, biographical, genealogical and local source material, including the publications of antiquarian and record societies. Other holdings include British Parliamentary Debates, Dáil and Seanad Debates, and publications of the Public Record Office, Historical MSS Commission, Irish MSS Commission and the Royal Commission on Historical Monuments. Other significant primary resource material include the *Monumenta Germanicae Historica*, *Patrologia Latina* and *Corpus Christianorum*.

GLUCKSMAN MAP LIBRARY

Basement, Ussher
(01-608-2087/1544; *fax:* 01-608-3537)
Email: map.library@tcd.ie
Open: Tue, Thu 1430-1645, Wed (Oct-Jun only) 0930-1300, closed Sep; other times by appointment
Map Librarian: Paul Ferguson
Contains the largest collection of printed maps and atlases in Ireland, holding over 650,000 items in paper, microform and digital formats. The collection is particularly strong on Ireland (including Northern Ireland) and Great Britain, but covers all areas of the world. The reading room also contains current atlases as well as a growing collection of reference works, gazetteers, catalogues, bibliographies, monographs and periodicals on maps and map-making, cartographers, the history of cartography, exploration and place-names.

THE HAMILTON LIBRARY

Hamilton Bldg (01-608-1805)
Open: term: Mon-Fri 0900-2200, Sat 0930-1600; vac: Mon-Fri 0930-1700, Sat 0930-1300
Sub-Librarian: Arlene Healy (arhealy@tcd.ie)
Houses the main book and journal collection for Life Sciences, Natural Sciences, Mathematics, Engineering, Computer Science and Pre-Clinical Medicine.

1937 READING ROOM

Open: term: Mon-Fri 0930-2200, Sat 0930-1300
The building functions as a Postgraduate Study Centre and does not house any collections.

Readers' Services is also responsible for:

THE INFORMATION SERVICE

Berkeley Library Bldg (01-608-1673; *fax:* 01-671-9003)
Email: infoserv@tcd.ie
Information Librarian: Deirdre Allen
Provides a fee-based information and document delivery service to members in the industrial, legal, financial and government sector. Specific services include manual searching of an extensive range of reference books and periodicals, database seaches in virtually all subject areas, and loans of books and photocopies of relevant documents subject to the provisions of the Copyright Act.

2. EARLY PRINTED BOOKS AND SPECIAL COLLECTIONS

East Pavilion, Old Library Bldg (01-608-1172)
Open: Mon-Fri 1000-2200 (-1700 during vacs), Sat 1000-1245
Keeper: Charles Benson (charles.benson@tcd.ie)
Responsible for all early printed books, including all books and periodicals printed before 1850, scarce and difficult-to-replace material printed from 1850-date, such as special collections, books of Irish interest, especially literary first editions, books printed in limited editions or by private presses, and some 19C and 20C newspapers and periodicals. The Department houses (along with the Berkeley Library), the Printed Catalogue of books received up to 1872. The department is also responsible for the Trinity Closet Press, a hand press which is used for teaching purposes as well as acting as a printing museum.

SPECIAL COLLECTIONS

Bender Collection (Californian private press books, 1920-50, c495 items); Bibliotheca Earberiana/Crofton Collection (political and economic pamphlets, especially Irish, 17C-18C, c2,000 items), Biblioteca Quiniana/Quin Collection (fine bindings, 16C-18C, 110 titles); Bonaparte-Wyse Collection (Provencal and Catalan literature, late 19C, 1,250 vols); Cuala Press Archive; Drama Collection (English and Irish drama, 17C-18C, 3,000 items); Fagel Collection (European history, politics and geography, 17C-18C, 20,000 items); Michael Freyer Dolmen Press Collection (1951-73, c466 items); Old Library Collections (17C-19C mathematics, philosophy, theology); Pollard School Book Collection (school textbooks, 18C-1910, 550 vols); Prout Collection (19C music); Purser Shortt Collection (liturgies and religious works, 18C-19C, c900 items); Sairseal agus Dill Collection (Irish language editions, 20C, 293 vols); Starkey Collection (hymnals and psalters, 18C-19C, 250 vols); Trinity College Historical Society Library (philosophy, history, literature, 18C, 350 vols); Yeats Collection (Anglo-Irish literature, 19C-20C, 194 items).

3. MANUSCRIPTS

West Pavilion, Old Library Bldg (01-608-1189)
Open: Mon-Fri 1000-1700, Sat 1000-1300
Keeper: Dr Bernard Meehan (bernard.meehan@tcd.ie)
Maintains the Library's MS collections, including some of its greatest treasures, including:

Book of Kells (c800); Book of Durrow (c675); Book of Armagh (807); Book of Dimma (8C); Book of Mulling (8C); Matthew Paris's Life of St Alban (12C); Fagel Missal (15C).

SPECIAL COLLECTIONS

Medieval insular MSS; James Ussher Collection; Greek and Egyptian papyri; Roman inquisitorial records (16C-18C); Petrie and Goodman Collections (Irish folk music); Ballet and Dallis Collection (lute books); as well as contemporary literary collections; 1798 Rebellion papers; numerous family and private papers.

Also responsible for Trinity College Dublin's own archives and muniments (16C-date).

The Library is a leading partner in ISOS (Irish Script on Screen/ Meamram Páipéar Ríomhaire), a co-operative venture dedicated to producing high-resolution digital images of Irish manuscripts for display on the World Wide Web.

4. COLLECTION MANAGEMENT

Keeper: Margaret Flood (margaret.flood@tcd.ie)
Based in the Berkeley/Lecky/Ussher Library, it accessions, catalogues and processes materials acquired by the Library. Also responsible for reprographic services, including microfilming, photography and digitisation.

OTHER SERVICES

VISITOR SERVICES

(01-608-2320; *fax:* 01-608-2090)
Staff Contact: Anne Marie Diffley (adiffley@tcd.ie)
The Long Room, Colonnades, Exhibition Area and Treasury in the Old Library are open to the public. Over 500,000 visitors see the building and the Book of Kells annually. The Library Shop has an extensive range of books and jewellery.

EXHIBITIONS

The Library mounts major exhibitions annually in the Colonnades area of the Old Library. A series of smaller scale exhibitions is held in the Long Room.

BRANCH LIBRARY

JOHN STEARNE MEDICAL LIBRARY

Trinity Centre for Health Sciences, St James's Hospital, James's St, Dublin 8, Ireland (01-608-2109/2724)
Open: term: Mon-Thu 0930-2145, Fri 0930-2030, Sat 0930-1300; vac: Mon-Fri 0930-1700
Medical Librarian: Thelma Pope (tpope@tcd.ie)

Subjects: core books and periodicals in clinical medicine, surgery, physiotherapy, nutrition, nursing and occupational therapy.
Stock: c10,000 books; 410 periodicals.
Services: photocopying; computer facilities, including internet.

SECTION 7 – IRISH PUBLIC LIBRARIES

Entries are arranged alphabetically under local authority names.

Public libraries are not generally open on bank holidays.

Telephone and fax numbers are given in the form of area dialling codes within the Republic of Ireland. To telephone the Irish Republic from outside the country, dial 00-353 followed by the number, minus the initial 0.

Entries are based on the library authorities' responses to the following questions:

	1. **Name of Library Service**
	2. **Full address of administrative headquarters or central library** *(incl. postcode)*
	Tel & Fax *(incl. STD code)*
Email:	**Electronic Mail**
Internet:	**Internet address**
Local Auth:	3. **Name of governing Local Authority**
Pop:	4. **Population served**
Cttee:	5. **Committee responsible for libraries**
	6. **Is library part of a larger department?** *(e.g., Amenities, Leisure Services)*
	If so please provide:
Larger Dept:	a) Name of department
Dept Chief:	b) Chief Officer *(give designation, name, qualifications)*
Chief:	7. **Chief Librarian/Officer** *(please state if responsible for a wider service than libraries alone)* Give designation, name, qualifications, email
Dep:	8. **Deputy** Give designation, name, qualifications, email
	9. **Other Senior Staff** Give designations, names, qualifications, email
Main Libs:	10. **District/Area/Regional/Divisional Libraries** Give addresses, postcodes, tel & fax, email
Branch Libs:	11. **Branch (or Community) Libraries** *(open for 20 or more hrs per week)* Give addresses, postcodes, tel & fax, email
Svc Pts:	12. **Number of service points**
PT:	a) Part-time libraries *(open less than 20 hrs per week)*
Mobile:	b) Mobile libraries
AV:	c) Service points with audiovisual stock
Computers:	d) Service points with computer facilities
Internet:	e) Service points with internet facilities
Other:	f) Other *(please specify)*
Collns:	13. **Special Collections** *(incl. BSI, EDC, & collns held as part of a national co-operative scheme, e.g., SCOLMA: Kenya, or STD: M-Mi)* Give collection name, subject(s), location, brief details
Co-op Schemes:	14. **Co-operative schemes in which library participates** *(incl. any listed in Q13, using acronyms where possible)*
ILLs:	15. **Inter-library loans**
Loans:	16. **Loan period** For books, audios, videos, CD-ROMs, other
Charges:	17. **Loan charges or subscription** *(if any)* For audios, videos, CD-ROMs, other
Income Gen:	18. **Other charges and income generation** *(not fees for equipment & facilities, for which see Q20)* For requests, reservations, lost tickets, other
Fines:	19. **Fines** *(if fine is distinguished from loan charge)* For books (adults, children, OAPs), audios, videos, CD-ROMs, other
	Groups exempt from fines *(e.g., registered blind)*
Equip:	20. **Equipment & facilities available to library users** *(give numbers, and fees per item if any)*
Disabled:	**Equipment for disabled** *(please specify, e.g., Kurzweil)*
Online:	**Online information service available** *(e.g., Dialog, give fees)*
	Other *(please specify)*
Offcr-in-Charge:	**Officer in charge of equipment purchases** Give designation, name, email

	21. **Stock & Issues**
Stock:	**Stock** (for 2000 & 2001)
Issues:	**Issues** (during 2000 & 2001)
ad lend:	a) Adult lending
ad ref:	b) Adult reference
ch:	c) Children *(excl. **d** below)*
schools:	d) Schools
instns:	e) Institutions *(e.g., prisons)*
audios:	f) Audios *(incl. cassettes & CDs)*
videos:	g) Videos
CD-ROMs:	h) CD-ROMs
periodcls:	i) Periodicals *(titles currently taken)*
archvs:	j) Archives *(specify unit e.g., linear, cubic metre)*
Acqs:	22. **Acquisitions** (during 2000 & 2001)
bks:	a) Books
AVs:	b) Audiovisuals
Source:	**Usual sources of acquisitions**
Co-op:	**Co-operative acquisitions programs**
Offcr-in-Charge:	**Officer in charge of acquisitions** Give designation, name, email
Classn:	23. **Classification method(s) used**
Cat:	24. **Catalogue**
Type:	**Type(s) of catalgue(s) used**
Medium:	**Medium on which the catalogue is kept**
Auto Sys:	25. **Automated Library system used** *(if any)*
Svcs:	**Services**
Extramural:	26. **Extramural services**
Info:	27. **Information services** *(please specify, e.g., business, community, careers, etc.)*
Other:	28. **Other services provided** *(please specify, e.g., open learning, etc.)*
Activs:	29. **Activities & Entertainments** *(on a regular basis)*
Offcr-in-Charge:	**Officer in charge** Give designation, name, email
Enqs:	30. **Enquiries handled** (during 2000 & 2001)
Staff:	31. **Staff establishment** *(give full-time equivalent for part-time staff incl. vacancies)*
	Total number of:
Libns:	a) Professional librarians
Other Prof:	b) Professional staff other than **a**
Non-Prof:	c) Non-professional staff
	32. **Finance** (for 2000 & 2001)
Inc from:	**Income from:**
local govt:	a) Local Government
fines/fees/sales:	b) Fines, Fees & Sales
total:	c) Total Income *(incl. a, b & any other income)*
Exp on:	**Expenditure on:**
bks:	a) Books & Printed Stock *(incl. binding)*
AV:	b) Audiovisual Stock *(incl. CD-ROMs)*
elec media:	c) Electronic media & Services *(incl. internet)*
activs:	d) Cultural activities
salaries:	e) Salaries & wages *(incl. superannuation & insurance & training)*
total:	f) Total Expenditure *(incl. **a** to **e** & any other exp)*
Proj:	33. **Capital projects** *(name any capital project approved for start in 2001 or 2002 and costing more than £100,000)*
Further Info:	34. **Additional Information**

Carlow

IP1 Carlow County Libraries

Carlow Central Lib, Tullow St, Carlow, Ireland
(0503-70094; *fax*: 0503-40548)
Email: carlowlib@hotmail.com
Internet: http://www.countycarlow.ie/services/
newLibrary.htm

Local Auth: Carlow County Council *Pop:* 45845
Chief: County Libn: Mr Thomas King (tking@
carlowcoco.ie)
Main Libs: CARLOW COUNTY LIB, addr as
above *Branch Libs:* MUINEBHEAG LIB, Main St,
Muinebheag, Co Carlow (0503-22208); TULLOW
LIB, The Courthouse, Barrack St, Tullow,
Co Carlow (0503-51497)
Svc Pts: Computers: 3 *Internet:* 3 *Other:* svc to
primary schools
Collns: Bruen Colln; Jackson Colln; Tyndall Colln;
Burton papers; Vigors Papers (all local studies
collns held at County Lib) *Loans:* bks/3 wks
Equip: copiers, computers (with internet, access
free)

Stock:	31 Dec 2000
ad lend:	49690
ch:	17630
schools:	6450
AVs:	1114
periodcls:	122

Issues:	2000
ad lend:	101058
ch:	48239
AVs:	4306

Acqs:	2000
bks:	7512
AVs:	114

Cat: Medium: auto *Auto Sys:* Dynix (Horizon)
Activs: ch's activs, temp exhibs, lectures
Staff: Libns: 3 *Non-Prof:* 12

Inc from:	2000
local govt:	IR£427926
fines etc:	IR£17249
total:	IR£457896

Exp on:	2000
bks:	IR£87566
salaries:	IR£214893
total:	IR£457896

Cavan

IP2 Cavan County Libraries

Cavan Lib, Farnham St, Cavan, Ireland (049-433-
1799; *fax*: 049-437-1832)
Email: cavancountylibrary@eircom.net
Internet: http://www.cavancoco.ie/services/
library.htm

Local Auth: Cavan County Council *Pop:* 53000
Cttee: Cavan County Lib & Arts Cttee *Chief:*
County Libn: Mrs Josephine Brady BA, DipLIS
Main Libs: CAVAN LIB, addr as above *Branch
Libs:* BAILIEBOROUGH LIB, Market House,
Bailieborough, Co Cavan (042-966-5779);
COOTEHILL LIB, Bridge St, Cootehill, Co Cavan
(049-555-9873)
Svc Pts: PT: 9 *AV:* 2 *Internet:* 6
Collns: comprehensive local hist colln, incl local
newspapers, photos & archvs

ILLs: county, natl & internatl *Loans:* bks &
audios/3 wks *Income Gen:* ILL request/€4
Fines: bks & audios/ad, ch & oap 25c per wk
Equip: 2 m-readers, fax, copiers, 12 computers
(all with wd-proc, internet & CD-ROM)

Stock:	31 Dec 2000
ad lend:	63482
ch:	53075
schools:	17365
AVs:	2407

Issues:	2000
ad lend:	48318
ch:	72700
schools:	11388
AVs:	1309

Acqs:	2000
bks:	11845
AVs:	194

Acqs: Source: lib suppl, publ & bksellers *Offcr-in-
Charge:* County Libn, as above
Classn: DDC *Cat: Type:* author & classified
Medium: auto *Auto Sys:* Horizon *Svcs: Extra-
mural:* schools, prison *Info:* business, EU, local
authority *Activs:* ch's activs, temp exhibs, lectures
Offcr-in-Charge: County Libn, as above
Staff: Libns: 3 *Non-Prof:* 17

Inc from:	2000
local govt:	IR£504160
fines etc:	IR£4956
total:	IR£528536

Exp on:	2000
all stock:	IR£66926
salaries:	IR£322549
total:	IR£528536

Clare

IP3 Clare County Libraries

Lib HQ, Mill Rd, Ennis, Co Clare, Ireland (065-684-
2461/682-1616; *fax*: 065-684-2462)
Email: mailbox@clarelibrary.ie
Internet: http://www.clarelibrary.ie/

Local Auth: Clare County Council *Pop:* 93914
Chief: County Libn: Mr Noel Crowley FLAI *Other
Snr Staff:* Exec Libn (Admin Svcs): Mr Ted Finn
(ted.finn@clarelibrary.ie); Exec Libn (IT Svcs): Mr
Anthony Edwards (anthony.edwards@
clarelibrary.ie); Exec Libn (Bibliographical Svcs):
Ms Carrie Stafford (carrie.stafford@clarelibrary.ie);
Exec Libn (Info Svcs): Ms Maureen Comber
(maureen.comber@clarelibrary.ie)
Main Libs: DE VALERA LIB, Harmony Row,
Ennis, Co Clare (065-684-6353); ENNISTYMON
LIB, The Square, Ennistymon, Co Clare (065-707-
1245); KILRUSH LIB, O Gorman St, Kilrush,
Co Clare (065-905-1504); KILLALOE LIB, The
Lock House, Killaloe, Co Clare (061-376062);
SEAN LEMASS LIB, Town Centre, Shannon,
Co Clare (061-364266) *Branch Libs:* DR
PATRICK J. HILLERY PUBLIC LIB, Ballard Rd,
Miltown Malbay, Co Clare (065-708-4822);
KILFINAGHTY PUBLIC LIB, Church St, Sixmile-
bridge, Co Clare (061-369678); NEWMARKET ON
FERGUS LIB, Kilnasoolagh Pk, Newmarket on
Fergus, Co Clare (061-368411); SWEENEY
MEMORIAL LIB, O'Connell St, Kilkee, Co Clare
(065-905-6034)
Svc Pts: PT: 6 *Computers:* 15 *Internet:* 15 *Other:*
LOCAL STUDIES CENTRE (see **IA55**);
SHANNON LANG CENTRE, at Sean Lemass Lib
Collns: Irish Ref Colln; local hist colln (both at
Local Studies Centre) *Co-op Schemes:* IJFR
ILLs: county, natl & internatl *Loans:* bks &
audios/4 wks *Charges:* annual sub for bks &
audio/ad €4.40, family €10, ch, oaps & registered
unemployed exempt *Fines:* bks & audio/ad & oap
35c per wk *Equip:* 3 m-readers, 3 m-printers, 8
copiers, computers (with internet) *Online:*
TalisInform (community info svc)

Stock:	31 Dec 2000
ad lend:	217420
ch: *	222261
audios:	2024
periodcls:	60

Issues:	2000
ad lend:	238598
ch: *	153665
audios:	930

* incl schools

Acqs:	2000
bks:	32322

Acqs: Source: lib suppl & bksellers *Offcr-in-
Charge:* Exec Libn (Bibliographical Svcs), as above
Classn: DDC *Cat: Type:* author, classified, subj &
title *Medium:* auto *Auto Sys:* Talis *Svcs:
Extramural:* schools *Info:* community, business,
arts; available on Lib web site *Activs:* ch's activs,
temp exhibs, author visits, storytelling, bk promotions
Staff: Libns: 8 *Non-Prof:* 31.1

Inc from:	2000
local govt:	IR£1258046
fines etc:	IR£70085
total:	IR£1356775

Exp on:	2000
bks:	IR£258570
AVs:	IR£4446
salaries:	IR£780136
total:	IR£1356775

Proj: new Scariff branch lib

Cork Corporation

IP4 Cork City Libraries

Cork Central Lib, 57-61 Grand Parade, Cork,
Ireland (021-427-7110; *fax*: 021-427-5684)
Email: citylibrary@corkcorp.ie
Internet: http://www.corkcitylibrary.ie/

Local Auth: Cork Corp *Pop:* 127000 *Cttee:* City
Lib Advisory Cttee *Chief:* City Libn: Ms Hanna
O'Sullivan FLAI *Dep:* Exec Libn (Admin): Ms Anne
Coleman BA, DipLT *Other Snr Staff:* Exec Libn
(Acqs & Cataloguing): Mr Eamonn Kirwan BA,
DipLib; Exec Libn (IT): Mr John Mullins
Main Libs: CORK CENTRAL LIB, as above
Branch (Community) Libs: DOUGLAS LIB,
Village Shopping Centre, Douglas, Cork (*email:*
douglas_library@corkcorp.ie); HOLLYHILL LIB,
Hollyhill Shopping Centre, Hollyhill, Cork (021-439-
2998; *fax*: 021-439-3032; *email:* hollyhill_library@
corkcorp.ie); MAYFIELD LIB, Murmont, Mayfield,
Cork (*email:* mayfield_library@corkcorp.ie); ST
MARY'S ROAD LIB, St Mary's Rd, Cathedral
Cross, Cork (*email:* stmarys_library@corkcorp.ie);
TORY TOP ROAD LIB, Tory Top Rd, Ballyphehane,
Cork (*email:* torytop_library@corkcorp.ie)
Svc Pts: Mobile: 1 *Other:* MUSIC LIB, at Central
Lib; LOCAL STUDIES DEPT, at Central Lib (see
IA20); HOUSEBND SVC, based at Mayfield Lib
Collns: IJFR: S; Cork Colln (local hist, at Central
Lib) *Co-op Schemes:* IJFR, SWAP, joint funding
of Douglas Lib with Cork County Council (see **IP5**)
ILLs: county, natl & internatl *Loans:* bks &
audios/2 wks *Charges:* registration/ad €12.50 pa,
students & conc €1.25 pa, ch, oap & disabled free;
audio sub/€50 pa *Income Gen:* reservations/cost
of postage *Fines:* bks & audios/ad 10c per wk, ch
5c per wk, oap & registered blind exempt *Equip:*
4 m-readers, 3 m-printers, 9 copiers, computers
(incl wd-proc, internet & CD-ROM) *Disabled:* 1
Kurzweil 1000, ZoomText *Online:* ENFO, IRIS,
Kompass

Stock:	31 Dec 2001
ad lend:	128000
ad ref:	30000
ch:	64100
audios:	20000

Issues: **2000**
all items: 693000

Acqs: *Source:* lib suppl & bksellers *Offcr-in-Charge:* Exec Libn (Acqs & Cataloguing), as above **Classn:** DDC **Cat:** *Type:* author, classified, subj & title *Medium:* auto *Auto Sys:* Dynix **Svcs:** *Extramural:* schools, prison *Info:* business, community, consumer **Activs:** ch's activs, temp exhibs, poetry readings, bk clubs, An Ciorcal Comhrá (Irish speaking group), literacy classes **Staff:** *Libns:* 13 *Non-Prof:* 41

Inc from:	**2000**
fines etc:	IR£364400

Exp on:	**2000**
bks:	IR£286000
AVs:	IR£30000
elec media:	IR£60000
culture:	IR£5000
salaries:	IR£1187100
total:	IR£1568100

Proj: new lib for the Blackrock/Mahon area

Cork

IP5 Cork County Library Service

Lib HQ, Cork County Lib, Farranlea Rd, Cork, Ireland (021-546499; *fax:* 021-343254)
Email: corkcountylibrary@eircom.net
Internet: http://www.corkcoco.com/cccmm/services/library/

Local Auth: Cork County Council *Pop:* 283116 *Cttee:* County Lib Cttee *Chief:* County Libn: Ms Ruth Flanagan BA, DipLib, ALAI *Dep:* Exec Libns: Mr Tim Cadogan BA, DipLib & Mr Joseph Higgins MA, DipLib
Main Libs: CORK COUNTY LIB, contact details as above *Branch Libs:* BALLINCOLLIG LIB, Village Shopping Centre, Ballincollig, Co Cork (021-487-3024; *email:* ballincolliglibrary@eircom.net); BANDON LIB, Shopping Centre, South Main St, Bandon, Co Cork (023-44830; *email:* bandonlibrary@eircom.net); BANTRY LIB, Bridge St, Bantry, Co Cork (027-50460; *fax:* 027-51389; *email:* bantrylibrary@eircom.net); CARRIGALINE LIB, Main St, Carrigaline, Co Cork (021-437-1888; *email:* carrigalinelibrary@eircom.net); CHARLEVILLE LIB, Main St, Charleville, Co Cork (063-89769; *email:* charlevillelibrary@eircom.net); CLONAKILTY LIB, Old Mill, Kent St, Clonakilty, Co Cork (023-34275; *email:* clonakiltylibrary@eircom.net); COBH LIB, The Arch Bldg, Casement Sq, Cobh, Co Cork (021-481-1130; *email:* cobhlibrary@eircom.net); FERMOY LIB, Connolly St, Fermoy, Co Cork (025-31318; *email:* fermoylibrary@eircom.net); KANTURK LIB, Main St, Kanturk, Co Cork (029-51384; *email:* kanturklibrary@eircom.net); KINSALE LIB, Methodist Hall, Market Quay, Kinsale, Co Cork (021-477-4266; *email:* kinsalelibrary@eircom.net); MACROOM LIB, Briery Gap, Cultural Centre, Main St, Macroom, Co Cork (026-42483; *email:* macroomlibrary@eircom.net); MALLOW LIB, Town Hall, Main St, Mallow, Co Cork (022-21821; *email:* mallowlibrary@eircom.net); MIDLETON LIB, Main St, Midleton, Co Cork (021-461-3929; *email:* midletonlibrary@eircom.net); MILLSTREET LIB, Council Offices, Town Hall, Millstreet, Co Cork (029-21920; *email:* millstreetlibrary@eircom.net); MITCHELSTOWN LIB, Council Offices, Georges St, Mitchelstown, Co Cork (025-24325; *email:* mitchelstownlibrary@eircom.net); SKIBBEREEN LIB, North St, Skibbereen, Co Cork (028-22400; *email:* skibbereenlibrary@eircom.net); YOUGHAL BRANCH LIB, Church St, Youghal, Co Cork (024-93459; *email:* youghallibrary@eircom.net)
Svc Pts: PT: 9 *Mobile:* 5
Collns: Cork Local Studies Colln (ref only); Choral Music Colln (sheet music, loan and/or ref), both at County Lib HQ *Co-op Schemes:* ILL, SWAP

Loans: bks & audios/2 wks, or 4 wks for snr citizens **Charges:** annual sub **Equip:** m-readers, m-printers, copiers, computers (with internet) *Online:* IRIS, UnCover, FactFinder

Stock:	**31 Dec 2000**	
bks:	1314143	
AVs:	6880	

Issues:	**2000**	**2001**
bks:	1284044	1256661

Acqs:	**2000**	**2001**
bks:	67558	45436

Acqs: *Source:* lib suppl & bksellers **Classn:** DDC **Cat:** *Medium:* m-form & auto *Auto Sys:* Dynix **Svcs:** *Extramural:* schools, prison, old people's homes *Info:* SWAP (South West Action Proj), business info svc at Bantry & Clonakilty Libs) **Activs:** ch's activs, temp exhibs, poetry readings, reading groups, writers' group (at Clonakilty Lib) **Staff:** *Libns:* 10 *Non-Prof:* 67

Inc from:	**2000**
fines etc:	IR£117477

Exp on:	**2000**
bks:	IR£650097
total:	IR£2961724

Donegal

IP6 Donegal County Council Library Service

County Lib Administrative Centre, Rosemount Ln, Letterkenny, Co Donegal, Ireland (074-21968; *fax:* 074-21740)
Email: library@donegalcoco.ie
Internet: http://www.donegal.ie/library/

Local Auth: Donegal County Council *Pop:* 137383 *Cttee:* Cultural Cttee *Larger Dept:* Cultural Svcs *Dept Chief:* Cultural Svcs Mgr: Mr Liam Ronayne BCL, DipLib, ALAI *Chief:* County Libn: Mr Liam Ronayne, as above *Other Snr Staff:* Asst Libns: Ms Eileen Burgess & Ms Geraldine McHugh
Main Libs: DONEGAL CENTRAL LIB, Oliver Plunkett Rd, Letterkenny, Co Donegal (*tel & fax:* 074-24950; *email:* dglcolib@iol.ie); BUNCRANA LIB, St Mary's Rd, Buncrana, Co Donegal (077-61941/64; *fax:* 077-61980; *email:* bunclibr@donegalcoco.ie) *Branch Libs:* CARNDONAGH COMMUNITY LIB, Courthouse, Carndonagh, Co Donegal; LEABHARLANN PHOBAIL NA ROSANN, Ionad Teampaill Chróine, Dungloe, Co Donegal; LIFFORD COMMUNITY LIB, Main St, Lifford, Co Donegal (074-41066); MILFORD COMMUNITY LIB, Main St, Milford, Co Donegal; MOVILLE COMMUNITY LIB, St Eugene's Hall, Moville, Co Donegal; RAMELTON COMMUNITY LIB, Old Meeting House, Back Ln, Ramelton, Co Donegal (074-51414)
Svc Pts: PT: 9 *Mobile:* 1 *AV:* 7 *Computers:* 9 *Internet:* 10
Collns: IJFR: short stories; Patrick McGill Colln (local author); Donegal Studies Colln (both at Central Lib) *Co-op Schemes:* IJFR *ILLs:* county, natl & internatl *Loans:* all items/3 wks *Charges:* audio sub/€17 pa; video sub/€15 pa *Income Gen:* requests/€5; lost ticket/€2 *Fines:* bks, audios & videos/ad & oap 50c per wk, ch exempt; audios, videos & CD-ROMs/50c per wk *Equip:* 3 m-form reader/printers, 5 fax, 7 video viewers, 5 copiers, 46 computers (all with wd-proc, internet & CD-ROM), room for hire

Stock:	**31 Dec 2000**
ad lend:	169836
ch:	134662
schools:	85478
audios:	6643
videos:	2640
periodcls:	227

Issues:	**2000**
ad lend:	86045
ch:	155533
audios:	10093
videos:	9015

Acqs:	**2000**
bks:	19774
AVs:	1114

Acqs: *Source:* lib suppl *Co-op:* IJFR *Offcr-in-Charge:* Asst Libn: Ms Eileen Burgess **Classn:** DDC (for lending) & categorisation **Cat:** *Type:* author, classified, subj & title *Medium:* auto *Auto Sys:* Genesis **Svcs:** *Extramural:* schools, old people's homes *Info:* business, community, careers *Other:* Open Learning, computer learning **Activs:** ch's activs, temp exhibs, poetry readings, reading groups, talks, author visits *Offcr-in-Charge:* Arts Organiser: Mr Traolach Ó Fionnáin **Staff:** *Libns:* 4 *Other Prof:* 4 *Non-Prof:* 29

Inc from:	**2000**	**2001**
local govt:	€1338576	€1548573
fines etc:	€38830	€51002
total:	€1424455	€1641838

Exp on:	**2000**	**2001**
bks:	€292484	€429536
total:	€1424455	€1641838

Proj: Bundoran Community Lib (started Aug 2002)

Dublin

IP7 Dublin City Public Libraries

Lib HQ, 138-144 Pearse St, Dublin 2, Ireland (01-674-4800; *fax:* 01-674-4879)
Email: dubcilib@iol.ie
Internet: http://www.iol.ie/dublincitylibrary/

Local Auth: Dublin Corp *Pop:* 495100 *Cttee:* Cultural Cttee *Chief:* Dublin City Libn: Mrs Deirdre Ellis-King BA, DipLib, MPhil, ALAI *Dep:* Dep City Libn: Mrs Margaret Hayes BA, HDipEd, DipLIS, ALAI *Other Snr Staff:* Divisional Libn (Reader Svcs): Ms Jane Alger; Divisional Libn (Staff & Training): Ms Miriam Leonard; Divisional Libn (Lifelong Learning & Outreach Programmes): Mr Alastair Smeaton BA, DipLib; Divisional Libn (Central Lib Svcs): Mr Michael Molloy; Divisional Libn (Bibliographical Svcs): Ms Sheila Kelly; Divisional Libn (Special Collns): Dr Maire Kennedy; Divisional Libn (Rsrch & Policy Development): Mrs Bernadette Cogan
Main Libs: CENTRAL LIB, ILAC Centre, Henry St, Dublin 1 (01-873-4333; *fax:* 01-872-1451) *Branch Libs:* BALLYFERMOT LIB, Ballyfermot Rd, Dublin 10 (01-626-9324/5; *fax:* 01-623-7365); BALLYMUN LIB, Ballymun Rd, Dublin 9 (01-842-1890); CABRA LIB, Navan Rd, Dublin 7 (01-869-1414; *fax:* 01-869-1412); CHARLEVILLE MALL LIB, Charleville Mall, North Strand, Dublin 1 (01-874-9619); COOLOCK LIB, Barryscourt Rd, Dublin 17 (01-847-7781); DOLPHIN'S BARN LIB, Parnell Rd, Dublin 12 (01-454-0681); DONAGH-MEDE LIB, Grange Rd, Dublin 13 (01-848-2833); DRUM-CONDRA LIB, Millmount Ave, Drumcondra, Dublin 9 (01-837-7206); FINGLAS LIB, Finglas Shopping Centre, Jamestown Rd, Dublin 11 (01-834-4906; *fax:* 01-864-2085); INCHICORE LIB, 34 Emmet Rd, Inchicore, Dublin 8 (01-453-3793); KEVIN ST LIB, 18 Lower Kevin St, Dublin 8 (01-475-3794); MARINO LIB, 14-20 Marino Mart, Fairview, Dublin 3 (01-833-6297); PEARSE STREET LIB, 138-142 Pearse St, Dublin 2 (01-677-2764); PEMBROKE LIB, Anglesea Rd, Ballsbridge, Dublin 4 (01-668-9575); PHIBSBORO LIB, Blackquire Bridge, Phibsboro, Dublin 7 (01-830-4341); RAHENY LIB, Howth Rd, Raheny, Dublin 5 (01-831-5521); RATHMINES LIB, 157 Lower Rathmines Rd, Rathmines, Dublin 6 (01-497-3539); RINGSEND LIB, Fitzwilliam St, Ringsend, Dublin 4 (01-668-0063); TERENURE LIB, Templeogue Rd, Terenure, Dublin 6 (01-490-7035); WALKINS-TOWN LIB, Percy French Rd, Walkinstown, Dublin 12 (01-455-8159) ☛

(Dublin City Public Libs cont)

Svc Pts: Mobile: 3 **Computers:** 32 **Internet:** 32 **Other:** BUSINESS INFO CENTRE, at Central Lib (01-873-3996/4333; *fax:* 01-872-1451; *email:* businesslibrary@dublincorp.ie); CH'S & SCHOOLS LIB SVC, at Kevin St Lib (01-475-8791; *email:* schollib@iol.ie); MOBILE LIB HQ, at Cabra Lib (01-869-1415; *fax:* 01-869-1412); MUSIC LIB, at Central Lib; PRISON LIB SVC HQ, Wheatfield Place of Detention, Cloverhill Rd, Clondalkin, Dublin 22 (*tel & fax:* 01-623-7434) **Collns:** Gilbert Lib (Dublin & Irish Collns); DIX Colln (early printed works & bindings); Yeats Colln (all at Pearse St); Dublin Newspapers (at Business Lib); IJFR: L-M **Co-op Schemes:** IJFR, BLDSC, SPRINTEL, MUMLIB **ILLs:** county, natl & internatl **Loans:** bks, audios & other/3 wks **Income Gen:** requests/cost of informing reader to collect; reservations/45c; ILLs/€4.40 **Fines:** bks, audios & other/ad, ch & oap 40c per wk **Equip:** m-reader, m-printer, video viewers, copiers (12c), 120 computers (all with internet), rooms for hire (free) **Disabled:** Kurzweil, ZoomText, JAWS **Online:** DPLNET, Mintel, ENFO

Stock:	31 Dec 2000	31 Dec 2001
ad lend:	1009020	* 1525082
ch:	171588	-
schools:	176928	-
audios:	60299	-
videos:	3407	-
periodcls:	572	-

Issues:	2000	2001
ad lend:	1535669	* 3132712
ch:	335384	-
schools:	930700	-
audios:	191237	-

* total for all items in 2001

Acqs:	2000
bks:	105909
AVs:	5635

Acqs: *Source:* lib suppl & bksellers *Offcr-in-Charge:* Divisional Libn (Bibliographical Svcs): Ms Sheila Kelly **Classn:** DDC **Cat:** Auto Sys: DS Galaxy 2000 **Svcs:** *Extramural:* schools, prison, hosps, old people's homes, housebnd *Info:* business, community, youth, NSSB, legal aid clinics *Other:* admin HQ for internatl IMPAC Dublin Literary Award, Open Learning Centre (at Central Lib), Ad Literacy Resource Centre (at Central Lib), Dublin Heritage Group Centre (at Ballyfermot Lib) **Activs:** ch's activs, bk sales, films, temp exhibs, poetry readings, reading groups, writers' groups, lectures, workshops, demos, ad literacy, lang exchange sessions *Offcr-in-Charge:* Divisional Libn (Lifelong Learning & Outreach Programmes), as above **Staff:** 394 total

Inc from:	2000
local govt:	IR£9748889
fines etc:	IR£608225
total:	IR£10721487

Exp on:	2000
bks:	IR£908000
AVs:	IR£162000
salaries:	IR£6579895
total:	IR£10721487

Proj: reconstruction & refurbishment of Pearse St Lib (incl Local Studies Colln), reopened Autumn 2001; new Branch Lib & Bibliographic Centre at Cabra, opened early 2001

Dún Laoghaire Rathdown

IP8 Dún Laoghaire Rathdown Public Library Service

Lib Svc HQ, 1st Floor, Duncairn House, 14 Carysfort Ave, Blackrock, Co Dublin, Ireland (01-278-1788; *fax:* 01-278-1792) **Email:** libraries@dlrcoco.ie **Internet:** http://www.dlrcoco.ie/library/

Local Auth: Dún Laoghaire-Rathdown County Council **Pop:** 200000 **Cttee:** County Council **Larger Dept:** Genl Purposes Dept **Dept Chief:** Snr Admin Offcr: Ms Kathleen Holdhan **Chief:** County Libn: Mr Muiris Ó Raghaill BSc, ALA (moraghaill@dlrcoco.ie) **Other Snr Staff:** Snr Libn (Info & IT): Ms Monica Boyle (mboyle@ dlrcoco.ie); Snr Libn (Admin & Staff): Ms Orla Gallagher BSocSc, DipLT (ogallagher@dlrcoco.ie); Snr Libn (Culture): Ms Marian Keyes (mkeyes@ dlrcoco.ie); Snr Libn (Bibliographic Control): Ms Joan Ann Lloyd (jlloyd@dlrcoco.ie) **Main Libs:** DÚN LAOGHAIRE LIB, Lower George's St, Dún Laoghaire, Co Dublin (01-280-1147; *fax:* 01-284-6141) **Branch Libs:** BLACK-ROCK LIB, Main St, Blackrock, Co Dublin (*tel & fax:* 01-288-8117); CABINTEELY LIB, Old Bray Rd, Cabinteely, Dublin 18 (01-285-5363; *fax:* 01-235-3000); DALKEY LIB, Castle St, Dalkey, Co Dublin (01-285-5317/5277; *fax:* 01-285-5789); DEANS-GRANGE LIB, Clonkeen Dr, Deansgrange, Dublin 18 (01-285-0860; *fax:* 01-289-8359); DUNDRUM LIB, Upper Churchtown Rd, Dundrum, Dublin 14 (01-298-5000; *fax:* 01-296-3216); SALLYNOGGIN LIB, Snr Coll, Pearse St, Sallynoggin, Co Dublin (*tel & fax:* 01-285-0127); SHANKILL LIB, Library Rd, Shankill, Co Dublin (01-282-3081; *fax:* 01-282-4555); STILLORGAN LIB, St Laurence's Pk, Stillorgan, Co Dublin (01-288-9655; *fax:* 01-278-1794) **Svc Pts:** PT: 1 Mobile: 7 stops AV: 10 Computers: 10, incl full multi-media at 5 branches Internet: 10 Other: HOME LIB SVC (run from Blackrock & Stillorgan Libs); SCHOOLS LIB SVC, contact Libn (Schools & Yng People): Ms Mary Mitchell (mmitchell@dlrcoco.ie) **Collns:** local hist colln; govt pubns (incl Acts of the Oireachtas); EU Colln (all at Dún Laoghaire Lib); Natl Social Svc Board (NSSB) files (at Deansgrange & Stillorgan Libs); County Council minutes (copies held at all branches) **Co-op Schemes:** IJFR, ISBN catalogue (Region K), ILL, BLDSC **ILLs:** county, natl & internatl **Loans:** bks & audios/3 wks; prints/3 months **Income Gen:** reservations/50c **Fines:** all items/ad 70c per wk, ch 55c per wk **Equip:** m-reader, m-printer, video viewers, copiers, computers (incl wd-procs, internet & CD-ROM), OPACs at each branch, rooms for hire (incl 2 music rooms at Dalkey Lib)

Stock:	31 Dec 2000	31 Dec 2001
all lend:	285000	272000
AVs:	13000	-
periodcls:	68	-

Issues:	2000
all lend:	669000
AVs:	47000

Acqs:	2000
bks:	29000

Acqs: *Source:* lib suppl, publ & bksellers *Offcr-in-Charge:* Snr Libn (Bibliographical Control), as above **Classn:** DDC **Cat:** *Type:* author, classified, subj & title *Medium:* auto **Auto Sys:** DS Galaxy 2000 **Svcs:** *Extramural:* schools, housebnd *Info:* community *Other:* music practice rooms (at Dalkey Lib) **Activs:** ch's activs, temp exhibs, poetry readings, musical festivals, lang exchange sessions (at Deansgrange Lib) *Offcr-in-Charge:* Snr Libn (Admin & Staff), as above **Staff:** Libns: 20 Non-Prof: 55

Inc from:	2000
fines etc:	IR£81451

Exp on:	2000
all stock:	IR£299872
total:	IR£2260835

Fingal

IP9 Fingal County Libraries

County Hall, Main St, Swords, Co Dublin, Ireland (01-890-5524; *fax:* 01-890-5599) **Email:** libraries@fingalcoco.ie **Internet:** http://www.iol.ie/~fincolib/

Local Auth: Fingal County Council **Pop:** 207000 **Larger Dept:** Dept of Environment, Parks & Public Libs **Dept Chief:** Dir of Svcs: Miss P.J. Howell **Chief:** County Libn: Mr Paul Harris (paul.harris@fingalcoco.ie) **Other Snr Staff:** Snr Libn (Personnel & Finance): Ms Anne Finn (anne.finn@fingalcoco.ie) **Branch Libs:** BALBRIGGAN LIB, George's Sq, Balbriggan, Co Dublin (01-841-1128; *fax:* 01-841-2101; *email:* balbrigganlibrary@yahoo.co.uk); BLANCHARDSTOWN LIB, Civic Centre, Blanchardstown, Dublin 15 (01-890-5560; *fax:* 01-890-5569; *email:* blanchlib@fingalcoco.ie); HOWTH LIB, Main St, Howth, Co Dublin (01-832-2130; *fax:* 01-832-2277; *email:* howthlibrary@ hotmail.com); MALAHIDE LIB, Main St, Malahide, Co Dublin (01-845-2026; *fax:* 01-845-2199; *email:* malahidelibrary@fingalcoco.ie); RATHBEALE LIB, Swords Shopping Centre, Rathbeale Rd, Swords, Co Dublin (01-840-4179; *fax:* 01-840-4417; *email:* rathbealelibrary@fingalcoco.ie); SKERRIES LIB, Strand St, Skerries, Co Dublin (01-849-1900; *fax:* 01-849-5142; *email:* skerrieslibrary@fingalcoco.ie) **Svc Pts:** PT: 2 Mobile: 4 Computers: 6 Internet: 6 Other: FINGAL MOBILE LIBS HQ, Unit 34, Coolmine Industrial Est, Coolmine, Dublin 15 (01-822-1564; *fax:* 01-822-1568); FINGAL SCHOOLS LIB SVC, Unit 34, Coolmine Industrial Est, Coolmine, Dublin 15 (01-822-5056; *fax:* 01-822-1568); HOUSEBND LIB SVC, Unit 34, Coolmine Industrial Est, Coolmine, Dublin 15 (01-860-4290; *fax:* 01-860-4291); COUNTY ARCHVS (see IA33); FINGAL LOCAL STUDIES COLLN, 3rd Floor, 11 Parnell Sq, Dublin 1 (01-878-6910; *fax:* 01-878-6919; *email:* local.studies@fingalcoco.ie) **Collns:** IJFRS: W; local studies; Travel Colln; Women's Studies Colln **Co-op Schemes:** IJFRS **ILLs:** county, natl & internatl **Loans:** bks, audios & videos/3 wks; prints/3 months **Income Gen:** reservations/35c **Fines:** bks/ad & ch 25c per wk or part of wk, oaps discretionary; audios & videos/ 25c per wk or part of wk; block loan scheme eliminates fines **Equip:** m-reader, m-printer (13c per pg), 8 fax, 2 video viewers, 7 copiers (13c per pg), 34 computers (incl 30 with internet), 20 addl internet PCs in Cyberskills Room, room for hire (€11 per hr) **Disabled:** 1 Kurzweil *Offcr-in-Charge:* Projs Libn: Mr Richie Farrell (ricfar21@ aol.com)

Stock:	31 Dec 2000
ad lend:	149115
ch:	78614
audios:	12968
videos:	599
periodcls:	89

Issues:	2000
bks:	602349
audios:	24305

Acqs:	2000
bks:	64602
AVs:	3299

Acqs: *Source:* lib suppl & bksellers *Offcr-in-Charge:* Snr Libn (Acqs & Circulations): Ms Rina Mullett (rina.mullett@fingalcoco.ie) **Classn:** DDC **Cat:** *Type:* author, classified, subj & title *Medium:* auto & online **Auto Sys:** DS Galaxy 2000 **Svcs:** *Extramural:* schools, housebnd, old peoples' homes, day centres *Info:* community, business, FACTfinder business database *Other:* lang courses, Cyberskills, computer self learning

Activs: ch's activs, temp exhibs, poetry readings, reading groups, writers' groups, ad literacy, quizzes, competitions, craft/art/music workshops *Offcr-in-Charge:* Development/PR Libn, Ms Yvonne Reilly (yvonne.reilly@fingalcoco.ie) *Staff: Libns:* 31 *Other Prof:* 1 *Non-Prof:* 72

Inc from:	2000
fines etc:	IR£56948

Exp on:	2000
all stock:	IR£487784
salaries:	IR£1634825
total:	IR£2580007

Proj: new lib at Blanchardstown

Galway

IP10 Galway Public Libraries

Lib HQ, Island House, Cathedral Sq, Galway, Ireland (091-562471; *fax:* 091-565039)
Email: info@galwaylibrary.ie
Internet: http://www.galwaylibrary.ie/

Local Auth: Galway County Council *Pop:* 178552 *Cttee:* County Lib Cttee (advisory) *Larger Dept:* Galway County Council *Chief:* County Libn: Mr Patrick McMahon DipLib *Dep:* Exec Libn: Miss Maureen Moran BA, FLAI
Main Libs: GALWAY CITY LIB, Hynes' Bldg, St Augustine St, Galway (091-561666; *fax:* 091-565039; *email:* info@galwaylibrary.ie) *Branch Libs:* BALLINASLOE LIB, Fair Green, Ballinasloe, Co Galway (0905-43464); CARRAROE LIB, An Scailp Chulturtha, Carraroe, Co Galway (091-595733); CLIFDEN LIB, Clifden, Co Galway (095-21092); LOUGHREA BRANCH LIB, Loughrea, Co Galway (091-847220; *email:* loughrealibrary@eircom.net); ORANMORE LIB, Oranmore, Co Galway (091-792117); PORTUMA BRANCH LIB, Portuma, Co Galway (0509-41261); TUAM BRANCH LIB, Tuam, Co Galway (093-24287)
Svc Pts: PT: 17 *Mobile:* 1 *Computers:* 25 *Internet:* 25 *Other:* postal cassette svc to the blind *Collns:* local hist colln (at Lib HQ) *ILLs:* county, natl & internatl *Loans:* bks & audios/3 wks *Charges:* annual sub/ad £5 pa, student & unemployed £2, ch & oap exempt *Fines:* bks & audios/10p per wk *Equip:* m-readers, m-printer, copiers (A4/10p, A3/15p), computers (incl internet) *Online:* Newsbank, Grove Dictionary of Music Online, Grove Dictionary of Art Online

Stock:	31 Dec 2000
bks:	442612
audios:	9844

Issues:	2000
bks:	325506
audios:	5527

Acqs:	2000
bks:	54401
AVs:	379

Acqs: Source: lib suppl *Offcr-in-Charge:* County Libn, as above
Classn: DDC *Cat: Type:* author *Medium:* cards & auto *Auto Sys:* Dynix (Horizon) *Svcs: Extramural:* schools, old people's homes *Other:* mobile lib svc to hosp in Ballinasloe *Activs:* ch's activs, temp exhibs, poetry readings, author visits, talks *Offcr-in-Charge:* Exec Libn, as above
Staff: Libns: 8 *Non-Prof:* 44

Exp on:	2000
total:	IR£1586724

Kerry

IP11 Kerry County Libraries

County Lib & Lib HQ, Moyderwell, Tralee, Co Kerry, Ireland (066-712-1200; *fax:* 066-712-9202)
Email: info@kerrycolib.ie
Internet: http://www.kerrycountylibrary.com/

Local Auth: Kerry County Council *Pop:* 132424 *Cttee:* County Kerry Lib Cttee *Chief:* County Libn: Mrs Kathleen Browne FLAI, ALA *Dep:* Exec Libn: Mr Patrick Walsh DipAdmSc
Main Libs: KERRY COUNTY LIB, addr as above *Branch Libs:* BALLYBUNION LIB, Ballybunion, Co Kerry (068-27615; *email:* ballybunion@kerrycolib.ie); CAHIRCIVEEN LIB, Cahirciveen, Co Kerry (066-947-2287; *email:* cahirciveen@kerrycolib.ie); CASTLEISLAND LIB, Castleisland, Co Kerry (066-714-1485; *email:* castleisland@kerrycolib.ie); DINGLE LIB, Dingle, Co Kerry (066-915-1499; *email:* dingle@kerrycolib.ie); KENMARE LIB, Kenmare, Co Kerry (064-41416; *email:* kenmare@kerrycolib.ie); KILLARNEY LIB, Killarney, Co Kerry (064-32655; *fax:* 064-36065; *email:* killarney@kerrycolib.ie); KILLORGLIN LIB, Killorglin, Co Kerry (066-976-1272; *email:* killorglin@kerrycolib.ie); LISTOWEL LIB, Listowel, Co Kerry (068-23044; *email:* listowel@kerrycolib.ie)
Svc Pts: Mobile: 1, plus 1 schools lib van *Computers:* 9 *Internet:* 9
Collns: IJFR: U (at Tralee Lib); An Canónach Ó Fiannachta Colln; Tomás Ághas Museum Colln; Cnosach Duibhneach Colln of bks related to Dingle Peninsula in English & Irish (all at Dingle Lib) *Co-op Schemes:* IJFR *ILLs:* county, natl & internatl *Loans:* bks & audios/30c per item or annual sub of €12, ch, 2nd level students & snr citizens exempt *Income Gen:* requests/postage *Fines:* bks/10c per wk *Equip:* 2 m-readers, 2 m-printers, 2 copiers, computers (with internet)

Stock:	31 Dec 2000
bks:	227743
audios:	5439
videos:	788

Issues:	2000	2001
all items:	276134	310877

Acqs:	2000
bks:	24343
AVs:	374

Acqs: Source: lib suppl & bksellers *Co-op:* IJFR
Classn: DDC *Cat: Type:* author & classified *Medium:* cards & auto *Auto Sys:* Dynix (Horizon), currently being installed *Svcs: Extramural:* schools, hosps, old people's homes *Other:* tourist; Kerry Archaeological & Historical Soc operates from HQ *Activs:* ch's activs, films, temp exhibs, poetry readings, reading groups
Staff: Libns: 8 *Other Prof:* 16 *Non-Prof:* 8

Inc from:	2000	2001
fines etc:	IR£37000	IR£67500

Exp on:	2000	2001
bks:	IR£192200	IR£195000
total:	IR£1317100	IR£1488500

Proj: new mobile lib introduced in 2001, another to come in 2003; new libs for Caherciveen & Castleisland in 2003

Kildare

IP12 Kildare Library and Arts Services

Riverbank, Main St, Newbridge, Co Kildare, Ireland (045-431486/1109; *fax:* 045-432490)
Email: kildarelibrary@kildarecoco.ie
Internet: http://www.kildare.ie/library/

Local Auth: Kildare County Council *Pop:* 150000 *Cttee:* Lib Cttee & Strategic Policy Cttee on Local Urban & Rural Development *Chief:* County Libn: Ms Breda Gleeson DipLIS, ALA (bgleeson@kildarecoco.ie) *Dep:* Exec Libn: Mr Michael Kavanagh FLAI
Branch Libs: ATHY LIB, The Courthouse, Emily Sq, Athy, Co Kildare (0507-31144; *fax:* 0507-31809; *email:* athylib@eircom.net); BALLITORE LIB & QUAKER MUSEUM, Mary Leadbeater House, Ballitore, Co Kildare (0507-23344; *email:* ballytorelib@eircom.net); CELBRIDGE LIB, St Patricks Pk, Celbridge, Co Kildare (01-627-2207; *email:* celbridgelib@eircom.net); LEIXLIP LIB, Newtown House, Captains Hill, Leixlip, Co Kildare (01-624-4240; *email:* leixliplib@eircom.net); MAYNOOTH LIB, Main St, Maynooth, Co Kildare (01-628-5530; *email:* maynoothlib@eircom.net); NAAS LIB, Canal Harbour, Naas, Co Kildare (045-879111; *fax:* 045-881766; *email:* naaslib@eircom.net); NEWBRIDGE LIB, Athgarvan Rd, Newbridge, Co Kildare (045-436453; *email:* newbridgelib@eircom.net)
Svc Pts: PT: 9 *Mobile:* 1 *Other:* SCHOOL LIB SVC, at Lib HQ; KILDARE HIST & FAMILY RSRCH CENTRE (see **IA82**)
Collns: IJFR: K *Co-op Schemes:* IJFR, LENDIT, LISTED, InfoCap 2000 *Loans:* bks, audios & videos/3 wks *Charges:* annual sub/ad €6, ch free, oap €2, family €12.50 *Fines:* all/10c per wk *Equip:* m-readers, m-printer, video viewers, faxes, copiers (A4/10c, A3/20c), computers (with internet)

Stock:	31 Dec 2000
ad lend:	249775
ch:	189030
schools:	20000
audios:	8607
videos:	1603

Issues:	2000
ad lend:	198712
ch:	158486
schools:	31000
audios:	13153

Acqs:	2000
bks:	27500
AVs:	750

Acqs: Source: lib suppl & bksellers
Classn: DDC *Cat: Type:* author *Medium:* cards & auto *Auto Sys:* Genesis *Svcs: Extramural:* schools *Info:* community *Other:* lang learning, computer software *Activs:* ch's activs, bk sales, films, County Arts Programme
Staff: Libns: 11 *Other Prof:* 29 *Non-Prof:* 20

Inc from:	2000
local govt:	IR£1265451
fines etc:	IR£62929
total:	IR£1372726

Exp on:	2000
bks:	IR£177971
salaries:	IR£816555
total:	IR£1372726

Kilkenny

IP13 Kilkenny County Libraries

Kilkenny County Lib HQ, 6 Rose Inn St, NIB Bldg, Kilkenny, Co Kilkenny, Ireland (056-91160; *fax:* 056-91168)
Email: katslibs@iol.ie
Internet: http://www.kilkennylibrary.ie/

Local Auth: Kilkenny County Council *Pop:* 74000 *Cttee:* Kilkenny County Lib Cttee *Chief:* County Libn: Mr James Fogarty DipLib, ALAI (james.fogarty@kilkennycoco.ie) *Dep:* Asst County Libn: Mr Declan Macauley BSc, DipLIS, DipEnDev
Main Libs: CASTLECOMER LIB, Kilkenny St, Castlecomer, Co Kilkenny (056-40055; *email:* comlibrary@eircom.net); GRAIGUENAMANAGH LIB, Convent Rd, Graiguenamanagh, Co Kilkenny (0503-24224; *email:* graiglib@eircom.net); KILKENNY CITY LIB, 6 Johns Quay, Kilkenny (056-22021/22606; *email:* citylib@eircom.net)
Branch Libs: LOUGHBOY LIB, Loughboy Shopping Centre, Waterford Rd, Kilkenny (056-22021/22606; *email:* lboylib@ireland.com); URLINGFORD LIB, The Courthouse, Main St, Urlingford, Co Kilkenny (056-31656; *email:* urlingfordlib@eircom.net)
Svc Pts: PT: 2 *Mobile:* 1 *Other:* 1 Schools' Lib Svc van ☞

(Kilkenny County Libs cont)
Collns: Local Studies Colln (see **IA61**); IJFR: Pa-Pk (both at Co Lib HQ) **Co-op Schemes:** IJFR
ILLs: county, natl & internatl **Loans:** bks, audios & videos/3 wks **Charges:** sub/ad €15 pa, families €25 pa, oaps & unemployed €6, students (14-18) €6, ch under 14 free **Income Gen:** reqs, res & lost ticket/cost of postage **Equip:** m-reader, m-printer, video viewer, fax, copiers, clr copier, 24 computers (with internet, €1.25 per half hr), rooms for hire

Stock:	31 Dec 2000
bks:	235168
schools:	55000
audios:	1289
periodcls:	200

Issues:	2000
bks:	306645
schools:	172000
audios:	11907

Acqs:	2000
bks:	15922

Acqs: Source: lib suppl, publ & bksellers
Classn: DDC **Cat:** Type: author & classified **Medium:** cards & printed **Auto Sys:** Genesis **Svcs:** Extramural: schools, hosps, old people's homes, housebnd **Info:** community, career, youth **Activs:** ch's activs, bk sales, films, temp exhibs, poetry readings, reading groups, author visits, homework clubs
Staff: Libns: 4 Non-Prof: 22

Inc from:	2000
fines etc:	IR£61352

Exp on:	2000
all stock:	IR£86685
salaries:	IR£552855
total:	IR£865384

Laois

IP14 Laois County Libraries
Lib HQ, Kea-Lew Business Pk, Mountrath Rd, Portlaoise, Co Laois, Ireland (0502-72340/1; *fax:* 0502-64558)
Email: library@laoiscoco.ie
Internet: http://www.laois.ie/libraries.asp

Local Auth: Laois County Council *Pop:* 53000
Chief: County Libn: Mr Gerry Maher
Branch Libs: PORTLAOISE LIB, Portlaoise, Co Laois (0502-22333; *fax:* 0502-63656); PORTARLINGTON LIB, Portarlington, Co Laois (0502-43751)
Svc Pts: PT: 10 *Computers:* 10 *Internet:* 10
Collns: IJFR: X; local studies **Co-op Schemes:** IJFR **Charges:** registration fee/ad €10 pa, ch & 2nd level students free **Income Gen:** BLDSC ILLs/€3.50; lost ticket/€1 **Fines:** bks/10c per wk; videos/50c pd **Equip:** m-readers, m-printers (50c per pg), copiers (10c per pg), computers (incl internet, €2.50 per half hr, €3.50 per hr, printouts 10c per sheet)

Stock:	31 Dec 2000
ad lend:	73889
ch:	49544
schools:	46825
audios:	3631
videos:	290

Issues:	2000
ad lend:	90521
ch:	65138
audios:	10685

Acqs:	2000
bks:	17251
AVs:	313

Cat: Medium: auto **Auto Sys:** Dynix **Svcs:** Info: community **Other:** ad literacy
Staff: Libns: 3 Non-Prof: 22

Inc from:	2000
local govt:	IR£458221
fines etc:	IR£44411
total:	IR£517990

Exp on:	2000
bks:	IR£86691
salaries:	IR£278126
total:	IR£517990

Leitrim

IP15 Leitrim County Libraries
Leitrim County Lib, , Ballinamore, Co Leitrim, Ireland (078-44012/424; *fax:* 078-44425)
Email: leitrimlibrary@eircom.net
Internet: http://www.leitrimcoco.ie/Services/Library/library.htm

Local Auth: Leitrim County Council *Pop:* 25815
Chief: County Libn: Mr Sean Ó Suilleabháin DipLT, FLAI, ALAI **Dep:** Asst Libn: Ms Gabrielle Flynn BA, DipLib
Branch Libs: BALLINAMORE LIB, Ballinamore, Co Leitrim (078-44012); CARRICK-ON-SHANNON LIB, Priest's Ln, Carrick-on-Shannon, Co Leitrim (078-20789); DRUMSHANBO LIB, Main St, Drumshanbo, Co Leitrim (078-41258); MANOR-HAMILTON LIB, Comprehensive School, Manor-hamilton, Co Leitrim (072-56180); MOHILL LIB, Castle St, Mohill, Co Leitrim (078-31360)
Svc Pts: PT: 2
Loans: bks & audios/4 wks; videos/1 wk
Charges: bks/ad 25c, ch free; videos/€1.27
Income Gen: requests/64c **Fines:** bks & audios/ad & ch 12c per wk **Equip:** 3 m-readers, 2 m-printers, fax, 2 copiers (12c), 14 computers (all with internet)

Stock:	31 Dec 2000	31 Dec 2001
ad lend:	45316	41988
ch:	22900	25000
AVs:	1350	-

Issues:	2000	2001
all items:	71852	69230

Acqs:		2001
bks:		7700

Classn: DDC **Svcs:** Extramural: schools, hosps, old people's homes **Activs:** ch's activs, films, temp exhibs, poetry readings **Offcr-in-Charge:** Asst Libn, as above
Staff: Libns: 2 Non-Prof: 3 FT, 8 PT

Inc from:	2000
fines etc:	IR£11528

Exp on:	2000
bks:	IR£32565
salaries:	IR£216728
total:	IR£358995

Proj: Ballinamore Lib HQ; Manorhamilton Lib

Limerick City

IP16 Limerick City Libraries
Limerick City Lib, The Granary, Michael St, Limerick, Ireland (061-314668; *fax:* 061-411506)
Email: citylib@limerickcity.ie
Internet: http://www.limerickcity.ie/

Local Auth: Limerick City Council *Pop:* 52043
Cttee: Cultural & Sporting Cttee **Chief:** City Libn: Ms Dolores Doyle BA(PubMgmt), FLAI, ALAI (ddoyle@limerickcity.ie) **Dep:** Exec Libn: Mrs Eileen McMahon BA, DipLIS (emcmahon@limerickcity.ie)
Main Libs: LIMERICK CITY LIB, addr as above
Branch Libs: ROXBORO BRANCH LIB, Roxboro Shopping Centre, Limerick (061-417906)
Svc Pts: Computers: 2 *Internet:* 2 *Other:* PRIMARY SCHOOLS LIB SVC, at City Lib
Collns: IJFR: O; local studies colln; Special GAA Colln; local newspapers on m-film from 1790 (all at City Lib) **Co-op Schemes:** IJFR **ILLs:** county, natl & internatl **Loans:** bks, audios & CD-ROMs/2 wks **Charges:** audios/€10 pa sub; CD-ROMs/€10 pa sub **Income Gen:** reqs & reservations/41c; British Lib ILLs/€6; lost ticket/€1 **Fines:** all items/1c pd (max €1 per item) **Equip:** 3 m-readers, 2 m-printers (10c per pg), 2 copiers (20c per pg), fax, 17 computers (incl wd-proc, internet & CD-ROM, access free) **Offcr-in-Charge:** City Libn, as above

Stock:	31 Dec 2000	31 Dec 2001
all items:	248609	254342

Issues:	2000	2001
ad lend:	140295	135033
ch:	58173	45338
audios:	15279	15321

Acqs:	2000	2001
bks:	10161	7500
AVs:	1982	1374

Acqs: Source: lib suppl, publ & bksellers **Offcr-in-Charge:** City Libn, as above
Classn: DDC **Cat:** Type: author, classified, subj & title **Medium:** auto **Auto Sys:** Dynix **Svcs:** Extramural: schools, prisons, play groups **Info:** Enterprise Centre, community, careers **Other:** Open Learning **Activs:** ch's activs, bk sales, temp exhibs, poetry readings, talks & lectures, ad literacy, computer courses **Offcr-in-Charge:** Exec Libn: Ms Deirdre O'Dea DipLIS (dodea@limerickcity.ie)
Staff: Libns: 5 Other Prof: 2 Non-Prof: 11

Inc from:	2000	2001
local govt:	€601700	€690400
fines etc:	€30133	€31768
total:	€718150	€777168

Exp on:	2000	2001
bks & AVs:	€120500	€144200
elec media:	€23200	€23300
culture:	€2000	€3000
salaries:	€319100	€348110
total:	€715150	€777168

Limerick

IP17 Limerick County Libraries
Lib HQ, 58 O'Connell St, Limerick, Ireland (061-214452; *fax:* 061-318570)
Email: libinfo@limerickcoco.ie
Internet: http://www.limerickcoco.ie/library/

Local Auth: Limerick County Council *Pop:* 113003 **Cttee:** Social & Cultural Cttee **Chief:** County Libn: Mr Damien Brady BA, DipLIS (dbrady@limerickcoco.ie) **Dep:** Exec Libn: Ms Helen Walsh DipLIS (hwalsh@limerickcoco.ie)
Main (Regional) Libs: ABBEYFEALE BRANCH LIB, Bridge St, Abbeyfeale, Co Limerick (068-32488); ADARE BRANCH LIB, Main St, Adare, Co Limerick (061-396822); DOORADOYLE BRANCH LIB, Crescent Shopping Centre, Dooradoyle, Co Limerick (061-301101); FOYNES BRANCH LIB, Foynes, Co Limerick (069-65835); NEWCASTLEWEST BRANCH LIB, Gorboy, Newcastlewest, Co Limerick (069-62273)
Svc Pts: PT: 21 *Mobile:* 2 *AV:* 4 *Computers:* 4 *Internet:* 8
Collns: IJFR: N (at HQ); ENFO pamphs & lit (from Dept of the Environment Lib in Dublin, at various locations); EU pamphs (from EU Lib in Molesworth

St, Dublin); NSSB files (from Natl Social Svc Board, at Newcastlewest & Dooradoyle Libs); local hist colln (at HQ) *Co-op Schemes:* IJFR *ILLs:* county, natl & internatl *Loans:* bks, audios & videos/2 wks *Income Gen:* lost ticket/€1 *Equip:* m-form reader/printer, fax, video viewer, 7 copiers, computers (incl wd-procs, internet & CD-ROM) *Disabled:* 2 Kurzweil (at Newcastlewest & Dooradoyle Libs)

Stock:	31 Dec 2000	31 Dec 2001
ad bks & AVs:	278070	289897
ch bks & AVs:	289652	307622

Issues:	2000
all items:	376226

Acqs:	2000	2001
bks & AVs:	31256	29797

Acqs: Source: lib suppl & bksellers *Offcr-in-Charge:* County Libn, as above
Classn: DDC *Cat: Type:* author, classified, subj & title *Medium:* cards & auto *Auto Sys:* Dynix (Horizon) *Svcs: Extramural:* schools, hosps, old people's homes, housebnd *Info:* local hist, genealogy, community, business, NSSB files, EU *Activs:* ch's activs, temp exhibs, poetry readings, arts activs on annual basis *Offcr-in-Charge:* Arts Offcr: Ms Joan McKernan BA
Staff: Libns: 11 *Non-Prof:* 40 + 7 support staff

Inc from:	2000
local govt:	IR£1138997
fines etc:	IR£6969
total:	IR£1177323

Exp on:	2000
bks:	IR£157690
AVs:	IR£31357
salaries:	IR£746230
total:	IR£1177323

Longford

IP18 Longford County Library and Arts Service

Lib HQ, Longford County Lib, Town Centre, Longford, Ireland (043-41124; *fax:* 043-48576)
Email: longlib@iol.ie
Internet: http://www.longfordcoco.ie/LIB/library.htm

Local Auth: Longford County Council *Pop:* 30166
Larger Dept: Community & Enterprise Directorate
Dept Chief: Dir: Mr Frankie Sheridan *Chief:* County Libn: Mrs Mary Carleton-Reynolds DipLIS, ALAI *Other Snr Staff:* Exec Libn: Ms Paula Mulry; Asst Libn: Ms Theresa O'Kelly
Main Libs: LONGFORD COUNTY LIB, contact details as above *Branch Libs:* DRUMLISH BRANCH LIB, Drumlish, Co Longford (043-24760); GRANARD BRANCH LIB, Market House, Granard, Co Longford (043-86164; *email:* granlib@eircom.net); LANESBORO BRANCH LIB, Lanesboro, Co Longford (043-21291; *email:* lanelib@eircom.net)
Svc Pts: PT: 2 *Mobile:* 1 *Computers:* 3 *Internet:* 3
Collns: Maria Edgeworth Colln; Oliver Goldsmith Colln; Padraic Colum Colln (works of local authors, all at Longford Lib HQ); local archival material, incl estate map colln; local newspapers on m-film (from 1837) *Co-op Schemes:* ILL *ILLs:* county, natl & internatl *Loans:* bks, audios & CD-ROMs/3 wks *Charges:* loan sub/ad €2.50 pa, ch free *Fines:* all items/6c per wk *Equip:* 4 copiers, 14 computers (all with wd-proc, internet & CD-ROM) *Offcr-in-Charge:* County Libn, as above

Stock:	31 Dec 2000	31 Dec 2001
ad lend:	71137	66554
ch:	43997	37229
schools:	46651	42888

Issues:	2000
all items:	115134

Acqs:	2000	2001
bks:	8666	9588

Acqs: Source: lib suppl, publ & bksellers *Offcr-in-Charge:* as above
Classn: DDC *Cat: Type:* author, classified, subj & title *Medium:* auto *Auto Sys:* Dynix Horizon *Svcs: Extramural:* schools, play groups *Info:* business, local hist *Activs:* ch's activs, temp exhibs, poetry readings, reading groups, writers' groups *Offcr-in-Charge:* Asst Libn, as above
Staff: Libns: 3 *Non-Prof:* 9

Exp on:	2000
total:	IR£446092

Louth

IP19 Louth County Libraries

Lib HQ, Dundalk Lib, Roden Pl, Dundalk, Co Louth, Ireland (042-933-5457/935-3190; *fax:* 042-933-7635)
Email: library@louthcoco.ie
Internet: http://www.louthcoco.ie/louth/html/library.htm

Local Auth: Louth County Council *Pop:* 92163
Cttee: Lib Cttee *Chief:* County Libn: Miss Ann Ward BA, DipLT
Main Libs: DUNDALK LIB, addr as above
Branch Libs: DROGHEDA LIB, Stockwell St, Drogheda, Co Louth (041-983-6649)
Svc Pts: PT: 3 *Mobile:* 1 *AV:* 6 *Other:* schools svc
Collns: Louth local hist (at Dundalk Lib) *Co-op Schemes:* IJFR, NERLG, BLDSC *ILLs:* county & internatl *Loans:* bks & audios/3 wks *Charges:* sub/ad €6.35 pa, conc €1.27, ch free *Fines:* bks & audios/ad 20c per wk, ch 5c per wk *Equip:* 4 m-readers, 2 m-printers (50c-75c), 2 fax, 5 copiers (15c), computers (incl wd-proc & internet)

Stock:	31 Dec 2000	31 Dec 2001
ad bks:	147759	113972
ch: *	147926	139546
audios:	7756	8197
videos:	706	715
CD-ROMs:	60	74
* incl schools		

Issues:	2000	2001
ad lend:	166356	172259
ch:	98217	102569
schools:	30720	37500
audios:	9139	10486

Acqs:	2000	2001
bks:	20117	21170
AVs:	625	633

Acqs: Source: lib suppl & bksellers *Offcr-in-Charge:* County Libn, as above
Classn: DDC *Cat: Type:* author, subj & title *Medium:* auto *Auto Sys:* Dynix *Svcs: Extramural:* schools, hosps, old people's homes *Info:* business (Enterprise Lib), local studies *Activs:* ch's activs, temp exhibs, author visits, bk readings *Offcr-in-Charge:* County Libn, as above
Staff: Libns: 6 *Non-Prof:* 21

Inc from:	2000	2001
local govt:	€853832	€1127515
fines etc:	€55808	€40388
total:	€1113980	€1205356

Exp on:	2000	2001
bks:	€219520	€253122
elec media:	€9949	€54678
salaries:	€504144	€600765
total:	€1081111	€1100413

Mayo

IP20 Mayo County Libraries

Lib HQ, Castlebar Lib, Mountain View, Castlebar, Co Mayo, Ireland (094-24444; *fax:* 094-24774)
Email: library@mayococo.ie
Internet: http://www.mayolibrary.ie/

Local Auth: Mayo County Council *Pop:* 110000
Cttee: Lib Cttee, Mayo County Council *Chief:* County Libn: Mr Austin Vaughan BA, DipLib (avaughan@mayococo.ie) *Dep:* Asst Libn: Mrs Mary Gannon DipLib
Main Libs: CASTLEBAR LIB, addr as above
Branch Libs: BALLINA LIB, Killala Rd, Ballina, Co Mayo (096-22180); BALLINROBE LIB, Main St, Ballinrobe, Co Mayo (092-41896); BALLYHAUNIS LIB, Clare St, Ballyhaunis, Co Mayo (0907-30161); BELMULLET LIB, American St, Belmullet, Co Mayo (097-82374); CLAREMORRIS LIB, Dalton St, Claremorris, Co Mayo (094-71666); CROSS-MOLINA LIB, Ballina St, Crossmolina, Co Mayo (096-31939); FOXFORD LIB, Main St, Foxford, Co Mayo (094-56040); KILTIMAGH LIB, Main St, Kiltimagh, Co Mayo (094-81786); SWINFORD LIB, Main St, Swinford, Co Mayo (094-52065); WEST-PORT LIB, The Cres, Westport, Co Mayo (098-25747)
Svc Pts: PT: 1 *Mobile:* 2 *Other:* 1 schools van
Co-op Schemes: ILL, Kaleidoscope Programme (EU scheme) *ILLs:* county, natl & internatl *Loans:* bks/3 wks *Charges:* registration fee/ad €3 pa, students & unemployed €1 pa, ch free *Equip:* m-readers, m-printers, video viewers, copiers, computers (with internet) *Disabled:* optical scanners, magnification & text-to-speech software

Stock:	31 Dec 2000
ad lend:	175742
ch:	133564
audios:	1250
videos:	308

Issues:	2000
ad lend:	255503
ch:	222451
audios:	19264

Acqs:	2000
bks:	112669
AVs:	220

Acqs: Source: lib suppl, publ & bksellers *Offcr-in-Charge:* County Libn, as above
Classn: DDC *Cat: Type:* author, classified, subj & title *Medium:* auto *Auto Sys:* Dynix *Svcs: Extramural:* schools *Info:* community, business, local govt, tourist, European, students *Activs:* ch's activs, temp exhibs, poetry readings, reading groups, writers' groups, talks, author visits *Offcr-in-Charge:* County Libn, as above
Enqs: 2000 (2001)
Staff: Libns: 4 *Non-Prof:* 25 plus 12 PT

Inc from:	2000
fines etc:	IR£63715

Exp on:	2000
bks:	IR£95000
AVs:	IR£9500
salaries:	IR£868785
total:	IR£1435000

Meath

IP21 Meath County Libraries

Lib HQ, Navan Lib, Railway St, Navan, Co Meath, Ireland (046-21134/451; *fax:* 046-21463)
Email: colibrar@meathcoco.ie
Internet: http://www.meath.ie/library.htm

Local Auth: Meath County Council *Pop:* 109000
Cttee: Meath County Lib Cttee *Chief:* County Libn: Mr Ciaran Mangan (cmangan@meathcoco.ie)
Main Libs: NAVAN LIB, contact details as above
Branch Libs: DULEEK LIB, Main St, Duleek, Co Meath (041-988-0700; *email:* duleeklib@meathcoco.ie); DUNSHAUGHLIN LIB, Main St, Dunshaughlin, Co Meath (01-825-0504); KELLS LIB, Maudlin St, Kells, Co Meath (046-41592); TRIM LIB, High St, Trim, Co Meath (046-36014)
Svc Pts: PT: 7
Collns: IJFR: T; local studies colln; Meath authors; MSS relating to Co Meath; music scores & tapes

PIRELAND
Meath
▼
Waterford
Public Libraries

(Meath County Libs cont)
Co-op Schemes: ILL, IJFR *Loans:* bks, audios & videos/2 wks *Charges:* annual sub *Equip:* m-reader, m-printer (10c per pg), copiers (10c per pg), computers (incl internet) *Disabled:* Kurzweil reader

Stock:	31 Dec 2000
bks:	374809
audios:	3431
videos:	913
periodcls:	72

Issues:	2000
bks:	203949
audios:	3879

Acqs:	2000
bks:	16238
AVs:	378

Classn: DDC *Cat: Medium:* auto *Auto Sys:* Horizon *Svcs: Extramural:* schools, hosps, old people's homes *Activs:* ch's activs, temp exhibs, poetry readings *Offcr-in-Charge:* Exec Libn
Staff: Libns: 5 *Non-Prof:* 23

Inc from:	2000
fines etc:	IRE£39412

Exp on:	2000
bks:	IRE£71785
AVs:	IRE£8239
salaries:	IRE£464482
total:	IRE£747524

Monaghan

IP22 Monaghan County Libraries
Lib HQ, Clones Lib, The Diamond, Clones, Co Monaghan, Ireland (047-51143; *fax:* 047-51863)
Email: moncolib@eircom.ie
Internet: http://www.monaghan.ie/html2/library.htm

Local Auth: Monaghan County Council *Pop:* 51266 *Chief:* County Libn: Mr Joseph McElvaney DipLIS (jmcelvaney@monaghancoco.ie) *Dep:* Asst Libn: Mrs Catherine Elliott BSocSc
Main Libs: CLONES LIB, addr as above *Branch Libs:* CARRICKMACROSS BRANCH LIB, Market Sq, Carrickmacross, Co Monaghan (042-966-1148); CASTLEBLAYNEY BRANCH LIB, Castleblayney Community Enterprise Centre, Dublin Rd, Castleblayney, Co Monaghan (042-974-0281); MONAGHAN BRANCH LIB, North Rd, Monaghan, Co Monaghan (047-81830)
Svc Pts: PT: 1 *Mobile:* 1 *Computers:* 5 *Internet:* 5 *Other:* SCHOOL MOBILE LIB SVC
Collns: local hist colln; local authors colln (both at Clones Lib) *Co-op Schemes:* ISBN Region K subscriber, NERS *ILLs:* county, natl & internatl
Loans: bks & audios/2 wks *Charges:* annual sub *Equip:* m-reader, m-printer, 3 copiers, 12 computers (with internet, access free) *Online:* ENFO, Mintel

Stock:	31 Dec 2000
bks:	184069
AVs:	4146

Issues:	2000
bks:	101747
AVs:	1279

Acqs:	2000
bks:	9144
AVs:	478

Acqs: Source: lib suppl & bksellers *Offcr-in-Charge:* County Libn, as above
Classn: DDC *Cat: Type:* author & classified *Medium:* cards *Svcs: Extramural:* schools, hosps, old people's homes *Info:* business, farming, health, cultural events, EU, environmental, tourist, social svcs, genealogy svc *Other:* local authority staff lib
Activs: ch's activs, temp exhibs, poetry readings, music recitals, workshops, public meetings *Offcr-in-Charge:* Snr Lib Asst: Ms Joan Ryan
Staff: Libns: 2 *Non-Prof:* 14.5

Exp on:	2000
bks:	IRE£66246
total:	IRE£431630

Offaly

IP23 Offaly County Library Service
Lib HQ, Tullamore Lib, O'Connor Sq, Tullamore, Co Offaly, Ireland (0506-46833/4; *fax:* 0506-52769)
Email: colibrar@offalycoco.ie
Internet: http://www.offaly.ie/librariesartsandculture/libraries.html

Local Auth: Offaly County Council *Pop:* 59000
Chief: County Libn: Miss Ann M. Coughlan
Main Libs: TULLAMORE LIB, addr as above (0506-46832/51274; *email:* tulllib@eircom.net)
Branch Libs: BIRR LIB, John's Mall, Birr, Co Offaly (0509-20961; *email:* birrlib@eircom.net); CLARA LIB, Clara, Co Offaly (0506-31389; *email:* clarlib@eircom.net); EDENDERRY LIB, J.K.L. St, Edenderry, Co Offaly (0405-31028; *email:* edenlib@eircom.net)
Svc Pts: PT: 5 *Computers:* 9 *Internet:* 9
Collns: Local Studies Colln *Co-op Schemes:* ILL
Loans: bks & lang videos/4 wks; videos & bks in heavy demand/1 wk *Income Gen:* membership sub/ad €10 pa, over-66 & FT students €3 pa, social welfare recipients, users of Ad Literacy programme & under-18s free *Equip:* 3 m-readers, m-printer, 7 copiers, fax, video viewer, 32 computers (all with wd-proc, internet & CD-ROM)

Stock:	31 Dec 2000
ad lend:	88027
ch:	68949
schools:	44834
audios:	658
videos:	666

Issues:	2000
ad lend:	79988
ch:	78759
schools:	12514
audios:	2274

Acqs:	2000
bks:	16966
AVs:	560

Cat: Medium: auto *Auto Sys:* Horizon *Svcs: Other:* Open Learning Centre *Activs:* ch's activs, writers' groups, author visits, ad literacy
Enqs: 9000 (2001)
Staff: Libns: 3 *Non-Prof:* 18

Inc from:	2000
local govt:	IRE£497513
fines etc:	IRE£41300
total:	IRE£564767

Exp on:	2000
all stock:	IRE£106768
salaries:	IRE£330524
total:	IRE£564767

Roscommon

IP24 Roscommon County Libraries
Lib HQ, Roscommon County Lib, Abbey St, Roscommon, Ireland (0903-37270 x184/186; *fax:* 0903-25474)
Email: roslib@eircom.net
Internet: http://www.roscommoncoco.ie/

Local Auth: Roscommon County Council *Pop:* 51897 *Chief:* Acting County Libn: Mr Eamonn Bolger DipLIS
Main Libs: ROSCOMMON COUNTY LIB, contact details as above *Branch Libs:* BALLAGHADERREEN BRANCH LIB, Main St, Ballaghaderreen, Co Roscommon (0907-77044; *email:* dbllib@eircom.net); BOYLE BRANCH LIB, King House, Boyle, Co Roscommon (079-62800; *email:* bbllib@eircom.net); CASTLEREA BRANCH LIB, Main St, Castlerea, Co Roscommon (0907-20745; *email:* cbllib@eircom.net); ELPHIN BRANCH LIB, Main St, Elphin, Co Roscommon (078-35775; *email:* ebllib@eircom.net); STROKESTOWN BRANCH LIB, Bawn St, Strokestown, Co Roscommon (078-34027; *email:* sbllib@eircom. net)
Svc Pts: PT: 1 *Other:* BUSINESS INFO SVC, at County Lib HQ (0903-37100; *fax:* 0903-25474); SCHOOLS LIB SVC
Collns: IJFR: V; local hist (at County Lib) *Co-op Schemes:* IJFR *ILLs:* county, natl & internatl
Loans: bks & audios/2 wks *Charges:* annual sub/ ad £3, under-18s free *Income Gen:* lost ticket/£1 *Fines:* bks & audios/ad, ch & oap 6p per wk, registered blind exempt *Equip:* 4 m-readers, 2 m-printers, fax, 7 copiers (10p), computers (incl wd-procs, internet & CD-ROM) *Online:* IRIS, UnCover, FactFinder

Stock:	31 Dec 2000
ad lend:	125592
ch:	65301
AVs:	11791

Issues:	2000
ad lend:	73267
ch:	43930
AVs:	8879

Acqs:	2000
bks:	16944
AVs:	764

Acqs: Source: lib suppl, publ & bksellers *Offcr-in-Charge:* Asst Libn: Mrs B. Gilligan
Classn: DDC *Cat: Type:* author, classified, subj & title *Medium:* auto *Auto Sys:* Dynix *Svcs: Extramural:* schools, old people's homes *Info:* business, community *Other:* Open Learning at all svc pts *Activs:* temp exhibs, poetry readings
Staff: Libns: 4 *Non-Prof:* 12.5

Inc from:	2000
local govt:	IRE£585809
fines etc:	IRE£11663
total:	IRE£613804

Exp on:	2000
all stock:	IRE£111769
salaries:	IRE£353339
total:	IRE£613804

Sligo

IP25 Sligo County Library Services
Lib HQ, Westward Town Centre, Bridge St, Sligo, Ireland (071-47190; *fax:* 071-46798)
Email: sligolib@sligococo.ie
Internet: http://www.sligococo.ie/

Local Auth: Sligo County Council *Pop:* 55000
Chief: County Libn: Mr Donal Tinney BA, DipLIS, ALAI (dtinney@sligococo.ie) *Dep:* Exec Libn: Ms Pauline Brennan (pbrenn@sligococo.ie) *Other Snr Staff:* Asst Libn & Database Administrator: Mr Fran Hegarty (fhegarty@sligococo.ie); Asst Libn (Lib Archvs & Admin): Mr Patrick Gannon (pgannon@sligococo.ie); Snr Lib Asst (Accounts): Ms Caroline Morgan (cmorgan@sligococo.ie)
Main Libs: CENTRAL REFERENCE LIB, The Courthouse, Teeling St, Sligo (071-42212)
Branch Libs: BALLYMOTE BRANCH LIB, Courthouse, Ballymote, Co Sligo
Svc Pts: PT: 2 *Other:* primary school svc

Collns: Yeats Colln (works & criticism of W.B. Yeats, at Sligo Lib HQ); Local Studies Colln (see **IA87**) *Co-op Schemes:* IJFR *ILLs:* county, natl & internatl *Loans:* bks, audios & videos/3 wks *Equip:* m-reader, m-printer, copier, computers (incl internet & CD-ROM) *Disabled:* Kurzweil

Stock:	31 Dec 2000
ad lend:	70104
ch:	43173
AVs:	983

Issues:	2000	2001
all items:	107600	120977

Acqs:	2000
bks:	9611
AVs:	220

Acqs: *Source:* lib suppl & bksellers *Offcr-in-Charge:* Asst Libn (Lib Archvs & Admin), as above **Classn:** DDC **Cat:** *Type:* author & classified *Medium:* cards **Svcs:** *Extramural:* schools, community groups *Activs:* ch's activs, temp exhibs *Offcr-in-Charge:* Snr Asst: Ms Caroline Morgan FLAI **Staff:** *Libns:* 3 *Non-Prof:* 12

Inc from:	2000
fines etc:	IR£16686

Exp on:	2000
bks:	IR£69739
AVs:	IR£6340
salaries:	IR£263989
total:	IR£102967

South Dublin

IP26 South Dublin Libraries

Lib HQ, Unit 1, The Square Industrial Complex, Tallaght, Dublin 24, Ireland (01-459-7834; *fax:* 01-459-7872)
Email: libraries@sdublincoco.ie
Internet: http://www.sdcc.ie/

Local Auth: South Dublin County Council *Pop:* 240000 *Larger Dept:* Corporate Svcs Dept *Chief:* County Libn: Ms Teresa Walsh BA, DipLIS (twalsh@sdublincoco.ie)
Main Libs: COUNTY LIB, Tallaght Town Centre, Tallaght, Dublin 24 (01-462-0073; *fax:* 01-414-9207; *email:* talib@sdublincoco.ie) *Branch Libs:* BALLYROAN LIB, Orchardstown Ave, Rathfarnham, Dublin 14 (01-494-1900; *fax:* 01-494-7083; *email:* ballyroan@sdublincoco.ie); CASTLETYMON LIB, Tymon North Shopping Centre, Tallaght, Dublin 24 (01-452-4888; fax 01-459-7873; *email:* castletymon@sdublincoco.ie); CLONDALKIN LIB, Monastery Rd, Clondalkin, Dublin 22 (01-459-3315; fax 01-459-5509; *email:* clondalkin@sdublincoco. ie); LUCAN LIB, Superquinn Shopping Centre, Newcastle Rd, Lucan, Co Dublin (01-621-6431; fax 01-621-6433; *email:* lucan@sdublincoco.ie)
Svc Pts: PT: 1 *Mobile:* 4 *AV:* at all branches *Other:* SCHOOL LIBS SVC, at Lib HQ (schools@sdublincoco.ie); MOBILE LIBS, at Lib HQ (mobiles@sdublincoco.ie)
Collns: IJFRS: J (at Lib HQ); Local Studies Colln (hist & heritage of South Dublin); Local Govt Colln (both at County Lib, Tallaght); Katherine Tynan Colln (at Castletymon Lib) *Co-op Schemes:* IJFRS *ILLs:* county, natl & internatl *Loans:* bks, audios & CD-ROMs/3 wks; videos/ref only; prints/3 months *Charges:* reqs & reservations/41c; lost ticket/no charge *Fines:* bks/ad & ch 21c per wk, oap discretionary; audios, CD-ROMs & prints/21c per wk *Equip:* m-reader, m-printer, 6 copiers (12c per pg), 5 fax, 5 video viewers, 40 computers (all with wd-proc, internet & CD-ROM), 3 rooms for hire *Disabled:* teletext *Online:* Pro Quest, Odyssey Marketing Direct (no fees)

Stock:	31 Dec 2000	31 Dec 2001
ad lend:	149959	187053
ad ref:	10103	11148
ch:	82169	106407
schools:	82886	74242
audios:	23305	25352
videos:	754	912
CD-ROMs:	729	800
periodcls:	100	110

Issues:	2000	2001
ad lend:	387844	514525
ch:	244719	362792
audios:	93040	90564
videos:	-	247
CD-ROMs:	5800	2042

Acqs:	2000	2001
bks:	56061	70023
AVs:	3576	3472

Acqs: *Source:* lib suppl, publ & bksellers **Classn:** DDC **Cat:** *Type:* author, classified, subj & title *Medium:* auto *Auto Sys:* DS Galaxy 2000 **Svcs:** *Extramural:* schools, housebnd, old people's homes, day centres *Info:* business *Other:* Open Learning Centre, lang learning facilities *Activs:* ch's activs, temp exhibs, poetry readings, reading groups, writers' groups, talks, author visits *Offcr-in-Charge:* snr libn in each branch **Staff:** *Libns:* 25 *Non-Prof:* 77

Inc from:	2000
fines etc:	IR£63700

Exp on:	2000
bks:	IR£265000
salaries:	IR£1667300
total:	IR£2882400

Tipperary

IP27 Tipperary Libraries

County Lib HQ, Thurles Public Lib, Castle Ave, Thurles, Co Tipperary, Ireland (0504-21555; *fax:* 0504-23442)
Email: info@tipperarylibraries.ie
Internet: http://ireland.iol.ie/~tipplibs/

Local Auth: North Tipperary County Council & South Tipperary County Council *Pop:* 133535 *Cttee:* County Tipperary Joint Libs Cttee (provides lib svcs for both North & South Tipperary) *Chief:* County Libn: Mr Martin Maher *Dep:* Exec Libn: Mrs Anne Corridan
Main Libs: CARRICK-ON-SUIR LIB, Fair Green, Carrick-on-Suir, Co Tipperary (*tel & fax:* 051-640591); CLONMEL LIB, Emmet St, Clonmel, Co Tipperary (052-24545; *fax:* 052-27336); NENAGH LIB, O'Rahilly St, Nenagh, Co Tipperary (067-34404; *fax:* 067-34405; *email:* nenagh@tipperarylibraries.ie); ROSCREA LIB, Birr Rd, Roscrea, Co Tipperary (*tel & fax:* 0505-22032); THURLES PUBLIC LIB, contact details as above; TIPPERARY LIB, Dan Breen House, Tipperary, Co Tipperary (*tel & fax:* 062-51761) *Branch Libs:* CAHIR LIB, The Square, Cahir, Co Tipperary (052-42075); CASHEL LIB, The Green, Cashel, Co Tipperary (062-63825; *fax:* 062-63948; *email:* cashel@tipperarylibraries.ie); TEMPLEMORE LIB, Town Hall, Templemore, Co Tipperary (0504-32421)
Svc Pts: PT: 4 *Computers:* 13 *Internet:* 13 *Other:* PRIMARY SCHOOLS LIB SVC, based at Lib HQ (covers 150+ schools)
Collns: IJFR: Y (at Thurles Lib); local studies colln *Co-op Schemes:* IJFR *ILLs:* county, natl & internatl *Loans:* bks, audios & videos/3 wks *Charges:* membership sub/ad €5 pa, oap €1.25 pa, ch free *Equip:* m-reader, fax, copiers, computer svc pts, computers (with internet) *Disabled:* speech synthesiser

Stock:	31 Dec 2000
ad lend:	359490
ch:	188126
audios:	6236
videos:	640
CD-ROMs:	104

Issues:	2000
ad lend:	238570
ch:	144355
AVs:	7594

Acqs:	2000
bks:	24073
AVs:	1334

Acqs: *Source:* lib suppl & bksellers *Offcr-in-Charge:* County Libn, as above **Classn:** DDC **Cat:** *Type:* author, classified & title *Medium:* cards **Svcs:** *Extramural:* schools *Activs:* ch's activs, temp exhibs, poetry readings, music recitals *Offcr-in-Charge:* each branch responsible **Staff:** *Libns:* 8 *Non-Prof:* 33

Inc from:	2000
fines etc:	IR£63852

Exp on:	2000
all stock:	IR£233822
salaries:	IR£683717
total:	IR£1187874

Waterford City

IP28 Waterford City Libraries

Lib HQ, 35 The Mall, Waterford, Ireland (051-860839; *fax:* 051-849704)
Email: library@waterfordcity.ie
Internet: http://www.waterfordcity.ie/library/

Local Auth: Waterford City Council *Pop:* 40345 *Larger Dept:* Dept of Housing & Corporate Affairs *Dept Chief:* Dir of Svcs: Mr Paddy Power *Chief:* City Libn: Ms Jane Cantwell BA, DipLIS (jcantwell@waterfordcity.ie) *Other Snr Staff:* Asst Libn: Ms Kathleen Moran BA, DipLIS (kmoran@waterfordcity.ie); Asst Libn: Ms Katherine Collins BA, HDipEd, DipLIS (kcollins@waterfordcity.ie)
Main Libs: WATERFORD CITY LIB, 31 Ballybricken, Waterford (051-309975; *fax:* 051-850031; *email:* library@waterfordcity.ie) *Branch Libs:* ARDKEEN LIB, Ardkeen Shopping Centre, Dunmore Rd, Waterford (051-849755; *fax:* 051-874100); BROWN'S ROAD LIB, Paddy Brown's Rd, Waterford (051-860840)
Svc Pts: AV: 3 *Computers:* 2 *Internet:* 2 *Collns:* Waterford Room Colln of local hist; archvs of the City & County Infirmary; Irish Colln (printed bks); genealogical colln (printed bks); genl fiction & non-fiction reserve store *Co-op Schemes:* IJFR, ILL *ILLs:* natl *Loans:* all items/3 wks *Charges:* membership charges/ad €6 pa, ch & snr citizens €2.50 pa *Income Gen:* reservations/35c; lost ticket/€1 *Fines:* bks, videos & CD-ROMs/ad & oap 12c pd, ch 1c pd; audios/12c pd; handicapped, disabled, blind, deaf, impoverished exempt *Equip:* m-reader, m-printer, copier (€1.25 per 10 copies), clr copier, computers (incl 17 with wd-proc & 17 with internet) *Online:* Grove Dictionary of Music

Stock:	31 Dec 2000	31 Dec 2001
ad lend:	51733	43331
ad ref:	-	8276
ch:	24363	22893
AVs:	7161	8983
periodcls:	96	96

Issues:	2000	2001
all items:	191933	195524

Acqs:	2000
bks:	12412
AVs:	408

Acqs: *Source:* lib suppl & bksellers *Offcr-in-Charge:* Asst Libn: Ms Kathleen Moran, as above

☞

(Waterford City Libs cont)

Classn: DDC *Cat: Type:* author, subj & title *Medium:* auto *Auto Sys:* Dynix *Svcs: Extramural:* schools *Info:* business, community *Other:* Open Univ *Activs:* ch's activs, bk sales, temp exhibs, poetry readings, author visits
Staff: Libns: 3 *Non-Prof:* 11

Inc from:	2000
local govt:	IR£422366
fines etc:	IR£26573
total:	IR£461624

Exp on:	2000
bks:	IR£68856
salaries:	IR£245189
total:	IR£461624

Proj: Arkdeen Lib; extension & refurbishment of Carnegie Lib at Lady Ln

Waterford

IP29 Waterford County Libraries

Lib HQ, Waterford County Lib, Main St, Lismore, Co Waterford, Ireland (058-54128; *fax:* 058-54877)
Email: libraryhq@waterfordcoco.ie
Internet: http://www.waterfordcoco.ie/

Local Auth: Waterford County Council *Pop:* 51296 *Cttee:* Libs Cttee *Larger Dept:* Council *Dept Chief:* County Mgr: Mr Donal Connolly *Chief:* County Libn: Mr Donal Brady BA, DipLT, ALAI *Dep:* Asst Libn: Eddie Byrne BA, DipLT
Main Libs: WATERFORD COUNTY LIB, contact details as above *Branch Libs:* DUNGARVAN CENTRAL LIB, Cois Mara, Davitts Quay, Dungarvan, Co Waterford (058-41231; *email:* dungarvanlibrary@waterfordcoco.ie); LISMORE BRANCH LIB, West St, Lismore, Co Waterford (058-54128; *email:* lismorelibrary@waterfordcoco.ie); TRAMORE BRANCH LIB, Market St, Tramore, Co Waterford (051-381479; *email:* tramorelibrary@waterfordcoco.ie)
Svc Pts: PT: 4 *Computers:* 8 *Internet:* 8 *Other:* SCHOOL LIB SVC (051-381479/058-54128; *email:* schoolslibrary@waterfordcoco.ie)
Collns: local studies colln; newspapers; photos *ILLs:* county, natl & internatl *Loans:* bks, audios & videos/2 wks *Equip:* m-reader, m-printer, video viewers, fax, copiers, computers (incl wd-procs, internet & CD-ROM), room for hire

Stock:	31 Dec 2000
ad lend:	50887
ch:	25593
audios:	2392
videos:	294
CD-ROMs:	20

Issues:	2000
all items:	171628

Acqs:	2000
bks:	10399
AVs:	466

Acqs: Source: lib suppl, publ & bksellers *Offcr-in-Charge:* Asst Libn: Ms Kate Murphy
Classn: DDC *Cat: Type:* author, classified, subj & title *Medium:* auto *Auto Sys:* Dynix *Svcs: Extramural:* schools, old people's homes *Info:* community, business *Other:* reading schemes *Activs:* ch's activs, bk sales, temp exhibs *Offcr-in-Charge:* Snr Lib Asst: Ms Anne Lenihan
Staff: Libns: 4 *Non-Prof:* 17

Inc from:	2000
local govt:	IR£435000
fines etc:	IR£15000
total:	IR£480000

Exp on:	2000
all stock:	IR£55000
elec media:	IR£20000
salaries:	IR£280000
total:	IR£480000

Proj: proposed mobile lib svc

Westmeath

IP30 Westmeath County Libraries

Lib HQ, Dublin Rd, Mullingar, Co Westmeath, Ireland (044-40781/2/3; *fax:* 044-41322)
Email: library@westmeathcoco.ie
Internet: http://www.westmeathcoco.ie/services/library/

Local Auth: Westmeath County Council *Pop:* 63000 *Cttee:* Housing, Cultural & Social Policy SPC *Chief:* County Libn: Ms Mary M. Farrell BA, HDipEd, DipLIS, ALAI (mfarrell@westmeathcoco.ie) *Other Snr Staff:* Exec Libn (Lib HQ): Ms Mary Stuart; Exec Libn (Athlone Lib): Mr Gearoid O'Brien; Asst Libn (Mullingar Lib): Mr Christopher Cox
Main Libs: ATHLONE BRANCH LIB, Fr Matthew Hall, Athlone, Co Westmeath (0902-92166; *fax:* 0902-94900; *email:* athlib@eircom.net); MULLINGAR BRANCH LIB, Church Ave, Mullingar, Co Westmeath (044-48278; *fax:* 044-42330; *email:* tcox@tinet.ie)
Svc Pts: PT: 4 *AV:* 4 *Computers:* 3 *Internet:* 6 *Other:* 1 school lib
Collns: IJFR: E; Westmeath Local Studies Colln; Westmeath authors or with Westmeath connections (Pakenham family, Lawrence of Arabia, Charles Howard Budy, explorer); Kirby Colln (illustrated eds of "Vicar of Wakefield"); Howard Bury Papers; John Broderick Colln *Co-op Schemes:* IJFR *ILLs:* county, natl & internatl *Loans:* bks & audios/3 wks *Fines:* all items/ad, ch & oap 10c per wk *Equip:* 5 m-readers, m-printer, fax, 3 copiers, 22 computers (free, all with wd-proc & internet) *Disabled:* equip for visually impaired

Stock:	31 Dec 2000
ad lend:	95155
ch:	37330
AVs:	2796

Issues:	2000	2001
all items:	214737	212711

Acqs:	2000	2001
bks & AVs:	16569	16712

Acqs: Source: lib suppl & bksellers *Offcr-in-Charge:* County Libn, as above
Classn: DDC *Cat: Type:* author, classified, subj & title *Medium:* auto *Auto Sys:* Horizon *Svcs: Extramural:* schools, old people's homes, play groups *Info:* business, student, Irish & local studies *Activs:* ch's activs, temp exhibs, writers' groups, author visits *Offcr-in-Charge:* County Libn, as above
Staff: Libns: 3 *Non-Prof:* 18

Exp on:	2000
total:	IR£741906

Proj: Castlepollard Lib (starting 2002)

Wexford

IP31 Wexford Public Libraries

Lib Mgmt Svcs, Kents Bldg, Ardcavan, Co Wexford, Ireland (053-24922/8; *fax:* 053-21097)
Email: libraryhq@wexfordcoco.ie
Internet: http://www.wexford.ie/library.htm

Local Auth: Wexford County Council *Pop:* 104000 *Cttee:* Cultural Strategic Policy Cttee *Chief:* County Libn: Ms Fionnuala Hanrahan BA, DipLIS, MLIS, ALA, ALAI *Dep:* Exec Libn: Ms Rita O'Brien BA, DipLIS
Main Libs: WEXFORD TOWN LIB, McCauley's Carpark, off Redmond Sq, Wexford, Co Wexford (053-21637; *fax:* 053-21641; *email:* wexfordlib@eircom.net) *Branch Libs:* ENNISCORTHY LIB, Lymington Rd, Enniscorthy, Co Wexford (054-36055; *fax:* 054-36164; *email:* enniscorthylib@eircom.net); NEW ROSS LIB, Barrack Ln, New Ross, Co Wexford (051-421877; *email:* newrosslib@eircom.net)
Svc Pts: PT: 2 *Mobile:* 2 *Other:* LOCAL STUDIES (see **IA1**); CH'S & SCHOOLS SVCS, at Lib Mgmt Svc; LOCAL AUTHORITY STAFF LIB
Collns: IJFR: Q *Co-op Schemes:* IJFR *ILLs:* county, natl & internatl *Loans:* 3 wks for all items
Income Gen: reservations/30c *Fines:* all items/5c per wk *Equip:* 2 m-readers, copier, computers (2-7 at each lib, incl wd-proc & internet), room for hire (free) *Online:* Internet access (free)

Stock:	31 Dec 2000
ad lend:	131300
ch:	30000
AVs:	6600

Issues:	2000
ad lend:	135400
ch:	73700
AVs:	9100

Acqs: Source: lib suppl & bksellers *Offcr-in-Charge:* Stock Acqs Libn: Ms Susan Kelly
Classn: DDC *Cat: Type:* author, classified, subj & title *Medium:* auto *Auto Sys:* Unicorn *Svcs: Extramural:* schools, old people's homes *Info:* community, career *Other:* archvs *Activs:* ch's activs, temp exhibs, poetry readings, community learning, lectures, community storytelling
Staff: Libns: 7 *Non-Prof:* 18

Exp on:	2000
bks:	IR£124500
total:	IR£791900

Proj: Gorey Lib; Bunclody Lib; mobile lib unit; computerisation with Unicorn sys

Wicklow

IP32 Wicklow County Council Library Service

Lib HQ, Wicklow County Lib, Boghall Rd, Bray, Co Wicklow, Ireland (01-286-6566; *fax:* 01-286-5811)
Email: wcclhq@eircom.ie
Internet: http://www.wicklow.ie/

Local Auth: Wicklow County Council *Pop:* 102417 *Cttee:* Social Policy Cttee (Social & Cultural) *Larger Dept:* Community & Enterprise *Dept Chief:* Dir: Mr Séamus Walker *Chief:* County Libn: Mr Brendan Martin (bmartin@wicklowcoco.ie) *Dep:* Exec Libns: Ms Carmel Moore (cmoore@wicklowcoco.ie) & Ms Noelle Ringwood (nringwood@wicklowcoco.ie)
Main Libs: WICKLOW COUNTY LIB, as above *Branch Libs:* ARKLOW PUBLIC LIB, Mary's Rd, Arklow, Co Wicklow (0402-39977); BALLY-WALTRIM PUBLIC LIB, Boghall Rd, Bray, Co Wicklow (01-272-3205); BRAY PUBLIC LIB, Eglinton Rd, Bray, Co Wicklow (01-286-2600); GREYSTONES PUBLIC LIB, Mill Rd, Greystones, Co Wicklow (01-287-3548); WICKLOW LIB, 37 St Mantann's Rd, Wicklow, Co Wicklow (0404-67025)
Svc Pts: PT: 8 *AV:* 6 *Computers:* 13 *Internet:* 13
Collns: IJFR: R; J.M. Synge Colln; Charles Stewart Parnell Colln; Oscar Wilde Colln; 1798 Colln; Local Hist Colln *Co-op Schemes:* IJFR *ILLs:* county, natl & internatl *Loans:* bks, audios & CD-ROMs/3 wks *Income Gen:* reqs & reservations/40c; ILLs/€3.80 *Fines:* all items/25c per wk or part thereof

Equip: m-form reader/printer (10c per sheet), copiers (10c per sheet), 33 computers (all with wd-proc, internet & CD-ROM, printouts 10c per copy, floppy disks €1.25 each) *Offcr-in-Charge:* County Libn, as above

Stock:	*31 Dec 2000*
ad lend:	188000
ch:	110000
audios:	4000
periodcls:	80

Issues:	*2000*	*2001*
all items:	334000	355000

Acqs: Source: lib suppl & bksellers *Offcr-in-Charge:* Exec Libn: Ms Carmel Moore, as above *Classn:* DDC *Cat: Type:* author, classified, subj & title *Medium:* cards & auto *Auto Sys:* Dynix *Svcs: Extramural:* schools, prison, hosps, old people's homes, day centres *Info:* business, community, tourist, careers, social welfare & health *Other:* Open Learning, lang learning *Activs:* ch's activs, bk sales, temp exhibs, poetry readings, reading groups, writers' groups, talks, author visits *Offcr-in-Charge:* Exec Libn: Ms Noelle Ringwood, as above *Staff: Libns:* 7 *Other Prof:* 9 *Non-Prof:* 9

Inc from:	*2002*
fines etc:	€35000

Exp on:	*2002*
bks:	€257000
AVs:	€20000
total:	€1500000

Proj: Newtownmountkennedy Branch Lib; mobile lib; disabled equip & facilities for Bray Lib; ongoing automation of catalogue

SECTION 8 – IRISH ARCHIVES AND LOCAL HISTORY

Entries are arranged alphabetically under town names. Institutions covered include governmental and local authority archives, local history and family history libraries and resources (both local authority and privately run), diocesan and other religious archives, museum archives, corporate archives and private archives.

Please note that many libraries also hold substantial archival and manuscript collections that are not listed in this section. See **Section 9 – Irish Special Libraries**, or consult the **Index** for specific named collections.

Access to many archives and record offices is restricted, and entry may require an appointment in advance. Often identification will be required and a special need to use the collections will have to be demonstrated.

Telephone and fax numbers are given in the form of area dialling codes within the Republic of Ireland. To telephone the Irish Republic from outside the country, dial 00-353 followed by the number, minus the initial 0.

Entries are based on the institutions' responses to the following questions:

	1. **Official name of Institution**	
Type:	2. **Type of Institution** *(see also Key to Symbols below)*	
	3. **Full postal address** *(incl. postcode)* Tel & fax numbers *(incl. STD code)*	
Email:	Electronic Mail	
Internet:	Internet address	
Gov Body:	4. **Governing body** *(if any, e.g., local authority, university)*	
Chief:	5. **Officer in charge** *(give designation, name, qualifications & email address)*	
Dep:	6. **Deputy** *(give designation, name, qualifications & email address)*	
Other Snr Staff:	7. **Other Senior Staff** *(give designation, name, qualifications & email address)*	
Assoc Offices:	8. **Associate or Branch Offices** *(if any, give address, tel, fax & email address, plus designation, name & qualifications of officer in charge)*	
Entry:	9. **Conditions for entry** *(e.g., reference only, advance appointment)*	
Open:	10. **Opening hours** *(please use 24-hour clock, e.g., 0930-1730)*	
Subj:	11. **Main subjects covered** Geographical area, main types of archives covered	
Collns:	12. **Special Collections** *(give subjects and brief details)*	
Bks & Pamphs:	a) Printed books & pamphlets	
Archvs:	b) Archives	
Other:	c) Other	
Co-op Schemes:	13. **Co-operative schemes** *(in which institution participates, if any)*	
Equip:	14. **Equipment & facilities available to users** *(give numbers, and fees if appropriate)*	
Disabled:	**Equipment for disabled** *(e.g., Kurzweil)*	
Online:	**Online information services** *(e.g., Dialog; give fees)*	
Offcr-in-Charge:	**Officer in charge of equipment purchases** *(give designation, name & email address)*	

Svcs:	15. **Services provided**	
Stock:	16. **Stock** *(give total quantities)*	
archvs	a) Archives *(specify unit e.g., by linear, cubic metre)*	
rec mgmt	b) Records management holdings *(specify unit e.g., by linear, cubic metre)*	
bks	c) Books *(incl bound periodicals)*	
periodcls	d) Current periodical titles	
photos	e) Photographs	
slides	f) Slides	
illusts	g) Illustrations	
pamphs	h) Pamphlets	
maps	i) Maps	
m-forms	j) Microforms	
audios	k) Audios	
videos	l) Videos	
CD-ROMs	m) CD-ROMs	
	n) Other *(please specify)*	
Acqs Offcr:	**Officer in charge of stock acquisitions** *(give designation, name & email address)*	
Classn:	17. **Classification method(s) used** *(if applicable)*	
Auto Sys:	18. **Automated Library system used** *(if any)*	
Pubns:	19. **Publications** *(e.g., guides & handlists; give titles & prices)*	
Staff:	20. **Staff establishment** *(give full-time equivalent for part-time staff incl. vacancies)* **Total number of:**	
Archivists:	a) Professional archivists	
Libns:	b) Professional librarians	
Other Prof:	c) Other professional staff	
Non-Prof:	d) Non-professional staff	
Exp:	21. **Finance** *(expenditure on documents and/or books, incl. purchase & conservation)* a) 1999-2000 b) 2000-01	
Proj:	22. **Capital projects** *(if any, starting in 2001 or 2002)*	
Further Info:	23. **Other Information**	

Key to Symbols

Academic/Educational	Corporate/Business	Governmental (incl local)	Medical/Health
Museum/Gallery	Photo/Film	Private	Religious

Ardcavan

IA1 🏛

Wexford County Council Public Library Service, Local Studies and Archives Section

Wexford Public Lib HQ, Kent Bldg, Ardcavan, Co Wexford, Ireland (053-24922; *fax:* 053-21097)
Email: libraryhq@wexfordcoco.ie
Internet: http://www.wexford.ie/

Type: local authority *Gov Body:* Wexford County Council (see **IP31**) *Chief:* County Libn: Ms Fionnuala Hanrahan BA, DipLib, MLIS *Other Snr Staff:* Exec Libn: Ms Rita O'Brien BA, DipLIS; Archivist: Ms Gráinne Doran BA, DipAS (grainne. doran@wexfordcoco.ie); Snr Lib Asst, Local Studies: Ms Celestine Rafferty BA, DIHS (celestine.rafferty@wexfordcoco.ie)
Entry: County Council archvs by appt only
Subj: Co Wexford: local authority archvs; parish records; estate archvs; family papers; business records; personal papers; records of parent org; local hist; genealogy *Collns: Bks & Pamphs:* local hist materials; 1798 Colln; John F. Kennedy Colln *Archvs:* archvs of Wexford County Council (1899-date); records of Rural Dist Councils, records of Town & Borough Councils; Grand Jury records for Co Wexford; records of Board of Guardians & Poor Law Commissioners; records of Board of Health & Public Assistance; records of Wexford Harbour Commissioners
Equip: 2 m-readers, m-printer (fees variable), copier *Svcs:* info, ref
Stock: archvs/figures unavailable; bks/8500; periodcls/20; pamphs/150; maps/100; m-forms/ 400; audios/150; videos/80; CD-ROMs/20; photos, slides & illusts/2000
Classn: DDC, ISAD(G) *Auto Sys:* Unicorn
Pubns: Mightier Than the Sword: The Culture of Wexford Revealed Through its Histories (€3); Out, Damned Spot! Preserving your Personal Papers & Memorabilia (€7); Publish & Be Damned: Some Practical Advice for the Community Publisher (€7); prices incl p&p
Staff: Archivists: 1 *Libns:* 1 *Non-Prof:* 1
See also WEXFORD CORPORATION ARCHVS (**IA98**)

Athlone

IA2 🔑

Roscommon Family History Society Library

Bealnamullia, Athlone, Co Roscommon, Ireland
Email: crfhs@eircom.net
Internet: http://www.geocities.com/Heartland/ Pines/7030/

Subj: Co Roscommon: local hist; family hist; genealogy; heraldry *Collns: Bks & Pamphs:* local pubns; family hist journals *Other:* census records; records of births, deaths & marriages; maps & photos; monumental inscriptions; family trees
Staff: run by volunteers
See also **IO41**

Ballinamore

IA3 🏛

Leitrim County Library, Archive Collections

Leitrim County Lib, Ballinamore, Co Leitrim, Ireland (078-44012; *fax:* 078-44425)
Email: leitrimlibrary@eircom.net

Gov Body: Leitrim County Council (see **IP15**)
Chief: County Libn: Mr Sean Ó Suilleabháin DipLT, FLAI, ALAI *Dep:* Asst Libn: Gabrielle Flynn BA, DipLib
Open: Mon-Fri 1000-1700
Subj: Co Leitrim: local authority archvs; estate archvs; business records; records of parent org
Collns: Archvs: minute bks of Boards of Guardians
Equip: 4 m-readers, 2 m-printers, copier, fax
Staff: Libns: 2 *Non-Prof:* 3

IA4 🔑

Leitrim Genealogy Centre

c/o Leitrim County Lib, Ballinamore, Co Leitrim, Ireland (071-964-4012; *fax:* 071-964-4425)
Email: leitrimgenealogy@eircom.net
Internet: http://www.irishroots.net/leitrim.htm

Chief: Chairman: Mr Josie Martin *Dep:* Sec: Mr Michael Whelan *Other Snr Staff:* Rsrcher: Ms Brid Sullivan
Open: Mon-Fri 1000-1300, 1400-1700, all year round
Subj: Co Leitrim: parish records; family hist; genealogy
Svcs: rsrch (fees)
Futher Info: The Centre carries out rsrch on Leitrim ancestors through a variety of computerised records, using the Irish Family Hist Foundation scale of charges; however, direct access to the computers is not available for the public

Blackrock

IA5 🙏

Congregation of the Irish Dominican Sisters, Archives

Dominican Convent, Sion Hill, Blackrock, Co Dublin, Ireland (01-288-8631; *fax:* 01-288-5260)
Email: siondoms2002@yahoo.com
Internet: http://www.cabraop.org/ireland/

Chief: Archivist: Sr Theophane Dwyer BA
Entry: by adv appt only
Subj: records of parent org *Collns: Bks & Pamphs:* religious bks of plays by Sir Joseph Lemass; some poetry *Archvs:* records & correspondence of the Congregation of the Irish Dominican Sisters (from foundation in 1836-date)
Staff: Non-Prof: 1 *Exp:* €100 (1999-2000); €100 (2000-01)

IA6 🙏

Missionary Sisters of Our Lady of the Holy Rosary, Archives

Generalate House, 23 Cross Ave, Blackrock, Co Dublin, Ireland (01-288-1708; *fax:* 01-283-6308)
Email: mshrgen@eircom.net

Chief: contact the Archivist
Subj: records of parent org *Collns: Archvs:* Missionary Sisters of Our Lady of the Holy Rosary, generalate archvs (19C-20C)

Bray

IA7 🏛

Wicklow County Libraries, Local Studies and Archives

County Lib HQ, Boghall Rd, Bray, Co Wicklow, Ireland (01-286-6566; *fax:* 01-286-5811)
Email: library@wicklowcoco.ie
Internet: http://www.wicklow.ie/

Gov Body: Wicklow County Council (see **IP32**)
Chief: County Libn: Mr Brendan Martin
Entry: ref only *Open:* Tue-Sat 1000-1300, 1400-1700; also open Wed-Thu 1800-2000
Subj: Co Wicklow: local authority archvs; poor law records; hosp records; local studies *Collns: Bks & Pamphs:* J.M. Synge Colln; Parnell Colln; 1798 Colln; various bks, journals & files relating to Co Wicklow *Archvs:* records of Wicklow County Council; Wicklow Borough & Town Commission minutes (1663-1888); Rural Dist Council minutes (1899-1925); Bray Urban Dist Council minutes (1857 onwards); Rathdrum Poor Law Union records; Shillelagh Poor Law Union records; Grand Jury Presentments (1819-1898); proceedings of Commissioner's Court (19C); misc hosp records (1930s) *Other:* local newspapers on m-film
Equip: m-reader, m-printer (10c per pg), copier (10c per pg), 6 computers (all with wd-proc & CD-ROM, 4 with internet) *Svcs:* info, ref
Stock: archvs/1000; m-forms/40; CD-ROMs/20
Classn: Local Hist *Auto Sys:* Dynix
Staff: Libns: 1 *Non Prof:* 1

Buncrana

IA8 🏛

Fort Dunree Military Museum, Archives

Dunree, Buncrana, Co Donegal, Ireland (074-936-1817; *fax:* 074-936-3922)
Email: dunree@eircom.net
Internet: http://www.dunree.pro.ie/

Gov Body: Dunree Fort Military Museum Company
Chief: Mgr: Mr David Magee BA(Hons) (davidmagee@utvinternet.com) *Dep:* Office Mgr: Ms Bernie Long
Entry: ref only *Open:* Jun-Sep: Mon-Sat 1030-1800, Sun 1300-1800; winter: Mon-Fri 1000-1630, Sat-Sun 1300-1800
Subj: Ireland, esp Co Donegal: military hist; local hist; military archvs *Collns: Other:* AV colln
Equip: 2 copiers, clr copier, fax, video viewer, 2 computers (both with wd-proc & CD-ROM, 1 with internet) *Offcr-in-Charge:* Mgr, as above *Svcs:* info *Acqs Offcr:* Mgr, as above

Carlow

IA9 🏛

Carlow County Libraries, Local Studies and Archives

Central Lib, Tullow St, Carlow, Co Carlow, Ireland (0503-70094; *fax:* 0503-40548)
Email: carlowlib@hotmail.com
Internet: http://www.countycarlow.ie/services/ newLibrary.htm

Type: local authority *Gov Body:* Carlow County Council (see **IP1**) *Chief:* Libn: Ms Monica Murphy
Entry: adv appt *Open:* Mon-Fri 0945-1300, 1400-1730
Subj: Co Carlow: local studies *Collns: Bks & Pamphs:* Bruen Colln; Jackson Colln; Tyndall Colln; bks of local interest; historical journals colln *Archvs:* Burton papers; Vigors Papers *Other:* census returns for Co Carlow (1901 & 1911); local newspapers (early 1800s onwards); map colln

IRELAND
Carlow
▼
Dublin
Archives

IA10 🖐

Kildare and Leighlin RC Diocesan Archives

Bishop's House, Dublin Rd, Carlow, Co Carlow, Ireland (0503-76725; *fax:* 0503-76850)
Email: chancellorkandl@eircom.net
Internet: http://www.dioceseofkildareandleighlin.ie/

Gov Body: RC Bishop of Kildare & Leighlin
Chief: Diocesan Archivist: Br Linus Walker FSP
Entry: accredited rsrchers by adv appt only with the Diocesan Chancellor; tel enqs for info cannot be entertained
Subj: Diocese of Kildare & Leighlin (incl parts of 7 counties in South East Ireland): diocesan records; some parish records; personal papers *Collns: Bks & Pamphs:* small colln of pubns by indiv clergy of the diocese; a few govt reports on church-related matters; copies of Maynooth Statutes (regulations made by Irish Hierarchy) *Archvs:* correspondence of bishops (c1745 onwards); notes, diaries & reports by clergy; correspondence with other Irish bishops & overseas clergy; some papers relating to religious orders working in the diocese; misc papers, incl obituary notices of clergy *Other:* some photos
Staff: Non-Prof: 1 PT *Exp:* €600 (2000-01); for archival preservation & storage materials only

Castlebar

IA11 🏛

Mayo Local History Department

Castlebar Central Lib, Castlebar, Co Mayo, Ireland (094-20193; *fax:* 094-26491)
Email: ihamrock@mayococo.ie
Internet: http://www.mayococo.ie/library/

Gov Body: Mayo County Council (see **IP20**)
Chief: Asst Libn (Local Hist): Mr Ivor Hamrock
Entry: ref only; adv appt advised *Open:* Tue-Wed 1000-2000, Thu-Fri 1000-1700, Sat 1000-1600
Subj: Co Mayo: local authority archvs; poor law records; parish records; local studies; family hist
Collns: Bks & Pamphs: 1798 Rebellion Colln; Waldron Colln (religion & Irish hist from 1870); works by & about local authors, incl: George Moore Colln; Michael Davitt Colln; George Birmingham Colln; local journals; official pubns; land surveys *Archvs:* Ballinrobe Poor Law Union records (1844-1926); parish records for Oughaval, Burrishoole, Achill & Ballycroy *Other:* Tithe Applotment Bks (c1830, m-film); Census of Ireland (1901-present); Griffith's Valuation (1855-1857); Photographic Archv, incl Wynne Colln (c2000 photos from 1870s onwards); postcards; map colln (incl 1839 OS); local newspapers; monumental inscriptions; Schools Folklore Colln for Co Mayo (1937-1938)
Equip: 2 m-readers, 2 m-printers, 2 copiers, 3 video viewers, 8 computers (all with wd-proc & internet) *Online:* catalogue *Svcs:* info, ref, exhibs
Acqs Offcr: County Libn: Mr Austin Vaughan (avaughan@mayococo.ie)
Classn: DDC *Auto Sys:* Horizon

Castlepollard

IA12 🔑

Tullynally Castle Archives

Castlepollard, Co Westmeath, Ireland (044-61159; *fax:* 044-61856)

Chief: contact the Archivist
Entry: adv appt only
Subj: Co Westmeath: estate archvs; family papers; personal papers; some local authority archvs *Collns: Archvs:* Pakenham family, Earls of Longford, family & estate papers (17C-20C); Langford Rowley family of Langford Lodge, papers (17C-18C); Cooke family of Cooksborough, correspondence & estate papers (17th-1912); correspondence & personal papers of Earls of Longford & other membs of the Pakenham family; Thomas Conolly papers (politician, 1735-1803); Lord Dunsany papers (Edward John Moreton Drax Plunkett, 18th Baron Dunsany, poet & dramatist, 1878-1957); papers of Co Westmeath militia & yeomanry (1796-1831); papers relating to Longford Borough (1677-1801)

Cavan

IA13 🏛

Cavan County Library, Archives and Local History Collections

County Lib, Farnham St, Cavan, Co Cavan, Ireland (049-433-1799; *fax:* 049-433-1384)
Email: cavancountylibrary@eircom.net

Type: local authority *Gov Body:* Cavan County Council (see **IP2**) *Chief:* County Libn: Mrs Josephine Brady BA, DipLIS
Entry: ref only for local hist materials *Open:* Mon, Thu 1100-1300, 1400-1700, 1800-2030, Tue-Wed 1100-1700, Fri 1100-1300, 1400-1700
Subj: Co Cavan: local authority archvs; estate archvs; personal papers; local hist *Collns: Bks & Pamphs:* comprehensive colln of local hist materials; Cavan-Monaghan Farmers Annuals; Cavan GAA Yearbks *Archvs:* Board of Guardian minute bks (1839-1921); Rural Dist Council minute bks (1899-1925); minutes & correspondence of Cavan Drama Festival (1945-1959); records of Bailieborough Model School (1860s-1900s); Co Cavan legal documents (18C-19C); Farnham Estate Archv; Barron Papers; Lanesborough Papers; Nugent Papers *Other:* Tithe Applotment Bks; Griffiths Valuation; census returns (1821, 1841, 1901 & 1911); local newspapers, incl: Anglo Celt; Cavan Weekly News; Cavan Herald; newspaper cuttings; maps (incl Downs Survey, 1835 OS & others); postcards & photos
Equip: 2 m-readers, 2 m-printers, 3 copiers, computers (incl internet) *Svcs:* info, ref
Stock: archvs/50; photos/100; maps/100; m-forms/100; videos/100; CD-ROMs/50
Classn: DDC *Staff: Libns:* 4 *Non-Prof:* 7

IA14 🔑

Co Cavan Genealogical Research Centre

Cana House, Farnham St, Cavan, Co Cavan, Ireland (049-436-1094; *fax:* 049-433-1494)
Email: canahous@iol.ie

Gov Body: Co Cavan Heritage & Genealogical Soc Ltd *Chief:* Mgr: Mrs Mary Sullivan DipLIS
Dep: Snr Rsrcher: Mrs Concepta McGovern
Entry: visitors welcome; enqs by tel, fax, email & in writing *Open:* Mon-Fri 0930-1700, Sat by appt
Subj: Co Cavan: diocesan records; parish records (incl church registers & school rolls); family papers; personal papers; parish hists; local hist; family hist; the Centre collects as much family hist & genea-logical info pertaining to Co Cavan as possible

Co-op Schemes: Irish Family Hist Foundation
Equip: Online: own genealogical database for Co Cavan, with 750000 records, incl: church & civil records of birth/baptisms, marriages & deaths/burials, census records, pre- & post-Famine land records & numerous other sources *Svcs:* full rsrch svc to those tracing their Cavan ancestry
Stock: archvs/244; periodcls/7; photos/82; pamphs/200+; maps/50+; m-forms/50; CD-ROMs/15 *Acqs Offcr:* Mgr, as above
Auto Sys: Préamh
Staff: Libns: 1 *Other Prof:* 2 researchers

IA15 🖐

Kilmore RC Diocesan Archives

Bishop's House, Cullies, Cavan, Co Cavan, Ireland (049-433-1496; *fax:* 049-436-1796)
Email: kilmdioc@eircom.net

Gov Body: Bishop of Kilmore *Chief:* Archivist: Rev G. Kelly CC
Entry: adv appt only *Open:* Mon-Fri 1000-1700
Subj: Diocese of Kilmore: diocesan records; parish records

Clonmel

IA16 🏛🏛

South Tipperary County Museum, Archives

Mick Delahunty Sq, Clonmel, Co Tipperary, Ireland (052-34550; *fax:* 052-80390)
Email: museum@southtippcoco.ie
Internet: http://www.southtippcoco.ie/

Gov Body: South Tipperary County Council
Chief: Curator: Ms Sarah Gillespie BA, MA (sgillespie@southtippcoco.ie) *Dep:* Outreach Offcr: Ms Jo Ronayne BA, MA (jronayne@southtippcoco.ie)
Entry: ref by adv appt *Open:* Tue-Sat 1000-1700
Subj: Tipperary South Riding County: local authority archvs; estate archvs; family papers; business records; personal papers; political papers (some quantities of each); local hist
Equip: copier, clr copier, fax, 8 computers (all with wd-proc & CD-ROM) *Svcs:* info, ref, rsrch
Stock: archvs/1000+; maps/c100
Auto Sys: Admuse
Pubns: T.F. Kiely bklet
Staff: Other Prof: 1 *Non-Prof:* 5
Further Info: South Tipperary County Council is in the process of establishing an archvs svc which will acquire the archvs of the council & the county; Archivist: Róisín Treacy

Cobh

IA17 🖐

Cloyne RC Diocesan Archives

Cloyne Diocesan Centre, Cobh, Co Cork, Ireland (021-481-1430; *fax:* 021-481-1026)
Email: cloyne@indigo.ie

Gov Body: RC Bishop of Cloyne *Chief:* Diocesan Archivist: Sr M. Cabrini Delahunty PhD
Subj: Diocese of Cloyne: diocesan records; parish records
See also MALLOW HERITAGE CENTRE (**IA75**)

Cork

IA18 🖐

Cork and Ross RC Diocesan Archives

Diocesan Office, Bishop's House, Redemption Rd, Cork, Ireland (021-430-1717; *fax:* 021-430-1557)

Gov Body: RC Bishop of Cork & Ross **Chief:** contact the Diocesan Sec
Entry: postal enqs only
Subj: Cork & Ross: diocesan records; personal papers **Collns:** *Archvs:* records of Cork & Ross Roman Catholic Diocese; personal papers of past RC Bishops of Cork

IA19
Cork Archives Institute
Christ Church, South Main St, Cork, Ireland (021-427-7809; *fax:* 021-427-4668)
Email: cai@indigo.ie
Internet: http://www.corkcorp.ie/facilities/facilities_archive.html

Type: non-profit org **Gov Body:** Exec Cttee; jointly funded by Cork Corp (see **IP4**), Cork County Council (see **IP5**) & Univ Coll Cork (see **IS27**)
Chief: contact the Archivist
Entry: adv appt only, rsrchers advised to provide 1 wk's notice of visit; group visits can be arranged
Open: Tue-Fri 1000-1300, 1430-1700
Subj: County & City of Cork: local authority archvs; estate archvs; family papers; business records; personal papers; poor law union records; trade union records; records of local clubs & socs
Collns: *Archvs:* Cork County Council archvs (1899 onwards); Cork Corp archvs (1901 onwards); large colln of Youghal Town records, incl Youghal Corp & Town Commissioners; records of Boards of Guardians; records of Urban Dist Councils & former Rural Dist Councils; Cork Port Sanitary Authority records (1898-1924); estate & family archvs, incl: Colthurst Family of Blarney; Newenham family of Coolmore & Carrigaline; Courtenay Family of Midleton; Coppinger Family of Ballyvolane & Carrigwohill; Bernard Family (Earls of Bandon); other estate collns relating to lands in North Cork; personal papers, incl: Richard Dowden (19C Mayor & philanthropist); Seamus Fitzgerald (1896-1972); J.J. Walshe TD (1880-1948); Barry M. Egan (1879-1954); Liam O Buachalla (Gaelic League teacher & Feis organiser, 1882-1941); Geraldine Cummins (spiritualist, 1890-1969); business records, incl: Beamish & Crawford Brewery (1787-1956); Cork Distillers (1795-1960); Cork Butter Market (1793-1904); Cork Gas Company (1857-1984); B&I (1871-1936, incl Cork Steam Ship Company, City of Cork Steam Ship Company, Coastlines Ltd & British & Irish Steam Packet Company Ltd); & others; Cork Coopers Soc records (1870-1968); Cork Typographical Union records (1868-1968); Cork Plumbers Union records (1868-1894); Cork Presbyterian Congregation records (1758-1822); Skiddy's Almhouse records (1809-43); Cork Grafton Club records (1888-1973); Cork Dist Model School records (1865-1980)
Proj: possible expansion & relocation to site at Albert Quay

IA20
Cork Corporation, Local Studies Department
Cork City Lib, 57-61 Grand Parade, Cork, Ireland (021-427-7110; *fax:* 021-427-5684)
Email: citylibrary@corkcity.ie
Internet: http://www.corkcorp.ie/

Gov Body: Cork Corp (see **IP4**) **Chief:** Asst Libn (Local Studies): Mr Kieran Burke
Assoc Offices: local archvs held at: CORK ARCHVS INST (see **IA19**)
Open: Tue-Sat 1000-1300, 1400-1730
Subj: County & City of Cork: local hist; geog; archaeo; antiquities; folklore **Collns:** *Bks & Pamphs:* local studies materials (Cork Colln)
Other: local newspaper archv; map colln; photo colln
Equip: m-reader, copier
Stock: archvs/5500 **Staff:** *Libns:* 1

IA21
University College Cork, Boole Library Archives Service
Boole Lib, Univ Coll, Cork, Ireland (021-490-3180; *fax:* 021-427-3428)
Email: c.quinn@ucc.ie
Internet: http://www.booleweb.ucc.ie/

Gov Body: Univ Coll Cork (see **IS27**) **Chief:** Archivist: Ms Carol Quinn BA, DipAA, RMSA
Assoc Offices: COLL ARCHVS, Coll Archivist: Ms Virginia Teehan (administers records relating to Coll itself)
Entry: adv appt **Open:** term: Mon-Fri 0930-1645; vac: Mon-Fri 0930-1615
Subj: estate archvs; family papers; personal papers; political papers **Collns:** *Archvs:* Grehan Estate Colln; Bantry House Colln; papers of George Boole FRS (1815-64); papers of Daniel Corkery/Donal Ó Corcora (1878-1964); AHIC Press Colln; Ryen of Inch Colln *Other:* photo collns, incl: Peters Photo Colln
Equip: m-reader, m-printer, copier, computers (incl internet & CD-ROM)
Classn: ISAD(G) **Auto Sys:** Innopac
Staff: *Archivists:* 2

Donabate

IA22
Newbridge House Archives
Donabate, Co Dublin, Ireland (01-843-6534/846-2184; *fax:* 01-846-2537)

Chief: contact the Curator
Entry: adv appt
Subj: estate archvs; family papers; personal papers; literary papers **Collns:** *Bks & Pamphs:* diary of Genl Sir Alexander Cobbe (1870-1931); journal of Charles Cobbe (Archbishop of Dublin, 1687-1765) *Archvs:* Cobbe family of Newbridge, family & estate papers (18C-19C); correspondence & memoirs of Laetitia Pilkington (18C poet & playwright); MS poems of Matthew Pilkington (18C Irish clergyman & poet)

Drogheda

IA23
Drogheda Port Company, Archives and Records
Maritime House, The Mall, Drogheda, Co Louth, Ireland (041-9838378; *fax:* 041-9832844)
Email: maritimehouse@droghedaport.ie

Type: semi-state body **Chief:** Chief Exec Offcr: Mr Paul Fleming
Entry: ref by adv appt **Open:** Mon-Fri 0930-1300
Subj: Drogheda: port records **Collns:** *Archvs:* Port minute bks (1790-date); correspondence (1790-date); vessel arrivals/departures; Harbour Master reports; surveys etc. *Other:* maps (1760 onwards); materials relating to River Boyne
Stock: archvs/50-60; maps/40-50; audios/various recorded interviews

Dublin

IA24
Allied Irish Banks plc, Archives
3-4 Foster Pl, Dublin 2, Ireland (01-677-6721)

Chief: contact the Archivist
Entry: adv appt only
Subj: banking; business records; records of parent org **Collns:** *Archvs:* records of Allied Irish Bank, dating back 150 years
Proj: transfer of archvs to a new, custom made facility in Bankcentre, Ballsbridge, Dublin 4

IA25
An Chartlann Náisiúnta (National Archives of Ireland)
Bishop St, Dublin 8, Ireland (01-407-2300; *fax:* 01-407-2333)
Email: mail@nationalarchives.ie
Internet: http://www.nationalarchives.ie/

Gov Body: Dept of Arts, Sport & Tourism **Chief:** Dir: Dr David Craig PhD (dcraig@nationalarchives.ie) **Dep:** Keeper: Mr Ken Hannigan BA (KHannigan@nationalarchives.ie) **Other Snr Staff:** Snr Archivist (with responsibility for Readers' Svcs): Ms Aideen Ireland MA, DipAS (aireland@nationalarchives.ie); Ms Catriona Crowe BA; Ms Frances McGee MA; Mr Tom Quinlan BA, DipAS
Entry: readers ticket granted on production of ID, ref only **Open:** Mon-Fri 1000-1700
Subj: Ireland: records of Irish Govt Depts (1922-date); records of Chief Sec's Office & related bodies (1790-1922); parish records (C of I); estate archvs; family papers; business records; political papers (mainly 20C); personal papers; records of parent org; census records; customs & excise records; genealogical abstracts; trade union archvs; hosp records; genealogy; local hist
Collns: *Bks & Pamphs:* small lib for staff use only; some frequently used pubns are available on open shelves in the Reading Room *Archvs:* numerous, incl: Natl School applications, registers & files (pre-1922); archvs of the Ordnance Survey of Ireland (partial, 1824-date); transportation records (transportation of convicts to Australia, 1788-1868); Ferguson MSS; Lodge's MSS; Rebellion Papers; materials relating to the Great Famine **Co-op Schemes:** various natl & internatl projs
Equip: 20 m-readers (incl 8 reader/printers), computer (with internet & CD-ROM) **Offcr-in-Charge:** various offcrs **Svcs:** info, ref, rsrch, genealogical consultation svc
Acqs Offcr: various offcrs
Classn: ISAD(G)
Pubns: Annual Reports of the Dir; Short Guide
Staff: *Archivists:* 13 *Non-Prof:* 22

IA26
Apothecaries Hall of Dublin, Archives
95 Merrion Sq, Dublin 2, Ireland

Gov Body: Apothecaries Hall of Dublin **Chief:** Registrar: Dr M. Powell MD, FRCPI
Open: Mon-Fri 0930-1230
Subj: records of parent org; generalities **Collns:** *Archvs:* Apothecaries Hall of Dublin minute bks (1745-date)
Svcs: ref

IA27
Archives of the Irish Sisters of Mercy
Catherine McAuley Centre, 27 Herbert St, Dublin 2, Ireland (01-638-7500; *fax:* 01-638-7511)
Internet: http://www.mercysisters.ie/

Gov Body: Sisters of Mercy **Chief:** Archivist: Ms Marianne Cosgrove
Assoc Offices: some secondary materials are held at: MERCY CENTRE INTERNATL, 64a Lower Baggott St, Dublin 2, Curator: Sr Maureen McGarrigle RSM (01-661-8061; *fax:* 01-676-5486; email: Archives@mercy-international.org)
Entry: adv appt
Subj: religion; Sisters of Mercy; personal papers; records of parent org **Collns:** *Archvs:* archvs of the Congregation of the Sisters of Mercy (19C-20C); correspondence & papers of Catharine McAuley (foundress of the order, 1787-1841)

IA28
Christ Church Cathedral, Archives and Library
Christ Church Pl, Dublin 8, Ireland (01-677-8099; *fax:* 01-679-8991)
Email: archives@cccdub.ie
Internet: http://www.cccdub.ie/archives/archives.html

Gov Body: Dean & Chapter of Christ Church Cathedral *Chief:* Hon Keeper of the Archvs: Dr Kenneth Milne, Historiographer for the Church of Ireland *Dep:* Hon Sec (Archvs, IT & Edu Cttee): Mr Stuart Kinsella MPhil
Assoc Offices: the bulk of the MS collns relating to the Cathedral are held at the REPRESENTATIVE CHURCH BODY LIB (see **IS131**)
Entry: by arrangement
Subj: Christ Church Cathedral (Cathedral of the united dioceses of Dublin & Glendalough, & Metropolitan Cathedral of the united Provinces of Dublin & Cashel): church hist; church music; cathedral records *Collns: Bks & Pamphs:* Dean Gilbert Mayes Colln (religious & liturgical bks); Journals of the C of I Genl Synod (1870-1996, except 1880-1); secondary works on hist of the Cathedral *Archvs:* m-film & photocopies of primary materials held elsewhere *Other:* printed music

IA29
Company of Goldsmiths Archives
Goldsmiths Hall, Dublin 2, Ireland (01-475-1286/478-0323; *fax:* 01-478-3838)
Email: assayirl@iol.ie

Chief: contact the Assay Master
Entry: adv appt *Open:* Mon-Fri 0830-1200, 1400-1600
Subj: assaying; records of parent org *Collns: Archvs:* records of the Dublin Guild of Goldsmiths (1637-1950)

IA30
Dublin City Archives
138-142 Pearse St, Dublin 2, Ireland (01-677-5877; *fax:* 01-677-5954)
Email: cityarchives@dublincity.ie
Internet: http://www.dublincity.ie/

Gov Body: Dublin City Council (see **IP7**) *Chief:* City Archivist: Ms Mary Clark BA(Hons), DipAS
Assoc Offices: CENTRE FOR DUBLIN & IRISH STUDIES, at same addr (see **IA31**)
Entry: adv appt *Open:* Mon-Fri 1000-1300, 1400-1700
Subj: Dublin City: local authority archvs; records of public bodies *Collns: Archvs:* historic records of municipal govt of city of Dublin (12C-date), incl: Royal Charters of City of Dublin (1171-1727); medieval cartularies, incl Liber Albus & Chain Bk of Dublin; Dublin City Assembly Rolls (1447-1841); minutes of Board of Aldermen (1567-1841); minutes of Sheriffs & Commons (1746-1841); Freedom of the City of Dublin Records (1576-1918); City Surveyor's Maps (1695-1827); Wide Streets Commission (1757-1849); records of Mansion House Fund for Relief of Distress in Ireland (19C); Urban Dist Council records of Rathmines, Rathgar & Pembroke areas (mid 19C-1930); records of Dublin Corp (1841-2002)

Equip: m-reader, video viewer, fax, copier *Svcs:* photographic svc
Stock: archvs/3000 linear m; rec mgmt/1000 linear m
Pubns: Dublin City Treasures (£3); A Vision of the City: The Wide Streets Commissioners (£3); The Dublin Guild Merchant Roll, 1190-1265 (£21.95); Directory of Historic Dublin Guilds (£7.95); Serving the City (£6.95); prices incl p&p
Staff: Archivists: 2 *Non-Prof:* 1

IA31
Dublin City Council, Centre for Dublin and Irish Studies
Pearse St Lib, 138-144 Pearse St, Dublin 2, Ireland (01-674-4999)
Email: dublinstudies@dublincity.ie
Internet: http://www.dublincity.ie/

Type: local authority *Gov Body:* Dublin City Council (see **IP7**) *Chief:* Divisional Libn (Special Collns): Dr Máire Kennedy MLIS, PhD
Assoc Offices: DUBLIN CITY ARCHVS, at same addr (see **IA30**)
Entry: ref only; reader's card can be obtained on arrival *Open:* to be confirmed
Subj: Ireland: Irish studies; local studies (Dublin); social, political & cultural hist of Ireland, esp Dublin; family hist; genealogy; personal papers; literary papers *Collns: Bks & Pamphs:* Gilbert Lib (MSS, bks & other materials accumulated by Sir John T. Gilbert, 19C historian of Dublin); early Irish printing & fine bindings, incl Dix Colln (c300 bks & pamphs); Irish Almanacks; Dublin directories (1761-1849); Yeats Colln; Irish periodcls *Archvs:* transcripts of municipal records of the City of Dublin & records of Dublin Guilds, incl minutes of Dublin Guild of Carpenters, Millers, Masons & Heliers (1513-64); MSS of John O'Donovan (Irish Scholar, 1809-1861); correspondence of Richard Caulfield & Thomas Crofton Croker (19C antiquaries) *Other:* rare early Dublin newspapers; maps & prints; m-film copies of Dublin parish registers (C of I); social & political ephemera
Equip: 6 m-readers, 5 m-printers (A4/25c) *Svcs:* info, ref, rsrch
Stock: archvs/100000; various photos, slides, illusts, pamphs, maps, m-forms, audios, videos & CD-ROMs
Classn: DDC *Auto Sys:* DS
Pubns: A Directory of Dublin for the Year 1738 (€12.70 paperback; €31.74 hardback); Catalogue of Books & Manuscripts ... of Sir John T. Gilbert (€45); Sir John T. Gilbert 1829-1898 (€25)

IA32
Dublin Diocesan Archives
Archbishop's House, Drumcondra, Dublin 9, Ireland (01-837-9253; *fax:* 01-836-8393)
Email: dco@iol.ie

Gov Body: RC Archdiocese of Dublin *Chief:* Diocesan Archivist: Mr David C. Sheehy BA, DipAA
Entry: adv appt *Open:* Mon-Fri 0930-1730
Subj: Archdiocese of Dublin: diocesan records; personal papers *Collns: Archvs:* records of the Archdiocese; collns of successive Archbishops of Dublin (1786-date); collns of priests & lay orgs
Equip: copier *Svcs:* info, rsrch
Stock: archvs/c500 linear m
Classn: ISAD(G) *Staff: Archivists:* 1

IA33
Fingal County Council, Archives Department
11 Parnell Sq, Dublin 1, Ireland (01-872-7968; *fax:* 01-878-6919)
Email: fincolib@iol.ie
Internet: http://www.iol.ie/~fincolib/archives.htm

Gov Body: Fingal County Council (see **IP9**)
Chief: Archivist: Ms Patricia McCarthy
Assoc Offices: FINGAL LOCAL STUDIES DEPT, at same addr, Libn: Mr Jeremy Black (01-878-6910; *fax:* 01-878-6919; *email:* local.studies@fingalcoco.ie)
Entry: adv appt essential *Open: Archvs:* Mon-Fri 1000-1300, 1400-1630; *Local Studies Dept:* Mon 1400-2030, Tue 1000-1715, Wed-Fri 1000-1700
Subj: former County of Dublin (area covered by Fingal, South Dublin & Dún Laoghaire-Rathdown County Councils): local authority archvs; personal papers; records of local orgs; local hist; Irish hist
Collns: Bks & Pamphs: wide variety of antiquarian & recent bks on all aspects of Co Dublin (in Local Studies Dept) *Archvs:* archvs of Dublin County Council (1898-1993); records of Grand Juries (19C); records of Boards of Guardians (1838-1930); records of Rural Dist Councils (1898-1930) *Other:* maps, newspapers, prints, photos, videos & ephemera (in Local Studies Dept)
Equip: m-reader, m-printer, copier, fax *Svcs:* info, ref, rsrch
Classn: DDC *Auto Sys:* Galaxy
Staff: Archivists: 1

IA34
Garda Síochána Archives and Museum
Record Tower, Dublin Castle, Dublin 2, Ireland (01-671-9597)
Email: gatower@iol.ie
Internet: http://www.geocities.com/CapitolHill/7900/museum.html

Chief: Archivist: Insp John Duffy DipAS
Subj: hist & development of policing in Ireland (19C-20C) *Collns: Bks & Pamphs:* historical lib containing police-related pubns, incl monthly Garda Pubn (1922-date) *Archvs:* departmental records dealing with personnel, crime & admin; archival materials relating to: Garda Síochána (natl police force, 1922-date); Irish Constabulary (1822-67); Royal Irish Constabulary (1867-1922); Dublin Police; Dublin Metropolitan Police (incl personnel registers, 1836-1970s)
Equip: m-reader

The Genealogical Office (Office of the Chief Herald of Ireland)
See NATL LIB OF IRELAND (**IL1**)

IA35
Guinness Ireland Archives
Guinness Storehouse, St James's Gate, Dublin 8, Ireland (01-408-4610; *fax:* 01-408-4737)
Email: guinness.archives@guinness.com

Chief: Archivist: Ms Eibhlin Roche
Assoc Offices: GUINNESS IRELAND RSRCH LIB (see **IS83**)
Entry: adv appt *Open:* Mon-Thu 0930-1700, Fri 0930-1630
Subj: Ireland: brewing; business records; local studies (Dublin & Ireland) *Collns: Bks & Pamphs:* lib of bks relating to brewing (from 19C); Guinness family hist *Archvs:* records of Arthur Guinness Son & Co Ltd, brewers (18C-21C), incl ledgers, accounts, letter-bks, correspondence, board minutes etc; minutes of Dublin Guild of Brewers & Maltsters (1696-1831); minutes of Dublin Guild of Coopers (1765-1836) *Other:* maps, drawings, photos, videos, film, memorabilia & other artifacts relating to company hist
Equip: copier, fax, video viewer *Disabled:* wheelchair access

IA36 🗝

The Irish Architectural Archive

73 Merrion Sq, Dublin 2, Ireland (01-676-3430; *fax:* 01-661-6309)
Email: iaa@archeire.com
Internet: http://www.archeire.com/iaa/

Chief: Archv Dir: Mr David James Griffin
Entry: open to all, no appt necessary *Open:* Tue-Fri 1000-1300, 1430-1700, closed Aug
Subj: 32 counties of Ireland: arch; architects; business records; personal papers *Collns: Bks & Pamphs:* RIAI Lib (arch, 18C-19C, 300 vols); Downes Colln (bnd arch journals) *Archvs:* RIAI Murray Colln (c11000 18C-19C drawings); Ashlin & Coleman Colln (c8000 drawings of RC Churches); Alfred Jones Biographical Index (2000+ biographical files on Irish architects); Dublin Artisans' Dwellings Company Colln; Emo Court Colln; Green Studio Colln; Alan Hope Colln; McCurdy & Mitchell Colln; Raymond McGrath Colln; Ormonde Loan Colln; Scott Tallon & Walker Colln; Workhouse Drawings Colln *Other:* arch models *Co-op Schemes:* ICA, ICAM
Equip: 2 copiers, fax *Svcs:* arch hist consultancy svc
Stock: archvs/c5000 MSS; bks/5000; periodcls/4; photos/500000; illusts/100000 arch drawings; maps/c2000
Pubns: Vanishing County Houses of Ireland (1988, £30); The Architecture of Richard & William Vitruvius Morrison (1989, £19.95); New Lease of Life: The Law Soc's Bldg at Blackhall Place (1990, £19.95); Daniel Grose (c1766-1838): The Antiquities of Ireland, a supplement to Francis Grose (1991, £19.85 pb, £30 hb); Drawings from the Irish Architectural Archv (1993, £12.95)
Staff: Archivists: 3 *Non-Prof:* 5

IA37 🎓 🎥

Irish Film Archive

Irish Film Centre, 6 Eustace St, Temple Bar, Dublin 2, Ireland (01-679-5744; *fax:* 01-677-8755)
Email: archive@ifc.ie
Internet: http://www.fii.ie/

Gov Body: Film Inst of Ireland *Chief:* Head of Irish Film Archv: Ms Kasandra O'Connell MA, HDipArc (Ko'Connell@ifc.ie) *Dep:* Curator: Ms Suriva O'Flynn (soflunn@ifc.ie) *Other Snr Staff:* Collns Archivist: Mr Eugene Finn (efinn@ifc.ie); Libn & Paper Archivist: Ms Antoinette Prout (aprout@ifc.ie)
Assoc Offices: TIERNAN MACBRIDE LIB (see **IS74**)
Entry: ref only by adv appt *Open:* Mon-Fri 1000-1600
Subj: Ireland: film & AV heritage; cinematic records; personal papers; records of parent org *Collns: Archvs:* extensive collns on film & magnetic tape (1897-date), incl: feature films; shorts; govt info films; travelogues & tourist promotional films; sports films (1940s-60s); educational & info films; early documentaries; newsreels (1917-64); commercials; missionary films; animations; amateur fiction & non-fiction films; the core colln consists of Irish films produced or distributed by the Natl Film Inst (precursor to Film Inst of Ireland); recent acqs incl: Irish Defence Forces Archv Film Colln (1929-date); Tom Maher Colln; Philip Donnellan Colln; Natl Museum of Ireland Colln; Radharc Colln; Guinness Colln; also holds the Paper Archv of the Film Inst of Ireland (managed by the Libn at the Tiernan MacBride Lib), incl: correspondence; production notes; programmes; press packs; press releases; reports; catalogues; postcards; invitations; flyers; newsletters; tickets; scripts; call sheets; all Film Inst of Ireland pubns & publicity materials; special collns incl: Lord Killanin Colln; Pat Murphy Colln;

material from Irish Film Soc; Tiernan MacBride Colln; Horgan Colln (Cork cinema exhibitor, 1918-43); Gael Linn Colln; archvs of the Film Inst of Ireland *Other:* stills & posters colln (managed by Libn at the Tiernan MacBride Lib)
Equip: copier; video viewers, computers (incl wd-procs, internet & CD-ROM), rooms for hire *Svcs:* info, ref, lending of prints from viewing copy colln for non-commercial & non-competitive festivals of Irish cinema
Stock: archvs/2000; film/20000+ cans
Auto Sys: InMagic
Staff: Archivists: 3 *Libns:* 1 *Non-Prof:* 3 *Exp:* IR£14500 (1999-2000); €22000 (2000-01)

IA38 🗝 🙏

Irish Jesuit Archives

35 Lower Leeson St, Dublin 2, Ireland (01-676-1248; *fax:* 01-676-2984)
Email: archives@s-j.ie
Internet: http://www.jesuit.ie/ (see under History)

Gov Body: Irish Jesuit Province *Chief:* Archivist: Rev Fergus O'Donoghue SJ
Entry: adv appt
Subj: Ireland, Australia, Hong Kong, Zambia: records of parent org (admin records of Irish Province, Soc of Jesus); papers of indiv Irish Jesuits *Collns: Archvs:* papers of Irish Jesuits in Australia, Hong Kong & Zambia; transcripts of Irish Jesuit records in all European repositories; transcripts of papers of Irish Colls in Spain, Lisbon, Rome & Poitiers *Other:* correspondence of Irish Jesuit chaplains in both World Wars
Equip: fax, computer (incl wd-proc)
Exp: no fixed budget

IA39 🏛 🙏 🗝

Irish Jewish Museum, Archives

3-4 Walworth Rd, Dublin 8, Ireland (*tel & fax:* 01-490-1857)

Gov Body: Irish Jewish Museum Cttee *Chief:* Curator: Mr Raphael V. Siev
Entry: a need to use the materials must be indicated *Open:* May-Sep: Sun, Tue, Thu 1100-1530; Oct-Apr: Sun 1030-1430; also by req or appt
Subj: Dublin & Ireland: family papers; business records; personal papers; records with Jewish interest or connection *Collns: Archvs:* documents, files & registers of Irish Jewish interest or connection; copies of some birth, marriage & death records relating to Ireland's Jewish community
Svcs: info, ref, rsrch
Stock: various bks, photos, pamphs, audios & videos *Acqs Offcr:* Curator, as above
Staff: Non-Prof: 4.5

IA40 🏛

Irish Labour History Society Museum and Archives

Beggars Bush Barracks, Haddington Rd, Dublin 4, Ireland (01-668-1071)
Email: info@ilhsonline.org
Internet: http://www.ilhsonline.org/

Gov Body: Irish Labour Hist Soc *Chief:* Historian: Ms Therese Moriarty
Entry: adv appt for archvs *Open:* Mon-Fri 1000-1600
Subj: Ireland: labour hist; trade union hist; personal papers; political papers
Equip: fax, copier, room for hire (limited availability) *Svcs:* info, ref, rsrch
Stock: archvs/5000; various periodcls, photos, pamphs, audios & videos
Pubns: Saothor (annual journal of the Irish Labour Hist Soc)
Staff: Non-Prof: 1

IA41 🗝

Irish Theatre Archive

c/o Dublin City Lib & Archv, 138-142 Pearse St, Dublin 2, Ireland (01-677-5877; *fax:* 01-677-5954)

Gov Body: Irish Theatre Archv Ltd *Chief:* Hon Archivist: Ms Mary Clark BA, DipAA
Entry: adv appt *Open:* Mon-Fri 1000-1300, 1415-1700
Subj: Ireland: theatre hist *Collns: Bks & Pamphs:* libs of theatre historians Gabriel Fallan, Michael O'Neill & Matthew Murtagh *Archvs:* papers & memorabilia of Jimmy O'Dea, Cecil Sheridan, Shelah Richards (actors); of Eddie Johnston (stage designer); of Irish Theatre Company, Dublin Theatre Festival, Brendan Smith Academy, An Damer; large colln of theatre ephemera
Equip: m-reader, video viewer, fax, copier
Stock: archvs/1000 linear m; other materials/250 linear m
Pubns: Prompts: Bulletin of Irish Theatre Archv, Issues 1-6 (£2 each)
Staff: Archivists: 2 *Non-Prof:* 1

IA42 🗝

Irish Traditional Music Archive

63 Merrion Sq South, Dublin 2, Ireland (01-661-9699; *fax:* 01-662-4585)
Internet: http://www.itma.ie/

Chief: Dir: Mr Nicholas Carolan
Entry: open to personal callers free of charge
Open: Mon-Fri 1000-1300, 1400-1700
Subj: Ireland & some overseas: folk music; Irish traditional music; personal papers *Collns: Bks & Pamphs:* chap bks; music collns; ref bks & periodcls *Archvs:* Breandán Breathnach Colln (foundation colln, recordings, printed items, MSS & papers); Hugh Shields Colln (Ulster recordings, 1966-81); Diane Hamilton Colln (recordings, 1955-62); Proinsias Ó Conluain Colln (printed items & recordings in Irish, 1963-82); Na Píobairí Uilleann Colln (recordings of uilleann pipers, 1970-90); Folkmusic Soc of Ireland Colln (reports & recordings, 1973-97); & others; misc printed & MS music; ballad sheets *Other:* photos, prints & drawings; video colln; ephemera; artifacts
Equip: video viewer, copier, audio listening equip, audio & video recording studio *Svcs:* info, ref, limited enqs svc by post or tel, recording svc
Stock: archvs/8000; periodcls/55; photos/5000; audios/12000 hrs; videos/750; ballad sheets/3000
Staff: 6 + volunteers

IA43 🏛

Land Commission, Records Branch

Bishop St, Dublin 8, Ireland (01-475-0766/7/8)

Gov Body: Dept of Agric & Food
Entry: subj to certain conditions laid down in the Land Acts & Rules, the solicitor for an owner may inspect deeds & get certified copies of deeds etc, but this svc is not available to the genl public
Subj: Ireland: estate archvs; records relating to land & Irish Land Commission proceedings
Staff: Non-Prof: 11

IA44 🏛

Land Registry

Chancery St, Dublin 7, Ireland (01-804-8006)
Internet: http://www.irlgov.ie/landreg/

Chief: Keeper of Records: Mr Danny McArt
Assoc Offices: 4 offices: LAND REGISTRY, Chancery St, Dublin 7 (01-670-7500); LAND REGISTRY, Nassau Bldg, Setanta Centre, Dublin 2 (01-670-7500); LAND REGISTRY, Block 1, Irish Life Centre, Lower Abbey St, Dublin 1 (01-670-7500); LAND REGISTRY, Cork Rd, Waterford, Co Waterford (051-303000) ☛

IRELAND
Dublin
▼
Galway
Archives

(Land Registry cont)

Entry: Names Index, folios & maps can be inspected by anyone on payment of the prescribed fee; instruments can only be inspected by the registered owner of the property, their personal representative or any person authorised by such persons or by an order of the court or by the Land Registration Rules (1972); please note that instruments are stored off-site & will not be available on the day of request *Open:* Mon-Fri 1030-1630
Subj: land registers for the 26 counties of Ireland; *Chancery St:* registers for Cavan, Donegal, Leitrim, Longford, Louth, Meath, Monaghan & Westmeath; *Setanta Centre:* registers for Clare, Dublin, Galway, Mayo, Roscommon & Sligo; *Irish Life Centre:* registers for Kildare & Wicklow; *Waterford:* registers for Carlow, Cork, Kerry, Kilkenny, Laois, Limerick, Offaly, Tipperary, Waterford & Wexford

IA45
The Military Archives
Cathal Brugha Barracks, Rathmines, Dublin 6, Ireland (01-497-5499; *fax:* 01-804-6237)
Internet: http://www.military.ie/

Gov Body: Defence Forces HQ/Dept of Defence *Chief:* Military Archivist: Comdt Victor Laing BA, DipAS *Dep:* Comdt P.B. Brennan BA, HDipAS *Other Snr Staff:* Systems Administrator: Pte A. Manning
Assoc Offices: DEFENCE FORCES LIB (see **IS28**)
Entry: adv appt only *Open:* Tue-Thu 1000-1600
Subj: Ireland: hist of the development of the Irish Defence Forces from the formation of the Irish Volunteers on 25 Nov 1913 to the present, incl Air Corps, Naval Svcs & svc with the UN from 1958; records of parent org (Dept of Defence, and files created by military branches); personal papers; military records; military hist *Collns: Bks & Pamphs:* rsrch lib of related printed materials, incl copies of handbks & military pubns, incl An t-Oglach (1918-30) & An Cosantoir (1940-date) *Archvs:* records of the Bureau of Military Hist (1913-21, comprising 1773 witness statements, 334 sets of contemporary documents, photos, voice recordings, press cuttings etc); Collins Papers (formation of the IRA, 1919-22); Liaison Papers (with British authorities, concerning the period between the Truce & the Civil War); Civil War operations & intelligence reports; records relating to the Special Infantry Corps & Railway Protection Corps; documents captured from Anti-Treaty forces dealing with operational & intelligence matters (1922-24); Army Census records (complete, 1922); Dept of Defence files (1922-25); records relating to Army Crisis (1924); Army Org Board records (1926); records of Military Mission to the USA (1926-27); Internees files (1934-39); records of Directorate of Intelligence, Directorate of Operations, Construction Corps, Air Defence Command, Marine & Coastwatching Svc, Look Out Post log bks & files (1939-45); Genl HQ Unit journals, minutes of GHQ conferences & Controller of Censorship files (1939-45); Dir of Operations records (1945-74); Air Corps records; Naval Svc records; records relating to UN svc (1958-84); personnel records for offcrs & other ranks; Army Pension Board files; 872 private collns of retired svc membs & persons involved with the Natl Army/Defence Forces; other materials relating to military

& intelligence activs in Ireland to date *Other:* maps, plans & drawings of military installations, disused or former barracks, incl some Martello Towers; photos; audio recordings; films & videos *Equip:* m-reader, m-printer, video viewer, copier, fax, 2 computers (with Military Archvs Data Retrieval System), various finding aids *Svcs:* ref *Stock:* archvs/26000+ linear ft; bks/110+ linear ft; photos/c15000; slides/200; maps/1200; m-forms/1125 reels; audios/a few; videos/550
Classn: ISAD(G)
Staff: Archivists: 2 *Libns:* 1 *Other Prof:* 2 *Non-Prof:* 3 *Exp:* €300000 (2000-01)
Proj: bldg refurbishment for storage

National Archives of Ireland
See AN CHARTLANN NÁISIÚNTA (**IA25**)

National Photographic Archive
See NATL LIB OF IRELAND (**IL1**)

IA46
Oifig An Ard-Chláraitheora (Office of the Registrar General)
Joyce House, 8-11 Lombard St East, Dublin 2, Ireland (01-635-4000; *fax:* 01-635-4440)
Internet: http://www.groireland.ie/

Gov Body: Dept of Health *Chief:* Registrar Genl *Dep:* Asst Registrar Genl
Entry: no appt necessary *Open:* Mon-Fri 0930-1230, 1415-1630
Collns: Archvs: registers of special events (births, deaths & marriages) in Ireland (1864-date) & Northern Ireland (1864-1921)
Staff: Other Prof: 47

IA47
Plunket Museum of Irish Education, Archive Collections
Church of Ireland Coll, Upper Rathmines Rd, Dublin 6, Ireland (01-497-0033; *fax:* 01-497-1932)

Gov Body: Board of Governors of the C of I Coll of Edu (see **IS49**) *Chief:* contact the Libn, C of I Coll of Edu: Ms Valerie Coghlan MSc, FLAI, FCLIP
Entry: by written application to the Libn, stating interest *Open:* by appt only
Subj: Ireland: hist of primary edu *Collns: Bks & Pamphs:* school textbks & tablets *Archvs:* school artifacts

IA48
South Dublin Local Studies Collection
c/o County Lib, Town Centre, Tallaght, Dublin 24, Ireland (01-462-0073; *fax:* 01-414-9207)
Email: talib@sdublincoco.ie

Gov Body: South Dublin County Council (see **IP26**) *Chief:* contact the Local Studies Libn
Assoc Offices: smaller collns held at other branch libs; local archvs held at: FINGAL COUNTY ARCHVS (see **IA33**)
Open: Mon-Thu 0945-2000, Fri-Sat 0945-1630
Subj: South Dublin: local hist; family hist *Collns: Bks & Pamphs:* local author collns, incl: Katharine Tynan Colln; Charles Lever Colln; Austin Clarke Colln; local directories; periodcls colln, incl archaeo & genealogical journals *Archvs:* minute bk of Tallaght Dispensary Cttee (1879-1899) *Other:* map colln (17C-20C); photo collns; video colln; topo-graphical prints; local newspapers (Tallaght Echo); info files on South Dublin civil parishes
Equip: computers *Online:* various genealogical resources on CD-ROM *Svcs:* info, ref, lectures & talks, local studies mailing list, annual Hist & Heritage Month (in Apr)

Stock: archvs/3500+
Pubns: Guide to the Local Studies Colln at the County Lib Tallaght; South Dublin Local Studies Colln: A Bibliography; Tracing Your Irish Ancestors: Some Resources at the County Lib Tallaght

IA49
University College Dublin, Archives Department
Lib Bldg, Belfield, Dublin 4, Ireland (01-716-7555; *fax:* 01-716-1146)
Email: archives@ucd.ie
Internet: http://www.ucd.ie/~archives/

Gov Body: Univ Coll Dublin (see **IS148**) *Chief:* Archivist: Mr Seamus Helferty
Entry: current readers' ticket required; adv appt essential *Open:* Mon-Thu 1000-1300, 1400-1700; closed Fri
Subj: Ireland: family papers; political papers; business records; personal papers; records of parent org *Collns: Archvs:* records of Univ Coll Dublin; records of bodies connected with the Coll, incl: Royal Coll of Sci for Ireland Archvs (1867-1929); records of the Royal Veterinary Coll of Ireland (1894-1977); Natl Univ Women Graduates' Assoc Archv (1903-85); Literary & Historical Soc Archv (1882-1992); rare MSS incl: Franciscan 'A' MSS; family collns incl: Bryan Family Papers; Caulfield Family of Drumcairn Papers; Cowen Family of Drumcondra Papers; Cox Family Papers; Fitzpatrick Family Papers (Earls of Upper Ossory & Barons Castletown); Hart-Synnot Family Papers; Herbert Family of Muckross Papers; Hutchinson & Synge Hutchinson Family Papers; Rice Family of Mountrice Papers; Upton Family of Coolatore & Glyde Court Papers; Wandesford Family Papers; political collns incl: Fianna Fáil Party Archv (1913-95); Archvs of the Cumann na nGaedheal & Fine Gael Parties (1922-75); personal papers incl: Eamon de Valera Papers; Michael Tierney Papers; Moss Twomey Papers; R. Dudley Edwards Papers; Conor Cruise O'Brien Papers; Eoin MacNeill Papers; T.M. Healy Papers; Michael Hayes Papers; Desmond & Mabel FitzGerald Papers; & others

IA50
Valuation Office Archives
Block 2, Irish Life Centre, Abbey St Lower, Dublin 1, Ireland (01-817-1000; *fax:* 01-817-1180)
Email: info@valoff.ie
Internet: http://www.valoff.ie/

Type: independent govt agency *Chief:* Asst Principal Offcr: Mr Pat McCarthy (patmccarthy@valoff.ie) *Dep:* Higher Exec Offcrs: Mrs Catherine English (catherine.english@valoff.ie) & Mrs Marion Richardson (marion.richardson@valoff.ie) *Other Snr Staff:* Record Keeper: Mr Geoff Farrell
Entry: open daily to the public *Open:* Mon-Fri 0930-1230, 1400-1630
Subj: valuation refs; genealogy *Collns: Archvs:* Griffiths Valuations (bks & maps, contact Geoff Farrell as above)
Equip: clr copier, computer (with CD-ROM) *Svcs:* info
Stock: archvs/2000; maps/3000
Classn: own *Staff: Non-Prof:* 2 FT

Dún Laoghaire

IA51
Dún Laoghaire-Rathdown Public Libraries, Local History Department
Dún Laoghaire Lib, Lower Georges St, Dún Laoghaire, Co Dublin, Ireland (01-280-1147; *fax:* 01-284-6141)
Email: patwalsh@dlrcoco.ie
Internet: http://www.dlrcoco.ie/library/lhistory.htm

Gov Body: Dún Laoghaire-Rathdown County Council (see **IP8**) **Chief:** Libn: Ms Pat Walsh **Assoc Offices:** local archvs held at: FINGAL COUNTY ARCHVS (see **IA33**)
Entry: open to public **Open:** Mon, Sat 1000-1300, 1400-1700, Tue, Thu 1315-2000, Wed, Fri 1000-1700
Subj: Dún Laoghaire-Rathdown: local hist; genealogy; local authority archvs (council minutes only) **Collns:** Bks & Pamphs: local hist materials, incl rare eds; local directories & registers (from 1758); govt pubns, incl: Acts of the Oireachtas (1922-date); Dáil & Seanad Debates (1994-date) **Archvs:** minutes of Township of Dún Laoghaire, Urban Dist of Dún Laoghaire, Borough of Dún Laoghaire & Dún Laoghaire-Rathdown County Council (from 1888); registers of electors (1942-73); Griffiths Valuation; census returns (on m-fiche, 1813-1911); Tithe Applotment Bks (on m-fiche) **Other:** newspaper colln (on m-film, from 1819); surveys, maps & charts (from 1730); audio colln; photo colln (photos, prints & drawings, 17C-date), incl: copies of Lawrence Colln & O'Connor Colln; Civil War Series (1922-23); Dún Laoghaire Harbour Colln; Karl Marx Colln; 1848 Colln
Svcs: info, ref, genealogical enqs

Dundalk

IA52
Louth Local Authorities Archives Service
Old Gaol, Ardee Rd, Dundalk, Co Louth, Ireland (042-933-9387; *fax:* 042-932-0429)
Email: archive@louthcoco.ie
Internet: http://www.louchcoco.ie/louth/html/archive.htm

Gov Body: Louth County Council (see **IP19**)
Chief: Archivist: Miss Lorraine Buchanan BA, HDipAS (lorraine.buchanan@louthcoco.ie)
Entry: adv appt
Subj: Co Louth: local authority archvs; port records **Collns:** Archvs: records of Louth County Council; records of Dundalk Port Company **Other:** map colln
Equip: copier, computer (with internet)
Stock: archvs/c142 sq m
Staff: Archivists: 1 Non-Prof: 1

Dungarvan

IA53
Dungarvan Museum Society, Archives and Library
St Augustine St, Dungarvan, Co Waterford, Ireland (058-45960)
Internet: http://www.dungarvanmuseum.org/

Gov Body: Dungarvan Museum Soc **Chief:** Curator: Mr Willie Fraher
Entry: ref only **Open:** summer (May-Sep): Mon-Sat 1000-1300, 1400-1700; rest of year: Mon-Fri 1000-1300, 1400-1630
Subj: Dungarvan & Co Waterford: local hist; genealogy **Collns:** Other: photographic hist of Dungarvan
Pubns: Desperate Haven – The Famine in Dungarvan; The Augustinians in Abbeyside – 1990; A Guide to Historic Dungarvan; Dungarvan – An Architectural Inventory

IA54
Waterford County Archives Service
Dungarvan Lib, Davitt's Quay, Dungarvan, Co Waterford, Ireland (058-23673)
Email: archivist@waterfordcoco.ie
Internet: http://www.waterfordcoco.ie/

Gov Body: Waterford County Council (see **IP29**)
Chief: County Archivist: Ms Joanne Rothwell BA HDipAS
Entry: adv appt **Open:** Tue 1000-1400, Fri 1300-1700
Subj: Co Waterford: local authority archvs; estate archvs; family papers; business records; personal papers; records of parent org; records of local groups & socs; poor law records **Collns:** Bks & Pamphs: political pamphs relating to Irish nationalism (1900-1960, part of Hugh Ryan Papers) **Archvs:** records of Waterford County Council (1899 onwards); Grand Jury records; records of Boards of Guardians for the Poor Law Unions of Dungarvan, Kilmacthomas, Lismore & Waterford; minutes of Rural Dist Councils for Lismore, Kilmacthomas, Youghal, Dungarvan, Clonmel, Waterford & Carrick-on-Suir; records of Dungarvan Urban Dist Council; Chearnley Papers (relating to Musgrave & Chearnley families, 1671-1915); Hugh Ryan Papers (local historian) **Other:** valuation bks; maps & plans; photo colln
Equip: m-reader, copier, computers (incl 4 with internet) **Svcs:** info, ref, rsrch
Stock: various archival holdings, photos, slides, pamphs, maps, m-forms & audios
Classn: ISAD(G) **Staff:** Archivists: 1 Non-Prof: 1
See also WATERFORD CITY ARCHVS (see **IA95**)

Ennis

IA55
Clare County Council, Local Studies and Archives
Local Studies Centre, The Manse, Harmony Row, Ennis, Co Clare, Ireland (065-682-6271; *fax:* 065-684-2462)
Email: clarelib@iol.ie
Internet: http://www.clarelibrary.ie/

Gov Body: Clare County Council (see **IP3**) **Chief:** Local Studies Libn: Mr Peter Beirne **Dep:** Snr Lib Asst: Ms Frances O'Gorman **Other Snr Staff:** Archivist: Ms Jacqui Hayes (065-682-1616; *email:* jhayes@clarecoco.ie)
Entry: ref only **Open:** Mon 0930-1300, 1400-1730, Tue-Fri 0930-1300, 1400-1700, Sat 1000-1400
Subj: Co Clare: local studies; local authority archvs; estate archvs; poor law records; land survey records; census records **Collns:** Bks & Pamphs: Clare Colln (c2000 titles on hist, archaeo & topography of Co Clare); Irish Colln (c8000 titles on all aspects of Irish soc); colln of historical & geographical journals **Archvs:** records of Clare County Council, Ennis Urban Dist Council, Kilrush Urban Dist Council & Kilkee Town Commissioners; Board of Guardian minute bks for Corofin Union, Ennis Union, Ennistymon Union, Kilrush Union & Tulla Union; minute bks of Corofin Rural Dist Council, Ennis Rural Dist Council & Ennistymon Rural Dist Council; records of Local Govt Board; records of Clare County Development Team; Board of Health registers; Corporation Bk of Ennis (1660-1810); Parliamentary Papers; Reports of Commissioners for enquiring into the condition of the Poorer Classes in Ireland (1835-7); Reports of the Commissioners of Natl Edu (1834-1920); Famine Relief records; Petworth House Colln (papers of Earls of Thomond, 17C-early 18C); Studdert Papers (Burton, Arthur, Lloyd, Studdert, North & other estates, 1880-1930); records of Our Lady's Hosp, Ennis; Tithe Applotment Bks (1828); Griffith's Valuation (1855); MSS on local folklore (compiled by school ch in 1930s) **Other:** local newspapers going back to 1824; map colln (1685 onwards); photos of Clare scenes, incl: Lawrence Colln (1870-1914); Westropp Colln (1900); McNamara Colln (1910); Irish Tourist Assoc Survey (1943); Bluett Colln (1940s-60s); O'Neill Colln (1950s)
Equip: 2 m-readers, copier, computers (incl 2 with internet)

Stock: archvs/10000+; photos/c4000
Classn: DDC
Staff: Archivists: 1 Libns: 1 Non-Prof: 1
Proj: establishment of County Archvs Svc

IA56
Killaloe RC Diocesan Archives
c/o Diocesan Office, Westbourne, Ennis, Co Clare, Ireland (065-28638)

Gov Body: RC Bishop of Killaloe **Chief:** Diocesan Archivist: Rev Neil Dargan
Entry: adv appt only
Subj: RC Diocese of Killaloe: diocesan records; parish records

Foxford

IA57
The Michael Davitt Memorial Museum, Archives
Straide, Foxford, Co Mayo, Ireland (094-31022)
Email: davittmuseum@eircom.net
Internet: http://www.museumsofmayo.com/davitt/

Type: non-profit specialist museum **Gov Body:** Michael Davitt Natl Memorial Assoc **Chief:** Curator: Ms Nancy Smyth **Dep:** Hon Sec: Ms Andrea Wills
Entry: small entry fee; adv booking for schools, clubs etc **Open:** Mon-Sun 1000-1800
Subj: family papers; personal papers; political papers **Collns:** Archvs: related to the life of Michael Davitt (1846-1906) & the Land League at the end of the 19C **Other:** artifacts related to the life of Michael Davitt & the Land League of Ireland
Equip: copier, video viewer, 4 computers (incl 1 with internet) **Svcs:** ref, rsrch, museum tours
Stock: various printed bks & photos
Classn: own catalogue
Pubns: Michael Davitt Memorial Museum, Straide: Hist of the Life of Davitt (€8)
Staff: Non-Prof: 10 **Exp:** IR£2000 (2000-01)

Galway

IA58
Galway Harbour Company, Archives and Records
Harbour Office, New Docks, Galway, Ireland (091-561874; *fax:* 091-563738)
Email: galwayharbour@eircom.net

Type: semi-state body **Chief:** Chief Exec Offcr: Mr Thomas O'Neill
Entry: adv appt **Open:** Mon-Fri 0930-1700
Subj: Galway: records of parent org; port records
Collns: Archvs: minutes of Galway Harbour Commissioners meetings; lists of Galway Harbour Commissioners
Pubns: Safe & Commodious: The Annals of Galway Harbour Commissioners 1830-1997, by Dr Kieran Woodman (2000)

IA59
Galway Public Libraries, Local History Department
Galway Public Lib HQ, Island House, Cathedral Sq, Galway, Co Galway, Ireland (091-562471; *fax:* 091-565039)
Email: info@galwaylibrary.ie
Internet: http://www.galwaylibrary.ie/

Gov Body: Galway County Council (see **IP10**)
Chief: Local Hist Libn: Mr Kieran Shaughnessy
Entry: adv appt advisable **Open:** Mon-Fri 0930-1300, 1400-1700

(Galway Public Libs, Local Hist Dept cont)
Subj: Co Galway: local hist *Collns: Archvs:* Poor Law Guardians' records (minute bks); Griffiths Valuation *Other:* map colln; historical photo colln; comprehensive colln of local newspapers (1820s onwards)
Equip: m-readers

IA60 🖐

Galway RC Diocesan Archives

Diocesan Office, The Cathedral, Galway, Co Galway, Ireland (091-23413; *fax:* 091-568333)

Chief: Archivist: T.M. May
Entry: adv appt
Subj: RC Diocese of Galway: diocesan records; some parish records *Collns: Archvs:* records of Galway Roman Catholic Diocese, incl parish property records
Staff: Non-Prof: 1 PT

Kilkenny

IA61 🏛

Kilkenny County Library, Local Studies Department

Kilkenny County Lib HQ, 6 Rose Inn St, NIB Bldg, Kilkenny, Co Kilkenny, Ireland (056-91160; *fax:* 056-91168)
Email: katlibs@iol.ie
Internet: http://www.kilkennylibrary.ie/local_studies.htm

Gov Body: Kilkenny County Council (see **IP13**)
Chief: County Libn: Mr James Fogarty DipLib, ALAI (james.fogarty@kilkennycoco.ie) *Dep:* Asst County Libn: Mr Declan Macauley BSc, DipLIS, DipEnDev
Entry: ref only; appt generally required for use of archvs & m-films *Open:* Mon-Fri 0900-1300, 1400-1700
Subj: Co Kilkenny (plus some regional sources): local authority archvs; diocesan records; parish records; business records; records of parent org; local hist; genealogy *Collns: Bks & Pamphs:* Kilkenny Colln (Kilkenny authors & people); Genealogical Colln; Kilkenny Lib Soc Colln; local hist pubns; local & regional periodcls; local directories *Archvs:* archvs of Kilkenny County Council; Kilkenny Corp archvs (misc unindexed records on m-film); archvs of rural dist councils; records of Board of Guardians (1850s-1920s); records of Callan Town Commissioners; records of Kilkenny County Lib; Grand Jury Presentments; Natl School Records for Co Kilkenny; Diocese of Ossory parochial records (19C, on m-film) *Other:* census returns & reports; electoral registers & poll bks; Tithe Applotment Bks; Griffith's Valuation; photo colln; topographical prints & drawings; local newspapers; UCD Folklore Colln for Co Kilkenny (1930s); various info files
Equip: 2 m-readers, 2 m-printers, copier *Offcr-in-Charge:* Asst County Libn: Mr Declan Macauley, as above *Svcs:* info, ref, rsrch
Stock: archvs/3058; periodcls/7; photos/1309; slides/50; illusts/30; pamphs/30; maps/250; m-forms/575; audios/20; videos/20; CD-ROMs/10
Acqs Offcr: Asst County Libn, as above
Classn: DDC & in-house *Auto Sys:* Genesis
Pubns: list of holdings (not for sale)

Staff: Libns: 1 *Non-Prof:* 1.5 *Exp:* €7000 (1999-2000); €10000 (2000-01)
Proj: new local studies facility established in 2002

Killarney

IA62 🖐

Kerry RC Diocesan Archives

Diocesan Office, Bishops House, Killarney, Co Kerry, Ireland (064-31168; *fax:* 064-31364)

Chief: contact the Diocesan Archivist
Entry: adv appt
Subj: RC Diocese of Kerry: diocesan records; personal papers *Collns: Archvs:* records of the RC Diocese of Kerry; some papers & correspondence of previous Bishops of Kerry, incl Francis Moylan (1735-1815)

Kilrush

IA63 🏛

Kilrush Town Council, Archives and Records

Town Hall, Kilrush, Co Clare, Ireland (065-905-1047; *fax:* 065-905-2821)
Email: kilrush@clarecoco.ie

Type: local authority *Gov Body:* Kilrush Town Council *Chief:* Town Clerk: Mrs Imy Whelan-Breen
Entry: adv appt *Open:* Mon 0930-1730, Tue-Fri 0930-1700
Subj: Kilrush: local authority archvs *Collns: Archvs:* records of Kilrush Town Council
Svcs: info

Kinsale

IA64 🏛

Kinsale Harbour Commissioner, Archives and Records

Harbour Office, Pier Rd, Kinsale, Co Cork, Ireland (021-477-2503; *fax:* 021-477-4695)
Email: kharbour@iol.ie

Type: port authority *Chief:* Capt Phil Devitt
Assoc Offices: DEPT OF COMMUNICATIONS, MARINE & NAT RESOURCES LIB (see **IS53**)
Open: Mon-Fri 0900-1730
Subj: Kinsale Harbour: harbour records; business records *Collns: Archvs:* records of Kinsale Harbour Commissioner; materials relating to cargo vessels entering Kinsale Harbour

Letterkenny

IA65 🏛

Donegal County Library, Donegal Studies Collection

Administrative Centre, Rosemount Ln, Letterkenny, Co Donegal, Ireland (074-21968; *fax:* 074-21740)
Email: library@donegalcoco.ie
Internet: http://www.donegal.ie/

Type: local authority *Gov Body:* Donegal County Council (see **IP6**) *Chief:* County Libn: Mr Liam Ronayne BCL, DipLib, ALAI
Assoc Offices: CATHAL O'SEARCAIGH LIB, Mín a'Leagha, Gort a'Choirce, Co Donegal (local author's personal lib of poetry & lit, maintained by Donegal County Lib in situ); for local archvs see: DONEGAL COUNTY ARCHVS (see **IA67**)
Entry: ref only
Subj: Co Donegal: local studies; literary papers
Collns: Bks & Pamphs: important colln of 18C bks; c300 vols printed before 1851; works by local

authors, incl: Patrick MacGill Colln; Peadar O'Donnell Colln; Seamus MacManus Colln; John Kells Ingram Colln; exhib catalogues; annual reports of local orgs *Archvs:* Cathal O'Searcaigh Archv (materials relating to local author & poet, incl MSS, publ work, broadcast material etc) *Other:* photo colln; prints; postcards; topographical drawings; map colln, incl Grand Jury Maps (1837 OS); ephemera colln relating to Co Donegal
Equip: m-reader, m-printer (70c per pg), copier (10c per pg), fax, 6 computers (all with wd-proc & internet) *Disabled:* optical scanners *Offcr-in-Charge:* County Libn: Mr Liam Ronayne, as above
Svcs: info, ref, rsrch *Acqs Offcr:* Asst Libn: Ms Eileen Burgess (eburgess@donegalcoco.ie)
Classn: DDC *Auto Sys:* Genesis
Staff: Libns: 1 *Other Prof:* 4 *Non-Prof:* 20

IA66 🖐

Raphoe RC Diocesan Archives

Diocesan Offices, Ard Adhamhnain, Letterkenny, Co Donegal, Ireland (072-21208; *fax:* 072-24872)
Email: raphoed@indigo.ie
Internet: http://www.raphoediocese.com/

Gov Body: RC Bishop of Raphoe *Chief:* Diocesan Archivist: Very Rev John Silke PhD
Other Snr Staff: Diocesan Sec: Fr Michael McKeever (to whom enqs should be directed in the first instance)
Entry: bona fide students & rsrchers by written appt only; contact the Diocesan Sec at above addr
Subj: Diocese of Raphoe: diocesan records; parish records

Lifford

IA67 🏛

Donegal County Archives

c/o Donegal County Council, 3 Rivers Centre, Lifford, Co Donegal, Ireland (074-72490; *fax:* 074-41367)
Email: nbrennan@donegalcoco.ie
Internet: http://www.donegal.ie/dcc/

Gov Body: Donegal County Council (see **IP6**)
Chief: Archivist: Dr Niamh Brennan PhD(Hist), HDipAS
Entry: adv appt *Open:* Wed 0900-1630, by appt
Subj: Co Donegal: local authority archvs; estate archvs; family papers; business records; personal papers; records of parent org; school records; records of local voluntary bodies *Collns: Bks & Pamphs:* local studies colln (Letterkenny area), held at Central Lib *Archvs:* minutes & other records of Donegal County Council (1899-1972); minutes & other records of Bundoran, Buncrana & Letterkenny Urban Dist Councils (1899-1972); minutes of Rural Dist Councils of Ballyshannon, Donegal, Dunfanaghy, Glenties, Inishowen, Letterkenny, Milford, Strabane No. 2 & Stranorlar (1899-1925); Donegal Board of Health & Public Assistance records (minutes & registers, 1924-1942, restricted access); Board of Guardian records (1841-1923); Grand Jury records (assizes, accounts, correspondence & maps, 1801-1898); minutes of Poor Law Unions of Bally-shannon, Donegal, Dunfanaghy, Glenties, Inishowen, Letterkenny, Milford & Stranorlar; minutes of Ballyshannon Town Commissioners (1896-1962); minutes of Ballyshannon Harbour Board (1887-1962); correspondence of County Donegal Cttee of Agric (1901-1930); Valuation records (1833-1969); school records (incl roll bks & registers, c1880-1960s); records of local Co-op & Agricultural Socs (1917-1945); records of Dist Nursing Assocs (1931-1974); Gweedore & Lough Swilly Hotels visitors bks (1842-1903); Andrews Linen Mills records (accounts, 1895-1951); records & papers of local figs, incl: Cathal Ó Searcaigh papers (poet, 1960-1990); Patrick MacGill papers (1917-1935);

Father Patrick Gallagher papers (1940-1980); Murray Stewart family papers (1749-1880); Captain Ernest Cochrane papers (1865-1899); Edward H. Harvey papers (from c1900) *Other:* oral hist interviews with Donegal people; OS maps of Donegal (1840-1881)
Stock: archvs/c300 sq m
Classn: ISAD(G) *Auto Sys:* CALM 2000+
Staff: Archivists: 1 *Exp:* €3000 (1999-2000); €4000 (2000-01)
Proj: new purpose-built Archvs Centre, yet to be funded; site donated by local business org for Archvs Centre; Proj Team set up in 2002

Limerick

IA68

Limerick Archives
The Granary, Michael St, Limerick, Ireland (061-415125; *fax:* 061-312985)
Email: archives@limerickcity.ie or archives@limerickcoco.ie

Gov Body: Limerick City Council (see **IP16**) & Limerick County Council (see **IP17**) *Chief:* City & County Archivist: Ms Jacqui Hayes
Assoc Offices: LIMERICK ANCESTRY (genealogical rsrch svc), at same addr; LIMERICK CITY LOCAL STUDIES COLLN (see **IA69**)
Entry: adv appt for archvs *Open:* Mon-Fri 0900-1300, 1400-1730
Subj: Limerick City & County: local authority archvs; parish records; estate archvs; family papers; business records; personal papers; records of parent orgs; local hist; family hist
Collns: Bks & Pamphs: small local & family hist lib *Archvs:* archvs of Limerick Corp; archvs of Limerick County Council; records of Poor Law Boards of Guardians; records of County Board of Public Health; records of Limerick Harbour Commissioners; de Vere estate records; Coote estate records; Monteagle estate records; RC, C of I, Methodist & Presbyterian parish records (computerised) *Other:* database (with 1.1 million entries); maps & plans; held on m-film: tithe bks; Griffiths Valuation; 1901 census; local newspapers
Equip: 3 m-readers, m-printer (no public access to m-form facilities), fax, copier, computers (incl 2 wd-proc) *Svcs:* info, rsrch
Stock: archvs/400 m
Pubns: The Poor Law of Counties Limerick, Clare & Tipperary (£2)
Staff: Archivists: 1 *Other Prof:* 0.5 *Non-Prof:* 2.2

IA69

Limerick City Local Studies Collection
Limerick City Lib, The Granary, Michael St, Limerick, Ireland (061-314668; *fax:* 061-411506)
Email: citylib@limerickcity.ie

Type: local authority *Gov Body:* Limerick City Council (see **IP16**) *Chief:* Ref & Local Hist Libn: Mr Michael Maguire (mmaguire@limerickcity.ie)
Assoc Offices: local archvs are held at: LIMERICK ARCHVS (see **IA68**)
Entry: ref only *Open:* Mon-Tue 1000-1730, Wed-Fri 1000-2000, Sat 1000-1300 (closed bank hols)
Subj: Limerick City & County: local studies; Irish hist; archaeo *Collns: Bks & Pamphs:* Seamus O'Ceallaigh Colln (hist of GAA in Limerick area); Jim Kemmy Colln (Irish hist, religion & politics, 30 vols); local & other journals relating to Irish hist, archaeo *Archvs:* copies of official documents, incl Parliamentary Papers (19C) & Acts of the Oireachtas (20C) *Other:* Local Studies Files (500+ items); local newspapers on m-film; photo colln; postcards; map colln, incl 1840 OS; Griffiths Valuation Maps (on CD-ROM); reports & ephemera

IA70

Limerick County Library, Local Studies Collection
1st Floor, County Lib HQ, 58 O'Connell St, Limerick, Ireland (061-214452; *fax:* 061-318570)
Email: colibrar@limerickcoco.ie

Type: local authority *Gov Body:* Limerick County Council (see **IP17**) *Chief:* County Libn: Mr Damien Brady BA, DipLIS (dbrady@limerickcoco.ie) *Dep:* Exec Libn: Ms Helen Walsh DipLIS (hwalsh@limerickcoco.ie) *Other Snr Staff:* Snr Lib Asst (Local Studies): Ms Margaret Franklin BA, DipLib (mfrankli@limerickcoco.ie)
Assoc Offices: local archvs are held at: LIMERICK ARCHVS (see **IA68**)
Entry: ref only *Open:* Mon-Fri 0930-1300, 1400-1630
Subj: Limerick County & City: local studies; Irish hist; family hist; genealogy; archaeo; arch; nat hist; geog; environment; folklore; biography; traditional music; art & artists; some parish records *Collns: Bks & Pamphs:* Archaeo Colln; Biography Colln; P.W. Joyce Colln (Irish music & hist); Irish Times Yng Historians Colln; works by Co Limerick authors; local & Irish journals, incl learned & parish journals; annual reports & pubns of Limerick County Council & Limerick County Lib; local directories *Archvs:* Grand Jury Presentments (1808-1900) *Other:* census reports & related lists & indexes, incl some dating back to 16C; Civil Survey (1654-56); Griffith's Valuation (1852); Tithe Applotment Bks (1823-38) on m-form; Fiants of the Tudor Sovereigns (1521-1603); O'Donovan Letters (1840 Ordnance Survey); monumental inscriptions; AV colln, incl Leitrim Genealogy Centre videos on traditional arts & crafts; map colln; local newspapers on m-film; photo colln
Equip: m-reader/printer (A4/10c, A3/15c), copier (A4/10c, A3/15c), fax, computer (with wd-proc, internet & CD-ROM) *Offcr-in-Charge:* Asst Libn: Mr Damien Dullaghan (ddullaghan@limerickcoco.ie) *Svcs:* ref, rsrch
Stock: various bks, periodcls, photos, pamphs, maps, m-forms, videos & CD-ROMs *Acqs Offcr:* Snr Lib Asst (Local Studies), as above
Classn: DDC

IA71

Limerick RC Diocesan Archives
Diocesan Office, 66 O'Connell St, Limerick, Co Limerick, Ireland (061-315856; *fax:* 061-310186)
Email: diocoff@eircom.net
Internet: http://www.limerick-diocese.org/

Gov Body: RC Diocese of Limerick *Chief:* Diocesan Sec: Rev Tony Mullins *Dep:* Asst Diocesan Sec: Rev Derek Leonard *Other Snr Staff:* Ms Aoife Bresnan; Ms Margaret Dalton
Assoc Offices: LIMERICK DIOCESAN PASTORAL CENTRE, Denmark St, Limerick, Dir: Rev Eamonn Fitzgibbon (061-400133; *fax:* 061-400601; *email:* ldpc@eircom.net)
Entry: strictly by prior appt with the Diocesan Office; a fee is charged for time-consuming searches, related to the time & staff involved
Open: Mon-Fri 0900-1700
Subj: Limerick Diocese: diocesan records; parish records; estate archvs; some business records; personal papers; local hist *Collns: Bks & Pamphs:* Lib of the late Bishop Newnam; local hist journals *Archvs:* records of the Diocese of Limerick, incl: records of 60 parishes; papers of bishops; old account bks; records of Diocesan happenings & events
Equip: copier, 5 computers (incl 4 with wd-proc & 1 with internet), room for hire *Disabled:* wheelchair access *Svcs:* info, ref, rsrch

Longford

IA72

Ardagh and Clonmacnois RC Diocesan Archives
Diocesan Office, St Michael's, Longford, Co Longford, Ireland (043-46432)
Email: archives@stmelscollege.ie

Gov Body: RC Bishop of Ardagh & Clonmacnois *Chief:* Diocesan Archivist: Rev. Tom Murray, c/o St Mel's Coll, St. Mel's Rd, Longford (043-46469)
Subj: Diocese of Ardagh & Clonmacnois: diocesan records; parish records

IA73

Longford County Libraries, Local Studies and Archives
County Lib HQ, Annaly Carpark, Longford, Ireland (043-41124/5; *fax:* 043-48576)
Email: longlib@iol.ie
Internet: http://www.longfordcoco.ie/

Type: local authority *Gov Body:* Longford County Council (see **IP18**) *Chief:* County Libn: Mrs Mary Carleton-Reynolds DipLIS, ALAI
Assoc Offices: small local hist colln at each branch lib
Entry: ref only *Open:* Mon-Thu 0930-1730, Fri 0930-1700
Subj: Co Longford: local authority archvs; estate archvs; poor law records; local studies *Collns: Bks & Pamphs:* Maria Edgeworth Colln (local author, 1767-1849); Oliver Goldsmith Colln (local author, 1728-1774); Padraic Colum Colln (local author, 1881-1972) *Archvs:* Longford County Council records; Longford Urban Dist Council records; Longford Rural Dist Council records; Ballymahon Rural Dist Council records; minutes of Ballymahon Poor Law Union, Granard Poor Law Union & Longford Poor Law Union; Grand Jury Presentments (1817-1895); King-Harman family of Newcastle, estate records (1810-1988); Longford Militia records; correspondence of Maria Edgeworth *Other:* Index to Parish Registers; Tithe Applotment Bks (1937); map colln, incl Down Survey (17C), OS (1833-44) & Co Longford estate maps; local newspapers (hard-bound & on m-film)
Equip: m-reader, m-printer (A4/12c, A3/24c), copier (A4/12c, A3/24c) *Svcs:* ref
Classn: DDC *Auto Sys:* Horizon

Loughrea

IA74

Clonfert RC Diocesan Archives
c/o St Brendan's Cathedral, Loughrea, Co Galway, Ireland (091-870063; *fax:* 091-847367)

Gov Body: Roman Catholic Diocese of Clonfert *Chief:* Diocesan Archivist: Rev Declan Kelly BD, HDipPastEd
Entry: adv appt with Archivist by letter or tel *Open:* Mon-Fri 1000-1300, 1400-1700
Subj: RC Diocese of Clonfert (East Galway): diocesan archvs; parish records; personal papers *Collns: Bks & Pamphs:* published pastoral letter & articles concerning diocesan personalities; diocesan coll magazines (1927-date); articles for journals by Clonfert clergy *Archvs:* records of the Diocese of Clonfert (mainly from 1884 onwards), incl: title deeds & legal documents relating to diocesan property; conference bks; registers of clergy; correspondence & personal papers of indiv bishops; papers relating to diocesan admin; Egan Papers (papers of the late Very Rev Dr Patrick K. Egan, former Diocesan Historian); papers of Rt Rev Msgr Fair (diocesan historical materials) ☞

(Clonfert RC Diocesan Archvs cont)
Equip: m-reader, copier, fax, room for hire *Online:* to be established *Offcr-in-Charge:* Diocesan Archivist: Rev Declan Kelly, as above *Svcs:* info, ref, rsrch
Acqs Offcr: Diocesan Archivist, as above
Staff: Non-Prof: 1 *Exp:* €1000 pa
Proj: completion of Diocesan Lib for use of students researching hist; diocesan web site incl access to archival data to be established by mid-2003; ongoing cataloging & classn of Egan Papers & Fair Papers

Mallow

IA75

Mallow Heritage Centre
27-28 Bank Pl, Mallow, Co Cork, Ireland (022-50302; *fax:* 022-20276)
Email: mallowhc@eircom.net

Gov Body: Mallow Catholic Church (RC Diocese of Cloyne) *Chief:* Rsrcher: Ms Martina Aherne
Open: Mon-Fri 1030-1300, 1400-1600
Subj: RC Diocese of Cloyne (46 parishes in North & East Cork): parish records; family hist; genealogy
Collns: Archvs: RC Diocese of Cloyne parish records (1757 onwards); C of I (Anglican/Episco-palian) records (North Cork area, from 1780) *Other:* Griffiths Valuation (1851-53); 1901 census; some monumental inscriptions
Svcs: rsrch
See also CLOYNE RC DIOCESAN ARCHVS (**IA17**)

Monaghan

IA76

Clogher RC Diocesan Archives
Bishop's House, Monaghan, Co Monaghan, Ireland (047-81019; *fax:* 047-84773)
Email: cloghdiocoff@mon.com

Gov Body: RC Diocese of Clogher *Chief:* RC Bishop of Clogher: Most Rev Dr Joseph Duffy MA, DD *Dep:* Diocesan Sec: Right Rev Mgr Liam S. MacDaid BA, HDipEd
Entry: Bishop's permission by adv appt *Open:* Mon-Fri 1030-1300
Subj: RC Diocese of Clogher: diocesan records; parish records
Equip: copier, fax
Staff: staffed by PT volunteers

Mullingar

IA77

Meath RC Diocesan Archives
Cathedral House, Mullingar, Co Westmeath, Ireland (044-48338)

Gov Body: RC Bishop of Meath *Chief:* Diocesan Archivist: Very Rev Seán Henry, Adm
Entry: adv appt
Subj: Meath: diocesan records; parish records
See also MEATH HERITAGE CENTRE (**IA93**)

IA78

Westmeath County Libraries, Local Studies Collection
County Lib HQ, Dublin Rd, Mullingar, Co Westmeath, Ireland (044-40781/2/3; *fax:* 044-41322)
Email: library@westmeathcoco.ie
Internet: http://www.westmeathcoco.ie/services/library/

Type: local govt *Gov Body:* Westmeath County Council (see **IP30**) *Chief:* County Libn: Ms Mary Farrell BA, HDipEd, DipLIS, ALAI *Dep:* Exec Libn (Lib HQ): Ms Mary Stuart
Entry: ref only *Open:* Mon-Fri 0930-1300, 1400-1700; other times by appt
Subj: Co Westmeath: local studies; Irish studies; local authority archvs; estate archvs; family papers; personal papers; poor law records; hosp records
Collns: Bks & Pamphs: local studies material, incl local directories, almanacs, topographical dictionaries, ecclesiastical & parish hists, GAA hists & unpublished theses & projs (c3500 items); Irish Colln (12000 vols on all aspects of Irish soc); Kirby Colln (c250 different eds of the 'Vicar of Wakefield' by Oliver Goldsmith); John Broderick Colln (local novelist); local journals; govt pubns (19C-date) *Archvs:* Westmeath County Council minutes (1899-1987); Rural Dist Council minutes for Athlone, Ballymore, Delvin, Kilbeggan & Mullingar; Board of Guardian minutes (19c-early 20C); Board of Health & Public Assistance minutes (1922-1942); Grand Jury Presentments (1802-1887); Belvedere Orphanage papers (1914-43); Westmeath County Infirmary records; Bury family, Earls of Charleville, family & estate papers (17C-20C); correspondence & papers of Earls of Charleville (18C-19C); Colonel Howard Bury Colln (various 19C diaries & papers); Marlay family of Belvedere, family & estate papers (19C-20C); Charles Marlay papers (landowner & politician, 1831-1912); correspondence of Henry Petty-Fitzmaurice (5th Marquess of Lansdowne, 1845-1927); Laurence Ginnell Papers (North Westmeath MP); Fr Paul Walsh Papers (historian & scholar); Burgess Colln (various materials relating to Athlone) *Other:* census materials (mainly 19C); land surveys; Tithe Applotment Bks (1828); Griffiths Valuations (1854); map colln (incl estate maps, 1837 OS & 1860 Geological Survey); OPW Sites & Monument record; local newspaper colln; photographic colln (c2500 prints); monumental inscriptions

Naas

IA79

Irish Family History Society, Reference Library and Archives
PO Box 36, Naas, Co Kildare, Ireland
Email: ifhs@eircom.ie
Internet: http://homepage.tinet.ie/~ifhs/

Type: membership org *Chief:* Chairman: Mr John Heueston *Dep:* Vice-Chairman: Mr Edward Brennan
Open: Mon-Fri 0930-1630
Subj: all Ireland (mainly secondary sources): local authority archvs; diocesan records; parish records; local hist; family hist; genealogy *Collns: Bks & Pamphs:* ref bks & indexes relevant to Irish family hist; journals from similar socs worldwide *Archvs:* mainly copies & secondary sources *Other:* IGI; LDS; Griffiths Valuation; family pedigree charts; OS maps; various materials on m-fiche
Equip: m-reader, copier, video viewer, computers (incl internet & CD-ROM) *Svcs:* info ref, rsrch (membs only)
Stock: archvs/100; periodcls/1000; maps/several dozen
Classn: own
Staff: Other Prof: 1 PT *Non-Prof:* 4 volunteers
See also **IO20**

Navan

IA80

Meath County Libraries, Local Studies and Archives
County Lib HQ, Railway St, Navan, Co Meath, Ireland (046-21451/134; *fax:* 046-21463)
Email: colibrar@meathcoco.ie

Gov Body: Meath County Council (see **IP21**)
Chief: County Libn: Mr Ciaran Mangan
Entry: ref only *Open:* Mon-Fri 0930-1700
Subj: Co Meath: local authority archvs; some estate archvs; poor law records; business records; local studies *Collns: Bks & Pamphs:* various bks & pamphs on Co Meath *Archvs:* Meath County Council records (1899-c1970), incl minutes, accounts, correspondence & valuation bks; archvs of Trim Town Commissioners & Trim Urban Dist Council (1880-1976); archvs of Kells Town Commissioners & Kells Urban Dist Council (1843-1966); archvs of Rural Dist Councils of Co Meath (1898-1925), covering Ardee, Dunshaughlin, Edenderry, Kells, Meath, Navan, Oldcastle & Trim; Board of Guardians records for the Poor Law Unions of Dunshaughlin, Kells, Navan, Oldcastle & Trim; Meath County Infirmary records (1809-1960); records of F&J Clayton Woollen Mills (woollen manufacturers, 1919-1966); various deeds & documents relating to Co Meath estates & instns *Other:* local newspapers (m-film); census records (1901 & 1911, on m-film)
Equip: m-reader, m-printer (10c per pg), copier, 7 computers (incl internet) *Disabled:* Kurzweil reader
Classn: DDC *Auto Sys:* Horizon
Staff: Libns: 6 *Non-Prof:* 8

New Ross

IA81

New Ross Port Company, Archives and Records
Harbour House, New Ross, Co Wexford, Ireland (051-421303; *fax:* 051-421294)

Type: semi-state body *Chief:* Chief Exec: Mr Thomas Meehan
Entry: adv appt *Open:* Mon-Fri 0900-1300, 1400-1700
Subj: New Ross: records of parent org; port records (1848-date)

Newbridge

IA82

Kildare History and Family Research Centre
Riverbank, Main St, Newbridge, Co Kildare, Ireland (*archvs:* 045-431611; *local hist:* 045-432690; *fax:* 045-431611)
Internet: http://www.kildare.ie/library/

Gov Body: Kildare County Council (see **IP12**) & Kildare Heritage & Genealogy Co *Chief:* Archivist: Ms Mary Fitzpatrick (kildarearchives@eircom.net); Local Studies Offcr: Mr Mario Corrigan (kildarelocalhistory@eircom.net) *Other Snr Staff:* Genealogist: Ms Karel Kiely (capinfo@iol.ie)
Subj: Co Kildare: local hist; local authority archvs; family papers *Collns: Bks & Pamphs:* Teresa Brayton Colln (bks, cuttings & personal items); Kildare Archaeological Soc journals (1891 onwards) *Archvs:* records of Grand Juries, Boards of Guardians & Rural Dist Councils; Ballitore MSS (correspondence, school notebks, drawings etc of Shackleton & other Quaker families of Ballitore, 19C) *Other:* Griffith's Valuation; Tithe Applotment Bks; map collns (incl OS maps of Co Kildare); photo colln (incl Lawrence Colln); local newspapers

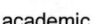

Auto Sys: Genesis
Pubns: local hist pubns incl: Tracing Your Ancestors in County Kildare; Lest We Forget: Kildare & The Great Famine; All That Delirium of the Brave: Kildare in 1798

Portlaoise

IA83
Laois County Libraries, Local Studies Collection

County Lib HQ, Kea-Lew Business Pk, Mount Rath Rd, Portlaoise, Co Laois, Ireland (0502-72340; *fax:* 0502-64558)
Email: library@laoisecoco.ie
Internet: http://www.laoisecoco.ie/

Gov Body: Laois County Council (see **IP14**)
Chief: contact the Local Studies Libn
Entry: ref only *Open:* Mon-Fri 0900-1300, 1400-1700
Subj: Co Laois: local studies; Irish studies; some estate papers; local authority archvs *Collns: Bks & Pamphs:* unique colln of material by local & Irish authors; journal of Royal Soc of Antiquities of Ireland (complete set); Kildare Archaeological Journal *Archvs:* Laois County Council Archvs (1880s onwards); Board of Guardian minute bks; Grand Jury Presentments (1845-1897); records of Petty Sessions (1851-96); records of Rural Dist Councils for Mountmellick, Abbeyleix, Cloney-gowan, Athy, Slievemargy & Roscrea (1899-1919) *Other:* Tithe Applotment Bks (1830s); Griffith's Valuation (1850s); local newspapers; photo collns, incl: Eason Colln; Lawrence Colln; Scully Colln; Redmond Colln; map colln, incl: Sir William Petty's maps (1685); Taylor & Skinner Road Maps (1778); 1841 OS maps
Proj: County Archv Svc currently under development; access to Archvs is via Local Studies Dept

Roscommon

IA84
Roscommon County Council, Local Studies and Archives

Roscommon County Lib, Abbey St, Roscommon, Co Roscommon, Ireland (0903-37285; *fax:* 0903-25474)
Email: roslib@eircom.net
Internet: http://www.roscommoncoco.ie/

Gov Body: Roscommon County Council (see **IP24**) *Chief:* Acting County Libn: Mr Eamonn Bolger DipLIS
Open: Tue, Thu 1300-2000, Wed 1300-1700, Fri-Sat 1000-1300, 1400-1700
Subj: Co Roscommon: local authority archvs; personal papers; local hist *Collns: Bks & Pamphs:* Douglas Hyde Colln (works of the Roscommon author & President of Ireland, 1860-1949) *Archvs:* minutes of Rural Dist Councils; minutes of Boards of Guardians; Roscommon Grand Jury records; Douglas Hyde, correspond-ence & photos; William Percy French Colln (composer & painter, 1854-1920); Crofton Family Papers *Other:* local newspapers; photo colln; map colln; extensive colln of local hist files
Equip: m-reader, computers

Slane

IA85
Francis Ledwidge Museum and War Memorial Centre, Archives

Jeanville, Slane, Co Meath, Ireland (041-982-4544)
Email: ledwidgemuseum@eircom.net

Chief: Museum Sec: Mrs Betty Tallon
Entry: adv appt *Open:* daily 1000-1700
Subj: relating to Francis Ledwidge (Irish poet): personal papers; literary papers *Collns: Archvs:* correspondence & MS poems of Francis Ledwidge (1891-1917) *Other:* memorabilia of WW1
Svcs: info
Pubns: Complete Poems of Francis Ledwidge (€7.50); Life of Francis Ledwidge (€9)

Sligo

IA86
Elphin RC Diocesan Archives

Diocesan Office, St Mary's, Sligo, Co Sligo, Ireland (071-62670; *fax:* 071-62414)
Email: elphindo@eircom.net

Gov Body: Roman Catholic Bishop of Elphin
Chief: Diocesan Offcr: Rev Patrick Lombard
Entry: adv appt *Open:* Mon-Fri 1000-1500
Subj: RC Diocese of Elphin: diocesan records; parish records; theology; scripture; Canon Law; ecclesiastical hist; Irish hist *Collns: Archvs:* Diocesan records from 1860; correspondence of Elphin bishops
Equip: room for hire
Staff: Non-Prof: 1 *Exp:* IR£400 (1999-2000); IR£400 (2000-01)
Proj: recent indexing of episcopal correspondence (2001)

IA87
Sligo County Council, Archives and Local Studies Collections

County Ref Lib, Westward Centre, Bridge St, Sligo, Co Sligo, Ireland (071-47190; *fax:* 071-46798)
Email: sligolib@sligococo.ie
Internet: http://www.sligococo.ie/

Gov Body: Sligo County Council (see **IP25**)
Chief: County Libn: Mr Donal Tinney BA, DipLIS, ALAI *Dep:* Exec Libn: Ms Pauline Brennan *Other Snr Staff:* Asst Libn (Lib Archvs & Admin): Mr Patrick Gannon (pgannon@sligococo.ie)
Entry: ref only; booking of m-readers advised
Open: Mon-Fri 1000-1250, 1400-1650
Subj: Co Sligo: local authority archvs; parish records; estate archvs; records of local clubs & socs; census records; legal records; local hist; genealogy; lit; antiquities *Collns: Bks & Pamphs:* Yeatsiana (photos, prints, letters, portraits, drawings, broadsheets & bks by & about the Yeats family); local directories, annuals & almanacs *Archvs:* records of Sligo County Council *Other:* maps; local newspapers; surveys; wills; Museum Colln (artifacts relating to Yeats, Constance Markievicz & to hist & archaeo of County Sligo)
Equip: m-reader, m-printer, copier, computers (incl internet & CD-ROM) *Svcs:* info, ref
Classn: DDC
Pubns: Sources of Local Hist (£7); Jack B. Yeats at the Niland Gallery Sligo (£9.99); The Yeats Brothers & Sligo (CD-ROM, £25)
Staff: Libns: 4 *Non-Prof:* 2

IA88
Sligo Harbour Commissioners, Archives and Records

Harbour Office, Ballast Quay, Sligo, Ireland (*tel & fax:* 071-61197)

Type: local authority *Chief:* Ms E. McDonnell
Open: Mon-Fri 0930-1700
Subj: Sligo: local authority archvs (port records)
Collns: Archvs: Sligo Harbour records (minute bks, maps, ledgers etc)
Equip: copier, computer (with wd-proc)
Staff: Non-Prof: 1

Thurles

IA89
Cashel and Emly RC Archdiocesan Archives

c/o Rev Christy O'Dwyer, St Patrick's Coll, Thurles, Co Tipperary, Ireland (0504-21201; *fax:* 0504-23735)

Gov Body: Archdiocese of Cashel & Emly Trust
Chief: Diocesan Archivist: Rev Christy O'Dwyer MA, STL
Assoc Offices: parish records for the Archdiocese are held at TIPPERARY FAMILY HIST RSRCH (see **IA91**); collns of secondary material preserved in ST PATRICK'S COLL, THURLES (see **IS201**)
Entry: by appt only
Subj: Archdiocese of Cashel & Diocese of Emly: diocesan records; personal papers; parish hists
Collns: Bks & Pamphs: large collns *Archvs:* papers of numerous Archbishops of Cashel & Emly
Equip: m-reader, m-camera, copier
Staff: Non-Prof: 1

IA90
Tipperary Local Studies Department

Tipperary Libs, Castle Ave, Thurles, Co Tipperary, Ireland (0504-21555; *fax:* 0504-23442)
Email: studies@tipperarylibraries.ie/
Internet: http://www.tipperarylibraries.ie/

Gov Body: Tipperary Libs (see **IP27**) *Chief:* Local Studies Libn: Mrs Mary Guinan-Darmody
Dep: Mr Pat Bracken
Entry: free access to public, ref only; adv appt advised for use of m-reader/printer *Open:* Mon-Fri 0930-1700; check in adv
Subj: Co Tipperary: local hist; family hist; Irish hist; genealogy; estate records; family papers *Collns: Bks & Pamphs:* major Tipperary pubns; parish & GAA pubns; bks by Tipperary authors (incl poetry & fiction); major antiquarian & historical journals, incl Journal of the Royal Soc of Antiquaries & Tipperary Historical Journal *Archvs:* Board of Guardian minute bks (1839-1926) & poor law rate bks; Grand Jury Presentments; Tithe Applotment Bks; Griffith's Valuation (1850-1851); estate materials *Other:* 1901 & 1911 census returns; genealogical indexes; prints & photos (incl Thurles Colln); Map Colln, incl: Down Survey Maps (1650s); Taylor & Skinner's Road Maps (1778); OS (from 1840s); Newspaper Colln, incl: Tipperary Star (m-film & hard copies, 1909-date); The Nationalist (m-film from 1890); Nenagh Guardian (1838-1960)
Equip: 2 m-readers m-printer (fees), copier (fees), computer (with wd-proc, internet & CD-ROM)
Svcs: info, ref, genealogical enqs (in writing)
Stock: various bks, periodcls, photos, maps, slides, m-fiche, m-film & archvs *Acqs Offcr:* Local Studies Libn, as above
Pubns: Tipperary Historical Journal
Staff: Non-Prof: 1

Tipperary

IA91
Tipperary Family History Research, The Excel Heritage Centre

(formerly Tipperary Heritage Unit)
Mitchel St, Tipperary, Ireland (062-80555)
Email: Research@tfhr.org
Internet: http://www.tfhr.org/

Type: charity *Gov Body:* The Excel Heritage Co Ltd *Chief:* Mgr: Mr Patrick McDonnell BBus *Dep:* Snr Rsrcher: Mrs Charlotte Crowe
Open: Mon-Fri 0930-1730

(Tipperary Family Hist Rsrch cont)
Subj: RC Archdiocese of Cashel & Emly (incl most of North & South Tipperary & parts of South East Limerick): diocesan records; parish records
Collns: *Archvs:* records of the RC Archdiocese of Cashel & Emly
Svcs: rsrch
Pubns: St Ailbe's Heritage: A Guide to the Hist, Genealogy & Towns of the Archdiocese of Cashel & Emly (€6 + p&p); see web site for full pubns list
Further Info: Tipperary Family Hist Rsrch is the diocesan centre for the area

Tralee

IA92 🏛
Kerry Local Studies and Archives Department
County Lib HQ, Moyderwell, Tralee, Co Kerry, Ireland (066-7121200; *fax:* 066-7129202)
Email: localhistory@kerrycolib.ie
Internet: http://www.kerrycountylibrary.com/

Type: local authority **Gov Body:** Kerry County Council (see **IP11**) **Chief:** County Libn: Mrs Kathleen Browne FLAI **Dep:** Exec Libn: Mr Pat Walsh **Other Snr Staff:** Ref Svcs Libn: Mr Michael Costello
Assoc Offices: other special collns are held at: DINGLE LIB, Dingle, Co Kerry
Entry: ref only **Open:** Mon-Fri 1000-1300, 1400-1700, Sat 1000-1230, 1430-1700
Subj: Co Kerry: local studies; hist; archaeo; family hist; genealogy; local authority archvs; diocesan records; parish records; estate archvs; family papers; business records; personal papers; poor law records; solicitors' records; records of parent org **Collns:** *Bks & Pamphs:* bks & journals relating to Co Kerry, incl many unavailable elsewhere; works by local authors; Daniel O'Connell Colln; special collns held at Dingle Lib: An Canónach Ó Fiannachta Colln (Celtic studies); Tomás Ághas Museum Colln; An Cnósach Dhuibhneach Colln (relating to Dingle peninsula) *Archvs:* Board of Guardian minute bks (1840s onwards); minutes of Rural Dist Councils of Cahirciveen, Dingle, Kenmare, Killarney, Listowel & Tralee; minutes of poor law unions for Cahirciveen, Dingle, Glin, Kenmare, Killarney, Listowel & Tralee; Dingle Harbour Commissioner records; Board of Health records; Reidy Family Papers; Ferris Papers (MSS relating to Kerry & Cork); Tom Crean Papers (Antarctic explorer); Thomas Ashe Colln; Roger Casement Colln; Kerry Archaeological & Historical Soc archvs **Other:** Irish Folklore Commission Schools Colln (1937, m-film); 1901 census on m-film; Tithe Applotment Bks (1820/30); Griffiths Valuation (c1850); local newspapers on m-film (1820s onwards) & hard copy (1931 onwards); map colln (1842 OS & rare Kerry maps); local historical photo colln, incl Kerryman newspaper archv (from 1958); audio colln; 19C prints
Equip: 2 m-readers, 3 m-printers, copier, fax, 7 computers (all with wd-proc & CD-ROM, 1 with internet) **Svcs:** info, ref
Acqs Offcr: Ref Svcs Libn, as above
Classn: DDC **Auto Sys:** Horizon
Staff: *Archivists:* 1 *Libns:* 2

Trim

IA93 🔑
Meath Heritage Centre
Town Hall, Castle St, Trim, Co Meath, Ireland (046-36633; *fax:* 046-37502)
Email: meathhc@iol.ie
Internet: http://www.iol.ie/~meathhc/

Gov Body: Trim Forum for Employment **Chief:** Dir: Mr Noel French **Dep:** Rsrcher: Ms Carmel Rice
Entry: adv appt **Open:** Mon-Fri 0900-1300, 1400-1700
Subj: Co Meath: parish records; local hist
Equip: m-reader, m-printer, copier, fax, computer (with wd-proc) **Svcs:** rsrch (fee-based)
Staff: *Non-Prof:* 2
See also MEATH RC DIOCESAN ARCHVS (**IA77**)

Tullamore

IA94 🏛
Offaly Local Studies and Archives Service
County Lib HQ, O'Connor Sq, Tullamore, Co Offaly, Ireland (0506-46834; *fax:* 0506-52769)
Email: libraryhq@offalycoco.ie
Internet: http://www.offaly.ie/

Type: local authority **Gov Body:** Offaly County Council (see **IP23**) **Chief:** County Libn: Miss Ann Coughlan
Assoc Offices: smaller collns at each local lib
Entry: ref only **Open:** Mon-Fri 0900-1700
Subj: Co Offaly: local studies; Irish studies; Irish lit; local authority archvs; estate archvs; personal papers; poor law records **Collns:** *Bks & Pamphs:* fiction by Irish authors; Local Authors Colln *Archvs:* archvs of local authority bodies in Offaly; various 19C & 20C public records; Grand Jury Presentments (1830-1878) **Other:** census data (incl 1st census in 1659); Tithe Applotment Bks (1823-1838); O'Donovan Letters (Ordnance Survey, 1839-40); Griffiths Valuation; local photographic archv; local newspapers (m-film & hardcopy); colln of local songs & ballads; map colln (incl Down Survey & OS); Schools Folklore Colln (1937-38); ephemera

Waterford

IA95 🏛
Waterford City Archives
c/o City Hall, The Mall, Waterford, Co Waterford, Ireland (051-843123; *fax:* 051-879124)
Email: archives@waterfordcity.ie
Internet: http://www.waterfordcity.ie/

Gov Body: Waterford City Council (see **IP28**)
Chief: City Archivist: Mr Donal Moore MA, HDipAS (dmoore@waterfordcity.ie)
Entry: ref only **Open:** Mon-Fri 0900-1300, 1400-1700
Subj: Waterford City: local authority archvs; family papers; estate archvs; personal papers; school records **Collns:** *Archvs:* records of Waterford Corp (1654-1990s), incl: minute bks; cttee records (1774-1940s); records of Town Clerk's Office (1700-1990s); records of Finance Office (1796-1980s); records of City Engineer's Office (1700-1990s); Corp estate records (incl database of expired leases, 1670s-1970s); records of local primary schools; over 70 small, private & institutional collns **Other:** photographic prints (1870s-date)
Equip: copier (at discretion of the City Archivist)
Svcs: info, ref

Stock: archvs/250 linear m; photos/2500+; maps/2500+
Pubns: The Royal Charters of Waterford (Waterford Corp, 1992); Waterford City Archvs: A New Svc, by Donal Moore (in Decies 54, 1998)
Staff: *Archivists:* 1 *Non-Prof:* 2
See also WATERFORD COUNTY ARCHVS SVC (**IA54**)

Wexford

IA96 🙏
Ferns RC Diocesan Archives
c/o St Peter's Coll, Wexford, Co Wexford, Ireland

Gov Body: RC Diocese of Ferns **Chief:** Diocesan Archivist: Rev Séamus S. de Vál
Entry: collns are only just being established; please contact the Diocesan Archivist for details of current availability
Subj: Diocese of Ferns & County of Wexford: diocesan records; parish records **Collns:** *Bks & Pamphs:* part of lib of House of Missions, Enniscorthy, Co Wexford (now closed), dealing mainly with hist & religion
Staff: *Non-Prof:* 1
Proj: establishment of Diocesan Archvs; acq of archival materials; cataloguing of existing holdings

IA97 🔑 🏛
Irish Agricultural Museum, Archives
Johnstown Castle, Old Farmyard, Wexford, Ireland (053-42888; *fax:* 053-42213)
Email: aosullivan@johnstown.teagasc.ie

Gov Body: Irish Agric Museum (J.C.) Ltd **Chief:** Curator: Dr A.M. O'Sullivan BSc, PhD **Dep:** Mr Adrian Stafford
Entry: adv appt with Curator **Open:** Mon-Fri 0900-1230, 1330-1700
Subj: 32 counties of Ireland: estate archvs; business records; agric; Irish rural life; rural crafts **Collns:** *Bks & Pamphs:* agric in the broadest sense; manufacturers' catalogues for farm machinery & household furnishings
Equip: copier, computer (with wd-proc) **Svcs:** info, ref, rsrch
Stock: archvs/25 m; bks/200 m; periodcls/10; photos/500; slides/11000; illusts/200; maps/50; AVs/10
Classn: UDC **Staff:** *Other Prof:* 1 *Non-Prof:* 2
Exp: IR£2500 (2000-01)

IA98 🏛
Wexford Corporation Archives
Municipal Bldgs, Wexford, Co Wexford, Ireland (053-42611; *fax:* 053-45947)
Email: info@wexfordcorp.ie

Gov Body: Wexford Corp **Chief:** Town Clerk: Mr Pat Collins
Entry: adv appt **Open:** Mon-Fri 0900-1700
Subj: Wexford Town: local authority archvs
Collns: *Archvs:* minute bks of Wexford Corp; Royal Charter
See also WEXFORD COUNTY COUNCIL, LOCAL STUDIES & ARCHVS (**IA1**)

SECTION 9 – IRISH SPECIAL LIBRARIES

Entries are arranged alphabetically under town names. Within this framework, libraries within the same institution are grouped together. Libraries covered include governmental libraries, academic libraries (universities, schools and institutes of higher and further education), hospital and other medical libraries, corporate libraries, commercial libraries, libraries held by museums and art galleries, churches and other religious organisations, and numerous private libraries such as those held by learned or professional bodies, charities and stately homes.

Access to many special libraries (including academic libraries) is restricted, and entry may require an appointment in advance. Often identification will be required and a special need to use the collections will have to be demonstrated.

Telephone and fax numbers are given in the form of area dialling codes within the Republic of Ireland. To telephone the Irish Republic from outside the country, dial 00-353 followed by the number, minus the initial 0.

Entries are based on the libraries' responses to the following questions:

	1. Official name of Library/Institution	
Type:	**2.** Type of Institution *(see also Key to Symbols below)*	
	3. Full postal address *(incl. postcode)* Tel & fax numbers *(incl. STD code)*	
Email:	Electronic Mail	
Internet:	Internet address	
Gov Body:	**4.** Governing body *(if any, e.g., local authority, university)*	
Chief:	**5.** Chief Librarian/Officer *(give designation, name, qualifications & email address)*	
Dep:	**6.** Deputy *(give designation, name, qualifications & email address)*	
Other Snr Staff:	**7.** Other Senior Staff *(give designation, name, qualifications & email address)*	
Assoc Libs:	**8.** Associate/Dependent Libraries *(if any, give address, tel, fax & email address, plus designation, name & qualifications of officer in charge)*	
Entry:	**9.** Conditions for entry *(e.g., reference only, advance appointment)*	
Open:	**10.** Opening hours *(please use 24-hour clock, e.g., 0930-1730)*	
Subj:	**11.** Main subjects covered	
Collns:	**12.** Special Collections *(give subjects and brief details)*	
Bks & Pamphs:	**a)** Printed books & pamphlets	
Archvs:	**b)** Archives	
Other:	**c)** Other	
Co-op Schemes:	**13.** Co-operative schemes *(in which library participates, if any)*	
Equip:	**14.** Equipment & facilities available to users *(give numbers, and fees if appropriate)*	
Disabled:	Equipment for disabled *(e.g., Kurzweil)*	
Online:	Online information services *(e.g., Dialog; give fees)*	
Offcr-in-Charge:	Officer in charge of equipment purchases *(give designation, name & email address)*	

Svcs:	**15.** Services provided	
Stock:	**16.** Stock *(give total quantities)*	
bks	**a)** Books *(incl bound periodicals)*	
periodcls	**b)** Current periodical titles	
photos	**c)** Photographs	
slides	**d)** Slides	
illusts	**e)** Illustrations	
pamphs	**f)** Pamphlets	
maps	**g** Maps	
m-forms	**h)** Microforms	
audios	**i)** Audios	
videos	**j)** Videos	
CD-ROMs	**k)** CD-ROMs	
archvs	**l)** Archives *(specify unit e.g., by linear, cubic metre)*	
rec mgmt	**m)** Records management holdings *(specify unit e.g., by linear, cubic metre)*	
	n) Other *(please specify)*	
Acqs Offcr:	Officer in charge of stock acquisitions *(give designation, name & email address)*	
Classn:	**17.** Classification method(s) used *(if applicable)*	
Auto Sys:	**18.** Automated Library system used *(if any)*	
Pubns:	**19.** Publications *(e.g., guides & handlists; give titles & prices)*	
Staff:	**20.** Staff establishment *(give full-time equivalent for part-time staff incl. vacancies)* **Total number of:**	
Libns:	**a)** Professional librarians	
Other Prof:	**b)** Other professional staff	
Non-Prof:	**c)** Non-professional staff	
Exp:	**21.** Finance *(expenditure on documents and/or books, incl. purchase & conservation)* **a)** 1999-2000 **b)** 2000-01	
Proj:	**22.** Capital projects *(if any, starting in 2001 or 2002)*	
Further Info:	**23.** Other Information	

Key to Symbols

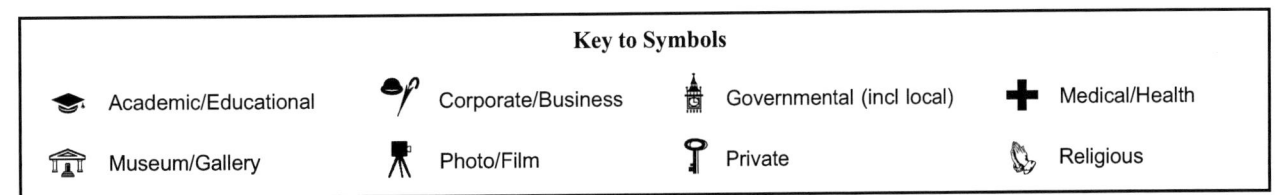

Academic/Educational   Corporate/Business   Governmental (incl local)   Medical/Health

Museum/Gallery   Photo/Film   Private   Religious

 **IRELAND**

Ardee
▼
Cork

Special Libraries

Ardee

IS1 ✚

St Brigid's Hospital Library

Mellifont Suite, St Brigit's Hosp, Kells Rd, Ardee, Co Louth, Ireland (041-685-7885; *fax:* 041-685-0669)
Email: marion.crosby@nehb.ie
Internet: http://www.nehb.ie/

Gov Body: North Eastern Health Board *Chief:* Libn: Ms Marion Crosby
Assoc Libs: other libs in NEHB Lib & Info Svc: MOTHER MARY MARTIN LIB (see **IS29**); CAVAN GENL HOSP LIB (see **IS16**); LOUTH COUNTY HOSP LIB (see **IS162**); MONAGHAN GENL HOSP LIB (see **IS186**); OUR LADY'S HOSP LIB (see **IS190**); ST DAVNET'S HOSP LIB (see **IS187**)
Subj: medicine
Equip: copier, computers *Online:* Medline, CINAHL, Cochrane, PsycInfo, BNI & others
Classn: DDC *Auto Sys:* Heritage

Athlone

IS2 🎓

Athlone Institute of Technology Library

Dublin Rd, Athlone, Co Westmeath, Ireland (090-642-4511; *fax:* 090-642-4626)
Email: library@ait.ie
Internet: http://www.ait.ie/

Gov Body: Athlone Inst of Tech *Chief:* Coll Libn: Ms Jo Corkery BA, HDipEd, DipLIS (JCorkery@ait.ie) *Dep:* Dep Libn: Ms Una O'Connor BA, DipLIS (UOConnor@ait.ie)
Entry: adv appt for external readers *Open:* term: Mon-Thu 0915-2145, Fri-Sat 0915-1700; vac: Mon-Fri 0915-1300, 1400-1700
Subj: all subjs; undergrad; postgrad; social sci; tech *Co-op Schemes:* BLDSC, ILL
Equip: 2 m-readers, 2 copiers, fax, 9 computers (incl 3 with internet & 6 with CD-ROM) *Online:* Science Direct, EBSCO, RAPRA, ABI Inform, FactFinder, Chemical Abstracts, Medline, Engineering Index, Infotrac Onefile *Svcs:* info, ref, biblio
Stock: bks/28200; periodcls/264; videos/300; CD-ROMs/various
Classn: DDC *Auto Sys:* Urica
Staff: Libns: 2 *Non-Prof:* 5 *Exp:* IR£41700 (1999-2000)

Ballintogher

IS3 🔑 ⚖ 🎓 🎓

Society of Irish Foresters, Library

Enterprise Centre, Ballintogher, Co Sligo, Ireland (071-916-4434; *fax:* 071-913-4904)
Email: sif@eircom.net
Internet: http://www.societyofirishforesters.ie/

Chief: Administrator: Mrs Paula Lahiff
Entry: membs only; ref by adv appt *Open:* Mon-Fri 1000-1600
Subj: forestry *Collns: Bks & Pamphs:* complete colln of Irish Forestry (Soc journal, 1942-date)
Equip: copier (10c per pg) *Online:* abstracts of all Soc articles & papers available on web site

Ballyjamesduff

IS4 🏛 🏛

Cavan County Museum Library

Virginia Rd, Ballyjamesduff, Co Cavan, Ireland (049-854-4070; *fax:* 049-854-4332)
Email: info@cavanmuseum.ie
Internet: http://www.cavanmuseum.ie/

Gov Body: Cavan County Council (see **IP2**)
Chief: Museum Curator: Mr Dominic Egan MA
Entry: ref only *Open:* Tue-Sat 1000-1700, Sun (Jun-Sep) 1400-1800
Subj: local study (Co Cavan): hist; geog; archaeo; geol
Equip: fax, video viewer, copier, clr copier, computers (incl wd-proc & internet) *Svcs:* info, ref
Stock: bks/200; periodcls/300; photos/500; slides/120; illusts/100; pamphs/100; maps/200; audios/80; videos/12
Classn: DDC *Staff: Other Prof:* 2 *Non-Prof:* 7

Ballyvaughn

IS5 🎓

Burren College of Art, Library

Newtown Castle, Ballyvaughn, Co Clare, Ireland (065-707-7200; *fax:* 065-707-7201)
Email: library@burrencollege.com
Internet: http://www.burrencollege.com/

Chief: Libn: Ms Marie Smart BA(Hons), DipLib
Entry: ref only except for membs of the Coll
Open: Mon-Thu 0930-1730
Subj: arts
Equip: copier, computers (incl wd-proc & internet)
Stock: bks/5000; periodcls/15; slides/1000; videos/50
Classn: UDC *Auto Sys:* EOSi
Staff: Libns: 1 *Non-Prof:* 1 both PT

Birr

IS6 🔑

Birr Castle Muniments Room

Birr Castle, Birr, Co Offaly, Ireland (0509-20023; *fax:* 0509-21583)
Email: info@birrcastle.com
Internet: http://www.birrcastleireland.com/

Gov Body: Birr Scientific & Heritage Foundation
Entry: open to Friends of Birr Castle Demesne, sub €55 pa *Open:* prior appt only
Subj: local studies (Counties Offaly, Tipperary, Wexford & Yorks); local ordinances; politics (late 18C), astronomy; eng; maths (astronomy & eng); arch; photography; hist (incl hist of sci); gardening & garden design; family papers *Collns: Bks & Pamphs:* Rosse on Christian Revelation (1834) & other religious works *Archvs:* archvs of the Parsons family from 1600, incl 16C & 17C papers & letters; materials relating to: politics; hist; 19C sci; construction of telescope; gardening; planting; expeditions to collect seed; also co-lateral branches of family: Messels of Nymans, Admiral Lord Hawke; estate mgmt & local interest *Other:* bnd portfolio of arch drawings of Samuel Cheaunley; miscellanea; structura; curiosa *Co-op Schemes:* some material on m-film in Public Records Office of Northern Ireland, Belfast (see **A41**); archv material loaned for exhibs at various insts, e.g., Ulster Museum (see **S146**)
Equip: m-reader
Pubns: Impressions of an Irish Countess (€15.25); The Astronomy of Birr Castle (out of stock); Reconstruction of the Rosse Six Foot Telescope (€5.75); From Galaxies to Turbines: Sci, Tech & the Parsons Family (€60); The Red Tree Trail (€3.20); prices excl p&p

Blackrock

IS7 🎓

Froebel College of Education Library

Sion Hill, Blackrock, Co Dublin, Ireland (01-288-8520; *fax:* 01-288-0618)
Email: library@froebel.ie
Internet: http://www.froebel.ie/

Chief: Libn: Ms Cora Gunter BA, DipLIS *Dep:* Lib Asst: Ms Angela Barrado
Open: Mon, Thu 0900-1730, Tue-Wed 0900-1900, Fri 0900-1630
Subj: phil; psy; religion; social sci; lang; sci; maths; arts; lit; geog; hist *Collns: Bks & Pamphs:* emphasis on methods of teaching subjs at primary/elementary level; large colln of bks for ch (fiction & non-fiction); small colln of printed bks, journals & pamphs on Froebel & the Froebel Foundation *Other:* colln of educational CD-ROMs for ch
Equip: 2 copiers, 3 computers (all with wd-proc, internet & CD-ROM) *Svcs:* info, ref, biblio
Stock: bks/10000; periodcls/40; pamphs/100; videos/200; charts/250
Classn: DDC *Auto Sys:* Alice for Windows
Staff: Libns: 1 *Non-Prof:* 1

IS8 🎓

Michael Smurfit Graduate School of Business, Library and Business Information Centre

Carysfort Ave, Blackrock, Co Dublin, Ireland (01-716-8069; *fax:* 01-716-8011)
Email: library.blackrock@ucd.ie
Internet: http://www.ucd.ie/~library/

Gov Body: Univ Coll Dublin (see **IS148**) *Chief:* Librarian-in-Charge: Mr John Steele BA, DipLib, MLIS, FLAI
Entry: registered staff & students of UCD *Open:* term: Mon-Fri 0930-2130, Sat 0930-1300; vac: Mon, Thu-Fri 0930-1730, Tue-Wed 0930-2130
Subj: business; commerce; psy; ethics; econ; banking; taxation; mgmt; accounting; marketing *Collns: Bks & Pamphs:* Irish & UK company annual reports (c4000 items, 1992-date); theses colln (c4000 items); East European colln; small theatre & drama colln (c1000 vols) *Co-op Schemes:* ILL
Equip: copier, computers (incl CD-ROM)
Stock: bks/c15000
Classn: DDC *Auto Sys:* Talis

IS9 🎓

St Catherine's College of Education for Home Economics, Library

Sion Hill, Blackrock, Co Dublin, Ireland (01-210-0221; *fax:* 01-283-4858)
Email: library@dna.ie

Chief: Coll Libn: Ms Dara Breaden BA(Mod), HDE, DipLIS, ALAI
Entry: letter of introduction *Open:* term: Mon-Thu 0900-2100, Fri 0900-1700; vac: Mon-Fri 0900-1700
Subj: genl; GCSE & A level; undergrad; phil; psy; religion; social sci; sociology; econ; edu; hist of fashion; lang; Irish lang; nutrition; food sci; cookery; sewing; textiles; textile arts; fashion design; Irish lit; geog (small colln); hist (small colln) *Collns: Bks & Pamphs:* curriculum lib *Other:* audio-visual colln (school & coll level) *Co-op Schemes:* BLDSC, Irish Health Libs network
Equip: m-reader, video viewer, copier, fax, computers (incl 1 with internet & 2 with CD-ROM)
Svcs: info, ref, biblio, indexing, abstracting, current awareness
Stock: bks/18000; periodcls/120; slides/3000; illusts/1000 posters; audios/100; videos/350
Classn: DDC *Auto Sys:* Heritage
Staff: Libns: 1 *Non-Prof:* 2
Proj: computerisation of stock

Carlow

IS10

County Carlow Chamber of Commerce, Library and Information Service

Upper Floor, Haddens Centre, Tullow St, Carlow, Co Carlow, Ireland (0503-32337; *fax:* 0503-30652)
Email: info@carlowchamber.com
Internet: http://www.carlowchamber.com/

Chief: Chief Exec Offcr: Ms Jacqui McNabb *Dep:* Office Administrator: Ms Caroline Wynne
Entry: membs of Chamber *Open:* Mon-Fri 0930-1750
Subj: business info
Equip: fax, copier, room for hire

IS11

Institute of Technology Carlow, Library

Kilkenny Rd, Carlow, Ireland (503-70567; *fax:* 503-70500)
Email: library@itcarlow.ie
Internet: http://www.library.itcarlow.ie/

Chief: Inst Libn: Mr Richard Lennon BA, DipLIS, ALAI (richard.lennon@itcarlow.ie) *Dep:* Asst Libn: Ms Elizabeth Hutton DipLIS (huttonl@itcarlow.ie)
Entry: full borrowing membership to Inst staff & students, external membership available for a fee; ref facilities free *Open:* term: Mon-Fri 0900-2200, Sat 0900-1300; vac: Mon-Fri 0900-1700
Subj: all subjs; undergrad; postgrad; phil; psy; social sci; lang; sci; maths; tech; arts; eng; business; computing
Equip: m-reader, 4 copiers (30 copies for €3), 6 video viewers, 250 computers (all with wd-proc, internet & CD-ROM) *Online:* various databases
Svcs: info, ref, biblio
Stock: bks/19865; periodcls/221; pamphs/1925; m-forms/6 sets; audios/2; videos/96; CD-ROMs/24; multimedia/27; e-journals/5000; dissertations/228
Classn: DDC *Auto Sys:* Millennium
Staff: Libns: 5 *Non-Prof:* 6

IS12

St Patrick's College Library

College St, Carlow, Ireland (0503-31114; *fax:* 0503-40258)
Email: info@carlowcollege.ie
Internet: http://www.carlowcollege.ie/

Gov Body: Trustees, St Patrick's Coll, Carlow
Chief: Libn: Mrs Martina Lennon BA, DipLS
Entry: adv appt for non-students *Open:* term: Mon-Thu 0915-2100, Fri 0915-1700; vac: Mon-Fri 0900-1630
Subj: phil; psy; religion; social sci *Collns: Bks & Pamphs:* 18-19C theological works; major theological & scriptural periodcls; some philosophical periodcls *Archvs:* 19C pamphs
Equip: copiers, computers (incl wd-proc, internet & CD-ROM)
Stock: bks/16000; periodcls/30
Classn: DDC *Staff:* Libns: 1 *Non-Prof:* 2

Cashel

IS13

The Bolton Library

GPA Bldg, John St, Cashel, Co Tipperary, Ireland (*tel & fax:* 062-61944)
Email: boltonlibrary@oceanfree.net

Gov Body: Dean & Chapter of Cashel *Chief:* Curator & Dean of Cashel Cathedral: The Very Revd Dean Dr Philip Knowles

---

Entry: open to public; small admission charge; students & rsrchers by adv appt *Open:* Mon-Fri 1000-1400 or by special arrangement; hrs subj to alteration
Subj: local studies (South Tipperary); generalities; phil; psy; religion; sci; lit; geog; hist *Collns: Bks & Pamphs:* Colln of William King (Archbishop of Dublin) & Theophilus Bolton (Archbishop of Cashel); 200 vols of 16C-17C pamphs; early (pre-1550) printed bks; significant holding of scarce STC & WING material *Archvs:* MSS (6 vols, c1200-1500); C of I parish records for part of Diocese (1654-date)
Svcs: info, ref
Stock: bks/c12000; photos/250; slides/150; various pamphs, MSS & maps
Staff: Non-Prof: 2 PT

Castlebar

IS14 ✚

Western Health Board, Castlebar Healthcare Library

St Mary's Inst, Mayo Genl Hosp, Castlebar, Co Mayo, Ireland (094-42635; *fax:* 042-29027)
Email: Julia.Reynolds@whb.ie
Internet: http://www.whb.ie/

Gov Body: Western Health Board *Chief:* Libn: Ms Julia Reynolds
Assoc Libs: WESTERN HEALTH BOARD LIB SVC (Lib HQ – see **IS168**); WESTERN HEALTH BOARD, EAST GALWAY/ROSCOMMON LIB SVCS, Portiuncula Hosp, Ballinasloe, Co Galway
Entry: WHB staff & students of St Mary's Inst
Open: Mon, Wed 1000-2000, Tue, Thu-Fri 1000-1700
Subj: medicine; health care *Collns: Bks & Pamphs:* official pubns (EU, Govt Depts, Health Boards etc) *Co-op Schemes:* Irish Healthcare Libs, other WHB libs
Equip: computers (incl internet) *Online:* Medline, Cochrane, CINAHL, CancerLit, Healthstar & others
Classn: DDC *Auto Sys:* Heritage

Castlerea

IS15

Clonalis House Library

Clonalis, Castlerea, Co Roscommon, Ireland (*tel & fax:* 0907-20014)
Email: clonalis@iol.ie

Chief: Libn: Mrs M. O'Connor
Entry: ref; by appt only *Open:* Mon-Fri 1030-1600
Subj: lit; geog; hist *Collns: Archvs:* social & historical colln of MSS
Further Info: This is a private colln located in a private house, but to which the public may come & carry out rsrch

Cavan

IS16 ✚

Cavan General Hospital, Medical Library

Lisdarn, Cavan, Co Cavan, Ireland (049-437-6114; *fax:* 049-433-1525)
Email: cavan.library@nehb.ie
Internet: http://www.nehb.ie/

Gov Body: North Eastern Health Board *Chief:* Regional Libn: Mrs Jean Harrison DipLIS *Dep:* Libn: Ms Dympna Lynch DipLIS
Assoc Libs: other libs in NEHB Lib & Info Svc: MOTHER MARY MARTIN LIB (see **IS29**); LOUTH COUNTY HOSP LIB (see **IS162**); MONAGHAN GENL HOSP LIB (see **IS186**); OUR LADY'S HOSP LIB (see **IS190**); ST BRIGIT'S HOSP LIB (see **IS1**); ST DAVNET'S HOSP LIB (see **IS187**)

Entry: NEHB staff only *Open:* Mon 0930-1930, Tue-Fri 0930-1730
Subj: medical ethics; psy; public health; child care; religion; sociology; medicine; nursing; mgmt
Collns: Bks & Pamphs: annual reports of Health Boards, hosps & other orgs; svc plans; legislation
Archvs: NEHB minutes *Other:* video colln, incl MRCP & Telemed *Co-op Schemes:* BLDSC, IHSLG
Equip: fax, copier, 6 computers (all with wd-proc & CD-ROM, 1 with internet) *Online:* Medline, CINAHL, Cochrane, PsycInfo, DARE, BNI; access free *Svcs:* info, ref
Stock: bks/c1000-1500; periodcls/55; pamphs/various; videos/30-40; CD-ROMs/10
Classn: DDC *Auto Sys:* Heritage
Staff: Libns: 1 *Non-Prof:* 1

Cork

IS17 🏛

Central Statistics Office Library

Skehard Rd, Cork, Ireland (021-453-5000; *fax:* 021-453-5555)
Email: info@cso.ie
Internet: http://www.cso.ie/

Chief: Exec Offcr: Ms Deirdre O Reardon
Open: Mon-Fri 0930-1245, 1430-1645
Subj: statistics; statistical rsrch
Svcs: info, ref *Stock:* bks/20000

IS18

Cork Euro Information Centre

Cork Chamber of Commerce, Fitzgerald House, Summerhill North, Cork, Ireland (021-450-9044; *fax:* 021-450-8568)
Email: tegwyn@corkchamber.ie
Internet: http://www.corkchamber.ie/

Gov Body: European Commission & Cork Chamber of Commerce *Chief:* Mgr: Ms Kate Geary *Dep:* Info Offcr: Mr Tegwyn Stephenson
Subj: business info; European info *Collns: Bks & Pamphs:* EU reports & pubns

IS19

Cork Institute of Technology Library

Rossa Ave, Bishopstown, Cork, Ireland (021-432-6501/2; *fax:* 021-454-5343)
Email: ddelaney@cit.ie
Internet: http://www.cit.ie/

Chief: Libn: Mr Derry Delaney BA, DipLIS *Dep:* Asst Libns: Mr Michael Costello BA, DipLIS & Ms Colette Fenton MSc, DipLIS
Assoc Libs: CRAWFORD COLL OF ART & DESIGN LIB (see **IS22**); CORK SCHOOL OF MUSIC LIB, Union Quay, Cork, Co Cork
Open: term: Mon-Fri 0915-2145, Sat 0930-1700; vac: Mon-Fri 0915-1730
Subj: all subjs; undergrad; postgrad *Co-op Schemes:* ILL
Equip: video viewers, 4 copiers, 40+ computers (incl wd-proc, internet & CD-ROM) *Svcs:* info, ref, biblio
Stock: bks/60000; periodcls/550
Classn: DDC *Auto Sys:* Millennium
Staff: 16.5 in total

IS20

Cork Public Museum, Library and Archives

Fitzgerald Pk, Mardyke, Cork, Co Cork, Ireland (021-427-0679; *fax:* 021-427-0931)
Email: museum@corkcorp.ie

(Cork Public Museum, Lib & Archvs cont)
Type: local authority *Gov Body:* Cork County Council (see **IP5**) *Chief:* Curator: Ms Stella Cherry *Dep:* Asst: Ms Samantha Melia
Entry: no entry conditions, but adv appt preferred for rsrch *Open:* Mon-Fri 1100-1300, 1415-1700 (-1800 Jun-Aug), Sun 1500-1700
Subj: local study (Cork City & County), mainly archaeo & hist *Collns:* Archvs: political hist (esp 1916-22), incl Peter Barry Colln (correspondence to & from Michael Collins); social hist (wide-ranging but mainly 18C-20C); archaeo archvs from recent excavations
Equip: fax, copier, 2 computers (incl wd-proc & CD-ROM) *Svcs:* info, ref

IS21

Cork University Hospital, Medical Library

Wilton Rd, Cork, Co Cork, Ireland (021-490-2976; *fax:* 021-434-5826)
Email: CUH.Library@ucc.ie
Internet: http://booleweb.ucc.ie

Gov Body: Univ Coll Cork (see **IS27**) *Chief:* Medical Libn: Ms Rosarii Buttimer (r.buttimer@ ucc.ie) *Other Snr Staff:* Nursing & Paramedical Libn: Ms Catherine Clehane (c.clehane@ucc.ie); Snr Lib Asst: Ms Anne Foley (a.foley@ucc.ie)
Entry: UCC staff & students; registered Southern Health Board staff from Cork Univ Hosp, St Finbarr's Hosp & Erinville Hosp; other healthcare profs may apply as external readers *Open:* Mon-Fri 0900-2030
Subj: medicine; nursing; health *Co-op Schemes:* BLDSC, Irish Healthcare Libs
Equip: 2 copiers, 9 computers *Online:* Biological Abstracts, CINAHL, Cochrane, ECO, ERIC, FSTA, Index to Theses, Medline, PsycInfo, Science Direct, World of Science

IS22

Crawford College of Art and Design Library

Sharman Crawford St, Cork, Co Cork, Ireland (021-496-6777; *fax:* 021-496-2267)
Email: mkenneally@cit.ie
Internet: http://www.cit.ie/

Gov Body: Cork Inst of Tech (see **IS19**) *Chief:* Snr Lib Asst: Mrs Margaret Kenneally *Dep:* Lib Asst (FT): Mr Francis Moore; Lib Asst (PT): Mr Charles Clarke
Assoc Libs: SLIDE LIB, at same addr
Entry: Coll students have ref & borrowing rights; external borrowers are limited to ref facilities during term, but summer membership is available Jun-Aug *Open:* term: Mon-Thu 1000-2000, Fri 0945-1645; vac: Mon-Fri 0945-1645
Subj: all subjs, esp: arts; design; fashion; art hist; arch; sculpture; ceramics; textiles; painting; print; photography *Collns:* Bks & Pamphs: artists' bks; art bks *Co-op Schemes:* ILL
Equip: video viewer, copier, computers (incl internet) *Svcs:* info, ref
Stock: bks/14000; periodcls/55; slides/30000 (in Slide Library); videos/100
Classn: DDC *Auto Sys:* Urica
Staff: Non-Prof: 2.5

IS23

The Crawford Municipal Art Gallery

Emmet Pl, Cork, Ireland (021-427-3377; *fax:* 021-480-5043)
Email: crawfordinfo@eircom.net
Internet: http://www.crawfordartgallery.com/

Gov Body: City of Cork Vocational Edu Cttee
Chief: The Curator
Entry: admission to lib for rsrch purposes by permission from curator *Open:* Mon-Sat 1000-1700; closed Sun & bank hols
Subj: arts
Stock: bks/1500; periodcls/3; slides/3000; videos/50

IS24

Erinville Hospital Library

Western Rd, Cork, Co Cork, Ireland (021-275211; *fax:* 021-275502)

Gov Body: Univ Coll Cork (see **IS27**)
Assoc Libs: UNIV COLL HOSP CORK, MEDICAL LIB (see **IS21**)
Entry: staff & students at hosp *Open:* Mon-Fri 0900-1700
Subj: medicine; obstetrics; gynaecology
Equip: video viewers, computers (to be acquired soon)
Further Info: Small hosp lib with limited facilities, although this currently changing

IS25 ✚

Mercy Hospital Medical Library

Grenville Pl, Cork, Co Cork, Ireland (021-427-1971; *fax:* 021-427-8815)
Email: library@mercy-hospital-cork.ie

Gov Body: Univ Coll Cork (see **IS27**) *Chief:* Libn: Mr Joseph Murphy BA, HDipEd, BSc(LIS) (joe.murphy@ucc.ie) *Dep:* Lib Asst: Ms Pamela Dummigan
Entry: staff & students of Mercy Hosp & Univ Coll Cork *Open:* Mon-Fri 0900-1700
Subj: medicine; nursing *Co-op Schemes:* Irish Healthcare Libs Network ILLs
Equip: fax, copier, 8 computers (all with wd-proc, internet & CD-ROM) *Online:* Medline, CINAHL (no charge) *Svcs:* info, ref, biblio
Stock: bks/1400; periodcls/60
Classn: DDC *Staff:* Libns: 1 *Non-Prof:* 1 *Exp:* IR£17000 (1999-2000)

IS26 ⚷ ✚

Potel Library

Bon Secours Hosp, College Rd, Cork, Co Cork, Ireland (021-480-1736; *fax:* 021-480-1661)
Email: tkenny@cork.bonsecours.ie

Type: private healthcare *Gov Body:* Bon Secours Healthcare System *Chief:* Libn: Ms Tara Kenny BSc, HDipLIS
Entry: hosp employees & students *Open:* Mon-Fri 0900-1700
Subj: social sci; medicine; healthcare *Co-op Schemes:* BLDSC, BMA, Health Scis Libs Group (Ireland)
Equip: fax, copier, video viewer, 4 computers (all with wd-proc & internet, 1 with CD-ROM) *Online:* Medline, CINAHL *Svcs:* info, ref, biblio
Stock: bks/2000+; periodcls/50
Classn: DDC *Staff:* Libns: 1 *Exp:* IR£30000 (1999-2000)

IS27

University College Cork, Boole Library

College Rd, Cork, Ireland (021-490-2794; *fax:* 021-427-3428)
Email: library@ucc.ie
Internet: http://booleweb.ucc.ie/

Chief: Libn: Mr John Fitzgerald (j.fitzgerald@ ucc.ie) *Dep:* Dep Libn (User Svcs): Mr Seamus McMahon (s.mcmahon@ucc.ie); Dep Libn (Support Svcs): Mr Ned Fahy (n.fahy@ucc.ie)
Assoc Libs: CORK UNIV HOSP, MEDICAL LIB (see **IS21**); BOOLE LIB ARCHVS SVC (see **IA21**); SPECIAL COLLNS, addr as above, Special Collns Libn: Ms Helen Davis (021-490-2282; *fax:* 021-427-3428; *email:* specialcollections@ucc.ie)
Entry: student or staff, of Univ; external membership available (various indiv & corporate fees) *Open:* 1st term: Mon-Thu 0830-2145, Fri 0830-2045, Sat 1000-1245; 2nd & 3rd terms: Mon-Thu 0830-2215, Fri 0830-2115, Sat 1000-1745 (-2145 in 3rd term), Sun (Mar-May) 1000-1745; summer vac: Mon-Fri 0830-1615, Sat 1000-1245; Xmas & Easter vacs: hrs may vary
Subj: all subjs; undergrad; postgrad *Collns:* Bks & Pamphs: EDC; Irish govt pubns; pre-1850 bks (c13000 bks & pamphs); St Fin Barres Cathedral Lib (3000 bks & pamphs); Torna Colln (Celtic studies, bks, journals & MSS); Munster Printing Colln; X Colln (rare post-1850 bks); Arnold Bax Colln (memorabilia); Cooke Lib (Hispanic studies, 4000 vols); Corkery Colln; de Courcy Ireland Colln; Friedlander Colln; Hawtin Bequest (socialism, economic hist, 8000 vols); Humour Colln; Langlands Colln; O'Kelly Offprint Colln (archaeo, 2000+offprints); O Riordain Colln; Senft Memorial Colln (social sci), 3500 vols); Cork Univ Press pubns; Attic Press pubns; various Irish journals; Irish & British parliamentary & state papers *Other:* primary sources for study of liturgy, hagiography & other aspects of medieval studies; various Gaelic & English MSS; maps (MSS, printed & m-form); other cartographical MSS; calendars & rolls; Griffith Valuation; censuses & surveys; newspapers (mainly on m-film) *Co-op Schemes:* BLDSC, ILL
Equip: 5 m-reader/printers, video viewers, copiers, computers (incl CD-ROM), audio listening booths *Online:* ABI/Inform, Analytical Abstracts, Biological Abstracts, BHI, CAB Abstracts, CETEDOC, CINAHL, Cochrane, ENKI, ERIC, ESTC, FactFinder, FAME, Food Science & Technology Abstracts, GeoBase, GPO, Historical Abstracts, Iconda, Inspec, JSTOR, Lexis-Nexis, Medline, MLA, OCLC FirstSearch, Philosopher's Index, PsycInfo, SIGLE, Social Sciences Index, Web of Science & others
Stock: bks/600000; periodcls/4000; videos/1744; AVs/3840
Classn: DDC *Auto Sys:* Innopac
Pubns: UCC Library News (2 pa); The Online Library (quarterly newsletter); resource guides
Staff: 120 in total (incl 6 at Medical Lib)

Curragh

IS28

Defence Forces Library

Defence Forces Training Centre, Curragh Camp, Curragh, Co Kildare, Ireland (*tel & fax:* 045-445871)
Email: dfl92@hotmail.com

Type: military *Gov Body:* Defence Forces HQ/ Dept of Defence *Chief:* Offcr in Charge: Comdt (Major) Rory Hynes BA, HDipLIS
Assoc Libs: THE MILITARY ARCHVS (see **IA45**)
Entry: membs only *Open:* Mon-Fri 0900-1700
Subj: generalities; phil; psy; lang; sci; maths; tech; geog; hist; military studies; military hist *Collns:* Bks & Pamphs: An Cosantoir (Defence Forces magazine) *Co-op Schemes:* ILL

Equip: 2 copiers, fax, 2 video viewers, 12 computers (all with wd-proc & CD-ROM, 8 with internet) *Offcr-in-Charge:* Comdt Rory Hynes, as above *Svcs:* info, ref, biblio, indexing, abstracting *Stock:* bks/10000; periodcls/60; videos/400; CD-ROMs/400 *Acqs Offcr:* Comdt Rory Hynes, as above *Classn:* DDC *Auto Sys:* InMagic *Staff:* Libns: 2 *Other Prof:* 3 *Non-Prof:* 2 *Exp:* €38000 (1999-2000); €38000 (2000-01)

Drogheda

IS29
North Eastern Health Board, Mother Mary Martin Library
Our Lady of Lourdes Hosp, Drogheda, Co Louth, Ireland (041-984-3696; *fax:* 041-984-3626) *Email:* linda.halton@nehb.ie *Internet:* http://www.nehb.ie/

Gov Body: North Eastern Health Board *Chief:* Regional Libn: Ms Jean Harrison BA, DipLib, DipIS *Dep:* Libn: Ms Linda Halton BA(Hons) *Assoc Libs:* other libs in NEHB Lib & Info Svc: CAVAN GENL HOSP LIB (see **IS16**); LOUTH COUNTY HOSP LIB (see **IS162**); MONAGHAN GENL HOSP LIB (see **IS186**); OUR LADY'S HOSP LIB (see **IS190**); ST BRIGIT'S HOSP LIB (see **IS1**); ST DAVNET'S HOSP LIB (see **IS187**) *Entry:* Health Board employees & GPs in area *Open:* Mon, Wed 0930-2000, Tue, Thu 0930-1800, Fri 0930-1700 *Subj:* psy; social sci; medicine; midwifery *Collns:* Bks & Pamphs: midwifery colln *Co-op Schemes:* Irish Health Libs Network, NULJ (UK), ILL *Equip:* video viewer, 2 copiers, clr copier, fax, 9 computers (all with wd-proc, internet & CD-ROM), digital camera, ultralite, clr printers, scanner, 2 laptops, 2 projectors *Online:* Infotrac, Medline, CINAHL, Cochrane, PsycInfo, BNI, Best Evidence, Proquest (all internet based) *Svcs:* info, ref, biblio, indexing, abstracting, internet & CD-ROM database training *Stock:* bks/c6000; periodcls/c145; videos/150; CD-ROMs/26; some slides, pamphs & audios *Classn:* DDC *Auto Sys:* Heritage *Staff:* Libns: 3 *Non-Prof:* 7 *Proj:* developing intranet, provision of online journals

Dublin

IS30
A&L Goodbody, Solicitors, Library
Internatl Financial Svcs Centre, North Way Quay, Dublin 1, Ireland (01-649-2000; *fax:* 01-649-2649) *Email:* jclavin@algoodbody.ie *Internet:* http://www.algoodbody.ie/

Chief: Libn: Ms Jane Clavin BA, DipLIS *Dep:* Ms Michelle Harnett *Assoc Libs:* ARCHVS, at same addr *Entry:* in-house access only *Subj:* law; business *Co-op Schemes:* ILL, BIALL *Equip:* copier, 5 computers (all with wd-proc, internet & CD-ROM) *Online:* LEXIS, FT Profile *Svcs:* info, abstracting *Stock:* bks/10000; periodcls/100; CD-ROMs/10 *Classn:* MOYS *Auto Sys:* TinLib *Staff:* Libns: 2 *Non-Prof:* 1

IS31
Adelaide and Meath Hospital and the National Children's Hospital, The Library
Tallaght, Dublin 24, Ireland (01-414-4852; *fax:* 01-414-3184) *Email:* library@amnch.ie

Gov Body: Board of Adelaide & Meath Hosp, incl the Natl Children's Hosp *Chief:* Chief Libn: Ms Anne Murphy BA(Hons), DipLIS *Entry:* hosp staff & Trinity Coll Dublin Health Faculty staff & students *Open:* Sep-Jun: Mon-Fri 0800-2145, Sat 0930-1330; Jul-Aug: Mon-Fri 0800-1700 *Subj:* social sci; tech; medicine *Co-op Schemes:* Irish Health Libs Network, ILL *Equip:* fax, video viewer, copier, computers (incl 5 with internet & 3 with CD-ROM) *Online:* biomedical colln (Medline etc) networked; various e-journals *Svcs:* info, ref, biblio, user edu *Stock:* bks/5000; periodcls/300 *Classn:* DDC *Auto Sys:* Heritage *Staff:* Libns: 3 *Non-Prof:* 1.4

IS32
Age Action Ireland, Library and Information Service
30-31 Lower Camden St, Dublin 2, Ireland (01-475-6989/6001; *fax:* 01-475-6011/6008) *Email:* library@ageaction.ie *Internet:* http://www.ageaction.ie/

Type: charity *Chief:* Head of Info & Publishing: Mr Paul Murray *Dep:* Libn: Mr Gerard Scully BA, MA, DipLIS *Entry:* ref only *Open:* Mon-Fri 0930-1730 *Subj:* ageing *Collns:* Bks & Pamphs: govt pubns; rsrch studies; conference proceedings *Equip:* Online: various CD-ROMs *Stock:* bks/4500; periodcls/80; videos/100 *Classn:* John Urquhart Classn *Auto Sys:* Catalist *Pubns:* Bulletin (monthly) *Staff:* Libns: 1 *Non-Prof:* 4

IS33
All Hallows College Library
Gracepark Rd, Drumcondra, Dublin 9, Ireland (01-837-3745) *Email:* library@allhallows.ie *Internet:* http://www.allhallows.ie/

Chief: Libn: Ms Brid O'Brien MA, DipLIS *Entry:* ref only, by adv appt *Subj:* religion; mission; phil; theology; lang; tech; arts; lit; geog; hist *Stock:* bks/20000; periodcls/100; audios/24; videos/24 *Classn:* DDC *Auto Sys:* Heritage

IS34
The Allen Library and Archival Centre
Edmund Rice House, North Richmond St, Dublin 1, Ireland (01-855-1077; *fax:* 01-855-5243) *Email:* allenlib@connect.ie *Internet:* http://www.allenlibrary.com/

Chief: Libn & Curator: Br Thomas Connolly BA *Dep:* Proj Co-ordinator: Ms Noelle Dowling BA(Hons), MA *Other Snr Staff:* Alison Duck BAppSc(Hons), DipCHM; Sinead Holland BA(Hons), DipAS *Entry:* adv appt; ref only *Open:* Mon-Fri 1000-1630 *Subj:* all subjs; Jnr & Leaving Cert; religion; social sci; arts; biography; Irish social, political & local hist; folklore; music; Irish lang; Irish lit; Irish ecclesiastical hist; GAA *Collns:* Bks & Pamphs: McGuirk Colln (Irish & local hist) *Archvs:* archvs relating to hist of the Congregation of the Christian Brothers & its founder Edmund Rice; papers relating to Irish political & historical figs, incl: Michael Collins; Roger Casement; Eamonn Ceant; Seán T. O'Kelly; P.H. Pearse; Frank Flood; Alice Milligan; Bryan Bolger; P.J. McCall; Grace Gifford; Fergus O'Connor *Other:* photographic & political poster database

Equip: copier, fax, 6 computers (all with wd-proc & CD-ROM, 1 with internet) *Offcr-in-Charge:* Libn & Curator, as above *Stock:* bks/30500; periodcls/501 no longer current; photos/3000; pamphs/2000; archvs/10000 items *Acqs Offcr:* Libn & Curator, as above *Classn:* in-house *Auto Sys:* Heritage *Pubns:* Mud Island: A Hist of Ballybough (€12.99); Edmund Rile's Dublin: Map & Heritage Trail (€5); To the Cause of Liberality: A Hist of O'Connell Schools (€5) *Staff:* Other Prof: 2 *Non-Prof:* 2 *Exp:* no budget for stock; new stock acquired primarily by donation *Proj:* upgrading of computers, shelving, security etc (€100000)

IS35
American College Dublin, Rooney Library
19 Lower Mount St, Dublin 2, Ireland (01-676-2992; *fax:* 01-676-9457) *Email:* library@amcol.ie *Internet:* http://www.amcol.ie/

Gov Body: Lynn Univ, Florida, USA *Chief:* Libn: Ms Breda Bennett MA, DipLib, DipInfSt (bbennett@amcol.ie) *Entry:* faculty, staff & students of coll *Open:* term: Mon-Thu 0830-2030, Fri 0830-1800, Sat 1000-1600; vac: Mon-Fri 0900-1700 *Subj:* undergrad; phil; psy; social sci; lang; tech; lit; geog; hist *Co-op Schemes:* BLDSC *Equip:* copier (100 por €10), 5 computers (all with internet, 4 with wd-proc & 4 with CD-ROM), room for hire *Online:* Proquest Direct *Svcs:* info, ref, biblio *Stock:* bks/8000; periodcls/200; videos/200 *Acqs Offcr:* Libn, as above *Classn:* DDC *Auto Sys:* Voyager *Staff:* Libns: 1 *Other Prof:* 2 *Exp:* €35000 (2000-01)

IS36
An Bord Altranais – Nursing Board of Ireland, Library
31-32 Fitzwilliam Sq, Dublin 2, Ireland (01-639-8510/1; *fax:* 01-661-4419) *Email:* library@nursingboard.ie *Internet:* http://www.nursingboard.ie/

Chief: Libn: Ms Cathy Zahra *Entry:* registered nurses *Open:* Mon-Tue, Thu-Fri 1000-1300, 1400-1700 *Subj:* medicine; nursing *Collns:* Archvs: nursing archv; small colln of minute bks *Other:* nursing info files; video colln *Co-op Schemes:* Irish Healthcare Libs Journal Holdings Index & ILL Co-op *Equip:* fax, copiers, computers (incl wd-proc, internet & CD-ROM) *Online:* CINAHL, Cochrane, BNI, PubMed *Svcs:* info, ref, current awareness *Stock:* bks/2660; periodcls/130+; videos/167; CD-ROMs/3 *Classn:* RCN Classn *Auto Sys:* InMagic *Pubns:* Current Awareness Bulletin (monthly); lib bklets: Lib Svcs; Journal Holdings; Video Catalogue *Staff:* Libns: 1 *Non-Prof:* 1.5

IS37
An Chomhairle Leabharlanna – The Library Council, Research Library
53-54 Upper Mount St, Dublin 2, Ireland (01-676-1167; *fax:* 01-676-6721) *Email:* info@librarycouncil.ie *Internet:* http://www.librarycouncil.ie/

Chief: Dir: Mrs Norma McDermott *Dep:* Rsrch & Info Offcr: Mr Alun Bevan MLib, ALA (abevan@librarycouncil.ie) *Entry:* adv appt only *Open:* Mon-Fri 0930-1300, 1415-1700

IRELAND
Dublin
▼
Dublin
Special Libraries

(An Chomhairle Leabharlanna, Rsrch Lib cont)
Subj: lib & info studies **Co-op Schemes:** BLDSC, ILL
Equip: m-reader, video viewer, copier, computer (with wd-proc, internet & CD-ROM) **Svcs:** info, ref, biblio
Stock: bks/3000; periodcls/200; videos/40; various slides & m-forms
Classn: DDC **Auto Sys:** Adlib
Pubns: Irish Lib News (monthly newsletter, free to Irish libraries/info units)
Staff: Libns: 1 Non-Prof: 1 **Exp:** IR£10500 (1999-2000)
See also **IO1**

IS38
APSO Resource Centre
Bishop's Sq, Redmond's Hill, Dublin 2, Ireland (01-478-9400; *fax:* 01-475-1006)
Email: jcarr@apso.ie
Internet: http://www.apso.ie/

Gov Body: Agency for Personal Svc Overseas (APSO) **Chief:** Libn: Ms June Carr
Entry: open to public, adv appt for groups over 3 people **Open:** Mon-Fri 0930-1300, 1400-1730
Subj: all subjs; developing countries & their living & working conditions; politics; econ; edu; health; agric; travel **Collns:** Bks & Pamphs: ref colln, incl travel info relating to developing countries in Africa, Asia, Eastern Europe, South & Central America, Middle East & Australasia
Equip: copier (10c per sheet), video viewer, fax, computers (incl 3 with wd-proc, 3 with internet & 3 with CD-ROM), slide projectors, light box, TV, tape/CD players **Svcs:** info, ref
Stock: bks/6000; periodcls/120; videos/1200; CD-ROMs/23; lang packs/100; 60 tape/slide sets
Classn: UDC **Auto Sys:** GLAS
Staff: Other Prof: 1 Non-Prof: 1 3 **Exp:** IR£30000 (1999-2000)

IS39
Archbishop Marsh's Library
St Patrick's Cl, Dublin 8, Ireland (01-454-3511; *fax:* 01-454-3511)
Email: keeper@marshlibrary.ie
Internet: http://www.marshlibrary.ie/

Type: rsrch lib; Ireland's 1st public lib **Gov Body:** Governors & Guardians of Marsh's Lib **Chief:** Keeper: Dr Muriel McCarthy MA, LLD **Dep:** Dep Keeper: Canon Rev C.R.J. Bradley MA
Assoc Libs: DELMAS CONSERVATION BINDERY, c/o Marsh's Lib at above addr
Entry: open to public; rsrchers must provide ref **Open:** Mon, Wed-Fri 1000-1300, 1400-1700, Sat 1030-1300
Subj: phil; psy; religion; lang; sci; music; medicine; travel; witchcraft **Collns:** Bks & Pamphs: Edward Stillingfleet Lib (Bishop of Worcester, 1635-1699, early printed works, c10000 vols); Archbishop Marsh Colln (1638-1713, mainly 17C sci, maths & music); Elias Bouhéreau Colln (1st Libn, Protestant theology & controversy, early Continental printing); John Stearne Colln (Bishop of Clogher, 1660-1745); substantial Irish hist colln **Archvs:** rare MSS, some dating back to 1400
Equip: computer with catalogue database **Svcs:** conservation advice
Stock: bks/25000; archvs/300 MSS

Pubns: exhib catalogues, incl: Leaves from the Past: Marsh's Botanical Books (€6, 2000); This Golden Fleece: Marsh's Lib 1701-2001 (€7, 2001); From Major to Minor: An Exhib of the Largest & Smallest Books in Marsh's Lib (€7, 2002)
Staff: Libns: 3 **Exp:** no budget for acqs

IS40
Astronomy Ireland Library
PO Box 2888, Dublin 5, Ireland (01-847-0777; *fax:* 01-847-0771)
Email: info@astronomy.ie
Internet: http://www.astronomy.ie/

Gov Body: Astronomy Ireland **Chief:** Libn: Mr David Moore BSc, FRAS
Entry: adv appt **Open:** Mon-Fri 0930-1730, Sat 1200-1800
Subj: astronomy; space **Collns:** Bks & Pamphs: magazines & star atlases
Equip: fax, copier, computer (staff use only) **Svcs:** info, ref
Stock: bks/500 **Staff:** Non-Prof: 2

IS41
Austin Clarke Library
Poetry Ireland, Bermingham Tower, Dublin Castle, Dublin 2, Ireland (01-671-4632; *fax:* 01-671-4634)
Email: poetry@iol.ie

Type: arts org **Gov Body:** Poetry Ireland **Chief:** Libns: Mr Joseph Woods & Ms Claire Doyle
Entry: ref only, adv appt **Open:** Mon-Fri 1400-1730
Subj: arts; lit; poetry; criticism **Collns:** Bks & Pamphs: Austin Clarke Colln (6000 vols); John Jordan Colln (2000 vols)
Equip: copier **Svcs:** ref
Stock: bks/8000+
Classn: card index & Poetry Ireland Lib Database
Pubns: Poetry Ireland Review (quarterly poetry journal, IR£5); Poetry Ireland News (newsletter, 6 pa); PI Pamph Series; occasional pubns, incl: Watching the River Flow: A Century in Irish Poetry (IR£13.99)
Staff: Libns: 2

S42
Beaumont Hospital Library
Beaumont Hosp, Dublin 9, Ireland (01-809-2531; *fax:* 01-836-7396)
Email: bhlibrary@rcsi.ie
Internet: http://www.rcsi.ie/library/

Gov Body: Royal Coll of Surgeons in Ireland (see **IS134**) **Chief:** Asst Libn: Mr James Molloy BSc, MLIS (jmolloy@rcsi.ie) **Dep:** Lib Asst: Ms Christina Doherty (cdoherty@rcsi.ie)
Entry: hosp staff; staff & students of RCSI; fee-based external membership available **Open:** term: Mon-Thu 0900-2200, Fri 0900-2000, Sat 0900-1300; vac: Mon-Thu 0900-2000, Fri 0900-1700
Subj: medicine; health care
Equip: copier, computers (incl wd-proc & internet) **Online:** Web of Science, Medline, CINAHL, PsycInfo **Svcs:** info, ref
Classn: DDC **Auto Sys:** Aleph 500
Staff: Libns: 1 Non-Prof: 1

IS43
CDVEC Curriculum Development Unit Library
Sundrive Rd, Crumlin, Dublin 12, Ireland (01-453-5487; *fax:* 01-453-7659)
Email: eva.hornung@cdu.cdvec.ie
Internet: http://www.curriculum.ie/

Chief: Libn: Miss Eva Hornung DipBibl, MLIS
Entry: ref only **Open:** Mon-Fri 0915-1700

Subj: post-primary edu; curriculum; citizenship; environmental edu; lifeskills edu **Co-op Schemes:** ILL
Equip: 3 copiers, fax **Svcs:** info, ref, biblio, translation (French/English), editing, web site design, internet & databases searching, internet tutoring
Stock: bks/13000; periodcls/100; videos/150; CD-ROMs/26; multimedia packs/200
Classn: DDC
Pubns: catalogue of c100 pubns available on demand (updated annually)
Staff: Libns: 1

IS44
Central Bank of Ireland Library
PO Box 559, Dame St, Dublin 2, Ireland (01-434-4416; *fax:* 01-434-4087)
Email: library@centralbank.ie

Type: central bank **Chief:** Libn: Ms Mairéad Ní Bhriain ACIS, MBA, Banking Dip **Dep:** Asst Libn: Mrs Mary Macken O'Neill
Assoc Libs: CENTRAL BANK OF IRELAND ARCHVS, Corporate Svcs Dept, PO Box 559, Dame St, Dublin 2, Records Offcr: Ms Maureen Murray BA
Entry: staff; others by appt **Open:** Mon-Fri 0930-1700
Subj: generalities; social sci; banking; econ; finance; sci; maths; tech; lit; geog; hist **Co-op Schemes:** BLDSC, ILL
Equip: copier, fax, 4 computers (all with wd-proc, internet & CD-ROM) **Online:** FT Profile **Svcs:** info, ref, biblio
Stock: bks/9000; periodcls/3000; maps/10; CD-ROMs/7
Classn: DDC **Auto Sys:** Libero
Staff: Other Prof: 1 Non-Prof: 4 **Exp:** IR£68000 (1999-2000); IR£78000 (2000-01)
Proj: lib computerisation

IS45
Central Catholic Library Association Inc
74 Merrion Sq, Dublin 2, Ireland (01-676-1264; *fax:* 01-678-7618)

Chief: Hon Libn: Mr Peter Costello **Dep:** Libn: Ms Teresa Whitington MA, DipLIS, DipTRANS
Entry: membs only (annual sub: €20, conc €10)
Open: Mon-Fri 1100-1830, Sat 1100-1730
Subj: local studies (Irish Counties); phil; psy; religion; arts; lit; geog; hist **Collns:** Bks & Pamphs: Christian art (2200 vols); 1200 printed bks (16C-1850) **Co-op Schemes:** ILL
Equip: fax (staff only), copier, computer (with wd-proc, staff only) **Svcs:** info, ref, biblio, translation (French/English)
Stock: bks/100000; periodcls/54; audios/196; videos/63
Classn: Brown Classn Scheme
Pubns: Bibliographical (newsletter of CCL) & other promotional material
Staff: Libns: 1 Other Prof: 1 Non-Prof: 25 volunteers

IS46
CERT – State Tourism Training Agency Library
CERT House, Amiens St, Dublin 1, Ireland (01-884-7700; *fax:* 01-855-6821)
Email: Mary.Penny@cert.ie
Internet: http://www.cert.ie/

Chief: Libn: Ms Mary Penny DipLIS, MBS **Dep:** Ms Suzie Rafter DipLIS
Entry: ref only; adv appt **Open:** Mon, Wed, Fri 1000-1230, 1300-1600, Tue, Thu 1000-1245, 1400-1700

Subj: generalities; phil; psy; social sci; lang; tech; lit; geog; hist; tourism; leisure studies *Co-op Schemes:* BLDSC, ILL
Equip: video viewer, copier, 7 computers (all with wd-proc & internet, 6 with CD-ROM) *Online:* Emerald, Proquest, EBSCO, Catchword, WHATT
Svcs: info, ref, biblio, indexing, abstracting
Stock: bks/10000; periodcls/130; videos/175; AVs/50
Classn: UDC *Auto Sys:* Heritage *Staff: Libns:* 2

IS47

The Chester Beatty Library

Dublin Castle, Dublin 2, Ireland (01-407-0750; *fax:* 01-407-0760)
Email: info@cbl.ie
Internet: http://www.cbl.ie/

Gov Body: Trustees of the Chester Beatty Lib
Chief: Dir: Dr Michael Ryan MA, PhD, FSA, MRIA
Entry: ref only, adv appt; reading ticket required for use of Reading Room *Open:* Mon 1000-1700 (May-Sep only), Tue-Fri 1000-1700, Sat 1100-1700, Sun 1300-1700
Subj: phil; psy; religion; lang; sci; maths; arts; lit; geog; hist *Collns: Bks & Pamphs:* Islamic, early Christian & Far Eastern MSS; incunabula; early printed bks; 18C political ephemera; Oriental & Western prints *Archvs:* relating to Sir Alfred Chester Beatty *Other:* decorative arts (Far Eastern)
Equip: 2 m-readers, m-printer, video viewer, copier, 2 computers (both with wd-proc & OPAC, 1 with CD-ROM), room for hire *Svcs:* info, ref
Stock: bks/7000; periodcls/16; slides/5000; m-forms/2500
Auto Sys: bespoke sys
Staff: Libns: 1 *Other Prof:* 9 *Non-Prof:* 12

IS48

Children's Books Ireland, Library

17 Lower Camden St, Dublin 2, Ireland (*tel & fax:* 01-872-5854)
Email: info@childrensbooksireland.com
Internet: http://www.childrensbooksireland.com/

Chief: Exec Dir: Ms Claire Ranson (claire@childrensbooksireland.com) *Dep:* Administrative Asst: Ms Liz Marshall (liz@childrensbookireland.com)
Entry: adv appt *Open:* office hrs
Subj: ch's lit *Collns: Bks & Pamphs:* ch's bks published in Ireland during the last 12 years; some older bks; colln donated by Joyce Padbury; some academic texts on ch's lit *Other:* completed questionnaires of the rsrch for "What's the Story? The Reading Choices of Young People in Ireland"
Stock: bks/3000
See also **IO5**

IS49

Church of Ireland College of Education Library

96 Upper Rathmines Rd, Dublin 6, Ireland (01-497-0033; *fax:* 01-497-1932)
Email: library@cice.ie

Chief: Libn: Ms Valerie Coghlan MSc(Econ), FLAI, FCLIP
Entry: students of CICE, others by appt *Open:* term: Mon-Fri 1000-1300, 1500-1800, 1900-2130; vac: varies, check by tel for details
Subj: phil; psy; primary edu; primary edu in Ireland; lang; arts; ch's lit; all subjs of the primary curriculum catered for in methodology & at curricular level *Collns: Bks & Pamphs:* Irish Primary Edu materials *Co-op Schemes:* BLDSC
Equip: video viewer, copier, computers (incl 1 with internet, 1 with CD-ROM & 3 OPACs) *Svcs:* info

Stock: bks/30000; periodcls/50; slides/5000; illusts/250 (incl charts); maps/100; audios/200; videos/500; rec mgmt/200
Classn: DDC *Auto Sys:* Alice (Softlink)
Staff: Libns: 1 *Non-Prof:* 1.3
See also PLUNKET MUSEUM OF IRISH EDU, ARCHV (**IA47**)

IS50

Colaiste Mhuire Marino Institute of Education Library

Griffith Ave, Dublin 9, Ireland (01-805-7753; *fax:* 01-833-5298)
Email: library@mie.ie

Gov Body: Marino Inst of Edu *Chief:* Libn: Ms Miriam Lambe BA, MA, DipAS, DipLIS (miriam.lambe@mie.ie)
Entry: registered students & staff of the Inst; ALCID membs; others by adv appt *Open:* term: Mon 1000-1800, Tue-Thu 1000-2130, Fri 1000-1700; vac: Mon-Fri 1000-1700
Subj: edu at undergrad level *Co-op Schemes:* BLDSC, ALCID
Equip: 2 copiers, 27 computers (all with wd-proc, internet & CD-ROM)
Stock: bks/14000; periodcls/20 *Acqs Offcr:* Libn, as above
Classn: DDC *Staff: Libns:* 1 *Non-Prof:* 1

IS51

The Contemporary Music Centre Ireland, Library and Archive Service

19 Fishamble St, Temple Bar, Dublin 8, Ireland (01-633-1922; *fax:* 01-633-1900)
Email: info@cmc.ie
Internet: http://www.cmc.ie/

Type: music info & promotion centre *Gov Body:* funded by Arts Council/An Chomhairle Ealaíon, the Arts Council of Northern Ireland & the Irish Music Rights Org *Chief:* Info Mgr: Mr Jonathan Grimes BMusEd, MA (jgrimes@cmc.ie) *Dep:* Music Info Offcr: Ms Anne-Marie Casey BA (amcasey@cmc.ie) *Other Snr Staff:* Dir: Ms Eve O'Kelly; Promotion Mgr: Ms Karen Hennessy
Entry: open to public without appt or charge *Open:* Mon-Fri 1000-1730
Subj: Irish contemporary music of the 20C & 21C *Collns: Bks & Pamphs:* Ref Lib of specialist periodcls & bks *Other:* Music Lib (scores by Irish composers); Sound Archv (incl rare early recordings); concert programmes, programme notes, photos; press clippings *Co-op Schemes:* IAMIC (Internatl Assoc of Music Info Centres)
Equip: computer (with internet & lib catalogue)
Disabled: wheelchair access *Offcr-in-Charge:* Info Mgr, as above *Svcs:* info, ref, biblio, indexing, music consultancy svcs
Stock: audios/5000; music scores/3000; various bks & periodcls *Acqs Offcr:* Info Mgr, as above
Classn: customised catalogue *Auto Sys:* Filemaker Pro
Pubns: New Music News (free newsletter, 3 pa, publ Feb, May & Sep); Directory of Irish Composers (annual, €8.50 + p&p); free info pack
Staff: Libns: 2 *Other Prof:* 5
Further Info: The Centre is Ireland's natl lib & archv for contemporary music

IS52

Department of Agriculture, Food and Rural Development Library

Agriculture House, Kildare St, Dublin 2, Ireland (01-607-2803; *fax:* 01-678-5213)
Email: mary.doyle@daff.irlgov.ie

Gov Body: Dept of Agric, Food & Rural Development *Chief:* Libn: Ms Mary Doyle DipIS
Assoc Libs: VETERINARY RSRCH LABORATORY LIB (see **IS153**)
Entry: by appt *Open:* Mon-Fri 0930-1245, 1430-1700
Subj: agric; food sci; rural development *Collns: Bks & Pamphs:* USDA & FAO pubns *Co-op Schemes:* ILL
Equip: m-reader, copier, computers (incl internet & CD-ROM) *Svcs:* info, ref, biblio
Stock: bks/100000; periodcls/1600; CD-ROMs/15
Classn: in-house *Auto Sys:* Cardbox
Staff: Libns: 2 *Non-Prof:* 3.5

IS53

Department of Communications, Marine and Natural Resources, Library

Leeson Ln, Dublin 2, Ireland (01-619-9200; *fax:* 01-661-8214)
Internet: http://www.dcmnr.gov.ie/

Chief: contact the Libn
Entry: open to bona fide rsrch workers *Open:* Mon-Fri 0915-1300, 1430-1730
Subj: communications; telecommunications; broadcasting; fisheries; marine environment; pollution; water quality; shipping *Co-op Schemes:* ILL, EURASLIC
Stock: bks/2500; periodcls/490; maps/100; m-forms/6000
Pubns: Annual Report; fisheries leaflets

IS54

Department of Education and Science, Library

Marlborough St, Dublin 1, Ireland (01-889-2202; *fax:* 01-889-2367)
Email: noeleen_edmonds@education.gov.ie
Internet: http://www.education.ie/

Chief: Libn: Ms Noeleen Edmonds
Subj: all subjs; edu; edu policy *Co-op Schemes:* ILL
Stock: bks/c8000; periodcls/c300

IS55

Department of Enterprise, Trade and Employment Library

23 Kildare St, Dublin 2, Ireland (01-631-2135; *fax:* 01-631-2827)
Email: carol_flynn@entemp.ie
Internet: http://www.entemp.ie/

Chief: Lib Mgr: Ms Carol Flynn
Subj: industrial development; tech; law; industry regulation; industrial relations; health & safety

IS56

Department of Foreign Affairs Library

Neagh House, 79-80 St Stephens Green, Dublin 2, Ireland (01-408-2836; *fax:* 01-478-5937)
Email: orla.gillen@iveagh.irlgov.ie
Internet: http://www.irlgov.ie/iveagh/

Gov Body: Dept of Foreign Affairs *Chief:* Libn: Ms Órla Gillen BA, MLIS
Entry: adv appt; access for non-membs of Dept is dependent on availability or otherwise of resources elsewhere *Open:* Mon-Fri 0915-1730
Subj: generalities; phil; psy; religion; social sci; lang; tech; arts; lit; geog; hist; internatl affairs; law; econ *Collns: Bks & Pamphs:* UN Colln; EU Colln; Legal Colln; lang learning materials *Co-op Schemes:* BLDSC

 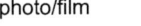

(Dept of Foreign Affairs Lib cont)
Equip: copier, clr copier, fax, video viewer, computer (with wd-proc, internet & CD-ROM)
Online: Factiva, Eurolaw, Oxford Analytica, EIO Country Reports, Profiles, various online journals
Svcs: info, ref, biblio
Stock: bks/20000; periodcls/200; pamphs/1000; maps/100; audios/50; videos/30; CD-ROMs/20
Acqs Offcr: Libn, as above
Classn: DDC *Auto Sys:* Unicorn
Staff: Libns: 1 *Non-Prof:* 4

IS57
Department of Health and Children, Library and Information Unit
Hawkins House, Hawkins St, Dublin 2, Ireland (01-671-4711)
Email: queries@health.irlgov.ie
Internet: http://www.doh.ie/

Gov Body: Dept of Health & Children
Entry: Dept of Health staff, others by adv appt
Subj: health care policy; mgmt; admin; econ; public health; social policy; public admin
Further Info: The Lib & Info Unit is being reorganised, to reopen in late 2003

IS58
Department of Social and Family Affairs, Library and Information Service
Floor 5, Aras Mhic Dhiarmada, Store St, Dublin 1, Ireland (01-704-3686)
Internet: http://portal.welfare.ie/

Chief: Libn: Ms Mary Lynam
Entry: ref only; adv appt
Subj: social policy; social svcs; employment; welfare
Stock: bks/12000; periodcls/100

IS59
Dublin Business School Library
13-14 Aungier St, Dublin 2, Ireland (01-417-7572/1; *fax:* 01-417-7595)
Email: library@dbs.edu
Internet: http://www.dbs.edu/lib/

Gov Body: Dublin Business School *Chief:* Acting Libn: Ms Aoife Doherty BA(Hons), MLIS (aoife@dbs.edu) *Dep:* Michèle Cashman BSocSc, MLIS (michele@dbs.edu)
Assoc Libs: DUBLIN BUSINESS SCHOOL ARTS LIB, 34-35 South William St, Dublin 2, Ireland, Libn: Ms Ritamary Bolton (01-648-5485)
Open: Mon-Thu 0830-2130, Fri 1000-1715, Sat 1000-1400
Subj: generalities; psy; social sci; lang; tech; accountancy; banking; business *Collns: Bks & Pamphs:* manuals for prof accountancy & banking exams, e.g., ACCA, CIMA, IATI *Co-op Schemes:* BLDSC, ILL with Trinity Coll Dublin Info Svc (see IL2)
Equip: copiers (50 units for €3), 6 computers (incl 4 with internet, 4 with CD-ROM & 2 OPACs)
Online: OPAC on website *Offcr-in-Charge:* Acting Libn, as above *Svcs:* info, ref, biblio

Stock: bks/10000; periodcls/100; videos/20; CD-ROMs/250 *Acqs Offcr:* Acting Libn, as above
Classn: DDC *Auto Sys:* Heritage
Staff: Libns: 3 *Non-Prof:* 4 *Exp:* IRE39900 (1999-2000)

IS60
Dublin City University Library
Dublin City Univ, Glasnevin, Dublin 9, Ireland (01-704-5212; *fax:* 01-704-5602)
Email: infodesk@dcu.ie
Internet: http://www.dcu.ie/~library/

Gov Body: Dublin City Univ *Chief:* Dir of Lib Svcs: Mr Paul Sheehan BA, LLB (paul.sheehan@dcu.ie) *Other Snr Staff:* Sub Libn (Info & Public Svcs): Ms Ellen Breen (ellen.breen@dcu.ie); Sub Libn (Colln Mgmt Svcs): Ms Geraldine McFeeley (geraldine.mcfeeley@dcu.ie); Sub Libn (Planning & Admin Svcs): Ms Miriam Corcoran (miriam.corcoran@dcu.ie)
Assoc Libs: ST PATRICK'S COLL LIB, Drumcondra (edu, see IS143)
Entry: membs of Univ; external membership available (grads of University €38 pa, others €126 pa); ref access for other 3rd level students via ALCID & other schemes; membs of local community may also apply for membership *Open:* term & Easter period: Mon-Thu 0830-2200, Fri 0830-2100, Sat 0930-1700; vac: Mon-Thu 0830-2100, Fri 0830-1645
Subj: all subjs; undergrad; postgrad *Collns: Bks & Pamphs:* annual reports of Irish public limited companies (printed & m-fiche); indexes & abstracts colln; EU colln; govt pubns; statistics colln *Other:* OS maps of Ireland (complete); historical Irish city maps *Co-op Schemes:* ALCID, ILL, IRIS
Equip: m-reader, m-printer, fax, video viewers, copiers (card operated), clr copier, computers (incl internet & CD-ROM) *Disabled:* Kurzweil, scanners, Braille printer, CCTV, various software incl Dragon Naturally Speaking, Duxbury, JAWS & TextHelp
Online: Infotrac, EBSCO, Web of Science, CINAHL, Cochrane, Compendex, Emerald FullText, ERIC, FactFinder, Inspec, JSTOR, Lexis-Nexis, LISA, MLA, Science Direct, Index to Theses etc; numerous e-journals *Svcs:* info, ref, biblio
Stock: bks/135000; periodcls/1500; videos/500; CD-ROMs/40
Classn: DDC *Auto Sys:* Talis
Pubns: Liblink (DCU lib newsletter); DCU Lib Strategic Plan
Staff: Libns: 16 *Non-Prof:* 30

IS61
Dublin Dental Hospital, Library and Archive
Lincoln Pl, Dublin 2, Ireland (01-612-7205; *fax:* 01-612-7298)
Email: aobyrne@dental.tcd.ie

Gov Body: Dublin Dental Hosp Board *Chief:* Libn: Ms Anne M. O'Bynre BSc, DipLIS
Entry: ref only for external readers *Open:* term: Mon-Fri 1000-2200, Sat 1000-1230; vac: Mon-Fri 1000-1700
Subj: medicine; dentistry; dental tech *Collns: Bks & Pamphs:* various in-house collns *Archvs:* Hist of Dentistry Colln; JRL Archv (from 1800s) *Co-op Schemes:* Irish Health Libs document delivery scheme
Equip: m-reader, fax, video viewer, copier, 20 networked computers (incl wd-proc, internet & CD-ROM) *Online:* Medline *Svcs:* info, ref, biblio
Stock: bks/3500, incl monographs + 4000 bound serials; periodcls/83; various photos, pamphs, videos & AVs
Classn: DDC *Auto Sys:* Dynix (Horizon)
Pubns: Lib Guide; Lib Guide to the Internet Series
Staff: Libns: 3 *Non-Prof:* 1 *Exp:* IRE83000 (1999-2000); incl salaries

IS62
Dublin Diocesan Library
Clonliffe Rd, Dublin 3, Ireland (01-874-1680; *fax:* 01-836-8920)

Chief: Libn: Mr Peter M. Folan
Entry: adv appt
Subj: religion; Irish hist; ecclesiastical hist *Collns: Bks & Pamphs:* Archbishop McQuaid Colln; Archbishop Ryan Colln *Archvs:* diocesan records
Co-op Schemes: ILL
Stock: bks/100000; periodcls/300; pamphs/5000; theses/40; printed music/500

IS63
Dublin Institute for Advanced Studies, School of Cosmic Physics Library
5 Merrion Sq, Dublin 2, Ireland (01-662-1333; *fax:* 01-662-1477)
Email: abyrne@cp.dias.ie

Gov Body: Dublin Inst for Advanced Studies
Chief: Libn: Ms Anne Byrne
Entry: adv appt; academics & students of relevant disciplines only
Subj: geol; seismology; palaeomagnetism & related subjs; astrophysics; nuclear physics
Equip: fax, copier
Stock: bks/5000; periodcls/60 *Staff:* Non-Prof: 3

IS64
Dublin Institute for Advanced Studies, School of Theoretical Physics Library
10 Burlington Rd, Dublin 4, Ireland (01-614-0104; *fax:* 01-668-0561)
Email: goldsmit@stp.dias.ie
Internet: http://www.stp.dias.ie/library.html

Gov Body: govt appointed *Chief:* Libn Exec: Ms A. Goldsmith BSc
Entry: membs only *Open:* Mon-Fri 0700-2300
Subj: sci; maths; physics *Co-op Schemes:* BLDSC
Equip: 2 m-readers, copier, computers *Svcs:* info, ref
Stock: bks/20000; periodcls/120
Classn: DDC *Auto Sys:* Cardbox
Staff: Other Prof: 0.5

IS65
Dublin Institute of Technology Library
Rathmines Rd, Dublin 6, Ireland (01-402-7800; *fax:* 01-402-7802)
Email: csu.library@dit.ie
Internet: http://www.dit.ie/library/

Gov Body: Dublin Inst of Tech *Chief:* Head of Lib Svcs: Mr Warrick Price *Other Snr Staff:* Snr Libns: Ms Ann McSweeney BA, DipLIS, MLIS; Ms Ursula Gavin BA, DipLIS, MLIS
Assoc (Branch) Libs: DIT AUNGIER ST LIB, Aungier St, Dublin 2, Faculty Libn: Ms Anne Ambrose BA, DipLIS (01-402-3068; *fax:* 01-402-3289; *email:* ast.library@dit.ie); DIT BOLTON ST LIB, Bolton St, Dublin 1, Faculty Libn: Mr Peter Cahalane BA, DipLib (01-402-3681; *fax:* 01-402-3995; *email:* bst.library@dit.ie); DIT CATHAL BRUGHA ST LIB, Cathal Brugha St, Dublin 1, Faculty Libn: Mr Brian Gillespie BA, DipLib (01-402-4423; *fax:* 01-402-4499; *email:* cbs.library@dit.ie); DIT KEVIN ST LIB, Kevin St, Dublin 8, Faculty Libn: Ms Mary Davis BSc, MLIS, MInfSc (01-402-4894; *fax:* 01-402-4651; *email:* kst.library@dit.ie); DIT LEARNING & TEACHING CENTRE LIB, 14 Upper Mount St, Dublin 2, Libn: Ms Diana Mitchell BA(Hons) (01-402-7889; *fax:* 01-676-7243; *email:* ltc.library@dit.ie);

DIT MOUNTJOY SQ LIB, 40-45 Mountjoy Sq, Dublin 2, Faculty Libn: Ms Ann Wrigley BA, DipLIS (01-402-4108; *fax:* 01-402-4290; *email:* mjs.library@dit.ie); DIT RATHMINES HOUSE LIB, 143-149 Lower Rathmines Rd, Dublin 6, Faculty Libn: Ms Ann Wrigley BA, DipLIS (01-402-3461; *fax:* 01-402-7854; *email:* rmh.library@dit.ie)
Entry: staff or student of Inst; external readers by appt *Open:* term: Mon-Fri 0930-2130, Sat 1000-1700, vac: Mon-Fri 0930-1715
Subj: all subjs; undergrad; postgrad; vocational *Co-op Schemes:* BLDSC
Equip: m-readers, m-printers, video viewers, copiers, computers (incl wd-proc, internet & CD-ROM) *Disabled:* ZoomText, Jaws for Windows, scanner, Braille printer *Online:* Dialog, Datastar, STN *Svcs:* info, ref, biblio
Stock: bks/200000; periodcls/2000
Classn: DDC *Auto Sys:* Innopac
Staff: Libns: 20 *Non-Prof:* 36 *Exp:* IR£1 mln (1999-2000)

IS66
Dublin Writers Museum Library
18 Parnell Sq, Dublin 1, Ireland (01-872-2077; *fax:* 01-872-2231)
Email: writers@dublintourism.ie
Internet: http://www.visualdublin.com/

Gov Body: Dublin Tourism *Chief:* Curator: Mr Robert Nicholson (rnicholson@dublintourism.ie) *Other Snr Staff:* Administrator: Ms Maria O'Callaghan (mooallaghan@dublintourism.io)
Entry: ref only; access to bks & other collns for reading, study & rsrch is by special arrangement *Open: Museum:* Mon-Sat 1000-1700, Sun 1100-1700
Subj: lit *Collns: Bks & Pamphs:* Leslie Shepard Colln (mainly 1st ed works by Bram Stoker, works about Stoker, Dracula, vampires & vampire lit, some related ephemera); Westmeath County Lib Goldsmith Colln (illustrated eds of Oliver Goldsmith's works); John O'Donohoe Colln (1st eds of bks by George Russel/AE, pamphs by him, periodcls ed by him, bks about him etc) *Archvs:* Rhoda McGuinness Colln (correspondence & papers relating to Nora McGuinness & Geoffrey Phibbs)
Equip: 2 rooms for hire (prices vary) *Offcr-in-Charge:* Administrator, as above *Svcs:* info
Acqs Offcr: Curator, as above
Staff: Other Prof: 2 *Non-Prof:* 3

IS67
Dunsink Observatory Library
Castleknock, Dublin 15, Ireland (01-838-7911/59; *fax:* 01-838-7090)
Email: astro@dunsink.dias.ie
Internet: http://www.dunsink.dias.ie/

Gov Body: Dublin Inst for Advanced Studies
Chief: Dir & Academic Libn: Prof E.J.A. Meurs
Dep: Sec: Ms Mary Callanan
Entry: permission from Dir *Open:* Mon-Fri 0930-1730
Subj: astronomy; astrophysics
Equip: copier, fax, computer (incl wd-proc)
Stock: bks/5000; periodcls/65; some photos & slides *Classn:* own

IS68
Economic and Social Research Institute Library
4 Burlington Rd, Dublin 4, Ireland (01-667-1525; *fax:* 01-668-6231)
Email: sarah.burns@esri.ie
Internet: http://www.esri.ie/

Chief: Libn: Ms Sarah Burns BSocSc *Dep:* Asst Libn: Mr Kevin Dillon BA, DipLIS

Open: Mon-Fri 1000-1300, 1400-1630
Subj: social sci; econ *Co-op Schemes:* ILL
Equip: copier
Stock: bks/25000; periodcls/150
Classn: DDC *Auto Sys:* CAIRS *Staff: Libns:* 2

IS69
Educational Research Centre Library
St Patrick's Coll, Drumcondra, Dublin 9, Ireland (01-837-3789; *fax:* 01-837-8997)

Gov Body: St Patrick's Coll, Drumcondra (see **IS143**) *Chief:* Libn: Ms Mary Rohan (mary.rohan@erc.ie) *Dep:* Ms Eileen Corbett (eileen.corbett@erc.ie)
Entry: adv appt
Subj: edu; psy; social sci; lang *Collns: Bks & Pamphs:* Irish school textbks; ch's bks *Co-op Schemes:* BLDSC, ILL
Equip: m-reader, m-printer, copier, computers (incl 1 with internet & 1 with CD-ROM)
Stock: bks/16500; periodcls/360; m-forms/200; CD-ROMs/30; theses/60
Classn: DDC *Auto Sys:* Adlib
Staff: Libns: 0.5 *Exp:* IR£60000 (1999-2000)

IS70
ENFO – The Environmental Information Service
17 St Andrew St, Dublin 2, Ireland (01-888-2001; *fax:* 01-888-3946)
Email: info@enfo.ie
Internet: http://www.enfo.ie/

Gov Body: Dept of the Environment & Local Govt *Chief:* Libn: vacant *Other Snr Staff:* Staff Offcr: Mr Colm O'Dowd (01-888-3913; *email:* colm_o'dowd@environ.irlgov.ie), responsible for day-to-day running of lib
Entry: public info svc *Open:* Mon-Sat 1000-1700
Subj: all aspects of the environment *Co-op Schemes:* BLDSC, ILL
Equip: 2 m-readers, 2 m-printers, 2 fax, 4 video viewers, 2 copiers, 12 computers (all with CD-ROM, 6 with wd-proc & 4 with internet); no charges except for fax *Disabled:* leaflets in Braille *Svcs:* info, ref, biblio
Stock: bks/20000; periodcls/100; pamphs/100; m-forms/400000; videos/300; teacher packs/150; environmental impact statements/1300
Classn: UDC *Auto Sys:* MS Access
Pubns: 100 pamphs, incl 20 on sustainable development, all free (also available on web site)
Staff: Other Prof: 12 *Exp:* IR£80000 (1999-2000)
Further Info: ENFO is the world's largest public access environmental info svc, with 50000 visitors per year

IS71
Enterprise Ireland, Client Knowledge Service
Glasnevin, Dublin 9, Ireland (01-808-2389; *fax:* 01-837-8854)
Email: infocentre@enterprise-ireland.com
Internet: http://www.enterprise-ireland.com/

Chief: Mgr: Mr Conor Fahy
Entry: prior appt preferred but not essential
Open: Mon-Fri 0915-1300, 1400-1700
Subj: marketing; trade; tech *Collns: Bks & Pamphs:* Irish & internatl business & market directories; company info; statistics; standards; reports; journals *Co-op Schemes:* ILL
Equip: fax, 2 copiers, 5 computers, 3 laser printers
Svcs: info, ref, enqs, photocopying
Stock: bks/12000; periodcls/450
Classn: UDC *Auto Sys:* Unicorn

IS72
Eye and Ear Hospital Medical Library
Adelaide Rd, Dublin 2, Ireland (01-678-5500)

Chief: contact the Hon Libn
Subj: ophthalmology
Equip: computer (incl internet)
Stock: bks/200; periodcls/9
Staff: 1 Hon Libn (memb of medical staff)

IS73
FAS – The Training and Employment Authority, Library and Technical Information Service
27-33 Upper Baggot St, Dublin 4, Ireland (01-607-0537; *fax:* 01-607-0634)
Email: library@fas.ie
Internet: http://www.fas.ie/

Chief: Libn: Ms Jennifer O'Mullane BA, DipLib, HDipEd (jennifer.omullane@fas.ie)
Entry: adv appt *Open:* Mon-Fri 0900-1230, 1330-1700
Subj: psy; social sci; econ; mgmt; business; training; edu; careers; employment; unemployment *Collns: Bks & Pamphs:* edu & business directories; yearbks; govt pubns; all pubns of the European Centre for the Development of Vocational Training (CEDEFOP). *Co-op Schemes:* ILL
Equip: fax, video viewer, copier, computers (incl wd-proc, internet & CD-ROM) *Online:* various commercial databases *Svcs:* info, ref, biblio, translation
Stock: bks/c15000, incl reports; periodcls/100
Classn: DDC *Staff: Libns:* 3 *Non-Prof:* 2

IS74
Film Institute of Ireland, The Tiernan MacBride Library
6 Eustace St, Temple Bar, Dublin 2, Ireland (01-679-5744; *fax:* 01-677-8755)
Email: info@ifc.ie
Internet: http://www.fii.ie/

Type: Natl Film Inst *Gov Body:* Film Inst of Ireland *Chief:* Libn: Ms Antoinette Prout
Assoc Libs: lib is a dept of the IRISH FILM ARCHV, at same addr (see **IA37**)
Entry: ref only *Open:* Mon-Tue, Thu-Fri 1400-1730, Wed 1400-1900
Subj: arts; film; cinema; Irish cinema; Irish film industry; film & cinema memorabilia *Collns: Bks & Pamphs:* all film-related pubns incl pamphs & bklets produced in Ireland; Irish & internatl film journals & periodcls; *Archvs:* Lib also manages the Paper Archvs of the Film Inst of Ireland, incl: Lord Killanin Colln; Pat Murphy Colln; Tiernan MacBride Colln; Gael Linn Colln; clippings relating to Irish film industry; production notes; press packs; press releases; reports; catalogues; scripts; ephemera; Film Inst of Ireland Archvs, incl correspondence & publicity materials *Other:* Stills & Posters Colln
Equip: copier, computers (with wd-proc, internet & CD-ROM) *Svcs:* info, ref
Stock: bks/2000; periodcls/12; *Stills & Posters Colln:* stills/1197; posters/467; transparencies/298; prints/123; video prints/21
Classn: UDC (mod, based on scheme used by BFI) *Auto Sys:* InMagic
Staff: Libns: 1 *Non-Prof:* 1
Proj: ongoing indexing of clippings, 'Film Ireland' & 'Film West'

IRELAND
Dublin
▼
Dublin

Special Libraries

IS75

Fisheries Research Centre Library

Marine Inst, Fisheries Rsrch Centre, Abbotstown, Dublin 15, Ireland (01-821-0111; *fax:* 01-820-5078)
Email: amanda.mahon@marine.ie
Internet: http://www.marine.ie/

Type: rsrch *Chief:* Libn: Mrs Amanda Mahon
Entry: adv appt *Open:* Mon-Fri 0930-1630
Subj: sci; freshwater & marine fisheries *Co-op Schemes:* ILL, BLDSC
Equip: m-reader, m-printer, 2 copiers, computer (with wd-proc, internet & CD-ROM) *Online:* ASFA, Fish & Fisheries Worldwide, Justis Celex, Waves, Current Contents
Stock: bks/11274; periodcls/800; maps/100; m-forms/10000; videos/25
Classn: DDC *Auto Sys:* CAIRS
Pubns: Fisheries Bulletin (free); Irish Fisheries Investigation (free); Marine Resource Series (free); fishery leaflets (free)
Staff: Libns: 1 *Exp:* IR£90000 (1999-2000)

IS76

Food Safety Authority of Ireland, Information Service

Abbey Ct, Lower Abbey St, Dublin 1, Ireland (01-817-1300; *fax:* 01-817-1301)
Email: info@fsai.ie
Internet: http://www.fsai.ie/

Chief: Libn: Ms Anne McMahon BA, DipLIS *Dep:* Info Exec: Ms Noeleen Murtagh
Entry: ref only; adv appt *Open:* Mon-Fri 0900-1700
Subj: food sci; food safety *Co-op Schemes:* Irish Healthcare Libs ILL, BLDSC, Trinity Info Svc, Leatherhead Food RA
Equip: copier (10c per copy), 2 computers (both with internet & CD-ROM) *Online:* Food Science & Technology Abstracts, CAB Abstracts, Aquatic Sciences & Fisheries Abstracts *Svcs:* info, ref
Stock: bks/2000; periodcls/110; videos/25
Classn: in-house *Auto Sys:* Unicorn

IS77

FORFÁS Library

Wilton Park House, Wilton Pl, Dublin 2, Ireland (01-607-3153; *fax:* 01-607-3276)
Email: burkeji@forfas.ie
Internet: http://www.forfas.ie/

Chief: Libn: Mr Jim Burke
Entry: closed to public *Open:* Mon-Fri 0900-1730
Subj: business; econ; industrial development
Equip: copier, computer (with internet) *Svcs:* info
Pubns: List of Trade Journals; Economic Material Statistics; Annual Reports
Staff: Non-Prof: 1

IS78

The Friends' Historical Library

Swanbrook House, Bloomfield Ave, Morehampton Rd, Donnybrook, Dublin 4, Ireland (01-687157)

Gov Body: Religious Soc of Friends in Ireland
Chief: Curator: Mrs Mary Shackleton
Open: Thu 1100-1300

Subj: Quakerism (esp Irish); Quaker life: religious, social, family, indiv (from mid-16C); Quaker work in Irish famine relief & anti-slavery campaign; schism of the White Quakers *Collns: Bks & Pamphs:* Life & Work of Anthony Sharp (12 vol MSS) *Archvs:* wills; marriage certs; legal documents; minute bks; diaries & biographical materials; 1700 MSS documents; 3000 letters of prominent Irish families *Other:* maps; Quaker dress examples; photos
Equip: copier, m-reader *Stock:* bks/1140

IS79

Geological Survey of Ireland Library

Beggars Bush, Haddington Rd, Dublin 4, Ireland (01-678-2867; *fax:* 01-678-2549)
Email: iversd@tec.irlgov.ie
Internet: http://www.gsi.ie/

Gov Body: Dept of Communications, Marine & Nat Resources (see **IS53**) *Chief:* Libn: Mr David Ivers
Entry: open to public *Open:* Mon-Thu 0930-1630, Fri 0930-1530
Subj: geol; surveying; cartography; earth sci
Collns: Bks & Pamphs: David Burdon Colln *Archvs:* historical archvs (1845 onwards), incl archival maps *Other:* aerial photo colln (charge for viewing); Open File Mineral Exploration Databases (60000 records on m-fiche) *Co-op Schemes:* ILL
Stock: bks/8000; periodcls/165; maps/500; m-forms/200

IS80

Goethe-Institut Library

37 Merrion Sq, Dublin 2, Ireland (01-661-1155; *fax:* 01-661-1358)
Email: library@goethe.iol.ie
Internet: http://www.goethe.de/dublin/

Gov Body: Head Office: Goethe-Institut Munich
Chief: Head Libn: Ms Monika Schlenger
Assoc Libs: GOETHE-INSTITUT LIB, London (see **S1147**) & Glasgow (see **S709**)
Entry: free access; borrowing requires Readers Card (issued on proof of ID) *Open:* Sep-May: Tue-Thu 1000-2000, Fri 1000-1430, Sat 1000-1330; Jun-Jul: Tue-Thu 1200-1800, Fri 1000-1430; closed Aug
Subj: lib serves as an info centre for the Federal Republic of Germany; all bks, magazines & other lib materials relate to Germany & German issues, incl: lit; hist; politics; social sci; art; cinema; music etc *Co-op Schemes:* ILL with other Goethe-Institut libs & academic libs in Germany
Equip: copier (15c per sheet), video viewer (available for groups e.g., secondary school classes), computer (incl CD-ROM) *Svcs:* info, ref, biblio, enq svc, lending, internet rsrch
Stock: bks/10000; periodcls/50; audios/700; videos/700
Classn: DDC (mod) *Staff:* Libns: 1 *Other Prof:* 1

IS81

The Grand Lodge Library and Museum

Freemasons' Hall, 17 Molesworth St, Dublin 2, Ireland (01-676-1337; *fax:* 01-662-5101)

Gov Body: The Grand Lodge of Freemasons of Ireland *Chief:* Libn: Mr Barry Lyons BA, DipLIS
Entry: membs, rsrchers *Open:* Mon-Fri 0930-1700
Subj: Masonic & related material *Collns: Bks & Pamphs:* various Masonic bks & pamphs *Archvs:* correspondence files to & from Grand Lodge (1820s onwards); membership registers (1760s onwards) *Co-op Schemes:* will lend, though not participants in any current sys

Equip: m-reader, m-printer, m-camera, copier
Stock: bks/6000+; photos/300+; some slides, illusts, pamphs, m-forms & videos (very limited specialised stock, too small to list)
Classn: locally applied sys
Pubns: Masonic Calendar & Directory (1 pa, €5)
Staff: Libns: 1 *Other Prof:* 1

IS82

Griffith College Dublin, Library

South Circular Rd, Dublin 8, Ireland (01-415-0490; *fax:* 01-454-9265)
Email: library@gcd.ie
Internet: http://www.gcd.ie/

Chief: Libn: Mr Robert McKenna BCL, DipLIS (robert.mckenna@gcd.ie) *Dep:* Asst Libn: Ms Margaret Kelly BA, MLIS (mags-kelly@gcd.ie)
Other Snr Staff: Lib & Info Svcs offcr: Ms Jane Farrelly BA, MLIS (jane.farrelly@gcd.ie)
Entry: student & staff of coll; ref only for others (letter of recommendation required) *Open:* term: Mon-Fri 0930-2130, Sat 1000-1600; vac: Mon-Fri 1000-1700
Subj: generalities; social sci; lang; sci; maths; tech; arts; lit; hist; geog *Collns: Bks & Pamphs:* large 19C colln *Archvs:* Leinster School of Music archvs (1700s-date), incl music MSS & bks *Co-op Schemes:* BLDSC, ILL
Equip: 3 copiers (card operated), 14 computers (all with wd-proc & CD-ROM, 11 with internet) *Online:* Lexis-Nexis, Eurolaw, Justis (free to lib users) *Offcr-in-Charge:* Libn, as above
Stock: bks/12000; periodcls/50; CD-ROMs/200; sheet music/5000 *Acqs Offcr:* Libn, as above
Classn: DDC *Auto Sys:* Alice
Staff: Libns: 3 *Non-Prof:* 1.5

IS83

Guinness Ireland, Research Library

Guinness Storehouse, St James' Gate, Dublin 8, Ireland (01-453-6700; *fax:* 01-453-4816)
Email: library@guinness.com

Chief: Libn: Ms Ann O'Sullivan BA, DipLIS *Dep:* Ms Amanda Woods BA, DipLIS
Assoc Libs: GUINNESS IRELAND ARCHVS, at same addr (see **IA35**)
Entry: employees of Guinness Ltd; rsrchers by appt *Open:* Mon-Thu 0930-1700, Fri 0930-1630
Subj: brewing sci *Svcs:* info, ref
Stock: bks/5000; periodcls/200; some videos & m-forms *Auto Sys:* CAIRS *Staff:* Libns: 2

IS84

Harden School Library

The King's Hosp, Palmerstown, Dublin 20, Ireland (01-626-5933; *fax:* 01-633-0349)
Email: khharden.ias@tinet.ie
Internet: http://www.kingshospital.ie/

Gov Body: Board of Governors *Chief:* School Libn: Mrs Vivien Bond ALA
Assoc Libs: SCHOOL ARCHVS, at same addr
Entry: ref only; prior appt required for Archvs
Open: term: Mon-Tue, Thu-Fri 1315-1415, 1530-1800, Wed 1330-1800
Subj: all subjs; leaving cert; local study (Ireland)
Collns: Archvs: held in separate dept: minutes, accounts, bldg records, headmasters' reports, lists of pupils etc (1669-20C)
Equip: video viewer, copier, 4 computers (incl wd-proc, internet & CD-ROM) *Svcs:* info, ref
Stock: bks/6000; periodcls/22; videos/30; CD-ROMs/10
Classn: DDC *Auto Sys:* Softlink
Staff: Libns: 1 PT *Other Prof:* 1 PT

 academic corporate *- 550 -* governmental medical

IS85

Health and Safety Authority Library

10 Hogan Pl, Dublin 2, Ireland (01-614-7000; *fax:* 01-614-7125)
Email: information@hsa.ie
Internet: http://www.hsa.ie/

Chief: Libn: post vacant
Entry: adv appt only; ref only *Open:* Mon-Fri 0915-1300, 1415-1700
Subj: occupational safety & health *Co-op Schemes:* Irish Health Sci Libs Holdings List
Equip: m-reader, video viewer, copier, computer (with internet & CD-ROM) *Svcs:* info, ref, biblio
Stock: bks/8000; periodcls/100; videos/50; CD-ROMs/5
Classn: in-house sys *Auto Sys:* Sirsi Unicorn
Staff: Libns: 1 *Non-Prof:* 4

IS86 🎓

Higher Education and Training Awards Council, Library

(formerly Natl Council for Educational Awards)
26 Mountjoy Sq, Dublin 1, Ireland (01-855-6526; *fax:* 01-855-4250)

Chief: Libn: Ms Margaret Purcell BA, MSc, DipLIS, ALAI
Entry: adv appt, for ref or photocopying *Open:* Mon-Fri 0915-1715
Subj: undergrad; postgrad; higher edu; technological & business edu; assessment; course recognition; accreditation; curriculum development; open learning; ref colln of material on edu systems & courses
Equip: m-printer, copier
Stock: bks/7000; periodcls/240; lang packs/5
Classn: DDC *Staff:* Libns: 1 *Exp:* IR£10000 (1999-2000)

IS87 🔑

Institute of Chartered Accountants in Ireland, Information and Research Services

87-89 Pembroke Rd, Ballsbridge, Dublin 4, Ireland (01-637-7228; *fax:* 01-668-0842)
Email: reillyg@icai.ie
Internet: http://www.icai.ie/

Gov Body: ICAI *Chief:* Libn: Mr Gerard Reilly
Assoc Libs: ICAI BELFAST LIB, 11 Donegall Sq South, Belfast, Northern Ireland, BT1 5JE, Lib Asst: Ms Lyndsey Riddell (028-9032-1600; *fax:* 028-9023-0071; *email:* riddelll@icai.ie)
Entry: adv appt required for non-membs *Open:* Dublin: Mon 0930-2000, Tue-Fri 0930-1730; Belfast: Mon-Fri 0900-1700
Subj: social sci; econ; taxation; accountancy; auditing; company law; mgmt; info tech *Collns: Other:* Irish company annual reports; Irish legislation; British legislation
Equip: copier, fax, computer (with CD-ROM)
Online: CABIN (Chartered Accountants' Business Index) *Svcs:* info, ref, biblio, indexing, rsrch
Stock: bks/c20000; periodcls/160; audios/200; videos/100
Classn: UDC *Auto Sys:* TinLib
Pubns: quarterly newsletter
Staff: Libns: 1 *Non-Prof:* 2

IS88 🔑 🎓

Institute of Public Administration Library

57-61 Lansdowne Rd, Dublin 4, Ireland (01-240-3600; *fax:* 01-668-9135)
Email: library@ipa.ie
Internet: http://www.ipa.ie/library/

Chief: Libn: Ms Patricia Trotter *Other Snr Staff:* Asst Libns: Ms Trudy Pirkl & Ms Marie Kilcullen
Entry: students, staff & membs of the Inst *Open:* term: Mon-Thu 0915-1300, 1415-2030 Fri 0915-1300, 1415-1730, Sat 1030-1430, Sun (tutorial weekends) 1200-1400; vac: Mon-Fri 0915-1300, 1415-1730
Subj: public admin *Co-op Schemes:* ILL
Svcs: postal svc for distance edu students
Stock: bks/40000; periodcls/330
Staff: 6 in total

IS89 🎓

Institute of Technology Blanchardstown, Library

Blancardstown Rd North, Blanchardstown, Dublin 15, Ireland (01-885-1046; *fax:* 01-885-1001)
Email: library@itb.ie
Internet: http://www.itb.ie/library/

Chief: Libn: Mr Aidin O'Sullivan (aidin.o'sullivan@itb.ie)
Entry: staff & students; a limited number of external users may become membs at the discretion of the Libn (annual fee payable) *Open:* term: Mon-Thu 0900-2000, Fri 0900-1700; vac: Mon-Fri 1000-1700
Subj: all subjs taught at Inst; English & Irish lit; travel; hobbies; fiction *Collns: Other:* annual reports & financial statements of Irish financial instns & public limited companies *Co-op Schemes:* ILL
Equip: copier, video viewers, 20 computers (incl internet & CD-ROM)
Classn: DDC *Staff:* 5

IS90 🎓

Institute of Technology, Tallaght, Library

Tallaght, Dublin 24, Ireland (01-404-2203; *fax:* 01-404-2700)
Email: library@it-tallaght.ie
Internet: http://millennium.it-tallaght.ie/

Chief: Libn: Ms Gillian Kerins BSocSc, DipLIS (gillian.kerins@it-tallaght.ie) *Dep:* Dep Libn: Mr Jerald Cavanagh BSc(Econ) (jerald.cavanagh@it-tallaght.ie)
Entry: membs of Inst; others ref only (letter of introduction from another lib required) *Open:* term: Mon-Fri 0800-2100, Sat 1000-1300; vac: Mon-Fri 0900-1700
Subj: all subjs; genl; undergrad; postgrad; generalities; phil; psy; social sci; business; sci; tech; computers; electronics; lang; heritage studies; mech eng; arts; AV studies; lit; geog; hist
Co-op Schemes: ILL
Equip: m-reader, m-printer, 2 video viewers, 2 copiers, 24 computers (all with wd-proc & internet, 1 with CD-ROM), self-svc checkout unit *Disabled:* Kurzweil, ZoomText, text magnifier, headphones, 2 scanners for PCs, 2 electric adjustable height computer desks *Online:* Infotrac, Emerald, Science Direct, British Standards Online, FactFinder, Health & Safety Online (OHSIS), Materials InfoBase *Offcr-in-Charge:* Libn, as above
Svcs: info, ref, biblio, indexing, abstracting
Stock: bks/23070; periodcls/382; audios/507; videos/305; CD-ROMs/11 *Acqs Offcr:* Dep Libn, as above
Classn: DDC *Auto Sys:* Millennium III
Staff: Libns: 4 *Non-Prof:* 8

IS91 🔑

Institution of Engineers of Ireland Library

22 Clyde Rd, Ballsbridge, Dublin 4, Ireland (01-668-4341; *fax:* 01-668-5508)
Email: info@iei.ie
Internet: http://www.iei.ie/

Chief: Libn: Mr John Callanan
Subj: eng *Collns: Bks & Pamphs:* historical eng colln
Stock: bks/5000; periodcls/75

IS92 🎓 🏛

Instituto Cervantes Library

58 Northumberland Rd, Dublin 4, Ireland (01-668-2024; *fax:* 01-668-8416)
Email: bibdub@cervantes.es
Internet: http://www.cervantes.es/

Gov Body: Spanish Govt *Chief:* Head Libn: Mr Santiago Díaz-Jove *Other Snr Staff:* Ms Elisabet Romero
Assoc Libs: INSTITUTO CERVANTES LIB, London (see **S1210**); INSTITUTO CERVANTES LIB, 322-330 (Unit 8) Deansgate, Campfield Ave Arcade, Manchester, M3 4FN (0161-661-4210)
Entry: open to public for ref & lending *Open:* Mon-Thu 1030-1400, 1600-1945, Fri 1000-1400
Subj: Spain & Latin America: Spanish lang; Spanish lit; hist; arts; social scis *Collns: Bks & Pamphs:* Spanish lang teaching resources; genl ref colln; works by Spanish authors *Co-op Schemes:* ILL
Equip: copier (10c per sheet), 2 computers (incl CD-ROM) *Svcs:* info, ref, biblio
Stock: bks/10500; periodcls/15; audios/600; videos/1200; DVDs/400 *Acqs Offcr:* Head Libn, as above
Classn: UDC
Staff: Libns: 1 *Other Prof:* 1 *Non-Prof:* 1

IS93 🔑

Irish Deaf Society Library

30 Blessington St, Dublin 7, Ireland (01-860-1878; *fax:* 01-860-1960)
Email: ids@indigo.ie
Internet: http://indigo.ie/~ids/

Gov Body: Irish Deaf Soc
Open: Mon-Fri 0900-1700
Subj: psy; social sci; sign lang; lit; hist; deaf issues
Equip: fax, copier *Svcs:* info, ref
Stock: various bks, photos, pamphs & videos
Staff: Non-Prof: 1

IS94 ✚

Irish Family Planning Association, Information Service and Archives

Solomons House, 42a Pearse St, Dublin 2, Ireland (01-878-0366; *fax:* 01-878-0375)
Email: post@ifpa.ie
Internet: http://www.ifpa.ie/

Type: charity *Chief:* Info Resource Offcr: Ms Karen Griffin
Entry: adv appt *Open:* Mon-Fri 1000-1700
Subj: sexual health; reproductive health issues; records of parent org *Collns: Bks & Pamphs:* sexual/reproductive health issues relevant to Ireland & worldwide; IFPA pubns for genl public on family planning; IFPA submissions to govt *Archvs:* newspaper articles from 1969 on IFPA & sexual/reproductive health issues in Ireland
Equip: copier (15c per sheet), fax (20c per sheet) *Disabled:* wheelchair access *Svcs:* info, ref
Stock: bks/200; periodcls/20; photos/50; pamphs/40; videos/20; archvs/c20 file drawers
Classn: own (by subj)
Pubns: The Irish Journey: Women's Stories of Abortion (€7); Always & Never: Submission in Response to Green Paper on Abortion (€3); Facing Up to Reality: Submission to Working Group on Abortion (€3); Contraception Factsheets (5c each + p&p)
Staff: Other Prof: 1

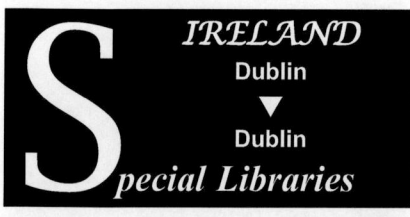

IS95

The Irish Historical Picture Co

5-6 Lower Ormond Quay, Dublin 1, Ireland (01-872-0144; *fax:* 01-878-3882)
Internet: http://www.irishhistoricalpics.ie/

Chief: Managing Dir: Mr Peter Holder MA
Open: Mon-Fri 0900-1800, Sat-Sun 0930-1700
Subj: local study (Ireland); Irish life (200 categories covering 800 townlands, villages, towns & cities throughout the 32 counties of Ireland); Irish hist; Irish geog & topography *Collns: Other:* 17000 prints from photos (many hand-tinted) taken 1895-1920 by over 80 photographers
Equip: viewing equip *Svcs:* ref, biblio
Stock: photos/17000 *Acqs Offcr:* Managing Dir, as above
Staff: Other Prof: 4 *Exp:* IR£6000 (1999-2000)

IS96

Irish Institute of Purchasing and Materials Management, Library

5 Belvedere Pl, Dublin 1, Ireland (01-855-9257/8; *fax:* 01-855-9259)
Email: iipmm@iipmm.ie
Internet: http://www.iipmm.ie/

Entry: membs only *Open:* Mon-Fri 0915-1700
Subj: purchasing; supply mgmt
Equip: video viewer, copier *Svcs:* info, ref
Staff: small lib administered by membs of Inst staff

IS97

Irish Management Institute, Information Centre and Library

Sandyford Rd, Dublin 16, Ireland (01-207-8513; *fax:* 01-295-9479)
Email: library@imi.ie
Internet: http://www.imi.ie/library/

Chief: Libn: Ms Elaine McMahon *Dep:* Mr Tom Mastin
Entry: IMI membs only *Open:* Mon, Wed, Fri 0830-1800, Tue, Thu 0830-2000, Sat (Oct-May) 1000-1400
Subj: social sci; mgmt; admin
Equip: copier (€2.50 per card), 6 computers (all with internet & CD-ROM) *Online:* InfoTrac, Proquest Direct, FactFinder *Svcs:* info
Stock: bks/8000; periodcls/200
Classn: UDC *Auto Sys:* GLAS
Staff: Libns: 2 *Non-Prof:* 1 lib asst

IS98

Irish Medicines Board (Bord Leigheasra na hEireann), Library

Earlsfort Centre, Earlsfort Ter, Dublin 2, Ireland (01-676-4971; *fax:* 01-676-7836)
Email: jim.healy@imb.ie
Internet: http://www.imb.ie/

Chief: Libn: Mr Jim Healy
Entry: staff only *Open:* Mon-Fri 1000-1300
Subj: medicine *Co-op Schemes:* Irish Health Lib Scis Group of the Lib Assoc of Ireland
Equip: computer (with wd-proc, internet & CD-ROM), room for hire *Offcr-in-Charge:* Ms Sinead Keenan *Svcs:* ref, biblio

Stock: bks/1000; periodcls/80; CD-ROMs/40
Acqs Offcr: Ms Sinead Keenan
Classn: DDC
Pubns: Annual Report & Accounts
Staff: Libns: 1

IS99

Irish Nurses Organisation, Library and Information Service

11 Fitzwilliam Pl, Dublin 2, Ireland (01-664-0614/9; *fax:* 01-661-0466)
Email: library@ino.ie
Internet: http://www.ino.ie/

Chief: Libn: Ms Muriel Haire BSc(Econ), DLS (muriel@ino.ie) *Dep:* Asst Libn: Ms Niamh Adams BA, HDipLIS (niamh@ino.ie) *Other Snr Staff:* Lib Assts: Ms Rhona Ledwidge (rhona@ino.ie)
Entry: membs of INO, non-membs contact lib in adv *Open:* Mon, Wed 0900-2000, Tue, Thu-Fri 0900-1700; also open every second Sat 0900-1300 (check with lib for details)
Subj: medicine; nursing; health *Collns: Bks & Pamphs:* official pubns relating to nursing & medicine *Other:* info files *Co-op Schemes:* BLDSC, IHSLG, NULJ
Equip: copier (€1.20 per 20 copies), clr copier, fax, 2 computers (both with wd-proc, internet & CD-ROM), room for hire *Online:* CINAHL, BNI, Medline, Cochrane *Offcr-in-Charge:* Libn, as above *Svcs:* info, ref, biblio, current awareness
Stock: bks/4955; periodcls/72; CD-ROMs/6 *Acqs Offcr:* Libn, as above
Classn: RCN *Staff: Libns:* 2 *Non-Prof:* 1 *Exp:* IR£IR25000 (1999-2000); €32000 (2000-01); figs are for total exp

IS100

The Irish Picture Library

69b Heather Rd, Sandyford Industrial Est, Dublin 18, Ireland (01-295-0799; *fax:* 01-295-0705)
Email: info@fatherbrowne.com
Internet: http://www.fatherbrowne.com/ipl/

Gov Body: limited company *Chief:* Mr Edwin Davison *Dep:* Mr David Davidson
Entry: appt required *Open:* Mon-Fri 0900-1700
Subj: arts; geog; hist *Collns: Other:* Fr Browne SJ Colln; Birr Castle Colln; early Irish photography
Stock: photos/6000

IS101

Irish Railway Record Society Ltd, Library and Archives

Box 9, Main Hall, Heuston Station, Dublin 8, Ireland
Internet: http://www.irrs.ie/

Chief: Hon Libn: Mr Tim Moriarty; Hon Archivist: Mr Joseph Leckey MSc(Econ), MSA
Entry: contact the Hon Libn or Hon Archivist
Subj: railways in Ireland; transport hist; railway law
Collns: Bks & Pamphs: Railway Law Colln (450 vols); financial reports; accident reports; statistics *Archvs:* business records of Irish railway companies; personal papers of Soc membs *Other:* railway timetables; railway photos; railway tickets
Stock: bks/16000, incl pamphlets; periodcls/600 current & no longer current; timetables/5500
Classn: DDC *Auto Sys:* LYBSIS

IS102

James Joyce Centre, Guinness Reference Library

35 North Gt George's St, Dublin 1, Ireland (01-878-8547; *fax:* 01-878-8488)
Email: joycecen@iol.ie
Internet: http://www.jamesjoyce.ie/

Type: cultural centre *Gov Body:* charitable instn
Chief: Chief Exec: Mr Robert Joyce
Entry: ref only *Open:* Mon-Sat 0930-1700, Sun & public hols 1230-1700
Subj: lang; lit (works of James Joyce); literary criticism; local studies *Collns: Bks & Pamphs:* James Joyce's works; criticism & translations of his works; bks relating to Dublin & Ireland
Equip: copier, fax, room for hire *Svcs:* info, ref
Stock: bks/2000

John Stearne Medical Library

See TRINITY COLL LIB DUBLIN (**IL2**)

IS103

The Judges Library

Áras Uí Dhálaigh, The Four Courts, Inns Quay, Dublin 7, Ireland (01-888-6777; *fax:* 01-872-6821)
Email: judgeslibrarystaff@courts.ie
Internet: http://www.www.courts.ie/

Gov Body: The Courts Svc *Chief:* Libn: Mr Joseph Donnelly MA, DipLIS (joedonnelly@courts.ie) *Dep:* Asst Libn: Ms Frances Keaney BA, HDip(Public Mgmt), MLIS (franceskeaney@courts.ie)
Entry: not generally open to the public; in special circumstances by adv appt *Open:* Mon-Fri 0930-1730; later if staff are on premises (often until 2100)
Subj: law *Collns: Bks & Pamphs:* law reports; legislation; digests; Oireachtas (Parliamentary) debates *Other:* newspaper cuttings *Co-op Schemes:* ILL, Trinity Coll Info Svc (see **IL2**), IALS, BIALL (Irish) Union Lists, Govt Libs Section Union List of Periodicals
Equip: 2 copiers, fax, 4 computers (all with wd-proc, 1 with internet & 1 with CD-ROM) *Online:* Lexis, Butterworths Direct, FirstLaw, Context Irish Reports, etc *Offcr-in-Charge:* Libn, as above
Svcs: info, ref, biblio, indexing
Stock: bks/c20000, incl law reports etc; periodcls/50; CD-ROMs/15 *Acqs Offcr:* Libn, as above
Classn: MOYS *Auto Sys:* Unicorn
Staff: Libns: 2 *Non-Prof:* 3

IS104

The Kimmage Mission Institute of Theology and Cultures Library

Kimmage Manor, Whitehall Rd, Dublin 12, Ireland (01-406-4456; *fax:* 01-455-7367)
Email: adminkmi@tinet.ie
Internet: http://www.kmitc.ie/

Chief: Libn: Ms Marie McGuinness
Entry: adv appt *Open:* Mon-Fri 0900-1700
Subj: phil; religion; theology; mission; social sci; culture; anthro
Stock: bks/14220; periodcls/108
Staff: Libns: 1 *Other Prof:* 1 *Non-Prof:* 1

IS105

King's Inns Library

Henrietta St, Dublin 1, Ireland (01-878-2119; *fax:* 01-874-4846)
Email: library@kingsinns.ie
Internet: http://www.kingsinns.ie/

Gov Body: The Honourable Soc of King's Inns
Chief: Libn: Mr Jonathan N. Armstrong BA, HDipEd, DipLIS, ALAI (jarmstrong@kingsinns.ie)
Dep: Asst Libn: Ms Isabel Duggan BA, MPhil, DipLIS (iduggan@kingsinns.ie) *Other Snr Staff:* Asst Libn (Cataloguing): Ms Ann Marie Brophy BA, DipLIS (ambrophy@kingsinns.ie)
Entry: adv appt *Open:* academic year: Mon-Thu 1000-2030, Fri 1000-1800, Sat 1000-1300; other times: Mon-Fri 1000-1800

Subj: regularly updated: law; no longer updated comprehensively: arts; lit; geog; hist; no longer updated: generalities; religion; lang *Collns: Bks & Pamphs:* 7000 17C-19C pamphs covering a wide variety of subj matter; 90 vols of printed Irish Appeals to British House of Lords (c1701-1860); rentals (1851-1914) under Encumbered Estates Act; 19C British Parliamentary Papers; Irish lang MSS *Archvs:* admission papers of barristers (1723-date) & of attorneys (1723-1867); records of the Honourable Soc of King's Inns *Other:* American Law Colln (American Jurisprudence 2nd; ALR 2nd, 3rd, 4th, 5th & Federal; Law Reviews etc.) presented by The Ireland Fund *Co-op Schemes:* 18C Short Title Catalogue; WING Short Title Catalogue; Incunabula Short Title Catalogue; BIALL Union Lists
Equip: m-reader, m-printer, fax, 2 copiers, 22 computers (all with wd-proc & internet, 2 with CD-ROM) *Online:* First Law *Offcr-in-Charge:* Libn, as above
Stock: bks/97000; periodcls/127; pamphs/7000; maps/100; m-forms/6 titles; CD-ROMs/8 *Acqs Offcr:* Libn, as above
Classn: MOYS *Auto Sys:* Unicorn
Pubns: The Honourable Society of King's Inns (free); King's Inns Portraits (€12)
Staff: Libns: 3 *Other Prof:* 1 PT archivist *Non-Prof:* 2 *Exp:* IR£74000 (1999-2000)

IS106
Law Library
Four Courts, Dublin 7, Ireland (01-872-0622; *fax:* 01-872-0455)
Email: brea@lawlibrary.ie
Internet: http://www.lawlibrary.ie/

Gov Body: The Bar Council of Ireland *Chief:* Libn: Mr Bernard Rea BL, MBA
Subj: law *Collns: Other:* Irish unreported judgements
Stock: bks/105000; periodcls/300
Staff: Libns: 4 *Other Prof:* 8 *Non-Prof:* 2

IS107
Law Society of Ireland Library
Blackhall Pl, Dublin 7, Ireland (01-672-4843/4; *fax:* 01-672-4845)
Email: library@lawsociety.ie
Internet: http://www.lawsociety.ie/

Chief: Libn: Ms Margaret Byrne *Dep:* Asst Libn: Ms Mary Gaynor
Entry: Law Soc membs & students only *Open:* Mon-Thu 0830-1800, Fri 0830-1700
Subj: law (Irish, English & EU); legislation *Collns: Bks & Pamphs:* law reports; govt pubns; Bills, Acts & Statutory Instruments; unreported judgements
Equip: copier, computers (incl internet & CD-ROM) *Online:* Lexis, own catalogue & database
Svcs: info, ref, biblio, document delivery
Stock: bks/15000; periodcls/120
Staff: Libns: 3 *Non-Prof:* 2

IS108
Library of the National Spiritual Assembly of the Bahá'ís of the Republic of Ireland
24 Burlington Rd, Dublin 4, Ireland (01-668-3150; *fax:* 01-668-9632)
Email: nsairl@iol.ie
Internet: http://www.bahai.ie/

Gov Body: Natl Spiritual Assembly of the Bahá'ís of the Republic of Ireland *Chief:* Libn: Mrs Ellen Fitzpatrick BA, DipEd *Other Snr Staff:* Archivist: Miss Diana Manuchehri BA
Entry: adv appt; ref only *Open:* any time convenient to staff & caretaker

Subj: religion; Bahá'í faith; world religions *Collns: Archvs:* records of the Natl Spiritual Assembly of the Bahá'ís of the Republic of Ireland
Equip: copier (no fee)
Acqs Offcr: Bookshop Mgr: Mrs Betsy Omidvaran (bahaibooks@tinet.ie)
Proj: refurbishment, with new rooms for lib & archvs; updating of lib & archv systems

IS109
Linguistics Institute of Ireland (Institúid Teangeolaíochta Éireann) Library
31 Fitzwilliam Pl, Dublin 2, Ireland (01-676-5489; *fax:* 01-661-0004)
Internet: http://www.ite.ie/leabh.htm

Chief: Librarian/Info Offcr: Ms Íosold Ní Dheirg MLitt, DipLT, ALAI (iosold@ite.ie) *Dep:* Lib Asst: Ms Orla Ní Chanainn (orla@ite.ie)
Entry: no restrictions on entry; lib membership available to postgrad rsrchers, teachers & academics *Open:* Tue-Fri 0930-1230, 1430-1700, closed Xmas & Easter
Subj: lang; linguistics; phonetics; phonology; sociology of lang; psy of lang; lang teaching *Co-op Schemes:* BLDSC, ILL
Equip: m-reader, copier, fax, computer (incl CD-ROM) *Svcs:* info, ref, biblio
Stock: bks/11000; periodcls/200; pamphs/500; audios/390
Classn: Lang Teaching Classn *Auto Sys:* Heritage
Pubns: Teangeolas (journal); List of Current Journals (annual); for registered readers only: Lib Accessions List (quarterly); Selected Articles from Lang Journals (quarterly)
Staff: Libns: 1 *Non-Prof:* 2

IS110
Médiathèque Tadhg O'Sullivan
(formerly La Médiathèque Française)
1 Kildare St, Dublin 2, Ireland (01-676-1732 x211; *fax:* 01-676-4077)
Email: biblio@alliance-francaise.ie
Internet: http://www.alliance-francaise.ie/

Gov Body: Alliance Française Dublin *Chief:* Libn: Ms Magalie Guigon BA
Entry: open to public *Open:* Oct-May: Tue-Thu 1000-1930, Fri 1000-1730, Sat 1000-1300; Jun-Sep: Tue-Thu 1000-1800, Fri 1000-1730
Subj: France: generalities; phil; psy; religion; social sci; French lang; sci; tech; arts; French lit; French geog; French hist *Collns: Other:* Children's Lib; Video & Music Lib (cassettes, CDs, videos & DVDs); French methodes with tapes & videos
Equip: copier, 2 video viewers, computers (incl 2 with wd-proc & 2 with CD-ROM, access free)
Svcs: info, ref
Stock: bks/10000; periodcls/41; audios/1180; videos/1145; CD-ROMs/21; DVDs/6 *Acqs Offcr:* Libn, as above
Classn: DDC *Auto Sys:* Bibal
Pubns: Living & Working in Ireland (free); Summer Work in France (free)
Staff: Libns: 1 *Other Prof:* 1

IS111
Met Eireann, Library and Information Service
Glasnevin Hill, Dublin 9, Ireland (01-806-4235; *fax:* 01-806-4247)
Email: library@met.ie
Internet: http://www.met.ie/

Gov Body: Dept of the Environment & Local Govt
Chief: Libn: Ms Jane Burns (jane.burns@met.ie)

Entry: Met Éireann staff; external users by appt with Libn *Open:* Mon-Fri 0915-1300, 1415-1700
Subj: meteorology; climatology; physics; statistics; computer sci *Collns: Bks & Pamphs:* World Meteorological Org Pubns *Co-op Schemes:* ILL (with some restrictions)
Equip: copier
Stock: bks/27000, incl reports; periodcls/50; CD-ROMs/10 *Classn:* UDC *Auto Sys:* Heritage

IS112
Milltown Institute of Theology and Philosophy, The Jesuit Library
Milltown Pk, Dublin 6, Ireland (01-269-8411; *fax:* 01-260-0371)
Email: jeslib@eircom.ie

Gov Body: Irish Province of the Soc of Jesus
Chief: Libn: Ms Patricia Quigley BA, DipLib
Entry: registered students of Milltown Inst, otherwise ref or by appt *Open:* Mon-Fri 0900-1700
Subj: undergrad; postgrad; local studies (Ireland); phil; psy; religion; social sci; lang; arts; lit; geog; hist *Collns: Bks & Pamphs:* bks & pamphs relating to religion in Ireland & Britain 16C-19C; bks by Jesuit authors; bks of the Irish Mission SJ (17C & 18C); political tracts of Irish interest *Archvs:* archvs of the Jesuit Community at Milltown since 1860
Equip: 2 copiers, 4 computers (incl CD-ROM)
Stock: bks/120000; periodcls/220; archvs/75 m
Classn: DDC, LC *Auto Sys:* Dynix
Staff: Libns: 1 *Other Prof:* 2 *Non-Prof:* 2

IS113
National Botanic Gardens Glasnevin Library
Natl Botanic Gdns, Glasnevin, Dublin 9, Ireland (01-804-0330; *fax:* 01-836-0080)

Gov Body: Dept of Arts, Heritage, Gaeltacht & the Islands *Chief:* Libn: Ms Sarah Ball BA, DBS, DipLIS (sball@ealga.ie) *Dep:* Clerical Offcr: Ms Colette Edwards BA (cedwards@ealga.ie)
Entry: for use of Natl Botanic Gdns staff & students, others admitted by appt for rsrch *Open:* Mon-Fri 0930-1300, 1400-1700
Subj: generalities; botany; hortic; parks; gardens; garden design; hist of botany & hortic; botanical art *Collns: Bks & Pamphs:* William Edward Gumbleton Bequest (fine illustrated botanical bks); Augustine Henry Colln (bks used during botanical exploration in China); Regina William Scully Colln (mainly Irish floristic works) *Archvs:* archvs relating to the hist of the Natl Botanic Gdns *Other:* Botanical Art Colln *Co-op Schemes:* BLDSC, ILL
Equip: m-reader, m-printer, fax, copier, 2 video viewers, 2 computers (both with wd-proc & CD-ROM, 1 with internet) *Offcr-in-Charge:* Libn, as above *Svcs:* ref
Stock: bks/45000; periodcls/350; slides/15000; videos/110; CD-ROMs/25; some maps, photos, illusts, pamphs, m-forms, archvs & MSS *Acqs Offcr:* Libn, as above
Classn: DDC *Auto Sys:* Cardbox
Pubns: Natl Botanic Gdns pubns available by exchange only through lib: Glasra, contributions from the Natl Botanic Gdns Glasnevin; Occasional Papers, Natl Botanic Gdns Glasnevin
Staff: Libns: 1 *Non-Prof:* 1

IS114
National Children's Resource Centre
Barnardo's, Christchurch Sq, Dublin 8, Ireland (01-454-9699; *fax:* 01-453-0300)
Email: ncrc@barnardos.ie
Internet: http://www.barnardos.ie/

(Natl Children's Resource Centre cont)
Type: charitable, voluntary **Gov Body:** Barnardo's
Chief: Info Offcr: Mr Peadar Cassidy BA, DipLIS
(peadar.cassidy@barnardos.ie) **Dep:** Lib Asst: Mr
Colm Carroll BA, DipLIS (colm.carroll@
barnardos.ie)
Assoc Libs: NATL CHILDREN'S RESOURCE
CENTRE ATHLONE, River Ct, Golden Island,
Athlone, Co Westmeath, Info Offcr: Ms Tina
Finneran (0906-479584; *fax:* 0906-479585; *email:*
ncrc@athlone.barnardos.ie); NATL CHILDREN'S
RESOURCE CENTRE CORK, 18 St Patrick's Hill,
Cork, Info Offcr: Ms Fiona Ellis (021-455-2100; *fax:*
021-455-2120; *email:* ncrc@cork.barnardos.ie);
NATL CHILDREN'S RESOURCE CENTRE
GALWAY, 41-43 Prospect Hill, Galway, Info Offcr:
Ms Fiona Morrissey (091-565058; *fax:* 091-565050;
email: ncrc@galway.barnardos.ie); NATL
CHILDREN'S RESOURCE CENTRE LIMERICK,
10 Sarsfield St, Limerick, Info Offcr: Mr Stephen
Doherty (061-208680; *fax:* 061-440214; *email:*
ncrc@midwest.barnardos.ie)
Entry: ref only; borrowing membership available
Open: contact each centre for opening hrs
Subj: children; families; childcare; childcare svcs;
childcare training; parenting; child psy; social
policy; child development; early edu; child
protection; family therapy; family support; family
breakdown; bereavement **Co-op Schemes:** Irish
Healthcare Libs, ILL
Equip: copier, fax, video viewer, computer (with
wd-proc, internet & CD-ROM), room for hire
Online: databases of childcare & parenting courses
Svcs: info, ref
Stock: bks/8000; periodcls/60; videos/150+; CD-
ROMs/20+
Classn: DDC **Auto Sys:** DBTextworks
Pubns: ChildLinks (journal, 3 pa); various bklets,
training manuals, info packs, reports etc; bk list
available on web site
Staff: Libns: 1 Non-Prof: 1

IS115
National College of Art and Design, Library
100 Thomas St, Dublin 8, Ireland (01-636-4200;
fax: 01-636-4207)
Internet: http://www.ncad.ie/

Chief: Head Libn: Mr Edward Murphy BA, DipLib,
MLIS **Dep:** Asst Libn: Ms Gemma Bradley BA,
MA, HDipEd, DipLIS
Assoc Libs: NATL IRISH VISUAL ARTS LIB,
Administrator: Ms Donna Romano BA, MA
Entry: Coll staff & students; others by written appt
Open: term: Mon-Fri 0930-2100; vac: Mon-Fri
0930-1700
Subj: social sci; arts; design **Collns:** Bks &
Pamphs: Natl Irish Visual Arts Lib (Irish art &
design) **Co-op Schemes:** ILL
Equip: 4 video viewers, 3 copiers, clr copier, 12
computers (incl 9 with internet & 3 with CD-ROM)
Svcs: info, ref
Stock: bks/63000; periodcls/300; pamphs/
c180000; audios/300; videos/300
Classn: DDC **Auto Sys:** Talis
Staff: Libns: 2 Other Prof: 1 Non-Prof: 9

IS116
National College of Ireland, Norman Smurfit Library
Internatl Financial Svcs Centre, Mayor St, Dublin 1,
Ireland (01-406-0590; *fax:* 01-406-0563)
Email: library@ncirl.ie
Internet: http://www.ncirl.ie/library_index.htm

Chief: Libn: Ms Mary Buckley BA, HDip, DipLIS
(mbuckley@ncirl.ie) **Dep:** Lib Asst: Ms Alison
Nolan BA, MSocSc, DLIS (anolan@ncirl.ie)
Assoc Libs: several Off Campus Centres (mini-
libs)
Entry: staff & students of Coll; external
membership available **Open:** term: Mon-Thu
0930-2100, Fri 0930-1930, Sat 0930-1700; vac:
Mon-Tue, Thu-Fri 1000-1700, Wed 0930-1930
Subj: undergrad; postgrad; psy; social sci;
organisational behaviour; sociology of work;
women's studies; industrial relations; trade union
studies; French lang; German lang; business
studies; human resource mgmt; accountancy;
marketing; labour hist; Irish hist **Co-op Schemes:**
ILL
Equip: fax, video viewer, copiers, computers (with
wd-proc, internet & CD-ROM) **Disabled:** height
adjustable tables **Online:** European Business
ASAP, Academic Abstracts, FactFinder, UnCover,
LEXIS/NEXIS **Svcs:** info, ref
Stock: bks/30000+; periodcls/220+; audios/90+;
videos/500+ **Acqs Offcr:** Snr Lib Asst: Mr Tim
Lawless (tlawless@ncirl.ie)
Classn: DDC **Auto Sys:** Dynix (Horizon)
Staff: Libns: 2 Non-Prof: 3
Proj: bldg of new Coll in Dublin Docklands area

IS117
National Disability Authority, Library and Archives
(formerly Natl Rehabilitation Board)
25 Clyde Rd, Ballsbridge, Dublin 4, Ireland (01-
608-0400; *fax:* 01-660-9935)
Email: library@nda.ie
Internet: http://www.nda.ie

Gov Body: Dept of Health & Children **Chief:**
Libn: Mr Michael Foley BEd, DipLIS (mfoley@
nda.ie)
Entry: adv appt **Open:** Mon-Fri 1000-1230, 1400-
1630
Subj: health & social sci, specifically disability
issues **Co-op Schemes:** BLDSC, Irish Medical
Libs ILL Scheme
Equip: copier (6c per copy), video viewer,
computer (with wd-proc, internet & CD-ROM)
Disabled: Kurzweil, JAWS, Dragon Dictate, Braille
embosser **Online:** Infotrac **Offcr-in-Charge:** Libn,
as above **Svcs:** info, ref
Stock: bks/10000; periodcls/230; audios/50;
videos/400; CD-ROMs/6; theses/30 **Acqs Offcr:**
Libn, as above
Classn: DDC **Auto Sys:** Lotus Notes
Staff: Libns: 1 Non-Prof: 1 **Exp:** €12000 (1999-
2000); €12000 (2000-01)
Proj: complete lib refurbishment completed 2002

IS118
The National Food Centre, Library
Dunsinea, Castleknock, Dublin 15, Ireland (01-
838-3222; *fax:* 01-838-3684)
Email: p.letellier@nfc.teagasc.ie

Type: semi-state org **Gov Body:** Teagasc (see
IS146) **Chief:** Libn: Mr Pascal Letellier DipLIS
Entry: adv appt **Open:** Mon-Fri 0900-1700
Subj: marketing (food industry); econ; statistics;
biochemistry; chemical analysis; food sci & tech;
food quality; nutrition; microbiology; physiology;
meat tech **Co-op Schemes:** ILL

Equip: m-reader, copier, computer (incl CD-ROM)
Online: FSTA CD-ROM, Current Contents
(diskette, updated weekly), BLAISE **Svcs:** info, ref
Stock: bks/4000; periodcls/122; m-forms/2
Classn: UDC **Staff:** Libns: 1

IS119
National Gallery of Ireland, Library and Archive
Merrion Sq West, Dublin 2, Ireland (01-663-3546;
fax: 01-661-5372)
Email: library@ngi.ie
Internet: http://www.nationalgallery.ie/

Gov Body: Natl Gallery of Ireland **Chief:** Libn: Ms
Andrea Lydon BA, MA, DipLIS (alydon@ngi.ie)
Other Snr Staff: Archivist: Ms Leah Benson BA,
HDipAS (lbenson@ngi.ie); Asst Libn: Ms Eileen
O'Brien BA, MLS (eobrien@ngi.ie)
Entry: ref only; adv appt **Open:** Mon-Fri 1000-
1900
Subj: arts; arch; Irish art (from Renaissance
onwards); Western European art (late Middle
Ages-1960s) **Collns:** Bks & Pamphs: exhib
catalogues from galleries worldwide; sales
catalogues; copies of Gallery's own pubns **Archvs:**
Natl Gallery of Ireland Archvs, incl: minute bks;
documents relating to hist of Gallery; papers of
indivs connected with Gallery **Co-op Schemes:**
ARLIS
Equip: copier (15c per sheet), clr copier (€3.50 per
5 copies), 2 computers (both with internet & CD-
ROM) **Online:** Bibliography of the History of Art,
SCIPIO Art & Rare Books Auction Catalogue
Svcs: info, ref, biblio
Stock: bks/30000; periodcls/60; pamphs/5000;
archvs/250 boxes, containing 10000+ MSS **Acqs
Offcr:** Libn, as above
Classn: DDC (mod) **Auto Sys:** Unicorn
Staff: Libns: 2 Other Prof: 1 Non-Prof: 3

IS120 ➕
National Medicines Information Centre
St James's Hosp, James's St, Dublin 8, Ireland
(01-473-0589; *fax:* 01-473-0596)
Email: nmic@stjames.ie
Internet: http://www.stjames.ie/ClinicalInformation/
NationalMedicinesInformationCentre/

Chief: Chief Pharmacist (Medicines Info): Ms
Claudine Hughes
Entry: healthcare profs only **Open:** Mon-Fri 0900-
1700
Subj: medicine; pharmacy
Equip: Online: Medline, Embase, Micromedex,
IPA (all on CD-ROM) **Svcs:** info, ref
Staff: Other Prof: 5 Non-Prof: 1

IS121
National Museum of Ireland, Library Service
Collins Barracks, Benburb St, Dublin 7, Ireland
(01-677-7444; *fax:* 01-677-7828)

Type: natl museum **Gov Body:** Dept of Arts,
Heritage, Gaeltacht & the Islands **Chief:**
Registrar: Ms Sylvia Frawley
Entry: ref only; adv appt **Open:** Mon-Fri 1000-
1700
Subj: museology; folk life; costume; military hist;
zoology; geol; decorative arts; archaeo; hist
Collns: Other: Dr J.K.S. St Joseph Colln of aerial
photos **Co-op Schemes:** BLDSC, ILL
Equip: m-reader, fax, copier
Stock: bks/23000; periodcls/260; pamphs/1100;
audios/1000 **Classn:** DDC

IS122
National Print Museum Library
Garrison Chapel, Beggars Bush, Haddington Rd, Dublin 4, Ireland (01-660-3770; *fax:* 01-667-3545)
Email: npmuseum@iol.ie
Internet: http://www.iol.ie/~npmuseum/

Gov Body: Natl Print Museum Cttee *Chief:* Libn: Mairéad White BA, MSc
Entry: ref only *Open:* May-Sep: Mon-Fri 1000-1230, 1430-1700, Sat-Sun 1200-1700; Oct-Apr: Tue, Thu, Sat-Sun 1400-1700
Subj: all aspects of printing; hist of printing; lit; hist
Equip: fax, video viewers, copier, computers (incl wd-proc, CD-ROM & internet), room for hire *Svcs:* ref
Stock: bks/c500 *Staff: Other Prof:* 1 *Non-Prof:* 6

IS123
Office of Public Works Library
51 St Stephen's Green, Dublin 2, Ireland (01-647-6023/4; *fax:* 01-661-3107)
Internet: http://www.opw.ie/

Chief: Libn: Ms Valerie M. Ingram MA, HDipEd, DipLT (valerie.ingram@opw.ie) *Dep:* Asst Libn: Ms Emma Poynton BA, MLIS (emma.poynton@opw.ie)
Assoc Libs: OFFICE OF PUBLIC WORKS FARMLEIGH LIB, Farmleigh Est, Phoenix Pk, Castleknock, Dublin 15, Ireland, Libn: Ms Julia Cummins BA, DipLIS (01-815-5908; *fax:* 01-815-5950; *email:* julia.cummins@opw.ie); collns at outstations around the country
Entry: Main Lib: Office of Public Works staff, public by appt; *Farmleigh Lib:* by appt only *Open: Main Lib:* Mon-Fri 0930-1230, 1400-1700
Subj: computing; social sci; flood relief; property mgmt; law; Health & Safety; econ; public admin; sci; tech; bldg construction; eng; drainage mgmt; arch; art; geog; Irish interest (at Farmleigh Lib)
Collns: Bks & Pamphs: govt reports; Guinness Colln (held at Farmleigh, on loan to state; Irish interest, incl lit & hist, rare bks, MSS & fine bindings) *Other:* arch plans & drawings *Co-op Schemes:* BLDSC, ILL
Equip: m-reader, m-printer, video viewer, fax, copier, clr copier, 6 computers (all with wd-proc & CD-ROM, 5 with internet) *Online:* Technical Indexes, UK & Irish Construction Info Svcs, Construction & Building Abstracts *Svcs:* info, ref, biblio, indexing
Stock: bks/24000; periodcls/1800; maps/2000; audios/300; videos/200; CD-ROMs/60; various photos, illusts, pamphs, m-forms & archival materials *Acqs Offcr:* Libn, as above
Classn: DDC *Auto Sys:* Cardbox Plus
Pubns: lib info leaflet
Staff: Libns: 4

IS124
Office of the Comptroller and Auditor General, Library and Archive
Head Office, Treasury Block, Dublin Castle, Dublin 2, Ireland (01-603-1000; *fax:* 01-603-1010)

Gov Body: Comptroller & Auditor Genl (constitutional office) *Chief:* Auditor (Corporate Svcs): Mr Derek Bracken BComm
Assoc Libs: INST OF PUBLIC ADMIN LIB (see **IS88**)
Entry: staff of Comptroller & Auditor Genl; membs of accountancy bodies; academic enqs
Subj: audit of public exp *Collns: Bks & Pamphs:* reports
Svcs: info, ref *Staff: Non-Prof:* 2

IS125
Office of the Director of Telecommunications Regulation, Library
Abbey Ct, Irish Life Centre, Lower Abbey St, Dublin 1, Ireland (01-804-9722; *fax:* 01-804-9680)
Email: info@odtr.ie
Internet: http://www.odtr.ie/

Chief: Info Offcr: Ms Patricia Dowling BA(Hons), MLIS (dowlingp@odtr.ie) *Dep:* Lib & Info Svc Asst: Ms Suzanne Behan BA (behans@odtr.ie)
Entry: primarily for ODTR staff; adv appt for others
Open: Mon-Fri 0900-1730
Subj: social sci; econ; law; communications; telecommunications tech; radio; electronics; mgmt
Collns: Bks & Pamphs: telecommunications pubns (CEPT, ERO, ETO, ITU); standards *Archvs:* ODTR Public Documents Archv *Co-op Schemes:* BLDSC, informal co-operation with local libs
Equip: copier, video viewer, 3 computers (all with wd-proc, internet & CD-ROM) *Online:* Dialog, Lexis-Nexis, Cullen Internatl, FirstLaw, ITU-T Recommendations, ITU-R Recommendations
Offcr-in-Charge: Info Offcr, as above *Svcs:* info, ref, biblio, indexing, current awareness (SDI), rsrch
Stock: bks/3000; periodcls/85; CD-ROMs/30; annual reports/100 *Acqs Offcr:* Info Offcr, as above
Classn: DDC *Auto Sys:* MS Access
Pubns: ODTR Annual Report 2000-01
Staff: Libns: 1 *Non-Prof:* 1 *Exp:* IR£85000 (2000-01)
Proj: acq of auto sys, Intranet, Lib Guide

IS126
Office of the Houses of the Oireachtas Library
Leinster House, Kildare St, Dublin 2, Ireland (01-618-3412; *fax:* 01-618-4376)
Email: lib@oireachtas.ie
Internet: http://www.gov.ie/oireachtas/

Type: parliamentary *Chief:* Libn: Ms Maura Corcoran
Subj: politics; public admin; parliamentary affairs
Equip: Online: LEXIZ-NEXIS, Eurolaw, JUSTIS UK Statutes
Stock: bks/100000; periodcls/130
Auto Sys: Unicorn

IS127
Old Dublin Society Library
58 South William St, Dublin 2, Ireland

Type: voluntary soc *Chief:* Editor: Mr Theo Mortimer
Entry: membs only *Open:* Tue-Sat 1000-1700
Subj: local studies; hist of Dublin *Collns: Bks & Pamphs:* printed bks on hist of Dublin; copies of the Dublin Historical Record (Soc journal)
Stock: bks/c3000; periodcls/1 *Acqs Offcr:* President: Rev D.A. Levistone Cooney
Pubns: Dublin Historical Record
Exp: €12000 (1999-2000); €12000 (2000-01)

IS128
Our Lady's Hospital for Sick Children, Library
Crumlin, Dublin 12, Ireland (01-409-6596; *fax:* 01-409-6049)
Email: olhsc.lib@udc.ie

Chief: Libn: Ms Suzanne Feeney MA, DipLIS
Dep: Asst Libn: Mr Ian O'Leary MA, DipLIS
Entry: open to all hosp staff & students; external readers by appt *Open:* Oct-Jun: Mon, Fri 0930-1700, Tue-Thu 0930-1900; Jul-Sep: Mon-Fri 0930-1700

Subj: medicine; paediatrics *Co-op Schemes:* BLDSC, Irish Healthcare Libs Journal Holdings List, NULJ (UK)
Equip: 2 copiers (€2.50 for 40 sheets), fax, 2 computers (both with wd-proc, internet & CD-ROM)
Svcs: info, ref
Stock: bks/1743; periodcls/100
Classn: DDC *Auto Sys:* DBTextworks (InMagic)
Staff: Libns: 2 *Non-Prof:* 1

IS129
Portobello College Library
South Richmond St, Dublin 2, Ireland (01-475-5811; *fax:* 01-475-5817)

Chief: Head Libn: Ms Nuala Canny MLIS (nuala@portobello.ie) *Dep:* Asst Libn: Ms Jane Buggle MLIS (jane@portobello.ie)
Entry: Coll membs only *Open:* term: Mon-Thu 0900-2100, Fri 0900-1700, Sat 0900-1400; vac: Mon-Fri 0900-1700
Subj: social sci; law; business; mgmt; econ; computer sci *Co-op Schemes:* ILL
Equip: 2 copiers (6c per copy); 4 computers (incl 3 with internet & 3 with CD-ROM) *Online:* Dialog Newsroom, CLI, VisionNet *Offcr-in-Charge:* Operations Offcr: Mr Donal O'Sullivan
Stock: bks/12000; periodcls/200; audios/20; videos/10; CD-ROMs/40 *Acqs Offcr:* Head Libn, as above
Classn: DDC *Auto Sys:* Heritage
Staff: Libns: 2 *Non-Prof:* 2 *Exp:* €60000 (1999-2000); €40000 (2000-01)

IS130
Radiological Protection Institute of Ireland, Library and Information Service
3 Clonskeagh Sq, Clonskeagh Rd, Dublin 14, Ireland (01-269-7766; *fax:* 01-269-7437)
Email: rpii@rpii.ie
Internet: http://www.rpii.ie/

Type: semi-state agency *Chief:* Info Offcr: Ms Marie Kelly BA(Mod), DipLIS (mkelly@rpii.ie)
Other Snr Staff: Mairead Connillan BA, DipLIS; Sandra Finlay Mulligan
Entry: ref only *Open:* Mon-Fri 0900-1700
Subj: radiation protection; nuclear sci & tech
Equip: m-reader, m-printer, copier, fax, 3 computers (all with wd-proc & CD-ROM, 2 with internet) *Svcs:* info, ref
Stock: bks/9500; periodcls/25 *Acqs Offcr:* Info Offcr, as above
Auto Sys: DBTextworks
Staff: Libns: 1 *Non-Prof:* 1

IS131
Representative Church Body Library
Braemor Pk, Churchtown, Dublin 14, Ireland (01-492-3979; *fax:* 01-492-4770)
Email: library@ireland.anglican.org
Internet: http://www.ireland.anglican.org/

Gov Body: C of I *Chief:* Libn & Archivist: Dr Raymond Refaussé BA, PhD
Open: Mon-Fri 0930-1300, 1400-1700
Subj: religion; ethics; theology; hist *Collns: Bks & Pamphs:* Watson Colln (prayer bks & associated liturgical works, 16-19C); parish, diocesan & cathedral records mainly from the Republic of Ireland (12C-20); misc ecclesiastical MSS (12C-20C) *Co-op Schemes:* BLDSC
Equip: m-reader, video viewer, copier, computers (incl 3 with wd-proc)
Stock: bks/40000; periodcls/75; m-forms/266; videos/500
Classn: DDC

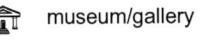

(Representative Church Body Lib cont)
Pubns: Parish Register Series; Texts & Calendars Series; A Lib on the Move: 25 Years of the Representative Church Body Lib in Churchtown (€2.50/IR£2); A Handlist of Church of Ireland Parish Registers in the Representative Church Body Lib (€2.50/IR£2); A Handlist of Church of Ireland Parish Vestry Minute Books in the Representative Church Body Lib (€2.50/IR£2) **Staff:** Libns: 2 Non-Prof: 1 **Exp:** €10000 (2000-01)
See also CHRIST CHURCH CATHEDRAL, LIB & ARCHVS **(IA28)**

IS132 ✚
Rotunda Hospital Library
Parnell Sq, Dublin 1, Ireland (01-817-1795; *fax:* 01-817-1708)
Internet: http://www.rotunda.ie/

Gov Body: Board of the Rotunda Hosp **Chief:** Libn: Ms Helen Delaney BSc, DipLIS (hdelaney@rotunda.ie) **Dep:** Asst Libn: Ms Jean Ryan BA, MLIS (jryan@rotunda.ie)
Entry: staff; students studying at the hosp; others by adv appt with the Libn **Open:** Mon, Wed-Thu 0900-1800, Tue 1230-1800, Fri 0900-1400 **Subj:** medicine; obstetrics; gynaecology; paediatrics **Collns:** Bks & Pamphs: clinical reports of Rotunda, Coombe & Natl Maternity Hosps; historical Rotunda pubns; staff pubns **Co-op Schemes:** BLDSC, BMA, IHLSG ILL Svcs **Equip:** copier (€1 per 20 copies), fax, 3 computers (all with wd-proc, internet & CD-ROM) **Online:** Medline, CINAHL, Cochrane, RCOG Dialog; no fees **Offcr-in-Charge:** Libn, as above **Svcs:** info, ref, biblio
Stock: bks/4000; periodcls/52; pamphs/20; videos/9; CD-ROMs/50 **Acqs Offcr:** Libn, as above **Classn:** DDC, NLM **Auto Sys:** Heritage **Staff:** Libns: 2

IS133 ♀ ✚
Royal College of Physicians of Ireland, Library and Archives
6 Kildare St, Dublin 2, Ireland (01-661-6677; *fax:* 01-676-3989)
Email: robertmills@rcpi.ie
Internet: http://www.rcpi.ie/

Gov Body: The Royal Coll of Physicians of Ireland **Chief:** Libn: Mr Robert W. Mills MA, ALA **Entry:** fellows & membs of Coll, others by adv appt **Open:** Mon-Fri 0930-1300, 1400-1700 **Subj:** medical hist **Collns:** Bks & Pamphs: Kirkpatrick Colln (Irish medical hist); Fleetwood Churchill Colln (obstetrics & gynaecology); Robert Travers Colln (fine bks) **Archvs:** Coll minutes (1692-date); Sir Dominic Corrigan Papers; Kirkpatrick Archv (biographical records of Irish doctors); Sir Patrick Dun's Hosp records; Westmoreland Lock Hosp records; St Ultan's Hosp records **Co-op Schemes:** ESTC **Equip:** fax, copier
Stock: bks/30000; periodcls/20; pamphs/5000; some photos, illusts & slides **Classn:** DDC (in progress), own sys still used for large part of stock **Auto Sys:** Alice (proposed) **Staff:** Libns: 1

IS134 ♀ ✎ ✚
Royal College of Surgeons in Ireland, The Mercer Library
Mercer St Lower, Dublin 2, Ireland (01-402-2411; *fax:* 01-402-2457)
Email: library@rcsi.ie
Internet: http://www.rcsi.ie/library/

Chief: Libn: Miss Beatrice M. Doran BA, DipLib, MBA, ALAI (bdoran@rcsi.ie) **Dep:** Dep Libn: Mr Paul Murphy BA, MLIS (pauljmurphy@rcsi.ie) **Other Snr Staff:** Archivist: Ms Mary O'Doherty MA, HDipEd, DipLIS (archivist@rcsi.ie) **Assoc Libs:** BEAUMONT HOSP LIB (see IS42) **Entry:** staff & students & grads of RCSI; Beaumont Hosp staff; others by appt; fee-based membership available **Open:** term: Mon-Fri 0900-2200, Sat 0900-2100, Sun 1300-1700; vac: Mon-Fri 0900-1700; Rare Bks & Archvs: Mon-Fri 0900-1230, 1400-1700
Subj: medicine; surgery; health care **Collns:** Bks & Pamphs: historical bk collns comprise c20000 vols, mainly 18C-19C; collns incl: Jacob Colln (medicine, travel, lit, 19C); Wheeler-Butcher Colln (mostly 18C historical material on medicine); Doolin Colln (hist of medicine); Barrington Colln; Bofin Colln; Logan Colln; Myles Colln; Pamph Colln (mainly 18C-19C); early medical & surgical journals **Archvs:** RCSI archvs; Dublin Hosp archvs; other collns relating to medicine in Ireland **Co-op Schemes:** BLDSC, IMLC
Equip: 2 m-readers, m-printer, 7 video viewers, 2 fax, 5 copiers, 60 computers (incl 55 with wd-proc, 55 with internet & 5 with CD-ROM), 2 rooms for hire **Online:** Web of Science, Medline, CINAHL, PsycInfo **Svcs:** info, ref
Stock: bks/69000; periodcls/650; photos/2000; pamphs/2000; videos/200
Classn: DDC **Auto Sys:** Aleph 500 **Staff:** Libns: 7 Non-Prof: 7

IS135 ♀
Royal Dublin Society Library
Merrion Rd, Ballsbridge, Dublin 4, Ireland (01-668-0866; *direct line:* 01-240-7288; *fax:* 01-660-4014)
Email: info@rds.ie
Internet: http://www.rds.ie/

Chief: Libn: Ms Mary Kelleher BA, DipIS, DipBR(Rome) (mary.kelleher@rds.ie) **Entry:** bona fide rsrchers with letter of introduction **Open:** Tue, Fri 1000-1700, Wed-Thu 1000-1900, Sat 1100-1700
Subj: arts; agric; sci; Irish interest **Collns:** Bks & Pamphs: Tighe Bequest; Preston Bequest; Hutton Bequest; Jacob Bequest **Archvs:** records of the Royal Dublin Soc (1731-date); correspondence & papers of George Fitzgerald (physicist, 1851-1901) **Co-op Schemes:** BLDSC, ILL **Equip:** video viewer, copier, computers (incl internet & CD-ROM)
Stock: bks/220000; periodcls/200; photos/2000; pamphs/70 vols; audios/200; videos/600; some slides, maps & m-forms **Classn:** DDC **Pubns:** Annual Report **Staff:** Libns: 4 Non-Prof: 3

IS136 ✎
Royal Horticultural Society of Ireland, Library and Archives
Marley House, Marley Pk, Grange Rd, Dublin 14, Ireland (*tel & fax:* 01-495-1770)
Internet: http://www.rhsi.ie/

Type: friendly soc **Chief:** Libn: Ms Natalie McGettigan MA, ALA **Entry:** Lending Lib: membs only; Ref Lib: non-membs by adv appt only **Open:** Lending Lib: evenings of Wesley House lectures (see fixtures list on web site); Ref Lib: Tue-Thu 1000-1300

Subj: hortic; gardening; floristry **Collns:** Archvs: minutes of the Royal Horticultural Soc of Ireland (incomplete, 1862 onwards) **Stock:** bks/c600; periodcls/10 **Classn:** own **Staff:** Libns: 1 volunteer **Exp:** €250 (2000-01)

IS137 ♀ ✎
Royal Irish Academy Library
19 Dawson St, Dublin 2, Ireland (01-676-2570/4222; *fax:* 01-676-2346)
Email: library@ria.ie
Internet: http://www.ria.ie/

Chief: Libn: Ms Siobhán O'Rafferty BA, HDipEd, DipLIS (s.orafferty@ria.ie) **Dep:** Dep Libn: Ms Bernadette Cunningham MA, DipLib (on leave of absence 2002-05) **Other Snr Staff:** Archivist: Ms Frances Clarke MA, HDipAS (f.clarke@ria.ie); Cataloguer: Mr Brendan Leen BEd, MA, MLIS (b.leen@ria.ie); Cataloguer: Ms Petra Schnabel MA (p.schnabel@ria.ie)
Entry: non-membs admitted on recommendation of membs, or with letter of introduction from faculty or another lib; open to ALCID card holders **Open:** Mon-Thu 1000-1730, Fri 1000-1700; closed 3 wks in late May/early Jun, 1 wk at Xmas, Good Fri to the Tue after Easter & all public hols
Subj: Ireland: local hist; Irish interest bks: hist; biography; linguistics; archaeo; nat hist; periodcls in physical & life scis & humanities **Collns:** Bks & Pamphs: Haliday Colln (pamphs & tracts); Bergin Colln; Moore Colln; Kirwan Colln; rare bk colln **Archvs:** 2500 MSS, incl sets of papers **Other:** various drawings & antiquarian sketches **Co-op Schemes:** BLDSC
Equip: m-printer (63c per copy), copier (38c per copy), 6 computers (incl 3 with wd-proc & 2 with CD-ROM), room for hire **Offcr-in-Charge:** Asst Exec Sec: Mr Hugh Shiels (h.shiels@ria.ie)
Stock: bks/50000; periodcls/1800; photos/2000; pamphs/30000; maps/110; m-forms/200; archvs/2500 MSS **Acqs Offcr:** Libn, as above **Classn:** LC **Auto Sys:** DBTextworks
Pubns: Notes on Important MSS (IR£1); postcards (20p each)
Staff: Libns: 4 Other Prof: 1 Non-Prof: 4-5 **Exp:** IR£30800 (1999-2000); €44442 (2000-01)
Proj: preservation m-filming proj (2002-08); major retrospective cataloguing proj (2002-05)

IS138 ✎ ♀
Royal Irish Academy of Music Library
36-38 Westland Row, Dublin 2, Ireland (01-632-5316; *fax:* 01-662-2798)
Email: philipshields@riam.ie

Chief: Libn: Mr Philip Shields BA(Mod), DipLIS **Dep:** Mr Fintan Quinn
Entry: ref only, by appt **Open:** term: Mon-Tue 1400-1800, Wed-Fri 1000-1300, 1400-1800, Sat 1100-1400; vac: closed mid-Jul to end of Aug
Subj: music; drama; poetry **Collns:** Other: choral & orchestral scores & parts of the Antient Concerts Soc (1834-63, acquired 1872); orchestral parts from the Dublin Anacreontic Soc (c1740-1865); Hudleston Colln of printed & MS guitar music; Monteagle Bequest; Joan Trimble Colln (printed music, historical eds of Irish traditional music) **Co-op Schemes:** ILL
Equip: m-reader, copier, 4 computers (incl wd-proc, internet & CD-ROM) **Svcs:** info, ref
Stock: bks/2500; periodcls/25; photos/50; audios/2000; videos/30; CD-ROMs/8; printed music/12000 items
Classn: DDC **Auto Sys:** Status
Pubns: "The Special Collns of the Royal Irish Academy of Music Lib", in To Talent Alone: The Royal Irish Academy of Music 1848-1998, ed by R. Pine & Charles Acton (1998)
Staff: 2 lib staff **Exp:** €20000 (2000-01)

 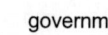

IS139
Royal Society of Antiquaries of Ireland Library
63 Merrion Sq, Dublin 2, Ireland (*tel & fax:* 01-676-1749)
Email: rsai@gofree.indigo.ie

Chief: Libn: Miss Nicole Arnould MA, HDipEd, DipLIS, FLAI
Entry: €4 per afternoon charged to non-membs
Open: Mon-Fri 1400-1700, closed Aug
Subj: Irish hist & archaeo *Collns: Bks & Pamphs:* archaeo & historical journals *Archvs:* Royal Soc of Antiquaries Archv; Weavers' Guild records *Other:* glass slide & photographic colln relating to hist & archaeo of Ireland
Equip: copier (A4/25c, A3/35c), fax (office only), room for hire *Svcs:* info, ref
Stock: bks/10000; various slides, photos & archvs
Classn: own
Pubns: Royal Soc of Antiquaries Journal (€33 pa)
Staff: Libns: 1 *Other Prof:* 1 *Exp:* IR£1000 (1999-2000)
Proj: computerisation

IS140
RTÉ Reference Library
Radio Telefis Éireann, Donnybrook, Dublin 4, Ireland (01-208-3327; *fax:* 01-208-3031)
Email: referencelibrary@rte.ie

Type: semi-state, natl broadcasting body *Gov Body:* Radio Telefis Éireann *Chief:* Ref Libn: Mr Malachy Moran BA, DipLIS (moranm@rte.ie)
Entry: contact Libn for access *Open:* Mon-Fri 0930-1730
Subj: all subjs; extensive broadcasting collns
Collns: Bks & Pamphs: RTÉ PUBNS & gray lit *Archvs:* Biographical Colln (mainly Irish, taken primarily from Irish newspapers & magazines) *Other:* Index of Irish Times newspaper (1969-2001)
Co-op Schemes: BLDSC
Equip: m-reader/printer, copier, 4 computers (all with wd-proc, internet & CD-ROM) *Online:* Lexis Nexis (staff only) *Svcs:* info, ref, biblio, indexing
Stock: bks/6000; periodcls/100
Classn: UDC *Auto Sys:* TechLib
Staff: Libns: 2 *Other Prof:* 1 *Non-Prof:* 1
See also RTÉ STILLS LIB (**IS141**)

IS141
RTÉ Stills Library
New Lib Bldg, Radio Telefis Éireann, Donnybrook, Dublin 4, Ireland (01-208-3127; *fax:* 01-208-3031)
Email: stillslibrary@rte.ie

Type: semi-state, natl broadcasting body *Gov Body:* Radio Telefis Éireann *Chief:* Stills Libn: Ms Emma Keogh *Other Snr Staff:* Asst Libns: Ms Peal Quinn & Ms Amy Kerr
Entry: adv appt *Open:* Mon-Fri 0915-1730
Subj: wide range of subjs relating to 20C Irish life; important coverage of Easter Rising, War of Independence & Civil War; travel; art; arch; design; photography; social hist; cultural hist *Collns: Bks & Pamphs:* illustrated bk colln *Other:* extensive archv of photos, slides & illusts, incl glass plates (early 1900s), contact prints, negatives, 35mm & lantern slides, clr & b&w prints; major collns incl: Cashman Colln (669 photos, 1913-66); Johnson Colln (Dublin City in 1950s, 950 items); Murtagh Colln (c400 photos, 1910s-1930s); Shard Collection/Cahill Colln (late 19C-early 20C middle class family life, 500 images); Stills Dept Colln (c200000 RTÉ copyright images, 1961-2001); Access Magazine Colln (c2000 hard copy prints from Access, the RTÉ staff magazine)
Equip: video viewer, copier, computer (with wd-proc, internet & CD-ROM), scanner, photographic printer

Stock: bks/3500; photos/300000; digital images/110000
Classn: UDC *Staff: Libns:* 1 *Non-Prof:* 2 *Exp:* IR£12000 (1999-2000)
See also RTÉ REF LIB (**IS140**)

IS142
St Luke's Institute of Cancer Research, Oncology Resource Centre
Highfield Rd, Rathgar, Dublin 6, Ireland (01-406-5224; *fax:* 01-497-4886)
Email: gay.doyle@slh.ie

Gov Body: St Luke's Inst of Cancer Rsrch & St Luke's Hosp *Chief:* Info Specialist: Ms Gabrielle Doyle BSocSc, MLIS
Entry: staff, students & rsrchers associated with St Luke's *Open:* Mon-Fri 0900-1645; also open 2 evenings per wk during term
Subj: medicine; nursing; oncology; cancer rsrch
Co-op Schemes: Irish Healthcare Libs Co-op Scheme
Equip: copier, 2 computers (both with wd-proc & CD-ROM) *Svcs:* info, ref, biblio
Stock: bks/2000; periodcls/70
Classn: DDC
Pubns: quarterly news update for lib users
Staff: Libns: 1 *Non-Prof:* 1 PT

IS143
St Patrick's College, Cregan Library
Drumcondra Rd, Dublin 9, Ireland (01-884-2174)
Email: info.library@spd.dcu.ie
Internet: http://www.spd.dcu.ie/library/

Gov Body: constituent coll of Dublin City Univ (see **IS60**) *Chief:* Libn: Mr Evan J. Salholm BA, MLIS, ALA (evan.salholm@spd.dcu.ie) *Dep:* Asst Libn: Ms Orla Nic Aodha BA, DipLIS, MA (oila.nicaodha@spd.dcu.ie)
Entry: open to public for ref purposes (apply at issue desk) *Open:* term: Mon-Thu 1000-2200, Fri 1000-1730, Sat 1000-1300; vac: Mon-Fri 1000-1300, 1400-1700
Subj: all subjs; undergrad; postgrad; local study (Ireland): lang; lit; hist; geog etc *Collns: Bks & Pamphs:* early school textbks; Dolmen Press bks; Three Candles Press bks *Co-op Schemes:* BLDSC
Equip: m-reader/printer (60 copies for €4), 5 copiers, clr copier, 15 computers (incl 4 with wd-proc, 4 with internet & 4 with CD-ROM, access free) *Svcs:* info, ref, biblio
Stock: bks/150000; periodcls/550; m-forms/1000
Classn: DDC *Auto Sys:* Talis
Staff: Libns: 2 *Non-Prof:* 8

IS144
St Vincent's University Hospital, Library
Edu & Rsrch Centre, Elm Pk, Dublin 4, Ireland (01-209-4921; *fax:* 01-283-3730)
Email: library.svh@ucd.ie
Internet: http://www.st-vincents.ie/

Gov Body: St Vincent's Univ Hosp Ltd *Chief:* Head of Lib & Info Svcs: Ms Niamh Lucey BA, MLIS (niamh.lucey@ucd.ie) *Other Snr Staff:* Lib Asst: Mr Greg Sheaf BA, DipLIS; Lib Asst: Ms Paula Maher BA
Entry: staff of St Vincent's Univ Hosp Group (incl Private Hosp & St Michael's Hosp); registered students & postgrads; local GPs by appt *Open:* term: Mon, Fri 0930-1730, Tue-Thu 0930-2100; vac: Mon-Fri 0930-1730; study area open 0730-2200 all wk
Subj: medicine; surgery; nursing; allied health; sociology; health svcs *Co-op Schemes:* BLDSC, Irish Medical Libs Group

Equip: m-reader, video viewer, fax, copier, 17 computers (incl wd-proc, internet & CD-ROM), 3 rooms for hire *Online:* Medline, BNI Plus, Science Direct, Synergy, CINAHL, Cochrane, PsycInfo
Offcr-in-Charge: Head of Lib & Info Svcs, as above
Svcs: info, ref, biblio, indexing, abstracting
Stock: bks/4000; periodcls/200; maps/2; videos/200; CD-ROMs/10 *Acqs Offcr:* Head of Lib & Info Svcs, as above
Classn: DDC *Auto Sys:* Heritage
Staff: Libns: 2 *Non-Prof:* 1
Proj: shelving proj; security sys installation

IS145
State Chemist Laboratory Library
Abbotstown, Dublin 15, Ireland (01-802-5800; *fax:* 01-821-7320)
Email: library@statelab.ie

Chief: Libn: Mr Michael O'Gorman (mogorman@statelab.ie)
Subj: analytical chem; toxicology; microbiology; environmental sci *Co-op Schemes:* ILL
Stock: bks/6000; periodcls/104; videos/70

IS146
TEAGASC Agriculture and Food Development Authority Library
19 Sandymount Ave, Ballsbridge, Dublin 4, Ireland (01-637-6000; *fax:* 01-668-8023)
Email: Library@hq.teagasc.ie

Chief: Libn: Ms Deirdre Brennan
Assoc Libs: NATL FOOD CENTRE LIB (see **IS118**)
Subj: sci; tech; agric; food sci; hortic *Co-op Schemes:* ILL, IFLA
Equip: Online: Lockheed, ESA, Cardbox
Stock: bks/37000; periodcls/1000; videos/160; bnd documents/300; theses/100; film/30

Trinity College Library Dublin
See **IL2**

IS147
Trocaire Library and Documentation Centre
169 Booterstown Ave, Dublin, Ireland (01-288-5385; *fax:* 01-288-3577)
Email: info@trocaire.ie
Internet: http://www.trocaire.org/

Type: NGO *Gov Body:* Board of Trustees *Chief:* Libn: Mrs Anne Kinsella BA, DipLib
Entry: adv appt preferred *Open:* Mon-Fri 0915-1300, 1400-1730
Subj: social sci; Third World development; human rights *Collns: Other:* photo colln; press cuttings
Equip: fax, copier, video viewers, computers (incl wd-proc, internet & CD-ROM), television *Online:* not for public use *Svcs:* info, ref, biblio
Stock: bks/8500; periodcls/90; videos/400; various photos, slides, pamphs & maps
Classn: UDC *Auto Sys:* own (in-house database)
Pubns: Trocaire Development Review; Trocaire World; Trocaire Campaigns Update
Staff: Libns: 1 *Non-Prof:* 1 PT

IS148
University College Dublin Library
Belfield, Dublin 4, Ireland (01-716-7583; *fax:* 01-283-7667)
Email: library@ucd.ie
Internet: http://library.ucd.ie/

Gov Body: Univ Coll Dublin *Chief:* Libn: Mr S. Phillips BA, ALA, ALAI *Dep:* Dep Libn: Ms P. Corrigan BA, DipLib ☛

(Univ Coll Dublin Lib cont)

Assoc Libs: EARLSFORT TER LIB (see **IS150**); MICHAEL SMURFIT GRAD SCHOOL OF BUSINESS LIB (see **IS8**); RICHVIEW LIB (see **IS151**); VETERINARY MEDICINE LIB (see **IS152**) *Entry:* open to those engaged in scholarly work & whose proposed use of lib is not detrimental to Coll users *Open:* term: Mon-Fri 0830-2200, Sat 0900-1700; vac: Mon-Thu 0830-2130, Fri 0830-1730 *Subj:* all subjs; undergrad; postgrad *Collns: Bks & Pamphs:* EDC; Zimmer Colln (Celtica); Curran Colln (Irish lit); Baron Palles Colln (law); O'Lochlainn Colln (Irish imprints); O'Kelley Colln (Irish imprints) *Archvs:* Patrick Kavanagh archv & papers *Co-op Schemes:* BLDSC, IRIS, ALCID *Equip:* 15 m-reader/printers, 12 copiers, 5 video viewers, 30 computers (all with wd-proc, 10 with CD-ROM) *Online:* Dialog, ESA/IRS, Datastar *Svcs:* info, ref *Stock:* bks/1000000; periodcls/6000; slides/1000; pamphs/20000; maps/3000; m-forms/120000; audios/2000; videos/500; archvs/100 MSS *Classn:* DDC *Auto Sys:* Talis *Staff: Libns:* 33.5 *Non-Prof:* 69.5 *Exp:* €3107050 (2000-01)

IS149 🎓
University College Dublin, Department of Irish Folklore Library
Belfield, Dublin 4, Ireland (01-706-8216; *fax:* 01-706-1144)
Email: seamus.ocathain@ucd.ie
Internet: http://www.ucd.ie/~library/

Gov Body: Univ Coll Dublin (see **IS148**) *Chief:* Head of Dept: Prof Séamus Ó Catháin *Entry:* open to public; adv appt for morning hrs *Open:* Mon-Fri 1430-1730, closed Aug *Subj:* local studies (Ireland); generalities; religion; social sci; lang; arts; geog; hist; Irish hist; Irish folklore; drama *Collns: Archvs:* oral folklore in MS form (collected over last century esp amongst rural pop of Republic of Ireland); School Collns (pertaining to primary schools, collected 1937-8); Dublin Urban Folklore Collns (c1980) *Co-op Schemes:* with main Univ Coll Lib *Equip:* m-reader, video viewer, copier, computer (incl wd-proc, internet & CD-ROM) *Svcs:* info, ref, biblio, indexing *Stock:* bks/45000; various photos, slides, pamphs, maps, audios & videos *Classn:* DDC *Auto Sys:* Talis *Staff: Non-Prof:* 3

IS150 🎓
University College Dublin, Earlsfort Terrace Library
Earlsfort Ter, Dublin 2, Ireland (01-706-7221)
Internet: http://www.ucd.ie/~library/

Gov Body: Univ Coll Dublin (see **IS148**) *Chief:* Sub-Libn: Ms Sheila Murphy BA, DipLib *Dep:* Asst Libn: Mr Paul Murphy *Open:* term: Mon-Fri 0930-2145, Sat 0930-1300; vac: Mon-Fri 0930-1700, Sat 0930-1300 *Subj:* sci; maths; civil eng; agric eng; medicine; nursing *Co-op Schemes:* BLDSC *Equip:* 3 m-readers, 2 m-printers, 3 copiers, 12 computers (incl 10 with internet & 2 with CD-ROM) *Svcs:* info, ref, biblio *Stock:* bks/60000; periodcls/800

Classn: DDC *Auto Sys:* Talis *Staff: Libns:* 4.5 *Non-Prof:* 8 *Exp:* €360000 (2000-01)

IS151 🎓
University College Dublin, Richview Library
School of Arch & Planning, Clonskeagh Rd, Dublin 14, Ireland (01-706-2741; *fax:* 01-283-0329)
Email: richview.library@ucd.ie
Internet: http://www.ucd.ie/~library/

Gov Body: Univ Coll Dublin (see **IS148**) *Chief:* Libn: Ms Julia Barrett BMus, DipLib, MBA (julia.barrett@ucd.ie)
Entry: staff & students of UCD *Open:* term: Mon-Thu 0930-2100, Fri 0930-1730, Sat 0930-1300; vac: Mon-Fri 0930-1730 *Subj:* arch; landscape design; construction; interior design; conservation; planning; housing; sociology; environmental studies *Collns: Bks & Pamphs:* product & trade lit *Other:* slide colln; map colln; county development plans; video colln *Co-op Schemes:* BLDSC *Equip:* 2 m-readers, m-printer, video viewer, 2 copiers, fax, computers (incl wd-proc & CD-ROM) *Online:* Dialog, ESA *Svcs:* info, ref, biblio, abstracting (in-house only), ARCHINFO (fee-based svc for arch practices in Ireland) *Stock:* bks/20000; periodcls/200; slides/c10000; pamphs/1000; maps/c15000; m-forms/2000; videos/200; AVs/500; archvs/50 ft (rare bks) *Classn:* DDC, CiSfb *Auto Sys:* Talis *Staff: Libns:* 3 *Non-Prof:* 4

IS152 🎓
University College Dublin, Veterinary Medicine Library
Veterinary Medicine Faculty Bldg, Univ Coll Dublin, Belfield, Dublin 4, Ireland (01-716-6208; *fax:* 01-716-6267)
Email: vetlib@ucd.ie
Internet: http://www.ucd.ie/~library/branches/vet/

Gov Body: Univ Coll Dublin (see **IS148**) *Chief:* Asst Libn: Ms Gwen Ryan BA, MLIS (gwen.ryan@ucd.ie) *Dep:* Snr Lib Asst: currently vacant *Entry:* ref & borrowing for registered users; ref only for others with a legitimate interest in the subj *Open:* term: Mon-Fri 0930-2130, Sat 0930-1230; vac: Mon-Fri 0930-1300, 1400-1730 *Subj:* genl sci; medicine; veterinary medicine; food sci *Collns: Bks & Pamphs:* bks on veterinary medicine (1900-date); some pre-1900 vols *Other:* video & slide collns *Co-op Schemes:* ILL, ALCID *Equip:* video viewer, 2 copiers, 8 computers (all OPACs with catalogue, 5 with internet, 1 with CD-ROM) *Disabled:* facilities based in main UCD Lib *Online:* Dialog (staff, postgrads & external readers only; fees vary) *Offcr-in-Charge:* Asst Libn, as above *Svcs:* info, ref *Stock:* bks/30000; periodcls/380; slides/81 sets; videos/263; archvs/8 m *Acqs Offcr:* Asst Libn, as above *Classn:* DDC *Auto Sys:* Talis *Pubns:* Lib Accessions List (free) *Staff: Libns:* 1 *Non-Prof:* 4 FTE

IS153 🏛
Veterinary Research Laboratory Library
Abbotstown, Castleknock, Dublin 15, Ireland (01-607-2869 x1001/2; *fax:* 01-821-3010)

Gov Body: Dept of Agric, Food & Rural Development (see **IS52**) *Chief:* Libn: Ms E. Gavin DipIS *Entry:* open to staff; visitors by appt only *Open:* Mon-Fri 0930-1730 *Subj:* veterinary medicine & related subjs *Co-op Schemes:* BLDSC, ILL *Equip:* video viewer, copier, computer *Svcs:* info, ref, biblio

Stock: bks/1692 + 4150 bnd journal vols; periodcls/109; videos/4 *Auto Sys:* Cardbox Plus *Pubns:* Veterinary Laboratory Svc Annual Report *Staff: Non-Prof:* 2

IS154 🎓
The Worth Library
Dr Steevens' Hosp, Kingsbridge, Dublin 8, Ireland (01-635-2446)
Email: charles.benson@tcd.ie

Chief: Libn: Dr Charles Benson *Entry:* adv appt, preferably in writing *Open:* Mon-Wed 0930-1230, 1330-1700 *Subj:* all subjs; genl *Collns: Bks & Pamphs:* Antiquarian Colln, not added to since the 1730s (genl interest, with emphasis on medicine, sci, classics & hist) *Archvs:* small colln of archival materials relating to the Lib *Svcs:* info, ref, biblio *Stock:* bks/4500; archvs/1 box *Staff: Libns:* 0.5

Dún Laoghaire

IS155 🎓
Dún Laoghaire Institute of Art, Design and Technology, Library, Information and Learning Resource Centre
Carriglea Pk, Kill Ave, Dún Laoghaire, Co Dublin, Ireland (01-214-4637; *fax:* 01-214-4700)
Email: library@iadt.ie
Internet: http://www.iadt.ie/

Chief: Libn: Ms Deirdre Judge *Entry:* staff & students *Open:* term: Mon-Thu 1000-2100, Fri 1000-1700 *Subj:* undergrad; postgrad; arts; design; tech *Collns: Bks & Pamphs:* exhib catalogues *Co-op Schemes:* ILL *Equip:* 12 video & DVD viewers, copiers, 2 clr copiers, 60 computers (incl internet), printers, scanner *Online:* Infotrac, FactFinder, Design & Applied Arts Index *Stock:* bks/c16000; periodcls/c80 *Classn:* DDC

IS156 💼
Dún Laoghaire Rathdown Chamber of Commerce, Library and Information Service
Kilcullen House, 1 Haigh Ter, Dún Laoghaire, Co Dublin, Ireland (01-284-5066; *fax:* 01-284-5034)
Email: info@dlrchamber.ie
Internet: http://www.dlrchamber.ie/

Chief: Memb Svcs Mgr: Mr Des Ryan *Open:* Mon-Fri 0930-1300, 1400-1700 *Subj:* Dún Laoghaire Rathdown & Dublin: econ; culture; business *Equip:* fax, copier, room for hire *Svcs:* info, ref *Stock:* small bk colln *Classn:* own (alphabetical & by category) *Staff: Libns:* 1 (main duty is as Member Svcs Mgr)

IS157 🔑 📿
Franciscan Library Killiney (FLK)
Dun Mhuire, Seafield Rd, Killiney, Dún Laoghaire, Co Dublin, Ireland (01-282-6760/6091; *fax:* 01-282-6993)

Gov Body: St Francis Trust, 4 Merchant's Quay, Dublin 8 *Chief:* Provincial Libn: Fr Ignatius Fennessey, OFM, BA, HDipEd *Assoc Libs:* IRISH FRANCISCAN ARCHVS, at same addr *Entry:* adv appt *Open:* Mon-Fri 1030-1700

Subj: Irish & Franciscan hist, principally ecclesiastical hist; Celtic studies *Collns: Bks & Pamphs:* rare bks colln, principally ecclesiastical & Irish pubns 1700-1850 (devotional lit & some other), 500 vols *Archvs:* Irish Franciscan Archvs *Co-op Schemes:* ILL
Equip: copier
Stock: bks/22000; periodcls/250; pamphs/900
Classn: Vatican Lib (mod)
Staff: Non-Prof: 2 *Exp:* approx IR£7500 pa

IS158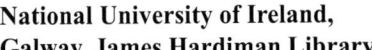
Irish Sea Fisheries Board (Bord Iascaigh Mhara), Library
PO Box 12, Crofton Rd, Dún Laoghaire, Co Dublin, Ireland (01-284-1544; *fax:* 01-284-1123)
Email: library@bim.ie

Chief: Lib Offcr: Ms Mary Cregg
Entry: adv appt *Open:* Mon-Fri 0915-1700
Subj: fisheries; marine aquaculture; fishery tech; market rsrch *Co-op Schemes:* EURASLIC
Stock: periodcls/150; various reports & theses
Pubns: Annual Report; Market Rsrch Series; Market Info Bulletin; Development Programme; edu posters; various technical & market related reports
Staff: Libns: 1

IS159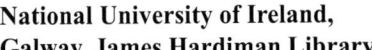
James Joyce Museum Library
Joyce Tower, Sandycove, Dún Laoghaire, Co Dublin, Ireland (*tel & fax:* 01-280-9265)
Email: joycetower@dublintourism.ie

Gov Body: Dublin City & County Regional Tourism Org *Chief:* Curator: Mr Robert Nicholson BA
Entry: Museum: paid admission; *Lib:* by adv appt
Open: Apr-Oct: Mon-Sat 1000-1300, 1400-1700, Sun & public hols 1400-1800; Nov-Mar: by appt (tel: 01-280-9265 or 01-872-2077)
Subj: James Joyce life & works; correspondence & info files of Joyce Tower; misc items of Joycean interest *Collns: Bks & Pamphs:* Joyce Tower Lib (eds of Joyce's works, incl some first & rare eds & many translations); critical & biographical works on Joyce *Archvs:* letters & photos
Stock: bks/300; archvs/1000 items
Classn: ACCESSION
Pubns: The James Joyce Tower (free); The Ulysses Map of Dublin (€1.27)
Staff: Other Prof: 1 *Non-Prof:* 0.5

IS160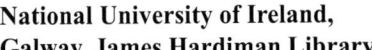
Maritime Institute of Ireland Museum and Library
Haigh Ter, Dún Laoghaire, Co Dublin, Ireland (*tel & fax:* 01-280-0969)
Internet: http://www.mii.connect.ie/

Type: grant-aided instn *Gov Body:* Maritime Inst of Ireland *Chief:* Chairman of Lib Cttee: Mr Des Branigan
Entry: membs; others by adv appt only
Subj: sea, naval forces & warfare; water transport; nautical eng; hist (Western Europe) *Collns: Bks & Pamphs:* Lloyds Register of Ships (1842-date); Halpin Colln; colln of 19C bks *Other:* charts; postcards of ships & boats
Equip: copier, fax, computer (incl wd-proc) *Svcs:* info, ref, biblio, genl rsrch
Stock: bks/4500; various periodcls, photos, pamphs, maps (in process of being recorded & catalogued)
Classn: DDC *Auto Sys:* InMagic
Staff: Libns: 1 *Other Prof:* 1 *Non-Prof:* 1 all PT
Exp: stock additions are by donations only
Proj: restoration of Mariners Church, with relocation of lib to basement with reading room & own entrance

Dundalk

IS161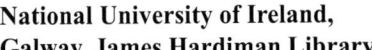
Dundalk Institute of Technology, Library
Dundalk, Co Louth, Ireland (042-937-0312; *fax:* 042-933-8313)
Email: librarian@dkit.ie
Internet: http://dkitlibs.dkit.ie/

Chief: Coll Libn: Ms Donna Ò Doibhlin BA, DipLIS (donna.odoibhlin@dkit.ie) *Dep:* Asst Libn: Ms Frances McKenna (frances.mckenna@dkit.ie)
Other Snr Staff: Asst Libn: Ms Concepta Woods BSc(Econ) (concepta.woods@dkit.ie)
Open: term: Mon-Thu 0900-2100, Fri 0900-1700; vac: Mon-Fri 0900-1700
Subj: all subjs; undergrad *Collns: Bks & Pamphs:* RTC Educational Policy & Practice; Irish business & mgmt; arch *Archvs:* Coll Archv; local theatre archv *Co-op Schemes:* BLDSC, ILL
Equip: m-reader, m-printer, 3 copiers, 2 fax, 2 video viewers, 120 networked computers (all with wd-proc & internet), public slide printer/viewer
Online: Dialog, New FirstSearch, Onefile, Emerald FullText, BSOnline, Technical Indexes CIS *Svcs:* info, ref, biblio, indexing
Stock: bks/33000; periodcls/313; photos/20; slides/40; audios/30; videos/205; CD-ROMs/122
Acqs Offcr: Asst Libn, as above
Classn: DDC *Auto Sys:* Innopac/Millennium
Pubns: Irish Business Index
Staff: Libns: 3 *Other Prof:* 1 *Non-Prof:* 6 *Exp:* IR£100000 (1999-2000); IR£163000 (2000-01)

IS162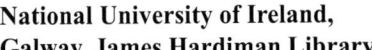
Louth County Hospital, Medical Library
Dublin Rd, Dundalk, Co Louth, Ireland (042-938-1135; *fax:* 048-932-9205)
Email: sandra.fanning@nehb.ie
Internet: http://www.nehb.ie/

Gov Body: North Eastern Health Board *Chief:* Libn: Ms Sandra Fanning
Assoc Libs: other NEHB Libs: MOTHER MARY MARTIN LIB (see IS29); CAVAN GENL HOSP LIB (see IS16); MONAGHAN GENL HOSP LIB (see IS186); OUR LADY'S HOSP LIB (see IS190); ST BRIGIT'S HOSP LIB (see IS1); ST DAVNET'S HOSP LIB (see IS187)
Subj: medicine
Equip: copier, computers (incl internet) *Online:* incl Medline, CINAHL, Cochrane, PsycInfo & BNI
Classn: DDC *Auto Sys:* Heritage

Ennis

IS163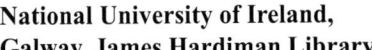
Our Lady's Hospital Library
Gort Rd, Ennis, Co Clare, Ireland (065-682-1414; *fax:* 065-684-0883)

Gov Body: Mid-Western Health Board *Chief:* Libn: Ms Fiona Gilligan
Subj: psy; medicine
Equip: computer *Svcs:* ref
Stock: small bk colln

Galway

IS164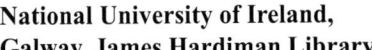
Galway Euro Information Centre
Galway Chamber of Commerce & Industry, Commerce House, Merchant's Rd, Galway, Co Galway, Ireland (091-562624; *fax:* 091-561963)
Email: elaine@galwaychamber.com
Internet: http://www.galwaychamber.com/euro.htm

Gov Body: European Commission, hosted by Galway Chamber of Commerce *Chief:* Info Offcr: Ms Elaine Wakely
Open: Mon-Fri 0900-1730
Subj: business development info; European info; economic development in Galway region *Collns: Bks & Pamphs:* official journals of the EU
Equip: fax, video viewer, copier, clr copier, computers (incl wd-proc, internet & CD-ROM)
Online: access to online resources with assistance of Info Offcr *Svcs:* info, ref
Stock: bks/1000; videos/5; CD-ROMs/1000
Classn: own *Staff: Other Prof:* 3 *Exp:* stock received free from European Commission

IS165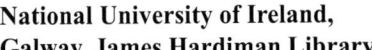
Galway-Mayo Institute of Technology Library
Dublin Rd, Renmore, Galway, Co Galway, Ireland (091-751107; *fax:* 091-742115)
Email: library@gmit.ie
Internet: http://www.gmit.ie/

Chief: Libn: Ms Ann Joyce Walsh BA, FLAI (ann.joyce@gmit.ie) *Dep:* Dep Libns: Ms Bernie Lally BA, HDip, DipLIS (bernie.lally@gmit.ie) & Margaret Waldron BA, HDip, DipLIS (margaret.waldron@gmit.ie)
Assoc Libs: CASTLEBAR CAMPUS LIB, Westport Rd, Castlebar, Co Mayo, Asst Libn: Ms Majella King BA, DipLIS (majeking@castle.gmit.ie); CLUAIN MHUIRE ART LIB, Munivea Rd, Galway, Librarian-in-Charge: Ms Ann Joyce Walsh (091-744009; *email:* teresa.keane@gmit.ie); LETTER-FRACK LIB, Connemara West, Letterfrack, Co Galway (095-41047; *email:* malhiggins@yahoo.com)
Entry: staff & students; ref only for external users
Open: 1st term: Mon-Thu 0900-2130, Fri 0900-1730; 2nd & 3rd term: Mon-Thu 0900-2200, Fri 0900-2100, Sat 1000-1300; vac: Mon-Fri 0930-1300, 1400-1700
Subj: all subjs; undergrad; postgrad; Irish heritage
Collns: Bks & Pamphs: Galway Diocesan Colln (c20000 bks & journals, mainly theology, also some hist, archaeo & lit) *Co-op Schemes:* BLDSC, ILL, Insts of Tech Consortium
Equip: 4 m-readers, 2 m-printers, 5 copiers, clr copier, 30 computers (all with internet & CD-ROM), room for hire, audio cassette player *Disabled:* Kurzweil *Online:* Art Abstracts, Infotrac Onefile, FactFinder, Proquest ABI Global, Emerald, Kompass, FirstLaw, Cambridge Scientific Abstracts, Science Direct & others; numerous online journals *Offcr-in-Charge:* Libn, as above
Svcs: info, ref, biblio, indexing, abstracting
Stock: bks/67000; periodcls/350; some slides, pamphs, maps, audios, videos, CD-ROMs & m-forms *Acqs Offcr:* Dep Libn, as above
Classn: DDC *Auto Sys:* Millennium
Staff: Libns: 2 *Non-Prof:* 8
Proj: new lib at Renmore for 2003

IS166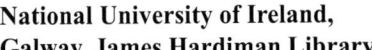
National University of Ireland, Galway, James Hardiman Library
University Rd, Galway, Ireland (091-524809; *fax:* 091-522394)
Email: library@nuigalway.ie
Internet: http://www.library.nuigalway.ie/

Chief: Libn: Mrs Marie Reddan DipLIS, DipSA, FLA, MCLIP (marie.reddan@nuigalway.ie) *Dep:* Dep Libn: Mr John Cox BA, MA, DipLib (john.cox@nuigalway.ie) *Other Snr Staff:* Sub-Libn (Systems): Mr Peter Corrigan BA, DipLIS (peter.corrigan@nuigalway.ie); Sub-Libn (Reader Svcs): Ms Ann Mitchell BA, ADipEd, DipLIS (ann.mitchell@nuigalway.ie); Sub-Libn (Info): Mr Niall McSweeney HDipEd, DipLIS (niall.mcsweeney@nuigalway.ie); Sub-Libn (Bibliographic Svcs): Mr Seamus Scanlon BSc, DipLIS (seamus.scanlon@nuigalway.ie)

(Natl Univ of Ireland Galway Lib cont)
Assoc Libs: MEDICAL LIB (see **IS167**); NURSING LIB, Univ Coll Hosp, Galway, Libn: Ms Maire O hAodha BA, DipLIS (091-524411 x87-4361; *fax:* 091-527214; *email:* maire.ohaodha@nuigalway.ie)
Entry: membs & grads of the Univ; specific svcs available to local community; fee-based svc available to external users **Open:** term: Mon-Fri 0900-2200, Sat 0900-1300; exam periods: Mon-Thu 0900-2300, Fri 0900-2200, Sat 0900-1700, Sun 0900-1600; vac: Mon-Fri 0900-1730; *Special Collns Reading Room:* Mon-Fri 0930-1315, 1400-1700
Subj: all subjs; generalities; phil; psy; religion; social sci; lang; sci; maths; tech; arts; lit; geog; hist; law; medicine; nursing **Collns: Bks & Pamphs:** ref colln of Irish govt & official pubns; EDC; special printed collns incl: Queen's Coll Galway Colln (pre-1850 bks); Gregory Colln (lib of Lady Gregory's works); Cairnes Colln (lib of economist John E. Cairnes); St Anthony's Lib Colln (theology, Irish & church hist, 20000+ items); particular strengths in the bks collns incl Irish lang, lit & hist, as well as 19C scientific material *Archvs:* over 300 collns; strengths incl: papers associated with NUI Galway; Irish lang & lit MSS; local authority records; estate archvs; political papers; personal papers (mainly relating to Co Galway); theatre & performing arts collns; named collns incl: Taibhearc Archv; Druid Theatre Archv; Galway Corp MSS (Galway's civic records, 1485-1818 & 1836-1922); Eyre Family Deeds (legal records, 1720-1857); Douglas Hyde MSS Colln (18C prose & poetry) *Other:* early newspapers in Irish & English **Co-op Schemes:** BLDSC, Medical Lib ILL Cartel
Equip: 8 m-readers, 5 m-printers (8c per pg), 10 video viewers, 15 copiers (8c per pg), clr copier (56c per pg), fax, 52 computers (all with internet & CD-ROM, 20 with wd-proc) *Disabled:* Dragon Naturally Speaking, JAWS, TextHelp, ReadWrite, Supernova, ZoomText, WYNN, Braille translator software *Online:* numerous databases via Dialog *Offcr-in-Charge:* PA to Chief Libn: Mrs Pauline Nic Chonaonaigh (pauline.nicchonaonaigh@nuigalway.ie) *Svcs:* info, ref, biblio
Stock: bks/443902; periodcls/1546; slides/390; maps/1539; m-forms/88930; AVs/2154; archvs/75 linear m **Acqs Offcr:** Sub-Libn (Bibliographic Svcs), as above
Classn: DDC, UDC **Auto Sys:** Aleph
Staff: Libns: 20 *Other Prof:* 1 *Non-Prof:* 83 *Exp:* IR£2986007 (1999-2000); IR£3133000 (2000-01); figs are for total lib exp

IS167 ● ✚
National University of Ireland, Galway, Medical Library
Clinical Sci Inst, Galway, Co Galway, Ireland (091-524411 x2791; *fax:* 091-750517)
Email: tim.collins@nuigalway.ie
Internet: http://www.library.nuigalway.ie/medlib.html

Gov Body: Natl Univ of Ireland, Galway (see **IS166**) **Chief:** Libn: Mr Tim Collins BSc, HDE, DipLib, DipSA, FLA **Dep:** Snr Lib Asst: Mr Edward O Loghlen
Assoc Libs: NURSING LIB, Univ Coll Hosp, Galway, Libn: Ms Maire O hAodha BA, DipLIS (091-524411 x87-4361; *fax:* 091-527214; *email:* maire.ohaodha@nuigalway.ie)

Entry: registered staff & students **Open:** term: Mon-Fri 0915-2200, Sat 0915-1300; vac: Mon-Fri 0915-1700
Subj: medicine **Collns: Archvs:** Richard Doherty Papers (obstetrics & gynaecology) *Other:* Grey Lit Colln **Co-op Schemes:** BLDSC, IMLC (Irish Medical Libs' Cartel), BMA, IRIS
Equip: video viewer, copier *Online:* Medline, Dialog, ESA-IRS, OCLC FirstSearch, UnCover, CINAHL, PsycInfo *Svcs:* info, ref, lit searches, CD-ROM training
Stock: bks/c5000; periodcls/140 + 520 no longer current **Staff:** 8 in total

IS168 ✚
Western Health Board Library Service
Edu Centre, Merlin Pk, Galway, Co Galway, Ireland (091-775327/46; *fax:* 091-779655)
Email: library@whb.ie
Internet: http://www.whb.ie/

Gov Body: Western Health Board **Chief:** Regional Libn: Mr Tony Linnane BA(Hons), DipCompSc, DipLIS (anthony.linnane@whb.ie) **Other Snr Staff:** Libn: Ms Julia Reynolds (julia.reynolds@whb.ie)
Assoc Libs: WESTERN HEALTH BOARD, CASTLEBAR HEALTHCARE LIB (see **IS14**); WESTERN HEALTH BOARD, EAST GALWAY/ROSCOMMON LIB SVCS, Portiuncula Hosp, Ballinasloe, Co Galway
Entry: WHB staff only **Open:** Mon-Fri 0930-1300, 1400-700
Subj: medicine; health care **Collns: Bks & Pamphs:** official pubns, incl EU, Irish Govt Depts & Health Boards **Co-op Schemes:** BLDSC for ILLs, Irish Healthcare Libs, other WHB libs
Equip: m-reader, fax, video viewer, copier, clr copier, 6 computers (incl 2 with wd-proc & 4 with internet), CD-ROM network *Online:* Medline, Cochrane, CINAHL, CancerLit, Healthstar & others *Svcs:* info, ref, biblio, indexing, copying svc
Stock: bks/25000; periodcls/190; CD-ROMs/100
Classn: DDC **Auto Sys:** Heritage
Staff: Libns: 2 *Non-Prof:* 1
Proj: 2 new libs

Greystones

IS169 ✚
Newcastle Hospital Library
Greystones, Co Wicklow, Ireland (01-281-9001; *fax:* 01-281-9323)

Gov Body: East Coast Area Health Board **Chief:** Clinical Dir & Hon Libn: Dr Brian O'Shea MB, BCh, BAO, FRCPsych
Entry: membs only **Open:** 24 hrs (by personal key)
Subj: psy; psychiatry; social sci; medicine **Collns: Archvs:** some old records relating to the hosp's TB days are held by Mrs P. Byrne (Area Mgr) at the hosp
Equip: fax, 2 copiers, clr copier, computer (with wd-proc, internet & CD-ROM) *Offcr-in-Charge:* contact Dr Justin Brophy *Svcs:* indexing (lib is basically a bench lib)
Stock: bks/240; periodcls/20 + 4 medical newspapers; slides/400; pamphs/100; videos/200; CD-ROMs/4 **Acqs Offcr:** Hon Libn, as above & Dr Justin Brophy
Classn: Idiosyncratic
Pubns: A Textbook of Psychological Medicine, ed P. O'Shea (4th ed, €1000), available via East Coast Area Health Board, Communications Dept, off Raphael Road, Bray, Co Wicklow
Staff: 1 Hon Libn *Exp:* €3500 pa
Further Info: Small lib for local use; Univ Coll Dublin Lib (see **IS148**) is available for reprint reqs

Kilkenny

IS170 🏛
Patents Office Library
Govt Bldgs, Hebron Rd, Kilkenny, Co Kilkenny, Ireland (056-772-0132; *fax:* 056-772-0100)
Email: patlib@entemp.ie
Internet: http://www.patentsoffice.ie/

Gov Body: Dept of Enterprise, Trade & Employment (see **IS55**) **Chief:** Info Offcr: Mr Declan Finlay
Entry: ref only **Open:** Mon-Fri 0945-1615
Subj: patents; trademarks **Collns: Bks & Pamphs:** govt acts; patents journals; legal texts relating to patents & trademarks *Archvs:* hard copies of Irish patents *Other:* many collns of CD-ROM Series of Internatl Patents
Equip: 5 computers (incl 1 with internet & 3 with CD-ROM) *Svcs:* info, ref
Pubns: Irish Patent & Trademark Journal; Annual Report
Staff: Non-Prof: 2

IS171 ✚
South Eastern Health Board, Library and Information Service
SEHB HQ, Lacken, Dublin Rd, Kilkenny, Ireland (056-51702; *fax:* 056-65270)
Email: tierneya@sehb.ie
Internet: http://www.sehb.ie/

Chief: Regional Libn: Ms Ann Tierney BA, DipLIS
Assoc Libs: WATERFORD REGIONAL HOSP LIB (see **IS210**); WEXFORD GENL HOSP LIB (see **IS211**)
Entry: SEHB staff only **Open:** Mon-Fri 0900-1700
Subj: phil; psy; social sci; medicine; health **Co-op Schemes:** Irish Healthcare Libs Network Journal Holdings Co-op
Equip: m-reader, fax, copier, computers (with wd-proc, internet & CD-ROM) *Svcs:* info, ref, biblio
Stock: bks/6500; periodcls/130; CD-ROMs/18
Classn: Bliss **Auto Sys:** Unicorn
Staff: Libns: 2 *Non-Prof:* 2

IS172 🗝 🙏
St Canice's Library
St Canice's Cathedral, Coach Hill, Kilkenny, Ireland (056-61910; *fax:* 056-51813)
Email: stcanicescathedral@eircom.net

Gov Body: C of I Diocese of Ossory **Chief:** The Bishop's Vicar **Dep:** Dep Libn: Mr Hugh Campbell
Entry: ref only, adv appt
Subj: generalities; phil; psy; religion; lang; sci; maths; arts; lit; geog; hist **Collns: Bks & Pamphs:** collns of two 17C-18C bishops *Other:* 15C-18C printings
Stock: bks/3300 **Staff:** Non-Prof: 1

Killarney

IS173 🗝
Muckross House Reference Library
The Natl Park, Killarney, Co Kerry, Ireland (064-35228; *fax:* 064-33926)
Email: library@muckross-house.ie
Internet: http://www.muckross-house.ie/

Gov Body: Trustees of Muckross House (Killarney) Ltd **Chief:** Rsrch & Edu Offcr: Ms Patricia O'Hare MA **Dep:** Asst: Ms Vivienne Heffernan BA
Entry: adv appt; completion of entry form **Open:** Mon-Fri 0900-1730, closed 24 Dec-2 Jan
Subj: Co Kerry: local studies; hist; geog; folklore; tourism; lang (Gaelic-speaking areas in Co Kerry); lit (Co Kerry authors); Irish social sci

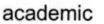

Equip: m-reader, m-printer, clr copier, 2 computers (incl wd-proc, internet & CD-ROM) *Svcs:* info, ref
Stock: bks/c10000; periodcls/10; photos/8000; slides/2000; maps/c1000; m-forms/c500; videos/100; AVs/1
Classn: DDC
Pubns: Muckross Newsletter (2 pa)
Staff: Other Prof: 5 *Exp:* IR£5000 (1999-2000)

Killybegs

IS174
Tourism College Killybegs, The Library
Killybegs, Co Donegal, Ireland (073-31120; *fax:* 073-31691)
Internet: http://www.tck.ie/

Gov Body: Donegal Vocational Educational Council & Letterkenny Inst of Tech (see **IS177**) *Chief:* Libn: Mr Michael Doheny (mdoheny@tck.ie) *Dep:* Asst Libn: Ms Terri McKenna BA, HDipEd (tmckenna@tck.ie) *Other Snr Staff:* Lib Asst: Ms Mairead O Kane (mokane@tck.ie)
Entry: staff & students *Open:* Mon-Thu 0900-2100, Fri 0900-1700
Subj: social sci; tourism; econ; food tech; food & beverages; mgmt; marketing; travel *Collns: Other:* Caterer & Hotelkeeper Journal *Co-op Schemes:* BLDSC
Equip: copier (10c per sheet), clr copier (30c per sheet), 10 computers (all with wd-proc, internet & CD-ROM) *Online:* Emerald, EBSCO, Croner *Svcs:* info, ref, indexing, abstracting
Stock: bks/3000; periodcls/30; pamphs/20; videos/106; CD-ROMs/35
Classn: DDC *Auto Sys:* Heritage
Staff: Libns: 1 FT *Non-Prof:* 1 PT
Proj: lib extension starting late 2002

Letterkenny

IS175
Donegal County Museum, Library and Archives
High Rd, Letterkenny, Co Donegal, Ireland (074-24613; *fax:* 074-26522)
Email: museum@donegalcoco.ie

Type: local authority *Gov Body:* Donegal County Council (see **IP6**) *Chief:* Curator: Ms Judith McCarthy (jmcarthy@donegalcoco.ie)
Entry: adv appt, ref only *Open:* Mon-Fri 1000-1230, 1300-1630, Sat 1300-1630
Subj: local studies (Co Donegal): archaeo; hist; associated subjs *Collns: Archvs:* archvs of Donegal Archaeological Survey, incl sketches, site plans & maps & written documentation *Other:* small slide colln
Equip: fax, copier *Svcs:* info
Staff: Other Prof: 3 *Non-Prof:* 1

IS176 ✚
Letterkenny Hospitals, Education Centre Library
St Conal's Hosp, Letterkenny, Co Donegal, Ireland (074-23729; *fax:* 074-23646)
Email: SCH.Library@nwhb.ie
Internet: http://www.nwhb.ie/

Gov Body: North Western Health Board *Chief:* Asst Libn: Mr Frank O'Deorain BSc, DipLib, ALA *Dep:* Snr Lib Asst: Mrs Anna Crowe *Assoc Libs:* associated with: SLIGO GENL HOSP LIB (see **IS197**)
Entry: NWHB staff & School of Nursing students only *Open:* Mon-Fri 0845-2200, but ring to check *Subj:* social sci; sociology; psy; medicine; psychiatry; nursing *Co-op Schemes:* BLDSC, Irish Heath Svcs Libs ILL scheme

---

Equip: copier (€1 for 20 copies); 3 computers (incl 1 with internet & 2 with CD-ROM) *Svcs:* info, ref
Stock: bks/5000; periodcls/120; CD-ROMs/4
Classn: LC *Auto Sys:* Cardbox
Staff: Libns: 1 *Non-Prof:* 2 *Exp:* IR£5000 on bk stock (2000-01); UK£35695 on journal subscriptions (2001); IR£2500 on CD-ROM Database subscriptions (2001)
Proj: tender for print journal subscriptions with associate lib; tender for supply of elec database provision in 2003

IS177
Letterkenny Institute of Technology Library
Port Rd, Letterkenny, Co Donegal, Ireland (074-64100; *fax:* 074-64111)
Internet: http://www.lyit.ie/

Chief: Chief Libn: Mr John Devlin BA, DipLIS (john.devlin@lyit.ie) *Dep:* Asst Libn: Ms Una Cronin BA, DipLIS, DBA (una.cronin@lyit.ie) *Assoc Libs:* ST CONAL'S LIB OF ART & DESIGN, Dep Libn & Head of Computer Svcs: Ms Maeve Diver BSc, HDipEd, MSc (maeve.diver@lyit.ie)
Entry: registered students of the Inst; also open to membs of public *Open:* term: Mon-Fri 0900-2130; vac: Mon-Fri 0900-1300, 1400-1730
Subj: all subjs; local hist (Donegal); Irish lang *Collns: Bks & Pamphs:* fine art colln *Other:* Irish Times (1971-date) on m-film; all England law reports dating back to 1558, Guinness Food Sci Collns (incl biochemistry, analytical chem, enzymology & bacteriology) *Co-op Schemes:* BLDSC, Insts of Tech Partnership
Equip: m-reader, 7 video viewers, copier, 90 computers (incl wd-proc, internet & CD-ROM) *Online:* Wilson General Science Online, Technical Index, Lexis Nexis, FactFinder, Design & Applied Art Index, Cambridge Scientific Abstract *Offcr-in-Charge:* Dep Libn & Head of Computer Svcs: Ms Maeve Diver, as above *Svcs:* info, biblio
Stock: bks/42000; periodcls/150; various maps, videos & AVs
Classn: DDC *Auto Sys:* Innopac
Staff: Libns: 3 *Non-Prof:* 3
Proj: ongoing implementation of Innopac

Limerick

IS178
Limerick Institute of Technology Library
Moylish Pk, Limerick, Ireland (061-327688; *fax:* 061-327696)
Email: Information@lit.ie
Internet: http://www.lit.ie/

Gov Body: Limerick Inst of Tech, Governing Body *Chief:* Coll Libn: Mrs Joan M. Minihan BA, DipLib, ALAI *Dep:* Asst Libn: Mrs Brid Foster DipLib *Assoc Libs:* ART & DESIGN LIB, Clare St Campus, Clare St, Limerick (under auspices of main Moylish Pk Lib, Libn: as above)
Entry: open to students & staff of Coll; others by appt *Open:* term: Mon-Fri 0930-2100; vac: Mon-Fri 0930-1700
Subj: undergrad; postgrad; computing; rsrch systems; econ; law; edu; lang (French, German, English, Irish, Spanish); maths; physics; chem; biology; microbiology; eng sci; elec eng; mech eng; auto eng; mgmt; bldg; arts *Collns: Bks & Pamphs:* product data (brochures) *Other:* m-fiche colln dealing with bldg, eng, hazardous chemicals, property & planning *Co-op Schemes:* ILL
Equip: m-readers, m-printers, video viewers, copiers, clr copier, computers (incl wd-proc & CD-ROM), scanner *Online:* Science Direct, Emerald, Medline, Iconda, Analytical Abstracts, Infotrac, Grove Dictionary of Art, Barbour Index *Svcs:* info, ref, biblio

---

Stock: bks/24000; periodcls/170; videos/700; large colln of slides; vast colln of m-forms; some audios & pamphs
Classn: DDC *Auto Sys:* Dynix
Pubns: Lib Guide
Staff: Libns: 3 *Non-Prof:* 6

IS179
Limerick Museum, Library and Archives
Castle Ln, Nicholas St, Limerick, Ireland (061-417826; *fax:* 061-415266)

Gov Body: Limerick City Council (see **IP16**) *Chief:* Curator: Mr L. Walsh MA
Entry: ref only, appt necessary *Open:* Tue-Fri 1000-1300, 1415-1700
Subj: North Munster: local hist & archaeo; genl antiquities *Collns: Bks & Pamphs:* locally printed 18C & 19C bks *Archvs:* misc indiv items of local interest
Stock: bks/1400; periodcls/13; photos/2700; slides/3000; illusts/200; pamphs/600; maps/250
Staff: Other Prof: 1 *Non-Prof:* 1 *Exp:* IR£2500 (1999-2000); €3000 (2000-01)

IS180 ✚
Limerick Regional Medical Library
Regional Hosp, Dooradoyle, Limerick, Co Limerick, Ireland (061-482414; *fax:* 061-482697)
Email: postgradlib@mwhb.ie

Gov Body: Univ of Limerick (see **IS182**) & Mid-Western Health Board *Chief:* Asst Libn: Ms Margaret Dillon BA, DipLIS
Entry: Mid-Western Health Board staff or affiliated staff & students *Open:* Mon-Thu 0900-1900, Fri 0900-1700
Subj: medicine; nursing *Co-op Schemes:* Irish Healthcare Libs Lending Co-op
Equip: copiers, computers (with CD-ROM) *Svcs:* info, ref, biblio
Stock: bks/5000; periodcls/155
Classn: DDC *Staff:* Libns: 0.5 *Non-Prof:* 2

IS181
Mary Immaculate College Library
South Circular Rd, Limerick, Ireland (061-314588; *fax:* 061-313632)
Internet: http://www.mic.ul.ie/

Gov Body: Bord Rialiathe *Chief:* Libn: Mr John Power BA, HDipEd, DipLib, ALAI (John.Power@mic.ul.ie) *Other Snr Staff:* Asst Libn (System & Technical Svcs): Ms Mary Brassil (Mary.Brassil@mic.ul.ie); Asst Libn (Info & User Svcs): Ms Geraldine Moloney (Geraldine.Moloney@mic.ul.ie)
Entry: membs of Coll & of Univ of Limerick *Open:* term: Mon-Fri 0930-2200, Sat 1400-1800; vac: Mon-Fri 0900-1700
Subj: all subjs; undergrad; postgrad; local study (Limerick area, geog & hist); generalities; phil; religion; social scis; Irish studies; media & communication studies; lang; sci; tech; arts; music; lit; geog; hist; edu *Collns: Other:* Irish Folklore Colln (m-film) *Co-op Schemes:* BLDSC, ILL
Equip: 3 m-readers, 3 m-printers, fax, 2 video viewers, 7 copiers, 10 computers (incl wd-proc, internet & CD-ROM) *Offcr-in-Charge:* Asst Libn (System & Technical Svcs), as above
Stock: bks/200000; periodcls/500; slides/c6000; illusts/c500; pamphs/some; maps/c500; m-forms/c4500; audios/c1000; videos/c800; CD-ROMs/some *Acqs Offcr:* Libn, as above
Classn: DDC *Auto Sys:* Talis
Pubns: Lib Guide; Classn Scheme Guide
Staff: Libns: 3 *Other Prof:* 3 *Non-Prof:* 15

IRELAND
Limerick
▼
Strokestown
Special Libraries

IS182

University of Limerick, Library and Information Services
Limerick, Ireland (061-202166; *fax:* 061-213090)
Internet: http://www.ul.ie/

Chief: Univ Libn: Mr John Lancaster
Entry: external membership available *Open:*
term: Mon-Fri 0830-2100, Sat 0900-1245; vac:
Mon-Fri 0900-1700
Subj: all subjs; undergrad; postgrad *Collns: Bks
& Pamphs:* Norton Colln; EDC; GPA Hist of
Aviation *Archvs:* Dunraven Papers; Glin Papers
Co-op Schemes: BLDSC
Equip: 3 m-printers, 10 copiers, clr copier, 4 video
viewers, 100 computers (all with wd-proc, internet
& CD-ROM) *Disabled:* Kurzweil *Online:* Dialog,
Datastar, STN, FT Profile, EU Databases,
UnCover, Web of Science, Science Direct, Lion,
JSTOR & others *Svcs:* info, ref, biblio
Stock: bks/200000; periodcls/2000; slides/1330;
maps/450; m-forms/1000 sets; audios/3000;
videos/540; AVs/450
Classn: DDC *Auto Sys:* Talis
Pubns: lib info leaflets
Staff: Libns: 14 *Non-Prof:* 44

Maynooth

IS183

National University of Ireland, Maynooth, Library
Maynooth, Co Kildare, Ireland (01-708-3884; *fax:*
01-628-6008)
Email: reader.services@may.ie
Internet: http://www.may.ie/library/

Gov Body: Natl Univ of Ireland, Maynooth *Chief:*
Libn: Agnes Neligan BA, HDipEd, MCLIP, ALAI
Dep: Dep Libn: Ms Helen Fallon MA, DipLIS, ALAI
Assoc Libs: RUSSELL RARE BK LIB, Libn-in-
Charge: Ms Penelope Woods BA, HDipEd, DipLib
Entry: membs of Univ, others ref only, adv appt for
Russell Lib *Open:* Mon-Fri 0830-2200, Sat 1000-
1700; *Russell Lib:* term: Mon-Thu 1000-1700
(closed Fri); vac: Mon-Fri 0900-1700
Subj: undergrad; postgrad; local studies
(Maynooth); generalities; phil; psy; religion; social
sci; lang; sci; maths; computer sci; arts; lit; geog;
hist *Collns: Bks & Pamphs:* incl those of St
Patrick's Coll Maynooth: pamph colln (18C-19C);
Hibernian Bible Soc, Bible colln; Furlong Historical
& Theological Colln; modern bks & pamphs, incl
official documents for Europe, Canada, Britain &
Ireland; Maynoothiana *Archvs:* part of Salamanca
Archvs (from the Irish Colls in Spain, c6000
documents) *Co-op Schemes:* BLDSC, ILL, OCLC
cataloguing, ESTC cataloguing proj, ALCID
Equip: 3 m-readers, 3 m-printers, video viewer,
fax, 6 copiers, clr copier, 50 computers (incl 38 with
internet & 4 with CD-ROM) *Online:* Web of
Science, FirstSearch *Svcs:* info, ref, biblio,
indexing
Stock: bks/400000; periodcls/4000; slides/10000;
pamphs/10000; maps/500; m-forms/20000; audios/
6600; videos/500; archvs/50000; MSS/600 *Acqs
Offcr:* Collns Mgr: Ms Valerie Seymour (valerie.
seymour@may.ie)
Classn: DDC *Auto Sys:* Aleph 500
Pubns: Annual Report; Lib Guide; Newsletter; A
Maynooth Book of Days (1996, €17.80)
Staff: Libns: 12 *Non-Prof:* 19

Monaghan

IS184

Monaghan Chamber of Commerce and Industry Ltd, Library and Information Service
29 Market St, Monaghan, Co Monaghan, Ireland
(047-71218; *fax:* 047-71241)
Email: moncom@eircom.net

Gov Body: Monaghan Chamber of Commerce &
Industry *Chief:* Info Offcr: Ms Jennifer Lambe
Entry: membership of Chamber only *Open:* Mon-
Fri 0930-1700
Subj: business; trade
Equip: fax, copier, computers (incl wd-proc,
internet & CD-ROM) *Svcs:* info, email req svc
(free-IR£100)
Stock: bks/100; periodcls/10; pamphs/1000;
videos/5; CD-ROMs/25

IS185

Monaghan County Museum, Research Library
1-2 Hill St, Monaghan, Ireland (047-82928; *fax:*
047-71189)
Email: comuseum@monaghancoco.ie

Type: local authority *Gov Body:* Monaghan
County Council (see **IP22**) *Chief:* Curator: Mrs
Roisin Doherty BA, PGDip, MPhil (rdoherty@
monaghancoco.ie) *Dep:* Exhibs Offcr: Mr Liam
Bradley BSc *Other Snr Staff:* Registrar: Ms
Donna Macklin (dmacklin@monaghancoco.ie);
Conservator: Mr Noel Breakey; Rsrcher: Mr
Padraig Clerkin; Administrative Asst: Ms Stephanie
Kelly; Edu Offcr: Ms Eileen McKenna
Entry: ref only, adv appt *Open:* Tue-Fri 1000-
1300, 1400-1700, Sat 1100-1300, 1400-1700
Subj: Co Monaghan: local studies (hist, arch,
folklife, economy); local social & economic hist;
religion (mostly secondary publ sources); industrial
arch; agric arch; lit (secondary sources & local
authors); broad range of mainly secondary sources
on local & genl Irish hist & geog *Collns: Bks &
Pamphs:* most of the contents are secondary
sources for genl & local historical & archaeo info
Archvs: some material, chiefly: estates, local govt,
family letters etc (main local govt archvs at County
Council HQ & County Lib *Other:* variable sources
of mainly local relevance; can be accessed by
written appl; quantity & quality can be determined
by staff search
Equip: fax, copier *Svcs:* info, ref
Stock: various bks, periodcls, photos, slides,
illusts, pamphs & maps
Classn: own
Staff: Other Prof: 3 *Non-Prof:* 4 *Exp:* €2539
(1999-2000); €2539 (2000-01)

IS186

Monaghan General Hospital, Medical Library
Monaghan, Co Monaghan, Ireland (047-81811;
fax: 047-72486)
Email: monaghan.library@nehb.ie
Internet: http://www.nehb.ie/

Gov Body: North Eastern Health Board *Chief:*
Lib Assistant/Clerical Offcr: Ms Kathleen
McGuinness
Assoc Libs: other libs in NEHB Lib & Info Svc:
MOTHER MARY MARTIN LIB (see **IS29**); CAVAN
GENL HOSP LIB (see **IS16**); LOUTH COUNTY
HOSP LIB (see **IS162**); OUR LADY'S HOSP LIB
(see **IS190**); ST BRIGIT'S HOSP LIB (see **IS1**); ST
DAVNET'S HOSP LIB (see **IS187**)
Entry: NEHB staff; GPs & other healthcare
employees *Open:* Mon-Fri 1400-1700

Subj: medicine; health care; nursing *Co-op
Schemes:* BLDSC, Irish & British Healthcare Libs
Networks ILL schemes
Equip: computer (incl wd-proc & internet) *Online:*
various databases, incl: Medline, CINAHL,
Cochrane
Classn: DDC *Auto Sys:* Heritage

IS187

St Davnet's Hospital Library
Monaghan, Co Monaghan, Ireland (047-81822;
fax: 047-81615)
Email: stdavnets.library@nehb.ie
Internet: http://www.nehb.ie/

Gov Body: North Eastern Health Board
Assoc Libs: other libs in NEHB Lib & Info Svc:
MOTHER MARY MARTIN LIB (see **IS29**); CAVAN
GENL HOSP LIB (see **IS16**); LOUTH COUNTY
HOSP LIB (see **IS162**); MONAGHAN GENL HOSP
LIB (see **IS186**); OUR LADY'S HOSP LIB (see
IS190); ST BRIGIT'S HOSP LIB (see **IS1**)
Subj: medicine
Equip: copier, computers (incl internet) *Online:*
Medline, CINAHL, Cochrane, PsycInfo, DARE, BNI
& others
Classn: DDC *Auto Sys:* Heritage

Murroe

IS188

Glenstal Abbey Library
Glenstal Abbey, Murroe, Co Limerick, Ireland (061-
386103; *fax:* 061-386328)
Email: librarian@glenstal.org
Internet: http://www.glenstal.org/

Gov Body: Glenstal Abbey *Chief:* Libn: Br
Colmán Ó Clabaigh
Entry: adv appt *Open:* contact the Libn
Subj: religion; theology; monastic studies; liturgy;
phil; arts; Irish lit; biography; geog; Irish hist
Collns: Bks & Pamphs: antiquarian bk colln (15C-
19C)
Equip: video viewer, copier, computers (incl wd-
proc & CD-ROM) *Svcs:* ref
Stock: bks/c58000; periodcls/100
Classn: DDC *Auto Sys:* ALS *Staff: Non-Prof:* 2

Naas

IS189

Naas General Hospital Library
Naas Genl Hosp, Naas, Co Kildare, Ireland (045-
897221 x393; *fax:* 045-874492)
Email: naashosplib@erha.ie

Gov Body: South Western Area Health Board
Chief: Lib Mgr: Ms Toody Gavin (toody.gavin@
erha.ie)
Entry: open entry *Open:* Mon-Fri 0930-1300,
1400-1730
Subj: medicine; healthcare *Co-op Schemes:* Irish
Healthcare Libs
Equip: copier, 2 clr copiers, 2 computers (both
with wd-proc, internet & CD-ROM) *Svcs:* info, ref,
biblio
Stock: bks/c500; periodcls/54; pamphs/10
Classn: DDC *Staff: Non-Prof:* 1 FT

Navan

IS190

Our Lady's Hospital, Medical Library
Navan, Co Meath, Ireland (046-78700; *fax:* 046-
73483)
Email: phil.moran@nehb.ie
Internet: http://www.nehb.ie/

Gov Body: North Eastern Health Board **Chief:** Libn: Mr Phil Moran
Assoc Libs: other libs in NEHB Lib & Info Svc: MOTHER MARY MARTIN LIB (see **IS29**); CAVAN GENL HOSP LIB (see **IS16**); LOUTH COUNTY HOSP LIB (see **IS162**); MONAGHAN GENL HOSP LIB (see **IS186**); ST BRIGIT'S HOSP LIB (see **IS1**); ST DAVNET'S HOSP LIB (see **IS187**)
Subj: medicine
Equip: copier, computers (incl internet) *Online:* databases incl Medline, CINAHL, Cochrane, PsycInfo, Infotrac, BNI
Classn: DDC **Auto Sys:** Heritage

IS191 🔑 🐾
St Columban's Library
Dalgan Pk, Navan, Co Meath, Ireland (046-21525; *fax:* 046-22799)
Email: collibr@iol.ie

Type: missionary soc **Chief:** Libn: Miss Linda Halton BA(Hons)
Entry: adv appt **Open:** Mon-Fri 0900-1300
Subj: the bible; theology; spirituality; mission studies; RC Church; other religions; geog & hist of Asia & Latin America
Equip: copier, fax, video viewer, computer (with wd-proc) **Svcs:** info, ref, indexing
Stock: bks/22000; periodcls/90; maps/90; videos/260
Classn: DDC **Auto Sys:** in-house **Staff:** Libns: 1

Newtownmountkennedy

IS192 🏛
Coillte Teoranta (Irish Forestry Board), Library
Rsrch & Development, Newtownmountkennedy, Co Wicklow, Ireland (01-201-1129; *fax:* 01-201-1199)
Email: ann.kehoe@coillte.ie
Internet: http://www.coillte.ie/

Chief: Libn: Ms Ann Kehoe MA, DipLIS
Entry: adv appt **Open:** Mon-Fri 0930-1700
Subj: sci; tech; forestry **Collns:** Other: main colln of forestry resources in Ireland **Co-op Schemes:** BLDSC, Trinity Coll Dublin Info Svc (see **IL2**)
Equip: fax, copier, computer **Svcs:** info, ref, biblio
Stock: bks/7000; periodcls/60
Classn: DDC **Auto Sys:** InMagic DBTextworks
Staff: Libns: 1 **Exp:** €25000 (2000-01)

Rathkeale

IS193 🔑
Irish International Arts Centre Library
Castle Matrix, Rathkeale, Co Limerick, Ireland (085-730-7760; *fax:* 069-63242)
Email: lysard@lycos.com

Gov Body: Irish Internatl Arts Centre **Chief:** Dir: Mrs Elizabeth O'Driscoll
Entry: only by special arrangement; adv appt in writing, providing two referees **Open:** usually Mon-Fri 1100-1300, 1400-1730; closed Easter & 15 Dec-15 Jan; note that staff/family may not always be available, hence prior arrangement required
Subj: genl; Ireland; local studies (Limerick & Cork: hist, geog & folklore); phil; psy; religion; symbolism; mythology; lang; tech; printing; graphic arts; arch; theatre; lit; Irish poets; Spenser; Celtic hist; Irish hist; European hist; archaeo; revolutions; genealogy; heraldry **Collns:** Bks & Pamphs: Wild Geese Colln (e.g., by Camille Desmoulins; French Revolution) Archvs: Wild Geese Documents; military archvs (16C-date) Other: heraldry texts (16C-

date); medieval heraldic MSS (Cooke's Ordinary of Arms, 1580); Irish mercenary documents
Equip: computer (with wd-proc) **Svcs:** info, ref
Stock: bks/12000; periodcls/6
Classn: by subj **Staff:** Other Prof: 1 Non-Prof: 1
Further Info: Lib temporarily in stasis late 2002 until new Trustees take over

Sherkin Island

IS194 🔑 🎓
Sherkin Island Marine Station, Library
Sherkin Island, Co Cork, Ireland (028-20187; *fax:* 028-20407)
Email: sherkinmarine@eircom.net
Internet: http://homepage.eircom.net/~sherkinmarine/

Type: NGO **Chief:** Dir: Mr Matt Murphy
Entry: open to visiting workers, not open to public
Open: 6 days per wk
Subj: marine biology; marine ecology; aquatic birds; aquatic insects; aquatic plants **Co-op Schemes:** EURASLIC
Stock: 100000 bks, maps, charts, m-forms, reports & reprints
Pubns: Bulletin of Sherkin Island; Ireland's Marine Life; Ireland's Bird Life; Sherkin Comment (4 pa); A Beginner's Guide to Ireland's Seashore; over 40 titles in total, incl proceedings & distribution maps

Sligo

IS195 🎓
Institute of Technology, Sligo, Library
Ballinode, Sligo, Ireland (071-55305; *fax:* 071-41996)
Email: foran.jim@itsligo.ie
Internet: http://www.itsligo.ie/

Chief: Libn: Mr James Foran MA, DipLib **Dep:** Asst Libn: Ms Sinéad Kelly
Entry: letter of introduction required; ref only
Open: term: Mon-Thu 1000-2200, Fri 1000-1700, Sat 1000-1400; vac: Mon-Fri 1200-1300
Subj: undergrad; postgrad; generalities; social sci; lang; sci; maths; tech; arts **Collns:** Bks & Pamphs: Irish Lang Colln; Quality Assurance Colln; Environmental Sci Colln **Co-op Schemes:** BLDSC
Equip: m-reader, m-printer, 3 copiers, 30 computers (all with wd-proc, internet & CD-ROM), room for hire *Online:* Dialog, STN (fees on cost recovery basis) **Svcs:** info, ref, biblio
Stock: bks/35000; periodcls/150; pamphs/4000; maps/100; m-forms/200; audios/50; videos/50
Classn: DDC **Auto Sys:** Millennium
Staff: Libns: 4 Non-Prof: 5

IS196 🍷 🎵
Sligo Euro Information Centre
Sligo Chamber of Commerce, 16 Quay St, Sligo, Co Sligo, Ireland (071-40017; *fax:* 071-60912)
Email: sligoeic@eircom.net

Gov Body: Sligo Chamber of Commerce **Chief:** Euro Info Offcr: Miss Laura Caslin BBS, MMII Grad
Open: Mon-Fri 0900-1700
Subj: European info; business info
Equip: fax, copier **Svcs:** info, ref
Staff: Other Prof: 1 FT **Exp:** stock received from European Commission

IS197 ✚
Sligo General Hospital, Research and Education Centre Library
Level 6, Genl Hosp, The Mall, Sligo, Co Sligo, Ireland (071-74604; *fax:* 071-69095)
Email: helen.clark@nwhb.ie
Internet: http://www.nwhb.ie/

Gov Body: North Western Health Board **Chief:** Lib & Info Svcs Mgr: Mrs Helen Clark BS(Hons), DipLib, MCLIP
Assoc Libs: LETTERKENNY HOSPS, EDU CENTRE LIB (see **IS176**)
Open: Mon-Wed 0800-1800, Thu 0900-2130, Fri 0900-1700
Subj: phil; psy; social sci; medicine; nursing; all health related subjs **Co-op Schemes:** BLDSC, Irish Health Scis Libs Group
Equip: video viewer, copier (charged), fax (free), 8 computers (all with wd-proc & internet, 7 with CD-ROM), scanner, digital camera, LCD maker, 2 rooms for hire *Online:* Medline, BNI, AMED, Cochrane & some full-text journals (access free, charge for printing) **Svcs:** info, ref, biblio
Stock: bks/5000; periodcls/140; videos/40; CD-ROMs/20
Classn: DDC **Auto Sys:** Heritage
Staff: Libns: 1 Non-Prof: 3 FTE **Exp:** €13000 on bks & €20000 on journals (2000-01)

IS198 🎓
St Angela's College Library
Lough Gill, Sligo, Ireland (071-43580 x215; *fax:* 071-44585)
Email: library@stangelascollegesligo.ie

Gov Body: Natl Univ of Ireland **Chief:** Libn: Mr Nicholas O'Sullivan BA, DipLIS (nosullivan@stangelascollegesligo.ie) **Dep:** Lib Asst: Mrs Andrea Mullen BA
Entry: external users ref only **Open:** term: Mon-Thu 0900-2100, Fri 0900-1700, Sat 1000-1330; vac: Mon-Fri 0900-1700
Subj: undergrad; postgrad; local studies (Sligo & Leitrim, incl local hist, tourism & archaeo); phil; psy; religion; social sci; sci; maths; tech; arts; lit; geog; hist **Collns:** Other: dissertations for BEd degree in Home Econ at St Angela's Coll (1984-date) **Co-op Schemes:** BLDSC
Equip: m-reader (students only), 2 video viewers, 3 copiers, 2 computers *Offcr-in-Charge:* Libn, as above **Svcs:** info, ref, biblio
Stock: bks/18000; periodcls/120; videos/300; CD-ROMs/50 **Acqs Offcr:** Libn, as above
Classn: DDC **Auto Sys:** Heritage
Staff: Libns: 1 Non-Prof: 1.5 **Exp:** IR£32000 (1999-2000); IR£35000 (2000-01)

Strokestown

IS199 🔑
Strokestown Park House, Library and Archive
Strokestown Pk, Strokestown, Co Roscommon, Ireland (078-33013; *fax:* 078-33712)
Email: info@strokestownpark.ie

Type: historic house **Chief:** Administrator: Mr Luke Dodd BA(Hons) **Dep:** Edu Offcr: Miss Rosaleen Cunningham BA
Entry: adv appt **Open:** by appt at all times
Subj: Co Roscommon & Pakenham: Mahon estate
Collns: Bks & Pamphs: historic colln of bks Archvs: Mahon estate correspondence Other: maps
Equip: fax, copier, computer (incl wd-proc), room for hire
Stock: bks/4000; periodcls/8; photos/1000; slides/300; illusts/300; pamphs/50; maps/200; audios/5; videos/25; archvs/9
Staff: Other Prof: 1 Non-Prof: 1

Templemore

▼

Wexford

Special Libraries

Templemore

IS200 🏛 🎓

Garda Síochána College Library

Training Centre, Templemore, Co Tipperary, Ireland (0504-35400; *fax:* 0504-32059)
Email: gdalibrary@eircom.net

Chief: Libn: Ms Angela Bergin
Entry: by appt *Open:* Mon-Thu 0900-1700, 1800-2100, Fri 0900-1700
Subj: law; policing; criminology; police training; mgmt *Collns: Other:* Irish newspapers; legislation; reports
Equip: m-reader, m-printer, video viewer, copier, computers *Svcs:* info, ref
Stock: bks/12000; periodcls/230; videos/20; theses/500; some CD-ROMs & m-forms
Classn: DDC

Thurles

IS201 🎓

St Patrick's College Library

Thurles, Co Tipperary, Ireland (0504-21201/21822; *fax:* 0504-23735)

Chief: Coll Libn: Rev Martin Hayes DipTheol, BSc, LPh *Dep:* Libn: Mr James O'Toole BA, DipLIS
Entry: letter of introduction required in adv *Open:* term: Mon-Fri 0900-2200; vac: Mon-Fri 1000-1700
Subj: generalities; Irish hist; genl hist; religion; theology; phil *Collns: Bks & Pamphs:* 18C theology; church affairs; 19C-20C Irish pamphs, covering Home Rule, Land War etc *Co-op Schemes:* informal loans with Tipperary County Lib (see **IP27**)
Equip: m-reader, 3 video viewers, copier, computer (incl wd-proc)
Stock: bks/65000; periodcls/70; pamphs/500; audios/70; videos/40
Classn: own *Staff:* Libns: 1 *Non-Prof:* 2

IS202 🎓

Tipperary Institute, Knowledge Resource Centre

Racecourse Rd, Thurles, Co Tipperary, Ireland (0504-28075; *fax:* 0504-28092)
Internet: http://www.tippinst.ie/

Chief: Knowledge Resource Centre Mgr: Mr Tom Deegan BA, HDipEd, MLIS, DipLIS (tedeegan@tippinst.ie) *Dep:* Info Specialist: Ms Marian Kelly (mlkelly@tippinst.ie) *Other Snr Staff:* Administrator: Mrs Angela Quinn (aquinn@tippinst.ie); Info Specialist: Ms Josephine Lambe (jclambe@tippinst.ie); Info Specialist: Mrs Marie Ryan (maryan@tippinst.ie)
Open: term: Mon-Fri 0900-2100, Sat 1000-1300, 1400-1700; vac: Mon-Fri 0900-1700
Subj: all subjs; genl; undergrad; postgrad; generalities; social sci; lang; sci; tech; rural development; business development; info & communications tech *Co-op Schemes:* BLDSC, Trinity Coll Lib Dublin (see **IL2**), BTIS
Equip: 2 m-readers, 2 copiers, 4 video viewers, 10 computers (all with wd-proc, internet & CD-ROM), room for hire *Online:* IEEE, Emerald, I-DOX *Offcr-in-Charge:* Knowledge Resource Centre Mgr, as above

Stock: bks/4597; periodcls/206; maps/100; m-forms/4; audios/9; videos/75; CD-ROMs/1000
Acqs Offcr: Knowledge Resource Centre Mgr, as above
Classn: DDC *Auto Sys:* Millennium
Staff: Libns: 2 *Non-Prof:* 4 *Exp:* IR£150000 (1999-2000); IR£150000 (2000-01)

Tralee

IS203 🗝 ✚

Bon Secours Hospital, Medical Library

Strand St, Tralee, Co Kerry, Ireland (066-714-9800; *fax:* 066-712871)
Email: enq@tralee.bonsecours.ie
Internet: http://www.bonsecours.ie/

Gov Body: Bon Secours Health System Ltd
Chief: contact the Libn *Other Snr Staff:* Hosp Mgr: Mr Paul Garnett
Entry: employees only *Open:* 24 hrs, Mon-Sun
Subj: health related
Equip: computer (with wd-proc, internet & CD-ROM) *Online:* various *Offcr-in-Charge:* Mr Steve Donnellan *Svcs:* info, ref

IS204 🎓

Institute of Technology, Tralee, Library

Clash, Tralee, Co Kerry, Ireland (066-714-5620; *fax:* 066-712-5711)
Email: john.cooke@ittralee.ie
Internet: http://libraryweb.ittralee.ie/

Gov Body: IT Tralee Governing Body *Chief:* Coll Libn: Mr Pat Doherty BComm, DipLIS (pat.doherty@ittralee.ie) *Dep:* Dep Libn: Ms Catherine Murray BA, DipLIS, HDipEd (catherine.murray@ittralee.ie) *Other Snr Staff:* Snr Lib Asst: Mr Gerard Griffin BA, DipLIS (gerard.griffin@ittralee.ie)
Entry: staff & students; external membership decided on indiv basis, contact Libn for details
Open: term: Mon-Thu 0900-2130, Fri 0900-1700, Sat 1000-1400; vac Mon-Fri 0900-1700
Subj: all subjs; sci; tech; business studies *Collns: Bks & Pamphs:* official pubns *Co-op Schemes:* BLDSC, ILL with Trinity Coll Lib Dublin (see **IL2**)
Equip: m-reader, m-printer, 2 copiers, clr copier, computers (incl internet & CD-ROM) *Online:* Infotrac, ECCH, ANBAR/CITIS, Current Contents Connect, ECCTIS, ANTEnet, CELEX *Svcs:* info, ref
Stock: bks/30000+; periodcls/200+; slides/20; pamphs/40; maps/20; videos/40
Classn: DDC *Auto Sys:* Horizon
Staff: Libns: 3 *Non-Prof:* 7

IS205 🎓

Irish College for the Humanities, Library

Kilteely House, Ballyard, Tralee, Co Kerry, Ireland (*tel & fax:* 066-712-0540)
Email: ichkerry@iol.ie
Internet: http://www.iol.ie/~ichkerry/

Chief: Administrator: Ms Kathryn Kissane BA(Arts)
Entry: adv appt; ref only
Subj: arts; art hist; world hist; Irish studies
Equip: fax, copier, computers (incl wd-proc & internet), overhead projector, slide projector, room for hire *Svcs:* info, ref
Stock: bks/10000; slides/12000
Classn: proprietary
Staff: Other Prof: 2 *Non-Prof:* 1

IS206 ✚

Tralee General Hospital, The Library

Tralee Genl Hosp, Tralee, Co Kerry, Ireland (066-718-4216)
Email: tghlibrary@shb.ie
Internet: http://www.shb.ie/

Gov Body: Southern Health Board *Chief:* Libn: Mr Patrick Fitzgerald BA, MA (fitzgeraldp2@shb.ie)
Assoc Libs: BANTRY GENL HOSP LIB, Bantry Genl Hosp, Bantry, Co Cork, Libn: Ms C. Doody (027-50133; *fax:* 027-52435); MALLOW GENL HOSP LIB, Mallow Genl Hosp, Mallow, Co Cork (022-21251)
Entry: membs only; visitors by appt *Open:* Mon, Fri 0915-1645, Tue-Thu 0915-2045
Subj: medicine *Co-op Schemes:* IHSLG
Equip: copier, fax, computers (incl 8 with wd-proc, 8 with internet & 8 with CD-ROM) *Online:* CINAHL, Medline, Cochrane etc *Svcs:* info, ref, biblio
Stock: bks/2000; periodcls/420
Classn: DDC *Staff:* Libns: 1 *Non-Prof:* 3

Tullamore

IS207 ✚

Midland Health Board, Central Library and Information Service

Midland Regional Hosp, Tullamore, Co Offaly, Ireland (0506-46170; *fax:* 0506-46207)

Gov Body: Midland Health Board *Chief:* Regional Libn: Ms Nicola Fay BA(Hons), DipLIS (nicola.fay@mhb.ie) *Dep:* Asst Libn: Ms Sandra Keating BA, DipLIS (sandra.keating@mhb.ie)
Assoc Libs: MIDLAND REGIONAL HOSP LIB, Portlaoise, Co Laois, Asst Libn: Ms Sandra Keating, as above (0502-78160; *fax:* 0502-78428); MIDLAND REGIONAL HOSP LIB, Mullingar, Co Westmeath, Asst Libn: Ms Margaret Morgan BA(Hons), HDip, DipLIS (044-39272; *fax:* 044-39282)
Entry: Health Board staff only *Open:* Mon-Fri 1000-1700
Subj: psy; social sci; medicine; nursing; allied health *Co-op Schemes:* Irish Health Scis Libs Group, BL
Equip: 3 copiers (€2.50 for 50 copies); 13 computers (incl 3 with wd-proc, 4 with CD-ROM & 6 with internet) *Online:* EBSCO Online (Medline, CINAHL) *Offcr-in-Charge:* Regional Libn, as above
Svcs: info, ref, biblio
Stock: bks/3500; periodcls/200
Classn: DDC *Auto Sys:* Heritage
Staff: Libns: 3 *Non-Prof:* 3.5 *Exp:* €118435 (2000-01); incl all print & elec resources

IS208 🗝 🎓

Offaly Historical and Archaeological Society, Library and Archives

Offaly Historical Centre, Bury Quay, Tullamore, Co Offaly, Ireland (*tel & fax:* 0506-21421)
Email: ohas@iol.ie
Internet: http://www.offalyhistory.com/

Chief: contact the Chairman: Mr Stephen McNeill
Entry: free admission to membs; public may access ref materials in the Public Reading Room
Subj: local studies (Co Offaly); archaeo; Irish hist & heritage; family hist; genealogy; church hist; women's hist; local business & industry; transport; family papers; business records; personal papers; records of local orgs *Collns: Bks & Pamphs:* extensive local hist ref colln *Archvs:* MS materials relating to the hist of Co Offaly, incl correspondence, diaries, minute bks, ledgers etc *Other:* extensive photographic colln, incl Hanley Colln & Magan Colln; map colln; local newspapers; films; audio recordings; postcards; memorabilia

 academic   corporate   **- 564 -**   governmental   medical

Svcs: photocopying, reprographic, rsrch
Stock: bks/10000; photos/20000, incl prints & postcards; various maps & MSS
Staff: staffed by volunteers
See also **IO40**

Waterford

IS209

Waterford Institute of Technology, Luke Wadding Library

Cork Rd, Waterford, Ireland (051-302840; *fax:* 051-302661)
Email: libinfo@wit.ie
Internet: http://www.wit.ie/library/

Gov Body: Waterford Inst of Tech (WIT) **Chief:** Inst Libn: Mr Ted Lynch (tlynch@wit.ie)
Assoc Libs: COLLEGE ST CAMPUS LIB, College St, Cork
Entry: students & staff of the Inst; by letter of introduction from other colls; external borrowing available **Open:** *Main Lib:* term: Mon-Thu 0915-2100, Fri 0915-1700, Sat 0915-1300; vac: Mon-Fri 0915-1700; *Coll Street Lib:* term: Mon-Thu 0915-2100, Fri 0915-1700; vac: Mon-Fri 0915-1700
Subj: all subjs; genl; A-level; undergrad; postgrad; local studies (Waterford) **Co-op Schemes:** LAMDA, BLDSC, ILL, Irish Health Libs Co-op
Equip: 4 m-readers, m-printer, 8 copiers (card operated), 2 video viewers, 200 computers (all with wd-proc, internet & CD-ROM) *Disabled:* Dragon software, JAWS *Online:* Web of Science, Science Direct, ABI Inform, Emerald, EI Compendex, Infotrac, Dialog *Offcr-in-Charge:* Inst Libn, as above **Svcs:** info, ref, biblio, indexing, info literacy training
Stock: bks/127804; periodcls/405; maps/120; audios/2662; videos/1092; music scores/2500
Acqs Offcr: Academic Liaison Team
Classn: UDC **Auto Sys:** Horizon
Pubns: Erga Journal (new, in print & online); Lib Bulletin (monthly, on web site)
Staff: *Libns:* 6 *Other Prof:* 5 *Non-Prof:* 17
Further Info: WIT Libs constitutes the largest 3rd level lib in South East Ireland

IS210 ✚

Waterford Regional Hospital, Library and Information Service

Dunmore Rd, Waterford, Co Waterford, Ireland (051-842434; *fax:* 051-848561)
Email: Library.WRH@sehb.ie

Gov Body: South Eastern Health Board **Chief:** Libn: Ms Emma Quinn MA, DipLIS **Other Snr Staff:** Lib Asst: Ms Bernadette Power
Assoc Libs: SOUTH EASTERN HEALTH BOARD LIB (see **IS171**); WEXFORD GENL HOSP LIB (see **IS211**)
Entry: SEHB staff only **Open:** Mon-Thu 0930-2100, Fri 0930-1700, Sat 1000-1400
Subj: medicine; nursing; psy; sociology; child care; biochemistry; genetics; biology; physiotherapy; nutrition; occupational therapy; health mgmt; medical law **Co-op Schemes:** BLDSC, BMA, RCSE, Irish Healthcare Libs Group
Equip: m-reader, 2 copiers (card operated), fax, video viewer, 8 computers (all with wd-proc, internet & CD-ROM) **Svcs:** info, ref
Stock: bks/4000; periodcls/130; slides/100; audios/10; videos/20; CD-ROMs/30
Classn: Bliss **Auto Sys:** Unicorn
Staff: *Libns:* 1 *Non-Prof:* 4

Wexford

IS211 ✚

Wexford General Hospital Library

Wexford Genl Hosp, Wexford, Co Wexford, Ireland (053-42233)

Gov Body: South Eastern Health Board **Chief:** Regional Libn: Ms Ann Tierney BA, DipLIS **Dep:** Lib Asst: Mrs Mary McDonald
Assoc Libs: SOUTH EASTERN HEALTH BOARD LIB (see **IS171**); WATERFORD REGIONAL HOSP LIB (see **IS210**)
Entry: SEHB staff only **Open:** Mon 1300-1600, Tue 1300-1730, Wed 1300-1530, Fri 1030-1530
Subj: health; medicine
Equip: copier, computer (with wd-proc & CD-ROM) **Svcs:** info, ref
Stock: bks/600; periodcls/45; CD-ROMs/2
Classn: Bliss **Auto Sys:** Unicorn
Staff: *Non-Prof:* 0.5

SECTION 10 – IRISH LIBRARY AND INFORMATION ORGANISATIONS

Entries are arranged alphabetically under organisation names. Organisations listed include professional societies and associations such as the Library Association of Ireland (along with branches and special interest groups), co-ordinating bodies, pressure groups, specialist information services, local and family history societies, and library and information studies departments of universities and colleges.

Irish organisations based in Northern Ireland are listed in **Section 5 – UK Library and Information Organisations**, but are cross-referenced from this Section.

While every effort is made to ensure that addresses and other contact details are accurate and up-to-date, it should be noted that a number of the following organisations can only be contacted via their senior officers, and that contact details may change following any turnover in these positions.

To telephone organisations within the Irish Republic from outside the country, dial 00-353 followed by the number, minus the initial 0.

Entries are based on the organisations' responses to the following questions:

	1. **a) Official name of organisation** **b) Acronym of organisation**
	2. **Full postal address** *(incl. postcode)* **Tel & Fax** *(incl. STD code)*
Email:	Electronic Mail
Internet:	Internet address
Type:	3. **Type of Organisation** *(see key to Symbols below)*
Gov Body:	4. **Governing body** *(if any)*
Chief:	5. **Chief Officer** *(incl. name, designation & email)*
Other Snr Offcrs:	6. **Other Senior Officers** *(incl. name, designation & email)*
Membs: indivs instns	7. **Members** *(if any)* **a)** individual **b)** institutional
Memb Req:	**Membership Requirements** *(if applicable, incl. subscription fees)*
Branches & Groups:	8. **Branch Organisations/Special Interest Groups** *(if any; give contact details & name & designation of officer in charge)*
Activs:	9. **Main activities/services of organisation**
Pubns:	10. **Publications** *(give Titles, Terms of issue, Prices)*
Further Info:	11. **Further Information**

Key to Symbols

 Academic/Educational	Corporate/Business	Governmental (incl local)
Museum/Gallery	Photo/Film	Private

Medical/Health

Religious

IRELAND
An Chomhairle
▼
Co Louth
Organisations

IO1

An Chomhairle Leabharlanna – The Library Council

53-54 Upper Mount St, Dublin 2, Ireland (01-676-1167/1963; *fax:* 01-676-6721)
Email: info@librarycouncil.ie
Internet: http://www.librarycouncil.ie/

Chief: Dir: Mrs Norma McDermott (nmcdermott@ librarycouncil.ie)
Activs: Acts as the advisory body on public library development to the Minister for the Environment and Local Government, and to public library authorities in Ireland. Provides an information service on libraries and librarianship. An Chomhairle Leabharlanna is the Regional Library Bureau for Ireland and operates the inter-library lending system for all of Ireland.
Pubns: Irish Library News (monthly newsletter, free to Irish libs & info units); annual report; TIPS (monthly current awareness svc for public lib staff); statistical series: Public Library Authority Statistics: Actual (annual, free); Public Library Authorities Annual Estimates of Expenditure (free); Public Library Statistics: An Analysis of Trends in Relation to Irish Public Libraries (irregular, free)
See also **IS37**

IO2

Books Ireland

11 Newgrove Ave, Dublin 4, Ireland (01-269-2185; *fax:* 01-260-4927)
Email: booksi@eircom.net

Chief: Publisher: Mr Jeremy Addis
Activs: Publisher of Books Ireland magazine, which reviews and lists books of particular Irish interest or provenance. It also includes seasonal lists of forthcoming titles, interviews with authors, publishers and other book professionals, and an annual index of books listed or reviewed by author, title and subject. Maintains an archive of books of Irish interest and bibliography.
Pubns: Books Ireland (9 pa, postal subscription €32, UK£20); Twelve Years of Irish Publishing (CD-ROM, index & biblio 1990-2001)

IO3 ⚷

British and Irish Association of Law Librarians, Irish Group [BIALL]

c/o Thérèse Broy, Libn, Arthur Cox, Earlsfort Centre, Earlsfort Ter, Dublin 2, Ireland (01-618-0870; *fax:* 01-618-0727)
Email: tbroy@arthurcox.ie

Gov Body: British & Irish Assoc of Law Libns (see **O72**) *Chief:* Sec: Ms Thérèse Broy, as above
Membs: 60 membs, from both jurisdictions
Activs: Acts as a forum for law librarians in Ireland; meets at least three times a year; runs the Irish Legal Reference Materials Course; publishes Union List of Periodicals & Union List of Law Reports.

IO4 ⚷ 🎓

Carlow Historical and Archaeological Society [CHAS]

c/o Rev Dermot McKenna, 20 Sherwood, Carlow, Co Carlow, Ireland (0503-30915)
Email: mckenna@itcarlow.ie

Gov Body: Offcrs & Cttee *Chief:* President: Dr Michael Conry *Other Snr Offcrs:* Hon Sec: Rev Dermot McKenna, as above
Membs: 248 indivs *Membership Req:* subscription: €10 pa
Activs: Promotes the study of the local history of Co Carlow; organises lectures during winter months and outings during the summer; maintains a local history museum in Carlow.
Pubns: Carlovonia (journal, €8)

IO5 ⚷

Children's Books Ireland

17 Lower Camden St, Dublin 2, Ireland (*tel & fax:* 01-872-5854)
Email: info@childrensbooksireland.com
Internet: http://www.childrensbooksireland.com

Type: arts org *Chief:* Exec Dir: Ms Claire Ranson (claire@childrensbooksireland.com) *Other Snr Offcrs:* Administrative Asst: Ms Liz Marshall (liz@childrensbookireland.com)
Membs: 400 indivs; 100 instns *Membership Req:* subscription: indivs €25 pa (students/ unwaged €15), overseas €45/US$40 pa, instns €35 pa, corps €300 pa
Activs: Provides an information service on all aspects of children's literature; organises three children's literature events for adults each year; runs the annual nationwide Children's Book Festival; runs the BISTO/CBI Book of the Year Awards.
Pubns: INIS (quarterly magazine, free to membs, €4.99 to non-membs); Chalk Talk (annual magazine for teachers, free to membs); Book Fest (annual festival pubn, free); Magic Books (annual festival pubn, free); Book Choice for Primary Schools (free to membs); Book Choice for Post-Primary Schools (free to membs); Big Guide 2: Irish Children's Books; various others
See also **IS48**

IO6 ⚷

Clé – The Irish Book Publishers' Association [CLÉ]

43-44 Temple Bar, Dublin 2, Ireland (01-670-7642; *fax:* 01-670-7393)
Email: cle@iol.ie
Internet: http://www.irelandseye.com/cle/ home.html

Type: trade assoc *Gov Body:* Cttee *Chief:* Exec Dir: Ms Orla Martin
Membs: 40 companies (publishers) *Membership Req:* open to publishers of bks (must have at least two titles published & an ongoing programme of pubn); associate membership open to indivs engaged in related work (proofreading, editorial, publicity or illustration work etc)
Activs: Brings together publishers in the Republic of Ireland and Northern Ireland to share expertise and resources and to solve common problems. Provides training in all areas of publishing, marketing services (e.g., World Book Day) and information, including international aid with contacts. Also provides copyright training and acts as lobby for members' interests on issues of copyright. Conducts a bi-annual statistical survey of the Irish book publishing industry.

IO7 ⚷ 🎓

Clondalkin History Society

c/o 13 New Rd, Newlands, Clondalkin, Dublin 22, Ireland (01-459-2049)

Chief: Chairperson: Mrs Josephine Byrne *Other Snr Offcrs:* Vice Chairman: Mr Martin Grace; Hon Sec & Archivist: Lt Col Padraig A. Murphy (pcomurchu@yahoo.co.uk); Hon Treasurer: Mr Philipp Brunkard
Membership Req: subscription: €13 pa (snr citizens & students €10)
Activs: Aims to research, study and publicise the pre-history and history of Clondalkin and its environs, and to encourage the preservation of areas and items of historic interest, and where appropriate to assist in such preservation.
Pubns: A Walk Through the Past: The Clondalkin Tourist Trail (o/p); The Catholic Parish of Clondalkin 630-2001 AD, by Padraig Murphy (2002, €8)

IO8 ⚷ 🎓

Cloyne Literary and Historical Society

c/o Ms Helen Duggan, 20 Laurel Ct, Midleton, Co Cork, Ireland (021-463-3143)
Email: super@iol.ie

Chief: Chairperson: Mr John McAuliffe *Other Snr Offcrs:* Sec: Ms Helen Duggan, as above; Treasurer: Ms Marie Guillot
Membs: 50 indivs *Membership Req:* subscription: €15 pa
Activs: Promotes the literary and historical heritage of Cloyne; organises lectures and outings to places of literary and historical interest; publishes books relating to the history of Cloyne.
Pubns: The Pipe Roll of Cloyne, ed by P. MacCotter & K. Nichols (1996, €57 + €6.50 p&p); The Gravestone Inscriptions of the Cathedral Cemetery of Cloyne, Co Cork, by Richard Henchion (1999, €15 + €6.50 p&p); walking map of Cloyne (forthcoming)

IO9 ⚷ 🎓

Co Donegal Historical Society

c/o Ms Kathleen Emerson, 61 Cluain Barron, Ballyshannon, Co Donegal, Ireland (072-51267)

Gov Body: President & Exec Cttee *Chief:* Chairman: Mr Anthony Begley, Carrickboy, Ballyshannon, Co Donegal *Other Snr Offcrs:* Hon Sec: Ms Kathleen Emerson, as above; Treasurer: Ms Una McGarrigle, Parkhill, Ballyshannon, Co Donegal
Membs: 950 indivs *Membership Req:* subscription: €20 pa
Activs: Study of Donegal local history, archaeology, geology and art; publication of an annual each year containing original research work on these subjects; maintains a small museum, at which lectures are sometimes held, including an annual seminar; also organises field days and an annual coach outing.
Pubns: Donegal Historical Society Annual (incl in annual membership fee, IR£8 + p&p to non-membs)

IO10 ⚷ 🎓

Co Louth Archaeological and Historical Society [CLAHS]

5 Oliver Plunkett Pk, Dundalk, Co Louth, Ireland (042-933-1679)

Gov Body: Council *Chief:* President: Mr John McCullen *Other Snr Offcrs:* Hon Sec: Ms D. Howard Russell; Treasurer: Mr K. Campbell; Editor: Mr M. Ross ☛

IRELAND
Co Louth
▼
Library

Organisations

(Co Louth Archaeo & Historical Soc cont)
Membs: 614 indivs; 64 instns *Membership Req:* subscription: €10 pa
Activs: Brings together those interested in the study of the local history and archaeology of Co Louth; organises lectures, seminars and excursions.
Pubns: Journal (1 pa, back-issues available, membs €9, non-membs €11); Monasterboice & its Monuments (€3); Council Book of the Corporation of Drogheda: Vol 1 1649-1734 (€13); Louth County Guide & Directory (membs €15.50, non-membs €23); Richardson's Map of the Commons of Ardee (€6.50); Ravell's Map of Drogheda (membs €19; non-membs €20.50); Journal of Henry McClintock (membs €38, non-membs €44.50); prices excl p&p

IO11 🔑 🎓
Co Roscommon Historical and Archaeological Society
c/o Ms Mary O'Connell, Tonrevagh, Castlerea, Co Roscommon, Ireland (0907-20013)
Email: miriamharlow@eircom.net

Chief: President: Mr John Brady *Other Snr Offcrs:* Joint Secs: Ms Mary O'Connell & Ms Miriam Harlow; Treasurer: Mr Shane Lynskey
Membs: 50 indivs *Membership Req:* open to all those interested in the heritage of Co Roscommon; subscription: families €20 pa, snr citizens €15 pa, students free, corporate membership €25 pa
Activs: Promotes the preservation of and research into the rich heritage of Co Roscommon; arranges a monthly meeting followed by a lecture on a topic related to the County, with speakers ranging from local researchers to professional academics; organises trips to museums and sites of archaeological interest. Members are actively involved in helping to protect the County's heritage, and take part in running the County Museum.
Pubns: journals (2 pa); museum info pubns

IO12 🏛
COLICO – Committee on Library Co-operation in Ireland
c/o 53-54 Upper Mount St, Dublin 2, Ireland (01-676-1167/1963; *fax:* 01-676-6721)
Email: cclery@librarycouncil.ie
Internet: http://www.librarycouncil.ie/colico.html

Type: advisory body, lib cttee for the whole of Ireland *Chief:* Chairman: Ms Siobhán O'Rafferty, Royal Irish Academy Lib (s.orafferty@ria.ie) *Other Snr Offcrs:* Sec: Ms Caroline Clery, Libn, An Chomhairle Leabharlanna, addr as above
Membs: 20 indivs; 8 instns
Activs: The advisory body on co-operation to both the Library and Information Services Council (Northern Ireland) and to An Chomhairle Leabharlanna (The Library Council). Provides a forum for the exchange of information and co-operation between libraries and library organisations in the Republic of Ireland and Northern Ireland; examines all aspects of library co-operation, develops policies, formulates proposals for action and encourages participation. The Committee meets three times a year.
Pubns: Annual Report (free, available from above addr)

IO13 🔑
Crumlin Historical and Preservation Society
c/o Ms Finola Watchorn, 39 St Agnes Rd, Crumlin, Dublin 12, Ireland (01-455-1758 or 01-450-2987)

Chief: Chairperson/Planning Offcr: Ms Finola Watchorn, as above *Other Snr Offcrs:* Hon Sec: Ms Peg Rawlins; Treasurer: Mr Christy Talbot
Membership Req: subscription: indivs €7 pa, families €9 pa
Activs: Collection and dissemination of historical data on Crumlin area and environs; production of books and booklets on local history; organises historical lectures, walks, outings, slide shows etc; active in the preservation and restoration of local buildings and sites of historical and archaeological interest.
Pubns: Crumlin & The Way It Was, by Finola Watchorn (1985, 2nd ed nearing completion); commemorative bklet on erection of replica of medieval village cross on original site

IO14 🔑
Dún Laoghaire Rathdown Heritage Society
Moran Pk House, Dún Laoghaire, Co Dublin, Ireland (01-280-6961 x238; *fax:* 01-280-6969)

Activs: Provides an information service for enquirers seeking information on their ancestors from Dún Laoghaire and the south County Dublin area. To date the Centre has computerised over 145000 records, including Roman Catholic, Church of Ireland and Presbyterian records.
Pubns: In the Mind's Eye: Memories of Dún Laoghaire; Dalkey: St Begnet's Graveyard; Dalkey: Medieval Manor & Seaport

IO15 🔑
Federation of Local History Societies of Ireland
c/o Mr Dermot Ryan, Winter's Hill, Kinsale, Co Cork, Ireland (0507-38181; *fax:* 0507-38459)
Email: dermotjosephkennedy@eircom.net
Internet: http://homepage.tinet.ie/~localhist/

Chief: President: Fr Sean Doherty PP *Other Snr Offcrs:* Chairperson: Ms Myra English; Sec: Mr Dermot Ryan, as above
Membs: c100 instns *Membership Req:* open to all Irish Local Hist Socs, Archaeological Socs, Field Groups, Folklore & Folk-Life Socs, Family or Genealogical Socs & local museums
Activs: Established in 1981 to promote the interests of amateur historians and voluntary museums and to represent their views. The aims of the Federation are: to encourage research in the fields of history, archaeology, folk-life and folklore; to exchange information among affiliated societies through the medium of newsletters, publications, seminars etc; to develop mutual support among affiliated societies; to encourage the publication of information of historical interest and the better utilisation of archives.
Pubns: Federation Journal (1pa); Newsletter, (4 pa, free to membs)

IO16 🔑
Genealogical Society of Ireland
11 Desmond Ave, Dún Laoghaire, Co Dublin, Ireland (01-284-2711; *fax:* 01-285-4020)
Email: GenSocIreland@iol.ie
Internet: http://www.dun-laoghaire.com/genealogy/main.html

Chief: contact the Hon Sec at the above addr
Membership Req: open to all those interested in Irish genealogy; subscription: €15 pa

Activs: The Society is an educational charity founded to promote an interest in genealogy in Ireland. Organises open meetings, lectures, workshops & publishes genealogical material. The Society does not undertake commercial genealogical research.
Pubns: Journal of the Genealogical Society of Ireland (quarterly, €5 each, membs €4.50); The Genie Gazette (monthly, €5); A Guide to the Articles & Sources Published by the Genealogical Society of Ireland 1992 – 1996 (€2.54); Memorial Inscriptions of Deansgrange Cemetery (Vols 1-5, €13 each); Irish Genealogical Sources Series (prices vary); various others; prices excl p&p

IO17 🏛
Information Society Commission
Dept of the Taoiseach, Govt Bldgs, Upper Merrion St, Dublin 2, Ireland (01-619-4344; *fax:* 01-619-4340)
Email: info@isc.ie
Internet: http://www.isc.ie/

Gov Body: Dept of the Taoiseach *Chief:* Chairman: Dr Danny O'Hare
Membs: 21 indivs
Branches & Groups: various advisory & working groups: E-BUSINESS GROUP; LEGAL ISSUES GROUP; TELECOMMUNICATIONS INFRA-STRUCTURE GROUP; E-GOVERNMENT GROUP; E-INCLUSION GROUP; LEARNING GROUP; FUTURES GROUP
Activs: An independent advisory body to Government, reporting directly to the Taoiseach. It plays a key role in shaping the public policy for the Information Society in Ireland, contributing to policy formulation, monitoring progress, and highlighting issues that need to be prioritised.

IO18 🔑
Ireland Literature Exchange (Idirmhalartán Litríocht Éireann) [ILE]
Irish Writers' Centre, 19 Parnell Sq, Dublin 1, Ireland (01-872-7900; *fax:* 01-872-7875)
Email: info@irelandliterature.com
Internet: http://www.irelandliterature.com/

Type: non-profit *Gov Body:* Board of Dirs *Chief:* Dir: Ms Dara O'Hare
Activs: Aims to increase the readership of the literature of Ireland, primarily through translation, in international markets; provides financial support for the translation of Irish literature from both English and Irish to other languages; acts as an information centre for Irish and foreign publishers.
Pubns: New Books from Ireland (free catalogue, 2 pa)

IO19 🔑
Irish Copyright Licensing Agency [ICLA]
Irish Writers' Centre, 19 Parnell Sq, Dublin 1, Ireland (01-872-9202; *fax:* 01-872-2035)
Email: info@icla.ie
Internet: http://www.icla.ie/

Type: reproduction rights org *Gov Body:* Board of Dirs (4 from Irish Writers' Union, 4 from Irish Bk Publishers' Assoc) *Chief:* contact Ms Órla O'Sullivan at above addr
Membs: 1300 authors; 106 publishers
Activs: Issues licenses for the photocopying of limited amounts of copyright material (books and journals); the money thus collected is distributed to the authors and publishers whose works have been photocopied.

IO20 ♟

Irish Family History Society (Cumann Stair Clann na hEireann)

PO Box 36, Naas, Co Kildare, Ireland
Email: heueston@iol.ie
Internet: http://homepage.tinet.ie/~ifhs/

Chief: Hon Chairman: Mr John C. Heueston
Membership Req: subscription: €20 pa for residents of the Republic of Ireland, €25 pa overseas
Activs: Aims to promote the study of Irish family history and genealogy and to promote the preservation, security and accessibility of archival materials; advises all those interested in seeking their Irish roots and encourages the repatriation of information from overseas on Irish emigration; organises lectures, seminars and workshops.
Pubns: Irish Family History Journal (€12, previous vols €6, surface postage free, airmail €4); Directory of Parish Registers (3rd ed, €5 + 50c surface p&p, airmail €2); Table of Church of Ireland Parochial Records (€5 + €3 surface p&p, airmail €8); Members' Interest Directory (free to membs); News Sheet (free to membs)
See also **IA79**

IO21 🏛

Irish Manuscripts Commission

73 Merrion Sq, Dublin 2, Ireland (01-676-1610; *fax:* 01-662-3832)
Email: irmss@eircom.net
Internet: http://www.irmss.ie/

Gov Body: Dept of Arts, Culture, Gaeltacht & the Islands *Chief:* Chairman: Prof Geoffrey Hand
Other Snr Offcrs: Sec: Ms Margaret Clancy
Membs: 21 indivs
Activs: Established to report on the nature, extent and importance of collections of manuscripts and papers of literary, historical and general interest, relating to Ireland, whether in private or public ownership and on the places in which such manuscripts and papers are deposited. The Commission also arranges for the preparation and publication of calendars, catalogues and editions of manuscripts.
Pubns: 140+ vols published since 1930, over 50 of which are still available in print

Irish Science Librarians' Group
See **O239** in UK Orgs

IO22 ♟

Irish Society for Archives (Cumann Cartlannaíochta Éireann)

c/o Ms Ursula Mitchell, Trinity Coll Lib Dublin, MSS Dept, College St, Dublin 2, Ireland (01-608-1189)
Email: umitchel@tcd.ie
Internet: http://www.ucd.ie/~archives/isa/isa-index.html

Chief: Chairperson: Dr Raymond Refaussé (rcblibrarian@ireland.anglican.org) *Other Snr Offcrs:* Hon Sec: Ms Ursula Mitchell, as above; Hon Treasurer: Mr Tom Quinlan (tquinlan@nationalarchives.ie)
Membership Req: open to anyone in Ireland & beyond interested in archvs; subscription: indivs €20 (students €10), instns €40
Activs: Exists to promote the place of archives in Irish society. Organises lectures on topics of interest and concern to archivists, the users of archives and the wider public.
Pubns: Irish Archives (journal, 1 pa); newsletter (2 pa)

IO23 ♟

Irish Translators' and Interpreters' Association [ITIA]

Irish Writers' Centre, 19 Parnell Sq, Dublin 1, Ireland (01-872-2014; *fax:* 01-872-6282)
Email: translation@eircom.net
Internet: http://www.translatorsassociation.ie/

Type: voluntary *Chief:* Mr Michael McCann
Other Snr Offcrs: Hon Sec: Ms Miriam Lee; Treasurer: Mr Robert Kortenhorst
Membs: 420 indivs; 23 corporate instns
Membership Req: subscription: indivs €30 pa (students €15), prof membs €55 pa
Activs: Aims to improve the development of the profession of translation and interpretation; offers information and advice to its members on a range of issues; arranges International Translation Day lectures, highlighting the varied history of translation in Ireland; has established Infotech and Translation Studies networks; offers an annual Prix de l'Ambassade Bursary for translators, in conjunction with the French Embassy.
Pubns: Translation Ireland (newsletter, 4 pa); Register of Members (1 pa)

IO24 ♟

Irish Writer's Union (Chomar na Scribhneoiri)

Irish Writers' Centre, 19 Parnell Sq, Dublin 1, Ireland (01-872-1302; *fax:* 01-872-6282)
Email: info@writerscentre.ie
Internet: http://www.ireland-writers.com/

Chief: Chair: Mr Conor Kostick *Other Snr Offcrs:* Hon Sec: Mr Anthony P. Quinn; Treasurer: Mr Sam McAughtrey; Administrator: Ms Katherine Moore
Membership Req: open to FT or PT writers who are Irish by birth, adoption or association; subscription: €45 pa; associate membership available for those not yet published
Activs: Aims to defend the rights of authors; campaigns for improvements in royalties, advances, contracts and conditions; provides confidential advice to members on contracts & publishing, as well as assistance in the event of a professional dispute; acts as a voice and forum for members; contributes to relevant educational policy; organises a programme of meetings and events throughout the year.
Pubns: Final Draft (monthly newsletter)

IO25 ♟ 🎓

Kerry Archaeological and Historical Society [KAHS]

c/o Ms Kathleen Browne, Kerry County Lib, Tralee, Co Kerry, Ireland (066-712-1200; *fax:* 066-712-9202)
Email: kahs@eircom.net
Internet: http://www.kerrycolib.ie/kahs/

Chief: President: Mr Emmet Kennelly *Other Snr Offcrs:* Hon Sec: Ms Kathleen Brown, addr as above; Hon Treasurer: Mr Gerry O'Leary
Membs: 500 indivs *Membership Req:* open to all those interested in the hist, topography & antiquities of Co Kerry; subscription: indivs €25 pa (students €13), families €38 pa, instns €50
Activs: Aims to promote and facilitate the collection, recording, study and preservation of the history and antiquities of Co Kerry; organises regular lectures and field outings.
Pubns: Journal (1 pa, free to membs, back issues €13 to membs, €19 to non-membs); Kerry Magazine (1 pa, free to membs, back issues €6 incl p&p)
Further Info: The Soc's lib & archvs are held at Kerry County Lib (see **IP11** & **IA92**)

IO26 ♟

Library Association of Ireland (Cumann Leabharlanna na hEireann) [LAI]

53 Upper Mount St, Dublin 2, Ireland (01-704-8500 or 086-607-0462; *fax:* 01-608-8700)
Email: admin@libraryassociation.ie
Internet: http://www.libraryassociation.ie/

Type: prof *Chief:* President: Ms Gobnait O'Riordan (president@libraryassociation.ie) *Other Snr Offcrs:* Hon Sec: Ms Geraldine McHugh (honsec@libraryassociation.ie); Admin Sec: Ms Eileen O'Donohoe
Membs: 510 indivs; 71 instns *Membership Req:* open to those employed in the profession of librarianship (incl lib assts); associate membership open to those interested in the work, progress & welfare of libs but who are not employed in the profession; institutional membership open to libs & other corporate bodies
Branches & Groups: ACADEMIC & SPECIAL LIBS SECTION (see **IO27**); ASST LIBNS' SECTION (see **IO28**); AUDIOVISUAL & IT SECTION (see **IO29**); CATALOGUING & INDEXING GROUP (see **IO30**); COUNTY & CITY LIBNS' SECTION (see **IO31**); GOVT LIBS SECTION (see **IO32**); HEALTH SCIS LIBS SECTION (see **IO33**); IRISH LANG GROUP (see **O261**); MUNSTER REGIONAL SECTION (see **IO34**); RARE BKS GROUP (see **IO35**); WESTERN REGIONAL SECTION (see **IO36**); YOUTH LIBS GROUP (see **IO37**)
Activs: Represents the profession of librarianship in the Republic of Ireland; promotes high standards of librarianship and of library and information services in Ireland; promotes greater co-operation between libraries; seeks to maintain the status of the profession of librarianship by requiring the observance of strict rules of personal professional conduct as a condition of membership; evaluates and gives recognition to degrees, diplomas and other professional qualifications in librarianship; conducts courses of study, sets examinations and issues diplomas; examines legislation affecting libraries and the profession in Ireland, and assists in the promotion of legislation necessary for the advancement of libraries; acts on behalf of the profession in dealing with Government and other bodies; collects and publishes information of service or interest to members; organises conferences and other functions to promote the interests of the Association.
Pubns: An Leabharlann – The Irish Library (quarterly, free to membs); Annual Report; conference proceedings; policy documents

IO27 ♟

Library Association of Ireland, Academic and Special Libraries Section

c/o Caitriona Sharkey, Ernst & Young, Ernst & Young Bldg, Harcourt Centre, Harcourt St, Dublin 2, Ireland (01-475-0555)

Type: prof *Gov Body:* Lib Assoc of Ireland (see **IO26**) *Chief:* Chairperson: Ms Caitriona Sharkey, addr as above *Other Snr Offcrs:* Sec: Ms Nicky Kilroy, KPMG (nicky.kilroy@kpmg.ie)
Membership Req: open to membs of the Lib Assoc of Ireland working or with an interest in the academic & special libs sector
Activs: Caters within the LAI for the needs of information professionals working in Universities, Institutes of Technology, Regional Technical Colleges, private third level colleges and research institutions, as well as the commercial, state and semi-state sectors. Provides a forum for discussion of issues relevant to academic and special librarians; organises seminars, workshops, talks and visits.

IO28 ⚷

Library Association of Ireland, Assistant Librarians' Section

c/o Mr Gerard Flannery, Tipperary Libs, Castle Ave, Thurles, Co Tipperary, Ireland (0504-21555; *fax:* 0504-23442)
Email: gflannery@tipperarylibraries.ie

Type: prof *Gov Body:* Lib Assoc of Ireland (see **IO26**) *Chief:* Chairperson: Ms Jess Codd, Tipperary Libs *Other Snr Offcrs:* Hon Sec: Mr Gerard Flannery, Tipperary Libs, as above
Activs: Caters for the needs of all grades of librarianship from Library Assistant to Executive Librarian, representing their interests within the LAI as a whole; maintains a strong interest in the provision of ongoing education and training for library staff; organises an annual conference, seminars and visits.

IO29 ⚷

Library Association of Ireland, Audiovisual and Information Technology Section [LAI AVIT]

c/o Ms Marie Burke, Univ Coll Dublin, Belfield, Dublin 4, Ireland (01-716-7614)

Type: prof *Gov Body:* Lib Assoc of Ireland (see **IO26**) *Chief:* Chairperson: Ms Marie Burke, at above addr
Activs: Special interest group of the LAI. Aims to provides members and others with a forum for discussion in the audiovisual and IT fields; to promote wide awareness of issues relevant to these fields; organises seminars, workshops and conferences.
Pubns: Newsletter

IO30 ⚷

Library Association of Ireland, Cataloguing and Indexing Group

c/o Mr Mícheál Ó hAodha, Univ of Limerick Lib, Limerick, Ireland (061-202166)

Type: prof *Gov Body:* Lib Assoc of Ireland (see **IO26**) *Chief:* Chairman: Ms Jane Gribbon, Univ of Limerick *Other Snr Offcrs:* Sec: Mr Mícheál Ó hAodha, at above addr
Activs: Advises the LAI on matters relevant to the fields of cataloguing and indexing; encourages the provision of training, education and professional development; facilitates the exchange of experience and ideas within the cataloguing and indexing fields; organises courses, workshops, seminars and visits.

IO31 ⚷

Library Association of Ireland, County and City Librarians' Section

c/o Ms Dolores Doyle, Limerick City Lib, The Granary, Michael St, Limerick, Ireland (061-314668; *fax:* 061-411506)
Email: doyledolores@hotmail.com

Type: prof *Gov Body:* Lib Assoc of Ireland (see **IO26**) *Chief:* Chairman: Mr Donal Brady, County Libn, Waterford County Lib *Other Snr Offcrs:* Sec: Dolores Doyle, City Libn, Limerick City Lib, as above
Membs: 32 indivs
Activs: Represents the interests of librarians working in city and county libraries in Ireland. Organises meetings, seminars, conferences and training.

IO32 ⚷

Library Association of Ireland, Government Libraries Section [LAI GLS]

c/o Ms Valerie Ingram, Office of Public Works Lib, 51 St Stephen's Green, Dublin 2, Ireland (01-647-6023; *fax:* 01-661-3107)
Email: valerie.ingram@opw.ie
Internet: http://www.libraryassociation.ie/sections/govtlibs/

Type: prof *Gov Body:* Lib Assoc of Ireland (see **IO26**) *Chief:* Chairperson: Mr Michael O'Gorman (mogorman@statelab.ie) *Other Snr Offcrs:* Minutes Sec: Ms Orla Gillen (orla.gillen@iveagh.irlgov.ie); Correspondence Sec: Ms Valerie Ingram, as above; Treasurer: Ms Ruth O'Flaherty (ruth.oflaherty@hsa.ie)
Membs: 57 indivs; 15 instns *Membership Req:* open to membs of the Lib Assoc of Ireland involved in the govt libs sector; no addl fee
Branches & Groups: COPYRIGHT & LICENSES FOR ELEC DATABASES, contact: Ms Mary Doyle (MaryP.Doyle@agriculture.gov.ie)
Activs: Represents the interests of all government library staff in Ireland; aims to develop and promote the role of libraries in the Civil Service and to promote co-operation between government libraries; organises meetings, training, visits, demonstrations and social events.
Pubns: GLINT (newsletter, irregular, free to membs)

IO33 ⚷ ✚

Library Association of Ireland, Health Sciences Libraries Section

c/o Ms Niamh O'Sullivan, Irish Blood Transfusion Svc Lib, Natl Blood Centre, James's St, Dublin 8, Ireland (01-432-2848)
Email: niamh.o'sullivan@ibts.ie

Type: prof *Gov Body:* Lib Assoc of Ireland (see **IO26**) *Chief:* Chair: Mr Bernard Barrett, South Eastern Health Board, Lacken, Dublin Rd, Kilkenny (056-84110; *email:* barrettb@sehb.ie) *Other Snr Offcrs:* Sec: Mr Timothy Collins, Medical Lib, Clinical Sci Inst, Natl Univ of Ireland Galway (091-524411 x2791); Communications Offcr: Ms Niamh O'Sullivan, as above
Membership Req: open to all membs of the Lib Assoc of Ireland
Activs: Represents the interests of librarians working in medical, health science, nursing and other health care libraries in Ireland. Provides a forum for health care library workers to meet, discuss issues of common concern, and find joint solutions to problems; ensures that the knowledge and practice of members informs national and, where appropriate, international policy; organises activities, meetings and training courses.

Library Association of Ireland, Irish language Group (Meitheál Oibre na Leabharlainnthe)

See **O261** in UK Orgs

IO34 ⚷

Library Association of Ireland, Munster Regional Section

c/o Ms Niamh Cronin, Cork County Lib, Farranlea Rd, Cork, Ireland (021-454-6499)
Email: niamhmary@hotmail.com

Type: prof *Gov Body:* Lib Assoc of Ireland (see **IO26**) *Chief:* Chairman: Mr Denis Murphy, Cork County Lib (dinjmurphy@hotmail.com) *Other Snr Offcrs:* Sec: Ms Niamh Cronin, as above
Membership Req: open to LAI membs working in the south of Ireland
Activs: Aims to inform and educate library staff in the region and to represent their interests; provides opportunities for social interaction; organises seminars, lectures, social gatherings, and visits to libraries and other places of interest.

IO35 ⚷

Library Association of Ireland, Rare Books Group

c/o Mrs Penelope Woods, Russell Lib, Natl Univ of Ireland Maynooth, Maynooth, Co Kildare, Ireland (01-708-3890; *fax:* 01-628-6008)
Email: penny.woods@may.ie
Internet: http://www.libraryaccociation.ie/sections/rarebooks/

Type: prof *Gov Body:* Lib Assoc of Ireland (see **IO26**) *Chief:* Chair: Mr Charles Horton, Chester Beatty Lib (horton@cbl.ie) *Other Snr Offcrs:* Sec: Mrs Penny Woods, as above; Treasurer: Dr Charles Benson, Trinity Coll Dublin (cbenson@tcd.ie)
Activs: Caters primarily for library staff working with early printed books and special collections within Ireland, but welcomes other library and information professionals with an interest in these materials; takes a particular interest in cultivating an awareness of the importance of such collections and in their care and preservation; organises informal talks, seminars and visits.
Pubns: Books Beyond the Pale: Aspects of the Provincial Booktrade in Ireland Before 1850, ed by Gerard Long (€13.35 + p&p); The Experience of Reading: Irish Historical Perspectives, ed by Bernadette Cunningham & Maire Kennedy (€19.05 + p&p)

IO36 ⚷

Library Association of Ireland, Western Regional Section [WLAI]

c/o Galway Public Lib, Hynes Bldgs, St Augustine St, Galway, Ireland (091-561666)
Email: margaret.waldron@gmit.ie
Internet: http://www.libraryassociation.ie/sections/westregion/

Type: prof *Gov Body:* Lib Assoc of Ireland (see **IO26**) *Chief:* Chairperson: Ms Margaret Waldron, Galway-Mayo Inst of Tech Lib *Other Snr Offcrs:* Sec: Ms Siobhan Arkin, Galway Community Coll Lib, Moneenageisha, Galway; Treasurer: Ms Majella King, Galway-Mayo Inst of Tech Lib
Membership Req: fees vary according to lib grade of memb
Activs: Represents the interests of LAI members working in the west of Ireland.

IO37 ⚷

Library Association of Ireland, Youth Libraries Group [LAI YLG]

c/o Ms Anne Gannon, Dublin City Public Libs, 138-144 Pearse St, Dublin 2, Ireland (01-674-4800)

Type: prof *Gov Body:* Lib Assoc of Ireland (see **IO26**) *Chief:* Chairperson: Ms Anne Gannon, as above
Membership Req: open to all membs of the LAI interested in ch's bks
Activs: Aims to promote children's books and reading activities; organises seminars, workshops and lectures related to children's books and libraries; organises the annual Children's Book Festival in association with Children's Books Ireland (see **IO5**).

IO38
Longford Historical Society
c/o Longford Museum & Heritage Centre, Lower Main St, Longford, Ireland (043-46153)
Email: jmulvey@tinet.ie

Chief: Chairman: Mr Luke Baxter (lbaxter@iol.ie)
Other Snr Offcrs: Hon Sec: Seamus Mulvey, as above
Membs: 280 indivs
Activs: Aims to promote an interest in the history, archaeology and customs of Co Longford, and to preserve its monuments, historical sites and traditions. Activities include educational lectures, arranging outings, collecting historical documents and artifacts, publications and generally acting as a watchdog in matters of local historical interest.
Pubns: Teathbha (Soc journal); newsletter (6 pa)

IO39
Meath Archaeological and Historical Society [MAHS]
c/o Mr Oliver Ward, Spiddal, Nobber, Co Meath, Ireland (046-52236; *fax:* 046-52453)

Chief: President: Mr John Gavin *Other Snr Offcrs:* Sec & Pubns Sec: Mr Oliver Ward, as above; Treasurer: Ms Ann O'Reilly; Editor: Mr Seamus MacGabhann; Public Relations Offcr: Ms Marie MacSweeney
Membs: 367 indivs; 25 Irish instns, 14 abroad
Membership Req: subscription: €20 pa
Branches & Groups: linked with 11 local socs in the County
Activs: Promotes the local history, family history and archaeology of Co Meath; organises 13 lectures annually, including lectures for 2nd Level students; arranges regional seminars and excursions and visits; provides an information service to members, students and family history researchers.
Pubns: Ríocht na Midhe (annual journal); Index to Ríocht na Midhe 1955-89 (currently being updated); Medieval Fonts of Meath, by Helen Roe; The High Crosses of Kells, by Helen Roe; Skryne & the Early Normans, by Elizabeth Hickey; St Finian of Clonard, by Elizabeth Hickey; The 1798 Rebellion in Meath, by Seamus Ó Loingsigh; Meath: Studies in Local History (14 articles, text for NUI Maynooth Local Hist course); several other pubns, now o/p

IO40
Offaly Historical and Archaeological Society [OHAS]
Offaly Historical Centre, Bury Quay, Tullamore, Co Offaly, Ireland (*tel & fax:* 0506-21421)
Email: ohas@iol.ie
Internet: http://www.offalyhistory.com/

Type: local historical soc *Chief:* Chairman: Mr Stephen McNeill *Other Snr Offcrs:* Sec: Mr Michael Byrne
Membs: 150 indivs; 10 instns *Membership Req:* open to all those interested in the heritage of Co Offaly; subscription: €25 pa

Branches & Groups: FAMILY HIST GROUP, contact Ms Margaret White c/o above addr
Activs: Aims to preserve, protect and understand the history of Co Offaly; organises an autumn/winter lecture programme and educational activities; maintains a bookshop, an exhibition centre and an extensive library and archive to facilitate research into the County's history.
Pubns: Newsletter (monthly, free to membs); wide variety of local hist pubns for sale (list available, contact the Offaly Historical Centre as above)
See also **IS208**

IO41
Roscommon Family History Society
Bealnamullia, Athlone, Co Roscommon, Ireland
Email: rendell@eircom.net
Internet: http://www.geocities.com/Heartland/Pines/7030/

Chief: Sec: M. Rendell
Membership Req: open to anybody with an interest in Co Roscommon
Activs: Aims to record and preserve information related to the people of Co Roscommon; to publish information on, about, and in connection with Co Roscommon; to build and maintain a library of such information; to assist researchers and family genealogists whenever possible within the confines of staff availability.
Pubns: Roscommon Family History Society Journal (1 pa, €16.50, £15 UK & Europe, $26 USA & rest of world); pubns of rsrch done by Soc membs, incl: Freeholders of Roscommon, Index of Surnames 1830; Freeholders of Roscommon, Index of Surnames 1831-33; Freeholders of Roscommon, Index of Surnames 1839; Convictions in Roscommon,1830-1832; Births, Deaths & Marriages, 1848-1854; Births, Deaths & Marriages, 1855-1859; Kelly Colln, Notes on Family of; Roscommon Soldiers Who Died in World War 1; Roscommon People
See also **IA2**

IO42
Society of Archivists, Ireland
c/o Ms Clare Hackett, Guinness Archv, Guinness Storehouse, St. James Gate, Dublin 8, Ireland (01-471-4557; *fax:* 01-408-4737)
Email: clare.hackett@diageo.com

Type: prof *Gov Body:* Soc of Archivists (see **O355**) *Chief:* Chairman: Mr Colum O'Riordan, Irish Architectural Archv, 73 Merrion Sq, Dublin 2 (iaa1@iaa.iol.ie) *Other Snr Offcrs:* Hon Sec: Ms Clare Hackett, as above
Membs: 120 indivs
Branches & Groups: LOCAL AUTHORITIES ARCHIVISTS GROUP
Activs: Regional body of the Society of Archivists, bringing together archivists working in the north and south of Ireland; organises social events and a full programme of training days and regular meetings.
Pubns: The 3rd Directory of Irish Archives; Standards for the Development of Archive Services in Ireland; both available from bookshops or directly from publishers (Four Courts Press, Dublin)

IO43
Society of Indexers, Irish Group
c/o Ms Helen Litton, 45 Eglinton Rd, Donnybrook, Dublin 4, Ireland (01-269-2214)
Email: helenlitton@clubi.ie

Type: prof *Gov Body:* Soc of Indexers (see **O377**) *Chief:* Sec: Ms Helen Litton
Membership Req: membs of the Soc of Indexers living or working in Ireland

Activs: Aims to promote the Society and its objectives; facilitates communication between Irish members of the Society; organises regular meetings, workshops and seminars.

IO44
Swords Historical Society Ltd / Fingal Genealogy
c/o Carnegie Lib, North St, Swords, Co Dublin, Ireland (*tel & fax:* 01-840-0080)
Email: swordsheritage@eircom.net

Chief: Chair: Ms Bernadette Marks, at above addr
Other Snr Offcrs: Dir: Ms Pauline Archbold
Membs: 10 indivs *Membership Req:* open to anyone interested in local & family hist; subscription: €10 pa
Branches & Groups: affiliated to the IRISH FAMILY HIST FOUNDATION
Activs: Promotes the study of local history and genealogy in the Swords area of Co Dublin; provides genealogical services for Fingal and North Dublin; engaged in local Oral History Project, providing tapes & publications of the reminiscences of elderly people; arranges exhibitions at the local museum.
Pubns: Swords Voices (annual oral hist pubn, 9th ed 2002)

IO45
University College Dublin, Department of Library and Information Studies
Belfield, Dublin 4, Ireland (01-716-7055; *fax:* 01-716-1161)
Email: deplis@ucd.ie

Gov Body: Univ Coll Dublin (see **IS148**) *Chief:* Head of Dept: Prof Mary Burke *Other Snr Offcrs:* Departmental Sec: Ms Noreen Hayes
Membs: 8 FT & 6 PT staff
Activs: Provides teaching and research in Library and Information Studies; programmes include:
i) 3 year undergraduate programme leading to Joint Hons BA/BSocSc with Information Studies;
ii) Postgraduate Diploma in LIS (1 year, DipLIS);
iii) Masters degree in LIS: (MA(LIS) and MLIS);
iv) Doctoral degree in LIS (MLitt/PhD).

INDEX

This is a combined index for all sections of the book, including:

Libraries, Archives and Organisations, including all bodies with entries in the Directory, as well as their governing bodies and major associate libraries. Public library authorities are listed, but individual public libraries are not, except where they have their own individual entries. Where possible, bodies that are part of one institution (such as the departmental libraries of a university) are grouped together under the heading of the main institution.

Subjects, including all major subjects covered by special libraries and archives. Specialisations within a subject are usually listed under the more general heading, e.g., for "electronic engineering", look up "engineering, electronic".

Collections, including named collections and collections relating to specific individuals or institutions. Where possible, some indication of the subject matter of the collection has been included. Collections that are part of co-operative schemes such as GLASS or JFR have been excluded. Collections named after an individual are indexed by surname (e.g., Newton, Sir Isaac, Colln), while collections named after an institution are listed as normal (e.g., Josephine Butler Soc Colln).

Please note that the subjects and collections included in the index are based on those listed by the libraries themselves in their entries. Some libraries with a wide subject coverage do not list their subjects individually, and those with a wide range of collections list only major or representative collections. Consequently, although the index is intended to be as comprehensive as possible, it is not exhaustive in its coverage of the collections held and subjects covered by all the libraries in the Directory.

Key to Index

libraries, archives, organisations and other institutions are listed in bold text
subjects are listed in normal text
collections are listed in italics

Index references are to entry numbers. Each reference, or group of references, is preceded by the appropriate section prefix:

L Legal Deposit Libraries   **A** Archives & Record Offices   **P** Public Libraries   **S** Special Libraries   **O** Library & Information Organisations

Irish libraries, archives and organisations are further prefixed with an **I**.

For instance, **IA**7; **IS**101, 107; **P**26; **S**413, 522, 1211 refers to entry entry IA7 in the Irish Archives section, entries IS101 and IS107 in the Irish Special Libraries section, entry P26 in the Public Libraries section, and entries S413, S522 and S1211 in the Special Libraries section.

Agency for Personal Svc Overseas, *see* IS38

Ághas, Tomás, Museum Colln, IA92; IP11

agribusiness, S476

agriculture, A86, 430; IA97; IS38, 52, 135, 146; S9, 16, 19, 49, 64, 65, 74, 78, 108, 114, 117, 123, 141, 150, 226, 263, 273, 280, 287, 341, 348, 420, 449, 452, 473, 476, 502, 515, 525, 578, 618, 625, 626, 628, 654, 772, 805, 844, 857, 940, 955, 959, 1110, 1246, 1319, 1370, 1499, 1540, 1564, 1582, 1601, 1603, 1610, 1622, 1647, 1735, 1788, 1793, 1801, 1837, 1848, 1850, 1882, 1887, 1955, 1971, 1991, 2000, 2045, 2123, 2139, 2160; American, S1653; biodynamic, S2000; co-operative, S1758; early, S786; Irish, S1653; organic, S2000; Scottish, S618; Ulster, S1653; *see also engineering, agricultural; farming; industry, land-based; land-based studies*

agronomy, S786

AHIC Press Colln, IA21

Ahier, Philip, MSS (author), S2190

AIDS, S1157, 1830

Ailesbury family & estate papers, A493

Ailsa Craig Archvs (motor boats), S94

Aimers McLean records (millwrights & engineers), A448

Aintree Lib & Info Resource Centre, S962

air conditioning, S1070

Air Corps records (Ireland), IA45

Air Defence Command, records (Ireland), IA45

air pollution, S233

air power, S1925, 2018

air traffic control, S691

Aircraft Rsrch Assoc Ltd, Lib, S111

Airdrie Weavers Colln, P126

Aireborough Urban Dist, records, A226

Airedale NHS Trust Lib Info Svc, S852

airports, S691

airships, S1342

AIT records (anarchist org), S1224

Aitken's of Falkirk, records (brewers), A179

Al-Furqan Islamic Heritage Foundation, O9; **Lib,** S989

Aladin, Alexis, papers (Russian hist), S1512

Albania, S1436

Albemarle, Earls of, papers, A215

Albert Sloman Lib, S482

Albinson, John, Colln (land surveyor), A57

Albion Archv, A48

Albright & Wilson, archvs (phosphorous manufacture), A51

Alcan Internatl Ltd, Technical Info Centre, S68

alchemy, S1964

alcohol & alcohol studies, S1157, 1189

alcohol & health, S1694

alcoholic beverages, S1694

alcoholism, S417, 1694

Aldam, W., MP Papers, A124

Alderney Lib, P215

Alderney Soc Museum Lib, S2183

Aldershot Military Museum, Lib & Archvs, A9

Aldine Colln, S788, 1512

Alexander Lib, S1725

Alexander, Samual, papers (phil), S1512

Alexandra Hosp Lib, S1852

Alfred Dunhill Archv, A249

algology, S32

Aligent Technologies UK plc, Rsrch & Development Lib & Info Svc, S1934

Alkan Soc Colln, S1154

All England Lawn Tennis & Croquet Club, *see* S1226

All Hallows Coll Lib, IS33

All Nations Bible Coll Archvs, S2081

All Nations Christian Coll Lib, S2081

All Nations Missionary Coll Archvs, S2081

All Nations Missionary Union Archvs, S2081

All Souls Coll, Codrington Lib, S1663

All Wales Health Info & Lib Extension Svcs, O10

Allchin Lib (Asian archaeo), S290

Allen & Hanbury Ltd, records (manufacturing chemists), A189

Allen Lib & Archival Centre, IS34

Allen, Edgar, archvs (tramways), S1539

Allen, Sir Hugh, Colln (music), S1728

Allen, William, papers (Quaker), A189

Allerdale Borough Council, *see* S858

Allestree Lib, *see* S1670

Alleyn, Edward, papers, S1117

Alliance & Leicester Group Archvs, A58

Alliance Française Dublin, *see* IS110

Allied Irish Banks plc, Archvs, IA24

Alloa Allotments Assoc records, A10

Alloa Brewery Co, records, A179

Alloa Grain Market records, A10

Alloway, Lord, correspondence, A20

Allsport Photo Colln, S645

Alma-Tadema Colln, S179

Almedingen, E.M., MSS, S1946

Alnwick Castle Archvs, A11

Alpine Club Lib, S990

Alport, Lord, Papers, S482

ALS Dickens Letters, S1113

Alston Papers, P126

Althorpe estate archv, A395

Altnagelvin Area Hosp, Multi-Disciplinary Edu Centre Lib, S1475

aluminium, S68, 153

Aluminium Federation, Lib & Info Svc, S153

Alverstoke Deanery, parish records, A423

Alyth Burgh records, A416

Alzheimer's Soc, Ann Brown Memorial Lib, S991

Amalgamated Eng Union, archv, S1887

Amateur Festivals Movement, Lib, S1493

Ambleside papers, S31

ambulance services, S1287

America & American studies, S482, 968, 1804

American Coll Dublin, Rooney Lib, IS35

American life, S1621

American Museum in Britain Lib, S97

American War of Independence, S1647

Amgueddfa Lechi Cymru, *see* S422

Amgueddfa Werin Cymru, *see* S419

Amish, S97

Amnesty Internatl Archvs, P110

Amnesty Internatl, Info Resources Program, S992

Amory Lib, S2042

Amy of Patier, family papers, S2190

An Bord Altranais – Nursing Board of Ireland, Lib, IS36

An Canónach Ó Fiannachta Colln (Celtic studies), IA92; IP11

An Chartlann Náisiúnta, IA25

An Chomhairle Ealaíon, *see* IS51

An Chomhairle Leabharlanna – The Lib Council, IO1; **Rsrch Lib,** IS37

An Cnósach Dhuibhneach Colln (Dingle peninsula), IA92

An Comunn Gaidhealach Colln (Gaelic & Highlands), P199

An Damer, archv (Irish theatre), IA41

anaesthesia, S548

anarchism, S1224, 1887

Anarchist Federation of Britain records, S1224

anatomy, L4; S79, 338, 1299, 1357, 1583, 1719; human, S1745; plant, S1862

Anchor Line, records, A176

Ancient India & Iran Trust Lib, S290

Ancient Near Eastern studies, S1747

Ancient Order of Foresters Heritage Trust, A458

Anders, Gen Wladyslaw, papers, S1327

Anderson Colln, S741

Anderson Colln (John Donne), L3

Anderson Colln (phil, edu), S1964

Anderson Press, records, A440

Anderson's Coll of Medicine, records, A176

Anderson, James, Colln, S863

Anderson, Lewis, Tartan Colln, A148

Anderson, Lindsay, Archv, S1978; *Private VHS Colln,* S731

Anderson, T. McLurg, Colln (physiotherapy), A177

Andover Museum, Local Studies Room, A14

Andrade Colln (lit, hist of sci), A37

Andrews Linen Mills, records, IA67

Andrews, M.C., Colln (cartography), S1363, 1364

Anglesey Aluminium records, A324

Anglesey County Record Office, A245

Anglesey Lib, Info & Archv Svc, P3

Anglesey Quarter Sessions records, A245

Anglia Support Partnership, Knowledge Lib Svcs, S829

Anglia Television, film & video archv, A277

Anglian Water plc, Lib, S830

Anglicanism, S1234, 1322, 1798, 1804, 2174

Anglo-American relations, S1621

Anglo-Ecuadorian Oilfields Ltd, records, A482

Anglo-European Coll of Chiropractic, Vilhelm Krause Memorial Lib, S205

Anglo-French Colln, S918

Anglo-German relations, S1144, 1751

Anglo-Japanese relations, S1221

Anglo-Judaica, S1238

Anglo-Polonica, S1328

Anglo-Zulu War, papers, A64

Angus Archvs & Local Studies Centre, A384

Angus Coll Lib, S39

Augus Libs, P4

Angus Lib (Baptist hist), S1760

Angus Trade Incorporation Records, A384

animal behaviour, S71

animal breeding, S1872

animal care, S270, 273, 348, 525, 772, 805, 844, 940, 959, 1499, 1540, 1622, 1882, 1955, 1971, 2045, 2123

Animal Health Info Specialists (UK & Ireland), O11

Animal Health Trust Lib, S1592

animal husbandry, S263, 1850

animal production, S1872

animal rights, S234, 820

animal sciences, S2045

animals & animal life, S637, 983, 1614, 2160

animation, S215

Ann Brown Memorial Lib, S991

Annan Colln, S1180

Anniesland Coll, The Metro, S693

Anstruther, Rev Godfrey, OP, papers (RC English martyrs), A252

Antarctica & Antarctic studies, S294, 339

Anthony, Gordon, Theatre Colln (photos), S1170

Anthrax Papers, S217

anthropology, A328; IS104; S492, 751, 1034, 1171, 1308, 1457, 1632, 1732, 1742, 1949, 1978, 1982; biological, S323, 1741; cultural, S1732; Greek, S1159; Mexican, S1447; Roman, S1159; social, S318, 323, 1732, 1741; *see also ethnography*

anthroposophy, S2000

Anti-Apartheid Movement, records, L4; *Scotland,* S701

Anti-Corn Law League, records, A194

anti-fascism, A365; S1517

anti-Methodism, A368; S264

anti-Semitism, S1195, 1517

anti-slavery, IS78; S1242; *see also slavery & the slave trade*

Anti-Slavery Soc, records, L4

Anti-Treaty Forces, documents, IA45

antibiotics, S1830

Antient Concerts Soc Colln (music scores), IS138

antiquarianism, A200, 400

antiques, S1944

antiquities, A37; IA20, 87; IS179; S98, 433, 530, 571, 807, 1028, 1396, 1584, 1789; classical, S1159; medieval, S1031

antisera, S1830

Antrim Grand Jury Presentments, A23

Antrim Healthcare Lib, S38

Antrim Presbytery Lib (16C-18C), S139

Antrobus family & estate papers, A493

apiculture, S416, 627; *see also beekeeping*

Apostleship of the Sea, records, A388

Apothecaries Hall of Dublin, Archvs, IA26

Appleby Colln (guitar music), S1154

Appleton Colln (19C printing & binding), S18, 19

APSO Resource Centre, IS38

aquaculture, S8, 32, 83, 543, 840, 849, 1488, 1822, 1898, 2123; marine, IS158; S638

Aqualate family papers, A467

aquatic resources, S1822

aquatic science, S1805

Arab studies, S672

Arab-Israeli conflict, S672

arachnids, S1359

Arapoff, C., Colln (inland waterways), A183

arboriculture, S273, 682, 772, 844; *see also forestry*

Arbours Assoc, records, A104

Arbroath Town Council, records, A384

Arbuthnott family & estate papers, A3

archaeology, A14, 37, 68, 86, 108, 151, 167, 236, 301, 303, 410, 420, 442, 455, 480, 483, 488, 508; IA20, 69, 70, 92; S56, 98, 146, 220, 246, 247, 283, 341, 355, 422, 436, 439, 450, 451, 472, 479, 502, 530, 545, 593, 612, 775, 807, 909, 919, 929, 941, 950, 956, 972, 1028, 1031, 1033, 1034, 1122, 1263, 1288, 1324, 1396, 1502, 1546, 1584, 1588, 1597, 1632, 1742, 1880, 1890, 1900, 1912, 1933, 1949, 1967, 2016, 2025, 2036, 2044, 2049, 2077, 2091, 2126, 2150, 2169, 2176, 2183, 2186, 2187, 2190; Anatolian, S1033; Ancient Near Eastern, S1033; Arabian, S1033; Asian, S290; British, S1396, 2162; Bronze Age, S1030, 1031; Causasian, S1033; Central Asian, S1033; classical, S325, 1030, 1747; Cycladic, S1030; Dark Age, S688; European, S1031, 1396, 1747; Greek, S1030, 1159; industrial, S146, 422, 530, 775, 956, 1933; Iranian, S1033; Irish, IS4, 20, 121, 137, 139, 175, 179, 193, 198, 208; Iron Age, S1031, 1963; Levantine, S1033, 1321; medieval, S1880; Mesopotamian, S1033; Middle Eastern, S1321; Minoan, S1030; Mycenaean, S1030; near-Eastern, S355; Neolithic, S1031; Palaeolithic, S1031; Palestinian, S1321; prehistoric, S1747; Roman, S1030, 1159, 1963; Scottish, S612, 980; social, S323; Welsh, A6, 504; *see also Egyptology*

Archbishop Marsh's Lib, IS39

Archdeacon Gordon James Lib, S426

Archdeacon Sharp Lib, S567

Archer of Tanworth, family & estate papers, A476

Archifdy Ceredigion, A5

Archifdy Meirion, A123

Archifdy Ynys Môn, A245

architects, IA36

Architectural Assoc Lib, S993

architecture, A151, 409, 455, 483; IA36, 70; IS6, 22, 119, 123, 141, 151, 161, 193; S12, 44, 56, 97, 102, 125, 263, 268, 324, 422, 448, 450, 466, 502, 523, 554, 561, 591, 594, 623, 707, 880, 937, 941, 955, 966, 969, 993, 996, 998, 1007, 1019, 1028, 1075, 1122, 1205, 1246, 1261, 1262, 1267, 1268, 1282, 1290, 1306, 1391, 1396, 1418, 1439, 1452, 1503, 1527, 1584, 1700, 1747, 1778, 1912, 2029, 2076, 2103, 2120; agricultural, IS185; church, S264, 952, 1057; domestic, S775; ecclesiastical, S320, 746, 775, 1102, 1459, 2174; industrial, IS185; Irish, S132; landscape, S12, 591, 594, 1235, 1912, 2160; naval, S1372, 2030; railway, S48; theatre, A267; vernacular, S419, 470, 1653; Welsh, A6

Architecture Libns Group, O12
Archv of Art & Design, A250; *see also* A353
Archv of British Publishing, S1848
Archv of Historical Textile & Business Records, *see* A148
Archv of the Actuarial Profession, S1188
Archv of the Diocese of Brentwood (RC), A65
Archv of the Dirs of Social Work, *see* S712
Archv of the Medical Assoc for the Prevention of War, S217
Archv of the Soc of Jesus in Britain, A251
Archv of Traditional Welsh Music, A24
Archvs Council Wales, O13
Archvs in Edu (Wales), *see* O372
Archvs of the Archdiocese of Southwark (RC), A252
Archvs of the Irish Sisters of Mercy, IA27
Archvs of the RC Archdiocese of Armagh, *see* A16
Archivists in Independent Television, O14
Archway Healthcare Lib, S994
Arctic, S339
Ardagh & Clonmacnois RC Diocesan Archvs, IA72
Ardee Rural Dist Council, archvs, IA80
Argyll & Bute Archvs, A248
Argyll & Bute Lib & Info Svc, P5; **Local Studies Colln,** A140
Argyll & Clyde Acute Hosps NHS Trust, S763
Argyll & The Isles, Episcopal Diocese of, records, A248
Aristotle Colln, S1756
Arkell Lib of Jurassic Geol, *see* S1738
ARLIS UK & Ireland, O15
Armachiana Colln, A15
Armagh Corp records, S41
Armagh County Museum, Archvs, A15
Armagh militia, records, S43
Armagh Observatory Lib, S40
Armagh Public Lib, S41
Armagh, RC Archdiocese of, archvs, A16
Armitage Colln, P75
Armitage of Kirklees Hall, family & estate records, A194
Armitt Lib & Museum Centre, Ambleside, S31
armoured vehicles, S2084
arms & armour, S913, 1455
arms control, S1213
Armstrong Gibbs, C., MSS (music), S25
Armstrong Lib, S470
Armstrong, J.R., Photo Colln, S470
army, British, A311; S1284, 1289; Colonial, S1289; Indian, S1289
Army Lib Svc, Prince Consort's Lib, S26; **Svcs Central Lib,** S995
Army Records Soc, O16
Arnell, Richard, MSS (music), S1428
Arnold Walker & Florence Mitchell Lib, S1349
Arnold, F.T., Bequest (18C music), L5
Arnold, Thomas, papers (historian), A511; S1879
Arrowe Park Hosp, McArdle Postgrad Medical Lib, S2133
Arrowsmith Firm, archv (cartography), S1364
art & arts, A17, 151, 152, 205, 220, 241, 265, 288, 313, 335, 349, 409, 428, 430, 465, 466, 480, 496, 508; IA70; IS5, 7, 11, 22, 23, 33, 34, 41, 45, 47, 49, 56, 74, 82, 90, 92, 100, 105, 110, 112, 115, 119, 123, 135, 141, 149, 155, 166, 172, 178, 181, 183, 188, 195, 198, 205; S2, 12, 31, 34, 44, 67, 70, 73, 76, 103, 108, 121, 150, 155, 156, 160, 180, 190, 198, 208, 215, 237, 238, 248, 258, 263, 269, 270, 275, 283, 296, 297, 325, 327, 332, 340, 347, 352, 355, 359, 382, 383, 415, 424, 430, 436, 442, 443, 469, 474, 478, 482, 495, 525, 530, 533, 540, 541, 545, 546, 561, 565, 588, 590, 593, 611, 633, 634, 661, 673, 674, 675, 677, 683, 687, 689, 698, 707, 713, 741, 743, 747, 788, 803, 810, 824, 834, 838, 855, 859, 866, 870, 879, 880, 885, 900, 901, 904, 907, 910, 918, 927, 950, 958, 966, 968, 969, 972, 993, 996, 997, 1002, 1009, 1015, 1016, 1018, 1028, 1032, 1043, 1050, 1059, 1060, 1075, 1085, 1102, 1104, 1108, 1115, 1123, 1127, 1148, 1161, 1169, 1170, 1217, 1227, 1232, 1243, 1246, 1254, 1255, 1260, 1261, 1262, 1266, 1272, 1274, 1282, 1286, 1287, 1288, 1297, 1298, 1306, 1310, 1323, 1333, 1339, 1340, 1344, 1347, 1362, 1378, 1391, 1403, 1421, 1452, 1455, 1465, 1467, 1491, 1493, 1497, 1498, 1501, 1503, 1512, 1525, 1529, 1544, 1552, 1562, 1565, 1572, 1577, 1581, 1597, 1599, 1611, 1617, 1630, 1632, 1637, 1641, 1652, 1654, 1659, 1678, 1693, 1728, 1745, 1760, 1767, 1806, 1807, 1810, 1816, 1828, 1847, 1853, 1874, 1886, 1887, 1889, 1907, 1911, 1912, 1919, 1923, 1942, 1944, 1949, 1966, 1969, 1978, 1979, 1983, 1999, 2001, 2036, 2038, 2042, 2045, 2046, 2049, 2050, 2056, 2059, 2061, 2064, 2067, 2076, 2093, 2094, 2095, 2096, 2103, 2120, 2122, 2127, 2130, 2144, 2145, 2147, 2148, 2150, 2168, 2169, 2171, 2176, 2179; Africa, S1632; Albanian, S1436; American, S97, 1632; Anatolian, S1033; ancient, S1033; Ancient Near Eastern, S1033; applied, S102, 146, 246, 1105, 1149, 1261, 1418, 1464, 1503; Arabian, S1033; Asian, S290; Austrian, S1006; Belarussian, S1135, 1436; botanical, IS113; S1367; British, S467, 1339, 1418; Bulgarian, S1436; Byzantine, S1747; Canadian, S1053; Causasian, S1033; Celtic, S688; Central Asian, S1033; Christian, IS45; church, S264, 952; classical, S1747; contemporary, S1105, 1693, 1889, 2076; Czech, S1436; decorative, IS121; S97, 102, 206, 238, 324, 422, 451, 612, 623, 705, 1290, 1396, 1418, 1455, 1503, 1900, 2033, 2176; East European, S1436; ecclesiastical, S320, 523, 1234, 1459, 2174; Estonian, S1436; ethnic, S1034; European, S206, 1031, 1455; expressive, S855; Far Eastern, S1290; fine, IS177; S102, 146, 155, 160, 206, 246, 324, 422, 474, 554, 577, 591, 611, 623, 673, 705, 707, 918, 960, 1018, 1032, 1049, 1050, 1060, 1075, 1122, 1255, 1261, 1282, 1290, 1418, 1455, 1589, 1745, 1747, 1848, 1900, 1978; Finnish, S1120, 1436; folk, S1653; foundation, S202; French, S716, 1455, 1690; German, IS80; S709, 1147; graphic, IS193; S2094; Greek, S1159; historic, S2076; Hungarian, S1436; in education, S1804; Indian, S1014, 1184, 1290; indigenous, S1632; Indonesia, S1632; Iranian, S1033; Irish, IS119; S132; Islamic, S989, 1386; Italian, S1216; Japanese, S576, 1220; Latvian, S1436; Levantine, S1033; Lithuanian, S1436; medieval, S1396; Mesopotamian, S1033; modern, S368, 467, 633, 1418, 1693; Moldavian, S1436; natural history, S1308; Oceania, S1632; of the book, S1290; oriental, S246, 328; performance, S1282; performing, A192, 326, 338; S22, 208, 478, 796, 838, 915, 1014, 1323, 1423, 1428; Polish, S1328, 1436; public, S1075; Roman, S1159; Romanian, S1436; Russian, S1393, 1436; Scottish, S611, 623, 633, 876; Slavonic, S327, 1436; Slovakian, S1436; South East Asian, S1290; Spanish, S1210; textile, IS9; Ukrainian, S1436; visual, S368, 673, 1082, 1272; Western European, IS119; Yugoslav, S1436; *see also design; history of art; painting; sculpture*
art history, *see history of art*
Art Libs Soc, O15
art technique, S1745
art theory, S1693, 1745
Art Workers Guild Lib, S996
Arthington Trust Colln (missionary work), P72
Arthur Estate Papers, IA55
Arthurian Colln, L3; P54
artillery, A285; S680, 1130
artistic societies, A254
artists, A63, 313, 349; IA70; S31, 160, 467, 677, 738, 1075, 1255, 1339, 1418, 2036, 2127; Scottish, S633; women, S1272
Artists Internatl Assoc Archv, A349
Arts & Crafts Exhib Soc archvs, A250
arts & crafts movement, S451, 996
Arts Archv (govt & politics), S1989
Arts Council England, Lib, S997; *see also* O324; S352, 1272, 1325, 1581
Arts Council of Ireland, *see* IS51
Arts Council of Northern Ireland, *see* IS51
Arts Council of Wales, *see* A24; S415, 432; *see also* L3
arts policy, S997, 1085, 1108
Arts Theatre Group Archv, A182
Arun Dist Council, *see* A236
Arundel & Brighton RC Diocesan Archvs, A207
Arundel Castle MSS, A452
Arundel family & estate papers, A493
Arundel MSS, L1
Arup Lib & Info Svcs, S998
asbestos, S606, 656
Asburton papers, L2
Ashbee, C.R., papers, S369
Ashbridge Colln (Marylebone), A268
Ashburnham, Earl of, records, A230
Ashby Lib, S347
Ashby-de-la-Zouch Museum, Archvs, A18
Ashe Colln, P36
Ashe, Thomas, Colln, IA92
Ashford & St Peter's Hosps NHS Trust, Health Scis Lib, S455
Ashford Lib Railway Colln, S48
Ashley Lib & MSS (19C English lit), L1
Ashley, Robert, Colln, S1281
Ashley-Cooper, F.S., Lib (cricket), S1276
Ashlin & Coleman Colln (arch drawings of RC Churches), IA36
Ashmole, Elias, Colln, P174
Ashmolean Lib, *see* S1747
Ashorne Hill Mgmt Coll Lib, S889
Ashrail Railways Colln, P67
Ashridge LRC, S149
Ashton, Edgar, colln (folk music), S598
Ashworth, Cornelius, of Ovenden, records (farmer & weaver), A194
Asia, S1095, 1344, 1377, 1443, 1804
Asian Libns & Advisors Group, O17
Askham Bryan Coll Lib, S2160
Aslib, The Assoc for Info Mgmt, O18; **Biosciences Group,** O19; **Charitable Info Group,** O20; **Econ & Business Info Group,** O21; **Eng Group,** O22; **European Business Opportunities Svc,** O23; **IT & Communications Group,** O24; **Knowledge & Info Mgmt Network,** O25; **Midlands Branch,** O26; **Multimedia Group,** O27; **Northern Branch,** O28; **One Man Bands Group,** O29; **Scottish Branch,** O30; **Social Scis Info Group & Network,** O31; **Technical Translation Group,** O32; *see also* O82
ASP records (anarchist publishers), S1224
Aspect Picture Lib, S999
Asperger Syndrome, S1293
Asquith, Herbert, papers, L4
Assam Oil Co Ltd, records, A482
assaying, IA29; S1149
Assembly of the States of Guernsey, records, A531
assessment, IS86
Assessment of Performance Unit, records, S1929
Assheton Family of Middleton papers, A364
Asst Masters Assoc, archvs, S1444
Associated Examining Board, Lib, S767
Associated Newspapers Ltd, Ref Lib, S1000
Associated Scottish Distilleries Ltd, records, A376
Associated Telegraph Co, records, A414
Assoc for Geographic Info, O33; **Scotland,** O34
Assoc for Sci Edu Archv, S918
Assoc of Anaesthetists of Gt Britain & Ireland, Lib & Archvs, S1001
Assoc of British Theatre Technicians, Lib & Archvs, S1002
Assoc of British Theological & Philosophical Libs, O35
Assoc of Chief Archivists in Local Govt, O36
Assoc of Child Care Workers, records, A53
Assoc of Commonwealth Univs, Ref Lib, S1003
Assoc of County & Metropolitan Authorities, archvs, S1250
Assoc of Dirs of Social Work Archv, S712
Assoc of Dist Councils, archvs, S1250
Assoc of Edu Committees Archv, S918
Assoc of Family Case Workers, records, A53
Assoc of Genealogists & Rsrchers in Archvs, O37
Assoc of Genl & Family Case Workers, records, A53
Assoc of Independent Libs, O38
Assoc of Info Offcrs in The Pharmaceutical Industry, O39
Assoc of Law Libns in Central England, O40
Assoc of Learned & Prof Soc Publishers, O41; *see also* O322
Assoc of Libns in Land-based Colls & Univs, O42
Assoc of Local Hist Tutors, O43
Assoc of London Chief Libns, O44
Assoc of Northern Ireland Edu & Lib Boards, O45
Assoc of Northumberland Local Hist Socs, O46
Assoc of Polish Prof Soldiers in Gt Britain, records, S1327
Assoc of Psychiatric Social Workers, records, A53
Assoc of Scottish Genealogists & Record Agents, O47
Assoc of Scottish Life Offices, records, S599
Assoc of Snr Children's & Edu Libns, O48
Assoc of Social Workers, records, A53
Assoc of the British Pharmaceutical Industry Lib, S1004
Assoc of Therapeutic Communities, records, A104
Assoc of UK Media Libns, O49
Assoc of Welsh Local Authorities, archvs, L3
Assoc of Workers for Children with Emotional & Behavioural Difficulties, records, A104
asthma, S1291
ASTIC Rsrch Associates Lib, S492
Aston Univ, Lib & Info Svcs, S154
Aston, W.G., Colln (Japanese bks), L5
Astorga Colln (Spanish bks), L2
AstraZeneca Rsrch & Development Charnwood, Info Sci, Lib & Archvs, S1480
astrology, S743, 1243
astronautics, S1020, 1026
Astronomers Royal for Scotland, papers, S621
Astronomical Inst of Edinburgh papers, S621
astronomy, IS6, 40, 67; L4, 5; S40, 331, 535, 556, 621, 1020, 1026, 1303, 1345, 1435, 1740, 1978, 2000
Astronomy Ireland Lib, IS40
astrophysics, IS63, 67; L4; S40, 331, 535, 1740
asylum, S1203
Athenaeum, Lib, S1005
Athenaeum, Liverpool, Lib, S963
Athlone Inst of Tech Lib, IS2
Athlone Rural Dist Council minutes, IA78
Atholl Colln (music), P144

Athy Rural Dist Council, records, IA83
Atkin, Lord, papers, S1150
Atkins, Anna, Colln (photography), S215
Atkinson Morleys Hosp Medical Lib, see S1410; see also A348
Atlas Preservative Co Ltd, records, A482
Atomic Weapons Establishment Lib, S1842
Attic Press pubns, IS27
Attlee, Clement, papers, L4
Aubrey Keep Lib, S818
Aubrey, John, MSS, S530
Auchinleck papers (military studies), S1512
Auchterarder Burgh records, A416
Auden, W.H., Colln, S593; MSS, S25
Audenshaw Colln (church & soc), S1512
audiovisual studies, IS90
Audit Commission Info Svc, S241
auditing, IS87, 124; S241, 624, 1193, 1292
Audley End Estate Colln, A442
Auerbach, Erich, Colln (music photos), S1170
Auld, Joan, Memorial Colln (labour hist), A137; S561
Austin Clarke Lib, IS41
Australia & Australasia, S1440, 1443, 1804
Austrian Cultural Forum London, Lib, S1006
Authors' Licensing & Collecting Soc, O50; see also O174
autism, S1293
automata, S1105
automatic control, S321
automation, S1530
Automobile Assoc Visual Archv, S266
automobiles, S266, 1346
Avalon Leather Board Co Ltd , records, A477
Avalon Lib Assoc, see S743
AVEC Archvs, S1776
Aventis Pharma UK, Lib, S2106
aviation, A505; S526, 691, 1007, 1316, 1342, 1343; civil, S1261; early, S1342; military, S1343, 1621, 1925
Aviation Picture Lib, S1007
Aviva Co Archv, A396
Avon & Western Wiltshire Mental Healthcare NHS Trust, Staff Lib, S242
Avon Local Hist Assoc, O51
Avon Univ Libs in Co-operation, O52
Avon, Lord, Papers, S179
Avoncroft Museum of Historic Bldgs, Lib, S268
Aydelotte-Kieffer-Smith Colln (US pubns), L4
Aylesbury Coll LRC, S55
Aylmer Colln (music), S413
Ayr Hosp, MacDonald Edu Centre Lib, S62
Ayrshire & Arran Acute Hosps NHS Trust, see S62
Ayrshire & Arran Health Board records, A20
Ayrshire Archvs, A20
Ayrshire Commissioners of Supply, records, A20
Ayrshire Commissioners of the County Bldgs, records, A20
Ayrshire Highway Authorities, records, A20
Ayrshire Justice of the Peace records, A20
Ayrshire Kirk Session records, A20
Ayrshire Medical Offcr reports, A20
Ayrshire Parochial Board records, A20
Ayrshire Poorhouse records, A20
Ayrshire School Boards & Edu Trusts, records, A20
Ayrshire Sound Archv (local hist), S66

B&I records, IA19
BAAS Geological Photo Colln, S1636
Babcock & Wilcox, records (boiler makers), A176
Babington family papers, S393
Babraham Inst Lib, S291
Background Colln (18C bks), P68

bacteriology, S1830
Baden-Powell, Major B.F.S., papers (early aviation), S1342
Baden-Powell, Robert, papers, A343
Badminton Colln (sports), S1989
Badminton family & estate records, A22; L3
Badminton Muniments, A22
Baeck, Leo, papers (rabbi), S1238
Bagot family papers, A467
Bagshaw family muniments, S1512
Bagshawe Colln, S1491
Baguley-Drewery Railcars, records, A467
Bahá'í faith, IS108
Baigent, Francis, papers (antiquary), A511
Bailey Pegg Archv (19C gun drawings), S680
Bailey, H. Hamilton, Colln (surgery), A336
Bailey, Sir Harold, Lib & MSS (ancient langs & lit), S290
Bailieborough Model School, records, IA13
Bain, George, archv (Celtic artwork), S688
Bainbridge of Newcastle, records (dept store), A470
Baines Colln (early ch's bks), S1444
Baines Colln (Sussex authors), P49
Baines, John Manwaring, Colln, A197
Baird, Gen Sir David, papers (Napoleonic Wars), S613
Baird, John Logie, correspondence, A197
Baker Bks Colln, S239
Baker, T.H., MSS, S530
Baker, Tom, Colln (Lincolnshire), S950
bakery, S915, 1850
BAL Drawings Colln, see S1019
Balcon, Michael, Colln (cinema), S1013
Baldwin, Stanley, papers, L5
Bale, Stewart, Photo Colln, A239
Balfour Bequest Lib (ornithology), S1247
Balfour Estate Papers, IL1
Balfour Handel Colln (early eds of Handel), L2
Balfour Lib, S319, 1742
Balint, Enid, Papers, S482
Balkan affairs, S2086
balladry, S373, 751
Ballantyne, J.W., Colln (foetal pathology), S616
ballet, A275, 331, 338; S1170; in education, A496
Ballet & Dallis Colln (lute bks), IL2
Ballet For All Archv, S1232
Ballet Rambert Ltd, see A321
Ballinrobe Poor Law Union records, IA11
Balliol Coll Lib & Archvs, S1664
Ballitore MSS (Quaker families papers), IA82
ballooning, S1342
Ballycroy parish records, IA11
Ballymahon Poor Law Union, minutes, IA73
Ballymahon Rural Dist Council records, IA73
Ballymena Local Studies Colln, P133
Ballymoney Special Colln, P133
Ballymore Rural Dist Council minutes, IA78
Ballyshannon Harbour Board, records, IA67
Ballyshannon Poor Law Union, minutes, IA67
Ballyshannon Rural Dist Council, records, IA67
Ballyshannon Town Commissioners, minutes, IA67
Baltic Coffee House & Chamber of Commerce, records, A135
Bandar Colln of Islamic Law, L4
Bandon, Earls of, estate & family archv, IA19
Bangor Cathedral Lib Colln, S76
Bank Mill, Styal, Cheshire, records, A367
Bank of England, Archv, A253; **Info Centre,** S1008

Bank of London & South America Dirs Lib, A300
Bank of Scotland Archvs Dept, see A147
banking, A147, 253, 271, 287, 300, 329, 363; IA24; IS8, 44, 59; S75, 1008, 1185, 1197, 1261, 1758; see also finance
Banking Info Group, O53
Banks, Sir Joseph, Archv, S1308; Colln, P75; S851; Lib, L1; papers, S1862
Bankside Gallery Archvs, A254
Bannister Hall Print Works, records, A470
Bantock, Granville, Colln (printed music), S158
Bantry Genl Hosp Lib, see IS206
Bantry House Colln, IA21
Baptist Historical Soc Lib, S1760
Baptist Missionary Soc Lib & Archvs, S534; see also S1760
Baptist Union Lib & records, S1760
Bar Council of Ireland, see IS106
Bar Lib, S119
Barb, Alfons A., papers, S1456
Barber Inst of Fine Arts Lib, S155
Barber Music Lib, see S179
Barber, Revis, Papers, S217
Barbirolli, Sir John, Colln (conducting scores), S1428
Barclays Group Archvs, A363
Barclays Univ Lib, S752
Baring Brothers & Co Ltd, archv (merchant bank), S1185
Baring Estate Papers, A297
Baring family estate papers (Barons Northbrook), S1185
Baring-Gould Ballad Colln, L3
Baring-Gould, Sabine, Colln, M20
Barking & Dagenham Lib Svcs, P77; **Archvs & Local Studies Centre,** A118
Barking & Dagenham Health Authority, see S84
Barking & Dagenham Primary Care Trust, Clock House Lib, S84
Barking Coll Lib & Info Svc, S1867
Barkworth Colln (microbiology), S1603
Barley Colln (antiquarian, botany), S1960
Barlow Colln (17C pamphs, theology), L4
Barlow Dante Lib, S1433
Barlow, H.M., Colln (medical bkplates), S1355
Barnard Lib, S1914
Barnardo's Archv, A972; see also S835
Barnardo's Lib, S835; see also IS114
Barnardo, Thomas J., MSS, S835
Barne family & estate papers, A215
Barnes Lib, S182
Barnes, Bishop, Papers, S179
Barnes, Gordon, Bequest (Victorian church arch), S1102
Barnes, John, & Co Ltd, records (dept store), A470
Barnes, William, Colln, S545
Barnet & Chase Farm Hosps NHS Trust, Barnet Medical Lib, S85
Barnet Archvs & Local Studies Centre, A255
Barnet Coll, Independent Learning Centre, S86
Barnet Libs, P78
Barnsley Archvs & Local Studies, A26
Barnsley Dist Genl Hosp NHS Trust, Staff Lib, S87
Barnsley Libs, P6
Barnstaple Borough Archvs, A27
Barnstaple, Archdeaconry of, parish records, A27
Barnwell, F.S., notebks (aviation design), S1342
Baron Ballet & Portrait Colln, S1170
Barrett-Lennard (Belhus) family & estate papers, A188
Barrie, James M., Colln, S876
Barrington Baker Colln (Irish lit & theatre), A37
Barrington Colln (medicine), IS134
Barrington Family, records, A195
Barrington-Simeon Colln (estate records), A392
Barron Papers, IA13

Barron, Arthur T., Colln (environment therapy), A104
Barry Coll, LRC, S92
Barry, Peter, Colln (Michael Collins), IS20
Bartholomew Archv (Edinburgh mapmaking firm), L2
Bartholomew Pamphs, L4
Bartholomew, John, Colln (atlases), L2
Bartle, George, Colln (edu), A216
Barts & The London NHS Trust, see A336
Baruch, Ludwig, Internment Archv (WW2), S217
Basildon Coll, see S758
Basildon Dist Council, see S94
Basildon Healthcare Lib, S93
Basingstoke Coll of Tech, LRC, S95
basketry, S1105
Bassano Colln (London photos), S1288
Bassetlaw Hosp, Staff Lib, S2152
Bassingbourn Parish Lib, S482
Bastard of Kitley estate archv, A419
Bateman Colln (20C labour movement), A77
Bates, H.E., Colln, P131
Bateson, William, Lib & Papers, S1624
Bath & North East Somerset Libs, P7
Bath & Wells Diocesan records, A487
Bath & West Soc Lib (agric), S106
Bath Info & Data Svcs, O61
Bath Nat Hist & Antiquarian Field Club Lib & Archvs, S98
Bath Record Office, A31
Bath Royal Literary & Scientific Instn Lib, S98
Bath Spa Univ Coll Lib, S99
Bath Univ, see Univ of Bath
Bathurst of Cirencester, family & estate records, A185
Battenburg Family Papers, S1946
Battersea Polytechnic, archvs, S776
Battle Abbey Estate Archv, A230
Bauza Colln (maps of South America), L1
Bawtree Family of Sutton Photo & Film Archv, A478
Bax MSS (music), S25
Bax, Arnold, Colln (memorabilia), IS27
Baxter Colln (early clr prints), P49
Baxter, L.A.J., Colln, A297
Baykov Lib, see S179
Bayly Papers, A419
Bayne Family of Kincardine Papers, A10
Baynes, Norman, Colln (Byzantine hist & culture), S1116
BBC Info & Archvs, S1009
BBC Northern Ireland Archvs, A205; see also S815
BBC Photograph Lib, S1010
BBC Press Cuttings Colln, S593
BBC Radio Brighton Tapes, P17
BBC Radio Merseyside Lib, A238
BBC Scotland Radio & TV Script Colln, A182
BBC Sheet Music Lib, S1011
BBC Sound Archvs, see L1
BBC South West Film Lib, A421
BBC World War II Sound Archv, A292
BBC Written Archvs Centre, A428
Beaford Photographic Archv (North Devon), A27
Beamish & Crawford Brewery, records, IA19
BEAMISH, The North of England Open Air Museum, Regional Resource Centre, S108
Bean Memorial Colln (William Blake facsimiles), S482
Beard, Capt Jack, Colln (sailing ship hists), A239
Bearsden & Milngavie Dist Council, records, A171
Béaslaí, Piaras, papers, IL1
Beato, Felice, Colln (images of 19C Asia), S1170
Beaton, Archbishop James, papers, A155
Beaton, Sir Cecil, papers (photographer), A250
Beatson Oncology Centre Lib, S694
Beaufort of Badminton, family & estate records, A185

Beaufort, Dukes of, papers, **A**22
Beaulieu Estate Archv, **A**78
Beaulieu Poor Law records, **A**78
Beaumont Archv (Welsh industry), **L**3
Beaumont Hosp Lib, IS42
Beaumont of Carlton, family & estate papers, **S**828
Beaumont of Whitley, family & estate records, **A**208
Beaumont papers (Coleorton Hall), **A**18
beauty, **S**22, 504, 915, 1969, 2079, 2103
Beaverbrook Papers, **A**286
Bechtel Ltd Lib, S1012
Becke, Major A.F., papers, **S**1130
Beckett's House Lib, S837
Beckett, Samuel, Colln, **S**1848
BECTU Oral Hist Colln, S1013
Bedale Museum, Local Hist Archv, A34
Bedales Memorial Lib, S1802
Beddoe, John, papers, **A**77
Bedford Archdeaconry records, **A**35
Bedford Coll Archvs, **S**651
Bedford Estate Archvs, A380
Bedford Estates, records, **A**161
Bedford Family & Estate (Woburn) archvs, **A**35; **S**2029
Bedford Level Corp, records, **A**87
Bedford MSS (music), **S**25
Bedford School Lib, S112
Bedford, Earls & Dukes of, Family Colln, **S**2029; papers, **A**11, 380
Bedford, Evan, Lib of Cardiology, **S**1355
Bedfordshire & Hertfordshire Health Lib, S2098
Bedfordshire & Hertfordshire Regiment archvs, **A**35
Bedfordshire & Luton Archvs & Record Svc, A35
Bedfordshire Historical Record Soc, O54
Bedfordshire Libs, P8
Bedfordshire Local Hist Assoc, O55
Bedlay of Chryston papers, **A**174
Beds & Bucks Info, O56
Beechams Pills Co Ltd, records, **A**464
Beedell, Charles, Colln (environment therapy), **A**104
beekeeping, **S**416, 627; see also apiculture
beer, **S**1694
Beerbohm, Max, Colln, **S**1692
Beetham Parish Lib, S883
Behan, Brendan, papers, **IL**1
behavioural science, **S**126, 603, 711, 1251; see also psychology
Beit Lib, S327
Beith parish papers, **A**176
Belarus, **S**1135, 1436
Belfast Edu & Lib Board, P132; see also **A**37
Belfast Harbour Commissioners, Archvs, A36
Belfast Inst of Further & Higher Edu, Lib & Learning Resources, S120
Belfast Lib & Soc for Promoting Knowledge, S121
Belfast Ulster & Irish Studies Lib, A37
Belford Hosp Lib, see S839
Belgian Underground Press Colln, **L**1
Belhaven, records (brewers), **A**179
Belhus family & estate papers, **A**188
Bell Coll of Tech, Dumfries Campus Lib, S550; **Hamilton Campus Lib, S**780
Bell Lib, S2143
Bell, Bishop, of Chichester papers, **S**1234
Bell, Gertrude, Papers (politics, arch), **S**1586; Photo Colln, **S**1588
Bell, Idris, Colln (papyrology, classics), **L**3
Bell, Joseph, Papers (surgery), **S**617
Bell, W.G., Colln (Plague & Gt Fire of London), **S**1288
Bell, William Blair, papers (gynaecology), **S**1352
Bellairs, George, MSS, **S**1512
Bellamy, Denis, Papers, **S**217
Bellew Estate Papers, **IL**1

Bellhouse, Billy, Colln (fairs & fairgrounds), **A**451
Bellmoor Colln (hist of Hampstead), **A**262
Belloc, H., Colln, **S**1839
Belvedere Estate Archv, **A**47
Belvedere Orphanage papers, **IA**78
Bemrose, Sir Henry Howe, Colln (Derbyshire), **A**122
benchmarking, **S**1098
Bendall, Cecil, Colln (Buddhist MSS), **L**5
Bender Colln (Californian private press), **IL**2
Benedictine Order, **S**1798
benefits, **S**1069, 1204
Bennet & Bidwell Colln (arch drawings), **S**937
Bennett Papers, **S**1572
Bennett, Arnold, papers, **S**1433
Bensley Colln (Hebrew, Arabic), **L**5
Benson Judaica Colln, **S**523
Benson, Arthur, correspondence, **A**516
Bensusan Colln, **S**482
Bent Diaries (classics), **S**1159
Bentham, George, papers, **S**1862
Bentham, Jeremy, Colln, **S**1433
Bentinck, Cavendish, Colln (rare bks), **S**1469
Bentley MSS, **S**393
bereavement, **IS**114; **S**557, 1409
Bergin Colln, **IS**137
Berington Family of Little Malvern Court Lib, **S**179
Berkeley, L., MSS (music), **S**25
Berkeley, M., MSS (music), **S**25
Berkshire Coll of Agric, LRC, S1499
Berkshire Lib & Info Partnership, O57
Berkshire Local Hist Assoc, O58
Berkshire Masonic Lib & Museum, S1924
Berkshire Record Office, A429
Berkshire Record Soc, O59
Berkshire, Archdeaconry of, parish records, **A**429
Bernal Peace Colln (peace movement), **S**1274
Bernal, J.D., papers, **S**1015
Bernard family & estate papers (Earls of Bandon), **IA**19
Bernard's of Edinburgh, records (brewers), **A**179
Bernstein, Sidney, Colln (theatre), **A**337
Berry, W.E., Poster Colln, **S**215
Berwick Salmon Fisheries Co records, **A**44
Berwick-upon-Tweed Record Office, A44
Besford Court School, archvs, **A**52
Bessemer, Sir Henry, Colln (19C engineer), **S**1200
Best family of Chatham/Boxley, family & estate papers, **A**435
Betham-Edwards, Matilda, Colln (19C France), **P**49
Bethlem Royal Hosp, Archvs & Museum, A33; **Multidisciplinary Lib, S**109
Bethnal Green Museum of Childhood, records, **A**353
Betjeman, John, Colln, **S**1161; Working Lib, **S**671
Betts, Tristam, Africa Colln, **S**1744
Betty & Gordon Moore Lib, see L5
Beudeker Colln (17C cartography), **L**1
Bevan-Naish Colln (Quakerism), **S**185
beverages, **IS**174
Beveridge Colln (Norway, Esperanto, apiculture), **S**1964
Beveridge, Sir William, Colln, **S**1241
Beverley, RC Diocese of, records, **A**224
Beverton, Raymond, Colln (fisheries), **S**1898
Bewdley Borough records, **A**518
Bewick, Thomas, Colln, **A**442; **P**121; **S**1576
Bexhill Museum Lib, S151
Bexley Coll Learning Centre, S148
Bexley Lib Svc, P79
Bexley Local Studies & Archv Centre, A47
BFI Natl Lib, S1013

BG plc, archvs, **A**500
Bhavan's Centre – Inst of Indian Art & Culture, Lib & Archvs, S1014
BHR Group Ltd, Lib, S503
BHR Hosps NHS Trust, see S1869
Bibas Colln (18C French works), **S**357
Bibby, records (shipping company), **A**239
biblical studies, **IS**191; **S**180, 320, 363, 396, 523, 596, 880, 1136, 1238, 1266, 1463, 1522, 1619, 1673, 1752, 1863
Bibliographical Soc, O60
bibliography, **S**322, 466, 569, 705, 738, 801, 952, 1234, 1443, 1627; ethnographic, **S**1034; Hebrew, **S**1701; Islamic, **S**989; Japanese, **S**2113; Jewish, **S**1701; Latin American, **S**1447
Biblioteca Quiniana (fine bindings), **IL**2
Bibliotheca Earberiana (political & economic pamphs), **IL**2
BICC records, **A**239
Bice Bellairs Colln of Revived Greek Dance, **A**192
Bicton Coll Lib, S273
Bidder Lib (marine biology), **S**1805
Biddulph, Gen Sir Robert, papers, **S**1130
BIDS: Bath Info & Data Svcs, O61
Biesenthal Colln (Hebraica), **S**5
Biggar Albion Foundation Ltd, see A48
Biggar, F.J., Lib & Archv (Irish hist & culture), **A**37; **P**132
Bignold Family Papers, **A**396
Bill Douglas Centre for the Hist of Cinema & Popular Culture, Lib & Archv, S661
Billington, Roy, papers, **S**360
Bilsborrow, James, papers (Archbishop of Cardiff), **A**94
binding, **S**1408
Bing, Gertrud, papers, **S**1456
Binnall, Canon P.G., Colln (stained glass), **S**1102
Binnell Colln, P75
biochemistry, **IS**118, 210; **L**4; **S**64, 78, 240, 303, 375, 376, 608, 784, 1300, 1380, 1541, 1697, 1830, 1862, 2087
biodiversity, **S**543, 844
Biodynamic Agricultural Assoc, Lib, S2000
biography, **A**156, 235, 260, 417, 420, 428, 507; **IA**70; **IS**34, 137, 188; **S**44, 88, 98, 156, 297, 415, 545, 676, 712, 738, 771, 907, 916, 1106, 1125, 1205, 1303, 1377, 1379, 1398, 1463, 1468, 1527, 1652, 1653, 1789, 1887, 2068, 2174; Arabic, **S**989; business, **S**1129; Catholic, **S**1057; ecclesiastical, **A**450; **S**1866; Indian, **S**1014; Islamic, **S**989; Jewish, **S**1701; medical, **S**617, 1355, 1357, 1381, 1755; military, **S**1130, 1954, 2084; missionary, **S**360; naval, **S**1827, 1954; political, **L**5; religious, **S**600, 1417, 1463; scientific, **S**1387; technical, **S**1387; theatre, **S**1340; Welsh, **A**480; **S**419
biology, **IS**178, 210; **L**4, 5; **S**16, 226, 240, 294, 475, 482, 558, 608, 612, 626, 844, 923, 927, 959, 1247, 1583, 1622, 1741, 1786, 1830, 1947, 1978, 2000, 2045, 2046, 2091, 2176; cell, **S**309, 313, 1300; fish, **S**1898; freshwater, **S**32, 1803; insect, **S**1359; marine, **IS**194; **S**8, 83, 849, 972, 1805, 1898, 1945, 2187; molecular, **S**291, 375, 377, 1192, 2136; plant, **S**1721; systematic, **S**422; see also botany; life science; natural history; zoology
biomaterials, **S**181
biomechanics, **S**1259
biomedicine, **S**142, 852, 1054, 1178, 1190, 1227, 1300, 1381, 1450, 1452, 1457, 1590, 1825, 1826, 1830
biophysics, **S**2087
bioscience, **S**649
biotechnology, **S**113, 117, 558, 1452, 1888, 2045, 2107; microbial, **S**1624; plant, **S**1624
Biotech & Biological Scis Rsrch Council, see S117, 786, 1570, 1623, 2020

Birchall English Civil War Colln, **P**57
Bird MSS, **A**202
Birdlife Internatl, Lib, S292
birds, see ornithology
Birkbeck Coll Lib, S1015
Birkbeck Lib (Quakerism), **S**918
Birkbeck Literary & Scientific Inst, records, **S**1015
Birkenhead & Wallasey magistrates records, **A**50
Birkenhead County Court records, **A**50
Birkenhead Quarter Sessions records, **A**50
Birkett, Sir Norman, papers, **S**1634
Birmingham & Dist Local Hist Assoc, O62
Birmingham & Midland Inst Lib, S156
Birmingham Black Oral Hist Proj Archv, **S**180
Birmingham Children's Hosp NHS Trust, Lib, S157
Birmingham City Archvs, A51
Birmingham City Rail Carriages & Wagons Co, records, **A**467
Birmingham Coll of Art Lib, see S160, 183
Birmingham Conservatoire, Lib Svcs, S158
Birmingham Flute Soc Colln (printed music), **S**158
Birmingham Heartlands & Solihull NHS Trust, see S159, 1931
Birmingham Heartlands Hosp Lib, S159
Birmingham Inst of Art & Design Lib, S160
Birmingham Law Soc Lib, S161
Birmingham Libs, P9
Birmingham Medical Inst Colln, **S**182
Birmingham RC Archdiocesan Archvs, A52
Birmingham Repertory Theatre Archv, **P**9
Birmingham School of Jewellery Lib, see S160, 183
Birmingham Soc for the Care of Invalid & Nervous Children, records, **A**104
Birmingham Univ, see Univ of Birmingham
Birmingham Women's Hosp NHS Trust, Trust Lib & Info Svc, S162
Birmingham, Diocese of, parish records, **A**51, 499, 503
Birmingham, George, Colln, **IA**11
Birr Castle Colln (photography), **IS**100
Birr Castle Muniments Room, IS6
birth defects, **S**1326
births, marriages & deaths, Australia, **S**1398; England, **A**310; **S**1312, 1398; Ireland, **IA**46; Isle of Man, **A**527; New Zealand, **S**1398; Northern Ireland, **A**39; Scotland, **A**146; **S**1398; Wales, **A**310; **S**1312, 1398
Bishop Auckland Coll Lib, S186
Bishop Auckland Genl Hosp Lib, S187
Bishop Burton Coll, Lib & Info Centre, S150
Bishop Grosseteste Coll, Sibthorp Lib, S950
Bishop Phillpotts Lib, S2054
Bishop's Waltham Deanery, records, **A**509
Bishopsgate Inst Lib, S1016
Black & Ethnic Minority Experience Oral Hist Archv, **S**515
Black Colln (Penicuik), **A**247
Black Country Chamber & Business Link, S227
Black Country Living Museum Archvs, A129
Black Country Local Hist Consortium, O63
Black Cultural Archvs, A256
Black Watch Museum, Regimental Archvs, A415
Black, W., Colln (geol), **S**307
Blackberry Hill Hosp Lib, S243
Blackburn Cathedral Chapter, see A55
Blackburn Clinical Lib, see S1840
Blackburn Colln (women's rights), **S**357

Blackburn Coll Lib, S188
Blackburn Museum & Art Gallery, S189
Blackburn with Darwen Community Hist Dept, A54; *see also* A425
Blackburn with Darwen Lib & Info Svc, P10
Blackburn, Diocese of, parish records, A425
Blacker Day Bks Colln, A15
Blackfriars Cambridge Lib, S293
Blackfriars Lib, S1665
Blackheath Justices of the Peace, records, A278
Blackie, Walter, & Son, Bk Colln (publishers), S797
Blackmore, R.D., papers, A164
Blackpool & the Fylde Coll, LRC, S192; Nautical Campus LRC, S685
Blackpool Borough Council, *see* A425
Blackpool Health Profs' Lib, *see* S193
Blackpool Maritime Colln, S192
Blackpool, Fylde & Wyre Health Lib, S193
Blackwood, William, & Sons, archv (Scottish publishers), L2
Blades, William, Lib (printing), S1408
Blaenau Gwent Libs, P11; *see also* A117
Blaenavon Co Ltd, records (coal, iron & steel), A117
Blaikie, Walter, Colln (Jacobitism), L2
Blaikley Colln of Michael Faraday MSS, A294
Blair Colln (nat sci), A508
Blair, Sir Robert, papers (educationalist), A148
Blairgowie & Rattray Burgh records, A416
Blairs Coll Colln (Scottish Catholicism), L2
Blaise Castle House Museum, *see* S246
Blake Facsimiles Colln, S410
Blake, William, Colln, P109; S918, 972, 1572
Blanco-White, Joseph (poet & Unitarian), Colln (South American & Spanish), S963; *papers,* S972, 1677
Blathwayt of Dyrham, family & estate records, A185
blending, A376
Blenheim Papers, L1
Blenkhorn Richardson, records (textile company), A148
Bletchley Par Archv, S1776
blind welfare, S1374
blindness, S984, 1374; *see also visual impairment*
Bliss Classn Assoc, O64
BLISS Lib Collns, *see* S1066
Bliss, Sir Arthur, papers & MSS, L5
Blok, Vladimir, Lib (Russian composer), A344
Blomfield, Sir Reginald, papers (architect), A511
Blondal, Sigfus, Colln (Icelandic studies), S593
Blondeau Colln (French drama), L3
blood products, S254, 632, 1830
blood transfusion, S254, 632
Bloom Colln (genealogy), S1996
Bloomfield Colln (MSS & early printed materials), P17
Bloomsbury Estate records, A380
Bloomsbury Healthcare Lib, S1017
Blue Circle Industries plc, *see* S762
blues, S511
Bluett Colln (photography), IA55
Blundell of Gt Crosby, family & estate papers, A425
Blundell of Ince Blundell, family & estate papers, A425
Blundell's School, Amory Lib, S2042
Blunden, Edmund, MSS, S1946
Blunkett, David, MP, papers, A452
Blunt papers, S355
Board of Commissioners for the Affairs of India, records, L1
Board of Deputies of British Jews, Archvs, A257
Board of Edu Inspectors Assoc, archvs, S1444

Board of Ordnance Colln (18C military maps), L2
Boardman, Pete, Colln (mountaineering photos), S2118
boating, S1898
Bobbin, Tim, Colln (dialect & prints), A434
Boby, Robert, records (engineers), A83
Bodichon, Barbara, papers, S357
Bodleian Lib, L4; *see also* Oxford Univ
BOEM Ltd, records (crushing industry), A209
Boer War Colln, S1005
Bofin Colln (medicine), IS134
Bogle Papers (tobacco merchants), A174
Bognor Regis Film Soc Colln, A71
Bohn, David, papers (physicist), S1015
Boldero Lib, S1361
Bolger, Bryan, papers, IS34
Bolingbroke Hosp Lib, *see* S1410
Bolingbroke Hosp, minutes, A348
Bollywood Colln, S215
Bolton Archv & Local Studies Svc Lib, A57
Bolton Community Coll, Learning Centres & Libs, S197
Bolton Cotton Spinners archvs, S1512
Bolton Inst of Higher Edu, Learning Support Svcs, S198
Bolton Libs, P12
Bolton Lib, IS13
Bolton School, Boys' Div, Chained Lib, S199
Bolton, 1st Baron, papers, A509
Bolton, Salford & Trafford Mental Health Partnership, Prof Lib, S1506
Bolton, Theophilus, Colln (Archbishop of Cashel), IS13
Bomberg, David, papers, A349
Bon Secours Hosp, Medical Lib, IS203; *see also* IS26
Bonaparte-Wyse Colln (Provencal & Catalan lit), IL2
Bonar Law Papers, A286
Bond, John, Lib (horticulture), S1367
Bond, Nathaniel, papers (politician), A511
Bonds of Norwich, records (dept store), A470
Bonham Carter family papers, A509
Bonnell Colln, S853
Bonthrone, Alexander, & Sons Ltd, records (maltsters), A376
Bk Aid Internatl, O65
Bk Development Council Internatl, *see* O321
Bk Hist Reading Group, *see* O107
Bk Industry Communications, O66
book trade, A440
Bk Trust, O67
bookkeeping, S1193
Bks Ireland, IO2
Bksellers Assoc of the UK & Ireland Ltd, O68; *see also* O262
bookselling, S1408
Boole Lib, IS27
Boole, George, FRS, papers, IA21
Boot, Henry, papers, A294
Booth Colln, S1241
Booth Museum of Nat Hist Lib, S229
Booth, E.T., Lib & MSS, S229
Booth, records (shipping company), A239
Booth, Valerie, Colln (ballet), A192
Booth, Vera Southgate, Colln (ch's lit), S1512
Bootham Park Hosp Lib, *see* S2173
Boothroyd, Betty, Papers, S1554
Boots Co plc, Co Archvs, A402
Borax Europe Ltd, Lib & Info Dept, S768
Bord Iascaigh Mhara, IS158
Bord Leigheasra na hEireann, IS98
Bord Rialtaithe, *see* IS181
Border Television, film & video archv, A277
Border Union Agricultural Soc records, A448
Borders Police records, A448
Borders Regional Council, records, A448

Borg Colln (Vikings), L3
Borough & County of the Town of Poole, *see* A125, 422; P147
Borough Road Coll, Southwark, records, A216
Borrow, W.H., Colln (postcards of Sussex & Kent), P49
Borthwick Inst of Historical Rsrch, Lib & Archvs, A522
Bosanquet family & estate records, A117
Bosanquet, Mary, MSS (Methodism), A368
Boston Coll, LRC, S203
Bosville family papers, A438
Boswell, James, Colln, P44, 174; S947
botany, A346; IS113; S16, 78, 146, 260, 294, 299, 348, 422, 615, 622, 626, 654, 756, 772, 831, 844, 1263, 1308, 1367, 1487, 1622, 1721, 1794, 2000, 2137, 2187; *agricultural,* S381; *economic,* S1862; *pre-Linnean,* S1862; *systematic,* S1862; *tropical,* S1862; *see also history of botany; plant science*
Botfield, Beriah, Lib & papers, S2086
Botfield, Thomas, & Co archvs, S1512
Bottomley, Gordon (poet & dramatist), Colln, P15; *correspondence,* A182
Boucherett family & estate papers, A215
Boucicault Colln (theatre), S410
Bouhéreau, Elias, Colln (Protestant theology), IS39
Boulton & Watt Archv of the Industrial Revolution, A51; P9
Boulton & Watt Drawings Colln (eng), S1208
Boulton, Matthew, papers & estate records, A51
Boundary Commission Papers (England & Wales), S482
Bounty Papers, S1169
Bourdillon Colln (French medieval lit), L3
Bourne, Hugh, papers (Methodism), A368
Bournemouth & Poole Coll, LRC, S1816
Bournemouth House Lib, *see* S1817
Bournemouth Libs, P13
Bournemouth Local Studies Colln, A59; *see also* A125
Bournemouth Poetry Soc papers, S1946
Bournemouth Univ, Lib, S1817; Oral Hist Rsrch Unit Archv, A60
Bournville Coll of Art Lib, *see* S160, 183
Bournville Coll of Further Edu, Lib Resources Centre, S163
Bowditch Papers, A297
Bowdler Family Colln (tracts), S880
Bowes & Bowes (Cambridge) Ltd, records (bksellers), A484
Bowes Museum, Ref Lib & Archvs, S206
Bowes, John & Josephine, Colln & Papers, S206
Bowlby, John, Papers, S1457
Bowley, Sir Arthur Lyon, papers (20C economist & statistician), A339
Bowling Iron Co, records, A62
Bowtell Colln (Cambridge), S351
Box Colln (Judaica & biblical hist), S1227
Boxall, Sir William, Papers, S1297
Boyd Historical Colln (anatomical slides), S338
Boyd, Eddie, Script Colln (Scottish theatre), A182
Boyd-Dawkins, W.M., Archv (caves & geol), S283
Boyd-Orr Archv, S13
Boyle, Robert, Colln, S311
BP Archv, A112
BP Exploration Operating Co Ltd, Map Lib, S2002
BPB Info Centre, S1481
Brace Colln, P75
Brackenridge & Graham, Solicitors, records, A20
Bracknell & Wokingham Coll, LRC, S208
Bracknell Forest Lib & Info Svc, P14

Bradfield, Nancy, Archv (costume historian), S103
Bradford Canal Co, records, A62
Bradford Cathedral Chapter Lib & Archvs, S211
Bradford Coll Lib Svcs, Grove Lib, S212
Bradford Dyers' Assoc Archv, S217
Bradford family papers, A467
Bradford Health Informatics Svc Lib, S1916
Bradford Hosps NHS Trust, Medical & Healthcare Lib & Info Svcs, S213
Bradford Inst of Tech Archv, S217
Bradford Mechanics' Inst Lib, S214
Bradford Public Libs, P15; *see also* A62
Bradford Technical Coll Archv, S217
Bradford, Diocese of, parish records, A62, 98, 194, 217, 393, 425; *records,* A226
Bradlaugh, Charles, Colln of MSS (secularism), S1016
Bradley, F.H., Colln, S1692
Bradshaw Colln (Irish materials), L5
Bradshaw-Isherwood family papers, A472
Brady Colln (theatrical ephemera), S1670
Braer Shipping Incident Colln, S1898
Bragg, W.H., MSS, S1371
Bragg, W.L., MSS, S1371
Braidwood Colln, P44
Braikenridge Colln (Somerset drawings), S2025
brain injury, S1616
Brain, Lord, papers, S1355
Braintree Coll Lib, S219
Braintree Dist Museum, Ref Lib, S220
Braithwaite & Kirt Photographic Archv (bridge bldg), A129
Brangwyn, Sir Frank, Art Colln, S76
Brasenose Coll, Lib, S1666
bravery awards, S1368
Bray Urban Dist Council minutes, IA7
Brayton, Teresa, Colln, IA82
Brazil, Angela, Colln, P31
Breathnach, Breandán, Colln (Irish music), IA42
Brechin Diocesan Lib & MSS (theology), A137; S561
Brechin Town Council, records, A384
Brecknock Museum & Gallery, Archvs, A63
Brecknock Soc records, A63
Brenchley, T.F., Colln (T.S. Eliot), S1692
Brendan Smith Academy, archv, IA41
Brent Community Hist Archv, A258
Brent Lib Svc, P80
Brentwood, RC Diocese of, records, A65
Brett Local Studies Colln (East Sussex), P49
Brett, Jacob, Papers, A294
Brett-Smith Colln (English drama), L5
Bretton Estate Archv, A496
Brewers & Licensed Retailers Assoc, *see* S1694
Brewery Hist Soc Archvs, A51
brewing, A76, 179, 358; IA35; IS83; S1609, 1694
Brewing Rsrch Group, *see* S1694
Brewster, David, papers (Scottish photographers), L2
Brian, Havergal, Papers, S1572
Bridewell Royal Hosp records, A280
Bridge Estates, records, A436
Bridge House Estates, records, A270
Bridge MSS (music), S25
Bridge, Sir Frederick, Lib (printed music), S1428
Bridgeman Art Lib, S1018
Bridgend Coll Lib, S223
Bridgend Lib & Info Svc, P16
Bridgend Local Studies Lib, A66; *see also* A97
Bridgend Postgrad Centre Lib, S224
Bridgewater Estate Archv, S1886
bridging, S444
Bridgnorth Coll LRC, *see* S1919
Bridgnorth Historical Colln, P163
Bridgwater Coll, LRC, S225

Bridie, James, Colln (dramatist & critic), A182
Bridon plc records, A124
Briggs Colln (early edu), S1647
Briggs Room (antiquarian bks), S1684
Briggs, Asa, Collection, S1861
Brighouse family & estate records, A194
Bright Colln (psychical rsrch), S1440
Brighton & Hove Libs, P17
Brighton & Hove Local Studies Lib, A67
Brighton & Hove Nat Hist Soc Lib, S229
Brighton & Sussex Univ Hosps NHS Trust, see S236, 795
Brighton Art Gallery & Museum, Lib & Archvs, A68
Brighton Coll of Tech, see S231
Brimelow, Lord, Papers, S482
Brinkley Colln, S880
Brinson, Peter, Colln (dance), S1232
Brisbane of Largs papers, A174
Bristol & Gloucestershire Archaeo Soc Lib, S450
Bristol Baptist Coll Lib, S244
Bristol Chamber of Commerce & Initiative, Lib & Info Svc, S245
Bristol Children's Hosp Lib, see S259
Bristol City Council Women's Unit, records, A75
Bristol City Libs, P18
Bristol City Museums & Art Gallery, Lib & Archvs, S246
Bristol Edu Soc, S244
Bristol Eye Hosp Lib, see S259
Bristol Genl Hosp Lib, see S259
Bristol Grammar School Lib, S247
Bristol Industrial Museum, see S246
Bristol Law Libns Group, O69
Bristol Oncology Centre Lib, see S259
Bristol Quarter & Petty Sessions, records, A72
Bristol Record Office, A72
Bristol Univ, see Univ of Bristol
Bristol Univ Coll, records, A77
Bristol Women's Centre, records, A75
Bristol, Archdeaconry of, records, A72
Bristol, Diocese of, records, A72, 493
Bristol, Marquisses of, family papers, A83
Britain & Ireland Assoc of Aquatic Scis Libs & Info Centres, O70
British Aerospace, records, A505
British Aircraft Corp, records, A505
British Alkaloids Ltd, records (manufacturing chemists), A446
British & Foreign Bible Soc, Lib & Archvs, see L5
British & Foreign School Soc Archv Centre, A216
British & Internatl Federation of Festivals, see S1493
British & Irish Archaeo Bibliography, O71
British & Irish Assoc of Law Libns, O72; **Irish Group,** IO3
British & Irish Steam Packet Co Ltd, records, IA19
British Antarctic Survey Lib, S294
British Architectural Lib, S1019
British Aristocracy Colln (illusts), S1789
British Assoc for Info & Lib Edu & Rsrch, O73
British Assoc for Local Hist, O74
British Assoc of Academic Phoneticians Archv, A169
British Assoc of Occupational Therapists, S1092
British Assoc of Paper Historians, O75
British Assoc of Picture Libs & Agencies, O76
British Assoc of Social Workers Archvs, A53; see also A114
British Astronomical Assoc Lib, S1020
British Balneological & Climatology Soc, archvs, S1381
British Beer & Pub Assoc, see S1694
British Board of Film Censors, archv, S1013

British Broadcasting Corp, see BBC
British Business Schools Libns' Group, O77
British Cartographic Soc, Map Curators Group, O78
British Cave Rsrch Assoc Lib, P36
British Cement Assoc, Centre for Concrete Info, S510
British Cocoa & Chocolate Co Ltd, records, S164
British Coll of Osteopathic Medicine Lib, S1021
British Commercial Gas Assoc Film Colln, A500
British Comparative & Internatl Edu Soc, archvs, S1444
British Computer Soc Lib, see S1206
British Copyright Council, O79
British Council of Churches Archv, A266
British Dam Soc Archvs, S1205
British Dental Assoc Info Centre & Museum Archvs, S1022
British Dyslexia Assoc Lib, S1843
British Electric Traction, archvs, S1539
British Electrotherapy Soc, archvs, S1381
British Empire & Commonwealth Museum, Lib & Archvs, S248
British Energy plc Corporate Lib, S745; see also S581
British Falconers' Club Lib, S1725
British Footwear Manufacturers Federation, records, A477
British Gas, archvs, A500
British Geological Survey, Lib & Archvs, S1636; **London Info Office,** S1023; see also S2072
British Geotechnical Soc Archvs, S1205
British Glass Lib, S1904
British Gynaecological Soc, archvs, S1381
British Homoeopathic Lib, Glasgow, S695
British Horological Inst Lib, S1567
British Industry Life Assurance Co, records, A320
British Inst of Internatl & Comparative Law, Grotius Lib, S1024
British Inst of Jazz Studies, Lib, S511; see also S360
British Inst of Learning Disabilities, Info & Resource Centre, S860
British Inst of Radiology, Lib & Info Svc, S1025
British Instn of Radio Engineers, records, A294
British Interplanetary Soc, L.J. Carter Lib, S1026
British Iron & Steel Federation records, A121
British Journal of Anaesthesia Lib, see S1001
British Kinematograph Sound & Television Soc Lib, S1043
British Laryngological, Rhinological & Otological Assoc, archvs, S1381
British Lib, L1
British Lib for Development Studies, S230
British Lib of Political & Economic Sci, S1241
British Linen Bank, records, A147
British Maritime Law Assoc Archvs, S1433
British Maritime Tech Lib, S2030; **Wallsend Rsrch Station Lib,** S2073
British Medical Assoc Lib, S1027
British Medical Informatics Soc, O80
British Medical Ultrasound Soc, see S1025
British Museum, Anthro Lib, S1034; **Central Archvs,** A259; **Central Lib,** see S1028; **Dept of Coins & Medals Lib,** S1029; **Dept of Greek & Roman Antiquities Lib,** S1030; **Dept of Libs & Archvs,** S1028; **Dept of Prehistory & Europe Lib,** S1031; **Dept of Prints & Drawings Lib,** S1032; **Dept of the Ancient Near East Lib,** S1033; **Paul Hamlyn Lib,** see S1028; see also A328
British Music Info Centre, S1035

British Music Soc Archv, S1428
British Mutual Life Assurance Soc, records, A320
British Mycological Soc Lib & Archvs, S1860
British Natl Space Centre, Lib & Info Unit, S1036
British Numismatic Soc Lib, S1375
British Official Pubns Collaborative Reader Info Svc, O81
British Official Pubns Current Awareness Svc, O82
British Optical Assoc Lib, S1037
British Ornithologists Union Lib, S1725; *Balfour Bequest Lib,* S1247
British Orthodox Church Lib, S1038
British Orthopaedic Assoc, meeting papers, S1698
British Power Boat Co Colln, S1943
British Psycho-Analytical Soc Lib & Archvs, S1039
British Psychological Soc Colln, S1040; see also S1989
British Records Assoc, O83
British Records Soc Ltd, O84
British Red Cross Museum & Archvs, A260
British School of Osteopathy Lib, S1041
British Ship Rsrch Assoc, reports, S2073
British Soc for the Study of Orthodontics Lib, A336
British Soc of Rheology Lib, S18
British Standards Instn, O85; **Lib,** S1042
British Sugar Business Info Centre, S1793
British Theatre Assoc Colln, S415
British Tourist Authority Lib, see S1454
British Trade Internatl, see S1424
British Univs Film & Video Council, Info Svc, S1043
British Waterways Archv, A183; see also A159; S749
British Widows Assurance Co Ltd, records, A320
British Xylonite Co records, A215
British-American Tobacco Info Centre, S1938
British-Israel Chamber of Commerce, Lib, S1044
British-Soviet Friendship Soc Archv, S1274
Brittain, Vera, Colln, P174; *MSS,* S1762
Britten, Benjamin, Colln, A361; P179; S25; *papers & MSS,* S25
Britten-Pears Lib, S25
Britton, John, MSS, S530
Bro Morgannwg NHS Trust, see S224, 1821
broadcasting, A293, 428; IS53, 140; S474, 1009, 1010, 1108; see also radio; television
Broadgreen Hosp, Edu Centre Lib, S964
Broadsides Colln of Ephemera, P193
Broadstairs & St Peter's Urban Dist Council, records, A128
Broadwater Colln (Churchill family), A88
Broadwood of Lyne, records (piano manufacturers), A513
Broadwood, Lucy, MSS, S1453
Brockbank Cricket Colln, S1512
Brocklebank, records (shipping company), A239
Broderick, John, Colln (Westmeath novelist), IA78; IP30
Brodie Castle Lib, S687
Brodie, Benjamin, MSS, A348
Brodsky, Adolph, Archv (music), S1528
Brogyntyn family & estate archv, L3
Broken Hill Secretariat records, A324
Bromhead Colln (hist of London), S1440
Bromley Coll of Further & Higher Edu, Lib, S267
Bromley Davenport family muniments, S1512
Bromley Hosps NHS Trust, see S1658
Bromley House Lib, S1637
Bromley Libs, P81

Bromley Local Studies Lib & Archvs, A79
Bronglais Hosp Lib Svcs, S15
Brontë Colln, P15; *family MSS,* S853; *papers & MSS,* S918
Brontë Parsonage Museum Lib, S853
Brontë Soc Colln, S853
Bronwydd family & estate archv, L3
Brook, G.L., Colln (theatre), S1512
Brooke Colln (17C-19C printed bks), S1444
Brooke, Gwydion, Bassoon Colln (music), S1528
Brooke, Rupert, papers, S369
Brookes, Beata, Papers, L3
Brooking Rowe Colln (brass-rubbings & bkplates), A164
Brooklands Museum Trust Ltd, Archvs, A505
Brooksby Melton Coll Lib, S1540
Broom's Barn Rsrch Station Lib, S280; see also S786
Broome, Christopher Edmund, Colln (botany & mycology), S98
Broomfield Hosp, Warner Lib, S447
Brotherton Colln (rare bks & MSS), S918
Brotherton Lib, S918
Brougham, 1st Lord of, Papers, S1433
Brown & Root Ltd, see S893
Brown Colln (travel in Morocco), S1363
Brown Family, records (millers of Houghton), A211
Brown Street Natl School Archv, A37
Brown, E.G., Colln (Arabic, Persian, Turkish), L5
Brown, Graham, Colln (alpine), L2
Brown, John, of Clydebank, records (shipbldg), A176
Brown, Kenneth, Railway Colln, S1512
Brown, Sadd, Lib (Women in the Commonwealth), S1469
Brown, Sir Edward, Lib (poultry sci), S1601
Brown, Thomas, papers (Bishop of Newport & Menevia), A94
Brown-Sequard, C.E., papers, S1355
Browne Lib (marine biology), S1805
Browne, Fr, SJ Colln (photography), IS100
Browning, Robert & Elizabeth Barrett, Colln, S2130
Brownrigg, Longfield & Murray Colln (18C Irish estate maps), IL1
Broxbourne Colln (incunabula, early printing), L4
Bruce Castle Museum Picture Colln, S1275
Bruce Glasier, John & Katharine, papers, S972
Bruce, William Speirs, Colln (oceanography, exploration), S593; *papers,* S612
Bruen Colln, IA9; IP1
Brunel Coll of Arts & Tech, S250
Brunel family papers, A77
Brunel Photo Colln (eng), S1208
Brunel Univ Lib, S2065; see also A216
Brunel, I.K., papers & sketch bks, S260
Brunner, John, Archv, S973
Brushfield Colln (Sir Walter Raleigh), A164
Bryan Family Papers, IA49
Bryant & May, records (match manufacturers), A281
Brynmor Jones Lib, S828
Bryson & MacAdam MSS (Irish lang), A37
BSA archvs, P165
BSTC Lib & Info Svcs, see S1793
BT Group Archvs, A261; **Lib,** S841
Bubbles Photo Lib, S1045
BUBL Info Svc, O86
Buccleuch, Duke of, Furness Estate Colln, A28
Buchan School, Cubbon Lib, see S2177
Buchan, Norman & Janey, Colln, S701
Buchan, Norman, MP, papers, S1782
Buchanan Bequest, P44
Buchanan Family of Milton of Campsie papers, A171
Buchanan, George, Colln, S1964

Buckingham Univ, see Univ of Buckingham
Buckingham, Archdeaconry of, records, A19
Buckinghamshire Archaeo Soc Lib, S56
Buckinghamshire Chilterns Univ Coll, Lib, S810
Buckinghamshire County Lib Svc, P19; see also A19
Buckinghamshire Health Authority Lib, S57
Buckinghamshire Local Studies Lib, see A19
Buckinghamshire Mental Health NHS Trust, Tindal Centre Lib, S58
Buckinghamshire Poor Law Unions, records, A19
Buckinghamshire Quarter Sessions records, A19
Buckinghamshire Record Office, see A19
Buckinghamshire Record Soc, O87
Buckland, William, papers (geol), S1738
Bucks Constabulary records, A19
Budden, George, Music Colln, S263
Buddhism, S180, 320, 1046
Buddhist Soc Lib, S1046
Budgen Bequest (slides of Eastbourne), P49
Budy, Charles Howard, Colln (explorer), IP30
Buffs Regiment records, A311
building, IS123, 178; S125, 470, 810, 865, 1122, 1155, 1205, 1515, 1824; see also construction
building materials, S470, 1481
building methods & techniques, S470; traditional, S268
building services, S865, 1070
Bldg Svcs Rsrch & Info Assoc, Lib, S209
building studies, S2103
buildings, church, S1102; farm, S1850; health, S911; historic, A93, 345; S268, 1298; listed, A483; public, S1298; religious, S1298; rural, S1850; Welsh, S419
Bulgaria, S1436
Bull, AH, Ltd, records (drapers & furnishers), A470
Bull, Frederick William, Colln (19C publicity material), P131
Bull, Sir William, Colln (antiquarian), A282
Bullar Colln (theology, hist, lit), S1946
Bullard Laboratories Lib, see S307
Bullard, E., Colln (geol), S307
Bullock Colln (early printed bks), S1512
Bullock Cttee, archvs, S1444
Bullock family & estate papers, A493
Bulman, O.M.B., Colln (geol), S307
Bulmer-Thomas Colln (hist of maths & sci), S1770
Bulmershe Lib, see S1848
Bult family correspondence, A282
Bulwer Lytton, Sir Edward, Colln, S877
Buncrana Urban Dist Council, records, IA67
Bund, Willis, Colln, P206
Bundoran Urban Dist Council, records, IA67
Bunting, Jabez, papers (Methodism), A368
Bunyan Meeting Free Church, S116
Bunyan, John, Colln, P8; S116
Burch, Cecil Reginald, papers, A77
Burchell Colln (British films), P73
Burdon, David, Colln (geol), IS79
Bureau of Military Hist, records (Ireland), IA45
Burges Salmon, Solicitors, Lib, S249
Burgess Colln (Athlone), IA78
Burgess, Thomas, Colln, S880
Burgh-by-Sands Parish Lib, S433
Burghley, Lord, papers, L1
Burgoyne, Gen Sir John, papers, S445
Burke, Edmund, papers, A452
Burkitt, Miles, Bequest (archaeo), S323
Burma Office, records, L1
Burmah Castrol Archvs, A482; see also A112
Burne Colln (family papers), A468
Burney Colln (17C-19C newspapers), L1
Burney MSS, L1
Burnley Clinical Lib, see S1840
Burnley Genl Hosp, Mackenzie Medical Centre Lib, S274
Burnley Grammar School Lib, S883
Burns Cottage Trustees Lib, S63
Burns, John, Colln (labour hist), S1440
Burns, Robert, Colln, A21; P44, 53, 56, 167; S63, 121, 876; MSS, L2
Burntwood Foundation School Lib, S1047
Burren Coll of Art, Lib, IS5
Burrishoole parish records, IA11
Burrows Colln (Greek & Byzantine studies), S1227
Burslem & Wolstanton Poor Law Union records, A473
Burt, Sir Cyril, papers (psychologist), S972
Burton Estate Papers, IA55
Burton Family Colln, A197
Burton Grad Medical Centre Lib, S276
Burton papers, IA9; IP1
Burton, Sir Richard, Colln (explorer), A433; P103; S1344
Burton-upon-Trent Methodist Circuit, records, A81
Burton-upon-Trent Poor Law Union, records, A81
Burton-upon-Trent, County Borough of, records, A81
Bury Archv Svc, A82
Bury Coll Lib, S278
Bury family & estate papers (Earls of Charleville), IA78
Bury Public Lib Svc, P20
Bury, Colonel Howard, Papers, IA78; IP30
Bus & Coach Council, archvs, S1539
Busby Lib (16C-17C academic bks), S1461
Bush, Alan, Colln (music scores), S1148
Bushnell, G.H.S., Bequest (archaeo), S323
business, A376; IS8, 11, 30, 59, 71, 73, 77, 90, 129, 156, 161, 184, 202; S12, 22, 33, 149, 221, 263, 271, 367, 430, 431, 478, 565, 572, 581, 610, 657, 676, 689, 737, 752, 780, 800, 824, 834, 869, 917, 968, 983, 1009, 1044, 1079, 1098, 1121, 1129, 1145, 1174, 1185, 1194, 1196, 1223, 1251, 1253, 1254, 1262, 1282, 1335, 1338, 1346, 1439, 1452, 1479, 1498, 1514, 1536, 1550, 1597, 1617, 1635, 1641, 1700, 1748, 1758, 1772, 1824, 1851, 1882, 1883, 1898, 1911, 1912, 1966, 2004, 2013, 2045, 2046, 2079, 2094, 2103, 2113, 2160, 2182; international, S476; see also business information; business studies
Business & Legal Info Network, O88
Business Archvs Council, O89; Business Hist Lib, S1048
Business Archvs Council of Scotland, O90
business information, A410; IS10, 164, 196; S1, 14, 129, 227, 245, 465, 518, 729, 845, 848, 967, 1218, 1635, 1834
Business Link Wolverhampton, see S227
business policy, S1098
business studies, IS116, 204; S42, 115, 144, 202, 208, 267, 469, 525, 675, 741, 810, 915, 940, 969, 1261, 1515, 1557, 1638, 1816, 1969, 2148
Bute Colln (English plays), L2
Bute County Council records, A174
Bute family & estate archv, L3
Butler Lib, S1986; see also S349
Butler, Josephine, papers, S972
Butterfield, William, papers (architect), A511
Butterfly Conservation, Lib, S2083
Butterworth & Co (Publishers) Ltd, Archvs, A490
Butterworth, George, MSS, S1453
Buttress Colln of Applied Biology, L5
Buxton Family papers, S2081
Buxton Museum & Art Gallery, S283
Buxton of Channons & Shadwell, family & estate papers, L5
Byam Shaw School of Art, Lib, S1049
Byrom, John, Lib, S1507
Byron, Lord, Colln, P138; MSS, S788; papers & MSS, S918
Bywater Colln (hist of classical scholarship), L4
Byzantine studies, S101

C&A Ltd Archv, S1255
C&J Clark Ltd, Shoe Museum & Archvs, A477
CAB International-Oxford Forestry Inst Info Svc, see S1721
CABi Bioscience Lib, S649
CABi Info for Development, O91
Cabinet Office, see S2163; Centre for Mgmt & Policy Studies, see S46
Cable & Wireless Archvs, A414
Cable Authority Archvs, A293
Cadbury family papers, A51
Cadbury Ltd, records, S164
Cadbury Papers, S179
Cadbury Schweppes Ltd, records, S164
Cadbury Trebor Bassett, Lib & Info Svc, S164
Cadbury, William, Colln (cocoa & South America), S164
Cadder Estate archv, A171
Cadell of Grange papers, L2
Cadw: The Welsh Historic Monuments Exec Agency, A93
Caernarvonshire Historical Soc, O92
Caerphilly County Borough Council Libs, P21; see also A97, 117
Caffyn Bks (relating to Percy Shelley), S239
Cahill Colln (photography), IS141
Cahirciveen Poor Law Union, minutes, IA92
Cahirciveen Rural Dist Council, minutes, IA92
Cahnn, Sir Julien, Lib (cricket), S1276
Cain, Arthur, Colln (public relations);, A399
Caird Lib, S1303
Cairn of Lochwinnoch Colln (local families), A413; P152
Cairnes, John E., Colln (economist), IS166
Cairney, John, Colln (Scottish theatre), A182
Cairngorm Club Lib, A3
Cairns Lib, S1749
Caithness County records, A213
Caithness Family Hist Soc Lib, A489
Caithness Genl Hosp Lib, see S839
Calderdale & Huddersfield NHS Trust, Lib & Info Svc, S778; see also S821
Calderdale Colls Corp, Campus Lib & Learning Centre, S779
Calderdale Libs Svc, P22
Calderdale Local Studies Section, see A194
Caldicott Classical Lib, see S247
Caleus of Windsor, records (dept store), A470
Callaghan, James, papers, L4
Callan Town Commissioners, records, IA61
calligraphy, S373, 1290, 1408
Calmady Papers, A419
Calman, Mel, Colln (cartoons), A91
Calthorpe, 3rd Baron, papers, A509
Calverley & Eccleshill, family & estate records, A62
Camanachd Assoc Archv, L2
Camberwell Coll of Arts, Lib & Learning Resources, S1050
Camborne Pool Redruth Coll Learning Centre, see S1856
Cambrian Archaeo Assoc Lib, S422
Cambridge Antiquarian Soc Colln, S323
Cambridge Arctic Shelf Programme Lib, S342
Cambridge Bibliographical Soc, O93
Cambridge Colln, L5
Cambridge Cttee for Christian Work in Delhi Archvs, S360
Cambridge Drama Colln (English plays), S1647
Cambridge Economic Club, S335
Cambridge Refrigeration Tech Lib, S295
Cambridge Regional Coll, LRC, S296
Cambridge Scientific Instrument Co Archvs, L5
Cambridge Shakespeare Colln, S1647
Cambridge South Asian Archv, S300
Cambridge Union Soc, Keynes Lib, S297
Cambridge Univ Lib, L5; African Studies Centre Lib, S298; Botanic Garden (Cory) Lib, S299; Centre of South Asian Studies, Lib & Archvs, S300; Computer Laboratory Lib, S301; Dept of Applied Econ Lib, S302; Dept of Biochemistry, Colman Lib, S303; Dept of Chemical Eng Lib, S304; Dept of Chem Lib, S305; Dept of Clinical Veterinary Medicine Lib, S306; Dept of Earth Scis Lib, S307; Dept of Experimental Psy Lib, S308; Dept of Genetics Lib, S309; Dept of Geog Lib, S310; Dept of Hist & Phil of Sci, Whipple Lib, S311; Dept of Materials Sci & Metallurgy Lib, S312; Dept of Pathology, Kanthack & Nuttall Lib, S313; Dept of Pharmacology Lib, S314; Dept of Physics, Rayleigh Lib, S315; Dept of Physiology Lib, S316; Dept of Plant Scis Lib, S317; Dept of Social Anthro Lib, S318; Dept of Zoology, Balfour & Newton Libs, S319; Divinity Faculty Lib, S320; Eng Faculty Lib, S321; English Faculty Lib, S322; Faculty of Archaeo & Anthro, Haddon Lib, S323; Faculty of Arch & Hist of Art Lib, S324; Faculty of Classics & Museum of Classical Archaeo Lib, S325; Faculty of Edu, Lib & Info Svc, S326; Faculty of Modern & Medieval Langs Lib, S327; Faculty of Oriental Studies Lib, S328; Faculty of Phil, Casimir Lewy Lib, S329; Faculty of Social & Political Scis Lib, S330; Inst of Astronomy Lib, S331; Inst of Continuing Edu Lib, S332; Inst of Criminology, Radzinowicz Lib, S333; Lang Centre Lib, S334; Marshall Lib of Econ, S335; Mill Lane Lib, S336; Pendlebury Lib of Music, S337; School of Anatomy Lib, S338; Scott Polar Rsrch Inst Lib, S339; Seeley Historical Lib, S340; Univ Colln of Air Photographs, S341; Anglo-Saxon, Norse & Celtic Dept Lib, see S322; Archvs, see L5; Betty & Gordon Moore Lib, see L5; Centre of Internatl Studies & Development Studies, see S336; Dept of Land Economy Lib, see S336; Latin American Studies Lib, see S336; Medical Lib, see L5; Scientific Periodicals Lib, see L5; Squire Law Lib, see L5; Veterinary Anatomy (Lovaton) Lib, see S338; see also A89; S290, 342, 355, 365, 367, 368, 370, 371, 386, 398, 399
Cambridge Univ Press, records, S1408
Cambridgeshire & Peterborough Mental Health Partnership NHS Trust, S356
Cambridgeshire County Record Office, A87; see also A211
Cambridgeshire Health Authority Lib, see S829
Cambridgeshire Libs & Info Svc, P23
Cambridgeshire Local Hist Soc, O94
Cambridgeshire Records Soc, O95
Camden & Islington Mental Health Trust, see S994, 1051
Camden & Islington NHS Trust, see S1259
Camden & Islington Primary Care Trusts, Lib & Info Svc, S1051
Camden Lib Svc, P82
Camden Local Studies & Archvs Centre, A262
Camden Soc, papers, S1366
Camden, William, Colln, S1459

Clackmannan Coll of Further Edu, Learning Resource Svcs, S27
Clackmannanshire Justices of the Peace, records, A471
Clackmannanshire Libs, P28
Clapham parish records, A296
Clare Board of Health, registers, IA55
Clare Coll, Forbes Mellon Lib, S346
Clare County Development Team, records, IA55
Clare County Libs, IP3; Local Studies & Archvs, IA55
Clare Folklore MSS, IA55
Clare Hall, Ashby Lib, S347
Clare Hall Laboratories Lib, *see* S1054
Clare Local Govt Board, records, IA55
Clare, John, Colln, P131; *Poetry Colln,* S1799
Clarendon Laboratory Lib, S1712
Clarendon Press Colln, L4
Clark Colln (travel & exploration), S310
Clark Papers, A419
Clark, C&J, Ltd, records (shoe manufacturers), A477
Clark, Dr David, papers (therapeutic communities), A104
Clark, Edward, Colln (hist of printing & publishing), S610
Clark, Grahame, Bequest (archaeo), S323
Clark, K.C., Slide Colln (radiology), S1025
Clark, Kenneth, papers, A349
Clark, Paul, Archv (design), A69
Clarke papers (Civil War MSS), S1778
Clarke, Adam, papers (Methodism), A368
Clarke, Austin, Colln (poetry), IA48; IS41
Clarke, Canon B.F.L., Colln (church bldg & restoration, 18C-19C), S1102
Clarke, Sir Fred, Colln (edu), S1444
Classical Schoolbk Colln, S2130
classics, S44, 199, 523, 553, 788, 1285, 1440, 1588, 1627, 1672, 1747, 1759, 1773, 1863, 2125, 2130
Clatterbridge Centre for Oncology Trust, *see* S2135
Clatterbridge Hosp, John A. Aitken Lib, S2135
Clay, Richard, Ltd of Bungay records (printers), A361
Clayton, F&J, Woollen Mills, records, IA80
Clé – The Irish Bk Publishers' Assoc, IO6
Clements Colln (heraldic bindings), S1290
Clements Estate Papers, IL1
Clemo, Jack, Colln, S671
Clerical Medical Investment Group Ltd, Archvs, A73
Clericetti Colln (15C Italian writers), P17
Cleveland & Teesside Local Hist Soc, O164
Cleveland Coll of Art & Design Lib, S1544
Cleveland County Council, archvs, A379
Cleveland Craft Centre, *see* S1546
Cleveland Social Survey archvs, S1982
Cleveland, Lt Gen Samuel, Colln, S1130
Click, John, Papers (locomotive engineer), S2165
Cliff, Clarice, Colln, A473
Cliffe Hill Granite Co Ltd records, A514
Clifford, Lady Anne, papers (17C), A217
Clifton House Archv, S121
Clifton RC Diocesan Archvs, A74
Clifton Suspension Bridge Trust Papers, A77
climatology, IS111; S294, 307, 1786, 2072
clinical effectiveness, S2069
clinical governance, S662, 1916
clinical science, S789, 935, 1227, 1749
Clinical Soc of London, archvs, S1381
Clinker Colln (railway hist), S2065

Clinton papers (military studies), S1512
Clockmaker's Co Lib, P99
clocks & clockmaking, S419, 1031
Clogher RC Diocesan Archvs, IA76
Clonalis House Lib, IS15
Clonbrock Estate Papers & Photo Colln, IL1
Clondalkin Hist Soc, IO7
Cloneygowan Rural Dist Council, records, IA83
Clonfert RC Diocesan Archvs, IA74
Clonmel Rural Dist Council, minutes, IA54
clothing, S1533
Clothing & Footwear Inst Colln, S1254
clothing production, S1254
Cloyne Literary & Historical Soc, IO8
Cloyne RC Diocesan Archvs, IA17; *see also* IA75
Cluain Mhuire Art Lib, *see* IS165
Clwyd-Powys Archaeo Trust, Archvs, A504
Clyde Navigation Trust, records, A174
Clydebank Blitz 1941 Colln, A110
Cnosach Duibhneach Colln (Dingle Peninsula), IP11
Co Cavan Genealogical Rsrch Centre, IA14
Co Cavan Heritage & Genealogical Soc Ltd, IA14
Co Donegal Historical Soc, IO9
Co Louth Archaeo & Historical Soc, IO10
Co Roscommon Historical & Archaeo Soc, IO11
Co-East, O165
Co-operation Colln, A434
Co-op Archv, *see* A370
co-operative movement, A370; P154; S1016, 1758, 1887
Co-operative Party Colln, A370
Co-operative Soc Archvs, S1016
Co-operative Women's Guild Colln, A370; *minutes,* S1016
coaching, S641
coal, S1172, 1885, 2068; *see also* mining
Coal Smoke Abatement Soc Colln, S233
Coalbrookdale Co, records, S2033
coastlines, S1306
Coastlines Ltd, records, IA19
Coates Lorilleux Info Dept, S1657
Coates, Eric, Colln, P139
Coats, J&P, records (Paisley thread manufacturers), A176
Cobbe Family of Newbridge, family & estate papers, IA22
Cobbe, Charles, journal (18C Archbishop of Dublin), IA22
Cobbe, Frances Power, Colln, L3
Cobbe, Gen Sir Alexander, diary, IA22
Cobbett, William, Colln, A167
Cobden Colln, P17
Cobham Colln (hist of Cyprus), L5
Cochrane Lib, S1785
Cochrane, Capt Ernest, papers, IA67
Cochrane, Douglas B., Colln (steam ship hists), A239
Cochrane, Prof Archie, Archv, S1785
Cock Colln (Thomas More), P99
Cock, Alfred, papers, S1634
Cocks, Joe, Studio Colln (theatre photos), S1996
codes of practice, S1042
Codrington Lib, S1663
Codrington of Dodington, family & estate records, A185
Codrington, Gen Sir William, papers, A311
coffee, S1212
Cohen Colln (Latin America), S385
Cohn Colln (European law), S1227
COI Footage File, *see* S1128
Coillte Teoranta, IS192
Coke of Weasenham Hall, family & estate papers, L5
Coke Press papers, A490
Coke, Thomas, papers (Methodism), A368
Colaiste Mhuire Marino Inst of Edu Lib, IS50
Colchester Borough records, A111
Colchester Inst, Learning Resources, Info & Student Svcs, S478

Cole Brothers of Sheffield, records (dept store), A470
Cole Family papers, A433
Cole Lib of Zoology & Hist of Medicine, S1848
Cole, Sir Henry, Colln, S1290
Coleg Garddwriaeth Cymry, S1556
Coleg Glan Hafren, Learning Centre, S414
Coleg Gwent, LRC, S1594
Coleg Menai Lib, S73
Coleg y Drindod Caerfyrddin, S440
Coleorton Hall papers, A18
Coleridge, Samuel Taylor, Colln, P112; S1161; *correspondence,* S34; *MSS,* S179; *papers,* A511
Colet, Dean, estate records, A307
Colfe, Abraham, Lib (17C Vicar of Lewisham), A357
COLICO – Cttee on Lib Co-operation in Ireland, IO12
Coliseum Theatre, London, archv, A276
Collar, A.R., papers, A77
collecting, S1028
collection care, S1680
Collns Picture Lib, S1089
collective bargaining, A319
Coll Farm records, S19
Coll of Arms, Archvs, A269
Coll of Falmouth Learning Centre, *see* S1856
Coll of Law, Birmingham Lib, S168; Chester Lib, S458; Guildford Lib, S769; London Lib, S1090; York Lib, S2161
Coll of North East London, Centenary Learning Centre, S1091
Coll of Occupational Therapists Lib, S1092
Coll of Radiographers, *see* S1025
Coll of St Mark & St John Lib, S1804
Coll of St Paul & St Mary, records, S454
Coll of The Ascension Lib, *see* S180
Coll of West Anglia Lib, S864; Faculty of Land-Based Studies Lib, S348
Colles Lib, S546
Collier, John, Colln (dialect & prints), A434
Collin, Fr, papers (Northampton Diocesan hist), A394
Collings Colln (20C Slavonic art), S1290
Collins, F.W., Papers, S1483
Collins, Michael, papers, IA45; IS34
Colman & Rye Colln, P123
Colne Valley Labour Party, archvs, S824
Colonial Life Assurance Co Archvs, records, A157
colonies, British, S1647
colour & coloration, S216, 1347
Colour Museum Lib, S216
Colquhouns of Luss, family & estate papers, A174
Colthurst Family of Blarney, papers, IA19
Colum, Padraic, Colln (Longford author), IA73; IP18
Colville, Duncan, Colln, S863
Colvin, Ian, papers (Katyn Massacre & Gen Sikorski's death), S1327
Colwyn Bay & Llandudno English Methodist Circuit, records, A244
Colwyn Bay & Llandudno Joint Water Supply records, A244
Colwyn Council records, A244
Colyton Local Hist Centre, *see* A161
Combe Farm, records, A278
Comben Colln (veterinary sci), S1387
Combined Regions, O166
Comfort Colln of Gerontology, S1381
Comhairle nan Eilean Siar, P199
commerce, A409; IS8; S419, 1044, 1145, 1253, 1298, 1378
commercial vehicles, A48; S266
commercials, television, S215
Commission for New Towns Lib, S969
Commission for Racial Equality Lib, S1093
Commission of the European Communities, London Lib, S1094

Commissioners for Enquiring into the Condition of the Poorer Classes in Ireland, reports, IA55
Commissioners of Natl Edu, reports (Ireland), IA55
Cttee for Overseas Lib Development, *see* O251
Cttee on Lib Co-operation in Ireland, IO12
Cttee on Standards in Public Life, papers, S482
Common Svcs Agency for the NHS in Scotland, *see* S589, 629, 632, 728
Common Svcs Agency, Info & Statistics Div Lib, S589
Common Wealth Party, papers, S239
Commonweal Colln (non-violent social change), S217
Commonwealth & Commonwealth studies, S248, 1095, 1123, 1440, 1443
Commonwealth Inst Resource Centre Collns, S248
Commonwealth Nurses Federation, records, A153
Commonwealth Secretariat Lib, S1095
communication & communication studies, IS181; S610, 614, 1452, 1911, 2004, 2046; human, S923; visual, S160
communications, A409, 414; IS53, 125, 202; S110, 208, 488, 1261; radio, S1334; *see also* telecommunications
communism, A365; S1274
Communist Party of Gt Britain Archvs, A365; *Scottish Cttee,* S701
community care, S87, 437, 493, 559, 1229, 1452, 1615
community involvement, S1294
Community of the Resurrection Lib, S1555; *see also* S2168
Community Practitioners & Health Visitors' Assoc, Info Resources & Lib, S1096
Community Relations Council Ref Lib, S122
community studies, S180, 923, 1526, 1597
community work, S1761
Company of Goldsmiths Archvs, IA29
Compaq Computers, advertising archv, A399
competition, S1097, 1313, 1314
Competition Commission, Lib & Info Centre, S1097
competitiveness, S1098
compulsory purchase, S1370
Computer Auditers Colln, P99
computers & computer science, A369; IS11, 90, 111, 123, 129, 178, 183; L4, 5; S12, 19, 42, 77, 208, 231, 241, 263, 270, 301, 310, 315, 430, 478, 482, 503, 525, 535, 593, 608, 610, 621, 675, 684, 691, 810, 839, 844, 865, 869, 959, 969, 995, 1082, 1084, 1180, 1193, 1206, 1261, 1282, 1284, 1405, 1422, 1439, 1452, 1498, 1541, 1550, 1597, 1617, 1713, 1788, 1804, 1816, 1830, 1854, 1898, 1911, 1912, 1925, 1934, 1940, 1945, 1978, 2004, 2046, 2079, 2087, 2094, 2103, 2121, 2141, 2168
Comte Colln, S972
Comtelburo Ltd records (telegraphic agents), A323
Conan Doyle, Sir Arthur, Colln, P50
Concerted Action on Mgmt Info for Libs in Europe, O167
Concerts of Ancient Music Lib, S1350
conciliation, S982
Concord Multi-Faith Colln, S915
concrete, S510
Confederation of British Industry Info Centre, S1098; *see also* A114
Conference of Regional & Local Historians, O168
conflict, S26, 1246
Conflict & Peace Rsrch Colln, S410
conflict resolution, S122
Congregation of the Christian Brothers, records, IS34
Congregation of the Irish Dominican Sisters, Archvs, IA5
Congregation of the Sisters of Mercy, archvs, IA27

Congregational Church, **S**397
Congregational Coll Colln (nonconformity), **S**1512
Congregational Lib, S1099; *see also* **S**1116
Connolly, T.W.J., papers (historian), **S**444
Conolly, Thomas, papers (18C politician), **IA**12
Conradiana Colln (Joseph Conrad), **S**1328
conservation, **A**93; **IS**151; **S**71, 72, 134, 146, 292, 348, 422, 515, 543, 612, 705, 772, 844, 1028, 1050, 1066, 1110, 1122, 1261, 1601, 1622, 1780, 1882, 1895, 1933, 1955, 2045, 2083, 2187; animal, **S**1474; art, **S**359; book, **S**1680; building, **A**345; **S**1102; countryside, **S**452; environmental, **S**654; fungal, **S**1862; landscape, **S**635; nature, **S**74, 341, 635, 1794, 1896; of built environment, **S**1088; paper, **S**1680; plant, **S**1862; textile, **S**2127
Conservation Trust Colln, **S**114
Conservative Party Archvs, **L**4
Conservative Party Lib, S1100
Consolidated Investment & Assurance Co, records, **A**320
Consolidated Zinc Corp records, **A**324
Consortium of Univ Rsrch Libs, O169
Consortium of Welsh Lib & Info Svcs, O170
constitutions, **S**1277
construction, **IS**123, 151; **S**22, 45, 209, 504, 510, 588, 591, 594, 702, 770, 838, 844, 852, 902, 969, 998, 1316, 1439, 1452, 1515, 1638, 1816, 1911, 1919, 1966, 1969, 2046, 2112, 2148; building, **S**2141; steel, **S**47; *see also building*
Construction Corps, records (Ireland), **IA**45
Construction Industry Info Group, O171
Construction Industry Training Board, Info Centre, S865
construction materials, **A**514
consumer affairs, **S**1313
Consumer Health Info Consortium, O172
consumer protection, **S**172
consumer science, **S**1623
consumer studies, **S**12, 554, 614, 701
Contemporary Art Slide Scheme Archv, **S**1075
Contemporary Art Soc Archv, **A**349
Contemporary Medical Archvs, **S**1457
Contemporary Music Centre Ireland, Lib & Archv Svc, IS51
contraception, **S**1134
contracting, **S**1845
control, **S**1545
Conurbation Lib & Info Plan, O173
Conway Lloyd, Lt Col Sir John, papers, **A**63
Conwy & Denbighshire NHS Trust, S1859
Conwy Archv & Modern Record Svc, A244
Conwy Lib, Info & Archv Svc, P29
Conwy Poor Law Union records, **A**244
Conwy Sites & Monuments Record, **A**504
Conyngham Estate Papers, **IL**1
Conze, Edward, Colln & Papers (oriental theology), **A**77
Cook Colln (early linguistics), **S**665
Cook, Capt, Colln, **P**115
Cook, Ernest E., Colln, **S**102
Cook, Thomas & John, correspondence (tourist agents), **A**418
Cook, Thomas, & Son Ltd, records (travel agents), **A**418
Cooke family of Cooksborough, correspondence & estate papers, **IA**12
Cooke Lib (Hispanic studies), **IS**27
Cooke, Peter, Colln of African Music (recordings), **S**598
Cooke, Sir William Fothergill, Papers (development of telegraph), **A**294
cookery, **IS**9; **S**97, 419; *see also catering*
Cookridge Hosp NHS Staff Lib, S899
Cookson, Catherine, Colln, **S**1586
Coolattin Estate Papers, **IL**1

Coombe Borough records, **A**219
Cooper Abbs Colln (18C), **S**2168
Cooper, Major Derek, papers (Middle East), **S**1744
Coote estate records, **IA**68
COPAC, *see* **O**169
Cope Colln (Hampshire & Isle of Wight), **S**1946
Copland, Aaron, Colln (scores), **S**2168
Copleston, Edward, papers (Bishop of Llandaff), **S**426
Coppinger Family of Ballyvolane & Carrigwohill, papers, **IA**19
copyright, **S**1100
Copyright Licensing Agency Ltd, O174
Copyright Tribunal Lib, S1101
Corbett Hosp Medical Lib, S1994
Corby Borough Council, County Ref Lib, S490
Corby Development Corp, records, **A**395
Cordell, Frank, MSS (music), **S**1428
Corder MSS, **P**180
Corinium Museum, Archvs, A108
Cork & Ross RC Diocesan Archvs, IA18
Cork Archvs Inst, IA19
Cork Boards of Guardians, records, **IA**19
Cork Butter Market, records, **IA**19
Cork Chamber of Commerce, *see* **IS**18
Cork City Libs, IP4
Cork Coopers Soc records, **IA**19
Cork Corp, Local Studies Dept, IA20
Cork County Lib Svc, IP5
Cork Distillers, records, **IA**19
Cork Dist Model School records, **IA**19
Cork Euro Info Centre, IS18
Cork Gas Co, records, **IA**19
Cork Grafton Club records, **IA**19
Cork Inst of Tech Lib, IS19; *see also* **IS**22
Cork Plumbers Union records, **IA**19
Cork Port Sanitary Authority records, **IA**19
Cork Presbyterian Congregation records, **IA**19
Cork Public Museum, Lib & Archvs, IS20
Cork School of Music Lib, *see* **IS**19
Cork Steam Ship Co, records, **IA**19
Cork Typographical Union records, **IA**19
Cork Univ Hosp, Medical Lib, IS21
Cork Univ Press Colln, **IS**27
Cork, Bishops of, papers, **IA**18
Cork, City of, Steam Ship Co, records, **IA**19
Cork, City of, Vocational Edu Cttee, *see* **IS**23
Corkery, Daniel, Colln, **IS**27; *papers*, **IA**21
Cornish Hist Rsrch Centre, S2056
Cornish Maritime Colln, **P**30
Cornish Studies Lib, A430
Cornwall Coll, Learning Svcs, S1856; *see also* **S**287
Cornwall County Council, minutes, **A**494; *records*, **A**420
Cornwall Lib Svc, P30
Cornwall Postgrad Centre Medical Lib, S2055
Cornwall Quarter Sessions records, **A**494
Cornwall Record Office, A494
Cornwall-Legh family muniments, **S**1512
Cornwallis Family Papers, **A**215
Cornwallis, 1st Marquis, letters, **A**215
Corofin Board of Guardians, minutes, **IA**55
Corofin Rural Dist Council, minutes, **IA**55
coronations, **S**1459
corporate governance, **S**1194
Corp of London Libs, P99; **Records Office, A**270; *see also* **A**280, 304; **S**1154, 1225, 1408
Corpus Christi Coll (Cambridge), Parker Lib, S349
Corpus Christi Coll (Oxford), Lib, S1672

Corrigan, Sir Dominic, Papers (medicine), **IS**133
Corson Colln (Sir Walter Scott), **S**593
Corus Colors Regional Records Centre, A121
Corus Northern Regional Records Centre, A377
Corus Rsrch, Swinden Tech Centre Lib, S1873; **Teesside Tech Centre Lib, S**1545
Cory Lib, S299
costume, **IS**121; **S**103, 815, 823, 1340, 1423, 1467, 1497, 2170; Welsh, **S**419
Coton, A.V., Colln (dance), **S**651
Cotswold Dist Council, *see* **A**108
Cottle, Basil, papers, **A**77
Cotton Colln (16C-17C governmental maps), **S**1545
Cotton Coll, archvs, **A**52
Cotton MSS, **L**1
Cottonian Colln Lib & Archvs, *see* **S**1810
Cottril Colln (archaeo), **A**301
Council for British Archaeo Lib, S2162; *see also* **O**71
Council for Environmental Edu, Lib & Resource Centre, S1844
Council for Learning Resources in Colls, O175
Council for Museums, Archvs & Libs, *see* **O**328
Council for Slavonic & East European Lib & Info Svcs, O176
Council for the Care of Churches Lib, S1102
Council for the Central Laboratory of the Rsrch Councils, Daresbury Laboratory, Chadwick Lib, S2087; **Rutherford Appleton Laboratory Lib, S**535
Council for the Principality, archvs, **L**3
Council for the Protection of Rural England Lib, S1103
Council for World Mission Archvs, **S**1449
Council of Academic & Prof Publishers, *see* **A**228
counselling, **S**180, 437, 475, 609, 676, 796, 1082, 1335, 1816, 1949
Countess of Chester Hosp, School of Nursing & Midwifery Lib, S459
countryside, **S**65, 74, 256, 263, 273, 348, 452, 1316, 1850, 1955, 1971
Countryside Agency Lib, S452
countryside care, **S**287, 525
Countryside Council for Wales, Lib, S74; *see also* **S**72
County Carlow Chamber of Commerce, Lib & Info Svc, IS10
County Durham & Darlington Primary Care Trust, Shared Svcs Lib, S568
County Record Office, Huntingdon, A211
Coupar Angus Burgh records, **A**416
couples, **S**1045
Courage Ltd, records (brewers), **A**76
course recognition, **IS**86
Court of Appeal (Civil Div), transcripts, **S**1416
Court Svc Agency, *see* **A**318; **S**1416, 1579
Courtauld Inst of Art Lib, S1104
Courtenay Family of Midleton, papers, **IA**19
Courtenay of Powderham, estate archv, **A**161
Courtney Lib & Cornish Hist Rsrch Centre, S2056
Courtney, Lord, of Penwith, papers (voting reform), **S**1277
Courts Svc (Ireland), *see* **IS**103
Coutts & Co, Archvs Dept, A271
Covenanters Colln, **S**876
Coventry City Archvs, A113
Coventry Diocesan Readers Lib, S890
Coventry Kersey Dighton Patmore Colln, **S**1647
Coventry Libs & Info Svcs, P31
Coventry Quarter Sessions records, **A**113
Coventry Univ, Lanchester Lib, S495; **Nursing & Midwifery Lib, S**496
Coventry, Diocese of, records, **A**503

Cowan Colln (Scottish liturgy), **L**2
Cowan, Joseph, Colln (19C radicalism), **P**121
Cowen Family of Drumcondra Papers, **IA**49
Cowen Lib, S1588
Cowes Lib & Maritime Museum, S500
Cowper & Newton Museum, Lib & Archv, S1652
Cowper, Earl, of Panshanger, family & estate archv, **A**204
Cowper, William, Colln, **S**1652
Cox Family Papers, **IA**49
Cox, C.W.M.C., Colln, **S**1695
Cox, E.S., Papers (locomotive engineer), **S**2165
CR Colln (nat scis), **L**4
Crace Colln (London plans & views), **L**1
Cracherode, Revd C.M., Lib, **L**1
crafts, **A**421, 526; **S**248, 268, 996, 1105, 1653, 1804; contemporary, **S**1105; rural, **IA**97; **S**578; textile, **S**1582; Welsh, **S**419
Crafts Council Resource Centre, S1105; *see also* **A**250
Craig, Edith, archv (theatre), **S**2037
Craig, Edward Gordon, Colln, **S**2037, 2130
Craigavon Healthcare Lib, S501
Craigavon Museum Svcs, Philip B. Wilson Lib, S502
Cranbrook, 1st Earl of, papers, **A**215
Crane, Walter, Colln, **S**1050
Cranfield Univ Lib, S113; **Silsoe Campus Lib, S**114; *see also* **S**118, 2021
Crawford Collns (15C-19C), **L**2
Crawford Coll of Art & Design Lib, IS22
Crawford Lib (astronomy), **S**621
Crawford Lib (philatelic lit), **L**1
Crawford Municipal Art Gallery, IS23
Crawford of Haigh family & estate papers, **A**228
Crawford, 26th Earl of, papers, **S**621
Crawley Coll, LRC, S504
Crawley Hosp, Lib & Info Svc, S505
Crean, Tom, Papers (Antarctic explorer), **IA**92
Creasey, John, Colln, **S**1889
Cregan Lib, IS143
Cresswell Maternity Hosp, archvs, **A**132
Cresswell, Beatrix, papers, **A**164
Crews Colln (Judaeo-Spanish material), **S**357
Cribb Colln (chem), **S**1380
Crichton Museum Archvs, A132
Crichton Royal Hosp, records, **A**132
cricket, **S**1276
Crickitt Colln (Hogarth engravings), **A**206
Cricklade Coll, LRC, S36
Crieff Burgh records, **A**416
crime, **S**137, 493, 712, 816
crime & punishment, **S**419, 1634
Crimean War, **S**1647
criminology, **IS**200; **L**4; **S**28, 333, 676, 881, 1162, 1163, 1634, 1710, 1711, 1722, 1877, 1949
Crippen, Hawley Harvey, records (murderer), **A**305
Crisp, Norman, MSS, **S**1946
criticism, drama, **S**415, 1340; literary, **A**235; **IS**41, 102; **S**973
Croda Universal Ltd, Lib, S825
Crofton Colln (political & economic pamphs), **L**2
Crofton Family Papers, **IA**84
Croker, Thomas Crofton, correspondence (19C antiquary), **IA**31
Crombie Colln (theology), **S**1964
Crompton, Samuel, Papers (inventor of spinning mule), **A**57; **P**12
Cromwell-Bush family papers, **A**211
Crone, J.S., Archv (Irish writer), **A**37
Crookshank Lib, **A**106
crop production & protection, **S**1601
Crosby Lib, Local Hist Unit, *see* **A**462
Crosby Ravensworth Parish Lib, **S**433

cross-community relations, **S**122
Crosse MSS (music), **S**25
Crossle Colln MSS (Newry families hist), **P**134
Crow Collns (early English lit), **S**410
Crow, John, Papers, **S**410
Crown Agents Philatelic Colln & Archv, **L**1
Crown Office Lib, **S**590
Crowther Hall Lib, see **S**180
Crowther, J.G., papers, **S**239
Croydon Airport Colln, **A**478
Croydon Coll Lib, **S**513
Croydon Health Promotion Lib, see **S**514
Croydon Health Scis Lib, **S**2040
Croydon Lib Svc, **P**83
Croydon Local Studies Lib & Archvs Svc, **A**115
Croydon Nat Hist & Scientific Soc Ltd, Lib, **S**1933
Croydon Primary Care Lib, **S**514
Crozier, W.P., papers (journalism), **S**1512
Cruising Assoc, Lib & Info Centre, **S**1106
Crumlin Historical & Preservation Soc, **IO**13
Crusades, **S**1287
cryogenetics, **S**608
Crystal Palace Colln, **P**81; *records*, **A**296
Cuala Press Archv, **IL**2
Cubbon Lib, see **S**2177
Cubitt Town Estate, records, **A**350
Cullen, William, correspondence, **S**616
Cullum Lib (18C-19C bks), **A**83; **P**179
cultural activity, **S**190
cultural diversity, **S**122
Cultural Heritage Natl Training Org, **O**177
cultural policy, **S**997, 1525
cultural studies, **S**22, 360, 591, 918, 969, 1272, 1282, 1851
cultural theory, **S**1282
culture & cultures, **IS**104; **S**190, 248, 263, 677, 1151, 1243, 1246, 1298, 1422; Africa, **S**1632; American, **S**1621, 1632; Arab, **S**672, 1386; Black, **A**256; French, **S**605, 716; French Canadian, **S**1053; Indian, **L**4; Indonesia, **S**1632; Irish, **IS**156; Islamic, **S**1386; Japanese, **L**4; **S**1851; Jewish, **S**1270; Manx, **S**2179; Middle Eastern, **S**672; Oceania, **S**1632; Polish, **S**1328; popular, **S**661, 1634; Scottish, **S**598, 631; South East Asian, **L**4; Ulster, **A**205; Welsh, **A**480; world, **S**909, 2076
Cumann Cartlannaíochta Éireann, **IO**22
Cumann Leabharlanna na hEireann, **IO**26
Cumann na nGaedheal Party Archvs, **IA**49
Cumann Stair Clann na hEireann, **IO**20
Cumber, John, papers (SCF Dir Genl), **A**342
Cumberland & Westmorland Antiquarian & Archaeo Soc Colln, **S**436; *transactions*, **S**433
Cumberland Infirmary, Edu Centre Lib, **S**435
Cumbria Inst of the Arts Lib, **S**436
Cumbria Lib Svc, **P**32
Cumbria Local Hist Federation, **O**178
Cumbria Local Studies Lib, Barrow, **A**28; **Whitehaven**, **A**507
Cumbria Picture Lib, see **S**854
Cumbria Record Office, Barrow, **A**28; **Carlisle**, **A**98; **Kendal**, **A**217; **Whitehaven**, **A**507
Cummings, Michael, Colln (cartoons), **A**91
Cummins, Geraldine, papers (spiritualist), **IA**19
Cunard Steam-Ship Co, records, **A**239; **S**972
Cunningham, B.K., Colln, **S**399
Cunninghame of Auchenharvie family papers, **A**20
Cunninghame-Graham, R.B., Colln, **S**1055

Cunnington, William, works & MSS, **S**530
Cupar Presbytery & Kirk Session, records, **S**1964
curatorship, **S**1122; *see also museology*
cureos, **S**1323
Currall, Ivo, Colln (G.B. Shaw), **S**1340
Curran Colln (Irish lit), **IS**148
current affairs, **A**205; **S**418, 1107, 1129, 1320, 1337, 1925; African, **L**4; Commonwealth, **L**4; French, **S**1231; Latin American, **S**1447; US, **L**4
curriculum development, **IS**86
Curtis Museum, Resource Room, **A**12
Curtis, W.M., Archv (botanist), **A**508
Curtius, Philippe, papers (wax modeller), **A**305
Curwen Press Archvs, **L**5
Curwen, Capt J., Lib, **A**217
customs, **A**409; **S**751; folk, **S**419; traditional, **S**1453; Ulster, **A**205
customs & excise, **S**1162, 1883
Cuthbert-Odgson Colln (early aeronautics), **S**1342
Cwmbran New Town Development Corp, archvs, **A**117
Cyfarthfa Archv (Welsh industry), **L**3
Cyngor Archifau Cymru, **O**13
Cyngor Cefn Gwlad Cymru, **S**74
Cyngor Llyfrau Cymru, see **S**20
Cyngor Sir Ynys Môn, see *Isle of Anglesey County Council*
Cyril Kleinwort Lib, see **S**1084
Cyril Parker Lib, **S**1861
cytology, **S**309
Czechoslovakia, **S**1436

D'Eon, Chevalier, Colln, **S**918
d'Hancarville, Baron, papers, **A**259
D'Oyly Carte Opera Co Archv, **A**272
Dadaism, **S**633
Dailuaine-Talisker Distilleries Ltd, records, **A**376
Daily Herald Photograph Archv, **S**215
Dairy Council, advertising archv, **A**399
dairy science, **S**64
dairying, **S**1850
Dalcroze Soc Archv, **A**192
Daley Colln, **S**1265
Dallas Pratt Colln (cartography), **S**97
Dallas, Sarah, Knitwear Archv, **S**103
Dalton Colln, **S**1241
Dalton, John, papers (hist of chem), **S**1512
Daly, Cardinal, Lib (theology, Irish hist), **S**42
Dalziel Colln (proof engravings), **A**262
Dambusters Colln, **A**505
dance, **A**192, 321; **S**115, 419, 469, 776, 923, 969, 1170, 1232, 1282, 1323; Indian, **S**1014; traditional, **S**1453
Dance Adv Archv, **A**192
Dance & the Child Internatl Archv, **A**192
Dandy, Morten, Colln, **S**1519
Danson Estate Archv, **A**47
Dante Colln, **S**1216, 1512, 1751
Darlington Centre for Local Studies, **A**119
Darlington Coll of Edu, records, **A**216
Darlington Coll of Tech, Info & Learning Technologies Centre, **S**519
Darlington Lib Svc, **P**33
Darlington Memorial Hosp Lib, **S**520
Darlington Poor Law Union records, **A**119
Darlington, C.D., Working Lib, **S**1624
Darnley of Cobham, family & estate papers, **A**435
Dart Colln (amenity rsrch), **S**1603
Dartford & Gravesham NHS Trust Lib, **S**521
Dartington Coll of Arts, Lib & LRC, **S**2050
Dartmouth family papers, **A**467
Darwin Coll Lib, **S**350
Darwin Lib, see **S**593
Darwin, Charles, Colln, **L**5; *correspondence*, **S**179; *letters*, **S**344, 1020, 1359; *papers*, **L**5
Darwin, Erasmus, Colln, **P**174
Darwiniana Colln, **S**1920
Davenport Lib (Oxfordshire), **A**412
David Ferriman Lib, **S**1309

David Hoffman Photo Lib, **S**1107
David Livingstone Centre, Lib, **S**196
David Owen Waterways Archv, **A**159; *see also* **S**749
Davidson, James, papers, **A**164
Davies MSS, **A**202
Davies, C.P., Wind & Watermill Colln, **S**410
Davies, Clement, Papers, **L**3
Davies, Dr Rupert, papers (Methodism), **A**368
Davies, Emily, papers, **S**357
Davies, Idris, Colln, **P**21
Davies, William, MSS (author), **S**2190
Davis, Henry, Colln (early printed bks), **S**484
Davis, Uri, Colln (Arab-Israeli Conflict), **S**672
Davison, Emily Wilding, papers, **S**1469
Davitt, Michael, Colln, **IA**11; *papers*, **IA**57
Davy, C., MSS, **S**1371
Dawkins Colln (Greek), **S**1751
Dawson Colln (illusts), **S**1789
Dawson, John, Lib (18C lib), **A**281
de Almeida, Antonio, Colln (printed music), **S**1428
de Beaumont, Robin, Colln (German Renaissance & 19C British bks), **S**1032
de Beer Colln (Charles Darwin), **S**1227
de Beer Papers, **S**1433
de Broke, Lords Willoughby, of Compton Verney, family & estate papers, **A**476
de Courcy Ireland Colln, **IS**27
De Freyne Estate Papers, **IL**1
de la Beche, Sir Henry Thomas, Papers (geol), **A**422
de la Mare, Walter, Colln, **P**81
De La Warr, Earl, records, **A**230
De Laszlo Colln (phytotherapy), **L**5
de Lloyd, David, Papers (Welsh folksongs), **S**18
De Montfort Univ Lib, **S**921; **Bedford Lib**, **S**115; **Charles Frears Lib**, **S**922; **Milton Keynes Info Centre**, **S**1550; **Scraptoft Lib**, **S**923; *see also* **S**70
De Morgan Colln (maths), **S**1440; *papers*, **S**1433
de Navarro, J.M., Bequest (archaeo), **S**323
De Quincey Colln, **P**112
De Ramsey of Romsey, Lords, family & estate records, **A**211
de Sausmarez Papers, **A**531
de Valera, Eamon, Papers, **IA**49
de Vere estate records, **IA**68
De Vesci Estate Papers, **IL**1
De Zoete, Beryl, Colln (dance), **S**1165
Deacon Archvs, **S**1945
deaf awareness, **S**1082
deafness, **IS**93; **S**1373
Deal Borough records, **A**128
Dean Clarke House NHS Lib, **S**662
Dean Savage Lib, see **S**945
Dean, Basil, papers (theatre), **S**1512
death, **S**1409
Deeside Coll, Multimedia Learning Centre, **S**522
defence, **S**289, 1009, 1284; civil, **S**2163
Defence Evaluation & Rsrch Agency, see **S**760
defence forces, **S**1284
Defence Forces Lib, **IS**28
Defence Geographic & Imagery Intelligence Agency, Lib & Info Centre, **S**684
Defence Medical Training Lib, **S**753
defence policy, **A**88, 298; **S**1213, 1284
defence studies, **S**1925, 2021
Delaney, Mary, MSS (18C), **P**122
Delmas Conservation Bindery, see **IS**39
Delvin Rural Dist Council minutes, **IA**78
Demarco, Richard, Archv, **S**633
dementia, **S**991
demography, **S**599, 1188, 1265, 1312, 1679, 1722, 1741; East European, **S**1436
Denbigh Community Coll Lib, see **S**485
Denbighshire Lib & Info Svcs, **P**34

Denbighshire Record Office, **A**441
Denbighshire Sites & Monuments Record, **A**504
Denham, Dixon, MSS (exploration), **A**334
Denmylne State Papers, **L**2
Dennis Vehicles, records, **A**513
Denny Lib, **S**1372
Denny, William, of Dumbarton, records (shipbldg), **A**176
Dent, Alan, Colln, **S**1996
Dent-Brocklehurst of Sudeley, family & estate records, **A**185
dentistry, **IS**61; **S**140, 170, 181, 261, 408, 428, 561, 617, 740, 918, 972, 1022, 1118, 1227, 1333, 1357, 1494, 1535, 1590, 1620, 1970, 2135, 2157
Dept for Culture, Media & Sport, Info Centre, **S**1108; *see also* **S**680, 913
Dept for Edu & Skills, Lib & Info Svc, **S**1109
Dept for Environment, Food & Rural Affairs, Nobel House Lib, **S**1110; *see also* **S**23, 1488, 1794
Dept for Gter London Archaeo, records, **A**301
Dept for Internatl Development, see **S**580
Dept for Transport, Info Svcs & Sources, see **S**1316; *see also* **S**1939, 2010
Dept of Agric & Rural Development (Northern Ireland), Lib, **S**123; *see also* **S**488
Dept of Agric, Food & Rural Development, Lib, **IS**52; *see also* **IA**43; **IS**153
Dept of Arts, Culture, Gaeltacht & the Islands, see **IO**21; **IS**113, 121
Dept of Arts, Sport & Tourism, see **IA**25
Dept of Communications, Marine & Nat Resources Lib, **IS**53; *see also* **IA**64; **IS**79
Dept of Culture, Arts & Leisure (Northern Ireland), see **A**41
Dept of Defence, see **IA**45; **IS**28
Dept of Economic Development Northern Ireland, see **S**124
Dept of Edu & Sci, Lib, **IS**54
Dept of Enterprise, Trade & Employment, Lib, **IS**55; *see also* **IS**170
Dept of Enterprise, Trade & Investment (Northern Ireland) Lib, **S**124; *see also* **S**128, 135
Dept of Finance & Personnel, Northern Ireland, Construction Svc Lib, **S**125
Dept of Foreign Affairs & Internatl Trade (Canada), see **S**1053
Dept of Foreign Affairs Lib, **IS**56
Dept of Health, Lib & Info Svcs, **S**1111; *see also* **S**911, 1256, 1280
Dept of Health & Children, Lib & Info Unit, **IS**57; *see also* **IA**46; **IS**117
Dept of Social & Family Affairs, Lib & Info Svc, **IS**58
Dept of Social Security, see **S**1112
Dept of State (US), see **S**1432
Dept of the Environment & Local Govt, see **S**70, 111
Dept of the Environment for Northern Ireland, see **S**136
Dept of the Taoiseach, see **IO**17
Dept of Trade & Industry, see **S**1097, 1314, 1315, 1334
Dept of Urban Archaeo, records, **A**301
Dept of Work & Pensions, Info Centre, **S**1112
Derby Borough records, **A**122
Derby Canal Co records, **A**122
Derby China Factory records, **A**122
Derby City Genl Hosp, Lib & Knowledge Svc, **S**524
Derby City Libs, **P**35
Derby Coll, Lib & Learning Resources, **S**525
Derby Local Studies Lib, **A**122
Derby Univ, see *Univ of Derby*
Derby, Diocese of, records, **A**375
Derby, Earls of, family & estate papers, **A**238, 425

Derbyshire Libs & Heritage, P36; *see also* S283
Derbyshire Local Hist Socs Network, O179
Derbyshire Local Studies Lib, A374
Derbyshire Record Office, A375
Dermatological Soc of London, archvs, S1381
dermatology, S1227, 1994, 2135
Derry RC Diocesan Archvs, A359
Derwentside Coll, LRC, S486
design, A69; IS22, 115, 141, 155; S12, 146, 160, 202, 208, 237, 238, 263, 430, 467, 495, 554, 591, 610, 673, 675, 677, 683, 689, 707, 803, 810, 838, 870, 958, 968, 969, 1009, 1018, 1059, 1060, 1073, 1075, 1122, 1255, 1261, 1282, 1290, 1378, 1418, 1452, 1503, 1544, 1577, 1597, 1617, 1630, 1641, 1804, 1828, 1840, 1847, 1911, 1969, 2094, 2103, 2127, 2148; 3D, S160, 474; aircraft, A505; automotive, S878; book, S1290, 1519, 1680; civic, S972; costume, A321; S1423; engineering, S430; exhibition, A250; Far Eastern, S1290; fashion, A250; IS9; S1254; furniture, A250; garden, IS6, 113; S772, 844, 1367, 1622, 2045; graphic, A250; S474, 702, 1255, 1282, 1408; Indian, S1290; interior, A250; IS151; S22, 150, 591, 702, 844, 1141, 1262, 1282, 1610; landscape, IS151; S226, 654, 1235, 1622, 2045; metalwork, A250; modern, S1031; product, S430, 901, 1060, 1282; South East Asian, S1290; sports building, S641; stage, S467, 1423; stained glass, A250; tank, S2084; textile, A250; theatre, S467, 1002; transport, S1268; urban, S594; *see also art & arts*
Design & Artists Copyright Soc Ltd, O180
Design Council, *see* A69
Design Hist Rsrch Centre Archvs, A69
Deutsches Archäologisches Institut (Rome) Photo Archv, S1747
developing countries, IS38; S1319, 1733, 1912
development, S234, 310, 1212, 1246, 1370; book, S1211; cell, S309; child, S1045; community, S133; economic, S124, 580, 723, 1151; educational, S364; industrial, IS55, 77; S628; information, S1211; international, S580; organisational, S133; pastoral, S1319; port, S638; rural, IS52, 202; S123, 230, 1319, 1758, 1991; sustainable, S1110; Third World, IS147
Development Colln (development studies), S217
development control, S341
development studies, S49, 114, 180, 230, 336, 1733, 1804
Devereux papers, S2086
Devon & Cornwall Record Soc, O181; *see also* A164
Devon & Exeter Instn, Lib & Reading Rooms, S663
Devon County Beekeeping Colln, S273
Devon County Council, records, A161, 420
Devon Hist Soc, O182
Devon Lib & Info Svcs, P37; *see also* A164
Devon Partnership NHS Trust, Wonford House Hosp Lib, S664
Devon Quarter Sessions records, A161
Devon Railway Studies Colln, P37
Devon Record Office, A161; *see also* A27, 163
Devonshire & Dorset Regiment Museum, Regimental Archvs, A162
Devonshire Assoc, proceedings, S1806
Devonshire Regiment archvs, A126
Devonshire, Duke of, Colln (Derbyshire local studies), A122
Devonshire, Earls & Dukes of, correspondence, S67
Dewar MSS, S1371
Dewsbury Coll Lib, S531
Dewsbury Health Care NHS Trust, *see* S532

DFID Lib, S580
diabetes, S1708
Diageo Ltd, Archvs, A376
Diageo plc, Brand Technical Centre Lib, S1541
dialects, A469; S419, 751
Diamond Colln (19C photos of psychiatric patients), S1381
Diana Princess of Wales Hosp, Trust Lib, S765
Dick, W.B., & Co Ltd, records (lubricating oil manufacturers), A482
Dick-Read, Grantly, papers, S1457
Dickens House Museum, Lib, S1113
Dickens, Charles, Colln, A435; P148; S156, 1823; *correspondence,* S179; *MSS,* S918, 1113, 1290
Dickinson, John, & Co Photo Archv (paper manufacturers), A204
Dickinson, Thorold, Cinema Colln, S1050
Dickson, Major Genl Sir Alexander, MSS, S1130
Die-Casting Soc Colln, S2085
Dieterichs Colln (German Reformation), L2
dietetics, S376, 818
Digbeth Centre for Arts & Digital Media Lib, *see* S177
Digital Health Rsrch Unit, *see* O163
Dilke Colln (Keats), S1225
Dillwyn, Lewis Weston, Colln (botany), L3
Dingle Harbour Commissioner records, IA92
Dingle Poor Law Union, minutes, IA92
Dingle Rural Dist Council, minutes, IA92
Dinosaur Trackways Collns, S545
Diocese of Arundel & Brighton (RC), Archvs, A207
Diocese of Derry (RC) Archvs, A359
Diocese of East Anglia (RC), Diocesan Archvs, A397
Diocese of Winchester, Thorold & Lyttleton Lib, S2120
diplomacy, A88; S1132
Direct Mail Assoc, archvs, A399
Directorate of Intelligence, records (Ireland), IA45
Directorate of Operations, records (Ireland), IA45
disability, IS117; S1138, 1430; child, S1296; learning, S58, 818, 860, 861, 1615, 1616, 1841, 1855
disaster relief, S1319
disasters, S2163
disease, Alzheimer's, S991; communicable, S728; foot-&-mouth, S2136; heart, S417; industrial, S656; infectious, S1331, 1462, 1755; musculoskeletal, S1698
Disease in Childhood Journal, archv, S1354
Disraeli, Benjamin, Colln, S812; *correspondence,* S1185; *papers,* L4
distilling, A178, 376; S1541
Ditton Park estate records, A78
Diver, Cyril, Colln, S543, 1786
divinity, *see religion & related subjects*
divorce, S1317
Dix Colln (early Irish printing), IA31; IL1; IP7
Doble Colln (Celtic hagiography), S2056
Docklands Lib & Archv, S1114
doctrine, S1125, 1463; Christian, S1752; Eastern Orthodox, S1685, 1686
Dodgson, Charles L., papers, A513
Doherty, Richard, Papers (obstetrics & gynaecology), IS167
Doig Colln (arch plans), A158; P119
Dolaucothi family & estate archv, L3
Dollar Academy Lib, S539
Dolmen Press Colln, IS143
domestic policy, US, S1432
Dominican Order of Friars Preachers, S293
Donald Mason Lib, S971
Donaldson Colln (classics & edu), S1964
Doncaster & Bassetlaw Hosps NHS Trust, S542

Doncaster Archvs, A124
Doncaster Coll, LRCs, S540
Doncaster Horse Racing Colln, P38
Doncaster Lib & Info Svcs, P38
Doncaster Museum & Art Gallery, Lib & Archvs, S541
Doncaster Railway Colln, P38
Doncaster Royal Infirmary, Medical & Prof Lib, S542
Doncaster Royal Infirmary Patients' Lib, *see* P38; S542
Doncaster, Archdeaconry of, records, A124
Donegal Archaeo Survey, archvs, IS175
Donegal Board of Guardian records, IA67
Donegal Board of Health & Public Assistance records, IA67
Donegal Co-op & Agricultural Socs, records, IA67
Donegal Cttee of Agric, records, IA67
Donegal County Archvs, IA67
Donegal County Council Lib Svc, IP6; Donegal Studies Colln, IA65
Donegal County Museum, Lib & Archvs, IS175
Donegal Dist Nursing Assocs, records, IA67
Donegal Grand Jury records, IA67
Donegal Historical Soc, IO9
Donegal Poor Law Union, minutes, IA67
Donegal Vocational Educational Council, *see* IS174
Doneraile Estate Papers, IL1
Donne, John, Colln, S1281
Donnellan, Philip, Colln (film), IA37
Doolin Colln (hist of medicine), IS134
Dorchester, 1st Marquis of, Lib, S1355
Dorman Museum Resources Room, S1546
Dormans Diesels, records, A467
Dorset Archaeo Collns & Records, S545
Dorset Archvs Svc, A125
Dorset County Hosp Lib, S544
Dorset Libs & Arts Svc, P39
Dorset Nat Hist & Archaeo Soc Lib, S545
Dorset Provincial Museum & Lib, S1818
Dorset Regiment archvs, A126
Dorville family & estate papers, A282
Douce Colln, L4
Doughty, C.M., papers, S358
Douglas Public Lib, P210
Dover Borough records, A128
Dover Harbour Board, records, A128
Dover Postgrad Medical Centre Lib, *see* S50
Dover Rural Dist Council, records, A128
Dowden, Richard, papers (19C Mayor of Cork & philanthropist), IA19
Dowlais Iron Co, records, A97
Down & Connor RC Diocesan Archvs, A38
Downes Colln (arch), IA36
Downey, W&D, Colln (court photos), S1170
Downing Coll, Maitland Robinson Lib, S351
Downside Abbey Lib, S101
Dowty Group, records, A185
Doyle, Lynn, Colln (Ulster writer), A37
Dr Johnson's House, Lib, S1115
Dr Pusey Memorial Lib, S1673
Dr Scholl Lib, S2177
Dr Shepherd's Lib, P71
Dr Thomlinson's Lib (18C bks), P121
Dr Williams' Lib, S1116; *see also* S1099
drainage, IS123
drama, A267; IS138, 149; S415, 424, 614, 726, 968, 969, 1043, 1059, 1082, 1139, 1154, 1282, 1340, 1390, 1423, 1527, 1797, 1816, 1887, 1923, 1996; Canadian, S1053; Cuban, S1447; Elizabethan, S1390, 1778; English, S1997; Scottish, A182; traditional, S1453; *see also theatre*
Drama Assoc of Wales Lib, S415
Drapers' Co Archv, A273
drawing, S1032

Drayton, Michael, Colln, P194
Dreadnought Lib, *see* S1439
dress, S103, 419, 1290
Drinkwater, John, MS works, A354
Driver & Vehicle Licensing Agency, Open Resource Centre, S2010
drives, S1530
Drogheda Port Co, Archvs & Records, IA23
Droitwich Borough records, A518
Drosophilia Offprint Colln, S309
drug abuse, S417
drugs, S222
Druid Theatre Archv, IS166
Drummond Colln (religious tracts), S1978
Drummond Lib, *see* S593
Drummond's of Lumb Lane, records, A62
Drummond, Archbishop Hay, Lib, S509
Drummond, William, Colln (lit), S593
Drummond-Hays of Seggieden, family & estate records, A416
Drumpellier Papers, P126
Drygrange Colln (Scottish Catholicism), P40
Du Mont Colln (19C photo illust), S104
Dublin Anacreontic Soc Colln (orchestral parts), IS138
Dublin Artisans' Dwellings Co Colln, IA36
Dublin Board of Aldermen, records, IA30
Dublin Boards of Guardians, records, IA33
Dublin Business School Lib, IS59
Dublin City & County Regional Tourism Org, *see* IS159
Dublin City Archvs, IA30
Dublin City Public Libs, IP7; Centre for Dublin & Irish Studies, IA31
Dublin City Univ Lib, IS60; *see also* IS143
Dublin County Council, archvs, IA33
Dublin Dental Hosp, Lib & Archv, IS61
Dublin Diocesan Archvs, IA32; Lib, IS62
Dublin Grand Juries, records, IA33
Dublin Guild of Brewers & Maltsters, minutes, IA35
Dublin Guild of Coopers, minutes, IA35
Dublin Guild of Goldsmiths, records, IA29
Dublin Hosp archvs, IS134
Dublin Inst for Advanced Studies, School of Cosmic Physics Lib, IS63; School of Theoretical Physics Lib, IS64; *see also* IS67
Dublin Inst of Tech Lib, IS65
Dublin Police & Metropolitan Police, records, IA34
Dublin Sheriffs & Commons, records, IA30
Dublin Theatre Festival, archv, IA41
Dublin Tourism, *see* IS66
Dublin Urban Folklore Collns, IS149
Dublin Wide Streets Commission, records, IA30
Dublin Writers Museum Lib, IS66
Duchy Coll Learning Centre, S287
Ducie family muniments, S1512
Ducie of Tortworth, family & estate records, A185
Dudley Archvs & Local Hist Svc, A130
Dudley Coll of Tech Lib, S547
Dudley Group of Hosps NHS Trust, Clinical Lib Svc, S548; Corbett Hosp Medical Lib, S1994
Dudley Health Authority Lib, S549
Dudley Lib Svcs, P40
Dudley papers, S2086
Dudley, Earls of, archv, A130; *Estate archv,* P40
Duff Colln of Pamphs (classics), S18
Duff House (Montcoffer) Papers, A3
Duff of Meldrum family & estate papers, A3
Dugdale Soc, O183
Duke of Edinburgh's Royal Regiment, records, A445
Duke of Norfolk's Lib, S44
Dulwich Coll, Wodehouse Lib, S1117

S12, 126, 928, 1157; higher, IS86; S253, 1003, 1395; Irish, IA47; language, S1061, 2175; lifeskills, IS43; media, A496; museum, S1653, 2076; non-formal, S364; non-sectarian, A216; outdoor, S1788; peace, S122; physical, S81, 115, 430, 584, 609, 968, 969, 1406; post-compulsory, S1439; primary, IA47; IS49; S504, 1550; progressive, A104; religious, A314; S1057, 1804, 1894; special needs, S1430; teacher, S1597, 1969; technological, IS86; visually impaired, S2145; women's, S357, 379, 651, 1763, 1768; see also teaching; training
education policy, IS54
education systems, IS86
Educational Dance-Drama Theatre Archv, A192
Educational Publishers Council, see O321
Educational Rsrch Centre Lib, IS69
Edward Boyle Lib, see S918
Edward Grey Inst of Field Ornithology, Alexander Lib, S1725
Edward VII Colln, S1706
Edwards, Amelia B., Lib & MSS, S1762
Edwards, Bob, papers (politics), A365
Edwards, R. Dudley, Papers, IA49
Edwards, Sir George, papers (aeronautical engineer), A505
Edyvean-Walker Medical Lib, S1876
Effingham family papers, A438
Egan, Barry M., papers, IA19
Egan, Very Rev Dr Patrick, Papers (Clonfert diocese), IA74
Egerton MSS, L1
Egerton, Baron, papers, A215
Egglishaw, H.J., Colln, S863
Egham Museum Lib, S650
Egypt Exploration Soc Lib, S1119
Egyptology, S612, 1119, 1324, 1747, 1759, 2016
Ehrenberg, Dr Victor, Antiquities Colln, S1159
Eidsworth & Mudford records (consulting engineers), A294
EIFF VHS Colln, S731
Eisler, Robert, literary papers, S1456
Eisteddfod, S419
Elder, Michael, Colln (Scottish theatre), A182
Eldon Lib, S1828
Eldon, 1st Earl of, papers (Lord Chancellor), A511
election studies, S1277
Electoral Reform Soc, archvs, S1277
Electrical Assoc for Women records, A294
electro-optics, S760
Electronic Knowledge Access Team, O193
Electronic Publishers Forum, see O321
electronics, IS90, 125; S315, 535, 621, 691, 760, 869, 1831, 1854, 2103, 2168; defence, A60; marine, S638; see also engineering, electronic
Elgar Birthplace Museum Archvs, A516
Elgar, Sir Edward, papers, A516, 518
Elgin Museum – Moray Soc, Lib, S652
Elham Parish Lib, S404
Elham Rural Dist Council, records, A128
Eli Lilly & Co Ltd, Info Centre, S2128
Elias Lib (hymnology), S401
Elias, Ney, MSS (exploration), A334
Elias-Jones, T.F., Colln (bacteriology, public health), S706
Eliot Colln (English lit), S2168
Eliot, George, Colln, P31, 194
Eliot, T.S., Colln, S410; papers, S369
Eliot-Phelips Colln (Spanish imprints), S1440
Elizabeth Blackwell Lib, see S252, 257
Elizabeth Gaskell Lib, see S1519
Elizabethan life, S1996
Elkoshi Colln (Hebrew lit), S1701
Ellen Terry Memorial Museum Lib, S2037
Ellermans Lamport & Holt, records (shipping company), A239
Ellingen Papers (civil eng), S1205
Elliott Theological Colln (15C), P17
Ellis Lib (19C), S17
Ellis, George, Photo Archv (Cornwall), A430
Ellis, John, papers (nat hist), S1247
Ellis, T.E., Papers, L3
Elmwood Coll Lib, S515
Elphin RC Diocesan Archvs, IA86
Elston Parochial Lib, S1647
Eltham Poor Law Union records, A128
Elton Colln (Industrial Revolution), S2033
Elton Lib, see S1723
Elton, Prof Sir Geoffrey, Lib, A522; papers, S1366
Elwyn-Jones, Lord, Papers, L3
Ely Colln (part of lib of Ely Cathedral), L5
Ely Diocesan Records, A89
Ely, Diocese of, records, A87, 89, 211, 400, 512; L5
EMB Technical Drawings Colln, S1539
Embassy of Finland, Press & Info Office, S1120
Emberton, Joseph, Archv (design), A69
Emden Colln (military hist), S1767
Emergency Planning Coll Lib, S2163
Emery, Walter, Colln (Bach MSS), S337
EMI Music Archvs, A201
emigration, S1303, 1328; Irish, S1653
EMMA/Midlands Dance Co Archv, A192
Emmanuel Coll Lib, S353
Emmwood, Vicky, Colln (cartoons), A91
Emo Court Colln (arch), IA36
employment, IS58, 73; S982, 1098, 1214, 1425, 1470
employment affairs, S1121
employment relations, S982
endocrinology, S1830, 1872
endovirology, S1830
energy, S848, 1172, 1704; gas, S1471; hydroelectric, S1471; nuclear, S1471; oil, S1471; solar, S1471; wind, S1471
energy policy, S581, 1098
energy use, S1070
Enfield Libs, P85; see also A302
ENFO – The Environmental Info Svc, IS70
engineering, IS6, 11, 91, 123; L4, 5; S12, 114, 208, 232, 263, 395, 425, 430, 495, 526, 535, 561, 593, 610, 701, 776, 780, 824, 834, 844, 880, 918, 972, 995, 1012, 1121, 1199, 1200, 1205, 1208, 1439, 1452, 1545, 1557, 1597, 1617, 1641, 1647, 1700, 1717, 1816, 1873, 1911, 1912, 1919, 1969, 2004, 2013, 2031, 2033, 2046, 2087, 2094, 2103, 2112, 2148, 2160; aeronautical, S869, 1180, 1342; aerospace, S111, 755, 1925; agricultural, IS150; S114, 117, 473, 1601; automated, IS178; S478, 2046; automobile, S1648; automotive, S266, 878; building services, S1070; ceramic, S1985; chemical, S304, 1180, 1541, 1545; civil, IS150; S125, 865, 869, 998, 1122, 1180, 1205, 1439, 1646, 1824, 2021, 2138; communications, A414; computer, S267; electrical, A294; S267, 321, 745, 998, 1180, 1206, 1824, 1925, 2021; electronic, A294; IS178; S77, 125, 482, 610, 969, 1180, 1206, 1824, 1925; environmental, S830, 1180; fluid, S503; food, S1110; gas, S1207; industrial, S998; manufacturing, S321, 1206; marine, S755, 969, 1199, 1372, 1898, 1935, 1944, 1945; materials, S1925; mechanical, IS90, 178; S113, 125, 267, 745, 869, 969, 998, 1180, 1208, 1580, 1824, 1925, 2021; military, S26, 444, 445, 1130, 1646; mining, S1580; motor, S515; motor cycle, S1557; nautical, IS160; naval, S2073; nuclear, S745; ocean, S2030; printing, A225; product, S1282; production, S869; railway, S48; rehabilitation, S719; structural, S125, 1209; transport, S1208, 1539; wind tunnel, S111
Eng & Physical Scis Rsrch Council, see S2020
Eng Employers' Federation Lib, S1121
England's Dreaming Punk Archv, S969
English Benedictine Congregation, records, S101
English Caroline Divines Colln, S433
English Domestic Politics Colln, S217
English Dominican Friars, see S1665
English Folk Dance & Song Soc, see S1453
English Goethe Soc Lib & Papers, S1445
English Heritage Lib, S1122; see also A483; S1217
English Local Hist Colln, S934
English Mission, papers, A356
English Music Theatre Co Archvs, S25
English Natl Ballet Archv, A275
English Natl Opera Archv, A276
English Nature, Info & Lib Svcs, S1794
English Opera Group Archvs, S25
English Regional Arts Boards Archv, S1591
English Table Tennis Assoc Archvs, S972
English Tourism Council Lib, see S1454
English, Donald, Archv, S1776
English, Raymond, Colln (anti-slavery), S1512
English-Speaking Union, Page Memorial Lib, S1123
engraving, S1275
Enk Colln (classics), S1227
Ennis Board of Guardians, minutes, IA55
Ennis Rural & Urban Dist Council, records, IA55
Ennistymon Board of Guardians, minutes, IA55
Ennistymon Rural Dist Council, minutes, IA55
enterprise, S1253
Enterprise Ireland, Client Knowledge Svc, IS71
entertainment, A404; S1009
entomology, S71, 786, 1263, 1308, 1359, 1576, 1669, 1738, 1895, 2083, 2089, 2137, 2187; early, S1359; marine, IS194
environment, IA70; IS70, 145; S33, 49, 123, 230, 234, 270, 336, 476, 478, 581, 628, 647, 723, 780, 805, 892, 1103, 1151, 1246, 1298, 1378, 1383, 1702, 1711, 1850, 1882, 1887, 1912, 2004, 2072, 2160; aquatic, S1786; built, S263, 628, 1088; coastal, S74; historic, S1108; marine, IS53; S74; terrestrial, S1786
environmental change, S756, 1750
environmental hazards, S656
environmental issues, S233, 1107, 1202
environmental policy, S1103, 1702
environmental protection, S1110
environmental science, L5; S9, 16, 78, 114, 310, 469, 682, 733, 940, 1439, 1488, 1803, 1804, 1982, 2139
environmental studies, IS151; S115, 525, 561, 968, 972, 1433, 1641, 1788, 2046
Enys Autograph Colln, S2056
enzymes, S1830
Ephemera Soc, O194
Epidemiological Soc, archvs, S1381
epidemiology, S417, 662, 1331, 1613
epigraphy, S1747; Graeco-Roman, S1159
Epping Forest Coll, LRC, S1484
Epsom Hosp, Sally Howell Lib, S658; see also S441
Epstein, Sir Jacob (sculptor), archv, S2076; papers, A349
equal opportunities, S1510
Equal Opportunities Commission, Info Centre, S1510
equestrianism, S226, 940, 1622
equine science, S263, 1837
equine studies, S19, 270, 273, 476, 772, 805, 1499, 1610, 1955, 1971, 2045
ERA Tech Ltd, Info Centre, S891
Erasmus Colln, S385
Eric Whitehead Photography, S854
Eric Young Memorial Lib, S2189
Erickson, John & Ljubica, Colln (Soviet Union), L2
Erinville Hosp Lib, IS24
Erkine Allon Colln (musical scores), S297
Erredge Colln (Brighton local hist), P17
Erskine Medical Lib, S595
Eshelby Colln (Yorkshire), S963
Eshton Hall Estate Papers, S918
esotericism, S743
Esperanto Assoc of Britain, Butler Lib, S1986
Essex Archaeo & Historical Congress, O195
Essex Colln (Chelmsford church hist), S448
Essex Jazz Archv Colln, P51
Essex Libs, P51; see also A360, 443
Essex Poor Law Unions, records, A100
Essex Quarter Sessions, records, A111
Essex Record Office, A100; Colchester & North East Essex Branch, A111; Southend Branch, A461
Essex Regiment Museum, Regimental Archvs, A101
Essex Rivers Healthcare NHS Trust, see S480
Essex Soc for Archaeo & Hist Lib, S479
Essex Soc for Family Hist Rsrch Centre, see A100
Essex Sound Archv, A100
Essex Univ, see Univ of Essex
Essex, James, papers (architect), A511
Esso Petroleum Co Ltd, see S892
estate agency, S1370
Estonia, S1436
ethics, IS8, 131; L4; S448, 523, 562, 844, 959, 1407, 1463, 1702; business, S1191; medical, IS16; S790, 1027, 1457; religious, S320
ethnic peoples, S2118
ethnic relations, S1195
ethnicity, S717
ethnography, S146, 451, 612, 1034, 1165, 1742, 1926, 2049; Slavonic, S1436; see also anthropology
ethnomusicology, A24; S751, 1742
ethology, S1872
Eton Coll Lib, S2130
Eugenics Soc, archv, S1457
Euing Collns of the Bible & Music, S738
Europe & European studies, S144, 263, 593, 1804, 1982; Eastern, S492
Europe, C of E Diocese in, records, A280
European Commission, see IS18, 164
European Community, A365; S1094
European Green Archv, S1548
European Info Assoc, O196
European Parliament, Lib, S1124
European Parliamentary Labour Party, records, A365
European School of Osteopathy Lib, S207
Eva Crane IBRA Lib, S416
Evangelical Lib Ltd, S1125
Evangelical Lutheran Church of England, see S400
evangelical movements, A368
evangelism, S1125, 1652, 1767
Evans & Bevin Archv (Welsh industry), L3
Evans Cotton Mill records, A122
Evans, Dom Illtyd, papers, S879
Evans, Gwynfor, Papers, L3
Evelyn Colln of Topographical Works, S2171
Evelyn Estate Papers, A297
Evening Standard Photo Colln, S1170
Everest Expedition Papers, A334; S1363
evolution, S1247, 1741; human, S1741
Ewing, Elizabeth, Archv (costume historian), S103
Ewing, John C., Colln (Scottish interest), P4
Excel Heritage Co Ltd, see IA91
exercise & exercise science, S584, 1982
Exeter Cathedral Archvs, A163; Lib, S665; see also S671

food quality, **IS**118
food safety, **IS**76; **S**1895
Food Safety Authority of Ireland, Info Svc, IS76
food science & technology, **IS**9, 52, 76, 118, 146, 152, 174; **S**12, 64, 65, 114, 117, 123, 141, 226, 430, 488, 638, 703, 844, 894, 1603, 1623, 1647, 1955, 2166
food studies, **S**515, 1848
Foot, Michael, papers (politics), **A**365
football, association, **S**1131; rugby, **S**2060
Football Assoc Lib, S1131
Foots Cray Place Estate Archv, **A**47
footwear, **S**1254
Forbes Colln of Callendar Muniments, **A**165
Forbes Mellon Lib, S346
Forbes, G.H., Colln (theology & liturgy), **S**1964
Forbes, J.D., Colln (sci), **S**1964
Forbes-Julian Letter & Autograph Colln, **S**2049
Ford et al, estate records, **A**44
Ford Motor Co, Dunton Technical Centre Lib, S878
Ford Motors Visual Archv, **S**266
Ford Railway Colln, **S**883
Ford, A.L., Lib (cricket), **S**1276
Ford, Thomas, Papers, **S**934
Fordham, Sir H.G., Colln (cartography), **S**1363, 1364
foreign affairs, **S**1009, 1369; British, **S**1647; Irish, **S**1647
Foreign & Commonwealth Office Colln (stamps), **L**1
Foreign & Commonwealth Office Lib, S1132; **Legal Lib, S**1133; *see also* **S**1442
foreign policy, **A**88, 365; US, **S**1432
Forest, Will, Colln (Scottish music recordings), **S**598
forestry, **IS**3, 192; **S**9, 71, 72, 74, 78, 114, 123, 336, 341, 403, 452, 476, 615, 682, 805, 810, 840, 940, 1319, 1370, 1721, 1788, 1882, 2052, 2160; tropical, **S**1786; *see also* arboriculture
Forestry Commission Lib, S682
Forfar Town Council, records, **A**384
Forfarshire Chamber of Commerce, records, **A**135
FORFÁS, IS77
Forgetfulness Colln (dementia), **P**94
Forman, Buxton, Colln (Keats), **S**1225
Forrester Cockburn Centre for Edu & Learning, Lib, S699
Forster Colln (18C English verse), **L**5
Forster Colln (lit), **S**1290
Forster Estate Papers, **A**297
Forster's Glass Co Ltd, records, **A**464
Forster, E.M., papers & MSS, **S**25, 369
Forster, W.E., papers, **A**62
Forston Clinic Staff Lib, see **S**544
Fort Augustus Benedictine Monastery Lib, **S**538
Fort Dunree Military Museum, Archvs, IA8
Fortescue of Castle Hill, estate archv, **A**161
Forth Valley NHS Health Board, Lib, S1977
fortification, **S**444, 680, 1130
Fortrose Council, minutes, **S**688
Forum for Interlending, O201
Foster Lib, S951
Foster, Sir Michael, Pamph Colln (physiology), **S**311
Foster-Probyn Lib, minutes (beer bottlers), **A**358
Fountains Abbey, family & estate records, **A**226
Four Parishes Rsrch Group, O202
Fowler Colln (antiquarian logic bks), **L**4
Fowler Lib (medieval & modern hist), **P**8
Fowler, Roy, Cinema Bk Colln, **S**215
Fowlers of Prestonpans, records (brewers), **A**179
Fox & Wallace Colln (Westoe family archvs), **P**170
Fox Papers, **A**419
Foxwell, Herbert Somerton, archv (econ), **S**335

Foyle Special Collns Lib, *see* **S**1227
Foyle, Gilbert, Dickens Colln, **S**239
Foz Photos Colln (news & features), **S**1170
FPA Lib & Info Centre, S1134
France, **IS**110; **S**716, 1231, 1690
Frances Perry Lib, S654
Francis Bacon Soc Colln, **S**1440
Francis Costello Lib, S1660
Francis Ledwidge Museum & War Memorial Centre, Archvs, IA85
Francis Skaryna Belarusian Lib & Museum, S1135
Francis, Tom, Colln of Mitcham Photos, **A**385
Franciscan 'A' MSS, IA49
Franciscan Lib Killiney (FLK), IS157
Franciscan Order, **A**92; **IS**157; **S**1676
Franciscan Order of Friars Minor, Archvs, A92
Frank, Sir Charles, papers, **A**77
Franklin, Marjorie, Colln (environment therapy), **A**104
Franz Bergel Lib, *see* **S**1192
Fraser Colln (tobacco), **S**972
Fraser Colln on Nuclear Disarmament, **S**217
Fraser of Westermains papers, **A**171
Fraser, Alexander Campbell, papers, **L**2
Fraser, Ronald, Oral Hist Colln (Spanish Civil War), **S**972
Fraser-Mackintosh Colln (Highland hist), **P**64
fraud, **S**1389
Frazer, James, Colln (anthro), **S**323
Frederick Oughton Colln (woodworking), **S**2038
Free Church of Scotland Coll Lib, S600
Free French Colln (La France Libre), **S**1231
Freedman, Barnett, archv (artist), **S**1519
Freedom of the City of Dublin, records, **IA**30
Freedom of the City of London, records, **A**270
Freedom Press Lib (anarchist movement), **S**1016
Freeman Hosp Lib, S1574
Freeman, E.A., papers (English historian), **S**1512
freemasonry, **IS**81; **S**602, 1240, 1818, 1924
French churches, **S**1169
French Enlightenment, **S**1751
French Hosp Friendly Soc, **S**1169
French Memoirs Colln, **S**934
French Protestant Church of London Lib, S1136
French Revolution Colln, **S**1512, 1647, 2086
French Salon Criticism Colln, **S**1747
French Spirituality Colln, **S**523
French, Cecil, Bequest (pottery & painting), **A**282
French, Field Marshal Sir John, papers, **A**289
French, John, papers (fashion photographer), **A**250
French, William Percy, Colln (composer & painter), **IA**84
Frenchay Lib & Info Svc, S252
Frere Colln of Hebrew MSS, **S**357
Frere, Sheppard, excavation archv, **S**1963
Freshwater Biological Assoc Lib, S32
Freud Museum, Lib & Archvs, S1137
Freud, Anna, Working Lib & Papers, **S**1137
Freud, Sigmund, Colln, **S**482; *Lib & Papers,* **S**1137
Frewen Archv, **A**230
Frewen Lib, S1829
Frewin, Richard, Bequest (rare bks), **L**4
Freyer, Michael, Dolmen Press Colln, **IL**2
Friarage Hosp Study Centre, Dist Lib, S1608
Friedlander Colln, **IS**27
friendly societies, **A**458
Friends of the Children of Gt Ormond Street Lib, S1138

Friends of The Natl Libs, O203
Friends' Historical Lib, IS78
Friends' Provident Life Insurance Archvs, A127
Friern Hosp Colln (psychiatry), **S**1360
Frimley Park Hosp NHS Trust, Health Scis Lib, S288
Frith Colln (Berkshire photos), **P**150
Frith, Francis, & Co Colln (Welsh photography), **L**3
Fritsch Colln of Algal Illusts, **S**32, 1786
Froebel Coll of Edu Lib, IS7
Frome Museum Lib, A168
Frost, Eunice, papers, **A**77
Frost, Maurice, Colln of Hymnody, **S**546, 1350
fruit, **S**2107, 2137
Fry Portrait Colln, **A**77
Fry, C.B., Colln (cricketer), **A**460
Fry, J.S., & Sons Ltd, records (chocolate manufacturers), **A**72; **S**164
Fry, Roger, papers, **S**369
fuel poverty, **S**1314
Fulbourn Hosp, Prof Medical Lib, S356
Fulham Bridge Co records, **A**282
Fulham Manorial records, **A**282
Fulham Papers (Bishops of London), **S**1234
Fulham Pottery, records, **A**282
Fuller Colln (hospitality & catering), **S**1700
Fuller Colln of Seals, **S**1440
Fuller Lib, **A**106
Fuller, Gen J.F.C., diaries, **S**2084
Fuller-Maitland Music Colln, **P**71
Fullhurst Community Coll Lib, S924
fundraising, **A**264; **S**1078
fungal distribution, **S**1862
Furness Coll LRC, S91
Furness Estate Colln, **A**28
Furness Railway records, **A**28
Furness Withy Archv, **S**1943
Furniss, Harry, Colln (illustrator), **P**49
furniture, **A**250; **S**419, 1105, 1141, 1261, 1282, 1290, 1455, 1515, 1653; *see also* design, furniture
Furse, Dame Katherine, correspondence, **A**77

GAA Colln, **IP**16
Gabby Kearney Lib, S1951
Gabell, Henry, papers (headmaster of Winchester Coll), **A**511
Gael Linn Colln (film), **IA**37; **IS**74
Gaelic Soc Lib, P64
Gaelic Soc of London Lib, **S**1433
Gainsborough's House Soc, Lib & Archv, S2001
Gainsborough, Thomas & family, papers, **S**2001
Gaitskell Papers, **S**1433
Galashiels Combined Technical School, records, **A**148
Gale, Keith, Lib (iron & steel industry), **A**129
Gallagher, Father Patrick, papers, **IA**67
galleries, **S**1108; *see also* museums
Galleries of Justice, Wolfson Resource Centre, S1634
Galsworthy, John, papers, **A**164
Galt, John, Colln, **A**21; **P**44
Galton, Sir Francis, Papers, **S**1433
Galway Chamber of Commerce, *see* **IS**164
Galway Corp MSS, **IS**166
Galway Diocesan Colln, **IS**165
Galway Euro Info Centre, IS164
Galway Harbour Commissioners, records, **IA**58
Galway Harbour Co, Archvs & Records, IA58
Galway Poor Law Guardians, records, **IA**59
Galway Public Libs, IP10; Local Hist Dept, **IA**59
Galway RC Diocesan Archvs, IA60
Galway-Mayo Inst of Tech Lib, IS165
gamekeeping, **S**273, 844
games, children's, **S**751; Irish, **A**16
Gandhi, Mahatma, Colln, **S**1184

Garda Síochána, Archvs & Museum, IA34; **Coll Lib, IS**200
Garden City Movement Colln, **S**937
gardens & gardening, **IS**6, 113, 136; **S**44, 687, 772, 1122, 1136, 1306, 1367, 2045; early, **S**2089; landscape, **S**226; professional, **S**2137; *see also* horticulture
Gardiner, Gen Sir Robert, papers, **S**1130
Gardner, James, Archv (design), **A**69
Gardner, Willoughby, Lib (early nat hist), **S**422
Garforth Urban Dist, records, **A**226
Garland Photographic Colln (Sussex rural life), **A**106
Garland, Nicholas, Colln (cartoons), **A**91
Garlick Colln, **S**1776
Garner Chemical Eng Lib, *see* **S**179
Garnet Colln (railway hist), **S**2065
Garrett Shakespeare Lib, **S**247
Garrett, Richard, & Sons records (engineers), **A**215
Garrick Club Lib, S1139
Garrick Colln (early English drama), **L**1
Garrick Hosp, Stranraer, records, **A**132
Garrick, David, Colln, **P**174
Garry Weston Lib, S1140
Garscube Estate Papers, **A**176
Gartnavel Genl Hosp, Staff Lib, S700
Gas Council, archvs, **A**500
Gascoigne Colln (military & naval hist), **P**72
Gaskell Colln, P112
Gaskell, Elizabeth, Colln, **S**405; *MSS,* **S**1512
Gaster Colln (Romanian lit), **S**1436
Gaster, Dr Moses, Colln (Judaica), **S**1512; *Papers,* **S**1433
gastroenterology, **S**648
Gateshead Arts & Libs, P55; *see also* **A**391
Gateshead Coll Centre4... Knowledge, S690
Gateway Theatre Archv, **A**182
Gatti Family Colln (ice & ice cream merchants), **S**1252
Gatty, Mrs, papers, **A**452
Gaudier-Brzeska, Henri, papers (sculptor), **S**368, 482
Gay Sweatshop Theatre Co Archv, **S**651
GEC Archvs, *see* **A**102
GEC Rugby Colln (photos of electrical manufacture), **A**294
Gedde, Sir Patrick, papers, **S**741
Geekie Family of Keillor, papers, **A**135
Geekie, Alexander, correspondence (17C-18C surgeon), **A**135
Geffrye Museum, Ref Lib & Archvs, S1141
Geikie, James, Colln (geol), **S**593
Gell of Hopton, family archv, **A**375
gender & gender studies, **S**42, 180, 230, 322, 1095, 1272, 1758
gender equality, **S**1510
Genealogical Office of Ireland, *see* **IL**1
Genealogical Soc of Ireland, IO16
genealogy, **A**8, 43, 54, 59, 97, 222, 269, 362, 366, 389, 407, 420, 443, 457, 476, 489, 501, 506; **L**1, 3; **S**407, 530, 775, 807, 951, 1398, 2009, 2044, 2190; Irish, **IA**1, 2, 4, 14, 25, 31, 50, 51, 53, 61, 70, 75, 79, 87, 90, 92; **IL**1; **IS**193, 208; **S**121, 1478; Manx, **A**530; Scottish, **A**1, 3, 21, 134, 138, 156, 158, 173, 190; **S**639; Welsh, **A**480; **S**419, 492; *see also* family history
geneaogy, Belarussian, **S**1135
Genl Accident Archvs, **A**396
Genl Bks Council, *see* **O**321
Genl Conference of the New Church Lib, S1142
Genl HQ Unit, records (Ireland), **IA**45
Genl Medical Council, minutes, **A**346
Genl Nursing Council, records, **A**153
Genl Photographic Agency Colln, **S**1170
general practice, **S**15, 276, 435, 1058, 1348, 1916, 2055
Genl Register Office, A310; **Northern Ireland, A**39; Scotland, **A**146

Genl Reversionary & Investment Co, records, A73
Genl Strike 1926 Colln, S1425
Genl Synod of the C of E, *see* S1102
Genl, Municipal & Boilermakers & Allied Trades Union, archv, S1887
Genetical Soc of Gt Britain Archvs, S1624
genetics, IS210; S309, 313, 536, 543, 608, 1300, 1457, 1719, 1741, 1862, 1872, 2045; classical, S1624; human, S608, 1719; medical, S1326; molecular, S608, 1624
Genizah Fragments, L5; S401, 1512
geochemistry, S307; applied, S1439
geodesy, S684
Geoffrey Evans Lib, S1348
geography, A17, 151, 152, 197, 218, 236, 273, 409, 414, 443, 455, 522; IA70; IS4, 7, 9, 13, 15, 28, 33, 35, 44, 45, 46, 47, 56, 82, 90, 105, 112, 123, 143, 166, 172, 173, 181, 183, 188, 198; S4, 10, 26, 32, 41, 67, 98, 108, 114, 115, 121, 131, 152, 156, 180, 194, 198, 220, 234, 258, 268, 269, 270, 295, 296, 297, 307, 310, 323, 330, 332, 336, 340, 382, 383, 404, 436, 442, 443, 450, 456, 469, 478, 479, 530, 540, 541, 565, 578, 593, 650, 652, 669, 687, 688, 698, 713, 727, 741, 749, 788, 813, 819, 838, 851, 859, 866, 869, 877, 879, 880, 910, 937, 950, 968, 969, 986, 1015, 1016, 1018, 1053, 1102, 1106, 1169, 1171, 1227, 1246, 1255, 1260, 1262, 1282, 1287, 1288, 1298, 1310, 1322, 1328, 1333, 1362, 1363, 1364, 1365, 1421, 1439, 1440, 1491, 1505, 1511, 1512, 1522, 1544, 1552, 1565, 1572, 1599, 1604, 1635, 1637, 1654, 1659, 1663, 1672, 1677, 1678, 1702, 1716, 1733, 1750, 1760, 1767, 1786, 1799, 1804, 1806, 1811, 1833, 1839, 1886, 1912, 1917, 1933, 1935, 1940, 1942, 1976, 1978, 1979, 1982, 2018, 2029, 2033, 2036, 2042, 2046, 2049, 2056, 2059, 2064, 2067, 2091, 2093, 2096, 2122, 2125, 2130, 2145, 2147, 2150, 2168, 2176, 2179, 2187; African, S30; ancient, S325; Antarctic, S30; Asian, IS191; S1344, 1377; Austrian, S1006; British, S310; economic, S2113; European, S310; Finnish, S1120; French, IS110; S310, 1690; Greek, S1159; historical, S310; Indian, S1184; Irish, A23; IA20; IS95, 100, 149, 185, 193; Italian, S1216; Japanese, S1220; Latin American, IS191; S1210; Middle Eastern, S1321; military, S1130; North American, S310; of Palestine, S1321; oriental, S328; Pacific, S310; physical, S1363, 2113; Roman, S1159; Russian, S310; Scottish, S628, 876; South American, S310; South Asian, S300, 310; Spanish, S1210; Turkish, S1429; US, S97; Welsh, S74, 419
geographical information systems, S1439
Geological Soc of London Lib, S1143
Geological Survey of Ireland Lib, IS79; *see also* S128
Geological Survey of Northern Ireland, Lib & Info Svc, S128
Geologist's Assoc Lib, S1433
geology, A187, 409, 420, 480; IS4, 63, 79, 121; S9, 74, 83, 98, 128, 146, 246, 283, 294, 307, 310, 342, 422, 530, 545, 592, 612, 807, 844, 849, 858, 909, 927, 1023, 1143, 1205, 1263, 1308, 1439, 1546, 1576, 1715, 1738, 1933, 1945, 2036, 2049, 2068, 2091, 2138, 2176, 2186, 2187, 2190; applied, S1180; Arctic, S342; Central Asian, S342; Chinese, S342; early, S260; economic, S1200; engineering, S1439; industrial, S1857; marine, S1945; Russian, S342; *see also earth science; palaeontology*
geomorphology, S310, 2072
geophysics, S294, 535, 684, 1345; marine, S1945
George Cross, A308
George Green Lib, *see* S1647
George Herdman Lib, P213
George III Maritime & Topographical Collns (cartography), L1
George Wiernik Lib, S1729
George, Stefan, Colln, S1445
Georgina Scott Sutherland Lib, S12
Gerhard, Roberto, papers & MSS, L5
geriatrics, S35, 559
Gerish, William Blyth, Colln (Hertfordshire), A204
German Historical Inst Lib, S1144
German-British Chamber of Industry & Commerce, Marketing Svcs, S1145
Germany & German studies, S709, 1147, 1195, 1445, 1647
gerontology, S1062, 1708
Getty Images, *see* S1170
Gibb Colln (civil eng), S1205
Gibbon, Lewis Grassic, Colln (lit), S593
Gibbs & Canning Co, minutes, A485
Gibbs, James, Bequest (rare bks), L4
Gibley Pamphs (agric, rural development), S1991
Gibson Colln (Thomas Moore), S139
Gibson family correspondence, S152
Gibson of Hexham & Blankenburg Photo Colln, A390
Gibson Papers, A442
Gibson, J.A., Colln, S863
Gibson-Craig of Riccarton, family & estate papers, A148
Gielgud, Sir John, Colln, S1390
Giffard family papers, A467
Gifford, Grace, papers, IS34
Gilbert & Sullivan Soc Lib, P99
Gilbert White Museum, S30
Gilbert, Sir John T., Lib (Dublin), IA31; IP7
Gild of the Holy Cross, records, A476
Gill, Eric, Colln, A106; *drawings,* S1408
Gill, T.P., papers, IL1
Gillespie & Scott Colln (arch), S1964
Gillies Archvs, A454
Gillies, W.G., RSA Bequest (artist), S623
Gillingham Lib, *see* S562
Gillinson Pamph Colln (Israel & Zionism), S1238
Gillis Centre Lib, S601
Gillow Archvs (furniture makers), A268
Ginnell, Laurence, Papers (North Westmeath MP), IA78
Girdlestone Orthopaedic Soc, meeting papers, S1698
Girl Guide Movement, A279
Girl Guides Assoc, records, A279
Girls' Day School Trust Archv, A456
Girton Coll Lib, S357
Gissing, George, Colln (Wakefield), P191
Give Peace A Chance Trust, S234
glaciology, S294, 307, 339
Gladstone, Robert, Colln (law), S963
Gladstone, W.E., Lib, S523
Gladstone, William, Colln, L3; *Papers,* L1
Gladstoniana Colln, S523
Glamorgan Record Office, A97
Glamorgan Univ, *see Univ of Glamorgan*
Glan Clwyd Hosp Lib, S1859
Glasgow & Galloway, Diocese of, records, A174
Glasgow & West of Scotland Coll of Domestic Sci, archv, S701
Glasgow & West of Scotland Family Hist Soc, Rsrch Centre, A173
Glasgow Caledonian Univ, Lib & Info Centre, S701; *see also* A170; S712
Glasgow City Archvs, A174
Glasgow City Libs, Info & Learning, P56
Glasgow Coll of Bldg & Printing, Laird Lib, S702
Glasgow Coll of Food Tech, Lib, S703
Glasgow Coll of Nautical Studies Lib, S704
Glasgow Coll of Tech, archv, S701
Glasgow Coll, archv, S701
Glasgow Corp, records, A174; *Technical Drawings Colln,* S1539
Glasgow Jewish Inst Players Archv, A182
Glasgow Medical Soc, records, S724
Glasgow Museums, Lib & Info Centre, S705
Glasgow Odontological Soc, records, S724
Glasgow Polytechnic, archv, S701
Glasgow Presbytery, records, A174
Glasgow RC Archdiocesan Archv, A175
Glasgow Royal Infirmary, Lib & Learning Centre, S706; *see also* A177
Glasgow School of Art Lib, S707
Glasgow School of Cookery, archv, S701
Glasgow Southern Medical Soc, records, S724
Glasgow Unity Theatre Archv, A182
Glasgow Univ Archv Svcs, A176; *see also* A177, 179; *see also Univ of Glasgow*
Glasgow Veterinary Coll, records, A176
Glasgow Women's Lib, S708
Glasgow, Earl of, papers, A20
glass, S1105, 1146, 1904, 1985, 2004
Glass & Glazing Federation, Lib, S1146
Glass, Thomas, Bequest (sci & medicine), S665
glassware, S1290
Glastonbury Abbey, records, S2086
Glaxo Wellcome Heritage Archvs, A189
GlaxoSmithKline, GSK Lib, S221
glazing, S1146
Glen Colln (Scottish music), L2
Glenfield Hosp NHS Trust, Medical Lib, S925
Glenochil Distillery records, A10
Glenrothes Coll Learning Resource Svc, Learner Development Centre, S744
Glenrothes Development Corp, records, A373
Glenstal Abbey Lib, IS188
Glenties Poor Law Union, minutes, IA67
Glenties Rural Dist Council, records, IA67
Glin Papers, IS182
Glin Poor Law Union, minutes, IA92
global issues, S234
globalisation, S230, 364
Gloucester Cathedral Lib, S746
Gloucester City Archvs, A185
Gloucester Railway Carriage & Wagon Co, records, A185
Gloucester, Diocese of, Archvs, A185
Gloucestershire Beekeepers Assoc Lib, S263
Gloucestershire Coll of Arts & Tech, Brunswick Campus Learning Centre, S747
Gloucestershire County Lib Svc, P57; **Gloucestershire Colln,** A184
Gloucestershire Guardians of the Poor, records, A185
Gloucestershire Highway Boards, records, A185
Gloucestershire Hosps NHS Trust Staff Lib, S453
Gloucestershire Local Hist Cttee, O204
Gloucestershire Naturalists Soc Lib, S263
Gloucestershire Quarter Sessions Archvs, A185
Gloucestershire Record Office, A185
Gloucestershire Regimental Archvs, A186
Gloucestershire Royal Hosp Lib, S748
Gloucestershire Rural Community Council Ltd, *see* O204
Gloucestershire School Boards, records, A185
Gloucestershire Univ, *see Univ of Gloucestershire*
Glynde Archv, A230
Glyndebourne Archv, A231
Glynne, Sir Stephen, Lib, S523
Glynne-Gladstone MSS, S523
Godden Colln (auction catalogues), S1944
Godmanchester Borough records, A211
Godwin, H., Colln (geol), S307
Godwyn Colln (18C hist), L4
Goehr, Alexander, papers & MSS, L5
Goethe-Institut Inter Nationes Lib, S1147
Goethe-Institut Lib, Dublin, IS80; **Glasgow,** S709
Goldberg Lib, S836
Golden Age Lit Colln, S1751
Golders Green Hippodrome Colln (theatre programmes), A255
Goldney Family Papers, A77
Goldsmith, Oliver, Colln (Longford author), IA73; IP18
goldsmithing, S1149
Goldsmiths' Coll Lib, S1148
Goldsmiths' Co Lib, S1149
Goldsmiths' Lib of Economic Hist, S1441
golf studies, S772
Gonning family & estate papers, A215
Gonville & Caius Coll Lib, S358
Good Hope Hosp NHS Trust, Edu Centre Lib, S2006
Good, Ronald, Botanical Archv, S543, 1786
Goodale Colln (cinema), S776
Goodricke, John, papers (astronomy), A525
Goodwin Family of Kirkintilloch papers, A171
Goodwood Estate records, A106
Goodyear Tyres, records, A515
Goossens Colln (oboe music), S1154
Gorddinog Estate Archv, A244
Gordon of Cairness family & estate papers, A3
Gordon, Major Gen Charles, correspondence, S1185; *papers,* S445
Gorer, Geoffrey, papers, S239
Gorrie Colln (socialism), S934
Gosport Deanery, parish records, A423
Gosport Museum, Local Resources Room, A187
Gosse Piracy Colln, S1303
Gosse, Sir Edmund, papers & MSS, S918
Gotch Family Colln, P131
Gott Bequest (16C-18C gardening), P72
Goudie, Gilbert, Colln (Shetlandiana), P162
Gough Colln (maps, prints, drawings), L4
Goulburn of Betchworth & Jamaica, family papers, A513
Goulding, R.W., Colln, P75
Gourock Ropeworks Co, records, A176
governance, S230
government, S132, 482, 1109, 1166, 1250, 1883, 1887; local, S241, 490, 723, 1151, 1250, 1316; regional, S1316; US, S1432
government & industry, S1098
Goya Colln (prints & drawings), S1032
GPA Hist of Aviation, IS182
GPVTS Colln, S1994
graduate recruitment, S1709
Gradwell Colln (theology), S968
Grafton, Dukes of, estate & family papers, A83
Graham, James Methuen, Papers (surgery), S617
Graham, Rigby, archv (artist), S1519
Grail Quest, S743
Grampian Health Board, *see* A4
Grampian Info, O205; **Business Group,** O206; **Health & Community Group,** O207; **Local Studies & Archvs Group,** O208; **Oil Group,** O209; **Sci Rsrch Group,** O210
Grampian Regional Archvs, A2
Grampian Television Lib, *see* S732
Granada Visual, A277
Granard Poor Law Union, minutes, IA73
Grand Lodge of Freemasons of Ireland Lib & Museum, IS81
Grand Lodge of Scotland Lib, S602
Grand Orange Lodge of Scotland, Cameron Lib, S710
Grand Theatre, Wolverhampton, records, A515

Grant, Henry, Colln (London photos), S1288
Grantham & Dist Hosp, Staff Lib, S757
Granville papers, S2086
Granville-Sharp slavery papers, A185
graphics, S1050, 1060, 2004; see also art & arts; design, graphic
Graves Early Sci Lib, S1433
Graves Lib (bricks, bldg), S1985
Graves, Robert, papers, A85
Gray Colln (theology, classics), L2
Gray family papers, A525
Gray's Inn Lib, S1150
Gray, Alan, music MSS, L5
Gray, Eileen, papers (designer), A250
Gray, Henry, Colln (ornithology), S1358
Gray, T., MSS, S382
Gt Exhib of 1851 Colln, S1290
Gt Famine Colln, IA25
Gt Yarmouth Borough Archvs, A400
Greater Glasgow NHS Board Archv, A177
Greater Glasgow Primary Care NHS Trust, Maria Henderson Lib, S711
Greater London Authority Rsrch Lib, S1151
Gter London Council, records, A304
Greater Manchester County Record Office, A364
Greater Manchester Police Museum, Lib & Archvs, S1511
Greaves, C. Desmond, Lib, S1887
Green Candle Dance Co Archv, A192
Green Coll Lib, S1675
Green Studio Colln (arch), IA36
Green Textiles Archv, S1075
Green, Archbishop, MSS, S523
Green, Francis, Colln (Welsh genealogy), P143
Green, Gordon, Colln (keyboard music), S1528
Green, J.R., papers (19C historian), S1681
Green, W.A., Colln, S815
Greenaway, Kate, Colln, A262; P82
Greene Lib (works by old Westminsters), S1461
Greene MSS (music), S25
Greenfield Medical Lib, see S1647
Greenham Common Colln, A75
Greening, E.O., papers (co-op movement), A370
greenkeeping, S515, 772
Greenough, G.B., Colln (mapping), S1364; papers (geol), S1143
Greenup, Mary, papers, A215
Greenwell Colln (mining, coal industry), L3
Greenwich Community Coll, Lib & LRC, S1152
Greenwich Labour Party, records, A278
Greenwich Libs, P86
Greenwich Local Hist Lib, A278
Greenwich Univ, see Univ of Greenwich
Greenwood, Walter, Colln, S1886
Greffe, Guernsey, A531; see also A532
Greffe, Sark, A535
Gregg's Quarry, records, A367
Gregory Colln (early sci & medicine), A3; S5
Gregory, Lady, Colln, IS166
Gregory, Sir Richard, papers, S239
Gregory-Hood of Stivichall, family & estate papers, A476
Gregynog Colln (printing), L3
Gregynog Press Colln, L3; P149; S422
Grehan Estate Colln, IA21
Greig, David, FRCSEd, papers (surgery in Crimean War), A135
Grenfell & Hunt Papyrological Lib, S1747
Grenfell Colln (physical edu), S1444
Grenville Lib (politics & lit), L1
Grenville, Lord, papers, S289
Gresham Coll Colln, P99
Gresham, Sir Thomas, estate records, A307
Grey, C.G., papers (early aviation), S1342
Greyfriars Lib, S1676
Grierson, John, Archv (documentary film maker), S1978

Grieve Colln (stage designs), S1440
Grieve, C.M., Colln (Hugh MacDiarmid), S593
Griffin, Charles, & Co Archv (publisher), S1408
Griffith Coll Dublin, Lib, IS82
Griffith Inst Lib & Archvs, see S1747
Griffiths, Trevor, Colln (cinema), S1013
Grigson, Jane, Colln, P99
Grimes London Archv (archaeo), A301
Grimsby Coll Lib, S766
Grindea, Miron, Lib (20C European lit), S1227
Groam House Museum, Lib & Archvs, S688
Grolier Colln, S853
Grosvenor Estate Archvs, A268
Grote Colln (classics), S1440
Grotius Lib, S1024
Group Analytic Soc, archv, S1457
Grove-Hills Colln (astronomical name bks), S1345
Groves, Sir Charles, Colln (contemporary scores), S1528
Guardian / Observer Rsrch Dept Lib, S1153
Guardian Archvs (journalism), S1512
Guardian Media Group plc, see S1153, 1516
Guernsey / Island Archvs Svc, A532
Guernsey Coll of Further Edu Lib, S2184
Guernsey Inst of Health Studies Lib, S2185
Guernsey Local Studies Colln, P216, 217
Guernsey Museum & Art Gallery, Lib & Archvs, S2186
Guernsey Sites & Monuments Record, S2186
Guernsey, Royal Court of, records, A531, 532
Guernsey, States of, records, A532
Guide Assoc Archv, A279
Guild of One-Name Studies, O211
Guild of St George Archv, A452
Guildford Coll of Further & Higher Edu, LRC, S770
Guildford Inst of The Univ of Surrey Lib, S771
Guildford, Diocese of, records, A513
Guildhall Lib, Manuscripts Section, A280
Guildhall Museum Roman & Mediaeval records, A301
Guildhall School of Music & Drama Lib, S1154; see also A270
guilds, S1441
Guille-Alles Lib, P217
Guinness Colln, IS123
Guinness Colln (film), IA37
Guinness Family Hist Colln, IA35
Guinness Food Sci Collns, IS177
Guinness Ireland, Archvs, IA35; **Rsrch Lib,** IS83
Guinness, Arthur, Son & Co Ltd, records, IA35
Gulf studies, S672
Gulf Wars, S672
Gumbleton, William Edward, Bequest (botany), IS113
Gundolf, Friedrich, Archv, S1445
Gunther Colln (Italian geol & antiquities), S1363
Gurney Lib, see A522
Gurney, Ivor, Colln, A184
Guthrie, Sir Douglas, Papers (surgery), S617
Guttman, Henry, Colln (photos), S1170
Guy's & St Thomas' Hosp NHS Trust, see S1279, 1415
Guy's Hosp, Info Svcs Centre, see S1227
Gwent County Hist Assoc, see O212
Gwent Healthcare NHS Trust Lib Svcs, S1595; see also S285
Gwent Healthcare Postgrad Lib, S285
Gwent Local Hist Council, O212
Gwent Quarter Sessions records, A117
Gwent Record Office, A117
Gwynedd Archvs & Museums Svc, A84; see also A123; S508
Gwynedd Lib & Info Svc, P58

Gynaecological Visiting Soc Archvs, S1352
gynaecology, IS24, 132; S1352, 1785
Gyosei Internatl Coll in the UK, see S1851
Gypsy Lore Soc Archv, S972
Gypsy Smith Colln, S1458

Haas, Ernst, Colln (images), S1170
Hack Colln, P17
Hackney Archvs Dept, A281
Hackney Community Coll, Lib & Learning Centre, S1155
Hackney Libs Svc, P87
Haddon Lib, S323
Haddon, Alfred, Colln (anthro), S323
Hadley Colln (French Revolution & Napoleonic era), S340
Hadley Family Papers, A297
Hadlow Coll Lib, S2045
haematology, S1830
Haggerston & Tillmouth, estate records, A44
Hagley Hall Estate records, A51
Haig of Dollarfield Papers, A10
Haig, Earl, papers, L2
Haig, John, & Co Ltd, records (whisky distillers), A376
Hailstone Colln, S2174
Haines Colln (Monmouthshire), P122
hairdressing, S22, 202, 504, 770, 915, 1254, 1816, 2079, 2093
Hakluyt Soc, O213
Haldane Colln, S1180
Haldane Papers, S1433
Haldane, J.B.S., papers, L2
Haldane, J.S., papers, L2
Haldane, Lord, papers, L2
Hale End & Brantham records, A215
Hale MSS, S1245
Hale, Matthew Blagden, Papers, A77
Halesowen Coll Lib & Learning Centre, S777
Half Moon Theatre Co Archv, S651
Halford-Mackinder Archv, S1750
halibut, S638
Haliday Colln (pamphs & tracts), IS137
Halifax Antiquarian Soc, records, A194
Halifax Colln (keyboard music), S1528
Halifax Genl Hosp Lib, see S778
Halifax Loyal Georgian Soc, records, A194
Halifax Parish Lib Colln, S2168
Halifax, Earls of, Archvs, A522
Hall Carpenter Archvs, S1241
Hall Place Estate Archv, A47
Hall, Basil, Colln, S1005
Hall, Edward, Colln, A228
Hall, Keith Clifford, Lib (optics), S1037
Hall, Rex, Colln (maritime), S2056
Hall, Richard, Colln (music), S1528
Hallam RC Diocesan Archvs, A450; see also A452
Halley Stewart Lib, S1409
Halliwell-Phillipps Colln (broadsides), S1507
Halliwell-Phillips Colln (drama), P17; S593
hallmarking, S1149
Hallward Lib, see S1647
Halpern, Joel Martin, Balkan Archv, S217
Halpin Colln (maritime), IS160
Halton Borough Council Lib Svc, P59
Halton Coll, Widnes, Lib, S2114
Halton Local Studies & Family Hist Collns, A439
Hambleden, Viscounts, family & estate papers, A484
Hambly & Rowe Colln, A430
Hamilton Colln (military hist, lit), S1227
Hamilton Colln (phil), S738
Hamilton Fairley Colln (tropical medicine), S1849
Hamilton Jenkin, A.K., Colln, A430
Hamilton Kerr Inst Lib, S359
Hamilton of Dalziel Papers, P126
Hamilton, Bishop, Colln, S1894
Hamilton, Diane, Colln (Irish music recordings), IA42
Hamilton, Duke of, Colln, P126
Hamilton, Emma, correspondence, A383

Hamilton, Eric, papers (teacher), A216
Hamish Hamilton Ltd Editorial & Historical Archv, A77
Hammersmith & Fulham Libs, P88; **Archvs & Local Hist Centre,** A282
Hammersmith & West London Coll, Hammersmith Learning Centre, S1156
Hammersmith Bridge Co, records, A282
Hammond, Sir John, Colln (nutrition), S306
Hampshire & Isle of Wight Strategic Health Authority Lib, S1941
Hampshire County Council Museums Svc, Lib, A508; see also A9, 12, 14, 29, 30, 107, 143, 166, 187, 198
Hampshire Field Club Lib (hist & archaeo), S1946
Hampshire Gardens Trust Lib, S1946
Hampshire Lib & Info Svc, P60
Hampshire Naval Colln, P60
Hampshire Ornithological Soc Lib, S1946
Hampshire Record Office, A509; see also A508, 510
Hampstead Manor records, A262
Hampstead Metropolitan Borough records, A262
Hanbury of Pontypool, family & estate records, A117
Hanbury, Daniel, letter bks (pharmacist), A189
Hanbury-Bateman families, papers, A215
handicap, mental, S356; multiple, S860; see also disability
Handley-Read Colln (Victorian decorative arts), S1019
Handover Bequest (hist of printing), S1763
Hanley Colln (photography), IS208
Hanley Lib, S1952
Hannah Colln (19C tracts), S466
Hannah Rsrch Inst Lib, S64
Hannam Clark Palestine Colln, P57
Hannington, Wal, Papers (labour & unemployment), S1274
Hansen Colln (20C Scandinavian music), S1528
Hansen Colln (images of ships), S2051
Hansford-Worth Photos of Dartmoor, S2049
Harcourt, Field Marshal William, papers, S289
Harden School Lib, IS84
Hardie, James Keir, Colln, P44
Harding Colln (songbks, poetry, drama), L4
Harding Law Lib, see S179
Harding, T., & Co, records (fishing industry), A209
Hardman, John, & Co, archvs (stained glass manufacture), A51
Hardy, Gathorne, papers, A215
Hardy, Sir Alister, Archv of Religious Experience, S879; papers, S879
Hardy, Thomas, Colln, P39; S2130; Memorial Colln, S545; MSS, S25
Hare, Julius, Colln (German theology, lit, phil), S393
Harefield Hosp Lib, S782
Harewood family & estate records, A226
Harford Colln, S880
Hargrave MSS (legal MSS), L1
Hargrave, Lawrence, papers (early aviation), S1342
Haringey Libs, Archvs & Museum Svc, P89
Haringey Museum & Archv Svc, A283
Harington Colln, S665
Harker, A., Colln (geol), S307
Harland & Wolff Ltd, records (shipbuilders), S815
Harland, Ben, Slide Colln, P17
Harleian Soc, O214
Harley MSS, L1
Harlow Bequest Colln, P81
Harlow Carr Garden Lib, see S1367, 2137
Harlow Coll Lib, S783

Harlow Local Hist Lib, A195
Harlow Poor Law Guardians records, A195
Harmer Lib (marine biology), S1805
Harold Bridges Lib, S886
Harold Cohen Lib, *see* S972
Harold Wood Hosp, Multi-disciplinary Lib & Info Svc, S1868
Harper Adams Univ Coll Lib, S1601
Harpur Crewe of Calke Abbey, family archv, A375
Harrington, T.C., papers, IL1
Harris Inst Archvs, S1840
Harris Manchester Coll Lib, S1677
Harris Opera Colln, S1154
Harris papers, A509
Harris, Howell, papers (18C evangelical), A368
Harrison Colln (Commonwealth die proofs), L1
Harrod Colln (19C illustrated bks), S1290
Harrow Coll of Higher Edu Archv, S1452
Harrow Libs, P90
Harrow Local Hist Colln, A196
Harrow School, Vaughan Lib, S788
Harrowby Manuscripts at Sandon Hall, A466
Harsnett Colln (16C-17C), P51
Harsnett Lib, S482
Hart Colln (early printing & medieval MSS), S189
Hart, Judith, papers (politics), A365
Hart-Synnot Family Papers, IA49
Hartlepool Borough Libs, P61; *see also* A379
Hartlepool Genl Hosp Medical Lib, *see* S790
Hartley Colln (hist & lit), S1946
Hartley Instn, archvs, S1946
Hartley Lib, S1946
Hartley, E.R., papers, A62
Hartley, L.P., MSS, S1512
Hartley-Victoria Coll, *see* S1526
Hartlib, Samuel, papers, S1912
Hartnett, Michael, papers, IL1
Harvard Core Business Colln, S1861
Harveian Soc of London, Archvs, A284
Harvey Besterman Edu Centre Lib, S2188
Harvey MSS (music), S25
Harvey, Edward H., papers, IA67
Harvey, Eliab, correspondence, S1352
Harvey, Gabriel, Colln, A442
Harvey, William, Colln, A284; S50
Harvie-Brown papers, S612
Harwood MSS (church composer), S546
Harwood, Carole, Greenham Common Archv, A75
Hasidism, S1238
Haskalah Colln (Judaica), S1512
Haskell Colln, S1747
Hasleden, W.K., Colln (cartoons), A91
Haslett, Dame Caroline, Papers, A294
Hasluck Colln (Albanian), S1751
Hassall Archv, S355
Hassall, John, Colln, S482
Hastings & Rother NHS Trust, Rosewell Lib, S1968
Hastings Corp & Borough Council Archvs, A197
Hastings Coll of Arts & Tech Lib, S1969
Hastings Museum & Art Gallery, Archvs & Lib, A197
Hastings Volunteer Fire Brigade, records, A197
Hastings, Sir Charles, Colln, S1027
Hatherton family papers, A467
Hatrics: The Southern Info Network, O215
Hattersley & Sons, records (loom manufacturers), A62
Hatton Colln (topography & hist), S934
Havant Deanery, parish records, A423
Havant Museum, Local Studies Room, A198
Haverfield Archv, S1747
Havering Coll of Further & Higher Edu Lib, S817
Havering Lib Svcs, P91

Havering Local Hist Colln, A437
Havinden, Ashley, Archv, S633
Hawick Farmers Club records, A448
Hawke, Admiral Lord, papers, IS6
Hawker Aircraft & Hawker Siddeley Aviation Ltd, records, A505
Hawker, Rev R.S., Colln, S2056
Hawkes Colln, L3
Hawkins Papers, A419
Hawkins' Hosp Chatham, records, A435
Hawkins, Gen Sir John, papers, S445
Hawtin Bequest (socialism, economic hist), IS27
Hay Fleming, David, Colln, P53; *Ref Lib & Papers (Scottish hist),* S1964
Hay of Leyes Papers, S1964
Hayes, Michael, Papers, IA49
Hayes, Revd W., papers, A188
HBOS plc Group Archvs, A147
Headford Estate Papers, IL1
Headlam-Morley Colln (WW1), S484
Heal & Son, records (bedding manufacturers & retailers), A250
Heal Colln (St Pancras), A262
healing, S1243; alternative, S743; complementary, S743
health, A409; IS21, 38, 99, 117, 144, 171, 197, 203, 207, 211; S15, 57, 60, 69, 79, 81, 105, 140, 187, 193, 208, 228, 230, 243, 252, 255, 263, 282, 420, 430, 438, 463, 469, 475, 499, 514, 521, 525, 550, 565, 568, 607, 610, 628, 629, 673, 676, 722, 753, 757, 778, 802, 818, 835, 837, 847, 850, 862, 867, 884, 898, 899, 905, 918, 922, 923, 928, 933, 939, 978, 979, 991, 994, 1004, 1082, 1111, 1158, 1227, 1243, 1256, 1282, 1309, 1351, 1401, 1486, 1504, 1531, 1543, 1583, 1590, 1595, 1600, 1607, 1608, 1612, 1613, 1617, 1633, 1658, 1662, 1708, 1722, 1729, 1796, 1849, 1865, 1869, 1871, 1876, 1882, 1911, 1916, 1952, 1974, 1981, 1982, 1987, 1988, 2006, 2027, 2028, 2034, 2048, 2055, 2066, 2069, 2080, 2090, 2098, 2103, 2108, 2133, 2143, 2156, 2168; animal, S1110, 1384, 1570, 1592; child, S126, 542, 1077, 1138, 1296, 1354, 1433; community, S126, 408, 818, 948; environmental, S728, 1065; maternal, S126, 1138; mental, S58, 87, 109, 480, 610, 664, 750, 818, 875, 948, 1283, 1356, 1560, 1585, 1615, 1616, 1825, 1826, 1855, 1921; primary, S1452; public, IS16, 57; S276, 417, 549, 662, 717, 843, 975, 1051, 1229, 1265, 1452, 1613, 1629, 1731, 1755, 1916, 2104; reproductive, IS94; sexual, IS94; S126, 1134, 1157; urban, S162, 417; women's, S162, 417, 1045; young people's, S417; *see also health care; health promotion; health science; health studies; medicine*
health & race, S1229
health & safety, IS55, 85, 123; S175, 200, 427, 653, 745, 796, 844, 857, 892, 1098, 1121, 1214, 1258, 1425, 1512, 1598, 2010, 2068, 2140, 2160; at sea, S638
Health & Safety Authority Lib, IS85
Health & Safety Exec Info Svcs, S200; Nuclear Safety Div, Info Centre, S201
Health Archvs Group, O216
health care, IS14, 26, 42, 134, 168, 186, 189; S38, 93, 169, 204, 236, 435, 455, 480, 504, 527, 542, 662, 670, 675, 692, 712, 734, 765, 785, 795, 796, 821, 826, 832, 834, 836, 852, 869, 954, 964, 969, 1017, 1096, 1332, 1410, 1439, 1490, 1534, 1559, 1758, 1784, 1813, 1816, 1855, 1875, 1897, 1922, 1927, 1972, 2012, 2092, 2116, 2158, 2173, 2188; evidence-based, S1785; independent, S1183
health care delivery, S939, 1993
health care policy, IS57; S1051
health care purchasing, S549
Health Edu Authority, Health Promotion Info Centre, S1157
Health Edu Board for Scotland, S603
Health First Learning Centre, S1158
Health Libs & Info Confederation, O217

Health Libs Network, O218
health policy, S109, 629, 785, 939, 1111, 1229, 1355, 1613, 1629, 1731, 1916
health promotion, S87, 126, 417, 514, 603, 662, 742, 837, 928, 938, 975, 1051, 1157, 1158, 1613, 1897, 2069, 2104
Health Promotion Lib, Scotland, S603
Health Promotion Wales, Lib, S417
Health Protection Agency, *see* S1888
health science, S24, 182, 482, 495, 735, 748, 1402, 1438, 1494, 1821, 1859, 1948, 2004, 2124, 2154
health service, IS144; S15, 455, 603, 939, 1229; mental, S881
health service policy, S662
Health Svcs Mgmt Centre & NHS Exec (West Midlands), Lib & Info Svc, S169
health studies, S241, 478, 810, 915, 1783, 2185
health visiting, S1096
Health Visitors' Assoc, archv, S1457
Healy, T.M., Papers, IA49
hearing loss, S1373
Hearne, Thomas, Colln, S1767
heat engines, S321
heat transfer, S295
Heatherbank Museum of Social Work, Lib & Archvs, S712
Heatherbank Press Colln, S712
Heatherwood & Wexham Parks Hosps NHS Trust, John Jamison Lib, S1927
Heatherwood Hosp Lib, *see* S1927
heating, S1070
Heaviside, Oliver, papers, A294; S1206
Hebblethwaites, records (land agents), A209
Heberden Coin Room Lib, *see* S1747
Heberden Colln (ancient music), S1666
Hebraica Libs Group, O219
Hebrew studies, S1266
Hedges, Anthony, Colln, P68
Hedley, John, papers (Bishop of Newport & Menevia), A94
Heelas Ltd, records (dept store), A470
Heffer, Eric, papers (politics), A365
Heinz, H.J., Co Ltd, advertising archv, A399
Hellenic & Roman Socs Joint Lib, S1159
Hellyer Brothers, records (fishing industry), A209
Hemel Hempstead Hosp Lib, S798
Henderson Colln (Cornish estates), S2056
Henderson, Murdoch, Scottish Music Colln, L2; P1
Hendy, Philip, Papers, S1297
Hengrave Hall MSS, L5
Henley Mgmt Coll, PowerGen Lib, S800
Henri, Adrian, papers, S972
Henrion, F.H.K., Archv & Rsrch Lib (design), A69
Henry Martyn Centre for the Study of Mission & World Christianity, Lib, S360
Henry Moore Foundation Lib, S1562
Henry Moore Inst Lib & Archvs, S900
Henry, Augustine, Colln (botany), IS113
Hensleigh Wedgwood Lib (philology), S179
Henson, Bishops H.H., papers, S569
Henty, G.A., Colln, P109
Henze MSS (music), S25
Hepworth, Dame Barbara, papers, A349
heraldry, A97, 156, 269; IA2; IL1; IS193; L1; S44, 407, 419, 466, 516, 529, 1102, 1398, 1627; *see also genealogy*
Heraldry Soc of Scotland, O220
Herbage, Julian, papers (Thomas Arne), S25
herbalism, S622, 1076, 1367, 1376
Herbert Family of Muckross Papers, IA49
Herbert of Llanarth, family & estate records, A117
Hercules Insurance Co, records, A320

Hereford Cathedral Lib & Archvs, S801
Hereford County Hosp, Nurse Edu Centre Lib, *see* S802
Hereford Local Studies Lib, A202
Hereford, Diocese of, records, A203
Herefordshire Clinical Lib, S802
Herefordshire Coll of Art & Design Lib, S803
Herefordshire Coll of Tech, LRC, S804
Herefordshire Libs & Info Svc, P62
Herefordshire Record Office, A203
Heriot-Watt Coll, records, A148
Heriot-Watt Univ Lib, S604; Archv, Records Mgmt & Museum Svc, A148; Martindale Lib, S689
heritage, IS90; Indo-Iranian, S290; industrial, S1857; Irish, IS165, 208; Jewish, S1270; natural, S635; Scottish, S631, 635; Welsh, A93
Heritage Lib (Inner City Trust), S1476
Heron-Allen Colln (Omar Khayyám), S1260
Heron-Allen Colln (string instruments), S1350
Herschel, Candice, Archv, S1345
Herschel, John, Archv, S1345; *Colln (astronomy),* S1020
Herschel, William, Archv, S1345; *Colln (astronomy),* P164; S1020
Hertford Coll (Oxford) Lib, S1678
Hertford Regional Coll, Lib & Learning Resources, S2082
Hertford, Archdeaconry of, records, A204
Hertford, Marquesses of, family papers, S1455
Hertford-Wallace Family MSS, S1455
Hertfordshire Archvs & Local Studies, A204
Hertfordshire Assoc for Local Hist, O221
Hertfordshire Libs, P63
Hertfordshire Nat Hist Soc Lib, S1433
Hertfordshire Partnership NHS Trust, Harperbury Lib Svcs, S1841
Hertfordshire Record Soc, O222
Hertfordshire Univ, *see Univ of Hertfordshire*
Hervey family papers (Marquisses of Bristol), A83
Hesketh Centre Lib, *see* S1951
Hesketh Colln (chamber music & song), S1528
Heskett, Lady, MSS, S1652
Heslop Colln (rare bks & pamphs), S179
Hetherington, Alastair, papers (journalism), S1512
Hewitt, John, Lib (Ulster poetry), S484
Hexham & Newcastle RC Diocesan Archvs, A388
Hexham Genl Hosp, Ryder Postgrad Medical Centre Lib, S809
Heygate Colln (Irish affairs), S1478
Heym, Stefan, papers, L5
Heythrop Coll Lib, S1160
Heywood Local Studies Lib, *see* A434
Hibernian Bible Soc Colln, IS183
Hibernica Colln (Celtic Ireland), S139
Hicks Beach of Coln St Aldwyn, family & estate records, A185
Higgins, L.G., Lib (entomology), S1738
Higginson Colln (field sports), S1260
High Peak Coll, *see* S284
Highbury Coll Portsmouth, Lib, S1824
Higher Edu & Training Awards Council, Lib, IS86
Higher Edu Funding Council for England, Knowledge Centre, S253
Higher Edu Statistics Agency, reports, S1395
Highgate Cemetery records, A262
Highgate Literary & Scientific Instn, Lib, S1161
Highland Council Archv, A213; *see also* A86
Highland Council Social Work Dept Colln, S839
Highland Distillers Co, records, A176
Highland Health Board Archvs, S839

Highland Health Scis Lib, S839
Highland Kirk Session Lib (hist & theology), P64
Highland Lib & Info Svcs, P64
Highland Theological Coll Lib, S538
Highlands Coll LRC, S2189
Highway Boards, records, A128
Higson Colln (early ch's bks), S934, 936
Hill & Adamson (photographers) Colln, P50; S215, 707; *records,* L2
Hill House Lib of Blackie Bks, S797
Hill, Dr William Henry, Colln (Glasgow), S725
Hill, Henry, papers (architect), A511
Hill, Roger, Tapes Colln (popular music), S965
Hill, Samuel, of Soyland, records (clothier), A194
Hilliard Colln (handicapped edu), S1512
Hillingdon Hosp NHS Trust Lib, S2066
Hillingdon Libs, Arts & Info Svc, P92
Hillingdon Local Studies & Archvs, A495
Hinchingbrooke Health Care NHS Trust, Edu Centre Lib, S832
Hinchliff, Peter, papers, S360
Hinduism, S180, 320
Hine, Reginald, Colln (Hitchin), A204
Hinshelwood, Dr Robert, papers (therapeutic communities), A104
Hinton, H.E., papers, A77
Hinton, Lord, papers (eng), S1208
Hipperholme family & estate records, A194
Hirsch, Paul, Colln (music), L1
Hisp Colln (16C-19C Spanish bks), L5
Hispanic & Luso-Brazilian Council, *see* S1055
Historic Commercial Vehicle Colln, P101
Historic Houses Archivists Group, O223
Historic Libs Forum, O224
Historic Soc of Lancashire & Cheshire Lib, A238
Historical Assoc, O225
Historical Assoc Pamphs Colln, S469
Historical Manuscripts Commission, O226; **Searchroom,** A431
historiography, S1144, 1366, 1730
history, A108, 151, 152, 167, 218, 273, 409, 430, 443, 466, 468, 507, 508, 522; IA92; IS6, 7, 9, 13, 15, 28, 33, 35, 44, 45, 46, 47, 56, 82, 90, 93, 105, 112, 121, 122, 131, 143, 149, 166, 172, 173, 181, 183, 198, 201, 205; L4; S4, 10, 26, 41, 44, 67, 108, 115, 121, 152, 156, 173, 179, 180, 198, 220, 234, 238, 247, 248, 258, 263, 264, 268, 269, 271, 296, 297, 323, 327, 330, 332, 336, 340, 382, 383, 404, 436, 442, 443, 456, 469, 478, 479, 482, 509, 523, 530, 540, 541, 552, 553, 565, 578, 612, 650, 652, 663, 669, 677, 680, 687, 698, 705, 710, 713, 741, 743, 776, 788, 801, 813, 823, 834, 838, 851, 859, 866, 869, 877, 879, 907, 909, 910, 919, 929, 937, 950, 951, 968, 969, 986, 1015, 1016, 1018, 1028, 1059, 1082, 1115, 1116, 1122, 1123, 1132, 1148, 1161, 1182, 1195, 1206, 1227, 1234, 1241, 1246, 1255, 1260, 1262, 1267, 1274, 1282, 1287, 1288, 1298, 1322, 1333, 1344, 1362, 1366, 1398, 1421, 1440, 1446, 1465, 1491, 1502, 1505, 1507, 1511, 1522, 1527, 1544, 1546, 1552, 1565, 1572, 1584, 1599, 1604, 1627, 1635, 1637, 1654, 1659, 1663, 1672, 1677, 1678, 1702, 1716, 1730, 1733, 1757, 1758, 1760, 1761, 1767, 1789, 1799, 1802, 1804, 1806, 1811, 1839, 1848, 1880, 1886, 1903, 1911, 1912, 1917, 1935, 1942, 1946, 1949, 1964, 1976, 1978, 1979, 2004, 2018, 2025, 2033, 2042, 2046, 2049, 2056, 2059, 2064, 2067, 2077, 2091, 2093, 2096, 2119, 2120, 2122, 2125, 2130, 2132, 2145, 2147, 2150, 2168, 2169, 2174, 2176, 2179, 2187, 2190; aeronautical, S1782; African, L4; agrarian, S1850; agricultural, A29; S246; Albanian, S1436; ambulance, S1287; American, S1621, 1653; ancient, S325, 1747; Anglican, S1102, 1234; Anglo-Japanese, S1221; antiquarian, IS154; architectural, S594; art, S1680; Asian, IS191; S738, 1377; Austrian, S1006; aviation, S1925; Baptist, S244; Belarussian, S1135, 1436; Black, A256; book, S1680; Bridgettine, S1932; British, S433, 665, 672, 1396, 1759, 1887, 1925; Bulgarian, S1436; business, A287; S260, 883, 1048; Canadian, S1053; canal, S1252; cathedral, S211, 746, 1798; Catholic, A52, 155, 388; S44, 179, 191, 391, 577, 1057; Celtic, IS193; S688; church, A1, 16, 17, 156, 252, 309, 450; IA28; IS208; S41, 98, 132, 179, 264, 320, 397, 448, 466, 502, 523, 538, 566, 577, 665, 801, 880, 952, 966, 1057, 1125, 1135, 1159, 1459, 1463, 1522, 1619, 1673, 1752, 1759, 1863, 1894, 1958, 2120, 2174; Commonwealth, L4; S248, 1443; Congregational, S397; contemporary, S1195; Cornish, S2056; costume, S1254, 2170; cultural, IA31; IS141; S1456; Czech, S1436; dockland, S1114; East Asian, S378; East European, S1436; Eastern European, S738, 1144; ecclesiastical, IA86; IS34, 62, 157; S404, 433, 596, 600, 945, 951, 1116, 1234, 1798; economic, A114, 147, 253, 300, 365, 469; IS185; S179, 419, 523, 739, 880, 1241, 1440, 1441, 1850, 1887; English, S746, 1144, 2174; Estonian, S1436; European, IS160, 193; S577, 1195, 1456, 1982; film, S1043; Finnish, S1120, 1436; Franciscan, IS157; S1676; French, IS110; S716, 1690; garden, S260; German, IS80; S1144, 1195; Greek, S1159; Highland, S1926; hospital, A33; S1922; Huguenot, S1169; Hungarian, S1436; Indian, L4; S1184; industrial, A129, 165, 220, 225, 444; S56, 246, 422, 955, 1114, 2033, 2051; intellectual, S1456; international, S1241; Irish, A16, 17, 23, 36; IA8, 31, 33, 69, 70, 86, 90; IS4, 20, 34, 39, 62, 95, 100, 116, 123, 137, 139, 149, 157, 175, 185, 188, 193, 201, 208; S121, 132, 502, 1217, 1653; Irish-American, S1653; Islamic, S989; Italian, S1216; Japanese, L4; S576, 1220, 1851; Jesuit, S191; Jewish, S1195, 1222, 1238, 1266, 1270, 1517, 1701; labour, A114, 365, 370; IA40; IS116; S828, 1016, 1214, 1274, 1512, 1591, 1761, 1887; Latin American, IS191; S327, 1210, 1735; Latvian, S1436; legal, L5; S883, 1245, 1634; Lithuanian, S1436; maritime, A36, 239; IS160; S248, 378, 446, 500, 704, 1106, 1303, 1827, 1944, 2051, 2056; media, S1817; medical, A4, 177; medieval, S404, 1730, 1880; Middle Eastern, S672, 1321, 1737; military, A9, 85, 96, 126, 160, 223, 234, 285, 288, 289, 290, 291, 292, 298, 308, 311, 333, 382, 517, 524; IA8, 45; IS28, 121; S26, 43, 88, 195, 248, 289, 423, 444, 445, 468, 502, 570, 612, 613, 672, 680, 946, 1130, 1182, 1284, 1289, 1327, 1621, 1663, 1925, 1954, 2063, 2084, 2170; mining, S1580; missionary, S360; modern, S1261, 1730, 1764, 1964; Moldavian, S1436; monastic, S101, 2036; Moravian, A309; museum, S1028; naval, S446, 1303, 1827, 1954; New Church, S1142; nuclear, A298; of actuarial science, S1188; of advertising, A399; of agriculture, S618, 772, 844; of alternative medicine, S1021; of amateur radio, S1831; of anaesthesia, S1001; of anarchism, S1224; of animal welfare, S820; of apiculture, S416; of architecture, S1396; of armoured warfare, S2084; of art, IS22, 205; S160, 324, 355, 424, 467, 611, 673, 870, 918, 1050, 1075, 1104, 1217, 1282, 1297, 1440, 1456, 1562, 1589, 1730, 1745, 1747, 2004, 2171; of art education, A496; of assaying, S1149; of astronomy, S621, 1020, 1345; of aviation, S1343; of banking, A287, 300, 329; S1197; of beekeeping, S416; of botany, IS113; S299; of brewing, A179; S1694; of British army, S1289; of building conservation, A345; of building economics, S1370; of canals, A183; of chemistry, S1380; of child abuse, S1304; of Church of England, S1234; of cinema, S661; of civil engineering, S1205; of classical tradition, S1456; of co-operation, A370; of Colonial armies, S1289; of communism, S1144; of computing, A369; of countryside, S844; of customs & excise, S1162; of dentistry, IS61; S740; of design, S160, 1141, 1282, 2127; of dress, S103; of Dublin, IA31; IS127; of Dulux, S1928; of Early Church, S1159; of East Asian science, S378; of Eastern Orthodox Church, S1685, 1686; of education, A216, 314; IA47; S718, 910, 936; of electrical engineering, A294; of electricity industry, S2017; of electronics, A60; of evangelism, A368; of fairs & fairgrounds, A451; of fans, S1126; of fashion, IS9; S103; of film, S215; of fire service, S1558; of firefighting, S1258; of fisheries, S759; of fishing communities, S759; of food, S1850; of football, S645; of forestry, S772; of freemasonry, S602; of furniture industry, S1141; of gas industry, A500; of geophysics, S1345; of German studies, S1445; of gold, S1149; of government, S1166; of gynaecology, S1352; of hallmarking, S1149; of herbalism, S1076; of horse breeding, S1593; of horseracing, S1593; of horticulture, IS113; S772, 844; of Indian army, S1289; of industry, A29; of inland waterways, A183; S749, 1252; of insurance, A396; S1072; of Irish Defence Forces, IA45; of Irish Diaspora, S1653; of Jews in Britain, S1222; of Knights Hospitallers, S1287; of Knights Templars, S1287; of land surveying, S1370; of laryngology, S1434; of libraries, S1066; of London, S1288, 1440; of magic, S1456; of marketing, A399; of mathematics, S1739; of mechanical engineering, S1208; of medicine, A336, 346; IS133; S179, 311, 378, 408, 561, 616, 617, 724, 738, 826, 899, 1001, 1287, 1352, 1355, 1357, 1381, 1457, 1656, 1755; of Methodism, A368; S1458, 1776; of military aviation, S1343; of military engineering, S444, 445; of military music, S2063; of military signalling, S195; of mining, S2068; of money, S1029; of motoring, S1346; of motorsport, S1346; of mountaineering, S990; of music, S726, 738, 1428; of music industry, A201; of natural history, S1576; of naval engineering, S755; of neurology, S1448; of neuroscience, S1754; of nonconformity, S1116, 1647; of nursing, A153, 336; S1351, 1583; of obstetrics, S1352; of oil industry, A112; S892; of optics, S1037; of optometry, S1037; of orthopaedics, S1698; of otology, S1434; of Palestine, S1321; of Parliament, S1166; of peace movement, S1052; of pharmacy, A346; S217; of philosophy, L4; of photography, S104, 215; of physical education, S115; of physiology, S316; of polar exploration, S339; of policing, IA34; of Polish Forces, S1327; of political song, A170; of poultry farming, S1601; of printing, IS122; S179, 1763, 1848; of psychiatry, S242, 1356; of psychoanalysis, S1137; of public health, S1265; of public houses, S1694; of public relations, A399; of publishing, A440; of quantum physics, S1387; of RAF, S1925; of railways, S1441; of religion, S244, 1456; of Royal Marines, S1954; of rugby football, S2060; of Salvation Army, S1463; of science, IS6; L4; S179, 311, 378, 612, 1247, 1371, 1379, 1387, 1440, 1456, 1624, 1730, 1739; of scientific instruments, S1739; of Scots law, S643; of Scottish football, S645; of shoe manufacture, A477; of silver, S1149; of social work, S712; of speech science, S1299; of syndicalism, S1224; of technology, A29, 60; S378, 612, 1205, 1371, 1387, 1440, 1739, 2033; of telecommunications, A261, 414; of television, S215, 1382; of temperance, S1189; of textiles, S689; of the British Empire, S248; of the British Museum, S1028; of the family, S407; of the hovercraft, S896; of tobacco, S1938; of tools, S1963; of tourism, A418; S1454; of trade, S1963; of transport, A29; S1268; of travel, A418; of tropical medicine, S1265; of veterinary medicine, S306, 1358; of veterinary science, S1384; of Western art, S1747; of Western European painting, S1297; of women's education, S357, 379, 1763, 1768; of working-class movement, S1274; oriental, S328, 738; paper, S1680; penal, S1877; Pictish, S688; Polish, S1328, 1436; political, A114, 428; IA31; IS34; S88, 508, 880, 1016, 1053, 1166, 1241, 1887; postal, A317; S110; Presbyterian, S397; psychiatric, S2070; Quaker, S1242; railway, S48; recusant, A424; regimental, A42, 45, 85, 96, 101, 154, 160, 162, 186, 214, 223, 234, 333, 382, 415, 426, 445, 502, 517, 524; S26, 43, 423, 445, 570, 946, 1130, 1284, 2084, 2131; regional, S1759, 1887; religious, S665, 1222; Roman, S1159; Romanian, S1436; Russian, S179, 1310, 1436, 1746; Scottish, A155, 156; S516, 598, 602, 612, 613, 628, 639, 688, 738, 876, 980, 1964; shipping, A299; Slavonic, S327; Slovakian, S1436; social, A114, 129, 205, 220, 225, 236, 292, 300, 365, 428, 442, 469; IA31; IS34, 141, 185; S88, 108, 220, 246, 451, 502, 508, 523, 545, 612, 705, 739, 823, 880, 955, 1106, 1222, 1241, 1298, 1340, 1440, 1457, 1517, 1546, 1827, 1900, 2036, 2068, 2126, 2170; South Asian, S300; South East Asian, L4; Soviet, S179, 738, 1310, 1746; Spanish, IS92; S1210; sport, S2060; Stuart, S523; textile, S2170; theatre, IA41; S1139, 1154, 1340, 1996; trade union, IA40; S1887; transport, IS101; S2051; Tudor, S523; Turkish, S1429; Ukrainian, S1436; US, L4; S97, 1123; Victorian, S523; Welsh, A6; S17, 74, 82, 419, 2051; Western European, S1446; women's, A365; IS208; S357; working class, S1761; Yugoslav, S1436; *see also oral history*
Hist of Advertising Trust Archv, A399
Hitchin Museum Resource Centre, S813
Hitchings Colln of Bibles, P57
HIV/AIDS Colln, P87
HM Customs & Excise, Lib & Info Svc, S1162, 1883
HM Govt Advertising Colln, A399
HM Inspector of Mines, reports, S1604
HMS Victory, logbks, A383
Hoadly, Benjamin, papers (Bishop of Winchester), A511
Hoare family & estate papers, A493
Hoare, Sir Richard Colt, works & MSS, S530
Hobbes, Thomas, MSS, S67
hobbies, IS89
Hobson, Bulmer, papers, IL1
Hochschule Lib (Judaism), S1238
Hockcliffe Colln (early ch's bks), S115
Hodgson, W.B., Colln (econ), S593
Hogarth MSS (Yorkshire RC clergy), A224
Hogarth, Paul, archv (artist), S1519
Hogg, A.G., papers, S360
Hogg, A.H.A., Colln (Welsh archaeo), A6
Hogg, A.R., Photo Colln, S146
Hogg, James, Colln, A448; *MSS,* L2; *papers,* S1978

Imperial Cancer Rsrch Fund, *see* S1054

Imperial Chemical Industries plc, Group HQ Lib, S1176

Imperial Coll Faculty of Medicine, Charing Cross Campus Lib, S1177; Hammersmith Campus, Wellcome Lib, S1178; St Mary's Campus Lib, S1179

Imperial Coll London, Central Lib, S1180; Natl Heart & Lung Inst Lib, S1181; Wye Campus, Kempe Centre Lib, S49; *see also* S1387

Imperial Inst Overseas Geological Survey, records, S1636

Imperial Internatl Communications Ltd, records, A414

Imperial Smelting Corp records, A324

Imperial War Museum, Dept of Art Archvs, A288; Dept of Documents, A289; Dept of Printed Bks, S1182; Film & Video Archv, A290; Photograph Archv, A291; Sound Archv, A292

imperialism, S248, 1203

Inchiquin Estate Papers, IL1

income distribution, S1112

Incorporated Soc of British Advertisers, archvs, A399

Independent Broadcasting Authority Archvs, A293

Independent Healthcare Assoc, Lib, S1183

Independent Order of Rechabites, Galston, records, A20

Independent Publishers Guild, O228

Independent Television Commission, Archvs, A293; *Lib,* S1013

Independent Television Commission, Records Mgmt Centre, A293

India, S328, 1184, 1246, 1449, 1647

India House Lib, S1184

India Life Assurance Co, records, A157

India Office Lib & Records, L1

Indian Film Cinema (Bollywood) Colln, S215

industrial affairs, S1009

industrial relations, A114, 319; IS55, 116; S498, 982, 1069, 1098, 1121, 1425, 1470, 1761, 1772, 2068

Industrial Soc, *see* S1470

industry, A129, 168, 300, 409, 421, 430, 480, 526; IS208; S108, 248, 420, 815, 937, 983, 1121, 1129, 1174, 1200, 1246, 1253, 1298, 1338, 1635; agricultural engineering, S1850; American, S1653; brewing, A179; S1694; ceramic, S2144; chemical, S1176, 1397; china clay, A463; coal, S2068; coffee, S1212; construction, S47, 969; cotton, A469; craft, S1850; creative, S1108; distilling, A376; electricity, S497, 1314, 2017; energy, S892; environment, S1071; film, IS74; S731; fishing, S37; food, IS118; S1793; furniture, S1141; gas, A500; S4, 1314; glazing, S1146; Irish, S1653; Irish linen, S960; iron, A121, 377; S1546; lace, S1491; land-based, S449, 473, 1540, 1564, 1610, 1837, 1955, 1960, 1991, 2139; linen, S960; mining, S1887, 2051; motor, S1648; music, A201; S965; nuclear, S581; oil, A112; S4, 11, 628, 892, 1202; petroleum, A482; S892, 1202; pharmaceutical, S1004; power, S1644; printers' engineering, A225; racing, S1593; recording, A201; regulation, IS55; rubber, S2100; Scottish film, S731; silk, S1497; slate, S82; steel, A121, 377; S889, 1546, 1873, 1905; telecommunications, S1315; textile, A148; S220; tobacco, S1938; Ulster, S1653; water, S172, 1071; Welsh, S82, 2051; *see also* history, industrial

industry & government, S1098

Info Automation Ltd, *see* O105

Info Cttee, O229

Info Focus for Allied Health, O230

Info for Energy Group, O231

Info for Social Change, O232

Info for the Mgmt of Healthcare, O233

Info Mgmt Rsrch Inst, O418

information science, S19, 1066, 1617

Info Svcs Natl Training Org, O234

Info Soc Commission, IO17

information studies, IS37; S1912

information technology, *see* technology, information

ING Barings: Info Centre, S1185

Ingham, Benjamin, papers (18C evangelical), A368

Inglis Colln (Scottish music), L2

Inglis, James, Colln (Scottish theatre), A182

Inglis, R.W., Free Lib, P4

Ingram, John Kells, Colln (Donegal author), IA65

Inishowen Poor Law Union, minutes, IA67

Inishowen Rural Dist Council, records, IA67

Inland Revenue Lib, S1186

Inn of Court of Northern Ireland, S119

Inner City Trust, *see* S1476

Inner London Archaeo Unit records, A301

Inner Temple Lib, S1187

Innerpeffray Lib, S509

Innes family papers, S1624

Innogy plc Info Centre, S2017

innovation policy, S235

Insch, James, Tea Lib (tea cultivation & hist), S1247

insects, *see* entomology

Instant Lib Ltd, *see* S1479

Institúid Teangeolaíochta Éireann, see IS109

Institut Français Archvs & Children's Lib, *see* S1231

Institut Français d'Ecosse Lib, S605

Inst & Guild of Brewing Lib & Archv Group, *see* S1694

Inst for Animal Health, Compton Lib, S1570; Pirbright Laboratory Lib, S2136

Inst for Orthodox Christian Studies Lib, S363

Inst for Scientific Info, O235

Inst for Supervision & Mgmt, *see* S944

Inst for the Study of Terrorism Colln, S934

Inst for Volunteering Rsrch Colln, S1294

Inst of Acoustics Lib, S1959

Inst of Actuaries, Historical Lib, S1188; Norwich Lib, S1679; *see also* S599

Inst of Advanced Legal Studies Lib, S1442

Inst of Agricultural Engineers Lib, *see* S114

Inst of Alcohol Studies Lib, S1189

Inst of Almoners, records, A53

Inst of Arable Crops Rsrch, *see* S280, 786

Inst of Archaeo Lib, *see* S1433

Inst of Biomedical Sci, Lib, S1190

Inst of Brewing, *see* S1694

Inst of British Foundrymen, *see* S2101

Inst of British Geographers, Archvs, *see* A334; Lib, *see* S1363

Inst of Business Ethics, Ref Lib, S1191

Inst of Cancer Rsrch Lib, S1192

Inst of Cast Metals Engineers, Lib, S2101

Inst of Chartered Accountants in England & Wales Lib, S1193

Inst of Chartered Accountants in Ireland, Info & Rsrch Svcs, IS87

Inst of Chartered Accountants of Scotland, *see* S624; *see also* L2

Inst of Chartered Secretaries & Administrators, Info Centre, S1194

Inst of Child Health Lib, *see* S1433

Inst of Civil Engineers Archvs, S1205

Inst of Classical Studies Lib, *see* S1159

Inst of Commonwealth Studies Lib, S1443

Inst of Contemporary Hist & Wiener Lib, S1195

Inst of Dirs, Business Lib, S1196

Inst of Edu, Newsam Lib, S1444; *see also* S1912

Inst of European Finance, Rsrch Lib, S75

Inst of Financial Svcs, Info Svc, S1197

Inst of Fisheries Mgmt, archvs, S1540

Inst of Food Rsrch, Lib & Info Svcs, S1623

Inst of Germanic Studies Lib, S1445

Inst of Grassland & Environmental Rsrch, Stapledon Lib & Info Svc, S16

Inst of Heraldic & Genealogical Studies, Lib, S407

Inst of Historical Rsrch Lib, S1446

Inst of Indian Art & Culture, *see* S1014

Inst of Laryngology & Otology Lib, S1434

Inst of Latin American Studies Lib, S1447

Inst of Leadership & Mgmt, Lib & Info Svc, S944

Inst of Leisure & Amenity Mgmt, Info Centre, S1845

Inst of Linguists Lib, S1198

Inst of Mgmt, *see* S489

Inst of Mgmt Svcs, *see* S489

Inst of Marine Eng, Sci & Tech, Marine Info Centre, S1199

Inst of Masters of Wine Lib, P99

Inst of Materials, Minerals & Mining, Lib & Info Svcs, S1200

Inst of Mechanical Engineers, transactions, S1199

Inst of Medical Social Workers, records, A53

Inst of Mining Engineers, transactions, S1604

Inst of Municipal Engineers Archvs, S1205

Inst of Neurology, Rockefeller Medical Lib, S1448

Inst of Occupational Medicine Lib, S606

Inst of Ophthalmology & Moorfields Eye Hosp, Joint Lib, S1201

Inst of Orthopaedics, Francis Costello Lib, S1660

Inst of Paper Conservation, O236; Judith Chantry Lib & Resource Centre, S1680

Inst of Petroleum Lib, S1202; *see also* O231

Inst of Phenomenological Studies, records, A104

Inst of Popular Music, Lib & Archvs, S965

Inst of Public Admin Lib, IS88; *see also* IS124

Inst of Public Relations, archvs, A399

Inst of Race Relations Lib, S1203

Inst of Revenues, Rating & Valuation Lib, S1204

Inst of Social & Cultural Anthro, Tylor Lib, S1732

Inst of Statisticians Archv, A339

Inst of Tech Blanchardstown, Lib, IS89

Inst of Tech Carlow, Lib, IS11

Inst of Tech, Sligo, Lib, IS195

Inst of Tech, Tallaght, Lib, IS90

Inst of Tech, Tralee, Lib, IS204

Inst of Terrestrial Ecology Colln, S756

Inst of Transport & Logistics, John Williams Lib, S491

Inst of Urology Lib, S1361

Inst of Virology & Environmental Microbiology, *see* S1669

Instn of Automobile Engineers, records, S1208

Instn of Civil Engineers, Lib & Info Svcs, S1205; *see also* S1275

Instn of Electrical Engineers Archvs, A294; Lib, S1206

Instn of Electronic & Radio Engineers Lib, *see* S1206

Instn of Electronic Engineers Archvs, A294

Instn of Engineers of Ireland Lib, IS91

Instn of Gas Engineers & Mgrs, Lib & Info Svcs, S1207

Instn of Gas Engineers, papers, A500

Instn of Locomotive Engineers, records, S1208

Instn of Manufacturing Engineers, *see* A294; S1206

Instn of Mechanical Engineers, Info & Lib Svc, S1208

Instn of Mining & Metallurgy, *see* S1200

Instn of Mining Engineers, transactions, S2068

Instn of Production Engineers, records, A294

Instn of Prof Civil Servants, records, A319

Instn of Profs, Mgrs & Specialists, *see* A319

Instn of Royal Engineers, *see* S444

Instn of Structural Engineers, Info & Lib Svc, S1209

Instituto Cervantes Lib, S1210; Dublin, IS92

instrumentation, S1545, 2022

insurance, A127, 320, 327, 396; S1072, 1188, 1249, 1261, 1679, 1758

intellectual property, S1068

Intensive Care Soc, archvs, S1001

interiors, S1122, 1306

internal displacement, S1744

international affairs, IS56; S289, 1369, 1764

Internatl Assoc of Music Libs, Archvs & Documentation Centres (UK), O237

Internatl Bee Rsrch Assoc, *see* S416

Internatl Bk Development Ltd, O238; Rsrch Lib, S1211

Internatl Brewers' Guild, *see* S1694

Internatl Brigade Lib & Archvs (Spanish Civil War), S1274

Internatl Centre for Distance Learning, Lib, S1551

Internatl Centre for Island Tech Lib, *see* S604

Internatl Coffee Organization Lib, S1212

Internatl Communications Industries Assoc Inc, *see* O227

Internatl Council for Kinetography Laban Archv, A192

Internatl Council for Nurses, records, A153

Internatl Development Centre Lib, S1733

Internatl Energy Agency, *see* S1172

Internatl Extension Coll Resource Centre, S364

Internatl Federation of Gynaecology & Obstetrics Archvs, S1352

Internatl Geographical Union papers, A334

Internatl Inst for Strategic Studies, Holinger-Telegraph Lib, S1213

Internatl Inst of Communications Lib, S1452

Internatl Labour Office, Ref Lib & Info Unit, S1214; *see also* S934

Internatl Life Assurance Soc, records, A320

Internatl Military Tribunal Nuremberg Colln, A292

Internatl Planned Parenthood Federation Lib, S1215

Internatl Postage Assoc, minutes, S1378

Internatl Public Relations Assoc, archvs, A399

international relations, A88; S26, 180, 1132, 1213, 1447, 1743, 1887, 2021

Internatl Rubber Study Group, Lib, S2100

international studies, S271, 336, 1195, 2004

Internatl Union of Food Sci Archv, S741

Internatl Wine & Food Soc Lib, P99

Inventory Archv, S1075

Inverclyde Archvs & Local Hist, A190

Inverclyde Libs, P65

Inverclyde Royal Hosp, Robert Lamb Lib, S763

Inverness Burgh records, A213

Inverness Coll, LRC, S840

Inverness-shire County records, A213

Invest Northern Ireland, Business Info Svcs & Euro Info Centre, S129
investment, A73, 147; S599, 1044, 1193, 1679
Ipswich Hosp NHS Trust, S842
Ipswich Local Studies Lib, see A215
Ipswich Medical Lib, S842
Ipswich Old Town Lib, P179
Ipswich Primary Care Trust, Suffolk Knowledge Svcs, S843
Iraq Petroleum Co Archv, A112
Ireland Lit Exchange, IO18
Ireland, Alexander, Colln, P112
Ireland, Phyllis, Colln (Norman England), S1866
Irish Agricultural Museum, Archvs, IA97
Irish Almanacks Colln, IA31
Irish Architectural Archv, IA36
Irish Army records, IA45
Irish Bk Publishers' Assoc, IO6; see also IO19
Irish Civil War, IA45; IS141
Irish Colln, IA55, 78; IP7, 28; L5; P135, 136; S484, 1887
Irish Coll for the Humanities, Lib, IS205
Irish Constabulary, records, IA34
Irish Convention, documents, S1758
Irish Copyright Licensing Agency, IO19
Irish Deaf Soc Lib, IS93
Irish Defence Forces, IA45
Irish Defence Forces Archv Film Colln, IA37
Irish Diaspora, S1653
Irish Dominican Sisters, records, IA5
Irish Family Hist Soc, IO20; Ref Lib & Archvs, IA79
Irish Family Planning Assoc, Info Svc & Archvs, IS94
Irish Famine, IS78
Irish Film Archv, IA37; see also IS74
Irish Film Soc Colln, IA37
Irish Folklore Colln, IS181
Irish Forestry Board, Lib, IS192
Irish Franciscan Archvs, IS157
Irish Historical Picture Co, IS95
Irish Inst of Purchasing & Materials Mgmt, Lib, IS96
Irish Internatl Arts Centre Lib, IS193
Irish Jesuit Archvs, IA38
Irish Jewish Museum, Archvs, IA39
Irish Labour Hist Soc Museum & Archvs, IA40
Irish Land Commission, records, IA43
Irish Linen Centre & Lisburn Museum, Lib & Archvs, S960
Irish Mgmt Inst, Info Centre & Lib, IS97
Irish Manuscripts Commission, IO21; see also A37
Irish Medicines Board, Lib, IS98
Irish Medium Colln (Irish lang), S144
Irish Military Mission to the USA, records, IA45
Irish Music Rights Org, see IS51
Irish Nurses Org, Lib & Info Svc, IS99
Irish Picture Lib, IS100
Irish Province of the Soc of Jesus, see IS112
Irish Railway Record Soc Ltd, Lib & Archvs, IS101
Irish Recess Cttee, documents, S1758
Irish Sci Libns' Group, O239
Irish Sea Fisheries Board, Lib, IS158
Irish Soc for Archvs, IO22
Irish Soc records (Ulster estates), A270
Irish studies, A37; IA31, 78, 83, 94; IS95, 141, 181, 205; S42, 121, 1839, 2064
Irish Theatre Archv, IA41
Irish Theatre Co, archv, IA41
Irish Times Young Historians Colln, IA70
Irish Tourist Assoc Photo Survey, IA55
Irish Traditional Music Archv, IA42
Irish Translators' & Interpreters' Assoc, IO23
Irish Travellers Colln, S484
Irish War of Independence, IS141
Irish Writer's Union, IO24; see also IO19
Irish-European links, A16

Irlam Urban Dist, records, A444
Ironbridge Gorge Museum Trust Lib, S2033
ironfounding, S165
Isaac Newton Inst for Mathematical Scis, Lib, S365
Isaacs, Rufus, papers, S1634
Isaacs, Susan, Colln (edu), A216
Isherwood Colln (ships' drawings), A459
Islam & Islamic studies, S180, 320, 328, 593, 672, 989, 1737
Islam Colln, P87, 106
Isle of Anglesey County Council, see A245; P3
Isle of Man Centre for Nurse Edu, Lib, S2178
Isle of Man Coll Lib, S2179
Isle of Man Dept of Edu, Noble's Lib, S2180; see also S2179
Isle of Man Family Hist Soc Lib, A530
Isle of Man Genl Registry, A527; see also A528
Isle of Man Govt, Tynwald Lib, S2181
Isle of Man Internatl Business School Lib, S2182
Isle of Man Public Record Office, A528
Isle of Mull Museum Trust, see S2044
Isle of Wight Coll, Victor Stevenson LRC, S1599
Isle of Wight County Record Office, A392
Isle of Wight Healthcare NHS Trust, Oliveira Lib, S1600
Isle of Wight Lib Svc, P66; see also S500
Islington Lib & Cultural Svcs, P94
Islington Local Hist Centre, A295
Islington Primary Care Trust, see S994, 1051
Israel, S1238, 1701
Italian Cultural Inst Lib, S1216
Italiener, Bruno, papers (rabbi), S1238
Ivanyi Colln (Hungarica), S1436
Iveagh Bequest, Kenwood, Lib, S1217
Ivory & Sime, records (investment trust mgrs), A176
Ivory Colln (maths & sci), A136; P42
IWA records (anarchist org), S1224

J. Rothschild Capital Mgmt Ltd, Lib, S1218
J.B. Morrell Lib, S2168
J.B. Priestley Lib, S217
Jack Taylor Lib, S1865
Jackson Colln, IA9; IP1
Jackson Colln (econ), S963
Jackson, Barry, Colln (theatre), P9
Jackson, J.W., Archv (caves & geol), S283
Jackson, T.A., Lib, S1887
Jacob Bequest, IS135
Jacob Colln (19C medicine, travel, lit), IS134
Jacob, F.H., Hist of Medicine Colln, S1647
Jacobean life, S1996
Jacobite Rising of 1745 Colln, S1647
Jacobson, Bishop, Colln, S456
Jaeger & Co Archvs, A268
James B.P. Ferguson Lib, S781
James Bridie Lib, S735
James Cameron-Gifford Lib, see S1647
James Clavell Lib, S1130
James Clerk Maxwell Lib, see S593
James Fawcett Edu Centre, Goldberg Lib, S836
James Hardiman Lib, IS166
James Herriot Lib, see S738
James Ireland Memorial Lib, S740
James Joyce Centre, Guinness Ref Lib, IS102
James Joyce Museum Lib, IS159
James McBey Art Ref Lib, S2
James Paget Healthcare NHS Trust, see S761
James Watt Coll of Further & Higher Edu Lib, S764
James, C.L.R., papers (West Indian politician & writer), S1443

James, J.G., Colln (civil eng), S1205
Jamieson, Menie, Colln (Scottish theatre), A182
Janiurek, Peggy, Colln (ch's lit), S2168
Japan & Japanese studies, L4; S328, 576, 1219, 1220, 1221, 1851
Japan Foundation Lib, S1219
Japan Info & Cultural Centre Lib, S1220
Japan Soc Lib, S1221
Jardine Matheson Archvs, L5
Jardine papers, S612
Jardine Skinner Archvs, L5
Jardine's Naturalist's Lib, S618
Jarrett Colln (Biblical), S390
Jarrow March Colln (photos), A457
jazz, A360; S511, 903
Jebb, Eglantyne, Papers (Save the Children Fund), A342
Jebb, Richard, papers (publicist & writer), S1443
Jee's Hartshill Granite & Brick Co Ltd records (quarry owners), A514
Jeffcote, Norman, papers (gynaecology), S1352
Jefferies, Richard, Colln, P183
Jefferson Lib, S1520
Jefferson, Dr G., Neurosurgical Colln, S1520
Jeffrey Ref Lib (fine bindings & illust), P56
Jeffreys, H., Colln (geol), S307
Jenner, Edward, correspondence, S1352
Jenyns, Rev Leonard, Colln (sci & nat hist), S98
Jerningham Letters, S179
Jersey Archv, A533
Jersey Lib, P218
Jersey Merchant Seamen's Benefit Soc Registers, S2190
Jersey Public Registry Office, A534
Jersey, Bailiff of, Occupation Files, A533
Jersey, Lt Governor of, Jersey, A533
Jersey, Royal Court of, records, A533, 534
Jerwood Lib, S394
Jerwood Lib of Performing Arts, S1428
Jessel Colln (hist of playing cards), L4
Jessops of Nottingham, records (dept store), A470
Jesuit Order, A251; IA38; IS112; S191
Jesus Coll (Cambridge), Quincentenary Lib, S366
Jesus Coll (Oxford) Lib, S1681
Jevons, W.S., papers (econ), S1512
Jevons, William, statistical papers (19C economist), A339
jewellery, S160, 1060, 1105, 1149
Jewish Archvs (Anglo-Judaism), S1946
Jewish Historical Soc Lib, S1433
Jewish Museum, London, Lib & Archvs, S1222
Jewish studies, S1238, 1266
Jewish-Christian relations, S343
Jews' Coll, see S1266
Jobbing Printing Colln, S1290
Jodrell Bank, Audio Colln, A109; Colln (hist of astronomy), S1512
John A. Aitken Lib, S2135
John Bunyan Museum & Lib, S116
John Campbell Trust, O240
John Creasey Museum, Salisbury Lib, S1889
John Dewar & Sons Ltd, Co Archvs, A178
John Fawcett Postgrad Medical Centre, Laxton Lib, S1796
John Howard Lib, S1168
John Innes Centre Lib, S1624
John Jamison Lib, S1927
John Levy Archv, see S598
John Lewis, Archv, A470; Business Info Dept, S1223
John McDermott Lib & LRC, S2024
John Price Lib & Archv, S1539
John Ross Postgrad Medical Lib, see S802
John Rylands Univ Lib of Manchester, S1512; see also A368; S54; see also Univ of Manchester
John Spalding Lib, S2157

John Squire Lib, S789
John Stearne Medical Lib, see IL2
John Wesley's House Lib, S1458
John Williams Lib, S491
John, Augustus & Gwen, Colln (artists), S2036
John, Gwen, papers, L3
Johnson Colln, P9
Johnson Colln (Dublin photos), IS141
Johnson Lib, S1903
Johnson, B.S., Colln (20C lit & poetry), S1227
Johnson, Barham, Colln, S1652
Johnson, Hewlett, Papers, S410
Johnson, John, Colln (ephemera), L4
Johnson, Johnny, MSS, S1652
Johnson, Samuel, Colln, P174; S947, 1756
Johnston, Denis, Colln (playwright & journalist), S484
Johnston, Eddie, papers (stage designer), IA41
Johnston, Thomas, papers, IL1
Johnstone Lavis Vulcanology Lib, S1433
Johnstone, Hilda, Lib, A106
Joint Academic Network User Group for Libs, O241
Joint Edu & Training Lib, S506
Joint Info Systems Cttee, O242; see also O61, 86
Joint Svcs Command & Staff Coll Lib, S2018
Jolly Colln (theology), L2
Joly Colln (Irish materials), IL1
Jones Brothers (Holloway) Ltd, records (dept store), A470
Jones Colln (art & manufacture), S1290
Jones of Llanarth, family & estate records, A117
Jones, Alfred, Biographical Index (Irish architects), IA36
Jones, Burne, papers, A282
Jones, D.W.K., Photo Colln (tramways), S1539
Jones, David, Colln (Wales), L3; correspondence, S368; papers, A85; L3
Jones, Ernest, Archvs (psychoanalysis), S1039
Jones, John Paul, Colln, S876
Jones, O.T., papers, L3
Jones, Peter, of London, records (dept store), A470
Jones, Thomas, CH Papers, L3
Jones, Thomas, Colln, P21
Jones, William Parry, Colln (psychiatry), A177
Jordan, John, Colln (poetry), IS41
Joseph Rowntree Foundation, Lib, S2164
Joseph, Stephen, papers (theatre), S1512
Josephine Butler Soc Colln & Archvs (prostitution, sexuality), S1469
Joule Lib, see S1536
Joule's Brewery, records, A467
Joule, James Prescott, Colln, S1536
journalism, A88, 316; S271, 1254, 1255
Joy, David, Drawings Colln (eng), S1208
Joyce Tower Lib, IS159
Joyce, James, Colln, IS102, 159; S1433; papers, IL1
Joyce, P.W., Colln (Irish music & hist), IA70
JRL Archv, IS61
Jubilee Gardens, records, A331
Judaism, S180, 320, 1222, 1238, 1266, 1270; Progressive, S1238
Judge Inst of Mgmt, Lib, S367
Judges Lib, IS103
Judith Chantry Lib & Resource Centre, S1680
justice, criminal, S1168, 1710; social, S185
JVZ Picture Lib, see S1310

Kabbalah, S1238
Kahn-Freund Colln (labour law), L4
Kanthack & Nuttall Lib, S313
Kantorowich Lib, see S1512
Kate Sharpley Lib, S1224

Kavanagh, Patrick, papers, IL1; IS148
Kay Colln (colonial revenue stamps), L1
Keats Memorial Lib, S1225
Keats, John, MSS, S1225
Keble Coll Lib, S1682
Keele Univ Lib, S1572; Air Photo Archive/Lib, A387; Health Lib, S1987
Keene, Richard, Colln (photography), A122
Keep Military Museum, Archvs, A126
Keiller, Gabrielle, Archv, S633
Keith Donaldson Lib, S1899
Keith of Kintore family & estate papers, A3
Keith, Arthur Berriedale, Colln (British Empire, Indian culture), S593
Keith, Arthur, Colln (surgery), S1357
Kelham Island Museum, Lib & Archvs, S1905
Kellogg Brown & Root Ltd, Info Resource Centre, S893
Kells Board of Guardians records, IA80
Kells Town Commissioners, archvs, IA80
Kelly Colln (18C-19C posters), P170
Kelly Colln (religion), P115
Kelmscott Press Colln (private press), A282; S1464, 1512
Kelsall, Charles, Colln, S1285
Kelvin, Lord, Collns, L5
Kelvinside Academy Lib, S713
Kemball, Bishop & Co Ltd, records (tartaric acid merchants), A446
Kemmy, Jim, Colln (Irish hist, religion & politics), IA69
Kempe Centre Lib, S49
Kendal Coll, LRC, S855
Kenmare Poor Law Union, minutes, IA92
Kenmare Rural Dist Council, minutes, IA92
Kennally Northern Ireland Archv, S217
Kennedy Colln (Japan & Far East), S1912
Kennedy of Kirkmichael papers, A20
Kennedy, John F., Colln, IA1
Kennedy, Margaret, MSS, S1762
Kenneth Ritchie Wimbledon Lib, S1226
Kenney Papers, S1631
Kenrick Colln (catalogues & design registrations), A129
Kensington & Chelsea Libs & Info Svcs, P95
Kent & Canterbury Hosp records, A128
Kent & Sussex Postgrad Medical Centre, MacDonald Lib, S2057
Kent Archaeo Soc Lib, S1502
Kent Arts & Libs, P67; see also A90, 128, 362, 372, 427, 449; S48
Kent County Council, records, A362, 435
Kent Hist Federation, O243
Kent Info & Lib Network, O244
Kent Inst of Art & Design Lib, S1503
Kent Postgrad Medical Centre, Linacre Lib, S408
Kent Univ, see Univ of Kent at Canterbury
Kents Cavern Excavation Archv, S2049
Keogh Colln (Irish photos), IL1
Keppel, Admiral Viscount, papers, A215
Keppel, Genl Sir William, papers, A215
Kern River Oilfields of California records, A324
Kerrison family & estate papers, A215
Kerry Archaeo & Historical Soc, IO25; see also IA92
Kerry Board of Guardians, minutes, IA92
Kerry Board of Health records, IA92
Kerry County Libs, IP11
Kerry Local Studies & Archvs Dept, IA92
Kerry RC Diocesan Archvs, IA62
Kerryman Newspaper Photo Archv, IA92
Keswick Museum & Art Gallery Lib, S858
Kettle's Yard Museum & Art Gallery, Lib & Archvs, S368

Ketton-Cremer Colln (East Anglia), S1631
Keynes Colln, L5
Keynes, J.M., Lib & papers, S369
Keynes, John Neville, archv (econ), S335
Keystone Colln (news & features), S1170
Kickstart Dance Co Archv, A192
Kidbrooke parish records, A278
Kidderminster Hosp Lib, S862
Kidson Colln (folk music), P56
Kiely, Benedict, papers, IL1
Kilbeggan Rural Dist Council minutes, IA78
Kildare & Leighlin RC Diocesan Archvs, IA10
Kildare Boards of Guardians, records, IA82
Kildare Grand Jury records, IA82
Kildare Hist & Family Rsrch Centre, IA82
Kildare Lib & Arts Svcs, IP12
Kilkee Town Commissioners, records, IA55
Kilkenny Board of Guardians, records, IA61
Kilkenny County Libs, IP13; Local Studies Dept, IA61
Kilkenny Grand Jury Presentments, IA61
Kilkenny Lib Soc Colln, IA61
Killaloe RC Diocesan Archvs, IA56
Killanin, Lord, Colln (film), IA37
Killarney Poor Law Union, minutes, IA92
Killarney Rural Dist Council, minutes, IA92
Kilmacthomas Board of Guardians, records, IA54
Kilmacthomas Rural Dist Council, minutes, IA54
Kilmartin House Trust, Marion Campbell Lib, S980
Kilmore RC Diocesan Archvs, IA15
Kilner Lib of Plastic Surgery, S1683
Kilrush Board of Guardians, minutes, IA55
Kilrush Town Council, Archvs & Records, IA63
Kilrush Urban Dist Council, records, IA55
Kimber Colln (lit), S1631
Kimmage Mission Inst of Theology & Cultures Lib, IS104
Kindrogan Field Centre Lib, S194
King Alfred's Coll, Martial Rose Lib, S2122
King Edward VI Coll, Lib & LRC, S1995
King Edward's Hosp Fund for London, S1229
King Lib (17C), S466
King William's Coll, Dr Scholl Lib, S2177
King's Coll (Aberdeen), archvs, A3
King's Coll (Cambridge) Lib, S369
King's Coll London, Info Svcs & Systems, 1227; Inst of Psychiatry Lib, S1228; see also A298; S109, 1326
King's Dragoon Guards, records, S423
King's Fund, Lib & Info Svc, S1229
King's Inns Lib, IS105
King's Lib of George III (hist, topography), L1
King's Lynn Borough Archvs, A400
King's Lynn Museum, Lib, S866
King's Mill Hosp Medical Lib, S2007
King's MSS (collected by George III), L1
King's Own Royal Regiment Museum, Regimental Archvs, A223
King's Own Scottish Borders Archvs, A45
King's Regiment Archv, A239
King's School in Macclesfield Lib, S1495
King's School Lib, S409
King, Charles, Colln (anaesthesia), S1001
King, David James Cathcart, Papers (medieval castles), A77
King, William, Colln (Archbishop of Dublin), IS13

King-Harman family of Newcastle, estate records, IA73
Kingam Hill Trust, S1311
Kingston Coll, LRC, S868
Kingston Libs, P96
Kingston Museum & Heritage Svc, Local Hist Room, A219
Kingston Univ Lib Svcs, S869; Knights Park Lib, S870
Kingston upon Hull City Libs & Archvs, P68
Kingswood Abbey Colln, A77
Kinnaid, Barons, of Inchture, family & estate records, A416
Kinnear Local Colln (Dundee), A137; S561
Kinross Burgh records, A416
Kinsale Harbour Commissioner, Archvs & Records, IA64
Kintyre Nat Hist Soc Lib, S863
Kipling Colln, P17
Kipling Soc Lib, S1230
Kipling, Rudyard, Colln, S1230; papers, S239
Kirby Colln, IA78; IP30
Kirby, Edmund, archvs (architects & surveyors), A238
Kirkby Urban Dist Council, minutes, A222
Kirkcaldy Dist Council, records, A373
Kirkcaldy Museum & Art Gallery, Archvs, A220
Kirkcudbright Hosp, records, A132
Kirkintilloch Dist Council, records, A171
Kirklees Libs, P69; see also A208; S823
Kirkpatrick Colln & Archv (Irish medical hist & biography), IS133
Kirriemuir Town Council, records, A384
Kirwan Colln, IS137
Kitchin Colln (Peterborough photos), A417
Kitching, Jack, Archv (edu inspection), S1444
Klugmann, James, Colln (early radicals & Chartists), S1274
Knebworth House, Lib & Archv, S877
Knight & Lee of Southsea, records (dept store), A470
Knight, Charles, Colln, S1647
Knight, Dame Laura, Photo Colln, S1272
Knight, Frank, Memorial Lib, S844
Knight, John Henry, Colln (photography), A167
Knightbridge Lib (Puritan theology & patristics), S448
Knights Hospitallers, S1287
Knights Templars, S1287
Knowsley Community Coll, Roby Centre Lib, S1864
Knowsley Lib Svc, P70
Knowsley Local Studies & Archvs, A222
Knussen MSS (music), S25
Knutsford, 2nd Viscount, papers, A336
Kodak Colln (photography), S215
Koestler, Arthur, Colln, S593
Kónyi, Manó, & Lónyay, Menyhért, Colln (Hungarian politics), S1436
Kopal, Zdenek, archv (hist of astronomy), S1512
Korea Lib Group, O245
Korean War, S1182
Kostoris Medical Lib, S1508
Kraszna-Krausz, Andor, Colln (photography), S215
Kray, R.E., Colln (archaeo notebks), A6
Krazy Kat Arkive (20C popular culture), A250
Krebs, Sir Hans, Lib & Papers (life sci), S1912
Kressel Colln & Archv (Jewish hist, lit & biography), S1701
Krishnamurti Colln, P50
Kunath, Siegward, Colln (archaeo artefacts), S1238
Kuwait Oil Co Archv, A112
Kvaerner Eng & Construction (UK), Info Svcs, S2112

L.J. Carter Lib, S1026
Laban Art of Movement Guild Archv, A192
Laban Lib & Archv, S1232
Laban, Rudolf, Archv, A192; Colln (dance), S1232
laboratory science, S839
Labour & Socialist Internatl, records, A365
Labour Heritage, O246
labour history, see history, labour
Labour Hist Archv & Study Centre, A365
labour movement, S1274, 1761, 1887
Labour Party Archvs, A365; Wales, L3
Labour Party Colln, S1512
Lackham Coll, see S473
Lady Margaret Hall Lib, S1684
Lady Spencer Churchill Coll Archv, S1776
LaFarge Cement UK, Quality Support Laboratory Lib, S762
Laing Colln (maths), S741
Laing Colln & MSS, S593
Laing Museum, Ref Lib, S516
Laing, Alexander, Lib, S516
Laird Lib, S702
Lakeman Lib for Electoral Studies, see S1277
Lakes Coll – West Cumbria, Lib, S2151
Lalor, James Fintan, papers, IL1
Lamb Colln (Dundee), A136; P42
Lamb, Charles, Colln, S1064
Lamb, William, Papers, A1946
Lambarde, William, Colln, A273
Lambeth Archvs Dept, A296
Lambeth Coll, Learning Resources Svc, S1233
Lambeth Healthcare NHS Trust, see S1402
Lambeth Libs, Archvs & Arts, P97
Lambeth Palace Lib & Archvs, S1234; see also S974
Lambeth Stoneware Pottery Colln, A296
Lanark State Hosp, Staff Lib, S881
Lanarkshire County Council records, A174
Lanarkshire Health Board, James B.P. Ferguson Lib, S781
Lancashire & Cheshire Antiquarian Soc, O247; Lib, S1513
Lancashire Authors' Assoc Colln, P71
Lancashire Coalfield Archvs, S1885
Lancashire Cotton Districts Relief Fund, records, A918
Lancashire Cotton Trade Colln, S1519
Lancashire County Libs, P71
Lancashire Dialect Colln, A57
Lancashire Local Hist Federation, O248
Lancashire Mining Museum, Salford, Ref Lib, S1885
Lancashire Quarter Sessions, records, A425
Lancashire Record Office, A425; see also A109
Lancashire Regiment, records, A426
Lancashire Teaching Hosps NHS Trust, Lib & Info Svc, S1835; Postgrad Edu Centre Lib, S475
Lancashire Theatre Organ Trust Colln (recordings), A109
Lancaster & Morecambe Coll Lib, S882
Lancaster Univ Lib, S883; see also S885
Lancaster, Joseph, Colln (19C educationalist & philanthropist), A216
Lancaster, Osbert, Colln (comic art, humour), S1290
Lancaster, RC Diocese of, Archv, S1839
Lanchester Coll LRC, see S486
Lanchester Lib, S495
Lanchester, F.W., papers, S495
Lanchester, Frederick, papers (eng), S1208
Lancing Coll Lib, S887
Land Commission (Ireland), Records Branch, IA43
Land Drainage & Commissioners of Sewers, records, A128

land economy, S336
Land League of Ireland, records, IA57
land registers, Ireland, IA44
Land Registry (Ireland), IA44
land use, S74, 635, 831, 1601, 1603, 1786, 1794, 1850, 1940; analytical, S756; rural, S476
land valuation, IA50
land-based studies, S263, 525, 1641; *see also agriculture; farming; industry, land-based*
Lands Improvement Co, records, A73
Landscape Inst Lib, S1235
landscapes, S1298, 1306; Welsh, S74
landscaping, S591, 594, 654, 772, 993, 1622, 1912, 2045, 2160; *see also architecture, landscape; design, landscape*
Lane, Sir Allen, Colln of Penguin Bks, S260; *papers,* A77
Lanesborough Papers, IA13
Lang, Andrew, Colln, A448; S1964
Lang, Matheson, Colln, A267
Langford Rowley family of Langford Lodge, papers, IA12
Langholm Lib, S888
Langlands Colln, IS27
Langley Colln (prints & drawings), S1459
Langside Coll, The Litehouse, S714
language, IS7, 9, 11, 28, 33, 35, 39, 46, 47, 49, 56, 59, 69, 82, 90, 102, 105, 109, 112, 166, 172, 181, 183, 193, 195, 202; S98, 116, 121, 154, 180, 208, 258, 269, 296, 297, 322, 332, 334, 336, 382, 436, 442, 443, 469, 478, 482, 523, 525, 540, 565, 610, 665, 698, 701, 713, 741, 743, 788, 810, 855, 859, 869, 879, 880, 910, 959, 969, 986, 1015, 1053, 1059, 1061, 1082, 1115, 1148, 1160, 1169, 1198, 1227, 1260, 1261, 1262, 1282, 1286, 1299, 1333, 1373, 1403, 1421, 1452, 1524, 1536, 1565, 1572, 1599, 1635, 1654, 1659, 1678, 1727, 1734, 1760, 1767, 1843, 1848, 1882, 1886, 1942, 1983, 2004, 2017, 2042, 2064, 2067, 2093, 2103, 2145, 2147, 2148, 2168; African, S1449, 1751; Albanian, S1436; ancient, S2119; Arabic, S989; Asian, S1344, 1449; Belarussian, S1135, 1436; biblical, S320, 880; Bulgarian, S1436; Celtic, S1926, 2056; classical, S1747; Continental, S327; continental, S1751; Cornish, S751, 2056; cuneiform, S1747; Czech, S1436; Dutch, S327; East European, S1436; English, IS178; S271, 504, 609, 838, 1123, 1726, 1804, 1911, 2046, 2103; Esperanto, S1512, 1986; Estonian, S1436; European, S327, 1751; Finnish, S1120, 1436; foreign, S2046; French, IS110, 116, 178; S267, 271, 495, 605, 716, 776, 838, 1804, 1982; French Canadian, S1053; Gaelic, IS173; S600, 688, 751, 1926; Gammon, S751; German, IS116, 178; S267, 495, 709, 776, 838, 1147, 1445, 1982; Germanic, S1440; Greek, S325, 1751; Hebrew, S1238, 1266; Hungarian, S327, 1436; Indian, L4; S1184; Indo-Iranian, S290; Irish, A16; IS9, 34, 143, 149, 177, 178; S121, 144, 1926; Italian, S267, 495; Japanese, S1219, 1220, 1851; Latin, S325; Latin American, S1751; Latvian, S1436; Lithuanian, S1436; medieval, S327; modern, S1440, 1727, 1751; modern Greek, S1751; Moldavian, S1436; oriental, S328; Pacific, S1449; Polish, S1328, 1436; Portuguese, S327; Romance, S1440; Romanian, S1436; Russian, S495, 776, 1436, 1751; sign, IS93; S1082; Slavonic, S327, 1436, 1751; Slovakian, S1436; South East Asian, L4; Spanish, IS92, 178; S267, 271, 495, 776, 1210, 1982; Swedish, S776; Turkish, S1429; Ukrainian, S1436; Welsh, S20, 82, 492, 751, 1882, 1926; Western European, S1727; Yugoslav, S1436; *see also linguistics*
Langs of Ulster Colln, S121
Lansdowne MSS, L1
Lansdowne, 5th Marquess of, correspondence, IA78

Lantra Lib, S857
Laois Board of Guardians, minutes, IA83
Laois County Libs, IP14; **Local Studies Colln,** IA83
Laois Grand Jury Presentments, IA83
Laois Petty Sessions records, IA83
Largo Field Studies Soc, records, A373
Larionov Colln (theatre & opera), S1290
Larkin, Philip, MSS, S828
Larman Colln (local & church hist, genealogy), S394
laryngology, S1434
LASER Foundation, O249
lasers, S535
Latimer, Barons, family papers, A11
Latin America & Latin American studies, S336, 482, 492, 972, 1055, 1440, 1447, 1735
Latin American Centre Lib, S1735
Lattice Group, archvs, A500
Lattimore, Owen, Colln (Mongolia & Central Asia), S328
Latvia, S1436
Lauder Coll Lib, S563
Lauder, Sir Harry, Colln (Scottish theatre), A182
Laughton-Le-Skerne Poor Law Union records, A119
Laurence Sterne Trust, *see* S2167
Laurence, Simon, archv (artist), S1519
Laurie & Whittle, archv (cartography), S1364
Lauriston Castle Colln (Scottish bks), L2
Lauterpacht Rsrch Centre for Internatl Law, Lib, S370
Laver Papers (fine art), S738
law, IS30, 55, 56, 103, 105, 106, 107, 123, 125, 129, 166, 177, 178, 200; L4, 5; S12, 119, 130, 132, 161, 168, 180, 212, 224, 241, 249, 263, 271, 272, 336, 431, 458, 476, 482, 553, 561, 571, 586, 593, 610, 630, 639, 640, 667, 671, 676, 725, 741, 769, 776, 790, 824, 835, 869, 918, 969, 972, 995, 1024, 1063, 1090, 1133, 1150, 1166, 1167, 1176, 1187, 1194, 1236, 1237, 1245, 1249, 1250, 1251, 1261, 1269, 1281, 1282, 1416, 1427, 1439, 1442, 1452, 1512, 1572, 1579, 1586, 1617, 1627, 1641, 1647, 1654, 1663, 1672, 1679, 1702, 1711, 1758, 1800, 1848, 1887, 1911, 1912, 1989, 2004, 2046, 2103, 2151, 2160, 2161; administrative, S1634; banking, S1197; building, S1370; business, S227; canon, IA86; S394, 801; charity, S1063; child care, S712; civil, S394; Commonwealth, S586, 630, 1187, 1236, 1245, 1416; company, IS87; S624, 1098, 1193, 1194; comparative, L5; S630, 1024; constitutional, S1634; construction, S45; contract, S45; criminal, S28, 816, 1389, 1634, 1710; early, S963; ecclesiastical, S1759; employment, S227, 982, 1069, 1470; English, IS107; S630, 1150, 1427; environmental, L5; European, IS107; S1024, 1133, 1237, 1281, 1416, 1427; family, S1304, 1711; foreign, S1132; housing, S1370; human rights, S1024; industrial, S1098; insurance, S1072; international, L5; S370, 1024, 1133, 1150, 1241, 1427; Irish, IS107; S1427; Islamic, S1449; Isle of Man, S2181; labour, S1214, 2140; land, S1370; marine, S1944; maritime, S1939; medical, IS210; S1711; naval, S1827; overseas territories, S1133; planning, S1383; private, S1634; railway, IS101; Roman, L5; Scottish, S630, 640, 643, 1427; Spanish, S1210; US, S1281; *see also legislation*
law & order, S137
Law Commission Lib, S1236
Law Lib, IS106
law reform, S630; Commonwealth, S1236
Law Soc of Ireland Lib, IS107
Law Soc of Northern Ireland Lib, S130
Law Soc's Lib, S1237
Lawes Chemical Co, records, A118

Lawes, John Bennet, & Co Ltd, records (citric & tartaric acid manufacturers), A446
Lawrence Batley Centre for the Natl Arts, Edu Archv, A496
Lawrence Colln (Irish photography), A17; IA51, 55, 82, 83; IL1
Lawrence, D.H., Colln, P36, 138, 139; S1647
Lawrence, Lord Justice, papers (Nuremburg trials), S1634
Lawrence, T.E., Colln, IP30; S1681, 1682, 1925; *correspondence,* S368
Lawson Lib, S906
Laxton Lib, S1796
Layton Colln of Local Studies (Hounslow), A206; P93
Le Marchant, Gen J.G., papers, S289
Lea Castle Centre Lib, S861
Leabharlainn nan Eilean Siar, P199
Leabharlann An t-Sabhail Mhòir, S1926
Leabharlann Náisiúnta na h-Éireann, IL1
Lead Development Assoc Internatl, S1473
leadership, S944; healthcare, S897
Leadhills Miners Lib, S152
League of Nations, documents, S18
Leake Colln (classics), S325
learning, online, S364
Learning & Teaching Scotland, Glasgow Lib, S715
Learning & Teaching Support Network, *see* O272
leather, S1105
Leatherhead Food Internatl, Lib, S894
Leathes, William, papers (ambassador), A215
Lebour Lib (marine biology), S1805
Leckford Estate Colln, A470
Ledwidge, Francis, papers (poet), IA85
Lee Lib, S402
Lee, Ann, drawings (botanical illust), S1862
Lee, Dr J. Alfred, Colln (anaesthesia), S1001
Lee, Harry, Colln (fairs & fairgrounds), A451
Lee, Jennie, Papers, S1554
Lee, John, papers, L2
Lee, John, Papers (trial documents), S1634
Lee, Vernon, MSS, S1762
Leech, Ralph, papers, S360
Leedale Colln (algal cytology), S32
Leeds Board of Guardians, records, A226
Leeds Coll of Art & Design Lib, S901
Leeds Coll of Bldg Lib, S902
Leeds Coll of Music Lib, S903
Leeds Coll of Tech Lib, S904
Leeds Diocesan Archvs (RC), A224
Leeds Friends Old Lib (Quakerism), S918
Leeds Genl Infirmary, Postgrad Medical Lib, S905
Leeds Grammar School, Lawson Lib, S906
Leeds Lib, S907
Leeds Lib & Info Svc, P72; *see also* A226
Leeds Liverpool Canal Co, records, A62
Leeds Local Edu Authority Archv, S918
Leeds Metropolitan Univ, Lib, S908; **School of Info Mgmt,** O250
Leeds Museum Resource Centre, S909; *see also* S900
Leeds Philosophical & Literary Soc Lib, S918
Leeds Public Assistance Cttee, records, A226
Leeds Russian Archv, S918
Leeds School Board, records, A226
Leeds Teaching Hosps NHS Trust, *see* S898, 899, 905, 914, 1662
Leeds Univ, *see Univ of Leeds*
Leeds, RC Diocese of, records, A224
Leek Coll of Further Edu, LRC, S920
Leesdale Colln, S1786
Leeson, Jack, Colln (photos of fairgrounds), A451

Lefevre, H.S., & Co records (merchant bankers), S1185
Lefroy, Lt Gen John, papers, S1130
Left Bk Club Colln, S1912
Left Pamph Colln (20C politics), S1912
legal systems, English, S1634; international, S1634
Legh Family of Lyme Hall papers, A364
Legh of Lyme family muniments, S1512
legislation, IS103, 107; S641, 2032; building, S125; education, S1929; environmental, S233; European, S130, 245, 1042; Ireland, S130; Isle of Man, S2181; Northern Ireland, S130; overseas territories, S1132; shipping, S1939; technical, S1042; UK, S130; US, S1432; *see also law*
Lehmann MSS (music), S25
Leicester City Libs, P73
Leicester Coll Lib, S926
Leicester Diplomatic Archv, S934
Leicester Frith Medical Lib, *see* S925
Leicester Genl Hosp Edu Centre Lib, S933
Leicester Medical Soc Colln, S934, 935
Leicester Multi-Faith Colln, S934
Leicester Museum & Art Gallery, S927
Leicester Univ, *see Univ of Leicester*
Leicester Univ Press Colln, S934
Leicester, Diocese of, records, A227
Leicester, Leicestershire & Rutland Health Promotion Agency Lib, S928
Leicestershire Archaeo & Historical Soc, Lib, S929
Leicestershire Libs & Info Svc, P74
Leicestershire, Leicester & Rutland Record Office, A227
Leigh Board of Guardians records, A228
Leigh Colln (French materials), L5
Leigh Municipal Borough Urban & Rural Districts, records, A228
Leigh Quarter & Petty Sessions records, A228
Leigh, Blanche, Colln (cookery), S918
Leigh, Lords, of Stoneleigh Abbey, family & estate papers, A476
Leighton Hosp, Joint Edu & Training Lib, S506
Leighton Lib, Dunblane, S553; *see also* S1978
Leighton, Archbishop Robert, Lib, S1978
Leighton, Kenneth, Archv (music), S597
Lein, Melanie, papers, S1457
Leinster School of Music Archvs, IS82
leisure & leisure studies, A526; IS46; S12, 22, 33, 65, 115, 208, 248, 273, 287, 419, 504, 515, 584, 609, 641, 654, 796, 805, 810, 834, 915, 1499, 1845, 1887, 1912, 2005, 2093, 2094, 2103; *see also recreation*
leisure policy, S584
Leitch Family of Kirkintilloch papers, A171
Leith Nautical Coll, records, A148
Leitrim Boards of Guardians, minutes, IA3
Leitrim County Libs, IP15; **Archv Collns,** IA3
Leitrim Genealogy Centre, IA4
Lemass, Sir Joseph, Colln (religious bks of plays), IA5
Lemoine, Serge, Colln (photos of royalty), S1170
Lempriére family papers (Channel Islands), A509
Leng Colln of Scottish Phil, S561
Lennox Estates archv, A171
Lenzie papers, A171
Leo Baeck Coll Centre for Jewish Edu Lib, S1238
Léon, Paul, Papers (James Joyce), IL1
Leonard, Hugh, papers, IL1
Leopold Muller Memorial Lib, S1701
lepidoptera, S2083
Les Cannon Memorial Lib, S1620
Lesbian & Gay Newsmedia Archv, S1282
Lesbian Archv & Info Centre, *see* S708
Leslie family & estate papers (Earls of Rothes), A373

Letchworth Garden City Heritage Foundation, see S937
lettering, S1105
Letterkenny Hosps, Edu Centre Lib, IS176; see also IS197
Letterkenny Inst of Tech Lib, IS177; see also IS174
Letterkenny Poor Law Union, minutes, IA67
Lever, Charles, Colln, IA48
Levy, John, Colln (ethnomusicological recordings), S598
Lewes Tertiary Coll, see S942
Lewis Colln (fine art), P17
Lewis Lib, see S1512
Lewis of St Pierre, family & estate records, A117
Lewis, John, Partnership Ltd, records, A470
Lewis, Sir Henry, papers, L3
Lewis, Sir John Herbert, Papers, L3
Lewis, Sir Thomas, papers, S1457
Lewisham Coll Learning Centre, S1239
Lewisham Deanery records, A297
Lewisham Hosp NHS Trust, S1438
Lewisham Lib Svc, P98
Lewisham Local Studies & Archvs, A297
Lewisham/Greenwich Board of Works, records, A297
Lews Castle Coll Lib, S1992
Leyton Borough records, A354
Liaison Papers (Irish War of Independence), IA45
Liberal Party Archvs, S1241; *Collns,* A77
Liberty & Co Archvs, A268; *Printed Catalogues Colln,* S1290
Liberty of Romney Marsh, records, A128
Libns' Christian Fellowship, O251
librarianship, S19, 969, 1066
libraries, S1108
Libs & Archvs Copyright Alliance, O252
Libs for Life for Londoners, O253
Libs for Nursing, O254
Libs North West, O255
Libs of Insts & Schools of Edu, O256
Libs Together: Liverpool Learning Partnership, O257
Lib + Info Show, O258
Lib & Info Svcs Council (Northern Ireland), O259
Lib & Info Statistics Unit, O260
library & information studies, IS37
Lib & Museum of Freemasonry, S1240
Lib & Museum of Modern Art, Oxford, see S1693
Lib Assoc of Ireland, IO26; **Academic & Special Libs Section,** IO27; **Asst Libns' Section,** IO28; **Audiovisual & Info Tech Section,** IO29; **Cataloguing & Indexing Group,** IO30; **County & City Libns' Section,** IO31; **Govt Libs Section,** IO32; **Health Scis Libs Section,** IO33; **Irish Lang Group (Meitheál Oibre na Leabharlainnthe),** O261; **Munster Regional Section,** IO34; **Rare Bks Group,** IO35; **Western Regional Section,** IO36; **Youth Libs Group,** IO37
Lib Bksellers Group of the Bksellers Assoc, O262
Lib Campaign, O263
Lib Council, IO1
Lib of Avalon, S743
Lib of Historic Advertising, S1282
Lib of Japanese Sci & Tech, S2113
Lib of Light-Orchestral Music, S1836
Lib of the Fellowship of St Alban & St Sergius, S1685
Lib of the House of St Gregory & St Macrina, S1686
Lib of the London School of Econ & Political Sci, S1241
Lib of the Natl Spiritual Assembly of the Bahá'ís of the Republic of Ireland, IS108
Lib of the Religious Soc of Friends, Britain Yearly Meeting, S1242
Lib of the Theosophical Soc in England, S1243
library science, S1066, 2113
Lib Svcs Trust, O264
Lichfield Cathedral Lib, S945
Lichfield City Council, see S947
Lichfield City Council archvs, A232
Lichfield Rural Dist Council archvs, A232
Lichfield, Diocese of, records, A232, 453, 467
Liddell Hart Centre for Military Archvs, A298
Liddell Hart Colln (fashion), S969
Liddell Hart, Capt Sir Basil, Colln (military hist), A298; S1227
Liddle Colln (WW1 papers), S918
Lieutenancy of London records, A270
life assurance, S599
Life File Photographic Lib, S1244
Life Guard, historical records, S2131
Life Insurance Co of Scotland Archvs, records, A157
Life of Christ Colln (Christology), P201
life science, S13, 78, 182, 221, 267, 427, 476, 593, 776, 1180, 1282, 1308, 1439, 1452, 1622, 1649, 2160; see also biology
lifeboats, S1819
lifestyles, S126, 983, 1174, 1338
Light Music Soc, see S1836
light railway systems, S1539
Lightfoot, Bishop J.B., Lib, S320; *papers,* S569
lighting, S1070
Lilburn Colln, P180
Lilleshall Co, records, S2033
Lilley & Skinner, records (shoe manufacturers & retailers), A250
Lilley, Lewis, Colln (music), S934
Lilly Industries Ltd, see S2128
Limavady Coll of Further & Higher Edu, Lib, S949
Lime Firms Ltd records (lime manufacturers), A514
Limerick Archvs, IA68
Limerick Art & Design Lib, see IS178
Limerick City Libs, IP16; **Local Studies Colln,** IA69
Limerick County Board of Public Health, records, IA68
Limerick County Libs, IP17; **Local Studies Colln,** IA70
Limerick Diocesan Pastoral Centre, IA71
Limerick Grand Jury Presentments, IA70
Limerick Harbour Commissioners, records, IA68
Limerick Inst of Tech Lib, IS178
Limerick Museum, Lib & Archvs, IS179
Limerick Poor Law Boards of Guardians, records, IA68
Limerick RC Diocesan Archvs, IA71
Limerick Regional Medical Lib, IS180
Limerick Univ, see Univ of Limerick
limnology, S32
Linacre Coll Lib, S1687
Linacre Lib, S408
Lincoln Cathedral Lib, S952
Lincoln Cathedral, Dean & Chapter records, A233
Lincoln Coll, Lib & Learning Resources Unit, S953
Lincoln Coll (Oxford) Lib, S1688
Lincoln County Hosp, Prof Lib, S954
Lincoln Univ, see Univ of Lincoln
Lincoln's Inn Archvs, S1245
Lincoln's Inn Lib, S1245
Lincoln, Diocese of, records, A233
Lincolnshire Archvs, A233; see also S951
Lincolnshire Knowledge & Resource Svc, S1897
Lincolnshire Libs, P75
Lincolnshire Record Soc Lib, S1798
Lincolnshire Windmill Archv, S955
Linder Bequest (Beatrix Potter), S1290
Lindholme HM Prison Lib, see P38
Lindley Lib, S1367
Lindley, John, Colln (horticulturalist), S1367
Lindsay, James Bowman, Colln, A136
Linen Hall Lib, S121
Linen Industry Rsrch Assoc, Lib & Archv, S960
Linfield Lib of Humour, S410
linguistics, IS109, 137; S322, 327, 482, 492, 776, 880, 1059, 1061, 1198, 1299, 1727, 1734, 1751; Asian, S1344; biblical, S1619; see also language
Linguistics Inst of Ireland Lib, IS109
Link Picture Lib, S1246
Linnaeus, Carolus, Colln (nat hist), S1308; *Lib & MSS,* S1247
Linnean Colln, S1862
Linnean Soc of London Lib, S1247
Linnell, John, Archv, S355
Linthorpe Art Pottery Colln, S1546
Lisbon Coll Colln & Archvs, S577
Lisburn Borough Council, see S960
Lismore Board of Guardians, records, IA54
Lismore Estate Papers, IL1
Lismore Rural Dist Council, minutes, IA54
Listening Bks, S1248
Lister Colln (antiseptic surgery), A177
Lister Hosp Lib, S1974
Lister Inst, archv, S1457
Lister of Shibden Hall, family & estate records, A194
Lister, Anne, travel journals, A194
Lister, Joseph, Colln, S1357; *correspondence,* S1352; *Papers,* S617, 724
Lister, Raymond, archv, S355
Liston, Sir Robert, papers, L2
Listowel Poor Law Union, minutes, IA92
Listowel Rural Dist Council, minutes, IA92
Literary & Philosophical Soc of Newcastle upon Tyne, Lib, S1575
literary theory, S322
literature, A17, 88, 205, 235, 289, 430, 466; IA87; IS7, 13, 15, 33, 35, 41, 44, 45, 46, 47, 56, 66, 82, 90, 93, 105, 112, 122, 143, 166, 172, 181, 183, 193, 198; S31, 34, 44, 67, 115, 116, 121, 131, 152, 156, 180, 198, 214, 238, 258, 260, 263, 264, 269, 296, 297, 322, 332, 336, 340, 373, 382, 383, 436, 442, 443, 456, 469, 478, 482, 509, 515, 540, 545, 565, 577, 677, 687, 698, 713, 741, 743, 771, 776, 788, 834, 853, 855, 859, 869, 877, 879, 880, 885, 904, 907, 950, 969, 995, 1015, 1018, 1059, 1064, 1081, 1082, 1106, 1113, 1115, 1116, 1123, 1127, 1136, 1148, 1160, 1161, 1169, 1182, 1227, 1230, 1243, 1260, 1262, 1274, 1282, 1333, 1362, 1373, 1421, 1465, 1505, 1527, 1552, 1565, 1572, 1575, 1599, 1630, 1637, 1652, 1654, 1659, 1663, 1672, 1677, 1678, 1727, 1760, 1767, 1778, 1789, 1802, 1806, 1807, 1811, 1823, 1848, 1886, 1887, 1889, 1907, 1912, 1923, 1942, 1944, 1978, 1979, 1983, 2004, 2025, 2029, 2036, 2042, 2046, 2049, 2064, 2067, 2068, 2093, 2095, 2120, 2122, 2125, 2145, 2147, 2167, 2168, 2174, 2179; African, S1751; Albanian, S1436; American, S322, 1804; ancient, S325; Arabic, S989, 1512, 1737; Asian, S1290, 1344; Austrian, S1006; Belarussian, S1135, 1436; Bulgarian, S1436; Canadian, S1053, 1751; Catholic, S1057; Celtic, S738, 1751, 1926; children's, A314; IS48, 49; S20, 144, 179, 326, 405, 410, 413, 457, 528, 609, 936, 950, 968, 972, 1373, 1393, 1451, 1472, 1519, 1597, 1611, 1616, 1655, 1789, 1848, 1899, 1949, 1979, 2019, 2175; Christian, S1125; classical, S963, 1136, 1747; Continental, S327; continental, S1751; Counter-Reformation, S2125; crime, S1634; Czech, S1436; early, S1234; East European, S1436; Elizabethan, S2049; English, IS89; S271, 322, 433, 523, 838, 968, 1440, 1726, 1761, 1804, 1949, 1978, 1996, 1997, 2130, 2174; Estonian, S1436; European, S523, 1290, 1751; fantasy, S973; Finnish, S1120, 1436; foreign, S963; French, IS110; S716, 968, 1637, 1690, 1978, 2130; Gaelic, S1926; German, IS80; S498, 709, 1147, 1445, 1751; Greek, S433, 553, 746, 1751; Hebrew, S553, 1701; Hungarian, S1436; Icelandic, S1726; Indian, L4; S1014, 1184; international, S322; Irish, IA94; IS9, 34, 89, 102, 123, 159, 173, 185, 188; S1217; Italian, S1216, 2130; Japanese, S576, 1220, 1851, 1978; Jewish, S1238, 1266, 1517; Latin, S433, 746; Latin American, S1210, 1751; Latvian, S1436; Lithuanian, S1436; medieval, S523; modern, S1751; modern Greek, S1751; Moldavian, S1436; Norse, S1726; oriental, S328, 738; Persian, S1512; Polish, S1328, 1436; Puritan, S600; Quaker, S961; Reformation, S2125; Reformed, S600; religious, S320, 1057; Romanian, S1436; Russian, S1436, 1746; science fiction, S973; Scottish, S63, 876, 1926, 1978; Slavonic, S1436; Slovakian, S1436; South East Asian, L4; Soviet, S1746; Spanish, IS92; S1210, 1978; Swiss, S1445; Turkish, S1429; Ukrainian, S1436; Victorian, S410, 413, 771, 1527; Welsh, S17, 20, 82; Western European, S1727; Yiddish, S1751; Yugoslav, S1436; see also drama; poetry
Lithgow, Sir James, papers (entrepreneur), A176
Lithgows of Port Glasgow, records (shipbldg), A176
Lithuania, S1436
Litill, Clement, Bequest (theology), S593
Little Bequest (illustrated ch bks), S1290
Little Magazines Colln, S1433
Little, Bryan, Papers, A77
Littlehampton Museum Local Studies Room, A236
liturgy, A450; IS188; S101, 320, 546, 577, 596, 966, 1057, 1412, 1752, 1798; Eastern, S1038; Jewish, S1238, 1266; Western, S1038
Liverpool Academy archvs, A241
Liverpool & Dist Scientific Industrial & Rsrch Lib Advisory Council, O265
Liverpool Cathedral, Radcliffe Lib, S966
Liverpool Chamber of Commerce & Industry, Business Info Svc, S967
Liverpool Church House Lib, S966
Liverpool Hope Univ Coll, S968; **Sheppard-Worlock Lib,** S968
Liverpool John Moores Univ, Centre for Info & Lib Mgmt, O266; **Learning & Info Svcs,** S969
Liverpool Libs & Info Svcs, P76
Liverpool Medical Instn Lib, S970
Liverpool Nautical Rsrch Soc records, A239
Liverpool RC Archdiocesan Archv, A237
Liverpool Record Office & Local Studies Dept, A238; see also A240
Liverpool Registers of Merchant Ships, A239
Liverpool School of Tropical Medicine, Donald Mason Lib, S971; see also S972
Liverpool Univ Lib, S972; **Sydney Jones Lib, Sci Fiction Foundation Colln,** S973; see also S462, 965
Liverpool, Bank of, records, A363
Liverpool, Diocese of, parish records, A228
Livesey Colln (temperance), S1840
livestock, S857, 1601, 1850, 2139, 2160
Livingston Development Corp Archvs, A242
Livingstone, David, Colln, S196; *MSS,* A334; *papers,* L2
Llandaff Cathedral Lib (theology), L3
Llandaff, Diocese of, parish records, A97
Llandinam Archv (Welsh industry), L3
Llandough Hosp NHS Trust, Cochrane Lib, S1785
Llandrillo Coll Lib, S485
Llanelli Port records, A99

Lloyd Dunn Colln (Cornish shipwrecks), S2056
Lloyd Estate Papers, IA55
Lloyd George Museum, Ref Lib, S508
Lloyd George, David, Colln, S410; *papers*, A286; L3; S508
Lloyd's Business Intelligence Centre, S1249
Lloyd's Marine Colln, P99
Lloyd's Register of Shipping, A299
Lloyd, A.L., Colln (ethnomusicology), S1148
Lloyd-Baker of Hardwicke Court, family & estate records, A185
Lloyd-Roberts Colln (hist of medicine), S427
Lloyds of London records, A280
Lloyds TSB Group Archvs, A300
Llyfrgell Amgueddfa Werin Cymru, S419
Llyfrgell Genedlaethol Cymru, L3
Llysfasi Coll of Agric Lib, S1882
Lobitos Oilfields Ltd, records, A482
local area networks, S301
Local Authorities Archivists Group, see IO42
Local Authorities Rsrch & Intelligence Assoc, see O7
Local Enterprise Development Unit, see S129
Local Govt Assoc, Lib & Info Centre, S1250
local history & local studies, Aberdeen, S2, 4; Alderney, S2183; Aldershot, A9; Anglesey, A246; Antrim, A23; Argyll, S980; Argyll & Bute, A140; Armagh, A15, 17; S42, 502; Avon, S450, 454; Ayrshire, A21; Barking & Dagenham, A118; Barnet, A255; Barnsley, A26; Bath, S98, 99, 102; Bedfordshire, A398; Belfast, A36, 37; S131; Berkshire, A429, 510; S1571, 1850; Bexhill, S151; Bexley, A47; Birmingham, S156, 163, 179; Blackburn with Darwen, A54; S189; Boston, S203; Bournemouth, A59; Bradford, S211, 214; Braintree, S220; Brent, A258; Bridgend, A66; Brighton, A67, 68; Brighton & Hove, A71; Bristol, S244, 246, 247, 250, 251, 264, 450; Bromley, S1659; Buckinghamshire, A19, 381; S56, 1652; Burnley, S275; Caithness, A489; Calderdale, A194; Cambridgeshire, A87, 398, 512; S297, 299, 358, 361, 385, 1798, 1799, 1800, 1967; Camden, A262; Canterbury, S404, 406; Carlow, IA9; Carmarthenshire, A439; Cavan, IA13, 14; IS4; Channel Islands, S2184, 2186, 2187; Channels Islands, S2183; Cheltenham, S451; Cheshire, A8, 238, 371, 439; S456, 1496, 1497, 1513, 1572; Chester, A456; Clare, IA55; Clerkenwell, S1287; Cleveland, S1544; Conwy, A244; Cork, IA20; IS20, 193; Cornwall, A414, 430, 463, 465; S663, 677, 1789, 1811, 1965, 2029, 2056; Cotswolds, S454; Croydon, A115; S1933; Cumbria, A28, 507; S31, 33, 433, 436, 854, 858, 859, 886, 1839; Darlington, A119; Derbyshire, A122, 374; S283, 528, 1647; Devon, A164, 218, 420, 492; S88, 663, 665, 669, 1804, 1806, 1811, 1954, 2029, 2042, 2047, 2049; Doncaster, S541; Donegal, IA8, 65; IS175, 177; Dorset, A422, 510; S545, 1915; Dublin, IA31, 33, 35; IS102, 127; Dudley, A130; Dumfries & Galloway, A134, 475; S552, 876; Dún Laoghaire-Rathdown, IA51; Dundee, A136; Dungarvan, IA53; Durham, A119, 389; S108, 186, 569, 1575, 1588; Ealing, A274; East Anglia, S578, 1621, 1631; East Dunbartonshire, A171; East Lothian, A193; East Midlands, S528, 1647; East Renfrewshire, A172; Eastleigh, A460; Edinburgh, A145; S588, S650; Egham, S650; Enfield, A302; England, S1398; Essex, A398, 443; S220, 471, 479; Exeter, S663, 665; Falkirk, A165; Farnborough, A9; Fenlands, A512; S361; Fife, A220, 373;

S516; Fingal, IA33; Forest of Dean, S483; Galway, IA59; Glasgow, A173, 174; S713, 724, 738; Glastonbury, S743; Gloucestershire, A108, 184; S247, 450, 451, 454, 483; Greenwich, A278; S1303; Guernsey, S2184, 2186, 2187; Hadlow, S2045; Halton, A439; Hammersmith & Fulham, A282; Hampshire, A12, 14, 29, 30, 107, 143, 166, 167, 187, 198, 460, 508, 510; S30, 680, 1946, 1954, 2122, 2126; Haringey, A283; Harlow, A195; Harrow, A196; S788; Hastings, A197; Havant, A198; Havering, A437; Herefordshire, A202; S2141; Hertfordshire, A204, 398; S813, 937, 1958, 1963, 1976; Highlands, A489; S840, 2023, 2041; Hillingdon, A495; Horsham, S819; Hounslow, A206; S851; Huddersfield, S823, 824; Humberside, A447; Huntingdonshire, S1967; Inverclyde, A190; Ireland, A17; IA25, 35, 79; IS34, 45, 84, 95, 112, 137, 143, 149; S138, 139; Isle of Man, A529; S2177, 2179; Isle of Wight, A392, 510; S500, 1599, 1946; Islington, A295; S1287; Kensington & Chelsea, A330; Kent, A71, 362, 372, 427; S48, 404, 406, 410, 1234, 1502, 1659, 1866, 1903, 1954, 2045, 2059; Kenwood, S1217; Kerry, IA92; IS173; Keswick, S858; Kildare, IA82; IS183; Kilkenny, IA61; Kingston upon Thames, A219; Kirkcaldy, A220; Kirklees, S823; Knowsley, A222; Lagan Valley, S960; Lake District, S854, 858, 859; Lambeth, A296; Lanarkshire, S152; Lancashire, A238, 366, 371; S189, 191, 275, 883, 886, 1513, 1837, 1838, 1839, 1840; Laois, IA83; Leeds, A225; S907, 909, 916; Leicestershire, A18; S477, 924, 927, 929, 1482, 1483, 1647; Leitrim, IS198; Letchworth, S937; Lewisham, A297; Lichfield, S947; Limerick, IA68, 69, 70, 71; IS179, 181, 193; Lincolnshire, A447; S203, 950, 951, 955, 956, 1487, 1647, 1900, 1901; Lisburn, S960; Liverpool, A238; S202, 963; London, A273, 300, 301, 317; S1016, 1081, 1082, 1114, 1130, 1141, 1161, 1217, 1266, 1267, 1285, 1288, 1346, 1362, 1405, 1440, 1468; London, City of, S1016; Londonderry, A23; S1476, 1478; Longford, IA73; Loughborough, S1482; Luton, S1491; Macclesfield, S1496, 1497; Manchester, A366, 367, 368, 371; S1507, 1511, 1517, 1518, 1519; Mayo, IA11; Meath, IA80, 93; Medway, A71, 435; S444, 1954; Merseyside, S963; Merthyr Tydfil, S1542; Merton, A385; Middlesbrough, S1546; Middlesex, S851; Midlands, A403; S156; Midlothian, A247; Milton Keynes, A381; Monaghan, IS185; Monmouth, A383; Moray, A158; S687; Mull, S2044; Nairn, S687; Neath Port Talbot, S1565; Newbury, S1571; Newcastle upon Tyne, S1577, 1584; Newham, A303; Newmarket, S1593; Norfolk, A398, 401, 512; S358, 578, 866, 1621, 1631, 2009; North East England, S883; North Lanarkshire, A116; North Lincolnshire, A447; North West England, S883; Northamptonshire, S1611, 1617; Northern Ireland, A15, 37, 43, 205; S119, 133, 146, 815, 960; Northumberland, A44, 389; S1575, 1582, 1588; Nottinghamshire, A407; S1637, 1638, 1645, 1647; Offaly, IA94; IS6, 208; Oldham, A408; Olney, S1652; Oxfordshire, A410; S1705, 1706, 1714, 1770; Paisley, S1782; Peak District, S283; Pembrokeshire, S2036; Perth & Kinross, S872, 1792; Peterborough, A417; S1798, 1799, 1800; Plymouth, A420; Poole, A422; Powys, A63; S1833; Radnorshire, S1833; Ramsgate, A427; Redbridge, A212; Renfrewshire, A413; Richmond upon Thames, A433; Rochester, S1866; Roscommon, IA2, 84; Ross-shire, S688; Rutland, S1647; Saffron Walden, A442, 443; Salford, A444;

Salisbury, S1890, 1892; Scotland, A1, 3, 21, 156, 173; S10, 194, 713, 724, 732, 741, 1604; Scottish Borders, A448; Sefton, A462; S202; Sevenoaks, S1903; Sheffield, S1905; Shrewsbury, A49; Shropshire, S1572, 1919, 1920, 2033, 2141; Sligo, IA87; IS198; Solihull, A455; Somerset, A168, 487, 488; S98, 101, 225, 247, 743, 2025, 2097; South Dublin, IA48; South Gloucestershire, A521; South Tyneside, A457; S1935; South West England, S1804, 1806; Southampton, A459; S1943; Southwark, A347; St Albans, S1958, 1963; St Helens, A464; St Ives, A465; Staffordshire, A468, 473, 485; S945, 947, 1572, 1990, 2077, 2141; Stevenage, S1976; Stoke-on-Trent, A473; S1990; Stratford-upon-Avon, A476; Sudbury, S2001; Suffolk, A398; S358, 2001; Surrey, A71, 505; S650, 775, 1215, 1234; Sussex, A67, 71, 197, 236; S470, 819, 941, 942, 1234; Sutton, A478; Swaffham, S2009; Swansea, A479, 480; Swindon, S2019; Tamworth, A485; Tavistock, S2029; Tayside, A136; Teesdale, S206; Thirsk, S2039; Thurrock, A188; Tipperary, IA16, 90; IS6, 13; Tiverton, S2042; Torbay, A491; S2049; Torquay, S2047; Totnes, A492; Tower Hamlets, A350; Trafford, A13; Tunbridge Wells, S2059; Wales, A25; S17, 74, 82; Walsall, A498; S2079; Waltham Forest, A354; Wandsworth, A355; Warrington, A501; Warwickshire, A503; S1996, 2091; Waterford, IA53; IS209; Wells, S2097; Wessex, S1915; West Country, S743; West Dunbartonshire, A110; West Lothian, A56; West Midlands, A129; S171, 2141; Westcountry, A164; Western Isles, A474; S1992; Westmeath, IA78; Westminster, A268; S1459; Wexford, IA1; IS6; Wicklow, IA7; Wigan, S2115; Wigtownshire, A475; Wiltshire, A510; S530, 1890, 1892, 2019; Wimbledon, S1468; Winchester Hampshire, S2126; Windsor, S2132; Wirral, S963; Woolwich, S1130; Worcestershire, S2141, 2144, 2150; York, S1905, 2169, 2170, 2172; Yorkshire, A34, 194; S211, 214, 541, 907, 909, 916, 917, 919, 1544, 2039, 2169, 2170, 2172
Lochmaben Hosp, records, A132
Lock, Max, Archv (architect), S1452
Lockerbie Air Disaster Archv, P41
Lockey, Francis, Colln (early calotypes), S98
Lockhart, J.G., MSS, L2
Lockton Liturgy Bequest, S2120
Lockwood, Sir John, papers, S1015
Locomotive Manufactures Assoc, records, S2165
Lodge's MSS, IA25
Loeb Classical Lib, P49
Logan Colln (medicine), IS134
Logan, Jimmy, Colln (theatre), A182
logic, L4
logistics, S113, 118, 491, 1925
London Aerial Photo Lib, S1625
London & Lancashire Insurance Co Ltd, records, A327
London & Middlesex Archaeo Soc Lib, A301; S1288
London Archaeo Archv & Rsrch Centre, A301; see also S1267
London Arts, see S1272
London Assay Office, records, S1149
London Bible Coll Lib, S1619
London Borough of Barking & Dagenham, see A118; P77
London Borough of Barnet, see A255; P78
London Borough of Bexley, see A47; P79
London Borough of Brent, see A258; P80
London Borough of Bromley, see A79; P81
London Borough of Camden, see A262; P82
London Borough of Croydon, see A115; P83, 107

London Borough of Ealing, see A274; P84
London Borough of Enfield, Archvs & Local Hist Unit, A302; see also P85
London Borough of Greenwich, see A278; P86
London Borough of Hackney, see A281; P87
London Borough of Hammersmith & Fulham, see A282; P88
London Borough of Haringey, see A283; P89
London Borough of Harrow, see A196; P90
London Borough of Havering, see A437; P91
London Borough of Hillingdon, see A495; P92
London Borough of Hounslow, see A206; P93
London Borough of Islington, see A295; P94; S1429
London Borough of Lambeth, see A296; P97, 107
London Borough of Lewisham, see A297; P98
London Borough of Merton, see A385; P100
London Borough of Newham, Local Hist & Archaeo Resource Centre, A303; see also A315; P101
London Borough of Redbridge, see A212; P102
London Borough of Richmond upon Thames, Lib & Info Svcs, P103; see also A433
London Borough of Southwark, see A347; P104
London Borough of Sutton, Lib Svcs, P105; see also A478
London Borough of Tower Hamlets, see A350; P106
London Borough of Waltham Forest, see A354; P108; S1464
London Borough of Wandsworth, see A355; P109
London Business School Lib, S1251
London Canal Museum Lib, S1252
London Chamber Business Info Centre, S1253
London Chamber of Commerce records, A280
London Chest Hosp records, A336
London Coll of Fashion Lib, S1254
London Coll of Printing, Lib & Learning Resources, S1255
London Corp Libs, see P99
London Directorate of Health & Social Care, Lib Info Centre, S1256
London Docklands Development Corp, records, S1114
London Excavation Council records, A301
London Film Productions, records, A320
London Film School Lib, S1257
London Fire Brigade Lib, S1258
London Foot Hosp & School of Podiatric Medicine Lib, S1259
London Guildhall Univ, see London Metropolitan Univ; Fawcett Lib, see S1469
London Hist Teachers Assoc, archvs, S1444
London Hosp "Old Londoner" Colln, A336
London Hosp Medical Coll Lib, see A336
London Inst, see S1050, 1060, 1075, 1254, 1255
London Internatl Film School, see S1257
London Libs Development Agency, O267; see also O271
London Lib, S1260
London Lock Hosp, archvs, S1357
London Mathematical Soc Lib, S1433
London Mechanics' Inst, records, S1015
London Metropolitan Archvs, A304; see also S1225
London Metropolitan Univ, City Campus Lib Svcs, S1261; **Dept of**

Applied Social Sci, O268; **North Campus Lib Svcs, S**1262; *see also* **S**1469
London Museums Agency, *see* **O**271
London Nat Hist Soc Lib, S1263
London Oratory Lib, S1264
London Port records, **A**226; **S**1114
London Record Soc, O269
London Regional Archv Council, O270; *see also* **O**271
London School of Econ & Political Sci, *see* **S**1241
London School of Hygiene & Tropical Medicine Lib, S1265
London School of Jewish Studies Lib, S1266
London School of Medicine for Women, records, **A**332
London Soc Lib, S1267
London Stereoscopic Colln (photos), **S**1170
London Stock Exchange records, **A**280
London Topographical Record, **S**1267
London Univ, *see* **Univ of London**
London Weekend Television, film & video archv, **A**277
London Zoo, records, **S**1474
London's Museums, Archvs & Libs, O271
London's Transport Museum, Ref Lib, S1268
London, City of, Lunatic Asylum/ Mental Hosp, records, **A**270
London, Corp of, *see* **Corp of London**
London, Corp of, River Cttee, minutes, **S**1114
London, Diocese of, records, **A**280, 304
London, Heinz, papers, **A**77
Londonderry family papers, **A**141
Londonderry Grand Jury Presentments, **A**23
Long Classics Colln, **P**17
Long family & estate papers, **A**215, 493
Long, B.K. , papers, **A**316
Longford Borough, papers, **IA**12
Longford County Lib & Arts Svc, IP18; **Local Studies & Archvs, IA**73
Longford Grand Jury Presentments, **IA**73
Longford Historical Soc, IO38
Longford Militia records, **IA**73
Longford Poor Law Union, minutes, **IA**73
Longford, Earls of, papers, **IA**12
Longleat House, Lib & Archvs, S2086
Longsdon of Longstone, family archv, **A**375
Lónyay, Menyhért, Colln (Hungarian politics), **S**1436
Lopes of Maristow estate archv, **A**419
Lord Barnby Foundation Lib, S1533
Lord Chancellor's Dept, HQ Lib, S1269; *see also* **A**432; **S**1236
Lord Coutanche Lib, S2190
Lord Gt Chamberlain, records, **A**286
Lord Warden of the Cinque Ports records, **A**128
Losey, Joseph, Colln (cinema), **S**1013
Lothian Coal Co, records, **S**1604
Lothian Health Svcs Archv, A149
Lothian NHS Board Lib & Resource Centre, S607
Lothian Regional Council, minutes, **A**56
Lotus Shoes, records, **A**467
Lough Fea Pamphs (17C), **IL**1
Loughborough Coll of Art & Design, records, **S**1483
Loughborough Coll of Edu, records, **S**1483
Loughborough Coll of Tech, records, **S**1483
Loughborough Coll, records, **S**1483
Loughborough Grammar School Lib, S1482
Loughborough Univ, Dept of Info Sci, O272; **Pilkington Lib, S**1483
Loughry Coll Lib, S488
Louth Archaeo & Historical Soc, IO10
Louth County Hosp (Ireland), Medical Lib, IS162
Louth County Hosp (Lincolnshire), Medical Lib, S1486
Louth County Libs, IP19

Louth Estate Papers, **IL**1
Louth Local Authorities Archvs Svc, IA52
Louth Museum (Lincolnshire), Lib, S1487
Louth Naturalists', Antiquarian & Literary Soc, *see* **S**1487
Lovat Scouts, records, **A**214
Lovaton Lib, *see* **S**338
Lovell Reeve, records (publishers), **S**1862
Lovell, Bernard, archv (hist of astronomy), **S**1512
Lovelock, William, MSS (music), **S**1428
Low Colln (theology), **S**1964
Low, David, Colln (cartoons), **A**91
Lowestoft Coll Lib, S1489
Lowestoft Local Studies Lib, *see* **A**361
Lowestoft, Port of, shipping records, **A**361
Lowrie, WP, & Co Ltd, records (whisky distillers), **A**376
Loyal Order of Ancient Shepherds records, **A**10
Loyal Regiment (North Lancashire), records, **A**426
Loyd Colln (alpine & mountaineering), **L**2
Lubavitch Lending Lib, S1270
Lucas & Pyke eng drawings, **A**294
Lucas of Wrest Park archvs, **A**35
Lucas, John, Literary Colln, **S**1483
Luckes, Eva, papers, **A**336
Lucknow Sparks Lib (Hindi, Urdu, Persian), **L**4
Lucy Cavendish Coll Lib, S371
Luke Wadding Lib, IS209
Lukis MS Colln (Guernsey archaeo), **S**2186
Lumsden of Arden, records (stationers), **A**176
Lumsden, James, Colln, **S**863
Luther King House Lib, S1526
Lutheranism, **S**400
Lutolawski MSS (music), **S**25
Luton & Dunstable Hosp Lib, S1490
Luton Libs, P111; *see also* **A**35
Luton Museum & Art Gallery, Ref Lib, S1491
Luton Univ, *see* **Univ of Luton**
Lydd Borough records, **A**128
Lyle, Keith, Colln (ophthalmology), **S**1849
Lynedock papers, **L**2
Lynn Marshland, Deanery of, records, **A**512
Lynn Univ, *see* **IS**35
Lyttleton, Gen Sir Neville, papers, **S**1333
Lytton family papers, **S**877
Lytton, 1st Lord, Colln, **S**877
Lytton, Earl, of Knebworth, family & estate archv, **A**204

M25 Consortium of Academic Libs, O273
Macadam Colln (baking & confectionary), **L**2
Macaulay Colln, **S**393
Macaulay Land Use Rsrch Inst Lib, S9
Macaulay, T.B., Photo Colln, **P**199
MacBean Jacobite Colln, **A**3; **S**5
MacBride, Tiernan, Colln (film), **IA**37; **IS**74
Macclesfield Coll, LRC, S1496
Macclesfield Museums, Lib & Archvs, S1497
Maccoll, Ewan, Archv, **S**1761
MacCormick Colln (Highlands), **S**1926
MacCurdy Psychopathology Lib (clinical psy), **S**308
MacDairmid, Hugh, MSS, **L**2
MacDonagh, Thomas, papers, **IL**1
MacDonald Lib, S2057
MacDonald, Donald, Tolsta Papers, **P**199
MacDonald, George, Colln (Huntley), **P**2
Macdouall Colln (lit, Sanskrit, philology), **S**139
MacEwan Colln (aseptic surgery), **A**177

Macewan, William, Papers (surgery), **S**724
Macfadyen, W.A., Colln (geol), **S**307
Macfie, Scott, Gypsy Colln, **S**972
MacGill, Patrick (Donegal author), Colln, **IA**65; *papers,* **IA**67
MacGillivray Colln (Scottish lit & hist), **S**1964
Machen, Arthur, Colln, **P**122
machine tools, **S**1208
machinery, **S**2045
MacIntosh, John, Colln (arch plans), **A**20
MacIntyre, Tom, papers, **IL**1
Mackay, Aeneas J.G., Bequest (Scots hist, lit, law), **S**593; *Colln,* **P**52
Mackay, George, Papers (surgery), **S**617
Mackenzie Colln, **S**1964
MacKenzie Colln (civil eng), **S**1205
Mackenzie Medical Centre Lib, S274
Mackenzie, Dr William, Lib (ophthalmology), **S**724
MacKenzie, Sir Compton, Colln, **S**1414
MacKenzie, Sir James, papers, **S**1355
Mackenzie, William Lyon, Canadiana Colln, **S**561
Mackinnon, Donald, Colln (Celtic studies, theology), **S**593
MacKintosh Colln (17C), **P**144
Mackmurdo, Arthur H., papers, **S**1464
MacLean, Alex, Colln (salon music), **P**130
MacLeod Colln (Scottish theatrical hist), **S**1978
Macleod, Alan, papers, **S**360
MacManus, Seamus, Colln (Donegal author), **IA**65
Macmillan, Harold, papers, **L**4
MacNeill, Eoin, Papers, **IA**49
Maconchy, Elizabeth, music MSS, **S**25, 1768
MacPherson Colln of Atlases, **S**1303
macroeconomics, **S**1319
Madame Tussaud's London, Archvs, A305
Madden Colln (broadside ballads), **L**5
Maddison, R.E.W., Colln & Papers (hist of sci & tech), **S**410
Madge, Charles, papers, **S**239
Madgwick Colln of Railway Photos, **A**67
Madingley Hall Archv, **S**332
MAFF Rsrch Station, Conwy, records, **A**244
Magan Colln (photography), **IS**208
Magdalen Coll (Oxford) Lib, S1689
Magdalen Hall Lib, **S**1678
Magdalene Coll (Cambridge), Lib, S372; **Pepys Lib, S**373
Magee Colln (Irish hist, lit & edu), **S**144
Magnum Photos Ltd, Photo Agency & Archv, S1271
Maher, Tom, Colln (film), **IA**37
Mahon Estate Archv, **IL**1; **IS**199
Maidstone & Tunbridge Wells NHS Trust, Maidstone Hosp Lib, S1504; **Pembury Hosp Lib, S**2058
Maidstone, Archdeaconry of, parish records, **A**362
Maindiff Court Hosp Lib, *see* **S**1595
Maison Française D'Oxford Lib, S1690
Maisoneuve Colln (French civilisation & culture), **S**345
Maitland Colln (early aeronautics), **S**1342
Maitland Robinson Lib, S351
Majut Colln (German), **S**934
MAKE Resource, S1272
make-up, stage, **S**1340
Malacological Soc Lib, **S**1433
Malaysia, **S**1449
Malaysian Rubber Rsrch & Development Board, *see* **S**808
Malcolm of Poltalloch Papers, **A**248
Malcolm, Gen Sir Neill, papers, **S**1764
Malden Borough records, **A**219
Maley & Taunton, technical drawings, **S**1539
Mallock of Cockington, estate archv, **A**161
Mallow Genl Hosp Lib, *see* **IS**206

Mallow Heritage Centre, IA75
Malmesbury, Earl of, papers, **A**509
Malone Colln (16C-17C lit), **L**4
mammalogy, **S**1576
management, **IS**8, 57, 73, 87, 97, 125, 129, 161, 174, 178, 200; **S**1, 12, 19, 28, 33, 42, 113, 114, 124, 149, 150, 154, 204, 208, 224, 241, 259, 271, 367, 437, 469, 476, 478, 489, 491, 515, 554, 572, 584, 609, 628, 629, 701, 737, 745, 752, 757, 776, 780, 787, 800, 810, 816, 835, 839, 841, 844, 857, 865, 889, 892, 944, 954, 968, 969, 995, 1112, 1121, 1176, 1180, 1193, 1194, 1206, 1214, 1227, 1250, 1251, 1253, 1254, 1255, 1258, 1261, 1282, 1284, 1318, 1420, 1452, 1500, 1515, 1536, 1583, 1597, 1617, 1700, 1748, 1758, 1772, 1800, 1816, 1824, 1845, 1851, 1877, 1912, 1925, 1927, 1940, 1949, 1966, 1978, 1993, 2004, 2010, 2079, 2094, 2095, 2103, 2134, 2160; aquatic resources, **S**1822; arts, **S**997, 1085; business, **S**796, 917; charity, **S**1063; coastal zone, **S**1822; collections, **S**1066; conservation, **S**543; construction, **S**45; countryside, **S**19, 263, 273, 348, 1971, 2045; defence, **S**2021; drainage, **IS**123; educational, **S**1430; environmental, **S**1071, 1098, 1822, 1857; estate, **S**1452, 1603; executive, **S**676; farm, **S**2107; fashion, **S**1254; fisheries, **S**32, 543, 638, 2045; health, **IS**16, 210; **S**12, 140, 455, 463, 480, 562, 568, 629, 785, 790, 837, 975, 1111, 1158, 1229, 1504, 1560, 1595, 1613, 1731, 2069; health & safety, **S**796; health care, **S**50, 109, 257, 734, 897, 1051, 1553, 1825, 1826; health service, **S**87, 178, 475, 549, 662, 763, 774, 781, 811, 829, 843, 862, 1835, 1921, 1922, 2014; hospital, **S**1968; hospitality, **S**12, 915, 1603, 2079; hotel, **S**22, 504, 1557, 1816, 1824, 1969, 2005; housing, **S**1370; human resource, **IS**116; **S**1772; industrial heritage, **S**1857; information, **S**614, 1066, 1772; land, **S**476; landscape, **S**2045; leisure, **S**33, 609, 654, 1837, 1912; mineral resource, **S**1857; natural resource, **S**114, 1439; personnel, **S**676, 982, 1069; project, **S**1370; property, **IS**123; **S**1370; quality, **S**491; recreation, **S**1406; retail, **S**1772; rural, **S**1603; rural resource, **S**1319; site, **S**45; supply, **IS**96; supply chain, **S**118, 491; turf, **S**226; wildlife, **S**74; woodland, **S**268, 2107; *see also* administration
Manchester & Lancashire Family Hist Soc, Lib & Study Room, A366
Manchester & Stockport Methodist Dist, records, **A**367
Manchester Archvs & Local Studies, A367; *see also* **A**364
Manchester Business School, Lib & Info Svc, S1514
Manchester Chamber of Commerce, records, **A**367
Manchester Christian Inst, *see* **S**1526
Manchester Coll of Art & Polytechnic, records, **S**1519
Manchester Coll of Arts & Tech, City Centre Campus Lib, S1515
Manchester Diocesan Archvs, **A**367
Manchester European Wind Lib (scores), **S**1528
Manchester Evening News Lib, S1516
Manchester Geographical Soc Colln, **S**1512
Manchester Jewish Museum, S1517
Manchester Legal Info Group, O274
Manchester Lib & Info Svc, P112
Manchester Literary & Philosophical Soc, Lib & Archvs, S1518
Manchester Medical Soc Colln, **S**1512
Manchester Metropolitan Univ, Dept of Info & Communications, O275; **Lib, S**1519; *see also* **A**371
Manchester Museum Colln, **S**1512
Manchester Oil Refinery (Holdings) Ltd, records, **A**482
Manchester Regiment records, **A**469
Manchester Royal Infirmary, Jefferson Lib, S1520

Manchester School of Physiotherapy Lib, S1521
Manchester Ship Canal Co records, A364
Manchester Soc of Architects, archvs, S1512; Colln, S1519
Manchester Studies Unit Oral Hist Colln, A469
Manchester Univ, see John Rylands Univ Lib of Manchester; Univ of Manchester
Manchester, Earls & Dukes of, family & estate records, A211
Mander & Mitchenson Theatre Colln, S1428
Mann Music Lib, S369
Mann, I., Colln (drawings & photos), S1201
Mann, Tom, Colln, P31
Manning, Thomas H., Polar Archvs, S339
Manor Hosp Postgrad Medical Centre Lib, S2075
Manor of Prescot, family & estate papers, A425
Manorial Soc of Gt Britain, O276
Mansfield Coll Lib, S1691
Mansfield Estate Papers, IL1
Mansion House Fund for Relief of Distress in Ireland, records, IA30
Manson, Sir Patrick, Colln & Papers (tropical medicine), S1265
Manson, T.W., papers (nonconformity), S1512
manufacturing, S113, 419, 491, 1208, 1378, 1479, 1887, 2103
Manx Colln, P210, 211, 212
Manx Dyslexia Assoc Colln, P211
Manx Natl Heritage Lib, A529
Mapperley Hosp Historical Archv, S1642
Marconi & GEC Archvs, A102
Marconi, records, A102, 414
Mardon, Heber, Colln (Napoleonic prints), A164
Mare, C.J., & Co records (shipbuilders), S1185
Margaret Beaufort Inst of Theology, Lib, S374
Margate Borough records, A128
Margate Local Studies Lib, A372
Margoliouth Lib (Arabic), L4
Maria Henderson Lib, S711
Maria Mercer Physics Lib, see S260
Marie Curie Centre – Warren Pearl, Lib, S1930
Mariko Mori Archv (art), S1075
Marine & Coastwatching Svc, records (Ireland), IA45
Marine Biological Assoc, see S1805
Marine Pollution Info Centre, see S1805
marine science, S83, 1649, 1832, 1944, 1945
Marine Soc, Seafarers Libs, S1273
Marino Inst of Edu Lib, see IS50
Marion Campbell Lib, S980
Marischal Colln (maps of Scotland), L2
Marischal Coll, archvs, A3
Marischal Museum, Lib & Archv, S10
Maritime & Coastguard Agency, Marine Info Centre, S1939
Maritime Info Assoc, O277
Maritime Inst of Ireland Museum & Lib, IS160
maritime studies, S2, 4, 88, 94, 685, 704, 969, 1439, 1489; see also history, maritime
market research, IS158; S997, 1202, 1312, 1424
marketing, A399; IS8, 71, 116, 118, 174; S1, 114, 208, 245, 491, 610, 865, 988, 1255, 1261, 1452, 1454, 1500, 1601, 1758, 1940, 2004, 2094, 2103; arts, S997
Markham Bequest (19C pamphs), S1894
Markham, Sir Clements, MSS (exploration), A334; papers, S1363
Markland Lib & Info Svc, see S1352
Marks & Spencer Co Archv, A306
Marks, Simon, papers (businessman), A306

Marlay Family of Belvedere, family & estate papers, IA78
Marlay, Charles, papers (landowner & politician), IA78
Marlborough family papers, A88
Marlowe Soc Colln, S1148
Marmion Colln (ch's lit), S1512
Marmorstein Colln (Judaica), S1512
marriage, S1317
Marrick Priory Papers, S918
Marriot Colln (political & economic hist), P208
Marsden, William, Colln, S1227
Marsh, Archbishop, Colln (17C sci, maths, music), IS39
Marshall Bequest (archaeo), S807
Marshall Lib of Econ, S335
Marshall Soc Archvs (econ), S335
Marshall, Alfred & Mary, archv (econ), S335
Marshall, Catherine, records (suffragist & pacifist), A98
Marshall, Sir John, Colln (Indian archaeo photos), S328
Martial Rose Lib, S2122
Martin Colln (19C ch's lit), S1440
Martin Family Papers, A278
Martin Kaye Lib, S1626
Martin, A.R., Colln (East London), A278
Martin, J.E., Colln (transport photos), S2051
Martin, Kingsley, papers, S239
Martin, Sir Richard Biddulph, MP, papers, A363
Martineau papers (Unitarianism), S1677
Martineau, Harriet, Papers, S179
Martinware Papers (ceramics), A274
Martyn, Henry, correspondence, S386
Marvell, Andrew, Colln, P68
Marwick Colln (Scottish economic & labour hist), A247; P116
Marwick Nat Hist Soc Lib, A197
Marx Memorial Lib, S1274
Marx, Karl, Colln, IA51
Marxism, S1274, 1887
Mary Evans Picture Lib, S1275
Mary Immaculate Coll Lib, IS181
Mary Marlborough Centre, see S1698
Marylebone Cricket Club Lib, S1276
Masefield, John, Colln, P62
Maskell, Dan, Papers, S1483
Mason Colln (rare bks, fine printing), L4
Mason, Charlotte, Archv, S33
Mason, Eudo, Colln (ch's bks), L2
Mason, Lord, papers, A26
Mass-Observation Archv, A70
Massey, Gerald, Colln (Victorian Chartist, poet, spiritualist & Egyptologist), P107
material culture, S1742
materials handling, S491
materials science, L4, 5; S113, 312, 321, 395, 1180, 1200, 1545, 1720, 2021
Mathematical Assoc Lib, S934
Mathematical Inst, Whitehead Lib, S1736
mathematics, IS6, 7, 11, 28, 44, 47, 64, 82, 150, 166, 172, 178, 183, 195, 198; L4; S12, 29, 40, 77, 78, 156, 232, 241, 263, 269, 271, 295, 296, 297, 301, 303, 315, 332, 365, 382, 404, 443, 456, 469, 478, 482, 495, 503, 515, 535, 540, 565, 593, 604, 610, 621, 665, 669, 681, 684, 713, 741, 755, 760, 776, 788, 810, 859, 869, 877, 893, 904, 910, 968, 969, 986, 1015, 1084, 1136, 1180, 1188, 1227, 1261, 1262, 1333, 1379, 1421, 1422, 1429, 1435, 1439, 1452, 1505, 1524, 1552, 1565, 1572, 1599, 1610, 1641, 1659, 1678, 1713, 1716, 1736, 1767, 1786, 1816, 1842, 1854, 1886, 1895, 1907, 1925, 1942, 1955, 1959, 1964, 1978, 1983, 2004, 2015, 2020, 2036, 2038, 2042, 2046, 2049, 2067, 2072, 2091, 2094, 2095, 2113, 2125, 2145, 2147, 2168, 2179; applied, L5; Greek, S1159; pure, L5; Roman, S1159
Mathews Colln, A422
Matthew Boulton Coll of Further & Higher Edu, Lib, S170

Matthews Colln (Hebrew & Oriental lit), P17
Matthews, C., MSS (music), S25
Matthews, D., MSS (music), S25
Mattison Colln (early socialism), S918
Mattli Archv (costume), S103
Mattuck, Israel, papers (rabbi), S1238
Maudsley Hosp, archvs, A33
Maugham, William Somerset, Lib, S409
Maurice Colln (military hist), S1227
Mavow Adams Family Papers, A297
Maw & Co, records, S2033
Maw MSS (music), S25
Mawson, Thomas H., papers (landscape architect), A217
Maxwell Davies MSS (music), S25
Maxwell of Monreith papers, L2
Maxwell, James Clerk, papers, L5
Maxwell-Constable of Everingham, family & estate papers, S828
Maxwells of Pollock, family & estate papers, A174
Mayall, W.H., papers (design), A69
Mayday Univ Hosp NHS Trust, see S2040
Mayes, Dean Gilbert, Colln (religion & liturgy), IA28
Maynard family & estate papers, A215
Maynard, Constance, Archv, S1333
Maynoothiana Colln, IS183
Mayo County Libs, IP20
Mayo Local Hist Dept, IA11
Mazarinades Pamphs (French studies), S1512
McArdle Postgrad Medical Lib, S2133
McAuley, Catharine, papers (foundress of Irish Sisters of Mercy), IA27
McBey, James, Ex Libris Colln, S2
McBurney, Charles, Bequest (archaeo), S323
McCall, P.J., papers, IS34
McColl Papers (fine art), S738
McColl/Seeger Colln (folk music), S1148
McConnel & Kennedy archvs, S1512
McCurdy & Mitchell Colln (arch), IA36
McDougall Lib for Electoral Studies, S1277
McEwan, James F., Colln (Scottish transport hist), A171; P45
McGill, Patrick, Colln (Donegal author), IP6
McGonagall, William, Colln, A136
McGowin Lib, S1756
McGrath, Raymond, Colln (arch), IA36
McGuinness, Rhoda, papers, IS66
McGuirk Colln (Irish & local hist), IS34
McIntyre Colln (X-rays), A177
McMillan, Margaret, Papers, A297
McNamara Colln (photography), IA55
McNeill, Eoin, papers, IL1
McQuaid, Archbishop, Colln, IS62
McRoberts Photo Colln, A239
McShane, Harry, papers (politics), A365
McWilliam, J.M., Colln, S863
Meadowbrook Dept of Psychiatric Medicine, Prof Lib, see S1506
meat & meat technology, IS118; S915
meat trade, S295
Meath Archaeo & Historical Soc, IO39
Meath County Infirmary records, IA80
Meath County Libs, IP21; Local Studies & Archvs, IA80
Meath Heritage Centre, IA93
Meath RC Diocesan Archvs, IA77
Meccano, records, A239
mechanics, S315, 321; fluid, S503, 526, 1208, 2030; quantum, S315; soil, S321, 2138
Medawar, Sir Peter, papers, S1457
media, A293; S12, 22, 208, 263, 271, 610, 677, 741, 747, 915, 988, 1043, 1255, 1282, 1452, 1516, 1577, 1597, 1978; digital, S474; print, S610
Media Archv for Central England, A403
media relations, A88
media studies, IS181; S19, 322, 469, 917, 969, 1254, 1261, 1804, 1824, 2004, 2103

Mediateque de l'Alliance Française de Glasgow, S716
Médiatèque de L'Institut Français, S1231
Médiathèque Tadhg O'Sullivan, IS110
mediation, S982
Medical Devices Agency Lib, S1278
Medical Rsrch Council Lib, S536; Dunn Human Nutrition Unit Lib, S375; Human Genetics Unit Lib, S608; Human Nutrition Rsrch Lib, S376; Laboratory of Molecular Biology Lib, S377; Social & Public Health Scis Unit, Lib, S717; see also S1300
medical science, S427, 475, 717, 1190, 1984, 1987, 2149
Medical Soc of London MSS, S1457
Medical Soc of London, Lib & Archvs, see A284
Medical Toxicology Unit Lib, S1279
Medical Women's Federation, archv, S1457
medicinal plants, S1076
medicine, A260, 346; IS1, 14, 16, 21, 24, 25, 26, 29, 31, 36, 39, 42, 61, 72, 98, 99, 120, 128, 132, 133, 134, 142, 144, 150, 152, 162, 163, 166, 167, 168, 169, 171, 176, 180, 186, 187, 189, 190, 197, 206, 207, 210, 211; L4; S7, 15, 24, 35, 50, 52, 59, 62, 69, 79, 85, 87, 90, 93, 96, 105, 140, 142, 143, 157, 159, 162, 167, 174, 178, 182, 184, 187, 193, 204, 205, 213, 221, 222, 224, 228, 236, 243, 252, 255, 257, 259, 263, 274, 279, 282, 285, 288, 376, 408, 411, 419, 427, 428, 435, 441, 447, 453, 455, 462, 463, 480, 499, 501, 505, 506, 520, 524, 527, 532, 542, 544, 548, 549, 553, 561, 562, 564, 579, 583, 593, 595, 610, 616, 619, 620, 648, 655, 658, 664, 668, 670, 691, 694, 700, 706, 711, 722, 724, 728, 734, 735, 742, 748, 753, 754, 757, 761, 763, 765, 774, 778, 781, 782, 785, 787, 789, 790, 794, 795, 798, 802, 809, 811, 821, 826, 832, 833, 836, 839, 842, 850, 852, 856, 862, 867, 873, 884, 898, 899, 905, 914, 918, 925, 933, 935, 954, 962, 964, 972, 975, 976, 978, 979, 994, 1009, 1017, 1021, 1027, 1041, 1058, 1086, 1087, 1136, 1164, 1177, 1179, 1180, 1215, 1227, 1280, 1299, 1309, 1333, 1348, 1349, 1352, 1355, 1360, 1381, 1388, 1410, 1415, 1419, 1422, 1457, 1462, 1475, 1479, 1486, 1492, 1494, 1504, 1506, 1512, 1520, 1521, 1523, 1532, 1534, 1535, 1538, 1543, 1553, 1569, 1574, 1578, 1590, 1595, 1600, 1607, 1608, 1612, 1615, 1620, 1639, 1647, 1651, 1654, 1656, 1658, 1660, 1662, 1668, 1671, 1675, 1698, 1708, 1729, 1749, 1783, 1784, 1785, 1795, 1796, 1809, 1813, 1821, 1825, 1826, 1830, 1835, 1841, 1849, 1852, 1855, 1858, 1865, 1868, 1869, 1875, 1876, 1884, 1893, 1902, 1908, 1913, 1914, 1922, 1927, 1931, 1936, 1941, 1947, 1948, 1951, 1952, 1962, 1968, 1970, 1974, 1977, 1981, 1982, 1984, 1987, 1988, 1993, 1994, 2006, 2007, 2008, 2011, 2014, 2027, 2034, 2040, 2046, 2048, 2055, 2057, 2058, 2066, 2075, 2090, 2092, 2098, 2099, 2102, 2105, 2106, 2108, 2116, 2124, 2133, 2134, 2135, 2143, 2149, 2152, 2156, 2157, 2158, 2185, 2188; alternative, S1021; antiquarian, IS154; cardiorespiratory, S1181; cardiothoracic, S782; clinical, IL2; L5; S176, 276, 970, 1179, 1361; community, S1402; complementary, S207, 695, 1452; early, S260, 616, 1759; East Asian, S378; equine, S1592; evidence-based, S662, 1897; forensic, S1333; herbal, S1076; high altitude, S990; military, S753, 754; occupational, S606; oral, S1118; oriental, S1457; paediatric, S699; public health, S84; renal, S441; respiratory, S782; social, S1349; sports, S641, 1259; tropical, S971, 1265, 1755; see also biomedicine; clinical science; dentistry; ethics, medical; general practice; health; history

of medicine; medical science; nursing; surgery
Medicines & Healthcare Products Regulatory Agency, Info Centre, S1280
Medicines Control Agency, Info Centre, *see* S1280
medieval thought, L4
Medway Archvs & Local Studies Centre, A435
Medway Lib, Info & Museum Svc, P113
Medway Naval Colln, A435
Medway NHS Trust Lib, S692
Medway Poor Law Union, records, A435
Medway Topographical Colln, A435
Medway Towns Methodists, records, A435
Mee, Arthur, Colln, P139
Mee, Margaret, drawings (botany), S1862
Meehan Papers, S741
Meissen Lib, S573
Melingriffith Co Ltd, records (tinplate manufacturers), S2051
Mellish Meteorological Colln, S1647
Mellor Memorial Lib, S1985
Melville Colln (theatre), S410
Mendham Colln (anti-Catholic lit), S404
Mendham Colln (law), S1237
Mental Aftercare Assoc, archv, S1457
mental health, *see* health, mental
Mental Health Svcs of Salford NHS Trust, *see* S1506
Mercantile Bank of India, records, A287
Mercer, Sir Walter, Papers (surgery), S617
Mercers' Co Archv, A307
merchandising, visual, S1255
Merchant Navy, S1303
Merck Pharmaceuticals Lib, S2105
Merck Sharp & Dohme Rsrch Laboratories, Rsrch Lib, S784
Mercy Centre Internatl, IA27
Mercy Hosp Medical Lib, IS25
Meredith-Jones, Betty, Colln (dance therapist), A192
Meriden Tea Co Ltd, records, S164
Meridian Television, film & video archv, A277
Merioneth Area Archvs Office, A123
Merrist Wood Coll, LRC, S772
Mersey Care NHS Trust, Gabby Kearney Lib, S1951
Mersey Docks & Harbour Co, records, A239
Merseyside Archvs Liaison Group, O278
Merseyside Development Corp archvs, A240
Merseyside Fire Svc, records, A240
Merseyside Maritime Museum, Maritime Archvs & Lib, A239
Merseyside Passenger Transport Exec, records, A240
Merseyside Poets Colln, S972
Merseyside Record Office, A240; *see also* A238
Merthyr Tydfil Coll, LRC, S1542
Merthyr Tydfil Libs, P114; *see also* A97
Merton Coll (Oxford) Lib, S1692
Merton Coll, Lib Learning Centres, S1557
Merton Lib & Heritage Svcs, P100; **Local Studies Centre,** A385
Merz Colln (sci, medicine), S1586
Messels of Nymans, papers, IS6
Met Eireann, Lib & Info Svc, IS111
Met Office, *see* A61; S210
metallurgy, S68, 153, 165, 312, 1200, 1473, 1720, 1857, 1873, 1905, 2033, 2087; ferrous, S1545
metalwork, A250; S1050, 1060, 1105, 1290
meteorology, A61; IS111; S83, 210, 294, 315, 1750, 1933, 2072
Methodism, A368; S127, 398, 1458, 1776, 2056
Methodist Archvs & Rsrch Centre, A368

Methodist Church in Ireland, *see* S127
Methodist Church Music Soc Lib, *see* S264
Methodist Colln of Modern Christian Art, S1776
Methodist Coll, Lib, S131
Methodist Conference, records, A368
Methodist Missionary Soc Archvs, S1449
Methuen family & estate papers, A493
Methuen Publishing, records, A440
Metro-Cammell Archv (railway rolling stock manufacture), A51
Metropolitan Police Visual Archv, S266
Meyerstein, E.H.W., MSS, S1726
Meynell, Sir Francis, papers, L5
Meyricke Lib, *see* S1681
Michael Bruce Cottage Museum, S872
Michael Davitt Memorial Museum, Archvs, IA57
Michael Loveitt Biomedical Lib, *see* S498
Michael Smurfit Grad School of Business, Lib & Business Info Centre, IS8
Michaelides Papyri (Arabic & Coptic), L5
Michelangelo Colln , S1032
microbiology, IS118, 145, 178; S32, 64, 313, 1300, 1331, 1541, 1669, 1787, 1830, 1888; aquatic, S32; marine, S849
Micronesia, S492
microscopy, electron, S1830
microwaves, S760
Mid Devon Dist Council records, A161
Mid Essex Hosps Health Svc Trust, *see* S447
Mid Glamorgan County Council, records, A97
Mid Staffordshire Genl Hosps NHS Trust, Postgrad Medical Lib, S1970
Mid Yorkshire Hosps NHS Trust, S1813
Mid-Cheshire Coll Lib, S1618
Mid-Kent Coll of Higher & Further Edu, Lib & Info Centres, S443
Mid-Kent Healthcare Trust Lib, *see* S1504
Mid-Western Health Board, *see* IS163, 180
Mid-Yorkshire Hosps NHS Trust, Lib & Knowledge Svcs, S532
Middle East & Middle East studies, S328, 593, 672, 1195, 1737
Middle East Centre Lib & Archvs, S1737
Middle East conflict, S672, 1182
Middle East Libs Cttee, O279
Middle Temple Lib, S1281
Middlesbrough Art Gallery, *see* S1546
Middlesbrough Coll, LRCs, S1547
Middlesbrough Libs & Info, P115; *see also* A379
Middlesbrough RC Diocesan Archvs, A378
Middlesex Hosp & Medical School, archvs, A351
Middlesex Regiment records, A311
Middlesex Univ, Info & Learning Resource Svcs, S1282; *see also* S655, 994, 1309
Middleton family & estate papers, A215
Middleton Local Studies Lib, *see* A434
Middleton, James & Lucy, papers, S1761
Middleton, Stanley, Colln, P138
Midland Bank, records, A287
Midland Health Board, Central Lib & Info Svc, IS207
Midlands Inst of Otology Colln, S182
Midlothian Chamber of Commerce, Business Info Svc, S518
Midlothian Council Lib Svc, P116
Midlothian Records Centre & Local Studies Dept, A247
midwifery, IS29; L5; S12, 50, 60, 66, 79, 87, 140, 184, 193, 204, 459, 496, 542, 550, 561, 583, 610, 673, 847, 869, 875, 922, 923, 1086, 1087, 1227, 1309,

1349, 1422, 1532, 1583, 1633, 1825, 1826, 1893, 1921, 1978, 2008, 2078, 2142, 2156
Migeod, F.W.H., MSS (exploration), A334
migration, S419, 1203; forced, S1744
Miles, Philip Napier, Papers, A77
Milestones Living Hist Museum, Local Resource Colln, A29
Milford Poor Law Union, minutes, IA67
Milford Rural Dist Council, records, IA67
Military Archvs (Ireland), IA45; *see also* IS28
Military Historical Soc Archvs, A308
military history, *see* history, military
military police, S468
military science, S1631, 1925, 2021; early, S913
military studies, IS28; S26
Mill Hill Historical Soc Colln, A255
Mill, John Stuart, Lib, S1762
Miller Colln (Scottish fishing industry), S37
Miller Inst Lib, P64
Miller, Frank, Colln, P41
Millest, John, Colln (art), S406
Milligan, Alice, papers, IS34
milling, S1850
Millner, J.W., Colln (photos of inland waterways), A183
Mills Observatory Lib, S556
Mills, Dr J.V., Colln (South East Asian maritime hist), S378
Milltown Inst of Theology & Phil, Jesuit Lib, IS112
Milner Colln, S1695
Milner, Isaac, Bequest (18C French maths), S385
Milner-White Colln (detective fiction), S2168
Milnes Walker Colln (early medicine), S2168
Milton estate archv, A395
Milton Keynes Coll LRC, S1552
Milton Keynes Council Lib Svc, P117
Milton Keynes Genl NHS Trust, Staff Lib, S1553
Milton Keynes Learning City Libs Network, O280
Milton Keynes Local Studies & Family Hist Lib, A381
Milton's Cottage Lib, S442
Milton, John, Colln, P9; S344, 442; *MSS,* S393; *Papers,* S442
Milton, Lord, papers, L2
MIND Lib, S1283
MIND, historical records, S1283
mineral processing, S1200, 1857
Mineral Waters Colln, P130
Mineralogical Soc of Gt Britain & Ireland Lib, S871
mineralogy, S146, 307, 871, 1200, 1308, 1481, 1715, 1738, 1857
Minerva Life Assurance Co, records, A157
Minet, William, Colln (Lambeth), A296
Mingana Colln (Arabic & Syriac MSS), S180
mining, A324, 420, 430, 507; S152, 540, 1200, 1580, 1604, 1857, 1885, 1989, 2015, 2115; coal, S1604, 1885, 2051, 2068; metalliferous, A494; S1885; opencast, S1885
mining communities, S1604
Ministry for Foreign Affairs, Finland, *see* S1120
Ministry of Agric, Fisheries & Food, *see* Dept for Environment, Food & Rural Affairs
Ministry of Defence HQ, Info & Lib Svc, S1284; *see also* A126, 486, 524; S684, 753, 754, 755, 995, 1646, 1925, 2018, 2063
Ministry of External Affairs, India, *see* S1184
Ministry of Foreign Affairs, France, *see* S1231, 1690
Ministry of Foreign Affairs, Italy, *see* S1216
Ministry of Foreign Affairs, Japan, *see* S1220
minority groups, S1203
Minter, R.A., papers, S360

Minto papers, L2
Minton, John, papers, A349
MIRA Ltd, Automotive Info Centre, S1648
Mirehouse Lib, S859
Mirfield Colln, S2168
Mission to Seamen Archvs, S759
Missionary Sisters of Our Lady of the Holy Rosary, Archvs, IA6
missionary studies & missiology, IS33, 104, 191; S180, 360, 1322, 2081
Missionary Training Colony Archvs, S2081
missionary work, S196, 360, 492, 534, 1463; overseas, S264
Mitchell, A.C., Colln (South Wales photos), S2051
Mitchell, Cosmo, Dance Colln, P1
Mitchell, W.R., Archv (Yorkshire Dales), S217
Mitford, Mary, Colln, P150
Mitrinovic Lib, S217
MLA West Midlands: The Regional Council for Museums, Libs & Archvs, O281
Mobil North Sea Ltd, Technical Lib, S11
Mocatta Lib of Anglo-Judaica, S1433
Modern 1st Editions Colln, S410
Modern Art Oxford, S1693
Modern Churchpeople's Union, Lib & Archvs, S974
Modern Movement Colln (arch), S1019
Modern Records Centre, A114
modernist movement, S1863; Catholic, S1964
Moeran MSS (music), S25
Moffatt Hosp, records, A132
Moir Lib, S627
Moir, Chasser, papers (gynaecology), S1352
Moldavia, S1436
Monaghan Chamber of Commerce & Industry Ltd, Lib & Info Svc, IS184
Monaghan County Libs, IP22
Monaghan County Museum, Rsrch Lib, IS185
Monaghan Genl Hosp, Medical Lib, IS186
monastic studies, IS188
monasticism, S569, 1880
Monifieth Town Council, records, A384
Monkhouse, A.N., papers (theatre), S1512
Monkhouse, P.J., papers (journalism), S1512
Monklands Hosp Lib, S24
Monmouth Castle & Regimental Museum, Archvs, A382
Monmouth, Diocese of, records, A117
Monmouthshire Antiquarian Assoc Lib, S422
Monmouthshire Commissioners of the Sewers, records, A117
Monmouthshire Libs & Info Svc, P118; *see also* A117
Monmouthshire Regiment, records, A64
monopolies, S1097
Mont St Michel Colln, A531
Montagu family & estate records (Earls of Sandwich), A211
Montagu family of Kimbolton records (Earls & Dukes of Manchester), A211
Montagu family papers, A78
Montagu, Lady Mary Wortley, papers, A466
Montague Graham-White Archv (motoring), S266
Montague, C.E., papers (theatre), S1512
Montague, Ivor, Colln (cinema), S1013
Monteagle Bequest (Irish music), IS138
Monteagle Estate Papers, IA68; IL1
Montefiore Colln (Hebrew MSS & bks), S1266
Montgomery, Field Marshal Viscount, of Alamein, papers, A289
Montrose Subscription Lib (travel & lit), P4
Montrose Town Council, records, A384
monuments, ancient, A93
Moore Colln, IS137
Moore of Bank Hall, family & estate papers, A238

Moore, A.S., Colln (Belfast local hist), A37
Moore, G.E., papers, L5
Moore, George (Irish author), Colln, IA11; papers, IL1
Moore, Henry, Archv, S1562
Moore, William, Colln (theology), S1964
Moorfields Eye Hosp Lib, S1201
Moorgreen Hosp Staff Lib, see S1941
Moorlands HM Prison Lib, see P38
Moorman, Bishop, Franciscan Lib & Papers, S523
Moral Welfare Workers Assoc, records, A53
Moran, Lord, papers, S1457
Morant, Philip, MSS (Essex), A111
Moravian Church Archv & Lib, A309; see also A77
Moray Coll LRC, S653
Moray Fishery Office, records, A158
Moray House Inst of Edu, Lib, S609
Moray Justice of the Peace, court records, A158
Moray Libs & Info Svcs, P119
Moray Local Heritage Centre, A158
Moray Soc Lib, S652
Morden Coll Lib, S1285
More Molyneaux of Losely Park, family papers, A513
More, Henry, letters, S344
Morecambe Bay Hosps NHS Trust, see S856, 884
Moredun Rsrch Inst Lib, S1787
Morfill Colln (Russian), S1751
Morgan Colln (Irish aerial photography), IL1
Morgan, Conwy Lloyd, papers, A77
Morgan, Edwin, Papers, S738
Morgan, F.C., Colln (photography), A202
Morison Colln (hist of freemasonry), S602
Morison, Stanley, Colln & papers (typography, palaeography, church hist), L5
Morley Borough records, A226
Morley Coll Lib & Ursula Hyde Learning Centre, S1286
Morley, Malcolm, Lib (stagecraft), S1440
Morpeth Records Centre, A386
Morrab Lib, S1789
Morris, Alfred Edwin, papers (Archbishop of Wales), S879
Morris, Henry, Colln (Irish material), S484
Morris, Sir Philip, papers, A77
Morris, William, Colln, A385; P100; MSS, S1464; papers, A282
Morrison, D.R., Scalpay Papers (Gaelic verse & journalism), P199
Morriston Hosp, Staff Lib, S2011; Nursing Lib, see S2015
mortality, S599
mosaics, S1105
Mosely Colln (British African stamps), L1
Moser Colln (19C watercolours), S1920
mosques, S1298
Moss Twomey Papers, IA49
Mostyn, Francis, papers (Archbishop of Cardiff), A94
Mother Mary Martin Lib, IS29
Motherwell Coll Lib, S1561
motor boats, S94
Motor Industry Rsrch Assoc, see S1648
motor racing, A505
motor vehicles, S22, 838
Motorboat Museum, Lib & Archvs, S94
motorcycles, S266
motoring, S266, 1346
Motoring Film & Video Lib, see S266
Motoring Picture Lib, see S266
motorsport, S266, 1346
Mott MacDonald Ltd, Lib, S232
Mottram Colln (English & American lit), S1227
Moulton Coll LRC, S1610
Mount Everest Foundation papers, A334

Mount Hermon Missionary Training Coll Archvs, S2081
Mount St Bernard Abbey Lib, S930
Mount Vernon Postgrad Medical Centre, Les Cannon Memorial Lib, S1620
mountaineering, S990, 1392, 1750, 2118; ski, S990
Mountbatten Lib, S1944
Mountbatten Papers, S1946
Mountmellick Rural Dist Council, records, IA83
movement, A192
Mowat Colln (Highland hist), P64
Moxon Colln (travel & ornithology), P146
Moylan, Francis, papers (Bishop of Kerry), IA62
Muckross House Ref Lib, IS173
Muggeridge Collns (photos of English windmills), S410
Mull Museum, Ref Lib & Archv, S2044
Muller, George, Colln (founder of Muller Soc Orphanages), S250
Mullingar Rural Dist Council minutes, IA78
Mumbles Railway, records, S2015
mummers, S751
Munby Colln (19C photos), S393
Munby Colln (lib & auction catalogues), L5
Munby family papers, A525
Municipal Tramways & Transport Assoc, archvs, S1539
Munn Colln (Londonderry), S1478
Munro Kerr, J.M., papers (gynaecology), S1352
Munrow, David, Lib (music), S1341
Munster Printing Colln, IS27
Muntz, Elizabeth & Hope, Colln, S545
Murchison, R.I., papers (geol), S1143
Murison Burns Colln, P53
Murphy, Pat, Colln (film), IA37; IS74
Murray Colln (18C military maps), L2
Murray Lib, see S2004
Murray Royal Hosp, Stalker Lib, S1790
Murray Stewart family papers, IA67
Murray, David, Colln (Glasgow hist), S738
Murray, Margaret, Colln, S1433
Murray, Sir George, papers, L2
Murray, Walter, Local Studies Colln (Clackmannanshire), A10; P28
Murtagh Colln (photography), IS141
Murtagh, Matthew, Lib (theatre historian), IA41
museology, A259, 353; IS121; S134, 146, 190, 422, 439, 470, 612, 631, 705, 1028, 1122, 1632, 1900, 1943, 2033, 2091, 2126; see also curatorship; museum studies
Museum & Lib of The Order of St John, S1287
Museum of Antiquities Lib, S612
Museum of Costume, Lib & Archvs, S103
Museum of Dartmoor Life, see A161
Museum of Edu, Scotland Street School, S718
Museum of Farnham, Local Studies Lib, A167
Museum of Lincolnshire Life, Lib & Archvs, S955
Museum of London, Lib & Archvs, S1288; see also A301; S1114
Museum of Methodism, Lib, S1458
Museum of Rugby, Lib, S2060
Museum of St Albans, see S1963
Museum of the Hist of Edu Lib, S910
Museum of the Queen's Lancashire Regiment, A426
Museum of the Staffordshire Regiment, Regimental Lib & Archvs, S946
Museum of the Welsh Woollen Industry, see S419, 422
Museum of Welsh Life Lib, S419
Museum of Worcester Porcelain, Lib & Archvs, S2144
Museum Resource Centre, Hitchin, S813
museum studies, S934

museums, S190, 470, 1085, 1108, 1653; folk, S470; Scottish, S631; see also galleries
Museums & Galleries of Northern Ireland, see A15
Museums Assoc, O282; see also S1433
Musgrave Family Papers, IA54
music, A32, 103, 231, 326, 331, 344, 360, 516; IS34, 39, 138, 181; L1, 5; S25, 80, 158, 337, 355, 373, 424, 432, 448, 469, 478, 511, 523, 571, 593, 610, 726, 738, 776, 824, 838, 869, 880, 903, 918, 945, 965, 968, 972, 1009, 1011, 1035, 1082, 1154, 1282, 1286, 1323, 1341, 1350, 1353, 1428, 1440, 1512, 1528, 1577, 1617, 1647, 1728, 1797, 1816, 1836, 1848, 1912, 1978, 1979, 2063, 2103, 2174; African, S965; American, S965; art, S597; blues, S511; Brazilian, S965; British, S1035; Cajun, S965; choral, S546; church, IA28; S466, 546, 569, 746, 801, 952, 2119; classical, S1035, 1575; contemporary, IS51; country, S965; disco, S965; early, S2119; ecclesiastical, S320, 1459; film, S965; folk, A24; IA42; S419, 751, 965; French, S605, 1231; funk, S965; German, IS80; Indian, S1014; instrumental, S751; Irish, IA42; IS51; S965; jazz, S511, 903, 965; Jewish, S1266; Latin American, S965; light-orchestral, S1836; military, S2063; modern, S1035; organ, S546, 1353; R&B, S965; reggae, S965; religious, S264, 1463; rock, S965; rockabilly, S965; Scottish, S63, 597, 598, 730; soul, S965; stage, S965; traditional, A24; IA42, 70; S597; vocal, S751; Welsh, A24; S432; Western, S597; world, S597, 965
music hall, A267
Music Performance Rsrch Centre, Archv, P99; Colln, S1428
music policy, S965
Music Preserved Colln (live music), S1428
Music Publishers Assoc, O283
musical instruments, S419, 1105, 1165, 1557, 1568
musicals, A263; S1797
musicology, S726, 738, 1428
Mutford & Lothingland Half-Hundred Court records, A361
Mutual & Genl Securities Co Ltd, records, A320
Muybridge, Eadweard, papers, A219
mycology, S31, 649, 756, 1860, 1862
Myers Colln (Russian sci fiction), S973
Myerscough Coll Lib, S1837
Myles Colln (medicine), IS134
mysticism, S1243, 1417
mythology, S193; S1243; Arthurian, S743

Na Píobairí Uilleann Colln (recordings of uilleann pipers), IA42
Naas Genl Hosp Lib, IS189
NACODS Colln, S2004
Nairn, James, Bequest (theology), S593
Nairnshire County records, A213
names, S419
Nance Colln (Cornish), S2056
Nantyglo & Blaina Ironworks Co Ltd, records, A117; S2051
Napier Shaw Lib, S315
Napier Univ Learning Info Svcs, S610; see also O337
Napier, A.S., MSS, S1726
Napier, Major Gen William, correspondence, S1185
Napoleonic Colln, P7, 68
Napoleonic Illusts Colln, S1789
Nash MSS (music), S25
Nash, Paul, papers, A349
Nasmyth Drawings Colln (eng), S1208
Nathan Colln (explosives & firearms), S1380
Nathaniel Waterhouse Charities, records, A194
Natl Acqs Group, O284
Natl Archv for Electrical Sci & Tech, see A294
Natl Archv for the Hist of Computing, A369

Natl Archvs, A432; Family Records Centre, A310; see also A431; O226
Natl Archvs Network User Rsrch Group, O288
Natl Archvs of Ireland, IA25
Natl Archvs of Scotland, A150
Natl Army Museum, Dept of Archvs, A311; Dept of Printed Bks, S1289; see also A308
Natl Art Lib, S1290; see also A250, 353
Natl Arts Edu Archv, see A496
Natl Assembly for Wales Lib, S420; Central Register of Air Photography of Wales, S421; see also A93; P188; S417
Natl Assoc of Aerial Photographic Libs, O285
Natl Assoc of Chief & Principal Nursing Offcrs, records, A153
Natl Assoc of Divisional Executives in Edu Archv, S1946
Natl Assoc of Lit Development, O286
Natl Assoc of State Enrolled Nurses, records, A153
Natl Asthma Campaign, Lib & Info Svc, S1291
Natl Audit Office Lib, S1292
Natl Autistic Soc Info Centre, S1293
Natl Bibliographic Svc, see L1
Natl Biological Standards Board, see S1830
Natl Birthday Trust Fund, archv, S1457
Natl Blood Svc (Bristol Centre) & IBGRL Lib, S254
Natl Botanic Gardens Glasnevin Lib, IS113
Natl Brewing Lib, S1694
Natl Bldgs Record (Wales), A6
Natl Campaign for the Arts Archv, S1148
Natl Cataloguing Unit for the Archvs of Contemporary Scientists, O287
Natl Centre for Athletics Lit Colln, S179
Natl Centre for Training & Edu in Prosthetics & Orthotics, Info Centre, S719
Natl Centre For Volunteering, Info Svc & Lib, S1294
Natl Childbirth Trust Lib, S1295
Natl Children's Bureau, Lib & Info Svc, S1296
Natl Children's Home Archv, S972
Natl Children's Hosp Lib, IS31
Natl Children's Resource Centre, IS114
Natl Co-op Archv, A370
Natl Coaching Foundation Colln, S653, 840
Natl Coal Board records, A128, 141, 452; Scotland, S1604
Natl Coal Mining Museum for England Lib, S2068
Natl Coll of Art & Design, Lib, IS115
Natl Coll of Ireland, Norman Smurfit Lib, IS116
Natl Commission on Edu, archvs, S1444
Natl Council for Civil Liberties, records, S828
Natl Council for Educational Awards, see IS86
Natl Council of Nurses, records, A153
Natl Council of the Pottery Industry, archvs, A473
Natl Council of Women, records, A153
Natl Council on Archvs, O288
Natl Council on Orientalist Lib Resources, O289
Natl Cycle Archv, A114
Natl Disability Authority, Lib & Archvs, IS117
Natl Eisteddfod, archv, L3
Natl Fairground Archv, A451
Natl Farmers' Union, Archvs, A312
Natl Film & Television Archv, see S1013
Natl Fisheries Rsrch Centre, S759
Natl Food Centre, Lib, IS118
Natl Forum for Info Planning & Co-operation, O290
Natl Foundation for Educational Rsrch, Lib & Info Svcs, S1929

Natl Gallery Lib & Archv, S1297
Natl Gallery of Ireland, Lib & Archv, IS119
Natl Gallery of Scotland Lib, S611; see also S633, 634
Natl Gas Archv, A500
Natl Grid Co plc, Info Learning Centre, S497
Natl Grid Transco, archvs, A500
Natl Heritage Archv of British Isles, S1298
Natl Heritage Lib, S1298
Natl Horseracing Museum, Lib & Archv, S1593
Natl Info Centre for Speech-Lang Therapy, Dept of Human Communication Sci Lib, S1299
Natl Inst for Biological Standards & Control, Lib, S1830
Natl Inst for Medical Rsrch, Lib & Info Svc, S1300
Natl Inst for Social Work, Lib & Info Svc, S1301
Natl Inst of Adult Continuing Edu, Lib, S931
Natl Inst of Agricultural Botany Lib, S381
Natl Inst of Economic & Social Rsrch Lib, S1302
Natl Inst of the Boot & Shoe Industry, minutes, A477
Natl Irish Visual Arts Lib, see IS115
Natl Jazz Archv, A360
Natl Liberal Club Papers, A77; S260
Natl Lib for the Blind, S1979
Natl Lib of Ireland, IL1
Natl Lib of Scotland, L2; see also O338
Natl Lib of Wales, L3
Natl Listening Lib, see S1248
Natl Literacy Trust, O291
National Lottery, S1108
Natl Marine Biological Lib, S1805
Natl Maritime Museum, Caird Lib, S1303
Natl Medicines Info Centre, IS120
Natl Memorial Fund, minutes, S1378
Natl Meteorological Archv, A61; Lib, S210
Natl Monuments Record, A483; Scotland, A151; Wales, A6
Natl Motor Museum, Lib of Motoring, S266
Natl Motorboat Museum, see S94
Natl Museum of Ireland Film Colln, IA37
Natl Museum of Ireland, Lib Svc, IS121
Natl Museum of Labour Hist, see A365
Natl Museum of Photography, Film & Television, Collns & Rsrch Centre (Insight), S215
Natl Museum of Sci & Industry, see S1387; see also S215, 2165
Natl Museums & Galleries of Northern Ireland, S146
Natl Museums & Galleries of Wales, Lib, S422; Dept of Industry Ref Lib, S2051; see also S419
Natl Museums & Galleries on Merseyside, see A239, 241; see also S972
Natl Museums of Scotland, Lib & Archvs, S612; see also S613
Natl Operatic & Dramatic Assoc, NODA Lib, S1797
Natl Orthotics Rsrch Eng, see S1698
Natl Photographic Archv of Ireland, see IL1
Natl Physical Laboratory Lib, S2031
Natl Police Lib, S816
Natl Portrait Gallery, Heinz Archv & Lib, A313
Natl Power plc Info Centre, see S2017
Natl Preservation Office, O292
Natl Print Museum Lib, IS122
Natl Radiological Protection Board Lib, S537
Natl Railway Museum, Lib & Archv, S2165
Natl Register of Archvs, A431
Natl Rehabilitation Board, see IS117

Natl Reports Colln, L1
Natl Resource Centre for Dance, Archvs, A192; see also S776
Natl Resources Inst Lib, see S1439
Natl School Records (Ireland), IA25, 61
Natl Screen & Sound Archv of Wales, see L3
Natl Secular Soc Lib, S1016
Natl Smelting Co records, A324
Natl Smoke Abatement Soc Colln, S233
Natl Soc Archvs & Lib, A314; see also S968
Natl Soc for Clean Air & Environmental Protection, Lib, S233
Natl Soc for the Prevention of Cruelty to Children, Lib & Info Svc, S1304
Natl Speleological Lib, P36
Natl Spiritual Assembly of the Bahá'ís of the Republic of Ireland, records, IS108
Natl Survey of Churches Archv, S1102
Natl Temperance Hosp archvs, A351
Natl Tramway Museum, John Price Lib & Archv, S1539
Natl Trust For Scotland Archvs, A152; see also S196, 687, 797, 876
Natl Trust Libs, S1305; Photographic Lib, S1306; see also S812, 1056, 2037
Natl Unemployed Workers Movement, papers, S1274
Natl Union of Boot & Shoe Operatives, records, A477
Natl Union of Mineworkers, Energy Rsrch Archv, S1912; records, A222, 473; S1604
Natl Union of Teachers, Lib & Info Unit, S1307
Natl Union of Women Teachers, archvs, S1444
Natl Univ of Ireland, Galway, James Hardiman Lib, IS166; Galway, Medical Lib, IS167; Maynooth, Lib, IS183; see also IS198
Natl Univ Women Graduates' Assoc Archv, IA49
Natl Viewers & Listeners' Assoc, archv, S482
Natl War Museum of Scotland, Lib & Archvs, S613
Natl Waterways Museum, Lib, S749; see also A159
Natl Youth Agency Lib, S932
Native Americans, S97
NATO Film & Video Lib, A290
Nat Environment Rsrch Council, see S71, 72, 294, 543, 756, 831, 1669, 1786, 1805, 1832, 1945, 2020, 2072
natural history, A14, 197, 409, 442, 480; IA70; IS137; S31, 56, 65, 98, 194, 229, 246, 247, 412, 451, 509, 530, 545, 552, 616, 680, 705, 807, 909, 1165, 1247, 1263, 1308, 1321, 1468, 1527, 1563, 1576, 1640, 1738, 1769, 1789, 1896, 1933, 2025, 2036, 2044, 2049, 2086, 2183, 2186; Scottish, S863; see also botany; wildlife; zoology
Nat Hist & Antiquarian Soc of Mid-Argyll Lib, see S980
Nat Hist Museum, Lib & Archvs, S1308
Nat Hist Soc of Northumbria Lib, S1576
Nat Movement Archv, A192
natural resource policy, S1098
natural resources, S114, 1103, 1439
nature, S1174, 1338, 1388
Nature Conservancy Colln (staff pubns), S756
NatWest Group Archvs, A329
Naughton, Bill, Archv (playwright), A57; P12
nautical studies, S1898
naval science, S1827
Naval Svc records (Ireland), IA45
naval studies, A420; IS160; S373, 1303
Navan Board of Guardians records, IA80
Navan Rural Dist Council, archvs, IA80
navigation, S1106, 1303, 1944
Navy Records Soc, O293; see also S1827
Nawn Colln (Irish & local hist), P136

Nazarene Theological Coll Lib, S1522
Nazism, S1195
Neal, Daniel, records (childrenswear chain), A470
Neath Abbey Ironworks Colln (eng drawings), A481
Neath Port Talbot Coll, Afan Campus Lib, S1820; Neath Campus Lib, S1565
Neath Port Talbot Hosp, Edu Lib, S1821
Neath Port Talbot Lib & Info Svcs, P120; see also A481
Needham Rsrch Inst, East Asian Hist of Sci Lib, S378
Neele, G.P., Diaries (railways), S2165
Neill Lib, S1711
Nell, P., Archv, S33
Nelson & Colne Coll, LRC, S1566
Nelson Lib, S1989
Nelson Museum & Local Hist Centre, A383
Nelson, Horatio, Colln, A385; P100; letters, S1303; papers, A383
neonatology, S143
Nestec York Ltd, Technical Info Svcs, S2166
Nettleship, E., papers, S1201
Network: Tackling Social Exclusion in Libs, Museums, Archvs & Galleries, O294
Neuberg Colln (religion), S934
Neuchatel Asphalte Co Ltd records, A514
Neurological Soc, archvs, S1381
neurology, S356, 608, 1448
neuroscience, S648, 1228, 1300, 1708, 1754; clinical, S1448
neurosurgery, S1448
Nevill Archv (Welsh industry), L3
Nevill family papers (Barons Latimer), A11
Nevill Forves Colln (Russian), S1751
Nevill Hall Hosp Postgrad Lib, see S1595
New Art Gallery Walsall, Art Lib, S2076
New Church, S1142, 1417
New Church Coll Lib, see S1142
New Coll (Oxford) Lib, S1695
New Coll (Swindon) Lib, S2019
New Coll (Worcester) Lib, S2145
New Coll Durham, Lib Svcs, S574
New Coll Nottingham, Basford Hall Learning Centre, S1638
New Craigs Hosp Lib, see S839
New Hall Coll, Rosemary Murray Lib, S379
New Kilpatrick Dist Council, records, A171
New Moon Lib, A132
New Romney Borough records, A128
New Ross Port Co, Archvs & Records, IA81
New Shakespeare Co, archvs, S1997
New Statesman Archv, S239
New Zealand House Lib, S593
Newall Colln (Scandinavia), S357
Newark & Sherwood Coll Learning Centre, S1568
Newark Hosp Medical Lib, S1569
Newbattle Colln (European lit & humanities), L2
Newbold Colln (fine arts), S2168
Newbridge House Archvs, IA22
Newbury Coll LRC, S1571
Newby Hall family & estate records, A226
Newcastle Coll Lib Svc, S1577
Newcastle Genl Hosp, Tomlinson Teaching Centre Lib, S1578
Newcastle Hosp (Ireland) Lib, IS169
Newcastle Law Courts Lib, S1579
Newcastle Libs & Info Svc, P121; see also A391
Newcastle Trust Papers, S523
Newcastle Univ, see Univ of Newcastle upon Tyne
Newcastle upon Tyne Hosps NHS Trust, see S1574, 1583
Newcastle, Diocese of, records, A386
Newcastle, North Tyneside & Northumberland Mental Health NHS Trust, see S1560, 1578, 1585

Newcastle-under-Lyme Coll, LRC, S1573
Newcome Colln, P75
Newenham family of Coolmore & Carrigaline, papers, IA19
Newhailes Lib (18C), L2
Newham Archv & Local Studies Lib, A315
Newham Libs, P101
Newham Museum Svc, Local Hist & Archaeo Resource Centre, see A303
Newman Colln (British road maps), L2
Newman Coll of Higher Edu Lib, S171
Newman Flower Colln of Handel MSS, P112
Newman, J.H., Colln, S171
Newman, Philip, Colln (music), S1528
Newmarch Colln (actuarial pamphs), S1188
Newmarch, William, papers (19C economist & statistician), A339
Newmarket Racing Colln, P179
Newnam, Bishop, Lib, IA71
Newnham Coll Lib, S380
Newport & Menevia, Bishops of, papers, A94
Newport Lib & Info Svc, P122; see also A117
Newry & Kilkeel Inst of Further & Higher Edu Lib, S1602
News Internatl Record Office, A316
Newsam Lib, S1444
Newspaper Soc, O295
NEWSPLAN Panel, O296
Newton Colln (medieval art), S2168
Newton Colln (ornithology), S319
Newton Lib, S319
Newton Stewart Burgh records, A475
Newton Stewart Hosp, records, A132
Newton, John, Colln, S1652
Newton, John, correspondence, S386
Newton, Lily, Papers (water pollution), S18
Newton, Rev John, papers, S1234
Newton, Sir Isaac, Colln, P75; S393; papers, L5; S369
NHS Estates Info Centre, S911
NHS Exec (West Midlands) Lib, S169
NHS Exec, London Regional Office, see S1256
NHS Lib & Knowledge Development Network, O297
NIAB Lib, S381
Nichol Colln (art), S561
Nicholl of Merthyr Mawr, family & estate records, A97
Nicholle, E.T., MSS (author), S2190
Nicholls, David, Colln (religion & politics), S1760
Nicholson, Ben, correspondence, S368; papers, A349
Nicholson, Marjorie, Papers (labour movement & the colonies), S1425
Nicholson, Nigel, papers, S239
Nicol, Dr H., Photo Colln (tramways), S1539
Nicoll, Allardyce, Colln (theatre), S1512
Nightingale, Florence, Colln, A153; correspondence, A336, 509; S1352
Ninewells Hosp & Medical School Lib, see S561
Nissa Torrents Video Colln, S1447
Nitrogen Fixation Laboratory Archvs, S1624
Noall, Cyril, Colln (maritime), S2056
Noble's Isle of Man Hosp, Postgrad Medical Lib, see S2178
Nolan Cttee, papers, S482
non-wovens, S895
Nonsuch Colln (archaeo), A301
Norfolk County Council Lib & Info Svc, P123; see also S1621
Norfolk Edu Authority, see S864
Norfolk Heraldry Soc Lib, S529
Norfolk Museums & Archaeo Svc, see S866
Norfolk Record Office, A400
Norfolk Rural Life Museum & Union Farm, Lib, S578
Norfolk, Dukes of, family & estate archvs, S44
Norman Reprint Colln, S319

health, **S**881, 1560; ophthalmic, **S**1201; orthopaedic, **S**1698; practice, **S**1096; psychiatric, **S**610, 1642; surgical, **S**429; veterinary, **S**263, 273, 940, 1499, 1837, 1971, 2045; *see also health; medicine*

Nursing Board of Ireland, Lib, IS36

nutrition, **IL**2; **IS**9, 118, 210; **S**13, 64, 375, 376, 614, 638, 1157, 1452, 1872; human, **S**1265

O Buachalla, Liam, papers (Gaelic League teacher & Feis organiser), **IA**19

Ó Conluain, Proinsias, Colln (Irish music), **IA**42

Ó Corcora, Donal, papers, **IA**21

Ó Fiaich, Cardinal Tomás, Lib & Papers, **A**16

*O Riordain Colln, IS*27

Ó Searcaigh, Cathal, papers (poet), **IA**67

O'Brien, Conor Cruise, Papers, **IA**49

O'Brien, J.F.X., papers, **IL**1

O'Brien, William, Colln (Irish political pamphs) & papers, **IL**1

O'Casey, Seán, papers, **IL**1

O'Ceallaigh, Seamus, Colln (GAA in Limerick), **IA**69

O'Connell, Daniel, Colln, **IA**92; *papers,* **IL**1

O'Connor Colln (photography), **IA**51

O'Connor, Fergus, papers, **IS**34

O'Connor, M.J., Photo Colln (tramways), **S**1539

O'Dea Colln (images of Irish railway transport), **IL**1

O'Dea, Jimmy, papers (actor), **IA**41

O'Dell Railway Colln, **A**3; **S**5

O'Donnell, Peadar, Colln (Donegal author), **IA**65

O'Donoghue, D.J., Archv (Irish libn & writer), **A**37

O'Donohoe, John, Colln (George 'AE' Russel), **IS**66

O'Donovan Letters (1840 Ordnance Survey), **IA**70, 94

O'Donovan, John, MSS (19C Irish scholar), **IA**31

O'Gowan, Dorman, papers (military studies), **S**1512

O'Hara Estate Papers, **IL**1

O'Kane Colln of Audio-Tapes (Irish War of Independence), **A**16

O'Kelley Colln (Irish imprints), **IS**148

O'Kelly Colln (religion in Ireland), **IL**1

O'Kelly Offprint Colln (archaeo), **IS**27

O'Kelly, Seán T., papers, **IL**1; **IS**34

O'Lochlainn Colln (Irish imprints), **IS**148

O'Neill Colln (photography), **IA**55

O'Neill, Michael, Lib (theatre historian), **IA**41

O'Searcaigh, Cathal, Lib & Archv (Donegal author & poet), **IA**65

Oak Hill Coll Lib, S1311

*Oakham Parochial Lib, S*1647

Oaklands Coll, Smallford Campus Lib, S1960

Oates Colln (slavery in West Indies), **S**1946

*Oates family papers, S*30

Oates Memorial Lib & Museum & Gilbert White Museum, S30

Oatley, Sir George H., & Partners, records (architects), **A**77

Oatridge Coll Lib, S270

Obstetrical Soc of London, archvs, **S**1381

obstetrics, **IS**24, 132; **S**1352, 1532, 1785

occultism, **P**109; **S**743; Western, **S**1243; *see also parapsychology; psychical research*

Occupational & Environmental Diseases Assoc, Lib, S656

occupational hazards, **S**656

OCE (UK) Ltd, see S526

Ocean PSNC, records (shipping company), **A**239

oceanography, **S**8, 32, 78, 83, 849, 1649, 1805, 1898, 1944; physical, **S**1832

*Odonto-Chirurgical Soc Papers, S*617

Odontological Soc of Gt Britain, archvs, **S**1381

Offaly County Lib Svc, IP23

Offaly Grand Jury Presentments, **IA**94

Offaly Historical & Archaeo Soc, IO40; **Lib & Archvs, IS**208

Offaly Local Studies & Archvs Svc, IA94

Office for Lib & Info Networking, see O405

Office for Natl Statistics Info & Lib Svc, S1201

Office of Fair Trading, Lib & Info Centre, S1313

Office of Gas & Electricity Markets Lib, S1314

Office of Public Works Lib, IS123

Office of Sci & Tech, see S2087

Office of Telecommunications Lib, S1315

Office of the Chief Herald of Ireland, see IL1

Office of the Comptroller & Auditor Genl, Lib & Archv, IS124

Office of the Dep Prime Minister & Dept for Transport, Info Svcs & Sources, S1316; *see also* **S**1558

Office of the Dir of Telecommunications Regulation, Lib, IS125

Office of the Houses of the Oireachtas Lib, IS126

Office of the Info Commissioner, O308

Office of the Registrar Genl, IA46

Office of Water Svcs Lib, S172

office skills, **S**2094

OFWAT Lib, S172

*Ogden, C.K., Lib, S*1433

*Ogdon, John, MSS (music), S*1528

*Ogilvy Colln (fisheries), S*8

Oglander family papers, **A**392

Oglander, Sir John, Colln (Isle of Wight), **A**392

Oifig An Ard-Chláraitheora, see IA46

old age, **S**1045

Old Brotherhood, records, **A**356

Old Chapter of England, records, **A**356

Old Dublin Soc Lib, IS127

Old Londoner Colln (London Hosp), **A**336

Old Manor Hosp Lib, see S1893

Old Royal Lib, **L**1

Old Straight Track Club, papers, **A**202

Oldaker Binding Colln, **S**1459

Oldbury & Smethwick Primary Care Trust, S2104

Oldcastle Board of Guardians records, **IA**80

Oldcastle Rural Dist Council, archvs, **IA**80

Oldchurch Hosp Lib & Info Svc, S1869

older people, **S**587

Oldham Coll Lib, S1650

Oldham Coroner records, **A**408

Oldham Lib & Info Svc, P140

Oldham Local Studies & Archvs, A408

*Oldham MSS (music), S*25

Oldham Poor Law Union records, **A**408

Oldham Textile Employers archvs, **S**1512

Oldham Walton Archv (Sir William Walton), **A**408

Olive Gibbs Centre, S1703

Oliver & Boyd, archv (Scottish publishers), **L**2

Oliver Colln (Surrey hist & topography), **S**651

Ollivant, Alfred, papers (Bishop of Llandaff), **S**426

Omagh Coll of Further Edu Lib, S1654

Ommaney, E., MSS (exploration), **A**334

Onchan Lib, P211

oncology, **IS**142; **S**259, 313, 411, 648, 694, 696, 1054, 1192, 1508, 1668, 1729, 1914, 2135; *see also cancer & cancer research*

One Plus One, Lib & Info Svc, S1317

One World Edu Lib, S234

Open & Distance Learning Quality Council, O309

open learning, **IS**86

Open Univ Colln, **S**1519

Open Univ Lib, S1554; *see also* **S**1551

Opening the Bk Ltd, O310

opera, **A**231, 272, 276, 331, 338; **S**1323; in education, **A**496; light, **S**1797

operating systems, **S**301

operational research, **S**1318

Operational Rsrch Soc Lib, S1318; *see also* **S**1180

ophthalmology, **IS**72; **S**259, 548, 608, 1201, 1697

Opie Colln (ch's lit), **L**4

Oppenheimer Colln (Hebrew lit), **L**4

optics, **S**331, 1020, 1037, 1201

optometry, **S**1037

OPW Sites & Monument Record, IA78

oral history, **A**60, 109, 292, 369; Scottish, **A**229

Oral Hist Soc, O311

Orange Order, **S**710

Ord & Maddison Ltd records (quarry owners), **A**514

Order of St John, see S1287

Ordnance Survey Archaeo Branch (Scotland), records, **A**151

Ordnance Survey Archaeo Div (Welsh section) Lib & records, **A**6

Ordnance Survey Lib, S1940

Ordnance Survey of Ireland Archvs, **IA**25

Ordnance Survey of Northern Ireland, Map Lib, S136

Organ Club Lib, S1341

organisation, **S**489

organisational behaviour, **IS**116

Oriel Coll Lib, S1699

Oriel Ynys Môn, Archvs & Local Studies Colln, A246

Oriental studies, **L**4; **S**328

Orkney Archvs, A221

Orkney Libs, P141

Orkney Sheriff Court, records, **A**221

Ormond Estate Papers, **IL**1

Ormonde Loan Colln (arch), **IA**36

Ormskirk Clinical Lib, see S1840

Ormskirk Hosp, Sanderson Lib, S1656

ornithology, **S**71, 292, 1263, 1308, 1563, 1576, 1725, 1769, 1896, 2187; marine, **IS**194

Orpington Coll Lib, S1659

Orpington Hosp Lib, see S1658

Orthodox Church, **S**363; Eastern, **S**1685

orthopaedics, **S**174, 1660, 1698, 2133

orthoptics, **S**1201

orthotics, **S**719, 1698

Ortiz, Joseph, Colln (opera), **S**1428

Orton, Joe, Colln, **A**295; *Papers,* **S**934

Orwell, George, Archv, **S**1433; *Colln,* **L**1

Osborne, John, Colln, **L**1

Oscott Coll archvs, **A**52

Osman-Gidal Colln (20C magazines), **S**1290

Osmond, Cecily, Colln (schools on early collective farms), **S**1393

Ossory, C of I Bishops of, Colln, **IS**172

Ossory, Diocese of, parochial records, **IA**61

osteopathy, **S**207, 1021, 1041

othopaedics, **S**1994

otology, **S**1434

otorhinolaryngology, **S**1434

Ottoman Empire, **S**1737

Oughaval parish records, **IA**11

Our Lady's Hosp (Ennis), Lib, IS163; *see also* **IA**55

Our Lady's Hosp (Navan), Medical Lib, IS190

Our Lady's Hosp for Sick Children, Lib, IS128

outdoor pursuits, **S**805

outdoor studies, **S**33

Outram, Lt Gen Sir James, papers, **A**311

overseas aid, **S**1319

overseas aid policy, **S**580

Overseas Archv (Irish in Europe), **A**16

Overseas Development Inst Lib, S1319

Owen Colln (classics), **S**325

Owen Lib, see S2013

Owen, Lord David, papers, **S**972

Owen, Richard, Colln (anatomy), **S**1357

Owen, Robert, Colln, **L**3; **S**1605; *papers,* **A**370

Owen, Wilfred, Lib, **S**1726; *MSS,* **S**25, 1726

Owens, Owen, archvs, **S**1512

Oxford Architectural & Historical Soc Lib, **S**1747

Oxford Bibliographical Soc, O312

Oxford Brookes Univ Lib, S1700; *see also* **S**1694

Oxford Centre for Enablement, see S1698

Oxford Centre for Hebrew & Jewish Studies, Leopold Muller Memorial Lib, S1701

Oxford Centre for Musculoskeletal Rsrch, see S1698

Oxford Centre for the Environment, Ethics & Soc, William Robbins Lib, S1702

Oxford Coll of Further Edu, Olive Gibbs Centre, S1703

Oxford Forestry Inst Info Svc, see S1721

Oxford Inst for Energy Studies, Lib, S1704

*Oxford Mountaineering Lib, S*1750

*Oxford Movement Colln, S*1673, 1769

Oxford Museum of Nat Hist, Hope Lib, S1738

Oxford Museum of the Hist of Sci, Lib & Archvs, S1739

Oxford Orthopaedic Eng Centre, see S1698

*Oxford Picture Lib, S*1705

Oxford Radcliffe Trusts, see S69

Oxford Union Soc Lib, S1706

Oxford Univ, Bodleian Lib, L4; **Bodleian Japanese Lib, see L**4; **Bodleian Law Lib, see L**4; **Bodleian Lib of Commonwealth & African Studies at Rhodes House, see L**4; **Botanic Garden Lib, S**1707; **Cairns Lib, Radcliffe Infirmary Branch, S**1708; **Careers Svc Lib, S**1709; **Centre for Criminological Rsrch Lib, S**1710; **Centre for Socio-Legal Studies, Neill Lib, S**1711; **Clarendon Laboratory Lib, S**1712; **Classics Lending Lib, see S**1747; **Computing Laboratory Lib, S**1713; **Dept for Continuing Edu Lib, S**1714; **Dept of Earth Scis Lib, S**1715; **Dept of Educational Studies Lib, S**1716; **Dept of Eng Sci Lib, S**1717; **Dept of Experimental Psy Lib, S**1718; **Dept of Human Anatomy & Genetics Lib, S**1719; **Dept of Materials, Materials Sci Lib, S**1720; **Dept of Plant Scis Lib & Info Svc, S**1721; **Dept of Social Policy & Social Work Lib, S**1722; **Dept of Zoology Lib, S**1723; **Eastern Art Lib, see S**1747; **Econ Lib, S**1724; **Edward Grey Inst of Field Ornithology, Alexander Lib, S**1725; **English Faculty Lib, S**1726; **Faculty of Modern Langs Lib, S**1727; **Faculty of Music Lib, S**1728; **George Wiernik Lib, S**1729; **Hist Faculty Lib, S**1730; **Hist of Art Lib, see S**1747; **Hooke Lending Lib, see L**4; **Indian Inst Lib, see L**4; **Inst for Chinese Studies Lib, see L**4; **Inst of Health Scis Lib, S**1731; **Inst of Social & Cultural Anthro, Tylor Lib, S**1732; **Internatl Development Centre Lib, S**1733; **Lang Centre, Lib, S**1734; **Latin American Centre Lib, S**1735; **Mathematical Inst, Whitehead Lib, S**1736; **Middle East Centre Lib & Archvs, S**1737; **Museum of Ethnography, see S**1742; **Museum of Nat Hist, Hope Lib, S**1738; **Museum of the Hist of Sci Lib, S**1739; **Nuclear & Astrophysics Lib, S**1740; **Nuffield Dept of Orthopaedic Surgery Lib, see S**1698; **Oriental Inst Lib, see L**4; **Pauling Centre for Human Scis Lib, S**1741; **Phil Lib, see L**4;

Oxford Univ (cont), Radcliffe Sci Lib, *see* L4; Pitt Rivers Museum, Balfour Lib, S1742; Politics, Internatl Relations & Sociology Lib, S1743; Refugee Studies Centre Lib, S1744; Ruskin School of Drawing & Fine Art, Lib, S1745; Russian & East European Centre Lib, S1746; Sackler Lib, S1747; Said Business School, Sainsbury Lib, S1748; School of Anthro, *see* S1742; School of Clinical Medicine, Cairns Lib, S1749, *see also* S1708; School of Geog & the Environment Lib, S1750; Social Studies Faculty, *see* S1724; Taylor Instn Lib, S1751; Theology Faculty Lib, S1752; Transport Studies Unit Lib, S1753; Univ Archvs, *see* L4; Univ Laboratory of Physiology Lib, S1754; Vere Harmsworth Lib, *see* L4; Wellcome Unit for the Hist of Medicine, S1755; Western Art Lib, *see* S1747; *see also* S1665, 1675, 1683, 1690, 1697, 1702, 1735, 1753, 1766, 1772, 1773, 1777, 1779
Oxford Univ Music Soc Colln, S1728
Oxford Univ Press Archvs, A411
Oxford, Diocese of, records, A19, 412, 429
Oxfordshire Lib Svc, P142; *see also* A410
Oxfordshire Local Hist Assoc, O313
Oxfordshire Oral Hist Archv, A410
Oxfordshire Record Office, A412
Oxfordshire Record Soc, O314
Oxfordshire Sites & Monuments Record, A410

P&O records (shipping company), S1303
PA Photos, S1320
Pacific, S492, 1443, 1449
pacifism, A292; S1182, 1242
packaging, A376; S491, 895, 2094
Padbury, Joyce, Colln (ch's lit), IS48
paediatrics, IS128, 132; S143, 157, 619, 1138, 1354, 1532, 1908, 1994, 2133
paganism, S743
Page Memorial Lib, S1123
Page, Harry, Colln (ephemera & bkplates), S1519
Page, Tim, Photo Colln, S1917
Paget family papers, A77, 467
Paget Papers, S1433
Paine, Thomas, Colln, P17, 123, 157; S1887
paint, S1928, 2032
Paint Rsrch Assoc Lib, S2032
painting, IS22; S97, 523, 591, 623, 880, 1297, 1455, 2004; *see also* art & arts
Paisley Burns Club Colln, P152
Paisley Coll Archv, S1782
Paisley Dean of Guild Plans, P152
Paisley Pamphs Colln, A413; P152
Paisley Poor Law records, A413; P152
Paisley Univ, *see* Univ of Paisley
Paisley Weavers, Hammermen & Tailors records, A413
Pakenham family & estate papers (Earls of Longford), IA12
Pakenham Family Colln, IP30
Palace House (Beaulieu) Archv, Montagu Ventures Ltd, A78
palaeoanthropology, S1031
palaeography, S569, 1440, 1730
palaeomagnetism, IS63
palaeontology, S146, 307, 592, 849, 1308, 1738, 1967, 2049; *see also earth science; geology*
Palestine, S1517
Palestine Exploration Fund, Lib & Archvs, S1321
Pallant House Gallery Lib, S467
Palles, Baron, Colln (law), IS148
palliative care, S274, 481, 557, 642, 660, 1409, 1671, 1930
Palmer, Christopher, Colln (Serge Prokofiev), A344
Palmleaf MSS, A512
Pamerston Papers, S1946
Paolozzi, Sir Eduardo, Krazy Kat Arkive (20C popular culture), A250; *papers*, A349

paper, S895, 1105, 1408, 1481
paper science, S1680
Papworth Hosp NHS Trust, Clinical Lib Svc, S1784
papyrology, S1159, 1512, 1747
Paquin Archv (costume), S103
paramedicine, S257, 496, 701, 763, 839, 1578
parapsychology, S1243, 1394, 1485; *see also occultism; psychical research*
parasitology, S313
parenting, IS114
Pares, Sir Bernard, Colln (Russian studies), S1436
Parikian Armenian Colln, S2130
Park Lane Coll Lib, S912
Parker Colln of Children's Bks, P9
Parker of Saltram estate archv, A419
Parker, Barry, Colln (arch drawings), S937
Parker, Charles, Archv (oral hist, folk music, politics), A51
Parker, Matthew, Bequest, S349
Parker, Robert, records (18C Halifax attorney), A194
Parker-Jervis Colln (family papers), A468
Parkes Lib (Jewish/non-Jewish relations), S1946
Parkes, Bessie, papers, S357
Parkhurst Bequest (theology), S773
parks, IS113; S1845
Parliament, S1166, 1167
Parliament for Wales Campaign, records, L3
parliamentary affairs, IS126; S1098, 1237
Parliamentary & Political Parties Archv Group, O315
Parliamentary Archvs, A286
Parliamentary Labour Party, records, A365
Parmenter, Geoffrey, papers (Catholic hist), A252
Parnell, Charles Stewart, Colln, IA7; IP32
Parry, Joseph, papers, L3
Parsons Family Papers, IS6
Parsons Lib, *see* S1577
participation, S230
Particle Physics & Astronomy Rsrch Council, S2020
Partington Colln (hist of chem), S1512
partnership, S1317
Partnership for Theological Edu, Luther King House Lib, S1526
Partnership House Mission Studies Lib, S1322
Pascall, James, Ltd, records (confectionery manufacturers), S164
Pascoe, F.P., Lib (entomology), S1738
Passfield Colln, S1241
pastoral care, S1057
pastoralia, S523
Patagonia, S82
Patent Office, Classn Lib, S1596
patents, IS170; S1068, 1408, 1596
Patents Office Lib, IS170
Paterson, T.G.F., Archv (Armachiana), A15
Pathological Soc of London, archvs, S1381
pathology, S313, 1357; plant, S381, 1624, 1895, 2137
patristics, S101, 448, 1412, 1673, 1752, 2096
Patterson, Sylvia, Jazz Colln, S965
Paul Hamlyn Lib, *see* S1028
Paul's Malt & Associated British Maltsters records, A215
Pauling Centre for Human Scis Lib, S1741
Paxton, Joseph, correspondence, S67
peace & peace studies, S185, 234
peace movement, S1052
peace-keeping, S1182
Peak Dist Mines Hist Soc Lib, P36
Peake, Mervyn, MSS, S1433
Pears House Colln (hist), S851
Pears, Peter, Colln & papers (music), S25
Pearse, Patrick, papers, IL1; IS34
Pearsie papers, A135
Pearson, Bishop, Colln, S456

Peart-Binns Christian Socialist Archv, S217
Peatling, Dr Albert, Colln (Carshalton), A478
Peckham, W.D., Lib (Sussex antiquarian), A106
Peel Colln of Irish Pamphs, S1167
Peel Town Commissioners, *see* P212
Peel, Sir Robert, Colln, P174
Peers, Edgar Allison, Colln (Spanish Civil War), S972
Peet Lib of Egyptology, *see* S1759
Pegg, W.E., Papers & others, S1483
Peirson Lib, S2146
Pembroke Coll (Cambridge) Lib, S382; *see also* L5
Pembroke Coll (Oxford), McGowin Lib, S1756
Pembroke Urban Dist Council records, IA30
Pembrokeshire & Derwen NHS Trust, S794
Pembrokeshire Coll Lib, S793
Pembrokeshire Libs, P143
Pembrokeshire Record Office, A199
Pembury Hosp Lib, S2058
Pen Dalton Archv (feminist posters), A75
Pen-Y-Fal Hosp records, A117
penal policy, S1330
Pencoed Coll Lib, *see* S223
Pendered, Mary, Colln (Northamptonshire writer), P131
Pendlebury Lib of Music, S337
Pengelly, Hester, Letter & Autograph Colln, S2049
Penguin Bks Colln, S410, 593
Penguin Bks Ltd Editorial Archvs, A77; S260
Peninsular War, S444, 1647
Penitentes, S97
Penn, William, Colln (Chigwell School), S471
Pennine Acute Hosps NHS Trust, Jack Taylor Lib, S1865; *see also* S279
penology, S676, 816, 1877
Penrice & Margam family & estate archv, L3
Penrose Colln (cookery bks), S1460
Penrose Papers, S1433
Penrose, Roland, Archv, S633
pensions, S599, 1112, 1679
Penton Family & Estate Papers, A295
Pentyrch Ironworks, records, S2051
People's Network ICT Content Group, *see* O306
Peoples' Coll, Nottingham, LRCs, S1643
Pepys, Samuel, Colln, P99; S373
Perceval, Spencer, papers, L5
Percy family papers (Dukes of Northumberland), A11
Percy, John, Papers (19C metallurgist), S1200
Percy, Thomas, Lib (18C lit), S139
performance studies, S1617
Performing Arts Lib, S1323
Periodical Publishers Assoc, O316; *see also* O322
Periodical Publishers Assoc, archvs, A399
Perkins Agricultural Lib, S1946
Perowne Colln (Knights of Malta), S349
Perry Lib, *see* S1400
Perry, Frances, Working Lib, S654
Pershore Coll Lib, *see* S805
personalities, S1170
Perth & Kinross Council Archv, A416
Perth & Kinross Libs, P144
Perth Coll, LRC, S1791
Perth Museum & Art Gallery, S1792
Perth Royal Infirmary, Gillingham Lib, *see* S562
Perthshire Nat Hist Soc Lib, S863
pest control, S649
pesticides, S626, 786, 1895
Peterborough Cathedral Lib, S1798; *see also* L5
Peterborough Dean & Chapter Archvs, S1798
Peterborough Gentlemen's Soc Lib, A417

Peterborough Hosp NHS Trust, S1796
Peterborough Libs, P145
Peterborough Local Studies Colln, A417
Peterborough Museum & Art Gallery, Lib & Archvs, S1799
Peterborough Regional Coll, Learning Resources & Lib Centre, S1800
Peterborough, Diocese of, parish records, A227, 395
Peterhouse, Perne Lib, S383; **Ward Lib**, S384
Peterhouse Coll, medieval MSS, L5
Peters Photo Colln, IA21
Petersfield Deanery, records, A509
Peto, Michael, Photo Colln, A137
Petre of Axminster, estate archv, A161
Petrie & Goodman Collns (Irish folk music), IL2
Petrie Museum of Egyptian Archaeo, Lib & Archvs, S1324
petroleum, A482; S1202
petrology, S307
Pettingell Colln (theatre), S410
Petty Colln (English Civil War), P130
Petty-Fitzmaurice, Henry, correspondence (5th Marquess of Lansdowne), IA78
Pettybridge Colln (potato lit), S558
Petworth House Colln (Earls of Thomond), IA55
Petworth House estate records, A106
Petyt MSS, S1187
Peugeot Talbot Visual Archv, S266
Pfizer Ltd, Records Mgmt, A446
pharmaceuticals, A189, 446; S221, 622, 1004, 1280, 1376, 1450, 1480, 2105, 2106; protein, S632
pharmacology, L4; S314, 784, 1697, 1755, 2128
pharmacy, A346; IS120; S12, 142, 622, 1376, 1450
Phelps, Barry, Colln, S1117
philately, A317; L1
Philbrick Colln (Cornish postal & turnpike records), S2056
Philip, G., archv (cartography), S1364
Philip, George, Ltd Colln (cartography), S1364
Philips Rsrch Laboratories, Info Centre, S1854
Philips, J.S., papers, S360
Phillimore Papers, S1670
Phillipps of Welcombe, family & estate papers, A476
Phillipps, Sir Thomas, Antiquarian Colln, A185; *Medieval MSS*, A215
Phillips, John, papers (geol), S1738
Phillips, Morgan, papers (politics), A365
Phillips, Reginald, Philatelic Colln, S239
Phillips, Thomas, Colln, S880
Phillpotts, Eden, Colln, A420; *papers*, A164
Philological Soc Lib, S1433
philology, S327; Indo-Iranian, S290
philosophy, IS7, 9, 11, 12, 13, 28, 33, 35, 39, 45, 46, 47, 49, 56, 90, 104, 112, 166, 171, 172, 181, 183, 188, 193, 197, 198, 201; L4; S41, 67, 121, 152, 156, 173, 180, 198, 238, 244, 258, 264, 269, 293, 297, 308, 323, 326, 329, 330, 332, 340, 368, 382, 383, 433, 436, 443, 448, 456, 482, 523, 538, 540, 553, 601, 670, 687, 698, 701, 713, 738, 741, 743, 776, 788, 810, 859, 877, 879, 930, 945, 950, 969, 1006, 1015, 1082, 1116, 1127, 1135, 1144, 1148, 1160, 1227, 1243, 1260, 1328, 1333, 1411, 1412, 1421, 1429, 1440, 1485, 1505, 1522, 1526, 1529, 1565, 1572, 1599, 1619, 1637, 1659, 1665, 1672, 1673, 1677, 1678, 1702, 1757, 1759, 1760, 1767, 1804, 1806, 1839, 1855, 1886, 1887, 1942, 1944, 1964, 1978, 2004, 2042, 2096, 2122, 2132, 2147, 2168, 2178; alternative, A104; ancient, S325; Asian, S1344; dissenting, A104; economic, S1758; French, IS110; S1690; Greek, S1159; Indian, S1014, 1184; Islamic, S989; Japanese, S1220;

Jewish, S1238, 1266; of ecology, S2000; of education, S1804; of geography, S310; of mathematics, S329; of medicine, S311; of physics, L4; of religion, S320, 1752, 1894; of science, L4; S311, 1440, 1624, 1887; of social science, S329; oriental, S328; political, S1758; Roman, S1159
Phoenix Assurance Archvs, L5
phonetics, IS109; S1734
phonology, IS109
Photo Union Colln (London photos), S1288
photogrammetry, S684, 1336, 1940
photography, IS6, 22, 141; S104, 146, 208, 215, 474, 591, 634, 645, 702, 834, 981, 983, 985, 999, 1007, 1010, 1018, 1045, 1050, 1060, 1089, 1107, 1170, 1171, 1173, 1174, 1175, 1244, 1246, 1255, 1271, 1286, 1306, 1310, 1320, 1338, 1365, 1388, 1418, 1503, 1597, 1614, 1705, 1912, 1917, 2004, 2023, 2094, 2111, 2118; aerial, A387, 483, 486; S136, 341, 421, 998, 1007, 1364, 1588, 1625; astronomical, S1020; Irish, IS100; medical, S429; snooker, S854
phrenology, S311
phycology, S32
Physical Edu Assoc, Archvs, S972; *Lib,* P161
Physical Soc Colln (hist of physics), S934
physics, IS64, 111, 178; L4, 5; S40, 315, 482, 593, 621, 776, 959, 972, 1180, 1206, 1481, 1512, 1649, 1712, 1964, 1978, 2031, 2046; accelerator, S2087; applied, S1205; atomic, S1712, 2087; condensed matter, S535, 1712; laser, S1712; marine, S1945; medical, S1914; molecular, S2087; nuclear, IS63; S535, 1740, 1842, 2087; particle, S535, 1740; solid state, S2087; theoretical, S1712; upper atmosphere, S294
physiography, S341
Physiological Soc, archv, S1457
physiology, IS118; L4; S64, 79, 291, 316, 376, 1300, 1357, 1479, 1754, 1872, 1982, 2156; fruit, S295
physiotherapy, IL2; IS210; S12, 174, 429, 478, 584, 614, 818, 1074, 1521, 1947, 2069; *see also therapy*
phytopathology, S626
Pick, Frank, Archv (London Transport), S1268
Pickard-Cambridge Lib (entomology), S1738
Picken Colln (early Bach eds), S337
Picken Colln (ethnomusicology), L5
Pickering Colln (printing), S1255
Picts, S688
Picture Post Colln (photos), S1170
Pier Arts Centre, Archv Lib, S1999
Piercefield Park papers, A117
Pigott Colln (Somerset drawings), S2025
Pike Ward Colln (Iceland), A164
Pilgrim Fathers Colln, P139
Pilgrim Hosp Staff Lib, S204
Pilkington Lib, S1483
Pilkington, Matthew & Laetitia, papers & MSS (18C Irish poets), IA22
Pilley Colln (Herefordshire), A202
Pinney Family Papers, A77; S260
Pinto Colln (directories), S1290
Piot Colln (pageantry), S1290
Piozzi, Hester, Colln, S947
Pipe Roll Soc, O317
Piper, John, papers, A349
Piper, Myfanwy, MSS, S25
Pipon family papers, S2190
PIRA Internatl, Info Centre, S895
piracy, S1303
Piranesi Colln, S1433
Pitlochry Burgh records, A416
Pitman Colln (shorthand sys), S106
Pitt Rivers Museum, Balfour Lib, S1742
Pitt Rivers, Gen A.L.F., papers, S1890
Pitt, Morton, Colln, S1005
Pitt-Rivers, A.H., Gift (archaeo), S323
Place, Francis, Colln (cuttings), L1
Plague Colln, S182
Plaid Cymru Archvs, L3
Plainsong & Medieval Music Soc Lib, S1440
Planned Environment Therapy Trust, Archv & Study Centre, A104
planning, IS151; S74, 256, 310, 420, 476, 554, 591, 594, 723, 993, 1122, 1316, 1370, 1452, 1700, 1794, 1848, 1911, 1912, 1933, 2160; countryside, S452; emergency, S2163; environmental, S1103; health, S939, 1229; health service, S662; physical, S628; regional, S1151, 1912; sports, S641; town, S452, 1205, 1383, 1912; urban, S594, 1151
planning control, S341
Planning Exchange, O318; **Info Unit,** S723
Planning Inspectorate, Lib & Info Centre, S256
Plant Breeding Inst Archvs, S1624
plant commissioning, S1070
plant distribution, S1862
plant science, L4; S317, 558, 682, 786, 1624, 1669, 2045, 2089, 2107; aquatic, IS194; *see also botany*
Plas Power Colln (lit, hist), L3
plastics, S1918
Plater Coll Lib, S1757
Platten Bequest (spelaeology), S2097
play, S1296, 1845
Player, John, Papers, A442
Playwrights Union of Canada Colln, S1053
Plomer, William, MSS, S25
Plowright Colln (ironmongering trade), S578
Plumbe-Tempest, family & estate papers, A238
Plume, Archdeacon Thomas, MSS, S1505
Plumpton Coll Lib, S940
Plunket Museum of Irish Edu, Archv Collns, IA47
Plunkett Foundation Ref Lib & Info Centre, S1758
Plunkett, Horace, diaries & letters, S1758
Plunkett, James, papers, IL1
Plymouth & West Devon Record Office, A419
Plymouth Athenaeum Lib, S1806
Plymouth Coll of Art & Design Lib, S1807
Plymouth Coll of Further Edu, Lib & Learning Resources Svc, S1808
Plymouth Dock Labour Board records, A419
Plymouth Hosps NHS Trust Staff Lib, S1809
Plymouth Instn, proceedings, S1806
Plymouth Latter Day Saints Genealogical Branch Lib, *see* A420
Plymouth Lib & Info Svcs, *see* P146
Plymouth Local & Naval Studies Lib, A420
Plymouth Marine Laboratory, *see* S1805
Plymouth Marine Laboratory, records, S1805
Plymouth Museum & Art Gallery, S1810
Plymouth Proprietary Lib, S1811
Plymouth RC Diocesan Archvs, A120
Plymouth Univ, *see Univ of Plymouth*
Plymouth, Archdeaconry of, records, A419
Pneumatic Despatch Co Ltd, records, A484
Pocknell Colln (shorthand), A164
podiatry, S170, 584, 818, 1259, 1808, 1949
Podro Colln of Judaica, S1238
poetry, A235; IS41, 138; S368, 636, 687, 1325, 1340, 1527, 1637; Elizabethan, S2049; international, S636; modern, S636; Restoration, S1647; Romantic, S1225; Scottish, S63, 636; war, S1182; *see also literature*
Poetry Ireland, *see* IS41
Poetry Lib, S1325
Poetry Soc Lib, S2168
poets, S858, 872, 1225; Irish, IS193; Romantic, S34
Poland, S1327, 1436
Polani Rsrch Lib, S1326
polar regions, S339
Police Museum, Lib & Archvs, S137
Police Svc of Northern Ireland, records, S137
policing, IS200; S28, 137, 816, 1163, 1511, 1634; Irish, IA34
Polish community, S1328
Polish Inst & Sikorski Museum, Ref Lib, S1327
Polish Lib, S1328
Polish Underground & Solidarity Colln, S1328
Political Advertising Colln, A399
political parties & movements, S1887
political science, S628, 1241, 1277
politics, A88, 205, 289, 365, 370, 409; IS6, 38, 126; L4; S26, 28, 132, 144, 202, 230, 271, 336, 442, 508, 523, 610, 739, 869, 969, 1009, 1095, 1100, 1109, 1132, 1166, 1170, 1182, 1224, 1250, 1251, 1261, 1274, 1284, 1320, 1337, 1441, 1465, 1527, 1627, 1702, 1704, 1735, 1743, 1764, 1887, 1978, 2004, 2046; Albanian, S1436; American, S1653; Asian, S1377; Belarussian, S1436; British, S1647; Bulgarian, S1436; Chilean, S1447; Commonwealth, S1443; Czech, S1436; East European, S1436; Estonian, S1436; Finnish, S1436; foreign, S1213; German, IS80; Highlands, S1926; Hungarian, S1436; industrial, A114; international, S1369; Irish, A17; S1647, 1653; Latvian, S1436; Lithuanian, S1436; Middle Eastern, S672, Moldavian, S1436; Polish, S1328, 1436; religious, S132; Romanian, S1436; Russian, S1436, 1746; sexual, S234; Slavonic, S1436; Slovakian, S1436; Soviet, S1746; Spanish, S1210; Ukrainian, S1436; Ulster, S1653; US, S1432; Welsh, S419; women's, A365; Yugoslav, S1436; *see also history, political*
Pollard Colln, S2004
Pollard School Bk Colln, IL2
pollution, IS53; S32, 72, 543, 831, 1805; air, S1786; marine, S1805
Polwhele, Rev R., Colln, S2056
polymers, S808, 1200, 1918, 1928
Pontefract Genl Infirmary, Health Lib, S1813
Ponting, H.G., Colln (images of Scott's Antarctic expedition), S1614
Pontypridd & Rhondda NHS Trust, *see* S979
Pontypridd Coll Learning Centre, S1814
Poole Colln (Irish photography), IL1
Poole Libs, P147
Poole Local Hist Centre, A422
Poole Museum Archvs, A422
Poole, Borough of, records, A125
Pope, Alexander, Colln, A433; P103
Popperfoto (Paul Popper Ltd), S1614
population & population studies, S1312, 1741
porcelain, S1455, 1985
Porritt & Dawson Lib, S1918
Port Erin Town Commissioners, *see* P213
Port of Lowestoft Rsrch Soc, records, A361
Port Royale Colln, S1682
Port Talbot Local Studies Colln, P120
Porter Colln (ornithology), S1647
Porter Colln (solicitors' records), A244
Porteus Lib, S1440
Portico Lib, S1527
Portland papers, S2086
Portland, 7th Duke of, estate records, A20
Portobello Coll Lib, IS129
Porton Colln (Judaism), P72
portraiture, A313; Scottish, S634
Portsmouth City Lib Svc, P148
Portsmouth City Museums & Records Svc, A423; *see also* S1823
Portsmouth Deanery, parish records, A423
Portsmouth Hosps NHS Trust Lib Svc, S1825; *see also* S1826
Portsmouth Naval Colln, P148
Portsmouth RC Diocesan Archvs, A424
Portsmouth Univ, *see Univ of Portsmouth*
Portsmouth, Diocese of, records, A392, 423, 509
Portugal, S492, 1055
Post Office Heritage, A317
Post Office Savings Bank, papers, A317
post-natal care, S1295
Postal Hist Soc Lib, S110
Poster Lit Colln, S1050
postgraduate study, S1709
Potel Lib, IS26
Potter, Beatrix, Colln, S1472
pottery, S1804
poultry, S65, 1601, 1872
poverty, S230, 1112, 1319
Powell, Cecil, papers, A77
Powell, George, Colln (lit, art, music), S18
Powell, James, & Son (Whitefriars) Ltd, records (stained glass manufacturers), A250
power generation, A294; S581
power supply, S1070
PowerGen Lib, S800
Powergen, Power Tech Centre Lib, S1644
Powerscourt Estate Papers, IL1
Powicke Colln (Cambridge Platonists), S185
Powis Castle estate archv, L3
Powys Brothers Colln, S545
Powys Colln, P39; S345
Powys County Archvs Office, A243; *see also* A63
Powys Lib & Archv Svc, P149
Powys Sites & Monuments Record, A504
Powys, John Cowper, papers, L3
Poynton Colln (early aeronautics), S1342
Prange, Gordon W., Colln, S576
Pratt's (Bon Marche Ltd), records (dept store), A470
Pratt, Lawson, Colln (photos of Wellingborough), P131
preaching, S538
pregnancy, S1045, 1295
prehistory, S1031, 2097
Premier Health NHS Trust, *see* S948
Presbyterian Church in Ireland, records, S138, 147
Presbyterian Church of England, archvs, S397
Presbyterian Church of Wales, *see* S17
Presbyterian Historical Soc, Lib & Archvs, S138
Prescot Grammar School archvs, A222
Prescot Urban Dist, minutes, A222
preservation, S996; food, S295; music, S1836
Preshome Chapel Lib (theology), L2
Press Assoc News Lib, S1329
press freedom & regulation, S1108
pressure vessels, S1208
Preston & Whiston Co-op Soc archvs, A222
Preston Bequest, IS135
Preston Blake Colln (William Blake), A268
Preston Colln (cookery), S918
Preston Coll, William Tuson Lib, S1838
Preston Parish Lib, S404
Preston, Thomas, Lib, S883
Pretyman, George, papers (Bishop of Lincoln & Winchester), A215
Pretyman-Tomline families, papers, A215
Priaulx Lib, P216
Price's Patent Candle Co Ltd, records, A50
Price, Harry, Lib of Psychical Rsrch, S1440
Prichard, Mervyn, Colln (early geog), L3
Prideaux, John, Lib (17C Bishop of Worcester), S2147
Priebsch-Closs Colln (18C-19C German texts), S1445

Royal Soc for Asian Affairs, Lib, **S**1377

Royal Soc for the Encouragement of Arts, Manufactures & Commerce, Lib, **S**1378

Royal Soc for the Prevention of Accidents, Lib & Info Svcs, **S**175; see also **S**972

Royal Soc for the Prevention of Cruelty to Animals, HQ Lib, **S**820

Royal Soc for the Protection of Birds Lib, **S**1896

Royal Soc Lib, **S**1379

Royal Soc of Antiquaries of Ireland Lib, **IS**139

Royal Soc of British Artists Archv, **A**250

Royal Soc of Chem, Lib & Info Centre, **S**1380

Royal Soc of Edinburgh Nat Hist Lib, **S**863

Royal Soc of Lit, **O**330

Royal Soc of Medicine Lib, **S**1381; see also **S**221

Royal Soc of Painter-Printmakers, archvs, **A**254

Royal Soc of Portrait Painters Archv, **A**304

Royal Soc records, **S**1379

Royal South Hants Hosp, Staff Lib, **S**1941

Royal Statistical Soc Archvs, **A**339; see also **S**482, 1433

Royal Surrey County Hosp, Edu Centre Lib, **S**774

Royal Sussex Regiment archvs, **A**106

Royal Television Soc, Lib & Archv, **S**1382

Royal Town Planning Inst Lib, **S**1383

Royal Tunbridge Wells & Council, archv, **S**2059

Royal Tyrone Militia, records, **A**160

Royal Ulster Constabulary, records, **S**137

Royal Ulster Rifles Museum, Lib & Archvs, **A**42

Royal United Hosp NHS Trust, Postgrad Centre Lib, **S**105

Royal Veterinary Coll Lib, **S**1384

Royal Veterinary Coll of Ireland, records, **IA**49

Royal Victoria Hosp For Children, records, **A**348

Royal Victoria Infirmary Lib, **S**1583

Royal Watercolour Soc, archvs, **A**254

Royal Welch Fusiliers Museum Archvs, **A**85

Royal Welsh Agric Soc, records, **L**3

Royal Welsh Coll of Music & Drama Lib, **S**424

Royal Wolverhampton Hosps NHS Trust, see **S**2143

royalty, **S**1170, 1320, 1614

Royston, Buntington & Bishops Stortford Primary Care Trust, see **S**2098

RR Colln (rare bks), **L**4

RSSPCC Children First Archvs, **S**701

RTÉ Ref Lib, **IS**140; Stills Lib, **IS**141

rubber, **S**808, 1200, 1918, 2100; synthetic, **S**2100

Rudler Colln of Pamphs (geol), **S**18

rugby, **S**2060

Rugby Coll, LRC, **S**1878

Rugby Football Union, see **S**2060

Rugby School, Temple Reading Room, **S**1879

Ruggles Gates Colln (genetics), **S**1227

Runciman Papers (19C-20C politics), **S**1586

Runnett Music Lib, see **S**1627

Runshaw Coll Lib, **S**943

Rural Hist Centre, **S**1850

rural life & society, **A**421; **S**452, 578, 1103, 1850; Irish, **IA**97; Welsh, **S**419

rural studies, **S**273

rural trades, **S**578

RUSI Collns (military maps), **L**1

Ruskin Coll Lib, **S**1761

Ruskin Gallery Lib, **S**1907

Ruskin Lib, **S**885

Ruskin School of Drawing & Fine Art, Lib, **S**1745

Ruskin, John, Colln, **S**885, 1907; *MSS,* **S**828, 885, 1907; *papers,* **S**31, 1512

Russell family, estate papers (Dukes of Bedford), **A**11

Russell Rare Bk Lib, see **IS**183

Russell, Dora, Colln (Women's Peace Caravan), **A**75

Russell, Eric Frank, Archv, **S**973

Russell, George (AE), MSS, **A**15

Russell, Joan, Archv (choreographer), **A**192

Russell, Ken, Colln (film-maker), **S**1944

Russells of Woburn, estate archvs, **A**35

Russia & Russian studies, **S**1310, 1436, 1746

Russian & East European Centre Lib, **S**1746

Russian Orthodox Church Colln (hist & doctrine), **S**1436

Ruth Gibbes Lib, **S**1671

Rutherford Appleton Laboratory Lib, **S**535

Rutherford, Lord, papers, **L**5

Rutland County Council Lib Svc, **P**156

Rutland Local Hist & Record Soc, **O**331

Ryan, Archbishop, Colln, **IS**62

Ryan, Garman, Art Colln, **S**2076

Ryan, Hugh, Papers (Waterford historian), **IA**54

Rycotewood Coll, LRC, **S**2038

Rye Borough Archv, **A**230

Ryen of Inch Colln, **IA**21

Saatchi & Saatchi Campaigns & Slides Colln, **A**399

Sabatier Colln (French monetary hist), **S**1441

Sabhal Mòr Ostaig Lib, **S**1926

Sacher, Harry, papers (journalist & barrister), **A**306

Sackler Lib, **S**1747

sacraments, **S**1057

Sacred Harmonic Soc Lib (early printed music), **S**1350

Saddleworth Museum Archv Dept, **A**409

Sadler's Wells Opera, archv, **A**276

Sadler's Wells Theatre Archv, **A**295

safety, **S**865

Saffron Walden Archv Soc, **O**332

Saffron Walden Coll, records, **A**216

Saffron Walden Literary & Scientific Inst Lib, see **A**443

Saffron Walden Museum, Archvs, **A**442

Saffron Walden Town Lib & Victorian Studies Centre, **A**443

Said Business School, Sainsbury Lib, **S**1748

Sainsbury Laboratory Archvs, **S**1624

Sainsbury Lib, **S**1748

Sairseal agus Dill Colln (Irish lang eds), **IL**2

Salamanca Archvs (Irish Colls in Spain), **IS**183

salaries, **S**1069

sales promotion, **S**988

Salford City Archvs Svc, **A**444

Salford Coll, LRCs, **S**1529

Salford Libs & Info Svc, **P**157

Salford RC Diocesan Archvs, **A**80

Salford Royal Hosps NHS Trust, **S**1884

Salford Univ, see Univ of Salford

Salisbury & South Wiltshire Museum, Stevens Memorial Lib, **S**1890

Salisbury Cathedral Lib, **S**1891

Salisbury Coll Lib, **S**1892

Salisbury Health Care NHS Trust, Staff Lib, **S**1893

Salisbury, Diocese of, records, **A**125, 493, 509

Salisbury, Marquess of, family & estate papers, **A**238

Sally Howell Lib, **S**658

Salmon Colln (19C edu), **A**216

Salmon, Morrey, Photo Archv (ornithology), **S**412

Salop, Archdeaconry of, parish records, **A**453

Salt, William, Colln, **A**468

Saltash Coll Learning Centre, see **S**1856

Salter/Slater Colln (edu & training), **S**2140

Salters' Co Archv, **A**340

Saltoun Manse Colln, **L**2

Saltoun papers, **L**2

Salts of Saltaire, records, **A**62

Salvation Army, Internatl Heritage Centre, **A**341; Territorial HQ Lib, **S**1385; Training Coll Lib, see **S**1463

Samuel Johnson Birthplace Museum Lib, **S**947

Samuel, Raphael, Working Papers (ltd access), **S**1016

Sancroft, William, Colln, **S**353

Sandars Colln (liturgy, fine bindings), **L**5

Sanders Colln, **S**456

Sanderson Colln (19C-20C fashion), **P**72

Sanderson Lib, **S**1656

Sanderson, R&A, records (textile company), **A**148

Sandgate Urban Dist Council, records, **A**128

Sandwell & West Birmingham Hosps NHS Trust, Sandwell Clinical Lib, **S**2102

Sandwell Coll, Smethwick Campus Learning Centre, **S**2085; Wednesbury Campus Learning Centre, **S**2095; West Bromwich Campus Learning Centre, **S**2103

Sandwell Community Hist & Archvs Svc, **A**499

Sandwell Healthcare NHS Trust, see **S**2102

Sandwell Lib & Info Svc, **P**158

Sandwell Primary Care Trusts Lib, **S**2104

Sandwich Borough records, **A**128

Sandwich, Earls of, family & estate records, **A**211

Sandys Colln (classics), **S**325

sanitaryware, **S**1985

sanitation, **S**1070

Sanofi-Synthelabo Rsrch Lib, **S**29

Sanquhar Burgh records, **A**133

Sark Court, records, **A**535, 536

Sark Militia, records, **A**536

Sark Seigneurie, **A**536

Sark, Ministers & Seigneurs of, papers, **A**536

Sarsfield Estate Papers, **IL**1

Sarum Coll Lib, **S**1894

Sasha London Theatre Colln (photos), **S**1170

Sassoon, Siegfried, papers & MSS, **A**289; **L**5

satire, **S**1032

Satow Colln (Buddhist lit), **L**4

Satow, Ernest, Colln (Japanese bks), **L**5

Saudi Arabia, **S**1386

Saudi Arabian Info Centre Lib, **S**1386

Saumarez, Admiral Sir James, papers, **A**215

Saunders Colln (Warwickshire), **S**1996

Saurat, Denis, MSS, **S**1231

Savage-Stevens Lib (early printed music), **S**1341

Save the Children Fund, Archvs, **A**342

Savile of Thornhill, family & estate records, **A**208

Savory Colln (Huguenot material), **S**139

Saxl, Fritz, papers, **S**1456

Saxton MSS (music), **S**25

Sayle, Robert, of Cambridge, records (dept store), **A**470

schizophrenia, **S**2069

Schillabeer, Paul, Photo Archv, **L**2

Schnitzler Press-Cuttings Archv, **S**671

Schnitzler, Arthur, papers, **L**5

School Lib Assoc, **O**333; Scotland, **O**334

School of Slavonic & East European Studies Archvs, **S**1436

Schools Council, archvs, **S**1444

Schottlander, Bernard, papers (design), **A**69

Schrumpf Colln (Armenian lit), **S**1344

Schulkind, Eugene W., Commune Colln (Paris Commune 1871), **S**239

Schwitters, Kurt, Colln & Archv (art), **S**1075

Scicluna Colln (hist of Malta), **L**4

science, **A**88, 480, 508; **IS**6, 7, 11, 13, 28, 39, 44, 47, 64, 75, 82, 90, 110, 123, 135, 137, 146, 150, 152, 166, 172, 181, 183, 192, 195, 198, 202, 204; **L**4; **S**12, 16, 29, 30, 49, 50, 67, 68, 78, 98, 107, 117, 121, 156, 165, 180, 229, 232, 269, 270, 271, 273, 295, 296, 297, 303, 316, 332, 347, 382, 404, 412, 433, 443, 456, 469, 473, 478, 482, 495, 498, 503, 505, 515, 525, 540, 541, 561, 565, 581, 593, 604, 606, 610, 616, 621, 652, 665, 669, 681, 701, 713, 733, 741, 755, 776, 780, 788, 805, 810, 813, 824, 825, 834, 838, 858, 859, 869, 877, 893, 904, 910, 918, 927, 969, 972, 986, 1009, 1015, 1053, 1076, 1084, 1106, 1110, 1135, 1180, 1200, 1202, 1227, 1243, 1251, 1262, 1266, 1333, 1338, 1362, 1371, 1379, 1388, 1421, 1429, 1433, 1435, 1480, 1487, 1505, 1512, 1524, 1536, 1540, 1546, 1552, 1565, 1570, 1572, 1582, 1597, 1599, 1610, 1623, 1636, 1637, 1639, 1641, 1644, 1647, 1654, 1659, 1678, 1716, 1767, 1780, 1786, 1792, 1799, 1800, 1804, 1806, 1816, 1822, 1837, 1842, 1848, 1854, 1855, 1881, 1886, 1895, 1900, 1907, 1911, 1912, 1942, 1955, 1959, 1966, 1969, 1971, 1976, 1978, 1983, 2010, 2015, 2020, 2031, 2036, 2038, 2042, 2045, 2049, 2059, 2067, 2091, 2094, 2095, 2103, 2113, 2120, 2125, 2130, 2145, 2147, 2168, 2176, 2178, 2179; antiquarian, **IS**154; applied, **S**113, 263, 430, 561; early, **S**433, 577; East Asian, **S**378; engineering, **IS**178; environmental, **IS**145; Greek, **S**1159; Islamic, **S**989; military, **A**292; **S**26; nuclear, **IS**130; Roman, **S**1159; *see also history of science; philosophy of science; also under individual sciences*

science & religion, **S**320, 1752

Sci & Tech Policy Rsrch Lib, **S**235

science & the media, **S**1043

Sci Fiction Foundation, see **S**973

Sci Museum Lib, **S**1387; see also **S**215, 2165

Sci Photo Lib Ltd, **S**1388

science policy, **S**235, 1379, 1457

Scientific Cttee on Problems of the Environment, papers, **S**482

Scientific Film Assoc, papers, **S**1043

scientific instruments, **S**1031

Scotland & Scottish studies, **S**593, 598, 645

Scotland Street Museum of Edu, **S**718

Scott family & estate papers, **A**282

Scott Polar Rsrch Inst Lib, **S**339

Scott Tallon & Walker Colln (arch), **IA**36

Scott, C.P., papers (journalism), **S**1512

Scott, Doug, Colln (mountaineering photos), **S**2118

Scott, John, papers (architect), **A**511

Scott, John, papers (Lord Chancellor), **A**511

Scott, Marion, Bequest (early Haydn scores), **L**5

Scott, Sir James George, Colln (South East Asian langs), **L**5

Scott, Sir Walter, Colln, **A**448; **S**1978; *papers & MSS,* **L**2; **S**918

Scottish Academic Libs Co-op Training Group, **O**335

Scottish Accountancy Rsrch Trust Lib, **S**624

Scottish Actors Co Archv, **A**182

Scottish Agricultural Coll Lib, **S**625; W.J. Thomson Lib, **S**65

Scottish Agricultural Sci Agency Lib, **S**626

Scottish Amicable Life Assurance Soc, records, **A**320

Scottish & Newcastle, records (brewers), **A**179

Scottish & Northern Bk Distribution Centre Colln, **S**701

Scottish Arts Council Archv, **L**2

Simms Colln (early Irish bks), S139
Simon Community Archv, S972
Simon, Lord, papers, A367
Simon, Oliver, Colln (fine printing), S19
Simonds, Gavin, papers (judge), A511
Simpson Colln (British floras), S317
Simpson, Alexander Russell, correspondence, S1352
Simpson, J.Y., Colln (obstetrics & gynaecology), S616
Simpson, Robert, Archv, S651
Simson, James, Colln (16C-18C), S1964
Singer Manufacturing Co Ltd Colln, A110
Singer's Art Metalworks, records, A168
Singh, Gurharpal, Archv (Punjabi communism), A114
Singleton Hosp Staff Lib, S2012
SINTO: The Info Partnership for South Yorkshire & North Derbyshire, O352
Sion Colln (theology, ecclesiastical hist), S1227
Sion Coll Colln & MSS, S1234
Sir Alister Hardy Foundation for Ocean Sci, *see* S1805
Sir Herbert Duthrie Lib, S427
Sir James Paget Lib, S761
Sir John Black Lib, *see* S499, 1876
Sir John Soane's House & Museum Lib, S1391
Sir Patrick Dun's Hosp, records, IS133
Sir William Burnett Lib, S754
Sisson, C.H., papers, A77
Sisters of Mercy, *see* IA27
Sitwell, Edith, papers & MSS, S25, 239
Six Towns, local authority archvs, A473
Sizewell 'B' Inquiry, records, A77
Sjöö, Monica, Archv (feminism), A75
Skeat & Furnivall Colln (early English lang & lit), S1227
Ski Club of Gt Britain Lib, S1392
Skiddy's Almhouse records, IA19
skiing, S1392, 2111
Skilliter Centre for Ottoman Studies, *see* S380
skills, S1098
Skishoot-Offshoot Picture Lib, S2111
Sladen Colln (letters & papers), P103
Sladen, Douglas, Colln (19C editor of Who's Who), A433
Slains Castle Colln (16C-18C), P56
Slaithwaite Parish Lib Colln, S2168
slavery & the slave trade, A239, 256; S248, 404, 1441
Slessor, Mary, Colln, A136
Slievemargy Rural Dist Council, records, IA83
Sligo Chamber of Commerce, *see* IS196
Sligo County Lib Svcs, IP25; **Archvs & Local Studies Collns,** IA87
Sligo Euro Info Centre, IS196
Sligo Genl Hosp, Rsrch & Edu Centre Lib, IS197
Sligo Harbour Commissioners, Archvs & Records, IA88
Sligo Museum Colln, IA87
Sloane, Sir Hans, Lib & MSS, L1
Slough Libs & Info Svc, P164; *see also* A429
Smallwood Clinical Lib, S176
Smart, C., MSS, S382
Smeatonian Soc of Civil Engineers Archvs, S1205
Smetham Colln (art), S1776
Smith Colln (printing & engraving), S2168
Smith Colln of Cartoon & Caricature Bks, S410
Smith family & estate papers (Viscounts Hambleden), A484
Smith O'Brien, William, papers, IL1
Smith, A&W, records (machinery manufacturers), A176
Smith, Adam, Colln, S593; *Lib,* S139
Smith, Charles Lesingham, Colln (early scientific bks), S344
Smith, Frank, Colln (civil eng), S1205
Smith, James, papers (politician), A511
Smith, Janet, & Dancers Archv, A192
Smith, John, Colln (17C maths), S385
Smith, John, Papers (surgery), S617
Smith, Kenneth M., Colln (virologist), S1669
Smith, Patrick, Colln (London photos), S1288
Smith, Sir Frank Ewart, papers (eng), S1208
Smith, Sir J.E., papers (nat hist), S1247
Smith, Sydney, letters, S1695
Smith, Thomas, Colln (Renaissance humanism), S385
Smith, W.H., & Son Ltd, records, A484
Smith, William, papers (geol), S1738
SmithKline Beecham Lib, S1966
SmithKline Beecham Pharmaceuticals Lib, *see* S221
SmithKline Beecham, advertising archv, A399
Smoke Abatement League of Gt Britain Colln, S233
smoking, S417, 1157
Smyth family of Ashton Court, records, A72
Snell, Philip, Colln (popular music), S965
Sneyd Papers, S1572
Sneyd-Kynnersley family papers, A467
snooker, S854
Snow, Brigadier, Papers (liberation of Channel Islands), A533
snowboarding, S2111
Snowden Colln, P15
Soane, Sir John, Lib & Papers, S1391
social affairs, S1009
social care, S208, 263, 504, 525, 565, 796, 834, 915, 991, 1096, 1600, 1788, 1816, 1882, 2103, 2149
Social Democratic Party Archvs, S482; *Scotland,* S701; *Wales,* L3
social history, *see history, social*
social issues, S1107, 1170, 1214, 1432
social policy, A264; IS57, 58, 114; S113, 133, 562, 717, 1112, 1151, 1294, 1420, 1702, 1722, 1978
social responsibility, business, S1191
social science, A328; IS2, 7, 9, 11, 12, 26, 29, 31, 34, 35, 44, 46, 56, 59, 68, 69, 73, 80, 82, 87, 90, 92, 93, 97, 104, 110, 112, 115, 116, 117, 123, 125, 129, 147, 149, 166, 169, 171, 173, 174, 176, 181, 183, 195, 197, 198, 202, 207; S7, 12, 42, 49, 50, 60, 73, 76, 79, 115, 121, 150, 156, 173, 198, 208, 224, 230, 234, 238, 244, 258, 263, 264, 271, 273, 288, 296, 297, 300, 302, 320, 323, 328, 330, 332, 336, 340, 382, 427, 429, 430, 436, 437, 442, 443, 469, 478, 490, 492, 495, 498, 505, 506, 515, 525, 540, 550, 559, 561, 565, 576, 587, 590, 591, 593, 603, 604, 610, 670, 675, 676, 681, 698, 701, 709, 713, 717, 723, 739, 741, 743, 757, 765, 776, 788, 790, 794, 810, 839, 847, 855, 856, 869, 870, 875, 879, 904, 910, 918, 923, 931, 932, 950, 969, 972, 982, 986, 1015, 1016, 1017, 1018, 1053, 1059, 1078, 1082, 1084, 1096, 1112, 1123, 1127, 1135, 1144, 1147, 1148, 1160, 1163, 1180, 1182, 1188, 1189, 1194, 1204, 1215, 1220, 1227, 1238, 1241, 1246, 1250, 1255, 1260, 1261, 1262, 1266, 1274, 1277, 1282, 1296, 1299, 1301, 1302, 1328, 1330, 1333, 1334, 1403, 1419, 1420, 1421, 1429, 1440, 1444, 1447, 1449, 1452, 1463, 1497, 1498, 1510, 1511, 1512, 1524, 1526, 1529, 1536, 1550, 1552, 1565, 1572, 1574, 1599, 1616, 1617, 1623, 1629, 1630, 1635, 1637, 1641, 1654, 1659, 1663, 1675, 1677, 1678, 1690, 1696, 1700, 1702, 1710, 1711, 1716, 1722, 1724, 1733, 1741, 1743, 1744, 1757, 1758, 1760, 1767, 1772, 1788, 1804, 1806, 1807, 1822, 1837, 1855, 1858, 1877, 1886, 1887, 1893, 1902, 1907, 1912, 1917, 1929, 1942, 1944, 1949, 1952, 1971, 1976, 1978, 1982, 1983, 1987, 2004, 2010, 2018, 2020, 2028, 2036, 2042, 2064, 2067, 2080, 2093, 2095, 2120, 2122, 2134, 2145, 2156, 2160, 2164, 2168, 2173, 2178, 2179; applied, S438; *see also sociology*
social security, S1112, 1679
social services, IS58; S1111, 1993; Salvation Army, S1463
social studies, L4; S1597, 1761, 1816, 1894, 1911; Indian, L4; South East Asian, L4
social theory, S310
social work, S140, 180, 267, 469, 492, 609, 628, 712, 723, 881, 923, 969, 1301, 1304, 1420, 1475, 1550, 1722, 1761
socialism, A370; S883, 1274, 1464, 1887; early, S1441; English, S1441; French, S1441
Socialist Medical Assoc, records, S828
Société Guernesiaise, Lib, S2187
Société Jersiaise, Lord Coutanche Lib, S2190
Soc for Co-operation in Russian & Soviet Studies, Lib, S1393
Soc for Lincolnshire Hist & Archaeo, O353; **Lib,** S956; *see also* A233
Soc for Name Studies in Britain & Ireland, O354
Soc for Psychical Rsrch Lib, S1394; *see also* L5
Soc for Rsrch into Higher Edu, Lib, S1395
Soc for Storytelling Lib, P163
Soc for the Diffusion of Useful Knowledge, archvs, S1433
Soc for the Furtherance of the Gospel, records, A309
Soc for the Protection of Ancient Bldgs, Archvs, A345
Soc for the Study of Diseases in Children, archvs, S1381
Soc of Anaesthetists, archvs, S1381
Soc of Antiquaries, Colln, A151; *papers,* S612
Soc of Antiquaries of London Lib, S1396
Soc of Antiquaries of Newcastle upon Tyne Lib, S1584; *see also* A390
Soc of Antiquaries of Scotland Lib, S612
Soc of Apothecaries Archvs, A346
Soc of Architectural Historians of Gt Britain, archvs, S1512
Soc of Archivists, O355; **Archvs for Edu & Learning Group,** O356; **Business Records Group,** O357; **EAD/Data Exchange Group,** O358; **East Midlands Region,** O359; **Eastern Region,** O360; **Film & Sound Group,** O361; **Ireland,** IO42; **London Region,** O362; **North West Region,** O363; **Northern Region,** O364; **Preservation & Conservation Group,** O365; **Records Mgmt Group,** O366; **Scotland,** O371; **South East Region,** O367; **South West Region,** O368; **Specialist Repositories Group,** O369; **Wales,** O372; **West Midlands Region,** O370
Soc of Authors, O373
Soc of Chemical Industry, Lib & Archv, S1397
Soc of Chief Libns in England & Wales, O374
Soc of Civil Eng Technicians Archvs, S1205
Soc of Coll, Natl & Univ Libs, O375
Soc of Dyers & Colourists, Colour Museum, Lib, S216
Soc of Genealogists, O376; **Lib,** S1398
Soc of Glass Tech Colln, S1912
Soc of Indexers, O377; **Irish Group,** IO43; **Scottish Group,** O378
Soc of Irish Foresters, Lib, IS3
Soc of Jesus in Britain, A251
Soc of Mental Welfare Offcrs, records, A53
Soc of Naval Architects & Marine Engineers, transactions, S1199, 2030
Soc of Petroleum Papers, S12
Soc of Public Info Networks, O379
Soc of Solicitors in the Supreme Court of Scotland (SSC) Lib, S640
Soc of Teachers Opposed to Physical Punishment, archvs, S1444
Soc of Technical Analysts Lib, P99
Soc of Writers to Her Majesty's Signet, S639
sociolinguistics, S419
sociology, IS9, 16, 144, 151, 176, 210; S12, 22, 109, 115, 180, 202, 310, 326, 336, 419, 482, 492, 562, 609, 628, 776, 787, 790, 838, 968, 995, 1082, 1210, 1243, 1304, 1328, 1349, 1407, 1430, 1439, 1475, 1560, 1616, 1702, 1743, 1783, 1978, 1982, 1993, 2008, 2046, 2113, 2158; medical, S717; of language, IS109; of religion, S1522, 1752; of work, IS116; *see also social science*
Sodor & Man, Diocese of, records, A529
software, S301
SOG Ltd, Heath Lib, S1881
Soho Square Hosp for Women, archvs, A351
Soil Mechanics Lib, S2138
soil science, S9, 72, 78, 310, 321, 341, 786, 831, 1882, 2000, 2072, 2137
Solihull Heritage & Local Studies Dept, A455
Solihull Hosp Lib, S1931
Solihull Libs, P165
Solomons, Bethel, papers (gynaecology), S1352
Solon Colln, A473
Somerset Archaeo & Nat Hist Soc Lib, S2025; *see also* A488; S98
Somerset Archv & Record Office, A487
Somerset Coll of Arts & Tech Lib, S2026
Somerset family & estate papers, A493
Somerset family papers (Dukes of Beaufort), A22
Somerset Libs, Arts & Info, P166
Somerset Miners Assoc Colln, A77
Somerset Poor Law Unions, records, A487
Somerset Postgrad Centre Medical Lib, S2027
Somerset Quarter & Petty Sessions, records, A487
Somerset Record Soc, O380
Somerset Studies Lib, A488
Somerset West Liberal Assoc, minutes, A477
Somerset, Dukes of, estate papers, A11
Somerset, Lord Fitzroy, papers, A311
Somerville Colln (maths), S357
Somerville Coll Lib, S1762
song, S419; English, S25; political, A170; traditional, S1453
Sorabji Archv, A32
Sorabji, Kaikhosru Shapurji, MSS (music), S1428
Soulby, J., Jobbing Printer, Colln, A28
Soutar, William, Lib (lit), P144
South Africa Colln (apartheid era), S1903
South Africa House Lib, S1399
South & East Belfast Health & Social Svcs Trust, *see* S126
South Asia Archv & Lib Group, O381
South Asian Dance Colln, A192
South Asian studies, L4
South Ayrshire Lib & Info Svcs, P167
South Ayrshire Scottish & Local Hist Lib, A21; *see also* A20
South Bank Board, S1325
South Bank Centre, exhib records, A331
South Bank Univ, Learning & Info Svcs, S1400; **East London Campus Lib,** S1401; **Essex Campus Lib,** S1871
South Birmingham Coll Lib Svcs, S177
South Birmingham Primary Care Trust, S176
South Buckinghamshire NHS Trust, Staff Lib, S35; *see also* S811
South Cheshire Coll Lib, S507
South Devon Coll Learning Centre, S2047
South Devon Dist Council records, A161
South Devon Healthcare NHS Trust Lib, S2048
South Downs Coll, LRC, S792
South Dublin Libs, IP26
South Dublin Local Studies Colln, IA48
South Durham Healthcare NHS Trust, *see* S187, 520
South East Asian studies, S828

South East Derbyshire Coll Lib, S838
South East Essex Coll, Study Centre, S1950
South East Film & Video Archv, A71
South East Museum, Lib & Archv Council, O382
South East Regional Archv Council, O383
South East Univ Libns, O384
South Eastern Edu & Lib Board, Lib Svc, P135
South Eastern Health Board, Lib & Info Svc, IS171; *see also* IS210, 211
South Essex Health Authority, Lib & Info Svc, S222
South Glamorgan County Council, records, A97
South Glasgow Univ Hosps NHS Trust, Central Lib, S734; James Bridie Lib, S735
South Gloucestershire Lib Svc, P168
South Gloucestershire Local Studies Svc, A521
South Humber Primary Care Resource Centre, S228
South Kent Coll Lib, S686
South Lanarkshire Libs & Community Learning Svc, P169; Archvs & Info Mgmt Svc, A142
South Lancashire Regiment, records, A426
South Leicestershire Coll, LRC, S2117
South London & Maudsley NHS Trust, Multidisciplinary Lib, S1402; *see also* S109
South Manchester Univ Hosps NHS Trust, Lib Svcs, S1531
South Nottingham Coll Lib, S1645
South of Scotland Central Technical Coll, records, A148
South Staffordshire Healthcare NHS Trust Lib Svcs, S948; Stafford Site, S1972
South Staffordshire Regiment, records, S946
South Thames Coll, Learning Centre, S1403
South Tipperary County Council, *see* IA16; IP27
South Tipperary County Museum, Archvs, IA16
South Tyneside Coll Lib, S1935; Hebburn Lib, S796
South Tyneside Healthcare NHS Trust, Edu Centre Lib, S1936
South Tyneside Libs, P170
South Tyneside Local Hist Lib, A457; *see also* A391
South Wales Borderers & Monmouthshire Regimental Museum, Archvs, A64
South Wales Coalfield Colln, S2015; records, A97
South Wales Inst of Engineers, Lib, S425
South Wales Miners' Lib, *see* S2015
South Warwickshire Medical Edu Centre Lib, S2090
South West Film & Television Archv, A421
South West Museums, Libs & Archvs Council, O385
South West Regional Archv Council, O386
South West Water Ltd, HQ Lib, S669
South West Yorkshire Mental Health NHS Trust, Fieldhead Hosp Lib, S2069
South Western Area Health Board, *see* IS189
South Western Regional Lib System, O387
South Yorkshire Access to Libs for Learning, *see* O352
South Yorkshire County Council, records, A452
Southall & West London Coll, Southall Learning Centre, S1937
Southampton Archvs Svcs, A459
Southampton City Coll Lib, S1942
Southampton City Cultural Svcs, Collns Mgmt Centre, S1943
Southampton City Libs, P171

Southampton Conservative Party, records, A459
Southampton Deanery, records, A459
Southampton Harbour Board, minutes, S1943
Southampton Inst, Mountbatten Lib, S1944
Southampton Labour Party, records, A459
Southampton Maritime Colln, P171
Southampton Medical Reading Club, records, S1946
Southampton Methodist Circuit, records, A459
Southampton Oceanography Centre, Natl Oceanographic Lib, S1945
Southampton School of Art, records, S1946
Southampton Univ, *see Univ of Southampton*
Southend Coll of Tech, *see* S1950
Southend Hosp, Edu Centre Lib, S2108
Southend on Sea Borough Libs, P172
Southern & South East Arts, *see* O324
Southern Derbyshire Acute Hosps NHS Trust, Lib & Knowledge Svc, S527; *see also* S524
Southern Edu & Lib Board, P134; Irish & Local Studies Lib, A17
Southern Health Board, *see* IS206
Southern Info Network, *see* O215
Southern Television Archv, S1013
Southey, Robert, MSS, A442; S858
Southgate Coll Lib, S1404
Southmead Lib & Info Svc, S257
Southowram family & estate records, A194
Southport & Ormskirk Hosp NHS Trust, Hanley Lib, S1952; *see also* S1656
Southport Coll Lib, S1953
Southport Lib, Local Hist Unit, *see* A462
Southward, John, Colln (printing tech), S1408
Southwark Coll Learning Centre, S1405
Southwark Diocesan Training Lib, *see* S1140
Southwark Libs, P104
Southwark Local Studies Lib, A347
Southwark, Diocese of, records, A304, 513
Southwark, RC Archdiocese of, records, A252
Southwell Diocesan Record Office, *see* A406
Southwell Minster Lib, S1956
Soviet Union, S482, 1310
Sowerby family & estate records, A194
Sowerby letters (zoology), S422
space & space science, IS40; S535, 1026, 1036, 1388, 1614
Spain & Spanish studies, S492, 1055
Spanish Civil War, S1016, 1182
Spanish Drama Colln, S1946
Spare Rib Colln, A75
Sparrow, John, Colln (works of Rev R. Polwhele), S2056
Sparrow, John, Colln of Cowper Bks, S1652
Sparshatt Archv (motoring), S266
Sparsholt Coll Hampshire, Lib & Info Centre, S2123
Special Infantry Corps, records (Ireland), IA45
Special Interest Group on Adverse Reactions, *see* O39
Special Interest Group on Legal Records, *see* O326
Special Libs Assoc (European Chapter), O388
special needs, S1430, 2179
Spectral Data Colln, S1512
speech & speech science, S1299, 1373
spelaeology, S2097
Spencer (Althorpe), estate archv, A395
Spencer Colln (early ch's bks), P71
Spencer Colln (early printed bks), S1512
Spencer Darien Scheme (17C Scottish colony in Panama), records, S738

Spencer Stanhope family papers, A452
Spencer, Jean, Archv (art), S1075
Spencer, Robert, Colln (music), S1341
Spencer, Sir Stanley, Colln, S1501; papers, A349
Spencer-Stanhope of Horsforth, family & estate records, A349
Speyburn Glenlivet Distillery Co Ltd, records, A376
spinal cord injury, S59
spirituality, IS191; S577, 1057, 1463, 1932
Spitalfields Mathematical Soc Lib, S1345
Spode Papers, S1572
sponsorship, S1406
sport, S65, 81, 287, 297, 584, 641, 645, 805, 838, 983, 985, 1106, 1108, 1131, 1170, 1226, 1276, 1298, 1320, 1338, 1392, 1406, 1499, 1614, 1622, 1845, 1978, 1982, 2060, 2103
Sport England, Info Centre, S1406
Sports Council papers, S179
sports science, S469, 641, 969, 1439, 1617, 1949, 2045, 2064
sports studies, S115, 180, 430, 796, 1610
sports turf, S1499
Sportscotland, Lib, S641
SPRI Picture Lib, S339
SPRIG: Promoting Info in Leisure, Tourism & Sport, O389
Spring Hill Coll Lib Colln (theology), S1691
Spring, Howard, MSS, S1512
Springdale Coll Lib, *see* S180
Springfield Hosp Staff Lib, *see* S1410
SPRU Lib, S235
Spurgeon's Coll Lib, S1407
Spurgeon, Charles, archv, S1407
Squire Law Lib, *see* L5
Sraffa Colln (hist of econ), S393
St Aidan's Theological Coll Lib, S966
St Albans City Hosp, Staff Lib & Info Svc, S1962
St Albans Museums Lib, S1963
St Albans, City of, archvs, S1963
St Albans, Diocese of, records, A35, 204
St Andrew's Group of Hosps Medical Lib, S1616
St Andrew's Hall Lib, *see* S180
St Andrews Presbytery & Kirk Session, records, S1964
St Andrews Univ, *see Univ of St Andrews*
St Andrews Univ Missionary Soc Colln, S1964
St Angela's Coll Lib, IS198
St Anne's Coll Lib, S1763
St Anthony's Lib Colln (theology, hist), IS166
St Antony's Coll Lib, S1764; *see also* S1735, 1737, 1746
St Asaph Cathedral Lib, L3
St Aubyn Estate Archv, A419
St Augustine's Lib of Theology, *see* S404
St Austell China Clay Museum Ltd, *see* A463
St Austell Coll Lib, S1965
St Bart's Hosp Rochester, records, A435
St Bartholomew's & The London Queen Mary's School of Medicine & Dentistry, Medical Lib, *see* S1333
St Benedict's Hosp, Tooting, records, A348
St Bernard's Hosp Patients' Lib, *see* P84
St Bride Printing Lib, S1408
St Brigid's Hosp Lib, IS1
St Cadoc's Psychiatric Hosp Lib, *see* S1595
St Canice's Lib, IS172
St Catharine's Coll (Cambridge) Lib, S390
St Catherine's Coll (Oxford) Lib, S1765
St Catherine's Coll of Edu for Home Econ, Lib, IS9
St Christopher's Hospice, Halley Stewart Lib, S1409
St Columb's Cathedral, Chapter House Lib, S1478
St Columba's Hospice, Clinical Lib, S642

St Columban's Lib, IS191
St Conal's Lib of Art & Design, *see* IS177
St Cross Coll Lib, S1766
St Davnet's Hosp Lib, IS187
St Deiniol's Residential Lib, S523; *see also* A200
St Edmund Hall Lib, S1767
St Edmund's Coll, 15th Duke of Norfolk Memorial Lib, S391
St Edmunds Coll, Ware, records, A356
St Edmundsbury & Ipswich, Diocese of, records, A83, 215, 361
St Fin Barres Cathedral Lib, IS27
St Francis Trust, *see* IS157
St George's Chapel, Chapter Lib, S2132
St George's Hosp (Essex), Aubrey Keep Lib, S818
St George's Hosp (London), Archv, A348; Medical School Lib, S1410
St George's Hosp (Northumberland), Mental Health Lib, S1560
St George's Medical & Surgical Soc, records, A348
St Helena Hospice, Millie Hare Lib, S481
St Helens Coll, SmithKline Beecham Lib, S1966
St Helens Lib & Info Svc, P173
St Helens Local Hist & Archvs Lib, A464
St Helier Hosp, Hirson Lib, S441
St Hilda's Coll Lib, S1768
St Hugh's Coll Lib, S1769
St Ives Town Council, *see* S1967
St Ives Trust Archv Study Centre, A465
St James Hosp, Balham, records, A348
St James's Univ Hosp Lib, *see* S918
St John Ambulance Brigade, *see* S1287
St John Nixon Colln (motoring), S266
St John's Ambulance Assoc, *see* S1362
St John's Coll (Cambridge) Lib, S392
St John's Coll (Durham) Lib, S575
St John's Coll (Lampeter) Archv, S879
St John's Coll (Oxford) Lib, S1770
St Johns Hosp Lib, *see* S447
St Joseph's Missionary Soc, Mill Hill Lib, S1411
St Joseph, Dr J.K.S., Colln (aerial photos), IS121
St Katherine Cree Sunday School Lib, A314
St Leonard, Shoreditch, parish records, A280
St Loye's School of Health Studies Lib, S670
St Luke's Inst of Cancer Rsrch, Oncology Resource Centre, IS142
St Margaret's (Lee), parish records, A297
St Margaret's Colln, P123
St Martin's Coll, Harold Bridges Lib, S886; Ambleside Lib, S33; Carlisle Lib, S438
St Mary's (Lewisham), parish records, A297
St Mary's Cathedral Chapter records, A388
St Mary's Coll, Info Svcs & Systems, S2064
St Mary's Hosp Medical School Colln, S1179
St Mary's Medical Lib, S1532
St Mary's Univ Coll Lib, S144
St Michael's Coll, Archdeacon Gordon James Lib, S426
St Michael's Hosp Lib, *see* S259
St Nicolas Hosp, Mental Health Lib, S1585
St Pancras Metropolitan Borough, records, A262
St Patrick's Coll, Carlow, Lib, IS12
St Patrick's Coll, Cregan Lib, IS143; *see also* IS69
St Patrick's Coll, Maynooth, Pamph Colln, IS183
St Patrick's Coll, Thules, Lib, IS201
St Paul's Cathedral Lib, S1412; *see also* A280
St Paul's Girls' School Lib, S1413

Swansea Lib & Info Svc, **P**182; **Local Studies Dept, A**479
Swansea Museum, Lib & Archvs, A480
Swansea NHS Trust, see **S**2011, 2012, 2014
Swansea Psychiatric Edu Centre Lib, S2014
Swanstock Colln (fine art images), **S**1173
Swarthmore MSS (Quakerism), **S**1242
Swedenborg Soc Lib, S1417
Swedenborg, Emanuel, Colln, **S**1417
Sweet, J.M., papers, **S**612
Swift, Jonathan, Colln (early eds), **IL**1
Swinburne, A.C., Colln, **P**109; *papers & MSS,* **S**918
Swindon Libs, P183
Swindon, Archdeaconry of, records, **A**493
Swinton Urban Dist, records, **A**444
Swords Historical Soc Ltd, IO44
Sydney Jones Lib, see **S**972, 973
Sykes of Sledmere, family & estate papers, **S**828
Sykes Pumps, records, **A**278
symbolism, **IS**193
Symonds, John Addington, Papers & MSS, **A**77
synagogues, **S**1298, 1517
Syndicalist Workers Federation records, **S**1224
Synge Hutchinson Family Papers, **IA**49
Synge, John Millington, Colln, **IA**7; **IP**32; *papers,* **IL**1
Syon Abbey Lib & Community Archvs, S1932; see also **S**671
systematics, **S**1247
Syvret, Marguerite, MSS (author), **S**2190

tableware, **S**1985
Tabley family muniments, **S**1512
Tackling Social Exclusion in Libs, Museums, Archvs & Galleries, O294
tactics, **S**26, 1130
Taibhearc Archv, **IS**166
tailoring, **S**1254
Tait Colln (political pamphs), **S**1978
Tait, James, papers (historian), **S**1512
Talbot family & estate papers, **A**467, 493
Talbot Lib, S1839
Talbot papers, **S**2086
Talbot, W.H.F., Colln & MSS (early photography), **S**215
Talis Info Ltd, O400
Tallaght Dispensary Cttee, minutes, **IA**48
Tameside Coll Lib, S53
Tameside Libs & Leisure, P184
Tameside Local Studies Lib, A469
Tameside Mechanics Insts, records, **A**469
Tameside Turnpike Trusts, records, **A**469
Tamworth & Lichfield Coll, John McDermott Lib & LRC, S2024
Tamworth Castle & Museum Svc, Archvs, A485
Tamworth Coll Lib, see **S**2024
Tamworth Court Rolls, **S**1572
Tangye, Sir Richard, Colln (Cromwelliana), **S**1288
Tank Museum, Ref Lib & Archv, S2084
Tanner Colln, **A**409
Tanner Lib & Archv, S102
Tanner, Robin, Papers, **A**77
Taphouse Colln (17C-18C music), **P**72
Tapling Colln (stamps), **L**1
Tarmac plc Archvs, A514
Tasker Colln (agric implement manufacturers), **A**29
Tasker, Joe, Colln (mountaineering photos), **S**2118
Tate Archv, A349; **Lib, S**1418
Tattersall Colln (concrete eng), **S**1912
Taunton & Somerset NHS Trust, see **S**2027
Tavistock & Portman NHS Trust Lib, S1419
Tavistock Inst Lib, S1420

Tavistock Subscription Lib, S2029
Tawney Soc archvs, **S**482
taxation, **IS**8, 87; **S**476, 624, 1112, 1162, 1186, 1193, 1204, 1426, 1883; land, **S**1370; property, **S**1370
taxonomy, **S**1247, 1738; fungal, **S**1862; insect, **S**1359; invertebrate, **S**32; plant, **S**1721, 1862; zoological, **S**612
Tay Valley Family Hist Soc, Rsrch Centre, A138
Taylor & Francis Archv (printer & publisher), **S**1408
Taylor Colln (games & simulation), **S**610
Taylor Instn Lib, S1751
Taylor Lib & Archvs, S1920
Taylor Psalmody Colln, **A**3
Taylor, R.A., Colln (fairs & fairgrounds), **A**451
Taylor, Simon, papers (Jamaican plantation owner), **S**1443
Taylor-Schechter Genizah Rsrch Unit, see **L**5
Tayside Health Board Archv, **A**137
Tayside Primary Care NHS Trust Lib, S559; see also **S**557, 1790
Tayside Regional Council, records, **A**135
teaching, **S**33, 212, 326, 438, 504, 715, 910, 969, 1307, 1597, 1899, 1949, 1969, 2079, 2103, 2145; language, **IS**109; **S**1061; see also education
teaching studies, **S**950
TEAGASC Agric & Food Development Authority Lib, IS146; see also **IS**118
Teasdale, Keith, Colln (socialism), **P**115
Tebbut Printed Music Colln, **P**131
Technical Info Centre Royal Engineers, S1646
technology, **A**88; **IS**2, 11, 28, 31, 33, 35, 44, 46, 55, 56, 59, 71, 82, 90, 110, 123, 146, 155, 166, 181, 192, 193, 195, 198, 202, 204; **L**5; **S**1, 11, 12, 21, 29, 50, 68, 73, 107, 108, 111, 113, 121, 124, 125, 154, 165, 198, 232, 246, 248, 269, 295, 296, 419, 436, 443, 460, 473, 478, 503, 540, 550, 565, 581, 588, 603, 604, 606, 621, 681, 698, 701, 702, 713, 741, 745, 755, 757, 760, 762, 776, 780, 788, 804, 810, 825, 841, 855, 869, 876, 891, 893, 904, 910, 969, 986, 1012, 1026, 1050, 1053, 1084, 1096, 1120, 1180, 1200, 1202, 1206, 1209, 1227, 1255, 1258, 1262, 1284, 1333, 1334, 1362, 1371, 1379, 1388, 1403, 1421, 1429, 1452, 1491, 1497, 1498, 1505, 1524, 1529, 1530, 1536, 1541, 1552, 1565, 1574, 1599, 1604, 1609, 1610, 1623, 1644, 1648, 1654, 1657, 1678, 1716, 1767, 1800, 1804, 1806, 1822, 1837, 1842, 1855, 1874, 1881, 1886, 1895, 1905, 1917, 1918, 1934, 1942, 1944, 1959, 1966, 1971, 1978, 1983, 2004, 2010, 2018, 2020, 2031, 2038, 2042, 2045, 2049, 2067, 2080, 2094, 2095, 2101, 2103, 2112, 2113, 2145, 2168, 2179; aeronautical, **S**1342; agricultural, **S**1850; broadcasting, **A**428; building, **S**45; cast metal, **S**2101; cast metals, **S**165; ceramic, **S**1200; chemical, **S**1180; chocolate, **S**164; clothing, **S**1254; coal mining, **S**2068; communications, **A**414; **IS**202; computer, **S**1541; dental, **IS**61; fishing, **IS**158; **S**8; fishing gear, **S**638; fuel gas, **S**1207; gas, **S**1207; glass, **S**1904; Greek, **S**1159; gypsum, **S**1481; information, **IS**202; **S**114, 208, 478, 491, 959, 968, 1206, 1251, 1261, 1282, 1541, 1788, 1882, 1957; ink, **S**1657; marine, **S**1199, 1372, 1944, 2073; media, **S**1043; medical, **S**7, 505, 632, 1278, 1583, 1984; metal, **S**1200; military, **S**26, 2021; musical instrument, **S**1557; nuclear, **IS**130; offshore, **S**1199; paint, **S**1928, 2032; pattern making, **S**2101; pharmaceutical, **S**1450; plaster, **S**1481; polymer, **S**1200; public transport, **S**1268; reproductive, **S**1134; Roman, **S**1159; rubber, **S**1200; seed, **S**381; ship, **S**1939; space, **S**1036;

telecommunications, **IS**125; theatre, **S**1002; tobacco, **S**1938; water, **S**669; weapons, **A**298; see also history of technology
technology policy, **S**235, 1098
teenagers, **S**1045
Teesside Archvs, A379
Teesside Univ, see Univ of Teesside
Tefal, advertising archv, **A**399
Teichman Bequest (prints of 18C Russia), **A**77
Teikyo Univ of Japan in Durham Lib, S576
telecommunications, **A**261, 414; **IS**53, 125; **S**841, 1206, 1315, 1934; see also communications
telegraphy, **A**294, 414
television, **A**95, 267, 293, 404; **IS**140; **S**215, 554, 731, 1010, 1013, 1382, 1831; see also broadcasting
television studies, **S**1043
Telford & Wrekin Libs, P185; see also **A**453
Telford Coll of Arts & Tech, LRC, S2035
Telford, Thomas, Colln & MSS (civil eng), **S**1205, 2033
Telfourd-Jones Colln (nat hist), **S**76
temperance, **S**1189, 1441, 1694
Tempest Colln (aerial photos), **S**2051
Tempest of Tong, family & estate records, **A**62
Temple Newsam, family & estate records, **A**226
Temple, William, Colln, **S**538, 1512
Templeton Coll, Info Centre, S1772
tenancy, **S**1370
Tenby Museum & Art Gallery, Lib & Archvs, S2036
Tenison Grove Colln (Londonderry), **S**1478
Tenison, E.M., Papers, **S**410
Tennant Caledonian, records (brewers), **A**179
Tennant Family of Neath, papers, **A**481
tennis, **S**1276; lawn, **S**1226
Tennyson family papers & correspondence, **A**235
Tennyson Rsrch Centre, A235
Tennyson, Alfred, Colln, **P**75; **S**413; *Lib & Papers,* **A**235; *MSS,* **S**393
Tennyson, Emily, journal, **A**235
Tennyson, George Clayton, Lib, **A**235
Terence Mortimer Postgrad Edu Centre Lib, see **S**69
Terry, Ellen, archv (theatre), **S**2037
Tertis, Lionel, Colln (music MSS), **S**1428
Textile Inst, Lord Barnby Foundation Lib, S1533
textiles, **A**148, 250, 409, 508; **IS**9, 22; **S**12, 103, 160, 419, 901, 960, 1050, 1060, 1105, 1254, 1282, 1290, 1497, 1533, 1582, 2127, 2170
Thackeray Colln, **S**393
Thames Colln, **P**202
Thames Conservancy records, **A**270, 429; **S**1114
Thames River, **S**1114
Thames Valley Univ, Centre for Info Mgmt, O401; **Learning Resource Svc, S**1421; **Westel House LRC, S**1422
Thanet Coll Lib, S265
Thanet Healthcare Trust Clinical Studies Lib, see **S**1538
Thanet Rural Dist Council, records, **A**128
Thatcher Papers, **A**88
theatre, **A**263, 267, 337; **IS**193; **S**115, 415, 591, 880, 1002, 1139, 1170, 1323, 1340, 1390, 1423, 1428, 1467, 1797, 1923, 2037; Elizabethan, **S**1117; English, **S**1997; in education, **A**496; Irish, **IA**41; Japanese, **S**1220; Kabuki, **S**1220; musical, **S**1059; Noh, **S**1220; Russian, **S**1393; Scottish, **A**182; Soviet, **S**1393; technical, **S**1154; see also drama
Theatre Info Group, O402
Theatre Museum Lib, S1423; see also **A**353
Theatre Proj Consultants Ltd, records, **S**651

Theatre Royal, Richmond, Playbill Colln, **A**433
Theodorakis, Mikis, Colln (Greek composer & activist), **S**965
theology, **A**224; **IA**86; **IS**12, 33, 104, 131, 188, 191, 201; **S**98, 101, 127, 147, 173, 179, 199, 293, 320, 360, 363, 374, 386, 388, 394, 400, 404, 426, 448, 466, 469, 509, 523, 538, 577, 596, 600, 801, 880, 945, 952, 966, 968, 1038, 1057, 1116, 1160, 1407, 1412, 1440, 1522, 1619, 1627, 1665, 1673, 1691, 1700, 1702, 1752, 1759, 1773, 1781, 1894, 1958, 2054, 2081, 2096, 2130; Catholic, **S**391, 1665, 1667; Christian, **S**180, 433, 553; historical, **S**1619; Jewish, **S**1266; Methodist, **S**1776; modern, **S**567, 1626; moral, **S**1057; Moravian, **A**309; pastoral, **S**1463; practical, **S**1522; Reformation, **S**773; social, **S**1522; Wesleyan, **S**1776; see also religion
Theosophical Soc in England, see **S**1243
therapeutic community work, **A**104
Therapeutical Soc, archvs, **S**1381
therapy, **S**178; art, **S**1560; beauty, **S**1254, 1816; creative, **S**356; environment, **A**104; family, **IS**114; **S**1304; language, **S**923; milieu, **A**104; music, **S**263; occupational, **IL**2; **IS**210; **S**12, 429, 478, 584, 614, 670, 818, 1092, 1560, 1700, 1947, 2069; speech, **S**614, 818, 923, 1059; see also physiotherapy; psychotherapy
thermodynamics, **S**321, 1208
Third Reich, **S**1195
Third World, **IS**147
Thirsk Museum, Lib, S2039
Thom, Alexander, Colln (genl interest), **IL**1
Thomas Cook Archvs, A418
Thomas Corson & Co, records (livestock auctioneers), **A**248
Thomas Danby Coll, Learning Centre Lib, S915
Thomas Hope Hosp, Langholm, records, **A**132
Thomas Lib (Sanskrit studies), **L**4
Thomas Plume's Lib, S1505
Thomas, Bertram, papers (traveller in Arabia), **S**328
Thomas, Dr K. Bryn, Colln (anaesthesia), **S**1001, 1849
Thomas, Dylan, Colln, **A**479; **P**182
Thomas, Edgar, Colln (agric econ), **S**1850
Thomas, Edward, Colln, **P**109; **S**413, 1414
Thomas, John, Colln (Welsh photography), **L**3
Thomas, Sir Eric, Lib (Mesoamerican arch), **S**1034
Thomas-Stanford Euclid Colln, **L**3
Thomason Tracts (17C), **L**1
Thomond, Earls of, papers, **IA**55
Thompson Lib, see **S**1989, 2013
Thompson Newspaper Colln, **S**1591
Thompson, D'Arcy Wentworth, Papers, **S**1964
Thompson, Dorothy, Colln (Chartism), **S**1989
Thompson, Francis G., Colln (hist of Highlands & Islands), **S**1992
Thompson, J Walter, advertising archv, **A**399
Thompson, John, Colln (plans), **S**1799
Thompson, John, records (Wolverhampton company), **A**515
Thompson, S.P., Lib, **S**1206
Thompson, Sam, Colln (Belfast playwright), **A**37
Thompson, Silvanus P., Colln, **A**294
Thoms Mineralogy Colln, **S**561
Thomson Corp, see **O**235
Thomson Herald King Pamphs, **A**3
Thomson, Sir J.J., papers, **L**5
Thoresby Soc Lib, S916
Thorkelin Colln (Scandinavia), **L**2
Thorneycroft & Day, Summers, shipbldg drawings, **S**1943
Thornhill Hosp, records, **A**132
Thornhill of Fixby, family & estate records, **A**208

Viner Colln (17C-18C), **L4**
Vint, Hill & Killick (Solicitors), records, **A62**
Virago Fiction Colln, **A75**
Virginia Henderson Lib, see **S1351**
virology, **S**313, 1300, 1669, 1787, 1830, 2136
Virus Rsrch Unit Archvs, **S1624**
VisitBritain, Thames Tower Lib, S1454
Visual Arts UK Archv, **S1591**
visual impairment, **S**984, 1374, 2145; *see also* blindness
visual science, **S1201**
vitamins, **S1059**
vitreous enamels, **S1985**
voice, **S1059**
Vokins Archv (design), **A69**
Volbach, Fritz, correspondence, **A516**
Voltaire Colln, **S1751**
voluntary sector, **A**264; **S1294**
volunteering, **S1294**
Von Hügel Colln (theology & phil), **S1964**
voting systems, **S1277**
voyages, **S1106**
Vulcan Locomotive Works, records, **A239**
Vulliamy Horological Colln, **S1205**

W.H. Smith Archv Ltd, A484
W.J. Thomson Lib, S65
Waddesdon Manor (Natl Trust), Lib, S61
Waddington Colln (fairs & fairgrounds), **A451**
Waddington Envlronment Lib, S647
Waddington-Feather Colln (Yorkshire lit), **S217**
Waddleton Colln (illustrated bks), **L5**
Wade Colln (18C military maps), **L2**
Wade Cooper Photo Colln, **S645**
Wade, Sir Henry, Papers (surgery), **S617**
Wade, Sir Thomas, Bequest (19C Chinese hist), **L5**
Wadham Coll Lib, S1775
wages, **S**1098, 1425
Wainright Colln (19C politics), **S1840**
Wainwright, Hilary, papers (politics), **A365**
Waitrose, records (supermarket chain), **A470**
Wake, Archbishop, papers, **S1670**
Wakefield & Pontefract Community Health Trust, S2070
Wakefield Coll Learning Centres, S2071
Wakefield Diocese, records, **A497**
Wakefield Libs & Info Svcs, P191; *see also* **A497**
Waldron Colln (religion & Irish hist), **IA11**
Wales & Welsh studies, **A**6, 479; **S**82, 492
Wales Euro Info Centre, see S413
Wales Higher Edu Libs Forum, O424
Walford & North Staffordshire Coll Lib, S1661
Walker Art Gallery Archvs, A241
Walker Family Papers, **A297**
Walker Lib, S1414
Walker Music Colln, **P1**
Walker, Charles, Colln (myths, magic, strange phenomena), **S1174**
Walker, Emery, Photo Colln (William Morris), **S1408**
Walker, Ted, Archv (Sussex poet), **S469**
walking, **S990**
Wallace Colln, Lib & Archvs, S1455
Wallace, Alfred Russel, Colln (nat hist), **S**1308; *Lib*, **S1247**
Wallace, Edgar, Colln, **P98**
Wallington Magistrates Court, records, **A478**
Wallis Colln (maths), **S1586**
Wallis, Alfred, correspondence, **S368**
Wallis, Sir Barnes, Colln (aeronautical engineer), **A505**
Walmer Urban Dist Council, records, **A128**
Walmisley MSS (church composer), **S546**
Walpole, Horace, Colln, **A433**

Walpole, Hugh, Colln (fine printing & literary MSS), **S409**; *MSS*, **S858**
Walpole, Sir Robert, Papers, **L5**
Walsall Archvs & Local Hist Centre, A498
Walsall Coll of Arts & Tech, European Design Centre Lib, S2079
Walsall Health Authority Dist Lib, S2080
Walsall Hosp records, **A498**
Walsall Hosps NHS Trust, S2075
Walsall Libs & Heritage, P192
Walsall Museum & Art Gallery, see S2076
Walsall, Archdeaconry of, records, **A467**
Walsgrave Health Scis Lib, S499
Walsh, Fr Paul, Papers (historian & scholar), **IA78**
Walsh, Micheline Kerney, papers, **A16**
Walshe, J.J., TD, papers, **IA19**
Walsingham Colln (entomology), **S1308**
Walter family of Bear Wood papers, **A316**
Walter Scott Lib, see S586
Walters Electrical Manufacturing Co Ltd records, **A294**
Waltham Forest Archvs & Local Studies Lib, A354
Waltham Forest Deanery, parish records, **A354**
Waltham Forest Libs, P108
Walthamstow Borough records, **A354**
Walton Colln, S1572
Walton Lib, S1590
Wandesford Family Papers, **IA49**
Wandsworth Libs, P109
Wandsworth Local Hist Svc, A355
Wansbeck Hosp Lib, S52
Wantage, Lord, papers (British Red Cross Soc), **A260**
war crimes, **A**289, 292
War Poetry Colln, **P9**
War Poets Colln, S610
Warburg Inst Lib, S1456
Warburg, Aby, papers, **S1456**
Warburg, Sir Siegmund, Colln, **S1413**
Warburton family muniments, **S1512**
Ward estate archv, **A392**
Ward Lib, P212
Ward, Gordon, Archv (historical ephemera), **S1502**; *Notebks (Sevenoaks)*, **A449**
Ward, Sir Adolphus, Colln (hist & English lit), **S384**
Warden Colln (shorthand), **L2**
Wardle Colln (silk industry), **P174**
warfare, **A**288, 289, 290, 291, 292, 409; **S**909, 913, 1130, 1170, 1182, 1614, 1925; air, **S**1621, 1925; armoured, **S**2084; naval, **IS**160; **S**1303; nuclear, **S**1052; *see also* history, military
Warlington Park Hosp, archvs, **A33**
Warlock, Peter, music MSS, **L5**
Warner Lib, S447
Warner, Sylvia Townsend, Colln, **S545**
Warren, Max, Colln (Church Missionary Soc), **S1322**
Warrilow Photos, **S1572**
Warrington Academy Colln, **P193**
Warrington Collegiate Inst, LRC, S2088
Warrington Guardian Archv, **A501**
Warrington Libs, Local & Family Hist Colln, A501
Warrington Lib & Info Svcs, P193
warships, **S1303**
Warwick Univ, see Univ of Warwick
Warwickshire County Record Office, A503
Warwickshire Lib & Info Svc, P194
Warwickshire Local Hist Soc, O425
Warwickshire Museum, Lib, S2091
Warwickshire NHS Trust, see S1876
Warwickshire Sites & Monuments Record, see S2091
waste water, **S**1071, 2022
Watchmeal Colln (West Dunbarton-shire), **A131**
water, **S**107, 172, 218, 543, 669, 830, 1071, 2022
water quality, **IS**53; **S2072**
Water Rsrch Centre Swindon, Lib, S2022

water resources, **S**1319, 2072
water supply, **S**1070, 2022
water treatment, **S2022**
Waterford Board of Guardians, records, **IA54**
Waterford City & County Infirmary, archvs, **IP28**
Waterford City Archvs, IA95
Waterford City Engineer's Office, records, **IA95**
Waterford City Libs, IP28
Waterford County Archvs Svc, IA54
Waterford County Libs, IP29
Waterford Finance Office, records, **IA95**
Waterford Grand Jury records, **IA54**
Waterford Inst of Tech, Luke Wadding Lib, IS209
Waterford Political Pamphs Colln, **IA54**
Waterford Regional Hosp, Lib & Info Svc, IS210
Waterston Lib, S1563
Waterston, A. Rodger, Colln, **S863**
waterways, inland, **A**159, 183; **S**749, 1106, 1252; *see also* canals
Waterways Trust, see A159, 183
Watford Genl Hosp Lib, S2092
Watkins, A., & Morgan, F.C., Photo Negative Colln, **P62**
Watkins, Alfred, Archv (photography) & Lib (beekeeping), **A202**
Watkins, Vernon, papers, **L3**
Watney Mann Archvs (brewers), **A268**
Watson Colln (liturgy), **IS131**
Watson Colln (labour hist), **S1978**
Watson, Graham, Colln (clr plate bks), **S353**
Watt Instn & School of Arts, records, **A148**
Watt, James, Archv, **A148**; *Colln*, **S764**
Watts Charity Rochester, records, **A435**
Watts, A., Colln (inland waterways), **A183**
Waverley Borough Council, see A167
Weald & Downland Open Air Museum, Armstrong Lib, S470
Weale, W.H., Colln, **S1290**
weaponry, **A298**
weapons, **S**419, 913, 1925, 1954; nuclear, **S1052**
Weatherill, Bernard, Papers, **S410**
Weavers' Guild records, **IS139**
Webbs (Aberbeeg) Ltd, records (brewers), **A117**
Webster, Thomas, Letters (19C geol), **S18**
Wedgwood Papers, **S1572**
Wedlake & Greening Colln (archaeo), **S1817**
Weegee Colln (American photojournalism), **S1170**
Weir, Viscount William, papers (entrepreneur), **A176**
Weis, Paul, papers, **S1744**
Weiss Colln of Beethoven Lit, **S597**
Weizmann, Chaim, correspondence (scholar & Zionist leader), **A306**
Welbeck Estates, records (7th Duke of Portland), **A20**
Welch Regiment Museum, Archvs, A96
Welch, R.J., Photo Colln, **S146**
welding, **S**395, 796
Welensky, Sir Roy, papers, **L4**
welfare, **IS**58; **S**757, 1298, 1722; animal, **S**263, 820, 1110, 1610; child, **S**835; social, **A**264; **S**204, 222, 562, 835, 1078, 1304, 1402, 1463, 1993
welfare state, **S493**
Wellcome Archvs, **S1457**
Wellcome Historical Medical Museum, archvs, **S1457**
Wellcome Inst, archvs, **S1457**
Wellcome Lib for the Hist & Understanding of Medicine, S1457
Wellcome Tropical Inst Collns, **S1457**
Wellcome Unit for the Hist of Medicine Lib, S1755
Wellcome, Sir Henry, papers, **S1457**
Wellesley, Arthur, correspondence, **S1185**
Wellesz MSS (music), **S25**
Wellesz, Egon, Colln (Byzantine music), **S1728**
Wellington Museum, records, **A353**

Wellington Pamphs & Papers, **S1946**
Wells Cathedral Lib, S2096
Wells Museum Lib, S2097
Wells, H.G., Colln, **A79**; **P81**; **S**1262, 1647
Welsh Almanacs Colln, **L3**
Welsh Arts Council, see Arts Council of Wales
Welsh Ballads Colln, **L3**; **S880**
Welsh Bks Council, Lib, S20
Welsh Church Commission, records, **L3**
Welsh Colln, **P163**; **S19**
Welsh Coll of Horticulture, LRC, S1556
Welsh Conservative & Unionist Assocs, records, **L3**
Welsh Development Agency, Lib & Info Unit, S431
Welsh Economy Press Cuttings, **S413**
Welsh Folk Museum, see S419
Welsh Historic Monuments Exec Agency, **A93**
Welsh Hymn Colln, **S880**
Welsh Industrial & Maritime Museum, see S2051
Welsh Liberal Party, records, **L3**
Welsh Music Info Centre, S432
Welsh Natl Council of the United Nations Assoc, records, **L3**
Welsh Political Archv, see L3
Welsh Portrait Archv, **L3**
Welsh Religious Hist Soc Records, **S879**
Welsh Slate Museum, see S422
Welsh Topographical Bks Colln, **S422**
Welwyn Dept Store, records, **A470**
Wennington School, records, **A104**
Wentworth of Woolley Hall Papers, **S918**
Wentworth Woodhouse Muniments, **A452**
Wentworth-Fitzwilliam Muniments, **A452**
Wesley & Methodist Studies Centre, Lib & Archv, S1776
Wesley Coll Lib, S264
Wesley Family, Colln, **A447**; **P127**; *papers & MSS*, **A368**
Wesley Historical Soc Lib & Archv, **S1776**
Wesley House Lib, S398
Wesley's Chapel Lib, S1458
Wesley, Charles, Lib & Papers, **A368**
Wesley, John, letters, **S1458**; *Lib*, **S1458**; *papers & MSS*, **A368**; **S264**
Wesley, S., MSS (church composer), **S546**
Wessex Film & Sound Archv, A510
Wessex Water Lib, S107
West Berkshire Libs & Info, P195
West Cheshire Coll, Lib & Learning Centre, S461
West Cheshire Postgrad Medical Centre Lib, S462
West Cumbria Coll, see S2151
West Devon Borough Council Archvs, **A419**
West Devon Borough Quarter Sessions records, **A419**
West Dorset Genl Hosp NHS Trust, see S544
West Dunbartonshire Libs, P196; Clydebank Central Lib - Local Colln & Archvs, **A110**; Dumbarton Lib - Info & Local Studies, **A131**
West End Local Hist Soc, Museum & Rsrch Centre, A460
West End School of Cookery, archv, **S701**
West Glamorgan Archv Svc, A481
West Hampshire NHS Trust, see S679, 1941
West Hertfordshire Coll, Teaching & Learning Resources Svc, Cassio Campus, S2093; Dacorum Campus, **S799**; Watford Campus, **S2094**
West Hertfordshire Hosps NHS Trust, see S798, 1620, 1962, 2092
West Hope Manor, records, **A104**
*West India Cttee Lib & Archv, S1443**
West Indies Papers (personal & estate records), **A77**
West Kent Coll, Lib Svcs, S2046
West Kent Postgrad Centre Lib, see S1658

West London Hosp records, **A**282
West Lothian Archvs & Records Mgmt Svc, A242
West Lothian Coll Lib, S977
West Lothian Council Libs, Local Hist Dept, A56
West Lothian Lib Svcs, P197
West Middlesex Univ Hosp NHS Trust, Lib & Info Svc, S850
West Midlands Creative Lit Colln, **P**163
West Midlands Regional Archv Forum, O426
West Nottinghamshire Coll, LRC, S1537
West of Scotland Community Relations Council Archvs, **S**1782
West Riding County Council, records, **A**497
West Riding Quarter Sessions records, **A**497
West Suffolk Coll, LRC, S281
West Suffolk Hosp, Edu Centre & Lib, S282
West Suffolk Local Studies Lib, **A**83
West Surrey Health Authority Lib, *see* **S774**
West Sussex Archvs Soc, O427
West Sussex Libs & Info, P198
West Sussex Record Office, A106; *see also* **A71**
West Thames Coll, LRC, S851
West Yorkshire Archv Svc, Bradford, A62; Calderdale, A194; Kirklees, A208; Leeds, A226; Wakefield, A497
West Yorkshire Metropolitan County Council, records, **A**497
West Yorkshire Regiment, records, **A**524
West, R.G., Colln (geol), **S**307
Westbury Manor Museum, Local Studies Room, A166
Westcott House Lib, S399
Westcott, Brooke Foss, Colln (religion), **S**399
Westcountry Studies Lib, A164
Western Antiquary Colln, **S**1806
Western Edu & Lib Board, P136; *see also* **S1477, 1653**
Western Genl Hosp Lib, S648
Western Health Board Lib Svc, IS168; Castlebar Healthcare Lib, IS14
Western Infirmary Lib & eLearning Centre, S742
Western Isles Health Unit, *see* **S1993**
Western Isles Hosp Lib, S1993
Western Isles Libs, P199; Local Hist Colln, A474
Western Isles School Board of Mgmt, minutes, **A**474
Western Morning News Photo Colln, **A**419
Western Regional Health Board, records, **A**177
Western Theatre Ballet Archv, **A**182
Western Women's Internatl Zionist Org, records, **A**306
Westfield Coll Archv, **S**1333
Westfield House Lib, S400
Westmeath Board of Guardian minutes, **IA**78
Westmeath Board of Health & Public Assistance minutes, **IA**78
Westmeath County Infirmary records, **IA**78
Westmeath County Libs, IP30; Local Studies Colln, IA78
Westmeath County Lib Goldsmith Colln, **IS**66
Westmeath Grand Jury Presentments, **IA**78
Westmeath Militia & Yeomanry, papers, **IA**12
Westminster Abbey, Lib & Muniment Room, S1459
Westminster Coll (Cambridge) Lib, S401
Westminster Coll (Oxford) Lib, *see* **S1700;** *see also* **S1776**
Westminster Conservative Assoc, records, **A**268
Westminster Diocesan Archvs, A356
Westminster Kingsway Coll Lib Svc, S1460
Westminster Libs, P110; *see also* **A268**
Westminster School Lib, S1461

Westminster, Diocese of, records, **A**268
Westminster, RC Archbishops of, papers, **A**356
Westmoreland Lock Hosp, records, **IS**133
Westmorland Genl Hosp, Edu Centre Lib, S856
Westmorland Quarter Session records, **A**217
Westoe Family Archvs (18C-19C), **P**170
Weston Coll Lib, S2109
Weston Park Hosp, Barnard Lib, S1914
Westropp Colln (photography), **IA**55
Westward Television Film Lib, **A**421
Westwood, J.O., Colln (entomology), **S**1738
Wetherall, Gen, Papers, **A**274
Wetherby Rural Dist Council, records, **A**226
Wethred, Audrey & Gardner, Chloë, Colln (movement therapists), **A**192
Wexford Board of Guardians, records, **IA**1
Wexford Board of Health & Public Assistance, records, **IA**1
Wexford Corp Archvs, IA98
Wexford Genl Hosp Lib, IS211
Wexford Grand Jury records, **IA**1
Wexford Harbour Commissioners, records, **IA**1
Wexford Poor Law Commissioners, records, **IA**1
Wexford Public Libs, IP31; Local Studies & Archvs Section, IA1
Wexham Park Hosp LRC, *see* **S1421**
Weymouth Coll Lib, S2110
Wharfdale Rural Dist, records, **A**226
Wharfedale Genl Hosp, Postgrad Medical Centre Lib, S1662
Wharncliffe, Earls of, family papers, **A**452
Wheat Colln (17C-19C law), **S**1912
Wheatstone Colln (19C maths & physics), **S**1227
Wheeler Colln, **P**75
Wheeler Colln (18C bks), **S**746
Wheeler, Sir Mortimer, excavation archv, **S**1963
Wheeler-Bennett, Sir John, papers, **S**1764
Wheeler-Butcher Colln (18C medicine), **IS**134
Wheler Colln (Warwickshire), **S**1996
Whewell MSS, **S**393
Whipple Lib, S311
Whipple, R.S., Colln (sci, maths), **S**311
Whipps Cross Univ Hosp, Multidisciplinary Lib Svc, S1462
Whipsnade Zoo, records, **S**1474
whisky, **A**178
Whistler, J.M., archv, **S**738
Whiston Rural Dist Council, minutes, **A**222
Whitaker Colln (maps), **S**918
Whitbread Brewing Archv Colln, **S**1694
Whitby Archvs & Heritage Centre, A506
White Colln (maths, physics, optics), **L**5
White family papers, **S**30
White, Gilbert, Colln, **S**30
White, R.F., Archv (UK's 1st advertising agency), **A**399
White, Robert, Colln (hist of Northumberland), **S**1586
Whiteabbey Flax Spinning Co, records, **S**815
Whitefield, George, papers (18C evangelical), **A**368
Whitehall Lib, S1736
Whitelocke papers, **S**2086
whitewares, **S**1985
Whitley Wildlife Conservation Trust Lib, S1780
Whitman, Walt, Colln, **A**57; **P**12
Whitney Colln (Church hist), **S**340
Whitney Colln of Photos, **A**211
Whitorn Burgh records, **A**475
Whittaker Library, **S**726
Whittet Colln (arch plans), **P**119
Whittinghams Colln (19C printing), **S**19
Whittington Hosp NHS Trust, S994
Whittington Press Colln, **S**454

Whittington, Richard, estate records, **A**307
Whitworth, Sir Joseph, papers (eng), **S**1208
Wick Harbour Trust Colln, **A**86
Wickham, William, papers, **A**509
Wicklow Commissioner's Court, proceedings, **IA**7
Wicklow County Council Lib Svc, IP32; Local Studies & Archvs, IA7
Wicklow Estate Papers, **IL**1
Wicklow Grand Jury Presentments, **IA**7
Widdowson, Dr Elsie May, Colln (nutrition), **S**376
Wiener Lib, S1195
Wier MSS (music), **S**25
Wigan & Leigh Coll, Learning Resources & Lib Svcs, S2115
Wigan & Leigh Medical Inst, Lib, S2116
Wigan Archvs Svc, A228
Wigan Board of Guardians records, **A**228
Wigan Clinical Lib, *see* **S1840**
Wigan Libs & Lifelong Learning, P200
Wigan Mining Lib, **S**1885
Wigan Quarter & Petty Sessions records, **A**228
Wightman Pamph Colln (archaeo, ancient hist), **S**1964
Wighton Colln of Natl Scottish Music, **A**136; **P**42
Wiglesworth Ornithological Colln, **S**260
Wigley, Dafydd, Papers, **L**3
Wigston Coll of Further Edu, *see* **S2117**
Wigtown Burgh records, **A**475
WILCO: Wiltshire Libs in Co-operation, O428
Wild Geese Colln (Irish mercenaries), **IS**193
Wilde, Oscar, Colln, **IP**32
wildlife, **S**74, 256, 1110, 1246, 1780, 1917; Welsh, **S**74; *see also natural history*
Wilkes, John, Colln, **P**99; *correspondence,* **S**1887
Wilkinson, Ellen, papers (politics), **A**365
Willats, Stephen, Archv (art), **S**1075
William Booth Coll Lib, S1463; *see also* **A341**
William Cookworthy Museum, Local Heritage Resource Centre, A218
William Harvey Hosp, Edu Centre Lib, S50
William Kenrick Lib, S183
William Morris Gallery, Ref Lib & Archvs, S1464
William Morris Soc Lib, S1465
William of Orange Colln, **S**1647
William Robbins Lib, S1702
William Salt Lib, A468
William Tuson Lib, S1838
Williams Colln (theatre), **S**1631
Williams, Alfred, Colln, **P**183
Williams, Cicely, papers, **S**1457
Williams, D.J., Colln (Welsh children's bks), **L**3
Williams, Emlyn, papers, **L**3
Williams, F.C., papers (computing), **A**369
Williams, G.O., papers (Archbishop of Wales), **S**879
Williams, Griffith John, Colln (Welsh & Celtic studies), **L**3
Williams, Isaac, Colln, **S**880
Williams, Peter, Colln (dance), **S**1232
Williams, Samuel, & Sons Ltd, records, **A**118
Williams, Sir John, Colln, **L**3
Williamson MSS (music), **S**25
Williamson, Henry, Colln, **P**98
Williamson, Henry, Colln & Papers (Devon author), **S**671
Williamson, John, Colln (US labour movement), **S**1274
Willis Museum, Archv Collns, A30
Willis, Constance, Peace Archv, **S**217
Willoughby, Francis, papers (17C naturalist), **S**1647
wills, **A**318

Wills Memorial Lib, *see* **S260**
Wills, W. David, Papers (environment therapy), **A**104
Wills, W.D. & H.O., Colln, **A**72
Wilmot-Horton of Catton, family archv, **A**375
Wilson Barrett Co Archv, **A**182
Wilson MSS Pedigrees, **S**907
Wilson of Bannockburn, records (tartan manufacturer), **S**613
Wilson, Admiral Knyvet, Colln, **S**2009
Wilson, Alexander, Bequest (photography), **A**136
Wilson, Bishop, Colln, **S**456
Wilson, Field Marshal Sir Henry, papers, **A**289
Wilson, George Washington, Photo Colln, **A**3; **P**1; **S**5, 215
Wilson, George, correspondence (Anti-Corn Law League), **A**367
Wilson, H.G., Pamph Colln (anti-slavery), **S**1512
Wilson, Harold, papers, **L**4
Wilson, J.B., Colln (London hist), **P**107
Wilson, John, Lib (theology), **S**952
Wilson, John, of Broomhead Papers, **S**918
Wilson, Reg, Colln (theatre photos), **S**1996
Wilson, Roger, papers, **A**77
Wilson-Todd Colln (WW1 stamps), **L**1
Wilton Family of Heaton Hall papers, **A**364
Wiltshire & Swindon Record Office, A493
Wiltshire Archaeo & Nat Hist Soc Lib, S530
Wiltshire Colln (Dublin photos), **IL**1
Wiltshire Coll, Chippenham Lib, S472; Lackham Lib, S473
Wiltshire Coll, Trowbridge Lib, S2053
Wiltshire Libs & Heritage, P201
Wiltshire Local Hist Forum, O429
Wiltshire Quarter Sessions Archvs, **A**493
Wiltshire Record Soc, O430
Wiltshire Regiment, records, **A**445
Wiltshire, Somerset & Waymouth Railway Co, records, **S**2165
Wimbledon Coll, Milward LRC, S1466
Wimbledon Mission, records, **S**1466
Wimbledon School of Art Lib, S1467
Wimbledon School, records, **S**1466
Wimbledon Soc Museum Lib, S1468
Wimborne Minster Chained Lib, S2119
Wimborne Papers (Churchill family correspondence), **A**88
Winchester & Eastleigh Healthcare NHS Trust, Healthcare Lib, S2124
Winchester Bishopric, estate records, **A**509
Winchester Coll Archvs, A511; Warden & Fellows' Lib, S2125
Winchester Diocese, Thorold & Lyttleton Lib, S2120
Winchester Museums Svc, Historical Resources Centre, S2126
Winchester School of Art Lib, S2127
Winchester, Diocese of, records, **A**509
Wind Colln (iconography), **S**1747
Windscale 1977 Public Enquiry papers, **S**482
Windsor & Maidenhead Lib & Info Svcs, P202; *see also* **A429**
Windsor, Dean & Canons of, *see* **S2132**
wine studies, **S**940
Winstanley, Henry, Colln (prints), **A**442
Wirral Archvs Svc, A50
Wirral Health Authority records, **A**50
Wirral Hosp NHS Trust, *see* **S2133, 2135**
Wirral Libs, P203
Wisbech & Fenland Museum, A512
Wisbech Literary Soc Lib, **A**512
Wisbech Town Lib, **A**512
Wisbech, Deanery of, records, **A**512
Wisley Garden Lib, *see* **S1367, 2137**
Witan Hall Lib, S1851
witchcraft, **IS**39
Witherby, H.F., Colln, **S**863